C000082525

Revised Edition

SWAP & DERIVATIVE Financing

About the Author

Satyajit Das is a leading international authority in the area of financial derivatives and treasury management.

Between 1988 and early 1994, he was the Treasurer of TNT Group, an Australian based international transport and logistics company. In this position, he had responsibility for the Global Treasury function, including liquidity management, corporate finance, capital markets, and financial risk management. He was also involved in the financial restructuring of the TNT Group in the early 1990s. Since early 1994, Mr Das has continued his relationship with TNT in a part-time capacity, in the position of General Manager, Financial Planning. In this capacity, he acts as an internal consultant to the TNT Group in the areas of financial strategy and policy, capital allocation/management and strategic risk management.

Prior to this, between 1977 and 1987, he worked in banking with the Commonwealth Bank of Australia, Citicorp Investment Bank and Merrill Lynch Capital Markets specialising in fund raising for Australian and New Zealand borrowers in domestic and international capital markets and risk management, involving the use of derivative products, including swaps, futures and options.

In 1987, Mr Das was a Visiting Fellow at the Centre for Studies in Money, Banking and Finance, Macquarie University where he was involved in teaching in the post-graduate Master of Applied Finance programme and consulted to various Australian corporations and international banks.

Mr Das is the author of "Swap Financing" (IFR Publishing Limited/The Law Book Company Limited, 1989) and editor of "The Global Swaps Market" (IFR Publishing Limited, 1991). He has published widely on financial derivatives, corporate finance, treasury and risk management issues in professional and applied finance journals (including *Risk*, *Journal of International Securities Markets* and *Euromoney Corporate Finance*).

He has presented seminars on financial derivatives (swaps, commodity and equity swaps, and advanced financial derivatives) and treasury management/corporate finance in Europe, North America, Asia and Australia.

Mr Das holds Bachelors degrees in Commerce (Accounting, Finance and Systems) and Law from the University of New South Wales and a Masters degree in Business Administration from the Australian Graduate School of Management.

Revised Edition

SWAP & DERIVATIVE Financing

The Global Reference to Products, Pricing, Applications and Markets

Satyajit Das

With chapters by
ALLEN ALLEN & HEMSLEY
AND
KPMG PEAT MARWICK
SYDNEY LONDON NEW YORK

McGraw-Hill

New York • San Francisco • Washington, D.C.
Auckland • Bogotá • Caracas • Lisbon • London
Madrid • Mexico City • Milan • Montreal • New Delhi
San Juan • Singapore • Sydney • Tokyo • Toronto

First published in Australia by The Law Book Company Limited, Sydney Australia, 1993.

McGraw-Hill

A Division of The ***McGraw-Hill*** *Companies*

ISBN 1-55738-542-4

Designed and edited by Tricia Dearborn

Typeset in Times Roman, 10 on 11 point, by Mercier Typesetters Pty Ltd, Granville, NSW

Printed in the United States of America

BB

6 7 8 9 0

For

my parents

Aparna and Sukumar Das

and

my friend

Jade Novakovic

Preface

Origins

Swap & Derivative Financing is, effectively, the second edition of *Swap Financing*. The original edition of *Swap Financing* was published in August 1989, simultaneously, by the Law Book Company Limited in Sydney, Australia and IFR Publishing Limited, internationally.

Since its publication, *Swap Financing* has established itself as a major reference work on swap and derivative instruments globally.

The success of *Swap Financing* and a related title, *Global Swap Markets* (published in 1991 by IFR Publishing Limited), which was a collection of essays on the swap and derivatives market (which I edited) have encouraged me to embark on this second edition of the book.

The primary motivating factors behind the second edition include:

- the significant product developments in the swap and derivative markets globally;
- significant changes in the technology of swaps with the development of newer and more interesting hedging and trading techniques;
- developments in the regulatory framework governing the derivatives market; and
- the extension of derivative instrument technology to the commodity and equity markets.

In approaching the second edition, I rapidly became aware of the impossibility of grafting sections onto the existing text. Such an approach to updating in the book did not, in my view, do justice to the complexity of the more recent developments requiring inclusion in the new edition. This necessitated a major reorganisation of the book and, eventually, an almost total rewrite of significant portions of the book. In fact, the second edition preserves only about 20% of the original text material.

In part, the extensive rewriting also allowed inclusion of new material and enabled me to alter the explanation of a variety of aspects of the swap market in a manner consistent with reader comments on the first edition.

Objectives

Swap & Derivative Financing continues, like its predecessor, to be ambitious in its objectives. The book seeks to bring together all aspects of the global swap and derivatives market within a comprehensive conceptual framework. This is designed to allow the structure, economics, pricing, hedging, trading, applications and institutional aspects of these instruments to be understood in an integrated and comprehensive manner.

A number of aspects of the book should be especially noted:

- The book does not confine itself to interest rate and currency swaps. The term "swaps and derivatives" is used to describe a variety of financial exchange contracts. Like the first edition, the book covers interest rate and currency swaps, forward rate agreements (FRAs), long-term forward exchange contracts (LTFX) and caps, floors and collars. In addition, the second edition covers a wide variety of interest rate and currency derivative hybrids as well as more recent extensions of derivative technology into the commodities and equities markets as well as more recent extensions into macro-economic risk management.

- The book continues to emphasise the integrated nature of the instruments examined. The book proceeds from the premise that all derivative instruments can be decomposed into more basic components, primarily forward and option contracts, and recombined into newer instrument structures. This method of unbundling and re-bundling is seen as the key to analysing and understanding various derivative structures.
- The book is, necessarily, global in focus. Swaps and derivative instruments are viewed as an integrating component of global capital markets. While US$ transactions are used as the base currency (at least, in the generic examples), the basic concepts are applicable to *every* swap market, irrespective of currency. In addition, to emphasise the global focus of the book, it draws on examples of transactions from almost every major swap market around the world.
- The book is written from a practical point of view. Its objective is to give the reader a fundamentally complete understanding of swap and derivative instruments. The structure of the book (described below) is designed to allow readers to seek an understanding of these instruments at a level commensurate with their requirements. The book is not only for the sophisticated user but will allow individuals seeking an introduction to the swap market to obtain their required level of understanding.
- Despite its practical focus, every attempt is made to analyse the structure and practice of the market in terms of financial economics theory to enhance the reader's understanding. This reflects the fact that swap and derivative instruments are increasingly more rigorously analysed and priced, according to the dictates of financial economics, and my belief that good theory and practice are totally integrated and complementary. This mix of practical and theoretical perspectives is ultimately designed to allow the reader to apply the basic swap concept as a problem solving instrument within his or her area of interest.
- The mathematical sophistication of the book is consistent with the explanation of the concepts covered. Inevitably, certain sections require knowledge of mathematics and finance theory. However, complex mathematical explanations are minimised, as far as possible, and practical examples, designed to allow the reader to master the mathematics necessary to utilise the instruments, are included.

Swap & Derivative Financing, like the first edition, continues to be intended primarily as a practical reference work for finance professionals. This includes commercial and investment bankers, either directly involved in swap and derivative transactions or with more general corporate finance responsibilities entailing advice to clients regarding funding and/or risk management. This also includes professional finance staff such as finance directors, chief financial officers, treasurers and treasury staff with the responsibility for the financial management of organisations in both the public and private sector. The book will also be relevant to accounting, consulting, legal, strategy, taxation and technology professionals involved in supporting these industries and specialisations.

The book is relevant to both experienced swap professionals and to less experienced practitioners.

For the experienced professional, the book offers:

- a useful reference volume encompassing a wide variety of transactions and structures from different markets;

- a summary of market conventions in different currencies and information on individual swap markets;
- historical statistical information on several aspects of the swap market (such as rate and spread data) in a number of currencies;
- an analytical perspective on the functioning of various aspects of the swap market which seeks to identify the economic logic and value characteristics of a variety of transactions; and
- a review of various aspects of hedging and trading swaps and derivative instruments, including advantages and disadvantages, as well as risks, of particular approaches, which can allow individuals to review their own practices.

For the less experienced professional, particularly those entering the derivative market, the book is designed to improve his or her knowledge of these instruments. Detailed descriptions of structures, economics, pricing, hedging and trading applications of these instruments will allow the less experienced professional to improve his or her knowledge base and their consequent capacity to undertake actual transactions. The accounting, taxation, legal or documentary requirements of swap transactions are also covered, providing less experienced practitioners with a complete overview of the functioning of this particular market.

This latter aspect of the book, which is reflected in its organisation, should allow the book to provide the basis for practical "in-house" training courses, such as banking and finance executive development seminars. In addition, the book should find a place in post-graduate programmes, such as MBA courses in financial management, or in advanced undergraduate courses in corporate finance in capital markets, primarily as supplementary or recommended reading. I hope that the availability of this book will encourage universities and other educational institutions to introduce either courses or modules within existing courses dealing with these important developments in capital markets.

Organisation

The overall structure of *Swap & Derivative Financing* requires some explanation.

As noted above, the book is predicated on two principal assumptions:

- swaps and financial derivatives constitute an integrated set of financial exchange transactions; and
- the basic concepts of swap and derivative instruments are consistent across currencies, albeit with some differences.

Against this background, the book does not differentiate between swap and derivative instruments in any particular currency or different swap structure seeking rather to develop a number of unified fundamental principles relating to the instruments as a whole, prior to analysing the actual products or individual markets themselves. The structure is consistent with this objective and strategy.

Part 1, The Function of Swap and Financial Derivative Transactions, provides a basic introduction to the book. The topics covered are primarily a historical background to and the evolution of swap and derivative markets. In addition, the fundamental function of swap and derivative instruments is analysed.

Part 2, Basic Swap and Financial Derivative Instruments, describes the basic swap instruments. The basic structures and key characteristics of different types of swap instruments such as interest rate and currency swaps, long-term forward exchange contracts, forward rate agreements, and caps, floors and collars is considered. A fundamental aspect of this part is the consideration of the relationship between different types of instruments and, in particular, the integrated nature of these instruments and transactions. The concept of "financial engineering", that is, the decomposition/recomposition of swap and derivative transaction structures into equivalent instruments through the reduction of instruments into their forward and option contract equivalents, is examined in detail.

Part 3, Economics and Pricing of Swaps and Financial Derivatives, analyses the economics, pricing and valuation of swap and derivative instruments. A general unified framework for pricing derivative transactions is developed. This is followed by a discussion of the pricing and valuation of individual structures such as interest rate and currency swaps, LTFX contracts, FRAs, and caps, floors and collars. As in Part 2 the various interrelationships between the different types of instrument, in the context of pricing such transactions, is explored in detail.

Part 4, Complex Non-Generic Swap and Financial Derivative Structures, examines structural variations and extensions of the basic instruments themselves. A number of structural variations (non-generic structures, basis/floating-to-floating swaps, options on swaps and interest rate and currency linked swap hybrids) are considered as are swaps involving assets as distinct from liabilities. More recent extensions of swap and derivative instrument concepts to commodity and equity markets are also discussed.

Part 5, Applications of Swaps and Financial Derivatives, focuses on the utilisation of swaps, primarily as a means for accessing funding on a more cost-effective basis (new issue arbitrage) as well as the utilisation of these instruments to manage asset liability portfolios.

Part 6, Global Swap and Financial Derivative Markets, analyses various global swap markets in a variety of currencies. All major swap markets are considered together with separate chapters analysing the global LTFX, FRA, cap/floor markets as well as the market for commodity and equity derivatives. The focus in this part is on the institutional structure and practice in different market segments, classified by currency or instrument.

Part 7, Hedging and Management of Swaps and Financial Derivatives Portfolios, focuses on the activity of financial institutions in making markets in (referred to as warehousing and portfolio management) and hedging and trading swap transactions. The rationale and economics for this type of activity as well as its risks are considered. Portfolio risk managment techniques for interest rate and currency swaps, LTFX, FRAs and caps are analysed in detail.

Part 8, Credit Exposure in Swaps and Financial Derivatives, examines the issue of credit exposure in swap transactions including coverage of techniques for measurement and management of credit exposures in swaps and financial derivative instrument transactions in detail. The recent development of special purpose derivative vehicles is discussed.

Part 9, Regulatory Aspects of Swaps and Financial Derivatives, examines the regulation of the derivatives market including analysis of the regulation of the swap and derivative market in relation to credit risk. In addition, more recent developments, including the BIS market risk directives linking capital requirements to interest rate and currency exposures assumed, are covered.

Part 10, Operational, Control, Accounting, Taxation and Legal Aspects of Swaps and Financial Derivatives, focuses on accounting, taxation, control and documentary aspects of such transactions. Back office, settlement, procedural, systems and control aspects of swap portfolio managment are firstly considered.

This is followed by discussion of the accounting and taxation aspects of such instruments. The final chapter in this part looks at legal and documentation issues arising from swap and derivative instrument transactions.

Part 11, Future Prospects for the Global Swaps and Financial Derivatives Market, concludes the book with a discussion of anticipated future developments within the global swap market.

The approach and overall methodology of the book remains consistent with that utilised in the first edition. Each chapter includes numerous exhibits which provide either diagrammatic expositions of particular structures or statistical and graphical data on various aspects of the swap market. All major mathematical and structural concepts discussed in the text are illustrated by detailed exhibits which predominantly feature actual transaction examples and transaction "walk-throughs" with detailed step-by-step explanation of the computations entailed. These examples should allow both experienced and inexperienced professionals to follow the structuring, pricing, hedging and economics of particular types of transactions. The book also includes an extensive bibliography and a detailed index. These features are designed to allow the book to continue to function as a valuable resource volume for professionals active in swap transactions.

The book was written in the period commencing late 1991 to early 1993. Every effort was made to extensively revise drafts to make the book as current as possible as at late 1993.

Changes from first edition

As noted above, *Swap & Derivative Financing* is, effectively, the second edition of the original publication, *Swap Financing*. The principal changes between the two editions are summarised in this section.

The approach of the book, as outlined above, is substantially faithful to the original publication. However, a number of general changes have been made. The major change in this regard is the use of US$ as the principal currency. The original edition of *Swap Financing* was intended primarily for Australian audiences. However, the book was adopted globally, with sales outside Australia being greater than those in Australia. In deference to the more international audience, the principal currency utilised in this edition is US$. This is also reflected in the use of US$ LIBOR as the primary floating rate index throughout the example.

The second edition is also significantly larger than its predecessor. The second edition has 45 chapters (as against 35 in the original edition) and is more than *twice* (!) the first edition in terms of total length. This expansion is not, hopefully, as a result of self-indulgence but rather dictated by the evolution of the market and the development of various techniques which have been included in this version of the text.

The principal changes from the first edition are summarised below:

- The introductory section has been expanded and now includes the material previously covered in the section on Evolution of the Swap Market.
- Part 3, Economics and Pricing of Swaps and Financial Derivatives, has been considerably expanded in the following areas:
  - The material on financial engineering involving decomposition and re-engineering of instruments utilising basic derivative products, namely forward and option contracts, has been expanded, reflecting its increased importance in structuring instruments and pricing, valuing and trading them.

- — The chapter on Valuation and Yield Mathematics has been completely rewritten with the addition of significant new material on valuation techniques, including detailed examples of calculation of zero coupon rates and stripping of yield curves. This addition reflects increasing focus on the valuation and mathematical procedures of swap transactions.
- — Significant additional material in the pricing, hedging and trading of debt options reflecting significant theoretical developments in this area.

- Part 4, Complex Non-Generic Swap and Financial Derivative Structures, has been significantly expanded and reorganised. The reorganisation primarily consists of dividing the chapter on non-generic structures into two self-contained chapters on Non-Generic Swap Structures and Basis and Floating-to-Floating Swaps. The chapter on Option Swaps has been restructured and retitled Interest Rate and Currency Linked Financial Derivatives and covers the variety of swap hybrids which have developed. There are new chapters covering commodity derivatives and equity index derivatives, reflecting the extension of swap techniques into these markets. The existing material in relation to complex/non-generic swap structures has also been significantly updated to cover the latest developments and examples of products and transaction structures current in the market place.

  The material in relation to complex/non-generic swap structures has been expanded to cover recent developments and examples of transaction structures in the market place including coverage of:
  - — index amortising swaps;
  - — index differential swaps;
  - — capped floater swaps/ratchet floater swaps;
  - — SURF swaps;
  - — new generation of options on swap products;
  - — new interest rate and currency linked swap hybrids including currency indexed and interest rate indexed swap structures;
  - — dual currency swaps;
  - — inverse FRN swaps;
  - — the new generation of option embedded securities and derivative securitisation structures.

- Part 5, Applications of Swaps and Financial Derivatives, has been significantly modified in the following respect:
  - — The chapter on New Issue Arbitrage includes material on the evolution of arbitrage funding practices including recent developments in response to the narrower arbitrage margins now achievable.
  - — The chapter on Asset Liability Management has been significantly expanded and a new chapter on more complex techniques of asset liability management involving derivatives has been added.

  The changes, particularly the new chapter on complex techniques of asset and liability management, reflect the application of financial engineering concepts to the management of debt and asset portfolios to achieve unique risk profiles or increase the return characteristics of these portfolios.

- Part 6, Global Swap and Financial Derivative Markets, has been significantly modified and expanded. The coverage of the main swap markets, discussed in the previous edition, has been extensively reworked and brought up-to-date. In addition, new chapters on various swap markets in Europe (French francs, Spanish pesetas, Italian lira, Luxembourg/Belgian francs, Portuguese escudos, Scandinavian currencies) as well as minor Asian swap currencies have been added.

In addition, a chapter on Global Commodity and Equity Derivative Markets is included.

- Part 7, Hedging and Management of Swaps and Financial Derivatives Portfolios, has also been significantly expanded. These changes include:
  - Consideration of the economics of swap market making and swap operations generally.
  - Enhanced coverage of the risks in swap market making and, in particular, coverage of integrated portfolio and risk management approaches.
  - The material on swap portfolio risk management techniques has been expanded and now covers two chapters, rather than one. More complex risk management techniques, entailing the use of duration and PVBP/generalised cash flow approaches to risk management are covered, including detailed examples. Additional material on earnings/profit and loss attribution on swap portfolios is included. New material on repo markets, particularly from the viewpoint of financing swap hedge positions, as well as valuation techniques applicable to buying and selling swap and derivative portfolios, is included.
  - An additional chapter covering management of floating rate portfolios within swap/derivative books is included for the first time.
  - The material on FRA portfolio risk management is expanded with detailed treatment of the use of strips of interest rate futures contracts, utilising Eurodollar futures as the paradigm case, included.
  - The chapter covering management of cap/floor/collar portfolios also includes significant new material on techniques for managing and trading such risk portfolios.
- Part 8, Credit Exposure in Swaps and Financial Derivatives, is expanded and modified in the following manner:
  - The material on swap credit exposure measurement and management issues has been expanded to include new material on portfolio and netting approaches to measuring swap credit exposure and option-based approaches to credit exposure measurement.
  - Additional material on techniques for credit risk management including collateralisation and mark-to-market has been added.
  - A new chapter has been added in which the emergence of special purpose derivative vehicles such as Merrill Lynch Derivative Products is analysed in detail.
- Part 9, Regulatory Aspects of Swaps and Financial Derivatives, has been totally rewritten. The chapter on the Bank of International Settlements capital adequacy accord has been totally reworked to include a detailed analysis of the impact of these regulations on the swap market. There is coverage of the new netting arrangements approved by regulators. A new chapter addresses new regulatory proposals on market risk issued by the BIS, and the EC Capital Adequacy Directives are also covered.
- Part 10, Operational, Control, Accounting, Taxation and Legal Aspects of Swaps and Financial Derivatives, has been extensively modified.

A new chapter covering "back office" issues including settlement, procedural, information systems and control aspects of swap portfolio management has been added reflecting the growing importance of this area for financial institutions.

The chapters on accounting, taxation and legal and documentation aspects have been updated. The legal and documentary issues include coverage of the *1992 ISDA Master Interest Rate and Currency Swap Agreement* with new material of all types of derivative instrument transactions.

- Part 11, Future Prospects for the Global Swaps and Financial Derivatives Market, has been modified to reflect the developments in the swap and derivatives market and focuses on the perceived future opportunities for participants in the market for these instruments.

The Bibliography has been expanded significantly. This reflects the rapid growth in literature on the swap and derivative markets generally in the period since the first edition was published. Similarly, the Index has been updated to reflect the expanded coverage of the book.

Acknowledgments

Contrary to my initial expectations, the preparation of the second edition proved to be as complex and as time consuming a task as the preparation of the original edition of this work. A wide variety of people contributed in various ways to the completion of this undertaking. I have tried to include and acknowledge the contribution of all relevant parties and I am hopeful that no contributor is unacknowledged. However, if I have neglected to acknowledge the contribution of any individual, I can only apologise. My debt to a variety of people in connection with the preparation of the first edition of this book was acknowledged in the preface to that publication. My debt to them remains as large as ever.

In relation to the preparation of the second edition, I would like to acknowledge the support of my employers, TNT Group, in particular David Mortimer (Managing Director and Chief Executive) and Colin Green (Chief Financial Officer) who allowed me to pursue this undertaking.

I am also grateful for the various students and professionals whom I have had the opportunity to teach at various times over the last few years. Their continued questioning of my various assumptions and the capacity to provide insights have been important in assisting me to clarify and to improve my approach to the subject matter. I am also grateful to readers of the first edition who were extremely generous in their comments, which were constructive and, I hope, have assisted in improving the quality of the book.

I am grateful to KPMG Peat Marwick, in particular John Buttle, Graham Bailey, Martin McGrath and Jenny Clarke who contributed the chapters on accounting and taxation. I am also grateful to Allen Allen & Hemsley, and particularly Ian Wallace who contributed the chapter on legal and documentary aspects of swap and derivative instrument transactions.

I would like to also thank a number of organisations and individuals within those organisations who made a variety of material available without which the book would be less satisfactory. These include: Per Akerlind (SEK), Keith Amburgey (formerly ISDA, now Morgan Stanley), Nadine Badra (BNP), Alberto L Basadonna (San Paolo Finance), Rod Beckstrom (C.ATS), Rosaris Benavides (Salomon Brothers), Peter Berckelman (UBS), Andrew Best (Chase Manhatten), Debbie Birch (Wardley Limited), Rajan Brotia (Citibank), Krishnan Chandrasekhar (IFC), Peter Colvin (BA), Greg Creecy (AIG), David Curry (BA), Michael Dorf (AIG), Whitney Drayton (Bain Refco), Mark Dunstan (BGL), Ron Erdos (formerly Westpac, now BA Asia), George Francois (ISDA), Robert Gumerlock (Swiss Bank Corporation), Reto Germann (UBS), Nigel Harvey (Barclays), Pers Hartland-Swann (USIS),

Sudhir Krishnamurti (World Bank), Philip Kelly (IBJ Australia), David Johns (Nomura), Bill Jones (Reserve Bank of Australia), Graham Jones (Hambros), John Kempler (J Aron & Sons), Richard Leibovitch (J P Morgan), Michael Lindstrom (Svenska Handelsbank), Bernd Luedecke (Mitsubishi Bank), John MacCormick (BA), Greg Manning (Market Data Corporation), John Masters (Price Waterhouse), Patricia McKea (Paribas), Colin McKeith (Citibank), Peter McLady (Bain Refco), Ulrike Minde (Deutsche Bank), Lyle Minton (ISDA), Catherine Moore (Telerate), Max Morley (Westpac), Witek Petrusewicz (NatWest Capital Markets), Andrew Price (Nomura Securities), Chris Reeve (Tullet & Tokyo), Deborah Rutherford (BA), Adrienne Sartori (UBS), R D Schultze (ABN-Amro), Susan Schultze (Deutsche Bank), John Secker (Royal Bank of Canada), Michael Staveley (Swiss Bank Corporation), Mark Steele (Goldman Sachs), Leon Tatevossian (Salomon Brothers), Dilip Thadani (Salomon Brothers), Eric Warner (formerly NatWest Capital Markets), Michael Witts (Deutsche Bank), and Halya Yilmarz (Westpac).

I am also grateful to a variety of individuals who read copies of draft chapters and whose comments were extremely valuable. I would like to acknowledge my debt to Michael Dorf (AIG Financial Products), Chris Fehon and Colin McKeith (Citibank), Bernd Luedecke (Mitsubishi Bank Australia) and Bill Jones (Reserve Bank of Australia).

I am particularly grateful to a variety of capable assistants who typed the manuscript for this book at various times. In particular, I would like to thank Sharon Williams, Sandra Ingram and Judy Payne who assisted in the preparation of the manuscript for this book.

I am grateful to the publishers, the Law Book Company, in particular, Victor Kline as Consultant and Anne Marie O'Neil as Publications Manager who were extremely helpful in preparing the second edition for publication. I would also like to thank the international affiliates of the Law Book Company, IFR Publishing Limited, in particular Anne O'Brien who assisted in ensuring the international distribution of this book. As well, I would like to thank Probus Publishing (Michael Jefers and Kevin Commins) who agreed to undertake a special edition for North America. I would like to thank Gillian Armitage (who oversaw production), Mark Webster (who edited part of the book) and John Ferrier (who co-designed the cover). Special thanks to Tricia Dearborn who co-designed the cover and edited the work. Tricia undertook the extremely complex task of co-ordinating this encyclopedic work with cheerfulness and exceptional dedication as well as professionalism. Her willingness to accept innumerable changes/amendments as markets changed and her commitment to a "perfect" end product was an important factor in the end work.

Last but by no means least, my thanks go to my family for their support. This book was written and edited in time which was literally stolen from them. Special thanks go to my friend, Jade Novakovic, who endured "yet another book" and the trials, anxieties and pressures which go with it. Thanks to my parents, my mother Aparna Das and my father Sukumar Das, for their support and encouragement. Thanks also to my "extended" family, Jade's parents, Stanislav and Smiljana Novakovic, for their encouragement.

It remains only to say that any remaining errors remain my sole responsibility.

SATYAJIT DAS

Sydney
December 1993

Table of Contents

Part 5

Applications of Swaps and Financial Derivatives

Part 6

Global Swap and Financial Derivative Markets

Part 7

Hedging and Management of Swaps and Financial Derivatives Portfolios

Part 8

Credit Exposure in Swaps and Financial Derivatives

Part 9

Regulatory Aspects of Swap and Financial Derivatives

Part 10

Operational, Control, Accounting, Taxation and Legal Aspects of Swaps and Financial Derivatives

Part 11

Future Prospects for the Global Swaps and Financial Derivatives Market

List of Exhibits

Exhibit

Abbreviations

For reasons of clarity, the following abbreviations have been used throughout the text.

Currencies

US$	United States dollars	ECU	European Currency Unit
A$	Australian dollars	ATS	Austrian schillings
NZ$	New Zealand dollars	BFR	Belgian francs
C$	Canadian dollars	DKR	Danish kroner
HK$	Hong Kong dollars	FMK	Finnish markkaa
GBP	Pound sterling	LIT	Italian lire
DEM	Deutschmarks	NKR	Norwegian kroner
FFR	French francs	PTA	Spanish pesetas
SFR	Swiss francs	SKR	Swedish kronor
Dfl	Dutch guilders	S$	Singapore dollars
JPY	Japanese yen	LUF	Luxembourg francs

Instruments

CD	Certificate of Deposit
CP	Commercial Paper
FRN	Floating Rate Note

Rates

BBR	Bank Bill Rate
LIBID	London Interbank Bid Rate
LIBOR	London Interbank Offered Rate

Miscellaneous

bps	Basis points (1bps = 0.01% pa)
% pa	Percentage per annum
% pa (S/A)	Interest rate expressed as percentage per annum compounding semi-annually
% pa (A)	Interest rate expressed as percentage per annum compounding annually
IRR	Internal Rate of Return
NPV	Net Present Value
PV	Present Value
PVBP	Present Value of Basis Point
OTC	Over The Counter
ET	Exchange Traded

Swap terminology

FRA	Forward Rate Agreement
FSA	Forward Spread Agreement
LTFX	Long-Term Foreign Exchange Contract

Organisations

AIDC	Australian Investment Development Corporation
BIS	Bank for International Settlements
ISDA	International Swaps and Derivatives Association
SEK	AB Svensk Exportkredit (Swedish Export Credit Corporation)
World Bank	International Bank for Reconstruction and Development

Selected Bibliography

"A Back Door to Fixed-Rate Loan", *Business Week*, 13 December 1982, p 63.

"Aetna Takes On Swap Insurance" (1986) (May) *Euromoney* 12-13.

"African Swap New Venture for the IFC" (1991) (June) *Corporate Finance, Euromoney Publications* 8-9.

"The Age of Entitlement" (1993) (January) 6 (No 1) *Risk* 26-30.

Aggarwal, Raj, "Assessing Risks in Interest Rate Swaps: The Role of Legal and Institutional Uncertainties" (1991) (May/June) *Journal of Cash Management* 15-18.

———, "True Cost of Default" (1991) (February) *Corporate Finance, Euromoney Publications* 12-13.

Allan, Richard, Elstone, Rob, Lock, Geoff and Valentine, Tom (1990) *Foreign Exchange Management*; Sydney: Allen & Unwin.

Alldis, Robert, "A Snapshot of Exposure" (1993) (January) 6 (No 1) *Risk* 6-8.

———, "No Sin But Ignorance" (1993) (June) 6 (No 6) *Risk* 7.

———, "It's An Ill Wind" (1993) (June) 6 (No 6) *Risk* 11.

Allen, Julie A and Showers, Janet L (April 1991) *Equity Indexed Linked Derivatives—An Investor's Guide*; New York: Salomon Brothers, Bond Portfolio Analysis Group.

Anderson, Torben Juul and Hasan, Rikky (1990) *Interest Rate Risk Management*; London: IFR Publishing Ltd.

Antl, Boris, "Pricing The Hedge To Cut The Cost" (1983) (May) *Euromoney* 230-233.

——— (ed) (1983) *Swap Financing Techniques*; London: Euromoney Publications Limited.

———, "Quantifying Risk in Swap Transactions" (1984) (December) *Corporate Finance, Euromoney Publications* 19-21.

——— (ed) (1986) *Swap Finance*; London: Euromoney Publications Limited, Volumes 1 and 2.

——— (ed) (1987) *Swap Finance Update Service*; London: Euromoney Publications Limited.

——— (1988) *Management of Interest Rate Risk*; London, England: Euromoney Publications.

——— (1989) *Management of Currency Risk—Volumes 1 & 2*; London, England: Euromoney Publications.

———, "All Kinds of Bells and Whistles" (August 1989) *Euromoney* 80-88.

Arak, Marcell, Estrella, Arturo, Goodman, Lawrie and Silver, Andrew, "Interest Rate Swaps: An Alternative Explanation" (1988) (No 2) *Financial Management* 12.

(1983) *Arbitrage Techniques*; London: The London International Financial Futures Exchange.

Armstrong, Robert and Sarwal, Arun, "Performing Or Not?" (1989) (October) 2 (No 9) *Risk* 23-27.

Arnold, Tanya S, "How to Do Interest Rate Swaps" (1984) (September-October) *Harvard Business Review* 96-101.

Asay, Michael R, "A Note on the Design of Commodity Option Contracts" (1982) 2 (No 1) *Journal of Futures Markets* 1-7.

———, "A Note on the Design of Commodity Option Contracts: A Reply" (1983) 3 (No 3) *Journal of Futures Markets* 335-338.

——— and Edelsburg, Charles, "Can a Dynamic Strategy Replicate the Return of an Option" (1986) 6 (No 1) *Journal of Futures Markets* 63-70.

"Asset Swap—How Denmark Dog Won Its Stars and Stripes" (1987) (December) *Corporate Finance, Euromoney Publications* 57.

"Asset Swap—The New Global Synthesis" (1986) (No 647, 8 November) *International Financing Review* 3314.

(1992) *The Australian Guide to Completion of AFMA/ISDA Standard Documentation*; Sydney, Australia: Australian Financial Markets Association.

Australian Securities Commission (July 1993) *Draft Report on Over-The-Counter Derivatives Markets.*

"Australian Swap—The Light Through the Window" (1986) (December) *Corporate Finance, Euromoney Publications* 18-19.

Baldoni, Robert, "Evolving Into a Service-Centre Treasury" (1993) (March) *Corporate Finance, Euromoney Publications* 15-17.

Balducci, Vince, Doraiswami, Johnson, Cal and Showers, Janet (September 1990) *Currency Swaps: Corporate Applications and Pricing Methodology*; New York: Salomon Brothers.

Ball, Colin and Ireland, Louise, "Swap Unwinds: What Are They Worth?" *Corporate Finance, Euromoney Publications* 15-17.

Banham, Russ, "On Bermuda's Horizon, 'Acts of God' Bonds" (1993) (September) *Global Finance* 82-86.

Bank of America, "Engineering Solutions to Financial Risk" (Sponsorship Statement) (1993) (March) *Global Finance* 21-25.

Bank of International Settlements, "Derivative Financial Instruments And Banks' Involvement in Selected Off-Balance-Sheet Business" (1992) (Autumn) 6 *Journal of International Securities Market* 279-292.

Bankers Trust Company, "The International Swap Market" (1985) (September) *Euromoney,* Specially Sponsored Supplement.

Bansal, Vipul K, Bicksler, James L, Chen, Andrew H, Marshall, John F, "Gains from Synthetic Financing with Interest Rate Swaps: Fact or Fancy?" (1993) (Fall) 6 (No 3) *Journal of Applied Corporate Finance* 91-94.

Bardwell, Tim and Ireland, Louise, "Swaps Checklist" (1988) (May) *Corporate Finance, Euromoney Publications* 21-25.

Barnaud, Frederic and Dabouineau, Jean, "Past Correction" (1992) (September) 5 (No 8) *Risk* 108-111.

Barrat, John, Moore, Gerald and Wilmott, Paul, "Inelegant Efficiency" (1992) (October) 5 (No 9) *Risk* 82-84.

Bartko, Peter, "BIS Plugs The Holes In Netting" (1991) (May) *Euromoney* 101-102.

Basle Supervisors Committee, "Proposals for International Convergence of Capital Measurement and Capital Standards".

Bates, "Documenting the Withholding Tax Risk in Swaps" (1988) *Journal of International Banking and Financial Law* 453.

Beckstrom, Rod, "Visual Magnitude" (1991) (October) 4 (No 9) *Risk* 25-27.

Beenstock, Michael, "The Robustness of the Black-Scholes Option Pricing Model" (1981) (July) 61 *The Investment Analyst* 12-19.

Beidelman, Carl R (1985) *Financial Swaps: New Strategies in Currency and Coupon Risk Management*; Homewood, Illinois: Dow Jones-Irwin.

——— (ed) (1990) *Interest Rate Swaps*; Homewood, Illinois: Business One Irwin.

——— (ed) (1991) *Cross Currency Swaps*; Homewood, Illinois: Business One Irwin.

———, Hilley, J L and Greenleaf, J A, "Alternatives in Hedging Long-Date Contractual Foreign Exchange Exposure" (1983) (Summer) *Sloan Management Review* 45-54.

Bennet, Rosemary, "Rocket Scientists Produce a Fresh Wave of Solutions" (1993) (March) *Euromoney* 46-54.

———, "Goldman Revisits The Triple-A Club" (1993) (November) *Euromoney* 12-14.

———, "Revenge of The Nerds" (1993) (December) *Euromoney* 22-24.

Bentley, Greg, "Mitigating Circumstances" (1989) (June) 2 (No 6) *Risk* 44-45.

Berg, Anthony, "The Safety In Numbers" (1992) (September) 5 (No 8) *Risk* 6.

"Beware of LIBOR in Arrears" (1988) 1 (No 5) *Risk* 2.

Bicksler, James and Chen, Andrew H, "An Economic Analysis of Interest Rate Swaps" (1986) (3 July) *Journal of Finance* 645-655.

Bierwag, Gerald O (1987) *Duration Analysis—Managing Interest Rate Risk*; Cambridge, Massachusetts: Ballinger Publishing Company.

———, Kaufman, George G and Toers, Alder, "Duration: Its Development and Use in Bond Portfolio Management" (1983) (July-August) *Financial Analysis Journal* 15-34.

"Big Leap in Canadian Dollar Market" (1986) (July) *Corporate Finance, Euromoney Publications* 44-45.

Binks, Tom, "Caps and Collars" (1984) (December) *Corporate Finance, Euromoney Publications* 29.

Black, Fischer, "The Pricing of Commodity Contracts" (1976) (March) 3 *Journal of Financial Economics* 167-179.

———, "The Holes in Black-Scholes" (1988) (March) 1 (No 4) *Risk*.

———, "How We Came Up With The Option Formula" (1989) (Winter) *Journal of Portfolio Management* 4-8.

———, "How to Use the Holes in Black-Scholes" (1989) 1 (No 4) *Continental Bank Journal of Applied Corporate Finance* 59.

———, "Living Up To The Model" (1990) (March) 3 (No 3) *Risk* 11-13k.

———, Derman, E, and Toy, W, "A One Factor Model of Interest Rates And Its Application To Treasury Bond Options" (1990) 46 (No 1) *Financial Analysts Journal* 33-39.

———, and Scholes, Myron, "The Pricing of Options and Corporate Liabilities" (1973) 81 *Journal of Political Economy* 637.

Blake, Victoria, "Swap Deal Closeouts" (1984) (December) *Corporate Finance, Euromoney Publications* 29.

Blitz, Stephen (3 June, 1987) *The Participating Interest Rate Agreement (PART): A New Tool For Liability Management*; New York: Salomon Brothers.

Bookstaber, Richard (1985) *The Complete Investment Book—Trading Stocks, Bonds, and Options with Computer Applications*; Glenview, Illinois: Scott, Foresman and Company.

———, Jacob, David P and Langsam, Joseph A (February 1986) *Pitfalls in Debt Option Models*; New York: Morgan Stanley.

Bowden, Roger, "It Lives" (1993) 6 (No 8) *Risk* 41-44.

Bowe, Michael (1988) *Eurobonds*; Homewood, Illinois: Dow Jones-Irwin.

Boyle, Phelim P, "Options: A Monte Carlo Approach" (1977) (May) 4 *Journal of Financial Economics* 323-338.

——— and Turnbull, Stuart M, "Pricing and Hedging Capped Options" (1989) 9 (No 14) *Journal Of Futures Markets* 41-54.

Brady, Simon, "Commodity Financiers Sharpen Up" (1989) (August) *Euromoney* 38-44.

———, "Dressing Up, Without A Killing" (1990) (April) *Euromoney* 77-80.

———, "How To Tailor Your Assets" (1990) (April) *Euromoney* 83-89.

———, "Time Runs Out For Low Rated Swappers" (1991) (February) *Euromoney* 9-10.

———, "Investors Get Into Embeddos" (1991) (July) *Supplement to Euromoney* 3-20.

———, "Riding The US Yield Curve" (1992) (April) *Euromoney* 12-14.

———, "The Ref Gets Rough" (1992) (April) *Euromoney* 25-30.

———, "Emerging Markets: Developing Derivatives" (1992) (June) *Euromoney* 16.

———, "Derivatives Sprout Bells And Whistles" (1992) (August) *Euromoney* 29-39.

——— and Murphy, Simon, "Exotic Cures for Currency Headaches" (1993) (October) *Corporate Finance, Euromoney Publications* 18-21.

Bralver, Charles and Kuritzkes, Andrew, "Risk Adjusted Performance Measurement in the Trading Room" (1993) (Fall) 6 (No 3) *Journal of Applied Corporate Finance* 104-108.

Brauer, Greggory A and Ravichandran, "How Sweet Is Silver" (1986) (Summer) *Journal Of Portfolio Management* 33-42.

Brodeur, Brian J, "Rate Swaps or Caps" (1985) (May) *Intermarket* 19-23.

Brookes, Martin, "The Search for a Better Model of Volatility" (1993) (March) *Euromoney* 55-56.

Brown, J, Dickson and Linegar, C, "Interest Rate and Currency Swaps in Company Financing" (1983) (January) *Rydge's* 100-102.

Brown, Keith C, "Forward Swaps, Swap Options, and The Management of Callable Debt" (1990) (Winter) *Journal of Applied Corporate Finance* 59-71.

Brown, Richard, "FRAs Move Into Market As Hedging Alternative" (1985) (January) *Corporate Finance, Euromoney Publications* 24.

Brown, Robert L (1986) *Some Simple Condition For Determining Swap Feasibility*, Working Paper No 27, Department of Accounting and Finance, Monash University.

Buchmiller, Jack, "Diversifying Interest Rate Indices With Basis Swaps" (1992) (August) *Corporate Finance, Euromoney Publications* 41-43.

———, "Segmenting The Yield Curve" (1992) (September) *Corporate Finance, Euromoney Publications* 37-39.

———, "Using Swaptions In A Low-Rate Environment" (1992) (October) *Corporate Finance, Euromoney Publications* 40-42.

———, "Floating Rate Strategies For Callable Debt" (1992) (November) *Corporate Finance, Euromoney Publications* 38-40.

———, "Fixed or Floating: Which is Cheaper?" (1993) (January) *Corporate Finance, Euromoney Publications* 13-15.

———, "Stripping Options from Callable Debt" (1993) (February) *Corporate Finance, Euromoney Publications* 11-13.

———, "Strategies for a Flattening Yield Curve" (1993) (April) *Corporate Finance, Euromoney Publications* 13-15.

———, "Managing The Effective Cost Of Debt" (1993) (May) *Corporate Finance, Euromoney Publications* 14-16.

———, "The 24 Commandments of the G-30" (1993) (September) *Corporate Finance, Euromoney Publications* 37-42.

Budd, Nicholas, "A Future Role For Commodity-Linked Securities" (1982) (November) *The Banker* 49-57.

———, "The Future Of Commodity Indexed Financing" (1983) (July-August) *Harvard Business Review* 44-46.

Burkett, Shannon, "Tightening Up on Swap Credit Risk" (1989) (March) *Corporate Finance, Euromoney Publications* 35.

Byrd, John and Zwirlein, Tom, "Environmental Protection and Forward Contracts: A Note on the New Sulfur Dioxide Emission Allowances" (1993) (Fall) 6 (No 3) *Journal of Applied Corporate Finance* 109-110.

"Calls Coming Through Loud and Clear for Kleinwort" (1987) (May) *Corporate Finance, Euromoney Publications* 22-24.

Cartledge, Peter C (1991) *A Handbook of Financial Mathematics*; London: Euromoney Publications.

Carverhill, Dr Andrew, "Interest Rate Derivative Products" (1989) (November) *The Treasurer* 39-41.

Celarier, Michelle, "The Biggest Banks in Derivatives" (1993) (August) *Global Finance* 27-34.

———, "New Catastrophe Scenarios Bedevil Derivatives" (1993) (October) *Global Finance* 60-66.

Chance, Don, "Leap into the Unknown" (1993) (May) 6 (No 5) *Risk* 60-66.

Chaplin, Geoff, "Not So Random" (1993) (February) 6 (No 2) *Risk* 56-57.

"Chase Rides The Rollers" (1991-2) (December-January) *Risk* 6-8.

Chesler-Marsh, Caren, "The Market Gets Choosy" (1990) (August) *Euromoney* 16-19.

———, "How To Play The Yield Curve" (1991) (July) *Supplement to Euromoney* 25-30.

———, "US Develops Taste For Municipal Swaps" (1991) (November) *Euromoney* 8-9.

———, "How Merrill Lynch Pitches For Top Swaps" (1991) (December) *Euromoney* 11-12.

———, "Deutsche Theorises On Credit Sensitive Swaps" (1992) (February) *Euromoney* 12.

———, "Nightmare On Wall Street" (1992) (February) *Euromoney* 23-30.

Chew, Lillian, "Warrants Fever" (1986) (May) *Corporate Finance, Euromoney Publications* 49-61.

———, "Grand Met's Costly Caps" (1988) (November) 1 (No 11) *Risk* 2-3.

———, "The Bespoke Approach" (1989) (May) 2 (No 5) *Risk* 12-14.

———, "Managing The Gap" (1989) (September) 2 (No 8) *Risk* 79-83.

———, "Enticing, But Dangerous" (1990) (April) 3 (No 4) *Risk* 31-33.

———, "Strip Mining" (1991) (February) 4 (No 2) *Risk* 20-29.

———, "Sex, Swaps and Arbitrage" (1991) (June) 4 (No 6) *Risk* 21-28.

———, "ELF and Efficiency" (1991) (October) 4 (No 9) *Risk*.

Chew, Lillian, "Now You're Talking" (1991) (October) 4 (No 9) *Risk* 92-98.
———, "A Bit Of A Jam" (1992) (September) 5 (No 8) *Risk* 82-93.
———, "Don't Worry be Happy" (1992) (December) 5 (No 11) *Risk* 8.
———, "Judgement of Salomon" (1993) (March) 6 (No 3) *Risk* 8-10.
———, "Quanto Leap" (1993) (April) 6 (No 4) *Risk* 21-28.
———, "Good, Bad and Indifferent" (1993) (June) 6 (No 6) *Risk* 30-36.
———, "Exploding The Myth" (1993) (July) 6 (No 7) *Risk* 10-12.
———, "Knowledge Transfer" (1993) (August) 6 (No 8) *Risk* 6-7.
———, "When The Snoozing Had To Stop" (1993) (August) 6 (No 9) *Risk* 72-79.
———, "Summer of Content" (1993) (October) 6 (No 10) *Risk* 28-35.
———, "Hedge of The Abyss" (1993) 6 (No 11) *Risk* 17-18.
———, Cookson, Richard, Falloon, William, Shireff, David and Westlake, Melvyn, "Five Years Of Risk" (1992) (December) 5 (No 11) *Risk* 35-56.
——— and Falloon, William, "Unpicking Haute Couture" (1992) (April) 5 (No 4) *Risk* 17-22.
Chiarella, Carl, "A Survey of Models for the Pricing of Interest Rate Derivative Securities", course presented by the School of Finance and Economics, University of Technology, Sydney, Australia (3-4 June 1992) 985.
Choie, Kenneth S and Novomestky, Frederick, "Replication of Long-Term With Short-Term Options" (1989) (Winter) *Journal of Portfolio Management* 17-19.
Clark, Ephraim, "More On Duration As a Risk Management Tool" (1988) (Spring) *Journal of International Securities Markets* 47-52.
——— and Rousseau, Patrick, "Bond Duration With Uncertain Cash Flows" (1991) (Spring) *Journal of International Securities Markets* 29-33.
Cohen, Edi, "No Overnight Solutions" (1988) (March) *The Banker* 21-29.
Cole, Joseph B (29 September, 1989) *Using Monte Carlo Methods to Price Options*; Chicago, Illinois: Drexel Burnam Lambert.
——— (11 December, 1989) *Cash Flow Management Using Asian Options*; Chicago, Illinois: Drexel Burnam Lambert.
Commins, Kevin, "The Best New Financial Products Of 1986" (1987) (January) *Intermarket* 17-24.
Cookson, Richard, "Cross Wise Companies" (1991) (September) 4 (No 8) *Risk* 4.
———, "The Only Way Is Up" (1992) (June) 5 (No 6) *Risk* 8.
———, "Models of Imperfection" (1992) (October) 5 (No 9) *Risk* 55-61.
———, "Stock Still" (1992) (November) 5 (No 10) *Risk* 27-33.
———, "Confused? You Will Be" (1992) (December) 5 (No 11) *Risk* 10.
———, "Yield Curves Bend Rules" (1993) (February) 6 (No 2) *Risk* 8-10.
———, "Dangerous Liaisons" (1993) (March) 6 (No 3) *Risk* 30-36.
———, "Stand and Deliver" (1993) (April) 6 (No 4) *Risk* 6-7.
———, "Marriage On The Rebound" (1993) (April) 6 (No 4) *Risk* 11.
———, "Rule Italia" (1993) (June) 6 (No 6) *Risk* 47-50.
———, "Britannia Waives The Rules" (1993) (September) 6 (No 9) *Risk* 7.
———, "Moving In The Right Direction" (1993) (October) 6 (No 10) *Risk* 22-26.
——— and Alldis, Robert, "Unfolding The Withholding" (1993) (July) 6 (No 7) *Risk* 12-13.
——— and Chew, Lillian, "Things Fall Apart" (1992) (October) 5 (No 9) *Risk* 44-53.
Cooper, Dale F and Watson, Ian R, "How to Assess Credit Risks in Swaps" (1987) (February) *The Banker* 28-31.
Cooper, Graham, "Margins Made Manageable" (1993) (September) 6 (No 9) *Risk* 10-13.
———, "Special FX" (1993) (October) 6 (No 10) *Risk* 42-48.
———, "Blossom Time" (1993) 6 (No 11) *Risk* 22-26.
———, ". . . And the One That Won't Stop" (1993) (December) *Risk* 8-10.
———, "All the Hits and More" (1993) (December) *Risk* 12-13.
Cooper, Martin, "Exploring Differential Swaps" (December 1991) *Treasury Management, Euromoney Publications* 15.
Cooper, Ron, "Swap Houses Switch to New Values" (1987) (January) *Euromoney* 32-33.
———, "Still Plenty of Room to Grow" (1988) (October) *Euromoney* 35.
———, "They're Teaching the Old Swap New Tricks" (1989) (April) *Euromoney* 43-52.

Coopers & Lybrands (1992) *Swap Series 1: Interest Rate Swaps*; IFR Publishing Limited: London.

Coopers & Lybrands (1993) *Swap Series 1: Currency Swaps*; IFR Publishing Limited: London.

Copeland, Thomas E and Weston, Fred J (1983) *Financial Theory and Corporate Policy* (2nd ed); Reading Massachusetts: Addison-Wesley Publishing Company.

Cornish, Martin, Mercer, Vincent and Thomas, Simon, "Quote, Unquote" (1992) (November) 5 (No 10) *Risk* 33-37.

Cornwall, John and Price, John, "The Wise, For Cure, On Exercise Depend" (1989) (October) 2 (No 9) *Risk* 10-14.

"Corporate Speculators' Loophole—or Noose?" (1987) (November) *Corporate Finance, Euromoney Publications* 17-18.

"Council Swaps Grab the Headlines" (1989) (April) *Corporate Finance, Euromoney Publications* 14-16.

Cox, John C, Ross, Stephen C and Rubinstein, "Option Pricing: A Simplified Approach" (1979) (September) 7 *Journal of Financial Economics* 229-263.

Cox, John C and Rubinstein, Mark (1985) *Option Markets*; Englewood Cliffs, New Jersey: Prentice-Hall Inc.

Crable, Matthew, "Clearing House for Swaps" (1986) (September) *Euromoney* 345-351.

Crapp, Harvey R and Marshall, John (1986) *Money Market Maths*; Sydney: Allen and Unwin.

Credit Suisse Financial Products, "Sponsorship Statement—Derivative Products In The 1990s" (1991) (July) *Supplement to Euromoney* 11-18.

Cunningham, Michael M (1987) *Selected Analysis Of Recently Issued Index-Linked And Option Embedded Securities*; unpublished research paper presented to course on *Swap Financing*, Centre for Studies in Money, Banking and Finance, Macquarie University.

Cunningham and Rogers, "The Status of Swap Agreements in Bankruptcy" in *Interest Rate and Currency Swaps 1987* (Practicing Law Institute, Corporate Practice Handbook No 564, 1987), p 417.

(1986), *Currency and Interest Rate Swaps*; New York: Merrill Lynch Capital Markets.

(1987), *Currency and Interest Rate Swaps: Accounting, Tax and Control Considerations*; Sydney, Australia: Peat, Marwick, Mitchell & Co.

Curry, "Bend The Rate With A Flexible Swap" (1991) (June) *Corporate Finance, Euromoney Publications* 48.

Dahl, Henrik, "Profile Matching" (1990) (November) 3 (No 10) *Risk* 35-39.

"The Dangers Of Neutrality" (1991) (November) 4 (No 10) *Risk* 48-49.

Danker, Stella, "Swapping Speculation For Sophistication" (1988) (November) 1 (No 11) *Risk* 32-33.

Das, Satyajit, "Interest Rate Swaps" (1983) (No 1) *JASSA* 10-13.

———, "Interest Rate Swaps" (1983-1984) (No 1) *Bulletin of Money, Banking and Finance* 1-40.

———, "Options on Debt Instruments for Australian Corporate Treasurers Parts 1 and 2" (1985) 99 (No 4) *The Australian Banker* 147-155 and (1985) 99 (No 5) 194-201.

———, "Options on Debt Instruments for Australian Investment Managers" (1985) (No 1) Journal of the Securities Institute of Australia 3-12.

———, "The Evolution of Swap Financing as an Instrument of International Finance" (1985-1986) (No 2) *Bulletin of Money, Banking and Finance* 1-68.

———, "Swaps as an Instrument for Asset/Liability Management" (1986) *The Australian Corporate Treasurer* (August) 8-11 and (October) 8-12.

———, "Granting Options: The Risk Management Process" (1987) 4 *Bulletin of Money, Banking and Finance* 1-77.

———, "Utilising Swaps as an Instrument for Dynamic Asset-Liability Management" (1987) 101 (No 2) *The Australian Banker* 63-68 and (1987) 101 (No 3) 108-114.

———, "Swap Arbitrages: An Analysis of the Economic Gains in Interest Rate and Currency Swaps" (1988) 1 *Bulletin of Money, Banking and Finance* 1-55.

———, "Option Swaps: Securitising Options Embedded in Securities Issues" (1988) (Summer) *Journal of International Securities Market* 117-138.

Das, Satyajit, (1989) *Swap Financing*; Sydney, Australia: Law Book Company; London: IFR Publishing Limited.

———, "Swap Strategies in the New Climate" (1989) (August) *Corporate Finance, Euromoney Publications* 12-13.

———, "Oil and Commodity Swaps" (Autumn 1990) 4 *Journal of International Securities Markets* 227-250.

———, "Equity Swaps and Related Derivatives" (1992) (Winter) 6 *Journal of International Securities Markets* 349-370.

———, "Differential Strip Down" (1992) (June) 5 (No 6) *Risk* 65-72.

———, "Differential Operators" (1992) (July-August) 5 (No 7) *Risk* 51-53.

———, "The Maturing of the Swaps Market" (1993) (January) *Corporate Finance, Euromoney Publications* 41-46.

———, "Forward March!" (1993) (February) 6 (No 2) *Risk* 41-49.

———, "The Futures of the Swaps Market" (1993) (February) *Corporate Finance, Euromoney Publications* 41-44.

———, "Operational Aspects of Swaps" (1993) (July) *Corporate Finance, Euromoney Publications* 39-43.

———, "Control Systems in Swaps" (1993) (August) *Corporate Finance, Euromoney Publications* 33-37.

——— (ed) (1991) *Global Swap Markets*; London: IFR Publishing Limited.

——— and Ferris, David, "Innovations in Bond Portfolio Management" (1983-1984) 164 *Bulletin of Money, Banking and Finance* 17-74.

——— and Martin, John, "The Gain in Spain" (1991) (June) 4 (No 6) *Risk* 12-16.

——— and Martin, John, "Protective Strategies" (1991) (September) 4 (No 8) *Risk* 93-97.

——— and Martin, John, "The Cost of Quality" (1991) (November) 5 (No 10) *Risk* 56-57.

Daugaard, Daniel (1991) *The Swaps Handbook*; Sydney, Australia: Financial Training and Analysis Services Pty Ltd.

———, "What Drives Swap Spreads?" (1992) 1 *Applied Finance Bulletin* 52-68.

——— and Jarrat, John D, "Dynamic Option Portfolio Management" (1990) 1 *Applied Finance Bulletin* 28-56.

Davidson, Clive, "Bunny Money" (1993) (December) *Risk* 46-49.

De Groen, David and Valentine, Tom, "Duration" (1990) 1 *Applied Finance Bulletin* 1-27.

Decovny, Sherree and Tacchi, Christine, (1991) *Hedging Strategies*; Cambridge: Woodhead-Faulkner.

Dembo, Ron and Rissin, Dan, "French Dressing" (1991) (November) 4 (No 10) *Risk* 55-61.

"Denmark TOPS Libor . . ." (1987) (March) *Corporate Finance, Euromoney Publications* 16-20.

(1993) (May) *Derivatives*, Supplement to May 1993 Edition of *Corporate Finance, Euromoney Publications*: London.

(1992) *The Derivatives Handbook*; New York: Global Finance.

"Derivatives Instruments: BIS And The Lawyers Further The Netting Cause" (17 November 1990) (Issue 853) *International Financing Review* 78.

"Derivatives Instruments: Merrill Sets Up Triple A-Rated Derivatives Unit" (16 November 1991) (Issue 904) *International Financing Review* 75-76.

(1991) *Derivatives: The Markets Mature* (Supplement to July 1991 Issue of Euromoney); London: Euromoney Publications.

(1993) *Derivatives: Principles and Practices*, Global Derivatives Study Group; Group of Thirty: Washington, DC.

Dew, James Kurt, "The Case For Interest Rate Swap Futures" (1987) (Winter) 1 *Journal of International Securities Markets* 149-155.

Dewynne, Jeff and Wilmott, Paul, "Partial To The Exotic" (1993) (March) 6 (No 1) *Risk* 38-46.

Dickens, Paul, "Fast Forward with FRAs" (1988) (April) *Corporate Finance* 27.

(1992) *Dictionary of Derivatives* (Supplement to June 1992 Issue of Euromoney); London: Euromoney Publications.

Discepolo, Alfred J and Burchett, Shannon B, "The Long Hedge is Here to Stay" (1984) (March) *Euromoney* 195-196.

Dolde, Walter, "The Trajectory of Corporate Financial Risk Management" (1993) (Fall) 6 (No 3) *Journal of Applied Corporate Finance* 35-41.
"Dollar Diplomacy" (1993) (February) 6 (No 2) *Risk* 23-25.
"Dollar Seekers Forsake Aussie for the Kiwi Route" (1987) (October) *Corporate Finance, Euromoney Publications* 22-25.
Duffy, Maureen, "Formidable Union" (1993) (February) 6 (No 2) *Risk* 66-68.
______, "Tower Systems" (1993) (April) 6 (No 4) *Risk* 18-19.
______, "Risque Business" (1993) (April) 6 (No 4) *Risk* 50-54.
______, "Blind Data" (1993) (June) 6 (No 6) *Risk* 61-62.
______, "Making Ends Meet" (1993) (July) 6 (No 7) *Risk* 34-38.
Dupire, Bruno, "Model Art" (1993) (September) 6 (No 9) *Risk* 44-49.
Dyer, Geoff, "The Polymaths of the Dealing Room" (1994) (January) *Euromoney* 65-68.
Dyer, Lawrence J and Jacob, David P, "A Practitioner's Guide To Fixed-Income Option Models" (1989) (Spring) *Journal of International Securities Markets* 23-48.
Eisenberg, Larry, "Somebody Else's Money" (1993) 6 (No 8) *Risk* 44-49.
______, "One Step Beyond" (1993) 6 (No 11) *Risk* 60-68.
"Engineering Swaps" (1986) (April) *Corporate Finance, Euromoney Publications* 25-34.
"Equity Linked Rules" (1992) (April) 5 (No 4) *Risk* 25-29.
"Equity Swaps and OTC Derivatives" (11 September 1991) Conference arranged by *Risk* Magazine, London.
Euro-Financing and Capital Markets, Conference organised by ITR Pty Ltd, 13 and 14 August 1986, Sheraton-Wentworth Hotel, Sydney.
"*Euromoney* 1990 Swaps Poll" (1990) (September) *Euromoney* 251-260.
"*Euromoney* 1991 Poll Liability Management" (1991) (September) *Euromoney* 123-126.
Evans, Ellen and Parente, Gloria M (1987), *What Drives Interest Rate Swap Spreads;* New York: Salomon Brothers Inc Bond Market Research.
Evans, Garry, "Lawyers Warn on Void Swap Deals" (1992) (April) *Euromoney* 14.
______, "Westpac Breaks Sovereign Ceiling" (1994) (January) *Euromoney* 14.
(1986), *The Explosive Growth of the Yen/Dollar Swap Market;* London: Nomura International Limited.
"FDIC Tells Swap Dealers Failed Banks' Swaps Would Likely Be Honored" (1989) 52 *Banking Report (BNA)* 320.
Fabozzi, Frank J, (1989) *The International Investor Focus on Investment Management;* Cambridge, Massachusetts; Ballinger Publishing Company.
______ and Pollack, Irving M (1983) *The Handbook of Fixed Income Securities;* Homewood, Illinois: Dow Jones-Irwin.
______ and Pollack, Irving M (1987) *The Handbook of Fixed Income Securities—Second Edition;* Homewood, Illinois: Dow Jones-Irwin.
Fall, William, "Caps versus Swaps versus Hybrids" (1988) 1 (No 5) *Risk* 21.
______, "Taking Off-Balance Sheet Products Into Account" (1989) (April) *Institutional Investor* 96-97.
Faloon, William, "The Corporate Problem Solver" (1987) (March) *Intermarket* 23-58.
______, "Will New Requirements Strangle Swaps?" (1987) (July) *Intermarket* 10-14.
______, "Curves and The Fuller Figure" (1992) (May) 5 (No 5) *Risk* 19-25.
______, "Texas Parries" (1992) (September) 5 (No 8) *Risk* 105-106
______, "International Rescue" (1992) (October) 5 (No 9) *Risk* 84-85.
______, "Better To Have Loved And Lost" (1992) (November) 5 (No 10) *Risk* 5.
______, "Marginal Improvements" (1992) (November) 5 (No 10) *Risk* 57-58.
______, "The Tower Of Garble" (1993) (January) 6 (No 1) *Risk* 58-63.
______, "Primary Colours" (1993) (February) 6 (No 2) *Risk* 33-39.
______, "Virtual Realty" (1993) (March) 6 (No 3) *Risk* 7-8.
______, "Close Encounters" (1993) (March) 6 (No 3) *Risk* 10-12.
______, "Do Not Pass Go" (1993) (April) 6 (No 4) *Risk* 8-10
______, "Crude Ambition" (1993) (May) 6 (No 5) *Risk* 7-8.
______, "Savings Grace" (1993) (May) 6 (No 5) *Risk* 8-11.
______, "Court In The Act" (1993) (May) 6 (No 5) *Risk* 23-27.
______, "Built On Sand" (1993) (May) 6 (No 5) *Risk* 43-49.
______, "Burnt Offerings" (1993) (June) 6 (No 6) *Risk* 11.

Falloon, William, "Fannie Foils IRS" (1993) (July) 6 (No 7) *Risk* 6-7.
———, "Golden Horizons" (1993) (July) 6 (No 7) *Risk* 24-25.
———, "Forex in Disneyland" (1993) (July) 6 (No 7) *Risk* 27-29.
———, "A Wealth of Stealth" (1993) (July) 6 (No 7) *Risk* 29-33.
———, "Hot Property" (1993) (August) 6 (No 8) *Risk* 8-10.
———, "Great Mines Think Alike" (1993) (September) 6 (No 9) *Risk* 114-116.
———, "Steady As She Goes" (1993) (October) 6 (No 10) *Risk* 17-20.
———, "Taxpayers One, Taxman Nil" (1993) 6 (No 11) *Risk* 13-15.
———, "Too Good To Refuse" (1993) 6 (No 11) *Risk* 29-36.
———, "Escape From The Provinces" (1993) 6 (No 11) *Risk* 57-58.
———, "Fairway to Heaven" (1993) (December) *Risk* 21-27.
——— and Chew, Lillian, "Performance and Promise" (1992) (October) 5 (No 9) *Risk* 31-41.
——— and Westlake, Melvyn, "American Excess" (1993) (March) 6 (No 3) *Risk* 25-29.
"The Fast-Moving World of the Asset Swap" (1986) (No 630, 12 July) *International Financial Review* 2043-4.
Ferron, Mark and Handjinicolaou, George, "Understanding Swap Credit Risk: The Simulation Approach" (1987) (Winter) *Journal of International Security Markets* 135-148.
Fetzer, Rodney and Janney, Den, "Zero Coupon Bond Swaps" (1984) (December) *Corporate Finance, Euromoney Publications* 24.
Figlewski, Stephen, Silber, William, L, and Subrahmanyam, Marti G (1990) *Financial Options: From Theory to Practice*; Homewood, Illinois: Business One Irwin.
(1989) *Financial Futures and Options*; London: IFR Publishing Limited.
(1982) *Financial Instruments Markets: Cash-Futures Relationships*; Chicago: Board of Trade of the City of Chicago.
"Financial Risk Measurement and Management of Derivatives" (28-29 April 1992) Conference arranged by IIR Limited, Le Meridien, London.
Finnerty, John D, "Measuring the Duration of a Floating Rate Bond" (1989) (Summer) *Journal Of Portfolio Management* 67-72.
———, "An Overview of Corporate Securities Innovation" (1992) (Winter) 4 (No 4) *Journal of Applied Corporate Finance* 23-39.
Finney, Robert, "Proceeding With A Commodity Swap" (1991) (September) *Corporate Finance, Euromoney Publications* 47-48.
Firth, Denys C, "Swaps with Warrants" (1984) (December) *Corporate Finance, Euromoney Publications* 24-25.
Fischer, Stanley, "The Demand For Index Bonds" (1975) 83 (No 3) *Journal Of Political Economy* 509-534.
Fisher III, F G (1988) *Eurobonds*; London, England: Euromoney Publications.
Fisher, Lawrence and Weil, Roman L, "Coping with the Risk of Interest Rate Fluctuations: Returns to Bondholders from Naive and Optional Strategies" (1971) 44 *Journal of Business* 418.
Fisher, Mark, "At Issue: The Interest Rate" (1993) (February) *Corporate Finance, Euromoney Publications* 29-33.
Fitzgerald, M Desmond (1983) *Financial Futures*; London, England: Euromoney Publications.
——— (1987) *Financial Options*; London: Euromoney Publications Limited.
——— (1992) *Financial Futures—Second Edition*; London, England: Euromoney Publications.
——— (1993) *Financial Futures, Second Edition*; London: Euromoney Publications.
——— and Rutterford, Janette, "Variations On A Theme" (1988) (June) 1 (No 7) *Risk* 30-31.
Flavell, Richard (1992) *Swaps*; London, England: Euromoney Publications.
Fong, Gifford, Vasicel, Oldrich and Yoo, Daihyun, "Omission Impossible" (1992) (February) 5 (No 2) *Risk* 62-65.

(1986) *Forward Rate Agreements Accounting, Tax and Control Considerations*; Sydney: Peat, Marwick, Mitchell and Co, Banking and Financial Services Group Briefing Notes.

(1986) *Forward Spread Agreements*; London: Fulton Prebon Capital Markets.

Fox, Mark, "Aspects of Barriers To International Integrated Securities Markets" (1992) (Autumn) 6 *Journal of International Securities Market* 209-218.

Frank, David, "Index Swaps Trade High Rates for Low Ones" (January 1992) *Global Finance* 18-20.

Fraser, K Michael, "Forex Derivatives Take A Wild Ride" (1992) (November) *Global Finance* 50-54.

———, "What It Takes To Excel in Exotics" (1993) (March) *Global Finance* 44-49.

(1992) *From Black-Scholes to Black Holes*; Risk Magazine Limited: London.

Frye, Jon, "Greek Alphabet Soup: A Recipe For Success" (1988) (March) 1 (No 4) *Risk* 6-9.

———, "Static Portfolio Replication" (1988) (November) 1 (No 11) *Risk* 22-23.

———, "The Real shape Of Convexity" (1990) (October) 3 (No 9) *Risk* 42-49.

———, "Underexposed And Overanxious" (1992) (March) 5 (No 3) *Risk* 41-45.

Gallant, Peter (1988) *The Eurobond Market*; Cambridge, England: Woodhead-Faulkner.

Garlock, David and Schenck, David, "Unforeseen Contingencies" (1993) (March) 6 (No 3) *Risk* 49-57.

Garman, Mark B, "The Duration Of Option Portfolios" (1985) 14 *Journal of Financial Economics* 309-315.

———, "Semper Tempus Fugit" (1989) (May) 2 (No 5) *Risk* 34-35.

———, "Charm School" (1992) (July-August) 5 (No 7) *Risk* 53-56.

———, "Spread The Load" (1992) (December) 5 (No 11) *Risk* 68, 84.

——— and Kohlhagen, Steven W, "Foreign Currency Option Values" (1983) 2 *Journal of International Money and Finance* 231-237.

Gentle, David, "Basket Weaving" (1993) (June) 6 (No 6) *Risk* 51-52.

Gerlardin, Jacques P and Swenson, David, "The Changing World of Swaps" (1983) (June) *Euromoney* 33-35.

Geske, Robert, "The Valuation of Compound Options" (1979) (March) 7 *Journal of Financial Economics* 63-81.

Giarraputo, Joseph D, "Over-the-Counter Derivatives: What the Experts Say" *Global Finance* 37-39.

"The Global Swaps Market" (1986) (June) *Corporate Finance, Euromoney Publications*, Supplement.

"Global Swaps—SEK Digs Up The Treasure Chest" (1988) (2 July) (Issue 731) *International Financing Review* 2134-6.

Gold, Michael, "Fancier Footwork By The World Bank's Derivatives Team" (1992) (November) *Global Finance* 70.

Gooch, Antony C and Klein, Linda B, "Damages Provisions in Swap Agreements" (1984) (October) *International Financial Law Review* 36.

——— (1986), *Swap Agreement Documentation*; London: Euromoney Publications Limited.

Goodhart, Will, "Spain's Hesitant Hedgers" (1992) (February) *Corporate Finance, Euromoney Publications* 29-32.

———, "When an Equity Derivative Becomes Applicable" (1992) (June) *Corporate Finance, Euromoney Publications* 13-16.

———, "Help In Hedging Balance Sheet Exposure" (1992) (November) *Corporate Finance, Euromoney Publications* 15-17.

Goodman, Laurie S, "Put-Call Parity With Coupon Instruments" (1985) (Winter) *Journal of Portfolio Management* 59-60.

———, "The Use of Interest Rate Swaps in Managing Corporate Liabilities" (1987) (Winter) *Journal of Applied Corporate Finance* 35-47.

Grabbe, J Orlin, "The Pricing of Call and Put Options on Foreign Exchange" (1983) (December) 2 *Journal of International Money and Finance* 239-253.

——— (1986) *International Financial Markets*; Holland: Elsevier Science Publishing Co, Inc.

"Grand Met Caps The Bill For Pillsbury" (1988) (November) *Corporate Finance, Euromoney Publications* 10-11.

Grannan, Lawrence and Levine, Matthew, "Rolling Your Own" (1989) (February) 2 (No 2) *Risk* 29-31.

Grant, Charles, "Why Treasurers are Swapping Swaps" (1985) (April) *Euromoney* 19-30.

———, "Can Caps Beat Swaps" (1985) (July) *Euromoney* 12-14.

Gray, Gavin, "Swaps Market Stalls" (1990) (December) *Corporate Finance, Euromoney Publications* 13-18.

———, "Growing Pains Of Commodity Swaps" (1991) (March) *Corporate Finance, Euromoney Publications* 9-13.

———, "Timing The Swap As Rates Peak" (1991) (April) *Corporate Finance, Euromoney Publications* 11-13.

———, "Seeking Solutions to Swap Counterparty Credit Risk" (1992) (January) *Corporate Finance, Euromoney Publications* 11-13.

———, "Swap Market Overcome by Optimism" (1992) (February) *Corporate Finance, Euromoney Publications* 21-24.

Gray, R W, Kurz, W C F and Strupp, C N, "Structuring And Documenting Interest Rate Swaps" (1982) (October) *International Financial Law Review* 14-18.

"The Great Derivatives Debate: Should There Be More Regulation?" A Risk/C.ATS Software Symposium at The Hilton, Park Lane, London, England on 1-2 December 1992.

Greenwich Associates, "Risk Management In Europe" (1992) (Autumn) 6 *Journal of International Securities Market* 261-278.

Grobel, Ronald A (September 1987) *Understanding The Duration Of Floating Rate Notes*; New York: Salomon Brothers Inc.

Gumerlock, Robert, "Applying Empirical Techniques to the Measurement of Swap Credit Risk" (1993) (Spring/Summer) 7 *Journal of International Securities Markets* 29-36.

———, "Double Trouble" (1993) (September) 6 (No 9) *Risk* 88-91.

Guth, Michael A S, "Exercise By Numbers" (1992) (February) 5 (No 2) *Risk* 33-37.

Hagger, Euan, "Making The Most Of Wide Spread Assets" (1993) (April) *Euromoney* 79-83.

Haghani, Victor J (4 April 1986) *Foreign Exchange Annuity Swaps*; New York: Salomon Brothers Inc.

——— and Stavis, Robert M (1986) *Interest Rate Caps and Floors: Tools for Asset Liability Management*; New York: Salomon Brothers Inc, Bond Portfolio Analysis Group.

Haider, Said N (16 January, 1989) *Understanding Duration And Convexity*; Chicago, Illinois: Drexel Burnham Lambert.

Hampton, Michael and Baker, Robin, "Spread The Load" (1991) (September) 4 (No 8) *Risk* 87-89.

Hanna, J, Britain, R and Parente, G M (1983) *The Case for Currency-Hedged Bonds*; New York: Salomon Brothers Inc, Bond Market Research.

Harrington, Henry, "The Wait Of Money" (1993) 6 (No 11) *Risk* 46-50.

Harris, Stephen, "Gulf Crisis Throws Spotlight On Jet Fuel Hedging" (1990) (September) *Airfinance Journal* 66-72.

Heath, D, Jarrow, R and Morton, A, "Contingent Claim Valuation With A Random Evolution Of Interest Rates" (1991) *Review of Futures Markets* 54-76.

———, "Bond Pricing And The Term Structure Of Interest Rates: A New Methodology For Contingent Claims Valuation" (1992) 60 (No 1) *Econometrica* 77-105.

———, "Easier Done Than Said" (1992) (October) 5 (No 9) *Risk* 77-80.

Hecht, Liz, "Dual Currency Dual Swaps in the Swiss Franc Market" (1985) (April) *Corporate Finance, Euromoney Publications* 13-14.

Henderson, John, "How to Create an Interest Rate Cap" (1985) (May) *Euromoney* 63-64.

Henderson, Schuyler K, "Termination Of Swaps Under US Insolvency Laws" (1984) (December) *International Financial Law Review* 17-21.

———, "The Constraints On Trading Swaps" (1985) (May) *Euromoney* 63-64.

———, "Exposure of Swaps and Termination Provisions of Swap Agreements" in Antl, Boris (ed) (1986) *Swap Finance*; London: Euromoney Publications Limited, Vol 2, p 125.

Henderson, Schuyler K, "Should Swap Termination Payments Be One Way Or Two Way" (1990) (October) *International Financial Law Review* 27-32.

——— and Klein, Linda B, "A User's Guide To ISDA Master Swap Agreements" (1987) (Autumn) *Journal of International Securities Markets* 41-45.

———, "Swap Credit Risk: A Multi-Perspective Analysis" (1989) 44 *Business Law* 365.

Heston, J Clark, "Land of Prudent Men" (1990-91) (December-January) 4 (No 1) *Risk* 17-23.

Hilley, J L, Beidleman, C R and Greenleaf, J A, "Does Covered Interest Arbitrage Dominate in Foreign Exchange Markets?" (1979) (Winter) *Columbia Journal of World Business* 99-107.

———, "Why There is 'No Long' Forward Market in Foreign Exchange" (1981) (January) *Euromoney* 94-103.

Ho, Richard, "Derivative Uses in Investment Management: Upside-Downside" *International Bond Investor* 6-1.

Ho, T S Y and Lee, S B, "Term Structure Movements And Pricing Interest Rate Contingent Claims" (1986) 41 (No 5) *Journal of Finance* 1011-29.

Hogan, Michael and Breidbart, Seth, "The Long-Term Behavior of Interest Rates and Option Pricing" (1990) (Spring) *Journal of International Securities Markets* 49-56.

Houghton, "Regulatory Provision on Off-Balance Sheet Capital Requirements: Netting Off Agreements—The Legal Perspective" (1987) 4 *Journal of International Banking Law* 241.

"How Big Swappers Can Offset Credit Risk" (1988) (No 2) *Risk* 50-51.

"How to Manage Exposures with Swaptions" (1986) (January) *Corporate Finance, Euromoney Publications* 51-52.

"How to Use the Global Swap Market" (1987) (January) *Corporate Finance, Euromoney Publications*, Supplement.

Hu, Henry, "Swaps: The Modern Process of Financial Innovation and the Vulnerability of a Regulatory Paradigm" (1989) (December) 138 *University of Pennsylvania Law Review* 333-435.

———, "Misunderstood Derivatives: The Causes of Informational Failure and the Promise of Regulatory Incrementalism" (1993) (April) 102 *Yale Law Journal* 1457-1513.

Hudson, Mike, "The Value In Going Out" (1991) (March) 4 (No 3) *Risk* 29-33.

Huertas, Thomas, "Making Capital Requirements Realistic" (1992) (July) *Corporate Finance, Euromoney Publications* 33-37.

Hull, John (1989) *Options, Futures, and Other Securities*; Englewood Cliffs, NJ: Prentice Hall.

——— (1991) *Introduction to Futures and Options Markets*: Prentice Hall: Englewood Cliffs.

——— and White, Alan, "Coming To Term" (1989-90) (December-January) 3 (No 1) *Risk* 21-25.

———, "Valuing Derivative Securities Using The Explicit Finite Difference Method" (1990) (March) 25 *Journal of Financial and Quantitative Analysis* 87-100.

———, "Root and Branch" (1990) (September) 3 (No 8) *Risk* 69-72.

———, "News Ways With The Yield Curve" (1990) (October) 3 (No 9) *Risk* 13-17.

———, "Modern Greek" (1990-91) (December-January) 4 (No 1) *Risk* 65-67.

——— (1992) (September) 5 (No 8) *Risk* 101-103.

———, "In The Common Interest" (1992) (March) 5 (No 3) *Risk* 64-68.

———, "Finding The Keys" (1993) (September) 6 (No 9) *Risk* 109-112.

Humphrey, Gary, "Discount Wars: A New Weapon Is Wheeled In" (1987) (February) *Euromoney* 17-18.

ISDA Market Survey Highlights (Various Issues); New York: International Swap Dealers Association, Inc.

Iben, Benjamin and Brotherton-Ratcliffe, Rupert, "Principals At Stake" (1991-92) (December-January) 5 (No 1) *Risk* 76-81.

"IFC Forges Hedging Line for Ghanaian Mine" (1991) (November) *Risk* 15-16.

"If It Doesn't Sell—Swap It" (1986) (April) *Euromoney* 1-13.

Inside the Global Derivatives Market (Supplement to November 1990 Issue of Euromoney); London: Euromoney Publications.

(1985) *Inside the Swap Market*; London: IFR Publishing Limited.

(1986) *Inside the Swap Market (2nd ed)*; London: IFR Publishing Limited.

(1988) *Inside the Swap Market (3rd ed)*; London: IFR Publishing Limited.

"Integration and Re-engineering of Technology in Trading Operations" Conference organised by IIR Conferences at Ramada Renaissance Hotel, Sydney, Australia on 1-2 April 1993.

(1986) *Interest Rate Caps*; United Kingdom: Peat Marwick, Banking and Finance Briefing Notes.

"Interest Rate Caps, Floors and Collars" Conference organised by Institute for International Research, 19 and 20 June 1986, 10 St James Square, London SW1.

Interest Rate Swaps; London: Credit Suisse First Boston Limited.

International Swap Dealer's Association Inc (1987) *User's Guide to the Standard Form Agreements.*

International Swap Dealers Association "Swap Default Survey" (1992) (Autumn) 6 *Journal of International Securities Market* 293-296.

Ireland, Louise, "Tax Drives SEK To Swap Pounds For ECUs" (1988) (May) *Corporate Finance, Euromoney Publications* 18-19.

———, "Dollar Caps Set to Top Swaps Market" (1988) (July) *Corporate Finance* 36.

———, "Call of the Swaptions Market" (1988) (July) *Corporate Finance* 38.

———, "Getting a Fix with Swaps" (1988) (October) *Corporate Finance, Euromoney Publications* 39-42.

———, "What Price Capital Adequacy" (1989) (January) *Corporate Finance, Euromoney Publications* 13-14.

———, "Calls: Buy'em Low, Sell'em High" (1989) (February) *Corporate Finance, Euromoney Publications* 15-16.

———, "Counting on Your Counterparty" (1989) (March) *Corporate Finance, Euromoney Publications* 31-34.

———, "Issuers Exploit The Liquidity Of Oil" (1989) (May) *Corporate Finance, Euromoney Publications* 18-20.

———, "Spread-Locks: Safe Combinations" (1989) (July) *Corporate Finance, Euromoney Publications* 11-13.

———, "Macquarie's Choice Offer" (1989) (July) *Corporate Finance, Euromoney Publications* 13-14.

———, "Designer Debt" (1990) (January) *Corporate Finance, Euromoney Publications* 22-24.

———, "Look Closely at Your Counterparty" (1990) (February) *Corporate Finance, Euromoney Publications* 10.

———, "SEK's Safety Net Under Nikkei Wire" (1990) (May) *Corporate Finance, Euromoney Publications* 15-17.

J P Morgan & Co Incorporated (1992) *Commodity-Linked Finance*; London: Euromoney Publications.

Jackson, John Howland, "Managing A Successful Derivatives Business" (Summer 1992) 6 *Journal of International Securities Markets* 161-165.

Jackson, Ted, "NationsBank Buys Big-League Status" (1993) (April) *Euromoney* 71-72.

Jacob, David P, Lord, Graham and Tilley, James A (April 1986) *Price, Duration, and Convexity of a Stream of Interest-Sensitive Cash Flows*; New York: Morgan Stanley.

Jacque, Laurent and Hawawini, Gabriel, "Myths and Realities of the Global Capital Market: Lessons for Financial Managers" (1993) (Fall) 6 (No 3) *Journal of Applied Corporate Finance* 81-90.

Jaffe, Violet, "Swap Fever: The Changing Shape of the Debt Markets" (1985) (October) *Institutional Investor*, Special Advertising Section.

James, Christopher and Wier, Peggy, "Are Bank Loans Different?: Some Evidence From The Stock Market" (1988) (Summer) *Journal Of Applied Corporate Finance* 46-54.

Jamshidian, Farshid, "Price Differentials" (1993) (July) 6 (No 7) *Risk* 48-51.

Jarratt, John (1987) *Simple Valuation Techniques and Advanced Valuation Techniques*; Notes Prepared for Securities Institute of Australia, Diploma Course, Options Markets and Trading.

Jarrow, Robert A and Rudd, Andrew (1983) *Option Pricing*; Homewood, Illinois: Richard D Irwin.

Jarrow, Robert and Turnbull, Stuart, "Drawing The Analogy" (1992) (October) 5 (No 9) *Risk* 63-71.

Jenkins, Richard and Dixon, Richard, "Equity Swaps For Index Exposure" (1992) (12 October) *Australian Derivative News, Macquaries Equities Limited* 10-12.

Jensen, Michael C and Ruback, Richard S, "Theory of the Firm: Managerial Behaviour, Agency Costs and Ownership Structure" (1976) 3 (No 4) *Journal of Financial Economics* 305-360.

Johnson, Cal (July 1989) *Options on Interest Rate Swaps: New Tools for Asset and Liability Management*; New York: Salomon Brothers.

Johnson, Mark, "From The Lion's Mouth" (1989) (October) *Corporate Finance, Euromoney Publications* 21-23.

Jonas, Stan, "Eurodollar Futures—How Swaps, Futures Markets Work in Parallel" (1987) (No 661, 21 February) *International Financing Review* 642-643.

Jones, Morven and Perry, Simon, "How To Hedge A Reverse Floater" (1990) (September) *Corporate Finance, Euromoney Publications* 47-48.

Jones, William R (1987) *Swap Agreements and the Bank of England Federal Reserve Proposal* Unpublished research paper, presented to course on *Swap Financing*, Centre for Studies in Money, Banking and Finance, Macquarie University.

Jory, Richard, "Pure Risk Management" (1993) (February) 146 *Airfinance Journal* 38-40.

"Judged By Their Peers" (1991) (September) *Risk* 99-105.

KPMG Peat Marwick, "Capital Adequacy and Market Risk" (1993) (September) *KPMG Peat Marwick (Australia) Banking and Finance Letter No 93-3* 1-7.

Kahn, Sharon, "Swap Futures Debut" (1991) (June) *Global Finance* 19.

Kalotay, Andrew J and Williams, George O, "How to Succeed in Derivatives Without Really Buying" (1993) (Fall) 6 (No 3) *Journal of Applied Corporate Finance* 100-103.

Kalvaria, Leon, "Financial Management with Swaps" (1984) (December) *Corporate Finance, Euromoney Publications* 21-24.

———, "You've Come a Long Way, Baby" (1985) (September) *Intermarket* 17-21.

Kapstein, Jonathan, "Meeting BIS Standards Takes Its Toll" (1992) (November) *Global Finance* 31-34.

Karsenty, Franck and Sikorav, Jacques, "Instalment Plan" (1993) (October) 6 (No 10) *Risk* 36-40.

Katsouris, Christina, "Filing Up With Gas" (1992) (March) 5 (No 3) *Risk* 21-27.

———, "The Base Players" (1992) (June) 5 (No 6) *Risk* 58-63.

———, "Writers' Block" (1992) (November) 5 (No 10) *Risk* 44-47.

Keller, Paul, "The Rocket Men Are Still At Work" (1989) (September) *Euromoney* 148-158.

Kemp, D S, "Hedging a Long-Term Financing" (1981) (February) *Euromoney* 102-105.

Kerr, William D, "UK/US Proposal On Swap Capital Requirements" (1987) (May) *International Financial Law Review* 19-23.

Kirby, Richard and Davies, Helen, "How Treasurers Can Swap Pitfalls for Potential" (1987) (August) *Corporate Finance, Euromoney Publications* 36-37.

———, "Getting The Measure Of Exposure" (1987) (October) *Corporate Finance, Euromoney Publications* 93-95.

Kish, Richard J and Livingston, Miles, "Estimating the Value of Call Options on Corporate Bonds" (1993) (Fall) 6 (No 3) *Journal of Applied Corporate Finance* 91-94.

Klaffsky, Thomas E (1982) *Coupon Stripping: The Theoretical Spot Rate Curve*; New York: Salomon Brothers Inc.

Klein, Linda, "Swap Agreement Terms Enforced" (1989) (April) *International Financial Law Review* 42.

Kleinbard, Duncan and Greenberg, "US Reduces Tax Risk for Swaps" (1987) (February) *International Financial Law Review* 26.

Klotz, Richard G (October 1985) *Convexity of Fixed Income Securities*; New York: Salomon Brothers Inc.

Knox, David M, "Australian Indexed Bonds" (1985) (October) *JASSA* 28-31.

———, Zima, Petr, Brown, Robert L (1984) *Mathematics of Finance*; Sydney: McGraw-Hill Book Company.

Koh, Kenny (1986) *Option Or Forward Swap Related Financing Structures* Unpublished research paper presented to course on *Swap Financing*, Centre for Studies in Money, Banking and Finance, Macquarie University.

——— (1986) *Reasons For Using And The Pricing of Commodity Linked Bonds* Unpublished research paper presented to course on *Swap Financing*, Centre for Studies in Money, Banking and Finance, Macquarie University.

Kolman, Joe, "The Sultans of Swap" (1985) (October) *Institutional Investor* 76-84.

———, "The Battles are Heating Up For Derivatives Advantage" (1991) (December) *Global Finance* 59-60.

Koniishi, Atsuo and Dattatreya, Ravi (eds) (1991) *The Handbook of Derivative Instruments—Investment Research, Analysis and Portfolio Applications*; Chicago, Illinois: Probus Publishing Company.

Kopprasch, Robert W (1983) *Understanding Duration and Volatility*; New York: Salomon Brothers Inc.

——— and Haghani, Victor J (1986) *Foreign Exchange Annuity Swap*; New York: Salomon Brothers Inc.

———, Macfarlane, John, Ross, Daniel R and Showers, Janet (1985) *The Interest Rate Swap Market: Yield Mathematics, Terminology and Conventions*; New York: Salomon Brothers Inc.

Kramer, Andrea S and Heston, J Clark, "An Overview of Current Tax Impediments to Risk Management" (1993) (Fall) 6 (No 3) *Journal of Applied Corporate Finance* 73-80.

Kreca, Michael E, "Pricing Versus Credit: An Art or a Science" (1986) (May) *Intermarket* 38-43.

———, "The Currency Swap—Sleeping Giant or Second Fiddle" (1986) (July) *Intermarket* 38-41.

Krzyzak, Krystyna, "Duration Package Zeroes In On Risk Management" (1987) (December) 1 (No 1) *Risk* 52-55.

———, "Swaptions Deciphered" (1988) (February) 2 (No 2) *Risk* 9-17.

———, "Don't Take Swaps At Face Value" (1988) (November) 1 (No 11) *Risk* 28-31.

———, "A Family Affair" (1989) (February) 2 (No 2) *Risk* 36-38.

———, "From Basis Points To Barrels" (1989) (May) 2 (No 5) *Risk* 8-12.

———, "Copper Bottomed Hedge" (1989) (September) 2 (No 8) *Risk* 35-39.

———, "Squaring A Circle" (1989) (November) 2 (No 10) *Risk* 21-28.

———, "Arbitraging on Destiny" (1990) (April) 3 (No 4) *Risk* 7-16.

———, "Gamma Raison" (1990) (May) 3 (No 5) *Risk* 21-27.

———, "Far From Crude" (1990) (June) 3 (No 6) *Risk* 5.

———, "Dizzy Heights" (1990) (July-August) 3 (No 7) *Risk* 27-31.

———, "Around The Houses" (1990) (September) 3 (No 8) *Risk* 51-57.

———, "Thoroughly Modern Hedging" (1990) (October) 3 (No 9) *Risk* 50-59.

———, "CBOT Swaps Seek Sponsor" (1991) (April) 4 (No 4) *Risk* 8-9.

———, "Under The Credit Cloud" (1991) (June) 4 (No 6) *Risk* 29-37.

———, "Australian Rules" (1991) (September) 4 (No 8) *Risk* 111-115.

———, "Paris Axes" (1991) (October) 4 (No 9) *Risk* 29-35.

———, "24-Carat Goldman" (1992) (April) 5 (No 4) *Risk* 6-8.

———, "Miracles Of The Market" (1992) (June) 5 (No 6) *Risk* 8-10.

———, "Sewing Up Materials" (1992) (June) 5 (No 6) *Risk* 11-13.

———, Chew, Lillian, and Metcalfe, Richard, "The Year of Bust and Boom" (1990-91) (December-January) 4 (No 1) *Risk* 32-50.

Lanchner, David, "Why New Converts Are Embracing Derivatives In Europe" (1992) (November) *Global Finance* 55-57.

Lassiter, Leslie, "Commodities Blue Print for Corporate Finance" (1991) (March) *Euromoney* 95-98.

Lecat, Oliver, "The BIS Risk Based Capital Guidelines: The Industry Response" Presentation to the ISDA Conference, New York City (29 July 1992).

Lecky Jr, Robert P (1987) *Synthetic Asset Handbook*; New York: First Boston, Derivative Product Groups.

Lee, Peter, "Cutting Back On Swaps" (1988) (September) *Euromoney* 215.

———, "Why Investors Are Missing Profits" (1989) (April) *Euromoney* 56-57.

Lee, Peter, "Securities Houses Face Capital Clampdown" (1992) (April) *Euromoney* 32-43.

———, "How To Exorcise Your Derivatives Demons" (1992) (September) *Euromoney* 36-48.

Leggett, Desmond, "Interest Rate Swaps—A New Financing Technique" (1983) (June) *The Bankers' Magazine* 101-103.

Leong, Kenneth, "In the Eye of the Beholder" (1990) (July-August) 3 (No 7) *Risk* 38-40.

———, "The Emperor's New Clothes" (1990) (September) 3 (No 8) *Risk* 11-15.

———, "Exorcising The Demon" (1990) (October) 3 (No 9) *Risk* 29-35.

———, "Solving the Mystery" (1990-91) (December-January) 4 (No 1) *Risk* 68-71.

———, "Estimates, Guesstimates and Rules of Thumb" (1991) (February) 4 (No 2) *Risk* 15-19.

———, "Mean Streets" (1991) (May) 4 (No 5) *Risk* 45-48.

———, "Price Vs Value" (1991) (November) 4 (No 10) *Risk* 22-26.

———, "Model Choice" (1992) (December) 5 (No 11) *Risk* 60-66.

Levis, Mario and Suchar, Victor, "What Those Guidelines Mean" (1989) (September) *Euromoney* 215-218.

———, "Basle Basics" (1990) (April) 3 (No 4) *Risk* 38-39.

Levy, Edmond, "Asian Arithmetic" (1990) (May) 3 (No 5) *Risk* 7-8.

———, "Capitalising On Correlation" (1991) (May) 4 (No 5) *Risk* 30-33.

——— and Turnbull, Stuart, "Average Intelligence" (1992) (February) 5 (No 2) *Risk* 53-59.

Lewis, Julien, "The Sheikhs Of Wall Street" (1990) (October) *Euromoney* 16-22.

———, "Oil Price Jitters? Try Energy Swaps" (1990) (December) *Euromoney* 90-92.

Lipsky, John and Elhabaski, Sahar (1985) *Swap-Driven Primary Issuance In The International Bond Market*; New York: Salomon Brothers Inc.

Locke, Jane, "Commercials Get Their Break" (1993) (September) 6 (No 9) *Risk* 8-10.

———, "Flight Into The Unknown" (1993) 6 (No 11) *Risk* 12-13.

"The London Code of Conduct—Part 2: The Swap Market" in Bank of England (1987) *The Regulation of the Wholesale Markets in Sterling, Foreign Exchange and Bullion*; London: Bank of England.

"A Look at all Kinds of Risk" (1992) (May) *Global Finance* 27-33.

Lowenstein, Jack, "Prompt Action Avoids Crisis In DFC Collapse" (1990) (March) 16.

Luedecke, Bernd, "Weather Eye On Theta" (1991) (May) 4 (No 5) *Risk* 35-38.

Lund, Gustav and Rantanen, Seppo, "Safe and Efficient Equity Plays" (1993) (June) *Corporate Finance, Euromoney Publications* 49-53.

Lynn, Leslie and Hein, Michael, "Interest Rate Caps and Collars" (1985) (December) *Corporate Finance, Euromoney Publications*, Special Sponsored Section.

McCrary, Ernest, "Pricing Emerging Market Derivatives" (1993) (August) *Global Finance* 47-51.

McDonald, Robert and Siegel, Daniel, "A Note on the Design of Commodity Option Contracts: A Comment" (1983) 3 (No 1) *Journal of Futures Markets* 43-46.

McDougall, Rosamund, "Switch or Shrink" (1988) (March) *The Banker* 23-29.

McGoldrick, Beth, "The Interest Rate Swap Comes of Age" (1983) (August) *Institutional Investor* 83-86, 90.

———, "New Life for Interest Swaps" (1983) (August) *Institutional Investor* 91-94.

———, "The Wild, Wild World of Interest Rate Swaps" (1984) (November) *Institutional Investor* 89-94.

———, "Some Tax Driven Swaps Are Legal" (1989) (April) *Euromoney* 49.

———, "Swaptions Have Charms for the Investors Too" (1989) (April) *Euromoney* 49.

———, "If You Feel Sure You Know Where LIBOR's Taking You, Lie Back and Float" (1989) (April) *Euromoney* 52.

McIver, Jeffrey, "Tree Power" (1993) (December) *Risk* 58-64.

McKenzie, A M (ed) (1992) *Risk Management With Derivatives*; London: MacMillan Press.

McQuilkin, Chris, "Outwitting Outrageous Fortune" (1992) (December) *Corporate Finance, Euromoney Publications* 58-62.

"Man Han Claims US$600m in One Year" (1989) (No 769, 1 April) *International Financing Review* 75.

"Managing Commodity Price Risk" (9-10 March 1991) Conference arranged by IIR Limited, Ramada Renaissance, Sydney, Australia.

Marki, Frederick R V (1986) *Size and Structure of Worlds Bond Markets Special Report No 14—Domestic and International Bond Markets (As of December 1985)*; New York: Merrill Lynch Capital Markets, International Fixed Income Research Department.

Marshall, John (1989) *Money Equals Maths*; Sydney: Allen & Unwin.

———, "The DPC That Dare Not Speak Its Name" (1993) (December) *Risk* 13-15.

———, "Open the Box" (1993) (December) *Risk* 34-38.

Marshall, John F and Bansal, Vipul K, (1992) *Financial Engineering: A Guide to Financial Innovation*; New York Institute of Finance: New York.

Marshall, John F, Bansal, Vipul K, Herbst, Anthony F and Tucker, Alan L, "Hedging Business Cycle Risk with Macro Swaps and Options" (1992) (Winter) 4 (No 4) *Journal of Applied Corporate Finance* 103-108.

Marshall, John F and Kapner, Kenneth R (1990) *Understanding Swap Finance*; Cincinatti, Ohio: South-Western Publishing Co.

Marshall, John S, "Index Linked Fixed Interest Securities" (1983) (October) *The Australian Accountant* 645-648.

Martocchio, Donald A, "Synthetic Alternatives for International Equity Investment" Presentation to the ISDA Conference, New York City (30 July 1992).

Marty, Wolfgang, "The Concept of Duration" (1992) 2 *Swiss Bank Corporation Prospects* 4-7.

Mason, R C, "Building on Black-Scholes" (1988) (November) 1 (No 11) *Risk* 13-17.

Massey, Les, "One Borrower's Experience of a Eurobond Issue Case Study of a Straight Issue and Swap", Paper presented at "Globalisation of Capital Markets" Conference organised by IIR Pty Ltd, 12 and 13 March 1987, Hilton International Hotel, Sydney.

(April 1993) *Measurement of Banks' Exposure to Interest Rate Risks—Preface to Consultative Proposal by the Basle Committee on Banking Supervision*; BIS: Basle.

Medero, Joanne and Schachter, Barry, "Will You Excuse US?" (1992) (December) 5 (No 11) *Risk* 58-59.

Meisner, James F, and Labuszewski, "Modifying the Black-Scholes Option Pricing Model for Alternative Underlying Instruments" (1984) (November-December) *Financial Analysts Journal* 23-30.

Merton, Robert C and Perold, André F, "Theory of Risk Capital in Financial Terms" (1993) (Fall) 6 (No 3) *Journal of Applied Corporate Finance* 16-32.

Metcalfe, Richard, "All Clear" (1989) (June) 2 (No 6) *Risk* 23-26.

———, "Roll Out The Barrels" (1990) (April) 3 (No 4) *Risk* 23-25.

———, "Taking The Bull By The Horns" (1990) (May) 3 (No 5) *Risk* 9-12.

———, "No Risk Please, We're Italian" (1990) (June) 3 (No 6) *Risk* 35-39.

———, "Out Of The Shadows" (1990) (October) 3 (No 9) *Risk* 40-42.

"Methodologies and Practical Applications of Pricing, Hedging and Trading Correlation" Conference organised by Risk Magazine Limited, at The Hilton on Park Lane, London W1, 29th April 1993.

Militello Jr, Frederick C, "Swap Financing—A New Approach to International Transactions" (1984) (October) *Financial Executive* 34-39.

Miller, Gregory, "Making a Market in Slightly Used Swaps" (1984) (November) *Institutional Investor* 99-104.

———, "When Swaps Unwind" (1986) (November) *Institutional Investor* 127-136.

Miller, Merton H, "Financial Innovation: Achievements and Prospects" (1992) (Winter) 4 (No 4) *Journal of Applied Corporate Finance* 4-12.

Millman, Gregory J and Kolman, Joe, "Are We Heading For A Swaps Meltdown?" (8 June 1992) 1 (No 2) *Derivatives Strategy and Tactics* 1-4.

Miron, Paul and Swannell, Philip (1991) *Pricing and Hedging Swaps*; London, England: Euromoney Publications.

Moerman, Filip, "Ruffles On The Level Playing-Field" (1993) (November) *Euromoney* 24.

Monet, Francois-Marie, "Swaps and The Swiss Bond Manager" (1990) (Winter) 4 *Journal of International Securities Markets* 323-331.

Monroe, Ann, "Hedging The Steep Yield Curve—And Profiting Besides" (1992) (September) *Global Finance* 18-19.

Monroe, Ann, "How Derivatives Are Changing Finance" (1992) (November) *Global Finance* 42-46.

(December 1991) *Moody's Rates The Counterparty Risk Of Merrill Lynch Derivatives Products, Inc*; Moody's Special Report.

Moore, Philip, "Cleaning Up The Town Hall Mess" (1991) (April) *Euromoney* 31-33.

Morris, John, "The Unsurest Insurance" (1984) (November) *Euromoney* 89-95.

"Mortgage Swaps Tax Regulators" (1988) (May) 1 (No 7) *Risk* 4-5.

Moynihan, Jon, "The Key To Survival" (1988) (June) 1 (No 7) *Risk* 12-14.

Mudge, Daniel T and Wee, Lieng Seng, "Truer to Type" (1993) (December) *Risk* 16-19.

Musiela, Marek, Ng, Philip and Byron, David, "Tree Surgery" (1992) (May) 5 (No 5) *Risk* 42-43.

Myers, Steve, "Basle Faulty" (1990) (July-August) 3 (No 7) *Risk* 12-17.

Nelken, Izzy, "Square Deals" (1993) (April) 6 (No 4) *Risk* 9.

Nevler, James, "A Crash Course in Structured Notes" (1993) (October) *Global Finance* 43-47.

"The New Face of the Eurobond Syndicate Desk" (1986) (December) *Euromoney* 113-120.

"No Paine, No Gain" (1993) (December) *Risk* 15.

(1986) *Nymex Energy Hedging Manual*; New York: The New York Mercantile Exchange.

O'Hara, Maureen, "Commodity Bonds and Consumption Risks" (1984) (March) 39 (No 1) *Journal Of Finance* 193-206.

Ogden, Joan, "Pension Funds' New Appetite For Derivatives" (1993) (August) *Global Finance* 42-45.

Ollard, Will, "How SEK Borrows at 50 Below" (1985) (May) *Euromoney* 13-23.

———, "Beating The Drums For Commodity Derivatives" (1992) (August) *Global Finance* 48-50.

"Options on Interest Rates" (9-10 March 1992) Conference arranged by IIR Limited, Hotel Inter-Continental, Sydney, Australia.

"The Paradigm Shifts In Derivatives" (1992) (November) *Global Finance* 79-82.

Parente, Gioia M (23 April 1986) *Fixed Income Opportunities: Create High-Yielding Eurodollar Floating-Rate Notes Through Asset-Based Interest Rate Swaps*; New York: Salomon Brothers.

Parkhurst, Charles H (June 1988) *Short-Term Liability Management Techniques*; New York: Salomon Brothers.

Parry, John, "Spanish Matadors Have a Fight on Their Hands" (1994) (January) *Euromoney* 111-114.

Parsley, Mark, "The Last Piece Of The Jigsaw" (1993) (November) *Euromoney* 29-32.

Partridge-Hicks, Stephen, and Hartland-Swann, Piers (1988) *Synthetic Securities*; London, England: Euromoney Publications.

Pattanaik, Swaha, "Corporates Are Learning To Value Derivatives" (1993) (March) *Corporate Finance, Euromoney Publications* 11-12.

Paul, Roger, "Tax treatment of Financial Products" Paper presented to Seminar Series "Corporate Debt Finance: Current Tax and Planning Issues" (16 and 30 April 1991), University of New South Wales, Faculty of Law, Continuing Legal Education.

Phillips, Chris, "How to Choose your Risk Management System" (1990) (September) 3 (No 8) *Risk* 59-61.

Picker, Ida, "Son of Swaps" (1991) (February) *Institutional Investor* 119-122.

Piggott, Charles, "Top Borrowers Take Advantage of EdP's Swap Window" (1993) (December) *Euromoney* 12.

Pitman, Joanna, "Swooping On Swaps" (1988) (January) *Euromoney* 68-82.

Pitts, Mark, "The Pricing Of Options On Debt Securities" (1985) (Winter) *Journal of Portfolio Management* 41-50.

——— and Goldstone, Rebecca, "Trading Strategies—Playing the Eurodollar Strip/US Treasury Note Spread" (1987) (No 662, 28 February) *International Financing Review* 746-747.

——— (October 1992) *The Valuation of Options on Fixed-Income Securities*; New York: Salomon Brothers Inc.

Platt, Gordon, "Swap: The Building Block" (1987) (October) *Intermarket* 39-41.

Platt, Robert B (1986) *Controlling Interest Rate Risk—New Techniques and Applications for Money Management*; New York: John Wiley & Sons.

"Policing a Permanent Revolution" (1988) 1 (No 5) *Risk* 14.

Pollard, "Treatment of Swaps in Bankruptcy" (1988) 3 *Butterworths Journal of International Banking and Finance Law* 514.

Powers, Mark and Vogel, David (1984) *Inside the Financial Futures Markets—Second Edition*; New York: John Wiley & Sons.

Price, John, "Modern Currency Exchange Financing Techniques" (1983) (October) *The Chartered Accountant in Australia* 30-34.

——— and Henderson, Schuyler K (1984) *Currency and Interest Rate Swaps*; London: Butterworths.

——— (1987) *Currency and Interest Rate Swaps* (2nd ed); London: Butterworths.

Price, John A M, Keller, Jules and Neilson, Max, "The Delicate Art of Swaps" (1983) (April) *Euromoney* 118-125.

Price Waterhouse (26 July 1993) *Price Waterhouse Client Memorandum: Group of Thirty Report on Derivatives*; Price Waterhouse: Sydney, Australia.

"Pricing and Structuring Energy Swaps" (2 March 1991) Conference arranged by IIR Ltd in association with Mitsubishi Finance International Plc, Gloucester Hotel, London.

Priestley, Sarah, "US and UK Companies Warm to DM Swap Market" (1985) (September) *Corporate Finance, Euromoney Publications* 40.

———, "Engineering Swaps" (1986) (April) *Corporate Finance, Euromoney Publications* 25-37.

Pringle, John J and Connelly, Robert A, "The Nature and Causes of Foreign Currency Exposure" (1993) (Fall) 6 (No 3) *Journal of Applied Corporate Finance* 61-72.

Pritchard, David, "Swap Financing Techniques: A Citicorp Guide" (1984) (May) *Euromoney, Special Advertising Section.*

———, "Swaps" in Perry, Simon (ed) (1985) *Euromoney Year Book '85*; London: Euromoney Publications, pp 187-191.

Privolos, Theophilos and Duncan, Ronald C (eds) (1991) *Commodity Risk Management and Finance*; Oxford: Oxford University Press.

(April 1993) *The Prudential Supervision of Netting, Market Risks and Interest Rate Risk—Preface to Consultative Proposal by the Basle Committee on Banking Supervision*; BIS: Basle.

Pucci, Fred, "Australia's Spin On Netting And Swaps Recycling" (1992) (November) *Corporate Finance, Euromoney Publications* 45-46.

Quinn, Lawrence, "Relationships Lose Out In Energy Risk Deals" (1991) (December) *Corporate Finance, Euromoney Publications* 11-15.

"REALs Rests Its Case" (1988) (March) 1 (No 4) *Risk* 2-3.

Raiti, Lisa M (May 1992) *Structured Finance: Credit Sensitivity Spurs DPC Growth*; Standard & Poor's: New York.

Ranganathan, V K (March 1991) *Interest Rate Trends & Comparisons*; New York, USA: Security Pacific National Bank.

Ravindran, K, "Low Fat Spreads" (1993) (October) 6 (No 10) *Risk* 66-67.

Rawls, Waite S and Smithson, Charles, W, "The Evolution of Risk Management Products" (1989) 1 (No 4) *The Continental Bank Journal of Applied Corporate Finance* 48.

Read, Pat, "Regulators Focus on Swap Dealers" (1987) (April) *Triple A* 75-79.

Reading, Ronald E, "Opportunities and Challenges for the Derivatives Market" Presentation to Conference on "Financial Risk Measurement and Management of Derivatives" (IIR Limited) London, 28 and 29 April 1992.

"Real Flavour of Synthetics" (1986) (July) *Corporate Finance, Euromoney Publications* 44-45.

"Recent Developments in the Swap Market" (1987) (February) *Bank of England Quarterly Bulletin* 66-79.

"Recent Trends, Latest Developments, New Techniques and Advanced Strategies in Swaps" Conference organised by IIR Pty Ltd, 1 November 1985, Hotel Inter-Continental, Sydney.

"Redland's Coup: Coupon Saving in Dollars on a Convertible" (1987) (September) *Corporate Finance, Euromoney Publications* 18-19.

"Reducing Risk Through FXNET" (1986) (July) *International Financial Law Review* 24.
Reed, Nick, "The Watchdog That Didn't Bark", (1993) (December) *Risk* 7-8.
———, "Long-Standing Room Only" (1993) (December) *Risk* 10-12.
"Regulation: Capital Punishment for Some?" (1987) (April) *Corporate Finance, Euromoney Publications* 27-31.
Reier, S, "The Enduring Appeal of Currency Swaps" (1981) (April) *Institutional Investor* 261-262.
———, "The Rise of Interest Rate Swaps" (1982) (October) *Institutional Investor* 95-96.
———, "The Boon in Long-Dated Forwards" (1983) (October) *Institutional Investor* 353-354.
Reiner, Eric, "Quanto Mechanics" (1992) (March) 5 (No 3) *Risk* 59-63.
Rendleman, Richard, "Share and Share Unlike" (1993) (February) 6 (No 2) *Risk* 50-54.
"Repackaging: Flying in the Face of Misfortune" (1987) (April) *Corporate Finance, Euromoney Publications* 54-66.
Revell, Stephen and Jakeways, John, "Local Authority Swaps: The Court of Appeal's View" (1990) (April) *International Financial Law* 20-22.
"The 'Revolving' Currency Swap" (1987) (June) *The Banker* 18.
Ricards, Trevor S, "Interest Rate Swaps Offer Flexible Financing, Lower Interest Costs" (1985) (March) *Australian Corporate Treasurer* 2-3.
"Riding The Yield Curve" (20 July, 1992) 1 (No 4) *Derivatives Strategy and Tactics* 1-4.
"Risk 1993 Rankings: The Great Pretenders" (1993) (September) 6 (No 9) *Risk* 31-49.
"The Risk and Devon Conference on Equity Derivatives: Pricing, Hedging and Risk Management" Organised by Risk Magazine Limited and Devon Systems International, at The Hilton on Park Lane, London W1, 9-10 February 1993.
"Risk Management: Man Han Claim US$600m In One Year" (1 April 1989) *International Financing Review Issue 769* 75.
"Risk Management Products" (1988) (March) *Risk* 14-16.
"Risk Rankings" (1992) (September) *Risk* 24-51.
Ritchen, Peter (1987) *Options—Theory, Strategy and Applications*; Glenview, Illinois: Scott, Foresman and Company.
Rivett, Phil and Speak, Peter (1991) *The Financial Jungle—A Guide to Financial Instruments*; London: IFR Publishing Limited.
Robb, Richard G, "The Black-Scholes Model and Common Sense" (1985) (July) *Intermarket* 49-51.
Robinson, Danielle, "Diff Swaps Tempt the Wary" (October 1991) *Euromoney* 10-11.
———, "Oiling The Wheels" (May 1992) *Euromoney* 117-120.
———, "Stuck At The Crossroads" (1992) (October) *Euromoney* 33-44.
———, "Cash Hungry Latins Love Equity Derivatives" (1993) (October) *Euromoney* 35-40.
Robinson, Nick, "The Merely Cosmetic Value of Reset Swaps" (1988) (September) *Corporate Finance, Euromoney Publications* 15-18.
Roche, Julian (1993) *Commodity Linked Derivatives*; London: IFR Publishing Limited.
Rogers, "Interest Rate Swaps: The Secondary Market" in *Interest Rate and Currency Swaps 1987* (Practising Law Institute, Corporate Law and Practice Handbook No 564, 1987), p 25.
Rombach, Ed, "Not So Perfect" (1990) (October) 3 (No 9) *Risk* 11-13.
———, "The Cost of Insurance" (1991) (May) 4 (No 5) *Risk* 12-14.
———, "Fear of Flying" (1991) (September) 4 (No 8) *Risk* 39-43.
Rowe, David, "Curves of Confidence" (1993) 6 (No 11) *Risk* 52-55.
Rowley, Ian, "Pricing Options Using the Black-Scholes Model" (1987) (May) *Corporate Finance, Euromoney Publications* 108-112.
———, "Option Pricing Models: How Good is Black-Scholes?" (1987) (June) *Corporate Finance, Euromoney Publications* 30-34.
——— and Neuhaus, Henrik, "How Caps and Floors Can Influence Desired Cash Flow" (1986) (July) *Corporate Finance, Euromoney Publications* 37-42.
Rubinstein, Mark, "Pay Now, Choose Later" (1991) (February) 4 (No 2) *Risk* 13.
———, "Options For The Undecided" (1991) (April) 4 (No 4) *Risk* 43.
———, "Two Into One" (1991) (May) 4 (No 5) *Risk* 49.

Rubinstein, Mark, "One For Another" (1991) (July-August) 4 (No 7) *Risk* 30-32.

———, "Double Trouble" (1991-92) (December-January) 4 (No 5) *Risk* 73.

——— and Leland, Hayne E, "Replicating Options With Positions in Stock and Cash" (1981) (July-August) *Financial Analysts Journal* 63-72.

——— and Reiner, Eric, "Breaking Down The Barriers" (1991) (September) 8 (No 9) *Risk* 28-35.

———, "Unscrambling The Binary Code" (1991) (October) 4 (No 9) *Risk* 75-83.

"Ruling Leaves Banks At A Loss" (1989) (November) *Corporate Finance, Euromoney Publications* 17-18.

Ruml, Elizabeth H, "Derivatives 101" Presentation to the Bank and Financial Analysts Association, 22nd Annual Banking Symposium (26 March 1992).

Rutterford, Janette, Sher, Anwer and Fitzgerald, Desmond, "Building Blocks" (1989) (July-August) 2 (No 7) *Risk* 42-43.

Ruttiens, Alain, "Classical Replica" (1990) (February) 3 (No 2) *Risk* 33-35.

Saber, Nasser, "Netting The Right Value" (1989-90) (December-January) 3 (No 1) *Risk* 35-37.

Satty, Glen, "Equity Index Option And Alternatives" Presentation to the ISDA Conference, New York City (30 July 1992).

Schaefer, Stephen, "Immunisation and Duration: A Review of Theory, Performance and Applications" (1984) 2 (No 3) *Midland Corporate Finance Journal* 41-58.

Schwartz, Eduardo S, "The Pricing Of Commodity-Linked Bonds" (1982) (May) 37 (No 2) *Journal Of Finance* 525-541.

Schwartz, Robert J and Smith, Jr, Clifford W (1991) *The Handbook of Currency and Interest Rate Risk Management*; New York, New York Institute of Finance.

Schwarz, Edward W, Hill, Joanne M and Schneeweis, Thomas (1986) *Financial Futures—Fundamentals, Strategies, and Applications*; Homewood, Illinois: Irwin.

Schwob, Robert, "Style Counsel" (1993) (December) *Risk* 41-45.

Scott-Quinn, Brian (1990) *Investment Banking: Theory and Practice*; London, Euromoney Publications.

Seigel, Lester, "When Noise Is A Positive Asset" (1990) (April) *Corporate Finance, Euromoney Publications* 9-10.

"Senate Judiciary Urged to Amend Bankruptcy Code to Honour Swap Contracts" (1989) 52 *Banking Reports* (BNA) 870.

Sender, Henry, "The Boom in Yen-Yen Swaps" (1988) (February) *Institutional Investor* 143.

"Set LIBOR in Arrears for Cheaper Funding" (1988) (April) *Corporate Finance* 27.

Shah, Ayesha, "Asset Swaps: The Repackaging Game" (1988) (Summer) *Journal of International Securities Markets* 83-88.

Shale, Tony, "How ISDA Got The Message" (1993) (April) *Euromoney* 75-76.

Shanahan, Terence, "Horses For Courses" (1990) (March) 3 (No 3) *Risk* 62-64.

———, "The Repo Market" (1991) (Summer) *Journal of International Securities Markets* 169-180.

——— and Durant, Jim, "Driving Factors" (1990) (November) 3 (No 10) *Risk* 14-21.

Sharpe, William F (1985) *Investments* (3rd ed); Englewood Cliffs, New Jersey: Prentice-Hall Inc.

Shastri, Kuldeep and Tandon, Kishore, "Options on Futures Contracts: A Comparison of European and American Pricing Models" (1986) 6 (No 4) *Journal of Futures Markets* 593-618.

Shegog, Andrew, "The Grey Dawn of Commodity Swaps" (1986) (December) *Euromoney* 9-11.

———, "Who's Top in Swaps?" (1987) (January) *Euromoney* 25-29.

———, "Riding Cross-Currents in Swaps" (1987) (September) *Euromoney* 222-226.

Sheridan, Elayne, "Giving A Dam" (1992) (October) 5 (No 9) *Risk* 73-75.

———, "Some Like It Hot" (1993) (January) 6 (No 1) *Risk* 48-53.

———, "The Mother of Invention" (1993) (May) 6 (No 5) *Risk* 28-37.

Shibata, Yoko, "Making The Grade in Japan By a Hair" (1992) (November) *Global Finance* 35-38.

———, "Japan's Love/Hate Relationship With Derivatives" (1992) (November) *Global Finance* 66-69.

Shimoko, David, "Bounds of Probability" (1993) (April) 6 (No 4) *Risk* 33-37.
Shirreff, David, "The Fearsome Growth of Swaps" (1985) (October) *Euromoney* 247.
———, "The Dangerous New Protection Racket" (1986) (March) *Euromoney* 26-40.
———, "Turning Down the Gaz de France Swap Credit Exposure" (1987) 1 (No 1) *Risk* 28-29.
———, "Les Derives Sont Arrives?" (1988) (July) 1 (No 8) *Risk* 24-29.
———, "What's In A Name?" (1988) (August-September) 1 (No 8) *Risk* 58-61.
———, "ISDA To Call For Capital Mitigation" (1989) (March) 2 (No 3) *Risk* 2-3.
———, "Documenting Caps" (1989) (March) 2 (No 3) *Risk* 6.
———, "The Taming Of The Swap?" (1989) (April) 2 (No 4) *Risk* 8-10.
———, "Unwise Councils" (1989) (April) 2 (No 4) *Risk* 13-16.
———, "The Hedge That Never Was" (1989) (May) 2 (No 5) *Risk* 16-1.
———, "All Clear" (1989) (June) 2 (No 6) *Risk* 23-27.
———, "Loosening The Chains?" (1989) (June) 2 (No 6) *Risk* 38-40.
———, "Big Capital Wins The Day" (1989) (July-August) 2 (No 7) *Risk* 9-13.
———, "In The Shadow Of The Mark" (1989) (November) 2 (No 10) *Risk* 43-49.
———, "One Man's Meat" (1989-90) (December-January) 3 (No 1) *Risk* 41-45.
———, "Save The Puppy" (1990) (February) 3 (No 2) *Risk* 43-47.
———, "Netting Nightmare" (1990) (March) 3 (No 3) *Risk* 15-23.
———, "Clearing The Decks" (1990) (March) 3 (No 3) *Risk* 25-27.
———, "Not So Sexy" (1990) (June) 3 (No 6) *Risk* 26-42.
———, "The Real Cost of Swaps" (1990) (June) *Global Finance* 37-40.
———, "Net Effect Unfair" (1990) (July-August) *Global Finance* 4-5.
———, "Lords of the Jungle" (1991) (February) 4 (No 2) *Risk* 4-6.
———, "Dealing With Default" (1991) (March) 4 (No 3) *Risk* 19-27.
———, "Now For The Debt Index Options" (1991) (April) 4 (No 4) *Risk* 4-5.
———, "Miracle Ingredients" (1991) (July-August) 4 (No 7) *Risk* 21-28.
———, "Holes In The Net" (1991) (September) 4 (No 8) *Risk* 4-5.
———, "A Small Umbrella" (1991) (September) 4 (No 8) *Risk* 6-10.
———, "Running In Neutra" (1991) (October) 4 (No 9) *Risk* 67-71.
———, "Merrill Plays Ratings Game" (1991) (November) 4 (No 10) *Risk* 5-8.
———, "No Rush To Copy Merrill" (1991-92) (December-January) 5 (No 1) *Risk* 8-9.
———, "Sitting Ducks for Canuck Bucks" (1991-92) (December-January) 5 (No 1) *Risk* 21-25.
———, "The Wins of Change" (1992) (February) 5 (No 2) *Risk* 19-25.
———, "Swap And Think" (1992) (March) 5 (No 3) *Risk* 29-35, 72.
———, "Battling The Barracudas" (1992) (April) 5 (No 4) *Risk* 5-6.
———, "ISDA And The Famous Four" (1992) (April) 5 (No 4) *Risk* 8-10.
———, "MIF And Reality" (1992) (June) 5 (No 6) *Risk* 19-25, 72.
———, "O & Y Swappers' License To Kill" (1992) (July-August) 5 (No 7) *Risk* 6.
———, "Swappers Win In DFC And NZ" (1992) (October) 5 (No 9) *Risk* 5-6.
———, "Germany's Warrantmania" (1992) (November) *Global Finance* 58-59.
———, "Noises From The Hedge" (1992) (November) 5 (No 10) *Risk* 21-25.
———, "A Question Of Judgement" (1992) (December) 5 (No 11) *Risk* 11.
———, "Glad To Be Gray" (1992) (December) 5 (No 11) *Risk* 19-24.
———, "A Nation Divided" (1993) (January) 6 (No 1) *Risk* 17-24.
———, "Making Ends Meet" (1993) (February) 6 (No 2) *Risk* 16-21.
———, "Uncommon Market" (1993) (March) 6 (No 3) *Risk* 49-57.
———, "The Sky Holds Up—Official" (1993) (April) 6 (No 4) *Risk* 7-8.
———, "Home and Away" (1993) (April) 6 (No 5) *Risk* 37-41.
———, "Lions or Lemmings" (1993) (December) *Euromoney* 41-44.
Showers, Janet L (October 1986) *Forward Currency Swaps—A Product for Managing Interest Rate and Currency Exposure*; New York: Salomon Brothers.
——— and Blanton, Peter B (February 1989) *Hedging and Financing Strategies for the Corporate Borrower—Liability Management Using Forwards, Futures, Options, and Swaps*; New York: Salomon Brothers.
"The Show Goes On . . ." (1987) (December) *Corporate Finance, Euromoney Publications*, Supplement.

Singh, Premjit, "Managing the Interest Rate Margin" (1993) (June) *Corporate Finance, Euromoney Publications* 14-17.

Smith, A L H (1986) *Trading Financial Options*; London: Butterworths.

Smith, Clifford W, Smithson, Charles W and Wilford, D Sykes, "Managing Financial Risk" (1989) 1 (No 4) *Continental Bank Journal of Applied Corporate Finance* 49.

Smith Jr, Clifford W and Wakeman, L Macdonald, "The Evolving Market for Swaps" (1986) (Winter) *Midland Corporate Finance Journal* 20-32.

Smith, Jr, Clifford W, Smithson, Charles W and Wakeman, Lee Macdonald, "The Market for Interest Rate Swaps" (1988) (Winter) *Financial Management* 34-44.

Smith, Jr, Clifford W, Smithson, Charles W and Wilford, D Sykes (1990) *Managing Financial Risk*; New York: Harper Business.

Smith, Jr, Clifford W and Smithson, Charles W (eds) (1990) *The Handbook of Financial Engineering: New Financial Product Innovations, Applications, and Analyses*; Harper and Row: New York.

Smith, David, "By The Bookstraps" (1990) (June) 3 (No 6) *Risk* 40-42.

Smith, Donald J, "Putting the Cap on Options" (1987) (January) *Corporate Finance, Euromoney Publications* 20-22.

———, "The Arithmetic of Financial Engineering" (1989) (Winter) *Journal of Applied Corporate Finance* 49-58.

———, "The Arithmetic of Financial Engineering" (1989) 1 (No 4) *Continental Bank Journal of Applied Corporate Finance* 49.

Smithson, Charles W, "A LEGO® Approach to Financial Engineering: An Introduction to Forwards, Futures, Swaps and Options" (1987) (Winter) *Midland Corporate Finance Journal* 16-28.

———, "Wonderful Life" (1991) (October) 4 (No 9) *Risk* 37-44.

Smithson, Charles W and Chew, Donald H, "The Use of Hybrid Debt in Managing Corporate Risk" (1992) (Winter) 4 (No 4) *Journal of Applied Corporate Finance* 79-89.

(April 1993) *The Supervisory Recognition of Netting For Capital Adequacy Purposes—Preface to Consultative Proposal by the Basle Committee on Banking Supervision*; BIS: Basle.

(April 1993) *The Supervisory Treatment of Market Risks—Preface to Consultative Proposal by the Basle Committee on Banking Supervision*; BIS: Basle.

———, "Something or Nothing" (1992) (December) 5 (No 11) *Risk* 70-74.

Sood, Arivinder, "Opportunities in Low Coupon Currency Swaps" (1987) (May) *Intermarket* 10-13.

———, "The Long and Short of Interest Rate Swap Spreads" (1988) 1 (No 5) *Risk* 24.

———, "Compelling Structures of US Issues" (1988) (October) *Corporate Finance, Euromoney Publications* 18-22.

Spender, Michael, "Interest Rate Swaps—The Great Futures Vs Treasury Yield Pricing Argument" (1986) (No 638, 6 September) *International Financing Review* 2683-4.

———, "Interest Rate Swaps—Further Thoughts on the Futures Pricing Model" (1986) (No 641, 27 September) *International Financing Review* 2922-3.

Stambaugh, Fred, "Put All Your Exposures In One Basket" (1993) (October) *Corporate Finance, Euromoney Publications* 22-23.

Stavis, Robert M and Haghani, Victor J (1987) *Puttable Swaps Tools for Managing Callable Assets*; New York: Salomon Brothers Inc.

Stigum, Marcia (1981) *Money Market Calculations—Yields, Break-evens, and Arbitrage*; Homewood, Illinois: Dow Jones-Irwin.

——— (1989) *The Repo and Reverse Markets*; Homewood, Illinois: Dow Jones-Irwin.

Stillit, Daniel, "Calls Coming Through Loud And Clear Klienwort" (1987) (May) *Corporate Finance, Euromoney Publications* 22-24.

———, "Switching on to Swaps" (1987) (May) *Corporate Finance, Euromoney Publications* 68-75.

———, "The Booker Prize To Warburg For Some Fairly Novel Work" (1987) (June) *Corporate Finance, Euromoney Publications* 20-21.

———, "The Imperceptible Nod Opens Windows for Yen/Yen Market" (1987) (August) *Corporate Finance, Euromoney Publications* 18-21.

Stillit, Daniel and Ireland, Louise, "Equity Warrants: Why Japanese Want That Negative Feeling" (1987) (July) *Corporate Finance, Euromoney Publications* 20-23.

Stoakes, Christopher, "Standardising Swaps Documentation" (1985) (March) *International Financial Law Review* 11.

———, "How to Terminate a Swap" (1985) (April) *Euromoney* 18.

Stott, Andrew and Jameson, Helen, "Refocusing Ambitions in Investment Banking: The View from London" (1993) (Spring/Summer) 7 *Journal of International Securities Markets* 121-138.

Strauss, Mel and Herman, Bernard, "Why Swappers Need Duration" (1988) (February) 1 (No 3) *Risk* 22-23.

Sturm, Frederick W, "Duration As A Risk Management Tool" (1987) (Autumn) *Journal of International Securities Markets* 17-32.

Suhar, V V and Lyons, D D, "Choosing Between a Parallel Loan and a Swap" (1979) (March) *Euromoney* 114-116.

(September 1989) *Survey of Australian Dollar Interest Rate and Currency Swap Market*; Sydney, Australia: Australian Swap Dealers Committee.

(September 1990) *Survey of Australian Dollar Interest Rate and Currency Swap Market*; Sydney, Australia: Australian Financial Markets Association.

"Survey Shows Losses are Low in Swap Market" (1988) (20 July) *American Banker* 2.

"Swap Credit Risk" (1989) (March) *Corporation Finance* 31.

"The Swap Market: ManHan's Answer To Reduce Risk Capital" (18 June 1988) *International Financing Review Issue 729* 1992-4.

"Swapping Past The Tax Man" (1991) (December) *Euromoney* 44.

"Swaps" (1984) (December) *Corporate Finance, Euromoney Publications* 15-29.

"Swaps" (1985) (November) *Corporate Finance, Euromoney Publications* 69-86.

(1986) *Swaps*; London: Orion Royal Bank Limited.

"Swaps" Conference organised by IIR Pty Ltd, 4 and 5 May 1987, Sheraton-Wentworth Hotel, Sydney.

"Swaps, Derivatives and Synthetic Products" Conference organised by IIR Pty Ltd, 28 and 29 April 1988, Hotel Intercontinental, Sydney.

"Swaps Software" (1990) (March) 3 (No 3) *Risk* 29-35.

"The Swaps that Unlock Credit", *Business Week*, 2 August 1982, p 39.

"Swaps: The Revolution in Debt Management Techniques" (1984) (December) *Corporate Finance, Euromoney Publications* 15-29.

"Swaps Trading: An Opportunisitic Trading Strategy in US Dollar Swaps" (19 December, 1987) *International Financing Review Issue 704* 4013-15.

"Swaps and Swap Derivatives" Conference organised by IIR Pty Ltd, 2 and 3 May 1989, Regent Hotel, Sydney.

"Swaps—New Moves" (1987) (July) *Euromoney* and (1987) (July) *Corporate Finance, Euromoney Publications*, Supplement.

"Swaps—SecPac's LIBOR Minus 5.2% 'Disaster' Rate" (1988) (2 January) *International Financing Review Issue 705* 55-58.

Synthetic Securities; London: Citicorp Investment Bank.

"TNT: Reverse Forward Swap Shaped to the Yield Curve" (1987) (January) *Supplement to Corporate Finance, Euromoney Publications* 23.

Tait, Simon, "It Takes Two to Tango" (1983) (February) *Euromoney* 75-81.

"Taux De Trop" (1992) (March) 5 (No 3) *Risk* 39-40.

Taylor, Barry W, "Swaps: A Creditor's Perspective on Rate Risk" (1987) (Autumn) *Journal of International Securities Markets* 33-39.

Taylor, Charles, "Practice Made Perfect" (1993) 6 (No 11) *Risk* 18-19.

Taylor, Jon and Smith, Matthew, "Options Replication" (1987) (December) *Intermarket* 16, 53-55.

Taylor, "The Magic Kingdom of Swaps: From Space Mountain to Dumbo—A Lawyer's Guide to Interest Rate and Exchange Rate Risk" in *Interest Rate and Currency Swaps 1987* (Practicing Law Institute, Corporate Law and Practice Handbook No 564, 1987), p 65.

"Tender Panel Fits into Grand Met Scheme" (1987) (June) *Corporate Finance, Euromoney Publications* 21-22.

Thomas, Bryan, "Something To Shout About" (1993) (May) 6 (No 5) *Risk* 56-58.
Tiner, John, "Bringing FRAs To Book" (1988) (April) 1 (No 5) *Risk* 52-53.
Tolhurst, A, Wallace, E and Zipfinger, F (1979) *Stamp Duties*; Sydney, Australia: Butterworths.
Tompkins, Robert, "Behind The Mirror" (1989) (February) 2 (No 2) *Risk* 17-23.
———, "The A-Z Of Caps" (1989) (March) 2 (No 3) *Risk* 21-41.
———, "Which Hedge Is Best" (1989) (April) 2 (No 4) *Risk* 49-53.
——— (1991) *Options Explained*; London: MacMillan Press.
Tracy, J R, and Goldstein, Gregg, "Swap Options: A Descriptive Approach" (1991) (August/September) 4 *Swiss Bank Corporation Economic and Financial Prospects* 1-4.
"Treasurers' Top Team in Derivatives" (1992) (May) *Corporate Finance, Euromoney Publications* 25-32.
"Treasury Swap Goes Native" (1987) 1 (No 1) *Risk* 6-7.
Tremble, Kerry and Sarwa, Arun, "Happiness Is A Full Net" (1991) (April) *Euromoney* 34-36.
(12 December 1991) *Trends in US$ Swap Spreads*; New York: Salomon Brothers.
Treves, Daniel, "The Case For The FRA" (1984) (November) *Euromoney* 196.
Tufano, Peter, "Financial Innovation and First Mover Advantages" (1992) (Spring) 5 (No 1) *Journal of Applied Corporate Finance* 83-87.
Turnbull, Stuart M, "Swaps: A Zero Sum Game?" (1987) (Spring) *Financial Management* 15-21.
———, "The Price Is Right" (1992) (April) 5 (No 4) *Risk* 56-57.
"Two More Innovations in Eurobond Year", *Asian Finance*, 15 September 1982, p 14.
"Unlocking Bonds from the Balance Sheet" (1988) (January) 1 (No 2) *Risk* 30-31.
"Unlocking Bonds from the Balance Sheet" (1988) 1 (No 2) *Risk* 2-3.
"Unravelling the Asset Swap" (1987) (April) *Corporate Finance, Euromoney Publications* 24-27.
Uren, David, "Swaps Come to the Company Tax Party" (1986) (August) *Triple A* 15-19.
———, "Westfield Rides a Non-Recourse Winner" (1987) (May) *Triple A* 15-17.
Van Horne, James C (1984) *Financial Market Rates and Flows* (2nd ed), Englewood Cliffs, New Jersey: Prentice Hall Inc.
Vann, Bradley, "Swaps and Statutory Authorities" (1991) (August) *The Australian Corporate Treasurer* 6-10.
Vecchi, Carlo, "When Is Duration Not Duration?" (1988) (July) 1 (No 8) *Risk* 37-39.
———, "Duration Defined" (1989) (March) 21 (No 38) *Risk* 30-33.
Verherstraeten, Maurits, "Risk Measurement And Quality Of Profits In The Foreign Exchange Market" (1992) (Winter) 6 *Journal Of International Securities Markets* 377-386.
"Volatility—Analysis, Pricing, Risk Management and Trading" Conference arranged by IIR Limited, Gloucester Hotel, London, 23-24 January 1992.
"Volatility in US and Japanese Stock Markets: A Symposium" (1992) (Spring) 5 (No 1) *Journal of Applied Corporate Finance* 4-35.
Wakeman, Lee Macdonald (16 May 1986) *The Portfolio Approach To Swaps Management*; New York: Chemical Bank Capital Markets Group.
Walker, Andrew and Warner, Eric, "A Strategy for High Deutschemark Interest Rates" (June 1992) *Corporate Finance, Euromoney Publications* 43-44.
"Equity Linked Rules" (1992) (April) 5 (No 4) *Risk* 25-29.
Walmsley, Julian, "Interest Rate Swaps: The Hinge Between Money and Capital Markets" (1985) (April) *The Banker* 37-40.
——— (1988) *The New Financial Instruments—An Investor's Guide*; New York: John Wiley & Sons.
Walther, Arthur, "Commercial Paper Swaps" (1984) (December) *Corporate Finance, Euromoney Publications* 25-28.
Walton, David (28 May 1991) *Backwardation in Commodity Markets*; Goldmans, Sachs & Co.
——— (30 August 1991) *Commodity Prices And Inflation*; Goldmans, Sachs & Co.
(1987) *Warrants and Options; Euromoney Publications*, London: IFR Publishing Limited.

Watkins, James A, "Legal Issues In Currency Swaps" (1982) (June) *International Financial Law Review* 26-28.

———, "Legal Issues In Currency Swaps" (1982) (September) *International Financial Law Review* 30-32.

Watson, Ian and Peerless, Simon (1987) *Taxation and Accounting for Financial Instruments*; London: IFR Publishing Ltd.

"The Way into Any Market" (1983) (November) *Euromoney* 60-75.

Weinberger, Ed, "The Letter Box" (1993) (June) 6 (No 6) *Risk* 54-55.

Weisweiller, Rudi (ed) (1986) *Arbitrage*; Cambridge: Woodhead-Faulkner.

Westlake, Melvyn, "Private Means" (1992) (November) 5 (No 10) *Risk* 48-54.

———, "Mountain Enthusiasm" (1993) (February) 6 (No 2) *Risk* 27-31.

———, "Fun In The Sun" (1993) (May) 6 (No 5) *Risk* 17-21.

———, "Private Party" (1993) 6 (No 8) *Risk* 35-40.

———, "Latin Lovers" (1993) 6 (No 9) *Risk* 51-60.

———, "Land of The Fee" (1993) 6 (No 9) *Risk* 61-64.

———, "Give'em Enough Hope" (1993) 6 (No 11) *Risk* 6-7.

———, "On Your Marks" (1993) (December) *Risk* 51-57.

Westminister Equity, "Building Confidence" (1990) (April) 3 (No 4) *Risk* 33-36.

Whalley, Elizabeth and Wilmott, Paul, "Counting The Cost" (1993) (October) 6 (No 10) *Risk* 59-66.

"When Anything Less Than Triple-A Is Not Enough" (1993) (February) *Euromoney* 52.

White, Daniel L, "Next In Corporate Finance: Index Linked Loans" (1981) (September-October) *Harvard Business Review* 14-22.

Whitelaw, John, "Quick Off The Benchmark" (1993) 6 (No 11) *Risk* 8.

Williams, Richard, "New Markets, New Products" (1992) (November) *Global Finance* 47-49.

Wilmott, Dewynne and Howison (1993) *Option Pricing: Mathematical Models and Computation*; Oxford Financial Press: Oxford.

Wilson, Thomas, "Infinite Wisdom" (1993) (June) 6 (No 6) *Risk* 37-45.

Wilson, Tom, "RAROC Remodelled" (1992) (September) 5 (No 8) *Risk* 112-119.

Wolf, Avner, "Fundamentals of Commodity Options on Futures" (1982) 2 (No 4) *Journal of Futures Markets* 391-408.

Wood, Alan, "The BIS Risk Based Capital Guidelines: The Industry Response" Presentation To The ISDA Conference, New York City (29 July 1992).

"The Worm in the Derivatives Apple" (December 1989) *Corporate Finance, Euromoney Publications* 13-14.

Yamada, H, "The Euroyen Swap Market—How Most Euroyen Issues Are Swapped" (1986) (No 649, 22 November) *International Financing Review*, Special Survey by Daiwa Europe Limited, pp ix-x.

Zucker, Jon, "Does The Swap Market Lead Or Lag The Bond Market?" (1992) (Summer) 6 *Journal of International Securities Markets* 121-124.

Part 1

The Function of Swap and Financial Derivative Transactions

Chapter 1

The Role and Function of Swap and Financial Derivative Markets

INTRODUCTION

The emergence of the international swap market represents an exciting and important development in finance. Unlike many other techniques which have emerged as specific responses to particular market conditions, including regulatory and tax factors, the development of swaps represents a fundamental change in the way in which capital markets function. It is this unique aspect of swap transactions which has been central to the rapid growth in swap volume. It has also allowed swaps to have a profound impact upon the development of financing techniques and financial markets generally.

The prominence obtained by swaps in global capital markets is evident from several perspectives:

- the size of the global swap market;
- the variety of participants utilising swaps;
- the variety of potential uses for swap transactions; and
- the range of swap instruments and their continued development and proliferation.

As outlined in more detail below, the swap market has grown from a negligible volume in the early 1980s to total swap outstandings of approximately US$4.6 trillion as at the end of 1992. Total annual volume currently is also significant, running at around US$3.5 trillion per annum.

The volume of swap transactions reflects the tremendous importance of this type of instrument in capital market transactions. In purely numerical terms, the volume of swap activity substantially exceeds other innovations in capital markets.

The importance of the swap market is also evidenced by the variety of participants. Almost every financial institution of any size has made some commitment to the swap market by establishing their own swap group or department committed to the promotion of swap products in the market.

The importance of swaps is also evident from the variety of users of these instruments. Swaps are a technique widely used by the world's most prestigious financial institutions, corporations, supranational or official institutions. Swap transactions are accepted as an established technique utilised as an integral part of the funding and risk management strategy of treasurers world-wide.

The importance of the role of the global swap market is in part predicated upon a range of potential applications. Swaps are utilised to undertake at least three general types of functions:

- undertake capital market arbitrage between various markets around the world to significantly lower the financing cost of borrowers or increase asset yields for investors;
- manage the risk, both interest rate and currency, of asset liability portfolios against sharp and unpredictable shifts in exchange and interest rates;
- circumvent adverse market conditions or regulations which would otherwise make standard capital market transactions difficult or impossible.

The utilisation of swap transactions in the management of asset and liability portfolios generally continues to evolve, with new applications emerging steadily.

A central element of the global swap market is the range of swap techniques and instruments that are available. The "core" swap instruments (interest rate and currency swaps, forward rate agreements (FRAs), long-term foreign exchange (LTFX), and long-dated options—caps, floors, collars etc) are well established as an integrated set of financial instruments.

However, the range of instruments has increased with the emergence of a whole range of derivative instruments within the basic swap framework, in response to evolving capital market opportunities and asset/liability management requirements. These include variations on the basic "core" swap instruments including development of markets in options on these basic instruments as well as extensions of these techniques to commodity and equity markets.

There is, in addition, increasing integration of the swap market into the market for derivative instruments generally.

These various dimensions of the swap market highlight the central role that this group of instruments has come to occupy in capital markets. It is fair to say that swaps, more than any other instrument, represent *the* key development in the evolution of global capital markets in the 1980s and the 1990s.

SIZE OF THE GLOBAL SWAP MARKET

Exhibit 1.1 sets out estimated total volume of interest rate and currency swap activity in the period from 1987 to 1992.

These statistics are gathered by the International Swaps and Derivatives Association (ISDA). ISDA gathers information on a semi-annual basis from its members, who represent most of the major participants in the global swap market. The ISDA statistics represent "quasi" official figures on the size of the global swap market.

Exhibit 1.1 highlights the extremely rapid growth in the global swap market. This rate of growth is even more astonishing if the period from the early 1980s when swap transactions commenced to the present time is considered. The growth in annual volume is in the order of a compound rate of growth of 25.30% pa.

Several aspects of the pattern of growth require comment:

- In terms of the total global swap market, North American currencies (US$ and C$) have decreased as a percentage of the total global market from approximately 70% as at 1987 (and even higher earlier in the 1980s) to approximately 50%. This reflects the strong growth in swap markets in Europe, Asia (primarily Japan) and Australasia.
- In terms of the global interest rate swap market, North American currencies, primarily the US$ interest rate swap market, are dominant. US$ interest rate swaps currently constitute approximately 50% of the global interest rate swap market which is down significantly from its approximately 80% share in 1987. The major reasons for this decline is the growth in interest rate swap market in European currencies and, to a lesser extent, Asian and Australasian currencies.
- In terms of currency swaps, North American currencies have declined in market share from approximately 48% in 1987 to approximately 40% in 1992. European, Asian and Australasian currencies constitute the major portion of the global currency swap market, with European currencies constituting the largest part with a total market share of approximately 40%.

Exhibit 1.1

Global Swap and Derivative Markets—Volume Statistics

TABLE 1

Total Interest Rate and Currency Swaps (US$ Million)

	1987	% of Market	1988	% of Market	Growth (%)	1989	% of Market	Growth (%)	1990	% of Market	Growth (%)	1991	% of Market	Growth (%)	1992	% of Market	Growth (%)
North American																	
US$	704,123	67.2%	997,643	60.7%	41.7%	1,365,365	56.7%	36.9%	1,701,008	49.1%	24.6%	2,090,258	44.7%	22.9%	1,547,992	44.1%	−25.9%
C$	20,375	1.9%	45,030	2.7%	121.0%	62,457	2.6%	38.7%	125,211	3.6%	100.5%	125,021	2.7%	−0.2%	88,961	2.5%	−28.8%
European																	
DEM	53,017	5.1%	90,445	5.5%	70.6%	148,250	6.2%	63.9%	265,675	7.7%	79.2%	358,589	7.7%	35.0%	367,696	10.5%	−2.5%
GBP	40,212	3.8%	69,969	4.3%	74.0%	135,489	5.6%	93.6%	291,130	8.4%	114.9%	328,351	7.0%	12.8%	237,059	6.8%	−27.8%
FFR	16,022	1.5%	24,049	1.5%	50.1%	56,959	2.4%	136.8%	74,980	2.2%	31.6%	132,864	2.8%	77.2%	225,482	6.4%	69.7%
SFR	44,959	4.3%	88,593	5.4%	97.1%	96,349	4.0%	8.8%	172,623	5.0%	79.2%	274,226	5.9%	58.9%	123,162	3.5%	−55.1%
ECU	21,939	2.1%	33,694	2.0%	53.6%	60,826	2.5%	80.5%	88,199	2.5%	45.0%	134,274	2.9%	52.2%	97,190	2.8%	−27.6%
Dfl	5,073	0.5%	8,250	0.5%	62.6%	16,686	0.7%	102.3%	26,852	0.8%	60.9%	31,214	0.7%	16.2%	29,658	0.8%	−5.0%
BFR	1,515	0.1%	2,421	0.1%	59.8%	3,981	0.2%	64.4%	9,218	0.3%	131.5%	14,401	0.3%	56.2%	11,894	0.3%	−17.4%
LIT	0	0.0%	0	0.0%		0	0.0%		21,645	0.6%		70,222	1.5%	224.4%	90,231	2.6%	28.5%
SKR	0	0.0%	0	0.0%		0	0.0%		17,674	0.5%		35,967	0.8%	103.5%	34,053	1.0%	−5.3%
DKR	0	0.0%	0	0.0%		0	0.0%		2,792	0.1%		3,711	0.1%	32.9%	6,737	0.2%	81.5%
PTA	0	0.0%	0	0.0%		0	0.0%		0	0.0%		0	0.0%		8,878	0.3%	
Australasian																	
JPY	100,244	9.6%	209,521	12.7%	109.0%	324,684	13.5%	55.0%	476,729	13.8%	46.8%	839,011	17.9%	76.0%	499,897	14.3%	−40.4%
A$	31,126	3.0%	61,978	3.8%	99.1%	128,211	5.3%	106.9%	144,749	4.2%	12.9%	158,863	3.4%	9.8%	76,796	2.2%	−51.7%
NZ$	8,366	0.8%	9,515	0.6%	13.7%	6,264	0.3%	−34.2%	6,828	0.2%	9.0%	9,885	0.2%	44.8%	1,281	0.0%	−87.0%
HK$	1,533	0.1%	2,738	0.2%	78.6%	2,700	0.1%	−1.4%	3,067	0.1%	13.6%	3,778	0.1%	23.2%	4,614	0.1%	22.1%
Other		0.0%		0.0%		0	0.0%		38,233	1.1%		68,762	1.5%	79.8%	54,741	1.6%	−20.4%
	1,048,504	100.0%	1,643,846	100.0%	56.8%	2,408,221	100.0%	46.5%	3,466,613	100.0%	43.9%	4,679,397	100.0%	35.0%	3,506,322	100.0%	−25.1%
Year	1987		1988			1989			1990			1991			1992		
Currency Blocks																	
North America	724,498	69.1%	1,042,673	63.4%	43.9%	1,427,822	59.3%	36.9%	1,826,219	52.7%	27.9%	2,215,279	47.3%	21.3%	1,636,953	46.7%	−26.1%
Europe	182,737	17.4%	317,421	19.3%	73.7%	518,540	21.5%	63.4%	970,788	28.0%	87.2%	1,383,819	29.6%	42.5%	1,232,040	35.1%	−11.0%
Australasia	141,269	13.5%	283,752	17.3%	100.9%	461,859	19.2%	62.8%	631,373	18.2%	36.7%	1,011,537	21.6%	60.2%	582,588	16.6%	−42.4%
Other	0	0.0%	0	0.0%		0	0.0%		38,233	1.1%		68,762	1.5%	79.8%	54,741	1.6%	−20.4%
Total	1,048,504	100.0%	1,643,846	100.0%	56.8%	2,408,221	100.0%	46.5%	3,466,613	100.0%	43.9%	4,679,397	100.0%	35.0%	3,506,322	100.0%	−25.1%

Source: International Swaps and Derivatives Association.

Exhibit 1.1—continued

TABLE 2
Interest Rate Swaps (US$ Million)

	1987	% of Market	1988	% of Market	Growth (%)	1989	% of Market	Growth (%)	1990	% of Market	Growth (%)	1991	% of Market	Growth (%)	1992	% of Market	Growth (%)
North American																	
US$	541,517	79.3%	728,166	72.1%	34.5%	1,011,199	65.7%	38.9%	1,272,653	55.1%	25.9%	1,505,995	49.1%	18.3%	1,335,809	46.0%	−11.3%
C$	6,494	1.0%	15,771	1.6%	142.9%	29,873	1.9%	89.4%	68,292	3.0%	128.6%	61,335	2.0%	−10.2%	54,659	1.9%	−10.9%
European																	
DEM	31,640	4.6%	56,466	5.6%	78.5%	94,241	6.1%	66.9%	193,365	8.4%	105.2%	263,411	8.6%	36.2%	317,185	10.9%	20.4%
GBP	29,706	4.4%	52,265	5.2%	75.9%	101,674	6.6%	94.5%	242,089	10.5%	138.1%	253,516	8.3%	4.7%	206,186	7.1%	−18.7%
FFR	11,195	1.6%	18,871	1.9%	68.6%	48,614	3.2%	157.6%	61,582	2.7%	26.7%	115,607	3.8%	87.7%	209,224	7.2%	81.0%
SFR	5,031	0.7%	14,610	1.4%	190.4%	31,405	2.0%	115.0%	80,539	3.5%	156.5%	137,620	4.5%	70.9%	80,351	2.8%	−41.6%
ECU	3,221	0.5%	9,197	0.9%	185.5%	20,882	1.4%	127.1%	40,367	1.7%	93.0%	72,822	2.4%	80.4%	67,505	2.3%	−7.3%
Dfl	1,086	0.2%	2,086	0.2%	92.1%	6,594	0.4%	216.1%	13,743	0.6%	108.4%	18,742	0.6%	36.4%	22,250	0.8%	18.7%
BFR	185	0.0%	554	0.1%	199.5%	916	0.1%	65.3%	3,523	0.2%	284.6%	7,523	0.2%	113.5%	8,466	0.3%	12.5%
LIT	0	0.0%	0	0.0%		0	0.0%		8,041	0.3%		34,321	1.1%	326.8%	63,728	2.2%	85.7%
SKR	0	0.0%	0	0.0%		0	0.0%		11,485	0.5%		18,233	0.6%	58.8%	13,019	0.4%	−28.6%
DKR	0	0.0%	0	0.0%		0	0.0%		1,054	0.0%		908	0.0%	−13.9%	4,237	0.1%	366.6%
ESP	0	0.0%	0	0.0%		0	0.0%		0	0.0%		0	0.0%		5,359	0.2%	
Australasian																	
JPY	40,498	5.9%	78,488	7.8%	93.8%	124,359	8.1%	58.4%	231,942	10.0%	86.5%	478,923	15.6%	106.5%	427,562	14.7%	−10.7%
A$	10,688	1.6%	29,341	2.9%	174.5%	66,975	4.4%	128.3%	67,342	2.9%	0.5%	72,339	2.4%	7.4%	57,635	2.0%	−20.3%
NZ$	292	0.0%	2,042	0.2%	599.3%	441	0.0%	−78.4%	1,013	0.0%	129.7%	3,399	0.1%	235.5%	624	0.0%	−81.6%
HK$	1,336	0.2%	2,348	0.2%	75.7%	2,147	0.1%	−8.6%	2,428	0.1%	13.1%	2,821	0.1%	16.2%	3,755	0.1%	33.1%
Other		0.0%		0.0%		0	0.0%		12,086	1.5%		17,550	0.6%	45.2%	25,053	0.9%	42.8%
	682,889	100.0%	1,010,205	100.0%	47.9%	1,539,320	100.0%	52.4%	2,311,544	100.0%	50.2%	3,065,065	100.0%	32.6%	2,902,607	99.8%	−5.3%
Year	1987		1988			1989			1990			1991			1992		
Currency Blocks																	
North America	548,011	80.2%	743,937	73.6%	35.8%	1,041,072	67.6%	39.9%	1,340,945	58.0%	28.8%	1,567,330	51.1%	16.9%	1,390,468	47.9%	−11.3%
Europe	82,064	12.0%	154,049	15.2%	87.7%	304,326	19.8%	97.6%	655,788	28.4%	115.5%	922,703	30.1%	40.7%	997,510	34.4%	8.1%
Australasia	52,814	7.7%	112,219	11.1%	112.5%	193,922	12.6%	72.8%	302,725	13.1%	56.1%	557,482	18.2%	84.2%	489,576	16.9%	−12.2%
Other	0	0.0%	0	0.0%		0	0.0%		12,086	0.5%		17,550	0.6%	45.2%	25,053	0.9%	42.8%
Total	682,889	100.0%	1,010,205	100.0%	47.9%	1,539,320	100.0%	52.4%	2,311,544	100.0%	50.2%	3,065,065	100.0%	32.6%	2,902,607	100.0%	−5.3%

Source: International Swaps and Derivatives Association.

Exhibit 1.1—continued

TABLE 3

Cross-Currency Swaps (US$ Million)

	1987	% of Market	1988	% of Market	Growth (%)	1989	% of Market	Growth (%)	1990	% of Market	Growth (%)	1991	% of Market	Growth (%)	1992	% of Market	Growth (%)
North American																	
US$	162,606	44.3%	269,477	42.5%	65.7%	354,166	40.8%	31.4%	428,355	37.1%	20.9%	584,263	36.2%	36.4%	212,183	35.1%	–63.7%
C$	13,881	3.8%	29,259	4.6%	110.8%	32,584	3.8%	11.4%	56,919	4.9%	74.7%	63,686	3.9%	11.9%	34,302	5.7%	–46.1%
European																	
DEM	21,377	5.8%	33,979	5.4%	59.0%	54,009	6.2%	58.9%	72,310	6.3%	33.9%	95,178	5.9%	31.6%	50,511	8.4%	–46.9%
GBP	10,506	2.9%	17,704	2.8%	68.5%	33,815	3.9%	91.0%	49,041	4.2%	45.0%	74,835	4.6%	52.6%	30,873	5.1%	–58.7%
FFR	4,827	1.3%	5,178	0.8%	7.3%	8,345	1.0%	61.2%	13,398	1.2%	60.6%	17,257	1.1%	28.8%	16,258	2.7%	–5.8%
SFR	39,928	10.9%	73,983	11.7%	85.3%	64,944	7.5%	–12.2%	92,084	8.0%	41.8%	136,606	8.5%	48.3%	42,811	7.1%	–68.7%
ECU	18,718	5.1%	24,497	3.9%	30.9%	39,944	4.6%	63.1%	47,832	4.1%	19.7%	61,452	3.8%	28.5%	29,685	4.9%	–51.7%
Dfl	3,987	1.1%	6,164	1.0%	54.6%	10,092	1.2%	63.7%	13,109	1.1%	29.9%	12,472	0.8%	–4.9%	7,408	1.2%	–40.6%
BFR	1,330	0.4%	1,867	0.4%	40.4%	3,065	0.4%	64.2%	5,695	0.5%	85.8%	6,878	0.4%	20.8%	3,428	0.6%	–50.2%
LIT	0	0.0%	0	0.0%		0	0.0%		13,604	1.2%		35,901	2.2%	163.9%	26,503	4.4%	–26.2%
SKR	0	0.0%	0	0.0%		0	0.0%		6,189	0.5%		17,734	1.1%	186.5%	21,034	3.5%	18.6%
DKR	0	0.0%	0	0.0%		0	0.0%		1,738	0.2%		2,803	0.2%	61.3%	2,500	0.4%	–10.8%
ESP	0	0.0%	0	0.0%		0	0.0%		0	0.0%		0	0.0%		3,519	0.6%	
Australasian																	
JPY	59,746	16.3%	131,033	20.7%	119.3%	200,325	23.1%	52.9%	244,787	21.2%	22.2%	360,088	22.3%	47.1%	72,335	12.0%	–79.9%
A$	20,438	5.6%	32,637	5.2%	59.7%	61,236	7.0%	87.6%	77,407	6.7%	26.4%	86,524	5.4%	11.8%	19,161	3.2%	–77.9%
NZ$	8,074	2.2%	7,473	1.2%	–7.4%	5,823	0.7%	–22.1%	5,815	0.5%	–0.1%	6,486	0.4%	11.5%	657	0.1%	–89.9%
HK$	197	0.1%	390	0.1%	98.0%	553	0.1%	41.8%	639	0.1%	15.6%	957	0.1%	49.8%	859	0.1%	–10.2%
Other		0.0%		0.0%		0	0.0%		26,147	2.3%		51,212	3.2%	95.9%	29,688	4.9%	–42.0%
	365,615	100.0%	633,641	100.0%	73.3%	868,901	100.0%	37.1%	1,155,069	100.0%	32.9%	1,614,332	100.0%	39.8%	603,715	99.4%	–62.6%
Year	1987		1988			1989			1990			1991			1992		
Currency Blocks																	
North America	176,487	48.3%	298,736	47.1%	69.3%	386,750	44.5%	29.5%	485,274	42.0%	25.5%	647,949	40.1%	33.5%	246,485	40.8%	–62.0%
Europe	100,673	27.5%	163,372	25.8%	62.3%	214,214	24.7%	31.1%	315,000	27.3%	47.0%	461,116	28.6%	46.4%	234,530	38.8%	–49.1%
Australasia	88,455	24.2%	171,533	27.1%	93.9%	267,937	30.8%	56.2%	328,648	28.5%	22.7%	454,055	28.1%	38.2%	93,012	15.4%	–79.5%
Other	0	0.0%	0	0.0%		0	0.0%		26,147	2.3%		51,212	3.2%	95.9%	29,688	4.9%	–42.0%
Total	365,615	100.0%	633,641	100.0%	73.3%	868,901	100.0%	37.1%	1,155,069	100.0%	32.9%	1,614,332	100.0%	39.8%	603,715	100.0%	–62.6%

Source: International Swaps and Derivatives Association.

Exhibit 1.1—continued

TABLE 4
Total Cap and Swaptions Volume (US$ Billion)

Year	1989	1990	Growth (%)	1991	Growth (%)	1992	Growth (%)
Caps	254	319	25.6%	317	−0.6%	323	1.9%
Floors	86	110	27.9%	129	17.3%	99	−23.3%
Combinations	39	38	−2.6%	23	−39.5%	35	52.2%
Total	379	467	23.2%	469	0.4%	457	−2.6%
Swaptions	72	94	30.6%	109	16.0%	91	−16.5%

Source: International Swaps and Derivatives Association.

TABLE 5
Interest Rate and Currency Swaps Outstanding at Year End 1992

Interest rate swaps				Currency swaps		
$ equivalent (million)	Currency as a % of total	% change over year end 1991	Currency	$ equivalent (million)*	Currency as a % of total	% change over year end 1991
1,760,231	45.7	16.89	US dollar (US$)	309,020	35.9	5.78
103,944	2.7	43.69	Australian dollar (A$)	47,996	5.6	10.94
14,170	0.4	88.36	Belgian franc (BFR)	5,199	0.6	51.18
98,570	2.6	60.71	Canadian dollar (C$)	45,392	5.3	42.55
140,412	3.6	2.03	Swiss franc (SFR)	69,527	8.1	1.79
344,430	8.9	30.76	Deutschmark (DEM)	53,332	6.2	12.07
5,080	0.1	459.47	Danish krone (DKR)	1,513	0.2	7.92
15,225	0.4	NA	Spanish peseta (PTA)	20,085	2.3	NA
139,113	3.6	20.33	French franc (FFR)	15,816	0.1	83.30
294,804	7.7	16.29	Sterling (GBP)	40,116	4.7	7.21
4,970	0.1	76.18	Hong Kong dollar (HK$)	731	0.08	52.66
58,222	1.5	69.64	Italian lira (LIT)	21,996	2.6	22.53
706,042	18.3	47.42	Yen (JPY)	154,295	17.9	−14.39
31,212	0.8	86.54	Dutch guilder (Dfl)	7,416	0.9	16.92
1,321	0.03	−61.14	New Zealand dollar (NZ$)	1,824	0.2	−43.77
22,229	0.6	26.68	Other currencies	15,236	1.8	−40.50
17,702	0.5	−2.91	Swedish krona (SKR)	14,931	1.7	68.38
93,128	2.4	27.86	European currency unit (ECU)	35,977	4.2	17.09
3,850,805		25.00		860,402		−6.00

* Total adjusted for double counting of both sides of a currency swap.

Source: International Swaps and Derivatives Association.

Exhibit 1.1—continued

TABLE 6

Equity, Commodity, and Multi-Asset Derivatives Outstanding at Year End 1992*

	Transactions Between Dealers	Transactions With End Users	Total Outstanding
Commodity Swaps			
Energy	5	10	15
Metals	—	3	3
Subtotal	5	13	18
Commodity Options			
Energy	2	3	5
Metals	2	5	7
Subtotal	4	8	12
Equity Swaps			
Indices (by Index Country)			
Japan	3	3	6
US	1	1	2
Other	—	1	1
Baskets and Individual Stocks	—	1	1
Subtotal	4	6	10
Equity Options			
Indices (by Index Country)			
Japan	11	9	20
US	3	8	11
UK	6	5	11
Germany	4	2	6
France	3	2	5
Other	2	2	4
Baskets	—	2	2
Individual Stocks	1	6	7
Subtotal	30	36	66
Multi-Asset Transactions	10	15	25
Combined Total	53	78	131

* Notional principal in billions of US dollars.

Source: International Swaps and Derivatives Association.

Exhibit 1.1—continued

COMPOSITION OF INTEREST RATE SWAPS

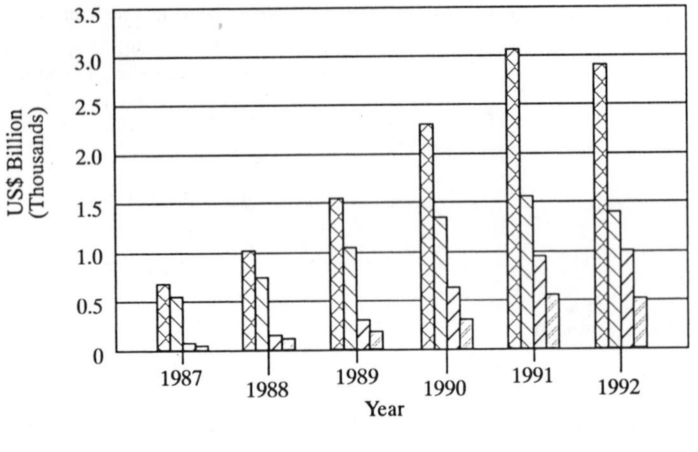

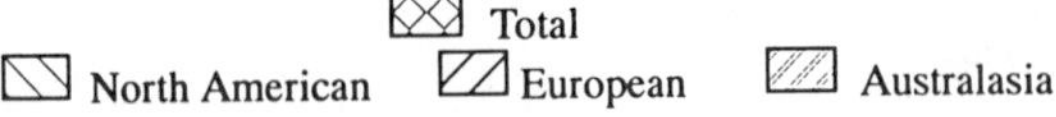

COMPOSITION OF CURRENCY SWAPS

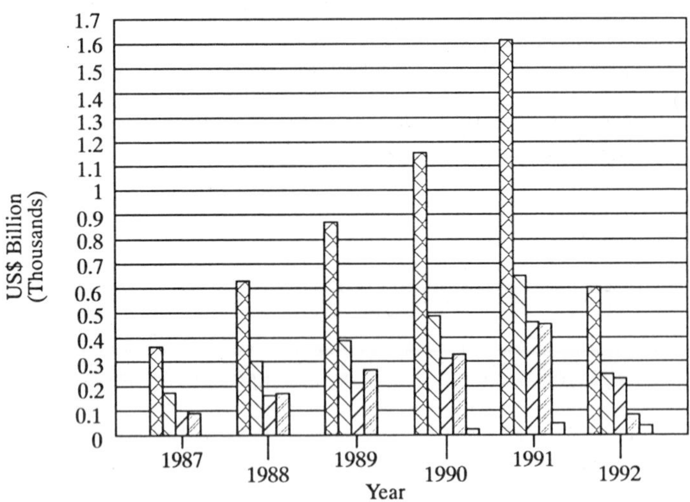

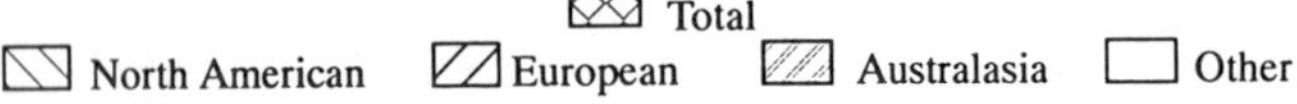

Exhibit 1.1—continued

COMPOSITION OF SWAP MARKET

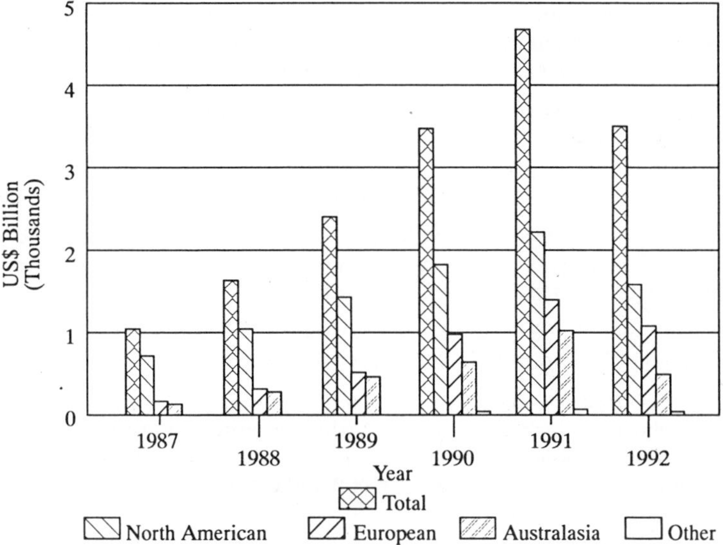

TOTAL SIZE OF SWAP MARKET

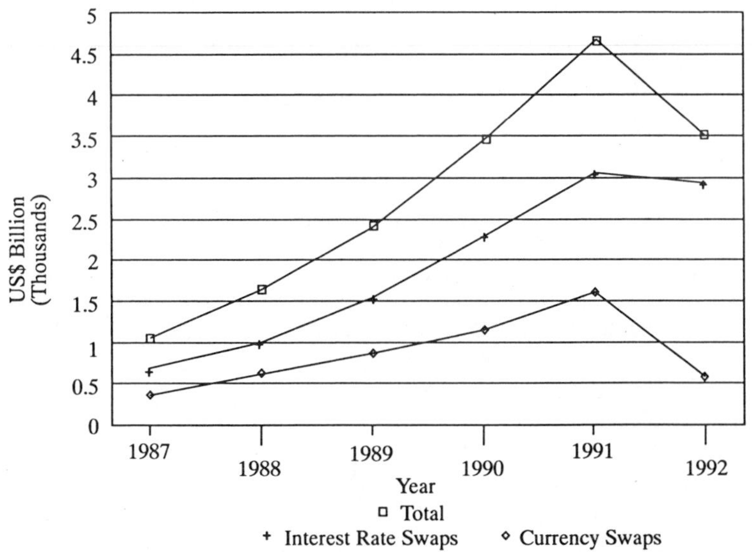

THE FUNCTION OF SWAPS

Swap instruments

The term "swap" in this book is utilised to describe a generalised class of financial exchange transactions in which counterparties simultaneously sell and purchase rights to streams of cash flows which vary in terms of the currency, interest rate basis and a number of other financial features.

The "core" swap instruments are interest rate swaps, currency swaps, FRAs, LTFX and caps/floors. These core swap instruments are well established as a fully integrated and interrelated set of financial instruments. These core swap instruments can be utilised for the purpose of management of both asset and liability profiles.

Increasingly, in response to evolutionary processes discussed in detail below, the range of swap instruments has increased. The development in the technical structure of swaps reflects two separate developments:

- the development of variations on basic swap instruments; and
- the extension of swap technique to other markets.

Variations on basic swap structures include evolution of a variety of non-generic swap arrangements which entail variation in the pattern and type of cash flows exchanged. For example, these include timing variations, maturity variations, notional principal variations (amortising etc) and other types of reconfigurations of the cash flow profile of such instruments. They also include a whole range of transactions focusing exclusively on floating rate cash flows such as basis swaps, yield curve swaps, arrears reset swaps and index differential swaps. In addition, a separate development is the growth of markets entailing the purchase and sale of options on swap transactions themselves. These include options on swaps (swaptions) as well as a variety of swap and option combinations.

Hybrid swap transactions, with embedded interest rate and currency option features have also emerged as a specific class of swap transactions.

An interesting development has been the extension of the basic concept and technique of swap transactions to other markets, primarily commodity and equity markets. Commodity and equity swaps, as well as the use of hybrid swap structures to securitise forward and option positions embedded in commodity and equity linked securities issues, are also an increasing element in the range of swap instruments.

The development of swap products and markets reflects the strong growth of the market for derivative instruments. Markets for derivative instruments, either those traded on organised exchanges (including stock, futures and option exchanges) or OTC markets, have evolved rapidly in response to the demand for risk transfer instruments. The development of swap products is increasingly an integral part of the broader development of derivative markets generally.

Function of swaps

Swap transactions have two major economic functions:

- to provide a vehicle for market linkage, integrating global capital markets; and
- to allow greater efficiency in the management of interest rate and currency exposures.

Swap transactions provide a classical bridge between markets, integrating different types of financial instruments, such as fixed and floating interest rates, and also linking various global capital markets.

This market linkage derives largely from the fact that swaps allow the extension of the theory of comparative advantage from the commodity and service markets to the world's capital markets. The theory of comparative advantage in trade states that each party should specialise in the production of those goods for which it has a relative comparative advantage. Having done so, the parties can exchange those goods through trade (if they desire) for a mix of commodities and hence increase their welfare beyond that which would have been possible had they attempted to provide for all their commodity needs directly.

Swap transactions fundamentally enable institutions to accomplish similar objectives in international capital markets allowing each institution to either borrow or invest where it has a relative comparative advantage and then obtain the desired interest rate or currency basis of the borrowing or investment through an accompanying interest rate or currency swap.

Swaps also enable institutions to take a much more flexible approach towards the management of assets and liabilities. Swaps enable institutions to manage these portfolios in the light of changed expectations as to interest rates and currencies in a flexible way, adjusting their portfolios to avoid potential losses or to lock in gains. In this regard, swaps are superior to alternative techniques for achieving similar objectives such as the early retirement of borrowings or the liquidation of asset portfolios.

The greater efficiency in managing asset liability portfolios possible through swap transactions derives from the unique characteristics of swaps which allow a fundamental unbundling of various aspects of borrowing or investment transactions. This unbundling element in swap transactions operates on two levels: first, swaps are separate from the underlying funding or investment transaction; and secondly, the swap transaction, being separate, is also independent from a timing perspective.

This separability of the swap transaction means that borrowers and investors can obtain liquidity or invest funds in a manner quite separate from the management of the interest rate and currency rate basis. A borrowing or investment transaction can be combined with an interest rate or currency swap to effectively generate the form of funding or investment desired by the borrower or investor.

The fact that the swap transaction is separate from the underlying funding or investment transaction in a timing sense allows existing liabilities or assets to be managed in the light of new information as to the future course of interest rates and currency values. By utilising a swap transaction, entered into sometime after the original funding or investment decision, the borrower or investor can transform the interest rate or currency basis of that liability or asset to better fit current expectations and performance objectives.

The development of currency swaps has also led to extension of the maturity of foreign exchange markets. Traditionally, foreign exchange markets have been limited to maturities of one and, at most, two years. However, the emergence and growth of swaps has added significant liquidity to the long-dated foreign exchange market whereby markets are routinely made in a wide variety of currencies for maturities of up to five years and in some cases for maturities of up to ten years. This growth in liquidity of the long-dated foreign exchange market allows greater flexibility in the management of future cash flows resulting from various contractual obligations enabling participants to hedge the currency risk of these future cash flows where they are denominated in a currency other than that of the borrower or investor.

The non-generic swap instruments function in a similar manner, facilitating arbitrage or allowing asset liability management strategies to be implemented. Commodity and equity swaps and derivatives facilitate the management of price risk in the underlying asset. In the case of equity swaps, these transactions also allow the simulation of exposure to equity markets, without the necessity for an actual investment in stocks or shares.

THE IMPACT OF SWAPS ON DEBT MARKETS

The development of highly liquid markets in interest rate and currency swaps has had a fundamental impact on the operation of primary debt markets throughout the world. Increasingly, primary debt markets have come to be swap-driven. A swap-driven transaction can be defined as a primary issue in a debt market, in the standard form of that market, where the borrower will have acquired an exposure in a currency or interest rate basis other than that of the issue through an interest rate or currency swap transaction undertaken in conjunction with the issuance of debt.

The availability of swaps has also fundamentally altered the activity of investors in the primary and secondary debt markets. The availability of asset swaps, whereby a swap transaction is combined with the purchase of an underlying security to create synthetic investments with cash flows tailored to specific investor requirements, in terms of currency or interest rate basis as well as desired linkages to a variety of indexes, has greatly increased the range of investments that can be engineered.

The emergence of swaps, therefore, has enhanced the fungibility of funds flows in capital markets for both asset and liability applications. For borrowers, swaps facilitate the transformation of borrowings in any given currency or interest rate basis into a liability in its desired currency or interest rate basis. Similarly, the availability of swaps allows investors to transform the currency in interest rate denominations of its investments, irrespective of the original structure and form of these obligations.

The fungibility and inherent ability to substitute securities facilitated by the availability of a whole class of financial instruments inevitably encourages the process of arbitrage *between markets*. These features of swaps essentially imply a greater degree of interrelationship between primary and secondary debt markets in different countries denominated in different currencies as well as within sectors of the debt market in the same currency. Consequently, swaps act as the "hinge" between almost every national and international market.

The availability of commodity and equity derivatives has impacted on debt markets in a more limited way. The availability of securities with embedded commodity and equity elements has facilitated the access of investors to assets which allow creation of specific exposures to these asset classes.

ORIGINS OF THE SWAP MARKET

The history of the development of swap transactions is a much debated and disputed one. However, there appears to be agreement that the concept of swaps originated from the GBP and US$ parallel loans arranged between British and American entities in the 1970s. It is important to note, however, that a type of currency swap transaction (involving foreign currencies and occasionally gold) has a long history. These transactions were usually undertaken between a number of key central banks and the Bank for International Settlements (BIS).

The central bank swap arrangements involved foreign currencies and, initially, monetary gold. They were and are similar to short-dated foreign exchange swaps combining a spot sale (purchase) of a currency with a simultaneous agreement to buy (sell) the currency at some time in the future. This swap network is designed to create additional international reserves through a cross-crediting system to facilitate central bank stabilisation of the international monetary system.

The genesis of modern swap structures is evident in the structure of these arrangements which sought to overcome structural regulatory barriers and which were predicated on the basis of risk-free, mutually beneficial but offsetting transactions as between the parties involved.

However, it was in the 1970s with the introduction of exchange controls in the United Kingdom that parallel and back-to-back loans were arranged, ultimately evolving into the first currency swap in 1976. In that transaction, Continental Illinois Limited (subsequently First Interstate Limited) and Goldman Sachs arranged a transaction between a Dutch (Bos Kalis Westminister) and British (ICI Finance) company involving the Dfl and GBP.

This transaction was followed by a transaction completed on behalf of Consolidated Goldfields in April 1977 and a transaction involving the government of Venezuela in connection with the construction of the Caracas Metro System involving a substantial US$ and FFR currency swap undertaken at about the same time.

The first currency swap transacted against a capital market issue was undertaken in 1979 by Roylease, the leasing subsidiary of the Royal Bank of Canada, involving a DEM issue swapped into C$. In this transaction, Roylease undertook a five year DEM60m issue with a coupon of 6.75% pa which was swapped into fixed C$ at a coupon cost under the borrower's target cost of 11.00% pa. The transaction was apparently structured as a series of foreign exchange contracts which were used to hedge all the DEM principal and interest payments first into US$ and then into the required C$.

However, it was not until August 1981 that currency swaps became an established feature of international capital markets when the World Bank swapped a US$290m bond issue into an equivalent amount of DEM and SFR provided by IBM under an arrangement devised by Salomon Brothers. A brief summary of this historic transaction is set out in *Exhibit 1.2*.

The first interest rate swaps were also undertaken in 1981, initially by Citibank and Continental Illinois. The first interest rate swaps included a number of private transactions culminating in 1982 with a much publicised US$300m seven year bond issue by Deutsche Bank which was swapped into US$ LIBOR.

From that landmark transaction onwards, the interest rate swap market was to expand at a much more sustained pace than its foreign exchange counterpart, the currency swap market.

While initial developments were in the US$ market, the potential of swaps was quickly recognised and markets in other currencies developed rapidly.

Exhibit 1.2
1981 World Bank—IBM Swap

Some years ago IBM needed to raise substantial funds and as the amount required was greater than could be raised in any one capital market, IBM launched a world-wide borrowing programme which included raising large amounts in the deutschmark and Swiss franc capital markets. The proceeds of these loans were sold for US$ and remitted back to head office where they were used for general corporate funding purposes. Coincidentally, the World Bank had (and still has) a declared policy of raising funds in currencies with low interest rates, such as the deutschmark and the Japanese yen. It is faced with a problem in that its demand for fixed rate funds in these currencies is greater than the capacity of the respective capital markets to support. The third ingredient to this transaction was that the US$ had appreciated substantially against the Swiss franc and the deutschmark from the time IBM borrowed these currencies to the time it entered into the swap transaction with the World Bank creating a significant unrealised foreign exchange gain.

IBM was approached to see if it would be interested in locking in the capital gain on its Swiss franc and deutschmark borrowings, and effectively converting these liabilities into simulated US$ liabilities. At the same time, the World Bank was asked whether it would like to complement its Swiss franc and deutschmark borrowing programme by raising US$s and converting the borrowing into Swiss francs and deutschmarks via a cross-currency fixed-to-fixed debt swap with IBM. The result was that the World Bank issued a two-tranche US$ fixed rate Eurobond with maturities exactly matching IBM's Swiss franc and deutschmark debt, and at the same time entered into a swap with IBM. Under the swap agreement, IBM agreed to pay all the future interest and principal payments on the World Bank's US$ Eurobonds in return for the World Bank agreeing to pay all future interest and principal payments on IBM's Swiss franc and deutschmark debt. The transaction is depicted diagramatically below.

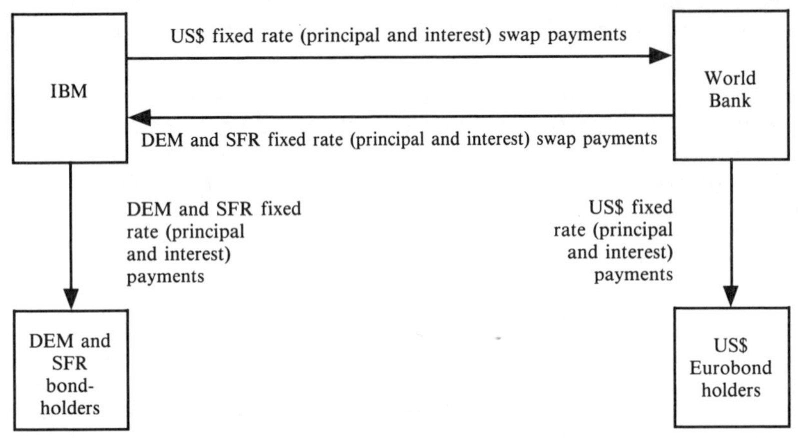

The detailed methodology can be illustrated utilising one of the key elements of the transaction—a 4.60 year (average life) US$210m issue by the World Bank to fund the swaps against the Swiss franc and deutschmark cash flows provided by IBM.

The calculation procedure was:

- to discount the Swiss franc and deutschmark cash flows at a negotiated interest rate;
- to convert the resulting present values into US$ at prevailing exchange rates;
- to construct matching US$ flows on the basis of prevailing dollar interest rates.

These three variables—the all-in cost in Swiss francs (or deutschmarks), the spot exchange rate, and the all-in dollar cost accepted by the bank's counterparty—were the key points of negotiation in the swap transaction.

Exhibit 1.2—continued

Following is the schedule of flows being exchanged through the swap.

Exchange date	**SFR amount**	**DEM amount**	**US$ amount**
30.3.82	12,375,000	30,000,000	20,066,667[1]
30.3.83	12,375,000	30,000,000	33,600,000
30.3.84	12,375,000	30,000,000	33,600,000
30.3.85	12,375,000	30,000,000	33,600,000
30.3.86	212,375,000	330,000,000	243,600,000
Compounding rate	8.00%	11.00%	16.80%[2]
Compounded value	191,367,478	301,315,273	205,485,000
Exchange rate	US$1.00: SFR2.18	US$1.00: DM2.56	US$1.00
Compounded value in US$	87,783,247	117,703,153	205,485,000

The compounded value of the US$ cash flows was then utilised to work back to the structure of the underlying World Bank issue. The coupon (16.00%) and the total discount from par to the bank on the issue (that is, the price of the issue less commissions and expenses) were given by the market. The per cent proceeds (that is 97.85%) could then be used to gross up the absolute dollar proceeds in order to obtain the par amount of notes to be issued, as follows:

$$\frac{\text{US\$205,485,000}}{0.9785} = \text{US\$210,000,000}$$

Notes:

1. The first dollar amount is reduced to take account of the partial first period on the dollar bond issue.
2. The yield to maturity on a 16.00% bond due on 30 March 1988 and purchased on 25 August is 16.61%.

Source: This discussion is based substantially on David R Bock, "Fixed-to-Fixed Currency Swap: The Origins of the World Bank Borrowing Programme" in Antl (1986), Vol 2, pp 218-223.

EVOLUTION OF THE SWAP MARKET

Key evolutionary factors

The rapid growth in the absolute size of the global swap market tends to mask the subtle changes in the nature of swaps as a category of financial instruments and in the patterns of the global swap market itself.

The key factors which have influenced the development and evolution of the swap market include:

- regulations and the regulatory environment—which created opportunities for capital market arbitrage;
- volatility of key financial market variables, such as interest rates, exchange rates and, more recently, commodity and equity prices—which prompted increased emphasis on risk management;
- the internationalisation of financial markets—which facilitated the globalisation of fund raising and investing activity;
- the regulation of the swap market itself through the BIS capital adequacy requirement—which affected the capacity of financial institutions to participate as intermediaries in swap transactions;

- the competitive market structure—which dictated the participation of financial institutions in the global swap markets and influenced the development in complementary markets for derivative products generally.

The evolution in the pattern of the swap market has largely been a response to development in these key factors. As would be expected, each of these factors and the corresponding evolution of the market are closely interrelated. This makes it difficult to decipher the precise cause-effect relationships in the evolution of the market.

Phase 1 (to 1982/83)—new product

The initial phase of the evolution of the global swap market was in the early 80s—in the period from approximately 1977/78 to 1982/83.

The major characteristics of this period included:

- low transaction volumes;
- highly structured transactions involving counterparties with exactly matching and opposite requirements;
- the presence of very substantial arbitrage profits from such transactions which provided significant returns to both the counterparties and the intermediaries involved in facilitating these transactions;
- limited product knowledge which was confined to a very few pioneering individuals in a small coterie of financial institutions;
- limited acceptance of the product with potential end users being usually sceptical and cautious about entering into such transactions; and
- the absence of a definitive framework for pricing, accounting and taxing of such transactions.

The major impetus to the market of this phase was very complex currency hedging requirements which could not be satisfied by traditional foreign exchange markets, primarily reflecting the lack of depth and liquidity in these markets beyond relatively short maturities (one to two years) at this point in time and the high cost of hedging currency exposures beyond this limited time horizon. An added impetus was the need for borrowers to manage the currency exposures on extremely attractively priced long-term export credit financing denominated in a variety of currencies where the borrower wished to change the currency denomination of the liability stream to match its currency requirements. For the financial community, the substantial fee-generating potential of such transactions provided significant incentive to promote these products.

Towards the end of the initial phase of the global swap market, the emphasis of the market changed significantly. The swap market began to have an increasingly primary market emphasis entailing the use of new issue arbitrage techniques to generate cost-effective funding. The currency management emphasis of the Consolidated Goldfields and IBM type of transaction was replaced by a focus on the arrangement of swaps combined with fund raising transactions to generate low-cost funding for the borrower.

In this initial phase, the primary impetus for new issue arbitrage came from highly rated global banks and other financial institutions. These institutions which had traditionally not issued Eurobonds because of their lack of requirement for fixed rate funding began to enter the market to issue fixed rate Eurobonds, primarily in US$, combined with an interest rate swap to generate funding at substantial margins below LIBOR. The benefits to the bank included the capacity to significantly lengthen the tenor of their liability portfolio in addition to the significant cost savings available. The fixed rate paying interest in such US$ interest rate swap transactions came from a variety of borrowers seeking to hedge their interest rate exposure under floating rate borrowings in response to the volatility of US$ interest rates.

Phase 2 (1983-1988/89)—growth

The second phase of the evolution of the swap market between approximately 1983 and 1989 entailed an unprecedented and extraordinary level of growth in the swap market. The major characteristics of this period included:

- the evolution of the function of swaps, including expansion of swap applications from capital market arbitrage to asset liability management;
- the evolution of swap structures themselves;
- the proliferation of currencies in which swap transactions were undertaken; and
- changes in the institutional structure of the swap market, including a dramatic growth in the type and number of swap market participants.

All of the above developments are closely interrelated. For example, the change of emphasis in the utilisation of swaps from pure capital market arbitrage to asset liability management resulted from the decreased arbitrage profits available from capital market arbitrage transactions and also the increased volatility of currency and interest rates which promoted the use of swaps as techniques of risk management. The erosion of profits from capital market arbitrage led to the development of various security issue structures designed to arbitrage capital markets which required the corresponding development of new swap structures to translate these arbitrage profits into the issuer's desired currency and interest rate basis.

The search for new arbitrage profits also prompted the opening of swap markets in a wide range of currencies. Simultaneously, the increased use of swaps as asset liability management tools prompted a number of financial intermediaries to enter into swaps on a principal basis while managing the risks entailed in swap trading through various hedging techniques.

The evolving function of swaps

Historically, swap transactions evolved in response to regulatory factors and opportunities for capital market arbitrage.

The impact of regulatory factors on the evolution of the swap market was both direct and indirect during this period. The economics of swap transactions derive, at least in part, from the existence of regulations. Government regulation influenced the evolution of the swap market indirectly through the imposition of restrictions on cross-border capital flows, such as withholding taxes, and restrictions on asset portfolio choice.

Capital market arbitrage as a basis for the development of the swap market operated on a number of bases:

- classical financial arbitrage;
- tax and regulatory arbitrage.

Classical financial arbitrage across different capital markets has and continues to be one of the basic factors driving the development of the swap market. This type of financial arbitrage is based on the fact that prices in various world capital markets are not mutually consistent and issuers can lower their borrowing costs by accessing the capital market with the lowest relative rates, borrowing there, and then swapping their exposure back into the desired currency thereby achieving lower cost funding than obtainable directly from borrowing in that market. For example, the development of interest rate swaps was predicated on a form of credit arbitrage based on the differential pricing of identical risks in between the fixed and floating rates debt markets.

The second type of arbitrage, tax and regulatory arbitrage, as noted above, relies on externally imposed restrictions on capital flows or investment choice. An important aspect of the development of the swap market has been the evolution of some extremely creative swap structures designed to in effect unbundle the currency and interest rate exposure from the regulation and tax rules applicable in certain markets.

An additional factor driving the development of the swap market was the increased volatility in currency and interest rates. Throughout the 1980s, financial markets experienced unprecedented volatility in currency and interest rates. In this environment, the capacity of swaps to allow firms to manage exposures to interest rates and/or currencies was quickly recognised. The capacity of interest rate swaps to function as forward interest rate contracts extending beyond the scope of organised futures markets in interest rates was increasingly useful to market participants as a means of managing asset and liability exposures. Similarly, the role of currency swaps in replicating conventional LTFX contracts, usually more efficiently, allowed the currency swap to be utilised as an instrument for the management of corporate foreign exchange exposures over extended periods.

Initially, swap transactions were, in the main, predicated on the exchange by one party of a benefit which it enjoyed in a particular market for a corresponding benefit available to another party in a different market. This advantage could be one of access or effective after-tax cost. Consequently, the swap market functioned as a new funding market utilised by a wide range of organisations to lower the cost of raising new funds.

The classical interest rate swap, for example, arbitraged the different risk and reward criteria of fixed rate investors against those of floating rate lenders. However, as in any type of arbitrage, the continuous and active exploitation of an identifiable arbitrage opportunity gradually eroded the arbitrage. For example, in the case of interest rate swaps, the market actions embodied in the transaction should result in the following:

- Direct fixed rate borrowing costs to fixed rate issuers (such as banks) would increase as they borrow more in the fixed rate market.
- Direct floating rate costs to fixed rate issuers would decrease as they borrow less in the floating rate market.
- Direct fixed rate costs to the lower rated companies would decrease as they borrow less in the fixed rate market.
- Direct floating rate costs to lower rated companies would increase as they borrow more in the floating rate market.

The actual outcome of market actions, for example, in the US$ market during this period, corresponded closely to the predictions of the theory. The use of interest rate swaps appears to have caused the predicted changes in pricing relationships.

The most obvious impact of such transactions has been in the Eurobond market. As the cost savings of funding via a fixed rate bond issue with an interest rate swap or (if appropriate) a currency swap attached became apparent, banks, particularly those with good credit standings, switched from the floating rate markets to the fixed rate market as a source of funds.

The switch had dramatic consequences for pricing relationships. In the floating rate markets traditionally used by banks to raise floating rate funds (primarily US$), such as the floating rate note (FRN) and floating rate certificate of deposit market, the absence of new issues meant that prices on existing issues increased with banks being able to issue new paper at lower spreads relative to LIBOR than ever before. Through 1985 and 1986, the margins on FRNs issued by prime quality issuers plummeted, precipitating a collapse of the FRN market in late 1986. In the fixed rate bond markets, the increased volume of new issues by bank names meant a marked increase in the yields demanded by investors to purchase bank issued fixed rate Eurobonds. The relative deterioration of the banks' collective standing in the Eurobond market was a factor of not only the increased supply of bank paper but of investors' belief that many bank Eurobond issues were being unrealistically priced to accommodate the swap integral to the transaction.

An associated, but not often recognised factor, which affected at least the US$ interest rate swap market over this period was the abolition of the United States withholding tax on interest rate payments to overseas investors in United States domestic securities. While the change, implemented in July 1984, did not spell the end, as indeed some had predicted, of the Eurobond market, which continued to survive and even prosper as a result of its qualities of innovation and superior speed relative to the United States market, it did reshape some historic pricing relationships.

The previously existing pricing differences between anonymous, bearer Eurodollar bonds and registered United States bonds were eroded as foreign purchases of United States government and corporate securities grew. The previous pricing pattern which had favoured virtually all credit-worthy borrowers in the Eurobond market was reversed as most international borrowers attracted comparable and sometimes higher yields on their Eurodollar bonds than the yield on United States government treasury bonds of a comparable maturity.

New Eurodollar offerings were no longer expected to trade consistently at lower yields than United States treasury bonds and the borrowers that can issue Eurobonds at yields below United States treasuries are extremely rare. Even the most coveted borrowers in the Eurobond market have seen their issues outperformed consistently by treasuries during the period since the abolition of withholding tax. For example, Eurodollar bonds with five year maturities issued by a selected group of United States corporations have traded, on average, at a yield of approximately 0.30% pa above five year United States treasuries since the change, compared to an average yield of 0.70% pa below comparable United States treasuries prior to the repeal of the withholding tax.

The increase in yields on Eurobonds eliminated, to a very significant degree, the advantage previously enjoyed by major international borrowers who could issue at a substantial margin under comparable United States treasuries and swap into floating rate US$ funds against a fixed rate borrower (usually a United States corporation of medium to low credit standing) pricing off treasuries as a benchmark to determine the alternative cost of US$ fixed rate funding.

The erosion of the arbitrage through market actions and the increased yields evident in the Eurobond market as a result of the change in United States withholding tax laws combined to reduce the gains from interest rate swaps. For example, whereas the first swap transactions routinely generated floating rate funds for banks at LIBOR less 0.625% pa to 0.75% pa, those same banks would now be struggling to achieve funding at LIBOR less 0.125% pa to 0.25% pa through a straight Eurodollar bond issue with an interest rate swap attached. As the arbitrage spread narrowed, the savings to fixed rate borrowers, who were utilising swaps to generate fixed rate funds, also diminished.

While the above analysis focuses primarily on US$ interest rate swaps, a similar erosion in the arbitrage savings from other segments of the interest rate and currency swaps was evident, as the arbitrage were exploited by market forces.

However, as the process of arbitrage erosion became evident, the swap market itself adapted by undergoing certain fundamental changes. The market developed in two different but complementary directions. The first development involved the search for "new" arbitrage opportunities and the development of transaction structures designed to exploit identified discrepancies to provide net economic gains to the parties involved. The second development was a change in the purpose for which swaps were utilised; instead of merely being an attractive way of reducing the cost of new funds to be raised, swaps were increasingly used as an instrument for actively managing an organisation's existing liabilities.

The search for new arbitrage opportunities primarily entailed increased effort to understand the economics of swap transactions and to identify the underlying comparative advantages which enable the arbitrage to be undertaken. As already noted, swap transactions are predicated on the central principle of the exchange of an advantage which a party enjoys in one market for an advantage enjoyed by a counterparty in a different market. Importantly, the advantage need not be absolute, it need only be comparative, that is, one party may in fact have an absolute advantage in both markets, but may have a comparatively greater advantage in one market. That advantage can be in terms of cost borrowing and/or availability of funds.

As market forces eroded the initial credit arbitrage between fixed and floating rate markets, the search for new opportunities focused on both temporary and sustainable arbitrage opportunities between various markets. Some short-lived arbitrage opportunities which appeared intermittently focused on the creation of securities issues and associated swap structures which appealed to niches of investors and borrowers at particular times. The experience of the Eurobond market, where it is common to think of the market in terms of "windows" (the term being used to characterise the moments in time when a particular type of security can be issued because the investors are "there") rapidly became equally relevant to the swap market.

Popular innovations of this type (at least for a time) included zero coupon bond swaps, debt warrant swaps and dual currency bond swaps. Just as the type of security and related swap changed in line with investor and borrower preferences, the relevant sector of the bond market which provided the most attractive swap also changed. During this period, markets as widely varied as the Eurosterling, Euroyen, European Currency Unit (ECU), EuroCanadian dollar, EuroNew Zealand dollar, Eurolira, EuroFrench franc, Eurokrone and the EuroAustralian dollar market at various times provided the basis of the most attractive swap transactions.

A particular feature of this change in the basic arbitrage nature of swap transactions was an unbundling process, primarily in straight interest rate swaps, whereby the securities issue used to raise the underlying debt and the swap transaction were separated in a timing sense. A borrower would issue into a particular market at the time when the market was most receptive to its issue with the swap being separately entered into later when the swap market was most attractive for the swap transaction. The order of transactions could also be reversed with the swap being put in place prior to the fund raising.

The process of unbundling or swap timing also saw borrowers seeking to engineer currency swap transactions in stages. For example, a borrower seeking to swap from fixed rate GBP to fixed rate A$ would first swap from fixed rate GBP to floating rate US$ (this transaction being timed to ensure the maximum position achievable under LIBOR) and subsequently swap from floating rate US$ to fixed rate achieved).

In this regard, floating rate US$, usually priced relative to LIBOR, emerged as a useful medium through which a large proportion of cross-currency swaps were transacted. This was, at least in part, a result of the emergence of a select group of currency swap market makers (see discussion below) who were willing to quote prices relative to US$ LIBOR, that is, an institution may make prices in Japanese yen whereby it would pay (receive) fixed rate yen in return for receiving (paying) US$ LIBOR.

As the classic arbitrage advantage of swaps diminished, there was, in addition to seeking out new arbitrage opportunities, a fundamental change in the purposes for which swaps were utilised. Currency and interest rate swaps came to be utilised as an instrument for the active management of an organisation's existing liabilities. At the same time, swap applications relevant to the asset side as opposed to the liability side of the balance sheet came increasingly to be recognised, enabling portfolio or investment managers to use interest rate and currency swaps to create synthetic securities which were otherwise unavailable, to provide both yield pick-up and portfolio diversification.

For the borrower, interest rate swaps had four major applications:

- to lock in the cost of floating rate debt;
- to create term floating rate debt; and
- to actively manage the cost of an organisation's fixed or floating rate debt in a manner consistent with interest rate expectations.

The continued use of interest rate swaps to generate a synthetic fixed rate liability, even when they are not necessarily a method of creating liabilities at rates more advantageous than a conventional capital market transaction (such as a direct fixed rate bond issue), highlighted the increased focus on factors other than cost savings in the decision to utilise swaps. The flexibility, speed and anonymity of swap transactions were increasingly major considerations in utilising swaps.

The flexibility of swaps derives from the fact that the swap transaction is separate from the underlying funding to be transformed. Swap transactions are also more flexible from a timing viewpoint. Unlike a major public bond issue, swaps may be specifically tailored to a company's exact requirements. For example, whereas a public issue requires the rate to be set at a single point of time (creating problems in timing the issue to obtain the most attractive interest cost) a strategy whereby a series of swaps are undertaken, perhaps incorporating some timing options, enabled an organisation to achieve a blended rate which may result in a lower average all-in cost.

Swap transactions, unlike a conventional fixed rate issue, also allow the underlying floating rate source of funds to be varied, for example, by switching between US$ LIBOR-based funding and United States CP funding, to take advantage of variations in the cost of funds to further reduce the overall costs to the borrower.

The primary feature of swaps is that they, unlike direct borrowings, are highly flexible and can be reversed. Effectively, unlike most public issues, swaps provide a borrower with an at-the-market call on its fixed rate debt enabling the company to manage its interest cost more actively than previously feasible. The fact that the restrictions in terms of covenants etc that swap transactions place on a borrower are generally less onerous relative to loan documents enhances this added flexibility.

In addition to their inherent flexibility, the speed with which swap transactions were increasingly able to be undertaken is relevant. The emergence of a select group of market makers who were willing to transact swaps as principals as distinct from agents structuring on behalf of other counterparties enabled swap transactions to rapidly become a financial commodity with transactions being completed over the telephone. The relative simplicity of swap documentation relative to the requirements for borrowing transactions, such as the formal registration, prospectus, reporting etc requirements usually associated with public issues, contributed to the speed with which transactions can be completed.

The fact that swaps enjoyed a high degree of anonymity by virtue of the fact that they are private transactions is also a consideration. Rating agencies tended to view swaps in a neutral manner, treating them as fixed rate obligations of the appropriate maturity and the relatively uncomplicated accounting and tax treatment of such transactions makes swaps an attractive financing alternative.

The above comments are equally relevant for currency swaps. However, as it encompasses a currency exchange, a swap provides a mechanism for managing long-term foreign currency exposure. For example, a currency swap can be used to transform the currency denomination of its borrowing relatively easily to lock in unrealised gains on foreign currency liabilities incurred during a period of favourable exchange rates or created by a rise in interest rates relative to the level at which the borrower obtained the foreign liability. By executing a currency swap, the borrower, depending on the currency into which the liability is transformed, alters or eliminates the exchange risk for the remaining life of the liability and therefore protects itself from a possible reversal of the gain or increase in any loss due to further currency and interest rate fluctuations.

For the investor, swaps emerged as an instrument for creating synthetic assets and as a means for more active portfolio management. Interest rate swaps could be utilised to effectively create a fixed rate investment using floating rate securities, or transform a fixed rate asset into a floating rate investment. Interest rate swaps could also be used to lock in capital gains or minimise losses arising from the impact of interest rate fluctuations on investment portfolios.

For portfolio managers, the impact of swap transactions on investment strategies in respect of holdings of debt securities was subtle. The active investment management approach of many portfolio managers seeking improved performance means that swaps did not alter their approach to portfolio management but rather changed the way in which active portfolio management could be undertaken. Swaps emerged as an alternative technique whereby existing investments could be transformed through swaps into selected currencies and/or interest rate basis without the need to physically trade the underlying security.

Evolution of swap structures

The evolution of the function of swap transactions from its original role as a tool of new issue arbitrage to a general asset liability management technique was accompanied by significant innovations in the technical structures of swaps. The technical evolution of swap structures was evident in three separate areas:

- development of new liability swap structures;

- development of asset swaps; and
- the emerging differentiation between primary and secondary market swaps.

The new liability swap structures evolved in response to the demand for enhancements to the classical swap structure to accommodate more complex asset liability management applications as well as structural innovations designed to accommodate the swapping of new types of securities issues structured to capitalise on available tax and regulatory arbitrages.

While many banks and corporations were competing fiercely to swap their liabilities into desired currency and interest rate bases, the realisation that assets could be swapped as readily and easily as liabilities prompted the development of the asset swap market. The term asset swap generally refers to an interest rate or currency swap combined with an asset designed to transform the interest rate and/or currency basis of the investment.

The development of the asset swap market was driven by two separate influences:

- yield considerations; and
- asset management considerations.

The early impetus to the asset swap market came from the potential to create higher yielding securities than those available directly. This was the direct reverse of the liability arbitrage which had originally created the currency and interest rate swap market. However, as the active exploitation of the asset swap arbitrage saw potential profits diminish, the asset swap became accepted as a technique for enhancing the flexibility and management of asset portfolios.

The technical evolution of the swap market as well as the altered function of swaps effectively created a two-tier market: a primary and a secondary market.

A primary market transaction usually refers to a transaction between two counterparties. In contrast, a secondary market transaction refers to subsequent transactions involving the original contract between the counterparties.

This secondary market in swaps has emerged for two reasons: first, the emergence of market makers (see below) who must eventually move to neutralise the temporary risk position (protected by hedges) created by entering into one side of the swap, by entering into an equal and opposite swap which provides the only perfect hedge; and secondly, the move by borrowers to actively manage their asset or liability portfolios by entering into swaps then subsequently terminating their initial position.

Development of global swap markets

As swap transactions increasingly unbundled the process of fund raising, separating the decision to raise funds in a particular market and the process of conversion of funds raised into the desired currency and interest rate basis, all the major global bond markets increasingly became arbitrage markets. With an ever-higher percentage of issues being swap-driven, the pricing in almost every segment of the international bond market came to be arbitrage-driven; the relevant pricing being not the absolute interest cost of an issue per se, but the pricing achievable in US$ terms in either fixed rate terms relative to United States treasuries, or more often in floating rate terms as a margin relative to LIBOR.

As the classic credit arbitrage in the Eurodollar sector of the Eurobond market eroded, each sector of the international bond market came to be regarded as a potential source of swap-driven issues. At various times, the Eurosterling, the Euroyen, the ECU, EuroCanadian dollar, EuroNew Zealand dollar, Eurolira,

EuroFrench franc, Eurokrone and the EuroAustralian dollar markets became the focus of large volumes of issues as borrowers without a legitimate direct interest in the market used the issue as an arbitrage-based vehicle to generate lower cost overall funding taking advantage of the particular circumstances that prevailed.

As the major global bond markets increasingly became swap-driven, swap markets in a wide variety of currencies also developed. The development of bond markets, in particular Eurobond markets in a wide variety of currencies, were dependent on the simultaneous development of corresponding currency swap markets. The liquidity in the bond and swap markets came to be closely related with pricing in one being closely related to pricing in the other.

Against this background, currency and interest rate swap markets developed in a wide range of currencies. As noted also, the US$ interest rate swap market continues to remain the largest single swap market. The outstanding volume of currency swaps, while less than that of interest rate swaps, showed greater growth.

Swap market participants

There are two broad classes of participants in the swap market: end users and intermediaries. An end user is a counterparty which engages in a swap in order to change its interest rate or currency exposure for some economic or financial reason. An intermediary (or a dealer) enters into a swap in order to earn fees or trading profits. In principle, end users and intermediaries are distinguished by their motivations. In practice, however, some institutions are active in both capacities.

A wide variety of end users became involved in the swap markets during this period. Banks and corporations around the world, savings and thrift institutions, insurance companies, government agencies, international agencies and sovereign entities all became active.

End users began to utilise the swap markets for a number of reasons:

- to obtain low-cost financing;
- to create high-yield assets;
- to hedge interest rate of currency exposure generated from the structure of normal business;
- to implement asset liability management strategies; and
- to speculate.

The World Bank was a major driving force in the development of the currency swap market. It sought low interest rate borrowings, mainly in Swiss francs or deutschmarks, since it wished to make loans in these currencies. The World Bank borrowed a considerable amount directly but at times wished to issue more debt in the Swiss and German markets than could be absorbed easily. On the other hand, it could borrow relatively cheaply in the larger US$ markets. These circumstances created a natural opportunity to carry out swaps with counterparties who had European currencies or good access to borrowings in Europe, but who needed US$ financing.

In the early part of this period of evolution, most intermediaries merely brought together the two swap parties and arranged swaps. At times, they also provided letters of credit or other forms of credit enhancement for weaker credits. As the variety of end users on both sides of the market increased, potential counterparties grew increasingly reluctant to accept the credit risks involved. This created the opportunity for large commercial and investment banks to take on the role of the intermediary by entering into two offsetting swaps.

The largest intermediaries in the swap market during this period included major United States money centre banks, major United States and United Kingdom investment and merchant banks, and major Japanese securities companies. Commercial banks in Australia, New Zealand, Canada, France, Japan, Sweden, Switzerland and the United Kingdom were also active. These institutions have undertaken dealing in swaps in order to earn fee income and to profit from trading opportunities. For both commercial and investment banks, swaps represented an attractive source of off-balance sheet earnings as well as a product which facilitated other types of business (for example, underwriting securities).

Commercial banks and investment banks developed different approaches to the swap market. Commercial banks tended to view swaps as an extension of more conventional banking business. For example, when a bank combines a floating rate loan with a swap, it is creating the equivalent of a fixed rate loan for a borrower. In the past, banks found it difficult to extend fixed rate loans outright because their fixed rate funding costs have been high, sometimes as high as those faced by some of their customers. Moreover, they felt obliged to accept prepayments on fixed rate loans when rates moved to the disadvantage of the borrower. By unbundling the components (the floating rate loan and the swap) banks were able to price each more efficiently. Commercial banks stressed that as swap market intermediaries they offered a large customer base and expertise in assuming long-term market and credit risks.

Investment or merchant banks tended to view swaps as tradeable securities. They were at the forefront of efforts to standardise swap contracts and market practices in order to improve the liquidity of the swap market. Investment banks also attempted to equalise the credit exposure on all swaps by incorporating collateral provisions in the contract. These provisions gave the investment bank (and sometimes the other counterparty) the right to call for an amount of collateral equal to the credit exposure on the contract. As intermediaries, investment banks sought to offer competitive pricing because of their trading and hedging expertise.

By the mid 1980s there was an active market in swaps between swap dealers that served to match end users in much the same way that the interbank Eurocurrency market connects non-bank depositors with ultimate borrowers. Thus, for example, a bank (which is not a swap specialist) would enter into a swap with an end user for which it has arranged a bond issue. It would cover itself by entering into an offsetting swap with a dealer, who in turn entered into an offsetting swap with another dealer. This second dealer might then have located a bank which wanted to offset a swap it had arranged with an end user. In this example, a swap between two end users gave rise to four intermediate swaps.

The move by intermediaries to act as principal or direct counterparties in swap transactions had two separate aspects. The intermediary could either be a genuine market maker in swaps willing to trade more or less continuously offering a relatively tight bid-offer spread or alternatively could enter into the swap utilising its balance sheet and then square its position with a market-making house.

Relatively few financial intermediaries sought, at least initially, to act as market makers in swap transactions routinely quoting two-way prices on swaps. The major emphasis amongst market makers was on interest rate swaps, particularly US$ interest rate swaps, although specialist market makers in interest rate swaps in a number of liquid swap currencies also developed. Simultaneously, a much smaller group of institutions emerged as market makers in cross-currency swaps in and between, inter alia, SFR, DEM, ECU, JPY, GBP, C$, A$, NZ$ and US$.

The smaller number of market makers in currency swaps reflected the smaller transaction volume and the complexity and difficulty of hedging and managing positions in this type of transaction.

The emergence of market makers in swap transactions required the development by the institutions concerned of techniques to manage the large temporary risk positions created in a variety of currencies where the institution transacted swaps as a principal when there was no immediately available counterparty. The risk confronting a swap market maker is that in providing one side of a swap transaction, it may not be able to profitably cover the other side in the market. This temporary risk position can be in the form of position taking in the swap market as a natural extension of position taking in other fixed interest or currency markets, or alternatively it can be viewed as a transient unmatched position, not entered into as an interest rate or currency (in the case of currency swaps) bet, but with the exposure to interest rates or currency values being hedged either through the physical securities market (for example, bonds, deposits, borrowings, etc) or in a corresponding futures market on the relevant underlying physical security. The latter is often referred to as swap "warehousing".

The development of market-making capabilities in interest rate swaps had two distinct implications for the potential swap participant:

- The availability of institutions willing to commit to an interest rate or currency swap without necessarily having a counterparty in position made possible a prompt execution capability which eliminated the delay necessitated where it was necessary to have precisely matched counterparties to complete a transaction.
- The availability of market makers making two-way prices on swap transactions provided the flexibility required to allow companies to reverse or unwind a swap transaction at the current market rate facilitating the use of swaps as a dynamic asset liability management instrument.

Phase 3 (1989 to present)—maturity

By 1989, the growth period in the evolution of the global swap market had reached its conclusion. During this period, the global swap market had evolved substantially into its modern form. The principle features of the global swap market which continue to the present day were substantially in place including:

- a broad range of swap financing instruments;
- swap markets in a wide range of currencies;
- well established applications of swap instruments covering both asset and liability management applications; and
- a deep and liquid market in swap instruments, in most currencies, supported by the active participation and involvement of a wide range of financial institutions and intermediaries.

However, as the market reached the end of the growth phase, a number of changes in the underlying dynamics of its operation emerged. The major factors underlying the changes coincident upon entering maturity included:

- lower profitability; and
- the increasing commodity nature of conventional swap instruments.

The rapid growth of the swap market during its growth phase attracted a wide variety of financial institutions to enter the market resulting in the inevitable pressure on margins in swap transactions. This was exacerbated by the tendency towards loss leading and cross-subsidising by a number of participants in an effort to gain market share as part of their overall strategy in the financial services industry.

The lower profitability of the swap market for financial institutions was attenuated by the increasingly commodity nature of the instruments themselves. The technology of swap financing proliferated throughout financial markets. In contrast to the early 1980s when relatively few practitioners possessed the product knowledge to identify, price and conclude such transactions, by the late 1980s understanding of the technology of swap financing was extremely widespread in the financial community. A major factor in the proliferation of this knowledge was the movement of personnel between institutions which at one stage reached almost epidemic proportions.

The combination of these two factors served to undermine the basic profitability of the swap business. That is not to say that institutions were not successful in earning adequate return from the swap businesses. A number of institutions continued to operate very profitably in the swap market. However, the source of their profits altered significantly.

Earnings from conventional swap transactions fell sharply with the bulk of earnings being generated either from specially structured swaps (where the competition amongst financial institutions was less intense reflecting the inability or unwillingness of the majority of institutions to assume the risk of such structures), or from speculative gains from foreign exchange and interest rate positions assumed as part of the market-making or warehousing functions for these instruments.

Maturity also coincided with a number of events which accelerated changes within the swap market itself. These included:

- rationalisation of the financial services industry;
- implementation of the BIS capital adequacy standards for off-balance sheet transactions; and
- deterioration of bank credit ratings.

The ambitious expansion of the banking sector throughout the 1980s in response to the perceived opportunities provided by financial deregulation in a variety of national markets came to an end. The need for rationalisation reflected the significant over-capacity in the global banking system resulting in retrenchment of banking capacity through a combination of bank mergers and a close-down of operations in selected products and market segments.

The swap market on the whole did not suffer a major retrenchment of capacity in this regard. Swaps and derivative products generally continued to be viewed as desirable areas of operation and consequently a number of institutions in fact directed additional resources to this area. However, the overall retrenchment of banking capacity forced increasing focus on and selection of particular areas or segments within the swap market as the favoured areas of operation for each institution.

Banking authorities throughout the world adopted the BIS Capital Adequacy Proposal (first issued in December 1987). These guidelines included a minimum capital level of 8% to be complied with by 1992 and the adoption of the concept of risk weighted assets applying a specified series of risk weights to all assets and *off-balance sheet exposures*. This required capital to be committed to swap transactions entered into by banks for the first time. While banks and other financial institutions had traditionally recognised the credit exposures entailed in transacting swaps, they had not been formally acquired to hold capital against such transactions until the implementation of the BIS Capital Adequacy Proposals.

During this period, bank credit ratings also deteriorated sharply. This reflected significant loan losses from lending to LDC countries, loans connected with highly leveraged transactions, exposures to real estate lending, loans to savings and loans institutions in the USA and higher bad debts in both personal and corporate lending as a result of the onset of recession in a variety of countries. These higher loan losses resulted in sharply reduced profitability of the banking sector reinforcing the need for rationalisation and retrenchment of capacity.

Against this background, the predominant themes of the swap market in its maturity include:

- increased product integration;
- changed product focus;
- increased emphasis on improved portfolio risk management techniques;
- focus on expanding applications of existing products; and
- rationalisation and restructuring market participants.

Product integration issues

A predominant theme in the maturity of the swap market is the focus on swaps as a component of the derivatives market generally and the resulting integration of swap operations into the institution's derivatives portfolio overall. Derivatives in this context refers to an instrument whose value depends on the values of other more basic underlying variables, primarily forward/futures or options on currencies, debt securities, commodities or equity securities.

In this context, the integration of swaps into other derivative operations focused on combining the swaps operation with other activities entailing, primarily, forward/options on currencies, futures and options on a wide range of underlying instruments traded on futures and options exchanges and forward/option contracts on commodities and equities.

This trend towards product integration is predicated on the underlying nature of swaps and other derivative instruments which are capable of being decomposed into two basic instruments: forward and option contracts. This is often referred to as financial engineering. This allied to the increasing trend in swaps and derivative transactions generally to complex instrument structures involving various combinations of forward and option contract elements necessitated a more integrated approach to the development, marketing, pricing, hedging and management of portfolios in these products.

This emphasis on product integration has increasingly extended to amalgamating and merging derivative operations within financial institutions. In the case of a number of larger banks, this has been taken further with the derivative operation, including swaps, being absorbed into and being viewed as an integral part of the institution's overall treasury and risk management functions.

This process of integration is predicated upon:

- perceived economies of scale and scope in combining these operations;
- the potential improvements in risk management and risk assessment technology deriving from these combinations;
- substantial cost saving from integrating support functions for these products, in particular, lowering the overhead costs of settlement support for each operation; and

- facilitating product development and customer financial and risk management problem solving.

Altered product focus

The product focus within some operations has changed significantly, reflecting the broader changes in the swap market. Swap products are capable of being classified as three separate but highly integrated sets of activity:

- *commodity products*—primarily, conventional interest rate and currency swaps, LTFX, FRAs and cap/floors;
- *value-added structures*—usually entailing non-generic swap structures (although a number of these are increasingly treated as commodities because of the capability of a wide variety of institutions to execute these transactions), highly structured innovative swap structures and complex customised asset liability management applications of these instruments; and
- *cross-market extensions of swap technology*—whereby basic swap concepts and techniques are increasingly applied to solving financial requirements in other market segments such as commodities and equities.

The basic commodity swap products are the essential building blocks for complex swap structures. As such, a capability to transact such instruments is a prerequisite to a presence in the market for more complex structured swap products.

There are two approaches to this commodity component of the swap market. A number of institutions are increasingly emphasising commodity products, basing their capacity to compete and earn satisfactory returns from such operations by a mixture of high volume (designed to compensate for the relatively low margins), reliance on complex proprietary hedging technologies designed to minimise hedging costs, and management of the capital committed to such operations.

Management of capital commitment in this regard typically entails tightly controlling the type of counterparty (seeking counterparties with a risk level less than the maximum risk weighting), control of the size of the portfolio (by assigning matching contracts etc) and utilising credit enhancement techniques (such as mark-to-market) to minimise capital utilisation. In addition, such institutions may seek to emphasise particular types of transactions, such as short-dated swap transactions which can be hedged utilising futures, taking advantage of the lower capital utilisation of such operations.

Other institutions have substantially de-emphasised commodity product operations except to the extent that participation in that component of the market is necessary to facilitate their activities in their preferred products. Such institutions will adjust the prices and margins for their commodity products to reflect their desire to participate in these sectors depending on underlying requirements from the rest of their operations.

An increasing number of institutions are focusing on value-added, highly structured swap products seeking to take advantage of the higher returns and margins available. These value added products relate typically to non-generic swap structures, option/swap combination and hybrid swap products. Such swap structures are particularly allied to new issue arbitrage transactions involving capital market issues structured to take advantage of particular investor requirements or complex asset liability applications designed to address individual risk management requirements.

The fact that design, pricing and hedging of these more complex swap structures requires more complex hedging technology and, generally, increased appetite and capacity to assume a variety of risks allows the institutions active in this product sector to establish some (albeit limited) barriers to entry for other market participants.

However, the lack of ability to totally control the proliferation of the technical knowledge necessary to undertake individual transactions, at least for substantial periods of time, typically results in a very short product life cycle for individual instruments with a rapid decline in profitability. These institutions seek to overcome the problems of a relatively short product life cycle by investing substantial resources in product development and in understanding and developing solutions to unusual and complex financial structuring requirements.

Increasingly, swap techniques are being extended to include a variety of transactions entailing commodities and equity markets. In part, this development is the inevitable result of increased product integration which allows increased cross-fertilisation of ideas and technology.

The major areas of these cross-market extensions are commodities (primarily energy products such as oil and gas) as well as equity markets. These product extensions primarily entail commodity and equity swaps as well as the development of swap structures to securitise options and forward positions embedded in a variety of customised securities with commodity and equity linkages.

The ability to adapt existing pricing and hedging technology of swaps for such product extensions has facilitated this development. The higher margins available from these products, at least initially, has provided impetus for the rapid expansion of these markets. Increasingly, it is evident that as the pricing and hedging technology proliferates, the market for these types of cross-market products will also become akin to other commodity-like financial instruments with the resulting compression of spreads and reduction in profitability.

Portfolio risk management

An important element of the swap market in its maturity is the increased emphasis on portfolio risk management. Portfolio risk management in this context refers to the management of the various risks entailed in operating portfolios of swaps and other derivative products. This encompasses pricing of transaction, the assessment of risks, hedging of risk, ongoing portfolio management, settlement of such transactions and the reporting of risk, profit/losses and cash flows from such activity.

The impetus of improved portfolio risk management derives from a variety of sources:

- the celebrated failures of risk management in a variety of institutions resulting in substantial losses;
- the complexity of non-generic swap structures with the corresponding demands on sound risk management practices;
- the higher risk within swap portfolios as a result of the more complex products which are transacted and must be hedged and the hedge managed over the life of transactions (in some cases, up to 30 years);
- the potential for creating competitive advantage by superior portfolio risk management techniques through lower hedge costs as well as the capacity to price and hedge esoteric instruments and structures;
- the need to ensure the integrity of reported earnings from derivative operations whose profile (from the perspective of accounting and tax treatment) is increasingly complex; and

- the need to minimise the cost of administration and settlement of transactions as these costs expanded rapidly resulting from the overall growth in the size of the swap market and the number of transactions within portfolios.

These factors, both positive (capacity to lower costs and create genuine competitive advantages) and negative (protect revenue and ensure appropriate control of risk), have forced institutions active in these markets to invest in often complex financial technology to understand and manage risks in these derivative portfolios.

An interesting aspect of this process has been the move by financial institutions to recruit a number of highly respected financial economists (including Fisher Black and Myron Scholes—the originators of the Black/Scholes Option Pricing Model) to assist with this process.

Applications focus

The range of applications of swap instruments continues to expand. The focus of swap applications continues to be new issue arbitrage to generate lower-cost funding and asset liability management.

The process of new issue arbitrage has changed markedly as between the growth and maturity period of the swap market. The arbitrage benefits which were reduced substantially through the growth period continue to shrink. Opportunities which occur are more transient, reflecting responses by investors to specific market movements and requirements for structured investments, usually in response to regulatory barriers to transacting directly in a variety of markets. The transience of opportunities has limited the scope of new issue arbitrage which has become confined to a relatively few, highly credit-worthy and market responsive borrowers.

In an interesting development, a number of borrowers have increasingly by-passed financial institutions in this process. For example, Swedish Export Credit (SEK) has increasingly internalised the risk management process in respect of complex commodity and equity linked securities, utilising an external consultancy specialising in risk management. The primary motive for this type of action is to capture a greater share of the arbitrage gains by reducing the costs (that is, the profit to the intermediary) in order to capture a bigger portion of the smaller available arbitrage gain by the borrower.

Asset liability management applications of swap instruments continue to evolve. A major focus in this regard is the increased use of financial engineering techniques to create complex asset and liability structures consistent with requirements of individual borrowers and investors.

There has also been an increase in the use of swaps to speculate or position to take advantage of anticipated movement in currencies and interest rates. An additional element in this regard has been the writing of options on a variety of swap structures to generate premium income in return for accepting a variety of risks. Dangers inherent in such strategies from the perspective of end users has been demonstrated in the tragic case of the United Kingdom Councils: see discussion below, Chapters 37 and 42.

Market participants

The maturity of the swap market has seen some rationalisation in market participation by financial institutions. This has derived from the following factors:

- overall rationalisation of the financial services industry;

- the focus on capital management; and
- reduced credit rating of a number of institutions.

The trend towards overall rationalisation and focus on capital management has led to a number of institutions withdrawing from or refocusing their involvement in the swap market. The deterioration in credit rating of a number of institutions has limited the scope for these institutions to participate in the swap market as more credit sensitive counterparties are unable, because of unavailability of credit limits, to transact with these institutions.

These developments have led to significant changes amongst market participants in the global swap market. A number of houses have withdrawn from all or certain segments of the market. A number of major swap houses have disappeared for a variety of reasons including bankruptcy (Drexel Burnam Lambert) and merger (Security Pacific, which has merged with Bank of America).

The withdrawal of a number of participants, either generally or from particular market segments, has been substantially offset by the entry into the global swap market of new participants. The new entrants fall into a variety of categories:

AAA rated banks

A number of highly rated banks have established or upgraded their swap/derivatives operations. This has been undertaken in two forms: upgrading the swap operation generally within the existing banks structure, or establishment of a separate operation specialising in swaps and other derivatives.

Deutsche Bank, for example, has significantly increased its profile in the global swap and derivatives market. This has been undertaken by upgrading the swap operation within the bank's capital market/treasury operations. In contrast, Credit Suisse has established a specialist unit—Credit Suisse Financial Products (CSFP)—outside the main structure of the bank, using a mixture of internal staff and recruits, most significantly from Bankers Trust, to establish a stand-alone derivatives operation.

Similarly, Swiss Bank Corporation (SBC) entered into, initially, a partnership with O'Connor Partners, a Chicago-based derivatives partnership, to form a specialist derivatives operation. Subsequently, SBC moved to full ownership of the derivatives operation.

More recently, in early 1993, NationsBank based in North Carolina (which resulted from the merger of NCNB and Souran Bank) acquired the Chicago Research and Trading Group (CRT). The acquisition satisfied the need for CRT to expand into OTC markets complementing its already strong presence in ET products while simultaneously facilitating NationsBank's entry into the derivatives market.

Japanese banks

A number of Japanese banks have created specialist derivatives operations outside the structure of the bank itself: these include Sumitomo Bank (Sumitomo Bank Capital Markets, Mitsui Taiyo Kobe (now called Sakura Bank) (Sakura Global Capital) and Dai-Ichi-Kangyo Bank (DKB Financial Products).

In the case of the Japanese banks, the primary motivation for establishing separate operations was that the banks desired to recruit externally, in particular, to recruit gaijin staff, who would have been reluctant to work for the bank itself. In some cases, such as Sakura Global Capital, these external recruits not only supply expertise to the operation but are significant shareholders.

Non-bank financial institutions

A number of financial institutions, primarily insurance companies, have taken advantage of perceived market opportunities and their relative freedom from regulations affecting banks and investment bank to establish swap and derivative operations.

The earliest of these ventures was by Prudential Life which established Prudential Global Funding as a stand-alone swap operation. Subsequently, similar operations have been established by the American Insurance Group (AIG Financial Products), General Reinsurance Company (General Re Financial Products) and New England Life Insurance Company (Mercadian Capital). Mercadian Capital itself experienced difficulties in 1993 when as a result of its declining credit ratings a large number of its staff defected to establish a similar operation within Republic Bank of New York.

These organisations have sought to use the leverage of their high credit rating (AA or better) to establish a position in the derivatives market at a time when traditional participants, such as banks, were disadvantaged by capital restraints and declining credit ratings.

The pattern of participation by institutions active in the swap market has also significantly altered in the maturity phase of the market. These include:

- Greater focus of individual swap operations on a specific range of products. The number of swap trading operations seeking to offer a truly complete range of financial instruments is increasingly limited. Institutions are relatively focused in the market segments in which they wish to participate seeking to generate competitive advantage from particular institutional attributes which allows them to build significant and sustainable competitive positions in the relevant market sectors.
- The increased concern about credit quality in the swap market has forced weaker participants to seek to establish specialised credit-enhanced vehicles to carry out swap activities. The most notable example of this type of development has been the establishment of a special purpose derivatives vehicle by Merril Lynch—Merril Lynch Derivatives Product—which is rated AAA. Competing United States investment bank Goldman Sachs has also established a specialised derivatives vehicle—Goldman Sachs Financial Products. In 1993, Salomon Brothers and Paribas also established AAA rated Special Purpose Derivative Vehicles.
- The credit concerns in the swap market have encouraged increasing use of exchange traded risk management instruments. The deposit and margining requirements of organised futures and options exchanges have become increasingly attractive to end users and to financial institutions active in the swap market as a mechanism for risk management of ultimate exposures or swap portfolio positions.

Despite the rationalisation described above, the participation in the global swap market and derivatives generally continues to be high amongst financial institutions. This derives primarily from the following factors:

- the relatively high earnings opportunities that are perceived; and
- the relatively low credit default risk in this market (despite the celebrated failures in recent years of Development Finance Corporation of New Zealand (DFC), Drexel Burnam Lambert and the United Kingdom Councils).

Participation from end users continues to increase. Notable developments in recent years has been the increased capacity of less developed countries to participate in the global swaps market. The increased relevance of swaps, particularly on commodities as well as on interest rates and currencies, to these entities has prompted supranational organisations, such as the International Finance Corporation (a subsidiary of the World Bank), to intermediate swaps for these counterparties.

In addition, the extention of the swap market to cover commodities and equities has allowed a wider variety of corporations with commodity exposures, as well as investors with equity investments, to participate.

SUMMARY

The emergence of deep and relatively liquid markets in swaps and related instruments represents an important and significant development in corporate finance in recent times. The use of these structures as part of financing strategies to take advantage of capital markets arbitrage opportunities as well as the utilisation for the management of interest rate, currency and, more recently, commodity and equity price risks has significantly altered the operation of global financial markets. The sheer size of the global swap market, the range of instruments encompassed, and the range of market participants and their varied reasons for involvement provide testament to the importance of these financial instruments.

Part 2

Basic Swap and Financial Derivative Instruments

Chapter 2

Financial Derivatives: Basic Structures and Key Characteristics

SWAP TRANSACTIONS: A CLASSIFICATION

The term swap is utilised to describe a variety of transactions. It can be used to refer to a specific type of transaction, such as an interest rate or currency swap. However, it can also be used generically to cover a range of specialised negotiated capital market transactions where two or more entities exchange or swap cash flows in the same or in two or several different currencies and/or interest rate bases for a pre-determined length of time.

It is useful to categorise swap transactions into two general categories:

- basic or "core" swap structures (which covers parallel or back-to-back loans, interest rate swaps, currency swaps and long-dated or long term forward foreign exchange contracts (LTFX), FRAs, caps, collars and floors); and
- non-generic and hybrid swap structures which entail variations on core swap structures and a variety of option/swap combinations.

In addition, there are separate categories of swap instruments involving commodities and equities.

In this chapter, the basic structures and, in particular, the key interrelationships between the various swap instruments are outlined. In addition, the capacity to decompose the various swap instruments into two more basic financial instruments, namely, forward and option contracts, are also outlined.

As will be evident from the discussion in Chapter 6 these basic structural interrelationships are central to the pricing and, ultimately, the hedging and trading of these instruments.

SWAP INSTRUMENTS: STRUCTURAL RELATIONSHIPS

Core swap instruments

Parallel or back-to-back loans (from which other types of swaps developed) represent a specialised technique which originally developed to avoid the investment premium on investments outside the United Kingdom imposed by foreign exchange regulations. The basic concept of a back-to-back loan has been adapted into a currency swap making the original structures largely redundant. However, while parallel and back-to-back loans are no longer commonly utilised, they remain a useful technique for mobilising otherwise potentially sterile cash balances in blocked funds situations.

Swap transactions, which evolved structurally from parallel and back-to-back loans, are the major type of swap financing transactions. They usually encompass three specific types of transactions: interest rates swaps, currency swaps and LTFX.

It is usual to classify LTFX transactions with swaps as they are functionally identical to a zero coupon currency swap. In essence, LTFX transactions can be used to replicate a fixed-to-fixed currency swap. LTFX transactions also represent an extension of the market in forward foreign exchange which operates in and between short-term money and foreign exchange markets across currencies.

The FRA market functions at a number of levels:

- a forward-forward deposit or borrowing market at rates nominated today;
- a short-term interest rate swap market, particularly in the two years and under maturity segment;
- an interest rate swap, dismembered into shorter time periods commencing some time in the future.

While the FRA market is largely a market in forward interest rates, in which respect it functions in a manner similar to a negotiated futures market in interest rates, it is closely linked with interest rate swap markets in the relevant currency.

This relationship arises from two separate sources. First, an interest rate swap and an FRA can be similar in that a series of FRAs locking in or fixing rates on future interest rate reset dates or "rolls" on a floating rate borrowing can be used as a substitute for a floating-to-fixed interest rate swap as both transactions effectively provide the party entering into the transaction with a known fixed cost of funding. Similarly, the reverse of this transaction can be utilised to generate a fixed-to-floating swap allowing a borrower to switch to a floating rate of interest on its borrowings.

The second type of linkage arises from the fact that an interest rate swap entered into can then be parcelled into known rates of interest for various periods within the term of the overall interest rate swap and sold into the market as FRAs. These two levels of linkage allow interest rate swaps and FRAs to coexist and complement each other within capital markets.

Interest rate caps, collars or floors are different from swap transactions. They represent the purchase or sale of options on interest rates over extended time frames. It is usual in such transactions to buy not one but a series of options.

For example, an interest rate cap places an upper limit on the interest cost of the purchaser. Under the usual transaction structure, the purchaser of the cap, in return for the payment of an upfront fee or premium, is protected against rises in interest rates on its floating rate borrowings beyond a certain nominated upper limit. If rates breach this cap level, the writer of the cap agrees to make payments to the purchaser designed to effectively reduce the cost of funding to the level of the cap. Analytically, this represents the purchase of a series of put options on the price of the relevant debt securities priced off a short-term interest rate index coinciding with rollover dates on the borrower's floating rate borrowings.

For a borrower, a collar places both a maximum and minimum rate on its borrowings and represents, analytically, the simultaneous purchase of a series of put options with the writing of a series of call options, representing the floor rate. In contrast, a floor agreement, usually utilised by investors, places a minimum yield constraint on the investor's portfolio of floating rate assets.

The market in caps, collars and floors is a subset of the market for debt options. However, these options markets are closely related to the market for interest rate swaps in the relevant currencies.

This linkage arises for a number of reasons. In particular, users of the swap market will usually view the cap or collar market as effectively a potential substitute for interest rate swaps and will constantly compare the price available in both markets to structure liability management transactions which best reflect their interest rate expectations.

In addition, the fact that analytically an interest rate swap can be characterised as the simultaneous purchase and sale of options provides a further basis for linkage between the two markets. For example, an interest rate swap where the entity in question pays the fixed rate in return for receiving the floating rate can be characterised as the purchase of a put option at the fixed rate with the simultaneous writing of a call option also at the fixed rate. This is effectively a collar with no difference between the floor and the cap rates. It is similarly possible to characterise a swap where the party in question is a receiver of the fixed rate as the simultaneous writing of a put option with the purchase of a call option.

An important aspect to note is that FRA, cap, collar and floor markets operate in a single currency. In this regard, FRAs and caps etc are similar to interest rate swaps while currency swaps usually bear a greater relationship to (historically) parallel or back-to-back loans and LTFX contracts.

Exhibit 2.1 illustrates diagrammatically the basic structural relationships of the above types of transactions.

Exhibit 2.1

Swap Instruments—Structural Interrelationships

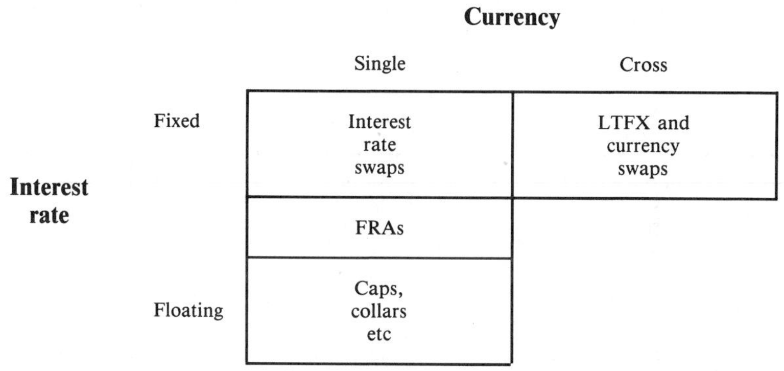

		Currency	
		Single	Cross
Interest rate	Fixed	Interest rate swaps	LTFX and currency swaps
		FRAs	
	Floating	Caps, collars etc	

Non-generic and hybrid swap instruments

Variations on basic swap structures have evolved in response to changing market requirements. The major types of variations on core swap instruments include:

- non-generic swaps;
- floating/floating or basis swaps;
- options on swap/swaptions;
- interest rate and currency linked hybrids; and equity and commodity swaps and derivatives.

In addition, there are swap instruments, typically conventional or structured swaps, combined with the purchase of an investment asset—described as asset swaps.

Non-generic swaps, generally, entail variations on conventional swap instruments. This includes variations in terms of notional principal, commencement date, other timing aspects, maturity variations as well as specific cash flow patterns embodied within the swap. Basis or floating/floating swaps encompass a special class of swap transactions where both streams of cash flow are variable, being priced off different indexes within the same currency or, in certain cases, different currencies.

Options on swaps/swaptions entail a variety of options on swap instruments, particularly on the fixed rate component of swap transactions. Another variation within options on swap/swaptions includes combinations of swaps and options.

Interest rate and currency linked, equity and commodity swap hybrids encompass variations on, or combinations of different derivative elements and product extensions into related markets. Interest rate and currency linked hybrids typically entail combinations of foreign exchange or interest rate options or forward contracts within the swap structure.

Commodity swaps, equity swaps and inflation swaps are closely interrelated. They typically entail either a portfolio of forward contracts on a commodity, equity (typically, market indexes) or an economic index (such as inflation rate embodied in a specific price series); or structured swap arrangements linked to security issues with embedded commodity or equity components.

Exhibit 2.2 sets out a schematic of the classification of non-generic and other hybrid swap structures.

Exhibit 2.2

Classification of Swap Structures

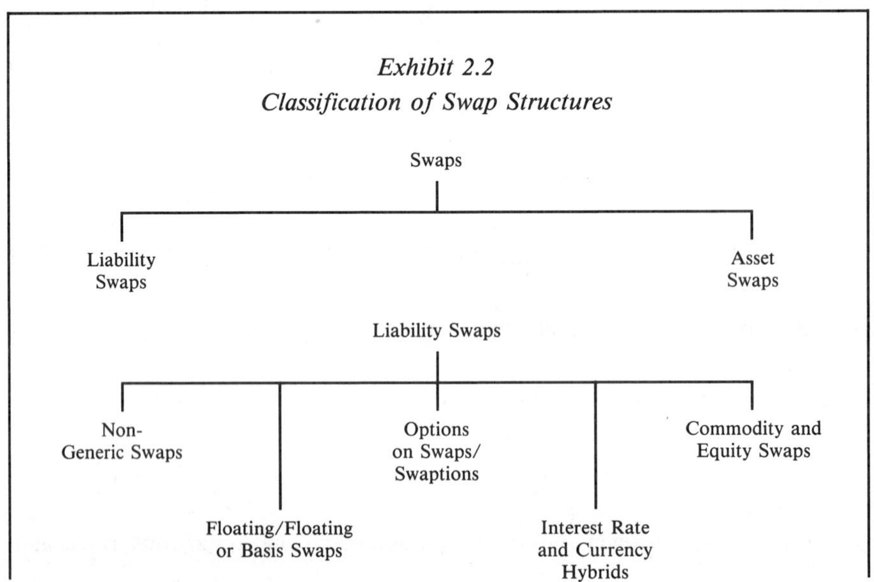

Exhibit 2.2—continued

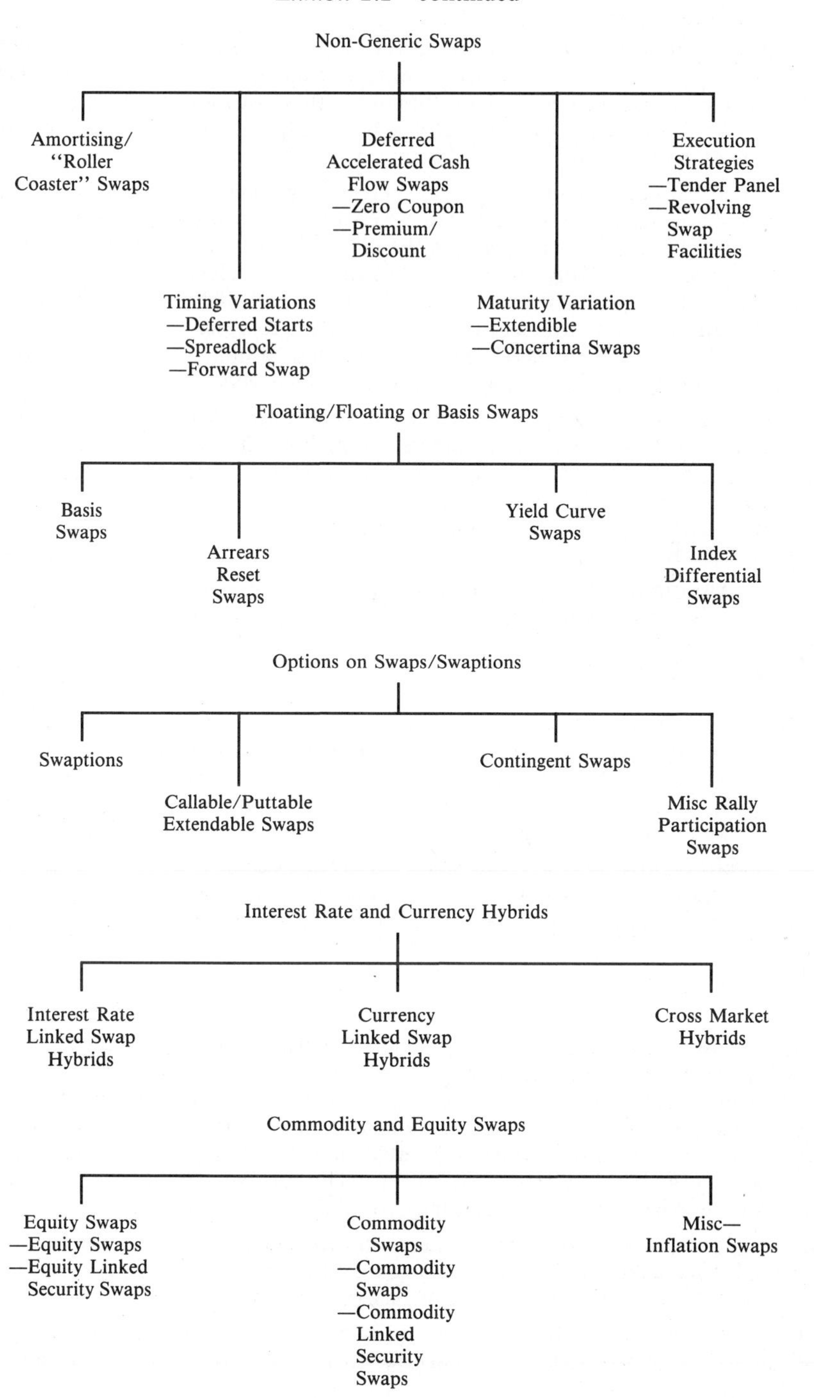

SWAPS AND FINANCIAL ENGINEERING[1]

As is evident from the above discussion, the various instruments, usually referred to generically as swap transactions, have significant economic interrelationships. However, it is in fact also possible to decompose these various instruments, that is, currency and interest rate swaps, LTFX, FRAs and caps, collars and floors, into two basic instruments: forward and option contracts.

The term "financial engineering" has increasingly come to be used as a general catch cry of financial markets. The wide variety of swap instruments available have, in particular, become synonymous with the use of the phrase *financial engineering*. While financial engineering in its purest form usually refers to the use of swap instruments to manage the cash flows of asset and liability transactions by borrowers and investors, the instruments themselves represent a form of financial engineering in that they are merely combinations and permutations of two relatively simple instruments, namely, forward and option contracts.

Decomposition of swap instruments into their basic elements and analysis of the interrelationships is essential in understanding both the structural and economic aspects of such transactions. In this regard, it is essential to deal with currency and interest rate swaps, LTFX, FRAs, caps, floors and collars and variations on these basic swap instruments not as separate instruments but as a highly integrated set of financial transactions.

In decomposing and then re-engineering swap transactions from their basic elements, it is necessary to first define forward and option contracts.

Forward contracts

A forward contract obligates the purchaser to buy a given asset on a specified date at a known price (known, usually, as the forward price). This forward price is specified at the time the contract is entered into. If at maturity the actual price is higher than the forward price, the contract owner will make a profit; if the price is lower, the owner suffers a loss.

A forward contract entailing the sale of a given asset on a specified date in the future at a known forward price is also feasible, representing the offsetting side of a forward purchase. In this case, the payoffs for the forward seller are clearly reversed.

The payoff (profit and loss profile) from a bought or sold forward contract are set out in *Exhibit 2.3*.

In the case of forward contracts in capital markets, the underlying asset will usually be either a security (either debt or equity) or a specified amount of foreign currency or commodity. Where the asset is a security, its price will reflect interest rates. Consequently, a forward contract on such an asset would essentially operate functionally as a forward contract on interest rates. Similarly, where the underlying commodity is a specified amount of the foreign currency, the forward contract essentially represents a forward currency contract.

From a functional perspective, a futures contract is identical to a forward contract in that a futures contract also obligates its owner to purchase or sell a specified asset at a specified forward price on the contract maturity date.

The major difference between futures and forward contracts relates to the institutional structure of the two markets. In the case of futures contracts, the

1. This discussion draws heavily on Smithson (1987).

Exhibit 2.3
Payoff Profiles for Forward Positions

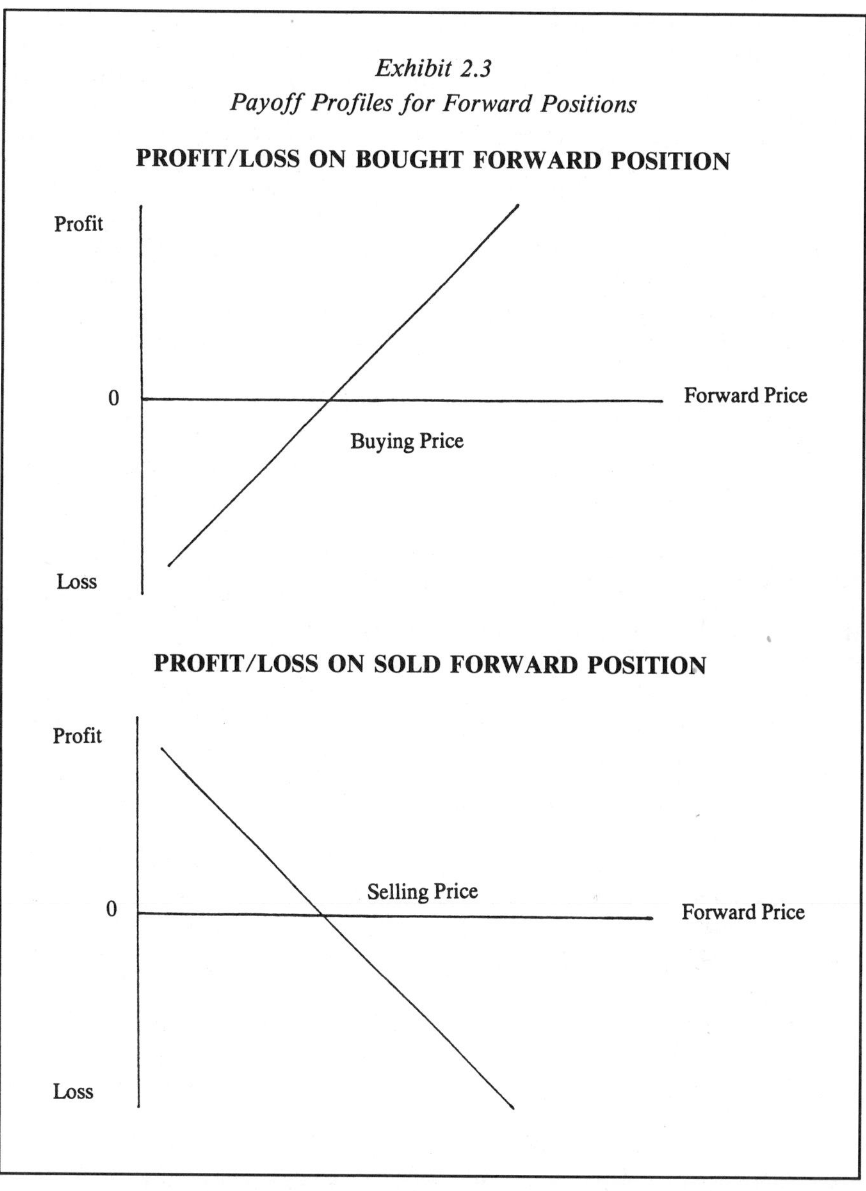

underlying asset to be traded is usually homogenised through a process of standardisation and the specification of nominated exercise dates (usually four per year). This is usually designed to enable the futures market to become relatively liquid. An additional difference of significance is the use of a futures exchange or clearing house which acts as a counterparty to each transaction. This is designed not only to facilitate liquidity but to reduce the likelihood of credit or default risk through a process of performance bonds, involving the posting of deposits and margins. Technically, a futures contract is a forward contract which is settled daily with a new forward contract being written simultaneously.

The relationship between interest rate swap contracts and forward contracts derives from the fact that, in effect, the swap contract is a series of forward contracts combined. As detailed in Chapter 3 an interest rate swap entails the exchange of specified cash flows determined by reference to two different interest rates. An interest rate swap can be represented by a series of cash inflows in return for a series of cash outflows. This contractual arrangement can be decomposed into a portfolio of simpler single payment contracts, which can in turn be decomposed into a series of forward contracts. Utilising this approach, it is possible to restate an interest rate swap as a series of implicit forward contracts on interest rates.

As noted above, an FRA contract is essentially a market in forward interest rates, in effect forward contracts on interest rates. Consequently, FRAs are logically linked to interest rate swaps in a manner identical to the linkage between forward contracts and interest rate swaps.

Option contracts

A forward contract, as specified above, entails an obligation to buy or sell the stated asset. In contrast, an option contract gives the purchaser the *right*, but not the *obligation*, to purchase or sell an asset. A call option gives the owner the right to purchase an asset while a put option gives the purchaser the right to sell the asset. In both cases, the purchase price or selling price is specified at the time the option contract is originated. This price is usually referred to as the exercise price. The financial price of the asset, as in the case of forward contracts, can be an interest rate, a currency exchange rate or the price of a security, commodity or equity market index.

The purchaser of a call option contract has the right to purchase the asset at the exercise price. Consequently, if the price of the asset rises above the exercise price, then the value of the option also goes up. However, because the option contract does not obligate the purchaser to purchase the asset if the price falls, the value of the option does not fall by the same amount as the price declines. A similar but reverse logic applies in the case of put options.

The pay-off profile for the party who has sold (written or granted) the call or put option is different. In contrast to the purchaser of the option, the seller of the option has the obligation to perform. For example, if the holder of the option elects to exercise her or his option to purchase the asset, the seller of the option is obligated to sell the asset.

The payoffs from a purchase or sale of a call and a put option are set out in *Exhibit 2.4*.

The relationship between option contracts and swap transactions operates at a number of levels:

- the relationship between option contracts and forward contracts;
- the relationship between option contracts and interest rate swaps.

As discussed in more detail in Chapter 6, it can be demonstrated that there are at least two interrelated linkages between options and forward contracts:

- A call option can be replicated by continuously adjusting or managing dynamically a portfolio of securities or forward contracts on the underlying asset (for example, securities or foreign exchange) and riskless securities or cash. As the price of the asset rises, the call option equivalent portfolio would contain an increasing proportion of the assets or forward contracts. As the financial price of the asset decreases, the call option equivalent portfolio would reduce its holding of the assets or forward contracts.

- Option contracts can be used to replicate forward contracts through a relationship known as put call parity (discussed in detail in Chapter 11). In terms of this relationship, the simultaneous purchase of a call option and the sale of a put option is equivalent to a forward purchase while the sale of a call option simultaneously combined with the purchase of a put option is equivalent to a forward sale.

These two levels of linkage between options and forward contracts imply a natural structural and economic relationship between the two instruments. In turn, option

Exhibit 2.4
Payoff Profiles for Option Positions

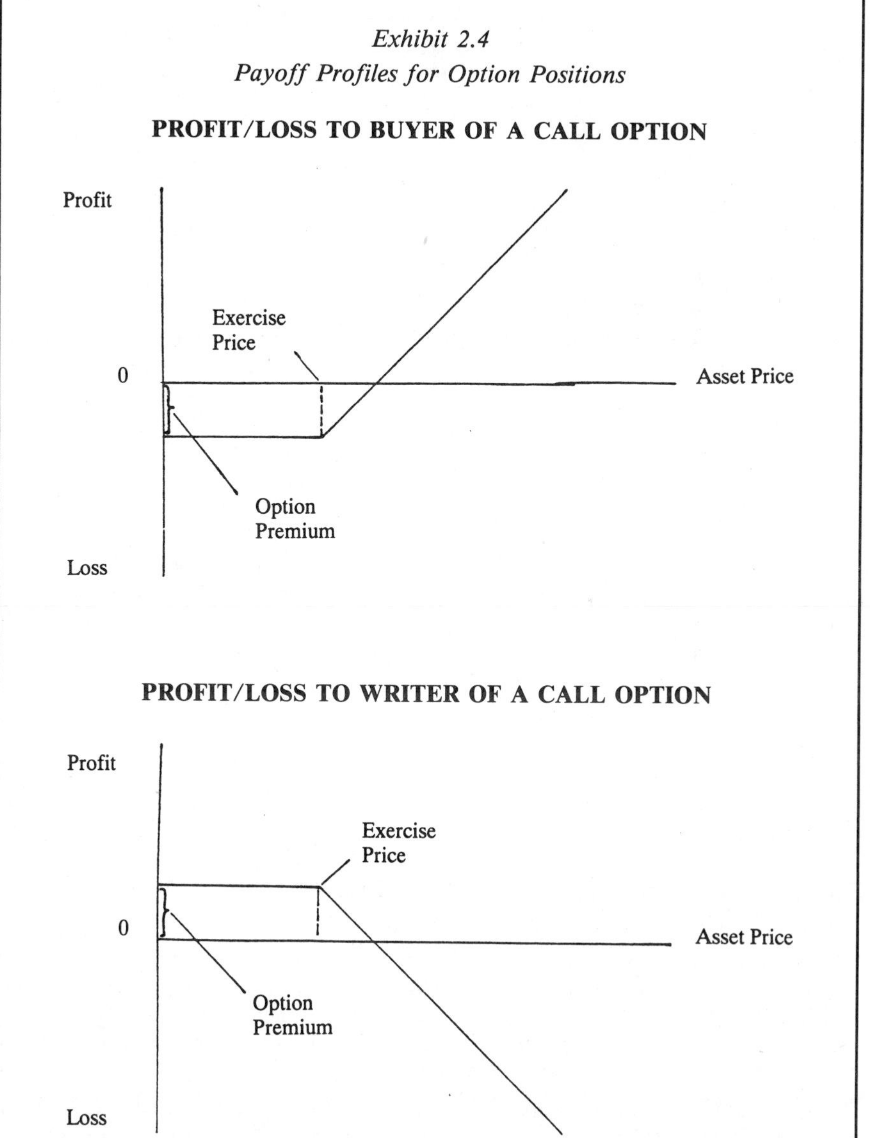

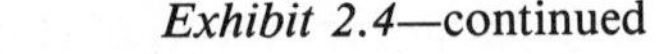

Exhibit 2.4—continued

PROFIT/LOSS TO BUYER OF A PUT OPTION

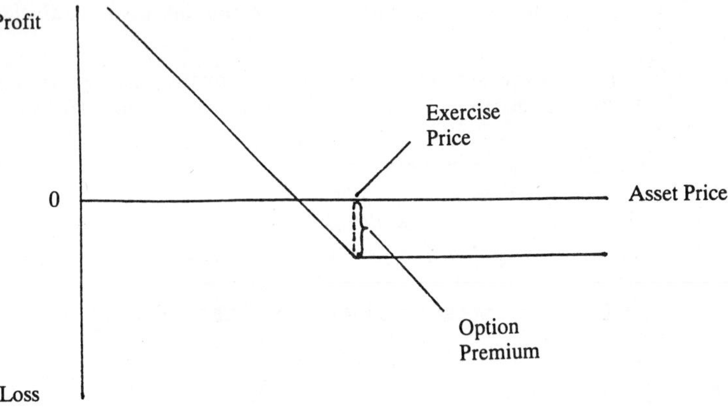

PROFIT/LOSS TO WRITER OF A PUT OPTION

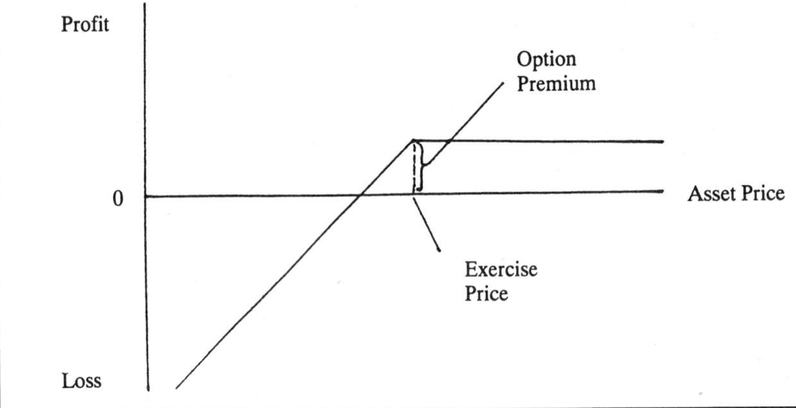

contracts impose a similar influence on interest rate swaps indirectly through their relationship with forward or futures contracts.

More directly, as noted above, options may have a direct relationship to interest rate swaps insofar as an interest rate swap can be characterised as a portfolio of purchased and sold options. This, of course, reflects the fact that an interest rate swap can be characterised as a series of forward contracts while forward contracts can be replicated through option contracts.

Swap instruments, such as caps, floors and collars are, in effect, a series of option contracts. This means that they are directly equivalent to underlying option contracts and consequently would enjoy a similar relationship to both forward and futures contracts or their customised equivalent FRAs as well as to interest rate swaps.

The discussion to date has confined itself to instruments in a single currency. However, the analysis is capable of extension to a multi-currency situation. A currency swap between two currencies is equivalent to a portfolio of currency forwards and futures or, alternatively, a portfolio of purchased and sold currency options. The currency forwards and currency options themselves are, first, linked to each other through option put call parity and relicating portfolio relationships, and, second, to the interest rate swap, forward and/or futures and option markets in their respective currencies.

This complex interrelationship between swap, forward and option markets is illustrated in *Exhibit 2.5* both in a single and multiple currency setting.

The process of decomposition of swap instruments into its basic constituent components—namely, forward and option contracts—is equally applicable to more complex non-generic and hybrid swap instruments. As is evident from the consideration of these types of swap structures in Part 4, each non-generic or hybrid swap structure is constituted from core swap instruments in *combination with* additional forward or option elements. This is particularly the case with non-generic swaps and options on swap/swaptions as well as interest rate and currency linked swap hybrids.

In the case of commodity and equity swaps, these instruments represent a forward contract on the underlying commodity or the equity market index. This dictates that there is a close relationship between equity and commodity swap contracts and forward and futures contract on the relevant commodity and equity market indexes.

Similarly, corresponding to the relationship between swaps, forward contracts/futures contracts, and options in interest rates and currency markets, the anticipated triangular relationship exists between equity and commodity swaps and forward and option markets in the relevant commodity or equity market. The basic nature of this relationship is almost identical to that which exists in interest rate and currency markets (as outlined above).

As illustrated, the capacity for swap transactions to be essentially dismembered into the basic constituent forward and option contracts is clearly evident. The ability to decompose swaps is not only elegant but highly useful for a number of reasons:

- the structural relationships allow the specific elements of individual transactions to be separated and recombined to create new instruments. This is particularly important in more complex liability and asset swap structures (see Part 4);
- the interrelationships form the basis of pricing swap transactions. The established technology of pricing forward and option contracts provides the basis for the pricing and economic analysis of swaps;
- the decomposition process also facilitates the trading and hedging of swap transactions where financial institutions make markets in these instruments.

Exhibit 2.5
Swap, Forward and Option Market Interrelationships

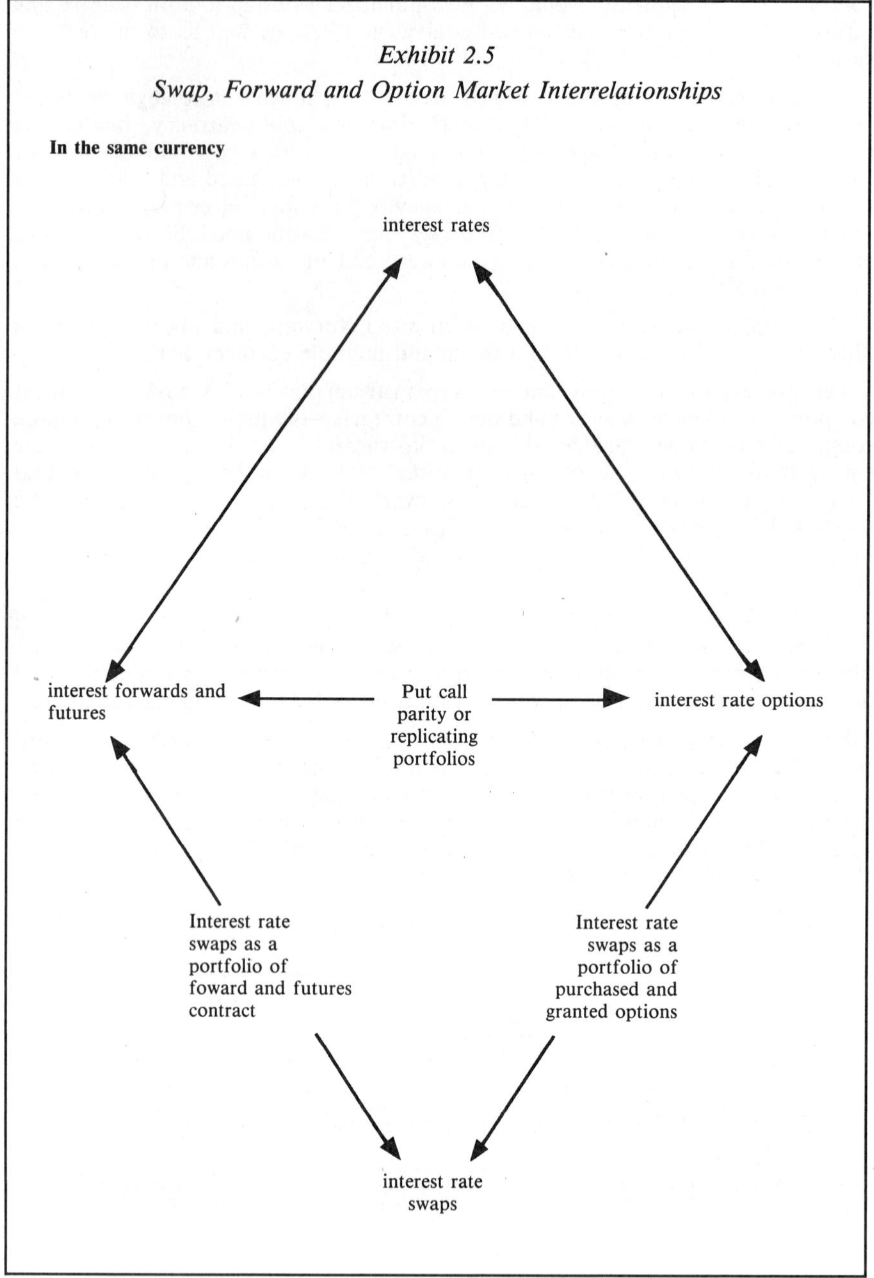

Exhibit 2.5—continued

As between two currencies (for example, A$ and US$)

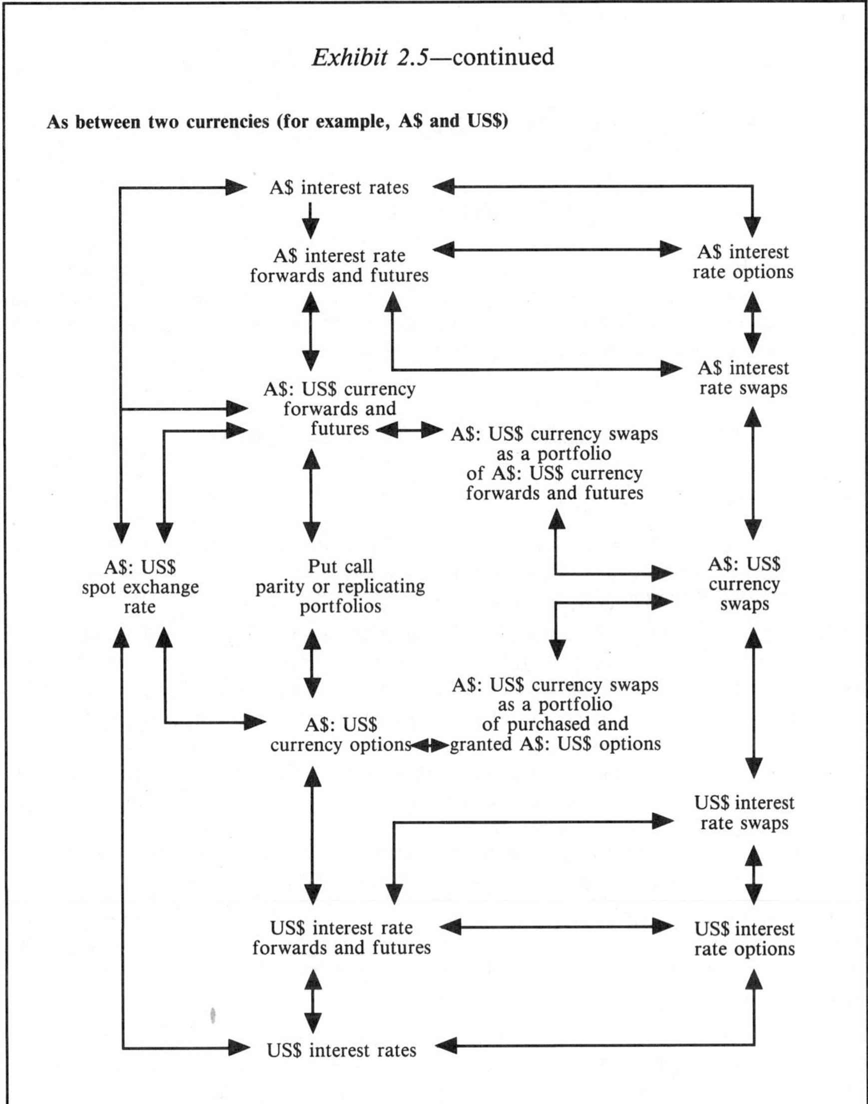

Chapter 3

Interest Rate and Currency Swap Structures

INTRODUCTION

Parallel or back-to-back loans and currency and interest rate swaps and LTFX represent two distinct categories of swap instruments. However, their historical relationship which is linked to the technical evolution of the various structures dictates that they are logically considered together.

PARALLEL OR BACK-TO-BACK LOANS

Parallel loans

Parallel loans involve two entities, with headquarters in different countries, each having subsidiaries in the other's country, and each having mirror-image liquidity positions and financing requirements.

For example, a United States parent company with a subsidiary in Australia may have surplus US$ liquidity or ready access to new US$ borrowings in the United States while its Australian subsidiary needs additional A$ financing. Simultaneously, an Australian parent company (or institution) may have surplus A$ liquidity or access to new A$ borrowings in Australia and may be seeking US$ financing for its United States subsidiary (or to support a portfolio investment). A parallel loan transaction consists of a US$ loan from the United States parent company to the United States subsidiary of the Australian parent, and a simultaneous A$ loan of an equivalent amount from the Australian parent company to the Australian subsidiary of the United States company.

This structure (set out in *Exhibit 3.1*) satisfies the respective financing objectives of both parties, while avoiding any relevant exchange control inherent in direct investment by each parent, any higher costs of independent borrowing by each subsidiary, and currency exposure on the investment.

Interest rates on the two parallel loans are usually set at a fixed rate corresponding to commercial rates prevailing for each currency at the time of closing and may be subject to local government regulations. The spread between the two interest rates is subject to negotiation but would be a function of general interest rate levels in the two countries as well as the current equilibrium or disequilibrium in the market between providers and users of either currency.

In the above example, if A$ rates were 15.00% pa and US$ rates were 10.00% pa and the transaction was for a maturity of five years, then the transaction cash flows would be that set out in *Exhibit 3.2*.

The 5.00% annual differential would be paid by the United States multinational company. From an economic perspective, the Australian company, in receiving the 5.00% pa differential, is essentially compensated for any opportunity loss that might otherwise be suffered as a result of A$ interest rates being higher than US$ interest rates.

Exhibit 3.1

Parallel Loan Structure

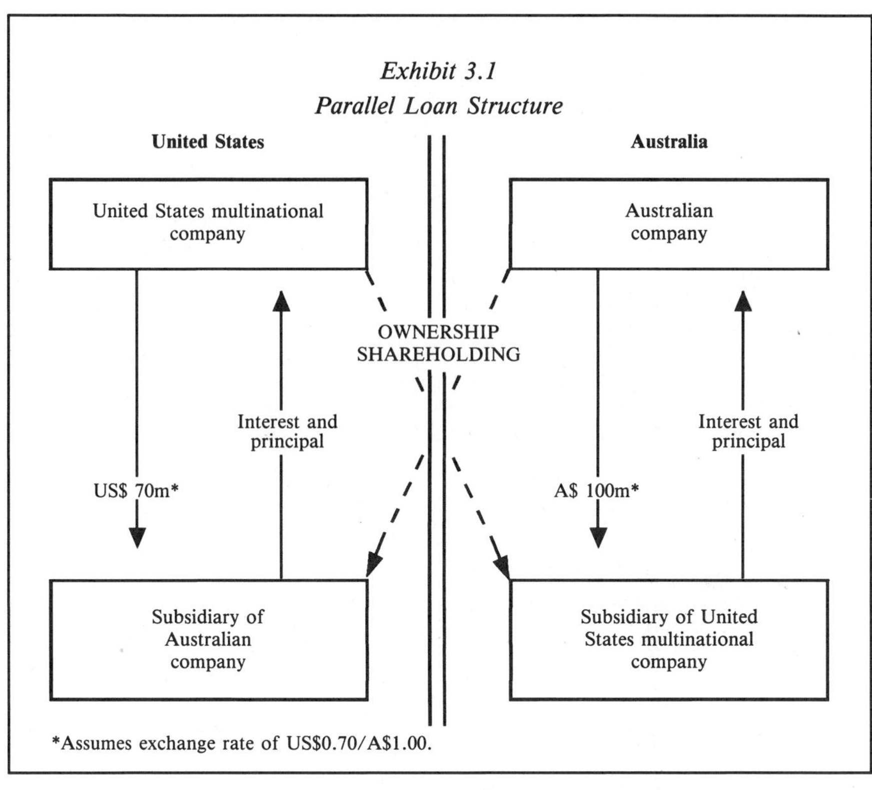

*Assumes exchange rate of US$0.70/A$1.00.

Exhibit 3.2

Parallel Loan: Cash Flows

Year	**Amount received by subsidiary of Australian company**	**Amount received by subsidiary of United States multinational company**
	US$	**A$**
0	+70	+100
1	− 7	− 15
2	− 7	− 15
3	− 7	− 15
4	− 7	− 15
5	{ − 7	{ − 15
	{ −70	{ −100

Note: Negative signs assume cash outflows.

Mechanically, the interest differential is generally paid in the form of an annual fee. In the case of the earliest swaps, this was structured as a series of forward currency sales by the party with the higher interest rate funding. However, subsequently the Bank of England specified an alternative formula (set out in *Exhibit 3.3*) which in effect required payment of the two interest rates at a gross rate which was converted into one currency using prevailing spot exchange rates and then netted.

Exhibit 3.3
Bank of England Interest Differential Fee Calculation

$$\text{Annual fee} = \text{US\\$ amount} \times \text{US\\$ interest \%} - \frac{\text{DEM amount} \times \text{DEM interest \%}}{\text{future US\\$/DEM exchange rate}}$$

Where: future exchange rate = US$/DEM exchange rate prevailing two days prior to fee payment date.

The following example illustrates the working of the formula and proves that it locks in local currency fixed rate financing costs.

Party A enters into a cross-currency fixed-to-fixed three year debt swap with party B under which party A agrees to sell DEM250 to party B in return for party B selling US$100 to party A. Both parties agree to the payment of an annual fee to be calculated in accordance with the Bank of England formula. Particulars of the swap are as follows:

Example
DEM amount = DEM250
US$ amount = US$100
DEM interest rate = 10.50%
US$ interest rate = 15.00%

Future exchange rate
Year 1 US$1 = DEM2.50
Year 2 US$1 = DEM1.25
Year 3 US$1 = DEM3.75

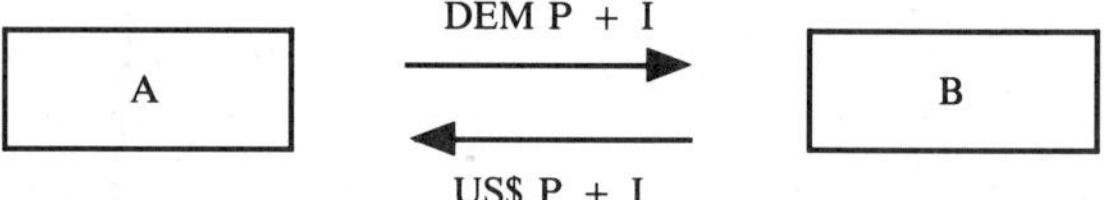

Calculation of fee

Year 1

$$\text{US\\$100} \times 15.00\% - \frac{\text{DEM250} \times 10.50\%}{\text{DEM2.5}} = \text{fee}$$

$$\text{US\\$15} - \text{US\\$10.50} = \text{US\\$4.50}$$

Therefore US$4.50 is payable by B to A.

Year 2

$$\text{US\\$15} - \text{US\\$21} = -\text{US\\$6}$$

Therefore US$6 is payable by A to B.

Year 3

$$\text{US\\$15} - \text{US\\$7} = \text{US\\$8}$$

Therefore US$8 is payable by B to A.

Total amount in dollar terms payable by B
(That is, deutschmark interest in dollar terms plus fee.)

(a) Deutschmark interest on bond at 10.50% payment	**(b)** Future exchange	**(a) ÷ (b) = (c)** Dollar equivalent	**(d)** Fee (see above)	**(c) + (d) = (e)** Total dollar
DEM		US$	US$	US$
26.25	2.50	10.50	4.50	15.00
26.25	1.25	21.00	−6.00	15.00
26.25	3.75	7.00	8.00	15.00

Exhibit 3.3—continued

As can be seen from the above calculations, the interest cost of servicing the simulated dollar loan, in dollar terms, is always US$15 (or 15.00%). Abolition of United Kingdom foreign exchange controls meant the Bank of England formula was no longer required. It is still used from time to time in order to simulate true borrowing cost. The same result is more customarily reached today by the parties agreeing to exchange defined amounts (determined implicitly by the parties agreeing to exchange defined amounts (determined implicitly by interest rates)) on the annual or semi-annual payment dates.

Source: Price and Henderson, *Currency and Interest Rate Swaps* (Butterworths, 1984), pp 13, 14.

It is also feasible to structure parallel loan transactions where the relevant interest rates are variable or floating if the rate is set at a fixed margin over a recognised indicator rate.

Maturities generally range from five to ten years, depending on the currencies involved, although shorter maturities are not uncommon. Maturities over ten years are unusual.

Interest payments on the two loans are usually made at the same intervals and in most cases take place simultaneously on both loans. For administrative simplicity, parallel loans are usually "bullet" loans, that is, they provide for no interim amortisation with the principal amount being repayable in full at the conclusion of the transaction. At maturity, the parallel loans are thus simply reversed.

Transactions providing for interim amortisation are feasible where an appropriate counterparty can be located. Prepayment provisions, though unusual, may be included to enable one party to prepay its loan without accelerating the other's payment.

The creditworthiness of the participants to the transaction is an important element in the transaction, and the credit risk may be mitigated by the inclusion of offset rights which allow each party the right to offset payments not received against payments due. Parallel loans (as distinct from back-to-back loans) do not include a right of offset. If either counterparty considers the other's subsidiary less than credit-worthy in its own right, specific security or a parent guarantee is usually negotiated.

A topping-up provision is often included to keep the principal amounts outstanding in balance where exchange rates move significantly during the life of the loans. A topping-up clause usually requires the lenders to make additional advances or repayments on one of the loans whenever the spot exchange rate moves past a trigger point, for example, in the A$ and US$ parallel loan example, additional A$ may have to be lent if the spot rate moves 10 cents lower, or paid back if the rate moves a corresponding amount higher.

Back-to-back loans

Parallel loans differ from back-to-back loans in that parallel loans do not include a right of offset or cross-collateralisation between loans, while back-to-back loans include a right of offset (see discussion below). As exchange control regulations of many countries prohibit rights of offset, parallel loans are more common than back-to-back loans.

The back-to-back loan differs from a parallel loan in structure as follows: under the back-to-back loan, the United States multinational company in the United States would lend to the Australian company in Australia whereas under a parallel loan structure the two parties would lend funds to their respective subsidiaries. This structure is set out in *Exhibit 3.4*.

Exhibit 3.4
Back-to-Back Loan Structure

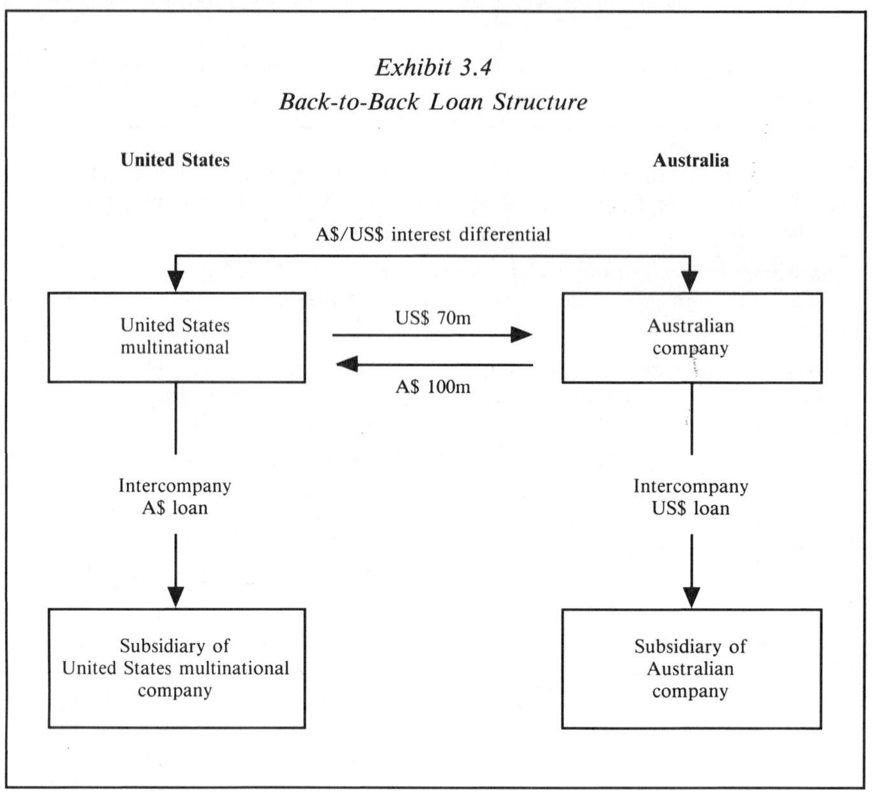

The back-to-back loan entails the United States multinational company lending US$ to the Australian company in return for the Australian company lending the United States company A$. This is accompanied by an intercompany loan to their respective subsidiaries. Both loans are priced in line with market yields in the respective markets. Consequently, the transaction can be regarded as an initial exchange of currencies with an accompanying agreement to repay the respective loans in a form which could be regarded as a forward sale of US$ for A$ on the one hand and a forward sale of US$ for A$ on the other.

Significant structural differences between parallel and back-to-back loans include:

- a back-to-back loan entails cross-border funds flows which raise withholding tax issues;
- there is only one loan document in a back-to-back loan.

The general terms of a back-to-back loan are very similar to those for a parallel loan, although protection against withholding taxes may be included.

A comparison of parallel, back-to-back loans and currency swaps

A parallel or back-to-back loan transaction and a currency swap (the structural successor to back-to-back loans) are similar techniques generally used to achieve similar objectives. In fact, currency swaps have, for most purposes, superseded parallel loans. However, a number of differences should be noted which might influence a company's choice between a parallel, back-to-back loan or a currency swap:

- Accountants differ on how parallel and back-to-back loans should be reported by the parent company on its balance sheet. Even if there exists a right of offset, some accountants feel that both loans should appear in the balance sheet rather than being treated as off-balance sheet items. Such treatment, which inflates the company's balance sheet, may produce adverse consequences under existing trust deeds or loan covenants and may therefore make a back-to-back loan or currency swap preferable. Where the back-to-back loan or currency swap does not entail new fund raising (that is, the party entering into the transaction has existing liquidity) the transaction entails the exchange of cash assets which effectively provides off-balance sheet financing as the future commitment to exchange currencies is analogous to a forward exchange contract which is not required to be reported on the balance sheet although it may require disclosure as a contingent liability or commitment.
- In a parallel loan transaction, each borrower has an unambiguous tax-deductible interest expense and each lender has taxable interest income. In a back-to-back loan or a currency swap, the annual payments paid by one party to the other (representing in effect the differential between the interest rates in the respective currencies) may or may not be tax-deductible depending upon local law. Either a parallel loan transaction or a back-to-back loan or currency swap might be preferable depending upon the tax position of each counterparty.
- An implied right of offset often exists in the case of a back-to-back loan or currency swap, whereas no such right exists between parallel loans. If this right of offset is important as a credit matter, a currency swap or back-to-back loan might be preferable.
- The constituting documents of certain potential counterparties may permit entry into a parallel loan but not into a back-to-back loan or currency swap or vice versa.
- Two major structural differences between parallel, back-to-back loans and currency swaps are significant:

  —in a currency swap, no initial cash movements are necessary, since the swap is normally based on prevailing spot rates thereby allowing each party to obtain the relevant currency through the spot foreign exchange (FX) market (this is considered in detail later in this chapter);
  —swaps offer greater flexibility than parallel or back-to-back loans.

The modern role of parallel or back-to-back loan structures

Parallel and back-to-back loan structures are best regarded as earlier technical forms of swap transactions. The evolution of parallel loans into back-to-back structures, and the recognition that these transactions could be unbundled essentially into spot and forward currency contracts provided some of the important insights which underpin the modern swap market.

However, despite its structural obsolescence, parallel loans, in particular, continue to enjoy a secular role in the context of freeing blocked funds. Harking back to its original rationale of bypassing exchange controls, parallel loans continue to be used to circumvent exchange restrictions in countries which do not allow the free transfer of capital across its boundaries.

The modern parallel loan tends to be more custom-designed to the needs of the transaction, although the basic structure remains very close to the original transaction mechanics. The market operates primarily against US$ although transactions not involving the US$ are not uncommon.

SWAP TRANSACTIONS STRUCTURES

Interest rate swap

An interest rate swap is a transaction in which two parties agree to exchange streams of cash flows based on a hypothetical (or notional) principal amount where one stream is calculated with reference to a floating interest rate and the other stream is calculated based on a fixed interest rate.

An interest swap can be used to transform one type of interest obligation into another and thereby enable a swap participant to tailor its interest obligations to meet its needs in a given rate environment.

Typically, the payment to be made by one party is calculated using a floating rate of interest (such as LIBOR, the Bank Bill Rate (BBR) etc) while the payment to be made by the other party is determined on the basis of a fixed rate of interest or a different floating rate.

In its most common form, an interest rate swap is undertaken by two parties: the first, for example, may be a borrower which wants to pay interest at a fixed rate but which has already borrowed at a floating rate and the second may be a borrower which wants to pay interest at a floating rate but which has already borrowed at a fixed rate. The borrower wanting to pay a fixed rate borrows the principal amount that it needs, but on a floating rate basis. The borrower wanting to pay a floating rate borrows an identical amount at fixed rates. If a borrower was entering into the swap with respect to an existing debt, it would not undertake a new borrowing.

The two then enter into an agreement in which each undertakes to make periodic payments to the other in amounts equal to, or determined on the same basis as, the other's interest cost. Only payments calculated in the form of interest are made; payments corresponding to principal amounts are not made by either party. The net result of this exchange is that each party is able to obtain the type of interest rate, fixed or floating, which it wants and on acceptable terms.

Exhibit 3.5 sets out in diagrammatic form the basic structure of an interest rate swap.

Exhibit 3.6 sets out the cash flows for a five year US$ interest rate swap where company A borrows US$100m for five years at a rate of 7.50% and enters into a swap with company B which borrows US$100m for five years on a floating rate basis at a cost of US$ six month LIBOR plus a margin of 0.50% pa. The swap is undertaken on the following terms: company B pays 7.50% pa in return for receiving US$ six month LIBOR.

Exhibit 3.5
Interest Rate Swap Structure

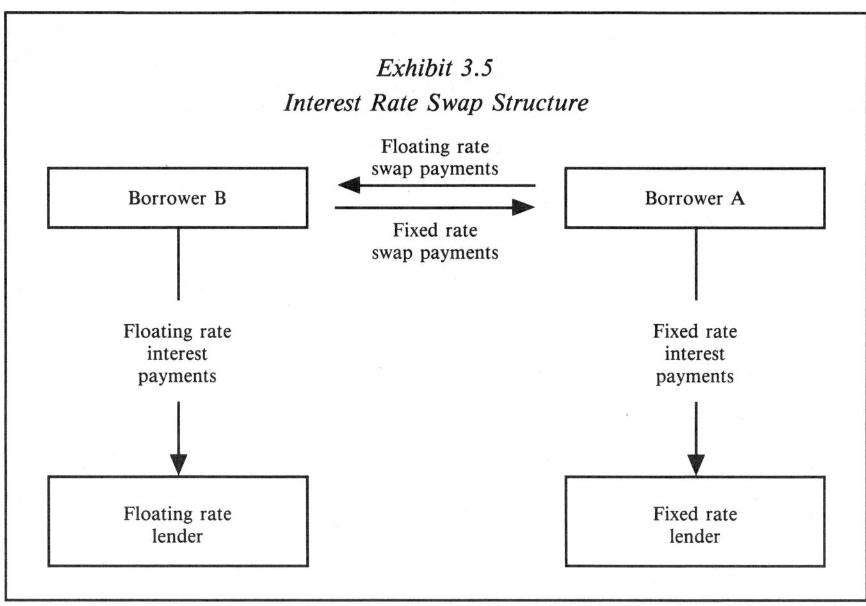

Exhibit 3.6
Fixed-to-Floating Interest Rate Swap: Cash Flows and Costs (in US$m)

	Company A				**Company B**			
	Amount received from	**Swap**		**Net cash**	**Amount received from**	**Swap**		**Net cash**
Year	**lender**	**Receipt**	**Payment**	**flow**	**lender**	**Receipt**	**Payment**	**flow**
0	+100	—	—	+100	+100	—	—	+100
0.5	−3.75	3.75	−LIBOR	−LIBOR	−LIBOR+.25	+LIBOR	−3.75	−4.00
1.0	−3.75	3.75	−LIBOR	−LIBOR	−LIBOR+.25	+LIBOR	−3.75	−4.00
1.5	−3.75	3.75	−LIBOR	−LIBOR	−LIBOR+.25	+LIBOR	−3.75	−4.00
2.0	−3.75	3.75	−LIBOR	−LIBOR	−LIBOR+.25	+LIBOR	−3.75	−4.00
2.5	−3.75	3.75	−LIBOR	−LIBOR	−LIBOR+.25	+LIBOR	−3.75	−4.00
3.0	−3.75	3.75	−LIBOR	−LIBOR	−LIBOR+.25	+LIBOR	−3.75	−4.00
3.5	−3.75	3.75	−LIBOR	−LIBOR	−LIBOR+.25	+LIBOR	−3.75	−4.00
4.0	−3.75	3.75	−LIBOR	−LIBOR	−LIBOR+.25	+LIBOR	−3.75	−4.00
4.5	−3.75	3.75	−LIBOR	−LIBOR	−LIBOR+.25	+LIBOR	−3.75	−4.00
5.0	−3.75	3.75	−LIBOR	−LIBOR	−LIBOR+.25	+LIBOR	−3.75	−4.00
	−100	—	—	−100	−100	—	—	−100

Notes: 1. (+) indicates a receipt, while (−) indicates a payment.
2. The accrual on the fixed rate payments assumes equal interest rate payments for simplicity.
3. LIBOR = six month LIBOR set each six months × 100 × (actual days/360). It is also assumed LIBOR on the loan and the swap are the same, that is, rates are (plus 0.50% in respect of the margin on the loan) set on the same day by the same rate setting or reference banks.

Exhibit 3.7 sets out the cash flows for a three year A$ interest rate swap where company A borrows A$100m for three years at a fixed rate of 14.00% pa (S/A) and enters into a swap with company B which borrows A$100m for three years on a floating rate basis at BBR plus 1.00% pa. The swap is undertaken on the following terms: company B pays 14.00% pa in return for receiving BBR flat.

Exhibit 3.7

Fixed-to-Floating Interest Rate Swap: Cash Flows and Costs (in A$m)

	Company A				Company B			
	Amount received from	Swap		Net cash	Amount received from	Swap		Net cash
Year	**lender**	**Receipt**	**Payment**	**flow**	**lender**	**Receipt**	**Payment**	**flow**
0	+100	—	—	+100	+100	—	—	+100
0.5	− 7	+7	−BBR	−BBR	−BBR+0.5	+BBR	−7.0	−7.5
1.0	− 7	+7	−BBR	−BBR	−BBR+0.5	+BBR	−7.0	−7.5
1.5	− 7	+7	−BBR	−BBR	−BBR+0.5	+BBR	−7.0	−7.5
2.0	− 7	+7	−BBR	−BBR	−BBR+0.5	+BBR	−7.0	−7.5
2.5	− 7	+7	−BBR	−BBR	−BBR+0.5	+BBR	−7.0	−7.5
3.0	− 7	+7	−BBR	−BBR	−BBR+0.5	+BBR	−7.0	−7.5
	−100	—	—	−100	−100	—	—	−100

Notes: 1. Negative signs assume cash outflows.
2. BBR = six month BBR set each six months × 100 × (actual days/365). It is also assumed BBR on the loan and the swap are the same, that is, rates are (plus 1.00% in respect of the loan) set on the same day by the same rate setting or reference banks.

A number of essential features of the interest rate swap should be noted:

- The transaction amount is referred to as the notional principal or amount. It is notional in the sense that it is not usually exchanged as both participants do *not* obtain the underlying liquidity or funding through the swap. In any case, an exchange would be meaningless as each counterparty would provide the other with the same amount in the same currency. The notional amount is very important, nevertheless, as it provides the basis for interest calculations under the swap. For example, in *Exhibit 3.6* the 7.50% and the LIBOR interest flows are calculated on US$100 which is the notional principal amount.
- The swap transaction is totally independent from any underlying borrowing transactions for either party. The swap merely affects the coupon flows of a separately undertaken liability.
- Neither lender is a party to the swap; each borrower continues to be obligated to its own lender for the payment of both principal and interest. In fact, the lenders would not necessarily be aware that the swap had been undertaken. Each swap party takes the risk that the other may not make its swap payments, which would leave the non-defaulting party with the interest cost of its own borrowing uncovered by the swap. The swap does not relieve either borrower from the obligation to pay both principal and interest on its own borrowing.

Exhibit 3.8 sets out sample transaction confirmations confirming entry by a company into interest rate swaps denominated in US$ and A$. Each sample confirmation details the typical terms and conditions of such swap transactions.

Exhibit 3.8
Interest Rate Swap Confirmations

Confirmation 1: US$ Interest Rate Swap

TO:	[BANK]
DATE:	18 MARCH 19X2
FROM:	[COMPANY]
SUBJECT:	*[COMPANY]—US$ INTEREST RATE SWAP CONFIRMATION*

[Company] confirms entering into the interest swap with your organisation as per the terms and conditions outlined below:

General

Parties:	[Company] and [Bank]
Notional Principal Amount:	US$100,000,000
Deal Date:	18 March 19X2
Commencement Date:	20 March 19X2
Termination Date:	20 March 19X7

Fixed Amounts

Fixed Rate Payer:	[Company]
Fixed Rate Payment Dates:	20 September 19X2 and thereafter each 20 March and 20 September up to and including the Termination Date (subject to the modified following business day convention).
Fixed Rate:	7.5254% pa
Fixed Rate Day Count Method:	Semi-annual Bond basis (30/360 day basis)

Floating Amounts

Floating Rate Payer:	[Bank]
Floating Rate Payment Dates:	Same as per Fixed Rate Payment Dates
Floating Rate:	Six Month US$ LIBOR (as quoted on Reuters Screen LIBO) rounded to the nearest fifth decimal place.
Floating Rate Day Count Basis Method:	LIBOR basis (actual/360 day basis)

Miscellaneous

Documentation:	Mutually acceptable documentation based on the standard ISDA contract
Governing Law:	English or New York
Conditions:	1. The obligation of [Company] to close the transaction contemplated herein is subject to the execution of mutually satisfactory documentation. 2. [Bank] enters into this transaction a firm basis acting as principal to the transaction. 3. No arrangement fee will be payable. 4. Each party will bear their own costs and expenses in the execution and documentation of this transaction.

Exhibit 3.8—continued

[Company] US$ Account details:	[Company Bank] Chips UID No: Account Name: Account No:
[Bank] US$ Account details:	Please advise US$ account details
Confirmation:	Please send confirmation to: [Company] Telex No: Fax No: Phone Nos:

If you have any queries in respect of any of the above, please call the undersigned.

Confirmation 2: A$ Interest Rate Swap

TO:	[BANK]
DATE:	1 APRIL 19X2
FROM:	[COMPANY]
SUBJECT:	*[COMPANY]—A$ INTEREST RATE SWAP CONFIRMATION*

[Company] confirms entering into the interest swap with your organisation as per the terms and conditions outlined below:

General

Parties:	[Company] and [Bank]
Notional Principal Amount:	A$100,000,000
Deal Date:	1 April 19X2
Commencement Date:	8 April 19X2
Termination Date:	8 April 19X5

Fixed Amounts

Fixed Rate Payer:	[Bank]
Fixed Rate Payment Dates:	8 July 19X2 and thereafter each 8 January, 8 April, 8 July and 8 October up to and including the Termination Date (subject to the preceding business day convention).
Fixed Rate:	10.075% pa
Fixed Rate Day Count Method:	Actual/365 day basis

Floating Amounts

Floating Rate Payer:	[Company]
Floating Rate Payment Dates:	Same as per Fixed Rate Payment Dates
Floating Rate:	Three Month Bank Accepted Bill Rate (as quoted on Reuters Screen BBSW) rounded to the nearest fifth decimal place.
Floating Rate Day Count Basis Method:	Actual/365 day basis

Exhibit 3.8—continued

Miscellaneous	
Documentation:	Mutually acceptable documentation based on the standard ISDA contract
Governing Law:	English or New York
Conditions:	1. The obligation of [Company] to close the transaction contemplated herein is subject to the execution of mutually satisfactory documentation. 2. [Bank] enters into this transaction a firm basis acting as principal to the transaction. 3. No arrangement fee will be payable. 4. Each party will bear their own costs and expenses in the execution and documentation of this transaction.
[Company] A$ Account details:	[Company Bank] Account Name: Account No:
[Bank] A$ Account details:	Please advise A$ account details
Confirmation:	Please send confirmation to: [Company] Telex No: Fax No: Phone Nos:

If you have any queries in respect of any of the above, please call the undersigned.

This "decoupling" of the interest rate characteristics of a transaction is essentially one of the key features of swaps. It essentially allows a number of aspects of financing transactions to be separated or unbundled, including:

- source of funding, that is, which market or lender;
- form of funding, that is, fixed or floating rate;
- timing of raising the required funding.

There are a number of common variations in interest rate swap structures, including:

- the incorporation of an intermediary;
- the use of structures not entailing entry by one party into the swap;
- the use of net as distinct from gross settlements under the swap.

In the basic structure (outlined above) both borrowers directly swap their obligations under their respective loans (refer *Exhibit 3.5*). Each borrower therefore takes the risk that the other may not make its swap payments.

However, under current market practice, most interest rate swaps do not utilise this direct structure. If either or both of the borrowers are unwilling to accept the risk of non-payment by the other, a third party, generally a bank or other financial institution, may be interposed between the borrowers to create an intermediated swap (refer *Exhibit 3.9*). Borrowers on both sides generally deal solely with the intermediary and have separate contracts with the intermediating bank. In this form the swap may be anonymous with the identity of both parties only being known to the intermediary.

Exhibit 3.9

Intermediated Interest Rate Swap Structure

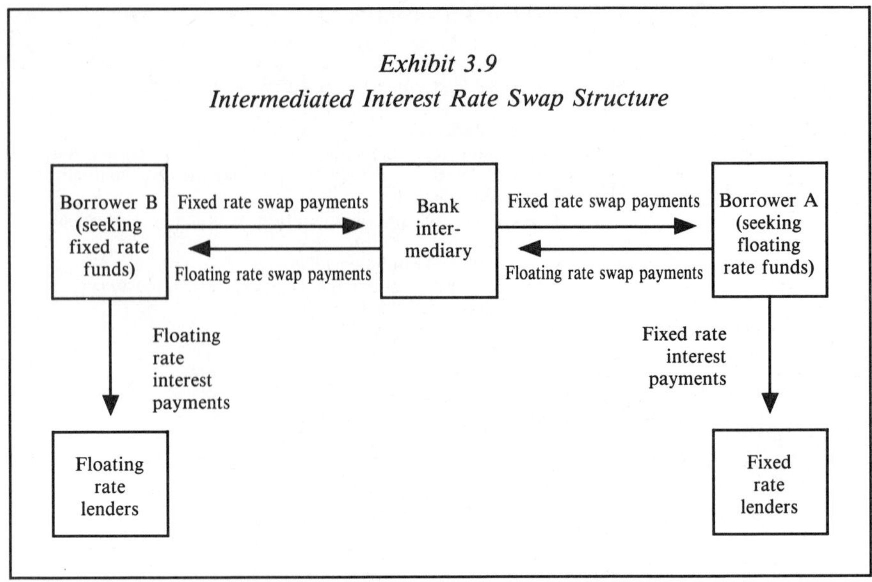

The interposition of an intermediary in an interest rate swap insulates each borrower from the other and in so doing the intermediary, for a fee, guarantees that each borrower will receive the swap payment due from the other. The exact risk assumed by the intermediary varies between transactions. In general, in the type of transaction considered to date, the intermediating institution's guarantee is limited to the interest or coupon obligations swapped. If either party to the swap fails to make a swap payment due to the intermediary, then the intermediary will not meet its corresponding payment under the swap. Consequently, the risk being assumed by the intermediary in respect of default is limited to any excess which the intermediary must pay to the other party over the payment to be received from the other party.

Where the swap encompasses exchanges of principal as well as interest or coupon obligations (see discussion of currency swap structures below), the intermediary may guarantee the principal amount in addition to the net swap payments. The fee payable to the intermediary is based on the principal amount of the borrowing covered by the swap and/or the amount of the interest swap payments received by it and reflects the extent of credit risk assumed.

The presence of an intermediary also eliminates the need for exact matching of the two legs of the swaps. At its simplest, the separation of contractual obligations would generally enable transactions involving different amounts and a number of parties with slightly different needs to be matched. For example, some economies of scale and price advantages may be achieved by structuring a transaction using a very large bond offering by a particularly creditworthy borrower and swapping the proceeds with a number of floating rate borrowers. Additional flexibility in respect of early termination etc may also be facilitated by the interposition of an intermediary. These advantages generally favour the intermediated form of interest rate swap and most transactions utilise this structure.

The credit exposure issues of swaps as well as the market making role of financial institutions in swap transactions are considered in detail in Parts 7 and 8.

In practice, certain transaction structures adopted make it unnecessary for borrowers to be parties to the interest swap itself. For example, if one borrower is unwilling or unable to enter into a swap, for example, for legal reasons, a special transaction structure may be adopted to enable the swap payments to be made between its lender and intermediary. Under this arrangement, the fixed rate borrower obtains fixed rate funds from the floating rate lender which converts its return to a floating rate basis through a swap with the intermediary which in turn enters into a complementary swap with the borrower (which seeks floating rate funds) which is willing to swap its fixed interest rate obligation for a floating rate obligation. Under this structure, the fixed rate borrower effectively achieves a conventional fixed rate loan although the payment flows and related risks and costs are determined to a large extent by the existence of the interest rate swap to which it is not a party. This type of transaction structure is depicted in *Exhibit 3.10.*

Exhibit 3.10
Interest Rate Swap Structure for Borrowers Not Wishing to Swap

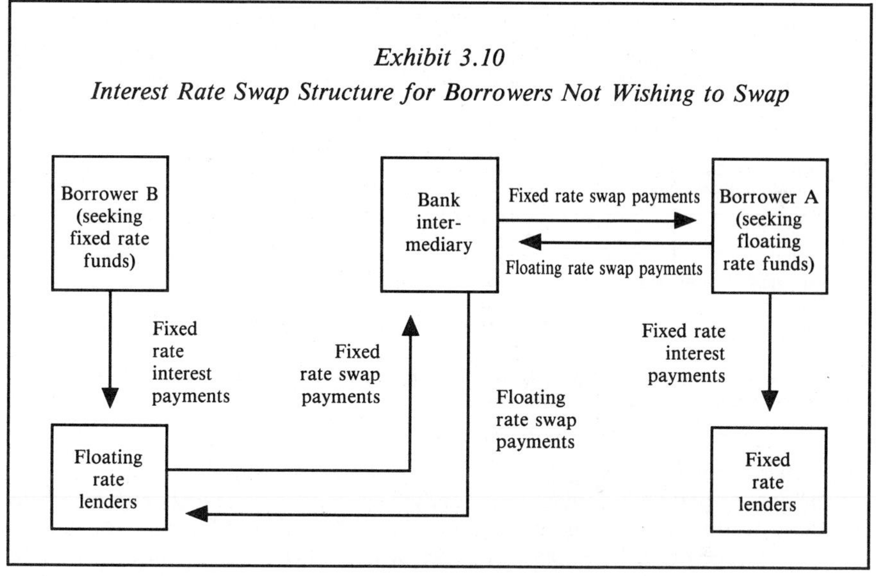

The third structural variation of importance is the use of net settlement terms under the swap. This is predicated on eliminating the flow of cash, representing the *full* interest payment to be made by each swap counterparty to the other. Instead, a *net* amount is either paid or received, representing the difference between the amount under the swap required to be paid to and the amount simultaneously due from the counterparty. *Exhibit 3.11* illustrates the use of the net settlement technique.

Some other structural variations should also be noted. The examples, to date, have focused on transactions entailing new liabilities which are specifically undertaken as the basis for the swap. In practice, swaps can also be undertaken against existing liabilities and even, in the extreme, against no liabilities. In the later case, the swap is purely speculative in nature. Similarly, the swap need not be undertaken for the full term of the underlying borrowings. For example, the first two years of a three year obligation could be swapped based on interest rate expectations.

Exhibit 3.11

Calculation of Swap Net Settlement Amounts

Assume the same terms as for the swap described in *Exhibit 3.7*. Examining the transaction from the perspective of company A, the net settlement amounts under the swap (based on a notional principal amount of A$100m) would be as follows:

Year	Assumed BBR	Swap flows Receipt (A$m)[1]	Payment (A$m)[2]	Net settlement amount (A$m)[3]
0.5	15.0%	7.00	7.50	−0.50
1.0	13.5%	7.00	6.75	+0.25
1.5	13.0%	7.00	6.50	+0.50

Notes: 1. The swap fixed rate is 14.00% pa (S/A).
2. The swap floating rate is calculated as BBR × Swap Notional Principal for the period of six months.
3. The (+) indicates a receipt, while a (−) indicates a payment.

These settlement amounts achieve the following effective interest commitments for each party.

Year	Interest paid (including margin if any) (A$m)	Net settlement amount from swap (A$m)	Effective interest payment (including margins if any) (A$m)	Effective interest rate (% pa)
Company A's position				
0.5	−7.00	−0.50	−7.50	15.00
1.0	−7.00	+0.25	−6.75	13.50
1.5	−7.00	+0.50	−6.50	13.00
Company B's position				
0.5	−8.00	+0.50	−7.50	15.00
1.0	−7.25	−0.25	−7.50	15.00
1.5	−7.00	−0.50	−7.50	15.00

As a result of the swap, company B ends up with an effective fixed interest rate of 15.00% pa and company A ends up with an effective floating rate of BBR.

Another structural variation of some importance is the use of discount instruments as part of the underlying funding for a swap. The difficulty relates to the fact that the proceeds of discount instruments, such as an A$ bank bill or promissory note or US$ commercial paper, are less than its face value or par. In order to allow exact cash flow matching under the swap, where a discount instrument is being used, it is necessary to structure the drawdown of, for example, bills such that the face value is varied to provide net proceed equal to the notional principal amount of the swap.

For example, in the example discussed in *Exhibit 3.7*, if BBR at commencement of the transaction was 16.00%, company B should have drawn down A$108.5 million face value of six month discounted securities. These bills would provide B with proceeds of $100 (the notional principal amount of the swap) if discounted at 17.00% pa (BBR plus the margin of 1.00%). This procedure would be repeated every six months to maintain the underlying funding at the required level.

Currency swaps

A currency swap is similar to a parallel or back-to-back loan. In a currency swap, the counterparties do not lend currencies to each other but sell them to each other with a concomitant agreement to reverse the exchange of currencies at a fixed date in the future.

The amount to be swapped is established in one currency, and the prevailing spot exchange rate is used to establish the amount in the other currency. Currency swaps entail interest payments which take the form of a periodical payment by the counterparty in the lower interest rate country to the counterparty in the higher interest rate country. The interest cost generally approximates the interest rate differential between the countries. These rates can be either fixed or floating.

All currency swaps involve the buying and selling of different currency cash flows in the future, each respective sale being contingent upon the other. This is an important point as it distinguishes a currency swap from a loan and, by definition, being a forward conditional commitment makes it a contingent obligation therefore an off-balance sheet item.

Consider the following example: company A borrows A$100m for five years at 14.00% pa payable annually while company B borrows the US$ equivalent of A$100m, say US$65m for five years at LIBOR plus a margin (say 0.50%) payable semi-annually (assume A$1/US$0.65).

The currency swap would operate in three distinct phases: initial principal exchange, interest payments coverage and a re-exchange of principal at maturity.

At commencement of the transaction, company A would sell the proceeds of its A$ issue to company B in return for company B selling the proceeds of its US$ borrowing to company A. This exchange is effected at the prevailing spot exchange rate.

Each party agrees to service the other party's debt, that is, company A would pay the interest on company B's loan and company B the interest on company A's loan. In this example, it is assumed that company A does not pay the spread over LIBOR on company B's loan.

At maturity the parties would merely reverse the initial exchange. In other words, company A would sell US$65m to company B in return for company B selling A$100m to company A.

Exhibit 3.12 sets out in diagrammatic form the basic structure of a currency swap.

Exhibit 3.13 sets out the detailed cash flows and effective cost calculations of the transaction described.

As indicated in the cash flow schedule company B's net cost of funds is 14.00% in A$ plus 0.50% spread over US$ LIBOR paid semi-annually while company A's cost is US$ LIBOR. This example does not allow for the front end borrowing costs for either company's borrowings. Assuming each company borrowed by way of a public issue, in calculating all-in costs one has to not only allow for front end issue fees but all other issue expenses.

It is important to note that the currency swap detailed in *Exhibits 3.12* and *3.13* does *not* totally eliminate company C's currency exposure as it receives US$ LIBOR but makes US$ LIBOR plus 0.25% pa payments every six months. This 0.25% pa US$ shortfall arises as a result of the normal economic structuring of the swap. However, in practice, company C would seek to eliminate the mismatch by introducing an intermediary which would allow company C to restructure the swap as follows: company C would pay, say, 14.65% pa on A$100m in return for receiving LIBOR plus 0.50% pa on US$65m. This would transfer the mismatch risk from company C to the intermediary.

The currency swap structure is very similar to that of an interest rate swap as described above. The major difference relates to the need to exchange principal amounts at the commencement and conclusion of a transaction. This exchange is designed to provide the parties to the swap with access to their desired currency for

Exhibit 3.12
Fixed-to-Floating Currency Swap Structure

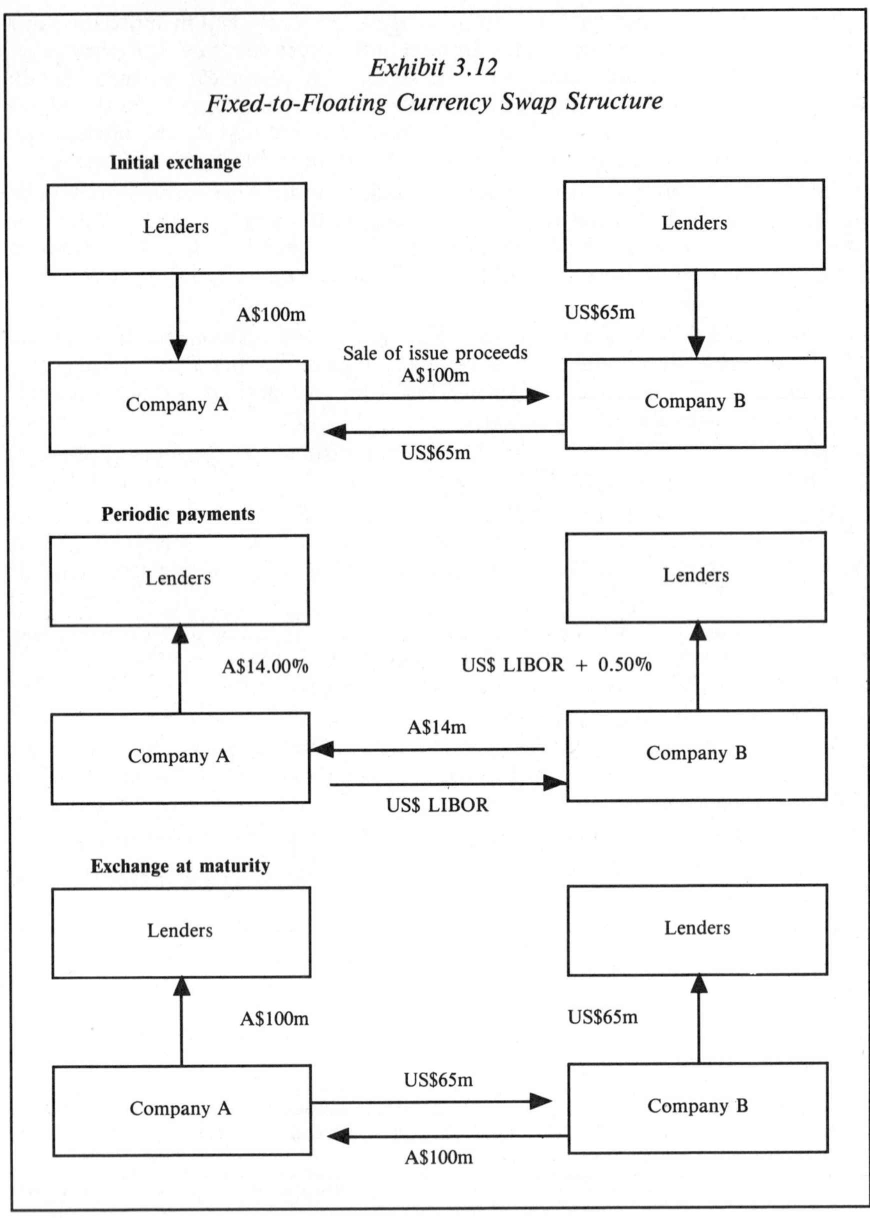

the life of the transaction while eliminating any foreign exchange exposure, other than in the nominated currency.

Exhibit 3.14 sets out sample transaction confirmations confirming entry by a company into currency and interest rate swaps as between SFR and US$ and JPY and US$. Each sample confirmation details the typical terms and conditions of such swap transactions.

Exhibit 3.13
Fixed-to-Floating Currency Swap: Cash Flows and Costs (in millions)

	Company A				Company B			
Year	Amount received from lender A$	Swap Receipt A$	Swap Payment US$	Net cash flow US$	Amount received from lender US$	Swap Receipt US$	Swap Payment A$	Net cash flow A$
0	+100	−100	+65	+65	+65	−65	+100	+100
0.5	—	—	−LIBOR	−LIBOR	−(LIBOR+0.25)	+LIBOR	—	−0.25
1.0	−14	+14	−LIBOR	−LIBOR	−(LIBOR+0.25)	+LIBOR	−14	−14.25
1.5	—	—	−LIBOR	−LIBOR	−(LIBOR+0.25)	+LIBOR	—	−0.25
2.0	−14	+14	−LIBOR	−LIBOR	−(LIBOR+0.25)	+LIBOR	−14	−14.25
2.5	—	—	−LIBOR	−LIBOR	−(LIBOR+0.25)	+LIBOR	—	− 0.25
3.0	−14	+14	−LIBOR	−LIBOR	−(LIBOR+0.25)	+LIBOR	−14	−14.25
3.5	—	—	−LIBOR	−LIBOR	−(LIBOR+0.25)	+LIBOR	—	−0.25
4.0	−14	+14	−LIBOR	−LIBOR	−(LIBOR+0.25)	+LIBOR	−14	−14.25
4.5	—	—	−LIBOR	−LIBOR	−(LIBOR+0.25)	+LIBOR	—	−0.25
5.0	−14	+14	−LIBOR	−LIBOR	−(LIBOR+0.25)	+LIBOR	−14	−14.25
	−100	+100	−65	−65	−65	+65	−100	−100

Notes: 1. Negative signs assume cash outflows.
2. LIBOR = six month LIBOR rate set each six months × US$65m × (actual days ÷ 365). It also assumes LIBOR on the loan and the swap are the same, that is, rates are (plus 0.50% in respect of the loan) set on the same day by the same rate setting or reference banks.

Exhibit 3.14
Currency Swap Confirmations

Confirmation 1: SFR/US$ Currency Swap

TO: [BANK]
DATE: 2 MAY 19X2
FROM: [COMPANY]
RE: [COMPANY]—
SWISS FRANC/US DOLLAR CROSS CURRENCY SWAP

[Company] confirms entering into a Swiss Franc (SFR)/US Dollar (US$) Cross-Currency Swap on the terms and conditions outlined below:

General

Parties:	[Company] and [Bank] (the Counterparty)
Swiss Franc Principal Amount:	SFR100,000,000
US$ Principal Amount:	The US$ equivalent of the Swiss Franc Principal Amount calculated at the Agreed Exchange Rate.
Agreed Exchange Rate:	The SFR/US$ spot exchange rate on 13 June 19X2 for value 15 June 19X2 (as agreed to by [Company] and the Counterparty).
Commencement Date:	15 June 19X2
Termination Date:	15 June 19X9
Payment Dates:	Every 15 June and 15 December, commencing 15 December 19X2 and ending on the Termination Date subject to adjustment in accordance with the Modified Following Business Day Convention.

Exhibit 3.14—continued

Exchanges of Principal

Initial Exchange: For value on the Commencement Date (such date being subject to the Modified Following Business Day Convention) [Company] shall pay to the Counterparty the US$ Principal Amount and [Company] will receive from the Counterparty the Swiss Franc Principal Amount.

Exchange at Maturity: For value on the Termination Day (such date being subject to adjustment in accordance with the Modified Business Day Convention) [Company] will receive from the Counterparty the US$ Principal Amount and [Company] shall pay to the Counterparty the Swiss Franc Principal Amount.

Swiss Franc Payments

Payments by [Company]: [Company] will pay to the Counterparty the Swiss Franc Interest Amount on every Payment Date.

Swiss Franc Interest Amount: An amount equal to interest at 7.65 percentage per annum payable semi annually of the Swiss Franc Principal Amount, calculated on a semi annual bond basis (30/360 day basis).

US$ Payments

Payments by Counterparty: The Counterparty shall pay to [Company] an amount equal to the US$ Interest Amount on every Payment date.

US$ Interest Amount: An amount equal to interest on the US$ Principal Amount at six month LIBOR (flat) calculated on an actual/360 day basis. The LIBOR amount is to be set with reference to the Reuters page LIBO (calculated to five decimal places).

Miscellaneous

Documentation: Mutually acceptable documentation based on the standard ISDA Contract.

Conditions:

1. The obligation of [Company] to close the transaction contemplated hereby is subject to the execution of mutually satisfactory documentation.
2. [Bank] is entering this transaction acting as principal.
3. No arrangement fee will be payable.
4. Each party will bear their own costs and expenses in the execution and documentation of this transaction.

[Company] Bank Account Details:

US$ Account
[Bank]
Chips UID NO:
Account Name:
Account No:
SFR Account
[Bank]
Account Name:
Account No:

[Bank] Bank Account Details: Please advise US$ and SFR Account details.

If you have any queries in respect of this transaction, please call the undersigned.

Confirmation 2: JPY/US$ Currency Swap

TO: [BANK]
DATE: 2 MAY 19X9
FROM: [COMPANY]
RE: [COMPANY]—
YEN/US DOLLAR CROSS CURRENCY SWAP

Exhibit 3.14—continued

[Company] confirms entering into a Yen (JPY)/US Dollar (US$) Cross-Currency Swap on the terms and conditions outlined below:

General

Parties:	[Company] and [Bank] (the Counterparty)
JPY Principal Amount:	JPY10,000,000,000
US$ Principal Amount:	The US$ equivalent of the JPY Principal Amount calculated at the Agreed Exchange Rate.
Agreed Exchange Rate:	The JPY/US$ spot exchange rate on 13 June 19X9 for value 15 June 19X9 (as agreed to by [Company] and the Counterparty).
Commencement Date:	15 June 19X9
Termination Date:	15 June 19X4
JPY Payment Dates:	Every 15 June commencing 15 June 19X0 and ending on the Termination Date subject to adjustment in accordance with the Modified Following Business Day Convention.
US$ Payment Dates:	Every 15 June and 15 December, commencing 15 December 19X9 and ending on the Termination Date subject to adjustment in accordance with the Modified Following Business Day Convention.

Exchanges of Principal

Initial Exchange:	For value on the Commencement Date (such date being subject to the Modified Following Business Day Convention) [Company] shall pay to the Counterparty the JPY Principal Amount and [Company] will receive from the Counterparty the US$ Principal Amount.
Exchange at Maturity:	For value on the Termination Day (such date being subject to adjustment in accordance with the Modified Business Day Convention) [Company] will receive from the Counterparty the JPY Principal Amount and [Company] shall pay to the Counterparty the US$ Principal Amount.

JPY Payments

Payments by [Bank]:	[Bank] will pay to the [Company] the JPY Interest Amount on every JPY Payment Date.
JPY Interest Amount:	An amount equal to interest at 6.50 percentage per annum payable annually of the JPY Principal Amount, calculated on an annual bond basis (30/360 day basis).

US$ Payments

Payments by [Company]:	The [Company] shall pay to [Bank] an amount equal to the US$ Interest Amount on every US$ Payment date.
US$ Interest Amount:	An amount equal to interest on the US$ Principal Amount at 6 month LIBOR minus the US$ margin calculated on an actual/360 day basis. The LIBOR amount is to be set with reference to the Reuters page LIBO (calculated to five decimal places).
US$ Margin:	0.00375% pa

Miscellaneous

Documentation:	Mutually acceptable documentation based on the standard ISDA Contract.
Conditions:	1. The obligation of [Company] to close the transaction contemplated hereby is subject to the execution of mutually satisfactory documentation.

Exhibit 3.14—continued

	2. [Bank] is entering this transaction acting as principal. 3. No arrangement fee will be payable. 4. Each party will bear their own costs and expenses in the execution and documentation of this transaction.
[Company] Bank Account Details:	*US$ Account* [Bank] Chips UID NO: Account Name: Account No: *JPY Account* [Bank] Account Name: Account No:
[Bank] Bank Account Details:	Please advise US$ and JPY Account Details.

If you have any queries in respect of this transaction, please call the undersigned.

The exchanges in a currency swap can be eliminated. Instead of an initial exchange, a spot FX transaction can allow each party to generate its desired currency (refer *Exhibit 3.15*). However, the elimination of the initial exchange does not obviate the need *to set* a reference spot rate between the relevant currencies. This rate is, of course, the rate at which the re-exchange at maturity is to be effected.

Exhibit 3.15

Currency Swap With No Initial Exchange

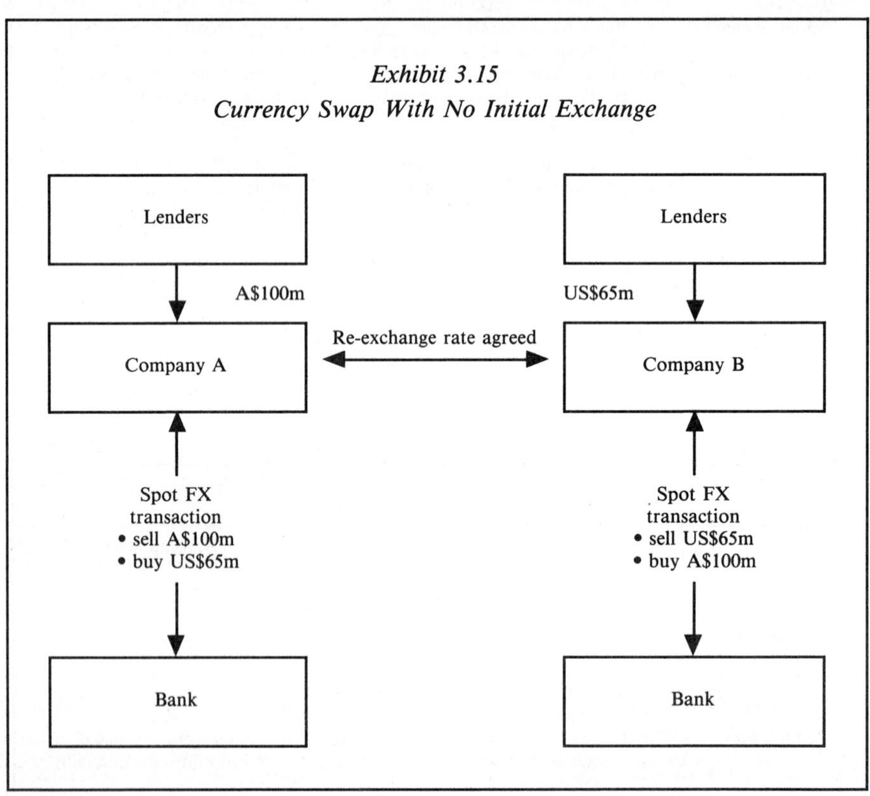

Where an initial exchange is not undertaken the spot rate must be set using a defined market rate as quoted by a specified bank at a particular time. Care is necessary to ensure that the definition used is the same for all parties, particularly where a multi-legged swap is sought to be transacted. A major problem relates to the fact that the swap counterparties, respectively buyers and sellers of the currencies, will by definition be on the "wrong" side of the bid-offer spread. These slight mismatches in amount are problematic as they may open unintentional currency exposures or, alternatively, will affect the all-in cost achieved.

The most common reason for not using an initial exchange is that the swap is being undertaken against existing borrowings where there are no new cash flows which can be used to support the swap exchange.

The final re-exchange can also be eliminated. This is achieved by the parties undertaking appropriate spot FX transactions and by a currency difference (reflecting the appreciation or depreciation of the currencies) being paid by one party to the other. The spot FX transaction, in conjunction with the settlement amount, will give the same result as if the re-exchange had been effected at the original nominated rate (refer *Exhibit 3.16*).

Exhibit 3.16

Currency Swap With No Re-exchange at Maturity

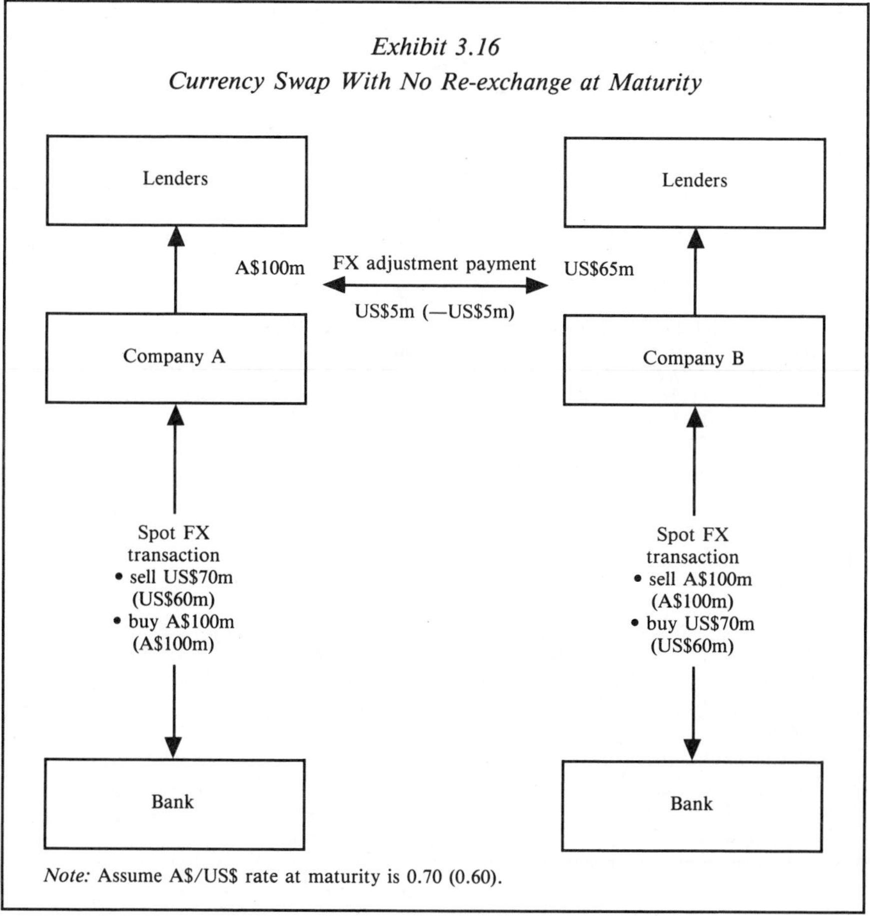

Note: Assume A$/US$ rate at maturity is 0.70 (0.60).

The analysis to date assumes that the initial exchange is undertaken at the prevailing swap rate. It is technically possible to structure currency swaps at off-market spot rates usually to accelerate or defer currency losses or gains. A variety of structures are feasible with the FX difference usually being incorporated in the interest rates under the swap.

The various structural differences discussed in the context of interest rate swaps are all also generally applicable to currency swap transactions. However, it is worth noting that net settlement procedures are less common in currency swaps and where utilised require the two swap flows to be translated into a common currency, usually US$.

LTFX agreements

Fixed-to-fixed currency swaps are similar conceptually to and can be used to effectively replicate LTFX transactions. In fact, technically a fixed-to-fixed currency swap is identical to a par forward FX contract (refer *Exhibit 3.17*).

Exhibit 3.17
Par Forward Contract

Scenario 1

A purchase of US$1m every month for four months:

Spot A$1: US$0.6600
forward points: 7.07.X7 – 50
7.08.X7 – 100
7.09.X7 – 150
7.10.X7 – 200

NORMAL FORWARD COVER			PAR FORWARD COVER		
Date	**Rate (A$1/US$)**	**Cost**	**Date**	**Rate (A$1/US$)**	**Cost**
7.07.X7	0.6550	A$1,526,717	7.07.X7	0.6476	A$1,544,163
7.08.X7	0.6500	A$1,538,461	7.08.X7	0.6476	A$1,544,163
7.09.X7	0.6450	A$1,550,387	7.09.X7	0.6476	A$1,544,163
7.10.X7	0.6400	A$1,562,500	7.10.X7	0.6476	A$1,544,163

Note:

Par forward rate = nominal rate + funding cost

$$\text{Nominal rate} = \frac{0.6550 - 0.6500 + 0.6450 + 0.6400}{4} = 0.6475$$

Funding cost = Cost or benefit to the company due to different cash flows. The cost to the company in the current example is A$785 which is compensated for in a benefit of one exchange point.
0.6475 + 0.0001 = 0.6476

Scenario 2

A purchase of US$1m one year forward can be transacted in one of the following ways:

- a forward purchase of US$1m for value in one year's time at US$0.6200 reflecting a spot rate of A$1/US$0.6600 and the one year forward premium of 0.0400 (that is, 7.00% pa);
- a par forward with the forward being transacted at the spot rate of US$0.6200 with deferred settlement at an interest cost of 7.00%.

LTFX agreements are outright forward transactions with no spot exchange taking place at time of closing. They are used primarily for hedging existing or anticipated exposures, such as long-term borrowings or future receivables. LTFX agreements normally call for a single specific exchange at a future date or a series of exchanges spread evenly over a number of years.

To illustrate, a United States company with A$ liability decides that its currency exposure is unacceptable and decides to buy A$ forward. At the same time, an Australian airline plans to purchase aircraft in the United States and wants to guarantee the A$ price of its investment. To satisfy the respective hedging needs of the two companies, an LTFX contract could be structured. The United States company sells US$ to and buys A$ from the Australian company. The Australian company, on the other hand, will use the acquired US$ to pay for its US$ denominated investments. In brief, the currency risk of the two companies has been eliminated at the cost of the forward premium discount between the two currencies.

Exhibit 3.18 sets out in diagrammatic form the structure of the LTFX transaction described.

Exhibit 3.18
LTFX Contract Structure

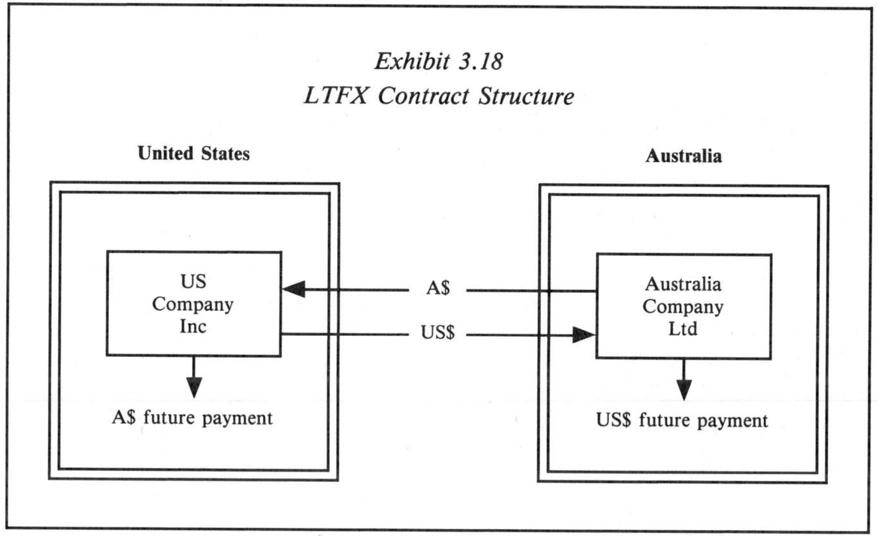

The prices on forward contracts, that is, the premiums/discounts, are negotiable but generally reflect the prevailing market interest rates for the two currencies for the same maturity. The longer the maturity in general, the wider the bid/ask spread, reflecting the thinness of the market in the longer maturity ranges. In terms of credit and FX risk, the obligation to perform is implied in a forward FX agreement, and its terms and conditions are usually negotiated between the two parties.

The forward exchange commitment leg of a currency swap transaction which simply entails the purchase and sale of foreign currency is very similar to that of a normal currency forward contract. However, currency swaps provide a greater degree of structural flexibility relative to a long-dated forward contract. For example, in a swap, the normal par forward structure (the reversal of the currency exchange is at the initial rate of exchange) means that the premium or discount built into the forward rate is settled through periodic payment which enables the parties to cover the interest flows in the underlying borrowings, and also has the advantage that, for balance sheet purposes, the reported size of the borrowing before and after the swap is the same as the forward rate corresponding to the spot rate at inception of the transaction.

Swaps are also probably easier to administer than a series of outright forwards, all at different rates and expressed as swap points deducted or added from the spot rate. Matching the cash flows in the foreign currency will mean uneven cash flows in the base currency.

Fixed rate currency swaps (both interest rates at fixed rates) also generally offer longer terms and better volume. Bid-offer spreads are, if anything, narrower in the swap market.

Exhibit 3.19 compares the actual cash flows for an identical currency swap and LTFX contract.

Exhibit 3.19

Currency Swap versus LTFX Cash Flows

Years	Currency swap cash flows			LTFX cash flows	
	A$	US$	Rate	A$	US$
	−150.00	+100	0.67	−150.00	+100
1	+22.50	−10	0.64	15.60	−10
2	+22.50	−10	0.61	16.40	−10
3	+22.50	−10	0.58	17.20	−10
3	+150.00	−100	0.58	172.40	−100
	67.50	−30		71.60	−30

Assumptions:

1. A$/US$ spot rate: 0.67
2. A$ interest rate: 15.00%
3. US$ interest rate: 10.00%
4. No bid or offer spread

LTFX contracts are particularly useful for transactions which entail uneven cash flows, either in amount or, alternatively, in a certain timing or spacing irregularity over the full maturity. In contrast, currency swaps are more suitable where even cash flow streams such as those in a borrowing are required to be transferred into another currency. LTFX contracts are also particularly useful where the transaction does not commence immediately but at some time in the future.

Types of swap transactions

The various types of swap transactions theoretically feasible are set out in *Exhibit 3.20.*

Two types of swaps require special comment: floating-to-floating currency swaps and cocktail swaps.

Theoretically cross-currency floating-to-floating swaps should not exist because a floating-to-floating swap is nothing more than a series of, for example, six month forward foreign exchange contracts rolled over every six months until maturity. In practice, however, a floating-to-floating currency swap can be a far better alternative to a forward foreign exchange transaction. This is because one avoids the spread between bid and offered rates every rollover date and the cash flow effect of the difference between the contracted forward rate and the spot rate at rollover.

Exhibit 3.20
Types of Swaps

Type	**Interest rate**		**Currency**	**Example**
	From	**To**		
Interest rate (coupon) swap	Floating	Fixed	Same	Swapping the interest cost of a floating rate Eurodollar loan into fixed rates
Cross-currency interest rate swap	Floating	Fixed	Different	Swapping fixed rate proceeds of a Swiss franc bond issue into floating rate US$
Fixed-to-fixed swap	Fixed	Fixed	Same	Swapping interest rate basis from a normal coupon fixed rate to a zero coupon fixed rate
Cross-currency fixed-to-fixed swap	Fixed	Fixed	Different	Swapping fixed rate proceeds of a Swiss franc bond issue into fixed rate US$
Floating-to-floating (basis) swap	Floating	Floating	Same	Swapping interest rate basis of floating rate US$ commercial paper funds into US$ LIBOR based funds
Cross-currency floating-to-floating (basis) swap	Floating	Floating	Different	Swapping interest rate basis of floating rate A$ bank bill funds into US$ LIBOR funds

Exhibit 3.21 sets out the structure of a floating-to-floating A$ and US$ currency swap.

It is possible to arrange a transaction, sometimes referred to as a cocktail swap, involving various types of swaps, including both interest and currency swaps and including also a bank as an intermediary. Examples of such transactions are shown in *Exhibit 3.22*.

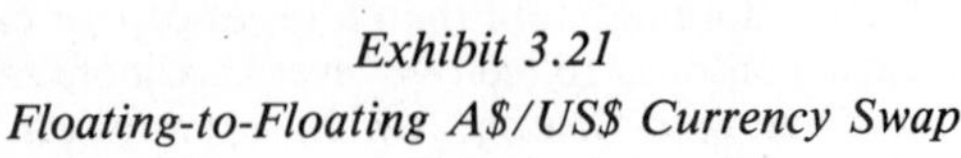

Exhibit 3.21
Floating-to-Floating A$/US$ Currency Swap

Initial exchange

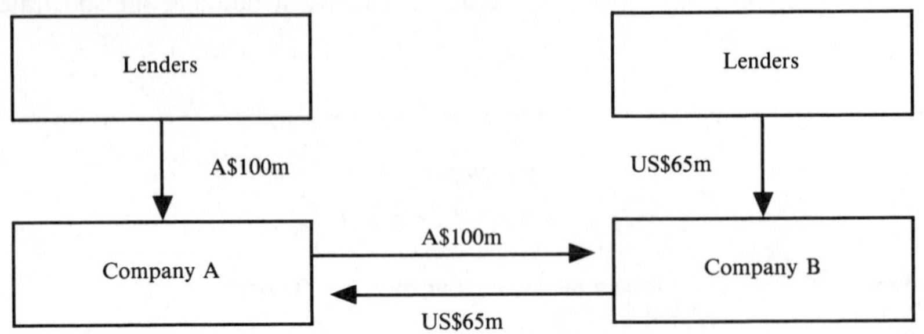

Future periodic (interest) payments

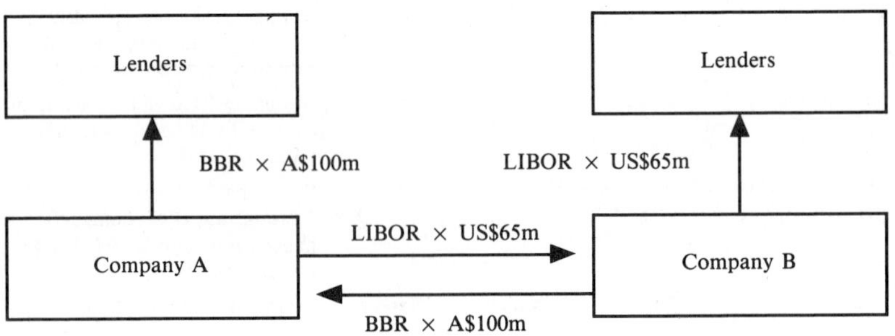

At maturity (principal) repayment

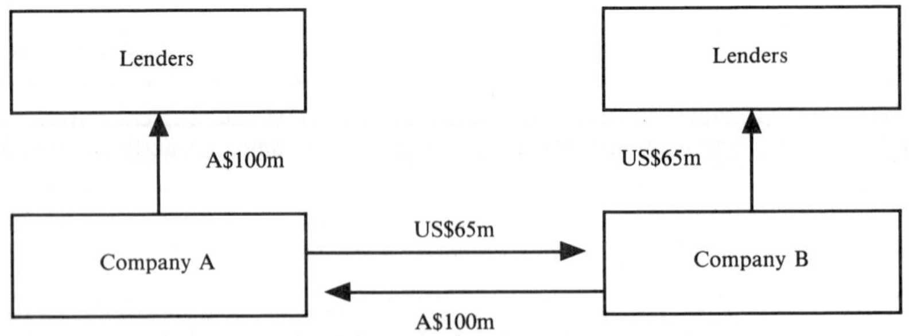

Note: The exchange rate assumed at commencement of the transaction is A$1.00/US$0.65.

Exhibit 3.22
Examples of Cocktail Swaps

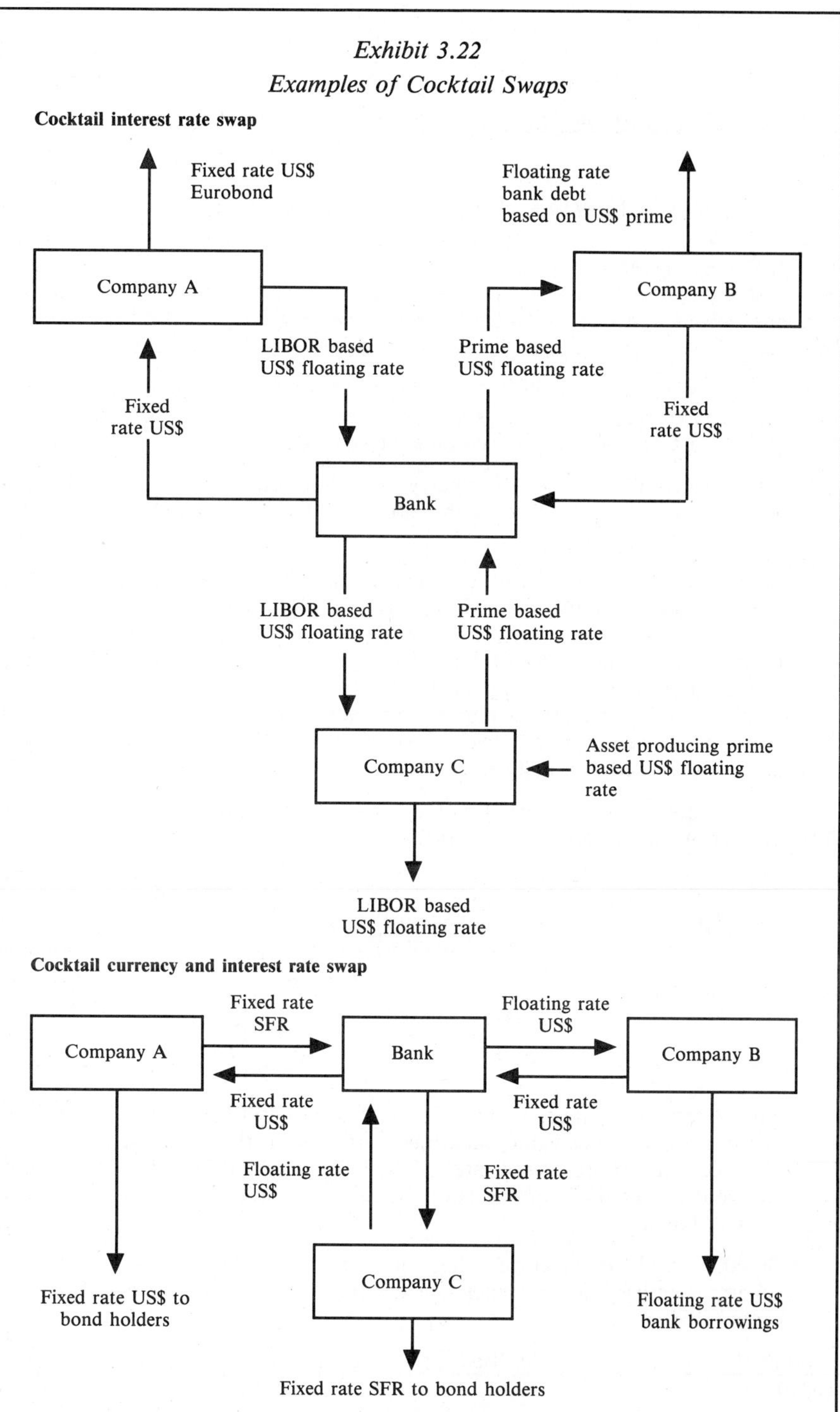

Chapter 4

Forward Rate Agreements

FORWARD RATE AGREEMENTS

An FRA is an agreement in respect of forward interest rates between two parties who wish to protect themselves against a future movement in interest rates. The parties involved agree on an interest rate for a specific period of time from a specified future settlement date based on an agreed principal amount.

The *buyer* is the party to the FRA wishing to protect itself against a future rise in the relevant interest rate. The *seller* is the party to the FRA wishing to protect itself against a future fall in the relevant interest rate.

No commitment is made by either party to lend or borrow the principal amount. The exposure to both parties is only the interest difference between the agreed rate and actual settlement rate.

Cash settlement takes place on the settlement date. The settlement rate procedure will be agreed. For example, in the US$ FRA market, the settlement rate is based on market rates, such as those displayed on Reuters screen page LIBO or its Telerate equivalent. Similarly, in the A$ FRA market, the settlement rate is based on market rates displayed on Reuters screen page BBSW. ISDA have attempted to standardise quotations for settlement of various money market rate indexes. Reuters screen ISDA sets out money market rates for common maturities for a wide variety of currencies as collected and collated by ISDA.

If the settlement rate is higher than the agreed rate the borrower will receive the difference from the lender or vice versa:

$$\text{Settlement amount} = \frac{\left\{\begin{array}{l}\text{The difference between}\\ \text{the settlement rate and}\\ \text{agreed rate}\end{array}\right\} \times \begin{array}{l}\text{contract}\\ \text{run}\end{array} \times \begin{array}{r}\text{principal}\\ \text{amount*}\end{array}}{(36{,}000 \text{ or } 36{,}500)^{**} + (\text{Settlement rate} \times \text{contract run})}$$

* For currencies or markets where the custom is to utilise discounted (that is net receipts less than par value) securities, this figure is the discounted amount of the face value of the agreed rate. For example, in A$ FRAs, this figure would be the discounted net proceeds of the relevant bank bill or promissory note transaction.

** 36,000 is used for currencies where the basis of calculation is actual/360 day; 36,500 is utilised for currencies where the basis for interest calculations is actual/365 days.

Some key terms usually utilised in connection with FRAs are set out in *Exhibit 4.1*.

Exhibit 4.1
FRA Terminology

FRA	A forward (or future) rate agreement.
Forward rate	A future rate of interest agreed between the parties at the outset. Sometimes called the agreed rate or the guaranteed rate.
Buyer (or borrower)	The party wishing to protect itself from a rise in interest rates.
Seller (or lender)	The party wishing to protect itself from a fall in interest rates.
Settlement date	The start date of the loan or deposit upon which the FRA is based.
Contract period	The period between the date the rate was agreed and the settlement date.
Maturity date	The date on which the FRA contract period ends.
Fixing date	For most currencies two business days before the settlement date. For same day value currencies (eg A$) this will be on the settlement date.
Settlement rate	The mean rate quoted by specified reference banks for the relevant period and currency. For most currencies LIBOR as shown on Telerate Page 3750 or Reuters Page LIBO. For A$ FRAs the interest rate will be the BBR shown on Reuters Page BBSW.
Run	Period or term of underlying investment or borrowing—normally 90 or 180 days, that is, a three or six month run.

FORWARD RATE AGREEMENTS: TRANSACTION EXAMPLES

Future deposit

Assume a company will have A$1m to deposit in three months for a six month period. The company treasurer is concerned that interest rates will fall over the next few months and therefore wishes to secure today's implied interest rate.

Assume FRAs three month against nine month or 3 × 9 (that is, the six month interest rate in three months from the present) are quoted 17.75-18.00% pa and that the client agrees to the forward rate of 17.75% pa.

Calculate the discount sum:

$$\frac{\text{face value} \times 36{,}500}{(\text{agreed rate} \times \text{days}) + 36{,}500} = \frac{1{,}000{,}000 \times 36{,}500}{(17.75 \times 182) + 36{,}500} = \text{A\$918,689.67}$$

- If in three months' time the settlement rate is 15.00% then the FRA provider will settle the difference in favour of the company as follows:

$$\frac{(17.75 - 15.00) \times 182 \times 918{,}689.67}{36{,}500 + (15.00 \times 182)} = \text{A\$11,720.72}$$

- If in three months' time the rate is 19.75% then the company will settle the difference in favour of the FRA provider as follows:

$$\frac{(19.75 - 17.75) \times 182 \times 918{,}689.67}{36{,}500 + (19.75 \times 182)} = \text{A\$8,340.37}$$

Future borrowing

Assume a company will need to borrow US$1m in one month for a six month period. The company treasurer thinks that interest rates may rise by the time the company borrows the money and wishes to fix the borrowing cost today.

Assume the company and the FRA provider agree on a 1 × 7 FRA rate of 8.50%.

If in one months' time the settlement rate is 10.00% the FRA provider will settle the difference in favour of the company as follows:

$$\frac{(10.00 - 8.50) \times 182 \times 1{,}000{,}000}{36{,}000 + (10.00 \times 182)} = \text{US\$7,218.40}$$

If in one months' time the settlement rate is 7.00% the company will settle the difference in favour of the TRA provider as follows:

$$\frac{(8.50 - 7.00) \times 182 \times 1{,}000{,}000}{36{,}000 + (7.00 \times 182)} = \text{US\$7,324.14}$$

Exhibit 4.2 sets out a number of confirmations on behalf of a company confirming entry into FRA transactions, detailing the typical terms and conditions of such transactions.

Exhibit 4.2

FRA Confirmations

To:	[Bank]
From:	[Company]
Fax No:	
Date:	

[Company] confirms the following Forward Rate Agreement as per the following details:

FRA Type	US$
Lender:	[Bank]
Borrower:	[Company]
Principal:	US$50,000,000
Fixed Rate:	4.625% pa
Settlement Date:	24 July 19X2
Maturity Date:	24 January 19X3
Rate Set Date:	22 July 19X2
Rate Reference:	US$ LIBOR (as per LIBO Screen)

To:	[Bank]
From:	[Company]
Fax No:	
Date:	

[Company] confirms the following Forward Rate Agreement as per the following details:

Exhibit 4.2—continued

FRA Type	A$
Lender:	[Company]
Borrower:	[Bank]
Principal:	A$10,000,000
Fixed Rate:	7.785% pa
Settlement Date:	15 June 19X2
Maturity Date:	15 September 19X2
Rate Set Date:	15 June 19X2
Rate Reference:	A$ Bank Bill Rate (as per BBSW Screen)

LONDON INTERBANK FORWARD RATE AGREEMENTS—RECOMMENDED TERMS

A significant proportion of FRAs are transacted under what have come to be known as "FRABBA"—FRA British Bankers' Association—terms. These terms were drawn up by the British Bankers' Association (BBA) in conjunction with market interests, including the Foreign Exchange and Currency Deposit Brokers Association, to provide recommended terms and conditions for such contracts and to provide guidance on market practice.

The BBA standard for FRA agreements, known as the FRABBA terms, are treated as normal market practice for interbank transactions falling within the categories covered. Banks are free to deal on other terms provided they make it clear to the counterparty that the transaction is not governed by the FRABBA terms. In the absence of such explicit clarification, banks and brokers in the London interbank market are expected to follow the FRABBA terms.

The FRABBA terms are summarised in the Appendix to this Chapter.

A major element of the FRABBA terms was the establishment of daily interest settlement rates to be fixed by reference to market rates for deposits in the London interbank market. These are calculated and published daily by Telerate on Screen Pages 3740-50. *Exhibit 4.3* sets out a copy of the page.

THE RATIONALE FOR FRAs

Some organisations use the futures market to protect themselves against interest rate fluctuations affecting their borrowings or investment. Assuming cancellation or reversal at the takedown date, the futures strategy to hedge a borrowing consists of selling financial futures, that is, contracting to sell a certain number of US$ LIBOR or A$ bills contracts for delivery at a future date simultaneously or as close as possible to when the company expects to borrow. At that time, if interest rates have increased, they will be offset by profits on the futures contract sale. If rates have dropped, the savings will cover the loss on the futures contract. The effect should be that the net interest cost (subject to basis risk) would be identical. In order to hedge the interest rate exposure on an investment, financial futures would be bought. The same effect can be achieved arguably more efficiently and effectively through the use of FRAs.

The principal advantages of FRAs over other methods of hedging interest rate risk, such as futures, include:

Exhibit 4.3

British Bankers Association/Telerate Interest Settlement Rates

	US$	Sterling	DEM	SFR	JPY	ECU	A$	FFR
1 month	3.18750	7.25000	8.62500	5.56250	3.81250	9.75000	5.68750	11.93750
3 months	3.31250	6.93750	8.43750	5.56250	3.68750	9.71875	5.81250	11.43750
6 months	3.43750	6.62500	8.06250	5.51563	3.54688	9.50000	5.90625	10.42188
9 months	3.62500	6.51563	7.75000	5.43750	3.50000	9.10156	6.12500	9.75000
12 months	3.81250	6.50000	7.53125	5.35938	3.50000	8.39750	6.32813	9.37500

Rates are as displayed on Telerate pages 3750/3740 at about 2 pm on Friday. They provide the basis for the settlement of all forward rate agreements (FRAs) and swaps written under BBA recommended terms. Unlike LIBOR (which is expressed in fractions and will continue to be available for other purposes), BBA rates are expressed to five decimal places. They are based on rates quoted by 16 BBA-designated banks as being, in their view, the offered rate at which deposits are being quoted to prime banks in the London interbank market at 11 am London time. After eliminating the two highest and the two lowest, the remaining four quotations are averaged and then (if necessary) the result is rounded upwards to five decimal places.

Source: Telerate/British Bankers' Association.

- As FRAs are not transacted through a futures exchange there is no requirement for deposits or margin variation calls, with a corresponding saving in administration costs and in the costs of financing deposit and margin calls.
- Whereas futures contracts are standardised as to amount, settlement day, etc FRAs can be negotiated to fit precisely the identified hedging requirements.
- The institution's exposure to credit risk is limited to the interest variation based on the principal and is not the full principal amount. The extent of the credit risk depends on the interest rate volatility.
- The FRA is settled by exchange of a cash sum and consequently does not gross up the balance sheet. This is in contrast to a forward deposit transaction (an agreement to place or take a deposit for a specified period at a specified value date) where funds equal to the principal of the deposit will be exchanged on the value date and the deposit will then be carried on the balance sheet throughout the hedge period.
- An FRA hedge can be closed out at any stage by entering into an equal and opposite FRA at a new price. This price will reflect the interest rate for the period at the time of closing the hedge.
- A company's borrowing rate and futures rate do not necessarily move in parallel. This basis risk can diminish the value of the hedge. FRAs can lock in a specific floating interest rate index regardless of fluctuations in other prevailing rates.
- For long-term hedging contracts, especially those having delivery dates months away or longer, the futures market may be thin. It may be difficult to buy and sell in significant amounts. Futures exchanges legislate maximum allowable daily price changes causing an unfavourable contract to be illiquid during extremely volatile periods. There is the risk of not being able to enter into or close off a hedge. FRAs eliminate some of the liquidity problem as a number of intermediaries guarantee to quote FRA transactions at any time.

However, FRAs do have two disadvantages when compared with financial futures including:

- There is no formal market in which FRAs can be traded and secondary market liquidity is therefore limited in the FRA market.
- FRAs carry the credit risk (although only for the settlement amount) of the counterparty, whereas for financial futures this is covered by substitution of the clearing house as the counterparty to a transaction which is in turn protected by the deposit and margins.

FRA VARIATIONS

There are a number of significant variations on the conventional FRA including:

- Using a "strip" or a series of FRAs to lock in the interest rate over a series of interest rate reset dates;
- using a combination of FRAs and foreign exchange forward contracts to create a synthetic FRA in a foreign currency;
- Forward Spread Agreements (FSA), a relatively recent variation designed to allow parties to lock in spreads or differentials between currencies.

A strip of FRAs can be utilised to create a fixed rate loan or investment. The FRAs act as a hedge guaranteeing the interest rate on each rollover date allowing determination at the outset of the interest rate over the whole period. An example of this type of transaction is set out in *Exhibit 4.4*.

It is important to note that where a strip of FRAs is used, particularly at regular intervals, the transaction is functionally identical to an interest rate swap for the term.

FRAs are not available in every currency. However, where they are unavailable, it is feasible to synthesise an FRA in the relevant currency utilising a combination of FRAs and FX forward transactions. An example of this type of transaction is set out in *Exhibit 4.5*.

Exhibit 4.4
FRA Strip Hedge

US$ LIBOR Strip Hedge

An investor seeks to hedge its exposure on US$10m of investments currently earning floating interest rates for a period of 18 months ending 15 October 19X3:

Maturity Dates	**Number of days**	**US$ FRA Rates %**	**US$ LIBOR Spot Rate on Repricing Dates %**	**FRA Settlement Cash Flow US$**
15.4.X2		—	4.75	—
15.10.X2	183	5.125	5.00	+6,164
15.4.X3	182	5.375	5.125	+12,386
15.10.X3	183			
	Net FRA Settlement			18,550
	Effective 18 month investment yield			5.15% pa

Exhibit 4.4—continued

A$ BBR Strip Hedge

A borrower seeks to hedge an exposure on a A$10m floating rate borrowing for a period of 12 months ending 4 June 19X8:

Maturity Dates	Number of days	A$ FRA Rates %	A$ BBR Spot Rate on Repricing Dates %	FRA Settlement Cash Flows A$
4.6.X8	91	—	12.00	—
3.9.X8	91	13.00	12.50	−12,089
3.12.X8	91	12.50	13.00	+12,074
4.3.X9	92	12.00	13.25	+30,489
4.6.X9				
	Net FRA Settlement			+30,474
	Effective 12 month borrowing cost			12.96% pa (payable quarterly)

Note: The effective borrowing cost is calculated as the compounded interest rates on the FRAs.

Exhibit 4.5
Synthetic FRA Transaction

A borrower wishes to lock in a two month borrowing cost in NZ$ for NZ$10m. Normally, the borrower would achieve this objective by buying a NZ$ 1 × 3 month FRA, that is, an FRA on two month NZ$ interest rates in one month's time. However, we assume that NZ$ FRAs are not directly available although A$ FRAs for the required term as well as A$ and NZ$ currency forwards are available.

The current market rates are:*

A$/NZ$	Spot:	A$1.00	= NZ$1.1660
	1 month forward		= NZ$1.1710
	3 months forward		= NZ$1.1840
A$ FRAs	1 × 3	13.24%	

In these circumstances the borrower could synthesise a NZ$ FRA as follows:

- buy NZ$10m against a sale of A$8,539,710 for value in one month at the quoted rate of NZ$1.1710;
- sell NZ$10,334,133 against a purchase of A$8,728,153 for value in three months at the quoted rate of NZ$1.1840;
- enter into a two month A$ FRA commencing in one month at a rate of 13.24% pa.

This series of transactions would provide the borrower with a known fully hedged cost of NZ$ funds.

Under the transaction, the borrower would draw down A$ funding for two months in one month at a rate of 13.24% pa guaranteed under the FRA. The A$ would be converted into NZ$ through the A$ and NZ$ foreign exchange contract. The A$ amount drawn down is determined by the need to generate NZ$10m of funding. At maturity, the borrower would repay NZ$10,334,133 which would be converted into A$8,728,153 through the forward contract. The A$ amount at maturity corresponds to the amount required to meet the principal and interest commitment on the A$ liability.

The overall transaction results in a guaranteed borrowing cost for NZ$10m for two months in one month's time of 20.05% pa.

* Bid-offer spreads are omitted for ease of exposition.

An FSA is an agreement between two parties seeking protection against potential future changes usually in the differential between London interbank interest rates for two different currencies, one of which will always be the US$ (the other one being known as the countercurrency).

The instrument is structured like a dual currency FRA but is closer to a currency swap such as a par value forward deal where the initial amount of currency at maturity is exchanged at the same rate as the initial exchange, and where a series of payments reflects the interest rate differential over the life of the swap. The instrument is seen as a competitor to swaps only in the short-term portion of the market where a simple structure and an even simpler type of documentation should prove advantageous.

An FSA is not designed to hedge foreign exchange risk. Typical users will be banks and corporates with assets in one currency and liabilities in another one. Such cross-currency funding entails the risk of rising interest rates in the funding currency while they decrease in the asset currency. This translates into an interest rate spread risk.

Those institutions willing to protect themselves against a narrowing of the spread between the US$ and the countercurrency interest rate will be sellers of an FSA, while those willing to hedge against a widening of the spread will be buyers of the new instrument. If the settlement spread is numerically higher than the forward spread, the seller pays the buyer the settlement sum, expressed in US$. If the settlement spread is numerically lower than the forward spread, then the buyer pays the seller the settlement sum.

An FSA trader will be receiving and paying the settlement amounts in US$. This does not involve foreign exchange exposure, but changes in the spot rate may have an impact on the profitability of a hedge. A firm hedging an interest rate spread (for example, the US$ and yen rate spread in the case of US$ assets and yen liabilities) is left with a small exposure when the settlement is made in US$. This is because the spot rate at the time of the settlement may be different from the spot rate at the time the FSA is entered into and this amount is decided upon. However, this small exposure may be hedged, as it is possible to track the influence of a move in the spot exchange rate (US$ and yen in this case) on the settlement amount made in US$.

Promoters of the FSA see a future for the product with banks or corporates running spread books as opposed to running the various legs separately. Institutions with non-US$ assets or liabilities can convert them into US$ terms and hedge that risk by combining an FSA with a US$ interest rate hedging instrument. FSAs are an alternative to forward-forward contracts, which express interest rate differentials as well, but entail a commitment in a loan or a deposit.

An example of an FSA transaction is set out in *Exhibit 4.6.*

Exhibit 4.6

Example of an FSA Transaction

On a given day, interest rates for three month deposits in Eurodollars and in Euroyen are as follows:

- for three month Eurodollars: 6.50%;
- for three month Euroyen: 4.50%.

The spread between interest rates for three month deposits in Eurodollars and in Euroyen will be −2.00% (or −200bps). If the rates are reversed, the spread will be 2.00% (or 200bps).

Exhibit 4.6—continued

A two-way market spread price would be quoted as, for example:

−205 (bid price) to −195 (offer price).

On 18 May 19X7, a party (the buyer) wishing to protect a forward spread of −1.95% (or −195bps) between interest rates for three month deposits or Eurodollars and in Euroyen placed on 18 November 19X7 could enter into an FSA where the forward spread is agreed at −195bps and where the settlement date is 18 November 19X7 and the maturity date is 18 February 19X7.

On 16 November 19X7 (the fixing date) the spread between three month deposits in Eurodollars and in Euroyen for value at 18 November 19X7 would be calculated and this spread would represent the settlement spread.

When the countercurrency rate is lower than the US$ rate:

Forward spread (per cent)	**Settlement spread (per cent)**	**Payer**
−1.95000	−1.53125	Seller
−2.05000	−2.53125	Buyer

When the countercurrency rate is higher than the US$ rate:

Forward spread (per cent)	**Settlement spread (per cent)**	**Payer**
1.95000	1.53125	Buyer
2.05000	2.53125	Seller

The *settlement sum* is the amount payable in US$ by the buyer or the seller on the settlement date. It is calculated as follows:

$$\frac{A}{100} \times \frac{D}{360} \times \text{notional principal sum} = \text{settlement sum}$$

where: A = the difference, expressed in all cases as a positive number in decimal form to five decimal places, between the numerical value of the forward spread and the numerical value of the settlement spread.

D = the actual number of days elapsed from (and including) the settlement date to (but excluding) the maturity date.

For an FSA with a settlement date of 18 November 19X7 and a maturity date of 18 February 19X7 (92 days) and a notional principle sum of US$25m, where the forward spread is −195bps (or −1.95%) and the settlement spread is −1.53125%, the settlement sum (payable by the seller to the buyer) would be as follows:

$$\frac{0.41875}{100} \times \frac{92}{360} \times 25{,}000{,}000 = \text{US\$}26{,}753.47$$

Source: *Introduction to Forward Spread Agreements* (December 1986, Fulton Prebon Capital Markets in conjunction with the Hong Kong and Shanghai Banking Corporation).

APPENDIX

FORWARD RATE AGREEMENTS ("FRABBA" TERMS) EXTRACTS*

B. *DEFINITIONS* (as denoted by initial capital letters in all texts in this booklet)

"BBA Designated Banks"	means the panel of not less than twelve banks as designated from time to time by the British Bankers' Association for the purpose of establishing the BBA Interest Settlement Rate.
"BBA Interest Settlement Rate"	means, in respect of the Contract Period, the rate calculated, and published, by the information vendor for the time being designated by the British Bankers' Association to make such calculation. The information vendor shall calculate such rate by taking the rates quoted to it by eight BBA Designated Banks as being in their view the offered rate at which deposits in the Contract Currency for such Contract Period are being quoted to prime banks in the London interbank market at 11.00 a.m. on the relevant Fixing Date for Settlement Date value and eliminating the two highest (or, in the event of equality, two of the highest) and the two lowest (or, in the event of equality, two of the lowest), taking the average of the remaining four rates and then (if necessary) rounding the resultant figure upwards to five decimal places.
"Broken Date"	means a Contract Period of a different duration from that used in the fixing of the BBA Interest Settlement Rate, and any Contract Period exceeding 1 year.
"Business Day"	means any day (other than a Saturday or a Sunday) on which banks are open for business in London.
"Buyer"	means the bank seeking to protect itself against a future rise in interest rates.
"Contract Amount"	means the notional sum on which the F.R.A. is based.
"Contract Currency"	means the currency in which the F.R.A. is based (see Appendix).
"Contract Period"	means the period from the Settlement Date to the Maturity Date.
"Contract Rate"	means the forward rate of interest for the Contract Period as agreed between the parties.

* *Source*: British Bankers' Association (in association with the Foreign Exchange and Currency Deposit Brokers' Association).

"Fixing Date"	means the day which is two Business Days prior to the Settlement Date except for Pounds Sterling for which the Fixing Date and the Settlement Date are the same.
"F.R.A."	means Forward Rate Agreement (sometimes referred to as Future Rate Agreement) as defined in Section D. 1.2 below.
"FRABBA"	means F.R.A.s written on B.B.A. terms as laid down in Section D of this booklet.
"Maturity Date"	means the date on which the Contract Period ends. If the Maturity Date originally agreed upon shall prove not to be both a Business Day and a day on which banks are open for business in the principal financial centre of the country of the Contract Currency, then the Maturity Date shall be the immediately succeeding day which is both a Business Day and a day in which banks are so open, unless, in the case of all currencies except Pounds Sterling, such date falls in the next calendar month in which case the Maturity Date shall be the immediately preceding day which is both a Business Day and a day on which banks are so open.
"Seller"	means the bank seeking to protect itself against a future fall in interest rates.
"Settlement Date"	means the date from which the Contract Period commences, being the date on which the Settlement Sum is paid. If the Settlement Date originally agreed upon shall prove not to be both a Business Day and a day on which banks are open for business in the principal financial centre of the country of the Contract Currency, then the Settlement Date shall be the immediately succeeding day which is both a Business Day and a day in which banks are so open, unless, in the case of all currencies except Pounds Sterling, such date falls in the next calendar month in which case the Settlement Date shall be the immediately preceding day which is both a Business Day and a day on which banks are so open.
"Settlement Sum"	means an amount equal to the difference between: (a) an amount representing interest calculated at the Contract Rate in respect of the Contract Amount for the Contract Period and on the basis of the actual number of days in the Contract Period and a year of 360 days (or 365 days where the Contract Currency is

Pounds Sterling, or any other currency where the period is so calculated in accordance with London market custom); and

(b) an amount representing interest calculated at the BBA Interest Settlement Rate in respect of the Contract Amount for the Contract Period on such basis,

which amount shall be discounted in accordance with the formula shown in Section D. 4.

C. *CONVENTIONAL STYLE OF PRICE QUOTATION*

The normal Contract Periods for F.R.A. quotations, unless otherwise specified, will be based on the conventional value dates applicable to each subsequent month for the currency concerned in the London interbank deposit market on the day of negotiation.

Any F.R.A. having a Contract Period with a duration different from the normal Contract Period, as described above, will be construed as a Broken Date F.R.A., which requires that the procedures followed shall be in compliance with Section D. 4.2.

D. *RECOMMENDED TERMS AND CONDITIONS*

1. *Scope*

1.1 These recommended Terms and Conditions shall apply to all Forward Rate Agreements (F.R.A.s) between participants operating in the U.K. interbank market and shall be deemed to be incorporated in any contract, whether oral or written, entered into relating to a F.R.A. Unless otherwise stated all F.R.A. deals will be regarded as having been written in "FRABBA terms". ANY VARIATION FROM THESE RECOMMENDED TERMS AND CONDITIONS MUST BE CLEARLY AGREED AT THE TIME OF THE DEAL AND SPECIFIED IN THE DOCUMENTATION.

1.2 A F.R.A. is an agreement between any two banks seeking to protect themselves against a future interest rate movement in the currencies listed in the Appendix, for an agreed Contract Amount, for a specified Contract Period at an agreed Contract Rate; and requires that settlement is effected between the parties in accordance with Section D. 4. For the purpose of the F.R.A. there is no commitment made by either party to lend or borrow the Contract Amount.

1.3 It is understood that both parties have entered into this F.R.A. in accordance with normal banking practice.

2. *Representations and Warranties*

Each party represents and warrants to the other that:—

(i) it has full power and authority (corporate and otherwise) to enter into this F.R.A. and to exercise its rights and perform its obligations hereunder and has obtained all authorisations and consents necessary for it so to enter, exercise rights and perform obligations and such authorisations and consents are in full force and effect;

(ii) the obligations expressed to be assumed by it under this F.R.A. are legal and valid obligations binding on it in accordance with their terms; and

(iii) as of the date of this F.R.A. all payments to be made by it hereunder may be made free and clear of, and without deduction for or on account of, any taxes whatsoever.

3. *Confirmation/Notification*

F.R.A.s may be entered into either orally or in writing and any demand may be made orally or in writing. Each of the parties shall be bound (but without prejudice to the binding nature thereof) to give confirmation in writing of any F.R.A. or demand concluded or made orally. Where such confirmation or demand is made or confirmed by letter it shall be deemed to have been properly made or confirmed to the counterparty, if posted, addressed to the counterparty's registered office or such other address as may be notified and shall be deemed to have been given or made at the time at which it would, in the ordinary course of post, have been delivered. Where such a confirmation or demand is made by telex (or other agreed telegraphic means) it shall be deemed properly made at the time of transmission provided the telex (or other transmission) was sent to the last published number of the recipient and, in the case of telex, the last published answer back of the recipient appears thereon. (For examples see Section F.)

4. *Settlement (for contract periods in excess of one year see Section E)*

4.1 Wherever two parties enter into a F.R.A. the Buyer will agree to pay to the Seller on the Settlement Date (if the Contract Rate exceeds the BBA Interest Settlement Rate), and the Seller will agree to pay to the Buyer on the Settlement Date (if the BBA Interest Settlement Rate exceeds the Contract Rate) an amount calculated in accordance with the following formula:

(a) when L is higher than R

$$\frac{(L - R) \times D \times A}{(B \times 100) + (L \times D)}$$

or (b) when R is higher than L

$$\frac{(R - L) \times D \times A}{(B \times 100) + (L \times D)}$$

where L = BBA Interest Settlement Rate (expressed as a number and not a percentage, e.g. 10.11625 and not 10.11625%)

R = Contract Rate (expressed as a number and not a percentage)

D = Days in Contract Period

A = Contract Amount

B = 360 except where the Contract Currency is Pounds Sterling (or any other currency where the contract rate is calculated on 365 days according to market custom) when "B" = 365.

4.2 *Broken Dates*

In the event that no BBA Interest Settlement Rate is available for the Contract Period, then it will be the responsibility of both parties to agree both the basis for establishing an alternative rate and the reference banks to be used for this purpose; and to specify the Settlement Date and the Maturity Date at the time of dealing.

4.3 *Subsequent Declaration of Non-Business Day*

If the Contract Period ceases to be eligible for settlement under recommended FRABBA terms owing to circumstances where the original Settlement Date ceases to be a normal business day (e.g. the announcement, subsequent to the contract date, of a public holiday and/or a market closure in London or in the other relevant financial centre) the settlement rate will be obtainable for the revised Fixing Date from a member of FECDBA (in liaison with members of the Sterling Brokers Association) as specified from time to time by their Hon. Secretary.

5. *Payment*

Any payments shall be made for value on the Settlement Date when due in the Contract Currency and be immediately available, freely transferable and freely convertible by credit to the counterparty's specified account.

6. *Cancellation/Compensation*

Subject to mutual agreement between both parties, an existing F.R.A. can be cancelled, at which time the method of calculating the Settlement Sum must be agreed by both parties. In the event that agreement cannot be reached there will be no cancellation.

7. *Events of Default*

7.1 The occurrence of any one or more of the following circumstances in respect of either party (the "Defaulting Party") shall be an Event of Default:

(i) an order of a competent court is made or an effective resolution is passed for the winding up or dissolution of the Defaulting Party other than for the purpose of a reconstruction or amalgamation previously approved in writing by the other party, such approval not to be unreasonably withheld; or

(ii) the initiation of proceedings under any applicable bankruptcy, reorganisation, composition or insolvency law by (in respect of itself) or against the Defaulting Party, provided that such proceedings have not been discharged or stayed within 30 days, or the appointment of a receiver over all or any part of the undertaking or any property, assets or revenues of the Defaulting Party; or

(iii) any representation made or warranty given by the Defaulting Party pursuant to Clause 2 is or proves to have been materially incorrect or misleading when made.

7.2 *Notice of Event of Default*

Each of the parties undertakes with the other that it will promptly notify the other of any occurrence which constitutes an Event of Default by it. Upon an Event of Default occurring in respect of either party, the other (the "non-Defaulting Party") may, by notice to the Defaulting Party, elect to terminate this F.R.A. immediately whereupon each party shall be released and discharged from its obligations hereunder, providing always that the foregoing shall be without prejudice to any rights, obligations or liabilities under this F.R.A. of the parties hereto which may have accrued up to and including the date of such notice.

8. *Indemnity*

The Defaulting Party shall fully indemnify (and keep indemnified) the non-Defaulting Party from and against any and all expense, cost, loss, damage or liability incurred by the non-Defaulting Party arising out of the termination of a F.R.A. pursuant to Clause 7 by the non-Defaulting Party which the non-Defaulting Party incurs as a consequence (directly or indirectly) of the occurrence of any Event of Default in respect of the Defaulting Party and/or such termination including, but without limitation, any legal or out-of-pocket expenses, and any amount required to compensate the non-Defaulting Party for any losses sustained and/or costs incurred by the non-Defaulting Party in making alternative arrangements to secure the financial equivalent of the payments and receipts contemplated by Clause 4. In each case, the certificate of the non-Defaulting Party as to the amount of any such costs and/or losses shall be conclusive in the absence of manifest error. Each party expressly recognises that the other is or may become party to one or more transactions which are the reverse of the transactions contemplated in this F.R.A. to which that party may refer for the purpose of computing its expenses, costs, losses, damage or liability.

9. *Rights and Remedies*

9.1 These Terms and Conditions shall be binding upon and enure to the benefit of both parties and their respective successors and assigns. The rights and obligations of each party may not be assigned (whether by way of charge or otherwise) or transferred without the prior written consent of the other party.

9.2 No delay or omission by either party in exercising any right, power or privilege conferred upon it by this F.R.A. shall impair the same nor shall any single or partial exercise thereof preclude any further exercise thereof or the exercise of any other right, power or privilege. The rights and the remedies herein provided are cumulative and not exclusive of any rights or remedies provided by law.

10. *Governing Law*

F.R.A.s entered into under these Terms and Conditions shall be governed by and construed in accordance with the laws of England.

E.

FORWARD RATE AGREEMENTS WITH A CONTRACT PERIOD IN EXCESS OF 1 YEAR

RECOMMENDED CALCULATION PROCEDURE

Example: 2½ year F.R.A.

L = Settlement rate (expressed as a number and not a percentage)
R = Contract Rate (expressed as a number and not a percentage)
A = Contract Amount
B = 36000 (or if Pounds Sterling 36500)
D1 = Number of days in year 1
D2 = Number of days in year 2
D3 = Number of days in year 3
SS1 = Discounted Interest Differential due for year 1
SS2 = Discounted Interest Differential due for year 2
SS3 = Discounted Interest Differential due for year 3

Formulae

$$\frac{(L - R) \times D1 \times A}{B + (L \times D1)} = SS1$$

$$\frac{(L - R) \times D2 \times A}{B + (L \times D2)} = SS2$$

$$\frac{(L - R) \times D3 \times A}{B + (L \times D3)} = SS3$$

$$\text{Settlement} = \frac{SS3}{\left(1+\left(\frac{D2 \times L}{B}\right)\right)\left(1+\left(\frac{D1 \times L}{B}\right)\right)} + \frac{SS2}{1+\left(\frac{D1 \times L}{B}\right)} + SS1$$

N.B.
The above formula calculates the discounted interest differential for each period (SS1, SS2 and SS3) and then discounts each discounted sum back to start date.

F. 1. *EXAMPLES OF CONFIRMATIONS*

PART I
To Be Used on the Agreement Date

F.R.A. CONTRACT *AGREEMENT DATE*
CONFIRMATION NOTICE
TO:—
FROM:—

We are pleased to confirm the following Forward Rate Agreement ("F.R.A.") made between ourselves as per FRABBA Recommended Terms and Conditions dated 1985. (Direct/Broker ....)

CONTRACT CURRENCY & AMOUNT ....

SETTLEMENT DATE.............. MATURITY DATE ....

CONTRACT PERIOD (DAYS) ....

CONTRACT RATE .... % per annum on an actual over 360/365 days basis (as applicable)

SELLER'S NAME ....

BUYER'S NAME ....

NON-STANDARD TERMS & CONDITIONS (IF ANY) ....

Any payment to be made to us under the F.R.A. hereby confirmed should be credited to our Account Number ....

at ....

PLEASE ADVISE BY TELEX, OR CABLE US IMMEDIATELY, SHOULD THE PARTICULARS OF THIS CONFIRMATION NOT BE IN ACCORDANCE WITH YOUR UNDERSTANDING.

Either:— Or:—

SIGNED .... TESTED TELEX CONFO
FOR AND ON BEHALF OF

....

F. 2. *EXAMPLES OF CONFIRMATIONS*

PART II
To Be Used on the Settlement Date

F.R.A. CONTRACT *AGREEMENT DATE*
CONFIRMATION NOTICE—*SETTLEMENT*
TO:—
FROM:—

We refer to the following Forward Rate Agreement ("F.R.A.") made between ourselves as per FRABBA Recommended Terms and Conditions dated 1985. (Direct/Broker ....)

CONTRACT CURRENCY & AMOUNT ....

SETTLEMENT DATE.................. MATURITY DATE ....

CONTRACT PERIOD (DAYS) ....

CONTRACT RATE .... % per annum on an actual over 360/365 days basis (as applicable)

SELLER'S NAME ....

BUYER'S NAME ....

NON-STANDARD TERMS & CONDITIONS (IF ANY) ....

SETTLEMENT RATE .... % per annum

SETTLEMENT SUM .... ($/£ etc.)

SETTLEMENT
INSTRUCTIONS:—

☐ WE PAY THE SETTLEMENT SUM ON THE SETTLEMENT DATE TO YOUR ACCCOUNT NO. .... AT ....

☐ WE RECEIVE THE SETTLEMENT SUM ON THE SETTLEMENT DATE AT OUR ACCOUNT NO. .... AT ....

Please tick as applicable

Either:— Or:—

SIGNED .... TESTED TELEX CONFO
FOR AND ON BEHALF OF

....

Chapter 5

Caps, Floors and Collars

CAPS, FLOORS AND COLLARS

Caps, floors and collars are all different types of usually long-dated option transactions designed to hedge interest rate exposure.

Caps

An interest rate cap is an agreement between the seller or provider of the cap and a borrower to limit the borrower's floating interest rate to a specified level for a period of time.

The borrower selects a reference rate to hedge (for example, US$ LIBOR or A$ BBR), a period of time to hedge (for example, 12 months, two years, five years, ten years), and the level of protection desired (for example, 10.00%, 11.50%, 12.00%). The seller or provider of the cap, for a fee, assures the buyer that its reference rate will not exceed the specified ceiling rate during the terms of the agreement. If market rates exceed the maximum rate, the cap provider will make payments to the buyer sufficient to bring its rate back to the maximum rate. When market rates are below the maximum rate, no payments are made, and the borrower pays market rates. The buyer of a cap therefore enjoys a fixed rate when market rates are above the cap and floating rates when market rates are below the cap.

Floors

An interest rate floor is similar to an interest rate cap agreement. An interest rate floor agreement is an agreement between the seller or provider of the floor and an investor which guarantees that the investor's floating rate of return on investments will not fall below a specified level over an agreed period of time.

The investor selects a reference rate to hedge, the period of time to hedge, and the level of protection desired. If market rates fall below the minimum or floor rate, the floor provider will make payments to the buyer sufficient to bring its rate back up to the agreed floor. When market rates are above the floor, no payments are made, and the investor enjoys market rates of return.

Collars

An interest rate collar is a variation on the cap agreement. The seller or provider of the collar agrees to limit the borrower's floating interest rate to a band limited by a specified cap rate and floor rate.

The borrower selects a reference rate to hedge (for example, LIBOR or BBR), a period of time to hedge (for example, 12 months, five years, ten years), and the level of protection desired (for example, 8.25-10.25%, 8.00-11.00%). The seller or provider of the collar, for a fee, assures the borrower that its reference rate will not exceed the specified cap rate nor be less than the specified floor rate during the term of the agreement. If market rates exceed the cap rate, the collar provider will make payments to the buyer sufficient to bring its rate back to the cap. If market rates fall below the floor, the borrower makes payments to the collar provider to bring its rate back to the floor. When market rates are between the floor and the cap, the borrower pays the market rate. The buyer of a collar, therefore has its borrowing rate confined to a band or collar, ranging from the floor to the cap.

Settlement mechanics

At the end of each settlement period (for example, monthly, quarterly, semi-annually etc as agreed depending on the type of index) during the term of a cap agreement, the market rate is compared to the ceiling rate. If the market rate is higher than the ceiling rate, the borrower will receive a cash payment equal to the difference between the market rate and the ceiling rate multiplied by the principal amount of the hedge. For example, suppose a borrower had a $10m three month LIBOR cap at 10.00% for two years. During a quarter when LIBOR is 12.00%, it will receive a payment of $50,556.

The market rate can be determined on a spot or average basis; that is, the spot rate on the first day of the period or the daily average during the period. The choice is usually made to match the nature of the underlying debt obligation being hedged. Sometimes longer or shorter settlement periods are chosen than are usually associated with the instrument being hedged (for example, annual settlement for three month LIBOR).

The settlement mechanics for floors and collars are similar.

Examples

Exhibit 5.1 sets out an example of a cap and floor transaction.

Exhibit 5.2 sets out confirmations for a series of cap, floor and collar transactions. In these confirmations, the bank confirms to its counterparties the purchase and sale of, variously, a US$ interest rate cap, a A$ interest rate floor and a US$ interest collar. Each confirmation details typical conditions relevant to such transactions.

Exhibit 5.1

Cap and Floor Transactions

US$ Cap Transaction

A borrower purchases a cap at a strike cap level of 8.00% pa on US$ 3 month LIBOR for a period of 12 months (commencing 1 June 19X2 and ending on June 19X3) to hedge its exposure to increasing interest rates on a US$10m floating rate borrowing which prices off 3 month LIBOR.

Maturity Date	Number of Days In Period	Cap Rate % pa	US$ 3 month LIBOR Spot Rates On Repricing Date % pa	Net Settlement Amounts US$
1. 6.X2			6.25	—
1. 9.X2	92	8.00	6.75	—
1.12.X2	91	8.00	8.35	8,750
1. 3.X3	90	8.00	7.80	—
1. 6.X3	92			

Effective borrowing cost over period: 7.45% pa

Exhibit 5.1—continued

A payoff diagram for this cap (effectively, a put option on the price of a security pricing off US$ 3 month LIBOR) is attached.

PROFIT/LOSS TO BUYER OF A CAP

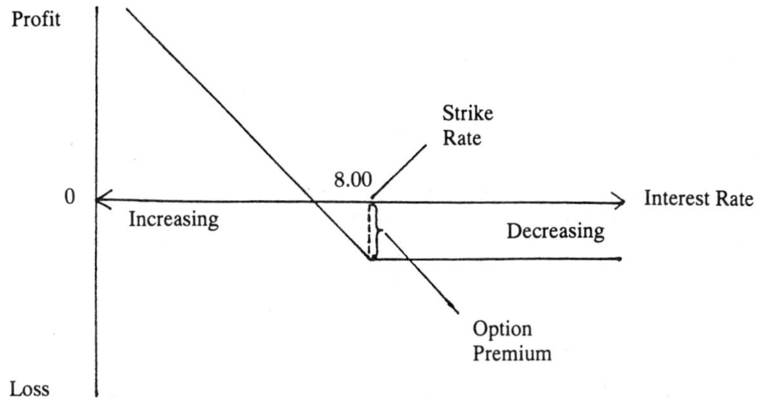

PROFIT/LOSS TO WRITER OF A CAP

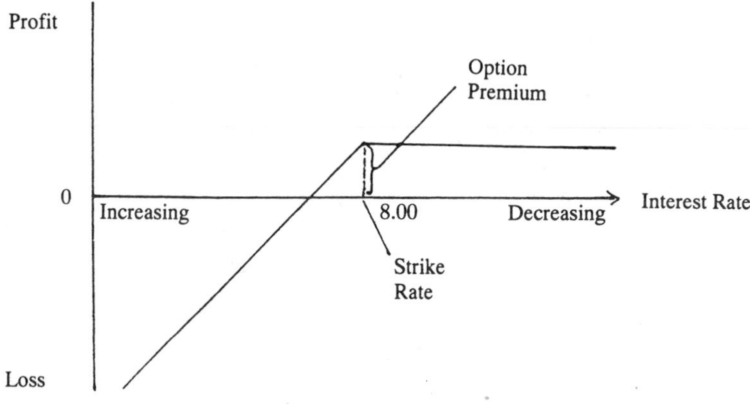

Notes:

1. Net Settlement Amount is calculated as:

   US$10m × (8.35% − 8.00%) × 90/360 = US$8,750

   Please note that the settlement amount assumes a constant face value borrowing as distinct from a discount instrument.

2. Effective borrowing yield is calculated as the US$ 3 month LIBOR rate (where it is below the cap rate) or the cap rate (where US$ 3 month LIBOR is above the cap rate) compounded over the period.

Exhibit 5.1—continued

A$ Floor Transaction

An investor purchases a floor at a strike floor level of 8.50% pa on A$ 3 month BBR for a period of 12 months (commencing 1 June 19X2 and ending 1 June 19X3) to protect its investment returns on A$10m of money market investments which is priced off 3 month BBR.

Maturity Date	Number of Days In Period	Floor Rate % pa	A$ 3 month BBR Spot Rates On Repricing Date % pa	Net Settlement Amounts A$
1. 6.X2			9.05	—
1. 9.X2	92	8.50	8.60	—
1.12.X2	91	8.50	8.25	+5,917
1. 3.X3	90	8.50	8.00	+12,095
1. 6.X3	92			

Effective investment return over period: 8.95% pa

A payoff diagram for the floor (effectively, a call option on the price of a security pricing off A$ 3 month BBR) is attached.

PROFIT/LOSS TO BUYER OF A FLOOR

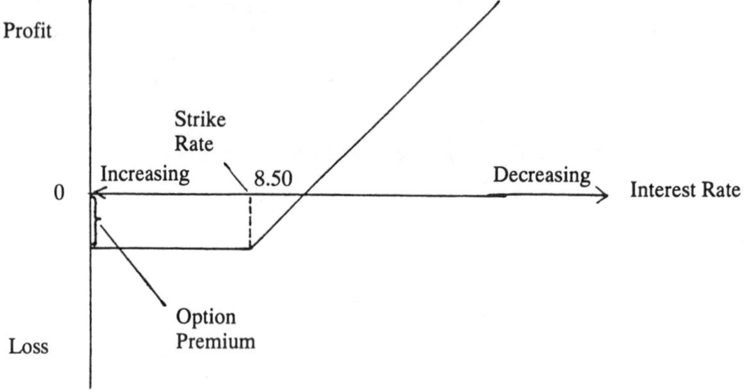

PROFIT/LOSS TO WRITER OF A FLOOR

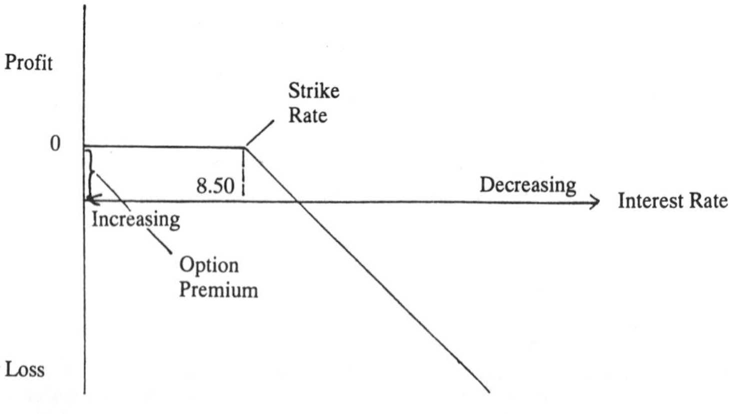

Exhibit 5.1—continued

Notes:

1. Net Settlement Amount is calculated as:

$$\frac{10,000,000}{1 + (8.50\% \times 90/365)} - \frac{10,000,000}{1 + (8.25\% \times 90/365)} = 5,917$$

This reflects the fact that the transaction is structured on the basis of a constant face value and varying present value reflecting the use of discounted instruments.

2. Effective investment return is calulated as the A$ 3 month BBR rate (where it is above the floor rate) on the floor rate (where A$ 3 month BBR is below the floor rate) compounded over the period.

Exhibit 5.2
Cap, Floor and Collar Confirmations

To:	[Company]
From:	[Bank]
Date:	18 August 19X2
Subject:	Interest Rate Option

[Bank] is pleased to confirm the following interest rate option transaction:

Type:	US$ Interest Rate Cap
Buyer:	[Company]
Seller:	[Bank]
Face Value Amount:	US$10,000,000
Strike Rate:	8.5000% pa
Transaction Date:	18 August 19X2
Maturity Date:	20 August 19X5
Option Premium:	1.25% (FLAT) on Face Value Amount payable by Buyer to the Seller for value 20 August 19X2.
Reference Rate:	US$ 6 month LIBOR (as quoted on Reuters Screen LIBO) rounded to the nearest fifth decimal place.
Rate Determination Dates:	Two business days prior to each 20 February and 20 August commencing 20 February 19X3 and terminating on 20 February 19X5, provided that if a Rate Determination Date is not a Business Day then the next succeeding Business Day will constitute the relevant Rate Determination Date.
Settlement Dates:	Each next Rate Determination Date or the Maturity Date.
Settlement Tenor:	Number of days between the Rate Determination Date and the Next Rate Determination Date are in respect of the last Rate Fixing Date the Maturity Date.

Exhibit 5.2—continued

Settlement Amount: On each Rate Determination Date:

1. If the Reference Rate is greater than the Strike Rate, the Seller shall pay to the buyer at the corresponding Settlement Date, an amount calculated as the difference between:

$$FV \times (1 \times SR \times \frac{D}{360})$$

and

$$FV \times (1 \times RR \times \frac{D}{360})$$

FV = Face Value Amount
SR = Strike Rate
RR = Reference Rate
D = Settlement Tenor

2. If the Reference Rate is less than or equal to the Strike Rate, Neither Party is obliged to make any payment to the other.

[Bank] Bank Account: [Bank]
Account Name:
Account No:

[Company] Bank Account: Please advise US$ account details.

Please confirm the terms of this agreement by return facsimile or telex stating "[Company] confirms entry into the Interest Rate Option Agreement with [Bank] on the terms and conditions set forth on your telex or facsimile of 18 August 19X2".

To: [Company]

From: [Bank]

Date: 18 August 19X2

Subject: Interest Rate Option

[Bank] is pleased to confirm the following interest rate option transaction:

Type: A$ Interest Rate Floor

Buyer: [Bank]

Seller: [Company]

Face Value Amount: A$10,000,000

Strike Rate: 6.5000% pa

Transaction Date: 18 August 19X2

Maturity Date: 20 August 19X5

Option Premium: 0.75% (FLAT) on Face Value Amount payable by Buyer to the Seller for value 20 August 19X2.

Reference Rate: A$ 6 month Bank Bill Rate (as quoted on Reuters Screen BBSW) rounded to the nearest fifth decimal place.

Exhibit 5.2—continued

Rate Determination Dates:	Two business days prior to each 20 February and 20 August commencing 20 February 19X3 and terminating on 20 February 19X5, provided that if a Rate Determination Date is not a Business Day then the next succeeding Business Day will constitute the relevant Rate Determination Date.
Settlement Dates:	Each next Rate Determination Date or the Maturity Date.
Settlement Tenor:	Number of days between the Rate Determination Date and the Next Rate Determination Date are in respect of the last Rate Fixing Date the Maturity Date.

Settlement Amount: On each Rate Determination Date:

1. If the Reference Rate is less than the Strike Rate, the Seller shall pay to the buyer at the corresponding Settlement Date, an amount calculated as the difference between:

   $$FV \times (1 \times SR \times \frac{D}{360})$$

   and

   $$FV \times (1 \times RR \times \frac{D}{360})$$

   FV = Face Value Amount
   SR = Strike Rate
   RR = Reference Rate
   D = Settlement Tenor

2. If the Reference Rate is greater than or equal to the Strike Rate, Neither Party is obliged to make any payment to the other.

[Bank] Bank Account:	[Bank] Account Name: Account No:
[Company] Bank Account:	Please advise A$ account details.

Please confirm the terms of this agreement by return facsimile or telex stating "[Company] confirm entry into the Interest Rate Option Agreement with [Bank] on the terms and conditions set forth on your telex or facsimile of 18 August 19X2".

To:	[Company]
From:	[Bank]
Date:	18 August 19X2
Subject:	Interest Rate Option

[Bank] is pleased to confirm the following interest rate option transaction:

Type:	US$ Interest Rate Collar
Buyer:	[Company]
Seller:	[Bank]

Exhibit 5.2—continued

Face Value Amount:	US$10,000,000
Cap Strike Rate:	9.000% pa
Floor Strike Rate	7.5000% pa
Transaction Date:	18 August 19X2
Maturity Date:	20 August 19X5
Option Premium:	0.25% (FLAT) on Face Value Amount payable by Buyer to the Seller for value 20 August 19X2.
Reference Rate:	US$ 3 month LIBOR (as quoted on Reuters Screen LIBO) rounded to the nearest fifth decimal place.
Rate Determination Dates:	Two business days prior to each 20 February, 20 May, 20 August and 20 November commencing 20 November 19X2 and terminating on 20 May 19X5, provided that if a Rate Determination Date is not a Business Day then the next succeeding Business Day will constitute the relevant Rate Determination Date.
Settlement Dates:	Each next Rate Determination Date or the Maturity Date.
Settlement Tenor:	Number of days between the Rate Determination Date and the Next Rate Determination Date are in respect of the last Rate Fixing Date the Maturity Date.
Settlement Amount:	On each Rate Determination Date:

1. If the Reference Rate is greater than the Cap Strike Rate, the Seller shall pay to the Buyer at the corresponding Settlement Date, an amount calculated as the difference between:

   $$FV \times (1 \times SR \times \frac{D}{360})$$

   and

   $$FV \times (1 \times RR \times \frac{D}{360})$$

   FV = Face Value Amount
   CSR = Cap Strike Rate
   RR = Reference Rate
   D = Settlement Tenor

2. If the Reference Rate is less than the Floor Strike Rate, the Buyer shall pay to the Seller on the corresponding Settlement Date an amount calulated as the difference between:

   $$FV \times (1 \times SR \times \frac{D}{360})$$

   and

   $$FV \times (1 \times RR \times \frac{D}{360})$$

Exhibit 5.2—continued

FV = Face Value Amount
FSR = Floor Strike Rate
RR = Reference Rate
D = Settlement Tenor

3. If the Reference Rate is less than or equal to the Cap Strike Rate on more than or equal to the Floor Strike Rate, Neither Party is obliged to make any payment to the other.

[Bank]
Bank
Account: [Bank]
Account Name:
Account No:
[Company]
Bank
Account: Please advise US$ account details.

Please confirm the terms of this agreement by return facsimile or telex stating "[Company] confirms entry into the Interest Rate Option Agreement with [Bank] on the terms and conditions set forth on your telex or facsimile of 18 August 19X2".

THE RATIONALE FOR CAPS, COLLARS AND FLOORS

Caps provide protection against rising interest rates without fixing rates. With its hedge in place, the buyer continues to borrow at the short-term end of the yield curve. When the yield curve is upward sloping, borrowing short-term results in considerable cost savings compared to fixed rate alternatives such as bonds or interest rate swaps, which are priced off the term yield curve.

Locking in a fixed rate in a positive yield curve environment results in an immediate increase in interest cost. The per annum cost of a cap may be much less than this immediate increment. The fixed rate borrower has no additional risk if rates rise, but enjoys no benefit if rates decline. If rates rise only moderately, or decline, the short-term borrower with a cap will tend to achieve substantial savings without unlimited risk.

Buyers of cap agreements generally pay an upfront fee determined by the cap level, the maturity of the agreement, the instrument being hedged and market conditions (see Chapter 11 for a discussion on how caps are priced). Cap providers will take the fee either up front or in instalments. The front end fees will depend upon how close to current rates the cap is set and the volatility of the index.

Collars provide protection against rising interest rates without fixing rates. They can be thought of as "interest rate swaps with a band". As in the case of cap agreements, buyers of collars continue to borrow at the short-term end of the yield curve and therefore may enjoy substantial cost savings compared to fixed rate alternatives, with only moderate upside risk. Collars are generally priced so that the all-in cost per annum of borrowing at the cap rate will be somewhat more than fixed rate alternatives, while the all-in cost at the floor will be considerably less than fixed-rate alternatives. The trade-off of the cost saving to the upside risk may be as much as five to one.

The chief disadvantage of collars versus cap only agreements is that they limit the possibility of profit from a decline in rates below the floor. Obviously, interest rate expectations drive potential users toward or away from collars. Because collars are two-way agreements, they entail credit considerations similar to interest rate swaps. In fact, collars are sometimes used as a complement to, or substitute for, swaps.

As in the case of cap only agreements, buyers generally pay an upfront fee determined by the ceiling and floor level, the maturity of the agreement, the instrument being hedged and market conditions. Fees for collars are lower than for ceiling only agreements with the cap at the same level. This is because the floor has value to the provider, which is passed on to the buyer in the form of a lower front end fee. The fee depends upon how close to current rates the cap rate and floor rate are set.

The growth of these markets reflects largely the corresponding growth in the market for debt options generally, including those traded on exchanges. Caps, floors and collars represent customised options similar in a number of respects to the debt options traded on exchange rates on the relevant indexes.

Consequently, it is possible to utilise options on the relevant index traded on a futures or options exchange to replicate a cap, floor or collar agreement. The major difficulty in utilising these exchanges include:

- Exchange traded options on floating rate indexes rarely trade out for more than two years. Some contracts are limited to nine months or a year. In practice, trading depth may not be present except in the nearest months. This restricts the construction of long-term hedges which would require the hedger to rollover contracts incurring the risk of changes in rate levels and volatility as well as basis changes.
- Options, like futures contracts, are standardised and do not allow participants interested in matching dates and structures to fully match their required dates on their underlying debt obligations with the option transaction.
- There are mechanical problems involving the posting of deposits and possible margin calls on option transactions on exchanges which adds to the cost and difficulty of administration of the use of these exchange traded options.

The major advantage of exchange traded options and of utilising these instruments for hedging purposes is that they do not require the purchaser to incur the credit risk of the seller of the option.

In practice, the existence of exchange traded options provides the basis for the development of the market in customised caps, floors and collars as they essentially provide a mechanism by which financial intermediaries willing to enter the market as direct sellers of these customised option products hedge their own exposures.

PREMIUM DYNAMICS OF CAPS, FLOORS AND COLLARS

Interest rate caps can be thought of as similar to a string of put options. The writer of the option (seller of the cap) determines a premium (fee) of the option desired based on the time remaining to the expiration of the option, the current market interest rate of the instrument being hedged, and the strike price (ceiling or cap rate). As with options, the further ''out-of-the-money'' the strike price is, the higher the cap is, and/or the shorter the time to expiration is, the lower the premium is.

Floors can be thought of as similar to call options. In effect in a collar agreement, a series of call options is being sold back to the provider of the cap, which reduces the premium, thus floor ceiling premiums are lower than agreements.

Providers of customised caps can price caps at almost any level. The problem for the prospective user is where to set the cap: tight, loose or in between. Clearly, the tighter the cap (the closer to current implied forward money market rates), the higher the fee will be and vice versa.

Borrowers using caps or collars as a substitute for fixed rate debt who are only willing to accept limited upside risk in return for cost savings if rates are stable or fall, will set their caps relatively close to current rates, say 100 to 150 basis points above them. The fee will be relatively high but the overall economics may be attractive. Other borrowers are more interested in "disaster insurance" that is protection against violent rate changes for a low front end fee. Such caps may be 300 to 400 basis points or more over current implied forward rates.

Because fees for caps tend to be priced in reference to options pricing theory, fees do not decrease proportionately as cap levels are raised. The relationship between premiums and strike prices are non-linear; for example, the premium on a put option does not decline proportionately as the strike price is raised out of the money. Therefore, the hedger does not get an equal amount of protection for its money when paying a low fee for a high cap compared to paying a high fee for a tight cap. This is a factor to keep in mind, although it may not necessarily influence the final decision, which will depend upon how much risk it is willing to bear and how much it is willing to pay for protection. The pricing of caps etc, is discussed in detail in Chapter 11.

VARIATIONS ON CONVENTIONAL CAP, FLOOR, COLLAR STRUCTURES

Conventional cap and floor structures have evolved, primarily, in response to asset liability management requirements of a variety of users.

These structural variations focus, basically, on two primary areas:

- timing, strike rate and cash flow variations on the conventional cap or floor structure; and
- combinations of cap and floor with additional interest rate optional elements.

The major variations include:

Step up/step down coupon cap or floor

Under this structure, the purchaser of the cap structures the strike rate such that it increases or decreases over time.

A step up coupon cap provides the maximum interest rate protection in the initial period, with the protection diminishing as the strike level of the cap is increased. This type of structure can be utilised to reduce the premium of purchasing a cap, particularly in a sharply positively sloped yield curve environment. This structure may be appropriate for a borrower that is concerned about its cash flow in the near term and is willing to trade-off additional risk against the lower cost of protection over longer time horizons.

A step down cap can be structured, with similar objectives, most appropriately in a negatively sloped yield curve environment.

Similar structures for floors to take advantage of the prevailing yield curve shape are also feasible.

Delayed cap/floor

A delayed cap or floor is a cap or floor which only becomes effective at a point in time in the future, often years after the date of purchase.

The delayed cap structure is designed to reduce the cost of the premium relative to a conventional cap of the same maturity. The reduction in premium is particularly effective in a negatively sloped yield curve environment.

Delayed start caps are typically utilised by companies in an environment when yield curves are positively sloped to allow them to enjoy the low prevailing short term money market interest rates with the delayed start cap providing protection in the future.

Variable notional principal structures

Caps and floors have been structured based on revolving notional amounts (primarily, to accommodate seasonal borrowing requirements) or on declining notional amounts to match funding for amortising assets. In each of these cases, the notional amount of the cap or floor contract is structured to accommodate the borrower or investor exposure profile.

Participating structures

A participating cap is equivalent to an interest rate swap under which the counterparty pays fixed rates combined with the purchase of a floor, covering at least part of the notional principal amount. This provides a participation element in the event that interest rates do not rise above the fixed rate on the swap. (This type of structure is discussed in detail in Chapter 15.)

This structure can also entail the counterparty purchasing a cap and selling a floor at the same price, but on a smaller notional amount prospectively providing it with protection against rates rising above the cap rate but limiting the degree of participation in the downward movement in interest rates in return for a lower premium.

A variation on this structure is the weighted collar. Under this structure, the floor level is set at a strike rate lower than the cap level, thus creating a collar or band around the strike rate. The weighted collar structure allows the counterparty to enjoy protection in the event of a rise in interest rate, but provides it with some participation if rates fall below the lower band rate.

Similar structures involving floors can also be constructed.

Corridor options

This type of structure entails the counterparty lowering the cost of the cap by simultaneously selling another cap at a higher strike rate. In a typical example, a borrower would purchase a cap at a strike rate of 8% and sacrifice some of its protection by selling a cap at 10%. Under this structure, the borrower is fully protected if interest rates increase up to 10%. The company therefore trades the lower cost (effectively the net cash flow from the amount paid for an 8% cap and the amount received for the sale of a 10% cap) for the risk that it will not be protected if rates move above 10%.

Similar corridor structures involving floors can also be constructed.

Captions

Captions are essentially options to purchase caps or floors at a specified price. That is, they represent options *on options.*

In the case of a caption, if cap prices increase, the company can exercise its option to buy the cap at a "below market" price. If cap prices have declined, the purchaser can let the caption expire.

Such captions allow purchasers to take highly leveraged positions as a hedge against interest rate movements. While generally captions are expensive (in premium terms), they allow purchasers to take positions in anticipated movements in not only absolute interest rate levels, but changes in the strip of forward prices (effectively, changes in the shape of the yield curve) as well as the volatility of caps and other interest rate options.

Similar structures involving floors are also available.

Part 3

Economics and Pricing of Swaps and Financial Derivatives

Chapter 6

Economics and Pricing: Overview

INTRODUCTION

The economics and pricing of swap transactions are central to the process of structuring, negotiating and completing such transactions. With the recent growth of the swap market, price indications for both interest rate and currency swaps in a wide variety of currencies are readily available. This increasing availability of swap prices is not matched by an equal level of understanding of key aspects of swap economics and the determinants of price for such instruments.

There is a widespread tendency to attribute such pricing behaviour to the relative "supply and demand conditions" in the particular market. While it is inevitably true that changes in supply and demand impact upon the pricing of such instruments, it is a truism to nominate the essential clearing mechanism, that is, the adjustment of supply or demand at a particular price level, as the cause or determinant rather than the eventual effect in the pricing of such transactions.

The key issues in the economics and pricing of swap transactions include:

- Pricing approaches.
- The pricing of interest rate and currency swaps versus pricing of other "core" swap instruments, such as LTFX, FRAs and caps, collars etc.
- The distinction between pricing of core swap instruments and the pricing/economics of variations on or extensions of core swap instruments.
- The distinction between the economics of swaps and pricing/yield mathematics.

As discussed in detail below, there are a number of alternative available approaches to pricing swap transactions. These include the decomposition of swap instruments into constituent elements (primarily, forward and/or option contracts) and pricing these constituent elements (often referred to as financial engineering). Alternatively, swap instruments can be priced on the basis of capital market arbitrage. The two approaches also have a complex series of interrelationships.

As discussed below, there are significant differences in the pricing of interest rate and currency swaps as against pricing of other swap instruments, namely, LTFX, FRAs and caps, floors etc. Interest rate and currency swaps are, typically, priced on the basis of capital market arbitrage. The other core swap instruments can either be priced on the basis of their pricing interrelationship with interest rate and currency swaps (see discussion in Chapter 2) or by decomposing these instruments themselves into their constituent forward or option elements.

Variations on core swap instruments are priced in a similar manner through either a process of decomposition into its constituent elements or through a process of capital market arbitrage.

An important distinction is between the economics of swaps and related transactions and the pricing/yield mathematics of such transactions. The distinction lies in the fact that swap economics emphasises the basic parameters which form the pricing framework of such transactions while pricing/yield mathematics emphasises the arithmetical procedures such as the IRR or net present value concepts. The arithmetical and technical steps utilised in pricing/yield mathematics associated with swap transactions are common to all financial transactions and not peculiar to swaps.

In this chapter, an overview of the framework within which swap pricing is undertaken is analysed. In particular, the interrelationships between pricing of various instruments is examined.

The remaining chapters in this Part, consider the various detailed issues of pricing and swap economics. Specific techniques of pricing interest rate and currency swaps utilising capital market arbitrage techniques is considered in detail in Chapter 7. Specific yield mathematics of valuing interest rate and currency swaps are outlined in Chapter 8. The specific pricing methodologies utilised to value FRAs, LTFX and caps/floors are considered in detail in Chapters 9, 10 and 11.

SWAP PRICING FRAMEWORK

Exhibit 6.1 sets out a framework for pricing swap transaction.

Exhibit 6.1

Swap Economics/Pricing: Overview

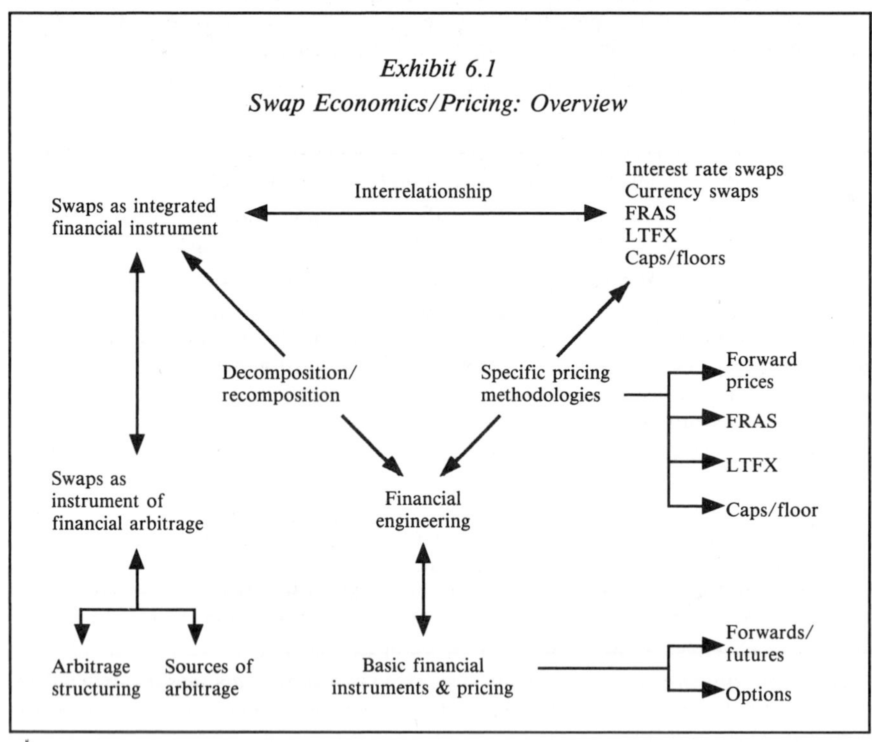

The key features of this framework include:

- alternative approaches to swap pricing;
- the pricing interrelationships and, consequently, capacity for arbitrage between instruments; and
- the coexistence of various approaches to pricing.

The framework outlined clearly identifies the two possible approaches to pricing swap transactions. Under the first approach, each swap instrument is decomposed into its basic constituent elements. These constituent elements will, as noted in Chapter 2, be either forward/futures contracts or option contracts. These constituent elements are then priced utilising available economic techniques to imply a price for the swap instrument.

For example, using this approach, an interest rate swap can be decomposed into a portfolio of forward contracts which are then priced utilising available techniques for pricing forward contracts to imply a price for the swap.

Under the alternative approach, swaps are regarded as instruments of financial arbitrage. This is particularly true of interest rate and currency swaps which, as discussed above, facilitate the exchange of comparative advantage across financial markets as between participants. Under this approach, the price for an interest rate swap or currency swap would be generated through the process of arbitrage. This overall interest rate or currency swap price would then be decomposed into equivalent prices for other core swap instruments, such as FRAs, LTFX and caps/floors. This process of decomposition/recomposition is essentially implied by the structural interrelationships between the various instruments whereby they exist as an integrated package of financial transactions.

This process is reinforced by the opportunity for arbitrage between instruments. For example, an interest rate swap can be replicated by entering into a series of FRAs. Similarly, a currency swap can be replicated by a series of LTFX contracts. This structural interrelationship facilitates substitution of instrument structures because of their functional equivalence. This dictates that the overall pricing of swap instruments thus, at a given point in time, must be mutually consistent. In the absence of such mutual consistency, the opportunity to arbitrage as between the prices of the various instruments would force convergence to equilibrium levels.

The process described implies coexistence of both approaches to swap pricing. In practice, swap pricing will gravitate to the theoretical forward and option contract prices implied by capital market rates prevailing at a given point in time. This can, in reality, be regarded as the theoretical or limit pricing of these instruments.

Opportunities for capital market arbitrage through financial exchange transactions will, generally, create opportunities to structure these transactions at rates *better* than those implied by theoretical forward or option prices. The generation of prices, superior to theoretical prices, as a result of capital market arbitrage in any one instrument will, within a very short time, result in adjustment in prices of all other instruments. This adjustment in the pricing structure is predicated upon the interrelationship between the instruments and the possibility of arbitrage in the event of mutually inconsistent prices of the various instruments.

In practice, swap pricing is largely driven by arbitrage opportunities to facilitate opportunities to create pricing levels away from theoretical forward and option pricing levels.

However, the specific technologies of pricing forward and option contracts are integral to the process of pricing swaps. They are integral to the process of decomposition/recomposition of instruments into constituent elements to price individual instruments within an overall pricing framework.

FINANCIAL DERIVATIVE PRICING—BUILDING BLOCKS

As noted above, swap transactions, indeed all derivative products, can be decomposed into two basic instruments: forward or futures contracts and option contracts. This process of decomposition and, its reverse, recomposition facilitates the process of pricing whereby the price of the relevant instrument can be built up from the theoretical price of the forward/futures and/or option contract.

The basic building blocks for swap pricing, utilising this approach, include:

- pricing of forward contracts;
- pricing of option contracts;
- put-call parity, which specifies mathematically the relationship between forward and option contracts.

Forward contracts are capable of being priced utilising a series of forward prices which is based on the theoretical cost of "carry" implied in the existing yield curve. Detailed discussion of the pricing of forward contracts is set out in Chapter 9 (in the context of pricing of FRAs).

Option contracts are capable of being priced utilising theoretical pricing models based on expectations of future distributions of the price of instruments. These pricing techniques include: the famous Black-Scholes Option Pricing Model and a variety of numerical/simulation techniques. A detailed discussion of the derivation and implication of pricing techniques through option contracts is set out in Chapter 11.

The final building block of swap pricing relates to the interrelationship between forward prices and option prices. This relationship can be stated in terms of the theoretical construct known as put-call parity whereby:

$$C(E) + PV(K) = P(E) + S$$

where

$C(E)$ = the price of the European call option

$PV(K)$ = the present value of the strike price of the option

$P(E)$ = a theoretical price of both European put option

S = the price of the underlying commodity

This relationship which holds for options of the same series (that is, identical maturity and strike prices) implies the following relationship:

> The purchase of a call and investment of the present value of the strike price of that option is identical to the value of a put option and the purchase price or value of the underlying commodity.

Rearrangement of elements of this theoretical relationship facilitates the creation of synthetic option and underlying asset positions.

For example, the purchase of a call and the sale of a put option (of the same series) is equivalent to a forward purchase of the underlying commodity. Similarly, the sale of a call and the purchase of a put (of the same series) is equivalent to a forward sale of the underlying commodity. A more detailed discussion of the theoretical elements of the put call-parity relationship is set out in Chapter 11.

Exhibit 6.2 sets out the return/payoff profiles for asset or forward contracts, option contracts as well as synthetic asset positions.

Exhibit 6.2
Theoretical Option—Forward Equivalencies

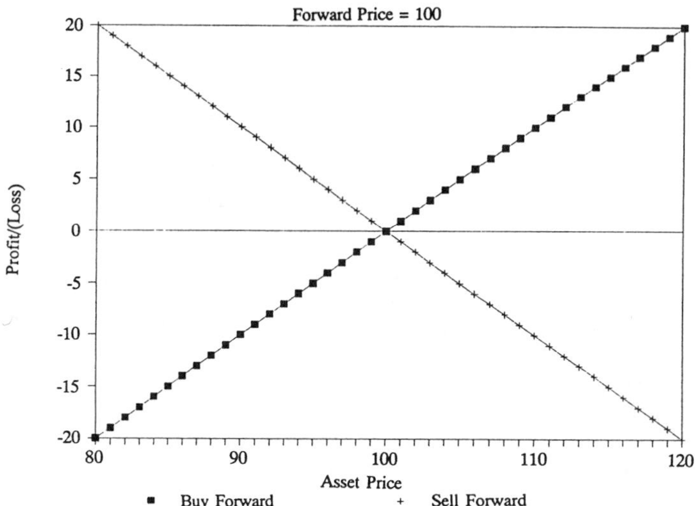

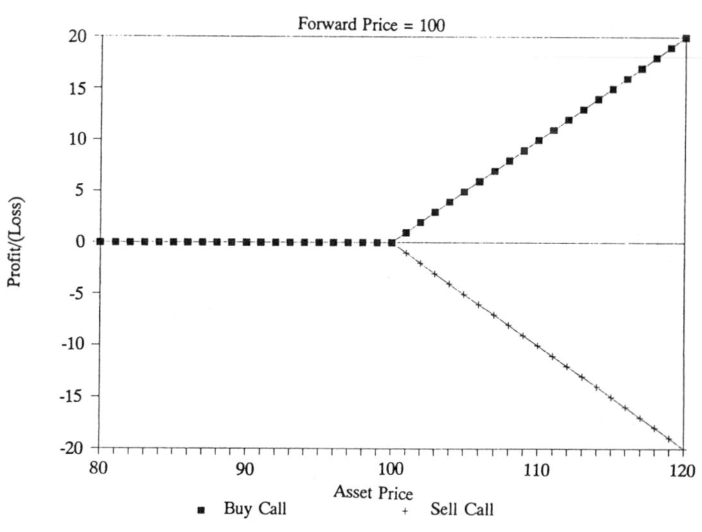

Exhibit 6.2—continued

PAYOFF DIAGRAM

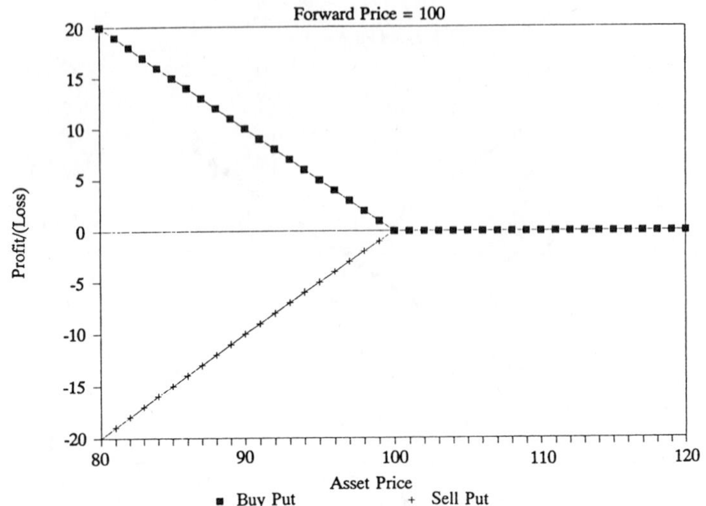

PAYOFF DIAGRAM—SYNTHETIC BOUGHT FWD

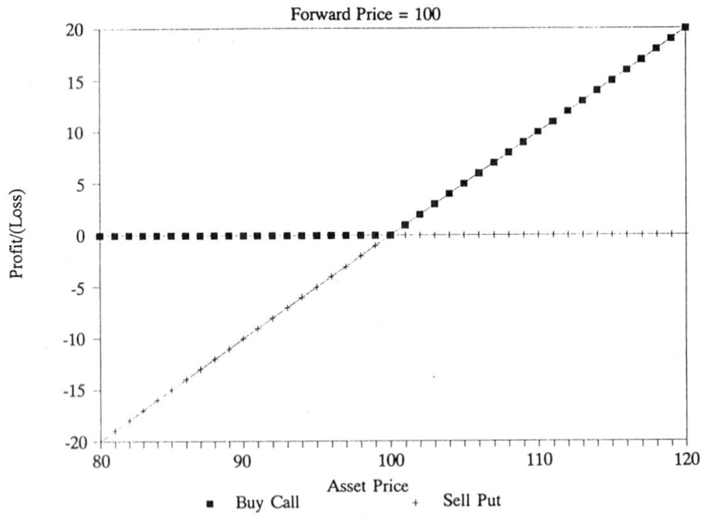

Exhibit 6.2—continued

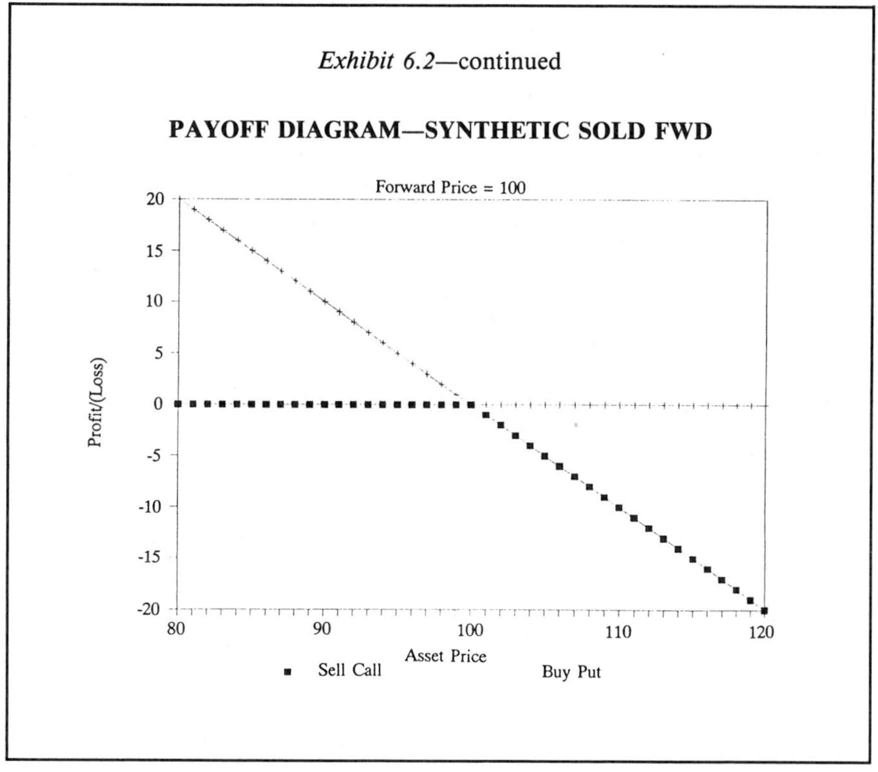

The application of these basic pricing technologies and interrelationships to swap transactions, particularly to core swap instruments, derives from the fact that these instruments can be characterised as portfolios of forward and option contracts. These theoretical structural relationships include:

- FRAs are equivalent to forward interest rates.
- LTFX or Forward Foreign Exchange contracts are equivalent to forward contracts on the relevant currency.
- Caps and floors can be decomposed into interest rate options.
- Interest rate swaps can be characterised as a portfolio of forward contracts or FRAs (refer *Exhibit 6.3*).
- Currency swaps can be characterised as a portfolio of forward FX contracts (refer *Exhibit 6.4*).
- Interest rate swaps can, alternatively, be characterised as a portfolio of interest rate options or caps and floors. For example, paying fixed/receiving floating interest rates in an interest rate swap is equivalent to buying a cap (put option) and simultaneously selling a floor (call option). Conversely, receiving fixed/paying floating rates under an interest rate swap is equivalent to buying a floor and selling a cap. Utilising this approach, an interest rate swap can be thought of as a combination of caps, floors (and, by implication, interest rate options) with a strike price equivalent to the swap rate.

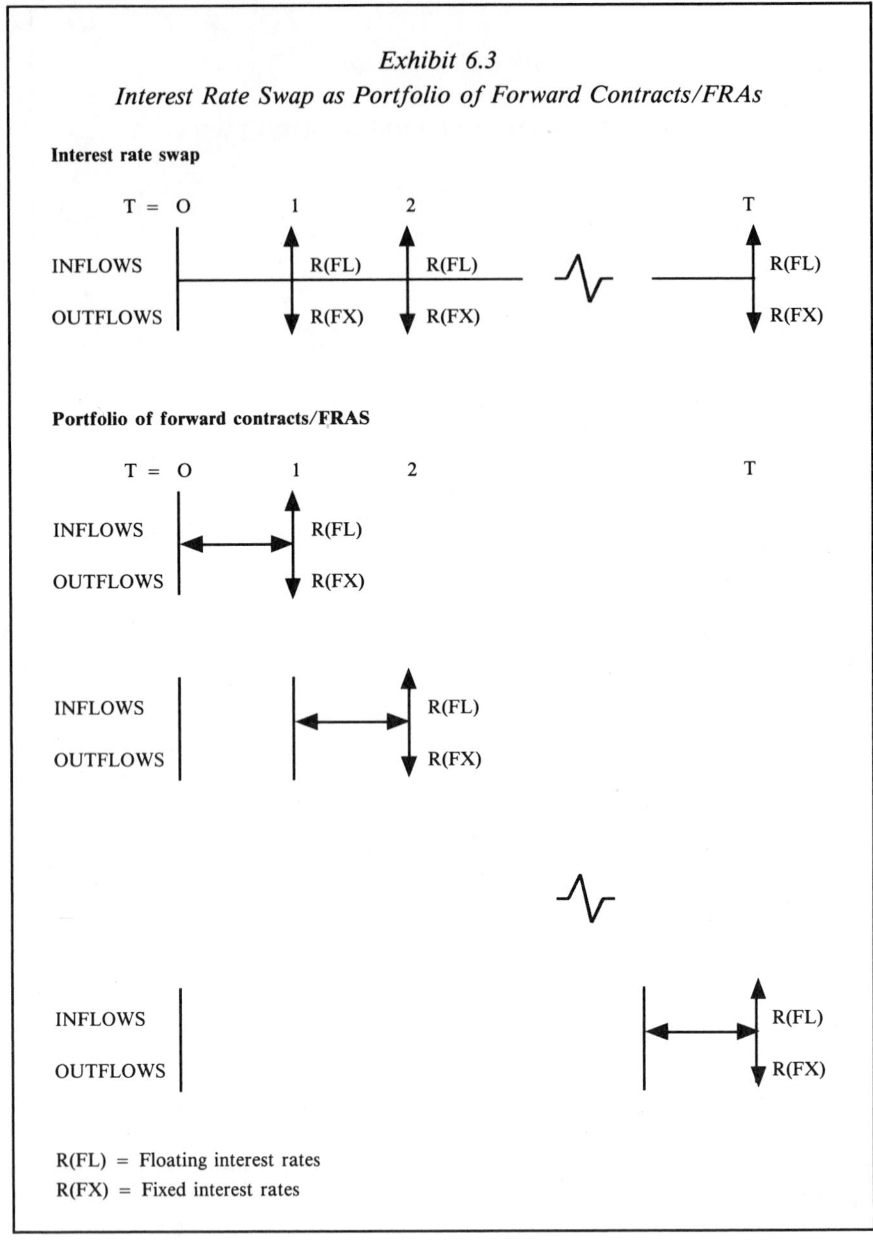

The structural interrelationships outlined above are identical to those discussed in Chapter 2.

The significance of this capacity of decomposition of swap instruments into its basic constituents, as outlined above, is that the constituent forward or option elements can be priced, utilising available financial technology and utilised to price the swap instrument itself.

Exhibit 6.4
Currency Swap as Portfolio of Forward FX Contracts

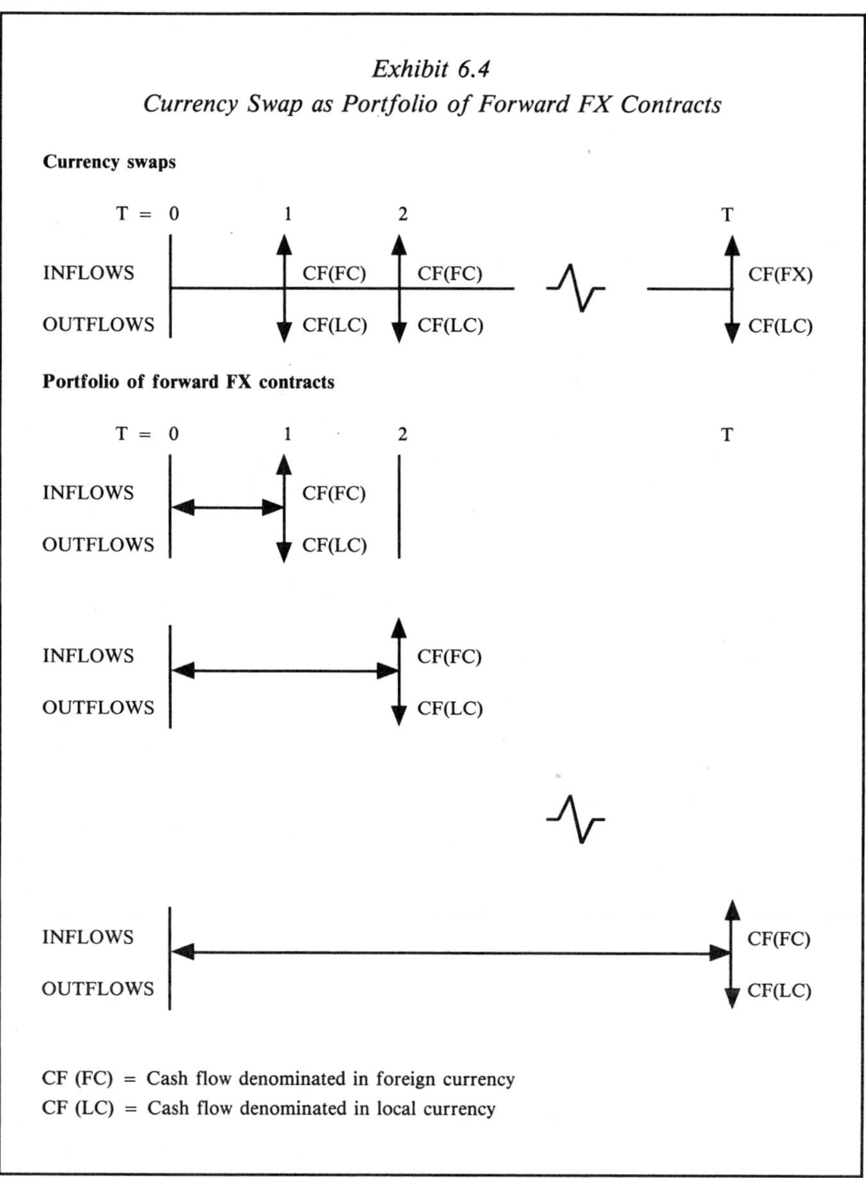

SWAP ECONOMICS AND PRICING—PRACTICAL INTERRELATIONSHIPS

The economics of swap transactions vary significantly as between individual instruments although, as noted above, there are significant interrelationships between the various transactions and consequently in the pricing between individual market segments.

It is useful to differentiate pricing mechanics as between the following categories of transactions:

- parallel or back-to-back loans;
- interest rate and currency swaps/LTFX;
- FRAs;
- caps, floors and collars.

Each of these transactions are usually priced on different bases. The parallel or back-to-back loan transactions are usually priced with reference to blocked fund situations or environments in which foreign exchange controls prevent the free movement of capital across national borders.

For example, the early parallel loans and back-to-back loan transactions arose out of the situation created both by exchange controls in the 1970s which prevented United Kingdom entities buying US$ on the spot basis and by the shortage of fixed rate GBP funding for the United Kingdom subsidiaries of United States companies. Pricing of these transactions was curiously devoid of any relationship to United States or United Kingdom government bond rates. Instead, the economics of these transactions responded freely to supply and demand factors in the market. The use of these types of transactions in more recent times, usually in response to foreign exchange controls in less developed countries, has been undertaken on a purely negotiated basis as between the counterparties with the pricing/economics responding to supply and demand factors.

In contrast, the market for swaps and LTFXs is highly responsive to arbitrage between various segments of the capital market.

These transactions provide for the extension of the theory of comparative advantage from the commodity and service markets to financial and capital markets enabling institutions to borrow in markets where it enjoys a relative comparative advantage then exchanging the funds raised for funds denominated in the desired currency and/or interest rate basis through the swap transactions. In this regard, swaps are similar to parallel or back-to-back loans in that they effectively entail a "barter" transaction between counterparties trading advantages or benefits such as availability of funds and/or after tax cost.

In addition, interest rates and currency swaps must, by definition, bear a strong relationship to the forward market price for the relevant underlying commodity, namely forward interest rates or forward exchange rates. This is wholly consistent with the characterisation of interest rate and currency swaps as portfolios of interest rate and currency forward contracts.

LTFX transactions (which as discussed above can be equated to zero coupon currency swaps) provide a further level of linkage between swap transactions and money and foreign exchange markets as LTFX pricing will generally reflect current interest rates and interest differentials between currencies.

The economics of FRAs and caps and collar transactions do not directly derive from capital market arbitrage. FRA pricing usually derives from forward-forward interest rates evident in the yield curve at any particular point in time which can be replicated by cash market transactions or in the rates implied in the purchase or sale of interest rate futures contracts.

Caps and collars represent option transactions which are priced utilising option pricing theories or models whereby premiums are related to a number of factors including, in particular, the time remaining to the expiration of the option, the current rate of the instrument being hedged, the strike price (the cap or floor rate) and its relationship to the current rate, and future expectations as to the distribution and volatility of interest rates.

Although the economics of the various types of transactions are predicated primarily on different pricing bases, a number of close interrelationships exist between the pricing of the different instruments (refer *Exhibit 6.5*). These pricing relationships are totally consistent with and are implied by the structural interrelationships between the various instruments outlined in Chapter 2 (refer *Exhibit 2.2*).

Exhibit 6.5
Pricing Interrelationships

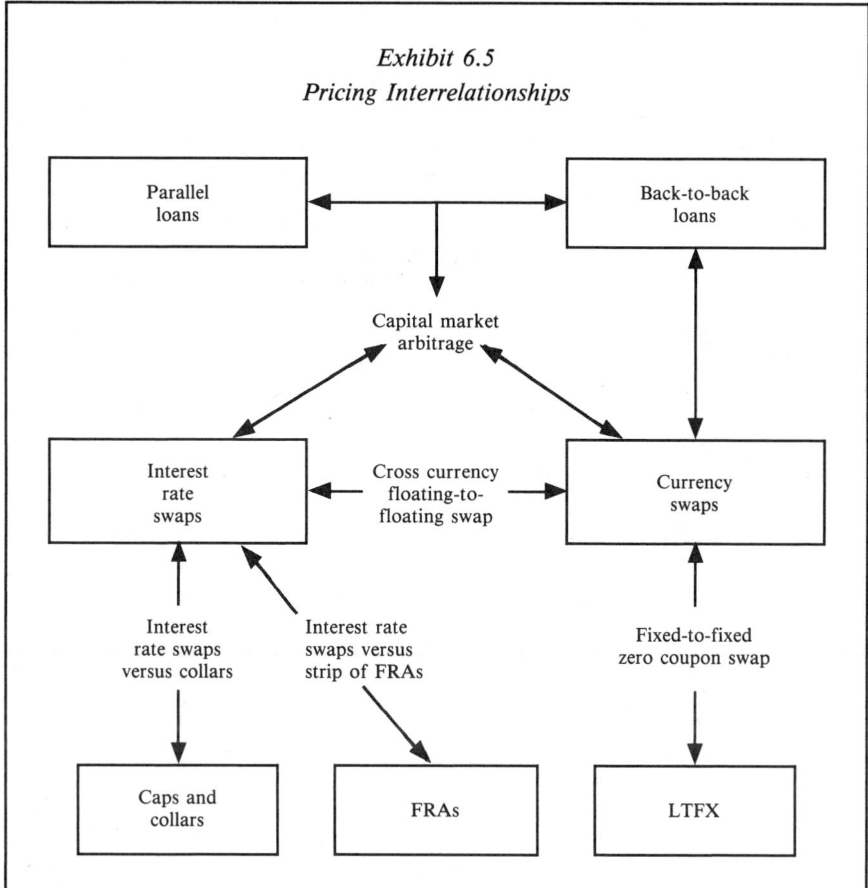

The pricing interrelationship between parallel or back-to-back loans with other transactions is relatively weak. However, back-to-back loans are, functionally, extremely similar to currency swaps and consequently the pricing between these two types of transactions is closely related, at least where a blocked fund situation is not involved.

Interest rate swaps and currency swaps are closely related in a pricing or economics sense to the other types of transactions identified. For example, an LTFX transaction is functionally identical to a fixed-to-fixed currency swap and the pricing between these two transactions must be, in theory, and indeed is, in practice, closely related.

Similarly, the pricing of an interest rate swap in a particular currency is closely related to the pricing on FRAs and caps and collars in the same currency. This relationship exists because interest rate swap transactions can effectively be replicated through a series of FRA transactions coinciding with the maturity and term of the interest rate swap. Similarly, the interest rate swap is functionally identical to a collar transaction where the cap level is set at the fixed rate level on the swap with the floor level being maintained at an identical level.

FRAs in turn are related to cap and floor prices because a combination of caps and floors can be used to replicate both a bought or sold FRA. For example, a synthetic long forward or sold FRA can be created by buying a floor and selling a cap at the desired forward level. Similarly, a bought FRA or synthetic short forward position can be created by selling a floor and buying a put at the desired forward rate level.

The detailed pricing interrelationship would operate in the following manner. Given yield curves in two currencies and a spot exchange rate between the currencies, it would be possible to derive theoretical prices for the full range of swap instruments. Given that swaps can be characterised as a portfolio of forward interest rate contracts, the existence of yield curves would allow the construction of interest rate swap prices in both currencies. This by implication would allow simultaneously the pricing of FRAs in the respective currencies as prices for these instruments would correspond to the forward interest rates evident in the yield curve. The availability of spot and forward interest rates could in turn form the basis of interest rate option prices for caps, collars etc, where the expected volatility of various interest rates could be supplied. Alternatively, given the capacity to characterise both interest rate swaps and FRAs as a portfolio of purchased and sold options, the prices for interest rate swaps and FRAs could be utilised as the basis for working back to option prices.

The availability of interest rates in both currencies and the spot exchange rate between the currencies would allow currency swap prices and LTFX prices also to be generated.

A striking feature of the pricing interrelationship between the various instruments is that as forward interest rates and exchange rates are a critical component of the pricing calculation, the economics of such transactions are determined not by intermediaries or the swap market per se but rather by competition from other capital market instruments and rates and flows. These rates and flows are reflected in the yield curves and spot exchange rates which are the only information needed to determine the pricing of most swap instruments. Given that the swap is, at its simplest, a package of forward contracts, the forward rates reflected in the swap must conform to the implied forward rates in the prevailing yield curve as otherwise arbitrage will become profitable. Consequently, the process of financial arbitrage will ensure that the pricing interrelationships described will inevitably be enforced.

The basic interrelationships in terms of pricing and economics as outlined above may be disrupted in practice by a number of factors including: barriers to capital flow which effectively prevent replication of particular transactions in other markets and also differential treatment under accounting, taxation or regulatory standards.

In examining the pricing interrelationships between the various types of transaction, it is important to recognise that, in practice, such transactions are often entered into, at least in the first place, by financial intermediaries rather than direct counterparties who are end users of the opposite leg of the trade. The financial intermediary enters into the transaction to provide liquidity in the relevant market, undertaking the transaction on a hedged basis in the expectation of eventually matching the transaction with an end user or other counterpart. This requirement for temporary hedging usually means that swap transactions, of any kind, are often priced on the basis of the economics of the underlying hedge rather than the pure economics of the transaction. This type of hedge based pricing will, by definition reflecting the choice of hedging instruments, conform to the pricing economics described.

The basic economics of each transaction cannot be violated for long periods without effectively inviting arbitrage which has the natural effect of restoring equilibrium pricing in the market. Consequently, while markets in these types of transactions may not always be in equilibrium, the basic economics dictate the framework within which the pricing of individual transactions must be effected.

The central role played by financial intermediaries in transactions involving these instruments, also facilitates the financial arbitrage which forces prices to their natural economic equilibrium. These financial intermediaries who are active in all the relevant capital market segments are ideally placed to take advantage of pricing discrepancies and to undertake transactions predicated on deviations from pricing equilibrium thereby forcing market prices towards their economic levels.

PRICING EXTENSIONS/VARIATIONS ON SWAP TRANSACTIONS

The above discussion focuses on, primarily, on the pricing of core swap instruments. The pricing of non-generic structures options on swaps and swap hybrids is essentially similar.

The approach to pricing such variations on swaps utilises the framework described above with individual transactions being priced, either, utilising financial engineering concepts with instruments being decomposed into forward and option contract elements, or through the process of capital market arbitrage.

Non-generic swap structures and floating-to-floating basis swaps are priced utilising a framework which is identical to that described above.

Options on swaps are, generally, priced utilising conventional option pricing models where the underlying commodity is the swap itself. However, in practice, pricing of options on swaps is influenced by capital market arbitrage. This reflects the fact that such options are utilised to securitise debt options embedded in securities issues. This dictates that the pricing of such options reflects opportunities for arbitrage in individual debt markets and the differential values placed on debt options as between issuers, investors and asset liability managers.

Swap hybrids entailing combinations of swaps with interest rate and currency option or forward elements are typically priced away from their theoretical values reflecting the arbitrage nature of such transactions. These swap structures are, in the main, utilised to secure and facilitate the trading of the forward or option contract elements of securities issued, designed to take advantage of capital market arbitrage opportunities.

Commodity and equity swap contracts are typically priced as portfolios of forward and/or option contract in the relevant commodity or equity market. In some cases, the pricing is driven by capital market arbitrage opportunities, primarily, in the form of commodity or equity option linked securities transactions structured to take advantage of particular investor requirements. The developing nature of markets in some commodity and equity indexes, particularly over longer terms, dictates that the pricing efficiency of these markets is somewhat lower than that which prevails in corresponding markets for interest rates and currencies.

The pricing techniques for variations on core swap instruments are very similar to the economics and pricing characteristics of conventional swaps, with pricing being driven by either opportunities for capital market arbitrage or the capacity to decompose instruments into their constituent element and price these elements utilising available technologies for pricing forward and option contracts.

SWAP ECONOMICS AND MARKET EFFICIENCY

The fact that the swap market is predicated on the exploitation of certain arbitrage opportunities within capital markets has already been alluded to. It is useful at this point to briefly outline the meaning of the phrase "efficient markets" as it is used here and the concept of arbitrage.

An efficient market by definition is one in which prices are set at levels whereby the resources traded in the market are allocated efficiently among the participants. This highly artificial construction of economic theory requires the satisfaction of a wide range of conditions:

- The costless availability of all relevant information to market participants.
- Highly efficient markets would, in addition, require that all participants agree on the implications of equally available information and its effect on the price of the resource or commodity being traded in the market. That is, the price import of the information would be unambiguous.
- The market structure would be such that the trading process would allow transmission of the impact of information into the price of the asset traded which implies the presence of many buyers and sellers.
- Efficient market theory requires that transaction costs, including market frictions such as taxes, regulation, or accounting impediments, are absent.

These conditions are, in practice, difficult to satisfy. The impact of taxation, regulation, and differences in these between national markets combined with differences in the perceived price impact of information, the perception of risk and the differential valuation of risk between capital markets or even segments of capital markets, create certain anomalies or inefficiencies which allow arbitrage transactions to take place.

Technically, arbitrage transactions are defined to mean one or more actions by market participants designed to exploit pricing inefficiencies or anomalies to earn profit from the inherent discrepancy in the pricing or valuation of assets as between markets. In its simplest form, arbitrage would involve the simultaneous purchase and sale of an identical asset in different markets. Where identical assets are employed in the process of arbitrage, the transaction involves no risk. However, in practice, the type of arbitrage described here entails the simultaneous purchase and sale of *similar*, although not identical, financial assets.

In pure arbitrage, profits are possible because of inefficiencies or differences in alternative markets for essentially the same asset. In the less restrictive form of arbitrage being considered here, profits are possible because of relative inefficiencies or differences in the pricing of *comparable* although not *identical* assets once adjustments are made for the relevant differences. That is, the transactions entail profit opportunities arising from anomalies among markets for assets that are close substitutes for each other.

Exhibit 6.6
Pricing of Swap Transactions

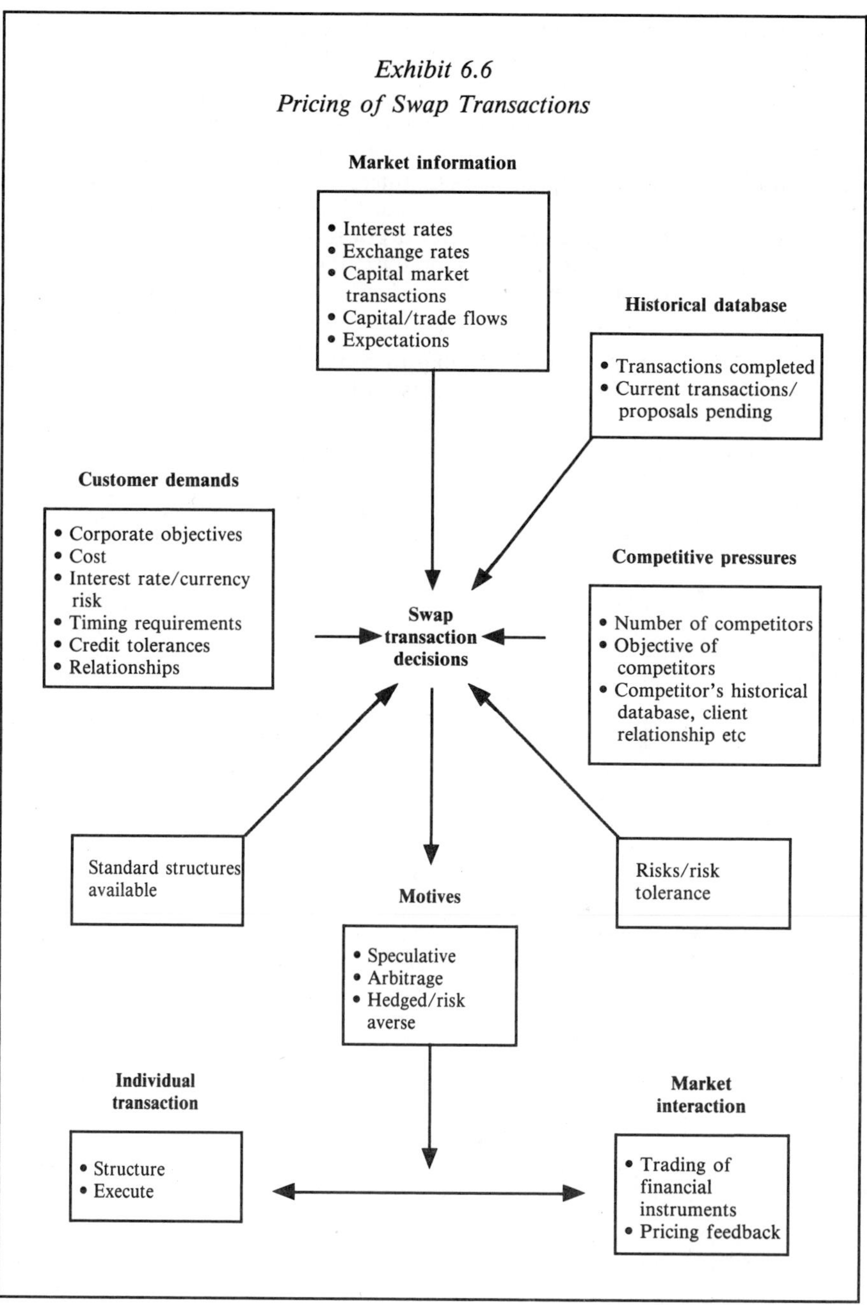

By definition, arbitrage transactions operate to eliminate their own incentive. Undertaking arbitrage transactions will inevitably move prices to eradicate the initial profit opportunity. However, where the profit opportunity is implied by externally imposed action such as taxation or regulation, the mere act of seeking to take advantage of the arbitrage opportunity may not adjust market prices to eliminate the opportunity which will persist until the offending regulation etc, is eliminated.

The pricing of the category of instruments referred to as swaps is complex. This complexity derives from the fact that it is multi-dimensional. As outlined above, at its simplest, swap prices may be calculated from financial asset price information freely available from the capital market. Interest rate swaps and currency swap pricings can be derived from available forward interest rate and currency prices. However, the relationship between forward prices and swap prices is merely one dimension in the swap pricing issue. In practise, the use of the swaps to engage in various types of financial arbitrage will overlay the forward price elements of such instruments.

Against this background, it is possible to construct a heuristic model for the pricing of swap transactions. This model is outlined in *Exhibit 6.6*.

Chapter 7

Economics and Pricing of Interest Rate and Currency Swaps

THE CONCEPTUAL FRAMEWORK

Popular literature on interest rate and currency swaps emphasises the ability of market participants to generate significant cost savings by combining an issue of securities with an interest rate or currency swap. The capacity to identify the source of this cost saving and a satisfying explanation of the underlying economics of such transactions is therefore essential to the pricing of swaps and also for a fundamental understanding of the market itself.

From a conceptual viewpoint, pricing of interest rate and currency swaps can be approached from two different viewpoints:

- analysing swaps as a series of forward prices;
- analysing swaps as a means for financial arbitrage.

As discussed in Chapter 6, forward interest rates and forward exchange rates are central to any interest rate and currency swap agreement respectively. It is clearly possible to characterise swap contracts as essentially a series of forward contracts which, in turn, implies that the forward rate embodied in a swap contract must correspond to the forward rates inherent in other corresponding financial instruments, primarily securities and futures contracts.

There are a number of problems with this particular approach. Attempting to price swaps on the basis of forward prices assumes the existence of the relevant forward price itself. For example, in the case of interest rate swaps, it assumes the existence of a continuous yield curve for securities of comparable characteristics, in particular, of comparable risk. In practice, such yield curves may not be available as in reality the swap may be predicated on the access or, conversely, lack of access to funding in a particular currency in a particular form. Similar considerations would apply in respect of currency swaps where the required forward exchange rates may not be available for particular market participants.

The problem of lack of availability of the relevant prices is merely symptomatic of the fact that the underlying process of arbitrage which would be required to force prices to their economic level is absent. The insufficiency of arbitrage for other than very short maturities reflects the fact that transaction costs and certain risks associated with arbitrage activity prevent the markets from operating at maximum optimal efficiency.

Transaction costs would include the bid/ask spread which in longer maturities may prevent efficient arbitrage. In a sense, the bid/ask spread is the demand for liquidity reflecting the cost of market making activities. The very wide spreads in longer maturities reflects the lack of liquidity in the market for instruments of that particular tenor. Other transaction costs include balance sheet holding costs and credit risk factors, some of which may be influenced by regulatory constraints, which once again add costs to the process of arbitrage and ultimately reduce the incentive to take advantage of price discrepancies.

An added problem in arbitrage over longer maturities is the fact that the instruments required to undertake this type of transaction would inevitably entail intermediate cash flows from holding of coupon securities which would require reinvestment. Uncertainty as to the reinvestment rate that may *actually* be achieved creates uncertainty as to the terminal cash value over the required holding period for securities which introduces an element of risk in the arbitrage transaction. This particular reinvestment problem is less acute in short-term arbitrage as generally discount instruments rather than coupon instruments are involved, eliminating any reinvestment risk.

However, even if the required forward prices were available, it is unlikely that the swap would conform to the market view of the forward price. This is because the existence of forward prices would imply that a market participant would be faced with two alternative means of achieving its objectives:

- a direct transaction to borrow funds in the relevant currency in the relevant form, that is, fixed or floating interest rates;
- an indirect transaction involving fund raising combined with an interest rate or currency swap to generate funding in the required currency and interest basis.

If swap prices were merely reflective of the forward rates which could be determined by competition from other credit market instruments, then there would be no direct cost incentive for the participant to utilise the swap as a means of obtaining its nominated objectives. There may be certain related advantages such as flexibility, particularly timing considerations, which would be difficult to quantify. These advantages of flexibility etc, may in fact also be offset by the additional credit risk assumed by the participant. This is because under the indirect option the organisation would have two levels of credit risk:

- the underlying securities transaction;
- the swap transaction.

This increased level of credit risk would impact upon the organisation's balance sheet as well as its available credit limits from banks and financial institutions. The funding transaction would be reflected on the balance sheet while the swap would be recorded as a contingent liability and both transactions would utilise credit lines available to the organisation. While the credit risk on swaps (see Part 8) does not equate to the notional principal amount of the swap, some credit limit utilisation would be entailed.

These problems with utilising forward prices in pricing swaps essentially mean that this price level operates as an upper bound to the pricing of interest rate and currency swaps at a given point in time. In essence, the swap price if it conforms to the forward price for either interest rates or currencies inevitably will represent an alternative means for an organisation to achieve its financing or risk management objectives which, however, does not provide any direct cost advantage.

The second approach to pricing interest rate and currency swaps is predicated on such transactions operating as a means of financial arbitrage across different capital markets. This approach implies that mutual cost savings are achievable primarily because prices in various world capital markets are not mutually consistent. Organisations can achieve lower borrowing costs by accessing particular markets with lower *relative* cost, borrowing there, and swapping their exposure, both interest rate and currency, back into their preferred form of funding, thereby achieving lower cost funding than that attainable from directly accessing the relevant markets. The basic sources of swap arbitrage include financial arbitrage, tax and regulatory arbitrage, as well as the existence of incomplete markets and the presence of transaction costs.

In summary, while from a conceptual viewpoint, it is possible to approach swap economics and pricing in terms of two different frameworks (namely, forward prices and financial arbitrage), in practice, to date, financial arbitrage has dominated swap pricing and economics. The main reason for this domination is the fact that financial arbitrage, unlike forward prices, creates a natural cost incentive for organisations to utilise swaps. If swaps were merely a means of replicating direct transactions with no cost advantage and, indeed, some level of additional cost, it is difficult to see the attraction of such transactions except for some qualitative benefits such as added flexibility.

In the remainder of this chapter, the detailed process of swap arbitrage is considered and the sources of swap arbitrage are detailed. The chapter concludes with a consideration of swap arbitrage in a specific capital market context (in this case, the A$ market) to further develop an understanding of the process by which the price of such transactions evolves.

SWAP ARBITRAGE

Interest rate swap arbitrage

All swap transactions are predicated on the exchange by one party of a benefit which it enjoys in a particular market for a corresponding benefit available to another party in a different market. The basic economics of a swap transaction are best illustrated by example.

Assume that a major international bank (bank A) can issue fixed rate US$ debt for five years in the form of a Eurodollar bond issue at an interest cost of 10.50% pa; bank A pays LIBOR for its floating rate US$ funds for an equivalent maturity. Contrast that with a medium rated company (company B), which because of its lower credit standing, can only issue five year fixed rate US$ debt (if at all) at 12.00% pa; company B can, however, raise five year floating rate funds from banks at LIBOR plus 0.75% pa.

The difference between the cost of funds for bank A and company B is: 0.75% pa in floating rate terms and 1.50% pa in fixed rate terms.

5 year funding	**Bank A**	**Company B**	**Interest cost differential**
Floating rate	LIBOR	LIBOR + 0.75% pa	0.75% pa
Fixed rate	10.50% pa	12.00% pa (if available)	1.50% pa

This disparity between the fixed and floating rate markets provides the arbitrage which is the basis of all interest rate swaps. The discrepancy is exploited as set out in *Exhibit 7.1*. Each party borrows from the market in which they get the best relative term (bank A in the fixed rate market and company B in the floating rate market) and then exchange their interest obligations to convert into their preferred form of funding.

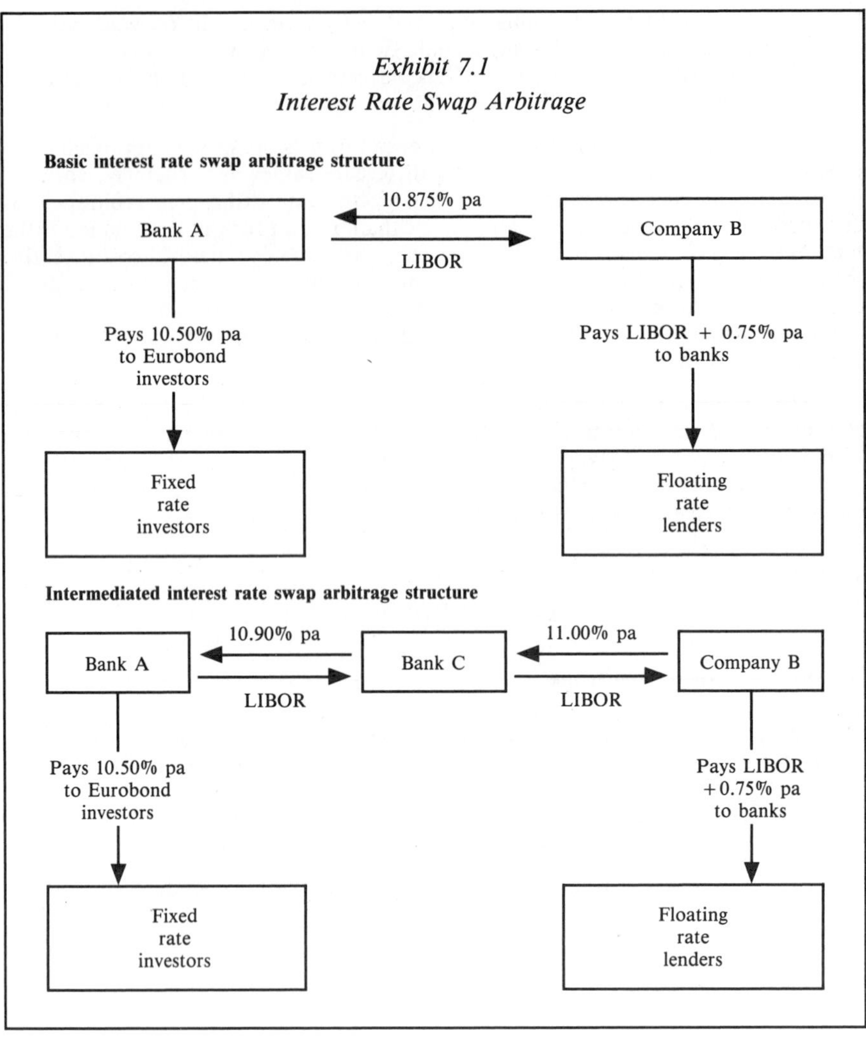

The net result of the transaction is as follows:

- bank A has raised floating rate US$ funds at LIBOR minus 0.375% pa, a saving of 0.375% pa;
- company B has raised fixed rate US$ fund at 11.625% pa, a saving of 0.375%.

Net costs	**Bank A**	**Company B**
Fixed rate outflow	10.50% pa	10.875% pa
Fixed rate inflow	10.875% pa	—
Floating rate outflow	LIBOR	LIBOR + 0.75% pa
Floating rate inflow	—	LIBOR
Net cost	LIBOR −0.375% pa	11.625% pa
Alternative cost	LIBOR	12.000% pa
Saving	0.375% pa	0.375% pa

The split between counterparties is driven mainly on the basis of supply and demand and on the basis of the cost of alternative available funding which are directly related to the credit standing of each party.

In the above example, the arbitrage gains are split equally between the two parties. In addition, the transaction structure assumes no intermediation by a bank or financial institution. A more realistic transaction structure, involving intermediation, is depicted in the intermediated swap arbitrage structure illustrated in the second part of *Exhibit 7.1*.

A similar type of analysis can be utilised for currency swaps.

Currency swap arbitrage

Assume that a major multinational (company A) has access to five year fixed rate Swiss francs at 5.00% pa; company A also can raise five year fixed rate US$ at 10.75% pa. In contrast, a company well known in the US$ domestic market but relatively unknown in the Swiss market (company B) has access to five year fixed rate Swiss francs at 5.50% pa, and five year fixed rate US$ at 11.00% pa.

The discrepancy between the cost of funds clearly provides the basis of an arbitrage transaction:

5 year funding	**Company A**	**Company B**	**Interest differential**
Fixed rate SFR	5.00% pa	5.50% pa	0.50% pa
Fixed rate US$	10.75% pa	11.00% pa	0.25% pa

Where company A is interested in raising US$ and conversely company B is interested in raising Swiss francs, the discrepancy can be exploited as set out in *Exhibit 7.2*. Company A raises Swiss francs and company B raises US$ and they then exchange their principal and interest obligations to convert into their preferred form of funding.

Net costs	**Company A**	**Company B**
US$ fixed rate outflow	10.625% pa	11.000% pa
US$ fixed rate inflow	—	10.625% pa
SFR fixed rate outflow	5.000% pa	5.000% pa
SFR fixed rate inflow	5.000% pa	—
Net cost	10.625% pa	5.375% pa
Alternative cost	10.750% pa	5.500% pa
Saving	0.125% pa	0.125% pa

Swap arbitrage: the general methodology

The basic process of swap arbitrage can be generalised.[1] As noted above, all swap transactions are predicated on the exchange by one party of a benefit which it enjoys in a particular market for a corresponding benefit available to another party in a different market. The economics and structuring of this process are usually undertaken in a series of discrete steps:

1. For an algebraic generalisation, see Turnbull (1987).

Exhibit 7.2
Currency Swap Arbitrage

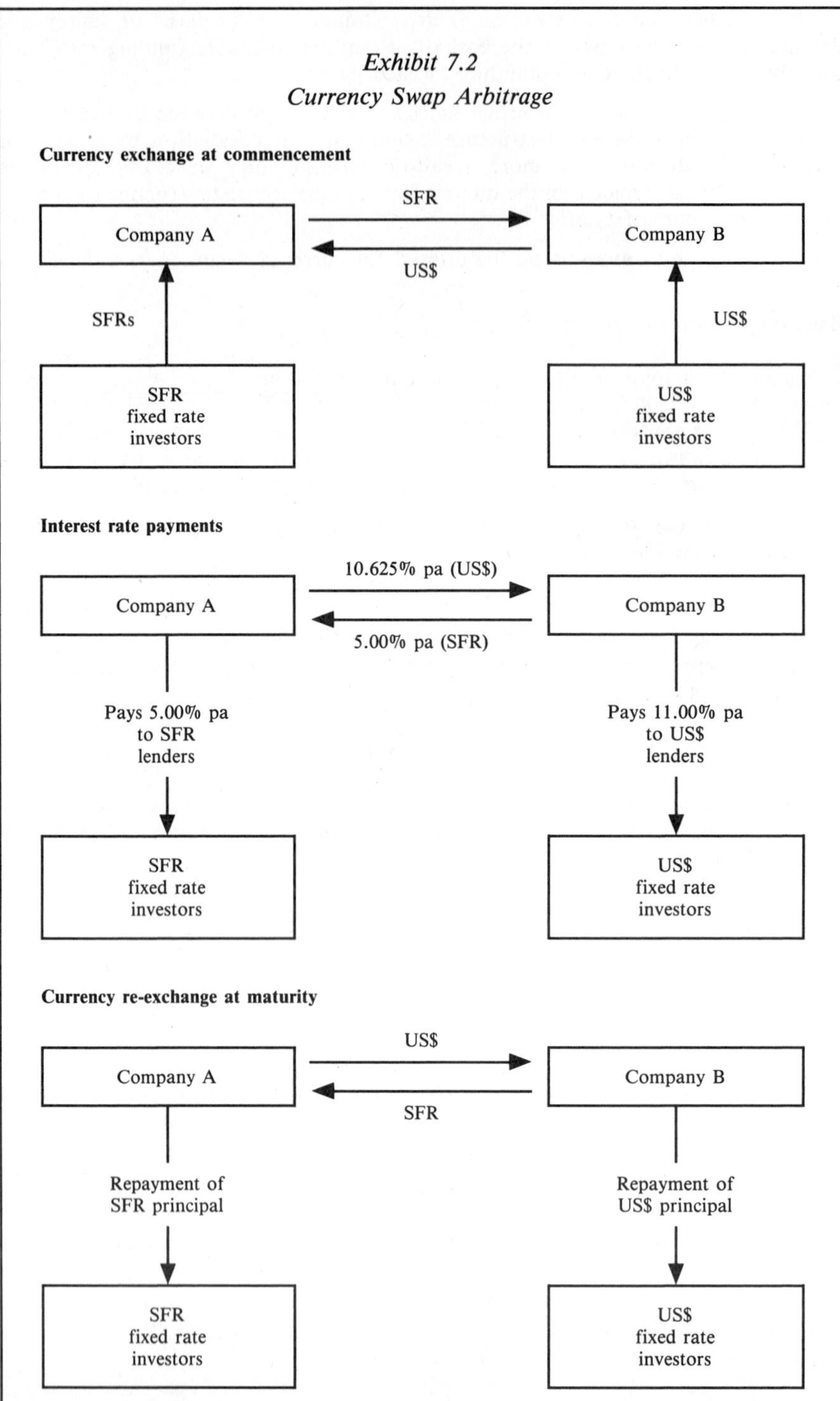

- creating the cost/access matrix;
- determining the comparative advantage of the respective parties;
- structuring the swap;
- pricing the swap.

To facilitate the determination of swap arbitrages, it is initially necessary to construct a matrix of the relative cost and availability of access to certain markets of the different borrowers. Once this cost/access matrix is created, interest cost differentials as between the parties can be determined allowing identification of relative comparative advantage.

The process of identifying the relative comparative advantages as between the two parties entails calculation of the differential cost of access to different markets. Structuring the swap arbitrage requires that the market in which each party has a comparative advantage be identified. Once this is completed, the swap can be structured on the basis that each party borrows in the market in which they enjoy a comparative advantage and the swap is structured to exchange their interest obligations to convert their liabilities into their preferred form of funding.

The pricing of the swap operates within the swap structure implied by the comparative advantage analysis. As the market in which each party will borrow is now known, it remains to calculate the swap price itself. The swap is calculated in two distinct parts:

- the maximum swap price for each party is determined;
- the arbitrage gain is split as between the parties.

Determining the outer limits of swap prices from both parties' perspectives requires the identification of the cost of direct access into the preferred form of funding. For example, utilising the data in our interest rate swap arbitrage example outlined above, company B would not pay a fixed rate of more than 11.25% pa against the receipt of LIBOR. This is because having borrowed in the market in which it enjoys a comparative advantage, namely the floating rate market at LIBOR plus 0.75% pa, and undertaking a swap as described at a rate of 11.25% would give it an all-in fixed rate cost for five years of 12.00% pa. This, not coincidentally, is its direct cost of access to fixed rate funds for five years. Similarly, utilising an identical methodology, the minimum swap pricing from the perspective of bank A could be determined as bank A receiving 10.50% pa against payment of LIBOR as this would equate to its direct cost of floating rate funds.

The determination of this pricing limit is important as it provides the outer bounds of the swap price at any one time as the price at which each party can create its preferred form of funding indirectly at no cost advantage.

The next part of the pricing phase is to then adjust the swap pricing on the basis of the split of the arbitrage gain implied. The arbitrage gain available for division between the parties to the swap is merely the differential cost of access to the two funding markets. In the interest rate swap example described above, the arbitrage profit is 0.75% pa, being the difference between the floating rate and fixed rate interest cost differentials.

This general methodology can be illustrated utilising an example in the US$ interest rate swap market. For example, assume the arbitrage in the US$ market is as follows:

	Fixed Rate Funding 3 Years	Floating Rate Funding 3 Years
US government	B	LIBOR – 40
AAA Sovereigns	B + 20	LIBOR – 20
Supra-National	B + 30	LIBOR – 20
Banks (AA or better)	B + 65	LIBOR – 15
Banks (A or BBB)	B + 95	LIBOR – 5
Prime Corporate	B + 120	LIBOR + 20
Lower Rate Corporate	B + 250	LIBOR + 75

Note: B + 30 means the prevailing US three year Treasury bond rate + 0.30% pa; LIBOR + 25 means six month US$ LIBOR + 0.25% pa.

A possible transaction is set out in *Exhibit 7.3*.

Exhibit 7.3
US$ Interest Rate Swap Arbitrage

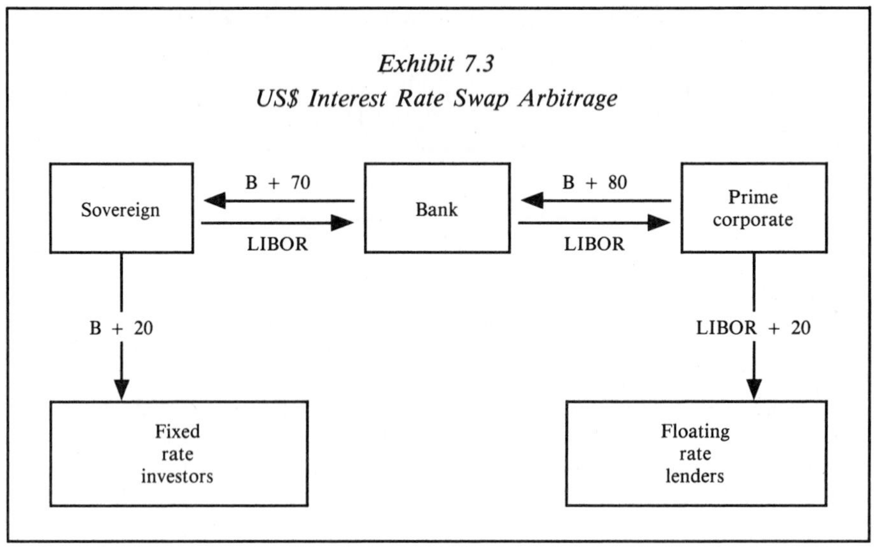

The swap arbitrage is structured as follows:

- It is first necessary to identify the two likely swap counterparties which are assumed in this case to be the AAA Sovereign entity and the prime corporate.
- On the basis of the cost/access matrix outlined, it is possible to identify that the interest cost differential in the fixed rate market between the sovereign and the prime corporate is 100bps in the fixed rate market as against 40bps in the floating rate market.
- The interest differentials imply that the sovereign entity enjoys a comparative advantage in the fixed rate market. It is, however, important to note that the sovereign in fact enjoys an *absolute* cost advantage in both markets. Suggesting that the sovereign enjoys a *comparative* advantage in the fixed rate market is to identify that its interest differential in the fixed rate market is greater than its interest differential in the floating rate market. In this bilateral arrangement, by implication, the prime corporate enjoys a *comparative* advantage in the floating

rate market which is to say that, relatively speaking, its absolute cost disadvantage is *least* in the floating rate market.

- Given the comparative cost structure, it is possible to structure the swap on the basis that the sovereign would borrow in the fixed rate funding market (the market in which it enjoys a comparative advantage) and the prime corporate would borrow in the floating rate funding market (the market in which it enjoys a comparative advantage). A swap would then be arranged whereby the sovereign would receive fixed rate and pay floating rate while the prime corporate would undertake the reverse.
- As noted above, the outer bound on the swap pricing is the level at which the two counterparties would be indifferent as to entering into the swap, that is, the swap price combined with the underlying funding equates to the cost of direct access to the respective markets. In this case, the outer bounds of the swap pricing are as follows:
  - sovereign would receive fixed rate at no lower than B + 40 and this would generate floating rate funding at its direct cost of LIBOR – 20;
  - prime corporate would not pay at a rate higher than B + 100 which equates to its direct cost of fixed rate funding.
- Within this outer bounds, the arbitrage gain of 60bps will be apportioned. This 60bps is the difference between the interest differential in the fixed rate funding market (100bps) and the differential in the floating rate market (40bps).

The relative bargaining powers of the two parties, supply and demand etc, will influence the manner in which the arbitrage gain is shared between the parties. A possible swap pricing in this environment is set out below:

Fixed side arbitrage: 30
Floating side arbitrage: 20
Cost of intermediation: 10
Likely swap pricing: B + 70/B + 80

Bank intermediation is assumed in this example.

The analysis of the US$ interest rate swap arbitrage highlights certain deficiencies in the general swap arbitrage methodology. The major deficiencies include the fact that the analysis is predominantly bilateral rather than multi-lateral. Additional deficiencies include the fact that the arbitrage analysis is mono-dimensional in that it is confined to a particular swap as between two markets. In addition, the arbitrage as portrayed is confined to the liability side of the respective participants' activities. The analysis does not take into account the possibility of the "reverse arbitrage" which allows the creation of higher yielding assets or assets not directly available, that is, an asset swap (see Chapter 18).

While swaps are bilateral transactions, the fact that there are more than two potential participants in the swap market at any given time means that the bilateral mode of analysis has a number of shortcomings. In practice, swap markets gravitate to an arbitrage driven by the two most likely participants at a given point in time. The most likely participants in swap transactions at a given time are determined by a wide range of factors including:

- the attractiveness in absolute terms of the swap arbitrage;
- the asset liability management requirements of both counterparties which may be driven by fundamental business considerations as well as interest rate and currency expectations;

- credit criteria which may limit the capacity of potential swap participants for transacting either directly or through a bank intermediary. In the latter case, the cost of intermediation essentially outweighs the benefits of the swap arbitrage;
- the investment objectives of fixed rate and floating rate investors across a wide range of currencies and their tolerance for particular credit risks as well as the state of their portfolios at a given point in time.

The major implications of a multi-lateral market is that the exploitation of the swap arbitrage inevitably means some change in the underlying cost/access matrix. This in a sense leads to a self-perpetuating series of evolving swap arbitrages. In essence, the swap arbitrage persists but in an ever-changing form.

The second level of deficiency relates to the fact that each participant in the swap market may have options beyond those capable of being captured within the swap arbitrage methodology outlined. For example, in our US$ interest rate swap example, the sovereign entity may not find a swap where it receives B + 70bps to generate LIBOR – 50bps attractive if it could issue A$ on a fixed rate basis and swap it first into floating rate US$ LIBOR at a superior rate to that achievable in the US$ interest rate swap market. Consequently, while swap arbitrage methodology may give indicative pricing within the context defined, the presence of other opportunities for funding arbitrages will to some extent determine the willingness of particular participants to transact at the levels implied.

The analysis also does not recognise the capacity for other market participants to enter into reverse arbitrages creating higher yielding assets. This can be illustrated in our US$ interest rate swap example. Assume that a comparable creditor to a sovereign entity is the intermediating bank. It is quoting a swap price of B + 70/80. This would allow an investor seeking sovereign assets to buy floating rate securities yielding LIBOR – 20 and swap them into fixed rate US$ assets yielding B + 50 by entering into a swap with the bank whereby it would pay LIBOR – 20bps and receive B + 50bps.

Provided the additional credit risk in respect of the swap is less than 20bps pa, the investor could create a higher yielding asset than that directly available in the form of fixed rate securities issued by the sovereign. This reverse arbitrage would impinge on the primary arbitrage process as essentially it would create demand for sovereign floating rate assets but decrease demand for fixed rate securities issued by sovereigns. Moreover, it would also have the effect of changing the swap pricing whereby the bank would gradually decrease the rate it is willing to pay from B + 70 to lower levels thereby squeezing out the arbitrage for the sovereign.

This complex process of interaction is evident from the analysis of some of the deficiencies of the basic swap arbitrage methodology. Some of these interactions are examined in greater detail in the section on swap arbitrages in the A$ market later in this chapter.

The method of analysis identified may, a number of commentators have argued, be fundamentally flawed. Turnbull (1987) argues that the type of simple comparison is misleading as a simple comparison of interest rates is insufficient if financial instruments differ in design and risk.[2] Theoretically, this proposition must be correct. However, if the financial instruments are identical (which is the implicit assumption in the method of analysis outlined) it is not clear why a simple comparison is *not* sufficient.

2. Turnbull (1987) gives the example of a comparison of issue of *callable* fixed rate debt against the issue of *non-callable* floating rate debt which is then swapped into fixed rate. This swap is, of course, inherently non-callable, although reversible at market rates.

Turnbull (1987) introduces the concept of present value into the analysis respecifying the swap arbitrage condition as the present value of its inflows being not less than the present value of the outflows. The introduction of present value is not necessarily helpful as it requires assumptions to be made either about the absolute level of future short-term interest rates or a stochastic process by which future interest rates are generated.

In essence, the borrower must, by definition, determine whether or not it requires a fixed or floating rate liability or the currency of such a liability. That decision is totally separate from the swap arbitrage analysis, being governed by factors such as interest and currency rate expectations, asset liability matching requirements etc. Swap arbitrage merely assists in creating the required liability.

The more relevant problem with this methodology may be the fact that it does not incorporate the credit exposure entailed in the swap itself. If a borrower utilises a swap to create a synthetic liability, it incurs credit exposures under both the borrowing and the swap thereby utilising a scarce resource, namely access to credit. While this additional credit exposure is *not* encompassed by the methodology outlined, the oversight is inconsequential insofar as the presence of this additional risk merely dictates that there must be sufficient cost benefits in the swap to offest the credit exposure entailed. In particular it serves to highlight that while swaps can be priced as a series of forward contracts, if the market traded swaps at that price there would be limited incentives for the existence of a viable swap market.

SOURCES OF SWAP ARBITRAGE

Swap arbitrage sources: a classification

Swap arbitrage methodology is predicated on the relative comparative advantages of various participants in the capital market to different sources of funding. The methodology itself is silent as to the underlying source of the comparative advantage. The theme common to all types of swaps is that they involve trading an advantage which a borrower or investor enjoys in one market for an equivalent advantage available to another company in a different market. This advantage, which drives the underlying economics, lies in one of two areas:

- post-tax cost;
- availability or access.

This principle applies equally to all types of swaps, including interest rate swaps and currency swaps. Application of this theme allows asset and liability managers to separate decisions on the market in which to invest or borrow from and decisions on the currency and interest rate basis of the investment or borrowing. In essence, the underlying swap arbitrage enables companies and investors to separate the source of liquidity from the management or the nature of the underlying asset or liability which is ultimately created.

The sources of the swap arbitrage are capable of classification into at least three separate categories:

- financial arbitrage;
- tax and regulatory arbitrage;
- miscellaneous arbitrages.

Financial arbitrage

Financial arbitrage in its purest form involves exploiting mutually inconsistent prices for securities of identical structural and issuer credit criteria in various world capital markets. The process of financial arbitrage as it applies to swap transactions entails a series of different types of arbitrage including:

- credit arbitrage (including the effect of name arbitrage and credit margin compression);
- supply and demand factors (including market segmentation, market saturation and diversification issues, sluggish communication and inadequate market liquidity etc).

Credit arbitrage

Credit arbitrage refers to a market anomaly which is predicated on differences in risk premium requirements across capital markets or alternatively, between different segments of a particular capital market. Credit arbitrage is made possible by an *intra* or *intermarket* dissimilarity in the assessment of credit risk and the resultant discrepancies of risk premium. The examples outlined above of interest rate and currency swap arbitrage all rely to some extent on credit arbitrage.

The difference in risk pricing reflects a number of different factors operating in the respective markets or market segments.

In the case of *intramarket* credit arbitrage, such as the interest rate swap arbitrages described above, a major factor in the differential risk pricing is the fact that the suppliers of funds are different as between the fixed and floating rate markets. The predominant suppliers of floating rate finance are banks and financial institutions. In contrast, the suppliers of fixed rate funding are direct rather than intermediated lenders, such as institutional and retail investors. The different lending groups have different capacities to assess and assume credit risk.

It is arguable that banks and financial institutions have a comparative advantage in credit risk assessment. These organisations operate sophisticated credit analysis systems and are able to analyse and accurately assess the credit risk of all borrowers. In particular, this allows them to assume credit risk in respect of lower rated borrowers more readily than direct investors.

This comparative advantage in credit risk assessment enjoyed by banks and financial institutions is certainly true in respect of retail investors who are ill-equipped to assess complex or difficult business organisations. However, capital markets have undergone significant changes in recent years with a marked institutionalisation of investment which has seen the concentration of investment decisions in professional money managers who could easily perform the evaluation of credit and investment opportunities which traditionally have been functions in which the banks have enjoyed an advantage. Consequently, while comparative capacities for credit risk assessment may explain the differential in risk pricing as between banks, financial institutions and retail investors, the argument is less compelling in respect of institutional investors.

Banks also enjoy the capacity to diversify their risk as between different borrowers, in terms of industry, geographic location etc. This allows banks to price risk premiums more competitively on a portfolio basis than investors. Again, while the diversification argument has considerable explanatory power in respect of retail investor pricing of risk, the capacity of large institutional fund managers to achieve diversification at a level comparable to that of banks and financial institutions means that the diversification argument does not fully explain the differential risk premiums as between banks and institutional investors.

The discrepancy in risk premiums between the public and bank markets, particularly in respect of institutional investors, is more probably capable of explanation in terms of the modern finance constructs of agency and contracting costs.[3] Under this approach, it can be argued that banks and other financial institutions, because of their large individual investments by way of debt funding for individual borrowers and the fact that borrowers usually deal with a relatively limited number of banks, are able to more effectively monitor loans. In contrast, the monitoring costs faced by individual institutional investors with relatively small holdings of debt securities are relatively higher and require costly contracting mechanisms such as trust deeds etc. The high monitoring cost faced by individual and institutional investors translates into a higher return required by such investors to provide loan funds to a firm of the stated risk profile relative to financial institutions giving rise to the differential in risk premiums.

Anecdotal evidence suggests that this argument is of substance. Typically, public securities issues are held in relatively small parcels of usually under US$3-5m for an individual issue and in some cases much smaller parcels. Bank loans etc extended by individual financial institutions to a particular borrower will usually be substantially larger than individual securities holdings.

The contracting and monitoring cost argument can also be extended to enforcement issues. For example, it can be argued that the absolute cost of enforcement of a particular creditor's claim is relatively fixed and consequently translates into a higher percentage amount relative to a small individual investment in public securities relative to the percentage cost on a larger bank loan. Additional factors in this regard would include the fact that as individual borrowers may deal with a limited number of banks as distinct from a large number of security holders, banks and financial institutions enjoy a significant advantage in managing and working out problem loans.

Underlying this enforcement problem is the fundamental nature of the contracting arrangements in intermediated and direct financing. In the case of intermediated financing, the bank or financial institution accepts a deposit which it undertakes to repay at maturity together with interest. The bank then in turn on-lends the funds to a borrower. Where the borrower gets into difficulties and is unable to repay the loan or to meet interest commitments, the bank's obligations to its depositors are quite separate from and in no way linked to the performance of the loan. This separation, which is achieved through interposition of the bank in the intermediation process, provides the bank with some flexibility in the management of problem loans. This is so particularly where with a diversified portfolio it is able to service its deposits, both interest and principal payments, without jeopardising its financial viability.

In contrast, an institutional investor has a different contractual arrangement with the beneficiaries of the funds under management. The fund manager acts in a fiduciary capacity managing funds on behalf of individual investors. Under these contracting arrangements, a failure by a borrower to perform under its loan conditions, in terms of repayment of principal or interest or other loan conditions, will directly impact upon the investor. This is because the fund manager does not independently guarantee or ensure the payment of interest or principal as does a bank in the intermediated finance case. This more direct relationship clearly limits

3. For an introduction to these concepts, see Jensen and Ruback (1976), pp 305-360.

the discretion of the fund manager, in particular, in the case of a problem loan requiring rescheduling and restructuring. This different contracting relationship may, inevitably, tend to bias fund managers to place a higher risk premium on less credit-worthy borrowers than banks and financial institutions.

These factors all have the following effects:

- Higher quality borrowers enjoy a comparative advantage in the public securities market, usually the fixed rate market, as investors for the reasons outlined are willing to pay a high price (or sacrifice yield) to purchase the securities of these entities which have a low default risk.
- Lower quality or less credit-worthy borrowers enjoy a comparative advantage in the floating rate market, which is predominantly a bank or financial institution lending market, based on the fact that these institutions have certain advantages in dealing with lesser quality credits.

Both factors tend to create differential risk premiums which facilitate swap arbitrage.

Intermarket credit arbitrage is driven by slightly different factors, predominantly spread compression and name arbitrage factors.

Spread compression refers to an intermarket anomaly whereby the risk premium is significantly different as between markets. In capital markets, a hierarchy of risk is assessed by security analysts or credit rating firms and the risk premium component of the yield is related to the credit-worthiness of issuers as ranked under this rating process in a more or less continuous scale of quality ratings.

For example, in the United States market a BBB rated credit would command a risk premium of say 1.50-2.00% greater than a higher quality AAA rated credit for term financing. This yield spread will vary significantly based on market conditions. However, in the European capital markets, such as Switzerland and West Germany, the risk premium between a AAA and a BBB credit may be as low as 0.40-0.60% pa. This lower risk premium may be related to the higher savings rates in particular countries, the liquidity levels in particular markets, the absolute yield levels in different currencies, as well as different normal financing practices. For example, in certain markets such as the Eurobond market, investors may be inclined to view a credit as either acceptable or unacceptable and behave accordingly in investment decisions without well defined attempts to differentiate between various degrees of credit-worthiness.

This intermarket spread compression phenomena is often allied to investor focus on the *name* or reputation of a borrower as distinct from its strict credit-worthiness. This phenomena of name arbitrage is particularly significant in Europe and the Euromarkets where a lower rated credit may enjoy superior access to funding at lower risk differentials than in its home market on the basis of the company being a producer of a well known and accepted product which enjoys everyday use, popularity and acceptance of the brand name. For example, companies such as Coca Cola, McDonalds and Eastman Kodak enjoy access to European capital markets at costs very favourable, relative to their actual credit-worthiness. This is particularly so in contrast to the relative cost of funding in their home markets, say the United States where the company's name and product association means far less in the credit analysis and subsequent rating of the firm's securities.

The related phenomena of spread compression and name arbitrage allows certain categories of borrowers to obtain funds in certain markets at significantly lower risk premiums than would be available in their traditional domestic or home markets, generating the comparative advantages which can form the basis of swap arbitrage.

Market segmentation

Market segmentation exists within individual national capital markets as well as between various world capital markets. Market segmentation can take the form of restrictions on investment choice imposed by regulation or internal management policy, which are dealt with in the section on tax and regulatory arbitrage.

Market segmentation exists at a number of levels. At the extreme, restrictions on cross-border capital flows create currency blockages which create attractive opportunities for participants who can circumvent capital flow restrictions by taking the opposite sides of desired transactions.

As discussed in Chapter 3, parallel and back-to-back loans, the precursors of interest rate and currency swaps, were largely an attempt to overcome government imposed currency restrictions on free cross-border capital flows. This type of market segmentation creates problems of funding availability encouraging swap arbitrage designed to exchange demand for a blocked currency for liquidity available in another capital market.

More typically, market segmentation reflects differing investor perceptions and preferences which manifest themselves in the form of risk pricing differentials similar to the spread compression issues discussed above. Market segmentation in this latter form appears to be predicated on administrative limitations on investment in certain instruments or participation in different sectors of markets.

The international market for debt security extends around the globe and is subdivided into numerous national, regional and international sectors. The major distinctions in the international bond market are between international and domestic bond issues. Domestic bond issues are offerings which are sold largely within the country of the borrower. In contrast, international bond issues are security offerings which are sold largely outside the country of the borrower. International bond issues may be further subdivided into two types of issues: Eurobonds and foreign bonds. Eurobonds are international bond issues underwritten by an international syndicate of banks and sold principally and, at times, exclusively in countries other than the country of currency in which the bonds are denominated. Foreign bonds, in contrast, are international bond issues underwritten by a syndicate of banks composed primarily of institutions from one country, distributed in the same way as domestic issues in that country, and denominated in the currency of that country.

The distinctions between the various market segments while accurate in theory are considerably more difficult to determine in practice. The major difficulty arises as a result of the nature of the securities which typically enjoy considerable liquidity as they can be freely bought and sold in an active secondary market. Consequently, one would expect that investors are able to purcase securities from different markets as and when their investment requirements dictate. This would lead to a breakdown in the strict categorisation proposed above and more importantly would lead to uniformity of pricing for comparable securities issued by the same borrower or same class of borrowers. In the early 1990s, the emergence of global bond issuance structures—effectively, the issue of securities, simultaneously in a number of markets combined with settlement, clearance and transfer mechanisms designed to facilitate trading in the securities—was an attempt to create a truly global market for securities. Global bond issues have been pioneered by the World Bank and issues completed in US$, C$, A$, JPY and a few other currencies.[4]

However, there is significant evidence to suggest that investors only participate in certain sectors of the respective markets worldwide for legal, liquidity and

4. See Kenneth G Lay and V Jan Wright, "Taming the Dollar Market Machine: Reducing Friction in Distribution and Trading of Non-Treasury Bonds" (1988) (Autumn) *Journal of International Securities Markets* 165-173.

convenience reasons. In fact, there is evidence to suggest that nearly two thirds of the international bond market is not readily accessible or liquid enough for active international participation.[5] This lack of freedom for international fund flows implies a significant level of market segmentation and resultant pricing anomalies which facilitate swap arbitrage.

One example of this type of market segmentation motivated swap arbitrage is in the US$ market as between the Eurodollar and Yankee bond markets.[6] The yield differential between Eurodollar and Yankee bond markets have varied significantly over time with numerous instances when yields of similarly structured Eurodollar and Yankee bonds issued by the same borrower differ by up to 0.50% pa in yield. These divergent trading patterns create significant swap opportunities for market participants.

The pricing differences as between the markets appear to be principally caused by the different credit perceptions and preferences of investors in the United States domestic and international market. These factors include:

- different maturity and issuer preferences;
- investor perceptions of credit quality of bond issuers;
- currency factors and their relevance to the investment decision.

The differing investor perceptions and preferences can be seen in the fact that bonds offered by a variety of high quality sovereign issuers, irrespective of credit rating, have generally enjoyed a less favourable reception in the Yankee market than in the Eurobond market. For example, debt issued by prime issuers such as the Kingdoms of Denmark, Sweden, Finland as well as the Government of New Zealand trade at a significantly higher yield in the Yankee market than in the Eurobond market. In contrast, Canadian issuers have languished in the Eurobond market but because of the proximity of the United States and Canada, have enjoyed an excellent reception in the United States domestic Yankee market.

The differential maturity preferences are evident in the fact that Eurodollar bonds with maturities over 20 years have fared very poorly in the international market. This reflects the fact that investors in the Eurodollar market have traditionally been composed of short to intermediate term security investors. This created significant pricing anomalies with the World Bank's 30 year Eurodollar bonds yielding an average of 30bps more than the 30 year Yankee bonds by the same borrower.

In addition, the Eurodollar bond market, in contrast to the Yankee market, demonstrates a high degree of sensitivity to the value of the US$. This appears to have contributed to wider spreads in the Eurodollar market relative to the domestic Yankee market. This differential partially reflects the fact that international (non-United States) investors in US$ view their investment as a currency as well as an interest rate play and consequently will price the same credit risk differentially according to their expectations on the future direction of the US$ relative to other major currencies.

This analysis highlights how segmentation of markets creates differential risk pricing which creates opportunities for swap arbitrages of the type described. While the discussion above has been confined to the US$ market, similar considerations apply to a significant number of other markets where similar opportunities are created by the different factors motivating investor participation in various segments of the international capital market.

5. See Marki (1986).
6. The foreign bond sector of the United States domestic bond market.

Supply and demand factors

A third category of financial arbitrage relates to supply and demand factors affecting an individual issuer's securities. In particular, imbalances in the supply and demand conditions create opportunities for arbitrage.

The simplest type of supply and demand factor giving rise to financial arbitrage opportunities is market saturation or its reverse, the scarcity value of an issuer's securities. An extreme case of supply and demand imbalance exists when a given capital market is unwilling to absorb any more debt of a given issuer. In this case, if the issuer still requires financing in the currency of that particular market, proxy borrowers who are acceptable to the saturated market must be sought with the borrower's financing objectives being met by exchanging the new obligations in the required currency for more easily saleable obligations in a currency where the market continues to have demand for the debt of the particular borrower.

Market saturation relates essentially to the relative elasticity or inelasticity of the demand curve for a particular issuer's securities. It is evident that the demand curve for a particular issuer's or risk class of securities, while relatively price insensitive when limited quantities of the issuers securities are on issue, tends to become inelastic and highly price sensitive when a certain saturation point is reached. In that case, additional sales of securities by that particular issuer can only be achieved at significant increases in the risk differential required to be paid to investors. The issue of market saturation, at least from the perspective of investors, appears to relate to:

- the portfolio or credit diversification objectives of investors;
- the financing requirements of the particular issuer relative to the size of the particular capital market.

Investors on the whole seek to limit credit exposure within their investment portfolios to any particular issuer or class of issuer to a relatively small percentage of the total portfolio. This has the consequence of forcing issuers requiring substantial financing in a particular currency, beyond the capacity of that particular sector or market to provide such financing, to pay a penalty if it persists in seeking to raise funds from that particular market. In essence, at the margin, once saturation point has been reached additional net investment in that issuer's securities will only grow in proportion to the total net growth in the funds available for investment as investors are unwilling to increase their investment on a percentage basis.

Scarcity value considerations have the converse effect that investors may be willing to purchase securities issued by *infrequent* issuers in that particular market or market sector at a much higher price (lower yield) than dictated by purely economic factors on the basis of scarcity which allows the investor to achieve a greater degree of portfolio credit risk diversification.

This problem can actually be illustrated with reference to a number of supranational organisations which persist in a borrowing policy which dictates raising funds in particular currency markets. This particular category of borrowers, primarily the World Bank, but also other development banks and the national agencies of a number of developed countries, are frequent borrowers in traditionally low coupon currencies such as Swiss francs, deutschmarks and Japanese yen.

In the case of the larger borrowers, particularly the World Bank, the substantial size of their borrowing requirement places a heavy burden on the debt markets in these low nominal interest rate currencies. Consequently, the World Bank tends to pay a bigger penalty for its frequent borrowings in a number of low coupon currencies. This problem has led over time to the World Bank evolving a policy which dictates diversification of funding sources by issuing in a wide range of different currency markets, thereby allowing it to reach investors who would not invest in the borrower's usual currencies, and then swapping the funds raised into the institution's preferred currency and interest rate basis.

A number of institutions, primarily sovereign entities or major international banks, have also sought to diversify their funding base by issuing in a wide range of currencies allowing them to reach investors other than in their traditional currencies on the basis that the funds raised are at an attractive relative rate allowing swaps back into the desired currency at an attractive rate relative to direct market access (see discussion of new issue arbitrage in Chapter 19).

Short run supply demand imbalances, often referred to as market "windows", also create significant opportunities for swap arbitrage. Global debt markets increasingly operate on an opportunistic basis. Windows of attractive opportunities close and open as investor sentiment as to currency and interest rate outlook alters in the light of new available information. High levels of volatility in currency and interest rates as well as improved global communications and information flows means that increasingly transactions are done on the basis of the specific short-lived opportunity which is predicated on investor demand which allows a particular security transaction because the market conditions are "right" and the investors are "there"!

In this type of market, rapidly changing investor demand for particular types of securities create short-run supply imbalances which creates a premium on timing. For example, assume investor expectations in respect of a currency, say the A$, have improved dramactically in the light of market information. In this environment, investors will be seeking to purchase A$ securities for short-term capital gains as a result of currency fluctuations. This creates a short-term excess of demand over the supply of A$ securities as usually the secondary market in A$ securities cannot meet the sudden upsurge in demand for investments. Under these circumstances, an opportunistic issuer may be able to take advantage of market sentiment to issue A$ securities at a relatively advantageous cost, fulfilling the supply gap in the market, creating a comparative cost advantage which may form the basis of a swap into its preferred currency.

A similar process would apply to an opportunistic issue of particular *types* of securities designed to capitalise on market opportunities. A number of the security structures described in Part 4 were created as a result of market demand for a specific type of security with characteristics designed to provide the investor with a particular return profile linked to specific market conditions existing at the time of issue. Opportunistic issuers have frequently been able to take advantage of this demand for particular types of securities to create borrowings at relatively low cost which have then been swapped into the borrower's preferred form of borrowing through a customised swap or derivative transaction.

Tax and regulatory arbitrage

Tax and regulatory arbitrage is predicated on the existence of artificially imposed restrictions on capital flows or the pricing of capital flows which artificially creates differential pricing or differential access for different classes of participants in capital markets. There are a number of classes of tax and regulatory arbitrage:

- withholding tax;
- investment asset choice;
- taxation differentials;
- subsidised funding sources.

Withholding tax

The presence of withholding taxes creates a wedge between yields on domestic securities and those on comparable securities issued outside the domestic market, primarily in the Eurobond market. The creation of swap arbitrage opportunities as a result of the presence of withholding tax relates essentially to the differential treatment of different classes of transaction under withholding tax legislation. This can be best illustrated by an example involving the A$ market.

Under currently applicable regulations, an international, that is, non-Australian investor purchasing A$ securities issued in the domestic market is subject to a withholding tax of usually 10.00% on interest payments. For example, a European investor purchasing Commonwealth government bonds yielding 13.00% pa would on each interest coupon date receive the equivalent of only 11.70% pa being the 13.00% coupon reduced by the mandatory 10.00% withholding tax. The European investor may be able to recover this withholding tax by way of a tax credit in its own country. Consequently, at best, the investor will recover the withholding by way of adjustments to its domestic tax liability which will usually entail a slight delay and some loss in yield or, at worst, the withholding will not be recoverable resulting in a significant yield loss.

Assume that the European investor can achieve its desired A$ investment objectives by purchasing A$ Eurobonds, issued by a European continental institution of high credit standing. The A$ Eurobond is free and clear of all withholding taxes as essentially it does not involve a resident to non-resident transaction for Australian tax purposes with fund flows taking place entirely outside Australia. Let us also assume that this Eurobond is priced at a yield *under* the equivalent Commonwealth government bond rate of 13.00%, say 12.50% pa. The investor will be attracted to the Eurobond on the basis that it does not realistically represent a yield loss of 0.50% pa relative to an alternative investment, the Commonwealth government bond, but rather an effective yield pick up of 0.80% pa relative to the realised yield where the investor is unable to take advantage of the tax withholding through a foreign tax credit mechanism.

In these circumstances, the issuer of A$ Eurobonds enjoys a comparative advantage in its access to A$ funding relative to domestic institutions and may, if it is not a direct user of A$, swap out of its A$ liability into another liability, say floating rate US$, which is its preferred form of funding. The swap would be effected with a domestic Australian counterparty who would exchange its floating rate US$ liability for lixed rate A$. As the domestic Australian swap counterparty would find its fixed rate debt trading at a significant margin above the Commonwealth government bond rate, the fact that the issuer has achieved a cost of funds under the bond rate should facilitate a significant cost saving in fixed rate A$ terms.

The swap arbitrage predicated on withholding tax in our example is, however, predicated on two important factors:

- the fact that the swap cash flows are free of withholding tax;
- that the Australian counterparty's underlying funding is free and clear of withholding tax.

In practice, swap payments are usually not subject to withholding tax thereby satisfying the first condition. For Australian borrowers, the US$ liability would in all probability be free of withholding tax under an alternative withholding tax exemption provision which provides for no withholding tax on transactions involving the issue offshore of widely distributed bearer securities. This exemption satisfies the second condition for the swap arbitrage involving withholding tax to be effective.

Another example of the impact of withholding tax on swap arbitrage opportunities is that which exists in the ECU market.

Under current Italian tax regulations, Italian government's Certificate Del Tresore in ECU (CTEs) are subject to a 12.5% Italian withholding tax. Consequently, CTEs must be issued at a gross yield above that of ECU Eurobonds (up to 75-100bps above comparable Eurobonds). However, many investors outside Italy are able to reclaim this withholding tax under tax credit arrangements between Italy and these countries. These circumstances create attractive tax arbitrage opportunities.

Investors, particularly those able to reclaim the Italian withholding tax, are aggressive buyers of CTEs which are then swapped into attractive floating rate assets. This demand by investors seeking to undertake asset swap CTE investments forces up the fixed rate payable in the ECU swap market, particularly relative to prevailing ECU Eurobond yields thereby providing issuing opportunities for borrowers who issue ECU Eurobonds and enter into a simultaneous swap to generate LIBOR related funding. *Exhibit 7.4* sets out this type of activity in the ECU swap market.

Exhibit 7.4
ECU Swap Market—CTE Arbitrage

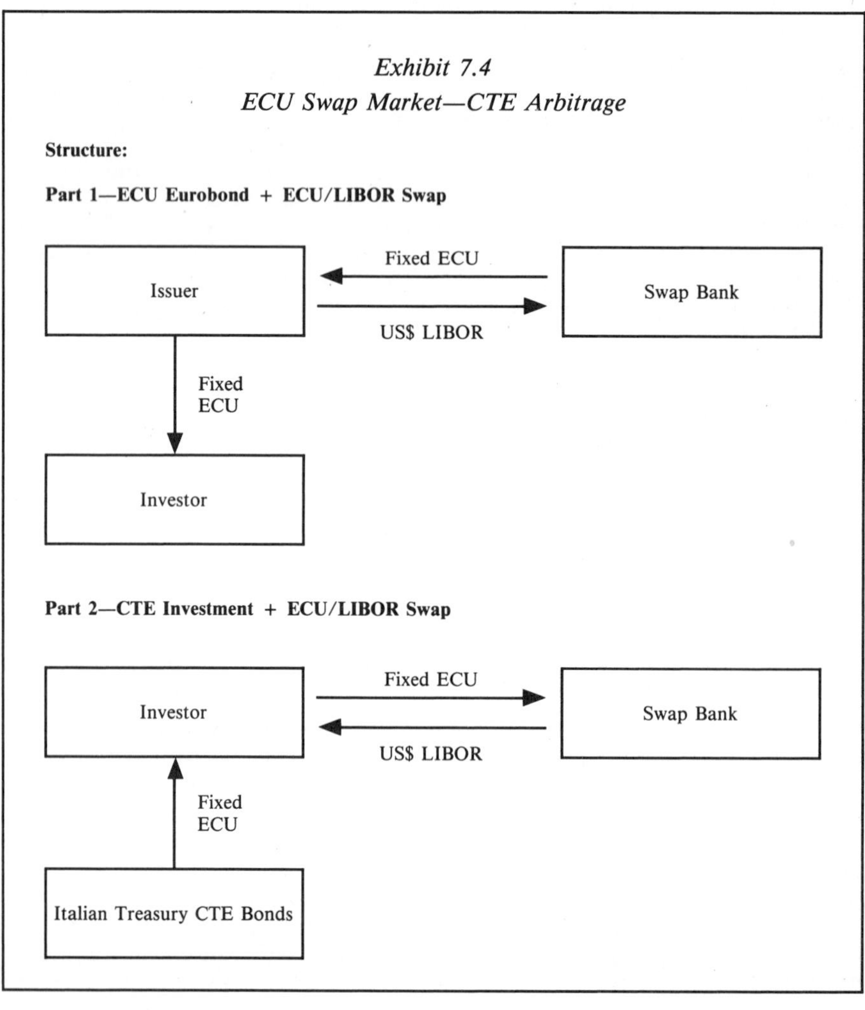

As a consequence of the existence of this tax arbitrage, issues of CTEs were, traditionally, followed by issuing activity in the primary ECU Eurobond market. However, the ECU swap market has become more efficient at anticipating this type of arbitrage, somewhat reducing arbitrage opportunities available.

Existence of the Italian withholding tax of 12.5% creates very similar arbitrage opportunities as between the Italian domestic bond market and the Eurolira bond market.

In summary, the presence of withholding tax impacts upon the pricing of capital flows across borders which may create significant differences in access and in the price of funding to different borrowers facilitating swap structures designed to arbitrage the withholding tax wedge.

Investment asset choice restrictions

Restrictions on choice of investment assets which usually limit fund managers from investing in certain types of instruments are common in a variety of markets. These restrictions are usually imposed either by regulatory authorities (both formally and informally) or by the fund itself based on prudential criteria. Restrictions usually operate on two levels:

- type of investment instrument, for example, use of futures or options may be restricted;
- currency and issuer location restrictions, for example, investment in foreign currency denominated investments or securities issued by foreign issuers may be subject to limitations.

Where such restrictions exist, particularly those imposed by regulatory authorities, fund managers often will undertake transactions designed to circumvent the limitations on investment choice to better achieve the fund's overall investment objectives. To achieve these objectives, the fund may undertake complex transactions designed to *indirectly* achieve what cannot be done *directly*. In these circumstances, the fund will inevitably undertake the transaction at a pricing level significantly above the market price level as the transaction cannot be undertaken directly resulting in arbitrage opportunities which can be exploited through swap structures.

In recent years the often byzantine nature of Japanese investment restrictions, during a period when Japanese fund managers and investors have sought to recycle substantial capital surpluses, has meant that the paradigm examples of these types of transactions entail Japanese investors. Several examples of these are outlined below. However, it is important to note that similar asset choice restrictions also pervade other markets and create equally attractive swap arbitrage opportunities from time to time.

In late 1984 and early 1985, Japanese investors sought to increase their exposure to foreign currency denominated securities. In particular, at that time, the high yields available on A$ securities made investment in A$ bonds particularly attractive. However, Japanese institutions were subject to a limitation which restricted investment in foreign currency securities to 10.00% of overall portfolios. At that time, the institutions' quota of foreign securities were close to or at the legal limit.

In early 1985, it became apparent that the 10.00% rule was subject to a minor exception. Issues of foreign currency denominated securities *by a Japanese resident company* did not, for some peculiar reason, count as part of the 10.00% foreign security quota. This exemption allied to the Japanese investors' appetite for A$

securities led to two issues by Japanese banks which were placed primarily with Japanese institutional investors. These issues were undertaken at substantially lower yields than the prevailing A$ government bond rates. The yield level accepted by investors reflected the fact that a comparison with domestic A$ interest rates was largely irrelevant as under existing rules they could not, had they desired to, invest in those instruments whereas they were able to purchase the A$ securities issued by the Japanese banks. The banks in turn converted their price advantage resulting from the demand for these A$ securities within Japan into low cost US$ funding by swapping with Australian domestic institutions who in turn achieved cost effective fixed rate A$ at levels unobtainable in the domestic A$, or indeed, any market at that point in time.

Another instance of tax and regulatory arbitrage entailing circumventing investment asset choice restrictions involves dual currency bonds. Until recently, under Japanese tax law, zero coupon bonds received extremely favourable treatment as the difference between the purchase price and the face value of the bond was treated as a capital gain and taxed at the favourable capital gains rate. However, the Ministry of Finance limited the amount a Japanese pension fund could invest in non-yen denominated bonds issued by foreign corporations. In response to these conditions, a number of issuers undertook issues of a zero coupon yen bond plus a dual currency bond with interest payments in yen and principal repayment in US$.

The Ministry of Finance ruled that the dual currency bonds qualified as a yen issue for purposes of pension fund investment restrictions, even though the dual currency bond had imbedded within it a US$ denominated zero coupon bond. Effectively, the zero coupon yen bond and dual currency yen and US$ bond combined respresented an investment in a normal coupon yen bond and an investment in a zero coupon US$ bond. However, this particular structure allowed issuers to capitalise on the desire of Japanese investors to diversify their portfolios internationally within the regulations imposed by regulatory authorities.

The fact that this particular structure allowed the investors to achieve an exposure otherwise not available to them, led to a pricing level which was particularly advantageous to the issuer who would usually swap the combined securities into a US$ exposure through a series of swap transactions. The cost achievable through that series of swaps was significantly better than that available from direct access to the US$ market.

In recent times, a wide variety of issue structures combining option, equity and commodity elements with securities have appeared. These option and forward embedded securities (which are discussed in more detail in Chapters 15, 16 and 17) have been structured to the specifications of investors, usually European or Japanese, who are unable to otherwise undertake futures and options transactions to hedge or position their portfolios. The fact that the direct alternative, that is, utilisation of futures and options contracts, are not directly available to these institutions has meant that they are willing to pay above market prices for the privilege of entering into these futures and options contracts indirectly. This cost benefit has usually been translated by the issuer of these securities into cheaper cost funding in the borrowers desired currency and interest rate basis through a number of swap transactions.

A non-Japanese example relevant in this context is the issue of US$ and A$ dual currency bonds in the United States domestic market designed to cater to the requirements of certain investor groups which have provided the basis for a number of swap arbitrage opportunities in recent times.

Tax differentials

Tax driven swap arbitrage usually focuses on the dissimilarity of taxation treatment across countries for similar financial instruments. Swap arbitrage involving withholding tax effects has already been discussed. The other two major categories of tax driven swap arbitrage are:

- the differential tax treatment of types of income in the hands of investors, or conversely the different characterisations and treatments of interest, expense etc, from the perspective of the borrower or issuer of securities;
- capital allowances, such as depreciation and one off large capital investment or expenditure allowances, made available by national governments to stimulate capital investment.

The second of these two sources of swap arbitrage predicated on tax factors is discussed in the later section on subsidised funding sources.

Swap arbitrage predicated on differential treatment of revenue and/or expense focuses on the fact that investors seek to maximise *after tax* income while borrowers seek to minimise *after tax* costs of funding. Where a particular issuance format, either entailing a particular combination of cash flows or the location of the borrower or investor in a particular tax jurisdiction, is tax effective, there is a natural incentive for both borrowers and investors to gravitate towards the particular format which respectively reduces after tax cost or increases after tax returns. This potential to enhance the economics of the transaction provides the essential arbitrage profit which can be allocated between the parties through a specially structured swap transaction. This process can be best illustrated with an example.

In the early 1980s, zero coupon securities emerged as an important financial instrument. While non-tax factors, such as reduction of reinvestment risk, call protection, price volatility and duration factors, were important in the emergence of these types of debt instruments, it was tax factors which were instrumental in the upsurge of interest in zero coupon securities.

Zero coupon securities were particularly attractive for investors who were either not taxed or who were taxed at concessional rates of interest on the discount (that is, the difference between purchase price and face value which constitutes the essential return to the investor). In a number of jurisdictions, such as Japan and several European countries, the difference between the investor's sale price and the purchase price of the discount security was treated as a non-taxable capital gain. In other jurisdictions, the discount was taxed at a concessional rate which was lower than the normal rate of taxation allowing investors to achieve significant improvements in return on holdings of zero coupon securities relative to normal coupon securities. Investors, as a result of these tax factors, were willing to purchase zero coupon securities at prices which were substantially higher (implying lower yields) than conventional securities. The higher price willing to be paid reflected the willingness of investors to share part of the return benefit on an after tax basis with the issuer.

Allied to the tax factors was the preference for the investors who enjoyed tax benefits of zero coupon securities to purchase bearer securities, usually Eurobonds, which allow holders to preserve their anonymity and also the lack of any withholding tax, which also favoured Eurobond issues. The particular investors were also concerned that the issuers be of a higher credit quality satisfying not only their normal credit requirements but the additional credit risk given that the full return on the investment was "back ended".

In this environment, borrowers satisfying the identified requirements were able to access fixed rate fundings on a zero coupon basis at significantly lower yield than through other sources. This cost advantage was able to be utilised as the basis for swap arbitrages. In particular, the fact that the issuers may not have wanted to use the funding generated in the particular cash flow pattern of a zero coupon security necessitated the development of particular swap structures designed to convert this all-in cost advantage to a more acceptable or preferable form. These structures are discussed in detail in the section on accelerated and deferred cash flow swaps in Chapter 12.

Other types of tax factors which create opportunities for swap arbitrage include:

- differential rates of income tax which create incentives for cross-border financial transactions conceived to defer or avoid income taxes;
- treatment for tax purposes of hedging transactions of different types;
- differential tax policies governing cross-border transfers;
- differential foreign tax credit systems.

Often tax factors are combined with other conditions which together provide opportunities for swap arbitrage.

Subsidised funding sources

A major source of swap arbitrage opportunities derives from the fact that particular borrowers may enjoy preferential access to subsidised financing sources. Examples of such subsidised financings include:

- export credit funding;
- tax based financing structures, including leasing.

Most developed nations exporting large amounts of capital goods have established agencies to assist their exporters in financing sales overseas. These agencies which are usually government departments or statutory bodies typically provide low cost finance, or interest subsidies, as an inducement to foreign purchase of major items of capital investment. This type of export credit financing is clearly linked to the purchase of the underlying capital goods but is usually also subject to significant restrictions as to the terms and conditions of the financing, in particular the currency and interest rate basis.

A purchaser of capital goods with access to export credit financing can, therefore, find itself in the position of having access to finance on preferential terms relative to the market but in a currency or on an interest rate basis which differs from its preferred liability structure. In these circumstances, the potential arbitrage profit locked into its preferential funding sources can be mobilised through a swap structure to allow the borrower to achieve its desired mix of liabilities.

Tax based financing opportunities, particularly in the area of leasing, function in a similiar way. As noted above, government policies designed to stimulate capital investment usually provide for large capital investment allowances in the form of depreciation or immediate write-offs. Potential users of equipment attracting such advantageous tax treatment, either directly through purchase or indirectly by some type of lease or hire arrangement, can usually structure financing arrangements designed to lower the all-in cost based on the available tax advantages. A limitation of this type of financing is that the tax advantage may dictate the financing being structured on a currency or interest rate basis other than the borrower's preferred liability structure. As in the case of export credits, this creates the opportunity for utilisation of swap arbitrage structures predicated on the tax-based financing arrangements generating a more attractive cost structure than normal financing arrangements.

Miscellaneous arbitrages

Two other sources of swap arbitrage require mention:

- incomplete markets;
- transaction costs.

The opportunity for swaps arbitrage is also partially predicated on the incomplete nature of capital markets. In this regard, swaps contribute to the integration of financial markets by allowing market participants to fill gaps left by the unavailability of particular types of financial instruments. The use of swaps to overcome institutional market limitations is particularly apparent in Australia. For example, the institutional structure of the Australian debt market did not encompass, until very recently, a substantial long-term fixed rate corporate debt market. A factor underpinning the growth of A$ swaps is that such transactions allow corporations to generate fixed rate A$ liabilities under circumstances where such transactions are not directly available.

Transaction costs as a source of swap arbitrage are more complex. Various types of transaction costs are identifiable including the requirement for confidentiality, queuing restrictions and the opportunity to lock in gains or minimise losses on particular borrowings.

There are many reasons why a borrower may want to keep its fund raising behaviour in a particular market confidential. Where confidentiality is an issue, the borrower's objectives can be accomplished by using proxy borrowers in the desired market which forms the basis of currency and/or interest rate swaps into the borrower's preferred form of liability. In these circumstances, the advantage of confidentiality manifests itself in the form of the willingness on the part of the borrower to pay a premium for access in this particular form which can form the basis of the swap arbitrage.

The requirement of confidentiality by particular borrowers may be motivated by such factors as the desire to avoid review by rating agencies or governmental bodies.

Another form of transaction cost is the queuing procedure often applied by different national governments which dictates the timing and order of access to particular capital markets. In essence, to control the flow of investment funds, financial authorities in many countries establish a quota of financing that is available to borrowers of particular types in each financing period. Borrowers apply for permission to borrow and, if approved, are placed in a queue until their turn to borrow arrives. In certain circumstances, the queue can be extremely lengthy, being as much as one year in length.

The existence of a queuing system creates problems in the sense that borrowers must be able to anticipate market conditions and their own financial requirements considerably in advance. Given the volatility of currency and interest rate markets, it is possible that even where the financial requirement has been anticipated in advance, the period between entering into the queue and being eligible to borrow may mean that market conditions have worsened significantly from those anticipated at the time the borrowing was contemplated.

In these circumstances, borrowers can either accelerate or defer borrowings when in a queue by entering into a swap with another borrower. To accelerate its borrowing, the borrower would usually enter into a swap with a party which has currently arrived at the head of the queue. Where the borrower seeks to defer its borrowing in the particular currency or on the interest rate basis previously contemplated, the borrower having reached the head of the queue would undertake the borrowing transaction and swap out of the liability into a preferred interest rate or currency basis more in line with its expectations and requirements at the time of issue.

In these circumstances, the borrower in the queue may be willing to pay a premium to accelerate or defer its transaction creating a natural arbitrage gain which can be the basis for swap transactions. A major factor underlying swaps predicated on queuing positions is that national regulatory authorities tend to take an unfavourable view of borrowers who, having positioned themselves in a queue, upon reaching the appropriate borrowing position do not undertake the originally contemplated transaction.

The desire of borrowers to lock in currency and interest rate gains or alternatively to minimise losses from market movements also creates the basis of swap arbitrage. Unless fully hedged, currency and interest rate transactions may result in accumulated gains or losses after their inception. Rather than run the risk that an unrealised book gain will be dissipated or a book loss increased by subsequent changes in market conditions, organisations may undertake swaps to lock in the size of the gain or loss at its present level. In this context, the use of swaps becomes relevant for a number of factors:

- Alternative means of covering the exposures may not be available. For example, the borrowing may not be able to be repaid because of contractual agreements or penalties. These transaction costs create an incentive for the borrower in question to pay a premium to undertake the swap facilitating the swap arbitrage.
- Even where eligible to undertake the transaction by alternative means, market protocol may dictate that the borrower should not, in order to preserve its access to the particular sector, retire or otherwise restructure its borrowings. In these circumstances, an incentive exists for the borrower to once again pay a premium to achieve its objectives thereby indirectly providing the arbitrage gain which can form the basis of swap transactions.
- The potential dissipation of any gain or aggravation of any loss, depending on the rate expectations of the organisation, and the likelihood of such an outcome eventuating may be so great that the borrowers are once again willing to pay a substantial premium which can provide the source of swap arbitrage.

Swap arbitrage sources: some comments

In considering the various sources of swap arbitrage, it is important to note that in a given market, several of the factors identified may coexist and combine to provide the basis of swap activity. Some aspects of this complex interaction of various elements are evident in the analysis of swap arbitrages in the A$ market later in this chapter.

A persistent problem in seeking to explain the economics and pricing of swaps in terms of arbitrage is the problem of arbitrage erosion. In classical arbitrage, the very process of exploiting this type of opportunity would soon eliminate it. However, a careful analysis of the various sources of swap arbitrage suggests that a substantial number of them are structural in nature. This essentially means that growth in swap activity while it may have the impact of reducing the scale of the arbitrage profit, does not of itself *eliminate* (as distinct from *reduce*) the arbitrage profit.

In the case of tax and regulatory arbitrage, in particular, there is no reason for the arbitrage opportunity to disappear, at least until the relevant tax or regulatory provisions are altered.

In summary, while opportunities for classical financial arbitrage employing swaps may be eroded by competition, several of the sources of swap arbitrage profit are embedded in the very structure of modern capital markets and, in particular, the imperfection of contracting arrangements and regulatory regimes particularly as between national markets.

SWAP ARBITRAGE IN THE A$ MARKET: A CASE STUDY

The complex process by which swap arbitrage operates in specific markets is best understood with reference to an actual example. The example utilised in this section is of swap arbitrage in the A$ market. The data utilised is hypothetical, although it is fairly typical of conditions which have existed in this market.

The various cost and access opportunities relevant to A$ currency swap arbitrage are set out in *Exhibit 7.5. Exhibit 7.6* sets out the various cost differentials as between various participants in the market.

Exhibit 7.5
A$ Currency Swap Arbitrage Matrix

Entity	**A$ fixed rate funding typical costs**	**A$ floating rate funding typical costs**	**US$ floating rate funding typical costs**
Sovereigns	B − 25	BBR − 35	LIBOR − 12.50
AAA/AA + "name" multinationals	B − 20	BBR − 25	LIBOR − 12.50
International banks	B − 10	BBR − 25	LIBOR − 6.25
Commonwealth of Australia	B	BBR − 10	LIBOR − 12.50
Semi-government instrumentalities	B + 90	BBR	LIBOR − 6.25
Australian banks	B + 100	BBR	LIBOR − 6.25
Finance companies	B + 140	BBR + 30	LIBOR + 25
Prime corporates	B + 140	BBR + 20	LIBOR + 10
Lower rated corporates	B + 250/ unavailable	BBR + 70	LIBOR + 125/ unavailable

Perusal of the two exhibits reveals the following distinguishing features of the cost of funding the various participants in the different market segments:

- In the A$ fixed rate funding market, there is minimal differentiation between four entities, namely, sovereign borrowers, multinational borrowers, international banks and the Commonwealth. There is also significant bunching in the typical A$ fixed rate funding costs as between semi-government instrumentalities (semis), banks (which are taken to be Australian banks), finance companies and prime corporates.
- In the A$ floating rate funding market, there appear to be three separate categories of borrower costs:
  - sovereigns, multinationals and international banks;
  - the Commonwealth, semis and Australian banks;
  - finance companies, prime corporates and lower rated corporates.

Exhibit 7.6

A$ Swap Arbitrage: Cost Differentials (bps)

	Sovereigns	AAA/AA + multinational	International bank	Commonwealth	Semi-government instrumentalities	Australian banks	Finance companies	Prime corporates	Lower rated corporates
Sovereigns	— — —	5 (10) [0]	15 (10) [6.25]	25 (25) [0]	115 (35) [6.25]	125 (35) [6.25]	165 (65) [37.50]	165 (55) [22.50]	275 (105) [137.50]
AAA/AA + "name" multinational			10 (0) [6.25]	20 (15) [0]	110 (25) [6.25]	120 (25) [6.25]	160 (55) [37.50]	160 (45) [22.50]	270 (95) [137.50]
International bank				10 (15) [−6.25]	100 (25) [0]	110 (25) [0]	150 (55) [31.25]	150 (45) [16.25]	260 (95) [131.25]
Commonwealth					90 (10) [6.25]	100 (10) [6.25]	140 (40) [37.25]	140 (30) [22.50]	250 (80) [137.50]
Semi-government instrumentalities						10 (0) [0]	50 (30) [31.25]	50 (30) [16.25]	160 (70) [131.25]
Australian banks							40 (30) [31.25]	40 (20) [16.25]	150 (70) [131.25]
Finance companies								0 (−10) [−15]	110 (40) [100]
Prime corporates									110 (50) [115]

Notes:

1. Figures without brackets refer to cost differentials in A$ fixed rate funding.
2. Figures in ( ) refer to A$ floating rate cost differentials.
3. Figures in [ ] refer to US$ floating rate funding differentials.

- In the US$ floating rate funding market, a number of dominant groupings emerge. These are the lower rated corporates, the prime corporates and finance companies, and all the other parties.

The differential access of the different groupings to different market segments appear to be predicated on a number of factors. One of the major determinants of the various cost differentials appears to be the distinction between onshore and offshore fund raising. For example, the A$ fixed rate and floating rate costs of sovereigns, multinationals and international banks are based on issues outside the A$ domestic market.

In the A$ fixed rate market, this distinction appears based on the presence of Australian withholding tax which leads investors outside of Australia to favour the purchase of issues structured as Eurobonds and thereby free of withholding tax in preference to the purchase of higher yielding securities issued in the A$ domestic market. The presence of withholding tax means that these investors are prepared to buy securities structured in this manner at substantial yield concessions to prevailing yields in the domestic market relative to the comparative credit standing of the parties. Additional factors include investor preference for the anonymity available in the form of bearer Eurobond securities as well as a preference for borrowers well known to the lenders. The fact that Australian organisations are not well known to the particular international investor groups attracted to A$ securities means that investors are willing to sacrifice yield in investing in securities issued by sovereigns, multinationals and international banks.

Similar conditions form the basis of the pricing differences of the A$ floating rate market. The substantially lower cost of A$ floating rate funding for sovereigns, multinationals etc, is predicated on the fact that these funds are supplied by offshore investors, primarily in Europe and Asia, seeking withholding tax-free investments in bearer form with a bias to well known issuers.

The factors identified to date do not of themselves indicate the reasons underlying the demand by overseas investors for A$ securities. This demand is clearly predicated on factors such as currency and interest rate expectations and portfolio diversification objectives. In particular, during the period in question, the fact that A$ securities yielded significantly higher nominal interest returns relative to securities denominated in other currencies, prompted investor demand on the basis that the currency risk intrinsic to the A$ investment was more than compensated for by the higher available yield.

In contrast, domestic A$ investors whose home currency is the A$ would continue to buy A$ securities for normal asset and liability matching reasons and the demand factors relevant to these investors are significantly different to those affecting international investors. The different investment motivations mean that if international investment sentiment changes, leading to a reduction in the demand for A$ securities, the different yields demanded by A$ investors in taking on A$ currency risk would change the typical A$ fixed rate and floating rate funding costs which would be reflected in the A$ currency swap arbitrage pricing.

Other factors affecting the structure of the pricing differentials include:

- the institutional structure of the A$ domestic market which dictates that a limited and relatively expensive term debt market for borrowers other than primarily the Commonwealth, semis and, to a lesser extent, banks exists. This means that prime corporates and lower rated corporates rely on swaps as a means of synthetically filling this market gap;

- the structure of international markets and investor preferences which favour non-Australian issuers of A$ securities in international markets forcing borrowers seeking fixed rate A$ to resort to swaps with borrowers such as sovereigns, multinationals etc, with preferential access to fixed rate A$;
- within the A$ market, credit arbitrage considerations which dictate that higher rated credits such as the semi-government instrumentalities enjoy preferential access to fixed rate A$ funding;
- spread compression in the floating rate US$ markets reflecting very small risk differentials predicated, in all likelihood, on excess market liquidity and competition between financial institutions seeking to obtain quality assets;
- a marked bias in the behaviour of international US$ lenders against lower rated Australian corporates.

Under these circumstances, the pricing structure as between the markets dictates that the most likely arbitrage transaction is likely to be between two groups: sovereigns, multinationals or international banks (as A$ fixed rate borrowers) and the semis, Australian banks, prime corporates etc (as users of fixed A$ funding). The focus of the arbitrage as between these two parties is dictated by the natural preferences of both groups of borrowers and the fact that the arbitrage gain, when adjusted for the differential credit risk that must be assumed through the swap, is at a relatively high level for this type of transaction.

Assume that at this time the swap arbitrage is being driven predominantly by international issuers and Australian semis. This reflects the fact that investors seeking A$ securities, primarily European investors, favour borrowers well known to them while the semis have an extensive A$ borrowing programme during the current period and they wish to diversify their sources of funding.

In these circumstances, currency swap structures similar to those set out in *Exhibit* 7.7 might evolve.

Exhibit 7.7

A$ Currency Swap Transaction

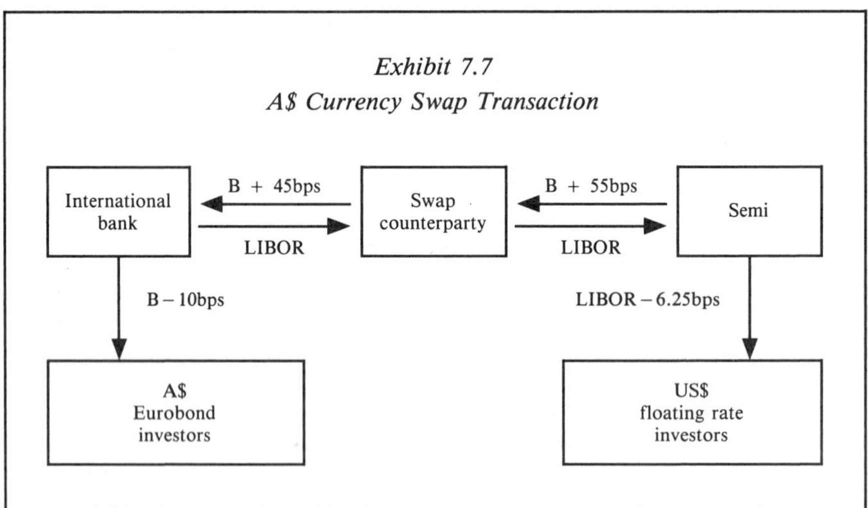

Under the structure depicted, the international bank achieves funding at LIBOR minus 55bps, while the semi achieves funding at a cost of bonds plus 48.75bps. The overall swap arbitrage gain of 100bps, reflecting the difference in the relative fixed

A$ funding costs as both parties have the same US$ floating rate funding costs, is split as follows:

Semi	41.25bps
International bank	48.75bps
Swap counterparty	10.00bps

The split of the arbitrage gain between the two parties is dictated by competitive factors, supply and demand etc. In this case, the division of the swap arbitrage gain, that is, the nominated sub-LIBOR level required by the international bank to undertake the issue on the basis of a swap into floating rate US$ will be driven by other swap arbitrage opportunities available to it. For example, it may at this point in time have available to it other swap driven issues in say yen, NZ$, C$ etc. The sub-LIBOR levels available in these other markets will to a large extent determine the level required to undertake an A$ issue. The riskiness of the issue and its likelihood of success, the state of the A$ Eurobond market etc, will also be relevant. For a more detailed analysis of the factors underlying the decision to take advantage of this swap arbitrage, see the discussion of new issue arbitrage in Chapter 19.

The swap pricing in this example will also be determined by the level of competition between the semi-government and Australian banks to raise fixed A$. For example, since the arbitrage gain as between the international bank and the Australian bank is slightly higher, 110bps as against 100bps, if the credit risk of the two entities is comparable or at least the credit risk premium is less than 10bps, an opportunity exists for the Australian bank to agree to a higher fixed A$ rate flow under the swap fundamentally altering the division of the arbitrage gain for the semi if it still wishes to transact the swap.

The swap transaction itself has a number of effects. In the first instance, the availability of the swap means that the A$ currency swap arbitrage matrix must be altered to reflect the changed A$ fixed rate funding cost for the semi and the altered US$ floating rate funding cost for the international bank. The change in cost structure of the matrix will result in consequential changes in the relative cost differentials as between the various parties. The matrix and the cost differentials can be reworked. The change in the relative status of different parties as a result of the undertaking of the swap transaction would of itself create new arbitrage opportunities as between various participants.

At a more fundamental level, the altered borrowing behaviour of various market participants will lead to a change in their relative borrowing costs. The increased volume of A$ securities on issue from international banks, both individually and as a group, as well as the reduction in A$ securities issued by semis in the domestic market will lead to an alteration in the pricing structure. Similar effects in the US$ floating rate market will be evident. These changes will also, by engineering changes in the relative cost differentials, lead to a reconfiguration of the arbitrage opportunities in the market.

Exogenous factors such as changed market expectations as to currency and interest rates will also impact on the process of currency swap arbitrage. For example, if A$ interest rates were expected to increase in absolute term or the A$, relative to the home currencies of the investors, is expected to depreciate, investor demand for A$ securities internationally would show a significant decrease. In terms of the currency swap arbitrage, this would manifest itself in the form of an altered A$ fixed rate funding cost for sovereigns, multinationals etc. This in turn, will alter relative cost differentials creating a different set of arbitrage opportunities.

The behaviour of market participants also has the scope to fundamentally alter the pattern of currency swap arbitrage described. For example, the swap counterparty could fundamentally alter the pricing levels in the market if it were willing to:

- Reallocate the fixed A$ funding to other parties, say lower rated corporations. This assumes that the swap counterparty is willing to assume the higher credit risk entailed.
- The swap counterparty could seek to unbundle the arbitrage and maximise its own earnings, for example, by transacting fixed A$ against floating rate A$ swaps with lower rated corporates where the potential arbitrage profit is at a very substantial level and managing the US$ and A$ risks by floating rate A$ and US$ swaps with say semis, Australian banks, finance companies or prime corporates. In this case, the dual level of credit risk must be factored into increased potential earnings from this unbundling process.

Other categories of market participants may also intervene in the pricing process. For example, a potential fixed rate A$ investor could create higher yielding investments by purchasing floating rate US$ securities issued by international banks and swapping them into a fixed rate A$ investment with the swap counterparty at a yield of approximately bonds plus 38.75bps. This is clearly superior to the investment return achieveable by direct purchase of A$ securities issued by the international bank at bonds minus 10bps. Implicit in this analysis is that the swap counterparty and the international banks are of a similar credit quality and that the liquidity of the underlying security plus swap package is comparable to that of the A$ security purchased directly. Alternatively, the higher yield is sufficient to more than compensate for any added credit risk and/or loss of liquidity.

The process of swap arbitrage, particularly the various levels of interaction, are both complex and difficult to model accurately. This is because the basic arbitrage process itself is subject to numerous, often unpredictable, factors which, furthermore, have complex interrelationships. The above example utilising the A$ currency swap market highlights some of the factors underlying this process of interaction which is fundamental in determining the economics of swap arbitrage.

Chapter 8

Swap Yield Mathematics and Swap Valuation

INTRODUCTION

The yield mathematics of interest rate and currency swaps encompasses the arithmetical and technical steps utilised to value individual swap transactions. In essence, the yield mathematics starts with a given swap price (driven by the underlying pricing economics discussed in Chapter 7) and translates it, mathematically, to an equivalent price for the specific swap being analysed.

The arithmetical and technical procedures utilised are common to all financial transactions and are not necessarily peculiar to swaps. However, swap transactions give rise to particular complexities which are considered in detail in this chapter.

The basic complexities of pricing swap transactions arise from two sources:

- the different methods for calculating yields in different markets; and
- the fact that swap transactions are seldom of a standard type.

Yield calculations vary significantly between markets as do a number of variables such as the manner in which interest payments are made, the frequency of payments, the relevant day basis and the compounding method used. In addition, standard market prices, such as those made available on Telerate, Reuters etc screens, are usually confined to transactions of a standard type. The most important variations cover commencement dates, transaction size, spreads above or below the floating rate indexes, various mismatches, premium or discounts or reimbursement of issue fees and expenses. Price adjustments are usually necessary to accommodate these variations.

SWAPS—PRICING CONVENTIONS

Exhibit 8.1 sets out examples of typical swap quotations in a number of currencies.

The cost of a typical interest rate swap is expressed in the rates on the fixed and floating interest payments. More specifically, the price on an interest rate swap of a given maturity is quoted as a fixed rate (for example, 10.00% pa) against a floating rate index, quoted flat (that is, with no margin over or under the index).

In a number of markets, the price on a generic interest rate swap is quoted as a spread over a fixed rate index against the floating rate index flat.

For example, in US$ interest rate swaps, an intermediary might quote the price on a seven year fixed rate US$ against LIBOR swap to a fixed rate payer as "the seven year treasury rate plus 60bps versus six month LIBOR". A$ interest rate swaps are priced relative to the State government bond curve against BBR flat as the floating rate index. A number of other markets also follow a similar quoting convention with the fixed rate being expressed usually as a margin over the appropriate government bond rate. However, in markets other than the US$ swap market, the relationship of swap rates to the comparable government securities rate may be inconsistent and weak.

Exhibit 8.1
Swap Market Quotations

Capital Markets Information Service

05/04 15:13 EDT (C) 1993 [MKT DATA CORP SOURCE: TULLETT & TOKYO] PAGE 19901

LDN 827-2345 TK 241-8771 [U.S. INTEREST RATE SWAPS] SYD 223-3500 NY 208-2160

PRICE	YIELD	YL MID	SPREAD	BOND SA 365	SEMI A 360	ANNUAL 360
2 Y 100.08 −082	3.743 − 739	3.741	22/19	3.96 − 3.93	3.91 − 3.88	3.94 − 3.91
3 Y 101.09 + −10	4.125 − 119	4.122	37/34	4.49 − 4.46	4.43 − 4.40	4.48 − 4.45
4 Y **		4.574	36/33	4.93 − 4.90	4.87 − 4.84	4.93 − 4.90
5 Y 100.13 + −136	5.028 − 026	5.027	27/24	5.30 − 5.27	5.22 − 5.20	5.29 − 5.26
7 Y 100.02 + HIT	5.486 HIT	5.486	34/31	5.83 − 5.80	5.75 − 5.72	5.83 − 5.80
10Y 102.16 −17	5.908 − 904	5.906	35/32	6.26 − 6.23	6.17 − 6.14	6.27 − 6.24

** − 4Y YLD Interpolated. SWAP Rates Calculated From YLD Midpoint. *B/E = Break Even

EURO $ DEPOSITS	1Y EURO$ B/E*	SHRT FWD B/E	FORWARD	FORWARD	SWAPS
6M 3.5000 −3.4500	JUN/JUN 3.47	2 − 26 4.08	1 − 3 5.04 −	4.94 1 − 5	5.84 − 5.74
1Y 3.5625 −3.4375	SEP/SEP 3.70	3 − 27 4.17	2 − 4 6.04 −	5.94 2 − 6	6.54 − 6.44
2Y 4.1875 −4.0625	DEC/DEC 3.98	4 − 28 4.26	3 − 5 6.71 −	6.61 3 − 7	7.08 − 6.98
3Y 4.7500 −4.6250	MAR/MAR 4.27	5 − 29 4.34	5 − 7 7.48 −	7.38 1 − 6	6.08 − 5.98
4Y 5.1875 −5.0625	* IMM. FROM	6 − 30 4.45	1 − 4 5.49 −	5.39 2 − 7	6.77 − 6.67
5Y 5.5625 −5.4375	1220-1900 GM 1	7 − 31 4.55	2 − 5 6.34 −	6.24 5 − 10	7.59 − 7.49
[STG 1.5655-60 YEN 110.25-29 DM 1.5753-63 AU$ 0.6983-93]				1 − 7	6.34 − 6.24

TELERATE Page 19901

US Dollar Interest Rate Swaps

- Live market prices and yields on US government securities: two years to 10 years; source: Cantor Fitzgerald.
- Live swap rates for semi-annual bond, annual and semi-annual money market interest rate assumptions.
- 1 Year IMM swap rates and break-evens.
- Short forward and forward forward swaps.
- Spot foreign exchange rates for STG, YEN, DM, and AU$.

24-hour coverage.

In markets where swaps are quoted on a spread basis, the precise definition of the benchmark bond rate can be the subject of dispute and will normally be agreed upon at the time of commitment. Generally, it is either:

- the yield on an actively traded security with the relevant maturity; if the swap's maturity lies between that of two actively traded securities, the yield must be interpolated; or
- the yield to maturity of a specific bond or bond with a maturity closest to that of the swap.

The second approach is often criticised because it does not exclude thinly traded securities with anomalous prices.

Exhibit 8.1—continued

Capital Markets Information Service

05/04 15:13 EDT (C) 1993 [MKT DATA CORP SOURCE: TULLETT & TOKYO] PAGE 19902
CURRENCY INTEREST RATE SWAPS [SEE ALSO 19901-08]

CHF (30/360) P.A.		ECU (30/360) P.A.		EURO FF (30/360) P.A.		STG/STG (A/365) SA	
[2 YR]	4.52 – 4.46	[2 YR]	7.47 – 7.42	[2 YR]	7.19 – 7.13	[2 YR]	6.73 – 6.70
[3 YR]	4.51 – 4.45	[3 YR]	7.47 – 7.42	[3 YR]	7.20 – 7.14	[3 YR]	7.19 – 7.16
[4 YR]	4.61 – 4.55	[4 YR]	7.47 – 7.42	[4 YR]	7.23 – 7.17	[4 YR]	7.57 – 7.54
[5 YR]	4.72 – 4.66	[5 YR]	7.47 – 7.42	[5 YR]	7.25 – 7.19	[5 YR]	7.76 – 7.74
[7 YR]	4.91 – 4.85	[7 YR]	7.66 – 7.61	[7 YR]	7.41 – 7.35	[7 YR]	8.14 – 8.09
[10 YR]	5.12 – 5.06	[10 YR]	7.71 – 7.66	[10 YR]	7.56 – 7.50	[10 YR]	8.38 – 8.33
DM/DM (30/360) P.A.		**YEN/USD (A/365) SA**		**YEN/YEN (A/365) SA**		**NLG (30/360) P.A.**	
[2 YR]	6.51 – 6.47	[2 YR]	3.76 – 3.68	[2 YR]	3.77 – 3.74	[2 YR]	6.53 – 6.47
[3 YR]	6.51 – 6.47	[3 YR]	4.14 – 4.06	[3 YR]	4.15 – 4.11	[3 YR]	6.58 – 5.51
[4 YR]	6.53 – 6.49	[4 YR]	4.57 – 4.49	[4 YR]	4.57 – 4.55	[4 YR]	6.63 – 6.57
[5 YR]	6.63 – 6.59	[5 YR]	4.77 – 4.69	[5 YR]	4.77 – 4.75	[5 YR]	6.73 – 6.65
[7 YR]	6.82 – 6.78	[7 YR]	5.00 – 4.92	[7 YR]	5.01 – 4.97	[7 YR]	6.90 – 6.83
[10 YR]	7.02 – 6.98	[10 YR]	5.09 – 5.01	[10 YR]	5.11 – 5.07	[10 YR]	7.05 – 6.98

LDN 827-2345		[STERLING]	[YEN]	[D/MARK]	SYD 223-3500
TOK 241-8771	FX SPOT	1.5655-60	110.25-29	1.5753-63	NY 208-2160

TELERATE Page 19902

Currency Interest Rate Swaps

- Fixed Swiss franc (CHF) to 6 month LIBOR.
- Fixed Eurocurrency Unit (ECU) to 6 month ECU LIBOR.
- Fixed French franc (FF) rate to 6 month FF LIBOR.
- Fixed British pound (STG) to 6 month STG LIBOR.
- Fixed Deutschemark (DM) to 6 month DM LIBOR.
- Fixed Japanese yen rate to 6 month YEN LIBOR.
- Fixed YEN rate to 6 month US dollar LIBOR.
- Fixed Dutch guilder (NLG) rate to 6 month NLG LIBOR.
- Spot STG, YEN, DM.

24-hour coverage.

The price of a typical currency swap is quoted in a manner very similar to that utilised in the case of interest rate swaps. Typically, the price of a currency swap of a given maturity is quoted as a fixed rate (expressed as either an absolute rate or as a spread over the relevant fixed rate index in the currency) against the receipt of US$ three or six month LIBOR. For example, A$ currency swaps might be quoted as 11% pa against US$ six month LIBOR. Alternatively, the same currency swap could be quoted as the relevant A$ bond plus a margin of 60bps versus US$ six month LIBOR flat.

Exhibit 8.1—continued

Capital Markets Information Service

05/04 15:13 EDT (C) 1993 [MKT DATA CORP SOURCE: TULLETT & TOKYO] PAGE 19903
CURRENCY INTEREST RATE SWAPS [SEE ALSO 19901-08]

AUS$ (A/365) S.A.		CURRENT CAD BONDS		YIELD	SPREAD	CAD (A/365) S.A.	
[2 YR]	5.97 – 5.90Q	[2 YR]	7.00 MAR 95	6.414	25/22	[2 YR]	6.664 – 6.634
[3 YR]	6.65 – 6.58Q	[3 YR]	6.50 AUG 96*	6.617	45/42	[3 YR]	7.067 – 7.037
[4 YR]	6.99 – 6.92S	[4 YR]	INTERPOLATE	6.728	58/54	[4 YR]	7.308 – 7.268
[5 YR]	7.26 – 6.18S	[5 YR]	6.25 FEB 98	6.839	58/54	[5 YR]	7.419 – 7.379
[7 YR]	7.65 – 7.58S	[7 YR]	INTERPOLATE	7.089	58/54	[7 YR]	7.669 – 7.629
[10 YR]	7.94 – 7.86S	[10 YR]	7.25 JUN 03	7.465	52/48	[10 YR]	7.985 – 7.945

JAPAN LTPR FLAT VS. 6M YEN LIBOR APR. 30		HK$ (A/365) Q.A.		U.S. GOVERNMENTS			SPOT FX	
[2 YR]	YLIB + 208/178	[2 YR]	4.30 – 4.20	2Y	100.081	3.741	STG	1.5653-63
[3 YR]	YLIB + 193/163	[3 YR]	4.90 – 4.80	3Y	101.096	4.122	YEN	110.26-32
[4 YR]	YLIB + 167/137	[4 YR]	5.45 – 5.35	5Y	100.13 +	5.028	DM	1.5752-62
[5 YR]	YLIB + 156/126	[5 YR]	5.85 – 5.75	7Y	100.02 +	5.486	CA$	1.2710-14
		[7 YR]	6.40 – 6.30	10Y	102.16	5.908	AU$	0.6983-93
		[10 YR]	7.00 – 6.90	30Y	104.026	6.802	FF	5.3095-15

[AUSTRALIA 612-223-3500] [HONG KONG 85-5-8107325/825-5-8107361]

[NEW YORK 208-2160] [TOKYO 241-8771] [LONDON 827-2345] [SYDNEY 223-3500]

TELERATE Page 19903

Currency Interest Rate Swaps

- Fixed Australian dollar rate to floating 90-day Australian bank bill rate.
- Fixed Canadian dollar rate (spread to Canadian treasury bill) to floating 90-day Canadian BAs.
- Fixed Hong Kong dollar rate to floating 90-day Hong Kong dollar LIBOR.
- Live trade prices and yields for active US government notes and bonds from Cantor Fitzgerald.
- Spot FX rates for STG, YEN, DM, CA$, AU$, FF.

24-hour coverage.

Exhibit 8.1—continued

Capital Markets Information Service

05/04 15:13 EDT (C) 1993	[MKT DATA CORP SOURCE: TULLETT & TOKYO]			PAGE 19904
STG 1.5653-63	US$ BASIS/INDEX SWAPS			[SEE ALSO 19901-08]
US $ PRIME/LIBOR	BASIS SWAP	STG LIBOR/US $ LIBOR		
TERM REC PAY	TERM	REC	PAY	VS
2 Y P−232 −237	3 Y		ST FLAT	6M FLAT
3 Y P−221 −227	4 Y	ST+ 1/16	ST FLAT	6M FLAT
4 Y P−211 −218	5 Y	ST+ 1/16	ST FLAT	6M FLAT
5 Y P−205 −212	7 Y	ST+ 1/8	ST FLAT	6M FLAT
7 Y P−192 −202	10 Y	ST+ 1/8	ST FLAT	6M FLAT
US PRIME/FIXED US	INDEX SWAP	US $ LIBOR/US $ LIBOR		
TERM REC PAY	TERM	REC	PAY	VS
2 Y P−251 −259	2 Y			6M FLAT
3 Y P−255 −264	3 Y	3M +5	3M FLAT	6M FLAT
4 Y P−244 −254	4 Y	3M +5	3M FLAT	6M FLAT
5 Y P−229 −239	5 Y	3M +5	3M FLAT	6M FLAT
7 Y P−223 −236	7 Y	3M +5	3M FLAT	6M FLAT

CANTOR FITZGERALD	2Y	3Y	5Y	7Y	10Y	30Y
U.S. GOV YIELDS	3.741	4.122	5.028	5.484	6.904	6.802

TELERATE Page 19904

US Dollar Basis/Index Swaps

- Floating US dollar prime rate (Federal Reserve H.15 Report) to US dollar LIBOR.
- British pound sterling (STG) LIBOR to US dollar LIBOR.
- Floating US dollar prime rate (Federal Reserve H.15 Report) to fixed US swap rate (spread to US Treasury).
- US dollar 30 month LIBOR to US dollar 6 month LIBOR, or other index as activity warrants.
- Live yields for active US government notes and bonds from Cantor Fitzgerald.
- Spot STG.

24-hour coverage.

Exhibit 8.1—continued

Capital Markets Information Service

05/04 15:13 EDT (C) 1993 [MKT DATA CORP SOURCE: TULLETT & TOKYO] PAGE 19905								
[LDN 827-2345]	[TOK 241-8771]	INT RATE BASIS SWAPS	[SYD 223-3500]	[NY 208-2160]				
FIXED TRSY YLO/COM PAPER			COMMERCIAL PAPER/US$ LIBOR					
	REC	PAY		REC	PAY	VS		
2 Y	+20	+14	2 YR	C.P.+05	C.P.+02	1M FLAT		
3 Y	+34	+28	3 YR	C.P.+06	C.P.+03	3M FLAT		
4 Y	+33	+27	4 YR	C.P.+06	C.P.+03	3M FLAT		
5 Y	+24	+18	5 YR	C.P.+06	C.P.+03	3M FLAT		
7 Y	+29	+23	7 YR	C.P.+08	C.P.+05	3M FLAT		
FIXED TRSY YLD/T BILLS			TREASURY BILLS/US$ LIBOR					
	REC	PAY		REC	PAY	VS		
2 Y	−8	−17	2 YR	TB +36	TB +30	3M FLAT		
3 Y		−9	3 YR	TB +43	TB +37	3M FLAT		
4 Y	−4	−15	4 YR	TB +48	TB +40	3M FLAT		
5 Y	−16	−26	5 YR	TB +50	TB +43	3M FLAT		
7 Y	−14	−27	7 YR	TB +58	TB +48	3M FLAT		
CANTOR FITZGERALD	3M	6M	1Y	2Y	3Y	5Y	7Y	
US GOV YIELDS	2.926	3.047	3.219	3.741	4.122	5.028	5.486	

TELERATE Page 19905

Interest Rate Basis Swaps

- Fixed US Treasury rate to floating commercial paper rate (Federal Reserve H.15 Report).
- Fixed US Treasury rate and spread to floating US Treasury bill rate (weekly auction).
- Floating commercial paper rate (Federal Reserve H.15 Report) to US dollar LIBOR.
- Floating 90-day US Treasury bill rate (weekly auction) rate to floating 6 month US dollar LIBOR.
- Live yields for active US government notes and bonds from Cantor Fitzgerald.

24-hour coverage.

Exhibit 8.1—continued

Capital Markets Information Service

05/04 15:13 EDT (C) 1993 [MKT DATA CORP SOURCE: TULLETT & TOKYO] PAGE 19906
INTEREST RATE CAPS AND FLOORS

[MTY	CCY	C/F	STRIKE	ROLL	BID	OFF	MTY	CCY	C/F	STRIKE	ROLL	BID	OFF]
2	USD	C	6.00	3 M	0.10	0.13	1	STG	C	6.00	3 M	0.36	0.39
2	USD	C	6.50	3 M	0.07	0.08	1	STG	C	6.50	3 M	0.20	0.23
2	USD	F	4.00	3 M	0.75	0.79	2	STG	C	7.00	3 M	0.96	1.03
3	USD	C	6.00	3 M	0.62	0.70	2	STG	C	8.00	3 M	0.52	0.58
3	USD	C	7.00	3 M	0.33	0.39	2	STG	F	6.00	3 M	0.43	0.50
3	USD	F	5.00	3 M	2.47	2.56	3	STG	C	7.50	3 M	1.99	2.11
4	USD	C	7.00	3 M	0.92	1.02	3	STG	C	8.50	3 M	1.29	1.40
4	USD	C	8.00	3 M	0.55	0.63	3	STG	F	6.00	3 M	0.69	0.78
4	USD	F	5.00	3 M	2.80	2.90	4	STG	C	8.00	3 M	2.96	3.13
5	USD	C	7.00	3 M	1.74	1.84	4	STG	F	6.50	3 M	1.48	1.63
5	USD	C	8.00	3 M	1.11	1.21	5	STG	C	9.00	3 M	2.94	3.19
5	USD	F	5.50	3 M	4.35	4.50	5	STG	F	6.50	3 M	1.72	1.92

STRIKES QUOTED AGAINST LIBOR PREMIUMS AS PERCENT OF PRINCIPAL

[LONDON 827-2346]	[TOKYO 231-4024]	[SYDNEY 223-3500]	[NEW YORK 208-2160]

TELERATE Page 19906

Interest Rate Caps and Floors

- Live bids and offers for interest rate caps and floors in US dollar and British pound denominations.
- Most active strike and roll prices.
- Strike prices quoted against LIBOR.
- Premium prices quoted as percent of principal.

24-hour coverage.

Exhibit 8.1—continued

Capital Markets Information Service

05/04 15:13 EDT (C) 1993 [MKT DATA CORP SOURCE: TULLETT & TOKYO] PAGE 19907
INTEREST RATE CAPS(C), FLOORS(F), AND SWAPTIONS(S)

[MTY	CCY	C/S	STRIKE	ROLL	BID	OFF	MTY	CCY	C/S	STRIKE	ROLL	BID	OFF]
1	DM	F	7.00	6 M	0.21	0.27	2	YY	C	4.00	6 M	17.00	19.00
2	DM	C	7.50	6 M	0.12	0.16	3	YY	C	4.50	6 M	16.50	18.50
2	DM	F	6.50	6 M	1.12	1.18	4	YY	C	5.00	6 M	14.50	16.50
3	DM	C	7.00	6 M	0.56	0.64	5	YY	C	5.00	6 M	13.50	15.00
3	DM	C	8.00	6 M	0.21	0.27	7	YY	C	5.00	6 M	11.50	13.00
3	DM	F	6.50	6 M	1.76	1.85	0	YY	C	5.50	6 M	8.50	10.50
4	DM	C	7.00	6 M	0.96	1.10	2	YY	F	3.50	6 M	18.50	21.00
4	DM	C	8.00	6 M	0.45	0.55	3	YY	F	4.00	6 M	17.50	20.00
4	DM	F	6.50	6 M	2.35	2.50	4	YY	F	4.50	6 M	16.00	18.00
5	DM	C	7.00	6 M	1.54	1.73	5	YY	F	4.50	6 M	14.50	16.50
5	DM	C	8.00	6 M	0.80	0.96	7	YY	F	4.50	6 M	12.50	14.50
0	OO	O	0.50	6 M	2.86	3.07	0	YY	F	4.50	6 M	9.50	11.50

30/04/1993 FRIDAY AM9 20 (YEN'S VOLA'S INDICATION)

[LONDON 827-2346]	[TOKYO 231-4024]	[SYDNEY 223-3500]	[NEW YORK 208-2160]

TELERATE Page 19907

Interest Rate Caps and Floors

- Live bids and offers for interest rate caps and floors in Deutschemark and Japanese yen denominations.
- Most active strike and roll prices.
- Strike prices quoted against LIBOR.
- Premium prices quoted as percent of principal.

24-hour coverage.

Exhibit 8.1—continued

Capital Markets Information Service

05/04 15:13 EDT (C) 1993 [MKT DATA CORP SOURCE: TULLETT & TOKYO] PAGE 19909
YEN SWAPS AND FRAS

YEN/YEN (A/365) SA	YEN/USD (A/365) SA	CHF/YEN (A/360) SA		
[2 YR] 3.77 – 3.74	[2 YR] 3.76 – 3.68	[2 YR]	—	LT PRIME 6.00
[3 YR] 4.15 – 4.11	[3 YR] 4.14 – 4.06	[3 YR]	—	ST PRIME
[4 YR] 4.57 – 4.55	[4 YR] 4.57 – 4.49	[4 YR]	—	DISC RATE 3.75
[5 YR] 4.77 – 4.75	[5 YR] 4.77 – 4.69	[5 YR]	—	
[7 YR] 5.01 – 4.97	[7 YR] 5.00 – 4.92	[7 YR]	—	
[10 YR] 5.11 – 5.07	[10 YR] 5.09 – 5.01	[10 YR]	—	

SPOT EX		1 YR SWAP YEN/YEN (A/360) VS 3MS	YEN FRA	
YEN	110.26-32		1×4 3.25 – 3.28	9×12 3.37 – 3.41
DM	1.5752-62	JUN/JUN 4.11 – 4.07	2×5 3.25 – 3.28	1×7 3.26 – 3.29
CHF	1.4200-16	SEP/SEP 4.40 – 4.35	3×6 3.24 – 3.28	3×9 3.26 – 3.29
AU$	0.6985-95	DEC/DEC 3.70 – 3.66	4×7 3.23 – 3.26	6×12 3.33 – 3.36
		MAR/MAR 3.85 – 3.80	6×9 3.25 – 3.28	3×12 3.32 – 3.36

[LONDON 827-2345]	[TOKYO 241-8771]	[SYDNEY 223-3500]	[NEW YORK 208-2160]

TELERATE Page 19909

Yen Interest Rate Swaps

- Fixed Japanese yen rates to 6 month yen LIBOR.
- Fixed yen to 6 month US dollar LIBOR.
- Japanese money market interest rates.
- One year IMM date yen swaps.
- YEN forward rate agreements.

Exhibit 8.1—continued

Capital Markets Information Service

05/04 15:13 EDT (C) 1993 [MKT DATA CORP SOURCE: TULLETT & TOKYO] PAGE 19910

FORWARD RATE AGREEMENTS (EXPRESSED AS OFFER—BID) [SEE ALSO PGS 19901-08]

FRA	US$	STG	DM	YEN	ECU	FFR	AU$	CHF
1×4	3.15-20	6.05-09	7.31-35	3.25-28	8.20-25	7.59-64	5.11-19	4.81-86
2×5	3.16-21	6.06-10	7.04-08	3.25-28	7.91-96	7.42-48	5.10-18	4.63-68
3×6	3.19-24	6.07-11	6.75-80	3.24-28	7.62-67	7.20-25	5.13-21	4.50-55
4×7	3.21-26	6.09-13	6.87-51	3.23-26	7.33-38	6.96-01	5.13-21	4.41-46
6×9	3.48-53	5.29-34	6.17-21	3.25-28	7.11-16	6.68-73	5.25-33	4.24-29
9×12	3.58-63	6.34-38	5.75-79	3.37-41	6.80-85	6.26-32	5.51-59	4.07-12
1×7	3.22-27	6.11-15	6.97-99	3.26-29	7.86-91	7.35-41	5.14-22	4.63-68
3×9	3.34-39	6.15-19	6.51-55	3.26-29	7.42-47	7.00-05	5.21-29	4.38-43
6×12	3.54-59	6.29-33	6.00-04	3.33-36	7.01-06	6.58-63	5.20-28	4.18-23
3×12	3.44-49	5.44-49	6.33-37	3.32-36	7.38-43	6.86-92		4.35-40

[AUS FRAS ARE LONDON PRICES ONLY, ACTUAL/360 BASIS]

TULLETT FORWARD RATE AGREE'S				SPOT FOREIGN EXCHANGE					
NY (US$)	208-2070	TOKYO	241-9957	STG	1.5653-63	ECU	1.2395-98	CHF	1.4200-16
NY (ALL)	208-2070	SYDNEY	223-3500	DM	1.5752-62	FFR	5.3085-15	CA$	1.2712-16
LONDON	827-2345	FFT	—	YEN	110.26-32	AU$	0.6985-95		

TELERATE Page 19910

Forward Rate Agreements

- Forward rate agreements in US dollars:
  STG, DM, YEN, ECU, FFR, AU$, CHF.
- Spot STG, DM, YEN, ECU, FFR, AU$, CHF, CA$.

Source: © 1993 MDC, Market Data Corporation, One Wall Street, 37th Floor, New York, New York 10005.

Under market convention, an offer (bid) swap price indicates the price at which the market is willing to receive (pay) the fixed rate under the swap. The dealer's spread, representing dealer earnings, is the difference between the offer and bid swap price. The terminology associated with swap price quotation is not uniform and some versions in common use are set out in *Exhibit 8.2*.

Exhibit 8.2
Swap Market Terminology

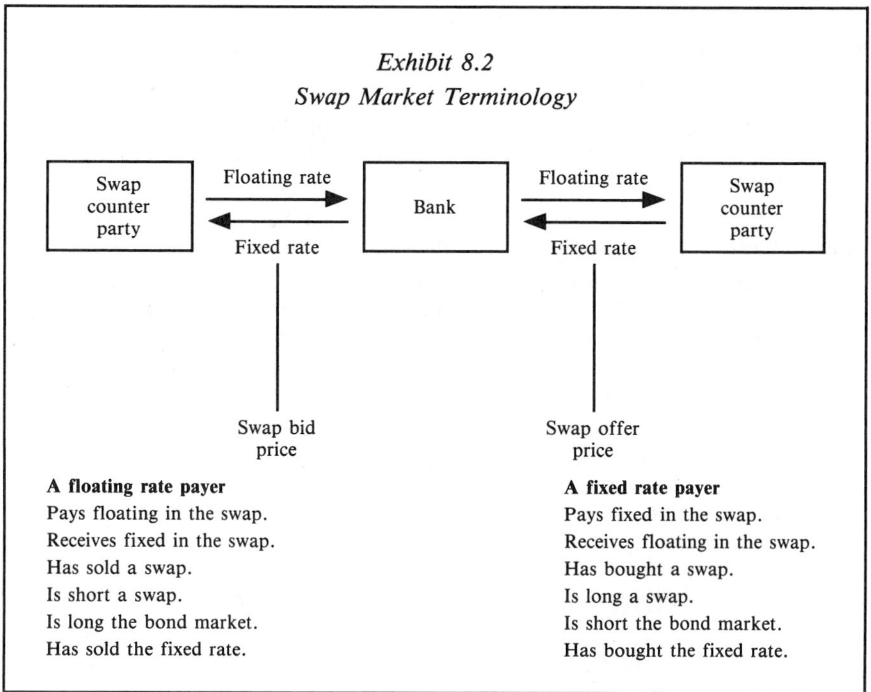

A floating rate payer
Pays floating in the swap.
Receives fixed in the swap.
Has sold a swap.
Is short a swap.
Is long the bond market.
Has sold the fixed rate.

A fixed rate payer
Pays fixed in the swap.
Receives floating in the swap.
Has bought a swap.
Is long a swap.
Is short the bond market.
Has bought the fixed rate.

The linkage between swap rates and government or other benchmark bond rates merits additional comment. The relationship, which arose originally in the US$ swap market, appears to be based upon two factors:

- spreads over a risk-free rate, such as the government bond rate, act as a proxy for credit risk differentials; and
- the use of government bonds to hedge swap transactions.

In highly developed capital markets, such as the US$ market, the risk premiums, embodied in spread differentials, for borrowers of different credit quality are relatively well established. Although these risk premiums change over time, the fact that they are readily determinable means that they can form the basis for swap arbitrage analysis. A result of this is that swaps, which function as a means of creating synthetic fixed and floating rate borrowings, tend to be priced "off" a benchmark risk free rate in a manner similar to that of pricing direct borrowings.

This thesis is confirmed to some degree by the fact that the relationship between swap prices and government bond rates is strongest in markets with highly developed risk premium structures. In markets where certain types of securities issues are not readily possible, the linkage is significantly weaker.

Swap prices are closely tied to the cost of hedging swap exposures (refer Part 7). Before a swap is matched with another swap, it is generally hedged with a combination of securities, futures contracts and some form of floating rate investment or funding such as repurchase agreements. For example, if the intermediary is the fixed rate payer on the swap, the hedge usually involves the purchase of an appropriate amount of government securities with the same maturity as the swap. The purchase of securities is in turn financed by borrowing in an appropriate market (in practice, the cash or, if available, the short-term repurchase agreement market). The government security creates a hedge against capital loss if long-term interest rates change, and also generates fixed rate income which matches the fixed payments of the swap. The floating rate income from the swap covers the floating rate cost of funding the purchase. Swaps of shorter maturity (usually up to two to three years) are more likely to be hedged in the short term interest rate futures market.

A number of other quotation conventions should be noted. The term "trade date" refers to the date on which the counterparties commit themselves to the swap.

The "effective date" on a swap is the date on which fixed and floating interest starts accruing. Normally, this is a period of up to five business days after the trade date depending upon market convention in the particular swap market. The "settlement date" is the date on which the transaction is priced for value. Normally in swap transactions this is the same as the effective date.

Swap agreements are executed on an "as of" basis; that is, the agreement is prepared and executed some time after the effective date. This custom enhances the liquidity of the swap market, but should a party fail before the contract is executed, the protection offered by the agreement, obviously, might not be present.

SWAP VALUATION—A FRAMEWORK

Exhibit 8.3 sets out the framework for the valuation of swap transactions.

The framework identifies a three stage valuation process:

- *Phase 1*—whereby relatively standard techniques of financial mathematics, interest rate/yield calculations and par or zero discount rates are derived to assist in the process of valuing specific swap structures.
- *Phase 2*—whereby valuation principles are applied to the cash flows applicable to generic or conventional swap structures, both interest rate swaps and currency swaps.
- *Phase 3*—whereby the identified valuation principles are utilised to price/cost the impact of variations from generic swap structures derive the price of non-generic swaps.

Each of these aspects of the valuation process are considered in detail below.

SWAP VALUATION PRINCIPLES

The basic principles of swap valuation emphasise conventional financial mathematics, interest/yield calculations and the derivation of discount rates to be utilised in valuing swaps. The arithmetical procedures are common to all financial transactions and are not necessarily peculiar to swaps. In practice, the calculations and analysis required is typically performed utilising a hand-held financial calculator (such as a Hewlett-Packard HP12C, HP17B or its equivalent) or spreadsheet programmes run on conventional personal computers (such as LOTUS 1-2-3, EXCEL or their equivalent).

Exhibit 8.3
Swap Valuation Framework

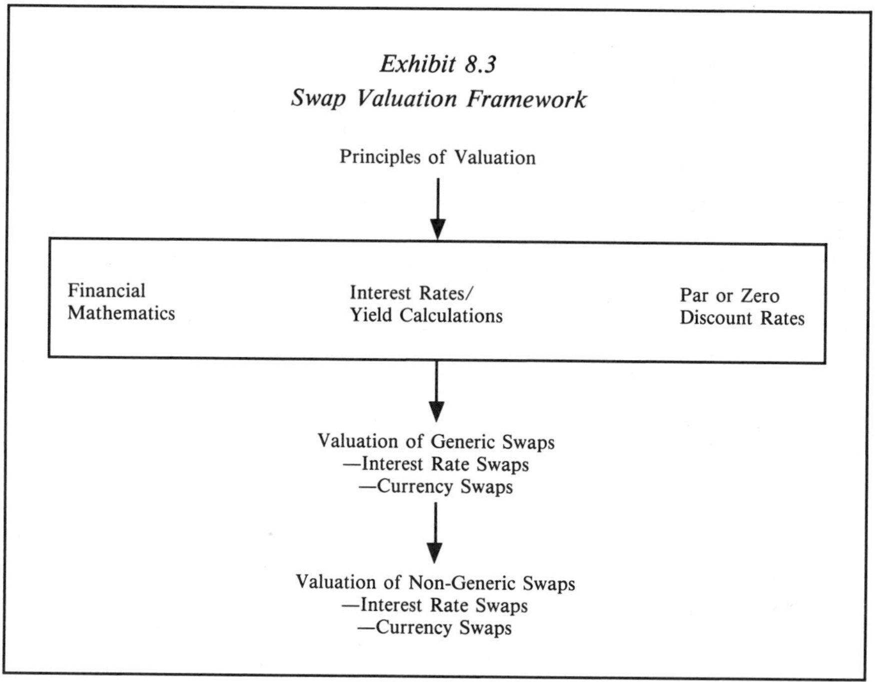

Financial mathematics

The basic financial mathematics required to value swap transactions utilise standard time value of money or net present value/discounted cash flow concepts. Parties to swap arrangements measure the relative attractiveness of the transaction through the calculation of the transaction's "all-in cost". This is, generally, equivalent to the present value of the cash flows utilising appropriate discount factors (generally based on zero coupon rates) in the relevant currency.

Swap cash flows are largely identical to cash flows under equivalent bonds or similar securities, either floating rate or fixed rate bonds. Consequently, the analysis of swap cash flows are substantively similar to the mathematics utilised to value bonds or similar transactions, utilising standard compound interest and present value concepts. Standard financial mathematics valuation concepts such as bond and annuity valuation are integral to the process of valuing swap transactions.[1]

1. The discussion in this section/chapter and the book assumes an understanding of net present value (NPV) and internal rate of return (IRR) concepts. For readers seeking to revise their understanding of these concepts, the following book provides a sound coverage of the basic techniques: Peter Cartledge, *A Handbook of Financial Mathematics* (Euromoney Publications, London, 1992).

Interest rate calculations

A complexity relating to interest rate calculations (as they are relevant to swaps) derives from three basic sources:

- Different yield calculation conventions—market convention on certain key aspects of interest rate calculations vary significantly between various domestic and international capital markets, with the primary differences being in the area of:
  —payment of interest (discount or coupon basis);
  —frequency of interest payments (annual, semi-annual, quarterly etc);
  —day basis factor used in accruing and compounding of interest; and,
  —accrued interest calculations.
- The requirement to convert interest rate/yield from one interest rate basis into another interest rate basis.
- The requirement to convert interest rates in one currency to its equivalent in another currency.

Yield calculation convention

Exhibit 8.4 summarises the major features of the primary methods of interest rate calculations, including annual bond basis, annual money market basis, semi-annual bond basis and semi-annual money market basis.

Exhibit 8.4

Interest Rate Calculations

1. Annual Bond Basis (AIBD or COUPON basis)

This calculation assumes a year of 360 days with 12 months each of 30 days. A normal security under this interest basis will pay interest in equal annual amounts (if fixed rate) irrespective of when the payment is made. Thus a security of $100m with a coupon of 8% will pay $8m on each anniversary prior to maturity. If a payment date falls on a non-business day, for example, the $8m will be paid on the next business day without additional interest in respect of the delay.

In the case of accrued interest the calculation then follows the 12 months × actual days rule.

Example: Last coupon date = 18.2.X5
Settlement Date = 23.8.X5
Number of Bond Days = 10 + 150 + 23 = 183

The accrued interest on the above security would be:

$8,000,000 × 183/360 = $4,066,666.67

It is important in swaps to clarify the payment calculation as there is a difference between Coupon basis and 30/360 basis.

2. Annual Money Market (Annual Cash)

Interest is calculated on an Actual/360 day basis. For example, an Annual Money Market rate of 5% on $100m would produce an annual coupon of $5,069,444.44 for a normal year of 365 days.

3. Semi-Annual Bond Basis

As in 1. above the interest calculation is on the basis of a year of 360 days and 12 months of 30 days. Thus, in the case of a semi-annual rate of 6% on a $100m, interest would be calculated as $3m per period.

Exhibit 8.4—continued

The difference between Semi-Annual Bond and 30/360 would be apparent on those occasions when the payment date is a non-business day. For example, if payment dates are 5th of January and June and 5 July falls on Saturday the interest would be calculated as 182 bond days (180 days for 5 January to 5 July plus 2 days for settlement on 7 July).

4. Semi-Annual Money Market

As in 3.0 above the interest calculation is worked on an Actual/360 day basis. For example, assuming a semi-annual interest rate of 5% for the period 5 January to 5 July the interest due would be $2,513,888.89 [$100m × 5% × 181/360].

Exhibit 8.5 summarises the calculation conventions in a variety of major domestic and international capital markets.

Exhibit 8.5
Yield Calculation Conventions

United States Dollar[1]	**Payment frequency**	**Compounding**	**Number of days**
Prime	—	—	365/360
US$ LIBOR	—	—	365/360
US$ treasury bill	—	—	365/360
US$ CD	—	—	365/360
US$ commercial paper	—	—	365/360
US$ federal funds	—	—	365/360
US$ bankers' acceptances	—	—	365/360
Money market[2]	—	A	365/360
Treasury bonds	S/A	S/A	365/365
Corporate bonds	S/A	S/A	360/360
Yankee bonds	S/A	S/A	360/360
Eurodollar bonds	A	A	360/360
Swaps	S/A	S/A	360/360
West German Deutschmark			
DEM LIBOR	—	—	365/360
DEM Frankfurt Interbank Offered Rate (FIBOR)	—	—	365/360
Schuldscheine	A	A	360/360
Domestic government bonds	A	A	360/360
EuroDEM bonds	A	A	360/360
Swaps	A	A	360/360
Swiss Franc			
SFR LIBOR	—	—	365/360
Foreign bonds (public issue)	A	A	360/360
Foreign notes (private placements)	A	A	360/360
Domestic government bonds	A	A	360/360
Swaps	A	A	360/360
United Kingdom Sterling			
GBP LIBOR	—	—	365/365
Gilt edged securities	S/A	S/A	365/365
Bulldog bonds	S/A	S/A	365/365
Eurosterling bonds	A	A	360/360
Swaps	S/A	S/A	365/365

Exhibit 8.5—continued

Canadian dollar			
C$ LIBOR	—	—	365/360
C$ bankers' acceptances	—	—	365/365
C$ treasury bill	—	—	365/365
Federal government bonds	S/A	S/A	365/365
Corporate bonds	S/A	S/A	365/365
EuroCanadian bonds	A	A	360/360
Swaps	S/A	S/A	365/365
Japanese Yen			
JPY LIBOR	—	—	365/360
Domestic government coupon bonds	S/A	A	363/365
Samurai bonds	S/A	A	365/365
Euroyen bonds	A	A	360/360
Swaps	S/A	S/A	365/365
Australian Dollar			
A$ Bank bill rate	—	—	365/365
A$ LIBOR	—	—	365/360
Commonwealth/Semi-government bonds	S/A	S/A	365/365
EuroAustralian bonds	A	A	360/360
Yankee Australian bonds	S/A	S/A	360/360
Swaps	S/A	S/A	365/365
New Zealand Dollar			
NZ$ Prime commercial bill rate	—	—	365/365
NZ$ LIBOR	—	—	365/360
Government bonds	S/A	S/A	365/360
EuroAustralian bonds	A	A	360/360
Yankee New Zealand bonds	S/A	S/A	360/360
Swaps	S/A	S/A	365/360
French Franc			
FFR Paris Interbank Offered Rate (PIBOR)	—	—	365/360
TAM (Taux Annual Monetaire)	—	—	365/365
Government bonds (OAT—Obligations Assimilables du Treror)	A	A	365/365
Euro Franc bonds	A	A	360/360
Swaps	A	A	360/360
Dutch Guilder			
Dfl Amsterdam Interbank Offered Rate (AIBOR)	—	—	365/360
Government bonds	A	A	360/360
Foreign Guilder notes	A	A	360/360
Euro Guilder notes	A	A	360/360
Swaps	A	A	360/360
European Currency Units			
ECU LIBOR	—	—	365/360
ECU Paris Interbank Offered Rate (ECUPIBOR)	—	—	365/360
ECU Eurobonds	A	A	360/360
Swaps	A	A	360/360

Exhibit 8.5—continued

Spanish Pesetas			
PTAS Madrid Interbank Offered Rate (MIBOR)	—	—	365/360
PTAS Eurobonds	A	A	360/360
Swaps	A	A	360/360
Swedish Krona			
Swedish treasury bill			
Stockholm Interbank Offered Rate (SIBOR)	—	—	365/360
Government bonds	A	A	360/360
Krona Eurobonds	A	A	360/360
Swaps	A	A	360/360
Danish Krone			
Copenhagen Interbank Offered Rate	—	—	365/360
Krone Eurobond	A	A	360/360
Swaps	A	A	360/360
Hong Kong Dollars			
HK Interbank Offered Rate (HIBOR)	—	—	365/360
HK$ CDs	Q	Q	365/365
Swaps	Q	Q	365/365
Italian Lira			
Milan Interbank Offered Rate	—	—	365/360
Rendiob	—	—	365/360
Rolint (average of MIBOR & Rendiob)	—	—	365/360
LIT LIBOR	—	—	365/360
Government bonds (BTPs)	S/A	S/A	360/360
LIT Eurobonds	A	A	360/360
Swaps	A	A	360/360

Notes:

1. The practice in the United States and certain other domestic bond markets is the semi-annual compounding of semi-annual bond coupons. In the Eurobond market the practice of the Association of International Bond Dealers (AIBD) is to compound annually either the annual or semi-annual bond coupons.
2. To convert rates from AIBD to United States money market basis, multiply by 360/365. To convert rates from United States money market to AIBD basis, multiply by 365/360.
3. Yield to maturity on yen bonds is calculated and quoted on a *non-compounded basis within Japan*. Outside Japan yields are usually calculated on a AIBD *or* United States basis.

Interest rate conversions

As noted above, in valuing swap transactions, it is frequently necessary to convert interest rates from one particular interest rate basis to its equivalent utilising a different interest rate basis. For example, it may be necessary to convert semi-annual yields to annual yields etc.

Exhibit 8.6 sets out the formulae for converting interest rates from a variety of bases into its equivalent utilising other interest rate yield bases.

Exhibit 8.6

Interest Rate Conversions (1)

Compounding Conversions

The generalised formula for converting interest rate to a different compounding basis is as follows:

(1) *Compounding to Annual Rate*

(1 + RN/N)N − 1 = RA

where:

RN = Interest Rate (in decimal form) compounded every N period.

RA = Interest Rate (in decimal form) on a pa annual compounding or effective basis.

(2) *De-compounding Annual Rate*

[(1 + RA) (1/N) − 1] × N = RN

where RA and RN are the same as above.

Bond/Money Market Conversions

(1) *Money Market to Bond Equivalent Basis*

RB = RMM x 365/360

where:

RB = Interest Rate on a bond equivalent (Actual/365 day) basis.

RMM = Interest Rate on a money market (Actual/360 day) basis.

(2) *Bond Equivalent to Money Market Basis*

RMM = RB × 360/365

where RB and RMM are the same as above.

Exhibit 8.7 sets out examples of calculating interest rate yield equivalents on different interest rate basis for a range of interest rates.

Exhibit 8.7

Interest Rate Conversions (2)

Example 1

Rate: 8.000%

Compounding Conversions

	Original Rate Compounding Period			
Rate Equivalent	Monthly	Quarterly	Semi-Annual	Annual
Monthly	8.0000%	7.9473%	7.8698%	7.7208%
Quarterly	8.0535%	8.0000%	7.9216%	7.7706%
Semi-Annual	8.1345%	8.0800%	8.0000%	7.8461%
Annual	8.3000%	8.2432%	8.1600%	8.0000%

Exhibit 8.7—continued

Day Count Conversions

Original Day Count Days	360	365
Day Equivalent Basis		
360	8.0000%	7.8904%
365	8.1111%	8.0000%

Example 2

Rate: 10.000%

Compounding Conversions

	Original Rate Compounding Period			
Rate Equivalent	Monthly	Quarterly	Semi-Annual	Annual
Monthly	10.0000%	9.9178%	9.7978%	9.5690%
Quarterly	10.0836%	10.0000%	9.8780%	9.6455%
Semi-Annual	10.2107%	10.1250%	10.0000%	9.7618%
Annual	10.4713%	10.3813%	10.2500%	10.0000%

Day Count Conversions

Original Day Count Days	360	365
Day Equivalent Basis		
360	10.0000%	9.8630%
365	10.1389%	10.0000%

Example 3

Rate: 12.000%

Compounding Conversions

	Original Rate Compounding Period			
Rate Equivalent	Monthly	Quarterly	Semi-Annual	Annual
Monthly	12.0000%	11.8820%	11.7106%	11.3866%
Quarterly	12.1204%	12.0000%	11.8252%	11.4949%
Semi-Annual	12.3040%	12.1800%	12.0000%	11.6601%
Annual	12.6825%	12.5509%	12.3600%	12.0000%

Day Count Conversions

Original Day Count Days	360	365
Day Equivalent Basis		
360	12.0000%	11.8356%
365	12.1667%	12.0000%

Foreign currency basis points

In the case of currency swaps, in addition to the different market conventions applicable to the relevant currencies, it will, generally, be necessary to calculate equivalencies as between currencies.

The necessity to adjust the different computational basis or market conventions between the different currency markets are identical to the process described above.

The adjustments required to ensure equivalencies as between currencies are more complex. The requirement to match flows between currencies occurs, usually, in the context of spreads above or below the floating rate index in a particular currency. This requirement to make payments of spreads/margins above or below the relevant floating rate index effectively requires the party making or forgoing such payments to either borrow or lend the foreign currency. Consequently, the transaction pricing and the required adjustment requires the borrowing and lending transactions to be encompassed in the pricing of the transaction. Pricing of these adjustments reflects essentially the prevailing interest rates in the two currencies.

In practice, these spreads above or below the relevant index can be priced on the basis of either assumed borrowing or lending transactions in the relevant currencies or alternatively as a string of forward foreign exchange contracts designed to convert exposure from one currency to another.

In practice, this conversion is effected as follows:

- The number of basis points being converted from one currency to the other is structured as an annuity stream for the relevant number of periods.
- This annuity stream is then present valued at the prevailing interest rate applicable to the relevant maturity.
- The present value equivalent of this annuity stream in one currency is then reconverted into an annuity in the second currency utilising the interest rate applicable to that currency for the relevant maturity.
- The annuity amount generated as a result of this procedure equates to the equivalent number of basis points in the second currency.

In theoretical terms, this technique seeks to equate the present value of x% pa in one currency payable periodically with y% pa in the second currency. *Exhibit 8.8* sets out the theoretical relationship reflecting interest rate differentials between y and x.

Exhibit 8.9 sets out a number of examples of computing equivalencies as between several currencies.

Exhibit 8.8
Calculation of Currency Equivalencies

The equation of value set out below equals the present value of x% pa is one currency, say US$, payable semi-annually with y% is another currency, say A$ payable semi-annually.

The theoretical relationship reflecting interest rate differentials between y and x is:

$$x/2 \; A_{\overline{n}|}^{US_n} = y/2 \; A_{\overline{n}|}^{A_n}$$

therefore:

$$y/x = \frac{A_{\overline{n}|}^{US_n}}{A_{\overline{n}|}^{A_n}}$$

where:

x = % margin in US$

y = equivalent % margin in, say, A$

US_n = US$ interest rate for relevant maturity

A_n = A$ interest rate for relevant maturity

n = Number of half years

$A_{\overline{n}|} = (1 - V^n)/i$

where:

$V^n = (1/(1 + i))^n$

Exhibit 8.8—continued

where:

n = as above

i = semi-annual yield/2

assume:

US_n = 10.0%

A_n = 14.05%

n = 7 years or 14 semi-annual periods

Utilising the above formula, the currency equivalency is as follows:

$V^{US} = (1/1.05)^{14} = 0.505068$

$V^{A} = (1/1.07025)^{14} = 0.386551$

$A\overline{n}\rceil 7^{US} = (1\text{-}0.505068)/0.05 = 9.898641$

$A\overline{n}\rceil 7^{A} = (1\text{-}0.386551)/0.07025 = 8.732372$

$y/x = 9.898641/8.732372$

$= 1.133557$

This means that 1bps in US$ is equivalent to 1.1335057bps in A$. Therefore:

US$ bps	A$ bps
25	28.338925
50	56.677850
100	113.3555701

Exhibit 8.9
Examples of Foreign Currency Basis Points Conversion

Examples of conversion foreign currency basis points are set out below.

The calculations are undertaken on the basis of converting a given number of bps in one currency into equivalent bps in another currency. The conversion is based on assumed interest rates in each country and a specified number of payments per year. This information is re-configured as the present value (PV) of the bps stream (as an annuity) (PMT) in the known currency (using the specified interest rate) (INT) over the relevant periods (Periods). The present value calculated is used to generate an annuity equivalent (using the specified interest rate). The present value calculated is used to generate an annuity (using the specified interest rate in that currency) which equates to the bps equivalency in the other currency.

FX Basis Points Conversion: Example 1

		Rates (%pa)	Period (per year)
Base currency:	DEM	9.580%	2
Foreign currency:	US$	7.250%	2
Term (years):	5		
bps equivalency	DEM	35.000bps	
	US$	33.038bps	

Calculations:

	PMT	INT	Periods	PV
DEM	17.50	4.790%	10	136.52
US$	16.52	3.625%	10	136.52

Exhibit 8.9—continued

FX Basis Points Conversion: Example 2

		Rates (%pa)		Period (per year)
Base currency:	JPY	7.320%		2
Foreign currency:	US$	7.850%		2
Term (years):	10			
bps equivalency	JPY	50.000bps		
	US$	51.198bps		
Calculations:				
	PMT	INT	Periods	PV
JPY	25.00	3.660%	20	350.22
US$	25.60	3.925%	20	350.22

Yield adjustment

The yield calculations utilised in swap transactions effectively require adjustments reflecting a variety of factors including: the impact of bid-offer spreads, the need to interpolate yields for specific maturities, adjustments for long or short first coupons, compounding of swap spreads, adjustment of floating rate spreads above or below the floating rate index etc.

Bid-offer spread

The use of government bonds or futures contracts, noted above, to hedge swaps has an important technical effect on the yield mechanics of pricing swaps. In practice, the underlying benchmark bond or futures contract will not trade at *one* given yield, rather, it will trade on a bid-offer spread where the bid price (the price at which the trader purchases the commodity) is lower than the offer price (the price at which the trader sells the commodity). The spread, that is the difference between the bid and offer price, reflects the traders return from the transaction.

Exhibit 8.10 sets out an extract from a screen for United States government treasury bonds highlighting the bid-offer prices for five year United States treasury which would typically be utilised to hedge a five year swap transaction.

Swap trader or counterparty will if it receives (pays) the fixed rate under the swap then seek to hedge by selling (buying) bonds or futures. The relevant bond or futures price should be used as the base or benchmark price and will correspond to the bid (offer) price of the market for those instruments plus the relevant swap spread.

Exhibit 8.11 highlights the impact of the bid-offer spread in the underlying pricing benchmark and the pricing of the swap transaction itself.

Yield interpolation

As noted above, in a number of markets, swaps are priced as a spread over a fixed rate index, typically government or equivalent bond interest rate. However, the maturity of the benchmark fixed rate index will not coincide precisely with the maturity of the swap.

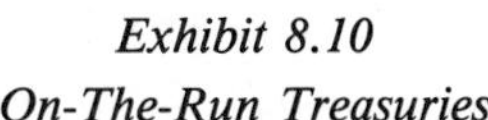

Exhibit 8.10
On-The-Run Treasuries

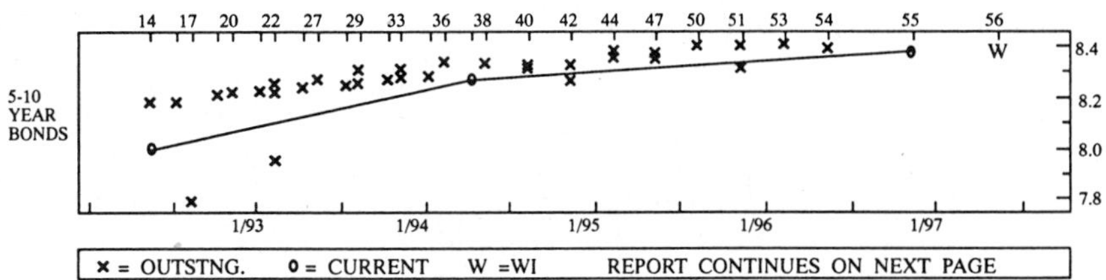

5 YR BONDS

Security			Bid	Ask	Yield
12⅜	4/91		114-11	114-13	8.05
8⅛	5/91		100- 7	100- 9	8.04
14½	5/91		121-24	121-26	8.07
13¾	7/91		119-22	119-24	8.11
7½	8/91		97-30	98- 0	8.06
14⅞	8/91		124- 2	124- 4	8.10
12¼	10/91		115- 0	115- 2	8.15
6½	11/91		94-11	94-13	7.99
14¼	11/91		122-29	122-31	8.10
11⅝	1/92		113- 9	113-11	8.15
6⅝	2/92		94-11	94-13	8.04
14⅝	2/92		125-11	125-13	8.12
11¾	4/92		114-11	114-13	8.16
6⅝	5/92	C	94- 8	94-10	8.01
13¾	5/92		122-16	122-18	8.19

Exhibit 8.11
Treasury Market—Impact of Bid-Offer Spread

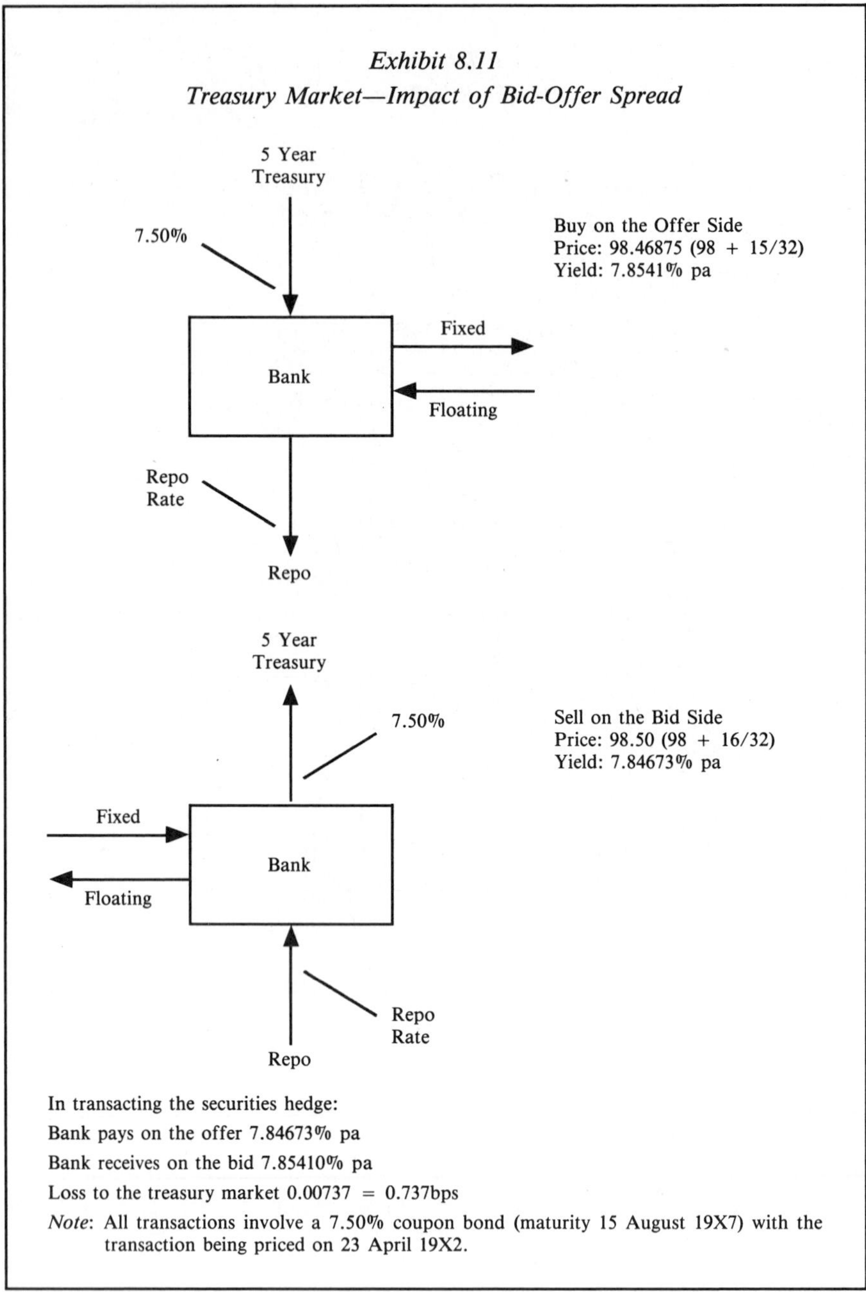

In transacting the securities hedge:

Bank pays on the offer 7.84673% pa

Bank receives on the bid 7.85410% pa

Loss to the treasury market 0.00737 = 0.737bps

Note: All transactions involve a 7.50% coupon bond (maturity 15 August 19X7) with the transaction being priced on 23 April 19X2.

Exhibit 8.12 highlights this potential maturity mismatch in the US$ swap market. This mismatch has two primary implications:

- It is necessary to interpolate yields for maturities corresponding to the relevant swap to allow transactions to be priced (the yield interpolation problem).

- The volatility and convexity of the bond utilised to price and hedge the swap will be different to that of the swap itself (the volatility/convexity matching problem).

Exhibit 8.12

Swaps vs Treasury/Bond Maturity Mismatch

Swap	Maturity	Treasury	Maturity	Mismatch	Mismatch as % of Transaction
3 year	28/5/X5	3 year	15/8/X5	+79 Days	7.2%
5 year	28/5/X7	5 year	15/2/X7	−102 Days	5.6%
7 year	28/5/X9	7 year	15/11/X9	171 Days	6.7%
10 year	28/5/Y2	10 year	15/2/Y1	−102 Days	2.8%

Note: All transactions are as of 28 May 19X2.

The convexity/volatility matching problem is discussed in detail in the context of trading and market making in swaps: see Chapter 32.

The problem of yield interpolation can be dealt with in a number of ways. It is important to note that the problem of yield interpolation is not unique to swap transactions. It arises generally in financial markets as a result of the fact that observable securities prices/yields only exist for certain securities with specific maturities, necessitating estimation of yield in between observable yield points on an essentially discontinuous yield curve.

Yield interpolation is always associated with a certain degree of risk. The observable yield curve is discontinuous which implies that the yield curve can change shape at each measurement point and can do so abruptly. However, most techniques of yield interpolation assume yield transitions from one maturity to another to be fairly smooth—that is, to be characterised by a continuous curve.

In practice, yield interpolation is undertaken utilising one of the following two methods:

- linear interpolation; and
- fitting yield curves utilising mathematical techniques.

Exhibit 8.13 and *Exhibit 8.14* set out a mechanism for linear interpolation of yields for both fixed rates and floating or short-term money market rates. Please note the technique for adjusting the rate uses factors to ensure the appropriate weighting of the relevant maturity.

The use of linear interpolation is not consistent with the assumption of a yield curve which changes shape continuously. An alternative method for estimating yield curves for maturities away from measurement points is to fit mathematical curves to the relevant yield points. A number of possible mathematical models of fitting such curves are set out in *Exhibit 8.15*.

Long or short first coupon

Commonly utilised techniques for calculating yield-to-maturity assume that all coupon periods are of equal length. In certain circumstances, the underlying government bond or swap itself will have a long or short first coupon.

Exhibit 8.13
Interpolation of Yields—Term Rates

Given the following seven and ten year treasury bond rates, the benchmark interpolated bond rate for an eight year swap is calculated as follows:

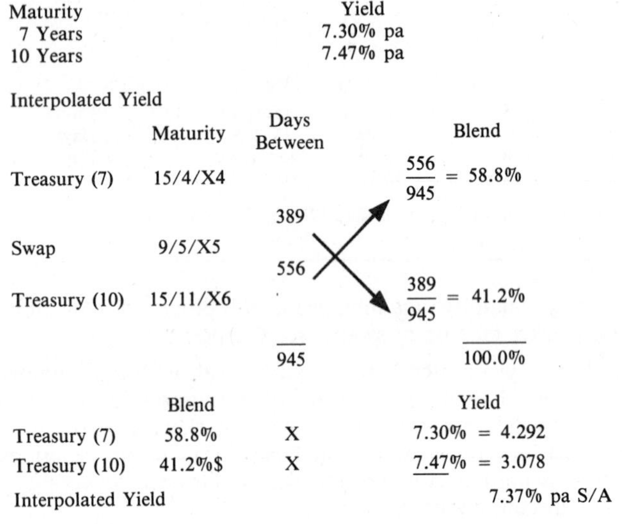

Maturity	Yield
7 Years	7.30% pa
10 Years	7.47% pa

Interpolated Yield

	Maturity	Days Between	Blend
Treasury (7)	15/4/X4		556/945 = 58.8%
		389	
Swap	9/5/X5		
		556	
Treasury (10)	15/11/X6		389/945 = 41.2%
		945	100.0%

	Blend		Yield
Treasury (7)	58.8%	X	7.30% = 4.292
Treasury (10)	41.2%$	X	7.47% = 3.078
Interpolated Yield			7.37% pa S/A

Exhibit 8.14
Interpolation of Yield—Short-Term Rates

Given a three and six month LIBOR rate, a four month LIBOR rate can be interpolated as follows:

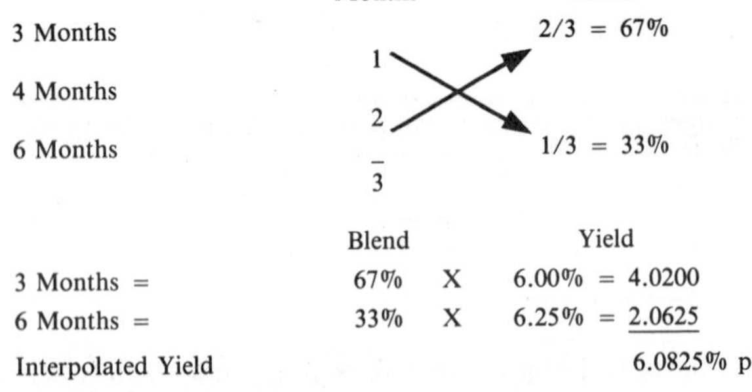

	Months	Blend
3 Months		2/3 = 67%
	1	
4 Months		
	2	
6 Months		1/3 = 33%
	3	

	Blend		Yield
3 Months =	67%	X	6.00% = 4.0200
6 Months =	33%	X	6.25% = 2.0625
Interpolated Yield			6.0825% pa

Exhibit 8.15
Mathematical Interpolation of Yield Curves

1. *Bradley-Crane Model*[1]
   The Bradley-Crane model has the form
   $\ln(1 + R_M) = a + b_1(M) + b_2\ln(M) + e$

   This implies values equal to the natural logarithm (ln) of one plus the observed yields for term to maturity of length M are regressed on two variables, the term to maturity and the natural log of the term of maturity. The last term represents the unexplained yield variation. Once the estimated values of a, b_1 and b_2 are obtained, specific maturities of interest can be substituted to obtain estimated yields at these maturity points.

2. *Elliot-Echols Model*[2]
   The Elliot-Echols model has the form:
   $\ln(1 + R_i) = a + b_1(1/M_i) + b_2(M_i) + b_3(C_i) + e_i$
   where R_i, M_i, and C_i are the yield to maturity, term to maturity, and coupon rate of the ith bond.

   The Elliot-Echols Model is useful where it is sought to fit yield curves directly to yield data for individual bonds rather than to homogenised yield series. This might be desirable as a means of avoiding possible distortions created in the process of arriving at the synthetic yield series.

3. *Laguerre Functions*[3]
   Laguerre functions consist of a polynomial multiplied by a polynomial decay function. For example,

   $1(t) = (a_0 + a_1 *t + a_2 *t^2 + \ldots + a_n *t^n) * e^{b*t}$
   is a Laguerre function where, a_i s and b are parameters and t is a measure of time.

   One obvious advantage of using Laguerre functions for term structure modelling is that as the decay function eventually dominates the polynomial component the long term rates, as predicted by a Laguerre function, stabilises. This property provides Laguerre models with an advantage over many other models whose long term predicted rates continued to either increase or decrease with time.

   The justification for the use of Laguerre functions in term structure studies is that they provide a range of flexible shapes which are consistent with observable interest rate data and that there is some theoretical justification for their applicability to interest rate data.

1. Stephen P Bradley and Dwight B Crane, "Management of Commercial Bank Government Security Portfolios: An Optimisation Approach under Uncertainty" (1973) (Spring) *Journal of Bank Research* 18.
2. Michael E Echols and Jan Walter Elliott, "A Quantitative Yield Curve Model for Estimating the Term Structure of Interest Rates" (1976) *Journal of Financial and Quantitative Analysis* 87.
3. B F Hunt, "Modelling The Term Structure" (Paper presented at Conference on Options on Interest Rates (organised by IIR Pty Ltd) at Sydney, March 1992).

For example, the five year treasury bond (which would normally pay interest semi-annually) may be structured so that the initial coupon is not paid for eight months and the initial eight month coupon is not properly compounded. A major reason for this type of structure is the desire to create fungible issues with matching coupons and interest payment dates.

The reduction in yield tends to be largest when the actual coupon payment is larger (that is, the coupon yield rate is high). In order to adjust for the impact of the long first coupon, it is necessary to calculate the precise number of calendar days from settlement to each cash flow and discount each cash flow by the appropriate discount factor based to the power of the *number of days* from settlement to that cash flow. This would typically allow the yield to be adjusted for the fact that the initial coupon period is larger and the initial coupon is not compounded.

Similarly, where the initial fixed rate period is shorter than the normal fixed rate period, it will be necessary to decompound the initial fixed rate.

For example, if the bond pays 8% pa (semi-annually) with the first payment due in one month. It is necessary to decompound the 8% pa semi-annual rate to its monthly equivalent (7.87%) to adjust the yield level.

Swap spread compounding

A common problem relates to the compounding of swap spreads. *Exhibit 8.16* sets out two possible techniques of compounding swap spreads—compounding the bond yield and then adding the swap spread or (the market convention) of compounding the sum of the underlying bond and swap spread. Please note the substantial difference in the effective all-in swap rate generated by the two techniques.

Exhibit 8.16

Compounding of Swap Spreads

Market Convention		**Alternative Approach**	
8.06%	S/A	8.06%	S/A
0.85%	spread	8.2224%	pa
8.91%		0.85%	spread
9.1085%	pa	9.0724%	pa

Note: All rates are compounded on a bond equivalent basis.

Floating rate spread above and below floating rate index

The presence of different day counts (between fixed rate and floating rate markets) and differential compounding interest periods affect the all-in cost of a swap transaction where a spread above or below the floating rate index is payable.

Exhibit 8.17 sets out an example of adjusting for a spread above or below a floating index. In that example, the bank is willing to pay bond plus 75bps against receipt of floating rate LIBOR. If the swap is to be restructured with counterparty paying the bank LIBOR minus 50bps, then the bank would be required to pay bond plus 24.241bps not bond plus 25bps reflecting the impact of the differential day count (money market versus bond basis) and interest compounding period (semi-annual versus annual rate).

Discount rates

Valuation of all swap transactions assumes the use of identified and specific interest rates or discount/present value factors to discount or present value cash flows identified with individual transactions.

Two alternative types of interest rates are available:

Exhibit 8.17
Adjusting for Spread Above or Below Floating Index

LIBOR – 50bps pa S/A (365/360 Money Market Basis) is equivalent to:
LIBOR – 50.694% pa S/A (365/365 Bond Equivalent Basis)
LIBOR – 50.759% pa A (365/360 Bond Equivalent Basis)

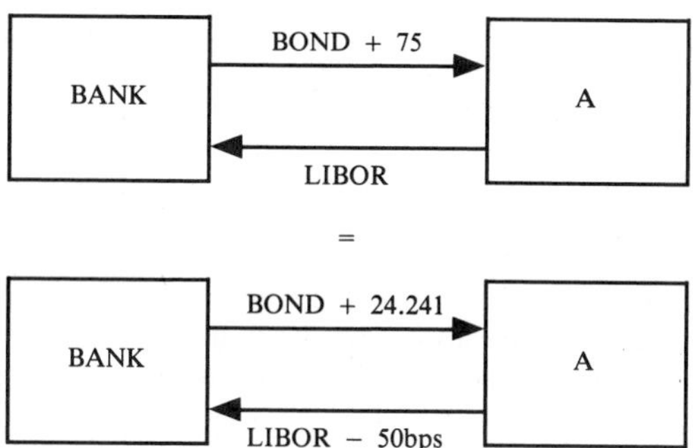

Note: Assumes fixed rate on swap is quoted as an annual rate.

- coupon or par yield to maturity—which is the standard internal rate of return formulae which discounts all payments on a coupon bond or instrument at the same interest rates; and
- spot rate or zero coupon rate (referred to as zero coupon rates)—which is the rate of exchange between a cash flow now and a cash flow at a single date in the future, that is, the yield on a pure discount bond or zero coupon security.

The coupon or par yield to maturity is usually directly observable, being the market quoted rate for the relevant securities of the required maturity. In the case of swap transactions, the relevant coupon or par yield to maturity is, typically, the quoted swap rate for the relevant maturity or, if unavailable, the interpolated yield based on available swap yield curve information.

In contrast, the zero coupon rate is *not* directly observable and is usually estimated from the existing par yield curve for the relevant instrument.

Traditionally, financial instruments are valued utilising coupon or par yield to maturity. However, use of coupon or par yields creates two problems:

- assumptions on reinvestment rates; and
- the absence of an unambiguous rate for each maturity.

Utilisation of the coupon or par yield techniques implies that the actual realised return only equals the normal redemption par yield to maturity if reinvestment rates on all intermediate cash flows, typically the coupons, are actually equal to the redemption yield. The realised yield, therefore, would only be equal to the par yield where the security is a zero coupon security, that is, a security which has *no* intermediate cash flows, as there is no potential reinvestment risk in the transaction. In practice, reinvestment rates on coupon cash flows will not equal the redemption yield. Theoretical forward rates (see below, Chapter 10) are the only true measure of available reinvestment rates, and even then, the forward rates implicit in the yield curves at any point in time do not guarantee that these reinvestment rates are *actually achieved.*

In addition, the use of coupon of par yields creates an ambiguous relationship between yields and maturities. The use of coupon or par yield technology does not facilitate the identification of the *unique* interest rate and, by implication, discount factor for a particular maturity. For example, assume the following yield curve exists:

Maturity (years)	Par yield % pa
0.25	7.25
0.50	7.55
1.00	7.92
1.50	8.23
2.00	9.05

Under these circumstances, a two year security, which pays intermediate coupons, say every six months, will be valued by discounting all payments at 9.05% pa. However, for an identical security, with a maturity of 1.5 years, all cash flows, including intermediate coupons, would be discounted at a different rate, namely, 8.23%. Consequently, the rates applicable for years 0.5, 1.00 and 1.5 can be, either, 9.05 or 8.23% pa depending, solely, on the final maturity of the security.

Consequently, coupon or par yield to maturity valuation does not imply an unambiguous relationship between the interest rate and the relevant maturity.

The problems of coupon or par yield to maturity technology are substantially overcome by utilising zero coupon rates.

As noted above, the zero coupon rate can be defined as the interest or discount rate which applies between a cash flow now and a cash flow at a single date in the future, which is equivalent to the yield on a pure discount bond or zero coupon security (hence, the reference to zero coupon rate). Utilising zero coupon rates allows, for example, a two year yield to be directly related to a pure two year security, being a pure zero coupon security with a single cash flow in two years time.

The use of zero coupon rates to discount or present value cash flows does not involve any assumptions as to the reinvestment rate applicable to any intermediate cash flows. In addition, the zero coupon rate has the advantage that each maturity is identified with a *single* unambiguous interest rate, being the rate of a pure single payment instrument. These factors allow zero coupon rates to be utilised to value and ultimately manage entire portfolios of financial instruments (swaps, hedges, cash etc) as a series of cash flows each of which is valued at a unique rate.

The actual computation of the zero coupon rate yield curve is complex. In theory, for each future payment of a coupon security, there exists a zero coupon rate that discounts that payment to its present value. These rates constitute the "zero coupon yield curve", points along which represent the yield to maturity of a zero coupon bond for the appropriate maturity rate. This zero coupon yield curve is estimated *from the existing par or coupon yield curve.* This is completed by calculating equilibrium zero coupon rates which value each component of the cash flow of conventional coupon securities in an internally consistent fashion, such that all par bonds would have the same value as the sum of their cash flow components. A detailed methodology for calculating zero coupon rates is set out in the Appendix to this chapter.

Both coupon or par yields to maturity and zero coupon rates require the existence of a known yield curve. This observable yield curve, in the swap market, is, generally, the combination of swap rates for given maturities. For example, in the US$ market, the swap yield curve is the treasury yield plus the swap spread quoted on a semi-annual bond basis for the relevant maturities.

In some markets, portions of the swap yield curve are taken from the yield curve implied by traded prices of futures contract on organised futures exchanges in the relevant currency.

For example, in the US$ market, the implied LIBOR yield curve from Eurodollar futures contracts is utilised as the swap yield curve for maturities up to approximately three years. As discussed in detail in Chapters 10 and 35, a strip rate is the implied yield of an investment or borrowing made in cash LIBOR up to the first futures contract and the rate on each successive futures contract thereafter. A strip yield curve is, usually, assumed to be the same as the swap yield curve because of the presence of arbitrage which would force the strip and swap yield curves to the same level.

The discount rates generated or utilised to calculate a discount factor which is essentially the present value of $1 at a specific future time. In theoretical terms, this is merely the price of the relevant zero coupon bond, discounted at the zero coupon rate (or, if appropriate, the par or coupon yield to maturity).

Mathematically, the discount factors are calculated as follows:

$$DF_{t1} = 1/(1 + R(t1))^{t1}$$

where

DF_{t1} = discount rate for time t

$R(t1)$ = The per annum discount rate at time t1

For example, for R(ti) = 10% and t1 = 1 year

$$DF(1) = 1/(1.10)^{1} = 0.909091$$

SWAP VALUATION—GENERIC SWAPS

The valuation methodology in respect of generic swaps entails two specific and distinct phases:

- the valuation of a generic (or "plain vanilla") swap; and
- the factoring in of the price/cost impact of variations from the generic structure to generate a price for the non-generic swap.

The pricing of non-generic swap structures is considered in the next section.

A generic swap structure refers to the underlying conventional swap structure which forms the basis for all swap transactions. Characteristics of a generic interest rate swap are summarised in *Exhibit 8.18*. Similarly, the corresponding characteristics of the generic currency swap are summarised in *Exhibit 8.19*.

Exhibit 8.20 summarises the approach to valuation of generic swap structures.

Exhibit 8.18

Characteristics of Generic Interest Rate Swap

Terms	**Definition**
Maturity	One to 15 Years.
Effective date	Depending on market convention, up to five business days from trade date. The effective date is such that the first fixed and first floating payment periods are full coupon periods (that is, no long or short first coupons).
Settlement date	Effective date.
All-in-cost	Depends on market convention, but usually the quarterly, semi-annual or annual equivalent of the internal rate of return of the fixed flows versus the floating index flat.
Premium or discount	None.
Fixed payment	
Fixed coupon	Current market rate.
Payment frequency	Either quarterly, semiannually or annually depending on market convention.
Day count	Based on market convention.
Pricing date	Trade date.
Floating payment	
Floating index	Certain money market indices.
Spread	None.
Determination source	Some publicly quoted source.
Payment frequency	The term of the floating index itself.
Day count	Based on market convention.
Reset frequency	The term of the floating index itself.
First coupon	Current market rate for the index.

Source: Adapted from Kopprasch et al, *The Interest Rate Swap Market: Yield Mathematics, Terminology and Conventions* (1985).

The basic valuation procedure for a generic interest rate swap is predicated on the transaction being characterised as an exchange of two securities: a fixed rate and a floating rate security. The swap can, therefore, be conceptualised as follows:

- a fixed rate payer is selling a fixed rate security and buying a floating rate security; or
- a fixed rate receiver is buying a fixed rate security and selling a floating rate security.

The valuation of the swap is, therefore, predicated on the valuation of the two different securities.

The two securities can be valued using traditional debt security valuation techniques based on present value concepts. Typically, the fixed rate security would be valued by solving the following equation:

$$P_o = \sum_{n=1}^{n} \frac{C_n}{(1 + i)^n} + \frac{P}{(1 + i)^n}$$

where P_o = the current market price of the instrument.
C_n = the expected cash flow (the periodic coupon) payable in period n.
P = the principal amount payable at maturity, period n.
n = the number of periods.
i = the yield to maturity, the discount rate or the internal rate of return.

Two factors complicate the basic valuation methodology:

- The interest rate swap involves neither an investment at commencement or a final maturity payment as only coupon flows are swapped.
- The expected cash flows under the floating rate security are not certain as they are contingent on the level of future interest rates.

Exhibit 8.19

*Characteristics of Generic Currency Swaps**

Terms	**Definition**
Maturity	One to 15 years.
Effective Date	Depending on market convention, two to five business days from trade date. The effective date is such that the first fixed and floating payments are full coupon periods (that is, no long or short first coupons).
Settlement Date	Effective date.
Contractual Exchange Rate	Exchange rate as between US$ and the relevant currency (or the two currencies if US$ is not involved) for value the effective date.
All-in-cost	Depends on market convention, but usually quarterly, semi-annual or annual equivalent of the internal rate of return of the fixed flows in the relevant currency versus US$ three or six month LIBOR flat.
Premium or Discount	None.
Currency	**Non-US$ currency.**
Notional Principal	US$ notional principal x contractual exchange rate.
Fixed Coupon	Current market rate in the relevant currency.
Payment Frequency	Either quarterly, semi-annual or annual depending on market convention.
Day Count	Based on market convention.
Pricing Date	Trade date.
Floating Payment Currency	**US$.**
Floating Index	US$ three or six month LIBOR.
Spread	None.
Determination Source	Some publicly quoted source (eg Reuters page LIBO).
Payment Frequency	The term of the floating rate index.
Day Count	Based on market convention (generally, Actual/360).
Reset Frequency	The term of the floating index itself.
First Coupon	Current market rate for the index.

* Most currency swaps are quoted and transacted as a fixed rate swap (in a non US$ currency) against US$ LIBOR and the terms set out here are for such a transaction.

Source: Adapted for Vince Balducci et al, *Currency Swaps: Corporate Applications and Pricing Methodology* (1990).

Exhibit 8.20

Generic Swap Valuation Methodology

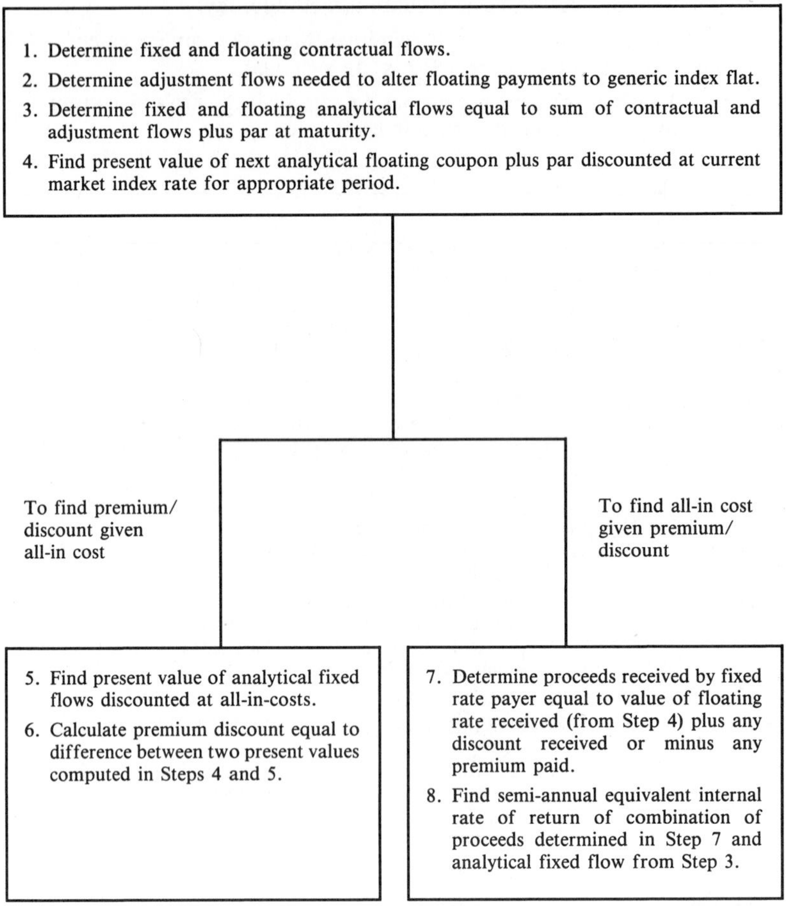

1. Determine fixed and floating contractual flows.
2. Determine adjustment flows needed to alter floating payments to generic index flat.
3. Determine fixed and floating analytical flows equal to sum of contractual and adjustment flows plus par at maturity.
4. Find present value of next analytical floating coupon plus par discounted at current market index rate for appropriate period.

To find premium/discount given all-in cost

5. Find present value of analytical fixed flows discounted at all-in-costs.
6. Calculate premium discount equal to difference between two present values computed in Steps 4 and 5.

To find all-in cost given premium/discount

7. Determine proceeds received by fixed rate payer equal to value of floating rate received (from Step 4) plus any discount received or minus any premium paid.
8. Find semi-annual equivalent internal rate of return of combination of proceeds determined in Step 7 and analytical fixed flow from Step 3.

Source: Kopprasch et al, *The Interest Rate Swap Market: Yield Mathematics, Terminology and Conventions* (1985).

The first consideration is not problematic as the party undertaking the swap simultaneously buys and sells the equivalent amount of a fixed rate and a floating rate security. This creates a netting of the two cash flows both at commencement and at maturity creating no net cash flow effect.

The uncertainty of the floating rate cash flow stream is more difficult and can be resolved utilising different approaches. Kopprasch et al (1985) resolve this issue simply. They argue that unlike a true floating rate security, a swap has two-way cash flows: fixed versus floating. This feature allows the swap market to value the relative attractiveness of a swap's floating index by bidding the accompanying fixed rate up or down. Consequently, the floating rate security may not require separate valuation. The value of the floating rate security is incorporated into the fixed cost quoted versus the floating payments. Therefore, valuation questions for swaps focus on the hypothetical fixed rate security.

In contrast, Bicksler and Chen (1986) argue that the pricing of the swap requires valuation of the floating rate security by incorporating assumptions as to the stochastic movements of short-term interest rates.

In practice, the former approach is utilised. This is because market participants assume that the floating rate component of a swap will tend to have a value close to par (its original value) because of its frequent repricing characteristic.

Available floating rate security pricing techniques, such as the simple margin, total margin, adjusted total margin or discount margin technique, are still required to adjust the floating rate security's return by quantifying an implicit change in the floating rate whenever the note deviates from par. These adjustments generally reflect minor price effects for swaps trading with a long or short coupon where the level of the floating rate index set is above or below the current market rate for the current coupon period. An example of this type of adjustment is set out in *Exhibit 8.21*.

The basic valuation procedure for an interest rate swap with a generic structure entails calculating the internal rate of return of the hypothetical fixed security cash flows. For analytical purposes these flows, from the perspective of the fixed rate payer, are the proceeds received from the sale of the hypothetical fixed rate security versus an outflow of the fixed rate payments plus the notional principal amount at maturity.

The proceeds, in this context, are not cash but instead are the value of the hypothetical floating rate security received in exchange. In a generic swap the value of the floating rate security is par. For non-generic swaps the proceeds are the net of the value of the floating rate security and any cash payment on the settlement date: see the discussion later in this chapter.

The internal rate of return (expressed as yield equivalent) of the hypothetical fixed security is quoted as the all-in cost versus the floating flows that constitute the index flat. The steps entailed in valuation are as follows:

- The cash flows of the two "securities" as specified in the swap contract are identified.
- Whether the floating payments are generic must be determined. If they are not, the floating cash flows must be adjusted to correspond to a stream of payments satisfying the generic standard. If the floating payments must be altered, the fixed cash flows must be adjusted by these equivalent dollar amounts (the adjustment flows) so that the swap's net cash flows remain unchanged.
- The final step in the process is to determine the internal rate of return (on a yield basis) of the analytical fixed flows. Because the floating cash flows were adjusted to be the generic standard, this internal rate of return is the swap's all-in-cost.

In practice, in a generic swap which is transacted at current market rates the prices of the exchanged "securities" are equal and, thus no net cash payment is exchanged upon settlement. In non-generic swaps, the prices may not be equal. In such a case, the net of the two purchase prices would determine the cash payment upon settlement or alternatively the adjustment to the swap rates themselves.

Exhibit 8.22 sets out examples of the valuation of generic interest rate swaps. *Exhibit 8.23* sets out examples of the valuation of generic currency swaps.

Exhibit 8.21

Pricing Adjustments for the Floating Rate Component of a Swap

For example, consider a swap with a floating side that resets and pays quarterly and floats off three month LIBOR. When priced with two months to the next floating payment, the discount rate should be the current two month LIBOR rate. The formula for the full price of the floating rate side, adjusted to be the index flat, is:

$$\text{Present value of the floating side} = \frac{100 + ER \times \dfrac{D_{PN}}{360}}{1 + \dfrac{CR}{100} \times \dfrac{D_{SN}}{360}}$$

where ER = the current rate in effect for the next floating coupon payment (expressed as a percentage).

D_{PN} = the actual number of days from the previous floating payment date to the next floating payment date.

CR = the current market rate of the index for the period from the settlement date to the next floating payment date (expressed as a percentage).

D_{SN} = the actual number of days from the settlement date to the next floating payment date.

The accrued interest portion of the full price of the floating side can be calculated using the following formula:

$$\text{Accrued interest on the floating side} = \frac{ER \times (D_{PN} - D_{SN})}{360}$$

To price the floating rate side of the base case swap with a settlement date of 1 June 19X5, assuming the current floating rate in effect was set at 8.9375% on 15 May 19X5, and that the current market rate for five and one half month LIBOR is 9%, the aforementioned formulas would be applied as follows:

$$\text{Full price of the floating side} = \frac{100 + \left(8.9375 + \dfrac{184}{360}\right)}{1 + \left(\dfrac{9.00}{100} + \dfrac{167}{360}\right)} = 100.377$$

$$\text{Accrued interest on floating side} = 8.9375 \times \frac{(184 - 167)}{360} = 0.422$$

Source: Kopprasch et al, *The Interest Rate Swap Market; Yield Mathematics, Terminology and Conventions* (1985).

Exhibit 8.22

Valuation of Generic Interest Rate Swap

The table below sets out the valuation of a five year US$ interest rate swap for $100m. The valuation focuses on the fixed rate payments only as the floating rate payments are assumed to have a value of $100m at commencement of the swap. The small deviation from zero net valuation (notional par value less the present value of the swap payments) is the result of rounding errors. Please note that the cash flows are valued at both par and zero coupon rates. The zero coupon rate valuation is different from the par yield valuation.

Generic Interest Rate Swap

Amount	$100,000,000	5 year bond	9.0100%
Start	27-Aug-X2	Spread	0.5400%
End	27-Aug-X2	Rate (% SA)	9.5500%
1st transaction	27-Feb-X3	Rate (% A)	9.7780%

Date	Days to cash flows	Semi Annual Tenor	Zero rates	Semi Annual Payments: Payments	Cash flow	NPV par yield	NPV Zero Rates	Annual Tenor	Annual Payments: Payments	Cash flow	NPV	NPV Zero Rates
27-Aug-X2	0	0.00			($100,000,000)	($100,000,000)	($100,000,000)	0.00		($100,000,000)	($100,000,000)	($100,000,000)
27-Feb-X3	184	1.01	7.000%	$4,814,247	$4,814,247	$4,593,082	$4,650,131	0.50		$0	$0	$0
27-Aug-X3	365	2.00	7.800%	$4,735,753	$4,735,753	$4,313,936	$4,386,903	1.00	$9,778,006	$9,778,006	$8,907,072	$9,057,727
27-Feb-X4	549	3.01	8.040%	$4,814,247	$4,814,247	$4,183,972	$4,275,994	1.50	$0	$0	$0	$0
27-Aug-X4	730	4.00	8.280%	$4,735,753	$4,735,753	$3,929,691	$4,026,417	2.00	$9,778,006	$9,778,006	$8,113,713	$8,313,426
27-Feb-X5	914	5.01	8.500%	$4,814,247	$4,814,247	$3,811,303	$3,908,404	2.50	$0	$0	$0	$0
27-Aug-X5	1095	6.00	8.730%	$4,735,753	$4,735,753	$3,579,671	$3,664,880	3.00	$9,778,006	$9,778,006	$7,391,019	$7.566,953
27-Feb-X6	1279	7.01	8.920%	$4,814,247	$4,814,247	$3,471,828	$3,545,867	3.50	$0	$0	$0	$0
27-Aug-X6	1461	8.01	9.110%	$4,761,918	$4,761,918	$3,278,004	$3,333,630	4.00	$9,804,795	$9,804,795	$6,749,416	$6,863,950
27-Feb-X7	1645	9.01	9.430%	$4,814,247	$4,814,247	$3,161,781	$3,178,148	4.51	$0	$0	$0	$0
27-Aug-X7	1826	10.01	9.760%	$4,735,753	$104,735,753	$65,676,086	$65,021,171	5.00	$9,778,006	$109,778,006	$68,837,905	$68,151,461
Totals				$47,776,164	$47,776,164	($645)	($8,454)		$48,916,820	$48,916,820	($876)	($46,484)

Exhibit 8.23

Valuation of Generic Currency Swap

The table below sets out the valuation of a five year US$/A$ fixed-to-fixed currency swap. The valuation focuses on the fixed rate payments in both currencies which are discounted back at the par and zero coupon rates for the relevant maturities. The value of the swap at commencement is zero (the slight deviation from zero is due to rounding errors). The valuation of a fixed-to-floating currency swap is identical with the exception that the floating rate component is assumed to a value equal to the notional value of the swap at commencement.

Generic Currency Swap—Fixed/Fixed Swap

Amount (US$)	$10,000,000
Deal date	25-Aug-X2
Start date	27-Aug-X2
Maturity	27-Aug-X7
1st transaction	27-Feb-X3
Swap exch rate (A$ = US$)	0.74
Current exch rate (A$ = US$)	0.74
Amount (A$):	$13,513,514
Current Swap Valuation (US$):	($9)

US$ Interest Rates	Original	Current
5 Year Swap (% SA)	9.5500%	9.5500%
Swap Rate (% A)	9.7780%	9.7780%

A$ Interest Rates	Original	Current
5 Year Swap (% SA)	8.8400%	8.8400%
Swap Rate (% A)	9.0354%	9.0354%

Date	Days to cash flows	S/A Tenor	US$ Payments (Semi-annual) US$ Zero Rates	Principal	Interest (Original)	Total	NPV @ 9.5500% (Current)	NPV @ Zero rates
27-Aug-X2	0	0.00		($10,000,000)		($10,000,000)	($10,000,000)	($10,000,000)
27-Feb-X3	184	1.01	7.00%		$481,425	$481,425	$459,308	$465,013
27-Aug-X3	365	2.00	7.80%		$473,575	$473,575	$431,394	$438,690
27-Feb-X4	549	3.01	8.04%		$481,425	$481,425	$418,397	$427,599
27-Aug-X4	730	4.00	8.28%		$473,575	$473,575	$392,969	$402,642
27-Feb-X5	914	5.01	8.50%		$481,425	$481,425	$381,130	$390,840
27-Aug-X5	1095	6.00	8.73%		$473,575	$473,575	$357,967	$366,488
27-Feb-X6	1279	7.01	8.92%		$481,425	$481,425	$347,183	$354,587
27-Aug-X6	1461	8.01	9.11%		$476,192	$476,192	$327,800	$333,363
27-Feb-X7	1645	9.01	9.43%		$481,425	$481,425	$316,178	$317,815
27-Aug-X7	1826	10.01	9.76%	$10,000,000	$473,575	$10,473,575	$6,567,609	$6,502,117
Total US$							($65)	($845)
Total A$							($87)	($1,142)
5 yr fwd rate								

Exhibit 8.23—continued

The Table below is a continuation of the Table on the previous page. The first three columns are repeated for convenience.

Generic Currency Swap—Fixed/Fixed Swap

Amount (US$)	$10,000,000
Deal date	25-Aug-X2
Start date	27-Aug-X2
Maturity	27-Aug-X7
1st transaction	27-Feb-X3
Swap exch rate (US$)	0.74
Current exch rate (A$)	0.74
Amount (A$):	$13,513,514
Current Swap Valuation (US$):	

Date	Days to cash flows	S/A Tenor	A$ Payments (Semi-annual) A$ Zero Rates	Principal	Interest (Original)	Total	NPV @ 8.8400% (Current)	NPV @ Zero rates
27-Aug-X2	0	0.00		($13,513,514)		($13,513,514)	($13,513,514)	($13,513,514)
27-Feb-X3	184	1.01	9.85%		$602,207	$602,207	$576,511	$573,713
27-Aug-X3	365	2.00	9.41%		$592,388	$592,388	$543,299	$540,345
27-Feb-X4	549	3.01	9.32%		$602,207	$602,207	$528,737	$525,098
27-Aug-X4	730	4.00	9.24%		$592,388	$592,388	$498,278	$494,478
27-Feb-X5	914	5.01	9.16%		$602,207	$602,207	$484,923	$481,219
27-Aug-X5	1095	6.00	9.09%		$592,388	$592,388	$456,987	$453,719
27-Feb-X6	1279	7.01	9.07%		$602,207	$602,207	$444,739	$441,322
27-Aug-X6	1461	8.01	9.06%		$595,661	$595,661	$421,334	$417,798
27-Feb-X7	1645	9.01	8.92%		$602,207	$602,207	$407,789	$406,383
27-Aug-X7	1826	10.01	8.78%	$13,513,514	$592,388	$14,105,902	$9,150,842	$9,177,188
Total US$							($56)	($1,665)
Total A$							($75)	($2,250)
5 yr fwd rate								

As noted above, a number of types of discount rates are available to present value swap cash flows to derive the valuation of a specific transaction. In particular, swap cash flows can be present valued utilising par or coupon yield to maturity or zero coupon rates. In the examples set out above, par or coupon yield to maturity are utilised to discount the cash flows. In each case, alternative values using zero coupon rates are also included. It is evident that there will be some discrepancy between the value generated utilising the par yields as against those generated by utilising zero coupon rates. In practice, a trader may speculate on any difference between the theoretical swap valuation, arrived at through pricing utilising zero coupon rates, and the market valuation of the swap based on par yields to maturity.

As discussed above and considered in detail in the context of hedging interest rate swaps (see above, Chapters 32 and 35), interest rate swaps with maturities up to approximately three years are typically priced of the implied LIBOR yield curve derived from Eurodollar futures contracts. The swap rate is an implied yield from a transaction, being a borrowing or lending transaction, undertaken in cash LIBOR up to the first futures contract and then at each successive rate of futures contracts thereafter. In the case where the commencement of the interest rate swap coincides with a futures contract date, then the interest rate swap is priced as the rate of the relevant futures contract. *Exhibit 8.24* sets out the pricing of a one year US$ swap priced off Eurodollar futures.

A similar technique can be utilised to price interest rate swaps in other currencies where there is an active short term interest rate futures market.

Exhibit 8.24

Pricing Short-Term Interest Rate Swap Off Eurodollar Futures Rates

Assume a bank is asked to price a one year (June 19X2/June 19X3) US$ interest rate swaps. IMM Eurodollar futures for the relevant months are trading as follows:

Contract	Contract Expiry	No of Days	Futures Price	Implied Yield (%PA)
June 19X2	15 June 19X2		92.60	7.40
September 19X2	14 September 19X2	91	92.28	7.72
December 19X2	14 December 19X2	91	92.04	7.96
March 19X3	12 March 19X3	88	91.85	8.15
	14 June 19X3	94		
			Average yield	7.8075

The yield on the one year swap can be calculated in two ways:

1. *Approximation—Quarterly Periods Assumed*

   The average yield of 7.8075% pa (quarterly) is compounded to an annual effective rate.

   $(1+0.078075/4)^4 - 1 =$ 0.080391
   or 8.0391% pa

   The 1 year swap price would be:

   Eurodollar Futures Strip: 8.0391% pa
   Bank Margin ± 0.05

   The bank would quote:

   7.9891/8.0891% pa

   The bank being prepared to pay 7.891% pa (receive 8.0891% pa) against receipt (payment) of three month US$ LIBOR.

Exhibit 8.24—continued

2. *Exact—Number of Days Used*

The above calculation assumed equal periods between the futures dates. In practice, the yield on the futures strip would be calculated as:

$(1+0.0740\times 91/365)\times(1+0.0772\times 91/365)\times(1+0.0796\times 88/365)\times$
$(1+0.0815\times 94/365) - 1$

= 0.080179 or 8.0179% pa.*

The bank would then quote:

7.9679/8.0679% pa

The difference of 0.02% on 2bps (using the spread mid point) is significant.

In practice, the exact day technique is to be preferred particularly, where a broken or stub period at the start and/on end of the swap is involved, making averaging inaccurate.

* A weighted average (using the number of days as the weighting factor) could also be utilised, yielding in similar results.

SWAP VALUATION—NON GENERIC SWAPS

The valuation of a swap can be affected by the introduction of variations in generic terms. A number of common variations include: delays in commencement date, altered payment frequency of floating rate cash flows, premium or discount structures, as well as valuation of unwinds or reversals of interest rate and currency swaps.

Deferred commencement

A common variation on standard swap structures relates to the delay in the effective date of commencement of the swap. *Exhibit 8.25* sets out the method for adjusting the swap rate for such a deferred start.

The basic technique for adjustment entails calculating the positive or negative accrual arising from the delay reflecting the difference in interest between the fixed rate on the swap transaction and the interest rate applicable for the period as between the normal commencement date and the delayed commencement date. In theoretical terms, the deferred start swap price reflects, quite simply, the implied forward price which can be derived from the swap yield curve itself.

Exhibit 8.25

Pricing Adjustment for Deferred Start

Assume a bank is asked to price a five year US$ interest rate swap where the bank receives fixed rate for a deferred start. The transaction date is 5 May 19X7. The normal effective or commencement would be 7 May 19X7, however the counterparty wishes the swap to commence from 7 June 19X7—a delay of 31 days.

The pricing adjustment for the delay can be derived in two ways:

1. Adjusting for the positive or negative accrual for the delay period—

This assumes that the bank enters into a normal 5 year swap at the time of committing to the delayed start swap to hedge its exposure.

Exhibit 8.25—continued

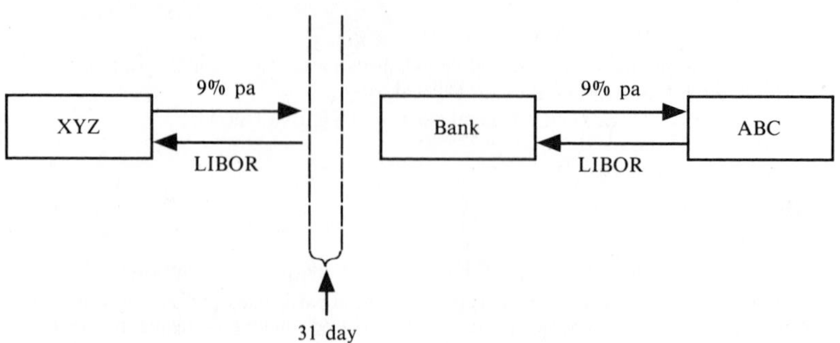

This creates a cash flow mismatch which must be valued. Assuming the six month LIBOR rate is 7.25% pa semi-annually, the adjustment is as follows:

S/A Bond Equivalent Basis (365/365)

Bank pays:	8.806% pa*
Bank receives:	7.351% pa#

*9.00% pa converted to semi-annual basis
#7.25% pa semi-annually (money market 365/360 day basis) converted to 365/365 day basis.

This results in the bank suffering a loss of 1.455% pa or 12.36bps over 31 days (calculated as 1.455% pa × 31/365). This 12.36bps is equivalent to 3.18bps pa when amortised over five years (the term of the swap) at the swap rate (9.00% pa).

The swap rate quoted is therefore 9.0318% pa.

2. Adjusting for the hedge cost—

The approach outlined above assumes the delayed start swap is hedged with a normal commencement swap. In practice, an alternative means of hedging the swap would be to sell a five year Government Bond and re-invest the proceeds for the delay period. The short bond position would be closed and a five year swap entered into effective 7 June 19X7 to hedge the delayed start swap. The gain on the Bond hedge would compensate for the movement in swap rates during the delay period.

Assuming the bond rate is 8.00% pa semi-annually and the repo (repurchase) rate is 6.00% pa semi-annually (the rate at which the bond proceeds are re-invested), the cost to the bank is 2.00% pa or 16.99bps over 31 days. This is equivalent to 4.367bps pa over the life of the swap resulting in an adjusted swap price of 9.0436% pa.

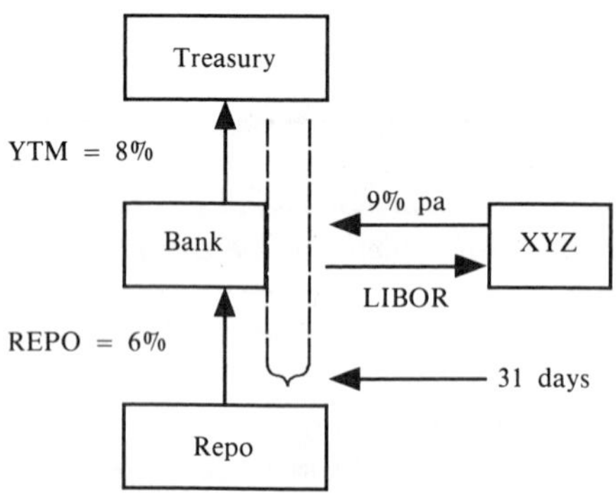

Payment frequency of floating rate index

Another common variation entails a mismatch in the payment frequency of the floating rate index. A reset frequency mismatch occurs when the reset frequency does not agree with the maturity of the floating rate index.

Exhibit 8.26
Payment Frequency of Floating Rate Index

Assume that a bank is asked to price a US$ interest swap for five years under which it receives fixed rate US$ and pays six month US$ LIBOR. The six month US$ LIBOR payments are, however, to be compounded and paid annually.

Assuming six month LIBOR is 4.50% pa (semi-annually), the compounded *annual* rate payable would be: 4.5506% pa. However, this implicitly assumes that the six month US$ LIBOR cash flow received (from the off-setting swap) and invested must yield, 4.50% pa semi-annually. In practice, this rate of return may not be available, necessitating an adjustment in the swap price.

The table below sets out the derivation of this adjustment. The pricing adjustment is calculated as follows:

- The investment (borrowing) rate is assumed (4%pa)
- The cash flow received (paid) at the end of six months period is discounted at the assumed investment rate.
- The *present value* of the cash flow to be paid at the end of one year is set at the present value of the six month cash flow. The future of this one year cash flow is then calculated at the assumed discount rate.
- The non-compounded LIBOR rate is then calculated based on the one year interest payment derived.

The difference in rates—4.5446% pa (non-compounded) versus 4.5506% pa (compounded)—of 0.6bps is used to adjust the fixed rate payable under the swap.

Payment Frequency of Floating Rate Compounding Analysis

Amount:	$100,000,000
Deal date:	25-Aug-X2
Start date:	27-Aug-X2
Maturity:	27-Aug-X7
LIBOR (6 M):	4.500%
LIBOR (12 M):	4.5506%
LIBOR (Non-compounded):	4.5446%

Date	No of days	Tenor (years)	Payments (LIBOR-6M)	Payments (LIBOR-1Y)	Difference	PV @ 4.00%
27-Aug-X2	0					
27-Feb-X3	184	0.5	$2,300,000	$0	($2,300,000)	($2,254,972)
27-Aug-X3	365	1.0	$2,262,500	$4,607,671	$2,345,171	$2,254,972
27-Feb-X4	549	1.5	$2,300,000	$0	($2,300,000)	($2,168,242)
27-Aug-X4	730	2.0	$2,262,500	$4,607,671	$2,345,171	$2,168,242
27-Feb-X5	914	2.5	$2,300,000	$0	($2,300,000)	($2,084,848)
27-Aug-X5	1095	3.0	$2,262,500	$4,607,671	$2,345,171	$2,084,848
27-Feb-X6	1279	3.5	$2,300,000	$0	($2,300,000)	($2,004,662)
27-Aug-X6	1461	4.0	$2,275,000	$4,620,423	$2,345,423	$2,004,662
27-Feb-X7	1645	4.5	$2,300,000	$0	($2,300,000)	($1,927,352)
27-Aug-X7	1826	5.0	$2,262,500	$4,607,671	$2,345,171	$1,927,352

For example, a reset frequency mismatch may entail six month LIBOR paid annually. *Exhibit 8.26* outlines the technique for adjusting the floating rate payments in a swap transaction where such a reset frequency mismatch occurs. In essence, the counterparty being asked to absorb the timing and reset mismatch is required to identify the reinvestment/borrowing costs applicable to the transaction and factor these into the price of the swap.

An alternative reset frequency mismatch which also occurs frequently is where under the terms of the swap the floating rate side is calculated as monthly resets of six month LIBOR. Such frequent resets will generally have a valuation effect as investors who have chosen a six month maturity have forsaken shorter maturities and more frequent repricing opportunities. Theoretically, on average the market expectation for the course of interest rates over the next six months will be incorporated in the six month rate. Therefore, altering the reset frequency will generally have valuation effects relative to the generic swap nature. As in the case of the six month LIBOR compounded and paid annually, specific valuation effects will vary with the expectations as to interest rates (the implicit reinvestment/borrowing rate assumptions) and portfolio considerations for the swap counterparty.

Off-market swaps—premium on discount structures

Another common variation to generic structures is the valuation of off-market swaps (also referred to as premium or discount structures). Under these types of arrangements, the interest rate coupons and, in the case of currency swaps, the currency rates utilised in the swap transaction are varied from current market rates. This necessitates payment, at the commencement of the transaction, by one counterparty to the other compensating for the off-market coupon or notional principal amounts.

Exhibit 8.27 sets out an example of an off-market interest rate swap.

Exhibit 8.27
Off-Market Swaps: Interest Rate Swaps

The tables below set out examples of the valuation of above and below market coupon swaps. These swaps are valued using two methods:

1. Matching Cash Flows—whereby the cash flows of an offsetting swap (at normal market coupon) is compared to the off market swap cash flows and the difference in cash flows are discounted.
2. Discounting Swap Cash Flows—whereby the cash flows of the off-market swap are discounted at current market rates to derive a premium or discount for the swap.

Please note the slightly different values of the swaps generated by the two methods as well as those derived from the use of zero coupon rather than par-yield rates.

Off Market Rate Interest Rate Swap: Example 1

	Input	Year	Input Zero Yields
Amount	$10,000,000	1	6.4500%
Deal date	25-Aug-X2	2	6.8400%
Start date	27-Aug-X2	3	7.0100%
Maturity	27-Aug-X7	4	7.3900%
1st cash flow	27-Feb-X3	5	7.8500%

Exhibit 8.27—continued

5 year bond	6.8000%	Swap Rate (% S/A)	7.4800%
Spread	0.6800%	Swap Rate (% A)	7.6199%
Off-mkt rate	5.0000%		

Approach 1—Matching Cash Flows

Date	No of Days	Tenor (Annual)	Payments (Off-Market) 5.0000%	Payments (Normal) 7.6199%	Difference −2.6199%	NPV @ 7.6199%	NPV @ Zero Rate
27-Aug-X2	0	0.00					
27-Feb-X3	184	0.50					
27-Aug-X3	365	1.00	$500,000	$761,988	($261,988)	($243,438)	($246,113)
27-Feb-X4	549	1.50	$0	$0	$0	$0	
27-Aug-X4	730	2.00	$500,000	$761,988	($261,988)	($226,202)	($229,516)
27-Feb-X5	914	2.50	$0	$0	$0	$0	
27-Aug-X5	1095	3.00	$500,000	$761,988	($261,988)	($210,186)	($213,800)
27-Feb-X6	1279	3.50	$0	$0	$0	$0	
27-Aug-X6	1461	4.00	$501,370	$764,075	($262,705)	($195,800)	($197,483)
27-Feb-X7	1645	4.51	$0	$0	$0	$0	
27-Aug-X7	1826	5.00	$500,000	$761,988	($261,988)	($181,439)	($179,511)
		Total	$2,501,370	$3,812,026	($1,310,656)	($1,057,064)	($1,066,422)

Approach 2—Discounting Swap Cash Flows

Date	No of Days	Tenor (Annual)	Payments (Off-Market) 5.0000%	Principal	Cash Flow	NPV @ 7.6199%	NPV @ Zero Rate
27-Aug-X2	0	0.00		($10,000,000)	($10,000,000)	($10,000,000)	($10,000,000)
27-Feb-X3	184	0.50	$0	$0	$0	$0	
27-Aug-X3	365	1.00	$500,000	$0	$500,000	$464,598	$469,704
27-Feb-X4	549	1.50	$0	$0	$0	$0	
27-Aug-X4	730	2.00	$500,000	$0	$500,000	$431,703	$438,028
27-Feb-X5	914	2.50	$0	$0	$0	$0	
27-Aug-X5	1095	3.00	$500,000	$0	$500,000	$401,137	$408,035
27-Feb-X6	1279	3.50	$0	$0	$0	$0	
27-Aug-X6	1461	4.00	$501,370	$0	$501,370	$373,681	$376,893
27-Feb-X7	1645	4.51	$0	$0	$0	$0	
27-Aug-X7	1826	5.00	$500,000	$10,000,000	$10,500,000	$7,271,759	$7,194,467
		Total	$2,501,370		$2,501,370	($1,057,122)	($1,112,873)

Off-Market Rate Interest Rate Swap: Example 2

	Input	Year	Input Zero Yields
Amount	$10,000,000	1	6.4500%
Deal date	25-Aug-X2	2	6.8400%
Start date	27-Aug-X2	3	7.0100%
Maturity	27-Aug-X7	4	7.3900%
1st cash flow	27-Feb-X3	5	7.8500%

5 year bond	6.8000%	Swap Rate (% S/A)	7.4800%
Spread	0.6800%	Swap Rate (% A)	7.6199%
Off-mkt rate	10.0000%		

Exhibit 8.27—continued

Approach 1—Matching Cash Flows

Date	No of Days	Tenor (Annual)	Payments (Off-Market) 10.0000%	Payments (Normal) 7.6199%	Difference 2.3801%	NPV @ 7.6199%	NPV @ Zero Rate
27-Aug-X2	0	0.00					
27-Feb-X3	184	0.50					
27-Aug-X3	365	1.00	$1,000,000	$761,988	$238,012	$221,160	$223,591
27-Feb-X4	549	1.50	$0	$0	$0	$0	
27-Aug-X4	730	2.00	$1,000,000	$761,988	$238,012	$205,501	$208,512
27-Feb-X5	914	2.50	$0	$0	$0	$0	
27-Aug-X5	1095	3.00	$1,000,000	$761,988	$238,012	$190,951)	$194,235
27-Feb-X6	1279	3.50	$0	$0	$0	$0	
27-Aug-X6	1461	4.00	$1,002,740	$764,075	$238,664	$177,881	$179,410
27-Feb-X7	1645	4.51	$0	$0	$0	$0	
27-Aug-X7	1826	5.00	$1,000,000	$761,988	$238,012	$164,835	$163,083
		Total	$5,002,740	$3,812,026	$1,190,714	$960,329	$968,831

Approach 2—Discounting Swap Cash Flows

Date	No of Days	Tenor (Annual)	Payments (Off-Market) 10.0000%	Principal	Cash Flow	NPV @ 7.6199%	NPV @ Zero Rate
27-Aug-X2	0	0.00		($10,000,000)	($10,000,000)	($10,000,000)	($10,000,000)
27-Feb-X3	184	0.50	$0	$0	$0	$0	
27-Aug-X3	365	1.00	$1,000,000	$0	$1,000,000	$929,196	$939,408
27-Feb-X4	549	1.50	$0	$0	$0	$0	
27-Aug-X4	730	2.00	$1,000,000	$0	$1,000,000	$863,406	$876,057
27-Feb-X5	914	2.50	$0	$0	$0	$0	
27-Aug-X5	1095	3.00	$1,000,000	$0	$1,000,000	$802,274	$816,069
27-Feb-X6	1279	3.50	$0	$0	$0	$0	
27-Aug-X6	1461	4.00	$1,002,740	$0	$1,002,740	$747,362	$753,786
27-Feb-X7	1645	4.51	$0	$0	$0	$0	
27-Aug-X7	1826	5.00	$1,000,000	$10,000,000	$11,000,000	$7,618,033	$7,537,061
		Total	$5,002,740		$5,002,740	$960,271	$922,381

In the case of a currency swap, use of an off-market coupon in either currency would necessitate a similar adjustment to that utilised in the case of the interest rate swap. However, it is also feasible to vary the currency rate embedded in the swap transaction. *Exhibit 8.28* sets out an example of valuation techniques for such a transaction. In this particular case, it is feasible to either compensate the relevant counterparty for the off-market exchange rate through an upfront payment or by altering the coupon flows on one or other payment side of the swap transaction.

Unwind/reversal valuations

Swap transactions, frequently, are required to be terminated prior to maturity. Such early terminations may be required for a number of reasons including:

- desire to take profit/minimise losses from the swap transaction;
- termination of the underlying business rationale (for example, the funding) to which the swap transactions related; or
- default by one counterparty, necessitating determination of the swap's liquidation value.

Exhibit 8.29 outlines the methodology for calculating the unwind or reversal value of the interest rate swap. *Exhibit 8.30* sets out a corresponding methodology for calculating the unwind value of a currency swap.

Exhibit 8.28

Off-Market Swaps: Currency Swaps

The Table below sets out an example of the valuation of a currency swap where the exchange rates utilised for the swap is different from the current market rate. Please note that the different notional principal amounts (resulting from the artificial exchange rates) results in off-market interest cash flows (*amounts* but not interest rates) in one currency. The currency swap is valued by discounting the swap cash flows at *current market swap rates* and converted at the *current exchange rate*.

Valuation of Off-Market Currency Swap—Fixed/Fixed Swap

Amount (US$)	$10,000,000	
Deal date	25-Aug-X2	
Start date	27-Aug-X2	
Maturity	27-Aug-X7	
1st transaction	27-Feb-X3	
Swap exch rate (A$1 = US$)	0.8000	
Current exch rate (A$1 = US$)	0.7400	
Initial Amount (A$):	$12,500,000	
Current Swap Valuation (US$):	Par yield	$749,987
	Zero rate	$750,695

US$ Interest Rates	Original	Current
5 Year Swap (% S/A)	9.5500%	9.5500%
Swap Rate (% A)	9.7780%	9.7780%

A$ Interest Rates	Original	Current
5 Year Swap (% S/A)	8.8400%	8.8400%
Swap Rate (% A)	9.0354%	9.0354%

Date	Days to Cash Flows	Semi-Annual Tenor	US$ Zero Rates	US$ Payments (Semi-Annual) Principal	Interest (Original)	Total	NPV @ 9.5500% (Current)	NPV @ Zero Rates
27-Aug-X2	0	0.00		($10,000,000)		($10,000,000)		
27-Feb-X3	184	1.01	7.00%		$481,425	$481,425	$459,308	$465,013
27-Aug-X3	365	2.00	7.80%		$473,575	$473,575	$431,394	$438,690
27-Feb-X4	549	3.01	8.04%		$481,425	$481,425	$418,397	$427,599
27-Aug-X4	730	4.00	8.28%		$473,575	$473,575	$392,969	$402,642
27-Feb-X5	914	5.01	8.50%		$481,425	$481,425	$381,130	$390,840
27-Aug-X5	1095	6.00	8.73%		$473,575	$473,575	$357,967	$366,488
27-Feb-X6	1279	7.01	8.92%		$481,425	$481,425	$347,183	$354,587
27-Aug-X6	1461	8.01	9.11%		$476,192	$476,192	$327,800	$333,363
27-Feb-X7	1645	9.01	9.43%		$481,425	$481,425	$316,178	$317,815
27-Aug-X7	1826	10.01	9.76%	$10,000,000	$473,575	$10,473,575	$6,567,609	$6,502,117
Total US$						NPV cash flows (US$):	$9,999,935	$9,999,155
Total A$						NPV cash flows (A$):	$13,513,426	13,512,371

Exhibit 8.28—continued

The Table below is a continuation of the Table on the previous page. The first three columns are repeated for convenience.

Valuation of Off-Market Currency Swap

Amount (US$)	$10,000,000
Deal date	25-Aug-X2
Start date	27-Aug-X2
Maturity	27-Aug-X7
1st transaction	27-Feb-X3
Swap exch rate (US$1 =)	
Current exch rate (US$1 =)	
Initial Amount (A$):	$12,500,000
Current Swap Valuation (US$):	

Date	Days to Cash Flows	Semi-Annual Tenor	A$ Payments (Semi-Annual) A$ Zero Rates	Principal	Interest (Original)	Total	NPV @ 8.8400% (Current)	NPV @ Zero Rates
27-Aug-X2	0	0.00		($12,500,000)		($12,500,000)		
27-Feb-X3	184	1.01	9.85%		$557,041	$557,041	$533,272	$530,685
27-Aug-X3	365	2.00	9.41%		$547,959	$547,959	$502,552	$499,819
27-Feb-X4	549	3.01	9.32%		$557,041	$557,041	$489,082	$485,716
27-Aug-X4	730	4.00	9.24%		$547,959	$547,959	$460,907	$457,393
27-Feb-X5	914	5.01	9.16%		$557,041	$557,041	$448,554	$445,127
27-Aug-X5	1095	6.00	9.09%		$547,959	$547,959	$422,713	$419,690
27-Feb-X6	1279	7.01	9.07%		$557,041	$557,041	$411,384	$408,222
27-Aug-X6	1461	8.01	9.06%		$550,986	$550,986	$389,734	$386,463
27-Feb-X7	1645	9.01	8.92%		$557,041	$557,041	$377,204	$375,904
27-Aug-X7	1826	10.01	8.78%	$12,500,000	$547,959	$13,047,959	$8,464,528	$8,488,899
Total US$						NPV cash flows (US$):	$9,249,949	$9,248,460
Total A$						NPV cash flows (A$):	$12,499,930	12,497,919

Exhibit 8.28—continued

The valuation procedure for off-market currency swaps where one or both coupons is set at rates away from current market rate is very similar to the procedure outlined in relation to interest rate swaps (*Exhibit 8.27*) with the off market swap flows being discounted at market rates *in the relevant* currency and converted at the current exchange rate. An example of this is set out in the table below:

Valuation of Off-Market Currency Swap—Fixed/Fixed Swap

Amount (US$)	$10,000,000	
Deal date	25-Aug-X2	
Start date	27-Aug-X2	
Maturity	27-Aug-X7	
1st transaction	27-Feb-X3	
Swap exch rate (US$1 =)	0.8000	
Current exch rate (US$1 =)	0.7400	
Initial Amount (A$):	$12,500,000	
Current Swap Valuation (US$):	Par yield	($1,016,786)
	Zero rate	($1,019,393)

US$ Interest Rates	Original	Current
5 Year Swap (% S/A)	8.0000%	9.5500%
Swap Rate (% A)	8.1600%	9.7780%

A$ Interest Rates	Original	Current
5 Year Swap (% S/A)	12.0000%	8.8400%
Swap Rate (% A)	12.3600%	9.0354%

Date	Days to Cash Flows	Semi-Annual Tenor	US$ Payments (Semi-Annual) US$ Zero Rates	Principal	Interest (Original)	Total	NPV @ 9.5500% (Current)	NPV @ Zero Rates
27-Aug-X2	0	0.00		($10,000,000)		($10,000,000)		
27-Feb-X3	184	1.01	7.00%		$403,288	$403,288	$384,761	$389,540
27-Aug-X3	365	2.00	7.80%		$396,712	$396,712	$361,377	$367,489
27-Feb-X4	549	3.01	8.04%		$403,288	$403,288	$350,490	$358,198
27-Aug-X4	730	4.00	8.28%		$396,712	$396,712	$329,189	$337,292
27-Feb-X5	914	5.01	8.50%		$403,288	$403,288	$319,271	$327,406
27-Aug-X5	1095	6.00	8.73%		$396,712	$396,712	$299,868	$307,006
27-Feb-X6	1279	7.01	8.92%		$403,288	$403,288	$290,834	$297,036
27-Aug-X6	1461	8.01	9.11%		$398,904	$398,904	$274,597	$279,257
27-Feb-X7	1645	9.01	9.43%		$403,288	$403,288	$264,861	$266,232
27-Aug-X7	1826	10.01	9.76%	$10,000,000	$396,712	$10,396,712	$6,519,411	$6,454,400
Total US$						NPV cash flows (US$):	$9,394,658	$9,383,855
Total A$						NPV cash flows (A$):	$12,695,484	12,680,885

Exhibit 8.28—continued

The Table below is a continuation of the Table on the previous page. The first three columns are repeated for convenience.

Valuation of Off-Market Currency Swap

Amount (US$)	$10,000,000
Deal date	25-Aug-X2
Start date	27-Aug-X2
Maturity	27-Aug-X7
1st transaction	27-Feb-X3
Swap exch rate (US$1 =)	
Current exch rate (US$1 =)	
Initial Amount (A$):	$12,500,000
Current Swap Valuation (US$):	

Date	Days to Cash Flows	Semi-Annual Tenor	A$ Payments (Semi-Annual) A$ Zero Rates	Principal	Interest (Original)	Total	NPV @ 8.8400% (Current)	NPV @ Zero Rates
27-Aug-X2	0	0.00		($12,500,000)		($12,500,000)		
27-Feb-X3	184	1.01	9.85%		$756,164	$756,164	$723,899	$720,387
27-Aug-X3	365	2.00	9.41%		$743,836	$743,836	$682,197	$678,488
27-Feb-X4	549	3.01	9.32%		$756,164	$756,164	$663,912	$659,343
27-Aug-X4	730	4.00	9.24%		$743,836	$743,836	$625,666	$620,895
27-Feb-X5	914	5.01	9.16%		$756,164	$756,164	$608,896	$604,245
27-Aug-X5	1095	6.00	9.09%		$743,836	$743,836	$573,819	$569,715
27-Feb-X6	1279	7.01	9.07%		$756,164	$756,164	$558,439	$554,148
27-Aug-X6	1461	8.01	9.06%		$747,945	$747,945	$529,051	$524,610
27-Feb-X7	1645	9.01	8.92%		$756,164	$756,164	$512,042	$510,278
27-Aug-X7	1826	10.01	8.78%	$12,500,000	$743,836	$13,243,836	$8,591,598	$8,616,335
Total US$						NPV cash flows (US$):	$10,411,445	$10,403,248
Total A$						NPV cash flows (A$):	$14,069,520	14,058,443

Exhibit 8.29

Unwind or Reversal Value: Interest Rate Swap

The table below sets out the method of valuation for an existing US$ interest rate swap where it is sought to reverse or unwind the transaction. The unwind valuation is calculated as follows:

- The *future* cash flows payable/receivable under the swap are identified.
- The cash flows for a matching but offsetting swap are identified using *current market rates*.
- The differences in cash flows are discounted back at the appropriate discount rates (par on zero coupon).

Please note the need to use a shortened or stub period in structuring the offsetting swap and the corresponding less than full interest period accrual on both the fixed and floating rate side.

Reversal/Unwind of Interest Rate Swap

				Year	Zero Yields
Amount (US$)	$10,000,000				
Deal date	25-Aug-X2	5 year bond	6.4800%	1	6.12%
Start date	27-Aug-X2	Spread	0.7500%	2	6.93%
Maturity	27-Aug-X7	Swap rate (%SA)	7.2300%	3	9.81%
Unwind date	15-Dec-X2	Swap rate (%A)	7.3607%	4	7.39%
1st transaction	27-Feb-X3			5	7.92%
Initial fxd	7.9500%	Current LIBOR	5.1250%		
Initial lib	6.8000%				

Date	Days to Cash Flows	Tenor (Annual)	Pay Fixed (Original)	Pay Fixed (Current)	Payments Out Profit/ (Loss)	Receive Floating (Original)	Receive Floating (Current)	Payments In Profit/ (Loss)	Total Profit/ (Loss)	NPV @ 7.3607%	NPV @ Zero Rates
27-Aug-X2	0	0.00									
15-Dec-X2	110	0.30									
27-Feb-X3	184	0.50				$347,556	$105,347	$242,208	$242,208	$238,746	$239,309
27-Aug-X3	365	1.00	$795,000	$514,239	($280,761)	$0	$0	$0	($280,761)	($267,169)	($269,348)
27-Feb-X4	549	1.50	$0	$0	$0	$0	$0	$0	$0	$0	$0
27-Aug-X4	730	2.00	$795,000	$736,068	($58,932)	$0	$0	$0	($58,932)	($52,234)	($53,276)
27-Feb-X5	914	2.50	$0	$0	$0	$0	$0	$0	$0	$0	$0
27-Aug-X5	1095	3.00	$795,000	$736,068	($58,932)	$0	$0	$0	($58,932)	($48,653)	($50,203)
27-Feb-X6	1279	3.50	$0	$0	$0	$0	$0	$0	$0	$0	$0
27-Aug-X6	1461	4.00	$797,178	$738,085	($59,093)	$0	$0	$0	($59,093)	($45,433)	($47,430)
27-Feb-X7	1645	4.51	$0	$0	$0	$0	$0	$0	$0	$0	$0
27-Aug-X7	1826	5.00	$795,000	$736,068	($58,932)	$0	$0	$0	($58,932)	($42,202)	($44,573)
Total			$3,977,178	$3,460,529					($274,441)	($216,946)	($225,520)

Exhibit 8.30

Unwind or Reversal Value: Currency Swap

The Table below sets out the valuation methodology for pricing the unwind or reversal of an existing A$/US$ fixed-to-fixed currency swap. The second Table sets out corresponding valuation methodology for a A$/US$ fixed A$ to floating US$ LIBOR currency swap.

The basic technique used is identical to that described in *Exhibit 8.29* with exception that it is necessary to convert cash flows in one currency into its equivalent in the other currency at *current exchange rates*.

Reversal of Fixed-to-Fixed Currency Swap

Amount (US$)	$10,000,000
Deal date	25-Aug-X2
Start date	27-Aug-X2
Maturity	27-Aug-X7
1st transaction	27-Feb-X3
Unwind date	2-Jan-X3
Swap exch rate (A$1 = US$)	0.78
Current exch rate (A$1 = US$)	0.745
Original amount (A$):	$12,820,513
Current amount (A$):	$13,422,819

US$ Interest Rates	Original	Current
5 Year Swap (% SA)	9.5500%	8.1250%
Swap Rate (% A)	9.7780%	8.2900%

A$ Interest Rates	Original	Current
5 Year Swap (% SA)	8.8400%	8.7500%
Swap Rate (% A)	9.0354%	8.9414%
Current swap valuation (US$)	Par yield	($998,426)
Current swap valuation (US$)	Zero rate	($987,831)

Date	Days to Cash Flows	Semi-Annual Tenor	Adjusted Tenor	US$ Payments (Semi-Annual): US$ Zero Rates	Principal	Interest (Original)	Total	Offsetting Swap: Total	Difference	NPV @ 8.1250% (Current)	NPV @ Zero Rates
27-Aug-X2	0	0.00									
2-Jan-X3	128	0.70									
27-Feb-X3	184	1.01	0.31	7.00%		$481,425	$481,425	$124,658	($356,767)	($352,434)	($353,021)
27-Aug-X3	365	2.00	1.30	7.80%		$473,575	$473,575	$402,911	($70,664)	($67,103)	($67,239)
27-Feb-X4	549	3.01	2.31	8.04%		$481,425	$481,425	$409,589	($71,836)	($65,531)	($65,592)
27-Aug-X4	730	4.00	3.30	8.28%		$473,575	$473,575	$402,911	($70,664)	($61,966)	($61,814)
27-Feb-X5	914	5.01	4.31	8.50%		$481,425	$481,425	$409,589	($71,836)	($60,514)	($60,047)
27-Aug-X5	1095	6.00	5.30	8.73%		$473,575	$473,575	$402,911	($70,664)	($57,222)	($56,349)
27-Feb-X6	1279	7.01	6.31	8.92%		$481,425	$481,425	$409,589	($71,836)	($55,881)	($54,554)
27-Aug-X6	1461	8.01	7.30	9.11%		$476,192	$476,192	$405,137	($71,055)	($53,122)	($51,321)
27-Feb-X7	1645	9.01	8.31	9.43%		$481,425	$481,425	$409,589	($71,836)	($51,592)	($48,980)
27-Aug-X7	1826	10.01	9.30	9.76%	$10,000,000	$473,575	$10,473,575	$10,402,911	($70,664)	($48,786)	($45,360)
Total US$										($874,151)	($864,277)
Total A$										($1,173,358)	($1,160,104)

Exhibit 8.30—continued

The Table below is a continuation of the Table on the previous page. The first three columns are repeated for convenience.

Date	Days to Cash Flows	Semi-Annual Tenor	Adjusted Tenor	A$ Payments (Semi-Annual)				Offsetting Swap	Difference	NPV @ 8.750% (Current)	NPV @ Zero Rates
				US$ Zero Rates	Principal	Interest (Original)	Total	Total			
27-Aug-X2	0	0.00									
2-Jan-X3	128	0.70									
27-Feb-X3	184	1.01	0.31	9.85%		$571,324	$571,324	$180,197	$391,127	$386,022	$385,400
27-Aug-X3	365	2.00	1.30	9.41%		$562,009	$562,009	$582,422	($20,412)	($19,308)	($19,229)
27-Feb-X4	549	3.01	2.31	9.32%		$571,324	$571,324	$592,075	($20,751)	($18,799)	($18,681)
27-Aug-X4	730	4.00	3.30	9.24%		$562,009	$562,009	$582,422	($20,412)	($17,724)	($17,587)
27-Feb-X5	914	5.01	4.31	9.16%		$571,324	$571,324	$592,075	($20,751)	($17,256)	($17,111)
27-Aug-X5	1095	6.00	5.30	9.09%		$562,009	$562,009	$582,422	($20,412)	($16,269)	($16,129)
27-Feb-X6	1279	7.01	6.31	9.07%		$571,324	$571,324	$592,075	($20,751)	($15,840)	($15,688)
27-Aug-X6	1461	8.01	7.30	9.06%		$565,114	$565,114	$585,639	($20,525)	($15,013)	($14,851)
27-Feb-X7	1645	9.01	8.31	8.92%		$571,324	$571,324	$529,075	($20,751)	($14,536)	($14,438)
27-Aug-X7	1826	10.01	9.30	8.78%	$12,820,513	$562,009	$13,382,522	$14,005,240	($622,718)	($418,088)	($417,530)
Total US$										($124,274)	($123,554)
Total A$										($166,811)	($165,844)

Exhibit 8.30—continued

Reversal of Fixed-to-Floating Currency Swap

Amount (US$)	$7,420,000	US$ Interest Rates	Original	Current
Deal date	25-Aug-X2	LIBOR (% S/A)	6.8750%	4.5625%
Start date	27-Aug-X2			
Maturity	27-Aug-X7			
1st transaction	27-Feb-X3			
Unwind date	2-Jan-X3	A$ Interest Rates	Original	Current
Swap exch rate (A$1 = US$)	0.742	5 Year Swap (% S/A)	10.5500%	10.1280%
Current exch rate (A$1 = US$)	0.7755	Swap Rate (% A)	10.8283%	10.3844%
Original amount (A$):	$10,000,000	Current swap valuation (US$)	Par yield	$533,031
Current amount (A$):	$9,568,021	Current swap valuation (US$)	Zero rate	$553,024

Date	Days to Cash Flows	Semi-Annual Tenor	Adjusted Tenor	US$ Payments (Semi-Annual): US$ Zero Rates	US$ Payments (Semi-Annual): Principal	US$ Payments (Semi-Annual): Interest (Original)	US$ Payments (Semi-Annual): Total	Offsetting Swap: Total	Difference	NPV @ 4.5625% (Current)	NPV @ Zero rates
27-Aug-X2	0	0.00									
2-Jan-X3	128	0.70									
27-Feb-X3	184	1.01	0.31	7.00%		$257,159	$257,159	$51,940	($205,219)	($203,803)	($203,064)
27-Aug-X3	365	2.00	1.30	7.80%		$0	$0	$0	$0	$0	$0
27-Feb-X4	549	3.01	2.31	8.04%		$0	$0	$0	$0	$0	$0
27-Aug-X4	730	4.00	3.30	8.28%		$0	$0	$0	$0	$0	$0
27-Feb-X5	914	5.01	4.31	8.50%		$0	$0	$0	$0	$0	$0
27-Aug-X5	1095	6.00	5.30	8.73%		$0	$0	$0	$0	$0	$0
27-Feb-X6	1279	7.01	6.31	8.92%		$0	$0	$0	$0	$0	$0
27-Aug-X6	1461	8.01	7.30	9.11%		$0	$0	$0	$0	$0	$0
27-Feb-X7	1645	9.01	8.31	9.43%		$0	$0	$0	$0	$0	$0
27-Aug-X7	1826	10.01	9.30	9.76%	$7,420,000	$0	$7,420,000	$7,420,000	$0	$0	$0
Total US$										($203,803)	($203,064)
Total A$										($262,803)	($261,849)

Exhibit 8.30—continued

The Table below is a continuation of the Table on the previous page. The first three columns are repeated for convenience.

Date	Days to Cash Flows	Semi-Annual Tenor	Adjusted Tenor	A$ Payments (Semi-Annual): A$ Zero Rates	A$ Payments (Semi-Annual): Principal	A$ Payments (Semi-Annual): Interest (Original)	A$ Payments (Semi-Annual): Total	Offsetting Swap: Total	Difference	NPV @ 10.1280% (Current)	NPV @ Zero Rates
27-Aug-X2	0	0.00									
2-Jan-X3	128	0.70									
27-Feb-X3	184	1.01	0.31	9.85%		$531,836	$531,836	$148,676	$383,160	$377,395	$377,549
27-Aug-X3	365	2.00	1.30	9.41%		$523,164	$523,164	$480,542	$42,622	$39,974	$40,152
27-Feb-X4	549	3.01	2.31	9.32%		$531,836	$531,836	$488,507	$43,329	$38,662	$39,007
27-Aug-X4	730	4.00	3.30	9.24%		$523,164	$523,164	$480,542	$42,622	$36,213)	$36,723
27-Feb-X5	914	5.01	4.31	9.16%		$531,836	$531,836	$488,507	$43,329	$35,025	$35,728
27-Aug-X5	1095	6.00	5.30	9.09%		$523,164	$523,164	$480,542	$42,622	$32,806	$33,679
27-Feb-X6	1279	7.01	6.31	9.07%		$531,836	$531,836	$488,507	$43,329	$31,730	$32,756
27-Aug-X6	1461	8.01	7.30	9.06%		$526,055	$526,055	$483,197	$42,858	$29,876	$31,009
27-Feb-X7	1645	9.01	8.31	8.92%		$531,836	$531,836	$488,507	$43,329	$28,737	$30,148
27-Aug-X7	1826	10.01	9.30	8.78%	$10,000,000	$523,164	$10,523,164	$10,048,563	$474,602	$299,723	$318,218
Total US$										$736,835	$756,088
Total A$										$950,142	$974,969

Bond swap packages

As noted above and discussed in detail in Chapter 19 (in the context of new issue arbitrage), swap transactions are frequently linked with securities issues as part of financing transaction. Such bond/swap packages entail a number of adjustments (encompassing many of the features identified above) to match the final cash flows of the bond/swap package to the exact requirements of the borrower.

Exhibit 8.31 sets out an example of a bond issue with attached interest rate swap transaction. *Exhibit 8.32* sets out a similar example of a bond issue with currency swap attached detailing the methodology for adjusting the market swap price to reflect the specific cash flow features dictated by the transaction.

Exhibit 8.31

Bond Issue Interest Rate Swap

Bond Issue Swap

Assume a US$100m bond issue with attached swap on the following terms:

Bond Issue:

Issuer:	ABC Bank (ABC)
Amount:	US$100m
Term:	Five years
Coupon:	8.00% pa (A)
Issue price:	100
Fees:	1.875% flat
Expenses:	US$125,000 or 0.125% flat
All-in issue cost:	8.5076% pa (A) or 8.3340% pa (S/A)
Payment:	In four weeks from launch

Interest Rate Swap

Type:	Interest rate swap
Structure:	ABC to receive fixed rate US$, pay six month US$ LIBOR
Market rate for standard:	Treasuries ("T") + 78/85 versus six month LIBOR
Swap:	T = 8.00% pa (S/A)
All-in swap quote:	8.78/8.85% pa (S/A)

Assume the swap structure requires reimbursement of fees and pricing adjustments.

The exact structure of the swap once adjusted will be as follows:

- Swap counterparty pays ABC US$2m at commencement of swap, that is, payment date.
- Swap counterparty will pay the following fixed rate versus six month LIBOR flat:

	% pa (A)
Annual swap rate[1]	8.92
Fee amortisation[2]	−0.51
Adjustment for delay[3]	+0.04
All-in swap payment	8.45

Notes:

1. The 8.92% pa (A) is the annualised equivalent of 8.78% pa (S/A). The full 19bps gross up is adjusted by 5bps reflecting the added reinvestment risk to the counterparty.
2. 0.51% pa represents the recovery of the 2.00% up front payment amortised over five years. The discount rate used is the swap rate (8.97% pa (A)) but could be higher or lower reflecting the cost of funding the payment to the swap counterparty.

Exhibit 8.31—continued

3. The 0.04% adjustment represents the positive carry or earning on the hedged or offsetting swap with immediate start. This represents an earning of 2.00% (based on short-term rates of 6.00% pa (S/A) versus bond rates of 8.00% pa (S/A)) which is equivalent to US$0.1538m over four weeks amortised over five years at the swap rate (8.97 % pa (S/A)).

The net result of the swap is that the counterparty pays 8.45% pa (A). However, the swap counterparty is required to make annual payments of 8.00% matching out the bond coupon and receives a spread under LIBOR. The swap counterparty receives LIBOR minus 44.33bps every six months.

The 0.67bps reflect the required adjustment to adjust the swap pricing to reflect the spread below the floating rate index. This adjustment is necessary unless the fixed rate and floating rate payments are calculated on the same daycount basis and paid on the same frequency. In this example, both conditions are not met.

A structural variation to improve swap pricing might be to reconfigure the bond to be issued at a premium, that is, the issue price could be 101, the coupon 8.25%, and a comparable yield of 8.5% pa. This may allow the issuer to improve its sub-LIBOR margin where the funding cost of the fees significantly exceeds the swap rate.

Exhibit 8.32
Currency Swap

Bond Issue Swap

Assume a A$50m bond issue with attached swap on the following terms:

Bond Issue:

Issuer:	German Bank (GB)
Amount:	A$50m
Term:	Five years
Coupon:	14.00% pa
Issue price:	101.25%
Fees:	2% pa
Expenses:	A$125,000 or 0.25% pa
Payment:	In four weeks from launch
All-in issue cost:	14.2933% pa (A) or 13.8161% pa (S/A)

Swap

Type:	A$ fixed: US$ floating currency swap
Structure:	GB to receive fixed rate A$ GB to pay floating rate US$
Market rate:	T + 60 T + 80 versus six month LIBOR
Swap:	T = 14.00% pa
All-in swap quote:	14.60/14.80% pa (S/A)

The swap can be structured in two separate ways:

Structure 1

Under this structure, the swap counterparty partially reimburses the issue fees up to par to GB to provide it with proceeds of A$50m.

The exact structure of the swap is as follows:

- At commencement (assuming exchange rate of US$0.70/A$1, effectively the four week A$/US$ forward rate as at the day the transaction is undertaken), GB will pay over issue proceed of A$49.5m to swap counterparty; in return, GB will receive: US$34.65m. GB will also receive US$0.35m being reimbursement of fees of 1.00% or A$0.5m.

Exhibit 8.32—continued

- Every year on the coupon payment date, GB will receive a payment of A$7m representing 14.00% on A$50m.
- At maturity, GB will receive A$50 to make the principal repayment to the bond-holders; GB will pay US$35m to the swap counterparty.

The pricing of the swap will be adjusted as follows:

	% pa (A)
Annual swap rate[1]	15.03
Fee amortisation[2]	−0.30
Adjustment for delay[3]	+0.05
All-in swap payment	14.68

Notes:

1. 15.03% pa (A) is the annualised equivalent of 14.60% pa (S/A) adjusted by 10bps pa for the increased reinvestment risk.
2. 0.30% pa represents the fee reimbursement of 1% over five years at 15.25% pa (A).
3. 0.05% pa represents the negative carry or accrual (based on short-term rates of 16.00% pa (S/A) versus bond rates of 14.00% pa (S/A)) for a period of four weeks amortised over five years at 15.25% pa (A).

The adjustments yield a swap price of 14.68% pa (A).

The swap structure requires payments of 14.00% pa (A) against receipts of six month LIBOR minus a margin. This margin is 55bps.

The 55bps reflects the US$ equivalent of A$ 68bps pa. It reflects the need notionally to borrow A$ to purchase a spot US$ investment which produces the necessary US$ flows to cover the periodic US$ shortfall over the life of the swap reflected in the sub-LIBOR US$ payments.

The adjustment is calculated to equate the present value of "off-yield curve" margin in A$ at current A$ rates with an equivalent off-yield curve margin in US$ at current US$ rates. In this example, the equivalency is calculated on the basis of A$ interest rate of 15.25% pa (A) and US$ interest rates 8.00% pa (S/A) for five years. In addition, the sub-LIBOR margin is then adjusted to a money market/LIBOR (360/365) day count basis.

Structure 2

This is identical to Structure 1 with the following major differences:

- In the initial exchange GB pays over A$49.5m and receives US$34.65m only.
- GB pays six month LIBOR minus a margin on US$34.65m.
- GB repays US$34.65m at maturity *but receives A$50m.*

The swap pricing adjustments are slightly different:

	% pa (A)
Annualised swap rate	15.03
Adjustment for delayed start	−0.05
Adjustment for A$ shortfall[1]	−0.15
Adjustment for lower A$ proceeds[2]	−0.14
All-in swap payment	14.69

Notes:

1. The 0.15% pa represents the amortised effect (at 15.00% pa (A)) of having notionally to invest A$ now to generate A$ at maturity to cover the extra A$ flow to GB.
2. The 0.14% represents an adjustment as the lower A$ proceeds received by the swap counterparty translates into a higher running coupon, that is,

$$\frac{\text{A\$7m}}{\text{A\$49.5m}} = 14.14\% \text{ pa}$$

The base swap price of 14.69% pa (A) is then adjusted as before to provide GB with sub-LIBOR margin equivalent of 56bps.

APPENDIX

CALCULATING ZERO COUPON RATES

1. *Basic Methodology*

The actual computation of the zero coupon yield curve requires some explanation. In theory, for each future payment of a coupon security, there exists a zero coupon rate that discounts that payment to its present value. These rates constitute the zero coupon yield curve, points along which represent the yield to maturity of a zero coupon bond for the appropriate maturity rate. It is possible to estimate the zero coupon curve from the existing par bond yield curve. This basically entails calculating equilibrium spot rates which value each component of the cash flow of a coupon security in an internally consistent fashion, that is, so all par bonds would have the same value as the sum of their cash flow components.

The zero coupon rates are calculated using an interative methodology whereby the zero coupon rate is determined from a known yield curve for the successive points in time (often referred to as "bootstrapping").

2. *Calculating Zero Coupon Rates*

The table below shows the simple calculation of a zero coupon rate. Given that a one year bond has a coupon and yield to maturity of 10.00% pa, a total price of $1m is derived. However, if the six month discount security has a yield of 5.00% (not 10.00%) and the first coupon is discounted accordingly at 5.00% (which is a zero coupon rate), the 12 month payments must be discounted at a rate higher than the rate (10.128% pa in this case) to maintain the equilibrium price of $1m.

Calculating Break-Even Spot Rates

Years	Par Yield (%pa SA)	Principal	Cash Flows Interest @ 10.000%	Total	Zero Coupon Rate (%pa Annual)	Zero Coupon Rate (%pa S/A)	PV at Zero Coupon Rate	PV at Par Rate	Difference
0.00				0					
0.50	5.000%		50,000	50,000	5.062%	5.000%	48,780	47,619	1,161
1.00	10.000%	1,000,000	50,000	1,050,000	10.385%	10.128%*	951,220	952,381	(1,161)
							1,000,000	1,000,000	

* 12 month break-even zero coupon rates

The above calculations are based on a 10.00% one year bond with a coupon of 10% pa payable semi-annually trading at par (100).

In a similar way, break even zero rates for each subsequent maturity can be derived interactively.

Mathematically, the equation being solved is as follows:

$$100 = \frac{5.00}{(1 + 0.05/2)} + \frac{105.00}{(1 + ZC_1/2)^2}$$

This can be restated as:

$$ZC1 = \left[\left[\frac{105.00}{100 - [5.00/(1 + 0.05/2)]}\right]^{1/2} - 1\right] \times 2$$

$$ZC1 = 10.128\%$$

The formula can be restated to calculate a 1.5 year zero coupon rate as follows:

$$ZC_{1.5} = \left[\left[\frac{1 + C_{1.5}}{(1 - C_{1.5} \times V_{0.5} - C_{1.5} \times V_1)}\right]^{1/N} - 1\right] \times N$$

where:

$C_{1.5}$ = Coupon at year 1.5
N = Compounding Period (2 = semi-annually)
V = $[1/(1 + Z^{ct}/_N)]^N$
ZC = Zero coupon rate for maturity N.

The zero coupon rate formula can be generalised as follows:

$$dfn = (1 - C_N^* \sum_{1=i}^{N-1} dfi)/(1 + C_N)$$

where:

dfn = the discount factor at time^n

$\sum$ dfi = the summation of all preceding discount factors

C_N = the yield-to-maturity coupon at time$_n$

dfn is then capable of conversion into the equivalent zero coupon rate RN as follows:

$$RN = \left[\left(\frac{1}{dfn}\right)^{1/tn}\right] - 1$$

where:

t_N = time elapsed to time n.

As an alternative method, it is possible to determine the zero coupon rate curve by using the forward rates implicit in the current yield curve and assuming compounding of intermediate cash flows at the implicit forward rates.

3. *Characteristics of Zero Coupon Rates*

The accompanying tables and graphs show examples of zero coupon rates for a number of yield curves.

The following characteristics of zero coupon rate and the corresponding zero coupon yield curve should be noted:

- Theoretical zero coupon rates are always above (below) the relevant par or coupon yield curve for a normal or positively (inverse or negatively) sloped yield curve.

  This reflects the fact that a coupon bond is a collection of zero coupon bonds and the yield to maturity on a coupon bond is simply the average of the zero coupon rates on the constituent zero coupon securities. Consequently, if yield is increasing in a normally sloped yield curve, each constituent zero element of the coupon bond will have a yield which is less than or equal to that on a zero with a maturity that is the same as the coupon bond dictating that the yield on the coupon bond must be less than a zero of the maturity. A reverse logic is applicable in the case of negatively sloped or inverse yield curves.

- The steeper the curve the more steep is the zero coupon rate curve.
- Zero coupon rates can be more volatile as each zero rate is dependent on each forward rate leading up to the maturity of the zero coupon rate. A movement in any of the rates results in a movement in the zero coupon rate.

Examples of zero coupon rate calculations

The accompanying schedules set on the derivation of zero coupon rates from a given yield curve utilising the interative methodology specified. The tables are calculated using the following assumptions:

- linear interpolation is used to determine the full yield curve;
- coupons (payable semi-annually) are assumed to equal the par yield applicable to a specified maturity.

The tables set out the full discounting procedure for all relevant cash flows.

Zero Yield Curve (Zero)

Based on the PV of future cash flows

Start	15-Dec-X2									
Maturity	15-Jun-Y3									
Par Yields	Term =	6 months	1 year	2 years	3 years	4 years	5 years	7 years	10 years	30 years
	% =	9.8500%	9.4200%	9.2500%	9.1100%	9.0800%	8.8400%	8.6500%	8.2100%	8.1700%
Zero rates	% =	9.8500%	9.4099%	9.2360%	9.0868%	9.0582%	8.7754%	8.5559%	7.9888%	

Date	# Days Payments	Semi-Annual Tenor	Par Yield	Coupons	Zero Yield	100 – Discounted Sum of Coupon Present Values	Periods 1	2	3
Total									
15-Dec-X2	0	0							
15-Jun-X3	182	1	9.85%	$4.93	9.85%				
15-Dec-X3	365	2	9.42%	$4.71	9.41%	95.51	4.49		
15-Jun-X4	547	3	9.34%	$4.67	9.32%	91.29	4.45	4.26	
15-Dec-X4	730	4	9.25%	$4.63	9.24%	87.34	4.41	4.22	4.03
15-Jun-X5	912	5	9.18%	$4.59	9.16%	83.60	4.37	4.19	4.00
15-Dec-X5	1095	6	9.11%	$4.56	9.09%	80.09	4.34	4.15	3.97
15-Jun-X6	1278	7	9.10%	$4.55	9.07%	76.64	4.33	4.15	3.97
15-Dec-X6	1461	8	9.08%	$4.54	9.06%	73.35	4.33	4.14	3.96
15-Jun-X7	1643	9	8.96%	$4.48	8.92%	70.56	4.27	4.09	3.91
15-Dec-X7	1826	10	8.84%	$4.42	8.78%	67.97	4.21	4.03	3.86
15-Jun-X8	2008	11	8.79%	$4.40	8.72%	65.28	4.19	4.01	3.83
15-Dec-X8	2191	12	8.75%	$4.37	8.67%	62.73	4.17	3.99	3.81
15-Jun-X9	2372	13	8.70%	$4.35	8.61%	60.32	4.14	3.97	3.79
15-Dec-X9	2556	14	8.65%	$4.32	8.56%	58.04	4.12	3.95	3.77
15-Jun-Y0	2739	15	8.58%	$4.29	8.46%	56.01	4.09	3.91	3.74
15-Dec-Y0	2922	16	8.50%	$4.25	8.37%	54.10	4.05	3.88	3.71
15-Jun-Y1	3104	17	8.43%	$4.22	8.28%	52.31	4.02	3.84	3.68
15-Dec-Y1	3287	18	8.36%	$4.18	8.18%	50.62	3.98	3.81	3.64
15-Jun-Y2	3469	19	8.28%	$4.14	8.09%	49.05	3.95	3.78	3.61
15-Dec-Y2	3652	20	8.21%	$4.11	7.99%	47.56	3.91	3.74	3.58
15-Jun-Y3	3834	21	8.21%						

4	5	6	7	8	9	10	11	12	13	14	15	16	17	18	19
3.83															
3.80	3.64														
3.80	3.64	3.48													
3.79	3.63	3.48	3.33												
3.74	3.58	3.43	3.28	3.14											
3.69	3.53	3.39	3.24	3.10	2.98										
3.67	3.51	3.37	3.22	3.08	2.97	2.8									
3.65	3.50	3.35	3.21	3.07	2.95	2.8	2.73								
3.63	3.48	3.33	3.19	3.05	2.94	2.8	2.72	2.61							
3.61	3.46	3.31	3.17	3.03	2.92	2.8	2.70	2.60	2.50						
3.58	3.43	3.28	3.14	3.01	2.90	2.7	2.68	2.58	2.48	2.39					
3.55	3.40	3.26	3.12	2.98	2.87	2.7	2.66	2.56	2.46	2.37	2.28				
3.52	3.37	3.23	3.09	2.96	2.85	2.7	2.64	2.53	2.44	2.34	2.26	2.19			
3.49	3.34	3.20	3.06	2.93	2.82	2.7	2.61	2.51	2.42	2.32	2.24	2.17	2.10		
3.46	3.31	3.17	3.04	2.91	2.80	2.7	2.59	2.49	2.39	2.30	2.22	2.15	2.08	2.01	
3.43	3.28	3.14	3.01	2.88	2.77	2.6	2.57	2.47	2.37	2.28	2.20	2.13	2.06	1.99	1.93

Zero Yield Curve (Zero)

Based on the PV of future cash flows

Start	15-Dec-X2									
Maturity	15-Jun-Y3									
Par Yields	Term =	6 months	1 year	2 years	3 years	4 years	5 years	7 years	10 years	30 years
	% =	7.0000%	7.7800%	8.2500%	8.6700%	9.0100%	9.5500%	10.1200%	10.9800%	11.3500%
Zero rates	% =	7.0000%	7.7952%	8.2805%	8.7318%	9.1102%	9.7571%	10.4676%	11.7694%	

Date	# Days Payments	Semi-Annual	Par Yield	Coupons	Zero Yield	100 – Discounted Sum of Coupon Present Values	Periods 1	2	3
Total									
15-Dec-X2	0	0							
15-Jun-X3	182	1	7.00%	$3.50	7.00%				
15-Dec-X3	365	2	7.78%	$3.89	7.80%	96.24	3.76		
15-Jun-X4	547	3	8.02%	$4.01	8.04%	92.42	3.87	3.71	
15-Dec-X4	730	4	8.25%	$4.13	8.28%	88.53	3.99	3.82	3.67
15-Jun-X5	912	5	8.46%	$4.23	8.50%	84.64	4.09	3.92	3.76
15-Dec-X5	1095	6	8.67%	$4.34	8.73%	80.74	4.19	4.02	3.85
15-Jun-X6	1278	7	8.84%	$4.42	8.92%	76.94	4.27	4.09	3.93
15-Dec-X6	1461	8	9.01%	$4.51	9.11%	73.18	4.35	4.17	4.00
15-Jun-X7	1643	9	9.28%	$4.64	9.43%	69.12	4.48	4.30	4.12
15-Dec-X7	1826	10	9.55%	$4.78	9.76%	65.07	4.61	4.42	4.24
15-Jun-X8	2008	11	9.69%	$4.85	9.93%	61.54	4.68	4.49	4.31
15-Dec-X8	2191	12	9.84%	$4.92	10.10%	58.09	4.75	4.56	4.37
15-Jun-X9	2373	13	9.98%	$4.99	10.28%	54.72	4.82	4.62	4.43
15-Dec-X9	2556	14	10.12%	$5.06	10.47%	51.44	4.89	4.69	4.50
15-Jun-Y0	2739	15	10.26%	$5.13	10.66%	48.24	4.96	4.75	4.56
15-Dec-Y0	2922	16	10.41%	$5.20	10.87%	45.13	5.03	4.82	4.62
15-Jun-Y1	3104	17	10.55%	$5.28	11.08%	42.11	5.10	4.89	4.69
15-Dec-Y1	3287	18	10.69%	$5.35	11.30%	39.18	5.17	4.95	4.75
15-Jun-Y2	3469	19	10.84%	$5.42	11.53%	36.35	5.24	5.02	4.81
15-Dec-Y2	3652	20	10.98%	$5.49	11.77%	33.62	5.30	5.09	4.88
15-Jun-Y3	3834	21	10.99%						

4	5	6	7	8	9	10	11	12	13	14	15	16	17	18	19
3.60															
3.69	3.52														
3.76	3.59	3.42													
3.83	3.66	3.49	3.32												
3.94	3.77	3.59	3.42	3.25											
4.06	3.88	3.70	3.52	3.34	3.15										
4.12	3.94	3.75	3.57	3.39	3.20	3.0									
4.18	3.99	3.81	3.62	3.44	3.25	3.0	2.89								
4.24	4.05	3.86	3.68	3.49	3.30	3.1	2.93	2.76							
4.30	4.11	3.92	3.73	3.54	3.34	3.1	2.97	2.80	2.64						
4.36	4.17	3.97	3.78	3.59	3.39	3.1	3.01	2.84	2.67	2.51					
4.42	4.23	4.03	3.83	3.64	3.44	3.2	3.05	2.88	2.71	2.55	2.39				
4.48	4.28	4.08	3.89	3.69	3.48	3.2	3.10	2.92	2.75	2.58	2.42	2.26			
4.55	4.34	4.14	3.94	3.74	3.53	3.3	3.14	2.96	2.79	2.62	2.45	2.29	2.14		
4.61	4.40	4.19	3.99	3.79	3.58	3.3	3.18	3.00	2.82	2.65	2.49	2.32	2.17	2.02	
4.67	4.46	4.25	4.05	3.84	3.63	3.4	3.22	3.04	2.86	2.69	2.52	2.35	2.20	2.04	1.89

Chapter 9

Pricing LTFX Contracts

LTFX PRICING METHODOLOGIES[1]

While the pricing of interest rate and currency swaps is largely dictated by capital market arbitrage between various borrowers and between various global capital markets, a number of specific theoretical pricing mechanisms are utilised for pricing distinct transactions such as LTFX, FRAs and caps and collars etc. In this chapter, the techniques for pricing LTFX contracts are discussed. Theoretical pricing mechanisms for pricing FRAs and caps and collars etc are discussed in Chapters 10 and 11.

LTFX transactions are usually priced in one of two ways:

- as forward foreign exchange contracts pricing off current interest rates and interest differentials between currencies for various maturities;
- as fixed-to-fixed zero coupon currency swaps.

Selection between the two approaches is dictated by the operating philosophies and the approach to LTFX adopted by individual institutions. In practice, both approaches co-exist.

INTEREST RATE DIFFERENTIAL PRICING MECHANISMS

The conceptual basis

The conceptual basis of utilising interest rate differentials to price forward currency contracts, irrespective of maturity, is based upon the concept of arbitrage between various foreign exchange and money markets. This approach predicts that the returns obtainable in any particular currency sold in the forward markets against a base currency would normally be equal to those obtainable in the base currency. If discrepancies occur and this condition does not hold, opportunities for risk free profit exist and are quickly exploited by market participants. This process of arbitrage forces the forward rates on currencies to reflect the interest rate differential between the respective currencies.

An example of forward currency rates pricing based on arbitrage between foreign exchange and money markets is set out in *Exhibit 9.1*. In this example, market participants are faced with two choices: an investment of A$10m yielding 12.00% pa and a US$7.2m investment yielding 7.50% pa. The different amount of initial investment reflects the current spot exchange rate between A$ and US$ at which the relevant currencies could be exchanged for each other to provide the initial investment capital. The two investments respectively provide a final termination value reflecting the return of principal plus interest earned of A$10.299m and US$7.355m respectively.

1. The discussion of LTFX pricing techniques draws on Antl (1983) and Antl, "Pricing of Long-Term Forward Foreign Exchange Contracts" in Antl (1986).

Exhibit 9.1

Arbitrage Between Foreign Exchange and Money Markets

Date:	28/9/X7	28/12/X7
A$ investment:	A$ 10.000[1]	
A$ return (principal and interest at 12.00% pa):[2]		10.299
US$ investment	US$ 7.200	
US$ return (principal and interest at 7.50% pa):		7.335
Spot exchange rate:	A$1.00/US$0.72	
Forward exchange rate:		0.7122

Notes

1. All amounts are in $m.
2. All rates are compounded annually and based on 365/365 day computational basis for simplicity.

This implies a forward exchange rate of A$1/US$0.7122 or a discount on spot of 0.0078. This discount equates the effective interest return capable of being earned between the two markets. This is because if the forward exchange rate does not reflect the existing interest rate differential then opportunities would exist for borrowing in one currency with a simultaneous investment in another to yield an arbitrage profit.

For example, if the forward exchange rate prevailing in the market for three months was A$1/US$0.7102, then it would be profitable to borrow A$10m, sell the currency spot for US$7.2m and lodge the US$ in an investment yielding 7.50% pa with the proceeds of the investment, both principal and interest (US$7.355m), being sold forward for value 28/12/X7 at the market forward rate. This series of transactions would provide the investor with an effective A$ termination value of A$10.328m, an increase of A$0.028m on a direct A$ investment or an effective yield of 13.14% pa which is significantly higher than the current market yield for A$ investment.

This potential arbitrage profit would encourage market participants to undertake the transaction described which would drive the market towards the equilibrium forward exchange rate as the increased supply of US$ for three months investment and also the emergence of increased numbers of forward sellers of US$ against A$ would force both the US$ interest rate and forward exchange rate to adjust.

Short-term versus long-term forward exchange contract pricing

The requirement that market participants exploit arbitrage opportunities for risk-free profit holds quite well for short-term forward exchange contracts. This is particularly so between freely convertible currencies in which there are well-developed money markets, especially when international markets in the relevant currencies also exist. The fact that the international markets are unregulated and outside the control of national authorities means that they are highly efficient and that the process of arbitrage does indeed force forward rates to reflect the interest rate differentials between currencies.

However, for LTFX contracts such arbitrage is more difficult and these rates do not necessarily reflect the activity of arbitrageurs between the various capital and foreign exchange markets.

The failure of arbitrage at longer maturities reflects, in the first instance, the reluctance of market participants to undertake long-term arbitrage because of the higher transaction costs involved. These higher transaction costs entail balance sheet holding costs for assets incurred in the process of arbitrage as well as the tying up of credit lines for extended periods of time. A major factor impeding arbitrage is the difficulty in locating securities or investments which are ideally suited to the requirements of the arbitrage process.

An analysis of the above example, which illustrates arbitrage between foreign exchange and money markets over a relatively short period, highlights that a number of conditions must exist for the arbitrage to be fully effective:

- There must be available appropriate securities or investments to allow participants to borrow and invest in the appropriate currencies to undertake the arbitrage.
- The securities or investments required must have particular cash flow characteristics, that is, they must have a *known terminal value* of the investment or borrowing cost.

The latter requirement is particularly problematic. In the case of short-term forward exchange contracts, the availability of discount instruments means that the terminal value of the investment or the cost of the borrowing is known in advance. However, once this simple one payment, one period situation is replaced by either a single payment, multi-period situation, or alternatively, a multi-period, multi-payment situation, the process of determining the terminal value of the investment becomes more complex.

This reflects the fact that where investments or borrowings are undertaken for periods in excess of, for example, one year, the required borrowing or lending transaction entails intermediate cash flows in the form of coupon payments. Intermediate cash flows must be compounded in multi-period situations to provide the required maturity values for the relevant transaction. However, unless zero coupon securities are utilised (as the interest rates at which the intermediate cash flows will have to be reinvested or borrowed is unknown in advance) there is uncertainty as to the maturity value.

There are two possible solutions to this problem. Under the first, it is usually assumed that reinvestment or funding in future periods will take place at current rates. This assumption, however, is speculative and there is no assurance that the assumed rate will in fact be realised. Alternatively, it is possible to produce a series of forward rates, as discussed in Chapter 10 in the context of FRA transactions, for the contemplated maturity. Under this approach, it is possible to compound the intermediate cash flows at the assumed forward rates. However, the forward rates assumed as the basis of any reinvestment or funding transaction in future periods may not in practice be realised. This is because while it is, on the basis of empirical evidence, an *unbiased* predictor of the future spot rate, the forward rate is not necessarily an *accurate predictor* of the *actual* future spot rate.

Numerous academic studies have indicated that, given certain assumptions, the forward rate does not produce a systematically biased estimate of the future spot rate. However, a number of factors may influence the behaviour of interest rates and cause realised interest rates to differ from the implied forward rates, including:

- changes in fiscal policy;
- changes in inflation rates;

- monetary policy factors;
- changes in the country's balance of payment situation;
- political developments and uncertainties.

Where the realised forward interest rates differ from implied annual rates, a number of possibilities exist:

- It is possible that the interest rate differential between the two currencies remains constant despite the fact that the actual realised interest rates differ from implied interest rates. Under the scenario, the LTFX contract rate is likely to be approximately the same as that implied by interest differentials.
- If the interest rate differential narrows as a result of the difference between realised and implied forward interest rates, the LTFX contract rate is likely to be higher on the basis of interest rate differentials than that achieved on the basis of reinvestment of intermediate cash flows.
- If, in contrast, the interest rate differential widens, the LTFX rate implied by the interest rate differentials at the time the transaction is undertaken is likely to be lower than that actually achieved as a result of reinvestment of intermediate cash flows.

These difficulties in applying standard arbitrage techniques involving interest rate differentials mean that there are a number of competing pricing techniques for LTFX contracts. The major ones include:

- current yield curve method;
- average forward rate method;
- exchange of borrowing and currency swap method;
- fully arbitraged cash flow method.

Each of the identified techniques for pricing LTFX contracts utilises interest rates derived from yield curves prevailing in the relevant currencies. The discussion so far does not specify the *specific* yield curves to be utilised.

The yield curves utilised to price a short term forward foreign exchange contract (such as that described in *Exhibit 9.1*), generally, utilises short term inter-bank interest rates; for example, US$ LIBOR rates or their equivalent in other currencies are utilised.

A debate on the specific yield curve utilised in pricing longer dated forward foreign exchange contracts has not been conclusively resolved. Alternative applicable yield curves include:

- a government security yield curve;
- inter-bank or bank borrowing rates with the relevant maturities;
- a swap yield curve.

The government security yield curve is typically not utilised as it does not embody appropriate credit risk margins. In addition, the government security yield curve and the rates applicable thereto do not, in practice, strictly relate to the underlying hedging transactions that may need to be effected by financial institutions in managing the risk of assumed LTFX positions. The inter-bank or bank rate yield curve is, generally, not available for all maturities, reflecting the banks' funding activities which are concentrated at the short end of the yield curve. Similarly, the increasing lack of homogeneity among banks, as a risk group, makes it difficult to use inter-bank borrowing rates as a relevant yield curve.

In practice, the swap yield curve represents the most suitable interest rate parameter for inclusion in pricing LTFX contracts. Swap yields are available for most maturities in a wide variety of currencies favouring the use of swap rate as the relevant interest rate pricing LTFX contracts.

The use of swap yield curve also allows the arbitrages in the swap market to be reflected in the pricing of LTFX contract: see discussion in Chapter 6.

Current yield curve method

The current yield curve method ultilises the technique for short-term forward exchange contracts to calculate LTFX rates. The forward rate is based on existing interest rate differentials for the relevant maturity and assumes that the same interest rate will prevail for the entire exposure period and, consequently, compounds the required investment or borrowing at the same rate for the same period. *Exhibit 9.2* sets out an example of the current yield curve method. The exhibit indicates that the five year forward rate can be calculated as equivalent to A$1 being equal to US$0.5067 or a discount of 0.1933 (1933) on the spot rate. The forward rate is calculated as follows.

Exhibit 9.2

Current Yield Curve Method

Assume the following market scenario:

Spot A$/US$ exchange rate = A$1.00/US$0.70

The interest rate structure is as follows:

Year	A$ interest rates (% pa (A))	US$ interest rates (% pa (A))
1	16.00	6.25
2	14.75	6.40
3	14.50	6.60
4	14.35	6.80
5	14.25	7.10

The forward rates using the various interest rate differentials would be as follows:

		US$ per A$1.00	Discount
Spot		0.7000	—
Forwards:	1 year	0.6412	0.0588
	2 years	0.6018	0.0982
	3 years	0.5649	0.1351
	4 years	0.5326	0.1674
	5 years	0.5067	0.1933

A$1m invested in A$ securities for five years at 14.25% pa should give a maturity value of A$1.9466m. This assumes reinvestment of any intermediate coupons at the assumed rate equivalent to the coupon of 14.25% pa. The same A$ amount converted in the spot market to give US$0.7m if invested for five years at 7.10% pa, the prevailing US$ rate for the maturity, would give a maturity value of US$0.9864m. The US$ maturity value also assumes compounding at the five year rate. The two investment maturity values imply a five year forward rate of A$1/US$0.5067 to prevent covered interest arbitrage between the two markets.

In this example, as in all the examples utilised in this chapter, bid-offer spreads are ignored to simplify the description of the concept. In practice, market participants would transact on either side of the implied five year forward rate with the difference between the rate at which it buys the currency and the rate at which it sells the currency representing its profit.

Average forward rate method

The average forward rate method assumes that the interest rates prevailing at the time the transaction is undertaken for the longest maturity contemplated are the best reflection of future yields and that reinvestment of funding of intermediate cash flows will be at the same rates. Utilising this method, forward rates will be calculated on the basis of interest rate differentials between the two currencies for the longest relevant maturities and by applying these differentials to each of the interim maturities to compute the forward rates.

Exhibit 9.3 sets out an example of average forward rate methodology. In this case, the five year interest rates for both currencies (refer *Exhibit 9.2*) are used throughout the five year period to generate the relevant forward rates.

Exhibit 9.3

Average Forward Rate Method

Year	A$ investments	US$ investments	Exchange rate (US$ per A$1.00)	Discount
0	1.0000	0.7000	0.7000	—
1	1.1425	0.7497	0.6562	0.0438
2	1.3053	0.8029	0.6151	0.0849
3	1.4913	0.8599	0.5766	0.1234
4	1.7038	0.9210	0.5405	0.1595
5	1.9466	0.9864	0.5067	0.1933

A number of aspects of the use of the average forward rate method should be noted:

- The forward rate for five years calculated under the average forward rate method is identical to that under the current yield curve method.
- The annual discount remains constant at the interest differential, 7.15% pa, for the entire period.

Exchange of borrowing and currency swap method

Under the exchange of borrowing and currency swap method, two parties with either existing or anticipated borrowings in two different currencies agree to swap their liabilities utilising the standard currency swap structure. Under this technique, the forward rates established reflect arbitrage between the two capital markets as all cash flows are matched and the reinvestment and funding problems, described above, do not create uncertainty as to the future values of assets or liabilities. An example of exchange of the borrowing and currency swap method is set out in *Exhibit 9.4*.

Exhibit 9.4

Exchange of Borrowing and Currency Swap Method

Borrowings	**A$m**	**US$m**
Face value:	100.000	70.000
Coupon:	14.250% pa	7.000% pa
Issue price:	100.125	100.000
Borrowing costs:	2.000%	1.875%
All-in-costs:	14.807% pa	7.463% pa
Net proceeds:	98.125	68.6875

Cash flows

Year	**A$m**	**US$m**	**Exchange rate (US$ per A$1.00)**	**Discount**
0	98.125	68.6875	0.7000	—
1	14.250	4.9000	0.3439	0.3561
2	14.250	4.9000	0.3439	0.3561
3	14.250	4.9000	0.3439	0.3561
4	14.250	4.9000	0.3439	0.3561
5	114.250	74.9000	0.6556	0.0444

As noted in Chapter 6, the process of arbitrage implied by the exchange of borrowing technique operates on the basis that it would be possible to replicate the transaction outlined by borrowing one of the currencies, converting the proceeds into the other currency utilising the spot foreign exchange market, investing the second currency proceeds in an instrument with the same interest payment dates and selling the interest payments and principal forward against the base currency.

Fully arbitraged cash flow method

The fully arbitraged cash flow method of pricing LTFX contracts seeks to overcome some of the deficiencies of other techniques, particularly the current yield curve and average forward rate method, by devising a structure which avoids any reinvestment risk on intermediate cash flows.

The fully arbitraged cash flow method, which was first described in Antl (1983), creates a set of fully arbitraged forward rates utilising the current yield curve. This is achieved by structuring a series of borrowings or investments spread out over the entire exposure period with the amount borrowed or invested for each maturity taking into account any intermediate cash flows, interest payments, due under borrowings or investments related to exposures in other periods. In essence, the total liabilities in each period, that is, the principal plus all interest payments received, are structured to equal all assets in that same period. This creates a series of self-liquidating cash transactions whereby all currency risk and investment risk is avoided.

Exhibit 9.5 sets out an example of the fully arbitraged method. In that example, fully arbitraged forward rates are created to cover future receipts of A$1m every year for five years.

As set out in the example, the self-liquidating cover must be structured by first computing the principal amount to be borrowed for the longest period. In this example, this is equal to A$0.8753m which reflects the exposure amount of A$1m discounted at the rate of 14.25% pa. This implies a cash flow in five years from commencement of the transaction equal to A$1m, being the sum of the principal plus the interest payment. This process is then repeated for each of the shorter periods. The amount borrowed for four years reflects the fact that the sum of the interest payment from the five year loan plus the final payment for the four year borrowing must equate to A$1m. Based on a four year interest rate of 14.35% pa, this is equal to A$0.7654m. This provides a maturity value (principal plus interest) of A$0.8753 which in conjunction with the interest payment of A$0.1247 on the five year borrowing provides the required A$ cash flow of A$1m. This process is repeated for each maturity. The total A$ borrowing can then be determined. In this example, this equates to A$3.394m.

Exhibit 9.5

LTFX—Fully Arbitraged Cash Flow Method

1. Constant Ratio Forward

Year	Exchange Rate (A$=US$) Rate	Discount	A$ Borrowing (A$)	US$ Investment (US$)
0	0.7000		3,393,997	(2,375,798)
1	0.5104	−0.1896	1,000,000	510,444
2	0.5447	−0.1553	1,000,000	544,720
3	0.5788	−0.1212	1,000,000	578,771
4	0.6157	−0.0843	1,000,000	615,739
5	0.6562	−0.0438	1,000,000	656,193

Year	A$ Receipts (A$)	A$ Borrowings Year / Rate	1	2	3	4	5	Total
		Rate	16.0000%	14.7500%	14.5000%	14.3500%	14.2500%	
0	3,393,997		502,217	582,572	668,501	765,434	875,274	3,393,997
1	1,000,000		(582,572)	(85,929)	(96,933)	(109,840)	(124,726)	(1,000,000)
2	1,000,000			(668,501)	(96,933)	(109,840)	(124,726)	(1,000,000)
3	1,000,000				(765,434)	(109,840)	(124,726)	(1,000,000)
4	1,000,000					(875,274)	(124,726)	(1,000,000)
5	1,000,000						(1,000,000)	(1,000,000)

Year	US$ Receipts (US$)	US$ Borrowings Year / Rate	1	2	3	4	5	Total
		Rate	6.2500%	6.4000%	6.6000%	6.8000%	7.1000%	
	Ratio		14.80%	17.16%	19.70%	22.55%	25.79%	100.000%
0	(2,375,798)		(351,552)	(407,800)	(467,951)	(535,804)	(612,691)	(2,375,798)
1	510,444		373,524	26,099	30,885	36,435	43,501	510,444
2	544,720			433,899	30,885	36,435	43,501	544,720
3	578,771				498,836	36,435	43,501	578,771
4	615,739					572,238	43,501	615,739
5	656,193						656,193	656,193

The other side of the hedge, the investment, operates as follows. The A$ borrowing proceeds are converted into US$, at the spot rate, and invested *in the same proportion as the borrowings undertaken*. In our example, the US$ proceeds, US$2.3758m, are invested in the amounts set out. For example, the amount invested for one year US$0.3515m equates to 14.80% of the total amount available for investment. This is the same proportion as the A$ borrowing for one year (A$0.5022m) as a percentage of the total A$ borrowing (A$3.3940m).

The proceeds of the investment are equal to the sum of investments maturing in each period plus any coupons received.

The forward exchange rates are then calculated as a function of the cash flows in the two currencies, that is, the A$1m receipts divided by the US$ amounts maturing each year.

In the above example, the US$ investments are invested *in the same proportion as the A$ borrowings undertaken*. However, in practice there is no need for the pattern of investment to be identical to the pattern of borrowing. By altering the proportion of the investment, an entirely new set of forward rates, which are capable of being totally hedged at market interest rates, can be created. These rates are often referred to as "slanted" LTFX rates. The specific ratios nominated can be manipulated to create a desired set of foreign exchange rate matching specific asset—liability management requirements. *Exhibit 9.6* takes the example previously discussed in *Exhibit 9.5* and alters the investment ratio to create a slanted set of LTFX rates.

Exhibit 9.6

LTFX—Fully Arbitraged Cash Flow Method: Creating Customised Forward Rates

1. Prescribed Ratio Forward

Year	Exchange Rate (A$=US$) Rate	Discount	A$ Borrowing (A$)	US$ Investment (US$)
0	0.7000		3,393,997	(2,375,798)
1	0.6418	−0.0582	1,000,000	641,777
2	0.5447	−0.1553	1,000,000	544,720
3	0.5860	−0.1140	1,000,000	585,980
4	0.5551	−0.1449	1,000,000	555,095
5	0.5187	−0.1813	1,000,000	518,661

Year	A$ Receipts (A$)		A$ Borrowings					
		Year	1	2	3	4	5	Total
		Rate	16.0000%	14.7500%	14.5000%	14.3500%	14.2500%	
0	3,393,997		502,217	582,572	668,501	765,434	875,274	3,393,997
1	1,000,000		(582,572)	(85,929)	(96,933)	(109,840)	(124,726)	(1,000,000)
2	1,000,000			(668,501)	(96,933)	(109,840)	(124,726)	(1,000,000)
3	1,000,000				(765,434)	(109,840)	(124,726)	(1,000,000)
4	1,000,000					(875,274)	(124,726)	(1,000,000)
5	1,000,000						(1,000,000)	(1,000,000)

Year	US$ Receipts (US$)		US$ Borrowings					
		Year	1	2	3	4	5	Total
		Rate	6.2500%	6.4000%	6.6000%	6.8000%	7.1000%	
	Ratio		20.00%	20.00%	20.00%	20.00%	20.00%	100.000%
0	(2,375,798)		(475,160)	(475,160)	(475,160)	(475,160)	(475,160)	(2,375,798)
1	641,777		504,857	26,099	30,885	36,435	43,501	641,777
2	544,720			433,899	30,885	36,435	43,501	544,720
3	585,980				506,044	36,435	43,501	585,980
4	555,095					511,594	43,501	555,095
5	518,661						518,661	518,661

The fully arbitraged cash flow method effectively creates forward foreign exchange rates utilising the zero coupon rates in the relevant currencies. A specific feature of the fully arbitraged cash flow method is the technique for pricing implicitly identifies the hedging transactions required it allows a party entering into these transactions to specifically construct hedges required to insulate it from any exposure to reinvestment rates in either currency.

Comparison of various methods

The forward rates calculations, utilising the different techniques, are summarised in *Exhibit 9.7.*

Exhibit 9.7

Comparison of LTFX Rates Utilising Different Methods

Year	Current yield curve method	Average forward rate method	Exchange of borrowings	Fully arbitraged cash flow
1	0.6412	0.6562	0.3439	0.5112
2	0.6018	0.6151	0.3439	0.5455
3	0.5649	0.5766	0.3439	0.5788
4	0.5326	0.5405	0.3439	0.6157
5	0.5067	0.5067	0.6556	0.6562

Note: All rates are US$ per A$1.00.

The significant differences in the forward rates require comment. The current yield curve method creates a set of forward rates which reflect the interest rate differentials for the various maturities at the inception of the transactions. In contrast, the average forward rate method creates an annual discount of the A$ which is consistent throughout the period. Depending on the actual structure of interest rates, the current yield curve method could, conceivably, produce a set of forward rates some of which are at a premium while others reflect a discount.

The exchange of borrowings technique provides a set of forward rates, which merely reflect the interest rate differentials embodied in the coupons of the two respective currencies, except in the final period when the repayment of principal is affected. All rates are at a discount on the A$ reflecting the fact that A$ five year interest rates exceed US$ five year rates.

The fully arbitraged method, in the example utilised, yields forward rates with increased discounts in the initial phase which are reduced for the more distant maturities, reflecting the shape of the yield curve in the two currencies whereby the interest differentials are greatest in the shorter maturities. Depending on the shape of the current yield curves, the fully arbitraged method may yield rates similar to those computed on the yield curve base and average rate methods as they are based on a similar principle and on the same rates, although the rates are combined in a different manner.

The variety of techniques and their different results prompts the question as to the most appropriate technique to utilise. There are no simple solutions to this problem although a consideration of some of the major differences between the techniques is instructive.

The current yield curve and average forward rate methods both ignore reinvestment risk as the forward rates derived by these two methods are not fully arbitraged rates. Pricing based on the current yield curve assumes that receipts and payments in each future period may be covered by separate transactions, the price of each of which is based on the interest rate differential for that period. In contrast, the average rate method, despite the advantage of simplicity, assumes that long-term interest rates are the best available predictor of future exchange rates and thereby ignores the shape of the current yield curve. However, in both cases, reinvestment of intermediate cash flows is assumed to take place at the then current interest rate creating uncertainty as to the actual maturity value achieved.

The exchange of borrowings technique provides a set of rates that is fully arbitraged. This is because by entering into a borrowing and investment transaction, an entity can create the desired set of forward rates without incurring any currency risk or reinvestment risk. This technique is suitable primarily for institutions undertaking borrowings which they seek to exchange for borrowings in another currency, that is, the classical process of swap arbitrage. From the perspective of other types of hedges, this pricing mechanism is less appealing in that all forward rates are identical, reflecting the coupon rate differential, except at maturity where the repayment of principal is taken into account. In this regard, the forward rates established using the exchange of borrowings techniques reflect notional forward rates which merely mirror the underlying cash flows at given rates.

The fully arbitraged cash flow technique, while not universally utilised, does have the advantage of providing a fully covered self-liquidating set of forward rates. The technique does not require any reinvestment risk to be assumed. A particular advantage of the fully arbitraged technique is that it is possible to create various sets of fully arbitraged forward exchange rates, by undertaking borrowing and investment transactions in which the *proportions* of the two sides of the transactions are mismatched, in terms of amounts or maturities. This manipulation of forward rates can allow institutions to create particular cash flow patterns which have applications in structuring patterns of income and expense consistent with the organisation's financial and tax requirements.

PRICING LTFX AS ZERO COUPON CURRENCY SWAP

As noted above, LTFX transactions can be priced as fixed-to-fixed zero coupon currency swaps. The use of currency swaps as a pricing basis here is similar to but not identical to the exchange of borrowing and currency swap methodology outlined above. The major difference lies in the fact that under the exchange of borrowing approach, the intention is to create a string of outright forward prices whereas where a fixed-to-fixed zero coupon currency swap is utilised, the intention is to create a single forward rate based on the compounding of the intermediate cash flows in the currency swap.

Exhibit 9.8 sets out an example of structuring and pricing a LTFX transaction as a fixed-to-fixed zero coupon currency swap. As set out in the example, the swap entails A$ 14.00% pa payable against receipt of US$ 7.00% pa on principal of A$100m based on a spot exchange rate of A$1.00/US$0.70. In the normal swap case, this would entail receipt of US$4.9m annually in exchange for payment of A$14m with the principal being exchanged at maturity. In the case of the zero coupon swap structure, intermediate cash flows are replaced with a single cash flow on maturity. The intermediate A$ payments of A$14m are compounded at the rate of 14.00% to give a maturity value of A$192.541m, reflecting compounded interest together with the repayment of the original principal received under the swap. Similarly, the intermediate US$ cash flows are compounded at the swap rate of 7.00% pa giving a maturity value of US$98.179m, reflecting principal plus compounded interest. This would imply a five year outright currency forward rate of A$1.00/US$0.5099 or a discount on the spot rate of 0.1901 or 1911 points.

Exhibit 9.8

Zero Coupon Currency Swap: Cash Flows

Assumes swap rates of A$14.00% pa payable against receipt of US$7.00% pa. All rates are on an annual compounding basis.

CONVENTIONAL US$ FIXED/A$ FIXED CURRENCY SWAP CASH FLOWS

Year	Swap cash flows	
	A$m receipts	US$m payments
0	+100	−70.0
1	−14	+4.9
2	−14	+4.9
3	−14	+4.9
4	−14	+4.9
5	−14 −100	+4.9 +70.0

ZERO COUPON US$ FIXED/A$ FIXED CURRENCY SWAP CASH FLOWS

Year	Swap cash flows					
	A$m receipts	A$m balance at start of period	Interest compounded on swap balance (A$m)	US$m receipts	US$m balance at start of period	Interest compounded on swap balance (US$m)
0	+100.000	+100.000	—	−70.000	70.000	—
1	—	114.000	14.000	—	74.900	4.900
2	—	129.960	15.960	—	80.143	5.243
3	—	148.154	18.194	—	85.753	5.610
4	—	168.896	20.742	—	91.756	6.003
5	−192.541	192.541	23.645	+98.179	98.179	6.423

A number of aspects of this transaction should be noted:

- If the initial cash flows are ignored, then the cash flow pattern entailing a receipt of US$ in exchange for a delivery of A$ at the end of five years is identical to a five year LTFX contract entailing the sale of A$ for US$. For example, a US$ borrower may have used this to hedge the principal repayment of a loan in this manner.
- The swap structure assumes compounding at the swap rate. In practice, the swap rate would have been adjusted to reflect reinvestment assumptions applicable under market conditions. This issue is discussed in greater detail in Chapters 32 and 33.
- The zero coupon currency swap is structured on the basis of exchanges of fixed rate cash flows in both currencies. This type of pricing cannot be applied to a currency swap between a fixed rate and floating rate as the floating rate cash flows

are uncertain and their maturity value unknown at the time the transaction is entered into. In practice, as most currency swaps are quoted against US$ LIBOR, the highly liquid US$ interest rate swap market can be utilised to imply fixed US$ rates which can form the basis of this pricing methodology.

- This technique is similar to the exchange of borrowing technique as described above, in that it reflects full arbitrage between the two capital markets in the same manner as the exchange of borrowings methodology.
- In this case, the price of the forward exchange contract for five years has been calculated. A similar methodology, utilising applicable zero coupon swap rates for the different maturities, could be utilised to engineer forward prices for all interim maturities.

Chapter 10

Pricing FRAs

APPROACHES TO PRICING FRAS

FRAs are priced off forward-forward interest rates. This forward-forward interest rate may be that implied in the cash market yield curve and capable of replication through cash market transactions, or, alternatively, through implied forward rates in an available interest rate futures market in the relevant currency.

Effectively, the pricing of FRAs reflects the FRA provider's capability, at least theoretically, to hedge the transaction either through the futures market or by undertaking the relevant cash market transactions.

FRAs can also be priced off a type of forward-forward arbitrage. This type of arbitrage is predicated on the fact that forward foreign exchange prices are determined by interest differentials between the relevant currencies reflecting the yield curves in the respective currencies. This therefore provides another mechanism to hedge by entering into an FRA to hedge the interest rate exposure under a covered interest rate arbitrage transaction, that is, to lock in the interest rate leg for the arbitrage.

FORWARD INTEREST RATES

Forward-forward rates

Forward interest rates can be calculated from the current yield curve. If suitably spaced yields and either synthetic or actual securities are available, then forward rates can be estimated.

The forward rates can be calculated based on the theoretical construct that securities of different maturities can be expected to be substitutes for one another.

Investors at any time have three choices. They may invest in an obligation having a maturity corresponding exactly to their anticipated holding period. They may invest in short-term securities, reinvesting in further short-term securities at each maturity over the holding period. They may invest in a security having a maturity longer than the anticipated holding period. In the last case, they would sell the security at the end of the given period, realising either a capital gain or a loss.

According to a version of the pure expectations theory, investors' expected return for any holding period would be the same, regardless of the alternative or combination of alternatives they chose. This return would be a weighted average of the current short-term interest rate plus future short rates expected to prevail over the holding period; this average is the same for each alternative.

Forward rates may be calculated from the currently prevailing cash market yield curve, as any deviation from the implied forward rates would create arbitrage opportunities which market participants would exploit. This arbitrage is undertaken by buying and selling securities at different maturities to synthetically create the intended forward transaction.

By simultaneously borrowing and lending the same amount in the cash market but for different maturities it is possible to lock in an interest rate for a period in the future. If the maturity of the cash lending exceeds the maturity of the cash borrowing the implied rate over the future period, the forward-forward rate, is a bid rate for a forward investment. Similarly, if the maturity of the cash borrowing exceeds the maturity of the cash lending, then the resulting forward-forward rate is an offer rate for a forward borrowing.

This process of generating forward rates is set out in *Exhibit 10.1*.

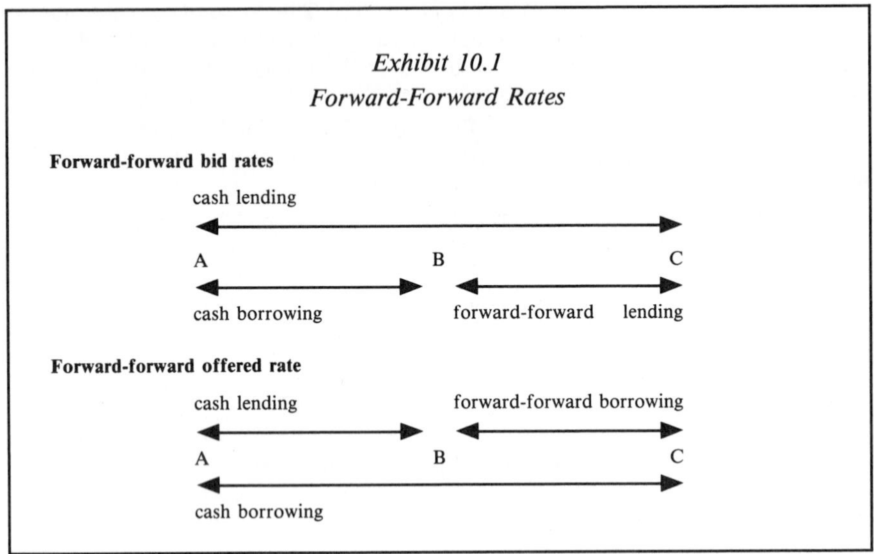

It is important to note that forward rates, when regarded as forecasts of future short-term interest rates, require a number of theoretical and practical assumptions. From a theoretical perspective, this approach assumes the absence of transaction costs and assumes the validity of the pure expectations theory of the term structure of interest rates. In particular, the forward rate as calculated from the current cash market yield curve contains no compensation for risk and, in particular, includes no liquidity premium.

Despite these theoretical objections, there is considerable behavioural support for this methodology of pricing forward rates and, therefore, FRAs. This is reflected in consistent arbitrage undertaken by market participants to drive FRA rates toward the implicit forward rates in the current cash market yield curve. It should, however, be noted that this process of arbitrage is not costless, involving the use of balance sheets, and consequently market efficiency is strongest in the shorter maturities.

A number of practical difficulties also exist. For example, it is difficult to obtain suitably spaced yields along the complete cash market yield curve. This difficulty is partially overcome by utilising fitted yield curves with forward rates being calculated off the fitted yield curve rather than the actual cash market curve. An additional problem relates to dealing spreads or bid-offer prices (effectively transaction costs) which will naturally distort forward rates.

Despite these minor difficulties, forward rates do bear a significant relationship to the current cash market yield curve although it is useful to bear in mind that forward bid and offer rates deviate sometimes from the implied forward rates and that the more distant the future period is, the greater the spread between the bid and offer rate and the divergence from the implied forward rate.

The actual yield curve utilised to derive the forward rate requires comment. The issues relating to selection of the specific yield curve to be utilised are similar to those discussed in the context of pricing LTFX rate: see above, Chapter 9.

In practice, forward rates are derived for shorter maturities (up to three years) from the inter-bank rate yield curve and from the swap yield curve for longer maturities.

The inter-bank rate yield curve, the swap yield curve and the implied futures strip curve, in most currencies, demonstrate a high degree of convergence in maturities up to two to three years. This reflects the process of arbitrage between cash and futures (see discussion below). Consequently, in practice forward rates, particularly, for the shorter maturities are those implied by futures contract and the implied futures yield curve of the relevant maturities.

Estimating forward rates

Forward rate structures are usually derived utilising the following equation:

$$(1 + R_{N-M})^{N-M} = \frac{(1 + R_N)^N}{(1 + R_m)^M}$$

where: $R,^{M},^{N}$ = interest rate for maturity M or N expressed as an interest rate pa

Exhibit 10.2 sets out examples of calculating forward rates. The forward rates implied in the first example by the yield curve are as follows:

1 × 3 (2 months in 1 months time): 6.627%
3 × 6 (3 months in 3 months time): 7.101%
6 × 9 (3 months in 6 months time): 7.716%
9 × 12 (3 months in 9 months time): 8.308%

On the basis of the above forward rates, FRAs would be priced at or about the implied forward rates. In practice, borrowing (investment) rates would be above (below) the implied forward rates reflecting hedging and transaction costs and the profit to the FRA provider.

FORWARD RATES IMPLIED BY SHORT-TERM INTEREST RATE FUTURES

Pricing of futures contracts

Short-term interest rate futures offer an alternative method for locking in interest rates over future periods. For example, the purchase of a three month interest rate futures contract (such as the Eurodollar contract) secures approximately a three month investment rate as of the futures delivery or settlement date whereas the sale of the same contract secures approximately a borrowing rate over the equivalent period. Futures contracts, in this regard, represent synthetic forwards and can be used as a substitute for the borrowing and lending transactions in the cash market which can be utilised to lock in an interest rate for a future period.

Exhibit 10.2

Calculation of Forward-Forward Interest Rates

Example 1

(1) Period (Years)	(2) Dates	Days	(3) Rates (Annual)	(4) $(1+R_{t1})^{t1}$	(5) $(1+R_{t0})^{t0}$	(6) (4)/(5)	(7) 1/(T1-T0)	Forward Rates Period T0-T1 $(6)^{(7)}-1$
0	01-Jul-X2	0						
0.085	01-Aug-X2	31	6.2500%	1.01600	1.00516	1.01078	5.98361	6.627%
0.252	01-Oct-X2	92	6.5000%	1.03372	1.01600	1.01744	3.96739	7.101%
0.504	01-Jan-X3	184	6.8000%	1.05284	1.03372	1.01850	4.05556	7.716%
0.751	01-Apr-X3	274	7.1000%	1.07400	1.05284	1.02010	4.01099	8.308%
1.000	01-Jul-X3	365	7.4000%	1.09478	1.07400	1.01934	3.96739	7.898%
1.252	01-Oct-X3	457	7.5000%	1.11570	1.09478	1.01911	3.96739	7.799%
1.504	01-Jan-X4	549	7.5500%	1.13682	1.11570	1.01894	4.05556	7.906%
1.751	01-Apr-X4	639	7.6000%	1.16532	1.13682	1.02507	4.01099	10.440%
2.000	01-Jul-X4	730	7.9500%					

Forward Rate Matrix

(1) Period (Years)	(2) Dates	Days	(3) Rates (Annual)								
0.000	01-Jul-X2	0									
0.085	01-Aug-X2	31	6.250%	6.627%							
0.252	01-Oct-X2	92	6.500%	6.912%	7.101%						
0.504	01-Jan-X3	184	6.800%	7.209%	7.405%	7.716%					
0.751	01-Apr-X3	274	7.100%	7.507%	7.705%	8.013%	8.308%				
1.000	01-Jul-X3	365	7.400%	7.592%	7.754%	7.974%	8.102%	7.898%			
1.252	01-Oct-X3	457	7.500%	7.628%	7.763%	7.930%	8.000%	7.848%	7.799%		
1.504	01-Jan-X4	549	7.550%	7.669%	7.786%	7.925%	7.977%	7.867%	7.852%	7.906%	
1.751	01-Apr-X4	639	7.600%	8.026%	8.161%	8.340%	8.464%	8.503%	8.708%	9.172%	10.440%
2.000	01-Jul-X4	730	7.950%								

Exhibit 10.2—continued

Example 2

(1) Period (Years)	(2) Dates	Days	(3) Rates (Annual)	(4) $(1+R_{t1})^{t1}$	(5) $(1+R_{t0})^{t0}$	(6) (4)/(5)	(7) 1/(T1-T0)	Forward Rates Period T0-T1 $(6)^{(7)}-1$
0	01-Jul-X4	0						
0.085	01-Aug-X4	31	10.2500%	1.02427	1.00832	1.01581	5.98361	9.843%
0.252	01-Oct-X4	92	9.9800%	1.04809	1.02427	1.02326	3.96739	9.550%
0.504	01-Jan-X4	184	9.7650%	1.07160	1.04809	1.02243	4.05556	9.415%
0.751	01-Apr-X4	274	9.6500%	1.09520	1.07160	1.02202	4.01099	9.130%
1.000	01-Jul-X4	365	9.5200%	1.11752	1.09520	1.02038	3.96739	8.333%
1.252	01-Oct-X4	457	9.2800%	1.14028	1.11752	1.02037	3.96739	8.329%
1.504	01-Jan-X4	549	9.1200%	1.16266	1.14028	1.01962	4.05556	8.200%
1.751	01-Apr-X4	639	8.9900%	1.18483	1.16266	1.01907	4.01099	7.872%
2.000	01-Jul-X4	730	8.8500%					

(1) Period (Years)	(2) Dates	Days	(3) Rates (Annual)	Forward Rate Matrix							
0.000	01-Jul-X4	0									
0.085	01-Aug-X4	31	10.250%	9.843%							
0.252	01-Oct-X4	92	9.980%	9.667%	9.550%						
0.504	01-Jan-X4	184	9.765%	9.574%	9.484%	9.415%					
0.751	01-Apr-X4	274	9.650%	9.452%	9.365%	9.271%	9.130%				
1.000	01-Jul-X4	365	9.520%	9.210%	9.104%	8.954%	8.728%	8.333%			
1.252	01-Oct-X4	457	9.280%	9.053%	8.948%	8.796%	8.594%	8.331%	8.329%		
1.504	01-Jan-X4	549	9.120%	8.926%	8.824%	8.678%	8.497%	8.288%	8.265%	8.200%	
1.751	01-Apr-X4	639	8.990%	8.788%	8.688%	8.543%	8.372%	8.184%	8.134%	8.035%	7.872%
2.000	01-Jul-X4	730	8.850%								

Note: The first Table in each example sets out the forward rate for the interval between each of the dates; that is, the three month rate in six, nine, 12, 15, 18 etc months. Details of the calculation are also specified. The second Table sets out a full matrix of forward rates based on the specified yield curve. Each column calculates the forward rates as of the earliest date to the final maturity (two years) in both examples); that is, the 21 month rate in three months' time; the 18 month rate in six months' time etc.

In their simplest form, futures prices are prices set today to be paid in the future for goods or securities. The price of a futures contract thus depends in part on an assessment of the future price of the underlying instrument at delivery, based on information currently available in the market. Part of this market information is the fact that for some securities, one can arrange to own the underlying instrument on the delivery date by buying it today at the current market price and storing it until that time. If this opportunity is available, the cost associated with immediate purchase and storage until delivery will certainly be an important factor in the price one is willing to pay for a futures contract. Holding the futures contract enables one to avoid the investment of cash and the storage, or carrying costs, that would be incurred if the good or security is bought early and stored until delivery.

Other important factors may influence the market's assessment of the futures price of the underlying instrument. These include:

- uncertainty in the supply or demand for the deliverable security between the date in which the futures price is set and the delivery date;
- any cash flows, such as dividends or interest payments, that one would receive if the security rather than the futures contract were held;
- any risks or uncertainties that futures contract holders are exposed to that makes them willing to pay less for a futures contract than they would in the absence of such risks.

These risks include basis risk which must be borne when using financial futures. This risk arises from fluctuations in the spread between the cash and futures price. Some movement in the basis is expected over the life of a futures contract. However, the underlying motivation for hedging is that the basis is much less volatile than the prices of the underlying security.

Another risk associated with futures positions is the need to immediately make good for losses in the value of a futures contract (referred to as marking-to-market). Uncertainty with respect to the exact instrument that will be delivered and the prices at the point of each settlement can also play a role in price determination for futures.

Calculating futures prices

Prices in the futures market for short-term interest rates are driven mainly by short-term interest rates for physical securities in the relevant currency. This is relevant to the futures market because the arbitrage which ensures an equilibrium futures price depends in part on a cash market position financed in the short-term market. An example of the so-called cash and carry trade will help make this clear.

In a competitive market, a risk-free arbitrage should earn a return equal to the risk-free rate. Using this principle, a risk-free position combining cash and futures can be established and the futures price determined such that the return on the combined position earns the risk-free rate over the holding period. Suppose the trade consists of a short position in the Eurodollar futures maturing in three months and a long position in the physical six months Eurodollar deposit market. The physical Eurodollar position is financed for three months (prior to its delivery into the contract) at the three month rate. In this trade, the cost of financing and the rate of return of the six month position are known. Arbitrage will determine the futures price. In equilibrium, it will be bid to a level such that the rate of return represented by the difference between the futures price and the deposit will be equal to the cost of financing the deposit over the three month period. This calculated rate is sometimes called the break-even borrowing cost.

If the futures price is greater than the equilibrium level, arbitrageurs will earn a positive return with no risk by purchasing the cash deposit, selling the futures and carrying the position at the three month rate. This will drive down the futures price relative to the cash price until the holding period return equals the cost of financing the trade. On the other hand, if the futures price is below the equilibrium price, arbitrageurs will buy the futures, sell the cash and invest the proceeds at a net positive spread. This will tend to drive the futures price up relative to the cash market, again resulting in an equilibrium price such that the rate of return on the trade equals the three month borrowing rate.

In both cases, the synthetic asset consists of cash deposits or equivalent securities which are either lengthened or shortened by going long or short in the futures market.

A long position in a futures contract or a strip of futures lengthens the cash position by purchasing deposits today for future delivery. On the other hand, a short futures position essentially sells off the back end of a cash deposit, thereby shortening it.

The cash and carry trade is an example of the latter variety; a long cash deposit is purchased and then delivered into a short futures position, producing a synthetic asset which matures on the expiration of the futures contract.

Examples of cash-futures arbitrage transactions involving the Eurodollar futures contract and also the A$ bank bill futures contract, are set out in *Exhibit 10.3*. These examples highlight the process of arbitrage through which futures and, by implication, forward prices are forced to equilibrium levels.

Exhibit 10.3

Examples of Cash Futures Arbitrage

Eurodollars

Assume the following trading condition exists on 1 September 19X2:

Eurodollar Rate for 195 days (to 15 March 19X3):	7.00% pa
Eurodollar Rate for 104 days (to 14 December 19X2):	6.34% pa

The implied equilibrium futures rate for the December 19X2 Eurodollar contract which expires on 14 December 19X2 is 92.25 or 7.75% pa. This futures price reflects the fact that the purchase of a 91 day investment (commencing 14 December 19X2) and the purchase of a 195 day deposit and the sale of the December Eurodollars contract are equivalent transactions.

Assume the December Eurodollar is trading at 92.59 (7.41% pa). Under these circumstances, it is feasible to structure a cash and carry cash-futures arbitrage transaction as follows:

- purchase a Eurodollar Deposit for 195 days at 7.00% pa;
- borrow Eurodollar for 104 days (to futures expiry) at 6.34% pa;
- sell the December Eurodollar contract at 92.59.

The results of these transactions (based on an assumed face value of US$1,000,000) are as follows:

Interest Earnings	*US$*
US$1,000,000 @ 7.00% × 195/360	37,916.67
Interest Expense	
$1,000,000 @ 6.34% × 104/360:	18,315.56
$1,000,000 @ 7.41% × 91/360:	18,730.83
	37,046.39
Net Gain	$870.28

The above calculation ignores the interest cost of funding the interest payment of US$18,315.56. Assuming a funding cost of 7.41% pa for 91 days, this equates to US$343.07 (US$18,315.56 @ 7.41% × 91/360). This reduces the net gain to $527.21.

Exhibit 10.3—continued

The party entering into the transaction can utilise the higher than equilibrium futures price to create a 195 day synthetic borrowing at a lower cost than the equivalent investment rate.

Alternatively, it would be possible to construct a synthetic 104 day investment at above market rates as follows:

	US$
Purchase one deposit at 7.00%: (future value at 15 March 19X3 of $1,037,916.67)	1,000,000.00
Sale of Eurodollar Deposit at 7.41% *(as at 14 December 19X2):	1,018,833.07
Gain	18,833.07

* Locked in rate through sale of December Eurodollar Contract.

This gain equates to a yield over 104 days of 6.52% pa, an arbitrage gain of 0.18% pa.

If the December Eurodollar Futures Contract is trading below equilibrium levels at 92.01, then a reverse cash and carry transaction could be engineered by purchasing a 104 day Eurodollar deposit, purchasing the December Eurodollar Contract and borrowing Eurodollars for 195 days.

The results of the transaction are as follows:

	US$
US$1,000,000 @ 6.34% × 104/360:	18,315.56
US$1,000,000 @ 7.99% × 91/360:	20,196.94
	38,512.50
Interest Expense	
US$ 1,000,000 @ 7.00% × 195/360:	37,916.67
Net Gain	595.83

The disequilibrium in the future price effectively allows the creation of a 195 day security yielding 7.11% pa, an arbitrage gain of 0.11% pa.

This calculation again ignores interest on the interim interest payment (in this case a receipt). This additional interest equates to US$369.92 (US$18,315.56 @ 7.99% × 91/360) increasing the net gain to US$965.75.

A$ Bank Bill Futures

Assume the following trading conditions exist on 1 May 19X2:

A$ BBR Interest Rates for 42 days (to 12 June 19X2):	6.85% pa
A$ BBR Interest Rates for 133 days (to 11 September 19X2):	7.12% pa

The implied equilibrium futures price for the June A$ Bank Bill Futures Contract is 92.76.

If the June A$ Bank Bill Contract is trading at 92.95 (or 7.05% pa), then a cash and carry transaction can be structured by purchasing a 133 day Bank Bill and selling the June Futures.

The results of the transaction (based on a principal face value of A$1,000,000) are as follows:

	A$
Purchase 133 day A$1,000,000 bill at 7.12% pa	974,711.97
Sell 91 day A$1,000,000 bill at 7.05% pa:*	982,726.89
Gain	8,014.93

* Locked in through rate of June BBR Futures Contract.

This gain equates to a yield over 42 days of 6.965% pa, an arbitrage gain of 0.115% pa.

The gains from the cash and carry arbitrage can alternatively be stated as follows:

Exhibit 10.3—continued

	A$
Interest Earnings	
Interest on A$1,000,000 bill @ 7.12% for 133 days:	25,288.03
Interest Expense	
Interest on A$1,000,000 @ 6.85% for 42 days	7,820.55
Interest on A$1,000,000 @ 7.05% for 91 days:	17,273.11
	25,093.66
Net Gain	194.37

The above result can be adjusted for the cost of financing the interim interest payment. This cost equates to A$137.46 (A$7,820.55 @ 7.05% × 91/365) reducing the gain to A$56.91.

If the June A$ Bank Bill Contract is trading at 92.45, then a reverse cash and carry transaction can be structured by purchasing a 42 day Bank Bill and purchasing the June Futures.

The results of the transaction are as follows:

	A$
Interest Earnings	
Interest on A$1,000,000 @ 6.85% pa for 42 days:	7,820.55
Interest on A$1,000,000 @ 7.55% pa for 91 days:	18,475.52
	26,296.07
Interest Expense	
Interest on A$1,000,000 @ 7.12% pa for 133 days:	25,288.03
Net Gain	1,008.04

The disequilibrium is the futures price effectively allows the creation of 133 day security yielding 7.217% pa, an arbitrage gain of 0.097% pa.

The net gain should be adjusted for interest on the intermediate interest payment. This adjustment equates to A$147.2 (A$7,820.55 @ 7.53% × 91/365) increasing the net gain to A$1,155.25.

Notes:

1. Bank Bills are discount securities and the A$ Bank Bill Contract is structured similarly.
2. The above examples ignore transaction costs such as bid-offer spreads, commission, deposits and margin calls.

Futures price and FRA prices

The relationship between the futures price and FRA prices is a complex one. The basic relationship is predicated on the FRA provider entering the futures market to hedge its exposure under the FRA itself.

For example, an FRA entered into to hedge a future borrowing or rollover entails the FRA provider having a forward purchase commitment or an exposure to rising rates which it can hedge by selling futures contracts. Consequently, the FRA provider may hedge itself in the relevant interest rate futures contract and therefore will price the FRA transaction on the basis of the corresponding price of the futures contract. However, the relationship is more complex as the terms of the FRA itself (the commencement date and its duration) may not coincide with those of the underlying interest rate futures contract being used to hedge the transaction. In this case, the futures price will be required to be adjusted to reflect these differences.

These adjustments are discussed in Chapter 35, in the context of market making in swap derivatives such as FRAs.

In summary, FRAs in any currency can be hedged utilising short-term interest rate futures contracts in the relevant currency, if such instruments are available. In fact, even if such short-term interest rate futures are not available in the relevant currency, it is in fact possible to replicate the desired instrument by a combination of futures and FRAs in a second currency and foreign exchange transactions as between the two currencies (refer *Exhibit 4.3*).

Chapter 11

Pricing Caps, Floors and Collars

CAPS, COLLARS ETC AS OPTIONS

Caps, collars etc are essentially customised versions of exchange traded options on short-term interest rates. Just as FRAs are a form of synthetic futures, caps and collars are option transactions which are customised in accordance with the requirements of purchasers.

As discussed above in Chapter 5 interest rate caps, floors and collars are essentially identical to a series of options. For example, an interest rate cap can be thought of as a series of put options. The writer of the option (seller of the cap) receives a fee (premium) for the cap (put options) from the purchaser of the option (purchaser of the cap). Similarly, floors can be thought of as a series of call options. A collar, in contrast, is in effect a combination of the above transactions with the purchaser of the collar buying a series of put options or caps whilst simultaneously selling back to the provider of the collar a series of call options or floors.

It is important to distinguish between options on the *interest rate index* as distinct from an option on *the price of the underlying debt security*. For example, an interest rate cap is equivalent to a series of *put options* on the *price* of the underlying debt security which is priced relative to short-term interest rate indexes. Alternatively, however, the cap can be thought of as a series of *call options* on the relevant *interest rate index*, such as six month LIBOR. Similarly, a floor can be thought of as a series of call options on the price of the underlying debt securities or, alternatively, a put option on the relevant interest rate index.

Considerable theory exists as to the pricing of option contracts. Predictably, fees for caps, floors and collars tend to be priced with reference to option pricing theory.

OPTION VALUATION CONCEPTS[1]

Option pricing nomenclature

In determining the value of an option, it is possible to distinguish between the *intrinsic value* and the *time value* of an option. An option's intrinsic value is based on the difference between its exercise price and the current price of the underlying debt instrument. If the option is currently profitable to exercise, it is said to have intrinsic value, that is, a call (put) option has intrinsic value if the current price of the instrument is above (below) the option's exercise price. Whether or not the option has intrinsic value, it may have time value (defined as the excess of the premium over the option's intrinsic value). The time value of the option reflects the amount buyers are willing to pay for the possibility that, at some time prior to expiration, the option may become profitable to exercise.

1. For an excellent discussion on option pricing see John Hull, *Option, Futures, and Other Derivative Instruments* (1989).

Three other option valuation terms merit comment:

- in-the-money;
- at-the-money;
- out-of-the-money.

It is customary for market participants to refer to particular options as belonging to one of the three groups. An option with an exercise price at or close to the current market price of the underlying security is said to be at-the-money. An option with intrinsic value is referred to as being in-the-money, while an out-of-the-money option is one with no intrinsic value, but presumably with some time value.

In using this option valuation terminology in the context of caps, floors and collars, it is necessary to recognise that the relevant current market price (or yield) of the underlying debt instrument is not the spot market price for the physical security. Instead, it is the *forward price* for the relevant security which is the relevant price benchmark.

For example, consider a three year interest rate cap agreement on three month LIBOR at a cap level of 10.00% pa. This agreement represents a commitment by the writer or seller of the interest rate cap that it will compensate the purchaser if, on specified quarterly dates over the three year period of the transaction, three month LIBOR exceeds the cap level of 10.00% pa. If current three month LIBOR rates are 8.00%, then it is tempting to argue that this interest rate cap is out-of-the-money. However, the cap level (the strike price of the option) must necessarily be compared with the current actual price of the security. This requires that the cap level be compared to the *forward* three month LIBOR rates over the full three year period of the agreement.

The agreement itself represents a series of 11 put options with a strike price equivalent to a yield of 10.00% on three month LIBOR commencing in three months time and terminating at the end of 36 months. Consequently, the strike price of 10.00% must be compared to the three month forward LIBOR rates on each of the relevant quarterly periods covered by the interest rate cap. Whether each option is in- or out-of-the-money will largely be determined by the shape of the yield curve: refer to the calculation technology for forward rates discussed above in Chapter 10.

Factors affecting option pricing

The fundamental direct determinants of option value include:

- the current price of the underlying instrument;
- the exercise price of the option;
- interest rates;
- the time to expiry;
- the volatility of prices on the underlying instrument.

Other factors affecting option valuation include the type of option (that is, whether the option is American or European) as well as payouts from holding the underlying instrument.

The general effect of each of the five major relevant variables on the value of an option (where all other variables are held constant) is summarised in *Exhibit 11.1*. The effect of changes in the spot price of the instrument, option strike prices, and time to expiry on the pricing of options are relatively easily understood.

Exhibit 11.1
Factors Affecting Option Valuation

Factor	Effect of increase in factor on value of	
	Call	**Put**
Strike price	Decrease	Increase
Spot price	Increase	Decrease
Interest rate	Increase	Decrease
Time to expiry	Increase	Increase (American option only)
Volatility	Increase	Increase

In the case of a call option, the higher the price of the underlying instrument, the higher the intrinsic value of the option if it is in-the-money and hence the higher the premium. If the call is out-of-the-money, then the higher the underlying instrument's price the greater the probability that it will be possible to exercise the call at a profit and hence the higher the time value, or premium, of the option. In the case of put options, the reverse will apply.

The impact of changes in exercise price is somewhat similar. For an in-the-money call option the lower the exercise price, the higher the intrinsic value, while for an out-of-the-money call the lower the exercise price the greater the probability of profitable exercise and hence the higher the time value. A similar but opposite logic applies in the case of put options.

The impact of time to expiration and option valuation is predicated on the fact that the longer an option has to run, the greater the probability that it will be possible to exercise the option profitably, hence the greater the time value of the option.

The impact of volatility derives from the fact that the greater the expected movement in the price of the underlying instrument, the greater the probability that the option can be exercised at a profit and hence the more valuable the option or its time value. In essence, the higher the volatility, the greater the likelihood that the asset will either do very well or very poorly which is reflected in the price of the option.

The impact of interest rates is less clear intuitively. The role of interest rates in the determination of option premiums is complex and varies from one type of option to another. In general, however, the higher the interest rate, the lower the *present value* of the exercise price the call buyer has contracted to pay in the event of exercise. In essence, a call option can be thought of as the right to buy the underlying asset at the discounted value of the exercise price. Consequently, the greater the degree of discount the more valuable is the right, hence, as interest rates increase and the degree of discount increases commensurately, the corresponding option value increases. In fact, a higher interest rate has a similar influence to that of a lower exercise price. A similar but opposite logic applies in the case of a put option. The higher interest rate decreases the value of the put option as it reduces the current (present valued or discounted) value of the exercise price that the buyer has contracted to receive.

OPTION PRICING THEORY

Approaches to mathematical option pricing

Mathematical option pricing models seek to calculate the price of particular options, utilising the identified fundamental determinants of option value and incorporating these within a defined formalised mathematical framework. The technological approach of formal valuation is the same regardless of the type of option being evaluated, whether it be an option on commodities, equity stock or market index currencies, or a debt instrument as well as futures contracts on each of these assets.

The development of mathematical option pricing models requires the following distinct steps:

- definition of certain rational arbitrage boundaries on the potential value of the option;
- specific assumptions as to the market and economic environment within which the option is sought to be valued as well as the likely price behaviour of the underlying instrument;
- derivation of a pricing solution, given the assumptions about economic environment and price behaviour within the valuation boundary constraints identified.

Boundary conditions to option values[2]

The first step in mathematical pricing is to identify certain boundaries that can be placed on the values of options based on arbitrage considerations. The concept of arbitrage in this context relies upon dominance whereby a portfolio asset is said to dominate another portfolio if, for the same cost, it offers a return that will, at least, be the same. The underlying assumption, in this context, is that if these boundary conditions are breached, arbitrage activity would force the prices of the underlying assets and options within the arbitrage boundaries as arbitrageurs would enter into transactions designed to take advantage of riskless profit opportunities.

In the interest of clarity, in this section, the boundary conditions to option value are stated with reference to generalised assets. Arbitrage conditions specific to options on debt instruments, that is, caps, floors and collars, are considered later in this chapter. However, it should be noted that the conditions discussed in this section are common to all options and the principles underlying the arbitrage conditions are fundamentally identical.

The following notation is used in outlining the boundary conditions:

S	=	asset price
K	=	strike price
T	=	time to maturity
RF	=	risk free interest rate
V	=	volatility of returns from asset
C(A)	=	price of American call
C(E)	=	price of European call
P(A)	=	price of American put
P(E)	=	price of European put

2. This discussion on boundary conditions is based substantially upon Rowley (1987).

AB = arbitrage boundary
VP = value of portfolio
PV(K) = present value of amount K

There are nine major arbitrage boundaries discussed in this section. Put-call parity for options is a special arbitrage condition which is discussed later in this chapter.

AB 1

$$C(A) \text{ or } C(E) \geq 0$$

AB 1 states that the value of the call option is greater than or equal to 0. Option exercise is voluntary, consequently, investors will never undertake an option transaction if they lose money which means that call prices cannot take on negative values.

AB 2

At maturity of the option:

$$C(A) \text{ or } C(E) = 0 \text{ or } S-K$$
$$P(A) \text{ or } P(E) = 0 \text{ or } K-S$$

At maturity, the value of a call or put option will be either 0 or its intrinsic value. If this condition is not satisfied, arbitrage opportunities exist. For example, if a call at maturity sells for less than $S-K$, arbitrageurs could lock in a profit by borrowing enough to purchase the call and exercising it immediately making a riskless profit after paying back the loan.

AB 3

Prior to maturity of the option,

$$C(A) \text{ will equal: } \geq 0 \text{ or } \geq S-K$$

$$P(A) \text{ will equal: } \geq 0 \text{ or } \geq K-S$$

AB 3 is an extension of AB 2. If at any time *prior* to maturity, an American option contract sells for less than its intrinsic value, an arbitrage opportunity exists to purchase the option and exercise immediately while buying or selling the physical asset to lock in a riskless profit.

AB 4

$$C(A) \geq C(E)$$
$$P(A) \geq P(E)$$

An American call should not sell for a premium value less than an identical European option because the American style of option provides all the benefits of the European contract with the addition of being able to be exercised at any time.

AB 5

An American call which has no intermediate cash flow should never be exercised before maturity; it is always better to sell the option.

The validity for this arbitrage condition can be established by constructing the following two portfolios:

VP 1: Buy C(E) and invest PV of strike price (PV(K))
VP 2: Buy S

The payoff from these two portfolios is set out below:

Portfolio	Current value	Value at maturity Out-of-the-money $Sm < K$	 In-the-money $Sm \geq K$
VP1	C(E) + PV(K)	0 + K	(Sm − K) + K
VP2	S	Sm	Sm
Relationship between portfolio values at maturity "m"		VP1 > VP2	VP1 = VP2

At maturity, VP1 is never worth less than VP2, so the current cost of VP1 can never be less than that of VP2. This implies that an American call option will usually never be exercised prior to maturity as the investor would only receive the intrinsic value of the option (S − K) which is less than $(S-K)E^{-RFT}$ for any positive interest rate. Consequently, AB 5 indicates that a rational investor will always sell a call option to somebody else rather than exercise the option.

AB 6

In the case of an American call where there are intermediate cash flows, early exercise is possible.

AB 6 is a variation of AB 5 which implies that where there are intermediate cash flows, an American option is capable of early exercise. The proof of this strategy can be established by constructing portfolios which are similar to above. The two portfolios are as follows:

VP3: Buy C(E) and invest PV of strike price (PV (K + D))
VP4: Buy S

Note that the amount invested is equal to the option's strike price and the intermediate cash flow.

Assuming that the intermediate cash flow is D, the payoff from these two portfolios will be as follows:

Portfolio	Current value	Value at maturity Out-of-the-money $Sm < K$	 In-the-money $Sm \geq K$
VP3	C(E) + PV(K + D)	0 + K + D	(Sm − K) + K + D
VP4	S	Sm + D	Sm + D
Relationship between portfolio values at maturity "m"		VP3 > VP4	VP3 = VP4

The payout table indicates that at maturity VP3 never pays less than VP4 and gives a higher return when the option expires out-of-the-money. Consequently, VP3 cannot sell for less than VP2. This means that whenever a European call is in-the-money prior to maturity the lowest value it can trade for will be equal to the stock price minus the investment required to receive an amount equal to the strike price plus any intermediate cash flow at maturity [S – PV (K + D)]. The lower limit on the value of the European call must be the lower limit on an American option's value.

This implies an optimal exercise policy for an American option on an asset with intermediate cash flows. If the lower limit on the call's value [S – PV (K + D)] is greater than the amount received by exercising (S – K), then it is better to sell than exercise. However, if [S – PV (K + D)] is less than (S – K), the American call should be exercised rather than sold if the position is to be closed down.

In general terms, an American call should therefore only be exercised early when the discounted value of the strike price and intermediate cash flows are worth more than the strike price. In essence, it is PV(D) that determines whether the option is sold or exercised. Early exercise is therefore more probable on American options where the underlying asset has high intermediate cash flows.

AB 7

$$C(E) \text{ or } C(A) \leq S$$

A call option cannot be worth more than the underlying stock because if the option were worth more than the stock, then a riskless arbitrage profit could be made by writing a call and using the proceeds to buy the stock. If the call is exercised, the stock can be delivered and the strike price received in return, while if the call is unexercised at maturity the stock which has a positive value will be held, thereby allowing the arbitrageur to make a positive profit without incurring any risk.

AB 8

C(E) or C(A) can never be worth more than an identical option with a lower exercise price.

P(E) or P(A) can never be worth more than an identical option with a higher exercise price.

In this case, the call with the low exercise price offers a greater chance of being in-the-money, consequently, it cannot sell for a price which is lower than an option which has less chance of being in-the-money. The reverse is true for put options.

AB 9

C(E) or C(A) cannot be worth less than an identical option with a shorter time to maturity.

Intuitively, the longer the maturity on the option, the greater the opportunity for there to be a sufficiently large change in the asset price to push the option into the money. Consequently, an option with a longer maturity cannot sell for less than an equivalent option with a shorter maturity. If this condition is violated, an arbitrage can be set up whereby the arbitrageur writes the shorter-dated option while purchasing the option with the longer maturity to lock in a riskless arbitrage profit.

Put-call parity

Put-call parity which defines the relationship between the price of a European call option and a European put option with the same exercise price and time to expiration is an additional arbitrage boundary on option values. Utilising the same notation as that used previously, put-call parity can be stated as follows:

$$C(E) + PV(K) = P(E) + S$$

This implies that buying a call and investing PV of K is identical to buying a put and buying the asset.

The proof of this relationship can be established by setting up two portfolios:

VP1: Buy C(E) and invest PV(K)
VP2: Buy P(E) and buy S

The payoffs on the two portfolios at maturity are as follows:

Portfolio	Current value	Value at maturity: Out-of-the-money $Sm<K$	Value at maturity: In-the-money $Sm \geq K$
VP1	C(E) + PV(K)	0 + K	$(S_m - K) + K$
VP2	P(E) + S	$(K - S_m) + S_m$	$0 + S_m$
Relationship between portfolio values at maturity "m"		VP1 = VP2	VP1 = VP2

At maturity, VP1 is equal to VP2 irrespective of whether the option expires in- or out-of-the-money.

The put-call parity condition can be restated as follows:

Synthetic call (reversal)

$$C(E) = P(E) + S - PV(K)$$

Synthetic put (conversion)

$$P(E) = C(E) - S + PV(K)$$

Long asset/forward

$$S = C(E) - P(E) + PV(K)$$

Short asset/forward

$$-S = P(E) - C(E) - PV(K)$$

For European options, arbitrage possibilities will exist if the put-call parity conditions are not fulfilled. An example of put-call parity arbitrage is set out in *Exhibit 11.2*.

It is important to note that the put-call parity theorem is only valid for European options. Synthetic positions for American options are not always pure. For example, if S decreases and P(A) is exercised, then you would lose the difference between K and S immediately, not at the forward date.

This means that put-call parity for American options can be stated as follows:

$$C(A) - S + PV(K) \leq P(A) \leq C(A) - S + K$$

Mathematical option pricing models: the conceptual basis assumptions underlying option pricing model

Mathematical option pricing models can be developed to synthesise the many factors which affect the option premium within the arbitrage boundaries identified. In order to develop such mathematical option pricing models, it is necessary to make a number of restrictive assumptions, including:

- no restrictions or costs of short selling;
- no taxes or transaction costs;

Exhibit 11.2
Put-Call Parity Arbitrage

Assume that the Sydney Futures Exchange (SFE) 90 day bank bill futures contract for the near month is trading at 86.14/86.15. Call options on the contract with strike price 86.00 on the contract are trading at 0.28/0.33. Put options with an identical strike price are trading at 0.02/0.07. In these circumstances, it is possible to create a synthetic 86.00 call at less than 0.28 as follows:

- buy 86.00 put at 0.07;
- simultaneously, buy futures at 86.15;
- sell 86.00 call at 0.28.

This transaction effectively creates a call at less than the 0.28 received. This can be proved as follows: the sold call and the bought put are equivalent to a synthetic short futures position at a price of 86.00. The position creates a net cash flow to the grantor of 0.21. Of the 0.21, 0.15 is lost through the bought bond futures position at 86.15 which is above the synthetic short price of 86.000. However, the futures loss of 0.15 is more than offset by the 0.21 gain on the option.

The analysis ignores the different value of points (0.01) at different yield levels.

- asset trading is continuous, with all asset prices following continuous and stationary stochastic processes;
- asset has no intermediate cash flows (for example, dividends, interest etc);
- the risk free rate of interest is constant over the option's life;
- the asset price moves around in a continuously random manner;
- the distribution of the asset's return is log normal;
- the variance of the return distribution is constant over the asset's life;
- the option is European.

Most of these assumptions are self-explanatory and are consistent with efficient capital market theory. Stochastic process refers to the evolution of asset prices through time modelled as random, characterised by continuous series of price changes governed by the laws of probability as prescribed. By continuous processes, it is usually implied that the price of the underlying asset can vary over time but does not have discontinuities or jumps, that is, the price movement over time of the asset could be graphed without lifting the pen from the paper.

The stationary stochastic process, as assumed, is one that is determined the same way for all time periods of equal length. Specifically, the traditional approach to option valuation assumed at the price of the underlying asset has a particular type of probability distribution, assumed to be a log normal distribution. It is also assumed that the standard deviation of this distribution is constant over time.

The "riskless hedge" concept

The derivation of the mathematical option pricing model also requires understanding of the concept of a riskless hedge. A riskless portfolio by definition consists of an asset and a corresponding option held in proportion to the prescribed hedge ratio, continuously adjusted, whereby the portfolio is perfectly hedged against movements in asset prices as changes in the call price and the asset price are mutually offsetting. Utilising the constructs of portfolio theory or the capital asset pricing model, it is predicted that a riskless portfolio should earn no more than a risk free rate of return. It is important to note that outside the context of this riskless hedge construct, the values derived by mathematical option pricing models are not meaningful.

Certain riskless portfolio positions are set out below:

- Position for hedging:
  - — long position in calls;
  - — short position in calls;
  - — long position in the stock;
  - — short position in the stock.
- How to hedge it:
  - — short stock for each call held;
  - — long stock for each all issued;
  - — short (1/△) of calls for each stock held;
  - — hold (1/△) of calls for each stock held.

The Black and Scholes option pricing model

Black and Scholes (1973) were the first to provide a close form solution for the valuation of European call options. The mathematical derivation of the Black and Scholes' option pricing model is beyond the mathematical capabilities assumed for this text.

Black and Scholes' option pricing model is usually specified as follows:

$$C(E) = S.\ N\ (d_1)\ - Ke^{-RF.T}\ .N\ (d_2)$$

where:

$$d_1 = \frac{\ln\ (S/K)\ +\ (RF\ +\ V^2\ /2)T}{v\ \sqrt{T}}$$

$$d_2 = \frac{\ln\ (S/K)\ +\ (RF\ -\ V^2\ /2)T}{v\ \sqrt{T}}$$

$N\ (d_1)$ and $N\ (d_2)$ are cumulative normal distribution functions for d_1 and d_2

ln is the natural logarithm

$Ke^{-RF.T}$ is the amount of cash needed to be invested over period or time T at a continuously compounded interest rate of RF in order to receive K at maturity.

The price of a European put option can be derived by utilising put-call parity.

Two aspects of the Black and Scholes' Option Pricing Model require comment:

- The calculation of the cumulative normal distribution function [N(D)] is undertaken either utilising a N(D) table or directly utilising numerical procedures. *Appendix A* to this chapter sets out a methodology for the calculating cumulative normal distribution function.
- The Model requires specification of the volatility of prices on the underlying instrument (parameter "V" in the above equation). Techniques for the estimation of volatility, including discussion of the various issues thereto, is detailed in *Appendix B* to this chapter.

Exhibit 11.3 sets out an example of utilising the Black and Scholes' Option Pricing Model to calculate the price of an option.

Exhibit 11.3

*Example of Using Black-Scholes Option Pricing Model**

Calculate the price for a call and put option on an asset based on the following information:

Asset Price	= S	= 105.00
Strike Price	= K	= 100.00
Time to Maturity	= T	= six months (0.5 yrs)
Risk Free Interest Rate	= RF	= 10% pa (0.10)
Volatility	= V	= 20% (0.20)

Using the above inputs, we can compute the call option price as follows:

$$d1 = \frac{\ln(105/100) + (0.1 + 0.20^2/2)\,0.5}{0.2\sqrt{0.5}}$$

$$= \frac{\ln(1.05) + (0.12)\,0.5}{0.2 \times 0.707107}$$

$$= \frac{0.108790}{0.141421} = 0.769263$$

$$d2 = \frac{\ln(105/100) + (0.1 - 0.20^2/2)\,0.5}{0.2\sqrt{0.5}}$$

$$= 0.627841$$

Using the Normal Cumulative Distribution Table

N(0.769263) = 0.7791
N(0.627841) = 0.7349

Therefore, the call option value is:

$$C(E) = 105 \times 0.7791 - 100 \times e^{-0.10 \times 0.50} \times 0.7349$$

$$= 105 \times 0.7791 - 95.123 \times 0.7349$$

$$= 11.900$$

The value of the call option is $11.90 or 11.33% of Asset Price.

The corresponding put option value is:

N(−0.769263) = 0.2209
N(−0.627841) = 0.2651

$$P(E) = 100 \times e^{-0.10 \times 0.5} \times 0.2651 - 105 \times 0.2209$$

$$= 2.023$$

The value of the put option is $2.023 or 1.9261% of Asset Price.

* This example is based on John Hull (1989), p 119.

Binomial option pricing

The binomial option pricing model utilises an identical logical approach to Black and Scholes. However, in contrast to Black and Scholes, the binomial approach assumes that the security price obeys a binomial generating process. The binomial approach also assumes that the option cannot or will not be exercised prior to expiration (that is, the option is European).

The valuation process begins by considering the possibility that the price can move up or down over a given period by a given amount. This enables calculation of the value of the call option at expiration of the relevant period (which is always the greater of zero or the price of the instrument minus the exercise price). The riskless hedge technique starts at expiration and works backwards in time to the current period for a portfolio consisting of the physical security sold short or one sold futures contract on the relevant asset and one bought call option on the relevant asset.

Since the portfolio is riskless, it, consistent with Black and Scholes, must return the risk free rate of return over the relevant period. The derivation of the value of the call option using this approach is predicated on the fact that the call option must be priced so that the risk free hedge earns exactly the risk free rate of return.

The binomial option pricing model contains the Black and Scholes formula as a limiting case. If, for the binomial option pricing model, the number of sub-periods are allowed to tend to infinity, the binomial option pricing model tends to the option pricing formula derived by Black and Scholes.

A significant advantage of the binomial approach is that it provides a solution not only for the closed form European option pricing problem but also for the more difficult American option pricing problems when numerical simulation approaches must be employed. In essense, the binomial pricing approach is useful as it can accommodate more complex option pricing problems.

Exhibit 11.4 sets details for utilising binomial option pricing techniques to price options.

Exhibit 11.4

Example of Binomial Option Pricing Model

The binomial option model is best illustrated by example. Assume the following:

Current asset price(S) = 100.

Possible Stock Price at Option Expiry = 110 or 90(± 10%) with equal probability of occurring.

Risk free rate (RF) = 8% pa.

This can be expressed diagrammatically as follows:

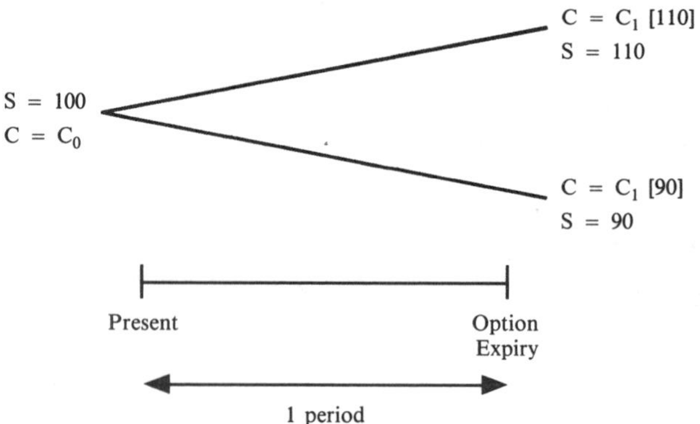

C_0 = Call Option Value at present.

C_1 [110] and C_1 = Call Option value in one month's time for asset prices of 110 and 90 at option expiry.

Exhibit 11.4—continued

The value of the call option is derived by establishing an arbitrage boundary whereby a riskless hedge portfolio consisting of a long or short position in the asset and an offsetting option (a portfolio which has no exposure to the underlying asset price) can only earn the risk free rate of return (this assumption is identical to the riskless hedge argument underlying Black and Scholes).

Assume the risk neutral hedge ratio is 0.50 for a European call option with strike price of 10.0. The detailed calculation of the hedge ratio is discussed below.

The value of the call option which avoids an arbitrage profit can be derived as follows (where C = Call Option Value).

	Time		
	Present	At Option Expiry	
Asset Price	100	90 *or*	110
Portfolio:			
−100 call*	100c	–	1,000
+50 assets#	5,000	4,500	5,500
Borrow at 8%	5,000 − 100c	(5,000 − 100c) × 1.08	(5,000 − 100c) × 1.08
Net Profit	0	0	0

* Signifies 100 written calls.

Signifies hedge position at the designated hedge ratio of 0.50.

The value for C which ensure no net arbitrage profits:

$$4{,}500 - (5{,}000 - 100c)\,(1.08) = 0$$
$$C = \$8.33.$$

The generalised option price with 1 period to expiration can be stated as =

$$C = (pCu + (1 - p)\,Cd)/RF$$

where
C = Call Premium
$Cu = \text{Max}\,(o,\ u\,s - x)$
$Cd = \text{Max}\,(o,\ d\,s - x)$
$RF = 1 +$ Risk Free Interest Rate
$u = 1 + \%$ up move
$d = 1 + \%$ down move
$$P = \frac{RF - d}{u - d}$$

The corresponding hedge ratio is:

$$\frac{Cu - Cd}{(u - d)\,S}$$

Based on the above example, we can calculate C as follows:

$$P = \frac{1.08 - 0.90}{1.10 - 0.90} = 0.90$$

$$C = [0.90 \times 10 + (1 - 0.90) \times 0]/1.08 = \$8.33$$

The hedge ratio is:

$$\frac{10 - 0}{(1.10 - 0.9)100} = \frac{1}{2} = 50\%$$

This equation can be extended for multiple periods utilising the same assumptions.

For example, a two step lattice might look something like this:

Exhibit 11.4—continued

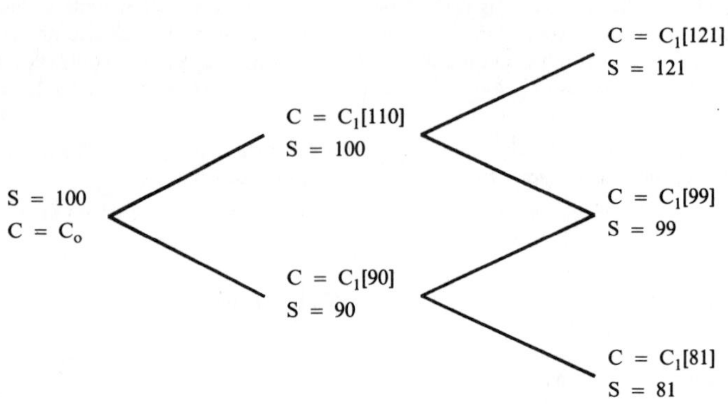

A multi-step binomial price path might look like this:

100

110

90

121

99

81

133.1 (one route)

108.9 (three routes)

89.1 (three routes)

72.9 (one route)

The general expression period binomial model can be written as:

$$C = \left[\sum_{J=O}^{N} \left(\frac{N!}{j!(N - S)!} \right) p^j (1 - p)^{N - J} \max\left[o, u^j d^{n - j} s - x\right] \right] / RF^N$$

This expression is usually solved iteratively backward to zero by working back through each node of the binomial lattice to derive the option value. Current practice is to break the period to option expiry into 50 or more sub-periods to provide good results.

Source: This example draws on F Desmond Fitzgerald, *Financial Options* (1988), pp 122-126.

Violation of Black and Scholes[3]

The major attraction of option pricing models such as Black and Scholes and its variations include:

- the fact that all input variables, other than volatility, are directly observable;
- the models do not make any reference to the investor's attitudes to risk.

3. This discussion is based substantially on Das (1987).

While the model plays a central role in option valuation trading, the underlying assumptions do not necessarily hold true in practice. In particular, major violations of the model's assumptions exist in the following areas:

- asset price behaviour;
- volatility measurement;
- constancy of interest rates;
- no intermediate cash flows;
- the issue of early exercise.

The key assumption that price changes are independent and log normally distributed over time with constant variance is violated in practice. The assumption of independence of asset price changes, as required by efficient market theory, is not wholly convincing. The empirical evidence and support for the log normal distribution of asset prices and its constancy over time is also not convincing. It is clear that option prices are sensitive to the stochastic processes assumed and changes in the assumptions produce significant, large percentage changes in option prices.

The violation of the asset price behaviour assumptions underlying Black and Scholes has prompted the development of variations on the basic model which make use of alternative stochastic processes, including absolute diffusion, displaced diffusion, jump processes and diffusion-jump processes. Empirical tests have tended to show that these alternative models are not able to provide better predictions of actual prices than the Black and Scholes type of model on a consistent basis. The price differences resulting from differing assumptions as to the underlying asset price movements in fact are *no* greater than the price differences that result from different assumptions of volatility.

The asset price volatility factor required as an input to option pricing models must be "forward looking", that is, a forecast of the probable size (although not necessarily the direction) of asset price changes between the present and the maturity of the option. The problem in volatility estimation (the determination of the true constant volatility of the asset price) is, in practice, sought to be overcome by utilising two types of volatility: historical and implied.

Historical volatility is based on past prices of the underlying asset computed as the standard deviation of log relatives of daily price returns (usually annualised) over a period of time. Utilising historical volatility requires the selection of the period over which price data is to be sampled. It is possible to utilise price information over long periods (up to five years or longer) to derive the volatility estimate. This assumes that volatility is constant over long periods. It is also possible to use a much shorter period (less than 30 days) to get a good estimate of the current level of volatility. It is necessary to adjust the volatility imput into the option pricing formula on a regular basis where short-term volatility is used on the basis that the volatility actually varies significantly.

Implied volatility is determined by solving an option pricing model (such as Black and Scholes) in reverse, that is, calculating the volatility which would be needed in the formula to make the market price equal to fair value as calculated by the model. Where this method is used, the implied volatility equates the model premium to the actual premium observed in the option market. An interesting problem with implied volatility measures is that options with different strike prices but with the same maturity often have different implied volatility.[4]

4. This discussion of volatility is based on Jarratt (1987).

Historical volatility is a measure of past, already experienced, price behaviour. To the extent the option pricing model is validated, implied volatility reflects market expectations of future price behaviour during the life of the option. Both measures are important, and comparing the two can reveal interesting insights into the market in the underlying asset. However, no normative rule for derivation of the volatility estimate is available. This means that in reviewing option premiums, particularly where the value of the option in question is sensitive to the volatility estimate utilised, any option price suggested by an option model must be regarded with caution.

Some attempted solutions to the volatility measurement model have sought to explicitly take into account the stochastic nature *of volatility* itself by using multi-factor numerical techniques which utilise two stochastic variables, namely, the asset and the volatility.

A detailed discussion of issues pertaining to estimation of volatility is set out in *Appendix B* to this chapter.

The model assumption regarding constancy of interest rates is also problematic. While option prices are relatively insensitive to interest rate fluctuations, Beenstock (1981) concludes that if interest rates are uncertain, Black and Scholes tend to underprice by approximately 4.00%.

The assumption that interest rates are constant is particularly problematic in the case of options on debt instruments. This is because interest rate changes drive asset price changes where the asset itself is an interest bearing security. In addition, the volatility of asset prices in the case of debt instrument is a function of remaining maturity and, in turn, interest rates which reflect the shape of the yield curve. As maturity diminishes, the volatility of the asset diminishes and constant variance cannot be assumed.

The impact of intermediate cash flows depends on the pattern of payments and the certainty with which the cash flows can be predicted. The Black and Scholes model does not appear to be very sensitive to assumptions about intermediate payouts which are certain. Where the intermediate cash flows are uncertain, however, the closed form Black and Scholes approach appears to break down and it is particularly difficult to compute American call prices.

The Black and Scholes model sets a lower limit for the price of the American call, but the model does not encompass the additional problem of determining the optimal time to exercise the option where the possibility of early exercise is not excluded. However, the model provides a reasonable approximation for the prices of American options.

Empirical tests of the Black and Scholes model indicate that the model is remarkably robust and provides accurate pricing for at-the-money options with medium to long maturity. The model appears to systematically misprice out-of-the-money and in-the-money options and also options where volatility increases or time to maturity is very short. In general, however, the model appears to successfully capture the essential determinants of option prices and United States studies show that traders cannot make consistent above normal returns on an after tax, post commission basis by setting up hedged portfolios.

Different models, which seek to overcome some deficiencies of Black and Scholes, essentially introduce new assumptions and do not necessarily produce improvements in pricing predictions.

The increased effort in improving and developing variations on available theoretical option pricing models creates the added problem of model selection.

Clearly, there is no simple basis for selecting between the various techniques as the actual benefit from a particular model will depend on the user's objective. The selection of any model, practically depends on the user's assumptions concerning the underlying asset price process. As there is no universal or true underlying process of asset prices, there can be no universal option pricing model and therefore no definitive fair value price for options.

The strength of the various option pricing models may ultimately lie in their capacity to compress the four observable variables into one other variable, implied volatility, which can then be interpreted. However, the problem of model pricing performance has led to option grantors utilising a range of pricing techniques and risk management techniques to manage the risk of writing options.

Hedge ratios: comparative statics

Mathematical option pricing models not only provide a neat closed form means of valuing option contracts, but, in addition, these models provide a wealth of additional data with respect to the various formula variables. For example, the delta, that is, the derivative of the option premium with respect to asset price, provides investors, portfolio managers or market makers with the exact hedge ratio required to hedge their portfolio position in options or in the underlying assets.

These derivatives allow market participants to identify the short-term sensitivity of option premiums to changes in the underlying security price, volatility, time to expiration etc. In mathematical terms, these sensitivities are derivatives of the premium with respect to these parameters.

These derivatives include:

- Price delta (delta): the change in the premium given a unit change in the underlying price. Deep out-of-the-money options have deltas close to zero because they are not very responsive to changes in the underlying asset price; deep in-the-money options have deltas close to 1 because they move in step with the underlying price; at-the-money options tend to have deltas close to 0.5 because of the interaction between time value and intrinsic value.
- Price gamma (gamma): the second derivative of the premium (delta is the first derivative) with respect to the underlying security price. It indicates how quickly delta will change as the underlying price changes, that is, the change in the price delta given the unit change in the underlying price. Gamma is generally maximised for at-the-money options which are close to expiration.
- Volatility delta (vega, kappa, or epsilon): the change in the premium given a one percentage change in the implied volatility. The absolute change in the option price for a given change in volatility is largest when the option is at-the-money with a long time to expiration.
- Time delta (theta): the decline in the premium given a one day passage of time. Theta increases as the option approaches expiry as this means that the time value of an option falls much more quickly as the time remaining to expiration diminishes.
- Interest rate delta (rho): the change in the option premium given a change in the risk-free rate.

Exhibits 11.5, *11.6*, *11.7* and *11.8* set out sample plots of the various derivatives and their behaviour over time.

Exhibit 11.5
Call Option Deltas

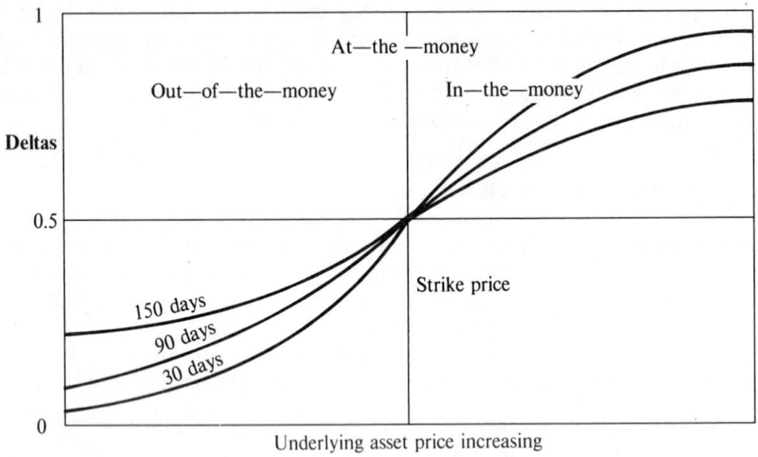

1
At—the —money
Out—of—the—money
In—the—money
Deltas
0.5
Strike price
150 days
90 days
30 days
0
Underlying asset price increasing

Exhibit 11.6
Option Gammas

High
30 days
90 days
Gamma
150 days
Strike price
Low
Underlying asset price increasing

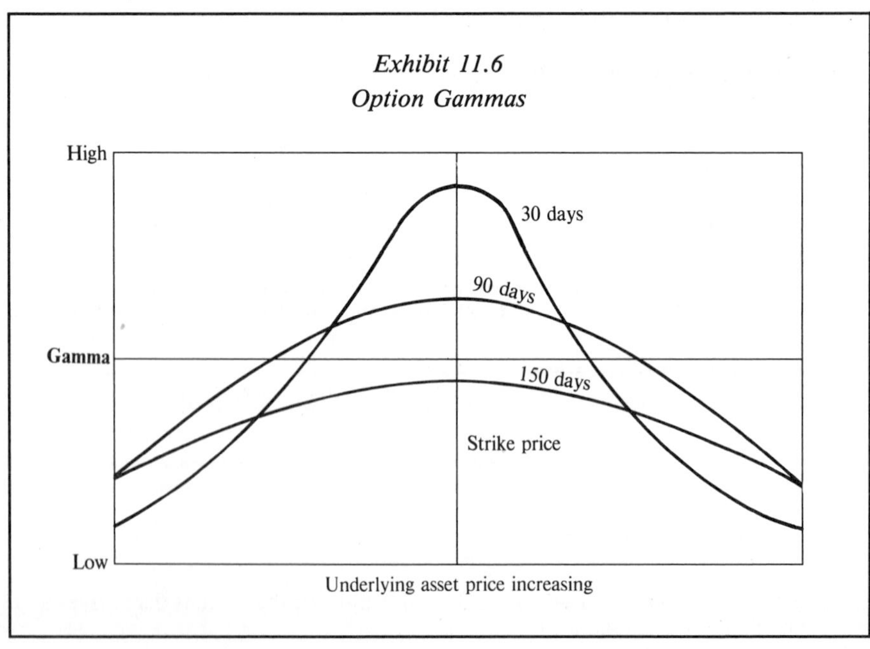

Exhibit 11.7
Option Vegas

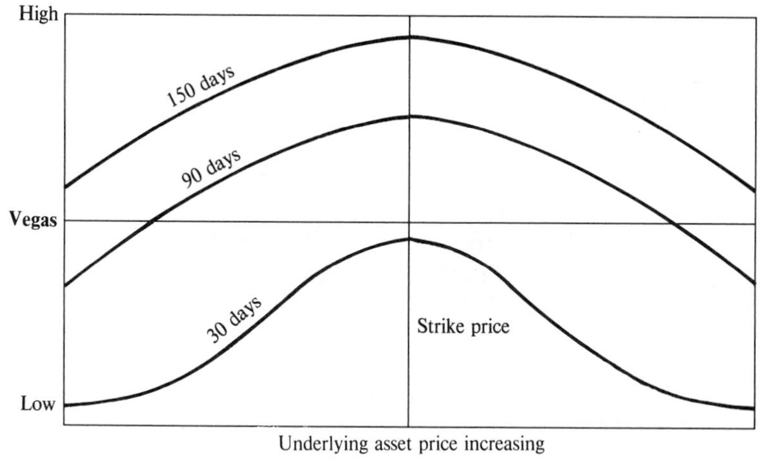

High
150 days
90 days
Vegas
30 days
Strike price
Low
Underlying asset price increasing

Exhibit 11.8
Option Thetas

High
30 days
Thetas
90 days
150 days
Strike price
Low
Underlying asset price increasing

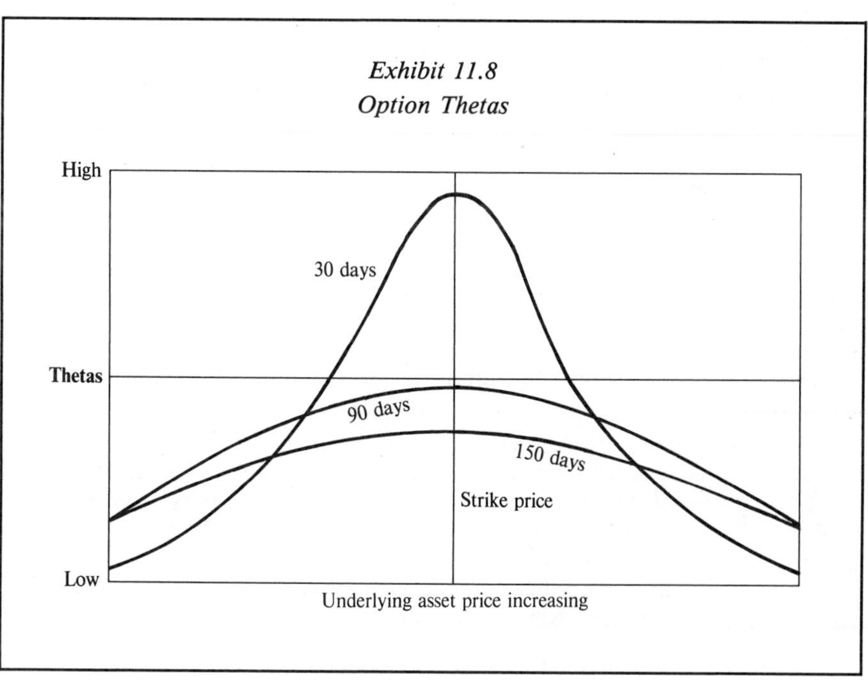

PRICING OF DEBT OPTIONS[5]

Distinctive features of debt options

The basic mathematical option pricing models, such as Black and Scholes, were originally developed in the context of equity options. The basic model requires significant amendments where it is used to value options on other instruments, such as futures contracts, currencies and also debt instruments. The pricing of options on interest rates and debt instruments are particularly complex and several distinctive features of debt instruments must be incorporated into the pricing of debt options.

The key features which require incorporation in the pricing mechanism include:

- Debt instruments, typically, have a defined maturity and their limited and declining life represents special problems in option pricing.
- The underlying security in the case of debt instruments usually involves payouts in the form of interest during the life of the option.
- The rate of interest cannot be assumed to be constant as, first, interest rate changes drive price changes in the underlying asset, and, secondly, most interest rate security values do not depend on a single random variable but on a number of random interest rates.
- Volatility of the underlying debt instrument cannot be assumed to be constant.

Most debt securities have a defined maturity. This is in contrast to other assets, such as equities, currencies and commodities which do not have fixed lines.

It is important to distinguish between two classes of options on debt instruments: options on the cash market debt instrument (that is, the actual physical debt security) and futures on the relevant debt instrument. In practice, both types of options coexist and are available. This is despite the fact that in any market, a cash market, a futures market and one options market (either on the cash market instrument or the futures contract) would usually be sufficient to fulfil all risk transfer possibilities since the option on the cash market and the option on the futures market will, generally, serve similar functions.

In practice, options on cash market or physical debt instruments takes one of two forms: *fixed deliverable*, whereby a debt instrument *with specified characteristics* is required to be delivered; or *variable deliverable*, whereby a *specified existing debt issue* is required to be delivered. For example, a six month call option on a 90 day Eurodollar deposit (90 days commencing from the expiry date of the option) is a fixed deliverable option. In contrast, a three month put option on the 8.5% August 2002 US treasury bond, which requires delivery on that specific security—irrespective of remaining term to maturity—is an example of a variable deliverable option.

Variable deliverable options create complex pricing issues. This reflects the fact that unlike other cash market assets which have infinite lives or futures contracts which are not based on a particular, wasting debt security (futures contracts have particular characteristics which are specified and constant), actual physical debt securities are affected by the passage of time in two respects:

- The underlying debt instrument itself has a shorter tenor or period to maturity as the option itself approaches expiration.

5. This discussion is based substantially on Hull (1989), Ch 10.

- At maturity, the value of the interest rate security converges to a known constant value (usually, par or face value) and the volatility of the security approaches zero.

The impact of intermediate cash flows on the underlying debt instrument will depend on whether the underlying asset for the debt option is a cash market debt security or a futures contract on the relevant instrument. Where the option is on a futures contract of the relevant debt instrument, the fact that there are no coupon interest payments and that the maturity of the particular debt securities is fixed, means that the general pricing technology applicable to options on futures contracts (see discussion below) can be utilised. However, where the option is on the physical debt security, the presence of intermediate cash flows can be problematic.

The assumption made by models such as Black and Scholes that there are no intermediate cash payouts can be relaxed using a modification of the formula which allows for payments that are proportional to the price of the underlying security. However, the normal type of adjustment utilised may not be appropriate in the case of debt options. Where the option is on an underlying security which bears a coupon, the accrued interest is continuously added to the full price of the bond representing a continuous payout to the holder of the debt security. As the coupons are fixed in dollar amount not proportional to the price of the underlying debt security, this type of modification proposed would be inappropriate.

As noted above, basic option pricing models assume that only one interest rate, the risk-free rate ("RF" in our equation) is relevant. However, at any given point in time, a variety of risk-free interest rates for different maturities are observable. Each of these interest rates and, consequently, the shape of the yield curve as a whole is subject to change over time.

A major difficulty in relation to the pricing of debt options relates to the fact that the price of the underlying asset (the debt security) itself is a function of interest rates. Moreover, it is unlikely depending on the type of option, that it is a function of the risk-free interest rate utilised to present value the exercise price of the option. An additional complication arises from the fact that where the option is a variable deliverable option (as defined above) the exact interest rate required to value the underlying debt instrument itself is subject to change with the passage of time.

These difficulties mean that the value of options on debt instruments or interest rates do not depend on a single random interest rate variable but may depend on a *number* of different random interest rates.

The effect of changes in interest rates and the time to expiration are particularly complex. For options on assets, such as shares, as the risk-free rate increases, the value of the call option increases as the present value of the exercise price in the event of exercise declines; that is, if the call option and the security itself are regarded as different ways for an investor to capture any gain on the security price, as rates rise the increased cost of carry on the underlying security will make the call more attractive leading to an increase in its value.

However, in the case of debt options, it is unreasonable to assume (as is usually done in the case of equity options) that the price of the underlying debt security is independent of the level of interest rates. Significant movements in the prices of the asset will occur as a result of changes in interest rates and, in general, any cost of carry consideration would be minor relative to the change in the value of the underlying security. For example, it would be reasonable to assume that rate increases will usually have a negative impact on the price of call options on debt instruments as a rise in interest rates will most likely cause a fall in the price of the underlying instrument or futures contract.

The constancy of the variance of volatility of the underlying debt instrument also cannot be assumed. This results from two factors:

- The stochastic process followed by interest rates appears to have a mean reversion quality—that is, there is an inbuilt drift that pulls them back to some long run average level.
- Volatility of debt securities (in the case of a variable delivery option) is likely to tend to zero, reflecting the fact that at maturity, the value of debt instrument itself must converge to a known value (usually, the par value of the security). An additional factor in this regard is that the price volatility of a security is itself a complicated funtion of the actual volatility of interest rates of varying maturity and the time to maturity at the security itself.

Consequently, the volatility of debt instruments will generally be a function of the assumed stochastic process of interest rate movement, assumptions about the shape and future movement of interest rate across the whole yield curve, and the remaining life of the security at a given point in time. These complexities dictate that constant variance cannot be assumed and it is probable that the volatility, itself, may also be stochastic variable.

The complexity of these interactions can be illustrated with reference to the effect of changes in time to expiration on such options. For options on assets with unlimited lives, an option with a longer time expiration will, generally, be worth more than a comparable option with a short term to expiry on the basis that it has all the attributes of the shorter dated option plus more benefits for the holder, that is, there is greater probability that the option can be profitably exercised. This property need not necessarily hold for debt options, particularly variable deliverable options, as depending on the relative magnitude of the time value and the intrinsic value, it is conceivable that under certain circumstances, an option with a longer time to expiration may be worth less than one with a shorter term. This would reflect the fact that securities usually begin to trade closer to par as the instrument approaches maturity. The greater price stability may distort the value of the option.

Approaches to pricing debt and interest rate options

In practice, the pricing of debt and interest rate options fall into two categories:

- Options on futures/forwards where the underlying asset is a standardised debt instrument—these types of options are valued in a manner consistent with the types of theoretical option pricing models outlined, in particular, the Black option pricing model discussed below, as some of the problems identified can be minimised.
- Options on physical debt instruments (particularly, on physical bonds)—are more problematic and usually entail the use of various numericals, usually binomial or latters, option pricing model.

The first type of approach is the one commonly used with pricing caps, floors and collars (as well as options on swaps/swaptions—see below, Chapter 14). This approach is described in detail below.

The major identified problems with pricing options on interest rates or debt instruments are most evident in pricing options on physical debt instruments, particularly medium- to long-term bonds. A variety of approaches have emerged towards pricing these types of options. A brief overview of some of these pricing approaches is summarised below.[6]

As noted above, the theoretical weaknesses of the conventional option pricing models in relation to interest rate options are most acutely evident in pricing option on bond. The various pricing approaches seeking to overcome the identified weaknesses are predicated on one of the following approaches:

- models based on bond price movements;
- models based on interest rate term structure movement;
- binomial/trinomial type of discrete time models;
- preference free approaches.[7]

The original model based on continuous time bond price dynamics was developed by Robert Merton (refer Merton (1973)) who examined the problem of pricing an option on equities where the interest rate is stochastic rather than deterministic as in the standard Black and Scholes framework. Merton's model does not explicitly indicate how specific properties of bonds, namely a fixed maturity and a known maturity value, are guaranteed.

Subsequent models, including Ball-Torous (refer Ball and Torous (1983)) and Schaefer-Schwartz (refer Schaefer and Schwartz (1987)) seek to overcome these deficiencies. The Schaefer-Schwartz model utilises a process whereby the bond price volatility is related to bond's duration as the basic model for the bond price dynamics. More recently, a variation on Merton (refer Bryis, Crouhy, and Schobel (1991)) has been developed predicated on the local expectations hypothesis whereby the expected rate of return for a unit of time on any bond is held equal to the short term rate.

The second class of pricing approaches which relates to models based on interest rate term structure movements seeks to overcome a clear deficiency in the continuous time models whereby there is no explicit assumptions or models of the term structure of interest rates as well as the lack of focus on the instantaneous riskless rate of interest in the option pricing model. These types of models, typically, make dynamic specification of the term structure of interest rate and the instantaneous riskless rate of return essential to the derivation of the option price. The models in this class include the following.

One state variable models—the major models include Vasick (1977), Courtadon (1982) and Cox, Ingersoll and Ross (1985).

Two state variable models—the major model is Brennan and Schwartz (1982).

Most of these models do not yield close form solutions for the term structure of interest rates and/or for the European call options. Accordingly, numerical procedures must be employed to solve for the price of the option.

The main difficulty with this approach is the requirement specifying a preference dependent function measuring the market price of risk of any non-traded state variables (for example, the instantaneous spot rate of interest). The estimation of this market price of risk expression which is required to solve these pricing formulae

6. A detailed treatment of these pricing approaches requires an understanding of mathematical techniques which are beyond the scope of this book. For readers interested in examining the details of the various approaches, see Hull (1989), Ch 10; Hull (1991); or the individual article in which the various pricing approaches were first described: see Selected Bibliography.
7. Classification utilised here is derived from and the brief explanation of individual models based upon: Carl Chiarella, "Pricing and Hedging Interest Rate Products" (paper presented to a conference "Options on Interest Rates", IIR Conferences, 9-10 March 1992, Sydney, Australia).

is difficult. This problem is complicated by the fact that option prices appear to be sensitive to changes in this parameter.

The difficulty with the term structure models requiring estimation of market price of risk functions prompted a number of approaches which sought to avoid the preference dependent market risk of price parameters by making use of the current yield curve. Two approaches are evident: the development of discrete time binomial lattice models and the use of Martingale concepts which underly the models of Hull-White and Heath-Jarrow-Morton.

The major preference free models are Hull and White (1990) and Heath, Jarrow and Morton (1990). The major discrete time models involving binomial and, more recently, trinomial lattices for interest rate and bond price movement inlcude Ho and Lee (1986) and the general binomial lattice pricing framework of Black, Derman and Toy (1990).

Most of these pricing models require numerical solution. For example, in the case of discrete time models the option is evaluated by starting at expiration and working backwards through the lattice or price tree utilising a procedure referred to as dynamic programming. Alternatively, numerical solutions of the partial differential equations developed utilising the various pricing approaches must be computed. These are sometimes undertaken utilising finite difference methods which value the option by solving numerically the differential equation that the option must satisfy by converting the differential equation into a set of different equations which are then solved iteratively.

A final approach to pricing debt options should be noted—namely, the use of monte carlo simulation techniques. Using this technique, a model of interest rates can be developed and the movement of the term structure of interest rates during the life of the option would then be repeatedly simulated assuming a distribution of interest rates conforming to the risk adjusted parameter levels. The simulation run would generate payoffs for the option which would then be discounted to the present time utilising the average short term rates. The value of the option would be arithmetic average of these discounted payoffs.

Model selection

The wide range of models available currently and the unsettled nature or the debate on pricing interest rate options forces the practitioner to confront the awkward question of which model to utilise.

In practice, the following trends are evident:

- Options on futures, particularly where the underlying debt instrument is a short term interest rate or security or the time to expiration is relatively short, particularly, in relation to the life of the underlying debt instrument, are priced using the Black model.
- The pricing of caps and floors is generally undertaken utilising the Black model.
- Options on swaps or swaptions are priced utilising the Black model, particularly, with the time to exercise it relatively short particularly, in relation to the life of the swap although numerical approaches, such as the Hull-White approach, are increasingly being utilised.
- Options on bonds are priced using Black's model where the time to expiry is short relative to the life of the underlying bond while for other bond options, a variety of approaches, particularly discrete time binomial or lattice type solutions are utilised.

- Other debt options, particularly long term options, such as those on callable and putable bonds, asset/mortgage-backed securities etc, are priced utilising predominantly discrete time binomial or lattice type models.

The statement of practice should not be regarded as comprehensive but rather indicative of market practitioners' approaches. For example, a number of practitioners are increasingly experimenting with binomial type models for pricing caps as well as swaptions.

The approach to pricing in practice reflects a variety of factors including:

- None of the option pricing models described is perfect *for all situations*.
- Users will typically utilise models which are easy to implement and which are not expensive to build or cumbersome to use. For example, a number of the pricing approaches requiring numerical solution require significant amounts of computer resources and can take a great deal of time to produce results (albeit, the increasing availability of very fast computers at ever decreasing costs is increasingly a factor).
- User considerations are particularly relevant as these models form the basis of pricing and risk management systems within financial institutions, who are active in trading and hedging these instruments. This dictates that the need to actively manage the risk exposure of positions in a rapidly changing market means the risk managers are willing to sacrifice some theoretical niceties in favour of speed and direct relevance of the information generated by the model.

In fundamental terms, the pricing of these complex instruments utilising often extremely complex mathematics must be taken in the context of market realities. In particular, the underlying market for debt instruments does not fully reflect the assumptions of perfect liquidity, no transaction costs and perfect information made in the pricing models themselves. Given these failures of the real market to conform to the theoretical constructions underlying option pricing models, no formula can be used risklessly to arbitrage mispricing. In addition, there are difficulties in evaluating the performance of individual models using rigorous empirical approaches.

As noted above, the difficulty in model selection necessarily makes the mathematical techniques merely indications of relative value of options on particular instruments.

A major advantage of Black and Scholes (and Black's variation thereto) is their capacity to compress four observable variables into one other variable, volatility, which can then be interpreted in the pricing, trading and hedging of these instruments. The enduring quality of the Black-Scholes model continues to be its ease of use, despite its theoretical shortcomings under certain conditions. This combined with the fact that its shortcomings are not as significant in the context of pricing caps, floors and swaptions (being the main relevant interest rate options dealt with) dictates that, the Black model is utilised predominantly throughout this book.

PRICING CAPS, FLOORS AND COLLARS

Approach

The discussion to date has focused on the generalised theory of option pricing as well as the pricing of general debt options. Within this framework, the pricing of cap, floor and collar agreements usually takes a definite form. The approach to pricing of such contracts reflects the fact that they are essentially European options on short-term interest rates. Consequently, they are analogous, for the most part, to European options on futures or forward contracts on short-term interest rates. This basic intuition is reinforced by the fact that caps, floors and collars are essentially simple, customised versions of options on short-term interest rate futures. There is considerable interaction between the two markets whereby the sellers of caps etc, utilise the futures and options on futures markets to hedge risk positions.

The Black option pricing model

This approach to pricing allows these contracts to utilise Black's version of the original basic Black and Scholes' model for a premium paid European option on a futures contract:

$$C(E) = e^{-RF.T}[F.N.(d_1) - K.N.(d_2)]$$

$$d_1 = \frac{\ln(F/K) + (1/2\, V^2 T)}{V\sqrt{T}}$$

$$d_2 = d_1 - V\sqrt{T}$$

All notation is as used elsewhere in this chapter except as follows:

F = forward or future prices of the underlying asset

The intuition behind the Black reformulation of the Black and Scholes option pricing model in the context of futures is that:

- Investment in a futures contract requires no commitment of funds (deposits, margins etc are ignored), whereas investment in the physical asset, for example, a share in the case of an equity option, imposes a cost. Consequently, nothing is paid or received (up-front) in setting up the hedge which entails buying or selling the futures contract.
- The value of a call option on a futures contract should be lower than the value of a call option on the physical asset, as the futures price should already impound the carrying costs associated with the physical commodity.

That is, the futures price is in essence the forward price which will naturally reflect any carry costs over the relevant period.

The price of a put option on the futures contract can be derived utilising standard put-call parity as follows for European put options:

$$P(E) = C(E) - (F - K)e^{RF.T}$$

The usual qualifications concerning early exercise of American options will, of course, apply.

The Black option pricing model involves the assumption that V—the volatility of the forward/futures contract—is constant. As noted above, this assumption is unlikely to hold in practice because of the mean reverting process. This dictates that when the period to option expiration is large, the price of the forward or futures contract is not greatly sensitive to current interest rates, but as the time to option expiry decreases, the current level of interest rates becomes progressively more important in determining the forward or futures price with the result that the volatility of the forward or futures price may increase with the effluxion of time.

In practice, the Black option pricing model can be applied if some adjustments designed to minimise impact of this phenomenon are adopted.

Utilising this approach, applied volatility for forward interest rates are calculated usually from traded futures options or from traded caps, floors etc. The debt option being valued is then priced utilising the implied volatilities generated. This multiple use of the Black model, first, to calculate implied volatility and, secondly, to price the option allows errors that may be caused by the use of the inexact model to be reduced. More importantly, they ensure that the calculated option prices are reasonably consistent with traded option prices.

In general, the mean reverting property of interest rates causes these implied volatilities to decrease with option maturity. Relationship between volatility and maturity of caps, floors and collars etc are difficult to observe since most of these over-the-counter instruments have maturities beyond the longest maturity of traded Eurodollar futures. However, in practice, this relationship can be extrapolated.

Exhibit 11.9 sets out an example of utilising the Black option pricing model to derive the price of an option on a forward contract.

Exhibit 11.9

*Example of Using Black's Option Pricing Model for Forward Contracts**

Calculate the price for a call and put option on an asset based on the following information:

Forward Price	= F	=	110
Strike Price	= K	=	100
Time to Maturity	= T	=	4 months (0.333 yrs)
Risk Free Interest Rate	= RF	=	9% pa (0.09)
Volatility	= V	=	25% (0.25)

Using the above inputs, we can compute the call option price as follows:

$$d1 = \frac{\ln(110/100) + (0.5 \times 0.25^2 \times 0.333)}{0.25\sqrt{0.333}}$$

$$= \frac{0.09531 + 0.010406}{0.144265} = 0.73279$$

$$d2 = 0.73279 - 0.25\sqrt{0.333}$$

$$= 0.58845$$

Using the N(x) table

N(d1) = N(0.73279) = 0.76816
N(d2) = N(0.58845) = 0.72187
N(−d1) = N(−0.73279) = 0.23184
N(−d2) = N(0.58845) = 0.27813

Therefore, the call and put prices are as follows:

$$C(E) = e^{-0.09 \times 0.333}[110 \times 0.76816 - 100 \times 0.72187]$$

$$= 0.9705 \times [84.4976 - 72.187]$$

$$= 11.9471$$

or 10.86% of Future Asset Value

$$P(e) = e^{-0.09 \times 0.333}[100 \times 0.27813 - 110 \times 0.23184]$$

$$= 2.2424$$

or 2.04 of Future Asset Value

* This example is based on Hull (1989), pp 147, 148.

The computational method where the Black model is used to price options *on futures contracts* for the price of the relevant options will differ depending on the type of margining system applicable. When the margining system dictates that proceeds are not paid up-front to option writers (for example, on the London and Sydney Futures Exchanges) prices have to be higher to compensate the seller for the fact that the premium is not received at the beginning and consequently it is not available for investment. If it is assumed initially that the premium is paid over to the seller of the option only at maturity, the premium would have to be increased by the additional interest that could have been earned over the life of the option if the premium was available for investment. Consequently, the value of the call option will become:

$$C(E) = F.N(d_1) - K.N(d_2)$$

In addition, the put-call parity relationship, where proceeds are not paid up-front for open futures contracts, is different:

$$P(E) = C(E) - F + K$$

In practice, the adjustment process is not simple, because if nothing changes, part of the premium will be paid over to the writer of the option as the time value decays to zero over the life of the option.

Utilising the Black option pricing model value caps, floors etc

Utilising the Black option pricing model to derive values for caps, floors and collars is essentially a two stage process.

In the first stage of the process, the Black model can be utilised to price a single period cap or floor as an individual call or put option. *Exhibit 11.10* sets out an example of using the Black model to price a single period cap and floor.

This single period approach is then extended to cover typical caps and floors which extend over multiple periods.

Exhibit 11.10

Example of Using Black's Option Pricing Model to Calculate Cap Prices

Yield Approach

*Example 1**

Calculate the premium for an 8% cap on three month LIBOR for one period of three months in one year's time where the forward rate for three month LIBOR in one year is 7% pa. This information can be reformulated for input into the model as follows:

F = 7.0% pa (0.07)
K = 8% pa (0.08)
T = one year (1.0)
RF = 6.5% (0.065)
V = 20% (0.20)

Using the above inputs, we can compute the cap price (call option on interest rates) as follows:

$$d1 = \frac{\ln(0.07/0.08) + (0.5 \times 0.20^2 \times 1.0)}{0.20\sqrt{1}}$$

$$= -0.5677$$

Exhibit 11.10—continued

$$d2 = -0.5677 - 0.20\sqrt{1}$$
$$= -0.7677$$

N(d1) = 0.285082
N(d2) = 0.221290

$$C(E) = e^{-0.065 \times 1.0} [0.07 \times 0.285082 - 0.08 \times 0.221290]$$
$$= 0.002111$$

In $ terms, per $1,000,000, we can restate the option premium as follows:

$$\left[\frac{t.FV}{(1 + F . t)} \right] \times C(E)$$

where:

t = the interest rate period = 0.25 (three months)
FV = face value of loan ($1,000,000)

$$\frac{0.25. 1{,}000{,}000}{(1 + 0.07 \times 0.25)} \times 0.002111$$

= $518.67 or 0.051867% of FV

The premium for an 8% floor (put option on interest rate) on similar term is calculated as follows:

N(−d1) =0.714918
N(−d2) =0.778710

$$P(E) = \left[\frac{t.FV}{(1 + F \times t)} \right] \times e^{-RF.T} [K.N(-d2) - F.N(-d1)]$$
$$= 245{,}700.25 \times e^{-0.065.1} [0.08 \times 0.778710 - 0.07 \times 0.714918]$$
$$= \$2{,}820.99 \text{ or } 0.2821\% \text{ of FV}$$

* This example is based on Hull (1989), pp 263, 264.

Example 2

Calculate the premium for a $100m 15% cap on three months LIBOR for one period of three months commencing in three months' time where the forward rate for three month LIBOR in three months' time is 15.016% pa and the three month risk free rate is 15.00% pa. This information can be reformulated for input into the model as follows:

F = 0.15016
K = 0.1500
T = 0.25
RF = 0.15
V = 0.17

The price of the cap can be calculated as follows:

$$d1 = \frac{\ln (0.15016/0.15) + (0.5 \times 0.17^2 \times 0.25)}{0.17\sqrt{0.25}}$$
$$= \frac{0.001066 + 0.007225}{0.085} = 0.055042$$
$$d2 = 0.055042 - 0.17\sqrt{0.25} = -0.029958$$

N(d1) = 0.5219
N(d2) = 0.4880

$$C(E) = \frac{0.25 \times 1{,}000{,}000}{(1 + 0.15016 \times 0.25)} \times e^{-0.1500 \times 0.25} \times [0.15016 \times 0.5219 - 0.15 \times 0.4880]$$
$$= 240{,}954.57 \times 0.963194 [0.005169]$$
$$= \$1{,}199.54 \text{ or } 0.1199\% \text{ of face value}$$

Exhibit 11.10—continued

The price of the equivalent floor (put on interest rates) is as follows:

$N(-d1) = 0.4781$
$N(-d2) = 0.5120$

$$P(E) = 240{,}954.57 \times e^{-0.15 \times 0.25} [0.15 \times 0.5120 - 0.15016 \times 0.4781]$$
$$= \$1{,}162.40 \text{ or } 0.1162\% \text{ of FV}$$

Price Approach

Example 3

Calculate the premium for Example 1 above using price volatility (0.343972%).

The model inputs are reconfigured as follows:

$F = 982{,}800.98$
$K = 980{,}392.16$
$T = 1.0$
$RF = 0.065$
$V = 0.00343972$

$$d1 = \frac{\ln(1.002457) + (0.5 \times 0.00343972^2 \times 1.0)}{0.00343972\sqrt{1}}$$
$$= \frac{0.002454 + 0.000006}{0.00343972} = 0.715174$$
$$d2 = 0.715174 - 0.00343972\sqrt{1} = 0.711735$$

$N(d1) = 0.7627$
$N(d2) = 0.7616$

$N(-d1) = 0.2373$
$N(-d2) = 0.2384$

Therefore, the cap premium (put option on price) is:

$$P(E) = e^{-0.065 \times 1} [980{,}392.16 \times 0.2384 - 982{,}800.98 \times 0.2373]$$
$$= \$474.92 \text{ or } 0.047492\% \text{ of FV}$$

Pricing caps, floors and collars utilising this approach entails the following steps:

- The cap, floor or collar agreement is analytically separated into a series of option contracts. For example, an interest rate cap agreement may be split up into a series of put option contracts on the relevant interest rate index.
- Each separate option is then valued utilising the identified model. In determining the price of each option, it is important to note that the input for the current spot price of the index is not the physical market price at the time the agreement is entered but the then current futures or forward price on the relevant index.
- The option premium for each contract is calculated and then summed to give the actual price for the overall contract. In the case of a collar, as the seller is simultaneously writing a series of put options while buying a corresponding set of call options from the purchaser of the collar, the price to the purchaser represents the value of the put options reduced by the value of the call option written.

Exhibit 11.11 sets out techniques for calculating the price of a cap, floor and collar on US$ LIBOR. *Exhibit 11.12* sets out an example of the calculation of cap, floor and collar prices on A$ BBR.

Exhibit 11.11
US$ Cap, Floor and Collar Pricing Example

Assume a bank is asked by one of its clients on 1/8/X2 to quote on an interest rate cap, floor and collar on the following terms:

Amount:	US$100m
Term:	One year (maturing 15/10/X3)
Cap Level:	7.50% pa
Reference Rate:	90 day on three month US$ LIBOR
Settlement:	Quarterly
Settlement Date:	3/8/X2

The bank is being asked to price the following series of options for the client:

Option:

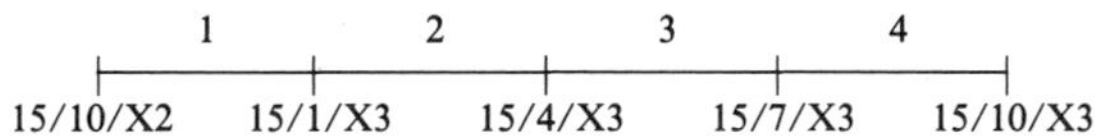

The following interest rate structure prevails:

	Maturity (year)	Yield to maturity (% pa)	Forward rates (% pa)
15/10/X2	0.200	4.875	5.616
15/1/X3	0.452	5.279	5.849
15/4/X3	0.699	5.480	6.549
15/7/X3	0.948	5.760	7.004
15/10/X3	1.200	6.020	

In this example, the bank is required to price four put options which it will grant to its customer. To evaluate this commitment the bank determines the forward interest rates (calculated from the yield curve—see above) and the volatility of interest rates. The option premium (the cap price) is then determined utilising the Black Option Pricing Model for an option on a forward or futures contract;

Expiry Date	Option Type	Strike Price (% pa)	Forward Rate	Price Volatility (% pa)	Option Price (% pa)
15/10/X2	Put	7.50	5.616	0.85	0.0193
15/1/X3	Put	7.50	5.849	0.85	0.0786
15/4/X3	Put	7.50	6.549	0.85	0.1744
15/7/X3	Put	7.50	7.004	0.85	0.2577

The total premium is 0.5300% flat in percentage terms. The dollar value of the cap (assuming a face value of US$100m) is US$529,984.

The floor is priced similarly. Assuming a floor level of 6.0% pa, the floor price is as follows:

Expiry Date	Option Type	Strike Price (% pa)	Forward Rate	Price Volatility (% pa)	Option Price (% pa)
15/10/X2	Call	6.00	5.616	0.85	0.2030
15/1/X3	Call	6.00	5.849	0.85	0.2414
15/4/X3	Call	6.00	6.549	0.85	0.2122
15/7/X3	Call	6.00	7.004	0.85	0.2076

The total premium is 0.8642% pa flat (US$864,181)

On this basis the bank would quote the following cap and collar prices:

Cap at 7.50% strike—53.00bps
Floor at 6.00% strike—86.42bps
Collar at 7.50/6.00% strike—(33.42)bps*

* Bank pays Client

Exhibit 11.11—continued

The effect of variations in cap and floor levels as well as volatility or cap and floor premiums (bps) for the transaction in this example are as follows:

	Price Volatility (% pa)		
	0.75	0.85	0.95
Cap:			
6.50% pa	76.58	87.39	98.29
7.00% pa	58.19	68.43	78.86
7.50% pa	43.63	53.00	62.69
Floor:			
5.50% pa	54.43	65.01	75.74
6.00% pa	75.46	86.42	97.44
6.50% pa	100.13	111.94	122.85

Exhibit 11.12

A$ Cap, Floor and Collar Pricing Example

Assume a bank is asked by one of its clients on 1/6/X3 to quote on an interest rate cap and a collar on the following terms:

Amount:	A$100m
Term:	3 years (maturing 1/6/X6)
Cap Level:	14.50% pa (300bps over the spot rate)
Reference Rate:	180 day BBR
Settlement:	SA
Settlement Date:	1/6/X3

The bank is being asked to structure the following series of options for the client:

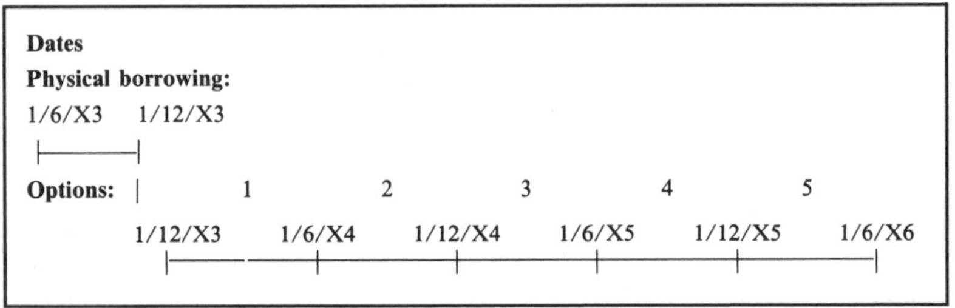

On 1/6/X3, the following interest rate structure prevails:

Date	**Maturity (year)**	**Yield to maturity (% pa)**	**Forward rates (% pa)**
1/12/X3	0.5	11.50	13.27
1/6/X4	1.0	12.36	12.93
1/12/X4	1.5	12.55	15.47
1/6/X5	2.0	13.27	14.67
1/12/X5	2.5	13.55	14.03
1/6/X6	3.0	13.63	—

Exhibit 11.12—continued

In this example, the bank is required to price five put options which it will grant to its customers. To evaluate this commitment the bank determines the forward interest rates (calculated from the yield curve—see above) and the volatility of interest rates. The option premium (the cap cost) is then determined utilising the Black Option Pricing Model for an option on a forward or futures contract:

Expiry date	Option type	Strike rate (% pa)	Forward rate (% pa)	Price Volatility (% pa)	Option price (%)
1/12/X3	cap	14.50	13.27	0.60	0.0154
1/6/X4	cap	14.50	12.93	0.60	0.0265
1/12/X4	cap	14.50	15.47	0.60	0.4445
1/6/X5	cap	14.50	14.67	0.60	0.2765
1/12/X5	cap	14.50	14.03	0.60	0.1893

The total premium is 0.9519% flat (in percentage terms). The dollar value of the cap is A$951,923.

The collar is priced in a similar manner. The main difference being that, in addition to the cap the floor element of the contract must necessarily be priced. Assuming that the floor is set at the level of the current spot rate for six months (11.50% pa), the floor price would be as follows:

Expiry date	Option type	Strike rate (% pa)	Forward rate (% pa)	Price Volatility (% pa)	Option price (%)
1/12/X3	floor	11.50	13.27	0.60	0.0036
1/6/X4	floor	11.50	12.93	0.60	0.0328
1/12/X4	floor	11.50	15.47	0.60	0.0011
1/6/X5	floor	11.50	14.67	0.60	0.0098
1/12/X5	floor	11.50	14.03	0.60	0.0324

The total premium is 0.0797% flat for the floor.

On this basis the bank would quote its client the following cap and collar prices. Cap set at 300bps above spot of 11.50% pa: 0.9519%; collar-cap at 300bps above spot of 11.50% pa; and floor set at spot: 0.8722%.

The effect of variations in cap and floor levels as well as volatility on cap and floor premiums (bps) for the transaction in this example are as follows:

	Price Volatility (% pa)		
	0.50	0.60	0.70
Cap:			
13.50	166.41	180.61	195.68
14.50	81.72	95.19	109.60
15.50	33.67	44.59	56.35
Floor:			
10.50	0.54	1.80	4.19
11.50	3.71	7.97	13.97
12.50	19.34	29.35	40.80

APPENDIX A

CUMULATIVE NORMAL DISTRIBUTION FUNCTION[1]

Tables for the cumulative normal distribution function (N) are attached. Alternatively, a polynomial approximation can be used:

$$N(x) = \begin{cases} 1 - N'(x)(a_1k + a_2k^2 + a_3k^3) & \text{when } x>0 \\ 1 - N(-x) & \text{when } x<0 \end{cases}$$

where

$$k = \frac{1}{1 + x}$$
$$= 0.33267$$
$$a_1 = 0.4361836$$
$$a_2 = -0.1201676$$
$$a_3 = 0.9372980$$

and

$$N'(x) = \tfrac{1}{2}\, e^{\frac{x2}{2}}$$

This provides values for N(x) that are usually accurate to about four decimal places and are always accurate to within 0.0002.

Table for N(x)

This table shows values of N(x) for $x \geq 0$. When $x<0$, the relationship $N(x)=1-N(-x)$ can be used. For example, $N(-0.12)=1-0.5478=0.4522$. The table should be used with interpolation. For example:

$$N(0.6278) = N(0.62)+0.78[N(0.63)-N(0.62)]$$
$$= 0.7324+0.78\times 0.0033$$
$$= 0.7350$$

x	.00	.01	.02	.03	.04	.05	.06	.07	.08	.09
0.0	0.5000	0.5040	0.5080	0.5120	0.5160	0.5199	0.5239	0.5279	0.5319	0.5359
0.1	0.5398	0.5438	0.5478	0.5517	0.5557	0.5596	0.5636	0.5675	0.5714	0.5753
0.2	0.5793	0.5832	0.5871	0.5910	0.5948	0.5987	0.6026	0.6064	0.6103	0.6141
0.3	0.6179	0.6217	0.6255	0.6293	0.6331	0.6368	0.6406	0.6443	0.6480	0.6517
0.4	0.6554	0.6591	0.6628	0.6664	0.6700	0.6736	0.6772	0.6808	0.6844	0.6879
0.5	0.6915	0.6950	0.6985	0.7019	0.7054	0.7088	0.7123	0.7157	0.7190	0.7224
0.6	0.7257	0.7291	0.7324	0.7357	0.7389	0.7422	0.7454	0.7486	0.7517	0.7549
0.7	0.7580	0.7611	0.7642	0.7673	0.7704	0.7734	0.7764	0.7794	0.7823	0.7852
0.8	0.7881	0.7910	0.7939	0.7967	0.7995	0.8023	0.8051	0.8078	0.8106	0.8133
0.9	0.8159	0.8186	0.8212	0.8238	0.8264	0.8289	0.8315	0.8340	0.8365	0.8389
1.0	0.8413	0.8438	0.8461	0.8485	0.8508	0.8531	0.8554	0.8577	0.8599	0.8621
1.1	0.8643	0.8665	0.8686	0.8708	0.8729	0.8749	0.8770	0.8790	0.8810	0.8830
1.2	0.8849	0.8869	0.8888	0.8907	0.8925	0.8944	0.8962	0.8980	0.8997	0.9015

1. See Abramowitz and Stegun, *Handbook of Mathematical Functions* (Dover Publications, New York, 1972).

Table for N(x)—*continued*

x	.00	.01	.02	.03	.04	.05	.06	.07	.08	.09
1.3	0.9032	0.9049	0.9066	0.9082	0.9099	0.9115	0.9131	0.9147	0.9162	0.9177
1.4	0.9192	0.9207	0.9222	0.9236	0.9251	0.9265	0.9279	0.9292	0.9306	0.9319
1.5	0.9332	0.9345	0.9357	0.9370	0.9382	0.9394	0.9406	0.9418	0.9429	0.9441
1.6	0.9452	0.9463	0.9474	0.9484	0.9495	0.9505	0.9515	0.9525	0.9535	0.9545
1.7	0.9554	0.9564	0.9573	0.9582	0.9591	0.9599	0.9608	0.9616	0.9625	0.9633
1.8	0.9641	0.9649	0.9656	0.9664	0.9671	0.9678	0.9686	0.9693	0.9699	0.9706
1.9	0.9713	0.9719	0.9726	0.9732	0.9738	0.9744	0.9750	0.9756	0.9761	0.9767
2.0	0.9772	0.9778	0.9783	0.9788	0.9793	0.9798	0.9803	0.9808	0.9812	0.9817
2.1	0.9821	0.9826	0.9830	0.9834	0.9838	0.9842	0.9846	0.9850	0.9854	0.9857
2.2	0.9861	0.9864	0.9868	0.9871	0.9875	0.9878	0.9881	0.9884	0.9887	0.9890
2.3	0.9893	0.9896	0.9898	0.9901	0.9904	0.9906	0.9909	0.9911	0.9913	0.9916
2.4	0.9918	0.9920	0.9922	0.9925	0.9927	0.9929	0.9931	0.9932	0.9934	0.9936
2.5	0.9938	0.9940	0.9941	0.9943	0.9945	0.9946	0.9948	0.9949	0.9951	0.9952
2.6	0.9953	0.9955	0.9956	0.9957	0.9959	0.9960	0.9961	0.9962	0.9963	0.9964
2.7	0.9965	0.9966	0.9967	0.9968	0.9969	0.9970	0.9971	0.9972	0.9973	0.9974
2.8	0.9974	0.9975	0.9976	0.9977	0.9977	0.9978	0.9979	0.9979	0.9980	0.9981
2.9	0.9981	0.9982	0.9982	0.9983	0.9984	0.9984	0.9985	0.9985	0.9986	0.9986
3.0	0.9986	0.9987	0.9987	0.9988	0.9988	0.9989	0.9989	0.9989	0.9990	0.9990
3.1	0.9990	0.9991	0.9991	0.9991	0.9992	0.9992	0.9992	0.9992	0.9993	0.9993
3.2	0.9993	0.9993	0.9994	0.9994	0.9994	0.9994	0.9994	0.9995	0.9995	0.9995
3.3	0.9995	0.9995	0.9995	0.9996	0.9996	0.9996	0.9996	0.9996	0.9996	0.9997
3.4	0.9997	0.9997	0.9997	0.9997	0.9997	0.9997	0.9997	0.9997	0.9997	0.9998
3.5	0.9998	0.9998	0.9998	0.9998	0.9998	0.9998	0.9998	0.9998	0.9998	0.9998
3.6	0.9998	0.9998	0.9999	0.9999	0.9999	0.9999	0.9999	0.9999	0.9999	0.9999
3.7	0.9999	0.9999	0.9999	0.9999	0.9999	0.9999	0.9999	0.9999	0.9999	0.9999
3.8	0.9999	0.9999	0.9999	0.9999	0.9999	0.9999	0.9999	0.9999	0.9999	0.9999
3.9	1.0000	1.0000	1.0000	1.0000	1.0000	1.0000	1.0000	1.0000	1.0000	1.0000
4.0	1.0000	1.0000	1.0000	1.0000	1.0000	1.0000	1.0000	1.0000	1.0000	1.0000

APPENDIX B

VOLATILITY ESTIMATION

Introduction

Mathematical option pricing models, such as Black and Scholes, requires estimation of the future volatility of the underlying asset price as this item is a parameter which must be input into the model. Volatility is calculated as the standard deviation of the assumed asset price distribution, which is assumed, in the case of Black and Scholes, to be log normal. Binomial models make similar distributional assumptions about future possible asset price movements and the volatility of these asset price movements.

Estimation approaches

Estimation of the true constant volatility of the underlying asset price is extremely difficult.[1] In practice, two alternative approaches are utilised:

- historical/empirical approach;
- implied volatility approach.

Under the historical or empirical approach, volatility estimates are calculated as the standard deviation of log relatives based on a sample of historical data for the asset price.

The implied volatility approach calculates volatility implied by the current market value of options. This is undertaken by specifying the option price and calculating the volatility which would be needed in a mathematical option pricing formula to derive the specified market price as a fair value of the option.

Empirical estimation procedures[2]

Calculation procedures

To estimate volatility empirically, the asset price is usually observed at fixed intervals of time (eg, every day, every week or every month). Define:

n: number of observations
S_i: asset price at end of ith interval ($i = 0, 1, \ldots, n - 1$)
t: length of time interval in years
U_i: In (S_i/S_{i-1})

Since $S_i = S_{i-1}, e^{ui}$, $^{\mathrm{i}}U_i$ is the continuously compounded return (not annualised) in the ith interval for $i = 1, 2, \ldots, n$. An unbiased estimate, s, of the standard deviation of the U_i's is given by:

1. Refer Cox and Rubenstein (1985), pp 255-260, 280-285 for a detailed discussion of volatility estimation techniques.
2. This section draws on Hull (1989), pp 88-90.

$$S = \sqrt{\frac{1}{n-1}\sum_{i=1}^{n} U_i^2 - \frac{1}{n(n-1)}\left(\sum_{i=1}^{n} U_i\right)^2}$$

where u is the mean of the U_i'S.

The standard deviation of the Ui'S is $\sigma\sqrt{t}$. The variable, s, is therefore an estimate of $\sigma\sqrt{t}$. It follows that itself can be estimated as s*, where:

$$s^* = \frac{s}{\sqrt{t}}$$

The standard error of this estimate can be shown to be approximately $\frac{s^*}{\sqrt{2n}}$

Example

Table 1 shows a possible sequence of asset prices over a 20 day period. Since:

$$\sum U_i = 0.01398 \text{ and } \sum^{20} U_i = 0.0087$$

an estimate of the standard deviation of the daily return is

$$\sqrt{\frac{0.0087}{19} - \frac{-0.01398^2}{380}} = 0.00674$$

Assuming that time is measured in trading days, and that there are 250 trading days per year, = 1/250 and the data give an estimate for the volatility pa of 0.00674 $\sqrt{250}$ = 0.10656. The estimated volatility is 10.656% pa. The standard error of this estimate is

$$\frac{0.10656}{\sqrt{2 \times 20}} = 0.0168$$

or 1.685% pa.

TABLE 1

Calculating Volatility from Historical Data—General Asset

Period	Asset Price	Price Relative (Si/(Si-t))	Daily Return Ui = ln(Si/(Si-t))	Ui^2
0	10.0000			
1	9.8750	0.98750	(0.01258)	0.00016
2	9.7240	0.98471	(0.01541)	0.00024
3	9.7500	1.00267	0.00267	0.00001
4	9.6875	0.99359	(0.00643)	0.00004

5	9.7210	1.00346	0.00345	0.00001
6	9.7055	0.99841	(0.00160)	0.00000
7	9.7212	1.00162	0.00162	0.00000
8	9.7489	1.00285	0.00285	0.00001
9	9.6750	0.99242	(0.00761)	0.00006
10	9.7846	1.01133	0.01126	0.00013
11	9.8225	1.00387	0.00387	0.00001
12	9.7468	0.99229	(0.00774)	0.00006
13	9.7853	1.00395	0.00394	0.00002
14	9.8225	1.00380	0.00379	0.00001
15	9.8578	1.00359	0.00359	0.00001
16	9.8125	0.99540	(0.00461)	0.00002
17	9.8468	1.00350	0.00349	0.00001
18	9.8828	1.00366	0.00365	0.00001
19	9.9224	1.00401	0.00400	0.00002
20	9.8612	0.99383	(0.00619)	0.00004
		Sum	(0.01398)	0.00087
Standard deviation (per period)			0.00674	
Annualised Volatility Days		250	0.10656	10.656%
Standard Error			0.0168	1.685%

Yield vs price volatility

The above example focuses on the volatility of *asset prices*. In the case of debt instruments, it is feasible to calculate the volatility of *both* asset prices (being volatility of the price of the underlying debt security) and *yield volatility* (being the volatility of the interest rate index itself).

In practice, as specified below, the two are related with the interest rate changes driving the changes in the price of the debt instrument.

Table 2 sets out calculation of both the price and yield volatility for a debt instrument (in this case a three month or 90 day discount instrument).

Converting yield volatility to price volatility

The following formula can be used to convert yield volatility (20%) into its price volatility equivalent:

Price Volatility

$$= \frac{(\triangle\text{Price}/\triangle\text{Yield})}{\text{Price}} \times \text{Yield} \times \text{Yield Volatility}$$

△Price/△Yield = 24.146851 for 0.0001% pa or 1 bps change in yield (per $1,000,000 face value of the security)

Therefore:

$$\text{Price Volatility} = \frac{24.146851}{982{,}800.98} \times 7.00 \times 20.00$$

$$= 0.000025 \times 7.00 \times 20.00$$

$$= 0.343972\%$$

TABLE 2

Calculating Volatility from Historial Data—Debt Security (91 Day Discount Securities)

Period	Interest Rate	Asset Price	Price Volatility Calculations: Price Relative (Si/(Si-t))	Price Volatility Calculations: Daily Return Ui = ln(Si/(Si-t))	Ui²	Yield Volatility Calculations: Price Relative (Si/(Si-t))	Yield Volatility Calculations: Daily Return Ui = ln(Si/(Si-t))	Ui²
0	8.450%	97.9590						
1	8.500%	97.9471	0.99988	(0.00012)	0.0000000146	1.00592	0.00590	0.00003
2	8.275%	98.0004	1.00054	0.00054	0.0000002954	0.97353	(0.02683)	0.00072
3	8.650%	97.9117	0.99909	(0.00091)	0.0000008204	1.04532	0.04432	0.00196
4	8.800%	97.8762	0.99964	(0.00036)	0.0000001311	1.01734	0.01719	0.00030
5	8.900%	97.8526	0.99976	(0.00024)	0.0000000582	1.01136	0.01130	0.00013
6	8.750%	97.8880	1.00036	0.00036	0.0000001310	0.98315	(0.01700)	0.00029
7	8.750%	97.8880	1.00000	0.00000	0.0000000000	1.00000	0.00000	0.00000
8	8.900%	97.8526	0.99964	(0.00036)	0.0000001310	1.01714	0.01700	0.00029
9	8.500%	97.9471	1.00097	0.00097	0.0000009324	0.95506	(0.04599)	0.00211
10	8.500%	97.9471	1.00000	0.00000	0.0000000000	1.00000	0.00000	0.00000
11	8.450%	97.9590	1.00012	0.00012	0.0000000146	0.99412	(0.00590)	0.00003
12	8.250%	98.0063	1.00048	0.00048	0.0000002335	0.97633	(0.02395)	0.00057
13	8.310%	97.9921	0.99986	(0.00014)	0.0000000210	1.00727	0.00725	0.00005
14	8.650%	97.9117	0.99918	(0.00082)	0.0000006743	1.04091	0.04010	0.00161
15	8.650%	97.9117	1.00000	0.00000	0.0000000000	1.00000	0.00000	0.00000
16	8.540%	97.9377	1.00027	0.00027	0.0000000705	0.98728	(0.01280)	0.00016
17	8.710%	97.8975	0.99959	(0.00041)	0.0000001685	1.01991	0.01971	0.00039
18	8.450%	97.9590	1.00063	0.00063	0.0000003942	0.97015	(0.03031)	0.00092
19	8.510%	97.9448	0.99986	(0.00014)	0.0000000210	1.00710	0.00708	0.00005
20	8.480%	97.9519	1.00007	0.00007	0.0000000052	0.99647	(0.00353)	0.00001
			Sum	(0.00007)	0.0000041170	Sum	0.00354	0.00964
Standard deviation (per period)				0.00047			0.02252	
Annualised Volatility (250 Days)				0.00736	0.736%		0.35608	35.608%
Standard Error				0.0012	0.116%		0.0563	5.630%

Issues in volatility estimation[3]

The estimation of the volatility of the underlying asset price is particularly problematic because it is the only parameter of most mathematical pricing models which is not observable directly. In this section, a variety of issues relating to the estimation of volatility is considered including: the key components of asset price volatility; problems with both historical/empirical and implied volatility approaches to volatility estimations; and, volatility estimation procedures in practice.

Factors determining volatility

Price volatility in asset markets are caused by a variety of factors, the most important of which is information releases. Information releases generally fall into two categories: anticipated and unanticipated information.

Anticipated information includes economic statistics as well as political or social information. This type of information release is anticipated. Market participants develop expectations regarding the content of the informational release. The impact of the information is, often, driven by whether or not it *corresponds to market expectations*. The impact of information releases can be analysed, particularly with reference to past releases. It may be possible to develop probabilistic expections of anticipated asset price volatility from the historical reaction of the market to prior actual data releases in combination with probabilities in relation to a variety of range outcomes for the relevant information release.

Unanticipated information releases typically relate to international events (wars, natural disasters etc) and other unanticipated or unanticipatable events. This type of information can have substantial and unpredictable impact on asset price volatility. The difficulty in predicting this type of informational release (by definition) makes it extremely complex to incorporate these types of factors in forecasting future asset price volatility.

In seeking to isolate factors generating asset price volatility, the linkages between volatility in various market segments or across markets should be noted. Analysis indicates that there may be implied and historical volatility relationships between different markets. For example, bond market volatility across various currencies show significant correlation. Similarly, in certain currencies, volatilities in the foreign exchange market are, often, useful indicators of volatility in credit markets in the relevant currencies.

Problems with historical/empirical approach

The historical/empirical techniques for volatility estimation seeks to quantify past market volatility and utilise this as a basis for forecasting *future* market volatility for asset prices.

The major difficulties with this approach include:

- assumed stationarity of volatility parameters.
- specifying the number of observations utilised.
- the availability of a variety of methods to calculate the price observations.

A major difficulty relates to the assumption implied by this technique that past volatility is a useful mechanism for deriving future asset price volatility. The

3. Portions of the discussion on volatility estimation issues are based on: Guy D Hargreaves, "Volatility in Interest Rate Options" (paper presented to a conference "Options on Interest Rates", IIR Conferences, 9-10 March 1992, Sydney, Australia).

assumed stationarity of the volatility estimate is neither logical nor supported by empirical evidence. Volatilities for a variety of assets demonstrate significant changes over time.

The period over which data is utilised to generate historical volatility is constantly debated. Proponents of utilising data over a very long period (say, five years) implicity assume that volatility is constant over long periods of time or, alternatively, tend towards a quantifiable *average* level of volatility. Proponents of utilising data over a shorter period (between one and three months) base their position on the implied view that volatility itself is not constant but varies significantly and prefers to use a shorter period to obtain a good estimate of the *current level of volatility*. This group would, as a consequence, adjust the volatility parameter imput into option pricing formulas regularly.

It is clear that the larger number of observations utilised to estimate volatility, the higher the probability that changes in, for example, general economic conditions or other exogenous factors, will impact upon the calculated volatility causing a violation of the assumption that the standard deviation of the asset's return is constant over the life of the option. The trade-off between increasing the period over which data is utilised in order to achieve more efficient estimates and the probability that the volatility has altered is essentially not resolvable within the context of the mathematical option pricing models discussed.

A further complication arises from the fact that the price data utilised can take a variety of forms including:

- close-to-close prices;
- open-to-close prices;
- close-to-open prices;
- high or low prices.

The use of close to close prices is the most common measure utilised. This measure allows the full daily movement of the asset price to be captured and the impact of all information released over the relevant 24 hour period to be captured. The impact of non-trading days (such as holidays and weekends) tends to distort the data series as information may be released and impact upon prices but is not captured until a later date. The process of annualisation utilised (see above) does not adjust for this phenomenon.

Open to close prices provide a measure of intraday volatility. Which shows reaction to all information released *during the trading day*. Use of open to close prices creates problems of annualisation as it is necessary, to be accurate, to adjust for the concentration of information released within an average 24 hour period.

Use of close to open prices allows a measure of *overnight volatility*. It shows reaction to information release outside trading hours and, in certain cases, measures the interrelationship between the domestic market and international market in other time zones. The close to open price series suffers from the same difficulties as the open to close price series because of difficulties of annualisation.

High to low prices again facilitate capturing of the range of full days price movements in the volatility estimate. It is typically useful to traders who have intraday positions or are hedging positions intraday.

The major value of the variety of price series and the different estimates of volatility that can be derived lies in the capacity to compare the relative price volatility of the various series.

Problems with implied volatility

The use of implied volatility is generally deficient in that it intrinsically sanctions a circular process. The volatility implied in options currently trading, which measures the volatility level required to clear the market at a given point in time, is treated as being the true constant asset price volatility parameter.

A major difficulty with implied volatilities is that options with different strikes with the same maturity often demonstrate different implied volatilities. In addition, where options of the relevant type or maturity are not traded, this technique is unavailable.

The major value of implied volatility techniques as a method of volatility estimation is that it provides an observable measure of the relevant option market expections as to volatility.

Volatility estimation in practice

Volatility estimation in practice is a complex activity, it requires an understanding of the following:

- the various volatility estimates available and their significance;
- behaviour of volatility parameters;
- the measurement of yield versus price volatility for debt instruments.

Multiple volatility estimates

In practice, market participants take into consideration the following types of volatility:

- implied versus historical volatility;
- implied versus predicted volatility;
- implied or historical volatility versus actual volatility.

The difference between implied and historical volatility is useful in predicting potential changes in market sentiment regarding volatility, while differences between implied versus predicated volatility determines a variety of trading strategies utilised by market participants. The relationship of the implied historical volatility versus actual realised volatility provides the basis for adjusting expectations of future asset price volatility.

In practice, the attitude to volatility estimation and the relative importance assigned to each of these methodologies will depend, to some extent, on the activities of the market participant and the risks sought to be managed. For example, an intraday hedger or trader will take a different view to a participant seeking to hedge longer term positions.

The volatility estimates available are, in practice, influenced by the underlying liquidity in assets. The lack of liquidity, signified by wider bid-offer spreads for particular securities, will generally be reflected in the pricing of options (that is, the implied volatility) for the securities.

Behaviour of volatility risks parameters

Two aspects of the behaviour of volatility estimates require comment:

- the behaviour of volatility relative to the strike price or yield of the option;
- behaviour of volatility relative to time to expiry.

In practice, at-the-money options, generally, trade with lower implied volatilities relative to out-of-the-money options.

This reflects a variety of factors including:

- Kurtosis of the price distribution, that is, deviation from the normal distribution assumption.

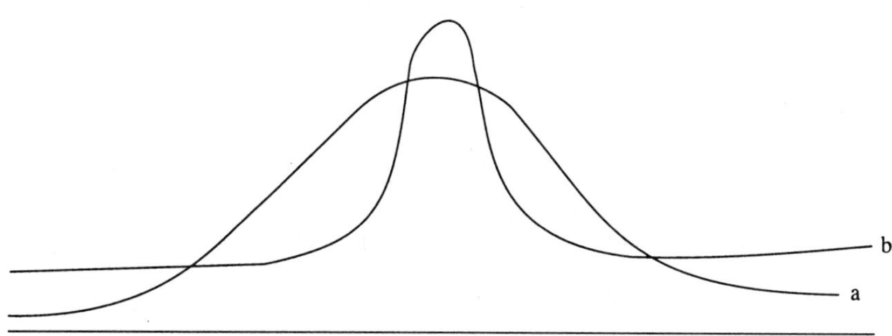

a Normal distribution of prices
b Actual distribution of prices

- The presence of "jump" risk, that is, non-stochastic movements in the price of the asset, dictates that out-of-the-money options are more difficult to hedge.

In general terms, volatility for shorter time to expiry option is higher than the volatility for options with longer times to expiry.

This usual term structure of volatility (often described as the *volatility cone*) is set out below:

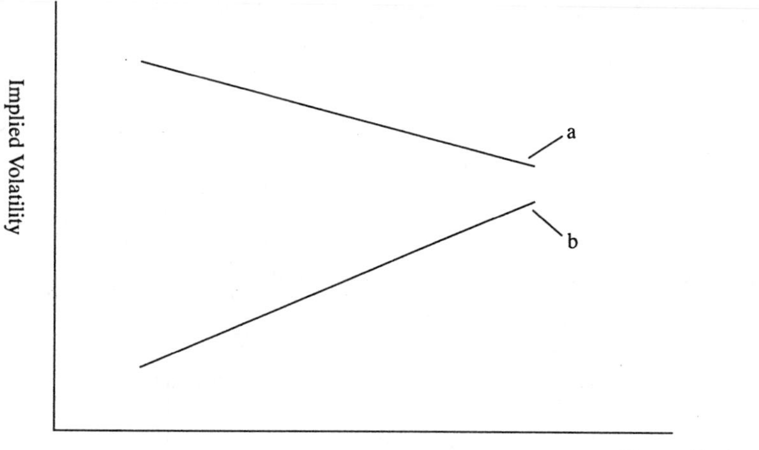

a Market expectation of volatility in near-term high
b Market expectation of volatility in near-term low

This pattern of decreasing volatility relative to option maturity essentially reflects the expectations of larger price movements in the very near future which drive the implied volatility levels to higher levels for short dated options.

Yield versus price volatility measures

Both yield based and price based measures of volatility are utilised for debt instruments. As described above, in theoretical terms, price volatility is proportional to absolute yield volatility and modified duration.

An observable feature of the relationship between yield and price volatility is that yield volatility increases in a market with decreasing yields where as price volatility decreases (for similar movements in outright yield).

In practice, both types of yields are utilised with the preferred volatility estimate parameter being driven, largely, by market convention.

In utilising yield volatility estimates, the following points should be noted:

- Yield volatility is usually assumed to be constant for fixed interest instruments of the same yield implying a flat yield curve which does not change shape and trades at constant yield volatility across all maturities.
- The use of yield volatility has the potential to create confusion where the yield curve shape is, itself, volatile.
- Yield volatility is not affected by the changing duration associated with fixed coupon bonds.

Utilising price volatility estimates for debt instruments, the following points should be noted:

- The price volatility constantly changes with changing duration of the underlying fixed interest instrument.
- It is necessary to clarify where the price volatility being calculated are the basis of a "clean" (ex interest) or "dirty" (cum accrued interest) price.

In practice, price volatility is utilised in markets where the underlying security is traded in price (for example, the US treasury bond market). In addition, yield volatility is utilised in preference to price volatility in a variety of markets for options on short term interest rates because price volatility of these instruments is very low.

Modelling asset volatility changes[4]

An important component of the process of estimating volatility is the modelling of volatility price changes. Increasingly, a variety of statistical/econometric techniques are being applied to volatility estimation. Once such technique is known as ARCH (an acronym for Auto Regressive Conditional Hetroskedasticity). A number of variations on ARCH techniques such as Generalised ARCH (GARCH), AGARCH, EGARCH, QGARCH), are also increasingly being utilised.

The basic insight underlying ARCH models is the concept that volatility follows clear patterns. Central to this approach is that the volatility of an asset *today* depends on the volatility of the asset *yesterday* and the "shock" in the price of the asset yesterday. A central tenet in this approach is that the intertemporal link in volatility changes over time is relatively constant or stationary. This implies that volatility changes are predictable on the basis of historical volatility. This approach is usually allied to an assumption that volatility regresses towards long-term long run means (that is, it shows a basic mean reversion tendency).

4. See, for example, Martin Brooks, "The Search For A Better Model of Volatility" (1993) (March) *Euromoney* 55-56.

ARCH models imply that the best estimate of volatility is not the volatility of the asset *today*. These models show how a "spike" in volatility persists and decays gradually (in a manner akin to the concept of half-life decay in nuclear physics). For example, an increase in asset price leads to an underlying increase in asset volatility with a gradual decrease towards a mean level.

The insight provided by ARCH-type models can be utilised to trade options on the basis of comparing implied volatility to ARCH model predictions. In addition, ARCH models can be utilised to price new options based on improved volatility estimates over the life of the option.

The variations on the basic ARCH concept incorporate specific assumptions on volatility changes. For example, EGARCH incorporates asymmetries in which volatility responds differently depending on whether the price of an asset rises or falls. This reflects Fischer Black's leverage effect in equity markets: a falling equity price leads to a further fall reflecting the increased risk from higher gearing resulting from the fall; a rise in equity prices reduces gearing and so partially offsets itself because of the lower risk.

An important element of ARCH models is that it more readily explains "fat tailed" and leptokurtic distributions of asset price changes.

The major applications of ARCH models, have, to date, been modelling correlations between assets and forecasting volatility. Specific applications have focused on:

- forecasting equity index volatilities;
- FX trading;
- hedging yield term trades;
- long-dated option volatility term structures;
- modelling asset betas.

Part 4

Complex Non-Generic Swap and Financial Derivative Structures

Chapter 12

Non-Generic Swap Structures

NON-GENERIC AND HYBRID SWAP STRUCTURES: AN OVERVIEW

The conventional swap structures discussed in Part 2 of this book form the basis of *all* swap transactions. However, an increasing proportion of swaps embody a wide variety of variations on the conventional swap concept. These variations are usually referred to as non-generic swap and/or hybrid structures.

Non-generic swap structures represent a response to the increased variety of uses to which swap transactions are put. These variations reflect, primarily, two factors:

- The variations in structure designed to accommodate the special features in underlying borrowings and securities transactions which were originated to take advantage of capital market arbitrage opportunities.
- The need to incorporate additional flexibility within the basic swap structure to cater for various asset liability management strategies.

The non-generic structures include both liability and asset swaps. While asset swaps do not necessarily require specific variations to the basic swap formula, it is useful to view asset swaps as a variation on the original liability swap idea.

Non-generic swap structures can be classified as follows:

Variations on conventional swaps

These involve simple variations on the basic parameters of interest rate and currency swaps such as: amortising notional principal; variations of the commencement date, such as deferred takedown swaps and forward swaps as well as spreadlocks; and, deferred or accelerated cash flow swaps such as zero coupon, deferred coupon, premium/discount and deferred coupon FRN swaps.

These also involve variations in the form of execution of swaps. Swap transactions are usually entered into with a principal, or, alternatively, arranged by a financial institution or broker which locates an appropriate counterparty. In recent times, a number of innovative execution strategies including tender processes and revolving swap facilities have also evolved to accommodate particular requirements of certain swap counterparties.

The above types of non-generic swap structures are considered in the remainder of this chapter.

In addition to these non-generic swap instruments, there are a number of other types of variations on core swap instruments including:

Floating/floating or basis swaps

These encompass a special class of swap transactions where both streams of cash flows are variable, being priced of different indexes within the same currency or, in certain cases, different currencies. These included floating-to-floating swaps in the same currency, arrears reset swaps, yield curve swaps and index differential swaps. Floating/floating or basis swap transactions are analysed in detail in Chapter 13.

Options on swaps/swaptions

Options on swaps/swaptions entail a variety of options on swap instruments, particularly on the fixed rate component of swap transactions. Options and swaps are considered in detail in Chapter 14.

Interest rate and currency linked swaps

These transactions evolved out of a number of innovative security structures, involving embedded options, which have developed, particularly in the Euromarket, in the period since 1985. The security structures required an option or forward element to be stripped and securitised. Options securitised through this particular technique included options on interest rates and currencies. In addition, stock index and commodity option/forward positions have been securitised through these hybrid swap structures (see below).

In recent times, the range of these types of swaps has been expanded to cover a variety of swap structures which include combination of conventional swap structures with interest rate and currency options.

Swaps entailing linkages to interest rate and currency options and/or forward positions are examined in detail in Chapter 15.

Commodity swaps, equity swaps and inflation swaps

Commodity swaps, equity swaps and inflation swaps are closely interrelated. They typically entail either a portfolio of forward contracts on a commodity, equity (typically, market indexes) or an economic index (such as the inflation rate embodied in a specific price series), or, structured swap arrangements linked to security issues with embedded commodity or equity components (typically, implicit forward or option positions in the relevant commodity or equity market).

Commodity and inflation swaps are described in detail in Chapter 16; equity swaps and related transactions are discussed in Chapter 17.

Asset swaps

As noted above, asset swaps are the converse of liability based swaps. This category of transactions is distinguished primarily by the fact that the underlying cash flows being transformed, whether in terms of currency or interest rate basis, are generated by an investment asset. Asset swap structures are considered in detail in Chapter 18.

It should be noted that the non-generic swap structures as described in this part of the book are *not* comprehensive, but rather represent the major types of variations to the basic swap concept. In addition, the grouping or classification of the various non-generic structures is subjective.

AMORTISING SWAPS

Concept and use

Amortising swaps entail swap transactions based on amortising (decreasing or increasing) notional principal amounts. This type of structure is used in connection with all types of non-bullet maturity assets and liabilities.

Amortising structures are feasible for both interest rate and currency swaps. The discussion below focuses primarily on interest rate swaps, for ease of exposition, but the basic concepts developed are equally applicable to amortising currency swaps.

Amortising swap transactions are relevant wherever non-bullet asset and liability structures are involved. For example, the conversion, in terms of interest rate or currency basis, of an amortising loan, either from the viewpoint of the borrower or the lender, would require an amortising swap structure to be utilised. A common example is lease transactions where lease rental payments include both a principal and interest component, often combined with a "balloon" residual value payment at maturity. Lessees can convert fixed rate lease rentals to a floating rate basis (or vice versa) while lessors can match fund lease receivables through amortising swaps to achieve the lowest cost funding available.

Asset funding for specific projects often entails a series of future drawdowns under a funding facility. Swaps with increasing principal balances can be utilised to fix the interest cost of the future schedule of liabilities. The most common application of this type of structure relates to construction funding where increasing notional principal swaps are used to fix the rate on a project which is to be funded with a floating rate facility. Where the construction funding facility has a specific principal amortisation schedule, the amortising swap may include both an increasing and decreasing principal basis giving rise to a "roller coaster" swap.

Other uses include asset swaps whereby amortising swap structures are used to convert amortising (via sinking fund or early redemption provisions) fixed interest securities into floating rate securities, or amortising swaps structured to match the expected prepayment schedule of mortgage backed securities or receivable backed securities to reduce reinvestment risk (see discussion below and in Chapter 14).

For example, in early 1992, amortising swap structures were utilised in the US$ capital market to take advantage of the prevailing historically steep yield curve. The structure utilised entailed issues of five year debt incorporating an amortising repayment schedule whereby half of the issue is paid down in year three and the remaining 50% in years four and five, giving an average life of approximately three years. The issue was then swapped utilising an amortising swap structure into floating rate US$ funding at rates better than that achievable for conventional three year bullet maturity issues.

The advantage derived from a market anomaly. While the debt issues have an average life of approximately three years, the amortising structure entails a concentration of cash flows in the final two years of the life of the bonds. The debt markets priced the bond slightly more attractively than an orthodox three year bullet issue. In contrast, the swap was priced (as described below) as a series of bullet notional principal swaps based on yields further along the yield curve.

In the market environment existing in February 1992, the amortising bond was priced against three year treasury note yielding approximately 5.60% while the swap was priced closer to the five year treasury note which was yielding 6.75%. Interestingly, the flatness of the swap yield curve between three and five years meant that it was only the steepness of the government bond curve which allowed this type of transaction.

Pricing amortising swap structures

Analytically, an amortising swap, whether an interest rate or currency swap can be replicated by a *series* of bullet notional principal swaps. *Exhibit 12.1* sets out, diagrammatically, the cash flow patterns for a five year amortising swap for a notional principal of US$50m with 20.00% annual (A$10m) straight line amortisation.

Consistent with this characterisation, amortising swaps are priced using current market swap spreads over the duration of the amortisation schedule. Within this framework, there are a number of available pricing approaches.

Exhibit 12.1
Five Year Amortising Swap

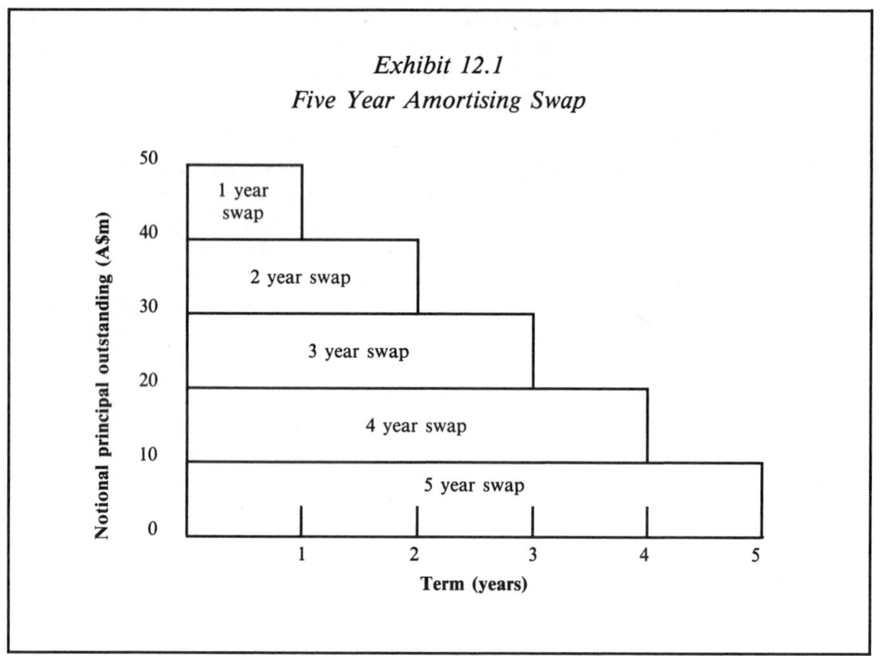

- *Blended rates*—whereby the swap is treated as *a number of separate* swaps with the total swap price reflecting a weighted average of these individual swap rates. *Exhibit 12.2* sets out an example of a blended rate pricing of a US$ floating-to-fixed interest rate swap. Under a variation to this technique, the transaction can be treated as a series of zero coupon swaps (see discussion below) and priced accordingly.
- *Duration or half-life pricing*—under this approach, the maturity characteristics of the amortising notional principal is reduced to a single measure. This measure is either the duration or the average life of the amortising swap (for an example of an average life calculation for an amortising swap see *Exhibit 12.3*). Once the duration or average life of the swap is calculated, the swap is then priced as a *bullet* swap with the maturity corresponding to the duration or half-life of the

Exhibit 12.2

Pricing an Amortising Swap

Pricing for a US$50m swap whose notional principal is amortising at the rate of US$7,142,857 every 12 months after six months:

Date	Tenor (years)	Notional Principal (US$)	Amortisation Amount (US$)	United States Treasury bond (% pa)	Spread (% pa)	All-in swap rate (% pa)	Tenor × amount (US$)*	Tenor × rate × amount (US$)*
30-Jun-19X5		50,000,000						
31-Dec-19X5	0.50	42,857,143	7,142,857	7.27	0.60	7.87	3,600,782.71	283,381.599
31-Dec-19X6	1.50	35,714,286	7,142,857	7.54	0.60	8.14	10,743,639.71	874,532.272
31-Dec-19X7	2.50	28,571,429	7,142,857	8.43	0.60	9.03	17,886,496.71	1,615,150.653
31-Dec-19X8	3.51	21,428,572	7.142,857	8.79	0.57	9.36	25,048,923.18	2,344,579.209
31-Dec-19X9	4.51	14,285,715	7,142,857	9.26	0.54	9.80	32,191,780.18	3,154,794.457
31-Dec-19X0	5.51	7,142,858	7,142,857	9.46	0.42	9.88	39,334,637.18	3,886,262.153
31-Dec-19X1	6.51	0	7,142,858	9.68	0.38	10.06	46,477,500.68	4,675,636.569
			50,000,000				175,283,760.34	16,834,336.91
						Weighted average rate:		9.604% pa

*The amount utilised is the amortisation amount of the swap for each date.

Exhibit 12.3

Calculating Average Life of an Amortising Swap

Amount: US$25m
Tenor: ten year
Grace: five year

Tenor (years) (A)	Balance (US$) (B)	Prepayment (US$) (C)	(D) = (A) × (C) (D)
0	25,000,000	0	0
1	25,000,000	0	0
2	25,000,000	0	0
3	25,000,000	0	0
4	25,000,000	0	0
5	25,000,000	0	0
6	20,000,000	(5,000,000)	(30,000,000)
7	15,000,000	(5,000,000)	(35,000,000)
8	10,000,000	(5,000,000)	(40,000,000)
9	5,000,000	(5,000,000)	(45,000,000)
10	0	(5,000,000)	(50,000,000)
		(25,000,000)	(200,000,000)

$$\text{Average life} = \frac{(200,000,000)}{(25,000,000)} = 8.000 \text{ years}$$

amortising swap. For example, if as in *Exhibit 12.3*, the average life of the amortising swap was eight years, the swap would be priced on the basis of a normal eight year bullet swap.

The blended rate technique whereby the amortising swap is treated as a series of bullet swaps is preferable primarily because it more accurately reflects the manner in which an amortising swap is matched off against offsetting counterparties. In practise, it is also common to include in the pricing a small additional risk premium which is based on the frequency or irregularity of the decline or increase in the notional principal balance.

Variations on amortising swaps

An interesting variation, utilising amortising swap structures developed in the steep yield curve environment, primarily in US$, that existed in late 1991 and 1992. These transactions involved variable amortisation structures (usually, referred to as index amortising swaps).

The rationale of these transactions was that in a very steep yield curve environment, borrowers were seeking to price their debt at the short end of the yield curve (that is, they prefer to be floating rate borrowers). In the yield curve environment that prevailed, borrowers could lower their interest cost by up to 200-250 basis points by issuing debt in longer maturities (five to ten years) and swapping it into a floating rate basis.

For the borrower, the benefit of this type of strategy included:

- The substantial savings on interest cost.
- The lack of liquidity risk as the underlying debt was medium to long-term.

- The interest rate savings (generated by the shape of the yield curve) gave the borrower protection against a future increase in the absolute interest rate levels or a change in the shape of the yield curve.

However, this type of strategy was disadvantaged by the fact that interest rate swap spreads in US$ fell sharply to historically low levels at this time. The variable amortising structure allowed borrowers to receive at higher interest rate swap spreads.

Under the arrangement, the borrower had the following cash flows:

- The borrower received a fixed rate from the swap counterparty.
- The borrower paid a floating rate payment to the swap counterparty usually, based on US$ LIBOR or US$ CP.
- The final maturity of the swap was between seven and 15 years (typically, around ten to 12 years).
- At the commencement of the transaction, an agreed amortisation schedule was agreed based on the prevailing level of treasury rates and on a stated final maturity.
- For the first five years (the so called "lock-up" period), the swap operated as a regular interest rate swap.
- After the expiry of the lock-up period, the swap works as follows:
  —The ten year rate on the swap is reset (for example, as the ten year constant maturity treasury as per the Federal Reserves H-15 rate).
  —The refixed ten year rate is then compared to the initial treasury rate assumed in the transaction. If the refixed ten year rate is higher than the assumed treasury rate, then there is a higher cash inflow to the borrower. If the refixed ten year rate is lower, then a lower net payment to the borrower results.
  —The higher or lower amounts are used to adjust the previously agreed amortisation schedule.
  —This process continues as at each rate setting days until the notional principal has been reduced to zero or the final maturity (say 15 years) is reached.

The variable amortisation structure results in a quicker (slower) amortisation depending on whether ten year rates increase (decrease). The major advantage of this type of structure was the increase in the swap spread achievable. For example, in late 1991, it was possible utilising this structure to increase the swap spread over treasury for maturities of ten to 12 years by an additional 25 to 30bps pa.

An example of an index amortising swap is set out in *Exhibit 12.4*.

The transaction structure had some appeal to borrowers as it was viewed as being self hedging from an economic perspective. This is because if ten year interest rates fell, the borrower benefited from lower interest costs creating additional cash flows which coincided with the slower amortisation of debt and the higher effective cost of borrowing.

Amortising currency swaps

Amortising currency swap structures are similar in structure to the amortising interest rate swaps described. In a typical amortising currency swap, the notional principal in one currency either decreases or increases in accordance with a specified schedule. The amortisation pattern in the particular currency is then treated in a manner very similar to an amortising interest *rate swap* in that currency and structured in price accordingly.

Exhibit 12.4
Index Amortising Rate Swaps

An index amortising rate swap entails a swap where the amortisation of the notional principal is linked in advance to the performance of interest rates.

Under this structure, as interest rates decrease (increase), the rate of prepayment or amortisation increases (decreases) in accordance with a predetermined pattern. In the extreme case, where rates increase sharply, the notional principal of the swap is not amortised until maturity.

Typically structures also included a "lock-out period" (say, the first two years of a five year swap) during which no amortisation can be effected.

The fixed rate under an index amortising swap is higher than for a conventional interest rate swap of the same maturity. This reflects that the receiver of fixed rates under this type of swap has written a series of options on interest rate swaps, the premium in respect of which is embedded in the higher swap rate.

Table 1 sets out an example of an index amortising swap.

Technically, a swap of this type has negative convexity which signifies that the swap loses value as interest rate decreases—*Table 2* summarises this feature of the transaction.

TABLE 1

Assume a transaction where the principal pays a fixed rate on a five year transaction with the following characteristics:

Notional amount: US$100 million

Fixed rate: 5.20% (two year US treasury @ $4.20% + 100bps).

Maturity: Five years.

Index: Three month LIBOR.

Initial base rate: 5.40% (to be set by the customer).

Lock-out option: No paydown of principal for the first two years.

Amortisation schedule: Subsequent amortisations are based on the difference between movements in the index and the initial base rate, with amortisations according to a matrix determined in advance. If future movements fall between the points indicated on the matrix, the annual amortisation rate (AAR) is determined by linear interpolation between the nearest points on the matrix.

Index change (bps)	Index (%)	AAR (%)	Average life (years)
−300 or lower	2.4	100	2.00
−200	3.4	100	2.00
−100	4.4	100	2.00
0	5.4	100	2.00
+100	6.4	80	2.89
+200	7.4	28	3.93
+300 or higher	8.4	0	5.00

Clean-up provision: The swap matures if the outstanding notional amount reaches 10% or less of the original notional amount.

Calculation of principal: If rates rise 100bps from the initial base rate of 5.4% on the first reset after the initial lock-up period (in this example the three month LIBOR rate from two years to two-and-a-quarter years is 6.4%) the new principal amount will be $80 million, derived as follows: Initial principal − (initial principal × annual amortisation rate ÷ number of

Exhibit 12.4—continued

periods per year) [in this case, four]. Thus $100 = ($100 million × 80% ÷ 4) = $80 million. Subsequent principal amounts will depend on the next reset rate and will be calculated on the remaining principal amount until the new principal reaches 10% of the original, when the clean-up provision takes effect.

Source: Sakura Global Capital in David Shirreff, "Making Ends Meet" (1993) (February) *Risk* Vol 6, No 2, p 17.

TABLE 2

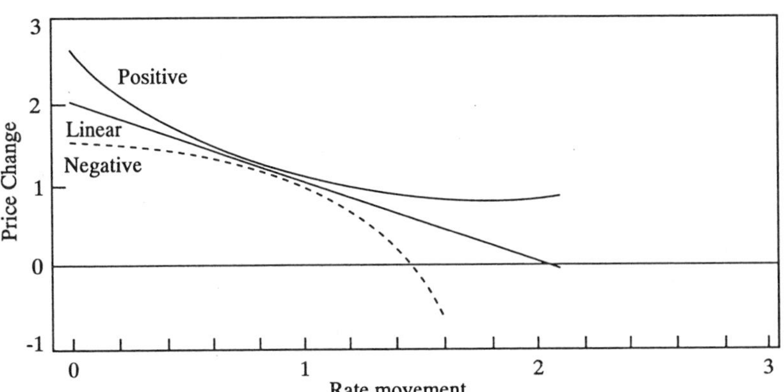

The convexity of an interest rate product describes the rate of change in its price for a movement in interest rates. If the rate of change is linear (it changes price in a constant ratio whether rates move up or down), the product has no convexity.

Fixed rate bonds and swaps (receiving fixed) have positive convexity: when rates rise, the rate of change in their price is slower relative to the interest rate move than when rates fall. Buying options will increase the convexity of an instrument or a portfolio.

Mortgage instruments and their imitations have negative convexity: when rates rise their price change is faster relative to the interest rate move than when rates fall. Selling options will reduce the convexity of an instrument or portfolio.

Index amortising rate swaps (receiving fixed) have negative convexity since they effectively involve the sale of put options to the fixed payer.

Source: Sakura Global Capital in David Shirreff, "Making Ends Meet" (1993) (February) *Risk* Vol 6, No 2, p 17.

A special case of amortising currency swaps is the foreign exchange annuity or amortising currency annuity swaps. This structure is utilised to exchange a set of constant even cash flows in one currency for an equivalent annuity cash flow in a second currency.

The pricing and structural considerations relevant to such a currency annuity swap is detailed in *Exhibit 12.5*. It will be evident that the structure outlined can be replicated quite simply by a series of LTFX contracts. The only major advantage of the annuity swap structure is that it avoids the impact of premiums and discounts on forward foreign currency rates (which would have the effect of creating an increasing or decreasing series of cash flows in one currency). Conceptually, the annuity swap structure is similar to the par forward foreign exchange contract arrangement described in Chapter 3.

Exhibit 12.5

Pricing an Amortising Currency or Annuity Swap

Assume Company A wishes to swap an annuity stream of US$1m pa over five years into an equivalent DEM annuity. This can be effected in two ways:

- by treating the US$ annuity as an amortising loan and executing an amortising principal US$/DEM currency or equivalent US$/DEM LTFX contracts; or
- transacting a currency annuity swap.

Assume A wishes to use a currency annuity swap.

Based on the interest rates prevailing, the normal forward currency rates are as follows:

TABLE 1

Calculating Currency Rates (US$1 = DEM)

Year	Zero Coupon Interest Rates US$	Zero Coupon Interest Rates DEM	Currency Rates (US$1 = DEM)	Premium/ Discount
0			1.6000	
1	4.500%	9.750%	1.6804	0.0804
2	4.950%	9.600%	1.7449	0.1449
3	5.400%	9.500%	1.7941	0.1941
4	5.850%	9.450%	1.8290	0.2290
5	6.250%	9.250%	1.8390	0.2390

The annuity swap rate is calculated as follows:

- Calculate the PV of the US$ annuity using the US$ zero coupon interest rates for each maturity.
- Calculate the PV of an equivalent DEM1m annuity using the DEM zero coupon interest rates for each maturity.
- Utilise the spot US$/DEM rate to convert the PV of the US$ annuity into DEM equivalent.
- Divide the DEM value of the US$ annuity by the PV of DEM annuity to generate the annuity swap rate.

TABLE 2

Calculating Annuity Swap Rates (US$1 = DEM)

Year	US$ Annuity	PV of US$ Annuity	DEM Annuity	PV of DEM Annuity
1	1.0000	0.9569	1.0000	0.9112
2	1.0000	0.9079	1.0000	0.8325
3	1.0000	0.8540	1.0000	0.7617
4	1.0000	0.7966	1.0000	0.6968
5	1.0000	0.7385	1.0000	0.6425

Annuity Period (years)		**1**	**2**	**3**	**4**	**5**
Present Value of US$ Annuity	US$	0.9569	1.8648	2.7189	3.5155	4.2540
Present Value of US$ Annuity	DEM	1.5311	2.9837	4.3502	5.6247	6.8064
Present Value of DEM Annuity	DEM	0.9112	1.7437	2.5053	3.2022	3.8447
Annuity Swap Rate	US$1 = DEM	1.6804	1.7112	1.7364	1.7566	1.7703

Exhibit 12.5—continued

In this example, the annuity swap rate is US$1 = DEM1.7703. Company A would enter into the annuity swap to exchange US$1m pa for DEM1.7703m pa.

The annuity swap rate is predictably somewhere in the range of outright LTFX rates. Part of the early cash flows are "borrowed" from later cash flows to create the annuity swap rate (which is higher than the outright LTFX rates). Where the interest rate differential is reversed, then the pattern of cash flow surplus is also reversed.

Change in the maturity of the annuity will have varying effect depending on the pattern of interest differentials. If the maturity is increased, then when swapping into a premium (discount) currency, the level of the annuity is increased (decreased) reflecting the fact that additional cash flows can be borrowed (forgone) from (to) later payments. Shortening the maturity of an annuity swap has the reverse impact.

Source: See Victor J Haghani (4 April 1986).

The foreign exchange annuity swap transactions are typically utilised by corporations with regular future inflows or outflows in a foreign currency arising from export sales, investments, known commitments to fund projects etc. A major advantage of this type of structure is that the expected foreign currency cash flows can be translated into its equivalent in the base currency of the organisation, providing certainty for planning purposes.

TIMING VARIATIONS

A conventional swap usually entails the transaction commencing within a short period after the agreement between the counterparties. Similarly the fixed rate payable under the swap is agreed to at the time the transaction is entered into. Both these terms of the swap can be varied.

Deferred start swap

Under a deferred or delayed start swap (also known as a forward commencement swap), if funding is not necessary immediately or a party wishes to more precisely match either a rollover date on an underlying borrowing, then a swap can be structured with an adjustment to the current fixed rate with accrual to begin at a mutually agreed rate, usually within six months. Under the deferred start structure, the fixed rate is agreed upon with accrual to commence at an agreed date in the future.

A forward swap is conceptually similar to a deferred start swap with the exception that the commencement date is usually deferred for a significant time frame, up to two to three years in the future (see discussion below).

Such deferred start swaps are usually priced as a standard swap with pricing adjustments reflecting the carry cost (the difference between the fixed rate on the swap and short-term rates) from the execution date to the forward start date.

This adjustment can be priced either as the difference between the current swap yield and current short-term rates or alternatively as the cost of undertaking a securities hedge and funding it. *Exhibit 12.6* sets out an example of pricing of a deferred start or takedown swap.

Exhibit 12.6
Pricing a Deferred Start Swap

Assume on 5 May 19X7 company A (A) approaches a bank (B) to enter into a five year swap whereby A pays US$ fixed rates against receipt of six month LIBOR. The transaction will commence on 7 June 19X7, as against a normal spot start of 7 May 19X7. Current market rates are as follows:

Five year swap rates:	13.40/13.50% pa (S/A)
Five year bond rates:	13.00/13.02% pa (S/A)
Six month LIBOR:	11.84% pa
One month LIBOR:	11.35% pa

If B enters into the deferred start swap it has two options:

1. It can enter into an offsetting *spot* start swap with another counterparty (C).
2. It can sell bonds to hedge its price risk and enter into an offsetting swap in 31 days' time.

Option 1

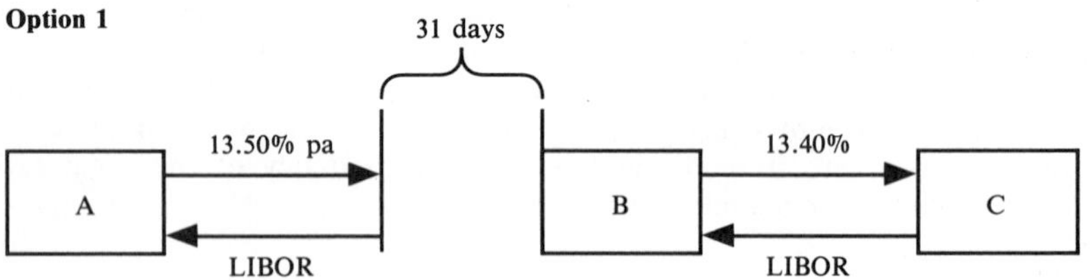

Under this structure, B is paying 13.40% pa for one month but *not* receiving the offsetting fixed rate accrual. The earning difference is as follows:

Fixed swap rate:	13.40% pa (S/A)
Six month LIBOR*	12.00% pa (S/A)
Difference	1.40% pa
or	11.89bps $\left(1.40 \times \frac{31}{365}\right)$

* Day count basis adjusted.

This difference is then amortised over the term of the swap at a discount rate equivalent to the swap offer rate (13.50% pa (S/A)) as a pricing adjustment of approx 3.347bps pa. Consequently, the deferred start swap price quoted to A would be 13.53347% pa (S/A) for a one month delayed start.

Please note:

- The discount rate is subjective and should reflect B's borrowing or investment opportunity cost.
- The price adjustment does *not* cover any risk of mismatches in reset dates arising from the delayed start.

Option 2

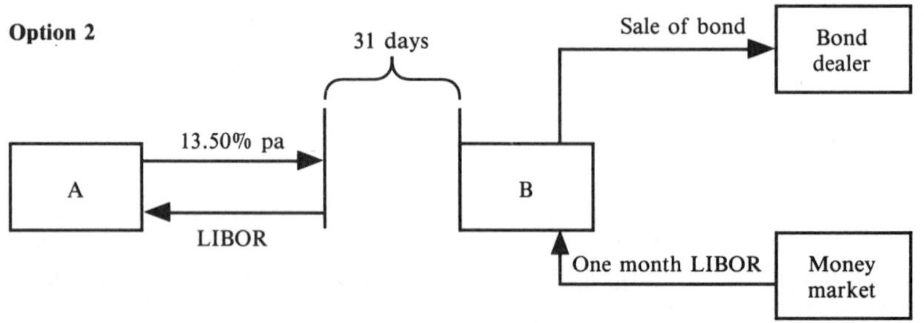

Exhibit 12.6—continued

Under this structure, B sells bonds and reinvests the proceeds at one month LIBOR, thereby lowering its interest accrual from the bond rate (13.02% pa) to one month LIBOR (11.78% pa—incorporating adjustment for day count basis and compounding period). This negative carry of 1.24 pa or 10.53bps over 31 days equates, when amortised at the swap rate, to 2.964bps or a one month deferred takedown swap price of 13.52964% pa (S/A).

This later structure, while it should cover any date reset mismatch risk does not protect B against movements in the swap spread.

Spreadlocks

A spreadlock or deferred *rate setting* swap is fundamentally different. Under the spreadlock structure, an institution may agree to provide the swap over a defined period (generally less than six months) at an agreed upon *spread* over a reference rate comparable to the maturity of the anticipated swap. The spreadlock is useful in guaranteeing the availability of the swap at a known *margin* over the relevant reference rate enabling the borrower to take advantage of any expected decrease in bare interest rates or movements in the swap spread. It is important to note that under a spreadlock, the party gaining the benefit of the spreadlock is obliged to enter into the swap. It merely has the option of determining the timing of setting the base fixed rate.

The pricing of the spreadlock is quite complex. For example, a swap counterparty may have paid out at bonds plus 45 for five years against six month LIBOR. It may have hedged this position by buying the appropriate amount of five year government securities. It can then enter into a spreadlock whereby it agrees to enter into a swap whereby its client pays and it receives bonds plus 60, with, however, the bond rate not being set for three months. In this case, the swap counterparty has locked in a spread profit of 15bps but is required to hold the hedge, that is the government securities, for up to three months. The spreadlock is then priced as the holding or carry cost of the bond for the relevant period.

An example of structuring/pricing a spreadlock is detailed in *Exhibit 12.7*.

A variation on the spreadlock structure entails utilisation of similar arrangements to undertake deferred rate setting in the context of bond issues. This type of transaction has been utilised by the World Bank.

In 1991, the World Bank commenced a programme of global bond issues, primarily in US$. Such transactions, entailing the issuance of large volumes of US$ debt securities (usually, at least, US$1,000m), exposed the World Bank to an exposure on the setting of the treasury rate. This related to the fact that a transaction was completed and priced on a single date. In order to lower this pricing risk, the World Bank developed a structure, analogous to spreadlocks, to defer the treasury price setting on its global bond issues over a more extended time frame.

Under this arrangement, the World Bank would undertake its global bond issue and price the transaction as usual at an agreed margin over US treasuries of the equivalent maturity. Simultaneously, or in a short period prior to the launch of the issue, the World Bank would purchase US treasuries of the equivalent maturity for an amount (up to) the full issue volume. The net result of these transactions was to leave the World Bank with an *agreed spread over treasuries* but with its underlying treasury rate yet to be determined.

Exhibit 12.7
Structuring/Pricing a Spreadlock

Assume that US$ five years swaps are trading at T+46/54. Company C (C) considers that the *spreads* are relatively low and wishes to lock in the pay or offer spread (54bps) for a period of three months, C enters into a spreadlock agreement with Bank B (B) to a payer spreadlock for a period for three months. At any time during the three month period, C can enter into a five year US$ interest rate swap where it pays the *then* prevailing five year US treasury rate plus 54bps (see discussion below) and receive three month US$ LIBOR.

The fee payable to B is determined by the cost of the hedge. The structure of the hedge is as follows:

- B enters into a five year three month swap under which it pays T+46 (assuming a current five year treasury of 7.60% pa and a swap rate of 8.06% pa).
- B hedges the five year treasury component of the swap by purchasing a five year three month (on equivalent treasury) and funding the purchase at the three month repo or other short term rate. This is designed to compensate for the fact that the swap with C under which B receives fixed rate has not commenced and the absolute rate has not been set.
- B sells the five year treasury purchased at the point in time that B exercises its right under the swap to enter into the swap.

The effective cost to B of providing the spreadlock is the cost of the treasury hedge. This hedge structure for both a payer and receiver spreadlock is set out below.

Pay Spreadlock Hedge

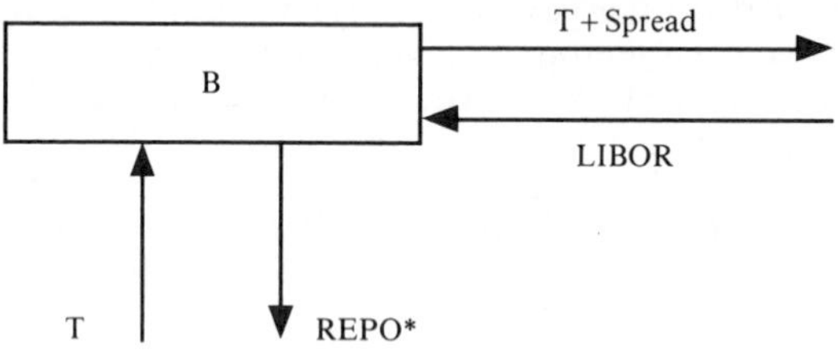

Receive Spreadlock Hedge

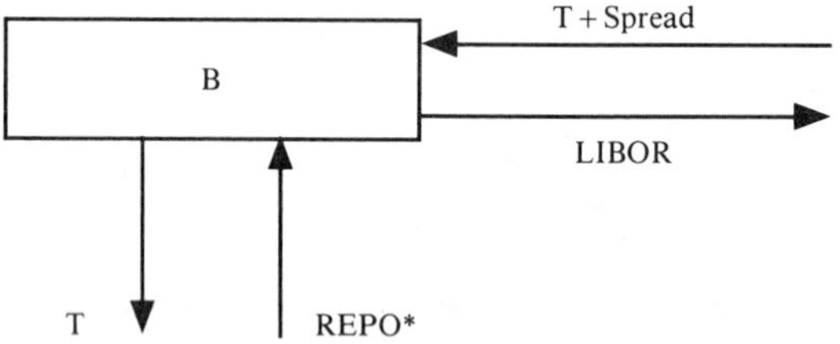

*REPO = Earning (cost) of lending (borrowing) bonds in the treasury repurchase market.

Assuming a cost of financing the treasury position is 6.5% pa then the treasury position generates earnings for B as follows:

Treasury Yield	7.60% pa
Financing Cost	6.50% pa
Gain	1.10% pa

The 1.10% pa is equivalent to 27.425bps over three months (1.10×91/365). If amortised over the life of the swap at the bond rate, this is equivalent to 6.797bps pa.

Exhibit 12.7—continued

This gain is substantially offset by the negative accrual under the swap entered into to hedge the payer spreadlock provided to C. This negative accrual is as follows:

Swap Fixed Rate (Paid)	8.06% pa
Swap Floating Rate (Received)	7.00% pa
Loss	1.06% pa

The 1.06% pa is equivalent to 26.427bps over three months (1.06×91/365). If amortised over the life of the swap, this is equivalent to 6.549bps pa.

The net benefit to B is 0.247bps pa. The spread in the spreadlock should be adjusted by this amount if B wishes to pass on this benefit to C.

The situation is reversed for a receiver spreadlock.

Several aspects of the structure and pricing of the spreadlock require comment:

- The spreadlock is set as a spread over the current treasury bond (normally the benchmark bond at the time the spreadlock is arranged). Where the spreadlock is of significant duration, there is a likelihood that the spreadlock will be affected by a change of benchmark (usually resulting from issuance of new treasury bonds and the changing maturity of the old benchmark). This necessitates that for longer spreadlocks, there is provision for a change in treasury benchmark during the life of the spreadlock whereby the agreed swap spread is adjusted by the difference in yields between the old and new benchmark bond. Typically, as the new treasury benchmark yields less than the old benchmark, the purchaser of a payer (receiver) spreadlock will incur a slight cost (benefit).
- B incurs an interest rate risk on the financing cost of the long treasury position or the cost of maintaining the treasury short position. This is because C can exercise its spreadlock at any time within the contract period. This generally means the treasury position is "rolled" on a short term basis.
- B's cash position is affected by the various accruals under the swap entered into to hedge the position as well as the treasury position. This is particularly significant where the spreadlock is of a significant duration.

For a pay spreadlock, during the period the spreadlock is in place prior to exercise, C's net cash flows are:

$$\text{LIBOR} - \text{REPO} - \text{Spread}$$

Assuming LIBOR ≥ REPO, at worst the cash flow deficiency will be equal to the swap spread for the relevant period.

For a receiver spreadlock, C's net cash flows are:

$$-\text{LIBOR} + \text{REPO} + \text{Spread}$$

Assuming Repo is low (as can be the case), the maximum net cash flow is spread minus LIBOR.

The actual rate quoted for a spreadlock would incorporate these factors or B's view on these rate relationships.

The World Bank then over a period of time would liquidate its treasury hedge position to gradually establish the effective borrowing cost. The gains and losses on the sale of treasury hedge would either increase or decrease the cost of borrowing, effectively adjusting the treasury rate set on the day the global bond issue was priced.

This type of arrangement, which is very similar to a spreadlock, allowed the World Bank to spread the treasury pricing risk over an acceptable period.

Timing variations on currency swaps

These types of variations on standard swap structures are also available for currency swaps. For example, it is possible to have deferred takedown or spreadlock arrangements on a currency swap. However, where these variations on currency swaps are utilised, care is taken to ensure that the spot exchange rate to be used at the commencement of the transaction is not fixed at the time the trade is entered into to ensure that an implicit currency forward or currency option is not created.

Pricing/hedging considerations

These variations on the classic swap structures are usually available from market makers in interest rate or currency swaps. These market participants price such swap transactions off their swap books and the pricing effectively reflects the cost of putting on the position and hedging it in conjunction with any profit margin to the swap provider. This is because it is unusual to be able to match out these specialised variations against capital market issues or against a direct counterparty. These variations are often also means by which these market makers manage certain mismatches within their swap books: see below, Part 8.

FORWARD SWAPS

Concept of forward swaps

A forward swap is an interest rate swap which commences at a specified time in the future. For example, a US$ interest rate swap commencing in two years from the time the transaction is entered into with final maturity three years from commencement or five years from the time the transaction is entered into is usually termed a forward swap.

As in a normal interest rate swap transaction, the party entering into the transaction can use the swap to convert floating rate liabilities into fixed rate liabilities or vice versa. There are two types of forward swaps:

- *forward swaps* in which the party entering into the transaction is a fixed rate payer;
- *reverse forward swaps* in which the party entering into the transaction is a payer of the floating rate.

Utilising forward swaps

Forward swaps are utilised for two general categories of transactions:

- forward rate setting transactions;
- structured capital market transactions, in particular, refinancing high coupon bonds.

Forward swaps are utilised, in the first type of transaction, to lock in fixed rates commencing at a specified time in the future. This type of rate setting is utilised in connection with projects with a known schedule of drawdowns extending several years into the future or to lock in a known fixed cost of funds for future funding. The rationale in both cases is the expectation that the general level of interest rates will increase between now and when the funding is required.

Forward swaps can also be used to extend existing swaps or fixed rate liabilities to suit a changing asset or liability profile. A reverse forward swap is utilised to convert an existing fixed rate liability into a floating rate liability at a point of time in the future. It is usually undertaken to take advantage of changes in the shape of the yield curve, changing spread differentials as between swaps and fixed rate liabilities, and existing profits or value in an entity's current portfolio of liabilities.

Exhibit 12.8 details an example of utilising forward swaps to take advantage of changes in yield curve shape to create value in a liability portfolio.

Exhibit 12.8
Utilising Forward Swaps

Assume a borrower Company A (A) has created seven year fixed rate debt at 7.75% pa. This fixed rate debt has been created by A converting a seven year US$ LIBOR based floating rate loan into fixed rate funding through a seven year US$ interest rate swap under which it pays fixed rate and receiving floating rate.

Shortly after this transaction is implemented, the yield curve steepens significantly as between five and seven years. The yield spread between five and seven years increases from approximately 15bps (at the time of the swap) to 45bps. This results in the rate for a two year swap commencing in approximately five years reaching 9.25% pa.

Under these circumstances, A can convert the rate advantage of approximately 150bps over years six and seven of the original financing by shortening the term of the original fixed rate borrowing from seven years to five years as follows. A enters into a forward swap for two years commencing in five years time where it receives fixed rate (at 9.25% pa) and pays floating rate.

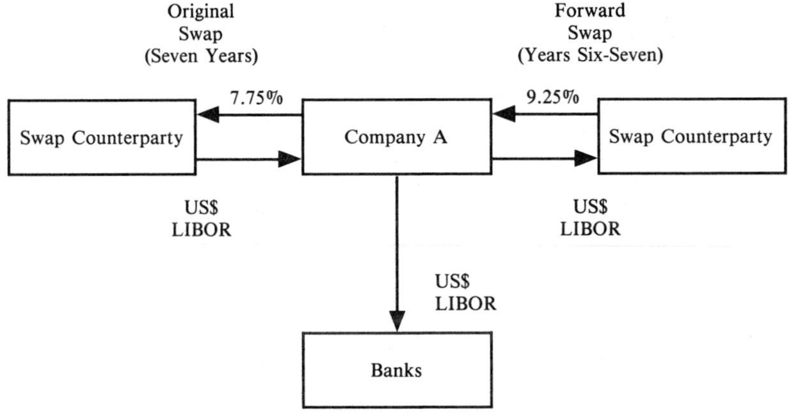

A can take the benefit in a number of ways:

1. A can leave the two swaps in place and maintain the underlying borrowing which is now at a rate of LIBOR minus 150bps in years six and seven.
2. A can close out the *last two years* of the original seven year swap which would generate a PV benefit of 1.82% of principal amount (using a discount rate of 8.00% pa). This benefit could be realised as an up-front cash benefit or as a reduction in the five year fixed rate payable under the swap of 45.6bps pa.

If A chose the first alternative, then it could potentially benefit from reversing *the forward swap* if the yield curve falls in absolute rate terms or it flattens in shape.

Irrespective of the alternatives selected, A would be left with a floating rate borrowing for two years in five years time. It would have the choice of either terminating the underlying funding (if a call option on the loan was available) or maintaining the borrowing.

The second category of applications evolved in early 1986 when a marked decline in US$ interest rates resulted in a corresponding increase in the value of call options on existing fixed rate bonds. In all cases, the call option on exisiting debt could not be exercised until some time in the future. This delay in the exercise of the call meant that its value was uncertain as an increase in interest rates between early 1986 and the time the call was capable of being exercised would erode or eliminate the value of the option.

In this environment, two particular types of transactions evolved:

- transactions which entailed ordinary callable fixed rate bonds; and
- transactions involving callable fixed rate bonds which had been swapped to generate sub-LIBOR floating rate funds.

In the first case, the issuers entered into a forward swap coinciding with the call option on the outstanding securities with the intention of calling the bond and simultaneously refinancing with new floating rate funds which, by virtue of the forward swap, would generate fixed rate funds at the current lower interest rates.

The second type of transaction was more complex. The borrowers had uncrystallised value from two sources: the value of the call and the value in the orginal interest rate swap written at rate levels above current market rates. In this environment, the borrower could call the original bond leaving it with an above market rate swap.

The value of the swap was realised by entering into a forward swap in which the borrower made payments to the forward swap counterparty corresponding to its fixed rate receipts from the original swap counterparty in return for receiving floating rate LIBOR payments which it passed onto the original swap counterparty. The forward swap simply reversed the original swap between the call and final maturity of the original fixed rate issue. This reversal left the borrower with a profit representing the movements in interest rates between the time the two swaps were entered into.

The value of the reversal was capable of being crystallised in a number of ways:

- as a periodic flow being the difference between the two swap rates; or
- as an up-front payment representing the present value of the future cash flows.

In one case, the difference was taken as a subsidy on a new issue and swap dramatically reducing the cost of funds to the borrower. In that case, the borrower chose to effectively prefund its call by issuing debt, swapped into floating rate funds, with a maturity coinciding with that on the original issue. The value of the forward reversal of the original swap was applied to the new issue. This prefunding of the call resulted in the borrower having additional cash for the period until the call on the original issue which was consistent with its financing requirements.

A number of these type of transactions, including a much publicised one for SEK, were concluded in early 1986.

Forward swap structures compete with deferred call debt warrant issues as a means of crystallising the current value in a call option not capable of being exercised until some time in the future.

Under the deferred call debt warrant structure, a borrower with a callable high coupon bond securitises the call option by issuing debt warrants. The warrants are exercisable, on the call date, into the borrower's debt on terms coinciding closely with the original callable issue. If interest rates fall the warrants are exercised. The borrower simultaneously calls the original issue being left with funding on largely identical terms but with a lower effective cost as a result of the premium received from the issue of warrants. If interest rates increase the warrants will expire unexercised, with the borrower using the premium received to lower its all-in borrowing cost.

The forward swap structure and the debt warrant were effectively different financial engineering techniques designed to achieve similar economic objectives. The choice between the techniques is usually a purely mathematical decision based on the market conditions and the resulting economics of the debt warrant and forward swap transactions.

Key market factors include:

- the shape of the swap yield curve which affects the pricing dynamics of the forward swaps;
- the value characteristics of the debt warrant which will be dependent upon:
  —the warrant exercise period (that is, the period until call);
  —the life of the back bonds underlying the warrants;
  —the exercise period for the warrant (that is, if the warrant is a "window" warrant designed to avoid doubling up of outstanding debt).

The attitude of the borrower is also critical. In particular, the issuer's attitude to doubling up debt until call etc, is important in determining the choice between the two techniques.

It is important to recognise that the concept of a forward liability can be replicated in the cash market by a borrowing, the proceeds of which are reinvested until needed to finance the call on the original bond. The technique of using physical instruments has the effect of increasing on-balance sheet commitments which may not be acceptable and also may be economically less attractive as a result of a negative spread between the borrowing and lending rates (although this will economically be factored into the price of the forward swap).

Pricing forward swaps

Forward swaps can be priced using one of two general approaches:

- constructing the forward swap as two separate but offsetting swaps mismatched as to maturity;
- treating the forward swap as a conventional swap with a delayed start.

The offsetting swap approach is illustrated in *Exhibit 12.9*. Additional examples are set out in *Exhibit 12.10*.

The all-in rate for the forward swap is calculated by allocating the net cash flow deficit in the first two years to the payments over the three years of the forward swaps on a present value basis using the swap rate as the relevant discount rate. The cost of the forward swap is dependent on the shape of the yield curve which determines the shortfall between the two swaps.

A reverse forward swap is priced in a similar manner. However, the price behaviour of a reverse forward swap is more attractive in a positive yield curve as there is a cash flow surplus in the early years of the swap which reduced the cost of the reverse forward swap by increasing the fixed rate inflow over its life.

Treating the forward swap as a deferred takedown conventional swap usually entails pricing the swap on the basis of the expected cost of the hedge. This approach is illustrated in *Exhibit 12.5*.

Exhibit 12.9
Pricing a Forward Swap

Assume company C (C) wishes to enter into a three year forward swap commencing in two years from the time of execution. The transactions can be broken into two separate swaps as follows:

- a five year swap where C pays a fixed rate and receives LIBOR;
- a two year swap where C receives a fixed rate and pays LIBOR.

Assuming that the swap rates are as follows:

Two years: 12.50/12.60% pa (S/A)
Five years: 13.60/13.70% pa (S/A)

the cash flows (A$m) to C for a A$100m forward swap would be as follows:

Period (years)	**Receives 12.50% pa**	**Pays LIBOR**	**Pays 13.70% pa**	**Receives LIBOR**	**Pays**	**Receives**
0.5	+6.250	−LIBOR	−6.850	+LIBOR	−0.600	—
1.0	+6.250	−LIBOR	−6.850	+LIBOR	−0.600	—
1.5	+6.250	−LIBOR	−6.850	+LIBOR	−0.600	—
2.0	+6.250	−LIBOR	−6.850	+LIBOR	−0.600	—
2.5			−6.850	+LIBOR	−6.850	+LIBOR
3.0			−6.850	+LIBOR	−6.850	+LIBOR
3.5			−6.850	+LIBOR	−6.850	+LIBOR
4.0			−6.850	+LIBOR	−6.850	+LIBOR
4.5			−6.850	+LIBOR	−6.850	+LIBOR
5.0			−6.850	+LIBOR	−6.850	+LIBOR

Where C does not wish to cover the cash flow shortfalls over the first two years, it may utilise a bank (B) to undertake the two swaps and create a customised forward swap for C. B will need to adjust the yield on the forward swap to reflect the funding required as a result of the shortfall from the combined swaps.

In this example, assuming that B uses a funding rate equivalent to the *five year* swap offer rate, the yield adjustment spread would be approximately 1.11% pa. This yield adjustment has the same net present value as the residual two year cash flow. Consequently, B would quote a rate of 14.81% pa (S/A) for a three year forward swap commencing in two years' time.

Exhibit 12.10

Pricing Forward Swaps Using Offsetting Swaps Technique: Examples

Example 1:

Swap Rates

Maturity (Years):	2	5
Rate (Bid):	10.450%	9.250%
Rate (Offer):	10.550%	9.350%

Forward Swap Cash Flows (Pay Fixed)

Period	Swap 1		Swap 2		Net Flows	
Years	Receives Fixed	Pays Floating	Pays Fixed	Receives Floating	Fixed	Floating
	10.450%		9.350%			
0.0						
0.5	5.225	(LIBOR)	−4.675	LIBOR	0.55	0
1.0	5.225	(LIBOR)	−4.675	LIBOR	0.55	0
1.5	5.225	(LIBOR)	−4.675	LIBOR	0.55	0
2.0	5.225	(LIBOR)	−4.675	LIBOR	0.55	0
2.5			−4.675	LIBOR	−4.675	LIBOR
3.0			−4.675	LIBOR	−4.675	LIBOR
3.5			−4.675	LIBOR	−4.675	LIBOR
4.0			−4.675	LIBOR	−4.675	LIBOR
4.5			−4.675	LIBOR	−4.675	LIBOR
5.0			−4.675	LIBOR	−4.675	LIBOR

Pricing Calculations

(1) Cash Flow Surplus (Deficiency) During Delay

FV	PMT	INT	Term	PV
−2.36	−0.55	4.675%	4	0

(2) Allocation of Surplus Over Swap Term

PV	PMT	INT	Term	FV
−2.36	−0.46	4.675%	6	0

Adjusted Forward Rate (Pay Fixed)

Spot Swap Rate:	9.350%
Forward Start Adjustment:	−0.920%
Forward Swap Rate:	8.430%

Forward Swap Cash Flows (Receive Fixed)

Period	Swap 1		Swap 2		Net Flows	
Years	Receives Fixed	Pays Floating	Pays Fixed	Receives Floating	Fixed	Floating
	10.550%		9.250%			
0.0						
0.5	−5.275	(LIBOR)	4.625	LIBOR	−0.65	0
1.0	−5.275	(LIBOR)	4.625	LIBOR	−0.65	0
1.5	−5.275	(LIBOR)	4.625	LIBOR	−0.65	0
2.0	−5.275	(LIBOR)	4.625	LIBOR	−0.65	0
2.5			4.625	LIBOR	4.625	LIBOR
3.0			4.625	LIBOR	4.625	LIBOR
3.5			4.625	LIBOR	4.625	LIBOR
4.0			4.625	LIBOR	4.625	LIBOR
4.5			4.625	LIBOR	4.625	LIBOR
5.0			4.625	LIBOR	4.625	LIBOR

Pricing Calculations

(1) Cash Flow Surplus (Deficiency) During Delay

FV	PMT	INT	Term	PV
−2.79	−0.65	4.675%	4	0

(2) Allocation of Surplus Over Swap Term

PV	PMT	INT	Term	FV
−2.79	−0.54	4.675%	6	0

Adjusted Forward Rate (Receive Fixed)

Spot Swap Rate:	9.250%
Forward Start Adjustment:	−1.087%
Forward Swap Rate:	8.163%

Exhibit 12.10—continued

Example 2:

Swap Rates		
Maturity (Years):	2	5
Rate (Bid):	6.500%	8.650%
Rate (Offer):	6.600%	8.750%

Forward Swap Cash Flows (Pay Fixed)

Period	Swap 1		Swap 2		Net Flows	
Years	Receives Fixed	Pays Floating	Pays Fixed	Receives Floating	Fixed	Floating
	6.500%		8.750%			
0.0						
0.5	3.25	(LIBOR)	−4.375	LIBOR	−1.125	0
1.0	3.25	(LIBOR)	−4.375	LIBOR	−1.125	0
1.5	3.25	(LIBOR)	−4.375	LIBOR	−1.125	0
2.0	3.25	(LIBOR)	−4.375	LIBOR	−1.125	0
2.5			−4.375	LIBOR	−4.375	LIBOR
3.0			−4.375	LIBOR	−4.375	LIBOR
3.5			−4.375	LIBOR	−4.375	LIBOR
4.0			−4.375	LIBOR	−4.375	LIBOR
4.5			−4.375	LIBOR	−4.375	LIBOR
5.0			−4.375	LIBOR	−4.375	LIBOR

Pricing Calculations

(1) Cash Flow Surplus (Deficiency) During Delay

FV	PMT	INT	Term	PV
4.80	1.13	4.375%	4	0

(2) Allocation of Surplus Over Swap Term

PV	PMT	INT	Term	FV
4.80	0.93	4.375%	6	0

Adjusted Forward Rate (Pay Fixed)

Spot Swap Rate:	8.750%
Forward Start Adjustment:	1.855%
Forward Swap Rate:	10.605%

Forward Swap Cash Flows (Receive Fixed)

Period	Swap 1		Swap 2		Net Flows	
Years	Receives Fixed	Pays Floating	Pays Fixed	Receives Floating	Fixed	Floating
	6.600%		8.650%			
0.0						
0.5	−3.3	(LIBOR)	4.325	LIBOR	1.025	0
1.0	−3.3	(LIBOR)	4.325	LIBOR	1.025	0
1.5	−3.3	(LIBOR)	4.325	LIBOR	1.025	0
2.0	−3.3	(LIBOR)	4.325	LIBOR	1.025	0
2.5			4.325	LIBOR	4.325	LIBOR
3.0			4.325	LIBOR	4.325	LIBOR
3.5			4.325	LIBOR	4.325	LIBOR
4.0			4.325	LIBOR	4.325	LIBOR
4.5			4.325	LIBOR	4.325	LIBOR
5.0			4.325	LIBOR	4.325	LIBOR

Pricing Calculations

(1) Cash Flow Surplus (Deficiency) During Delay

FV	PMT	INT	Term	PV
4.38	1.02	4.375%	4	0

(2) Allocation of Surplus Over Swap Term

PV	PMT	INT	Term	FV
4.38	0.85	4.375%	6	0

Adjusted Forward Rate (Receive Fixed)

Spot Swap Rate:	8.650%
Forward Start Adjustment:	1.690%
Forward Swap Rate:	10.340%

In the case of a forward swap, the swap counterparty would usually hedge by selling or shorting bonds. The price of the hedge would reflect the difference in investment yield as between the bond sold and the alternative short-term investment reflecting the deferred start of the swap. Where the yield curve is positive (negative), the lower (higher) investment return would translate into a higher (lower) forward swap rate relative to a conventional swap with an immediate start.

In the case of a reverse forward swap, the logic is identical. However, the hedge would be effected by purchasing bonds and the forward swap rate would reflect the positive or negative carry cost on the holding.

The two approaches are comparable and would usually yield comparable forward swap rates. However, the shape of the physical security yield as compared to the swap yield curve and differences in transaction costs entailing physical securities such as differential funding costs investment opportunities as well as the balance sheet impact of physical transactions create divergences between the two approaches.

Exhibit 12.11 summarises a matrix of forward swap rate for a given series of yield curves.

Forward currency swaps

Forward currency swaps are very similar, structurally, to forward interest rate swaps. As with forward interest rate swaps, forward currency swaps are utilised to:

- lock in future fixed rate funding costs in the relevant currency;
- as part of a refinancing or refunding operation on callable foreign currency debt transactions.

Other uses include management of currency exposures within an asset or liability portfolio or for the purposes of new issue arbitrage across different markets.

Exhibit 12.12 details an example of utilising forward currency swaps to hedge future financings. *Exhibit 12.13* sets out an example of utilising forward currency swaps to refund high coupon callable debt.

Exhibit
Forward Swap

Forward/Forward Interest Rate Swap Pricing

Date	No of Days	Year	S/A Periods	Swap Rate (% pa S/A)	Start Date (Years)						
15-Jun-19X2		0				10.0	9.5	9.0	8.5	8.0	7.5
15-Dec-19X2	183	0.50	1.003	9.85%	0.5	7.397%	7.528%	7.616%	7.736%	7.823%	7.911%
15-Jun-19X3	365	1.00	1.995	9.71%	1.0	7.278%	7.409%	7.495%	7.615%	7.700%	7.784%
15-Dec-19X3	548	1.50	2.995	9.58%	1.5	7.158%	7.290%	7.374%	7.493%	7.576%	7.657%
15-Jun-19X4	730	2.00	3.989	9.42%	2.0	7.048%	7.181%	7.263%	7.383%	7.463%	7.541%
15-Dec-19X4	913	2.50	4.989	9.31%	2.5	6.927%	7.060%	7.139%	7.259%	7.335%	7.408%
15-Jun-19X5	1095	3.00	5.984	9.21%	3.0	6.800%	6.935%	7.010%	7.128%	7.198%	7.264%
15-Dec-19X5	1278	3.50	6.984	9.07%	3.5	6.690%	6.827%	6.898%	7.018%	7.083%	7.143%
15-Jun-19X6	1461	4.00	7.984	9.01%	4.0	6.532%	6.667%	6.729%	6.843%	6.895%	6.937%
15-Dec-19X6	1644	4.50	8.984	8.87%	4.5	6.421%	6.558%	6.615%	6.729%	6.772%	6.800%
15-Jun-19X7	1826	5.00	9.978	8.65%	5.0	6.396%	6.545%	6.608%	6.737%	6.789%	6.825%
15-Dec-19X7	2009	5.50	10.978	8.51%	5.5	6.316%	6.473%	6.535%	6.674%	6.723%	6.752%
15-Jun-19X8	2191	6.00	11.973	8.38%	6.0	6.237%	6.405%	6.466%	6.619%	6.666%	6.686%
15-Dec-19X8	2374	6.50	12.973	8.24%	6.5	6.189%	6.378%	6.446%	6.631%	6.698%	6.744%
15-Jun-19X9	2556	7.00	13.967	8.13%	7.0	6.104%	6.314%	6.382%	6.608%	6.697%	6.787%
15-Dec-19X9	2739	7.50	14.967	8.04%	7.5	5.968%	6.195%	6.247%	6.518%	6.608%	
15-Jun-20X0	2922	8.01	15.967	7.95%	8.0	5.808%	6.058%	6.066%	6.428%		
15-Dec-20X0	3105	8.51	16.967	7.86%	8.5	5.601%	5.872%	5.703%			
15-Jun-20X1	3287	9.01	17.962	7.74%	9.0	5.549%	6.040%				
15-Dec-20X1	3470	9.51	18.962	7.65%	9.5	5.057%					
15-Jun-20X2	3652	10.01	19.956	7.52%							
15-Dec-20X2	3835										

Forward/Forward Interest Rate Swap Pricing

Date	No of Days	Year	S/A Periods	Swap Rate (% pa S/A)	Start Date (Years)						
15-Jun-19X2		0				10.0	9.5	9.0	8.5	8.0	7.5
15-Dec-19X2	183	0.50	1.003	7.60%	0.5	9.727%	9.607%	9.507%	9.460%	9.404%	9.326%
15-Jun-19X3	365	1.00	1.995	7.75%	1.0	9.829%	9.707%	9.607%	9.564%	9.511%	9.435%
15-Dec-19X3	548	1.50	2.995	7.84%	1.5	9.936%	9.813%	9.714%	9.675%	9.626%	9.554%
15-Jun-19X4	730	2.00	3.989	7.92%	2.0	10.047%	9.923%	9.824%	9.792%	9.748%	9.681%
15-Dec-19X4	913	2.50	4.989	8.01%	2.5	10.159%	10.035%	9.937%	9.911%	9.874%	9.813%
15-Jun-19X5	1095	3.00	5.984	8.16%	3.0	10.248%	10.121%	10.022%	10.001%	9.970%	9.912%
15-Dec-19X5	1278	3.50	6.984	8.24%	3.5	10.367%	10.238%	10.141%	10.130%	10.110%	10.062%
15-Jun-19X6	1461	4.00	7.984	8.35%	4.0	10.471%	10.340%	10.244%	10.243%	10.234%	10.197%
15-Dec-19X6	1644	4.50	8.984	8.48%	4.5	10.558%	10.423%	10.325%	10.333%	10.337%	10.311%
15-Jun-19X7	1826	5.00	9.978	8.72%	5.0	10.524%	10.370%	10.253%	10.253%	10.243%	10.193%
15-Dec-19X7	2009	5.50	10.978	8.80%	5.5	10.627%	10.466%	10.347%	10.362%	10.372%	10.343%
15-Jun-19X8	2191	6.00	11.973	8.95%	6.0	10.629%	10.446%	10.302%	10.312%	10.312%	10.253%
15-Dec-19X8	2374	6.50	12.973	9.02%	6.5	10.739%	10.543%	10.391%	10.425%	10.464%	10.450%
15-Jun-19X9	2556	7.00	13.967	9.07%	7.0	10.908%	10.707%	10.558%	10.659%	10.833%	11.175%
15-Dec-19X9	2739	7.50	14.967	9.21%	7.5	10.855%	10.590%	10.352%	10.401%	10.491%	
15-Jun-20X0	2922	8.01	15.967	9.29%	8.0	10.946%	10.623%	10.283%	10.310%		
15-Dec-20X0	3105	8.51	16.967	9.35%	8.5	11.159%	10.780%	10.255%			
15-Jun-20X1	3287	9.01	17.962	9.40%	9.0	11.612%	11.304%				
15-Dec-20X1	3470	9.51	18.962	9.50%	9.5	11.921%					
15-Jun-20X2	3652	10.01	19.956	9.62%							
15-Dec-20X2	3835										

12.11
Rate Matrix

Forward Swap Matrix (% pa)
Final Maturity (Years)

7.0	6.5	6.0	5.5	5.0	4.5	4.0	3.5	3.0	2.5	2.0	1.5	
7.998%	8.106%	8.246%	8.376%	8.516%	8.747%	8.890%	8.940%	9.081%	9.174%	9.276%	9.444%	9.56
7.868%	7.974%	8.115%	8.245%	8.386%	8.631%	8.777%	8.815%	8.960%	9.044%	9.130%	9.321%	
7.736%	7.840%	7.981%	8.110%	8.252%	8.516%	8.669%	8.688%	8.840%	8.905%	8.939%		
7.617%	7.718%	7.862%	7.992%	8.139%	8.432%	8.601%	8.605%	8.791%	8.872%			
7.477%	7.574%	7.718%	7.846%	7.992%	8.322%	8.511%	8.471%	8.709%				
7.324%	7.413%	7.554%	7.674%	7.814%	8.194%	8.413%	8.234%					
7.194%	7.276%	7.418%	7.535%	7.674%	8.173%	8.591%						
6.962%	7.014%	7.125%	7.183%	7.215%	7.756%							
6.803%	6.828%	6.914%	6.896%	6.673%								
6.835%	6.880%	7.034%	7.118%									
6.740%	6.760%	6.950%										
6.636%	6.571%											
6.700%												

Forward Swap Matrix (% pa)
Final Maturity (Years)

7.0	6.5	6.0	5.5	5.0	4.5	4.0	3.5	3.0	2.5	2.0	1.5	
9.184%	9.139%	9.074%	8.921%	8.846%	8.591%	8.458%	8.347%	8.273%	8.113%	8.028%	7.961%	7.90
9.291%	9.252%	9.191%	9.034%	8.963%	8.689%	8.550%	8.436%	8.365%	8.183%	8.090%	8.020%	
9.407%	9.375%	9.322%	9.161%	9.098%	8.801%	8.657%	8.541%	8.481%	8.265%	8.161%		
9.532%	9.510%	9.467%	9.304%	9.255%	8.928%	8.780%	8.667%	8.641%	8.369%			
9.661%	9.654%	9.624%	9.460%	9.432%	9.069%	8.918%	8.816%	8.914%				
9.755%	9.759%	9.742%	9.569%	9.562%	9.120%	8.919%	8.719%					
9.903%	9.933%	9.948%	9.783%	9.844%	9.320%	9.120%						
10.035%	10.097%	10.156%	10.004%	10.208%	9.521%							
10.138%	10.241%	10.369%	10.247%	10.900%								
9.948%	10.023%	10.104%	9.600%									
10.065%	10.235%	10.613%										
9.792%	9.860%											
9.723%												

Exhibit 12.12

Utilising Forward Currency Swaps to Hedge Future Financings

Assume Company A (A) has a funding commitment of DEM100m in two years time to fund the acquisition of a DEM asset (eg a contractual obligation to acquire a portion of a partly owned German business from its existing proprietors).

In order to lock in the funding rate on the financing as well as the US$ equivalent of the DEM purchase price, A enters into the forward currency swap on the following terms:

- A enters into a five year currency swap *commencing in two years time.*
- Under the swap, A agrees to:

  —pay fixed rate DEM at 8.25% pa

  —receive floating rate US$ at US$ six month LIBOR
- A agrees with the swap counterparty that the exchange rate applicable will be the two year US$/DEM forward rate of US$1 = DEM1.7074 (against spot of US$1 = DEM1.600). This implies an initial and final principal amounts to be exchanged of US$58.569m and DEM100.0m.

The execution of the transaction takes the following form:

Initial Exchange (two years from present)

A raises US$58.569m through a bank loan or a US$ FRN issue at say LIBOR plus 0.75% pa. A pays the US$ borrowing proceeds to the swap counterparty and, in return, receives DEM100m which is used to make the committed DEM payments.

Periodic Interest Payments (Years 3-7 inclusive)

A pays approximately DEM4.125m semi-annually (8.25% pa on the DEM100m principal) to the swap counterparty in return for receiving US$ six month LIBOR on US$58.569m semi-annually. The US$ LIBOR receipts covers the US$ payments (excluding the margin) on A's floating rate US$ borrowing. A's DEM outflows are presumably offset by DEM earnings/surplus cash flow from its DEM assets.

Final Exchange/Re-Exchange of Principal (Year 7)

A pays DEM100m to the counterparty and receives US$58.569m from the counterparty upon maturity of the swap. A uses the US$ receipts to repay the US$ floating rate borrowing. The DEM100m may be funded by liquidation of the asset or by re-financing in DEM (either directly or indirectly via a borrowing converted to DEM via another currency swap).

The structure of the transaction is set out diagrammatically below:

Initial Exchange (Year 2)

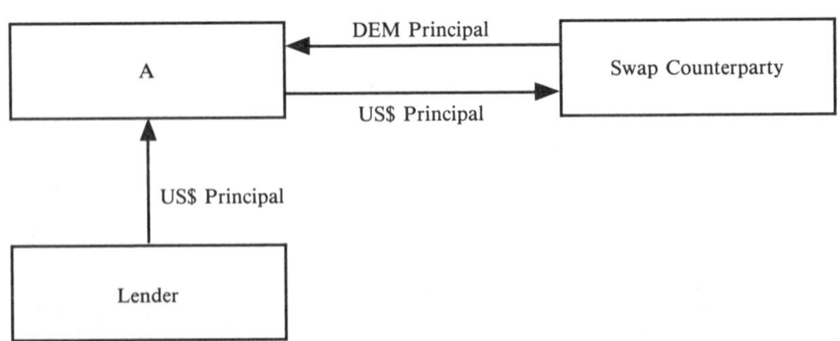

Exhibit 12.12—continued

Interest Payments/Re-Exchange (Years 3-7)

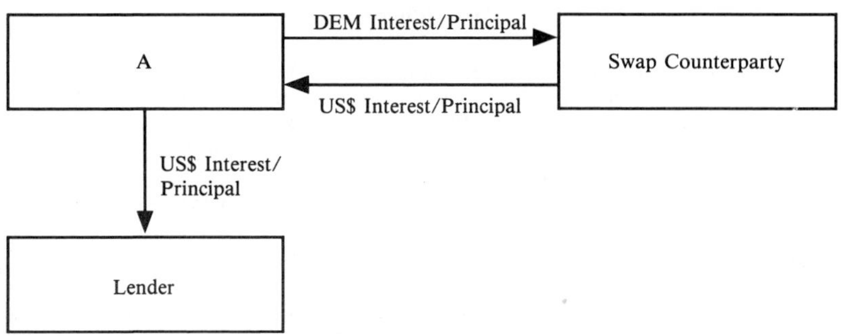

The transaction cash flows are summarised below:

Utilising Forward Currency Swaps to Hedge Future Financings Transaction Cash Flows (m)

	Year	US$ Borrowing		Forward Currency Swap-Cash Flows				Net Cash Flows
		Principal (US$ m)	Interest (US$ m) *	Principal (US$ m)	Interest (US$ m)	Principal (DEM m)	Interest (DEM m)	(DEM m) #
Entry into Forward Swap	0.0							
	0.5							
	1.0							
	1.5							
Forward Swap Commences	2.0	58.569		(58.569)		100.000		100.000
	2.5		(2.050)		1.830		(4.125)	(4.262)
	3.0		(2.050)		1.830		(4.125)	(4.262)
	3.5		(2.050)		1.830		(4.125)	(4.262)
	4.0		(2.050)		1.830		(4.125)	(4.262)
	4.5		(2.050)		1.830		(4.125)	(4.262)
	5.0		(2.050)		1.830		(4.125)	(4.262)
	5.5		(2.050)		1.830		(4.125)	(4.262)
	6.0		(2.050)		1.830		(4.125)	(4.262)
	6.5		(2.050)		1.830		(4.125)	(4.262)
Forward Swap Terminates	7.0	(58.569)	(2.050)	58.569	1.830	(100.000)	(4.125)	(104.262)

Effective DEM Borrowing Cost: 8.5245%

Notes: * US$ six month LIBOR is assumed to be 6.250%

The US$ margin shortfall has been converted into DEM at US$1 = DEM1.6000 the spot rate at the time the transaction is entered into for illustrative purposes.

The forward currency swap transaction allows A to guarantee itself financing in DEM at 8.25% pa in two years time. Similarly, it locks in a US$/DEM rate of US$1 = DEM1.7074. A will benefit (lose) if DEM five year interest rates rise (fall) or the US$ depreciates (appreciates) vis-à-vis the DEM.

It should be noted that the effective rate achieved by A is equivalent to 8.25% pa plus the margin over LIBOR of 0.75% pa (which must be translated from US$ into a DEM equivalent).

As in the case with forward interest rate swap, A can take no action or pre-fund in DEM and place the DEM raised on deposit until required in two years.

The first course leaves A exposed to rises in DEM rates and a depreciation in the US$.

The pre-funding alternative has similar economics to the forward currency swaps (being functionally its economic equivalent), it incurs costs by way of balance sheet utilisation and the impact of the differential between borrowing and deposit interest rates. (Apart from the loss of the bid-offer spread, the differential can be positive or negative depending on the shape of the yield curve and whether A is paying or receiving a particular interest rate under the forward swap.)

Exhibit 12.13

Utilising Forward Currency Swaps to Refund High Coupon Callable Debt

As at June 19X2 Company A (A) has an outstanding JPY20,000m issue with a coupon of 6.5% pa maturing in June 19X8. The JPY issue was swapped into floating rate US$125.0m funding at a rate of US$ six month LIBOR minus 0.20% pa at the time the issue was undertaken. The issue is callable as at June 19X4 at 102% of par value.

JPY interest rates have fallen since the time the issue was undertaken resulting in there being value in the call option. This value can be realised by A through entry into a JPY/US$ forward currency swap.

A seeks to realise the call value by entering into a forward currency swap in June 19X2 as follows:

- A enters into a four year forward currency swap commencing in approximately two years time (June 19X4).
- Under the terms of the swap:

—A agrees to pay fixed rate JPY at a rate of 5.50% pa annually

—A agrees to receive US$ six month LIBOR flat semi-annually.

A agrees with the swap counterparty that the exchange rate applicable will be the two year US$/JPY forward rate of US$1 = JPY138.0 implying an initial and final exchange amount to be exchanged of US$144.928m and JPY20bn.

This transaction has the effect of locking in a positive spread between the original JPY/US$ currency swap and the forward currency swap in the period between June 19X4 (the date of commencement of the forward swap) and June 19X8 (the maturity date of the original swap).

The transaction will operate as follows:

Initial Cash Flows (June 19X4)

A calls the bond issue and pays the bond investor JPY20.4bn (102 of par value) to redeem the issue.

A simultaneously enters into a four year new US$ borrowing whereby it borrows US$144.928m. Assume A completes this refinancing at a rate of US$ LIBOR flat.

The US$ proceeds of the new borrowing are delivered to the swap counterparty who in return provides JPY20.0bn to A who uses it to fund the call on the JPY bond.

There is a shortfall of JPY400m (US$2.899m at US$1 = JPY138.00) which is funded by A out of general resources.

Periodic Interest Flows (December 19X4 to June 19X8)

On 20 June (commencing June 19X5 and ending June 19X8), A receives JPY1,300m (under the original swap) and pays JPY1,100m (under the forward swap) resulting in a cash surplus of JPY200m as at each payment date.

On 20 June and 20 December (commencing December 19X4 and ending June 19X8), A has the following US$ cash flows:

- A pays US$ six month LIBOR on US$144.928m (on its four year borrowing);
- A receives US$ six month LIBOR on US$144.928m (under the forward currency swap);
- A pays US$ six month LIBOR minus 20bps on US$125.00m (under the original swap).

The net result is A pays US$ six month LIBOR minus 20 bps on US$125.0m.

Final Cash Flows (June 19X8)

A repays the US$144.928m borrowing of four years undertaken in June 19X4.

Under the two swaps, the following principal exchanges are completed:

- A receives JPY20.0bn (under the original swap) and pays JPY20.0bn (under the forward swap);
- A receives US$144.928m (under the forward swap) and pays US$125.0m (under the original swaps).

Exhibit 12.13—continued

The net result is A has a net cash outflow of US$125.0m representing its original borrowing. This amount is funded by liquidating the asset acquired (eg repayment of a loan funded through this transaction in the case of a financial institution) or by re-financing the US$ borrowing. The structure of the transaction is set out diagrammatically below:

As at June 19X2

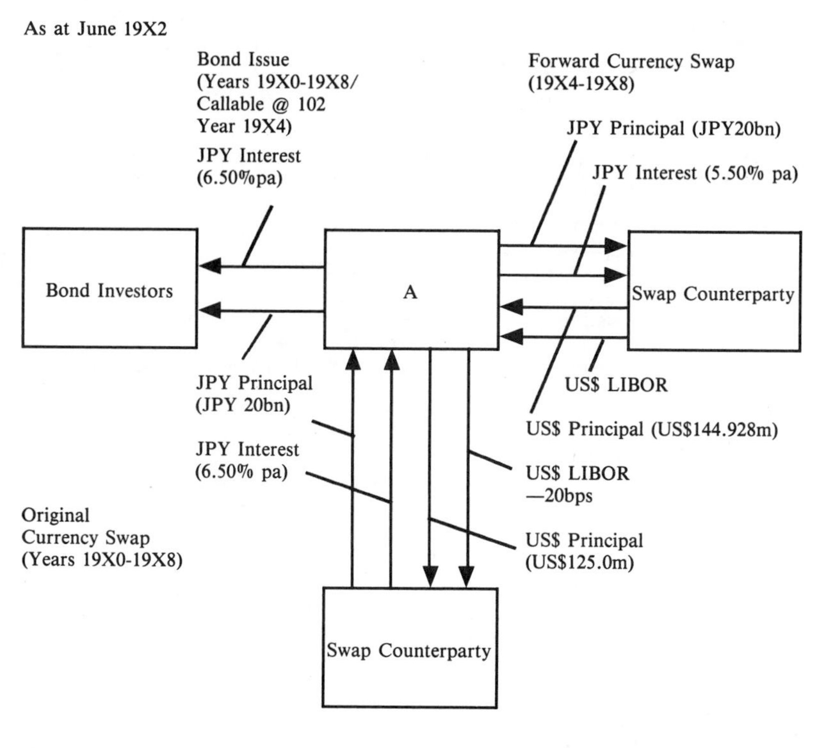

Exhibit 12.13—continued

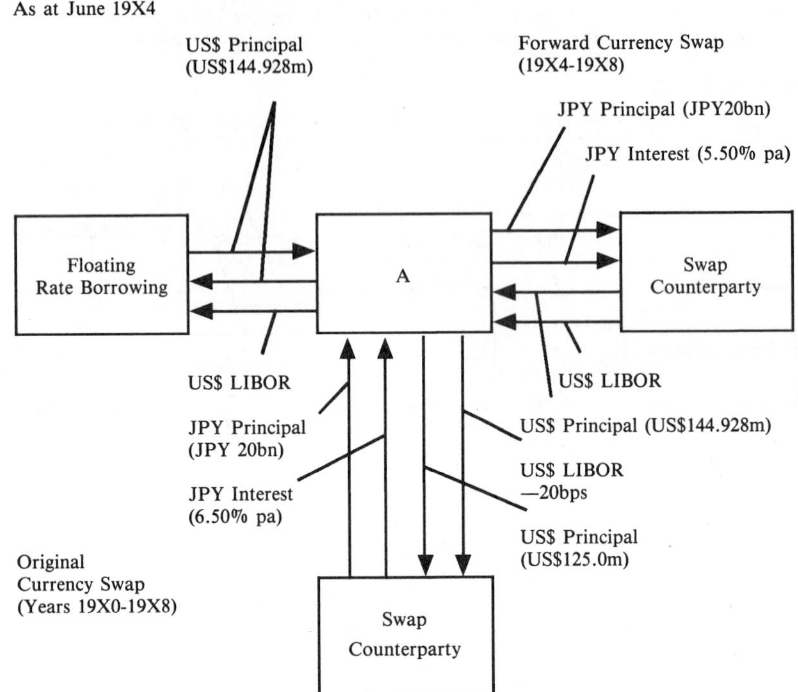

The net result of the transaction is A continues to have a borrowing of US$125m at an interest cost of US$ six month LIBOR minus 20bps.

In addition, it has a series of JPY flows whereby it has a JPY400m outflow (the call premium) as at June 19X4 and a series of JPY200m inflows on June 19X5 to June 19X8 (the difference between the JPY swap rates). These JPY flows if present valued to June 19X2 (at a JPY rate of 5.50% pa for year 19X4 to 19X8 and a rate of 5.35% pa for the year 19X2 to 19X4) is equivalent to JPY271.2m (US$2.009m assuming a spot rate of US$1 = JPY135). This is equivalent to an annuity of US$0.193m over 12 semi-annual periods using a US$ interest rate of 4.50% pa. Based on the borrowing amount of US$125m, this is equivalent to 30.9bps pa.

Consequently, the locked in interest gain on the JPY swaps can be used to lower A's borrowing cost from LIBOR minus 20bps to LIBOR minus 50.9bps.

In the period prior to the call (that is, to June 19X4), A enjoys an additional trading opportunity whereby if JPY interest rates rise, then it may be able to close the forward currency swap and maintain the bond issue and the related swap. The gain or the swap closeout further lowers A's borrowing cost.

Exhibit 12.13—continued

Utilising Forward Currency Swaps to Refund High Coupon Callable Debt

Transaction Cash Flows (m)

	Year	**JPY Bond** Principal	Call Premium	Interest	**Original Currency** Principal	Interest	**Swap-Cash Flows** Principal	Interest	**US$ Borrowing** Principal	Interest	**Forward Currency** Principal	Interest	**Swap-Cash Flows** Principal	Interest	**Net Cash Flows**	
		(JPY m)	(JPY m)	(JPY m)	(US$ m)	(US$ m) *	(JPY m)	(JPY m)	(US$ m)	(US$ m) *	(US$ m)	(US$ m) *	(JPY m)	(JPY m)	(JPY m)	(US$ m)
Entry into Forward Swap	0.0															
	0.5					(2.688)										(2.688)
	1.0			(1,300.0)		(2.688)		1,300.0								(2.688)
	1.5					(2.688)										(2.688)
Forward Swap Commences	2.0	(20,000.0)	(400.0)	(1,300.0)		(2.688)		1,300.0	144.928		(144.928)		20,000.0		(400.0)	(2.688)
	2.5					(2.688)				(3.261)		3.261				(2.688)
	3.0					(2.688)		1,300.0		(3.261)		3.261		(1,100.0)	200.0	(2.688)
	3.5					(2.688)				(3.261)		3.261				(2.688)
	4.0					(2.688)		1,300.0		(3.261)		3.261		(1,100.0)	200.0	(2.688)
	4.5					(2.688)				(3.261)		3.261				(2.688)
	5.0					(2.688)		1,300.0		(3.261)		3.261		(1,100.0)	200.0	(2.688)
	5.5					(2.688)				(3.261)		3.261				(2.688)
Forward Swap Terminates	6.0				(125.000)	(2.688)	20,000.0	1,300.0	(144.928)	(3.261)	144.928	3.261	(20,000.0)	(1,100.0)	200.0	(127.688)

Note: * US$ six month LIBOR is assumed to be 4.500%.

Structurally, forward currency swaps are similar to forward interest rate swaps. Under the terms of the forward currency swap, no payments occur until the forward start date, at which time interest payments start to accrue although all the terms of the swap, including forward start dates, principal amounts, implicit exchange rates, interest rates, payment amounts and payment dates are agreed to at the time of forward currency swap is arranged. Forward currency swaps can be structured as fixed rate to floating rate, fixed rate to fixed rate or floating rate to floating rate, as required. Typically, the basic form of the forward currency swap involves a forward currency swap between a fixed rate in the non US$ currency and floating rate US$ LIBOR.

It should be noted that forward currency swaps are capable of being unbundled into a series of LTFX contracts and a forward interest rate swap in one currency.

For example, consider the case of a borrower seeking to engineer a forward A$ fixed rate against US$ LIBOR floating rate swap where it wishes to pay floating rate US$. The transaction is to commence in two years with a final maturity three years from commencement. The cross-currency forward swap would take place in two stages.

- The borrower would create a three year deferred synthetic US$ liability commencing in two years by entering into a series of LTFX contracts (buying A$ and selling US$) which would convert the A$ cash flows into a synthetic US$ liability. This liability would have a known fixed cost as the US$ outflows to generate the A$ to fully cover the A$ outflows would be known at the outset. This known US$ cost could be translated into a yield or IRR figure which would then form the basis of the second part of the operation.
- The borrower would enter into a three year US$ forward swap commencing in two years to convert the fixed rate US$ liability into floating rate US$.

DEFERRED OR ACCELERATED CASH FLOW

Types of deferred or accelerated cash flow swaps

An important variation on the conventional swap structure, both interest rate and currency, involves swaps with significant changes in the structure of coupons relative to the even coupon cash flow associated with normal transactions.

The major types of deferred or accelerated cash flow swaps include:

- zero coupon swaps;
- deferred coupon swaps;
- deferred coupon FRN swaps;
- premium and discount swaps.

Applications of deferred or accelerated cash flow swaps

The demand for this type of swap structure is driven by three separate influences:

- unusual coupon structures of securities issues;
- taxation factors;
- cash flow considerations.

In recent times, a number of securities issues have been structured with unusual coupon payment patterns. In the extreme, securities which pay no interest until maturity (zero coupon bonds) have been issued. Other variations include graduated coupon bonds as well as high premium or high discount bond structures. These securities have generally been created to satisfy demand from investors seeking protection from reinvestment risks or seeking to take advantage of some particular tax treatment on discounts or premiums.

The *issuers* of these securities have generally, however, sought to be protected from the reinvestment or funding requirement implied by the security structure. This desire on the part of issuers has prompted the development of deferred and accelerated cash flow swaps which are designed to shield the issuer from the cash flow peculiarities of the issue while translating the overall yield advantage achievable through these securities into the desired currency and interest rate basis.

Tax factors have also played an important part in the restructuring of swap cash flows. Such structures involving either the deferral or acceleration of interest receipts or payments have primarily been utilised to influence the tax liabilities of the counterparty.

Tax-driven applications of deferred or accelerated cash flow swaps can be illustrated with the example of a tax loss company (a type of transaction utilised in the late 1980s and early 1990s in Australia). The tax loss company may have available tax credits which are due to expire shortly. In these circumstances, the tax loss company can "refresh" its existing tax losses utilising the swap structure depicted in *Exhibit 12.14*.

Exhibit 12.14
Tax-Driven Accelerated Cash Flow Swap

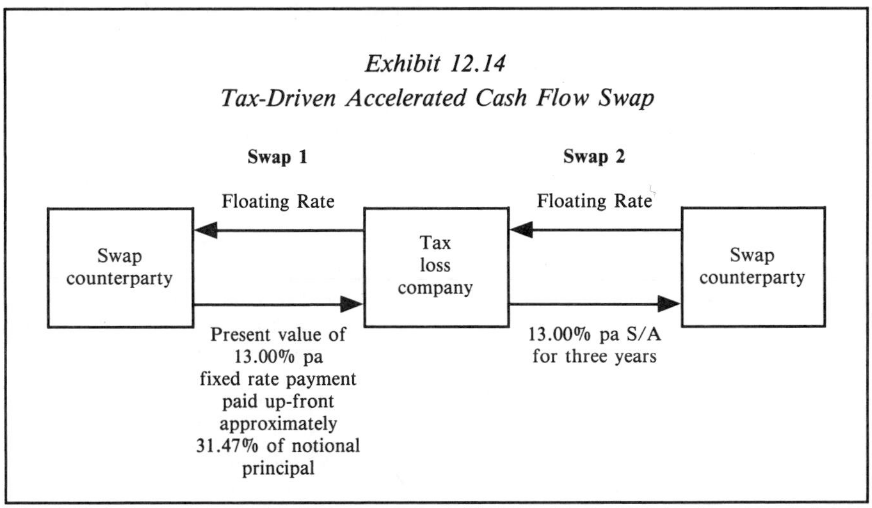

Under the structure, the tax loss company receives, in effect, a lump sum on settlement which is sheltered by tax losses. The company essentially repays this payment by way of the fixed rate payments under the swap over its full maturity. These payments, which are assumed to be deductible, allow the tax loss company to essentially renew its tax losses. Where, for example, the tax loss company hopes to return to profitability and tax paying status in future years, an additional element of tax arbitrage arises from the asymmetric treatment of the lump sum and the fixed rate swap payments which are respectively tax free and tax deductible.

This type of structure requires *sets* of swaps to be undertaken to essentially offset the floating rate exposure otherwise created by the transaction. Alternatively, this floating rate exposure can be notionally hedged against floating rate receipts from day to day investment operations or by hedging the floating rate component utilising futures agreements.

Such tax driven applications of accelerated or deferred cash flow swaps are predicated on the treatment of swap payments on a cash (that is, due and payable) as against an accrual basis. Where taxation on swap payments is on a cash basis, deductions (assessable income) on payments (receipts) arise when the swap payment is incurred. This allows the type of transaction described to be undertaken to manage tax liabilities. The position is less clear for entities deemed to be market makers or traders in swaps, such as financial institutions, including banks. There are widespread differences between the tax treatment of payments under swap agreements, particularly as to timing, across jurisdictions.

Irrespective of any tax impact, the capacity of accelerated and deferred cash flow swaps to generate or conserve cash flow has been a significant factor in their utilisation.

For example, in early 1987, an Australian company Westfield Capital Corporation arranged a funding package to finance its investments in a number of companies including Coles Myer and ACI. As the dividend yields on the investments were well below the interest coupons on the debt financing, Westfield utilised a zero coupon interest rate swap to generate fixed rate funding on which no payment was due until five years in the future. The zero coupon swap deferred the cash outflow, overcoming the problem of the negative spread as between dividend income and interest expense in the short run and was consistent with Westfield's objective of achieving capital growth on its share investments.

Another interesting example of utilising the cash flow patterns of zero coupon swaps relates to currency risk management considerations in cross border leasing.

The use of these structures, motivated, primarily, by currency risk management considerations, represents an excellent example of the utility of zero coupon currency swaps.

During the 1980s, cross-border leasing structures out of Japan were developed. Under these arrangements, Japanese equity investors in leveraged lease transactions purchased capital equipment and leased them to corporations who were non-residents of Japan. The basic rationale for the transaction was the utilisation of the depreciation and other capital allowances available to the Japanese investors as well as the interest deductions, resulting from the debt component of the leveraged lease, to generate a lower effective implicit interest rate yield to the non Japanese lessee. Such transactions were typically pure financing entailing no exposure for the Japanese lessor to the residual value of the asset as it was intended that the lessee would acquire the asset at the end of the transaction or would indemnify the lessor against any financial risk on disposal of the equipment at the end of the lease term.

The lease stream payable by the lessee under such transactions was typically denominated in a currency relevant to the lessee (typically, US$) matching the debt component of the leveraged lease. However, the lease structure required some JPY rentals to be paid, usually towards the maturity of the lease term. Often these JPY payments were structured as effectively the final residual value payment to the lessor.

The JPY payment, typically, created a currency exposure for the lessee. Initially, this exposure was hedged by the lessee placing a deposit (denominated in JPY) at the commencement of the transaction with Japanese financial institutions who would then assume the JPY obligations under the lease (effectively eliminating the cash and currency exposure of the lessee).

The deposit accepting institution in order to hedge their own interest rate exposure under this arrangement then sought to hedge themselves by utilising the following transactions:

- By entering into a JPY interest rate swap whereby it exchanged a stream of periodic payments (usually matching income generated by depositing the JPY on a short term basis earning JPY LIBOR or some other relevant money market rate) in exchange for a receipt of a lump sum at maturity matching the payment to be made under the lease.
- Alternatively, a number of institutions, particularly non Japanese institutions effectively utilised the JPY deposit as a means of generating low cost US$ funding by, simultaneously, entering into a JPY zero/US$ floating LIBOR swap whereby it received the JPY zero amount (required to service its commitment under the lease) while paying floating rate US$ LIBOR (usually at a margin under LIBOR).

As the lessees grew in sophistication, a number of them bypassed the deposit process and entered into the zero JPY/US$ LIBOR swap directly. This allowed the lessees to insulate itself from any currency exposure as the zero JPY amount received under the currency swap at maturity effectively matched the cash outflow under the lease payments.

Pricing of deferred or accelerated cash flow swaps

These structural departures from conventional interest rate or currency swaps effectively require the swap provider to either assume reinvestment risks or alternatively to fund payments to the swap counterparty which are then recovered over the life of the swap. The latter type of transaction can be equated to a loan transaction by a swap provider to the party entering into the swap. The pricing of these deferred and accelerated cash flow swaps reflects the assumptions as to reinvestment rates and funding costs.

The simplest way of pricing a zero coupon swap is to utilise the forward rates implicit in the prevailing yield curve. Under this approach, intermediate cash flows under the swap are reinvested at these forward rates, which, theoretically are unbiased estimators of expected forward rates. An example of this technique is set out in *Exhibit 12.15*. An additional example is set out in *Exhibit 12.16*.

Exhibit 12.15

Pricing a Zero Coupon Swap

Assume that the three year US$ interest rate swap market is priced at 14.85/14.95% pa (S/A) versus six month LIBOR. Bank A (A) is requested to quote on a US$10m zero coupon swap where it pays the fixed rate.

The swap is to be priced on the basis of the implicit forward reinvestment rates in the swap curve which are as follows:

Maturity	Interest rates (% pa S/A)	Forward rates (% pa S/A)
0.5	15.25	14.75
1.0	15.00	13.50
1.5	14.50	12.51
2.0	14.00	14.75
2.5	14.15	14.75
3.0	14.25	—

Exhibit 12.15—continued

These forward rates are then used to reinvest the cash flows to determine the zero coupon swap pricing:

Maturity	Fixed rate swap flow	Interest at forward rate	Accumulated balance
0.5	0.7425	—	0.7425
1.0	0.7425	0.0548	1.5398
1.5	0.7425	0.1039	2.3862
2.0	0.7425	0.1493	3.2779
2.5	0.7425	0.2417	4.2622
3.0	0.7425	0.3143	5.3190

This equates to a compounded swap rate on the zero swap rate of 14.73% pa (S/A) as against 14.85% pa (S/A) for a conventional swap (a cash difference of US$0.050m).

Exhibit 12.16

Pricing a Zero Coupon Swap: Example

Par Coupon Swap Rate: 8.740%

Zero Coupon Swap Rate: 8.497%

Date	Days	Periods (S/A)	Rate (pa S/A)	Forward Rate	Par Swap Coupons	Coupon Interest	Compounding Balance
01-Jul-19X2		0					
01-Jan-19X3	184	1.01	7.600%	7.471%	4.406		4.406
01-Jul-19X3	365	2.00	7.500%	8.803%	4.334	0.163	8.903
01-Jan-19X4	549	3.01	7.850%	8.477%	4.406	0.395	13.704
01-Jul-19X4	730	4.00	7.980%	8.574%	4.334	0.576	18.614
01-Jan-19X5	914	5.01	8.050%	8.767%	4.406	0.805	23.825
01-Jul-19X5	1095	6.00	8.150%	9.266%	4.334	1.036	29.195
01-Jan-19X6	1279	7.01	8.270%	8.608%	4.406	1.364	34.964
01-Jul-19X6	1461	8.01	8.290%	10.076%	4.358	1.501	40.823
01-Jan-19X7	1645	9.01	8.450%	11.617%	4.406	2.074	47.303
01-Jul-19X7	1826	10.01	8.740%		4.334		51.637
					43.724	7.913	

This type of pricing does not of course guarantee that the predicted return on the transaction is realised because the actual reinvestment rates achieved may differ substantially from the prevailing forward rates at the time the transaction was entered into. The risk can be sought to be managed in a number of ways:

- utilising pricing adjustments whereby conservative reinvestment rates or high borrowing rates are assumed;

- neutralising reinvestment risks by entering into hedging transactions and locking in the required maturity value. This may entail entering into, for example, forward rate agreements or forward swaps against the exposure created by the accelerated or deferred cash flow swap.

Some of the structures in respect of these transactions discussed in detail below seek to minimise the swap provider's exposure to these risks.

The utilisation of forward swaps to neutralise reinvestment risk in hedging a zero coupon swap structure requires additional comment. Such a structure may be devised as follows:

- The arrangement is predicated on the fact that the zero coupon swap is hedged (as described in *Exhibit 12.15*) with a normal coupon interest rate swap of equivalent maturity.
- The coupon inflows represent a cash surplus which is then invested in short term floating rate securities (such as US$ LIBOR Eurodollar deposits).
- In order to hedge the interest rate exposure on these deposits, it would be necessary to enter into a *series* of forward swaps whereby the party seeking to hedge itself would be receiving fixed rate and paying floating rate (corresponding to its floating rate earnings on its short term investments).
- The principal amount of the forward swap would be increasing reflecting the build up in cash flow from the receipt of coupons under the normal par interest rate swap. This would be covered by either entering into an accreting forward swap (essentially a reverse amortisation structure) or by entering into a *series* of forward swaps of decreasing life but increasing period to commencement.

Alternatively, a series of FRAs on an increasing principal (representing the investment of the coupons and accumulated interest on the coupons) could be utilised to guarantee the investment return and eliminate any reinvestment risk.

The hedging structures outlined above effectively seek to replicate a zero coupon swap rate for the relevant maturity. Consequently, the zero coupon swap, itself, may be priced utilising the zero coupon swap yield curve. However, in order to neutralise reinvestment or borrowing rate risks entailed in assuming such a structure, the party providing such a swap would enter into the arrangements described above to insulate itself from the interest rate risk.

The complex structure of such transactions means that pricing a reversal of the zero coupon swap entails certain special considerations. *Exhibit 12.17* sets out an example of pricing a zero coupon swap reversal which highlights the technical complexities of pricing such a transaction.

Exhibit 12.17

Pricing a Zero Coupon Swap Reversal

Assume Investor A entered into a zero coupon swap whereby it paid US$ six month LIBOR semi-annually in return for receiving a zero coupon GBP amount at maturity. The basic term of this swap is:

Commencement Date:	1 February 19X0
Termination Date:	1 February 19Y0
US$ Amount:	US$62,464,251
GBP Amount:	GBP37,972,189
Exchange Rate:	GBP1.00 = 1.6450

Exhibit 12.17—continued

Cash Flows:

1. Initial: At commencement date, A receives the US$ amount from the counterparty and pays the GBP amount to the counterparty.
2. Interest: On every 1 February and 1 August commencing 1 August 19X0 and up to and including the termination date, A pays US$ six month LIBOR on US$ amount.
3. Final: At termination date, A pays the US$ amount to the counterparty and receives the following GBP amounts:
   —the GBP amount;
   —a fixed payment of GBP (being compounded interest on the GBP amount at an interest rate of 10.1675% pa).

The swap has a special feature in respect of the floating rate US$ LIBOR payments whereby the interest on the principal amount is to be compounded at the relevant US$ six month LIBOR rate and only paid to the swap counterparty at maturity. This provision, which is quite common in zero coupon swaps, is designed to reduce the credit risk on the transaction for A.

Assume that A wishes to unwind this swap effective 15 June 19X2. The prevailing market rates as at the date are:

GBP1 = US$1.6800

US$ LIBOR (to 1 August 19X2) = 4.5625

GBP Swap Yield Curve:

Maturity (years)	Par Swap Yield (% pa)	Zero Coupon Rates (%)
0.5	7.07	7.0700
1.0	7.57	7.5795
2.0	8.21	8.2456
3.0	9.08	9.1947
4.0	9.12	9.2126
5.0	9.16	9.2430
6.0	9.40	9.5389
7.0	9.64	9.8501
8.0	9.65	9.8433
9.0	9.67	9.8428
10.0	9.68	9.8469

The zero coupon swap rate (using the forward rates inherent in the above yield curve as the relevant re-investment rate) is set out below:

Pricing Zero Coupon Swap

Par Coupon Swap Rate: 9.660%

Zero Coupon Swap Rate: 9.823%

Date	Days	Periods (S/A)	Rate (pa S/A)	Forward Rate	Par Swap Coupons	Coupon Interest	Compounding Balance
15-Jun-19X2		0					
15-Dec-19X2	183	1.00	7.070%	1.555%	4.843		4.843
01-Feb-19X3	231	1.27	7.570%	5.190%	1.270	0.010	6.123
01-Aug-19X3	412	2.26	7.890%	9.206%	4.790	0.158	11.071
01-Feb-19X4	596	3.27	8.210%	10.271%	4.870	0.514	16.455
01-Aug-19X4	777	4.26	8.650%	11.300%	4.790	0.838	22.083
01-Feb-19X5	961	5.27	9.080%	9.337%	4.870	1.258	28.211
01-Aug-19X5	1142	6.26	9.100%	9.539%	4.790	1.306	34.308
01-Feb-19X6	1326	7.27	9.120%	9.501%	4.870	1.650	40.827
01-Aug-19X6	1508	8.26	9.140%	9.651%	4.817	1.934	47.578
01-Feb-19X7	1692	9.27	9.160%	10.584%	4.870	2.315	54.762
01-Aug-19X7	1873	10.26	9.280%	11.002%	4.790	2.874	62.427
01-Feb-19X8	2057	11.27	9.400%	12.659%	4.870	3.462	70.759
01-Aug-19X8	2238	12.26	9.640%	10.097%	4.790	4.442	79.991
01-Feb-19X9	2422	13.27	9.650%	9.798%	4.870	4.071	88.932
01-Aug-19X9	2603	14.26	9.650%	10.128%	4.790	4.321	98.043
01-Feb-20Y0	2787	15.27	9.660%	10.064%	4.870	5.006	107.919
01-Aug-20Y0	2969	16.27	9.670%		4.817	5.416	118.151
				Total	78.577	39.575	

Utilising the calculated zero coupon swap rate of 9.823% pa, the swap can be revalued as follows:

Exhibit 12.17—continued

Reversal of GBP Zero Fixed to US$ Floating Currency Swap

A Pays US$ Floating
Receives GBP Zero Fixed

Amount (US$)	62,464,251
Deal Date	01-Feb-19X0
Start/LIBOR Set Date	01-Feb-19X2
Maturity	01-Feb-20Y0
Unwind Date	15-Jun-19X2
Exch Rate (GBP1 = US$)	
Swap Rate	1.6450
Current	1.6800
Original Amount (GBP):	37,972,189
Current Amount (GBP):	37,181,102

US$ Interest Rates	Original	Current
LIBOR (% SA)	4.2500%	4.5625%
Margin (% SA)	0.0000%	0.0000%

GBP Interest Rates	Original	Current
Swap Rate (% SA)	9.9214%	9.8230%
Swap Rate (% A)	10.1675%	10.0642%

Current Swap Valuation (US$)—Par Yield	$18,317,809
Current Swap Valuation (US$)—Zero Rate	$18,290,767

Exhibit 12.17—continued

Date	Days to Cash Flows	Semi-Annual Tenor	Adjusted S/A Tenor	Adjusted Annual Tenor	US$ Payments (Semi-Annual): US$ Zero Rates	US$ Payments (Semi-Annual): Principal	US$ Payments (Semi-Annual): Interest (Original)	US$ Payments (Semi-Annual): Total	Offsetting Swap (Receive): Total	Difference	NPV @ 4.5625% (Current)	NPV @ Zero Rates
01-Feb-19X2	0	0.00										
15-Jun-19X2	135	0.74	0.00	0.00	0.00%							
01-Aug-19X2	182	1.00	0.26	0.13	4.56%		(1,323,729)	(1,323,729)	366,977	(956,751)	(951,210)	(951,210)
01-Feb-19X3	366	2.01	1.27	0.63	0.00%		0	0	0	0	0	0
01-Aug-19X3	547	3.00	2.26	1.13	0.00%		0	0	0	0	0	0
01-Feb-19X4	731	4.01	3.27	1.63	0.00%		0	0	0	0	0	0
01-Aug-19X4	912	5.00	4.26	2.13	0.00%		0	0	0	0	0	0
01-Feb-19X5	1096	6.01	5.27	2.63	0.00%		0	0	0	0	0	0
01-Aug-19X5	1277	7.00	6.26	3.13	0.00%		0	0	0	0	0	0
01-Feb-19X6	1461	8.01	7.27	3.63	0.00%		0	0	0	0	0	0
01-Aug-19X6	1643	9.00	8.26	4.13	0.00%		0	0	0	0	0	0
01-Feb-19X7	1827	10.01	9.27	4.64	0.00%		0	0	0	0	0	0
01-Aug-19X7	2008	11.00	10.26	5.13	0.00%		0	0	0	0	0	0
01-Feb-19X8	2192	12.01	11.27	5.64	0.00%		0	0	0	0	0	0
01-Aug-19X8	2373	13.00	12.26	6.13	0.00%		0	0	0	0	0	0
01-Feb-19X9	2557	14.01	13.27	6.64	0.00%		0	0	0	0	0	0
01-Aug-19X9	2738	15.00	14.26	7.13	0.00%		0	0	0	0	0	0
01-Feb-20Y0	2922	16.01	15.27	7.64	0.00%	(62,464,251)	0	(62,464,251)	62,464,251	0	0	0
								Total US$			($951,210)	($951,210)

Exhibit 12.17—continued

Date	Days to Cash Flows	Semi-Annual Tenor	Adjusted S/A Tenor	Adjusted Annual Tenor	GBP Receipts (Zero Coupon Annual)				Offsetting Swap (Pay)	Difference	NPV @ 9.8230% (Current)	NPV @ Zero Rates
					GBP Zero Rates	Principal	Interest (Original)	Total	Total			
01-Feb-19X2	0	0.00										
15-Jun-19X2	135	0.74										
01-Aug-19X2	182	1.00	0.26	0.13	7.07%		0	0	0	0	0	0
01-Feb-19X3	366	2.01	1.27	0.63	7.58%		0	0	0	0	0	0
01-Aug-19X3	547	3.00	2.26	1.13	7.91%		0	0	0	0	0	0
01-Feb-19X4	731	4.01	3.27	1.63	8.25%		0	0	0	0	0	0
01-Aug-19X4	912	5.00	4.26	2.13	8.71%		0	0	0	0	0	0
01-Feb-19X5	1096	6.01	5.27	2.63	9.19%		0	0	0	0	0	0
01-Aug-19X5	1277	7.00	6.26	3.13	9.20%		0	0	0	0	0	0
01-Feb-19X6	1461	8.01	7.27	3.63	9.21%		0	0	0	0	0	0
01-Aug-19X6	1643	9.00	8.26	4.13	9.23%		0	0	0	0	0	0
01-Feb-19X7	1827	10.01	9.27	4.64	9.24%		0	0	0	0	0	0
01-Aug-19X7	2008	11.00	10.26	5.13	9.39%		0	0	0	0	0	0
01-Feb-19X8	2192	12.01	11.27	5.64	9.54%		0	0	0	0	0	0
01-Aug-19X8	2373	13.00	12.26	6.13	9.69%		0	0	0	0	0	0
01-Feb-19X9	2557	14.01	13.27	6.64	9.85%		0	0	0	0	0	0
01-Aug-19X9	2738	15.00	14.26	7.13	9.85%		0	0	0	0	0	0
01-Feb-20Y0	2922	16.01	15.27	7.64	9.84%	37,972,189	62,027,811	100,000,000	(77,324,409)	22,675,591	10,903,458	10,887,361
								Total GBP			10,903,458	10,887,361
								Total US$			18,317,809	18,290,767

Exhibit 12.17—continued

The analysis indicates that A would receive a cash payment of approximately US$18.3m to cancel the swap at the assumed rates.

In addition to the above, A would have to pay to the swap counterparty the accumulated floating rate interest (which has been compounded but not paid). This is calculated as follows:

Date	Days to Cash Flows	S/A Tenor	US$ LIBOR	US$ Principal	US$ Interest	Cumulative Balance
01-Feb-19X0	0	0.00	6.125%	62,464,251		62,464,251
01-Aug-19X0	181	0.99	5.750%		1,897,245	64,361,496
01-Feb-19X1	365	2.00	5.375%		1,865,602	66,227,097
01-Aug-19X1	546	2.99	4.875%		1,765,224	67,992,322
01-Feb-19X2	730	4.00			1,670,935	69,663,256
			Total		7,199,005	
			Accumulated Surplus Interest (US$)			7,199,005

This amount of US$7.2m would need to be paid to the swap counterparty on termination.

The "gain" on the reversal of the zero swap is somewhat misleading as it must be offset against the accrual of the discount foregone as a result of the cancellation of the swap:

	US$
Forgone Accrual [calculated as GBP37,972,189 at the original rate of 10.1675% pa for 2.26 year =GBP9,289,205 translated at GBP1=US$1.68]	15,605,865
Swap Gain (using Zero Coupon Rate)	18,290,767
Real Economic Gain	2,684,902

While the focus hitherto has been largely on interest rate swaps, the methodology in respect of currency swaps is identical. This reflects the fact that accelerated or deferred cash flow structures affect the coupons *in each currency*. Consequently, the currency basis of the transaction is not strictly speaking affected by the manipulation of the coupon flow. However, once a zero coupon swap rate has been established for the particular currency, it is still necessary to translate that into the specific cash flows of the transaction. An example of the pricing of a zero coupon currency swap is set out in *Exhibit 12.18*.

It should be noted that a zero coupon swap, as noted above, is structurally identical to an LTFX contract.

Zero coupon swaps

Under certain conditions in the 1980s, yields on zero coupon Eurodollar bonds were significantly lower than full coupon conventional bonds because of strong demand by foreign investors wanting to, for example, lock in relatively high yielding US$ interest rates (avoiding the reinvestment rate risk implicit in a normal coupon paid bond or take advantage of favourable tax treatment of the discount).

For example, in August 1984, a prime quality borrower would have been able to issue a ten year Eurodollar bond at an all-in cost of 30bps pa over a comparable United States treasury bond and swapped the fixed debt for floating debt at 55bps over a comparable United States treasury bond resulting in a cost of 25bps under LIBOR. The same company could have issued a ten year Eurodollar zero coupon bond at an all-in cost of at least 60bps pa *below* a comparable United States treasury. This significant saving on issuing yield on a zero coupon bond was available for swap transactions but required a special structure constructed to match the cash flow characteristics of a zero coupon security.

Exhibit 12.18

Pricing Zero Coupon NZ$ Issue and Cross-Currency Swap

Assume that the five year zero swap rate for fixed NZ$ and US$ LIBOR is 16.50% pa (A) versus six month LIBOR flat.

Also assume that the current spot exchange rate is NZ$1/US$0.58. For a NZ$ zero coupon issue with face value of NZ$100 with a maturity of five years yielding 16.50% pa (A), the current price of the issue would be NZ$46.598 giving net proceeds of US$27.027.

All-in issue pricing would be as follows:

Net proceeds:	US$27.0270m	= NZ$46.5983m
Reserve fund to generate sub-LIBOR margin:[1]	US$ 0.2698m	= NZ$ 0.4651m
Expense (US$125,000):	US$ 0.1250m	= NZ$ 0.2155m
Issue fees:		= NZ$ 0.6591m
Total:		= NZ$47.9380m
Swap fee:	US$ 0.500m	= NZ$ 0.8621m
		NZ$48.8001m

The gross proceeds required for the issue is therefore NZ$48.8001.

This translates into an issue yield of 15.43% pa (A) for a five year NZ$100 issue.

Note:

1. Based on sub-LIBOR margin of 25bps which equates to US$67,568 pa (0.25% of US$27.027). This is then discounted at 8.00% pa (A) (the current US$ interest rate) for five years to produce a present value amount of US$0.2698m.

Two possible types of zero coupon interest rate swap structures are outlined in *Exhibit 12.19* and *Exhibit 12.20*. Both transactions are designed to enable a borrower to issue zero coupon bonds and to enter into swaps such that the borrower's net cash flow is largely identical to that it would have had if it had instead issued a low cost coupon paid floating rate instrument.

The transaction outlined in *Exhibit 12.19* entails the borrower issuing a zero coupon Eurobond, for example, a ten year issue, net proceeds of US$50m, and a face value of US$135.7m which implies an interest rate of 10.50% pa on an annual basis. This issue is then swapped in two stages entailing two distinct transactions:

- *Transaction A*—Whereby the issuer enters into a conventional interest rate swap (with counterparty A) based on a notional principal amount of US$50m for a term of ten years under which the issuer pays floating rate interest at a margin under LIBOR while it receives fixed rate interest payments annually at a rate of 10.60% pa.
- *Transaction B*—Whereby the issuer reinvests the fixed interest rate payments received under the interest rate swap to guarantee a maturity value equal to the face value of the bonds to meet the repayment obligations to bond holders at maturity. Transaction B effects this as follows: the required maturity value is generated by the issuer entering into a commitment to deposit each fixed rate

Exhibit 12.19
Zero Coupon Interest Rate Swap Structure (1)

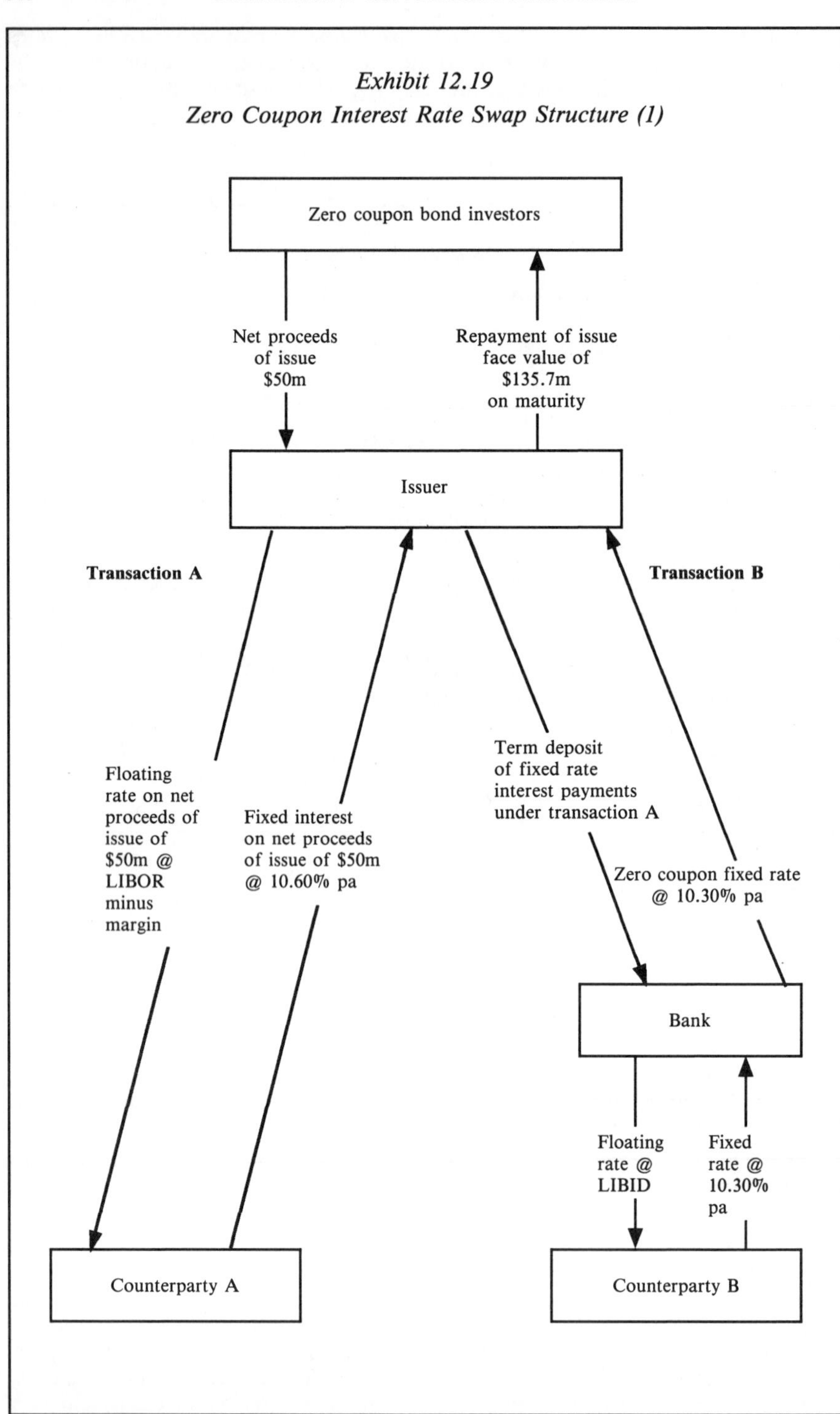

interest receipt under the swap with a bank. The bank in turn enters into an interest rate swap (with counterparty B) to fix the yield on the floating rate deposit. The size of the deposit increases and the corresponding notional principal under the swap increases over the term of the transaction. The swap with counterparty B enables the bank to guarantee the issuer a fixed rate on its deposits which continue to roll forward until the final maturity of the bond.

Exhibit 12.20 sets out an alternative structure.

Exhibit 12.20

Zero Coupon Interest Rate Swap Structure (2)

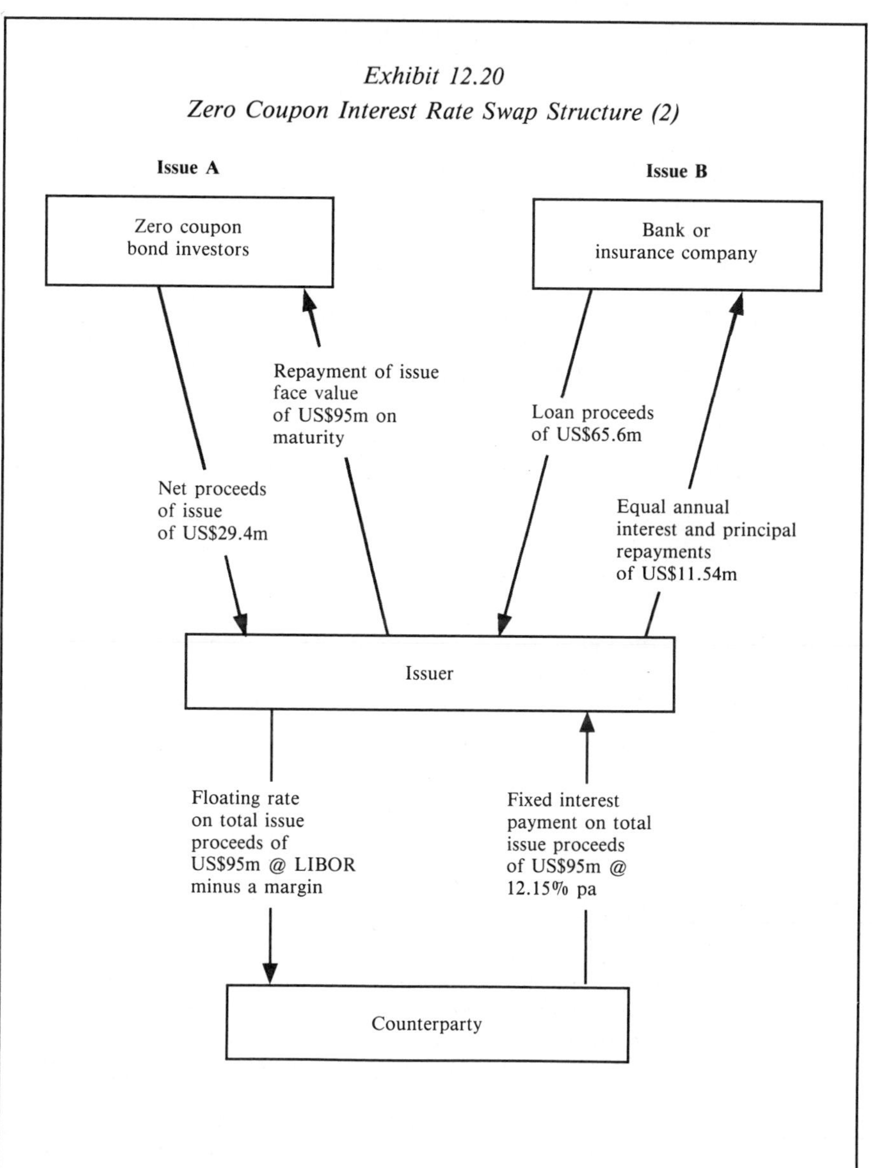

The transaction entails two separate issues:

- *Issue A*—An issue (usually public) of zero coupon Eurobonds, for example, ten year, net proceeds of $29.4m (after fees), and a face value of US$95m which implies an interest rate of 12.44% pa on an annual basis.
- *Issue B*—An annuity loan (usually arranged as a private placement) whereby the amount of the loan is repaid at the end of each year until maturity by equal level repayments composed of interest and annual redemption of principal, for example, a ten year loan for US$65.6m repayable by annual instalments of net US$11.54m which equates to an interest rate of 11.85% pa on an annual basis.

The overall package provides the issuer with total net proceeds of US$95m (net proceeds US$29.4m from the zero coupon Eurobond issue and net proceeds of US$65.6m from the annuity loan), an annual commitment for nine successive years to make payments of US$11.54m (corresponding to the interest and principal repayments under the annuity loan) and a final repayment of US$106.54m after ten years (equalling the repayment of the US$95m face value of the zero coupon issue and the final US$11.54m instalment of the annuity loan). The overall package implies a net interest cost to the issuer of 12.15% pa on an annual basis.

The issuer then undertakes a conventional interest rate swap transaction with a counterparty to the effect that the counterparty pays the issuer, on each annual interest date, US$11.54m corresonding to the instalments under the loan annuity and the issuer pays the counterparty every six months an amount equivalent to six months interest on the aggregated net proceeds of the two issues (US$95m), at a rate equalling LIBOR minus a margin.

An example of a zero coupon currency swap is set out in *Exhibit 12.21*. The transaction depicted is an A$200m zero coupon A$ Eurobond issue and associated currency swap and LTFX transaction undertaken by Eastman Kodak Company in early 1987. The transaction is particularly interesting in that it entailed two separate swap transactions to convert the issuer's A$ zero coupon exposure into fixed rate US$. Part of the issue proceeds were hedged into A$ utilising LTFX contracts.

The difficulty in creating the zero coupon swaps lies both in the reinvestment risk for the fixed rate payer and in the credit exposure which the floating rate payer has on the fixed rate payer, since no fixed payment is received until maturity. Some banks with large balance sheets avoid the reinvestment risk by ignoring the cash flow issues and by using duration analysis to determine the appropriate maturity for an offsetting conventional swap. In order to minimise the credit exposure of the floating rate payer, in some instances trust vehicles were established into which the floating rate payments would be made. The floating payments would then be held over time with interest accruing until the maturity of the swap.

Deferred coupon bond swaps

Deferred coupon bond swaps are architecturally similar to zero coupon swaps. Deferred coupon bonds entail the issue of a security with, say, maturity of seven years with a coupon of 8.00%. The issue structure requires a payment of the coupon for the first four years at the end of that period as a rolled up lump sum of 32.00% of the principal value of the bond with level 8.00% coupon payments thereafter. Designed to circumvent regulations against the purchase of zero coupon securities by Japanese investors, deferred coupon bonds had similar cash flow characteristics to zeros, at least for the first part of its life, and the swap structures utilised were largely similar to those utilised with zero coupon bonds.

Exhibit 12.21
Zero Currency Swap Structure

Initial exchange

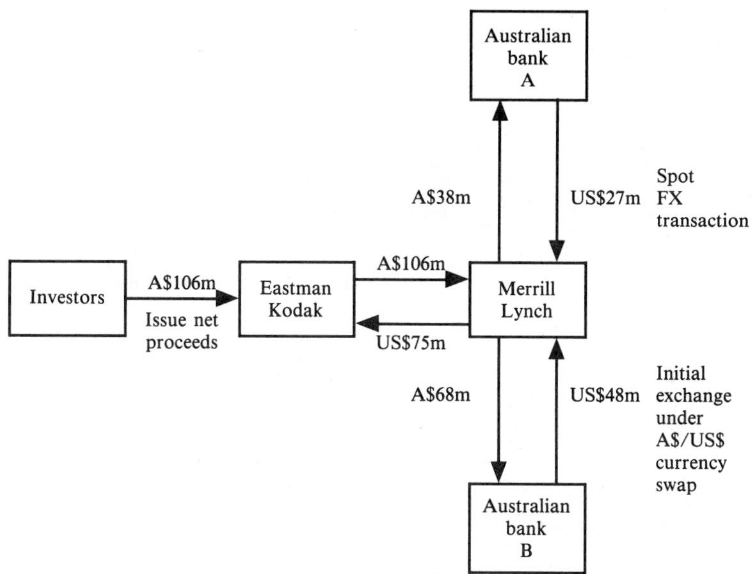

Exchange rate is US$0.7075/A$1.00.

Interest payments

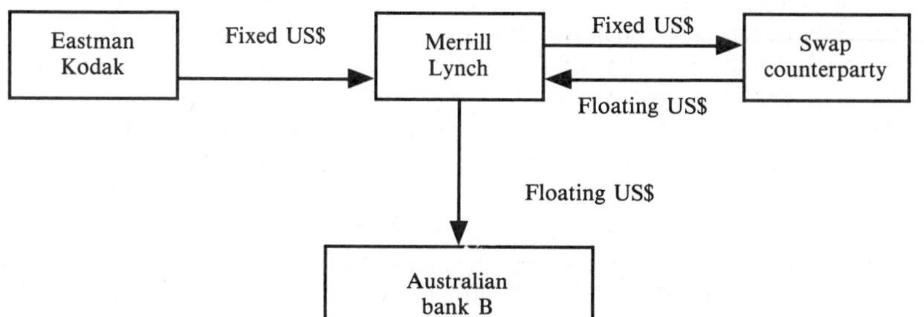

Exhibit 12.21—continued

Final exchange

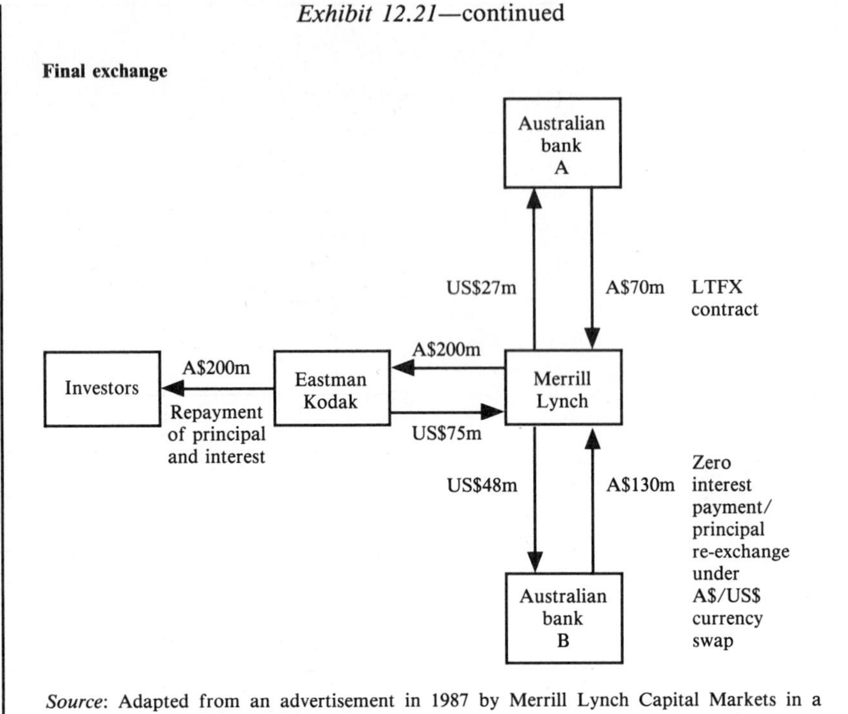

Source: Adapted from an advertisement in 1987 by Merrill Lynch Capital Markets in a number of financial journals.

Deferred coupon FRN bond swaps

Deferred coupon FRN structures emerged in early 1986. Typical issues had a maturity of approximately five years. The coupon structure required that the issuer made no coupon payment for the first two years but paid a relatively high margin of, say 4.50% over six month LIBOR for years three to five. The security issues were tailor-made for Japanese investors presumably seeking to defer income into future periods.

The issuers, however, sought to use the deferred coupon FRNs as the basis of swaps to obtain sub-LIBOR funding. The swap structure is complex but entails the swap provider covering the cash flows under the security issue in return for receiving a substantial margin under LIBOR throughout the five years. Under the structure, the swap provider has a positive cash flow initially followed by a negative cash flow. This cash surplus which turns into a deficiency presents the swap provider with a reinvestment risk. This risk can be partially managed, potentially, by utilising the positive cash flow in years one and two to purchase zero coupon securities maturing in the later period so as to service the 4.50% spread.

A variation on the deferred coupon FRN structure is the high initial spread FRN which reverses the cash flow pattern with large payments in the early years and absent or very low payments in the distant years. These transactions were similarly swapped but provided the opposite problem for the swap provider in that it required it to fund large payments in the early years which were recovered in the latter half of the transaction.

Premium or discount swaps

Premium or discount swaps entail either an up-front payment by the swap provider in return for higher running coupon payments or its reverse, that is, swaps entailing an up-front payment to the swap provider in return for lower subsequent swap payments. The basic rationale for such transactions is the acceleration or deferral of interest payment for cash flow or tax advantages.

An example of an off-market swap is set out in *Exhibit 12.22*. See also discussion on discount and premium swap structures in Chapter 8.

Exhibit 12.22

Structuring an Off-Market Interest Rate Swap

Assume current markets for five year US$ interest rate swaps are 13.25/13.35% pa (A). A borrower (B) wishes to transact an interest rate swap where it pays fixed rate of 15.00% pa (A) on US$25m for five years.

The value of the 15.00% pa swap at current market rates is as follows:

Period (years)	Generic swap flows (US$m)	Off-market swap flows (US$m)	Difference (A$m)
0	+25.00	+25.00	—
1	− 3.338	− 3.75	0.413
2	− 3.338	− 3.75	0.413
3	− 3.338	− 3.75	0.413
4	− 3.338	− 3.75	0.413
5	−28.338	−28.75	0.413

Utilising the offered swap rate (13.35% pa) as the relevant discount rate, the off-market swap is valued at US$26.439 which implies a payment of US$1.439m *to* B. This can be arrived at by discounting back the difference @ 13.35% pa *or* discounting back the off-market swap flows @ 13.35% pa and subtracting the value of a generic swap (US$25m).

As the swap counterparty is essentially lending B the up-front payment to be recovered via the higher than market swap payments, a higher discount rate may be appropriate. A discount rate of 14.35% pa (the offered swap rate plus 1.00% pa) reduces the up-front payment to US$0.553m.

MISCELLANEOUS SWAP STRUCTURES

The extraordinary flexibility of swap structures have made them relevant to a wide variety of new issue structures. A particular example of this was an issue by Halifax Building Society undertaken in May 1987. At that time, the best interest rate swaps in GBP were available in three year maturities. But the Bank of England did not allow Eurosterling issues with maturities of less than five years. Consequently, Halifax Building Society issued GBP50m of debt based on a fixed coupon for the first three years and a variable rate over LIBOR for the remaining two years. The building society which was seeking floating rate funding then swapped the first three year fixed rate coupon to floating. The three year swap was extremely attractive and allowed Halifax to swap into floating rate funding at a sufficient margin under LIBOR to generate sub-LIBOR funding for the whole five year life of the transaction.

As is evident from the inherent structure of interest rate and currency swaps, such transactions have a clearly identified maturity. Increasingly, swap transactions are utilised to manage asset and liabilities with uncertain maturities (such as mortgage-backed and asset-backed securities). The swap structures entailed typically involve options on swaps and are described in detail in Chapter 14. However, such structures involve securities with a known *range of final maturities*.

In 1987, Redland Capital, a subsidiary of the UK Building Group Redland, undertook a swap against a *convertible issue* by the company. The equity option inherent in the convertible bond means that the debt element of the convertible may be extinguished at any time during the relevant conversion period. However, Redland undertook a swap, albeit for the first five years of the 15 year life of the convertible, from GBP into US$. This was undertaken utilising a number of transactions:

- Redland undertook the currency swap against a GBP60m 15 year convertible issue.
- Redland also had an existing GBP60m (face value) zero coupon bond issue maturing in five years time.
- The swap from fixed rate GBP into fixed rate US$ was undertaken on a notional principal of GBP60m for a maturity of five years.

Existence of these various liabilities allowed Redland to manage the risk of conversion on the convertible issue. For example, in the event that conversion took place thereby extinguishing the debt component against which the swap is notionally undertaken, the GBP principal amount received at the end of the currency swap can be utilised to repay the existing zero coupon bond issue.

Redland argued that the transaction, while not riskless had limited exposure for the company as, to some extent, it is able to control the timing of conversion by adjusting dividends on its equity or forcing conversion by calling the bonds or increasing the dividend.

The major advantage to Redland of undertaking this swap against the convertible was to allow it to create a US$ liability to match existing US$ assets and income and to benefit from the substantial interest rate differential between GBP and US$ interest rate that existed at that time.

In 1993, Kreditanstalt Fuer Weideraufbrau (KFW) undertook a particularly interesting swap. KFW issued US$500m of five year bonds and entered into a series of swaps designed to get US$200m of the issue as ten year funds. The swaps, undertaken with Deutsche Bank, were as follows:

- KFW swapped US$200m of the issue paying US$ LIBOR against receipt of fixed rates covering the fixed interest cost of the bond.
- KFW entered into a swap where it pays fixed US$ rates for ten years against receipt of US$ LIBOR on US$200m.
- KFW entered into a deferred rate setting for US$200m of the proceed at 18bps over US treasuries. This is akin to a spreadlock and the deferred rate setting transaction used by the World Bank and effectively allows KFW to lock into a fixed rate liability of its choice before the expiration of the rate setting period.
- US$100m of the issue was left in fixed rate US$.

The first two swaps in combination allowed KFW to lock in ten year fixed rates (at below current ten year swap rates). KFW will have to refinance US$200m of the bonds at maturity. KFW's cost of finance is fixed as long as it refinances at US$ LIBOR flat; any improvement in its funding cost under LIBOR will improve its cost of funds.

The transaction achieved KFW's objective of ten year financing at a time when market conditions would have made a ten year issue expensive for the German State guaranteed agency.

MISCELLANEOUS VARIATIONS ON BASIC SWAP STRUCTURES

An interesting variation on basic swap structures focuses on the mechanism by which swap transactions are executed. Conventionally swaps are executed either directly with a counterparty, inevitably a financial institution or through the medium of an arranger or a broker who procures a counterparty. In recent years a number of innovative arrangements have been developed to arrange swap transactions reflecting, primarily, the size and complexity of the particular entities swap requirements.

Innovations in the area of swap execution commenced in 1984 when Morgan Grenfell arranged a US$50m Euronote facility for the Export Finance and Insurance Corporation of Australia. The facility included a tender panel which allowed members to bid for the right to swap the floating rate debt raised by the notes into fixed rate funding.

Subsequently, the Export Credit Guarantee Department in the United Kingdom and Grand Metropolitan, both of whom were faced with very large swap programmes, utilised a swap arranger to put together swap programmes with a number of counterparties.

The Grand Metropolitan transaction illustrates the basic concept. The company was faced with the need to put a programme of US$ interest rate swaps totalling US$750m. In order to avoid the administrative complexity of dealing with separate counterparties, given certain timing constraints, Grand Metropolitan appointed SG Warburg a United Kingdom investment bank, to arrange the programme. The structure of the Grand Metropolitan swap tender panel is set out in *Exhibit 12.23*.

SG Warburg were also instrumental in developing the revolving swap facility. In this case, the transaction was arranged for Booker, the international food distribution and health products business company, which had an ongoing need to convert US$ assets into GBP. The structure of the revolving currency swap facility is set out in *Exhibit 12.24*. In late 1987, the Mass Transit Railway Corporation of Hong Kong arranged a similar revolving currency swap facility to convert liabilities from a variety of other currencies into Hong Kong dollars.

In late 1989, SG Warburg were prominent in arranging swap programmes totalling approximately GBP2,500m for two highly leveraged transactions in the UK—Magnet and Isosceles. In each case, to avoid the risk of adverse market movements in GBP swap rates, SG Warburg acted as a *arranger* of the required swaps for and on behalf of the borrowers. In this case, rather than utilising a swap tender panel structure, SG Warburg directly sourced swap counterparties by arranging receivers of GBP fixed rates in the new issue market, either through public bond issues or private placements, taking advantage of buoyant market conditions in GBP. In this way, by creating a natural demand for the receipt of fixed rate GBP in the new issue market, SG Warburg was able to reduce the potential impact on GBP swap rates as a result of these transactions.

Exhibit 12.23

Grand Metropolitan Swap Tender Panel Structure

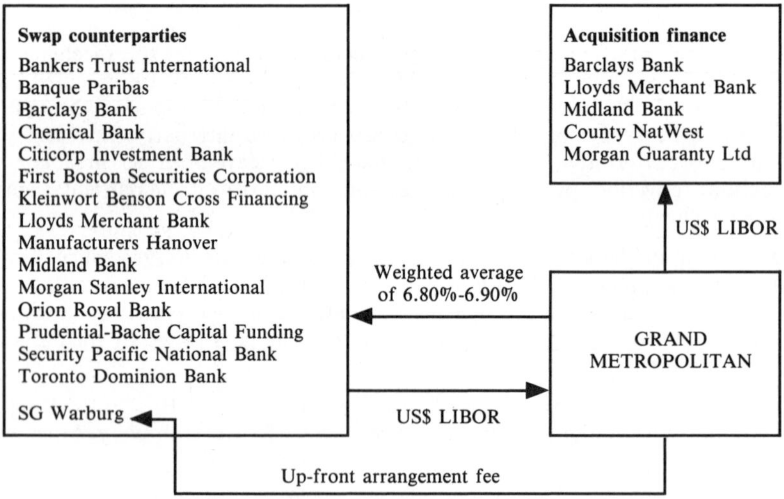

Swap counterparties
Bankers Trust International
Banque Paribas
Barclays Bank
Chemical Bank
Citicorp Investment Bank
First Boston Securities Corporation
Kleinwort Benson Cross Financing
Lloyds Merchant Bank
Manufacturers Hanover
Midland Bank
Morgan Stanley International
Orion Royal Bank
Prudential-Bache Capital Funding
Security Pacific National Bank
Toronto Dominion Bank
SG Warburg
Acquisition finance
Barclays Bank
Lloyds Merchant Bank
Midland Bank
County NatWest
Morgan Guaranty Ltd
US$ LIBOR
Weighted average of 6.80%-6.90%
GRAND METROPOLITAN
US$ LIBOR
Up-front arrangement fee

Source: Corporate Finance, Euromoney Publications.

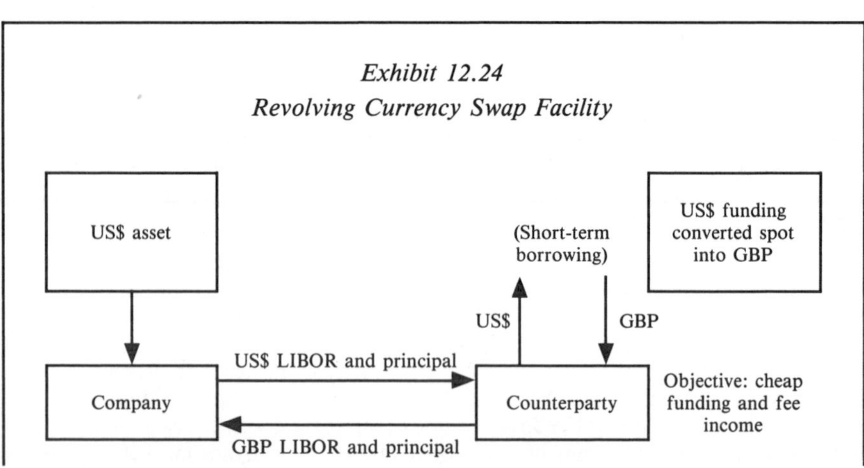

Exhibit 12.24

Revolving Currency Swap Facility

US$ asset
(Short-term borrowing)
US$ funding converted spot into GBP
US$
GBP
US$ LIBOR and principal
Company
Counterparty
Objective: cheap funding and fee income
GBP LIBOR and principal

Exhibit 12.24—continued

The company:

- pays US$ LIBOR and receives GBP LIBOR minus a spread;
- pays the US$ principal amount and receives the GBP principal amount at maturity;
- determines the date where the swap is entered into (facility is drawndown);
- determines the date where the swap is terminated.

The counterparty arranges the maturities of its funding so as to match possible termination dates chosen by the company.

Source: Corporate Finance, Euromoney Publications.

In late 1991/early 1992, a further variation on the execution of large swap programmes emerged with the utilisation of a specialist swap broker—Intercapital—by the African Development Bank to arrange approximately US$1,200m of interest rate and currency swaps. The African Development Bank was interested in executing this programme of currency swaps to correct an asset/liability mismatch in its liability portfolio and to rebalance its currency mix. Swaps required to be undertaken included: two fixed rate JPY/fixed rate US$ swaps for a total of US$475m; US$600m of swaps to fixed rate FFR; cancellation of two swaps totalling DEM200m; and assignment of one SFR150m swap. Transactions ranged in maturity from three to nine years.

Intercapital arranged transactions for and on behalf of the African Development Bank with a number of major international banks in return for receipt of a brokerage fee.

Chapter 13
Basis and Floating-to-Floating Swaps

CONCEPT OF BASIS/FLOATING-TO-FLOATING SWAPS

Basis or floating-to-floating swaps encompass a special class of swap transactions which are distinguished by the characteristic that both streams of cash flows exchanged as part of the transaction are variable, being priced off different indexes within the same currency or, in certain cases, different currencies.

There are four general types of basis of floating-to-floating swap transactions:

- basis or floating-to-floating interest rate swaps;
- arrears reset swaps;
- yield curve swaps;
- index differential swaps.

Each of these types of transactions are examined in this chapter.

BASIS SWAPS

Concept

Basis swaps (or floating-to-floating interest rate swaps) entail the conversion of one floating rate index into another in the same currency. Basis swaps function in much the same way as a fixed or floating interest rate swap, except that instead of one rate being held constant for the life of the transactions, both rates are reset throughout, relative to the agreed notional principal amount. As with a conventional interest rate swap, the notional principal is never exchanged.

The market in basis swaps, which is almost exclusively confined to US$, originally developed primarily between the United States prime rate and LIBOR. These transactions arose because non-United States banks were often members of lending syndicates with prime based (priced) loan assets which had to be funded in the LIBOR market, which was their traditional funding source. By entering into a swap where they paid a specified margin under United States prime and, in return, received LIBOR, these banks were able to match their assets and their liabilities and lock in the profit margin on the prime related loans.

The other forms of basis swaps developed in and between, inter alia, LIBOR, United States treasury bills (T-Bills), commercial paper (CP), certificate of deposit (CD) rates, bankers acceptance (BA) rates, federal funds rates, etc. *Exhibit 13.1* sets out the basic market quotations for the main types of basis swaps.

The various basis swap markets vary significantly as to liquidity and debt. The LIBOR/CP and the LIBOR/T-Bills are by far the most common markets. This reflects the popularity of United States CP as a form of short-term funding for high quality borrowers who use these short-term funds as the underlying liquidity for US$ interest rate swaps. In the case of T-Bills, the requirements of a number of prime borrowers, such as Sallie Mae, for T-Bill funding provides this market with liquidity.

Exhibit 13.1
Basis Swap Quotations

UNITED STATES MONEY MARKET INDEX SWAPS

	Receive	**Pay**
Prime/LIBOR		
1 year	+258	+253
2 years	+238	+233
3 years	+228	+223
4 years	+223	+216
5 years	+216	+206
T-Bills/LIBOR		
1 year	+20	+27
2 years	+24	+30
3 years	+28	+34
4 years	+34	+39
5 years	+38	+45
Commercial Paper/LIBOR		
1 year	+1	+3
2 years	+1	+3
3 years	+2	+5
4 years	+2	+5
5 years	+2	+5
Federal Funds/LIBOR		
1 year	+24	+30
2 years	+24	+30
3 years	+23	+28
4 years	+23	+28
5 years	+22	+27

Source: Euro Brokers Ltd, New York, as quoted in *International Financing Review*.

Applications

The initial application of basis swaps entailed borrower's obtaining funding in particular markets without the necessity for specifically entering those markets directly. For example, some non-United States companies utilised LIBOR and CP swaps to convert LIBOR funding to a CP base without needing to qualify themselves (for example, obtaining credit ratings etc) to issue in the CP market. Conversely, United States companies with available CP lines used these swaps to generate LIBOR based funding for their European operations. Financial institutions were particularly active in basis swaps, using their relative funding power in different markets to generate funding at attractive rates in other markets to better match asset liability portfolios.

The second application was predicated on the fact that when transforming a floating rate liability into a fixed rate basis the all-in fixed rate cost ultimately generated consists of two components: first, the fixed rate payment flow under the swap; and second, the spread between the floating rate payment flow under the swap and the floating rate funding cost. Where the latter is positive, that is, if the cost of the borrower's underlying variable rate funds is lower than the floating rate payment received from the counterparty, the fixed rate cost to the borrower is reduced.

A substantial market developed in transactions whereby companies fixed for several years the cost of short term borrowings through the United States CP market. The interest rate swaps used, however, were linked to LIBOR rather than the CP rate allowing the borrower to lower its fixed cost where its cost of CP is below the LIBOR floating rate payment it receives under the swap. As the swaps are generally linked to six month LIBOR but are effectively funded by 30 day CP and as six month LIBOR has exceeded the cost of 30 day A1/P1 CP, the borrower could, provided the historical pattern of rates is replicated during the term of the swap, sometimes achieve funding at a relatively attractive margin over the equivalent United States treasury rate at the commencement of the transaction. *Exhibit 13.2* sets out an example of this type of swap structure.

Exhibit 13.2

United States Commercial Paper and LIBOR Funding Arbitrage

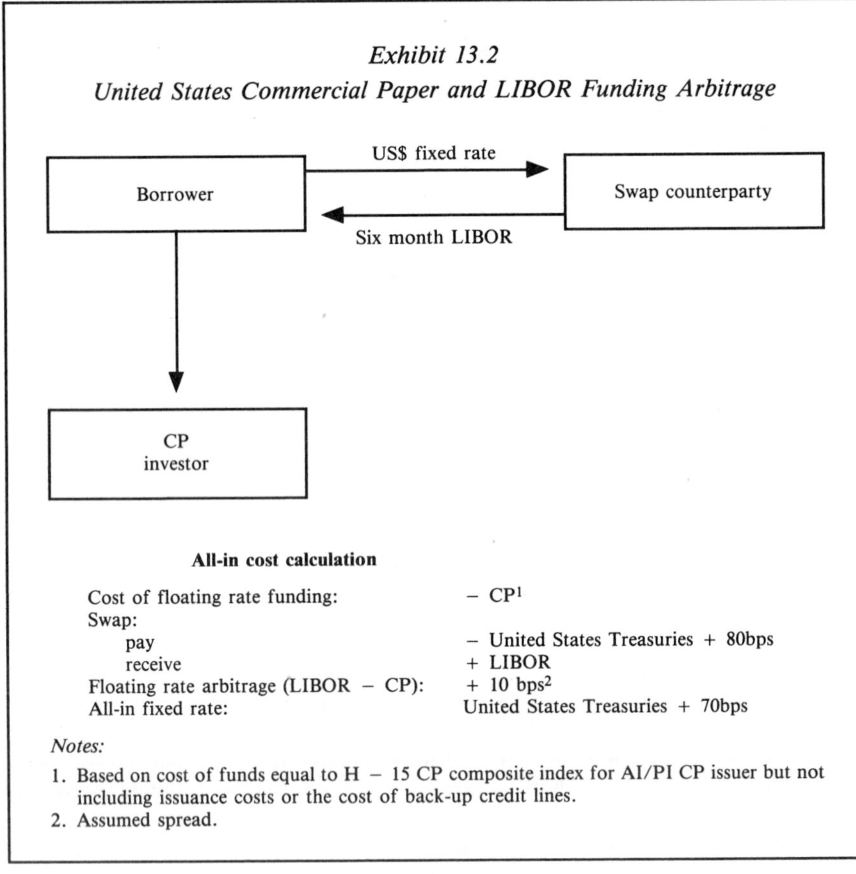

All-in cost calculation

Cost of floating rate funding:	– CP[1]
Swap:	
pay	– United States Treasuries + 80bps
receive	+ LIBOR
Floating rate arbitrage (LIBOR – CP):	+ 10 bps[2]
All-in fixed rate:	United States Treasuries + 70bps

Notes:

1. Based on cost of funds equal to H – 15 CP composite index for AI/PI CP issuer but not including issuance costs or the cost of back-up credit lines.
2. Assumed spread.

This transaction structure entails the borrower running the basis risk that CP rates will rise relative to LIBOR and, more importantly, that the shape of the yield curve may change, for example, an inverse yield curve where 30 day CP rates are above six month LIBOR, will increase its effective cost. The latter risk, in some transactions, is sought to be eliminated through a particular type of basis swap known as a "reset" swap which moderates the maturity risk that the cost of borrowing for 30 days will rise between the six monthly rate setting dates for LIBOR by sampling the six month LIBOR at more frequent (usually monthly) intervals. For example, a typical five year interest rate swap against six month LIBOR would entail ten LIBOR rate setting and payment dates. A reset swap will have ten *payment* dates but the rate that is paid every six months will be *the average of six monthly (a total of 60) rate settings of six month LIBOR*.

An alternative means of taking basis risk unhedged entails arbitraging the yield spreads between various floating rate indexes and the pricing margins on basis swaps. For example, where the spread between LIBOR and the CP rate narrowed and was accompanied by a lower than usual swap spread in switching from LIBOR based to CP based funding, a borrower could take advantage of its expectation that the spread between LIBOR and CP would widen by transacting a swap under which it receives LIBOR and pays CP plus a margin.

Exhibit 13.3 sets out a number of graphs setting out margins between a number of US$ short term money market interest rate indexes.

This form of risk-controlled arbitrage is increasingly the rationale for basis swaps, with borrowers and investors shifting to floating rate indexes which they believe will be more attractive over a particular time horizon. For example, if concern about the credit quality of the banking system could have an adverse impact on the LIBOR rate, then borrowers who have structured their borrowings with a LIBOR benchmark would experience an increased cost of funding. These borrowers may be

Exhibit 13.3

Commercial Paper versus LIBOR Spreads

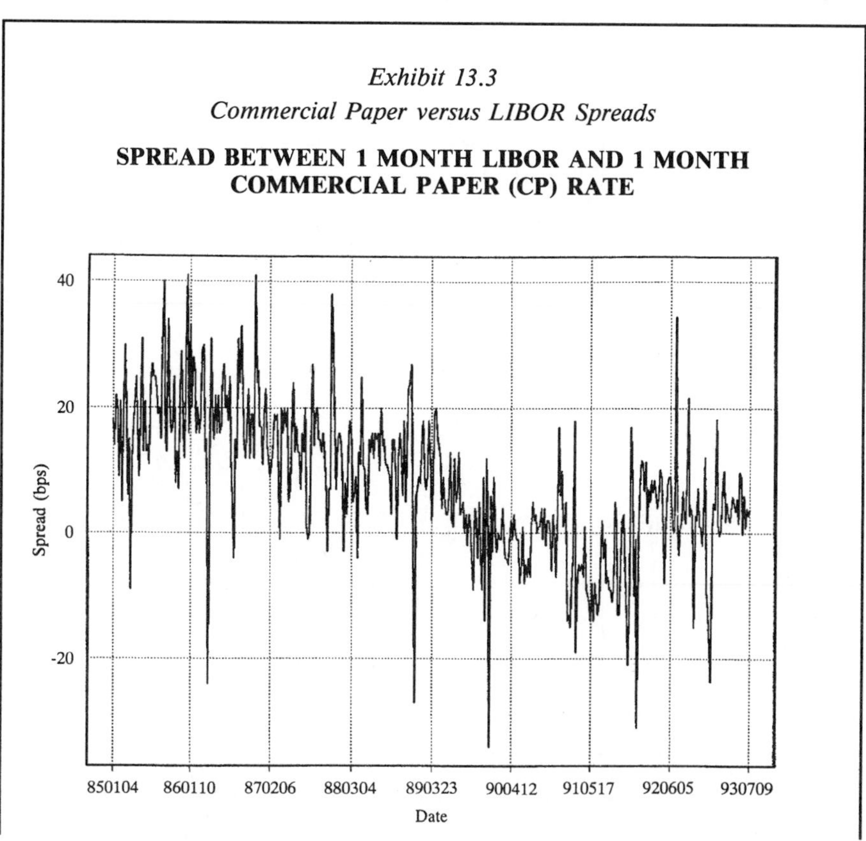

Exhibit 13.3—continued

SPREAD BETWEEN 3 MONTH LIBOR AND 3 MONTH COMMERCIAL PAPER (CP) RATE

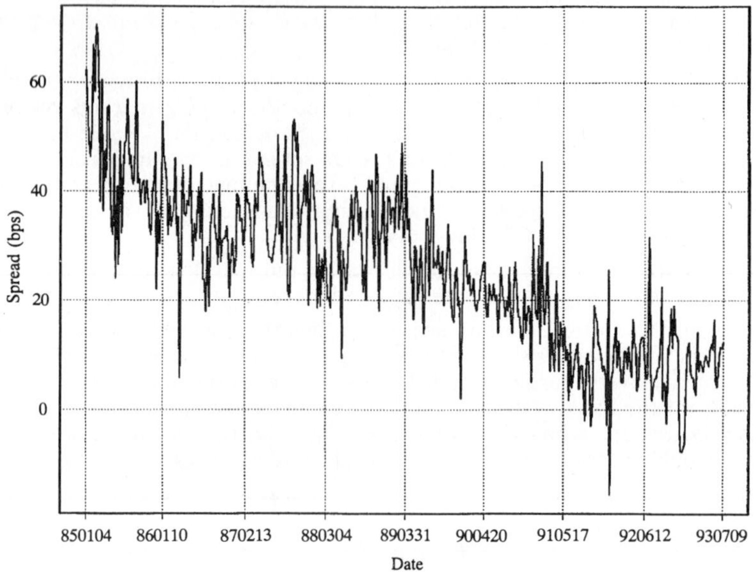

SPREAD BETWEEN 6 MONTH LIBOR AND 1 MONTH COMMERCIAL PAPER (CP) RATE

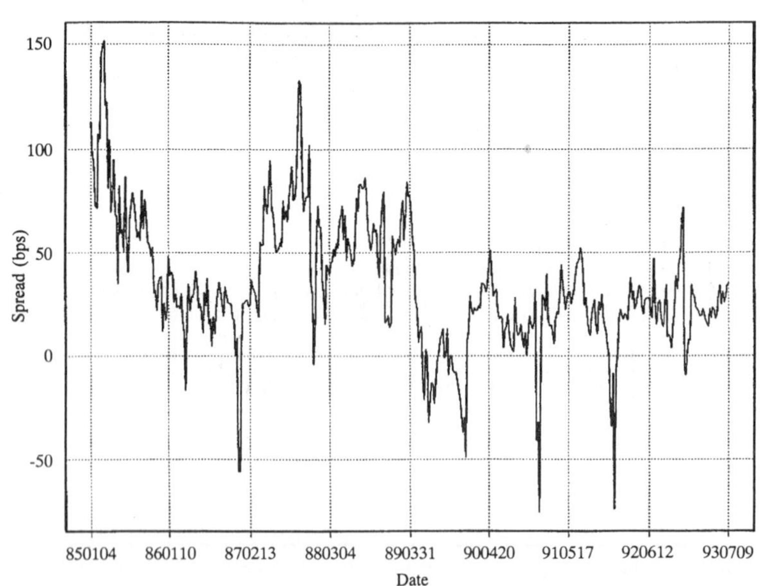

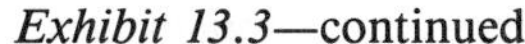
Exhibit 13.3—continued

SPREAD BETWEEN 6 MONTH LIBOR AND 3 MONTH COMMERCIAL PAPER (CP) RATE

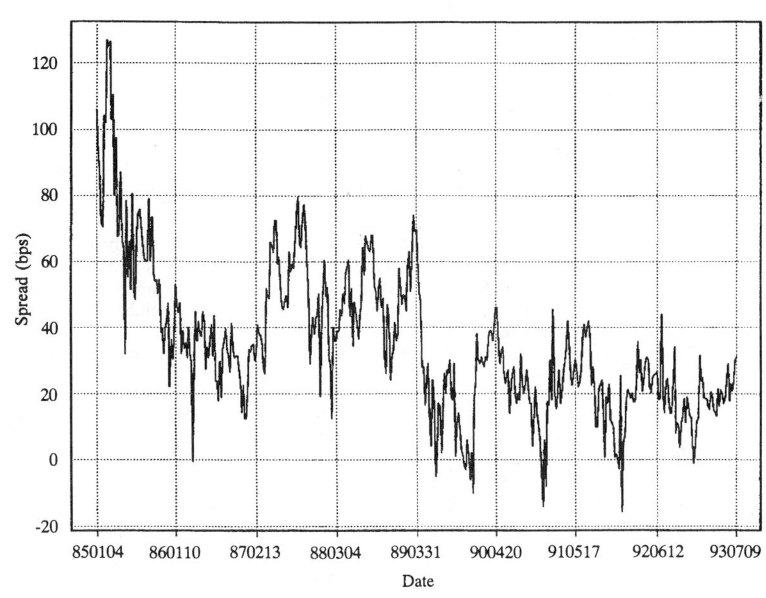

Source: Salomon Brothers—Derivatives Research.

able to obtain more attractive funding by entering into a basis swap which effectively converts their existing LIBOR linked funding to one tied to other benchmark rates, such as the United States treasury bill or CP index.

Basis swaps were also entered into by borrowers seeking to diversify away from a single floating rate index. For example, if a European corporate with extensive United States CP borrowings wishes to decrease its sensitivity to fluctuations in CP rates, it may do so by employing basis swaps which convert the debt into United States treasury bills or US$ LIBOR. It can thereby diminish its basis risk through diversification.

Swaps, which allow a borrower to convert three or six month LIBOR funds to one month LIBOR funds or vice versa, are a subset of basis swaps. These types of basis swaps are used extensively by banks. For example, the Australian Industries Development Corporation initiated one of the first basis option swaps when it requested that banks provide it with bids for a US$ interest rate swap against either one, three or six month LIBOR payments. This swap provided the Australian Industries Development Corporation with the option to pay on any of three floating rates consistent with its asset liability requirements.

Pricing considerations

Several major international banks run active books in basis swaps. Since basis swaps involve only a net interest exchange equal to the difference in short-term rate indices, the associated default risk is extremely low (see discussion in Chapter 37).

Market makers write such basis swaps against residual positions or mismatches arising from other swaps. For example, a market maker could have two swaps whereby it received fixed against six month LIBOR but had paid fixed against one month CP. The market maker could then write a basis swap paying CP against receipt of LIBOR to close off its mismatch. *Exhibit 13.4* sets out an example of the construction of a basis swap involving the United States prime rate and US$ LIBOR.

Exhibit 13.4

Engineering a US$ Prime and LIBOR Basis Swap

Bank X, which has access to floating rate funds through the London interbank market, has a prime based asset for which it seeks matched funding. It then enters into a swap whereby it receives an amount linked to LIBOR and pays an amount related to prime. The two offsetting counterparties could be company Y, swapping between a fixed rate and LIBOR, and company Z, swapping between prime and a fixed rate. The two fixed rates can then be arranged to cancel each other, leaving a residual position which is prime against LIBOR.

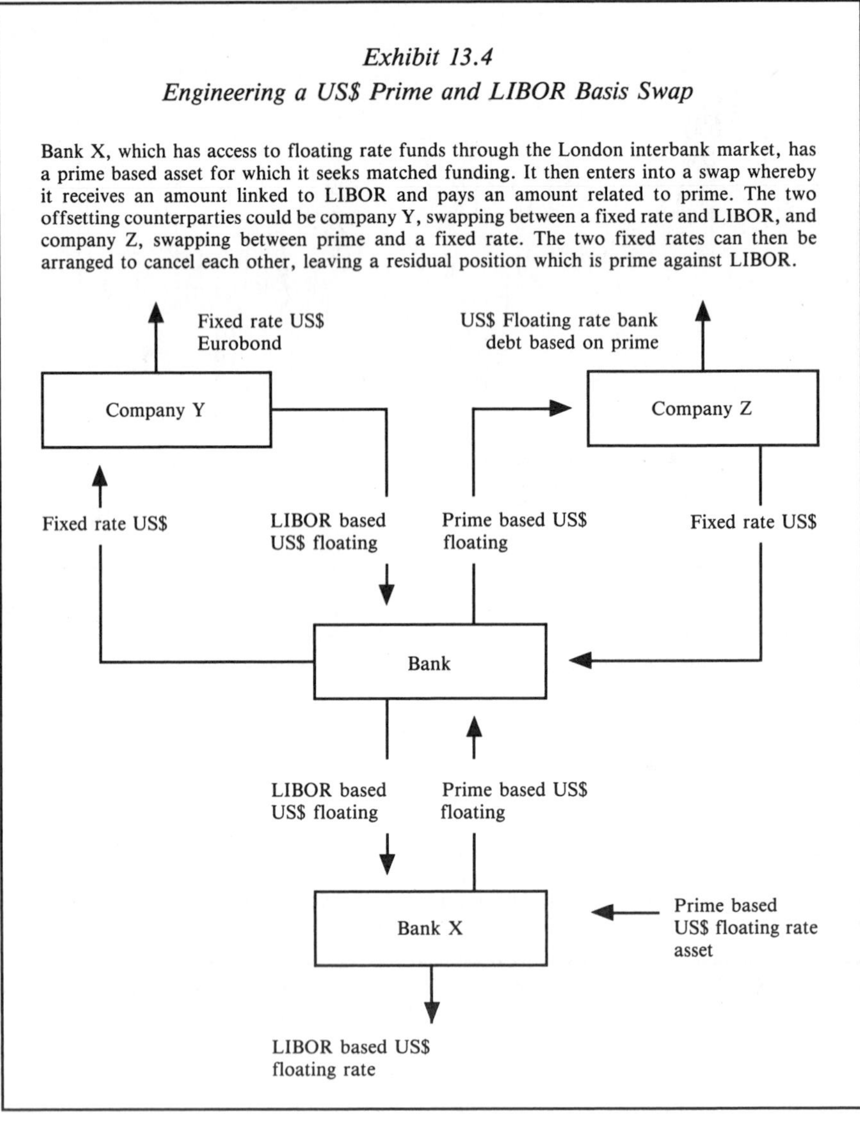

Pricing of basis swaps thus tends to be on the basis of existing swap position mismatches as well as market arbitrage positions. In addition, the historical relationship between the two floating rate indexes is also relevant.

ARREARS RESET SWAPS

In September 1987, AIG Financial Products engineered a swap involving an arrears reset on floating rate US$ LIBOR. Under the arrears reset structure, floating rate payments were based on LIBOR *set two days before the payment date*, whereas on a normal swap, LIBOR would be set *six months and two days prior to the payment date.*

Exhibit 13.5 sets out an example detailing the pricing/hedging considerations applicable to an arrears reset swap structure.

Exhibit 13.5
Pricing/Hedging an Arrears Reset Swap (ARS)

1. *Theoretical Pricing Considerations*

The pricing of an ARS revolves around extracting the value embedded in a strongly positively shaped yield curve in forward/forward interest rates which are above prevailing spot rates.

This can be seen in *Table 1* which sets out the cash flows of a ARS and a corresponding conventional interest rate swap. The net cash flows of a ARS is:

LIBOR (t0)-LIBOR (t4)

TABLE 1

Time (t)	Year	Cash Flows: Arrears Reset Swap		Conventional Swap		Net Cash Flow
		Fixed	Floating	Fixed	Floating	
1	0.5	F	L(t1)	F	L(t0)	L(t0)-L(t1)
2	1.0	F	L(t2)	F	L(t1)	L(t1)-L(t2)
3	1.5	F	L(t3)	F	L(t2)	L(t2)-L(t3)
4	2.0	F	L(t4)	F	L(t3)	L(t3)-L(t4)

F = Fixed Rate payable under swap.
L(t) = US$ six month LIBOR at time t.

Therefore, if US$ six month LIBOR (as at time t4) is greater (less) than spot US$ six month LIBOR, then a floating rate payer under a ARS structure gains (losses).

The approximate size of the gain on cost is:

[LIBOR (t4)-LIBOR (t0)] × Notional Amount × (No of days/360)

2. *Example*

Assume the following yield curve exists:

Date	No of days	Yield %	Zero Rate %	Forward Rate (%)
15-Dec-X0				
15-June-X1	182	6.00	6.0000	7.140
15-Dec-X1	365	6.55	6.5590	8.659
15-June-X2	548	7.25	7.2825	10.074
15-Dec-X2	731	7.95	8.0203	9.436
15-June-X3	913	8.25	8.3292	

Based on the above yield, the benefit of the ARS structure can be estimated as follows:

$(9.436 - 6.00) \times \$100 \times 182/360$
$= \$1.7371$ or 1.7371%

This gain can be amortised over the two year swap (at the swap rate equivalent to 7.95% pa annual) as 0.4774% every six months or 0.9548% pa. This can be built into the fixed rate side of the swap whereby the fixed rate payer increases the rate paid by 95.48bps (from 7.95% to 8.9048% pa).

Exhibit 13.5—continued

3. *Pricing In Practice*

The approximation of the ARS benefit is only accurate where the yield curve is flat and all zero coupon rates are the same. In practice, the exact adjustment is based on using the theoretical forward rates to generate the actual ARS cash flows (relative to cash flows under a conventional swap) which are then discounted using the zero rates. *Table 2* sets out this analysis for the above swap.

As set out below in *Table 2* the benefit derived (on a net present value basis) is 1.6538% or 90.904bps pa.

4. *Hedging*

For a swap counterparty, the exposure into a ARS transaction can be hedged as follows:

- The change in the PV of the cash flows of the ARS (eg in *Table 2* below, p 359) for a 1bps movement in interest rates is measured.
- To offset the ARS swap risk, the counterparty maintains a hedge (utilising a portfolio of physical securities and/or futures) to offset the NPV change in the ARS transaction.
- This hedge portfolio is adjusted periodically to align it with changes in the net value of the ARS.

Alternatively, the swap counterparty can structure hedges utilising either FRAs or deferred start swaps to seek to structure offsetting cash flows to immunise the ARS.

The arrears reset structure was designed to create value from a positively sloped yield curve where implied forward rates lie successively higher above the physical yield curve. However, higher implied forward rates are only an unbiased estimate of actual future interest rates, and the actual spot rate at the relevant future date may differ from that implied by the forward rate.

This means that the arrears reset structure may be attractive to a counterparty who expects that short-term rates will remain stable or decrease. Such a counterparty would under this structure receive fixed rates under the swap against payment of floating rates receiving the benefit of the higher implied forward rate, in the form of a higher fixed rate flow under the swap. If, however, LIBOR increases from one payment period to the next, the savings on the arrears reset structure could be offset by the higher LIBOR rate. This feature dictates that the arrears reset structure is unsuitable where the borrower is seeking to match fund assets.

While initial arrears reset structures were structured as a fixed rate against floating rate (calculated in arrears) transactions, increasingly, these type of swaps are unbundled into a floating-to-floating swap structure. Under this floating-to-floating structure, one floating leg is set in arrears while the other is calculated normally.

YIELD CURVE SWAPS

A yield curve swap is a floating-for-floating interest rate swap (similar conceptually to a basis swap—see above). Under the structure, the swap counterparty pays (receives) US$ LIBOR and receives (pays) the *ten or 30 year Treasury yield plus/minus a spread*. Both rates are reset either quarterly or semi-annually and the term of the yield curve swap ranges from three to ten years.

Exhibit 13.5—continued

TABLE 2

Pricing an Arrears Reset Swap

Date	No of days	Yield	Zero Rate	Forward Rate	Cash Flows ARS	Cash Flows Normal	Cash Flows Net	Discount Factor	Discounted Cash Flows	Change in Value (1bps)
15-Dec-19X0										
15-Jun-19X1	182	6.000%	6.000%	7.140%	3.6097	3.0333	0.5763	0.9714	0.5598	0.5598
15-Dec-19X1	365	6.550%	6.559%	8.659%	4.4017	3.6295	0.7722	0.9384	0.7246	0.7246
15-Jun-19X2	548	7.250%	7.283%	10.074%	5.1210	4.4017	0.7193	0.8998	0.6472	0.6472
15-Dec-19X2	731	7.950%	8.020%	9.436%	4.7966	5.1210	(0.3243)	0.8568	(0.2779)	(0.2778)
15-Jun-19X3	913	8.250%	8.329%							
								SUM	1.6538	1.6537
							Change in value (per 100m per 1bps rise)			($13,338.38)

The yield curve swap was introduced in July 1987. Conceptually, the transaction is similar to the basis swap except in so far as one of the interest indexes is a long term rate, although it is reset frequently.

Yield curve swaps have the following characteristics:

- They are generally insensitive to the absolute level of interest rates.
- Yield curve swaps are very sensitive to the shape of the yield curve.

Yield curve swaps create an exposure to the slope of the yield curve. Under a typical arrangement, where the counterparty receives the ten or 30 year treasury yield and pays US$ LIBOR, if the yield curve steepens (flattens or inverts) its net receipt under the yield curve swap will increase (decrease). *Exhibit 13.6* sets out the structure of a yield curve swap diagrammatically. *Exhibit 13.7* sets out an example of the mechanics of the yield curve swap.

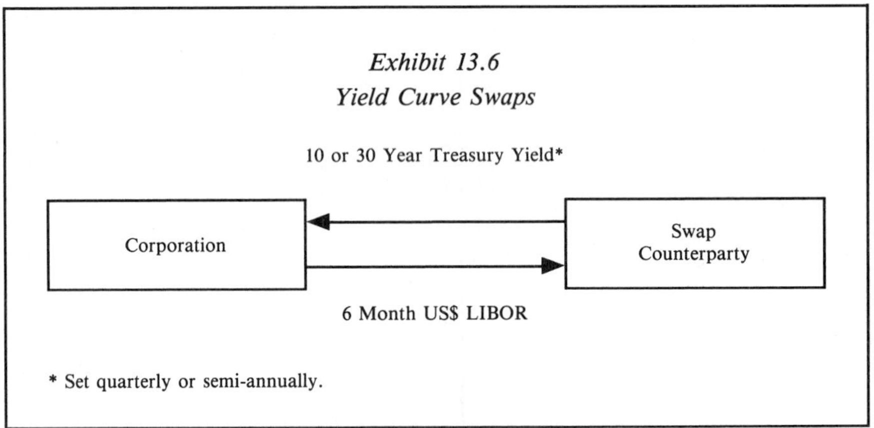

Exhibit 13.6
Yield Curve Swaps

Yield curve swaps allow the counterparty receiving the term rate to price of the long rather than the short end of the yield curve. The major application of this type of arrangement includes:

- Investors converting the return on a floating rate asset from a short-term rate index to a long-term rate by receiving the term rate and paying out US$ LIBOR which is matched by the income from the underlying floating rate asset.
- Hedging liabilities floating off the ten or 30 year treasury bond rate. These types of exposures are incurred by insurance companies and the yield curve swap payment received under such transactions offsets the liability floating off the long-term rate thus converting it into a LIBOR based liability.
- An example of this type of liability is US insurance company GIC's Guaranteed Investment Contracts whose return is pegged to the ten year treasury rate.
- An index diversification technique for investors to convert floating rate assets away from short term indexes to long term indexes.
- Positioning or trading the shape of the yield curve. For example, an investor expecting the yield curve to steepen would receive the ten year or 30 year rate and pay short-term rates or vice versa. Similar strategies can be developed for borrowers.

Exhibit 13.7
Example of Yield Curve Swap

Corporation A enters into a five year yield curve swap to pay six month LIBOR and receive the ten year treasury plus five basis points.

Trade Date	10/1/X9
1st Rate Setting Date	11/1/X9 (Next business day)
Effective Date	13/1/X9 (2 business days later)
2nd Rate Setting Date	11/7/X9 (6 months after 1st rate setting)
First Payment Date	13/7/X9 (6 months after effective date)

The ten year (or, if relevant, 30 year) rate utilised will be the Constant Maturity Treasury (CMT) rate for the relevant term as calculated by the US Treasury and the Federal Reserve Bank of New York by a process of interpolation from the existing yield curve (see discussion in Chapter 15).

Both LIBOR and the treasury rate are set as of the rate setting date. The treasury rate will not be known until the following Tuesday, after the release of the Fed H-15 report with calculation of the first payment being made until the release of the report.

Treasury Maturity	10 years
Payments per Year	2
Term	5 years
Swap Maturity Date	13/1/X4
Notional Principal	$100 million
Current 6 Month LIBOR	9.56% (Actual/360)
Current 10 year Treasury	9.23% (S/A bond equivalent)
Yield Curve Swap Spread	5bps

Each payment date the customer receives the following payment:

$$\$100\text{m} \times (10 \text{ year rate} + \text{spread}) \times \frac{\text{Actual days in period}}{365}$$

The customer pays the following:

$$\$100\text{m} \times \text{LIBOR} \times \frac{\text{Actual days}}{360}$$

Using the above formulas, the first payment to the customer is as follows (for the 181 day period 13/1/X9-13/7/X9):

$$\$100\text{m} \times \left[\left((9.23\% + .05\%) \times \frac{181}{365}\right) - \left(9.56\% \times \frac{181}{360}\right)\right]$$
$$= \$204,693.$$

The customer pays this amount on the first payment date, 13/7/X9.

Yield curve swaps developed rapidly to become commonly utilised products, particularly among investors, in the US$ swap market. Subsequently, it has been applied in a number of other markets, including the DEM and A$ swap market sectors, allowing investors of a liability managers and financial institutions to take advantage of the prevailing shape of the yield curve.

Exhibit 13.8 sets out a graphical analysis of the historical yields and spreads for six month LIBOR versus ten and 30 year treasury yield over an extended period of time.

Exhibit 13.8
Yield Curve Spreads

SPREAD BETWEEN 10 YEAR US TREASURY NOTE AND 3 MONTH LIBOR

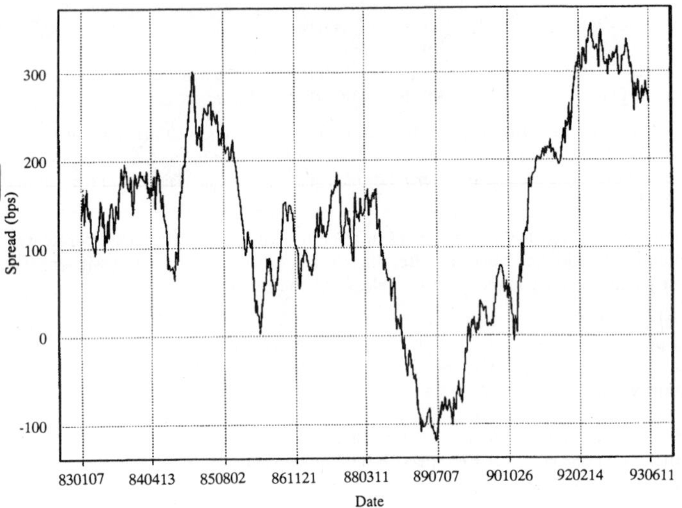

SPREAD BETWEEN 30 YEAR US TREASURY BOND AND 3 MONTH LIBOR

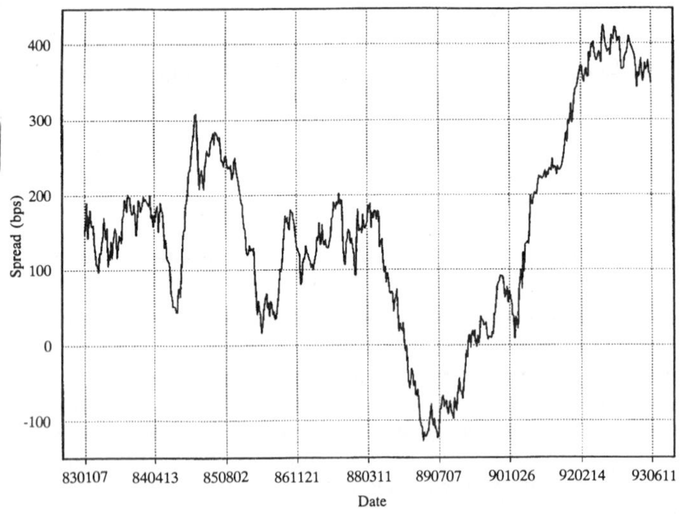

Source: Salomon Brothers—Derivatives Research.

The economic structure of yield curve swaps is driven, largely, by the shape of the yield curve in the relevant currency. The pricing of such transactions derives from the implicit forward rates embodied in the yield curve. In effect, the transaction pricing is generated by calculating the implied *term* "forward interest rates" (for example, the ten year rate in six, 12, 18, etc months) relative to the implied six month rates implied in the same yield curve (for example, the six month rate is six, 12, 18, etc months). The interaction of these two sets of implied forward rates determines the margin above or below the term interest rate component of the yield curve swap.

A number of variations on the standard yield curve swap structure have also emerged. Yield curve swaps, as between various term interest rates (for example, five year against ten year, etc) have been undertaken. A major variation has been the emergence of options on yield curve shapes. This type of instrument, effectively, allows traders, borrowers and investors to buy and sell volatility on the *shape* of the yield curve.

Another variation entails yield curve swaps being embedded in securities issues. The most notable example of this structure is an issue format known as SURFs (Step Up Recovery Floaters). The detailed structure of SURFs and its relationship to yield curve swap transactions is discussed in detail in Chapter 15.

INDEX DIFFERENTIAL SWAPS

Differential swaps—structure

Definition and general description

The differential swap structure is designed to allow financial managers to capture existing and expected differentials in floating or money market rates between alternative currencies without incurring any foreign exchange exposure. In a typical differential swap, the party entering into the transaction will:

- Agree to receive payment in a particular currency on a specific principal amount for a specified term at the prevailing floating money market rate in that currency.
- In exchange, it will make payments on the same principal amount, in the same currency, for the same term, based on the prevailing floating money market rate in an alternative or different currency.

The major features of this arrangement include:

- Both payments and receipts (which are based on the same notional principal amount) are on a floating rate basis, with the rate being reset at specified intervals (usually quarterly or semi-annually).
- All payments under the transaction are made in the counterparty's nominated currency thereby eliminating any foreign exchange exposure.
- Consistent with its status as a single currency transaction, no exchange of principal amounts is required.

Example

The following numerical example illustrates the concept utilising a transaction whereby a borrower elects to enter into a DEM/US$ differential swap seeking to benefit from the fact that floating money market rates in the US$ sector are currently well below equivalent floating money market rates in the DEM sector.

Exhibit 13.9 sets out the structure of this differential swap. The counterparty enters into a differential swap for a term of three years in which it agrees to pay interest in DEM which will be calculated by applying the nominal six month US$ LIBOR rate to a notional principal amount of DEM160.0m (based on an exchange rate of US$1 = DEM1.60, equivalent to US$100.0m). The counterparty will receive interest in DEM which will be calculated by applying the nominal six month DEM LIBOR rate to DEM160.0m.

Exhibit 13.9

Differential Swap—Structure

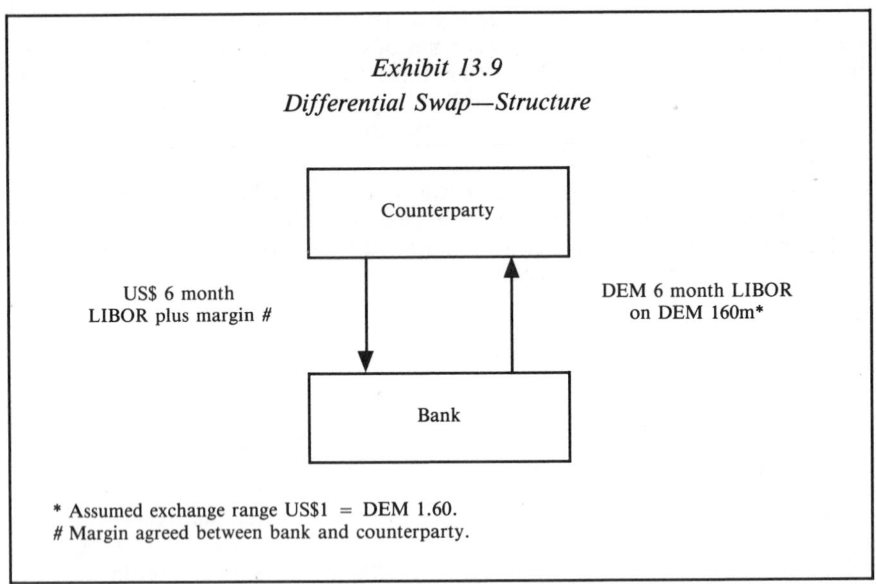

* Assumed exchange range US$1 = DEM 1.60.
\# Margin agreed between bank and counterparty.

The counterparty, under this differential swap, will pay interest under this transaction at a rate equivalent to the six month US$ LIBOR rate plus a margin (assumed to be 2.15% pa or 215bps in DEM). The margin represents, primarily, the differential between interest rates of the relevant maturity (three years) in US$ and DEM markets as well as the hedging costs to the bank. The derivation of this margin is discussed below in the section on pricing and hedging.

The cash flows under this differential swap transaction from the perspective of the counterparty is summarised in *Exhibit 13.10*.

Exhibit 13.10

Differential Swap—Cash Flows

Assumptions

Structure:	Pay	US$ LIBOR
	Rec	DEM LIBOR
FX currency:	US$	100,000,000
Base currency:	DEM	160,000,000
Exchange rate:		1.6000

Exhibit 13.10—continued

Term (years):		3					
Start date:		01-Mar-X2					
Maturity date:		01-Mar-X5					
Interest rates:							
Term swap:	US$	7.20%					
	DEM	8.70%					
Floating rates period		1	2	3	4	5	6
6 month LIBOR	US$	4.25%	4.38%	4.13%	4.75%	5.13%	5.50%
6 month LIBOR	DEM	9.50%	9.35%	9.62%	9.00%	8.63%	8.25%
Differential		5.25%	4.98%	5.50%	4.25%	3.50%	2.75%
Pricing margin (bps):	+	215	215	215	215	215	215
US$ LIBOR + margin:		6.40%	6.53%	6.28%	6.90%	7.28%	7.65%

Cash Flows

Period	Days	Counterparty Payments (DEM)	Counterparty Receipts (DEM)	Net Receipt or Payment (−) (DEM)
01-Mar-X2				
01-Sep-X2	184	5,237,033	7,768,889	2,531,856
01-Mar-X3	181	5,252,202	7,521,556	2,269,353
01-Sep-X3	184	5,134,811	7,867,022	2,732,211
01-Mar-X4	181	5,553,869	7,240,000	1,686,131
01-Sep-X4	184	5,952,589	7,053,333	1,100,745
01-Mar-X5	181	6,157,202	6,636,667	479,464

At the end of each interest period (semi-annually), the counterparty makes payments on DEM160.0m at the six month US$ LIBOR rate (plus the differential swap margin) and receives payment on DEM160.0m at the six month DEM LIBOR rate. The net settlement amount calculation is as follows:

Settlement Calculation—1 September 1992[1]

Counterparty—

Pays DEM160,000,000 @ US$ six month LIBOR plus margin (4.25% + 2.15% = 6.40%) × 184/360 days:	DEM(5,237,033)
Receives DEM160,000,000 @ DEM six month LIBOR (9.50%) × 184/360 days:	DEM7,768,889
Net Receipt	DEM2,531,856

Based on these assumed rates, as at the first settlement date, the bank would pay to the counterparty the net settlement sum of DEM2,531,856.

Exhibit 13.10 sets out the settlement sums for each of the remaining interest periods over the life of the swap based on assumed US$ and DEM LIBOR rates.

Under the terms of this differential swap, the counterparty will receive a net settlement amount which equates to the net differential between DEM and US$ LIBOR rates adjusted for the margin. If the US$ LIBOR rate inclusive of the margin is below the DEM six month LIBOR rate, then the counterparty receives a net settlement payment. Conversely, if the six month US$ LIBOR rate plus the margin rises to a level above the then prevailing DEM six month LIBOR rate on any

1. Cash flows are based on full precision of margin which is 2.153981% pa.

particular rate setting date, the counterparty will pay to the bank the difference in the two nominal interest rates in DEM.

It is evident from this example, all payments are made in the nominated base currency (DEM) on a net settlement basis.

From the viewpoint of the counterparty (assumed to be a DEM borrower) the transaction results in the following:

- The borrower has created a DEM liability with nominal US$ six LIBOR rate as the interest benchmark. This, necessarily, means that it benefits where US$ six month LIBOR rates are below DEM six month LIBOR rates by more than the margin.
- From mechanical perspective, this reduction in interest cost is achieved by the net settlement amounts under the swap which reduce the borrower's interest payments under its underlying DEM borrowing.
- The borrower has achieved a conversion of its DEM based liability to a US$ based liability without incurring any foreign exchange exposure as all its payments continue to be in DEM.

An identical transaction could be utilised by an asset manager to convert an underlying US$ asset yielding a floating rate of return linked to US$ LIBOR into a US$ asset yielding a return linked to DEM six month LIBOR.

Under this transaction structure, the base currency would be restructured to be US$100.0m (equating to DEM160.0m at the assumed exchange rate). The investor would pay US$ six month LIBOR on US$100.0m and receive DEM six month LIBOR *less* a specified margin on US$100.0m in US$. Under the terms of this transaction, all payments would be in US$ to insulate the investor from any foreign exchange risk. Such a transaction would allow the investor to benefit from the positive differential between DEM floating rates and US$ floating rates while maintaining its underlying US$ investment position.

Exhibit 13.11 summarises the structure of this differential swap from an investor perspective.

Exhibit 13.11

Differential Swap—Alternative Structure for Investor

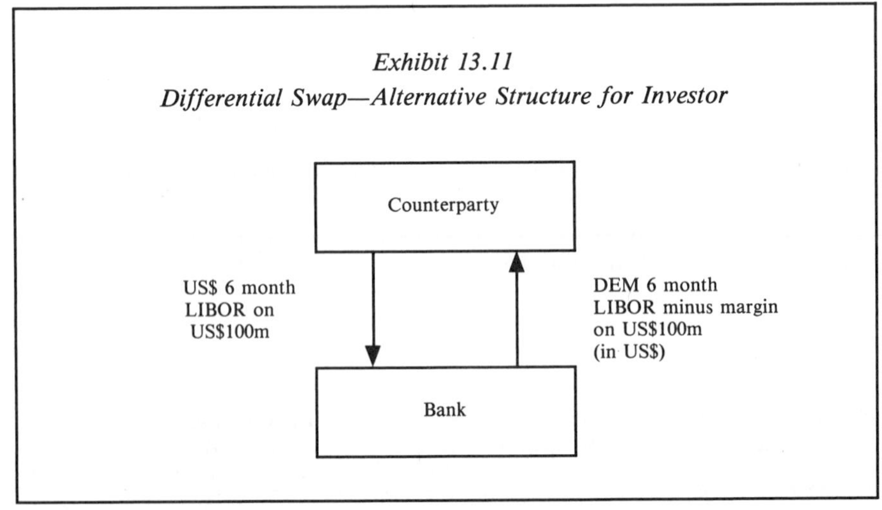

Pricing and hedging considerations

The pricing of a differential swap transaction is integral to and is derived from the techniques utilised by the bank to hedge its own exposures as a result of entering into a transaction with its counterparty.

The essential structure of the hedge for a differential swap entails two discrete steps:

- entry by the bank into two separate interest rate swap transactions to generate the cash flow stream of a differential swap;
- management of a complex series of foreign exchange exposures which are created in structuring the hedge.

Each of these two steps is considered in detail below. The analysis of pricing and hedging considerations is based on the numerical example of the DEM/US$ differential swap discussed above.

Hedging structure

In order to hedge its underlying position (refer *Exhibit 13.9*), the bank would enter into two three year interest rate swaps to replicate the cash flows of the differential swap. These swaps to be entered into by the bank would be as follows:

- A three year DEM160.0m interest rate swap under which the bank:
  - pays 8.7% pa on DEM160.0m (payable semi-annually on an actual/365 basis); and
  - receives DEM six month LIBOR on DEM160.0m.
- A three year US$100.0m interest rate swap in which the bank:
  - pays US$ six month LIBOR; and
  - receives 7.2% pa (payable semi-annually on an actual/365 basis).

The fixed rate on the US$ and DEM swaps are the prevailing market swap rates. The currency parities between the US$ and DEM interest rate swaps is established by the assumed US$/DEM exchange of US$1:DEM1.60 (the market rate at the time the transaction is entered into).

The overall hedging structure is illustrated in *Exhibit 13.12*.

For analytical purposes, the structure of the hedge can be simplified in two steps:

- In order to assist in deriving the spread over US$ LIBOR payable by the counterparty, the US$ interest rate swap is restructured to an off-market rate basis with the fixed rate under the US$ swap being restructured to match the fixed coupon of 8.7% pa payable under the corresponding DEM interest rate swap.

  This necessitates the bank paying the present valued equivalent of 1.5% pa at the commencement of the swap. The upfront payment required to restructure the swap is US$3,845,463 (equivalent DEM6,152,741). *Exhibit 13.13* sets out the derivation of this upfront payment.

  Please note that for convenience the swap rate has been utilised to present value the cash flow differences as between the 8.7% pa fixed rate payments required and the on market rate of 7.2% pa. In practice, zero coupon rates would be utilised adjusted for the fact that the US$ swap portfolio is essentially accepting a deposit over the life of the transaction which is repaid in the form of annuity by way of the higher coupon under the US$ interest rate swap requiring assumption of a reinvestment risk on these cash flows.

Exhibit 13.12
Differential Swap—Hedging Structure (1)

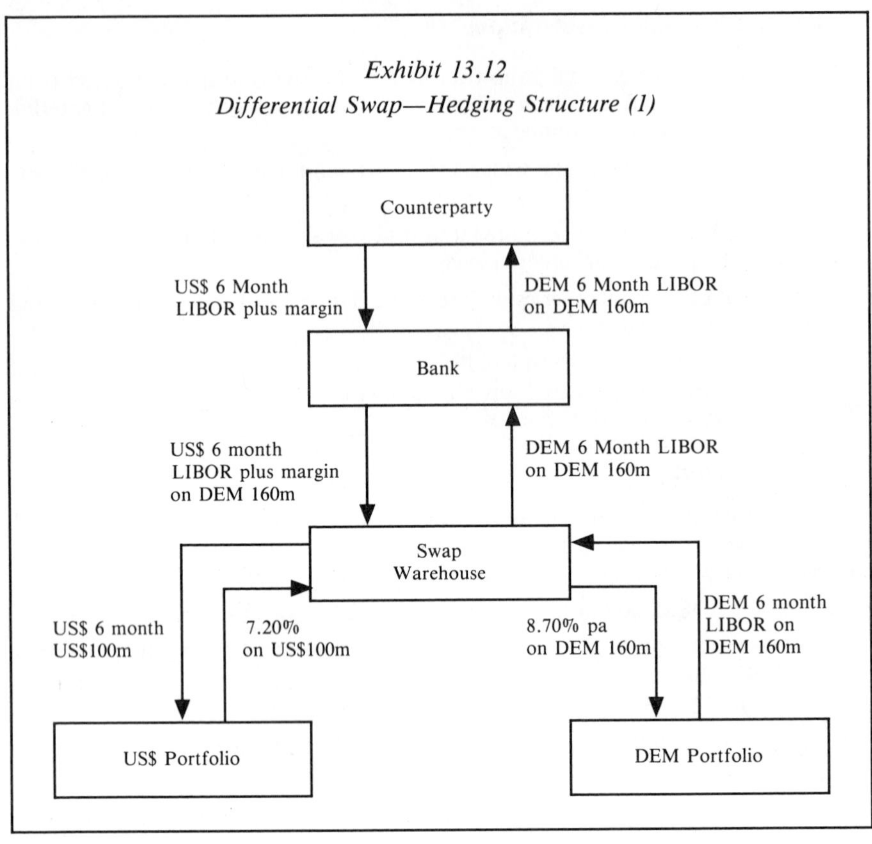

Exhibit 13.13
Differential Swap—Rewriting Swaps To Equate Coupons

Period	Days	US$ Payments @ Market 7.20% (US$)	US$ Payments @ Off-Market 8.70% (US$)	Payment Difference (US$)	PV of Payment Difference (US$)
1-Mar-X2					(3,845,463)
1-Sep-X2	184	3,629,589	4,385,753	(756,164)	
1-Mar-X3	181	3,570,411	4,314,247	(743,836)	
1-Sep-X3	184	3,629,589	4,385,753	(756,164)	
1-Mar-X4	181	3,570,411	4,314,247	(743,836)	
1-Sep-X4	184	3,629,589	4,385,753	(756,164)	
1-Mar-X5	181	3,570,411	4,314,247	(743,836)	

Exhibit 13.14 sets out the cash flow structure of the hedge following the restructure of the US$ interest rate swap flows.

- A review of *Exhibit 13.14* illustrates that two sets of cash flows completely offset each other in the hedge. The DEM six month LIBOR received on DEM160.0m by the swap warehouse is exactly matched by the corresponding payments required to be made to the counterparty. These cash flows which cancel or offset each other can be ignored for the purposes for the hedge and are eliminated. *Exhibit 13.15* sets out the remaining cashflows.

Exhibit 13.14

Differential Swap—Hedging Structure (2)

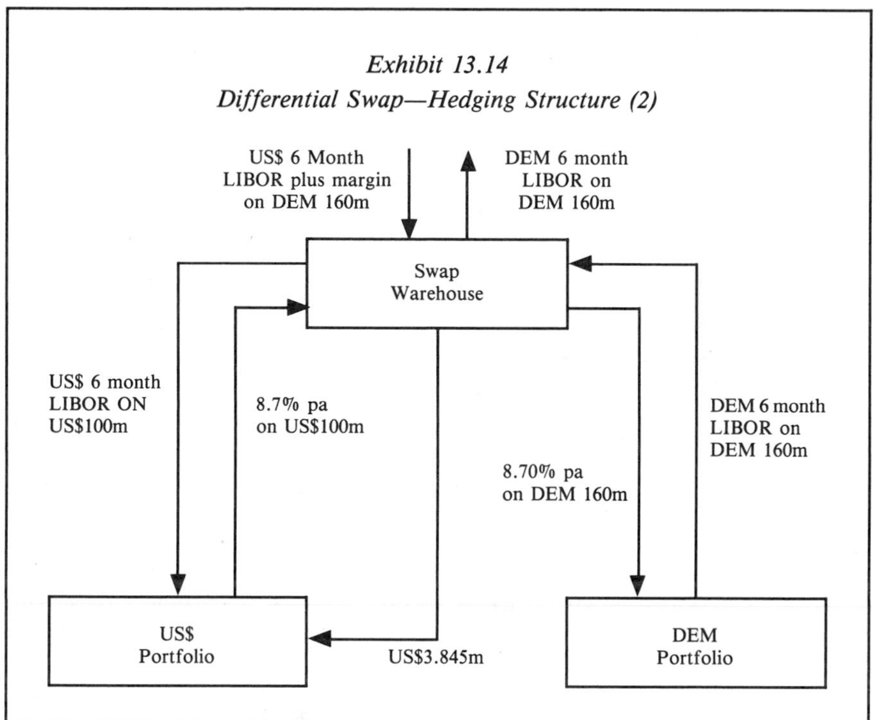

Currency risk management

Exhibit 13.15 clearly identifies the foreign exchange exposures inherent in the hedge structure. The bank, under the terms of the differential swap, has a complex foreign exchange exposure to movements in the US$/DEM interest rates reflecting the fact that the bank has a series of US$ and DEM cash flows to manage.

The unique aspect of this currency risk management position is that:

- The bank's US$ and DEM net cash flows as at each settlement date is determined by an exogenous factor—US$ six month LIBOR (which is not known until the rate is set at the commencement of the relevant interest period).
- The nature of the exposure to the US$/DEM rate *changes* depending upon the nominal level of six month US$ LIBOR.

Exhibit 13.15
Differential Swap—Hedging Structure (3)

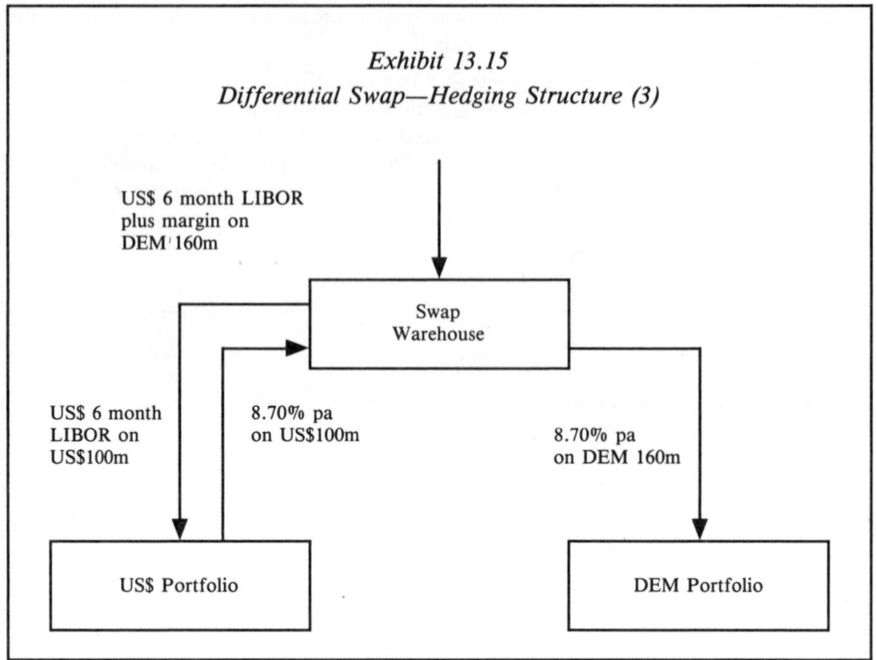

Exhibit 13.16 analyses the net cash flow exposures experienced by the bank (within its swap portfolio) as at the first settlement. Please note that while this discussion focuses on the first settlement date only, a similar problem exists in respect of each of the remaining five interest periods and settlement dates.

As evident from a review of *Exhibit 13.16*, if US$ six month LIBOR is less than 8.7% pa (the fixed rate payable under the DEM swap), then the bank will have a net receipt of US$ which will be needed to fund a net DEM outflow. Conversely, if US$ six month LIBOR exceeds 8.7% pa, then the bank has a net DEM inflow which is required to fund a net US$ outflow.

Consequently, the bank's swap portfolio, in hedging its exposure under the differential swap, is required to make a number of payments in one currency (either DEM or US$) while receiving the equivalent cash flow in the other currency. This complex foreign exchange exposure must be managed by the bank.

In analysing the complex foreign exchange exposures generated by the hedge structure, any exposure in regard to the *margin* over US$ six month LIBOR payable by the counterparty in DEM is ignored. In practice, part of the margin (see below) will represent an annuity designed to recover the upfront US$ payment made as part of restructuring the cash flows of the US$ interest rate swap to equate the fixed rate payable under the DEM interest rate swap. In practice, this exposure can be eliminated quite simply by the following strategies:

- The swap structure could have been realigned by *reducing* the DEM coupon to equate to the US$ interest rate swap coupon of 7.2% pa.
- Alternatively, the DEM equivalent of the US$ payment to the US$ swap portfolio could have been "borrowed" from the DEM swap portfolio with the borrowing being repaid by the margin payable by the counterparty (in DEM).

Exhibit 13.16

Differential Swap—Currency Exposure Analysis

FX Hedge Management Analysis (First Settlement)

Case 1: US$ 6 month LIBOR less than 8.70% pa

US$ LIBOR (%)	Receipts (DEM)	Payments (DEM)	Payments (US$)	Receipts (US$)	Net DEM Flow (DEM)	Net US$ Flow (US$)	FX Rate	Net Cash Flow (US$)
4.25%	3,475,556	(7,017,205)	(2,172,222)	4,385,753	(3,541,650)	2,213,531	1.6000	0
4.25%	3,475,556	(7,017,205)	(2,172,222)	4,385,753	(3,541,650)	2,213,531	2.0000	442,706
4.25%	3,475,556	(7,017,205)	(2,172,222)	4,385,753	(3,541,650)	2,213,531	1.8000	245,948
4.25%	3,475,556	(7,017,205)	(2,172,222)	4,385,753	(3,541,650)	2,213,531	1.4000	(316,219)
4.25%	3,475,556	(7,017,205)	(2,172,222)	4,385,753	(3,541,650)	2,213,531	1.2000	(737,844)

Case 2: US$ 6 month LIBOR greater than 8.70% pa

US$ LIBOR (%)	Receipts (DEM)	Payments (DEM)	Payments (US$)	Receipts (US$)	Net DEM Flow (DEM)	Net US$ Flow (US$)	FX Rate	Net Cash Flow (US$)
10.50%	8,586,667	(7,017,205)	(5,366,667)	4,385,753	1,569,461	(980,913)	1.6000	0
10.50%	8,586,667	(7,017,205)	(5,366,667)	4,385,753	1,569,461	(980,913)	2.0000	(196,183)
10.50%	8,586,667	(7,017,205)	(5,366,667)	4,385,753	1,569,461	(980,913)	1.8000	(108,990)
10.50%	8,586,667	(7,017,205)	(5,366,667)	4,385,753	1,569,461	(980,913)	1.4000	140,130
10.50%	8,586,667	(7,017,205)	(5,366,667)	4,385,753	1,569,461	(980,913)	1.2000	326,971

FX Hedge Position Analysis (at different US$ LIBOR rates)

US$ LIBOR Rate	4.250%	5.250%	6.250%	7.250%	8.250%	9.250%	10.250%	10.500%
US$ Cash Flows	2,213,531	1,702,420	1,191,309	680,198	169,087	(342,024)	(853,135)	(980,913)
DEM Cash Flows	(3,541,650)	(2,723,872)	(1,906,094)	(1,088,317)	(270,539)	547,239	1,365,017	1,569,461
Break-Even Exchange Rate	1.6000	1.6000	1.6000	1.6000	1.6000	1.6000	1.6000	1.6000

This exposure is ignored in the remainder of this analysis.

As is evident from *Exhibit 13.16*, if US$ six month LIBOR is less than 8.7% pa, then the bank has a net positive US$ cash flow which is utilised to fund a net cash outflow. If US$ six month LIBOR (for the first settlement) is set at 4.25% pa, then the bank has a net US$ inflow of US$2,213,531 and a net DEM outflow of DEM3,541,650. If the US$/DEM exchange rate remains at US$1:DEM1.6000 (the rate of the commencement of the transaction), then the bank's net cash flow position is zero; that is, the DEM equivalent of the net US$ inflow exactly matches the bank's DEM shortfall. However, the bank has a currency gain if the DEM depreciates against the US$ and has a currency loss if the DEM appreciates against the US$. The cash flows realised by the bank under alternative currency rate is summarised in *Exhibit 13.16*.

The bank's exposure to an appreciating DEM is *reversed* where US$ six month LIBOR is greater than 8.7% pa. As set out in *Exhibit 13.16*, where US$ six month LIBOR is greater than 8.7% pa, the bank has a net US$ outflow which must be funded from a net DEM cash surplus. As a consequence, the bank's exposure is to a depreciating DEM relative to the US$.

The difficulty in managing this exposure is the inherent linkage between the nature of the underlying currency exposure to the US$ six month LIBOR rate for any interest period during the life of the differential swap (refer *Exhibit 13.16*).

In practice, this exposure is treated as one which is similar to those incurred under currency options and hedged through the use of foreign exchange options.

To structure the currency option hedge it is necessary to make assumptions regarding the anticipated maximum and minimum future level of the six month US$ LIBOR rate over the life of the differential swap transaction. This is because the exact quantum of the cash flows to be hedged is generated by the actual level of US$ six month LIBOR as at any rate set date.

For the purpose of illustration, assume that it is anticipated that US$ six month LIBOR will never be set below 4.25% or above 10.5% over the three year term of the differential swap. Utilising this assumption, to fully hedge against losses, the bank would need to purchase the following options:

1. *Purchase of DEM call/US$ put option—*

   The bank would purchase a series of six DEM call options (with maturities corresponding with the payment date under the differential swap structure) at a strike price equal to the prevailing spot rate of US$1:DEM1.6000.

   The bank would purchase the DEM call on approximately 2.21% of the US$100.0m notional principal amount. The amount of DEM calls required is calculated by taking the difference between the assumed minimum LIBOR rate and the break even US$ six month LIBOR rate (which equates to the US$ swap rate payable under the swap) to generate the US$ cash inflow.

2. *Purchase of DEM Put/US$ call—*

   To hedge its exposure where US$ six month LIBOR is greater than 8.70% pa, the bank would purchase a series of six DEM put options with strike price of US$1:DEM1.6000. The bank would purchase DEM puts on approximately 0.98% of the US$100.0m notional principal amount of the transaction.

As is evident, the structure of this currency hedge is far from efficient. In particular, the effectiveness of the hedge depends on the forecasting accuracy of the minimum and maximum US$ six month LIBOR rates over the life of the differential swap. For example, even if the bank is accurate in prescribing the minimum and maximum levels of US$ six month LIBOR over the swap, there will be certain circumstances in which the hedge will not be accurate.

In periods in which US$ six month LIBOR is between the minimum level assumed (4.25%) and the break-even rate (8.7%), if the DEM strengthens against the US$, the DEM call/US$ put option purchased by the bank will generate a higher gain than the actual cash flow loss incurred by the bank under the swap. Similarly, the bank will be over-hedged where US$ six month LIBOR is between 8.7% pa and the assumed maximum of 10.5% pa and the US$ strengthens.

A common approach to avoid overhedging is for the amount of the options required to be calculated on the maximum and minimum rates which US$ six month LIBOR is expected to *average* over the life of the transaction, rather than the lowest and highest possible US$ six month LIBOR rate over the term of the transaction.

A problem in structuring the hedge which lowers hedge efficiency is the inherent assumption that movements in US$ six month LIBOR rate is not correlated to movements in the US$/DEM exchange rate. In practice, there will be some correlation between movement in US$ six month LIBOR rate and the US$/DEM rate which will necessarily influence the *actual* exposure under the differential swap.

A number of institutions utilise proprietary hedging techniques designed to improve the efficiency of the currency hedge necessitated by the differential swap. Improving the efficiency of the currency risk management process necessarily minimises the cost of implementing and maintaining the hedge.

For example, if it is assumed that increases in US$ LIBOR are likely to coincide with a stronger US$, the hedge structure could be adjusted to lower the effective level of protection against a depreciation of the US$ against the DEM. This could entail the bank purchasing a lower face value amount of DEM call/US$ put option (in the extreme case, this exposure could be left unhedged).

The correlation concepts underlying the derivation of the option value are common to a whole class of emerging derivative instruments usually referred to as quanto (or quantity adjusting) options. The central feature of these instruments is the uncertainty underlying the *value* or *amount of cash flow* required to be hedged.

An example other than differential swaps of this class of instrument is currency hedged equity warrants. Under this type of transaction, the warrant purchaser receives the value of any appreciation (in the case of a call option or warrant) in a nominated foreign equity market index in its base currency, *that is, without currency risk*.

This type of transaction is equivalent to a purchase of a relevant option on the foreign equity market index and the simultaneous entry into a derivative transaction to hedge the return on the warrant into its base currency usually at rates prevailing at the commencement of the transaction. Given the uncertainty in the value of the foreign equity market and therefore the maturity value of the option, the currency hedge must be structured to cater for the uncertainty of the value to be hedged. In effect, the hedge needs to recognise the correlation between the change in value of the foreign equity market index and the movements in the currency relativities. The problem is similar to that in the case of the index differential swaps where the underlying currency exposure is linked to the interest rate relativities as between the currencies.

Mathematical pricing models for valuing quanto options or derivatives of this type have been developed. Reiner (March 1992) and Rubinstein (May 1991) outline two valuation approaches. Increasingly, the approach to pricing quanto options is to utilise the correlation between the relevant variables as a parameter in the pricing of the option. For example, in the context of the currency hedged warrant structures, the relevant correlation is that between the returns on the relevant currency values and the return on the foreign market index in the currency *of the index*. In the case of index differential swaps, the relevant correlation is that between the relevant currencies and the interest rate *differential* between interest rates in the relevant currencies. A problem underlying this approach to pricing is the need to assume stability of the relationship between the variables.

An alternative approach would be for the bank to hedge its currency exposure by purchasing *options on the relevant currency options*. Where options of whatever type are utilised, the bank may choose not to actually purchase the identified options but utilise dynamic hedging techniques to synthetically create the requisite option position.

In practice, quanto option pricing approaches are utilised by major financial institutions active as differential swap market makers.

Margin determination

The actual margin payable under the differential swap requires the amortisation over the life of the transaction of the following items:

- the upfront payment required to be made by the bank to rewrite one of the interest rate swap coupons;
- the cost of purchasing or creating the options designed to hedge the foreign exchange exposure.

In the above example, the total cost that must be amortised over the life of the transaction is as follows:

Upfront payment in respect of US$ interest rate swap: US$3,845,463

Option premiums: US$1,029,348

This total cost of US$4,874,811 (DEM7,799,698) is amortised over the six payments (three years of semi-annual payments) and equates to approximately 2.15% pa or 1.08% pa semi-annually (refer *Exhibit 13.17*).

Based on these calculations, the pricing of the differential swap requires the counterparty to pay US$ six month LIBOR plus 2.15% pa on a notional principal amount of DEM160.0m in return for receiving DEM six month LIBOR on DEM160.0m. Accordingly, the counterparty would benefit from the transaction as long as US$ six month LIBOR was, at least, 2.15% pa below DEM six month LIBOR over the term of this transaction.

In general, pricing of a differential swap will closely approximate the net difference in swap rates in the relevant currencies for the maturities relevant to the desired term of the differential swap plus the cost of hedging the currency risk entailed for the bank in the transaction.

The margin component relating to the net difference in the swap rates will, typically, be similar for most institutions. However, the cost of management of the currency risk position may vary between institutions.

The actual imputed price for management of the currency risk will depend, initially, on the approach of the institution—that is, whether the institution will accept the currency risk or seek to neutralise the risk. In the event that the institution seeks to neutralise the risk, the premium charged to cover the cost of hedging will depend upon a variety of factors including: the assumptions regarding the future path of the relevant floating rate index and the exact structure of the currency hedge (particularly, the level of protection through currency options—irrespective of

Exhibit 13.17

Differential Swap—Margin Determination

Differential Swap Margin Adjustment									
(1) Option Cost									
	Face Value (US$)	Premium (US$)	Period (% of FV)	1	2	3	4	5	6
US$ Put/DEM Call	2,123,531	533,006		2.60%	3.30%	3.80%	4.40%	5.50%	5.50%
US$ Call/DEM Put	980,913	496,342		5.00%	7.30%	8.70%	9.50%	10.00%	10.10%
Total		1,029,348							
(2) Total									
		(US$)	(DEM)						
Swap PV Amount		3,845,463	6,152,741						
Hedging Costs		1,029,348	1,646,957						
Total		4,874,811	7,799,698						
Amortised Equivalent	US$ (SA)	1,029,038	1,723,185						
	BPS (SA)	1.03%	1.08%						
	BPS (A)	2.06%	2.15%						

whether they are outright purchases or synthetically created—utilised in the structure).

The cost of hedging the currency risk will generally depend on the shape of the yield curve of the two relevant currencies. The wider the interest differential between the two currencies over the life of the transaction, the higher the hedging costs (or benefits). The importance of this factor relates to the fact that the strike price of the relevant options will be set at the prevailing spot rate at the commencement of the transaction but the prevailing forward rate (determined by interest differentials) will dictate whether the options are in or out-of-the-money and, therefore, their relative cost.

For example, in the above example, because of the positive interest rate differential in favour of the DEM, forward rates for the purchase of DEM against sales of the US$ will be lower than the prevailing swap rate of US$1:DEM1.60. This means that DEM call/US$ puts with the strike rise of DEM1.60 required to be purchased will be out-of-the-money options, thereby, reducing the cost of the option. Conversely, the DEM put/US$ calls required to hedge the bank's cashflow mismatch where US$ six month LIBOR is greater than 8.7% will be in-the-money commensurately increasing the cost.

Consequently, the pricing of the differential swap in terms of the margin components will be most favourable where the net difference in swap rates between the two respective currencies for the relevant maturities is low and the shape of the yield curve for the two currencies means that the cost of hedging the currency risks is minimal.

Differential swaps—hedging/pricing in practice

The complexity of hedging and pricing differential swap transactions has, in practice, led to a multiplicity of approaches to the management of the underlying risks of such transactions. The concern about the methodology for pricing and hedging such transactions has been exacerbated by persistent rumours of large profits and losses incurred by major providers of such instruments as well as concern regarding the difficulties in hedging such exposures particularly in periods of increased volatility in markets, for example, during the realignment/breakup of Europe's Exchange Rate Mechanism (ERM).

For institutions active in financial derivatives generally who are large traders/providers of index differential swap products, a portfolio approach to risk management has generally been assumed. Under this approach, the risk of differential swap transactions is aggregated into portfolios of other interest rate and currency transactions and the net position hedged. As noted above, these institutions generally utilise the quanto option methodology to price the currency risk management component of such transactions.

Under an alternative approach,[2] the risks of differential swaps are separated into two specific components:

- exchange rate risk based on current yield curves in the relevant currencies and exchange rates; and
- a contingent exposure based on future yield curves.

This approach also seeks to manage and hedge the exchange rate and interest rate risks of differential swaps separately, the rationale being that this facilitates more efficient management of these risks.

2. See letter to the Editor by Jeremy Putley, Lehmann Brothers, New York (1993) (March) *Risk* Vol 6, No 3, p 12.

Under this approach, the amounts to be received and paid under the differential swaps are determined utilising the forward rates in the relevant currencies implied by the respective yield curves. For example, in the example utilised previously, the six month DEM LIBOR and the six month US$ LIBOR implied at the relevant points in time (for example, six, 12, 18, etc months in the future) from the existing yield curve would be determined. The determination of the forward rates would allow the differential to be paid or received under the differential swap to be established.

Once the net payments are established, the net amounts of a particular currency to be paid or received can be present valued to a current sum with the resultant payable or receivable amount being hedged by an offsetting spot position in the currency. This hedge is then dynamically adjusted as the yield curve in both currencies changes and the currency rates alter. This procedure allows the currency exposure of the transaction to be hedged but does not hedge the interest rate risk.

The contingent exchange rate risk which is driven by changes in interest rate risks is immunised, if required, through option transactions.

The approach described only enables a perfectly immunised position to be created instantaneously at a given point in time. Maintenance of the hedge requires future transaction costs to be incurred which will be driven by the volatility of interest rates, foreign exchange rates and, most importantly, the correlation between these variables. The major difficulty with this approach is that the risk of interest rates movements and currencies are, for all practical purposes, closely related and there are limited opportunities for hedging this correlation with liquid instruments.

An alternative method of hedging would entail utilising securities with the embedded differential swap positions (see discussion below) as a potential instrument to immunise exposures entered into by financial institutions in transacting differential swaps. However, the limited level of outstanding differential bonds greatly restricts the opportunities to manage portfolio exposures in such transactions in this manner.

A more promising avenue of hedging these transaction exposures is the emerging market in spread differential options which is discussed below.

Applications

Potential applications of differential swaps reflect its capacity to be utilised to capitalise on existing expected differences in short-term interest rates between currency sectors without incurring any currency exposure. The differential structure also allows counterparties to engineer yield curve positions whereby it assumes an exposure to future short-term interest rate differentials as against long-term interest differentials in the relevant currencies.

Both liability and asset managers can utilise differential swaps to manage underlying liability and asset portfolios.

A central aspect of differential swaps is that entry into these types of transactions are predicated on the counterparty assuming an interest rate risk position across currencies. The transaction is by its inherent nature not free of risk as changes in interest rate differentials will increase the cost of borrowing or reduce the return to investors utilising such transactions.

Differential swaps can, by their very nature, be utilised to trade the shape of the yield curve as between two currencies. For example, an existing differential swap position can be traded and unwound to lock in gains where the change in the yield differential (in the long-term interest rates in the relevant currencies which determine the differential swap margin) alter in favour of the counterparty. An issue in trading differential swaps is the relatively higher bid-offer spread which may increase the cost of such trading in these instruments.

In this regard, differential swaps are not dissimilar to another cross-market derivative product—spread differential warrants (see discussion below).

Liability management

Differential swaps are primarily utilised by liability managers to assume short-term interest rate positions (without incurring currency risk) designed to reduce the interest cost on borrowings.

For example, in the example outlined above, the counterparty has effectively converted a three year DEM160.0m floating rate liability into a DEM liability on which it pays interest rates calculated as US$ six month LIBOR plus 2.15%.

For example, as at the first settlement date, assuming DEM six month US$ LIBOR is set at 9.5% and US$ six month LIBOR set at 4.25%, the counterparty locks in a positive margin of 3.10% pa (the LIBOR differential of 5.25% adjusted for the differential swap margin of 2.15%). This has the impact of reducing its borrowing cost by 3.10% to 6.40% pa (in DEM) as opposed to a borrowing cost of 9.5% pa if it had not entered into the differential swap. *Exhibit 13.18* illustrates this transaction.

The counterparty benefits from transacting this differential swap against underlying DEM borrowing as long as US$ six month LIBOR is, at least, 2.15% pa below DEM six month LIBOR.

Exhibit 13.18

Liability-Based Differential Swap Structure

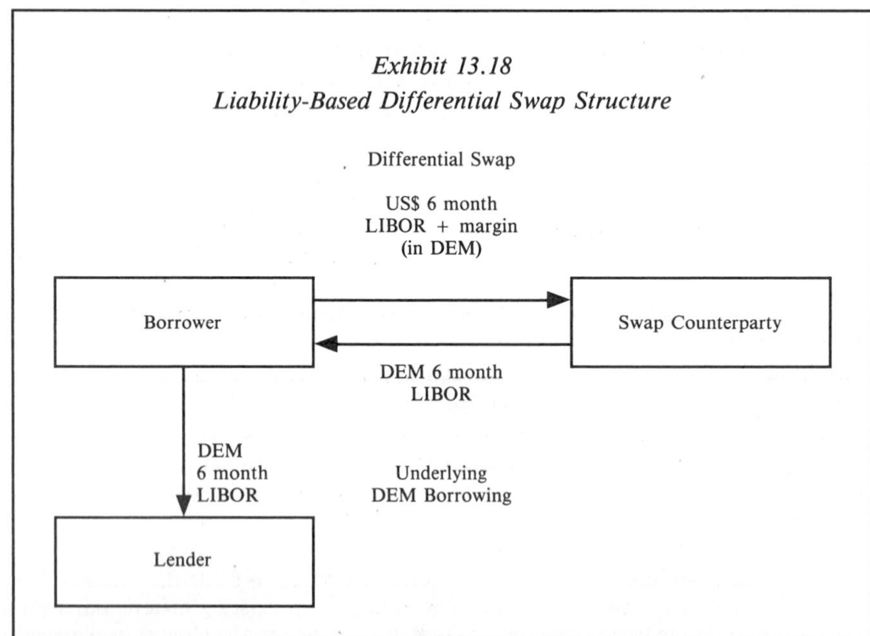

In a number of high short-term (at various times during recent years) interest currencies (primarily, DEM, GBP, JPY and C$), the benefit of the differential swap has been incorporated in the underlying loan transaction. Such loans (referred to a cross rate loans) entail a borrowing in a high short-term interest rate currency (such as JPY, DEM, CAN or GBP) on which the interest payable is calculated with reference to a lower interest rate currency such as US$ plus a cross rate spread.

Exhibit 13.19 illustrates the structure of such cross rate loan financings. The structure essentially entails the funding bank entering into a differential swap to restructure the normal single currency loan flows to create the cross rate loan.

Exhibit 13.19
Cross-Rate Loan Transaction

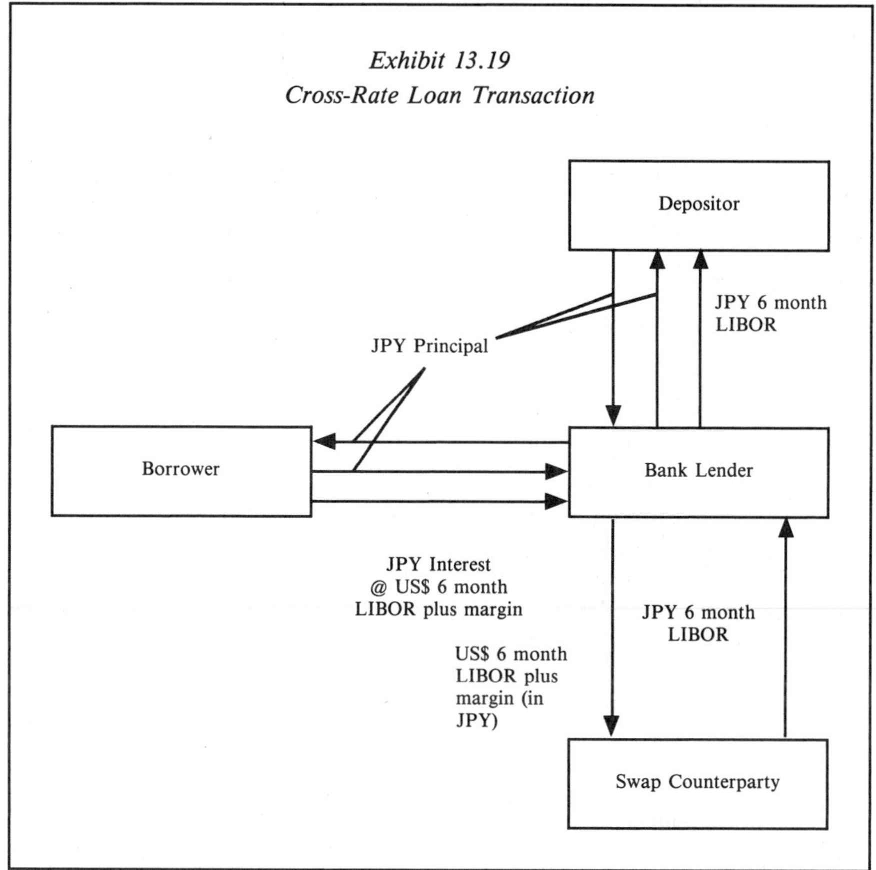

In a similar structure arrangement, number of security issues (primarily private placements and a few public issues) have been undertaken with embedded differential swap characteristics. In a typical issue, the borrower issues securities (say in US$) which carry an interest coupon in a high short-term rate currency (say DEM six month LIBOR minus a spread). The borrower, in turn, enters into a differential swap with a bank to convert its payments stream linked to DEM six month LIBOR to a US$ six month LIBOR related payment at a margin below its normal funding costs. *Exhibit 13.20* sets out an example of this type of structure.

Exhibit 13.20
Differential Swap Embedded Security (1)

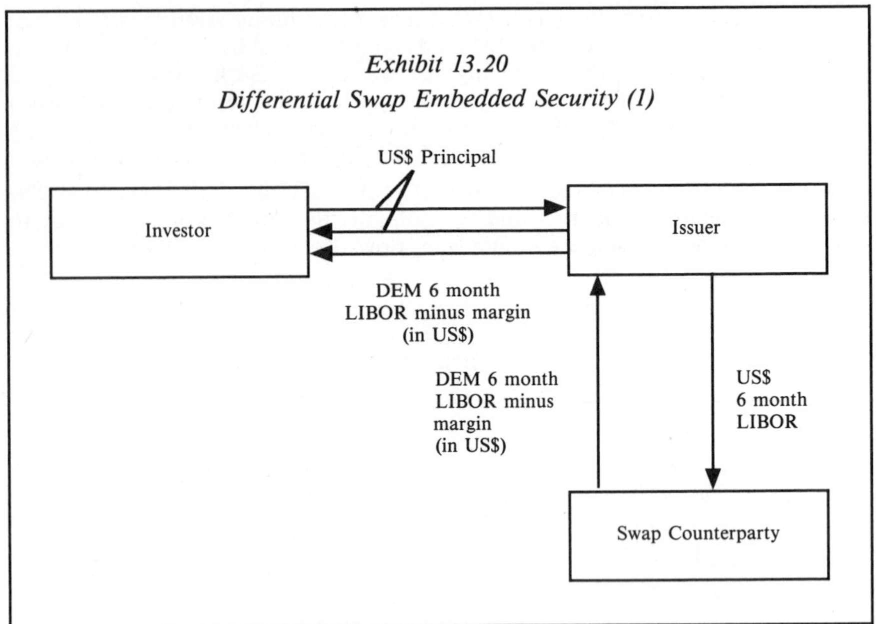

Differential swap transactions can also be embedded in Reverse Floating Rate Note (FRN) issues. In such a transaction, the investor would receive an interest rate on its investment of, say, 18.00% pa minus US$ LIBOR plus a margin, with all payments being in A$. The issuer of the A$ Reverse FRN would convert its borrowing onto a conventional basis by entering into two swaps:

- a differential swap under which it pays US$ LIBOR plus a margin and receives A$ LIBOR (all payments in A$);
- a conventional A$ interest rate swap on *double the total amount of the face value of the Reverse FRN* whereby it receives a fixed A$ rate (say, 2 × 9.50% pa = 19.00% pa) and pays A$ LIBOR (2 × A$ LIBOR).

The result of these swaps would be to leave the issuer with a borrowing (equivalent to the face value of the FRN) at a margin under A$ LIBOR (in this example, 1.00% pa). *Exhibit 13.21* sets out an example of this structure.

An interesting potential application of differential swap relates to existing interest rate swaps. For example, where corporations have entered into an interest rate swap, say in US$, to hedge underlying borrowings, the shape of the yield curve in that currency, currently, results in the borrower incurring substantial cost. This cost is represented by the differential between short-term US$ six month LIBOR rates and medium- to long-term swap rates payable in US$ (a differential of approximately 3% to 4% pa depending on maturity). The yield curve cost under such US$ interest swap transactions can be managed using differential swaps as follows:

- the borrower enters into a US$ interest rate swap where it pays a fixed rate and receives a floating rate (US$ six month LIBOR);
- simultaneously, the borrower enters into a differential swap for the same US$ notional principal amount whereby the borrower agrees to pay US$ six month LIBOR and receive DEM six month LIBOR less a margin (in US$).

Exhibit 13.21
Differential Swap Embedded Security (2)

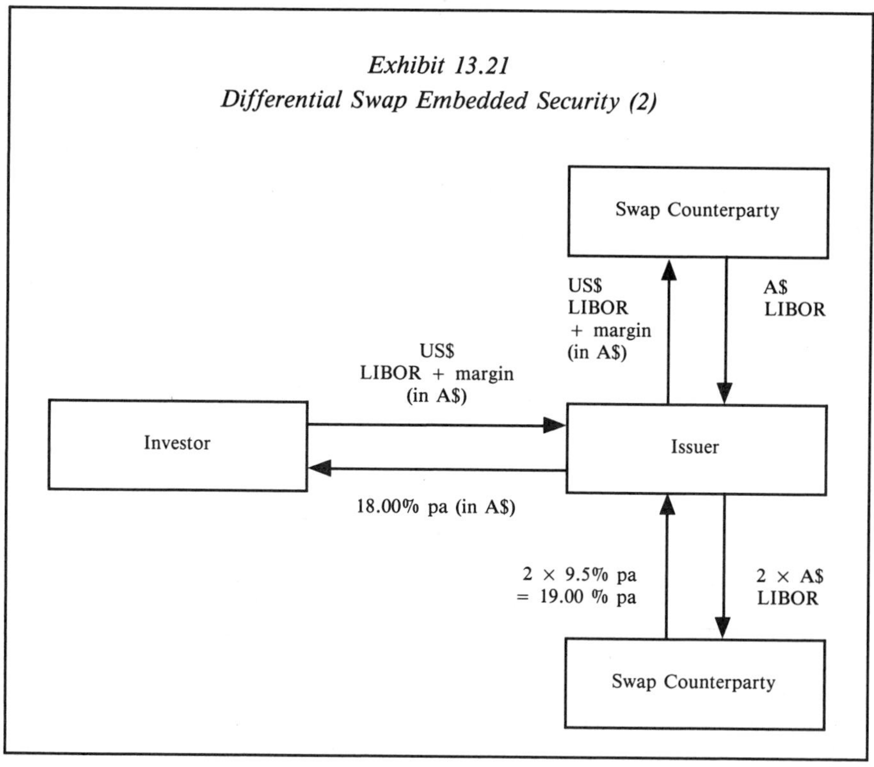

The result of this transaction is to increase the floating rate receipts under the US$ interest rate swap as long as DEM six month LIBOR adjusted for the differential swap margin exceeds US$ six month LIBOR. This has the impact of lowering the effective fixed rate cost to the borrower. *Exhibit 13.22* sets out this particular application.

Asset management

A significant impetus for differential swaps derives from investors seeking to increase returns on money market interest related investment assets. Asset managers, willing to take positions interest rate differentials between currencies, have utilised differential swaps to enhance returns on investment assets in currencies where money market rates have dropped to relatively low levels, such as US$ short-term investments.

Asset managers in this case would enter into a differential swap whereby it would receive DEM six month LIBOR minus differential swap spread (in US$) and pay US$ six month LIBOR.

Under this structure, the US$ six month LIBOR flows would be matched by the return accruing to the investor from its underlying US$ investment asset. The overall return to the investor would be based on DEM six month LIBOR rates. Accordingly, the investor would benefit from utilising the differential swaps where DEM six month LIBOR minus the differential swap margin exceeded US$ six month LIBOR over the life of the transaction.

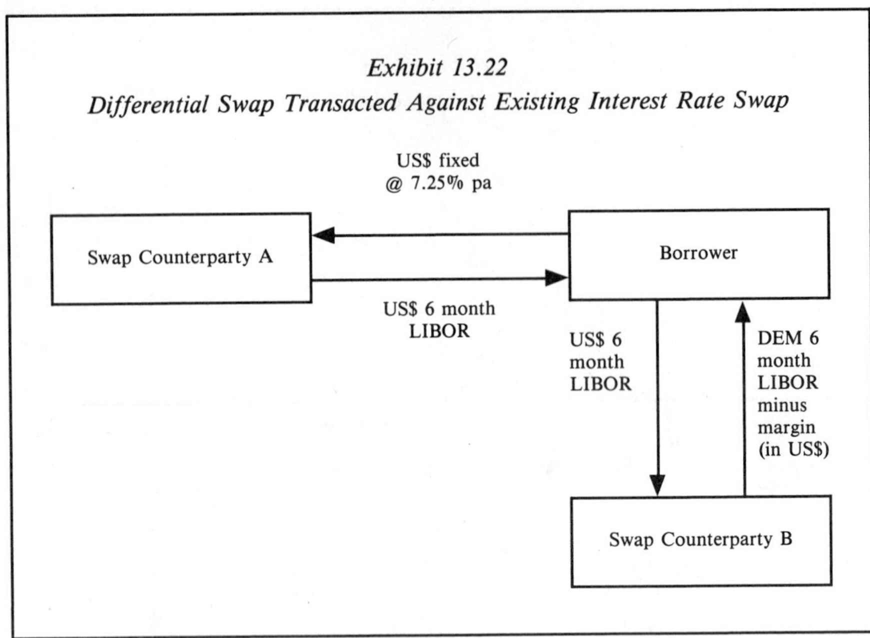

Exhibit 13.23 sets out an example of a differential swap structure which can be utilised by an asset manager.

As an alternative to entering into the differential swap, investors can benefit from the structural advantages of this type of transaction by purchasing securities where

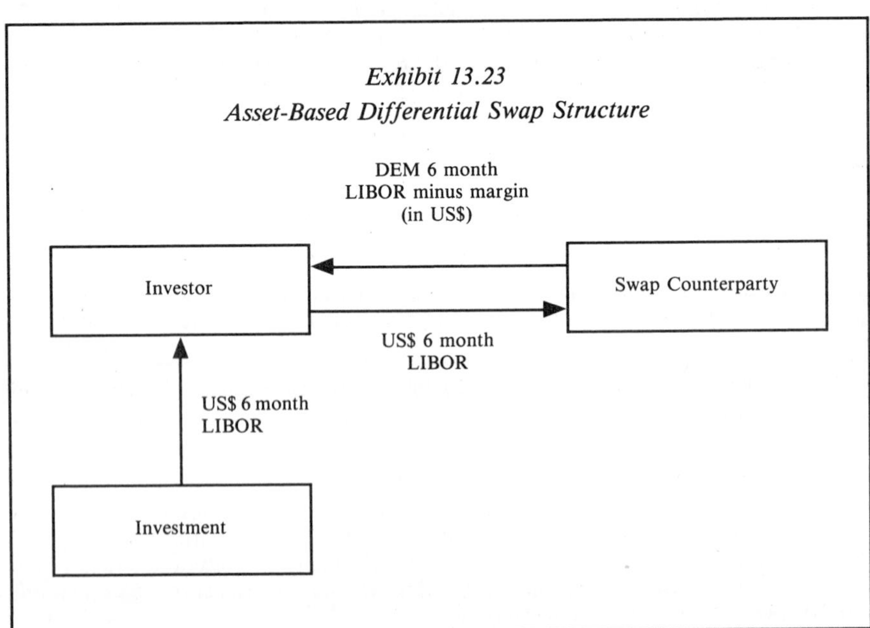

the differential swap cash flow profile is embedded into the bond to provide the anticipated interest rate differential benefit. *Exhibits 13.20* and *13.21* outline the structures of such securities.

An additional advantage for asset managers of differential swap structures is that they allow investors to take positions in interest rate differentials *as between any two currencies* without incurring currency exposures. For example, an investment manager with a predominant US$ investment portfolio could seek to take advantage of anticipated movements in the differential between DEM and JPY interest rates by entering into a DEM/JPY differential swap (where all payments are in US$) to create the required exposure to DEM/JPY interest differentials.

Market for differential swaps

The market for differential swaps is of relatively recent origin. The first differential swap was undertaken in late 1990/early 1991. The differential swap has increased in popularity with significant levels of transactions being completed in the latter half of 1991 and early 1992.

The major impetus to the market has been the prevailing structure of global interest rates. In the present environment, the difference in short-term interest rates as between a number of currencies is significantly different from the differential in long-term rates in these currencies. In addition, the prevalence of flat or inverted yield curves in a number of currencies (primarily European currencies) and the corresponding incidence of sharply positively sloped yield curves in some currencies (for example, US$) has assisted in creating differential swap opportunities.

The incidence of this type of interest rate environment has allowed differential swaps to be structured for two main types of capital market participants.

A major group of participants has been asset managers seeking to enhance returns on relatively low yielding US$ denominated investment assets yielding US$ money market related rates of return. These investors have entered into differential swaps where they pay US$ LIBOR and receive in US$ DEM, SFR, GBP and (until recently) JPY LIBOR minus the differential swap margin. Asset managers have sought to benefit from differential swap structure either directly by entering into such transactions or, indirectly, through purchasing securities in which the differential swap structure is embedded.

Another major class of participant in the differential swap market has been borrowers in currencies in which short-term money market rates have been relatively high. These borrowers have entered into differential swaps where they receive, for example, DEM, SFR or GBP six month LIBOR and pay US$ six month LIBOR plus the differential swap margin. These transactions are designed to reduce the borrowers' interest cost by seeking to capitalise on the interest differential as between the relevant currencies.

One group of borrowers who have been active in utilising the differential swap structure have been smaller Japanese companies who have restructured their liabilities to carry interest rates which are related to US$ floating rates seeking to capitalise on the favourable interest differential between US$ and JPY.

The development of a market in differential swaps is still in its early stages. The technology necessary to hedge and manage the currency exposures entailed by such transactions is confined to a relatively small group of financial institutions. Major providers of differential swaps include Bankers Trust, CS Financial Products, Merrill Lynch, JP Morgan and Morgan Stanley.

However, as transaction volumes grow and the hedging technology, inevitably, proliferates, other institutions are likely to enter the market with a resultant drop in bid-offer spreads thereby decreasing the cost for participants in transacting differential swaps.

Differential swaps and spread warrants

Spread differential warrants

Differential swaps belong to a category of transactions often referred to as cross-market financial derivatives. The key feature of these instruments is that the value of such instruments depends on the price of at least two financial variables. In the case of differential swaps, the relevant variables are money market rates in two different currencies.

An alternative means of capturing existing and expected differentials in interest rates between two currencies are spread differential warrants. Spread differential warrants are equivalent to options on the price differentials between two debt instruments. The rationale of such transactions is that the two underlying assets are related via the concept of demand substitution. For example, investors may look at two bond markets (and, indirectly, interest rates in those markets) as substitute investments for funds under management.

Exhibit 13.24 sets out an example of a spread differential warrant transaction.

The major relationship between spread differential warrants and differential swaps exists at two levels:

- hedging differential swaps; and
- improving the efficiency of pricing of differential swap transactions.

As noted above, the pricing on a differential swap is, to a large extent, driven by the interest differential as between the two relevant currencies. As also discussed above, this differential generates a complex currency hedging problem in the management of the risks of a differential swap.

In practice, where differential warrants or options on short term interest rate differentials are actively traded, a portfolio manager with a position in differential swaps could, by purchasing or selling such warrants or option, structure hedges to immunise its own differential swap portfolio position.

Exhibit 13.24

Spread Differential Warrants

In November 1991, Mitsubishi Finance International launched an issue of cross-currency yield spread warrants between gilts and bunds.

The terms of the issue were as follows:

Issuer:	Mitsubishi Finance Intl.
Number of warrants:	Seven tranches, each consisting of 100,000 puts warrants and 100,000 call warrants.
Issue price:	GBP33.00 per warrant.
Exercise:	Each warrant is exercisable into the spread differential between notional yields calculated by reference to the long gilt futures contract and the Bund futures contract listed on LIFFE.
Gearing:	5 times.

Exhibit 13.24—continued

Exercise style:	American.
Exercise period:	20 December 1991 to 27 May 1992.
Exercise level:	0bps, 50bps, 100bps, 167.5bps, 200bps, 250bps, 300bps.
Issue price:	Warrant with strike of 167.5bp-GBP33 per warrant, calls and puts, equivalent to 33bps in yield spread. Other issue prices available from Mitsubishi Finance.
Listing:	London.
Payment date:	19 December 1991.
Lead manager:	Mitsubishi Finance.

The warrant prices for different yield spreads are summarised below:

Price	-100	-50	-25	-10	0	10	25	50	100
Calls	5	13	21	27	33	40	49	66	106
Puts	106	66	49	40	33	27	21	13	5

The implied yields of the futures contracts are calculated by defining the contracts as theoretical constant maturity bonds, the long gilt as a 9% semi-annual coupon 20 year bond and the Bund as a 6% annual coupon ten year bond.

The notional bond terms are close to the terms of the futures contracts listed on LIFFE. Market professionals may choose to calculate the implied yield using the maturity of the cheapest to deliver for each contract. However, given this can change from day to day, it is probably unworkable as the basis for a spread warrant.

Each basis point of widening or narrowing in the yield spread away from the strike spread at issue provides a pay-off on exercise equivalent to GBP.

An example of the return to a call warrant investor is summarised below:

	Yields at launch (%)	**Yields exercise (%)**
Gilts	9.67	10.50
Bunds	8.00	8.00
Difference (strike yield)	1.67	2.50

On exercise, the holder of the call warrant is entitled to receive (250 – 167) = GBP83 per warrant.

Prior to maturity, warrant holders can expect to sell their warrants to realise not just the intrinsic value, but also any inherent time value.

The return to a put warrant investor is summarised below based on a strike yield of 167bps:

Gilt yield	9.67%	7.67	5.67	3.67
Bund yield	8.00	8.00	8.00	8.00
Difference	1.67	0.33	2.33	5.33
Put exercise value (GBP)	0.00	33.00	233.00	533.00

The value of the puts on exercise continues to increase, even when notional gilt yields are below bund yields. There is no theoretical maximum value for the puts, as bund yields can rise almost infinitely.

Warrants are traditionally analysed by reference to premium or gearing. To calculate the premium and gearing, the level of the underlying needs to be known.

$$\text{Premium of calls} = \left[\frac{(\text{warrant price} + \text{strike price})}{\text{level of underlying}} - \frac{1}{n}\right]\%$$

$$\text{Gearing} = \frac{(\text{warrant price})}{\text{level of underlying}} \times (\text{times})$$

The level of underlying of the at-the-money tranche of this issue was 167bps, giving a premium of 19.8% and a gearing of 5 times. However, the gearing of the tranche with a strike rate of 0bps would be infinity and the premium zero.

An alternative method is to look at the face amount of each gilt or bund future controlled by the warrant. In this case, a one basis point change in yield is equivalent to a GBP1 change

Exhibit 13.24—continued

in the intrinsic value of the warrant. An investor holding GBP1.234 of 15 year, 9% coupon bearing gilts would have a GBP1 change in the value of the holding for a one basis point change in yield. The premium is then 2.67% and the gearing 37.4 times.

This methodology makes it possible to compare warrants with different strikes, including a strike of zero. It also ties in with options on bonds, which have similarly low premiums and high gearings. However, it would be unrealistic as a methodology for currency, commodity or equity spreads. This is because the potential price range of a currency, commodity or equity is constrained on the put side on the downside, particularly in the case of equity values where the company is in liquidation.

If the investor has a view on the spread itself, the warrants provide a considerable degree of gearing. A GBP1,000 investment in the puts would show a 20% gain from a 10bps narrowing in the yield spread.

The Table attached shows the comparative performance of two portfolios. Portfolio "a" consisting of a GBP1,000 investment in the 11.75% Jan 2003/07 UK gilt and a second portfolio "b + w" also of GBP1,000 made up of one warrant and the remainder in the same gilt.

TABLE

Gilt yield s/a	**Gilt yield %**	**Value of a gilt portfolio with no warrants**	**Value of a gilt portfolio with 1 put warrant**	**Puts price at different gilt yields**	**Warrant portfolio value**	**Diff**
		a	b		w	a − (b + w)
		855.21	826.99			
10.07	111.076	984.61	952.12	21.00	21.00	(11.49)
9.92	112.152	993.82	961.02	27.00	27.00	(5.80)
9.82	112.875	1,000.00	967.00	33.00	33.00	0.00
9.72	113.61	1,006.29	973.08	40.00	40.00	6.79
9.57	114.72	1,015.78	982.26	49.00	49.00	15.48

Mitsubishi Finance probably used the available futures contacts to hedge the warrant. The specification of the gilt future has been changed to allow new issues to be delivered into the June 1992 contract. Mitsubishi will have to bear the risk that new issues with radically different coupons will cause large movements in the long gilt.

Source: "Product Analysis" (1991) (November) *International Financing Review* Issue 905, 82-83.

At a more general level, the theoretical work completed on pricing spread differential warrants is of assistance in pricing this element of differential swap transactions. This theoretical work is summarised below.

Pricing of spread differential options

The major features of pricing spread differential options and warrants includes:

- complexity of the hedge and, consequently, pricing problems;
- the existence of negative vegas (that is, lower volatility may produce higher option prices); and
- the non-log normal distribution of the underlying asset which creates pricing problems.

To date, two general approaches to pricing spread or differential options have emerged:

- The first approach treats the spread between the two variables as an asset price.
- The second approach utilises two factor spread pricing models.

Under the first approach, the spread is treated as an asset price, in its own right. This allows application of Black and Scholes type option pricing approaches. The major difficulty with this approach relates to the underlying assumptions of the Black and Scholes option pricing models.

In this context, the model implies through the log normal distribution assumption that the spread cannot be negative. In addition, the log normal assumption implies that spread fluctuation sizes would increase for larger spreads and decrease for smaller fluctuation sizes (phenomena not supported by evidence or experience). The above assumptions are clearly not realistic.

In addition, this type of approach requires that a commodity convenience yield (see discussion in Chapter 16) on the spread must be assumed and, in practice, is usually set at zero. In addition, this approach implies a single delta as a basis for hedging. This is particularly problematic where the spread is between assets of different volatility.

Deficiencies of this single factor approach has led to the development of two factor models which utilise the arithmetic difference between the log normally distributed asset prices as the spread. The input parameters for such models include:

- volatilities of both assets;
- the correlation between the two assets;
- the convenience (or other yield or earnings rate) of each asset.

The two factor models proclude multiple outputs including two deltas, multiple gammas, and two vegas.

An interesting aspect of these spread differential option pricing models is that they often generate negative vegas, as noted above. This means that the lower volatility of the underlying asset produces, on occasions, higher option prices. This reflects the fact that where the price of one asset increases and the price of the other asset increases at a slower rate reflecting diminished volatility in the price of that asset, the spread increases and the value of the option spread increases reflecting the increase in the spread itself, despite the lower volatility of one asset.

The two factor approach, which is similar to the quanto pricing approaches discussed previously, enables more accurate hedges and, therefore, more accurate pricing of these instruments to be structured.

The major implication of these theoretical developments in relation to pricing index differential swap transactions is that they increase the potential techniques available to a portfolio manager to hedge the underlying exposure incurred in trading in index differential swap transaction. For example, by trading in the underlying index differential options, the portfolio manager can immunise a component of the currency risk under the index differential transactions. Where the cost of structuring the interest rate hedge is lower than the cost of transacting in the relevant currency options, the hedge structure devised is more efficient and reduces the cost to the trader. In addition, the existence of a market in interest differential products facilitates reallocation of the interest rate spread risk component of differential swaps to participants willing to accept such risks for an appropriate price.

Chapter 14

Options on Swaps

INTRODUCTION

Coincidental with the growth in the market for swaps, transaction structures which combined features of swaps and options rapidly emerged. These types of instruments are referred to as options on swaps.

Options on swaps or swaptions entail an option on the fixed rate component of a swap transaction. A variety of structures, known variously as swaptions, callable, putable, collapsible, extendible etc swaps, are available.

While generally regarded as distinct and different types of transactions by market participants, the above structures are very similar. Each structure effectively represents an option to either enter into or provide the swap at a known price over a specified period. In essence, options on swaps combine the features of interest rate options with swap transactions.

It should be noted that the terminology associated with options on swaps is far from standardised. There are significant differences in usage as between jurisdictions. For example, as discussed in greater detail below, in the United States a putable swap would imply an option whereby the holder, a payer of fixed rates under a swap, would have the right to terminate a swap. In contrast, a callable swap would imply the right of the holder to enter into a swap as a payer of fixed rates. In some other jurisdictions terminology is exactly opposite with a callable swap giving the right to terminate the swap arrangement.

OPTIONS ON SWAPS

Terminology

An option on a swap usually entails an option on the fixed rate component of a swap. It is designed to give the holder the benefit of the strike rate (that is, the *fixed* rate specified in the agreement) if the market rates are worse, with the flexibility to deal at the market rates if they are better.

An option on a swap provides the purchaser or holder of the option with the right, but not the obligation, to enter into a swap where it pays fixed rates against receipt of a floating rate index as at a future date. The reverse type of transaction where the holder of the option on the swap will, if the option is exercised, receive the fixed rate is also feasible.

The terminology associated with options on swaps is as follows:

- *Receiver options on swaps*—whereby the purchaser or holder has the right to *receive* fixed rates under the swap.
- *Payer options on swaps*—whereby the purchaser or the holder has the right to *pay* fixed rates under the swap.
- *American style*—a swap option which can be exercised on any business day within the swap option exercise period.

- *European style*—a swap option which can be exercised only on the expiry date.
- *Exercise or strike price*—the specified rate at which the buyer has the right to enter into the swap.
- *Premium*—the consideration paid by the buyer for the swap option.
- *Expiry date*—the last date on which the swap option can be exercised and the effective date (if exercised) the fixed and floating components of the swap begin to accrue.

Characteristics of options on swaps

Options on swaps primarily offer protection against interest rate uncertainty in a manner analogous to a conventional debt option. The user of options on swaps is able to limit its downside risk in switching from fixed to floating interest rates or vice versa, without limiting potential benefits associated with unforeseen *favourable* interest rate movements. In return for this opportunity, the purchaser of an option on a swap pays a fee, that is, the swap premium.

An important aspect of options on swaps is that for certain classes of borrower, where they would ultimately be users of swaps, the emergence of options on swaps provides them with greater flexibility and certainty in managing their assets or liabilities. This can be seen from the fact that before the emergence of these instruments, the only management tool for asymmetric risk management available to customers were exchange traded options, usually on government bond rates or, to a lesser extent, over the counter markets in options on government bond rates.

There are a number of specific characteristics of options on swaps which make these instruments particularly useful for asset or liability managers seeking in managing interest rate exposures. These include:

- *Maturity*—options on swaps are available with periods to expiration of (up to) ten years, which is significantly longer than the maturity of options available on futures exchanges and other over-the-counter options.
- *Options on term interest rates*—in contrast to caps and floors which are long dated options on *short-term rates*, options on swaps represent options on intermediate and long-term rates adding an extra dimension to interest rate risk management for asset and liability managers.
- *Corporate spread component*—options and swaps provide an option on the all-in fixed cost of funds for borrowers (or return for investors) as they incorporate a corporate spread component (being the swap spread). This allows borrowers or investors who traditionally use swaps to manage their portfolios to avoid exposure to changing spreads between swap rates and underlying government bond rates on which, generally, exchange traded and over the counter options are available.
- *Flexibility*—options and swaps, like other over-the-counter products, are extremely flexible with the user being able to specify exercise dates, amounts, specific strike rates and other structural aspects without the constraint of standardised exchange options and administrative procedures such as deposits and margins.
- *Currencies*—increasingly, options on swaps are available in a wide range of currencies facilitating their use.
- *Liquidity*—the market for options on swaps is increasingly liquid, particularly in major swap currencies such as US$, DEM, GBP, JPY etc which further facilitates their utilisation.

TYPES OF OPTIONS ON SWAPS—FUNDAMENTAL EQUIVALENCES

As noted above, the various swap structures, referred to variously as swaptions, callable, putable, collapsible, extendible etc swaps are ultimately versions of options on swaps. Most importantly, they are essentially equivalent transactions. The structuring, pricing, trading and hedging of these various types of instruments are based on the fundamental equivalence of these transactions and the capacity to decompose them into either the receiver or payer options on swaps.

The structural features of the various types of options on swaps that are available are summarised below:

- *Swaptions*—swaptions are a common term utilised to describe options on swaps. Receiver and payer swaptions correspond precisely to receiver options on swaps and payer options on swaps.
- *Callable swaps*—under this structure, the fixed rate payer is allowed to enter into, at its option, swaps, up to a maximum amount, at a known cost, up until the end of the expiry of the option under the terms of which it pays a fixed rate and receives a floating rate. A callable swap is identical to a payer option on a swap. The reverse structure is also possible allowing the purchaser or holder of the option to, upon exercise, require the counterparty to *pay* fixed rate under the swap.
- *Extendible swap*—this represents a variation on the callable swap structure. Under the terms of an extendible swap, the fixed rate payer or receiver has the option to require the counterparty to continue the swap (upon existing terms) for a fixed period beyond the term of the original swap. Analytically, an extendible swap can be unbundled as follows:
  - —A payer extendible swap is equivalent to conventional interest rate swap, under which the party pays fixed rates and receives floating rates, combined with the purchase of a payer option on a swap, where the expiry date of the option coincides with the maturity of the interest rate swap.
  - —A receiver extendible swap is identical to the payer extendible swap except that holder receives fixed rates under the original interest rate swap and purchases a receiver option on a swap.
- *Putable swap*—under this structure, a fixed rate payer has the option to terminate the swap at some future date without penalty. Analytically a putable swap is identical to entry into an interest rate swap, under which the holder pays fixed rates and receives floating rates, combined with the purchase of a receiver option on a swap whereby the purchaser has the right to receive fixed rates and pay floating rates. The expiry date of the receiver option on a swap coincides with the date at which the fixed rate payer wishes to have the choice of terminating the interest rate swap. Upon exercise of the receiver option on a swap, the fixed rate and floating rate flows under the original interest rate swap and the swap entered into as a result of exercise of the receiver option on a swap match and offset each other, thereby effectively terminating the original transaction.
- *Cancellable/collapsible swap*—under this structure, a fixed rate payer provides the swap counterparty with the right to terminate the transaction. Effectively, the fixed rate payer in an interest rate swap for a specified term, sells a payer option on a swap (whereby it receives fixed rates and pays floating rates) on an underlying swap which commences sometime during the life of the original interest rate swap and matures as of the maturity of the original interest rate swap.

• *Contingent swap*—this structure is identical to a receiver option on a swap. This type of structure is utilised both with interest rate swaps and currency swaps and linked to contingent assets and liabilities such as call options on debt instruments in the form of warrants or options.

(The various structures described above are, by no means, a comprehensive listing of variations available. In addition, definitions of the various structures are not universal and variations in usage persist between jurisdictions and markets and even sectors within markets.)

It should be noted that the party entering into structures such as the callable, putable, extendible etc structures usually compensates the provider of the option on the swap, for the additional flexibility and option element, either by payment of an upfront premium or, more typically, by an adjustment built into the swap rate (reflecting the amortisation of the option premium at a nominated funding cost).

UTILISING OPTIONS ON SWAPS FOR ASSETS—LIABILITY MANAGEMENT

The use of options on swaps by asset and liability managers are similar to the strategies employed with other interest rate options. In this section, basic asset and liability management applications entailing the purchase and sale of options on swaps are examined. Other applications related to the use of options on swaps in conjunction with capital market issues (to either securitise embedded interest rate options or to create synthetic securities with particular characteristics) is considered in subsequent sections. It should be noted that the categorisation of applications is arbitrary. The strategies utilised are similar and analytically related.

Basic applications: examples

Two examples of utilising options on swaps are set out in *Exhibit 14.1*.

While the discussion to date has focused primarily on options on interest rate swaps, similar structures involving options on interest rates on a particular currency can be devised in currency swaps. Such structures can entail an interest rate swap alone or, whether the exchange rate on the currency swap at which the initial and final exchange are to be transacted are known in advance, an option on currencies can also be created. This type of option is sometimes structured as a contingent swap which is discussed in detail later in this chapter.

Anticipatory/contingency hedging applications

The most fundamental application of options on swaps relate to anticipatory and contingency hedging problems.

Both borrowers and investors can utilise options on swaps to hedge the future borrowing costs and investment returns. In this type of anticipatory hedging, a borrower may enter into a payer option on a swap to guarantee its funding cost in relation to known financing requirements. Conversely, an investor may utilise a receiver option on a swap to guarantee itself a return on an identified investment which is to be made in the future. In this regard, the purchase of options on swaps function as a means of providing asymmetric protection against forward movements in interest rates.

Exhibit 14.1
Using Options on Swaps

Example 1

Company A (A) has a six month US$ LIBOR facility for US$100m. The company is tendering to construct a plant estimated to cost US$100m.

The project manager needs to submit a fixed cost of funding this project to the finance director on 15 January 19X6. However, studies will not be completed until 31 March 19X6, and the contract will not be awarded until 15 April 19X6. The project manager needs to fix the cost of five year funds based on current information for a project that will not begin for at least three months, and will not necessarily be awarded to the company.

On 15 December 19X5 it was decided that there was no need to buy a swaption because of wasted time value. The swaption could be purchased, it was decided, next month at a lower premium. One month later the finance director agreed to buy a European style swaption at a premium of 2.00% of the principal. The company on exercise will pay a fixed interest rate of 10.00% pa and will receive LIBOR semi-annually for five years. The exercise date is 15 April 19X6.

On 15 April 19X6 the contract is awarded to A. The pay off to A in this case would be as follows:

Scenario 1

Interest rates increase to 12.00% therefore A agrees to exercise swaption.

Current interest rate:	12.00%
Swaption rate:	10.00%
Benefit from exercising swaption:	2.00%
2.00% × $100,000,000 × five years	US$10,000,000
Less cost of premium	– US$ 2,000,000
Total savings (on an undiscounted basis)	US$ 8,000,000

Cost of swap funding will be approximately 10.528% pa, 1.45% less than the current interest rate of 12.00%. A has ensured through the swaption that the cost of funding for the project will not be greater than the presumably acceptable level of 10.528% pa.

Scenario 2

Interest rates decrease to 8.00%. A abandons the swaption and enters into a swap transaction at a fixed rate of 8.00%.

Cost of funding achieved is 8.528% by taking advantage of lower interest rates.

Example 2

Interest charges on the US$ floating debt of company B (B) increased in the past year. B is considering actions to rectify this situation, but is unwilling to swap the floating debt into fixed debt because it believes interest rates will drop.

On 15 January 19X6 B purchases a European style option on a rate of 10.00% whereby the company on exercise will pay an annual fixed rate of 10.00% and will receive LIBOR semi-annually for five years. The premium is 2.00% of US$25m. The exercise date is 1 July 19X6.

On 1 July 19X6, B decide to exercise the option because rates have increased to 14.00%. This will allow B to fix its swap cost of funds for five years at 10.00%.

The benefits of this strategy are as follows:

4.00% × $25,000,000 × five years	US$5,000,000
2.00% premium	– US$ 500,000
Total savings (on an undiscounted basis)	US$4,500,000

The company achieves fixed rate funding at a rate of 10.528% pa after incorporation of the premium cost. If rates had fallen, B could have let the option lapse taking advantage of lower available market swap rates. For example, if swap rates fell to 6.00% pa, B would achieve an all-in swap cost of 6.528% pa.

Under these strategies, both borrowers and investors would only exercise the options on the underlying swaps where interest rates move adversely, for example, the borrower (investor) would not exercise the payer (receiver) options on a swap unless interest rates had increased (decreased) in the event that interest rate had decreased (increased), the borrower (investor) would allow the option on the swap to lapse unexercised and would fund (invest) at lower (higher) interest rates than that would have been achievable through the option on the swap.

Example 2 in *Exhibit 14.1* outlines an example of anticipatory hedge by a borrower utilising an option on a swap.

Options on swaps, because of their asymmetric risk profile for the purchaser, also provide a flexible means for hedging *contingent* funding requirements—that is, financing or investment requirements that are subject to some uncertainty. Options on swaps allow borrowers and investors to hedge these interest rate exposures at a known cost. Example 1 in *Exhibit 14.1* sets out an example of a contingency hedging problem.

An alternative type of anticipatory hedging transaction is commonly utilised in regard to export credit funding or other subsidised financing available in relation to the acquisition of large capital goods, such as aircraft, ships, power generation equipment etc. Such financing agencies often guarantee a known cost of funding for the beneficiary of the subsidised financing—effectively, granting a free interest rate option. However, because of lags and leads in the adjustment of export financing rates relative to movements in market rates, the subsidy element may effectively increase or decrease (in extreme cases, it may be eliminated) as a result of interest rate movements between the time of commitment and the time funding is drawn down. This exposure is often hedged utilising options on swaps. *Exhibit 14.2* sets out an example of this type of application of options on swaps.

Options on swaps have also proved to have considerable utility in financial institution asset-liability management. Asset liability managers in financial institutions have utilised options on swaps to manage balance sheet interest rate exposures (often known as "gap positions").

For example, where a balance sheet is structured such that long duration assets are funded with short duration liabilities (with the result to exposure to increases in interest rates), asset liability managers have purchased payer options on swaps to manage the gap exposure. Similarly, in the reverse position, purchases of receiver options on swaps have been used to hedge balance sheets that contain short duration assets funded with long duration liabilities.

The latter type of problem is particularly important where the financial institutions asset portfolio contains a significant proportion of callable assets, such as mortgages or credit card receivables, whose duration, typically, shortens in a low interest rate environment as a result of prepayments. In this context, options on swaps should be considered as an alternative to the use of conventional interest rate swap transactions and/or other types of options, primarily interest rate caps and floors as a means for facilitating the risk management objectives identified.

Writing options on swaps

The sale of options on swaps, either directly for premium income or, indirectly, by way of adjustment to the fixed rate under the swap, generates incremental income that may be consistent with the asset liability manager's objectives. Applications of options on swaps entailing granting or selling these instruments have evolved out of the more basic applications entailing purchase of such options on swaps.

Exhibit 14.2
Utilising Options on Swaps to Hedge Subsidised Export Credit Financing

Company A (A) has entered into a contract to acquire heavy machinery, with delivery scheduled in 12 months. The contractual arrangements incorporate a subsidised export credit financing package whereby A has the *option* to enter into an export credit loan in 12 months time for a period of five years at a rate of 6% pa. The interest rate on the loan is approximately 2% pa below normal market rates (the equivalent forward rate in 12 months time).

A has the following alternatives available to maximise the value of the subsidised financing:

1. *Do nothing*—A may suffer an opportunity loss if as a result of a fall in interest rates the subsidy implicit in the financing is eroded.
2. *Sell its interest rate option implicit in the export credit loan*—A would be exposed to increases in interest rates which may adversely affect the economics of the project.
3. *Enter into a forward start swap*—This would lock in the subsidy at current level.
4. *Purchase a receiver option on a swap*—This alternative is considered below.

Assume that A chooses alternative 4. Under this alternative A enters into an option on a five year interest rate swap to receive fixed rate at 8% pa and pay US$ LIBOR exercisable to one year's time.

The payoffs from this strategy are as follows:

- If rates rise, then the option is not exercised and A utilises the export credit financing, the value of which has increased.
- If rates fall, then the option is exercised to lock in the subsidy level.

Note that the above assumes that A wishes to finance on a floating rate US$ LIBOR basis. However, even if A wishes to finance on a fixed rate basis, the changes in value of the option on the swap preserves the subsidy value of the export financing.

Assuming a price of the one year option on the five year swap of 1.25% payable by A, then A will benefit where interest rates increase by approximately 0.338% pa (that is, five year rates increase to 8.338% pa). If rates fall, then the option on the swap locks in a subsidy value of 1.662% pa (being the 2.00% pa subsidy adjusted for the premium).

As in the case of options, transactions entailing writing or selling options on swaps can be either:

- *Naked*—not related to any underlying position in the instrument and designed purely as a means for capturing value from an anticipated movement in interest rates.
- *Covered*—that is, designed as a partial hedge against underlying risk positions in the asset liability portfolio such that exercise of the option would offset existing positions within the portfolio.

Naked writing of options on swaps to generate income is necessarily more risky than covered writing of such options. This reflects the fact that covered sales of options on swaps, typically, would only result in an *opportunity* cost rather than a pure and portfolio unrelated exposure to movements in the underlying interest rate.

Covered writing of options on swaps, which is the most common strategy employed, typically takes the form of targeted buying or selling of interest rates.

For example, a borrower may consider selling an out-of-the-money option on a swap to pay fixed rate where the fixed rate is below the prevailing current or forward rate for the relevant option maturity date. The borrower receives premium income for the sale of the option. In the event that interest rates do not fall the premium income received assists in reducing the borrowing cost of the portfolio. In the event that interest rates fall and the payer option on a swap is exercised by the purchaser, the borrower will have converted a portion of its floating rate debt into fixed rate. The rationale of such a transaction is that the borrower would be prepared to swap its floating rate borrowings into a fixed rate at the strike rate of the option on the swap and would therefore consider the risk of this transaction acceptable.

Investors can similarly utilise the sale of receiver options on swaps to convert floating rate asset returns to fixed rates. In each case, the effective rate achieved would be the fixed rate under the swap adjusted for the option premium element arising from the sale of the option on the swap.

A variation on this type of targeted buying or selling entails the use of cancellable swaps. Under this structure, borrowers would enter into a swap for, say, five years, where it pays fixed rates and receives floating rates. It would simultaneously sell the swap counterparty the right to terminate the swap at the end of, say, two years (effectively, the sale by the borrower of a payer option on a swap for a three year swap commencing in two years time). Premium received from the sale of the cancellation right would effectively lower the fixed rate payable under the swap.

Under this arrangement, the borrower has fixed rate borrowings for a period of either two or five years. The counterparty has the right to cancel the swap after two years and will, economically, do so if interest rates increase. Consequently, the borrower has an uncertain duration fixed rate borrowing albeit at an attractive rate, resulting from the subsidy element created by the sale of the option.

This type of structure was utilised by borrowers to aggressively reduce interest expense in near term fiscal periods in return for taking maturity risk on the term of the fixed rate. An additional factor in entering into such transactions was the capacity to generate upfront premiums (where the premium for the option on the swap was not amortised over the life of the transaction). A common reason for entering into such transactions for borrowers was to meet specified management interest cost targets which could not be met directly as interest rates were above target levels.

Popular structures late in 1989 and the early 1990s included, typically, five, seven or ten year swaps which could be terminated after two years. The structure described above allows a "one time" cancellation option. This creates less uncertainty for the borrower. However, a number of borrowers entered into transactions where the counterparty would have the right to cancel at six monthly intervals after two years. This type of transaction created additional value for the borrower as a result of the sale of a *series* of options on swaps.

As described in the section on pricing below, the extent to which value can be extracted from this type of structure would depend on the shape of the yield curve and the relationship of forward swap rates to spot swap rates for the relevant maturity.

The sale of options on swaps or, indirectly, in the form of cancellable, extendible etc swap structures, are not without risk. In fact, the risks are identical to those encountered in the sale of any options. The sale of options on swaps in covered transactions is less risky as the loss is an *opportunity loss* only (although the economic loss is none the less real).

Dangers of utilising sales of options on swaps to generate upfront option premium income as a source of cash flow was highlighted dramatically with the transactions involving the councils in England which collectively wrote an astonishing volume of swaptions merely to generate income speculating on future interest rate movements: see below, Chapters 37 and 44.

UTILISING OPTIONS ON SWAPS FOR CAPITAL MARKET ARBITRAGE

Capital market valuation of debt options

While the asset liability management applications of options on swaps are an important component of the market for such instruments, the primary impetus for their development has been the use of options on swaps to securitise embedded debt options in capital market issues. In fact, such capital market arbitrage transactions are central to the supply and pricing of such instruments.

Central to the use of options on swaps for capital market arbitrage is the relative valuation of options in the fixed interest and swap markets. Transactions entailing the securitisation of embedded options in debt instruments rely on the capacity to securitise relatively lower priced options implicit within fixed interest instruments which are then sold, through the means of the option on the swap, at a higher price in a different market segment. This apparent anomalous pricing of such options and the sources of relative value of such transactions merit comment.

Existence of this discrepancy of pricing suggests that implied volatility in the fixed interest market for corporate securities is lower than that in the swap market itself. Research on fixed interest markets indicates that the implied volatility of fixed interest markets, particularly corporate securities, may be lower than historical realised volatility for a number of reasons:[1]

- Investors focus on securities yields rather than on their total return thereby systematically undervaluing the call option implicit in a callable bond.
- Investors often evaluate securities on the basis of their yield to worst or cash flow yield, implicitly assuming that interest rate volatility is zero.
- Investors have a different information set regarding the probability of corporate bond calls than that which is incorporated in the market model which provides an estimate of an option's value from the investor's point of view by assuming that any call will be exercised with perfect economic efficiency. This additional information about individual issuers' behaviour may reduce the value of the option being reflected in the lower implied volatility.
- Investors expect realised volatility to decrease from the unusually elevated level of the 1980s, in view of the fact that realised volatility levels during the 1960s and 1970s were lower than that which prevailed in the 1980s.

Additional factors which may dictate the differences in relative value include yield curve differences between the swap and corporate market and relative value of synthetic securities created utilising options on swaps embeds a quality spread differential *within the corporate market*.

Research on yield curve relationship between the swap and corporate market, primarily undertaken in the US$ swap market, tends to indicate that swap spread track "A" or "AA" corporate spreads, although the relationship is not exact: see discussion in Chapter 23.

The difference in implied volatilities between the corporate bond market and the swap market may be explainable, at least in certain circumstances, by the shape of the yield curve and the implied forward rate structure in the swap curve relative to the corporate bond market curve. For example, if the three year swap rate seven

1. William M Boyce, Webster Hughes, Peter S A Niculescu and Michael Waldman, (January 1988), *The Implied Volatility of Fixed-Income Market* (Salomon Bros Inc Research Department, NY).

years forward is lower than the corresponding forward corporate rate, then the swap option will, utilising option theory, be worth more than the embedded call, even if their implied volatilities are equal.

Anecdotal evidence, during various periods in which swap market activity focused on options on swaps (see discussion below), indicate that such activity coincides with differences in the shape of the swap yield curve relative to the corporate bond yield curve. For example, in early 1989, the swap curve was inverted while the corporate bond curve was not inverted. This implies that when forward rates are lower in the swap market (generally, when the swap curve is inverted relative to the corporate curve), options to receive fixed in the swap market will be worth more than call options in the corporate market. Conversely, when forward rates are higher in the swap market, options to pay fixed in the swap market will be worth more than put options in the corporate market.

This discrepancy between the shape of the swap and corporate bond yield curve facilitates the type of capital market arbitrage described in greater detail below.

The second factor relates to an embedded quality spread differential within the corporate market. The swap market typically, operates on the following pattern (see Chapter 7):

- low quality issuers issue floating rate debt and swap into fixed rate debt utilising an interest rate swap.
- high quality issuers issue fixed rate debt which is then swapped through an interest rate swap into a floating rate debt.

This pattern implies that, for the investor, the swap market is an attractive source of high quality fixed rate assets through the purchase of highly rated floating rate assets which can then be swapped into fixed and, conversely, an attractive source of low quality floating rate assets created primarily through asset swaps entailing purchase of lower quality fixed rate bonds which are then swapped into floating rate basis.

Given that synthetic callable and putable securities can be created through the combination of actual physical non-callable or non-putable securities combined with options on swaps (described in detail below), the synthetic component (that is, the part which relies on the underlying swap) that can be created will, by definition, be as follows:

- where the synthetic component is floating rate, the asset is more likely to be attractive when the underlying corporate security is low quality; and
- when the synthetic part is fixed rate, the asset is likely to be attractive when the underlying corporate security is high quality.

This embedded quality spread differential again implies under pricing of volatility in the corporate bond market, particularly for issuers of high quality.[2]

In the remaining portion of this section, a variety of structures entailing the combinations of options on swaps and fixed interest securities with embedded debt options are examined.

Callable and putable swap structures have been utilised, primarily, in two situations:

- in conjunction with capital market issues which have implicit call and/or put options on the underlying debt security;
- in conjunction with asset swaps where the underlying fixed rate security has an uncertain life, as a result of call options embedded in the original issue terms.

2. Johnson (1989), pp 5-6.

Callable and putable swaps have been utilised usually in conjunction with callable or putable capital market issues. In this regard, these transactions represent the initial attempts to securitise the value of options embedded in debt securities, a process which has culminated in the transactions described in detail in Chapter 15.

Debt warrants/callable or putable bonds

The earliest examples of these structures emerged where a number of floating rate payers entered into transactions allowing them to enter into additional amounts of a swap, under which they received fixed rates in return for paying floating rates, during a specified period of sometimes up to five years. One of the first such swaps allowed the counterparty to call additional amounts of the swap when fixed rates fell in the future. These swaps were created to allow issuers to undertake bond issues with attached warrants for additional bonds. If the warrants were exercised, additional amounts of the swap could be called to convert the fixed rate funds into floating rate debt. The counterparty, who was effectively providing a call option, received an up-front premium for providing the option in return for absorbing the risk that rates might fall and the warrants would be exercised. The callable swap served to guarantee the borrower's spread below LIBOR on the additional funds raised. Debt warrant swaps are examined in Chapter 15.

These early callable and putable swap structures were eventually combined with issues of callable debt in highly sophisticated and complex transactions designed to effectively arbitrage the value of interest rate options between various markets. In 1986 and 1987 and again in early 1989, a significant volume of transactions, primarily in US$, combined a callable issue of debt securities with an associated putable swap.

The basic structure entailed a borrower issuing say five, seven or ten year debt securities which were non-callable for three or five years. After the expiry of the call protection period, the borrower could redeem the issue usually at par or with the payment of a premium. The borrowers, in these cases, utilised these fixed rate issues as a basis for creating a synthetic floating rate borrowing. Consequently, the borrower would inevitably enter into a simultaneous swap wherein it received fixed rates and paid floating rates. The interest rate swaps, however, had an additional feature whereby the swap counterparty, paying fixed rates, had the right to terminate the swap at a future date, coinciding with the call date of the underlying bond. For example, in the situation described above, the five year issue might be swapped with the counterparty who agreed to pay fixed rates for five years and receive floating rate but with the added right to cancel the swap after three years.

The economics of such transactions was predicated on the swap counterparty paying a premium to the borrower who thereby achieved a lower floating rate cost of funding. If interest rates fell, the swap counterparty would exercise its option and cancel the agreement. Simultaneously, the borrower would then have the right to terminate the overall borrowing by exercising its call option on its debt securities. If, however, interest rates rose, the swap counterparty would be unlikely to terminate the swap which would run its full term and the borrower would have achieved a cheaper cost of funding than it might otherwise have had available to it over the full five year term.

The internal economics of these transactions relied on the borrower's call option on its debt essentially offsetting the put option on the swap that it was creating in favour of the swap counterparty. Logically, investors should demand a higher yield on callable bonds because of the interest rate risk they assume and it would be expected that this increase in yield would offset any premium received from the swap counterparty for the cancellation rights. However, the fact was that the amount investors charged, by way of higher yields on the securities, for providing the borrower with a call option was substantially below what the swap counterparties were willing to pay for the right to cancel the swap. Consequently, the opportunity existed to securitise the call option on the debt securities via the putable swap to effectively allow the borrower to achieve a lower all-in cost of funding: see discussion on relative option values above.

The counterparties for these swaps were borrowers seeking to hedge interest rate risk but also seeking some capacity to benefit from a favourable rate movement. However, some counterparties entered into such putable swaps merely to buy the underlying call option on interest rates implicit in the putable swap.

For example, in November 1987, Salomon Brothers, in a difficult market, brought approximately US$1.85 billion of fixed rate debt involving putable swaps to market. While the rationale for these transactions was not made public, observers speculated that the transactions were driven by an internal need by Salomon Brothers to purchase call options on United State treasuries. Under one theory, the US Investment Bank was using the options to hedge positions in its proprietary option book whereby it had previously sold treasury bond options or interest rate options positions. Under an alternative theory, Salomon Brothers was using the putable swaps to hedge prepayment of mortgage backed securities, either in its own portfolio, or a portfolio which it had sold to a client.

An example of a transaction involving a putable swap is set out in *Exhibit 14.3*.

In early 1987, Banque Nationale de Paris (BNP) undertook an interesting variation on this basic structure which also coincidentally was one of the first callable interest rate swaps denominated in GBP. In this transaction, BNP issued a seven year GBP bond with a coupon of 10.00%, callable after five years at 100.25, with the call premium declining by 0.125% pa. BNP simultaneously entered into a five year GBP swap to generate floating rate GBP funding. The only unusual feature of this swap was that it was for a period of *five years*. BNP also entered into a forward GBP interest rate swap commencing in five years' time for a period of two years. This forward swap commenced at the call date of the underlying bond and at the maturity of the five year GBP interest rate swap. Both swaps were on identical terms.

The provider of the GBP forward swap, Kleinwort Benson, simultaneously purchased the right to terminate a two year interest rate swap in five years' time. This putable option on the swap somewhat confusingly allowed Kleinwort to put or terminate the swap with BNP. In effect, if Kleinwort Benson chose at the end of five years not to enter into the two year swap, BNP would merely call its underlying GBP bonds, thereby eliminating any exposure as a result of the expiry of the original swap. From the perspective of BNP, the premium received for the provision of this putable swap was significantly greater than the higher yield it paid on the bonds for the right to retire the securities after five years. This allowed BNP to achieve significant reductions in its overall cost borrowing in this transaction. The BNP transaction is set out in *Exhibit 14.4*.

Other variations include issues of callable fixed rate debt (say seven year with a call right as at year 3 combined with a *three year* swap under which it receives fixed rate and pays a floating rate. Simultaneously, the issuer sells the option for a counterparty to pay fixed rates under a swap *commencing at year 3*. If interest rates fell and the option to enter into the swap at year 3 was not exercised, then the issuer called the underlying debt. If the option on the swap was exercised, then the issue

Exhibit 14.3
Callable Bond Issue Combined with Putable Swap

Terms of bond

Issue date:	15/10/X1
Maturity:	15/10/X8
Coupon:	10.00% pa
Call provisions:	At par on 15/10/X6 and 15/10/X7
Issue price:	100

Terms of putable swap

Maturity:	15/10/X8
Fixed rate:	10.00% pa
Floating rate:	LIBOR—25bps
Put provisions:	At par on 15/10/X6 and 15/10/X7
Swap premium:	1.25% pa flat

The combined transaction results in the following case flows for years one to five of the transaction:

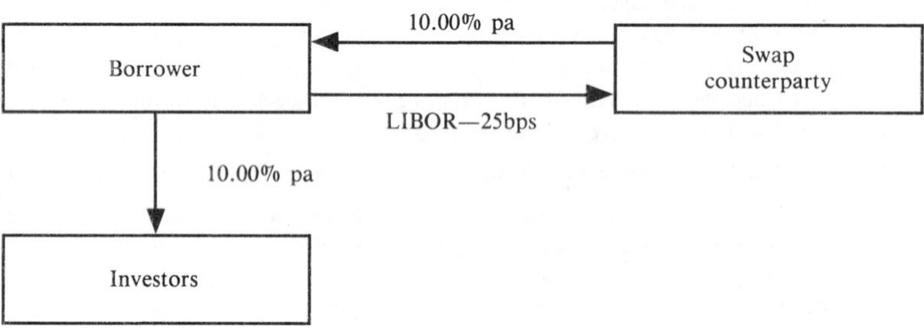

The all-in cost of funds to the borrower, after the proceeds of the up-front premium are factored in, is LIBOR—51bps (assuming a discount rate of 10.25% pa).

If the swap is cancelled under the put on the swap, the borrower calls the underlying bond which means it achieves lower cost funding but for a shorter period:

six years:	LIBOR—54bps
five years:	LIBOR—58bps

was *not* called and the issuer enjoyed floating rates for the full term of the issue at a favourable rate. This type of structure is particularly attractive in an environment when borrowers seek protection against potential interest rate increases but are anxious to preserve the opportunity to benefit from decreases in rates.

In another variation, during a number of periods in recent years, issues of putable debt have been undertaken. Such transaction entails the borrower issuing a fixed interest security for a maturity of say five to ten years with the investor having the right to terminate the transaction and put the bonds to the issuer prior to maturity, say, at the end of three years. In return for receiving the right to put the bonds to the issuer, the investors accept a lower return on the investment. In economic terms, the investor is purchasing a combination of a fixed interest security (with the final maturity of the bond) and a call option on interest rates or a put on the price of the bond. The option acquired by the investor has an expiry date coinciding with the put date and has a strike price equivalent to face value of the bond. The option premium is built into the coupon of the security.

Exhibit 14.4
BNP Sterling Callable Bond Issue with Putable Swap

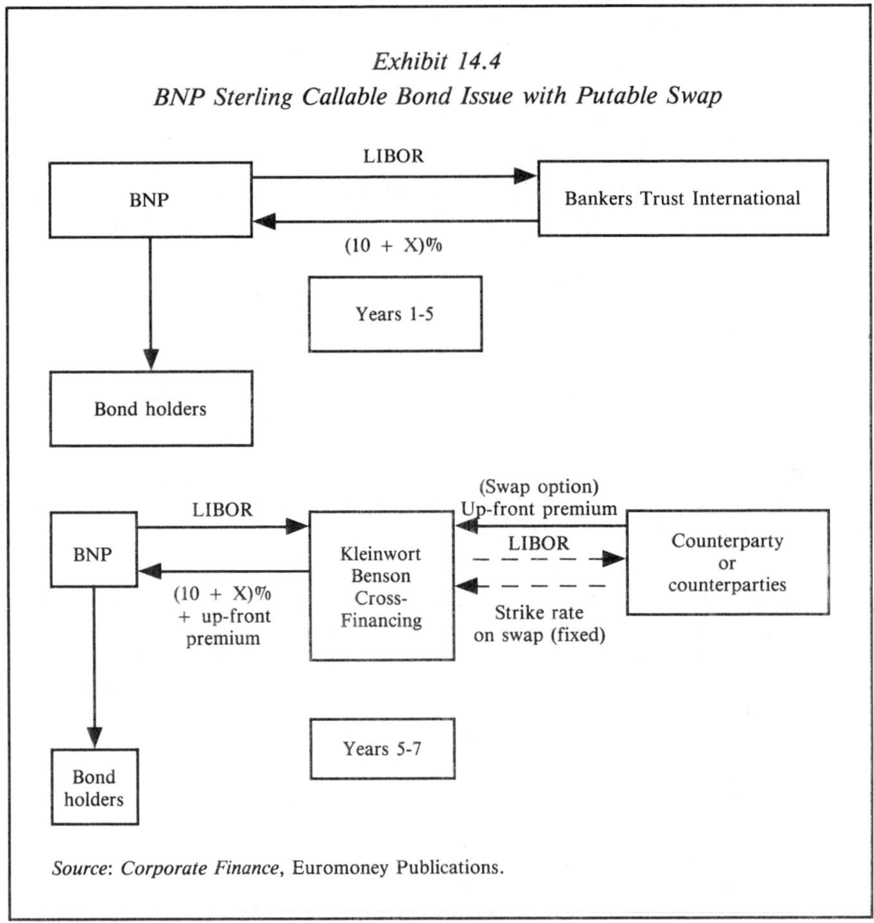

Source: *Corporate Finance*, Euromoney Publications.

Investors sought this type of security structure as a means from seeking protection from increases in interest rates. If rates increase, investors would be able to protect the capital value of its investment by terminating the borrowing transaction as at the put date and reinvesting in higher yielding securities.

Some issuers of these putable securities were willing to absorb the liquidity and interest rate risks resulting from the potential shorter life of the security (if interest rates rose). However a number of issuers used this security structure as a basis for generating lower cost floating rate funding by swapping the issue proceeds into a floating rate basis. This entails the use of extendible swaps whereby the issuer entered into a swap whereby it received fixed rates and paid floating rates for a maturity coinciding with the put date on the security and simultaneously purchased a receiver option on a swap to receive fixed rates (at the same rate) under a swap which commenced as at the put date and extended to the final maturity of the putable security.

In the event that interest rates fell and the put option was not exercised, the issuer exercised its option under the extendible swap or the receiver option on the swap to continue to maintain its status as a floating rate borrower. The lower coupon on the putable bond allowed the issuer to, at least, cover the cost of the purchase of the extendibility option or the receiver option on the swap.

Asset swaps involving callable bonds

Putable swaps have also been utilised in asset swapped transactions where the underlying asset is a callable bond. The putable swap allows investors to enter into transactions whereby a fixed rate bond, which is callable, is swapped into a floating rate basis. If the bond is called, then the investor can terminate the original swap by cancelling or putting the swap to the provider of the putable swap option. This allows the investor to terminate the swap at the time the underlying fixed rate security is called away.

Such asset based putable swap transactions were extremely important in the development of this particular type of swap structure. As discussed in detail in Chapter 18, asset swaps where synthetic floating rate assets at attractive spreads relative to LIBOR are created have been an important component of the growth of the swap market. However, there has been a limited universe of non-callable fixed rate bonds. As a result many of the bonds used in the asset based swaps have embedded call options.

When in 1986, interest rates fell sharply, the assets were called away with investors being left with interest rate swap positions with high fixed coupons. In the lower interest rate environment, similar quality, high yielding replacement assets were not available and the swaps were expensive to reverse, creating losses for investors. Putable swaps were structured as a means of mitigating these losses resulting from early redemption in asset swap transactions.

In addition, this type of structure can be utilised to swap assets which have uncertain lives. This can be particularly important in structuring asset swaps against mortgage and receivable backed securities. An example of an asset based putable swap is set out in *Exhibit 14.5*.

Exhibit 14.5

Asset-Based Putable Swaps

Terms of bond

Maturity:	15/3/X7
Coupon:	10.00% (S/A)
Call provisions (date and price):	15/3/X4 to 14/3/X5 @ 103 15/3/X5 to 14/3/X6 @ 102 15/3/X6 to 14/3/X7 @ 101 15/3/X7 @ 100
Bond price:	102.50

Terms of putable swap

Maturity:	15/3/X7
Up-front payment:	2.50 paid to investor (swap buyer pays fixed)
Fixed coupon:	10.00% (S/A)
Floating coupon:	LIBOR + 136

Exhibit 14.5—continued

Put provisions (date and price):	15/3/X4 to 14/3/X5 for three points 15/3/X5 to 14/3/X6 for two points 15/3/X6 to 14/3/X7 for one point
Option type:	Deferred American
All-in cost of non-putable swap:	8.00%
Cost of put option:	24bps

The initial cash flows under this transaction are as follows:

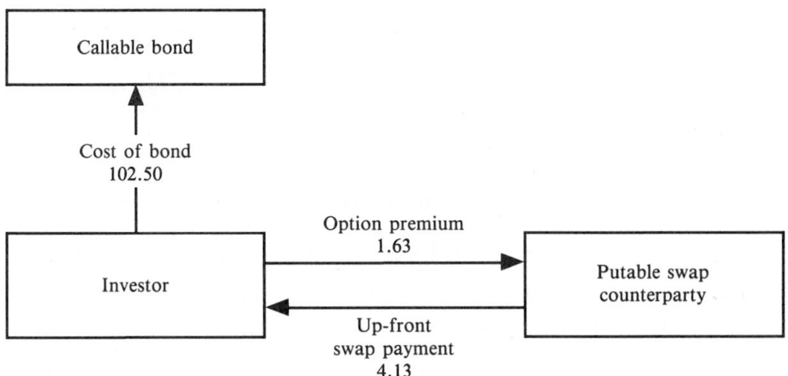

Net up-front payment to investor: 4.13 − 1.63 = 2.50.
Net cost to investor: 102.50 + 1.63 − 4.13 = 100.00.
The up-front payment of 2.50% to the investor represents the net of the up-front swap payment that the investor would *receive* for agreeing to pay what is effectively an above market fixed coupon, and the fact that the investor must *pay* for the put option on the swap.

The investor's cash flow on each interest payment date will be as follows:

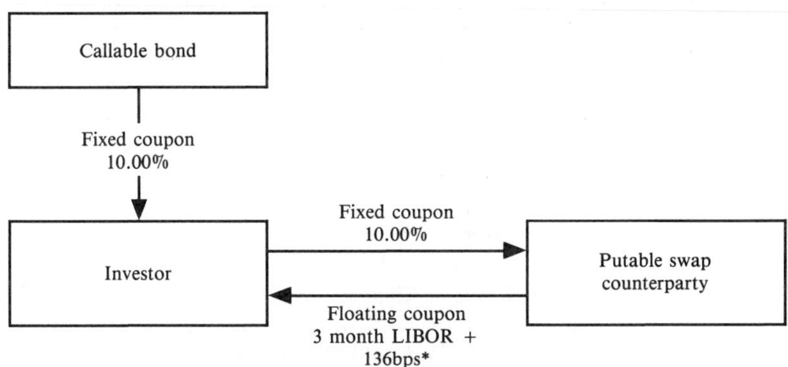

* Coupon is adjusted for put cost.

Note that, in fact, the 136bps amount is based on the assumption that the investor exercises its right to put the swap if and only if the underlying bond is called. However, the investor may be able to exercise its put option, even if the bond is not called, and buy another swap at more favourable terms. It may also be possible that when the issuer calls the bond, the investor would do better by selling the swap in the market than by exercising its put to cancel the swap.

Exhibit 14.5—continued

If the bond is called as per the schedule, say on 15 March 19X4, the investor is paid 103.00% by the issuer, but passes 3.00% to the swap counterparty for the right to cancel the swap. This effectively gives the investor back its initial investment of 100.

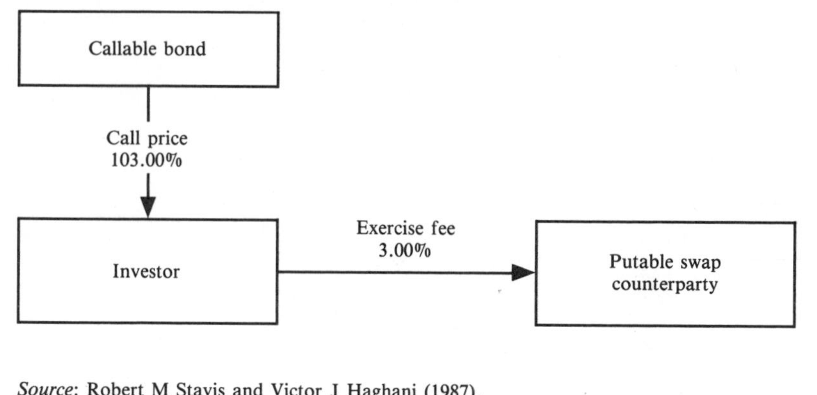

Source: Robert M Stavis and Victor J Haghani (1987).

Options on cross-currency swaps

While the discussion to date has been confined to callable and putable swaps in one currency, it is possible to extend the concept to currency swaps. For example, in 1987, Deutsche Bank undertook an issue of GBP75m for ten years. The issue was callable after seven years. Deutsche Bank swapped the sterling funds raised into US$ LIBOR by entering into a *ten year* GBP/US$ LIBOR currency swap. Kleinwort Benson, the swap counterparty, however, required the right to terminate the swap after seven years. Deutsche Bank received a substantial up-front premium in return for selling Kleinwort the right to terminate the swap, presumably utilising the proceeds to lower its cost relative to US$ LIBOR. The call option implicit in the GBP bond issue protected Deutsche Bank against any exposure from the exercise of the cancellation option under the swap as if the underlying currency swap was to be terminated, Deutsche Bank would merely call the GBP bonds to eliminate any currency exposure. The cross-currency putable swap is set out diagrammatically in *Exhibit 14.6*.

Creating synthetic callable/putable bonds

In an interesting example of reverse financial engineering, the development of substantial and liquid market in options on swaps has allowed both investors and borrowers to synthetically create callable/putable structures consistent with their own interest rate expectations and portfolio requirements. In particular, disparities in pricing as observed above, between the fixed interest and swap markets has allowed the creation of these synthetic callable and putable structures at values superior to those obtainable directly from the fixed interest market.

This type of activity is most prevalent in the US$ swap market. However, the principles are capable of extension and application to debt markets in any currency.

Exhibit 14.6
Deutsche Bank Cross-Currency Putable Swap

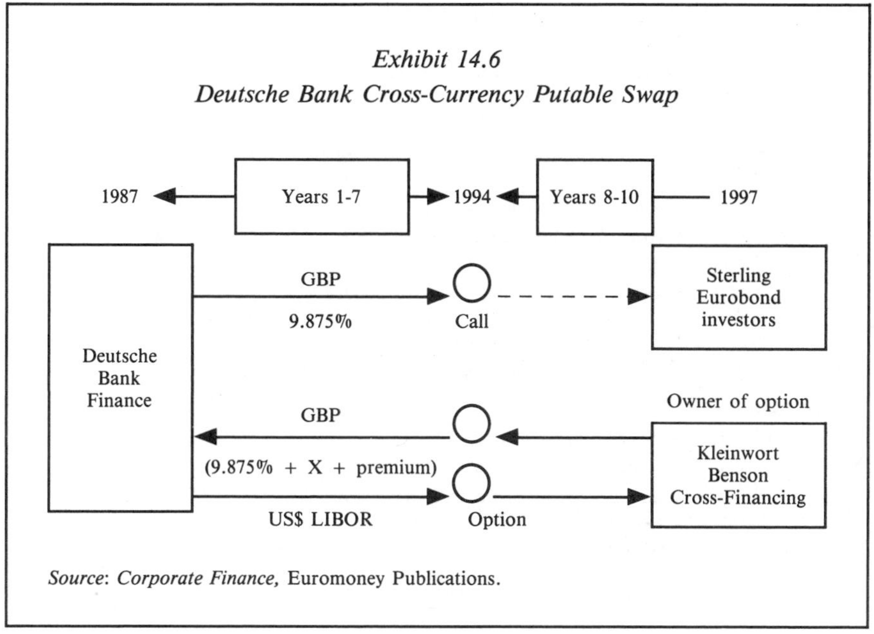

Source: *Corporate Finance,* Euromoney Publications.

Asset management

Asset managers can create synthetic callable or putable bonds by using a number of alternative combinations of physical securities and options on swaps.

For example, an asset manager can create a synthetic callable bond investment in at least three ways:

- purchase a long-term straight bond and sell a receiver option on a swap;
- purchase a floating rate note, enter into a swap under which it receives fixed/pays floating and sells an option to cancel the swap;
- purchase a short term bond and sell a payer option on a swap.

Exhibit 14.7 details creating a synthetic callable bond utilising each of these methods.

Similarly, an investor can create synthetic asset structures involving putable bonds. For example, an investor can create a synthetic putable bond by either:

- purchasing a long-term conventional bond and purchasing a payer option on a swap whereby it pays fixed and receives floating;
- purchase a short-term bond and purchase a receiver option on a swap whereby it receives fixed and pays floating.

The reverse of the above transactions whereby callable and putable bonds are converted into synthetic conventional non-call or non-put securities are also feasible. For example, *Exhibit 14.8* sets out an example of creating a synthetic conventional bond from a putable bond.

As is evident, the synthetic structures can be created utilising a variety of combination strategies which are, by definition, economically equivalent. The availability of these alternative structures, however, allows the creation of the most

Exhibit 14.7
Utilising Options on Swaps to Create Synthetic Callable Bonds

Assume Investor A (A) wishes to create a synthetic callable bond to match its portfolio requirements.

Assume the following market conditions exist:

Five year AA corporate bonds with a one time par call at three years are trading at 7.60% pa.

Five year AA corporate *non-callable* bonds are trading at 7.50% pa.

An option on a two year swap to receive 7.50% pa against payments of US$ LIBOR exercisable in three years time is valued at 180 bp premium payable immediately.

A can create a synthetic callable bond as follows:

1. *Alternative 1*

A enters into the following transactions:

- purchase five year non-callable bond;
- sell a receiver option on the swap whereby the counterparty can require A to pay 7.50% pa and receive US$ LIBOR for years four and five (if interest rates decrease).

The diagram below sets out the position:

Years 1-3 (Years 4-5 if Option on Swap Unexercised)

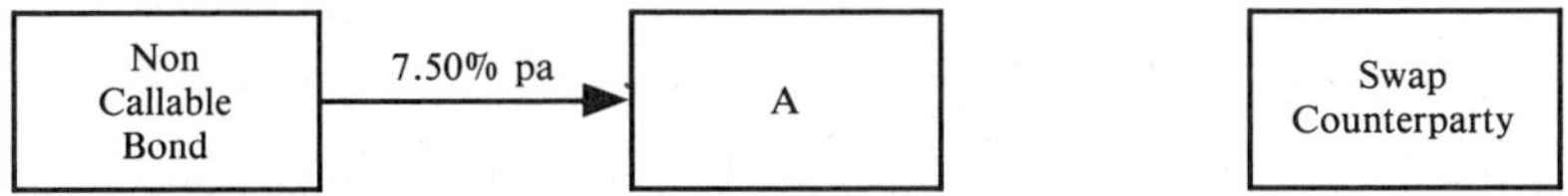

Years 4-5 (if Option on Swap Exercised)

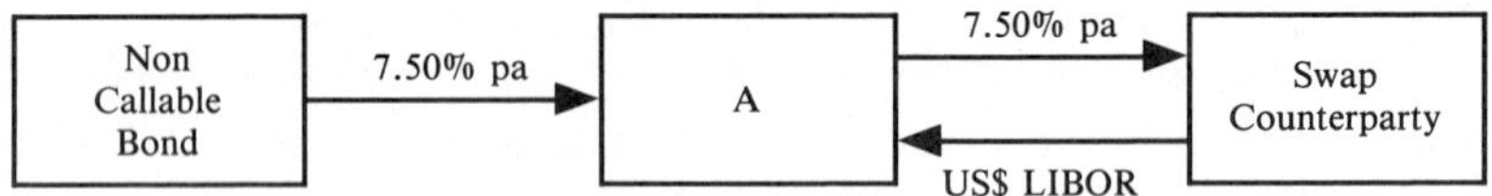

If interest rates rise, then the option on the swap is unexercised and A continues to receive the fixed coupon of 7.50% pa. If interest rates fall, then the option on the swap is exercised and A earns a floating rate of interest (at prevailing money market rates) on its investment. The return characteristics are identical to those under an actual callable bond.

The effective return to A incorporating the premium received is:

Over three years—8.192% pa.

Over five years—7.945% pa.

2. *Alternative 2*

A enters into the following transactions:

- purchases a five year floating rate asset yielding US$ LIBOR;
- enters into two swaps transactions:
  1. five year swap under which it receives 7.5% pa;
  2. sells a receiver option on a swap as in *Alternative 1*.

(Steps 1 and 2 can be combined in a cancellable swap whereby A's swap counterparty can cancel the swap under which it pays fixed (presumably, if interest rates fall) after three years.)

The diagram below sets out the position:

Exhibit 14.7—continued

Years 1-3 (Years 4-5 if Option on Swap Unexercised)

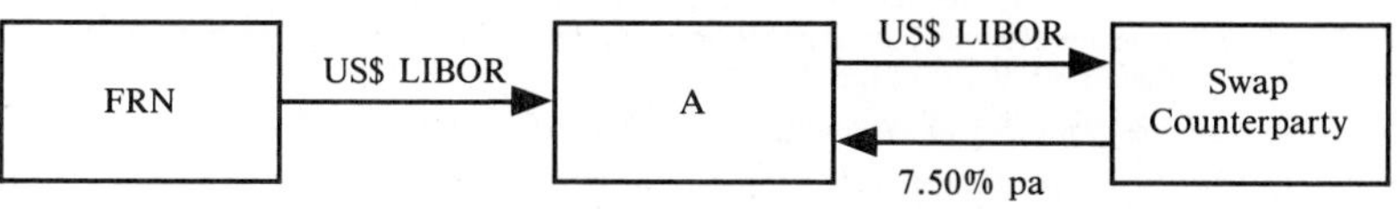

Years 4-5 (if Option on Swap Exercised)

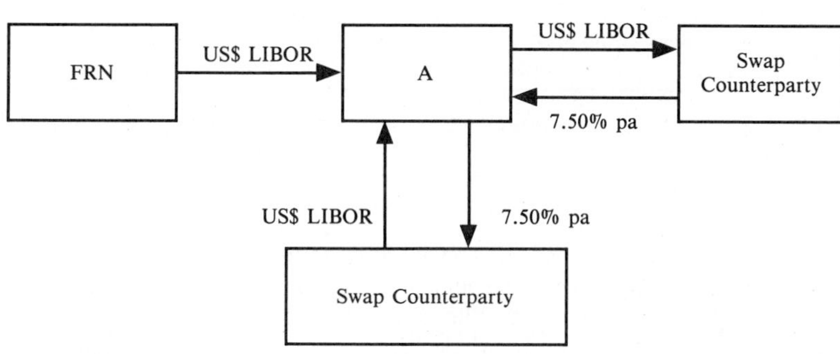

The result for A is identical to that in *Alternative 1.*

3. *Alternative 3*

A enters into the following transactions:

- purchases a three year non-callable AA corporate bond which yields 7.50% pa (for convenience, a flat yield curve is assumed);
- sells a payer option on a swap whereby the counterparty can at its option pay 7.50% pa and receive US$ LIBOR for years four and five (if interest rates decrease).

The diagram below sets out the position:

Years 1-3

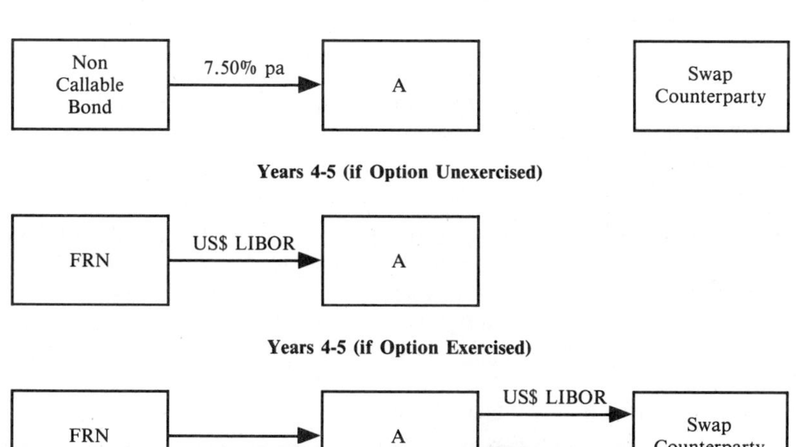

Exhibit 14.7—continued

The return to A under various interest rate scenarios is identical to those in *Alternatives 1* and *2*.

For convenience, the above examples assume flat yield curves and the returns from the different strategies are identical. In practice, considerable scope exists to extract additional value from one or other of the alternatives based on:

- the slope of the swap and/or corporate bond yield curves;
- the structure of forward rates implicit in the two yield curves;
- different implied volatilities and anomalies in the pricing of options on swaps; and
- capacity to enhance return by earning *above* US$ LIBOR return on floating rate investments.

Source: The above discussion draws on Johnson (1989).

efficient structure to take advantage of relative value considerations at any given point in time.

Liability management

In a manner analogous to that of the investor, liability managers can create synthetic debt structures at attractive value levels to manage liability portfolios. For example, borrowers can create the following security structures:

- *Synthetic non-callable debt*—through issue of callable debt which is then converted into a synthetic non-callable issue by neutralising the embedded call by entering into an option on a swap whereby it sells the right to receive fixed (a receiver option on a swap).
- *Synthetic putable bonds*—entailing the issue of a conventional bond combined with the sale of a payer option on a swap whereby an issuer pays fixed, exercisable when the debt matures effectively extending the maturity of the debt.
- *Synthetic portfolio shortening*—by selling payer options on swap, whereby the issuer has the right to pay fixed, thereby converting callable debt to fixed rate debt effectively maturing at the call date. Through this transaction, the issuer has purchased a call (embedded in the callable debt) and sold a put (the option on the swap is a put on the market), which effectively equates to a forward repurchase of the debt.

A major feature of these types of strategies is the capacity to tailor the strike price level (effectively the fixed rate under the swap) as well as other aspects of the transaction to specifically atune the synthetic liability structure to its specific requirements.

Contingent swaps

A contingent swap is an option to enter into a swap which is designed to hedge a contingent liability which generally takes the form of a call option on debt instruments, such as warrants exercisable into fixed rate bonds, issued either in conjunction with a host bond or on a naked or stand-alone basis. The call option embedded in the debt instrument may also take the form of an option to extend an existing issue.

There are two types of contingent swaps:

- a contingent interest rate swap;
- a contingent currency swap.

Exhibit 14.8

Utilising Options on Swaps to Create a Synthetic Non-Putable Bond

Assume Investor A (A) has purchased a ten year AA corporate bond which is putable to the issuer at year five. The putable bond yields 7.00% pa (versus the comparable yield on conventional ten year non putable ten year AA corporate bond of 7.50% pa).

In order to synthetically create a non-putable security, A simultaneously sells an option on a swap transaction whereby the counterparty can pay 7.50% pa in return for receiving US$ LIBOR (if rates increase).

The diagram below sets out the position:

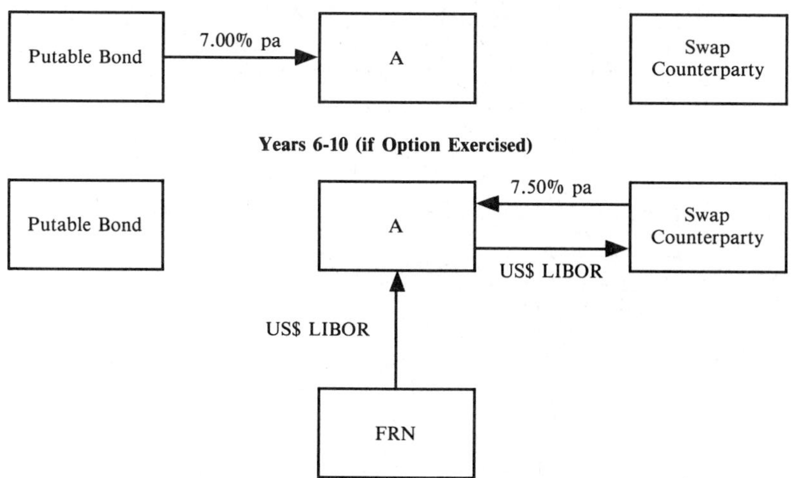

If interest rates fall, then A does not put the bonds as at year five, the option on the swap is unexercised and A receives the coupon of 7.00% pa for the full ten years. If interest rates rise, then A puts the bond to the issuer at par, the proceeds are re-invested at a floating rate asset yielding US$ LIBOR and the option is exercised converting the floating rate investment into a fixed rate investment yielding 7.50% pa.

The effective return to A (incorporating an option premium of 4.00% flat) is:

If option unexercised: 7.583% pa.
If option exercised: 7.794% pa.

Source: The above example draws on Johnson (1989).

The contingent interest rate swap entails purely an interest rate option. A contingent currency swap may entail either a purely interest rate option, or alternatively a combined interest rate and currency option.

A contingent swap structure designed to hedge a naked debt warrant issue illustrates the mechanics of a contingent swap. In this example, a contingent swap is tied to debt warrants exerciseable at interest rates below current market levels.

When the warrants are issued, the two parties enter into a contingent swap agreement and the fixed rate payer receives an up-front fee from the issuer of the warrants. The swap becomes effective if and when the warrants are exercised and is identical to a traditional interest rate or currency swap.

If interest rate levels rise or remain constant, it is likely that the warrants will expire unexercised and the contingent swap provider will keep the premium. If, however, interest rates fall, the warrants are likely to be exercised and the two parties will enter into the swap as the contingent swap is triggered.

The contingent swap structure generates significant savings compared to a standard swap. This saving is generated from two sources:

- The fixed interest rate on a contingent swap is generally substantially below the current market level.
- The fixed rate payer receives an up-front premium which, if the warrants expire unexercised, will be retained as income, or, if the warrants are exercised, will lower the all-in cost of the swap.

The issuer of the warrants, meantime, is insulated from the fixed rate level on the swap. If the warrants are exercised it immediately translates its fixed rate funding into floating rate funds, usually at a predetermined margin under a floating rate index, which compares favourably to its alternative cost of floating rate funds.

An example of a naked warrant issue and accompanying contingent swap is set out in *Exhibit 14.9*.

Exhibit 14.9

Naked Warrants Issue and Contingent Swap Structure

Institution A (A) issues warrants exercisable into A$ bonds on the following terms:

Back bonds

Amount:	A$50m
Term:	Five years
Coupon:	14.00% pa (A)

Warrants

Number of warrants:	50,000 (based on assumed exchange rate) each exercisable into A$1,000 bonds on above terms.
Assumed exchange rate:	US$0.70/A$1.00 (see discussion below).
Warrant price:	(See discussion below).
Expiry date:	The warrants will expire, unless exercised approximately one year after issue (that is, February 19X7). The warrant can be exercised at any point in time before expiry.

Institution B (B) provides a contingent currency swap on the following terms:

Amount:	A$50m
Term:	Five years
B to pay A:	14.00% pa (A)
B to receive from A:	Six month LIBOR
Up-front fee:	(See discussion below)
Commencement date:	The swap can be triggered at any time within one year after issue (that is, by February 19X7) at the option of A.

The rationale for the transaction is as follows:

- issuer (A) is indifferent as, if warrants are exercised, it triggers contingent swap to achieve a margin under LIBOR;
- purchaser of warrant gets a highly leveraged A$ interest rate play (possibly a currency play if exchange rate is fixed: see below);
- contingent swap provider (B) gets attractively priced funding if the contingent swap is called upon.

Exhibit 14.9—continued

From B's perspective:

- B can obtain funding at say 14.70% pa (S/A) (15.24% pa (A)) for six years (the A$ bond rate);
- B can obtain funding for one year (the swap option period) at 17.00% pa (S/A);
- consequently, if B can obtain funding at less than 14.24% (S/A) (14.75% pa (A)) in one year from now, it can effect a cost saving.

The pricing dynamics of the transaction are complex. Assume:

- A requires LIBOR minus 25bps; and
- B requires 13.75% pa (A) (13.25% pa (S/A)) if warrants and contingent swap are triggered to undertake the transaction.

Given these assumptions, it is possible to structure the transaction:

- B requires 25bps under 14.00%:
  - —25bps on A$50m = A$125,000 pa;
  - —discounted back at 15.24% pa (A) (the bond rate) this equates to A$416,649 (US$291,654 at the assumed exchange rate);
  - —however, the swap may not be exercised for up to a maximum of one year, that is, B gets investment earning at 15.24% pa (A) for this period, therefore allowing the up-front payment to be reduced (PV at 15.24% pa) to A$361,549 (US$253,084);
  - —therefore, depending on assumption of timing of warrant and swap exercise, B would need between US$253,084 to US$291,654 to achieve 13.75% pa (A).
- A requires 25bps under LIBOR:
  - —25bps on US$35m (A$50m @ US$0.70/A$1.00) = US$87,500;
  - —discounted back at 10.00% pa (A) this equates to US$331,694;
  - —depending on assumption of timing of warrant and swap exercise (see above discussion) A would need between US$301,540 and US$331,694 to achieve 25bps spread under LIBOR.

Given the size of the up-front payment to A and B the warrants would have to be sold for at least:

$$\left[\frac{(\text{US\$253,084} + \text{US\$301,540})}{50{,}000}\right] = \text{US\$11.09}$$

$$\left[\frac{(\text{US\$291,654} + \text{US\$331,694})}{50{,}000}\right] = \text{US\$12.47}$$

Any price over and above that amount would be profit for the investment bank structuring and executing the transaction.

B may, in fact, require a considerably higher payment to enter into the contingent swap if it analyses the transaction in terms of option theory to price the implicit interest rate option it is creating.

Assume that the warrants are sold for US$24.00 per warrant (net of fees, commissions and expenses). This will result in a net inflow of US$1,200,000 (50,000 warrants @ US$24.00 each). The warrant proceeds received are utilised as follows:

- A is paid US$331,694 for acting as the issuer of the warrants.
- B is paid US$291,654 for entering into the contingent swap.
- The surplus of US$576,652 is retained by the investment bank.

The position for all participants in this transaction under different interest rate scenarios, is as follows:

Exhibit 14.9—continued

Scenario	**Warrant holder or buyer**	**Warrant issuer or seller**	**Contingent swap provider**
Bond rates increase above 14.00% pa (A)	Warrants not exercised	Retains up-front payment US$0.30m	Retains up-front payment of US$0.25-US$0.30m
Bond rates decrease below 14.00% pa (A)	Warrants exercised	Obtain funding at LIBOR less 25bps	Obtain fixed rate funding at 13.75% pa: A provided it funds at LIBOR flat; *only* if rates have gone below 13.75% pa for five years would B register an *opportunity* loss

For the contingent swap provider, the opportunity loss may not be relevant, say where it has an ongoing need for substantial fixed rate funding or is running an asset liability gap, for example, for a bank with high yielding fixed rate loans on its books, it may be happy to take on the liability at an appropriate rate in any case.

As a variation, the A$/US$ exchange rate on exercise of the warrant can be fixed at or near the spot rate on the date of launch or settlement.

This has the following effects:

- The purchaser of the warrants has a currency option as well as an interest rate option, that is, if the A$ appreciates irrespective of interest rate movements, the warrant may have value. The purchaser gives up the opportunity of paying less US$ to buy the bond if the A$ depreciates, but the decline in A$ is reflected in the lower US$ value of the underlying bond.
- The issuer is indifferent because it knows the maximum cost of US$ funding it is obtaining, if the exchange rate is not fixed:

  —if the A$ appreciates, it gets less US$ and achieves a higher margin under LIBOR;

  —if the A$ depreciates it gets more US$ and achieves a lower margin under LIBOR.
- The contingent swap provider is in this case granting a foreign exchange option on the A$/US$ rate. Consequently, it has an exposure to an appreciation in the A$ where it would suffer a loss as it would receive less A$ or conversely it would have to borrow more US$ to support the currency swap if it was to be triggered.

Contingent swaps have special appeal to organisations with specific fixed rate financing targets below current market levels. A contingent swap entered into at the target level can provide such organisations with attractive fixed rate funding. Alternatively, organisations with large swap requirements can use contingent swaps as one component of a swap programme.

The concept of an interest rate swap which is contingent is easily extendible to a currency swap. However, the translation of the contingent swap concept into the domain of currency swaps need *not* entail a foreign exchange option. However, where the underlying debt warrants are exercisable into foreign currency bonds and say the US$ amount required to buy the relevant bonds is fixed at the outset, the warrants entail both a specific interest rate and currency option which is usually covered by the contingent currency swap.

In late 1985, a true currency option swap was created by Credit Commercial de France (CCF). CCF structured such a swap by issuing a US$ floating rate note for the first counterparty with attached warrants into an ECU issue. A contingent swap was then written with a second counterparty who wished to borrow ECU. If the warrants are exercised, then the contingent swap is invoked and the second counterparty pays the fixed rate coupons on the ECU bonds. The first counterparty then pays US$ LIBOR to cover the second counterparty's interbank funding cost. The investors purchased the warrants for a premium which reflected their estimation of the potential currency and interest rate option value. Since the ECU bond warrant premium is shared by both counterparties, the first party effectively raises dollars at a sub-LIBOR rate while the second counterparty raises fixed rate ECU at a borrowing cost well below current market levels, assuming that the warrants are exercised.

The earliest type of currency option swaps were those written by banks which allowed a corporate counterparty to increase the face amount of a currency swap at any time during the first six to 12 months of the transaction. The primary value of this type of option is that it gives the counterparty the opportunity to wait until spot currency rates are favourable. Although the interest rates on additional amounts of the swap remained unchanged under these transactions, the incremental principal amounts were calculated at the new exchange rates. Thus they can perhaps best be referred to as interest rate option swaps and not true currency option swaps.

Contingent currency swaps involving deutschmarks were also pioneered by CCF with an issue of 250,000 warrants to buy a 6.375% deutschmark bond attached to a US$250m floating rate note issue. If the warrants are exercised, a swap is automatically triggered whereby a counterparty agrees, in return for an option premium, to assume the fixed deutschmark liability on CCF's behalf and receive US$ coupon payments. CCF has thus hedged its currency exposure into US$ should the warrants be exercised. Similar deals were undertaken by Swedbank and PK Banken.

The swap market has developed the concept of contingent swap off-warrant issues into a more pragmatic structure, providing both corporations and banks with the opportunity to convert liabilities from one currency into another if they choose over a period of time. One variation on the contingent swap theme is the contingent basis swap, where floating debt in one currency may be exchanged for floating debt in another currency.

Option on swap arbitrage—market phases

It is evident that the opportunities the securitising options implicitly in debt issues is not available continuously. For example, within the deepest and most liquid options on swaps market in US$, the opportunities for this type of transaction occur relatively spasmodically. For example, in the US$ market, option on swap activity occurred in a number of distinct phases:

- late 1986;
- second half 1987;
- second half 1988;
- late 1989/early 1990.

This is not to suggest that *no* options on swaps entailing securitisation of debt options were undertaken outside these periods. However, there was a significant concentration of activity during these periods.

A possible explanation is existence of market factors (see discussion on relative value of options above) which were conducive to this type of arbitrage activity. The various phases of activity were also significantly different in terms of market sector and type of transaction undertaken.

For example, the period in second half 1987 was focused on the US domestic bond market and involved five year/three year non-call issues and three year/two year non-call structures. The issuers were generally banks and financial institutions, both US and foreign, which were issuing deposit notes.

This contrasts with other periods of activity which have been focused on the Euromarkets with the issues being targeted to investors (primarily, Japanese institutions) which were seeking to generate higher running coupon yields than that achievable through conventional transactions. For example, the activity in late 1989, early 1990 was focused on investors interested in high running yield and willing to trade off yield for maturity. These investors were primarily Japanese regional banks and leasing companies. These transactions took the form of Eurobonds with final maturity of ten years, with a call at three years.

As the arbitrage opportunities in the conventional debt option stripping market were reduced through the systematic arbitrage process involving the use of options on swaps, a variety of other security structures evolved:

- Through 1990, a number of fixed-floating notes were issued. The typical structure entailed an issue with a floating rate coupon (priced relative to US$ LIBOR) for years one to three and then a fixed coupon for the remaining life of the transaction (typically, seven to ten years). Such transactions were linked to the purchase by the issuer of receiver options on swaps designed to swap the fixed rate coupon commencing in year three through to maturity into a floating rate basis.
- In June 1992, a number of US federal agencies undertook issues in the US domestic market which were known as "step-up" bonds. The step-up structure allows the issuer to call the bonds after a specified period or increase the coupon by 100 or so bps for the remainder of the term. In many cases, the call option was securitised through a putable swap structure. The transactions typically were five year maturity callable at two years or seven years maturity callable at three years, although other combinations were also utilised.

In an effort to meet aggressive sub-LIBOR targets, a number of sovereign or semi-sovereign borrowers resorted in the early 1990s to elaborate structures entailing the use of options on swaps. For example, in order to improve the sub-LIBOR margins, a number of sovereigns issued fixed rate bonds in one or other currency and swapped into floating rate US$ at a cost of funds, say, LIBOR minus 35bps per annum. To further enhance the sub-LIBOR rate, the issuer agreed with the bank that at every six month interest period, the counterparty would have the right to fix the US$ payment stream at a rate determined at the time the issue was launched. In late 1989 and first half 1990, the sale of an option on a swap had the impact of reducing the borrower's floating rate cost to, say, LIBOR minus 55bps. The structure was somewhat cosmetic in that it was designed to allow the issuer to use the swaption to raise aggressively priced US dollars to meet its target levels. In the event that the swap option is exercised, that is, US$ interest rates fall, the argument was that the issuer had an attractive absolute fixed rate for the life of the transaction (typically, at a relatively attractive spread over treasuries at the time of launch).

A variation on this theme was a transaction undertaken for the Kingdom of Belgium, in late 1989. Belgium issued a ten year US$400 million FRN at US$ six month LIBID. In order to lower its cost, the Kingdom, according to market sources, simultaneously sold an option on a swap whereby the counterparty could oblige the Kingdom to pay treasuries plus 80 basis points for years five to ten of the life of the FRN, should the option on the swap be exercised. The impact of the option on the swap premium resulted in a saving of around 30bps pa over five years, generating sub-LIBOR funding at a level of LIBOR minus 42.5bps for the first five years of the transaction.

As noted above, options on swaps are also available in a number of other currencies (for example, the transactions in GBP outlined above). However, the level of activity in other currencies, with minor exceptions, is more sporadic, less systematic and linked to particular market conditions that prevail from time to time. Despite this more limited scope of activity, options on swaps, linked to capital markets issues, are relatively common in a variety of other currencies including GBP, JPY, DEM, SFR etc.

The pattern of activity in options on swaps in the DEM swap market are illustrative of the pattern of activity generally outside the US$ swap market.

The German option on swap market has been driven by the German Federal Government and its entities' appetite for fund raising. In an attempt to keep coupons below 9% pa, German issuers have offered investors in Schuldscheindarlehen (often referred to as Schuldscheine) the ability to put these bonds back after one, two and three years. Investors purchasing the Schuldscheine typically strip the put option and sell it to the option on swaps market. The government's role as essential suppliers of long-term options on government securities, through this put option, effectively facilitated the development of the DEM option on swaps market.

In contrast, the option on swap market in a variety of other currencies such as GBP and FFR, for example, remain relatively undeveloped due to the lack of supply of debt options by investors through callable bond etc structures.

PRICING OPTIONS ON SWAPS

Pricing/premium characteristics

Options on swaps represent combinations of the primary features of swaps and options on interest rates. Consequently, the pricing of options on swaps, predictably, is based on traditional option pricing theories. In essence, an option on a swap is the purchase or sale of an option on the fixed rate component of the swap.

The pricing of options on swaps reflects the underlying options embodied within the swap structure. This option price is usually captured as the option premium on an appropriate put or call option on government bonds in the relevant currency. This reflects the fact that these option are sometimes used to hedge positions created by writing options on swaps.

For example, where a counterparty provides a corporation with a putable swap, it may hedge its exposure by purchasing a call option on the appropriate government security. Similarly, a market maker may hedge its exposure under a callable swap by purchasing an appropriate put option on a government security.

It is important to note that the purchase of options on government securities is not necessarily a perfect hedge as effectively options on swaps entail separate options on interest rates on government securities and on the swap spread. The option on the swap spread is usually more difficult to hedge.

The primary determinants of the price or premiums payable on options on swaps include:

- the effective fixed rate level;
- swap maturity;
- exercise payments;
- time outstanding until exercise.

The level of effective fixed rates on the swap are one of the key determinants of the value of the option on the swap. For example, the higher the effective fixed coupon (fixed rate minus any spread relative to the variable index) under the swap, the greater the value of being able to put the swap back to the counterparty and, conversely, the lower the value of being able to enter into the swap. Consequently, if all other parameters are held constant, the higher the fixed rate payable under the swap, the more valuable (less valuable) is the option to, at some future date, terminate (enter into) the swap for a fixed exercise fee.

However, the net effect on the total cost to a borrower or investor is more complex. For example, in the case of a putable swap, while the value of the put option rises as the effective fixed rate on the swap is increased, the premium generated up-front by a higher effective coupon on the underlying swap increases at a faster rate. Consequently, although an increase in the fixed rate raises the cost of the put option, the net effect on the package may be a decrease in the up-front fee paid by the purchaser of the putable swap.

The greater the exercise payment that must be paid to exercise the option, the lower is the value of the option on the swap. In essence, a large positive exercise payment can be equated to an increasingly out-of-the-money option with the consequent impact on the value of the option on the swap.

Generally, the longer the time to final maturity of the underlying swap as at the exercise date of the option on the swap, the more valuable the option on that swap will be. This reflects the increased price sensitivity of the swap with the longer maturity.

The impact of outstanding time until exercise in the case of options on swaps can be complex. For example, if the time to expiration of a European swap option is extended, holding the maturity of the swap constant, a variety of factors begin to influence its value. While the increasing period to expiration of the option increases the premium, the fact that the underlying swap is aging over the life of the option may, in fact, lower the value of the put option. In the limiting case, where the expiration date of the option equals the maturity date of the swap the option will, in theory, have no value.

Pricing swaptions—approach

The basic pricing methodology is derived from the underlying option elements of option on swaps and utilises basic option pricing techniques.

The pricing of swaptions is undertaken in a number of discrete steps:

1. *Calculate forward swap rates*

   This requires calculation of forward swap rates implicit *in the swap yield curve*. This is because the underlying asset of the swaption is effectively *a forward swap*: see Chapter 12.

2. *Calculate the swaption price*

   This requires: (a) the specification of the various inputs (necessary to determine option prices); and, (b) incorporating these into the selected option pricing model and calculating the price.

Pricing swaptions—example

The examples below are based on the interest rate swap rate specified in *Exhibit 14.10*. The forward swap rates are calculated using the forward/forward rate formula outlined previously.

Exhibit 14.10
Forward/Forward Interest Rate Swap Rate

Year	No of Days	S/A Periods	Date	Swap Rate (% pa S/A)	Forward Swap Rate (% pa S/A)	Forward (1/4) Swap Rate (% pa S/A)	Forward (3/5) Swap Rate (% pa S/A)
0			2-Sep-X1				
0.50	182	0.997	2-Mar-X2	7.60%			
1.00	366	2.011	2-Sep-X2	7.75%	8.1686%	8.7587%	
1.50	547	3.005	2-Mar-X3	7.84%	8.1363%		
2.00	731	4.016	2-Sep-X3	7.92%	8.4196%		
2.50	912	5.011	2-Mar-X4	8.01%	8.5003%		
3.00	1096	6.022	2-Sep-X4	8.16%	9.2078%		9.8333%
3.50	1277	7.016	2-Mar-X5	8.24%	8.8643%		
4.00	1461	8.027	2-Sep-X5	8.35%	9.4299%		
4.50	1643	9.027	2-Mar-X6	8.48%	9.7534%		
5.01	1827	10.038	2-Sep-X6	8.72%	11.3005%		

Example 1

Calculate the price of the following swaption:

Type:	Payer Swaption
Fixed Rate:	9.00% pa (S/A)
Swap Term:	three years (from commencement)
Term of Swaption:	one year (expiring for value 2 September 19X2)

To calculate the price of the option, we need to determine the following:

- *Type*—Buyer has the right *to pay* fixed rates. This is effectively a put option (the buyer benefits if rates increase).
- *One/four year forward rate*—The underlying commodity is a three year swap commencing in one years time. The one/four year forward rate calculated using the methodology specified above is: 8.7587% pa (S/A).

The above information allows the specification of the inputs into the option pricing model (see below in respect of selection of model type):

Underlying Asset Price (S):	100.624727%
Strike Price (K):	100.0%

This requires some explanation:

- S is calculated as the present value (PV) of a three year swap paying 9.00% pa (S/A) discounted at the forward rate (8.7587% pa).
- K is set out par as it is the PV of the swap at the swap rate of 9.00% pa.

Time to Expiration (T):	366 days.
Risk Free Interest Rate (RF):	7.10% pa (S/A) (the one year T-Bill Rate).
Volatility (V):	5.00%

(Please note the relevant volatility is the annualised volatility of the asset—that is, the price volatility of a three year swap.)

Holding Cost (H): 0.

This is because the holding cost of a forward contract is typically assumed to be zero.

Model Specification: see discussion below.

Option Type: European (exercisable only at maturity).

Exhibit 14.11 summarises the price of the relevant swaption. At the assumed volatility, the swaption price is:

1.5931% (flat)
US$1,593,100 per US$100m face value.

Exhibit 14.11

Swaption Price Calculator

Asset Price:	100.62%		
Strike Price:	100.00%		
Time to Expiration:	366		
Risk Free Interest Rate:	7.10%		
Volatility:	5.00%	6.00%	7.00%
Holding Costs:	0		
Option Type:	European put		
Swaption Price:			
—Payer	1.5931%	1.9647%	2.3369%
—Receiver	2.1763%	2.5479%	2.9201%

Exhibit 14.12 summarises the swaption premiums (% flat) for a range of strike prices and volatilities for both European and American style exercise rights.

Please note how the swaption premium decreases as the strike price moves above the implied forward swap rate (that is, it effectively moves out-of-the-money).

Exhibit 14.12

European and American Payer Swaption Prices—Summary

European Payer Swaption Prices—Summary

Strike Price		Volatilities (% pa)		
% pa	Price	5.00%	6.00%	7.00%
8.50%	99.330%	2.1876%	2.5563%	2.9258%
8.76%	100.000%	1.8645%	2.2373%	2.6100%
9.00%	100.625%	1.5931%	1.9647%	2.3369%
9.25%	101.272%	1.3421%	1.7074%	2.0755%

American Payer Swaption Prices—Summary

Strike Price		Volatilities (% pa)		
% pa	Price	5.00%	6.00%	7.00%
8.50%	99.33%	2.1876%	2.5563%	2.9258%
8.76%	100.00%	1.8645%	2.2373%	2.6100%
9.00%	100.62%	1.5931%	1.9647%	2.3369%
9.25%	101.27%	1.3421%	1.7074%	2.0755%

Example 2

Calculate the price of the following swaption:

Type:	Receiver Swaption
Fixed Rate:	9.50% pa (S/A)
Swap Term:	two years (from commencement)
Term of Swaption:	three years (expiring for value to 2 September 19X4)

To calculate the price of this swaption, we need to calculate the following:

- *Type*—Buyer has right to receive the fixed rate, effectively a call option (the buyer benefits if rates decrease).
- *Three/five year forward rate*—the three/five year forward rate calculated is: 9.8333% pa (S/A).

The option model components are therefore as follows:

Asset Price:	99.408%
Strike Price:	100.0%
Time to Expiration:	1,096 days
Risk-Free Interest Rate:	7.60 pa (S/A) (three year treasuries rate)
Volatility:	5.00%
Holding Costs:	0
Model Specification:	See discussion below
Option Type:	European (exerciseable only at maturity)

Exhibit 14.13 summarises the price of the relevant swaption. At the assumed volatility, the swaption price is:

2.5339% (flat)
US$2,533,900 per US$100m face value.

Exhibit 14.13
Swaption Price Calculator

Asset Price:	99.41%		
Strike Price:	100.00%		
Time to Expiration:	1096		
Risk Free Interest Rate:	7.60%		
Volatility:	5.00%	6.00%	7.00%
Holding Costs:	0		
Option Type:	European call		
Swaption Price:			
—Payer	3.0090%	3.5605%	4.1120%
—Receiver	2.5339%	3.0854%	3.6369%

Exhibit 14.14 below summarises the swaption premiums (% flat) for a range of strike prices and volatilities for both European and American style exercise rights.

Please note again the increase in option premiums as the option strike price moves into-the-money (that is, the fixed rate to be received increases relative to the forward swap rate).

In the examples used, there is no significant difference between the prices for European and American options. However, there will be occasions in which there will be significant differences in the price depending upon the option type (see discussion below).

Exhibit 14.14

European and American Receiver Swaption Prices—Summary

European Receiver Swaption Prices—Summary

Strike Price		Volatilities (% pa)		
% pa	Price	5.00%	6.00%	7.00%
9.50%	99.408%	2.5339%	3.0853%	3.6369%
9.83%	100.000%	2.7732%	3.3274%	3.8813%
10.00%	100.296%	2.8977%	3.4525%	4.0070%
10.25%	100.740%	3.0906%	3.6451%	4.1999%

American Receiver Swaption Prices—Summary

Strike Price		Volatilities (% pa)		
% pa	Price	5.00%	6.00%	7.00%
9.50%	99.408%	2.5339%	3.0853%	3.6369%
9.83%	100.000%	2.7732%	3.3274%	3.8813%
10.00%	100.296%	2.8977%	3.4525%	4.0070%
10.25%	100.740%	3.0906%	3.6451%	4.1999%

Pricing issues

Swaption model choice

The swaption premium calculations are derived utilising the Modified Black-Scholes Option Pricing Model, consistent with general market convention. The Modified Black-Scholes formula relaxes some of the assumptions applicable to the original Black-Scholes formula. However, the following restrictive assumptions remain:

- the prices are for European option *only*;
- the option is not exercised before expiration date;
- the underlying asset prices are log-normally distributed;
- the short term interest rate is fixed over the life of the option;
- dividend payments (in the case of equity options) are not discrete, but continuous.

In the case of a swaption, the major breakdowns in the assumptions are that the underlying asset price may not be log normally distributed and the fact that interest rates are fixed over the life of the option. A number of alternative approaches which seek to address these problems are available: for those interested in examining these approaches, refer Chapter 11.

European versus American swaptions

The option model choice problem is compounded where the underlying swaption is American rather than European. This is primarily because of the possibility of early exercise. For example, with a call option on interest rates, there is always a possibility of early exercise if the holding costs are below the short term rate assumed.

The examples above for American swaptions, consistent with normal market practice, are calculated using the Modified Black-Scholes American Option Pricing Formula. This is the same as the Modified Black-Scholes European Option Pricing Formula except that the Black-Scholes American Formula checks to see if the value it is returning is below the intrinsic value of the option.

Where the Black-Scholes European Option value is below the intrinsic price of the option then the Modified Black-Scholes American Formula returns the intrinsic value of the option. That is:

Black-Scholes American Option Value = Maximum (Black-Scholes European Value, Intrinsic Value)

A possible alternative is to use quadratic approximation methods to value American swaptions. Under this approach, it is assumed that an American option is equal to a European option plus a separate early exercise option. The quadratic approximation method determines the early exercise option value and then adds it to the value calculated by the Modified Black-Scholes European Formula. The early exercise option value is determined by an iterative process.

Volatility estimation

Volatility estimation for swaptions is usually undertaken using one of the following methods:

- implied volatility (determined from market swaptions);
- historical volatility.

In the case of historical volatility, it is theoretically necessary to get the volatilities of the appropriate forward swap prices. In practice, the volatility of spot swap rates for the relevant maturity (in the above examples, the two and three year swap rates) are utilised.

A variety of alternative approaches are utilised in practice including:

- the volatility of government securities for the relevant maturity with an added element for swap spread volatility;
- the volatility of interest rate futures contracts (particularly where the underlying swap is of a relatively short maturity—less than two/three years—reflecting the use of interest rate futures to hedge the position).

Exhibit 14.15 summarises historical volatilities on US$ options on interest rate swaps.

Pricing swaptions in practice

In practice, the pricing of swaptions is subject to a number of constraints:

- The level of liquidity in the market; the higher the level of liquidity, the closer the premium to theoretical swaption values.
- The depth and trading levels in the specific swaption market and the availability of good two-way transaction flow which facilitates the assumption and hedging of exposures.
- The availability of hedging instruments and their cost and the efficiency of the hedge that can be achieved.

Swaption markets vary significantly between currencies. However, a number of general trends are apparent.

Shorter swaptions (that is, those with periods to expiry of less than one/two years) tend to be priced close to their theoretical values. This reflects the following factors:

- the opportunity for arbitrage to force the prices to theoretical levels;
- liquidity of the market which facilitates position clearing;
- the availability of a wide variety of hedging instruments including:
  —options on traded interest rate futures contracts;

—the capacity to generate forward/forward positions in interest rate swap portfolios;

—availability of option and forward markets in government securities in the relevant currencies.

Exhibit 14.15

US$ Option on Swap Volatility

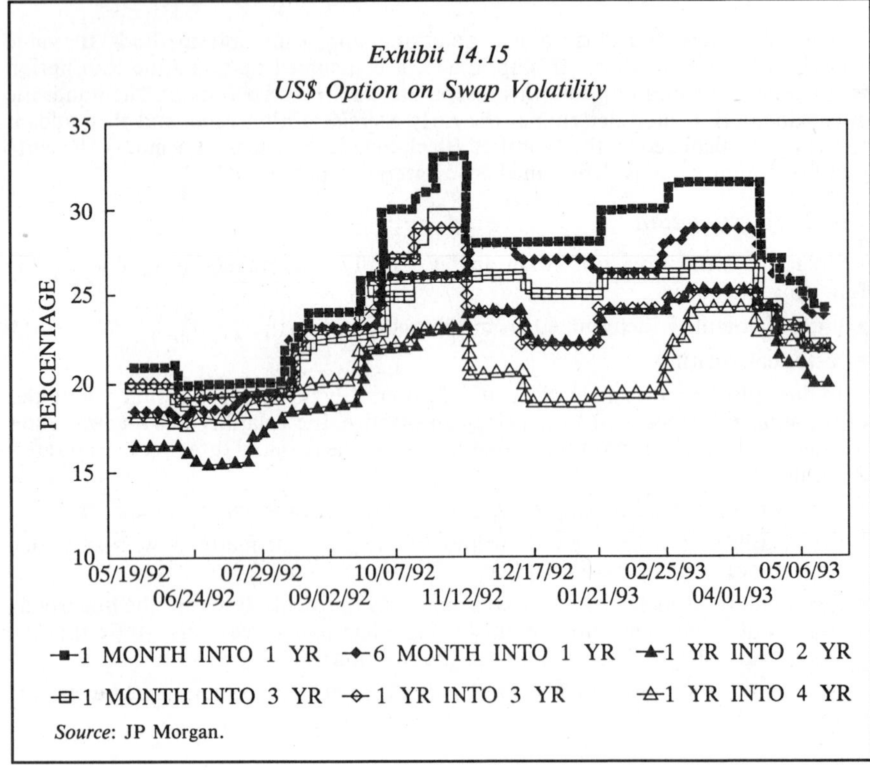

Source: JP Morgan.

Swaptions with longer maturities (that is, with periods to expiry in excess of two years) are more problematic. This reflects the difficulty of hedging the swaption positions. Consequently, these types of swaptions tend to be driven by capital market arbitrage and, in particular, the stripping of options from capital market instruments, such as callable bonds and mortgage-backed securities.

Pricing swaptions versus caps

Swaption prices are often compared to the pricing of interest rate caps. This is particularly misleading for the following reasons:

- A swaption is a *one-time* option which can be exercised into a swap to either receive or pay the fixed rate for the full term of the underlying interest rate swaps. In contrast, a cap or floor is a *series* of options on a short term interest rate index (such as three or six month LIBOR)
- A swaption provides protection against the adverse movement in interest rates for the period of the swaption. At the end of this period, the swaption must be exercised or allowed to lapse. If the swaption is exercised into the underlying

swap, then the purchaser is "locked into" the relevant fixed rate (in the case of a payer swaption). If the swaption is allowed to lapse, then the purchaser has no further protection.

In contrast, a purchaser of a cap receives the difference between market rate and the strike or protection level of the cap *over the full life of the contract*. In addition, the purchaser of the cap benefits where interest rates fall as its interest rate is priced at market levels which are lower than the strike level on the cap.

In summary, a swaption is priced as a one period option allowing exercise into an underlying swap. In contrast, a cap is a series of options on the relevant interest rate index.

There are, nevertheless, a number of linkages between the two instruments. These derive, primarily, from the fact that an interest rate swap is effectively a combination of a cap and floor contract.

For example, paying fixed rate/receiving floating rate under a swap is equivalent to buying a cap and selling a floor at the relevant swap rate. Conversely, receiving fixed under a swap equates to the purchase of a floor and a sale of a cap at the swap rate. Consequently, swaptions can be characterised as *options on interest rate caps/floors*. For example, the purchaser of a payer swaption can be decomposed into a:

- purchase of an option on an interest rate cap;
- sale of an option on interest rate floor.

The strike price of both the underlying cap and floor are equal to the strike rate of the swaption.

This method of decomposition allows the creation of compound options (that is, options on options) on interest rate indexes.

Another method of decomposition relates to the nature of interest rates swaps which entail exchanges of fixed rate cash flows for floating rate cash flows. This means that for a fixed rate payer under a swap, the only cash flow risk of the transaction is the fact that the short-term interest rate (on which the floating rates are calculated) average below the fixed rate of the swap, thereby requiring cash settlement on each relevant payment date.

Consequently, the purchaser of a payer swaption may protect its own risk under the transaction by purchasing a series of floor contracts corresponding to the floating rate interest rate sets on the underlying swap. Conversely, the seller of the swaption could hedge its own position by the purchase of interest rate caps, the cash flow under which would cover any cash payments due under the swaptions (if exercised). However, in practice, it is likely that these methods of hedging would be extremely expensive and render the swaption itself uneconomic.

Chapter 15

Interest Rate and Currency Linked Financial Derivatives

EVOLUTION OF INTEREST RATE AND CURRENCY LINKED HYBRID SWAP TRANSACTION

The evolution of derivative embedded securities

The emergence of hybrid swap structures, entailing linkages to interest rates and currency values, is related to a new class of securities which emerged in international capital markets in about 1985. These security structures involved bonds and other securities with forward, option and other derivative contract features *embedded* in the basic structure. The embedded derivative features are structured as variable redemption features, either on the principal amount or on interest coupons, where the amount payable by the issuer is linked to movements in the price of an external financial asset.

The options embedded in the capital market issues included options on debt instruments and interest rates, currencies and, more recently, commodities and equity indexes. In most cases, the transaction structure insulated the borrower from the derivative element embedded in the structure of the security itself. This was achieved through hybrid swap structures which were executed simultaneous to the securities issue itself.

These types of structures elicited considerable interest from investors and issuers. From the viewpoint of issuers, the fact that they typically have no exposure to the derivative element effectively created has meant that high quality issuers have utilised these types of securities issues as the vehicle for classical new issue arbitrage: see below, Chapter 19.

In contrast, investors have been attracted to these securities for more complex reasons including:

- The inability of certain key groups of investors, such as Japanese institutions and German institutional and retail investors, to purchase or write forwards, options or other derivatives on financial instruments because of regulatory restrictions which have the effect of restricting their portfolio management strategies.
- Several investors have sought to use these types of securities to hedge offsetting positions in the underlying commodity or instrument.
- Such transactions typically create derivative instruments for longer periods than are otherwise available thereby increasing the risk transfer opportunities for various market participants.

An important aspect of utilising capital markets to create these particular types of derivatives is that these transactions are usually based upon arbitraging various segments of the market seeking to capitalise on the differing values placed on the same instrument by different participants.

It is evident that on a number of occasions investors appear to have created options or forward positions, implicit in the securities purchased, below their theoretical fair economic value. This has allowed the creator of the derivative position to effectively purchase the position from the investor below fair market value and offset the position by securitising or on selling into the capital market, in another form. For example, in a number of the currency option transactions involving capital market issues (see below) high option premiums in the short-term markets have allowed option purchases to strip-off and buy the option created through the issue and recoup the bulk of the premium by granting options different in maturity as part of an ongoing currency option portfolio management programme.

The anomalous pricing features of these transactions are not readily explainable. They are similar to the mispricing of interest rate options discussed in the context of options on swaps: see above, Chapter 14. The reasons discussed, in that context, are equally applicable in regard to these structures. In addition, it is possible that investors may view the purchase of a derivative linked security fundamentally different to trading in options or forward. Key factors in this regard include the relative liquidity of the instruments, the income stream attaching to a security as distinct from an option, as well as attitudes towards and capacity to absorb risk.

Interest rate and currency linked swap structures

The hybrid swap structures discussed in this chapter and Chapters 16 and 17 entail, primarily, combinations of swaps with other derivative instruments—typically forward and option positions. In a number of cases, these types of transactions are, strictly speaking, not swap transactions at all as they entail, primarily, a series of forward or option transactions in the relevant currency.

However, coverage of these types of transaction structures is included for the following reasons:

- It is very common to incorporate a swap within the overall transaction structure to change the currency or interest rate basis of the borrowing as the derivative element in the transaction is merely designed to create the basis for a lower cost borrowing transaction for the issuer.
- The interest rate and currency linked hybrids are usually originated, structured and executed by the swap desks of financial intermediaries. This reflects the increasing integration and generalised focus of the derivative operations of major financial institutions which are focusing simultaneously on the structuring, pricing, hedging and distribution of derivative instruments covering interest rates, currencies, commodities and equities.
- The basic underlying premise of such transactions, involving arbitrage between various sectors of the capital market, as discussed below, is identical with the rationale of other types of swap transactions.
- It should be noted that the swap transactions incorporated in such arrangements, either interest rate or currency, commonly involves a considerable degree of structuring in itself. For example, it is common to utilise a premium or discount swap structure or a swap with accelerated deferred cash flows to match the uneven pattern of cash flows generated by the underlying derivative related security.

Types of interest rate and currency linked swap transactions

The hybrid swap structures can be divided into two distinct categories:

- the structures, which developed originally, to facilitate the securitisation of forward and option positions embedded in securities issues;
- hybrid swap structures, entailing specifically engineered linkages to interest rates, currencies, commodities or equity indexes, designed to facilitate identified asset liability management requirements, *independent of capital market issues*.

The latter category of hybrid swap structure has evolved strongly over recent years in response to the demand by borrowers and investors for complex synthetic liability and asset structures to facilitate particular portfolio management objectives.

This type of hybrid swap structure entails linkages, generally, to the following external variables:

- interest rates;
- foreign exchange or currency values;
- a wide range of commodities, including price series or inflation indexes;
- equity or stock indexes.

In addition, more complex structures involving linkages to more than one financial market variable, referred to as cross-market derivatives, have also emerged.

In this chapter, interest rate and currency linked swaps are considered. Swap structures with specifically engineered linkages to commodities and equity indexes are discussed in Chapters 16 and 17 respectively.

It is important to distinguish the derivative embedded capital market transactions and the accompanying hybrid swap structures, discussed in this and following chapters, from a totally different class of capital market transactions. These originally emerged in late 1986 and early 1987 and entailed the issue of debt accompanied by commodity or currency warrants.

These transactions were designed to take advantage of particularly attractive spreads between wholesale or institutional option prices and what retail customers and investors were willing to pay for similar options. For example, in late 1987, a number of United States investment banks arranged issues of foreign currency options, mainly US$ and JPY or US$ and DEM currency options in the United States domestic market as well as in the Eurobond markets. The issuer in each case hedged its own exposure under the currency option element by buying an identical option from professional market makers in such options, typically financial institutions. The profits from these transactions resulted from the fact that purchasers at a retail level for these options were willing to pay significantly higher amounts for these options than the premium at which the issuer could cover the exposure by the purchase of an identical option in the inter bank or wholesale market. *Exhibit 15.1* sets out an example of this type of transaction.

These types of transactions have made spasmodic reappearances in the international capital markets. At various times, issues with attached interest rate, commodity etc options have been issued to take advantage of, primarily, retail investor demands for speculative assets in the relevant commodity seeking to benefit from anticipated price movements.

Exhibit 15.1
Swapping an Issue of Bonds with Attached Currency Warrants

Assume that Issuer A (A) undertakes the following issue of fixed rate Eurobonds with attached DEM/US$ Currency Warrants:

Bonds

Amount: DEM200m

Maturity: five years

Coupon: 6% pa

Issue Price: 110

Fees/Commission: 2.00%

Warrants

The investor receives one currency warrant for every DEM5,000 bond purchased. The warrants have the following characteristics:

Type: US$ Call/DEM Put

Strike: US$1.00 = DEM1.85

Exercise Period: two years

The position of the investor in these bonds/currency warrants is as follows:

- The investor pays DEM5,500 (110% of par) for DEM5,000 face value of bonds yielding 6% pa.
- The investor acquires an option to purchase US$2,500 at a cost of DEM4,625.
- The implicit cost of the option is DEM500 (being the difference between the issue price and par value of the bonds).

The investor gains under the terms of the option where the US$ appreciates against the DEM. The investor profits where the US$ increases in value beyond US$1 = DEM2.09 (the term of the warrant adjusted for the DEM600 implicitly option premium).

The issuer's position in respect of the currency warrants is as follows:

- A has written the US$ call/DEM put and is exposed to an appreciation of the US$.
- A hedges its exposure under the currency option by purchasing an equivalent option from a trader or traders in currency options.
- A purchases the option for approximately DEM5 per DEM100 face value of the option, effectively creating a cash surplus of DEM5 per DEM100 which effectively lowers its borrowing cost.

The difference between the option premium paid by A and the sale price of the warrants reflects a number of factors including:

- The options are purchased wholesale and sold retail.
- The warrants are listed securities and have a degree of liquidity being capable of being traded over-the-counter.
- The targeted investors (in this transaction, German retail investors) under German gambling laws are not permitted to purchase or sell options unless they are listed securities.

These factors dictate that the investors are willing to pay a higher premium than the fair economic value for the option.

A's position under the transaction is as follows:

Year	Issue Cash Flows (DEMm)	Fees/ Commissions (DEMm)	Option Premium Paid (DEMm)	Net Cash Flow (DEMm)
0	+220.0	(4.4)	(10.0m)	205.6
1	(12)			(12)
2	(12)			(12)
3	(12)			(12)

Exhibit 15.1—continued

Year	Issue Cash Flows (DEMm)	Fees/ Commissions (DEMm)	Option Premium Paid (DEMm)	Net Cash Flow (DEMm)
4	(12)			(12)
5	(212)			(212)

This equates to an effective cost for A of 5.347%.

At the time of issue, the equivalent Germany Schuldscheine rate was approximately 6.00% pa. The issuer would have, if it wanted, translated the cost advantage under the issue, arising from the subsidy provided by the currency option premium differential, into attractively priced sub-LIBOR funding, either in DEM or US$, through an interest rate or currency swap.

INTEREST RATE DERIVATIVE EMBEDDED SECURITIES AND RELATED SWAPS

Interest rate linked swaps involving embedded derivative elements on debt instruments and interest rates, include reverse or inverse FRNs, issues of capped FRNs and certificates of deposit (CD), issues of debt warrants, either on a stand-alone (or naked) basis or in conjunction with the issue of debt securities, and issues of securities where the redemption amount is linked to fluctuations in the value of an identified debt security.

Reverse/inverse FRN swap structures

In early 1986, during a period of sustained decreases in interest rates, investors seeking the benefit from expected declines in short-term interest rates sought an instrument whose yield increased as interest rates fell. The "bull" or reverse or inverse FRN was one such instrument. The bull FRN carried an interest coupon which was a fixed rate (say, 17.25% pa) less six month US$ LIBOR. As LIBOR decreases, the return payable under the note increases commensurately. However, the instrument held little attraction for issuers who would be disadvantaged if short-term interest rates fell. However, a particularly ingenious swap structure designed to protect the issuer from increases in its effective cost of funds was advised. Under this structure, the issuer undertook conventional interest rate swaps for *double* the amount of the FRN issue to create a synthetic floating rate liability. The bull or reverse FRN issue and swap structure are set out in *Exhibit 15.2*.

The basic concept was varied with the "bear" FRN which carried a coupon of two times LIBOR minus a fixed rate which was designed to appeal to investors concerned about future increases in short-term interest rates.

The bear FRN structure together with accompanying swap is set out in *Exhibit 15.3*. Under this structure, as in the bull FRN, the issuer is insulated from any interest rate risk as a result of fluctuations of interest rates achieving floating rate funding related to LIBOR at an all-in cost below its normal floating rate funding cost.

The concept of bull or bear (also referred to as reverse or inverse) FRNs enjoyed a significant resurgence in the early 1990s. Initially, in late 1990, transactions were undertaken in US$ and C$ as well as GBP. However, the majority of such transactions, during this period, were undertaken in DEM. These transactions, undertaken in the early 1990s, were slightly different to those structures originated in the late 1980s. *Exhibit 15.4* details an example of a DEM Inverse FRN issue and swap structure from that period.

Exhibit 15.2
Reverse FRN Issue and Swap Structure

The issue structure entails a FRN issue on the following terms:

Amount:	US$100m
Term:	five years
Interest payment:	The issue carries an interest rate of 17.25% (calculated on bond basis payable S/A) less six months US$ LIBOR flat. At no time will there be negative interest for the investor, that is, if US$ six month LIBOR reaches 17.25% pa or above, the investor will not be required to make any payment to the issuer
Fees:	0.25% flat

The issue structure is designed to provide investors with an investment on which the return increases as short-term interest rates decline.

The underlying FRN issue is swapped utilising the following swap structure:

Transaction structure:	Conventional US$ interest rate swap
Notional principal amount:	US$200m
Issuer pays swap counterparty:	LIBOR − 0.125% pa
Issuer receives from swap counterparty:	8.625% pa S/A

The total transaction can be depicted as follows:

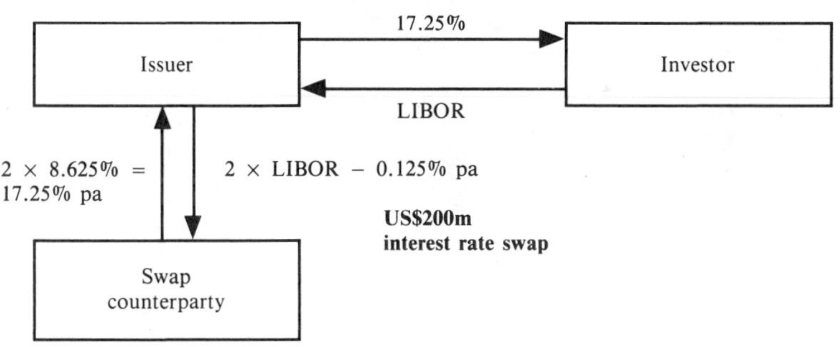

The net effect of the transaction is to generate LIBOR less 25bps on a principal borrowing of US$100m for the issuer.

Importantly, this result is achieved so long as LIBOR is less than 17.25% pa, that is, the basic fixed interest coupon on the FRN issue. Where LIBOR exceeds 17.25% pa S/A, the sub-LIBOR margin to the issuer is eroded. At a LIBOR level of 17.25% pa S/A, the issuer achieves funding at a level equivalent to LIBOR, that is, the sub-LIBOR margin is eroded.

The underlying cash flows of the issue and related swaps are set out in the following table.

Exhibit 15.2—continued

		Issue cash flows			Swap cash flows		
(1) Level of six month LIBOR (% pa S/A)	(2) 17.25% pa S/A on US$100 (S/A payment)	(3) Six month LIBOR on US$100m (S/A payment)	(4) Cost to issuer (return to investor) [(2) – (3)]	(5) Issuer receives 8.625% pa S/A on US$200m (S/A payment)	(6) Issuer pays US$ six month LIBOR minus 0.125% pa on US$200m (S/A payment)	(7) Net swap cash flow [(5) – (6)] (S/A payment)	(8) Net cost to issuer [(4) – (7)]
4.0625	8,625,000	2,031,250	6,593,750 (13.1875% pa S/A)	8,625,000	3,937,500	+4,687,500	1,906,250 (3.8125% pa S/A LIBOR – 25bps)
8.1250	8,625,000	4,062,500	4,562,500 (9.125% pa S/A)	8,625,000	8,000,000	+ 625,000	3,937,500 (7.875% pa S/A LIBOR – 25bps)
12.1875	8,625,000	6,093,750	2,531,250 (5.0625% pa S/A)	8,625,000	12,062,500	–3,437,500	5,968,750 (11.9375% pa S/A LIBOR – 25 bps)
17.2500	8,625,000	8,625,000	0	8,625,000	17,125,000	–8,500,000	8,500,000 (17.00% pa S/A LIBOR – 25 bps)
17.5000	8,625,000	8,625,000	0	8,625,000	17,137,000	–8,750,000	8,750,000 (17.50% pa S/A LIBOR)
21.5625	8,625,000	8,625,000	0	8,625,000	21,437,500	–12,812,500	12,812,500 (25.625% pa LIBOR + 406.25bps)

Exhibit 15.3
Bear FRN Issue and Swap Structure

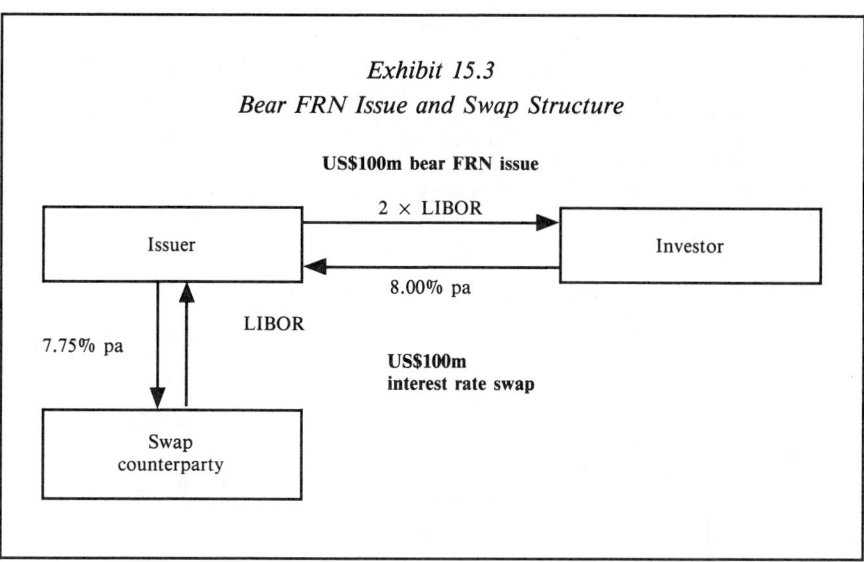

Exhibit 15.4
Deferred Inverse FRN Issue and Swap Structure

Issuer A undertakes a deferred inverse floater denominated in DEM on the following terms:

Amount: DEM100m

Maturity: 10 years

Interest: Years 1-3
Fixed at 9.00% pa
Years 3-10
Floating calculated as:
16.00% minus six month DEM LIBOR
The coupon cannot be negative.

The investors in this instrument will benefit in years 4-10 if DEM LIBOR falls. For example, the return to the investor at varying DEM LIBOR levels is set out below:

DEM LIBOR (% pa)	Investor Return (% pa)
9.00	7.00
8.50	7.50
8.00	8.00
7.50	8.50
7.00	9.00
6.50	9.50
6.00	10.00
5.50	10.50
5.00	11.00

The issuer is indifferent to whether rates rise or fall as it hedges itself against the inverse characteristics of the structure by entering into the following swaps:

- A forward DEM interest swap for seven years commencing three years forward whereby A receives fixed DEM at 8.85% pa and pays six month DEM LIBOR.
- A also purchases a deferred seven year cap commencing in three years at a strike price at 16.00% pa for a premium of 25bps.

Exhibit 15.4—continued

The cap is designed to protect A from the contingency that DEM LIBOR rises above 16.00% pa as the coupon cannot be negative. If DEM LIBOR rises above 16.00% then the investor receives no interest on the bond, A must pay DEM LIBOR under the terms of the forward interest rate swap. A's payment under the swap is effectively hedged by the cap which generates the shortfall where DEM LIBOR is above 16.00% pa.

The issue and accompanying swap structure is set out below:

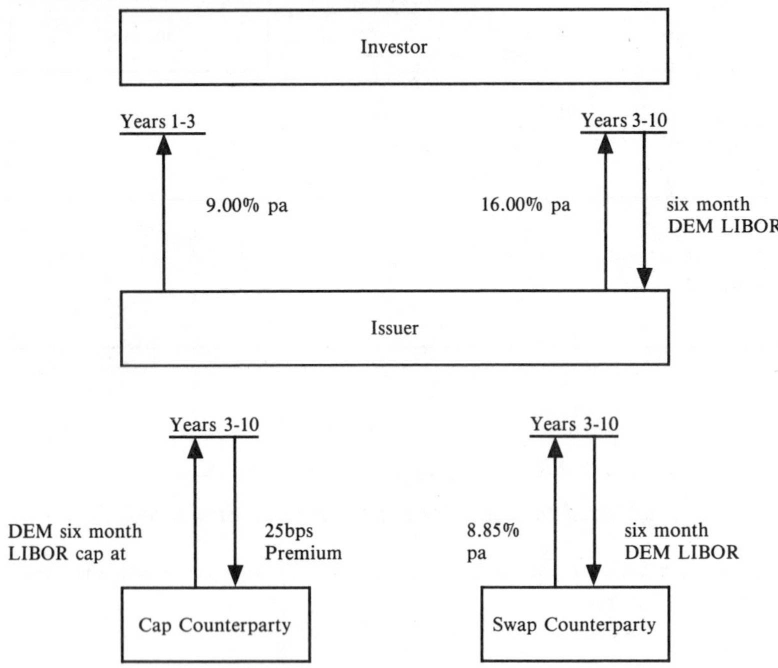

The all-in cost to the issue of the transaction is 7.86% pa (before any issue fees or the cost of the cap). Assuming issue fees of 1.25% and a cap premium of 25bps, the all-in cost of the transaction to A of approximately 8.09% pa.

In the event that A wishes to generate floating rate funding, A would enter into a ten year DEM interest rate where it receives DEM fixed at 8.75% pa and pays six month DEM LIBOR.

The issue and swap structure is set out below:

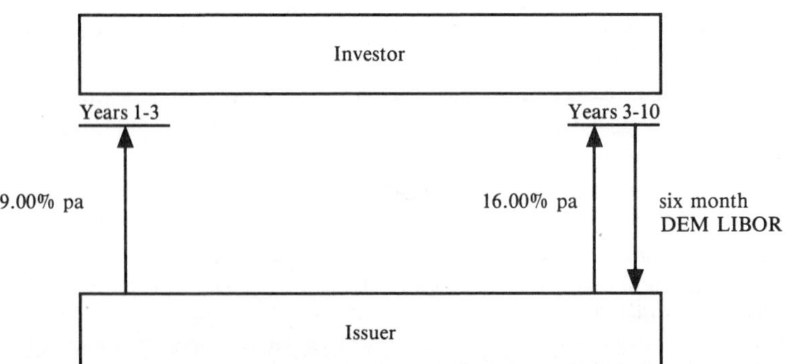

Exhibit 15.4—continued

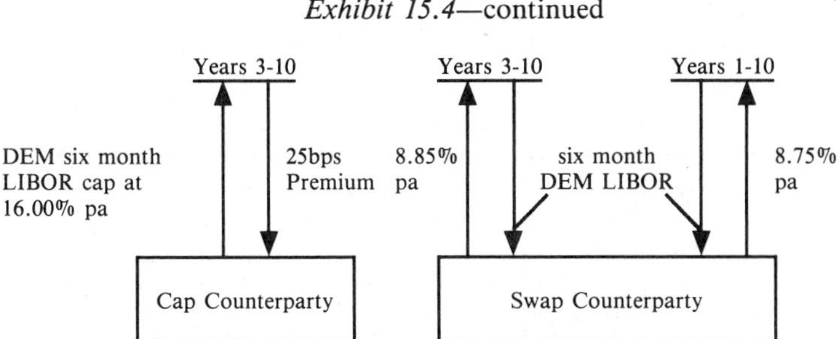

The all-in cost of this structure to A is DEM six month LIBOR minus 68.5bps pa.

This margin is generated as follows:

Years 1-3 — DEM LIBOR + 25bps (9.00% pa − 8.75% pa)

Years 4-10 — DEM LIBOR − 160bps (16.00% pa − (8.75% pa + 8.85% pa))

This generates a blended margin below DEM LIBOR of 90.7bps. Adjusted for issue expenses and the cap premium (an amortised annuity amount of 22.2bps pa), A's cost equates to DEM LIBOR minus 68.5bps pa.

Capped, mini-max, collared and floor FRNs

In the case of capped FRN and CD issues, typically, the issues were seven to 12 year FRN or two to five year CD issues with ceilings on interest payments undertaken by highly rated borrowers, primarily banks or sovereign entities. Investors in the issues, in return for accepting a ceiling on their yield, received a higher than normal current coupon or margin on the FRNs and CDs.

Capped FRN issues were initially undertaken in June 1985 in US$ in the Euromarkets. This was followed by the emergence of a capped floating rate CD market which has enjoyed more sustained interest. The capped FRN concept has also been extended beyond US$ with a series of issues in deutschmarks and in Dutch guilders. Later variations include delayed cap FRNs where the maximum interest rates do not operate for the first three to four years.

A variation on the capped FRN structure was the maximum rate notes (MRNs). MRNs involved the issue of fixed rate debt combined with a nominated cap rate on a floating rate index (such as six month LIBOR). If six month LIBOR exceeds the cap rate, the fixed rate coupon decreases by the same amount. Functionally, MRNs operate in the same way as capped FRNs.

The concept of a capped FRN issue has been utilised in a variety of other markets. For example, in late 1987, the State Electricity Commission of Western Australia issued a capped FRN in A$ with effectively, a cap on the Australian BBR. The cap implicit in the transaction was securitised in much the same way as similar issues in other markets. A number of other private transactions in the Australian domestic market as well as in JPY, GBP and DEM are known to have been completed.

The ceiling, which is structually identical to a put option on the price of a short-term security priced off the underlying short-term interest rate index, is sold to third parties with the proceeds of the sale, the option premium, in effect, lowering the issuer's borrowing cost, usually below market rates. Where the market rates exceed the capped rate, the investor's return is limited to the specified ceiling allowing the purchaser of the cap to receive the difference between the cap and market rate from the issuer, thereby allowing it to establish a known maximum cost of funding.

The detailed structure of the transaction is more complex. For example the Banque Indosuez transaction, arranged by Shearson Lehman Brothers, which opened this market, was an issue of 12 year US$200m FRNs carrying an interest coupon of 0.375% over three month LIMEAN. The FRN coupon was capped at 13.0625%. It should be noted that the cap level on LIMEAN is equivalent to 12.6875% (13.0625% pa minus the 0.375% pa margin). Shearsons arranged for the sale of the cap (with a strike of 12.6875% pa on LIMEAN) to a United States corporation. Indosuez pays out LIMEAN plus 0.375%, or 13.0625% to the holders of the FRNs if three month LIMEAN exceeds 12.6875% pa. For example, if LIMEAN go to 14.0625%, Indosuez pays 13.0625% to the FRN holders and 1.375% to Shearsons who passes it on to the purchaser of the cap to compensate it for rates rising above the cap level. Indoseuz is compensated for the cap by a payment of 0.375% pa of the principal amount (effectively, the option premium). Indoseuz wanted this flow as a continuous quarterly flow, although it could have received it as a discounted lump sum. This brought Indosuez's cost of funds down to LIMEAN. To avoid any credit risk, the purchaser of the cap paid Shearsons a lump sum which was reinvested in some treasury zero coupon securities which produced the quarterly income stream equivalent to 0.375% pa. The structure of such a transaction is set out in *Exhibit 15.5*.

In an extension of this concept, an issue of securitised caps, effectively an issue of put options or warrants, was arranged by Banque Paribas Capital Markets in early 1987.

The structure of the capped FRN and its derivatives is that the issue was engineered such that the investors created out-of-the-money caps. Analytically, the investor has written a *series* of put options expiring every three or six months until maturity on the underlying index. The premium paid to the investor is the higher spread on the FRN.

Studies undertaken to evaluate the pricing structure have concluded that the values implied for the caps are all low compared with theoretical values derived from historical levels of volatility. This undervaluation provided a significant arbitrage opportunity whereby certain organisations active in writing customised caps, usually by creating synthetic options (see discussion in Chapter 29) for higher premiums, purchased these caps stripped from the FRNs, etc to effectively hedge their risk exposures.

A variation on the capped FRN was the mini-max FRN structure whereby the investor was subject to both maximum and minimum rates of interest.

The first mini-max issue, undertaken by Goldman Sachs for the Kingdom of Denmark, was a ten year US$250m FRN with a coupon of 0.1875% pa over LIBOR subject to a minimum rate of 10.00% and a maximum rate of 11.875% pa. A series of issues for SEK, Commerzbank and Christiana Bank followed before investor interest evaporated.

Just as the maximum or cap interest rate was identical to a series of caps or put options, the minimum interest rate was analytically identical to a floor or a series of call options. These options, which were granted by the issuer in return for the investor accepting a maximum rate of interest on the security, were then presumably stripped off and sold separately. In the case of these mini-max issues, in a number of cases, the issuer eliminated any exposure under the call options or floors granted by in turn purchasing a floor from a financial intermediary.

Exhibit 15.5

Capped FRN Issue and Cap Securitisation Structure

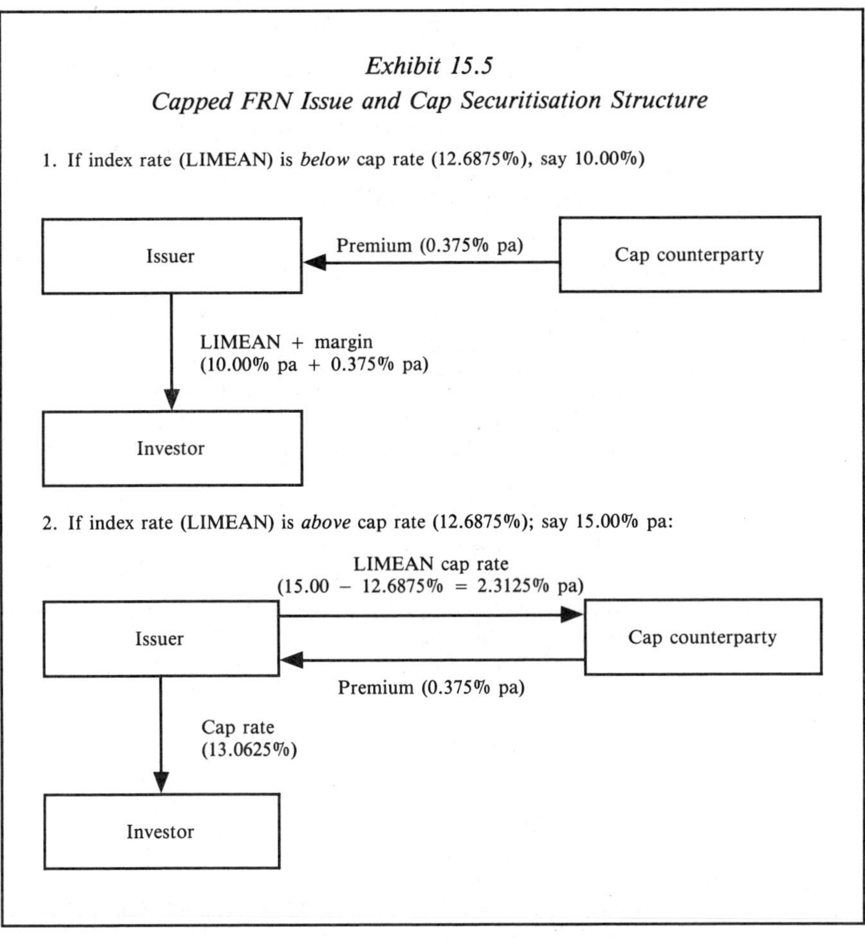

The mini-max FRN concept re-emerged in 1992/93 in the form of collared FRNs. In an environment of low nominal interest rates and a steeply sloping, positively shaped yield curve, investors seeking higher short-term money market interest rates fuelled a series of issues of FRNs with both a minimum and maximum interest rate. These structures, which effectively combined a normal FRN with an interest rate collar (a purchased cap and sold floor on the relevant interest rate index), were used to extract value from the positively shaped yield curves. *Exhibit 15.6* sets out a detailed analysis of collared FRN structures.

Exhibit 15.6

Collared Floating Rate Notes (FRNs)

BACKGROUND/ORIGINS

The collared FRN structure has its origins in the capped FRN and Mini-Max FRN transactions completed in the middle 1980s. The collared FRN market emerged around August 1992 when

Exhibit 15.6—continued

Kidder Peabody, the US investment bank, reintroduced the concept with issues for, amongst others, JP Morgan and Credit Local de France.

The market re-emerged in an environment of declining US interest rates. A particular feature of the market, at this time, was the relatively steep slope of the US$ interest rate yield curve.

STRUCTURE AND ECONOMICS

Structure

The basic structure of the collared FRN entails a normal FRN structure with an interest coupon related to US$ LIBOR (either three or six month). The interest rate coupon is subject to a minimum and maximum interest rate level of 5% pa and 10% pa respectively. The initial issues were undertaken for maturities of ten years.

The initial transactions undertaken were subordinated FRNs (designed to be treated as Tier II Capital for BIS capital adequacy purposes). However, a number of subsequent issues were senior rather than subordinated issue structures.

Table 1 sets out the term of the JP Morgan issue, one of their first transactions to be undertaken.

TABLE 1

JP Morgan and Co Inc

Amount:	US $200m of subordinated FRNs.
Maturity:	Ten years (due 19 August 2002).
Spread:	Three month LIBID flat.
Fixed re-offer price:	99.85.
Minimum interest:	5%.
Maximum interest:	10%.
Amortisation:	Bullet.
Call option:	None.
Listing:	Luxembourg.
Governing law:	New York.
Denominations:	US$5,000, US$100,000.
Commissions:	0.50% (management & underwriting 0.25%; selling 0.25%).
Payment:	18 August.
Swap:	Undisclosed.
Negative pledge:	No.
Cross default:	No.
Pari passu:	Yes.
144a option:	No.
Outstanding rating:	Aa2 (Moody's), AA+ (S&P).
Lead manager:	Kidder Peabody Intl (books).
Co-lead managers:	JP Morgan Securities, Merrill Lynch Intl, Salomon Brothers Intl, CSFB.
Co-managers:	Lehman Brother Intl, Goldman Sachs Intl, Morgan Stanley Intl.
Pre-market price:	100.10, 100.25.

Source: (1992) (August) *International Financing Review* Issue 940, 56.

Economics

The basic economics of the collared FRN is driven by the fact that it combines a standard FRN transaction with a US$ LIBOR interest rate cap and floor. Based on the structure described, the investor purchases a package consisting of:

- a normal ten year US$ LIBOR related coupon FRN;

Exhibit 15.6—continued

- sells a cap on US$ LIBOR at the maximum interest rate (say, 10% pa);
- purchases a US$ interest rate floor at the minimum interest rate level (say, 5% pa).

(The sale of the cap and purchase of the floor equates to, effectively, a sold interest rate collar on US$ LIBOR.)

The position of the issuer is the exact opposite of that of the investor. The issuer has borrowed utilising a US$ LIBOR-based FRN while simultaneously purchasing a US$ LIBOR interest rate cap and selling a US$ LIBOR based floor (a purchased interest rate collar on US$ LIBOR).

As described in detail below, the issuer hedges this exposure under the collar by onselling the cap and purchasing the floor to generate normal US$ LIBOR-based funding.

The economics of the transaction are driven, substantively, by the shape of the US$ yield curve. The strongly positive nature of the yield curve means that forward rates in US$ are significantly above the prevailing rates for particular maturities. For example, the rate for US$ three or six month LIBOR in three, six, nine, 12 etc months is significantly above the prevailing LIBOR or bank borrowing rates for the corresponding maturities. This merely reflects the steepness of the yield curve itself.

The steepness of the yield curve and the fact that the US$ LIBOR forward rates implied from the curve are significantly above the observed yield curve dictates the respective values of the cap and floor which, in turn, dictate the economics of the transaction.

The fact that forward US$ LIBOR rates are significantly above current yield curve rates means that the US$ LIBOR floors purchased by the investors while significantly in-the-money in the initial periods are out-of-the-money for much of the life of the transaction. In contrast, the higher US$ LIBOR forward rates implied in the yield curve dictate that the US$ interest rate cap is closer to the strike price of the maximum interest rate level (effectively, the cap strike level) of the collared FRN structure. This relativity of the minimum and maximum rates (effectively, the strike rates for the floor and cap respectively) determines their relative value.

At the time these transactions were undertaken, based on the yield curves prevailing, the market price for the cap and floor suggest that the investors were forgoing approximately 50bps pa in value from the transaction; in other words, collared FRN had an implied yield of approximately LIBOR minus 50bps pa. This forgone value effectively allowed the issuer to create attractively priced funding as described in detail below.

Investor perspective

The major demand for these collared FRNs were from money market investors, primarily money market funds seeking the benefit of the minimum coupon. With US$ short-term interest rates at historically low levels and, at that time, appearing still to be falling, investors were prepared to trade off the forgone profit of the cap for the high short-term current coupon income generated by the floor implicit in the minimum interest level. In effect, the investors were willing to sell the cap, at a lower than theoretical value level, as firstly, they placed a greater importance on current income and, secondly, their expectations of forward interest rates on US$ LIBOR were significantly below those implied by the current yield curve.

Initial demand for collared FRNs concentrated among Swiss and Far Eastern money market investors. However, as the market developed rapidly, German, United Kingdom and United States investors joined Swiss and Asian purchasers of these collared FRN transactions.

Issuer perspective

From the perspective of the issuer, these transactions were fully hedged into normal US$ LIBOR-based funding, typically, at relatively attractive borrowing rates. The issuer who had effectively purchased a US$ interest rate cap at the maximum rate and sold the investor an interest rate floor at the minimum interest rates hedged their exposure by simultaneously onselling the interest rate cap and purchasing a corresponding interest rate floor to immunise itself from the risk of the transaction. These interest rate cap and floor transactions were typically undertaken by the issuer directly with the arranger of the transaction or alternatively a third party cap/floor trader.

The attractive funding cost for the issuer was generated by the fact that, as noted above, the investors were valuing the collar element of the transaction at a level which was lower than the economic value of the separate interest rate cap and floor. This allowed issuers to typically

Exhibit 15.6—continued

onsell the interest rate cap and purchase the interest rate floor for premiums which generated a net cash inflow to the issuer which reduced their borrowing costs in some cases by as much as 50bps pa.

From the issuer's perspective, the transactions were particularly attractive as they generated attractively priced funding for long terms, typically, ten years, at a time when arbitrage opportunities in traditional bond markets were relatively scarce. An additional advantage, particularly for banks, was the capacity to structure a number of these transactions as subordinated issues, thereby allowing these institutions to raise cost effective Tier II Capital to enhance their capital adequacy positions.

MARKET EVOLUTION AND PRODUCT VARIATIONS

The market developed extremely rapidly with some US$2-3 billion of collared FRNs being issued in August 1992 after the re-emergence of this market. Interestingly, public issues of these instruments were augmented by a substantial number of private placement transactions, often in the context of continuously offered medium-term note programmes.

As the market developed, a number of variations on the basic product concept also emerged. These variations focused on a number of elements of the transactions:

- variations on the interest formula utilised;
- transaction in currencies other than US$;
- securitisation of the option elements of the transaction; and
- development of a whole new class of transactions.

Initially, the collared FRN market operated around the basic formula described in *Table 1* above with minor variations for the differences in credit quality of the issuer as well as fluctuations in the price of the cap or floor element reflecting changes in the shape of the US$ yield curve. However, as the arbitrage margins in such transactions narrowed, a number of transactions sought to maximise available opportunities with changes in the interest rate formula utilised.

The first such variation was to adjust the maximum interest rate level. In order to extract more value from the shape of the forward US$ LIBOR yield curve, the maximum interest rate was "tiered", with the rate increasing over time. For example, in a transaction completed for Abbey National Treasury Services Plc in late August 1992, the maximum interest rate was set at 6% pa in years 1 and 2, 7% in years 3 and 4 and 8% in year 5. A similar structure was utilised in an issue for Bayerische Hypotheken und Wechsel Bank with the maximum interest rate rising from 7% to 9%, albeit with a lower minimum interest rate of 4%. A central feature of these transactions requiring the tiered maximum interest rate was the issuers' desire for shorter maturities. This necessitated adjustments to the maximum interest rate level to generate premiums from the sale of interest rate caps to subsidise the floor of purchases required.

The other major change in the interest rate formula of such instruments emerged later in September 1992 as changes in yield curve shape dictated a reduction in the maximum interest rate to levels around 8-8.25% pa to extract the required value from the forward rates in the yield curve.

The lower band level was repeated in March 1993 as the flatter shape of the US$ yield curve forced a lowering of the maximum interest rate or cap strike level to generate the necessary premiums to allow these transactions to proceed.

A secondary development as the market evolved was the proliferation of these structures into other currencies, with transactions being undertaken in C$, DEM and A$.

As the market evolved, an interesting product variation focused on securitising the option elements of the structure. Under this arrangement, the issue of FRNs was combined with a maximum interest rate but was sold in conjunction with the issue by the borrower of floor certificates which were detachable. The floor certificates were effectively the minimum interest rate element of the transaction and allowed the investor to freely trade in the floor certificates quite separate from the capped FRN itself.

Table 2 sets out an example of this particular variation detailing the terms of an issue for the World Bank completed in March 1993.

Exhibit 15.6—continued

TABLE 2

World Bank: Capped FRN

Amount:	DEM200m of FRNs.
Maturity:	Ten years (due 28 April 2003).
Coupon:	Six month LIBOR plus 0.25% payable semi-annually on 28 April and 28 October.
Maximum interest:	7.25% as from the beginning of the fifth interest period.
First interest determination date:	26 April.
Issue price:	100%.
Amortisation:	Bullet.
Call option:	None.
Listing:	Frankfurt SE.
Denominations:	DEM10,000 and DEM250,000 (global note).
Commissions:	0.20% (management and underwriting combined 0.10%, selling 0.10%).
Governing law:	German.
Negative pledge:	Yes.
Cross default:	Yes.
Force majeure:	IPMA clause 2.
Pari passu:	Yes.
Launch date;	11 March.
Payment:	28 April.
Security number:	403 270 German, 429 49 04 Common Code.
Lead manager:	Commerzbank (books).
Co-managers:	ABN Amro Bank, BBL, Bayerische Landesbank, Bayerische Vereinsbank, CSFB Effectenbank, Deutsche Bank, Kidder Peabody Intl, Merrill Lynch Bank AG, JP Morgan GmbH, Morgan Stanley GmbH, Paribas GmbH, Salomon Brothers AG, Sanwa Bank (Deutschland), Schweizerische Bankgesellschaft (Deutschland), Schweizerischer Bankverein (Deutschland), Trinkaus & Burkhardt, WestLB.
Pre-market price:	99.80, 99.90.

World Bank: Floor Certificates

Issuer:	World Bank.
Number:	20,000 certificates.
Exercise:	Each certificate entitles the holder to payment on 28 April and 28 October corresponding to the positive difference between 7% and six month LIBOR. Each certificate relates to DEM10,000.
Issue price:	DEM 695 per certificate.
Expiration:	28 April 2003.
Selling concession:	0.25%.
Listing:	Frankfurt SE.
Governing law:	German.
Launch date:	11 March.
Payment date:	28 April.
Security numbers:	886 030 German, 429 49 63 Common Code.

Exhibit 15.6—continued

Lead manager:	Commerzbank (books).
Pre-market price:	DEM720, 740.

Source: (1993) (March) *International Financing Review* Issue 970, 72.

The structure is, in addition, interesting for a number of other features including:

- The deferral of the maximum interest level which only operates from the beginning of the fifth interest rate period (effectively, 2.5 years into the term of the ten year transaction). This reflected the fact that DEM LIBOR was higher than the maximum rate at the time of issue.
- The maximum interest rate which is lower than the then prevailing DEM LIBOR rate, reflecting the inverse slope of the DEM yield curve and the different pattern of forward DEM LIBOR rates implied.
- The structure of the floor certificates which have a strike rate at a level of 7% (which is unusually close to the maximum interest rate level) and operate for the full life of the transaction, again reflecting the particular shape of the DEM yield curve.

A number of variations entailing hybrid products have also evolved. Principal among these are one way or ratchet FRNs as well as a variety of structures linked to the ten year Constant Maturity Treasury (CMT) rate (known as Step Up Recovery FRNs—SURFs). These product variations seek to take advantage of the prevailing interest rate environment in a manner similar to collared FRNs extracting value from the higher forward US$ LIBOR rates implicit in the steep yield curve which is translated into a higher current income level through the purchase of a floor by the investor.

The one way or ratchet FRN offers investors a yield around three or six month US$ LIBOR plus 35bps, with a floor equal to the previous coupon and a cap equal to the previous coupon plus 25bps. The floor locks in any increase in LIBOR while the cap allows LIBOR to rise moderately. Effectively, the structure creates a "ratcheting" return for the investor. For example at the time these transactions were undertaken around late November/early December 1992, the first interest payment was set at around 4.2875% pa. This effectively means that given that the interest rate on the issue can rise by 0.25% for 20 semi-annual interest periods, the issue had an increasing cap which peaks at 9.2875% pa for the last interest rate period. *Table 3* sets out the terms of a typical ratchet FRN issue for Credit Local de France.

TABLE 3

Credit Local de France

Amount:	US$100m.
Maturity:	Five years (due 23 December 1997).
Coupon:	Three month LIBOR plus 0.35%. The coupon cannot be increased by more than 0.25% per interest reset and cannot be decreased.
Issue price:	101.625.
Fixed re-offer price:	100.
Amortisation:	Bullet.
Call option:	None.
Put option:	None.
Listing:	Luxembourg.
Denominations:	US$10,000, US$100,000, US$1m.
Commissions:	1⅞% (management & underwriting 0.05%; selling 1.825%).
Stabilisation:	SIB.
Payment:	23 December.
Swap:	Into a variety of fixed rate European currencies.
Governing law:	English.
Negative pledge:	Yes.
Cross default:	Yes.

Exhibit 15.6—continued

144A eligible:	No.
Tefra D Reg S Cat 1:	Yes.
Sales restrictions:	US, UK, France.
Outstanding rating:	Aaa (Moody's), AAA (S&P).
Lead managers:	Morgan Stanley International (books).
Co-managers:	Daiwa Europe, Merrill Lynch.
Pre-market price:	99.95.

Source: (1992) (December) *International Financing Review* Issue 958, 58.

The value in the ratchet structure is driven by the interaction in the premium levels of the tiered cap relative to that of the tiered floor which operates in such transactions. This type of structure yields the most economic value for the issuer where the slope of the yield curve and the pattern of forward rates implied are at a level where the interest rate caps sold by the investor through the ratchet structure are substantially more in-the-money or closer to the strike price of the ratcheting caps while the corresponding floors are to a large degree out-of-the-money.

A number of one way or ratchet FRNs were completed both in the US domestic market as well as a number of transactions in the Euromarket.

The sustained fall during 1986 and again in the early 1990s, in US$ interest rates served to highlight the option nature of the minimum coupon traditionally included in FRN issues. The minimum rate is to be understood not as the minimum reference rate, but as the sum of that rate plus the spread. These minimum coupons, usually set at 5.25% pa, effectively call options written by the issuers, gained in value as LIBOR rates fell. In a number of cases, investors holding a portfolio of FRNs stripped off and sold the minimum coupon as a floor (analytically, a call option) to investors seeking to protect returns on floating rate LIBOR based assets or to financial intermediaries who used the purchased floors to effectively hedge risk positions created by writing customised floor agreements.

The concept of securitising the call option element or floor was taken to its logical conclusion with issues of FRNs with floor warrants. These floor warrants are sold by the issuer to lower its floating rate cost of funds. The holders of the warrants are entitled to periodically receive, over the life of the warrants, an amount in US$ which is calculated with reference to the amount by which actual LIBOR rates are below the nominated floor rate.

The concept was introduced in February 1986 by Banque Paribas in an issue for BATIF which was repeated in July 1986. An issue for Bank of Montreal, via Morgan Guaranty, was undertaken in June 1986.

More recently, the concept of securitised floors in conjunction with an issue of FRNs has been utilised in the GBP market with the issue of FRNs with detachable Additional Detachable Interest Rights (ADIRs). The first issue for Britannia Building Society, arranged by Samuel Montagu in June 1993, entailed a GBP100m FRN at three month GBP LIBOR plus 15 bps in combination with ADIRs which entitled holder to receive 5% pa less three month GBP LIBOR where GBP LIBOR is less than 5% pa. The ADIRs were effectively floors on GBP LIBOR with a strike price equivalent to 5% pa and, in structure, securitised the minimum coupon on the FRN. The ADIR structure was utilised to create additional value for the issuer to allow a higher price for the minimum coupon element to be realised. In addition, the use of ADIRs avoided potential ultra vires problems regarding the capacity of the UK Building Society issuer to separately sell a 5% floor.

The put and call options created by the capped, mini-max, etc issues were, in fact, bought, substantially, by institutions active in the creation and sale of customised debt option facilities, usually in the form of floor, cap or collar agreements. The securitised options were purchased to match out the portfolio risk exposures of the market makers, allowing them to unwind (or reverse out of) other less efficient hedges.

These types of structures continue to be utilised from time to time. For example, in late 1991 and 1992, the sharp fall in interest rates in US$ as well as the steepness of the US$ yield curve encouraged investors seeking yield improvements on their short-term money market portfolios to purchase capped and collared FRNs in US$ (see discussion above).

A variety of other structures have also emerged which entail derivative return characteristics, particularly in the low nominal interest rate and steep yield curve environment of the early 1990s. An interesting example of these innovations is the Step Up Recovery FRNs (SURFs). This structure entails a floating rate bond where the interest return is linked to the return on the theoretical Constant Maturity ten year treasury bond rate. A detailed analysis of the SURF structure together with the accompanying swap arrangements, which incorporate a Yield Curve Swap (see Chapter 13), is set out in *Exhibit 15.7*.

Exhibit 15.7
SURFs (Step Up Recovery FRNs)

In early 1993, a series of structured FRNs—introduced as SURFs—were issued in the Eurobond market. The first issues were undertaken for the World Bank and Eurofima by Lehman Brothers. The issues of SURFs in the Eurobond market followed approximately US$1 billion of issues in the US domestic market.

SURF STRUCTURE

The basic structure is a floating rate bond where the interest rate is calculated in accordance with a formula linked to the theoretical ten year US treasury bond rate.

The terms of the World Bank transaction are summarised in *Table 1*.

TABLE 1

ISSUER

World Bank

Amount:	US$100m
Maturity:	Five years (due 17 March 1998).
Coupon:	(Constant Maturity Treasury × 0.5) plus 1.45%. CMT is a theoretical ten year treasury yield.
Minimum coupon:	4.6%.
Maximum coupon:	25%.
Issue and fixed re-offer price:	100.
Amortisation:	Bullet.
Call option:	None.
Put option:	None.
Listing:	Luxembourg.
Denominations:	US$1,000, US$10,000, US$100,000.
Commission:	0.4% (management and underwriting 0.15%; selling 0.25%).

Exhibit 15.7—continued

Payment:	17 March.
Swap:	Into floating rate deutschmarks.
Lead managers:	Lehman Brothers Intl (books).
Co-lead managers:	CSFB, Kidder Peabody Intl, Merrill Lynch Intl, Salomon Brothers Intl, SBC.
Pre-market price:	100, 100.15.

Source: (1993) (February) *International Financing Review* Issue 967, 59.

Yields on treasury securities at "constant maturity" are interpolated by the US treasury from the daily yield curve. This curve, which relates the yield on a security to its time from maturity, based on the closing market bid yields on actively traded treasury securities in the over-the-counter market. These market yields are calculated from composites of quotations reported by five leading US Government Securities dealers to the Federal Reserve Bank of New York. The constant maturity yield values are read from the yield curve at fixed maturities: currently one, two, three, five, seven, ten and 30 years. According to the Federal Reserve, this method would provide a yield for a ten year maturity, for example, even if no outstanding security has exactly ten years remaining to maturity.

The return to investors in a SURF is dependent on the CMT yield. For a LIBOR based investor, the return on the SURF is attractive.

For example, on the World Bank transaction, the CMT on the day of launch was just below 6.30%, meaning that the bonds would pay their minimum interest rate of 4.6%. This compared to three month dollar LIBOR of around 3.25%.

The return to the investor over the life of the transaction will continue to be attractive where the shape of the US$ yield curve remains positive. Based on a price formula of [(CMT × 0.5) + 1.45% pa], the investor's return on a SURF continues to be superior to LIBOR and the CMT rate is not less than approximately 35bps at the interest rate levels prevailing at the time of the issue (ignoring the minimum coupon level). The degree of yield curve steepness needed for the SURF to outperform a LIBOR-based FRN increases as the LIBOR level increases (see *Table 2*).

TABLE 2

Surf Bond Returns—Yield Curve Risks (Ignoring Minimum Rate)

LIBOR	CMT Margin	Breakeven Ten year CMT	SURF Yield	Breakeven LIBOR—CMT Spread (bps)
2.000%	1.450%	1.100%	2.000%	−90.0
2.500%	1.450%	2.100%	2.500%	−40.0
3.000%	1.450%	3.100%	3.000%	10.0
3.250%	1.450%	3.600%	3.250%	35.0
3.500%	1.450%	4.100%	3.500%	60.0
4.000%	1.450%	5.100%	4.000%	110.0
4.500%	1.450%	6.100%	4.500%	160.0
5.000%	1.450%	7.100%	5.000%	210.0
5.500%	1.450%	8.100%	5.500%	260.0
6.000%	1.450%	9.100%	6.000%	310.0
6.500%	1.450%	10.100%	6.500%	360.0
7.000%	1.450%	11.100%	7.000%	410.0
7.500%	1.450%	12.100%	7.500%	460.0
8.000%	1.450%	13.100%	8.000%	510.0
8.500%	1.450%	14.100%	8.500%	560.0
9.000%	1.450%	15.100%	9.000%	610.0
9.500%	1.450%	16.100%	9.500%	660.0
10.000%	1.450%	17.100%	10.000%	710.0
10.500%	1.450%	18.100%	10.500%	760.0
11.000%	1.450%	19.100%	11.000%	810.0

Exhibit 15.7—continued

LIBOR	CMT Margin	Breakeven Ten year CMT	SURF Yield	Breakeven LIBOR—CMT Spread (bps)
11.500%	1.450%	20.100%	11.500%	860.0
12.000%	1.450%	21.100%	12.000%	910.0
12.500%	1.450%	22.100%	12.500%	960.0
13.000%	1.450%	23.100%	13.000%	1010.0

SURF Bond Returns

Ten Year CMT Yields	SURF Yield (Unadjusted for Minimum Rate)	SURF Yield (Adjusted for Minimum Rate)
4.000%	3.450%	4.600%
4.500%	3.700%	4.600%
5.000%	3.950%	4.600%
5.500%	4.200%	4.600%
6.000%	4.450%	4.600%
6.500%	4.700%	4.700%
7.000%	4.950%	4.950%
7.500%	5.200%	5.200%
8.000%	5.450%	5.450%
8.500%	5.700%	5.700%
9.000%	5.950%	5.950%
9.500%	6.200%	6.200%
10.000%	6.450%	6.450%
10.500%	6.700%	6.700%
11.000%	6.950%	6.950%
11.500%	7.200%	7.200%
12.000%	7.450%	7.450%
12.500%	7.700%	7.700%
13.000%	7.950%	7.950%
13.500%	8.200%	8.200%
14.000%	8.450%	8.450%
14.500%	8.700%	8.700%
15.000%	8.950%	8.950%
15.500%	9.200%	9.200%
16.000%	9.450%	9.450%
16.500%	9.700%	9.700%
17.000%	9.950%	9.950%

The minimum or floor rate means that where the CMT rate is less than 6.30%, then the investor receives the minimum rate. This means that for CMT levels lower than or equal to 6.30%, LIBOR has to be below 4.60% (a yield spread of 170bps) for the SURF to outperform a LIBOR based FRN.

In essence, the SURF will outperform LIBOR-based FRNs where the yield curve remains positive and relatively steep. The major risk to the investor is a flattening or inversion of the US$ yield curve.

SWAP STRUCTURE

The issuer of the SURF will, typically, seek to insulate itself from the full impact of the coupon structure. The issuer will seek to swap the issue into US$ LIBOR-based funding.

The swap structure entails two separate transactions:

- A five year yield curve swap on 50% of the total amount of the SURF issue where the issuer receives CMT minus a margin and pay US$ LIBOR.
- A conventional five year US$ interest rate swap where the issuer receives fixed rates and pay US$ LIBOR.

Algebraically, the position is as follows:

Net Borrowing Cost = SURF Coupon − Yield Curve Swap Payment − Swap Payments.

Exhibit 15.7—continued

This translates into:

– [CMT * 0.5 + M(S)] + 0.5 [CMT – M(YCS) – LIBOR]
+ 0.5 [SR – LIBOR]

Where:

M(S) = SURF Margin

M(YCS) = Yield Curve Swap Margin

SR = Swap Rate

The equation simplifies to:

– LIBOR – M(S) + 0.5 (SR – M(YCS))

Assuming a transaction of US$100m where:

M(S) = + 145bps

M(YCS) = – 155bps

SR = 650bps (or 6.50% pa)

The net borrowing cost is:

LIBOR – [145 + 0.5 (650 – 155)]

= LIBOR – 102.5bps

This is equivalent to a borrowing cost of LIBOR – 102.5bps.

This cost does not include the cost of the floor at 4.6% pa designed to insulate the issuer from the risk of the minimum rate in the SURF. This floor is on the ten year CMT rate rather than on six month LIBOR, reflecting the interest formula of the SURF structure. Given the steeply positive shape of the US$ yield curve, the bulk of the value in the floor is in the initial periods. The higher forward rates implicit in the yield curve dictate that the floors as structured are inititally in-the-money; however, the longer dated floors are substantially out-of-the-money and are consequently relatively inexpensive.

In the above case the issuer has available, assuming a sub-LIBOR target of 50bps pa, 52.5bps pa (or 2.19% pa flat in present value) to cover the floor premium.

The 25% cap is more intriguing. CMT rates would have to rise above 47.1% pa for the SURF coupon to reach the cap level. The 25% pa cap, which the issuer can sell, is also not of any significant value and therefore does not assist in reducing the cost of the floor premium. One theory is that the Euromarket transactions are priced in accordance with US domestic transactions where such a cap was necessitated to avoid the cost of the SURF rising above legal upper limits on borrowing cost (for example, Fannie Mae has an official 24% cap on its borrowing cost).

The swap arrangements underlying the SURF issue highlight the price dynamics. The SURF pricing depends on the interaction of the following variables:

- the price for yield curve swaps;
- the price for interest rate swaps;
- the cost of the CMT floors.

The variables reflect the prevailing yield curve shapes in the relevant markets.

Variations on the above structure have been undertaken. Seven year transactions with a higher minimum rate (5.00% pa) emerged reflecting market opportunities as the US$ yield curve shifted.

Debt options and warrants

A substantial market in fixed rate bonds with attached warrants has emerged. The holders of the warrants acquire the right to purchase *further* fixed rate bonds of the issuer on predetermined terms. Issues of naked warrants, not linked to an issue of debt securities but usually accompanied by a contingent swap, have also been undertaken: see above, Chapter 14.

The warrants are effectively call options on the debt of the issuer created in exchange for the receipt of an explicit or implicit premium (that is, the premium may be built into a lower than market cost on a related issue of debt). From the borrower's viewpoint, the sale of warrants produces cash which reduces the cost of the borrower's total funding programme. This advantage can be translated into floating rate funding or funding in other currencies through a series of swaps, specially structured to accommodate the warrant issues.

In most transactions involving the issuance of debt options and warrants, the underlying funding has been swapped. The specific swap structure used can vary significantly depending on the overall structure of the debt warrant package. There are basically three general categories of swaps.

The first category is usually associated with naked warrant issues where a contingent swap is arranged: see above, Chapter 14.

The second and third categories of warrant swaps relate specifically to issues of warrants in conjunction with debt utilising one of two alternative arrangements:

- where the total package has an uncertain level of proceeds over its life and/or an uncertain maturity;
- debt warrant packages where the amount of debt remains relatively constant and the cost to the issuer does *not* change when and if the warrants are exercised.

The latter two categories of debt warrant swaps require elaboration.

For example, during 1984, expectations of falling rates saw a number of issues entailing the offering of fixed rate bonds with attached warrants which allowed the holder of the warrant the right to further purchase fixed rate bonds of the issuer at a predetermined coupon. The warrants which had lives of anywhere between one and seven years allowed the cost of the initial fixed rate debt to be reduced by the proceeds of the warrants. This resulted in a saving in yield of between 50 and 100bps relative to a conventional issue. The issuer was simultaneously exposed to issuing further debt at a coupon cost equal to that of the fixed rate bonds into which the warrants can be exercised which is generally 25 to 50bps lower than the host coupon bond. Given that there are no issuance costs or fees on issuance of the warrant bonds, the cost of the warrant bond can be 70 to 100bps below the issuer's current fixed rate cost.

The overall yield savings (anywhere up to 100bps compared to a conventional fixed rate offering) was achieved at the expense of not being able to determine in advance how many of the warrants which create additional debt will be exercised, or indeed when they will be exercised. The issuer therefore had a known cost of debt, but an uncertain amount of debt over the life of the transaction. For fixed rate issuers with absolute interest rate targets, the uncertainty regarding the amount of debt was not problematic. However, certain issuers were only attracted to a warrant issue on the basis of the underlying issue being swapped into floating rate US$.

If the borrower could insulate against the cost of the prospective issuance of additional fixed rate debt as a result of the warrants being exercised, by being able to swap it into floating rate, then both parties could be accommodated simultaneously. The borrower no longer has an exposure to fixed interest rates, only to the uncertain amount of debt which might be outstanding at any time.

The perfectly matched interest rate swap allowed the issuer to swap the host issue immediately into floating rate US$ and provided for the swap facility to be increased at any time to accommodate further amounts of fixed debt created by the exercise of warrants. In the first few transactions of this type, the warrant issuer was matched against a United States company with a sizeable requirement to swap from floating to fixed rate funds which had set itself interest rate hurdles at which it was willing to fix its cost of funds. It was then willing to effectively create a series of options on interest rate swaps whereby it was committed, where a bond holder exercised a warrant, to enter into a swap with the bond issuer on predefined terms, regardless of interest rate levels prevailing in the market at the time the warrant was exercised. This structure allowed the issuer to substantially shift the exposure of warrant exercise to the swap counterparty.

The cost of creating a swap which can be increased in size at a fixed known interest rate level could, however, outweigh most or even all of the advantages gained by issuing warrants. Consequently, the structure of warrant swaps increasingly began to trade off the quantum of the spread below LIBOR and warrant exercise risk. Typical warrant swap structures designed to provide cost savings and limit risk would feature a seven year host bond issue callable at par at any time after four years with attached warrants into a four year bond with a life of three years. This structure was predicated on the assumption that warrants are not usually exercised until near to their expiry date and at their expiry date the host issue can be called. This capacity to call the host bond, allows the issuer to have a degree of control over the amount of debt outstanding, enabling it to keep the total volume of paper on issue constant. The issue is combined with a standard seven year swap to convert the fixed rate into floating with the value of the warrants being used to subsidise the cost of the swap.

While originally the warrant swap structures proved popular, such transactions required the willingness of a prime counterparty to commit to a swap with a call option and as these counterparties found alternative outlets, the underlying warrant structures had to be considerably refined. The structure developed was the harmless debt warrant.

Pioneered by the Kingdom of Denmark, debt and warrant issue packages were created to ensure that the amount of the debt outstanding remained relatively constant and the cost of the issue did not change significantly if the warrants were exercised. The host bond was made callable at any time should warrants be exercised to ensure that the amount of debt outstanding remains constant enabling a standard interest rate swap to be executed. This alternative entails a higher cost of the host issue in terms of both coupon (approximately 0.125% pa) and call premium (approximately 1.00%). However, depending on the value of the attached warrants, the floating rate cost obtainable with this structure can be considerably better than a standard fixed rate issue without warrants. Under this structure, a conventional interest rate or (if applicable) currency swap could be utilised as the security issue's cash flows resemble a straight bond issue. This type of issue structure has increasingly gained in popularity.

This structure essentially gave borrowers access to cheap funds designed in most cases to be swapped into floating rate at extremely competitive levels with extremely limited exposure to the implicit call option. This is illustrated in *Exhibit 15.8* with the example of an issue for Westpac Banking Corporation.

A variation on the traditional warrant issue is the case of the putable bond or, its securitised extension, an issue of "put" warrants. Based on similar rationale to debt warrants, the proceeds of the implicit or securitised put option is designed to lower the borrower's cost of funds. As these issue structures provide the investor with the mechanism whereby, at its option, it can sell the bond back to the issuer at an agreed price, the structure creates a maturity uncertainty which is impossible to immunise. Where such issues have been swapped, the issuer would, where the basic debt is swapped, seek to protect its own exposure under the swap with an agreement with the swap counterparty to terminate the swap where the underlying debt was put back to the borrower: see examples in Chapter 14.

Exhibit 15.8

Westpac "Harmless" Debt Warrant Issue and Swap

The Westpac issue was on the following terms:

- US$100m ten year (maturing 1996) 10.00% pa coupon issued at 100⅞ with 2.00% fees; issue callable after five years at 101½, declining by 0.50% pa to par.
- 200,000 warrants @ US$50 each; two warrants are exercisable after five years into one 11.25% non-callable bond due 1996 at par (that is, US$100 per bond); during the first five years, the warrants pay 10.00% interest, and, if not exercised, they are each redeemable @ US$50 in 1996.

The table below shows the cash flow (US$m) to Westpac if the warrants are, or are not, exercised. It is assumed that the host bonds will be called if the warrants are exercised in years six to ten; the warrants will automatically be redeemed at maturity if they are not exercised.

		Year warrants are exercised (assume warrants exercised at year end)					
Year	**Not exercised**	**5**	**6**	**7**	**8**	**9**	**10**
0	108.875	108.875	108.875	108.875	108.875	108.875	108.875
1	−11.000	−11.000	−11.000	−11.000	−11.000	−11.000	−11.000
2	−11.000	−11.000	−11.000	−11.000	−11.000	−11.000	−11.000
3	−11.000	−11.000	−11.000	−11.000	−11.000	−11.000	−11.000
4	−11.000	−11.000	−11.000	−11.000	−11.000	−11.000	−11.000
5	−11.000	−12.500	−11.000	−11.000	−11.000	−11.000	−11.000
6	−10.000	−11.250	−11.000	−10.000	−10.000	−10.000	−10.000
7	−10.000	−11.250	−11.250	−10.500	−10.000	−10.000	−10.000
8	−10.000	−11.250	−11.250	−11.250	−10.000	−10.000	−10.000
9	−10.000	−11.250	−11.250	−11.250	−11.250	−10.000	−10.000
10	−120.000	−111.250	−111.250	−111.250	−111.250	−111.250	−111.250
All-in cost in Westpac as margin relative bps pa to United States Treasuries:							
	43	43	27	13	0	−8	−8

Note: Assumes host bonds are called from the end of year five. In the no-exercise case, warrants are redeemed at $50.

From the table, it is apparent that *the issue is structured such that the issuer is guaranteed a maximum rate, which can only decrease if the warrants are exercised.* Through this structure Westpac paid a *maximum* of 9.82% pa (9.59% S/A, or T+43), a saving of approximately 20-25bps.

The issue was swapped into, at least initially, floating rate US$ LIBOR using a conventional US$ interest swap which *may* have been structured to accommodate the unusual cash flow pattern.

Interest rate linked securities

The concept of embodying interest rates derivatives in capital market transactions has been extended in recent times to transactions where the implicit interest rate forward or option is engineered through a variable redemption amount (originally introduced in the form of Treasury Indexed Notes).

This type of transaction is best illustrated by an example. The basic transaction entails the issue of debt securities bearing a higher than market coupon. However, the redemption amount, that is, the amount repaid to the investor at maturity, is linked to price fluctuations (and by implication yield movements) on an identified debt instrument, usually the 30 year United States treasury bond. In a typical transaction, the coupon was 10.00% pa (approximately 200 to 250bps above the market yield) for three years with the redemption formula being as follows: if the benchmark 30 year United States Treasury bond at the end of three years (the maturity of the debt instrument) is at a break-even yield (say 7.10% pa) the bonds are redeemed at par (100), but if the yield is above (below) the break-even yield, the amount received by the investor will be less (greater) than par. In any case, the redemption amount cannot be less than zero.

Implicit in the variable redemption formula inherent in this particular structure are (European) options on the 30 year United States Treasury bond with a maturity of three years. The structure of the transaction entails the investor granting a put option on the 30 year bond with a strike yield of 7.10% pa and simultaneously purchasing a call option with an identical strike yield (effectively, a forward purchase of the 30 year treasury bond in three years).

The forward position is securitised through the swap to effectively insulate the issuer from the risk of variations in the redemption amount. The swap usually generates funding at an attractive margin relative to a floating rate index such as LIBOR.

The economic logic underlying the transaction would appear to be as follows: the investor (in the example) would usually be writing a put which was substantially in-the-money (by about 40bps) and buying an out-of-the-money call (for example, by the same margin). The swap provider would sell the put on the 30 year bond at a higher premium than the outlay needed to purchase the call with the difference being used to subsidise the higher than usual payments on the swap (remembering that the issue coupon would be substantially above the market). The swap thus behaves like a high coupon premium swap transaction.

The swap structure could be simulated, as an alternative to trading options, as an equivalent forward position by holding an appropriate amount of 30 year bonds purchased at market price (the yield would be approximately 7.50% pa) for the three years and liquidating them at market rates at the end of that period. The variable redemption structure would lock in the 40bps profit on the bonds which could be used to subsidise the swap.

The fact that the swap structure can be simulated through a long forward position with the underlying securities, merely reflects the fact that a transaction which involves the simultaneous purchase of a put option and the granting of a call option is equivalent to a short forward position in the relevant security.

Where the issuer does not wish to alter the currency or interest rate basis of the borrowing, the transaction need *not* technically be a swap, but merely a series of option trades or forward transaction. This is basically a consequence of the fact that buying put options and selling call options at the same strike price is economically identical to paying fixed rates under a swap.

The concept was introduced in two issues launched in April 1987 by Nomura International for GMAC and Mitsui and Co (USA). The GMAC issue was subsequently withdrawn due to problems with tax regulations. The basic concept has been extended to other structures, including dividing the issue into two tranches with one tranche providing the upside potential and the other the downside potential to better attune the structure to individual investor's interest rate expectations.

The detailed underlying transaction logic for such transactions is illustrated utilising a transaction for Quatrain, a vehicle guaranteed by the South Australian Financing Authority, set out in *Exhibit 15.9*.

Exhibit 15.9
Treasury Indexed Security and Option Swap Structure

Quatrain Co, through Nomura International, made a three year, 10.00% US$100m issue of treasury indexed bonds on 15 May 1986. Redemption value is linked to the 9.25% of 2016 series of United States treasury bonds via the following formula:

$$R = US\$100{,}000{,}000 \times \left(\frac{MIP - 26.491782}{100}\right)$$

where

R = redemption value in US$

MIP = market index price of the 9.25% of 2016 United States treasury bond at maturity of the issue

This exposure to 30 year treasuries is passed on by Quatrain to Nomura via the option swap.

Nomura can hedge its exposure, equivalent to taking on a short forward treasury position, through either the purchase of a 30 year treasury bond which is then funded and held for three years or by entering into a simultaneous forward commitment to buy US$100m 9.25% 2016 bonds in three years' time. Assume Nomura purchases the underlying treasury and funds it for three years at a rate not higher than the yield on the 30 year bond. Nomura can buy the 30 year treasuries at the current market yield of 7.65% pa and lock in a corresponding three year funding cost, probably through a repurchase agreement, at or less than 7.65% pa.

The profit dynamics are as follows:

- Assume 30 year United States treasury bond yield is 7.65% pa; and three year United States treasury bond yield is 7.50% pa.
- Nomura's net profit position from the purchase which is offset by the short forward position (bond price of US$118 equivalent to a yield of 7.65% pa) is:

$$\text{Profits} = US\$100{,}000{,}000 \times \left(\frac{I - 118}{100}\right) + \$100{,}000{,}000 \times \left(\frac{126.491782 - I}{100}\right)$$

$$= US\$100{,}000{,}000 \times \left(\frac{8.491782}{100}\right)$$

$$= US\$8{,}491{,}782 \text{ at maturity}$$

where I = MIP at maturity.

- Nomura's US$8,491,782 profit is equivalent to a US$2,628,526 annuity for three years at an interest rate of 7.50% pa. This annuity of US$2,628,526 can be used to reduce the treasury indexed bond's interest cost from US$10m (that is, 10.00% of $100m) to US$10,000,000—US$2,628,526 = US$7,371,474, so that effective interest cost is US$7,371,474/US$100,000,000 or 7.37% pa, which is *below* the equivalent three year treasury rate.
- In reality, the annuity stream will only be used to reduce the effective cost to a level at which the issuer's sub-LIBOR target is satisfied with the surplus representing Nomura's profit from the transaction.
- The accompanying US$ interest rate swap will entail Quatrain receiving the fixed rate equivalent of US$10m or 10.00% pa and paying LIBOR minus the agreed margin. Notice the off-market rates necessitated a premium swap structure.

The concept of embodying interest rate derivatives in capital markets which were then securitised through the swap structure was particularly popular, at least, for a time in relation to Japanese interest rates.

These types of transactions, basically, took the following forms:

- Bull-bear structures, involving the creation of offsetting tranches designed to appeal to bullish and bearish investors which produced a known maximum cost of funds to the issuer.
- High coupon JPY issue where the redemption formula was calculated with reference to future Japan Government Bond (JGB) futures prices to engineer an implicit forward interest rate position into the security.

Exhibit 15.10 sets out an example of a JPY bull-bear JGB linked bond and swap structure. *Exhibit 15.11* sets out an example of a JPY JGB linked bond issue and swap.

These structures were specifically designed for particular institutional investors seeking to create synthetic interest rate derivative positions to manage asset positions within their investment portfolios.

Exhibit 15.10
JPY Bull-Bear JGB Linked Bonds and Swap Structure

In February 1988, Societe Generale issued JPY10bn of five year bonds underwritten by Nikko Securities with the redemption value linked to the Tokyo Stock Exchange (TSE) Japanese Government Bond (JGB) December 1992 futures price. The bonds carried a coupon of 7% pa, compared to five year JGB yield of approximately 4.40/4.50% pa.

The issue consisted of two tranches: a JPY5bn bear tranche and a JPY5bn bull tranche.

The redemption value of the bonds were indexed to the December 1992 JGB futures price as follows:

Bear Tranche:
R = 195.45% of principal minus TSE JGB December 1992 futures price.

Bull Tranche
R = TSE JGB December 1992 futures price minus 20.55%

where R = redemption amount

TSE JGB = Tokyo Stock Exchange Japanese Government Bond

Minimum price = zero. Maximum price = 17.90%.

The offsetting nature of the two tranches and the counter balancing changes in the value of the tranches ensures that Societe Generale are immunised from the risk of the JGB linked redemption feature of the bond.

For example the TSE JGB December 1992 price = 125%.

Bear Tranche:

R = (195.45% − 125%) of JPY5bn

= 70.45% of JPY5bn

= JPY3,522,500,000

Bull Tranche:

R = (125% − 20.55%) of JPY5bn

= 104.45% of JPY5bn

= JPY5,222,500,000

Total redemption payout = JPY3,522,500,000 + JPY5,222,500,000 equals JPY8,745,000,000

TSE JGB December 1992 price = 75%

Bear Tranche:

R = (195.45% − 75%) of JPY5bn

= 120.45% of JPY5bn

= JPY6,022,500,000

Exhibit 15.10—continued

Bull Tranche:

R = (75% − 20.55%) of JPY5bn

= 54.45% of JPY5bn

= JPY2,722,500,000

Total redemption payout = JPY6,022,500,000 + JPY2,722,500,000 equals JPY8,745,000,000.

The structure results in the issuer repaying less than par on the bonds.

If Societe Generale borrows JPY10bn and is only required to repay JPY8,745,000,000 it has an effective book profit of JPY1,255,000,000.

At the risk-free five year JGB rate of 4.4%, this profit of JPY1,255,000 equates to an annual annuity of JPY229,862,335 each year for five years.

Incorporating the annuity of JPY229,862,335 benefit, the net funding cost of the issue equals JPY470,137,665 or 4.0% pa. This rate is 30bps above the comparable JPY risk-free rate but is well below the coupons offered on conventional Euro-Yen issues raised at this time which were 4⅞-5.00% allowing Societe Generale to swap into attractive floating US$ funding at a substantial margin below LIBOR.

Source: Michael M Cunningham (1988).

Exhibit 15.11
Yen JGB Linked Bond Issue and Swap

In January 1988, Societe Generale undertook an issue, through Mitsui Finance International of JPY7bn five year bonds. The issue's redemption value was linked to the value of TSE December 1990 JGB futures price. The issue carried a 7% pa coupon which was significantly above the equivalent five year JGB rate which was 4.40/4.50% or equivalent Euro-Yen yields which were in the range of 4.875/5.00% pa for comparable issues.

The redemption value of the bond was calculated in accordance with the following formula:

R = 193.60% minus opening TSE JGB December 1990 futures price.

The redemption payment is calculated on the JGB futures index two years hence but not payable for a further three years. This allows both the issuer and investor to know in advance the payout profile of the debt and so take appropriate funding decisions.

The issue was targeted specifically at Japanese institutional investors as the issue is designed as a hedge for holders of Japanese bonds should rates increase markedly. This is reflected in the structure whereby as the JGB futures price falls (ie the interest rates increase) the redemption payout increases, presumably compensating the investor for losses on its physical JGB portfolio.

This redemption structure effectively embeds a forward position in the December 1990 JGB futures contract. The issuer (investor) benefits from a general decrease (increase) in Japanese interest rate structures and a commensurate rise in the index price two years hence. While the investor would have had to accept the symmetric nature of the exposure, Societe Generale would have sought to insulate itself from the risk of the implicit JGB futures position through the structure of its swap with Mitsui.

Mitsui can hedge and securitise the inherent forward position in two ways:

- It could arrange for a counterparty eg a Japanese institutional investor, to take a long forward JGB futures December 1990 position two years hence. By arranging this hedge, Mitsui could expect to receive JPY420m (6% of JPY7bn) as payment for its services. Therefore a fall in the JGB December 1990 futures price in two years time will work against Societe Generale on the redemption repayment, however this impact will be offset by the short position it has been allocated by Mitsui (who matched out the position by establishing a corresponding long position for a counterparty).

Exhibit 15.11—continued

- Mitsui could also strip and securitise the embedded option position. Mitsui could sell at-the-money two year call on the JGB December 1990 futures contract. Mitsui could expect to receive JPY455m (6.5% of JPY7bn) for this position, considering the lack of "long-term" option hedging tools for Japanese institutions.

The funds received JPY875m (JPY420m for the forward position, plus JPY455m for the option) equals JPY1,085,201,902 after five years using the risk free rate of 4.4%, which equates to a yearly annuity of JPY198,762,584.

This annuity when offset against Societe Generale's annual interest cost of JPY490m results in an annual effective coupon cost of JPY291,237,416 equivalent to a nominal borrowing cost of 4.16%, 24bps below the risk free rate. Based on JPY swap rates of approximately 4.60/4.80% pa, Societe Generale would have been able to obtain funding at a substantial margin under LIBOR through a JPY/US$ currency swap.

Source: Michael M Cunningham (1988).

FOREIGN CURRENCY DERIVATIVE EMBEDDED SECURITIES AND RELATED SWAPS

Foreign currency linked swaps securitising the derivative component of securities featuring embedded foreign currency, forwards or options have also been undertaken.

Dual currency bond swap structures

A dual currency bond involves an issue where the interest coupon is denominated in a different currency to the underlying principal of the bond. For example, a dual currency US$/Swiss franc bond would have interest payable in Swiss francs and the principal in US$.

Alternative structures include dual currency bonds with interest payable in US$ and principal in Japanese yen (often referred to as a reverse dual currency bond as it contrasts with the usual structure whereby the coupon is payable in a low interest rate currency) which are designed to appeal to Japanese investors' eagerness to enjoy high current yield while minimising exposure to possible long-term devaluation of the US$ against the yen.

Other dual currency bond structures have been undertaken in: C$ and Swiss francs; A$ and yen; NZ$ and yen; Dutch guilders and US$.

The structure of a swap against a dual currency issue entails a number of separate steps usually involving separate currency or interest rate swaps and a series of LTFX contracts. For example, for a dual currency issue with coupons denominated in Swiss francs and principal in US$, the swap would entail the following separate transactions: a series of LTFX contracts to hedge the Swiss francs into US$ to create a synthetic US$ liability which could then be swapped into floating rate US$ through an interest rate swap or into an alternative desired currency or interest rate basis through a currency swap. Alternatively, the US$ principal could be hedged back into Swiss francs to create a synthetic Swiss franc liability which could then be swapped into US$ through a Swiss franc and US$ swap.

In the case of a reverse dual currency bond issue, the swap structure would include a conventional US$ interest rate swap to convert the borrower's interest commitment to floating rate US$ and a long-dated foreign exchange forward contract purchasing Japanese yen against US$ to lock in the fully hedged floating rate US$ cost to the issuer.

Exhibit 15.12 sets out an example of a yen and A$ dual currency bond issue undertaken in 1987 with the proceeds being swapped first, into US$ and, finally, into fixed rate A$.

Exhibit 15.12
JPY/A$ Dual Currency Bond and Swap Structure

In early 1987, an Australian borrower undertook a JPY/A$ dual currency bond issue on the following terms:

Amount:	JPY10 billion
Term:	five years
Issue price:	102.50%
Interest rate:	8.00% pa payable in yen and calculated on the yen denominated principal.
Redemption amount:	A$119.2m (implied redemption exchange rate of A$1/JPY83.92)
Fees:	2.00% flat

The borrower did *not* want a yen exposure but wished to create a synthetic A$ liability utilising the dual currency bond issue as the basis for an arbitrage funding transaction.

The issue was swapped in three stages:

1. The following series of LTFX contracts to create a synthetic fixed rate US$ liability:
   - sell spot JPY10.05 billion and buy US$70m;
   - buy forward at yearly intervals JPY800m and sell US$5m;
   - buy 5 year forward A$119.2m and sell US$68m.

2. A US$ interest rate swap to convert the fixed rate US$ liability into floating rate US$ as follows:
   - receive US$5m annually for five years;
   - pay LIBOR minus a margin (M) semi-annually for five years plus US$2m at maturity.

3. An A$ fixed to US$ floating currency swap to convert the floating US$ liability into fixed rate A$ as follows:
   - at commencement pay US$70m and receive A$100m;
   - over the life of the transaction receive US$ LIBOR—M semi-annually for five years and pay A$ fixed rates at the Australian bond rate (B) plus a margin (M*);
   - at maturity, receive US$70m and pay A$100m.

The overall effect of the forward contracts and swaps is to convert fixed yen payments to, first, fixed US$ payments, then to floating rate US$ payments and finally to end up with fixed A$ payments at an effective Commonwealth bond rate + M*. This rate represented a significant cost saving to the borrower.

The cash flows for the total transaction are set out in the table below:

Exhibit 15.12—continued

CASH FLOWS

Period (years)	Bonds	LTFX contracts JPYm	LTFX contracts US$m	Swap 1 Receive US$m	Swap 1 Pay US$m	Swap 2 Pay A$m	Swap 2 Receive US$m
0.0	+JPY10,055m	−10,055m	+70	—	—	−US$70.0m	+A$100m
0.5					−LIBOR—M	B+M*	+LIBOR—M
1.0	−JPY800m	+800	−5.0	+5.0	−LIBOR—M	B+M*	+LIBOR—M
1.5					−LIBOR—M	B+M*	+LIBOR—M
2.0	−JPY800m	+800	−5.0	+5.0	−LIBOR—M	B+M*	+LIBOR—M
2.5					−LIBOR—M	B+M*	+LIBOR—M
3.0	−JPY800m	+800	−5.0	+5.0	−LIBOR—M	B+M*	+LIBOR—M
3.5					−LIBOR—M	B+M*	+LIBOR—M
4.0	−JPY800m	+800	−5.0	+5.0	−LIBOR—M	B+M*	+LIBOR—M
4.5					−LIBOR—M	B+M*	+LIBOR—M
5.0	−JPY800m	+800	−5.0	+5.0	−LIBOR—M	B+M*	+LIBOR—M
	−A$119.2m	+A$119.2	−68.0		+US$2.0m	−A$100m	+US$70.0m

Exhibit 15.13 sets out an additional example of a JPY/A$ dual currency swap outlining detailed pricing and hedging issues related to such transactions.

The dual currency bond swap layers a complex initial transaction with a series of foreign exchange and swap transactions basically designed to generate, at least initially, cost-effective floating rate US$ funding.

Exhibit 15.13

Pricing/Hedging a JPY/A$ Dual Currency Swap

Assume Bank B is asked to price a JPY/A$ Dual Currency Swap in connection with the following issue:

Term: 10 years.

Principal Amount: JPY20,000m.

Coupon: 8.00% pa payable annually.
The coupon is payable in A$ calculated on the A$ equivalent of the JPY principal amount at the A$/JPY rate at the time of issue (assumed to be A$1 = JPY118).

Redemption Amount: JPY20,000m (payable in JPY).

The A$/JPY dual currency issue is targeted to investors seeking an interest coupon higher than that prevailing in JPY in return for accepting currency risk on the coupons (but not the principal amount of the investment).

Table 1 below sets out the issue cash flows together with the realised return to the investor under three A$/JPY exchange rate scenarios:

- The A/JPY rate remains at the level at the time of issue of A$1 = JPY118;
- the prevailing A$/JPY forward rates;
- a steady depreciation of the A$/JPY exchange rate by 5% pa.

The issuer of the bond wishes to be completely immunised from the dual currency characteristics of the transaction, seeking to use it as a basis for generating sub-LIBOR US$ floating rate funding. B enters into a structured currency swap whereby the issuer:

- At closing, pays the JPY20bn proceeds to B in return for receiving the equivalent amount of US$129,728,814 (based on a spot exchange rate of US$1 = JPY154.17).

Exhibit 15.13—continued

TABLE 1

Dual Currency Bond Issue

Issue Terms

Type:	
Principal Currency:	JPY
Principal Amount:	20,000,000,000
Coupon Currency:	A$
Coupon Rate:	8.000%

Exchange Rates (A$/JPY):	118.0000
Exchange Rates (A$/US$):	0.7654
Exchange Rates (US$/JPY):	154.1678

Issue cash flows and return to investors

Period	Bond Cash Flows		Realised Return to Investors Case 1: Steady Currency		Realised Return to Investors Case 2: Forward Currency Rates		Realised Return to Investors Case 3: 5% Depreciation	
	Principal JPY	Interest A$	JPY/A$ Rate	Bond Cash Flows (in JPY)	JPY/A$ Rate	Bond Cash Flows (in JPY)	JPY/A$ Rate	Bond Cash Flows (in JPY)
0	(20,000,000,000)		118.00	(20,000,000,000)	118.00	(20,000,000,000)	118.0000	(20,000,000,000)
1		13,559,322	118.00	1,600,000,000	109.35	1,482,730,506	112.1000	1,520,000,000
2		13,559,322	118.00	1,600,000,000	101.55	1,376,936,365	106.4950	1,444,000,000
3		13,559,322	118.00	1,600,000,000	94.23	1,277,681,719	101.1703	1,371,800,000
4		13,559,322	118.00	1,600,000,000	86.94	1,178,804,337	96.1117	1,303,210,000
5		13,559,322	118.00	1,600,000,000	81.27	1,178,804,337	91.3062	1,303,210,000
6		13,559,322	118.00	1,600,000,000	75.85	1,101,984,082	86.7408	1,238,049,500
7		13,559,322	118.00	1,600,000,000	70.84	1,028,539,295	82.4038	1,176,147,025
8		13,559,322	118.00	1,600,000,000	65.48	960,483,943	78.2836	1,117,339,674
9		13,559,322	118.00	1,600,000,000	60.89	887,826,856	74.3694	1,061,472,690
10	20,000,000,000	13,559,322	118.00	21,600,000,000	56.39	20,764,671,668	70.6510	20,957,979,103
	Realised JPY Yield			8.000%		5.787%		6.392%

Exhibit 15.13—continued

- Over the life of the transaction, A pays US$ six month LIBOR minus a margin (say 20bps pa) semi-annually in return for receiving A$13,559,322 being the exact A$ coupon due to the bond holders thereby eliminating any currency exposure.
- At maturity the initial exchange is reversed with the issuer paying US$129,728,814 to B in return for receiving JPY20bn covering the redemption of the dual currency issue.

In order to hedge its exposure under the transaction with the issuer, B will enter into two sets of transactions:

- A conventional JPY fixed US$ floating LIBOR swap under which it receives JPY at the market rate of 5.78% pa and pays US$ six month LIBOR minus 20bps.
- A series of A$/JPY LTFX contracts selling JPY1,156m/buying the equivalent A$.

The structure of the hedge and the detailed cash flows from the viewpoint of B are summarised below in *Table 2*, p 458.

The JPY/US$ currency swap (which matches the US$ floating cash flows) leaves B with net cash flows where it is long JPY (JPY1,156.0m) and short A$ (A$13,559,322) on each bond coupon date.

The LTFX contracts are designed to cover this exposure. The LTFX contracts results in a distinctive pattern of cash flows whereby B is short A$ in the early years (reflecting the fact that the JPY surplus does not at the relevant LTFX rate cover the A$ outflow) and long A$ in later years (reflecting the falling A$/JPY LTFX rates which result from the interest rate differential between A$ and JPY).

In essence, B has to fund this shortfall in the early years and recover the shortfall together with the funding cost from the surplus in late years.

Based on the assumed zero coupon interest rates, B generates a profit (on a PV basis) of A$1,912,861 from this transaction. This profit is additional to any earning generated by B from the JPY/US$ swap on the LTFX contracts (presumably, the bid-offer) or the dual currency issue itself.

Source: This example draws on Maxwell G W Morley, "Swapping An Australian Dollar/Yen Dual Currency Bond Issue" in Satyajit Das (1991).

Foreign currency linked bonds and related swaps

In 1985, an issue of indexed currency option notes (ICONs) saw for the first time the combination of a conventional fixed rate debt issue with a currency option. The ICON structure is very similar, conceptually, to and, in fact, predated the Treasury Indexed Note structure described above.

The initial issue, for the Long Term Credit Bank of Japan, entailed the issuer paying the investor a higher than usual coupon, in return for which the investor creates what is effectively a currency option. The investor, in that case, granted a European style ten year yen and US$ call option with a strike price of JPY169.

The redemption structure of the ICON effectively simulated the characteristics of a call option on yen (which can also be expressed as a put option on US$ relative to yen) with the investor (the grantor of the option) losing as the yen strengthens relative to the US$ and conversely the purchaser gaining.

The currency option was implicit in the redemption terms of the issue whereby notes were to be redeemed at par (100) if the yen and US$ rate was equal to JPY169 or more at maturity. If the US$ was below JPY169 at maturity, the redemption amount received by the investor was reduced on a sliding discount from par.

Analytically, the investor had granted a foreign currency option in exchange for the higher coupon on the transaction (approximately 55 to 65bps pa) which represented the option premium.

Exhibit 15.13—continued

TABLE 2

Dual Currency Swap Structure and Pricing

Period		Swap Pay		Cash Flows Receive	Hedge Transactions (1) JPY/US$ Swap Receive (JPY) @ 5.780%	Hedge Transactions (1) JPY/US$ Swap Pay (US$)	(2) Net Flows JPY	(2) Net Flows A$	Zero Coupon Interest Rates JPY	Zero Coupon Interest Rates A$	LTFX Rates	Net Cash Flow A$	PV A$
0	JPY	20,000,000,000	US$	(129,728,814)	(20,000,000,000)	129,728,814					118.0000		
1	A$	(13,559,322)	US$	LIBOR-margin	1,156,000,000	(LIBOR-margin)	1,156,000,000	(13,559,322)	6.840%	15.290%	109.3514	(2,987,896)	(2,591,635)
2	A$	(13,559,322)	US$	LIBOR-margin	1,156,000,000	(LIBOR-margin)	1,156,000,000	(13,559,322)	6.720%	15.040%	101.5491	(2,175,661)	(1,643,969)
3	A$	(13,559,322)	US$	LIBOR-margin	1,156,000,000	(LIBOR-margin)	1,156,000,000	(13,559,322)	6.590%	14.890%	94.2290	(1,291,340)	(851,518)
4	A$	(13,559,322)	US$	LIBOR-margin	1,156,000,000	(LIBOR-margin)	1,156,000,000	(13,559,322)	6.340%	14.780%	86.9368	(262,309)	(151,129)
5	A$	(13,559,322)	US$	LIBOR-margin	1,156,000,000	(LIBOR-margin)	1,156,000,000	(13,559,322)	6.290%	14.520%	81.2713	664,637	337,425
6	A$	(13,559,322)	US$	LIBOR-margin	1,156,000,000	(LIBOR-margin)	1,156,000,000	(13,559,322)	6.250%	14.370%	75.8548	1,680,325	750,794
7	A$	(13,559,322)	US$	LIBOR-margin	1,156,000,000	(LIBOR-margin)	1,156,000,000	(13,559,322)	6.180%	14.210%	70.8357	2,760,135	1,088,934
8	A$	(13,559,322)	US$	LIBOR-margin	1,156,000,000	(LIBOR-margin)	1,156,000,000	(13,559,322)	6.020%	14.120%	65.4772	4,095,670	1,423,741
9	A$	(13,559,322)	US$	LIBOR-margin	1,156,000,000	(LIBOR-margin)	1,156,000,000	(13,559,322)	5.910%	13.990%	60.8855	5,427,134	1,670,205
10	A$	(13,559,322)	US$	LIBOR-margin	1,156,000,000	(LIBOR-margin)	1,156,000,000	(13,559,322)	5.840%	13.950%	56.3945	6,939,118	1,880,014
	JPY	(20,000,000,000)	US$	129,728,814	20,000,000,000	(129,728,814)							
												Profit	1,912,861

The net result of the transaction is that the issuer, Long Term Credit Bank of Japan, has purchased a ten year European put option on the US$ against the yen with the strike price of US$1/JPY169 from the investors in the security. Given that it was interested in securitising the option, using the proceeds from the sale to reduce its borrowing costs, the issuer is likely to sell the option position to a financial intermediary, such as the originator of the transaction. The purchaser will compensate the issuer for the option either in the form of an up-front payment or, usually, through an annuity payment which will be designed to lower the all-in funding costs of the issuer. This will usually be built into the accompanying swap for the transaction.

The financial intermediary purchasing the option has a number of alternatives to securitise this currency option:

- The intermediary can, in turn, sell this currency option.
- Given that the market for long-dated currency options is limited, as an alternative to selling the option on identical terms, the intermediary could write short-term US$ put options against the yen and roll the position at maturity of each series of options. In this case, while the high level of premium for short-term options may allow the financial intermediary to recover the price it pays for the option in a relatively short time, the cash flow mismatches suggest that it may not be able to ensure a profit from the transaction and, in fact, it may even incur a loss if exchange rates move substantially against it, given that it cannot effectively exercise the currency option securitised through the ICON issue.
- Alternatively, the financial intermediary can utilise the US$ put option position as part of the hedge for a straight Euroyen debt issue for a counterparty who wants US$ funding.

The final structure noted is almost inevitably the most attractive means of securitising the option. This structure is set out, in the case of the ICON issue, in *Exhibit 15.14*.

A variation on this basic structure was undertaken in an issue for IBM (nicknamed "Heaven and Hell") whereby in return for taking a risk of loss if the yen strengthens beyond US$1/JPY169, the investor would receive a higher redemption payment if the yen is weaker than US$1/JPY169 at maturity.

Exhibit 15.14

ICONs and Swap Structures

The ICON issue was lead managed by Bankers Trust (BT) for the Long Term Credit Bank of Japan (LTCB). The issue was for US$120m for ten years with coupon of 11.50%. The redemption value was calculated according to the following formula if the JPY strengthened beyond JPY169/US$1:

$$R = US\$120{,}000{,}000 \times \left(1 - \frac{169 - S}{S}\right)$$

where

R = redemption value in US$

S = JPY/US$ spot exchange rate on 21/11/1995

If the JPY/US$ exchange rate was weaker than JPY169/US$1, investors would receive the face value of the notes.

Under the terms of the accompanying US$ interest rate swap, LTCB achieved an all-in cost of approximately LIBOR minus 40-45bps. The swap structure effectively securitises the

Exhibit 15.14—continued

currency option. BT purchases this US$ put option against the JPY on US$120m at a strike price of JPY169/US$1.

To securitise the option position, BT will arrange either directly or indirectly for a JPY issue at 6.65% pa for ten years for JPY24,240m, exchange the proceeds for US$120m on the spot market, hedge the interest commitments forward, leave the capital redemption unhedged and charge the counterparty 10.70% for the US$120m loan.

The profits dynamics of the transaction are as follows:

- Assume ten year United States treasury bond rate is 10.50% pa; yen risk free rate (the ten year Japanese government bond) is 6.50% pa; JPY/US$ spot exchange rate as at November 1985 was JPY202/US$1.
- Assume forward exchange rates were:

1 year forward	JPY194.6878/US$1;	6 year forward	JPY161.911/US$1;
2 year forward	JPY187.64/US$1;	7 year forward	JPY156.05/US$1;
3 year forward	JPY180.8476/US$1;	8 year forward	JPY150.401/US$1;
4 year forward	JPY174.3013/US$1;	9 year forward	JPY144.956/US$1;
5 year forward	JPY167.9918/US$1;	10 year forward	JPY139.956/US$1.

- At maturity, the worst case exchange rate BT will have to repay its JPY commitment is JPY169/US$1, therefore the shortfall in JPY amount on that date if the worst case rises is: JPY24,240,000,000 – JPY20,280,000,000 = JPY3,960,000,000. This shortfall translates into an annual payment of JPY293,454,573.
- Therefore, BT has to hedge the interest payment of JPY1,611,960,000 + JPY293,454,573 = JPY1,905,414,573 forward annually.
- Cash flows from the JPY24,240m debt issue are as follows:

Year	Yen interest commitment (JPY)	Annuity for capital redemption (JPY)	US$ amount to hedge cash flows (US$)	Counterparty interest payments (US$)	BT's profits (US$)
		@JPY202/$1 →			
0	24,240,000,000			120,000,000	
1	1,611,960,000	293,454,573	9,787,026	12,840,000	3,052,974
2	1,611,960,000	293,454,573	10,154,629	12,840,000	2,685,371
3	1,611,960,000	293,454,573	10,536,024	12,840,000	2,303,976
4	1,611,960,000	293,454,573	10,931,729	12,840,000	1,908,271
5	1,611,960,000	293,454,573	11,342,307	12,840,000	1,497,693
6	1,611,960,000	293,454,573	11,768,284	12,840,000	1,071,716
7	1,611,960,000	293,454,573	12,210,282	12,840,000	629,718
8	1,611,960,000	293,454,573	12,668,896	12,840,000	171,104
9	1,611,960,000	293,454,573	13,144,779	12,840,000	– 304,779
10	1,611,960,000	293,454,573	13,638,443	12,840,000	– 798,443
	24,240,000,000	– 3,960,000,000	@JPY169/$1 →	120,000,000	

- BT's profits from the above transaction, at a discount rate of 10.50% pa, will, after ten years, be US$25,564,688, equivalent to a US$1,566,024 annuity over ten years.
- This annuity can then be used to reduce LTCB's borrowing cost from US$13,800,000 (11.50% of US$120m) to US$12,233,976 pa (US$13,800,000 – US$1,566,024) which translates to an effective interest rate of US$12,233,976/US$120,000,000 or 10.20% pa, a rate under the equivalent United States treasury rate if all the profits are distributed to the issuer (an unlikely scenario).

The redemption arrangements analytically constitute a yen and US$ call granted by the investor and the simultaneous purchase of a yen and US$ put. Both options have a strike rate of US$1/JPY169 and a term of ten years. In the IBM transaction the issue was structured in two tranches: a fixed rate and a floating rate issue. In the fixed (floating) rate portion, the investor received approximately 70bps (25bps) in extra yield in return for the variable redemption arrangement. In this structure, a two-way currency option was created, one written by the investor and one by the issuer. Both options again were capable of being sold separately combined into a synthetic currency forward position to reduce the overall borrowing cost of its issues.

The detailed structure of the Heaven and Hell issue and accompanying currency linked swap is set out in *Exhibit 15.15*.

Exhibit 15.15
"Heaven and Hell" Notes and Swap Structure

The first issue of Heaven and Hell notes was lead managed by Nomura International for IBM Credit Corporation. The IBM issue was to raise US$50m for ten years, with a maturity date of 4 December 1995. To entice investors to invest in this bond, IBM had to pay a rich coupon of 10.75% pa, payable in US$, which was equivalent to 84bps over treasuries. In a prior comparable issue, IBM had only paid 14bps over treasuries for a straight Eurodollar issue. The redemption amount for the issue, payable in US$, will vary according to the following formula:

$$R = \text{US\$}50{,}000{,}000 \times \left(1 + \frac{S - 169}{S}\right)$$

where

R = redemption amount in US$
S = JPY/US$ spot exchange rate at maturity of the bonds

If the JPY/US$ exchange rate at maturity was stronger than JPY84.5/US$1, investors will get no principal return.

IBM securitises the options implicit in the transaction to Nomura in return for payments which effectively lower its cost of funds.

From the IBM Heaven and Hell debt issue, Nomura will have a short US$ position in ten years time at a forward price of JPY169/US$1 for US$50m. To utilise this forward position effectively, Nomura will issue JPY10,212,500,000 at 6.70% pa for a counterparty who wants ten year US$ funds. Nomura would exchange the JPY proceeds on the spot market, hedge the interest commitments forward and leave the final capital redemption amount unhedged. Nomura will charge the counterparty approximately 10.25% pa for the US$ funds.

The profit dynamics of the issue are as follows:

- Assume JPY ten year risk free interest rate is 6.50% pa; ten year United States treasury interest rate is 10.00% pa; JPY/US$ spot exchange rate is JPY204.25/US$1.
- Assume forward exchange rates were:

1 year forward	JPY197.751/US$1;	6 year forward	JPY168.230/US$1;
2 year forward	JPY191.459/US$1;	7 year forward	JPY162.877/US$1;
3 year forward	JPY185.367/US$1;	8 year forward	JPY157.695/US$1;
4 year forward	JPY179.469/US$1;	9 year forward	JPY152.677/US$1;
5 year forward	JPY173.759/US$1;	10 year forward	JPY147.819/US$1.

- At maturity, Nomura will exchange the US$ into JPY at the rate of JPY169/US$1. This will give Nomura JPY8,450,000,000 to repay the JPY10,212,500,000 JPY loan, leaving a shortfall of JPY1,762,500,000. This shortfall translates into an annual payment of JPY130,609,517 at the risk free rate of 6.50% pa.
- Nomura has therefore to enter into an annual forward agreement to hedge JPY814,847,017 annually (JPY684,237,500 + JPY130,609,517).

Exhibit 15.15—continued

- The cash flows involved are as follows:

Year	Yen interest commitment (JPY)	Annuity for capital redemption (JPY)	US$ amount to hedge cash flows (US$)	Counterparty interest payments (US$)	Nomura's profits (US$)
		@JPY204.25/US$1			
0	10,212,500,000	——————→		50,000,000	
1	684,237,500	130,609,517	4,120,571	5,125,000	1,004,429
2	684,237,500	130,609,517	4,255,987	5,125,000	869,013
3	684,237,500	130,609,517	4,395,858	5,125,000	729,142
4	684,237,500	130,609,517	4,540,322	5,125,000	584,678
5	684,237,500	130,609,517	4,689,524	5,125,000	435,476
6	684,237,500	130,609,517	4,843,649	5,125,000	281,351
7	684,237,500	130,609,517	5,002,837	5,125,000	122,168
8	684,237,500	130,609,517	5,167,234	5,125,000	−42,234
9	684,237,500	130,609,517	5,337,065	5,125,000	−212,065
10	684,237,500	130,609,517	5,512,465	5,125,000	−387,465
	10,212,500,000	−1,762,500,000	@JPY169/US$1 ——→	50,000,000	

- Nomura's profits from the above transaction, using a discount rate of 10.00% pa, will, at the end of ten years, be US$7,291,912, equivalent to a US$457,534 annuity over ten years.
- The annuity will be used to reduce IBM's annual interest cost of US$5,375,000 (10.75% of US$50m) to US$4,917,467 (US$5,375,000 − US$457,533) which will reduce IBM's interest cost down to US$4,917,467/US$50,000,000 = 9.835% (a rate below United States treasuries).
- However, because investors of the IBM Heaven and Hell issue also purchased a US$ put option with a strike price of JPY84.5/US$1, Nomura will be left with a residual foreign currency risk should the JPY/US$ exchange rate strengthen beyond JPYUS$84.5/US$1. Nomura can leave this position unhedged or hedge this residual exposure, by buying a customised US$ put option with a strike price of JPY84.5/US$1 or it could delta hedge the position to create a synthetic option.

The currency options implicit in these transactions are effectively securitised usually through a swap transaction structurally similar to that described above in connection with the Treasury Indexed Note structure.

The ICON type structure which yields currency options which are securitised and on-sold has been extended in a number of directions, for example:

- variability linked to currency rates has been extended to coupon amounts thereby creating a stream of currency options;
- mini-max notes where the variable redemption amount operates *only* if the currency rates are outside a stated band;
- inclusion of ICON features in dual currency issues; and
- variable redemption structures linked to both currency and interest rates.

The ingenuity of these currency linked variable redemption bonds and also their creators, primarily, the Japanese securities houses, is best illustrated by two examples. *Exhibit 15.16* sets out the intricate and elegant combination of an issue by OKB and BFCE which allowed simultaneous foreign currency options to be securitised. *Exhibit 15.17* sets out the structure of "duet" bonds where the linkage to currency rates has been extended to coupon amounts.

Currency linked swap structures continue to be utilised to securitise the implicit currency forward or option positions embedded in security issues. The demand for capital market issues with such embedded elements fluctuates. However, from time to time investor demand for particular currency related characteristics are evident. For example, in early 1992, General Electric Capital Corporation utilised its medium term note programme to issue US$33m five year 10.9% notes whose interest and principal are payable in US$ but the amount of principal repaid is pegged to a formula reflecting relationships between the US$, A$ and JPY. Simultaneous to the issue of debt, General Electric entered into a currency linked swap arrangement with Morgan Stanley, the arranger of the debt issue, to insulate itself from the currency linked redemption features. The total transaction generated attractively priced funding for General Electric.

Exhibit 15.16

JPY/US$ Variable Redemption Reverse Dual Currency Bond and Swap Structure

On 15 April 1986, Oesterreichische Kontrollbank (OKB) issued a JPY20 billion, ten year variable redemption bond. The coupon was 8.00% pa payable in JPY. Redemption was in US$ based on the following formula:

$$R = US\$114{,}155{,}252 \times \left(1 + \frac{S - 169}{S}\right)$$

where

R = redemption amount in US$
S = JPY/US$ spot exchange rate at maturity of the bonds

If JPY strengthens beyond JPY84.5/US$1, investors will not receive their principal back.

On the same date, Nomura also lead managed a reverse dual currency bond issue worth JPY20 billion, with a maturity of ten years for Banque Française du Commerce Exterieur (BFCE). This issue involved BFCE paying a 7.50% pa coupon, payable in US$ at a fixed exchange rate of JPY179/US$1. Redemption amount, payable in JPY, is at par as long as exchange rates are above JPY84.5/US$1, declining below par as JPY strengthened beyond JPY84.5/US$1. The foreign currency options implicit in the two issues were securitised by Nomura.

The OKB and BFCE issues complement one another as the redemption amount in the OKB issue is in US$ while the redemption amount of the BFCE issue is payable in JPY. The redemption formula of both issues *jointly* give a short US$ position at a forward price of JPY169/US$1.

Interest payment of the OKB issue is in US$ but that of the BFCE issue is in JPY, therefore, if BFCE wants US$ funding. Nomura will have to hedge the JPY interest commitments of the BFCE issue forward. To capitalise on the short US$ position obtained from both issues, Nomura would not hedge the capital redemption of OKB's JPY redemption amount forward.

The profit dynamics of the transaction are as follows:

- Assume JPY ten year risk-free interest rate is 6.50% pa; United States ten year treasury interest rate is 8.50% pa; JPY/US$ spot exchange rate is JPY175.2/US$1.
- Assume forward exchange rates were:

1 year forward	JPY171.97/US$1;	6 year forward	JPY156.69/US$1;
2 year forward	JPY168.8/US$1;	7 year forward	JPY153.81/US$1;
3 year forward	JPY165.65/US$1;	8 year forward	JPY150.97/US$1;
4 year forward	JPY162.63/US$1;	9 year forward	JPY148.19/US$1;
5 year forward	JPY159.64/US$1;	10 year forward	JPY145.46/US$1.

- Interest flows for BFCE are as follows: assuming OKB pays Nomura the equivalent of 8.30% pa (a rate under United States treasuries), BFCE pays an interest flow to Nomura of [(JPY20 billion/175.2) × 8.30%] = US$9,474,886. Nomura will have to pay investors

Exhibit 15.16—continued

[(JPY20 billion × 7.50%) JPY179/US$1] = US$8,379,888. Therefore, Nomura will obtain an annual profit of US$1,094,998 from this part of the transaction.

- Interest flows for OKB are as follows: assuming it pays Nomura the equivalent of US$8.30% pa, BFCE will pay Nomura US$9,474,886 [(JPY20 billion/175.2) × 8.30%] and Nomura will have to pay investors JPY1,600,000,000 [JPY20 billion × 8.00%]. Nomura will have to hedge this obligation forward to limit any losses.
- The interest flows under the OKB transaction are as set out below.

Year	OKB JPY interest commitment (JPY)	US$ amount to hedge cash flows (US$)	OKB's interest payments (US$)	Nomura's profits (US$)
1	1,600,000,000	9,303,949	9,474,886	170,937
2	1,600,000,000	9,478,673	9,474,886	-3,787
3	1,600,000,000	9,656,588	9,474,886	-181,722
4	1,600,000,000	9,838,283	9,474,886	-363,417
5	1,600,000,000	10,022,551	9,474,886	-547,685
6	1,600,000,000	10,211,245	9,474,886	-736,379
7	1,600,000,000	10,402,445	9,474,886	-927,579
8	1,600,000,000	10,598,132	9,474,886	-1,123,266
9	1,600,000,000	10,796,950	9,474,886	-1,322,084
10	1,600,000,000	10,999,588	9,474,886	-1,524,722

- Nomura's net profit position from the two transactions is:

Year	Profit from BFCE (US$)	Profit from OKB (US$)	Net profit (US$)
1	1,094,998	170,937	1,265,935
2	1,094,998	-3,787	1,091,211
3	1,094,998	-181,722	913,276
4	1,094,998	-363,417	731,581
5	1,094,998	-547,685	547,313
6	1,094,998	-736,379	358,619
7	1,094,998	-927,579	167,419
8	1,094,998	-1,123,266	-28,268
9	1,094,998	-1,322,084	-227,086
10	1,094,998	-1,524,722	-429,724

- At the US$ risk-free interest rate of 8.50% pa, the compounded value of this net profit cash flow at year 10 is US$8,368,408.
- Redemption amount which OKB and BFCE will pay Nomura at maturity = US$114,155,252 × 2 = US$228,310,504.
- Premium from OKB issue JPY300,000,000 and for BFCE, it is JPY350,000,000 which totals to US$3,710,045 at JPY175:US$1 (both issues were made at premiums to par).
- Total amount of cash available to Nomura to repay investors = US$8,368,408 (Nomura's profit) + US$228,310,504 (principal repayments in US$ by OKB and BFC) + US$3,710,045 (issue premium) = US$240,388,957.
- Amount owed by Nomura to investors of both issues at maturity if spot exchange rate is weaker than JPY84.5/US$1 depends on the following formula:

$$R = \text{JPY20 billion}/179 \times \left(1 + \frac{S - 169}{S}\right) + \text{JPY20 billion}/S$$

where

R = redemption amount in US$
S = JPY/US$ spot exchange rate

Therefore, Nomura's profit is as follows:

Exhibit 15.16—continued

Spot rate (S)	Cash available to Nomura (US$)	Redemption amount (US$)	Gain (US$)
300	240,388,957	227,188,083	13,200,874
200	240,388,957	229,050,280	11,338,677
150	240,388,957	230,912,477	9,476,480
100	240,388,957	234,636,872	5,752,085
90	240,388,957	235,878,337	4,510,620
85	240,388,957	236,608,610	3,780,347
84.5	240,388,957	236,686,391	3,702,566
80	240,388,957	235,937,500	4,451,457
60	240,388,957	197,222,222	43,166,735

- From the above profit table, we observe that it is possible for Nomura to reduce the cost of borrowing of both entities to below United States treasuries and still not incur a loss on the capital redemption amount at maturity.

Exhibit 15.17
Duet Bond and Swap Structure

The first duet bond was issued for the Kingdom of Denmark and managed by Dai-Ichi Kangyo Bank (DKB). It was a five year debt issue worth US$100m issued on 8 August 1986. The coupon, payable in US$, is based on the following formula:

$$C = \$100{,}000{,}000 \times 0.165 - \left[\frac{\text{JPY}16{,}300{,}000{,}000 \times 0.065}{S}\right]$$

where

C = coupon payable in US$
S = JPY/US$ exchange rate at coupon date

The capital redemption amount, also payable in US$, is calculated using the following formula:

$$R = \text{US}\$100{,}000{,}000 \times 2 - \left[\frac{\text{JPY}16{,}300{,}000{,}000}{S}\right]$$

where

R = redemption amount in US$
S = JPY/US$ exchange rate at maturity of the bonds

From the formula, it is clear that Denmark has an exposure to the JPY/US$ exchange rate on each coupon date and at maturity of the bonds. These currency options were securitised by DKB.

Under the swap structure, Denmark effectively sells the options implicit in the structure to DKB. DKB assume an annual exposure to JPY coupon payments as a result of the duet bond's coupon payment formula. In addition, DKB will have a short US$ forward exposure for US$100m in five years' time, at a forward rate of JPY163/US$1.

To capitalise on this position, DKB arranges a JPY issue, for a counterparty wanting US$ funding, with an annual coupon payment equivalent to JPY1,059,500,000. If the JPY interest rate on the issue is 5.20%, then DKB will have to issue JPY20,375m, principal amount pa of bonds.

The duet bond, because of the amount issued, will only support US$100m or JPY16,300m of the JPY issue to be perfectly hedged, therefore, JPY4,075m from the JPY issue will be unhedged. DKB has to undertake a five year forward agreement to purchase JPY to hedge this exposure.

The profit dynamics of this transaction are as follows:

- Assume five year JPY interest rate is 5.00% pa; five year US$ interest rate is 7.50% pa; spot exchange rate is JPY163/US$1; the five year forward rate is JPY144.9078/US$1.
- Therefore, DKB will require JPY4,075,000,000/JPY144.9078 = $28,121,329 to hedge the JPY4,075,000,000 JPY forward exposure.

Exhibit 15.17—continued

- If DKB charges counterparty 7.70% pa for US$ funding, the borrower will therefore have to pay DKB US$9,625,000 (7.70% of US$125,000,000) and DKB will be committed to pay JPY1,059,500,000 (at JPY163/US$1) (5.20% of JPY20,375,000,000) for the straight JPY debt. The duet bond coupon formula will cover this, leaving DKB with US$3,125,000 (US$9,625,000-US$6,500,000) annually for the next five years. This will accumulate to US$18,151,222 at the end of five years, at the interest rate of 7.50% pa.
- At maturity, DKB will have US$125m to pay off the JPY20,375m straight JPY debt. The duet bond will hedge JPY16,300m (equivalent to US$100m) and the forward agreement will hedge the remaining JPY4,075m. This amount will be covered by the US$18,151,222, from the coupon receipts and US$25m, from the capital redemption amount. This will leave DKB with US$25,000,000 + US$18,151,222 − US$28,121,329 = US$15,029,893 profits at maturity.
- This profit at maturity (US$15,029,893) would be used to reduce the duet bond's interest cost. The US$15,029,893 plus the US$1,625,000 premium from the issue of duet bonds will give an annuity of US$2,989,260 over five years at 7.50%. Interest cost of the duet bond = 10.00% of US$100,000,000 = US$10,000,000. Effective interest cost of the bond after deducting the annuity is: (US$10,000,000 − US$2,989,260)/US$1,000,000,000 = 7.02%, a rate under the equivalent United States treasury bond rate, if the full benefit is passed on to the borrower.

INTEREST RATE AND CURRENCY LINKED SWAPS[1]

Rationale

The interest rate and currency linked swap hybrids identified above are highly specific transactions designed to securitise forward and option positions implicit in capital market issues. The potential for creating hybrid swap structures, independent of capital market issues, evolved from these structures. The major impetus to such developments included:

- The financing and investment needs of borrowers and investors who are increasingly seeking to generate synthetic asset liability management instruments to match their portfolio requirement.
- The efforts by financial institutions to "bundle" packages of derivative products—in financial engineering combinations—to generate "value added" solutions to asset liability management requirements of their clients.

The interest rate and currency linked swap structures that evolved were essentially combinations of various swap instruments—primarily, forwards and options—specifically structured to create the required payoff profile, which, in turn, was linked closely to the interest rate or currency expectations of the potential user of the structure.

The analysis of these types of hybrid instruments is complicated by two factors:

- By their very nature, the structures developed are highly customised to individual users specifications and are not necessarily duplicated, although similar transactions may be undertaken.
- The nomenclature of the structures is highly individualised as between specific financial institutions who use their own trademark names for these structures.

1. This section draws on Colin McKeith and Jim L'Estrange, "Variation on Conventional Swap Structures—Swap Option Combination" in Satyajit Das (1991).

In the sections which follow, a number of common interest rate and currency linked swap structures which have developed are examined. It should be noted that the structures examined are by no means comprehensive but are, merely, indicative of the structuring possibilities available to satisfy individual risk management requirements.

Interest rate linked swaps

In this section, three interest rate linked swap hybrids are examined:

- participating cap or swap transactions;
- flexible or contingent swap transactions;
- super floater swaps.

Participating cap or swap transactions

Exhibit 15.18 sets out an example of the participating cap transaction (such transactions are often also referred to as participating swaps).

Exhibit 15.18
Participating Cap Transaction

Assume US$ three month LIBOR rates are at 6% pa. Company A (A) seeks protection from higher short-term interest rates on its short term floating rate debt, but would like to benefit, at least in part, from any potential decline in rates.

To achieve its objectives, A enters into a participating cap transaction.

The participating cap is structured as follows:

- A selects the cap interest rate level.
- The bank works out the effective participation ratio.

There is a trade-off between the cap level and the participation ratio. The higher the cap level A accepts the higher will be the participation in a fall in rates:

Cap level (% pa)	7.10	7.35	7.60	7.85	8.10
Participation rate (%)	0	23	41	55	64

The lowest cap level available for zero participation in a drop in rates is equivalent to paying fixed/receiving floating under an interest rate swap. The corresponding cap level is the equivalent of the offered rate on a three year swap. Where A wants 100% participation in a decrease in rates, it would be fully unhedged.

For a given participation rate and cap level, the effective rate to the institution, when LIBOR is under the cap level, is determined by the following formula:

Effective rate = Cap level − Participation rate × (Cap level-LIBOR)

If, for example, A chose a worst case level of 7.85%, the corresponding participation rate in a fall in rates would be 55%.

Thus if LIBOR is at 4%, the previous example gives an effective rate determined by:

Effective rate = 7.85% − 0.55 (7.85% − 4%) = 5.7325%

Therefore, if LIBOR should rise above 7.85%, then A's cost would be capped at that level. If LIBOR falls to 4% its effective cost of funds would be 5.7325% for that period. If three month LIBOR stays at 6.1875%, the cost of funds would be 6.9356%. A would therefore pay LIBOR to its lenders and the difference between 6.9356% and 6.1875% to the bank on the interest payment date. A effectively under this structure would have purchased protection at no up-front premium and yet still benefit if interest rates decline further.

Exhibit 15.18—continued

55% PARTICIPATING CAP AT 7.85% vs SWAP

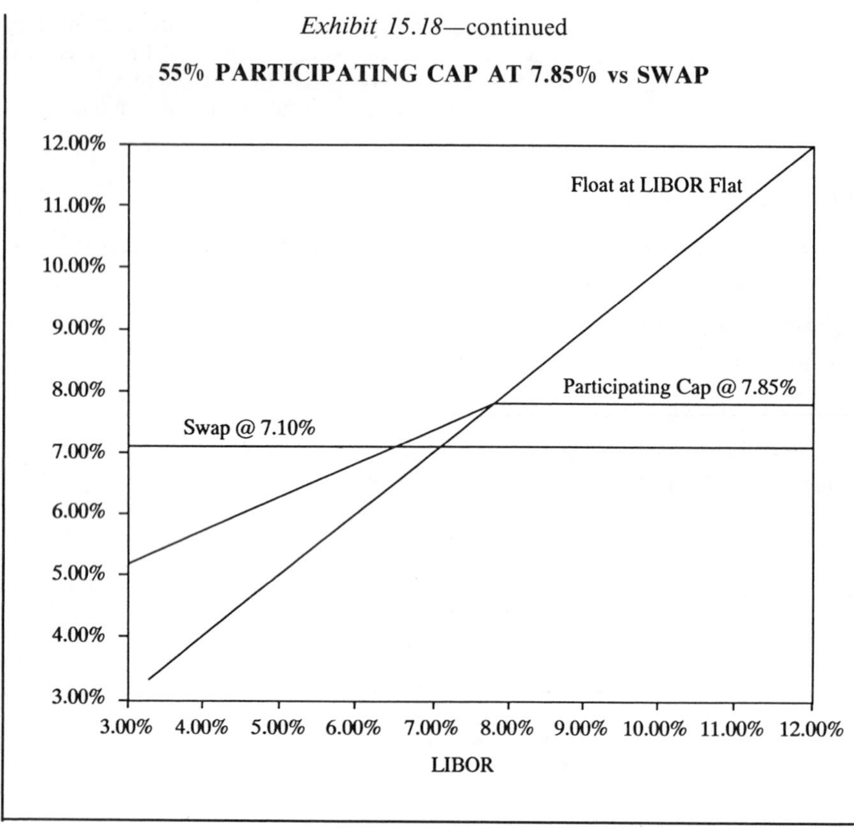

Borrowers with liabilities priced off short-term rates can hedge their interest rate exposure through entering into a swap (paying fixed/receiving floating) or purchasing a cap. The swap effectively means that the borrower incurs a cost where short-term interest rates are above long-term interest rates. This is exacerbated where the yield curve has a strong positive slope. The interest rate swap provides the borrower with certainty of its borrowing cost but allows it no opportunity to benefit from lower short-term interest rates. Cap transactions overcome the deficiencies of the interest rate swap but require payment of an explicit upfront premium which a number of borrowers dislike. This premium can, in part, be defrayed by simultaneously selling a floor as part of a collar transaction. The participating cap transaction seeks to address these specific concerns.

Under the participating cap structure, the borrower's cost is "capped" at a chosen maximum interest rate level, but, simultaneously, the borrower is allowed to benefit from lower interest rates on a *proportion* of the borrowing when rates are below the capped level. The cost of the participating cap structure lies in the quantum or the proportion of the total borrowing which is allowed to float below the maximum cap level (that is, the participation rate). This provides the participating cap structure with its attraction for borrowers as it combines the benefit of an interest rate swap which allows interest rate to be fixed with no explicit premium payment and interest rate caps, which allows participation in interest rates below the cap level.

Analytically, the participating caps transaction is essentially equivalent to the purchase of an out-of-the-money cap with the simultaneous purchase of a floor on a proportion of the principal value of the cap. Alternatively, the transaction can be decomposed into entry into an out-of-the-money interest rate swap with the simultaneous purchase of a floor on a proportion of the notional principal value of the swap.

The pricing of the participating cap transaction focuses on entry into an interest rate swap (whereby the borrower pays fixed and receives floating) on a proportion of the liability at a rate above the current swap rate for the relevant maturity. The fact that the swap rate, embedded in the participating cap structure, is above the prevailing swap curve creates a net credit to the purchaser which is used to purchase an interest rate cap, which is set at the same interest rate level as the out-of-the-money swap, on the remaining portion of the liability. Determination of the participation rate is derived from the amount of the total liability covered by the cap.

The pricing characteristics evolve around how far the embedded swap rate of the participating cap is set above the swap curve. The further out of the money the swap rate is relative to the prevailing swap curve, the higher the net credit and, therefore, cash available to purchase a cap on a proportionately larger portion of the amount to be hedged. Conversely, the lower the net credit, the lower the participation rate.

The behaviour of the participating cap transaction reflects this pricing characteristic:

- As the participation rate level increases corresponding to an increase in the maximum rate level under the structure, the instrument starts behaving more like an out-of-the-money cap.
- As the maximum rate level is reduced to a level closer to the prevailing swap curve, the participation rate is reduced and the participating cap's behaviour approximates that of an interest rate swap.

The participation cap structure can be utilised in a wide variety of currencies and on a variety of interest rate indexes.

This type of transaction has significant appeal for a variety of groups including:

- borrowers with a relatively large amount of short-term debt who are particularly exposed to short-term interest rate swings but who also want to minimise the initial cash outflow from the purchase of an interest rate cap;
- property developers and constructors seeking protection from sharp swings and short-term interest rates during the construction period;
- financial institutions seeking to maximise the benefits of positive gaps in their asset-liability portfolio without increasing the interest rate exposure of the portfolio beyond acceptable levels.

Flexible swap transaction

Exhibit 15.19 sets out an example of a flexible swap structure.

This type of structure evolved in response to borrowers, particularly in Europe and Asia, who were suspicious of or were not allowed to purchase or grant interest rate options who were seeking to take advantage of expectations of a gradual decline in interest rates in the relevant currency.

Exhibit 15.19
Flexible Swap Transaction

Assume Company A (A) has US$100m of floating rate debt priced at US$ six month LIBOR plus 0.50% pa. US$ swap rates for three years (A's hedging time horizon) are 7.59% pa (semi-annual). A expects that US$ rates will fall gradually over the next three years to around 7.00-7.10% pa.

A enters into the following three year flexible swap to hedge its interest rate exposure:

- The flexible swap is for US$100m for three years with semi-annual payments/settlements.
- A receives US$ LIBOR from the swap counterparty as at cash settlement date.
- A pays, at the counterparty's option, as at each settlement date the higher of:

—Fixed Rate: 7.05% pa; or

—Floating Rate: US$ six month LIBOR less 54bps pa.

A's interest cost under this structure is summarised in the Table below.

Flexible Swap Transaction: Borrower's Interest Cost

US$ six month LIBOR	**Borrower's Interest Cost**		
	Unhedged Floating Rate Borrowing	**Interest Rate Swap**	**Flexible Swap**
6.00%	6.50%	8.09%	7.55%
6.25%	6.75%	8.09%	7.55%
6.50%	7.00%	8.09%	7.55%
6.75%	7.25%	8.09%	7.55%
7.00%	7.50%	8.09%	7.55%
7.05%	7.55%	8.09%	7.55%
7.25%	7.75%	8.09%	7.21%
7.50%	8.00%	8.09%	7.46%
7.75%	8.25%	8.09%	7.71%
8.00%	8.50%	8.09%	7.96%
8.25%	8.75%	8.09%	8.21%
8.50%	9.00%	8.09%	8.46%
8.75%	9.25%	8.09%	8.71%
9.00%	9.50%	8.09%	8.96%
9.25%	9.75%	8.09%	9.21%
9.50%	10.00%	8.09%	9.46%
9.75%	10.25%	8.09%	9.71%
10.00%	10.50%	8.09%	9.96%

A's borrowing costs are set out on three bases:

- floating rate;
- fixed rate—utilising a three year swap;
- flexible swap.

Under the flexible swap, A has an interest cost of:

- 7.55% pa if US$ LIBOR falls below 7.05% pa;
- US$ LIBOR minus 54bps if rates are above 7.05% pa.

A benefits most where US$ LIBOR rates are above 7.05% pa and below 8.13% pa (the break-even upper US$ LIBOR as rates would have to be above 8.13% pa (8.13% pa less the negative margin of 54bps)).

Exhibit 15.19—continued

BORROWER'S INTEREST COST UNDER FLEXIBLE SWAP

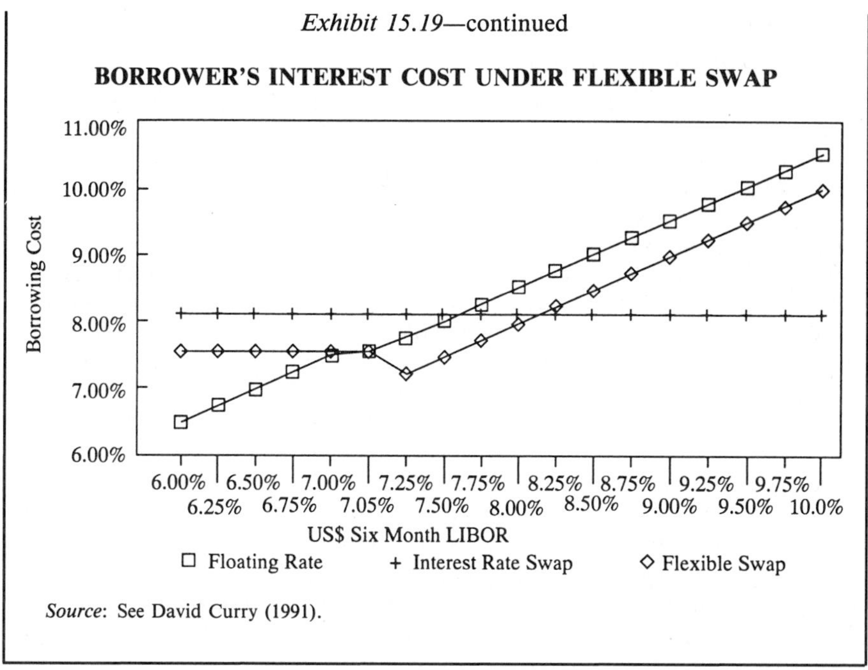

Source: See David Curry (1991).

These borrowers were reluctant to enter into interest rate swaps at the prevailing level as they believed interest rates would decline over the relevant time horizon. The flexible swap structure developed by financial institutions for these borrowers operated as follows:

- The company entered into a swap agreement with the bank.
- Under the terms of the agreement, the bank paid the client a floating rate.
- In return, the company was obliged to pay, *at the option of the bank*, either: a floating rate minus a margin or a fixed rate.
- The bank had these alternative payment receipt rights as at each coupon date over the life of the transaction.

From the viewpoint of the borrower, if interest rates behaved in accordance with its expectations and decreased gradually, the borrower's cost of funds was reduced until such time as rates fell below the fixed rate payment option. The fixed rate that the bank could, at its option, require the company to pay was significantly lower than the swap rate for the equivalent maturity prevailing *at the time the transaction was entered into*. It represented a rate and equivalent borrowing cost which the borrower found acceptable.

In the event that interest rates increase, the fact that the borrower was paying a margin under the floating rate index provided some protection against unforeseen increases in interest rates.

Analytically, this structure was identical to the sale of a floor at the implicit fixed rate under the flexible swap to the bank. The premium receipt was incorporated into the margin under the floating rate index and the adjustment to the flexible fixed rate to a level below the prevailing swap rate for the maturity.

Super floater swap

Exhibit 15.20 sets out an example of a super floater swap.

The super floater swap structure was utilised by borrowers seeking protection against higher interest rates. In addition to the fixed rate payable under the conventional swap transaction, the borrower selected an upper and lower strike rate with the floating rate on the reset dates under the swap being scaled (by a preselected multiplier) to changes in floating rates. For example, if floating interest rates increased above the upper strike level, assuming a multiplier factor of two, for each basis point that floating rates increased above the selected strike, the borrower would receive two basis points increase in floating rate. Conversely, in the event that the floating rate falls below the lower strike rate, the floating rate paid to the borrower will fall at a predetermined rate, say 1.3 to one, depending upon the tenor of the swap and where the strike rate is set. In effect, the borrower's cost increases as rates fall below the lower strike band but decreases as rates increase above the upper strike level.

The structure was designed to provide interest rate protection and the ability to significantly benefit from increases in short-term rates for borrowers who anticipated sharp rises in short-term floating rates.

Analytically, this type of structure entailed combining a conventional interest rate swap (under which the borrower paid fixed and received floating) with the simultaneous purchase of a cap at the upper strike level the sale of a floor at the lower strike level. Notional principal values of the cap and floor were determined by the selected multiplier and also whether or not the borrower wished to structure the package on a zero cost basis or with an upfront premium payable.

As an alternative, the structure could be designed with the swap rate payable being set at a level above the prevailing conventional swap yield curve to create a cash flow surplus for the counterparty bank which would be utilised to meet the option costs (conceptually, this is similar to the participating cap structure discussed above).

Exhibit 15.20
Super Floater Swap Transaction

Assume Company A (A) is a A$ floating rate borrower. A anticipates that short-term A$ interest rates will rise and enters into a super floater swap to hedge its borrowing costs on the following terms:

Amount:	A$100m
Maturity:	Two years
Swap Fixed Rate:	16.00% pa (quarterly)
Super Floater Terms:	
—Upper Strike:	18.35% pa
—Upper Multiplier:	2×
—Lower Strike:	14.00% pa
—Lower Multiplier:	1.7×

Under the swap, A's cash flows are as follows:

- A pay fixed under the swap at 16.00% pa;
- A receives A$ Bank Bill Rate under the swap as calculated below.

Exhibit 15.20—continued

The A$ Bank Bill Rate received is calculated as follows:

If BBR is between 14.00% pa and 18.35% pa—

A receives the A$ BBR rate.

If BBR is higher than 18.35% pa (say 19.35% pa)—

A receives the following adjusted floating rate:

18.35 + (2 × (19.35 − 18.35)] = 20.35% pa

If A$ BBR is less than 14.00% pa (say 13.00% pa)—

A receives the following adjusted floating rate:
14.00 − [1.7 × (14.00 − 13.00)] = 12.3% pa

A's interest cost under this structure is summarised in *Table 1*.
A's borrowing cost shows the following characteristics:

- Between A$ BBR of 14.00% and 18.35% (the upper and lower strike level), A's cost is the swap rate.
- If A$ BBR increases above the upper strike level of 18.35%, then the higher floating rate receipts reduce the cost of the swap fixed rate.
- If A$ BBR decrease below 14.00%, then the reduced floating rate receipts increase the cost of the swap fixed rate.

Super Floater Swap Transaction: Borrower's Interest Cost

Swap Fixed Rate:	16.00%
Upper Strike:	18.35%
Upper Multiplier:	2.00
Lower Strike:	14.00%
Lower Multiplier:	1.70

A$ six month BBR	Unhedged Floating Rate Borrowing	Super Floater Swap Payments: Pay Fixed Rate	Super Floater Swap Payments: Receive Floating Rate	Effective Fixed Rate Under Swap
12.00%	12.00%	16.00%	10.60%	17.40%
12.50%	12.50%	16.00%	11.45%	17.05%
13.00%	13.00%	16.00%	12.30%	16.70%
13.50%	13.50%	16.00%	13.15%	16.35%
14.00%	14.00%	16.00%	14.00%	16.00%
14.50%	14.50%	16.00%	14.50%	16.00%
15.00%	15.00%	16.00%	15.00%	16.00%
15.50%	15.50%	16.00%	15.50%	16.00%
16.00%	16.00%	16.00%	16.00%	16.00%
16.50%	16.50%	16.00%	16.50%	16.00%
17.00%	17.00%	16.00%	17.00%	16.00%
17.50%	17.50%	16.00%	17.50%	16.00%
18.00%	18.00%	16.00%	18.00%	16.00%
18.35%	18.35%	16.00%	18.35%	16.00%
18.50%	18.50%	16.00%	18.65%	15.85%
19.00%	19.00%	16.00%	19.65%	15.35%
19.50%	19.50%	16.00%	20.65%	14.85%
20.00%	20.00%	16.00%	21.65%	14.35%
20.50%	20.50%	16.00%	22.65%	13.85%

Exhibit 15.20—continued

BORROWER'S INTEREST COST UNDER SUPER FLOATER SWAP

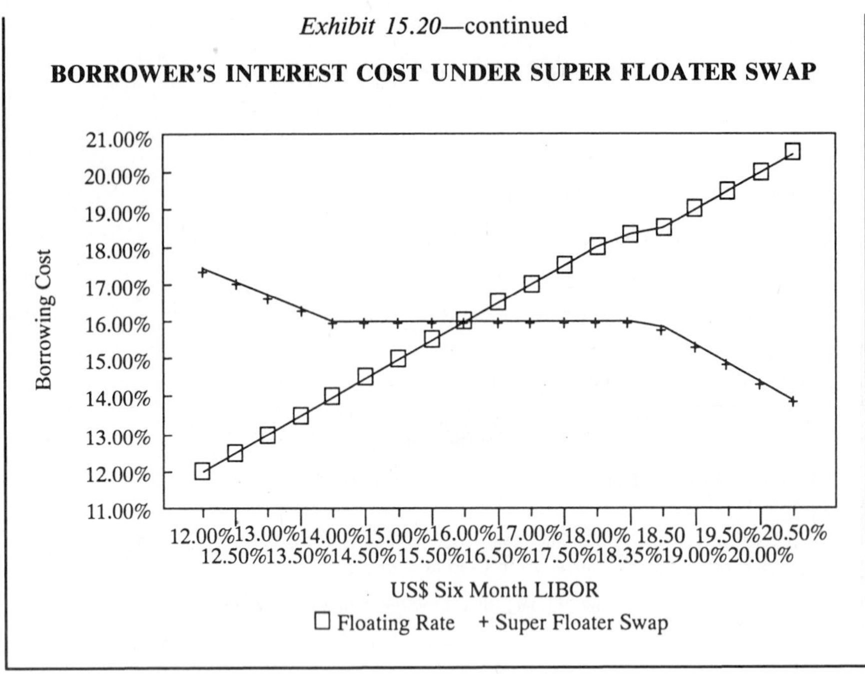

These types of structures were developed in a variety of currencies in environments where borrowers expected floating interest rates to increase sharply. The structure is quite flexible and can be tailored to suit individual borrowers' requirements. A major advantage of this particular structure was the flexibility with which it could be reversed at any time.

For example, if short-term interest rates increased sharply, the floor component of the super floater structure could be repurchased at minimal cost thereby eliminating the penalty incurred if interest rates were to fall over the life of the transaction.

Currency linked swaps

The currency linked swap structures which evolved were similar to the interest rate linked swap hybrids identified above. The major element to such transactions was, typically, the sale of foreign currency options with the proceeds being utilised to adjust the interest rate coupon level under the swap.

The earliest versions of currency linked swaps that evolved were essentially cross market option structures whereby borrowers and investors essentially financed interest rate option purchases by granting currency options or vice versa. This type of structure was designed to take advantage of perceived stability in one market (say currency) and/or high volatility levels to subsidise the cost of options in another market. This type of strategy was particularly attractive to market participants with known cash inflows or outflows in particular currencies where the option position could be structured as a hedge against these currency cash flows. A variety of structures have evolved and are considered below.

Contingent coupon currency swaps

This type of transaction typically took the following form:

- The borrower arranged a fixed rate financing for a term of, say, five years.
- Simultaneously, the borrower would enter into a swap with a counterparty whereby the borrower would agree to receive fixed rate in the currency of the financing (say, US$) and pay floating rate in its selected currency (say, A$) at a rate of say A$ BBR minus a margin per annum.
- Typically, following the first interest period at every interest rate reset date, the counterparty has the right to receive interest at *either* A$ BBR minus 200bps or US$ LIBOR minus 200bps.

The counterparty has a one time election to switch its interest receipts to US$ LIBOR. In the event that the counterparty elects to exercise this option, then it would be forced to receive US$ LIBOR for the remaining term of the swap. It is not able to switch from A$ to US$ and reverse the selection during the life of the loan.

This structure effectively embeds a A$ put/US$ call option into the currency swap. The borrower has written the A$ put/US$ call. In the event that the A$ declines in value relative to the US$, the swap counterparty will make an election under its swap to receive US$ thereby crystallising the foreign exchange gain. The premium due to the borrower for creating this option, is embedded into the swap structure by way of a lower margin under the relevant floating rate indexes.

A particular feature of this type of arrangement is that the option is very complex reflecting the fact that the amounts in both currencies are dependent on the relevant interest rates in A$ and US$. In essence, it is an option on an uncertain amount (often referred to as a quanto) and poses hedging problems similar to those identified in the context of index differential swaps: see above, Chapter 13.

A number of variations on this type of structure exist including arrangements whereby the swap counterparty has an independent and separate election as to the currency of its receipt *as at each interest rate reset date*. This merely means that the borrower is creating a series as distinct from a single option. In another variation, the borrower may grant the swap counterparty a "one-off" option to switch as at specified time during the life of the transaction, such as the first interest rate reset period (which is analogous to an option on a currency swap).

These types of structures were utilised to exploit, as discussed below in the context of dual coupon or currency indexed swaps (which are similar), to the natural currency portfolio positions of borrowers or investors with known cash inflows or outflows.

Dual coupon or currency indexed linked swaps

Exhibit 15.21 sets out an example of a dual coupon or currency indexed coupon swap.

The dual coupon swap structure (often also referred to as the currency indexed swap) is similar conceptually to the type of currency linked swap hybrid identified above. The dual coupon swap combines an interest rate swap with a strip of currency options whereby the interest rate is reduced in consideration for interest being paid either in the base currency or a nominated alternative currency at a predetermined exchange rate. The product utilises the currency option embedded in the coupons to lower the interest rate payable under the swap.

Exhibit 15.21

Currency Indexed Coupon Swap Transaction

Assume Company A (A) has A$100m of floating rate borrowings which it intends to swap into fixed rate for three years. The current three year A$ swap rate is 12.50% pa (quarterly). In order to lower the effective swap rate, A enters into a currency indexed coupon swap on the following terms:

Amount:	A$100m
Term:	Three years
Fixed Rate:	11.50% pa (quarterly)
FX Index:	0.7200—current spot

The swap effectively entails A writing a series of 12 A$ put/US$ call option with a strike price of A$1 = US$0.72 with expiry dates coinciding with the interest payment dates under the swap. In return for granting the currency options, the swap rate is reduced by 1.00% pa.

The swap operates as follows:

- The swap counterparty pays A$ BBR in A$ as under a conventional swap.
- The fixed rate payable by A under the swap is indexed in accordance with the FX index as described below.

The fixed rate payable is calculated as follows:

A$1 > US$0.72

As the A$ is higher than the strike price the option is not exercised.
A pays 11.50% pa on A$100m as under a normal swap.
A$100m × 0.1150 × 0.25 = A$2,875,000
A pay the A$2,875,000 in A$ normally.

A$1 < US$0.72

As the A$ is below the strike price, the option is exercised against A requiring it to purchase A$ and deliver US$ at the strike rate of 0.7200.

The payment amount is calculated as above:
A$100m × 0.1150 × 0.25 = A$2,875,000.

However, A must either:

- pay the US$ equivalent of A$2,875,000 at A$1.00 = US$0.72, that is US$2,070,000; or
- pay the A$ equivalent of US$2,070,00 the current exchange rate (say, A$1.00 = US$0.70), that is A$2,957,143.

This calculation must be done at each interest payment date.

The borrowing cost of A in A$ term is either 11.50% pa or higher if the A$ declines in value below the strike level. The Table below sets out the interest cost of A at varying A$/US$ exchange rate levels. As is evident, A gains when the exchange rate at each payment date averages above A$ = US$0.6600.

Where A has underlying US$ receivables and is a natural buyer of A$, it is likely that where the exchange rate is below the strike level, A will service the swap payments from its US$ receivables. This means that it is prepared to purchase A$ at US$0.72 and suffer any opportunity loss where the A$ declines below this level, trading off the exchange rate loss against the swap interest rate gain.

Where the option is not exercised, A would sell its US$ receivables at the prevailing exchange rate.

Currency Indexed Coupon Swap Transaction: Borrower's Interest Cost

Amount (A$):	100,000,000
Maturity:	3
Payment Frequency:	4
Swap Fixed Rate:	11.50%
Option Strike:	0.7200

Exhibit 15.21—continued

Exchange Rate (A$1 =)	Swap Fixed Rate Payment (A$)	(US$)	Effective Borrowing Cost	
0.7400	2,875,000	2,070,000	11.50%	11.50
0.7350	2,875,000	2,070,000	11.50%	11.50
0.7300	2,875,000	2,070,000	11.50%	11.50
0.7250	2,875,000	2,070,000	11.50%	11.50
0.7200	2,875,000	2,070,000	11.50%	11.50
0.7150	2,895,105	2,070,000	11.58%	11.58
0.7100	2,915,493	2,070,000	11.66%	11.66
0.7050	2,936,170	2,070,000	11.74%	11.74
0.7000	2,957,143	2,070,000	11.83%	11.83
0.6950	2,978,417	2,070,000	11.91%	11.91
0.6900	3,000,000	2,070,000	12.00%	12.00
0.6850	3,021,898	2,070,000	12.09%	12.09
0.6800	3,044,118	2,070,000	12.18%	12.18
0.6750	3,066,667	2,070,000	12.27%	12.27
0.6700	3,089,552	2,070,000	12.36%	12.36
0.6650	3,112,782	2,070,000	12.45%	12.45
0.6600	3,136,364	2,070,000	12.55%	12.55
0.6550	3,160,305	2,070,000	12.64%	12.64
0.6500	3,184,615	2,070,000	12.74%	12.74

CURRENCY INDEXED COUPON SWAP

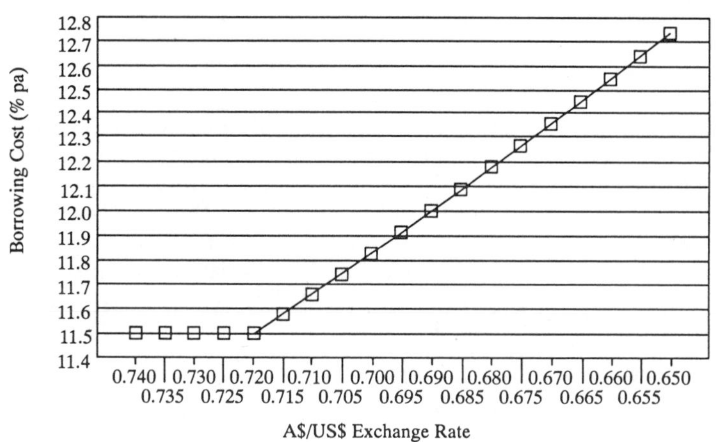

As with the contingent coupon currency swap structure, the dual coupon swap can be an effective management tool for borrowers or investors with currency exposures which can be utilised as the basis for the currency options created. For example, Australian companies with A$ debt and US$ receivables have been prolific users of this type of hybrid swap structure.

More complex currency linked swap hybrids

The range of currency linked swap hybrids that can be created is, effectively, infinite, constrained only by the requirements of borrowers and investors. Possible combinations include combinations of currencies, absolute and relative (that is, yield curve) interest rate as well as option elements entailing commodities and equities etc.

This type of innovation is best illustrated by the following example. A transaction which has been completed combines a conventional cross currency swap with a yield curve differential option. Under this transaction, a conventional cross currency swap is combined with an option which pays an agreed amount of, say, US$ for each basis point by which the difference between a set point on the GBP yield curve exceeds a set point on the US$ yield curve. The combination of the yield curve option with the cross currency swap allows the company entering into this transaction to improve the ongoing cash flow position generated by entering the swap (where the company is paying GBP/receiving US$—reflecting the substantial yield curve differential in favour of the GBP at the time of writing).

This type of transaction was utilised by a company with substantial net assets/equity in a GBP denominated asset which was, under current accounting standards, subject to variations in the US$/GBP exchange rate.

The company had entered into a conventional cross currency swap, where under if paid GBP, to hedge this balance sheet exposure. The combination of the swap and the option, in effect, enabled the potential benefit that can be derived from the event that GBP rates fall below US$ rates to be captured; effectively, foregoing the potential benefit of US$ rates exceeding GBP rates sometime during the life of the transaction.

This type of complex synthetic asset or liability structure created by a combination of currency and interest rate option and swap instrument reflects the requirement for complex hedging structures to match precisely particular portfolio requirements of borrowers and investors.

CROSS-MARKET DERIVATIVE STRUCTURES

The evolution of complex interest rate currency linked swap hybrids has provided the basis for development of a new class of hybrid instrument referred to as "cross-market derivatives". The key feature of cross-market derivatives is that the value of the instrument is dependent on the price of at least two financial variables.

The emergence of cross-market derivatives relates to the increasing focus on the correlation between various financial market variables, contingent hedging problems (that is, the relationship between the various financial exposures encountered by operating entities) as well as a desire by investors to capture "pure" returns (for example, capturing the return in an equity market outside its base currency without exposure to currency risk).

The major structural variations within cross-market derivatives relate to:

- assets which are related by demand substitution, such as European bonds or various types of substitutable commodities; or
- assets which are related via transformation potential, for example, the energy "crack" spreads as between crude oil and finished petroleum products.

The major types of cross-market derivatives to emerge include:

- products related to interest rate differentials between currencies;
- implicit interest rate spreads, such as options on forward foreign exchange premiums and discounts;
- commodity spreads, particularly "crack" or crude-product spreads in the oil market as well as spreads between various oil pricing indexes such as Brent, West Texas Intermediate, Tapis Crude spreads.

A variation relates to cross-market options not dissimilar to the more complex currency linked swap hybrids noted above. An example of this type of structure might entail options on currencies whose behaviour is dictated by movements in other markets. For example, a US$ call option which is triggered if US$/DEM six month interest rate spreads reach a particular level.

The major cross-market products in interest rate and currency markets have been instruments related to interest rate spreads as between currencies. The major example of this type of structure is index differential swaps: see the detailed discussion in Chapter 13. A variation on this structure, effectively providing the means for capturing interest differentials at the longer end of the yield curve as between two currencies, are spread differential warrants (refer *Exhibit 13.24*). Another example of a cross-market structure entailing interest rate differentials between currencies involves foreign exchange forwards, where the interest differential option is an implicit rather than explicit one.

A more direct example of this type of structure is set out in *Exhibit 15.22*, which illustrates an example of a currency option based on floating interest rates. An alternative structure (set out in *Exhibit 15.23*) links the rate of amortisation on a transaction to movements in currency rates (effectively creating a *currency linked* index amortising swap—described in Chapter 12).

Exhibit 15.22

Currency Options with Floating Interest Rate Structures

Concept and rationale

Companies when they undertake long-term currency forward or option transactions are not typically given a choice of fixed versus floating interest rates.

When a bank quotes a currency option to a client, it is based on the existing and fixed interest differential between the fixed rates in both currencies. It is feasible to modify the option structure and base the price on a floating interest rate.

When corporations enter into forward FX contracts for long tenors, such as par forwards, they may prefer to transact on the basis of a floating interest rate for one or both of the currencies.

Generally they do so because, either:

- they have a view on the direction of interest rates; or
- a floating rate provides a better hedge of their underlying exposure.

To create additional value on the currency option (that is, increasing the value of granted options, or decreasing the value of bought options) the client agrees to enter into an interest rate swap in that currency that has a strike price that is "in-the-money" from the bank's point of view; for example, the client will receive fixed US$ for three years at 4.00% pa when the market rate is 4.70% pa, against an expectation that the floating rate over the period of the swap will average below 4.00% pa.

The benefit from the in-the-money swap is converted to an equivalent adjustment to the option premium.

The structure yields maximum value where actual rates differ significantly from rates currently implied in the existing yield curve.

This is best illustrated by an example.

Example—an exporter

When hedging forward, the exporter receives A$ fixed rate, and pays US$ fixed rate. If exporter expects the A$ rates to be above the current fixed level, or US$ floating rates to be below their current fixed level, the company should float one or both of the currencies.

In a scenario of upward sloping yield curves and falling interest rates around the world, the rate on the pay side of the transaction should be floated. With rapidly rising rates the receiver side of the transaction should be floated.

Pricing: three year A$ call/US$ put

Client buys:

Spot 0.6640
Strike 0.6500
Premium (standard option): 4.3% of strike = US$430,000
Principal amounts at strike: US$10,000,000/A$15,384,615

Exhibit 15.22—continued

US$ swap amount: US$8.7 m @ 4.84% pa annual (on a present value basis)
Value at 4.00% pa annual fixed rate: US$179,000 (present value)
Premium (floating option): 2.60% of strike.

During the life of the transaction, the client will pay the floating rate (three monthly LIBOR, which is currently 3.50% pa) and receives the fixed rate of 4.00% pa.

The first rate set will result in a net settlement to the client of US$15,000 which is paid at the end of the first rate set period.

Similarly in subsequent periods there is a net settlement based on the US$ LIBOR rate compared to the strike rate. Provided that US$ LIBOR is no higher, on average, over life, than the strike rate, the client will retain the full benefit of the higher premium at inception.

Source: Citibank Australia.

Exhibit 15.23

Index Amortising Swap Structure Linked to Currency Value Movements

Assume a US company is a major exporter with strong foreign sales (in DEM). Growth in export sales has created increased working capital requirements which must be financed. The company seeks to borrow on a fixed rate basis in US$ to take advantage of low US$ interest rates. However, it seeks protection from a higher US$/DEM exchange rate which could reduce its export competitiveness and its foreign DEM sales thereby reducing its working capital funding requirement.

The company has two hedging options:

- It enters into a US$ interest rate swap which is callable; or
- It enters into an index amortisation swap (IAS) where amortisation is linked to the US$/DEM rate.

Under the first option, the position is as follows:

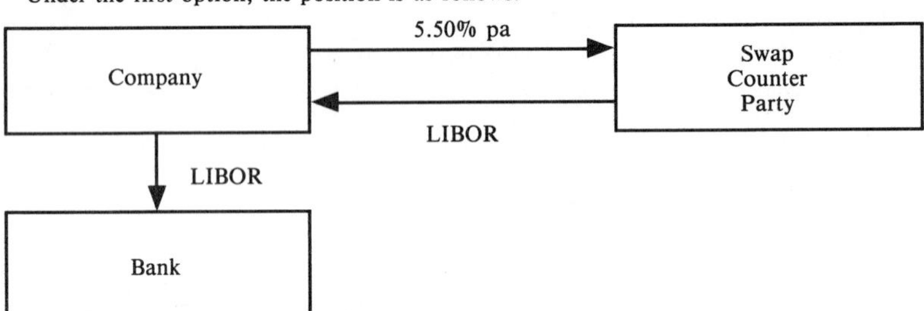

The swap is for five years and can be terminated at any time. However, the company may be incurring additional cost (the premium for the option on the swap) which may not be required.

Under the second option, the position is as follows:

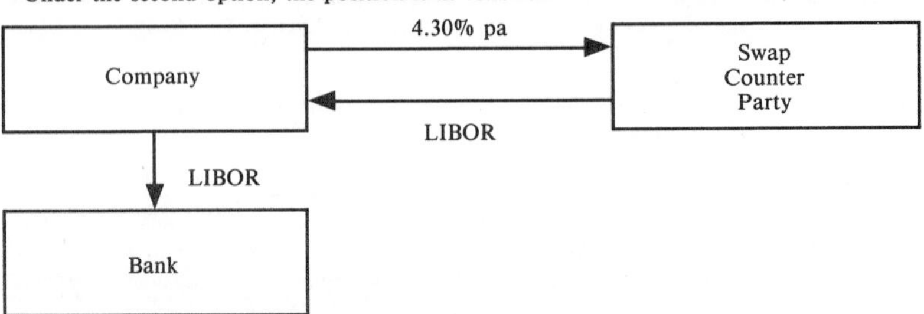

Exhibit 15.23—continued

The IAS swap would link amortisation of the principal amount of the swap to movements in the US$/DEM rate in accordance with the following schedule:

US$/DEM Spot Rate	Average Life of US$ Interest Rate Swap (Years)
2.1722	2
1.9833	3
1.8299	4
1.7000	5

As the US$ appreciates against the DEM, the US$ interest rate swap effectively shortens its life (the notional principal reduces) facilitating early repayment of the underlying loan. This structure provides the required hedging arrangement to offset the reduced need for working capital as a stronger currency reduces foreign sales revenue flows.

There are a number of examples of these structures being embedded in securities, linking the risk management transaction to the underlying financing. A good example of this type of structure involving Walt Disney is set out in *Exhibit 15.24*. While these examples deal with cross-market structures involving interest rates and currencies, more complex linkages involving commodities, equities and, ultimately, macro-economic variables are feasible (see Chapter 16).

Exhibit 15.24

Security Issue with Embedded Interest Rate/Currency Linkage

Walt Disney in 1992, under its US Securities and Exchange Commission Shelf Registration, issued US$36 of medium-term notes where the coupon payments of the notes were linked to the US$/GBP currency rate. The financing was in two tranches.

The notes, both principal and interest, are denominated in US$. The quarterly coupons, however, increase (decrease) where the GBP appreciates (depreciates) against the US$. The coupon has a cap and floor of 20% pa (if the GBP appreciates) and 4% pa (if the GBP depreciates). The notes entails a series of currency put and call option transactions which are effectively used to reduce the cost of financing (see the example of the currency indexed coupon swap in *Exhibit 15.21*). In this case, Walt Disney has undertaken the following options:

- a US$/GBP put option spread (buying a put near the prevailing exchange rate and selling another at a lower strike);
- a US$/GBP call option spread (selling a call at one strike rate and buying a call at a higher level).

The transaction combines a hedge of Walt Disney's GBP revenues and embeds the option premium benefit in the note coupon. If the GBP strengthens (weakens), then Disney's GBP revenues are higher (lower) in US$ terms effectively offsetting the increased (decreased) interest cost. It is rumoured that the company has used similar covered currency option embedded notes to hedge revenues denominated in FFR and JPY from overseas operations. The structure, combining the currency option and the note, may have been designed to achieve certain desired accounting outcomes.

Source: "Forex in Disneyland" (1993) (July) *Risk* Vol 6, No 7, pp 27-29.

The emergence of these cross-market derivative products is particularly exciting as it provides the basis for expansion of derivative activities into the area of correlation risk and its management. Correlation risk is relevant to products such as the cross-market products discussed in this section as well as currency protected structures such as quanto options (see discussion in Chapter 13). In addition, development of correlation risk approaches to hedging would be significant to the management of portfolios of interest rate, currency, commodity and equity derivatives (see discussion in Part 7).

Chapter 16

Commodity Swaps and Related Derivatives

INTRODUCTION

As noted in Chapter 1, swap techniques have been extended, in recent times, to entail a variety of transactions entailing commodity and equity markets. In this chapter, swaps and related derivatives linked to commodity price movements are examined.

The evolution of commodity linked swap transactions has occurred in two phases:

- In the first phase, commodity linked securities, whereby forward and/or option positions were embedded in the design of the debt security, were developed and special swap structures designed to securitise the derivative element were structured. These types of transactions were very similar to and based upon transactions securitising interest rate and foreign exchange derivative positions described in Chapter 15.
- In the succeeding phase, commodity swap transactions, entailing the creation of portfolios of forward contracts on commodity prices, developed. The development of commodity swaps as an over-the-counter forward contract on commodities paralleled the evolution of swap instruments as the over-the-counter equivalent to exchange traded futures and options on currencies and interest rate.

In addition to the above, a variety of commodity based derivatives, entailing options on commodity swaps and various combinations of forward and options on commodity prices, have also developed paralleling the proliferation of interest rate and currency based swap products.

Swaps and derivatives are available, increasingly, covering a wide variety of commodity types including crude oil and various refined oil products, gas, precious metals (gold, silver, and platinum), base metals (copper and aluminium) and a variety of agricultural products such as wheat. In addition, commodity swaps and derivatives have increasingly been extended to other products such as electricity.

A special type of commodity related swap transaction is macro-economic swaps. These transactions entail the hedging of business cycle risk or exposure to major macro-economic variables through derivatives which are close structurally to commodity swaps where the commodity is the relevant macro-economic index. An example of these structures is inflation swaps. In these transactions, the underlying commodity is a generalised price series (such as the US Consumer Price Index or Producer Price Index series, the UK Retail Price Index or the Australian Consumer Price Index series).

In this chapter, commodity linked securities and related swaps are considered in the following section. This is followed by an analysis of commodity swap transactions, with particular reference to pricing of commodity swaps. The final section examines the evolving market in macro-economic, particularly inflation, swap transactions.

COMMODITY LINKED SECURITIES AND RELATED SWAPS

Evolution of commodity linked derivatives

As noted above, commodity swaps and related derivatives evolved in response to the requirement to securitise commodity derivatives embedded in commodity linked security transactions.

Commodity linked bond transactions have been undertaken for a considerable period of time. During the inflationary period of the 1970s and early 1980s, a variety of commodity linked structures evolved in response to the demand for, effectively, price inflation linked securities. These types of investments were sought by investors seeking to protect the value of their investment capital *in real terms*. Amongst the earliest of these transactions were two issues undertaken in early 1980 by Sunshine Mining of the US which entailed the issue of US$25m of 8.5% coupon 15 year silver backed bonds. The bonds were to be redeemed at maturity at par or the market price of silver, whichever was higher. Each US$1,000 bond was redeemable either at par or the market price of 15 ounces of silver.

The attraction for the issuer was a relatively low nominal interest rate payable on the bonds (8.5% pa rather than the prevailing market interest rate of around 13-14% pa). The borrower absorbed the redemption risk of the issue. This reflected the fact that if the price of silver went up, thereby increasing the redemption price of the bonds, Sunshine Mining's revenues would have also appreciated reflecting the higher market value of its production. If, however, the price of silver stagnated or fell, the company would have borrowed money at a rate of interest substantially below market levels at the time of issue.

The Sunshine Mining issue is typical of the commodity linked bond transactions undertaken at this time. Other issues included an issue by Refinement International, in February 1981, entailing the issue of bonds indexed to the price of gold. Additional issues were undertaken by Barrick-Cullaton Gold Trust and a variety of small Australian gold miners. In a variation on this theme, the Mexican Government Agency, NAFINSA'S, issued bonds whose redemption price was linked to the price of Mexican crude oil.

The demand for commodity linked securities has primarily been driven by:

- investors seeking "inflation proof" investments in an attempt to preserve the purchasing power of their monetary assets;
- investors seeking "pure" commodity exposure;
- investors seeking exposure to commodities in a balanced portfolio where commodity assets are treated as a unique asset class;
- investors seeking to speculate on future price movements of the underlying commodity.

A factor in the demand for commodity linked security has also been the psychological element implicit in owning monetary assets supported by tangible commodities, which in some way is seen to safeguard future redemption of the bonds.

In contrast, issuers of commodity linked bonds were, originally, commodity producers or users motivated by the following reasons:

- Creating hedges against underlying commodity positions entailing the future sale or purchase of the relevant commodity.

- Commodity producers utilising the value of its commodity resources as the basis of raising capital to finance its extraction and production.
- Transfer potential profits or gains from appreciation or depreciation in the commodity price to investors in return for lower borrowing costs.

The original type of commodity linked bonds, which did not necessitate or involve commodity swaps or related derivatives, were based on matching investor demand and issuers with underlying positions in the relevant commodity. However, it rapidly became evident that demand for commodity linked securities out-stripped borrower interest in issuing such instruments. This necessitated the creation of *purely financial* commodity transactions which allowed issuers to offer investors the desired commodity exposure while simultaneously insulating themselves from the risk of commodity price movements through specially structured derivative transactions.

The central focus of these purely financial commodity transactions was arbitrage issuers (see discussion in Chapter 19) who were willing to undertake issues of commodity-linked transactions on the basis that their own commodity exposure was hedged by the swap counterparty. Central to this type of "new" commodity linked bond structure was the transference of specific forward or option positions in the underlying commodity via the swap structure from one segment of the capital market to another.

Types of commodity linked transactions

The various types of commodity linked securities and related swaps encompass the following categories:

- issues where the borrower accepts the commodity price risk;
- issues where the issuer's commodity price risk is transferred through the swap mechanism;
- issues of warrants or other options on the underlying commmodity price.

The first type of issue where the borrower accepts commodity risk is similar to those described above in the context of the evolution of commodity linked securities. A recent example of this type of structure was a series of issues undertaken in middle 1986 by the Standard Oil Company, the US arm of British Petroleum.

Under the structure, Standard Oil issued:

- US$300m 15 year, 6.3% coupon bonds priced at 74.7% of face value.
- Simultaneously, detachable oil indexed notes were issued as follows:
  —US$37.5m due December 1990; and
  —US$37.5m due March 1992.

The oil indexed notes have a strike price of US$25 per barrel (based on West Texas Intermediate Crude oil (WTI)). The oil indexed warrants were capped at a WTI market price of US$40 per barrel.

The result of the transaction is that Standard Oil borrows US$224.1m (being effectively the discounted proceeds of the US$300m face value bonds) at normal market rates. Simultaneously, it receives US$75m in return for the issue of the oil indexed notes (effectively call options on oil) to investors. This US$75m can be treated as reducing the cost of the 15 year bond issue or can be utilised to retire other debt.

For the investor in the oil index notes, if the WTI price is US$25 or below, the options will expire unexercised and the investor will receive the face value of the notes from Standard Oil. In the event that WTI is above US$25 per barrel, the investor will receive an indexed amount reflecting the appreciation in the oil price equating to the appreciation in the value of the call option.

From the perspective of Standard Oil, it achieves a lower cost of funding through the sale of the WTI call options. In the event that oil prices appreciate, its cost of borrowing increases reflecting the higher redemption payout under the oil indexed notes. However, this added borrowing cost should be offset by the increased revenue and earnings resulting from the higher oil price.

This type of structure does not, as noted above, require inclusion of a specially structured swap to securitise the commodity element in the issue or to insulate the issuer from commodity price risk.

The second type of commodity linked bond issue where the issuer is insulated from the commodity price movements is fundamentally different in the following respects:

- The issuer utilises the transaction as a means for generating lower cost funding in its desired currency (generally, at a nominated margin under US$ LIBOR). Accordingly, the issuer seeks complete insulation from the commodity price elements of the transaction which is shifted through the swap structure to the swap counterparty and ultimately to the commodity derivatives sector of the capital market.
- Unlike, the commodity linked bond structures described above, the *investor* absorbs the risk of the commodity price movement by either creating a forward or option on the relevant commodity *in favour of the issuer* of the security. The accompanying swap structure securitises this derivative element by selling it in another sector of the capital market. This effectively creates a lower cost borrowing for the issuer by arbitraging the price paid to the investor for the derivative element relative to the value obtainable for the forward or option on the commodity price in the capital market.

This type of transaction is best illustrated by example. *Exhibit 16.1* sets out a transaction undertaken by SEK where the redemption value of the bond is linked to the price of WTI crude. As described in detail in the Exhibit, the issue embodies a one year European style put option on WTI which is securitised through the accompanying swap structure allowing SEK to generate funding at a margin of around 60 to 70bps per annum under LIBOR.

Exhibit 16.1

Oil Indexed Bond Issue and Related Swap Structure

In April 1989, SEK undertook an issue of FUELS (an acronym for "Fixed US dollar Energy Linked Securities") through Salomon Brothers. The principal terms of the issue were as follows:

Amount:	US$100m.
Maturity:	1 year.
Coupon:	20% pa.
Issue Price:	100.875.
Commissions:	0.875%.
Redemption:	The redemption value of the bonds was linked to the following formula:
	— If the price of the oil index at maturity was greater than the redemption strike price of the oil index, then the redemption value is par.

Exhibit 16.1—continued

— If the price of the oil index is below the redemption strike price per barrel then the bondholder will receive less than par on his principal determined as below per US$1,000 bond:

$$1{,}000 \times \frac{\text{Reference Price}}{\text{Redemption Strike}}$$

For the purpose of the redemption formula:

Reference (Crude Type): West Texas Intermediate (WTI).

Redemption Strike Setting: The New York Mercantile Exchange Settlement Price per barrel on 19 April 1989 for the WTI light sweet crude oil futures contract for delivery during the month of June 1989, as quoted in the price source multiplied by a factor of 0.89. Approximately US$17.50.

Reference Price: The arithmetic average of New York Mercantile Exchange Settlement Prices for WTI light sweet crude oil futures contract for delivery during the month of June 1990, as quoted in the Price Source, for the three New York Mercantile trading days immediately preceding but excluding two days prior to the maturity date.

Price Source: The Wall Street Journal.

Settlement: Cash payment as per redemption formula above.

The redemption formula embodied a one year European style put option on WTI at a strike price of around US$17.50 per barrel. The put option was granted by the investor in favour of the issuer.

The issuer on sold the one year WTI European put to the arranger/swap counterparty—Salomon Brothers or its related entity Phibro Energy. The proceeds from the sale of the option allowing the issuer to reduce its costs below LIBOR.

The structure of the swap was as follows:

- The basic structure was that of a one year US$ interest rate swap.
- The swap counterparty pays 20% pa and receives US$ LIBOR minus a margin, quarterly or semi-annually.
- At maturity:
  - — If the reference price for WTI is above redemption strike price (US$17.50), then there are no cash flows under the swap and the issuer repays the bondholder the par value of the bonds.
  - — If the reference price for WTI is below redemption strike price (say, US$15.00), then the cash flows will be as follows:
    1. The issuer repays the bondholder in accordance with the redemption formula 85.714% of par calculated as follows:

       $1{,}000 \times (15.00/17.50) = 857.14$

       This is equivalent to US$85,714,286.
    2. The difference between par and the redemption value of US$14,285,714 is paid by the issuer to the swap counterparty representing the value of the option at maturity.

The volatility implicit in the embedded put option sold by the investor was estimated at around 23% pa. This compares to prevailing market levels for the volatility on comparable options of around 30% pa. This represents a difference in premium levels of approximately US$2.0-2.5m.

If the full benefit of this margin on the option is passed on by the swap counterparty to the issuer, SEK achieves a funding cost of around 8.30-8.80% pa, compared to one year LIBOR of 10.8125% pa. It is understood that SEK achieved funding of around 60-70bps under LIBOR.

Exhibit 16.2 sets out a similar transaction undertaken by SEK where the redemption price is linked to movements in the price of silver. In this structure, the investor enters into a forward position in silver to purchase a commodity at a price significantly above the effective forward price of silver prevailing in the over-the-counter or exchange traded market allowing SEK to generate attractively priced funding.

Exhibit 16.2

Silver Linked Bond Issue and Related Swap Structure

Structure of Commodity Linked Issue

The example outlined below is based on an issue undertaken by Svensk Export Kredit (SEK) named BISONs (Bull Index Silver Opportunity Notes). The terms of the commodity linked issue are summarised in *Table 1*.

TABLE 1

Terms of Commodity Linked Issue

Amount (US$):	100,000,000.
Term (Years):	1.
Coupon (% pa):	6.50%.
Redemption:	Amount × [1 + (SPM-4.46)/4.46)] Where: SPM = Silver Price (US$/ounce) at Maturity.
Swap Rate For Term (% pa):	6.78%.

Under the terms of the issue, the issuer undertakes for US$100.0m for one year. This borrowing carries a coupon of 6.5% pa.

The issue is structured to include a variable redemption feature whereby the redemption amount payable by the borrower is linked to movements in the price of silver. *Table 2* sets out the redemption payment to be made by the issuer to the investor based upon a range of market prices of silver at the maturity of the issue.

TABLE 2

Investors Return Profile

SPM	Redemption Amount (US$)	Redemption Amount (%)	Return (% pa)
1.46	32,735,426	32.7354%	−60.76%
1.96	43,946,188	43.9462%	−49.55%
2.46	55,156,951	55.1570%	−38.34%
2.96	66,367,713	66.3677%	−27.13%
3.46	77,578,475	77.5785%	−15.92%
3.96	88,789,238	88.7892%	−4.71%
4.46	100,000,000	100.0000%	6.50%
4.96	111,210,762	111.2108%	17.71%
5.46	122,421,525	122.4215%	28.92%
5.96	133,632,287	133.6323%	40.13%
6.46	144,843,049	144.8430%	51.34%
6.96	156,053,812	156.0538%	62.55%
7.46	167,264,574	167.2646%	73.76%
7.96	178,475,336	178.4753%	84.98%
8.46	189,686,099	189.6861%	96.19%

From the perspective of the investor, an investment in these notes combines two specific elements:

- investment in the US$100.0m debt instrument which pays 6.5% pa.
- a forward position in silver whereby the investor agrees to purchase (or is long) silver at US$4.46 per ounce for delivery at the maturity of the notes (that is, 1 year forward).

Consequently, the investor's return is linked to the prevailing price of silver at maturity. For example, the investor will only realise 6.5% pa (nominal return on the debt instrument) where the price of silver at maturity is US$4.46 per ounce. In the event that the price of silver is below the embedded forward price of US$4.46 per ounce, investor's return will be lower than 6.5% pa and, conversely, if the price of silver is above US$4.46 per ounce, the investor's return

Exhibit 16.2—continued

will be correspondingly higher. The rates of return accruing to the investor at varying closing prices of silver at maturity are summarised in *Table 2*.

Economics of the Transaction

The economics of the transaction derive, substantially, from the fact that the forward price embedded in the redemption structure is *above* the forward price prevailing for silver at the time of issue.

At the time of issue, the price of silver was as follows:

US$4.16 per ounce (spot)

US$4.40 per ounce (one year forward price based on one year Comex futures)

This "off-market" forward rate embedded in the security generates an arbitrage gain which forms the basis of the borrowing cost saving to the issuer and the profit to the intermediary arranging the transaction.

The amount of this arbitrage gain is US$1,345,291. This gain derives from the fact that the issuer (or the intermediary arranging the swap—see below) can "lock in" this US$0.06 difference in the forward prices. In order to achieve this, the party seeking to implement the hedge would purchase 22,421,525 ounces of silver (calculated as US$100.0m—US$4.46 per ounce) for delivery one year forward coinciding with the maturity of the notes. This transaction could be undertaken as an over-the-counter forward contract with a commodities dealer or, alternatively, as a futures transaction on Comex.

The issuer or the intermediary which is long silver in the forward market has a corresponding short position (at a forward price of US$4.46 per ounce) under the structure of the security (see detailed cash flow under the swap). This effectively locks in a gain of US$1,345,291 (being US$0.06 × 22,451,525 ounces).

The rationale for the investor purchasing silver forward at a rate some 1.36% above the actual forward price, which drives the arbitrage process, may be predicated on a number of factors:

- The investor may be a consumer or trader who anticipates having to purchase the relevant amount of silver in one year and wishes to create a hedge against its position in the underlying commodity.
- The investor anticipates a sharp recovery in silver prices and is willing to pay a premium for an instrument specifically structured to provide a return geared to this commodity outlook.

The US$ interest rate swap itself would typically be hedged using "strip" of Eurodollar futures contracts or FRAs.

Forward Silver Hedge

In additional to the US$ interest rate swap outlined above, the swap counterparty would enter into an agreement whereby it would cover the issuer's difference in cash flow between the actual amount borrowed (US$100.0m—the par value of the bonds) and the redemption amount calculated in accordance with the silver linked redemption formula.

These cash flows are more complex:

- In the event that the silver price at maturity of the notes is above the US$4.46 per ounce, then swap counterparty will make a payment to the issuer. The issuer, in turn, will repay to the investor the principal borrowed (US$100.0m) plus the redemption payment received from the swap counterparty. For example, if the silver price at maturity is equalled to US$4.96 per ounce, then the redemption value of the bonds will be US$111,210,762. The issuer will repay the US$100.0m received from the investor at the commencement of the transaction together with the US$11,210,762 received from the swap counterparty.
- In the event that the silver price at maturity is less than US$4.46 per ounce, then the issuer will repay the redemption amount of less than par (that is, less than US$100.0m) to the investor with the difference between the par value of the bond and the redemption amount being paid to the swap counterparty. For example, if the silver price at maturity is equal to US$3.96 per ounce, then the issuer will repay US$88,789,238 to the investor (in accordance with the redemption formula) and make a payment of US$11,210,762 to the swap counterparty.

These cash flows are set out in *Table 3*.

Exhibit 16.2—continued

TABLE 3

Swap Structure (Intermediary Perspective)

Case 1: Silver Price at Maturity Equal to US$4.46 per ounce

Dates	Days	Bond Cash Flows Interest	Bond Cash Flows Principal	Interest Rate Swap Payments	Interest Rate Swap Receipts	Redemption Payment	Forward Silver Hedge @ US$4.40/ounce	Net Cash Flow
1-Jun-92								
1-Sep-92	92							
1-Dec-92	91							
1-Mar-93	90							
31-May-93	91	6,500,000	100,000,000	(7,033,585)	7,033,585	0	1,345,291	1,345,291

Case 2: Silver Price at Maturity Equal to US$4.96 per ounce

Dates	Days	Bond Cash Flows Interest	Bond Cash Flows Principal	Interest Rate Swap Payments	Interest Rate Swap Receipts	Redemption Payment	Forward Silver Hedge @ US$4.40/ounce	Net Cash Flow
1-Jun-92								
1-Sep-92	92							
1-Dec-92	91							
1-Mar-93	90							
31-May-93	91	6,500,000	111,210,762	(7,033,585)	7,033,585	(11,210,762)	12,556,054	1,345,291

Case 3: Silver Price at Maturity Equal to US$3.96 per ounce

Dates	Days	Bond Cash Flows Interest	Bond Cash Flows Principal	Interest Rate Swap Payments	Interest Rate Swap Receipts	Redemption Payment	Forward Silver Hedge @ US$4.40/ounce	Net Cash Flow
1-Jun-92								
1-Sep-92	92							
1-Dec-92	91							
1-Mar-93	90							
31-May-93	91	6,500,000	88,789,238	(7,033,585)	7,033,585	11,210,762	(9,865,471)	1,345,291

Exhibit 16.2—continued

For the swap counterparty, the redemption cash flow payments are offset by its forward silver hedge whereby it has entered into a contract for the forward purchase of silver to match its position whereby it is selling silver forward to the issuer to cover the embedded forward silver contract in the commodity linked security. The overall position is summarised in the diagram below.

Commodity Linked Swap Structure

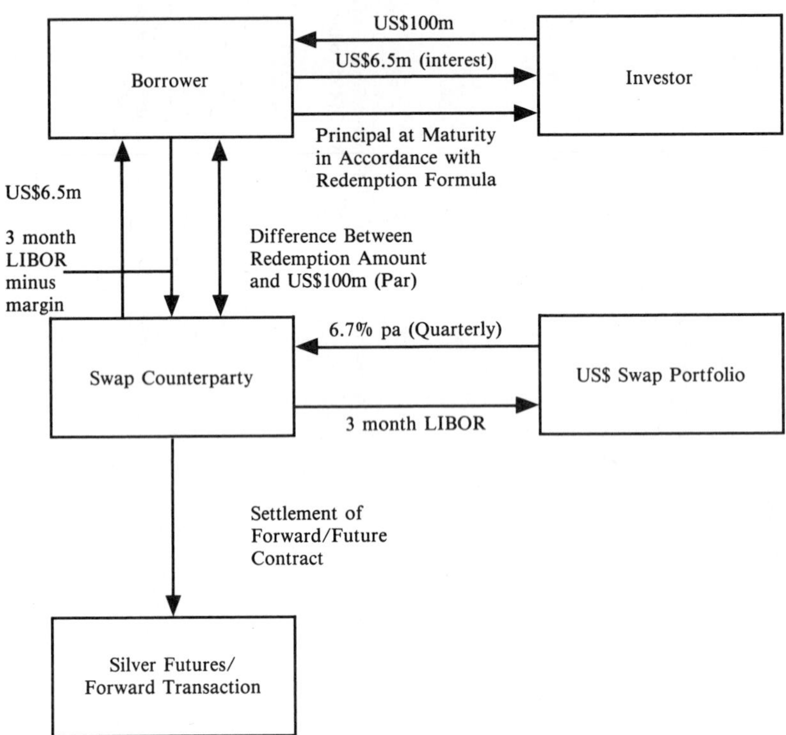

Arbitrage gain

The US$0.06 per ounce difference between the forward price achieved by the swap counterparty in its forward/futures hedge relative to a forward price embedded in the security and corresponding swap will result in a net gain to the swap counterparty. This gain (refer the diagram above) will reflect the net cashflow difference between the gain on the futures hedge position and the payment to be made to the issuer *or* the payment received from the issuer relative to the loss under the futures hedge.

This arbitrage gain is available for the following purposes:

- profit to the swap counterparty;
- to further lower the interest cost of the issuer;
- in practice, this arbitrage gain would be shared between swap counterparty and the issuer.

Assuming an equal share between the swap counterparty and the issuer (that is, US$672,645 each), the issuer's cost of funds from this transaction can be reduced by an additional approximately 66.34bps pa. This would result in the borrower achieving a borrowing cost in the vicinity of three month US$ LIBOR less 1.19% pa.

Commodity linked bonds where the issuer is totally insulated from the commodity price risk and the investor creates a derivative position in the commodity are now the predominant type of commodity-linked bonds utilised. Issues of these types have been undertaken from time to time in recent years. Issuance activity has tended to be spasmodic.

The earliest issues of this type were undertaken in the Swiss franc capital market in middle 1987 with a number of issues of Swiss franc notes with attached oil warrants being completed. The second phase of issuance of these types of securities was in middle 1989 with a substantial number of issues denominated in US$ linked to oil prices being completed.

In subsequent periods, sporadic issuance of notes with embedded commodity elements (covering a wide variety of commodities) has been undertaken. Increasingly, as described in more detail in Chapter 19, issuance of these types of structured securities is undertaken in the form of private placements within the continuously offered format of Medium Term Note programmes to satisfy specific investor requirements.

In addition, a number of syndicated loan transactions for less developed countries (such as Algeria and China) have been undertaken. Commodity, primarily oil, options have been utilised to reduce the margin on these syndicated loan transactions.

The final type of commodity linked security transaction has been the issue of warrants on the price of a variety of commodities, primarily energy commodities. These issues of warrants have been structured as either naked warrants or warrants issued in conjunction with debt.

In a number of cases, the issue of warrants linked to debt has been in transactions designed to take advantage of substantial spreads between retail and wholesale market prices for commodity options (the transaction structures are similar to those described in Chapter 15: refer *Exhibit 15.1*).

Where stand-alone options are issued, there is typically no accompanying swap required to insulate the issuer or to securitise the option element provided. In general, the issuer of these warrants has been a financial institution seeking to satisfy investor demand for instruments sensitive to commodity price movements. The financial institutions have hedged their own exposure under the derivative transactions by purchasing offsetting instruments in the wholesale market or by undertaking synthetic option hedging transactions: see discussion in Chapter 36.

COMMODITY SWAPS

Commodity swaps have evolved parallel to the transaction structures entailing the use of hybrid swaps to securitise commodity derivative elements embedded in securities. The development of commodity swaps, which are essentially over-the-counter forward contracts on the relevant commodity, have developed in response to increased awareness of commodity price risk management and as an adjunct to exchange traded futures and options markets in particular commodities, particularly oil and related energy products.

Commodity swaps—structure and mechanics

Commodity swap is a term utilised to refer to a special class of financial exchange transactions in which counterparties agree to exchange cash flows related to commodity prices with the objective of managing commodity price risks. The term "commodity swap" is utilised, typically, to cover a wide range of transaction structures, including: fixed-for-floating commodity price swaps, commodity price-for-interest swaps, and extensions thereof.

There are two basic types of commodity swaps:

- a fixed-for-floating commodity price swap;
- commodity price-for-interest swap.

The majority of activity relates to fixed-for-floating commodity price swaps. There are also a number of variations on these generic structures.

In addition, a substantial market in over-the-counter (OTC) options on commodities also exists, including commodity price caps, floors and other derivative products.

Fixed-for-floating commodity price swap

A fixed-for-floating commodity price swap is an agreement whereby an end user (producer) fixes the purchase (sale) price of its commodity relative to an agreed established market pricing benchmark for the commodity for an agreed (usually extended) period of time.

This type of agreement is used to fix the price of the commodity from both the perspective of the producer and user.

Exhibit 16.3 sets out in diagrammatic form the basic structure of a fixed-for-floating commodity price swap. In the example set out the commodity utilised is oil. *Exhibit 16.4* sets out the underlying transaction cash flows.

Exhibit 16.3

Fixed-for-Floating Oil Price Swap—Structure

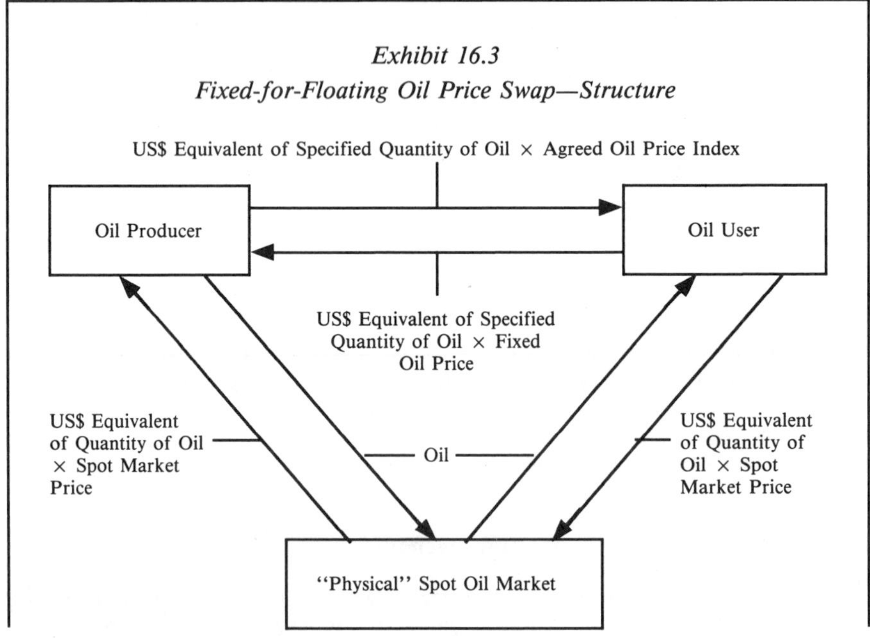

Exhibit 16.3—continued

"Hypothetical" Terms

The terms of the above swap are:
Specified Quantity of Oil — 6,000,000
Agreed Fixed Price Index — US$25.00/barrel
Agreed Oil Price Index — WTI Crude Oil
Term — Three years
Settlement Basis — Cash settlement based on spot WTI price semi-annually

Exhibit 16.4
Fixed-for-Floating Oil Price Swap—Cash Flows

Oil Producer

Year	WTI Price (US$1 Barrel)	Amount Received (US$) From Spot Oil Transaction	Commodity Swap Receipts (US$)	Commodity Swap Payments (US$)	Net Cash Flow
0.5	WTI	+ [1m × WTI]	+ [1m × US$25]	− [1m × WTI]	+ [1m × US$25m]
1.0	WTI	+ [1m × WTI]	+ [1m × US$25]	− [1m × WTI]	+ [1m × US$25m]
1.5	WTI	+ [1m × WTI]	+ [1m × US$25]	− [1m × WTI]	+ [1m × US$25m]
2.0	WTI	+ [1m × WTI]	+ [1m × US$25]	− [1m × WTI]	+ [1m × US$25m]
2.5	WTI	+ [1m × WTI]	+ [1m × US$25]	− [1m × WTI]	+ [1m × US$25m]
3.0	WTI	+ [1m × WTI]	+ [1m × US$25]	− [1m × WTI]	+ [1m × US$25m]

Oil User

Year	WTI Price (US$1 Barrel)	Amount Paid For Spot Oil Transaction (US$)	Commodity Swap Receipts (US$)	Commodity Swap Payments (US$)	Net Cash Flow (US$)
0.5	WTI	− [1m × WTI]	+ [1m × WTI]	− [1m × US$25]	− [1m × US$25]
1.0	WTI	− [1m × WTI]	+ [1m × WTI]	− [1m × US$25]	− [1m × US$25]
1.5	WTI	− [1m × WTI]	+ [1m × WTI]	− [1m × US$25]	− [1m × US$25]
2.0	WTI	− [1m × WTI]	+ [1m × WTI]	− [1m × US$25]	− [1m × US$25]
2.5	WTI	− [1m × WTI]	+ [1m × WTI]	− [1m × US$25]	− [1m × US$25]
3.0	WTI	− [1m × WTI]	+ [1m × WTI]	− [1m × US$25]	− [1m × US$25]

Notes

1. Positive signs refer to cash inflows; negative signs refer to cash outflows.
2. WTI is the spot price (US$/barrel) for WTI crude at the specific point of time ie WTI price at year 0.5 etc (typically, an average of the price over the period would be utilised).
3. The oil producer is assumed to undertake a spot transaction selling 1m barrels of oil at six monthly intervals at the prevailing WTI spot market price.
4. The oil user is assumed to purchase 1m barrels of oil at six monthly intervals at the prevailing WTI spot market price.
5. The commodity swaps flows are calculated with reference to the terms specified in *Exhibit 1* whereby: the Oil Producer (User) pays (receives) the US$ equivalent of 1m barrels at the WTI crude price (the agreed price index) against receipt (payment) of the US$ equivalent of 1m barrels at US$25/barrel (the agreed fixed price).
6. The net cash flows are the accumulation of the various cash flows incurred at that specific point of time.

In the example, in order to manage its exposure to oil price fluctuations, an oil producer enters into an oil price swap to "lock in" a fixed price for WTI crude oil. The opposite side of this oil price swap is taken by an oil user who seeks, similarly, to lock-in a fixed price for its oil purchases over an identical period.

Under the terms of the oil price swap, the oil producer and oil user agree to exchange cash flows (typically denominated in US$) whereby the oil producer receives US$25 per barrel on 1,000,000 barrels and agrees to pay its counterparty the floating oil price index (agreed to be the WTI Price Index) on an identical number of barrels. The counterparties agree that settlement will be on a cash basis based on spot WTI prices on a semi-annual basis.

As set out in *Exhibit 16.4*, the transaction effectively allows both the oil producer and oil user to lock in a price of US$25 per barrel on 1,000,000 million barrels of oil priced off the WTI Index every six months (or 2,000,000 annual production or purchase).

Under the terms of the swap, both the oil producer and the oil user continue to operate normally in the spot oil market. For example, the oil producer continues to produce oil normally and sell it into the spot oil physical market *at current market prices*. In this example, it is assumed these sales take place at six monthly intervals (a swap can be tailored to cover gradual sales over the six month period by utilising an average settlement mechanism—see below). Similarly, the oil user continues to purchase its oil requirement from the spot market at prevailing market prices. However, the US$ receipts and payments under the oil price swap has the effect of fixing the purchase or sale price of oil to allow both producer and user to achieve guaranteed prices.

Exhibit 16.5 sets out the actual settlement mechanics on one specific settlement date. The settlement mechanism allows both producer and user to achieve a guaranteed price, as agreed, of US$25/barrel. The final price achieved by producer and user is subject to basis risk (see discussion below) depending on the degree of correspondence between the hedge or commodity swap index used and the pricing basis of the physical market transaction.

A number of essential features of the fixed-for-floating commodity price swap structure should be noted:

- The commodity price swap is purely financial, that is, there is no physical exchange of commodities between the counterparties. The transaction assumes that both parties continue to operate in the spot market for the commodity normally to purchase or sell the required amount of oil or other commodity being swapped. The commodity price swap itself is totally independent of these underlying physical transactions and the purchaser or seller in the spot transaction does not enter into contractual relationships with the commodity swap counterparty and, in fact, would not necessarily be aware that the commodity swap had been undertaken.
- The financial nature of the transaction allows the "decoupling" of the acquisition or sale of the commodity with the setting of the effective price at which the transaction is undertaken (at least, after the commodity swap payments are factored into the overall transaction). This unbundling of the price setting and the physical transactions has advantages and disadvantages. A major advantage is the ability to time pricing decisions to exploit market cycles in a manner which is both flexible and retains confidentiality from physical suppliers. The major disadvantage is that the price at which the physical transaction is undertaken is assumed to be identical to the level of the agreed commodity price index against which settlement is determined (this problem of basis risk is discussed below).

Exhibit 16.5
Fixed-for-Floating Oil Price Swap—Settlement Mechanics

Assume that on the first settlement date of the transaction set out in *Exhibits 1* and *2*, the Agreed Oil Price Index (WTI Crude) is above (US$26.55) or below (US$17.37) the fixed price agreed. The net settlement amount would be calculated as follows:

Case	(1)	(2)
WTI Price (US$/barrel):	26.55	17.37
US$ Equivalent of 1,000,000 barrels at US$25/Barrel (US$)	25,000,000	25,000,000
US$ Equivalent of 1,000,000 barrels at current WTI Price (US$)	26,550,000	17,370,000
Net Settlement Amount	(1,550,000)	7,630,000

In Case (1) (where the WTI index is above the agreed fixed price) the oil producer pays the net settlement sum of US$1,550,000 to the oil user. In Case (2) (where the WTI index is below the agreed fixed price), the oil producer receives from the oil user the net settlement sum of US$7,630,000.

The impact of the settlement payments on the total overall position of the counterparties is summarised below:

Case	(1)	(2)
WTI Price (US$/barrel):	26.55	17.37
Oil Producer	*US$*	*US$*
Physical Transaction (US$ proceeds of sale of 1m barrels at *current* WTI price):	26,550,000	17,370,000
Oil Price Swap Settlement:	(1,550,000)	7,630,000
Net Receipt:	25,000,000	25,000,000
Net Effect: Oil Producer Receives	US$25/barrel	US$25/barrel
Oil User		
Physical Transaction (US$ cost of purchase of 1m barrel at *current* WTI price)	(26,550,000)	(17,370,000)
Oil Price Swap Settlement:	1,550,000	(7,630,000)
Net Payment	(25,000,000)	(25,000,000)
Net Effect: Oil User Pays	US$25/barrel	US$25/barrel

- The financial settlement undertaken is on a net basis only. The amounts owed to and from each counterparty are netted as at each settlement date with the party owing the greater amount paying the difference to the other party. There are no intermediate cash flows and the commodity price swap would not generally be subject to any margin or mark-to-market requirement.

The commodity price swap structure requires the counterparties to agree *precisely* on several aspects of the transaction including:

- *Quantity/quality*

  A specified quantity of the relevant commodity would be agreed to by the counterparties. For example, in the case above, the oil user wishes to hedge against price movements on 1,000,000 barrels every six months for three years (a total of 6,000,000 barrels over the period). This requirement could be structured in a number of ways such as a 2,000,000 barrel oil price swap settling *annually*; (the actual transaction described) an oil price swap for 1,000,000 barrels settling semi-annually; or, an oil price swap for 500,000 barrels settling quarterly.

The commodity will also need to be defined with great precision (for example, closing level of the WTI near month contract on the New York Mercantile Exchange (NYMEX)) as the value/price of the product may vary significantly depending on its specifications.

- *Term*

  The term of the transaction needs to be agreed between the counterparties.

- *Commodity Price Index*

  The settlement payment associated with the commodity price swap is based typically, on an agreed price index. This can be a closing futures price, an actual physical selling price, or an established price index.

  For example, for a typical oil swap, a suitable index might be the NYMEX light sweet WTI crude oil price, the Brent price (for North Sea oil), or other product price indices such as heating oil, jet fuel, naphtha etc for which there is not an established futures market but which are routinely traded and reported in industry journals such as Platts Oilgram.

  Major considerations in nominating the index include: it should be readily available; it should reflect a fair basis (that is, it corresponds closely to actual physical commodity transactions to be taken by the producer or user); and it is fair/impartial and not readily capable of artificial manipulation.

  This agreed price index is used to calculate the "floating" price under a fixed-for-floating commodity price swap.

- *Settlement methods*

  Settlement can be effected against the agreed commodity price index on a specific day or, alternatively, against *an average of the index for each trading day during the settlement period* (in the above example, the six month period). Under the averaging process, at the end of the period, the floating price for the settlement calculation would be derived from the simple arithmetic average of all the closing prices for each business day during the period.

  The averaging method is utilised for a number of reasons including:

  — producers and users particularly seek to match the swap with the underlying physical transactions which are likely to be undertaken *over the settlement period*, rather than at a spot date. This means that the average settlement price method would provide a better hedge than a one day settlement price.

  — the averaging method is more likely to reflect actual movements in crude oil prices during the period than taking the spot price at the end of the period as it reduces the impact of short term "spikes" in commodity prices and also lessens the impact of any temporary market distortions which may occur.

- *Miscellaneous requirements*

  In a number of jurisdictions, regulatory requirements may necessitate a maximum and/or minimum level of the agreed commodity price index to be nominated to place a maximum on the size of the settlement amount which might be payable under the transaction. In practice, these "cap" and "floor" prices are set some distance away from the agreed fixed prices. While legally necessary, these cap/floor prices are rarely economically significant.

The structure depicted details a commodity producer and user directly contracting with each other to guarantee the commodity price for the purchase and sale transaction. Such a structure would require each party to accept the credit exposure on the transaction of its counterparty.

In practice, most transactions utilise an intermediary, usually a bank or other financial institution such as a commodity trading house, with each counterparty separately contracting with the intermediary

This contractual structure, as with other derivative products, is designed to ensure confidentiality, insulation of the counterparties from counterparty credit risk as well as eliminating, where the intermediary agrees, the need for exact matching of the two legs of the commodity price swap. The separation of the contractual obligations enables transactions involving different amounts and a number of parties with different needs to be matched. The insertion of the intermediary also allows economies of scale and price advantages to be generated as well as allowing additional flexibility in respect of early termination.

Commodity price-for-interest swap

The commodity price-for-interest swap is a variation on the commodity price swap structure. Under a commodity price-for-interest swap, a commodity producer and a commodity user agreed to exchange a fixed amount of the specified commodity for floating rate (usually related to US$ LIBOR) payments.

The primary objective of the commodity price-for-interest swap is as follows:

- The commodity producer obtains protection from increases in its financing cost relative to commodity prices for its product; that is, the structure directly hedges its natural position of being "long" the commodity and "short" interest expense/rates.
- The commodity user locks in the price of its commodity purchases on a long term basis.

Exhibit 16.6 sets out the structure of a typical commodity price-for-interest swap. *Exhibit 16.7* sets out the detailed cash flows of an oil price-for-interest swap transaction.

Exhibit 16.6

Commodity Price-for-Interest Swap: Structure

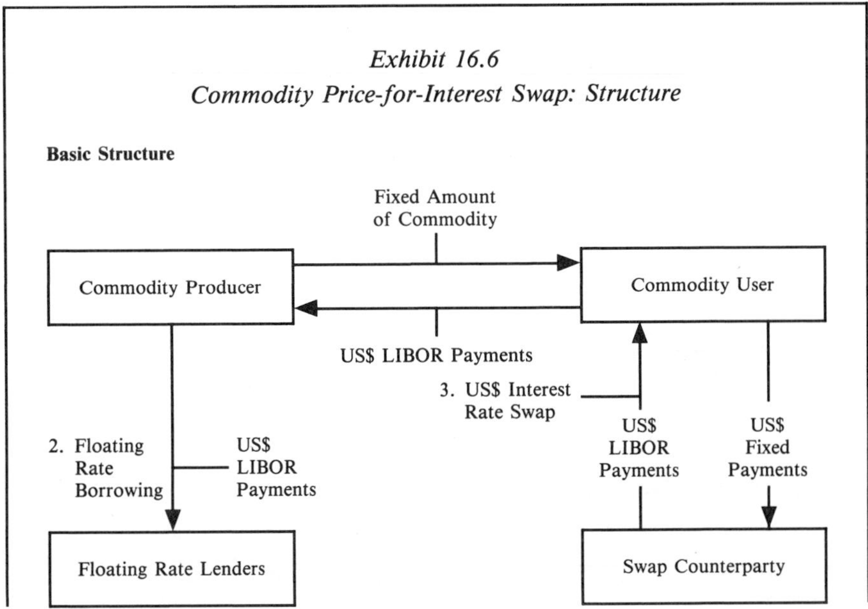

Exhibit 16.6—continued

The transaction is made up of three distinct components:

1. *A Commodity Price-for-Interest Swap*—whereby the commodity producer agrees to pay to the commodity user a fixed amount of a specified commodity in exchange for receiving US$ LIBOR payments on an agreed notional principal amount.
2. *A Floating Rate Borrowing*—whereby the commodity producer undertakes a US$ LIBOR floating rate borrowing to finance its production of the commodity.
3. *A US$ Interest Rate Swap*—whereby the commodity user enters into a US$ interest rate swap to lock in the fixed US$ cost of its commodity forward purchase.

Commodity Price-for-Interest Swap Using Notional Commodity Flows

It is common to structure commodity swaps in terms of notional flows rather than actual physical commodity flows. Under this structure (set out below), the specified fixed amount of the commodity is substituted with a notional amount (calculated as the US$ equivalent of Agreed Commodity Volume at the Agreed Price Index for the Commodity. In addition, both parties are required to undertake physical transactions.

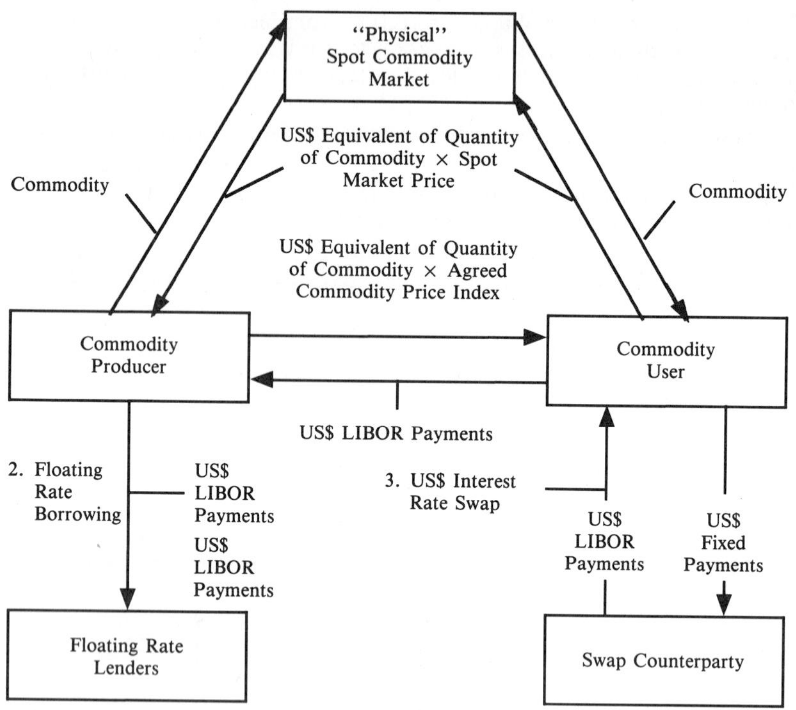

Commodity Price-for-Interest Swap Intermediated Structure

In practice, the commodity price-for-interest rate swap would be "unbundled" into a series of separate transactions: see below. A primary factor dictating such unbundling is the fact that from the viewpoint of the commodity user, the transaction is identical to a fixed-for-floating commodity price swap.

Exhibit 16.6—continued

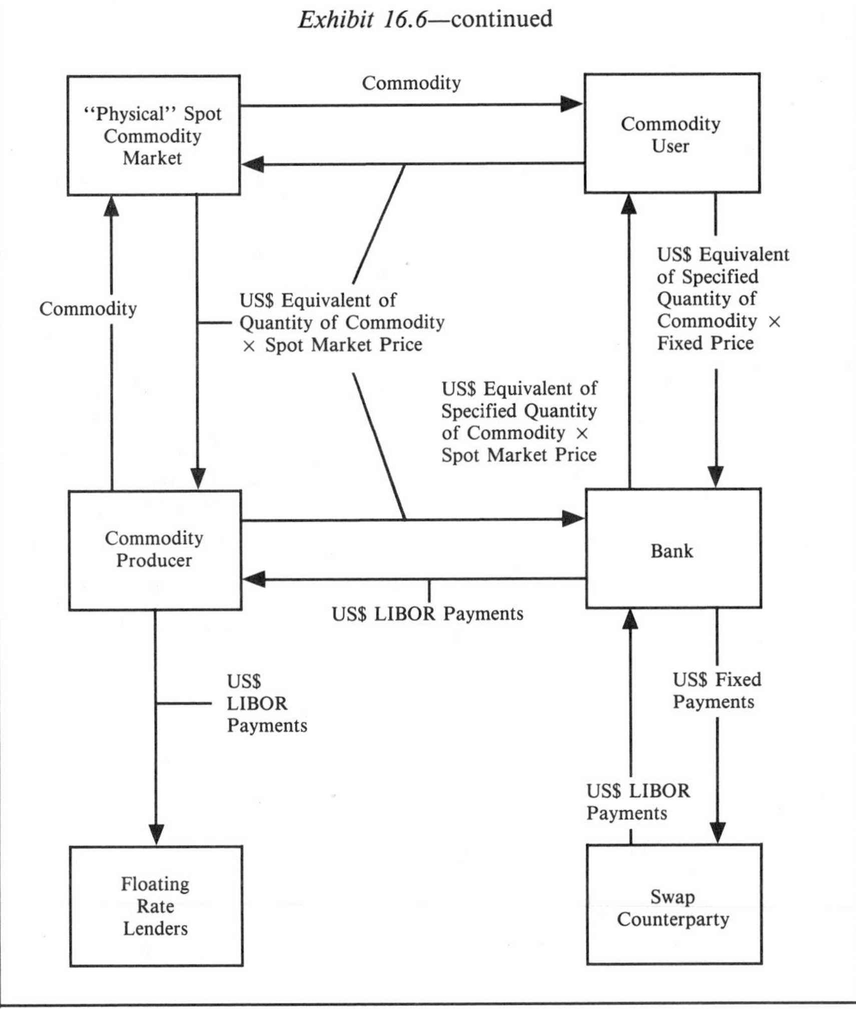

Exhibit 16.7
Commodity Price-for-Interest Swap: Example

1. *The Transaction*

Assume the following parameters for an oil/interest rate commodity price-for-interest swap:

Annual Fixed Amount of Oil:	1,000,000 barrels
Fixed Price of Oil:	US$25/barrel
Term:	Two years
Settlement:	semi-annual settlements
Fixed US$ Interest Rate Swap Rate (for two year maturity):	8.5% pa (semi-annual)
Current Six Month LIBOR:	8.25% pa

Exhibit 16.7—continued

Notional Principal Amount For Transaction:	[fixed amount of oil × fixed price] divided by two year swap rate = [1m × US$25]/0.0850 = US$294,117,647

2. *Implied Cash Flows at Commencement*

This implies initial semi-annual (the selected settlement period) cash flows as at the date the transaction is entered into as follows:

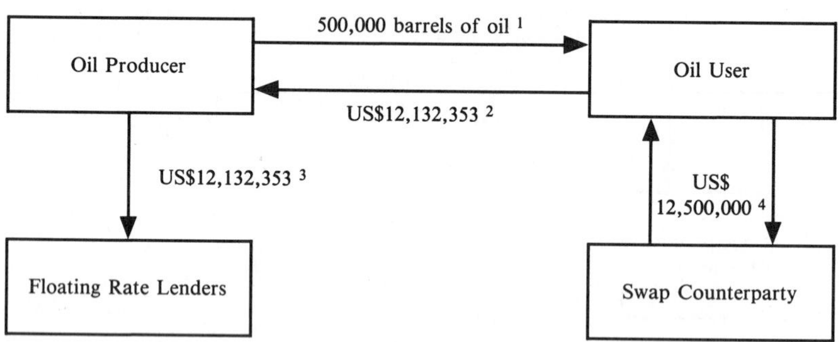

3. *Settlement Cash Flows* [5]

If US$ LIBOR increases to 10% pa:

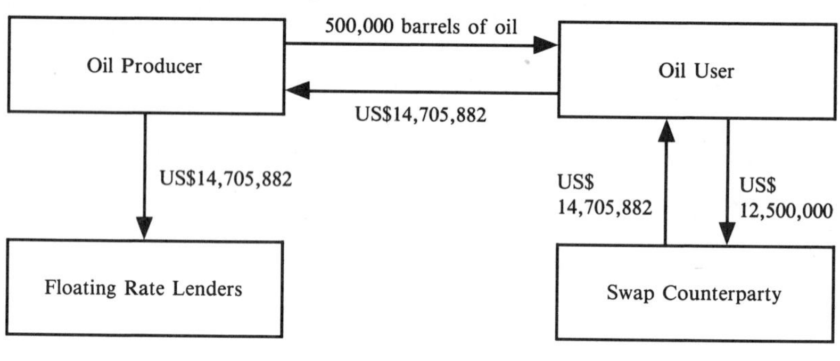

If US$ LIBOR falls to 6% pa: [5]

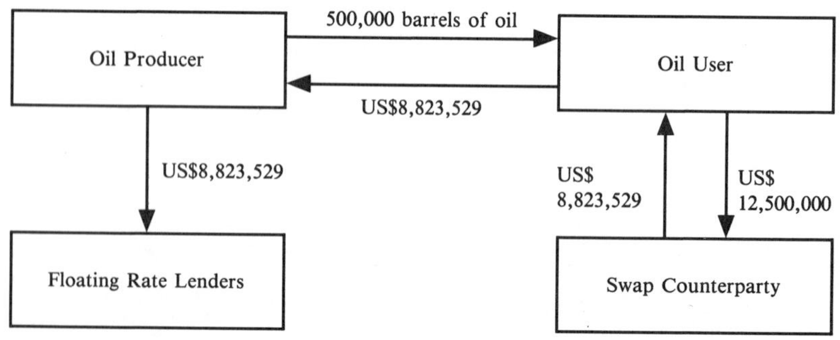

Exhibit 16.7—continued

Notes:

1. The semi-annual equivalent of the 1,000,000 barrels pa agreed to be delivered.
2. Calculated as US$294,117,647 (the Notional Principal Amount) at 8.25% (six month LIBOR) for six months.
3. Calculation is same as 2 and assumed to be the LIBOR payments on debt incurred by the oil producers (please note that is a notional calculation and does not in any way imply that the oil producer borrowed the notional principal amount to finance the production of the agreed amount of oil).
4. Calculated as US$294,117,647 (the notional principal amount) at 8.50% pa (the two year fixed rate) for six months.
5. All calculations are as in the implied cash flows at commencement except six months US$ LIBOR rates are reset at the assumed higher and lower level.

The analysis of the commodity price-for-interest swap is complex:

- In the example (refer *Exhibit 16.7*), the commodity user has effectively locked in a price 1,000,000 barrels of oil per annum for a period of two years at an agreed price of US$25 per barrel. This guaranteed rate is achieved as follows:

	*Physical Commodity***	*US$ Flows*
1. Oil Price-For-Interest	+0.5M barrels	−LIBOR (US$12,132,353)*
2. Interest Rate Swap		
Fixed Rate—		−8.50% (US$12,500,000)
Floating Rate—		+LIBOR (US$12,132,353)
	+0.5M barrels	−US$12,500,000

Net effect: oil user pays US$25/barrel

* Based on implied cash flows at commencement

** Likely to be a dollar amount based on 0.5m barrels × prevailing commodity price

Under the structure, irrespective of the level of US$ LIBOR, the oil user is guaranteed a price of US$25 per barrel.

- From the perspective of the oil producer, the commodity price-for-interest swap is more complex. The oil producer has converted its floating rate US$ denominated debt into effectively *commodity denominated borrowings*. It has synthesised a commodity loan notionally selling forward its production to service its debt. A structure entailing the amortisation of principal is also feasible.

  The payments received by the commodity producer under the swap are utilised to service its US$ denominated floating rate borrowings. If interest rates rise, then payments received under the price-for-interest swaps increases and would presumably offset the higher interest payments incurred by the commodity producer on its floating rate borrowings. The converse would occur if interest rates fell.

  The commodity producer's revenue stream is now variable, being a function of interest rates (US$ LIBOR related). The producer effectively makes debt payments using a commodity rather than US$. The commodity producer is now immunised against variations in US$ interest rates but risks opportunity losses if commodity prices exceed those implied in the swap. The difficulty lies in relating the amount/payments under the swap to the underlying level of borrowings, production costs, etc which would determine the total profitability of the producer.

The structure may have additional advantages in that where actual physical delivery of the commodity is required, the commodity user may be attracted to the transaction as it can gain assurance of obtaining fixed amounts of raw material on a long-term basis at guaranteed prices. Conversely, the commodity producer may be attracted to this particular structure because of the capacity to link its debt service to the production and delivery of its own commodity allowing it to benefit from increased certainty in terms of management of currency exposures, management of its debt portfolio, particularly its debt repayment schedule and planning of production. However, where physical delivery is not of special interest to the counterparties, these advantages can be retained in a notional swap structure together with flexibility of supply.

Despite its intellectual elegance and practical utility, commodity price-for-interest swaps are not as common as fixed-for-floating commodity swaps.

Pricing of commodity swaps

Commodity swaps as a portfolio of forward contracts

The pricing of derivative instruments is based on the ability to decompose all derivative products into a number of basic instruments (forwards or futures contracts and/or option contracts) for which well developed pricing methodologies exist. The pricing of commodity swaps is based on the essential insight that a commodity swap transaction (particularly, a commodity fixed-for-floating swap) can be decomposed into a portfolio of forward contracts on the commodity.

For example, in the case referred to in *Exhibit 16.3*, the oil producer (user) enters into a *series* of forward contracts to sell (buy) an agreed quantity of oil at a fixed price. The oil producer agrees to sell one million barrels of oil every six months at an agreed price of US$25 per barrel. Conversely, the oil user agrees to purchase one million barrels of oil every six months at a price of US$25 per barrel. Essentially, the oil producer and oil user have entered into six forward contracts with maturities between six months and three years to undertake forward purchases and sales of oil.

The basic concept of a commodity swap as a forward purchase or sale contract may require some minor variations depending upon the terms of the transaction itself. For example, where the settlement mechanism under the commodity swap requires the floating oil price to be the average for the preceding six months, the commodity swap must be decomposed into a series of *daily* forward contracts, (not six monthly forward contracts) to derive the appropriate pricing.

Based on the intuition that a commodity swap consists of a portfolio of forward purchase or sale contracts, a pricing model for this type of transaction can be developed. *Exhibit 16.8* sets out a conceptual model for the pricing of fixed-for-floating commodity swaps.

Forward price determination

The "pure" forward price of commodity is usually determined in accordance with an arbitrage-based forward pricing model (this is similar to the theory of pricing forward interest rates discussed in Chapter 10).

Exhibit 16.8
Commodity Swaps—Pricing Model

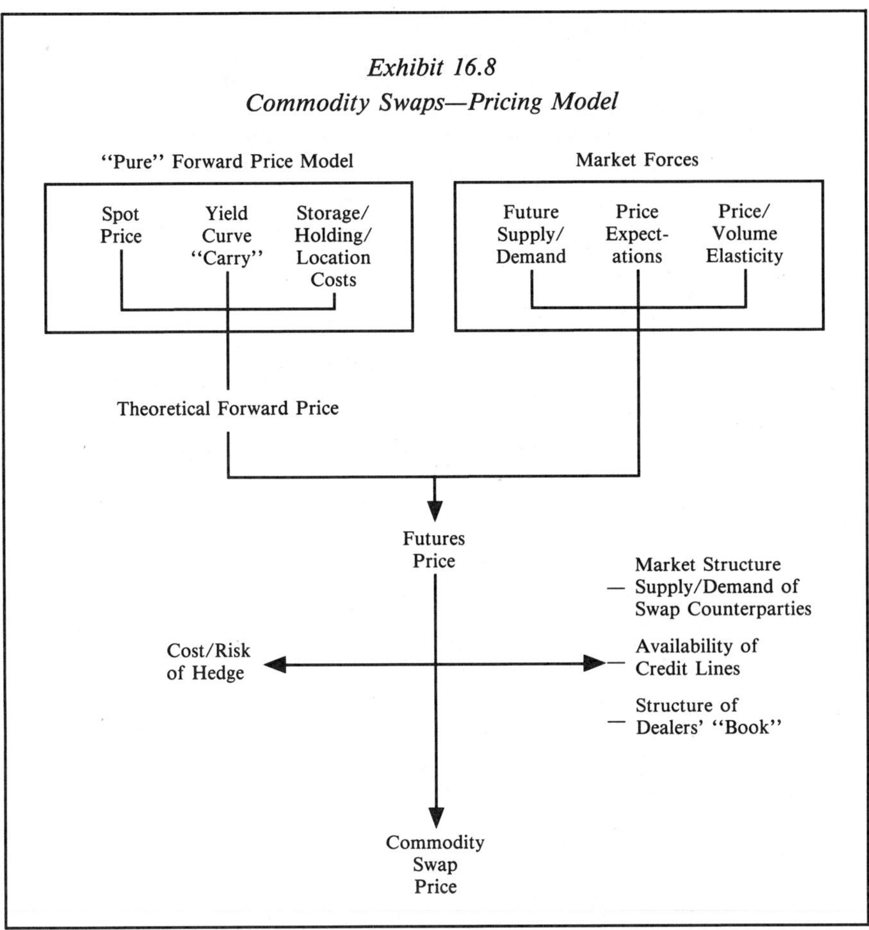

The forward price of a commodity is a price set today to be paid in the future for the purchase or sale of the identified commodity. This price depends in part on an assessment of the future price of the underlying commodity at delivery, utilising information available in the market at the time the forward contract is entered into. The major factors determining the "pure" forward price are:

- the spot price of the commodity;
- current interest rates as embodied in the yield curve or the "carry" cost;
- storage, holding and "location" or transportation costs, including any special factors relevant to the commodity such as perishability, seasonally etc.

This information, which is available in the market, can be utilised to calculate the forward price, utilising the essential condition that a forward contract can be replicated by entering into a series of transactions which would have the same economic effects as the forward contract.

For example, a forward purchaser of a commodity could arrange to purchase the required quantity of the commodity *today* at the current market price, fund and store it until the delivery date, and deliver the commodity to the forward purchaser on the agreed forward date. A forward seller could replicate a forward sale by selling the commodity on the spot market and investing the proceeds until the forward purchase date, when the maturing investment could be utilised to fund the purchase of the agreed amount of the commodity. The cost associated with the immediate purchase and funding and storage until delivery, therefore, forms a basis of the pricing of the forward contract.

Exhibit 16.9 sets out a simple example where the forward price of a commodity is calculated using the pure forward price model.

Exhibit 16.9
Forward Price of a Commodity

Assumptions

Assume that the spot price of WTI crude oil is US$18/barrel. The yield curve for US$ securities is as follows:

Years:	*Interest Rates (% pa)*
0.5	8.00
1.0	8.375
1.5	8.625
2.0	8.875
2.5	9.000
3.0	9.125

Storage/holding costs of oil are (approx) 0.50% pa (a hypothetical estimate).

Forward Price

Based on the above date, the following forward prices of WTI crude can be derived:

Year	Forward Price (Excluding Storage Costs) *US$/barrel*	Forward Price (Including Storage Costs) *US$/barrel*
Spot	18	18
0.5	18.71	18.75
1.0	19.51	19.60
1.5	20.38	20.52
2.0	21.34	21.53
2.5	22.33	22.58
3.0	23.39	23.71

Notes

1. The forward price is calculated using the following relationship
Forward Price = Spot Price + Carrying Cost

$$FP = SP \times [1 + (i + h)]^t$$

where

FP = the forward price in t period
SP = spot price
i = the annualised interest rate
h = the annualised holding cost of the commodity
t = period

Relationship between spot and forward commodity price—the commodity price curve

The relationship between spot and forward commodity prices at a given point in time, often referred to as the commodity price curve, can take three basic shapes:

- *Contango*—forward price higher than the spot price.
- *Backwardation*—forward price lower than the spot price.
- *Flat*—the spot price is the same as the forward price.

Exhibit 16.10 sets out possible shapes of the commodity price curve.

Exhibit 16.10
Commodity Price Curve

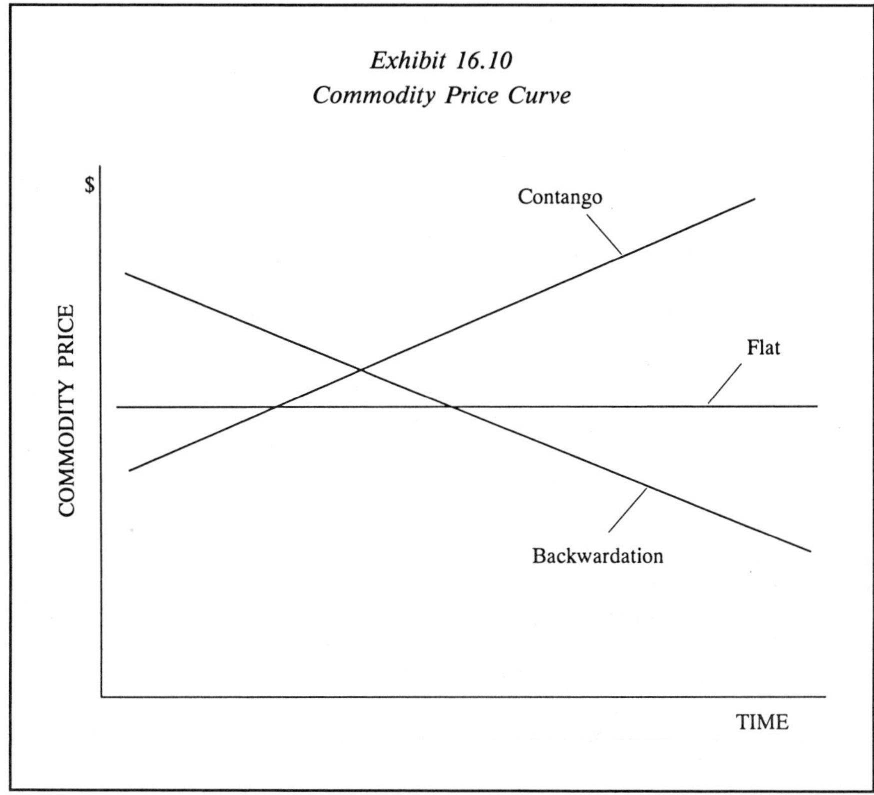

As shown in *Exhibit 16.9*, the forward price of commodity should always be above the spot price that is, in contango. This reflects the fact that the process of replication of the forward position will normally incur holding costs.

The major component of the holding cost is the interest expense of funding the holding of the spot commodity. In addition, the holding of a position in the physical commodity will result in expenditure on storage costs. These costs will include not only the physical storage and (possibly) the physical loss of the commodity through wastage and deterioration of the *quality* but also "location" costs. Location costs describe the fact that the consummation of a physical purchase or sale may require the commodity to be transported to a specific location. This may be in the form of actual physical transportation of the relevant commodity or, more probably, a "location swap" whereby specific amounts of a commodity *in different locations* are exchanged between two counterparties. These location swaps may incur costs, which must be factored into the forward price.

However, actual forward market prices for commodities are often lower than the spot price, that is, in backwardation.

For example, in early 1990 the forward price of oil implied from the NYMEX futures contract on WTI crude oil was as follows:

WTI Crude Oil Prices on NYMEX

	(US$/barrel)
March 1990	21.59
June 1990	20.10
September 1990	19.22
March 1991	18.67
June 1991	18.52

All prices are based on the forward price implied from the NYMEX futures contracts on WTI crude in January 1990.

The forward prices of oil implied from the NYMEX contract on WTI crude imply a market in backwardation. For example, the June 1991 contract implies that the forward price of oil is at a 16.6% pa discount to the current spot price.

Theoretical basis for relationship between spot and forward commodity prices

The factors determining the relationship between spot and forward commodity prices is complex.

Under the expectation hypothesis, the current price of a forward contract should be equal to the market consensus expectation of the spot price on the delivery date. This is based on the condition which implies that speculators can neither expect to win or lose from a position in the forward market. Alternatively, the net hedging theory suggests that the relationship between the spot and forward market will depend on the variable net hedging demand in the market. Both these theories would imply that the forward prices will sometimes be higher and sometimes lower than the current spot price of the commodity.

The normal contango shape of the commodity price curve is usually based on the following:

- the pure carry cost model described above;
- the fact that the market is net long hedgers and speculators have to be enticed to take short positions.

This implies that the forward price must exceed current spot price.

The theoretical attempts to explain the phenomenon of backwardation in the commodity market are more complex and varied. They include:

- the institutional structure of commodities markets which impedes the arbitrage process whereby the forward price is forced to its contango equilibrium level;
- the impact of futures supply/demand expectations;
- price expectations;
- price/volume elasticity of the commodity;
- the theory of normal backwardation put forward by John Maynard Keynes (termed normal backwardation).

As noted above, the pure forward price model would imply that the price for oil in forward months would be at a *premium* to the spot price. The arbitrage process underlying the derivation of the theoretical forward price of the commodity would, in the circumstances, imply an attractive arbitrage process whereby the forward price would be forced to its theoretical equilibrium.

Where the forward price is at a discount to the theoretical forward price, this arbitrage process would be as follows: the arbitrageur would sell the commodity in the spot market, and, simultaneously, repurchase an identical amount of the commodity *in the forward market*. The proceeds of the sale would be invested in an interest bearing investment until the maturity of the forward contract with the proceeds being utilised to fund the forward purchase. This process, in the circumstances described, would yield the arbitrageur a clear risk free profit and force the market forward price to increase.

A number of factors dictate that the actual forward price deviates significantly from that derived utilising the pure forward price model. These factors include: the difficulty of undertaking arbitrage transactions of the type described and the presence of certain market forces or factors which are not properly incorporated in the pure forward price model.

The process of arbitrage to force forward prices to their equilibrium level assumes:

- free purchase and sale of securities including short sales of commodities;
- availability of storage and holding facilities for commodities;
- absence of market frictions such as trading costs and taxes.

Many of these conditions are not satisfied in the traded market for commodities. A major violation is the inability of arbitrageurs (with the possible exception of large commodity producers and a few large trading companies) of entering into short sales of commodities. Where short sales are possible, the cost of financing or borrowing a commodity to be sold short is prohibitively high. In essence, it is only possible to be "long" or "flat" commodities. A fact which effectively eliminates certain types of arbitrage activities. The only economic means of creating a short position in a commodity is in the futures market for the commodity, if one exists.

These inadequacies in the institutional structure of commodities markets dictates that the arbitrage process which otherwise would be expected to force prices to their theoretical equilibrium forward levels does not function in accordance with the dictates of the theory.

A common explanation for the occurrence of backwardation is a shortage of supply of a commodity for immediate delivery. An adverse supply shock or a positive demand shock that raises the price of commodity also encourages consumers to substitute future consumption away from that commodity and producers to increase planned output. These anticipated supply and demand responses in reaction to a shock may cause the current spot to increase by more than anticipated future spot prices leading to backwardation.

The actual forward price of commodities, therefore often reflects *anticipated* changes in the *future supply and demand* of a particular commodity.

For example, increases in production in most commodities cannot be affected instantaneously. Where supply falls short of demand, the price in the spot market will increase to market clearing levels. However, simultaneously, production levels of the commodity may also increase. However, the increases in production and the resulting increase in supply in the spot market, may be subject to considerable time lags. The backwardation in the forward market may reflect this lag whereby the increased supply of the commodity is *expected* to more accurately balance demand and result in lower prices.

In addition, a number of commodities are subject to seasonal pricing cycles which may also impact upon the actual levels of forward prices and the premium or discount to the spot price.

A major factor influencing the level of forward prices will be the price/volume elasticity of the commodity. For example, the *absolute* level of prices for a particular commodity will reflect the nature of the demand for it.

For example, following the oil shocks of the 1970s, consumers of energy products have made considerable advances in structuring their energy consumption in a manner which allows them to switch between different energy products. A price rise in oil products may result in switching behaviour whereby major consumers of oil increase their purchase of coal or natural gas products in preference to oil based energy sources. Similarly, a fall in oil prices may induce a reverse switching behaviour. The forward price must impound expectations as to these types of changes in the supply and demand for commodities.

Backwardation in commodity markets may reflect the price expectations of investors anticipating a fall in commodity prices. Where investors anticipate prices of the commodity will fall because of and improvement in the supply/demand balance for a particular commodity, they will tend to defer their consumption of the commodity, awaiting the price fall.

Keynes advanced a further reason for backwardation in commodity markets—termed normal backwardation. Under this theory it is argued that the long run average futures price for a commodity would, in general, be below the long run average spot price. This reflects the fact that commodity producers would be prepared to pay a positive insurance premium—the difference between expected or current spot price and current forward price—to guard against the risk of unforeseen adverse price movements.

This theory of normal backwardation is interesting in that it does not depend on any deficiency in the commodity market but suggests that backwardation exists because the commodity forward market provides a mechanism by which a group of risk averse participants—namely producers who are committed to supplying the commodity subject to price uncertainty seek insurance from another group of risk averse traders—investors. The positive risk premium, being the difference between the anticipated futures spot price and the forward price, is simply an insurance premium paid by producers to investors to entice investors to undertake forward purchases.

The theory of normal backwardation implies that the degree of backwardation will be a function of:

- the volatility of commodity prices;
- the degree of risk aversion of producers and investors;
- the cost of trading and inventories.

Typically, backwardation tends to be greatest in markets where commodity prices are very volatile, producers are very sensitive to commodity price fluctuations and where it is costly to have large holdings of inventories. This is the characteristic of markets in oil, hogs and cattle. If any of these conditions fail to hold, the excess return will diminish. Consequently, backwardation is usually greatest in markets in which commodities are consumed as they are produced and holdings of stocks are small because they are expensive to store or unsuitable for storage. As a result, these particular commodities are more prone to supply disruptions and, as a result, physical possession often commands a premium, embedded in the spot price.

A feature of backwardation in commodity markets is that investors, who have no desire to hold physical quantities of commodities are able to make investments in commodity markets yielding, theoretically, returns above the riskless rate. Assuming reasonable stability in the price curve over time, an investor can buy a distant forward contract for a commodity and then transfer this contract into a more distant month as the original contract approaches maturity, thereby generating a running yield on the commodity holding. The size of the interest-like earning accruing to the investor would depend on the degree of backwardation.

The complexity of the factors which need to be incorporated in the forward price dictate that the theoretical price predictions of the pure forward price model is likely to be only one of a number of factors which will dictate the physical forward price. In practice, the market consensus forward price is best impounded in the futures contract prices for a variety of commodities which are traded on organised futures and options exchanges.

The concept of convenience yield

The complexity of the relationship between spot and forward commodity prices has resulted in a more complex construct of the relationship embodied within the commodity price curve. This is commonly referred to as "convenience yields". Utilising this basis, the spot-forward commodity price relationship can be specified as follows:

$$FP = SP \times (1 + (I + H - C))^{T}$$

where

FP = forward price at t period
SP = spot price
I = annualised interest rate
H = annualised holding cost of the commodity
C = the convenience yield
T = the period

The concept of convenience yield is equivalent to a "net" earning or yield accruing to the owner of a physical commodity.

For example, in a backwardated market, the discount evident in forward prices relative to the spot price represents a positive (negative) yield for oil consumers (producers). Conversely, in a contango market, the premium of forward prices over spot prices represents a negative (positive) yield to oil consumers (producers). In the case of a market in contango, it is possible that the convenience yield can be made positive depending upon the cost of holding the commodity (interest, storage etc). At a holding cost of less than the premium, a positive yield to producers exists.

Convenience yield estimates can be obtained by several means:

- from analysis of historical data;
- by fitting convenience yield process to current observe sets of forward prices; and
- research undertaken indicates that convenience yields are inversely related to the level of inventories. In addition, there is some evidence of a mean reversion process for convenience yields.[1]

The availability of estimates of convenience yields allows forward prices to be derived by applying the adjusted carry cost model, incorporating the convenience yield parameters, to generate a series of forward prices for a particular commodity as required.

It should be noted that there is some evidence of significant differences in the levels of convenience yield as between commodities. For example, oil and base

1. Based on research undertaken by Dr Desmond Fitzgerald presented in a paper "Pricing Energy Derivatives" at the conference "Pricing and Structuring Energy Swaps", IIR Pty Ltd, in London, England on 2 March 1992.

metals, such as copper, are industrial commodities which are consumed shortly after production and, in contrast, precious metals which are held as "repositories of value" in anticipation of future price appreciation. This means that certain commodities are not consumed and the bulk of production continues to exist.

In commodities which are rapidly consumed, the market is backwardated, in general, reflecting (as noted above):

- the relatively low levels of stocks of the commodity;
- the lack of infrastructure to store the commodity;
- the high possession value of the commodity, particularly during periods of market dislocation.

For example, in the oil market, most independent refiners are inherently capital constrained and are forced to rely on near-term surety of supply rather than longer-term hedging strategies. This results in a persistent pattern of purchasing crude at a time close to the consumption requirement. This necessitates that these independent refiners sacrifice the added "yield" from capturing the natural backwardation of the market.

In a variety of industries which are regulated, the impact of the regulatory framework effects the level of convenience yields. For example, in industries where consumers are assured supply or a regulatory mechanism exists allowing higher prices of the commodity to be passed on to the ultimate consumer, buying activities are concentrated in the near months forcing a backwardated curve with the resultant convenience yield structures. Similarly, in markets which are structured as cartels or supply is regulated, short term demand shocks or supply shocks may lead to sharp backwardation with the expectation of increased future production and/or consumer conservation as the regulatory body is expected to move to equalise demand and supply in the market.

Exhibit 16.11 sets out estimates of historical commodity convenience yields.

Valuation of commodity swaps

The derivation of the value of a commodity swap is based on combining a series of forward prices. The process requires completion of a series of distinct steps:

- Selection of the appropriate forward contract dates corresponding to the fixing dates on the swap. Typically, forward contract dates correspond to the expiry of the relevant futures contracts which are utilised to hedge the transaction. As discussed below, adjustments may be necessary where the fixing dates of the commodity swap do not coincide with the expiry date under the relevant futures or forward contracts.
- The futures equivalent barrels discounted is determined by discounting the barrels per month forward position utilising the identified discount factor applicable to the fixing date (a discount factor derived in a manner identical to that identified in Chapter 8).
- The commodity swap futures equivalent value is calculated by multiplying the underlying quantity by the futures price adjusted by the discount factor.
- The commodity swap futures equivalent value is then divided by the barrels discounted futures equivalent to give the weighted commodity swap value.

The valuation of a commodity swap where the swap fixing periods match futures contracts dates is set out in *Exhibit 16.12*. An example of the valuation of the swap where calculation periods do not match futures contracts dates is summarised in *Exhibit 16.13*.

Exhibit 16.11

Historical Commodity Convenience Yields

Continuously Compounded Returns

	GSCI		GSNE		GSEN		GSLV		GSAG		GSIN		GSPM	
	Spot	Total	Spot	Total	Spot	Total	Spot	Total	Spot	Total	Spot	Total	Spot	Total
1970	4.79%	14.06%	4.80%	14.06%	N/A	N/A	−5.71%	5.80%	17.73%	24.39%	N/A	N/A	N/A	N/A
1971	6.48%	19.13%	6.47%	19.14%	N/A	N/A	18.76%	35.70%	−8.31%	−1.11%	N/A	N/A	N/A	N/A
1972	27.35%	35.36%	27.35%	35.36%	N/A	N/A	18.43%	27.84%	38.65%	43.79%	N/A	N/A	N/A	N/A
1973	39.65%	55.94%	39.64%	55.94%	N/A	N/A	17.54%	11.12%	55.89%	90.68%	N/A	N/A	47.61%	49.74%
1974	18.82%	33.30%	18.82%	33.30%	N/A	N/A	−18.83%	−26.04%	36.83%	62.53%	N/A	N/A	30.44%	28.26%
1975	−36.41%	−18.90%	−36.41%	−18.90%	N/A	N/A	8.79%	35.87%	−60.35%	−50.30%	N/A	N/A	−5.38%	−8.96%
1976	−14.88%	−12.69%	−14.88%	−12.68%	N/A	N/A	−15.49%	−8.05%	−14.67%	−19.81%	N/A	N/A	3.57%	2.79%
1977	0.77%	9.86%	0.77%	9.86%	N/A	N/A	8.81%	30.22%	−7.01%	−11.29%	−5.64%	−8.43%	9.94%	8.55%
1978	19.21%	27.46%	19.21%	27.46%	N/A	N/A	24.33%	39.10%	12.32%	14.34%	16.41%	12.55%	29.76%	27.67%
1979	20.84%	29.13%	20.84%	29.13%	N/A	N/A	5.88%	18.87%	26.35%	29.85%	39.25%	46.20%	103.88%	102.86%
1980	12.21%	10.51%	12.21%	10.51%	N/A	N/A	2.10%	−0.10%	27.63%	26.35%	−19.51%	−18.26%	−7.79%	−9.72%
1981	−28.70%	−26.15%	−28.70%	−26.15%	N/A	N/A	−17.34%	−13.78%	−37.58%	−35.87%	−13.39%	−16.25%	−44.57%	−45.10%
1982	−0.09%	10.94%	−0.09%	10.94%	N/A	N/A	15.13%	39.82%	−17.28%	−20.29%	−8.33%	−11.71%	14.75%	13.66%
1983	7.03%	15.06%	9.31%	15.67%	0.38%	12.25%	4.44%	20.22%	19.20%	17.68%	−3.88%	−7.17%	−16.16%	−16.82%
1984	−10.02%	1.05%	−9.15%	−0.85%	−11.98%	5.57%	0.55%	8.36%	−18.02%	−7.49%	−15.81%	−17.70%	−25.56%	−26.25%
1985	0.26%	9.54%	−2.41%	1.04%	6.64%	29.71%	−10.61%	−10.10%	5.10%	12.43%	11.47%	11.75%	6.03%	6.47%
1986	−20.77%	2.02%	−11.81%	10.98%	−45.02%	−24.85%	−5.01%	20.28%	−24.60%	−2.38%	−4.79%	−3.12%	19.05%	19.74%
1987	3.13%	21.33%	11.53%	31.03%	−4.68%	12.46%	1.70%	38.50%	14.52%	14.20%	73.40%	93.16%	17.02%	16.42%
1988	11.53%	24.64%	17.08%	22.80%	5.10%	28.03%	14.51%	20.86%	25.66%	25.42%	6.16%	58.01%	−13.71%	−13.19%
1989	11.68%	32.41%	−4.12%	5.39%	28.49%	61.48%	4.53%	14.50%	−10.95%	−2.92%	−23.35%	0.06%	−3.38%	−1.44%
1990	5.96%	25.52%	−7.24%	8.83%	16.60%	37.34%	−0.02%	23.58%	−18.68%	−12.12%	9.37%	37.55%	−6.26%	−5.52%
1991	−21.78%	−6.33%	−4.46%	2.17%	−37.21%	−13.71%	−12.29%	0.23%	12.26%	12.32%	−23.65%	−18.74%	−11.97%	−11.45%
1992	2.28%	4.33%	0.44%	7.57%	4.25%	1.03%	7.84%	23.19%	−9.07%	−8.87%	5.16%	5.83%	−5.06%	−4.36%
AVERAGE	2.58%	13.81%	3.01%	12.72%	−3.74%	14.93%	2.96%	15.48%	2.85%	8.76%	2.68%	10.23%	6.18%	5.80%
STD DEV.	17.80%	18.59%	17.05%	18.03%	21.47%	23.99%	12.06%	18.07%	26.61%	30.35%	24.26%	31.40%	28.29%	28.25%
MINIMUM	−36.41%	−26.15%	−36.41%	−26.15%	−45.02%	−24.85%	−18.83%	−26.04%	−60.35%	−50.30%	−23.65%	−18.74%	−44.57%	−45.10%
MAXIMUM	39.65%	55.94%	39.64%	55.94%	28.49%	61.48%	24.33%	39.82%	55.89%	90.68%	73.40%	93.16%	103.88%	102.86%

GSCI—Goldman Sachs Commodity Index
GSEN—Goldman Sachs Energy Index
GSAG—Goldman Sachs Agricultural Index
GSPM—Goldman Sachs Precious Metals Index

GSNE—Goldman Sachs Non-Energy Index
GSLV—Goldman Sachs Livestock Index
GSIN—Goldman Sachs Industrial Metals Index

Exhibit 16.11—continued

Historical Annual Returns

	GSCI	T-BILL	GSCI + T-BILL	SP500	GBOND
1948	−10.88%	0.80%	−10.08%	5.36%	3.34%
1949	−3.87%	1.11%	−2.76%	17.22%	6.21%
1950	9.05%	1.17%	10.22%	27.56%	0.07%
1951	3.22%	1.47%	4.68%	21.52%	−4.02%
1952	−4.70%	1.67%	−3.03%	16.86%	1.15%
1953	1.61%	1.79%	3.40%	−0.99%	3.53%
1954	−1.35%	0.88%	−0.46%	42.28%	6.95%
1955	−11.55%	1.53%	−10.02%	27.43%	−1.32%
1956	7.69%	2.43%	10.12%	6.35%	−5.74%
1957	1.10%	3.12%	4.22%	−11.41%	7.20%
1958	−1.62%	1.49%	−0.13%	36.02%	−6.32%
1959	−6.41%	2.92%	−3.50%	11.29%	−2.26%
1960	3.36%	2.64%	6.00%	0.47%	12.88%
1961	0.65%	2.08%	2.73%	23.81%	0.98%
1962	3.02%	2.71%	5.73%	−9.13%	6.66%
1963	−4.19%	3.11%	−1.08%	20.54%	1.21%
1964	−2.99%	3.47%	0.48%	15.26%	3.44%
1965	10.58%	3.85%	14.43%	11.73%	0.70%
1966	−4.56%	4.65%	0.08%	−10.61%	3.58%
1967	−0.29%	4.14%	3.85%	21.49%	−9.63%
1968	0.49%	5.08%	5.56%	10.49%	−0.25%
1969	8.47%	6.36%	14.84%	−8.89%	−6.22%
1970	−5.15%	6.32%	1.17%	3.93%	11.43%
1971	6.02%	4.31%	10.32%	13.38%	12.43%
1972	16.46%	3.74%	20.20%	17.38%	5.52%
1973	45.68%	6.70%	52.38%	−15.85%	−1.12%
1974	21.47%	7.73%	29.20%	−30.75%	4.26%
1975	−8.20%	5.63%	−2.56%	31.63%	8.79%
1976	2.50%	4.94%	7.44%	21.38%	15.49%
1977	4.80%	5.00%	9.80%	−7.45%	−0.66%
1978	9.82%	6.95%	16.77%	6.35%	−1.17%
1979	41.62%	9.87%	51.49%	16.92%	−1.23%
1980	15.32%	10.65%	25.98%	28.08%	−4.02%
1981	−7.02%	13.71%	6.70%	−5.03%	1.82%
1982	−3.14%	10.02%	6.88%	19.40%	33.91%
1983	−3.07%	8.44%	5.38%	20.30%	0.67%
1984	−5.59%	9.39%	3.81%	6.08%	14.34%
1985	−0.61%	7.43%	6.83%	27.88%	26.98%
1986	−32.03%	5.98%	−26.05%	16.95%	21.87%
1987	7.91%	5.32%	13.23%	5.10%	−2.73%
1988	5.30%	6.16%	11.46%	15.54%	9.22%
1989	11.08%	8.04%	19.12%	27.38%	16.63%
1990	5.40%	7.53%	12.92%	−3.22%	5.99%
1991	−17.11%	5.44%	−11.67%	26.66%	17.62%
1992	2.29%	3.45%	5.74%	7.39%	7.75%
AVERAGE	2.46%	4.92%	7.37%	11.65%	5.04%
STD DEV.	12.63%	2.98%	13.61%	14.98%	8.80%
MINIMUM	−32.03%	0.80%	−26.05%	−30.75%	−9.63%
MAXIMUM	45.68%	13.71%	52.38%	42.28%	33.91%

GSCI historical index uses 1992 weights

Exhibit 16.11—continued

Notes: The Goldman Sachs Commodity Index (GSCI) measures the total unleveraged return of world production-weighted basket of commodity futures contracts. The Index includes both commodity spot return and commodity yield components. The spot return reflects spot price changes in the underlying constituent commodities. The yield includes two aspects of commodity futures return not reflected in spot price movements—roll yield and T-Bill yield. Roll yield results from the selling of near-dated futures contracts and the purchasing of far-dated contracts at a premium (negative roll yield) or discount (positive roll yield). T-Bill yield is calculated assuming 100% of the value of the Index is held in a margin account earning the three month treasury rate. The computation basis of the various sub-indices is very similar.

Source: Goldman Sachs/J Aron & Company.

Exhibit 16.12
Valuing Commodity Swaps (Swap Matched to Futures Dates)

Amount (barrels per month):	1,000,000
Transaction Date:	15-Nov-X2
Start Date:	21-Nov-X2
Term (months):	12.00
Swap Price ($/barrel):	$21.98

Period	Date Swap Commences	Date Swap Ends	Swap Settlement Date	Futures Settlement Date	No of Days (Calendar) From Entry	No of Days (Business) in Swap Period	Futures Contract Month	Interest Rate (% pa)	Interest Rate (% pa daily)	Discount Factor	Barrels per month	Futures Price ($/Barrel)	Barrels PV Equivalent	Oil Swap PV Equivalent
	15-Nov-X2													
1	21-Nov-X2	21-Dec-X2	22-Dec-X2	21-Dec-X2	36	21	Jan-X3	3.8750%	3.8020%	0.9963	1,000,000	$21.25	996,257	21,170,468
2	22-Dec-X2	21-Jan-X3	22-Jan-X3	21-Jan-X3	67	23	Feb-X3	4.0000%	3.9223%	0.9928	1,000,000	$21.28	992,826	21,127,347
3	22-Jan-X3	22-Feb-X3	23-Feb-X3	22-Feb-X3	99	22	Mar-X3	4.0625%	3.9824%	0.9893	1,000,000	$21.45	989,257	21,219,567
4	23-Feb-X3	22-Mar-X3	23-Mar-X3	22-Mar-X3	127	22	Apr-X3	4.1875%	4.1024%	0.9858	1,000,000	$21.69	985,828	21,382,609
5	23-Mar-X3	20-Apr-X3	21-Apr-X3	20-Apr-X3	156	21	May-X3	4.2500%	4.1624%	0.9824	1,000,000	$21.72	982,368	21,337,039
6	21-Apr-X3	20-May-X3	21-May-X3	20-May-X3	186	22	June-X3	4.2500%	4.1624%	0.9790	1,000,000	$21.78	979,013	21,322,912
7	21-May-X3	22-Jun-X3	23-Jun-X3	22-Jun-X3	219	23	Jul-X3	4.3750%	4.2823%	0.9746	1,000,000	$22.02	974,635	21,461,468
8	23-Jun-X3	22-Jul-X3	23-Jul-X3	22-Jul-X3	249	22	Aug-X3	4.4125%	4.3182%	0.9710	1,000,000	$22.18	970,973	21,536,184
9	23-Jul-X3	20-Aug-X3	21-Aug-X3	20-Aug-X3	278	21	Sep-X3	4.5000%	4.4020%	0.9670	1,000,000	$22.28	967,031	21,545,441
10	21-Aug-X3	21-Sep-X3	22-Sep-X3	21-Sep-X3	310	22	Oct-X3	4.6250%	4.5215%	0.9623	1,000,000	$22.55	962,328	21,700,505
11	22-Sep-X3	20-Oct-X3	21-Oct-X3	20-Oct-X3	339	21	Nov-X3	4.7500%	4.6409%	0.9578	1,000,000	$22.70	957,815	21,742,399
12	21-Oct-X3	19-Nov-X3	20-Nov-X3	19-Nov-X3	369	22	Dec-X3	4.8125%	4.7006%	0.9536	1,000,000	$22.89	953,593	21,827,752
												Total	11,711,926	257,373,690

Exhibit 16.13
Valuing Commodity Swaps (Swap Not Matched to Futures Dates)

Amount (barrels per month):	100,000
Transaction Date:	28-Nov-X2
Start Date:	10-Dec-X2
Term (months):	6.00
Swap Price ($/barrel):	$22.19

Period	Date Swap Commences	Date Swap Ends	Swap Settlement Date	Futures Settlement Date	No of Days (Calendar) From Entry	No of Days (Business) in Swap Period	No of Days (Business) in Period	Futures Contract Month	Interest Rate (% pa)	Interest Rate (% pa daily)	Discount Factor	Barrels per month	Barrels per Futures Period	Futures Price ($/Barrel)	Barrels PV Equivalent	Oil Swap PV Equivalent
	28-Nov-X2															
1	10-Dec-X2	21-Dec-X2	23-Dec-X2	21-Dec-X2	23		8	Jan-X3	3.8750%	3.8020%	0.9976	100,000	36.364	$21.37	36,277	775,231
	22-Dec-X2	9-Jan-X3	11-Jan-X3	20-Jan-X3	42	22	14	Feb-X3	4.0000%	3.9223%	0.9955		63,636	$21.57	63,350	1,366,456
2	10-Jan-X3	20-Jan-X3	22-Jan-X3	20-Jan-X3	53		8	Feb-X3	4.0625%	3.9824%	0.9942	100,000	36,364	$21.57	36,154	779,841
	21-Jan-X3	9-Feb-X3	11-Feb-X3	22-Feb-X3	73	22	14	Mar-X3	4.1250%	4.0424%	0.9919		63,636	$21.74	63,124	1,372,315
3	10-Feb-X3	22-Feb-X3	24-Feb-X3	22-Feb-X3	86		9	Mar-X3	4.1875%	4.1024%	0.9904	100,000	45,000	$21.74	44,567	968,890
	23-Feb-X3	9-Mar-X3	11-Mar-X3	22-Mar-X3	101	20	11	Apr-X3	4.2500%	4.1624%	0.9885		55,000	$21.95	54,370	1,193,426
4	10-Mar-X3	22-Mar-X3	24-Mar-X3	22-Mar-X3	114		9	Apr-X3	4.3750%	4.2823%	0.9867	100,000	39,130	$21.95	38,611	847,502
	23-Mar-X3	9-Apr-X3	11-Apr-X3	20-Apr-X3	132	23	14	May-X3	4.5000%	4.4020%	0.9842		60,870	$22.54	59,908	1,350,333
5	10-Apr-X3	20-Apr-X3	22-Apr-X3	20-Apr-X3	143		7	May-X3	4.5625%	4.4618%	0.9827	100,000	35,000	$22.54	34,394	775,230
	21-Apr-X3	9-May-X3	11-May-X3	20-May-X3	162	20	13	Jun-X3	4.6875%	4.5812%	0.9799		65,000	$22.74	63,692	1,448,351
6	10-May-X3	20-May-X3	22-May-X3	20-May-X3	173		9	Jun-X3	4.7500%	4.6409%	0.9782	100,000	39,130	$22.74	38,279	870,466
	21-May-X3	9-Jun-X3	11-Jun-X3	22-Jun-X3	193	23	14	Jul-X3	4.9125%	4.7960%	0.9750		60,870	$22.95	59,345	1,361,978
														Total	592,071	13,110,021

The basic methodology outlined is utilised to value all types of commodity swaps and certain variations on the basic commodity swap structure. The basic process can be adapted to pricing *forward* commodity swaps—effectively, a normal fixed-to-floating commodity swap with the deferred commencement date. An example of pricing a forward start commodity swap is set out in *Exhibit 16.14*.

Pricing in practice

The relationship of commodity swap prices to futures prices is based on:

- the fact that the futures price reflects a consensus between market participants of the current expected forward price (given that these market participants are the primary users of commodity swaps); and
- the use of commodity futures by financial institutions in hedging commodity swap positions.

As noted above, the majority of commodity swaps are transacted via a financial intermediary who assumes both the credit risk of and responsibility for arrangement of counterparties for each particular transaction. Where a commodity swap trader is approached to provide a price for a particular transaction, he or she will have two options in offsetting the risk of undertaking a commodity swap:

- locate and transact the offsetting component of the swap with a counterparty;
- if a counterparty is not readily available, enter into the commodity swap with the risk being assumed in one of two ways:
  - —assume the price risk and leave the position unhedged until a counterparty can be located;
  - —hedge the risk of movements in the price of the commodity by entering into a series of transactions in the physical or forward/futures market for the commodity to provide a temporary hedge until a counterparty can be located.

In practice, few dealers take pure price risks in entering into commodity swap transactions. Typically, the dealer will hedge the *absolute* price risk of a transaction by utilising the best available hedge instrument. In this way the dealer assumes the risk *of the hedge* in preference to *the risk of short-term movements in the price of the commodity*.

This behaviour of the trader necessarily means that the commodity swap price will reflect the market structure at the *point in time* as well as the cost and risk of a temporary hedge. Important market structure factors which may influence the commodity swap provider's price includes: the perceived supply/demand of swap counterparties; the availability of credit lines to enter into transactions with counterparties; and the structure of the dealer's book.

The cost or risk of the hedge will be calculated as the cost of setting up the hedge involving the physical commodity or the forward/future, the basis risk of the hedge, the liquidity of the hedging instrument utilised, and the time period for which the hedge is expected to be held.

The process of utilising futures to neutralise the risk of entering into commodity swaps is, in practice, subject to certain limitations. The hedging costs and risks differ between commodities where futures markets in the relevant commodity exist and commodities where liquid futures market do not exist or the futures markets that are an existence do not exactly match the hedging requirements of the commodity swap.

In the case where relatively liquid and deep futures markets exist, problems in using futures contracts to hedge commodity swap positions include:

- the costs of hedging, including variation margins and the risk of rolling futures positions;

Exhibit 16.14

Valuing Forward Commodity Swaps (Swap Matched to Futures Dates)

Amount (barrels per month):	1,000,000
Transaction Date:	7-Jan-X0
Start Date:	21-Nov-X2
Term (months):	12.00
Swap Price ($/barrel):	$21.96

Period	Date Swap Commences	Date Swap Ends	Swap Settlement Date	Swap Settlement Date	No of Days (Calendar) From Start	Swap Period (Business) in Swap Period	Contract Contract Month	Interest Rate (% pa)	Interest Rate (% pa daily)	Discount Factor	Barrels per month ($/Barrel)	Futures Price	Barrels PV Equivalent	Oil Swap PV Equivalent
	7-Jan-X0													
1	21-Nov-X2	21-Dec-X2	22-Dec-X2	21-Dec-X2	1444	21	Jan-X3	4.3750%	4.2823%	0.8442	1,000,000	$21.25	844,169	17,938,584
2	22-Dec-X2	21-Jan-X3	22-Jan-X3	21-Jan-X3	1475	23	Feb-X3	4.5000%	4.4020%	0.8370	1,000,000	$21.28	837,046	17,812,335
3	22-Jan-X3	22-Feb-X3	23-Feb-X3	22-Feb-X3	1507	22	Mar-X3	4.8125%	4.7006%	0.8236	1,000,000	$21.45	823,605	17,666,334
4	23-Feb-X3	22-Mar-X3	23-Mar-X3	22-Mar-X3	1535	22	Apr-X3	4.9000%	4.7840%	0.8178	1,000,000	$21.69	817,766	17,737,347
5	23-Mar-X3	20-Apr-X3	21-Apr-X3	20-Apr-X3	1564	21	May-X3	5.1200%	4.9936%	0.8074	1,000,000	$21.72	807,383	17,536,365
6	21-Apr-X3	20-May-X3	21-May-X3	20-May-X3	1594	22	Jun-X3	5.3750%	5.2359%	0.7956	1,000,000	$21.78	795,614	17,328,462
7	21-May-X3	22-Jun-X3	23-Jun-X3	22-Jun-X3	1627	23	Jul-X3	5.5500%	5.4019%	0.7860	1,000,000	$22.02	786,021	17,308,181
8	23-Jun-X3	22-Jul-X3	23-Jul-X3	22-Jul-X3	1657	22	Aug-X3	5.6250%	5.4729%	0.7800	1,000,000	$22.18	780,020	17,300,838
9	23-Jul-X3	20-Aug-X3	21-Aug-X3	20-Aug-X3	1686	21	Sep-X3	5.8200%	5.6574%	0.7700	1,000,000	$22.28	770,047	17,156,644
10	21-Aug-X3	21-Sep-X3	22-Sep-X3	21-Sep-X3	1718	22	Oct-X3	5.9750%	5.8038%	0.7610	1,000,000	$22.55	760,977	17,160,021
11	22-Sep-X3	20-Oct-X3	21-Oct-X3	20-Oct-X3	1747	21	Nov-X3	6.1200%	5.9405%	0.7525	1,000,000	$22.70	752,535	17,082,542
12	21-Oct-X3	19-Nov-X3	20-Nov-X3	19-Nov-X3	1777	22	Dec-X3	6.1875%	6.0041%	0.7466	1,000,000	$22.89	746,555	17,088,646
												Total	9,521,737	209,116,299

- the institutional structure of the futures market;
- the liquidity of the futures market;
- the seasonality of commodity prices.

In practice, pricing commodity swap off the hedge in the futures market requires a number of elements to be factored in. The major factor here is the cost of the bid-offer spread in the futures market itself (as a hedger must deal at the market price), the cost of deposits and variation margins required by the institutional structure of futures markets etc.

A major risk in undertaking futures hedges is the requirement that positions must be "rolled"—that is, due to the absence of liquidity in distant months, hedges are taken out in a near month and must be closed and re-opened. The necessity to roll a futures hedge essentially requires the hedger to estimate the "spread" between the near and far months (essentially, the commodity price curve) over the life of the transaction. Variations in the spread, which are unanticipated, can greatly effect the efficiency of the hedge.

The spread is a particularly significant factor where the commodity swap pricing dates do not exactly match the futures pricing dates. This necessitates that the futures contract be closed out prior to maturity often incurring additional spread costs and also creates a mismatch between the pricing date on the commodity swap and the futures contract necessitating additional costs in the hedging process.

Exhibit 16.15 sets out an analysis of spreads in WTI near against far month contracts which highlight the difficulties in rolling contracts.

Exhibit 16.15

WTI Price Relationships

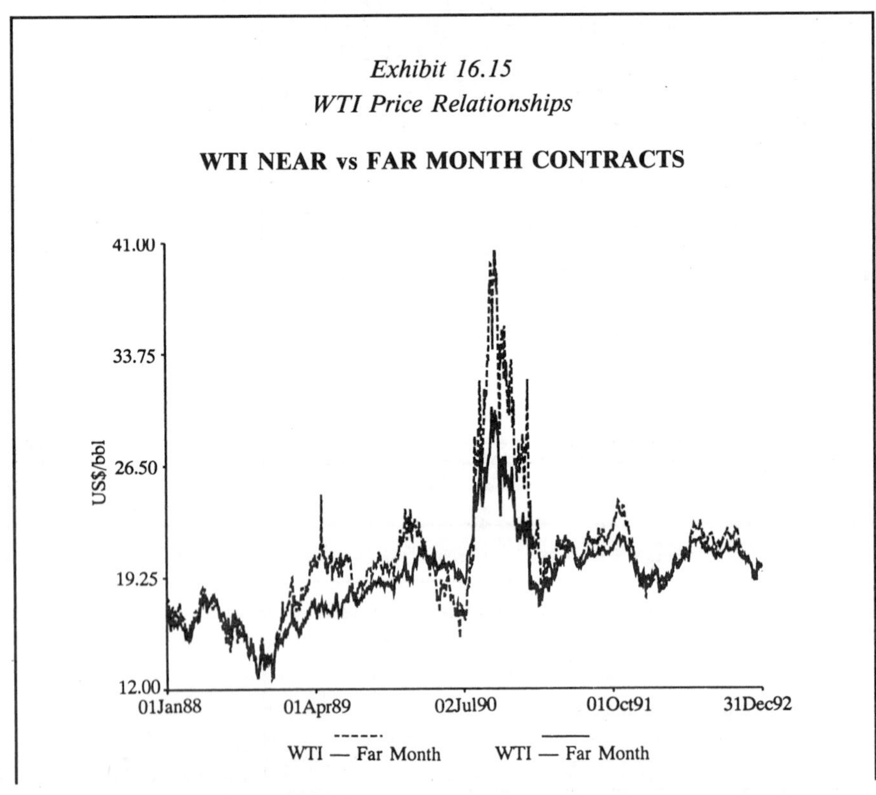

Exhibit 16.15—continued

WTI NEAR vs FAR MONTH CONTRACTS SPREAD HISTORY

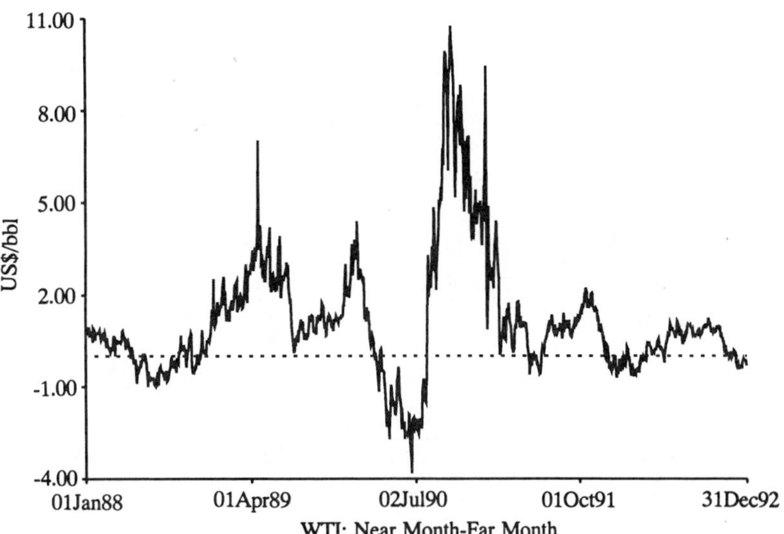

WTI NEAR vs FAR MONTH CONTRACTS

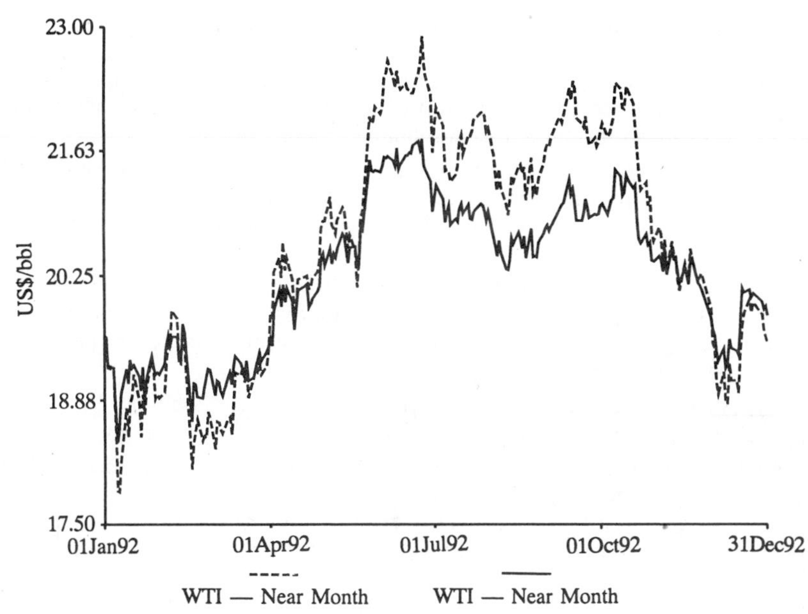

Exhibit 16.15—continued

WTI NEAR vs FAR MONTH CONTRACTS SPREAD

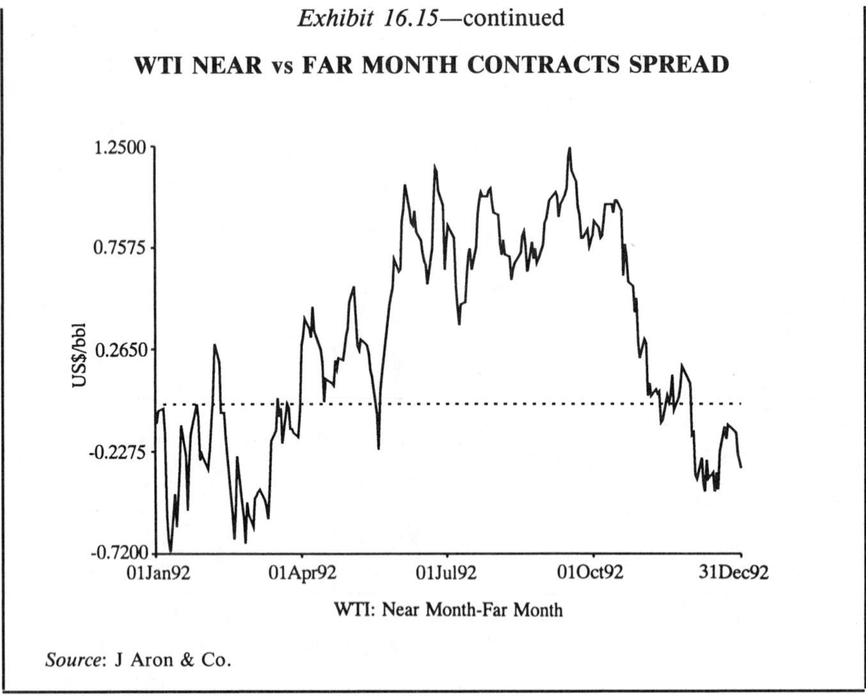

Source: J Aron & Co.

Additional costs incurred in the utilisation of futures to hedge include futures brokerage commissions.

A factor which influences the efficiency of the hedge is that many commodities exhibit seasonal variations in prices due to structural changes in supply and demand. Seasonality of commodity prices is a factor in pricing short dated swaps where the pricing must be adjusted to take account of the seasonal effect. Seasonality is not a significant problem in longer dated commodity swap pricings.

In practice, the bid-offer spread on the commodity swap must cover the financial institution entering into the transaction for the identified hedging costs as well as to compensate for the credit risk incurred, utilisation of capital, administrative costs and profit.

The position is somewhat complicated where the commodity futures market does not exactly match the terms of the commodity swap; that is, the futures market lacks depth or liquidity to effect the required hedge, or a futures market in the relevant commodity does not exist.

The types of solutions adopted under these circumstances include:

- The use of "stack" hedges whereby hedges are taken out in near month contracts, to avoid the problems associated with lack of liquidity in distant months with the aim of rolling the hedge as the expiry date of the futures contract (in which the hedge is placed) is approached. This exposes the hedger to the spread risk associated with rolling of the hedges identified above: see discussion in Chapter 35.
- The use of basis hedges whereby a commodity with similar characteristics to the commodity of the commodity swap is utilised to establish a hedge against price movements. The basis risk, in this case arises, in the hedging of one commodity

with a similar but distinctly different commodity. For example, the Nymex WTI crude or heating oil (no 2) contract can be utilised to hedge the price of jet fuel based on the correlation in prices of the two commodities, which although not exact is substantial. *Exhibit 16.16* sets out a graph comparing the movements in the price of jet fuel relative to WTI and heating oil to illustrate the volatility of the basis. This highlights the difficulty of establishing and managing surrogate hedges of this type.

In summary, the pricing of a commodity swap is a far from exact science. It reflects the influence of a number of factors. The principal factor influencing the commodity swap price is the prevailing forward/futures price of the commodity which reflects the fact that a commodity swap can be decomposed into a portfolio of forward contracts. The forward/futures price itself reflects both the theoretical forward price as generated by the arbitrage based pure forward pricing model and the influence of market forces on the forward price of the underlying commodity.

Pricing commodity price-for-interest swaps

The methodology discussed above relates primarily to fixed-for-floating commodity swap. The pricing of a commodity price-for-interest swap is intrinsically more complex.

Pricing a commodity price-for-interest swap can be separated into a number of distinct steps:

1. pricing the fixed purchase price for the commodity from the perspective of the commodity user;
2. price the interest rate swap;
3. price the amount of commodity to be exchanged for the US$ LIBOR payments.

Pricing of steps 1 and 2 can be readily generated. The fixed forward purchase price for the commodity user will conform closely to the price of a fixed-for-floating commodity swap. This is because from the perspective of the commodity user the two transactions are direct substitutes.

The interest rate swap price is freely available given the presence of a substantial, liquid and freely traded market in the instrument.

The final pricing step—step 3—can be forced out once steps 1 and 2 are known.

In practice, from the perspective of the commodity user there is no difference between a straight fixed-for-floating commodity price swap and a commodity price-for-interest swap (except for possible assurance of supply) and the commodity user may in fact prefer to structure the transaction as a straight fixed-for-floating commodity price swap.

However, the complex impact of the commodity price-for-interest swap on the commodity producer and, in particular, the asymmetric profile of the transaction (the impact on the producer will not necessarily mirror that of the user because of difference between producers in terms of capital structure, debt availability, debt structure, production costs etc) dictates that the actual transaction price will deviate, often significantly, from the theoretical price. In this respect, the pricing of commodity price-for-interest swap entails a greater "barter" or "exchange" element whereby the exact supply and demand of counterparties may significantly influence pricing at any point of time.

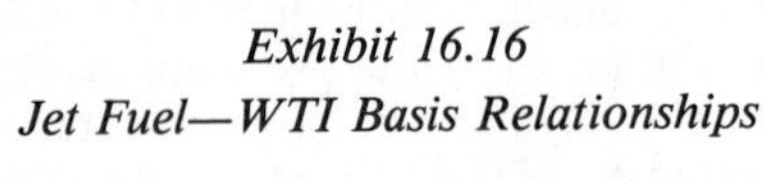

Exhibit 16.16
Jet Fuel—WTI Basis Relationships

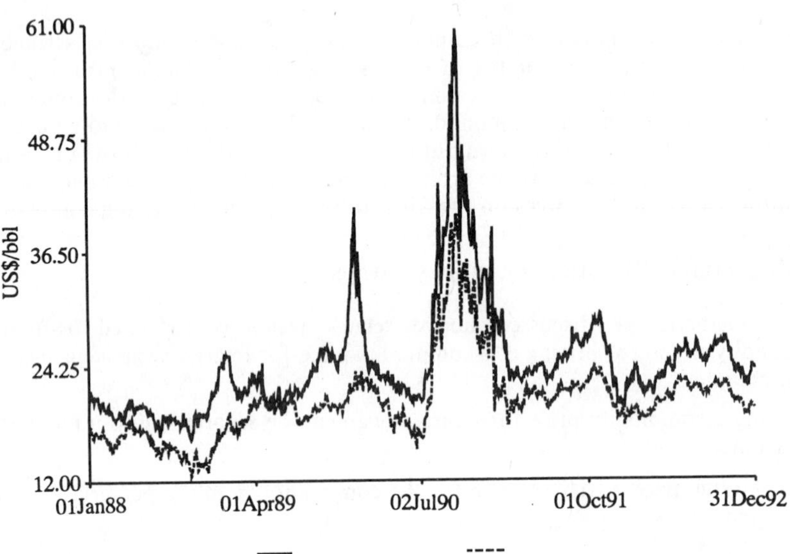

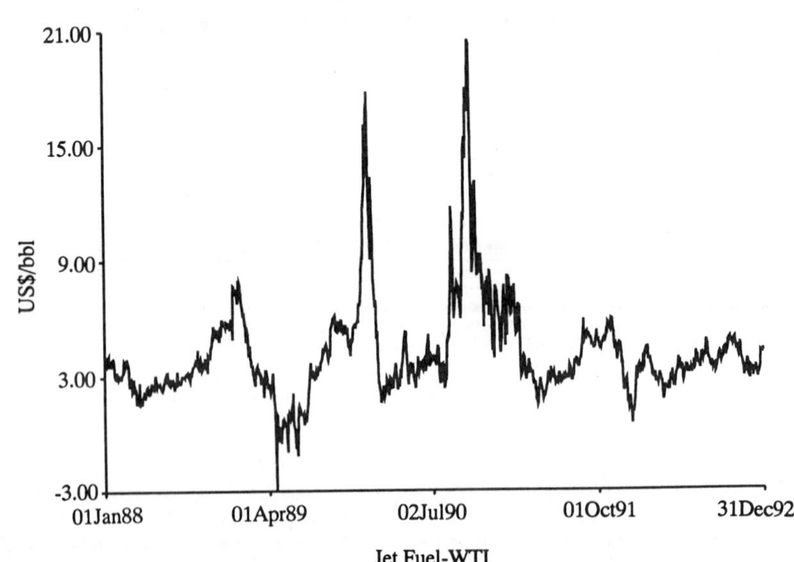

Exhibit 16.16—continued

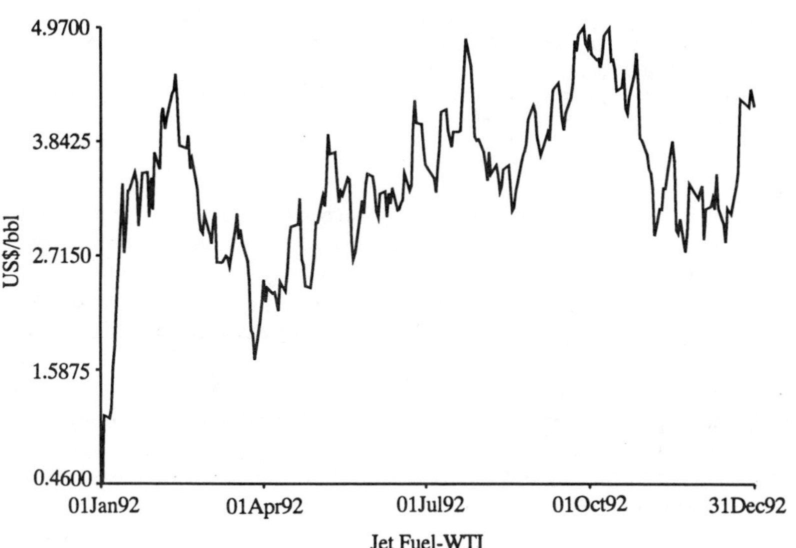

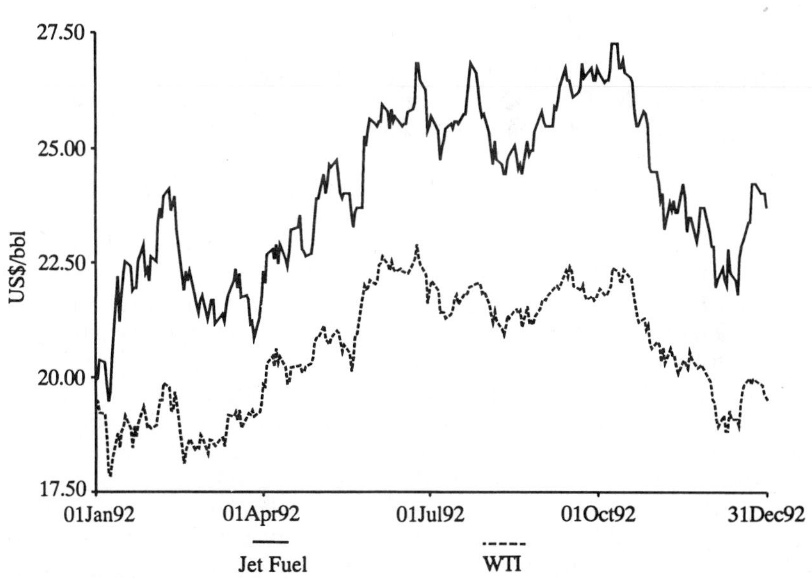

Source: J Aron & Co.

Commodity swaps versus commodity futures

Commodity swaps have evolved as a preferred method of managing commodity price risk for both producers and users because of certain structural inadequacies of commodity futures markets in the relevant commodities.

As noted above, futures markets in a wide variety of commodities have been available for some time. However, the use of futures while well suited to hedging individual transactions is not as useful in hedging typical corporate cash flows underlying commodity transactions. The major advantages of commodity swaps over futures transactions include:

Term

Commodity futures are typically traded for periods up to two years. However, only the near month contracts (up to three and, at most, six months out) are sufficiently traded and liquid to provide a basis for hedging exposures.

In contrast commodity swap transactions can be structured over a longer horizon for periods up to ten years (most commodity swaps are for maturities around six months to three years).

Futures contracts can be utilised to cover longer dated exposures but require that the hedge be rolled over periodically (eg monthly or quarterly). This rollover process is administratively clumsy as it requires cash settlements to be made at the time of rollover as well as exposing the hedger to the risk of the changing basis between the relevant futures contract.

Administrative simplicity

Commodity swap transactions, unlike future contracts, do not require initial deposits and, in most cases (subject to the credit standing of the counterparty), margin calls as the contracts are not marked to market periodically.

Basis risk

Hedging with commodity futures involves the hedger assuming basis risk. This risk arises from the fact that the commodity futures contract design must be specified precisely and the contract months are preset with no flexibility to depart from these contract standards.

Wherever the hedger utilises the traded futures contract to hedge a product related to *but not identical to* the commodity specified in the contract *and/or* seeks to cover an exposure in a month not coinciding exactly with the futures traded month, the hedger must assume basis risk. These risks can be classified as follows:

- *Product basis risk*—that is, the hedging of one commodity with a related but different commodity, for example, covering an exposure to jet fuel utilising WTI crude oil futures.
- *Timing risk*—that is, hedging an exposure in a month in which the commodity futures contract is not traded or, alternatively, is not sufficiently liquid to allow its utilisation requiring the hedger to structure the hedge by trading in a contract expiring in a different time period to its actual exposure.
- *Commodity location risk*—that is, where the subject of the futures contract is deliverable at a different location to the delivery requirements of the actual physical commodity transaction being hedged. For example, hedging WTI crude on a CIF New York basis with a Brent crude FOB product delivered in Rotterdam.

- *Commodity futures currency risk*—that is, the difference between the currency denomination of the commodity futures contracts (typically in US$) and the actual currency in which the hedge is required which may be in the producer or user's local currency (other than US$).

A major advantage of commodity swaps is that they can be tailored to overcome these basis risks. For example, each commodity swap can be tailored precisely to the requirements of the producer or user to overcome each of the basis risks identified. This would allow the hedger to assure itself of better performance of its hedge relative to its underlying physical transaction, relative to the situation where it was forced to utilise the commodity futures contract which did not conform to its physical transaction requirements.

Design flexibility

As is evident from the above, a major advantage of a commodity swap is that it can be tailor-made to suit the specific cash flow, commodity product type and time frame requirements of producers and users.

Exhibit 16.17 sets out a comparison between using a commodity swap and commodity futures.

Exhibit 16.17
A Comparison of Commodity Swap and Commodity Futures Transactions

Set out below is a comparison of equivalent hedging strategies in WTI crude entailing the use of a commodity swap and, as an alternative, a series of futures transaction (entailed trading the future strip).

In both cases, the hedge to be established is for 500,000 barrels covering the period from 1 January 19X2 to 30 January 19X2.

The prevailing swap price is US$20.45/barrel, based upon NYMEX settlement prices prevailing 5 June 19X1.

The futures strip price is as follows:

Date	Trading Days	Futures 2nd mth WTI	Price	Futures Contracts
Jan 1-21	13	March	20.69	51
22-31	8	April	20.65	32
Feb 1-20	13	April	20.65	52
21-29	6	May	20.62	24
Mar 1-20	15	May	20.62	59
21-31	7	June	20.60	28
Apr 1-21	15	June	20.60	59
22-30	7	July	20.59	28
May 1-19	13	July	20.59	52
20-31	7	August	20.59	28
Jun 1-22	16	August	20.59	63
23-30	6	September	20.59	24
	126	Average:	20.617	500

Both the oil swap and the futures settle off the second WTI reference month.

In the case of the futures strip, in order to replicate the swap to where it was based on average prices, it would be necessary to buy back an equal number of contracts through the life of the swap. It would be necessary to close four contracts per trading a day over the life of the transaction. These contracts would be closed on a Market on Close (MOC) basis to match the settlement basis of the swap.

Exhibit 16.17—continued

The additional cost of the future strip would be:

- Brokerage on the futures transaction.
- Financing the cost of the deposit. NYMEX allows lodgment of interest bearing US treasury bills (T-Bills) to cover contract deposit requirements.
- Financing of mark-to-market margin calls; debit margins earn no interest while variation margins earn interest as T-Bills minus 1.50% pa.

The impact of these additional costs on the above transaction are calculated as follows:

		US$/barrel
Average Price Sell Strip		20.6170
Brokerage[1]		(0.0300)
Cost of Deposit[2]		(0.0056)
Cost of Margin[3]		(0.0406)
—Debit Margin	(0.0625)	
—Credit Margin	0.0219	
	(0.0406)	
Net Futures Strip Price		20.5408

The adjusted futures price is superior to the swap price in this instance, with the added costs totalling US$0.0762/barrel which is not sufficient to eliminate the US$0.167 barrel margin.

The futures strip price is sensitive to the margin requirements and the cost of funding of deposits and margins.

The above analysis does not encompass the following:

- *Credit risk*—either the use of credit lines to execute the swap or the fact that the counterparty risk on the futures contract (the clearing home) is lower.
- *Price*—there may be "slippage" in the execution of the futures contract, although, the swap price embodies a premium for the risk that the swap provider cannot itself hedge its risk in the futures market—the magnitude of the price slippage relative to market marker's premium may differ.
- *Severability*—component contracts within the futures strip can be traded seperately unlike a swap which can only be managed as an entire transaction.

Notes:

1. Based on a brokerage cost of US$30.00 per round twin.
2. The cost of the deposit is calculated as the spread cost between the rate earnt (T-Bills) and the borrowing cost of the funds. Assuming a deposit requirement of US$1,500 per contract and a total requirement of 500 contracts, the total cash requirement is US$750,000. However, this amount decreases as the futures strip is unwound. Assuming a negative spread of 1.50% pa, the cost is:

   US$375,000 @ 1.50% pa for six months
   =US$2,813
   or $0.0056/barrel

   The US$375,000 deposit amount equates to the average deposit amount lodged.
3. Maintenance margins are calculated daily and must be covered in cash. Assume that the hedge is in deficit for 50% of the period (six months—reflecting the fact that the futures contracts are in place from 5 June 19X1 to maturity in 30 June 19X2). The deficit amount assumed is $5.00/barrel. The futures contracts are assumed to be in credit for the remaining six months to an amount of US$2.50/barrel. Note, as in the case of the deposit, the exposure declines over time and consequently the average exposure is used in calculation. Based on a T-Bill rate of 5% pa, the cost is as follows:

   Interest Cost ($2.50 @ 5.00% for six months)
   =US$0.0625/barrel.

Source: The above draws substantially on Richard Wilcox (17 June 1991) *A Comparison of Hedging Methods—Futures Strip Versus Oil Price Swap* (Bain Refer Commodities Limited, Sydney, Australia).

The features of commodity swaps which make them particularly attractive are similar to the features of interest rate and currency swap transactions which differentiate them from interest rate and/or currency futures. Essentially, commodity swaps function as an over-the-counter forward contract on specific commodities just as interest rate and currency swaps function as over-the-counter forward contracts on interest rates and currencies respectively.

These similarities extend to the mechanical/settlement features of the two types of transactions, particularly in the case of fixed-for-floating commodity price swaps.

However, despite these similarities, the relationship between the two types of transactions should *not* be overstated. The market for commodity swaps does not (at least currently) incorporate the more complex integrative and financial arbitrage functions of currency and interest rates swaps.

Currency and interest swaps function in a highly distinctive manner linking capital markets in various currencies as well as linking segments within individual capital markets. Interest rate and currency swaps provide this linking function by allowing comparative advantage theory to be extended from the market for goods and services to the market for financial assets and liabilities.

In contrast, commodities swaps, as they are structured currently, function purely as a mechanism for the transfer of risk between producers and users of commodities as well as speculators. In this regard, the market for commodity swaps is regarded more accurately as an extension of the forward/futures markets in the respective commodities.

VARIATIONS ON COMMODITY SWAPS

Commodity swap—extensions

As in the case of interest rate and currency derivatives, a variety of extensions to the basic concept have emerged. These product extensions include variations on commodity swap structures, commodity option structures and commodity hybrids (discussed in the following sections).

The primary extensions on commodity swap structures include:

- forwards/deferred start commodity swaps;
- basis swaps;
- crack spread swaps;
- "roll" or "curve lock" commodity swap (often also referred as time spread swaps).

Forward or deferred start swaps in commodities are identical in structure to forward/deferred start interest rate or currency swaps. The structure is typically used to hedge known forward consumption or production of a commodity to reduce the commodity price risk of the transaction. An example of a forward/deferred start commodity swap is set out above in *Exhibit 16.14*.

Basis swaps

The concept of a basis swap in commodities is very similar to that of an interest rate basis swap. Under a basis risk commodity swap structure, the party entering into the transaction receives a commodity price related to a certain index and pays prices based on an alternative index. For example, in the case of oil, a basis commodity swap can be structured between jet fuel and WTI or other crude index.

This type of structure is designed to allow the participant to capture value from anticipated movements in the "spread" (that is, the relative price of, for example, the relevant oil grades/products). Basis commodity swaps are utilised primarily by traders and producers seeking to take advantage of anticipated changes in spread relationships between various products within a particular commodity range. To date, this type of structure has been most commonly utilised in energy products where a wide variety of location and price reference indexes facilitates such transactions.

An example of an oil basis swap involving WTI and Tapis indexes is set out in *Exhibit 16.18*.

Exhibit 16.18

Oil Basis Swap

Assume Tapis crude (an Asian crude oil price index) is trading at a discount. An oil producer who sells a Tapis-based crude decides to hedge his sales prices but chooses to utilise a WTI swap to take advantage of the prevailing price differential between WTI and Tapis. This necessarily means that the producer assumes the basis risk between WTI and Tapis which while correlated will not necessarily move exactly together.

The producer's position after completing the swap is set out below:

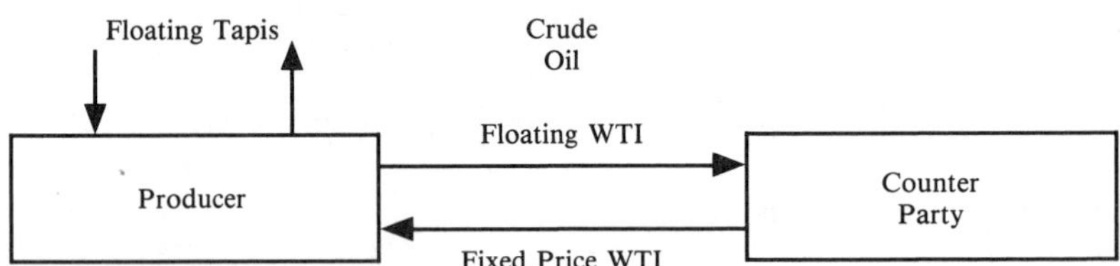

The producer may look to later eliminate the WTI-Tapis mismatch through a basis swap. Ideally, this transaction would be undertaken when the WTI-Tapis spread decreases from the level prevailing at the time the original hedge is established to allow the producer to exploit the basis changes between the two markets.

The producer's position after completing the basis swap is set out below:

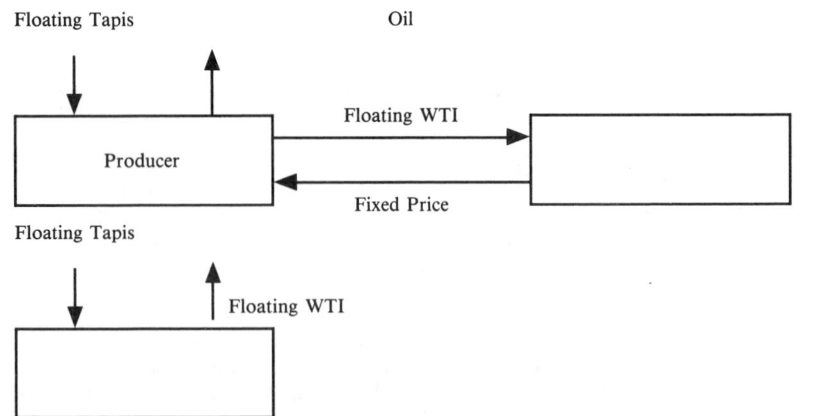

Exhibit 16.18—continued

The risk and opportunities in positioning in relation to the WTI-Tapis spread is evident from the historical movements in this relationship which is summarised below:

TAPIS-WTI SPREAD

Weekly Data 4/11/91-5/3/93

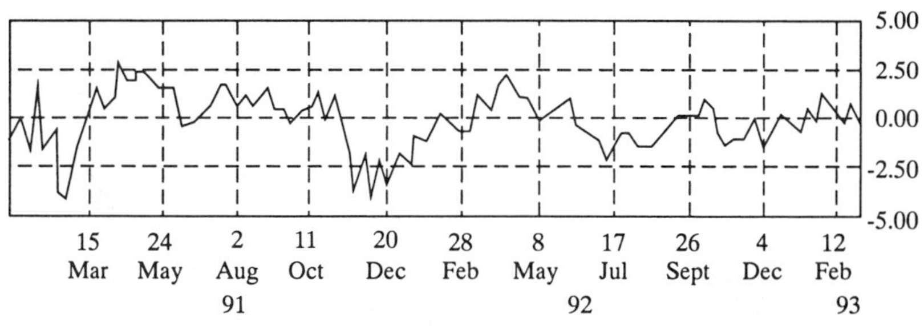

Source: Westpac Banking Corporation.

Crack spread swaps

A variation on the concept of the basis swap is the crack spread swap unique to energy markets. This type of transaction is primarily utilised by refiners and fixes profit margins through locking in the relative spread between the purchase price of crude oil (of whatever type) and refined products (heating oil, gasoline, jet fuel etc). Crack spread swaps are designed to guarantee the refiner a known spread between the price of the crude and refined products.

Curve lock swaps

The roll or curve lock commodity swap is predicated upon guaranteeing the party entering into the transaction the spread between the near and far month prices in the commodity price curve. In essence, it is a transaction designed to guarantee the interest rate/convenience yield factor in the commodity price yield curve. This type of product structure is designed to capture value from the degree of backwardation in the commodity price curve. This structure is best illustrated by an example taken from the oil market.

For example, assume as at a given point in time near month WTI contract is trading at US$23.80/barrel while the contract in one years time is trading at US$21.40/barrel. While the backwardation results in forward purchase one year out being relatively "cheap" relative to the current spot price, consumers may be reluctant to hedge at the current absolute prevailing price levels for oil. However, the degree of backwardation in the current price curve may be attractive.

Based on this assumption, the consumer could enter into a roll or curve lock swap whereby it locks in the spread between the near month and the far month. For example, a consumer could lock in a spread of WTI less US$2.00. The WTI contract in this case would be the agreed contract sometime in the future. At any time between entry into the roll or curve lock commodity swap and the expiry of the nominated contract month, the party entering into the swap could trigger the curve lock and lock into a price based on the then prevailing WTI price in the relevant contract month.

Assume that the transaction is entered into as at December 19X2 where the spot month price of WTI US$23.80/barrel. Under the terms of the curve lock, the consumer agrees to pay the March 19X3 WTI price minus US$2.00. Assume that the March 19X3 contract is trading at the time of entry into the transaction at US$22.90/barrel. If the anticipated price movement eventuates and the oil price weakens by US$3/barrel, then the consumer could trigger curve lock at: US$22.90—US$3 (decrease in price)—US$2.00 (the curve lock margin) equivalent to US$17.90/barrel.

This type of structure allows the consumer to benefit from a fall in the absolute price of the commodity while still benefiting from the degree of backwardation captured for the curve lock margin.

The value of this structure is based on the expectation that if commodity prices, particularly oil, fall sharply, the movement is most marked in the current spot price and the shape of the commodity price curve changes significantly. For example, in the situation envisaged above, it is likely that a fall in price, presumably due to an exogenous supply or demand factor of US$3.00/barrel, would be most marked in the near WTI futures month and may lead to a shift in the commodity price curve shape from a backwardated curve to one which is contango. This means that the party seeking to enter into a swap after the absolute price fall may be penalised because of the shape of the commodity price curve. The roll or curve lock swap allows capture of the value in backwardation (for the consumer) without commitment to the absolute price level which backwardated price is generated.

While the above example focuses on a consumer, similar structures can be developed for producers. Producers can benefit from this type of structure particularly when the market is less backwardated or in contango.

Commodity swap—real estate derivatives

An interesting extension in commodity swap structures entails transactions involving real estate price indexes.

In early 1993, Morgan Stanley made public a transaction involving a Boston-based pension fund and an insurance company. The transaction involving a property investment management firm, Aldrich, Eastman and Waltch, entailed a US$20m five year swap transaction on behalf of a major United States corporate pension fund which allowed the fund to balance its overall portfolio by reducing its exposure to real estate investments. The transaction was designed to allow the pension fund to reduce its exposure to real estate and allow it to reallocate these investment funds into other asset classes such as equities and United States treasury notes. A brief summary of the transaction is set out in *Exhibit 16.19*.

The attraction of this swap exists at a number of different levels. Its importance is that it opens up the possibility of other real estate linked commodity swap transactions facilitating reallocation of exposure to real estate price movements. Given the size of the global market in real estate, the potential of this particular market sector is clearly significant. However, the further importance of this innovation, lies in the fact that it opens the way for swaps involving *any* index of prices for a particular asset class.

Exhibit 16.19
Commodity Swap—Real Estate Index

Structure

The transaction entailed a five year US$20m deal completed by Morgan Stanley in late January 1993, with Aldrich, Eastman and Waltch (AEW) acting as the qualified pension asset manager (QPAM).

One counterparty to the overall transaction (a large United States corporate pension fund) agreed to pay Morgan Stanley a rate linked to the Frank Russell-National Council of Real Estate Investment Fiduciaries (NCREIF) property index. In return it will receive a LIBOR-based rate. The other counterparty (a medium-sized life insurance company with between US$20bn and US$40bn in assets) pays a LIBOR-based rate in exchange for payments based on the performance of the NCREIF index (see flow chart).

The corporate pension fund will reallocate the cash flows from this swap into a synthetic international equity investment for three years. This will enable the pension fund to "equitise" the cash flow generated from the swap as part of a strategic asset allocation decision. AEW indicated that the pension client isolated a real estate portfolio that represented "a microcosm of the NCREIF". The portfolio was specifically selected to match the risk/return characteristics of the index's underlying assets.

The structure is set out in the attached diagram.

Mechanics/pricing

The swap is priced off the NCREIF index, which tracks 1,800-2,000 United States properties with a combined market value of $21bn. The index includes five categories: residential apartment complexes, office buildings, retail properties, research and development/office facilities, and warehouses. The NCREIF is repriced through market appraisals. Roughly 25% of the index is reappraised quarterly and the new value is usually released ten weeks after the quarter ends. Minor adjustments of less than 1% are sometimes made after the revised index has been published.

The mechanism for dealing with any problems relating to the appraisal based character of the index or alternative arrangements where the index data is not published or released have not been disclosed. Several approaches are possible including an agreement by the parties to effectively share the impact of any adjustment in the index.

One problem relates to the potential problem that an initial overvaluation in the appraisal-based index might be built into the accounting of the swap. One approach would be to "discount the index at inception and amortise the difference to build in a credit over the life of the swap".

Structure of first real estate swap

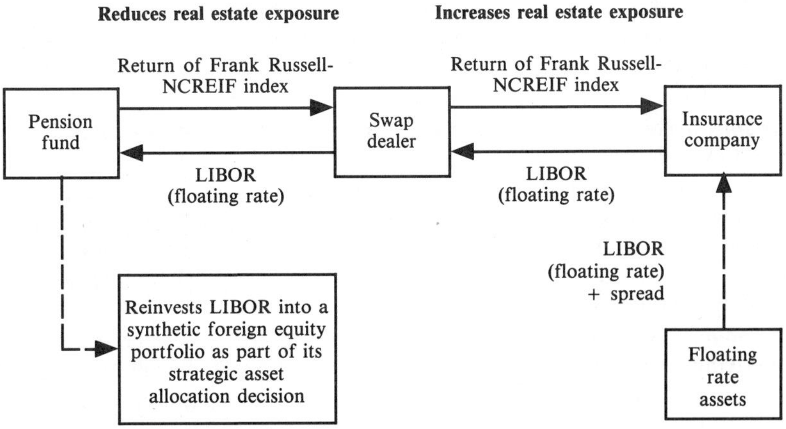

Source: William Falloon, "Virtual Realty" (1993) (March) *Risk* Vol 6, No 3, pp 7-8.

Commodity option structures

A variety of structures entailing options on commodity prices have also evolved. These commodity option structures generally take the following form:

- Options on commodity swaps (analogous to options on swaps—see Chapter 14).
- Paralleling the growth in exchange traded commodity options markets, over-the-counter market for commodity options—such as caps, floors and collar pricing arrangements—have also evolved.

The demand for over-the-counter commodity option structures such as caps, floors etc reflects user demand for asymmetric risk protection structures. For example:

- Consumers of commodities are frequent buyers of commodity priced caps (effectively call options on the commodity price) in order to lock in the maximum price they will have to pay for the commodity. Conversely, producers are purchasers of commodity price option floors (effectively put options of the commodity price) to preserve the value of future production and sales.
- Commodity consumers also frequently structure commodity price collars to guarantee itself a known range of prices for its commodity consumption requirements, while reducing the cost of the cap required to be purchased by selling a floor on the commodity price which limits its opportunity to benefit from future falls in the price of the commodity. Conversely, the producers often use reverse collars combining a purchased put with a sold call whereby it foregoes the benefit of future appreciation in the price of the commodity beyond the implicit call price level embedded in the collar in order to reduce the cost of the put.

A variety of more complex option structures have also evolved. These reflect similar more exotic option structures which have developed in interest rate and currency markets and include:

- *"Look back" options*—where the holder of the option has the opportunity to take advantage of the most favourable exchange rate recorded over the whole life of the option whereby the purchaser of the lookback call (put) can buy (sell) a fixed amount of commodity at a price equal to the minimum (maximum) price recorded over the options life time.
- *Average rate options*—whereby the value of the option at maturity is calculated not by the strike product at expiration but the average price since the option was purchased. This type of structure is particularly useful for commodity producers and consumers looking to hedge a series of recurrent cash flows over a nominated time period.
- *Variable strike options*—where the exact strike price is known only when the option expires.
- *Barrier options*—whereby the option is either operational from commencement but lapses as soon as the underlying price reaches a specified, predetermined level or "barrier", or, its reverse, whereby the option does not become effective or exercisable until the commodity price hits a certain level, where upon the option becomes "activated"
- *Compound options*—whereby the purchaser acquires the right to acquire an underlying asset which is itself an option—that is an option on an option.

The pricing of commodities options is very similar to the pricing of interest rate options: refer Chapter 11. Commodity options, consistent with their typical structure as options on forward contracts, are priced utilising the Black Options Pricing Model (which was developed originally to price futures contracts).

In utilising the Black Option Pricing Model to price commodity options, the following points should be noted:

- The asset price utilised is the forward price of the commodity as at the expiry date of the option and must be calculated taking into account convenience yields.
- A major issue in regard to pricing commodity options is the higher possibility of nonstochastic "jumps" (which are quite common in commodity markets) necessitating the use of different option pricing models incorporating jump price processes: see discussion in Chapter 11.

The calculation of volatility in commodity price markets follows the conventions utilised in regard to interest rate options and options generally. The methods utilised to calculate commodity option volatility include:

- historical volatility—which is estimated by calculating average price variation measures over short periods, typically, 60 days;
- analysis of implicit volatility in current set of actual option prices;
- historical analysis of implicit volatility of at-to-the-money options.

The difficulties of volatility estimation and commodity prices is similar to those experienced in volatility estimation generally. There is evidence to indicate that volatility, in commodity priced markets, demonstrates a mean reversion tendency. In addition, there appears to be a clear term structure of volatility, following the volatility cone structures described in the context of interest rate option volatility.

Commodity hybrids

A number of commodity hybrid structures, entailing combinations of interest rate and currency swaps with commodity swaps or derivatives, have also emerged.

In the first type of structure, commodity swaps or option elements are embedded into financing arrangements. This may typically be structured as follows:

- An underlying financing (in the currency of the borrower's choice) would be arranged, typically as a private placement.
- Simultaneous to entry into the financing transaction, the borrower would enter into specially structured swap arrangements under which, either, the coupons and/or the redemption principal under the currency swap was linked to commodity price movements. The commodity price element is typically an embedded commodity swap or option intended for the borrower, typically a commodity consumer or producer, designed to hedge its underlying position in the commodity.

The alternative structure, which is similar to the currency coupon or index linked swap (described in Chapter 15), whereby the interest rate under the swap arrangement was linked to commodity price movements. The linkage to the commodity is designed specifically for the swap counterparty consistent with its underlying commodity positions.

A series of transactions entered into by the VAW Australia, a German aluminium producer with an investment in the Tomago aluminium smelter in New South Wales, highlights the structural possibilities of this type of linkage. The first transaction, completed in late 1991, entailed a five year US$31m loan facility which was swapped into A$. The financing related to VAW's 6% share in the expansion of the Tomago smelter. Interest payments under the loan facility, which commenced some 18 months after the start of production (scheduled for January 1993) are indexed to the average London Metal Exchange (LME) price for aluminium.

As aluminium prices increase, the VAW's interest costs increase. However, the arrangement is subject to an upward limit (consistent with VAW's own price forecast for aluminium over the life of the facility) such that at the upper end of the aluminium price range nominated by VAW, the company will be paying approximately prevailing market rates at the time the transaction was entered. In the event that aluminium prices fall, the VAW will pay slightly higher rates than prevailing at commencement of the transaction.

Analytically, VAW has granted a series of options on the price of aluminium, subject to a cap level. The premium received effectively subsidises VAW's cost of funding.

Subsequent to the VAW transaction which was concluded with Bankers Trust Australia, the company entered into a further transaction with Citibank entailing entry into US$35m aluminium linked interest rate swap. The transaction, with a term of three years, linked the interest rate cost of the swap with aluminium prices. Under the structure, if the price of aluminium rises above the reference price (an average rise from the LME), then VAW pays a margin over LIBOR, and, if the price falls below the rate payment is LIBOR minus a margin.

The two transactions concluded by VAW highlight the interesting possibilities of engineering linkages between commodity prices and interest rate and currency structures.

MACRO-ECONOMIC HEDGING

Concept of macro-economic hedging

Macro-economic derivatives represent a special case of commodity derivatives. These transactions are structurally very similar to commodity swaps with the commodity in the relevant macro-economic derivative being an economic index. The most common type of macro-economic derivative currently is inflation swaps.

The concept of macro-economic derivatives is linked to the concept of macro-economic hedging. The basic concept relates to hedging business cycle risks or exposure to major macro-economic variables such as gross national product and gross domestic product, growth rates, rates of industrial production, retail sales, price indices, consumer confidence indexes etc.

Macro-economic risk management represents a shift from the traditional hedging focus, in relation to commodities, which focuses on price to a focus on quantity or volume. Macro-economic hedging, therefore, seeks to manage the volatility of business revenues as a result of quantity variations as a result of changes in the business cycle, technological developments and competitive market position. The conceptual basis and practice of macro-economic hedging is still in its infancy.

To date, two approaches to macro-economic hedging are evident:

- correlation based hedges;
- specific macro-economic derivatives.

The earliest approaches to macro-economic hedging were predicated on correlation-based hedges. Under this approach, adjustments are made to an entity's currency, interest rate, commodity or equity position based on assumed correlation with macro-economic variables. For example, adjustments in financial structure (capital structure, debt levels, fixed/floating or debt repricing structure) can be utilised to cover a business's correlation to business cycles.

An entity whose business performance is highly correlated to business cycles (such as certain service industries) can create economic hedges by having a larger proportion of floating rate debt than businesses whose performance is not as correlated to the broad business cycle movements. The basis for this approach is that strong growth in the economy, in general terms, will be correlated with increasing interest rates, which, in turn, will increase the cost of finance for the floating rate borrower. However, the higher interest expense of the entity will be offset by increased cash flow from higher earnings, reflecting the entity's performance correlation with the business cycle. The reverse applies where the business cycle turns down and interest rates fall.

Approaches based on correlation or multi-variate regression techniques have been utilised by a number of corporations to develop this type of macro-economic hedging structure.

However, the development of specific macro-economic derivatives may provide a more direct means of hedging this type of risk exposure.

Macro-economic swaps and derivatives

The basic structure of a macro-economic swap would entail a financial exchange between a stream of payments linked to changes in the level of a specified macro-economic variable and a stream of payments linked to an interest rate index or a fixed coupon level.

An example of a hypothetical macro-economic swap is set out in *Exhibit 16.20.*

Conceptually, variations on such macro-economic swaps would include options on macro-economic variables.

Exhibit 16.20
Macro-Economic Swap

Consider a fixed-for-floating swap in which the floating leg is tied to an Index of Consumer Confidence (ICC), such as the University of Michigan's Consumers Sentiment Confidence. The assumed ICC is based on a scale of 0 (absolutely no confidence) to 100 (perfect confidence), and it is asssumed that it currently stands at 80. Assume further that the notional principal of the macro swap is US$10m, the coupon rate is 20%, and the payments are scheduled to occur quarterly.*

In such a case, the floating and fixed rate legs would be calculated as follows:

Dealer Pays (Floating) = ((100 − ICC)/100) × (US$10m) × (0.25)

End User Pays (Fixed) = 20.0% × (US$10m) × (0.25)

Table 1 shows the first eight quarterly payments that would result from such a swap assuming our hypothetical ICC declined steadily during the first year and then recovered in the next.# In this case, the net cash flow to the firm from the macro swap over the entire two year period would be a positive US$350,000.

TABLE 1

Hypothetical Cash Flows on an ICC Swap

Calendar Quarter	Average ICC	Dealer Pays (Million)	Firm Pays (Million)	Net Flow (Million)
1st 19X1	80.00	$0.500	$0.500	$0.000
2nd 19X1	78.00	0.550	0.500	0.050
3rd 19X1	74.00	0.650	0.500	0.150
4th 19X1	70.00	0.750	0.500	0.250
1st 19X2	70.00	0.750	0.500	0.250
2nd 19X2	78.00	0.550	0.500	0.050
3rd 19X2	84.00	0.400	0.500	−0.100
4th 19X2	92.00	0.200	0.500	−0.300

Exhibit 16.20—continued

TABLE 2

Hypothetical Cash Flows on an ICC-based Floor

Calendar Quarter	Average ICC	Dealer Pays (Million)
1st 19X1	80.00	$0.000
2nd 19X1	78.00	0.025
3rd 19X1	74.00	0.075
4th 19X1	70.00	0.125
1st 19X2	70.00	0.125
2nd 19X2	78.00	0.025
3rd 19X2	84.00	−0.000
4th 19X2	92.00	−0.000

If the firm's profits exhibit the expected cyclical behaviour and the ICC proves to be an accurate gauge of general economic conditions, the swap illustrated above would offset most, if not all, of the firm's losses due to a weak economy and reduced sales. If the firm's profits instead decline far more sharply than the index, then the hedge would be only partly effective. The hedge would actually penalise the firm in the opposite set of circumstances—that is, if the index rose sharply instead of falling, and the firm's profits failed to increase as expected.

As this example illustrates, the effectiveness of a macro swap in reducing a firm's quantity risk depends ultimately on the degree of correlation between the swap's underlying macro-economic variable and the firm's sales and profitability. Given a strong and predictable correlation, the macro swap should enhance the firm's profits in an economically weak market.

As with any swap or derivative security, the end user can enter into a macro swap to hedge during a period of expected market downturn or temporarily heightened market uncertainty. But it is also important to recognise that swap dealers will price general market expectations into the swap. That is, the expected payoff (net of the dealer's commission) to both parties, dealer and user, should be zero at the outset of the contract. For end users, this means that, at any given time, a macro swap will be priced to yield payoffs only to the extent the actual decline in the economy exceeds the decline currently anticipated by the consensus of market participants.

* Determining how the coupon rate is established is beyond the scope of this example.

The ICC values reported can be assumed to be the average values that prevailed during the three months spanned by each calendar quarter.

Source: John F Marshall, Vipul K Bansal, Anthony F Herbst and Alan L Tucher, "Hedging Business Cycle Risk with Macro Same and Options" (1992) (Winter) *Journal of Applied Finance* Vol 4, No 4, 103-108.

Inflation swaps

Consumer price index or inflation swaps represent a special category of macro-economic swaps.

An inflation swap entails exchange of payment streams one of which is linked to an accepted inflation index and the other linked to a floating rate money market index. For example, a typical structure would entail swapping a payment stream linked to the US Consumer Price Index Series against US dollar LIBOR or, in Australian dollar terms, swapping a payment stream linked to the Australian Bureau of Statistics Consumer Price Index Series against A$ BBR.

Inflation swaps have evolved primarily in the United Kingdom and in Australia. The primary rationale for these structures include:

- to hedge "real" rather than nominal interest rates;
- convert inflation indexed income streams (such as inflation indexed bonds or inflation index rents, income etc) to nominal interest rates;
- to provide a basis for creating inflation indexed investment products, such as inflation indexed superannuation policies or annuities;
- to create hedges in relation to business cycle risks.

The activity in inflation swaps is still relatively modest. The basis for this activity in both the United Kingdom and in Australia is the presence of significant market in CPI or, in the United Kingdom, the Retail Price Index (RPI) linked government securities. In Australia, there is an additional substantial market of quasi sovereign infrastructure projects which have issued CPI linked bonds to create a linkage between interest payments and revenues, which are explicitly or implicitly linked to the inflation rate.

The transaction structures developed include:

- Index linked securities issues with accompanying swaps designed to convert the borrower's liability stream into nominal interest rate terms. For example, Merril Lynch arranged an issue for the Australian Trade Commission which swapped its CPI linked payments under a bond issue into floating rate US$ payments.
- Stand-alone swap transactions entailing exchanges of CPI index payment streams against floating rate interest payments.

It is important to distinguish this type of inflation swap transaction from a special class of CPI index linked bonds which emerged in the late 1980s which were designed as a form of tax arbitrage between the differential treatment between interest receipts and the inflation gain under these structures in certain jurisdictions.

The structure and pricing of these types of transactions are predicated on:

- counterparty transactions utilising inflation indexed income streams (primarily inflation indexed rents in property transactions, or inflation indexed income);
- utilising the cash flow streams in inflation indexed securities such as those available in the United Kingdom and in Australia;
- transactions which are hedged utilise inflation futures (such as the Commodity Research Board CRB Index futures in the United States), where available.

The market for inflation swaps is largely counterparty driven because of the difficulty of hedging inflation swap transactions. This reflects the fact that indexes typically moved in a "lumpy" way because it is not continuously calculated. For example, in Australia, inflation statistics are issued monthly, but accurate statistics only appear quarterly. Consequently, warehousing or hedging of inflation swaps would require the creation of a correlated surrogate CPI index using various commodity markets which is likely to be difficult.

In addition, the market growth is constrained in terms of the level of counterparty transactions because of the absence of people willing to swap CPI linked payment streams to nominal interest rates. For example, in Australia most borrowers with CPI index debts utilise it as a hedge against their, presumably, inflation adjusted income stream and are consequently not willing to exchange inflation indexed borrowing costs for normal interest costs.

Hedging macro-economic derivatives

Macro-economic swap and other derivative transactions are in their early stage of development and promise to be an interesting growth area in the global swap market.

As noted above, the primary focus to date has been on counterparty transactions based on opposing hedging requirements.

The concept of market making in macro-economic derivatives is still evolving. Tentative hedging techniques based on cross-hedging utilising correlations between financial market variables—primarily, interest rates, currency, commodity and equity indexes—and macro-economic variables are being tentatively explored.

Hedging macro-economic derivatives is subject to a number of difficulties:

- The cash value of the underlying economic variable is, generally, discontinuous as they are released at discrete intervals.
- Macro-economic releases are, often, subject to revisions at a later date.
- The basis for calculation of macro-economic releases are, generally, quite arbitrary and are capable of alteration at short notice.

An important aspect of the further development of this market in macro-economic derivatives will be, undoubtedly, the development of macro-economic futures. The development of futures in macro-economic indicators will provide market makers in these derivatives with the basic tools, provided the liquidity in the relevant futures markets is adequate, to manage risk exposures entailed in structuring transactions such as macro-economic swaps. In addition, greater awareness of macro-economic risk and interest in hedging this corporate risk aspect will also provide further impetus to this market.

Chapter 17

Equity Swaps and Related Derivatives[1]

EVOLUTION/DEVELOPMENT

The development of equity swaps and related derivatives parallels, to a substantial degree, the development of similar instruments in relation to commodities. However, there are significant differences both in the pattern of the development and in the instruments themselves.

Equity derivatives have a long history. Traditional forms of equity derivatives include equity options, convertible securities and, more recently, exchange traded options as well as futures contracts on equity indexes.

In recent years, these traditional equity derivative instruments have been complemented by the following instruments:

- hybrid equity linked securities and related swap structures designed to neutralise or securitise the derivative elements embedded in the security (these structures are very similar to those considered in relation to interest rates, currencies and commodities—refer Chapters 15 and 16); and
- equity index swaps.

The major difference between traditional and recent innovations in equity derivatives include:

- Traditional equity derivatives focus on *individual* stocks rather than market indexes.
- Traditional forms of equity derivatives were developed as means for providing capital raising opportunities for corporations as part of customised financing strategies.
- Modern equity derivatives tend to be equity market index oriented.
- Modern equity derivatives, insofar as they relate to individual corporations, are usually incorporated in the process of fund raising through new issue arbitrage techniques.
- Modern equity derivatives are directed primarily towards investors/portfolio managers, rather than corporations.

TYPES OF EQUITY LINKED DERIVATIVES

Equity index linked derivatives can be defined as a financial instrument whose return is linked to the performance of an equity market index. There are, basically, three major types of equity linked derivative structures:

- equity linked securities which are typically fixed interest securities where the principal repayment of the note at maturity and/or coupon payments throughout the life of the transaction are linked to the performance of an equity index;

1. The material in this chapter draws upon Julie A Allen and Janet L Showers (1991).

- equity index swaps where the counterparties enter into a contractual arrangement to exchange a stream of payments linked to the performance of a specified equity index against a stream of returns linked to a short-term interest rate index;
- equity options and warrants which are primarily call and put options on the equity market index.

As noted above, equity linked derivatives are linked to the performance of an equity market index. This is particularly true in relation to equity embedded securities and equity index swaps. In principal, there is no reason why such structures cannot be based on the performance of an individual equity security, such as the shares of an identified corporation and there are some examples of transactions of this type. A substantial market exists in options and warrants on individual or baskets of shares, paralleling the substantial market in options and warrants on equity market indexes.

RATIONALE

The development of modern, as distinct from traditional, equity linked derivatives reflects a number of factors:

- Investors can utilise these instruments to simulate purchase of an entire equity index as an alternative to direct investment in the relevant equity market with certain return and cost benefits.
- Equity index linked derivatives, which replicate the characteristics of derivative instruments, allow investors to circumvent investment constraints prohibiting entry into forward or option transaction on equities.
- These instruments allow investors to create highly customised structures creating a specific pattern of exposure to the relevant equity index.
- The structures are also capable of being customised in terms of exposure to exchange rates allowing investors to maintain currency exposure on foreign equity investments or to eliminate the foreign currency risk on the investment.
- Index instruments are attractive to investors who are primarily passive asset managers seeking exposure to the relevant equity market index.

A substantial portion of the attraction of these instruments focuses on the alternative to direct investment in the underlying equity markets. The major advantages relating to simulated, as distinct from direct, investment in equity markets include:

- *Asset allocation strategies*

  A substantial proportion of investors currently seek to achieve the required return in their portfolios through asset allocation strategies based on identifying particular markets in which to invest, as distinct from specific individual equity share selection. The investment strategy of these investors is focused on purchasing shares in order to create a portfolio that replicates the return on an index. Equity index linked derivatives are particularly suitable for this type of investment strategy as they facilitate the purchase of an entire index *with a single transaction*.

  Exhibit 17.1 summarises some of the most common equity market indexes utilised in equity linked derivative transaction.

Exhibit 17.1
Major Global Equity Market Indexes

Country	**Equity Index**	**Description**
Australia	All-Ords	All-Ordinaries Index. Capitalisation-weighted index of more than 250 companies, mostly industrial.
Canada	TSE-35	Toronto Stock Exchange 35 Index. Capitalisation-weighted index of 35 stocks.
France	CAC-40	Capitalisation-weighted index based on 40 of the 100 most highly capitalised companies listed on the forward segment of the official list. Calculated by the Societe des Bourses Francais.
Germany	DAX	Deutsche Aktien Index. Capitalisation-weighted, total rate-of-return index of 30 blue-chip stocks.
Great Britain	FTSE-100	Financial Times Stock Exchange 100-Share Index. Based on the 100 largest companies by market capitalisation.
Hong Kong	Hang Seng	Capitalisation-weighted index of 33 stocks, including four financial, nine property, six utility, and 14 commerce and industry.
Japan	TOPIX	Tokyo Price Index. Capitalisation-weighted index of all shares listed on the first section of the Tokyo Stock Exchange.
	NIKKEI-225	Price-weighted index of 225 Japanese blue-chip stocks that are traded on the first section of the Tokyo Stock Exchange.
The Netherlands	EOE	European Options Exchange Dutch Stock Index. Based on prices quoted on the Amsterdam Stock Exchange for 25 leading Dutch stocks.
Spain	FIEX	Capitalisation-weighted index of the 35 most liquid companies quoted on the four Spanish stock exchanges (Barcelona, Bilbao, Madrid and Valencia).
Sweden	OMX	Capitalisation-weighted index of 30 stocks quoted on the A1 list of the Stockholm Stock Exchange. The composition of this index changes quarterly according to trading volume.
Switzerland	SMI	Swiss Market Index. Capitalisation-weighted index currently consisting of 22 Swiss companies.
United States	S&P 500	Standard & Poor's Index of 500 widely held common stocks, including 400 industrial, 40 public utility, 40 financial and 20 transportation issues.

Source: Julie A Allen and Janet L Showers (1991).

- *Return enhancement*

The use of equity indexed securities can, in certain circumstances, result in improved returns to the investor. This return improvement derives from the following sources:

—depending upon the shape of the forward curve for equity index prices in the relevant market, simulated investment through equity indexed transactions can result in higher net returns relative to direct equity investment.

—improved returns may also be achieved reducing the cost that would typically be incurred by an investor in replicating an index through direct equity investments, including the cost of stamp taxes, portfolio rebalancing costs etc.

Exhibit 17.2 sets out an estimate of cost associated with direct equity ownership in a number of major markets.

Exhibit 17.2

Costs of Direct Equity Investment in Major Equity Markets[1]

	Round-Trip Costs[2]		Annual Costs	
Equity Index	Stamp Taxes and Commissions	Dealer Spread[3]	Portfolio Rebalancing[4]	Custody[5]
All-Ords	1.60%	1.60%	0.32%	0.15%
CAC-40	0.90	1.40	0.23	0.15
DAX	0.50	1.40	0.19	0.15
FTSE-100	0.90	1.20	0.21	0.15
TOPIX	0.80	0.90	0.17	0.15
EOE	0.75	1.50	0.23	0.15
SMI	0.80	1.50	0.23	0.15
S&P 500	0.25	0.70	0.10	0.05

Notes:

1. These are estimated costs to a United States investor. Actual costs may vary significantly.
2. Round-trip costs are transaction costs that occur when the shares of the equity portfolio are purchased and later sold.
3. Assumes that investor pays one half of the market spread on entry plus one half on exit.
4. Rebalancing costs assuming 10% portfolio turnover because of round-trip costs.
5. Estimate of annual safekeeping, dividend collection, reporting, and other miscellaneous expenses.

Source: Julie A Allen and Janet L Showers (1991).

- *Cross border investments*

  Equity index linked derivatives are particularly useful where the investor is undertaking investments in foreign markets. The use of these types of instruments enables the investor to avoid some of the physical transactions that would otherwise be required including foreign exchange transactions, rebalancing of the portfolio, tracking error, reinvestment of dividend income, as well as the avoidance of costs of custodial arrangements to hold the equities and stamp taxes etc.

- *Specialisation of asset management expertise*

  Equity index linked transactions also have the potential to improve the return to the investor by allowing specialisation in the management of one class of assets.

  For example, an investment manager with a relative advantage in managing short-term, fixed interest portfolios can create an asset allocation position in a specified equity market index by entering into an equity index swap against a portfolio of floating or fixed rate assets. The investor can out-perform the equity index where its performance in the management of the portfolio floating rate asset results in returns greater than the cash flows required to be paid by the investor under the equity index swap, thereby enhancing its return.

  Conversely, an investor with strong skills in equity investment management can seek to out-perform the return on fixed interest portfolios by utilising its comparative advantage in the management of equity portfolios through the reverse of this transaction. In this way, investors can *transfer* asset management expertise across markets.

A major factor underpinning the development of these types of derivatives in equity markets is the capacity to customise the pattern of returns from the relevant investment. Investment managers can utilise these specially tailored structures to position portfolios to profit from anticipated moves in equity market values, often within the constraints of investment portfolio management guidelines.

An additional factor is the capacity of these structures to be tailored to the foreign exchange risk management requirements of individual investors. Returns from investment in foreign equity markets, which are increasing, are a function of changes in value in both the equity market and in the exchange rate. Investment managers increasingly seek to customise their degree of exposure to the currency element of foreign equity market investments. The process of positioning currency hedges to achieve these objectives are more easily encompassed within equity index linked derivatives.

EQUITY LINKED SECURITIES AND RELATED SWAPS

The concept of creating debt securities whose performance is linked, in some way, to the performance of underlying equity asset has traditionally been embodied in convertible securities. More recently, a variety of equity index linked note structures has evolved.

The concept of creating and subsequently securitising derivatives, typically, forward or option positions, on the relevant equity market index has evolved from the various structures identified in relation to interest rates and currencies and more recently commodities: see above, Chapters 15 and 16.

The driving force behind these types of issues is investor demand for tailored exposure to specific anticipated equity market movements. The earliest examples of these types of transaction were driven by demand, primarily, from Japanese and continental European investors, for forward or option positions in the underlying equity market index. These investors were not able to take positions in the relevant derivative instruments due to investment restrictions: see discussion in Chapter 15. This prohibition meant that investors were willing to pay prices in excess of fair market value for these derivative instruments enabling the creation of securities issues as the basis of new issue arbitrage transactions.

The typical issuers of these equity linked securities were highly rated and well known sovereign, multi-national and financial institutions who utilised the transaction as a means of obtaining lower cost funding. This necessitated the issuers insulating themselves from any exposure to the performance of the underlying equity market index through a structured hybrid swap designed to transfer the equity market risk elements to the swap counterparty and ultimately to participants seeking this exposure.

The equity linked security structures that evolved were of two types:

- bull-bear type structures entailing the creation of offsetting tranches designed to appeal to bullish and bearish investors which produced a known maximum cost of funds for the issuer;
- securities whose principal and/or coupon payments were linked to the performance of an identified equity index.

Bull and bear bonds in all currencies have been structured to include offsetting tranches with the redemption value of each tranche being directly linked either positively (in the case of the bull bond) or inversely (in the case of the bear bond) to the value of the relevant index. From the viewpoint of the investor in a bull or bear bond, the fact that the redemption value upon maturity is determined by the level of the relevant index at some point of time in the future allows the investor to participate in index movements consistent with its expectations. It is however important to note that in almost all bull and bear bonds, the structure embodies a cap on the final pay out as well as a floor. In this regard, the characteristic pay off of a bull or bear bond approximates but is not a true option.

From the perspective of the issuer, there is no underlying risk to movements in the relevant index. This is because the two tranches are designed to be perfectly offsetting and to provide the issuer with a known fixed stream of cash flow payments into the future. The issuer effectively assumes no risk to movements in the relevant index as changes in the redemption value of one tranche (say the bull tranche) are offset by the asymmetric changes in the redemption value generated by the other tranche (in our example, the bear tranche).

An example of the type of stock index bull-bear issue involving the Nikkei Keisan Shimban Index on the Tokyo Stock Exchange is set out in *Exhibit 17.3*.

Exhibit 17.3

Yen Bull and Bear Bonds Linked to Nikkei Stock Index and Related Swap Structure

AB Svensk Exportkredit (SEK) on 25 July 1986 issued a series of JPY bull and bear bonds. The SEK issue involved two tranches, each for five years. The bull tranche involved an issue of JPY10,000m and pays a rich coupon of 8.00% to compensate investors for the additional risks that they have undertaken. The redemption value of the bonds were indexed to the Nikkei Keisai Shimbun index in the following manner.

For the bull bonds:

$$R = \text{JPY}10{,}000{,}000{,}000 \times (I + \frac{I - 26{,}067}{22{,}720})$$

For the bear bonds:

$$R = \text{JPY}10{,}000{,}000{,}000 \times (I + \frac{I - 19{,}373}{22{,}720})$$

where

R = redemption value in JPY
I = Nikkei stock average at maturity of the bonds

R is subject also to the following constraint: if I is greater than 28,461 at maturity, R = JPY6,000,000,000; if I is less than 16,979 at maturity, R = JPY11,054,000,000.

SEK's net position is a function of the underlying option position created which was securitised by Daiwa Securities, the lead manager of the issue.

For Daiwa, the bull bonds represent a five year (European) bear option spread where Daiwa purchased a call with a strike price of 28,461 and wrote a call with a strike price of 16,979, both of which expire in five years' time. The bear bonds resemble a bull spread for Daiwa where the strike price of the purchased call is 16,979 and the strike price of the written call is 28,461.

The offsetting nature of the two tranches allows Daiwa to stay perfectly hedged with no exposure to the stock index. Mathematically, this can be represented as follows:

- Redemption value of both the bull and bear tranches where I is the index at maturity is:

$$\text{JPY}10{,}000{,}000{,}000 \times [(1 - \frac{I - 19{,}373}{22{,}720}) + (1 + \frac{I - 26{,}067}{22{,}720})]$$

$$= \text{JPY}10{,}000{,}000{,}000 \times (\frac{22{,}720 - I + 19{,}373}{22{,}720} + \frac{22{,}720 + I - 26{,}067}{22{,}720}$$

$$= \text{JPY}10{,}000{,}000{,}000 \times (\frac{38{,}746}{22{,}720})$$

= JPY17,053,697,183

Exhibit 17.3—continued

- Therefore, profit for Daiwa
  = JPY20,000,000,000 − JPY17,053,697,183
  = JPY2,946,302,817
- For example, profit if the Nikkei Index is greater than 28,461 is:
  - for Bear bond: JPY10,000,000,000 − JPY 6,000,000,000 = JPY4,000,000
  - for Bull bond: JPY10,000,000,000 − JPY11,054,000,000 = JPY1,054,000

  Profit for Daiwa = JPY2,946,000
- Profit if Nikkei Index is less than 16,979 is:
  - for Bear bond: JPY10,000,000,000 − JPY11,054,000,000 = JPY1,054,000
  - for Bull bond: JPY10,000,000,000 − JPY 6,000,000,000 = JPY4,000,000

  Profit for Daiwa = JPY2,946,000

The profit dynamics of the issue are as follows:

- The bull bear bonds pay a rich JPY coupon of 8.00% which, in JPY terms is: JPY20,000,000,000 × 0.08 = JPY1,600,000,000
- At a five year JPY risk free rate of 6.50%, the profit of JPY2,946m translates into an annuity of JPY517,419,347 for five years.
- Therefore, effective interest cost to SEK is JPY1,600,000,000 − JPY517,419,347 = JPY1,082,580,653 which translates into 5.413% pa (JPY1,082,580,653/JPY20,000,000,000).
- From the above derivation, we observe that the bull and bear structure can reduce interest cost to below the JPY risk free rate. In fact, the all-in cost achieved represented a saving of approximately 55bps on a comparable Euroyen issue. SEK, desiring floating rate US$ funding, undertook a JPY/US$ swap generating funds at an attractive margin under LIBOR.

From the perspective of the issuer, the only reason for undertaking a bull or bear bond is that the overall locked-in fixed cost of funds generated is significantly lower than that achievable by a straight conventional transaction in the relevant market. That is, the issuer takes no final redemption risk (although the investor does) and is able to lock in a cheaper cost of borrowing no matter what the level of the relevant index is upon maturity.

This lower cost of borrowing achievable through the bull or bear bond can be translated across markets. That is, the issuer could effectively swap out of the currency or interest rate basis of the underlying bull or bear transaction to generate an attractive cost of funds in its desired currency or interest rate basis.

It is important to note that, from the viewpoint of the issuer, there is nothing apart from the relative cost to distinguish a bull or bear transaction from a conventional borrowing and the swap transaction is entirely conventional.

The only variation from a standard interest rate or cross-currency swap may flow from differential coupons etc (relative to market levels). For example, in one issue for SEK, the coupon on the bonds was an above market 8.00% pa (relative to the market rate that would have had to be paid by SEK of 6.00%). This higher coupon was compensated for by an effective redemption value at maturity of less than par (once the offsetting tranches were taken into account). If SEK had desired to undertake a swap against this bond issue then the peculiar high coupon cash flow structure would have had to be matched under the corresponding swap.

It is important to note that several important variations on the basic bull and bear structure are feasible such as undertaking a transaction where the linkage between the relevant index and the redemption value of the bond is structured on the basis that the maturity of the bond is longer than the period over which the final payout to be distributed to the investors in the various tranches is determined. For example, a number of transactions have been undertaken on the basis that on a five year maturity bond, the final redemption amount is determined by the movement in the index for a period of say one year. Under this structure, if the index appreciates, the bull tranche investor has a higher redemption value which crystallises and is guaranteed after one year although not payable until maturity of the bond. Conversely, the exact opposite applies to an investor in the bear tranche.

The equity indexed securities, where principal redemption at maturity is linked to the performance of an equity index are closer, structurally, to that of the Treasury Indexed Notes or ICONs (discussed in Chapter 15). Two types of structures have evolved entailing either the creation by the investor of options on the underlying equity index or, alternatively, the purchase by the investor of an option embedded in the security on the underlying equity market index.

Exhibit 17.4 sets out an example of a Nikkei Index Linked Bond and related swap structure. This type of transaction was extremely common in the late 1980s and early 1990s and essentially highlights the various structural elements of these types of securities and the related swaps.

Exhibit 17.4

Nikkei Linked Security Issue and Related Swap

1. *Terms of Issue*

Issuer:	AA Rated Financial Institution
Principal:	JPY5bn
Coupon (Annual (30/360)):	16.50%
Issue Price:	100.25%
Fees:	0.25%
Maturity:	One year
Redemption formula:	In yen at maturity based on:

$$100 - \frac{(\text{Nikkei at Maturity} - \text{Nikkei at launch})}{\text{Nikkei at launch}}$$

Maximum Redemption Amount = 100%

Minimum Redemption Amount = 0%

2. *Structure of Issue*

The pay-off structure of the issue (assuming the Nikkei Index at launch was 22,950) is set out in the Table below:

	Nikkei Linked Bond Issue High Coupon Structure		**Nikkei at Launch:**	**22,950.0**
Nikkei Index at Maturity	**Nikkei Index at Maturity (% of current)**	**Bond Redemption (% of principal)**	**Coupon Payment (% of principal)**	**Total Repayment (% of principal)**
11,475.0	50%	100%	16.50%	116.50%
13,770.0	60%	100%	16.50%	116.50%
16,065.0	70%	100%	16.50%	116.50%
18,360.0	80%	100%	16.50%	116.50%
20,655.0	90%	100%	16.50%	116.50%
22,950.0	100%	100%	16.50%	116.50%
25,245.0	110%	90%	16.50%	106.50%
27,540.0	120%	80%	16.50%	96.50%

Exhibit 17.4—continued

Nikkei Linked Bond Issue High Coupon Structure			Nikkei at Launch:	22,950.0
Nikkei Index at Maturity	**Nikkei Index at Maturity (% of current)**	**Bond Redemption (% of principal)**	**Coupon Payment (% of principal)**	**Total Repayment (% of principal)**
29,835.0	130%	70%	16.50%	86.50%
32,130.0	140%	60%	16.50%	76.50%
34,425.0	150%	50%	16.50%	66.50%
36,720.0	160%	40%	16.50%	56.50%
39,015.0	170%	30%	16.50%	46.50%
41,310.0	180%	20%	16.50%	36.50%
43,605.0	190%	10%	16.50%	26.50%
45,900.0	200%	0%	16.50%	16.50%

Under the structure embedded in the bond (via the redemption formula), the investor writes a call on the Nikkei 225 Index in favour of the issuer in return for the higher coupon.

If the Nikkei Index rises above the strike rate (the Nikkei Index at launch), then the principal repayed to the Investor is reduced in accordance with the formula.

3. *Structure of the Swap*

The swap structure entails two separate components:

(1) The JPY/US$ currency swap to convert the issue into floating rate US$ funding.

(2) The securitisation of the Nikkei Index Call.

3.1 *JPY/US$ Currency Swap*

Assume the rate structure at the time of launch is as follows:

JPY/US$ rate (one month forward): US$1 = JPY133.50

JPY/US$ swap rate (one year swap; one month forward start)

— Counterparty pays JPY8.09% pa (30/360 day basis);

— Counterparty receives US$ LIBOR *less* 0.25% pa (the issuer's sub-LIBOR target).

3.2 *Nikkei Index Call*

At the time of launch, the arranger procures a buyer for the (year approx) Nikkei Index Call Option to be sold in return for receipt of a premium of 8.25% (flat).

3.3 *Combined Cash Flows*

The combined cash flows (as between the issue and the arranger) are as follows:

Day 1—Payment Date

The issuer receives JPY5,012,500,000 (representing issue proceeds inclusive of the issue premium) from the issuer. The arranger receives JPY12,500,000 representing the issue fees out of the proceeds.

The issuer is party to the following payments with the arranger:

- issuer pays to the arranger JPY5,000,000,000;
- issuer receives from the arranger: US$37,453,184 ("the US$ Principal Amount").

The arranger, in turn, enters into two separate contracts:

- a conventional JPY/US$ currency swap (to match the cash flow between the arranger and the issuer);
- an option sale agreement whereunder the option buyer pays an amount of JPY412,500,000 (US$3,089,888) to the arranger (representing the option premium).

The option premium is then reinvested (typically via the currency swap) to generate the total JPY coupon payment under the issue.

Day 183 (six months after launch) US$ Interest Payment

Issuer pays arranger (who in turn makes a corresponding payment to swap counterparty) US$ interest at the rate of six month LIBOR less 0.25% pa (on the US$ principal amount).

Day 365 (Maturity)

US$ Interest Payment

Issuer pays arranger US$ interest at rate of six month LIBOR less 0.25% pa.

Principal/Redemption Payments
Case 1: Nikkei Index < Strike Level

(1) Arranger undertakes following payments:

Exhibit 17.4—continued

- The bond redemption amount is 100% of original face value. There is no payment obligation to the option buyer.
- Pays to issuer JPY5,825,000,000 (representing JPY5,000,000,000 (principal) and JPY825,000,000 (interest @ 16.50% pa)).
- Receives from issuer US$37,453,184

These cash flows are matched by offsetting cash flows with the swap counterparty.

(2) The issuer uses the JPY received in *Step (1)* to fulfil its obligation to the investor under the terms of the bond.

Case 2: Nikkei Index > Strike Level

The Bond Redemption Amount *is less than* 100% of original face value. The Nikkei Index Call Option is in-the-money and the option buyer is entitled to receive a payment under the option contract (based on a cash settlement arrangement).

The cash flows are the same as for Case 1 with the following adjustments:

- The arranger reduces the payment to the issuer. The amount of the payment is adjusted in accordance with the redemption formula with the issuer receiving exactly the JPY amount corresponding to its obligation to the investor.
- The balance of the JPY (the difference between the face value of the bond and the actual amount owed to the investor in terms of the redemption formula) is paid to the option buyer under the settlement terms of the option.

For example, if the Nikkei Index at maturity is 29,835 (130% of launch level), the arranger makes the following payments:

— To the issuer: JPY3,500,000,000 (70% of JPY5,000,000,000).

— To the option buyer: JPY1,500,000,000 (30% of JPY5,000,000,000).

The above arrangement ensures that the issuer and the arranger are protected from the fluctuations in the value of the option which are borne by the investor.

The structure of the cash flows are set out in diagrammatic form below:

NIKKEI LINKED BOND ISSUE SWAP STRUCTURE

Transaction Structure

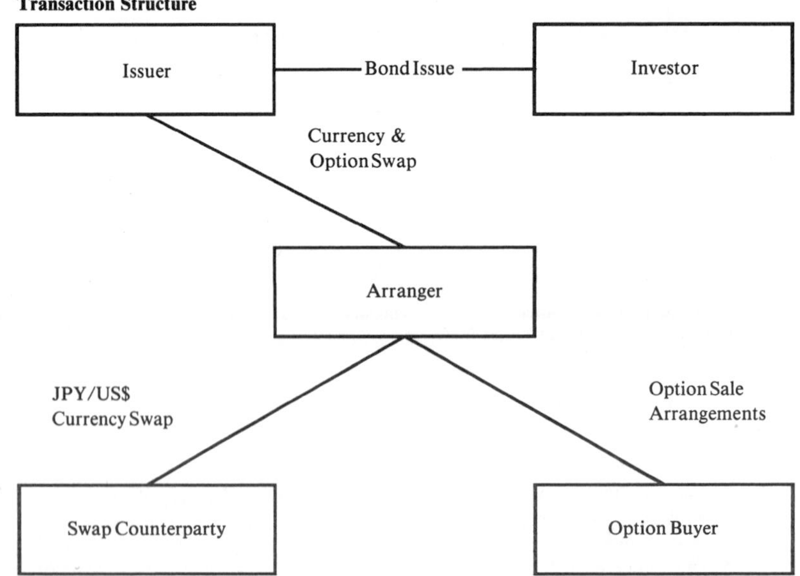

Exhibit 17.4—continued

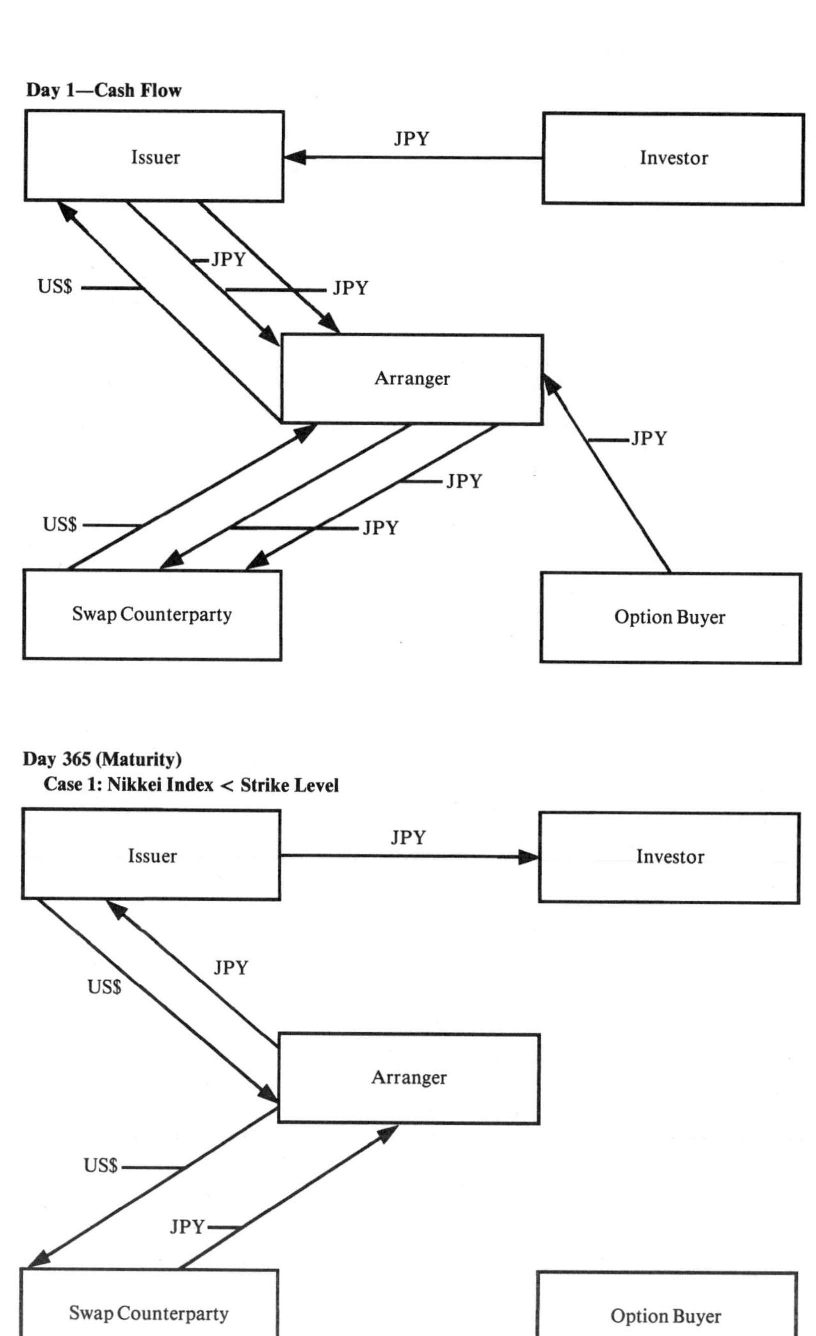

Exhibit 17.4—continued

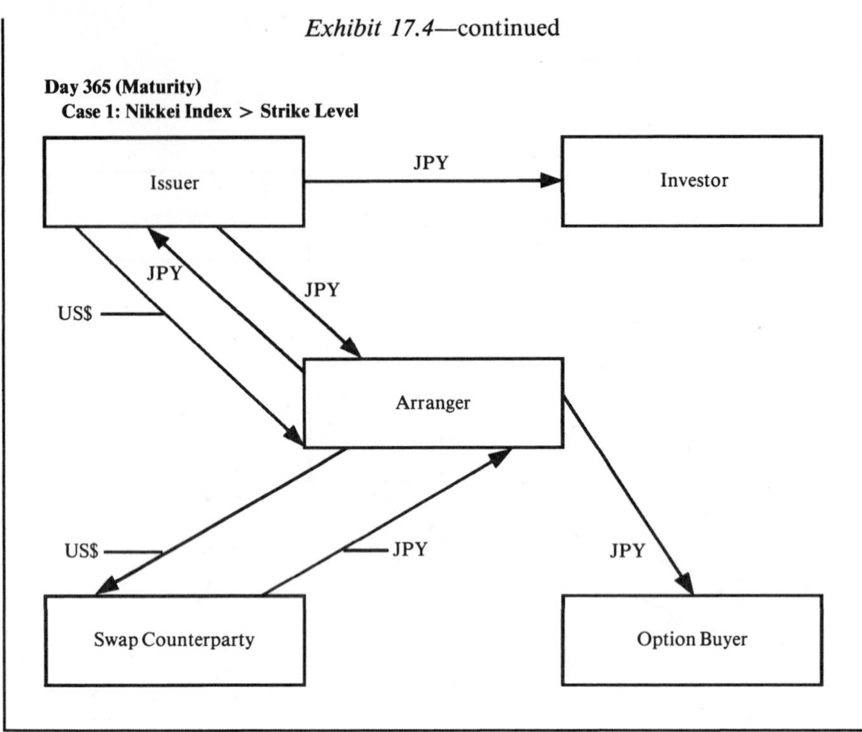

A transaction entailing the investor acquiring an option on the underlying equity market index is detailed in *Exhibit 17.5*. The transaction described is the issue of A$50m of All Ordinary Share Price Riskless Index Notes (ASPRINs) issued by the New South Wales Treasury Corporation in November 1986. This transaction illustrates this alternative type of structure as well as examining some of the pricing and structuring aspects of such securities and related swaps.

Exhibit 17.5

Australian All Ordinaries Share Price Indexed Notes and Related Swap Structure

In November of 1986, Bankers Trust Australia Limited (BTAL) launched an issue of A$50m of All Ordinaries Share Price Riskless Index Notes (ASPRINs) on the following terms:

Issuer:	New South Wales Treasury Corporation, guaranteed by the New South Wales government.
Amount:	A$50m
Maturity:	4 years (due 21 December 1990)
Coupon:	0%
Issue Price:	100
Redemption Price:	100 *or* $FV \times \frac{I(t4)}{I(t0)}$

Exhibit 17.5—continued

where:

FV = Face Value Amount

I(t4) = All Ordinaries Index at close of business 20 December 1990

I(tO) = All Ordinaries Index at time of issue set at 1372.00

From the viewpoint of the investor, the transaction operates as follows:

The investor is guaranteed return of its initial investment. That is, if A$100 is invested at maturity, then the investor receives at least A$100. The investor's final cash receipt, that is, the redemption amount, is linked to the All Ordinaries Share Price Index such that if the index appreciates over a stated level (1,372) and stands at this level upon maturity of the security, the investor receives a redemption amount which is calculated as the face value amount multiplied by the All Ordinaries Index at maturity divided by the initial share index level of 1,372. Thus, if the index doubles over the four year life of the bonds, investors simply double their original investment, if the index declines under the strike price, investors will receive back their original investment.

In substance, the investor has bought a four year European call option on the All-Ordinaries Index with a strike price of 1,372. The effective cost of the call is the income *forgone* on the funds invested.

This income forgone can be stated as: the forgone dividend receipts on the stock which constitute the index (around 3.00% pa); *or*, the interest income on equivalent four year comparable risk fixed interest investments (around 14.70/75% pa). In theoretical terms, the effective cost equates to the say, 14.70% pa forgone, interest which is equivalent to a A$ option cost of 42.83% of face value or A$21.42m for the A$50m call.

The issuer's perspective is different. The issuer saves approximately 14.70% pa, that is, the full coupon on conventional debt. However, the issuer assumes a final redemption risk as it has an exposure to the level of the All Ordinaries Share Price Index at maturity. The issuer uses a portion of its saving on interest cost to purchase an option which effectively hedges its exposure of the final redemption amount on the securities through the purchase of an (European) option on the All Ordinaries Index at a strike price of 1,372 with an expiry date in four years.

The options were arranged by BTAL and were apparently written by institutional investors. BTAL provided the New South Wales Treasury Corporation with the option and in turn purchased an offsetting option from the institutions. The institutions granting the option undertook the transaction as part of a programme of covered call writing against their equity portfolios.

The structure of the transaction for the issuer was as follows: New South Wales Treasury Corporation paid, it is estimated, 41% of face value (A$20.5m) to BTAL to cover its exposure under the equity index call. This effectively leaves New South Wales treasury with a four year zero coupon borrowing—face value A$50m; present value or net proceeds of A$29.5m (59% of face value). This equates to an effective yield of 14.10% pa—an estimated saving of approximately 60bps pa on its normal cost of funding.

At maturity, New South Wales Treasury Corporation repaid A$50 to the investors if the All Ordinaries Share Price Index was below 1372.0. If the index was above 1372.0, then BTAL made payments to the issuer covering the additional amounts as calculated under the redemption formula payable by New South Wales Treasury Corporation to the investor.

The economic basis of the ASPRINs issue was the differential value placed on the four year equity index call by the investor (the purchaser of the option) and the equity portfolio fund managers (the ultimate grantor of the option).

The value of the call option on the exercise price is estimated as follows:

OPTION PREMIUM (%)

Assumed	Dividend Rate (% pa)				
Volatility (% pa)	0	1.00	2.00	3.00	4.00
20	41.98	38.77	35.68	32.72	29.90
25	43.51	40.41	37.43	34.57	31.85
30	45.40	42.37	39.47	36.69	34.02

Exhibit 17.5—continued

The option fair value estimated is based on the following assumptions:

Market Index (at launch/closing):	1,372
Strike:	1,372
Time to Expiry:	4 years
Risk Free Rate:	13.90% (4 year government bond rate)

As is evident, the option price is sensitive to the assumed market dividend rate and volatility level. Based on an assumed market volatility level of 20% and a market dividend rate of around 3-4% pa, it is possible to establish a range of values for the option of 29.90-32.70%.

The investors in the ASPRINs transaction are clearly paying around 30% more for the call option on the market index, relative to its estimated fair value. Assuming that the institution granting the option priced the option at close to its theoretical price, then there is a maximum arbitrage margin of around 9-11% to be divided between the issuer and the arranger of the transaction.

A number of variations on these basic structures have also evolved including:

- Introduction of a gearing element into the principal or coupon indexation process whereby the value of the security changes by a multiple (usually higher than one, say 2 ×) for a move in the underlying equity market index.
- Hybrid structures where the performance of the underlying security is linked to not one but a variety of indexes. For example, the investor will receive a return based on the most favourable movement within a specified basket of indexes.

Stock indexes utilised for such transactions include the New York Stock Exchange Index, the New York Standard and Poors Index, the Japanese Nikkei Stock Average and Topix Index, the German FAZ and Dax Share Index, the Swiss SMI Index, the Hong Kong Hang Seng Index as well as the Sydney All Ordinaries Stock Index.

EQUITY INDEX SWAPS

Structure

The development of equity index swaps is a more recent feature of the market for equity linked derivatives. Equity index swaps are, structurally, similar to commodity swaps, although there are some significant differences. For example, commodity swaps, as discussed in Chapter 16, are utilised, typically, to hedge the price risk on forward purchasers or sales of commodities. In contrast, equity swaps are utilised *to simulate* an exposure to the relevant market index as a proxy for direct investment in the relevant equity market.

Structurally, an equity index swap entails a contractual agreement to exchange a stream of payments linked to the performance of an equity market index against a stream of payments based on a short term interest rate index.

Exhibit 17.6 sets out the structure of a typical equity index swap.

The key features of the structure of an equity index swap are:

- The payments are based on a notional principal amount but no principal is actually exchanged. The notional principal amount (which may be variable—see discussion below) is utilised for calculating the payment amounts.

Exhibit 17.6
Equity Swap—Structure

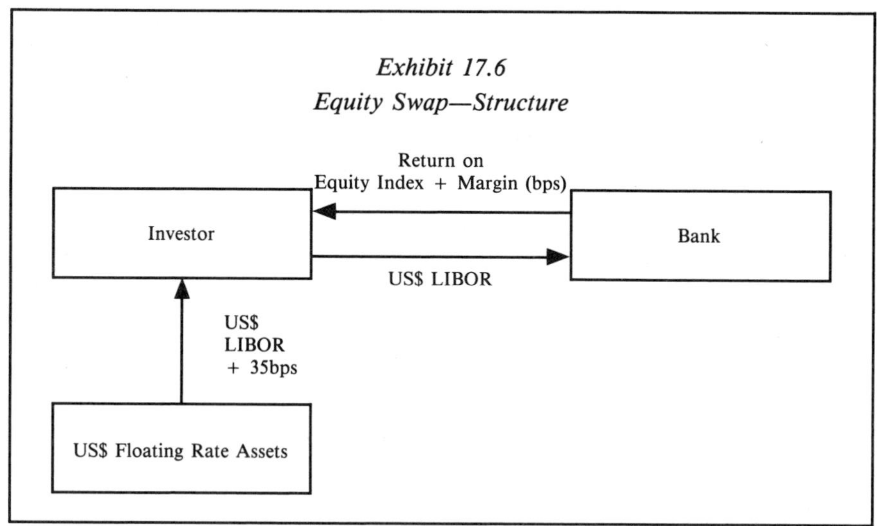

- As noted above, the exchange is based on two streams of cash flows:
  - *Stream based on a nominated equity market index*

    Party entering into the equity index swap will, typically, pay or receive the return on the equity market index plus or minus a spread (specified as a number of basis points). The actual spread or margin relative to the index reflects the equity index pricing and depends on market conditions, such as the prices in the futures market in the equity market index, and the particular structure of the transaction.

    The investor receives the total return of the index, defined as a percentage change in the index, where the return is positive. The investor will, in contrast, be required to make a payment to the counterparty in addition to the floating rate payment (*where it is the equity index return receiver under this equity index swap*) where the return over the period is negative.
  - *Payment stream based on short term interest rates*

    The party receiving (paying) the equity market index will as its other cash flow stream pay (receive) an amount calculated with reference to a nominated money market index. In a typical transaction, US$ LIBOR in the currency in which the swap is denominated is utilised.

    For example, floating rate payments in a US$ denominated swap would be based on US$ LIBOR; a Japanese yen denominated swap would be based on JPY LIBOR etc.

    The floating rate is set at the beginning of each payment period for the cash flow that occurs at the end of the period. The day count convention utilises the standard convention applicable to the relevant market.
- Payment exchanges are based on:
  - agreed reset frequency (typically, quarterly or semi-annual);
  - agreed maturity or termination date.

- As noted above, the payments under the equity index swap are based on a nominated notional principal amount. As discussed below, an equity index swap can be based on either a variable or fixed notional principal amounts. Typically, such swaps are structured with variable notional principal amounts which increase or decrease by the index return payment made or received. This type of structure is utilised to simulate the cash flows of a direct equity investment in the relevant market.

  Where a fixed notional principal amount is utilised, the principal amount is set on the swap settlement date and remains unchanged throughout the life of the swap. This type of structure simulates direct equity investment where the investor seeks to keep the equity investment constant and therefore is required to liquidate part of the equity portfolio whenever the market rises and invest more in the underlying equities whenever the market falls to maintain the investment in the index constant.

- The currency of the cash flows must be nominated. The streams of cash flows can be denominated in the same or in different currencies. In an equity index swap in a single currency, the index return is determined in the currency selected. In an equity index swap which is structured as a cross-currency transaction, the return associated with the transaction incorporates both the change in the index and the change in exchange rates between the index and swap currencies.

  The investor has the option of maintaining its exposure to the currency of the equity market index. Alternatively, the investor may hedge this foreign currency exposure by requesting currency hedge return payment. In this case, the return to the investor will be based on movements in the index adjusted for the cost of hedging the index returns back into the investor's specified currency.

Terms and conditions of equity index swaps

Exhibit 17.7 sets out the typical terms for a generic equity index swap.

The key terms and conditions include:

- The notional principal amount must be specified and a choice must be made as to whether it is fixed or variable.
- In relation to the equity index return payment, the specific equity index to be utilised, the spread, whether or not the index return is in the currency of the underlying index or currency hedged, and whether the dividends are to be reinvested must be specified.
- In relation to the floating rate payment, the specific floating rate index and the currency must be nominated.
- Other items to be clearly specified include:

  —final maturity;

  —commencement date;

  —reset frequency;

  —payment frequency;

  —payment dates.

Exhibit 17.7
Principal Terms of Basic Equity Swaps

Notional Principal:	Variable or fixed principal amount.
Maturity:	One to ten years.
Settlement Date:	Day on which floating interest starts to accrue.
Reset Frequency:	Periodicity with which indexes are reset, which is typically the term of the floating rate index.
Payment Frequency:	Periodicity of the exchange of payments, depending on the reset frequency: one, three, or six month intervals starting from settlement date.
Payment Date:	Date on which payments are exchanged; two business days following reset.
Index-Return Payment	
Equity Index:	Equity index on which return payments are based.
Spread:	Number of basis points to be added to or subtracted from the return payment.
Currency:	Currency in which payments are denominated.
Currency Hedge:	Foreign exchange rate risk is hedged or unhedged.
Floating-Rate Payment	
Floating Index:	Money market index on which floating payments are based.
Day Count:	Market convention (for example, Actual/360 for US$ LIBOR)
Currency:	Currency in which payments are denominated.

Source: Julie A Allen and Janet L Showers (1991).

Equity index swaps—alternative structures

The alternative types of equity index swap structures are dictated by variations in the following:

- variable or fixed notional principal;
- single or cross currency;
- currency exposure of equity market index hedged or unhedged.

The mechanical structure of alternative types of equity index swap transactions are set out in *Exhibit 17.8* to *Exhibit 17.11* (inclusive).

Exhibit 17.8 sets out an example of a variable notional principal single currency equity index swap. *Exhibit 17.9* sets out the structure of a fixed notional principal, single currency swap. *Exhibit 17.10* sets out the structure of a variable notional principal, cross-currency equity index swap. *Exhibit 17.11* sets out the structure of a variable notional principal, cross-currency swap where the equity index return is currency hedged.

The currency hedged equity swap structures incorporate, in effect, adjusting/compensating principal or quanto options: see discussion in the context of index differential swaps in Chapter 13.

Exhibit 17.8

Equity Swap Structure—Variable Notional Principal, Single Currency Cash Flows

1. Transaction Structure

Assume an investor enters into the following equity swap to convert a portfolio of DEM floating rate assets into a DAX Index linked investment. The terms of the swap are as follows:

Initial Notional Principal:	DEM100m
Term:	Two year (quarterly settlement)
Investor Pays:	DEM LIBOR
Investor Receives:	DAX Index + 0.10% pa

All swap cash flows are denominated DEM.

The cash flows under this swap (based on assumed DAX index and DEM LIBOR rates) are attached. All cash flows (in terms of receipts and payment) are analysed from the viewpoint of the bank counterparty (this is the case in *Exhibit 17.8* to *Exhibit 17.11* inclusive).

The methodology utilised in calculating the equity swap cash flows is summarised below.

2. First Settlement

The first settlement under the swap is effected on 2 May 19X2. The floating rate payment by the investor is calculated as follows:
Principal Amount × Floating Rate × No of Day/360
DEM100,000,000 × 9.45% × 90/360 = DEM2,362,500

The payment linked to the DAX Index is calculated as follows:
Principal Amount × (Index (t+1) − Index (t))/Index (t)
DEM100,000,000 × (1,912.5 − 1,900.6)/1,900.6 = DEM626,118.

The margin calculation is similar to the floating rate payment:
DEM100,000,000 × 0.10% pa × 90/360 = DEM25,000.

The net payment by the investor (to the counterparty) is:
DEM2,362,500 − DEM626,118 − DEM25,000 = DEM1,711,382.

The payment flows on all subsequent settlement dates are calculated in an identical manner.

3. Variable Notional Principal

The concept of variable notional principal is predicated on the concept that the investor purchases DEM100m of the equity index and does not add to or liquidate the investment and re-invests all dividends in the index over the term of the swap.

This, in practical terms, operates as follows:

- At the beginning of the swap, the investor purchases DEM100,000,000 of assets yielding, at least, DEM LIBOR. Through the swap, the investor has an equivalent purchase of DEM100,000,000 of shares in the DAX Index.
- As at the first settlement date, the DEM LIBOR income on the DEM100,000,000 of floating rate assets matches the outflow under the swap. The cash inflow of DEM626,118 (representing the appreciation of the index) is utilised to purchase an additional DEM626,118 of assets, increasing the notional principal under the transaction to DEM100,626,118.
- The notional principal under the swap is adjusted as at each payment date. The notional principal increases, that is, additional floating rate assets are purchased, where the index return is positive. The notional principal decreases, that is, floating rate assets are sold, where the index return is negative.
- At maturity, the swap payments (interest and index return) are calculated as normal. However, in addition, the floating rate assets mature or are sold for face value of DEM102,099,377 (the notional principal as at 2 November 19X3—the penultimate payment date). This together with the last index return payment of DEM115,753 generates a total investment value of DEM102,215,090 which equates the terminal value of an investment in the DAX Index over the two year period.

Exhibit 17.8—continued

Structure: DAX Index vs DEM LIBOR Swap
Variable Notional Principal

Terms:

Maturity (Years): 2

Periods per Year: 4

Initial Notional Principal: 100,000,000

Cash Flows—

Pay: DAX Index + 0.100%

Receive: DEM LIBOR

Cash Flows

Date	Days	Cumulative Days	Years	DAX Index	DEM LIBOR	Notional Principal (DEM)	Equity Swap Flows DAX Index (DEM)	Margin (DEM)	DEM LIBOR (DEM)	Net Payment (DEM)
02-Feb-X2				1,900.6	9.450%	100,000,000				
02-May-X2	90	90	0.25	1,912.5	9.375%	100,626,118	(626,118)	(25,000)	2,362,500	1,711,382
02-Aug-X2	92	182	0.50	1,875.9	9.250%	98,700,410	1,925,708	(25,716)	2,410,834	4,310,826
02-Nov-X2	92	274	0.75	1,860.5	9.480%	97,890,140	810,270	(25,223)	2,333,168	3,118,215
02-Feb-X3	92	366	1.00	1,885.4	9.100%	99,200,253	(1,310,113)	(25,016)	2,371,552	1,036,423
02-May-X3	89	455	1.25	1,885.8	8.520%	99,221,299	(21,046)	(24,525)	2,231,730	2,186,160
02-Aug-X3	92	547	1.50	1,892.7	8.240%	99,584,342	(363,043)	(25,357)	2,160,378	1,771,979
02-Nov-X3	92	639	1.75	1,940.5	8.010%	102,099,337	(2,514,995)	(25,449)	2,097,025	(443,420)
02-Feb-X4	92	731	2.00	1,942.7		102,215,090	(115,753)	(26,092)	2,089,973	1,948,128

Exhibit 17.9

Equity Swap Structure—Fixed Notional Principal, Single Currency Cash Flows

1. Transaction Structure

Assume the same transaction structure as in *Exhibit 17.8* with the exception that the swap is on a fixed notional principal amount—that is, the investor seeks a constant asset allocation strategy requiring the DEM100,000,000 principal of the swap to be constant.

The cash flows under this swap structure are attached. The methodology used to calculate the equity swap cash flow is summarised below.

2. First and Subsequent Settlement

The first settlement under the swap effected on 2 May 19X2 is as in *Exhibit 17.8* entailing a payment by the investor to the counterparty of DEM1,711,382.

However, at this date, the notional principal amount is not reset (as in *Exhibit 17.8*) and remains at DEM100,000,000. This means that the cash flows as at the second settlement date of 2 August 19X2 are as follows:

Floating Payment—
DEM100,000,000 × 9.375% × 92/360 = DEM2,395,833

Index Return—
DEM100,000,000 × (1,875.9 − 1,912.5)/1,912.5 = DEM(1,913,725)

Spread—
DEM100,000,000 × 0.10% × 92/360 = DEM25,556

The net payment by the investor to the counterparty is DEM4,284,003 (note the difference to the settlement amount in *Exhibit 17.8*).

As at each settlement date, the DEM LIBOR and DAX Index rates are reset to the new levels. The principal amount is never reset.

3. Fixed Notional Principal

The concept of fixed notional principal is predicated on maintaining the level of exposure to the equity market at a constant level. This, in practical terms, operates as follows:

- At the beginning of the swap, the investor purchases DEM100,000,000 of assets yielding DEM LIBOR.
- As at the first settlement, the DEM LIBOR receipt matches the equivalent outflow under the swap. The cash inflow of DEM626,118 (representing the appreciation of the index) means that the investment in the index is valued at DEM100,626,118. In order to maintain the DAX Index investment level at DEM100,000,000, part of the equity is sold, in conceptual terms, and would, in the case of direct investment in the index provide the investor with cash (the cash inflow under the equity swap corresponding to this).
- The notional principal stays constant as at each settlement date. Where the index return is positive, the investor receives a cash inflow (conceptually, the proceeds of the sale of part of the equity investment). Where the index return is negative, the investor experiences a cash outflow (conceptually, additional investment in the index to maintain the investment constant).
- At maturity, the investor receives DEM100,000,000 from the maturing floating rate assets or from the sale of these assets. In addition, the investor receives DEM113,373 reflecting the index return in the period 2 November 19X3 to 2 February 19X4. This amount equates to the market value of the investment in the DAX Index which could be realised through liquidation of the equivalent equity investment.

Exhibit 17.9—continued

Structure: DAX Index vs DEM LIBOR Swap
Fixed Notional Principal

Terms:

Maturity (Years): 2
Periods per Year: 4

Initial Notional Principal: 100,000,000

Cash Flows—

Pay: DAX Index + 0.100%

Receive: DEM LIBOR

Cash Flows

Date	Days	Cumulative Days	Years	DAX Index	DEM LIBOR	Notional Principal (DEM)	Equity Swap Flows DAX Index (DEM)	Margin (DEM)	DEM LIBOR (DEM)	Net Payment (DEM)
02-Feb-X2				1,900.6	9.450%	100,000,000				
02-May-X2	90	90	0.25	1,912.5	9.375%	100,000,000	(626,118)	(25,000)	2,362,500	1,711,382
02-Aug-X2	92	182	0.50	1,875.9	9.250%	100,000,000	1,913,725	(25,556)	2,395,833	4,284,003
02-Nov-X2	92	274	0.75	1,860.5	9.480%	100,000,000	820,939	(25,556)	2,363,889	3,159,273
02-Feb-X3	92	366	1.00	1,885.4	9.100%	100,000,000	(1,338,350)	(25,556)	2,422,667	1,058,761
02-May-X3	89	455	1.25	1,885.8	8.520%	100,000,000	(21,216)	(24,722)	2,249,722	2,203,784
02-Aug-X3	92	547	1.50	1,892.7	8.240%	100,000,000	(365,892)	(25,556)	2,177,333	1,785,885
02-Nov-X3	92	639	1.75	1,940.5	8.010%	100,000,000	(2,525,493)	(25,556)	2,105,778	(445,270)
02-Feb-X4	92	731	2.00	1,942.7		100,000,000	(113,373)	(25,556)	2,047,000	1,908,072

Exhibit 17.10

Equity Swap Structure—Variable Notional Principal, Cross-Currency Cash Flows

1. Transaction Structure

Assume an investor enters into the following equity swap to convert a portfolio of US$ floating rate assets into a DAX Index linked investment denominated in DEM. The terms of the swap are as follows:

Initial Notional Principal:	DEM100m
Term:	Two year (quarterly settlement)
Investor Pays:	US$ LIBOR
Investor Receives:	DAX Index + 0.15% pa
Exchange Rate at Commencement:	US$1 = DEM1.6425

The cross-currency nature of this transaction adds an extra layer of complexity. In the single currency (DEM), variable notional principal transaction (described in *Exhibit 17.8*), the market value of the swap was adjusted as at each settlement date by the return or the DAX Index. Most importantly, the DEM principal amounts for both the floating rate and the DAX Index payments were the same.

In the cross-currency swap, the process is similar but because of changes in the US$/DEM exchange rate over the life of the swap the US$ principal amount is likely to diverge from the DEM principal amount. This requires the market value of the swap to be adjusted as at each settlement date. This adjustment reflects the DAX Index return (in DEM) plus the change in value of the US$ principal over the period. This additional payment is made or received by the investor. In this case, if the DEM appreciates (depreciates) against the US$ relative to the level prevailing at the commencement of the transaction, then the investor receives (makes) the payment from (to) the counterparty.

The cash flows under this swap are attached. The methodology utilised in calculating the equity swap cash flow is summarised below.

2. Initial Principal Amounts

The initial DEM notional principal amount is specified at DEM100,000,000. The corresponding US$ notional principal amount is determined by converting the DEM notional principal amount to US$ at the US$/DEM rate current *at the commencement of the transaction.*

Assuming an exchange rate of US$1 = DEM1.6425, the US$ notional principal amount would be set at US$60,882,801.

On each subsequent settlement date, the notional principal amount is adjusted as follows:

- The DEM notional principal is adjusted by the DAX Index return.
- The US$ notional principal is reset to equate to the DEM notional principal amount *at the exchange rate prevailing at the settlement date.*

3. First Settlement

The first settlement under the swap is effected on 2 May 19X2 and is calculated as follows:

US$ Floating Rate
US$60,882,801 × 4.375% × 90/360 = US$665,906

US$ Spread
US$60,882,801 × 0.15% × 90/360 = US$22,831

Index Return
DEM100,000,000 × (1,912.5 − 1,900.6)/1,900.6 = DEM626,118

The investor pays US$643,075 (US$665,906 – US$22,831) and receives DEM626,118 from the counterparty.

The principal amounts are adjusted as follows:

- DEM notional principal is reset at DEM100,626,118.
- US$ notional principal is reset as per the following calculation:

  DEM100,626,118 @ US$1 = DEM1.7870 = US$56,310,083.

Exhibit 17.10—continued

- The difference between the original US$ notional principal and new reset US$ notional principal is made up of:

Movement in the original US$ notional principal		US$4,923,092
Movement in the DAX Index	=	US$(350,374)
Total	=	US$4,572,718

The exchange rate loss represented by the movement in the original principal (US$4,923,092) is paid by the investor to the counterparty.

The payment calculations for the next period are based on the reset DEM and US$ notional principal amounts calculated above.

The payment flows in all subsequent periods are determined in an identical manner.

4. Variable Notional Principal

The concept of variable notional principal is identical to that set out in *Exhibit 17.8* and assumes the reinvestment of dividends in the equity index and no change in investment during the term of the swap.

This, in practical terms, operates as follows:

- At the beginning of the swap, the investor invests in US$60,882,801 of floating rate US$ LIBOR yielding assets. Through the swap the investor has an equivalent purchase of DEM100,000,000 of shares in the DAX Index.
- As at the first settlement date, the US$ LIBOR receipt offsets the equivalent payment under the swap. There is, in addition, a positive cash flow of DEM626,118 (representing the return on the index) and a cash outflow of US$4,923,092 (representing the appreciation of the US$). The investor adjusts the US$ notional principal value of the floating rate assets by selling US$4,572,718 of these assets. This amount is paid to the counterparty, leaving the investor with no net cash flow.
- On subsequent settlement dates, the process is repeated. The US$ LIBOR payments are matched. Where the DAX Index return plus the change in the US$ value of the DEM investment is positive (negative), the investors purchases (sells) US$ floating rate assets to equate the value of the US$ floating rate assets to equal the DEM market value of the index at the settlement date.
- At maturity, the final swap payments (interest and index return) are calculated as normal. The investor has a total cash position of:

US$ floating rate assets	–	US$61,119,028
US$ Principal Adjustment	–	US$ 3,114,590
Total	–	US$64,233,618
DAX Index Return	–	DEM115,753 (US$72,825)

This equates to a total of US$64,306,442 or DEM102,215,090 which is equal to the terminal value of an investment in the DAX Index over the two year period.

Exhibit 17.10—continued

Structure:	DAX Index vs US$ LIBOR Swap Variable Notional Principal
Terms:	
Maturity (Years):	2
Periods per Year:	4
Initial Notional Principal:	DEM 100,000,000
Exchange Rate (US$/DEM):	1.6425
Cash Flows—	
Pay:	DAX Index + 0.150%
Receive:	US$ LIBOR

Cash Flows

Date	Days	Cumulative Days	Years	DAX Index	US$ LIBOR	US$/DEM	DEM Cash Flows		US$ Cash Flows		Spread (US$)	Principal Adjustment (DEM)
							Principal (DEM)	DAX Index (DEM)	Principal (US$)	US$ LIBOR (US$)		
02-Feb-X2				1,900.6	4.375%	1.6425	100,000,000		60,882,801			
02-May-X2	90	90	0.25	1,912.5	4.450%	1.7870	100,626,118	(626,118)	56,310,083	665,906	(22,831)	4,923,092
02-Aug-X2	92	182	0.50	1,875.9	4.750%	1.8795	98,700,410	1,925,708	52,514,185	640,371	(21,586)	2,771,313
02-Nov-X2	92	274	0.75	1,860.5	5.120%	1.8802	97,890,140	810,270	52,063,685	637,464	(20,130)	19,551
02-Feb-X3	92	366	1.00	1,885.4	4.975%	1.8647	99,200,253	(1,310,113)	53,199,041	681,224	(19,958)	(432,770)
02-May-X3	89	455	1.25	1,885.8	5.250%	1.8380	99,221,299	(21,046)	53,983,296	654,311	(19,728)	(772,804)
02-Aug-X3	92	547	1.50	1,892.7	5.480%	1.6820	99,584,342	(363,043)	59,205,911	724,276	(20,694)	(5,006,774)
02-Nov-X3	92	639	1.75	1,940.5	5.750%	1.6705	102,099,337	(2,514,995)	61,119,028	829,146	(22,696)	(407,583)
02-Feb-X4	92	731	2.00	1,942.7		1.5895	102,215,090	(115,753)	64,306,442	898,110	(23,429)	(3,114,590)

Exhibit 17.11

Equity Swap Structure—Variable Notional Principal, Currency Hedged

1. Transaction Structure

Assume the same structure as in *Exhibit 17.10* with the exception that the investor is insulated by the counterparty from movements in the US$/DEM exchange rate. In return for absorbing the exchange risk of the transaction, the swap margin is adjusted to *minus* 0.60% pa.

The margin adjustment reflects the cost of hedging the currency risk (representing the prevailing interest rate differential in favour of the DEM). An additional cost element of the transaction is the fact that the required forward currency contracts must be structured as *quantity adjusting* and *off-market* reflecting the uncertainty as to future DEM cash flows to be hedged (which are dependent on the level of the DAX Index).

Assume that the variable notional principal amount is set at US$100,000,000.

The cash flows under this swap structure are attached. The methodology used to calculate the equity swap cash flows is summarised below.

2. First Payment

The first settlement under the swap effected on 2 May 19X2 will entail the following cash flows:

Floating Payments—
US$100,000,000 × 4.375% × 90/360 = US$1,093,750

Index Return
US$100,000,000 × (1,912.5 − 1,900.6)/1,900.6 = US$626,118

Spread—
US$100,000,000 × 0.60% × 90/360 = US$150,000

The net payment by the investor to the counterparty is US$617,632.

The index for the subsequent settlement period is set at the level prevailing on 2 May 19X2. The notional principal amount is set at US$100,626,118.

This process is repeated as at each settlement date.

3. Variable Notional Principal

This type of transaction functions as a combination of a variable notional principal investment in the DAX Index (dividends reinvested and no change in investment over the swap term) and a (quantity adjusting) currency forward contract to convert DEM to US$ in two years at the initial exchange rate.

This, in practical terms, operates as follows:

- At the beginning of the swap, the investor purchases US$100,000,000 of assets paying interest at US$ LIBOR. Through the swap, the investor purchases an equivalent number of shares in the DAX Index (@ US$1.6425 = DEM164,250,000).
- On the first payment date, the US$ floating rate interest flows from the investment and the swap offset each other. There is a positive index return equivalent to US$626,118 which used to purchase additional floating rate assets increasing the notional principal underlying the swap. Through the swap, the investor has an investment in the DAX Index of DEM165,278,399 which, if converted at the initial exchange rate, is equal to US$100,626,118.
- On subsequent settlement dates, the pattern is repeated. The US$ interest rate cash flows continue to be offsetting. Where the index return is positive (negative), additional US$ floating rate assets have to be purchased (sold) to equate the value of the US$ floating rate investments to the market value of the index, converted to US$ at the initial exchange rate.
- At maturity, the interest flows and return on index are calculated as for all settlement dates. The US$ assets mature or are liquidated for US$102,104,193 which together with the final payment of US$110,897 equates to the value of the corresponding DAX maturity value of DEM167,888,285 which at the original, currency hedged rate, is equal to US$102,215,090.

Exhibit 17.11—continued

Structure:	DAX Index vs US$ LIBOR Swap Variable Notional Principal Currency Hedged	
Terms:		
Maturity (Years):		2
Periods per Year:		4
Initial Notional Principal (US$):		100,000,000
Exchange Rate (US$/DEM):		1.6425
Cash Flows—		
Pay:	DAX Index + −0.600%	
Receive:	US$ LIBOR	

Cash Flows

Date	Days	Cumulative Days	Years	DAX Index	US$ LIBOR	US$/ DEM	Principal US$	DAX Index US$	US$ LIBOR US$	Spread US$	Net Payment US$
02-Feb-X2				1,900.6	4.375%	1.6425	100,000,000				
02-May-X2	90	90	0.25	1,912.5	4.450%	1.7870	100,626,118	(626,118)	1,093,750	150,000	617,632
02-Aug-X2	92	182	0.50	1,875.9	4.750%	1.8795	98,700,410	1,925,708	1,144,343	154,293	3,224,344
02-Nov-X2	92	274	0.75	1,860.5	5.120%	1.8802	97,890,140	810,270	1,198,113	151,341	2,159,724
02-Feb-X3	92	366	1.00	1,885.4	4.975%	1.8647	99,200,253	(1,310,113)	1,280,838	150,098	120,824
02-May-X3	89	455	1.25	1,885.8	5.250%	1.8380	99,221,299	(21,046)	1,220,094	147,147	1,346,195
02-Aug-X3	92	547	1.50	1,892.7	5.480%	1.6820	99,584,342	(363,043)	1,331,219	152,139	1,120,315
02-Nov-X3	92	639	1.75	1,940.5	5.750%	1.6820	102,099,337	(2,514,995)	1,394,623	152,696	(967,676)
02-Feb-X4	92	731	2.00	1,942.7		1.6820	102,215,090	(115,753)	1,500,293	156,552	1,541,092

OTHER EQUITY DERIVATIVE INSTRUMENTS

Predictably, a number of variations on the basic equity derivative structures have evolved. For example, equity index swap structures combined with a variety of options as well as equity index swaps combined with offsetting futures positions to synthesise money market securities or neutralise futures roll exposures have developed.

A parallel and extremely substantial market in over-the-counter equity index options and warranties have also developed. These equity index options and warranties include call or put options on the market index. These equity index options are typically utilised by asset managers to hedge portfolio returns or to generate income by targeted put selling or covered call writing against existing equity investments in particular markets.

In addition to the basic option structures, a variety of more complex equity option structures have evolved including:

- *Currency hedged equity index options*

  These instruments are designed for investors whose domestic currency differs from that of the equity index and who seek protection from adverse fluctuations in the exchange rate. The currency hedged equity index option also often referred to as a quantity adjusted currency hedge or quanto essentially hedges this exchange risk. This ensures that the return of the option will depend solely on the performance of the equity index and the underlying amount is denominated in a specified currency. As a consequence of this type of transaction, the foreign equity return received at expiration is converted into the specific currency of the spot exchange rate when the transaction was entered into.

- *Compound equity index options*

  This type of structure entails an option on an equity index where the strike level is set in a currency other than that of the index currency. This type of compound option, allows asset managers to participate in equity market returns *in currency terms other than that which the equity indexes denominated.*

These types of structures and others (such as those discussed in the context of other underlying commodities—see Chapters 15 and 16) are evolving as asset managers increasingly seek solutions to the complex problems of managing equity exposures within their investment portfolios.

EQUITY SWAPS—PRICING

Pricing of equity swaps, effectively, is similar to the pricing of commodity swaps. An equity swap is, in its basic form, equivalent to a portfolio of forward contracts on the relevant equity index.

Consequently, the technique for pricing and valuing commodity swaps is, substantively, also applicable to the pricing of equity swap transactions.

In practice, the pricing of equity swap transactions is driven, to a large degree, by the means through which a dealer or market maker in such instruments can hedge its own exposure. Typically, the market maker in equity swaps will hedge the exposure in one or other of the following markets:

- the equity swap will be hedged in the futures market on the relevant stock market index;

- through the replication of the index by the market maker who will transact in the underlying physical shares constituting the index; or
- by matching the transaction with an exact but offsetting counterparty.

In practice, the predominant technique for hedging equity swap positions is the futures market in the relevant stock price index (at least, where index futures are available). In the absence of an index futures market, actual replication of the physical index can be utilised, although it is usually expensive.

The pricing of equity swaps hedged in the relevant stock index futures is a function of a number of factors:

- The liquidity in the futures market and, in particular, the liquidity in contracts other than near month contract. In practice, in a number of futures markets liquidity is confined to the near month stock index futures contract which necessitates the execution of "stack" hedges (see discussion in Chapter 35). Under this approach, a term equity index swap may be hedged by the market maker taking an offsetting position in the liquid near month futures contract. The market maker then periodically rolls the contract upon expiry assuming the risk of changes in the inter-contracts/inter-month spread between the relevant stock index futures contracts.
- Shape of the futures price curve in the relevant stock index. The arguments discussed in the context of commodities regarding the relationship between the spot and future price of a commodity are relevant. However, in practice, the capacity to arbitrage equity market indexes will generally ensure that it approximates the forward price behaviour of typical financial assets although backwardation in equity market index futures is not unknown nor indeed uncommon.
- Establishment of a hedge in the equity index futures contracts will require an estimate of a number of factors including:
  - the market impact of establishment rolling and closing of the futures position;
  - the basis risk between the equity swap and the futures contracts in which the position is hedged;
  - the cost of rolling futures contracts, in particular where, as noted above, a stack hedge entailing hedging a term swap in the near month liquid stock index futures contract is utilised (in this regard, it is useful to note that the relationship between contract months and, consequently, cost of rolling positions in futures markets is notoriously volatile and difficult to predict);
  - the cost of financing initial deposit and of margin payments;
  - the dealer's estimate of the risk of the hedge itself.

Additional factors relevant to pricing equity swaps include:

- In the case of cross-currency equity swaps, the base price of an equity swap in a single currency will be adjusted by the price of a cross-currency floating-to-floating swap. This may create value or reduce value in this specific transaction.
- In the case of currency hedge structures, the cost of hedging will incorporate, amongst other things:
  - the interest differentials between the currencies;
  - the yield curve shape between the relevant currencies;
  - the nature of the currency exposure to be hedged.

In regard to the nature of the currency exposure being hedged, where the investor seeks to capture a totally currency risk-free return on a foreign equity market index, in its home currency, the necessity for a quantity adjusting currency hedge creates additional costs. As noted above and discussed in detail in Chapter 13 (in the context of index differential swaps), such hedges, often referred to as "quanto hedges", require the hedge to operate in respect of *an uncertain amount*. In the context of capturing hedged equity market returns, the actual return component (the amount) is unknown and therefore a fixed quantity hedge cannot be structured. The cost of such quantity adjusting or quanto hedges is driven by the need to structure dynamic and correlation based hedges. The costs of these quanto options or hedges are incorporated into the currency hedged structures of equity swaps.

Chapter 18

Asset Swaps

THE CONCEPT OF ASSET SWAPS

The underlying concept of liability swaps can be extended to transactions involving the creation of synthetic assets.

"Asset swap" is a generic term for the repackaging of a security paying fixed interest rates into floating interest rates, or from floating into fixed, or from interest and principal payments in one currency to interest and principal payments in another currency.

The market for synthetic assets exists primarily for one of two basic reasons:

- An arbitrage (similar to a liability arbitrage) exists to enable the creation of a higher yielding security than one directly available in the market.
- The unavailability of a particular security with the desired credit, interest rate or currency characteristics in conventional form creates the opportunity to generate a synthetic security.

In essence, asset swaps are predicated on the fact that investors often require a set of *cash flows* that is unavailable directly in capital markets. In order to create the desired cash flows, the investor combines existing cash market instruments with an accompanying swap to create the synthetic asset.

In this chapter, techniques for structuring asset swaps, the market for synthetic assets, as well as private and public securitised asset swap structures are examined. The focus in this chapter is typically on transactions in which the asset and the accompanying swap have the same maturity, being designed to fully hedge the investor's underlying exposures into an acceptable form. However, it is clearly possible to structure transactions to provide any particular mismatch the investor requires and in practice, market timing or outlook, or any combination of both can greatly influence the structure of a synthetic asset transaction.

STRUCTURING AN ASSET SWAP

Asset swap mechanics

The basic mechanics of an asset swap are very similar to those of a liability swap. The asset swap will usually entail three distinct phases:

- the underlying physical security is purchased for cash;
- the cash flows, both interest and principal (in the case of a cross-currency asset swap), are linked to either an interest rate or a currency swap to change the interest rate or currency denomination of the investment into the desired form;
- the overall package is then held by the investor or, if assembled by a financial institution, is sold to an ultimate investor as an asset in its synthetic form.

Exhibit 18.1 sets out the basic structure of an asset swap involving an interest rate swap. The underlying transaction in this case is the purchase of a fixed rate US$ bond with a maturity of three years and a coupon of 10.00% pa. The fixed rate US$ bond is then swapped into a synthetic FRN, yielding LIBOR plus 25bps through an interest rate swap.

Exhibit 18.1

Asset Swap Involving Interest Rate Swap

Fixed Rate US$ Bond Swapped to Synthetic FRN

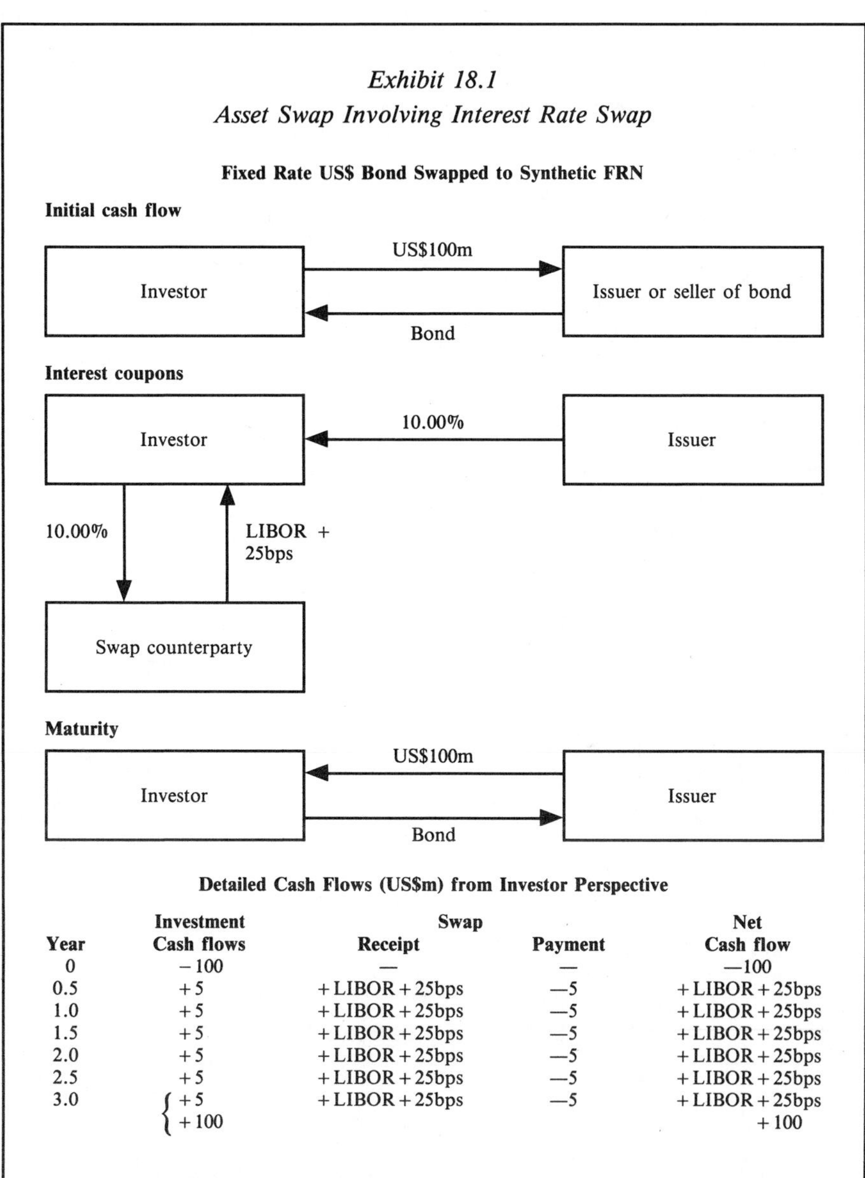

Detailed Cash Flows (US$m) from Investor Perspective

Year	Investment Cash flows	Swap Receipt	Swap Payment	Net Cash flow
0	−100	—	—	—100
0.5	+5	+LIBOR+25bps	—5	+LIBOR+25bps
1.0	+5	+LIBOR+25bps	—5	+LIBOR+25bps
1.5	+5	+LIBOR+25bps	—5	+LIBOR+25bps
2.0	+5	+LIBOR+25bps	—5	+LIBOR+25bps
2.5	+5	+LIBOR+25bps	—5	+LIBOR+25bps
3.0	+5 +100	+LIBOR+25bps	—5	+LIBOR+25bps +100

Exhibit 18.2 sets out the basic structure of an asset swap involving a currency swap. In this case, the underlying transaction is an investment in an A$ bond where the return is swapped to create a synthetic US$ FRN. The underlying A$ bond is

for three years with a coupon of 14.00% pa which when combined with an A$ and US$ LIBOR currency swap results in the creation of a US$ asset yielding LIBOR plus 45bps.

Exhibit 18.2
Asset Swap Involving Currency Swap

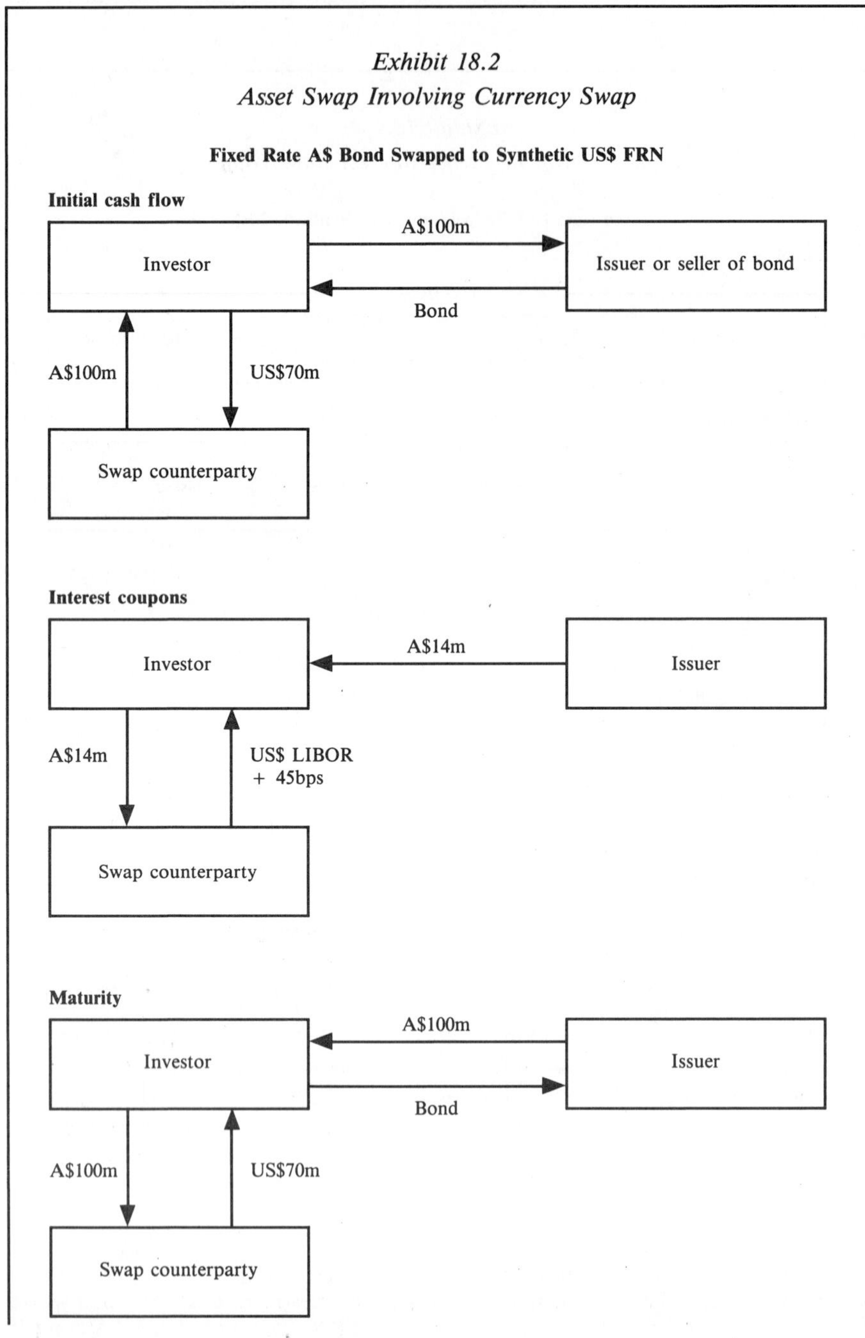

Exhibit 18.2—continued

Detailed Cash Flows from Investor Perspective

Year	Investment Cash flows ($Am)	Swap Receipt (US$m)	Swap Payment (A$m)	Net Cash flow (US$m)
0	—100	—70	+100	—70
0.5	+7	LIBOR+45bps	—7	LIBOR+45bps
1.0	+7	LIBOR+45bps	—7	LIBOR+45bps
1.5	+7	LIBOR+45bps	—7	LIBOR+45bps
2.0	+7	LIBOR+45bps	—7	LIBOR+45bps
2.5	+7	LIBOR+45bps	—7	LIBOR+45bps
3.0	+7 +100	LIBOR+45bps +70	—7 —100	LIBOR+45bps +70

In practice, the structuring of an asset swap is rarely this simple. The structural problems are usually created by factors such as accrued interest on the underlying security and any discount or premium reflecting differences between the coupon of the security and the current market yield for the asset. Given the preference of investors in synthetic assets for essentially a clean security where the investment is at par with the yield coupons equating to the purchase yield of the synthetic asset, it is usually necessary to significantly adjust the swap to convert the cash flows of the security to the desired pattern. *Exhibits 18.3* and *18.4* set out examples of structuring an asset swap in these circumstances.

Exhibit 18.3

Structuring an Asset Swap (1)

Assume the following scenario exists as of 23 March 19X2:

- A US$ Eurobond is trading in the secondary market on the following terms:

Amount:	US$10m
Maturity:	21 August 19X6
Coupon:	7.50% pa (Annual 30/360 day basis)
Yield:	9.21% pa
Settlement:	30 March 19X2
Price:	93.96385 or US$9,396,385.14
Accrued interest:	4.56250 or US$456,250.00

- The US$ swap market is trading at the following level for a final maturity of 21 August 19X6:

  8.23/8.30% pa (annual bond basis) versus six month US$ LIBOR

An investor decides to purchase the bonds and create a synthetic US$ FRN as follows:

- On 30 March 19X2, the investor pays US$9,852,635.14 to purchase the bonds.
- To convert the investment into the desired synthetic US$ FRN at an investment value of US$10m on par, the following swap is also transacted:
  - —Investor pays swap counterparty an additional US$147,364.86 on 30 March 19X2 to bring its investment to US$10m.
  - —Investor pays swap counterparty US$750,000 every 21 August commencing 21 August 19X2 and ending 21 August 19X4 (note that the first payment reflects the full annual coupon rather than the accrual from settlement).

Exhibit 18.3—continued

—Investor receives from swap counterparty, a margin over three month LIBOR based on a principal amount of US$10m (first payment 21 May 19X2 (broken period) and then quarterly thereafter).

The margin relative to three month LIBOR is calculated as follows:

	% pa[1]
Swap rate	−8.30
Fixed rate receipt	+7.50
Adjustments	
—full first coupon[2]	+1.1920
—additional initial payment[3]	+0.3939
—adjusted margin:	0.7859

The margin of 0.7859% pa is on an annual bond basis and must be converted to quarterly money market basis:

0.7859% pa (Annual) = 0.7836% pa (Quarterly)
= 0.7729% pa (Quarterly money market basis)

Notes:

1. All rates on an annual basis.
2. Calculated as US$456,250 discounted back to 30 March 19X2 (at five month LIBOR of 5.875% pa) and then amortised over each coupon date at swap bid rate (8.23% pa).
3. Amortisation of US$147,364.86 over the life of the swap.

Exhibit 18.4
Structuring an Asset Swap (2)

Assume the following scenario exists as of 19 May 19X7:

- An A$ bond is currently available in the secondary market on the following terms:

Amount:	A$10m
Maturity:	15 August 19X2
Coupon:	12.50% pa (S/A)
Yield:	14.90% pa (S/A)
Settlement:	26 May 19X7
Price:	91.4402 or A$9.1440m
Accrued interest:	3.4530 or A$0.3453m

- The A$ interest rate swap market for the relevant maturity is showing the following price: 14.30% pa/14.00% pa versus three month BBR.

An investor decides to purchase the bonds and swap them into a synthetic A$ FRN as follows:

- On 26 May 1987, the investor pays A$9.4893m to purchase the bonds.
- The investor simultaneously enters into a structured swap on the following terms:

An investor decides to purchase the bonds and swap them into a synthetic A$ FRN as follows:

—Swap counterparty pays A$0.3453m (accrued interest) on 26 May 19X7.

—Investor pays swap counterparty A$0.625m every 15 February and 15 August commencing 15 August 19X2 ending 15 August 19X2. Note that the first payment reflects the full coupon rather than the accrual from settlement.

—Investor receives from swap counterparty, a margin over three month BBR based on a notional principal of A$9.1440m (the original investment).

—At maturity, investor makes a payment of A$0.8560m to swap counterparty reflecting the difference between purchase price and face value of bond.

Exhibit 18.4—continued

The margin relative to BBR is determined as follows:

	% pa (S/A)
Swap rate	−14.30%
Actual fixed rate receipts[1]	+13.67%
Adjustment for principal payment at maturity[2]	+ 1.12%
Adjustment for carry cost on coupon[3]	− 0.01%
Adjusted margin:	0.48% pa

Notes:

1. Calculated as A$6.25m ÷ A$9.1442 or 13.67% pa.
2. Calculated as A$0.8560m amortised over each coupon date at the equivalent of 16.00% pa (S/A) on assumed principal of A$9.1442m.
3. Assuming a negative 4.00% pa over the 81 days to the first coupon on A$0.3453m amortised over each coupon date at the swap rate.

The adjustments required in structuring an asset swap are identical to the usual yield mathematics of such transactions as set out in Chapter 8.

Variations on basic asset swap structure

The basic asset swap structures entail swapping of a fixed rate asset into a floating rate of return or vice versa. Alternatively, it entails the swapping of the currency denomination of the asset as well as the interest rate basis. However, a number of variations of the basic asset swap structures are also feasible. Typically, these more complex types of asset swaps fall into the following categories:

- variations resulting from differences in the underlying securities utilised as the basis of the asset swap;
- adjustment swaps involving alteration of the basic cash flow of the security, usually utilising some type of non-generic liability swap structures (see Chapter 15).

An example of the first type of transaction may be a floating-to-floating asset swap where a basis swap transaction is utilised to convert a LIBOR-based floating rate certificate of deposit into a floating rate asset yielding a return relative to United States CP rates. Another variation may involve an asset swap with an amortising or sinking fund provision or a call option where the underlying instrument must be swapped utilising an amortising and a putable swap structure respectively. Some of the various types of underlying securities utilised in asset swaps and the variations resulting therein are discussed later in this chapter.

The concept of an adjustment swap is more complex. Typically, certain types of investors for reasons such as tax or accounting treatment may prefer to change the cash flow characteristics of the underlying security. For example:

- An investor buying a fixed rate bond or FRN at a substantial discount may seek to convert it into a par security by entering into an interest rate swap in which the investor pays fixed or floating at a rate equal to the coupon on the security. This rate will usually be less than the market rate on the swap of that maturity and in return for paying less than a market return, the investor will make a one-time up-front cash payment to the swap counterparty equal to the difference between the par value and the purchase price of the security. This difference compensates the swap counterparty for receiving a submarket coupon with the up-front payment being repaid to the investor over the life of the swap in the form of a premium on the swap payments it receives.

- In the opposite situation, an investor buying a bond at a premium may choose to pay an above market rate on the swap equivalent to the bond coupon in return for an up-front payment from the swap counterparty equal to the premium on the bond. This payment is recovered by the swap counterparty by the fact that the investor pays an above market coupon under the swap.

These types of adjustment swaps, which are increasingly common, allow investors to smooth out and adjust the cash flows connected with specific investments. In essence, swap coupons can be set equal to bond coupons while margins above or below market coupons can be exchanged for up-front or, in some cases, backended payments allowing the investor to rearrange cash flows from an investment into a structure that, for any reason, the investor finds more attractive.

Some examples of these types of adjustment swaps include:

- Par/par flat swap where a customer wishing to invest in a par asset at a stated return with no accrued interest needs to convert a security trading at a discount through this specific swap structure (for example, see *Exhibit 18.3*).
- A zero coupon issue swapped into a three or six month floating rate coupon.
- A discount floating rate coupon swapped to full floating coupon, for example, where a FRN can be bought at a substantial discount to par but the investor wants current income and therefore wants to buy the bonds at par and receive the current market yield to maturity spread rather than the difference between the purchase price and face value of the notes at maturity.
- A zero coupon bond swapped to a full fixed coupon, for example, where the zero coupon is priced attractively but the investor desires to shorten the duration and improve the cash flow of the investment.

Exhibit 18.5 illustrates an adjustment swap involving swapping of the discount on a FRN to a full floating coupon.

Exhibit 18.5
Adjustment Asset Swap

An investor has the opportunity to buy the following FRN:

Amount:	US$5m
Maturity:	30 June 19X9
Interest rate:	six month LIBOR, net and payable semi-annually
Price:	98.80
Yield to maturity spread:	LIBOR + 34bps
Current coupon:	7.3125%
Settlement date:	30 June 19X5

However, the investor has a preference for current income and thus would prefer to purchase the FRN at par and receive the current market yield to maturity spread as coupon income. The investor achieves this by entering into an asset swap whereby:

- The investor pays the counterparty six month LIBOR flat semi-annually as well as an up-front payment of 1.20% or US$60,000.
- In return, the investor receives six month LIBOR plus 35.74bps semi-annually over the life of the transaction.

The spread over LIBOR earned by the investor equates to the 1.20% being amortised over the outstanding life of the security at an assumed reinvestment rate of 8.80% pa (S/A).

THE MARKET FOR ASSET SWAPS

The structure of the market

The concept of asset swaps is best understood with reference to the underlying market for these types of transactions. The market for asset swaps which has evolved over the period since 1982 has a number of clearly identifiable dimensions:

- the type of asset swap transaction, classified by category of investor;
- types of underlying securities utilised in structuring the asset swap;
- private asset swap structures versus public or securitised asset swaps. Private asset swap structures themselves can be separated into two further categories: investor made swaps and synthetic securities.

The basic asset swap structures utilised are largely dictated by the interaction of these various structural dimensions.

Types of asset swaps

The types of asset swaps that are usually undertaken are dictated almost totally by the investor base for such synthetic assets. In turn, the investor base for these types of asset swaps is motivated to enter into such transactions for some clearly identifiable reasons.

The main factor in this context has been the increasing securitisation of capital markets which has led to borrowers increasingly issuing securities to raise money on more competitive terms than available by borrowing from financial intermediaries, primarily banks. This has created a significant shortage of conventional loan assets. As a result many banks face a dwindling asset base as they lose their historic customer base to the securities markets.

An additional factor which is relevant was the substantial improvement in yields that were achievable by creating synthetic assets relative to the purchase of direct investments. In essence, the right conditions existed for a basic arbitrage which created the opportunity for yield pick-ups where, importantly, there was a ready-made market for these synthetic assets primarily among banks.

A further factor is the use of asset swaps to achieve an increased level of diversification of a financial institution's asset portfolio.

Since the development of these markets, similar factors have attracted other more traditional investors such as institutions, pension funds etc to this market.

The basic types of asset swaps include:

- assets denominated in any currency which are swapped into synthetic US$ LIBOR based FRNs which are sold primarily to banks;
- asset swaps which entail the creation of synthetic fixed rate bonds, in currencies such as yen, utilising either fixed or floating rate securities in a variety of currencies for sale to institutional investors;
- asset swaps designed to create synthetic FRNs in currencies other than US$ to match demands for non-US$ floating rate assets;
- a number of variations on the above usually entailing special structured transactions including:
  —insurance company deposit transactions;
  —matched zaitech transactions.

Exhibit 18.6 sets out an analysis of repackaged issues by currency and type (fixed or floating rate). (These statistics are based on *public* repackaged asset swap issue (see discussion below) and do not include *private* transactions and consequently can only be regarded as indicative.) The statistics are for the period 1985 to 1990 which was probably the most active period for public repackaging issues.

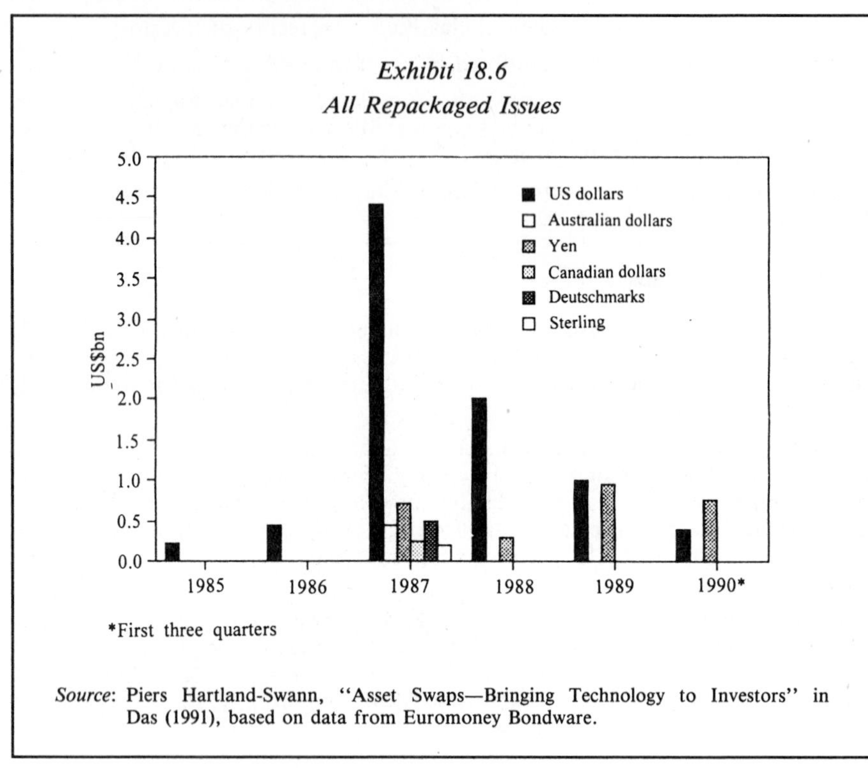

Exhibit 18.6

All Repackaged Issues

Source: Piers Hartland-Swann, "Asset Swaps—Bringing Technology to Investors" in Das (1991), based on data from Euromoney Bondware.

Asset swaps involving the creation of synthetic US$ LIBOR based FRNs constitute by far the most significant sector of the asset swap market. It constitutes probably 80-90% of all asset swaps undertaken. The predominance of this type of structure primarily reflects the nature of the underlying investment demand which comes from commercial banks seeking floating rate loan assets which can be match funded. The continued need for high quality and relatively high yield assets by a large group of commercial banks seeking asset growth, provides a significant impetus to this particular market segment. *Exhibit 18.7* sets out an analysis of repackaged issues by type. (These statistics only cover public repackagings in the period 1985 to 1990.)

Traditionally, demand for asset swap investments has been dominated by Japanese, Far Eastern, Middle Eastern, United States regional and Australasian banks. The participation of Japanese and United States regional banks, in particular, have declined in recent years. Their place has been taken by German banks, particularly the Landesbanks, as well as Benelux and Italian banks and United Kingdom building societies (to a lesser extent).

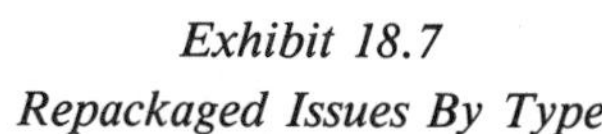

Exhibit 18.7
Repackaged Issues By Type

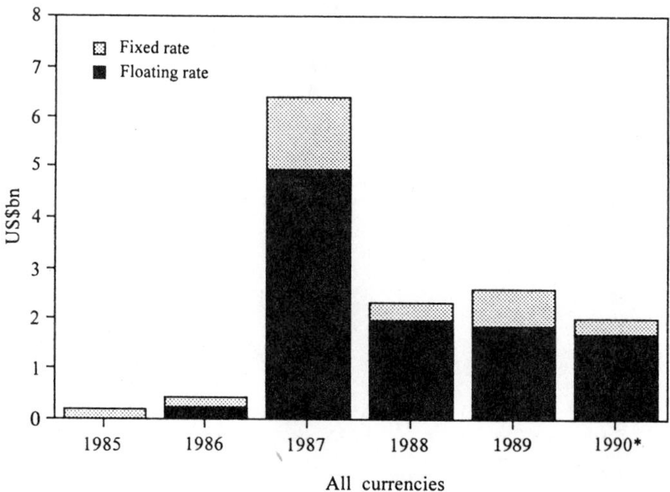

*First three quarters

Source: Piers Hartland-Swann, "Asset Swaps—Bringing Technology to Investors" in Das (1991), based on data from Euromoney Bondware.

The extent of the yield improvements achievable by investing in asset swaps as against direct purchase of floating rate assets can be gauged from the analysis set out in *Exhibits 18.8* and *18.9*. As indicated, the synthetic assets not only offer substantial yield pick-ups compared with the return available on equivalent direct investments but as an additional incentive they offer an investor greater flexibility to diversify its portfolio by allowing investment in issuers who do not usually undertaken FRN issues.

Exhibit 18.8
Return Comparison of Synthetic vs Direct US$ FRN

1. 1986

Issuer	**Rating**	**Maturity (years)**	**Margin over six months LIBID in basis points** Estimated in public FRN market	Available on synthetic FRN	**Absolute yield pick-up**
Republic of Austria	AAA	6	−5.0	+22.5	+27.5
Bank of Tokyo[1]	AA	5	+4.0	+25.0	+21.0
Credit Anstalt Bank Verein		5	+5.0	+27.5	+22.5
Kingdom of Denmark	AA+	6	−5.0	+25.0	+30.0

Exhibit 18.8—continued

Issuer	Rating	Maturity (years)	Margin over six months LIBID in basis points: Estimated in public FRN market	Available on synthetic FRN	Absolute yield pick-up
Industrial Bank of Japan[1]	AAA	6	+3.0	+25.0	+22.0
Royal Bank of Canada		6	+6.0	+27.5	+21.5
Oesterreichische Landesbank		3	+5.0	+25.0	+20.0
Mitsubishi Corporation	AAA(AA+)	8	+12.5	+30.0	+17.5
PK Banken		5	+6.0	+27.5	+21.5
Deutsche Bank	AAA	9	−2.0	+27.5	+29.5
Development Finance Corporation (New Zealand)	AA	9	0.0	+30.0	+30.0

2. May 1988

Issuer	Rating	Maturity (years)	Margin over six months LIBID in basis points: Estimated in public FRN market	Available on synthetic FRN	Absolute yield pick-up
Republic of Austria	AAA	1	0	+27	+27
Bank of Tokyo[1]	AA	7	+30	+47	+17
Credit Anstalt Bank Verein		5	−5	+23	+28
Kingdom of Denmark	AA+	3	0	+39	+39
Royal Bank of Canada		6	+6	+27.5	+21.5
Oesterreichische Landesbank		3	+5	+25	+20
Mitsubishi Corporation	AAA(AA+)	5	0	+42	+42
PK Banken		5	+10	+30	+20
Deutsche Bank	AAA	9	0	+30	+30
Development Finance Corporation (New Zealand)	AA	9	5	+55	+60

3. June/July 1993

Issuer	Rating	Maturity (years)	Margin over six months LIBID in basis points: Estimated in public FRN market	Available on synthetic FRN	Absolute yield pick-up
Republic of Italy	A	5-7	+47.5	+62.5	+15
IMI Bank	A	3-5	+50.5	+57.5	+17
CBA	AA	5-7	+27.5	+37.5	+10
Treasury Corp of Victoria	A	5	+27.5	+47.5	+20
Finland	AA	5	+32.5	+47.5	+15
Republic of Ireland	AA	8-10	+17.5	+32.5	+15
Abbey National	AA	5	+12.5	+35.5	+33
National & Provincial	A	5	+37.5	+52.5	+15
Kansallis Osaki Pankki	BBB	3	+82.5	+102.5	+20
World Bank	AAA	7-10	−2.5	+25.0	+27.5
EIB	AAA	7-10	−2.5	+25.0	+27.5

Note:
1. Similar returns are available on corporate bonds with bank guarantees.

Source: 1986 and 1988 data supplied by Citicorp. 1993 data supplied by Swiss Bank Corporation.

Exhibit 18.9
Return Available on Asset Swaps

1. Asset Swaps (Average LIBOR Spread (bp) by credit rating)

Sovereigns and supranationals	
AAA	1
AA1	13
AA2	33
AA3	49
Financial institutions	
AAA	6
AA1	22
AA2	30
AA3	50
Corporate issues	
AAA	7
AA2	23
A1	80
A2	134

As of 19 March 1993. Includes C$, DEM, FFR, GBP, LIT, JPY, US$, ECU.

Source: Paribas Capital Markets.

2. Selected Asset Swaps

Issuer	Amount available	Term	Rating	Libor + margin
Crédit Foncier	JPY1.5 billion	22.12.94	AAA	JPY + 3 bps
City of Gothenburg	SFR14 million	10.12.99	Aa3	SFR + 40 bps
Finland	US$10 million	24.11.97	Aa2	US$ + 42 bps
Portugal	JPY1 billion	12.2.98	A1	JPY + 26 bps
Ontario	SFR10 million	27.1.03	Aa2	SFR + 50 bps
National Bank of Hungary	DEM5 million	16.9.96	BB1	DEM + 210 bps
Victoria Finance	GBP10 million	11.8.99	A1	GBP + 50 bps
Soc Gen (France)	FFR100 million	14.1.03	Aa1	PIBOR + 37.5 bps
SBAB	SKR57 million	20.9.95	Aa3	US$ + 50 bps
Finnish Export Credit	SFR10 million	12.3.98	Aa2	SFR + 42 bps
Abbey National	GBP5 million	22.4.97	Aa2	GBP + 25 bps
Allied Lyons	GBP5 million	25.2.99	A2	GBP + 60 bps
Aerospatiale	LIT10 billion	16.12.96	AA	LIT + 40 bps
Lufthansa	DEM10 million	5.4.00	NR	DEM + 110 bps
Hoogovens	DEM10 million	1.6.95	NR	DEM + 350 bps
Eutelsat	GBP15 million	11.3.97	Aa1	GBP + 35 bps

Counterparty for asset swaps is Deutsche Bank Frankfurt. Source: Deutsche Bank London, 12 March 1993.

Source: Euan Hagger (1993).

It is also worth noting that part of the attraction of synthetic US$ FRNs relates to the call features on normal FRNs which allow the borrower to redeem the issue prior to maturity. In recent years, the absence of high quality assets and competition among financial intermediaries has led to decreasing levels of call protection on FRN issues. For example, in the first half of 1986, a number of major FRN borrowers exercised their calls and retired outstanding FRN issues and utilised alternative sources of funding to refinance—primarily, the rapidly developing Euro CP market. As a result, FRNs with protection against calls have tended to trade at substantial premiums to par therefore causing a significant erosion in margins as well as causing certain cash flow mismatches which may be unattractive to investors. Against this background, synthetic FRNs have proved particularly attractive as the underlying asset has in most cases provided higher levels of call protection.

The creation of fixed rate bonds for sale, in the main to Japanese investors, has been a more recent, and often transient, phenomenon. The essential motivation here is the substantial yield improvements achievable for these institutions by directing investment funds to synthetic as against direct yen assets. The concept of creating fixed rate bonds in a particular currency through an asset swap is not unique to the yen market and transactions involving other currencies have also been completed.

From time to time, substantial demand for non-US$ floating rate assets has existed. This has primarily reflected the asset demand of various banks with attractive funding in usually their home currency. Added demand has come from investors seeking to take advantage of currency fluctuations without necessarily creating a simultaneous interest rate exposure. The paradigm example of the creation of synthetic FRNs in other currencies is the Stars and Stripes transaction involving the creation of two synthetic FRNs, in deutschmark and GBP (see discussion below).

The concept of creating synthetic assets has particular found a market in specially structured transactions involving demand for specific assets to match a particular investor requirement. This investor requirement is usually dictated by an offsetting transaction elsewhere in the investor's portfolio or by regulatory considerations. While technically these types of transactions are similar to the other transactions described they nevertheless represent an interesting variation on the basic asset swap concept.

One of the earliest examples of this type of specially structured asset swap were insurance company deposit transactions. In this case, Japanese insurance companies were the primary factor behind such transactions because of their need to invest substantial volumes of funds in assets denominated in currencies other than yen. This particular investment requirement could usually not be satisfied directly because:

- the institution in question could not actually undertake foreign investments and was limited to domestic investments within Japan, such as bank deposits;
- these institutions, despite the fact that they were allowed to invest overseas, had already reached or were near the maximum limit imposed by the Ministry of Finance, which is the early half of the 1980s was 10% of their overall portfolio;
- direct investment in a foreign market was problematic because of unfamiliarity with the credit quality of issuers of the underlying securities, settlement difficulties and the impact of withholding tax on cross-border interest flows.

In these circumstances, a number of ingenious transactions were developed to circumvent some of these difficulties. In a typical transaction, an insurance company would make a deposit in the desired currency, say C$, with a Japanese bank. The Japanese bank in turn would buy a matching synthetic asset in C$ which provided the necessary cash flows to make interest payments and repay the original principal invested by the institution. The synthetic C$ asset would usually consist of floating rate US$ assets, either a US$ FRN or US$ CD which were rolled over on maturity, combined with a US$ LIBOR and C$ fixed currency swap.

This particular structure satisfied all the necessary requirements. For instance, the deposit with the Japanese bank was usually within the allowed investment categories of the investor and, moreover, the deposit with the Japanese bank did not usually constitute a foreign security for Ministry of Finance purposes and therefore did not represent utilisation of the 10% foreign asset allocation. It should, however, be noted that this rule deficiency was later rectified.

An additional benefit of this structure was that the Japanese bank, usually one of the major city or trust banks, was in a better position to assess the underlying credit of the security purchased as well as the credit of the swap counterparty. Settlement was also made relatively easy and the swap cash flows were not usually subject to withholding tax. This type of transaction involving deposits was undertaken in a wide variety of currencies including C$, A$ and NZ$.

The practice of zaitech transactions is a more recent phenomenon relating particularly to the period 1986 to 1990. The term zaitech derives from the Japanese word *zaiteku* which means financial engineering. The practice of zaitech financing refers to the activities of major Japanese corporations who increasingly found themselves involved in financial arbitrage transactions to generate profits to subsidise basic business earnings in a period when the appreciating yen led to severe downturns in the profitability of their export businesses.

A popular practice during this time was for these companies to undertake borrowing transactions where the funds raised were immediately reinvested at usually a higher return to provide a locked in annuity stream of earnings for the issuer. One form of this transaction was the issue of bonds with attached equity warrants which because of the equity option element led to the cost of financing being significantly reduced for the issuer, allowing it to generate substantially spread earnings by reinvesting the funds raised. In extreme cases, particularly in 1987, a number of borrowers actually were able to generate a negative cost of funds in yen. The funds raised were usually reinvested in yen assets. Some of these yen assets were, in fact, asset swaps, usually with the final synthetic asset being a fixed rate yen bond.

An example of a insurance company deposit transaction is set out in *Exhibit 18.10*. An example of a matched zaitech transaction is set out in *Exhibit 18.11*.

Exhibit 18.10
Insurance Company Deposit Transaction

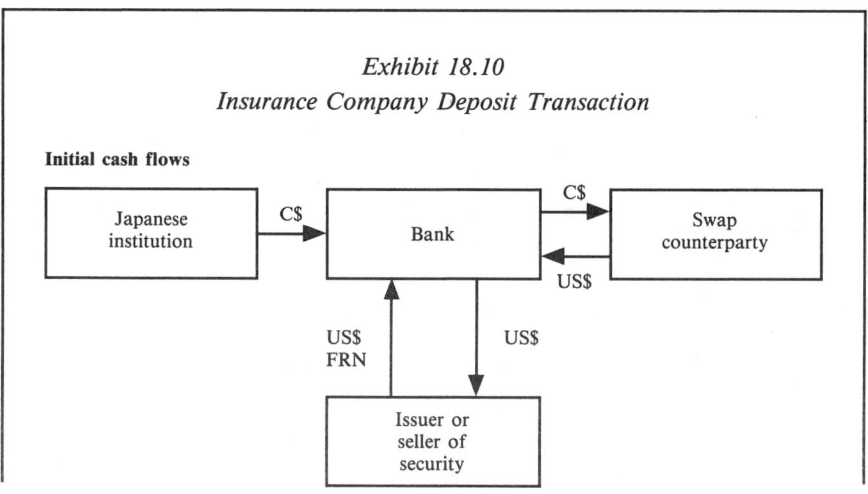

Exhibit 18.10—continued

Interest flows

Japanese institution ← C$ interest ← Bank ← C$ interest ← Swap counterparty

Bank → US$ Interest → Swap counterparty

Issuer → US$ interest → Bank

Maturity cash flows

Japanese institution ← C$ principal ← Bank ← C$ principal ← Swap counterparty

Bank → US$ principal → Swap counterparty

Issuer → US$ principal → Bank

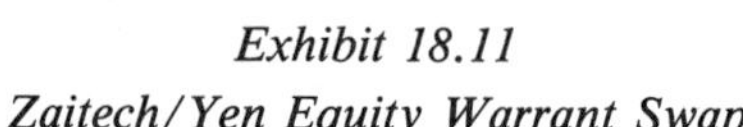

Exhibit 18.11
Zaitech/Yen Equity Warrant Swap

Assume that a Japanese corporation undertakes a US$ debt with equity warrants issue for a five year maturity with a coupon of 1.00% pa.

Assume that the following market rates are applicable:

US$ swap rate:	8.00% versus six month LIBOR
JPY/US$ swap rate:	4.77% versus six month LIBOR
US$/JPY spot:	140.00
US$/JPY five year forward:	114.80%

Under these conditions, the issuer's JPY cost is equal to approximately −2.03% pa (4.77% − (8 × 0.85) where 0.85 is the JPY/US$ conversion factor).

The issuer can undertake the swap in one of two ways:

- A series of interest rate and currency swaps.

Exhibit 18.11—continued

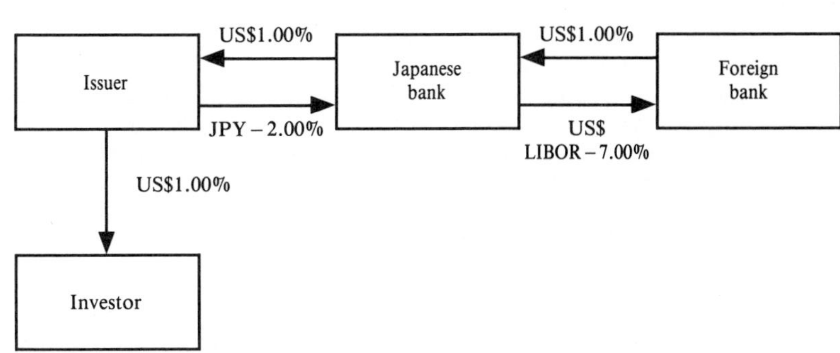

- A combination of LFTX contracts and a structured interest rate swap.

Year		Year	
0	US$100m	0	US$100m
1	1% × US$100m	1	1% × US$100m
2	1% × US$100m	2	1% × US$100m
3	1% × US$100m	3	1% × US$100m
4	1% × US$100m	4	1% × US$100m
5	1% × US$100m + $US100m[1]	5	1% × US$100m + $US30m

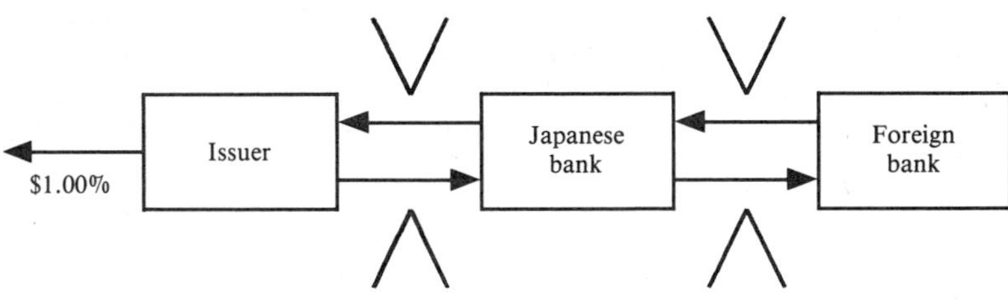

Year		Year	
0	US$100m × spot	0	US$70m
1	2% × JPY14 billion	1	LIBOR flat × US$70m
2	2% × JPY14 billion	2	LIBOR flat × US$70m
3	2% × JPY14 billion	3	LIBOR flat × US$70m
4	2% × JPY14 billion	4	LIBOR flat × US$70m
5	2% × JPY14 billion + JPY14bn	5	LIBOR flat × US$70m

The issuer would then purchase a fixed rate JPY asset to lock in a spread.

Note:
1. Japanese bank makes up the $70m difference ($100m – $30m) by selling JPY. Five year forward: $70m × (140 – 25.2) = JPY 8 billion.

Source: *Corporate Finance*, Euromoney Publications.

Types of securities used in asset swaps

The availability of the underlying securities is essential to the asset swap process. It is also essential that there be a discrepancy in the price of the asset and/or the relationship between the asset yield and swap prices. These discrepancies form the basis of the higher returns available on synthetic asset transactions.

The discrepancies in asset prices may arise from differential pricing between various market segments. This may reflect different credit criteria or restrictions on asset choice which create supply and demand imbalances leading to asset prices which provide opportunities for arbitrage. For example, in 1986, the margins on FRNs were bid to unsustainably low levels as the supply of FRNs dwindled and the opportunity for short-term capital gains attracted a variety of investors. As similar factors were not present in the fixed rate market, a discrepancy between the prices of assets emerged as between the FRN and fixed rate market creating the opportunity for arbitrage entailing the creation of synthetic FRNs which yielded significant margins over those available on comparable FRNs trading in the market.

Discrepancies in the relationship between asset yields and swap prices are more complex. Opportunities for arbitrage emerge when asset yields move to a level which allows them to be swapped, given the prevailing structure of swap rates, to generate a coupon stream in excess of that on equivalent non-synthetic securities. The process effectively is one of transferring the particular security from one market segment to another to equalise supply and demand at a given price.

As in the liability swap market, a major factor in asset swap arbitrage is the leads and lags between various market segments in the same currency. For example, lags between the domestic United States and Eurodollar market can sometimes be as long as several days. Just as a nervous or bearish United States treasury market opens the conventional liability swap window allowing issuers to swap their fixed rate new issues into sub-LIBOR funds, a rallying or bullish United States treasury market with United States treasury yields and swap rates falling, creates fixed-to-floating asset swap opportunities. If this asset swap is attractive vis-à-vis the conventional floating rate asset market, the asset swap arbitrage is undertaken.

The types of securities used in asset swaps are readily identifiable:

- ex-warrant debt component of a bond with equity warrants issue;
- illiquid or mispriced bonds available in the primary or secondary market;
- mortgage or asset backed securities;
- new issues specifically designed to be asset swapped.

More recently, there have been two additional sources of securities utilised in asset swaps:

- perpetual FRNs;
- tax advantaged securities.

Exhibits 18.12 and *18.13* set out an analysis of securities utilised in asset swaps. *Exhibit 18.12* sets out an analysis of repackaged issues by floating rate source bond. (These statistics only cover public repackaged issues in the period 1985 to 1990.)

By far the largest source of securities for asset swap transactions has been the ex-warrant debt component of a debt with equity warrants issue package where, in the main, the issuer is a Japanese corporation. In many cases, the Japanese issuer's own credit is enhanced by the availability of a bank guarantee or letter of credit securing the debt component of the issue.

During the sustained rally in the equity markets globally in the period leading up to the stock market crash in October 1987, particularly over 1986 and 1987, a substantial volume of debt with equity warrants was issued by Japanese entities.

Exhibit 18.12

Repackaged Issues by Fixed Rate Source Bond

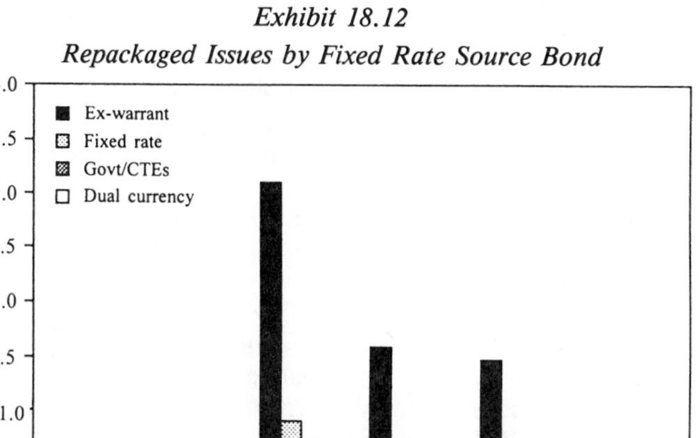

*First three quarters

Source: Piers Hartland-Swann, "Asset Swaps—Bringing Technology to Investors" in Das (1991), based on data from Euromoney Bondware.

Exhibit 18.13

Repackaged Issues by Floating Rate Source Bond

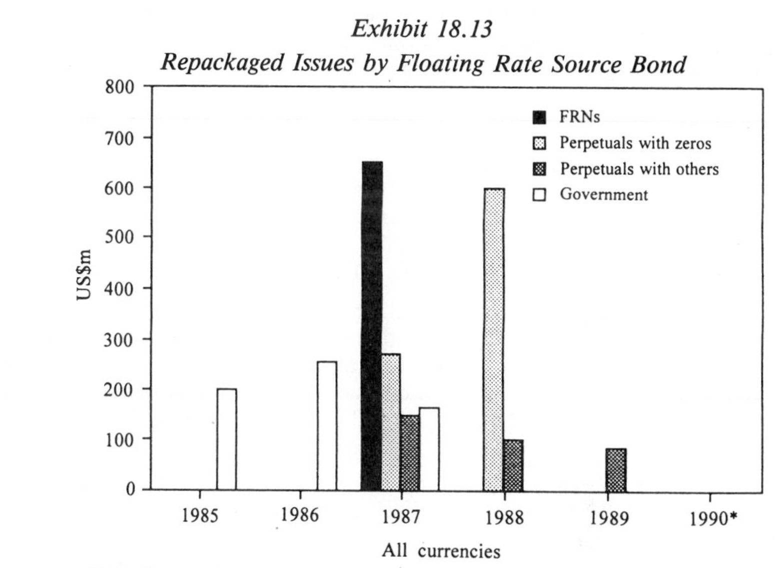

*First three quarters

Source: Piers Hartland-Swann, "Asset Swaps—Bringing Technology to Investors" in Das (1991), based on data from Euromoney Bondware.

Issuance of debt with equity warrants by Japanese companies continued strongly in the post 1987 crash period through till 1990/91. This reflected the fact that the Japanese equity markets were largely insulated from the impact of the crash initially until domestic factors, including a tight monetary policy regime, led to a slowdown in the Japanese economy and a sharp correction in the Nikkei.

The primary attraction of these packages was the equity warrants which were in the main stripped off and sold separately from the underlying debt component. The debt component itself usually has a very low coupon and consequently traded at substantial discount to its face value shortly after issue once the warrants had been stripped off and sold. The ex-warrant bond would usually trade at a yield primarily reflecting its illiquidity and discount structure despite its usually strong credit quality.

The Japanese securities houses who were the main financial intermediaries arranging these equity warrant issues essentially became involved in the process of repackaging many of these issues for sale primarily to commercial bank investors as high yielding US$ LIBOR based FRNs. As discussed more fully below, the swapping of ex-warrant bonds formed the basis of the large market in public or securitised asset swap structures which developed and existed in the period 1987 to 1990.

A major source of securities for asset swaps has been relatively illiquid or mispriced Eurobond issues. This lack of liquidity which facilitates the asset swap of arbitrage is predicated on a number of factors including:

- the pattern of trading in Eurobonds generally;
- the introduction into the securities markets of innovative security structures, many of which met with investor resistance.

The trading behaviour of a liquid, high credit quality, US$ straight Eurobond issue, can be utilised to illustrate the trading pattern of most international bonds. During its life, in terms of its yield spread relative to a benchmark, such as United States treasuries, the trading history of the security generally approximates the following pattern.

The spread, which is totally credit related, is greatest at issue date and declines over the life of the transaction to almost zero close to maturity when the credit risk is negligible. This assumes an issue which is originally successfully priced and placed and has considerable liquidity reflecting the underlying size of the issue, the quality of the issuer and the presence of a substantial number of major market makers willing to make consistent two-way prices in the issue throughout its life.

However, more typically, most bonds while they may be launched at the same spread relative to treasuries as the above liquid issue are less popular with a resultant drift to wider spreads over time vis-à-vis the underlying benchmark. This usually reflects the lack of liquidity in the issue which itself is a function of the size and the quality of the issuer, as well as the lack of market makers in the particular issue.

As the price of these issues falls relative to more liquid and better traded issues, the high yield on these bonds facilitates the asset swap arbitrage. This arbitrage is particularly facilitated by the fact that the investors in floating rate assets will traditionally be commercial banks or other financial intermediaries who match fund their assets, usually through the short-term money market at a cost relative to LIBOR. These institutions are seeking good quality loan assets and therefore will be less concerned about the factors which are leading to the bond's poor performance in the secondary market.

While the above example focuses on US$ Eurobonds, the situation is similar with bonds denominated in other currencies where the problems identified above are usually more acute in their influence on secondary market performance.

An additional factor assisting in the availability of asset swap fodder in recent years has been the competitive environment in international capital markets which has seen a consistent pattern of mispriced bonds being brought to market primarily to accommodate the new issue swap arbitrage, on the liability side, for the issuer. Many new issues now traditionally begin to trade shortly after launch at substantial spreads below issue price. Such aggressively priced, poorly syndicated and, most importantly, poorly distributed issues have tended to have a particularly poor trading performance as they have failed to attract any investor interest (the celebrated "dog" or "canine" issue).

An additional factor has been the incredible array of security structures which have been introduced into various markets in recent years as investment bankers have sought to create completely new types of securities to satisfy perceived investor requirements, usually predicating the issuer's involvement on the basis of a new issue arbitrage. Many of these issues have not attracted significant investor support. These issues on the whole have proved difficult to sell in their original form and have been combined with swaps to create a synthetic asset which is more attractive to investors.

A good example of this type of repackaging of what would otherwise have been unsaleable securities is the case of the reverse FRN. As discussed in Chapter 15 these types of issues were designed to appeal to investors seeking to benefit from falling short-term rates. A number of these issues proved to be disastrously unsuccessful as investors shunned the structures. Such issues were usually repackaged as floating rate assets for commercial bank investors. *Exhibit 18.14* sets out such a repackaging of a reverse FRN for an investor.

Exhibit 18.14
Reverse FRN Repackaging

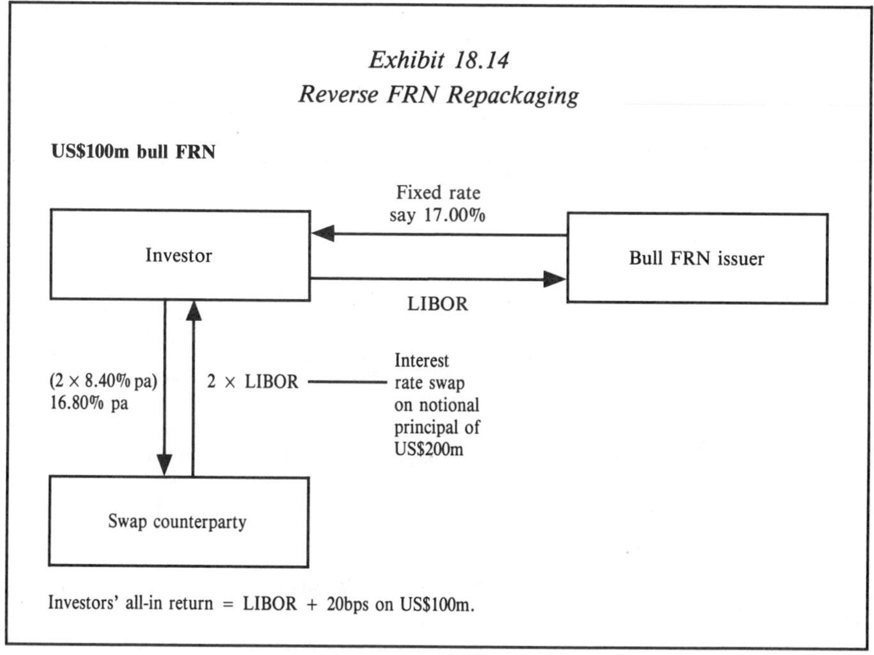

Investors' all-in return = LIBOR + 20bps on US$100m.

Another example of this process of repackaging involved a variety of dual currency and reverse dual currency issues, placed originally with primarily Japanese investors, which had to be "reverse engineered" to be replaced with other investors.

A central feature of the repackaging of these complex security structures is that it is, typically, the only way to generate liquidity for the holder. The re-engineered security usually has more general and broader appeal to investors facilitating disposal of the asset by the original investor.

An increasingly important source of securities for asset swapping is mortgage backed securities. Mortgage-backed and asset-backed securities have been particularly important sources of assets for such transactions because they have typically offered much higher yields than comparable corporate or financial institution paper. This added return, however, has been in return for the investor in the securities accepting an additional element of risk relating to the risk of prepayment. If interest rates fall, the underlying mortgages or assets tend to be prepaid effectively resulting in the mortgage backed security itself being called.

However, this risk of prepayment has not precluded the use of these securities for asset swaps with the underlying prepayment risk being essentially hedged through the use of putable swaps to convert the mortgage backed security to a floating rate asset (see description of putable swaps in Chapter 14). The fact that the spread differential between the coupon on the mortgage backed security and the fixed rate payable on the swap has in fact been consistently wide enough to create a substantial spread over LIBOR (even after immunising, usually within certain boundaries, the prepayment risk utilising a putable interest rate swap) has continued to make this particular type of asset swap extremely attractive. An example of this type of asset swap is set out in *Exhibit 18.15*.

Exhibit 18.15

Mortgage Backed Security Asset Swap

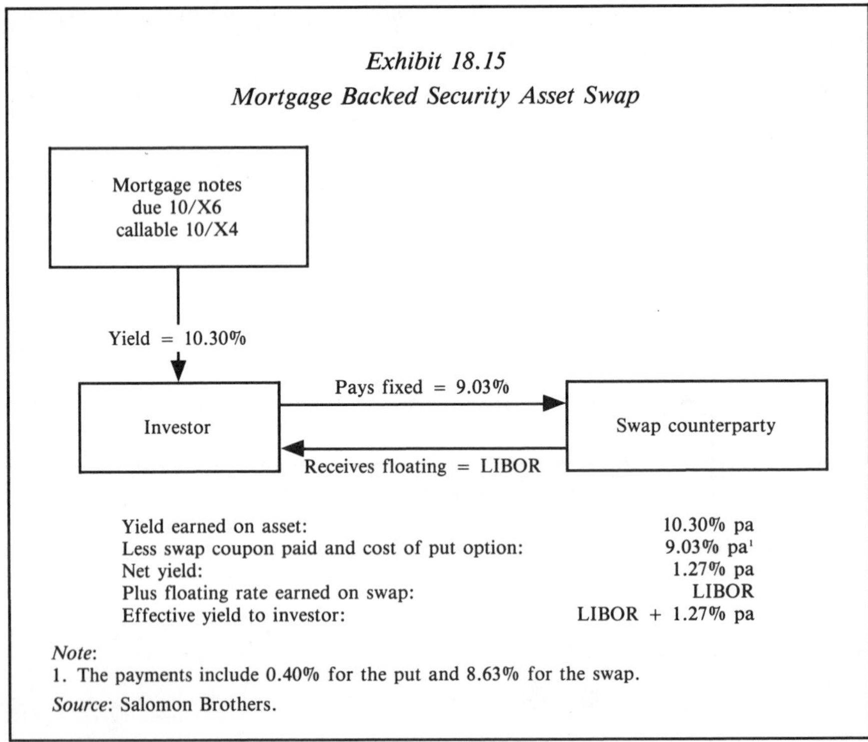

Yield earned on asset:	10.30% pa
Less swap coupon paid and cost of put option:	9.03% pa[1]
Net yield:	1.27% pa
Plus floating rate earned on swap:	LIBOR
Effective yield to investor:	LIBOR + 1.27% pa

Note:
1. The payments include 0.40% for the put and 8.63% for the swap.

Source: Salomon Brothers.

As swap technology has improved, a number of financial institutions have assumed the risk of prepayment through specially structured Collateralised Mortgage Obligations (CMO) swap arrangements. Under these structures, the investor swaps the CMO issue into floating rate return with no prepayment risk. The swap counterparty, in return for paying a lower floating rate return to the investor, absorbs the duration risk of the transaction whereby if rates fall the duration of the swap will correspondingly decline as mortgagors accelerate their principal repayment in order to refinance at lower interest rates.

Asset-backed securities, particularly short-term credit card and auto receivables, where these are utilised in asset swaps, have produced different problems. Shorter term receivables have demonstrated a more volatile and random repayment pattern.

This has necessitated the swaps designed to convert income streams from these securities into floating rates for investors to be structured on the basis of an assumed repayment schedule for the underlying debt. As actual repayments occur, the swap counterparty is forced to assume the residual position generated by variations from the *assumed* repayment schedule.

In the event that interest rates decrease and prepayments are higher than anticipated in the repayment schedule, the swap counterparty may end up with an out-of-the-money swap as the swap related to the asset backed issue is extinguished before its scheduled maturity. Swap market makers can utilise options on swaps to neutralise this risk of prepayment at a cost.

Another category of securities used in asset swaps are new securities issues specifically designed to be sold in synthetic asset form. Over the last several years, a number of asset swap-driven issues have been brought to market. These issues are usually for less creditworthy names allowing then to tap the fixed rate market from which they would be otherwise precluded with the fixed rate bond being sold in synthetic form as a US$ LIBOR FRN primarily to bank investors. *Exhibit 18.16* sets out an example of an issue specifically designed to be asset swapped.

Following the collapse of the market for perpetual FRNs (which had been utilised by banks to raise subordinated quasi capital), these types of floating rate securities came to be utilised in asset swaps. The use of perpetual FRNs in asset swaps was facilitated by the fact that they were trading, at one stage, at 60-70% of face value.

The asset swap structures devised were, typically, as follows:

- The investor purchased the perpetual FRN at, say, 70% of face value.
- The investor simultaneously invested approximately 26.70% of face value of the notes in a high credit quality deposit or commercial paper yielding around LIBOR. This deposit was for a term of three or six months with the intention of re-investing the sum at maturity of the deposit and repeating the procedure over the life of the transaction.
- Simultaneously, the investor entered into a 15 year zero coupon interest rate swap on a notional principal amount equivalent to the amount of the deposit (26.70% of the face value of the notes). Under the terms of the swap, the investor had the following cash flows:

  —The investor paid, either quarterly or semi-annually, LIBOR to the swap counterparty.

Exhibit 18.16

New Issue Designed to be Asset Swapped

Hotel Parker Meridien Capital Corporation

Guarantor:	Mitsubishi Bank
Amount:	US$60m
Maturity:	ten year (due 11 February 1997)
Coupon:	8.375%
Issue price:	10.25
Yield:	8.34% (gross), 8.55% (less selling concession)
Amortisation:	Bullet
Call option:	Of the issuer—for tax reasons only. Callable by the guarantor in certain circumstances at par
Listing:	Luxembourg
Denominations:	US$5,000 and US$50,000
Commissions:	2.00% (management, underwriting 0.625%, less 0.125% praecipum; selling 1.375%)
Expenses:	US$100,000
Stabilisation:	IPMA recommendations
Selling deadline:	9 January
Payment:	11 February
Governing law:	New York
Negative pledge:	Of the issuer only
Cross-default:	Of the guarantor only
Pari passu:	Yes
Lead managers:	Morgan Guaranty (books), Mitsubishi Finance
Co-managers:	BBL, Bear Stearns, Chemical Bank Int, Fuji Int, LTBC Int, Mitsubishi Trust Int, Mitsui Trust Int, Societe Generale, Sumitomo Trust Int, SBCI
Pre-market price:	Less 1.75, less 1.50

Launched at 144bps over treasuries, this deal is asset swappable producing AAA floating rate paper at around 20bps over LIBOR (although lead manager MGL reported some success in placing bonds in their pristine form). The deal amounts to a placement as the amount is obviously too small to provide liquidity.

The issuer is a special purpose company formed to finance the construction of the eponymous hotel in Manhattan by the Jack Parker Corporation. A first mortgage on the property has been assigned to the guarantor.

In an overall good performance, the bonds were quoted at less 1.75, less 1.50 by the lead manager Wednesday.

Source: *International Financing Review.*

—At maturity, the investor received, from the counterparty, a sum equivalent to the accumulated interest on the notional principal amount of the swap (assuming an interest rate of 9.00% pa payable semi-annually this equates to 100% of the face value of the notes—26.70% from the maturing deposit together with 73.30% being the accumulated zero coupon interest under the swap).

The net effect of the transaction was to create a *fixed term* (generally 12-15 year) conventional bank FRN at an attractive floating rate yield.

In the example above, assuming the perpetual FRN had a coupon of LIBOR plus 0.25% pa, the investor, under the asset swap was able to create a 15 year floating rate asset at a cost of 96.70% of face value. This is equivalent to an effective asset yield of around LIBOR plus 0.65% pa, which was an attractive return for what was usually good credit quality bank obligations.

Transactions of this type were undertaken both in the form of private asset swaps as well as public securitised repackaging transactions of the type discussed below.

This type of repackaging activity was short lived as bank regulations requiring bank investors to deduct holdings of subordinated bank obligations from their own capital (almost all perpetual issues were subordinated debt) made them unattractive assets for banks under capital constraints.

The other class of asset to be utilised in asset swaps relied on inconsistent tax treatment of obligations. The most notable example of this type of transaction utilises Certificates del Tresor in ECU (CTEs), securities denominated in ECU issued domestically by the Italian government.

CTEs have been issued since 1982. The original issues of CTEs were free from withholding tax for foreign investors. However, in September 1986, the rules were altered and the Italian government imposed a 6.25% (subsequently, increased to 12.5%) withholding tax on interest payments. The interest withholding tax may be recoverable under a number of double taxation treaties between Italy and the country of residence of the relevant investor.

CTEs have, generally, traded at a *pre tax* yield which is significantly above that of comparable ECU Eurobonds (CTEs trade on *a net of withholding tax* basis at yields below equivalent *tax free* ECU Eurobonds). This facilitates the use of CTEs to structure asset swaps generating floating rate returns to investors in a specified currency. This is achieved by combining a purchase of CTEs with an interest rate or currency swap.

The structure of the swap is as follows:

- The term of the swap exactly matches that of the underlying CTE.
- The investor makes fixed rate ECU payment equal to the gross coupon of the CTE. The investor will only receive 87.5% of the coupon and will need to recover the 12.5% withholding through an offsetting tax credit. The tax credit will be available after a delay resulting in a funding cost to the investor which will need to be incorporated in the return calculation. (This structure has proved more efficient than seeking to recoup the tax from the Italian authorities.)
- The investor will receive a floating rate return on its investment in its currency of choice.
- A principal exchange at commencement and at maturity will be required, using the principal cash flows of the underlying CTE, where the asset created is in a currency other than ECUs.

This type of structure has been attractive to investors for a number of reasons:

- The attractive returns available—CTE asset swaps have offered yield pick-ups of around 30-40bps pa relative to comparable FRN assets.
- CTEs are highly rated assets reflecting Italy's AAA credit rating. In addition, CTEs represent Italian sovereign risk and are attractive investments under the BIS capital adequacy regulations.

As the asset swap market has developed a number of problems associated with utilising particular assets have also become apparent.

For example, the use of CTEs in asset swaps has created some difficulties in regard to the following:

- Some asset holders have, it is understood, experienced difficulties in recovering the withholding tax from the Italian (other than where there is an Italian tax liability) and Swedish authorities resulting in a reduction in the yields on the transaction.

- Recovery of the interest withholding requires the investor to have taxable profits over the life of the transaction. As circumstances have changed, some investors have found themselves unable to use the credit due to changes in their underlying tax position.

However, the major difficulties that have arisen relate to the credit quality of the underlying securities used in the asset swap. As demand for asset swap investments increased and the yield gains were arbitraged down, asset swaps entailing the use of lower credit quality debt become common. This led to problems where the corporation issuing the underlying debt experienced financial difficulties.

For example, in May 1990, British and Commonwealth, a United Kingdom company, experienced financial difficulties with serious implications for holders of its GBP70 million seven year issue which had been asset swapped and placed with, primarily, bank investors. Concerned at the prospect of owning defaulted bonds and having an obligation under the related swap which would continue to run, investors rushed to cancel the swaps which were in-the-money to offset the loss on the bonds whose market value had fallen.

PRIVATE ASSET SWAP OR SYNTHETIC SECURITY STRUCTURE

A critical element in creating an asset swap, even where the security is available and an investor for the synthetic asset can be located, relates to the specific structuring of the swap in a form acceptable to the investor. The asset swap can be on a private or synthetic security basis or, alternatively, a public or securitised asset swap structure can be utilised. In this section, private asset swap structures are considered.

Where the asset swap is to be structured as a private transaction, there are two possible structures:

- a private or investor made asset swap;
- the creation of a synthetic security.

Exhibit 18.17 sets out, in diagrammatic form, the two structures.

Under the investor manufactured asset swap structure, the investor specifically purchases the underlying cash or physical security and enters into the swap to convert the return into its preferred form. The implications of this particular structure include:

- The investor is responsible for multiple sets of cash flows, including the coupon on the bond and the flows under the swap.
- The credit risk on this transaction is quite complex with the investor having credit risk on both the issuer *and* the swap counterparty. Conversely, the swap counterparty has a risk on the investor and will usually treat the transaction as an allocation of credit lines to the investor, potentially imposing a constraint on future transactions.
- The accounting and most importantly the revaluation structure of this package will be complex as both the bond and the swap will need to be treated separately. This may result, depending on the accounting techiques used, in discrepancies which distort the reporting of the investment.

Exhibit 18.17
Investor Asset Swap versus Synthetic Securities

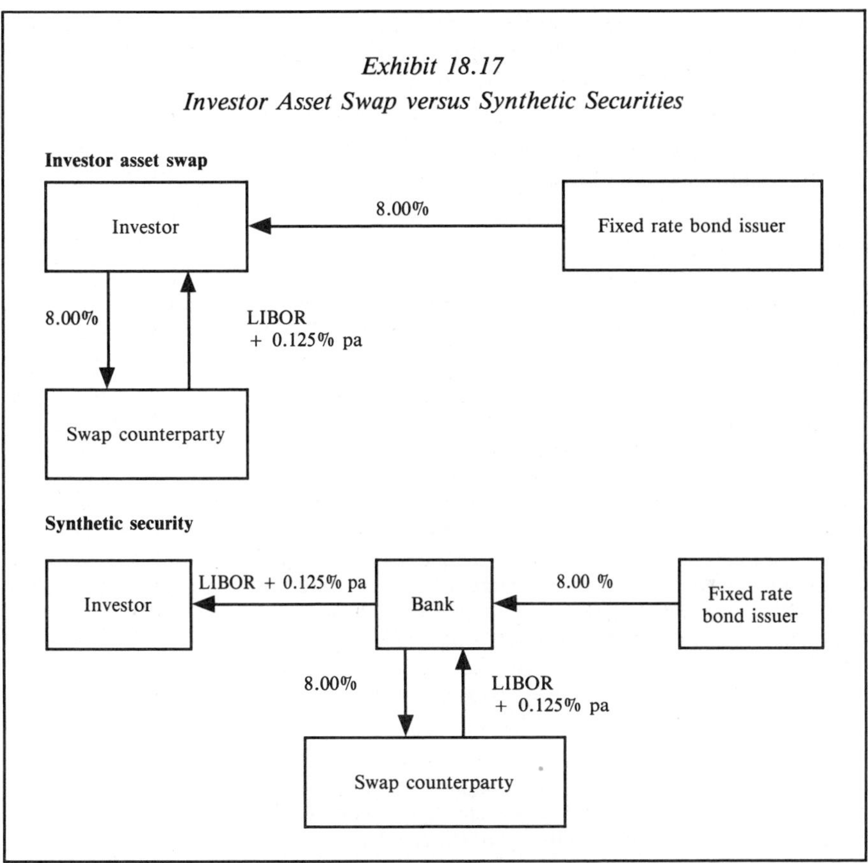

- The liquidity of this investment will be a factor of both the liquidity of the bond and the swap. The cost of liquidating the investment will essentially be the sum of the cost of the bid-offer spread for both the bond and the swap. Depending on the liquidity of the underlying security, the cost of selling the bonds may range from 0.50% to 1.00% of the price of the bond. Similarly, the cost of reversing the swap will typically be between 0.10% and 0.20% pa or up to 1.50% flat of the notional principal value of the swap, depending, of course, on maturity. The combined cost of liquidating both the bond and swap can therefore rage from 1.30% to as much as 2.50% of the principal value of the transaction.

These factors dictate that investor manufactured asset swaps are usually the preserve of highly sophisticated investors with the expertise to assemble and account for these structures and who moreover have no significant need for any secondary market liquidity of the package.

The synthetic security structure is specifically designed to overcome some of the difficulties of the first structure and to provide investors with the benefit of a simpler structure, lower transaction costs and enhanced liquidity.

The synthetic security structure was originally developed by Citicorp Investment Bank Limited (Citicorp). Under the structure, Citicorp effectively interposes itself between the issuer and the investor with regard to the cash flows of the transaction.

Citicorp strips and collects the fixed coupon from the bond and simultaneously arranges the swap, usually with an internal swap "warehouse". Under the structure Citicorp pays the investor a synthetic floating rate coupon.

The major structural advantages of the synthetic security include:

- The cash flows are considerably simplified by the marriage of the bond and the swap resulting in only one cash flow for the investor.
- The credit risk factors are, effectively, identical to a normal asset swap.
- The accounting and revaluation requirements for the investor are greatly simplified and the investor should, in most cases, be able to account for, and revalue the synthetic FRN as a normal FRN. This may have certain administrative advantages as existing accounting procedures and systems may be capable of being utilised for the investment.
- The major advantage of the synthetic security is that it is likely to be more liquid than the investor manufactured asset swap. This is because the permanent marriage of the bond to the swap should, in theory, create a tradeable package which can be traded as such thereby eliminating the requirement to liquidate the bond and swap separately. An additional factor is the absence of counterparty risk on the investor which should in theory allow the synthetic securities to be traded as between investors in the secondary market (provided that some sort of a master synthetic securities agreement is entered into by the investors). Synthetic securities, as traded by Citicorp, trade on a bid-offer spread in discount yield terms of 0.03% to 0.05% pa which is equivalent to approximately 0.125% in price terms, which is comparable with the typical 0.10% bid-offer price spread on a conventional FRN. This cost is significantly lower than the cost of liquidating a specifically manufactured asset swap.

The importance of Citicorp's synthetic security structure lies less in the structural simplicity and enhancement of the original investor manufactured asset swap than in its tentative attempts to securitise the asset swap. In fact, the synthetic security structure has to a large extent been superseded by the emergence of public or securitised asset swaps which are discussed below.

PUBLIC OR SECURITISED ASSET SWAP STRUCTURE

Until September 1985, asset swaps had been traditionally undertaken as private transactions, being structured as either investor manufactured swaps or as synthetic securities. However, since 1985, a substantial market in securitised asset swaps has developed. In essence, the reasons behind the growth of asset swaps in this particular form are almost identical to those dictating the development of the synthetic security structure itself.

In September 1985, the concept of the public or securitised asset swap was introduced with two transactions, one led by Hill Samuel and the other by Merrill Lynch Capital Markets. An analysis of the Merrill Lynch transaction provides an insight into the mechanics of the securitised asset swap.

Towards the end of September 1985, the United Kingdom raised US$2.5 billion through the issuance of seven year FRNs, due October 1992. The notes were originally priced at 99.70% of face value, net of fees, with a coupon of three month US$ LIBID and were non-callable for three years from the time of issuance. Following the launch of this issue, the sales force of Merrill Lynch, a United States investment bank, noted that there was considerable interest from its investors in *fixed rate* United Kingdom government US$ denominated debt. In particular, the sales force had reported a coupon of approximately 9.375% pa for a three year maturity as acceptable to these investors. However, no fixed rate United Kingdom government debt denominated in US$ was available. Consequently, the Merrill Lynch swap and Eurobond syndicate desk set about designing, at that time, the largest securitised asset swap.

The structure of the transaction was as follows:

- Merrill Lynch bought US$100m of United Kingdom FRNs.
- The US$100m of United Kingdom 1992 FRNs were then sold into a special purpose vehicle known as Marketable Eurodollar Collateralised Securities Limited (MECS).
- Simultaneously, Merrill Lynch arranged a swap with Prudential Global Funding Corporation between MECS and the swap counterparty under which MECS made payments of US$ LIBID every three months in return for Prudential making payments equivalent to 9.375% pa to MECS. This effectively converted the floating rate US$ cash flow that MECS trust earned from the United Kingdom FRNs into a fixed rate US$ flow.
- Merrill Lynch then arranged a Eurodollar bond issue in the name of MECS with a coupon of 9.375% pa and a final maturity of October 1988. The bonds issued by MECS were collateralised with the assets of the trust which was a holding of US$100m of United Kingdom FRNs and also the contingent liability reflecting the interest rate swap with Prudential. Essentially, the package constituted a high quality (AAA) credit risk.

This structure is set out in *Exhibit 18.18*.

The two transactions undertaken, both involving the United Kingdom government US$2.5 billion 1992 FRN, clearly demonstrated the advantages of securitising the underlying asset swap to improve the liquidity and marketability of the investment.

However, the market for public asset swap structures remained stagnant for almost one year. In September 1986, Morgan Guaranty Limited undertook a US$250m repackaging of a subsequent US$4 billion United Kingdom FRN. Significantly, in September 1986, Banque Paribas Capital Markets undertook the first securitised synthetic asset transaction involving a currency swap whereby, utilising a vehicle known as Republic of Italy Euro Repackaged Asset Limited (dubbed Ferraris), the French Investment Bank utilised approximatly ECU200m of Italy 1993 Treasury certificates as the basis of a synthetic asset US$, paying a coupon of LIMEAN.

It was in early 1987 that the securitised asset swap market entered its growth phase. Bankers Trust International undertook two transactions within one month of each other which created the environment for rapid growth in these transactions. Utilising a vehicle known as Trust Obligation Participating Securities (TOPS), Bankers Trust first repackaged Kingdom of Denmark 7.00% 1988 bonds into US$200m of two year FRNs paying a coupon of LIBOR plus 0.0625% pa and, perhaps more significantly, swapped a portfolio of Japanese bank guaranteed ex-warrant bonds into a US$100m five year US$ FRN paying LIBOR plus 0.125% pa. The structure of the second transaction was significant in that for the first time it utilised ex-warrant bonds, mainly from Japanese issuers with, usually, bank guarantees, in a public securitised asset swap transaction.

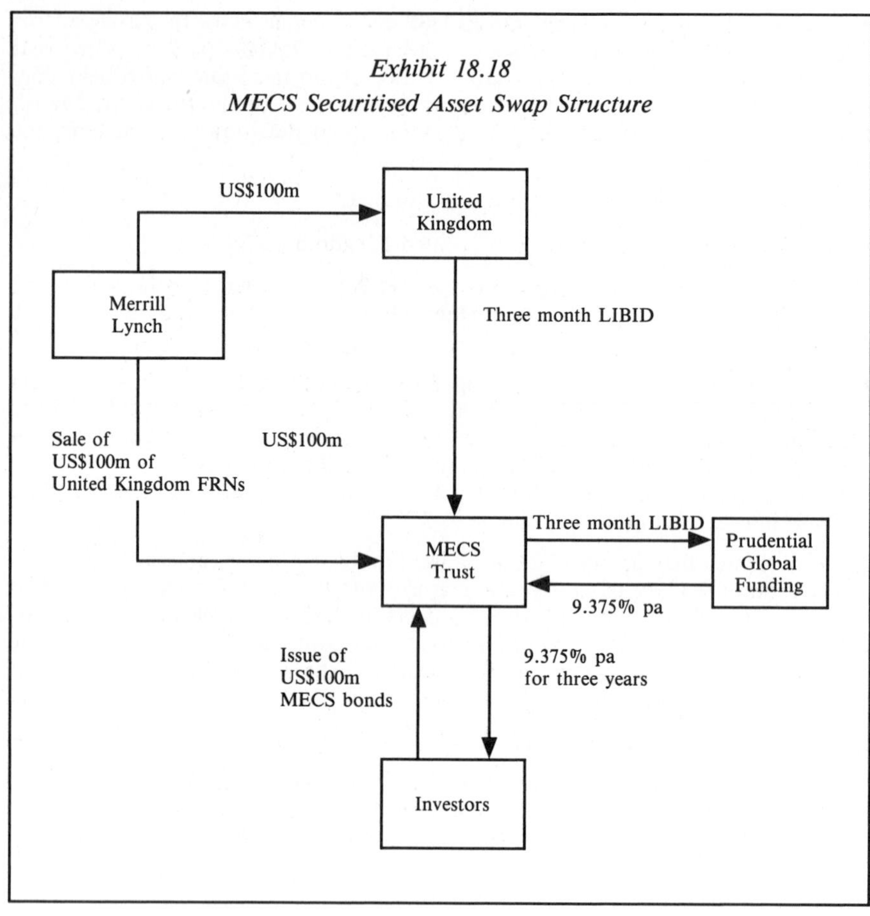

Exhibit 18.18
MECS Securitised Asset Swap Structure

The structure of the TOPS 2 transaction was extremely complex because the package of ex-warrant bonds contained a variety of maturities requiring the issue of FRNs to incorporate a complex sinking fund provision which detracted from its underlying liquidity. However, the transaction aroused sufficient interest from Japanese regional banks seeking US$ floating rate assets to allow further transactions to be undertaken.

In the period January to December 1987, approximately US$4 billion of public securitised asset swap transactions were undertaken. These transactions fell into two distinct categories:

- the repackaging of Japanese ex-warrant bonds for sale to commercial bank investors;
- other usually more complex transactions involving a variety of currencies.

The main factors operating in the market at this time appeared to be:

- the unsustainable decline in yields in the FRN market and the subsequent calamitous fall in and loss of liquidity in the main FRN market;

- the hugh volume of Japanese equity warrant issues being brought to market creating vast amounts of ex-warrant bonds which were proving increasingly difficult to sell;
- an interest rate environment where expectations of increased interest rates, primarily in US$, was forcing investors to seek refuge in floating rate assets.

The combination of these factors served to create a particularly conducive environment to this type of securitised asset swap activity. The repackaging of Japanese ex-warrant bonds into US$ FRNs for placement with bank investors quickly became a highly standardised issue structure dominated by the Japanese securities houses and the subsidiaries of Japanese banks who were the primary players in the equity warrant markets themselves. Initial problems involving the varieties of maturities requiring repackaging was solved simply and elegantly by bringing bunches of equity warrant issues with the same maturity and coupon dates to actually facilitate the repackaging process. The availability of a number of market makers willing to structure discount swaps to generate the required even coupon and maturity date cash flows also assisted in this process.

Exhibit 18.19 sets out the volume of ex-warrant bonds utilised in public repackaging/asset swaps in the public market in the period 1985 to 1990.

Exhibit 18.19

Repackaged Ex-Warrant Issues

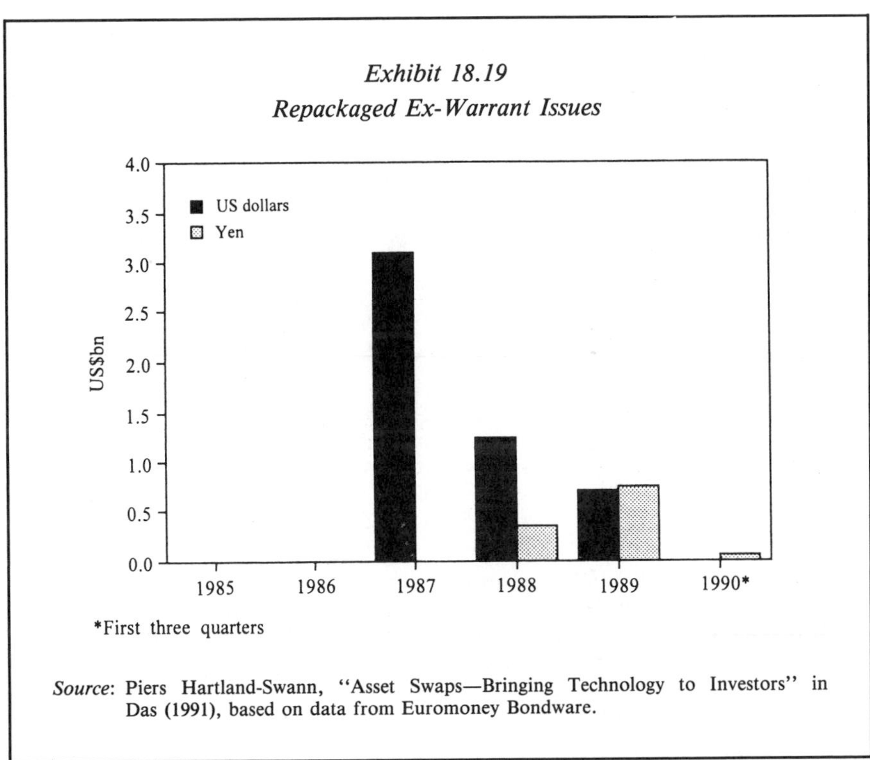

*First three quarters

Source: Piers Hartland-Swann, "Asset Swaps—Bringing Technology to Investors" in Das (1991), based on data from Euromoney Bondware.

The other category of securitised asset swaps was considerably more complex. In particular a large part of the activity appeared to be repackaging of originally unsuccessful issues into saleable form.

The most notable example of this type of transaction was the repackaging of the hallmark Kingdom of Denmark 1996 US$ FRN which had carried a coupon of 0.125% pa *below* LIBID, the lowest coupon on a US$ FRN in history. The transaction which met with considerable criticism appeared, ultimately, never to have found sufficient favour to be considered firmly placed with end investors. The original lead manager, Morgan Guaranty, elegantly repackaged the issue to produce deutschmark and GBP synthetic FRNs by combining the original US$ FRN with a deutschmark and US$ floating-to-floating currency swap and a GBP and US$ floating-to-floating currency swap respectively.

Taking advantage of a weakening US$, the general depression in FRNs and a window in the currency swap market, Morgan Guaranty placed the two synthetic assets, nicknamed Stars and Stripes, with different investor groups. The deutschmark FRN was mainly distributed into Europe, including German funds, while the GBP FRN, was sold to some banks as a commercial banking asset but also met with substantial demand from British building societies requiring floating rate assets.

Interestingly, subsequent repackaging included the restructuring of a number of highly complex dual currency bond transactions undertaken earlier (see discussions in Chapter 15) which were repackaged in more conventional form.

Ironically, the repackaging of bonds to create a tradeable instrument itself came under severe criticism for one of two reasons:

- The argument that the repackaging in the public or securitised asset swap form created liquidity rapidly disintegrated as investors tended to hold the security as a term asset thereby limiting the development of a secondary market.
- The repackaging activity was seen by a number of observers as a means of improving individual investment banks' standing in the "league table" (comparisons in terms of volume of new issues brought to market). In particular, there was an element of double counting as investment banks essentially got credit for the original bond issue as well as the repackaged security, where the latter was publicly syndicated.

The yields achieved on these public securitised asset swap transactions merit comment. They provide some indication of the shifts in the pattern of pricing within the asset swap market as a whole (which is difficult to discern given that a high portion of activity is private).

In the initial stages, the arbitrage spreads were particularly large and margins of LIBOR plus 0.30-0.40% pa were available on *AA/AAA rated sovereign risk*. However, as the demand for asset swapped investments developed and the asset swapped ex-warrant bond became the staple of the market, margins on securitised asset swaps stabilised in the range 0.125% to 0.25% over LIBOR (depending on the underlying credit quality of the banks guaranteeing the ex-warrant bonds).

The spreads declined to a low of around 0.10% to 0.15% in late 1986/early 1987. However, the spreads have since widened to 0.25% to 0.50% over LIBOR reflecting credit pressures within the global banking system, capital constraints and reduced asset growth targets. The exact change in margin levels is difficult to assess because of the decline in the level of public repackaging transactions which, in turn, reflects reduced Japanese debt with equity warrant issuance.

ASSET SWAPS: IMPLICATIONS FOR CAPITAL MARKETS

The emergence of asset swaps as an important aspect of capital market activity has considerable implications for issuers, investors, and financial intermediaries.

For borrowers, the significance of asset swaps lies in the fact that effectively it points to the existence of a particular investor clientele seeking to purchase securities issued by the relevant borrower but in a form other than that currently available. Consequently, one possible response would be for the borrower to issue a security similar in substance to the synthetic asset directly to the investor base.

The potential for asset swaps entailing securities issued by a particular borrower also points to potential arbitrages and mispricing of issues. By definition, a synthetic security should not be possible at least where the borrower has issued similar instruments which are outstanding in the market unless the investors could through the asset swap obtain a higher return. In this way, asset swaps point to potential mispricing of transactions.

Asset swaps also often allow borrowers to undertake transactions which would otherwise not be feasible. For example, a low rated corporation may not have direct access to fixed rate bond markets. However, where a high yielding fixed rate bond can be swapped into a synthetic FRN which would be attractive to certain investors, the borrower may be able to proceed with the direct fixed rate bond issue which otherwise would not be feasible. However, inevitably in these cases the transaction undertaken is inefficient from an economic and pricing viewpoint as the issuer pays a premium to gain this type of access to particular market segments.

The potential impact of asset swaps involving poorly performing outstanding issues on the issuer's capacity to access certain markets and/or the cost of such access is discussed in Chapter 19. However, it is evident that the availability of poorly trading bonds in the secondary or primary market which lends itself to repackaging is of obvious concern to issuers.

Some issuers have sought to control the opportunity to repackage their outstanding debt by repurchasing the available bonds. This is an option which is available where the issuer has the cash or liquidity resources to fund these repurchases.

In an interesting variation on this theme, Swiss Bank Corporation in late 1991 undertook the following transaction. Swiss Bank offered to repurchase *on its own account* two outstanding Commonwealth of Australia issues (11% May 1995 US$83 million outstanding and 11.5% October 1995 US$147m outstanding) at a spread of 65bps over the relevant US treasury bond. This spread was considered to be at least 20/25bps better than the bid spread relative to treasuries that would have been received from professional Eurobond traders. In addition, Swiss Bank offered other banks a 50bps commission for locating and submitting the bonds through a tender panel mechanism.

It is understood that the repurchased bonds were then swapped to create a US$ floating rate asset yielding LIBOR flat. It is not clear whether the asset was held by Swiss Bank Corporation or re-placed with investors as an attractive three year sovereign floating rate investment.

Swiss Bank subsequently launched a similar repurchase offer for an outstanding bond issued by the Australian Wheat Board. This issue was then capable of being swapped into a two year floating rate asset at around LIBOR plus 10bps. This compares to euro-commercial paper issues by the same borrowers at yields of *LIBID flat/minus 2/3 bps*.

In contrast, for investors, the emergence of a significant market for asset swap allows them to purchase or create investments yielding higher than normal returns or, alternatively, customised to precisely match the cash flow requirements of the particular investor. An additional advantage for investors is that the presence of asset swaps allows a greater degree of portfolio diversification by allowing investors the opportunity to better manage the composition of credit risks in a portfolio without necessarily being constrained by the types of securities actually on issue.

However, advantages have to be traded off against the problems of liquidity and added credit risk that must sometimes be assumed in purchasing synthetic assets as investments. In particular, the wide variety of synthetic asset structures and their differing liquidity dictates that investors must be discriminating in their choice of synthetic asset *structure* in order to be able to liquidate the investment in a timely and cost effective manner. The differences in credit risk between the structures also dictates that various types of synthetic asset structures must be evaluated with a view to optimising the utilisation of available credit lines.

A less obvious consequence of the growth of asset swaps is that the emergence of this market provides an upper bound to the price fluctuations or yield differences of securities held in a particular portfolio. The fact that bonds can have their basic structure altered through swaps and therefore be placed with a different group of investors tends to place bounds on its value. For example, a fixed rate bond will have its trading performance bounded by its relativity to swap market spreads as if the yield on the bond increases too rapidly then the bond can be repackaged as a floating rate asset at an attractive spread and placed with a particular investor who will accept the issuer's credit risk but would prefer the asset in a floating rate form. This influence on the trading performance of securities is of significance not only to investors but to financial institutions.

The first category of financial institutions affected by asset swaps are investment banks active in new issue markets or in trading bonds in the secondary market. Essentially, the value bounding process of the underlying asset arbitrage means that relatively illiquid issues or offerings which have for a variety of reasons performed poorly and proved difficult to place can be repackaged for sale in a new form to a group of investors to whom the security in its new form is attractive. This effectively creates a new option for investment banks to reduce their risk in new issue activity and in trading as it, at least in theory, provides them with an additional mechanism for selling and distributing securities.

For financial institutions active in swaps, the emergence of asset swaps provides an interesting new dimension in their activities. At the most basic level, asset swap activity creates additional transaction volume which increases the underlying liquidity of the relevant swap market. It provides the other end to the liability swap arbitrage and thereby creates an incentive for swap activity during periods when the liability swap arbitrage window is not operating. This additional liquidity improves the pricing performance and efficiency of the basic swap market.

In essence, the asset and the liability swap can, in many instances, be the opposite ends of the same transaction. This is because many new issues, as discussed previously, are undertaken on a fixed rate basis with an accompanying swap whereby the issuer receives the fixed rate to service the issue and pays floating rates. The pattern of payment under the liability swap, in this new issue arbitrage, is exactly the opposite side of the swap needed to generate synthetic assets, whereby, usually the purchaser of the asset will choose to pay a fixed rate in return for receiving a floating rate of return. Essentially, the presence of the asset swap therefore enables financial institutions active in swaps, particularly in swap warehousing and market making, to operate more or less continuously in the expectations of liquidity generated from both ends of the arbitrage.

For swap counterparties, the evolution of the form of the asset swap is also significant. Of particular significance is the development of the public or securitised asset swap structure. The major advantage to swap counterparties is the changing credit risk implications of this particular structure.

From the swap counterparties' perspective, the public or securitised structure through a special purpose vehicle significantly reduces its exposure to the investor. This is because the issue vehicle is almost always collateralised by the bonds being repackaged and the swap counterparty usually has first call on that collateral. This allows swap counterparties to enter into the structuring and sale of synthetic assets to investors whose credit may not have been acceptable to the swap counterparty directly. In essence, under the public or securitised asset swap structure, the investor takes a risk on the swap counterparty but the swap counterparty removes exposure to the investor. This absence of credit risk which would otherwise be present essentially improves the pricing efficiency of the swap market quite considerably.

Part 5

Applications of Swaps and Financial Derivatives

Chapter 19

New Issue Arbitrage

THE CONCEPT OF NEW ISSUE ARBITRAGE

Swaps can be utilised as an instrument for new issue arbitrage as well as an efficient asset and liability management device. New issue arbitrage refers to the role of swaps as a cost competitive *new* fund raising technique whereby combining the issuance of debt with a concurrent interest rate or currency swap can create a synthetic liability that, in the specific circumstances, can provide financing at a cost less than that available through conventional direct access to the relevant market.

The possibility of new issue arbitrage is self-evident in the basic origin of swaps and in the fundamental economics of swap transactions. In essence, new issue arbitrage usually refers to the fact that the swap transaction allows the party seeking to raise funds to arbitrage differential access and relative cost across different markets. Where the borrower wishes to raise funds in a market where the terms available to that specific borrower are *relatively* less favourable, it may be less expensive to issue debt in a market where the terms are more favourable and combine the issuance of new debt with an interest rate or currency swap thereby creating a liability corresponding to the borrower's favoured form of funding.

Analysis of the process of new issue arbitrage requires consideration of three major issues:

- the approach and economic criteria for profitable new issue arbitrage;
- the concept of arbitrage funding, the most developed form of new issue arbitrage; and
- the impact of these techniques on the primary debt markets and on the practices of borrowers and financial institutions.

APPROACH TO NEW ISSUE ARBITRAGE

New issue arbitrage transactions, at their simplest, entail the issuance of new debt combined with a swap transaction. The basic types of arbitrage involve:

- transactions in the same currency involving swapping fixed-to-floating and vice versa;
- transactions across currencies involving swapping of debt in a particular currency to another, usually, at least initially, into US$ floating rate funding.

A basic pattern permeates the types of new issue arbitrage undertaken. The predictions of the economic theory of swaps would suggest that highly rated borrowers would utilise their comparative advantage in fixed rate markets to swap their liabilities to a more cost effective floating rate basis within the same currency or, alternatively, issue in a foreign currency then exchange the liability for funds in the desired form in its own currency. Similarly, the theory would predict that lower rated borrowers would generally raise floating rate funding and swap it into fixed in the same currency or, alternatively, into floating or fixed in a foreign currency.

These predictions are consistent with actual market practice where this pattern is evident.

The analysis of new issue arbitrage tends, on the whole, to focus on term borrowings. The process of arbitrage, however, can exist in short-term markets. An obvious example of this type of transaction would entail the issue of say 90 day short-term securities in one currency with the simultaneous execution of a spot and forward currency contract to convert the liability into a different currency on the basis that the all-up achieved cost is superior to direct access to the relevant currency.

The process of new issue arbitrage also tends to over emphasise the role of securities. For example, it is commonplace to talk about swap-driven primary issue markets or swap-driven securities issues. This reflects the fact that the basic debt underlying swap transactions has in recent times involved the issue of securities. This reflects general trends in capital markets where the use of securities, particularly for highly rated borrowers, has become commonplace. The fact that the highly rated borrowers who, arguably, provide the driving force to new issue arbitrage enjoy strong access on cost advantageous terms to securities markets throughout the world is an important factor in this association. However, the whole concept of new issue arbitrage operates independently of the underlying source of the funding, although it should be noted that the basic access to direct funding through securities issue is, at least in part, the basis of the cost differences which allow the process of arbitrage to take place.

The process of new issue arbitrage, as its very title exemplifies, is primarily cost-driven. However, in practice, the process of new issue arbitrage is considerably more complex. The factors motivating new issue arbitrage include:

- minimisation of borrowing cost;
- diversification of funding sources;
- the success of the borrowing transaction and ensuring continued market access;
- specific factors inhibiting access to particular capital markets;
- flexibility of liability management.

The identified factors operate in a number of ways. Minimisation of cost operates as a first order factor which provides the initial incentive for new issue arbitrage. In contrast, the other identified factors act as qualifications to the basic cost minimisation objective and usually serve to set up minimum arbitrage profit targets which must be satisfied before a new issue funding involving a swap can be undertaken.

The cost minimisation objective is self-evident. However, this objective alone is not satisfactory because it does not of itself provide guidance as to the desirability of a transaction per se. For example, the concept of cost minimisation only has significance within a defined asset liability management requirement profile. Only where the relevant currency and interest rate exposure basis of the borrowing has been specified can cost be considered a factor. The overall specification of the asset liability management profile is usually generated by the nature of the underlying assets that are being funded. Other relevant factors may include the desired maturity profile of debt and liquidity considerations.

An additional problem in cost minimisation as the basis for new issue arbitrage is the need to set a minimum improvement on the cost of funds before undertaking the swap-driven new issue arbitrage transaction. This is because the cost minimisation argument in extremis would dictate that even a very marginal improvement in cost would dictate undertaking a swap-driven transaction. However, given that a particular funding transaction may have implications for future access to the market and hence future arbitrage possibilities, it is necessary to consider some of the other identified factors.

A further consideration is that at a given point in time a number of competing swap-driven arbitrage opportunities may exist. The borrower may have the choice of a number of issues in various formats which can be swapped to provide cost effective funding. The likelihood of success of individual transactions in terms of market reception etc may vary significantly. Consequently, the complexity of the cost minimisation objective increases as the risks of a transaction must be considered against the potential cost savings of individual transactions.

A critical factor shaping the process of new issue arbitrage appears to be the desire on the part of borrowers to diversify their sources of funding on a global basis. The need to diversify the sources of funding for a particular borrower through broadening the investor base in its debt is self-evident. This problem is exacerbated in the case of a number of borrowers whose borrowing requirements relative to the size of their domestic capital market are large. Given that this type of imbalance is one of the key factors underlying swap arbitrage profits (see Chapter 7) the process of new issue arbitrage must seek to balance carefully the supply and demand for an issuer's debt both on a global and a market by market basis.

The issue of diversification of investor base is a complex and controversial one. In theory, distinctions between markets, particularly given the increased trend towards global markets, should not be severe. The nature of debt securities (which are bonds which typically enjoy considerable liquidity being able to be freely bought and sold in an active over the counter secondary market) should of itself ensure distribution to the potential investors. This is so despite restrictions involving registration and listing etc which, theoretically, impede the distribution process into selected markets. There is evidence to suggest that investors are able to purchase securities from different markets as and when their investment requirements dictate. This would, in theory, lead to an automatic diversification of a borrower's investor base as individual suppliers of capital would diversify their portfolios in terms of borrower credit risk by buying the existing securities on issue of a particular borrower irrespective of which market the securities were originally issued in.

However, there is evidence to suggest that international investors only participate in certain sectors of the respective markets. This appears to be motivated primarily by reasons of legal restrictions, liquidity and convenience factors. In fact, there is evidence to suggest that nearly two thirds of the total size of the international bond market is not readily accessible or liquid enough for active international participation. This lack of freedom for international fund flows means that borrowers can tap different classes of investors by issuing in different currencies and utilising different instruments as well as by adopting different issuing formats in an attempt to appeal to particular investor clientele. These factors dictate that borrowers need to identify potential clientele for their securities and specifically seek to target these investor bases with the objective of finely balancing supply and demand to each segment with a view to maximising their arbitrage profits.

The availability of continued market access is particularly relevant. This dictates that an issue must be perceived as successful by the market at large to allow the borrower to return to access this particular investor base at a future point in time. This requirement while largely vouchsafed by borrowers has in recent times been sadly neglected with issuers grossly mispricing issues to accommodate their cost targets with resultant investor backlash. This issue is discussed in detail below.

The need to ensure success of the transaction and to maintain continued market access relates to the desire of borrowers to maximise their arbitrage gains from a particular market segment which is receptive to it in terms of credit-worthiness etc over a medium to long time horizon.

In looking at the underlying forces of new issue arbitrage, it is vital to recognise a number of restrictions which may impact upon individual institutions' capacities to enter into certain types of transactions. The major restriction of relevance is regulatory factors such as registration requirements in particular markets which must be satisfied as a precondition to the issue of debt securities. For example, a full public issue in the United States domestic market requires a full Securities and Exchange Commission registration, an onerous and time consuming process. In contrast, the self-regulated Eurobond market does not require such registration processes and the documentary and listing requirements are considerably less onerous than in certain domestic markets. An additional factor may be the operation of a queuing system whereby issuers must formally register their intention to undertake a securities transaction in the particular market.

In certain jurisdictions taxation factors, like the imposition of withholding tax, may limit the capacity to enter into new issue arbitrage transactions. In the case of Australian borrowers, the need to get an exemption from withholding tax under the provisions of s 128F of the *Income Tax Assessment Act* 1936 (Cth) means that the issue must satisfy certain structural constraints. This may have the effect of inhibiting certain types of arbitrage transactions.

An additional factor relevant to the new issue arbitrage decision is the difference in flexibility between a direct borrowing and a borrowing combined with a swap. This difference in flexibility may derive from a number of sources and may be both positive or negative in impact.

For example, where a fixed rate debt issue is swapped into floating rate funding, in the same or a different currency, the rollover or repricing timing of the floating rate debt is fixed at the time at which the original swap transaction is undertaken. There are minor exceptions to this as the timing of the repricing dates can be varied either through a separate swap, special arrangements within the swap transaction itself, or by utilising other instruments such as actual direct borrowings and lendings or future/forward interest rate transactions. This underlying inflexibility may detract from a party entertaining a new issue arbitrage transaction which must be matched up against an existing portfolio of assets whose characteristics do not align totally with those of the synthetic liability being created.

The use of a swap may also enhance flexibility. Where floating rate funding is swapped into fixed rate funding, the opportunity to vary the underlying source of liquidity can be seen as adding flexibility for the borrower. Other issues relating to flexibility include the potential to terminate both types of transaction as well as the opportunities for early redemption etc which may vary between a direct borrowing and a synthetic liability entailing the use of a swap.

The complex series of factors which underlie the process of new issue arbitrage necessarily dictate that the decision to undertake a particular arbitrage transaction requires a balance between these competing considerations. In practice, these factors are summarised in a target swap level set relative to a particular funding benchmark. Common funding benchmarks in this regard include US$ LIBOR or the relevant floating rate benchmark in the relevant currency rates as well as fixed rates relative to government securities, such as United States treasuries or its equivalent in the particular currency.

In deference to the complexity of determining the pricing of any new issue arbitrage transaction, swap targets are set at levels, in cost terms, substantially below the level of funds available from alternative sources. This additional arbitrage margin which is built in is designed essentially to capture in quantitative terms factors such as diversification, the utilisation of scarce market access, restrictions of access to particular markets as well as flexibility concerns. These benchmarks evolve over time reflecting the changing conditions in the capital market in general with benchmarks usually being adjusted up or down primarily as a result of changing market opportunities for arbitrage funding.

The whole approach to new issue arbitrage can be best understood in the context of a special category of borrower, referred to as arbitrage funders, who represent the most developed case of new issue arbitrage practices.

ARBITRAGE FUNDING

Arbitrage funding: the concept

The concept of arbitrage funding is merely an extreme case of new issue arbitrage. Specifically, it refers to the practice by a borrower of a highly opportunistic borrowing strategy which entails accessing almost any market at short notice on the basis that the issue proceeds will be swapped into the borrower's desired form of funding at a cost lower than a nominated benchmark. The basic concept is best exemplified by the title of an article published in *Euromoney* in 1985, "How SEK Borrows at Fifty Below (LIBOR)".

The concept is best illustrated by example. In essence, it involves a highly rated borrower who is attuned and exposed to market innovations and movements and is prepared to take advantage of short-term windows to issue debt in particular forms, currencies and/or structures with a view to generating cheaper funding elsewhere. The common operational benchmark in this regard is US$ floating rate LIBOR. Arbitrage funders usually nominate a margin *under* LIBOR as the relevant benchmark which must be surpassed if they are to transact. For example, to take the example of SEK, given a benchmark of LIBOR minus 50bps, SEK would be prepared to issue say NZ$ securities provided the accompanying swap could generate US$ floating rate funding at a cost of LIBOR minus 50bps or better.

The clearest distinguishing feature of arbitrage funding is the willingness of the borrower to issue debt on a swapped basis almost totally unfettered by asset liability management considerations. For example, the maturity of the debt or the availability of offsetting assets may not be major constraints on particular new fund raising structures. In particular, arbitrage funders may borrow on a purely opportunistic basis to optimise their costs of borrowings irrespective of asset funding requirements with the resultant funds being matched against specifically acquired investments which are later exchanged for normal business assets such as loans or other infrastructure required for the relevant business.

These requirements for effective use of arbitrage funding limit the types and numbers of entities which can engage in the practice. A number of key requirements to undertake arbitrage funding activities can be readily identified.

The most important criterion would appear to be that the borrower enjoy a very high credit standing, usually an AA or AAA rating. This limits the scope of arbitrage funding for entities other than major banks, sovereign or quasi-sovereign entities, supra-national organisations and a select group of corporations.

An additional important requirement is the capability for setting targets in terms of universally acceptable interest rate benchmarks. The setting of a benchmark such as LIBOR minus 50bps implicitly assumes that such a cost is, first, relevant to the institution in question, and, second, that the nominated cost level is a realistic estimation of a significant cost advantage.

The need to nominate this benchmark immediately assumes that the entity has assets priced off the same benchmark in the case of financial institutions or, in the case of non-financial institutions, that the benchmark represents an alternative source of funding for the borrower.

The benchmark issue is clear cut in the case of banks who may have substantial portfolios of loans etc priced off a number of indexes against which they can match opportunistic borrowings which represent significant cost savings relative to alternatives to funding these assets. However, in the case of non-financial institutions, the argument is more complex as it assumes that the funding cost achieved is better than an alternative source of funding priced against the same benchmark but has little to say about the relative attractiveness of a number of benchmarks. This difficulty arises largely because non-financial institutions tend not to have financial assets on the asset side of the balance sheet thereby creating more complex asset liability management matching requirements.

The benchmark issue also assumes that the borrower has a relative diverse range of funding facilities or instruments available allowing the borrower to establish alternative costs of borrowing directly in a number of markets. This tends to limit arbitrage funding practices, once again, to highly rated borrowers.

As noted earlier, the traditional benchmarks for arbitrage funding are nominated relative to indexes such as US$ LIBOR or the relevant floating rate benchmark in a particular currency. Alternatively, the benchmark may be represented as a spread above or below the relevant government bond rate in the currency.

The important role of US$ LIBOR in arbitrage funding necessitates comment. Its role derives partially from the fact that it is a major market benchmark of interest rates but also that the entities which practice arbitrage funding usually have loan assets or, alternatively, can readily acquire loan assets priced relative to this index creating the opportunity to match off opportunistic borrowings against these investments.

An additional reason underlying the use of LIBOR in this particular role relates to the fact that US$ LIBOR functions very much as a central hub against which all currency swaps are transacted. As discussed in Part 8, currency swaps tend to be quoted as a fixed rate against US$ LIBOR.

Adoption of arbitrage funding approaches requires that the borrower is of a critical portfolio mass which allows it to readily absorb new opportunistic borrowings into its overall balance sheet with little dislocation or additional mismatches.

For example, a very attractive funding opportunity may be less attractive if the particular pattern of repricings etc on the floating rate funding generated creates significant mismatches against the borrower's asset portfolio. The resultant exposure on the portfolio may more than offset the cost advantage achieved. This means that borrowers with substantial portfolios are at a distinct advantage in using this pattern of financing as their portfolios are likely to be large enough to absorb particular fundings without creating this type of additional exposure. In addition, such borrowers are likely to be less sensitive as to the types of liability, maturity, rate reset details etc, as the marginal effect of a new borrowing on the overall portfolio is limited.

An additional requirement may be the capacity of such entities to take on new liabilities because of their attractive pricing and to match them off against specifically purchased investments to lock in the arbitrage spread between the borrowing and the investment. This type of activity can be undertaken on a short-term basis with the intention of ultimately selling off the short-term investments with a view to acquiring the basic assets required to be funded. This necessity means that the borrower's balance sheet must be capable of absorbing significant size transactions without creating undue gearing or other balance sheet pressures.

A critical element in utilising arbitrage funding is the capability of responding flexibly and, most importantly, quickly to market opportunities. This requires a management structure which is market sensitive and capable of reacting to short-lived opportunities in capital markets. A key requirement in this regard is a management team with the necessary knowledge and experience to work with financial intermediaries and to tap into market linkages whereby they have sufficient exposure to market innovations and information to take advantage of opportunistic borrowings possibilities.

The range of borrowers who can be truly called arbitrage funders is relatively limited. The group is primarily limited to a number of supra-nationals and sovereign or quasi-sovereign issuers. As mentioned above, borrowers such as the World Bank, SEK, the Swedish Export Agency, and the Kingdom of Denmark have largely developed this concept. A number of major highly rated banks are also practitioners of these types of funding techniques.

In addition, a number of government borrowing agencies and highly rated corporates operate on the basic principles of arbitrage funding although the nature of their portfolios and range of activities provide some limits to the extent to which they can operate as purely opportunistic borrowers.

The impact of new issue arbitrage practices on the debt portfolios of these borrowers can be best illustrated by some examples. *Exhibit 19.1* summarises the debt portfolio (before and after swaps) of the World Bank as at 1992. The analysis clearly highlights how the use of swaps has allowed the World Bank to significantly broaden its funding base and yet to achieve its desired mix of currencies at the lowest possible cost. In addition, the World Bank has utilised swaps to provide it with flexibility in acquiring and managing its portfolio of liabilities.

Exhibit 19.1

International Bank for Reconstruction and Development

Borrowings, after swaps, fiscal year 1992
(amounts in US$ million equivalent)

	Before swaps			Currency	After swaps			
Item	Amount	%	Maturity (years)	swaps (amount)	Amount	%	Maturity (years)	Cost (%)
Medium- and long-term borrowings								
US dollars	4,008.0	34	6.7	156.0	4,164.0	35	6.7	7.00
Japanese yen	3,618.7	31	8.0	0.0	3,618.7	31	8.0	5.72
Deutschmark	478.6	4	6.9	2,250.1	2,728.7	23	7.5	7.63
Swiss francs	465.1	4	3.0	769.7	1,234.8	11	7.4	6.30
Others[1]	3,218.3	27	8.4	(3,175.8)	42.5	0	8.4	10.48
Total	11,788.7	100	7.3		11,788.7	100	7.3	6.69

Exhibit 19.1—continued

	Before swaps			Currency	After swaps			
Item	Amount	%	Maturity (years)	swaps (amount)	Amount	%	Maturity (years)	Cost (%)
Short-term borrowings outstanding								
Central bank facility								
(US dollars)	2,600.0	48	0.6					4.30
COPS (Swiss francs)[2]	24.5	1	0.1					7.66
Discount notes (US dollars)[3]	2,749.1	51	0.3					3.20
Total as of 30 June 1992[4]	5,373.6	100	0.5					3.75

Notes: Details may not add to totals because of rounding.

1. Represents borrowings in European currency units. French francs, Hong Kong dollars, Italian lire, Portuguese escudos, Spanish pesetas, and Swedish kronor.
2. Continuously offered payments rights in Swiss francs.
3. Includes other short-term market borrowings in US dollars.
4. Short-term borrowings outstanding on 30 June 1991 totalled $5,367.0 million.

Source: International Bank for Reconstruction and Development—Annual Report 1992.

Exhibit 19.2 sets out the debt portfolio (both before and after swap transactions) of SEK and highlights the use by this borrower of swaps to generate low cost funding through opportunistic borrowings in different currencies without sacrificing the maintenance of its desired currency mix.

Exhibit 19.2

SEK's Total Long-Term Borrowing

As per 31 December 1992

Currency	Distribution before currency swaps	Distribution after currency swaps
US$	37%	69%
ECU	13%	4%
JPY	14%	3%
GBP	8%	5%
C$	6%	—
SKR	4%	2%
SFR	4%	5%
A$	3%	—
DEM	—	8%
Others	11%	4%
	100.0%	100.0%

1 January 1993-30 June 1993

Currency	Distribution before currency swaps	Distribution after currency swaps
US$	49.4%	76.8%
SFR	16.5%	15.0%
LIT	12.1%	—
C$	10.4%	—
SKR	5.6%	5.4%
Other	6.0%	2.8%
	100.0%	100.0%

Source: AB Svensk Exportkredit.

The opportunities available through new issue arbitrage has encouraged large/substantial borrowers, with high credit ratings, to operate an arbitrage funding strategy with most public issues being linked to interest rate and currency swaps to generate, at least initially, floating rate US$ at substantial margins under LIBOR. In the case of borrowers seeking funding in currencies other than US$, subsequent swap transactions are utilised to convert the funding advantage relative to LIBOR into lower cost funding in the desired currency or interest rate basis.

Central to this fundraising approach are the following:

- an opportunistic approach to borrowing with willingness to raise funds at short notice with excess liquidity being invested at a positive spread in anticipation of future funding requirements;
- significant internal expertise and understanding of capital markets and the capacity to analyse and execute complex transactions within a relatively short time frame to take advantage of market opportunities;
- receptivity to new issue structures and instruments which are innovative by nature, being designed to take advantage of specific investment requirements of particular investors;
- capacity to use swaps and other derivatives to manage the total debt portfolio.

In the case of arbitrage funders, a review of the list of issues undertaken (particularly, the types of structures etc) highlight the fact that the currencies and issues structures utilised are, often, totally at odds with the basic currency and interest rate basis of the requirement of each entity. These discrepancies can only be explained on the basis that the issues are primarily designed to generate lower cost funds in each entities preferred currency and to allow these borrowers to diversify their fund raising activities.

Arbitrage funding: a case study[1]

Background

The process of arbitrage funding is best illustrated by use of an example. In this section, an example of a Euroyen bond issue with accompanying currency and interest rate swap is used as the basis for discussion of a number of general issues relevant to arbitrage funding.

Assume that the borrower or issuer in this example is a major Australian bank. The bank operates both in Australia and internationally and has substantial asset portfolios, primarily loans, denominated in two main currencies: A$ and US$. The bank is an opportunistic borrower willing to access a variety of markets to obtain cost effective funding to support its asset portfolio.

Major sources of funding for the bank (apart from shareholders' equity) include the following facilities:

- Domestic borrowings:
  - —negotiable certificates of deposit (NCDs) issued into the wholesale money market at a pricing of approximately BBR for the relevant maturity;
  - —retail and wholesale interest bearing deposits primarily for short terms up to six months at rates at least 30 to 40bps below BBR;

1. The author would like to acknowledge the assistance of Stephen Sloan (AIDC) in the preparation of this case study.

—sundry issues of term certificates of deposits and private placements to generate funds at the Australian government bond rate plus a margin.

- International facilities:

—public issues, primarily Eurobond issues in a variety of currencies as well as some foreign bond issues, primarily in Switzerland, swapped into usually US$ or A$. The margins on these borrowings achieved have been in the range US$ LIBOR minus 25bps to US$ LIBOR minus 45bps;

—inter-bank US$ deposits at around LIBOR;

—a Euro-Commercial Paper (ECP) facility, allowing for the issue of ECP or EuroCDs at rates around US$ LIBID/LIBID plus 4 to 6bps;

—a US CP programme which generates very short-term 30 to 45 day funding at a small margin under US$ LIBOR. The margin varies according to the US CP/LIBOR funding spread.

The major restrictions on the bank undertaking an international securities issue on a swapped basis include:

- the need to satisfy s 128F of the *Income Tax Assessment Act* to obtain exemption from Australian withholding tax which requires the borrower to satisfy the widely spread debenture issue requirements of the legislation (this is only relevant where the funding is to be used in its Australian operations);
- the fact that the bank does not have a current registration in the United States domestic market and consequently cannot undertake a domestically targeted issue in that and certain other markets.

The specific opportunity which currently exists involves the issue of a Euroyen bond with an accompanying swap into US$ LIBOR to produce funding for the bank at LIBOR minus 38bps. The transaction has been originated by a Japanese securities house which has approached the bank with the full package: bond and swap.

In practice, the opportunity could have arisen in a different manner. For example, an approach by a securities house or investment bank to undertake a Japanese yen issue may have provoked interest whereupon the bank may have made enquiries about Japanese yen/US$ LIBOR swap rates. Alternatively, a particularly attractive or aggressive swap opportunity may have led the bank to pursue the question of undertaking a securities issue on the back of the particular swap.

In this case, the transaction satisfies the general asset liability management requirements of the bank and there is a reasonable assurance of a successful reception for the issue. The bank has decided to proceed with the transaction.

The details of the proposed yen issue and the accompanying swap are detailed in *Exhibit 19.3*.

Negotiating and executing the transaction

Negotiating the terms of the bond package is more complex because the two elements must be separately negotiated but must correspond to fuse together into a seamless cohesive funding transaction.

The key elements in negotiating the actual bond issue include the following:

- *Selection of lead manager*—selection of the lead manager will depend upon the particular borrower's attitudes. Some borrowers may have established lead managers in particular markets whom they will try to utilise for this particular transaction. Alternatively, the borrower may award the mandate to a reputable investment bank on the basis of its all round abilities despite the fact the borrower

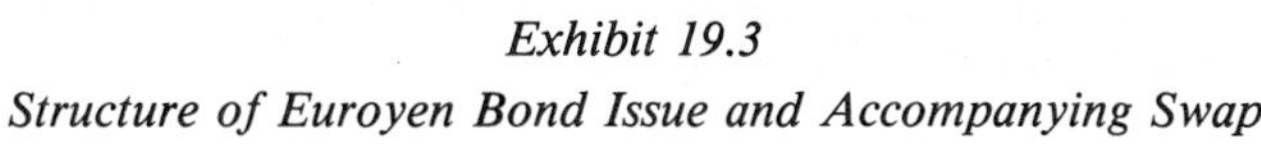

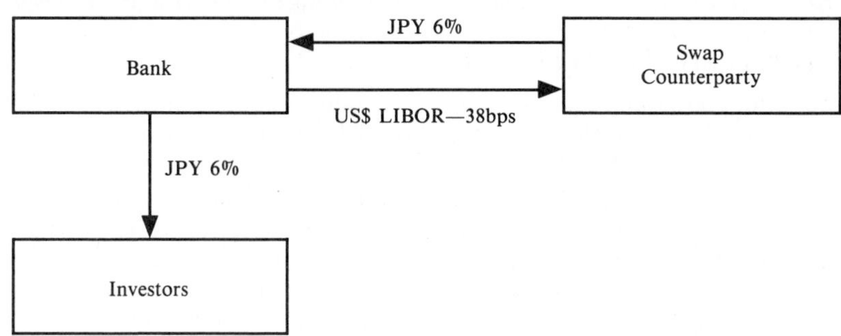

Detailed cash flows

Date	Bond issue	Swap		Net
		Receipts	Payments	
	(JPY billion)	(JPY billion)	(US$m)	(US$m)
26/3/X6	+19.675[1]	−19.675	+139.54[2]	+139.54
26/9/X6	—	—	(−LIBOR−38bps)[3]	(−LIBOR−38bps)
26/3/X7	−1.2[4]	+1.2	(−LIBOR−38bps)	(−LIBOR−38bps)
26/9/X7	—	—	(−LIBOR−38bps)	(−LIBOR−38bps)
26/3/X8	−1.2	+1.2	(−LIBOR−38bps)	(−LIBOR−38bps)
26/9/X8	—	—	(−LIBOR−38bps)	(−LIBOR−38bps)
26/3/X9	−1.2	+1.2	(−LIBOR−38bps)	(−LIBOR−38bps)
26/9/X9	—	—	(−LIBOR−38bps)	(−LIBOR−38bps)
26/3/X0	−1.2	+1.2	(−LIBOR−38bps)	(−LIBOR−38bps)
26/9/X0	—	—	(−LIBOR−38bps)	(−LIBOR−38bps)
26/3/X1	−1.2	+1.2	(−LIBOR−38bps)	(−LIBOR−38bps)
26/9/X1	−20.0	+20.0	−139.54	−139.54

Notes:

1. The initial yen receipts are calculated based on an issue amount of JPY20 billion, issued at 100.375 with fees of 2.00% giving net issue proceeds of JPY19.675 billion (JPY20 billion × 98.375%).
2. The US$ amount on initial exchange is calculated at an exchange rate of US$1.00/JPY141.00.
3. The US$ LIBOR flows are based on a US$ borrowing of US$139.54. For example, assuming LIBOR of 7.875, the actual interest payment for the relevant six month period is approximately US$5.555m.
4. Based on yen interest rate of 6.00% pa.

has no relationship with this bank in this particular market segment. The institution which has brought the opportunity to the attention of the bank will usually be awarded the mandate. "Deal shopping" is not well regarded by market participants and may lead to the borrower not being shown future attractive borrowing possibilities by the relevant institution.

- *Pricing and negotiating details of the bond issue*—the lead manager bringing the deal to the attention of the bank will inevitably provide indicative pricing which will be progressively refined as the deal nears execution. The focus will be on the all-in borrowing cost which in this type of transaction will inevitably mean the final sub-LIBOR margin achieved by the bank.

The bank may in fact seek a second opinion on pricing for the bond issue from another independent investment bank with whom it has a relationship in this particular market. This is usually done to mitigate the risk of a mispriced transaction. The strategy is risky as each house may try to denigrate its competitors and will tend to talk its own "book".

Important terms and conditions such as default conditions, negative pledges as well as the issuing vehicle to be used and credit support, such as guarantees (if applicable), must be agreed upon.

- The negotiation process will inevitably lead to the lead manager providing firm final pricing prior to agreement to undertake the issue. The need to provide firm pricing inevitably requires the transaction to be structured as a "bought deal", that is, the lead manager submits a firm offer to the borrower with an underwriting syndicate to be formed only after the borrower has accepted this offer. The technique of the bought deal is designed to transfer the entire market risk from the borrower to the lead manager to ensure that the securities transaction underlying the swap is assured. A "best efforts" or classical "open priced" bond transaction to be swapped would expose the issuer to a market risk of price movements on the bond and/or swap which most borrowers regard as unacceptable.

Typical offer and acceptance telexes for the Eurobond component of the transaction are set out in *Exhibit 19.4*.

Exhibit 19.4

Euroyen Issue Terms

Issuer:	Bank.
Lead manager/book runner:	Japanese securities company.
Co-lead managers:	Up to three co-lead managers recommended by the lead manager.
Principal amount:	JPY 20 billion
Maturity:	26 March 19X1.
Coupon:	6.00% pa.
Issue price:	100.375.
Gross commissions:	2%.
Out-of-pocket expenses:	Reimbursable lead managers expenses to be a maximum of US$60,000.
Form and denomination of notes:	To be specified.
Optional redemption:	None, except in the event of the imposition of withholding taxes and then in whole but not in part.
Payments:	All payments of principal and interest will be made without deductions or withholding for, or on account of, any present or future taxes or duties of whatever nature.
Governing law:	The law of England.
Conditions precedent:	Japanese Ministry of Finance approval to proceed with issue.

- *Selection of Eurobond management group for the Eurobond issue*—it is usual to offer the provider of the swap to the bond issue the opportunity to join the lead management group for the securities transaction. Other lead managers may be selected by virtue of their market presence in the relevant sector or relationships with either the issuer or the book running lead manager.

  Underwriters and co-managers will be selected similarly with regard to relationships with the borrower and lead manager as well as with reference to their placement power and market making capabilities in the particular market. Frequent borrowers to a particular market segment will have favoured co-management groups based on experience gained through the course of a number of transactions. Additions and deletions from this co-management group may be designed to create flexibility for particular transaction structures as well as to create incentives for improved performance.

The key points of negotiation on the swap component of the transaction will include a range of equally important but significantly different issues. These include:

- *Acceptability of counterparty*—it will be necessary to assess the creditworthiness of the swap counterparty as the issuer will be exposed, in a credit sense, to the swap counterparty for the life of the transaction.
- *Negotiating pricing, terms and conditions*—as in the case of the bond issue, the bank will negotiate the terms and conditions as well as the pricing of the swap leading up to final commitment. A particular problem may be getting swaps on truly comparable terms because of the variety of swap structures that can be utilised in connection with a particular issue (see further comments below). In addition, where a complex series of swaps are entailed, the necessity to match different elements of the securities transaction, the initial swap and any subsequent swap creates an extra level of complexity. For example, in this example, the bank could swap the yen issue into US$ LIBOR and then subsequently swap into A$ either on a fixed or floating basis.

  A key issue in negotiating the important terms and conditions of the swap will be the necessity from the view point of the borrower to ensure that the swap is conditional on the successful closing of the underlying securities transaction to minimise any market exposure for the bank. Swap counterparties usually attempt to resist this condition as it merely transfers the market risk from the issuer to the swap counterparty.

  An additional issue may be the question of structuring the swap to provide for front end recoupment of issue expenses. A number of borrowers who seek to minimise tax expenses in a given year will seek recovery of issue expenses and costs. The issue of front end recoupment is discussed in the context of the yield mathematics of swaps in Chapter 8.

  Once the final negotiations are completed and prices are agreed upon, the parties will exchange telexes detailing the terms of the swap agreed upon. A sample of this type of swap telex is set out in *Exhibit 19.5*.

It is customary for both offers on the securities and swap transactions to be confirmed by a return telex by the borrower agreeing to the terms on which the whole transaction is proposed to be undertaken.

The timing in negotiating a particular arbitrage funding transaction can vary significantly. In this particular case, the yen issue plus currency swap were negotiated in a period of approximately two to three days. However, for a first issue, the process may take several months depending upon the organisational and

Exhibit 19.5
JPY/US$ Currency Swap Terms

(Valid until 28 February, Tokyo time.)

Yen payer:	A counterparty acceptable to bank (counterparty).
US$ payer:	Bank.
Commencement date:	26 March 19X6.
Maturity date:	26 March 19X1.
Optional redemption:	Non-callable.
Initial yen amount:	JPY19.675 billion.
Initial US$ amount:	US$ equivalent of yen 19.675 billion for delivery on 26 March 19X6 as determined between bank and counterparty 10 am Tokyo time on launch date.
Annual yen payments:	JPY1.2 billion corresponding to yen coupon payments payable by bank on its Euroyen issue.
US$ payments:	Semi-annual payment on 26 March and 26 September in arrears based on 38bps less than six month LIBOR (the arithmetic mean of six month LIBOR quoted two London business days before start of each semi-annual interest payment period in Reuter LIBO page rounded upward to the nearest one bps) and calculated on the US$ amount.
Principal re-exchanges:	1. On 26 March 19X6 bank to pay counterparty JPY19.675 billion (as above) and counterparty to pay bank the US$ amount (as above). 2. On 26 March 19X1 bank to pay counterparty the US$ amount (as above) and the counterparty to pay bank the JPY20 billion.
Governing law:	The law of England.
Condition precedent:	Successful closure of bank's JPY20 billion Eurobond issue.

management styles of the parties and the specific transaction being proposed. The normal period of negotiation for experienced arbitrage funders is extremely short and would not be longer than a few days and may be as short as a few hours for a specific transaction.

Frequent issuers, who utilise arbitrage funding practices, usually seek indicative pricing from particular market segments on a regular basis, usually weekly for major markets and on a more opportunistic basis in other markets. This means the borrowers are well attuned to market movements and are well placed to react to particular opportunities within a relatively short time frame.

The timetable for the particular issue completed by the bank is summarised in *Exhibit 19.6*. The transaction will also entail a significant level of documentation and housekeeping. Some of the key documents required to be completed as well as some major housekeeping tasks required to be undertaken by the bank in our example are outlined in *Exhibit 19.7*.

Some of the key problems and difficulties encountered with arbitrage funding transactions include:

- *Price negotiations*—a key to price negotiations is the capacity to compare a wide variety of offers on a standardised basis. This is particularly so where bidding is relative to a benchmark.

  For example, US$ issues as well as US$ interest rate swaps are usually quoted at a spread to United States treasuries of a comparable maturity. However, because of potential significant differences between the benchmark, that is, United States treasury bond rate, assumed by different institutions quoting the transaction, the actual all-in rate for both swap and bond issue may not be clear and thereby inappropriate conclusions can be drawn.

Exhibit 19.6
Timetable for the Issue

Day	Activity
−3	Identify a specific opportunity for an issue and swap Check alternatives Price negotiations and obtain internal approvals
0	Agree final terms and conditions Form syndicate group
5	Japanese Ministry of Finance approval obtained Launch of issue Oral invitation to and acceptances from selling group
6	Formal telex to invite selling group Obtain quotes for fiscal agency services
8	Appoint fiscal agent
9-22	Receive draft documents—review and negotiate
10	Formalise any necessary internal approvals
11	Submit taxation applications (if applicable)
20	Obtain tax clearances (if required)
22	Sign subscription agreement Receive first audit comfort letter Exchange legal opinions
22-28	Finalise documents to be signed at the closing
28	Closing of the issue • sign fiscal agency and swap agreements • issue temporary global note • receive proceeds of issue • receive second audit comfort letter • exchange of principal amounts on swap transactions and any necessary rate sets • appoint process agent

Source: Massey (1987).

Exhibit 19.7
Bond/Swap Documentation and Housekeeping

Pre-closing

1. Appointing fiscal agent:
   - competitive quotes;
   - appointment;
   - documentation.
2. Telexes:
   - offer and acceptance, both for issue and swap(s);
   - selling and underwriting group;
   - allotment.

Exhibit 19.7—continued

3. Agreements:
   - subscription;
   - selling and underwriting group;
   - fiscal agency;
   - trustee (if applicable);
   - swap(s);
   - masters.
4. Taxation approvals.
5. Other documents:
   - legal opinions domestic and foreign counsel;
   - extel cards and prospectus;
   - stock exchange listing requirements;
   - consent for service of process;
   - press release.
6. Auditors comfort letters:
   - on signing subscription agreement;
   - at closing.
7. Housekeeping:
   - agree and ensure receipt of correct proceeds from the issue;
   - agree and settle swap(s) up-front cash flows.

Post-closing

1. Note printing:
   - temporary global note;
   - definitive notes.
2. Tax certificates.
3. Box advertisement (London Stock Exchange only).
4. Tombstones:
   - issue;
   - swap(s).
5. Maintain diaries:
   - reset dates for interest rate and/or currency fixes;
   - payments to noteholders and swap counterparty;
   - for callable issues:
     —redemption notice dates;
     —prepare draft public notices.

Source: Massey (1987).

An example of swap prices quoted in relation to United States treasuries is set out in *Exhibit 19.8*. In this particular case, the final bids received are anomalous as the major market makers in United States treasuries quote standard bid-offer spread of approximately 1.5bps. Consequently, the difference between the two quotes of 6bps is inexplicable given that the maximum can only, by definition, be approximately 3bps.

The variation between the relative and absolute bids can, in these circumstances, also be the result of different interest rate assumptions in the interest rate calculation for the absolute rate, different assumptions as to day counts as well as different discount rates used when up-front payments or other swap structure refinements are incorporated.

Exhibit 19.8

Swaps—Standardised Basis for Comparison

Firm prices quoted in relation to United States treasury bonds as at 10.00 am London time

Counterparty	Rate (spread to United States treasuries)	
A	+88	
B	+87	
C	+90.5	spread = 0.5bps
D	+90	
E	+89	
F	+84	
G	+86	

Based on these results C and D were invited to rebid their final absolute rate (against which the issuer would pay LIBOR.)

Counterparty	Bid rate	
C	8.77	difference = 6bps
D	8.71	

Solution may be to buy reference United States treasuries and sell to successful counterparty on swap.

Source: Massey (1987).

- *Issue pricing*—a critical consideration for a regular issuer in the particular market segment may be the requirement that the issue be regarded as fairly priced and trade successfully. This is a particularly vexed issue and is commented on separately below. However, one approach to overcoming these difficulties should be noted. A number of borrowers now disaggregate the securities issue and the swap, with the book running lead manager not being allowed to bid for the swap. This disaggregation is intended to provide fair pricing for both elements of the transaction as the lead manager is not allowed to cross-subsidise one element of the transaction with profits on the other.
- *Legal issues*—some of the particular problems in arbitrage funding relate to a number of legal considerations including differences in default conditions in the securities transaction and the swap as well as jurisdictional differences between the securities transaction and the swap. Care should be taken to ensure that required linkages between the swap and the issue are inserted into the documentation. Tax effects of the transaction must also be carefully considered.
- *Returning to the market sector*—most frequent issuers will wish to preserve the opportunity to return to a particular sector to undertake a future issue. Consequently, issuers inevitably analyse and rate the performance of participants in a particular transaction. Both the issue and the swap performance are analysed with reference to independent benchmarks. The performance of the management group on the securities transactions as well as the swap provider must be recognised and rewarded or punished as merited. One problem may be dealing with unsuccessful bidders as well as those parties not invited to form part of the management group for the issue, a particular problem for a well received transaction.

The risks of arbitrage funding

While the use of opportunistic arbitrage funding practices can be utilised by high quality borrowers to achieve significant cost savings, the practice also has inherent risks.

The major risk is rigid adherence to target spreads without flexibility. This may encourage mispricing of securities transactions resulting in poor secondary market performance and poor distribution ultimately damaging the borrower's reputation and capacity to access the market over a longer time frame. In essence, the argument is that a rigid arbitrage funding approach with insufficient emphasis on the success of the underlying borrowing transaction may reduce borrowing costs in the short-term but may, in fact, through reduced longer-term market access, cause the borrower's cost of funding to rise. This problem may be exacerbated where the borrower is slow in adjusting target spreads in rapidly moving market conditions.

An often bitter controversy surrounding the borrowing programme of the Kingdom of Denmark highlights some of the risks in respect of arbitrage funding.

The Kingdom of Denmark has established a reputation as one of the premier borrowers in international markets. Denmark approached the Eurobond market alone 32 times in 1986 raising the equivalent of 45 billion krone. Denmark established a reputation as a highly opportunistic arbitrage funder utilising swap-driven securities issues as a means of lowering its all-in cost of borrowings. The debt strategy of Denmark is highlighted in an explanatory note which was released by the Ministry of Finance and is set out as *Exhibit 19.9*.

Exhibit 19.9

Kingdom of Denmark Foreign Debt Management Strategy

The Kingdom of Denmark (KoD) is one of the most important sovereign borrowers with, in 1986, its gross foreign borrowing reaching a record of US$6.5 billion.

The KoD, that is the Ministry of Finance, does not go abroad to finance the budget (which showed a surplus for 1986) but is a residual or buffer borrower.

The Danish authorities do not want to adapt domestic economic policies to whatever change there may be in private capital movements which are free, except for certain short-term financial transactions.

Private capital movements have, indeed, shown big shifts, for example, from 1985 to 1986 when foreign borrowing by Danish businesses and movements of securities, especially domestic Danish krone bonds, made a swing of about US$7 billion. Furthermore, the borrowing activity in recent years had been enlarged because of prepayments ranging from US$1.5 billion to more than US$3 billion. In 1984, the KoD in fact reduced the outstanding debt whereas in 1987 net borrowing will amount to US$3 billion, assuming that there will be no private capital net inflow.

By the end of 1986 the total foreign debt of the KoD was US$15 billion, corresponding to 18.00% of GDP. For the country as a whole net foreign debt amounted to US$33 billion or nearly 40.00% of GDP.

The KoD and the Euromarket

The Euromarket has developed remarkably during the last few years. Because it is flexible and characterised by non-bureaucratic requirements for documentation, it is here that the growing competition among banks has been most visible and here that changes in borrowing techniques and products have gone furthest. The KoD has, since 1983, raised between 80% and 85% of its new funds in the Euromarket and we see no reason for immediate change.

Exhibit 19.9—continued

"Normal" loans and "profit" loans

The KoD conceptually divides its borrowings into two parts, the so-called "profit loans" and the "normal loans". The profit loans are those which would be undertaken even in the absence of a financing need, because it would be possible to place the proceeds at a higher yield. Unfortunately only something like one quarter to one third of the borrowing needs have been covered in this way, and it has been necessary to supplement these with normal market transactions. The difference in the cost of funds between the two types of borrowing was around 40bps in 1986.

It might be asked whether it would not have been better to relax the target for profit borrowing somewhat and thus increase the volume forthcoming, but it has been found that when the KoD through normal transactions had covered the substantive needs it could set relatively high standards for further transactions and exploit its unusually quick decision process to take advantage of possibilities cropping up in the markets.

Use of swaps to cheapen and balance the debt

Until 1983 the KoD used relatively traditional instruments in fund raising. The tremendous development in the swap markets and the willingness, indeed eagerness, of banks to make firm offers for an issue have changed the situation dramatically. Therefore, a borrower can tap the markets where its relative advantage is greatest and reach the desired currency and interest structure through swaps, knowing in advance precisely what the result will be.

The KoD made its first swap-driven new issue in 1983. In the beginning most transactions were fixed rate US$ issues transformed into floating rate money. In later years there has been a rise, especially in swap transactions from yen but also A$, NZ$ and C$. Altogether one third of the amounts raised by the Kingdom in the period 1983-1986 have been through transactions with simultaneous swaps mostly into floating rate US$.

This has left the KoD with a big proportion of dollars in the debt. To avoid the risk which lies in having too much debt in one currency, the KoD in 1986 began to make secondary market swaps out of floating rate dollars into fixed rate European currencies, with a view to a combination of relatively low interest rates combined with the low risk of dramatic exchange rate increases. In 1986 through May 1987 the KoD has swapped more than US$2 billion.

Even stronger change has been caused by the decline in the dollar exchange rate so the KoD's dollar debt fell from 67.00% in 1983 to 46.00% at the end of 1986. Since then it has been further reduced to 40.00%. It is difficult to determine where to go from there, but tentatively it is felt that the share of US$ in present circumstances should be reduced still further, perhaps to around one third of the debt.

While most of our deutschmark and Swiss franc debt has been raised through swaps from US$, ECU debt is provided through direct issues in the Eurobond market. This is due to the fact that it is cheaper getting ECU directly than through swaps. The KoD has normally only raised ECU when the interest rate has been lower than the one which could be theoretically calculated on the basis of the market rates for debt in the component currencies.

Avoiding being seduced by options

Many offers look advantageous because the underlying issue has some particular feature in which there is, at least temporarily, a special investor interest, for instance options, especially warrants. Our view is, however, that proceeds from the sale of the warrants cannot be deducted when determining the cost of the loan unless the warrants are covered in some way. This is not to say that the KoD will in no circumstances issue warrants which are harmless but to say that the question is whether the price for the warrants is high enough to cover the risk. The KoD has made seven transactions with attached warrants, of which five have been harmless.

Eurokrone market stabilisation

In 1985 the KoD began raising funds in the Euromarket for its own currency, the krone. It was not caused by a wish to include Danish krone in the portfolio, but rather to reduce the possibilities for arbitrage operations in which a foreign (or other Danish) entity would make Eurokrone issues and place the proceeds in domestic krone bonds at a higher yield. So whenever the interest differential between the Euromarket and the domestic market exceeds a certain level the KoD is disposed to move with a view to reduce the spread.

Source: (1987) (May) *International Financing Review* Issue 673, 1596, 1597.

The opportunistic borrowing strategies of Denmark made it the "darling" of investment bankers in the Eurobond market. Denmark's willingness to undertake innovative borrowing structures provided certain cost targets could be met provided these bankers with the opportunity to introduce innovations in security structures and accompanying swaps into the Euromarkets through 1985 and 1986. However, by 1986, there were disturbing signs suggesting some difficulties with this particular strategy.

Denmark through 1986 brought to the market a series of aggressively priced transactions. The result was a series of securities which, by general consensus, performed particularly poorly both in syndication and in secondary market trading. The difficulties encountered appeared to be motivated by a combination of factors including:

- aggressive pricing, often irrationally so, from underwriting banks competing for international bond business and "league table" status;
- Denmark's use of competition among Eurobond underwriters to lower its borrowing costs.

While Denmark utilised market conditions brilliantly, arguing that the banks making such aggressively priced offers to it must be the ultimate arbiter of how its securities could be sold and distributed in the international market, there was by the end of 1986 signs that the strategy had the potential to damage Denmark's reputation with the investor community and capital markets generally.

These signs were manifested in two particular ways:

- private indications from a number of major investment banks to the effect that they had no wish to lead manage or indeed participate in any Danish issue while this particular type of debt strategy prevailed;
- the recurrent appearance of a series of repackaged, usually asset swapped, Danish securities issues at pricing levels which were clearly undermining Denmark's future price levels in certain market segments.

The two factors were clearly interrelated. The willingness of Denmark to issue in response to aggressively priced offers from major investment banks led to a series of sometimes ill-conceived transactions which proved profitable only to the lead manager or, in a number of cases, to nobody other than Denmark. Problems of structure and pricing rapidly led to other underwriters and market makers becoming extremely reluctant and reticent to participate in Danish issues which resulted in poor syndication and poor subsequent secondary market trading performance. The poor trading performance allowed financial institutions to repackage Danish securities at very attractive prices *to the investor*. By early 1987, these repackaged issues included the following transactions:

- a US$300m fixed rate issue from Morgan Stanley International which represented a remarketing of a US$300m fixed-to-floating issue undertaken late in 1986;
- a US$200m synthetic FRN, dubbed TOPS, created by Bankers Trust International out of a US$1 billion two year fixed rate Eurobond launched late in 1986 by Shearson Lehman Brothers International;
- an elegant repackaging by Morgan Guaranty Limited of a historic US$1 billion ten year FRN priced at 0.125% *under* LIBID (the lowest priced FRN in history) into deutschmarks and GBP FRNs respectively totalling DEM300m and GBP100m.

Apart from these public repackagings, a series of privately repackaged Danish issues was also placed amongst investors. In each case the repackaging was made feasible by the poor original syndication of the host debt as well as its poor secondary market trading. The secondary market trading suggested that the real price for Danish securities was much lower than that being obtained by Denmark's relentless use of competitive pressures to clinch the tightest terms each time it came to market. The poor secondary market performance was, however, translated through the repackaging exercises into market clearing levels at which the issues, at least in their repackaged form, could be placed with genuine investors.

However, what was particularly disturbing was that the repackaged issues, whether private or public, emerged at a much higher yield than what market sources estimated Denmark would have attained on any direct borrowing in the particular market segment. For example, on the repackaged deutschmark and GBP FRNs (known as Stars and Stripes) the coupons were set at 0.1875% pa and 0.20% pa over deutschmark and Sterling LIBOR respectively. These levels, at the time, were significantly above the levels at which Denmark could have issued directly on a floating rate basis in DEM and GBP.

Essentially, the terms of the repackaged debt had dramatically impacted on Denmark's ability to tap those market segments in future as investors had available to them a supply of richly priced assets of Danish risk against which any future Danish transaction would be compared. The repackaged issues were essentially determining Denmark's future pricing in the relevant markets.

The repackagings also had implications for the relationship between Denmark and its investment bankers, underwriters and investors. Its use and reliance on unfettered competition between market participants had inevitably eroded any direct loyalty between borrower, intermediary, and lender. This is evident in the fact that in the case of the repackagings, the transactions were undertaken with minimum consultation with Denmark. Consequently, Denmark had effectively largely lost control of the secondary market trading and repackaging of its debt which ultimately would influence the terms on which Denmark could hope to access particular markets in the future.

Denmark issued a strongly worded reply to these allegations. This reply is reproduced in full in *Exhibit 19.10*.

However, despite this refutation defending its behaviour, there was evidence that Denmark was aware of the problems in this regard and was looking at means of ensuring a more orderly market for its securities transactions.

The case of the Kingdom of Denmark's debt strategy and the controversy surrounding it is not presented as a particular paradigm or case of particular notoriety. However, the controversy does highlight some of the risks of arbitrage funding. It is difficult, however, to disentangle the problems of Denmark's debt strategy from the particular market environment which prevailed in the mid to late 1980s. During this period, intense competition between financial institutions seeking to carve out market shares in the highly competitive international bond business as well as unprecedented growth in capital market activity and generally favourable market conditions may have to a large extent influenced events. With the market downturn in the late 1980s, following the collapse of global equity markets, the change in market environment, from a borrower's market to a lender's market, dictated changed attitudes which mitigated the more extreme aspects of arbitrage funding.

Exhibit 19.10
"Is the Kingdom of Denmark's Debt Strategy Going Badly Wrong?": A Reply

"If 'Big firms' do not want to do business with the Kingdom, it would be more business-like to tell us so directly, rather than do it in a defaming way under the cover of IFR. We have never received a message like that from any bank. On the contrary several prime banks have strongly asked us to be invited to bid for the next deal. By the way, only in eight out of 32 issues made in 1986 competitive bidding was used.

Furthermore, your article touches upon the performance of our issues when they come to market. As everybody knows forecasting the reception of the market is very difficult. However, that key point in bond issuing cannot be avoided so it is no wonder that banks in the market put their very best resources to tackle those problems. From time to time the market is not as good as expected but I fail to see how we are to be blamed, especially when considering that our knowledge and feeling of the market cannot be as deep as is the case for the prime banks.

That brings us to the next issue. Is it true that Danish bonds perform poorly in the secondary market? We do not think so. If you consider the major fixed rate issues we did in 1986, we think they perform reasonably satisfactorily. As far as the US$1 billion Morgan Guaranty FRN is concerned, we must admit that it has never performed well. But we think, as you also mention in the article, that there has been some special reasons for that, especially the United Kingdom super-jumbo FRN a few days later and the general development in the FRN market.

Thirdly, the question of repackaging our issues, which the article take[s] as writing on the wall. It should be noted that a lot of repackaging takes place in the market. It is not only bonds of the Kingdom of Denmark that are involved in such operations. Even the FRN from the United Kingdom has been used in such an operation. We do not think that repackaging operations necessarily is a bad thing. The Euromarket has over the years been very successful. One of the reasons is that the players accept innovations and arbitrage and repackaging is precisely an effort to overcome imperfections of the market. Looking from the borrowers' point of view repackaging could have a positive effect since the neutralising of the repackaged bonds may make it easier for us to sell new issues.

The article mentioned that we are considering to ask the Danish Central Bank to act as 'a purchaser of last resort'. For information, I can say that our line of thinking is different. The purpose of such operations would be to improve the market efficiency and to make a profit by making purchases in some of the old illiquid outstanding issues.

To sum up it is our conclusion that our strategy has been fairly successful. Quite often in the past the IFR has quoted sources saying that our strategy would backfire and make it difficult for us to place new issues at reasonable prices. Consistently this view has been shown to be erroneous since subsequent issues have been on advantageous conditions. We believe that it will be no different in the future. Quite another matter is that the ultra-competitive phase of the markets may well pass so that profit margins for the banks will improve."

Source: (1987) (March) *International Financing Review* Issue 663, 781.

However, there is little doubt that the opportunistic basis of arbitrage borrowings will continue to exist as a legitimate part of borrowers' strategies as it essentially derives from the basic economic fundamentals which give rise to these types of transactions in the first place. In essence, despite the risks of arbitrage funding, its impact on primary debt markets and the way in which new borrowing activity is conducted is not likely to change significantly.

EVOLUTION OF NEW ISSUE ARBITRAGE FUNDING PRACTICES[2]

Key evolutionary factors

New issue arbitrage practices are, predictably, not static. The opportunistic borrowing behaviour of key borrowers in global capital markets has evolved significantly in response to a variety of market and competitive factors.

The key elements of the initial development and growth of new issue arbitrage funding practices are the environment of growth and innovation that prevailed in the middle to late 1980s. The prevalence of the bought deal, with the frequent resultant mispricing of new issues, and the intense competition between new issue underwriters provided a strong basis for the development of these techniques. This was assisted by the strong growth in the swap market and the high levels of competition that existed among financial institutions seeking to build strong competitive positions in the market for swaps and other derivative products.

However, the significant changes in the global banking system resulting from the deteriorating quality of their asset portfolios, lower profitability and BIS capital requirements have forced significant changes in the business emphasis of banks and in the environment is debt and derivative markets. These changes have, in turn, forced changes in arbitrage funding techniques.

The changing competitive dynamics are not confined, merely, to financial institutions. Increased competition for lower cost funding from an increasingly larger group of borrowers has also greatly impacted upon arbitrage funding practices.

There are approximately five clearly identifiable phases in the evolution of new issue arbitrage practices. Each of these are considered below.

New issue arbitrage—pre-swap age

The predominant characteristics of this period were highly regulated markets, close relationships between borrowers and the lead manager or underwriter.

Borrowing transactions were, typically, negotiated over extended periods of time. Critical elements in determining pricing advantages depended upon the skills of the borrower, the appropriateness of the selection of the lead underwriter and timing of the issue. The ability to ensure liquidity of the borrowers' debt and engineer good distribution of securities were a major determinant of pricing and continued access to markets on a long-term basis.

New issue arbitrage—early swap age

The emergence of swaps in the early 1980s (primarily, as purely counterparty transactions) began to alter the funding equation for high quality borrowers.

The critical element in achieving lower cost funding in this period was the capacity and sophistication of borrowers in understanding swap transactions and their ability to negotiate bond/swap packages.

For market participants with no experience of this period, it is difficult to appreciate the radical changes that swap transactions, when linked to bond issues, necessitated. Borrowers needed to decide upon a whole variety of unfamiliar

2. This section draws substantially on Bernt Ljunggren, "New Issue Arbitrage—Designing Bond/Swap Packages at SEK" in Satyajit Das, *Global Swap Markets* (1991).

considerations, including calculations and valuation of cash flows, counterparty credit risks as well as negotiating highly individualised swap transactions where even trivial matters, such as day count and business days conventions, were not yet standardised and needed to be negotiated on a transaction by transaction basis. An added risk derived from the fact that the borrowing transaction and the accompanying swap would need to be negotiated and completed simultaneously.

Only a few borrowers, at this point in time, were able to develop the necessary expertise in swap technology to take advantage of the significant cost savings available from these transactions. The transactions undertaken at this point in time were extremely conventional in nature, usually taking the form of straight bond issues in various currencies with accompanying interest rate or currency swaps to generate funding in the borrowers desired currency or interest rate basis.

New issue arbitrage—the growth of swaps

As the swap market grew the understanding and knowledge of swap techniques proliferated, the practice of new issue arbitrage funding enjoyed rapid growth.

Standardisation within the swap market and a general pattern whereby financial institutions presented bond/swap packages to borrowers allowed greater numbers of borrowers to take advantage of opportunistic funding techniques.

From the borrowers' perspective, the principal requirements were reaction time and capacity to understand innovation. Swap market opportunities to generate low cost funding were still relatively plentiful but the borrower's reaction time became a crucial factor enabling a particular borrower to take advantage of a market opportunity. Particular borrowers were seen as being receptive to and capable of reacting within an appropriate time horizon leading financial institutions to focus their efforts on these borrowers. Similarly, receptivity to innovation allowed borrowers to take advantage of arbitrage opportunities. A number of borrowers encouraged innovation and were willing to undertake innovative transactions allowing them to benefit from a substantial reduction in borrowing costs.

The concept of a sub-LIBOR margin emerged but the competitive conditions were such that it was still possible to bring issues to market with an accompanying swap where it was not essential to aggressively misprice the bond allowing the borrower the opportunity to both achieve a successful bond issue as well as an acceptable cost of funds.

New issue arbitrage—maturity of the swap market

By the late 1980s, the commoditisation of swaps and the intensity of competition among financial institutions as well as borrowers to take advantage of new issue arbitrage opportunities led to a significant deterioration in opportunistic funding practices.

As more and more borrowers understood the advantages of new issue arbitrage and sought to take advantage of funding opportunities, the arbitrage opportunities themselves became more limited and the funding cost achievable and the arbitrage gain reduced. An additional factor, in this regard, was the increased sophistication on the part of investors who learned, through the development of the asset swap market, to look through the packages of bonds and swaps to the floating rate equivalent return of any transaction.

The borrowers role became one of nominating a sub-LIBOR target and waiting for investment banks and other financial institutions to structure a bewildering variety bond/swap packages which met these sub-LIBOR targets. Financial institutions now could meet investment demand with a list of borrowers of comparable high credit rating with estimated borrowing targets, all capable of entering into transactions at relatively short notice. As the list of borrowers with their targets increased, the sub-LIBOR targets themselves were eroded and some degree of trading between credit risk and sub-LIBOR margin began to occur.

For the intermediaries, this phase of the evolution of the new issue arbitrage market had both positive and negative features. The positive feature was that the increasing indifference of borrowers to the type of bond issue and the swap (provided the borrower's sub-LIBOR target could be met) allowed the development of a variety of financial instruments, usually with derivative elements embedded. A small group of banks developed expertise in the more esoteric instruments and concentrated in developing these structures where profit margins continued to be high.

A larger group of banks, without the technical expertise to engineer these more innovative bond/swap packages, were, in the face of increased competition, caught in a profit squeeze on both the underlying bond and the swap. The result was often grotesque mispricing of the bond and/or the swap as financial institutions competed with almost prehistoric voracity in an effort to win mandates and execute transactions.

New issue arbitrage—the late maturity of the swap market

By the late 1980s and early 1990s, a combination of more limited arbitrage opportunities and the presence of a substantial number of borrowers actively seeking to take advantage of such opportunities greatly reduced the scope for new issue arbitrage. That is not to say that arbitrage transactions were still not completed, rather, transactions that were completed were fewer in number, the savings in funding costs lower and the types of transaction utilised to generate funding advantage more varied.

An increasing feature of this period was the withdrawal of a large number of institutions from various elements of the new issue arbitrage business—namely, the debt underwriting side as well as the swap/derivative side: refer Chapter 1. This rationalisation of the level of competition, as part of the overall rationalisation of the financial services industry generally, ushered in a new competitive environment.

The market environment was characterised by a greater degree of rationality then at any time since the early 1980s. In the debt markets, a number of trends were evident:

- In the mainstream bond markets, increased focus on underwriting, pricing and distribution practices led to changes in market practice with the introduction of the fixed price re-offer structure in preference to the bought deal. This had the impact of avoiding some of the gross mispricing practices on bond transactions in the past. The bought deal continued to be utilised but the worst of the excesses of the late 1980s were avoided. The trend was also to very substantial issue sizes with increased focus on credit quality and issue liquidity, including the development of globally fungible distribution settlement and trading in particular issues.

- Bond markets in a variety of new, relatively minor currencies, developed in conjunction with parallel swap markets in those currencies. Swap arbitrage opportunities in these markets continued to be available and were a feature of the activity of arbitrage funders during this period.
- The use of continuous issue formats for borrowers, usually in the form of medium term note (MTN) programmes became increasingly popular. The major component of issues under these programmes was structured quasi-private placements of highly customised securities usually incorporating currency, interest rate, equity and commodity market derivatives, specifically designed to individual investor specifications. These issues were typically combined with specifically engineered swap structures to generate sub-LIBOR funding for borrowers. MTN programmes came rapidly to be viewed as effectively pre-packaged and pre-documented issuance format as structured private placements with substantial proportions of issuance under these programmes taking the structured formats identified.

In essence, debt markets bifurcated into a market for large scale issuance in traditional bond issuance format but based on increasingly negotiated pricing environment where underwriters would agree on the appropriate pricing of the bonds with controls binding underwriters in terms of syndication and after market pricing, and, a second tier market for debt issuance of a more structured or exotic kind in minor currency or entailing the MTN format (in major reserve currencies).

In the early 1990s, major borrowers were extremely active in altering their funding practices to fit these new markets exigencies.

This phase of the market evolution, which is still continuing, also required a significant alteration in the approach of new issue arbitrage borrowers. New issue arbitrage borrowers continued to function, very much as before, seeking to fund opportunistically and establishing the debt formats outlined above to allow them to take advantage of market opportunity. This approach continued to emphasise rapidness of reaction time (to allow borrowers to take advantage of market windows) and this activity and expertise analysing innovative debt issuance formats.

A particular development was the increasing need for borrowers to accept, as part of the new issue arbitrage process, some risk elements of these transactions. These risk elements included:

- *amount uncertainty*—whereby the borrower would not be certain of the amount of funding generated by the transaction although its cost would be predetermined;
- *maturity uncertainty*—whereby the borrower was certain of the amount of funding, its cost but not of its precise maturity, although the possible range of maturities would be known;
- *interest basis uncertainty*—that is, whether the borrowing was on a fixed or floating rate basis;
- *currency uncertainty*—whereby the borrower was subject to uncertainty about the currency in which the borrowing was denominated.

The presence of these risk elements dictated that new issue arbitrage borrowers were increasingly forced into risk reward trade-offs in undertaking these particular transactions. Sophisticated borrowers were usually prepared to accept some of these risks. Most large borrowers were prepared to accept uncertainty in respect of amount and/or maturity which could be absorbed into their overall liability portfolios. A number of large borrowers, particularly sovereign entities, were prepared to accept uncertainty as to the fixed or floating nature of the underlying funding generated. A limited number of borrowers were willing to accept the currency uncertain of certain types of transactions.

However, a smaller group of borrowers were willing to extend their opportunistic funding practices to seek to capture the profits of financial institutions actively packaging these complex debt/derivative packages in an effort to further reduce borrowing costs, albeit at the expense of an increased risk profile.

This latter type of approach is exemplified by SEK who in late 1989 entered into arrangements with a specialist risk management consultancy firm, Westminster Equity, to initially, analyse and subsequently to design and manage suitable risk positions utilising dynamic hedging and risk management techniques.

Utilising this approach, SEK was prepared to enter into transactions whereby the borrower issued debt instruments with embedded derivative elements as required by investors. The major difference was that instead of immediately immunising itself from the risk of the derivative structure by simultaneous execution of a swap which passed the risks of derivative elements on to a financial institution, SEK, in conjunction with Westminster Equity, assumed the risk of the position and sought to manage it dynamically.

The major advantages to SEK is the capacity to generate the funding and significant margins under LIBOR (claimed to be in the range of 200-300bps below LIBOR).

This approach which essentially seeks to disintermediate the financial institutions from the structuring and risk management role in these types of transaction has not been adopted by a large number of borrowers, presumably, because of the increased risks involved.

IMPACT OF NEW ISSUE ARBITRAGE ON PRIMARY DEBT MARKETS

Swap-driven primary issues

As swap transactions increasingly unbundle the process of fund raising, separating the decision to raise funds in a particular market and the process of conversion of the funds raised into the desired currency and interest rate basis, all the major global debt markets increasingly became arbitrage markets. This resulted in the development of a unique class of debt instruments that could be characterised as "swap-driven primary issues". By definition under such structures, despite the fact that the primary issuance of debt involved may well be a standard, publicised securities issue, the borrower acquired an exposure in a currency and interest rate basis other than that of the borrowing.

The emergence of swap-driven primary issues had two major implications:

- the pricing approach to the issuance of new debt changed radically;
- swap-driven primary issues resulted in a radical change in the currency distribution of international bond issues.

With an ever-higher percentage of issues being swap-driven, the pricing in almost every segment of the international bond market came to be arbitrage driven with the relevant pricing being *not* the absolute interest cost of an issue per se, but the pricing achievable in US$ terms in either fixed rate relative to United States Treasuries, or more often, in floating rate terms as a margin under LIBOR. In this regard, as noted above, floating rate US$, usually priced relative to LIBOR, emerged as a useful medium through which a large proportion of cross currency swaps were transacted. The exact pricing in US$ terms, be it in fixed or floating rates, did not matter as the existence of deep liquid markets in US$ interest rate swaps meant that floating rate could be converted to its fixed rate equivalent and vice versa.

The lack of reliable and comprehensive data on swap driven new issuance limits the analysis of swap driven primary issuance in international bond markets. However, the extent to which new issue markets are swap driven is evident from *Exhibit 19.11* which highlights a very rapid growth in swap driven new issue transactions. However, the true extent of swap driven transaction is probably higher as the statistics in *Exhibit 19.11* only consider currency swap driven issuance.

The extent to which the issue markets are dominated by swap activity is also evident from *Exhibit 19.12* which shows swap driven primary issues by currency of issues for the period 1981 to 1991, in terms of numbers of issues, dollar value of issues and the relative shares in currency terms of swap driven issuance. *Exhibit 19.13* reinforces the latter setting out an analysis of swap driven primary issues by nationality of issuers, for the same period, in terms of numbers of transactions, currency value of transaction and the relative share by nationality of issuer.

The data in *Exhibits 19.12* and *19.13* highlights several aspects of the impact of swaps on debt markets:

- The emergence of swap-driven primary issues of debt appears to have promoted or assisted in the development of international bond markets in a number of currencies, previously unknown outside their national markets. For example, international debt markets in A$, NZ$, French francs, Scandinavian currencies, lira, pesetas etc owe at least their rapid expansion to the existence of substantial currency swap markets which provide the basis for new issue activity in these market sectors.
- The pattern of swap-driven issuance in individual currencies is extremely volatile with significant changes in the relative share of swap-driven primary issuance in terms of currency of issue from one period to the next. This, in all probability, reflects investor appetite for securities in a particular currency dictated by anticipated movements in interest rate and currency values.
- The nationality of issuers in terms of swap-driven primary issues shows penetration of arbitrage funding practices to a wide variety of countries but with a significant concentration amongst supra-nationals, multi-nationals and OECD countries.

The impact on the primary debt markets, however, extended well beyond these factors and included certain effects on the characteristics of bonds which themselves started to evolve in response to their function as the host debt for often complex swap-driven fund raising exercises. The primary changes to the characteristics of the bonds included:

- the increased use of non-callable bullet maturities designed to help match counterparties in the swap transaction;

Exhibit 19.11
Swap-Driven New Issue Volume

New Issue Volume (US Dollar Million Equivalent) Swapped in International Markets (1981-1993)

	1981	1982	1983	1984	1985	1986	1987	1988	1989	1990	1991	1992	TOTAL
Non-US Dollar Issuance Volume	18,515	25,705	32,711	39,549	66,337	105,099	111,366	142,848	112,170	145,707	203,946	219,502	1,223,455
Non-US Dollar Issuance Swapped	217	729	1,934	3,440	16,069	26,403	33,212	26,201	39,371	41,758	54,067	55,001	298,402
% of Non-US Dollar Issuance Swapped	1.2%	2.8%	5.9%	8.7%	24.2%	25.1%	29.8%	18.3%	35.1%	28.7%	26.5%	25.1%	24.4%
US Dollar Issuance Volume	28,926	52,262	40,943	77,904	104,448	121,581	63,017	77,442	118,962	78,998	93,091	125,014	982,588
US Dollar Issuance Swapped	790	1,511	1,526	2,460	3,563	8,703	12,270	27,165	82,505	25,352	31,143	31,920	228,908
% of US Dollar Issuance Swapped	2.7%	2.9%	3.7%	3.2%	3.4%	7.2%	19.5%	35.1%	69.4%	32.1%	33.5%	25.5%	23.3%
Total Issuance Volume	47,441	77,967	73,654	117,453	170,785	226,680	174,383	220,290	231,132	224,705	297,037	344,516	2,206,043
Total Issuance Swapped	1,007	2,240	3,460	5,900	19,632	35,106	45,482	53,366	121,876	67,110	85,210	86,921	527,310
% of Total Issuance Swapped	2.1%	2.9%	4.7%	5.0%	11.5%	15.5%	26.1%	24.2%	52.7%	29.9%	28.7%	25.2%	23.9%

Source: Salomon Brothers Inc.

Exhibit

Swap-Driven Primary Issues

Volume (US Dollar Million Equivalent) of Swap-Driven Primary Issues by Currency of Issue (1981-1993)

	1981	% of Total	1982	% of Total	1983	% of Total	1984	% of Total	1985	% of Total	1986	% of Total
Australian Dollars	0	0.0%	0	0.0%	0	0.0%	132	2.2%	1,850	9.4%	3,822	10.9%
Austrian Schilling	0	0.0%	0	0.0%	0	0.0%	41	0.7%	53	0.3%	0	0.0%
Belgian Franc	0	0.0%	0	0.0%	0	0.0%	0	0.0%	0	0.0%	117	0.3%
Canadian Dollar	61	6.1%	71	3.2%	174	5.0%	330	5.6%	722	3.7%	1,444	4.1%
Dutch Guilder	0	0.0%	0	0.0%	0	0.0%	33	0.6%	0	0.0%	91	0.3%
Danish Krone	0	0.0%	0	0.0%	0	0.0%	0	0.0%	105	0.5%	61	0.2%
Deutschmark	0	0.0%	0	0.0%	197	5.7%	132	2.2%	1,034	5.3%	1,244	3.5%
ECU	0	0.0%	0	0.0%	432	12.5%	839	14.2%	2,971	15.1%	2,638	7.5%
Finnish Markka	0	0.0%	0	0.0%	0	0.0%	0	0.0%	0	0.0%	0	0.0%
French Franc	86	8.5%	0	0.0%	0	0.0%	0	0.0%	167	0.9%	334	1.0%
Hong Kong Dollar	0	0.0%	0	0.0%	0	0.0%	0	0.0%	0	0.0%	0	0.0%
Italian Lire	0	0.0%	0	0.0%	0	0.0%	0	0.0%	0	0.0%	35	0.1%
Luxembourg Franc	0	0.0%	0	0.0%	0	0.0%	0	0.0%	36	0.2%	45	0.1%
New Zealand Dollar	0	0.0%	0	0.0%	7	0.2%	0	0.0%	889	4.5%	736	2.1%
Spanish Peseta	0	0.0%	0	0.0%	0	0.0%	0	0.0%	0	0.0%	0	0.0%
Swedish Kronor	0	0.0%	0	0.0%	0	0.0%	0	0.0%	0	0.0%	43	0.1%
Swiss Franc	70	7.0%	514	22.9%	1,047	30.3%	1,296	22.0%	2,226	11.3%	4,874	13.9%
UK Sterling	0	0.0%	0	0.0%	77	2.2%	355	6.0%	422	2.1%	438	1.2%
US Dollar	790	78.5%	1,511	67.5%	1,526	44.1%	2,460	41.7%	3,563	18.1%	8,703	24.8%
Japanese Yen	0	0.0%	144	6.4%	0	0.0%	282	4.8%	5,594	28.5%	10,481	29.9%
Portuguese Escudo	0	0.0%	0	0.0%	0	0.0%	0	0.0%	0	0.0%	0	0.0%
Irish Punt	0	0.0%	0	0.0%	0	0.0%	0	0.0%	0	0.0%	0	0.0%
Norwegian Kroner	0	0.0%	0	0.0%	0	0.0%	0	0.0%	0	0.0%	0	0.0%
Total	1,007	100.0%	2,240	100.0%	3,460	100.0%	5,900	100.0%	19,632	100.0%	35,106	100.0%

Number of Swap-Driven Primary Issues by Currency of Issue (1981-1993)

	1981	% of Total	1982	% of Total	1983	% of Total	1984	% of Total	1985	% of Total	1986	% of Total
Australian Dollars	0	0.0%	0	0.0%	0	0.0%	4	3.8%	52	15.8%	77	18.2%
Austrian Schilling	0	0.0%	0	0.0%	0	0.0%	1	1.0%	2	0.6%	0	0.0%
Belgian Franc	0	0.0%	0	0.0%	0	0.0%	0	0.0%	0	0.0%	1	0.2%
Canadian Dollar	1	7.1%	2	5.3%	3	4.7%	6	5.7%	12	3.6%	19	4.5%
Dutch Guilder	0	0.0%	0	0.0%	0	0.0%	1	1.0%	0	0.0%	1	0.2%
Danish Krone	0	0.0%	0	0.0%	0	0.0%	0	0.0%	5	1.5%	1	0.2%
Deutschmark	0	0.0%	0	0.0%	4	6.3%	3	2.9%	14	4.2%	14	3.3%
ECU	0	0.0%	0	0.0%	10	15.6%	20	19.0%	63	19.1%	33	7.8%
Finnish Markka	0	0.0%	0	0.0%	0	0.0%	0	0.0%	0	0.0%	0	0.0%
French Franc	1	7.1%	0	0.0%	0	0.0%	0	0.0%	2	0.6%	5	1.2%
Hong Kong Dollar	0	0.0%	0	0.0%	0	0.0%	0	0.0%	0	0.0%	0	0.0%
Italian Lire	0	0.0%	0	0.0%	0	0.0%	0	0.0%	0	0.0%	1	0.2%
Luxembourg Franc	0	0.0%	0	0.0%	0	0.0%	0	0.0%	6	1.8%	7	1.7%
New Zealand Dollar	0	0.0%	0	0.0%	1	1.6%	0	0.0%	35	10.6%	18	4.3%
Spanish Peseta	0	0.0%	0	0.0%	0	0.0%	0	0.0%	0	0.0%	0	0.0%
Swedish Kroner	0	0.0%	0	0.0%	0	0.0%	0	0.0%	0	0.0%	1	0.2%
Swiss Franc	2	14.3%	17	44.7%	25	39.1%	30	28.6%	40	12.1%	68	16.1%
UK Sterling	0	0.0%	0	0.0%	2	3.1%	5	4.8%	6	1.8%	7	1.7%
US Dollar	10	71.4%	17	44.7%	19	29.7%	31	29.5%	36	10.9%	71	16.8%
Japanese Yen	0	0.0%	2	5.3%	0	0.0%	4	3.8%	57	17.3%	98	23.2%
Portuguese Escudo	0	0.0%	0	0.0%	0	0.0%	0	0.0%	0	0.0%	0	0.0%
Irish Punt	0	0.0%	0	0.0%	0	0.0%	0	0.0%	0	0.0%	0	0.0%
Norwegian Kroner	0	0.0%	0	0.0%	0	0.0%	0	0.0%	0	0.0%	0	0.0%
Total	14	100.0%	38	100.0%	64	100.0%	105	100.0%	330	100.0%	422	100.0%

Source: Salomon Brothers Inc.

19.12

(by Currency of Issue)

1987	% of Total	1988	% of Total	1989	% of Total	1990	% of Total	1991	% of Total	1992	% of Total	Total	% of Total
6,866	15.1%	3,036	5.7%	3,555	2.9%	1,648	2.5%	1,213	1.4%	2,025	2.3%	24,147	4.6%
98	0.2%	0	0.0%	0	0.0%	145	0.2%	376	0.4%	453	0.5%	1,166	0.2%
0	0.0%	0	0.0%	0	0.0%	0	0.0%	0	0.0%	0	0.0%	117	0.0%
2,978	6.5%	5,385	10.1%	6,507	5.3%	2,322	3.5%	8,779	10.3%	9,575	11.0%	38,348	7.3%
50	0.1%	146	0.3%	831	0.7%	56	0.1%	477	0.6%	2,978	3.4%	4,662	0.9%
205	0.5%	50	0.1%	39	0.0%	125	0.2%	0	0.0%	104	0.1%	689	0.1%
1,179	2.6%	834	1.6%	2,689	2.2%	3,345	5.0%	6,576	7.7%	9,226	10.6%	26,456	5.0%
2,926	6.4%	1,987	3.7%	3,794	3.1%	5,224	7.8%	9,042	10.6%	7,701	8.9%	37,554	7.1%
67	0.1%	0	0.0%	0	0.0%	430	0.6%	292	0.3%	0	0.0%	789	0.1%
265	0.6%	248	0.5%	633	0.5%	148	0.2%	2,156	2.5%	2,773	3.2%	6,810	1.3%
64	0.1%	0	0.0%	64	0.1%	77	0.1%	0	0.0%	130	0.1%	335	0.1%
132	0.3%	202	0.4%	1,399	1.1%	2,009	3.0%	4,598	5.4%	3,493	4.0%	11,868	2.3%
88	0.2%	8	0.0%	168	0.1%	1,243	1.9%	1,280	1.5%	1,945	2.2%	4,813	0.9%
1,933	4.3%	659	1.2%	1,203	1.0%	307	0.5%	189	0.2%	136	0.2%	6,059	1.1%
158	0.3%	0	0.0%	1,256	1.0%	482	0.7%	981	1.2%	763	0.9%	3,640	0.7%
0	0.0%	0	0.0%	282	0.2%	118	0.2%	609	0.7%	805	0.9%	1,857	0.4%
2,788	6.1%	3,774	7.1%	2,361	1.9%	7,275	10.8%	6,515	7.6%	7,227	8.3%	39,967	7.6%
2,703	5.9%	1,979	3.7%	4,481	3.7%	907	1.4%	3,565	4.2%	3,162	3.6%	18,089	3.4%
12,270	27.0%	27,165	50.9%	82,505	67.7%	25,352	37.8%	31,143	36.5%	31,920	36.7%	228,908	43.4%
10,712	23.6%	7,893	14.8%	10,109	8.3%	15,759	23.5%	7,199	8.4%	2,286	2.6%	70,459	13.4%
0	0.0%	0	0.0%	0	0.0%	57	0.1%	220	0.3%	124	0.1%	401	0.1%
0	0.0%	0	0.0%	0	0.0%		0.0%	0	0.0%	64	0.1%	64	0.0%
0	0.0%	0	0.0%	0	0.0%	81	0.1%	0	0.0%	0	0.0%	81	0.0%
45,482	100.0%	53,366	100.0%	121,876	100.0%	67,110	100.0%	85,210	100.0%	86,890	100.0%	527,279	100.0%

1987	% of Total	1988	% of Total	1989	% of Total	1990	% of Total	1991	% of Total	1992	% of Total	Total	% of Total
150	27.7%	63	11.3%	63	7.4%	27	4.0%	10	1.4%	18	2.9%	464	9.4%
2	0.4%	0	0.0%	0	0.0%	2	0.3%	5	0.7%	6	1.0%	18	0.4%
0	0.0%	0	0.0%	0	0.0%	0	0.0%	0	0.0%	0	0.0%	1	0.0%
47	8.7%	69	12.4%	64	7.5%	26	3.8%	69	10.0%	60	9.5%	378	7.7%
1	0.2%	2	0.4%	8	0.9%	1	0.1%	3	0.4%	20	3.2%	37	0.8%
5	0.9%	1	0.2%	1	0.1%	2	0.3%	0	0.0%	2	0.3%	17	0.3%
13	2.4%	12	2.2%	34	4.0%	34	5.0%	78	11.3%	93	14.8%	299	6.1%
31	5.7%	19	3.4%	45	5.3%	37	5.5%	36	5.2%	40	6.3%	334	6.8%
1	0.2%	0	0.0%	0	0.0%	7	1.0%	5	0.7%	0	0.0%	13	0.3%
3	0.6%	3	0.5%	7	0.8%	1	0.1%	12	1.7%	14	2.2%	48	1.0%
1	0.2%	0	0.0%	1	0.1%	1	0.1%	0	0.0%	2	0.3%	5	0.1%
3	0.6%	2	0.4%	14	1.6%	13	1.9%	33	4.8%	18	2.9%	84	1.7%
11	2.0%	1	0.2%	18	2.1%	66	9.8%	67	9.7%	63	10.0%	239	4.9%
40	7.4%	13	2.3%	12	1.4%	7	1.0%	6	0.9%	3	0.5%	135	2.7%
2	0.4%	0	0.0%	14	1.6%	5	0.7%	13	1.9%	7	1.1%	41	0.8%
0	0.0%	0	0.0%	5	0.6%	2	0.3%	8	1.2%	9	1.4%	25	0.5%
37	6.8%	43	7.7%	37	4.3%	108	16.0%	113	16.3%	123	19.5%	643	13.1%
29	5.4%	14	2.5%	32	3.8%	5	0.7%	22	3.2%	14	2.2%	136	2.8%
78	14.4%	187	33.6%	328	38.5%	128	18.9%	161	23.3%	129	20.5%	1,195	24.3%
87	16.1%	127	22.8%	168	19.7%	203	30.0%	46	6.6%	6	1.0%	798	16.2%
0	0.0%	0	0.0%	0	0.0%	1	0.1%	5	0.7%	1	0.2%	7	0.1%
0	0.0%	0	0.0%	0	0.0%	0	0.0%	0	0.0%	1	0.2%	1	0.0%
0	0.0%	0	0.0%	0	0.0%	0	0.0%	0	0.0%	1	0.2%	1	0.0%
541	100.0%	556	100.0%	851	100.0%	676	100.0%	692	100.0%	630	100.0%	4,918	100.0%

Exhibit

Swap-Driven Primary Issues

Number of Swap-Driven Primary Issues by Nationality of Issuer (1981-1993)

	1981	% of Total	1982	% of Total	1983	% of Total	1984	% of Total	1985	% of Total	1986	% of Total
Supranational	5	35.7%	4	10.5%	6	9.4%	5	4.8%	16	4.8%	25	5.9%
Multinational	1	7.1%	1	2.6%	0	0.0%	1	1.0%	3	0.9%	3	0.7%
Argentina	1	7.1%	0	0.0%	0	0.0%	0	0.0%	0	0.0%	0	0.0%
Australia	0	0.0%	0	0.0%	4	6.3%	17	16.2%	19	5.8%	14	3.3%
Austria	1	7.1%	6	15.8%	5	7.8%	10	9.5%	10	3.0%	11	2.6%
Belgium	0	0.0%	0	0.0%	2	3.1%	2	1.9%	8	2.4%	12	2.8%
Bulgaria	0	0.0%	0	0.0%	0	0.0%	0	0.0%	0	0.0%	0	0.0%
Canada	2	14.3%	7	18.4%	12	18.8%	8	7.6%	13	3.9%	27	6.4%
Cayman Islands	0	0.0%	0	0.0%	0	0.0%	0	0.0%	0	0.0%	0	0.0%
China	0	0.0%	0	0.0%	0	0.0%	0	0.0%	0	0.0%	0	0.0%
Denmark	0	0.0%	0	0.0%	1	1.6%	5	4.8%	13	3.9%	11	2.6%
Finland	0	0.0%	0	0.0%	0	0.0%	1	1.0%	8	2.4%	18	4.3%
France	0	0.0%	3	7.9%	4	6.3%	2	1.9%	22	6.7%	19	4.5%
Greece	0	0.0%	0	0.0%	0	0.0%	0	0.0%	0	0.0%	0	0.0%
Germany	0	0.0%	0	0.0%	2	3.1%	6	5.7%	19	5.8%	43	10.2%
Hong Kong	0	0.0%	0	0.0%	0	0.0%	0	0.0%	1	0.3%	1	0.2%
India	0	0.0%	0	0.0%	0	0.0%	0	0.0%	0	0.0%	0	0.0%
Ireland	0	0.0%	0	0.0%	0	0.0%	0	0.0%	0	0.0%	1	0.2%
Italy	0	0.0%	0	0.0%	0	0.0%	0	0.0%	7	2.1%	17	4.0%
Japan	2	14.3%	4	10.5%	6	9.4%	26	24.8%	48	14.5%	45	10.7%
Korea	0	0.0%	0	0.0%	0	0.0%	0	0.0%	0	0.0%	0	0.0%
Luxembourg	0	0.0%	0	0.0%	0	0.0%	0	0.0%	0	0.0%	2	0.5%
Netherlands	0	0.0%	2	5.3%	1	1.6%	2	1.9%	13	3.9%	13	3.1%
Norway	0	0.0%	0	0.0%	3	4.7%	1	1.0%	10	3.0%	9	2.1%
New Zealand	0	0.0%	0	0.0%	0	0.0%	1	1.0%	2	0.6%	1	0.2%
Portugal	0	0.0%	0	0.0%	0	0.0%	0	0.0%	0	0.0%	0	0.0%
Soviet Union	0	0.0%	0	0.0%	0	0.0%	0	0.0%	0	0.0%	0	0.0%
Spain	0	0.0%	0	0.0%	1	1.6%	0	0.0%	1	0.3%	0	0.0%
Sweden	0	0.0%	0	0.0%	2	3.1%	4	3.8%	11	3.3%	11	2.6%
Switzerland	0	0.0%	0	0.0%	1	1.6%	0	0.0%	0	0.0%	0	0.0%
Thailand	0	0.0%	0	0.0%	0	0.0%	0	0.0%	0	0.0%	0	0.0%
United Kingdom	1	7.1%	1	2.6%	5	7.8%	4	3.8%	10	3.0%	14	3.3%
United States	1	7.1%	10	26.3%	9	14.1%	10	9.5%	96	29.1%	125	29.6%
Brazil	0	0.0%	0	0.0%	0	0.0%	0	0.0%	0	0.0%	0	0.0%
Mexico	0	0.0%	0	0.0%	0	0.0%	0	0.0%	0	0.0%	0	0.0%
Malaysia	0	0.0%	0	0.0%	0	0.0%	0	0.0%	0	0.0%	0	0.0%
South Africa	0	0.0%	0	0.0%	0	0.0%	0	0.0%	0	0.0%	0	0.0%
Indonesia	0	0.0%	0	0.0%	0	0.0%	0	0.0%	0	0.0%	0	0.0%
Turkey	0	0.0%	0	0.0%	0	0.0%	0	0.0%	0	0.0%	0	0.0%
Total	14	100.0%	38	100.0%	64	100.0%	105	100.0%	330	100.0%	422	100.0%

Source: Salomon Brothers Inc.

19.13

(by Nationality of Issuer)

1987	% of Total	1988	% of Total	1989	% of Total	1990	% of Total	1991	% of Total	1992	% of Total	Total	% of Total
32	5.9%	15	2.7%	51	6.0%	49	7.2%	48	6.9%	65	10.3%	321	6.5%
3	0.6%	1	0.2%	4	0.5%	3	0.4%	0	0.0%	0	0.0%	20	0.4%
0	0.0%	0	0.0%	0	0.0%	0	0.0%	0	0.0%	0	0.0%	1	0.0%
20	3.7%	24	4.3%	36	4.2%	12	1.8%	10	1.4%	6	1.0%	162	3.3%
20	3.7%	17	3.1%	23	2.7%	19	2.8%	18	2.6%	21	3.3%	161	3.3%
13	2.4%	5	0.9%	16	1.9%	8	1.2%	14	2.0%	10	1.6%	90	1.8%
0	0.0%	0	0.0%	1	0.1%	0	0.0%	0	0.0%	0	0.0%	1	0.0%
36	6.7%	22	4.0%	53	6.2%	32	4.7%	22	3.2%	21	3.3%	255	5.2%
0	0.0%	0	0.0%	1	0.1%	4	0.6%	0	0.0%	3	0.5%	8	0.2%
0	0.0%	1	0.2%	0	0.0%	0	0.0%	0	0.0%	0	0.0%	1	0.0%
12	2.2%	8	1.4%	27	3.2%	15	2.2%	6	0.9%	4	0.6%	102	2.1%
8	1.5%	17	3.1%	49	5.8%	49	7.2%	30	4.3%	11	1.7%	191	3.9%
48	8.9%	46	8.3%	62	7.3%	82	12.1%	80	11.6%	56	8.9%	424	8.6%
0	0.0%	0	0.0%	1	0.1%	1	0.1%	0	0.0%	1	0.2%	3	0.1%
80	14.8%	38	6.8%	34	4.0%	41	6.1%	52	7.5%	56	8.9%	371	7.5%
2	0.4%	0	0.0%	0	0.0%	0	0.0%	2	0.3%	0	0.0%	6	0.1%
0	0.0%	1	0.2%	0	0.0%	0	0.0%	0	0.0%	0	0.0%	1	0.0%
1	0.2%	0	0.0%	1	0.1%	3	0.4%	4	0.6%	2	0.3%	12	0.2%
15	2.8%	18	3.2%	30	3.5%	16	2.4%	9	1.3%	7	1.1%	119	2.4%
48	8.9%	211	37.9%	296	34.8%	195	28.8%	270	39.0%	225	35.8%	1,376	28.0%
0	0.0%	0	0.0%	1	0.1%	3	0.4%	2	0.3%	3	0.5%	9	0.2%
3	0.6%	2	0.4%	2	0.2%	4	0.6%	1	0.1%	2	0.3%	16	0.3%
19	3.5%	8	1.4%	10	1.2%	16	2.4%	8	1.2%	15	2.4%	107	2.2%
29	5.4%	21	3.8%	21	2.5%	12	1.8%	7	1.0%	7	1.1%	120	2.4%
7	1.3%	3	0.5%	2	0.2%	1	0.1%	0	0.0%	0	0.0%	17	0.3%
1	0.2%	0	0.0%	1	0.1%	0	0.0%	1	0.1%	0	0.0%	3	0.1%
0	0.0%	0	0.0%	2	0.2%	0	0.0%	0	0.0%	0	0.0%	2	0.0%
1	0.2%	1	0.2%	3	0.4%	0	0.0%	0	0.0%	3	0.5%	10	0.2%
25	4.6%	30	5.4%	44	5.2%	40	5.9%	23	3.3%	29	4.6%	219	4.5%
5	0.9%	5	0.9%	9	1.1%	8	1.2%	15	2.2%	10	1.6%	53	1.1%
0	0.0%	1	0.2%	0	0.0%	0	0.0%	0	0.0%	0	0.0%	1	0.0%
21	3.9%	25	4.5%	36	4.2%	22	3.2%	25	3.6%	23	3.7%	187	3.8%
92	17.0%	36	6.5%	35	4.1%	40	5.9%	41	5.9%	44	7.0%	539	11.0%
0	0.0%	0	0.0%	0	0.0%	0	0.0%	0	0.0%	1	0.2%	1	0.0%
0	0.0%	0	0.0%	0	0.0%	0	0.0%	3	0.4%	2	0.3%	5	0.1%
0	0.0%	0	0.0%	0	0.0%	0	0.0%	1	0.1%	0	0.0%	1	0.0%
0	0.0%	0	0.0%	0	0.0%	0	0.0%	0	0.0%	2	0.3%	2	0.0%
0	0.0%	0	0.0%	0	0.0%	1	0.1%	0	0.0%	0	0.0%	1	0.0%
0	0.0%	0	0.0%	0	0.0%	1	0.1%	0	0.0%	0	0.0%	1	0.0%
541	100.0%	556	100.0%	851	100.0%	677	100.0%	692	100.0%	629	100.0%	4,919	100.0%

Exhibit 19.13—

Volume (US Dollar equivalent) of Swap-Driven Primary Issues by Nationality of Issuer (1981-1993)

	1981	% of Total	1982	% of Total	1983	% of Total	1984	% of Total	1985	% of Total	1986	% of Total
Supranational	560	55.6%	705	31.5%	399	11.5%	273	4.6%	1,048	5.3%	2,613	7.4%
Multinational	50	5.0%	50	2.2%	0	0.0%	43	0.7%	150	0.8%	195	0.6%
Argentina	50	5.0%	0	0.0%	0	0.0%	0	0.0%	0	0.0%	0	0.0%
Australia	0	0.0%	0	0.0%	126	3.6%	709	12.0%	1,170	6.0%	1,245	3.5%
Austria	86	8.5%	333	14.9%	379	11.0%	655	11.1%	878	4.5%	828	2.4%
Belgium	0	0.0%	0	0.0%	100	2.9%	132	2.2%	581	3.0%	2,188	6.2%
Bulgaria	0	0.0%	0	0.0%	0	0.0%	0	0.0%	0	0.0%	0	0.0%
Canada	107	10.6%	234	10.4%	590	17.1%	525	8.9%	603	3.1%	2,668	7.6%
Cayman Islands	0	0.0%	0	0.0%	0	0.0%	0	0.0%	0	0.0%	0	0.0%
China	0	0.0%	0	0.0%	0	0.0%	0	0.0%	0	0.0%	0	0.0%
Denmark	0	0.0%	0	0.0%	100	2.9%	422	7.2%	733	3.7%	982	2.8%
Finland	0	0.0%	0	0.0%	0	0.0%	30	0.5%	322	1.6%	1,319	3.8%
France	0	0.0%	168	7.5%	222	6.4%	96	1.6%	1,247	6.4%	2,158	6.1%
Greece	0	0.0%	0	0.0%	0	0.0%	0	0.0%	0	0.0%	0	0.0%
Germany	0	0.0%	0	0.0%	96	2.8%	194	3.3%	819	4.2%	1,913	5.4%
Hong Kong	0	0.0%	0	0.0%	0	0.0%	0	0.0%	40	0.2%	60	0.2%
India	0	0.0%	0	0.0%	0	0.0%	0	0.0%	0	0.0%	0	0.0%
Ireland	0	0.0%	0	0.0%	0	0.0%	0	0.0%	0	0.0%	94	0.3%
Italy	0	0.0%	0	0.0%	0	0.0%	0	0.0%	251	1.3%	1,206	3.4%
Japan	100	9.9%	213	9.5%	325	9.4%	1,614	27.4%	2,953	15.0%	3,440	9.8%
Korea	0	0.0%	0	0.0%	0	0.0%	0	0.0%	0	0.0%	0	0.0%
Luxembourg	0	0.0%	0	0.0%	0	0.0%	0	0.0%	0	0.0%	62	0.2%
Netherlands	0	0.0%	22	1.0%	75	2.2%	147	2.5%	406	2.1%	612	1.7%
Norway	0	0.0%	0	0.0%	93	2.7%	20	0.3%	496	2.5%	944	2.7%
New Zealand	0	0.0%	0	0.0%	0	0.0%	47	0.8%	96	0.5%	90	0.3%
Portugal	0	0.0%	0	0.0%	0	0.0%	0	0.0%	0	0.0%	0	0.0%
Soviet Union	0	0.0%	0	0.0%	0	0.0%	0	0.0%	0	0.0%	0	0.0%
Spain	0	0.0%	0	0.0%	100	2.9%	0	0.0%	100	0.5%	0	0.0%
Sweden	0	0.0%	0	0.0%	81	2.3%	195	3.3%	547	2.8%	819	2.3%
Switzerland	0	0.0%	0	0.0%	79	2.3%	0	0.0%	0	0.0%	0	0.0%
Thailand	0	0.0%	0	0.0%	0	0.0%	0	0.0%	0	0.0%	0	0.0%
United Kingdom	30	3.0%	50	2.2%	306	8.8%	216	3.7%	477	2.4%	1,219	3.5%
United States	24	2.4%	465	20.8%	389	11.2%	582	9.9%	6,715	34.2%	10,451	29.8%
Brazil	0	0.0%	0	0.0%	0	0.0%	0	0.0%	0	0.0%	0	0.0%
Mexico	0	0.0%	0	0.0%	0	0.0%	0	0.0%	0	0.0%	0	0.0%
Malaysia	0	0.0%	0	0.0%	0	0.0%	0	0.0%	0	0.0%	0	0.0%
South Africa	0	0.0%	0	0.0%	0	0.0%	0	0.0%	0	0.0%	0	0.0%
Indonesia	0	0.0%	0	0.0%	0	0.0%	0	0.0%	0	0.0%	0	0.0%
Turkey	0	0.0%	0	0.0%	0	0.0%	0	0.0%	0	0.0%	0	0.0%
Total	1,007	100.0%	2,240	100.0%	3,460	100.0%	5,900	100.0%	19,632	100.0%	35,106	100.0%

continued

1987	% of Total	1988	% of Total	1989	% of Total	1990	% of Total	1991	% of Total	1992	% of Total	Total	% of Total
3,339	7.3%	1,491	2.8%	4,462	3.7%	8,281	12.3%	9,573	11.2%	11,213	12.9%	43,957	8.3%
255	0.6%	40	0.1%	435	0.4%	150	0.2%	0	0.0%	0	0.0%	1,368	0.3%
0	0.0%	0	0.0%	0	0.0%	0	0.0%	0	0.0%	0	0.0%	50	0.0%
1,456	3.2%	1,672	3.1%	2,863	2.3%	585	0.9%	544	0.6%	358	0.4%	10,728	2.0%
1,469	3.2%	1,221	2.3%	2,953	2.4%	1,745	2.6%	2,509	2.9%	4,244	4.9%	17,300	3.3%
1,441	3.2%	371	0.7%	1,239	1.0%	573	0.9%	941	1.1%	638	0.7%	8,204	1.6%
0	0.0%	0	0.0%	75	0.1%	0	0.0%	0	0.0%	0	0.0%	75	0.0%
2,828	6.2%	1,361	2.6%	3,430	2.8%	2,632	3.9%	5,965	7.0%	7,990	9.2%	28,933	5.5%
0	0.0%	0	0.0%	103	0.1%	214	0.3%	0	0.0%	185	0.2%	502	0.1%
0	0.0%	118	0.2%	0	0.0%	0	0.0%	0	0.0%	0	0.0%	118	0.0%
1,495	3.3%	481	0.9%	2,189	1.8%	1,330	2.0%	370	0.4%	300	0.3%	8,402	1.6%
710	1.6%	757	1.4%	2,783	2.3%	3,003	4.5%	2,949	3.5%	1,311	1.5%	13,184	2.5%
4,557	10.0%	3,122	5.9%	5,496	4.5%	5,320	7.9%	7,996	9.4%	6,304	7.3%	36,686	7.0%
0	0.0%	0	0.0%	150	0.1%	388	0.6%	0	0.0%	548	0.6%	1,086	0.2%
3,982	8.8%	2,221	4.2%	2,907	2.4%	2,864	4.3%	5,970	7.0%	8,013	9.2%	28,979	5.5%
264	0.6%	0	0.0%	0	0.0%	0	0.0%	136	0.2%	0	0.0%	500	0.1%
0	0.0%	106	0.2%	0	0.0%	0	0.0%	0	0.0%	0	0.0%	106	0.0%
142	0.3%	0	0.0%	137	0.1%	298	0.4%	331	0.4%	221	0.3%	1,223	0.2%
2,004	4.4%	1,470	2.8%	5,531	4.5%	1,557	2.3%	1,427	1.7%	1,011	1.2%	14,457	2.7%
5,431	11.9%	28,090	52.6%	70,936	58.2%	25,694	38.3%	31,306	36.8%	23,851	27.5%	193,953	36.8%
0	0.0%	0	0.0%	50	0.0%	332	0.5%	225	0.3%	228	0.3%	835	0.2%
110	0.2%	116	0.2%	153	0.1%	195	0.3%	14	0.0%	91	0.1%	741	0.1%
1,129	2.5%	410	0.8%	749	0.6%	820	1.2%	686	0.8%	1,757	2.0%	6,813	1.3%
2,263	5.0%	1,318	2.5%	1,610	1.3%	772	1.2%	1,740	2.0%	2,131	2.5%	11,387	2.2%
901	2.0%	397	0.7%	167	0.1%	179	0.3%	0	0.0%	0	0.0%	1,877	0.4%
82	0.2%	0	0.0%	53	0.0%	0	0.0%	107	0.1%	0	0.0%	242	0.0%
0	0.0%	0	0.0%	171	0.1%	0	0.0%	0	0.0%	0	0.0%	171	0.0%
101	0.2%	36	0.1%	483	0.4%	0	0.0%	0	0.0%	1,968	2.3%	2,788	0.5%
2,292	5.0%	2,014	3.8%	3,146	2.6%	2,957	4.4%	2,253	2.6%	4,103	4.7%	18,407	3.5%
350	0.8%	403	0.8%	851	0.7%	775	1.2%	2,181	2.6%	1,579	1.8%	6,218	1.2%
0	0.0%	137	0.3%	0	0.0%	0	0.0%	0	0.0%	0	0.0%	137	0.0%
2,019	4.4%	2,888	5.4%	4,909	4.0%	2,553	3.8%	2,636	3.1%	2,781	3.2%	20,084	3.8%
6,862	15.1%	3,126	5.9%	3,846	3.2%	3,663	5.5%	4,782	5.6%	5,561	6.4%	46,466	8.8%
0	0.0%	0	0.0%	0	0.0%	0	0.0%	0	0.0%	40	0.0%	40	0.0%
0	0.0%	0	0.0%	0	0.0%	0	0.0%	321	0.4%	217	0.2%	538	0.1%
0	0.0%	0	0.0%	0	0.0%	0	0.0%	190	0.2%	0	0.0%	190	0.0%
0	0.0%	0	0.0%	0	0.0%	0	0.0%	0	0.0%	211	0.2%	211	0.0%
0	0.0%	0	0.0%	0	0.0%	80	0.1%	0	0.0%	0	0.0%	80	0.0%
0	0.0%	0	0.0%	0	0.0%	150	0.2%	0	0.0%	0	0.0%	150	0.0%
45,482	100.0%	53,366	100.0%	121,877	100.0%	67,110	100.0%	85,152	100.0%	86,854	100.0%	527,196	100.0%

- the issuance of securities in odd amounts in order to match the proceeds of the borrowing to the underlying swap because if one side of a currency swap is kept to a round amount, it produces, almost inevitably, an odd total in the other swapped currency;
- the emergence of a series of "exotic" security structures designed to appeal to small groups of investors with specific objectives, which were structured around the underlying swap transactions, which were increasingly complex and designed to insulate the issuer from some of the characteristics of the securities being issued;
- the phenomena of increasingly aggressive and tight pricing on swap-driven primary issues reflecting both the demand for the specific issuer's debt in the primary market being accessed but also aggressive bidding by investment banks and underwriters who were seeking to maximise their profits on a larger set of transactions, which included both the securities issue and the accompanying swap transactions.

Impact on the new issue business

The emergence of swap-driven primary issues also had a profound impact on how the new issue business itself operated. The increased realisation that issuers saw the actual securities issuance or debt transaction as the basis for an accompanying swap, meant that the financial institutions active in raising new funds for clients had to increasingly acquire a new set of skills. For intermediaries traditionally strong in the issuance of securities, it meant the acquisition of swap skills while for a number of major innovators in the swap market, it provided an opportunity to increase their new issue business on the back of their swap prowess. Financial institutions like JP Morgan, Banque Paribas Capital Markets and Bankers Trust are powerful examples of the second group.

As the practice of arbitrage funding, involving bond swap packages as well as easily defined funding targets developed, the basic approach to originating securities transactions and investment banking business was forced to evolve.

In the first place, the financial institutions were increasingly required to provide the total package with an all-up cost of funds stated as a margin under US$ LIBOR. In addition, as markers became increasingly volatile with issuance opportunities or windows opening and closing at relatively short notice and as swaps evolved from highly structured counterparty driven corporate finance transactions to standardised commodity products dealt off trading desks, the origination business moved rapidly into a trading room environment.

The whole process of originating securities transactions which had previously often stretched out over a period of months and in some cases years involving the client being courted by investment bankers gave way to highly opportunistic securities transactions on a swapped basis driven by the existence of short-lived opportunities. These opportunities came increasingly to be offered to potential borrowers through the medium of small units working closely with the securities issuance or syndicate desk and swap desks to develop all-in funding packages.

These units, referred to variously as "debt transactions group" (Merrill Lynch), "capital market services" (Salomon Brothers), "frequent issuers desks" (Citicorp and Nomura Securities), "financing desk" (Lehman Brothers) etc, would stay in touch with the borrower advising them of changing opportunities in the international capital markets and, in particular, the relatively rapid changes in estimated arbitrages available via primary market transactions in various currencies.

As the practice of arbitrage funding on a purely opportunistic basis grew, a number of financial institutions focused almost exclusively on these borrowers offering them various opportunities as and when they arose. This type of approach to the new issue business is evident from an advertisement in *Euromoney* in late 1987 placed by Bankers Trust Company which was headed: "If your bank has never delivered money at 200 points below LIBOR, try the one that has." The advertisement also indicated that: "over the last two years, Bankers Trust has lead managed 10 issues for SEK. We were book runners not only on their history-making US$200 million Eurobond issue at more than 200 basis points below LIBOR, but also on the US$200 million 40 year Eurobond issue—the longest term ever done."

Given the status of SEK as perhaps the premier arbitrage funder in the world, this strategy of Bankers Trust of centralising its resources to originate capital markets transactions by focusing the attention of various specialists, in a small unit delivering bond swap packages to key arbitrage funders is self-evident.

However, the impact on the new issue business of swap-driven primary issues also has a darker, more disturbing aspect. The emergence of primary issues which were swap-driven changed forever the profit equation on capital market business. As there were two sources of earnings, the securities issue and the swap, the financial institution involved had the opportunity to maximise its own earnings from the transaction by separating the pricing of the two elements to its own advantage. Increasingly through the 1980s, the underlying securities issue was often priced aggressively, sometimes beyond the tolerance of the market, reflecting aggressive pricing by the book running lead manager who, if it provided the swap, used the swap fees to compensate for the terms on the bond and who was essentially relying on competition for market share by co-managers to limit the lead manager's underwriting commitment and therefore its risk of loss on the securities transaction.

This changing profit equation led increasingly to mispriced issues which traded poorly and were not effectively distributed. These mispriced issues allowed substantial opportunities for asset swap transactions and repackaging of issues into alternative formats, usually involving a swap, to be undertaken. This aspect is considered in detail in the context of asset swaps in Chapter 18.

This practice is particularly true of a number of currency segments of the bond and swap market where lead managers take their earnings on the swap, which is clearly accruing to them, while structuring a tightly priced securities issue with the objective of syndicating the risk to lower any potential risk on placement of the securities. *Exhibit 19.14* sets out a numerical example of the cross-subsidisation of a new issue transaction.

However, the historical pattern of mispricing on the bond side with the lead manager laying off bonds on the syndicate and making money on the swap has undergone some revision in recent times. The swap has more often recently become the vehicle for the subsidy. This has been particularly true, indeed for some years, in certain swap market segments such as the Japanese yen where subsidies on the swap as a means of "buying business" has been a common, though often heatedly denied, practice.

Exhibit 19.14
Cross-Subsidisation of New Issue Transactions

Consider the interest swap transaction related to a new issue detailed in *Exhibit 8.30*. Assume the issuer has a sub-LIBOR target of 50bps under LIBOR.

The transaction structure generates a sub-LIBOR rate of LIBOR minus 44.33bps (below the target level). The bank arranging the swap can seek to improve the borrower's cost of funds in the following way:

- increase the rate paid under the swap; or
- lower the yield on the bond issue.

The structure and economics of the alternative strategies are set out below.

Adjusting the Swap Rate

The borrower's sub-LIBOR target could be met if the swap counterparty was willing to pay 8.504% pa (A) (based on the structure utilised). Assuming the adjustments are constant, this equates to an equivalent swap rate of 8.974% pa (A) or 8.829% (S/A) (adjusted by the 5bps reinvested risk premium for the semi-annual-annual conversion).

This rate is equivalent to the mid-point of the bid-offer spread in the market and translates into a subsidy on a present value basis equivalent to approximately US$194,914 (using 8.78% pa (S/A) as the discount rate).

Adjusting the Bond Yield

The borrower's sub-LIBOR target could be met if the yield on the bond issue could be adjusted by approximately 5bps. This could be achieved in a number of ways (adjusting coupon as well as issue price) and the method outlined below is only one manner in which this adjustment is effected.

Assume the bond is restructured as follows:

Coupon:	8% pa (A)
Issue Price:	100.25
Fees & Expenses:	2.00%

This is equivalent to a yield (net of fees) of 8.44% pa (A).

The equivalent swap rate is:

	% pa (A)
Assume Swap Rate[1]	8.92
Fee Amortisation[2]	−0.45
Adjustment for delay[1]	+0.04
	8.51

Notes:

1. See *Exhibit 8.30*.
2. 1.75% (necessary to gross up proceeds to par value) amortised over five years at 8.97% pa (A).

This equates to sub-LIBOR margin to the issuer of approximately 50.56 bps where the swap counterparty pays 8.00% matching the bond coupon.

The economic cost of this transaction to the financial institution will depend on a variety of factors:

- whether the institution is providing the swap only or is underwriting the bond (and, if so, the underwriting commitment).

Exhibit 19.14—continued

Assume the following:

- the swap counterparty underwrites, as bookrunning lead manager, US$20m of the issue.
- the investor demands a return of 8.48% pa (A) to purchase the bond (implying a bond price in new issue trading of 98.125-0.25 outside full-fees of 1.875).

The swap counterparty in relation to its underwriters incurs a loss of US$50,000 (0.25% of US$20m), which is presumably acceptable as it is covered by the earnings on the swap (approximately US$0.278m—based on the full bid offer spread on the swap).

The other underwriters will, in this situation make commensurately higher relative losses depending on their fee entitlement (which may be lower).

As issuers, concerned with market reputation and the desire to maintain longer term access to debt markets, dictate terms on the securities transactions to guard against mispricing, financial institutions, given that the borrower still wishes to satisfy certain cost targets, must increasingly build the subsidy into the swap. This shift in the profit equation has an interesting subsidiary effect as lead managers can only subsidise to the extent of the proportion of the new issue they control. This has resulted in book runners tending to control and distribute a very high percentage of issues with allotments to other underwriters and selling group participants being confined to relatively small amounts.

This was evident in a celebrated case where Credit Suisse First Boston pulled out of a syndicate for an issue lead by County Natwest for the Kingdom of Belgium on the basis that County, the book running lead manager, was holding back too much of the issue for itself in order to offset the reputedly substantial subsidy on the swap it had provided to win the particular mandate.

This change in the distribution of profits between the securities and the swap is not without its critics who point out that it might be more desirable to take a loss on the mispriced bonds than to book an offmarket rate swap because the latter is a term commitment which will stay on the books of the particular institution and will require capital to be held against it over the full term.

As noted above, the change in environment in international capital markets as at the end of the 1980s and in the early 1990s eliminated the worst of the excesses identified above. Reduced competition in between financial institutions and investor unwillingness to purchase mispriced securities and, essentially, subsidise financial institutions and borrowers, have led to broadly more rational new issuance practices. The adoption of the fixed price re-offering system and the trend to consensus pricing represents manifestations of this general movement. These developments do not, obviously, ensure that all bonds are appropriately priced or that no element of subsidisation is present in bond/swap combination transaction. In reality, subsidisation and mispricing of issues continues to be a factor, albeit a less important one than previously, in capital markets.

The fundamental underpinning of the securities issuance business by swap-driven primary issues has required market participants to adjust their business practices to the new environment. While changes to market environment have lead to some changes in the origination process for new transactions, the basic impact of swaps is likely to persist. This reflects the fact that while the continued growth of swap-driven primary issuance is not likely to continue at the explosive pace of growth recorded in the immediate past, it is nevertheless an established and important part of the structure of the international capital market and financial institutions operating in this market must necessarily recognise and adapt to it.

Chapter 20

Utilising Swaps for Asset and Liability Management: Basic Techniques

SWAPS AND ASSET LIABILITY MANAGEMENT

The use of swaps in asset and liability management is predicated on the capacity of such instruments to convert fixed rate exposures to floating rate and vice versa, and, in the case of currency swaps or LTFX, to convert assets and liabilities from one currency to another. This capacity makes swaps an important potential means of managing interest rate and currency exposures on *existing* assets and liabilities. In contrast to new issue arbitrage which focuses on utilising swaps to create synthetic liabilities on the basis of cost advantages, where swaps are used as instruments of asset and liability management, the economic or price benefit is subsumed to other objectives. In this regard, swaps function, as noted above, as an over-the-counter futures or forward contract on interest rates and currencies.

The key factors in the emergence of swaps as an asset liability management instrument include:

- The incomplete nature of market structures whereby swaps are utilised to fill in gaps in the range of available instruments.
- Swaps allow unbundling of funding (or investment decisions) from currency or interest rate basis determination.
- Non-economic benefits such as flexibility, lower critical transaction size, execution speed, anonymity, ease of documentation and absence of regulatory requirements.

The utilisation of swaps for asset and liability management is evident at two levels:

- the use of swaps in asset/liability management applications predicated on utilising swaps to convert fixed rate exposures to floating rate and vice versa and/or to convert asset and liabilities from one currency to another;
- the use of swaps for financial engineering applications utilising swaps to construct innovative asset and liability structures featuring combinations of traditional instruments (such as fixed interest bonds, floating rate notes, and other funding instruments) and derivative products (including all types of swap transactions as well as swap derivatives).

The first application (which can be described as basic techniques for asset and liability management) is covered in this chapter. This type of application is generally utilised to neutralise risk or, in certain circumstances, create limited risk positions.

The financial engineering application of swaps is necessarily more complex. It entails the use of swaps to generate synthetic asset and liability structures intra- and inter-currency as part of overall portfolio management strategies. These types of financial engineering application have, in particular, been applied to liability portfolios. Such techniques are equally applicable to asset portfolios, although their utilisation for these purposes is less wide spread. The financial engineering applications of swaps in the context of asset and liability portfolio management are considered in detail in Chapter 21.

The primary focus of this chapter is to outline potential uses of swaps in the active management of asset and liability portfolios. The use of interest rate and currency swaps are considered in detail first. The use of swap derivatives, such as FRAs, LTFX, caps and collars, etc, are then considered. The discussion, in respect of utilising the swap derivatives, focuses on the major differences between these derivatives and interest rate and currency swaps which usually motivate the use of these instruments.

The use of swaps as an instrument for active *asset* management requires some preliminary observations.

As the fundamental changes in the swap market began to manifest themselves, swap applications relevant to the asset side of the balance sheet came increasingly to be recognised. This enabled portfolio and investment managers to use interest rate and currency swaps to create synthetic securities which were otherwise unavailable and to provide both yield pick-up and portfolio diversification. The detailed structure and market for asset swaps is considered in detail in Chapter 18. However, in this chapter, the use of swaps as a means for *active* management of asset portfolios is considered.

The difference between a liability and an asset swap is minimal. The advantages of flexibility, speed and anonymity, which are significant considerations in liability swaps, are equally relevant to asset swap transactions. An added dimension, however, is the opportunity to trade swaps in a manner similar to more traditional debt instruments.

The use of swaps as a surrogate debt instrument for the purposes of investment and trading are predicated on their cash flow similarities to fixed interest securities. Under certain circumstances, the yield advantage on swaps (where they are at attractive margins relative to comparable debt securities), the absence of significant funding costs as well as favourable treatment (in some jurisdictions) from the perspective of withholding tax makes swaps attractive when compared to conventional securities.

For the investor, swaps have emerged as an instrument for creating synthetic assets and as a means for more active portfolio management. Interest rate swaps can be utilised to effectively transform a fixed rate asset into a floating rate investment. Interest rate swaps can also be used to lock in capital gains or minimise losses arising from the impact of interest rate fluctuations on investment portfolios.

Currency swaps, against underlying asset and investment portfolios, enable portfolio managers to create fixed or floating rate securities in currencies different to that of the underlying securities in which funds are invested. They can also be used to manage the foreign exchange risk of investments as well as protecting portfolios from possible reversals of gains arising from investments made during a period of favourable interest or exchange rates.

Swaps against assets and investments may be utilised to generate improvements in yields relative to conventional investment alternatives or to structure investments of a type not otherwise available. Even where higher yields and/or security availability is not a consideration, factors such as the flexibility, speed and anonymity of portfolio operations entailing swaps instead of purchases and sales of securities, have increasingly forced portfolio managers to view swaps as an investment management instrument. For example, the problems of an illiquid security held in a portfolio can be overcome, in part, by utilising swaps against that asset.

UTILISING INTEREST RATE AND CURRENCY SWAPS

Liability-based interest rate swaps: examples

Interest rate swap transactions can be utilised as an instrument for managing liabilities as follows:

Creating synthetic fixed or floating rate liabilities

The classic use of interest rate swaps is to create synthetic fixed or floating rate liabilities.

For example, where a corporate treasurer believes interest rates will increase, a swap can be used to create a synthetic fixed rate liability. Under the swap, the corporation pays a fixed rate and receives a floating rate thus locking in the cost of short-term debt: see *Exhibit 20.1*.

Exhibit 20.1
Synthetic Fixed or Floating Rate Liability

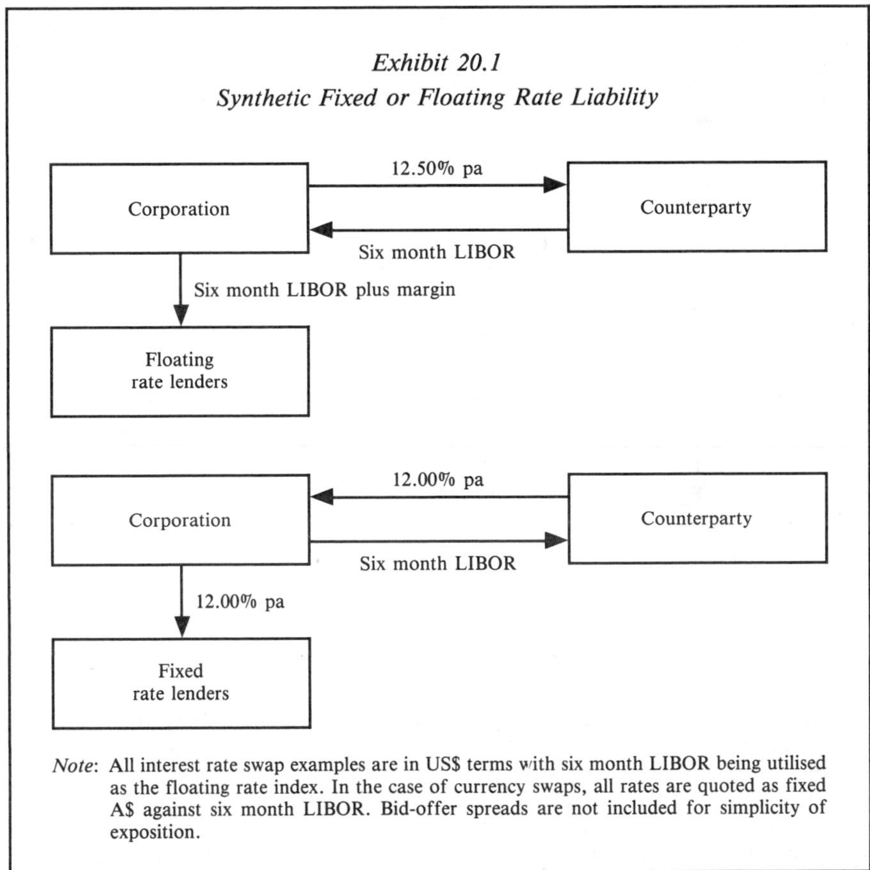

Note: All interest rate swap examples are in US$ terms with six month LIBOR being utilised as the floating rate index. In the case of currency swaps, all rates are quoted as fixed A$ against six month LIBOR. Bid-offer spreads are not included for simplicity of exposition.

The converse of this transaction entails the swap being undertaken against a fixed rate issue or borrowing to create synthetic floating rate term debt: see *Exhibit 20.1*. This type of transaction may be undertaken where a corporate treasurer believes that floating interest rates (given that these are priced at the shorter end of the yield curve) will provide the borrower with lower interest cost funding over the relevant time horizon.

Unlocking the high cost of existing fixed rate liabilities

An interest rate swap can be utilised to unlock (or unhinge) the cost of existing high coupon debt, enabling a company to achieve significant cost savings. This can be achieved either where the previous fixed rate debt was the result of a borrowing on fixed rate terms, or alternatively, was the result of an earlier swap transaction to convert floating rate liabilities to fixed rate.

For example, a borrower may have existing fixed rate debt at 14.00% pa. The current market swap rate for the borrower to receive fixed rate and pay floating rate for the remaining maturity of the original fixed rate liability, say five years, is 12.50%. The borrower can, under these circumstances, enter into a swap whereby it receives fixed at 12.50% pa (that is, 1.50% pa below its current fixed interest rate on its debt) and pays six month LIBOR: see *Exhibit 20.2*. As a result of the transaction, the borrower would achieve an effective floating rate liability at 1.50% pa over LIBOR. If six month LIBOR averages less than 12.50% pa over the five year remaining term of the underlying liability the borrower would achieve an absolute interest cost saving equivalent to the margin by which six month LIBOR is less than 12.50% pa.

Exhibit 20.2

Unlocking or Unhinging High Coupon Debt

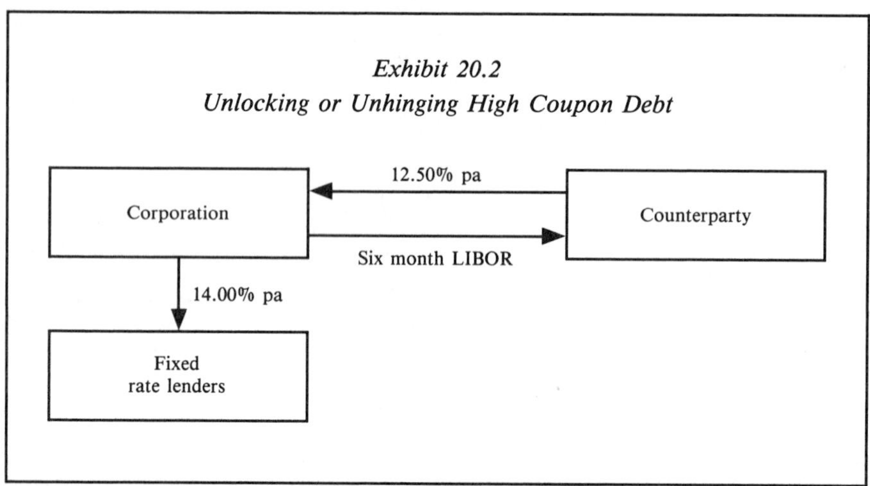

This type of transaction would be utilised, for example, where the borrower expected that a floating interest rate would provide it with lower cost funding for the relevant term. The use of a swap to unlock the high cost of existing fixed rate debt may be particularly attractive where the relevant borrowing cannot be repaid and, subsequently, refinanced or alternatively, where the prepayment penalties applicable and/or the costs associated with refinancing would be significant.

Managing the cost of floating rate liabilities

Interest rate swaps can be utilised by a borrower to manage the cost of its existing floating rate liabilities. For example, where a borrower is currently borrowing on a floating rate basis in the expectation that this will minimise its interest cost in a normally sloped yield curve environment, interest rate swaps can be utilised to lower its floating rate interest cost.

Transaction 1. The borrower enters into an interest swap where it pays a fixed rate in exchange for receiving LIBOR. The initial swap is then reversed at a later date by the borrower entering into a further swap where it *receives* a fixed rate in exchange for *paying* LIBOR. Provided that fixed interest rates have risen to a level above the rate at which the initial swap was entered into, the borrower would achieve a lower floating rate cost: see *Exhibit 20.3*.

Exhibit 20.3
Managing the Cost of Floating Rate Liabilities (1)

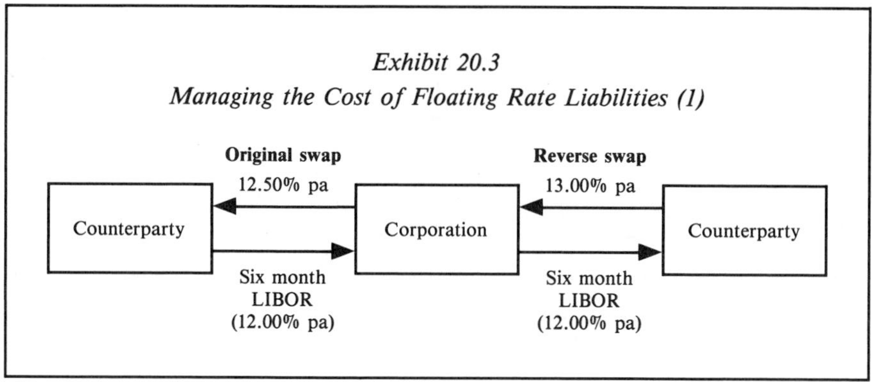

For example, if the fixed rate payable under the first swap was 12.50% pa and the swap could be reversed at a rate of 13.00% pa, the borrower would achieve a floating rate funding at 0.50% *below* LIBOR.

This cost saving represents the difference between the rates payable on the successive swaps. However, the all-up benefit must be calculated on the basis of factoring in the higher interest cost incurred during the period the borrower pays fixed rates under the first swap. This cost will vary depending on the shape of the yield curve, the period between the initial swap and its reversal and the remaining term of the borrowing.

In the above example, if six month LIBOR was 12.00% pa at the time the transaction was entered into, the time elapsed between the first and second transaction was six months, and the remaining term of the borrowing was five years, the net cost saving after factoring in the higher interest cost of six months would be equivalent to 0.425% pa below LIBOR.

Transaction 2. Where the borrower is currently borrowing on a floating rate basis, it bears the risk of a change in the shape of the yield curve, particularly an inversion of the yield curve.

For example, where the yield curve is negatively sloped, that is, six month LIBOR is at 15.00% pa while the swap rate for a party to pay fixed rate is 12.50% pa, the borrower could lower its funding cost by entering into a swap under which it pays a fixed rate of 12.50% pa and receives six month LIBOR. When the yield curve returns to a normal positive slope, the initial swap can be reversed by entering into an offsetting swap where the borrower receives fixed rate in return for paying six month LIBOR: see *Exhibit 20.4*.

Exhibit 20.4
Managing the Cost of Floating Rate Liabilities (2)

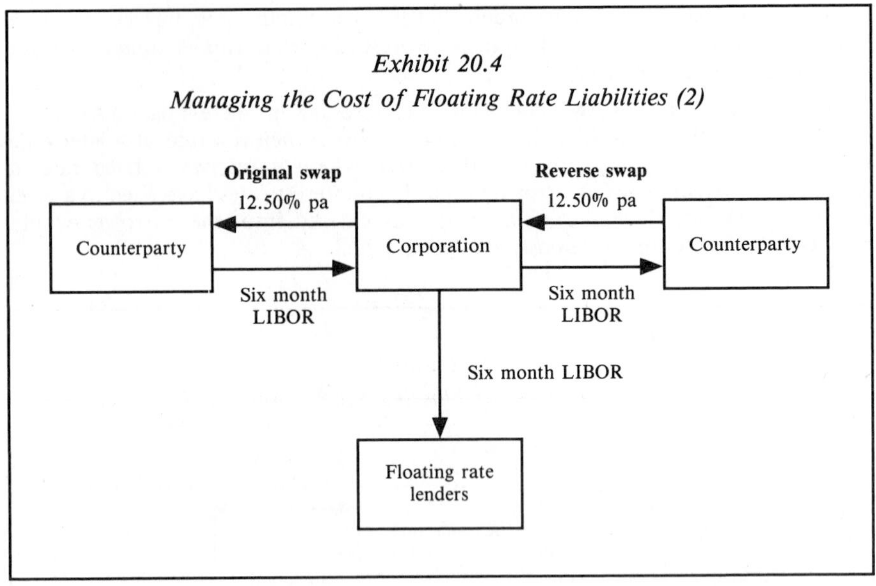

The saving achieved (in this example 2.50% pa) is realised as long as the fixed rate for the remaining maturity of the swap has not moved significantly from its previous level. For example, in the example used, if the initial transaction was for a maturity of three years and was reversed after six months, the borrower would realise an interest cost saving as long as the rate at which the reversal was achieved was greater than 11.902% pa.

Managing the cost of fixed rate liabilities

Interest rate swaps can be used by borrowers to also manage the cost of its *fixed rate* borrowings, created as a result of either a fixed rate borrowing or a previous interest rate swap.

For example, assume a borrower has fixed rate debt at 10.00% pa with a remaining term to maturity of five years. Current market fixed interest rates for five years are 12.50% pa but are expected to decline. The borrower normally would pay LIBOR plus a margin of 0.50% pa for its floating rate borrowings.

The borrower can, in these circumstances, utilise interest rate swaps to manage the cost of its fixed rate funding as follows. The borrower initially enters into a swap where it receives a fixed rate and pays six month LIBOR. This effectively generates floating rate funding at 2.50% *under* LIBOR enabling it to achieve a saving of 3.00% on its usual floating rate interest cost. If after six months, fixed rates decline as expected, to say 11.50% pa for four and a half years, the borrower can reverse the initial swap, swapping back into fixed rate funding. The reversal effectively generates fixed rate fundng at 9.00% pa: see *Exhibit 20.5*.

This particular transaction enables the borrower to preserve the value of its below market fixed rate funding even in a declining rate environment.

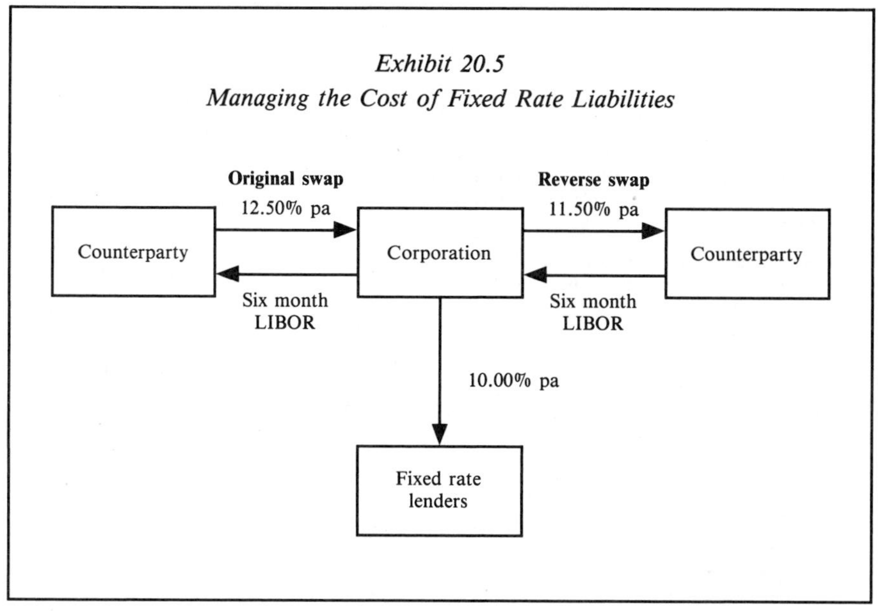

Exhibit 20.5
Managing the Cost of Fixed Rate Liabilities

Liability based currency swaps: examples

Currency swap transactions, whereby an interest rate exchange is combined with a currency exchange, can be utilised to expand the range of possible uses of swaps as follows.

To hedge foreign currency exposures

For example, where the borrower has an existing liability in a currency, say US$, which is expected to strengthen, it can hedge its exposure by entering into a currency swap to convert the currency denomination of its liability into say, A$.

Currency swaps can also, of course, be used to lower the cost of debt by converting existing liabilities in a particular currency to a liability in a different currency on either a fixed or floating rate basis in line with expectations on foreign exchange and interest rates.

To "lock in" foreign currency gains or minimising losses on foreign currency borrowings

For example, if the borrower had borrowed in US$ and the US$ had depreciated (appreciated) against the A$ since the liability was incurred, the borrower could enter into a currency swap whereby it converted its exposure from US$ into A$ and would, by virtue of the fact that the initial currency exchange and subsequent re-exchange would be undertaken at the then prevailing US$/A$ exchange rate, enable the foreign exchange gain (loss) to the borrower to be locked in (limited) irrespective of subsequent movements in the exchange rate.

The use of currency swaps to manage existing liabilities is illustrated by an example set out in *Exhibit 20.6*.

Exhibit 20.6

Managing Foreign Currency Liabilities Utilising a Currency Swap

The example relates to a US$/A$ currency swap. The company involved has an outstanding US$ issue which it now seeks to convert into an A$ liability in order to lock in the economic gains resulting from favourable movements in currency and interest rates since the liability was incurred.

The counterparty's A$ issue is specifically designed to match the principal amount, maturity and interest payment dates of the outstanding US$ issue. The terms of the borrowers' respective borrowings are as follows:

	Company's existing US$ issue	**Counterparty's new A$ issue**
Principal amount (millions)	US$50,000	A$75,000
Exchange rate (at time of issue)	A$1.50/US$1.00	—
Maturity (years)	5 (Remaining life of existing 8 year US$ issue)	5
Interest:		
Coupon rate	8.25%	12.50%
Payment frequency	Annual	Annual
Sinking fund	None	None
Issue price		100.00%
Less:		
Issuing and other issue expenses		2.125%
Net proceeds to issuer		97.875%
Net cost of money (annual)		13.11%

Assume that the counterparty has a US$ target rate of 10.00% pa. However, under the swap agreement, the counterparty will service the company's 8.25% US$ issue. Therefore, the counterparty will be required to compensate the company for the rate differential. In order to avoid any currency exposure, the compensation is in the form of an initial transfer payment.

Through its A$75m borrowing, the counterparty obtains net proceeds of A$73,406,250. By converting these proceeds in the spot market (at A$1.25/US$1.00), the counterparty obtains US$58,725,000. However, the net present value of the US$ payment stream to be assumed discounted at the counterparty's 10.00% pa target rate, is US$46,683,062. Therefore, the counterparty must pay the difference, A$15,052,423 (or US$12,041,938) to the company. This initial transfer payment effectively raises the counterparty's all-in US$ cost while lowering the company's A$ cost.

This initial transfer payment to the United States company represents the net present value (@ 10.00% pa) of the following:

- the difference between the current interest rate on US$ debt of the relevant maturity 10.00% pa and the coupon on the existing US$ issue of 8.25% pa;
- the exchange gain on the borrowing arising from the fact that the A$/US$ rate has moved from A$1.50/US$1.00 when the borrowing was undertaken to A$1.25/US$1.00.

The all-in US$ cost to the company is determined by translating the US$ principal amount of the seasoned issue into A$ at the spot rate and adjusting this amount to reflect original issuance costs (A$73,406,250, assuming issuing cost of 2.125%). In addition, the company must take into account the initial transfer payment which it receives from the counterparty (A$15,052,423) and the A$ payments it has agreed to make to cover the counterparty's A$ obligations of A$9,375,000 in years one through four and A$84,375,000 at maturity. The company would therefore effectively raise A$ at an all-in cost of 8.00% pa.

The all-in US$ cost to the counterparty consists of the US$ proceeds of US$58,725,000 resulting from its own A$ issue less the US$ transfer payment it makes to the company

Exhibit 20.6—continued

(US$12,041,938) and the US$ payments it has agreed to make to cover the company's US$ obligations of US$4,125,000 in years one through four and US$54,125,000 at maturity. The counterparty thus effectively raises US$ at an all-in cost of 10.00% pa.

Year	Cash flow on outstanding US$ issue	Effective A$ flow
0	(46,683,062)	(88,458,673)
1	4,125,000	9,375,000
2	4,125,000	9,375,000
3	4,125,000	9,375,000
4	4,125,000	9,375,000
5	54,125,000	84,375,000

Asset based interest rate swaps: examples

Interest rate swap transactions can be utilised as an instrument for managing investment portfolios as follows:

Creating synthetic fixed or floating rate assets

The classic use of interest rate swaps in asset or investment based transactions is to create synthetic fixed or floating rate securities which best satisfy return and portfolio requirements.

For example, a portfolio manager can transform existing or newly acquired floating rate investments (such as a bank deposit, FRN, floating rate CD or other variable rate asset) into a term fixed rate of return by entering into an interest rate swap whereby it pays a floating rate and receives a fixed rate: see *Exhibit 20.7*.

In the example, the transaction transforms the floating rate asset to provide an effective rate of return equal to approx 12.75% pa while maintaining the flexibility and liquidity of the underlying asset. An investment manager may undertake this type of transaction to increase the yield on its floating rate portfolio in a positively sloped yield curve environment.

The converse of this transaction entails an investor undertaking a swap, whereby it pays a fixed rate in return for receiving a floating rate, to transform the yield on a fixed rate asset (such as a bond, fixed rate CD or other fixed rate asset) into a floating rate: see *Exhibit 20.7*. This type of transaction may be undertaken where an investor believes short rates are going to rise and/or a negative yield curve is going to prevail or, alternatively, to change the mix of the investment portfolio. For example, in the example below, the investor generates an effective return of LIBOR plus 1.25% pa.

"Locking in" gains and minimising losses on fixed rate investments

Interest rate swaps can be utilised to "lock in" unrealised profits (or minimise losses) on the capital value of fixed rate investments resulting from interest rate fluctuations, irrespective of whether the underlying asset is a fixed rate security or a synthetically created fixed rate asset.

Exhibit 20.7
Synthetic Fixed or Floating Rate Assets

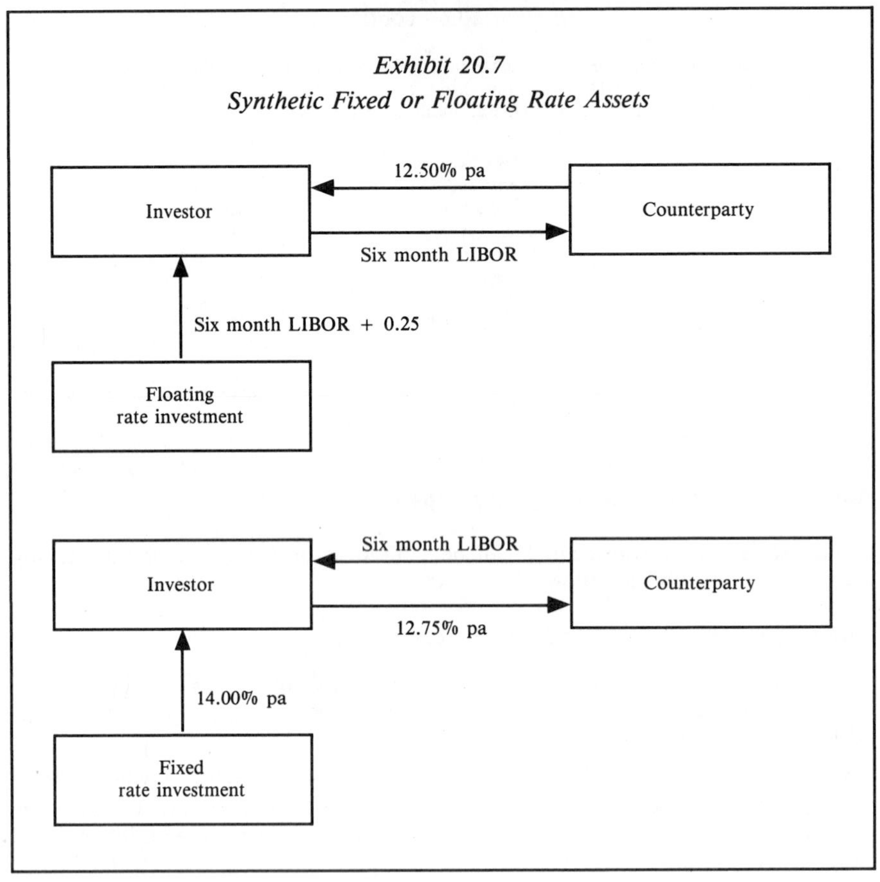

Transaction 1. For example, where the investor is holding fixed interest securities, yielding say 12.00% pa, and interest rates have fallen to 10.00% pa, the investor can protect itself from a possible reversal of gain due to further rate fluctuations as follows. The investor enters into an interest rate swap where it pays a fixed rate of 10.00% pa and receives a floating rate, six month LIBOR. This effectively generates a floating rate return of 2.00% pa over LIBOR. If rates for the relevant maturity increase to say 12.00% pa, it can reverse the original transaction by entering into a swap where it receives 12.00% pa and pays six month LIBOR. The net effect of the transaction is to provide the investor with a yield of 14.00% pa thereby using the swap transactions to "lock in" the unrealised capital gain to boost portfolio yield: see *Exhibit 20.8*.

The improvement in portfolio yield achieved is affected by the period between the two swaps and the slope of the yield curve, that is, the yield loss (if any) during the period that the investor has a floating rate asset. In the above example, if six month LIBOR averages 12.00% pa during the period until the first swap is reversed, no yield loss results. Assuming that the period between the initial swap and its reversal is six months and the underlying fixed rate investment was for a maturity of three years, the six month LIBOR rate would have to average less than 4.05% pa for the transaction to result in an overall loss of portfolio yield.

Exhibit 20.8
Locking In Gains on Fixed Rate Investments

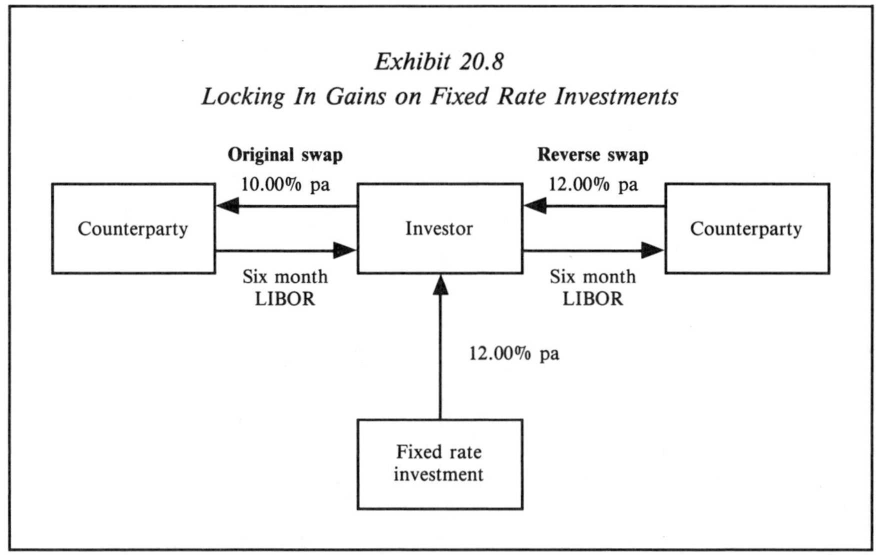

Transaction 2. Where the slope of the yield curve changes, interest rate swaps can be used to insulate the portfolio against capital losses.

For example, where a trader holds fixed interest securities by funding its investment through shorter-term borrowings, an inversion in the yield curve would result in the trader sustaining a loss as its cost of funding would, at least during the period the yield curve remained negatively sloped, exceed the earnings on the fixed interest security. Under these circumstances, the investor could protect itself by entering into a swap, whereby it receives a floating rate, six month LIBOR, in exchange for paying a fixed rate, as such a transaction would enable it to match its short-term funding cost with short-term investments. The initial transaction could then be reversed by a swap, whereby it pays six month LIBOR and receives a fixed rate, when the yield curve reverts to its normal slope: see *Exhibit 20.9*.

The risk for the investor is that the fixed interest rate on the swap transactions may move adversely in the period between the time when the original swap is entered into and its reversal. This risk must be weighed against the saving in funding costs during the period during which the yield curve is inverse. In the present case, assuming that the original fixed rate investment was for three years, and the period between the two swaps was six months, the rate payable on the second fixed rate swap would have to be less than 10.15% pa (a decrease of 0.35% pa) for the transaction to result in a loss to the investor.

An alternative means of achieving similar objectives would be to undertake yield curve (or maturity) switches utilising interest rate swaps rather than physical purchases and sales of securities: see discussion below. This would lengthen or shorten the term of the portfolio consistent with rate expectations to maximise the gains and/or minimise the losses resulting from yield curve changes.

Improving investment performance

Interest rate swaps can be utilised by investment managers, to improve portfolio performance on both fixed rate and floating rate assets.

Exhibit 20.9
Minimising Losses on Fixed Rate Investments

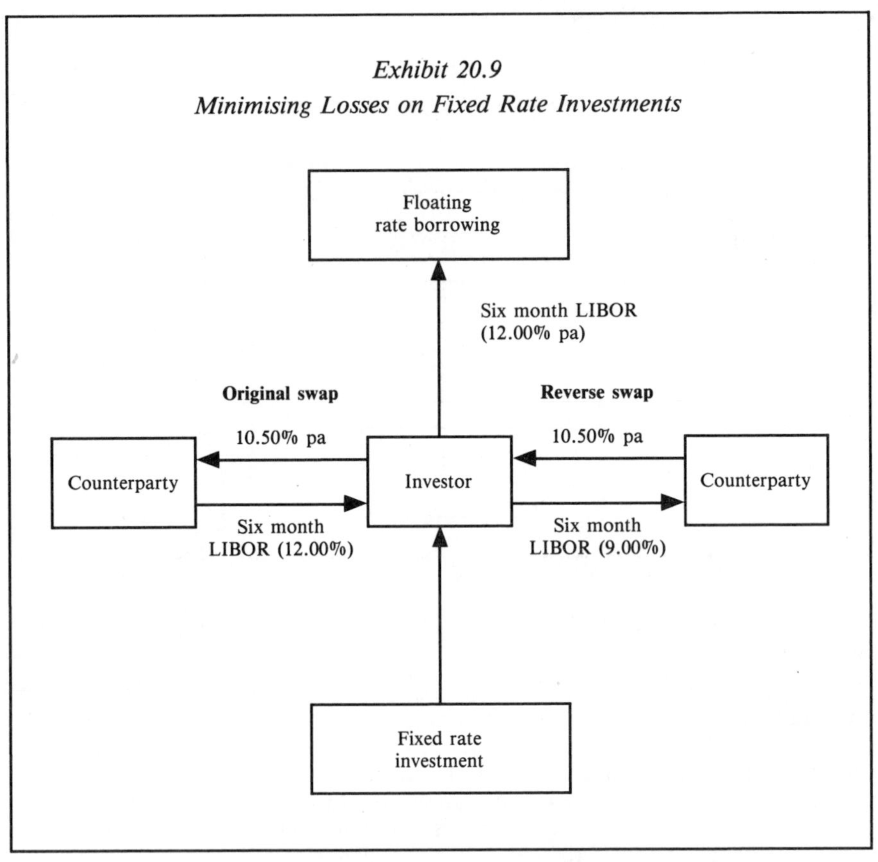

Transaction 1. Where an investor has an underlying portfolio of floating rate investments it can boost the investment yield on these assets by undertaking and then reversing interest rate swaps: see *Exhibit 20.10.* The investor would initially enter into a swap where it pays a floating rate, say six month LIBOR and receives a fixed rate of 11.50% pa. This swap is later reversed by a subsequent transaction whereby the investor receives six month LIBOR and pays a fixed rate. If the fixed rate paid under the second transaction is lower than the fixed rate on the first transaction, the investor enhances the return on its floating rate investment. For example, if the reversal is done when the fixed rate is 10.50% pa, the effective return after the two transactions to the investor is LIBOR plus 1.00% pa. Where the yield curve is positively sloped, the investor may, in addition, benefit from the increased earnings received under the swap during the period until the initial swap is reversed.

Transaction 2. Conversely where the investor has a fixed rate investment portfolio, it can enhance portfolio return by initially entering into a swap where it pays a fixed rate and receives six month LIBOR. This transaction is then reversed by a new swap under which the investor receives a fixed rate and pays floating rate. If the fixed rate paid under the initial swap was 10.50% pa and the fixed rate received at the time of the reversal is higher, say 11.50% pa, the investor will have achieved an effective increase in portfolio yield from 10.50% pa to 11.50% pa: see

Exhibit 20.11. The yield pick-up achieved is affected by the slope of the yield curve and the period between the two swap transactions. Where the yield curve is positively sloped the investor will incur a loss in earnings as it will receive the lower floating interest rate until the initial swap is reversed.

Exhibit 20.10

Managing Floating Rate Investments

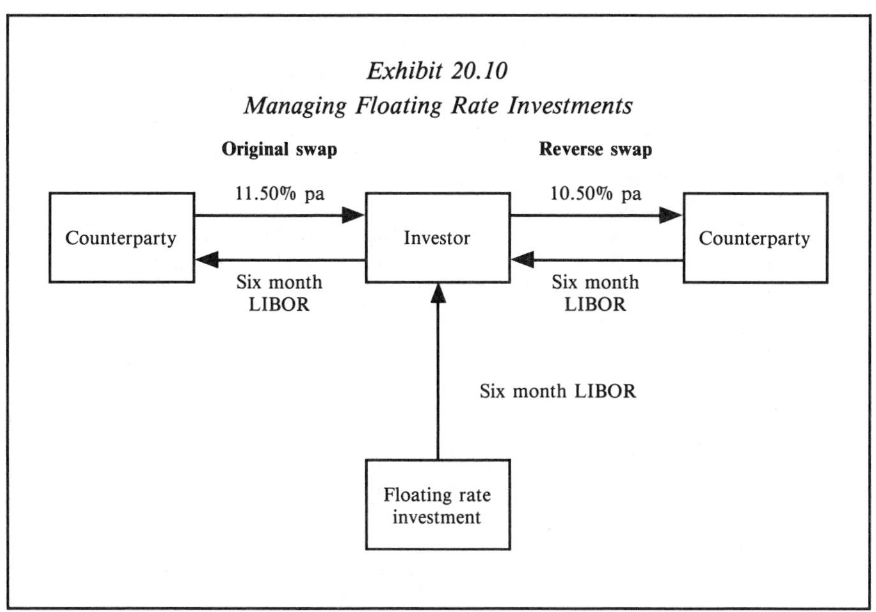

Exhibit 20.11

Managing Fixed Rate Investments

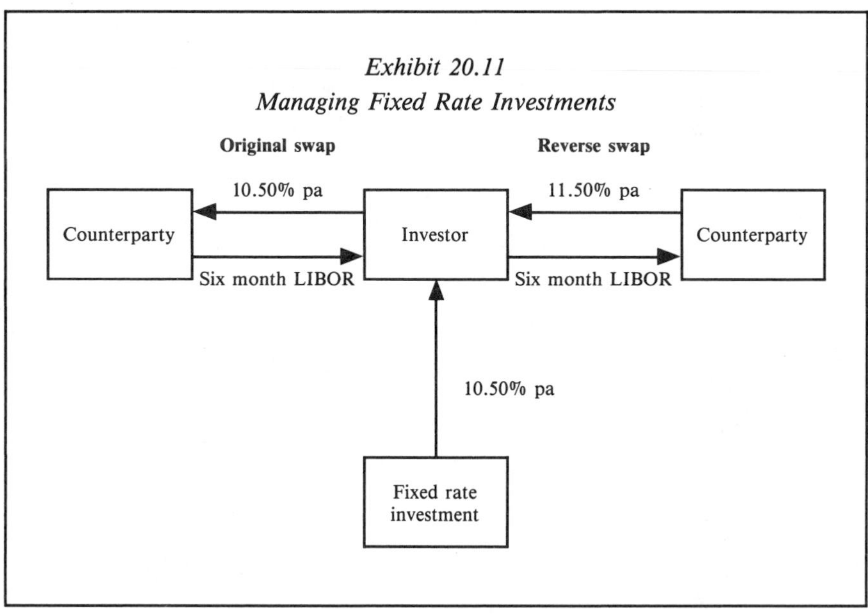

Transaction 3. Additional investment performance improvements can be achieved by the use of interest rate swaps to create synthetic yield curve switches with the maturity of the fixed rate investments being lengthened or shortened in an effort to maximise investment portfolio earnings.

For example, an investor holding a three year fixed interest security yielding 10.50% pa can create a synthetic five year asset by *simultaneously* entering into two interest rate swaps (effectively creating a forward swap) whereby, under the first it pays 10.50% pa for three years in return for receiving six month LIBOR, while under the second it receives 12.00% pa for five years while paying six month LIBOR: see *Exhibit 20.12*. These transactions may be reversed when the yield curve shifts have occurred. Where the switch is not reversed, after three years (when the fixed rate investment and the three year swap matures) the investor is left with the outstanding two years to maturity of the original five year swap. This swap can be left as a "naked" interest rate position or converted into a two year fixed rate security by the investor utilising the proceeds of the maturing investment to purchase floating rate securities yielding a rate relative to LIBOR which will generate a fixed return of 12.00% pa for two years.

Exhibit 20.12

Synthetic "Lengthening" Yield Curve Switch

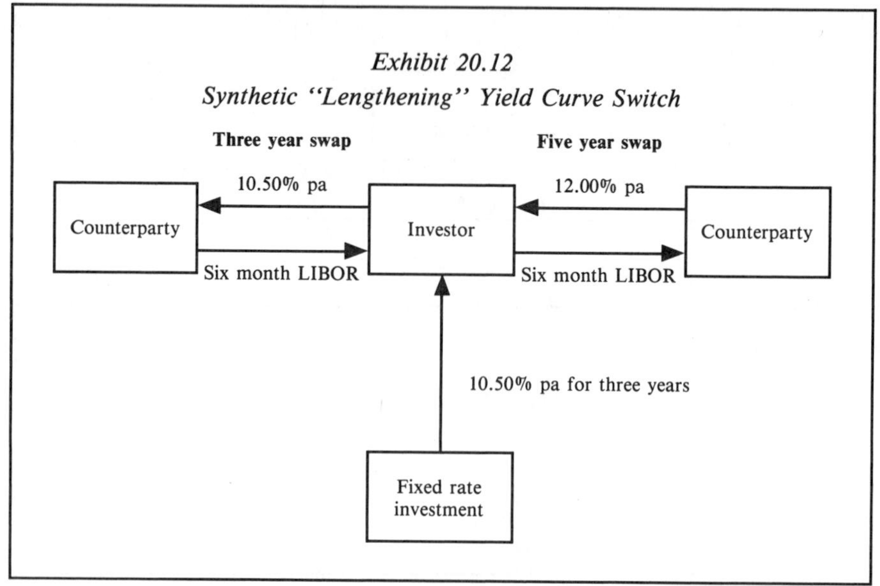

Conversely, an investor can shorten the maturity of its investment portfolio using two interest rate swaps. As in the case of a lengthening switch, the swap transactions can be reversed, for example, when the anticipated yield curve shifts have occurred. Where the switch is not reversed, at the end of three years the investor is left with a floating rate investment yielding LIBOR: see *Exhibit 20.13*.

Asset-based currency swaps: examples

Currency swaps can be utilised to expand the range of possible uses of swaps for portfolio managers as follows.

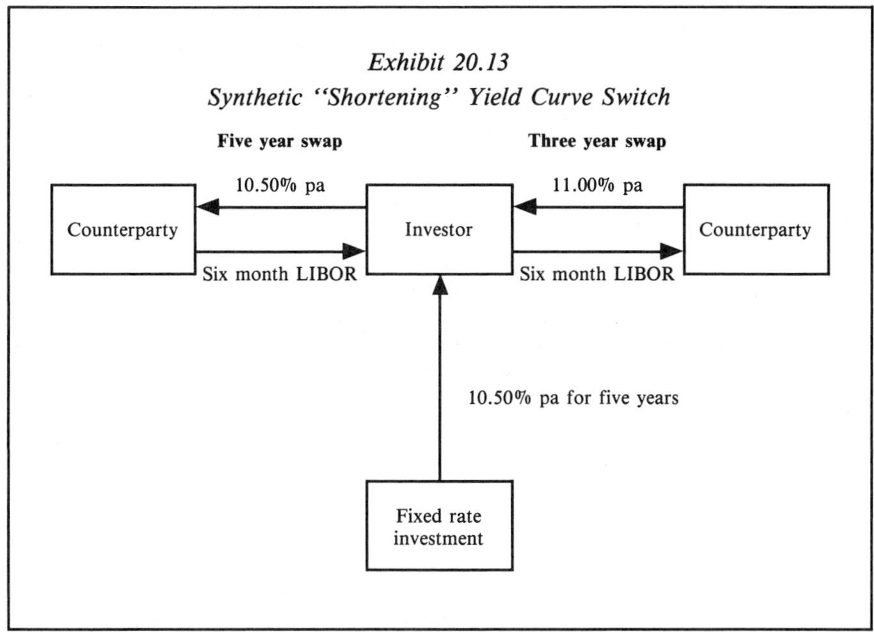

To create synthetic foreign currency assets

For example, where an investor has an existing asset in a currency, say US$, it can create a synthetic A$ asset by entering into a currency swap to convert the currency denomination and interest receipts of its assets. Under the swap, the investor would initially switch from US$ into A$, an exchange which would be reversed at the conclusion of the transaction. During the term of the swap the investor would pay interest rate related to US$ and receive interest flows calculated with reference to A$ interest rates.

This type of transaction structure may be particularly useful in avoiding the implications of withholding tax on a transaction or alternatively to create securities synthetically where equivalent securities may not in reality exist.

To lock in foreign currency gains or minimise losses on foreign currency investments

For example, if an investor had purchased US$ fixed interest securities and the US$ had appreciated against the A$ since the investment was undertaken, the investor could enter into a currency swap where it pays US$, corresponding to the interest flows from its existing US$ investment in return for receiving interest flows in A$. The swap transaction would, by virtue of the fact that the initial currency exchange and subsequent re-exchange would be undertaken at the then prevailing US$/A$ exchange rate, thereby eliminate any exchange risk for the investor for the remaining life of the investment. Therefore the investor protects itself from a possible reversal of the gain due to further currency and/or interest rate fluctuations.

Swap reversals

The use of swaps as an instrument of active asset or liability management requires the capacity to enter into and subsequently reverse the original transaction. Where an organisation trades its swaps to effectively neutralise any swap position so as to capitalise on market opportunities, it can either reverse or sell swap transactions as follows.

Reversing swaps

Assume a company completes the swap described below (the original swap) paying 10.50% pa and receiving LIBOR, and all rates increase by 50bps. If the company wished to reverse the swap in the new rate environment, the company would write a reverse swap, under which it would receive a fixed payment and make a LIBOR payment. When combined with the first swap, the company would achieve a 50bps pa profit between the fixed rate it receives and the fixed rate it pays and would pass the LIBOR it receives through as the LIBOR it pays: see *Exhibit 20.14*.

Swap sale or assignment

As an alternative, the company could assign or sell its position in the existing swap to a third party. The fair market value (cash payment) of the swap is determined by the present value of the difference between the fixed rate on the original contract (10.50% pa) and the fixed rate applicable to a new contract (11.00% pa). In this example, because interest rates have risen since the original swap was priced, the company could realise a substantial cash payment by selling the original swap: see *Exhibit 20.14*.

The difference between the two techniques is that under a reverse swap, the company will recognise its profit or loss over the remaining term of the mirror contracts whereas if it sells or assigns the original contract, this profit or loss will be recognised immediately. It should also be noted that the market tends to value the two techniques differently.

The assignment structure may be advantageous for reasons of income recognition in the current period, prepayment or sale of the underlying asset or liability being hedged, and interest cost management. It also eliminates the original credit exposure whereas the swap reversal structure creates an additional credit exposure.

The rationale behind the vast majority of assignments has been recognition as income of the cash payment in the current period. The assignment technique is particularly advantageous where the front end cash payment receives a favourable tax treatment, for example, as a capital amount.

The practice of income recognition in the current period has come under the scrutiny of the Financial Accounting Standards Board and the Federal Home Loan Bank Board in the United States, both of whom have discouraged the current period recognition of income or expense except when the underlying asset and/or liability has been eliminated. They recommend that any gain or loss be recognised over the remaining life of the underlying asset or liability to which the swap was tied. Accounting treatment elsewhere in the world is still relatively undefined.

The above examples relate to the reversal of interest rate swaps. A similar logic is applicable in the case of currency swaps which can be undertaken either as reversals/mirror currency swaps or currency swap sales, assignment or buy-outs.

The difference in the case of currency swaps is that, in addition to any interest rate differential, there may be foreign exchange gains or losses in the original currency swap position which must be valued.

Exhibit 20.14
Interest Rate Swap Reversals and Assignments

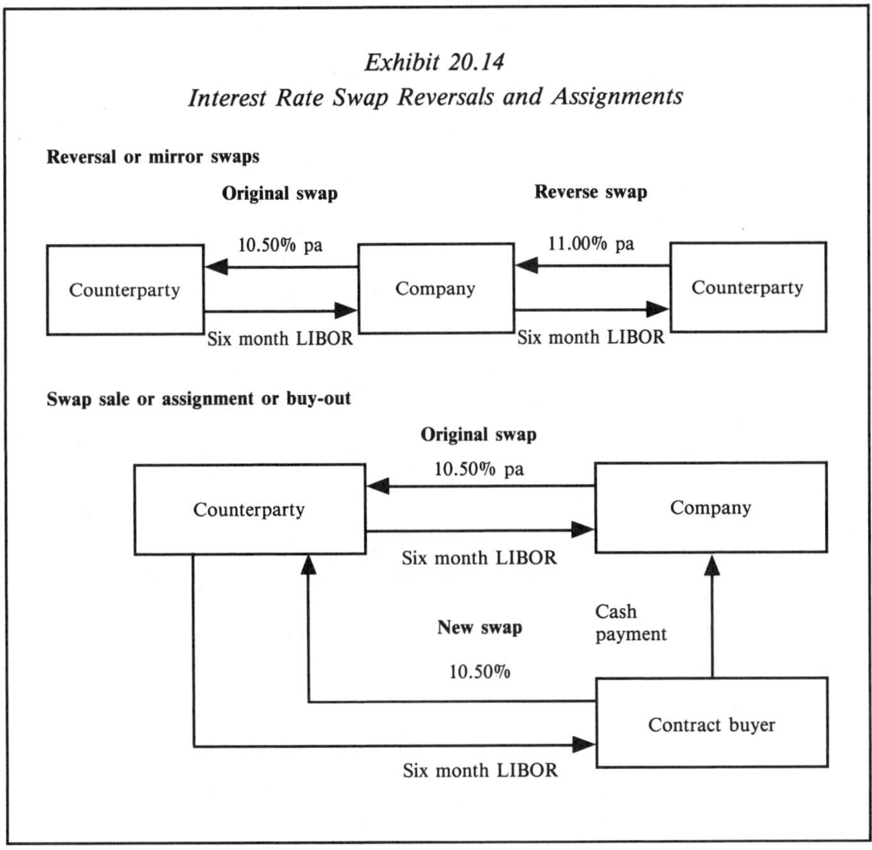

Exhibit 20.15 sets out a particularly innovative structure for the realisation of the present foreign exchange gain or loss in a currency swap reversal.

The valuation of swap unwinds or reversal entail assessing the economic value of an existing position in accordance with the concepts outlined in detail in Chapter 8: refer *Exhibit 8.29* to *Exhibit 8.30.*

UTILISING FRAs AND LTFX CONTRACTS

FRAs and LTFX versus interest rate and currency swaps

FRAs and LTFX contracts have similarities with interest rate swaps and currency swaps respectively. Consequently, it would be expected that FRAs and LTFX contracts could be utilised in a manner analogous to the use of these instruments for asset liability management purposes. The major difference between the two classes of instruments include:

- FRAs and LTFX contracts entail the management of *single* cash flows as distinct from interest rate and currency swaps which entail the exchange of a *series* of future cash flows.

Exhibit 20.15
Currency Swap Reversals

Assume that Company A has undertaken the following currency swap:

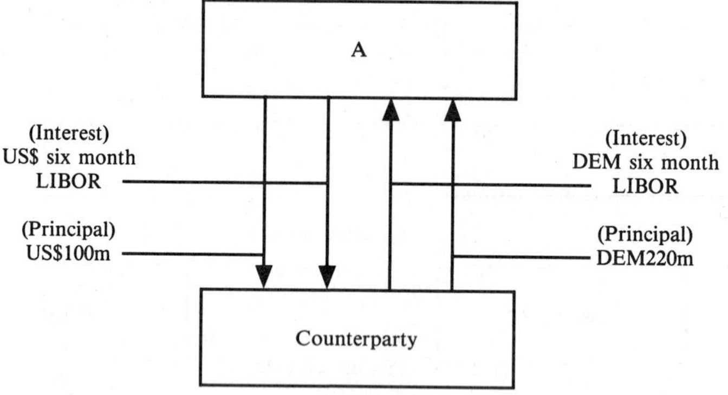

Original Term:	7 years
Remaining Term:	4 years
Original Currency Rate:	US$1 = DEM2.20
Current Currency Rate:	US$1 = DEM1.60

(Please note that the currency swap has been assumed to be a floating-to-floating currency swap in order to minimise interest rate valuation effects—particularly where the reversal is completed on an interest payment date.)

The depreciation in the US$ against the DEM results in an unrealised profit under the swap which A now seeks to realise. A can crystallise its gain utilising one of the following alternative structures:

- cancel the swap with the existing counterpary (the cancellation or buyout);
- assign or novate the existing swap to a third party for an up-front payment or receipt (the assignment);
- enter into an offsetting currency swap with a *new* counterparty to exactly match the cash flows under the existing swap (the mirror swap);
- enter into a new currency swap *at current market rates* with a new counterparty (the market swap).

Under the cancellation on assignment alternatives, A would receive the gain on the currency movements at the time of reversal. This gain would, in this case, represent the currency movement present valued to the date the swap is cancelled. (We have assumed that there is no gain or loss on the floating rate interest legs of the swap. In practice, there would be some difference in the accrued interest on the floating legs resulting in a net payment or receipt. In the case of a swap with fixed rates in one or other currency, movements in rates will result in an additional gain or loss which will be calculated and settled.)

The gain in this case would be approx as follows:

Currency Rates (US$1 =)	2.20	1.60
US$ Amount (M)	100.0	100.0
DEM Amount (M)	220.0	160.0

The gain is DEM60.0m or US$37.5m (at current rates). Present valued at 7.50% pa, this is equivalent to US$28.1m.

Exhibit 20.15—continued

The mirror swap alternative is similar to the cancellation or assignment alternatives and would be utilised, in general, only where the swap value generated by the *new* counterparty is better than that otherwise available. A disadvantage of the mirror swap alternative is that it does not reduce A's utilisation of credit lines (as in the cancellation or assignment) but *increases* them.

The market swap alternative is more novel:

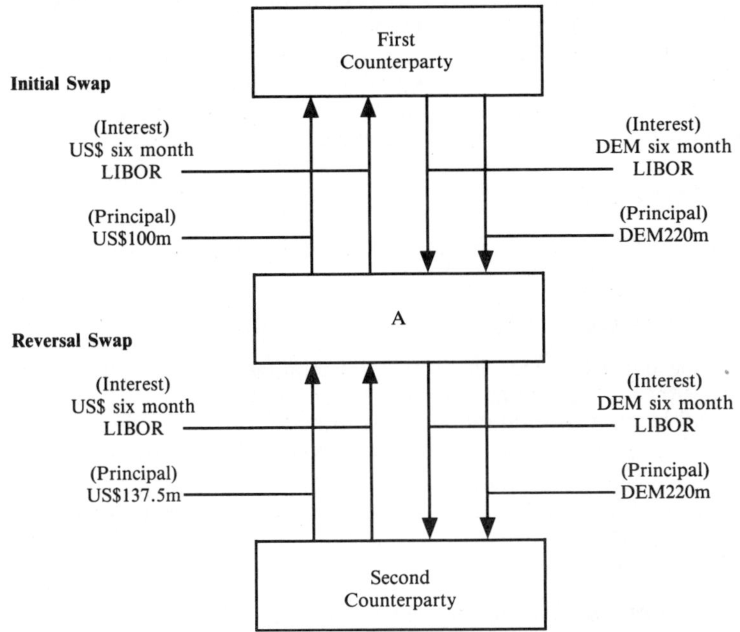

As is evident, A enters into a currency swap *at current market rates* which has the following effect:

- A's cash flows under the initial swap are matched as to principal and interest flows.
- A receives an amount of US$37.5m (being the *undiscounted* currency gain) in the final exchange.

Please note that the interest payments are calculated on the market principal amounts resulting in the US$ receipts being calculated on the higher US$ principal.

The market swap structure can be used where there are benefits in deferring the receipt of the gain.

- The pricing structure of FRAs and LTFX contracts vary with essentially the FRA or LTFX rate being above or below the current spot rate while in an interest rate or currency swap, this difference is built into the different interest rates on the two sets of cash flows which are exchanged.

The differences between the two classes of instruments dictate, to a large extent, how FRAs and LTFX contracts are utilised in asset liability management. There are three main classes of use of FRAs and LTFX contracts in managing existing portfolios of assets and liabilities:

- FRAs and LTFX contracts are ideal to manage uneven cash flows. Where cash flows are of different amounts or are not at regular periodic intervals, FRAs and LTFX contracts are relatively more flexible in changing the interest rate and currency basis of these cash flows. In contrast, where evenly spaced equal sets of cash flows are involved, it is usually more economical to utilise interest rate and currency swaps to effect the interest rate or currency basis conversion.
- FRAs and LTFX contracts allow each cash flow, where a stream of cash flows is involved, to be managed individually. In contrast interest rate and currency swaps convert all the relevant cash flows.
- FRAs and LTFX contracts can be more flexible than interest rate or currency swaps in adjusting or optimising a hedge. This is because it allows each cash flow, as noted above, to be treated independently but also allows the cost of the hedge to be attuned to particular market environments.

Utilising FRAs: examples

FRAs can be utilised as an instrument for managing assets and liabilities as follows.

Locking in future borrowings

FRAs can be utilised to lock in or fix or guarantee a future rollover rate or repricing on either a loan or an investment. Generally, the underlying loan or investment will be on a floating rate basis with the FRAs being utilised to lock in future borrowing or investment rates on the relevant repricings on the loan.

The FRA could be utilised (as noted above in Chapter 4) to fix the borrowing or investment return for a single period or, alternatively, a series of FRAs can be utilised to lock in the rates on a series of repricing dates to lock in investment or borrowing rates for an extended period.

Creating exposures to floating interest rates

FRAs can also be used to create an exposure to floating rates for an investor or borrower with a fixed rate investment or borrowing. A borrower with fixed rate debt can create synthetic floating rate exposure for the period of the borrowing by selling FRAs. Similarly, a fixed rate investor can create a synthetic floating rate investment by buying FRAs. As in the case of interest rate swaps, due to anomalies in the forward markets, it may be possible to create cheaper borrowings or high-yielding investments through these strategies.

Locking in future reinvestment rates

FRAs can also be utilised to lock in future reinvestment rates on intermediate cash flows, such as interest coupons, on a term borrowing. In this context, the FRAs function in a manner similar to zero coupon swaps where a periodic coupon flow is swapped for a lump sum amount payable at maturity. This type of strategy is applicable not only to investment managers seeking to eliminate reinvestment risk within their asset portfolios but also to corporate liability managers creating sinking funds for the repayment of future liabilities.

Trading static yield curves

A more complex strategy utilising FRAs entails using FRAs to trade a static yield curve. Where interest rates are expected to be static at or about current levels, investors and borrowers can both potentially benefit from utilising FRAs under certain circumstances. This type of strategy is predicated on the fact that the forward rate yield curve lies above or below the current physical market yield curve.

For example, if the yield curve is normal or upwards sloping, the forward rate yield curve lies above the cash market yield curve. Where the yield curve is inversely shaped or downwards sloping, the forward rates lie below the cash market yield curve. In an environment where the yield curve is not expected to change significantly, borrowers and investors can benefit where they plan to undertake short-term borrowing or lending activities.

In the case of investors, where the forward rate curve lies above the cash market yield curve, it may be profitable to lock-in forward investment rates as if the yield curve does not change significantly, then the forward rate achievable will be higher than the likely cash market rate at the time the investment must be undertaken. For borrowers, the reverse applies with borrowers being able to benefit by locking in lower forward borrowing costs for short time frames than would be physically possible in the cash market, provided that the inverse yield curve which prevails is not expected to shift significantly. It should be stressed that these strategies are not riskless but entail a form of limited risk yield curve trading or asset liability management.

Trading against interest rate swap

A more sophisticated kind of transaction would entail trading FRAs, usually a strip of FRAs against an interest rate swap. This type of strategy is predicated on the fact that the real cost of an interest rate swap for a payer of fixed rate is the difference between the fixed rate paid and the average floating rate cost over the life of the transaction. Where an inverse yield curve prevails, a fixed rate payer under an interest rate swap may simultaneously execute a series of sold FRA positions to lock in a fixed rate, usually higher than the swap rate for at least a part, sometimes a substantial part, of the life of the interest rate swap. This would lock in a spread between the rate being paid under the swap and the rate locked in through the sold FRAs. As the full term of the underlying interest rate swap is not covered, a residual exposure towards the latter end of the life of the swap, the "tail", will remain exposed.

In essence, the party undertaking the transaction is speculating that the spread locked in over the initial period of the swap will not be lost over the tail period where it must pay the fixed rate under the swap. In a reversal of the strategy, particularly where a positive yield curve exists, a transaction where the entity receives the fixed rate under the swap and offsets part of the risk exposure through buying FRAs, at least over part of the life of the swap, can be devised. Examples of this type of strategy are set out in *Exhibit 20.16*. It should be understood that these strategies are also not risk free but entail the assumption of certain risks related to the shape of the yield curve as well as underlying interest rate expectations.

Exhibit 20.16

FRAs versus Interest Rate Swap Arbitrage

Assume the following market rates are available:

- US$ interest rate swaps for three years are quoted at 14.00/13.90% pa versus six month LIBOR flat.
- Current LIBOR is 16.00% pa.

Exhibit 20.16—continued

- The following FRAs are available:

  6×12: 15.10/15.00
  12×18: 14.85/14.75
  18×24: 14.35/14.25

A financial institution (F) undertakes the following transaction:

- F enters into an interest rate swap where it pays 14.00% pa against receipt of LIBOR.
- F simultaneously sells three FRAs:

  one 6×12 at 15.00% pa
  one 12×18 at 14.75% pa
  one 18×24 at 14.25% pa

The net results of the FRA sales when combined with current LIBOR of 16.00% pa means that F has locked in a fixed rate of 15.00% pa for two years as against payments under the swap of 14.00% pa.

On a present value basis (assuming a discount rate of 15.00% pa) this locked in spread between the fixed rate being received and paid is valued at 1.77% at the commencement or a future value equivalent of 2.34% pa.

This implies that where the *net* payment in year three under the swap is *less than* approximately 2.62% pa (assuming a reinvestment rate for year three of 12.00% pa) then F will gain. For example if LIBOR averages 12.00% in year 3, then F will pay 2.00% pa (14.00% pa less 12.00% pa) under the swap generating net cash inflow of approximately 0.62% pa.

Utilising LTFX: some examples

LTFX contracts can be used as a substitute for currency swaps in a manner analogous to that of using FRAs as a surrogate for interest rate swaps. LTFX transactions can be utilised for managing assets and liabilities with great effect in the following situations:

- LTFX contracts can be used to change the currency basis of future cash flows in a particular currency. An LTFX contract can be utilised in respect of a future payment due on a loan or receipts generated from an investment. As with FRAs, a series of LTFX contracts can be simultaneously transacted to lock in the currency rate on payments or receipts relative to a base currency.
- A sophisticated use of LTFX contracts may be to undertake a type of risk arbitrage between currency swaps and a series of LTFX contracts. This particular technique is discussed in detail in the context of hedging LTFX books or market making in respect of LTFX contracts: see Chapter 32.

The main advantage of using LTFX contracts in preference to currency swaps is the capacity to alter the currency basis of *some* but not *all* cash flows in a foreign currency. An added advantage which is equally applicable to FRAs relates to the flexibility available to reverse hedges in line with evolving market expectations of future currency and interest rates. In the case of LTFX contracts, as each contract relates to a specific cash flow, individual payments can be hedged and unhedged. In contrast, under a currency swap, the whole swap must be lifted or reversed necessarily unwinding the hedge in respect of *all* future cash flows.

The method of pricing LTFX contracts, whereby they are priced in terms of points reflecting premiums and discounts relative to the spot exchange rate can provide potential advantages. For example, the cost of the hedge can be optimised in terms of points lost or gained rather than transferring the cost of the hedge to the interest rate differential received or paid in the case of a currency swap. This may provide potential advantages depending on the shape of the yield curve in the two relevant currencies which may create potential advantages for using LTFX contracts over currency swaps. This method of pricing LTFX contracts can also be particularly useful in accelerating or deferring income or expense items invoiced in different currencies for purposes of taxation treatment as well as balance sheet presentation.

UTILISING CAPS, COLLARS AND FLOORS

Symmetric versus asymmetric risk management instruments

Caps, collars and floors as species of options on interest rates belong to a class of asymmetric risk management instruments. This characteristic of caps, floors and collars necessarily means that there are some significant differences as well as similarities in their use in managing asset and liability portfolios. In particular the risk profiles and payoffs to buyers and sellers of these instruments are fundamentally different. As with all options, the purchaser of the cap, floor or collar enjoys the insurance features of such a transaction which limits their risk from adverse changes in interest rates but without the need to give up any potential benefits from a favourable movement in rates. In contrast, the seller of a cap or floor assumes a potentially unlimited liability, dependent only on movements in the benchmark rate, in exchange for a reward equal to the premium or fee received. These differences in payoffs dictate to a large extent the uses of this particular class of instrument in asset liability management.

There are two general classes of users in caps and floors:

- Purchasers of caps and floors utilise these instruments as an alternative to price fixing mechanisms such as interest rate swaps and FRAs. The basic intention is to establish a *maximum* cost of borrowings or *minimum* rate of return on investments while maintaining the possibility of lower costs or higher returns if favourable movements in the rate structure occur.
- Sellers of caps and floors seek to gain (particularly in stable market environments) from the premium received from option writing activities which can be speculative or written against offsetting portfolio positions. The premium acts as a means of lowering borrowing costs or enhancing investment returns while providing a cushion or limited hedge against minor market movements.

An example of the first type of transaction would entail a borrower taking out a cap as an alternative to swapping floating rate debt into a fixed rate liability as protection against potential increases in interest rates. Some examples of the sale of caps and floors as a technique for portfolio management are considered in detail below.

Caps and collars versus swaps

A fundamental issue in utilising symmetric versus asymmetric risk management instruments is the relative attractiveness of each technique under different market scenarios. *Exhibit 20.17* compares the cost of a number of hedging alternatives for a particular borrowing transaction.

The results of the selected hedging alternatives (outlined in *Exhibit 20.17*) at various rate levels indicate that there is no single preferred hedging strategy. Fixed rates prove to be the best protection against very high interest rates in the future, while no hedge appears to be the best strategy if rates fall. Caps or collars provide protection against high costs at high rate levels but allow the borrower to participate in falls in interest rates. While break-evens at any particular rate level are simple to ascertain, the true benefits of these alternative hedges can only be determined with reference to actual interest rates achieved over the life of the transaction. As future interest rates cannot be forecast accurately, many organisations seek to diversify the hedge by blending techniques. Alternatively, it is possible to simulate outcomes over time utilising different interest scenarios.

Exhibit 20.17

Utilising Caps and Collars versus Interest Rate Swaps

The following example compares the cost of four hedging alternatives on a five year, six month LIBOR based obligation. (All-in cost calculations do not include the borrower's credit spread, which would be the same in all cases; front end fees are converted to per annum equivalents using a discount rate of 11.00% pa.) At the time of the example six month LIBOR was 8.81% and five year treasuries were yielding 10.88%.

Alternatives

- No hedge.
- Interest rate swap (fixed rate of 11.68%, semi-annually, against six month LIBOR).
- Ceiling rate agreement, cap at 11.31% (2.5% higher than spot rate), fee 5.1% (equivalent to 1.37% pa).
- Floor-ceiling rate agreement, cap at 11.31%, floor at 8.81% (spot), fee 3.2% (equivalent to 0.87% pa).

All-in borrowing costs per annum

Market rate						
(six month LIBOR)	6.00%	8.00%	10.00%	12.00%	14.00%	20.00%
No hedge	6.00%	8.00%	10.00%	12.00%	14.00%	20.00%
Interest rate swap	11.68%	11.68%	11.68%	11.68%	11.68%	11.68%
Cap rate agreement						
Market rate	6.00%	8.00%	10.00%	12.00%	14.00%	20.00%
Cap rate refund	—	—	—	(0.69%)	(2.69%)	(8.69%)
Fee amortisation	1.37%	1.37%	1.37%	1.37%	1.37%	1.37%
Total	7.37%	9.37%	11.37%	12.68%	12.68%	12.68%
Collar agreement						
Market rate	6.00%	8.00%	10.00%	12.00%	14.00%	20.00%
Cap rate refund	—	—	—	(0.69%)	(2.69%)	(8.69%)
Floor rate payment	2.81%	0.81%	—	—	—	—
Fee amortisation	0.87%	0.87%	0.87%	0.87%	0.87%	0.87%
Total	9.68%	9.68%	10.87%	12.18%	12.18%	12.18%

A possible means of analysing these hedging positions is to take a probabilistic approach to future interest rate scenarios. But utilising assumptions of the future mean and volatility (standard deviation) in the level of interest rates, it is theoretically possible to calculate the expected cost or benefit of any particular hedging strategy. For example, in *Exhibit 20.17*, the problem of hedging floating rate debt against the potential increase in interest expense as a result of increasing interest rates can be analysed in terms of first establishing the economics of each hedging alternative and then calculating expected values for the outcome with various instruments. Applying this approach, it is necessary to first specify the actual economic cost of each alternative. The economics of the various hedging alternatives considered can be summarised as follows:

- The economics of a swap into a fixed rate can be specified in terms of a borrower incurring a cost if the floating rate remains *below* the fixed rate, on average, for the term of the swap. Conversely, an economic gain to the borrower accrues where the floating rate averages a level above the fixed rate paid under the swap.
- The economics of the purchase of a cap relates to the cost of the cap with an economic gain accruing to the borrower if the floating rate remains above the cap rate on average for the term of the transaction, after adjustment for the fee.
- The economics of the collar is similar to the economics of the cap combined with the sale by the borrower of the floor. The sale results in a premium being paid to the borrower which partially offsets the cost of the cap with an economic loss arising if the floating rate index remains below the floor rate agreed under the collar agreement.

In each case, for the purpose of constructing a mathematically analytical model, the expected loss or gain over the life of each transaction can be calculated based on an assumed probability distribution of interest rates for the relevant index.

The calculation of expected values of hedging with the different instruments would take the following form:

- In the case of the interest rate swap, the expected gain or loss equals the floating rate minus the fixed rate swap multiplied by the probability of that level of floating rate occurring. The total expected gain or loss of the swap will equal the probability weight of the sum of the gains and losses for all possible levels of the floating rate. This expected value will be a function of the mean level of the floating rate index, the current level of the floating rate and its volatility, or standard deviation.
- For the interest rate cap or collar, the expected gain or loss will be a function of the floating rate minus the cap rate or the floor rate minus the floating rate multiplied by the probability of that floating rate occurring. Once again, the expected overall gain or loss is equivalent to the probability weight and sum of the gains or losses for all possible interest rate levels.

This type of probabilistic analysis enables comparison of the relative cost effectiveness of different hedging strategies as a function of interest rate expectations using different probability estimates and levels of confidence. The framework allows outcomes to be simulated, utilising techniques such as monte carlo simulation.

Utilising caps and collars: examples

Caps, floors and collars can be utilised as an asset liability management technique in a number of ways.

A number of the applications outlined below are predicated on the capacity to create equivalent swap positions by combinations of caps and floors. In essence, they entail dismembering a swap into constituent cap and floor elements or, alternatively, combining caps and floors into the equivalent swap position to achieve a particular asset or liability management objective.

Structured caps and collars

Sophisticated insurance structures involving deferred or staggered caps can be devised. Under this type of arrangement, borrowing interest rates, for example, could be capped at increasing or decreasing levels or banded within upper and lower limits for individual periods within the overall term of the liability. This type of structuring can be utilised to achieve two objectives:

- To protect the borrower's cash flow capacity or interest cost levels relative to its resources by essentially insuring via the purchase of the cap or collar, that certain interest cost and/or cash flow levels are maintained. For example, caps and collars are utilised extensively in connection with real estate projects as well as leveraged buy-outs in the United States for these types of reasons.
- To adjust the cost of protection at levels consistent with the project's or borrower's capacity to bear risk.

Creating synthetic floating rate liabilities

A fixed rate borrower can create an exposure to a floating interest rate index by purchasing a floor at a level equal to the cost of its fixed rate debt. If interest rates fall, the borrower benefits by an amount equivalent to the difference between the market level of the index relative to the floor level, adjusted for the amortised purchase price of the floor. This type of strategy means that the borrower participates in any rate declines below the floor level on the relevant index, while having no exposure to rate increases because if the floating rate index exceeds the floor level, its cost of funds equate to its fixed rate debt costs. This type of strategy, which is identical to purchasing a cap, is illustrated in *Exhibit 20.18*.

Exhibit 20.18

Purchasing Floors to Create a Synthetic Floating Rate Liability

Assume a borrower has a five year fixed rate borrowing at 14.00% pa. The borrower purchases a five year floor on LIBOR at a floor level of 14.00% pa for a fee of 5.00% (equivalent to 1.46% pa utilising a discount rate of 14.00% pa).

All-in borrowing costs per annum

LIBOR	10.00%	12.00%	14.00%	16.00%	18.00%
Fixed rate borrowing	14.00%	14.00%	14.00%	14.00%	14.00%
Floor rate agreement					
Fixed rate borrowing	14.00%	14.00%	14.00%	14.00%	14.00%
Floor rate refund	(4.00%)	(2.00%)	—	—	—
Fee amortisation	1.46%	1.46%	1.46%	1.46%	1.46%
Total	11.46%	13.46%	15.46%	15.46%	15.46%

A conceptually similar strategy can be utilised by a fixed rate investor holding a portfolio of fixed rate assets, such as bonds, who engineers an exposure to floating rates by purchasing a cap where the cap level is set at the level of interest receipts on the fixed rate portfolio. If interest rates on the relevant index increase, the investor receives cash inflows equal to the excess of the index above the cap rate level (adjusted for the premium) thereby allowing it to participate by way of increased interest earnings if rates increase while maintaining a floor on portfolio interest earnings as the portfolio will earn a minimum of the fixed interest rate accruing on the portfolio.

This type of strategy can also be utilised by investors who may buy deferred or staggered floors or collars designed to guarantee minimum portfolio earnings or cash inflows to match expected liabilities in particular periods.

Selling caps and floors

A floating rate borrower can seek to lower its cost of borrowing while simultaneously achieving a modicum of protection from rate increases by selling floors against its liabilities. Under this type of strategy, if interest rates decline, the borrower does not participate in the fall in interest rates beyond the floor level as it must make payments to the purchaser of the floor which brings its cost of funding to the floor level adjusted to the premium received. If rates increase, however, the borrower has limited protection equal to the amortised premium level which partially offsets increased costs. However, if rates increase sharply, the borrower is exposed to increased interest cost under the strategy. An example of this type of transaction is set out in *Exhibit 20.19*.

Exhibit 20.19

Selling Floors to Manage Floating Rate Liabilities

Assume a borrower has floating rate liabilities for five year pricing "off" to six month LIBOR. The borrower sells a five year floor on LIBOR at a floor level of 12.00% pa for a fee of 2.40% (equivalent to 0.67% pa utilising a discount rate of 12.00% pa). The current level of LIBOR is 13.00% pa.

All-in borrowing costs per annum

LIBOR	10.00%	12.00%	14.00%	16.00%	18.00%
Floating rate borrowing	10.00%	12.00%	14.00%	16.00%	18.00%
Sale of floor rate agreement					
Floating rate borrowing	10.00%	12.00%	14.00%	16.00%	18.00%
Floor rate payments	2.00%	—	—	—	—
Fee amortisation	0.67%	0.67%	0.67%	0.67%	0.67%
Total	11.33%	11.33%	13.33%	15.55%	17.33%

In an asset-based variation of the last strategy, an investor holding a portfolio floating rate assets may seek to enhance the yield on the portfolio by selling caps. Under this strategy, if interest rates increase above the cap level, the investors return is limited to the level of the cap adjusted for the premium received. However, if rates drop, the investor earns the market interest rate adjusted for the premium which allows it to earn a margin above the usual floating rate earnings that would accrue to the investor.

The above strategies outlined are not comprehensive. The use of caps, floors and collars is still evolving. Additional uses and strategies for asset liability management utilising caps, floors and collars are likely to emerge.

Chapter 21

Utilising Swaps for Asset and Liability Management: Financial Engineering[1]

SWAPS AND FINANCIAL ENGINEERING APPLICATIONS

The basic techniques for asset and liability management utilising the basic swap instruments outlined in Chapter 20 highlight the use of these instruments to convert fixed rate exposures to floating rate and vice versa, and to convert asset and liabilities from one currency to another. The basic strategies discussed are not complex and are designed, generally, to limit the risk of the party entering into the transaction to adverse movements in interest rates and exchange rates. Even where the strategies outlined are not purely risk averse, the level of risk assumed is quite limited—the transactions belonging to a class of transactions usually referred to as risk arbitrage transactions.

However, increasingly paralleling the technical or product evolution of the swap market, the application of swaps to asset—liability management problems has also evolved. This more recent applications focus is often referred to as "financial engineering", a term utilised, in this context, to describe the construction of synthetic asset and liability structures featuring combination of traditional instruments (such as fixed interest bonds, floating rate notes, and other funding instruments) and derivative products (such as interest rate and currency swaps, caps, floors, collars, FRAs etc).

In this chapter, consideration is given to the utilisation of swap transactions for this type of financial engineering purpose. The major example of financial engineering application of utilising swaps occurs in the management corporate liability portfolios. This reflects the increased focus on active management of, particularly, debt portfolios by corporations seeking to minimise borrowing costs or maximise risk-return trade-offs. The principles outlined are equally applicable to the management of purely *asset portfolios*, such as institutional fixed income portfolios.

The use of many of the financial engineering structures identified are predicated on a fundamental decision to alter the interest rate and/or currency basis of an underlying asset or liability. The financial engineering structures outlined do not, of themselves, dictate the underlying decision to alter the interest rate or currency basis of the liability. The underlying decision to alter the interest rate or currency of the asset or liability will, more typically, be dictated by:

- changes in fundamental business circumstances, such as the purchase and sale of assets denominated in particular currencies.
- interest rate and/or currency exposure management considerations whereby the financial engineering structure is devised to convert the underlying portfolio to a basis more consistent with current interest and currency rate expectations.

1. This chapter is based on Satyajit Das and John Martin, "Corporate Liability Portfolio Management—Using Swaps and Swap Derivatives" in Satyajit Das (1991).

EVOLUTION OF ASSET/LIABILITY MANAGEMENT APPLICATIONS

The role of swaps in asset/liability management has undergone significant changes in recent years in response to changes in the market environment: see Chapter 1. The major influences include:

- increased volatility of interest and exchange rates;
- growing acceptance of the concept of "zaitech";
- a shift in corporate philosophies whereby the minimisation of financing costs came increasingly to be viewed as a component of the competitive positioning of an entity.

The unprecedented volatility of interest and exchange rates through the 1980s forced most organisations to focus closely on their exposure management practices. This focus, initially, encouraged the utilisation of swaps and other derivative instruments to protect profitability and cash flow from substantial fluctuations as a result of movements in interest and exchange rates. The shift to increasingly active management of asset liability portfolios also resulted in an increased understanding of the profit opportunities created by financial markets volatility.

The trend to more active management was allied to an increasing acceptance by a wide variety of corporations of the concept of zaitech.[2] The concept, at least, in its most common form, was seen to legitimise the active management of an organisation's financial flows in a manner designed to generate profits *in its own right*. This included, in its most extreme form, corporations entering into transactions for purely speculative reasons, totally unconnected to its underlying business activities or, in more modest forms, to organisations actively trading specific exposures generated by its core business activities in an effort to generate profits as a by-product to the actual minimisation of exposures that was the primary motivating factor in such activity.

The increasing globalisation of industry and increased competition across a variety of industries also forced, at or about the same time, an increased focus on minimisation of financing costs, as well as, in its most extreme form, the generation of zaitech profits, as a component of the competitive positioning of particular organisations.

These developments had significant implications for the management of swap portfolios. The coalescence of these complex and interrelated factors created an environment within which organisations came to view their underlying liability and derivative portfolios as streams of cash flows capable and demanding of active management on an ongoing basis.

Traditionally, users undertook swap transactions which were matched to the characteristics of the underlying asset or liability portfolio. The swap was completed and maintained until maturity. The only exception to this pattern of activity was where changes in the underlying business or debt portfolio necessitated that the swap be terminated or restructured.

However, corporations in particular increasingly came to view their swap transactions as a coherent portfolio of cash flows that must be managed separately

2. For a discussion of the concept of zaitech, see Kumiko Yokoi and Philip N Hubbard, "Zaitech: The Japanese Perspective on Financial Engineering" (1988) (Spring) 2 *Journal of International Securities Markets* 67-72; Satyajit Das, "Key Trends In Treasury Management" (1992) (April) *Corporate Finance* (Euromoney Publications) 40-43; Satyajit Das, "Key Trends In Treasury Management" (1992) (May) *Corporate Finance* (Euromoney Publications) 33-39.

or in conjunction with the corporation's underlying asset or liability portfolio. The major impetus for this change in approach to swap portfolio management was the changing nature of new issue arbitrage and asset liability management applications to which swap transactions were being put.

For example, as new issue arbitrage transactions increased in complexity, each transaction increasingly embodied a variety of option and/or other derivative products with specific value characteristics. Moreover, the value characteristics of these components evolve specifically in response to movements in financial market rates. The fact that each of these elements had value which could change depending upon the particular direction and quantum of movements in interest and/or exchange rates creating specific profit opportunities or potential opportunity gains or losses forced corporations to view these swap transactions on an individual basis, requiring separate and active management.

Similarly, the increased trend towards active asset liability management, as described above, forced organisations to focus on their swap portfolios as potential sources of value. The increasingly complex dictates of asset liability management necessitated the use of a wide variety of swap derivatives. The increasing complexity of the underlying instruments and the various component elements generated value creation opportunities (as with new issue arbitrage transactions as discussed above) which could not be ignored.

Additional impetus to this "new" approach to swap portfolio management came from a number of additional factors:

- Growth in the number of transactions undertaken by large corporations meant that these entities had swap and derivatives portfolios totalling hundreds of millions and, in a few cases, billions of dollars.
- Increased liquidity of the swap and derivatives market and the availability of market makers capable of structuring swaps transactions on customised cash flow requirements allowed new and more flexible transaction structures to be generated.

SWAP/DERIVATIVE PORTFOLIOS—THE ANALYTICAL FRAMEWORK

There are two fundamental issues in developing a framework for the management of corporate or end user swap portfolios:

- development of an analytical framework within which the swap/swap derivative portfolio is considered, in particular, its relationship to the underlying liability portfolio;
- theoretical/pricing techniques utilised to assess the value of these transactions and to examine restructuring opportunities.

Alternative analytical frameworks

There are two potential approaches to corporate swap portfolio management:

- *The integrated portfolio approach*

The swap/derivatives portfolio is regarded as an integral part *of the liability portfolio*; that is, the underlying debt in conjunction with the swaps equate to *a synthetic debt portfolio*. Under this approach, portfolio management focus is on *the end cash flows* to be managed. The separate debt and swap cash flows are ignored except insofar as they constitute the unified synthetic debt portfolio.

- *The separate portfolio approach*

  The underlying debt and swap/derivatives portfolios are treated as *two separate portfolios*. Each set of transactions is then assumed to have:

  —Different cash flow characteristics.

  —Different value characteristics which are moreover totally time specific. The transient values (for example, gains or losses, including opportunity gains or losses) are a function of movements in interest and exchange rates. These values are capable of being captured or released *by specific action being taken in respect of the debt and/or swap/derivatives portfolios.*

Exhibit 21.1 sets out a schematic overview of the two potential approaches.

The exhibit highlights a number of key differences between the two approaches:

- The impact of changes in interest and exchange rates is different under the two approaches. Under the integrated portfolio approach, the changes in value of the synthetic liability portfolio and its relationship to changes in the value of the asset portfolio are the primary focus. In the separate portfolio approach, the changes in value of three portfolios—the asset, the debt, and swap portfolio—and their interrelationships are the primary focus.
- Under the separate portfolio approach, it is probable that for a given movement in interest or exchange rates the value of the debt and swap portfolios will change *in opposite directions*. This is because, by definition, the cash flows in the swap will be designed *to offset* the debt cash flow to effect a transformation of the interest rate basis and/or currency denomination.
- Under the separate portfolio approach, the *quantum* of the change in the value of the debt and swap portfolios will often vary. This is because different factors will invariably impact upon the respective markets at a given point in time.[3]
- Under the separate portfolio approach, the relationship between the asset portfolio and the various components of the liability portfolio are more complex. This relationship is capable of being affected by external action taken to alter: (1) the debt portfolio; (2) the swap portfolio; or, (3) the synthetic debt portfolio.
- In the case of the integrated portfolio approach, the risk dimensions of the relationship between the asset and the "total" liability portfolios is clearly defined.
- In the case of the separate portfolio approach, the risk interrelationships between the asset and the "total" liability portfolios is extremely complex. Any change in the debt, swap or synthetic debt portfolios will alter the total risk profile and also its evolution path over time in response to changes in interest and exchange rates.

The two approaches to corporate swap portfolio management are environment or organisation specific.

The integrated portfolio approach is more suitable for *passive* asset liability portfolio management. Under this approach, the organisation practices a high degree of asset liability matching in terms of interest and exchange rate sensitivity. The liability portfolio is then created either through direct debt issuance or debt

3. This represents a temporary or permanent disequilibrium condition arising from a failure of market efficiency. This market inefficiency may result from a number of factors including: restrictions on free capital flows; institutional deficiencies in market structure; the presence of taxes; the imperfect flow of information; and/or short-term market frictions, such as supply-demand imbalances.

issuance combined with swap transactions to generate a preferred liability profile. The ultimate synthetic liability profile is then managed in response to changes in the characteristics of the asset portfolio it supports.

The separate portfolio approach is more suitable for *active* asset liability management. This type of asset liability manager will specifically manage its portfolio on a risk-reward trade-off basis. The liability portfolio constructed will match the corresponding asset portfolio but will explicitly take into account interest rate and/or exchange rate expectations. The active risk manager will then manage the underlying debt and swap portfolios separately, seeking to optimise the value *of both* sets of cash flows within its evolving interest rate and exchange rate expectations to preserve and maximise the value of *each* portfolio.

The objective of maximising the value of the debt and swap portfolios *independently* often will necessitate the deliberate creation of exposures relative to the asset portfolio being funded. For example, the closing out of an interest rate swap in order to lock in an unrealised gain may increase the overall risk of the asset liability portfolio. This is because unless rates move in the anticipated manner allowing the swap to be re-established at rates equivalent to or better than the closeout levels the overall portfolio will have an increased level of interest rate risk.

The separate portfolio management approach is significantly different from the integrated portfolio management methodology:

- it is inherently a higher risk approach, trading off an increased risk profile for higher earnings possibilities;
- it more truly realises the potential of swaps and derivative products, as it allows the maximum benefit to be derived from the de-coupling of liquidity from currency and interest rate selection.

This chapter focuses primarily on the separate portfolio management approach.

Exhibit 21.1

Corporate Liability Portfolio Management Analytical Frameworks

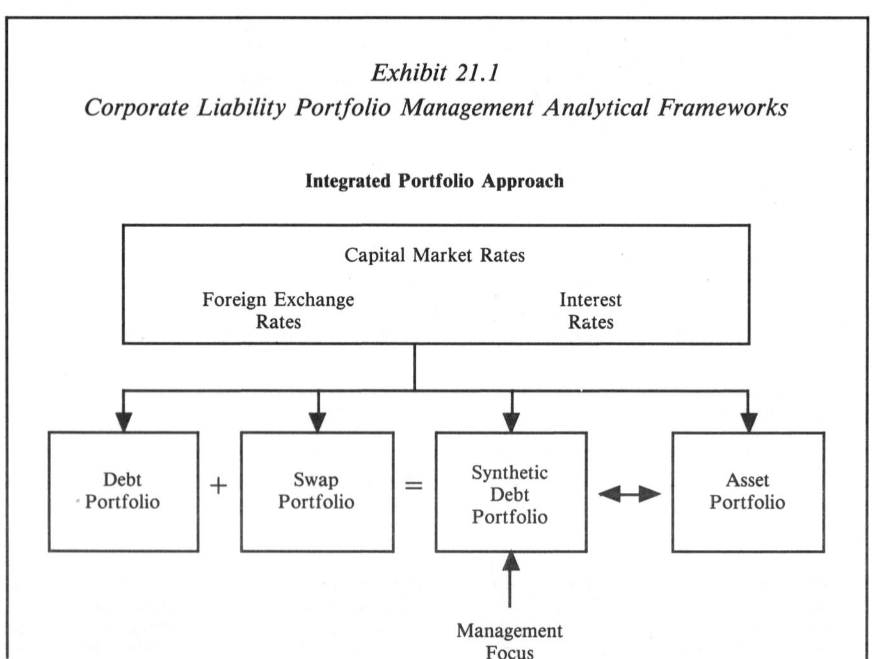

Exhibit 21.1—continued

Separate Portfolio Approach

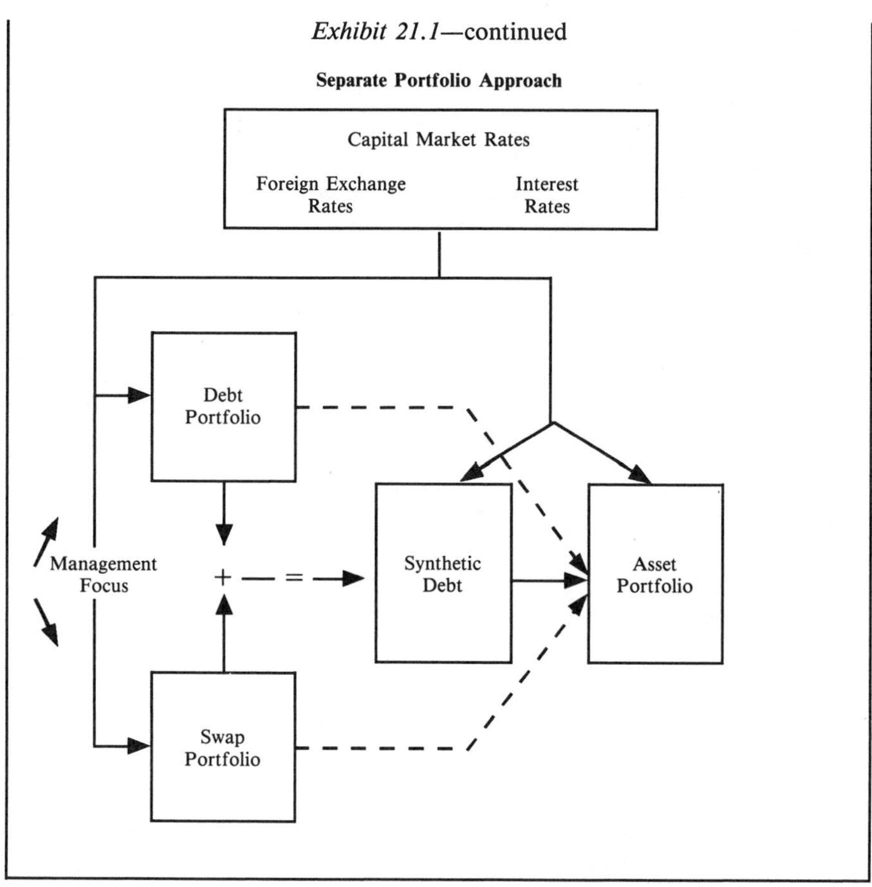

Management of swap/derivative portfolios—the separate portfolio approach

The separate portfolio approach to management of corporate swap portfolios is characterised by the following features:

- Separation of:
  - —debt portfolio (which provides the base funding/liquidity) *from*
  - —swap/derivatives portfolio (which is used to structure the portfolio's currency and interest rate basis).
- The debt and swap/derivative portfolio are valued and managed separately to maximise the value of the two portfolios as *independent* sets of transactions.

Under this approach, the management objectives applied to the two portfolios are different.

Management of the debt portfolio is predicated upon the following principles:

- The debt portfolio, ideally, is on a floating rate basis in one or more currencies of choice of the borrower. Typically, this would be in floating rate US$ (priced off LIBOR) and/or in the base currency of the borrower.

- The major objective of debt portfolio management is to provide assured liquidity through:
  —maintenance of an appropriate maturity structure.
  —appropriate diversification of funding sources.
- Minimisation of the after tax borrowing cost of the debt portfolio, requiring minimisation of the credit margin payable on the borrowings and appropriate tax planning.
- Maximisation of portfolio flexibility in terms of repayment/prepayment rights etc.

Management of the swap/derivatives portfolio is guided by a different set of principles:

- The swap transactions are utilised to restructure the currency and interest rate basis of the debt portfolio to achieve the desired currency/interest rate basis to match the characteristics of the assets to be funded.
- The value of the swap portfolio will be sensitive to currency/interest rate movements (its value may change quite differently to that of the underlying debt portfolio for a given change in market rates).[4]
- Ongoing management of the swap portfolio will be dictated by:
  —expectations of interest and current exchange rate movements over the relevant time horizon;
  —the organisation's asset liability interrelationship and in particular, the evolving characteristics of the asset portfolio;
  —the risk/reward attitude of the organisation.

Portfolio management—valuation issues

The separate portfolio approach requires the capacity to construct innovative liability structures by combining various swap derivative products to create desired risk-return configurations. This process, often referred to as "financial engineering" relies on the capacity to decompose the various debt instruments, swaps and derivative products into basic financial instruments whose value and pricing characteristics are well understood.

The separate portfolio approach requires the independent valuation of:

- the debt instruments;
- the swaps/derivatives.

The valuation of debt instruments is relatively straight forward and utilises conventional present value and internal rate of return concepts as embodied in standard bond pricing techniques. Gains and losses are measured as the present value of the differential between the original issuance rate and current market rates.

The valuation of debt instruments for the purposes of portfolio management require two additional factors to be taken into consideration:

- Currency gains and losses resulting from changes in currency parities between the reporting (or home) currency of the borrower and the currency denomination of the debt. In addition, there may be cross rate currency gains and losses resulting

4. Analytically, the delta and gamma of the debt portfolio with respect to interest rate and currency movements is different to the delta and gamma of the swap portfolio reflecting inherent structural differences between the instruments, in particular their cash flow characteristics.

from the movements in the values of the asset and liability portfolios relative to each other and to the borrowers reporting currency.

- Changes in the value of derivative elements embedded in the structure of the debt instrument. This may take the form of option components such as the right to prepay or call the debt (an implicit call option on the underlying debt granted by the investor to the borrower) or other specifically tailored elements of the transaction.

Swap/derivative instruments can typically be decomposed into and priced as:

- forward contracts;
- option contracts;
- combinations of forward and option contracts (refer Chapters 2 and 6).

This basic ability to dismember swap transactions into the basic constituent forward and option contracts is the basis for valuation and structuring of more complex asset liability applications of these types of transactions.

As is evident from the examples set out in the next section, these structural relationships allow the specific elements of individual transactions to be separated and revalued. Values contained in particular segments of the transaction can be released by reconfiguring the transaction to create new instruments. This process (often described as the "additivity aspect of swap transactions") facilitates the trading and hedging of swap transactions for more complex asset liability management applications.

CORPORATE LIABILITY MANAGEMENT UTILISING SWAPS—EXAMPLES

In this section, a number of examples of corporate liability portfolio management utilising swaps and swap derivatives are discussed. The examples illustrate the theoretical principles outlined in detail above. The examples discussed cover both new issue arbitrage and asset liability applications of swaps.

Example 1—balance sheet management

Initial position

Company B (a United States based corporation) has acquired a German company for a total consideration of DEM200m.

The acquisition is financed as follows:

1. Company B undertakes a ten year SFR bond issue in the Swiss capital market.
2. Company B enters into a ten year currency swap under which it receives fixed rate SFR (matching the SFR outflows under the bond issue) and, in exchange, make DEM payments.

The combination of the two transactions generates attractive DEM funding for Company B to finance its acquisition. The details of the transaction are set out in *Exhibit 21.2*.

The funding structure adopted by Company B reflects a number of important considerations:

Exhibit 21.2
Example 1—Detailed Structure

1. **Assumptions**

Currency rates

US$1 = DEM1.8000
US$1 = SFR1.5000
DEM1 = SFR0.8333

Interest rates

10 year DEM swap rate = 8.80% pa
10 year SFR swap rate = 8.00% pa

Company B's borrowing costs for a ten year maturity are as follows

DEM = 9.00% pa
SFR = 8.00% pa

2. **Transaction Structure**

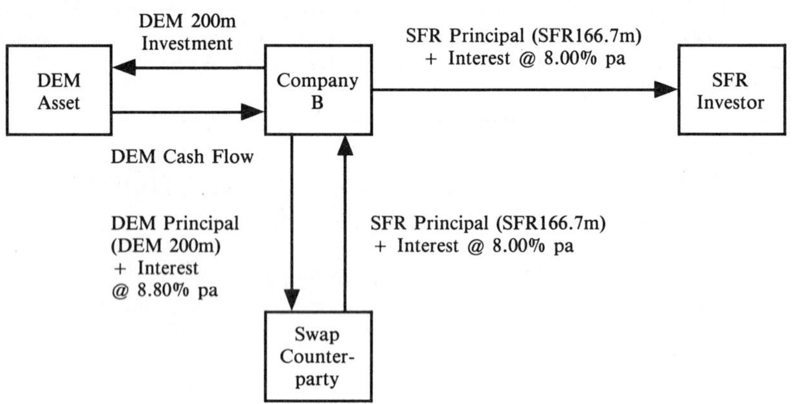

3. **Funding Economics**

The total funding structure economics are as follows:

	SFR (% pa)	DEM (% pa)
1. *Bond issue*		
Payment to SFR lenders	(8.00)	
2. *Currency swap*		
SFR receipts	8.00	
DEM payments		(8.80)
	+0.00	(8.80)

*Figures in ( ) represent payments.

The net DEM borrowing cost is (approx) 8.80% pa.

The funding cost raising to Company B is 0.20% pa (calculated as DEM borrowing costs of 9.00% pa less the DEM borrowing cost generated by the swap of 8.80% pa).

Exhibit 21.2—continued

4. Currency Exposure—Initial Position

The translation exposure position for Company B is summarised in the table below:

Item	Foreign Currency Amount (million)	Exchange Rate (US$ 1 =)	US$ Equivalent (US$m)
Assets			
DEM Investment	DEM 200.0	DEM1.80	111.1
Liabilities			
SFR Borrowing	SFR(166.70)	SFR1.50	(111.1)
DEM/SFR Swap			
—DEM Payments	DEM(200.0)	DEM1.80	(111.1)
—SFR Receipts	SFR 166.7	SFR1.50	111.1
Net			0

- *Currency exposure*

  The use of a synthetic DEM liability to match fund the DEM asset minimises any currency exposure. Company B operates an active approach to currency exposure management policies which allow the company to "match" or "proxy hedge" by funding assets within a particular currency block with other currencies within the same currency block.

  In the past, Company B has funded DEM assets with SFR liabilities on the basis of: (1) strong correlation between the two currencies; and (2) lower interest cost in SFR relative to DEM (which provides a "cushion" against adverse movement in the DEM/SFR exchange rate).

  On this occasion, Company B prefers to minimise its exposure by financing in DEM on the basis that the DEM is expected to weaken against the SFR and the interest advantage of borrowing a SFR relative to DEM is minimal.

- *Funding*

  The funding structure reflects the fact that Company B has good access to the Swiss Capital Market, based on a series of successful transactions undertaken over a number of years. In contrast, the company is not well known in the German Capital Market. These factors are reflected in the fact that the transaction structure has allowed B to generate DEM funding at a rate approx 0.20% pa below the funding cost achievable through a direct DEM funding transaction: refer *Exhibit 21.2*.

Current position

Assume that over the next six months, the SFR appreciates against the DEM (from DEM1 = SFR0.833 *to* DEM1 = SFR0.7692). During this period the DEM and SFR interest rates remain unchanged.

Company B's position is set out in *Exhibit 21.3* at the new exchange rates. Its position can be summarised as follows:

- The *net* position remains unchanged, although the specific components of its asset/liability position have changed significantly.

- The DEM investment has appreciated by approximately US$7.2m (reflecting the weaker US$ against the European currencies). However, this gain in the asset is offset by an equivalent but opposite change in the value of its DEM liabilities.
- The specific components within the liability portfolio have, predictably, moved in equal but opposite directions.
- The SFR borrowing shows an unrealised loss equivalent to US$17.1m. This unrealised loss on the SFR borrowings is offset by a gain on the DEM/SFR swap equivalent to the US$9.9m (SFR12.9m).
- The net change in the liability position (the SFR borrowing combined with the DEM/SFR currency swap) shows a net unrealised loss of US$7.2m which exactly matches the gain on Company B's DEM asset.

Exhibit 21.3

Example 1—Impact of Currency Fluctuations

Currency Rates

US$1 = DEM1.6905
US$1 = SFR1.3000
DEM1 = SFR0.7692

Interest Rates

As before.

Currency Exposure—Current Position

The translation exposure position for Company B at the current market rates is summarised in the Table below:

Item	Foreign Currency Amount (million)	Exchange Rate (US$1 =)	US$ Equivalent (US$m)
Assets			
DEM Investment	DEM200.0	DEM1.6905	118.3
Liabilities			
SFR Borrowing	SFR(166.70)	SFR1.3000	(128.2)
DEM/SFR Swap			
—DEM Payments	DEM(200.0)	DEM1.6905	(118.3)
—SFR Receipts	SFR166.7	SFR1.3000	128.2
Net			0

Portfolio management alternatives

Company B can, if it chooses, *realise* the gain on the currency swap or alternatively, protect this gain from being eroded by utilisation of one of a number of methods including:

- cancelling the swap;
- purchasing SFR put/DEM call option;
- selling a SFR call/DEM put option.

Some of these above techniques can be combined, for example, by writing a swaption whereby Company B agrees to receive fixed rate SFR and pay fixed rate

DEM with the exchange rate being agreed to as being the current prevailing SFR/DEM spot rate.

Each of these methods are analysed in detail below.

Swap cancellation

Under this alternative, Company B would enter into the following transactions:

- cancellation of the existing DEM/SFR currency swap;
- maintenance of the SFR borrowing, which provides the underlying liquidity to fund the DEM investment.

Cancellation of the currency swap would result in Company B realising a gain of US$9.9m (SFR12.9m). This realised gain and the resulting cash asset would offset the *net* unrealised loss of the same amount in the books of Company B on its DEM investments and the SFR liabilities funding the investment. The balance sheet position of Company B is summarised in *Exhibit 21.4*.

Exhibit 21.4

Example 1—Impact of Swap Cancellation

Following cancellation of the DEM/SFR currency swap, the translation exposure position for Company B is summarised in the table below:

Item	Foreign Currency Amount (million)	Exchange Rate (US$ 1 =)	US$ Equivalent (US$m)
Assets			
DEM Investment	DEM200.0	1.6905	118.3
Gain from Swap Cancellation	US$9.9		9.9
			128.2
Liabilities			
SFR Borrowing	SFR(166.7)	1.3000	(128.2)
Net			0

Purchase SFR put/DEM call option

A currency swap transaction can be decomposed into its currency option components. In this case, the position under the DEM/SFR currency swap equates to Company B currency purchasing a SFR call/DEM put option and granting a SFR put/DEM call (both with a strike price of DEM1 = SFR0.8333).

Company B can protect the unrealised gain under the currency swap by purchasing a SFR put/DEM call option with the strike price as equal to the current spot exchange rate DEM1 = SFR0.7692.

The purchased SFR put/DEM call option protects Company B's unrealised gain in the currency swap as follows:

- If the SFR continues to appreciate against the DEM, the option would expire unexercised, thereby allowing it to enjoy the continuing appreciation in the value of the swap corresponding to the increase in the value of the SFR against the DEM.

- If the SFR weakens against the DEM, then Company B can exercise its option to preserve a portion of its previously unrealised gain on the swap.

Company B can either purchase the option until the maturity of the swap (that is, 9.5 years) or, alternatively, purchase short term insurance via the purchase of a SFR put/DEM call option for a period shorter than the final maturity of the swap.

Exhibit 21.5 sets out a detailed analysis of this strategy.

Sell SFR call/DEM put option

Utilising the same decomposition analysis outlined above, as an alternative to the purchase of a SFR put/DEM call option, Company B could securitise the purchased SFR call/DEM put component of the original currency swap by granting a SFR call/DEM put with the strike equivalent to the DEM/SFR exchange rate at the time these transactions were initiated (DEM1 = SFR0.8333). Company B receives a premium for writing a deeply in-the-money option.

This strategy has the following impact:

- The premium received (together with interest earnings on the premium) has the effect of:
  —reducing the cost of the DEM funding generated by Company B.
  —providing a cushion against adverse currency movements (that is, further appreciation of the SFR against the DEM).
- If the SFR continues to appreciate against the DEM, then the SFR call/DEM put option will be exercised against Company B. This would effectively close out the foreign exchange component of the currency swap. In fact, Company B could, where the option is exercised, simultaneously cancel the currency swap.
- If the SFR weakened against the DEM, then the option would not be exercised. Under these circumstances Company B would be entitled to retain the premium, although the unrealised gain under the swap would be diminished.

Exhibit 21.5

Example 1—Hedging Swap Currency Gain via Purchase of SFR Put/DEM Call

By purchasing a SFR put/DEM call, Company B is ensuring it will at least realise the current foreign exchange gain in its existing SFR/DEM currency swap. If the SFR should depreciate against the DEM, then Company B is able to exercise the option and the gain realised will go toward offsetting the opportunity loss in the swap. Whereas, if the SFR should continue to appreciate, then the option is left to expire unexercised while the currency gain within the swap increases. The option premium represents the cost of this insurance and has considerable influence on the economics of the transaction.

Company B could purchase a SFR put/DEM call for the remaining term of the swap (9.5 years) or it could purchase insurance from short-term fluctuations (say a six month term). The current market prices for these options are as follows:

Type	*Term*	Strike (*1DEM* =)	Premium (% *of face value*)	(*DEMm*)
Buy SFR put/DEM call	6 months	SFR0.7692	1.6%	3.2
Buy SFR put/DEM call	9.5 years	SFR0.7692	9.0%	18.0

Exhibit 21.5—continued

By purchasing the option a substantial portion of the current FX gain within the swap is given away. In fact the premium for the 9.5 year option exceeds the value of the current gain. However, the options provide different terms of insurance and in fact if the premium is expressed as an increase in borrowing cost over the term of the transaction, then it will have the following result:

Effective DEM Borrowing Cost (before currency effect)

Term	*DEM Funding Cost* (*% pa*)	*DEM Funding Cost With Premium* (*% pa*)
6 months	8.8	9.01
9.5 years	8.8	10.21

The increase in DEM borrowing cost reflects the cash outflow of the option purchased. The increase in the overall borrowing cost is lower where the maturity of the option is short. However, this lower total borrowing cost is at the cost of a shorter period of protection against a decline in the SFR relative to the DEM. Such a decline, without the protection of the option, would result in an erosion in the unrealised value within the original currency swap.

The combined impact of the underlying borrowing, currency swap and currency option is demonstrated in the table below. This calculates the profit and loss impact of purchasing the option 9.5 year over a range of exchange rates at the maturity of the SFR put/DEM option:

Payoff Table (Currency Gain and Loss)
*US$m**

Exchange Rate at Option Maturity (1 DEM =)	SFR Borrowing	Swap	Option	Combined Total
SFR0.6667	(27.7)	27.7	(10)	(10)
SFR0.7143	(18.5)	18.5	(10)	(10)
SFR0.7692	(9.3)	9.3	(10)	(10)
SFR0.8333	0	0	(0.7)	(0.7)
SFR0.9091	9.3	(9.3)	8.6	8.6
SFR1.000	18.5	(18.5)	17.8	17.8

* Assumed exchange rate US$1 = DEM1.8

This payoff table demonstrates the three possible outcomes of this strategy:

- If the SFR continues to appreciate against the DEM, then the swap continues to offset the loss on the SFR borrowing hedging the DEM asset. However, as the option expires unexercised the premium represents a cost.
- If the SFR depreciates against the DEM, then the loss on the SFR liability is reduced and the swap gain is reduced while the option value increases.
- If the SFR remains steady, then the only impact is the loss of income due to premium paid.

As in the case of the SFR put/DEM call option, the option could be sold for a maturity coinciding with the maturity of the swap (9.5 years) or for a shorter maturity.

Exhibit 21.6 analyses the detailed economics of this alternative.

Portfolio management alternatives—comparison

Each of the alternative methods of *crystallising* the unrealised gain in the currency swap is predicated on the willingness of Company B to accept a currency exposure. This exposure entails the funding of a DEM asset *with a SFR liability*.

Exhibit 21.6

Example 1—Hedging Swap Currency Swap with Sale of SFR Call/DEM Put

In this case, Company B is willing to give up any further currency gains in the swap for the receipt of an upfront premium. If the SFR continues to appreciate until maturity of the option, then the option will be exercised against Company B. If the exchange rate remains stable or the SFR depreciates, then the option expires unexercised and Company B earns the premium.

As in the previous scenario, Company B can write short-term options against the underlying borrowing and swap or it can match up to the 9.5 year term of the underlying structure:

Type	*Term*	Strike (1 DEM =)	Premium % *of face value*	*(DEMm)*
SFR call/DEM put	6 months	0.8333	9%	18
SFR call/DEM put	9.5 years	0.8333	19%	38

Both options are substantially "in-the-money" and have a high delta (particularly the six month option).

The premium earned provides some protection against this eventuality and provides a cushion against further SFR appreciation. The extent of this cushion is calculated below and is referred to as the strategy's "break-even":

Term	SFR Appreciation Break-even (1DEM)
6 months	0.7645
9.5 years	0.6874

Further, if the exchange rate should remain steady then the premium provides a substantial reduction in DEM interest cost:

Term	DEM Borrowing Cost (% pa)	Effective DEM Borrowing Cost/ Including Premium (% pa)	Interest Saving (% pa)
6 months	8.80	8.10	0.70
9.5 years	8.80	7.32	1.38

The payoff of this strategy if 9.5 year options are granted are demonstrated in the table below:

Payoff Table—FX Gain and Loss

(US$m)*

Exchange Rate at Option Maturing (1DEM =)	SFR Borrowing	Swap	Option	Combined Total
0.6667	(27.7)	27.7	(6.7)	(6.7)
0.7143	(18.5)	18.5	2.6	2.6
0.7692	(9.3)	9.3	11.9	11.9
0.8333	0	0	21.1	21.1
0.9091	9.3	(9.3)		
1.000	18.5	(18.5)	21.1	21.1

* Assume 1US$ = 1.8DEM

As opposed to the bought option strategy, the preferred outcome is that the SFR/DEM exchange rate remain steady or decline.

Company B may be willing to acccept this exposure (as discussed above) for the following reasons:

- the belief that the SFR provides a sound long-term hedge for its DEM assets, that is, there is a strong correlation between the two currency units;
- the willingness to accept the risk of fluctuations in the DEM/SFR exchange rate on the basis of the lower interest cost in SFR which provides a "cushion" against adverse movements in the DEM/SFR exchange rate.

While each of the strategies discussed is predicated on this willingness to accept a DEM/SFR currency mismatch, the individual alternatives have different risk profiles. The optimal strategy is contingent upon Company B's expectation of future movements in the DEM/SFR exchange rate over the remaining life of the transaction.

Exhibit 21.7 sets out a comparison of the economic impact of the three alternatives discussed above.[5]

Exhibit 21.7

Payoff Diagram of Reversal Strategy

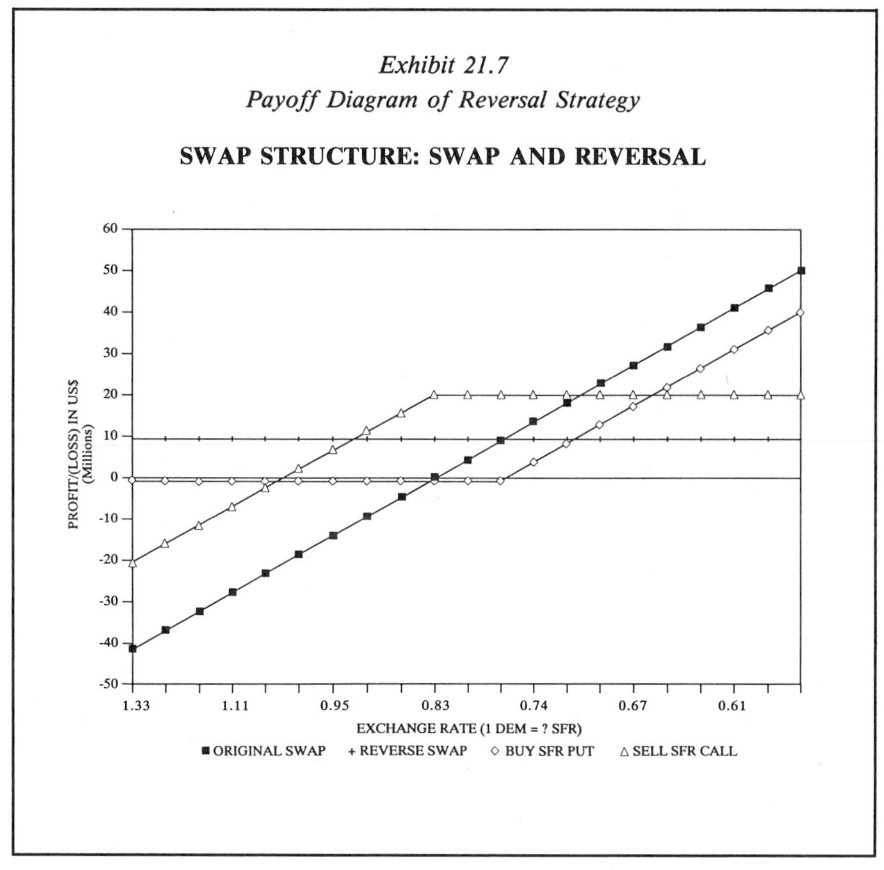

5. For a similar case study involving DEM and PTAs see Satyajit Das and John Martin (June 1991); the alternative case illustrates the impact of differing yield curves and interest rate differentials on the portfolio management alternatives.

In summary, the analysis indicates the following:

- *Swap cancellation*

  The swap cancellation is the optimal strategy if the SFR depreciates against the DEM over the remaining life of the transaction. If the swap is cancelled and, contrary to expectations, the SFR continues to appreciate against the DEM, Company B will be exposed to foreign exchange losses under the SFR borrowings which are not offset by corresponding gains under the currency swap. This will result in a net total unrealised loss to the company as the increase in value of its DEM investment is more than offset by unrealised losses on its SFR borrowings.

- *Purchase of a SFR put/DEM call option*

  The purchase of the option is the preferred strategy where the SFR is expected to continue appreciating against the DEM but protection is sought against a sudden and unexpected reversal in this appreciation. This strategy is the most risk-averse of the alternatives. It locks in a gain at maturity of the currency swap but as the swap is not cancelled, Company B is not exposed to potential currency losses on the mismatch on its DEM investment and the supporting SFR borrowing.

- *Sale of a SFR call/DEM put option*

  The option granting strategy is the preferred alternative if the SFR/DEM exchange rate remains relatively constant and oscillates within a tight band around its current level (DEM1 = SFR0.7692). However, if the SFR continues to appreciate, then the option would be exercised forcing Company B to terminate the currency swap and open a currency exposure. In contrast, if the SFR depreciates against the DEM from its current levels, then although Company B retains the premium received for the granting of the option, but it suffers a loss as the value of the currency swap deteriorates over time, potentially eliminating all the present unrealised gain.

Example 2—floating rate liability management

Initial position

Company A has an existing US$ interest rate swap for a notional principal amount of US$100M within its portfolio. Under this swap, Company A pays 9% pa semi-annually and receives six months LIBOR. The swap has a maturity of five years and was entered into to convert part of its floating rate borrowings into a fixed rate liability.

At the time of entry into this swap, the interest rate structure for US$ was as follows:

six month LIBOR: 8.00% pa.

five year swap rate: 9.0% pa (semi-annually).

Current position

Over the next six months, US$ interest rates rise rapidly across the maturity spectrum to the following levels:

six month LIBOR: 13.0% pa.

4.5 year swap rate: 11.00% pa (semi-annually)

As a result of the increase in interest rates, existing swap position is currently showing an unrealised gain. This gain (in present value terms) is approximately US$7.0m.[6]

Portfolio management alternatives

Company A may choose to manage its swap position to preserve its *unrealised* gain, utilising some of the following strategies:

- cancellation of the swap;
- purchase or sale of caps/floors.

Swap cancellation

Company A could choose to reverse or cancel any existing swap. This reversal would generate up-front gain equivalent to US$7.0m (or 7.0% of the principal value of the transaction), which is equivalent to 2.00% pa over the remaining 4.5 years of the transaction.

However, reversal of the swap has the following impact on Company A's position:

- Company A's interest cost rises immediately to the level of current six month LIBOR 13.0% pa (an increase of 4.0% pa from its existing fixed level of 9.0% pa). The up-front gain (together with interest earnings thereon), provides a degree of protection against the immediate rise in interest cost. The up-front gain provides "cushion" equivalent to 2.00% pa over the remaining life of the transaction.
- Company A, as a result of unwinding its swap, has no protection against interest rate increases above current market levels or an inversion of the yield curve. However, it benefits where six month LIBOR averages lower than 11% pa over the next 4.5 years.

Cap/floor strategies

These strategies are based on Company A's swap transaction being bundled into a series of option transactions.

Paying fixed rates and receiving floating rates under an interest rate swap can be characterised as buying a cap and simultaneously selling a floor with a strike price equivalent to the fixed rate under the swap, that is 9% pa.

Using this theoretical construct, Company A can manage its existing position by entering into a series of option transactions; for example, writing caps, buying floors or writing caps and buying floors (selling collars) or, alternatively, purchasing or granting options on the fixed rate portion of the swap.

These strategies revolve around a contingent nature of options. They allow the benefit of the original swap to be maintained while protection against unfavourable movements can be purchased or additional income generated through the sale of options.

6. The gain on the swap results from the fact that Company A can enter into a swap whereby it receives 11.0% pa (the current swap rate) thereby locking in a margin of 2.0% relative to the existing swap where it pays 9.0% pa the floating rate (six month LIBOR) legs under the swap would offset. Typically, the original swap would be cancelled or "bought out" with the counterparty making a payment to Company A representing the present valued equivalent of the margin of 2.00% pa.

Purchasing options

Company A could implement the following strategies:

- Purchase a swaption whereby Company A can elect to receive fixed rate (at 11% pa) against payment of six month LIBOR. The swaption purchased by Company A has an expiration date in six months time. The swaption purchased affords Company A protection from a decline in swap rates over the six month period. If swap rates decline, then the value of the swaption increases offsetting the loss of value in the underlying swap position.
- Purchase floors whereby Company A would benefit if six month LIBOR declined below the strike level (say 11% pa) over the term of the floor. Utilising this strategy, Company A, in return for the payment of an up-front premium, repurchases the sold floor or call option component of the swap. The purchase allows Company A to switch back to floating rate funding if six month LIBOR falls below the strike yield level.

Assume the current market rates are as follows:

Swaption

Type:	Purchase of option on swap (swaption) to receive the four year fixed rate and pay floating rate under an interest rate.
Strike rate:	11% pa (semi-annually).
Floating rate index:	six month LIBOR.
Option expiry:	six months.
Premium:	0.87% (flat).

Interest Rate Floor

Type:	Interest rate floor agreement (call options).
Floating rate index:	six month LIBOR.
Strike level:	11% pa.
Term:	4.5 years.
Settlement:	six monthly in arrears against spot six month LIBOR.
Premium:	2.00% (flat).

The swaption allows Company A to reverse its swap in six months time *if swap rates decline*. Exercise of the swaption will reverse the original swap for an upfront gain of US$5.5m. This up-front gain is lower than an immediate cancellation of the swap because the present value of interest flows has declined with the elapse of six months and a premium of US$0.87m was paid for the swaption. For this strategy to be the preferred alternative the decline in swap rates has to occur during the term of the swaption.

The floor also hedges Company A from an interest rate decline. However, the payoff profile differs to that under the swaption. Under the floor, Company A receives a net payment should six month LIBOR fall below 11% pa over the remaining term of the swap (4.5 years). Under this arrangement, Company A continues to pay fixed rates under the swap and maintain its protection against interest rate increases. The cost of the floor has the effect of increasing the effective swap rate by 0.58% pa (the amortised premium) to 9.58% pa.

The use of floors and swaptions to manage the existing swap position entails an element of *yield curve risk*.

It is possible that swap rates decline back to 9.0% pa while LIBOR does not fall below 12% (the strike level of the floor). In this case, the swap gain is extinguished but is not offset by a gain on the floor transaction. On the other hand, while a swap reversal through the exercise of the swaption exposes Company A to any future increase in interest rates, the combination of the swap and floor affords protection from any upward move in interest rates but allows it to benefit from any fall in short-term rates.

In essence, the combined position is a type of "cross-yield-curve" cap. Put-call parity suggests that a bought call (the floor) and a "short" underlying position (the swap) give us a bought put (an interest rate cap). It is a "cross-yield-curve" cap because A is protected from an upward movement in both swap rates and LIBOR while it only benefits when rates fall if LIBOR declines.

The effectiveness of realising the gain in this manner depends on the shape of the yield curve. The maximum gain is achieved if short-term rates fall further than swap rates (that is, the yield curve moves to a positive shape). A lesser gain is realised on the swap reversal if swap rates decline more than LIBOR (that is, the yield curve becomes more inverted).

Another interesting aspect to the strategy entailing a floor is that it could be purchased over a shorter period, say one year, effectively purchasing back the call option component of the original swap for only a portion of the remaining term.

Selling options

Instead of purchasing options to manage its existing swap position, Company B can sell options (interest rate caps or swaptions) to manage its existing swap portfolio. The sale of options has a radically different risk profile as they leave Company A exposed to any upward movement in interest rates and provide a small benefit from a fall in rates.

The impact of selling options on the six month LIBOR and fixed rate element of the swap is set out below.

Assume the following market rates:

Swaption

Type:	Sale of option on swap (swaption) to receive the four year fixed rate and pay floating rate under an interest rate.
Strike rate:	11% pa (semi-annually).
Floating rate index:	six month LIBOR.
Option expiry:	six months.
Premium:	0.60% (flat).

Interest Rate Cap

Type:	Interest rate cap agreement (put options).
Floating rate index:	six month LIBOR.
Strike level:	11% pa.
Term:	4.5 years.
Settlement:	six monthly in arrears against spot six month LIBOR.
Premium:	1.5% (flat).

The sale of the swaption has the following impact:

- Company B receives the premium equivalent to 0.60% which is equivalent to 0.17% pa and subsidises Company A's borrowing costs.
- If swap rates continue to increase, then the swaption will be exercised. Exercise of the swaption will result in cancellation of the swap realising a gain of US$6.3m to Company A (US$ 6.9m inclusive of the swaption premium). However, there is an opportunity loss as Company A could have closed down the swap at effecively a higher gain. In addition, upon cancellation of the swap, Company A has no further protection from increases in interest rates as it has effectively reverted to a floating rate borrowing.
- If swap rates decline, then the swaption will not be exercised. However, the fall in swap rates will result in an erosion of value in the existing swap position which will only be partially offset by the premium received.

The securitisation of the fixed rate component of the swap through the sale of the cap has the following impact:

- Company A receives the premium equivalent to 1.5% of the contract value at the commencement of the transaction. This is equivalent to an annualised amount of 0.43% pa which has the effect of subsidising Company A's borrowing costs.
- If six month LIBOR rates fall, then the cap is not exercised. The premium received lowers the effective fixed rate under the swap but there is, however, an opportunity lost to Company A if rates average less than 8.57% pa for the remainder of the life of the swap transaction (that is, 4.5 years).
- If rates increase above the strike level, 11% pa, then the cap is exercised and Company A is required to make payments to the cap purchaser that effectively transforms its borrowing into a floating rate liability at a rate equivalent to six months LIBOR less 0.43% pa (the amortised premium). Consequently, Company A has no protection against increases in six month LIBOR rates if LIBOR rates average greater than 11.43% pa for the next 4.5 years.

The sale of option strategies seeks to exploit the potential for further gains within the swap instead of "locking in" the existing gain resulting from market interest rate movements to date.

The sale of these interest rate options effectively prevents Company B from benefiting from any further rises in interest rates. Company A forgoes its protection in return for the receipt of a premium.

In these cases, Company A's maximum benefit is realised if interest rates remain at or about current level for the term of the option as it continues to receive the interest cost saving generated by the original swap and benefit from the premium received from the sale of options.

Portfolio management alternatives—comparisons

The alternatives for managing the interest rate swap portfolio considered above relate to situations where an increase in interest rates creates an unrealised gain in the existing swap portfolio.

Similar management techniques are applicable to where due to a fall in interest rates the existing swap position shows an opportunity loss.[7]

7. See Satyajit Das (1989) (August).

As discussed above in *Example 1* each of the alternatives available to manage an existing swap position implies an inherently different risk/reward profile. The basic management alternatives are all predicated on the following assumptions:

- The willingness/capacity of Company A to convert part of its portfolio from fixed to floating rate. This presumes:
  - —Company A has a sufficiently large portfolio of fixed and floating rate borrowings where a change from fixed to floating of US$100m has no significant strategic impact on the competitive position of the company.
  - —The company's assets and revenue flows are sensitive to and correlated with interest rate movements.
- The willingness to actively manage the fixed/floating mix of the portfolio within pre-established risk-reward parameters to minimise the group's interest costs.

As will be evident from a consideration of the above, the choice between alternatives is complex. *Exhibit 21.8* sets out a comparison of the various strategies outlined under different interest rates scenarios. The selection between alternatives is driven substantially by Company A's expectation of future interest rate movements, including the expected shape of the yield curve.

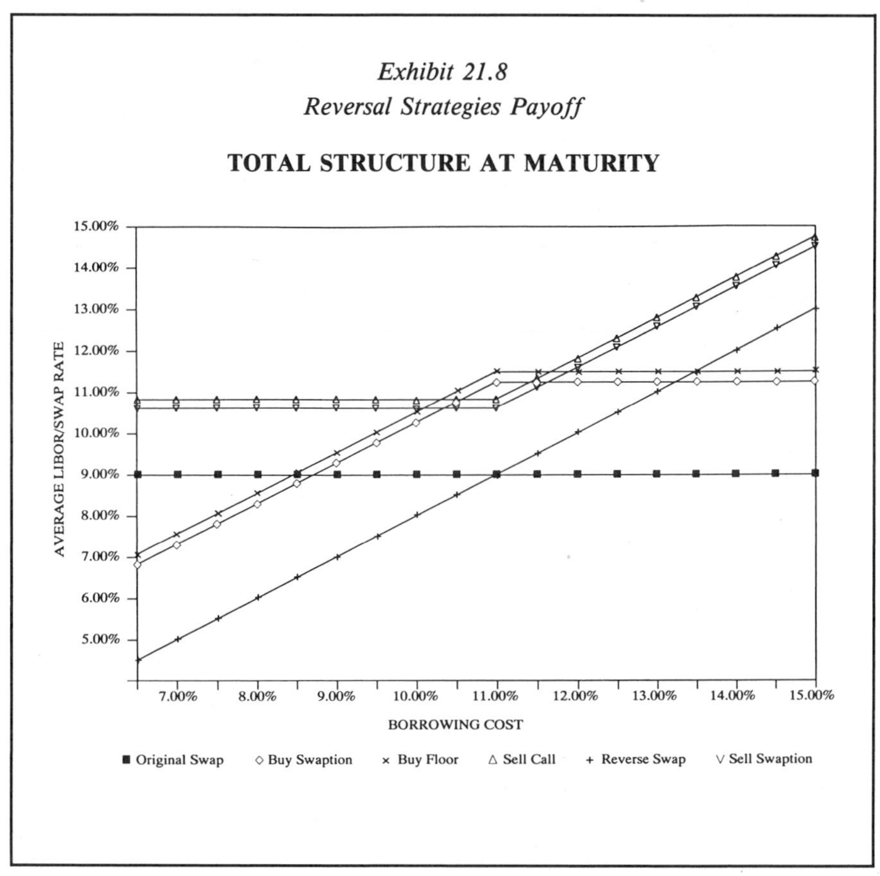

Exhibit 21.8
Reversal Strategies Payoff

In summary, Company A's selection between the alternatives would be influenced by the following factors:

- If interest rates are expected to decline across the yield curve, then the maximum benefit is realised by reversing the existing interest rate swap today.
- If, however, the interest rate decline is expected to take some time, an alternative may be to reverse part of the swap by entering into a forward swap to reverse say the last two or three years of the existing five year swap. This would leave Company A protected for the first two to three years but would convert it into a floating rate borrower for future periods when interest rates are expected to be lower.
- If interest rates are expected to decline but there is considerable uncertainty as to the timing or degree of the decline, then the purchase of the floor or swaption are the preferred alternatives. The selection between the floor and swaption will be dictated by expectations on the anticipated shape of the yield curve of the future.
- If rates are expected to increase, then no action needs to be taken although a floor or swaption may be purchased to protect against a failure of these expectations to be realised.
- If rates are expected to remain relatively static at or around current levels, then the sale of caps/swaptions is the economically superior alternative.

Example 3—floating rate liability management

Initial position

Company C purchases a US$100m interest rate cap to hedge its portfolio of floating rate US$ borrowings. The terms of the cap are as follows:

Type:	Purchase of interest cap (put options) on US$ LIBOR.
Floating rate index:	three month LIBOR.
Strike level:	9% pa.
Option term:	two years (spot start).
Premium:	0.44% (flat).
	The market rate structure at the time of entry into the transaction was as follows:
Three month LIBOR:	8% pa.
Two year swap:	8.5% pa.

The interest rate cap purchased is 0.5% pa out-of-the-money (being 0.5% pa above the two year swap rate or implied forward rate on three month LIBOR).

The purchased interest rate cap provides protection for Company C against interest rate increases above 9.24% pa (implied by the strike rate together with the amortised premium paid). If at each settlement date, three month LIBOR averages over 9.24% pa, then Company C benefits from a cost of funds which is lower than that which would have been applicable in the case when Company C did not purchase its protection. *Exhibit 21.9* summarises the payoff profile of the interest rate cap and contrasts it with that of an interest rate swap for the same maturity.

Exhibit 21.9
Example 3—Interest Rate Cap Payoffs

Average Three Month LIBOR (% pa)	*Gain (Loss) Under* Two Year Interest Rate Swap (% pa)	Two Year Interest Rate Cap (% pa)	*Company C Interest Cost* Two Year Interest Rate Swap (% pa)	Two Year Interest Rate Cap (% pa)
6	(2.5)	(0.24)	8.50	6.24
7	(1.50)	(0.24)	8.50	7.24
8	(0.50)	(0.24)	8.50	8.24
9	0.50	(0.24)	8.50	9.24
10	1.5	0.75	8.50	9.24
11	2.5	1.76	8.50	9.24

Current position

Over the next three months, United States interest rates rise to the following level:

Three month LIBOR: 11% pa.

1.75 year swap: 10% pa.

As a result of the increase in interest rates, the interest rate cap position is currently showing an unrealised gain.

Portfolio management alternatives

Company C can choose to manage its existing interest cap position to preserve its unrealised gain utilising some of the following strategies:

- the purchase or sale of caps/floors;
- entry into interest rate swaps.

The strategies outlined are based on similar interrelationships between interest rate swaps and interest rate caps/floors as those identified in *Example 2*.

Sale of cap

Company C could choose to liquidate its interest rate cap by selling the position.

Under current market conditions, the cap (now for a term of 1.75 years) can be sold for 2.31% pa (flat). This represents a gain of 1.87% or US$1.87m on the transaction.

Where the cap is sold, Company C reverts to a floating rate US$ borrowing. This borrowing is at a cost of three month LIBOR less 1.18% pa. This margin under LIBOR represents the gain on the sale of the cap amortised over the remaining life of the original transaction.

Where the cap is sold, Company C benefits where three month LIBOR averages less than 10.18% pa over the remaining 1.75 years of transaction.

Entry into interest rate swap

As an alternative to selling the cap, Company C could lock in the gain on its cap position by entering into an interest rate swap for a notional principal amount of US$100M whereby it receives fixed rates (at 10.0% pa the current market rate) and pays three month LIBOR.

This transaction has the following impact:

- The swap locks in a gain of 1.0% pa (the difference between the swap rate and the cap rate) on each of the remaining seven quarterly periods. This equates to a present value benefit of 1.59% flat, which adjusted for the premium paid for the cap is equivalent to 1.15%.
- Company C has no protection where interest rates increase from current levels.
- Where interest rates decline, entry into this interest swap has the affect of leveraging the returns to the company. This is because receiving fixed under an interest rate swap is the equivalent of selling a series of interest rate put options and simultaneously purchasing a series of interest rate call options. This transaction, the sold put embedded in the swap is offset by the previously purchased interest rate cap. This leaves Company C with a purchased call option or interest rate floor which increases in value if interest rates decline. The payoffs from this particular strategy are summarised in *Exhibit 21.10.*

The use of the swap to reverse the interest rate cap position is a particularly useful alternative where sale of the interest rate cap cannot be affected at or about its true economic value.

Exhibit 21.10

Example 3—Reversal of Cap Width Interest Rate Swap

Average Three Month LIBOR (% pa)	Interest Rate Cap (% pa)	*Gain (Loss) Under* Interest Rate Swap (% pa)	Total (% pa)	Company C Total Interest Rate Cost (% pa)
7	(0.24)	3.0	2.76	4.24
8	(0.24)	2.0	1.76	5.24
9	(0.24)	1.0	0.76	8.24
10	0.76	0.0	0.76	9.24
11	1.76	(1.0)	0.76	10.24
12	2.76	(2.0)	0.76	11.24

Buy floor

Company C could seek to lock in its gain, without sacrificing protection against further interest rate increases, by purchasing a floor for a term of 1.75 years at a strike price of 10.0% pa for a premium of 0.51% (flat) or 0.32% pa.

Exhibit 21.11 sets out the return from the strategy.

The table indicates that Company C remains protected against further increases in interest rates, albeit at a slightly higher level, but continues to benefit from future falls in interest rates.

Sell floor

Company C could protect its gain under the cap by writing a floor. This written floor combined with the bought put (interest rate cap) equates to an interest rate swap whereby Company C paid fixed rates and received three month LIBOR.

Exhibit 21.11

Example 3—Hedging Cap With Purchased Floor

Average Three Month LIBOR (% pa)	Interest Rate Cap (% pa)	*Gain (Loss) Under* Interest Rate Floor (% pa)	Total (% pa)	Company C Total Interest Rate Cost (% pa)
8	(0.24)	1.68	1.44	6.56
9	(0.24)	0.68	0.44	8.56
10	0.76	(0.32)	0.44	9.56
11	1.76	(0.32)	1.44	9.56
12	2.76	(0.32)	2.44	9.56

Where rates are anticipated to remain steady or increase, then the premium resulting from the sold floor would decrease the cost of borrowing for Company C, partially offsetting the previously incurred cost of purchasing the interest rate cap. *Exhibit 21.12* sets out the payoff of the strategy.

Exhibit 21.12

Example 3—Hedging Cap With Sold Floor

Average Three Month LIBOR (% pa)	Purchased Interest Rate Cap @ 9% (% pa)	*Gain (Loss) Under* Sold Interest Rate Floor @ 9% (% pa)	Total (% pa)	Company C Total Interest Rate Cost (% pa)
7	(0.24)	(1.87)	(2.11)	9.11
8	(0.24)	(0.87)	(1.11)	9.11
9	(0.24)	0.13	(0.11)	9.11
10	0.76	0.13	0.89	9.11
11	1.76	0.13	1.89	9.11
12	2.76	0.13	2.89	9.11

As in the case of *Examples 1* and *2* the management alternatives identified are all predicated on the willingness of Company C to switch between fixed and floating rate borrowings. Each individual strategy, however, has different risk profiles. For example, if interest rates are expected to continue to increase, the purchased or sold floor alternative would be the preferred method of management of this portfolio. However, if interest rates are expected to decline, then the sale of the cap, entry into an interest rate swap where Company C received fixed and paid floating rates or the purchase of the floor would represent the optimal economic mechanism by which the portfolios value would be maximised.

SUMMARY

Increasing attention has focused on the utilisation of swaps and derivatives in the management of asset and liability portfolios. This process, often referred to "financial engineering", has resulted from increased attention, particularly by corporate financial officers on the active management of corporate debt portfolios to minimise the borrowing costs of the entity within specified risk-reward guidelines. The potential to extend these concepts and techniques to the active management of asset portfolios is self evident.

The interrelationships between interest rate swaps and other derivatives and the capacity to compose and decompose synthetic liability and asset structures by complex combinations of these instruments are increasingly being utilised to exploit value creation opportunities within existing portfolios of debt and derivative instruments maintained by large corporations.

Continuing high levels of volatility in financial market rates—both currency and interest rates—together with increased focus on utilising corporate financial management expertise to generate value seems likely to ensure that these developments will continue to increase in importance.

Part 6

Global Swap and Financial Derivative Markets

Chapter 22

Global Swap and Derivative Markets

OVERVIEW

Like most other new financial instruments, swap and derivatives transactions are not executed in a physical market. Participants in the swap and derivatives market vary in terms of location, character and motivations in undertaking swap transactions. However, the total sum of activities of participants in the swap market gives it some of the characteristics of a classical financial market connected to an integrated underlying capital, money and foreign exchange markets.

As swaps are counterparty transactions, any structure or currency is possible for which there is a participant with an offsetting requirement. However, characteristics of most transactions are within the following ranges:

Currencies

- *North American*—United States dollars; Canadian dollars.
- *European*—pounds Sterling, deutschmarks, Dutch guilders, Belgium and Luxembourg francs, French francs, Spanish pesetas, Portugese escudos, Swiss francs, Italian lira, Austrian schillings, Swedish, Norwegian and Danish kroner, Finnish markkaa, and Irish pounds.
- *Asian*—Japanese yen, Hong Kong dollars, Singapore dollars, Thai bhats, Malaysian ringgits, Indonesian rupiahs.
- *Australasian*—Australian dollars, New Zealand dollars.

Maturities

The maturities of transactions available vary significantly between individual swap currencies. In the major swap currencies, maturities of (up to) ten years are readily available. In certain currencies, such as US$ or GBP longer maturities, in isolated cases, of up to 30 years have also been transacted. In the less developed swap markets, maturities tended to be shorter, being in the region of one to three years.

Amounts

Individual transaction sizes vary significantly between currencies. In the major currencies, amounts of (up to) US$100-200m (or its equivalent) can be transacted relatively easily. In the more liquid currencies, transactions of up to US$500m (equivalent) can be executed. In the less common swap currencies, individual transaction sizes are usually lower, being in the range of US$5-25m (or its equivalent).

Product range

The range of swap products available in individual currencies, particularly non-generic variations on standard structures, available in individual currencies varies significantly. The swap and derivatives markets in major reserve currencies are characterised by deep and liquid markets featuring a wide variety of the variations identified in Part 4. In the less common swap currencies, the product range is much more limited. In these currencies, the major instruments available, typically, cover LTFX, FRAs and, as the market develops, interest rate and currency swaps.

The global trend in swap markets is for swap and derivative products to become available in an ever increasing number of currencies, for longer maturities, higher individual transaction amounts and broader product ranges.

The market for "core" swap products is complemented by increasingly active parallel markets in swap derivatives, primarily option products, such as caps, floors and collars. In addition, in more recent times, markets in commodity swaps and related commodity derivatives and equity market index swaps and equity derivatives have also developed rapidly. The market for commodity and equity market index products, while to a degree independent of the market for basic swap products, is increasingly linked to the global swap and derivatives market. This linkage derives primarily from the desire of users of these products to simultaneously manage interest rate and currency exposures as part of the management of commodity and equity market index value risks necessitating the structuring of hybrid products.

THE STRUCTURE OF SWAP MARKETS

The mainstream swap markets tend to operate at two levels: an interest rate swap and a currency swap market. The distinction between these two market segments arises from the fact that the interest rate swap market, particularly in US$ and, to a lesser extent, in other swap currencies, behaves as a highly liquid and well traded market paralleling fixed interest markets in the relevant currency. In contrast, the currency swap market tends to be a less liquid, more structured market driven by new issues entailing the exchange of comparative advantage in terms of price and/or access to the market segment.

The difference between the two tiers of the swap market largely reflects the character of participants in the two different segments. The fact that a significant number of participants trade or make markets in interest rate swaps generates considerable liquidity in the interest rate swap markets. This reflects the use of interest rate swaps as a highly flexible mechanism for positioning, arbitrage and portfolio management activities. This generates considerable liquidity as both a primary and secondary market in interest rate swaps operate.

In contrast, the currency swap market operates as a primary market with limited secondary market activity. Although, in recent years, secondary market currency swap activity entailing restructuring and hedging of current debt portfolios, cash flows or investments has emerged, the currency swap market continues to be biased towards the primary market entailing the issue of securities accompanied by a swap to generate more attractive funding than that available directly.

A primary influence in the difference is the fact that market making in currency swaps, although growing, is still not as widespread as in the interest rate swap market. This reflects the difficulties in managing open currency swap positions. In particular, the difficulty of covering the interest rate risks in certain currencies while the swap is in position is considerable: see Part 7.

For example, a currency swap market maker can cover the foreign exchange risks associated with writing a position in a given currency. However, the market maker may not be able to cover against a movement in interest rates for that currency or is often forced to use poor surrogate cover as currency swap rates, in a given currency, may not move parallel to movements in local government bond market rates. This reflects the fact that in a number of currency swap markets, currency swap rates reflect the laws of supply and demand rather than relationships to interest rate movements in the relative market.

This means that the currency swap markets tend to be driven by liquidity in the underlying bond markets with a relatively lower proportion of secondary market activity.

The swap market in each currency would usually have at least three components:

- an interest rate swap market in the currency;
- a cross-currency market usually between the fixed rate in the currency and US$ LIBOR.
- a cross-currency floating-to-floating swap market.

This structure reflects the basic nature and objectives of participants in each swap market. While generally reflecting the pattern described, there are significant variations between markets which should be kept in mind.

The interest rate swap market usually reflects credit arbitrage in the local domestic capital market. In extreme cases, the absence of a substantial corporate bond market may foster the development of an interest rate swap market.

The cross-currency fixed to US$ floating market reflects the development of the Eurobond market in a wide number of currencies. The development of these multi-currency Eurobond markets in turn reflects the desire for portfolio diversification, in currency terms, by investors as well as investor preferences for Eurobonds or other types of international bond issues in preference to accessing domestic markets directly. This may reflect market frictions, such as withholding taxes, or investor preferences dictated by convenience and policy: see Chapter 7.

In addition, this type of cross-currency swap component reflects the existence of a wide variety of highly rated issuers who may be characterised as arbitrage funders. These issuers, primarily sovereigns, supranationals, and banks, are willing to issue in a wide range of currencies provided the issue can be swapped to generate funding at a rate, usually expressed as a margin relative to LIBOR. This margin, usually under LIBOR, reflects the degree of cost saving required by the issuer relative to other sources of borrowing, which will prompt the issuer to lend its name to a bond issue in a particular currency or utilising a particular structure: see Chapter 19.

These two developments have dictated the development of a cross-currency market where a floating rate leg usually paid by the issuer is priced relative to US$ LIBOR. The fact that US$ LIBOR based funding is increasingly available to most borrowers in almost every national market, allows these borrowers to utilise the other side of such swaps to obtain fixed rate funding in the relevant currencies at significant cost savings.

The floating-to-floating cross-currency swap structure is generally a by-product of the first two components of the swap market. For example, in Australia, this type of swap is usually utilised to cover the mismatch between A$ floating rate payments and US$ LIBOR receipts. However, on occasions, deliberate floating-to-floating cross-currency swaps have been engineered. The most notable example of this was the issue of A$ and NZ$ floating rate notes at significant margins under the A$ and NZ$ BBRs in the two countries in the Yankee market in 1986 and, briefly, in 1987.

While the structure of global swap markets has traditionally been dictated by the activities of liability managers, increasingly, asset swaps have come to influence these structures. In particular, asset swaps have, as discussed in Chapter 18, to a large extent contributed to the enhanced liquidity in certain segments of the swap market. This increased liquidity is most apparent in the interest rate swap and the cross-currency market between the fixed rate in one currency and US$ LIBOR. Asset swaps have generated a significant volume of fixed rate payers in these two market segments, reflecting the preference for the major category of investors in synthetic assets, commercial banks, for floating rate assets. This paying interest, in fixed rate terms, has provided an alternative supply of fixed rate payers under the swap, at times, particularly, when traditional paying interest from corporations or other borrowers has been absent due to either the absolute level of interest rates or the level of actual swap spreads.

The availability of asset swaps complements liability swap activity in the global swap markets. For example, when swap spreads, in a given currency, increase, this generally facilitates new issue arbitrage activity entailing liability swaps. This is made possible by the fact that increasing spreads on swaps, relative to spreads on new issuance of securities, enables the issue of fixed rate obligations which can be swapped into substantial margin under the relevant floating rate index. In contrast, if swap spreads decrease relative to spreads on securities, both in the new issue market and in secondary market trading, this enables the underlying debt to be swapped into floating rate assets at attractive yields over the relevant floating rate index. In this way, asset and liability swap transactions complement each other, effectively bounding value movements in securities markets and provides financial institutions active in swap transactions with a good two-way flow of transactions.

The other major component of swap markets is the basis swap. Again, the basis swap tends to be a residual position generated as a by-product of other swap activities, particularly mismatches in floating rate books of market makers in the relevant swap currency. The major basis swap market is in US$ reflecting the wide diversity of indexes in use in the US$ market.

In all swap markets, the bulk of activity entails standard or plain vanilla swaps, usually with minor variations to accommodate particular end user requirements. The alternative types of swap structures usually constitute a relatively small portion of the total swap market. In particular, these enhancements are responses to market situations, usually investor demand for particular types of securities issues, which generally have short life spans.

The generic structure of individual swap markets is set out, in diagrammatic form, in *Exhibit 22.1*.

The structure of individual swap markets outlined only examines the linkage between interest rate and currency swaps and, to a limited extent, variations within these product genres. Parallel markets in LTFX, FRAs, as well as caps, floors and collars exist. As described in detail in Chapters 2 and 6, these instruments have clear linkages to interest rate and currency swap transactions and provide a further structural component to the design of individual markets.

Additional layers of transactions and instrument structures flow from the presence of non-generic, complex or hybrid swap instruments. In addition, commodity and equity market products, as noted previously, have linkages to the interest rate and currency swap market as, in particular, currency risk management elements are embedded in commodity and equity market index swap and derivative transactions.

Exhibit 22.1
Structure of Individual Swap Markets

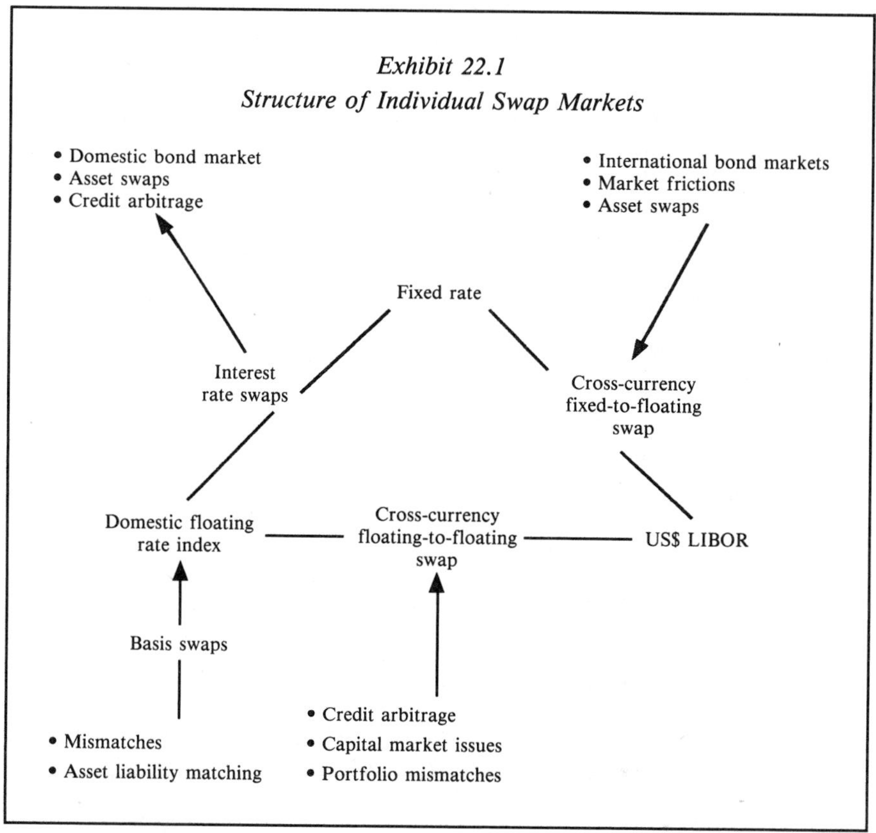

PRIMARY VERSUS SECONDARY MARKETS

The technical evolution of the swap market has effectively led to the creation of a two tier market in individual swap currencies—a *primary* and a *secondary* market.

A *primary market* transaction is usually defined as a transaction between two counterparties, typically, an end user and a financial institution active in market making in the relevant currency. A *secondary market* transaction refers to subsequent transactions based on, involving or predicated upon the original contract entered into between the original counterparties.

The secondary market in swaps has emerged for a number of reasons:

- the emergence of market makers who must eventually move to offset temporary risk positions (protected by surrogate hedges) assumed when entering into one side of the swap, by entering into an equal and opposite swap which provides the only perfect hedge to the original transaction;

- the move by end users to actively manage asset and liability portfolios by entering into swaps and subsequently reversing or unwinding their initial transactions.

Both types of transactions outlined can be accomplished by one of two methods. The reversal can be completed by entering into a mirror or identical but reverse position at current market rates. Alternatively, the reversal is done by effectively selling, at the prevailing market rate, the existing swap obligation to another market participant, effectively assigning or transferring the original obligations in their entirety. An added dimension to such secondary market transactions is when an end user of a swap seeks to cancel the transaction. The cancellation can be effectively accomplished, as is the case outlined for a market maker, by either entering into a mirror identical but reverse transaction or by cancelling, selling or assigning its position.

The economic consequences of such secondary market transactions, irrespective of the method adopted, will depend upon market conditions with the transaction resulting in a gain or loss depending upon the original transaction structure, the obligations of the party, and the movement in rates since the initial transaction is entered into. The major differences between the various approaches focuses on:

- credit risk considerations;
- recognition of profit and losses;
- competitive positioning.

Where a transaction is, effectively, covered by a market maker or reversed by a market maker or end user through an offsetting transaction, the credit risk of the original *as well as the new transaction* is assumed by the party. This essentially leads to a compounding chain of credit exposures in the swap market: refer Part 8 which considers credit exposure in swap transactions.

In contrast, sale of the existing transaction, cancellation or assignment through the transfer of all the obligations of the original transaction, does not increase the credit risk of the chain of transactions as it terminates the original swap obligations.

A further difference between the various techniques is that under a reversal or mirror swap, the profit or loss will usually be recognised over the remaining life of the matched contracts. In contrast, in the case of a sale or assignment of the original contract, the profit or loss on the transaction is crystallised immediately. This value equates to the net present value of the swap contract which is either payable or receivable when the transaction is sold or assigned.

Competitive aspects of the secondary market in swap transactions is quite complex. If one counterparty to an existing swap transaction seeks to terminate its obligations, a transaction structure entailing cancellation as between the two counterparties reduces the scope for competitive bidding. However, where the transaction structure is designed as an assignment, as a third party can bid to take over the obligations of one of the original two counterparties to a swap, competing market makers can determine the price of the transfer of obligations through the bidding process to become the replacement counterparty on the swap.

In this context, assignments which are more complex, because of credit considerations as well as documentary requirements, are an important component in facilitating competitive determination of the value of existing contracts and of providing liquidity from the perspective of existing counterparties to particular transactions.

The secondary market in swaps in individual currencies, therefore, includes a number of distinct types of transactions:

- swap sales (or assignments) to a new counterparty;
- voluntary swap terminations or cancellations;
- reverse or mirror swaps.

Swap sales or assignments are directly analogous to the secondary market and securities.

Such secondary market transactions constitute a significant proportion of activity in swap markets, with the specific proportion varying as between individual currencies. In well developed swap markets, secondary market transactions represent up to 30-40% of total activity.

The secondary market in swap and derivative transactions has developed relatively unevenly. The major factors impeding development include credit considerations, documentary factors and, at least initially, the absence of standard pricing and market benchmarks.

The credit considerations typically focus on the fact that the original counterparty to a potential swap assignment may, and often does, object to the assignment because it would assume a different counterparty credit risk. The first counterparty may be unacceptable for some reason or outstanding credit lines to that counterparty may be fully utilised, the latter factor being an increasing consideration in recent times.

Increasingly standardised documentation has overcome the problems that existed in the early phases of the swap market, of customised documentation which made assignments cumbersome or, at least on occasions, made it difficult to find parties willing to assume the swap at all.

Standardised pricing indexes and benchmarks, as well as size and maturities have developed sufficiently, at least in the major global swap markets, to allow the depth and liquidity of the secondary market to increase significantly.

The liquidity of the secondary swap markets is constantly debated. Liquidity in the sense of being able to realise assets or liquidate positions at the prevailing market price without substantial risk of loss is not, at least directly, applicable to swap markets. Swaps, particularly as they become increasingly customised and the utilisation of complex/non generic structures increases, are not capable of attaining the liquidity levels of standardised securities in the public or, in some instances, private placement market. However, the increasing volumes in individual swap currencies, the ever increasing size of individual transactions, the wide variety of transactions which are entered into, the availability of a wide range of market makers as well as end users and increasing market maturity enabling absorbtion of temporary disruptions all have assisted in increasing the liquidity of the secondary market in such instruments.

INDIVIDUAL SWAP MARKETS: OVERVIEW

The largest swap market in the world, although ironically not the oldest sector, is the US$ interest rate swap market. The most important currencies in the currency swap market in rough order of decreasing magnitude are Japanese yen, deutschmarks, Swiss francs, ECU (until recently), GBP, C$, A$ and NZ$.

The Swiss franc, yen and deutschmark swap markets have, at least historically, derived their impetus from their relatively low interest rates and the relative ease of access by a wide range of issuers to private and public debt in the international and domestic markets for these currencies. Many supranational and sovereign borrowers find their access to the debt markets of such currencies constrained relative to their sometimes very large requirements and therefore make active and frequent use of the currency swap market. These entities usually lend in these currencies and are therefore covering or matching assets with liabilities or are trying to diversify their debt portfolios away from the US$.

In recent times, changing interest rate relativities which have seen Swiss franc, yen and deutschmark interest rates rise sharply, have significantly changed the role of the capital markets in these currencies and the corresponding role of the swap markets. Continued dominance of these three capital markets has, increasingly, been predicated on their major capital surpluses and the need for investors in these markets to invest these capital resources. As access to the Swiss franc, yen and deutschmark bond and funding markets has developed, the corresponding swap markets have been utilised by borrowers of these currencies to convert the currency and interest rate basis of their financings to their specific requirements.

In contrast, the ECU swap market is predicated on the value of the ECU as a currency hedge for both investor and borrower and the fact that access to the ECU bond market is limited to a relatively small number of prime quality borrowers who provide the bulk of the fixed rate bond issues against which swap transactions are undertaken.

The high interest currencies, such as A$ and NZ$, GBP, C$, and, more recently, ESP, LIT, FFR and some Scandinavian currencies derive their role in the swap market primarily as speculative vehicles for aggressive debt portfolio managers or companies in the local market which would have to pay a premium to access fixed rate debt. These phenomena account for the very rapid development of Eurobond markets in these currencies and the corresponding development of relatively liquid currency swap markets.

As noted previously, the emergence of bond and financing markets in a number of currencies has been closely linked to the emergence of swap markets in those currencies. This symbiotic relationship between bond and swap markets has driven the development and growth in a variety of European currencies.

Additional factors underlying these developments include:

- The desire for investors to increasingly diversify the currency risk of their investment portfolios and to maximise returns by directing funds to where the risk adjusted returns are highest.
- The deregulation, progressively, of individual capital markets through the 1980s and 1990s which has facilitated free capital flows which, in turn, has provided the basis for swap market in those currencies.

The currency swap market is still dominated by the US$ on one side of the swap but increasingly, many direct currency combinations are developing rapidly. The most important among these include yen and deutschmark or Swiss franc, yen and ECU, deutschmark and Swiss franc etc.

Parallel markets, in each of these currencies, for swap derivatives have also developed. Often driving off mismatches or opportunities within overall swap books, substantial markets in FRAs and LTFX have developed complementing growth in mainstream markets in interest rate and currency swaps. Markets for long-dated interest rate options, in the form of caps, floors and collars, have emerged.

In the remaining chapters in this Part, major swap markets in individual currencies are considered. Swap markets in US$ and C$ are considered in Chapter 23.

Swap markets in Asia, primarily JPY and HK$, but including discussion of emerging swap markets in a variety of other Asian currencies, are considered in Chapter 24. Chapters 25 and 26 examine European swap markets. Chapter 27 analyses Australasian swap markets, primarily in A$ and NZ$. Chapter 28 examines the structure and features of the market globally for LTFX, FRAs and caps/floors. Chapter 29 examines the market for global commodity and equity derivatives.

Chapter 23

North American Swap and Derivative Markets: US$ and C$

US$ SWAP/DERIVATIVES MARKET

Overview

The US$ interest rate swap market is the largest single element of the global swap market. There is naturally no currency swap market in US$ as the US$ itself functions as the other side of almost all currency swaps.

The size of this market reflects a number of factors including the size of the United States capital market itself and particularly the size of the market for fixed rate obligations, primarily United States treasuries but also a very sizeable corporate bond market both within the United States and outside in the Eurobond market. An additional factor contributing to the size of the US$ interest rate swap market is the fact that a large proportion of global financing flows continue to be denominated in US$. The infrastructure which provides the US$ interest rate swap market with its depth and liquidity depends on these factors.

For example, the presence of a substantial number of market makers in US$ interest rate swaps contributes to the size and liquidity of the market. Their presence in turn, is predicated largely on the existence of a substantial and sophisticated market in United States treasury bonds and United States treasury futures and options which allows these participants to hedge their risk position in unmatched swaps. The practice of pricing US$ obligations as a margin relative to United States treasuries also contributes to the capacity of these market makers to trade or warehouse interest rate swaps and also, in a number of cases, make substantial capital commitments to the swap market.

The US$ interest rate swap market exhibits many of the characteristics of a mature financial market:

- a large number of participants with relatively clearly defined roles;
- the presence of several subsectors within the market;
- the presence of both a primary and secondary market; and
- the existence of considerable depth and liquidity.

In this regard, this market is by far the most sophisticated and structurally well developed of global swap markets.

Market structure

Market classification

The US$ interest rate swap market can be broadly classified into two sectors:

- The primary market, which itself can be further subdivided into two distinct segments in terms of maturity—under, say, three years and over.
- A secondary market.

Short-term US$ interest rate swaps

The distinction within the primary market is largely predicated on the factors driving activity, pricing and the method of hedging risk positions in these two segments. The under three year sector functions as an extension of financial futures markets in US$ interest rates. The key participants in this short-term sector are a group of United States and non-United States banks, both of which provide fixed rate US$, usually through their access to fixed rate Eurodollar deposits or to the fixed rate CD market in London and New York. They also act as payers of the fixed rate in these swaps. The activity in this area is largely driven by the structure of the bank's asset liability portfolio and the primary motivation is either balance sheet management or speculative in nature.

The pricing in this segment of the market largely reflects the hedging practice whereby risk positions in the short swaps are usually managed by executing futures transactions in US$ interest rate futures typically, Eurodollar futures, in the United States and London financial futures markets. Market makers in the short swaps traditionally utilise Eurodollar futures markets as the standard hedging vehicle for short-dated interest rate swaps. For example, a dealer entering into a swap whereby it receives fixed rate and pays floating rate for say two years will offset the risk on the swap by positioning a series of sold or short Eurodollar futures positions, that is, a "sold Eurodollar futures strip".

This segment of the market tends to be extremely volatile in price, largely reflecting its close proximity in maturity to the volatile US$ money markets. This price volatility of financial futures based swaps requires a high level of execution skills to undertake transactions in markets susceptible to very quick and sharp movements. A particular characteristic of this section of the market is a very substantial level of speculative interest whereby experienced dealers take positions on both absolute rate movements as well as spread movements between various indexes.

This type of speculative trading usually relates to the triangular relationship in this segment of the market between:

- the yield on the relevant United States treasury note;
- the implied rate on the Eurodollars futures strip;
- the prevailing swap spread over the treasury note.

In view of the fact that given any two of these variables, the remaining one is uniquely determinable, traders often trade the spread between the two year Eurodollar strip and two year United States treasury note. The primary objective of this type of trading is to profit from a correct prediction of the change in the spreads of the two or three year treasury note relative to the implied rate on the two or three year Eurodollar strip (in the jargon of the market: "trading the TED (Treasury Eurodollar) spread"). For example, if a trader expects the TED to narrow, he or she would buy Eurodollar futures and sell two year treasury notes, while conversely, if the trader expected the spread to widen he or she would sell Eurodollar futures and buy two year treasury notes.

This type of activity, which requires participants to establish and unwind these positions rapidly to maximise profits, has greatly increased the liquidity in the futures markets and, indirectly, contributed to the depth and liquidity in these types of swaps.

Exhibit 23.1 sets out the relationship over recent years between the two and three year Eurodollars strips and two and three year treasury note yields.

Exhibit 23.1

Two and Three Year US$/Eurodollar Strip Rate Spreads to US Treasury Notes

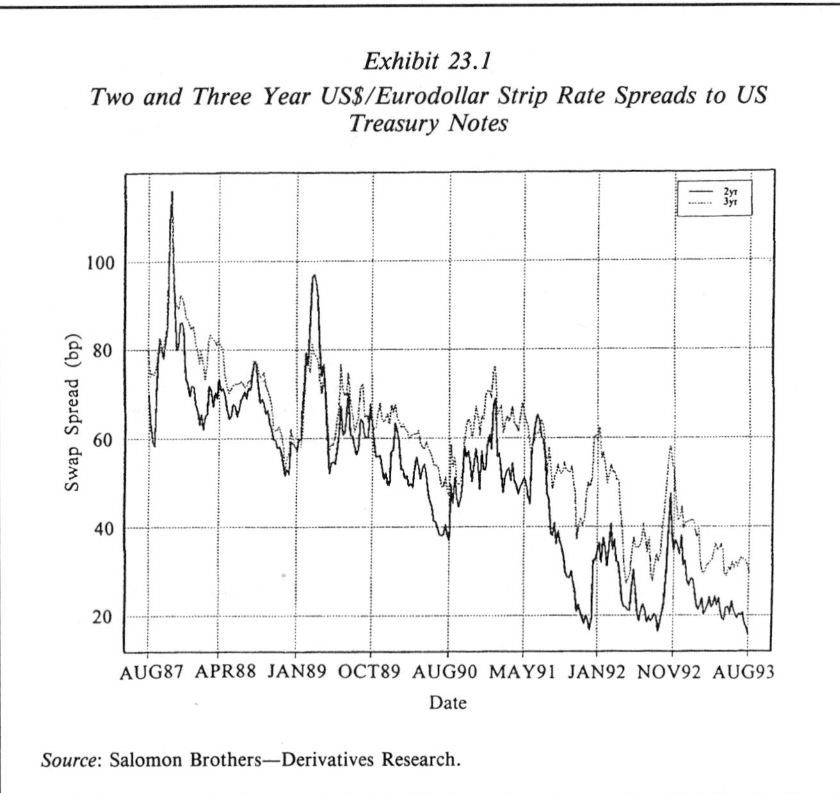

Source: Salomon Brothers—Derivatives Research.

The use of strips of Eurodollar futures contracts to hedge US$ interest rate swap positions is discussed in detail in Chapter 35. In practice, the correlation between US$ interest rate swap and Eurodollar strip prices is extremely close. *Exhibit 23.2* highlights the correlation between interest rate swaps and Eurodollar strip prices. Correlation is highest at the short end of the yield curve. The relationship is reduced as maturity is increased due to a variety of factors including decreased liquidity in the "back" Eurodollar months, increased futures execution risk and interest rate volatility.

One problem (discussed in detail in Chapter 35) in using Eurodollar futures to hedge interest rate swap positions is that the PVBP of Eurodollars are fixed regardless of the level of absolute rates. The PVBP of an equivalent swap will change according to the level of interest rates. Effectively, Eurodollars are non-convex whereas interest rate swaps are convex creating the necessity to rebalance the Eurodollar futures hedge, periodically, resulting in a loss of hedge efficiency.

With the extension of Eurodollars futures trading dates out to five years, several US$ interest rate swap dealers now use strip prices to price swaps beyond five years. This is usually done by pricing theoretical contracts out to ten years by extending the linear relationship in the furthest Eurodollar contract. These theoretical contracts would be hedged by using stack hedging techniques in the furthest Eurodollar contract: see discussion in Chapter 35.

Exhibit 23.2
Correlation Between Swap and Strip Prices

1991

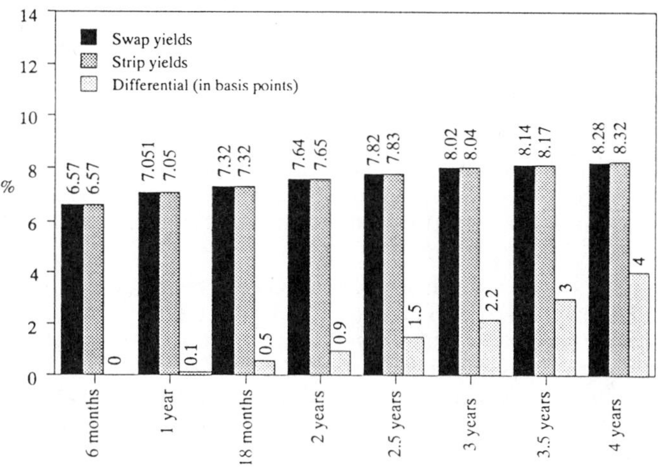

Assumes 14% volatility

AUGUST 1993

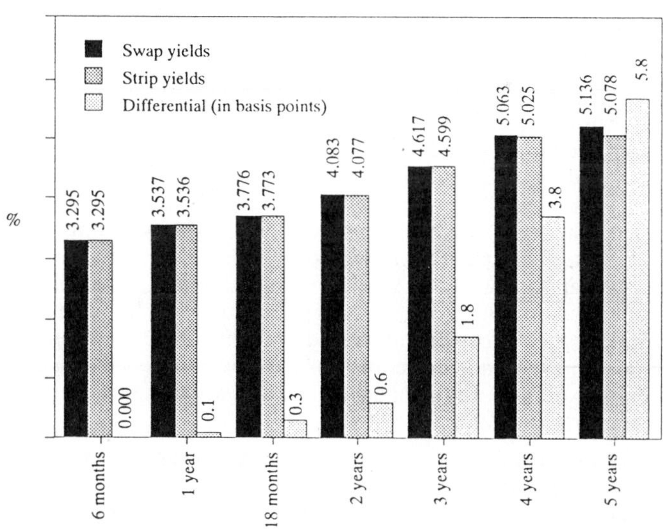

Assumes 20% volatility

Source: JP Morgan.

Medium/long-term US$ interest rate swaps

The longer maturities, beyond two to three years, in the US$ interest rate swap market are dominated by securities transactions, primarily the issuance of fixed rate bonds in the United States domestic and Eurodollar bond market. These debt markets and the parallel United States interest rate swap market enjoy a symbiotic relationship with ever-increasing volumes of new debt issuance being predicated on the accompanying swap. An important aspect of this complementary relationship is that the existence of the swap market has meant that the underlying US$ bond market now need never close despite the absolute levels of interest rates as issuers who would not come to market because of high interest rates can do so now to the extent that a swap is available.

Pricing in the longer term US$ interest rate swap market is almost exclusively related to the United States treasury rates for comparable maturities. These are therefore quoted on a spread to treasuries basis. The swap spreads are marked by relative stability, at least for short periods of time, that is, relative to the short-term swap markets.

Given the large size of most debt issues, usually in excess of US$100m, and the oversupply of entities able and willing to approach the Eurobond market to swap into floating rate funds, most issue related swaps are now entered into with a swap warehouse without, necessarily, a counterparty on the other side. The market maker usually hedges its risk position which traditionally leaves the warehouse manager with a spread risk. In periods of relative stability of spreads and a positively sloped yield curve allowing for positive carry, the market has functioned reasonably well with only occasional periods of severe oversupply in any particular maturity. Bids for bond issue related swaps tend to differ between major swap houses by only a few basis points, differences in the order of fourth or fifth decimal point are not unusual.

In the late 1980s and early 1990s, the fundamental factors driving liability arbitrage in US$ swaps changed substantively. The spreads on corporate bonds increased dramatically and, in particular, the spread differential between corporate bonds and swaps changed in structure.

A fall in bond issuance, decrease in liquidity, deterioration of bank credit quality, the collapse of the LBO market, event risk issues and balance sheet constraints resulted in corporate bond spreads rising relative to treasuries as well as the spread differential as between different qualities of credits widening significantly. As corporate spreads increased, the swap spreads lagged behind being driven by the relatively lower volatility of sovereign credit spreads. The widening in the spread differential minimised new issue arbitrage opportunities and therefore reduced the opportunities for liability swaps. In addition, the rising cost of funding for banks meant that traditional purchasers of asset swap securities were less aggressive in their purchase of these assets. The widening spread available on asset swapped corporate securities was also substantially offset by the banks own increasing funding costs as well as the impact of new capital adequacy rules which allocated a 100% risk weighting to corporate bonds.

The declining opportunities for liability arbitrage swaps as well as declining opportunities for asset swap transactions, utilising new issue or secondary market securities, has been partially offset by increased utilisation of these instruments for asset and liability management by financial institutions as well as corporations. A factor underlying the utilisation of swaps for asset liability management by banks has been the increased focus on *off-balance sheet* instruments, such as swaps and derivatives, to overcome balance sheet constraints on financial institutions. In addition, swaps have the additional advantage that they are accounted for by most such institutions on a mark-to-market basis (as distinct from bonds etc which are in some cases accounted for on an accrual basis) enabling the financial institution to effectively realise the mark-to-market value when transaction is closed (as distinct from accruing gains and losses over the life of the transaction). This capacity to realise gains has also contributed to the use of swaps by bank asset and liability managers taking absolute rate positions.

The volumes and structure of the medium/long-term US$ interest rate swap market has, historically, been driven by specific factors, some of which have only been operative for relatively short periods of time. For example, in the period between the mid and late 1980s, growth in volume in US$ interest rate swaps and other derivatives were driven, substantially, by Savings and Loan Association activity as well as leveraged buy out (LBO) activities. Investments banks, in particular, were active in structuring asset swaps, based on high yield/junk bond issues, that were placed with S & Ls. Similarly, large volume of swaps were undertaken in the context of LBOs where, under the terms of the financing, the LBO company was required to hedge a substantial portion of its borrowings. These end user transactions had a substantial multiple effect on the swap market as a whole as banks offset these positions with one another.

More recently, a major factor in US$ interest rate swaps has been longer-term (10-12 year, and on limited occasions, longer) swap structures related to aircraft lease transactions and real estate financing arrangements.

Secondary market

The secondary market in US$ interest rate swaps is inherently more complex. The primary rationale for activity in this market segment is that as interest rates fluctuate, a fixed rate payer or receiver may find that a substantial profit can be realised by reversing the original swap or cancelling the original swap in return for an up-front cash payment. With, at times, wild fluctuations in US$ interest rates, secondary market activity in US$ swaps has grown rapidly although there are a number of factors which continue to retard even stronger growth including:

- Market participants who undertake swaps as part of complex new issue funding arbitrages will not usually be susceptible to reversing the original swap position.
- While swap counterparties are likely to take profits in a reversal, given the "zero sum" game nature of the market, the fact that the counterparty with an offsetting loss would be less likely to reverse its original position, unless there are compelling arguments to the contrary, necessarily detracts from the liquidity in the market.
- The requirement of exactly matching the original swap creates a problem of "odd dates" which are often difficult to match off in the market and the pricing adjustments necessitated may erode any profits in the transaction.

Despite these problems, secondary market liquidity in swaps is constantly growing. A major factor in this regard is the increasing sophistication of market makers in US$ interest rate swaps who can accommodate the structural complexities of such reversals. The move by such swap houses from perfect matching to portfolio approaches to swap book management has largely contributed to this development: see Chapter 33.

Pricing relationships in US$ interest rate swaps

The pricing structure in US$ interest rate swaps is well developed. This reflects in part the mature nature of the underlying capital market and the well defined structure of credit differentials (based on credit agency rating levels) that prevails in the US$ bond and securities markets.

The major determinants of US$ interest rate swap prices/spreads include:

- volume and type of fixed rate bond issuance in US$, particularly in the US$ Eurobond market;
- corporate bond spreads relative to US$ treasury bonds;
- absolute interest rate levels and interest rate expectations.

Sovereign, international agency and, to a lesser extent, corporate and financial institution debt issues, particularly in the Eurobond market, are swapped into floating rate US$ LIBOR via the US$ interest rate swap market. Liability swaps linked to such new issues, particularly from higher quality issuers, are driven by the issuer's final objective of financing at margins well under LIBOR: refer discussion in Chapter 19. Such bonds are typically sold to institutional investors on the basis of "total-rate-of-return". High volumes of issuance of high quality straight US$ Eurobond with the corresponding entry by the issuers into liability swaps typically creates a large demand on US$ interest rate swap market makers to *pay* fixed rates, thereby inducing downward pressure on swap spreads. Periods of strong issuance of the US$ debt, both in the Euromarkets and United States domestic market (where the level of issues swapped into floating rate is somewhat lower) therefore impacts significantly on US$ swap prices.

Conversely, asset based swap transactions, arising from newly issued or seasoned bonds, typically lower rated (A or below) which are placed on an asset swapped basis with banks or financial institutions create demand for market makers to *receive* fixed rate in US$. A high level of demand for asset swapped securities can, therefore, place downward pressure on US$ swap spreads.

The underlying arbitrage nature of all swap markets dictates that the level of corporate bond spreads relative to the corresponding US treasury rates and, in turn, the relationship to swap spreads forces adjustments to US$ swap prices. Changes in spreads, particularly in the corporate market, can lead to significant changes in swap spread levels. Such changes can be driven by a variety of factors. For example, high levels of corporate bond issuance to refinance high coupon fixed rate debt or to take advantage of low absolute rate levels can change fixed rate bond spreads to US treasuries and impact upon swap spreads.

The absolute level of interest rates as well as expectations of interest rates movement can influence swap spread levels: see detailed discussion below.

Some additional factors which may influence US$ swap spread levels include spreads on long-term fixed rate bank liabilities as well as in the asset backed or mortgage backed securities markets. This reflects the fact that banks frequently fund on a long-term fixed rate basis which is then swapped into floating rate LIBOR in order to match their predominantly LIBOR based assets. Changes in the perceived credit standing of the bank sector generally can change the risk premiums on bank instruments, and, in the process, exert upwards or downwards pressure on US$ swap spreads. Changes in the level of spreads for asset and mortgage-backed instruments influences swap spreads because of their increased use as the basis for asset swaps where these securities are placed on a floating rate basis with a variety of investors.

Historically, though this is less relevant currently, Savings and Loan mortgage instruments spreads have played a significant role in the determining swap spreads in US$. This reflected the fact that the Savings and Loan tended to have fixed rate mortgage assets which they, in turn, swapped into LIBOR-based floating rate assets via the swap market.

The price of shorter-term interest rate swaps, as discussed previously, is substantially influenced by short-term interest rate futures market movements reflecting activity in trading the TED spread.

In 1987, Salomon Brothers Bond Market Research published an analysis of US$ interest rate spreads: see Evans, Ellen and Parente (1987). The research identified a number of key influences:

- Yield levels and spreads and movements in these parameters, particularly for corporate borrowers in public debt markets such as the United States domestic corporate, Yankee and Eurodollar bond markets, were a major factor in swap spread levels. Specifically, swap spreads approximate the spreads over United States treasuries on investment grade corporate securities, usually in a 20 to 30bps range defined by AA and A rated spreads.
- Swap spreads appeared to be influenced by interest rate expectations. For example, as set out in *Exhibit 23.3*, the historical data on changes in the absolute levels of rates show that swap spreads move inversely to treasuries: swap spreads tend to widen when treasury yields fall and narrow when treasury yields increase.

  The relationship between absolute interest rate levels, interest rate expectation and swap spreads requires elaboration. For example, if the absolute interest rate level is high, there, typically, is downward pressure on US$ swap spreads reflecting the increased supply of fixed rate receivers as borrowers refrain from fixing their interest cost at what they consider to be high absolute rate levels. Conversely, where interest rate levels are low, swap spreads experience upward pressure reflecting the increased supply of fixed rate payers as borrowers seek to fix their interest costs.

Exhibit 23.3

Relationship Between US$ Swap Spreads and Interest Rate Levels

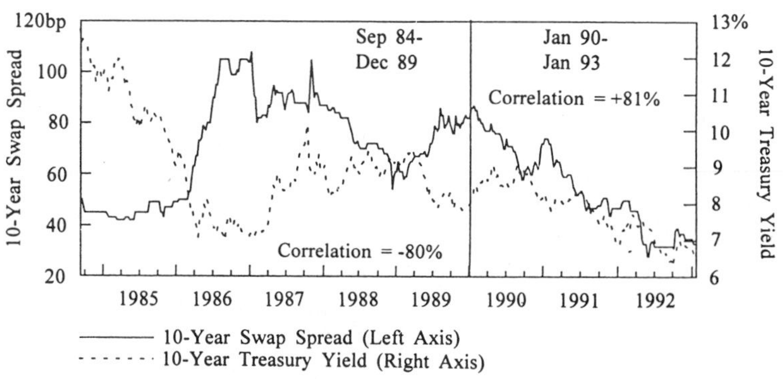

bp Basis points.

Exhibit 23.3—continued

RELATIONSHIP BETWEEN INTEREST RATE LEVELS AND SWAP SPREADS

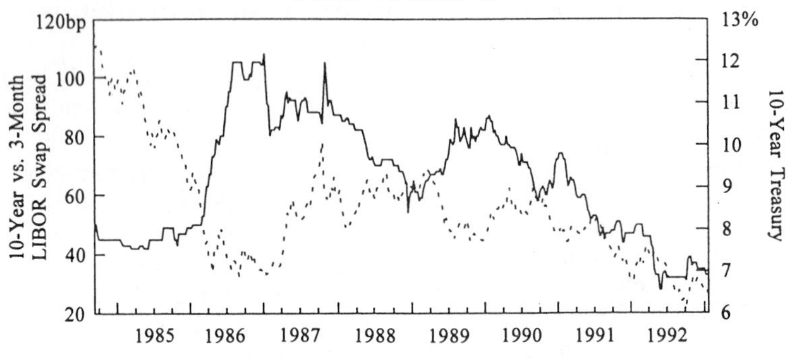

——— 10-Year vs. 3-Month LIBOR Swap Spread (Left Axis)
- - - - - - 10-Year Treasury (Right Axis)

bp Basis points. LIBOR London Interbank Offered Rate.

RELATIONSHIP BETWEEN SWAP SPREADS AND SLOPE OF THE YIELD CURVE, SEP 84-JAN 93

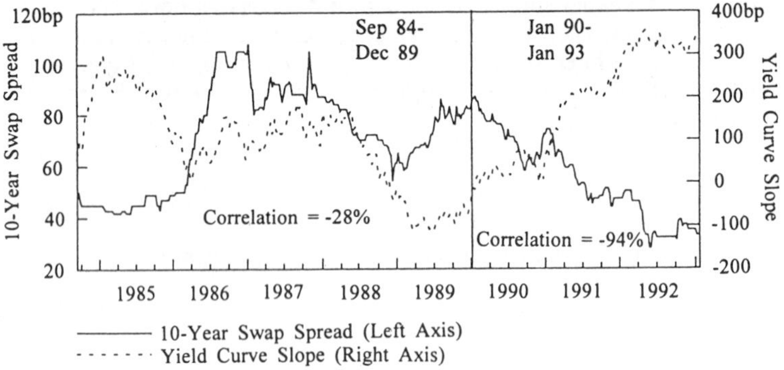

——— 10-Year Swap Spread (Left Axis)
- - - - - - Yield Curve Slope (Right Axis)

bp Basis points.
Source: Salomon Brothers Inc.

Similarly, where there is an *expectation* that interest rates will increase, swap spreads experience upward pressure as the supply of fixed rate payers tends to increase with borrowers seeking to lock in interest rates. Conversely, expectations of falling rates creates downward pressure on swaps spreads as there is a decreased supply of fixed rate payers with borrowers delaying entry into transactions to fix their interest costs.

- The changing use of swaps and the evolving cast of participants, particularly the development of asset swaps, by influencing the supply and demand of fixed rate payers, has been a major determinant of swap spreads.
- Technical factors, such as hedgings costs, have influenced spread changes.

Exhibit 23.4 sets out the swap spread curve at various periods. *Exhibit 23.5* sets out the historical levels of swap rates and spreads in a number of key maturities.

Exhibit 23.4
US$ Interest Rate Swap Spread Curve

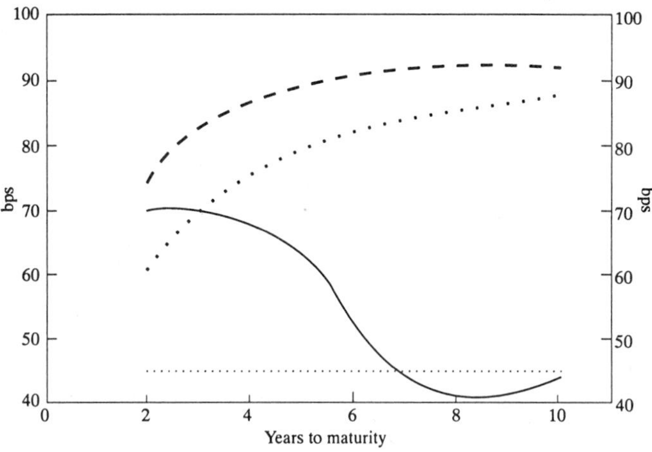

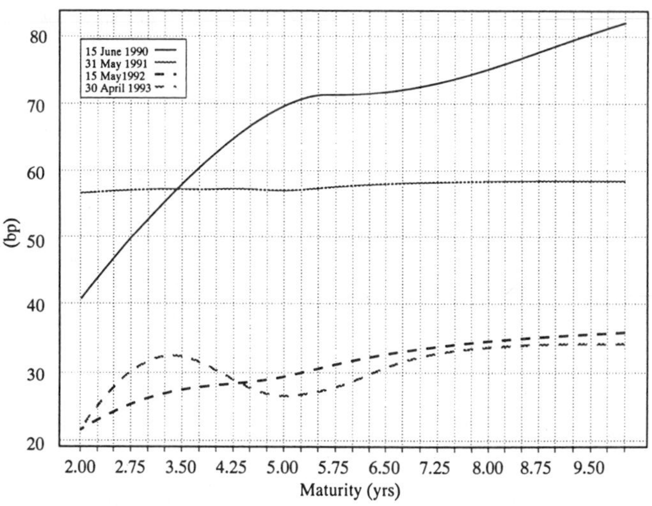

Source: Salomon Brothers Inc.

Exhibit 23.5
US$ Swap Rates and Spreads

SWAP SPREADS (AUG 87-JUNE 93)

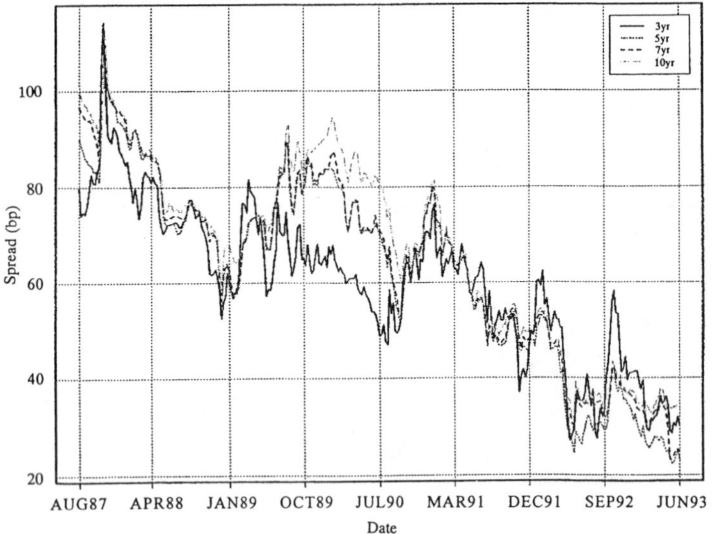

SWAP RATES (AUG 87-JUNE 93)

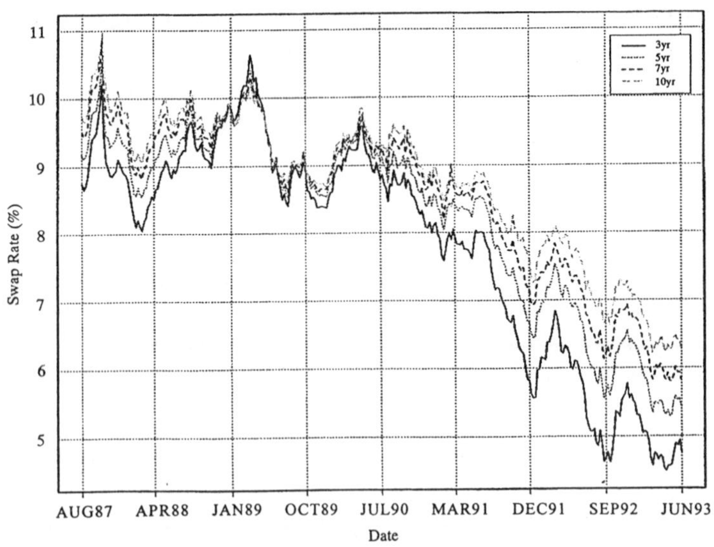

Source: Salomon Brothers Inc.

The swap spread curve data indicates that the swap market has been characterised by a number of phases:

- Third quarter 1984 to early 1986, when the swap spread curve was flat or negative, reflecting a similar pattern of spread to that prevailing in the primary corporate debt markets.
- At the end of the first quarter 1986, the swap spreads showed a sharp increase, particularly at longer maturities, with the swap yield curve gradually steepening. This reflected higher volumes of corporate debt issues to take advantage of lower absolute rates and increases in maturity risk premiums in the corporate debt market.
- In the first quarter 1987, swap spreads were exceedingly volatile, fluctuating by as much as 20bps, although the shape of the swap yield curve did not change.
- In the second quarter 1987, swap spreads rose, including a particularly sharp increase after the equity market collapse in October 1987 and then declined to previous levels. The swap yield curve also flattened significantly. The major underlying factor appeared to be persistent weakness in the US$ and expectations of interest rate increases which led to investors shunning US$ fixed rate issues. The rally in the US$ in early 1988 and easier interest rates led to increased corporate debt issuance levels and significant declines in the swap spread levels.
- In the late 1980s and early 1990s, the relatively stable relationship, previously existing, between AA corporate bond spreads and swap spreads has begun to break down. Corporate bond spreads increased in level as well as volatility. As noted previously, major factors underlying this increase in corporate spread was the decrease in liquidity in the corporate bond market, the deterioration of bank credit quality resulting in margins relative to LIBOR on asset swaps increasing, the collapse of LBO structures, event risk issues and balance sheet constraints, exacerbated by the new BIS rules which favoured investments in instruments bearing less than 100% risk weightings. As the spreads on bank paper increased, swap spreads lagged behind, influenced by the relative stability of sovereign industrial credit spreads. *Exhibit 23.6* compares the movement of corporate issuance spreads relative to swap spreads during this period.

Exhibit 23.6
Corporate Issuance Spreads Relative to Swap Spreads

RELATIONSHIP BETWEEN SWAP SPREADS AND A-RATED BOND SPREADS (SEP 84-JAN 93)

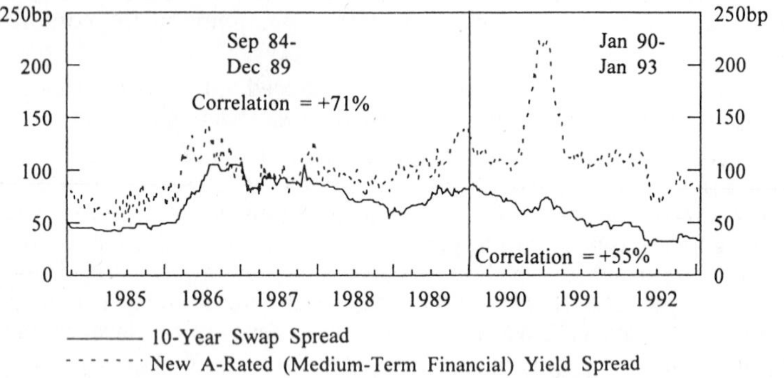

bp Basis points.
Source: Salomon Brothers Inc.

MOVEMENT OF CORPORATE ISSUANCE SPREADS BY INDUSTRY GROUP (JAN 90-MAR 91)

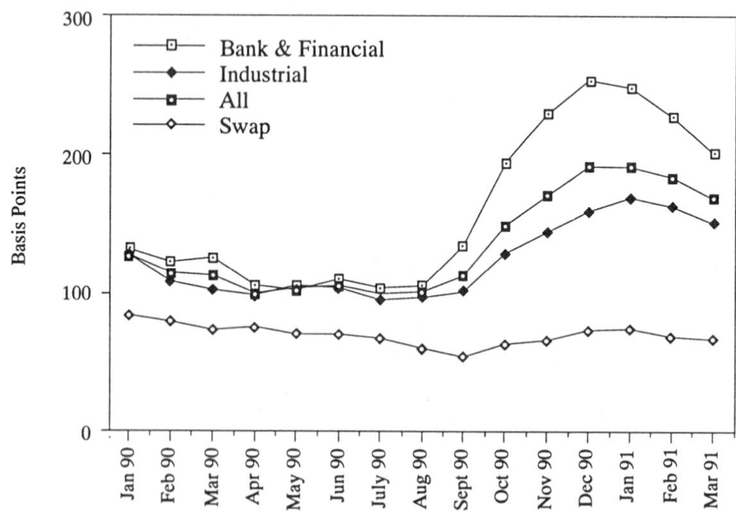

Source: JP Morgan.

Exhibit 23.6—continued

MOVEMENT OF CORPORATE ISSUANCE SPREADS BY INDUSTRY GROUP (MAR 92-JUN 93)

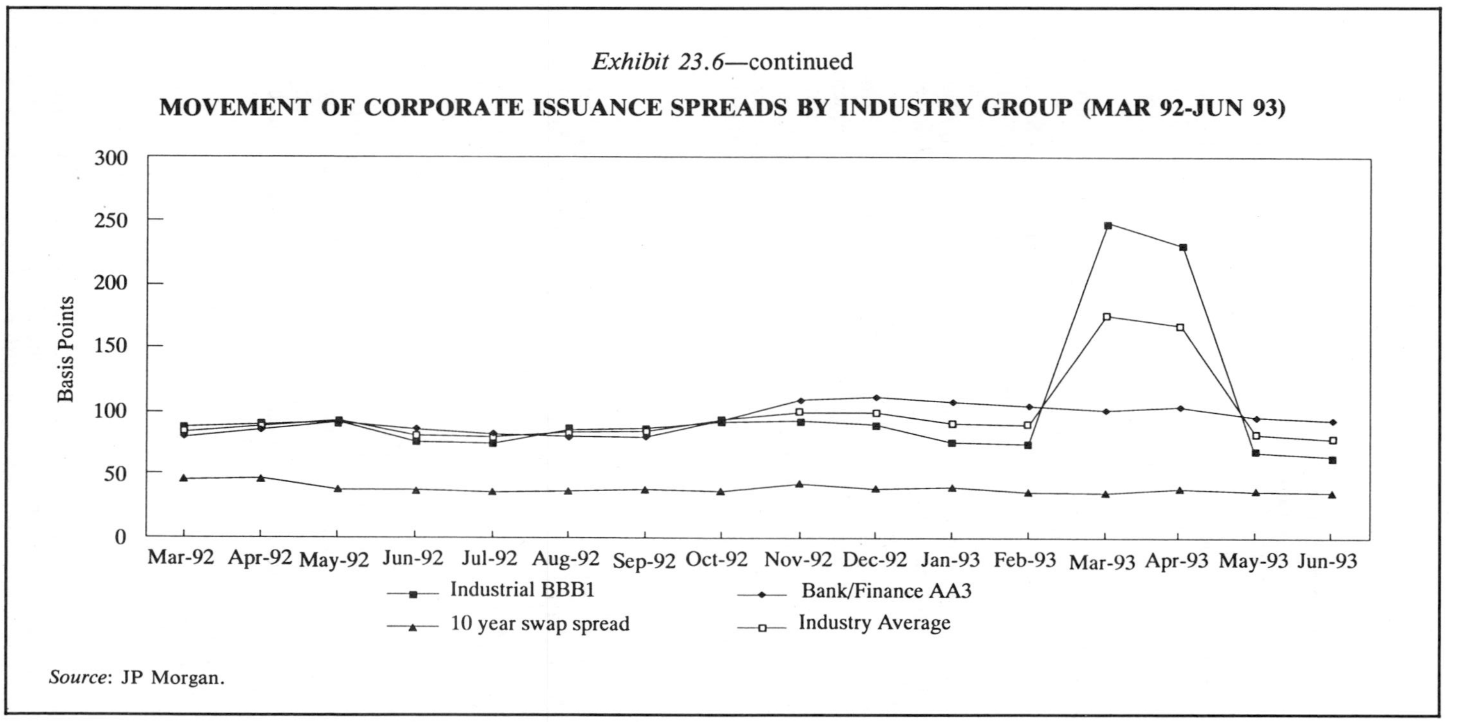

Source: JP Morgan.

- Another characteristic in the behaviour of swap spreads has been the uneven nature of movements in spreads across the yield curve. This has been particularly apparent for longer maturities, as the declining credit quality of financial institutions combined with the BIS capital adequacy requirements for swap transactions has limited the number of participants active in longer dated transactions. This diminished liquidity in the longer end of the US$ swap market combined with demand pressures from time to time from special structures, such as the aircraft lease and real estate transactions noted above, have affected the term structure of swap spreads. In particular, the swap spread curve has remained steep beyond ten years as a result of the continued high volumes of fixed rate payers and the relative scarcity of fixed rate receivers for maturities beyond ten years.
- Over recent years, US$ swap spreads in all maturities have, broadly, decreased. It is probable that the narrowing of spreads will continue for the foreseeable future. This reflects, in part, the fact that traditional bank lending has become increasingly expensive. This allied to the fact of a continuing level of high quality new issuance in US$ will ensure that new issue spreads are relatively low, ensuring that bank lending margins will be a major determinant of US$ swap spreads. This impact of bank lending margins is evident through the fact that lower rated borrowers will force swap spreads to a spread indifference level where their cost of fixed rate issuance versus their cost of funding on a floating rate from banks and swapping these funds into fixed rate are broadly equal. Consequently, as bank lending margins over LIBOR have increased, as a result of, among other things, BIS capital adequacy rules and bank's own increasing cost of funds, there has been a downward pressure on swap spreads as floating rate borrowers will be able to receive lower fixed rates under swap transactions and still achieve better results than conventional bank funding.

Products

The US$ interest rate swap market offers a wider variety of structures than almost any other swap/derivatives market. The maturity of the market together with the presence of a substantial number of market makers with large swap portfolios means that, increasingly, almost every variety of non-generic and hybrid swap structure are available. A major factor in this regard is the existence of substantial markets in physical and derivative products (including futures, forwards and options) on the underlying United States treasury bond market which allows hedging of risks entailed in a wide variety of swap transactions.

A major aspect of the US$ interest rate swap market is the presence of a substantial and, almost unique, market in basis rate swaps in and between the various US$ interest rate indexes. A heterogeneous population of participants and the resultant mismatches created in the books of swap market makers have fuelled the growth in this segment of the market.

In recent years, the US$ swap market has responded, consistent with other swap markets, to increased demands for innovation. Two major areas of innovation have included variable principal redemption swaps and tax exempt swap transactions.

The demand for variable principal redemption swaps have come from asset swap structures based on securities, such as mortgage and asset-backed securities, where there is some level of uncertainty in regard to the underlying cash flows. The major uncertainty relates to potential prepayment risk whereby, particularly in the case of collateralised mortgage obligations (CMO) transactions, as interest rates drop, these obligations tend to be repaid earlier as mortgagors seek to refinance their obligations at lower rates. This has the effect of shortening the life of the CMO obligation and, potentially, leaving the investor in the asset swap involving the CMO with an out-of-the-money swap where the duration of the CMO is shortened.

Increasingly, a number of swap market makers in US$ interest rate swaps are involved in structuring transactions where CMOs are swapped on a prepayment risk-free basis in exchange for a slight reduction in yields to the investor. As noted in Chapters 12 and 14, this essentially involves index amortising structures as well as structuring options on swaps to absorb the prepayment risk.

These types of variable principal redemption swaps have enabled other obligations, principally based on short-term receivables such as auto loans whose prepayment histories are more random to be asset swapped. Under these arrangements, swaps are structured based on the anticipated repayment schedule of the underlying security. As actual repayments take place over the life of the transaction, any deviations from the expected schedule become residual swap positions for the financial institution who transacted the swap. As in the case of the CMO swaps, these transactions entail the financial institutions writing and hedging series of options on swaps to manage the exposure of such transactions.

A similar example of innovation relates to swaps related to bank investment contracts (BICs). Under these BIC arrangements, investors lodge a deposit which is tailored specifically to meet the requirement of long term investors such as pension funds. These BICs can be withdrawn under certain circumstances. Structured swaps are utilised to cover the risk of early withdrawal on BIC contracts which banks have converted into a floating rate deposit with certain cash flows through a normal interest rate swap.

The tax exempt municipal swap market is unique to the United States. The tax exempt market involves bonds issued by municipalities that are not taxed on the local, State and federal levels of the State within which they are issued. The market orginally grew in late 1986 when issuers of tax exempt debt created synthetic funding through swapping their floating rate financing into fixed rate debt. Since that time, the market has grown rapidly. The original users of such transactions, the municipalities themselves who are motivated by obtaining cheaper fixed rate funding, are now complemented by investors seeking to generate attractive asset swaps using older tax exempt bonds that are trading at attractive levels relative to the swap curve. Other users of the municipal swap market include fixed rate receivers deriving attractive funding on a tax adjusted basis.

The standard structure of the tax exempt municipal swap is one in which one counterparty pays a fixed rate and receives a floating rate tax exempt rate, usually priced of the JJ Kenny Index of 35 thirty day municipal notes. The index measures the bid-side yield of a variety of high grade one month tax exempt paper evaluated on a daily basis. Alternative floating rate indexes exist in this market including, primarily, the New York tax exempt daily interest rate and the tax exempt note rate.

A tax exempt swap can be decomposed into a conventional interest rate swap and a tax exempt floating rate/LIBOR basis swap requiring such transactions to be priced on the basis of the floating rate basis risk that must be managed. This spread is driven by the yield differential between the taxable swap and the tax exempt municipal yield curves. Market makers in municipal swaps hedge themselves with either cash municipal bonds or the municipal bond futures contract. Typical contracts have maturities between one and ten years. This creates a problem in the sense that the municipal bond futures contract is based on an underlying *20 year* security creating hedging difficulties.

Participants

The US$ swap market is centred in New York with primary trading being undertaken in the "golden triangle" of New York, London and Tokyo. The factors which contribute to the size of the US$ interest rate swap market also dictate that a large number of participants with wide and varied interests participate in this particular swap market. Participants include corporations, supranational and sovereign borrowers, investors, financial institutions etc.

An important aspect of the US$ interest rate swap market is the participation of entities of widely different nationalities. Highly rated credits from a wide variety of jurisdictions participate in the US$ interest rate swap market as part of their arbitrage funding activities while less credit-worthy corporates with substantial US$ debt utilise this segment of the swap market as a means of either hedging existing floating rate debt or raising fixed rate debt on more competitive terms.

The role of banks and other financial institutions is particularly noteworthy. Banks play a fundamental part in the US$ interest rate swap market both as issuers of fixed rate debt which is then swapped into floating rate or as payers of fixed rate to hedge asset liability mismatches in addition to their role as swap warehouses or market makers. The participation of United States investment banks as market makers, both as brokers and as principals, has also been a significant factor in the evolution of the US$ interest rate swap market in terms of distributing transactions and, in particular, the ability to move positions quickly due to price volatility and risks inherent in the market.

A major group of financial institutions in the US$ interest rate swap market are United States thrifts. The entry of thrifts into the US$ swap market to manage asset liability mismatches contributed significantly to the liquidity of the market. Their entry was in a large part made possible by the creativity of United States investment banks, who pioneered collateral of swaps with high quality securities, enabling the participation of these less creditworthy institutions in the swap market.

In recent years, financial difficulties of the Savings and Loans Industry and the difficulties experienced by a wide variety of companies which undertook LBO transactions has meant the level of default in the US$ swap market has increased dramatically. In particular, the crisis in the Savings and Loan industry has left, literally, billions of US$ in swaps booked to, effectively, insolvent organisations. The Resolution Trust Corporation (RTC) has taken on the task of unwinding a huge portfolio of off balance sheet positions relating to the insolvent Savings and Loan Association. The RTC has worked closely with swap dealers to unwind some US$8 billion notional principal value of swap transactions to date.

An added factor in the market has been the deterioration in the credit-worthiness of US money centre banks. While no major bank swap counterparty has yet defaulted, the well publicised demise of Drexel Burnham and Lambert (see discussion in Chapter 38) highlights the considerable stresses on the US$ swap market.

Reflecting the maturity of the product itself and the depth and liquidity of the US$ interest rate swap market, the range of applications is very broad. New issue arbitrage as well as sophisticated asset liability management and interest rate risk management purposes is evident. An increasingly significant factor in the US$ interest rate swap market is the emergence of a substantial asset swap market in US$. The evolution of this particular market segment has provided greater liquidity to the US$ swap market overall as it has increased the supply of fixed rate payers, primarily commercial banks, who swap fixed rate assets into high yielding floating rate assets for portfolio purposes.

Market evolution

Initially, the US$ interest rate swap market was driven by two factors:

- the presence of United States withholding tax;
- a classic credit arbitrage.

The presence of United States withholding tax essentially allowed prime rated United States corporates to issue Eurodollar bonds for much of the early part of the 1980s at spreads under or comparable to United States treasuries. This discrepancy facilitated the initial growth of the swap market. Allied to this fact was the absence of banks and highly rated financial institutions from the fixed rate sector of the Eurobond market. These institutions who had little or no use for term fixed rate funds were attractive as issuers of fixed rate debt because of their scarcity values as investors sought to diversify the credit risk element in their portfolio.

The initial growth of US$ interest rate swaps saw these banks and financial institutions enter the market as issuers of fixed rate debt which was then swapped into floating rate US$ funding consistent with their general asset liability management requirements. However, the exploitation of the arbitrage as well as the legislative changes in United States withholding tax, led to this original rationale for US$ interest rate swaps declining in importance. It is clear that sub-LIBOR spreads available to issuers declined as the market became more efficient in pricing the relative value of the swap. While in the initial phase of the market, a AAA issuer could reasonably expect to achieve up to 75 to 100bps below LIBOR on a US$ straight bond issue and accompanying swap, by 1986, the same issuer might only expect to achieve a spread of 25 to 30bps below LIBOR on a plain vanilla bond issue and swap. Arbitrage spreads have continued to diminish.

The change in the arbitrage profits was also influenced by a number of less obvious factors. First, the growth of non-US$ international bond markets saw United States entities seeking fixed rate funds turning to sectors other than the US$ as a means of achieving the most cost effective US$ funding. In essence, the US$ interest rate swap market competed as an arbitrage market with other available opportunities in different currencies.

An additional factor was the change in relationship between the United States CP and LIBOR rates. The CP and LIBOR spread which was approximately 100bps in 1984 narrowed significantly. This meant that the situation whereby a United States corporate could pay 60bps over treasuries on a swap and receive LIBOR whilst being funded in the CP market at or about LIBOR minus 100 thereby allowing it to achieve an all-in cost of funds of treasuries minus 40bps, evaporated.

The final factor was the decline in interest rates during the 1985 to 1986 period which led to an oversupply of fixed rate payers with borrowers crowding in to fix debt costs at the lower absolute rates. A basic structural change also occurred with the increasing importance of asset swaps which added to the oversupply of fixed rate payers in the US$ interest rate swap markets.

Under these pressures, the fundamental structure of US$ swap rates changed dramatically, predominantly showing both an increase in the spread levels as well as a significantly higher degree of volatility in the swap spreads. Perversely, the changing pattern of swap spreads and the increase in underlying volatility of these spreads prompted innovations such as options on swaps, options on swap spreads, spreadlocks etc. The volatility also attracted trading interest, initially from United States investment banks, who came to view swaps as another trading instrument which, via the medium of the spread, allowed them to trade the relativities of different sectors of the capital market.

However, this basic speculative or positioning interest still needed to be fed by activity in the primary segment of the US$ interest rate swap market which inevitably meant the engineering of new issues. The primary focus in this regard was the creation of bond structures which offered the fixed rate issuer lower costs and therefore a better spread below LIBOR which in turn required additional engineering on the basic interest rate swap.

In addition to this requirement of creativity was a more highly developed sense of timing in bringing issues to market and in executing the accompanying swap. While finding a window in primary debt markets has always been a feature of a successful issue, with the advent and development of the US$ interest rate swap market, the Eurodollar bond market began to function in terms of a complex interaction of investor demand and swap spread windows. Given that the long-term US$ interest rate swap market operated on a relatively stable, at least in the short-term, spread level versus US$ treasuries, issuers sought to locate a spread window for a particular type of issuer usually predicated on timing leads and lags in the behaviour of various sectors of the markets, such as reaction lags as between the US$ domestic and Eurodollar markets.

The more recent history of the US$ swap market has been dominated by credit risk considerations. A central concern, in this regard, has been, as previously noted, the decline in credit quality of major bank participants in the swap market as well as a financial crisis among a number of end users.

A by-product of this increasing focus on credit in the US$ swap markets has been to reduce the market share of United States money centre banks and investment banks, who historically have dominated this market.

Even among the more credit-worthy market participants, the fact that swap credit exposures are approaching the limit of intra-dealer trading lines as well as the decision by many end users of swaps to restrict their counterparty credit quality to AA or better credit rated institutions has become a major factor in the structure of the market and the pattern of activity. This has created opportunities for strong non-United States banks, particularly European financial institutions to increase market share in US$ interest rate swaps, particularly at the longer end of the yield curve: see discussion in Chapters 1 and 43.

Consistent with general developments in other swap markets, the increasingly commodity nature of conventional swap products in the US$ has reduced profit margins forcing institutions to emphasise innovation or proprietary trading. A central feature of the US$ swap market has been the increased assumption of risk by dealers and market makers in an effort to continue to maintain strong earnings streams.

The United States domiciled swap market has itself been under threat of regulation from the Commodity Futures Trading Commission (CFTC). The possibility that exemption from CFTC regulation of most swap transactions would be removed had threatened to force the US$ swap market *outside the USA*. The major impetus to removing the exemption has come, predictably, from the powerful United States Futures Exchanges lobby who see the exemption as benefiting the OTC swap market and forcing business away from the organised futures and options exchanges. The exchanges sought maintenance of the current CFTC status quo, pending a full scale review of swap and other OTC activity. However, in

September 1992, congressional members finally approved the CFTC re-authorisation bill reducing concerns that a law court in theory may refuse to enforce swap contracts on the grounds there were unregulated futures contracts (under the terms of the legislation futures contracts *must* be traded on an organised exchange).

A recent problem to emerge in the US$ swap market has been increasing concern over the United States Internal Revenue Service's (IRS) tax treatment of derivatives. The traditional policy of the IRS regarding the treatment of hedges has focused on the original purposes of derivative transactions. If the transactions are undertaken for investment/speculation, then gains or losses are treated as capital; if they are intended to hedge ordinary expenses or income, then gains or losses are treated as ordinary business income or losses.

This historical position was thrown into doubt as an indirect result of a 1988 court case, *Arkansas Best v Commissioner of Internal Revenue*. This case tested the "business motives" doctrine that companies had, traditionally, used to justify ordinary taxation for their hedge transactions. The United States Supreme Court's ruling in that case as interpreted by the IRS dramatically restricted the types of transaction eligible for treatment as ordinary business income or loss. That case reversed an earlier decision and decreed that only hedges that act as substitutes or surrogates for inventory were eligible for ordinary taxation. The result of this interpretation was that liability hedges and other types of hedges would be treated as capital assets, thereby rendering a capital loss on a hedge non-deductible despite the fact that it was offsetting an ordinary business transaction.

The IRS interpretation of *Arkansas Best* has created significant controversy with US companies and trade associations. Seven US future exchanges, the Futures Industry Association and the American Bankers Association have protested about "a tax-induced disincentive [to] using risk-reducing, prudent business practices".

The IRS approach, together with a number of other cases which are at various stages of litigation in the United States, creates significant uncertainty. For example, the *Arkansas Best* decision may, ironically, create disadvantages for futures and options contracts traded on formal exchanges.

Exchange based commodity hedges, under the *Arkansas Best* approach, will only be available, at least where ordinary income tax treatment is required, for hedges of future purchases of inventory. However, while the IRS takes the view that short hedges of the value of inventory do not qualify for ordinary treatment, over-the-counter forward contracts, satisfied by delivery of the physical product, should not produce capital gains or losses. The delivery of inventory against the contract should be viewed as an ordinary sale of the product.

Similarly, for US$-based interest rate hedges, the IRS approach creates an incentive to use periodic exchanges under notional principal contracts rather than futures, forwards or cash market transaction in treasury bonds. This is because periodic payments may still be considered ordinary.

This approach creates a positive incentive in favour of over-the-counter products. However, the approach is not wholly favourable to the over-the-counter market itself. For example, termination and assignments of swaps may be treated as capital transactions by the IRS, forcing participants to offset transactions with a third party without recognising gains or losses on the original swaps (that is, transacting mirror transactions). As noted above in Chapter 21 this creates problems of pyramiding of credit risk within swap markets.

The uncertainties created by the IRS interpretation of the *Arkansas Best* decision together with the complexities of the IRS' foreign tax credit provisions create a number of impediments for US-based hedgers. This uncertainty clearly creates an adverse environment for the further development of this market. In late 1993, the IRS reversed its position and withdrew its opposition to the *Arkansas Best* decision. However, it is still some way from recognising the true economic basis of hedging, particularly on a portfolio basis. A detailed discussion of tax issues regarding swap and derivative transactions in the United States is set out in Chapter 41.

In summary, it is useful to distinguish between phases in the history of the US$ interest rate swap market.

- An initial period when substantial arbitrage gains provided the primary driving factor behind the growth of the market.
- A second, necessarily more complex, phase when in the face of declining arbitrage profits but ironically increasing depth and liquidity as various participants entered the market, the structure of the market broadened to widen the range of instruments available as well as basing the activity in the primary level of the market on development of new and innovative bond structures or on timing considerations.
- The current, more mature phase characterised by typical factors expected to be experienced at maturity, such as declining profit margins, credit risk and regulatory concerns, consolidation among participants and lower volume growth.

C$ SWAP MARKET

Origins

The involvement of United States banks and corporations in Canada and vice versa made the emergence of a C$ swap market inevitable. A natural demand for cross-currency swaps, primarily between C$ and US$, existed and interest rate swaps soon followed and now predominate.

The C$ swap market commenced in about 1980. The initial participants were the Canadian banks who sought to use swaps as a means of managing mismatches between assets and liabilities within their own portfolios. Currency swaps were also used to hedge foreign exchange positions. The growth in the market from these tentative beginnings was initially slow with the banks being followed into the market by the Crown agencies, such as the Federal Business Development Bank, who sought to utilise swaps as a method of generating cheaper floating rate funds to replace liabilities such as CP. The initial impetus to a faster rate of growth in the market came from a period of increased interest rates in the early 1980s when Canadian corporations and, more recently, trust and insurance companies entered the market. The participation of this last group was to primarily utilise swaps as a method of interest risk management as well as currency risk management.

Market structure

Structurally, the fixed rate side of the C$ swap market is dominated by the EuroCanadian dollar bond market. As in the case of a number of currencies, the availability of swaps has helped create a deeper C$ bond market, both domestically and internationally, while, simultaneously, the growth of the bond market has been critical to the further development of the swap market. Since 1985, increased international appetite for C$ securities, primarily in the form of EuroCanadian dollar issues, has helped sustain the C$ swap market. Investors have sought C$

investments as a yield pick-up relative to the US$ market or as an alternative to high yielding currencies such as the A$, NZ$, GBP and, more recently, some European currencies.

C$ swaps usually entail at least three specific sets of transactions:

- a cross-currency swap (C$ fixed/US$ LIBOR) typically transacted against a Euro-Canadian issue where the issuer swaps issue proceeds into floating rate US$ LIBOR;
- a C$ interest rate swap (C$ fixed/floating C$ BAs) transacted with corporate, provincial, public utilities of institutional clients;
- a floating-floating cross currency swap (US$ LIBOR/C$ BAs) transacted between the bank and, typically, a corporation raising funds in US$ converting its liability into floating rate C$.

The floating-floating currency swap leg can entail the bank, providing the swaps, absorbing the transaction to generate C$ funding within its own liability portfolio. Alternatively, this leg can be driven by an arbitrage whereby some Canadian companies are prepared to pay a margin of 8-15bps to get US$ LIBOR funding.

Exhibit 23.7 sets out the structure of the C$ swap market.

Exhibit 23.7

Euro-Canadian Dollar Swap Market Structure

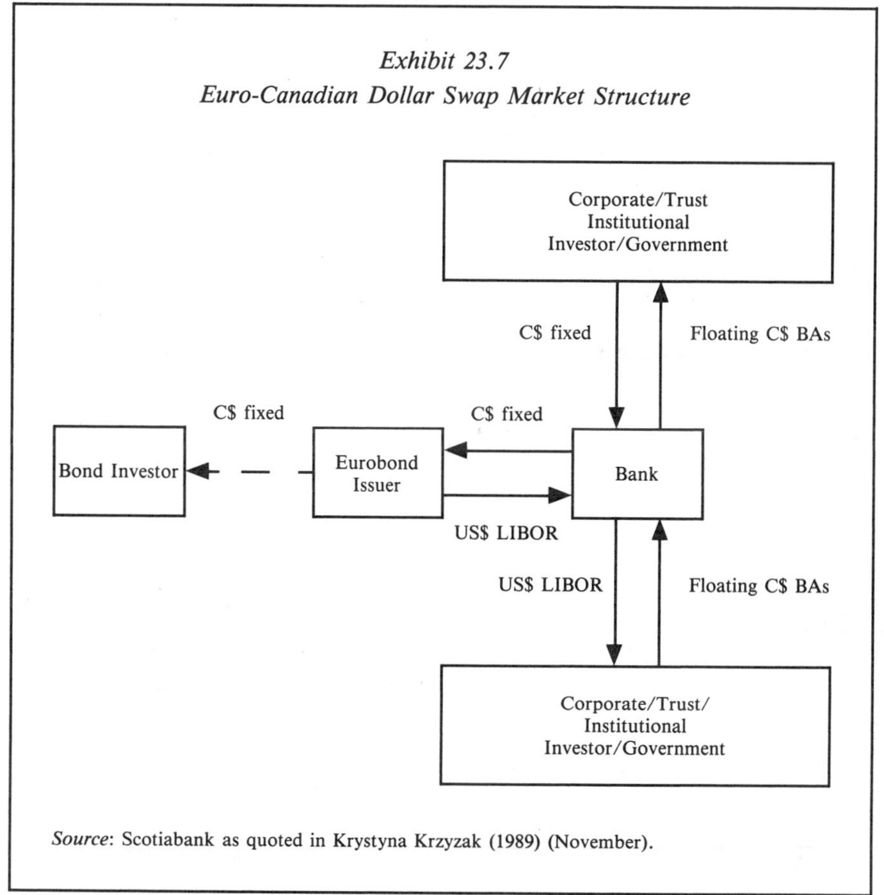

Source: Scotiabank as quoted in Krystyna Krzyzak (1989) (November).

Alternative sources of fixed rate funds for swap transactions have come from specially structured one off issues in the domestic Canadian market such as a home oil index debenture issued in 1986 or, until recently, the presence of a substantial fixed rate preference share market. As discussed in Chapter 18, C$ swaps have also been utilised in deposit-based asset swap transactions primarily in Japan.

However, with about half of the EuroCanadian issues currently being undertaken by non-Canadians, the primary driving force behind the growth of the market remains the continuing international demand for C$ securities.

Pricing/market conventions

Canadian dollar swaps are usually quoted on the fixed rate side as a margin over the yield on government of Canada bond issues of comparable maturities. The floating rate side is usually set in relation to the C$ bankers acceptances as the floating rate index, typically for 30, 60 or 90 days, or against US$ LIBOR set every three or six months, in the case of cross-currency swaps. The typical spread between the bid and offer price is 0.07/10% pa for interest rate swaps and 0.125/15% pa for currency swap.

Exhibit 23.8 sets out the historical levels of swap rates and spreads for C$ swaps in a number of key maturities.

Exhibit 23.8
C$ Interest Rate Swap Rates and Spreads

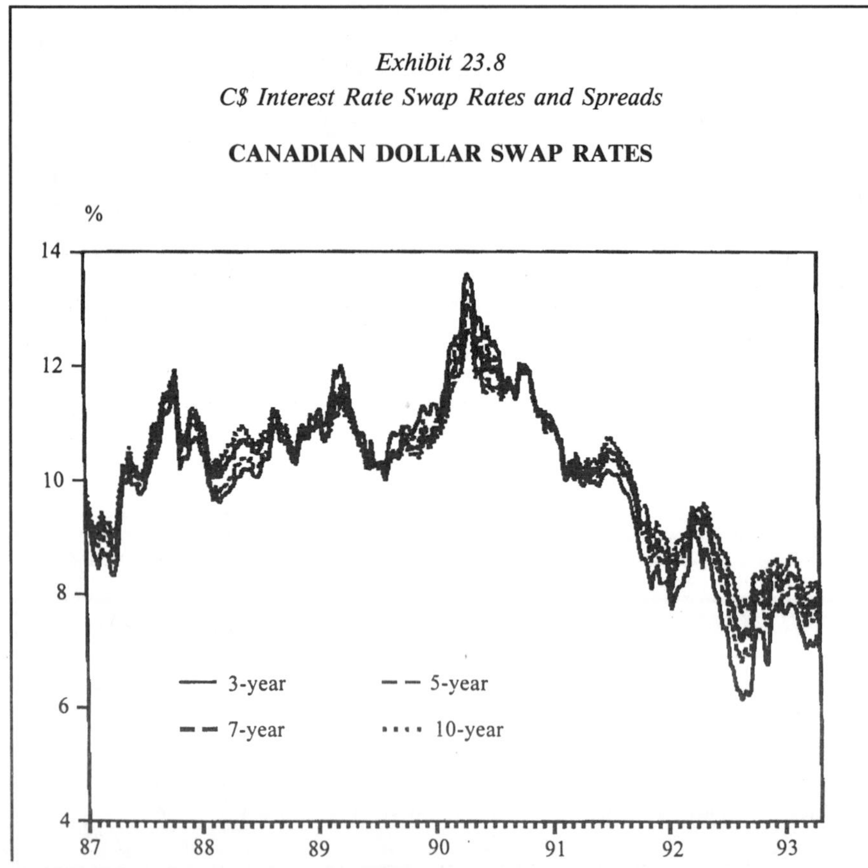

Exhibit 23.8—continued

CANADIAN DOLLAR SWAP SPREADS

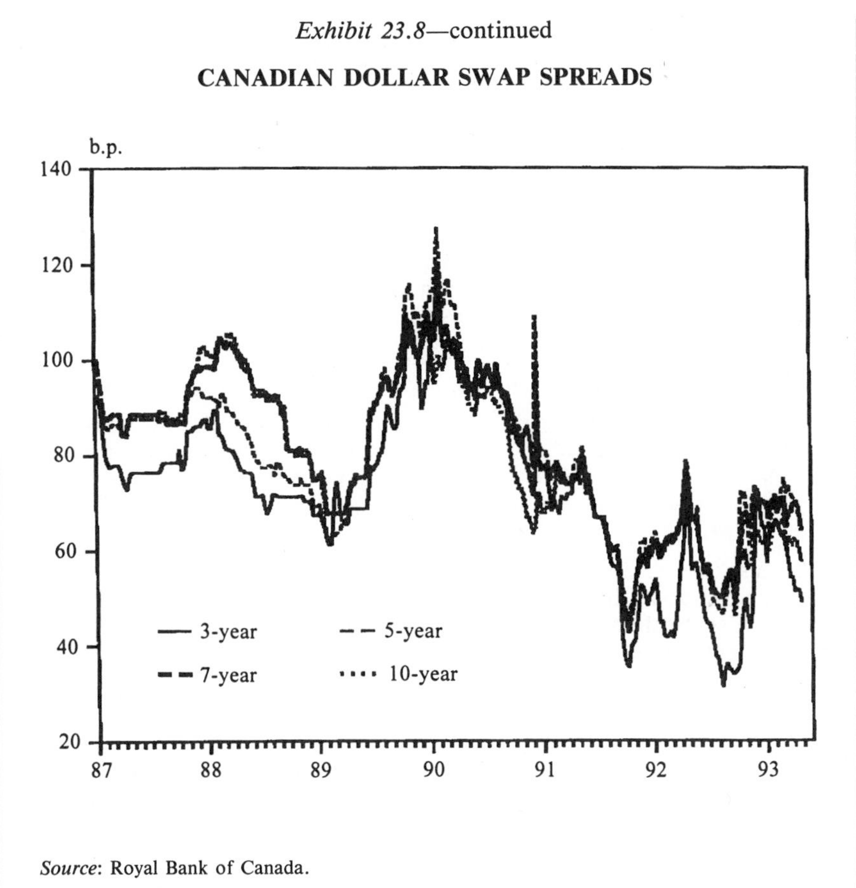

Source: Royal Bank of Canada.

Swaps vary hugely in size, ranging from C$5m to over C$100m. The normal size for a domestic transaction is in the range C$10-50m while Eurobond related swaps in C$ start at C$50m.

The nature of the investor base in C$ securities as well as the pattern of non-Canadian issuers has dictated the presence of some curious currency swap combinations between, inter alia, C$, yen, deutschmarks, Swiss francs, ECUs, GBP and, at least on one occasion, A$. Inevitably, however, the transactions involve a US$ LIBOR leg.

A factor in the C$ swap market is the difficulties of hedging a swap position reflecting the lower liquidity levels in the C$ bond market, compared to, say, the United States treasury note/bond market. An added problem in this regard is the relatively limited number of major market players where it is difficult for swap hedges to be executed without the knowledge of other major market participants because of the size of transactions that must be executed in the C$ bond market.

An added difficulty is that the absence of regular auctions of C$ government bonds which creates difficulty for trading as the bond used to hedge may be replaced by a new issue in the relevant series creating yield discrepancies.

The futures market in C$ BAs is developing increasingly allowing the shorter end of the C$ swap market to be priced of futures strips.

Additional difficulties derive from the fact that Canada lacks a true repo market creating difficulties in financing or shorting bonds to hedge swap risk positions.

Products

The C$ swap market is relatively well developed with a wide variety of instruments available, although trading depth and liquidity is not as high as in the US$ swap market. For example, a significant market in C$ swaptions exists and are primarily utilised by end users to monetise interest rate expectations.

Participants

The market is dominated by the major Canadian banks such as the Royal Bank of Canada, Canadian Imperial Bank of Commerce, Toronto Dominion and the other chartered Canadian banks with the major foreign participants being the United States banks with substantial activities in Canada, such as Citibank and Bankers Trust.

Other market participants include securities houses with an active presence in the Euro-Canadian dollar bond market as debt underwriters. However, activity from these financial institutions is spasmodic, being related to activity levels in the Euro-Canadian debt markets.

Domestic activity, particularly in C$ interest rate swaps, is dominated by Canadian corporations, government and quasi-government institutions and financial institutions. A major factor in recent years has been borrowing requirements of the provincial administrations and their crown corporations which have increased enormously. These entities are active in managing their increasing liability portfolios. Trust companies with big mortgage portfolios together with banks with their own asset liability management requirements are significant factors.

An unusual feature of the C$ swap market is the participation of the Bank of Canada, the Canadian Central Bank, which uses the domestic swap market principally to swap fixed rate government debt issues into floating rates.

Chapter 24

Asian Swap and Derivative Markets: Yen, HK$ and Other Currencies

JAPANESE YEN SWAP/DERIVATIVES MARKETS

Overview

The Japanese yen swap/derivatives market is among the largest swap markets in the world. While the yen market enjoys many structural similarities with other major swap/derivatives markets around the world, a major difference is that the arbitrage which drives swap transactions in yen tends to be more structural than the traditional forms of credit or other arbitrages which drive swaps in other markets.

A key factor underlying this type of structural arbitrage is the regulatory framework governing the activities of financial institutions within Japan. For example, the classification of Japanese financial institutions between city banks and long-term credit banks creates an artificial segmentation which leads to asset liability mismatches which to some extent have been arbitraged utilising swap transaction structures. Similarly, the regulation of interest rates and the complex inter-relationships between various interest rates within the Japanese market also underly the basic swap arbitrages undertaken.

Deregulation of the Japanese financial system, to an increasing extent, has reduced the rigid structural barriers which have determined the framework of the yen swap market. However, elements of this regulatory framework continue to exist.

Origins and evolution

The history and development of the yen swap market can be divided into two distinct phases: pre- and post-liberalisation and deregulation of the Euroyen bond market in 1984.

The earliest yen swaps were arranged in the early 1980s. During this period, the yen swap market consisted of back-to-back transaction mostly related to investment or borrowing transactions whereby large multinational corporations sought to hedge their forward payables or receivables of a commercial, rather than a financial nature.

In 1981, this was followed by a series of bond issues, primarily by French institutions, which were swapped into yen. The motivation for these transactions was primarily a large French foreign exchange borrowing requirement which the French authorities preferred to handle through private placements. Consequently, a public or private placement would be arranged; simultaneously, a swap into yen would be executed with Japanese investors who would thereby create an artificial yen asset.

At the same time, a number of Japanese entities created synthetic yen liabilities. For example, Japan Development Bank and Japan Airlines issued bonds in 1981 in

US$ which were swapped into yen. The source of the yen for these swaps were largely airline leases. For example, in one of these early transactions, a United States airline with a yen-based lease transaction, desiring to swap into US$, provided the yen part of one transaction. During this period the overall liquidity of the market was extremely low with spreads of over 1.00%.

The major expansion of the yen market came in 1984 with the liberalisation and deregulation of the Euroyen bond market. While the Euroyen market had begun in spectacular fashion in 1977 with an issue by the European Investment Bank, the Japanese Ministry of Finance only authorised six issues per year. In December 1984, non-Japanese residents were permitted access to the Euroyen market. Supranationals, sovereigns, government agencies and local governments with an A rating or better and all corporates with a AA rating or better as well as some lesser corporates were allowed to issue Euroyen bonds. Simultaneously, non-Japanese houses and subsidiaries of Japanese banks were allowed to lead manage Euroyen issues. The Ministry of Finance also allowed, for the first time, swaps on Euroyen issues.

These measures led to a dramatic increase in the volume of issues denominated in yen. This growth is evidenced by the fact that the yen rapidly became the second major currency, after the US$, in the international bond market.

In April 1986, further liberalisation took place with eligibility for Euroyen borrowers being relaxed further. The rule that Euroyen bonds could not be sold into Japan until 180 days had elapsed since issue was also replaced with a shorter restriction period of 90 days. More recently, foreign commercial banks were allowed to undertake Euroyen transactions. In July 1986, Euroyen subordinated bonds were also approved.

This expansion of the Euroyen market and in the resulting volume of yen funds that were being supplied led to a rapid expansion of the yen swap market. The impetus came primarily because a high proportion of Euroyen issues launched were swapped, primarily, into US$. In fact, because of the presence of withholding tax as well as a direct prohibition on some Japanese issuers undertaking borrowings, the Euroyen market until recently was primarily used by borrowers who utilised the yen funding as part of arbitrage funding practices to generate cheap funding in a variety of currencies. The legitimacy of the yen swap market was well and truly established in 1984 when a transaction was arranged for the World Bank, whereby it swapped an existing US$ liability into yen.

The majority of these swaps were undertaken by the issuers of Euroyen securities with the Japanese banks, in particular, the trust banks. These banks were the main payers of yen in any swap. The factors underlying the ultimate utilisation of the fixed rate yen funding generated are, however, more complex. The Japanese banks themselves are significant users of the fixed rate funds for their own asset liability management purposes. Similarly, the clients of the banks utilised significant quantities of this fixed rate yen funding, either directly through a swap against an existing liability or alternatively in the form of a fixed rate yen loan provided by a bank.

In recent years, a significant portion of the demand for yen funding via these swaps has come from Japanese corporations who have increasingly raised capital, denominated in non-yen currencies, outside Japan.

In the period through until 1991, when the Japanese equity market went into a protracted period of decline, Japanese corporations, primarily industrial companies or trading houses, raised substantial volumes of financing through equity warrant linked issues in international markets. In addition, Japanese corporations were significant borrowers of conventional bond issues in a variety of currencies. A significant proportion of the US$ liabilities created (either directly or indirectly by swapping the primary issue into floating rate US$ LIBOR) were, subsequently, swapped into fixed rate yen. As previously outlined in Chapter 18, on a number of occasions the borrowers, particularly in the heady days of 1987, were able to complete these transactions to create borrowings at *negative* interest rates.

Foreign borrowers have also utilised swaps as a vehicle for accessing fixed rate yen funding. The reasons for this are largely structural and relate to the eventual effective cost of the yen liability. For example, the World Bank has been a significant user of yen swaps because of its continuing high levels of demand for fixed rate yen funding.

The nature of the investor base in Euroyen securities has largely limited issuers to sovereign, semi-sovereign or prime corporate entities. The conservative nature of the investor base and their concern about changing financial conditions within the corporate sector has led over time, at least once the rarity value of corporate bonds decreased, to great limitations on the range of issuers whose securities were purchased. This has meant that a number of corporate borrowers, seeking yen funding, have found it more advantageous to utilise swaps to generate fixed rate yen liabilities.

In recent times, a significant proportion of yen swap business has related to: asset swap structures and swaps relating to Samurai issues/structured private placements within Japan.

The growth of asset swaps as a driving force in the yen swap markets relates to, originally, the issuance of equity warrant linked debt issues by Japanese corporations. While demand for the warrants themselves was strong reflecting the demand for leveraged exposure to the then rapidly increasing value of the Nikkei Index, demand for the debt component was relatively weak. This reflected in part the structure of the debt which because of its low coupon dictated that the ex-warrant bonds traded at an immediate discount. As noted in Chapter 18, a significant proportion of the debt component of equity warrant linked issues was repackaged through asset swaps and placed as floating rate US$ assets. However, a significant proportion of these ex-warrant bonds were also placed with Japanese clients *as yen assets*. Under these asset swap structures, the Japanese investor purchased the US$ bond and entered into a US$ fixed/JPY fixed swap to convert the return to a yen basis. A decline in equity linked debt issuance has reduced but not eliminated asset swap structures as a component of the yen market. Japanese investors increasingly purchase foreign securities repackaged into yen for reasons of portfolio diversification or yield enhancement.

An additional source of yen swap transactions has been the resurgence in Samurai issues, yen issues for foreign issuers taken in the Japanese domestic capital markets. Most foreign issuers, typically, swap the yen proceeds of Samurai issues into, initially, floating rate US$ LIBOR and, ultimately, into its desired currency and interest rate basis.

Complementing the Samurai issues are a wide variety of structured private placements which are inevitably accompanied by a swap transaction. The structured private placements are generally based on specific investor demand for particular security structures (such as those discussed in Chapters 15, 16 and 17). They include dual currency and reverse dual currency issue structures (see discussion below) which require complex structured swaps to insulate the issuer from the cash flow characteristics of the issue and its risk.

Structure of yen and US$ swap market[1]

There are two distinct and separate yen and US$ swaps markets, both of which are linked to either the Euroyen or the Eurodollar bond markets:

- the fixed yen versus floating rate US$ swap markets;
- the fixed yen versus fixed US$ market (that is, the LTFX market).

These two markets have traditionally not been closely connected because of the different ways the swaps are constructed and the different pricing variables.

Fixed yen and US$ LIBOR swaps

The typical structure of a fixed yen and US$ LIBOR swap against an issue is set out in *Exhibit 24.1*.

Exhibit 24.1
Structure of Yen and US$ LIBOR Swap Market

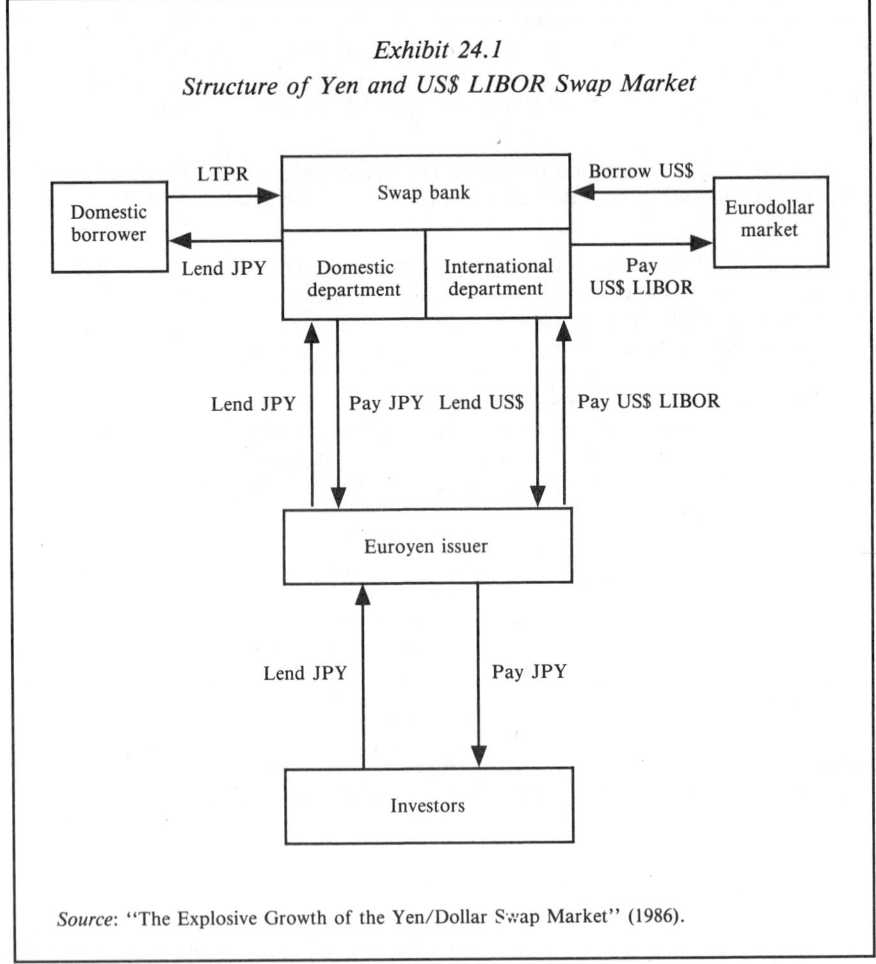

Source: "The Explosive Growth of the Yen/Dollar Swap Market" (1986).

1. This discussion of the structure of yen swaps draws heavily on "The Explosive Growth of the Yen/Dollar Swap Market" (1986).

The structure of this segment of the market is largely dictated by the type of participants while pricing is closely linked to their ability to borrow long-term yen funds.

Pricing for fixed yen and floating US$ swaps is determined principally by the long-term prime rate (LTPR). The LTPR is part of the regulated interest rate structure within Japan, and is connected to the Japanese government bond coupon via the bank debenture rate. An overview of the Japanese interest rate structure is set out in *Exhibit 24.2*.

The rate the swap bank will pay is typically a margin below LTPR (say 10-15bps). The final rate may depend upon expectations of future movements in the domestic bond market and LTPR. Consequently, swap rates depend very heavily on current demand from borrowers which, in turn, depends upon market expectations.

There is a division between certain types of banks within the Japanese domestic market. City banks have access to short-term (up to two years) funds which has meant that they have historically concentrated on short-term lending. The long-term banks and trust banks, in contrast, have access to long-term debt primarily through the issue of bank debentures and they have specialised in providing long-term loans to industry. Therefore the long-term and trust banks predominate as payers of fixed rate yen. More recently, however, in order to create fixed rate long-term yen liabilities to match their domestic long-term loans the city banks have played a more active role as payers of fixed rate yen in fixed yen and floating US$ swaps.

The principal source of potential arbitrage is the differential between the LTPR and Euroyen bond yields. The LTPR is dependent upon domestic Japanese government bond market conditions whereas Euroyen bond yields are subject to conditions in both the Japanese government bond market and the international bond markets as well as exchange rate expectations. Further, as Euroyen bond yields are substantially more volatile than the LTPR, the interest differentials between these two rates can widen substantially to create attractive swap arbitrages for Euroyen issuers.

The reverse of the first type of transaction is where the swap bank receives fixed rate yen, typically to convert a Eurodollar bond or "sushi" issue into fixed rate yen funding. This type of structure is set out in *Exhibit 24.3*.

In these cases, city banks are in a better competitive position as they can fund the yen receipts by utilising their very cheap deposit base. The banks are often prepared to risk the asset liability maturity mismatch for historical as well as strategic reasons. Trust banks and long-term banks will either match their long-term lending (via the swap) to their long-term funding or use their deposit base like the city banks.

There were a number of sources of arbitrage in these transactions. The swaps were often "hara-kiri" swaps; that is, the swaps were priced at off-market rates.

It was often assumed by non-Japanese observers, including other financial institutions, that the swap bank was making a loss. In reality, the bank providing the hara-kiri swap was not making an actual loss, but an "opportunity" loss (that is, it could have lent the funds at a higher rate), as the banks' funding cost (via cheap deposits) was below the rate at which they were lending via the swap.

An additional factor here was that the swap bank usually sought to time its entry into a swap to coincide with the large interest cost differential between the Japanese domestic and the Euroyen market. For example, there were periods when the volume of swap-driven issues rocketed. The first being between December 1985 and January 1986 when there was a wide gap between LTPR and the cost of Euroyen issues. At this time, LTPR was expected to rise and so Japanese corporations rushed

Exhibit 24.2

Japanese Interest Rates—Structural Interrelationships

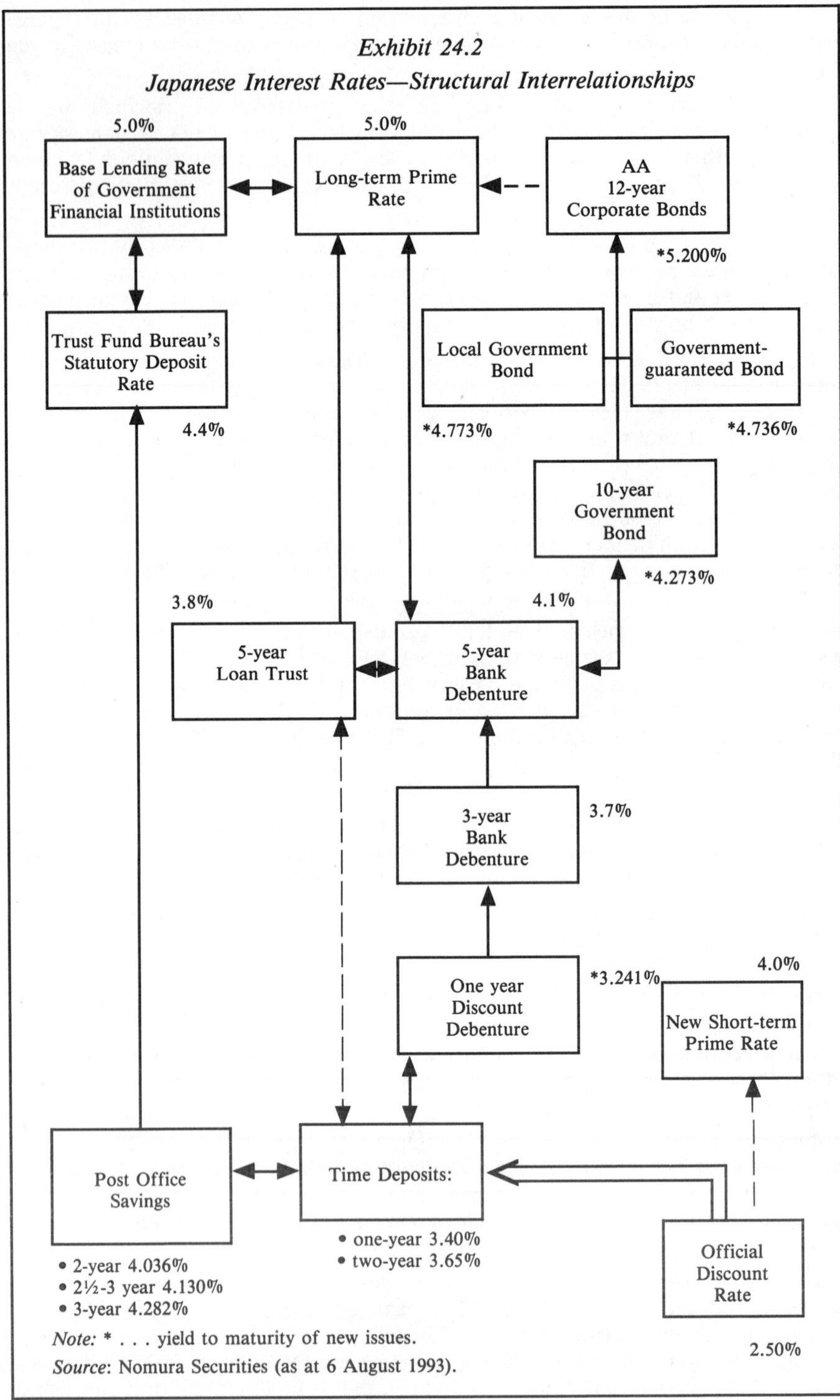

Note: * . . . yield to maturity of new issues.

Source: Nomura Securities (as at 6 August 1993).

to borrow from the banks. Similar conditions prevailed again in March and April 1986. During these periods, what may have appeared to the observer as extraordinarily aggressive yen swap rates were primarily temporary imbalances in the supply and demand of fixed rate yen funding creating attractive swap opportunities.

Exhibit 24.3

Structure of Yen and US$ Swap for Eurodollar or Sushi Issue

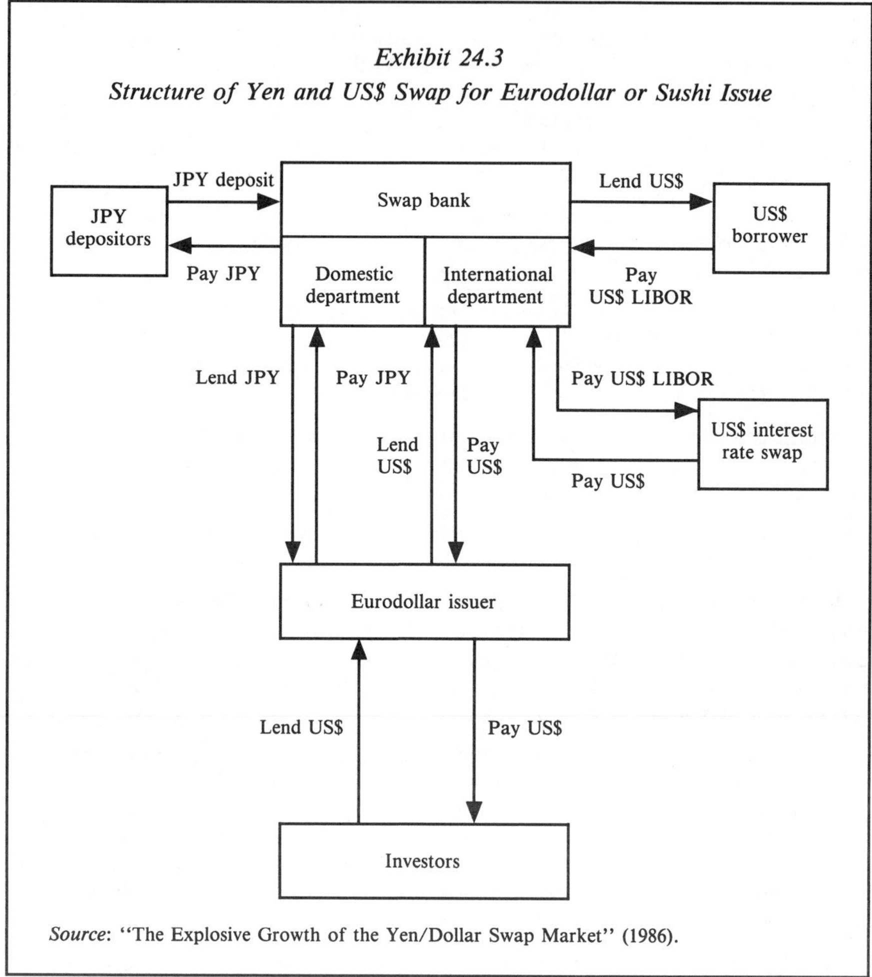

Source: "The Explosive Growth of the Yen/Dollar Swap Market" (1986).

An additional more nebulous consideration is that as the lending rate is virtually determined by the bank, it is necessary to consider whether the Japanese banks were able to manipulate LTPR to essentially prevent large losses from their aggressive swap positions.

It is also clear that the so-called hara-kiri swaps were typically provided to obtain a coveted co-lead management position in a Eurodollar issue for a Japanese corporation (a sushi issue), and/or to maintain or improve relationships with its own clients. To an extent, the aggressive swap pricing is explainable on the basis of the aggressive competition between the Japanese banks and securities houses. The banks were seeking to establish a foothold in the London market either as lead or co-lead managers for Eurobond issues. Simultaneously, the Japanese securities companies were also pricing swaps particularly aggressively as it provided them with the opportunities, via the Euroyen market, to establish relationships with prime non-Japanese borrowers.

A further element of arbitrage was that bonds issued by Japanese borrowers were exempt under Japanese regulations from inclusion in holdings of foreign securities by insurance companies and pension funds. As these investors were in the process of rapidly expanding their US$ denominated portfolios these sushi bonds became particularly attractive. As demand for the bonds exceeded supply, Japanese issuers were able to borrow at substantially cheaper rates than non-Japanese borrowers in the Eurodollar market.

The combination of hara-kiri swaps with the sushi bond issues produced very favourable terms for the issuers, certainly more favourable than those available in the domestic market.

As detailed in the discussion below, yen swap rate show a stronger correlation to Euroyen and LTPR rates. In particular, the five year swap rate has a strong historical relationship between LTPR and is closely monitored by Japanese banks active in yen swaps who seek to arbitrage the markets.

Recent changes in the financial structure of Japanese markets has assisted in the integration of the various market segments. However, the complex interrelationships between the markets continues to be a major factor.

Fixed yen and fixed US$ LTFX

The historical pattern of involvement of various participants in the foreign exchange market largely determined the existence of this parallel market. The trust banks and long-term banks are more active in the long-dated foreign exchange markets while the city banks, except for the Bank of Tokyo, have concentrated more on the spot and short-dated forward markets.

In addition, prior to 1971, the Ministry of Finance strictly controlled access of Japanese banks to the international markets. Class A banks, which included the large city banks, Bank of Tokyo and Industrial Bank of Japan, were permitted to open overseas branches, representative offices and subsidiaries. Class B banks, which included trust banks, local banks, and other types of financial institutions, were limited to foreign exchange dealing in Tokyo, trade financing and correspondent bank relationships.

The trust banks and long-term banks have used their long-dated foreign exchange dealing capabilities to develop their corporate relationships, both within and outside of Japan, and are therefore often prepared to offer attractive LTFX swaps if they are linked to public Eurobond transactions.

Pricing for fixed yen and fixed US$ swaps is determined principally by the interest rate differential between United States treasury bonds and Japanese government bonds, although because the yen and US$ LTFX market is relatively illiquid, it is also dependent to a large extent on supply and demand. Because of lags between price and yield movements in the United States treasury market, which is relatively volatile, and movements in rates in the LTFX markets, which are relatively stable, it is possible to pick up attractive arbitrage opportunities.

The source of the arbitrage, therefore, is the US$ and yen interest differential implicit in the yen and US$ spot and forward rates and the yield on United States treasuries.

Structure of the yen interest rate swap market

The yen interest rate swap market is the most recent stage of development of the Japanese yen swap market. The yen interest rate swap market evolved in the middle of 1986 and by the end of 1986 had become an important component of the Japanese capital market.

The growth in yen interest rate swaps is predicated on the following factors:

- the structure of the banking system within Japan;
- the asset liability management requirements of Japanese corporations.

Central to the growth of yen interest rate swaps has been the tacit approval by the Ministry of Finance to these types of transactions which implicitly portend crossing of traditional banking divides within Japan. These types of transactions have been utilised by the Japanese city banks as an entree into long-term lending, an area, as noted above, to which they have previously been denied access. These city banks have utilised swaps as a means of generating synthetic fixed rate funding to match off their exposure on fixed rate lending to Japanese corporations. The long-term trust banks, at least in theory, should provide the opposite side to these transactions as they are able to generate floating rate funding, pricing off short-term interest rates to fund their growing short-term lending business.

This role of yen interest rate swaps in bank asset liability management contributes to the fact that a high proportion of the activity is between financial institutions. However, there is a growing interest among Japanese corporations in utilising yen interest rate swaps. Liability management concerns predominate in attracting these participants into the yen interest rate swap market.

The participation of non-financial institutions in yen interest rate swaps is usually based on one of the following reasons:

- Fixed rate funding opportunities for companies with lower credit ratings. This is precisely the type of credit arbitrage which dominates many other swap markets. For example, steel and shipping companies as well as leasing companies have been active as payers of fixed rates in yen interest rate swaps.
- The use of interest rate swaps to unhinge high coupon yen borrowings into floating rate liabilities to lower the absolute interest levels on outstanding loans. This particular type of transaction has been popular because of the reluctance of Japanese corporations to repay existing loans at high fixed interest rates because of the complex relationship between lenders and borrowers in Japan. Against this background, by converting long-term fixed rate liabilities into floating rate through the swap market, Japanese corporations have sought to reduce their annual interest cost without having to risk falling out with their traditional house relationship bank.
- As liquidity has developed, corporations have sought to trade interest rates by entering into interest rate swaps to take advantage of the differential between fixed and floating interest rates and also to seek to capitalise on interest rate movements. The fact that swaps are off-balance sheet transactions requiring no margin calls or cash payment has made this type of positioning activity increasingly popular.

Market participants

The principal participants in the yen swap market include:

- International issuers of Euroyen bonds who utilise yen currency swaps convert yen funding into floating rate US$ LIBOR based financing.
- Japanese financial institutions, primarily Japanese city banks, who utilise swaps to both hedge their natural interest rate positions and for reasons of proprietary trading. The city banks who are traditionally restricted to funding through short-term deposits of maturities of less than one year, typically, utilise interest rate swaps to allow them access to longer term funding improving their asset-liability profile.
- Japanese corporations, insurance companies and other end users who either utilise swaps to convert foreign currency funding into yen or utilise yen interest rate swaps to generate fixed rate funding or to assume trading positions on interest rates.
- Financial institutions active in market making in yen swap and derivative product.

Major market makers in yen swaps are the larger Japanese banks, both city and long term credit banks, who are active for internal asset-liability management reasons, proprietary trading purposes as well as servicing end user demand. A number of foreign institutions maintain significant yen swap portfolios, although a substantial proportion of these are related to new issue transactions in the Euroyen bond market.

Securities houses, such as Nomura Securities, Diawa, Nikko Securities and Yamaichi Securities, have traditionally acted as arrangers of swaps rather than principal traders/market makers. However, under increased competitive pressure, these institutions are increasingly active as principals in the yen swap market.

The yen swap market is increasingly global in terms of trading activity, spanning the trading hours in Tokyo, London and New York. However, activity, generally, is still concentrated in the Tokyo time zone and, during the relevant times of the year, during the overlap of trading hours between Tokyo and London.

Products

The product range in the yen swap market has increasingly broadened and now approaches those available in the more developed swap currencies. Traditionally, foreign banks, based on their expertise and product range in other markets, have introduced innovations in yen swaps. However, increasingly Japanese banks have bridged the technology gap and are capable of product development/innovation at a level comparable to foreign banks active in yen swaps. In particular, Japanese institutions, with their intimate knowledge of investor and client requirements, have been instrumental in creating complex and hybrid swap structures: see discussions in Chapters 15, 16 and 17.

Structured non-generic swap transactions, including amortising, zero coupon and other arrangements are now available. Option based products such as options on swaps are also available. In particular, the sale of options on swaps as a source of premium income is common. In addition, options on swaps have been utilised to monetise the call options on yen private placements and Euroyen issues from time to time.

In recent years, hybrid swap structures primarily related to private placement activity, have emerged. Popular loan structures, at least for a time, have included reverse floater transactions, yen/A$ or other currency dual currency structures as well as transactions with embedded options covering currencies, interest rates, commodities or equities.

Pricing yen swaps

Market conventions

The yen market has, in recent years, matured significantly with pricing techniques for yen swaps having achieved a higher degree of standardisation than had previously existed.

Average maturities are around three years for interest rate swaps and around five years for currency swaps. Average transaction sizes are around JPY3/3.5 billion for interest rate swaps and JPY4/5 billion for currency swaps. The longer maturity and greater average size of currency swaps reflect their use in connection with new issues in the Euroyen market where issuers inevitably swap the proceeds into US$ LIBOR initially.

Market liquidity has improved significantly with spreads of 10bps pa in yen interest rate swaps and 12.5/15bps pa in yen currency swaps having narrowed significantly to around 5/7.5bps pa in both interest rate and currency swaps.

As discussed below, the yen swap market continues to trade as an absolute rate market, rather than a spread market as is the case, for example, in US$ or C$.

A further peculiarity of the Japanese market which affects participants in yen swaps is that Japanese institutions do not utilise present value accounting methods for profit and loss calculation. This limitation affects the hedging of swap transaction with cash bonds, futures or other instruments. This results in an asymmetry whereby the loss or gain on the hedge instrument cannot be offset by compensating mark-to-market profit from the transaction being hedged. This effectively restricts hedging practices.

Pricing relationships

As noted above, both yen interest rate and currency swaps are traded on an absolute rate basis. In practice, swap rates are not significantly correlated to the Japanese government bond market. This results in a low correlation between swap yields and the Japanese government bond (JGB) yields. Statistical work undertaken indicates the correlation between swap yields and JGB yields on a daily basis is less than 30%.

This lack of correlation between JGB and swap yield reflects a variety of factors:

- The JGB market focuses on one benchmark bond, typically of ten years maturity. JGBs of other maturities are not sufficiently liquid nor are their interest rate movements predictable enough to be utilised as a basis for swap pricing.
- Structural restrictions mean that it is almost impossible to short sell JGBs, except through the futures market.
- The lack of continuous supply of government bonds has meant that no consistent yield curve exists over which swaps can be quoted making relative valuation more difficult and creating inefficiencies in market pricing movements.
- Cash JGBs are subject to withholding tax for foreign entities further limiting their utilisation hedging yen swaps.
- As an alternative to the cash JGB market, the JGB futures markets are subject to limitations as well. The liquid JGB futures contract traded in Tokyo is subject

to a transaction tax. In contrast, the JGB future traded on LIFFE in London has insufficient liquidity to provide an adequate hedge.

The structural difficulties mean that it is not, for all practical purposes, possible to utilise JGBs to hedge and price yen swaps. In any case, as noted above, the lack of recognition of present value concepts would make it difficult for Japanese banks to utilise hedging instruments for accounting reasons.

In any case, even if JGBs could be utilised, the fact that the only relevant benchmark, either cash or futures, is the *ten year* JGB, would make it difficult to utilise this benchmark as a basis for hedging swaps *across the entire yield curve*.

In practice, the spread between ten year JGBs and yen interest rate swaps, in particular, is one of a number of factors considered by swap traders who seek to take positions on the spread for proprietary trading purposes. In particular, because of foreign interest in yen swaps, movements in *yen swap rates* tends to anticipate changes in yen JGB rates.

Yen swap rates are more strongly correlated to Euroyen interest rates. Highly credit-worthy Euroyen bonds and ten year swap rate trade at relatively consistent spread levels. Another additional benchmark which has emerged is the relationship between the five year yen interest rate swap level and the LTPR rate. LTPR rate, as noted above, governs where long term credit banks can issue five year debentures in the domestic Japanese retail market (a prime funding source for these banks). This relationship is evidenced by the degree of correlation between the LTPR and five year yen interest rate swap rates.

Exhibit 24.4 sets out yen swap rates for various maturities and the spreads between the swap rate and the then current ten year JGB rate.

Exhibit 24.5 sets out an analysis of yen swap rates compared to AAA Euroyen yields for comparative maturities. *Exhibit 24.6* sets out comparison of the five year yen interest rate swap rate versus LTPR. The pricing of the domestic yen interest rate swap market provides the basis, in part, of the pricing of yen currency swaps.

The yen LIBOR/US$ LIBOR floating-to-floating currency swap market rate is implied by the difference between the yen interest rate and yen currency swap rates. Historically, this market has remained at a level of between −3 and +10bps pa in favour of yen LIBOR (the market pays more to receive yen LIBOR/pay US$ LIBOR).

The complex pricing interrelationships in the yen swap market creates significant difficulties in hedging risk positions in yen swaps. This has led to innovative approaches being adopted by certain institutions to yen swap pricing and arbitrage (discussed in the following section).

In practice, yen swap market makers hedge their portfolio positions utilising the following instruments:

- Short-term interest rate swaps are hedged utilising the Euroyen futures short term interest rate contract.
- Longer-term swap positions are either hedged utilising the futures market in JGBs or through the use of curve hedging whereby a swap in a particular maturity is hedged by undertaking an opposite swap in *another maturity* on a duration or PVBP consistent basis.

The inefficiency of the hedge instruments available, in turn, contributes to the volatility of Japanese swap rates and spreads relative to the various benchmarks.

Exhibit 24.4
Japanese Yen—Swap Rates and Spreads Against JGBs

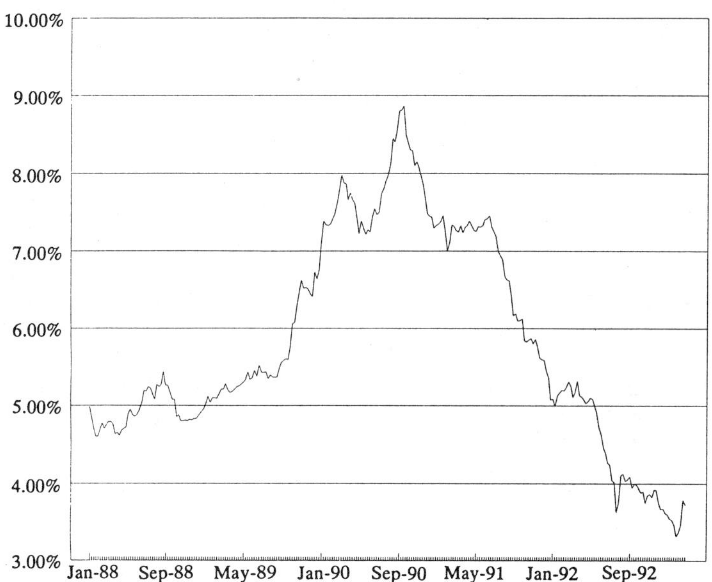

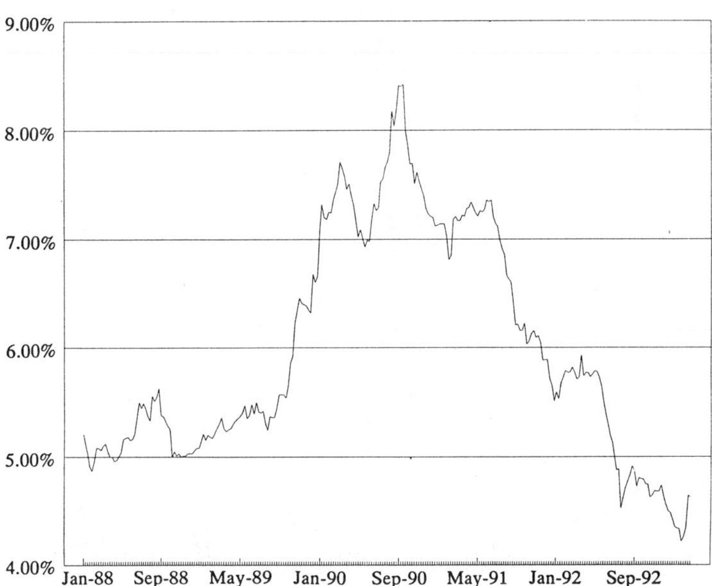

Exhibit 24.4—continued

FOUR YEAR YEN/YEN SWAP RATE

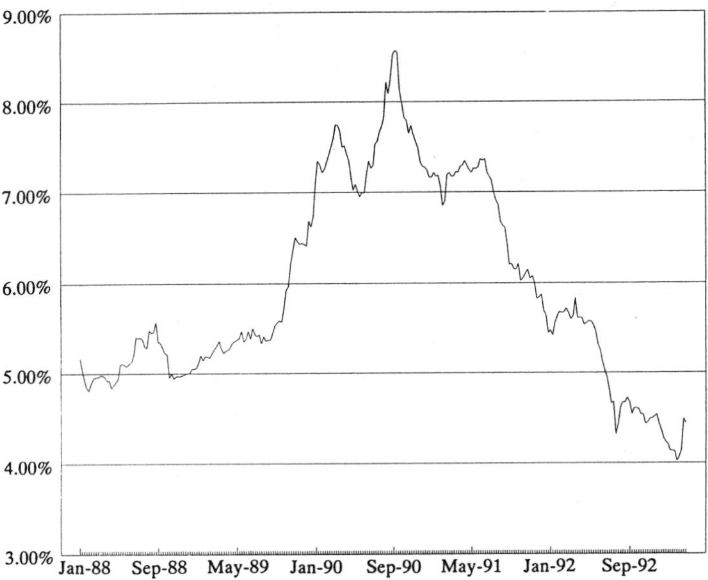

FIVE YEAR YEN/YEN SWAP RATE

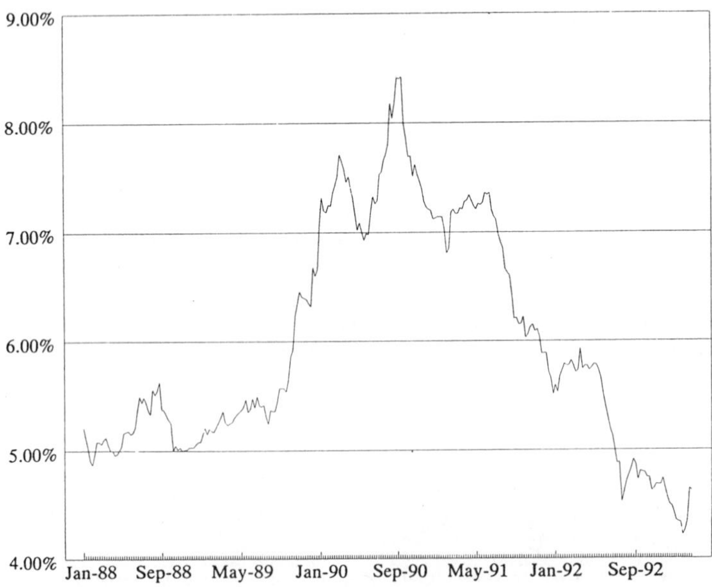

Exhibit 24.4—continued

SEVEN YEAR YEN/YEN SWAP RATE

TEN YEAR YEN/YEN SWAP RATE

Exhibit 24.4—continued

TWO YEAR YEN SWAP RATE—FIVE YEAR BENCHMARK JGB

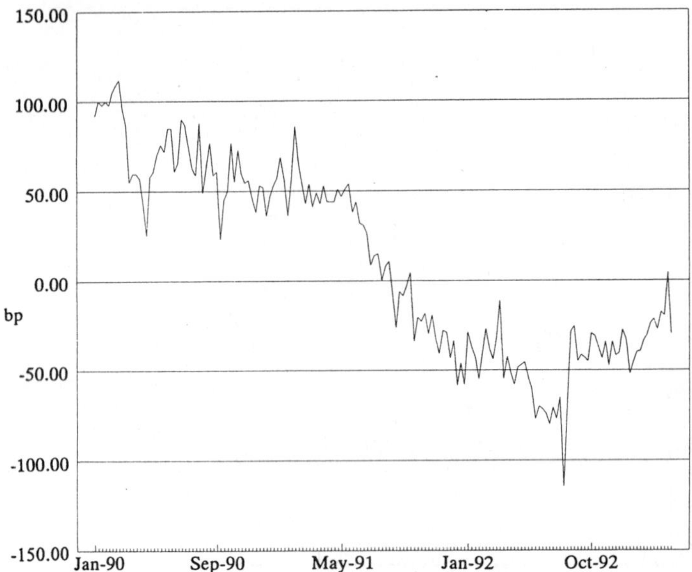

THREE YEAR YEN SWAP RATE—FIVE YEAR BENCHMARK JGB

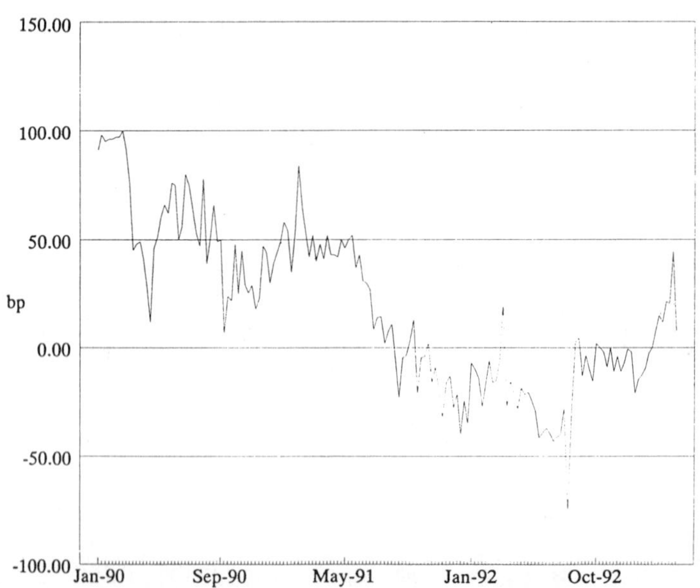

Exhibit 24.4—continued

FOUR YEAR YEN SWAP RATE—FIVE YEAR BENCHMARK JGB

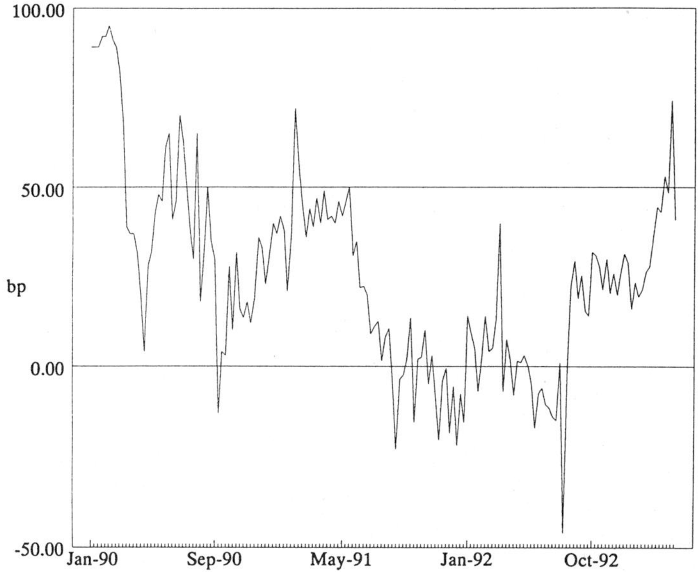

FIVE YEAR YEN SWAP RATE—FIVE YEAR BENCHMARK JGB

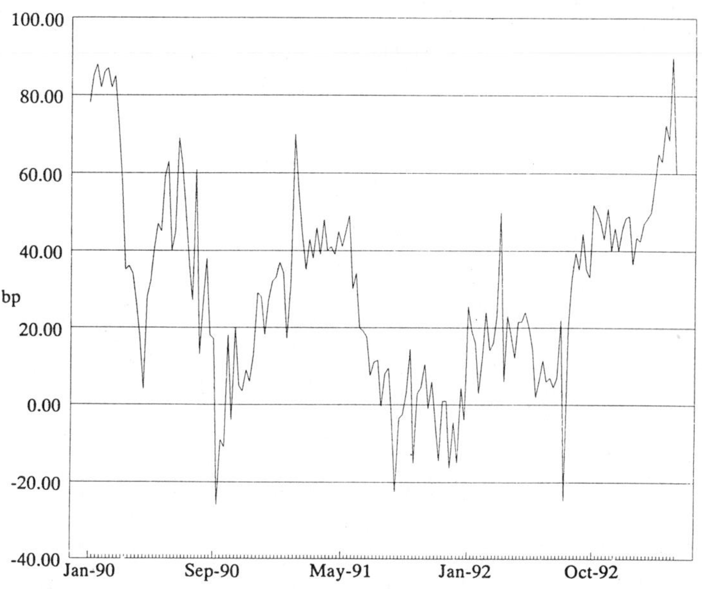

Exhibit 24.4—continued

SEVEN YEAR YEN SWAP RATE—TEN YEAR BENCHMARK JGB

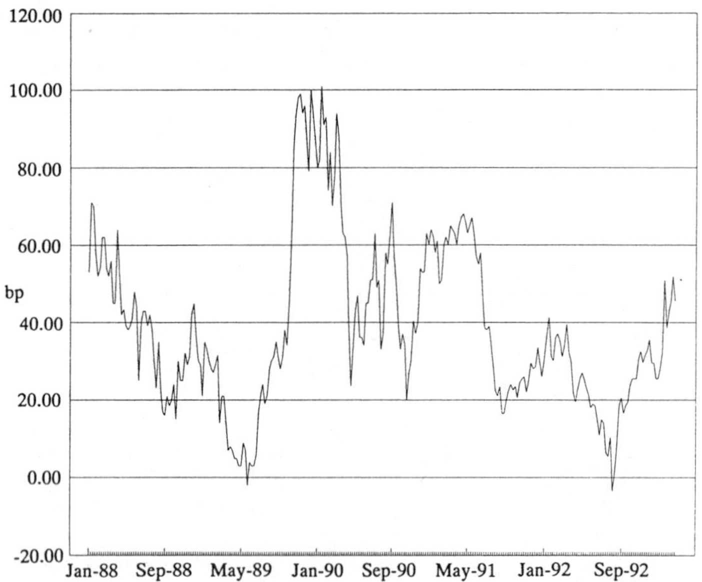

TEN YEAR YEN SWAP RATE—TEN YEAR BENCHMARK JGB

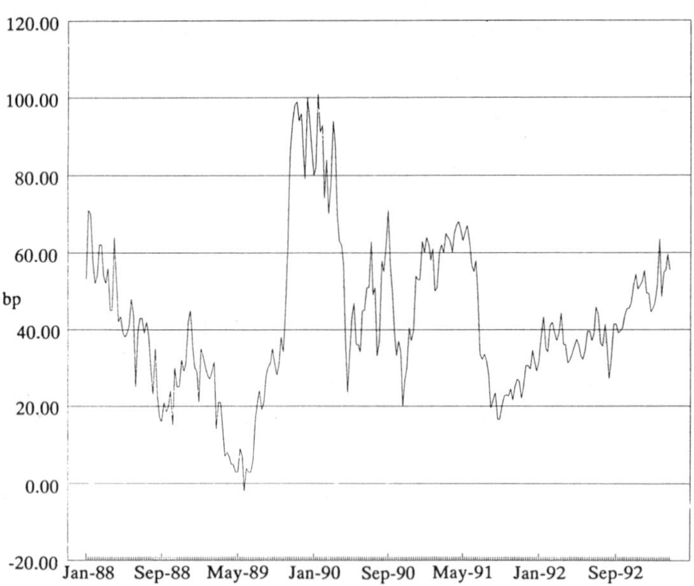

Source: Industrial Bank of Japan.

Exhibit 24.5

Japanese Yen Swap Rates and Spreads Against Euroyen Rates

TWO YEAR YEN SWAP RATE—FIVE YEAR AAA EUROYEN

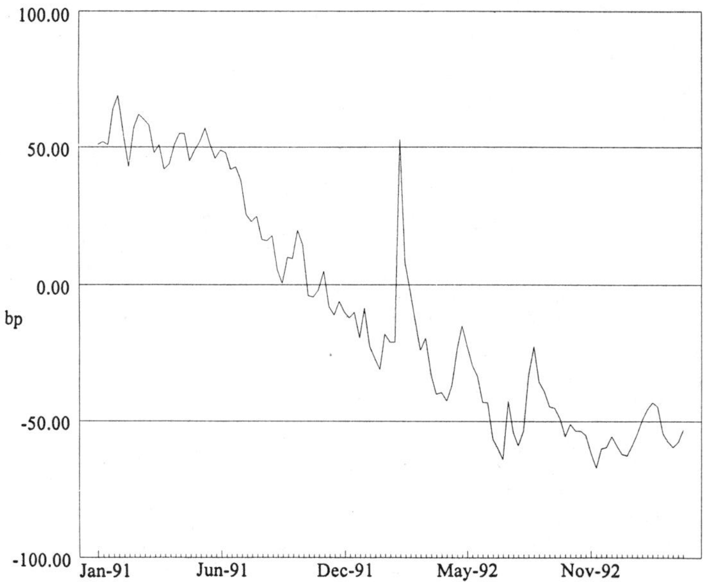

THREE YEAR YEN SWAP RATE—FIVE YEAR AAA EUROYEN

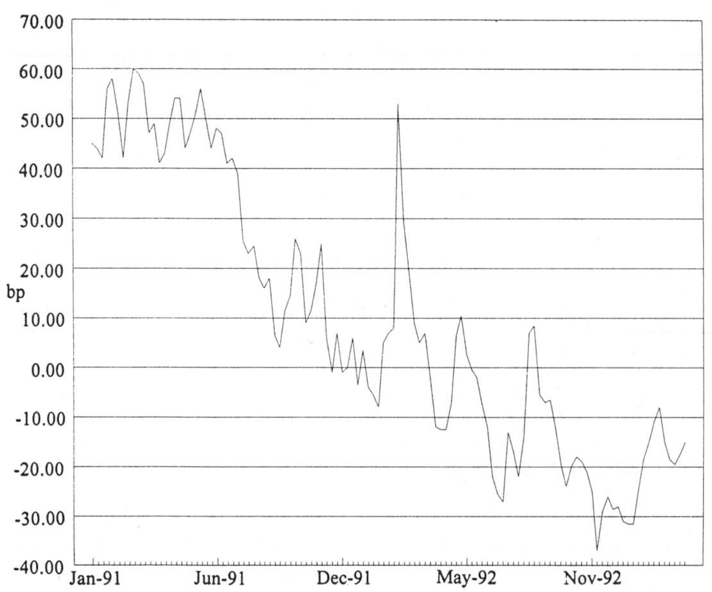

Exhibit 24.5—continued

FOUR YEAR YEN SWAP RATE—FIVE YEAR AAA EUROYEN

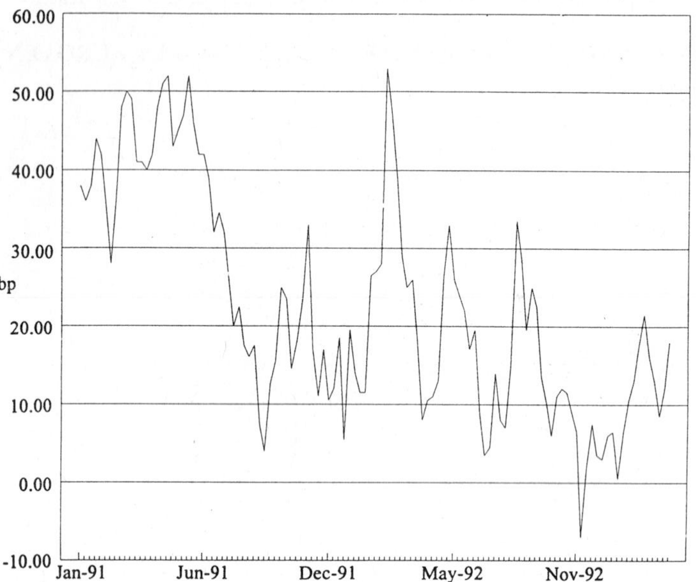

FIVE YEAR YEN SWAP RATE—FIVE YEAR AAA EUROYEN

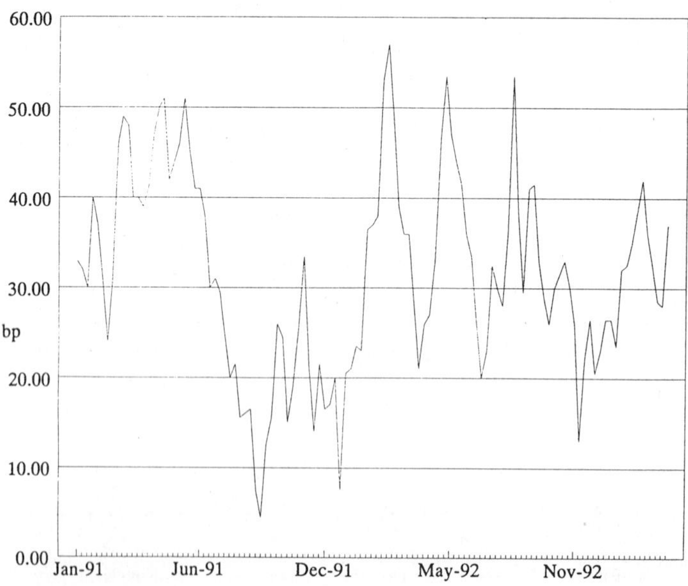

Exhibit 24.5—continued

SEVEN YEAR YEN SWAP RATE—TEN YEAR AAA EUROYEN

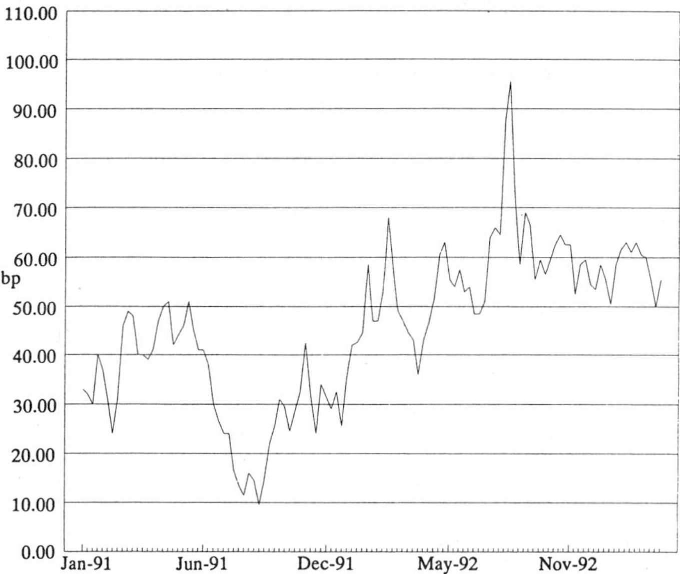

TEN YEAR YEN SWAP RATE—TEN YEAR AAA EUROYEN

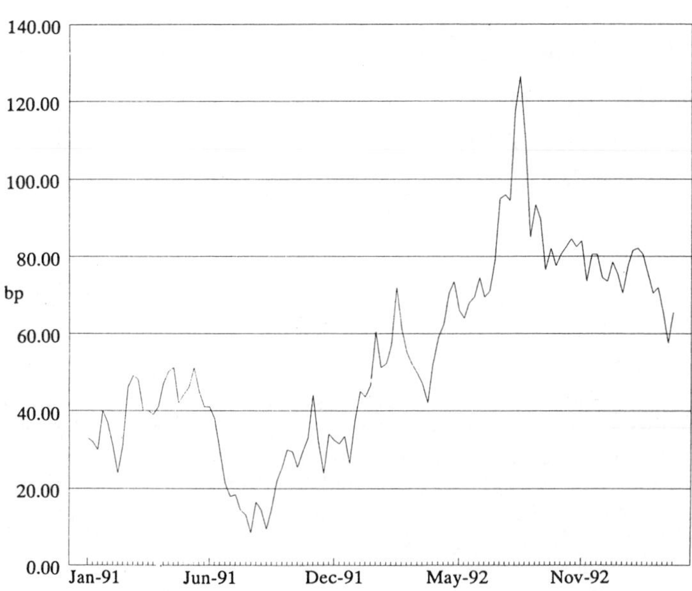

Source: Industrial Bank of Japan.

Exhibit 24.6

Japanese Yen Five Year Swap Rate Spreads to Yen LTPR

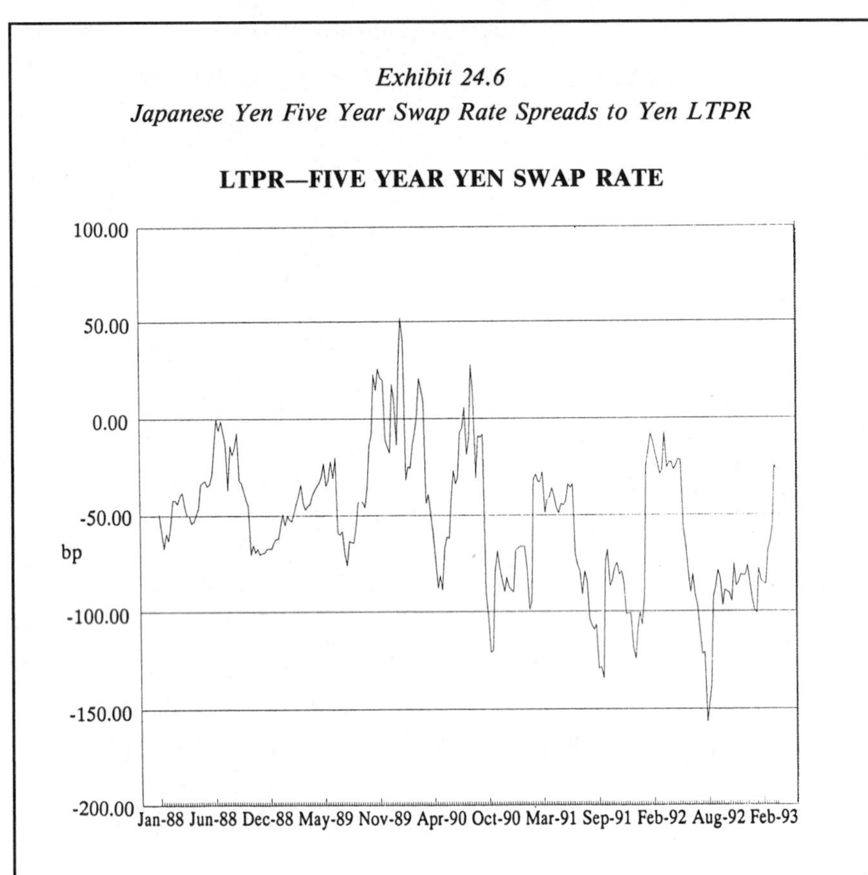

Source: Industrial Bank of Japan.

Approaches to yen swap pricing and arbitrage

The more complex factors driving swap arbitrages in yen means that the approaches to pricing yen swaps is not as readily identifiable as in the US$ market. Instead, the market is dominated by mismatches and arbitrage or position-driven pricing relationships.

As discussed above, one of the most serious obstacles to liquidity and the development of the market is the difficulty that market makers in yen swaps have in hedging their swap positions. Unlike other markets such as the US$ market, the number of hedging tools available are limited. While there is a substantial Japanese government bond market and an increasingly liquid yen bond futures contract traded in Tokyo, certain structural factors limit the potential to use these instruments to hedge swap positions.

As noted above, swap market makers tend to either take positions onto their books *unhedged*, utilise the futures market in yen government bonds or utilise curve hedging techniques which necessarily means the market maker assumes a significant amount of basis risk on the transaction.

Additional inefficiencies result from the method by which, for example, yen interest rate swaps are quoted. Currently, yen interest rate swaps are quoted on the basis of fixed yen interest rate payments against *Euroyen LIBOR*. Given that Euroyen LIBOR does not exactly correspond to the short-term funding rates for Japanese banks, there is necessarily a mismatch when such swaps are utilised to create synthetic assets or liabilities.

These structural problems within the yen swap market have led to two particular responses from the financial institutions who dominate activity in this area:

- A large number of participants maintain substantial swap books acting as market makers or warehouses for yen swaps.
- The development of new approaches to yen swap arbitrage primarily by the Japanese securities houses who, traditionally, have largely refrained from entering into such swaps on a market making or trading basis, although this practice has undergone change.

The approach to yen swaps by institutions has also been dictated by declining profitability and changes in the pattern by which swaps are transacted. Initially, the earnings from yen swaps were approximately 0.50% flat on the total notional principal of the swap and the spread between the bid and offer was 30 to 40bps pa. However, as the market developed, these spreads were rapidly squeezed and the profitability for financial institutions declined significantly. Simultaneously, while initially, the market had operated on an indicative basis with open timing, speed of execution rapidly became necessary to effect the underlying arbitrages.

Against this background, the larger Japanese city and long-term credit banks began to maintain large swap warehouses in yen. A number of foreign banks, including Citicorp, Bankers Trust, Morgan Guaranty, AIG, Salomon Brothers and Paribas, drawing on their experience in other global swap markets, also operate marketmaking facilities in yen swaps.

However, the Japanese securities houses, primarily Nomura Securities, initially the most aggressive of the Japanese securities houses in swap transactions, rapidly evolved a totally new approach to the yen swap market. This approach was predicated on a very complex process of multivariate risk management and a marked emphasis on innovation.

Nomura's approach to swap arbitrage was predicated on the fact that a swapped new bond issue, especially across currencies, provided numerous prospects *to exploit market opportunities*.

For example, in a Euroyen issue swapped into deutschmark there are typically six variables which directly determine the final deutschmark cost of funds to the issuer, including:

- Euroyen bond yields;
- yen and US$ spot rates;
- yen and US$ forward rates;
- United States government treasury note yields;
- US$ fixed and float swap spreads;
- fixed deutschmark and floating US$ swap rates.

Not only is the number of variables that can be arbitraged larger in a cross-currency swapped bond issue than in a single currency swapped issue, but their interrelationships are also significantly more complex.

The interrelationship between the variables for a fixed rate Eurodollar bond issue swapped into floating rate US$ are relatively stable over a typical 24 to 48 hour period. However, in the case of a fixed rate Euroyen issue swapped into a European currency, the relationship between the variables within the period of one working day is potentially very volatile.

Nomura would price and underwrite to the issuer the sum of the swaps (but not necessarily individual swaps) at an agreed break-even rate on cost to the borrower. The break-even rate could also be termed the natural arbitrage and is the statistically most probable economic relationship between the variables over a specified period of time. Nomura would take this multivariate risk onto its books.

Nomura would not normally lock in all the swap arbitrages or the swaps simultaneously. The reasons for this are complex.

First, in Euroyen issues, there was a time delay (originally three to ten days, subsequently reduced to 48 hours and then abandoned) between being awarded a mandate and the Japanese Ministry of Finance giving approval for the issue to be launched. In addition the time overlap between the major swap countries is limited. It would be common in a single transaction for the fixed yen and fixed US$ swap to be concluded in Japan, the US$ interest rate swap to be concluded in the United States and the floating US$ and fixed deutschmark to be concluded in Europe.

Second, and more importantly, time delays create not only additional risks, but also opportunities to improve both the borrower's cost of funds and the investor's yield. The variables have a different level of correlation, that is, particularly over a period of 12-24 hours, some of the variable interrationships will be stochastic. For example, within one day, the implied interest differential inherent in the yen and US$ spot and forward rates are unlikely to widen or narrow precisely in line with charges in the yields of United States government treasury bond and Japanese government bonds.

Over a specific period of time, the movements of the variables tend to be cyclical and are likely to return to the natural arbitrage position. The swaps or the swap arbitrages will therefore be locked in at the optimum point during the cycles of adjustment between the variables.

Nomura's approach involved the *positioning* and *trading* of the underlying swap arbitrages in a way designed to optimise the pricing of the swaps for the issuer as well as seeking to provide the best terms to the investor. Explicit in the approach was the fact that Nomura wished to maintain the ability to benefit from or conversely not lose from changing market conditions. This risky strategy was only possible because of Nomura's capacity to operate globally with detailed knowledge of individual markets as well as using time zones to its advantage wherever possible.

The second approach which was developed contemporaneously was the introduction of a number of innovations in securities structures. Many of the swap structures, described in Chapter 15, involving securitising derivative elements embedded in swaps are a direct outcome of these efforts. Each of the instruments identified were designed to meet specific investor portfolio requirements while providing borrowers with a competitive cost of funds, usually in floating rate US$. The investors in question were clients of the major European, Japanese and United States investment banks who were regular investors in a wide variety of assets. However, the approach was to identify particular portfolio requirements and to develop hybrid debt instruments to satisfy these requirements. Inevitably, the instruments combined conventional bond structures with arbitrage instruments, primarily forwards and options, which were then securitised through the swap specially structured for that specific purpose.

This development in yen swaps was an important response to the structural uncertainties of the yen market because from the viewpoint of the financial institutions the fact that they could be firmly placed at launch, as they were specifically matched to identified investor requirements, meant that they were not subject to the vagaries of short-term market movements of more conventional swap structures.

Interestingly, this combination of approaches allowed the major Japanese securities houses to operate highly successfully as mainstream *arrangers* of swaps in the yen market. However, as the market has matured, the Japanese securities houses have developed market making capacities in the swap market and now trade selectively as principals to complement their agency role.

HK$ SWAP MARKET

Origin/development

The HK$ swap market developed in the middle 1980s. Development of the HK$ swap market parallels the rapid development of Hong Kong's domestic capital market. The major impetus to HK$ swaps has been corporate appetite to fix interest rates, primarily during periods of very low interest rates. Parallel demand for converting revenue streams derived from exports into HK$ has provided the basis for market development.

Structure/market conventions

Structurally, the HK$ market has three specific components:

- Corporations seeking to fix interest rates on floating rate funding. For example, when long term prime interest rates fell from a peak of 17% pa in 1980 to only 7% pa at the end of 1985, a number of large Hong Kong companies, with substantial debt portfolios, sought to carry out swaps to lock in their cost of funding over the medium to long term.
- Activity in the domestic fixed rate CD market is also an integral part of swap activity. Banks and financial institutions issue fixed rate CDs and swap the relatively cheaply priced fixed rate funding into either floating rate US$ LIBOR based financing or floating rate HK$ funding at an attractive margin relative to the Hong Kong interbank offered rate (HIBOR).
- Currency swap/LTFX demand typically involving Hong Kong exporters looking to convert foreign currency revenues, primarily in US$ into HK$ to match its HK$ financing base. Conversely, the opposite side of the demand for the currency swap/LTFX contract is from foreign companies exporting goods to Hong Kong seeking to match its US$ LIBOR based funding with its HK$ revenues.

Two further, more recent, elements of the HK$ market have emerged. These are basis swaps between the Hong Kong Prime Rate (used for local syndicated loans) and the Hong Kong Interbank Offered Rate (HIBOR) which international banks prefer. In addition, export credits, denominated in foreign currency usually provided by agencies such as the United Kingdom's Export Credit Guarantee Department and Japan's Ex-Im Bank, occasionally prompts a swap from GBP or JPY into HK$.

Against this background, the market is segmented into three quite distinct components:

- The short-term swap market, that is, swaps maturing in less than two years. This is the most liquid component of the market reflecting the fact that the government issues securities in this maturity sector and therefore provides a suitable hedging facility for swap market makers.
- The medium-term market, comprising swaps of between two and five years in maturity. This market segment, traditionally, is related to CD issues and medium-term swap activities are dependent on the level of CD issuance.
- The long-term market, that is, swaps of between five and ten years in maturity. This is the least active sector of the market and is traditionally related to particular transactions. For example, the issue in late 1992 of a ten year HK$ bond by the Asian Development Bank which was swapped into, at least initially, floating rate US$ allowed the swap curve to be extended.

HK$ swaps are priced as an absolute rate versus HIBOR as a floating rate index. HIBOR is fixed daily using the HIBOR screen on Reuters or Telerate 9898. Accruals on both fixed and floating rate sides are calculated on the basis of actual numbers of days in a year of 365 days. The variable rate is fixed on the first day of the calculation period, unlike US$ LIBOR which is set two days in advance. The fixed rate, in HK$ swaps, is typically quoted on a quarterly basis (actual days over 365).

The HK$ swap market trades in round lots of approximately HK$50 million to HK$100 million. However, interbank trade of HK$300-500 million are possible, depending on market conditions. Broker bid-offer spreads are around 5bps for maturities up to three years, 10bps for maturity of four to five years and 15bps for longer maturities. However, it is probable that spreads on an actual deal transacted are slightly wider than these broker bid-offer spreads.

Pricing

Pricing of HK$ swaps is closely related to activity and yield movements relating to the market for bank issued fixed rate CDs. The pricing tends to be a function of the rate achievable on a fixed rate CD adjusted for the sub-HIBOR margin required by the issuing bank. This tends to create an absolute rate market, where the fixed rate is quoted against HIBOR.

A significant factor in the HK$ swap market is the absence of an active domestic government bond market (at least, beyond short-term maturities) and difficulties in hedging swap positions. In practice, swap positions are hedged as follows:

- Short dated swaps are hedged utilising the short term interest rate HIBOR contract on the Hong Kong Futures Exchange. However, the lack of significant liquidity outside the front two months requires the use of stack hedging techniques and the assumption of significant basis risk in using this instrument to hedge swap rate movements.
- Longer dated swaps can be hedged, at least temporarily, utilising US government bonds. This is predicated on the stability of the exchange rate for HK$ versus the US$ and assumes stability in the relationship between US government yields and HK$ interest rate swap rates.

The use of US$ swap rates to hedge HK$ swaps and the political risk premium required for long-term swaps, reflecting uncertainty about the future of Hong Kong beyond the British lease of the colony which expires in 1997, merit comment.

The use of US$ based hedges for HK$ swaps is predicated on the special nature of the HK$ exchange rate mechanism. Under this mechanism, the HK$ is pegged at HK$7.80/US$1. This provides interesting arbitrage and hedging opportunities.

Predicated on the stability of this relationship, market makers buy and sell US$ treasuries as a common form of hedge against HK$ swap positions. However, the spread is not constant although market makers prefer the spread risk to the absolute rate risk of running of unhedged positions.

Historically, the spread of HK$ swaps versus US treasuries has been around 70-75bps. However, the volatility of the spread is evident, particularly in times of crisis. For example, following the 1989 Tiananmen Square shootings in China, the spread increased to 130-150bps.

An added element in pricing is the political risk premium for any transaction where the maturity is beyond 1997 when Hong Kong reverts to Chinese sovereignty. There is currently an implicit 40-50bps liquidity premium for any transaction beyond 1997. This spread varies and has recently traded in the range of 40-70bps. The political risk premium increases with maturity. For example, the differential between a transaction maturing in, say, 1997/98 and beyond the turn of the century could be as high as 100-150bps. This contrasts with an almost zero risk premium which prevailed in 1992 following the conclusion of the Sino-British Agreement.

The political risk premium is designed to cover for the risk that the Chinese Government will, following reversion of sovereignty, uncouple the HK$ from the US$. It also reflects the fact that HK$ interest and currency rates will, following closer integration with China, reflect Chinese inflation.

Exhibit 24.7 sets out graphically HK$/US$ exchange rates. *Exhibit 24.8* sets out the spreads between HK$ and US$ interest rate swaps for the relevant maturity.

Exhibit 24.7
HK$ Versus US$

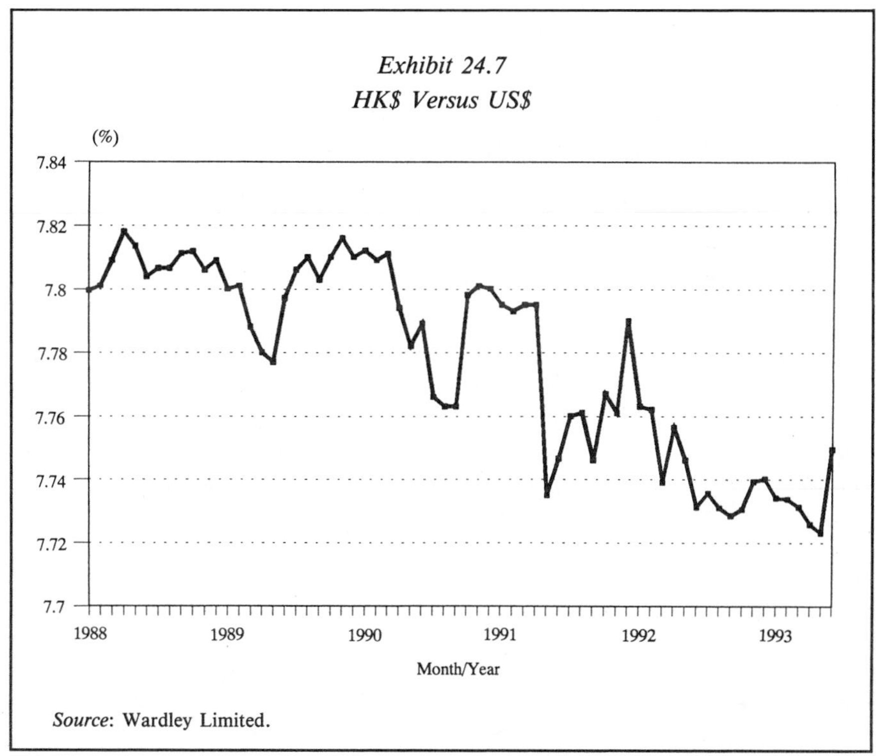

Source: Wardley Limited.

Exhibit 24.8
Spreads Between HK$ and US$ Interest Rate Swaps

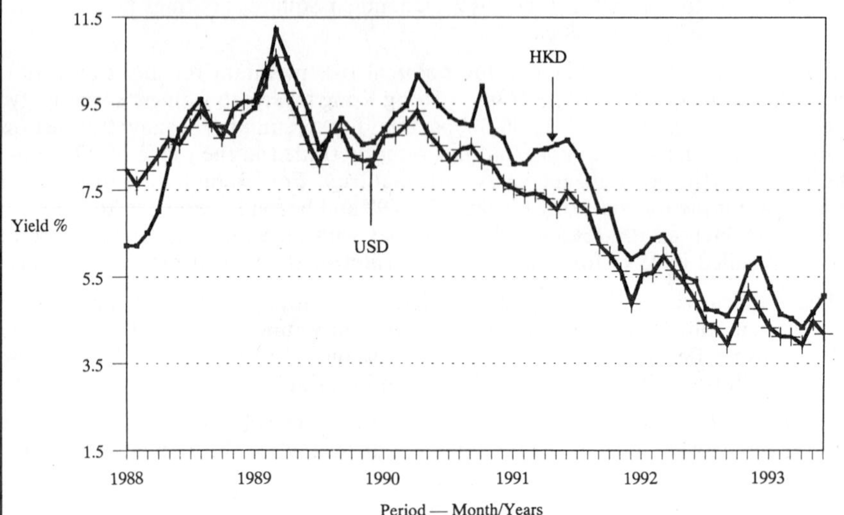

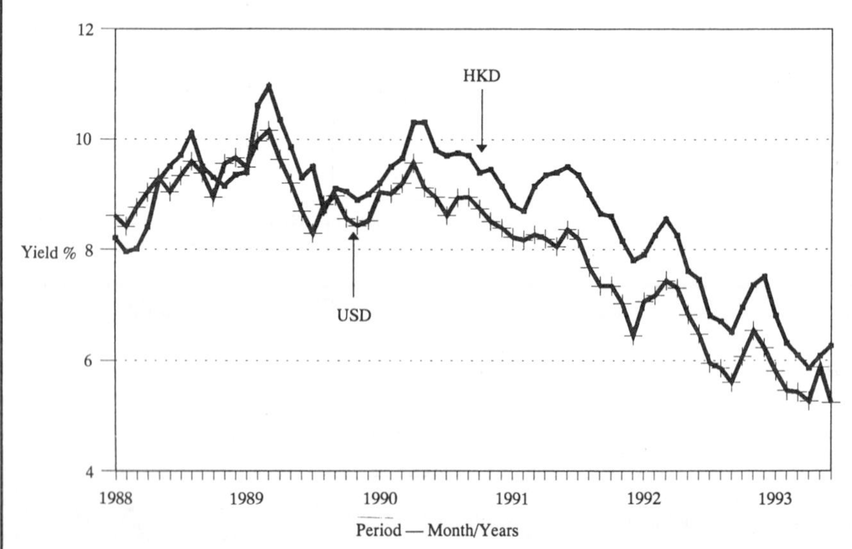

Exhibit 24.8—continued

LIBOR vs HIBOR (JAN 88 TO JUNE 93)

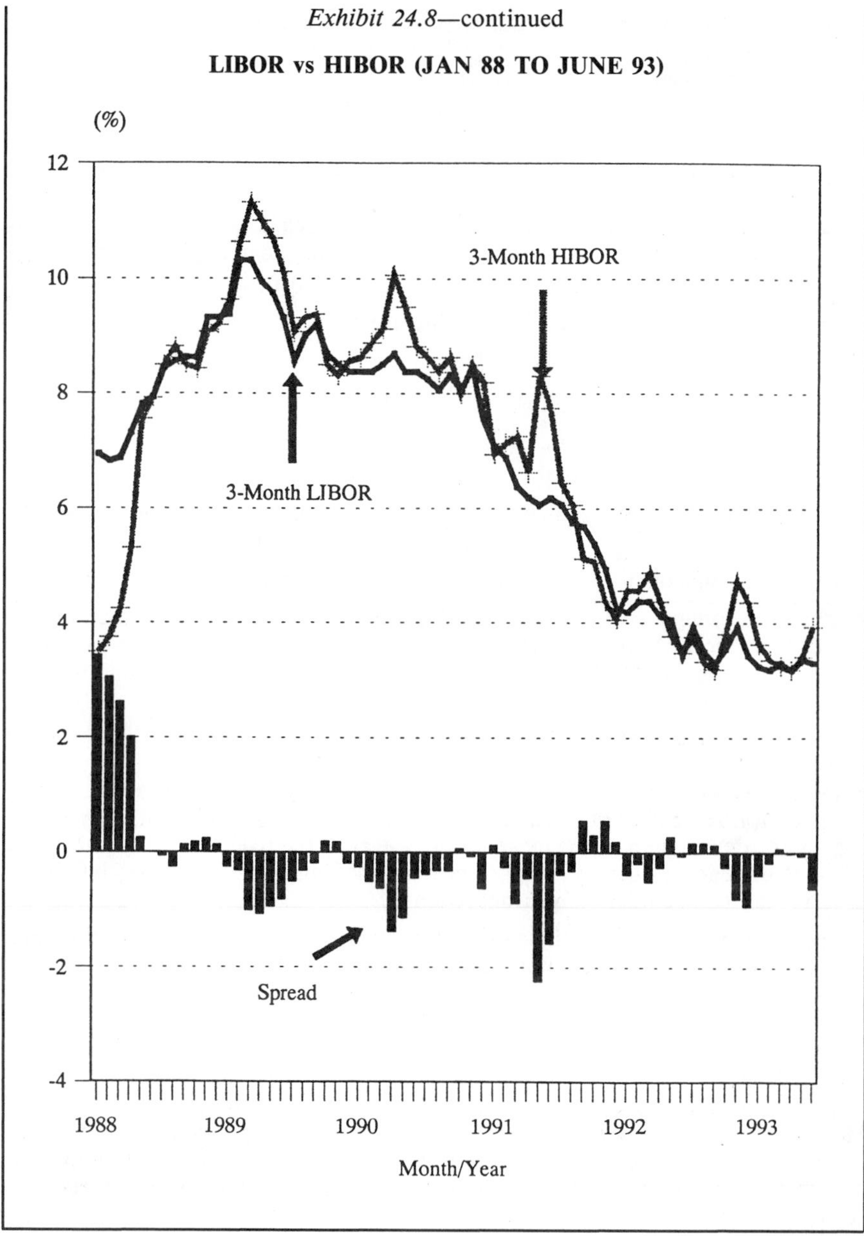

Participants

The market in HK$ swaps is largely driven by the larger Hong Kong corporations including Hong Kong Land, Mass Transit Railway Corporation, China Light and Power, Jardine Mathieson, Kesco and Eastern Energy. A significant inter-bank swap market between financial institutions active in HK$ swaps has also emerged. Major participants among the financial institutions include Hong Kong banks such as the Hong Kong and Shanghai Bank, Wardley and Standard Chartered as well as a number of foreign banks including Chase Manhattan, Citibank, Manufacturers Hanover (now Chemical), and Paribas.

OTHER ASIAN SWAP/DERIVATIVES MARKETS

In recent years, embryonic swap markets have begun to develop in a variety of other Asian countries. In part, this reflects strong economic growth in these countries and their increased integration into international trade and finance.

The major currencies, in this regard, include:

- Singapore dollars;
- Thai bahts;
- Malaysian ringgits;
- Indonesian rupiah.

Other currencies in the region which are developing include Taiwanese dollars and South Korean won.

The major impetus to the growth of swap markets in these currencies includes:

- Increased foreign investment by international corporations in these countries, reflecting location of factories and other production plants in many of these locations, creating foreign currency exposures for the parent corporations who have sought to hedge their currency risk.
- Increased reliance by these countries on borrowings denominated in foreign currencies. These borrowings (often of a subsidised nature) from commercial sources as well as from development agencies have typically been in foreign currencies. A number of Asian borrowers have, following substantial losses as a result of devaluation of the local currency against the relevant foreign currency, adopted policies whereby foreign currency liabilities are converted into local currencies through derivative transactions.

The form and structure of these swap markets is, as previously noted, embryonic. These markets exist principally in the form of:

- LTFX markets for maturities up to one to three years;
- short-term interest rate swap markets, primarily in the form of FRA transactions and interest rate swaps for maturities out to three years.

Transaction amounts remain small and vary significantly between currencies. Maturities are inevitably short. Liquidity is limited with transactions typically being undertaken on a matched counterparty basis or with financial institutions who absorb the risk of the transaction into their general operations in the relevant currency.

These swap markets exist in rudimentary structural form with their growth constrained by a variety of factors including the relatively undeveloped status of the individual capital markets in these countries as well as the highly regulated structure of financial markets and capital flows in these economies.

Exhibit 24.9 summarises key aspects of these emerging Asian currency markets.

The major steps that are necessary to allow further developments of swaps/derivative markets in these currencies include:

- The liberalisation of foreign exchange control. For example, Singapore and Malaysia restrict the volume of forward positions, in their respective currencies, that may be held with any one counterparty.
- The development of active inter-bank money markets in these currencies. The absence of a substantial inter-bank market reflects the fact that domestic banks in these countries have traditionally funded themselves through a substantial retail base limiting the necessity for activity in an inter-bank deposit market, at least, beyond very short maturities. The development of an inter-bank market is essential to create a genuinely market determined benchmark interest rate. In these currencies, the reliance on domestic bank debt where interest payments on most loan facilities are set on the prime lending rate of the bank, which is determined by the bank itself or a domestic banking cartel, dictate that these indicator rates are not purely market driven.
- The development of a well defined yield curve across a wider range of maturities. The absence of liquid bond markets in most countries, particularly beyond very short maturities, has denied both lenders and borrowers a benchmark yield curve. In addition, the absence of long-term fixed rate debt markets in the domestic currency further restricts the development of the markets.

Exhibit 24.9

Asian Currency Markets—Key Aspects

	FX control	Current FX spot (foreign per US$1)	Indicative 6 month rate	Indicative 3 year bond yield	Interest rate swap	Withholding tax on loans
Hong Kong dollar	No	7.732	3.50%	3.80%	Yes	0%
Indonesian rupiah	No	2070.00	13.00%	14.75%	Yes	15%
Korean won	Yes	793.6	12.00%	10.00%	No	20%
Malaysian ringgit	Yes	2.618	7.51%	7.12%	Yes	30%
Singapore dollar	Yes	1.647	2.13%	3.875%	Yes	30%
Taiwan dollar	Yes	28.5	7.50%	7.95%	No	20%
Thai bhat	Yes	25.4	6.15%	8.25%	Yes	15%

Source: Merrill Lynch.

However, as the level of experience and expertise of local financial institutions grow, allied to the gradual liberalisation of these markets, development of derivative markets in these Asian currencies is likely.

One factor facilitating development of derivative markets in these currencies currently is the linkages of some of these Asian currencies, implicitly or explicitly, to US$ exchange rates. Research indicates that there are definite correlations between these currencies and the US$. In a number of these currencies, there is also the process of managed depreciation, over time, against the US$.

Based on this relationship, there are increasing levels of interest from, primarily, international investors seeking higher investment returns, in investing in Asian markets through derivative structures. A number of complex transactions seeking to take advantage of the forward convergence of European currencies (primarily FFR and DEM) and Asian interest rates have been completed. The structures have usually been undertaken in the form of structured MTN notes. These notes have been purchased by investors seeking the higher yields available in currencies linked to the US$.

This interest allied to the rapid transfer of technology in modern financial markets is likely to create the environment for further development of Asian currency derivatives. This development will benefit both foreign corporations with operations or clients in the region as well as Asian borrowers, both public and private sector. Additional beneficiaries will be investors, both Asian and international.

Chapter 25

European Swap and Derivative Markets: Swiss Franc, Deutschmark, Pound Sterling and ECU

OVERVIEW

The European swap/derivatives market is made up of a large number of separate markets in different currencies which have a complex pattern of similarities and differences. The main European markets are, at least historically, the Swiss franc, deutschmark, pound sterling and ECU markets.

In addition to these major European swap markets, in recent times, markets for swaps have developed in a wide range of other European currencies including Dutch guilders, French francs, Luxembourg and Belgian francs, Swedish and Danish kroner, Finnish markkaa, Italian lire, Spanish pesetas, Portuguese escudos and Irish pounds. These new emerging swap markets are driven by a complex series of factors including:

- the development of international, primarily Eurobond, markets in a number of these currencies;
- the development of futures markets in some of these currencies;
- special regulatory factors which affect financial transactions in the currency.

A number of the minor European swap markets owe their existence to the recent development of bond markets, primarily outside the domestic market, driven by international investor interest in securities denominated in the particular currency. For example, international bond markets in Luxembourg francs, Swedish and Danish kroner, Italian lire, Spanish pesetas and Portuguese escudos have emerged as international investors have sought easy access to securities in these currencies. A number of arbitrage funders have sought to issue securities in these currencies on the basis of an accompanying swap into "cheap" US$ floating rate funding at attractive margins relative to LIBOR. The main counterparties to these swaps have been institutions, primarily in the domestic markets, seeking cost-effective fixed rate funds in the particular currency.

Against this background, these particular swap markets have developed on the back of periodic investor appetite for international securities denominated in the particular currency.

The recent introduction in a number of markets of futures contracts on interest rates has facilitated the development of shorter-term swap markets in the relevant currency. For example, the emergence of relatively liquid futures markets in French francs, lire and pesetas has allowed a number of financial institutions to offer short-dated swaps denominated in these currencies with the risk positions being offset in the futures market.

An additional factor influencing these minor European swap markets has been the regulatory framework within the individual currency. For example, in Italy, until recent changes, the presence of substantial foreign exchange controls created segmented markets where a small group of institutions, the state agencies, have been able to transact currency swaps off the back of international lira issues.

These factors are in addition to more traditional swap arbitrages such as the credit arbitrage between the fixed and floating segments of the capital market as well as market frictions such as withholding tax which have created opportunities for swap arbitrage.

The origins, structure, pricing patterns as well as participants in various European currency swap markets are discussed in this chapter and in Chapter 26. In this chapter, the Swiss franc swap market, the deutschmark swap market, the pound sterling swap market, and the European Currency Unit swap market are analysed. In Chapter 26, the Dutch guilder, French franc, Italian lira, Spanish peseta, Scandinavian currencies and other European currency swap markets are considered.

SWISS FRANC SWAP/DERIVATIVES MARKET

Origins

The Swiss franc market is one of the oldest "modern" swap markets. As described in Chapter 1 the hallmark swap between the World Bank and IBM involved Swiss francs.

Traditionally, the Swiss franc swap market has been primarily related to new issue activity in the Swiss franc bond market. However, as the market has matured swaps related to hedging of existing Swiss franc liabilities, asset swaps and swaps structured to assist with the management of Swiss franc bond portfolios have become more important components of market activity.

The Swiss franc swap market has, traditionally, been driven by new issues in Swiss francs. Structurally, the market is dominated by two groups:

- A group of Swiss franc bond issuers, usually highly rated corporations or sovereigns as well as a number of popular, well known United States and Japanese corporations with good name recognition among investors, who utilise the issue as a basis for an arbitrage into a more desired currency, primarily US$ and, to a lesser extent, yen.
- A group of swap counterparties, primarily supranationals and some lower rated sovereign borrowers, who provide the major interest in paying fixed rate Swiss francs under the swaps.

The receptivity of the Swiss franc market to some types of borrowers on terms not directly related to their credit rating has for many years formed the basis of the fundamental credit arbitrage which underlies this market. For example, a wide variety of well known United States corporations which are household names among the traditional retail investor base within Switzerland have been able to issue bonds denominated in Swiss francs on yield differentials which are substantially below the risk premiums they would have to pay in other markets, such as the US$ market. These institutions have utilised this differential access to Swiss franc funding to generate cheaper US$ debt. While the precise cost savings vary from time to time, cost savings for these lower rated United States corporations has often been up to 50bps, although the more typical number is 15-30bps.

Some very highly rated sovereign borrowers with no direct requirement for Swiss francs have also been periodic issuers as part of swap transactions. These borrowers, whose paper carries considerable scarcity value, have been able to generate cost savings in other markets through the vehicle of the Swiss franc issue from time to time.

The payers of fixed rate Swiss francs in the swaps have in the main been supranationals, such as the World Bank and Asian Development Bank, who have from time to time been able to use swaps to generate more cost effective Swiss franc funding. The substantial demand from such borrowers for low coupon funding has meant that a strategy of diversifying their source of funds and converting some of their non-Swiss franc liabilities into Swiss francs through swaps has proved an important aspect of their liability management.

Another group of swap counterparties are lower rated sovereigns and corporations who cannot undertake direct issues of debt. This group, including a number of South East Asian countries, have swapped against liabilities, usually US$ borrowings, diversifying the currency basis of their governmental debt portfolios.

As noted above, Swiss franc swaps unrelated to new issue activity have become an increasingly important component of the market. One of the major areas of activity is the use of swaps, particularly currency swaps, to hedge existing Swiss franc liabilities.

Historically, foreign borrowers in Swiss francs have tended to leave their liabilities denominated in Swiss francs. The currency risk associated with this strategy was accepted on the basis of, traditionally, low Swiss franc interest rates in comparison to interest rates in their base currencies. This type of activity relates primarily to borrowers hedging existing liabilities either to take advantage of favourable movements in exchange rates between the base currency and Swiss francs or to prevent the value of the liability increasing as the Swiss franc appreciates against the relevant currency.

A further area of growth has been asset swaps connected with Swiss franc or foreign currency denominated bonds. In its original phase, this market was illiquid reflecting the lack of liquidity in the Swiss franc bond market itself. However in the late 1980s, and early 1990s the rapid erosion in credit standing of a number of borrowers resulted in bond prices for these issuers falling sharply. This created attractive arbitrage opportunity whereby Swiss franc bonds were purchased from existing investors and re-placed, usually, as US$ LIBOR based assets with commercial banks at attractive yields. A major impetus to this market was the pressure on investment portfolio managers to divest certain securities once the price of these bonds had declined below certain levels for prudential purposes.

A parallel market where foreign bonds are swapped into Swiss francs and placed with Swiss institutional investors has also developed. The primary motivation for this sector of the market is Swiss franc investors who are seeking yield improvements in comparison to Swiss franc issues or are seeking to diversify the risk of their portfolios.

A major use of Swiss franc interest rate swaps is to manage the interest rate risk of bond investment portfolios. Increasingly, investment managers utilise such transactions to hedge against interest rate risk, to match the maturities of assets and liabilities and change the duration or maturity of their portfolios. This sector of the market has grown rapidly in recent years.

Market convention

The average size of a Swiss franc swap is around SFR50m, reflecting the predominantly capital market transaction driven nature of this currency sector. This is particularly so for Swiss franc currency swaps. If Swiss franc currency and interest rate swaps are aggregated, the average size of a transaction is around SFR25m.

Maturities for Swiss franc swaps are up to ten years, although transactions for longer periods have been completed. Volume is concentrated in the five to ten year region.

Swiss franc swaps are quoted on an absolute rate basis against six month SFR LIBOR or six month US$ LIBOR. Interest calculations are: bond basis (30/360) for fixed rate payments and money market basis (actual/360) of floating rate payments.

The market for SFR swaps is reasonably liquid with bid-offer spreads being approximately 10bps pa for maturities up to five years and between 10 and 15bps pa for maturities beyond five years. Interestingly, the difference in bid-offer spreads between interest rate and currency swaps is small in Swiss franc swaps compared with other currencies, reflecting the relatively high percentage of currency swaps to interest rate swaps in this market segment.

Pricing

The Swiss franc swap market is an absolute rate market. There is no base interest rate over which Swiss franc swaps are priced, unlike other markets such as US$, C$, A$, DEM or GBP swap markets.

In fact, swap rates are the defacto of benchmark interest rates for Swiss francs *generally*. This reflects the fact that the Swiss franc government bond market is illiquid and consequently, swap rates which are more actively traded and reflect changing yield requirements of borrowers and investors, are more indicative of movements in Swiss interest rates. This is reflected by the fact that, increasingly, derivative products designed to give international participants opportunities to hedge against or position for Swiss franc interest rate movements utilise swap rates in that currency as a benchmark.

Exhibit 25.1 sets out Swiss franc swap rates for different maturities.

Swiss franc swap rates are driven by bond yields in the currency, particularly in the new issue market. This reflects the fact that where swap rates are high relative to the coupon that a borrower, particularly a *foreign* borrower, must pay to access the Swiss franc capital market creates windows of opportunities for foreign issuers to undertake swap driven issues. Such issues are typically swapped, immediately, into floating rate US$ LIBOR. Such opportunities for new issue arbitrage in Swiss francs occurs, increasingly, with reduced frequency and when such windows occur for very short periods of time.

This pattern of new issue activity related to swaps reflects radical differences in the structure and regulation of the bond market compared with the swap market in Swiss francs. This reflects, in turn, the domination of the primary market for bond issuance by a cartel of major Swiss banks who effectively regulate issuance practices. The second characteristic which effects the timing of windows of opportunity is the illiquidity of the secondary market for Swiss bonds which is exacerbated by the Swiss stamp tax.

An interesting feature of the Swiss franc market is the fact that issues swapped into sub-US$ LIBOR financing often occur even when there is *seemingly* no window of opportunity. This reflects the fact that, based on the interest rate expectations of the swap counterparty, actual quotes to clients may be more or less aggressive than general market rates as these institutions utilise swaps to generate or hedge internal asset or liability positions.

Exhibit 25.1

Swiss Franc Swap Rates (based on CHF150 mio with 4 weeks delay)

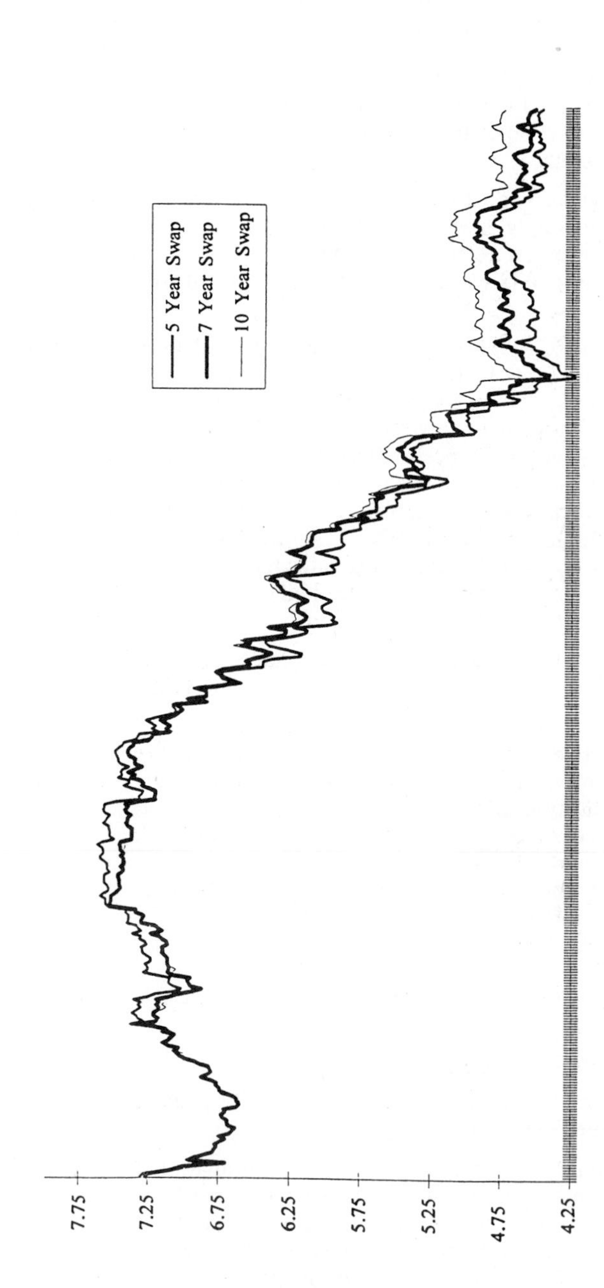

Source: Union Bank of Switzerland.

Exhibit 25.2 sets out swap arbitrage window opportunities comparing the all-in cost of bond issues versus swap rates. This exhibit plots weekly indications of all-in costs for five year issues against five year swap rates. The average difference is plotted as a reference point. Labels indicate the number of issues brought to market during that week by foreign borrowers which were swapped at the time of issue. The data supports the hypothesis that foreign borrower activity in the Swiss franc bond and swap market tends to occur when swap levels are high relative to the all in cost of the new issue.

While Swiss franc capital exports remain a prime driving factor behind swap pricing, increasingly asset swap activity also influences pricing. For example, if the swap rates are low relative to bond levels, Swiss franc bonds are increasingly repackaged into US$ synthetic FRNs for placement with investors *outside the Swiss market*.

The advent of the Swiss Options and Financial Futures Exchange (SOFFEX) is anticipated to assist in further developing the market. SOFFEX has commenced trading a medium term interest rate futures, since October 1991. The underlying security is a synthetic bond with a five year life and 6% coupon, the value of which is determined with reference to Swiss francs swap rates. The settlement price of the contract corresponds to the value of the underlying synthetic bond which is based on the hypothetical annual interest rate payments and the payment of the bond after five years. In addition, SOFFEX in March 1992 launched CONF-Future, a future on Swiss government bonds. This reflected a response to the increased level of government bond issuance to finance higher levels of government debt in the early 1990s.

SOFFEX introduced a short-term interest rate future (SIF) in March 1991. However, this contract was discontinued in June 1993. A three month Euro-Swiss franc future is still traded at LIFFE.

The effective structure of the market dictates that when there is good two way business flow as underlying Swiss franc payers and receivers establish positions, market liquidity is adequate. However, liquidity is fragile and can evaporate very quickly as the market becomes dominated by either paying or receiving interest. This reflects, in part, the difficulty for market makers of hedging their risk positions given the absence of a tradeable underlying government bond market.

Market participants

Market participants encompass a number of specific categories:

- issuers of Swiss franc bonds;
- bond market investors;
- Swiss corporates and multi-currency liability managers using Swiss franc swaps for treasury management.

The bond issuers (typically, sovereigns, supranationals, State guaranteed entities, corporates and large foreign banks) are receivers of fixed rate Swiss francs against new issues. Bond market investors are effectively risk managers seeking to, typically, pay fixed Swiss franc rates when bond yields are expected to rise, effectively hedging their bond investments, and reversing these positions when interest rates are expected to fall. The last category, covering both banks, both large and small, finance companies and corporations, typically, provide fixed rate Swiss franc payers which underlie the swap market as part of the conduct of their general asset liability management.

Exhibit 25.2

Swiss Franc Bond/Swap Arbitrage

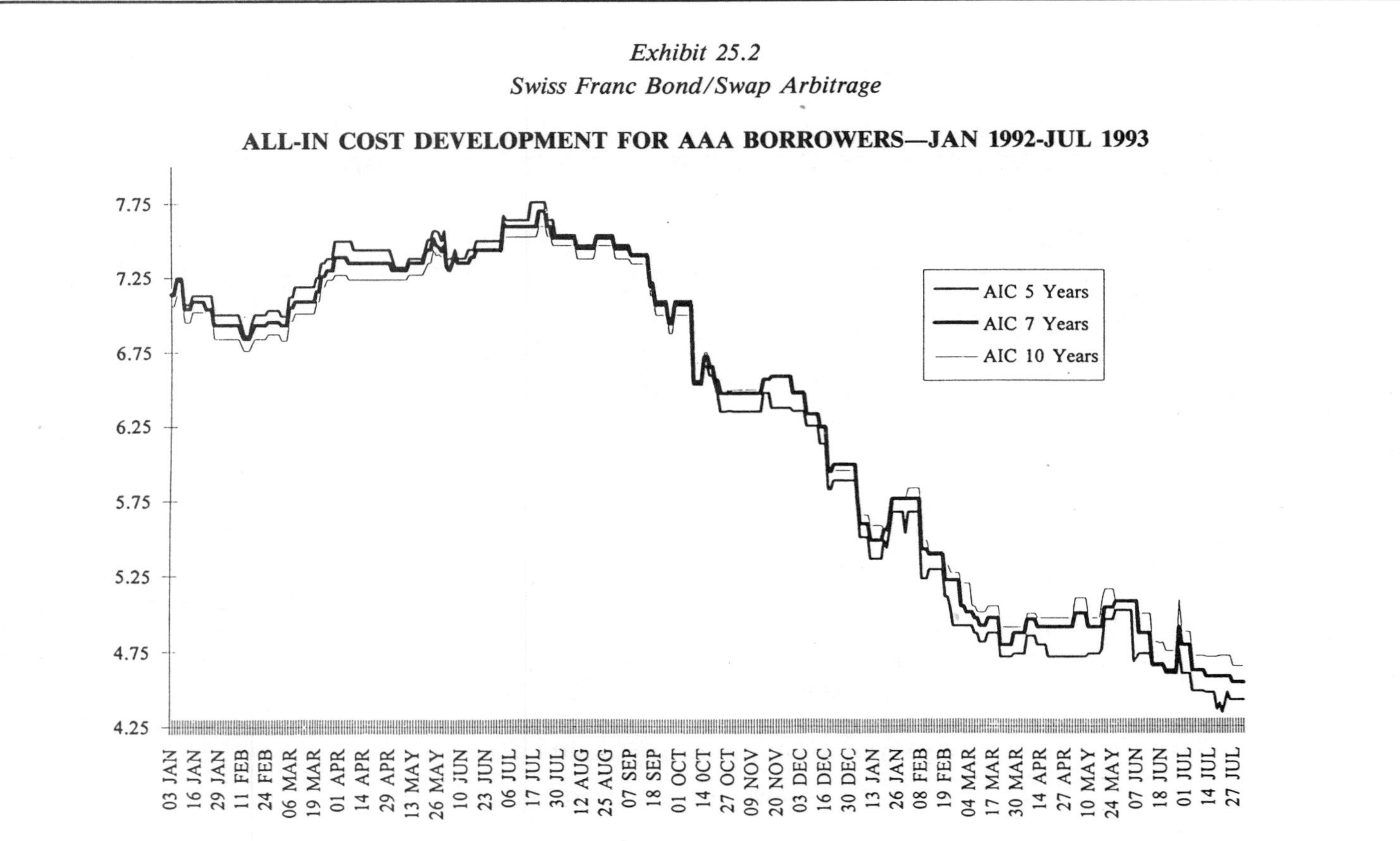

Exhibit 25.2—continued

SWISS FRANC BOND/SWAP ARBITRAGE

Swap Window Monitor
Based on indicative pricing for CHF 150 Mio.
Period: August 1992-July 1993

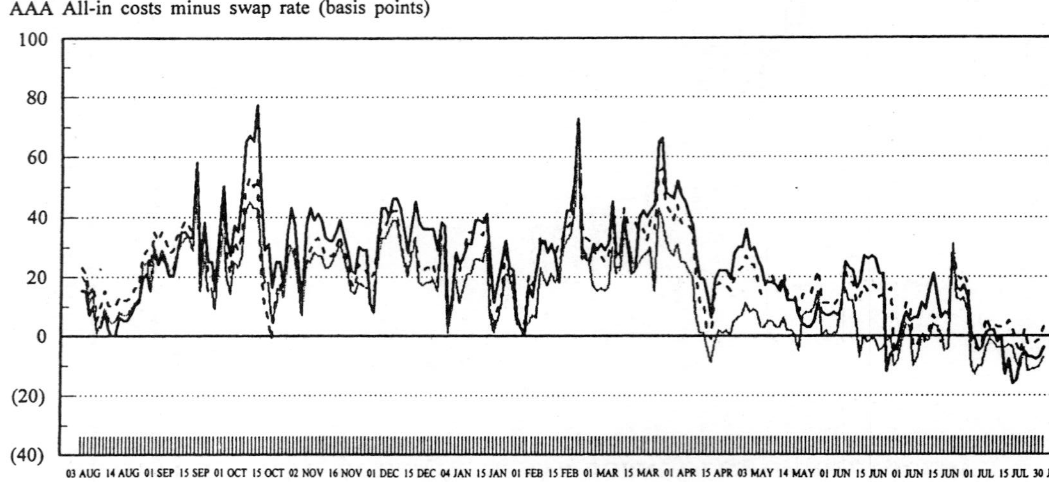

Source: Union Bank of Switzerland.

Major market makers in Swiss franc swaps are, as would be anticipated, the major Swiss universal banks. Swiss Bank Corporation, Credit Suisse and Union Bank of Switzerland dominate market making with a number of other institutions, primarily major foreign banks, such as Paribas, JP Morgan etc also being active. Increasingly, these foreign banks, particularly the United States money centre investment banks, have found themselves squeezed out of market making and acting as swap principals by the Swiss universal bank's insistence on high credit quality counterparties. This means that foreign participants are prevented, unless they are of high credit standing, from relying on the interbank market to hedge their risk positions making their participation highly risky in the absence of good two way business flows.

A significant feature of the market is that a great majority of both interest rate and currency swaps are concluded in the interbank market. Predictably, Swiss domestic corporations and investment managers are more active in interest rate swaps, while foreign corporations and asset managers are more active in the cross currency section. Currently, the growth in Swiss franc interest rate swaps is higher than that for currency swaps, reflecting, in part, a decline in the Swiss franc new issue market opportunities for swap arbitrage.

Product range

Swiss franc market is relatively sophisticated with a variety of structures available. Many of these structures have evolved in response to innovations in the bond market, such as zero coupon swaps, dual currency swaps etc, where non-standard new issue formats have dictated development of corresponding non generic swap arrangements.

DEUTSCHMARK SWAP/DERIVATIVES MARKET

Origins

The deutschmark swap market is similar to the Swiss franc swap market, although it is of more recent origin. The deutschmark swap market has its origins in the German Bundesbank's decision in 1984 to deregulate the deutschmark debt markets and lift a specific prohibition on deutschmark issues intended to be swapped. Prior to this period, a number of banks had, however, disregarded the rules. During the initial phase of deregulation, Bundesbank restrictions, such as a new issue calendar and a registration process to be completed two days before the end of the month preceding the launch, greatly restricted the flexibility of this market. However, recent changes greatly liberalising the issue procedures have given the market considerable impetus.

Structure

The structure of the deutschmark swap market has historically been very similar to that of the Swiss franc market with swaps being transacted primarily against new issues. The primary receivers of fixed rate deutschmark are either highly rated sovereign or corporate names sought after by investors and well known, but not necessarily highly rated, United States corporate names which enjoy good access to this particular market segment. This pattern in the new issue market reflects the fact that a significant portion of investors in deutschmark issues come from the traditional Swiss franc investor base.

The pattern of swap counterparties is also similar to those active in Swiss franc swaps. Supranationals as well as lower rated sovereigns often utilise deutschmark swaps to either achieve more cost efficient deutschmark funding or alternatively to avoid excessive access to this market segment however, there is an additional group of fixed deutschmark payers who are primarily motivated by asset liability management concerns. For example, a typical counterparty might be a Dutch company with heavy US$ borrowings and significant deutschmark assets. Another typical counterparty may be a German company seeking fixed rate deutschmark debt without accessing the public deutschmark markets. Both groups are highly active from time to time in the deutschmark market. The level of activity tends to be driven by the absolute levels of deutschmark rates as well as the DEM/US$ exchange rate.

Increasingly, as the deutschmark swap market has matured, the range of participants has increased to encompass most asset-liability management applications of sovereigns, supranational, corporate and other institutions. A feature of the market more recently has been the active participation of medium-sized as well as large German corporations and the regionally based Landesbanks and mortgage banks.

The new issue emphasis of the deutschmark swap market does not detract from the relative depth and liquidity in deutschmark swaps. Over recent years, liquidity has significantly increased with the emergence of newer participants as well as a number of major market makers.

Market conventions

Deutschmark swaps are typically quoted as an annual fixed rate on a bond basis (30/360 days basis) against six month deutschmark or US$ LIBOR.

Increasingly, there is a growing trend for DEM interest rate swaps to be undertaken against the Frankfurt Interbank Offered Rate (FIBOR). This trend, originally, reflected the growth in the issuance of FRNs in the deutschmark new issue market in late 1990 reflecting uncertainty over the direction of German interest rates. The trend to FIBOR-based swaps was strengthened by further deregulation of the market in 1992-1993.

The major difficulty with utilising FIBOR is its spread relative to DEM LIBOR. FIBOR is, typically, lower than LIBOR, with the spread between the two rates varying between 1/2bps to 12.5bps pa. This, in turn, is reflected in the difference in the fixed rate quoted relatively to FIBOR as against LIBOR.

FIBOR is a purely domestic rate and is driven largely by German cash markets. The fact that FIBOR is sometimes lower than LIBOR represents some problems for FIBOR-based interest rate swaps. For example, for DEM interest rate swaps, if participants may prefer to pay FIBOR/receive DEM fixed in contrast to LIBOR, then the transaction flow between fixed rate payers and receivers becomes unbalanced.

The lack of ability to hedge FIBOR has limited the size and liquidity in FIBOR swaps.

Pricing

A key factor in the deutschmark swap market is the difficulty of hedging swap risk positions through activity in the German government bond market (the Bunds).

This is particularly so in relation to creating short positions in the Bund market to cover risk positions in the corresponding swap.

Initially, short positions were created by selling bonds through Euroclear, which has a seven day clearing mechanism, and repurchasing the same bond through the German Kassenverein, which has two day clearing. This effectively allowed creation of a five day short position.

An additional mechanism by which initially, market makers hedged swap risk positions was by combining swap activities with their bond portfolio positions. Swaps were held against the bank's own bond inventory position to create "inhouse" hedges. This practice is clearly not efficient, particularly for foreign banks not active in the German domestic bond markets.

Availability of futures contracts from German interest rates has, increasingly, facilitated the hedging of deutschmark swap positions.

Since 1987, there has been a bond index future for Dutch government bonds in Amsterdam which was used as a surrogate for deutschmark bond price movements (reflecting the close interrelationships between the two markets). This, in turn, superseded the use of synthetic hedging techniques whereby United States treasury notes and US$/DEM foreign exchange contracts were used to hedge deutschmark swaps.

More recently, since late 1988, the London International Financial Futures Exchange (LIFFE) has traded a deutschmark government bond futures contract. A bond futures contract is also available on the DTB, the German Futures Exchange. The liquidity of the bond futures contract and the low bid-offer spread in the futures markets relative to the cash market for Bunds has made the contract a popular hedging mechanism for market makers in deutschmark swaps.

Availability of Bund futures contracts on both LIFFE and DTB creates certain problems. For example, the DTB has allowed bonds from the East German Treuhandanstalt to be deliverable into its ten year Bund contract. In contrast, LIFFE made the opposite decision refusing to allow the Government Guaranteed Treuhand Bonds to be delivered into its contract until it heard that the Bund might stop issuing ten year bonds for the near future. Consequently, for a futures contract maturity until the June 1993 contract, the LIFFE and Bund futures had different underlyings and trade at a differential spread (currently, about one tick).

DTB and LIFFE have also introduced a futures contract on BOBBL which is emerging as an important hedge for medium-term swaps.

The DTB is currently considering introducing a three month interest rate future based on FIBOR. This contract would compete with LIFFE's three month contract on DEM LIBOR, which in reality has a far more liquid underlying physical market. The development of the FIBOR contract should, at least in the long run, complement the DEM LIBOR contract. This will be particularly so where the FIBOR market is further developed with good liquidity in swaps and FRAs priced off FIBOR. Development of these short-term interest rate futures contracts in DEM should facilitate product development and more efficient hedging practices at the shorter end of the swap curve in deutschmarks.

As the deutschmark swap market has matured, swaps are increasingly compared to the domestic German index known as Schuldscheine. Schuldscheine are fixed rate promissory notes issued by German banks and corporations with maturities of one to ten years. Schuldscheine rates represent real interest rates reflecting current market conditions and are advantageous in that for potential participants, the swap rate can be related to current market levels for direct issuance of debt facilitating rate comparisons. The use of Schuldscheine as a guide for German swap pricing reflects a number of factors:

- The Bund market has structural deficiencies which prevent its utilisation as a hedging instrument. Bunds have original maturities of ten years and liquidity is concentrated in the most recent issue. Similarly, the Bund futures contract has had the effect of concentrating further liquidity in the ten year maturities diminishing the utility of Bunds to hedge shorter dated swaps, at least without incurring significant yield curve risks.
- Schuldscheine loans constitute over 50% of public sector debt. In addition, such transactions are used by major participants in the German market, the Landesbanks (State banks) as an important source of floating rate funding by issuing fixed rate Schuldscheine and swapping into floating rate DEM funding.
- The internal structure of the German bank funding system ensures the importance of Schuldscheine rates as a bank making a market in deutschmark swaps will, typically, ensure that the price of quotes for a deutschmark swap in exchange for a floating rate US$ LIBOR is linked to the cost of funds in the domestic market.
- Activity focusing on Schuldscheine-based asset swap arbitrage (buying Schuldscheine and swapping into LIBOR). This type of activity is largely the preserve of banks because of the lack of liquidity in the Schuldscheine market.

These factors have dictated that Schuldscheine rates will often be utilised as a guide for pricing swaps, particularly in maturities where the Bund market is less liquid.

In practice, the predominant pattern is for banks active in DEM swaps to use the Bund futures to hedge portfolio positions. A factor in this is the lack of liquidity in the repo market which could otherwise be used to finance hedge portfolios.

Exhibit 25.3 sets out deutschmark swap rates over recent times. *Exhibit 25.4* sets out the relationship of deutschmark swap rates relative to domestic German bond market rates.

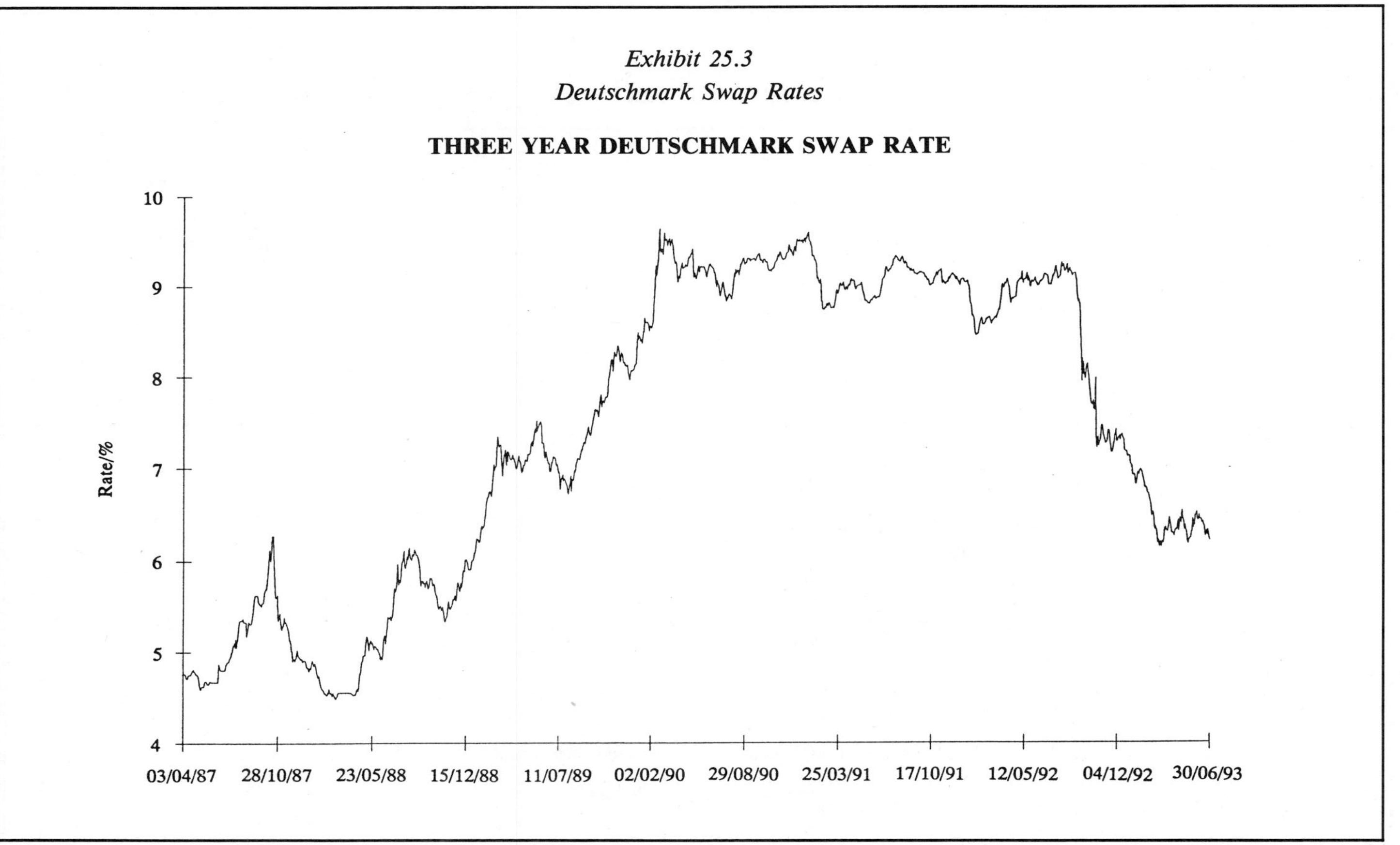

Exhibit 25.3
Deutschmark Swap Rates

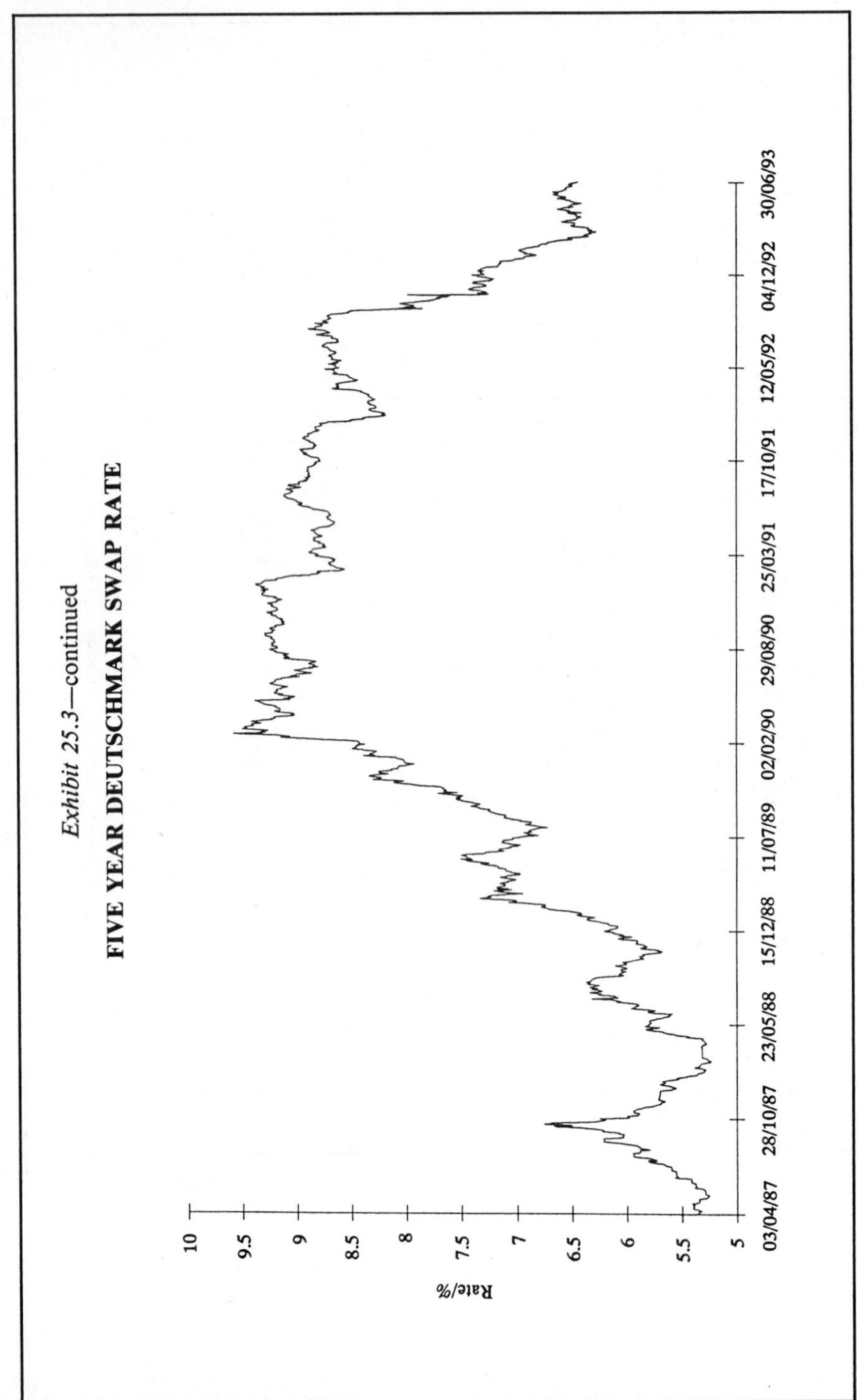
Exhibit 25.3—continued
FIVE YEAR DEUTSCHMARK SWAP RATE
Rate/%
10
9.5
9
8.5
8
7.5
7
6.5
6
5.5
5
03/04/87
28/10/87
23/05/88
15/12/88
11/07/89
02/02/90
29/08/90
25/03/91
17/10/91
12/05/92
04/12/92
30/06/93

Exhibit 25.3—continued

SEVEN YEAR DEUTSCHMARK SWAP RATE

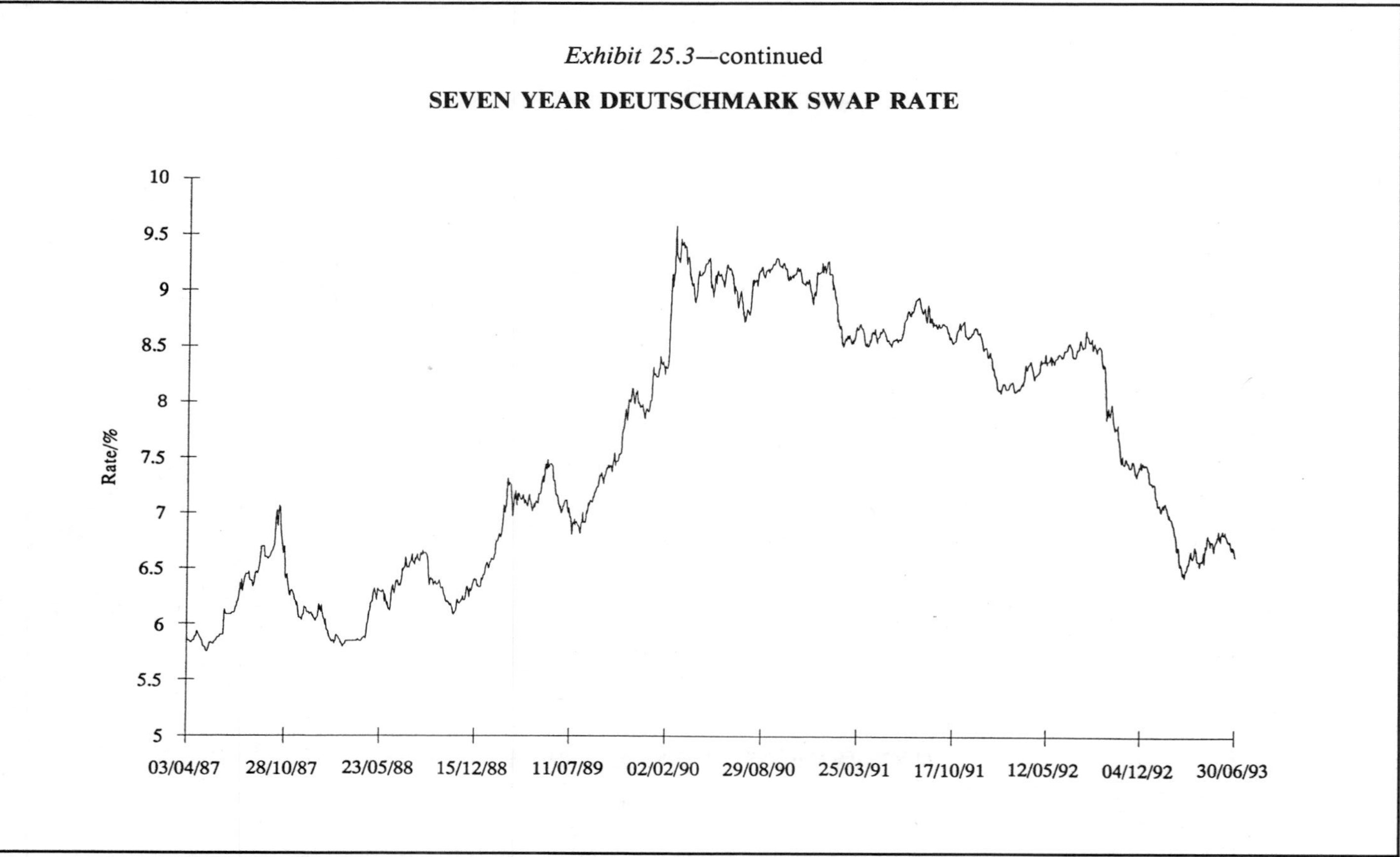

Exhibit 25.3—continued

TEN YEAR DEUTSCHMARK SWAP RATE

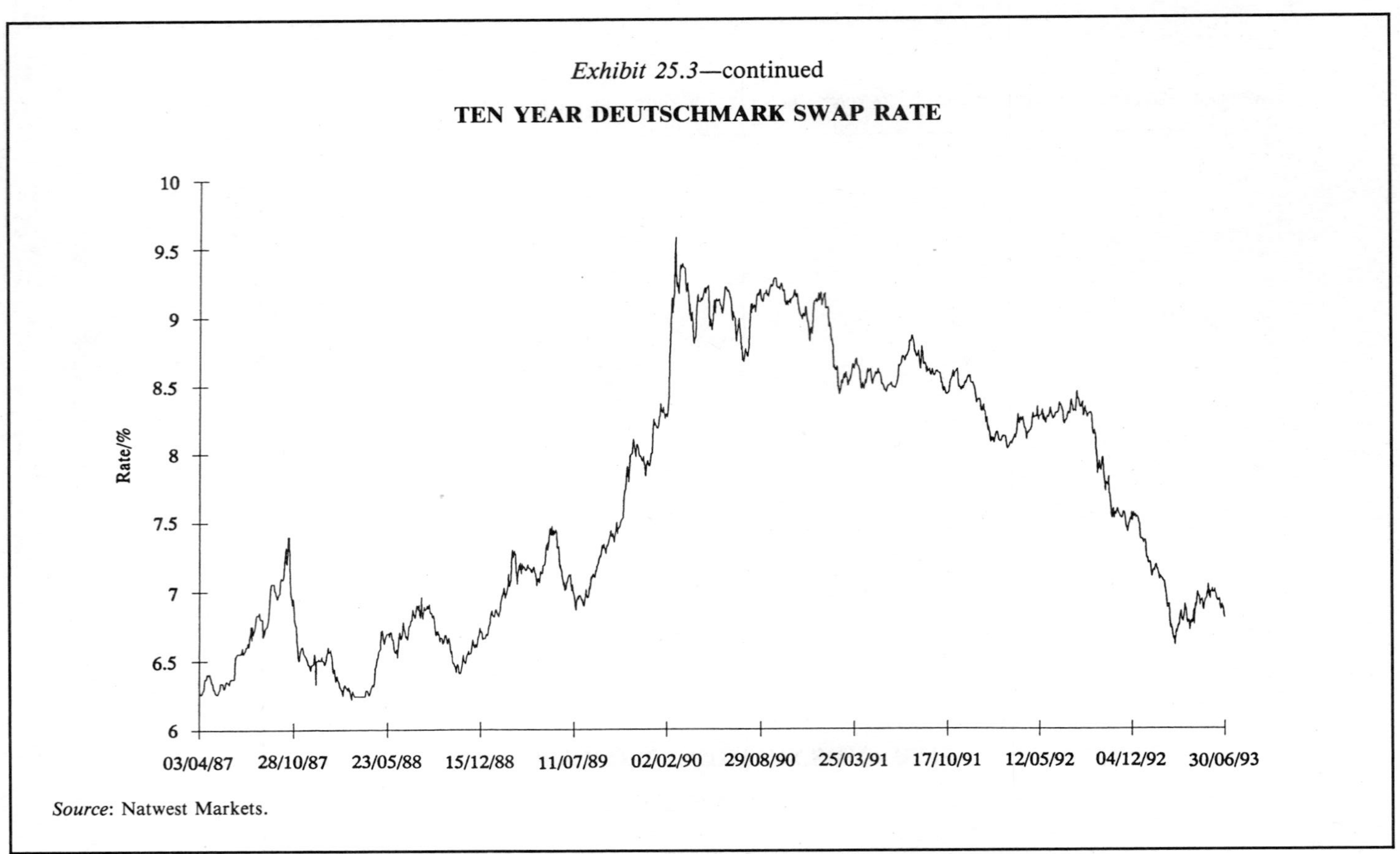

Source: Natwest Markets.

Exhibit 25.4

Deutschmark Swap Spreads

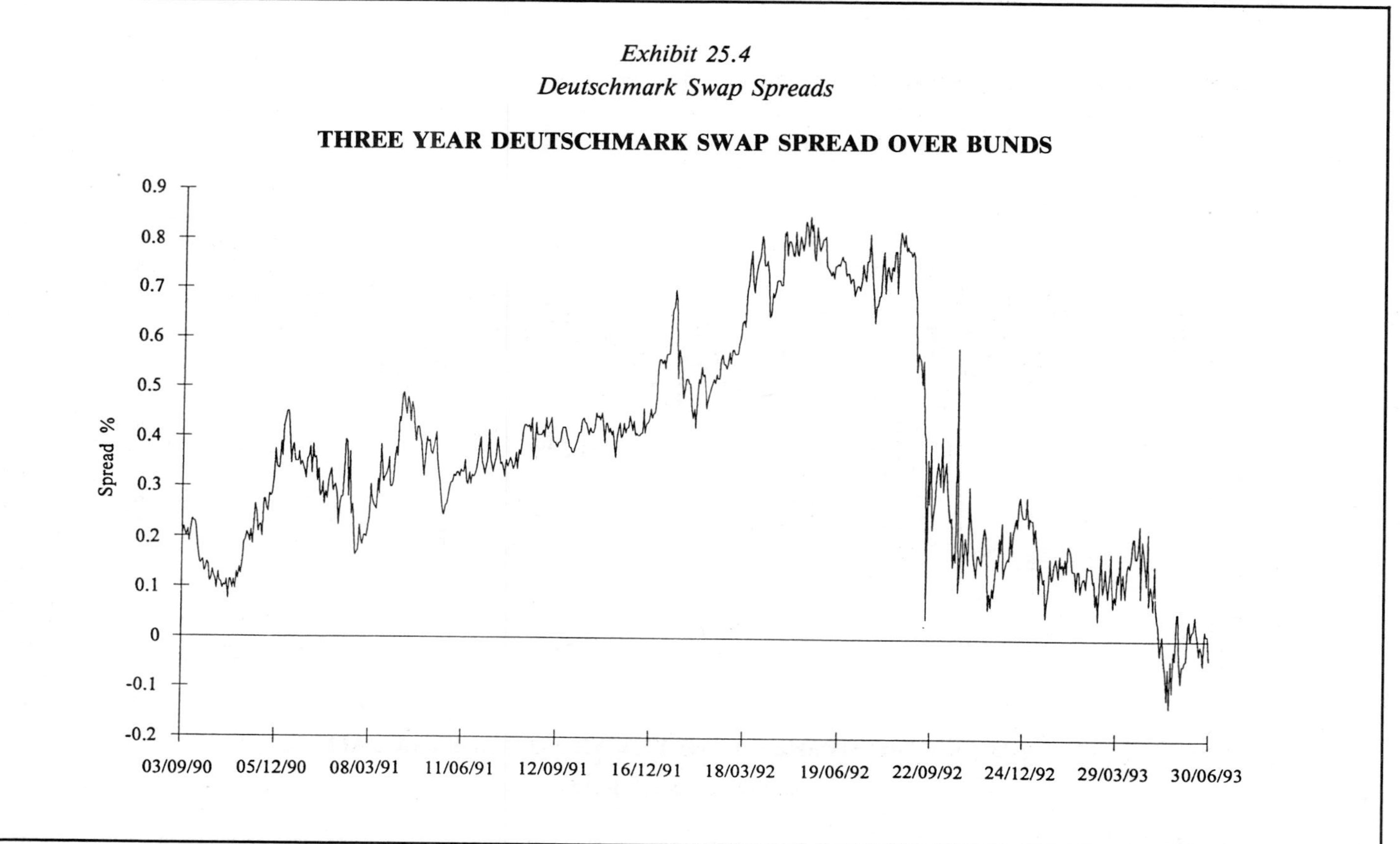

Exhibit 25.4—continued

FIVE YEAR DEUTSCHMARK SWAP SPREAD OVER BUNDS

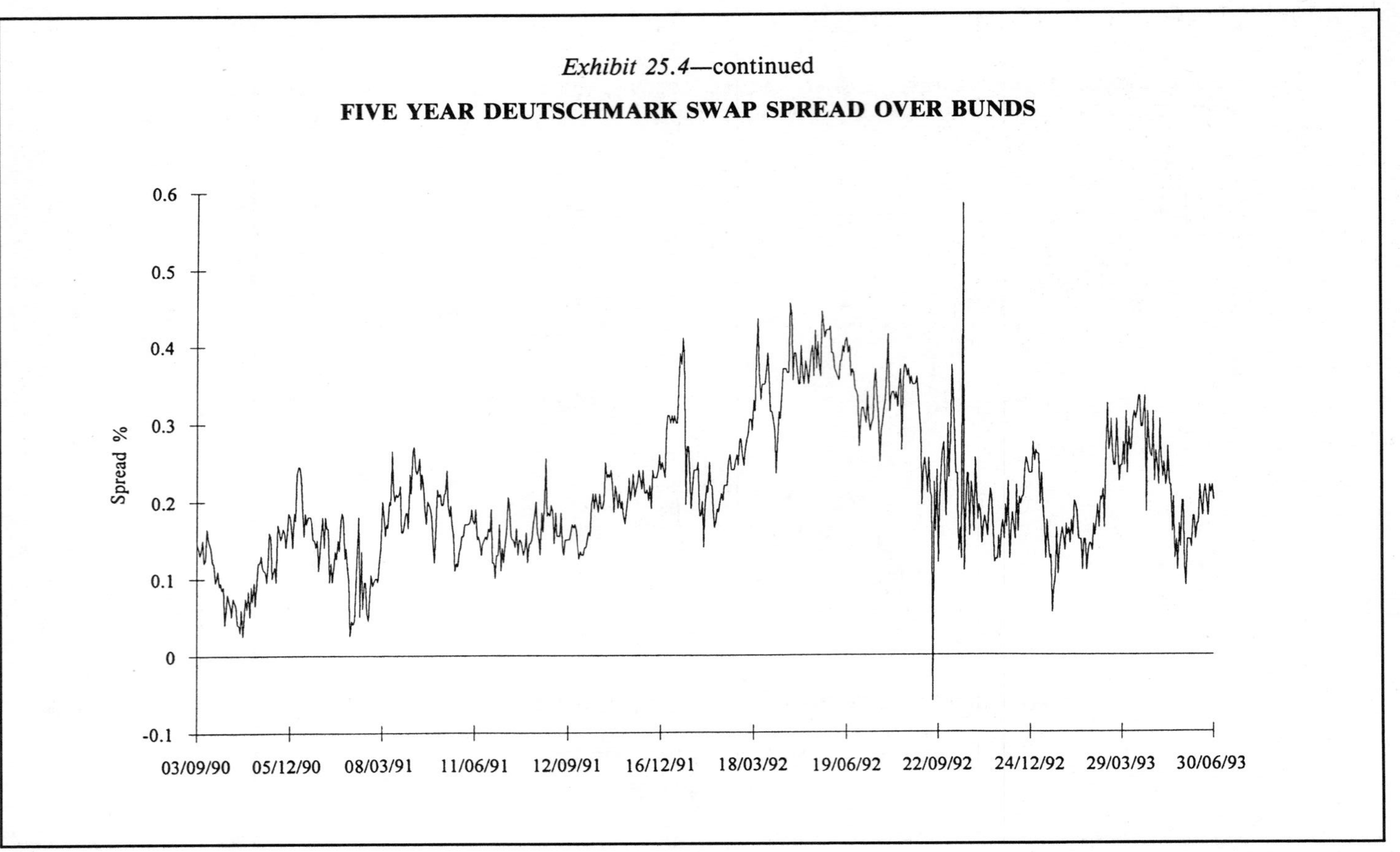

Exhibit 25.4—continued

SEVEN YEAR DEUTSCHMARK SWAP SPREAD OVER BUNDS

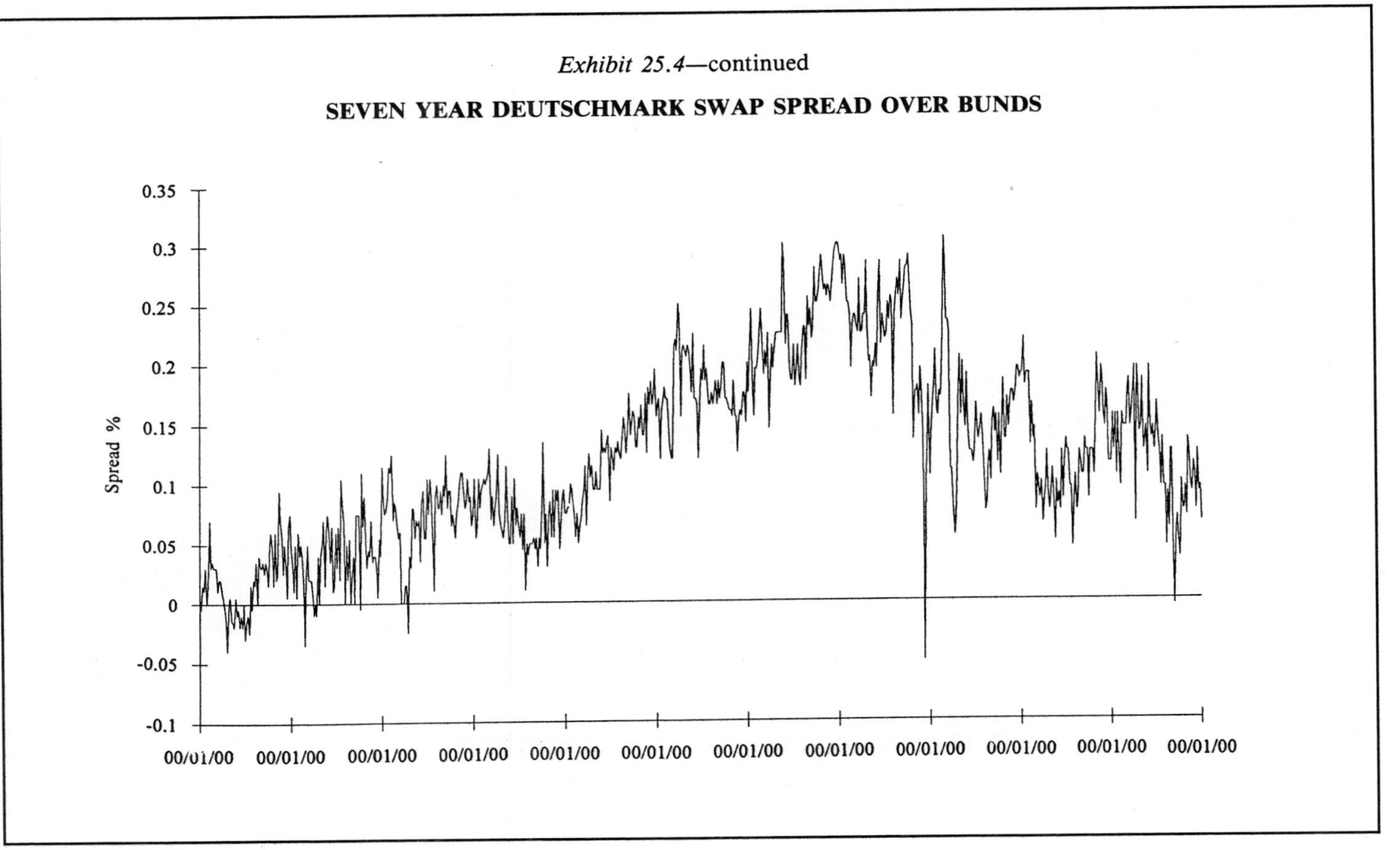

Exhibit 25.4—continued

TEN YEAR DEUTSCHMARK SWAP SPREAD OVER BUNDS

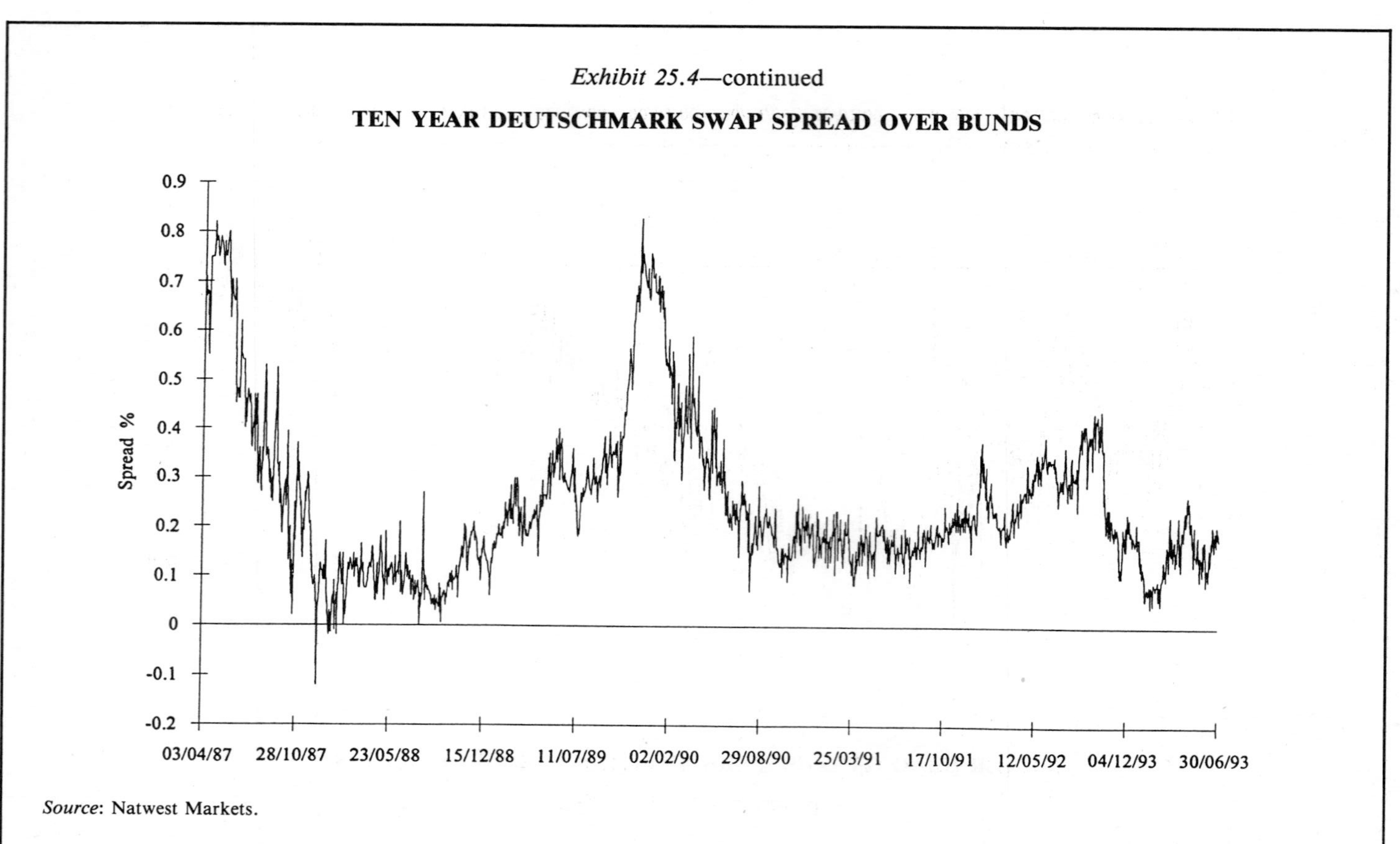

Source: Natwest Markets.

Exhibit 25.5 sets out a correlation matrix as between DEM, DEM swaps and Schuldscheine, Bund and Bund future rates. The analysis highlights the hedging relationships between the various benchmark rates and illustrates some of the difficulties of hedging in the deutschmark swap market. In practice, the predominant pattern would be for swap rates to drive other market rates in DEM, particularly Schuldscheine rates rather than the reverse.

Exhibit 25.5

Deutschmark Swap-Hedge Correlation

15 September, 1992	**2 year swap**	**5 year swap**	**10 year swap**	**10 year Schuldscheine**	**10 year bond**	**Bund future**
2 year swap	1	0.9120	0.8290	0.7650	0.5999	0.6720
5 year swap		1	0.9612	0.8998	0.6843	0.6265
10 year swap			1	0.8941	0.7661	0.6907
10 year Schuldscheine				1	0.6709	0.4639
10 year bond					1	0.6759
Bund future						1

4 November, 1992	**2 year swap**	**5 year swap**	**10 year swap**	**10 year Schuldscheine**	**10 year bond**	**Bund future**
2 year swap	1	0.9891	0.9810	0.9331	0.6645	0.9546
5 year swap		1	0.9953	0.9613	0.6542	0.9300
10 year swap			1	0.9566	0.6734	0.9330
10 year Schuldscheine				1	0.5985	0.8373
10 year bond					1	0.7193
Bund future						1

Source: West LB as quoted in David Shirreff (1993) (January).

A difficulty in pricing and hedging DEM swaps is the accounting and reporting practices imposed upon German banks by German supervisors and auditors. Under German accounting practice, unrealised losses are required to be recognised, although unrealised gains are not recognised. This is so even if a gain and a loss are part of a matched hedge position. This asymmetric and extremely conservative treatment often creates incentives for German banks to cash an in-the-money hedge when prudence dictates maintenance of the hedge position. German banks and their auditors are currently campaigning to have this accounting practice changed to a portfolio system in which unrealised with some success gains and losses in balance portfolio can offset each other.

This accounting practice has forced many derivative market makers to maintain multiple forms of accounting for their portfolios using mark-to-market calculations for their daily risk managements and accrual accounting for bank supervisors and auditors although this is becoming less important.

Ironically, anomalies on certain tax, accounting, capital and legal issues create incentives for some product innovations, in reality to the detriment of an overall transparent efficient market. Issues of capped warrants—pairs of puts and calls on indexes like the DAX (the Frankfurt Stock Market Index), currency rates, or bond prices with issue prices discounted to yield a zero coupon type return—rely on a tax anomaly whereby price gains are tax-free but interest income is taxed. Similar distortions persist in the treatment of certain option positions. However, the

German Finance Ministry has implemented new regulations which will prevent income being disguised as a capital gain through the use of cap warrants and other structures.

Market participants

The deutschmark swap market has a wide variety of participants. The principal categories of participants include:

- Sovereign and supranational borrowers, together with large, high credit quality corporate and bank/financial institutions, who are typically receivers of fixed rate DEM in connection with new issues in the currency. In addition, some sovereign, supranational and corporate borrowers who, as part of a multi-currency liability portfolio, will pay fixed rate deutschmark as a means of generating liabilities in that currency on a cost effective basis.
- Major corporations, both domestic and foreign, active in the German market which will borrow on a floating rate basis and utilise DEM interest rate swaps to manage interest rate risk.
- Domestic German banks and leasing companies which will often utilise DEM interest rate swaps to manage the asset liability mismatch, as a result of their fixed rate loans or leases, through the swap market.

Increasingly, smaller German financial institutions, primarily Landesbanks, Sparkssen (savings banks), Volksbankens (co-operative banks) and Hypotheken-banken (mortgage banks) are increasingly important participants.

Financial institutions, particularly the German universal banks, play an important role as market makers in the German swap market. The market is dominated, predictably, by banks such as Deutsche Bank and Dresdner Bank. Other German participants include Commerzbank, WestDeutsche Landesbank and Trinkaus and Burkhardt (now a subsidiary of Hong Kong Bank). Foreign Banks, including Bankers Trust, JP Morgan, Citibank, the Swiss Banks, Paribas and a number of other major participants in the global swap market, are also active. The presence of these market makers provide significant liquidity to the market.

Product range

The product range in the German market has developed rapidly over recent years. Various types of non-generic swap structures are increasingly feasible as well as growing markets in options and other swap derivatives.

An increasing area of growth has been the market for options on swaps in DEM. As previously discussed in Chapter 14, a principal factor underlying the growth of this market is a development of Schuldscheine bonds with embedded put options whereby investors have the right to resell the bonds to the issuer after one, two and three years. Investors have typically purchased the Schuldscheine bonds and stripped out the put option and sold it through the option on swaps market. This development has been an important factor in allowing the rapid development of the option on swaps market in DEM.

POUND STERLING SWAP/DERIVATIVES MARKET

Origins

The GBP swap market is an important European swap market which differs significantly from the Swiss franc and deutschmark swap markets in a number of respects.

The GBP swap market has its origins in the foreign exchange restrictions in the late 1960s and early 1970s when a thriving back-to-back or parallel loan market involving GBP on one side developed. The modern GBP swap market has its origins in the early 1980s when local authorities were being offered cheap subsidised fixed rate funds from the public works loan board. The subsidised nature of the funding provided the basis of a very attractive arbitrage for these public authorities into floating rate GBP allowing them to make significant savings or realise an immediate profit on a positive yield curve. While government action removed this pricing distortion, the GBP swap market has continued to develop. In recent years, an increasing market for Eurosterling bond issues has been a major component in the growth of the corresponding swap market. However, rather uncharacteristically, the swaps of Eurosterling issues are not necessarily exclusively into floating rate US$ with a number of issues being swapped instead into floating rate GBP.

The Eurosterling market itself is far from constant, operating spasmodically in response to the differential between GBP interest rates and comparable interest rates on other currencies as well as the future outlook for the GBP in foreign exchange markets. Investor demand for GBP, particularly outside the United Kingdom, tends to be driven by a mixture of portfolio diversification and short-term trading objectives. Expectations of interest rate falls or appreciation in the GBP creates short-term demand pressures for GBP assets which are usually quickly satisfied by bringing Eurosterling issues to market.

The issuers of Eurosterling securities on a swapped basis include typical arbitrage funders as well as the United Kingdom branches or subsidiaries of international banks and United Kingdom building societies. The foreign bank branches and building societies are primarily motivated by asset liability matching considerations and are seeking to generate cost effective floating rate funds in GBP at a cost better than that achievable directly. For United Kingdom building societies in particular, GBP interest rate swaps represent an alternative form of funding to more traditional techniques, such as the issuance of CDs or retail deposits.

The counterparties for these receivers of fixed rates have traditionally been corporations seeking to lock in their cost of funding over medium term maturities. The main corporates in this group include organisations without the ability to directly tap the Eurosterling market because of credit rating considerations or other entities whose funding requirements do not warrant a full scale Eurobond issue.

Corporate participation has, gradually, developed to encompass asset-liability management as well as, to a more limited degree, positioning on outright sterling interest rate movements. Corporate participation has increasingly been complemented by the involvement of institutional investors, such as insurance companies and pension funds. These organisations increasingly utilise the sterling swap market to manage their asset portfolios as well as take advantage of spread differentials between the swap and sterling government bond market.

The development of the sterling swap market has been impeded by the now infamous local councils affair. Previously, the local councils were active users of the sterling swap market as well as other derivative product markets. However, in 1985, the London Borough of Hammersmith and Fullham became unable to honour its outstanding swap and option derivatives contracts.

The Borough, one of the United Kingdom's local authorities, had been active in the sterling swap market, initially for the purpose of interest rate risk management but, as became evident much later, for speculative purposes. A major component of this speculative activity was the generation of premium income through the sale of options on swaps.

Eventually, it emerged that Hammersmith and Fullham had total sterling swap and option contracts totalling GBP6,000m in 1988 against the council's underlying debt of only GBP300m. Hammersmith and Fullham's district auditor ruled the Council's activity in these markets was beyond its powers as conferred by statute on the authority. After a complex series of legal proceedings, the decision of the district auditor was upheld in the House of Lords: see discussion in Chapter 44. This ruling resulted in losses to the swap counterparties, primarily banks and financial institutions, estimated at anywhere between GBP250 to GBP500m.

The subsequent withdrawal of the local councils and concern about the power of local authorities to enter into swap transactions have significantly impeded continuing development of the market. In particular, volumes in the option on swaps market in sterling have been reduced.

Market convention

The average size of sterling swaps are around GBP10m. Amounts up to GBP25 to 50m can be readily transacted. The average size of swaps has increased in recent times, particularly those in relation to new issues.

Maturities up to 10-12 years are readily available. An increasing feature of the sterling market is the ability to transact swaps for extremely long maturities, as far out as 25-30 years, although, it must be said that transactions of this maturity are not common.

For example, the Guaranteed Export Finance Corporation (GEFCO), the financing vehicle for the United Kingdom's Export Credit Guarantee Department swapped the proceeds of its GBP250m 21 year Eurobond issue without significant difficulties. Similarly, in the late 80s and early 90s, large GBP hedging programmes have been completed for leveraged buyout transaction (most notably Magnet and Isosceles). In addition, in early 1992, Charterhouse Bank in London completed a GBP1,700m interest rate swap.

Market spreads have decreased significantly in recent years. A typical bid offer spread is 5bps pa for maturities up to five years, 7bps pa up to ten years, with spreads widening significantly for maturities beyond ten years reflecting the lack of liquidity and credit concerns for transactions of those maturities.

Pricing

Sterling swaps are traditionally priced at a margin over a United Kingdom government security (referred to as "gilts") of the relevant maturity. However, the relationship between the swap rate and the underlying gilt is volatile with spreads fluctuating widely even as between market makers.

Major issues in relation to pricing sterling swaps include:

- The primary determinant of spread volatility appears to be changes in the interest rate on the underlying gilt rather than specific changes in the conditions of the swap market. The traditional relationship between spreads and absolute swap levels tends to be, in broad terms, inversely proportional. This reflects the fact that when interest rates are at relatively low levels, borrowers are prepared to pay fixed rates to fix funding costs thereby pushing up swap spreads. Conversely, when rates are perceived to be relatively high, the lack of demand for fixed rate funding puts downward pressure on swap spreads.
- The interrelationship between the Eurosterling market and the swap market is complex. For example, if swap spreads increase while the relationship between the

Eurosterling and gilt market remain static, a new issue window emerges allowing arbitrage funders to issue fixed rate sterling and swap into either floating rate sterling or into US$ LIBOR.

- The Bank of England policy whereby licensed gilt market makers are the only parties who can take short positions in the gilt market and borrow the relevant security to cover their short position means that a number of swap counterparties are prevented from hedging their swaps, except where they are already holders of the particular stock. This results in swap market makers being reluctant to take on certain positions where a gilt has to be shorted as a hedge because of a reluctance to utilise the gilt futures contracts (see discussion below) with its relevant risks. This exacerbates the volatility of spreads.
- Spread volatility relates in part to a lack of consistency and general agreement on the particular gilt in the relevant maturity to be utilised as the benchmark. This reflects, in part, the lack of liquidity in the gilt market and the fact that it is almost impossible to avoid hedging with gilts that are trading at a substantial premium or discount to par. This has resulted in a standard practice whereby the same gilt is used as a benchmark for each calendar year necessitating adjustments to the amounts of the bond used for hedging depending on the maturity mismatch.
- Further anomalies exist including the introduction of gilts that are free of tax to overseas residents which creates distortions in the yield curve further confusing the swap gilt spread relationship.

A significant problem is recent years has been the reduction in the supply of gilt stocks. In the Thatcher years, the public sector borrowing requirement was transformed into the public sector debt repayment programme. A combination of high tax revenues and the proceeds of the government's privatisation programme forced the Bank of England to become net buyers of gilt stocks reducing the total amount of outstanding debt by over 20%. This overall decrease in the size of the gilt market created an artificial scarcity of supply of hedging stock as investment managers became reluctant sellers of stock. Under these circumstances, gilt yields were lower forcing swap spreads to, unrealistically, high levels and further exacerbating its volatility.

The scarcity of gilts and the difficulties with utilising the gilt futures contract (discussed below) has forced market participants to look at Eurosterling bonds as an alternative hedge. The emergence of a number of large benchmark issues increasing liquidity has created an impetus for these discussions although considerations of credit rating on such securities has prevented significant progress.

In practice, sterling interest rate swaps are hedged in two ways:

- Shorter term transactions (up to two to three years) are now hedged through the LIFFE short dated sterling contract (effectively a futures contract on three month sterling interest rates). The extension of the trading months for the short-term sterling interest rate contract to a third year has encouraged the use of this contract for these hedging purposes.
- Longer dated swaps are hedged by a mixture of gilts of the relevant maturity and the gilt futures contract. A major problem in utilising the gilt futures contract is the long maturity of the gilt security underlying the futures contract. The use of the futures to hedge swap positions, consequently, results in significant yield curve risk being assumed.

Exhibit 25.6 sets out sterling swap rates for a number of maturities over recent years compared to the relevant gilt benchmark.

Exhibit 25.6

Sterling Swap Rates

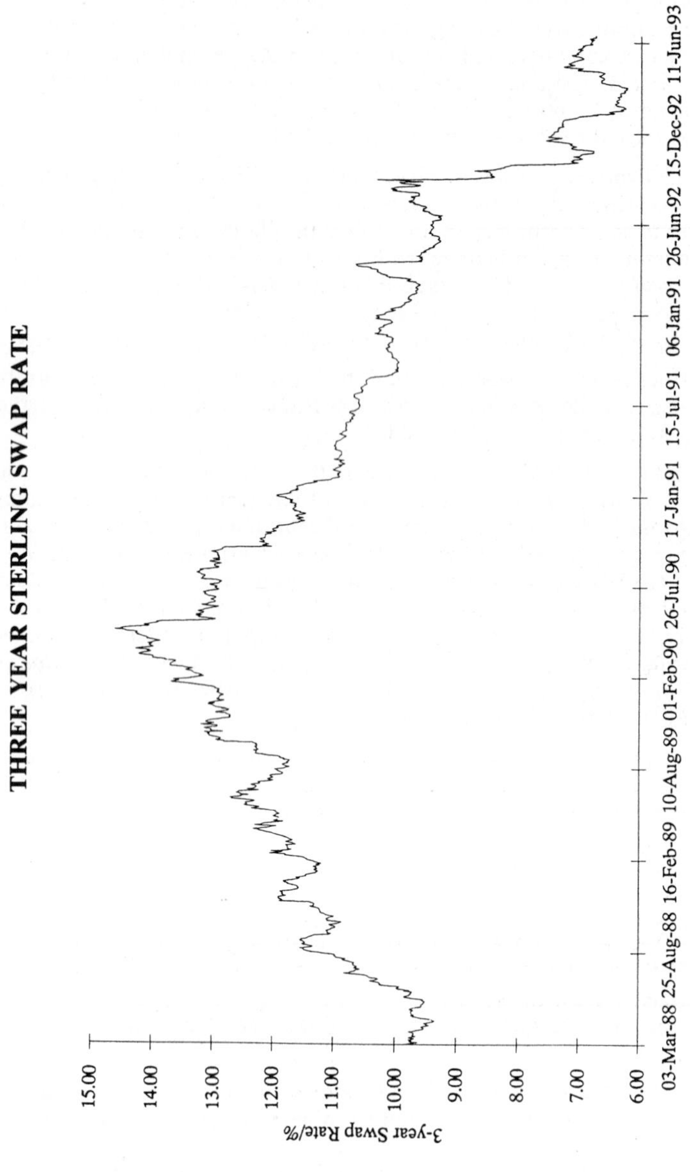

THREE YEAR STERLING SWAP RATE

3-year Swap Rate/%

15.00
14.00
13.00
12.00
11.00
10.00
9.00
8.00
7.00
6.00

03-Mar-88 25-Aug-88 16-Feb-89 10-Aug-89 01-Feb-90 26-Jul-90 17-Jan-91 15-Jul-91 06-Jan-91 26-Jun-92 15-Dec-92 11-Jun-93

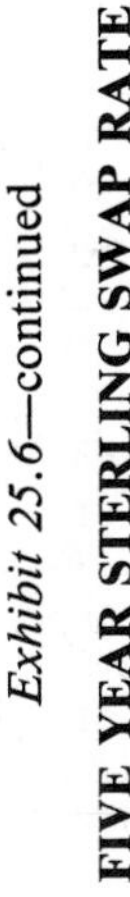

Exhibit 25.6—continued

FIVE YEAR STERLING SWAP RATE

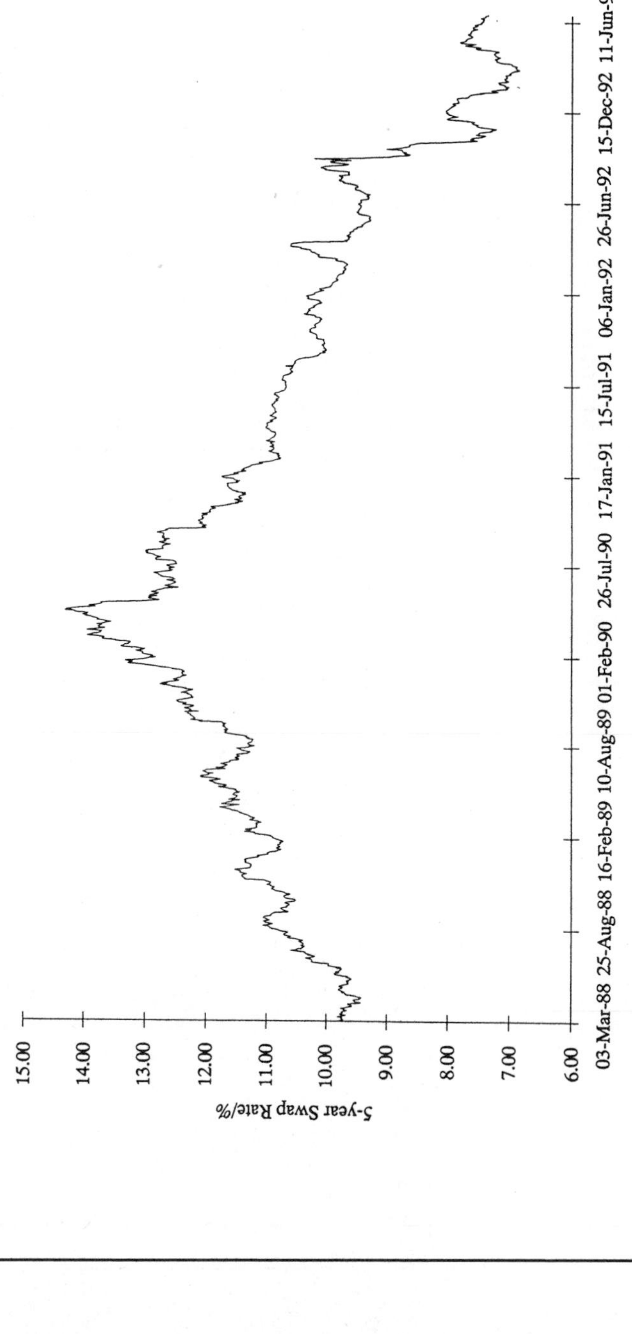

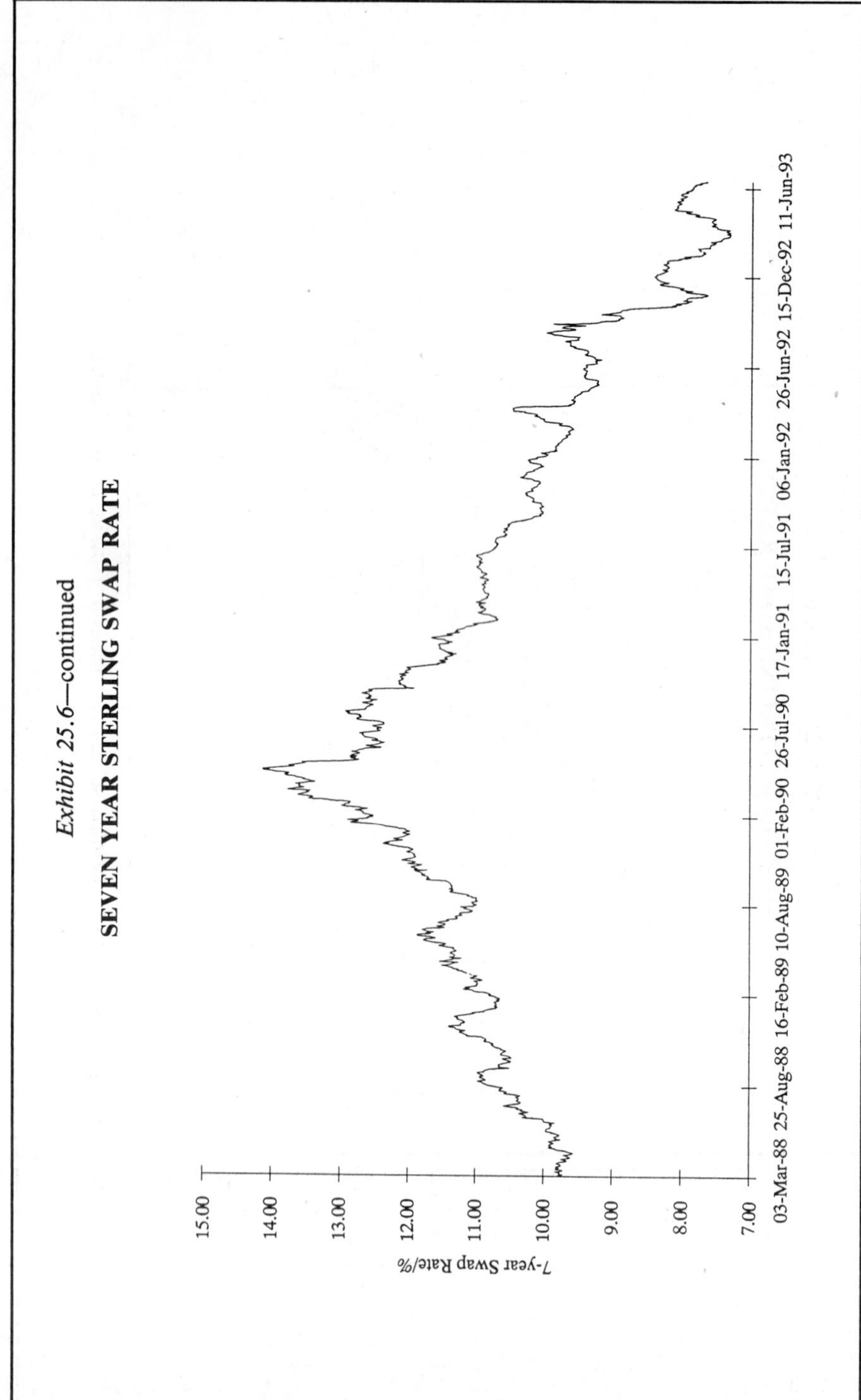

Exhibit 25.6—continued

SEVEN YEAR STERLING SWAP RATE

Exhibit 25.6—continued

TEN YEAR STERLING SWAP RATE

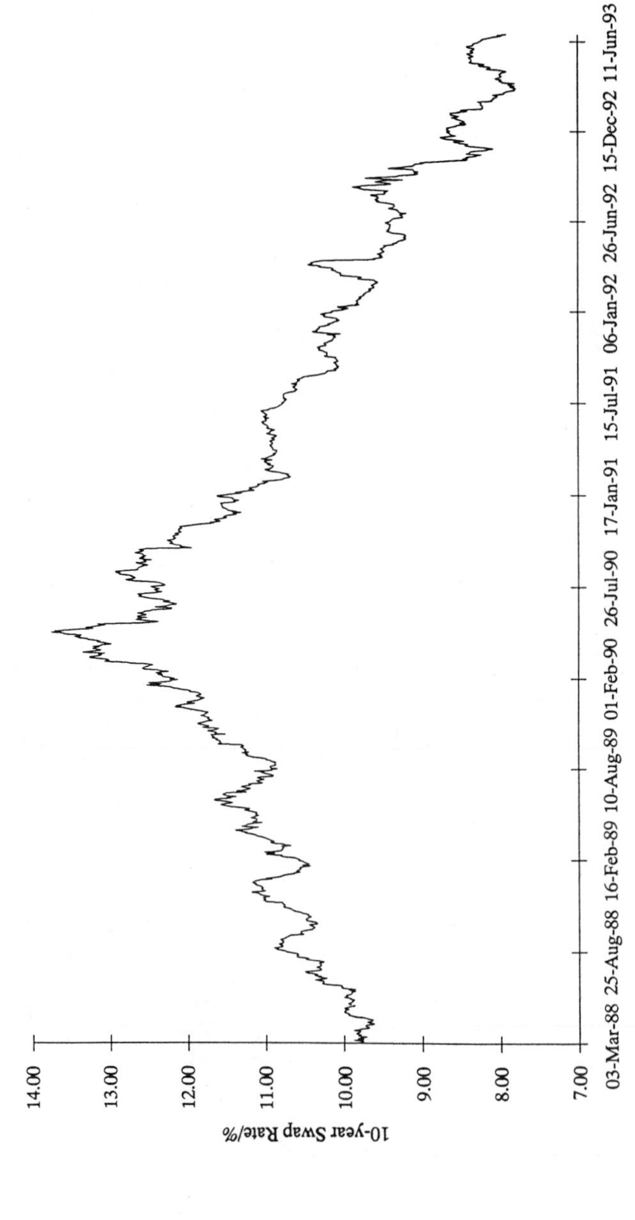

10-year Swap Rate/%

14.00
13.00
12.00
11.00
10.00
9.00
8.00
7.00

03-Mar-88 25-Aug-88 16-Feb-89 10-Aug-89 01-Feb-90 26-Jul-90 17-Jan-91 15-Jul-91 06-Jan-92 26-Jun-92 15-Dec-92 11-Jun-93

Exhibit 25.6—continued

THREE YEAR STERLING SWAP SPREAD OVER GILT

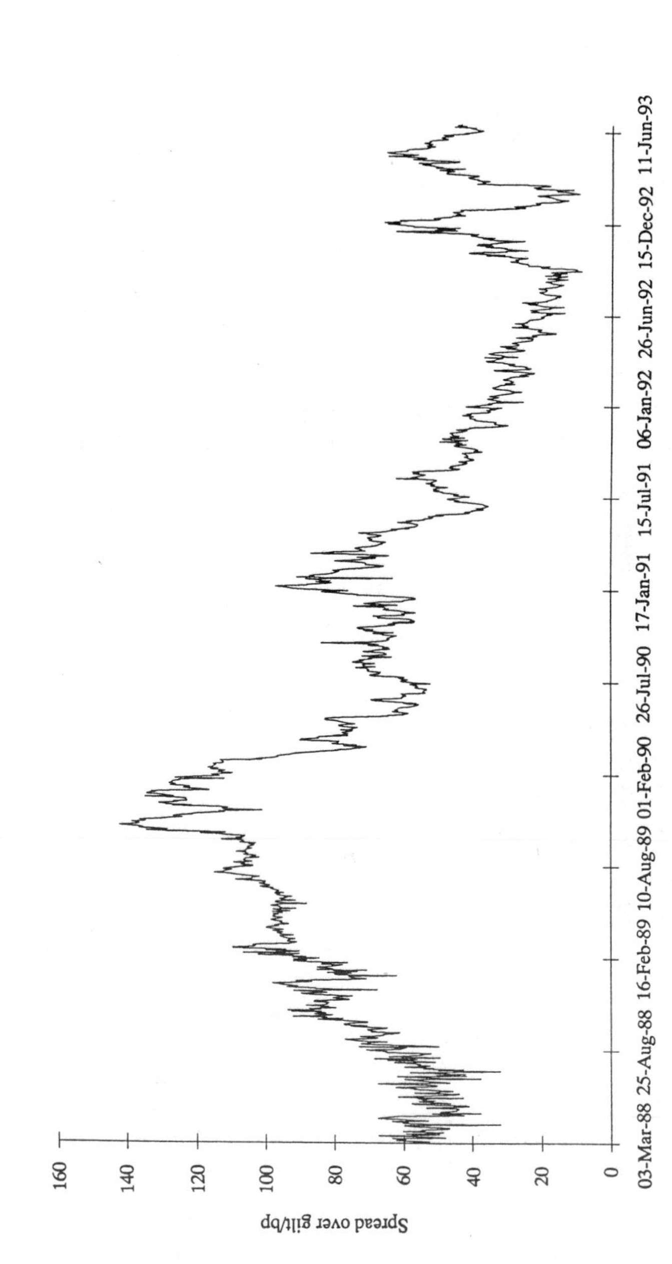

Exhibit 25.6—continued

FIVE YEAR STERLING SWAP SPREAD OVER GILT

Exhibit 25.6—continued

SEVEN YEAR STERLING SWAP SPREAD OVER GILT

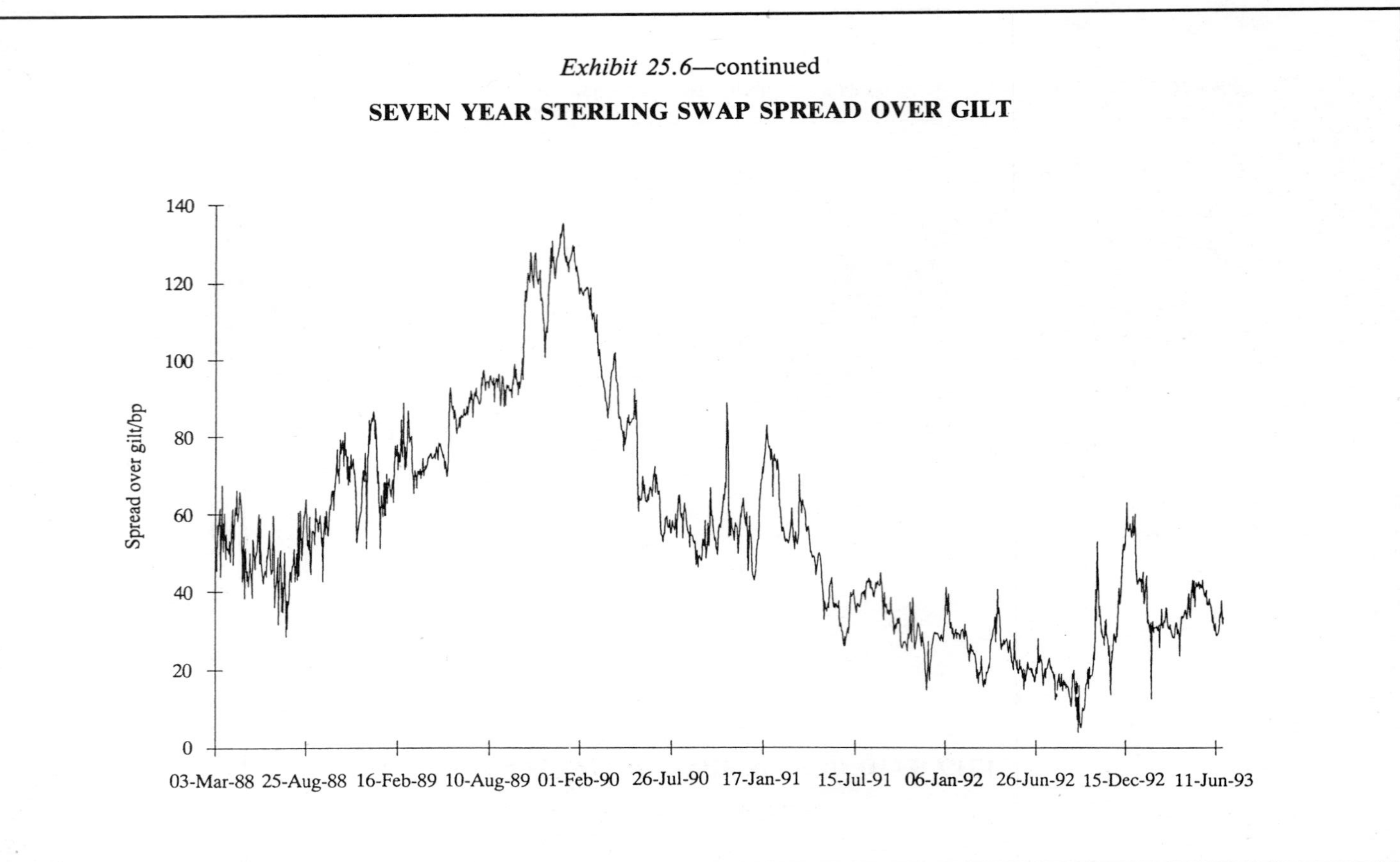

Exhibit 25.6—continued

TEN YEAR STERLING SWAP SPREAD OVER GILT

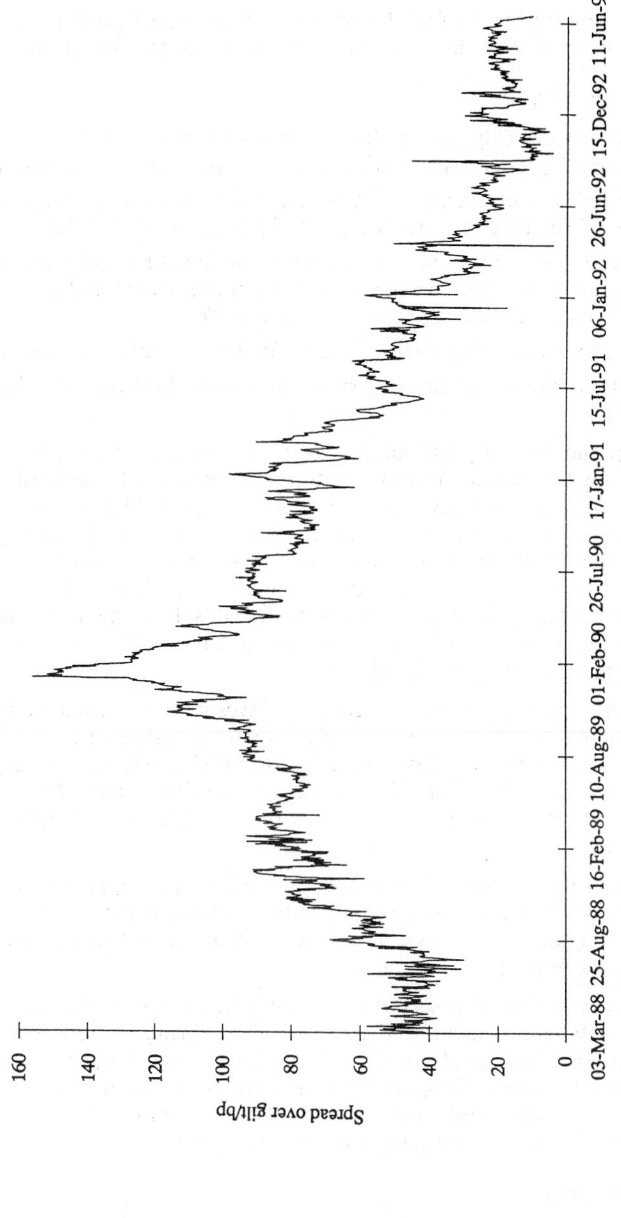

Spread over gilt/bp

160
140
120
100
80
60
40
20
0

03-Mar-88 25-Aug-88 16-Feb-89 10-Aug-89 01-Feb-90 26-Jul-90 17-Jan-91 15-Jul-91 06-Jan-92 26-Jun-92 15-Dec-92 11-Jun-93

Source: Natwest Markets.

Exhibit 25.7 sets out the interrelationship between changes in sterling swap rates and sterling interest rate movements highlighting inverse relationship noted above.

The GBP swap market also shows a reasonable amount of secondary market activity. The secondary market activity has tended to be generated out of the interbank market where banks holding gilt portfolios have utilised swaps to effectively short the gilt market. Because of difficulties in physically selling short, banks have, utilising the fact that swaps price off a particular gilt, paid out the fixed side as an alternative means of creating the short physical position.

Market participants

As noted previously, the sterling swap market enjoys active participation from a wide range of participants. Major categories of participants include:

- Issuers of sterling Eurobonds who are active receivers of fixed rate sterling and payers of floating rate sterling or floating rate US$ LIBOR.
- Financial institutions, primarily banks and building societies, which utilise the sterling swap market for interest rate risk management and positioning within an overall asset liability management framework.
- Corporations utilising sterling swaps for interest rate risk management.
- Institutional investors utilising swaps to manage long term pension and insurance liabilities.

The spread volatility and anomalies in pricing is a particularly significant factor in attracting the participation of institutional investors. These institutions have large asset portfolios designed to fund long-term liabilities. Increasingly, these organisations trade the spread differential between swaps and gilts, seeking to enhance the return on fixed interest portfolios. Under this approach, the institution may sell the underlying gilt and replace its cash flows with a swap of similar maturity, investing the cash proceeds of the gilt sale in the money markets to cover the floating rate side of the swap transaction. From time to time, the yield enhancement achieved is significant.

Further participation by institutional investors, particularly at their favoured longer end of the yield curve, is problematic for a variety of factors including credit risk considerations, liquidity, (most importantly) investment rules governing these institutions, as well as inability of these institutions to handle swap transactions from an administrative and accounting point of view (a deficiency which is being overcome).

The volatility of spreads has also assisted in the development of a significant market in sterling asset swap usually entailing transformation of under performing Eurosterling bonds into floating rate assets which are then placed, primarily, with the banking market.

The sterling market is served by a significant number of active market makers. Major participants include the large UK clearing banks—Barclays, National Westminster, Midland/Hong Kong Bank and Lloyds. The merchant banks, Baring Bros, Morgan Grenfell/Deutsche Bank, Hambros etc are active, although their share of the sterling swap market has declined. A number of foreign banks, such as Bankers Trust, JP Morgan, AIG etc are also active.

Product range

The sterling swap market is sophisticated with most non-generic structures being available.

Exhibit 25.7

Relationship Between Gilt Yield and Swap Margin (adjusted to show correlation)

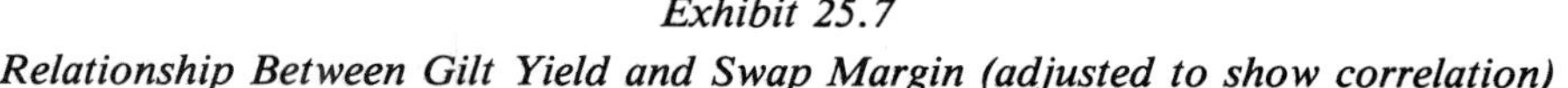

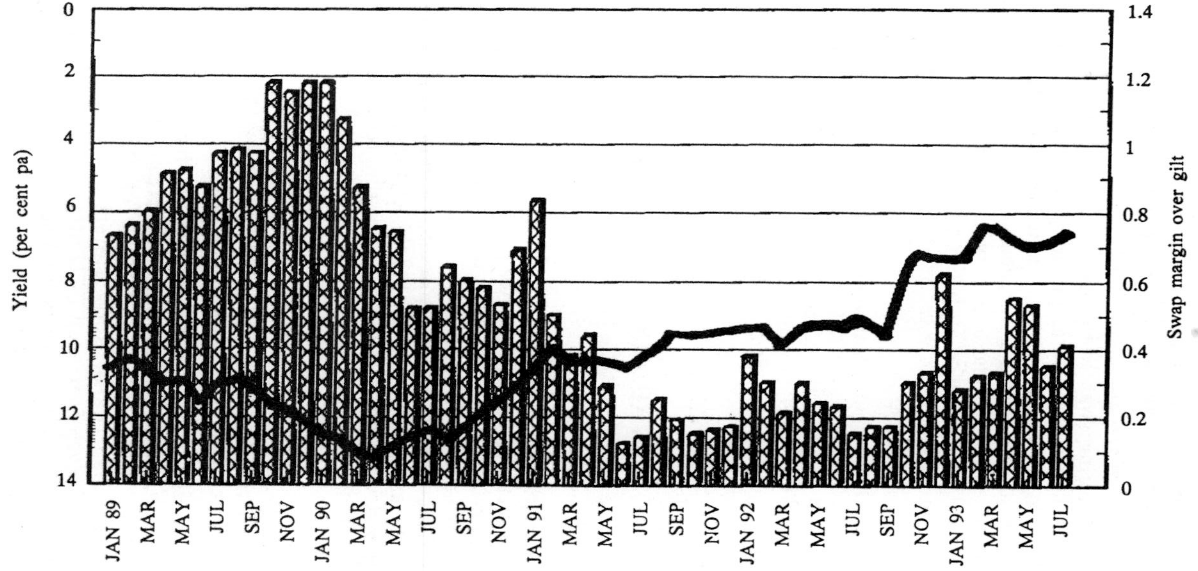

Note: The Scale on the left hand vertical axis has been inverted to illustrate the correlation between tightening gilt yields and swap margins.

Source: Hambros Bank.

An interesting aspect of the product range of the sterling swap market is the attempts to develop a basis swap market in sterling, entailing exchanges of sterling LIBOR for base rate or mortgage rate linked flows. This reflects reasonable demand from the United Kingdom building society sector, the bulk of whose lending is at the mortgage rate (which in turn is base rate linked), who have significant financings in sterling LIBOR. However, development of this market has been impeded by the fact that there is no natural end user of the opposite side to this transaction.

A significant feature of activity among market participants has been corporations seeking to unwind existing swap positions to realise up-front gains based on an expectation that sterling interest rates are likely to decline. Similarly, issues of certificates of deposits for relatively short maturities (up to two to three years) by banks and building societies seeking to generate funding at substantial margins below LIBOR have emerged. These two types of activities have provided an important supplement to the market in periods when Eurosterling market activity has been subdued, providing natural receivers of fixed rate maintaining ongoing market liquidity.

As noted above, the option on swaps market in sterling has suffered a significant decline due to the local councils affair. There continues to be a small group of banks who make markets in such instruments. Interest continues for such instruments from the corporate sector as well as from financial institutions. All options on swaps currently are settled on a cash basis rather than being exercised into a swap, with only minor exceptions.

ECU SWAP/DERIVATIVES MARKET

Background

The ECU swap market has a number of unique features although in its emphasis on new issue swap activity it demonstrates considerable similarity with the Swiss franc and deutschmark swap markets. This unique status derives from the fact that because of the artificial nature of the ECU, unlike most other bond markets, there is no natural benchmark against which absolute swap rates can be quoted as there are no ECU government bonds. Structurally, this creates a problem insofar as ECU swaps are inherently difficult to hedge with the resultant effect that most transactions are counterparty driven.

Structure

The ECU swap market structure is dictated by a close interrelationship between the ECU Eurobond market and the swap market itself.

The demand for ECU bonds comes principally from investors seeking high yielding securities with relatively low exchange rate risk. Since the ECU is a weighted basket of currencies composed of a mixture of "hard" currencies (such as deutschmark, Dutch guilder) and "soft" currencies (typically with higher yields, such as sterling, lira, French franc etc)[1] ECU offers yields somewhere between soft and hard currency levels. Investors typically come from the hard European currency countries seeking the added return without full exposure to the currency risk that would be entailed by direct investments in the soft European currencies. Additional investment comes from private retail clients primarily in the Benelux countries and Switzerland. In recent years, there has been some demand for ECU investments

1. Both sterling and lira withdrew from the ERM (the Exchange Rate Mechanism) in September 1992.

from Japanese investors reflecting the international demand for high yielding bonds providing high current income rather than capital gain.

A significant characteristic of the investors in the ECU bond market is their credit concerns and sensitivity. This has historically limited access to the ECU Eurobond market to a relatively limited range of borrowers. The main borrowers of ECUs include:

- Various official entities of the European Common Market, including supranational entities such as the European Investment Bank (EIB) and the European Coal and Steel Community (ECSC), as well as member countries such as France, Italy and Ireland. This group is largely motivated by the need to support the concept of the ECU as part of the EEC concept, the capacity to borrow outside their domestic market with a currency linked to their own and generally at a cheaper cost.
- Sovereign and semi-sovereign borrowers from a wide variety of countries, including Australia, who are motivated by objectives of diversification in terms of both currency and investor base.
- Corporations, both European and non-European, that have European assets and are seeking to incur liabilities in ECU as a means of match funding their balance sheets.
- A small group of opportunistic entities seeking to arbitrage the ECU versus other domestic markets. This type of activity is based on the fact that the ECU can often represent an opportunity to generate liabilities in currencies which cannot be obtained directly and, above all, offers the possibility to take advantage of discrepancies between yields of the component currencies and the ECU rate itself.

Potential borrowers in ECU do not, however, enjoy equal access to ECU funding. The major investor base in ECU, which in recent times has included a substantial Japanese element seeking a yield pick-up relative to the deutschmark (given that the deutschmark is a major component of the ECU), are highly credit sensitive. This means that access to the ECU bond market itself is available only to a relatively select group of borrowers. This necessarily means that several of the identified users of ECUs, primarily corporations seeking ECU funding either for asset liability management purposes or as an arbitrage to a component currency as well as some lesser rated sovereign borrowers seeking diversification, are forced to utilise ECU swaps usually against receipt of floating rate US$ to achieve their desired ECU exposures. Their interest in paying fixed rate ECU essentially drives new issue activity in the ECU Eurobond market.

The issuers of ECU Eurobonds are predominantly new issue arbitrage funders seeking cheap US$ floating rate funding. The type of issuer is influenced by investor demand which has from time to time favoured good quality United States names with good investor recognition. The fact that these often lesser ranking but well known borrowers can obtain funding on relatively attractive credit differentials in the ECU market relative to other borrowing avenues allows them to issue relatively cheap ECU debt which is then swapped into cheaper floating rate US$.

CTE tax arbitrages

A feature of the ECU swap market is a complex arbitrage between ECU Eurobonds and Certificates di Credits del Tresoro (CTE) denominated in ECU issued by the Republic of Italy.

This arbitrage transaction operates as follows: a borrower issues ECU Eurobonds and simultaneously enters into an ECU and US$ currency swap with a bank active in ECU swaps whereby it receives fixed rate ECU and pays US$ LIBOR. The bank generates the mirror reverse side of the swap by purchasing ECU CTEs and repackaging them via an asset swap into a US$ LIBOR FRN and placing the asset with an investor. The asset swap requires the investor to pay fixed rate ECU (the receipts from the CTEs) and receive US$ LIBOR neatly covering the bank's exposure under the original ECU swap.

The yield differential between ECU CTEs and AAA rated Eurobonds can be as much as 100bps pa, resulting in attractive swap arbitrage opportunities. This arbitrage differential may allow issuers to generate US$ funding at up to 40-50bps under LIBOR and investors to generate Republic of Italy assets at up to 40bps over LIBOR.

The crucial element driving CTE based swaps is withholding tax factors. CTEs issued prior to 20 September 1986 are tax exempt; issues prior to August 1987 are taxed at the rate of 6.25% on the coupon payment; all issues after August 1987 are taxed at a withholding tax rate of 12.50%. Investors in certain countries are exempt under a withholding tax exemption agreement between the Republic of Italy and the relevant country or, alternatively, are eligible to recover any withholding tax via a tax credit.

Market convention/pricing relationships

ECU swaps are typically quoted on an annual Eurobond basis (30/360 day basis) against six month ECU or six month US$ LIBOR (the floating side is quoted on a money market basis—365/360 day basis).

Average transaction volumes are large, reflecting the new issue driven nature of the market. Market activity encompasses maturities (up to) ten years. Major activity is concentrated on maturities up to five years.

The major trading centre for ECU is London and Paris with transaction activity being concentrated during the European time zone. A significant structural deficiency of the ECU market is the absence of an underlying government bond market which facilitates market makers hedging their own positions. The absence of such a market dictates that swap market makers have no efficient means of hedging swap risk position other than through offsetting swaps or by positioning the institution's swap portfolio to take advantage of anticipated movements in ECU fixed rates.

The structural constraint dictated, in the evolving phase of the market, that the majority of transactions were undertaken on a pure counterparty basis with financial institutions obtaining mandates from issuers based on an all-in cost target in the swap currency and then seeking to take advantage of ECU bond market conditions and the availability of swap counterparties to engineer the transaction.

However, as the market has developed, a number of institutions (see discussion below) began to provide liquidity by running unmatched swap warehousing operations allowing participants to transact swaps unrelated to a new issue. These financial institution made markets in ECU swaps either on the basis of positioning or utilising surrogate hedges for swap portfolio positions. For example, on occasions, these financial institutions would purchase deutschmark bonds to hedge the swap position. The risk linked to this activity was substantial because the only means to generate a short position in ECU itself was to launch an ECU issue when market conditions allowed.

The emergence of the CTE tax arbitrage has assisted in increasing market making flexibility as the capacity to buy and sell CTEs as part of asset swap package has allowed swap market makers to increasingly efficiently hedge their swap risk positions. However, it should be noted that any such hedge is subject to significant risks.

The emergence of the ECU three month interest rate contract futures on LIFFE and the Marche a Terme des Instrumentes Financiers (Matif) has assisted in hedging shorter dated ECU swaps. In addition, Matif has introduced an ECU bond contract which, theoretically, provides a means for hedging ECU swap positions. However, these futures contracts, currently, have limited liquidity which detracts from the use to manage swap portfolios.

Increasingly, market makers in ECU swaps utilise baskets of ECU constituent currencies to hedge risk positions. However, the liquidity of all but the deutschmark, sterling and French franc bond markets makes this inefficient. Consideration has also been given to using large benchmark ECU Eurobonds for the purposes of hedging such swaps.

Exhibit 25.8 sets out ECU swap rates in a number of maturities over recent years relative to theoretical ECU interest rates for the relevant maturities. *Exhibit 25.9* sets out the relationship of new ECU issue volume to the spread on ECU swap rates relative to the theoretical ECU yields.

The ECU market continues to be strongly dependent upon the primary bond market with a substantial proportion of the ECU Eurobonds being swapped. The cycles in ECU swaps being largely explainable on the basis of this interdependence. For example, at a given time, the exchange rate levels would trigger strong demand from counterparties wishing to convert their debt into ECU and this would, if market conditions were favourable, be met by a number of swapped bond issues. Usually, a surfeit of issues would create an oversupply in the primary bond market and force primary market yield to a level which would close off this particular arbitrage. Conversely, at other times, the demand for ECU bonds could rise to such a level that the lack of swap counterparties would induce a shortage of bond issues and an exaggerated decrease of primary market yields.

As noted above the emergence of the CTE tax arbitrage has to some extent diminished the volatility of ECU swap activity, corresponding to volume cycles in the ECU Eurobond market. The emergence of the CTE tax arbitrage asset swap has meant that activity now focuses on issues of CTEs which are followed by an increase in new issue activity in the primary ECU Eurobond market. However, as the markets have adjusted to this change in pattern of activity, the swap and bond markets are increasingly efficient at anticipating CTE issuance and have effectively reduced the new issue arbitrage opportunities available.

A practice which influences the pricing of ECU swaps is the use of ECU swaps to create hedges in minor European currencies where swap markets are either unavailable or are not liquid. Under this type of strategy, participants enter into an ECU swap then match off the ECU transaction against a subset basket of currencies creating a net position in the desired currency. A number of participants also enter into these sorts of transactions as a form of risk controlled arbitrage seeking to trade theoretical ECU yields against swap rates.

Market participants/product range

The nature of the market participants in ECU swaps has been commented on above. The major institutions active in market making in ECU swaps include a number of French, German, Swiss and international swap market participants. A strong relationship exists between market making in ECU swaps and position in the primary ECU Eurobond market because of the close interrelationship between activity in these two areas.

The product range in the ECU swap market is relatively limited. Although a number of non-generic structures have evolved. This limitation on the range of products reflects the fact that ECU Eurobond investors prefer large benchmark liquid conventional securities limiting the scope for innovative bond structures. This limitation in the form of primary securities to be swapped has acted as a restraint on innovation. In addition, the fact that the ECU is not a natural currency has also constrained product innovation.

The future of the ECU market—post-September 1992

In September 1992, the ECU market experienced significant difficulties following the collapse of the ERM. Following a period of protracted weakness in the GBP and LIT, both currencies were withdrawn from the ERM for an indefinite period. This withdrawal allied to considerable uncertainty about the ratification of the treaty on monetary union (the so called Maastricht Treaty), lead to considerable speculation against a number of European currencies, primarily, the Scandinavian currencies, the French franc and the Irish punt. This process culminated in a revision of the ERM in mid 1993 which altered the fluctuation bands to ±15% around the agreed parities. The uncertainties within the ERM were reflected in the ECU market in diminished issuing volume and the loss of liquidity in the swap market, which as noted above is heavily reliant on the primary equity Eurobond market.

Increasingly, through 1993, it became apparent that the ECU bond market's prospects would improve. Despite continuing strains within the ERM, the European Economic Community itself, through its agencies, was, it became apparent, seeking to access the ECU market to use its prestige and power to resuscitate activity in this sector. As investors became more sanguine about the prospects of a new, more volatile ECU, primary market underwriters increasingly looked to the EEC to provide a lead in the re-establishment of the ECU as an important European currency.

This process is still ongoing and, to a substantial degree, will be an important factor in the ongoing development of the ECU swap and derivative market.

During early 1993, there were some signs of resurgence in the ECU swap market. This reflected, in part, arbitrage between ECU rates and those in other European currencies such as DEM, BFR/LUF and Dfl. Another area of activity which emerged was the use by liability managers of the ECU-based index differential swaps. Under these structures, the borrowers receive ECU LIBOR to offset the payment of an underlying financing and paid US$ LIBOR plus a margin. Both legs were, as is the case with standard index differential swaps, calculated on an ECU notional principal amount. Based on the then prevailing ECU LIBOR of around 9.25% and an US$ LIBOR of around 3.5%, the ECU/US$ index differential structure generated potential savings over the first interest period of over 3.5%. The attraction of these products for ECU-based borrowers created a natural demand for ECU interest rate swaps as part of the index differential structure creating much needed impetus for the moribund ECU market.

Exhibit 25.8

European Currency Units—Swap Rates and Spreads

HISTORICAL DATA FROM 1 JANUARY 1991 TO 13 JULY 1993

3Y Theoretical
3Y ECU Swap

11.0000
10.5000
10.0000
9.5000
9.0000
8.5000
8.0000
7.5000
7.0000
6.5000
6.0000

01/01/91
31/05/91
28/10/91
26/03/92
23/08/92
20/01/93
19/06/93

Exhibit 25.8—continued

HISTORICAL DATA FROM 1 JANUARY 1991 TO 13 JULY 1993

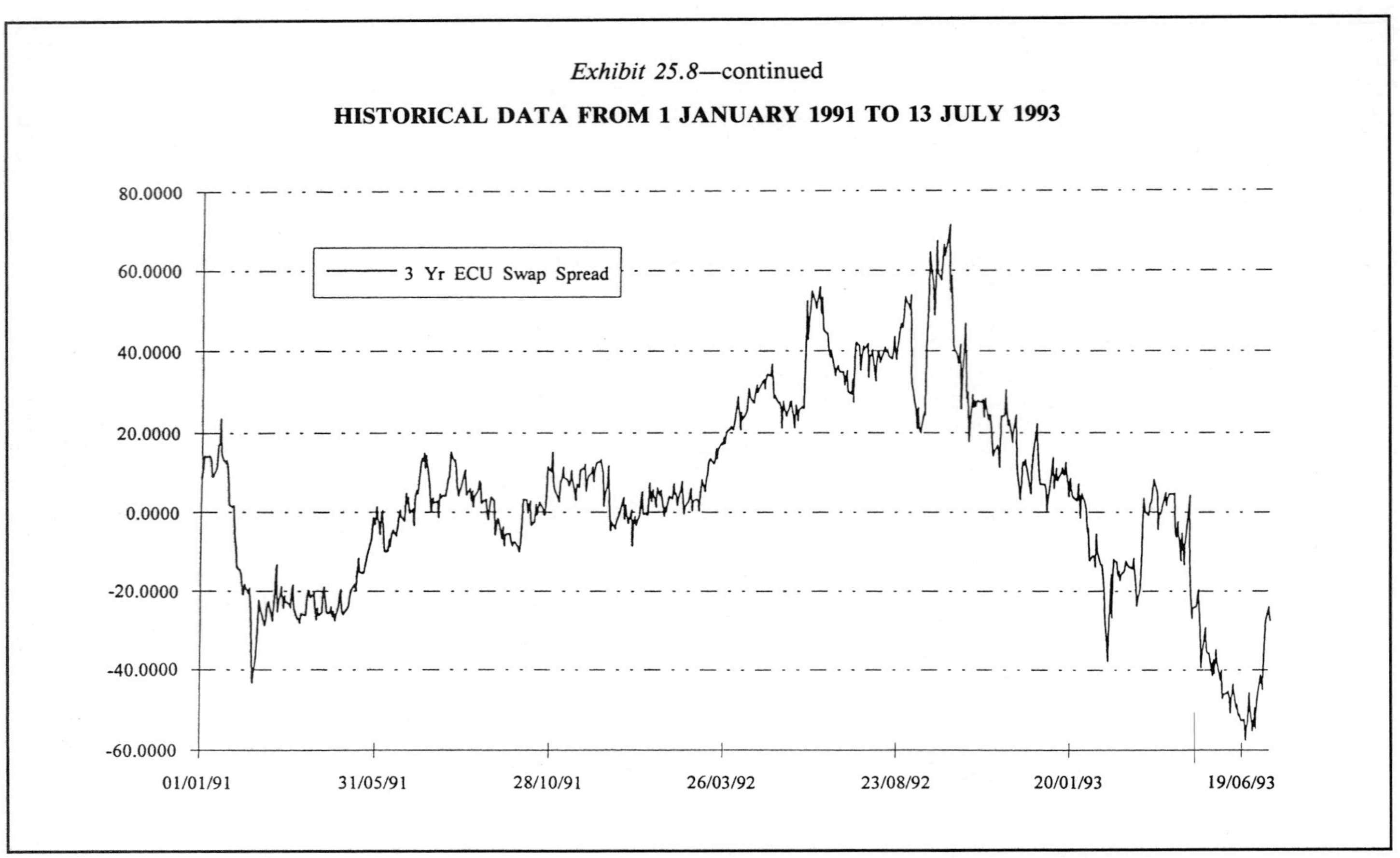

Exhibit 25.8—continued

HISTORICAL DATA FROM 1 JANUARY 1991 TO 13 JULY 1993

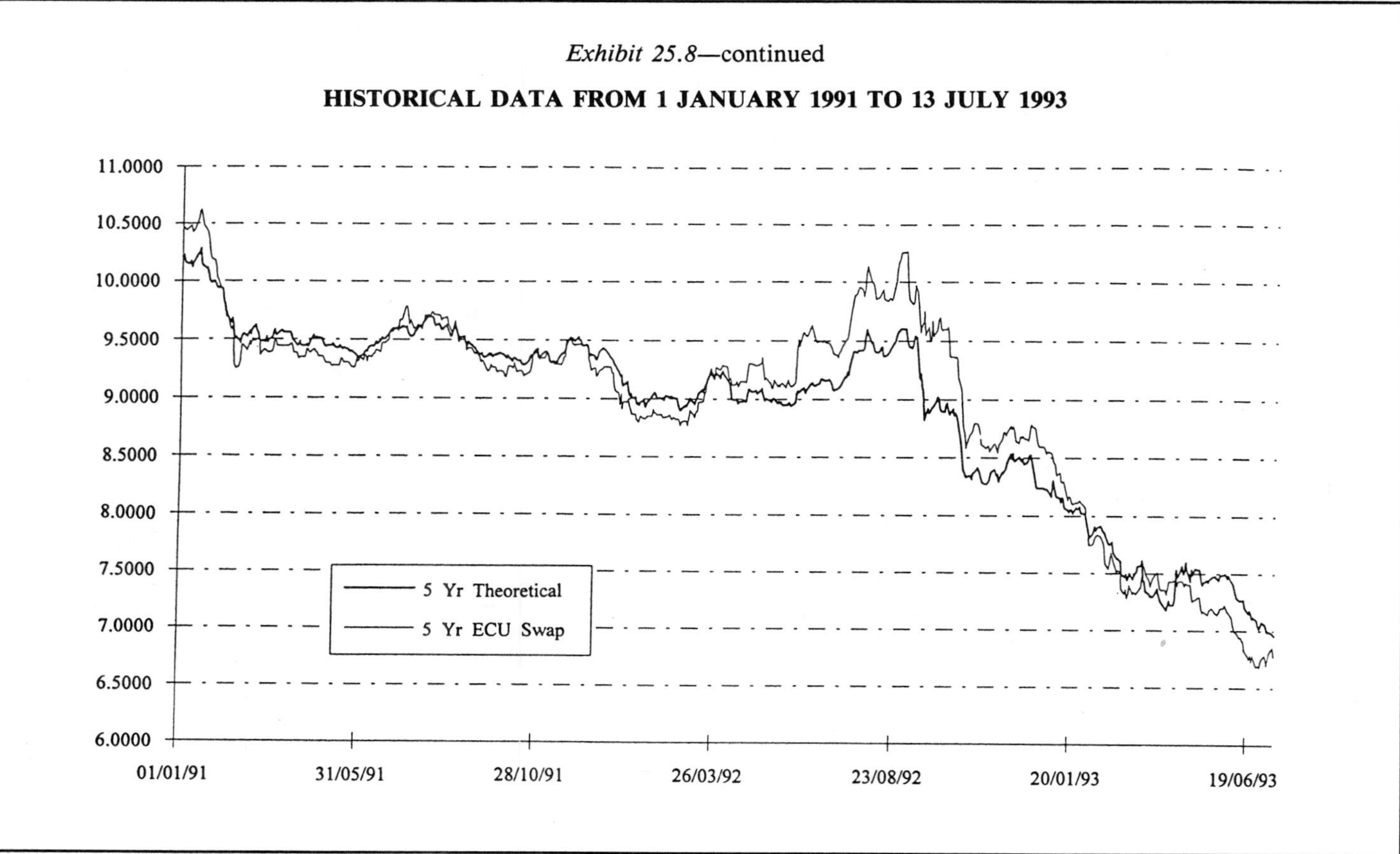

Exhibit 25.8—continued

HISTORICAL DATA FROM 1 JANUARY 1991 TO 13 JULY 1993

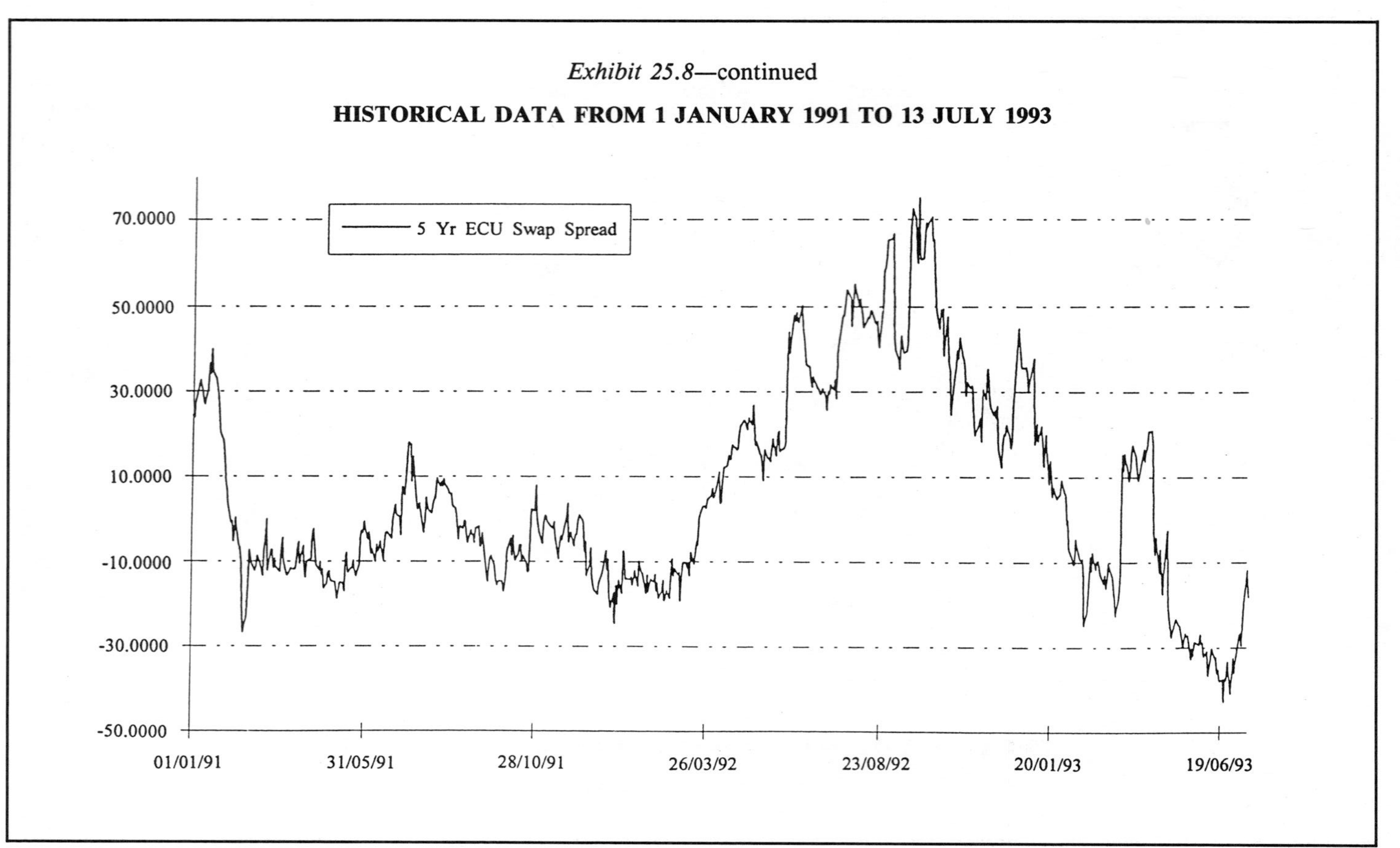

Exhibit 25.8—continued

HISTORICAL DATA FROM 1 JANUARY 1991 TO 13 JULY 1993

11.0000
10.5000
10.0000
9.5000
9.0000
8.5000
8.0000
7.5000
7.0000
6.5000
6.0000

01/01/91 31/05/91 28/10/91 26/03/92 23/08/92 20/01/93 19/06/93

—— 7 Yr Theoretical
—— 7 Yr ECU Swap

Exhibit 25.8—continued

HISTORICAL DATA FROM 1 JANUARY 1991 TO 13 JULY 1993

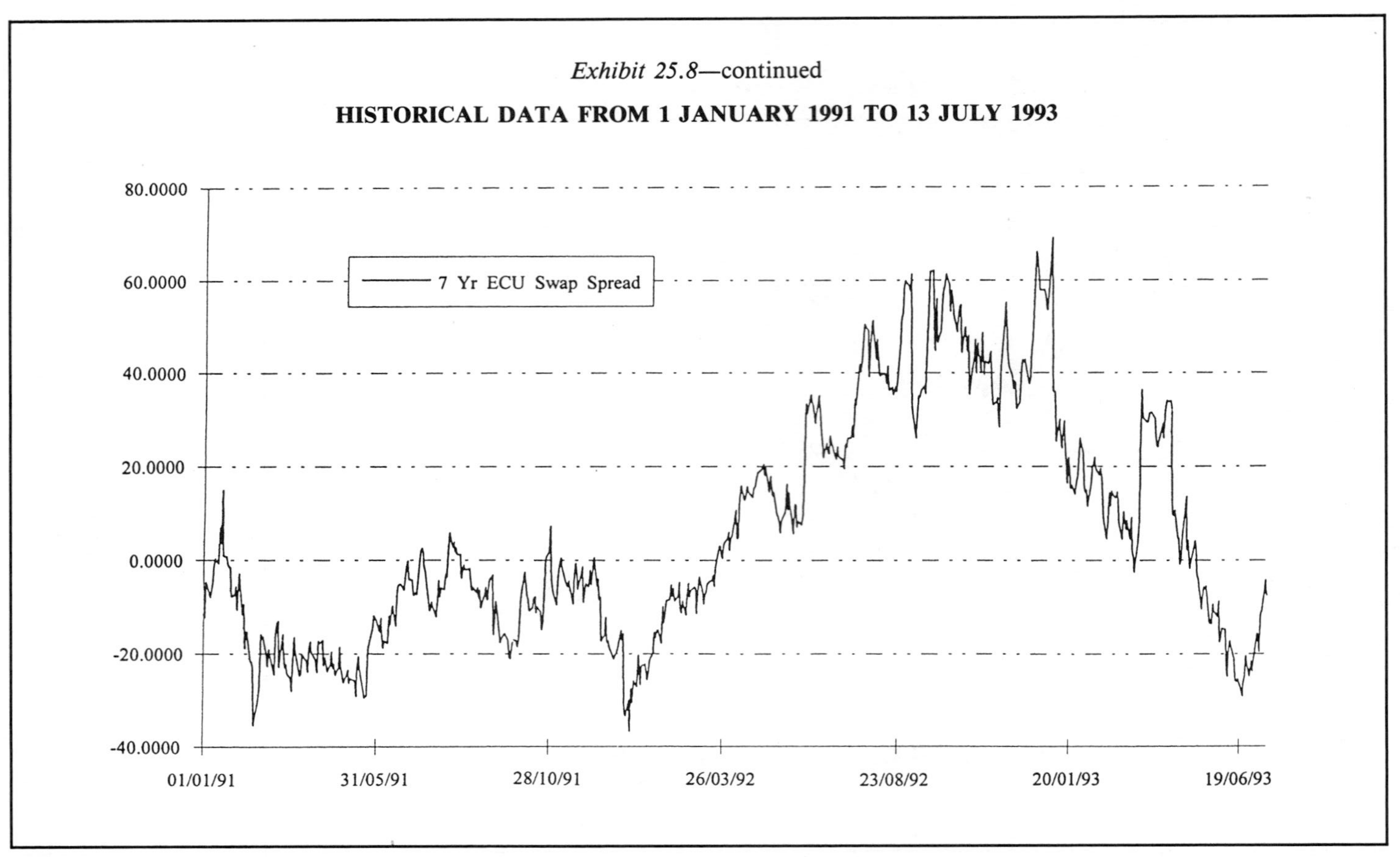

Exhibit 25.8—continued

HISTORICAL DATA FROM 1 JANUARY 1991 TO 13 JULY 1993

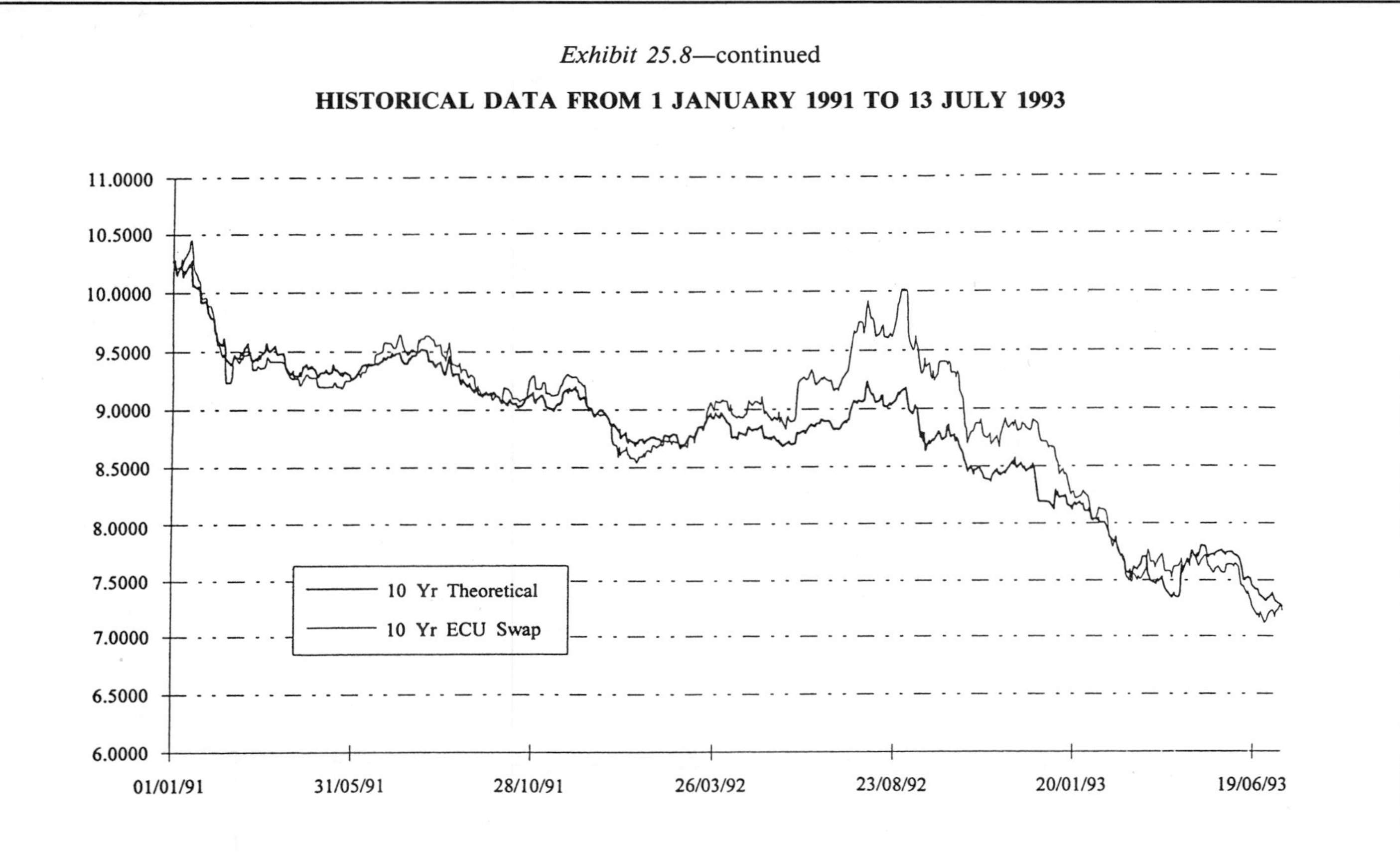

Exhibit 25.8—continued

HISTORICAL DATA FROM 1 JANUARY 1991 TO 13 JULY 1993

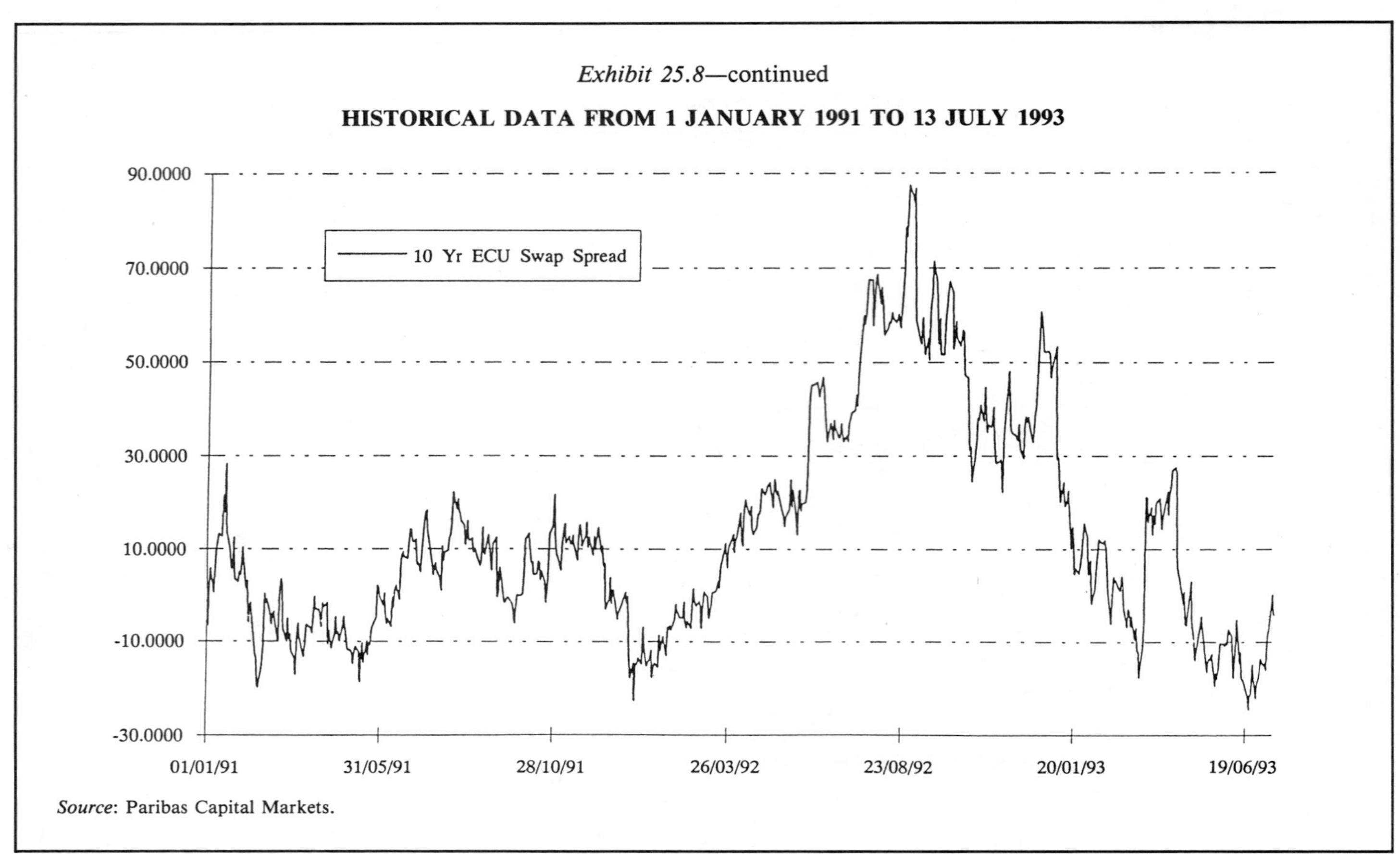

Source: Paribas Capital Markets.

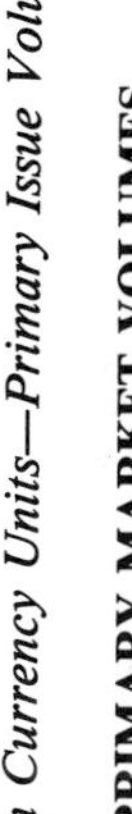

Exhibit 25.9

European Currency Units—Primary Issue Volumes

PRIMARY MARKET VOLUMES

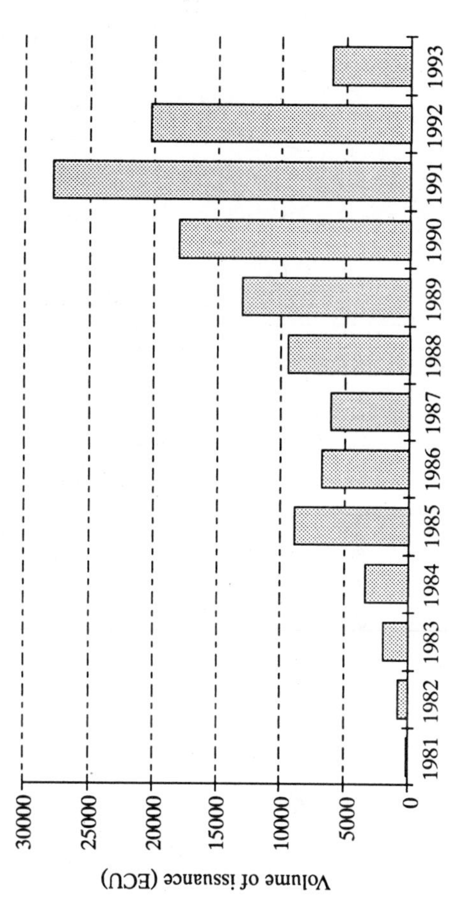

Exhibit 25.9—continued

PRIMARY MARKET VOLUME IN RELATION TO SPREAD

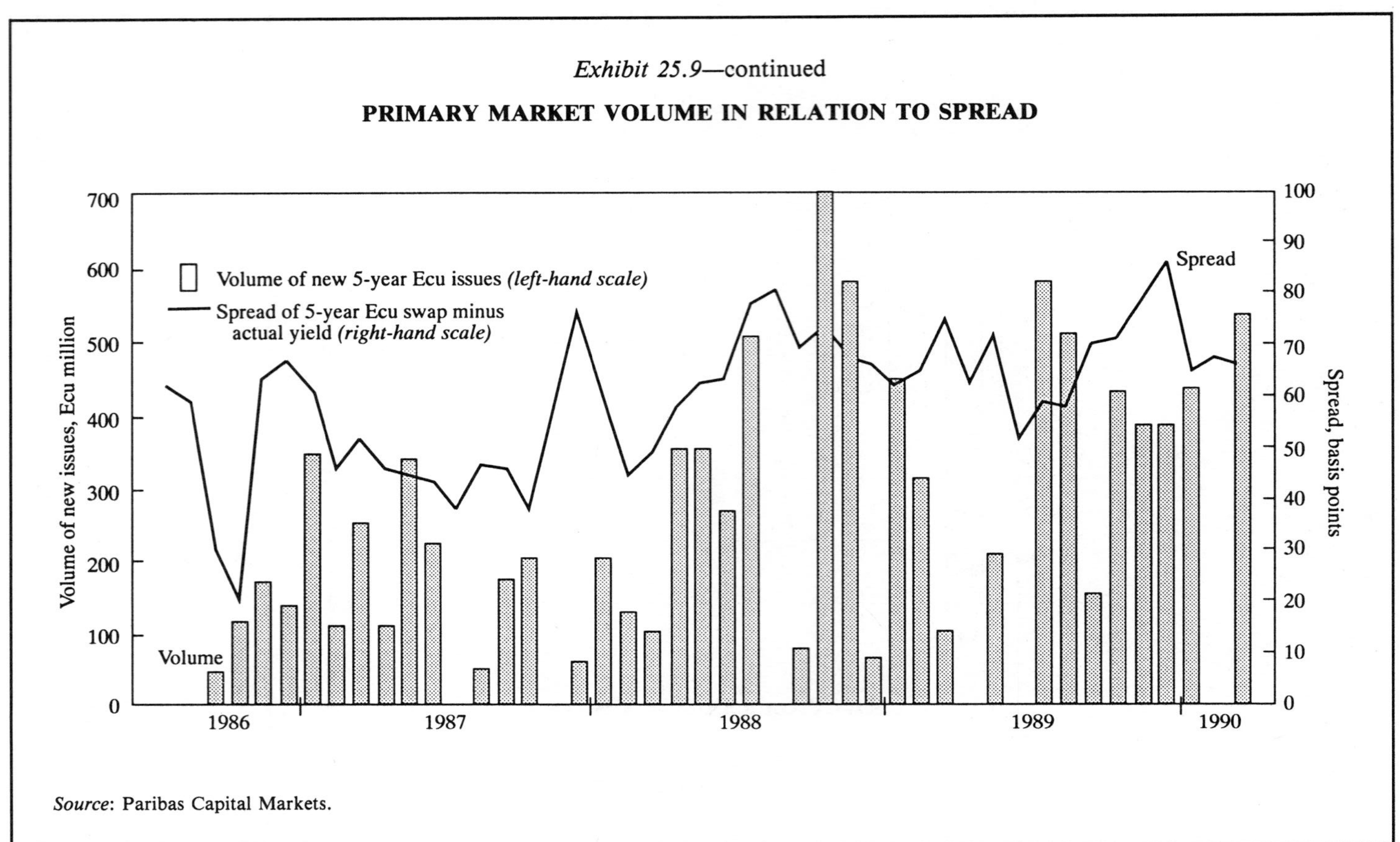

Source: Paribas Capital Markets.

Chapter 26

European Swap and Derivative Markets: French Franc, Dutch Guilder, Italian Lira, Spanish Peseta, Belgian/Luxembourg Franc and Scandinavian Currencies

BACKGROUND

In this chapter, the structure, market conventions, pricing characteristics and other related features of other European swap/derivatives markets are considered. Markets considered include: the French franc swap market, the Dutch guilder swap market, the Italian lira swap market, the Spanish peseta swap market, Belgian/Luxembourg franc and Scandinavian currency swap markets and other European swap markets.

The markets considered in this chapter are diverse in origin and structure. Most of these swap currencies have evolved relatively recently for specific reasons and are still developing.

FRENCH FRANC SWAP/DERIVATIVES MARKETS

Structure/participants

The French franc swap market is traditionally more domestically orientated than a number of other European currency swap markets.

The structure is dictated by a variety of factors including:

- limited participation by corporations and non-bank institutions;
- the dominant role of interbank transactions which total as much as 70-80% transaction volume;
- the use of the swap market to hedge domestic bond issues and also to arbitrage the domestic bond market with futures and options contracts on Matif.

The domestic focus of the French franc swap market is gradually decreasing. Corporate and non-bank participation is also increasingly evident.

An interesting feature of the French franc market is the relatively high proportion of long term (over seven years) transactions reflecting the use of swaps to hedge bond issues which have a minimum seven year maturity for a domestic French franc bond issue as well as the role of swaps as a component of arbitrage against futures and option contracts on Matif and the government bond market.

The range of participants is increasingly broad covering:

- banks, including the major French banks as well as smaller banks and related financial institutions;
- large corporations, either in their own capacity or through their finance arms;

- state enterprises; and
- insurance companies.

Applications of swaps correspond to those found in other markets such as new issue arbitrage and asset/liability management. A feature of the French market is the use of swaps for the purposes of positioning against anticipated movements in interest rates.

Market making is dominated by the major French banks, such as BNP, Paribas, CCF, Societe Generale, Indosuez etc. Foreign banks are active participants in selected market sectors. A unique feature of the French franc market is the participation of the so called arbitrage banks (Banques d'arbitrage or Banques du Tresorerie).

A significant group of participants in the French franc swap market is the SICAVs and Fonds communs de placement (FCPs). These institutional investors and mutual funds are natural users of derivatives to manage portfolios of debt instruments and asset swaps.

Market conventions

The French franc market involves two distinct and, to an extent, separate sectors: domestic swaps (fixed rate against TAM swaps or fixed rate against TAG floating rate swaps) and international swaps (fixed rate swaps against PIBOR). Each of these structures are considered below.

Fixed rate versus TAM swaps

Fixed rate against TAM swaps entail swaps of fixed French franc rates against a floating rate index known as the TAM (Taux Annuel Monetaire—annual money market rate). TAM is, effectively, the monthly compounded average of the annual overnight money market rate which is calculated and published ex post. The usual benchmark utilised is Telerate page 3205. TAM can only be used as a floating index for a 12 month period beginning and ending the first of the month. This rate is calculated every first Paris business day of the month, on the daily rates of the last 12 elapsed calendar months, allowing payment on the second Paris business day of the month.

TAM should be contrasted with the official overnight money market rate known as TMP (Taux Moyen Pondere—weighted average rate) which is published daily at 11.30 am: refer Reuters page BDFB.

The floating rate of a broken period, if any, under a fixed rate against TAM swap can be the T4M (Taux Moyen Mensuel du Marché Monetaire) or the more accurate TAG (Taux Annuel Glissant—sliding annual rate) which is the monthly compounding of the last sliding T4M of the period (Telerate page 20050 or Reuters page AFBP).

The definitions of TAG and T4M and their interrelationships with TAM is set out in *Exhibit 26.1*.

Fixed rate on a TAM swap is usually calculated on an actual/actual day count basis except where the swap is for a less than one year where an actual/money market basis or 360 days is utilised. The floating rate for TAM or, indeed, TAG is on an actual basis. However, for T4M it is calculated on actual/360 or money market basis.

Exhibit 26.1
French Franc Interest Rate Definition

1. **TAM Rate**

   TAM (Taux Annuel Monetaire—Annual Money Market Rate) is the monthly compounded average of the official overnight money market rate.

2. **TMP Rate**

   TMP (Taux Moyen Pondere—Weighted Average Rate) is the official overnight money market rate. The TMP is published daily at 11.30 am by the Banque de France on Reuter page BDFB.

Hence:

$$1 + TAM = \prod_{j=1}^{12} \left[1 + T4Mj \frac{Nj}{360} \right]$$

where Nj is the actual number of days of month j and T4Mj (= TMMMM = Taux Moyen Mensuel du Marché Monetaire) = Average Monthly Money Market Rate of the jth month.

$$\text{defined as } T4M = \frac{1}{Nj} \sum_{i=1}^{Nj} TMPi \text{ (published each month on BDFB)}$$

3. **TAG Rate**

   T4M is the accurate TAG (Taux Annuel Glissant—sliding annual rate) which is the monthly compounding of the last sliding T4M of the period (Telerate pay 20050 on AFBP).

Source: Jean Dominjon and Sebastien Cahen, "The French Franc Swap Market" in Satyajit Das (1991), Ch 8.

TAM swaps are traded for a standard value date of the first date of the current month if the transaction takes place between the first and 14th of the month and the first of the following month if the transaction takes place between the 15th and 31st of the month. This rule can be avoided by special negotiation between the parties and is usually negotiated where the transaction is dealt very close to the middle of the month.

TAM swaps typically have durations for an even number of months and extends over a year or more up to ten to 15 years.

Fixed rate against TAG swaps

The TAG swaps are a derivative of the TAM swap. The major difference relates to the value date and the periods. TAG swaps are spot transactions with the value date being the first business date following the date of the transaction. This means that the annual or monthly periods of the swap do not coincide with calendar months. Therefore, the floating rate is calculated as the TAG rate in accordance with the calculation of the French Banking Association as published on Telerate Page 20050 according to the TAM calculation rules. All other characteristics of TAG swaps are very similar to those of TAM swaps.

Fixed rate against PIBOR swaps

The swaps against the Paris Interbank Offered Rate (PIBOR) are similar to those applicable to standard interest rate swaps in other currencies.

The floating rate in these transactions is PIBOR (three or six months). Standard quotation of PIBOR is as per Telerate page 20041 or the Reuters page PIBO.

PIBOR swaps are for any term freely agreed between counterparties and are typically concentrated in the maturities up to ten years.

Transactions are usually for value the first business day following the day the transaction takes place. Floating rate date settings take place on the Paris business day preceding the beginning of each period (a variation from LIBOR which is two days prior to relevant date). PIBOR floating rate basis payments are calculated on actual/360 day basis while fixed rate is on an actual/actual day basis.

The debate between TAM and PIBOR swaps

The French franc swap market while it is substantial in size is, as previously noted, substantively domestic in its focus. However, as the process of integration of international markets proceeds, particularly within the European monetary system currencies, there is an increasing attempt to promote the French franc swap market as a more international market.

A significant component of this debate is that regarding the use of TAM versus PIBOR as the floating rate component of French franc swaps.

Currently, PIBOR swaps are between 30 to 50% of all French franc swaps. Although, PIBOR swaps as a component are growing, domestic borrowers tend to undertake TAM swaps, while, in contrast, international Eurobond issuers utilise PIBOR as their floating rate index. This emphasis has the effect of segregating the two markets reflecting the fact that French franc Eurobond activity is concentrated in the two to five and seven year maturities, while domestic bonds have a minimum maturity of seven years and extend out to as long as 15 years.

Both TAM and PIBOR swaps have their advocates. An advantage of TAM swaps over PIBOR is that TAM swaps by combining the nominal and accrued index has no sensitivity to changes in interest rates allowing the swap market maker to manage the duration of the fixed rate swap. In addition, it is the benchmark that is used by most of the smaller French banks and many corporations. A problem with TAM is that it is not an index which is familiar to foreign institutions used to quoting off an interbank rate.

In contrast, PIBOR swaps are more consistent with international practice and PIBOR market makers also have the advantage of utilising the three month PIBOR futures and options on the futures listed on Matif as a hedging vehicle. TAM market makers in contrast, utilise a liquid market in short term TFM swaps to offset positions.

The different basis of the market has created different average transaction sizes. PIBOR swaps tend to be around French francs 50m plus with transactions of FFR100-200m not being uncommon. In contrast, TAM swaps average around FFR25m.

Occasional arbitrage opportunities present themselves as a result of the existence of these two benchmarks. However, the advantages of arbitrage are largely outweighed by the problems of fragmented liquidity which this division creates.

In an effort to improve the use of PIBOR and to eliminate anomalies the Association de Banques (AFB) announced in late 1993 procedures for verifying the

PIBOR calculation. PIBOR will continue to be calculated as the arithmetic average of eight out of 16 quotes from banks as at 11 am each morning with the four highest and lowest quotes being eliminated. A new committee made up of representatives of AFB, the Banque de France and the Forex and Bank Treasurers' Association will check the process with the power to exclude any quote which, in its opinion, is not following proper procedures.

Pricing

French franc swap pricing is related to the underlying rates in the French franc bond market. However, the structure of the French franc interest rate swaps, divided between TAM and PIBOR swaps, produces two distinct swap yield curves. The spread between the two curves typically fluctuates between 3-5 and (up to) 20bps. The spread is largest for shorter maturities.

French franc swaps are hedged either in the physical bond or Matif futures markets. Physical hedging instruments include:

- BTANS—(Bons a Taux Annuel Normalise)—treasury notes with standard maturities of two and five years.
- OATS—(Obligations Assimilables du Tresor)—fungible government bonds with maturities in excess of five years.

Futures contracts on OATS, BTAN and on PIBOR as noted above, are traded on Matif. Turnover is relatively high and the contracts are sufficiently liquid to allow them to be used for hedging purposes. However, derivatives houses typically prefer to use the cash BTAN and OAT market and the associated repo market to hedge portfolio positions.

The swap yield curve in French francs demonstrates certain anomalies from time to time reflecting the use of different securities for hedging purposes. For example, BTANs are used to hedge maturities of up to five years while OATS are utilised to hedge longer term swaps. Differences in accounting and tax rules between the instruments mean that the yield curve is not continuous and often shows a distinct change in rate levels between five and seven year swap rates.

Consistent with other markets, the behaviour of swap spreads relative to BTANs and OATS interacts with new issue markets. Narrowing of the swap spread leads to a deteriorating condition for the new issue bond market generally encouraging French franc borrowers to issue in other currencies and swap into French francs. Conversely, increases in swap spreads leads to a surge of new issue activity.

The movement in spreads between swaps and the French bond market also allows periods of asset swap activity. *Exhibit 26.2* sets out an example of asset swaps at the short end of the yield curve.

Exhibit 26.3 sets out TAM swap rates for various maturities as well as PIBOR swap rates for a number of maturities.

Product range

The product range in French franc swaps is expanding with a number of non-generic swap structures available in other currencies becoming increasingly available. Markets for swap derivatives, including option based products, are also expanding.

Exhibit 26.2

French Franc BTF Asset Swaps

The spread between French Treasury Bills (Bons de Tresór à Taux Fixe—BTFs) and short-term interest rate swap rates are volatile (0-100bps) allowing asset swap activity. This asset swap activity is designed to allow money market investors to outperform the TMP average call money rates.

The asset swap is conducted in two stages:

- When the swap/BTF spread is narrow (say, zero) the investor buys BTFs and pays fixed locking in a return of TMP.
- When the spread increases, this reverses the trade to lock-in a return above BFFS, often by a significant margin.

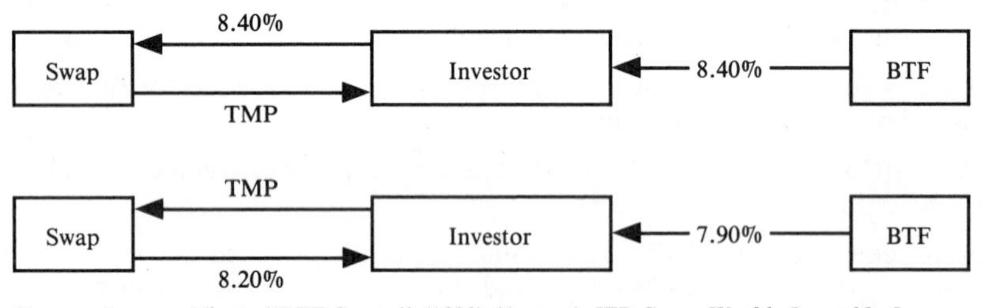

Source: Jacques Ninet, "BTF Swaps" (1993) (August) *IFR Swap Weekly* Issue 30, 5.

A feature of the French market in recent years has been the development of asset-backed swap structures reflecting the increasing trend to securitisation of assets in the French domestic market.

DUTCH GUILDER SWAP MARKET

Structure/participants

The Dutch guilder swap market has, predictably, had close parallels with and is related to the deutschmark swap market. Structurally, the market is similar to the deutschmark sector.

Major participants include major Dutch corporates such as Philips, Royal Debt Shell, Unilever and the large number of non-Dutch companies operating in the domestic market. The open nature of the economy and the nature of corporations based in Holland dictates activity not only in pure interest rate swaps but also in cross currency transactions, typically to hedge currency exposures.

The major Dutch banks dominate the Dutch guilder market. The major player is, predictably, the merged ABN-AMRO bank group. Rabobank and the newly merged NMB/Postbank are also likely to emerge as significant players. Foreign banks active include Paribas, Citicorp, JP Morgan, Swiss Bank Corporation and Bankers Trust among others. However, the interest of foreign banks in the Dutch guilder swap market is related to end client interest and, if appropriate, activity in the Dutch guilder bond market for foreign issuers.

Exhibit 26.3

French Franc Swap Rates and Spreads

HISTORICAL DATA FROM 1 JUNE 1989 TO 13 JULY 1993

PIBOR 6M

FFR 3YR SWAP

14.0000
13.0000
12.0000
11.0000
10.0000
9.0000
8.0000
7.0000
6.0000

02/04/89
19/10/89
07/05/90
23/11/90
11/06/91
28/12/91
15/07/92
31/01/93
19/08/93

Exhibit 26.3—continued

HISTORICAL DATA FROM 1 JUNE 1989 TO 13 JULY 1993

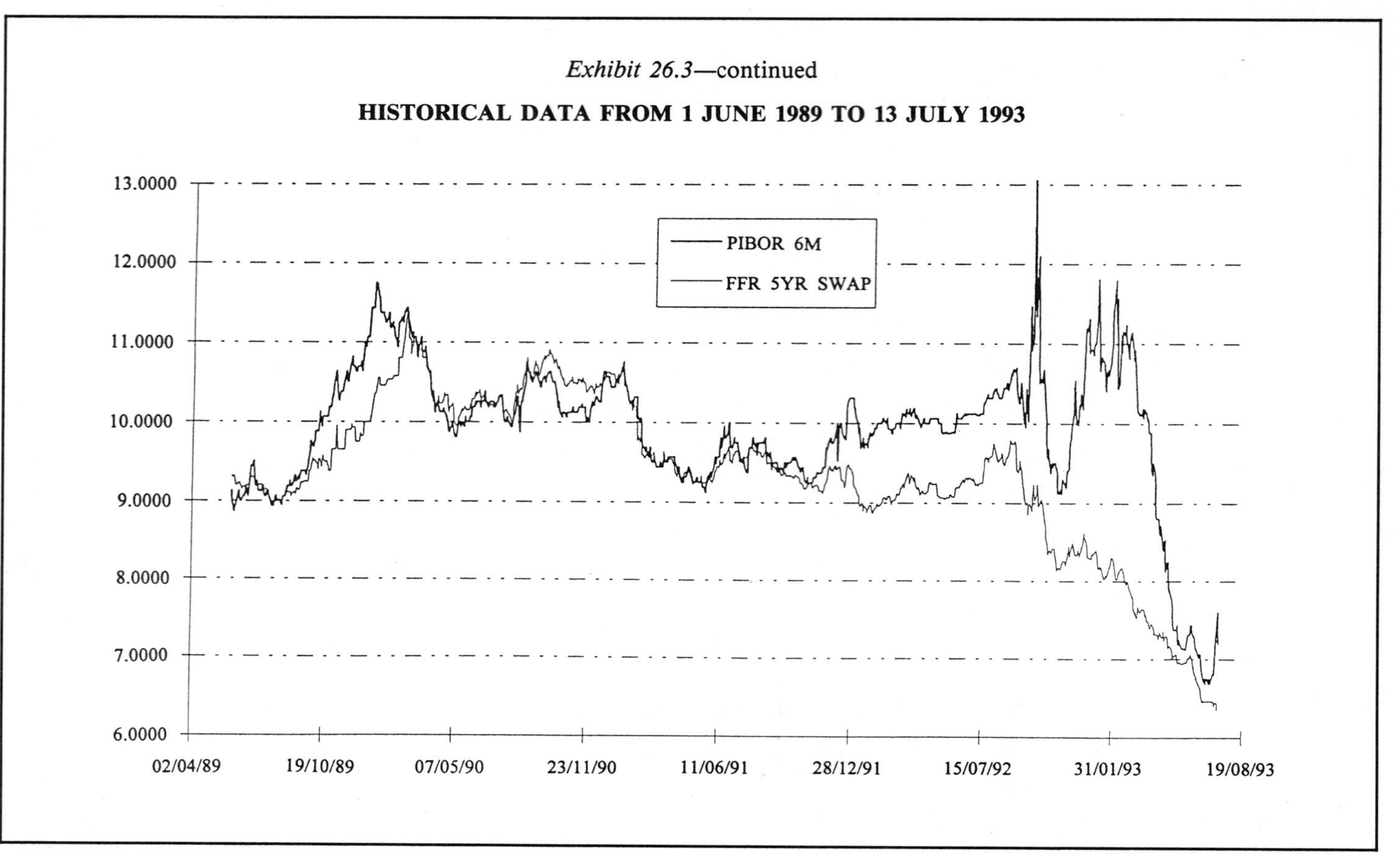

Exhibit 26.3—continued

HISTORICAL DATA FROM 1 JUNE 1989 TO 13 JULY 1993

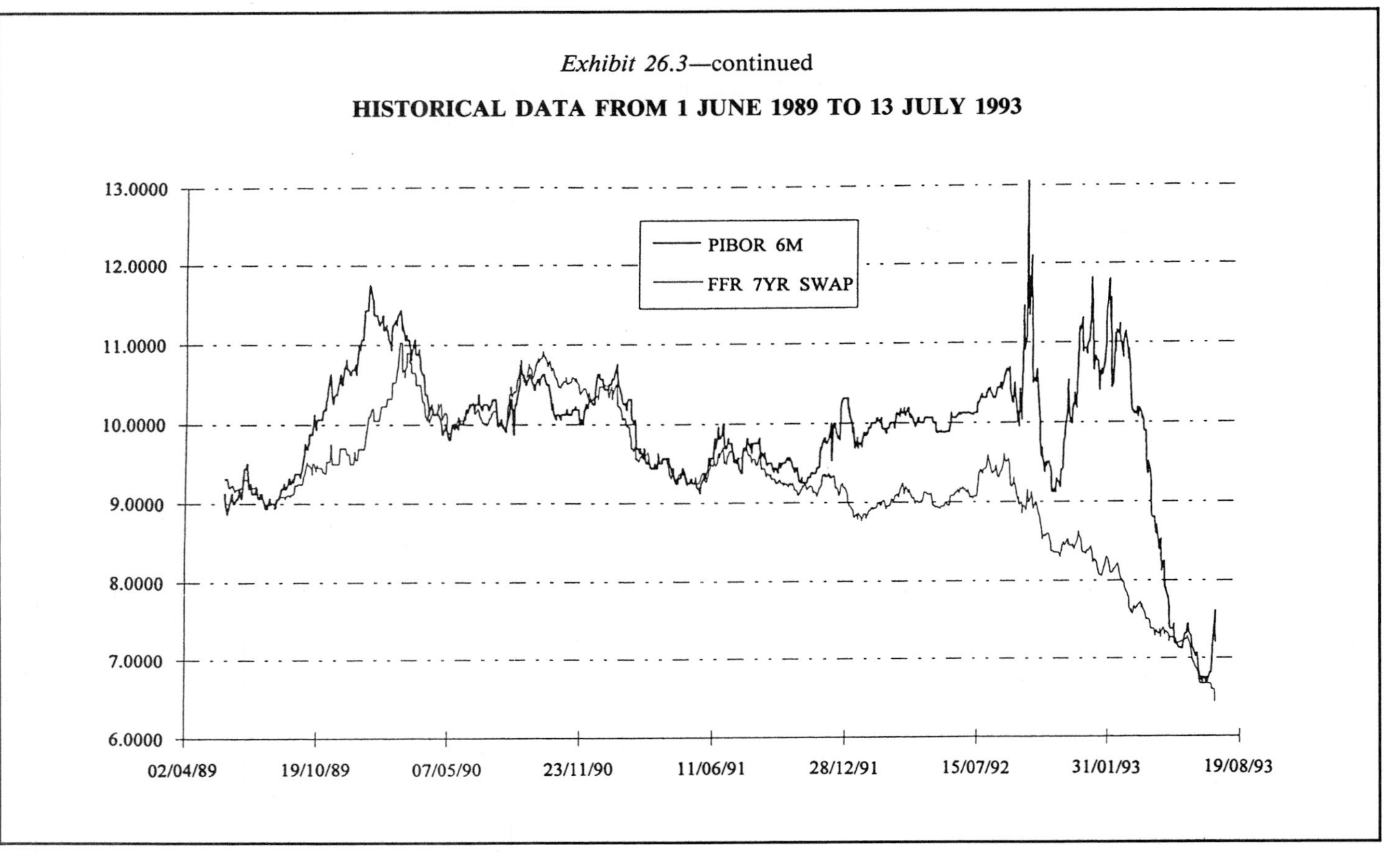

Exhibit 26.3—continued

HISTORICAL DATA FROM 1 JUNE 1989 TO 13 JULY 1993

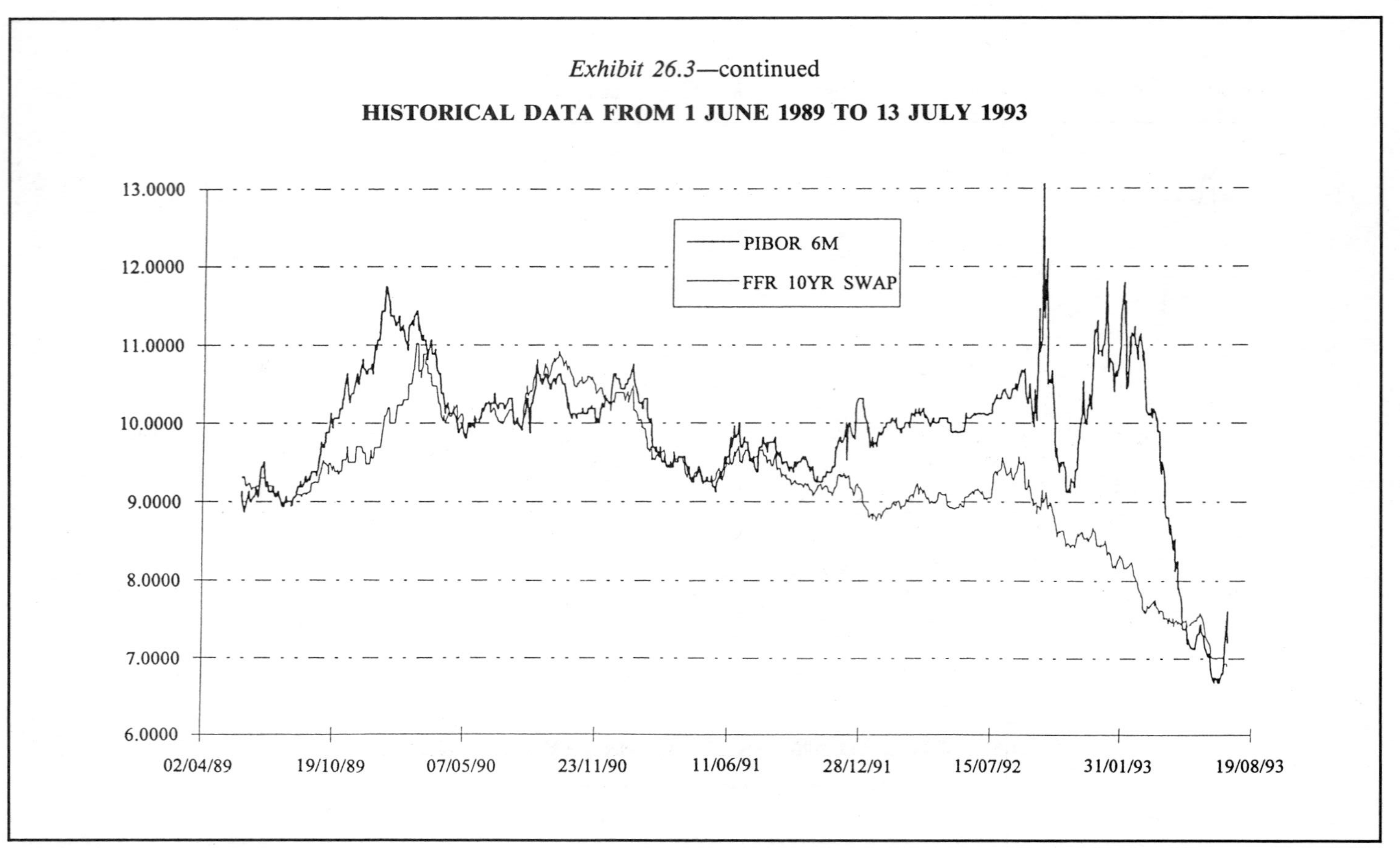

Exhibit 26.3—continued

HISTORICAL DATA FROM 2 JANUARY 1987 TO 13 JULY 1993

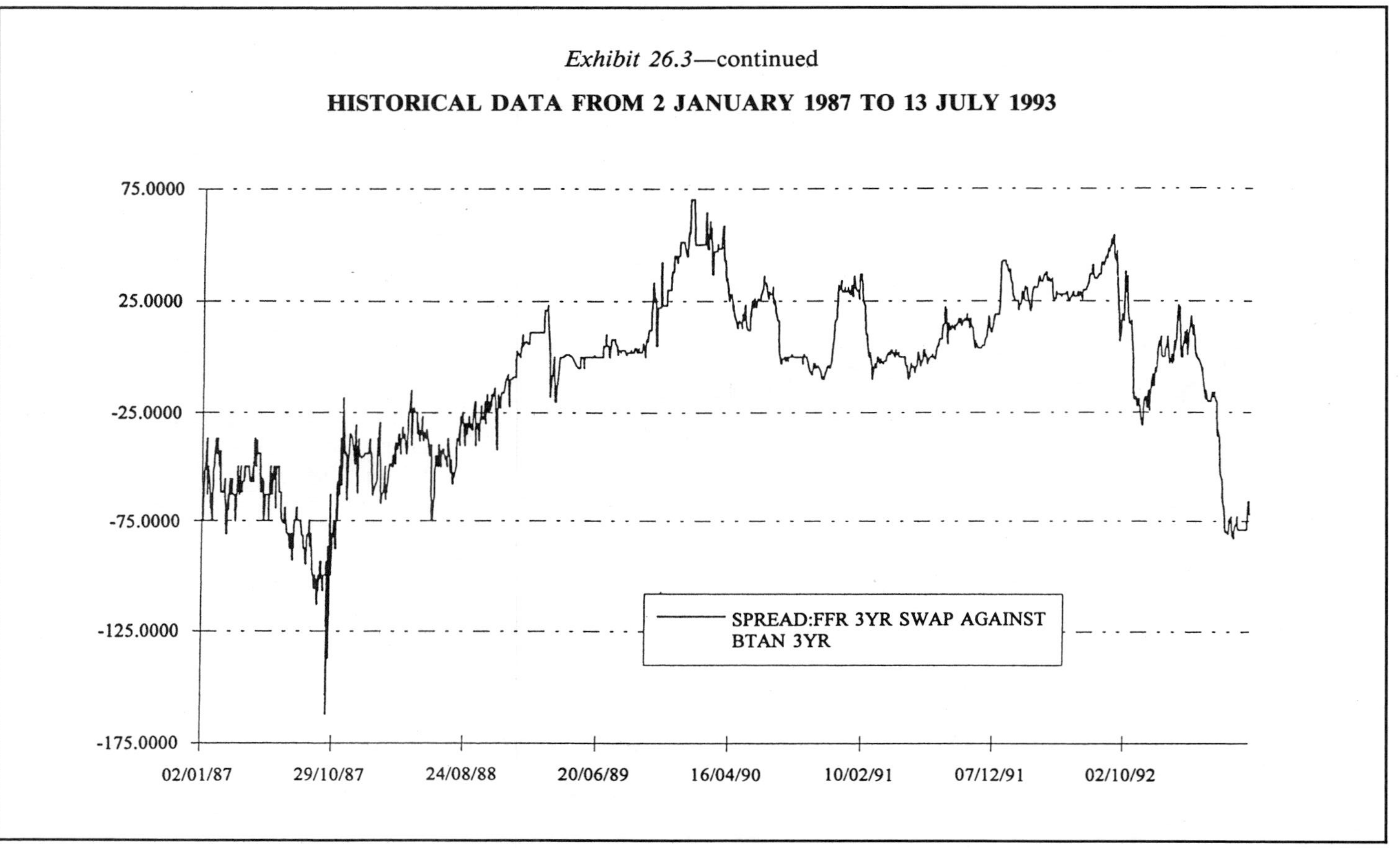

Exhibit 26.3—continued

HISTORICAL DATA FROM 2 JANUARY 1987 TO 13 JULY 1993

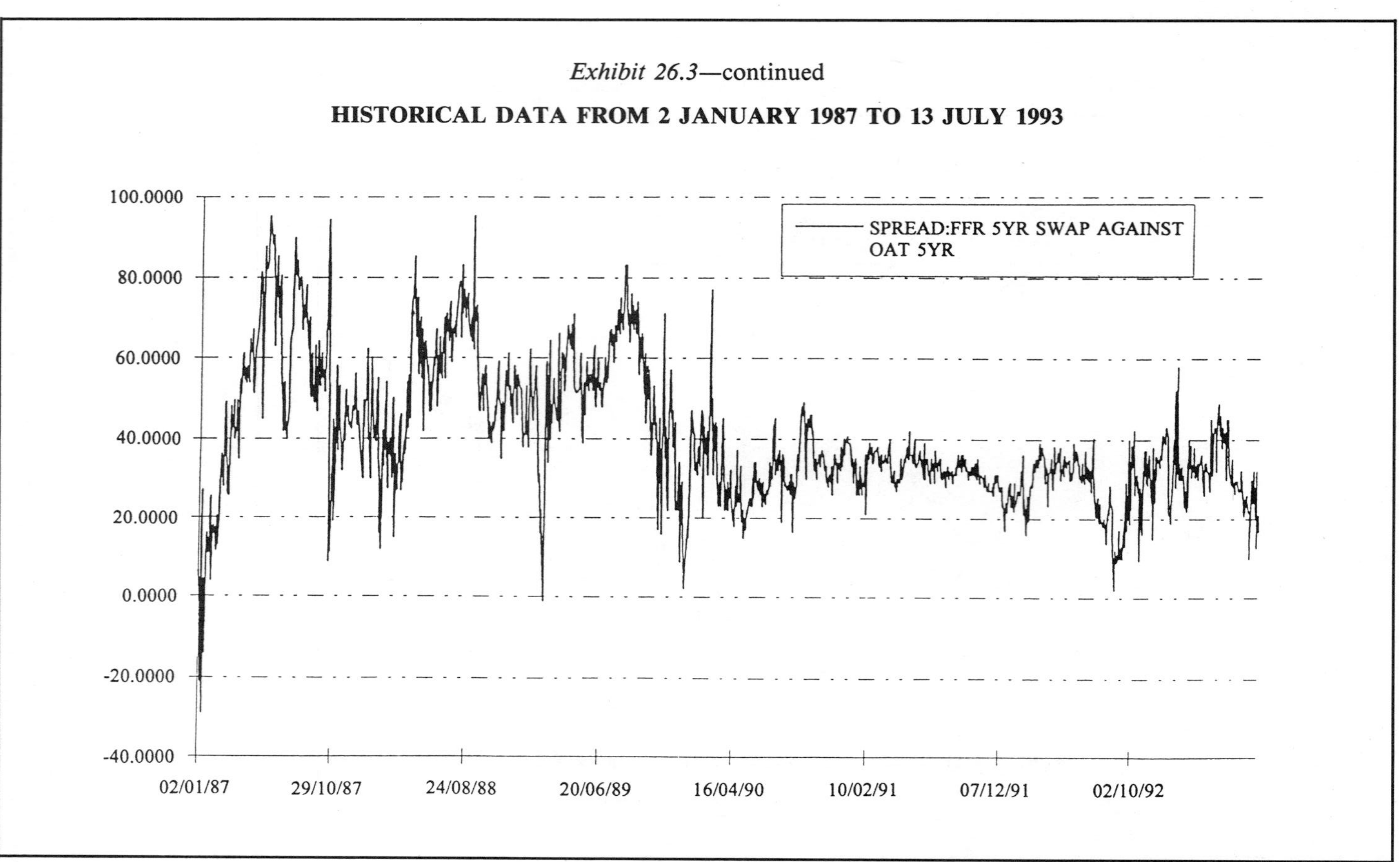

Exhibit 26.3—continued

HISTORICAL DATA FROM 2 JANUARY 1987 TO 13 JULY 1993

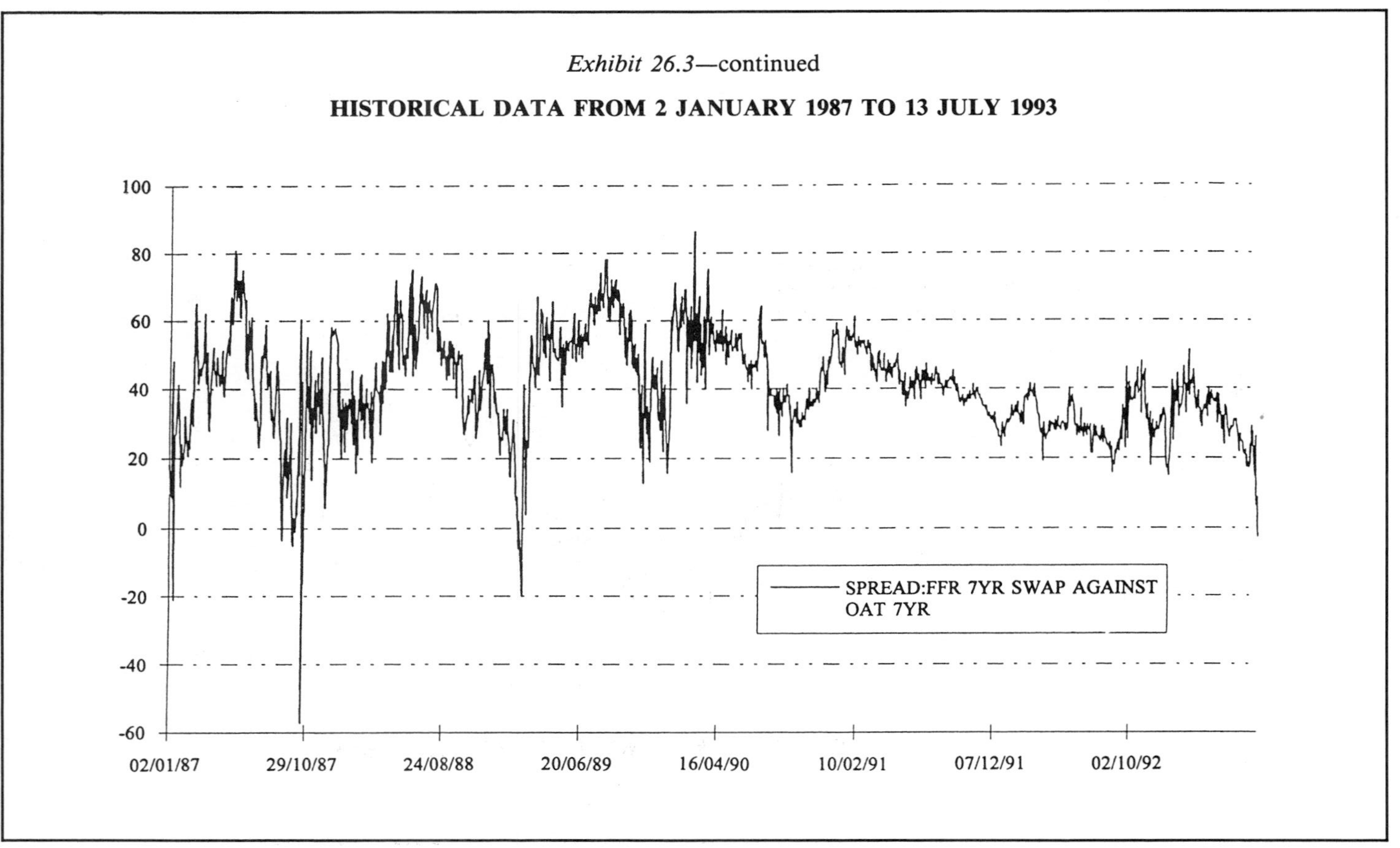

Exhibit 26.3—continued

HISTORICAL DATA FROM 2 JANUARY 1987 TO 13 JULY 1993

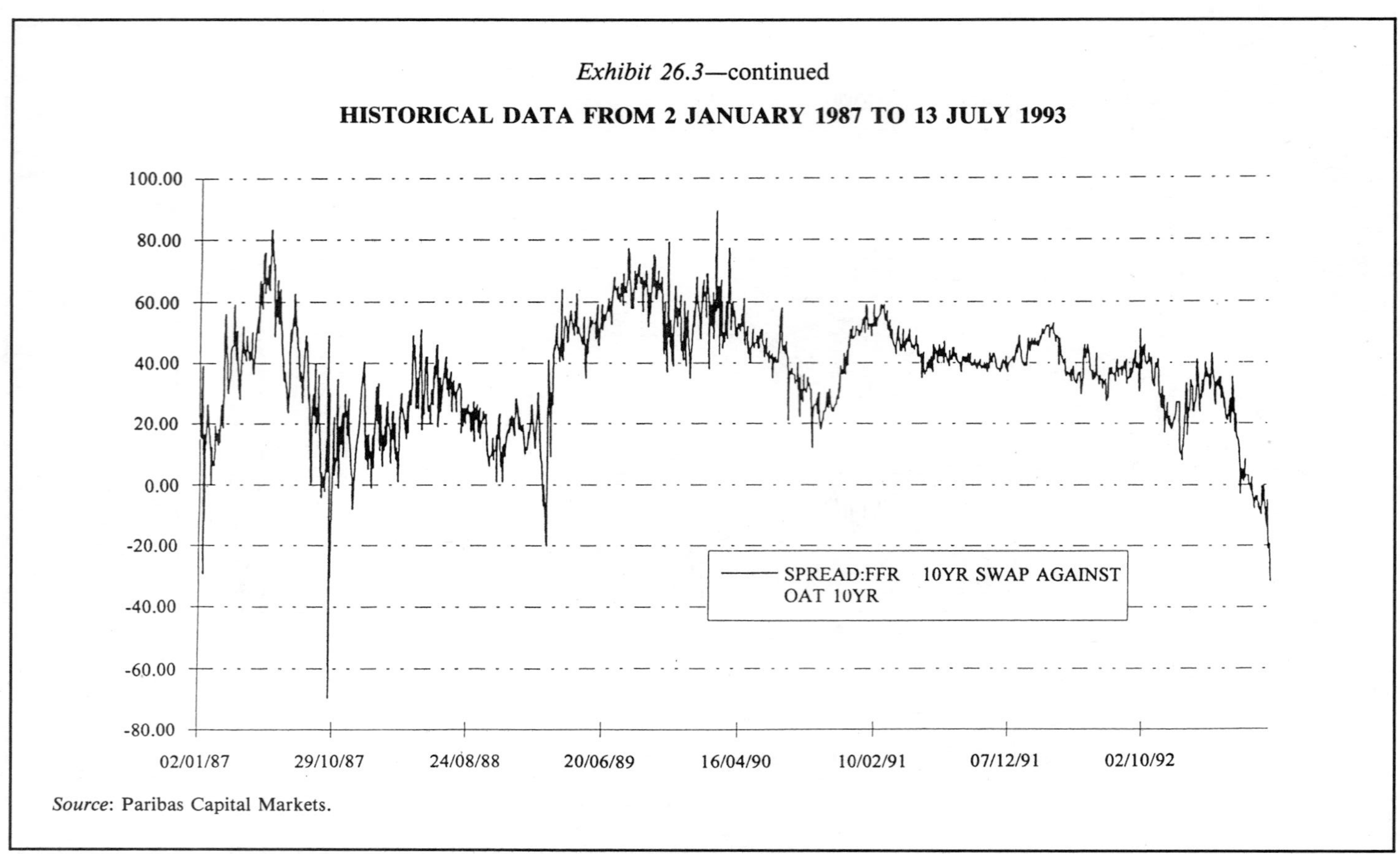

Source: Paribas Capital Markets.

Market conventions/pricing

Dutch guilder swaps are quoted on annual fixed rate basis with interest calculations undertaken under Eurobond conventions (30/360 day basis) against six month Dutch guilder rates (typically, priced off the Amsterdam Interbank Offered Rate (AIBOR)) or US$ LIBOR.

The Dutch guilder market is not priced off the international new issue market in Dutch guilders. The number of Euroguilder and international issues in the domestic market are relatively modest. This reflects, in part, the difficulty of arbitraging out of Dutch guilders because the relationship between the swap market and the government bond market is efficiently priced. Consequently, Dutch guilder swaps are driven by domestic banks and the fixed rates they are prepared to pay relative to the prevailing interest rates on Dutch State loans. The bank use of the swap market to generate floating rate funding drives swap rate.

Dutch guilder swaps are typically hedged with Dutch government bonds—effectively the Dutch state loan issues. Other instruments include the Bund futures or deutschmark swaps. The Dutch guilder bond futures contract is typically not utilised because of declining liquidity and wide bid-offer spreads.

A number of market makers, largely foreign banks, often operate Dutch guilder swap portfolios *in conjunction with their deutschmark portfolios*. Effectively, these market makers utilise the strong correlation between the two markets to provide hedges for positions in the respective portfolios. For example, a swap portfolio manager with the position in deutschmarks will often undertake a guilder swap to partially hedge its position.

Historically, the Dutch and German interest and swap rates have traded in unison with a premium ranging between 20 and 50bps. This relationship was disrupted towards the end of 1989 as Germany moved towards unification with its resultant large need to raise capital to finance the absorption of East Germany into what was previously West Germany. This resulted in the premium between Dutch and German rates declining to around 15 to 20bps. This volatility in the relationship between deutschmark and guilder rates has in fact reduced liquidity in the guilder market as market makers are cautious of the risks associated with cross-market positions between guilders and deutschmarks.

Exhibit 26.4 sets out Dutch guilder swap rates over recent years. *Exhibit 26.5* sets out historical relationships between Dutch guilder and deutschmark swap rates.

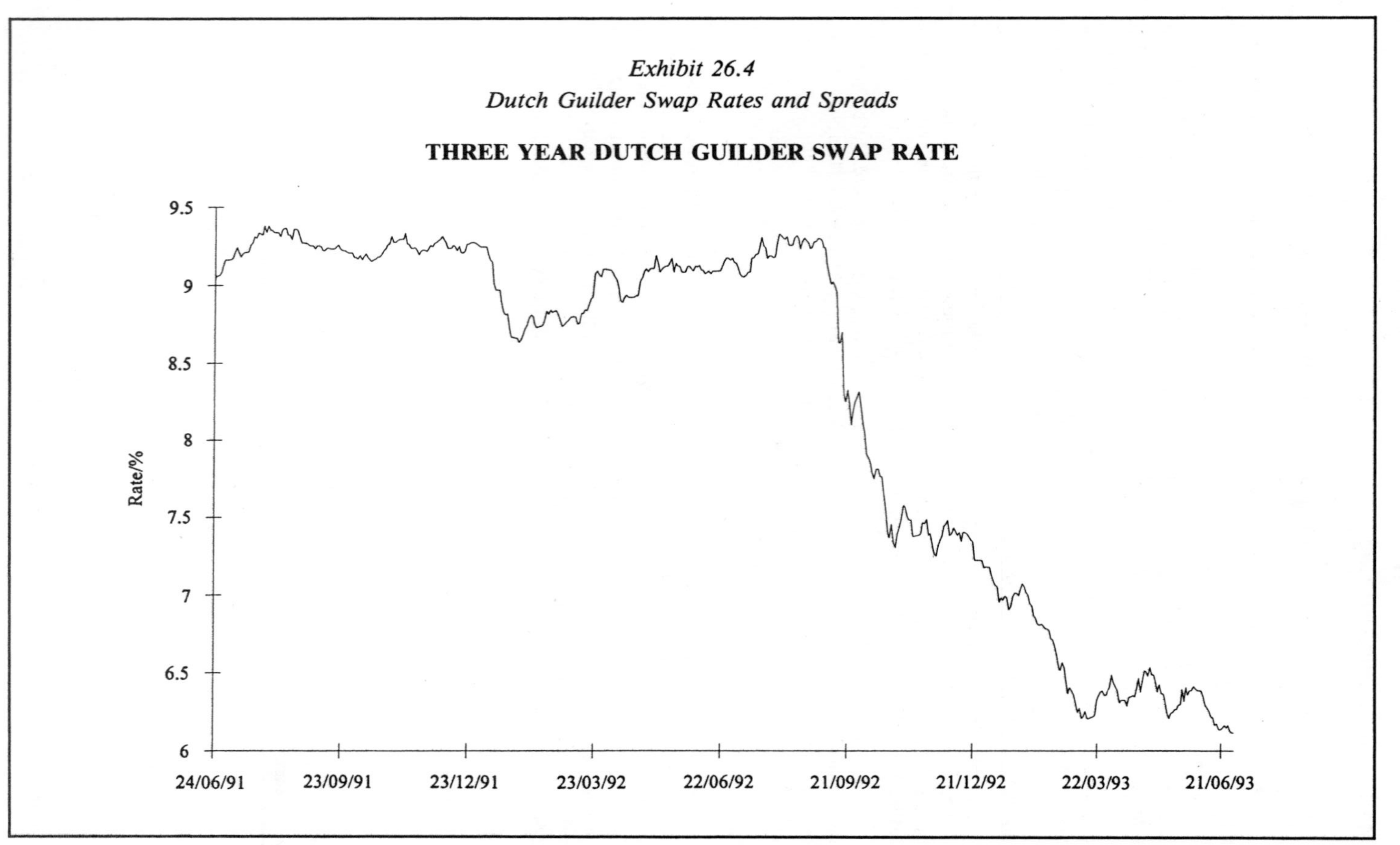

Exhibit 26.4
Dutch Guilder Swap Rates and Spreads

Exhibit 26.4—continued

FIVE YEAR DUTCH GUILDER SWAP RATE

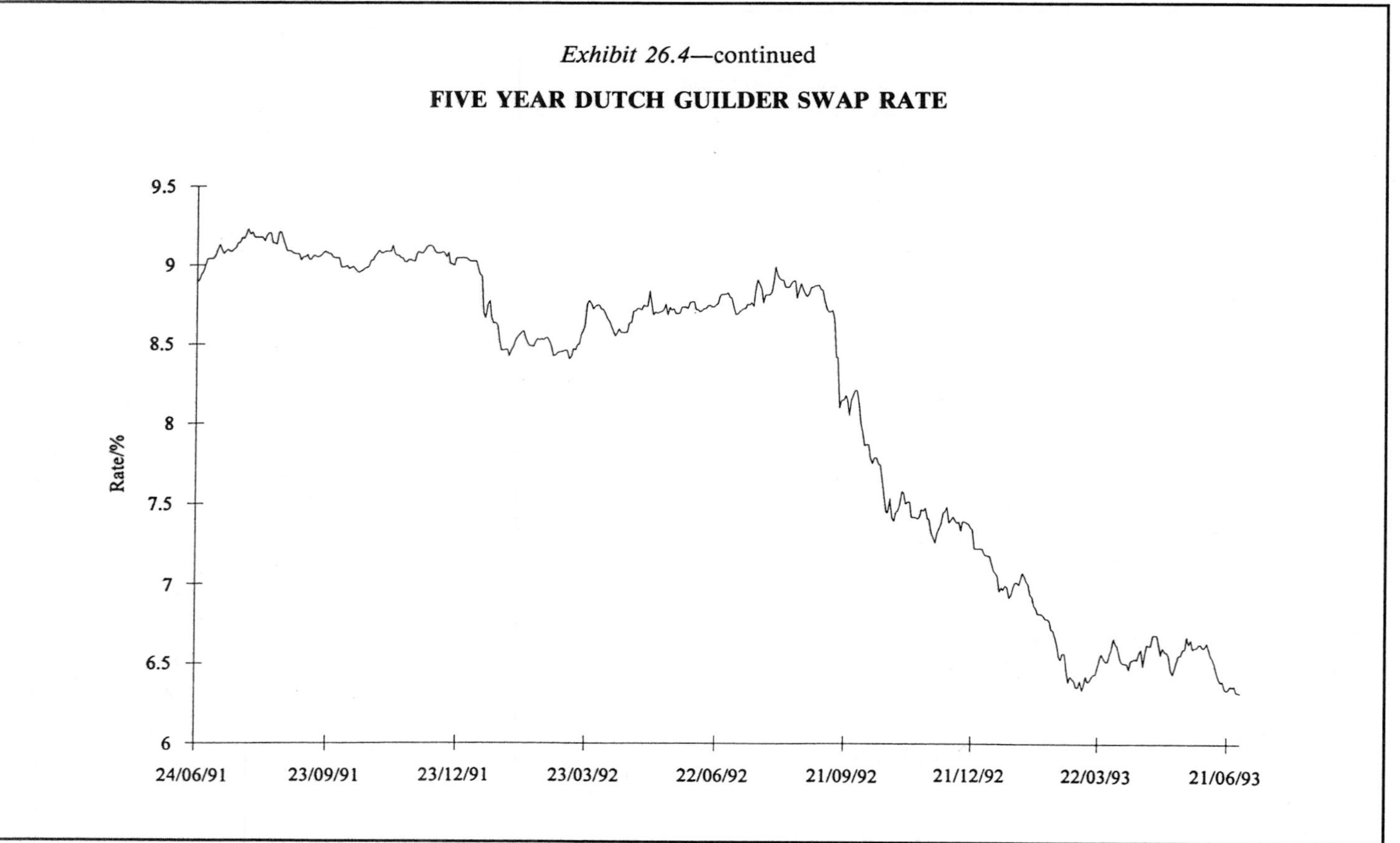

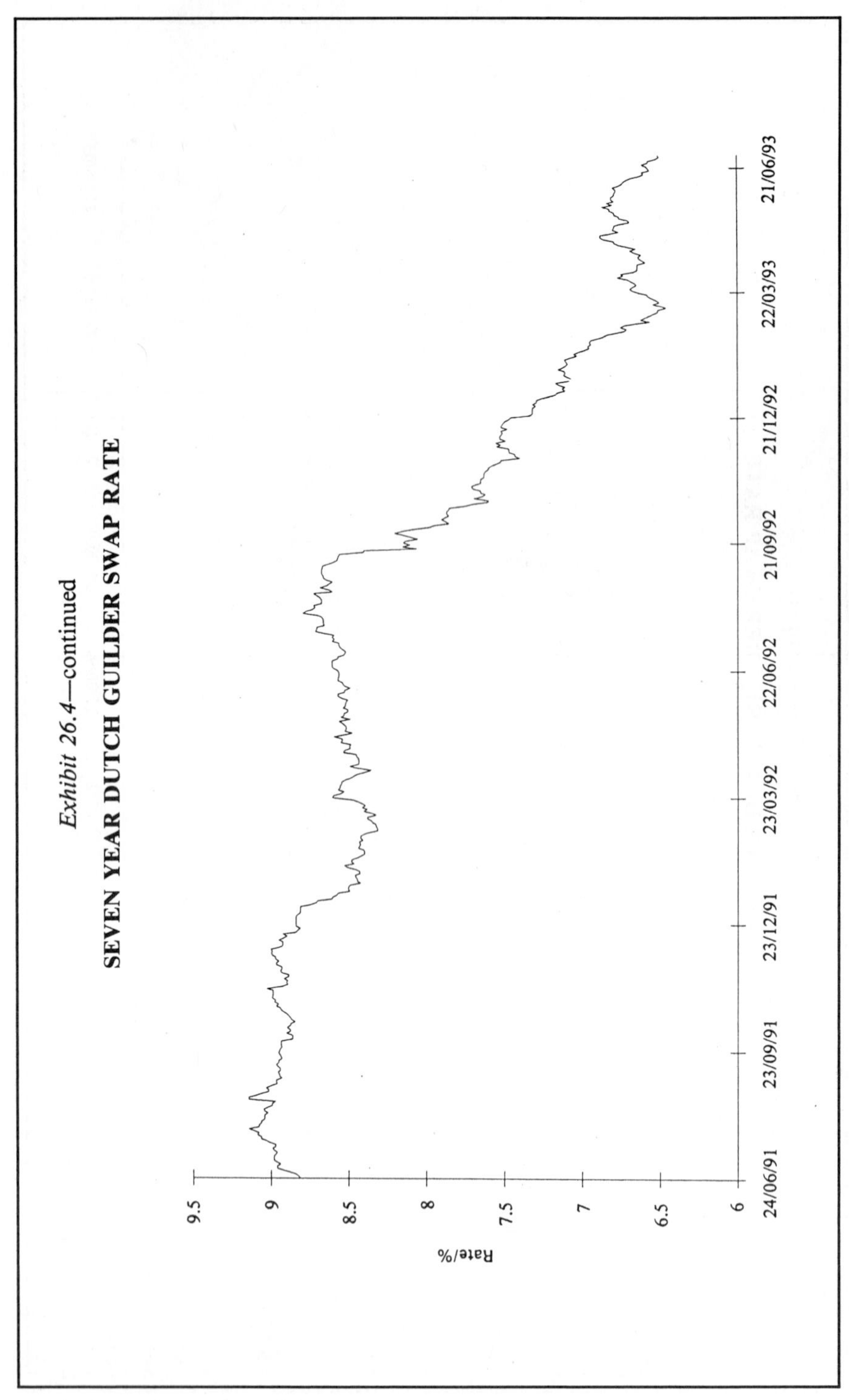

Exhibit 26.4—continued

SEVEN YEAR DUTCH GUILDER SWAP RATE

Exhibit 26.4—continued

TEN YEAR DUTCH GUILDER SWAP RATE

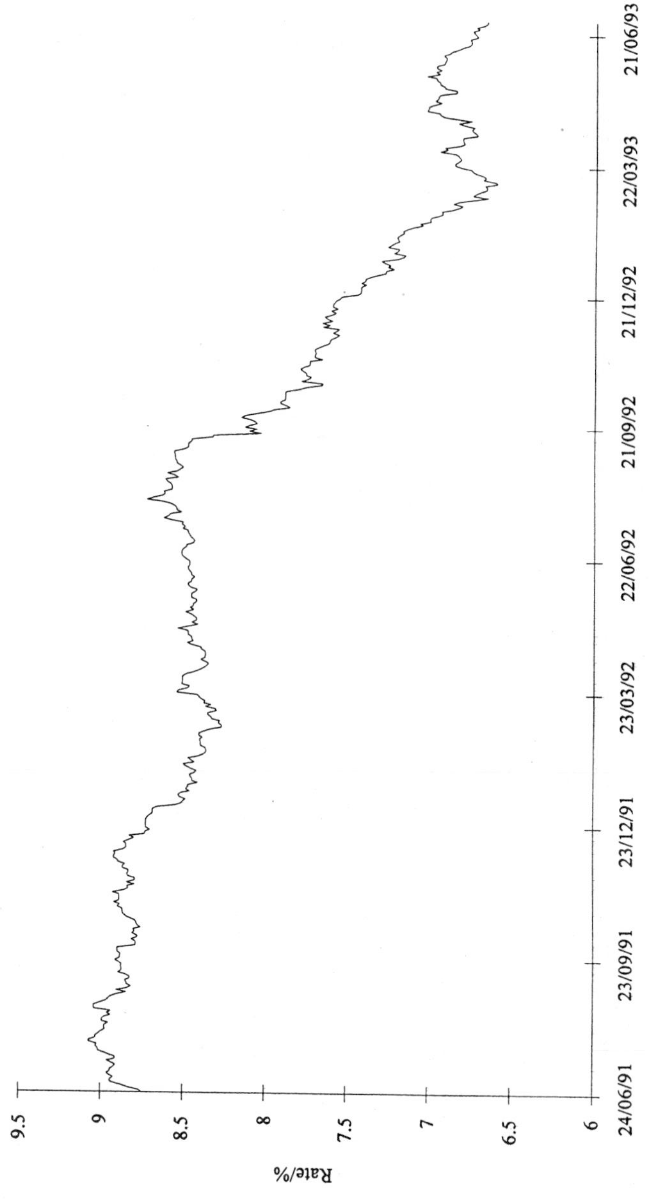

Rate/%

9.5
9
8.5
8
7.5
7
6.5
6

24/06/91 23/09/91 23/12/91 23/03/92 22/06/92 21/09/92 21/12/92 22/03/93 21/06/93

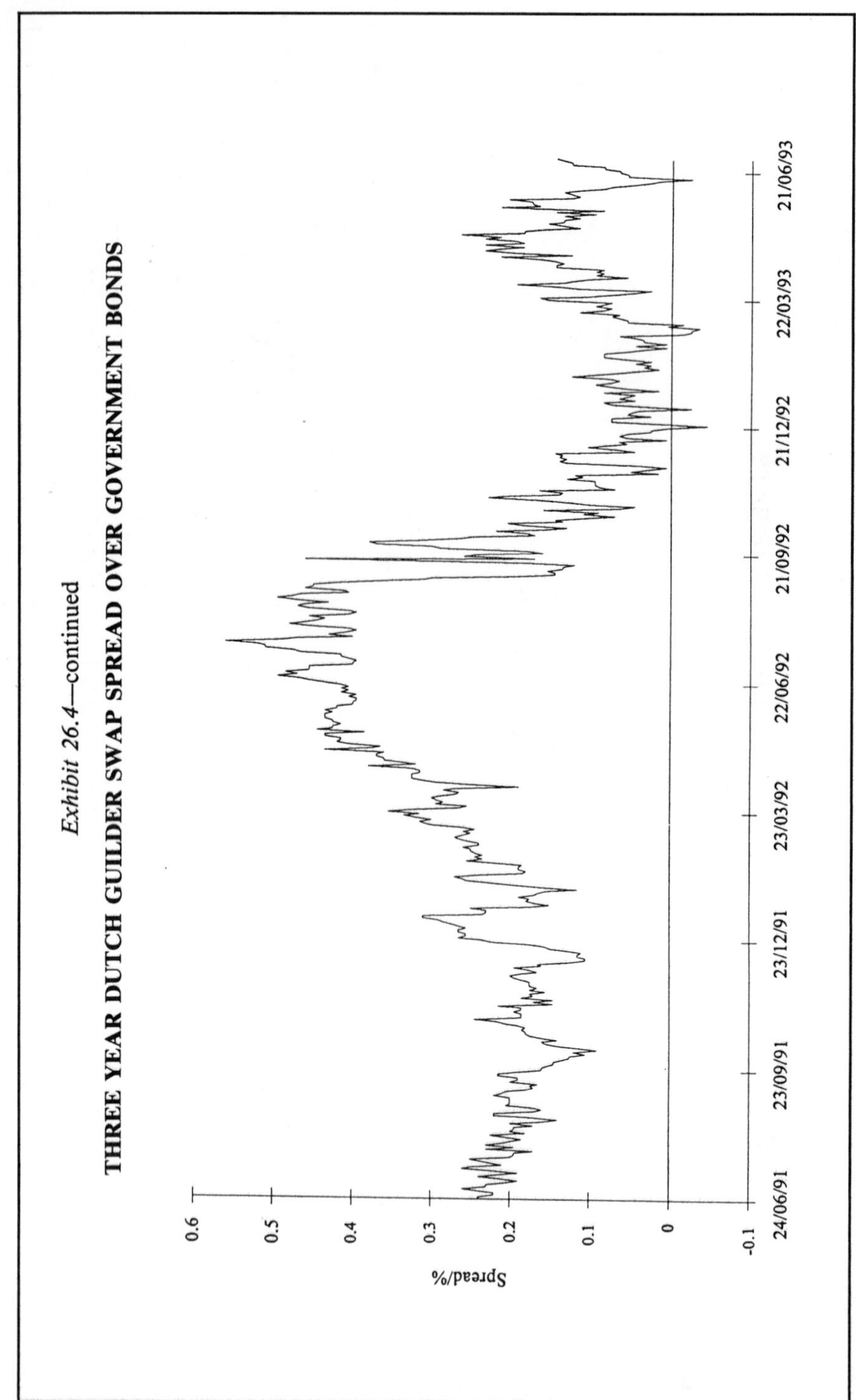

Exhibit 26.4—continued

THREE YEAR DUTCH GUILDER SWAP SPREAD OVER GOVERNMENT BONDS

Exhibit 26.4—continued

FIVE YEAR DUTCH GUILDER SWAP SPREAD OVER GOVERNMENT BONDS

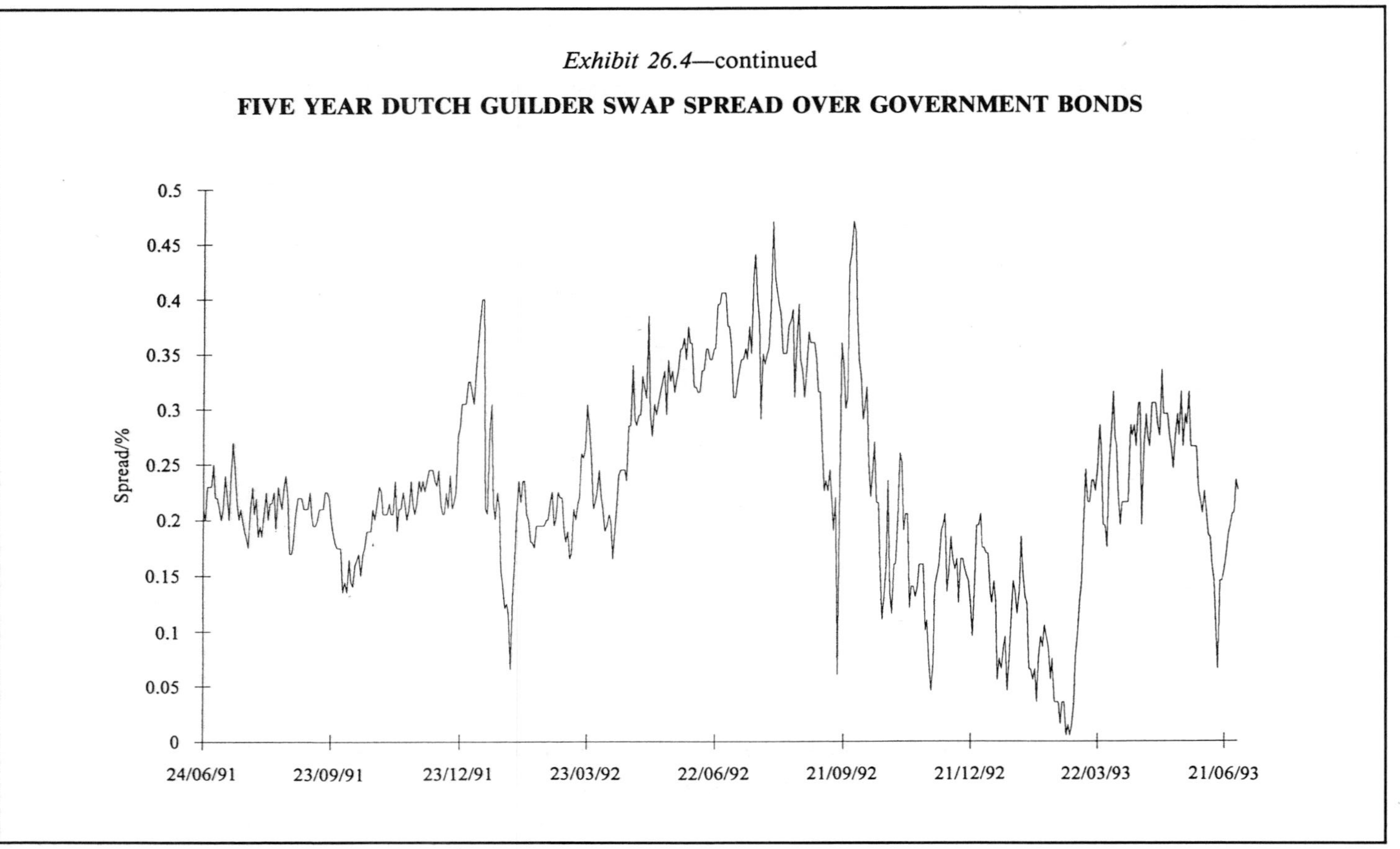

Exhibit 26.4—continued

SEVEN YEAR DUTCH GUILDER SWAP SPREAD OVER GOVERNMENT BONDS

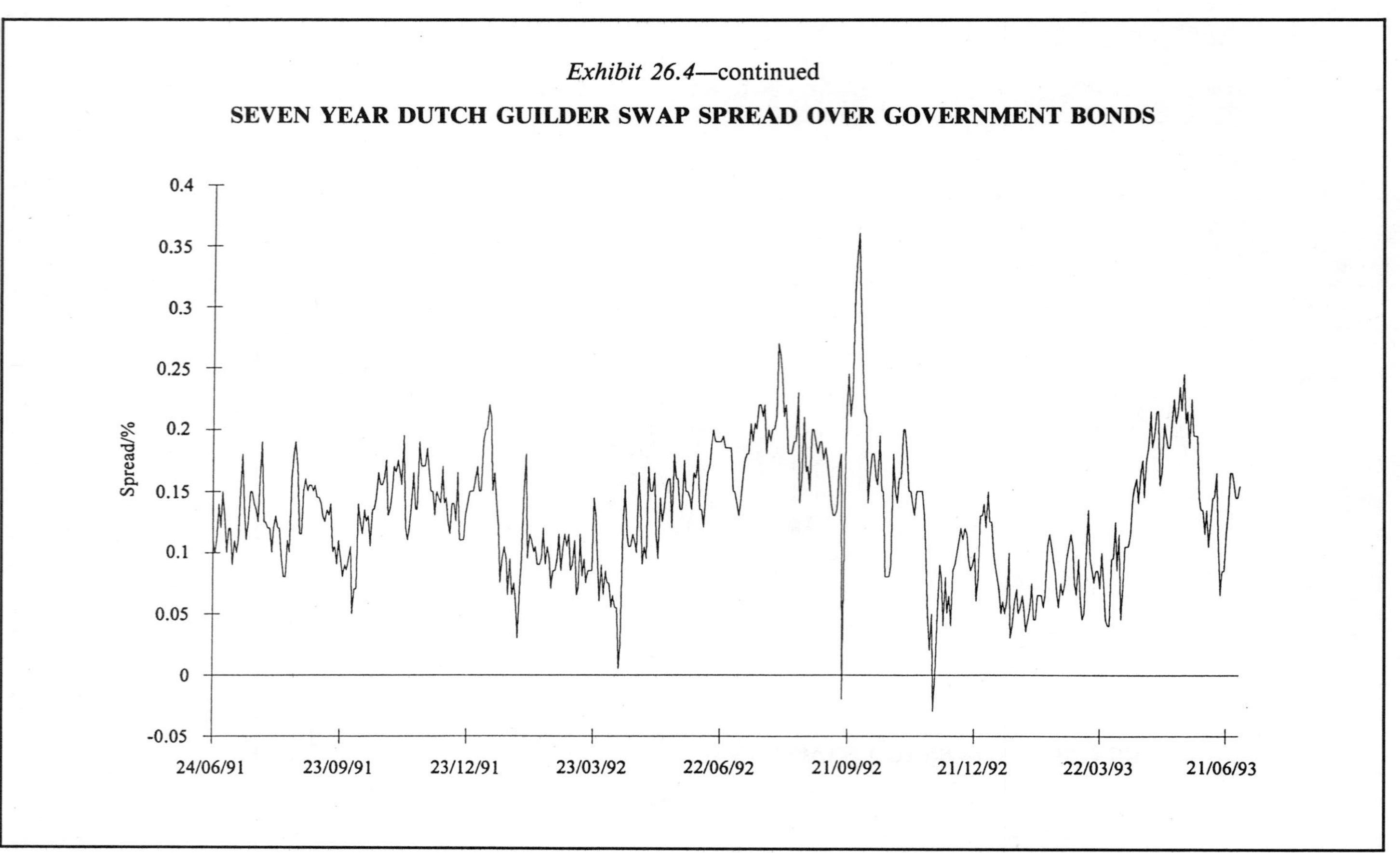

Exhibit 26.4—continued

TEN YEAR DUTCH GUILDER SWAP SPREAD OVER GOVERNMENT BONDS

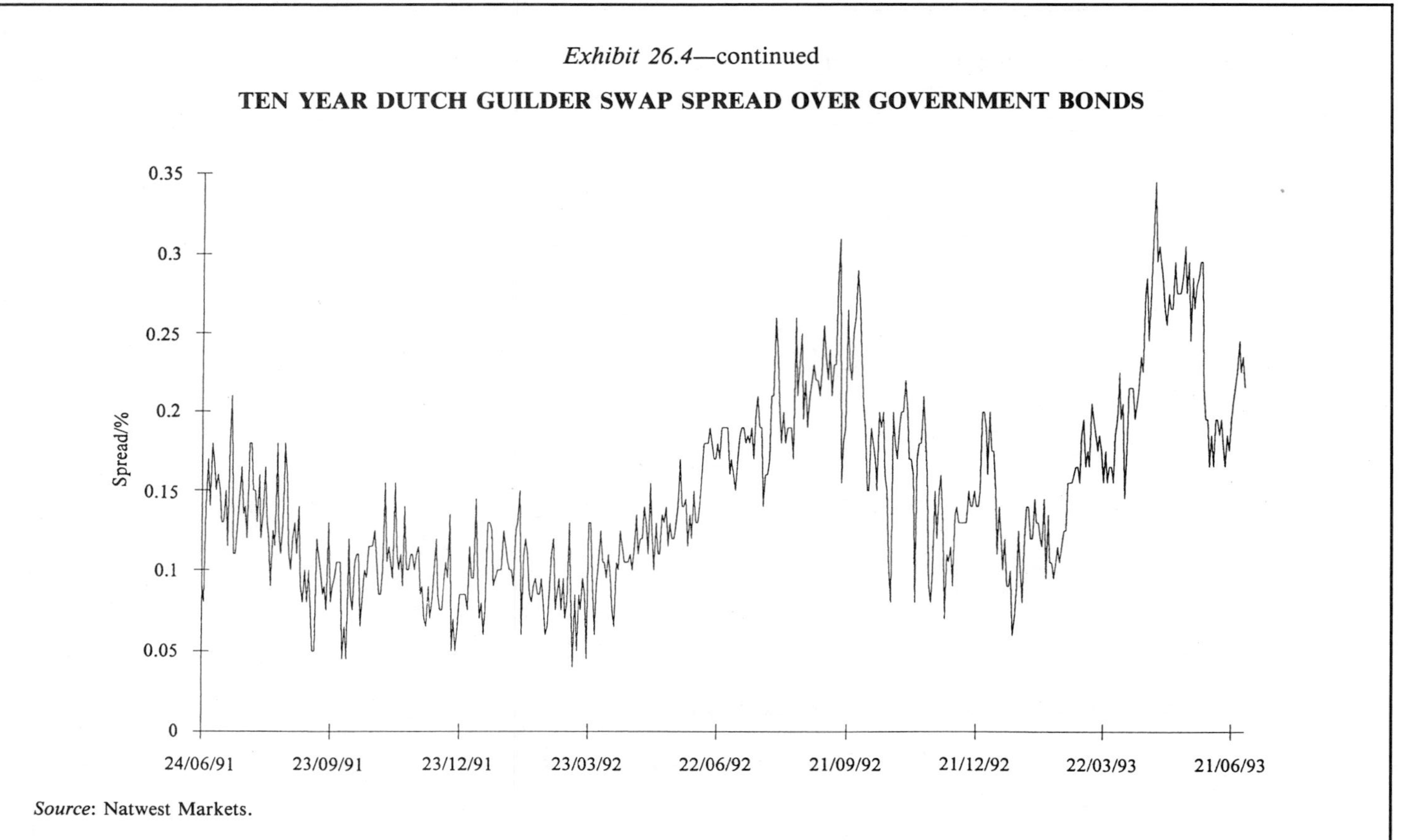

Source: Natwest Markets.

Exhibit 26.5

Dutch Guilder vs Deutschmark Swap Rates

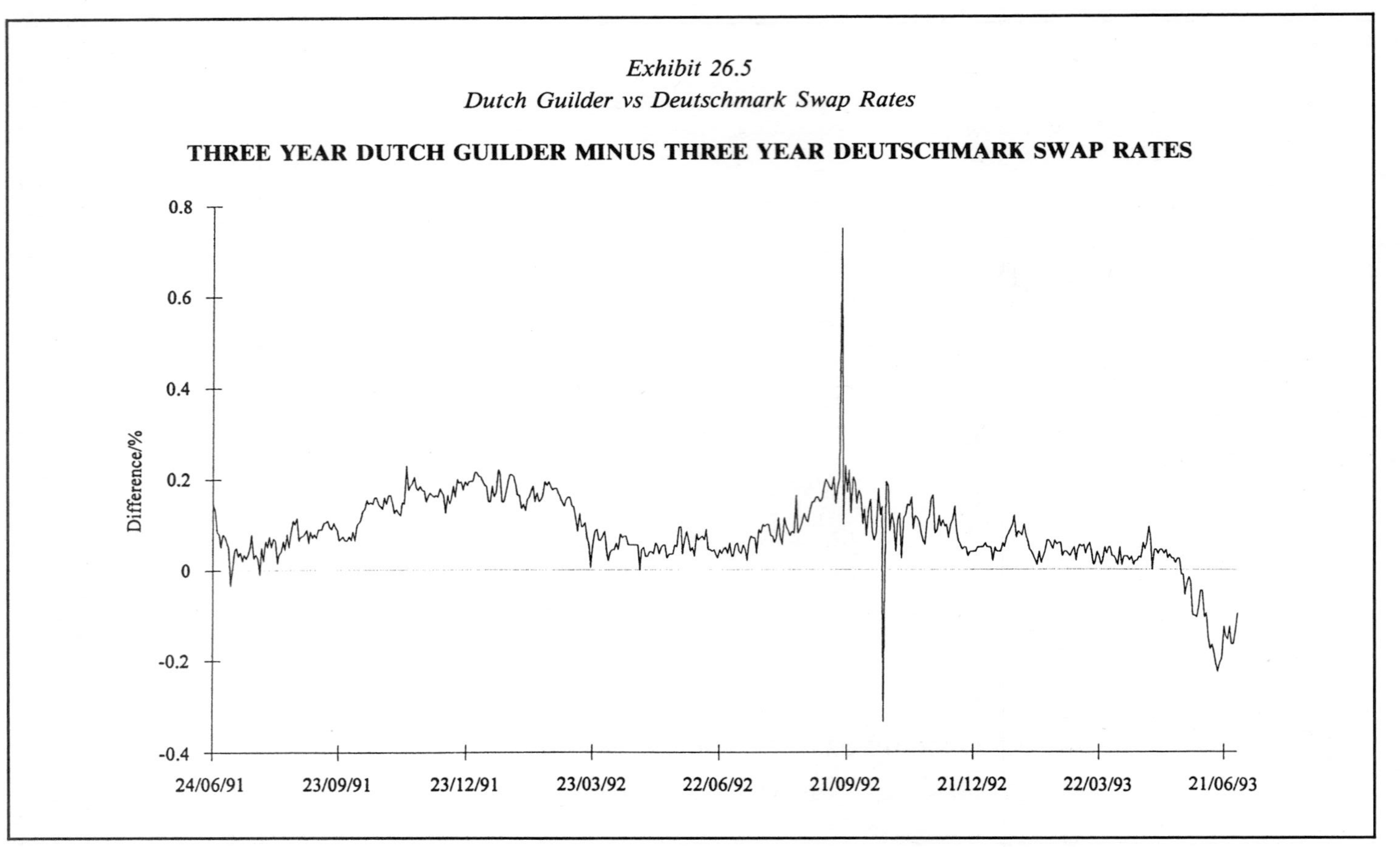

Exhibit 26.5—continued

FIVE YEAR DUTCH GUILDER MINUS FIVE YEAR DEUTSCHMARK SWAP RATES

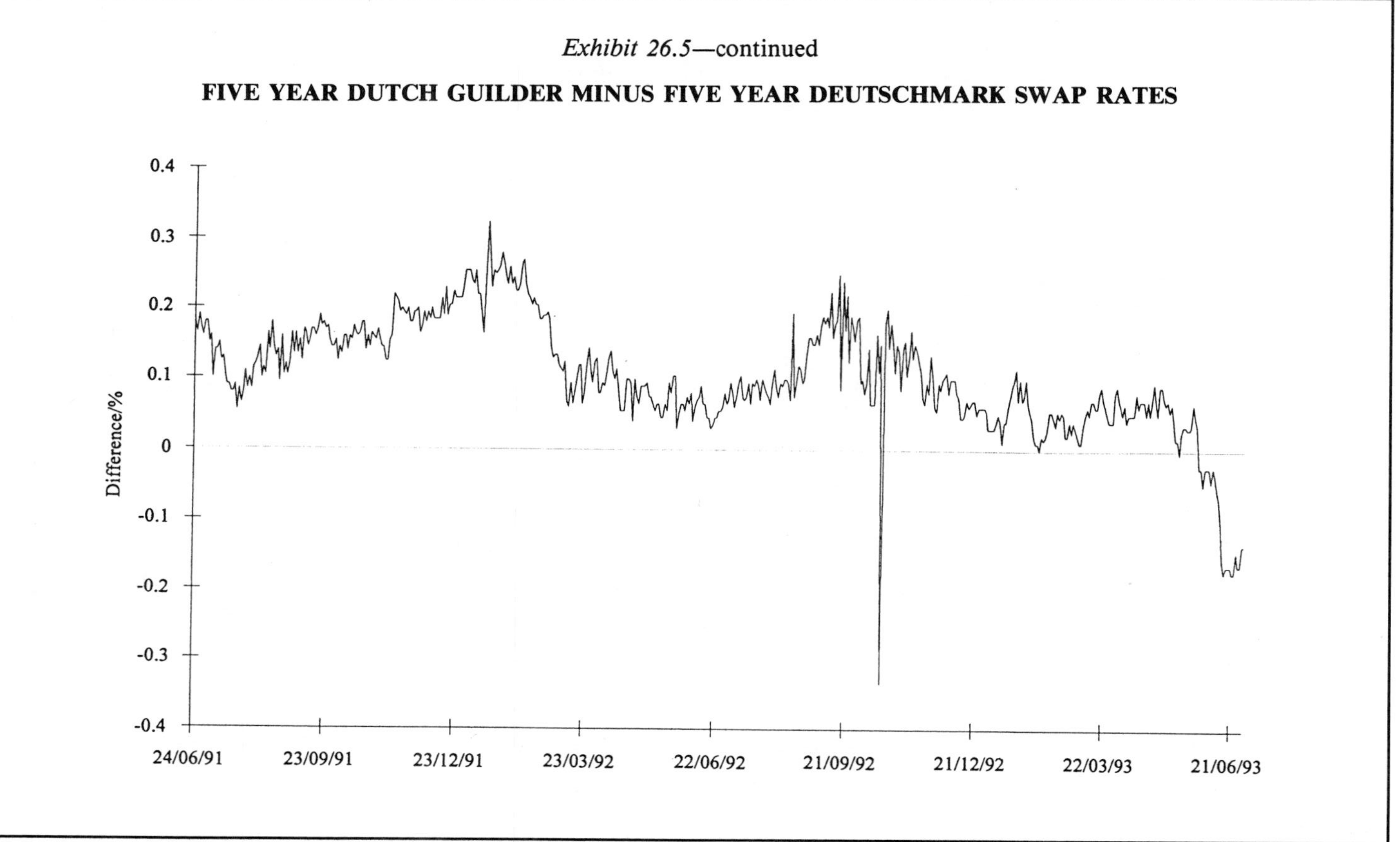

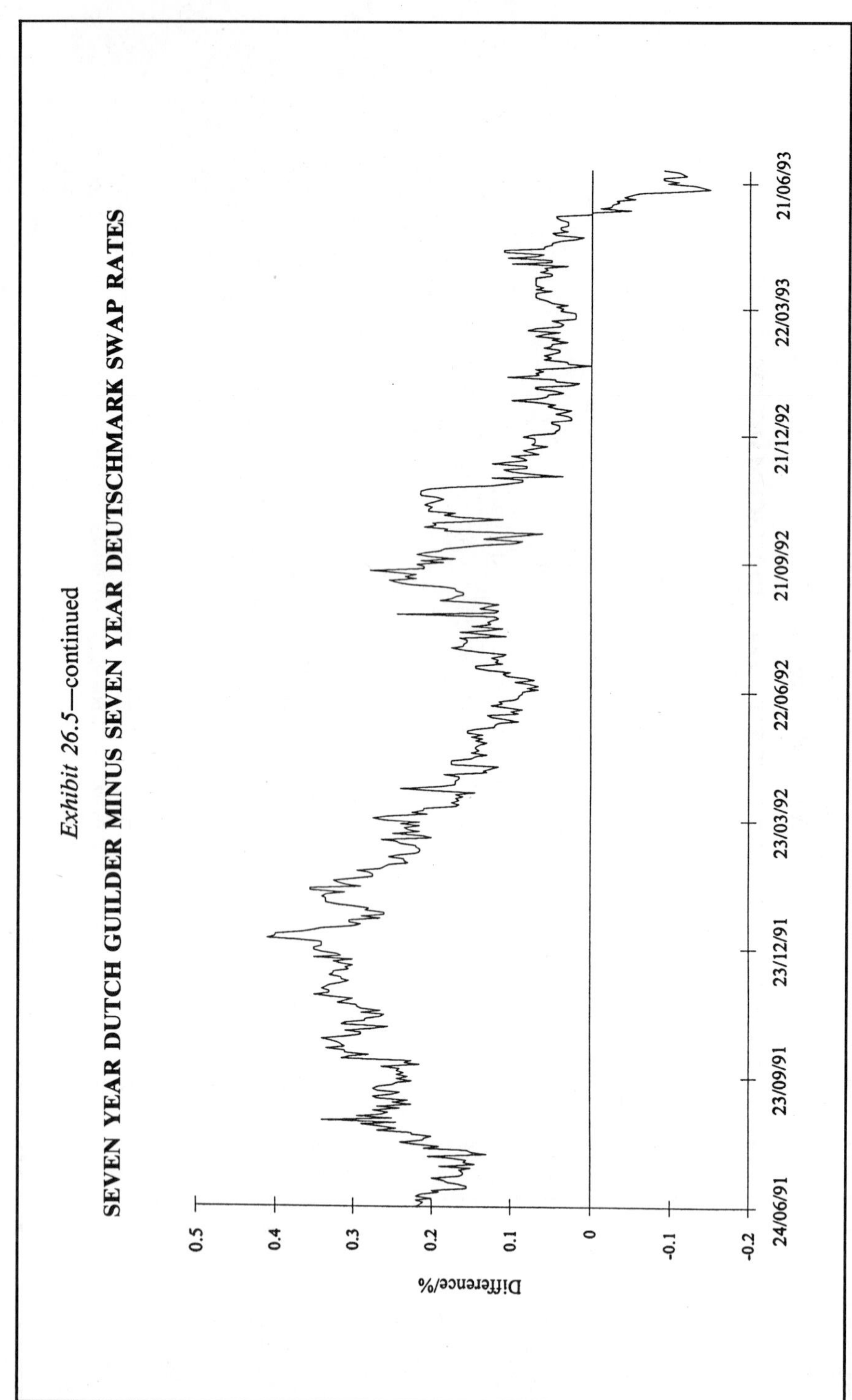

Exhibit 26.5—continued

SEVEN YEAR DUTCH GUILDER MINUS SEVEN YEAR DEUTSCHMARK SWAP RATES

Exhibit 26.5—continued

TEN YEAR DUTCH GUILDER MINUS TEN YEAR DEUTSCHMARK SWAP RATES

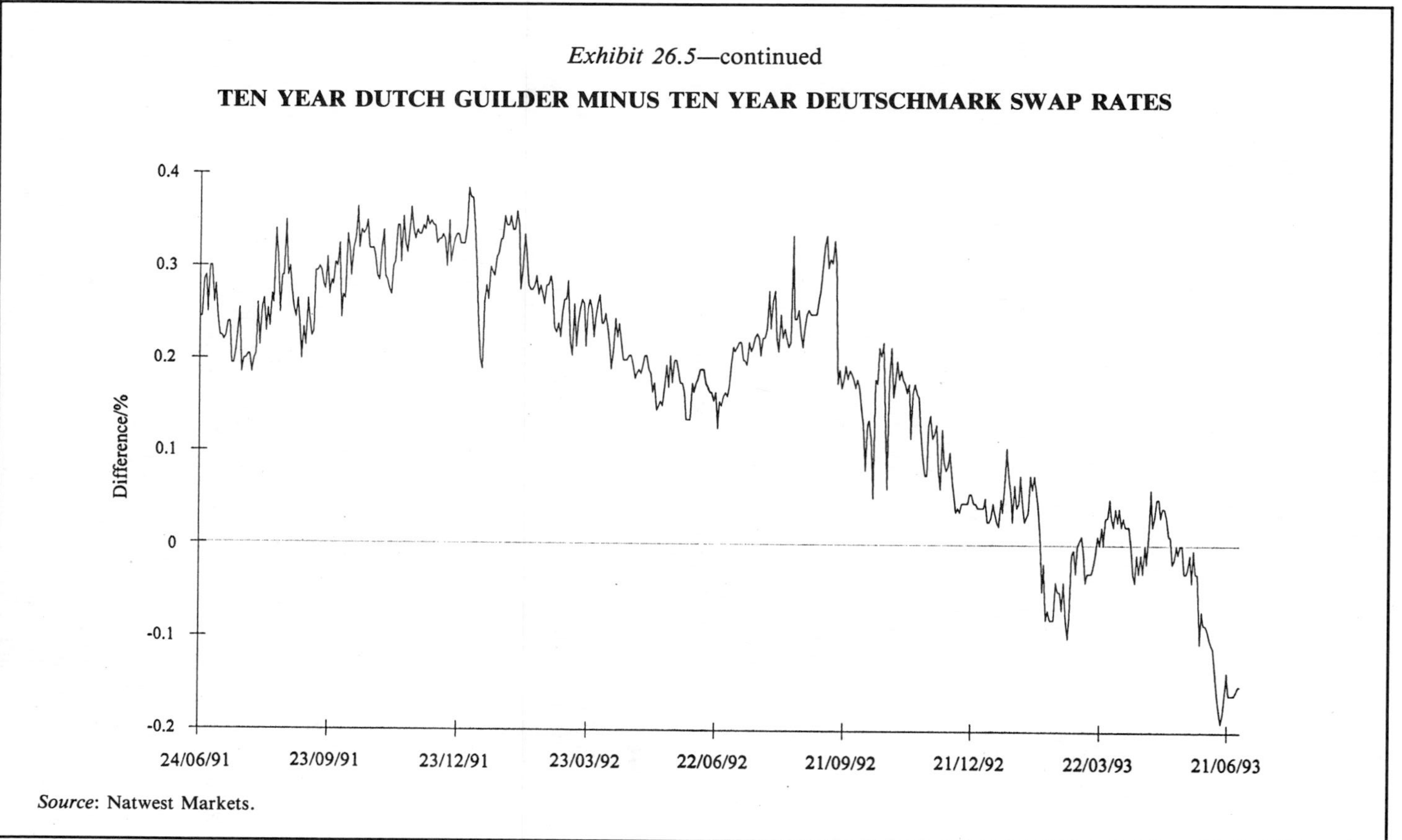

Source: Natwest Markets.

ITALIAN LIRA MARKET

Origins

The lira swap market is of relatively recent origin. Its development has been driven by a variety of factors including:

- The relaxation of the Italian regulatory framework which has facilitated risk management by Italian companies.
- The development of a small but growing Eurobond market in lira for international issuers.
- The existence of the Italian government bond market (the third largest in the world) which allows creation of synthetic assets based on government bonds.

The tax factors driving the lira market are both complex and volatile. The major relevant tax regulation is the 30% tax payable on Eurolira bond issues by foreign borrowers held by Italian investors and the exemption from withholding tax of bond issues by the three Italian State entities (Enel, Ferrovi and Creidiof) and four supranational entities (World Bank, EIB, CECA and Euratom). In late 1992 the Italian government ended the tax exemption for Italian residents investing in Eurobonds issued by certain supranational and Italian government borrowers. In addition, a uniform 12.5% withholding tax is, currently, to be applied to all bonds regardless of the nature of the borrower.

Such deregulation will effectively increase the efficiency of the market taking away the disadvantage for Italian investors to buy Eurolira bonds issued by foreign issuers, facilitating further growth in the lira swap market. However, in the short term, creation of "grandfathered" issues etc creates significant market anomalies.

Structure

The lira swap market has two distinct and, to a degree, separate components: the domestic interest rate swap market and the Eurolira currency swap market. It is anticipated that as the system of regulation is relaxed, the markets will continue their current trend of merging.

The domestic lira swap market operates as a market for fixed rates against three variable rate indexes:

- *Milan Interbank Offered Rate (MIBOR)*—quoted by Associazione Tesorieri Istituzioni Creditizi (ATIC) (this rate is quoted on Reuters page ATIA).
- *Rendiob*—which is the rate at which long-term credit institutions borrow term funding in the domestic market.
- *Rolint*—the average of MIBOR and Rendiob.

MIBOR trades, typically, at a margin above Eurolira LIBOR. This is reflected in a higher fixed rate for domestic interest rate swaps relative to Eurolira swap fixed rates.

Swaps are settled on a quarterly basis with both fixed and floating rates being calculated quarterly on a money market (365/360 day) basis.

Domestic lira swaps are transacted for maturities of between one and four years. Increasingly, swaps are available for maturities up to seven years reflecting the availability of Italian government bonds of that maturity, facilitating hedging of these types of swaps. Market liquidity is greatest maturities up to three years.

Under stable conditions, dealing spreads are in the range 10-20bps. However, in periods of volatility or uncertainty, dealing spreads can widen sharply to as much as 40bps, causing liquidity to diminish sharply.

The Eurolira or currency swap market basically functions in response to the existence of the lira Eurobond market. The market is typically a fixed lira versus US$ LIBOR market although increasingly lira interest rate swaps priced against the British Bankers Association lira LIBOR page (Telerate page 3740) have emerged.

In the Eurolira swap market, rate differences between lira interest rate swaps and lira currency swaps can be as high as 15bps pa. Typical maturities are up to ten years. As with the domestic market, liquidity is greatest in shorter maturities, in the Eurolira market, particularly for maturities up to five years.

The Eurolira market is dominated by lira Eurobond issuers seeking to swap fixed rate liabilities into either floating rate lira or US$. The fixed rate pay interest typically comes from asset swap transactions, corporations and domestic Italian lending institutions. Participation of domestic Italian lending institutions and commercial banks is particularly important at longer maturities.

Major market makers active in the lira market are the major Italian banks, although foreign banks as well as non-bank financial institutions play prominent roles in certain sectors of the market.

Market participants, amongst the financial institutions, can be divided into two groups. The first group involves a relatively small number of banks which are permitted by the Bank of Italy to lead Eurolira bond issues. The second group involves a much larger range of institutions, both domestic and foreign, who are involved in all other sectors of the lira market.

Participation by non-bank financial institutions, including foreign participants, in the lira swap market will be effected by a stock exchange reform law (the SIM or Societa Di Intermediazione Mobiliare Law). The SIM aims to clarify the roles of various financial intermediaries. Under current interpretations of the SIM law in regard to off balance sheet products, these transactions are treated as securities which means that only SIMs can either act as brokers or principal dealers. Consequently, all brokers and principals have to convert their operations into SIMS. Foreign banks have, to a large extent, either set up SIMs companies in Milan or alternatively have stopped soliciting businesses in Italy preferring to operate out of their London operations.

Pricing

Lira swaps are priced off the underlying Italian government bond market. This reflects the use of government bonds for the purposes of hedging swap positions.

The major instruments utilised to hedge include:

- BTPs (Buoni Del Tesorie Poliennali);
- CTOs (Certificati Del Tesoro Con Opzione).

The CTOs also have a put option which are occasionally stripped out and resold facilitating a small market in lira interest rate options.

The major problem with using the underlying government bond market is lack of fungibility between various government debt issues and the variety of types of bonds and bills which are in existence.

New issue ("on the run") bonds are usually sufficiently liquid to provide reasonable hedges for swap risk positions. Short positions in lira government bonds are usually accomplished by selling bonds from an existing or from a synthetic asset portfolio.

The spread relationship between the underlying BTP rate and swap rates is extremely volatile. This reflects the trading pattern in the lira government bond market where significant changes in interest rate levels gives rise to *uniform price changes* along the whole yield curve. This volatility creates active trading opportunities but creates a significant loss of hedge efficiency.

Exhibit 26.6 sets out lira swap rates as well as spread relationships to the underlying bond markets.

The lira swap market is increasingly utilising futures contracts as a hedging mechanism. This reflects the launch of a new government bond futures contract on these Mercato Italiano de Futures (MIF) as well as Italian short and medium term interest rate contracts launched by LIFFE. LIFFE's three month Eurolira interest rate contract is still relatively illiquid but offers, particularly as liquidity improves, opportunities to hedge short term interest rate swaps.

The ten year government bond futures contract on LIFFE and corresponding contract on MIF is reasonably liquid. The availability of the bond futures contract provides an alternative means for swap portfolio managers to hedge their swap risk positions, although the mismatch in maturities between the underlying BTP and swap transaction maturity creates a high degree of yield curve risk.

As is the case with the French franc swap market, separation of the domestic and international swap market components detracts from the overall development of lira swaps. However, there is evidence that the domestic interest rate swap, based on MIBOR, is now, to a large extent, superseded by the lira LIBOR based Eurolira swap market. The increasing popularity of LIBOR lira based swaps includes:

- The number of international swap market makers who have opened Eurolira swap portfolios.
- The greater liquidity of the Eurolira deposit markets relative to the domestic interbank market.
- The fact that the Eurolira deposit market more closely approximates the borrowing cost of corporations.
- Traditional users of MIBOR as a funding base are not active in lira interest rate swaps.
- The spread between MIBOR and Eurolira LIBOR has narrowed in recent times to around 15-20bps. With the withdrawal of withholding tax and domestic interbank deposits, the only theoretical difference between MIBOR and LIBOR should be the Italian banks minimum reserve requirements, assisting the rates in converging.

Product range

The product range in the lira swap market while still relatively basic is improving. A variety of option based products is gradually emerging, including options on swaps as well as caps, floors and collars.

An essential part of the lira swap market is the market for asset swaps facilitating creation of Italian government floating rate deposits priced of Eurolira LIBOR, MIBOR or US$ LIBOR which are increasingly placed with both domestic and international investors.

Exhibit 26.6

Italian Lira Swap Rate

LIRA THREE YEAR SWAP RATE

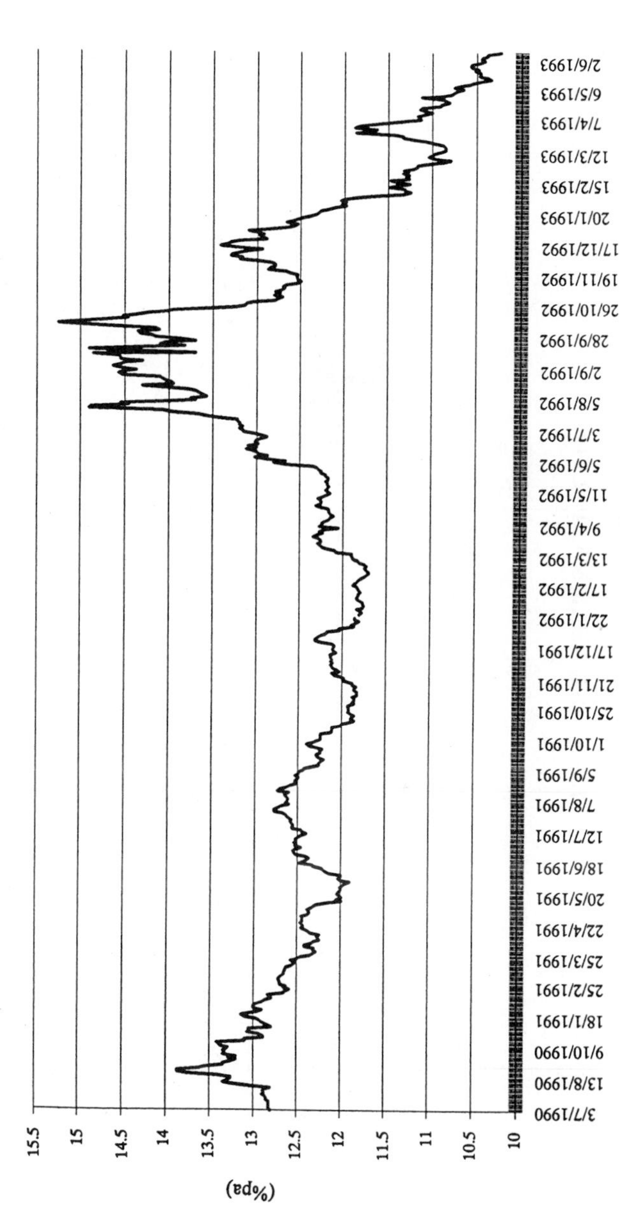

Exhibit 26.6—continued

LIRA FIVE YEAR SWAP RATE

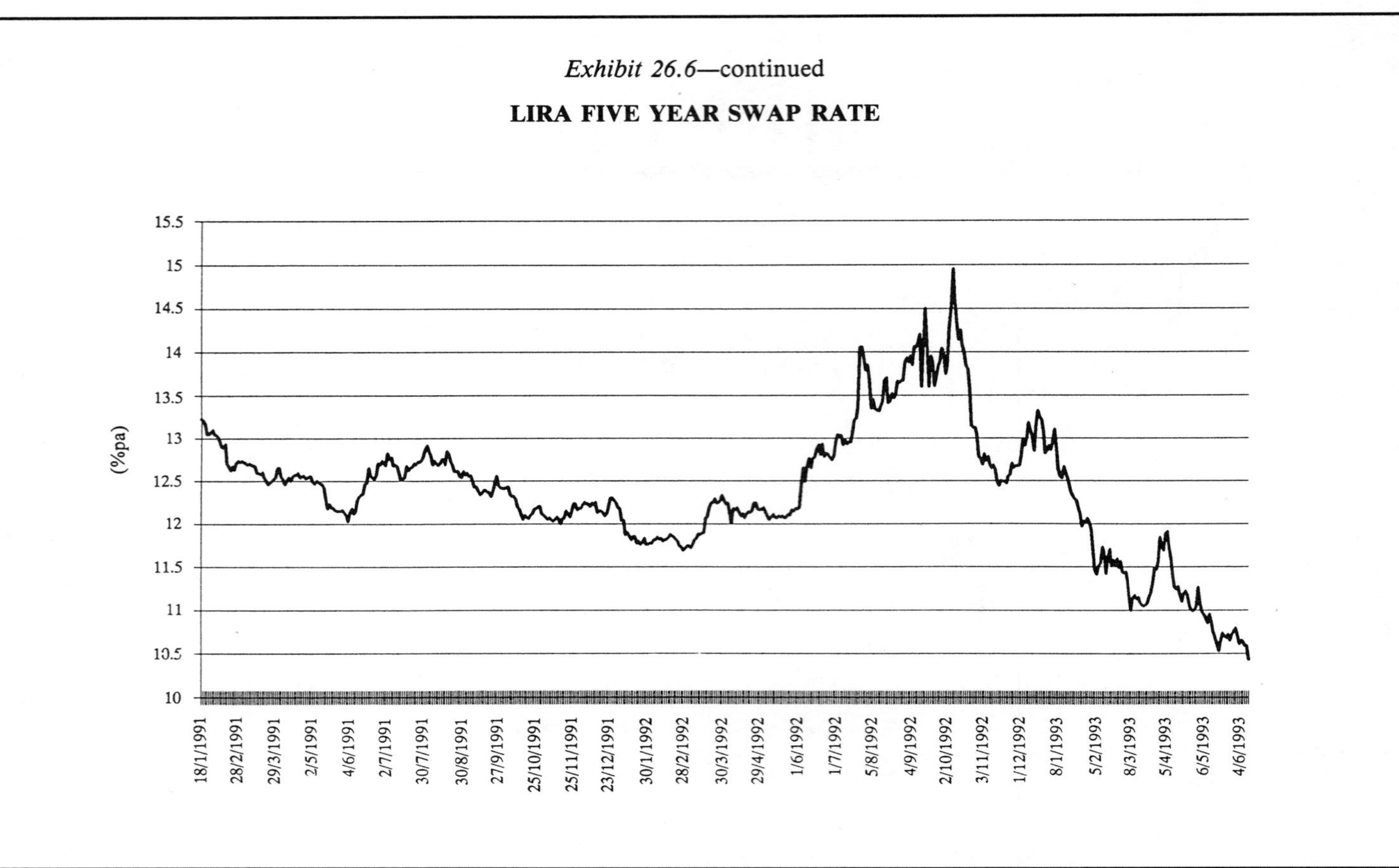

Exhibit 26.6—continued

LIRA SEVEN YEAR SWAP RATE

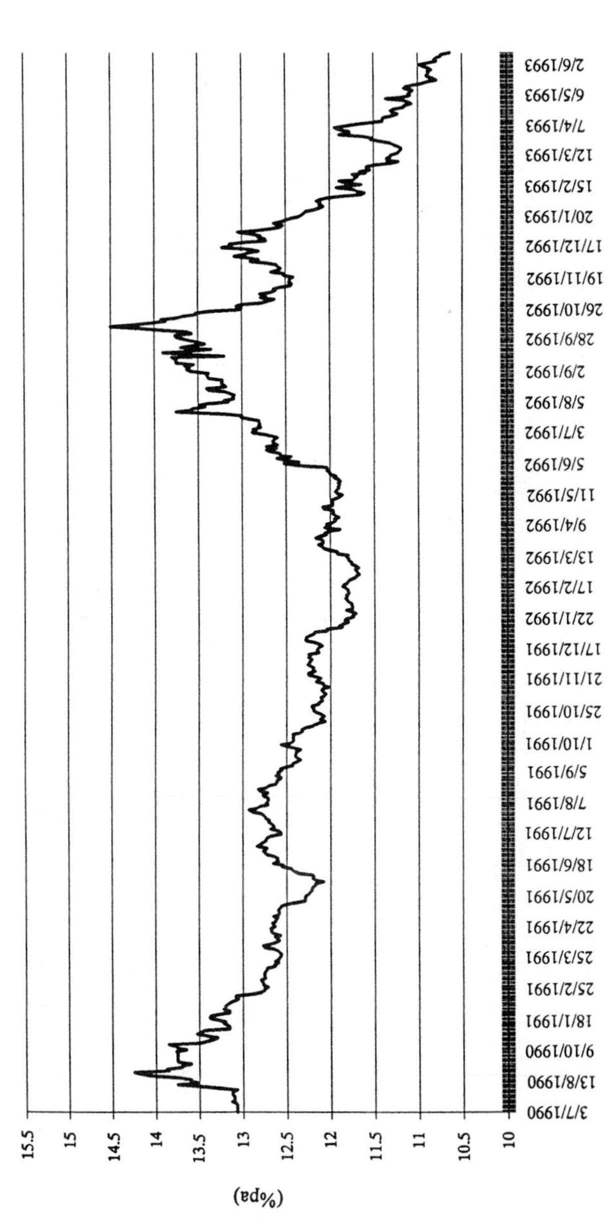

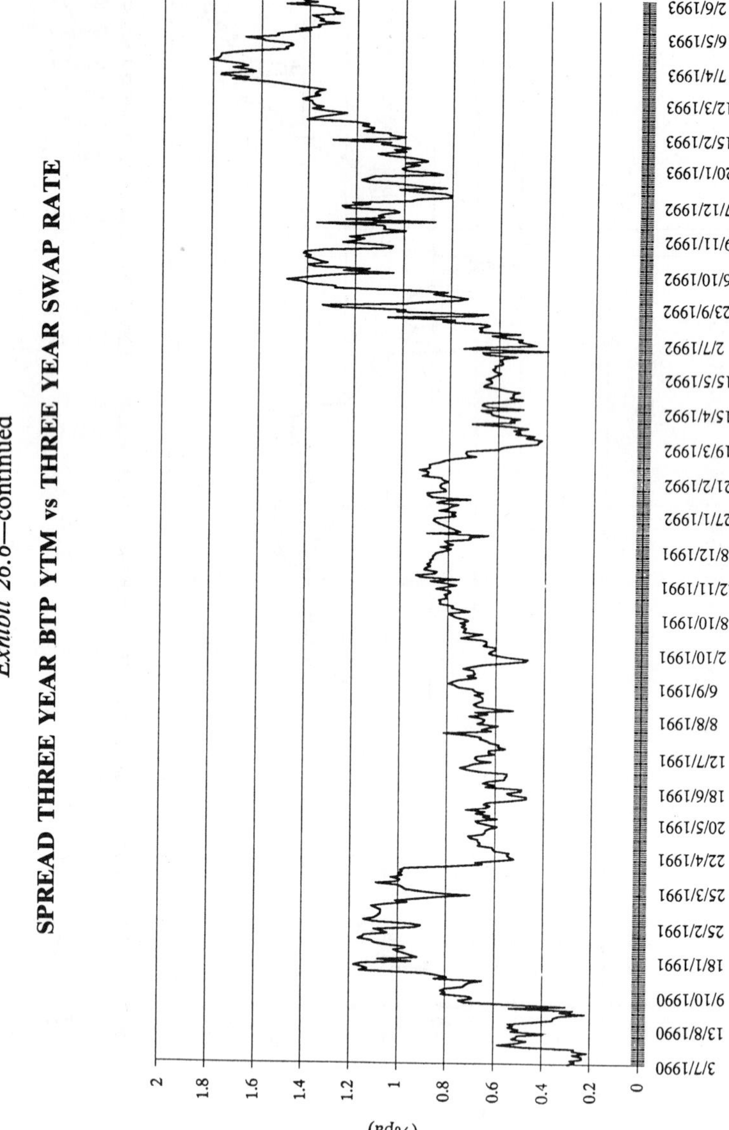

Exhibit 26.6—continued

SPREAD THREE YEAR BTP YTM vs THREE YEAR SWAP RATE

Exhibit 26.6—continued

SPREAD FIVE YEAR BTP YTM vs FIVE YEAR SWAP RATE

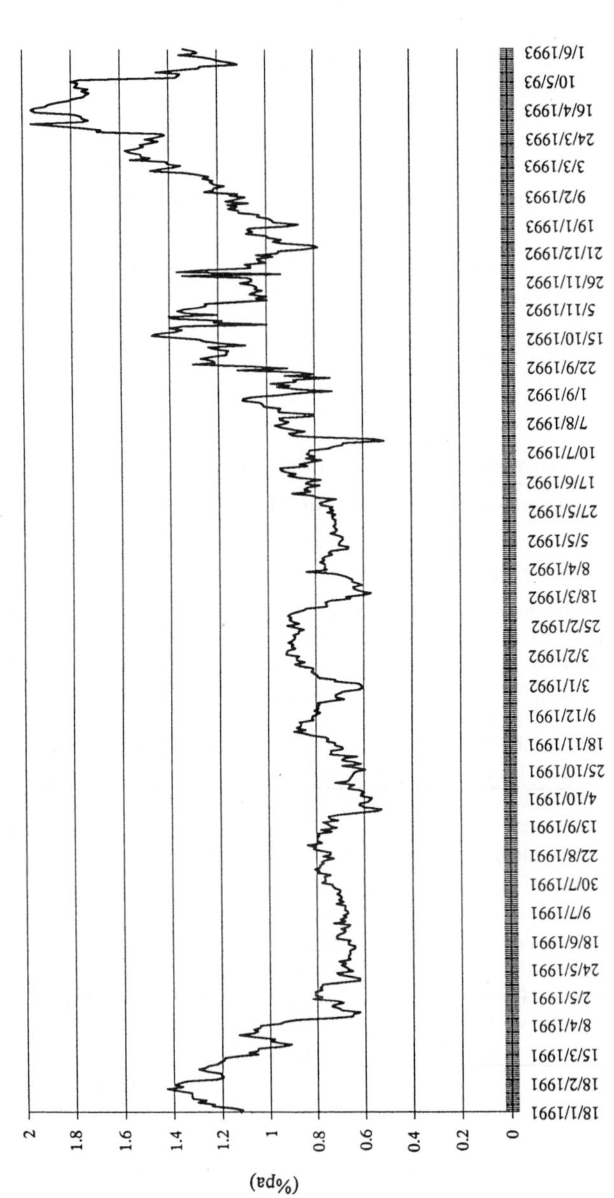

Source: Sanpaolo Finance SPA—Milano.

SPANISH PESETA SWAP MARKETS

Origins

The origins of the Spanish peseta swap market can be traced to middle 1987 when a syndicate of Spanish financial institutions lead by Caja Madrid, Caja de Barcelona and Caja de Zaragoza signed the first ever domestic interest rate swap (dubbed Cari Pesetas—Convenio de Ajuste Reciproco de Intres). The fixed-to-floating transaction was for PTA1,500m (approximately US$12m) for a maturity of ten years linked to a buyer credit facility under a scheme to promote exports of Spanish capital goods.

Since 1987, the peseta market has grown under the influence of the following factors:

- the development of the Spanish peseta bond market, particularly the emergence of the Matador market, that is the market for international issuers in pesetas;
- risk management requirements of local Spanish corporations as well as foreign corporations with investments and trade transactions with Spain.

Structure

The Spanish peseta market has three specific sectors:

- interest rate swaps in the domestic market;
- currency swaps from fixed rate pesetas into US$ LIBOR;
- basis swaps between domestic and Europeseta deposit rates.

Each component of the Spanish peseta swap market has a distinct range of participants. However, the peseta swap market overall is dominated, in terms of market making, by Spanish banks for both economic and regulatory factors. A major barrier for foreign banks is that few if any non-Spanish banks have access to all necessary components of the market and Spanish foreign exchange regulations, which have been relaxed but are still imposed from time to time, make it difficult for foreign banks to transact swaps freely. Spanish foreign exchange regulations have now been completely removed. However, the way that the Bank of Spain requires banks active in Spain to report their operations monthly makes some types of derivative transactions difficult.

The domestic peseta interest rate swap market is primarily a market between fixed peseta rates transacted against a domestic Madrid interbank offered rate (MIBOR). Activity is centred on Madrid with most transactions being in maturities up to five years. The maturity preference reflects the domestic bond market where the most active maturity is the three year Bonos del Estado. This market is typically utilised by Spanish corporations as a means of managing interest rate risk or the creation of fixed rate loans by Spanish banks for clients.

A significant proportion of peseta interest rate swaps are driven by Spanish banks lending fixed rate peseta to their corporate clients and funding on a floating rate basis. The Spanish banks then have a significant appetite to pay fixed/receive floating rate pesetas to manage the underlying asset liability mismatch in their treasury books. Banks therefore pay attractive fixed rates facilitating swapping of peseta fixed rate bond issues.

The peseta currency swap sector is driven by the Matador International bond market. This market is typically transacted in fixed rate pesetas against floating rate US$ LIBOR. The major components of this sector are international issuers, primarily supranational borrowers such as the World Bank, Council of Europe and the EIB, and, more recently sovereign borrowers, who issue fixed rate peseta Matador bonds which are accompanied by a swap into floating rate US$ LIBOR. The fixed rate peseta payments are generally driven by foreign corporations seeking peseta funding or creating a balance sheet hedge against assets denominated in pesetas arising from investments in Spain. A major group of fixed rate peseta payers in the currency swap market has been European manufacturers as well as the European subsidiaries of United States manufacturers establishing Spanish production plants to take advantage of lower labour costs in Spain. The Matador market is tightly controlled by the Bank of Spain and activity is sporadic.

The last component of the peseta swap market entails arbitrage of floating rate domestic peseta rates against Europeseta deposit rates. The spread between domestic MIBOR and Europeseta deposit rates has historically ranged between 5 and 10bps pa (down from 25-75 bps reflecting the elimination of foreign exchange controls). Domestic MIBOR rates are usually higher reflecting the reserve requirements (currently 3.5%) imposed by the Bank of Spain and the relative illiquidity of the domestic market.

The MIBOR/LIBOR segmentation is largely historical in origin and is increasingly less significant. However, the spread can fluctuate significantly (up to 40bps) with LIBOR rates rising *above MIBOR*, reflecting the fact that LIBOR rates are driven by the forward FX market.

The major market makers in the Spanish peseta swap market include large Spanish banks such as Central Hispano, BBV, Banco Santander. Foreign banks, such as Bank of America, Citibank and JP Morgan are also active.

A major structural feature of the Spanish peseta market is the relatively confused tax situation. Certain transactions are exempt under the Spanish government's double tax agreements. For example, in the absence of double tax treaty exemptions for withholding tax, cross-border swap transactions can be subject to significant withholding taxes as is the case with government bond holdings. However, this tax confusion is increasingly being addressed.

Market conventions

Spanish peseta swaps are most commonly quoted as fixed pesetas on an annual actual 360 basis against floating rate MIBOR for same day value (MIBOR is a same day fixing). Europeseta swaps are quoted on an annual 30/360 day basis for a two day settlement basis.

The market, at least theoretically, trades out to ten years, although maturities beyond five years are not common.

Market spreads are around 10-15bps pa for Europeseta currency swaps and 15-20bps for domestic peseta swaps. Bid-offer spreads are volatile and can narrow or widen significantly depending on trading conditions.

Other active segments of the peseta market include MIBOR and peseta LIBOR FRAs. MIBOR FRA bid-offer spreads are 5-10bps while peseta LIBOR FRAs are dealt on bid-offer spreads of around 10-15bps. Standard transaction size are PTA1-3 billion, with most activity concentrated in the 3-12 month dates (for MIBOR FRAs) and 3-6 month dates (for peseta LIBOR FRAs). MIBOR FRAs are currently transacted against the MIBOR CEMM (Commission d'estudios del Mercados Monetarios) contract. However, given the rapid growth in the peseta LIBOR FRA market, London-based banks are increasingly seeking to transact peseta FRAs on FRABBA terms.

Pricing

Pricing of peseta swaps is largely related to rate movements in the Matador bond market. Hedging utilises Spanish government bonds (bonos) but because of the impact of withholding tax, only domestic institutions typically use physical bonds as a hedge.

Increasingly, the peseta market is looking to hedge through interest rate futures and options traded on Madrid's Mercado de Opciones (MOFEX) and Barcelona's Mercado de Futuros Financieros (MEFF). Structured under a joint holding company, there will be little overlap, ultimately, between the two exchanges with MOFEX handling equity derivatives and MEFF interest rate and currency derivatives. Currently, MOFEX trades options contracts on three and five year notional government bonds and three month MIBOR while MEFF trades futures contracts on the same underlying instruments. The growing volume in the futures markets increasingly allows swap portfolio managers to use these futures as a means for hedging swap portfolio positions.

Exhibit 26.7 sets out peseta swap rates for different maturities.

Product range

Predictably, the product range in pesetas is relatively narrow with non-generic product structures slowly evolving.

Exhibit 26.7
Spanish Peseta Swap Rates

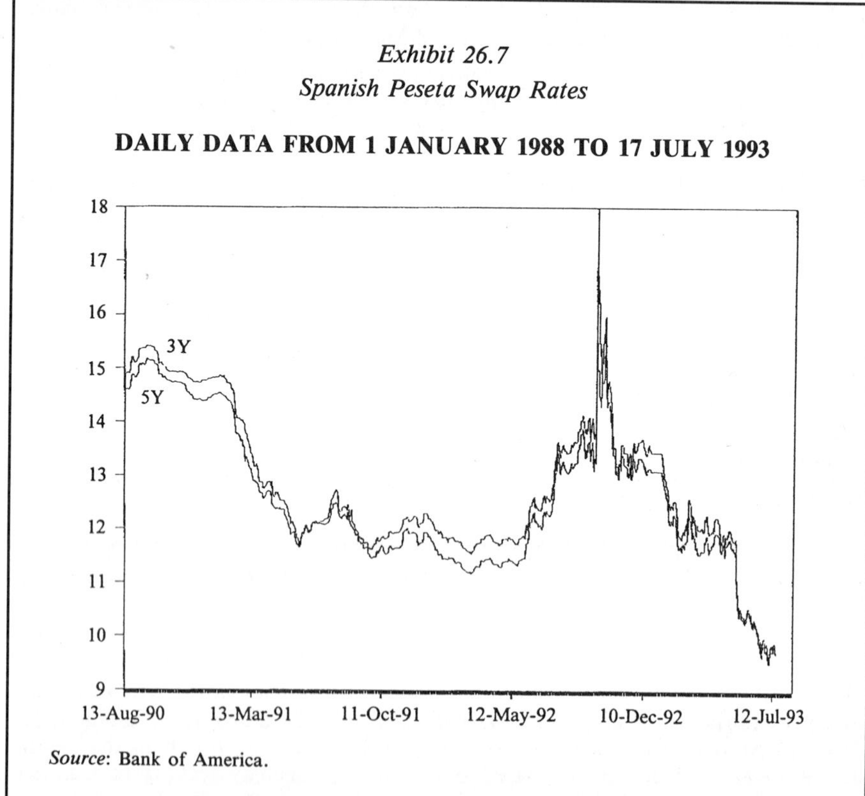

Source: Bank of America.

BELGIAN FRANC/LUXEMBOURG FRANC SWAP/DERIVATIVE MARKETS

Origins

The BFR/LUF swap market is quite unique. The markets in the two currencies are highly integrated reflecting a number of special factors.

The integrated structure is dictated by the following:

- Belgium and Luxembourg are connected through the Union Economique Belgo-Luxembourg (UEBL or BLEU) under which the two currencies are linked to one another and currency, monetary policy, central bank and exchange regulations are common to the two countries (see discussion below).
- The BFR market is subject to a variety of restrictions including:
  - — withholding tax of 10% (prior to 1990, withholding tax level was 25%);
  - — restrictions by the Belgian authorities preventing the development of a Eurobond market in BFR and active discouragement of disguised Euro-BFR offerings.

Historically, an additional factor creating an impetus for the particular market structure has been foreign exchange controls imposed by the Belgian Central Bank whereby it operated a dual-currency exchange rate system consisting of the controlled rate for commercial transactions (BEC) and the free, financial rate (BEF). This restriction on foreign exchange transactions was abolished in March 1992 in line with the harmonisation within the EEC which took place in 1992. From this time onwards, the BFR and LUF have traded in parallel with DEM.

Structure

The BFR/LUF swap market is driven almost exclusively by the Luxembourg franc bond market. This bond market owes its existence to the Belgian withholding tax, the Belgian restriction preventing the issue of BFR Eurobonds and the linkage between the two currencies.

Issuers of LUF Eurobonds/private placements, with minor exceptions, swap the proceeds of the issue. The swaps are undertaken primarily into US$ LIBOR (approximately 50-60%) and floating rate BFR, priced off the Belgian Interbank Offered Rate (BIBOR) (approximately 10-20%). Swaps out of LUF into DEM and FFR have been an increasing feature of the market, reflecting issuance of senior and subordinated debt by European banks.

The BFR/LUF swap market is dominated by the following products:

- fixed BFR/floating US$ LIBOR currency swaps; and
- fixed BFR/floating rate BIBOR interest rate swaps.

Historically, issuers of LUF bonds have assumed the political risks represented by the currency linkage between Belgium and Luxembourg. This risk has been assumed by transacting a BFR swap against an LUF issue which exposed the issuer to the risk of decoupling of the exchange rate and the resultant inefficiency of the hedge against the bond payments. In recent years, a number of issuers have transferred this risk to the provider of the swap which has structured the swap as an LUF swap, absorbing the BFR/LUF relativity risk into its portfolio for some additional margin on the transaction.

More recently, a small market in fixed LUF against floating LUF has commenced. The difficulty with this market is the absence of a true market short-term interbank rate in LUF. The Luxembourg Interbank Offered Rate (LUXIBOR "LXBO" screen on Reuters) is extremely illiquid and not a true market benchmark, creating a number of difficulties for these types of transactions.

The market dynamics of the BFR/LUF swap market is driven by demand for fixed rate BFR funding. The payers of fixed rate BFR typically raise floating rate BFR (priced off BIBOR) or US$ LIBOR funding and swap it into fixed rates through the swap. The swap, in turn, provides the driving mechanism for the LUF bond market.

The major payers of fixed rate BFR include:

- a number of Belgian state utilities and authorities (particularly at long end of maturity curve);
- Belgian corporations (2-5 year maturities);
- foreign corporations with operations in the Benelux countries (2-7 years); and
- Belgian banks and foreign banks with Belgian operations active, particularly, in mortgage lending.

The primary impetus to paying fixed rates in these swaps is classical asset-liability management requirements. For example, Belgian state utilities and corporations would typically utilise the swap to generate cost-effective fixed rate funding for their portfolios. Foreign corporations would utilise currency swaps to typically hedge their balance sheet exposures in the currency. In a similar manner, Belgian banks would utilise swaps either for balance sheet management purposes to match portfolios of fixed rate assets such as mortgage loans or to position their portfolios for interest rate movements.

Additional demand for paying fixed rate in these swaps is generated by asset swaps entailing repackaging of both seasoned LUF bonds from the secondary market as well as BFR government bonds. As discussed below, depending on swap rates, opportunities to repackage these assets at attractive spreads above LIBOR which are then placed with banks as floating rate investments are an important component of the market.

Paying interest also exists from banks seeking to position/arbitrage within the ECU basket and also to trade BFR/LUF relativities relative to the DEM. An additional source of speculative interest relates to trading BFR/LUF swaps against the Belgian futures market. This segment of the market is developing, a major factor being the activity of Benelux asset managers who increasingly enter into asset swaps as between Belgium government bonds and DEM or NLG swaps or Bunds with BEF/LUF swaps. International investors active in asset swaps often also exert significant influence on the market.

Market/pricing conventions/hedging

BFR/LUF swaps are quoted, generally, on 30/360 day annual basis for new issues and actual 365 for interest rate swaps. The floating rate component, where it is BFR, is priced off BIBOR (Reuters Screen "BEZO").

The BFR/LUF swap market prices off the LUF bond market and new issue activity in that sector. The LUF bond market is a unique market driven by the nature of the investors, tax factors and the interest rate relationships as between the BFR/LUF bloc and the development in DEM interest rates.

The LUF bond market remains a predominantly retail market. Investor demand traditionally focuses on corporate issuers (particularly those with high name recognition) in the 3-5 year maturity section and high credit quality bank or sovereign/supra national issuers in longer maturity. The inverse yield curve environment of the early 1990s has somewhat altered this investment pattern with significant demand for longer-term issues in the 7-12 year sector. The investor market does not appear to differentiate between senior and subordinated debt, making the LUF market one of the cheapest source of Tier II bank capital, albeit in small amounts.

Investor activity is dominated by tax factors—withholding taxes and, more importantly, inheritance taxes. The desire to avoid inheritance taxes of 25-35% is a central feature of this market.

The market has also been affected by cross-border fund flows from Germany. As a result of fiscal and tax changes in Germany, a substantial amount of retail DEM investment funds shifted into Luxembourg. This funds flow supported the DEM Euro-market as well as German issuers of subordinated LUF bonds. This German investment was primarily recycled into Germany through the Luxembourg banks and the Luxembourg subsidiaries of German banks.

Pricing in the BFR/LUF swap market is influenced by the yields on Belgian government bonds. Another major factor is DEM rates with movements in German rates having an often major influence on LUF bond yields.

Belgium has a reasonably developed market for government obligations. These bonds, known as OLO (Obligations Lineaires-Lineaire Obligaties), modelled on the French OAT.

The relativities between the BFR government bond yields, swap rates and the yields on the LUF issues are closely related. Where the swap rate rises relative to the BFR government bond rate and the LUF bond yields, the availability of an arbitrage window leads to an increase in a new issue activity. Issuers undertake LUF issues which are swapped into floating rate funding. Where the swap rate decreases relative to the BFR bond rate and the LUF bond yields, opportunities exist to purchase either BFR government bonds and seasoned LUF issues to repackage them as asset swaps for the banking market at attractive yields over LIBOR or BIBOR, as noted above.

The major participants in the BFR/LUF swap market are the Belgian banks, Belgian subsidiaries of major French banks and, primarily, London-based swap/derivative houses with active European operations.

Swap positions in BFR/LUF are typically hedged utilising Belgian government bonds. However, increasingly, swap positions are hedged utilising BIBOR futures and the Belgian government bond futures traded on the Belgian Futures and Options Exchange (BELFOX) which commenced operations in September 1991 in co-operation with the European Options Exchange in Amsterdam. In addition, the availability of asset swaps is often utilised by market makers to hedge their risk positions to the purchase of seasoned LUF issues with the objective of repackaging these assets.

A constraint in market making in the BFR/LUF market is that where a dealer takes on a significant position where it is paid fixed LUF against receipt of BIBOR or US$ LIBOR creates a significant surplus cash position in LUF. The difficulties with investing the LUF, because of the illiquidity of the LUF interbank market, creates difficulties in managing this position.

Future directions

The major issue for the BFR/LUF swap market is the future status of the UEBL or BLEU relationship between the two countries. In early 1993, it was announced that, consistent with European Community policies, Luxembourg was considering creating an independent central bank with an independent currency and monetary policy. This announcement created significant uncertainty in the BFR/LUF swap market as well as in the LUF primary/new issues market. A decoupling of the currency would, to a substantial degree, rob the LUF primary market of its rationale and result in significant realignments of swap rates. Even before this announcement, a number of participants in the swap market have, as a policy matter, refused to take on the BFR/LUF realignment risk and consequently do not make markets in swaps in this sector except where transactions can be exactly matched.

A possible outcome could be that to comply with the terms of the European Monetary Union which requires Luxembourg to have its own central bank, the Luxembourg Central Bank could be a "branch" of the Belgian Central Bank. The medium-term structural implication of these developments are clearly likely to be of significance.

SCANDINAVIAN CURRENCY SWAPS

Scandinavian swap market consists of, primarily, markets in Swedish and Danish krona swaps. In addition, a market in Norwegian krone and Finnish markka also exists. These markets are relatively small reflecting the relative sizes of domestic and international capital markets in the relevant currencies.

Scandinavian swap markets experienced significant difficulty in the context of tensions within the ERM in late August/early September 1992. As a result of action by Swedish authorities to defend the currency, marginal overnight rates were pushed up to 75% pa. This had the impact of effectively paralysing activity in the swap market in not only Swedish krona but in other Scandinavian currencies. Interbank swap trading almost totally ceased and payers of floating rate Swedish krona were forced to endure floating rate resets for periods of three months at 27% pa (as high as 500% pa was reached). Bid-offer spreads widened to over 100bps pa.

Orderly trading eventually resumed with rates reverting to pre-crisis levels. Whether these events have the impact of causing long-term damage to the Scandinavian swap market remains to be seen.

Swedish krona swap market

Swedish krona interest rate swap market originated in 1986 with initial transactions entailing payments of an annual fixed rate against receipt of three month Swedish treasury bill rates. Subsequently, the development of the Stockholm Interbank Offered Rate (STIBOR), effectively a LIBOR equivalent domestic Swedish krona deposit rate, has replaced treasury bill rates as a floating rate reference standard.

The Swedish krona swap market developed further following abolition of exchange controls in 1989. Cross-currency Swedish krona swaps also developed, complementing Swedish krona interest rate swaps, reflecting the following factors:

- Emergence of basket arbitrage reflecting the fact that the Swedish krona was fixed to a trade weighted basket of 15 currencies. The opportunity to lower interest rates, reflecting the lower weighted interest rates of the underlying currency baskets, approximately 2-3% lower than equivalent Swedish krona interest rates, facilitated the use of swaps as a cost effective means to manage liabilities.

- The emergence of a small market in Swedish krona Eurobonds which has complemented the domestic fixed rate market, where borrowings were dominated by the Kingdom and Swedish mortgage institution.
- The high degree of international involvement of Swedish corporations and corresponding need for active foreign exchange risk management.

The Swedish krona interest rate swap market has also benefited from interest rate volatility in the Swedish economy which has focused attention on interest rate risk management.

Swedish krona interest rate swaps are generally priced off either benchmark Swedish government bonds, available for maturities between one and sixteen years as well as mortgage bonds launched by banks and mortgage institutions. Complementing these cash hedging tools are futures and options contract traded through the Stockholm Options Market (OM). Futures contracts based on five, seven and ten year notional government bonds are traded on the options market as are option contracts on five year notional government bonds. The short end of the maturity range, futures on treasury bills are also actively traded.

Swedish krona swap rate typically used to track mortgage bond yields. However, government bond yields have become more important as a benchmark in recent years. *Exhibit 26.8* sets out historical information on Swedish swap rates.

Danish krone swap market

This market has its origins in 1985 when the first Danish krone interest rate and currency swap was completed against one of the first Eurobond issues denominated in Danish krone undertaken by the World Bank. Since that time, the market has developed amongst financial institutions, municipally owned regional Danish gas companies and Scandinavian corporations. In addition, the Kingdom of Denmark itself has made extensive use of swaps in connection with portfolio management of its borrowings to finance its activities as well as the balance of payments deficit.

Danish interest rate swap markets utilise the Copenhagen Interbank Offered Rate (CIBOR) as the official floating rate Danish interbank reference rate. The market structure encompasses three separate tiers:

- the interest rate swap market in Danish krone (fixed rate against CIBOR (the largest sector));
- currency swaps encompassing fixed krone against floating six month US$ LIBOR (this market is not as big as Swedish krona/US$ LIBOR swaps);
- currency swaps entailing fixed krone against floating six month DEM LIBOR.

The market has grown dramatically in recent years with narrowing bid offer spreads with larger amounts and maturity dates stretching out to ten years with some transactions of even longer maturities being completed. Currently, Danish krone interest rate and currency swap transactions are quoted for any amount between DKR25m and DKR1,000m (average size DKR100m).

The Danish krone swap market, like its Scandinavian counterpart, relies significantly on the government bond market as well as on interest in the corporate bond market, domestically. The Danish krone swap rates reflect the fixed rate in these markets.

Exhibit 26.8
SEK/SEK Interest Rate Swap

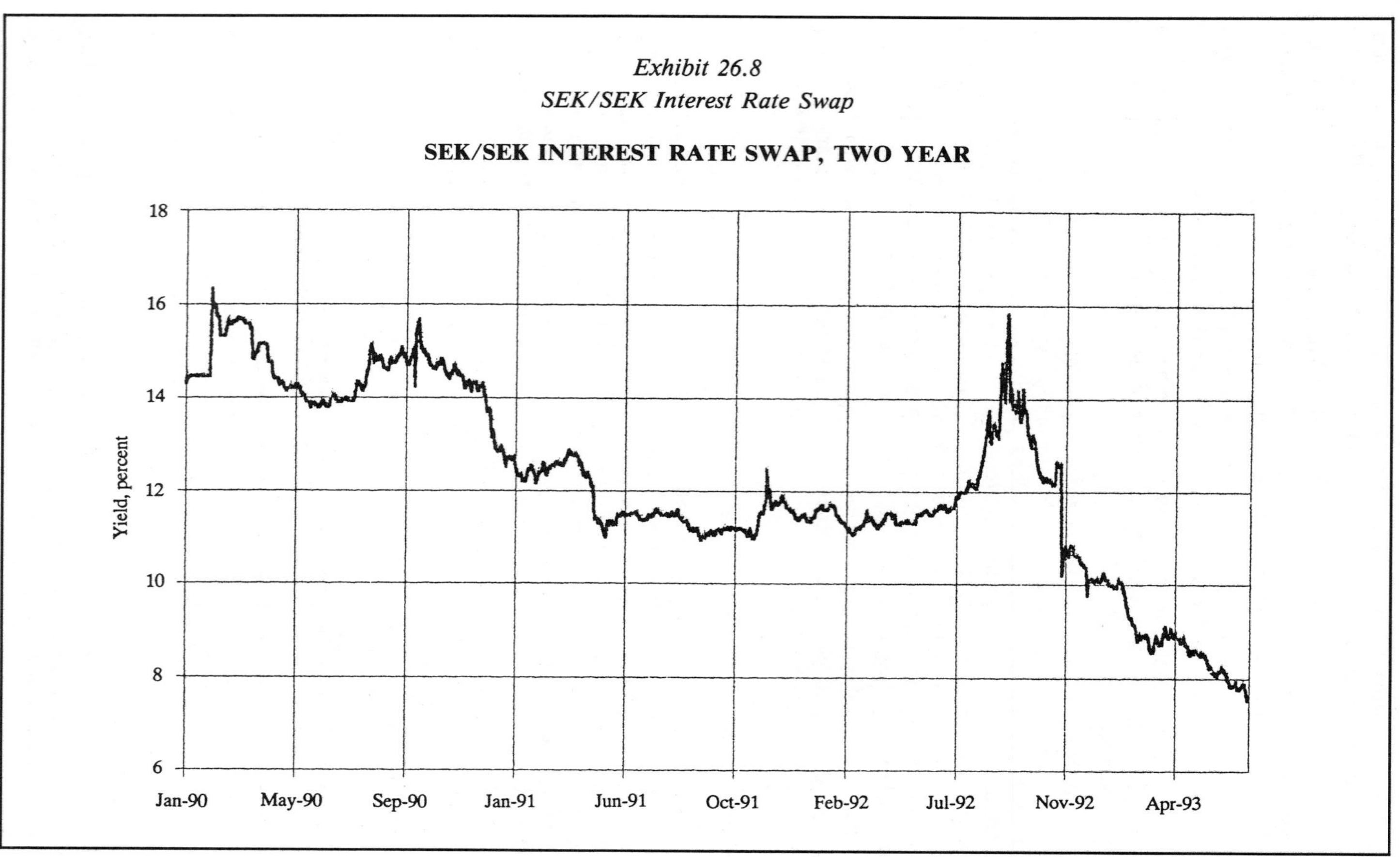

Exhibit 26.8—continued

SEK/SEK INTEREST RATE SWAP, FIVE YEAR

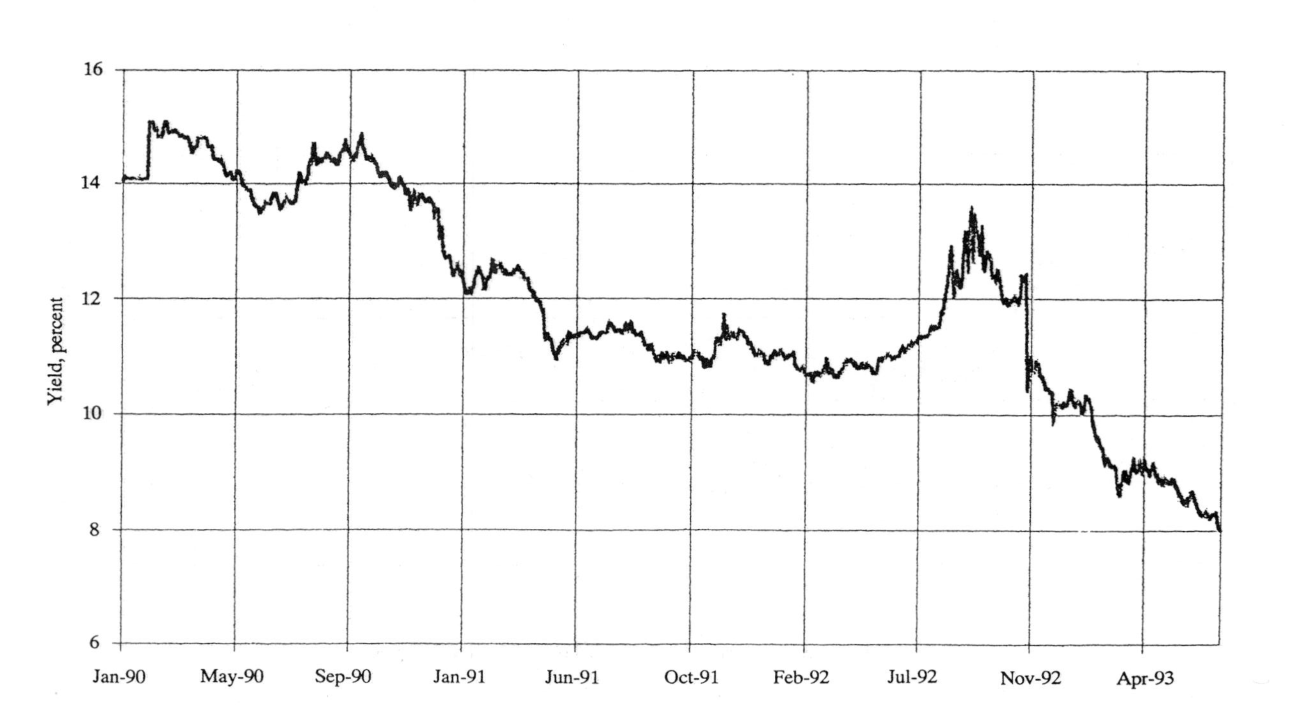

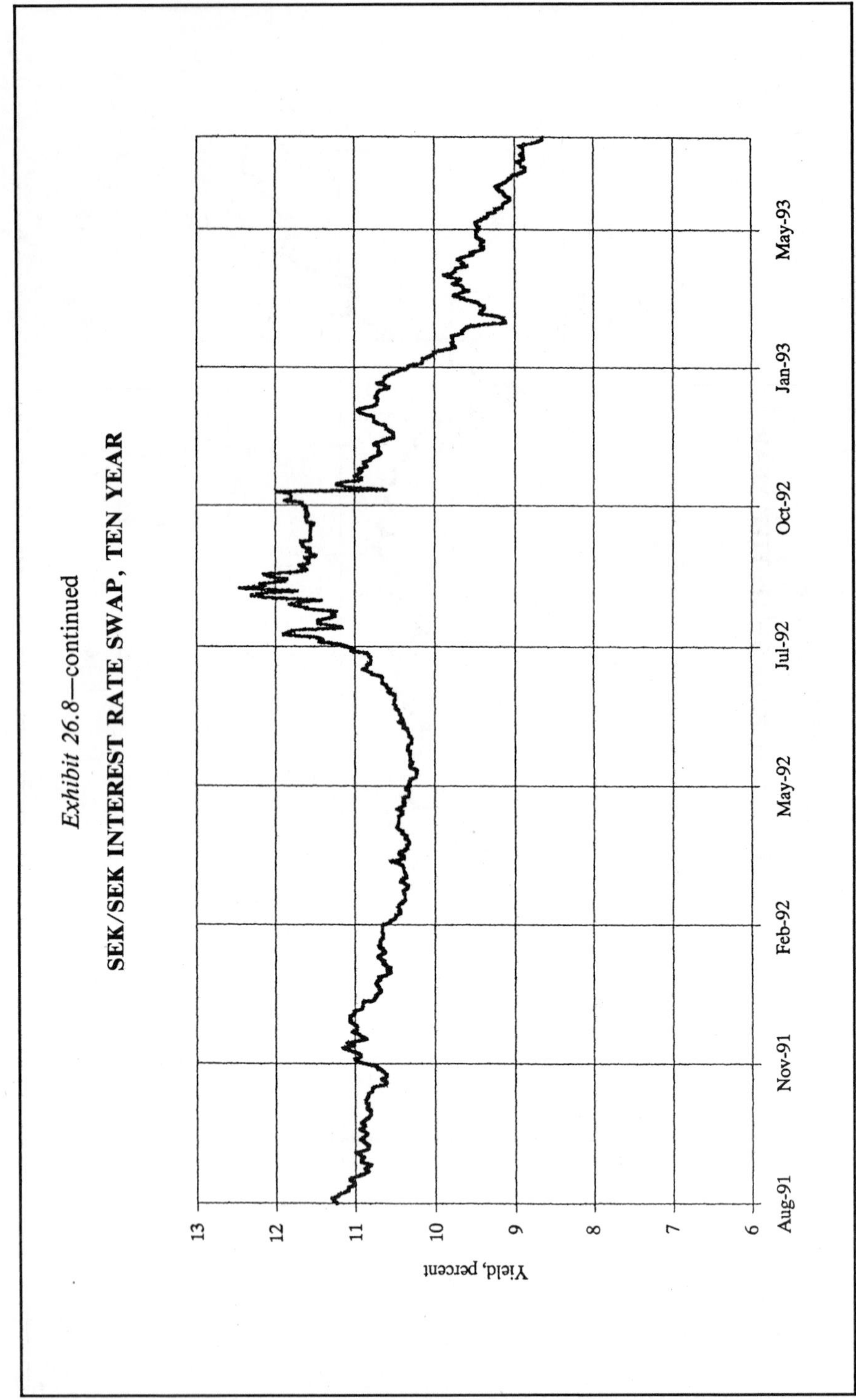

Exhibit 26.8—continued

SEK/SEK INTEREST RATE SWAP, TEN YEAR

Exhibit 26.8—continued

SPREAD BETWEEN FIVE YEAR SEK/SEK SWAP AND FIVE YEAR GOVERNMENT BOND

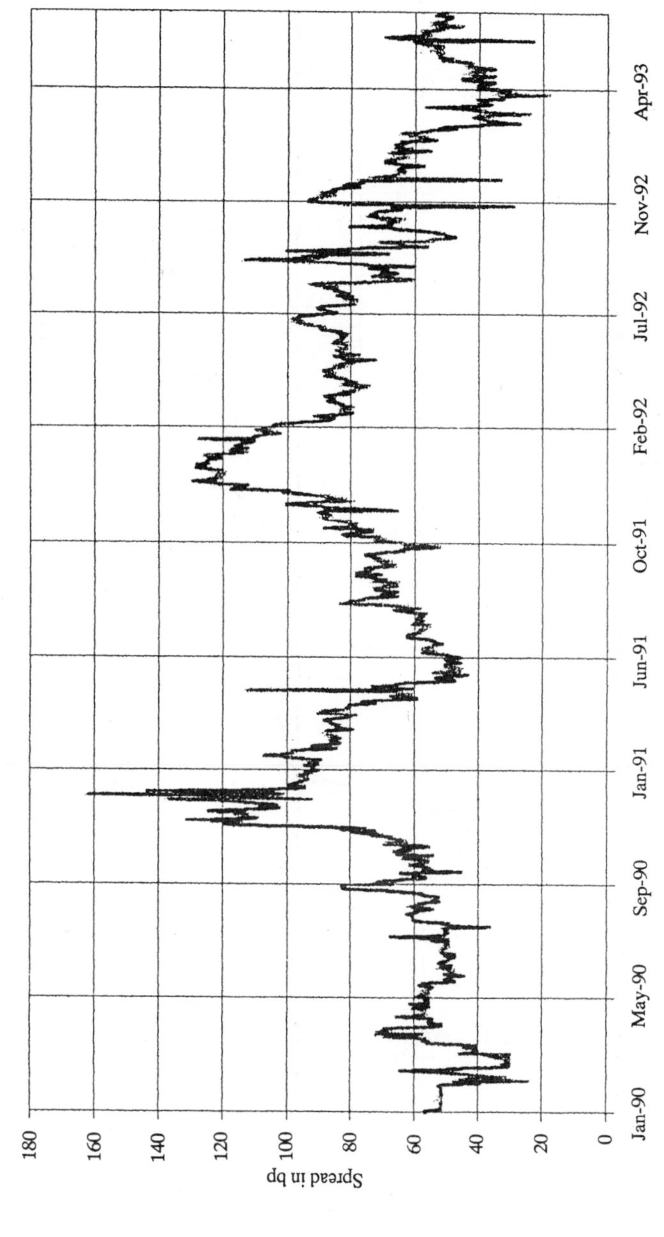

Exhibit 26.8—continued

SPREAD BETWEEN FIVE YEAR SEK/SEK SWAP AND FIVE YEAR MORTGAGE BOND

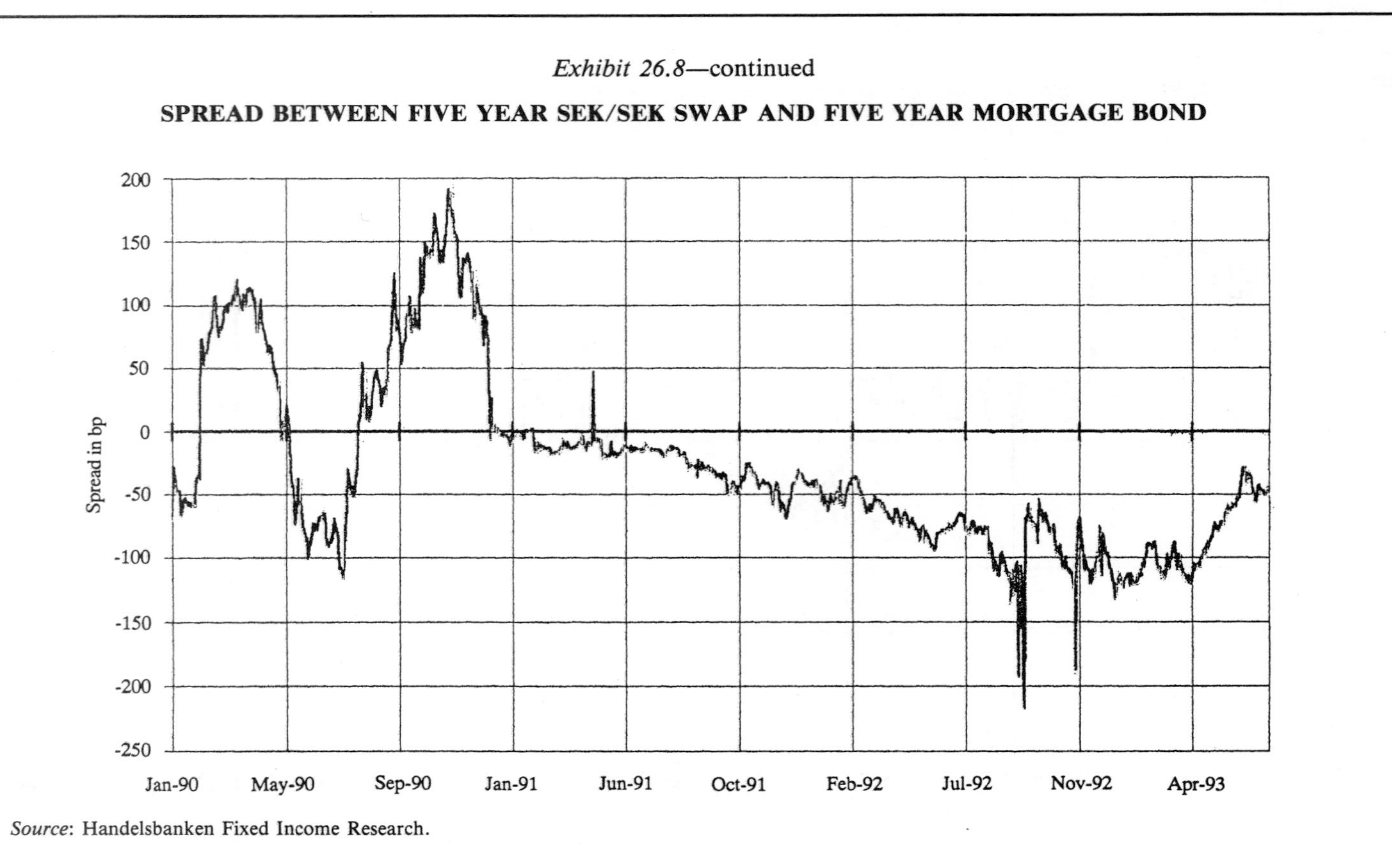

Source: Handelsbanken Fixed Income Research.

Market sophistication in Danish krone is increasing reflecting growing interest from a number of Dutch corporations who have begun to utilise interest rate and currency swap markets for asset liability management purposes. Newer products such as krone caps and floors and a variety of other derivative instruments have also evolved.

OTHER EUROPEAN CURRENCY SWAPS

Nascent swap markets exist in a variety of other currencies. The major relevant currencies include the Portuguese escudo, Irish punts and Finnish markka.

These relatively young and developing markets are motivated by different factors.

The Portuguese escudo swap market is driven by the increasingly internationalised escudo bond market, dubbed the Navigator Market. Swaps from escudos into US$ LIBOR transacted by these new issue arbitrage participants against interest from Portuguese companies seeking fixed rate escudos as well as foreign corporations seeking to hedge escudo exposures as a result of business investments in Portugal.

Small markets in Irish punt interest rate and, to a lesser extent, currency swaps exist.

Emerging markets include the Greek drachma market where longer-dated foreign exchange transactions are evident.

Major factor driving the emergence of these swap markets, particularly the pace of development will be the process of deregulation of capital markets in these currencies.

A factor facilitating the development of swap currencies in the minor European currencies, at least where the country is a member of the EEC and European monetary system, is the capacity to simulate swap transactions in the relevant currency by means of an ECU swap where exposures to certain currencies are neutralised by transacting opposite swaps in those currencies: see discussion in Chapter 25.

Chapter 27

A$ and NZ$ Swap and Derivative Markets

A$ SWAP AND DERIVATIVE MARKETS

History and development

Origins

The A$ swap market "proper" commenced in the second half of 1983, with two transactions between, first, the Commonwealth Trading Bank (as it was then known) and the Australian Industries Development Corporation (AIDC) and a subsequent transaction between the Commonwealth Trading Bank and the Primary Industries Bank of Australia (PIBA).

In the first of these transactions, the Commonwealth Bank entered into a five year interest rate swap with AIDC for a notional principal of A$30m, whereby the Commonwealth Bank paid AIDC fixed rate A$ in return for receiving floating rate A$, priced off BBR, the interbank floating money market rate benchmark being the rate at which major bank accepted bills are traded. The swap, significantly, was undertaken against a EuroAustralian dollar bond issue launched by AIDC. The issue was for five years for A$30m with a coupon of 14.00% pa and an all-in semi-annual cost to the issuer of about 14.10% pa. This was in a market environment where the prevailing market rate for five year Australian government bonds was approximately 15.20-15.30% pa.

The motivation for the swap was the need by AIDC to convert its fixed rate A$ funding into floating rate A$ to match its portfolio of A$ loans which were on a floating rate basis pricing off BBR. The Commonwealth Bank entered into the transaction locking in fixed rate funding at an attractive spread *under* the then prevailing government bond rate. The fixed rate funding generated was available either for on-lending to clients, for the bank's balance sheet for asset liability management purposes, or as part of a specific arbitrage whereby Commonwealth government securities could have been bought to lock away an attractive arbitrage spread. The rationale for the PIBA transaction was almost identical.

The two transactions which commenced the A$ swap market were significant for a number of reasons:

- They established clearly a linkage to primary debt markets in A$, most notably the EuroAustralian dollar bond market.
- They highlighted an unsatisfied requirement for instruments to enable a wide category of institutions to better match their asset liability portfolios.
- The transactions pinpointed a number of pricing anomalies as between the domestic A$ and offshore A$ markets.

It is significant that these concerns which allowed the initial transactions in the A$ market to be undertaken have continued to dominate this sector of the global swap market. An interesting aspect of these transactions was that the A$ swap market commenced with *interest rate swaps* rather than currency swaps which have historically opened swap markets in a number of currencies.

It should be noted that prior to August 1983, more precisely since 1981, a substantial market in short-term interest rate swaps had already existed within Australia. These were transactions involving the purchase and sale of bills at fixed rates, that is, essentially interest rate swaps. These forward sales and purchases of bills were undertaken by a small number of financial institutions with the price risk being hedged through the 90 day bank bill interest rate futures contract which had traded on the Sydney Futures Exchange since October 1978.

Phases of development

The development of the A$ swap market can be divided into two distinct phases:

- 1983 to 1984 when the major receivers of fixed rate A$ in swap transactions were AIDC, PIBA and the Australian Resources Development Bank (ARDB) as well as semi-government institutions;
- mid to late 1980s when the major receivers of fixed rate A$ were non-Australian issuers of A$ securities in the Eurobond and, more recently, Yankee markets;
- post 1989 which was characterised by declining Australian dollar Eurobond new issuance and the emergence of State semi-government authorities, the A$ domestic bond market and highly structured private placement transactions has the major receivers of fixed rate A$.

The distinction between the two periods is, in practice, less clearly delineated than might be assumed.

To 1983/84

The key factor underlying the evolution of the A$ swap market has been the development of an international market in A$ securities. Although international purchases of A$ securities commenced in the mid 1970s, until 1985 the primary issuers were Australian entities with a genuine demand for A$ funding. For example, during 1983 and 1984, AIDC and PIBA issued over A$200m of securities in the Eurobond market. These two issuers accounted for almost half the EuroAustralian dollar issues in that period. Both entities used their access to these cost effective fixed rate A$ to generate floating rate funding to support their asset portfolio utilising A$ interest rate swaps. Both PIBA and ARDB also swapped off the relatively cheap domestic fixed rate retail funding basis which they possessed.

During this period, the other major receiver of fixed rates in the A$ swap market were the semi-government authorities. These entities which enjoyed good access to fixed rate funding in the domestic market had predominantly fixed rate debt portfolios and a number of innovative statutory authorities took the opportunity to convert some of their debt into a floating rate basis via interest rate swaps as part of an overall restructuring of the interest rate basis of their debt.

During this period, the primary interest in paying fixed rates came from financial institutions interested in raising fixed rate funding to close out gaps in their asset liability portfolios and from corporations without alternative access to fixed rate A$ funding. Given that for much of this period the yield curve was sharply inverse, a natural cost incentive existed for undertaking such transactions.

Mid to late 1980s

However, in 1985 international demand for A$ securities reached an unprecedented level. Attracted by the high level of A$ interest rates as well as opportunities for currency diversification, successive waves of investors began to purchase A$ securities, primarily in the form of EuroAustralian dollar bonds, in unprecedented volumes. These investors included European retail and institutional investors, Japanese institutions, and United States institutions.

Within Europe itself, interest in A$ securities expanded from investors in the Benelux countries to other more substantial investors groups, such as retail German investors and the Swiss market.

This evolution in the investor base created a bias which prompted further growth in the A$ swap market. The new investors in A$ securities had a preference for bearer Eurobonds, free of any withholding tax, issued by organisations with which the investor base was familiar. This investor preference dictated to a large extent the form (Eurobond) and the type of issuer which now came to dominate the international A$ market. When in 1986, United States investors joined the numbers of investors seeking A$ securities, this clientele effect was also evident because United States domestic investors had a strong preference for United States Securities Exchange Commission registered issues, criteria which very few Australian borrowers could satisfy.

This shift in the structure of the A$ securities market meant that A$ borrowers ceased, almost totally, to directly borrow in A$, relying instead on a swap undertaken with an issuer who utilised the A$ securities issue as part of a new issue arbitrage transaction. These new issuers included a number of sovereign and supranational borrowers including the World Bank, a number of international banks, primarily German banks reflecting the underlying investor demand within Germany, as well as a number of well known United States corporations with good name recognition among European retail investors. Examples of the last category include companies such as Pepsico, McDonald's and IBM.

International interest in A$ securities after the initial surge proved to be volatile, although the A$ established itself as a significant, though minor, international currency. Interest rate movements, particularly interest rate differentials relative to the other major currencies and the behaviour of the A$ exchange rate shaped the pattern of investment and disinvestment from this sector of the international bond market. For example, in the second half of 1985, 1986 and 1987, A$ Eurobond activity slowed and, on a number of occasions, ceased completely. During these periods, borrowers with access to domestic fixed rate A$, primarily the semi-government authorities, moved quickly to resume their roles as major receivers of fixed rate A$ in swap transactions.

Late 1980s to present

As noted previously, the structure of the A$ swap market altered significantly in the late 1980s. The major change was the declining A$ Eurobond issuance levels which reduced the importance of this particular sector as receivers of fixed rate A$. The reduction in demand for levels of A$ Eurobond issues caused the funding arbitrage available to issuers to diminish and A$ Eurobond related swap activity declined. Initially, this development in the market put pressure on A$ swap spreads.

However, certain changes in the domestic fixed interest market and in overseas demand for A$ securities caused the nature of A$ fixed rate receivers to alter. During this period, the State semi-government authorities emerged as a significant receiver of fixed A$ as well as A$ payers as they became aggressive asset liability managers. In addition, fixed rate A$ receiving interest emerged in connection with the resurgence in the domestic A$ bond markets as well as the emergence of large volumes of swapped structured private placements, primarily A$/yen dual currency debt issues, placed with Japanese investors.

While the influence of the private placements into Japan for the development of the A$ swap market has diminished, the State semi-government authorities and issuers in the A$ domestic bond market continue to be major influences in the pattern of activity in the A$ swap market.

Structure of A$ swap market

The structure of the A$ swap market corresponds closely to that of the US$ market. The market is essentially split into two segments:

- short-dated interest rate swaps, primarily under two years;
- longer-dated swaps, usually with maturities between three and ten years, with a marked concentration in the three to five year range.

The difference between the two segments lies in the hedging mechanisms utilised and the consequent price behaviour. As in the United States market, the short-dated swaps tend to be hedged through the A$ interest rate futures market. This market is both liquid and volatile with interest rates showing a close correspondence to changes in money market conditions and movement in short-term interest rates. The long-term swap market is priced off Commonwealth and, more recently, semi-government government bonds and hedged by buying and selling these securities.

The A$ swap market, particularly in the over two year segment, is made up of three separate segments:

- fixed A$ and US$ LIBOR currency swaps;
- fixed A$ and floating A$ interest rate swaps; and
- floating A$ and floating US$ currency swaps.

The structure of the A$ swap market is set out in *Exhibit 27.1*.

The participants in each sector of the swap market are slightly different.

In the late 1980s, issuance of A$ Eurobonds declined sharply. This reflected a variety of factors including:

- a narrowing yield differential between A$ and European currencies;
- a shift in emphasis from European retail investors who became pre-occupied with continental political developments;
- increased concern among investors about the currency risk entailed in A$ Eurobond issues.

As demand for A$ Eurobond issues declined, the structure of the A$ swap market altered. Several new classes of aggressive fixed rate A$ receivers emerged including:

- the State semi-government authorities;
- issuers of A$ bonds in the domestic bond market;
- issuers of structured private placements.

The State semi-governments have always been active participants in the A$ swap markets. In the late 1980s, semi-governments increased both the level and pattern of participation. This reflected a number of factors:

- The establishment by several states of centralised borrowing authorities, such as the New South Wales Treasury Corporation, with the objective of undertaking more active and efficient debt and liability management.
- A shift in the public sector borrowing requirement from the federal or Commonwealth government to the States. This was reflected in a decline in the

Exhibit 27.1
Structure of A$ Swap Market

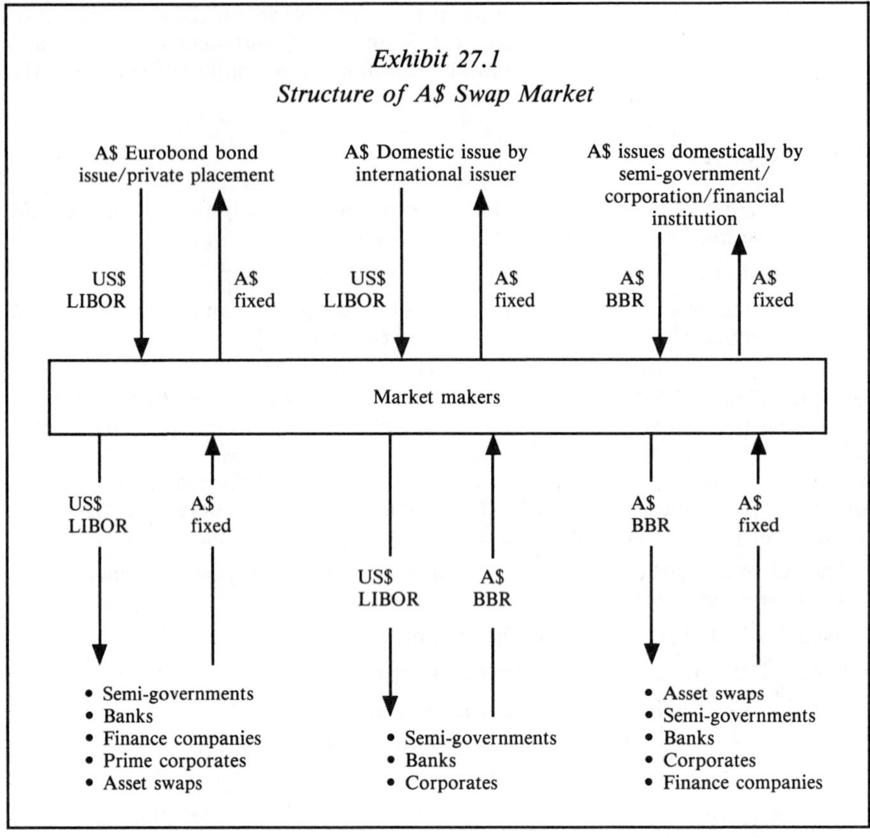

level of Commonwealth bonds outstanding which allowed the States to emerge as the most active issuers of high quality fixed rate obligations.

- An active approach to asset-liability management.

These factors manifested themselves in the form of a substantial proportion of the fixed rate debt of State and semi-government authorities being consolidated into a few large liquid lines of inscribed stock (colloquially referred to as "hot stocks"). A second feature was the active use of the A$ swap market for asset-liability management with these authorities being both fixed rate payers and receivers as they actively traded the spread between the swap rate and their own fixed rate debt on issue: see discussion below.

In the late 1980s, the domestic fixed interest market for corporate and financial institution debt re-emerged. Issuance was dominated by bank term Certificates of Deposits (transferable CDs), mortgage-backed securities and government-backed/guaranteed bonds (typically, from Commonwealth or State government owned entities). Small levels of issuance from corporations was evident, at least in the initial phase of the market, although corporate interest in the domestic corporate bond market has been very limited.

This market evolved, in 1991, into a market for the issuance of securities by non-Australian entities in the domestic market. Issues by the World Bank, Eurofima,

SEK and EIB, among others, were completed. This market was dubbed the "Matilda" bond market.

The emergence of the domestic bond market provided a new supply of fixed rate A$ receivers. A number of issuers, particularly international issuers in the Matilda market, typically swapped fixed rate A$ funds raised into either floating rate A$ or into US$ LIBOR. Conversely, the lack of access for industrial corporations to the corporate bond market meant that these corporations continue to utilise swaps to generate cost effective fixed rate funding as part of general interest rate risk management. The resurgence of the domestic bond market also opened up opportunities for asset swaps involving debt on issue in the domestic market.

In the period between late 1988 and early 1990, a large variety of structured issues, targeted to Japanese investors, were completed. These transactions which took, generally, the form of A$/JPY dual currency bonds and variations thereon were designed for investors seeking an interest rate yield pick up in exchange for assuming limited currency risk. These transactions provided a further supply of fixed rate receivers, particularly at the longer end of the yield curve. The importance of these structured private placements is high, with probably 50 to 60% of A$ currency swap business being driven by transactions of this type during the relevant period.

The payers of fixed rate A$, however, vary significantly between the various market segments. The main payers of fixed rate A$ against receipt of US$ LIBOR tend to be financial institutions, semi-government authorities, finance companies or a number of major corporations. In the case of financial institutions, the swap may be taken on as part of the bank's own balance sheet funding or alternatively as a position which will be shifted to clients either directly or indirectly by unbundling the swap into various components.

The participation of semi-governments as fixed rate payers is considerably more complex: see discussion below. Historically, many of the semi-government entities borrowed offshore in foreign currencies. The marked depreciation in the A$ in the 1985 to 1986 period led the semi-government entities, which had suffered severe currency losses, to change their liability management practices to undertake new funding, primarily in A$, as well as hedging their existing foreign currency exposures.

These entities also have annual allocations to borrow overseas which they have sought to utilise to achieve a greater degree of diversification of their funding sources. These factors have driven the semi-government entities to enter into swaps where they pay fixed rate A$ against receipt of US$ LIBOR to essentially hedge foreign currency borrowings back into A$. This is particularly so given that the semi-government entities have themselves become new issue arbitrage funders undertaking issues in overseas markets to generate cost-efficient floating rate US$ funds priced relative to LIBOR which are subsequently swapped back into A$. These fixed rate A$ may ultimately be swapped out into floating rate A$ depending on the liability management requirements of the particular institution.

Finance companies and corporations in the early 1980s began to enjoy significant access to floating rate US$ funding through note issuance facilities, transferable loan certificate facilities and other types of floating rate funding instruments. A number of finance companies and corporations, particularly where they did not have foreign currency denominated assets, swapped these US$ liabilities into fixed rate A$ liabilities through swaps.

A major incentive for all groups was the significantly lower fixed A$ cost achievable through these transactions. The significant swap arbitrage profits available in the A$ swap markets have allowed borrowers to achieve cost savings in the vicinity of 40-50bps pa on alternative direct sources of A$ funding.

The payers of fixed rate A$ against receipt of floating rate A$ have predominantly tended to be lower-rated corporates. The primary motivation for this group is their need to lock in fixed rates of interest on predominantly floating rate borrowings. In the negatively sloped yield curve environment of the early 1980s, an additional motivation was to ride down the yield curve with an extension of maturity to lower the absolute coupon borrowing cost. These transactions are structured either as interest rate swaps or as fixed rate bank bill facilities. Inevitably, these transactions are undertaken with a swap market maker, usually a bank or financial institution, on one side.

The floating US$ and floating A$ currency swap market has been dominated primarily by financial institutions, mainly banks, semi-government entities as well as a number of Australian corporates. This group enjoys access to relatively cost effective US$ funding, either through note issuance facilities, EuroCP facilities in the international money markets or United States CP programmes. A number of this group have converted these floating rate US$ liabilities into floating rate A$ liabilities on a term basis utilising this type of swap. Again, the all-in cost of floating rate A$ raised in this manner is typically lower than the cost of raising A$ in the domestic market.

A major impetus to this particular segment of the market came from the banking regulations applicable (now changed) which dictated that funds raised outside Australia did *not* attract the statutory reserve deposit reserve requirement. This made it particularly attractive for Australian banks to raise US$ overseas and swap them in this way into term A$ funding. However, recently announced changes which will see the phasing out of the statutory reserve deposit requirement will make this particular factor less relevant.

The floating US$/floating A$ swap market enjoyed a brief but spectacular period of growth in early 1986 when a series of A$ denominated FRNs, bearing margins substantially under BBR, were launched in the United States domestic market. These issues were swapped with Australian domestic institutions, primarily banks, who utilised the swaps to generate cost-effective A$ floating rate funding for their portfolios. Investor demand for these securities proved short-lived, closing this window very rapidly.

A substantial asset swap market in A$ provides a considerable volume of transactions whereby financial institutions pay fixed rate A$ against receipt of either A$ BBR or US$ LIBOR. The underlying assets being swapped are primarily fixed rate bonds, issued by finance companies and, to a lesser extent, semi-governments and corporations which are swapped into a floating rate basis as banking assets for a wide variety of financial institutions, primarily, a number of new licensed banks operating in Australia since 1985 and a significantly larger number of merchant banks that have commenced operations in the same period. Pricing anomalies in the highly illiquid secondary market for EuroAustralian dollars and Yankee A$ securities have also created sporadic asset swap opportunities which have fueled activity in the A$ swap market.

An increasing factor in the overall activity levels and structure of the A$ swap market has been interest in purely trading interest rate swaps. For example, during late 1986 and again in late 1987 when the EuroAustralian dollar bond market closed, a number of corporates unwound existing swaps to realise a capital profit to utilise the benefits as a subsidy on their net cost of funding. The windfall profits motivated a number of entities to begin trading swaps purely and simply on the basis of expected appreciation dictated by interest rate and, to a lesser extent, currency movements.

An additional source of volume has come from banks with substantial fixed asset portfolios held for reserve ratio purposes who have sought to hedge their investments against capital losses by entering into swaps to effectively create short positions against their bond portfolios in periods of increasing interest rates.

As previously noted, State government authorities, through the State treasury corporations, play a pivotal role in the pattern of activity in the A$ swap market. Led by the NSW Treasury Corporation which has established itself as the benchmark semi-government issuer by virtue of its credit rating as well as the liquidity in its securities, these authorities influence swap market in two ways:

- through the issuance of debt;
- the use of swaps and derivatives for asset liability management.

Major borrowing authorities utilise issuance of debt to regularly consolidate issues into substantial lines of securities to maintain liquidity and actively exploit pricing inefficiencies by repurchasing debt and thereby exert an influence on the benchmark against which swaps are priced. As discussed in greater detail below, the A$ swap market now prices off the NSW Treasury Corporation benchmark rates.

These borrowers complement their debt issuance activities through the use of swaps to manage its asset and liability portfolio in a number of ways:

- liability swaps to convert fixed rate issuance into floating-rate debt at substantial margins below the benchmark bank bill rate;
- asset related activity entailing the repurchase of debt by paying fixed rate against issuing floating-rate debt through the issue of promissory notes or commercial paper in the domestic money market.

Authorities typically use this activity to manage the swap-to-authority debt spread and to exploit market inefficiencies as a means for generating value. For example, the NSW Treasury Corporation has often taken advantage of the spread on its own securities increasing relative to swap spreads as lines of stock become shorter in maturity or less liquid as they are supplanted by newer hot stock lines. Under these circumstances, the corporation has sought to generate value by purchasing its short-dated stock in the secondary market and paying fixed in the swap market effectively lower the cost of its borrowings.

The role played by the State treasury corporations in the A$ swap market is unusual and, probably, without parallel in the global swap market.

Market conventions/pricing A$ swaps

Australian dollar interest rate swaps are priced off Commonwealth/State government bonds and are quoted as a spread relative to a comparable benchmark security. Interest rates are quoted against the 90 or 180 day BBR, usually determined with reference to Reuters screen "BBSW". Cross-currency swaps are quoted with reference to 90 or 180 day US$ LIBOR. The shorter end of the swap market is priced primarily off a strip of interest rate futures contracts.

While traditionally, A$ swaps have been priced off Commonwealth government bonds, in recent years, the swap to Commonwealth bond spread has been replaced by the swap to NSW Treasury Corporation (referred to as T-Corp) spread. The dominant role of the NSW Treasury Corporation and the State borrowing authority market has already been commented upon. This development reflects a variety of factors including:

- the reduction in the level of Commonwealth Government Bonds outstanding in the late 1980s reflecting Commonwealth government budget surpluses and reverse tenders designed to reduce federal debt;
- the substantial volume of semi-government debt issuance and their central role in the A$ swap market.

The pricing of A$ swaps is driven, to substantial degree, by hedging practices in the swap market. In practice, swap market makers utilise a variety of hedging instruments for hedging swap positions:

- use of the A$ bank bill interest rate futures contract (traded on the Sydney Futures Exchange (SFE)) to hedge short dated swaps up to two to three years in maturity;
- the use of Commonwealth government bonds or, more typically, semi-government bonds as well as interest rate futures contracts on three and ten year Commonwealth bonds traded on the SFE to hedge swaps of a longer maturity.

The SFE bank bill interest rate futures contract is now traded out to three years although liquidity continues to be concentrated in the front months. The lack of liquidity in the distant months has meant that short-dated swaps are priced either as strips of bank bill futures (often requiring stacking of the hedge) trading the swap as an absolute spread against the underlying semi-government, or less frequently Commonwealth government, bond of the same maturity.

Competition between these two methods of hedging tends to create a "kink" in or about the three year maturity point in the yield curve to mark the transition from swaps hedged in the bank bill interest rate futures to longer dated swaps priced against semi-government securities.

Longer-dated swaps with maturities of around three to five years are typically hedged against the three year Commonwealth bond futures contract. Longer-dated swaps are commonly hedged utilising the ten year Commonwealth bond futures contract. Both contracts have adequate liquidity in near months to facilitate hedging of temporary swap portfolio positions.

As an alternative, semi-government "hot stocks" are also used to hedge swap risk positions. The use of semi-government security as a hedging instrument has improved since the establishment by the State treasury corporations of very active security lending programmes which has facilitated short selling of these securities. The security lending programmes are not true "repo" arrangements and are fee based rather than market price driven. At times, this allows swap portfolio managers to short sell physical stocks at levels which are cheaper than the theoretical cost of running the short position, creating pricing anomalies in the swap market.

The strong correlation between the T-Corp bond market and swap spreads has encouraged the SFE to attempt to introduce a five year semi-government futures interest rate contract. However, after several attempts, the contract failed partly due to difficulties in making the contract deliverable.

Exhibit 27.2 sets out swap rates and spreads (relative to various underlying benchmarks) for A$ swaps of different maturities over recent years.

As is evident, A$ swap spreads relative to the underlying benchmarks can be volatile. However, in recent years the aggressive activity of the State treasury corporations, particularly T-Corp, has had a substantial impact on spread movements.

Exhibit 27.2

A$ Swap Rates and Spreads

TWO YEAR SWAP RATE

18 January 1991 to 16 April 1993

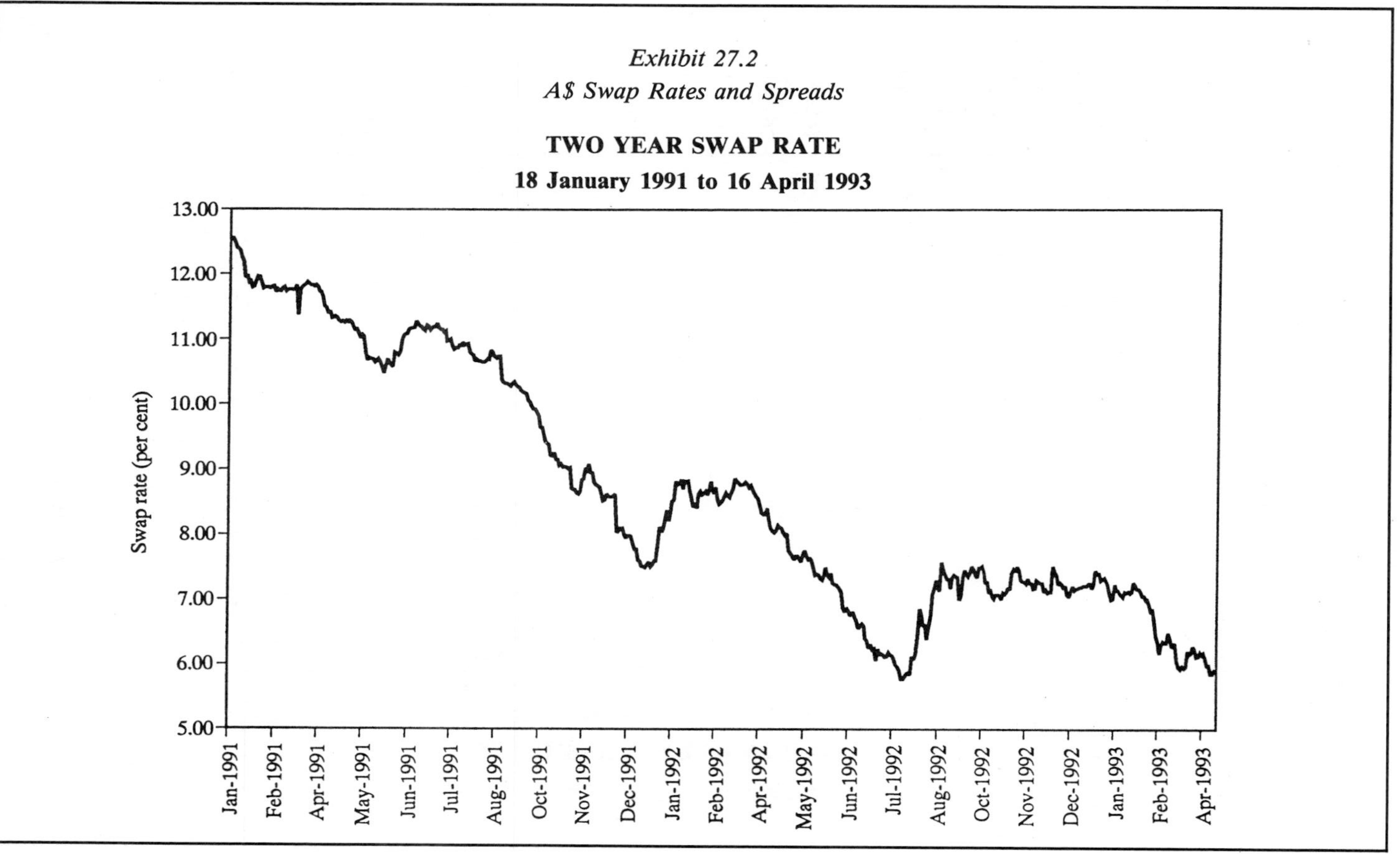

Exhibit 27.2—continued

THREE YEAR SWAP RATE

18 January 1991 to 16 April 1993

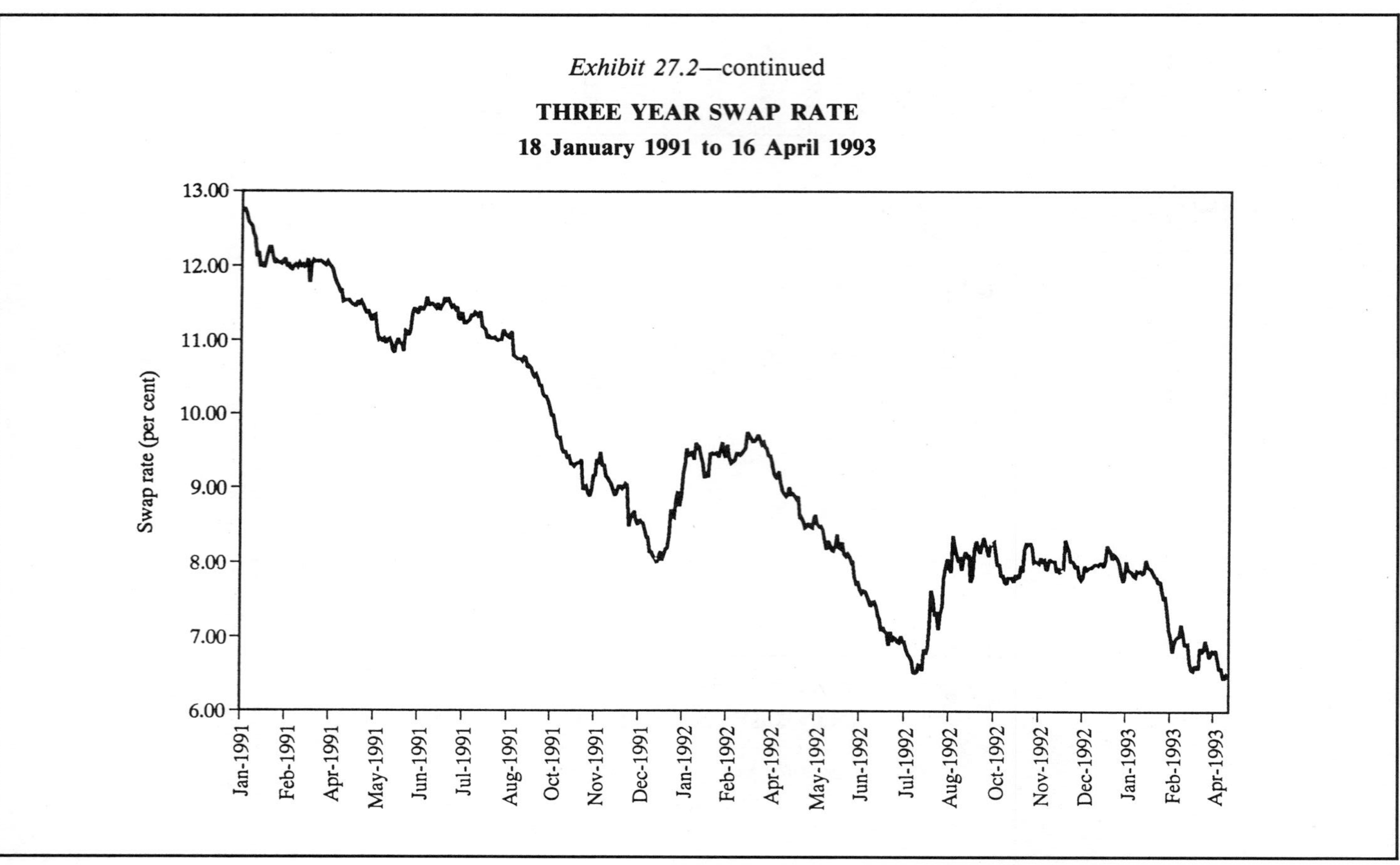

Exhibit 27.2—continued

FIVE YEAR SWAP RATE

18 January 1991 to 16 April 1993

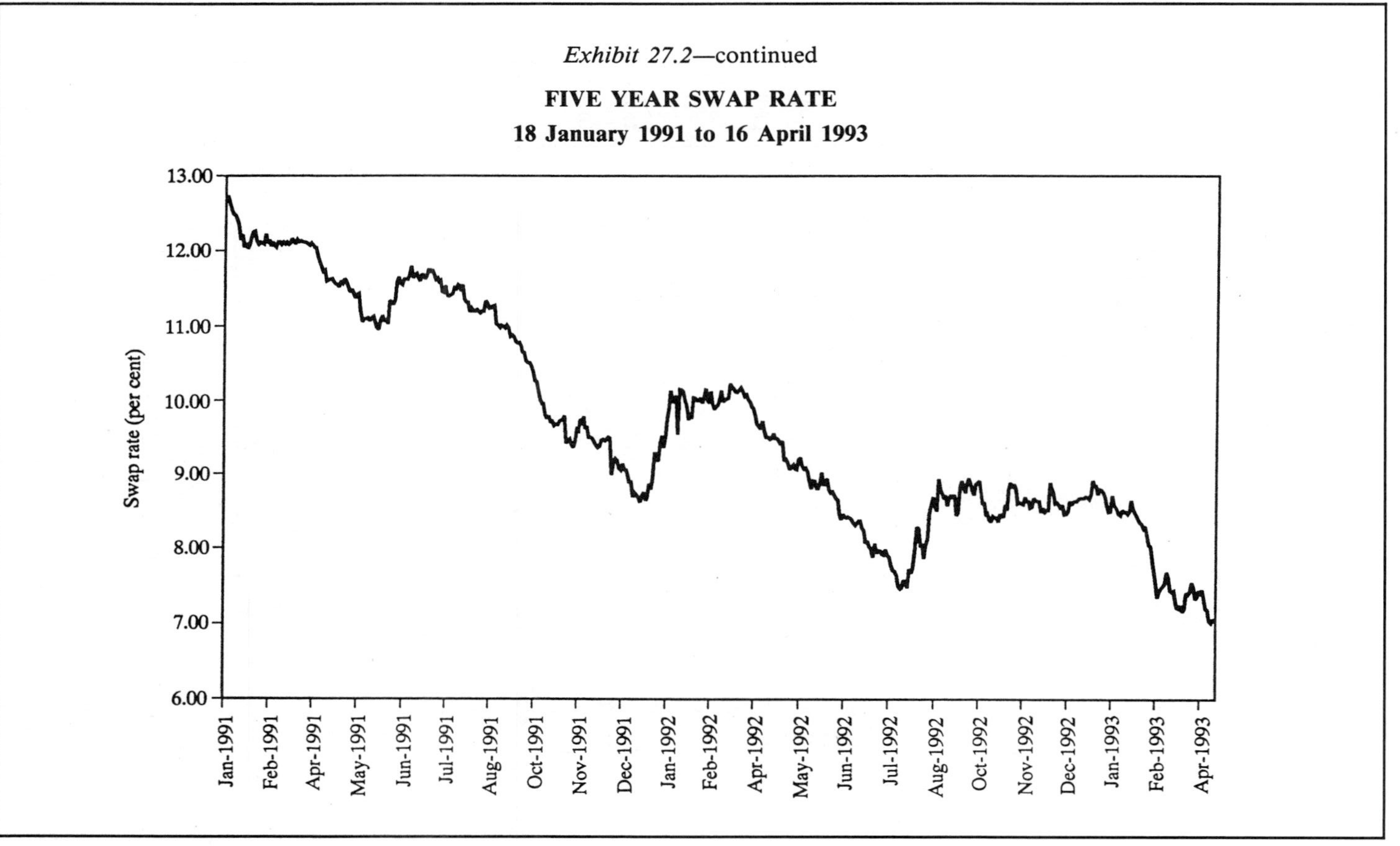

Exhibit 27.2—continued

SEVEN YEAR SWAP RATE

18 January 1991 to 16 April 1993

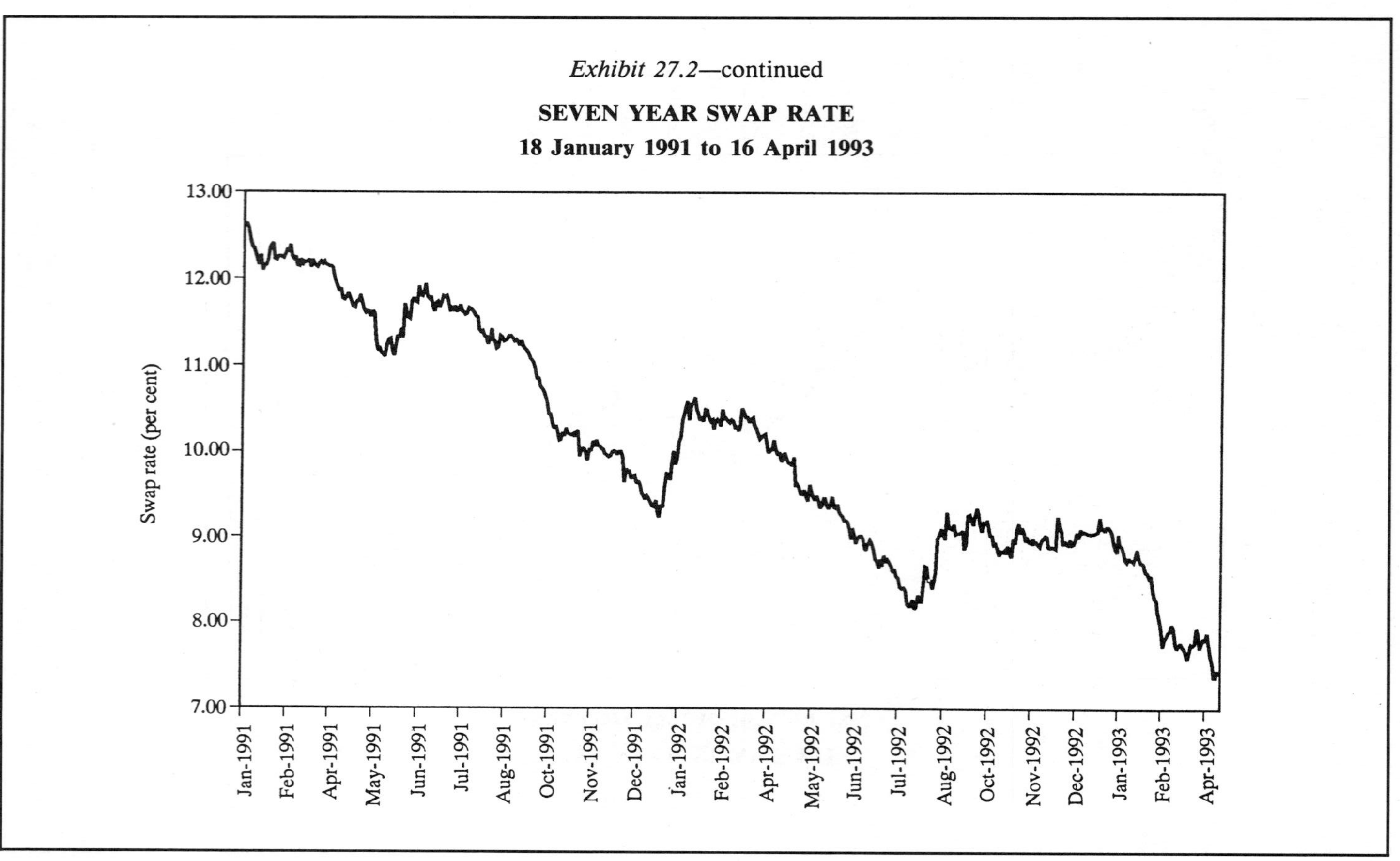

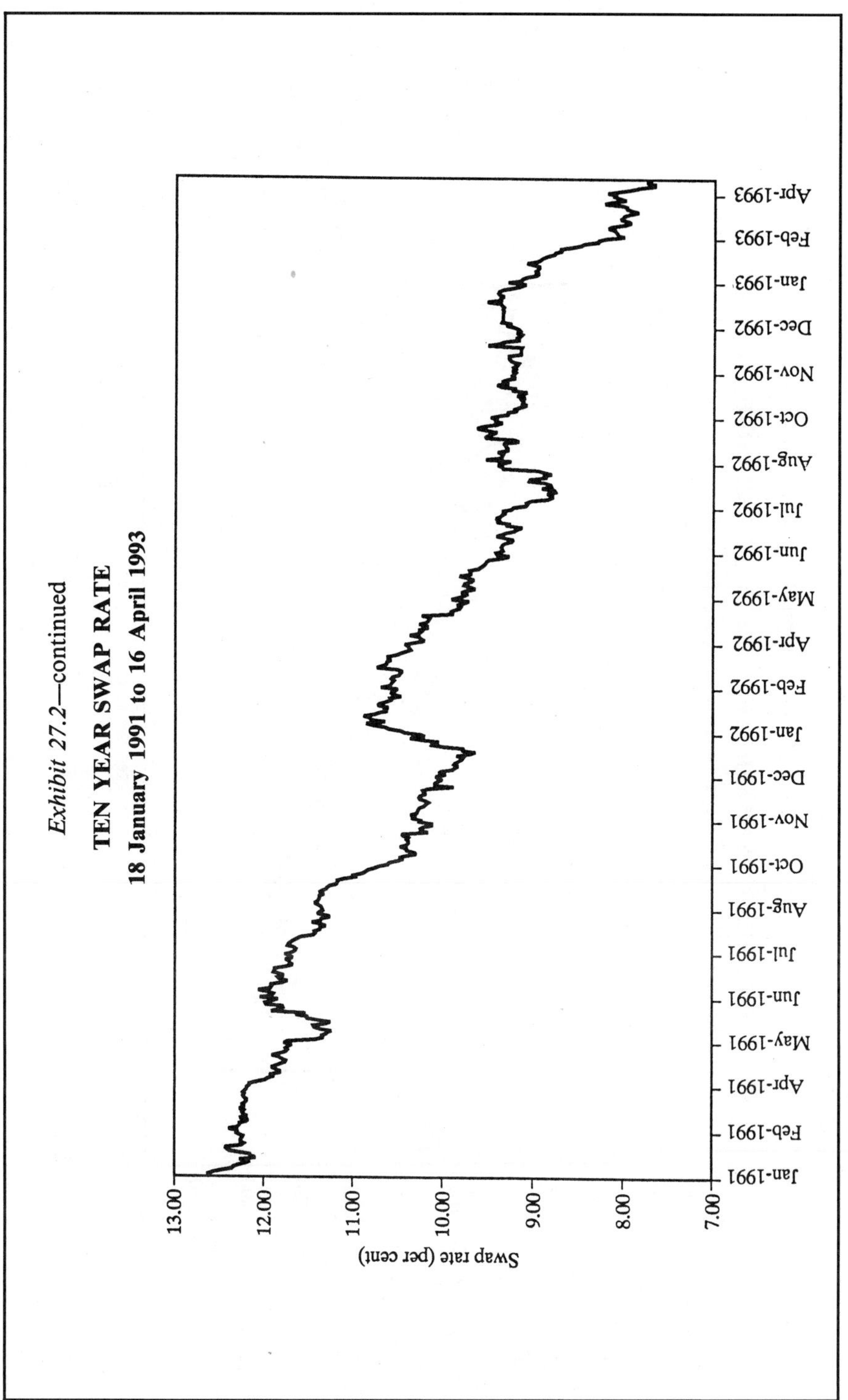

Exhibit 27.2—continued

TEN YEAR SWAP RATE

18 January 1991 to 16 April 1993

Exhibit 27.2—continued

TWO YEAR SWAP SPREAD OVER TWO YEAR BOND

13 April 1992 to 16 April 1993

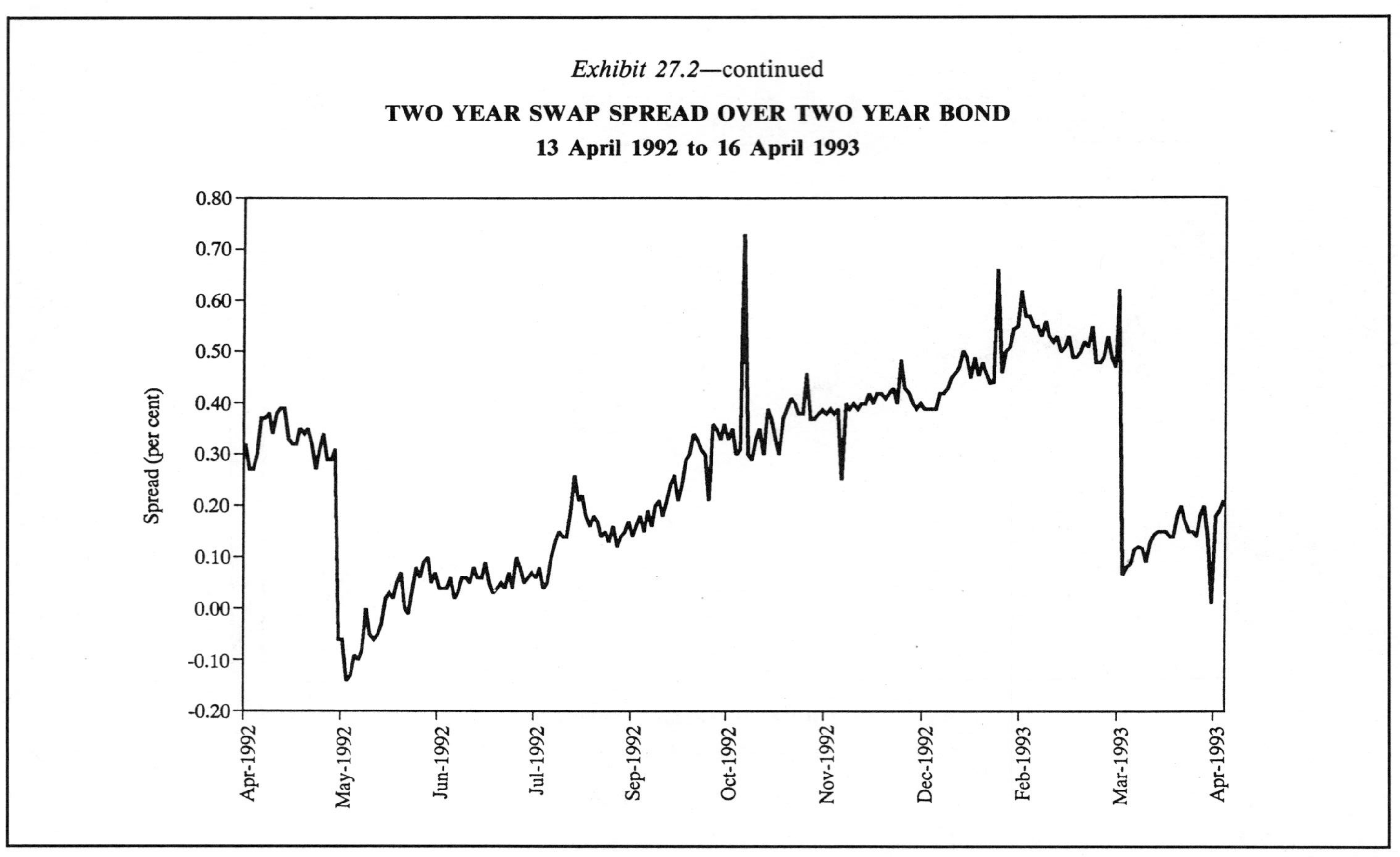

Exhibit 27.2—continued

THREE YEAR SWAP SPREAD OVER TWO YEAR BOND

13 April 1992 to 16 April 1993

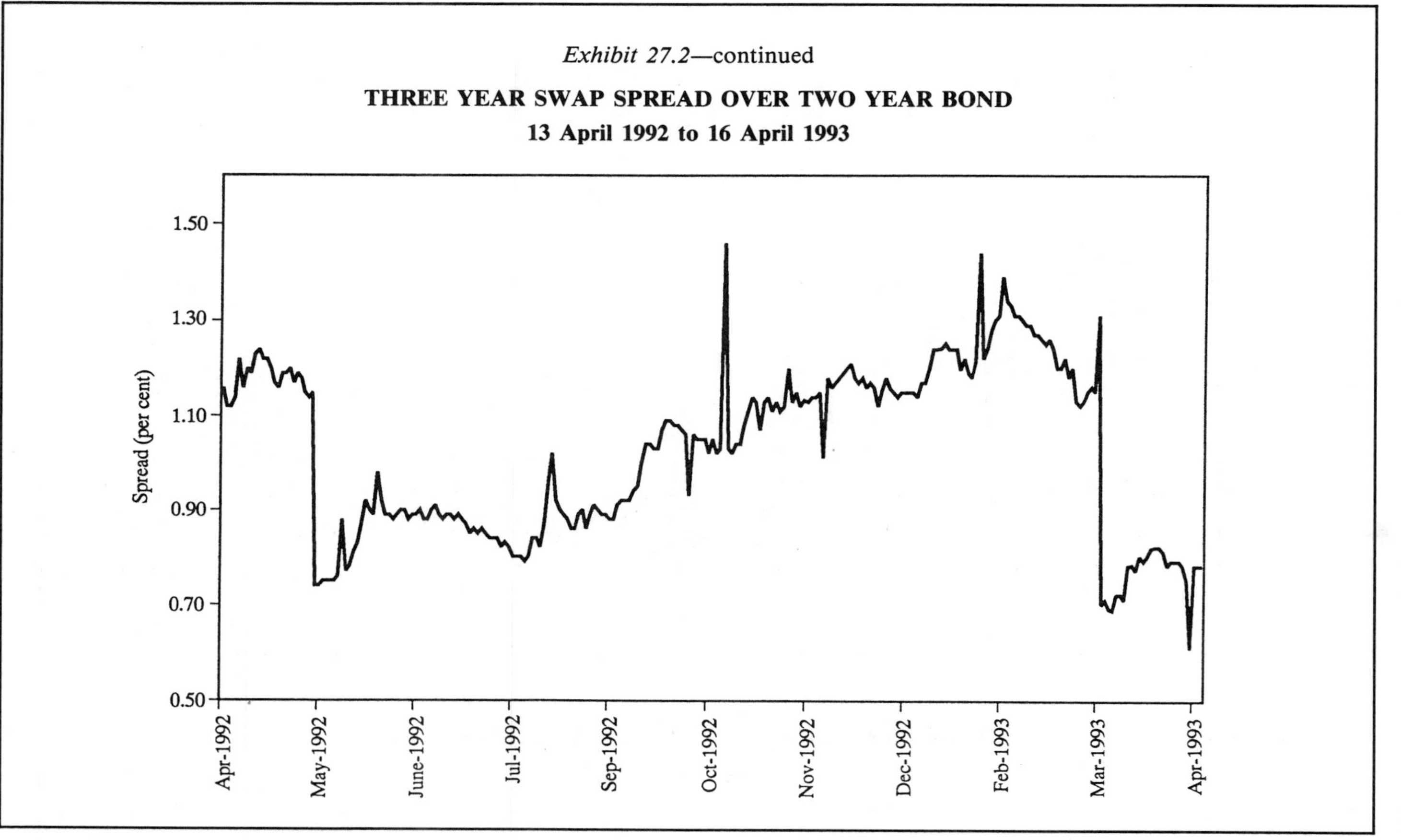

Exhibit 27.2—continued

FIVE YEAR SWAP SPREAD OVER FIVE YEAR BOND

13 April 1992 to 16 April 1993

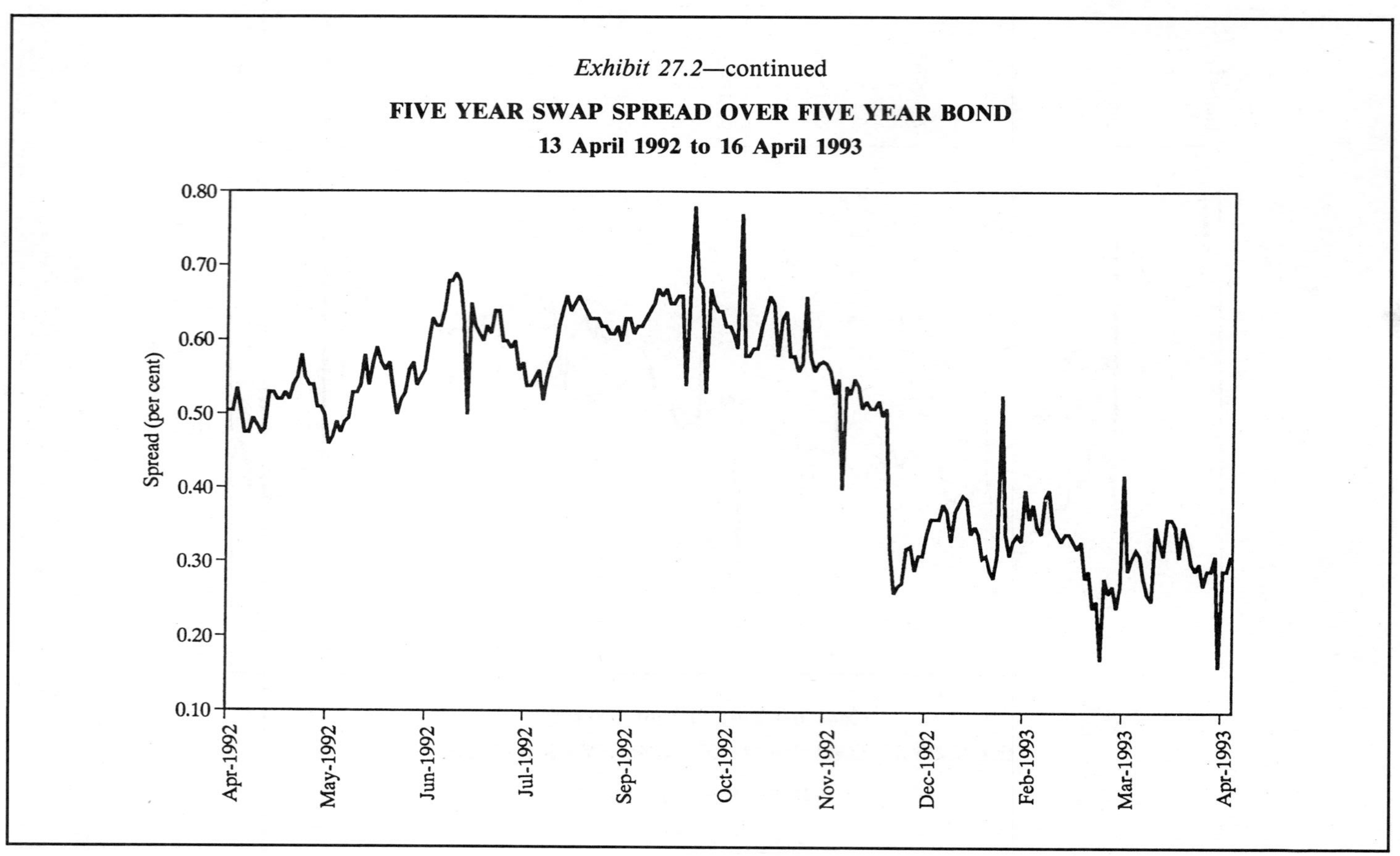

Exhibit 27.2—continued

TEN YEAR SWAP SPREAD OVER TEN YEAR BOND

18 January 1991 to 31 March 1993

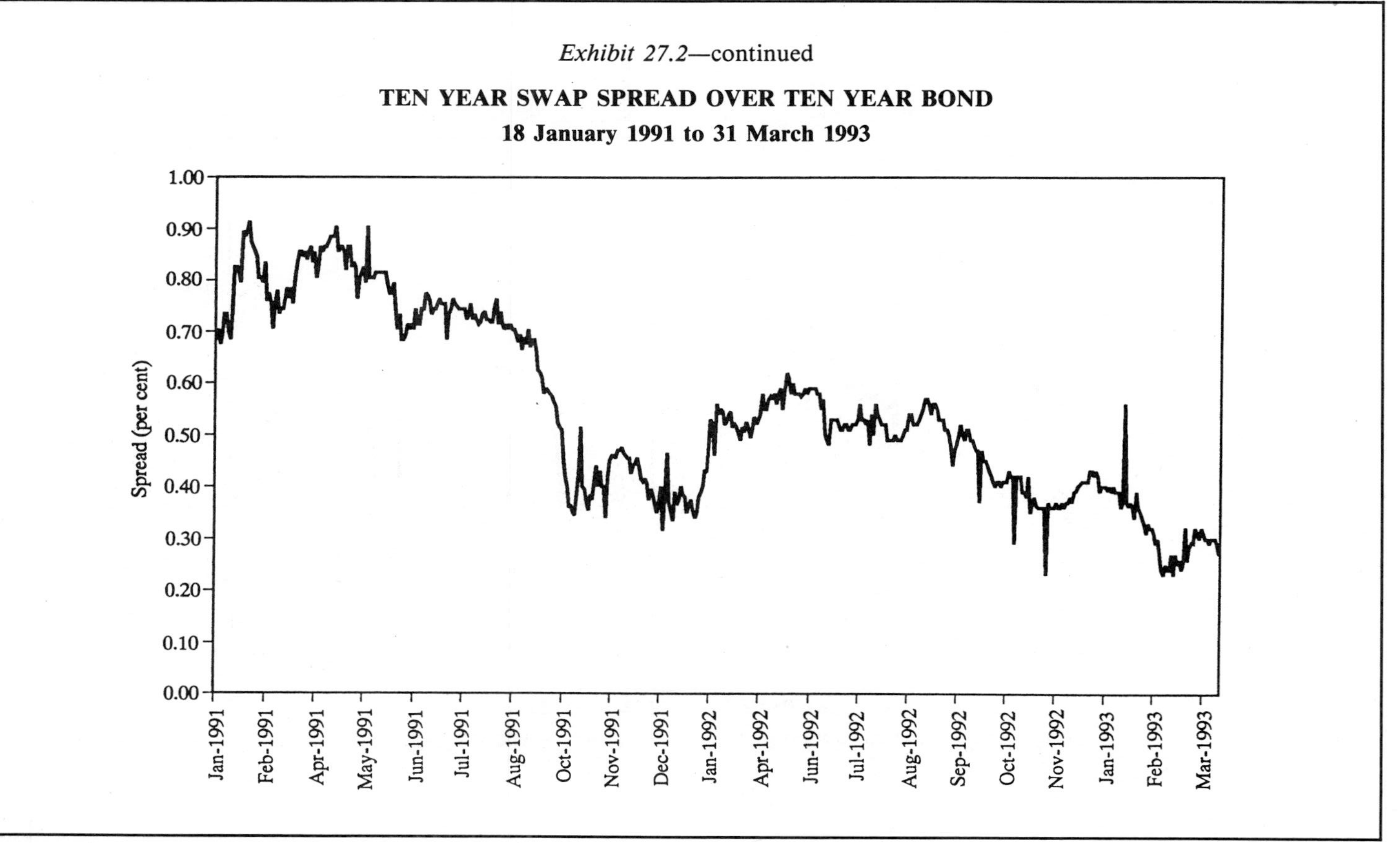

Exhibit 27.2—continued

THREE YEAR SWAP SPREAD OVER THREE YEAR FUTURES

13 April 1992 to 16 April 1993

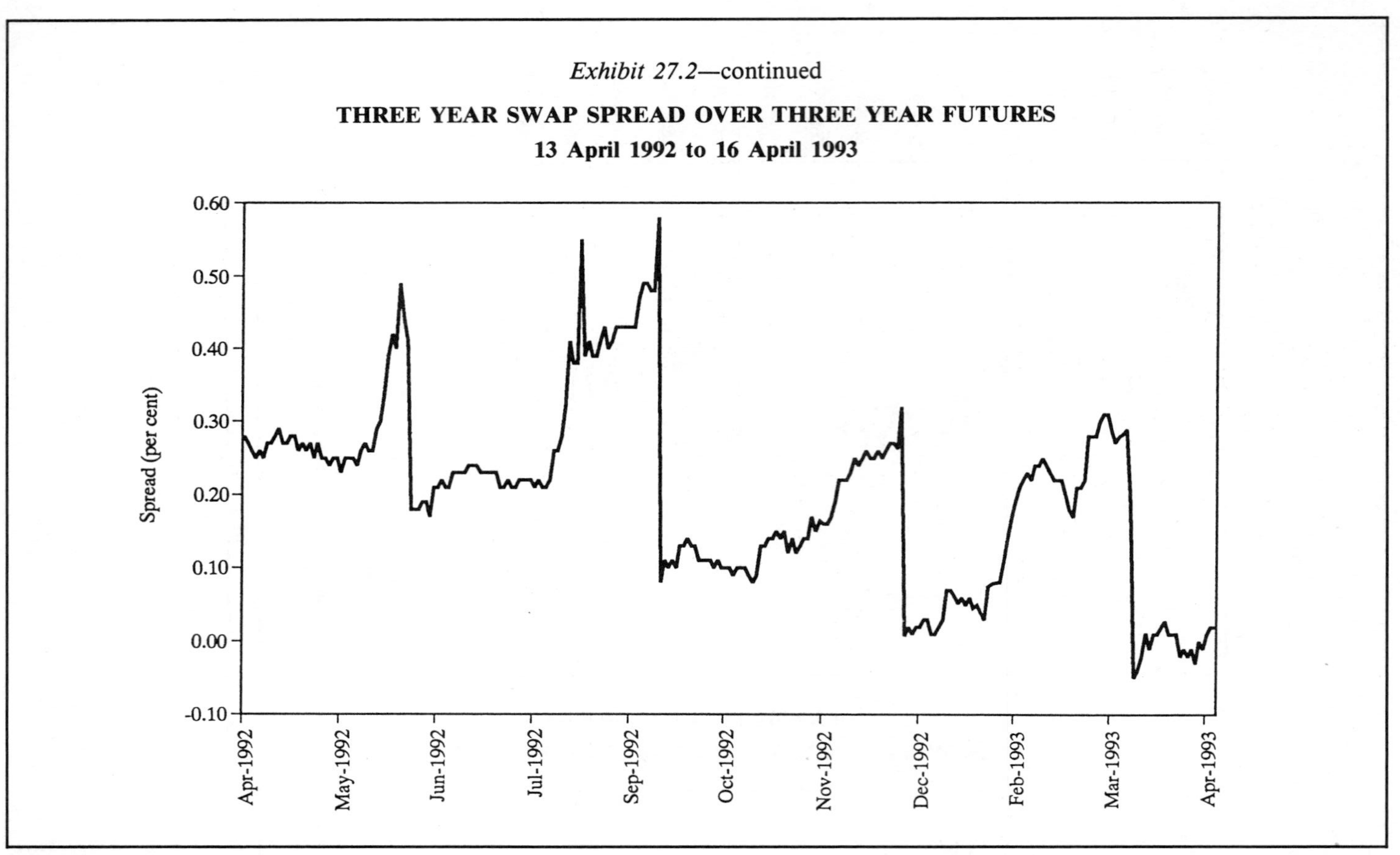

Exhibit 27.2—continued

FIVE YEAR SWAP SPREAD OVER THREE YEAR FUTURES

13 April 1992 to 16 April 1993

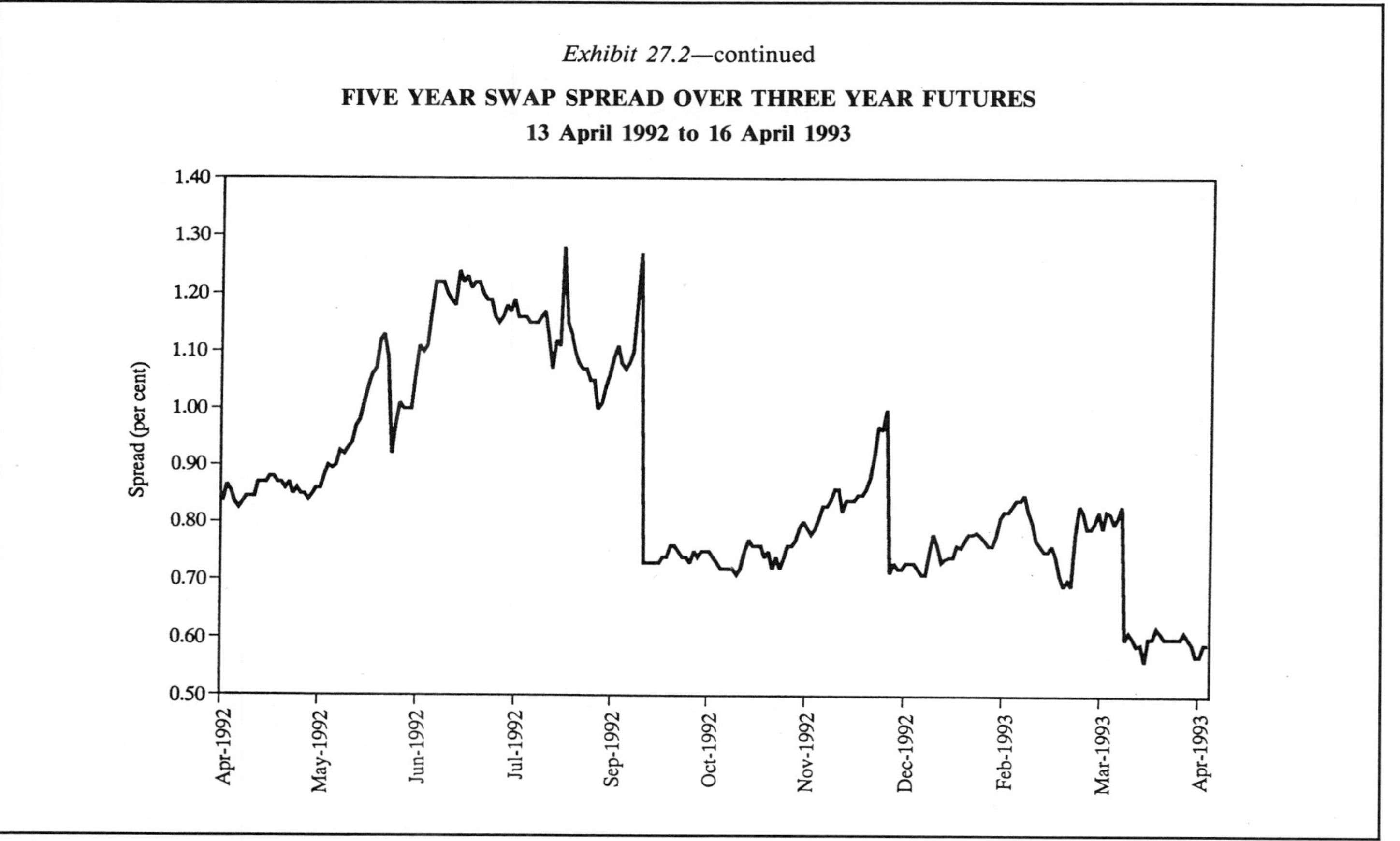

Exhibit 27.2—continued

SEVEN YEAR SWAP SPREAD OVER TEN YEAR FUTURES

13 April 1992 to 16 April 1993

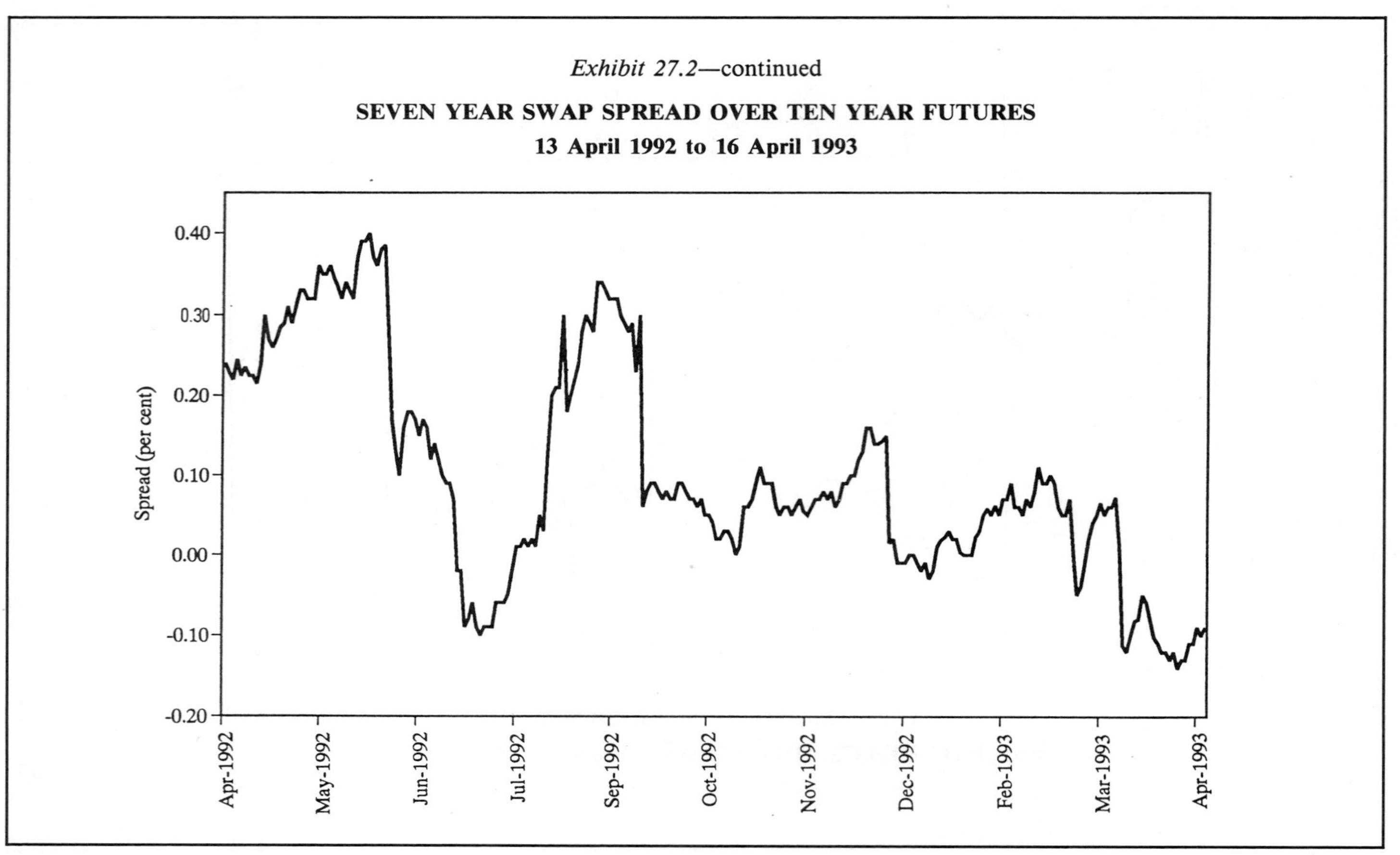

Exhibit 27.2—continued

TEN YEAR SWAP SPREAD OVER TEN YEAR FUTURES

13 April 1992 to 16 April 1993

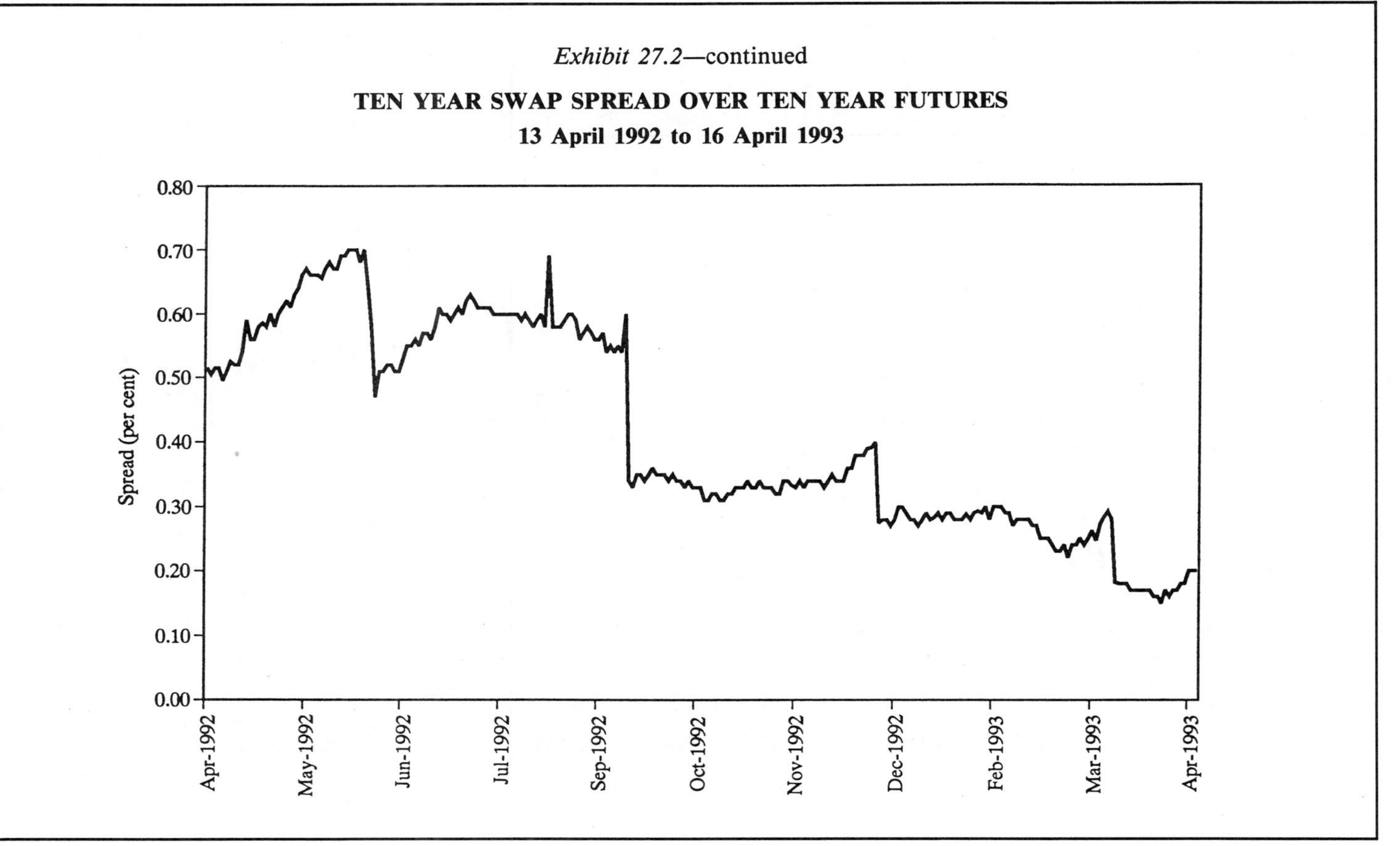

Exhibit 27.2—continued

TWO YEAR SWAP SPREAD OVER FIVE YEAR SEMI-GOVERNMENT BOND

13 April 1992 to 16 April 1993

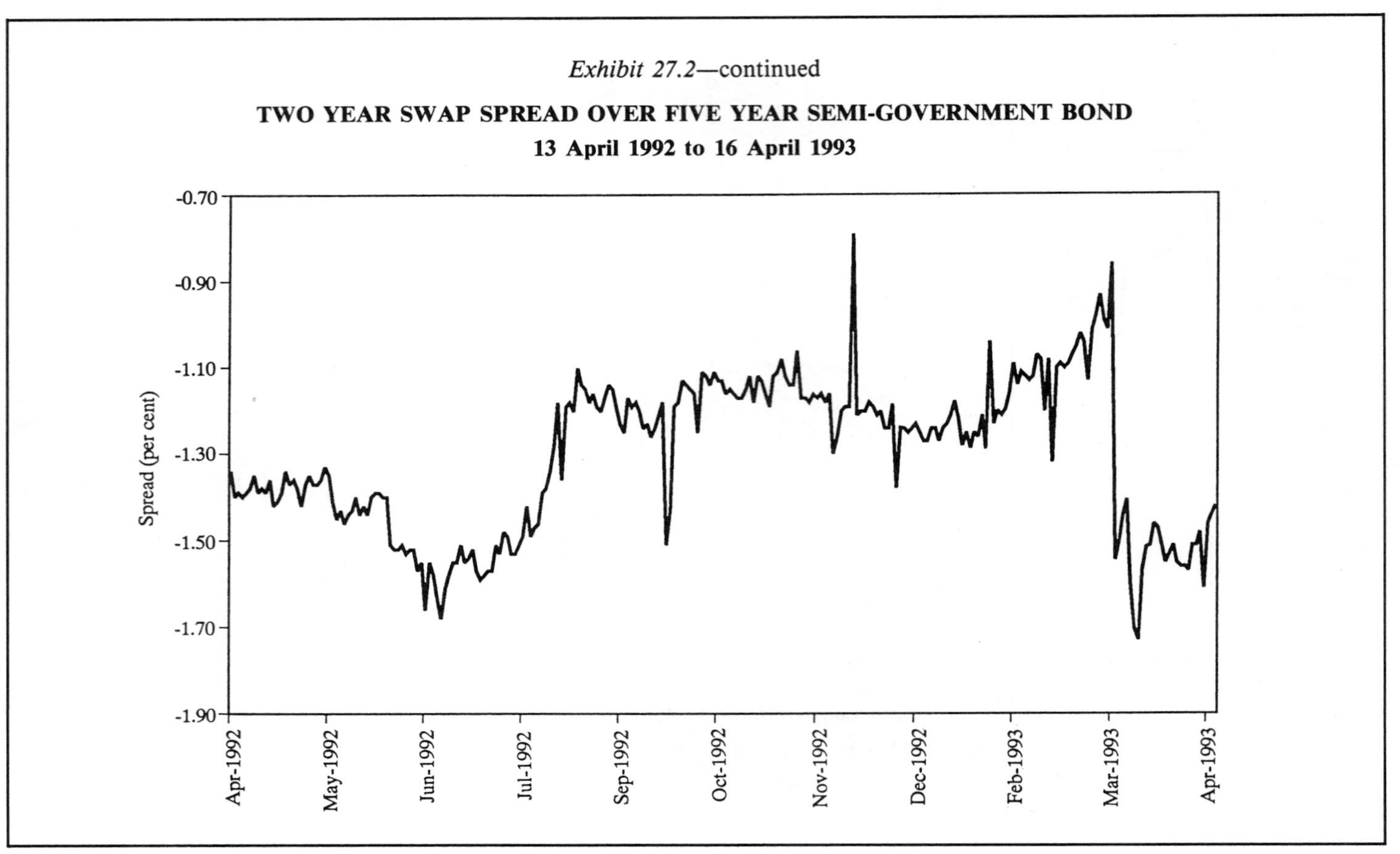

Exhibit 27.2—continued

THREE YEAR SWAP SPREAD OVER FIVE YEAR SEMI-GOVERNMENT BOND

13 April 1992 to 16 April 1993

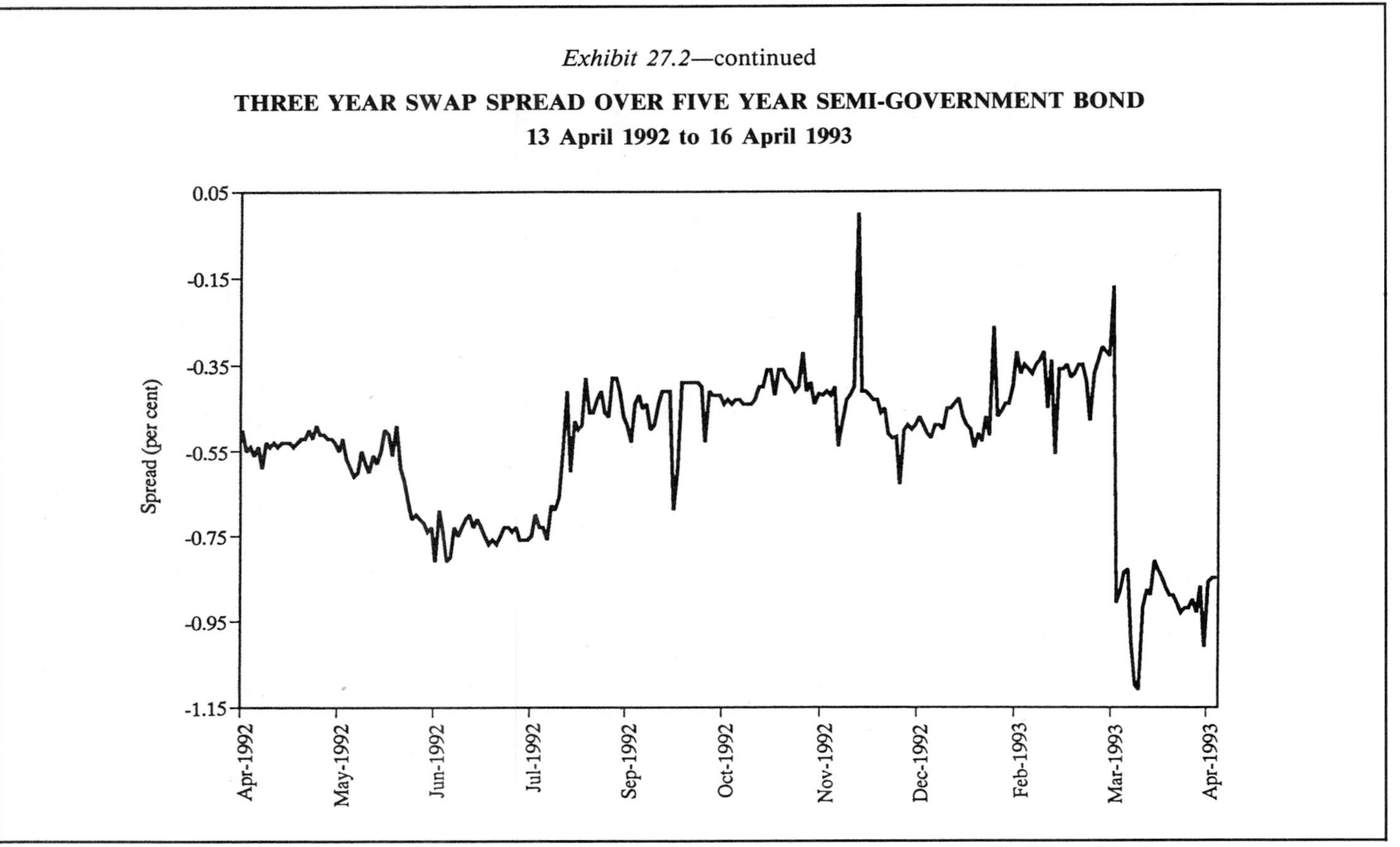

Exhibit 27.2—continued

FIVE YEAR SWAP SPREAD OVER FIVE YEAR SEMI-GOVERNMENT BOND

13 April 1992 to 16 April 1993

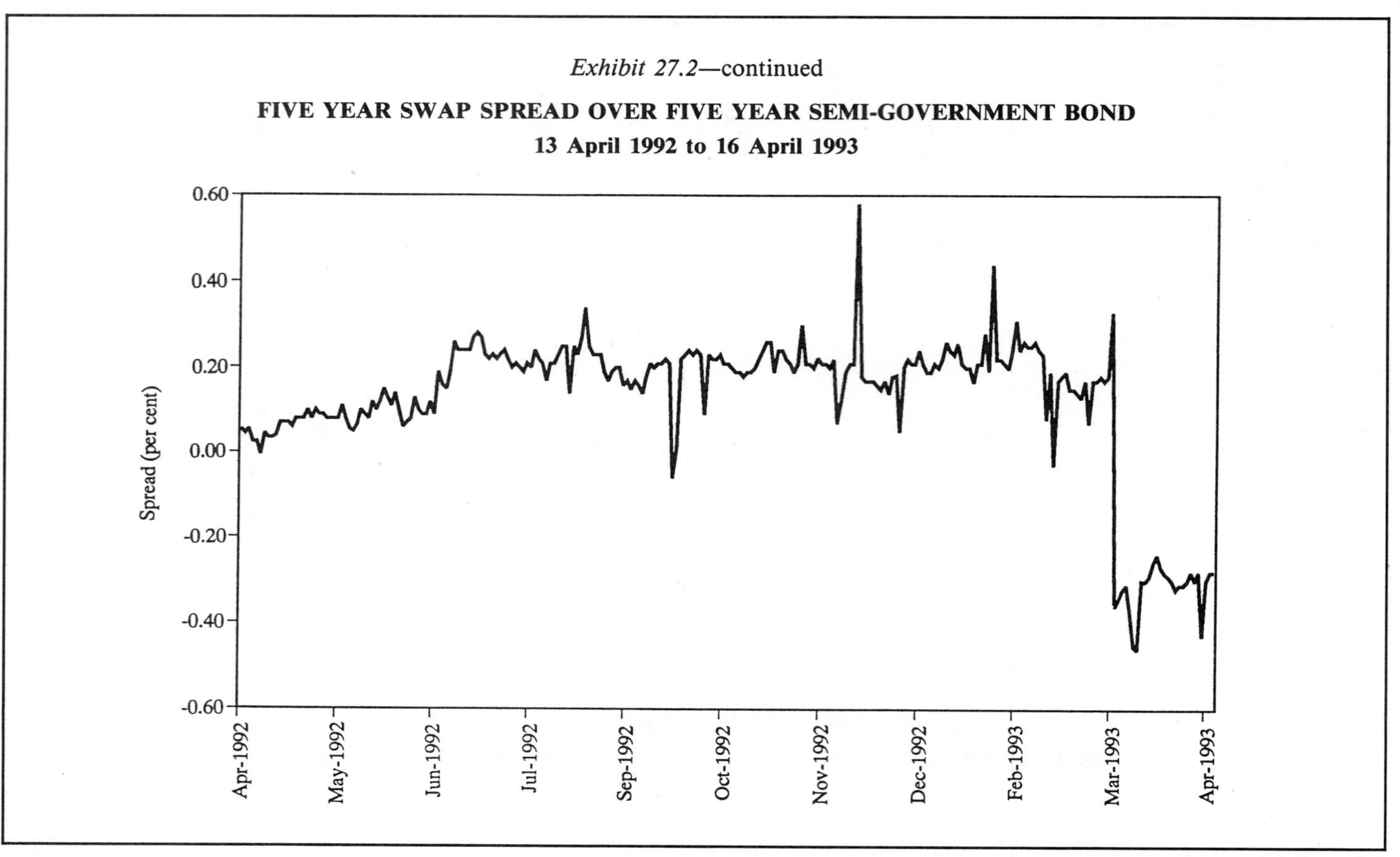

Exhibit 27.2—continued

SEVEN YEAR SWAP SPREAD OVER FIVE YEAR SEMI-GOVERNMENT BOND

13 April 1992 to 16 April 1993

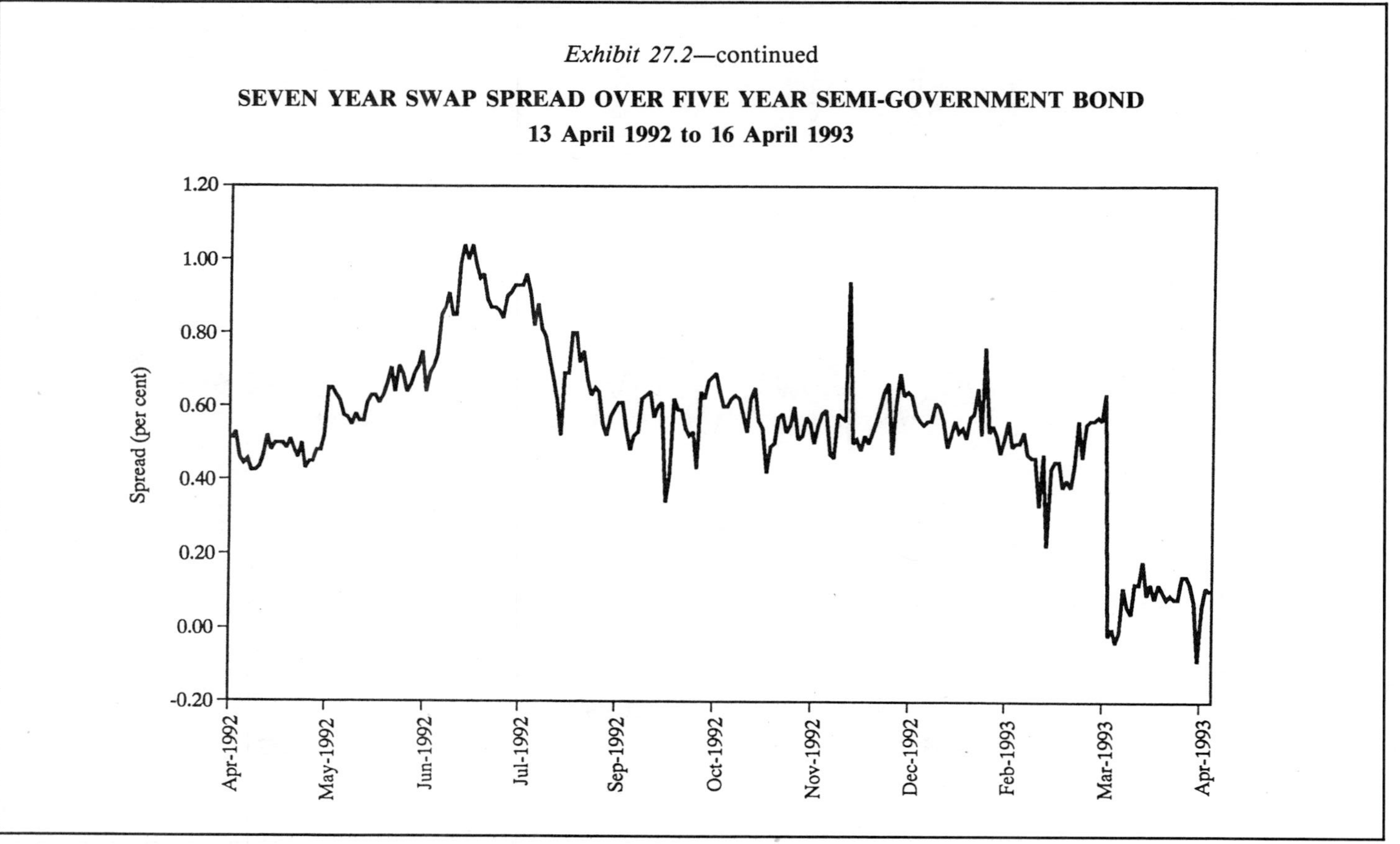

Exhibit 27.2—continued

TEN YEAR SWAP SPREAD OVER FIVE YEAR SEMI-GOVERNMENT BOND

13 April 1992 to 16 April 1993

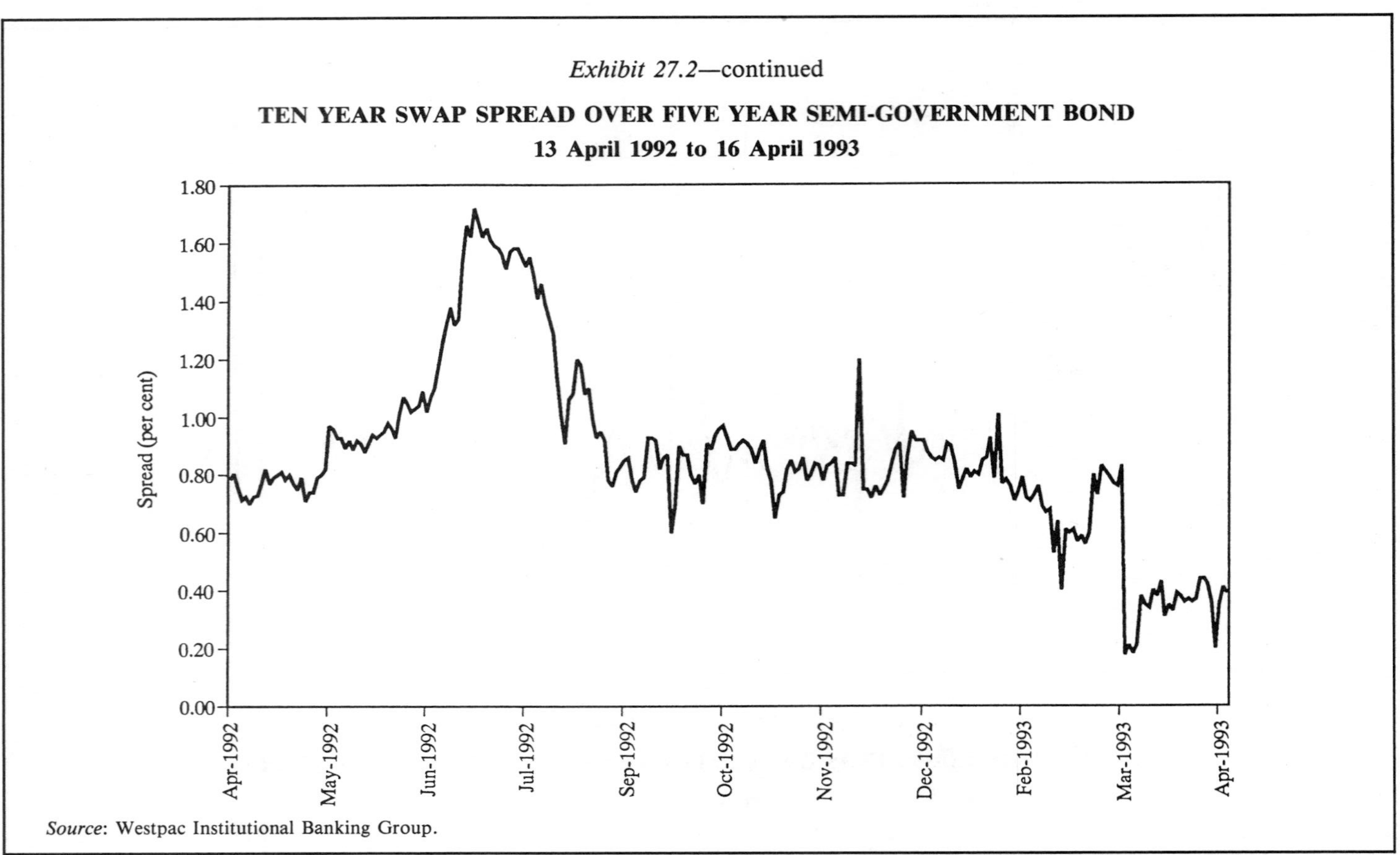

Source: Westpac Institutional Banking Group.

The pattern of spread movements over recent years has been dictated by a mix of the following factors, one or other of which has prevailed at a given point in time:

- The volumes of semi-government debt issuance and participation in the swap market, either as a fixed rate payer or receiver which has been dictated by the pricing level of their specific securities relative to swap rates.
- Corporate fixed rate paying interest, as part of interest rate risk management, which has declined in the period since 1990 reflecting falling interest rates and the onset of recession and resultant reduction in debt levels.
- Spasmodic periods of activity focusing on specific types of issues, such as the A$/JPY dual currency bond issue which has the capability of forcing swap spreads, in particular maturities, to behave in a particular fashion. For example, as a direct result of this type of activity, the ten year swap rate traded below semi-government yields for a large part of 1990 until issuance of these types of private placements declined in volume.
- Asset swap activity focus on swapping semi-government and bank debt, typically issued in the form of term CDs in the domestic bond market, into floating-rate assets for financial institutions.
- The dramatic shift in the shape of the yield curve from steeply inverse (November 1989) to a flat and, finally, positive yield curve by 1990 reflecting aggressive using of monetary policy by the Australian Central Bank. Aggressive receiving interest in short-dated swaps reduced swap spreads at the shorter end of the yield curve during this period of transition.

Participants/product range

As is evident from the discussion of the pattern and structure of the A$ swap market, market participants represent a heterogeneous group of financial institutions, government authorities and corporations. The A$ swap market is surprisingly international reflecting the important role of A$ debt securities issued in overseas markets or issuance of A$ securities by international issuers in the domestic A$ market.

A number of institutions are active in the A$ swap market in a market-making capacity. These include major Australian banks, such as Westpac, Commonwealth Bank, ANZ and the National Australia Bank. The activity of these institutions is complemented by the involvement of a number of foreign banks including Citibank, Bankers Trust as well as selective participation international swap market participants, such as Merrill Lynch and AIG.

The A$ swap market is well developed and has a diverse and, in some respects, complex product range. A wide variety of variations on basic structures are now available. A central feature of the market is its capacity to innovate, accommodating complex structured private placements such as the A$/JPY dual currency issues previously mentioned, as well as a variety of complex currency and interest rate option embedded hybrid structure designed to accommodate the requirements of Australian exporters and commodity producers. Long periods of sustained inverse yield curve structures have also provided an impetus to innovation focusing on management of corporate debt portfolios under such conditions utilising swap and derivative products.

NZ$ SWAP MARKET

The NZ$ swap market bears a close resemblance to the A$ swap market although it is a fraction of its size.

The NZ$ swap market, from a structural viewpoint, is primarily a currency swap market of fixed rate NZ$ against US$ LIBOR with a limited interest rate swap and an even more limited floating US$ and floating NZ$ currency swap component. A major reason for this particular structure is the relatively undeveloped state of the New Zealand domestic market where no clear dominant floating rate exists, although the prime commercial bill rate has increasingly begun to take on this role.

The NZ$ swap market, like its A$ counterpart, has historically been dominated by new issues of NZ$ Eurobonds as well as NZ$ Yankee issues. Driven by spasmodic investor interest in NZ$ securities from European and United States investors attracted by the high yields on NZ$ bonds, the market is largely predicated on the presence of 15.00% interest withholding tax, which creates significant pricing anomalies, and the lack of alternative sources of fixed rate NZ$ funding.

In the late 1980s and early 1990s, the NZ$ swap market contracted under the combined influence of sharply lower interest rates, reduced new issue activity in NZ$ Eurobonds, and the onset of a severe and long prolonged economic recession in the domestic economy. The only major activity, in recent years, has been:

- swaps related to investment by foreign, usually Australian, corporations where currency swaps have been utilised to hedge the NZ$ investment;
- liability management activities of fixed rate issuers such as the various state owned enterprises (as Electrocorp, New Zealand Telecom, Government Property Services, Housing Finance Corporation etc);
- the hedging requirements of project or infrastructure financing;
- sporadic activity in the NZ$ Eurobond market.

Primary issuers of NZ$ bonds are the classical arbitrage funding institutions such as sovereigns and semi-sovereign entities and a number of major international banks and well known corporations. For example, the Swedish export agency, SEK and BP are major issuers of NZ$ securities while Japanese institutions like Honda Finance have undertaken a number of issues which have been placed with Japanese investors. The major attraction for issuers is the significant arbitrage gains achievable from issuing in NZ$. For example, in the early days of the NZ$ swap market, swap rates were a significant margin *under* the corresponding government bond rate. This allowed issuers to swap their fixed rate NZ$ into huge margins under LIBOR; margins of around 80-100bps were not unknown. While the pricing relationships have gradually changed, the arbitrage profits from this sector of the swap market continue to be large, although inconsistent investor demand means the amount of funds available from this source are relatively restricted.

The primary payers of fixed NZ$ have been New Zealand state agencies and a number of large New Zealand corporates seeking fixed rate funding. Most of these institutions enjoy access to floating rate US$ funding which they transform through the swap into fixed rate NZ$. A major motivation during the period of high interest in the 1980s for a number of corporations entering into these types of swaps has been to lower their absolute cost of funds in the negatively sloped yield curve environment which has persisted in the NZ$ market in recent years. In addition, in the early days of the NZ$ swap market, a number of financial institutions merely undertook swaps on their own books purchasing government bonds as an offsetting investment to lock-in margins of up to 1.00 to 1.25% pa.

In recent years, the character of the domestic participants has changed as the shape of the yield curve has flattened and absolute yield levels have fallen. Increasingly, major participants such as the State-owned enterprises and domestic corporations utilise swaps to manage their floating-rate debt consistent with normal asset liability management practices.

While NZ$ swaps are, in theory, priced off New Zealand government rates, sometimes at a negative margin to the government bond rate, the volatility of the spread as well as the lack of liquidity in the NZ$ bond market dictates that the market primarily operates as an absolute rate market with prices being quoted relative to US$ LIBOR and, in the more limited interest rate swap market, against prime commercial bill rates.

As the NZ$ swap market has contracted, liquidity has decreased. The market is currently dominated by few market makers such as Bank of New Zealand (which is now a subsidiary of National Australia Bank), Westpac with participation by ANZ, Bankers Trust and Citibank. Bid-offer spreads are volatile with spreads of 15-25bps pa being common.

A major difficulty in pricing NZ$ swaps is the lack of liquidity in the underlying NZ$ government bond market. Low turnover, often as low as NZ$20m per day in the bond market, makes it increasingly difficult to hedge swaps utilising underlying government bonds. Similarly, a lack of liquidity in the three year government bond interest rate futures contract as well as the five year government interest rate bond contract makes hedging complex and risky.

In addition, structurally the NZ$ government bond market has inherent maturity restrictions with few, if any, stocks beyond five years. This contributes to a lack of liquidity of NZ$ swap maturities longer than five years.

Swap spreads tended to trade between 75-90bps pa above government yields in the five years and longer maturities while spreads in the shorter maturities generally are around 20-40bps pa over the two to three year NZ$ government bond yields. NZ$ swap spreads at the shorter end, have, in recent years, been influenced by one to two year swaps designed to arbitrage exporter's foreign exchange receipts and has, on occasion, forced short-term swap rates to levels comparable to government yields.

Short-term swaps in NZ$ are hedged in the relatively active New Zealand prime commercial bill interest rate futures market which facilitates strip hedging out to one year.

The behaviour of NZ$ swap rates and spreads is set out in *Exhibit 27.3*.

Exhibit 27.3
NZ$ Swap Rates and Spreads

NEW ZEALAND TWO YEAR SWAP RATE
2 March 1992 to 30 April 1993

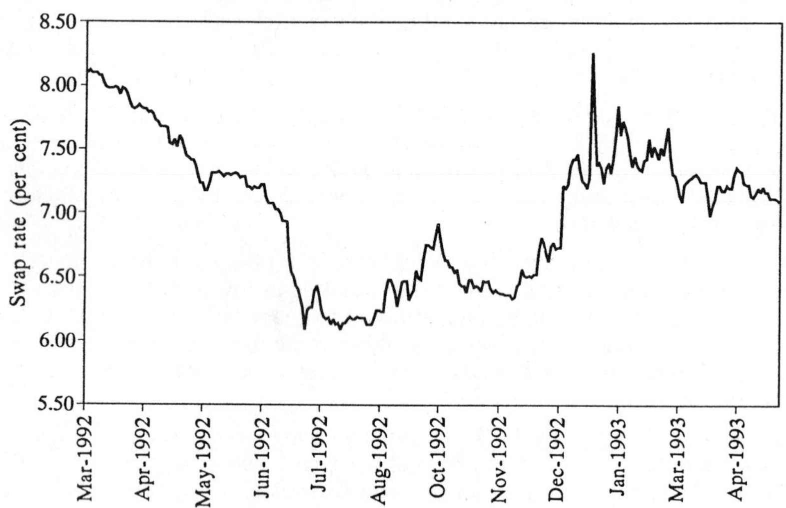

NEW ZEALAND THREE YEAR SWAP RATE
2 March 1992 to 30 April 1993

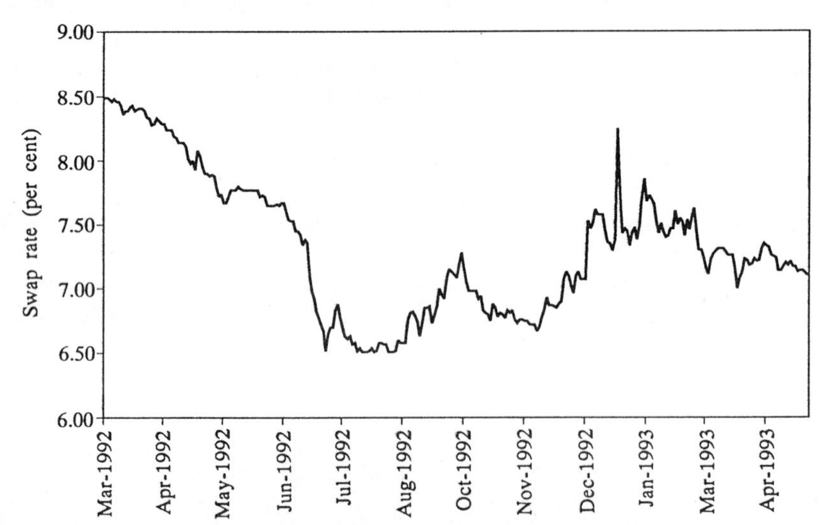

Exhibit 27.3—continued

NEW ZEALAND FIVE YEAR SWAP RATE

2 March 1992 to 30 April 1993

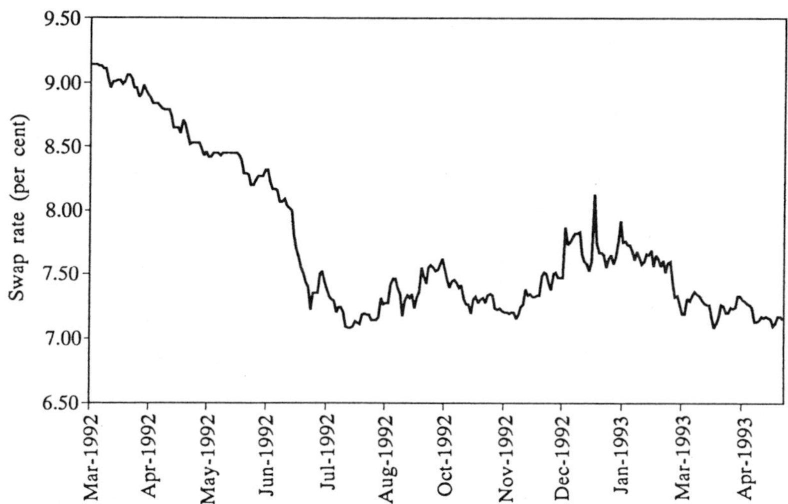

NEW ZEALAND TWO YEAR SWAP SPREAD OVER TWO YEAR TREASURY BOND

13 April 1992 to 30 April 1993

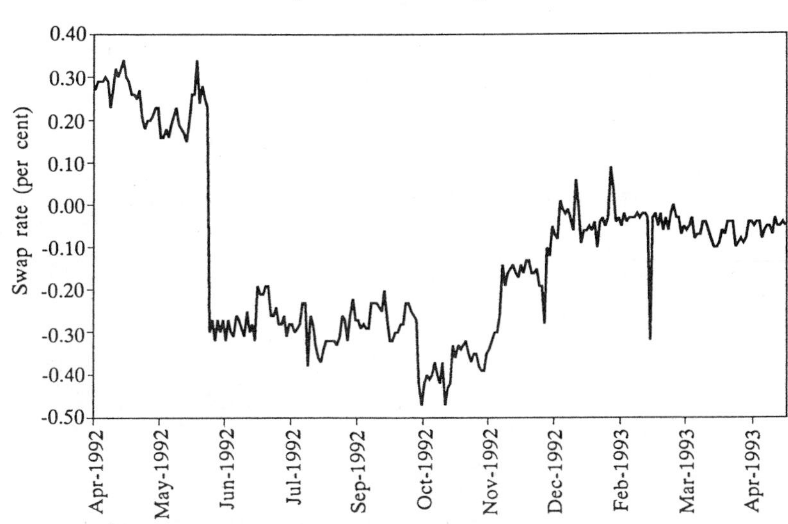

Exhibit 27.3—continued

NEW ZEALAND THREE YEAR SWAP SPREAD OVER TWO YEAR TREASURY BOND

13 April 1992 to 30 April 1993

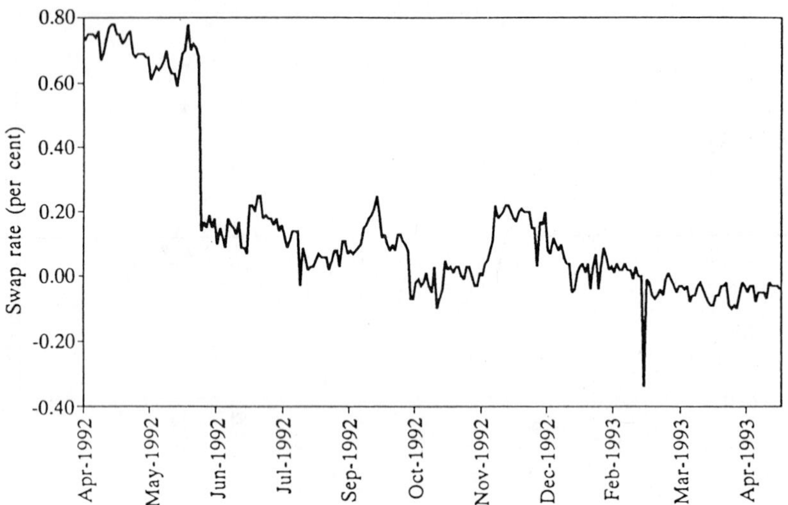

NEW ZEALAND FIVE YEAR SWAP SPREAD OVER FIVE YEAR TREASURY BOND

13 April 1992 to 30 April 1993

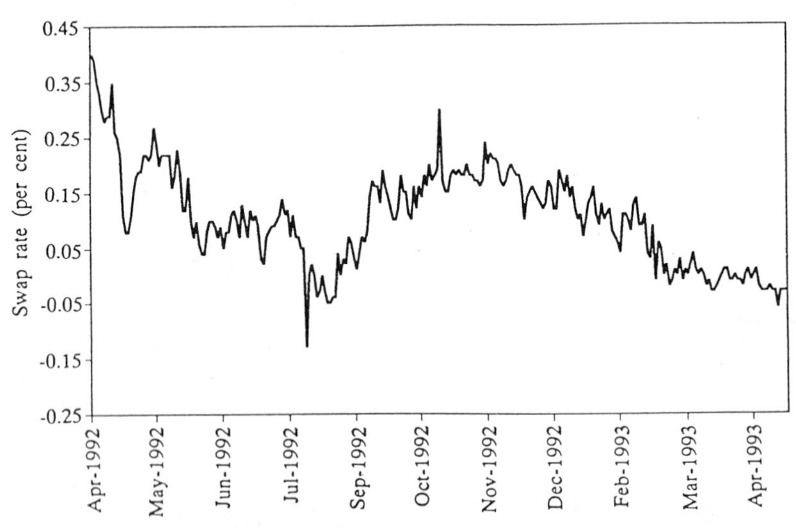

Source: Westpac Institutional Banking Group.

Chapter 28

Global LTFX, FRA and Cap and Collar Markets

OVERVIEW OF SWAP DERIVATIVE MARKETS

The markets for swap derivatives all have highly individual histories. For example, markets in LTFX contracts and FRAs have, in many cases, predated markets in interest rate and currency swaps in that currency. However, despite these historical nuances, it is evident that the market for these types of swap derivatives has grown strongly, paralleling the growth in mainstream swap instruments.

This growth has been accompanied by the development of significant interrelationships between the various market segments. These interrelationships cover a number of areas including:

- pricing relationships;
- consolidation of the trading in the various instruments into integrated units within financial intermediaries which quote and deal in the full range of swap instruments with a concentrated focus on utilisation of these instruments for corporate finance and risk management applications;
- the integration of the instruments allowing each to be used to complement others and to create and manage risk positions in one through activities in another instrument. For example, utilising a cap transaction to hedge an open risk position in the swap.

LTFX MARKETS

The LTFX market has operated largely parallel to and in some cases has predated the currency swap market in the relevant currency. The market participants usually include corporations and government institutions as well as financial intermediaries. Most corporations or government institutions enter into LTFX contracts for a number of reasons including:

- hedging capital market transactions;
- hedging trade flows;
- hedging capital flows denominated in other currencies associated with projects or capital acquisitions in other countries;
- hedging of asset exposure from cross-border investments;
- hedging foreign currency exposures on portfolio investments by institutional investors.

The development of reasonably liquid markets in currency swaps has significantly reduced the use of LTFX contracts in connection with capital market transactions. Some minor exceptions persist due to institutional or structural reasons. However, LTFX contracts continue to be used for the other applications. The major advantage of LTFX contracts relative to currency swap transactions is the capacity to tailor them to hedging uneven, in terms of amount and timing, currency cash flows. This capacity of LTFX contracts to be tailored to a specific size and date requirement has meant that LTFX contracts have continued to complement currency swap structures.

The main providers of LTFX contracts have been financial institutions, primarily commercial and investment banks. A number of these institutions quote prices between, inter alia, US$, deutschmarks, Swiss francs, yen, pound sterling, French francs, etc for various maturities up to ten years although for a number of currencies, only quotes for shorter periods are available. In addition, there is an active broker market for LTFX contracts.

Up to approximately 1982, almost all LTFX transactions were perfectly matched counterparty-driven transactions with participants seeking to cover foreign exchange exposures on future cash flows related to capital or trade transactions but in opposite directions. However, since that time, a number of institutions have started transacting LTFX business without necessarily having an offsetting position. In fact, currently in excess of 90-95% of LTFX transactions are executed by financial intermediaries without having an offsetting counterparty. In view of the interrelationship in pricing terms between swaps and LTFX contracts, most major financial intermediaries active in the area have integrated their LTFX and currency swap activities.

However, despite this increased participation by financial intermediaries which has added to the depth and liquidity of the market, the LTFX market, defined as all forward foreign exchange contracts with a maturity beyond one year, is considered less efficient and liquid than corresponding markets in foreign exchange forward contracts with shorter maturities. A principal reason underlying this reduced level of liquidity is the difficulty of undertaking arbitrage in longer-term markets and the absence of speculators who contribute to market depth.

The volume of LTFX transactions is significantly lower than that for short-dated foreign exchange forward contracts. The average size of an LTFX contract is US$10-20m with maturities concentrated in the three to five year range. A small group of financial institutions, primarily the United States money centre banks and a number of major investment banks as well as the major foreign exchange banks in each currency, are the principal participants in the LTFX markets. The increased participation by a range of institutions has contributed to the development of a growing interbank market in LTFX wherein banks can offset positions created through customer-driven transactions.

Pricing on LTFX contracts is generally based on interest rate differentials between the relevant currencies. Analysis of actual bid-offer spreads as well as comparison of *actual* forward market prices against theoretical market spreads suggests a highly efficient market. In general, the *actual* forward market prices could not profitably be made by making a market through covered interest arbitrage. This suggests that financial intermediaries do not use covered interest arbitrage but rather match offsetting LTFX transactions. The matching transaction can be a currency swap which is unbundled into its LTFX components by the financial intermediary. Actual LTFX bid-offer quotes suggest that the prices are largely similar to the calculated theoretical forward rates utilising the current yield curve method (based increasingly on zero coupon rates). Commission rates between dealers are similar with little differences in spreads between the major participants in the market.

An active secondary market in LTFX contracts is gradually developing with corporations trading their existing LTFX contracts as their underlying exposure positions alter or if market movements necessitate restructuring of the hedge.

The pattern of activity in LTFX varies significantly between markets. Major differences in this regard exist between the following markets:

- major reserve currencies;
- commodity driven currencies;
- the currencies of emerging economies.

LTFX markets in the major reserve currency are both substantial in size and enjoy a high degree of liquidity. This reflects participation from a wide variety of entities, related to substantial underlying transactions involving investments, both business and portfolio, as well as trade in goods and services.

The currency markets and the corresponding LTFX markets in a number of currencies are, to a substantial degree, commodity driven. Examples of these types of currencies include the A$. This reflects the fact that the underlying economy has substantial commodity exporters/producers and the fact that most, if not all, commodities are priced in currencies other than the home currency of the country. This creates a pattern of activity whereby commodity exporters seek to utilise LTFX contracts to convert long term streams of revenues into their base currency. The requirements of exporters, for converting foreign currency revenues into their home currency, can usually be offset by capital importers seeking to take out currency hedges against foreign exchange exposure on their borrowings denominated in foreign currencies.

LTFX contracts in emerging economies may be impacted by some of the factors noted above. An additional factor, generally, is the higher degree of regulation of the currency market in the relevant economy. The central banks of these emerging economies often plays a very active role in managing foreign exchange reserves and may regulate the commercial currency market. Under these conditions, the liquidity of LTFX contracts, the terms for which transactions can be completed and the process by which such transactions are undertaken, including the necessity to obtain governmental approvals, are important aspects of these markets.

FRA MARKETS

There has been, in recent times, significant growth in the market for FRAs.

The size of the global FRA market is extremely difficult to estimate due to problems of classification. For example, strips of FRAs are often reported as interest rate swaps, or, conversely, interest rate swaps are reported as FRAs. Similarly, fixed rate loan transactions which may be structured as a floating rate loan and a series of forward securities purchase obligations may or may not be reported as FRAs.

Despite the difficulties of estimation, the market globally is estimated at over US$1,000 billion pa.

FRAs are available in a wide variety of currencies including major North American currencies, all major European currencies, major Asian currencies and Australasian currencies.

FRA trading is concentrated in three distinct time zones—European, North American and Asian. In European trading hours, London is the dominant trading centre not only for sterling, but also for most other currencies. For example, London is the dominant trading focus for US$ and yen FRAs in the European time zones. Other European financial centres have significant trading roles, but typically in their own currency. For example, Frankfurt is the dominant trading centre for deutschmark FRAs while Paris dominates trading in French franc FRAs.

North American trading is dominated by New York. A smaller market exists in Toronto but with a strong focus on Canadian dollars, although because of the cross-border flows between Canada and the United States of America, substantial volumes of US$ FRAs are also traded. New York is the dominant trading centre during North American hours for not only US$ FRAs but for FRAs in a wide variety of currencies including yen, deutschmark, sterling and Swiss francs.

Within the Asian time zone, a number of centres compete for business including Tokyo, Hong Kong, Singapore and Sydney, Australia.

United States dollar FRAs are by far the largest segment of the market, totalling between 60 and 70% of the total FRA market. Initially, FRAs were only available for round periods such as three against six months. However, as the US$ FRA market matured, the range of dates for which FRAs are quoted has broadened substantially. Currently, for US$ FRAs it is possible to obtain quotes for practically any period, although the greatest liquidity is, predictably, with standard periods. In the current market environment, US$ FRAs amounting to US$50-500m can be readily executed.

Major market participants in the FRA market include:

- corporations as well as the treasuries of supranational, sovereign and other governmental agencies active in the management of interest rate risk exposure on borrowings;
- institutional investors seeking to manage the interest rate risk on money market portfolios;
- banks and financial institution managing interest rate exposures within their various liquidity and trading portfolios.

A feature of the FRA market is the substantial interbank component. Financial institutions utilise FRAs, aggressively, to not only manage the institution's interest rate risk positions but also to:

- undertake cash-futures and cash-forward arbitrage;
- manage the risk of the interest rate component of forward foreign exchange contract portfolios;
- position for anticipated changes in interest rates.

For example, in US$, substantial speculative interest exists in the FRA market where interbank traders utilise this instrument to seek to trade movements in Eurodollar interest rates.

An interesting feature of interbank activity in FRAs is that participation of banks and financial institutions varies significantly between trading centres. For example, a branch of a particular bank may be a very active participant in the FRA market in the European time zone but will be a less active participant through other branches outside this time zone.

The pattern of participation in the FRA market, particularly from end users, is also different in terms of geographical locations. For example, FRAs are particularly popular in Europe and Asia where they are traditionally favoured because of their various advantages as the preferred means for a short-term interest rate risk management.

In the United States, use of exchange traded futures contracts by non-banks is well established and the FRA is, therefore, comparatively less attractive. There is limited investment bank involvement in FRAs, either for their own account or as market makers. Commercial banks use FRAs for their own account.

The growth of FRAs has been assisted by the relative ease with which commercial banks have been able to provide FRAs for clients by combining this activity with their own deposit taking and lending operation. Banks have particularly utilised FRAs to shorten or lengthen their own liability profile. The availability of usually liquid markets in short-term interest rate futures in a number of currencies has allowed financial institutions to write FRAs which are then hedged through the futures markets.

Market pricing of FRAs in each currency reflects the cost of alternative ways of constructing a similar hedge either through a combination of the cash deposit and lending market, the interest rate futures market and the term interest rate swap market itself. Bid-offer spreads on FRAs have narrowed from approximately 0.10 to 0.125% pa in early 1986 to 0.02 to 0.05% pa currently (for major currencies).

The liquidity of the FRA market, predictably, varies significantly as between currencies and trading centres. The only truly global FRA currency appears to be US$. US$ FRAs are traded 24 hours a day and the market is extremely liquid, even outside North American trading hours.

Liquidity in other currencies varies. Liquidity of FRAs in major European currencies, C$, yen and A$ are reasonably liquid.

The liquidity of FRA markets is linked, not surprisingly, to the existence of liquid markets in short term interest rate futures in the relevant currency. For example, the deutschmark FRA market has improved significantly, in liquidity terms, since the introduction of the Eurodeutschmark futures contract on LIFFE. Similarly, Swiss franc and ECU FRAs have also improved in liquidity with the growth of interest rate futures contracts in those currencies.

There is no evidence that widespread profitable arbitrage opportunities exist between the FRA and deposit markets after taking into account transaction costs. Nevertheless, the FRA rate in any of the available currencies can at times be sufficiently different from the implied forward-forward rate for one means of hedging to be preferable to the other.

Arbitrage opportunities involving placing and taking of deposits do appear to exist for the banks active in writing FRAs, allowing these banks usually to fund themselves at relatively attractive rates under the interbank rate. This appears to be particularly the case for longer maturities such as nine against 12 months. This type of arbitrage involving deposits is not usually attractive, however, for banks with return on asset requirements since the interest differential can only be enjoyed for three months while the transaction would have to be placed on-balance sheet with consequent gearing and reserve costs for a full 12 month period.

Interestingly, in recent times, swap market makers and warehouses have emerged not only as market makers of FRAs but as users of the instrument. These market makers have utilised FRAs to hedge their own risk positions or to reallocate the risk arising from mismatches within their swap books.

CAP, FLOOR AND COLLAR MARKET

The market for caps, floors and related derivatives has, historically, been dominated by transactions in US$. Over recent years, markets in these types of transactions have spread to a variety of other currencies including the major European currencies, C$, yen and A$ as well as a number of minor currencies. However, the US$ cap and floor market is still the most significant proportion of the global market in these instruments.

The difference between the US$ sector and the other currencies is most marked in terms of:

- size, depth and liquidity of market which outside the US$ sector is variable;
- maturities, features and special structures which are also limited outside the US$ sector;
- the range of cap and floor derivatives available is more limited for currencies other than US$.

The primary focus in this section is on the US$ cap market reflecting its size and importance. However, increasingly over recent times, the markets for these instruments in those other currencies have developed rapidly and some of the characteristics of the US$ cap/floor market are to be found in the markets for these instruments in other currencies.

US$ caps, floors and collars have a significant history. The market originated in the early 1980s in the form of insurance against increases or decreases in interest rates. In the early 1980s, Merrill Lynch was one of the first institutions to offer a cap facility utilising the proprietary title ''Interest Rate Protection''. Other financial institutions such as Citicorp and Salomon Brothers joined Merrill Lynch as providers of this type of facility. A number of commercial banks and, interestingly, a number of insurance companies and commodity brokers also began providing these types of facilities. However, for many of these participants, the experiment was short-lived in that a number of providers of caps ultimately discontinued their involvement. However, their early efforts created the basis for the market itself to develop and ultimately prosper.

The growth in the cap market reflects the complex interaction of a number of factors including client demand for these types of risk management instruments as well as the increased availability of providers. However, the rapid development of options markets generally and in particular exchange traded options on interest rates have assisted in the overall growth. The emergence of exchange traded options has been critical in that it has allowed participants in the cap market who act as providers of these instruments to, at least partially, reallocate their risk through the exchange rated options market. In this regard, the cap market operates in a manner which is largely analogous to the relationship between the futures markets in short-term interest rates and FRAs.

Customer demand for caps, floors and collars has been motivated primarily by the asymmetric risk profile of the instrument. The capability of these caps or collars to provide protection against adverse movements in interest rates while allowing the user to benefit from favourable movements has become particularly attractive given the sharply increased *volatility* of interest rate structures in the global capital market.

Typical users of caps etc have included:

- companies involved in leveraged buyouts and leveraged acquisitions;
- real estate developers concerned with capping construction interest costs;
- project financing sponsors;
- financial institutions utilising them for asset liability management;

- floating rate borrowers who have sought to place a cap on borrowing costs for specific periods of time based on rate expectations, exposure levels or as an alternative to interest rate swaps.

Historically, major demand for caps and similar products has come from thrift institutions, particularly in the United States, and from corporations seeking interest rate risk protection in the context of highly leveraged acquisitions or leveraged buyouts.

The demand from thrift institutions is generated by the inherent asset-liability mismatch entailed in financing long-term fixed rate assets with short-term floating rate liabilities. Thrifts, given this basic imbalance in their asset liability management structure, utilised caps to manage this interest rate risk. However, with the crisis in the Savings and Loans Associations, the fall in interest rates and the shift to more positive yield curves, demand from this source has declined.

The second category of demand identified related to corporate floating rate debt funding for acquisitions and undertaking leveraged buyouts. In a substantial number of cases, the parties providing the financing, as part of the terms of the loan, required the borrowers to implement interest rate risk protection in the form of swaps or caps. In the vast majority of cases, the risky nature of the transactions and the lower credit quality of the borrowers meant that the swap market was excluded from the range of interest rate risk management possibilities for credit reasons. This meant that caps were the only avenue for hedging the substantial interest rate risk entailed in these transactions.

In recent times, corporate liability managers have emerged as substantial purchasers of caps as part of general interest rate risk management. This reflects a variety of factors including:

- the steepness of the yield curve in a number of currencies which favoured borrowing short-term or pricing-off floating-rate short-term interest rate indexes with, typically, out-of-the-money caps being purchased to protect against unanticipated rises in the absolute levels of rates or an inversion of the yield curve;
- product innovation with the introduction of "zero cost" or "free" collars to eliminate the need for corporations to incur the premium cost of such transactions;
- at least for United States borrowers, the availability of products utilising the commercial paper rate as the interest rate index for the cap or floor transactions reflecting the fact that this was a more prevalent index for United States domestic corporate borrowers.

A key factor in the growth of the cap market has been the increased availability of providers of these types of facilities. Ironically, as noted above, many of the early participants in the market have ceased to participate due in no small part to losses sustained in the early 1980s when interest rates rose sharply.

The ranks of providers of caps, at least in a principal capacity, are dominated by a handful of commercial and investment banks. The less active participants may act as brokers, marking up a cap provided by another principal or by supplying caps stripped from a debt issue in the market: see discussion below. An important factor limiting the range of cap providers is credit risk. Given that the cap provider must be able to make payments over a number of years when and if market rates exceed the cap rate, the provider of the cap must be of very high credit standing. This naturally limits the range of financial institutions who would be acceptable as a counterparty to such transactions.

The main attraction to providers of these types of instruments include:

- the fact that there is no credit risk by the purchaser of the cap allows these financial institutions to deal with a wider range of market participants;
- potential profit from these particular transactions has been perceived as being significant;
- caps etc complement other risk management services offered by these institutions;
- developments in hedge technology have allowed a number of these participants to create mechanisms for reallocating the risk of managing cap portfolios within acceptable risk limits.

The providers of caps, floors or collars fall into one of a number of categories:

- brokers or matched back-to-back providers;
- traders or positioners;
- customised cap providers utilising theoretical delta-based or synthetic option hedge strategies;
- providers of stripped caps who distribute the cap element from capital market issues that they have originated;
- synthetic swap providers.

The brokers or matched providers of caps or floors usually source their supply of caps etc either from stripping operations related to capital market issues or with genuine customer demand for the offsetting form of the transaction. In the case of financial institutions, often the customer is the bank's own treasury which seeks to write options as part of their asset and liability management process. A number of providers write caps, floors and collars purely based on interest rate expectations, seeking to profit from a view that the floor or cap level will not be breached during the life of the transaction.

The third category of provider is by far the most dominant one. This group is made up of a number of financial intermediaries who utilise option theory, in particular delta hedging, whereby they hedge the cap positions utilising a mixture of cash, securities and futures contracts. For shorter maturities, these financial intermediaries often utilise exchange rated options markets to cover their own exposures and the cap or collar agreements.

As discussed in Chapters 11 and 36, the risks associated with providing caps on this basis are not inconsiderable. While theoretically tractable, this type of technique has a number of practical problems which can lead to losses particularly where interest rates prove volatile, as in the 1980s. These problems have led a number of participants to initially enter and ultimately withdraw from the market.

Institutions active in providing options have been frustrated by a number of factors including:

- the fact that caps have proved too cheap in the market relative to theoretical option values;
- the need to provide for hedging and transaction costs.

The need to factor in the fair value of the option plus the requisite mark up for risk and transaction costs has made the prices of these financial institutions for caps and collars relatively expensive and out of the market. This problem has in recent times been exacerbated by the emergence of a substantial market in stripped caps.

This market developed in June 1985 when capped FRNs were introduced. As discussed in Chapter 15 in the context of securitising options through option swaps, these capped FRN issues embodied cap and/or floor elements which were capable of being separated and sold in securitised form. In the second half of 1985, in excess of US$4 billion of floating rate paper with caps were issued. These caps were then stripped and sold into the market.

The emergence of the stripped caps provided institutions active in writing customised caps using delta hedging technology with significant competition. These competitive pressures derived from the fact that the presence of stripped caps attracted a whole new class of participants. The fact that these caps involved no positioning or trading risk allowed a variety of financial institutions to act as brokers distributing these caps to end customers. While the emergence of stripped caps and the entry of new participants assisted in greatly increasing the awareness of these instruments among potential corporate and financial institution clients, the fact that the premiums for these stripped caps tended to be consistently lower than those quoted by financial institutions for customised transactions created a new source of competitive pressure.

The stripped caps available were, in reality, not ideal for corporate or investor risk management applications. Typical stripped caps available were of two varieties:

- Seven or 12 year caps with a strike level of around 12.50-13.25% pa with the reference index being three or six month LIBOR. These caps were stripped-off capped FRN issues in the Euromarkets.
- Three or five year caps with strike levels of 11.875-12.50% pa again with the reference rate being LIBOR. These caps were stripped off variable rates CD issues primarily undertaken by Japanese banks in the New York or Far East market.

The caps provided by these issues were often too high or too long in maturity for most corporate applications. For example, FRN caps were bought by United States thrifts. In addition, the lack of flexibility as to term, structure and level available make the stripped caps relatively unattractive. Inability to customise the transaction to the end customer's need in terms of a client's rollover dates on its underlying borrowing, variable settlement bases, a choice of indices as well as special features such as deferred starts, amortisation, variable principal, etc to a large extent mitigated the competitive impact of the stripped caps.

The supply of stripped caps from capital market issues has also been less than consistent. Supply from this source is dependent upon investor willingness to create securities with the requisite features. In fact, shortly after this market was born, investor demand for capped Eurocurrency FRNs and, to a lesser extent, for variable rate CDs evaporated significantly creating a shortage of supply from this particular source. However, as detailed in Chapter 15, the market for stripped caps and floors has re-emerged in 1992/93. The difference between the customised caps sold by financial institutions and the stripped cap market should not be overstated. This is because, in fact, the bulk of caps created by capital market issues were, in fact, bought by financial institutions which utilised these caps as hedges against open positions in their own cap books.

A growing source of cap providers have been financial institutions who are active in providing interest rate swaps on a principal basis through their swap warehouses. This is because, as outlined in Chapter 2, an interest rate swap can be characterised as a simultaneous purchase and sale of a cap and a floor with the same strike price. Utilising this basic economic relationship, a number of swap warehouses have started to write caps and collars while simultaneously hedging the inherent risks through their swap books. This area promises to be a growing source of supply of these types of instruments.

The technology for hedging the risk on cap and floor transactions has developed substantially in recent years. Availability of options on swaps has also provided market makers in caps with new techniques for hedging risk positions. A number of dealers increasingly utilise options on swaps to reduce the degree to which their cap portfolios were net sellers or purchasers of volatility. A major factor underlying this development was the fact that, at particular times, because of the supply of options on swaps, primarily related to securitising call options in bond issues, dealers were allowed to hedge their cap portfolios at substantially lower implied volatilities than those in the cap and floor market. This resulted in the overall level of implied volatilities in caps and floors in US$ declining from levels of around 20% in the middle 1980s to levels around 10-15%, by the late 1980s and early 1990s.

The other major development in hedging technology has been increased willingness of various capital market participants to, themselves, write caps or floors. For example, the late 1980s, United States thrift institution undertook of super floater swaps (see discussion in Chapter 15) which entailed the institution selling, effectively, out-of-the-money caps to generate the required economic profile of these transactions. More recently, Japanese financial institutions, including banks and institutional investors, have emerged as substantial sellers of caps and floors seeking to generate current income. This trend is also evident, to a lesser extent, among financial institutions, corporations and, in some cases, sovereign borrowers in other countries. For example, one common strategy is for borrowers to sell floors to lower their floating rate cost of funds or to sell out-of-the-money caps against fixed rate liabilities to generate premium income.

An interbank market in caps and collars, primarily in New York and London, has emerged. The market is dominated by three to four participants who are the primary market makers. An additional 15 to 20 financial institutions also participate in this market. A number of commodity traders, such as Cargill of Minnesota, are also active in this market. A number of active brokers also participate. The market is primarily in three to five year caps and the depth and liquidity of the market is increasing. The geographical distribution of all cap activity irrespective of currency, is interesting with the United States dominating with a total of around 50% of total activity. The other major centres include the United Kingdom (20%), France and Germany (both approximately 5-10%) and the remainder of the world, which includes Europe and Australasia contributing the remainder.

An interesting feature of the global cap market is the significant differences in the way a number of these markets, at least initially, commenced. For example, the deutschmark and Dutch guilder cap markets were purely created off the back of capped FRN issues in those particular currencies.

In recent years, the market for caps, floors and similar instruments has grown more rapidly in currencies other than US$. The growth in these instruments in currencies such as deutschmarks, sterling and yen have reflected a variety of factors including:

- the rapid transfer of technology from the US$ cap market;
- volatility of interest rates in these currencies which has created an environment prompting increasing focus on utilising these instruments for interest rate risk management;
- the growth in and proliferation of financial instruments in these markets generally.

Outside of these currencies, markets in caps and similar instruments exist in a wide variety of currencies although the markets are more spasmodic and limited in scope.

As noted previously, the major differences between the major and minor markets is in terms of individual transaction amounts which can be executed, maturities (markets other than the major markets tend to have shorter maturities generally out to three years) and limited liquidity.

Chapter 29

Global Equity and Commodity Derivatives Markets

BACKGROUND

The markets for equity and commodity derivatives are of more recent origin and are, consequently, still in the early stages of evolution.

The market for commodity and equity derivatives has a number of significant differences to the market for other swap products with their emphasis on interest rate and currency risk elements. These differences include:

- These products are not, at least to the same extent, an integrated set of transactions as are other swap instruments (that is, the interrelationships between swaps, FRAs, LTFX and caps etc). There is, however, relatively strong integration in relation to commodity products relating to a *specific commodity*.
- While commodity and equity derivatives are predicated on and, to a substantial extent, draw on basic swap instruments, there is little or no linkage between commodity and equity products and traditional swap instruments. The only linkages relate to where commodity or equity products are currency hedged or interest rate or currency elements are embedded in the instruments.
- The commodity markets are truly global and are not restricted by national boundaries as the commodities themselves do not have a country based origin. In contrast, equity derivatives more closely resemble currency markets as they are basically financial instruments linked closely to particular national markets. Ironically, despite their more recent origin, markets in commodities and equities have existed for significantly longer than other swap derivatives, albeit in a different form.

The basic rationale for markets for commodity and equity derivatives differs as between the two classes of instruments:

- Commodity derivatives are predicated on, to some substantial extent, commodity price-risk management considerations.
- Equity derivatives represent different ways of capturing equity market returns or alternative methods for the management of portfolios of equity investments.

COMMODITY SWAPS

Origins/development

The earliest commodity swap is thought to have been transacted in 1986. The technique is thought to have been pioneered by Chase Manhattan as well as a number of other institutions.

The market has grown rapidly under the influence of a variety of factors identified in the following section. While measurement of the size of the market is difficult, it is estimated that the total notional amount of commodity derivative transactions undertaken annually is around US$80-100bn pa. The primary component is energy derivatives where transaction volumes are around US$40-60bn pa (approximately half in crude oil and the remainder in oil products and natural gas). Activity can be volatile with estimates indicating that following the invasion of Kuwait by Iraq and the resultant Gulf war, activity in commodity derivatives rose to levels approaching US$40-50bn *per month*.

The market for commodity derivatives and its structure has been dictated, primarily, by the increased focus on commodity risk management. However, market structure and growth has also been influenced by a number of specific factors such as the impact of airlines hedging fuel costs, the Gulf war and investor interest in assuming commodity risk.

The development of commodity swaps has been affected by the actions of regulators, particularly the United States Commodity Futures Trading Commission (CFTC).

In 1987, following Chase Manhattan's advertisement of their services in *The Wall Street Journal* and the publication of a brochure on commodity swaps by the bank, the CFTC subpoenaed the manager of Chase Manhattan's Commodity Index Swaps and Financing Group as part of its investigative action to consider whether it should regulate the market. The agency also released an advance notice of proposed rule-making on hybrid instruments which viewed commodity swaps as a form of futures contract which could only be traded on a recognised exchange. The impact of the decision was that the commodity swap market essentially moved overseas and United States banks were only allowed to participate in this market through overseas subsidiaries.

The CFTC position led to a number of transactions, including a gold-linked certificate of deposit issue by Wells Fargo Bank, having to be withdrawn.

However, in 1989 the CFTC reversed its stance and accepted the position that commodity swaps do not fall under its jurisdiction; consequently it discontinued its investigative actions. In a policy statement (dated 14 July 1989) the Commission set out the features which characterised the swap market and accepted that, provided the transaction meets a number of conditions, they are in a "safe harbour" and outside the CFTC's regulatory ambit. These conditions (which largely reflect existing market practice) include:

- transactions must be individually tailored;
- transactions do not have the credit support of a clearing organisation nor are they marked-to-market or use a variation settlement system which eliminates individual credit risk;
- transactions are undertaken as part of the participant's general line of business;
- transactions are not offered to the retail public.

The only criteria which creates difficulty is the second. Increasingly, swap transactions (both in the commodity swap market and in similar products such as interest rate and currency swaps) resort to mark-to-market and/or collateralisation provisions as a means of reducing counterparty credit exposures for capital adequacy purposes. However, there are significant differences between the daily mark-to-market mechanisms of a futures contract and those applied in connection with commodity and related swaps. These differences have allowed most transactions to satisfy the "safe harbour" provisions specified by the CFTC.

Key structural factors

Commodity risk management

The commodity derivatives market reflects the influence of a number of factors, including:

- increasing sophistication of corporate financial management and focus on commodity risk management;
- improvements in financial engineering technology;
- increased commodity price volatility.

The level of financial risk in the environment in which companies operate has increased dramatically in the last two decades. Unanticipated changes in financial market rates for foreign currencies, interest rates, and commodity prices rapidly impact upon corporate profitability. The increased focus on commodity price risk management is part of the increased focus on financial risk management within corporations.

This more widespread awareness of commodity price risk management also coincides with increasing volatility in commodity markets.

Exhibit 29.1 plots the history of prices for major commodities. The graphs indicate that the prices of major commodities including petroleum products, metals, etc, have been increasingly volatile. For example, basic commodity prices in the 1970s rose sharply, reflecting high rates of inflation in the global economy. The declining purchasing power of monetary assets increased the demand for commodities, resulting in an increase in the prices of real goods (including commodities) relative to financial assets. The major impact of this period was the massive transfer of wealth from commodity users to commodity producers, particularly oil producing countries.

However, high real interest rates in the late 1970s and throughout much of the 1980s meant that the relationship between commodity prices and financial assets changed dramatically. As real interest rates rose, the opportunity costs of holding inventories of commodities increased, resulting in a shift out of commodities and into financial assets.

The late 1980s and early 1990s have been characterised by a period of high *real* but low nominal interest rates (particularly, outside the European currency block) in a period of declining inflation. These trends, combined with outlook for lower rates of economic growth globally has resulted in significant declines in commodity prices. The exception to this overall decline has been the extreme volatility of energy prices particularly as a result of the Gulf war.

The increased volatility in commodity prices prompted the development of a number of commodity risk management products. These included, initially, forward/futures markets in many commodities. However, the market also evolved a variety of highly customised commodity risk management products including commodity indexed securities, commodity warrants and commodity swaps.

Exhibit 29.1

History of Prices for Major Commodities

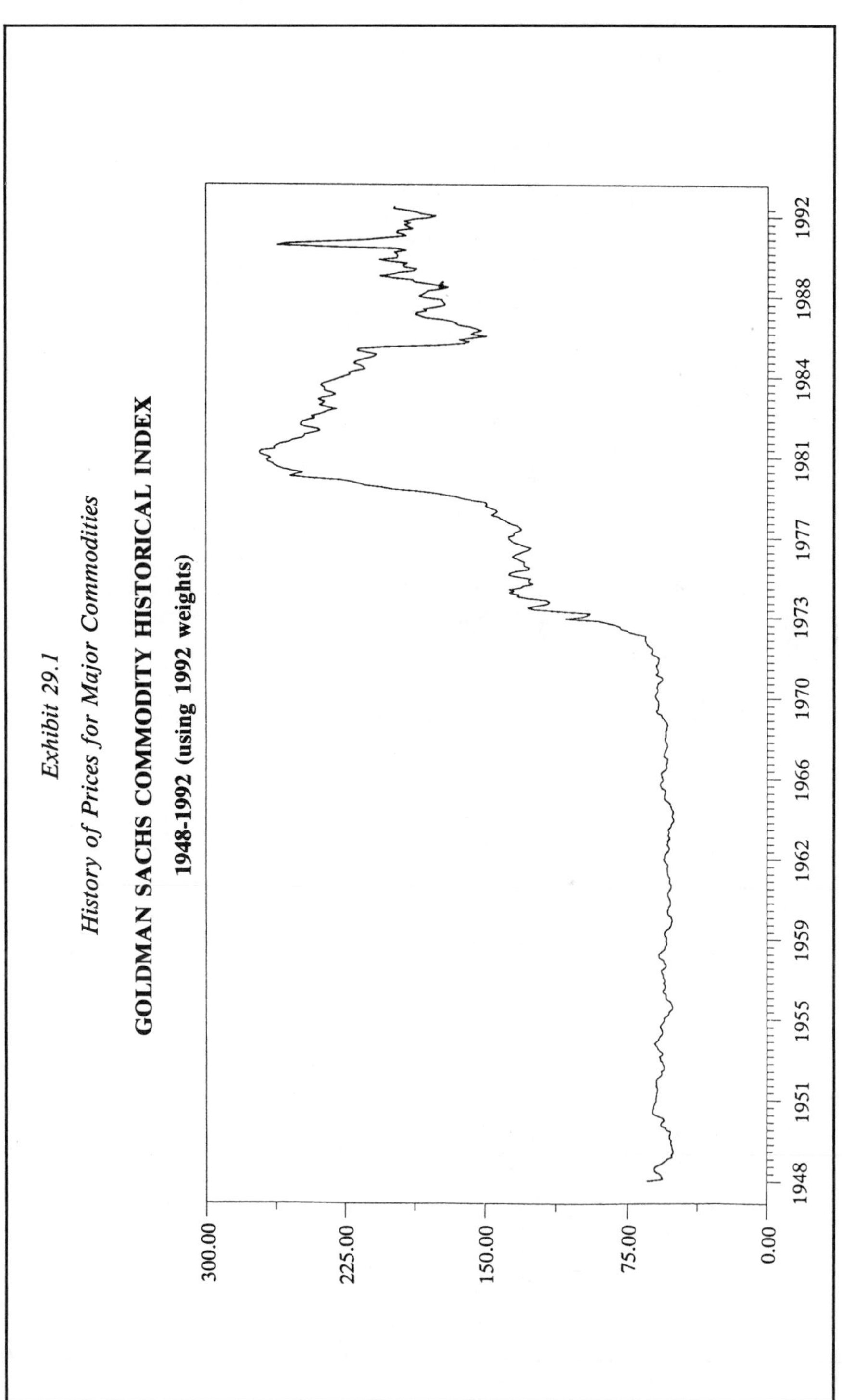

Exhibit 29.1—continued

GOLDMAN SACHS COMMODITY INDEX ANNUAL % CHANGES

1948-1992

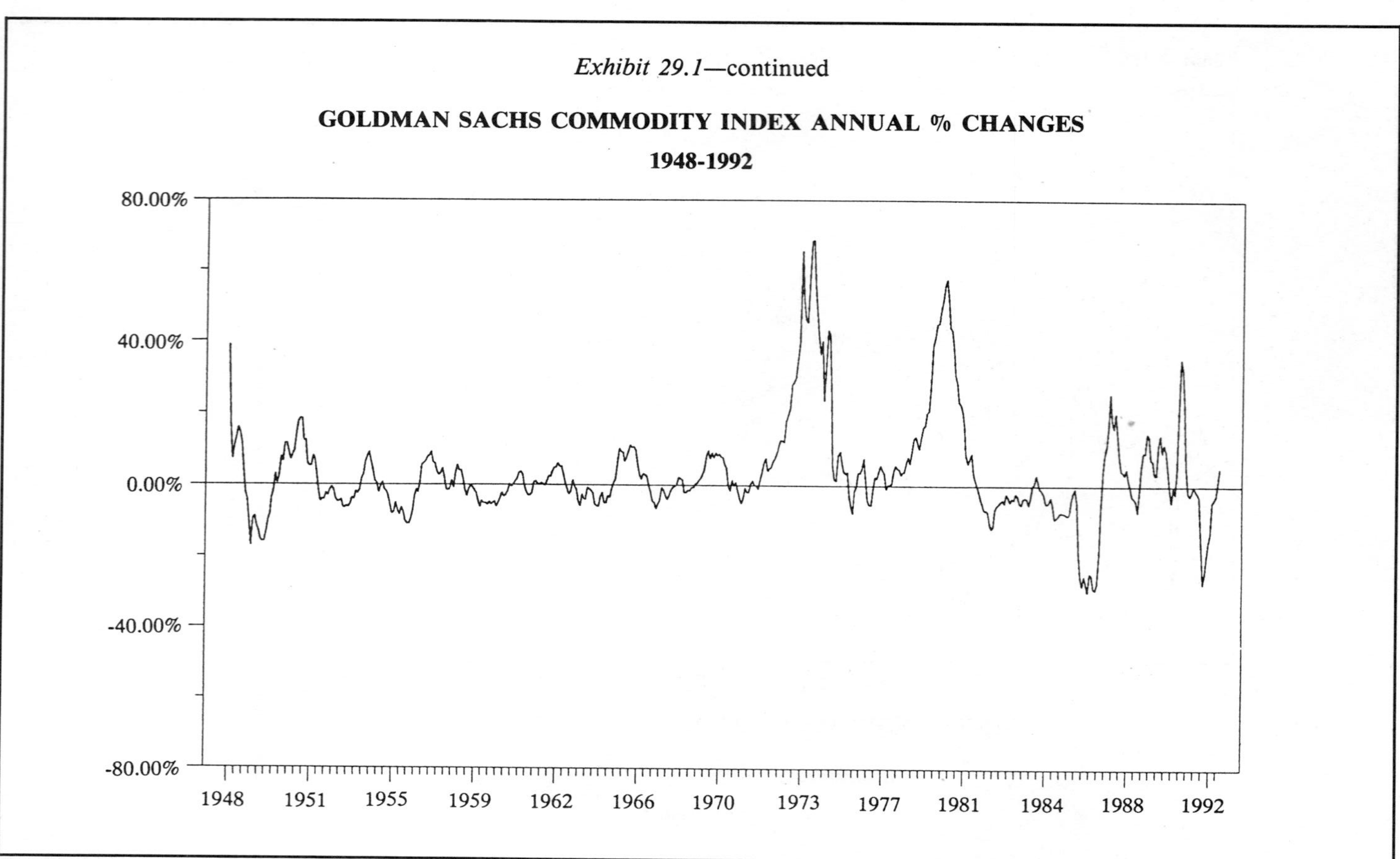

Exhibit 29.1—continued

GOLDMAN SACHS NON-ENERGY HISTORICAL INDEX

1948-1992 (using 1992 weights)

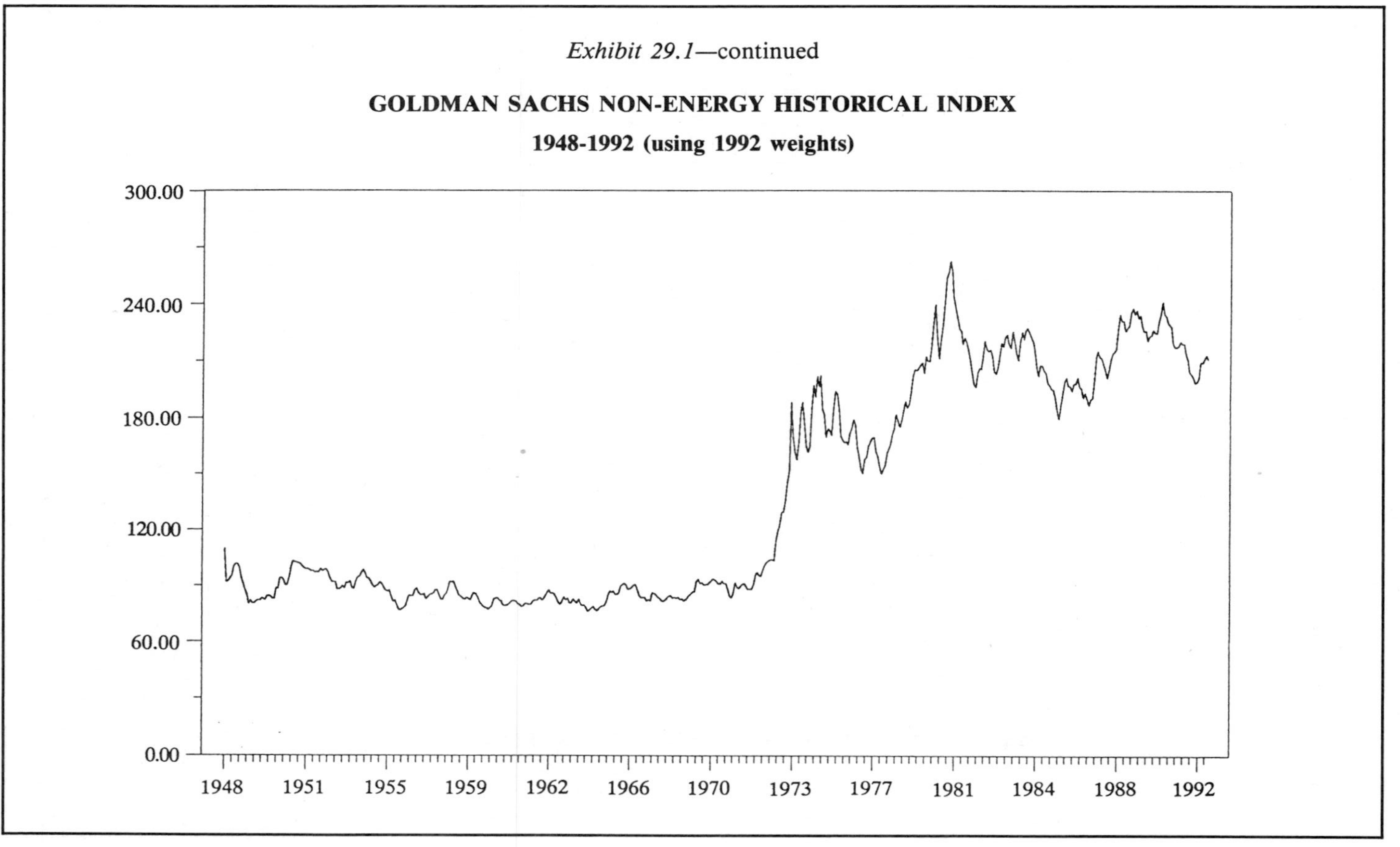

Exhibit 29.1—continued

GOLDMAN SACHS NON-ENERGY ANNUAL % CHANGES

1948-1992

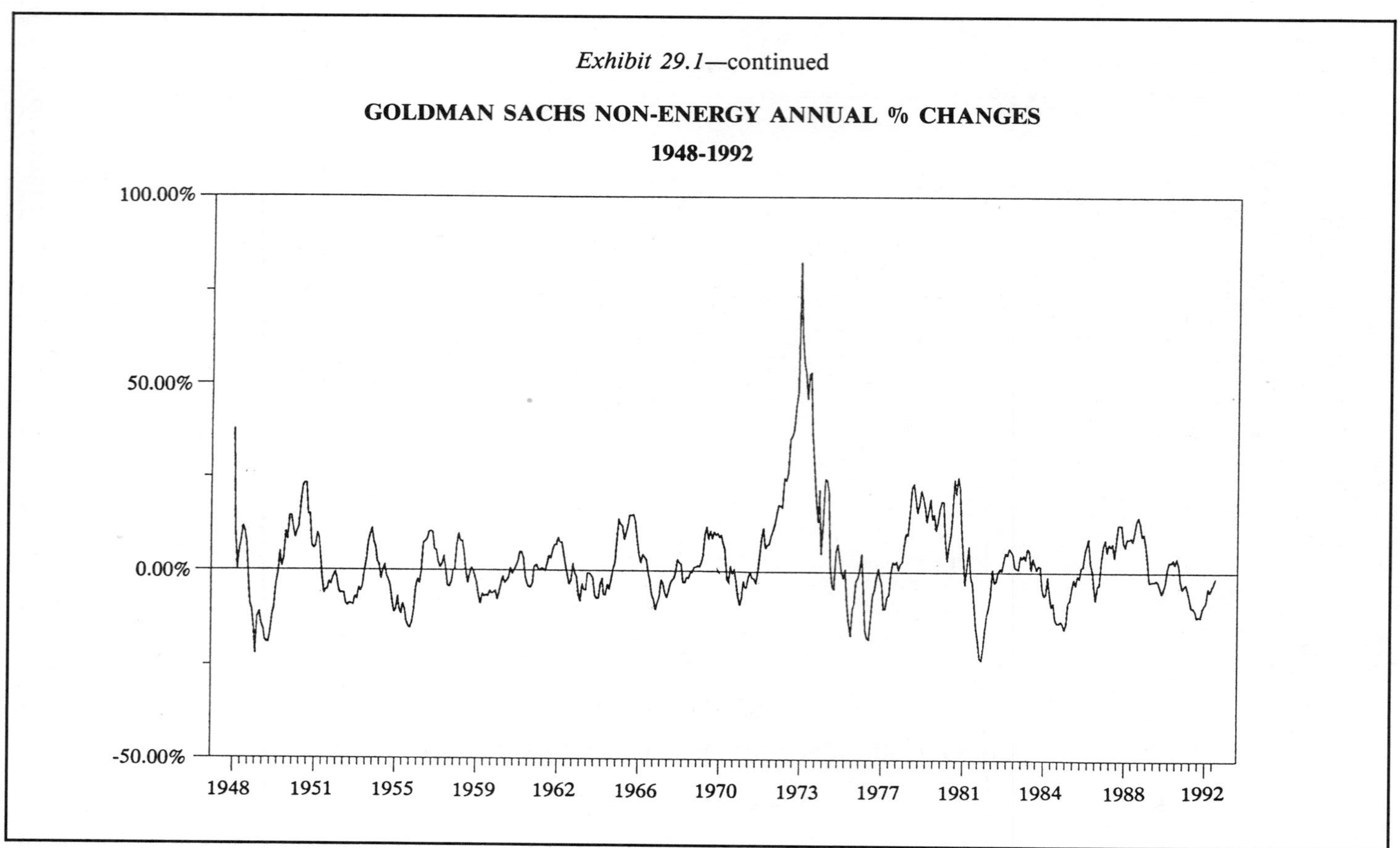

Exhibit 29.1—continued

GOLDMAN SACHS ENERGY HISTORICAL INDEX

1948-1992 (using 1992 weights)

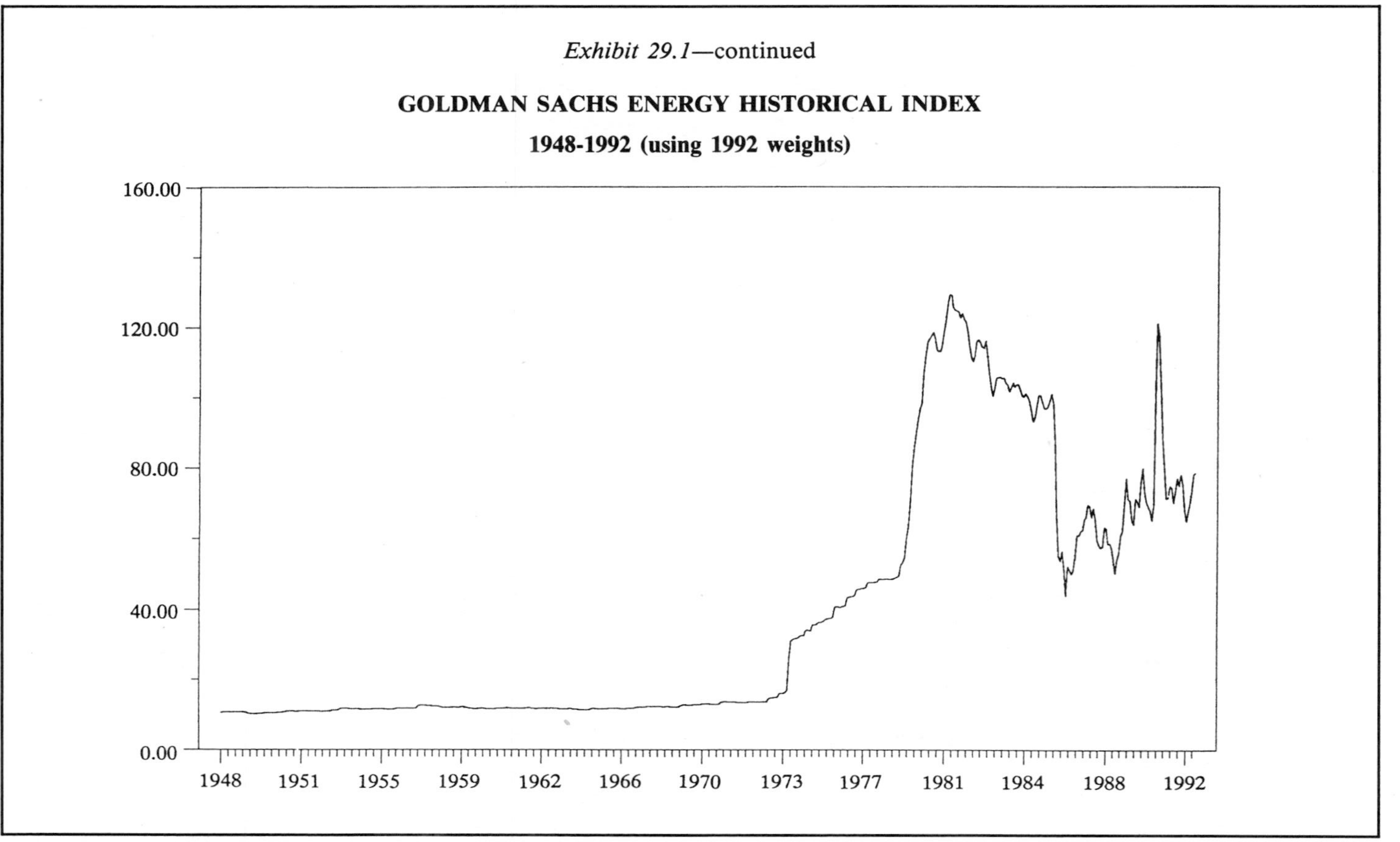

Exhibit 29.1—continued

GOLDMAN SACHS ENERGY INDEX ANNUAL % CHANGES

1948-1992

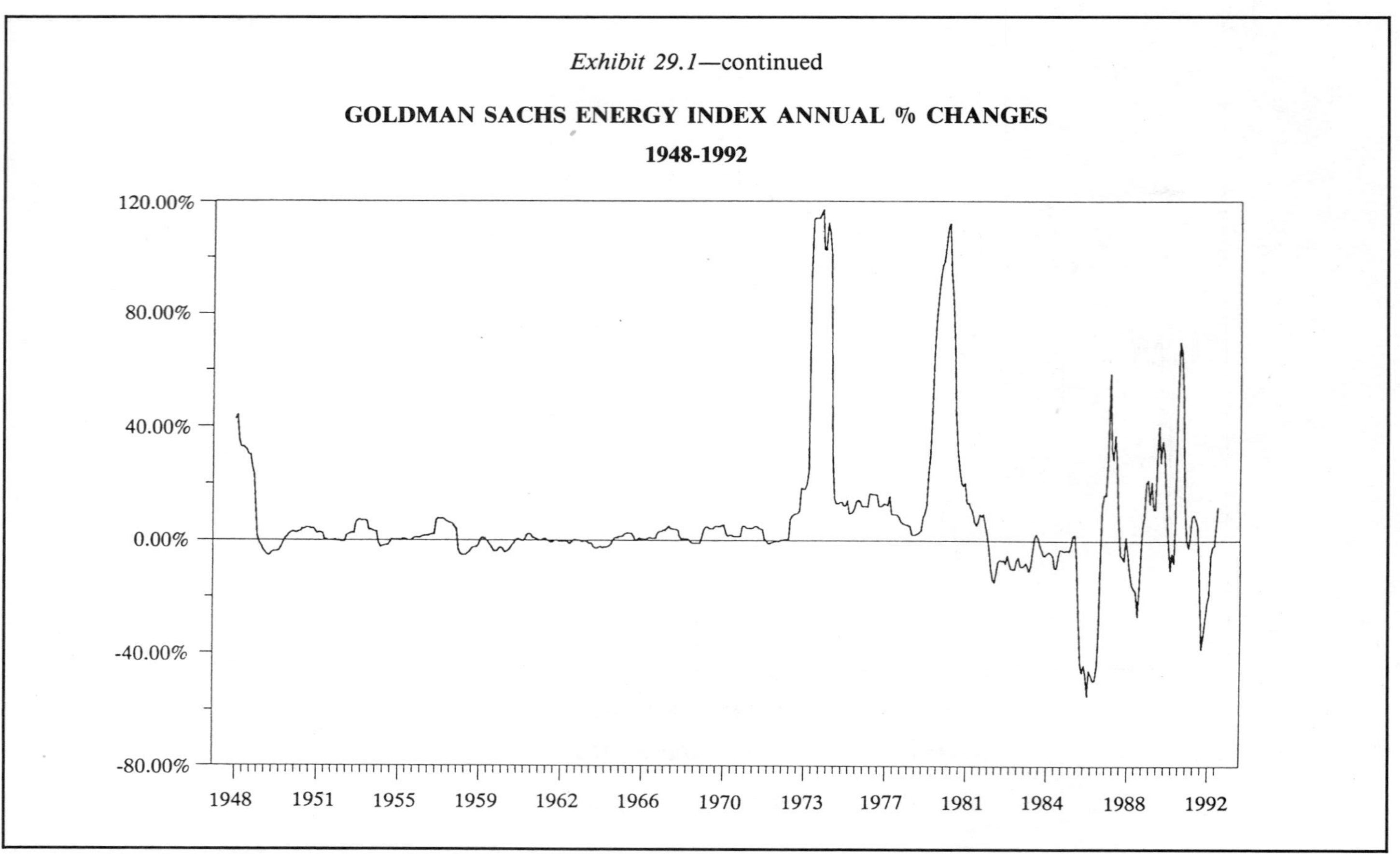

Exhibit 29.1—continued

GOLDMAN SACHS LIVESTOCK HISTORICAL INDEX

1948-1992 (using 1992 weights)

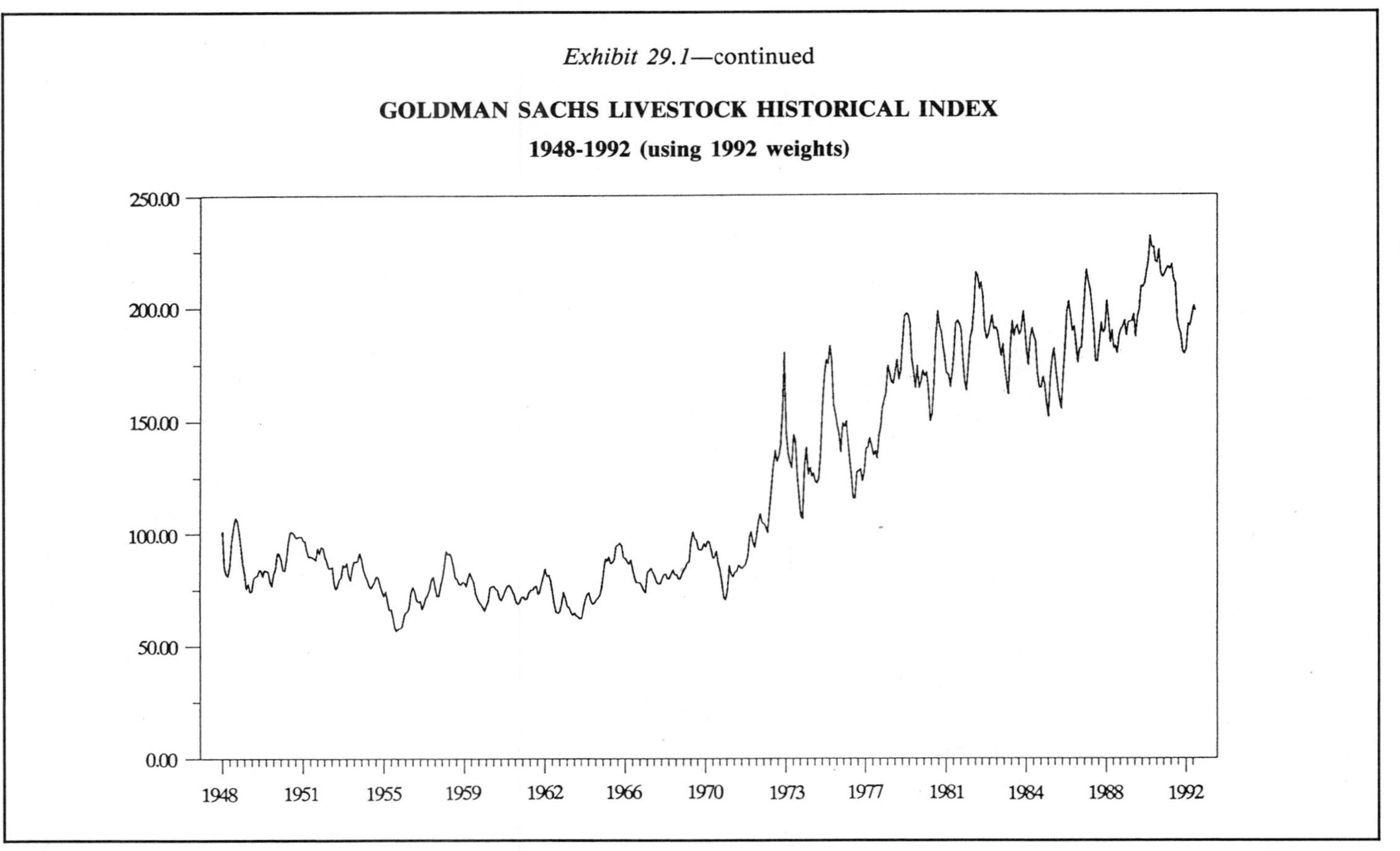

Exhibit 29.1—continued

GOLDMAN SACHS LIVESTOCK INDEX ANNUAL % CHANGES

1948-1992

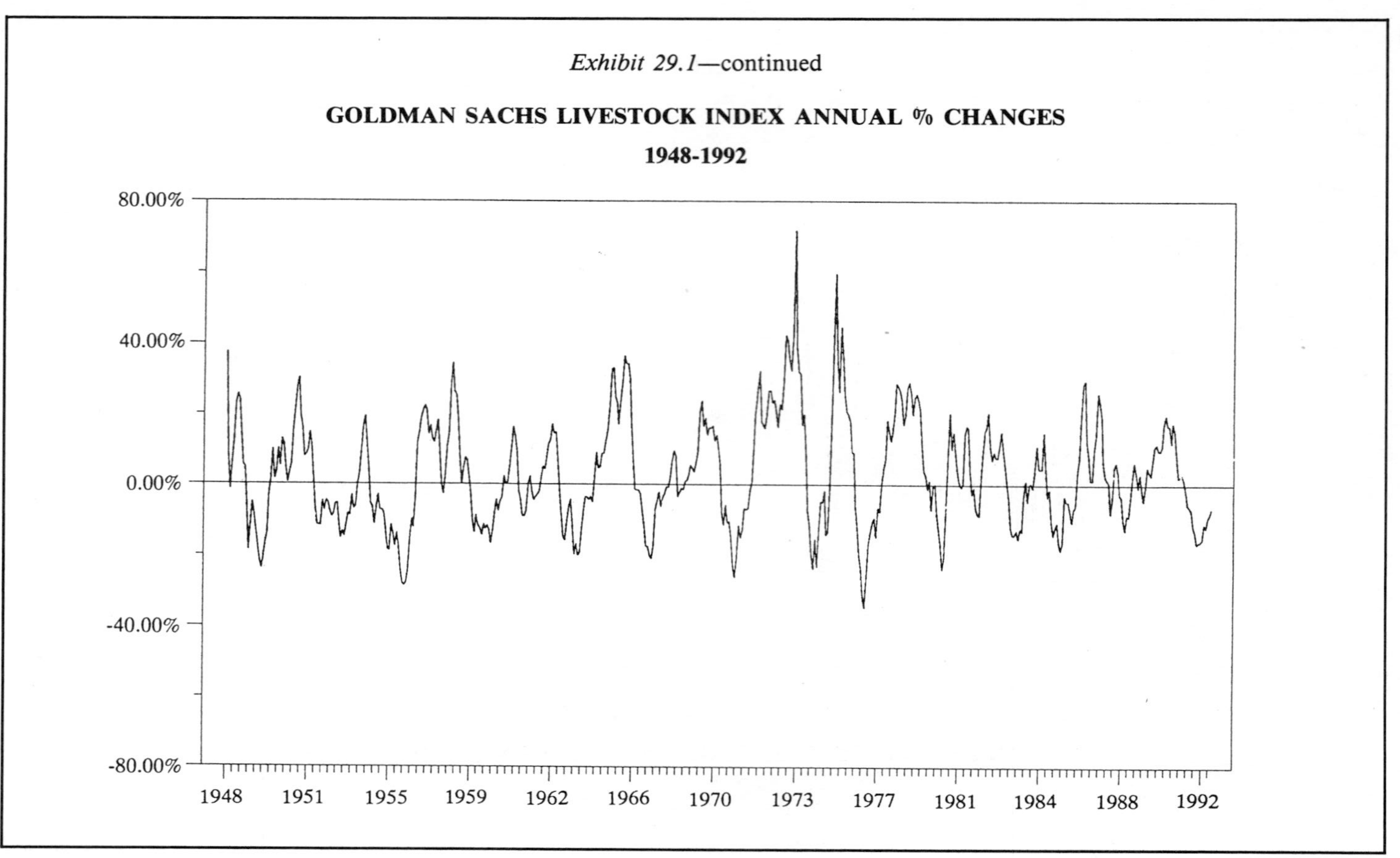

Exhibit 29.1—continued

GOLDMAN SACHS AGRICULTURAL HISTORICAL INDEX

1948-1992 (using 1992 weights)

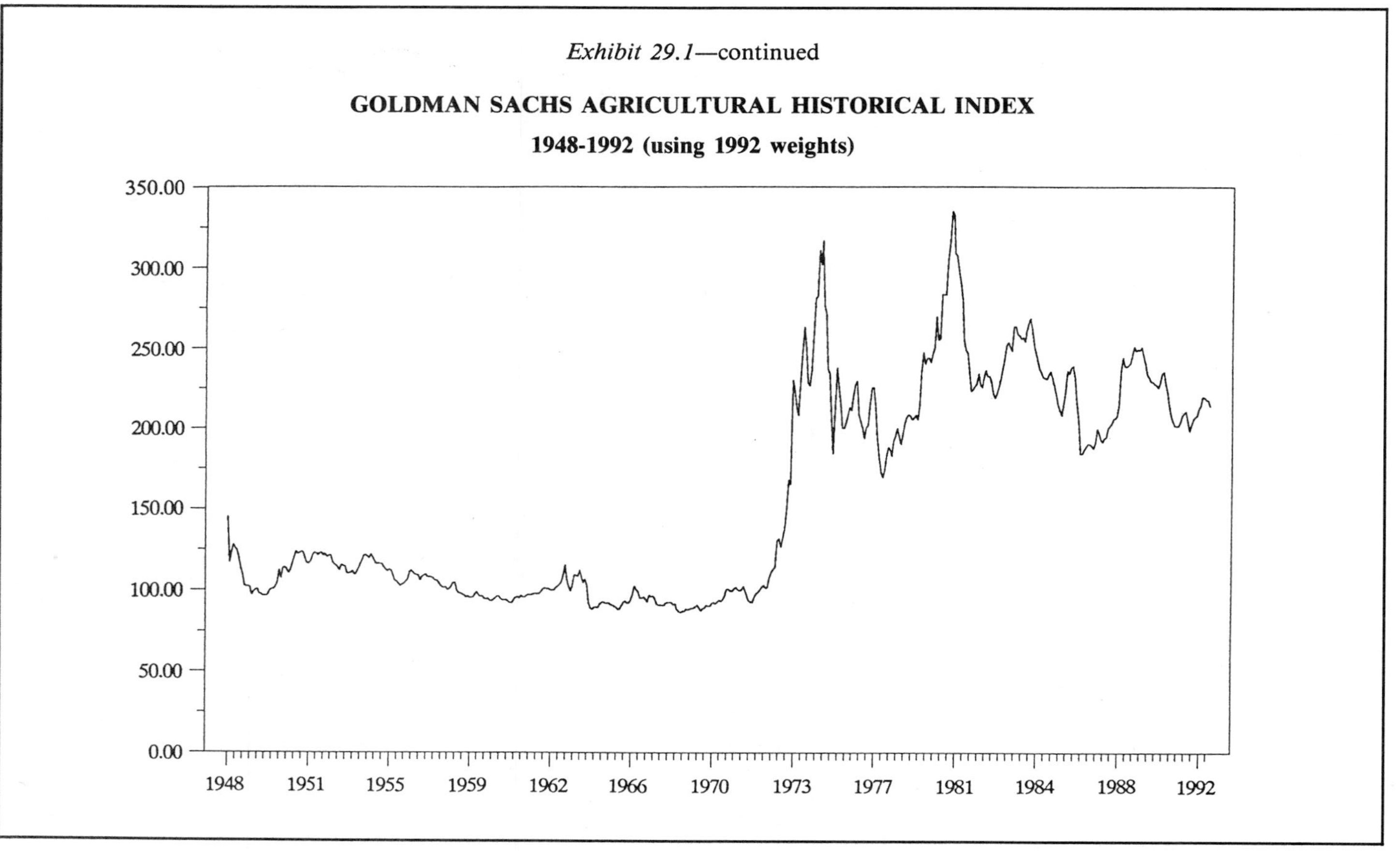

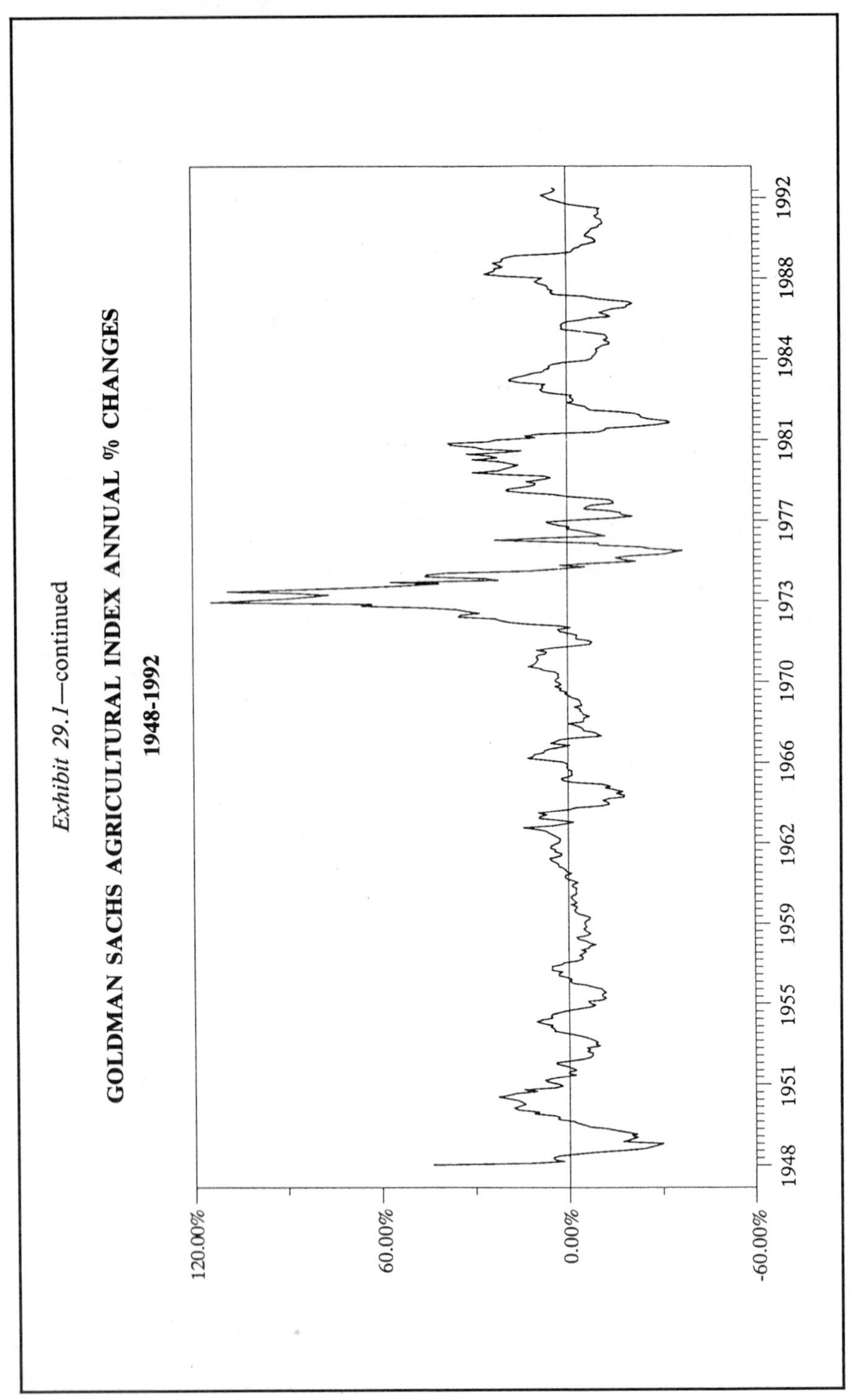
Exhibit 29.1—continued
GOLDMAN SACHS AGRICULTURAL INDEX ANNUAL % CHANGES
1948-1992
120.00%
60.00%
0.00%
-60.00%
1948
1951
1955
1959
1962
1966
1970
1973
1977
1981
1984
1988
1992

Exhibit 29.1—continued

GOLDMAN SACHS INDUSTRIAL METALS HISTORICAL INDEX

1948-1992 (using 1992 weights)

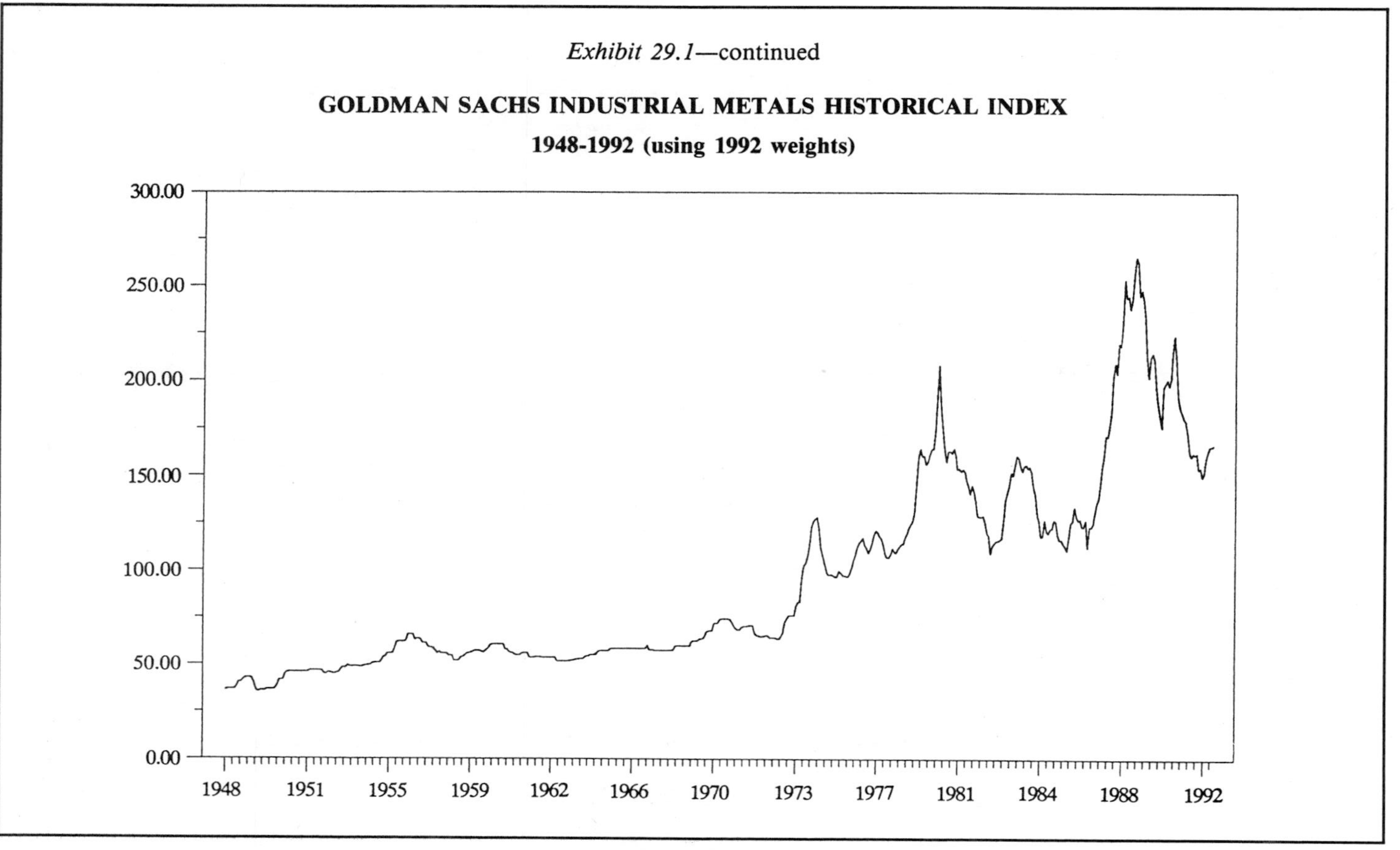

Exhibit 29.1—continued

GOLDMAN SACHS INDUSTRIAL METALS INDEX ANNUAL % CHANGES

1948-1992

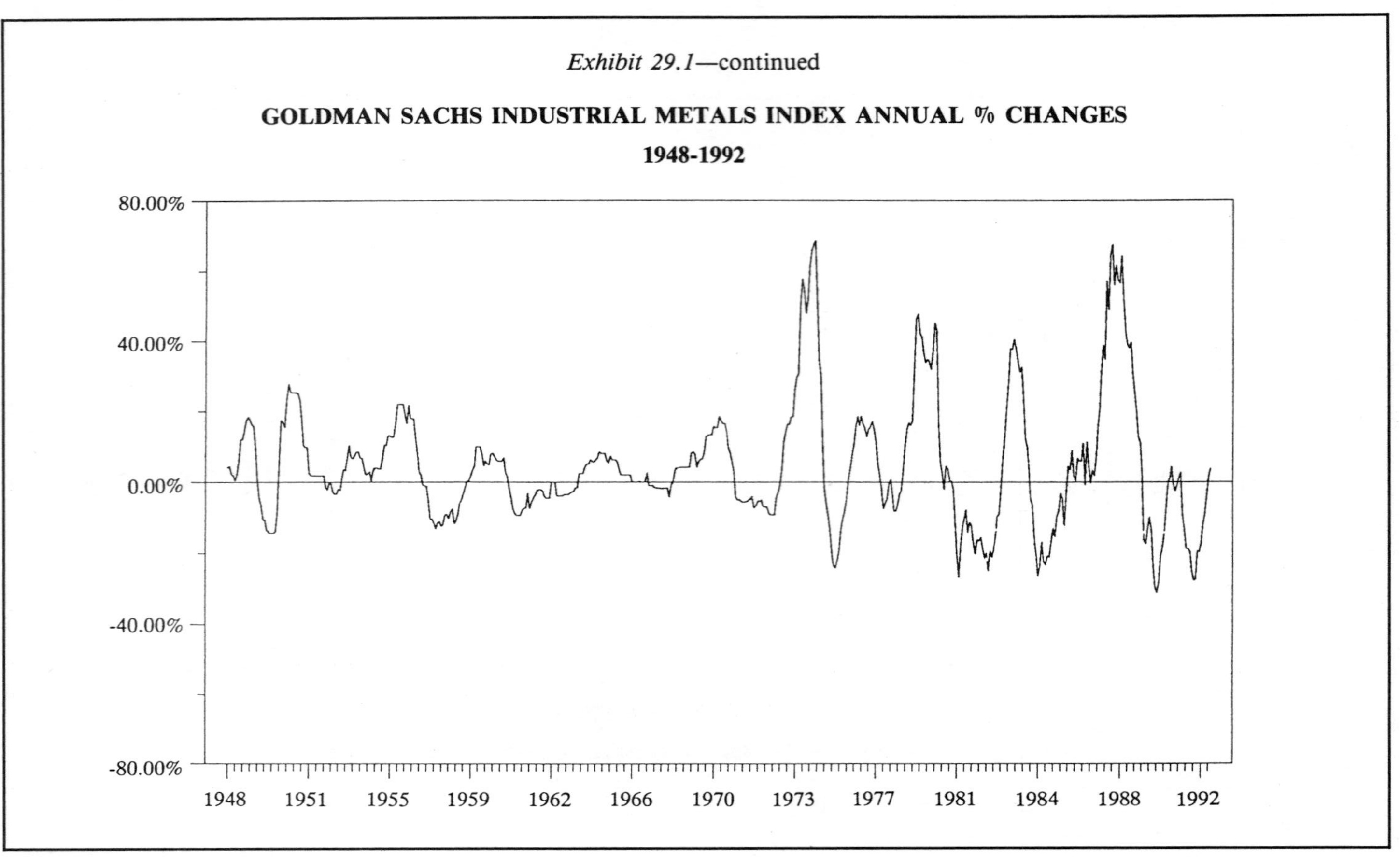

Exhibit 29.1—continued

GOLDMAN SACHS PRECIOUS METALS HISTORICAL INDEX

1948-1992 (using 1992 weights)

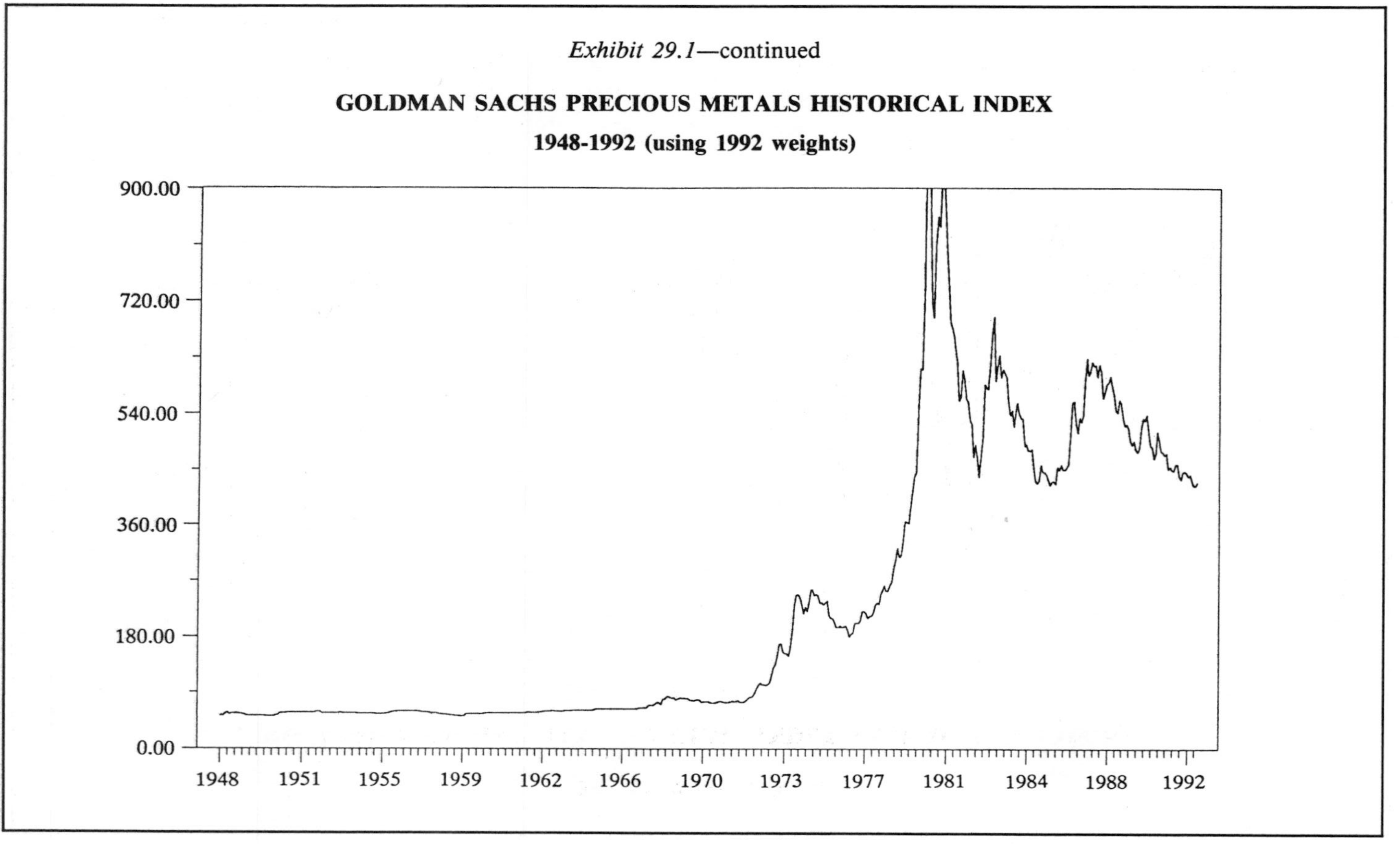

Exhibit 29.1—continued

GOLDMAN SACHS PRECIOUS METALS INDEX ANNUAL % CHANGES

1948-1992

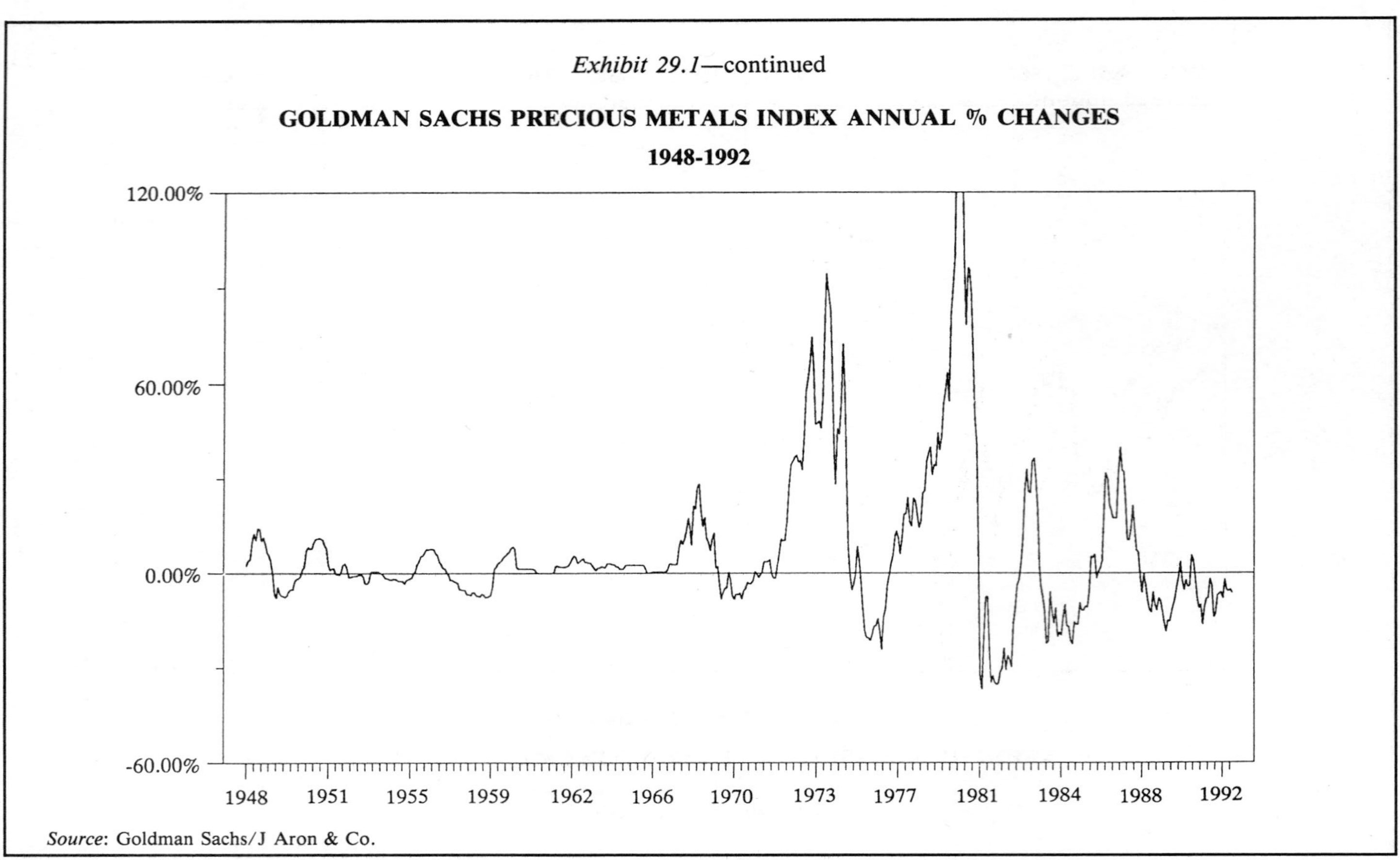

Source: Goldman Sachs/J Aron & Co.

Impact of specific factors

As noted previously, the structure and rate of development of the commodity markets has been influenced by a number of specific factors. The demand for energy price hedging instruments by airlines is one of these specific factors.

Factors underlying the demand for aviation fuel hedging techniques from airlines reflect the complex interplay of a number of factors:

- the fact that jet fuel costs comprise a significant component (up to 30-40%) of the cost structure of airlines;
- the volatility of oil prices and the influence of specific political factors which contribute to the volatility;
- the competitive structure of the airline industry with its volatile profitability and increased global competition as a result of deregulation in a variety of markets which has forced airlines to seek to generate competitive advantage from any available source.

Against this background, the airlines, led by the major United States carriers, major European airlines (British Airways, Air France, KLM and Scandinavian Airlines), and large Asia-Pacific airlines, such as Singapore Airlines and the major Japanese carriers, have sought various mechanisms to hedge their fuel oil exposure. In fact, the first significant commodity swap was reputedly for an Asian airline where the transaction was structured to provide the carrier with the capacity to exchange a floating price for jet fuel for a fixed price for the commodity for a period of six months.

The impetus for airlines managing their fuel price exposure has been given additional impetus by the Gulf war where jet fuel prices increased dramatically resulting in unhedged airlines suffering substantial operating cost increases and, in a number of cases, very significant losses.

The second factor which has influenced the development of the commodity derivatives market was the Gulf war itself. The Gulf war had the effect of focusing the attention of corporate financial risk managers upon the substantial impact of commodity price volatility on earnings and financial performance. In addition, the Gulf war which created, at times, extreme volatility in the oil price markets attracted interest from a wide variety of investors seeking to speculate on oil price movements.

The immediate impact of the Gulf war was to highlight the advantages of fuel price hedging for airlines. However, it allowed a wide variety of producers, ranging from the large global oil companies to medium-sized producers, to take advantage of rises in oil prices to lock in forward sale price of petroleum product, in some cases for significant periods of time.

The volatility of oil prices and the potential impact of higher oil prices on global inflation levels, among the oil-consuming countries, highlighted the interrelationship between commodity price movements and returns on other financial instruments. Institutional investors were forced to review their attitudes to commodity price risk and to incorporate commodity assets and the risk of price movements of these assets as a specific component of their asset portfolios which required management.

Recognition of this complex interrelationship created a significant demand for, initially, oil market related commodity derivatives targeted at investors seeking to take positions in commodity price markets to either hedge underlying portfolio risks or to take positions in respect of anticipated price movements. A component of this demand came from retail investors seeking to speculate on anticipated commodity price movements.

The gradual recognition of commodities as a specific class of investment assets is a final factor which has influenced the structure of commodity derivative markets.

Types of commodities/product structures

The major commodity involved has, traditionally, been oil and related energy products. Commodity swaps are available in a variety of energy products including WTI, Brent, heating oil, jet fuel, naphtha and bunker fuel. More recently, commodity swap products in natural gas have also been introduced. *Exhibit 29.2* sets out WTI oil swap prices between October 1989 and September 1992.

Exhibit 29.3 sets out an example of a natural gas swap transaction. *Exhibit 29.4* sets out an example of a British Thermal Unit swap (BTU swap) which is predicated on using a heat conversion pricing mechanism to allow utilities and co-generators to reproduce the effect of buying the cheapest form of fuel at a given point in time. Such transactions are structured on the basis of the commodity swap dealer taking the basis risk between oil and gas prices. Designing such transactions relies on agreeing a conversion rate enabling direct comparison of fuel and oil prices. These transaction structures highlight the unique facets of each commodity derivative market and the special elements influencing pricing and structure in relation to specific commodities.

Commodity swap transactions in a variety of metals are also available. The major commodity is copper but transactions involving zinc, aluminium, and nickel are also possible. Commodity swaps involving precious metals such as gold, silver, platinum, etc, have also been available.

The fungibility of precious metals, which approximates the characteristics of currency markets, has allowed this market to evolve more rapidly.

Products involving grains, particularly wheat, are available. Products involving other commodities such as sugar, coffee, cocoa, etc as well as wood products (paper pulp) are also increasingly available to market participants. A market in products such as orange juice (involving orange juice swaps) as between producers and consumers (primarily, soft drink concentrate manufacturers) has developed.

A number of factors determine whether commodity derivatives in a particular commodity are feasible. These include:

- prices fixed by market forces with reliable transparent reporting mechanisms;
- liquid spot market, the presence of a liquid futures market in the commodity is helpful although not essential;
- opposing price expectations for consumers and producers of the commodity, and sufficient numbers of both; and
- price volatility.

Some commodities, such as diamonds or wool (at least, until recently) where the supply and price are tightly controlled, are not suitable for commodity derivative transactions.

In theory, commodity derivative transactions for maturities as long as 10-12 years are available for oil products. However, in practice trading in oil derivatives is concentrated in maturities between six months and three years, although traded maturities are increasing in tenor. Maturities available for other commodities are significantly shorter with a concentration of transactions in the shorter maturities.

Exhibit 29.2
WTI Oil Swap Prices
(prompt start)

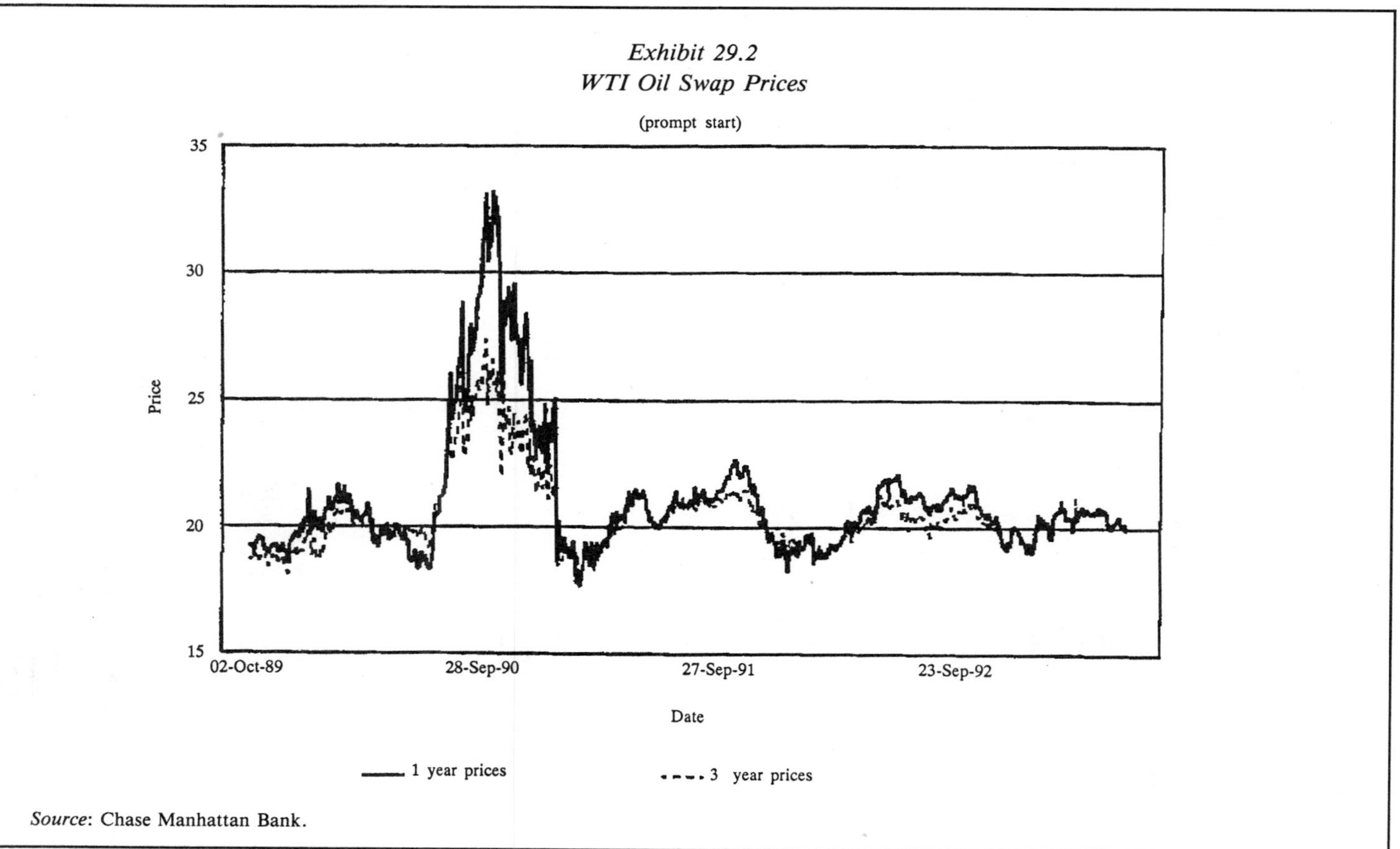

Source: Chase Manhattan Bank.

Exhibit 29.3
Natural Gas Swaps

Natural gas is typically sold in one of three ways. With *firm contracts* the producer must deliver an agreed amount of gas at a fixed price, or pay the difference if supply problems mean that the consumer must buy in the market. With *baseload contracts* the producer must also deliver an agreed volume at an agreed price, unless prevented by events beyond its control (in which case there is no financial penalty). With *swing sales* prices and volumes are subject to renegotiation by either the buyer or the seller.

Swing sales account for some 30-40% of all US natural gas transactions. And baseload contracts can even turn into swing contracts if limited demand means that producers have no other way of selling their gas.

Swing contracts can assist producers, marketers, distributors and consumers to cope with supply disruptions, or help producers pick up additional business; but they can also subject counterparties to extreme price volatility and uncertainty of supply.

1. Nymex deal with swing sale

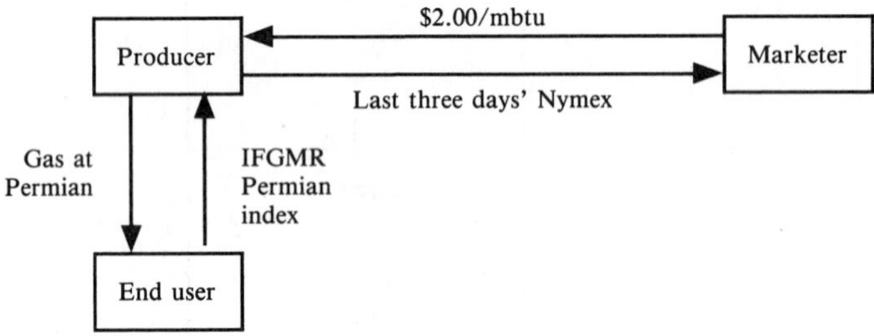

2. Firm physical deal

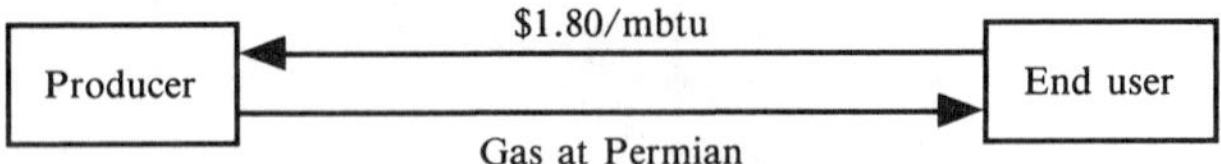

3. Nymex deal with basis swap and firm sale

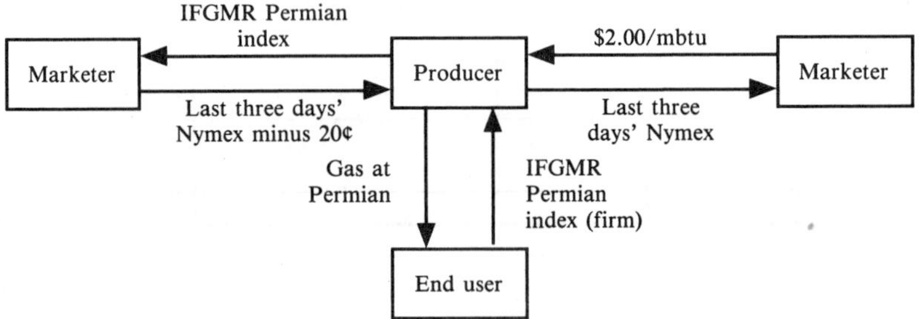

Source: Enron Risk Management.

For example, figure 1 demonstrates the problem faced by producers that used Nymex-based swaps to hedge swing sales of natural gas last May. Basis risk between the price of gas in the Permian Basin and Nymex-linked prices cost some producers as much as 30c/mbtu when the price differential shifted. At the same time, Permian gas end users also renegotiated swing sale

Exhibit 29.3—continued

prices that were as much as 70c lower, as Permian physical prices fell. The result: a $1/mbtu loss.

In contrast, the other figures demonstrate the cash flows seen by a producer that used either a firm, fixed price physical deal at $1.80/mbtu (figure 2) or a basis swap combined with a firm indexed deal (figure 3) to avoid both basis and swing risks. In both instances, the producer achieved its desired price of $1.80/mbtu. However, figure 3 involves transaction costs on three trades, versus the single transaction cost of figure 2.

Source: William Falloon (1993) (June), p 24.

Exhibit 29.4
BTU Swap

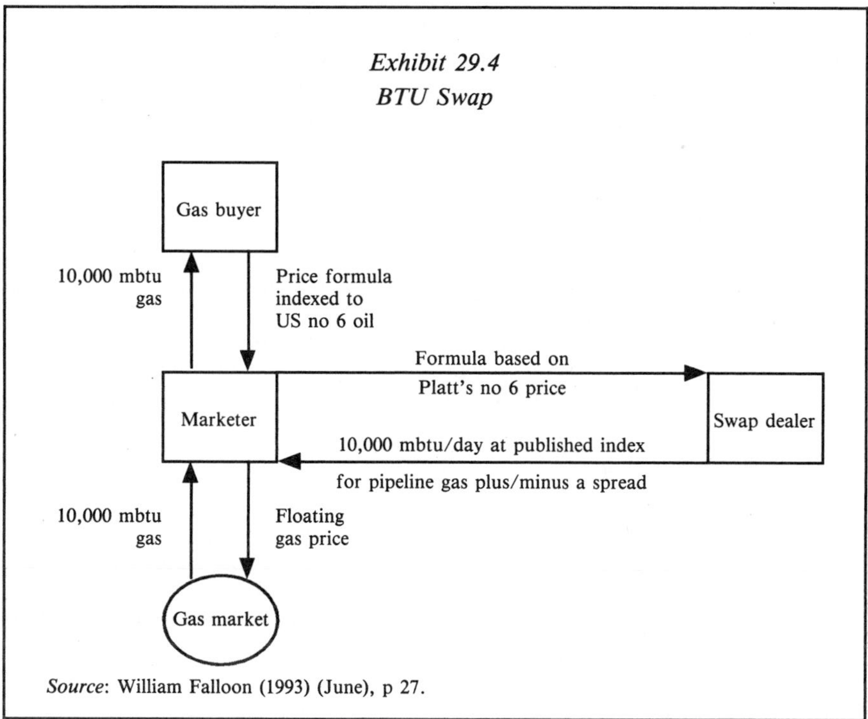

Source: William Falloon (1993) (June), p 27.

The individual transaction amounts which can be executed varies significantly, again, between commodities. In the oil market, it is feasible to undertake transactions up to ten million barrels (equivalent to approximately US$200m in notional principal) with relative ease. However, in practice average transaction sizes are well below these levels. The amount for transactions in other currencies reflects the liquidity of the underlying market for the commodity and specific trading practices.

Market participants

General

Predictably, the major participants in the commodity swap market have been commodity producers and users. Others include financial institutions and, to a lesser extent, major commodity trading houses who have been active in facilitating transactions between producers and users.

The major motivations for using commodity swaps (for both commodity producers and users) have included:

- Seeking protection against commodity price volatility—commodity swaps have offered both producers and users the ability to lock in the price of commodity purchases or sales.

  For the producer, it has the benefit of fixing revenue for a given maturity, often allowing it to use the "locked-in" receipts to ensure the viability of an operation. This is of particular importance to high cost producers who, by sacrificing the potential windfall gains of higher productions prices, have gained protection against a price fall that could, in the extreme, result in pressure to close production of a high cost pit or field.

  For the user, these transactions have guaranteed prices for the purchases of essential raw materials, often allowing profit margins on end products to be determined.

- In the case of commodity price-for-interest swaps in particular, the transaction may also assure both producer and user of a guaranteed market or availability of an essential commodity.
- Additional financing flexibility—the availability of commodity swaps ensures that producers can increase the certainty of cash flows, thereby allowing the organisation to raise funds against guaranteed revenues. This is particularly important in the case of commodity producers in less developed countries (LDCs) seeking financing for resource and other (typically non-recourse) projects (see discussion below).

The market for commodity swaps has grown as more producers and consumers have become attracted to these financing instruments.

Traditionally, companies avoided hedging on the basis that commodity price movements are firstly, a common competitive position of each participant in the industry; secondly, can be passed onto customers; and, thirdly, producers, in particular, often argued that their shareholders sought an exposure to the underlying commodity price volatility. However, as market structures have changed, companies have had to rethink their strategies.

A number of aggressive commodity producers and users have tried to use commodity swaps and related techniques to generate competitive advantage by, for example, guaranteeing revenue flows for projects that are extremely sensitive to price fluctuations and might have otherwise been foregone. Commodity users and producers may also use these instruments to take views upon and position themselves for the long-term price cycles by buying or selling forward production at what is believed to be attractive prices (relative to what is expected to prevail).

As participants within a given industry begin to use certain instruments to generate potential competitive advantages, competitors are increasingly forced to focus on the desirability of similar strategies as commodity price fluctuations do not affect all competitors equally and impede the possibility of transferring the risk to consumers.

An example of this type of industry behaviour is to be found in the airline industry where a number of airlines have used commodity swaps on crude oil or jet fuel to lock-in cost structures, allowing them to price airline fares in advance without assuming exposure to fuel price changes.

Commodity swaps have evolved as a preferred method of managing commodity price risk for both producers and users because of certain structural inadequacies of commodity futures markets in the relevant commodities.

The pattern of participation in commodity derivatives is evident from a consideration of the oil market. The original users of commodity derivative included oil producers, refiners as well as users, primarily airlines and shipping operators. For example, the United Kingdom based cruise line, Cunard, is an active participant hedging approximately 50% of its oil requirements.

As the market has developed, a variety of other users have also emerged. These include the Metropolitan Atlanta Rapid Transit Authority (MARTA) which has utilised commodity derivatives to lock-in the price of fuel needed to run its buses. Other public utilities have also sought to implement similar hedging programmes. Other participants include such entities as the United States railway carrier Amtrak which hedges its substantial diesel fuel requirements.

The pattern of hedging has also become increasingly sophisticated. For example, charter airlines usually operate packaged holiday programmes where they have a significant exposure from the time of the sale of the ticket (which is usually booked and paid for in advance) to the time the actual travel is undertaken. As the price of the holiday package is fixed, the airline operator has an exposure to changing fuel costs. Consequently, a number of operators have utilised hedges structured to protect them from movements in their underlying cost structure to ensure profitability on their operations. This contrasts with regular passenger transport carriers which must seek to manage their fuel oil exposures in a more general sense, seeking where possible to pass on cost rises to passengers.

Another group whose participation in the oil hedging market has evolved is that of sovereign entities. For example, the Portuguese government, through its oil entity Petrogal, has undertaken hedging of energy price risk in relation to its oil purchases abroad.

In a different context, the State of Texas, in late 1992, commenced a programme of hedging its exposure to oil which manifests itself as fluctuations in oil tax revenues on which the State government is heavily dependent. This represents the first instance of an oil producing State using energy derivatives to manage the impact of oil price fluctuation on their revenues. Major sovereign consumers, primarily United States energy consuming States and municipal transit authorities, have, as mentioned above in the context of MARTA, implemented energy hedging programmes to manage their exposure to changes in commodity prices.

The pattern of evolution of participation in other commodity markets is similar. Reflecting similar concerns and considerations, producers and consumers in a variety of industry have begun to recognise the benefits of having active commodity price hedging programmes.

These range across a wide variety of industries including:

- bakeries in various parts of the world who have a clear exposure to movements in the price of grain such as wheat;
- producers of asphalt who have an indirect exposure to changes in oil prices;

- users of silver, primarily photo processing companies, such as Eastman Kodak and Qualex, who have utilised silver price hedging to manage the cost of key component in their process.

The role of financial institutions

Financial institutions as well as, to a lesser extent, a number of commodity trading houses have acted as facilitators of commodity swap transactions. Moreover, a number of producers (for example, British Petroleum and ELF) have set up units to market commodity swap transactions.

The role played by these institutions in the commodity swap market is quite similar to that played by institutions in the market for other derivative products (including interest rate and currency swap transactions and other derivative products).

These institutions provide:

- credit enhancement to the transaction by acting as a counterparty to both end users; and
- speed and flexibility in execution by allowing each party to:
  —structure the transaction to suit its specific requirements;
  —enter into the transaction at its option in terms of timing irrespective of the availability of a counterparty.

The number of entities willing to price and enter into commodity swap transactions on a "principal" basis are relatively few.

Institutions active in running books in, or warehousing, commodity derivatives are relatively limited. They fall into two categories:

- traditional banks and financial institutions;
- major oil and commodity trading houses.

The market share as between these two groups is approximately equal.

The major financial institutions active in commodity derivatives include commercial banks (Chase Manhattan, Paribas, Bankers Trust, JP Morgan, Credit Suisse Financial Products etc) as well as investment banks (Morgan Stanley, Merrill Lynch etc) as well as specialised entities such as AIG.

The major oil and commodity traders include both traditional oil producers (BP International, Hedge Oil—the marketing arm for ELF Aquitaine), commodity traders (Cargill, Louis Dreyfuss) as well as the commodity trading arms of a number of investment banks such as Salomon Bros (Phibro) and Goldman Sachs (J Aron).

These institutions will enter into commodity swaps without necessarily having an opposite and exactly matching counterparty. The risk assumed as a result of an individual transaction is absorbed into their overall commodity swap book with the residual price risk being hedged by transactions in the physical or forward/futures market in the commodity—a practice referred to as "warehousing".

For example, a commodity swap provider entering into a swap with an oil user whereby the swap provider guarantees a series of forward purchase prices to the oil user, would require it to enter the spot or futures market for oil to purchase an appropriate amount of the commodity to hedge its exposure as a result of the transaction.

Conversely, where a transaction guarantees an oil producer a forward sale price, the commodity swap provider would necessarily need to create a short position in the physical or futures market to hedge its exposure.

However, as discussed in Chapter 16, the fact that the commodity swap entails a series of forward contracts would require a provider to enter into a series of futures contracts to precisely match up the actual forward contracts embedded in the commodity swap. In practice, such exact matching of the hedge to the transaction may not be feasible because of the parameters of the swap transaction. The residual risk must then be carried by the entity until such time as an opposite swap can be entered into in order to offset its position.

The operation of a commodity swap warehouse is essentially very similar to the function of operating an interest rate and currency swap warehouse. Both function as a risk management mechanism whereby temporary risk positions are managed through a series of surrogate hedges until the opposite side to a swap transaction can be arranged. However, there are important differences between the two types of warehouses:

- Banks do not typically carry commodity price risks on their balance sheets in the same way as they face inherent interest rate and currency risks as a result of normal banking transactions, and this reduces the capacity of a bank to benefit from economies of scope and scale in the operation of a commodity swap warehouse.
- The significant differences in the structure of commodity markets relative to foreign exchange and securities markets restrict hedging practices.

These factors may restrict participation in commodity swaps to a greater extent than, for example, in interest rate and currency swaps. In addition, for commodity trading houses that are active participants in the physical market for the commodity, operating commodity swap warehouses may bring significant advantage.

However, bank/financial institutions have competitive advantages particularly where commodity derivative transaction must be combined with interest rate and currency risk management products. For example, this occurs most frequently in the context of currency hedge structures and currency derivatives. In addition, banks/financial institutions continue to play a role in being able to absorb the credit risk of counterparty in relation to commodity derivative transactions.

The presence of institutions willing to make markets in commodity swaps in a variety of currencies is an extremely important development in the evolution of the commodity swap market. An absence of market makers would severely impede the growth of this market as seasonal, geographical and other discrepancies are such that offsetting counterparties may not necessarily be available, particularly at the required point in time to facilitate a liquid and efficiently traded market in commodity swaps.

Project financing

A major area of potential growth in commodity swaps is the integration of such transactions into natural resource project financings, particularly for the LDC resource producers. Commercial bank financing for economically self-sufficient projects has been extremely difficult. A recent transaction completed by Banque Paribas for the Mexican copper producer Mexicana de Cobre (see *Exhibit 29.5*) may well form the basis of other transactions where commodity price management instruments are used as part of corporate financing packages to fund projects.

The use of commodity derivative structures to manage the product price risk on resource projects is increasing, in part in response to the insistence of project financiers making the loan subject to a condition that appropriate price hedging action is implemented. A major factor facilitating the use of such commodity derivatives in the context of project financing, particularly in LDC resource projects, is the increased involvement of supranational bodies, such as the International Financing Corporation, a subsidiary of the World Bank, as a credit counterparty through whom such transactions are routed to allow these entities access to the global commodity derivatives markets.

Future outlook

The prospects for growth of commodity derivatives is extremely positive. It is probable that growth in traditional areas will continue with a number of new commodities, particularly soft commodities, becoming available. This growth will reflect increased producer and consumer understanding of the benefits of commodity price risk hedging and transference in the relevant markets.

This growth in traditional areas will be complemented by:

- growth in the incorporation of commodity hedging arrangements in the context of project financing transactions (see discussion above);
- the increased utilisation of commodity priced hedging techniques by sovereign entities and municipal authorities, such as that mentioned above.

Exhibit 29.5

Case Study: Mexicana de Cobre Copper—Commodity Indexed Financing

Mexicana de Cobre (MDC) is the owner and operator of Mexico's largest open pit mining and metallurgical copper complex.

In July 1989, MDC entered into an innovative commodity swap-related pre-export financing, arranged by Banque Paribas (Paribas).

The transaction (set out in the diagram) had three components:

1. A syndicated loan (arranged by Paribas and provided by European and Mexican banks) for \$210m for a maturity of 38 months. The loan carried interest at a rate of 11.48% pa (based on interbank rates for three years and a margin of 3%). The loan is to be repaid through 12 equal quarterly payments.
2. MDC entered into a forward-rate arrangement for its production with SOGEM SA of Belgium. Under the terms of the contract, SOGEM committed to purchase 4,000 tonnes of copper from MDC per month for 38 months at the average London Metal Exchange (LME) price.
3. MDC entered into a fixed-for-floating commodity swap with Paribas whereby it paid floating rates linked to the average LME price (matching its receipts under the sale contract with SOGEM) and received an agreed fixed price for copper.

The combined result for the series of transactions is that MDC achieves guaranteed sales of its copper production at a known fixed price, with the proceeds of the sale being used to effect repayment of the loan.

The structure of the financing effectively protects lenders against the project risks:

- the risk of sale of the copper production is covered by the SOGEM purchase contract;
- the price risk on future sales of copper is hedged via the commodity swap;
- the major risk borne by the lenders is that of failure of MDC to produce the required amount of copper.

Exhibit 29.5—continued

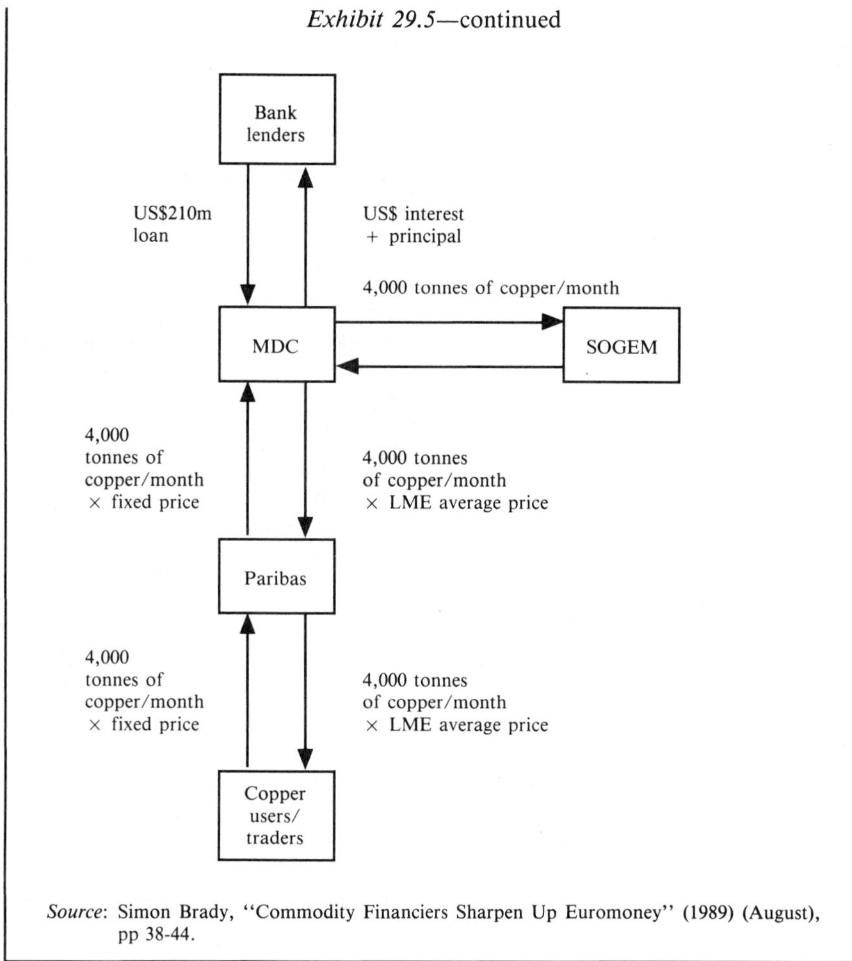

Source: Simon Brady, "Commodity Financiers Sharpen Up Euromoney" (1989) (August), pp 38-44.

A number of aspects of the likely future evolution of the market should be noted:

- An increasing element of the commodity derivative markets will be the construction of hedging instruments which are sold in the form of commodity assets, primarily as investments for selected institutional and retail investors seeking exposure to the commodity price risk. The examples of the transactions outlined in Chapter 16 are typical of the types of structure which are likely to evolve. As noted above, investor demand for "pure" commodity price exposure is likely to be a significant factor in the growth of these instruments.

- The pattern of geographic expansion will be interesting. Key markets where commodity derivative growth is likely to occur includes Germany and Japan, both substantial consumers of commodity products. Neither group are significant users, at this stage, of commodity derivatives. For example, Japanese participation in the oil derivatives market is relatively limited despite Japan's significant exposure to changes in the price of oil products. Similarly, the German industrial companies have significant commodity price exposure in a variety of energy as well as ferrous and non-ferrous metals. The participation of these companies, at this stage, is still limited. Growth in the participation of both these groups, either directly or through trading companies, is anticipated.

Major commodities in which growth is anticipated includes wood products, primarily pulp, reflecting significant volumes (estimated at around US$120bn of wood pulp alone) which is traded globally. Other areas of growth include other wood pulp derivatives such as newsprint. In addition, development of other soft commodities such as grains, sugar and orange juice are anticipated. Similarly, strong growth is expected in markets for electricity, cement and even some semi-finished goods, such as paint. Growth in these new commodities will complement anticipated growth in existing energy products as well as non-ferrous metals.

A factor assisting in future growth will be the increased standardisation of documentation for these transactions with the introduction of the revised ISDA Master Swap Agreement, which is designed to incorporate commodity derivative transactions. While, in its current form, the agreement incorporates commodity derivative transactions in a limited range of commodities, it is anticipated that ultimately, this documentation will incorporate standardised pricing references and documentation for a wide variety of commodities reducing a significant impediment to further growth in the market for these products.

The similarity between commodity derivatives and other swap transactions, essentially interest and currency related derivatives, necessitates an assessment of the likely growth potential of commodity derivatives generally.

The features of commodity derivatives which make them particularly attractive are similar to the features of interest rate and currency swap and derivative transactions which differentiate them from interest rate and/or currency futures. Essentially, commodity swaps function as an over-the-counter forward contract on specific commodities just as interest rate and currency swaps function as over-the-counter forward contracts on interest rates and currencies respectively.

These similarities extend to the mechanical/settlement features of the two types of transactions, particularly in the case of fixed-for-floating commodity price swaps.

However, despite these similarities, the relationship between the two type of transactions should not be overstated. The market for commodity swaps and derivatives does not (at least currently) involve the more complex integrative and financial arbitrage functions of currency and interest rate swaps.

Currency and interest rate swaps operate in a highly distinctive way. They link together not just capital markets in various currencies, but also segments within individual capital markets. This is because through swaps comparative advantage theory is extended from the market for goods and services to the market for financial assets and liabilities.

In contrast, commodity swaps and derivative transactions as they are structured currently, function purely as a mechanism for the transfer of risk between producers and users of commodities as well as speculators. In this regard, the market for commodity swaps is regarded more accurately as an extension of the forward/futures markets in the respective commodities.

EQUITY DERIVATIVES

Origins/development

The evolution of the market for equity derivative is driven by very different factors to those underlying the development of the commodity derivatives market.

Traditional forms of equity derivatives, primarily equity options on individual stocks have been available for a substantial period of time. More modern versions of equity derivatives, particularly index-linked transactions, evolved in the late 1980s. The first equity swap transactions were concluded in late 1989/early 1990.

The modern equity derivatives market has developed in response to a number of factors:

- the internationalisation of equity investment;
- the growth of equity indexed portfolios and management techniques;
- the demand for equity hedging instruments;
- investor demand for highly engineered equity instruments.

A key element underlying the development of equity derivatives has been the gradual internationalisation of equity investment. Increase in cross-border equity investment to take advantage of opportunities that exist in other equity markets and to obtain the advantages associated with increased portfolio diversification has created demand for instruments such as equity swaps which provide investors with international equity exposure without the necessity of actual investment in foreign equity markets.

Internationalisation of equity investment is related to the rise of equity indexed funds. Investors seeking to invest in a foreign equity market often seek exposure to the *entire* equity market index in the relevant currency. Modern equity derivative instruments, with their emphasis on equity market index products, facilitate these investor objectives. Investors can utilise equity swaps or equity indexed securities to simulate the outright purchase of an entire equity index while avoiding necessity of actually investing in the foreign equity market.

The increased focus on indexing techniques and index funds and portfolios in the investor's *home market* has also created demand for these equity derivative products in the context of more generalised portfolio management.

The increased focus on maximising portfolio performance has dictated that investors are seeking to more actively manage their investment portfolios. This active management takes the form of the capacity to alter market exposures or to protect the value of their investment portfolios with a view to out-performing the relevant equity market benchmark. A variety of equity derivatives, such as equity swaps as well as equity indexed bonds and equity index or basket options have been developed in response to these specific investor requirements.

The last factor driving the development of these equity investors has been the increased demand by investors for highly structured or engineered equity exposure through derivative instruments. For example, investors have sought to purchase financially engineered securities giving a specific risk profile in relation to the exposure to an underlying equity market index. In part, this demand has been dictated by the preference for investors to assume certain equity market risks but also to circumvent regulatory constraints regarding the types of instruments in which transactions can be undertaken to manage the investment portfolio.

An added factor in regard to customised solutions to equity market investment problems has been the increased demand for currency-hedged equity market investment structures. Under these arrangements, investors seek exposure to the foreign market index with or without the currency risk of the investment in the relevant country. A variety of equity derivative instruments have developed which customises the currency exposure of such investments precisely to investor requirements.

This pattern of development of equity market indexed derivatives highlights certain differences and similarities with the market for commodity derivatives.

The major similarities relate to the form of these instruments. For example, the structure of commodity and equity derivatives are very similar and the specific classes of transactions (swaps, derivative embedded securities etc) are basically identical.

The major difference between the two markets is that equity derivative activity can be motivated by arbitrage opportunities. This reflects the fact that equity derivatives allow an investment manager to transfer her or his expertise in managing one class of assets to enhance the returns available from investment in another class of assets. This is best illustrated by example.

For example, a portfolio manager, with specialist skill and a relative comparative advantage in managing fixed-income investments, can improve the performance of her or his equity investment portfolio by undertaking an index linked swap transaction which is funded with the portfolio of fixed rate investments. The capacity of the investment manager to achieve performance levels superior to the benchmark on the fixed rate asset portfolio will be translated, effectively, into a higher return in the equity market investment portfolio. Conversely, an investment manager with expertise in the management of domestic or foreign equities can, through equity derivative transactions, effectively transfer the skill and take advantage of her or his comparative advantage in the management of equities to generate above market returns from the institution's money market or fixed interest portfolios.

This capability of transferring expertise across asset classes can be accentuated, in certain jurisdictions, by the tax treatment of equity returns (treatment of capital gains, dividends and withholding tax or other international tax issues). Differences in tax treatment as between different types of investors which results in differential after tax returns can create attractive arbitrage possibilities.

This capacity to transfer skills provides opportunities for arbitrage between specific expertise and management of investments in particular asset classes.

Product range

Developed markets

Reflecting the developing nature of the market for equity derivatives, the product range of instruments is still evolving.

The principal indexes in which such derivative transactions are undertaken include the United States equity market index, the Standard & Poor's 500; and the Japanese-Nikkei 225. Other indexes in which there are significant activity include: Germany's DAX index; France's CAC-40; Switzerland's SMI; and, to a lesser extent, the United Kingdom's FT-SE100.

Transactions in other indexes are also undertaken, although the volumes in these indexes are somewhat lower.

The principal type of equity derivative utilised is the equity index swap with investors receiving or paying index return in exchange for payments or receipts or a floating or fixed-rate coupon. Other common products include equity indexed bonds and equity market index option.

The major areas of product development include:

- Transactions entailing composite indexes. For example, American investors wishing to gain exposure to overseas markets have transacted a number of equity swaps involving a "basket" of major European indexes, or, as an alternative, utilised composite index such as the Morgan Stanley EAFE (Europe, Australia and the Far East) Index.
- Product innovations include equity indexed transactions entailing blended return from two equity market or structures where the investor receives the highest return as between a nominated series of markets.

An increasing feature of the product range of equity derivative instruments is the demand for highly engineered derivative instruments. For example, there is increasing interest in equity index swaps incorporating option elements. For example, the investor may wish to embed a call option on the equity index to eliminate any exposure to declines in the index. Alternative structures embedding a collar within the equity market index swap are also evident.

As noted previously, the other area requiring engineered solutions has been the management of currency risks in relation to investments in foreign equities. Undertaking an equity market index swap or option transaction does not eliminate the underlying currency risk, although there is, proportionately, less risk in such transactions relative to physical equity market investments. This reflects the fact that for an investor undertaking, say, a Nikkei equity market index swap, the only currency exposure relates to the net difference between US$ LIBOR and the yen denominated Nikkei market return. However, increasingly investors are seeking currency hedged structures to combine specifically tailored currency exposure with the desired equity market exposure profile.

A typical transaction entails amounts between US$50m and US$100m with occasional transactions of (up to) US$500m (although these are relatively rare).

Maturities are concentrated in the three months to three years region, although transactions of longer maturities, say, five years and, the occasional longer transaction, have been transacted.

The market is gradually standardising its practices; for example, payment frequencies are generally quarterly with transaction structures being either variable notional amounts or constant notional structures.

Emerging markets

An interesting component of the equity derivative market is the market for emerging market derivatives. This market has several components:

- derivatives on LDC/emerging market debt
- derivatives on emerging market equities.

The first market is primarily in OTC options on the prices of LDC debt, including various debt obligations associated with debt restructuring programmes (for example, Brady Bonds, Argentine Guaranteed Re-financing Agreements (GRAs),

Venezuela Debt Conversion Bonds (DCBs, etc). These instruments are generally call or put options on the price of the underlying securities.

The second market is necessarily more complex. One component of the market is OTC options on either individual equities or indexes in emerging markets. Equity swaps or equity indexed structures where the underlying equity index relates to an emerging market have been completed. These transaction structures are primarily designed to allow investors to create exposure to the relevant market.

A parallel market involving stock sales and equity swaps designed to allow emerging market borrowers to raise capital have also emerged. An example of this type of structure is set out in *Exhibit 29.6*.

Exhibit 29.6

Emerging Market Equity Swap Structure

A particular example of the emerging market equity derivative transactions is the stock trade or equity swap.

The structure combines a sale of stock with an equity swap. The structure is set out in the diagram below:

Stock sale with equity swap

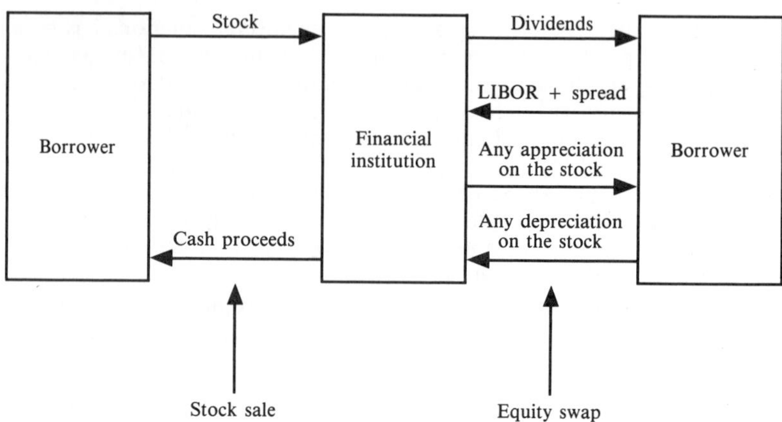

The essential features of this structure are as follows:

- The borrower sells the stocks to the financial institution to generate financing.
- The stock acts as a hedge for the financial institution which enters into an equity swap. The value of the stock portfolio is utilised as the notional principal amount for the equity swap. The price agreed for the stock portfolio is utilised as the entry price for the equity swap. The stock sale and the equity swap are usually entered into simultaneously.
- The structure of the equity swap is quite conventional:

—The borrower pays US$ LIBOR plus a spread.

—The financial institution pays the borrower the return on the stock. Any appreciation (depreciation) over the price agreed for the stock at commencement is paid by the financial institution (borrower).

—At maturity, the financial institution sells the stock either to the borrower or liquidates it in the market. The sale price, in either case, determines the termination price for the swap.

Exhibit 29.6—continued

These types of transactions are popular with borrowers in emerging markets, such as Mexico and Argentina. The objective of the borrower is to generate cost-effective financing through liquidation (on a permanent or a term basis—in the case of a buy-back structure) of an equity portfolio or a corporation's own stock.

In 1993, a typical transaction would have allowed a Mexican borrower to pay US$ LIBOR plus 150-200bps through the equity swap as against a normal borrowing cost of US$ LIBOR plus 200-250bps. Argentinian corporations during this period would have paid US$ LIBOR plus 250-300bps in the swap structure compared to normal borrowing costs of US$ LIBOR plus 300-350bps.

Source: Danielle Robinson (1993) (October), p 36.

Market participants

General

The major participants in the equity derivatives market fall into a number of categories:

- the end asset holders, who are typically holders of equity assets or managers of equity portfolios;
- organisations involved in equity market arbitrage;
- financial institutions active in either facilitating equity derivative transactions or as users of equity derivatives to manage their market making activities.

The major asset holders include insurance companies and other institutional investors, fund managers involved in the management of equity or equity index funds, as well as corporations who have equity exposure through strategic holdings of stock in other corporations.

The major application for these equity asset owners of equity derivatives is to either create exposure to specific equity indexes or to hedge their exposure to specific equity markets, from time to time. In addition, these asset holders may seek to generate premium income by undertaking covered option writing strategies against their equity portfolios.

The asset owners may be constrained by a variety of factors in their participation in these markets including:

- holding period requirements;
- regulatory limitations on participation in equity derivative transactions;
- liquidity considerations;
- the impact of cost issues which may prevent these asset holders from undertaking physical transactions in particular markets.

Arbitrageurs include market makers in equity products, principal traders in futures and options markets as well as specialised funds seeking to generate above average returns from money market or equity portfolios. The arbitrageurs are a significant factor in the equity derivatives markets because of their substantial capital resources which allow this group to absorb certain risk elements in the market and enhance overall market liquidity. An example of this type of risk taking capacity relates to futures roll risk which is important in pricing equity index swaps: see discussion in Chapter 17. A number of principal futures and options players will take risk positions in relation to futures roll risk enhancing the capacity of market makers to price and hedge transactions.

The role of financial institutions extends to both facilitating equity derivative transactions as well as utilising equity derivatives to hedge market making positions. The role of financial institutions in this context is considered in detail below.

The participation of asset holders in the equity derivative markets is growing. United States institutional investors and fund managers have become active, reflecting their involvement with more traditional equity derivatives such as stock index futures and equity options on specific stocks. European institutional investors have been slower to utilise the equity derivatives market although their participation is increasing.

Increased recognition of the often higher returns available through such transactions as well as savings on commission and withholding tax are key factors underlying this increased interest.

The application of equity swaps to corporate risk management is still in its developmental phase. Corporations, typically, have significant equity exposure arising from either long-term strategic investments in other corporations or from temporary equity risk positions resulting from merges and acquisitions activity.

Role of financial institutions

Financial institutions play an important role in the equity derivative market both as market makers but also as end users of equity derivative products to hedge internal risk positions.

The role of financial institutions encompasses a variety of functions:

- *arranger*—arranging swap transactions between market participants;
- *market making*—facilitating liquidity by acting as a market maker in equity derivative products, facilitating the flow of such transactions by smoothing the demand/supply pattern of activity;
- *proprietary trading*—encompassing position taking as an adjunct to other trading positions.

A key area of demand for equity derivatives, particularly equity swaps, is generated by the activity of market makers in long-term equity options. A key issue for long-dated equity option market makers is the ability to create long-term long or short equity positions in the relevant market. Equity swap transactions provide an extremely effective means of creating such exposures. In contrast, an alternative method of hedging such equity option positions over long periods would require running long or short equity index futures positions against the option necessitating rolling of the futures positions with its attendant risks. As a consequence, the price of equity index swaps substantially reflects the activity of such equity option market makers.

A major constraint in markets where there are no futures contracts on the relevant index is the necessity to hedge index transactions through physical stocks. Use of physical stocks to hedge is made more complex by the inability to borrow stock efficiently or to short the relevant equity markets in a number of major markets. For example, in Germany, the cost of borrowing equities for the purpose of shorting costs 2.5% which is very inefficient compared with the United States market, where borrowing stock costs 0.5%. Similarly, the fact that the cost of borrowing stock can be highly variable has to be taken into account in this context.

The major financial institutions active in equity derivatives include:

- *Leading equity brokers*—these include major United States investment banks such as Goldman Sachs, Morgan Stanley, Salomon Brothers and Merrill Lynch as well as European firms, such as Barclays De Zoete Wedd.
- *Major financial institutions active in the international swaps and options markets*—this includes Bankers Trust, Credit Suisse Financial Products, Swiss Bank Corporation, Deutsche Bank, JP Morgan, Societe Generale etc.
- *Specialised financial derivative firms*—these include firms such as AIG Financial Products.

The competitive market dynamics as between the major participants is interesting. The major equity brokers utilise their strengths in the various underlying equity markets through their strong execution capabilities to derive competitive advantage in these products. In contrast, more traditional financial institutions and banks utilise a broader range of strategies. For example, a number of institutions, such as Credit Suisse Financial Products and Bankers Trust focuses on highly structured equity index products. In contrast, other institutions seek to build market share in equity derivatives by quoting tight bid-offer spreads and building a strong market making position, particularly in the more liquid and mature markets. This particular strategy appears to be pursued by firms such as JP Morgan and Societe Generale.

Other firms have sought to differentiate themselves by:

- proprietary risk management techniques and a corresponding emphasis on proprietary positions;
- emphasis on high credit ratings and concentration on longer-dated transactions.

The rapid growth in the equity derivatives markets is attracting added participation from financial institutions. This has had an impact on pricing and margins reflecting increased competition as financial institutions seek to establish market share as well as strong competitive positions in what is generally perceived to be an important and profitable sector of the global derivatives market in the long term.

Part 7

Hedging and Management of Swaps and Financial Derivatives Portfolios

Chapter 30

Financial Derivative Portfolio Management

COUNTERPARTY TRANSACTIONS VERSUS MARKET MAKING IN SWAPS AND DERIVATIVES

Many of the developments in swap and derivative markets, in terms of both the greater range of structures that have emerged and the changes in the way swaps and derivatives are used, were made possible by fundamental changes in the way the market operated.

The earliest transactions were purely counterparty transactions where a commercial or investment bank structured a transaction on behalf of two (or more) counterparties with matched but mirror reverse requirements. However, as the market matured, the major participants in the market moved to being principals in transactions rather than only agents structuring transactions on behalf of counterparties. This shift accelerated the creation of a secondary market in swaps as these institutions began to act as market makers routinely quoting two-way prices on swaps.

The change in emphasis from counterparty transactions to intermediated transactions, where financial institutions enter into swaps as principals, took place on two separate levels:

- bank intermediation in a matched counterparty transaction;
- principal trading without matching counterparty.

These two different approaches were predicated on quite different considerations. Bank intermediation in a matched transaction was utilised as a form of credit enhancement. In contrast, principal trading entailed market making, that is, willingness to buy or sell swaps at a price. Market making was usually undertaken as part of positioning and arbitrage strategies or on a fully hedged basis, involving entry into a temporary unmatched swap position until a counterparty could be located while hedging the risks entailed.

Principal trading can, but need not necessarily, merge the market making function with the credit intermediation role.

Against this background it is possible to set out a taxonomy of swap arrangement techniques. Swap arrangers can act in any of the following capacities:

- *Brokers* instantaneously arrange perfectly matched swaps acting solely as agents by introducing complementary swap partners to one another. Brokers collect a small arrangement fee for their services.
- *Intermediated swap arrangers* serve as principals to instantaneously priced, exactly matched swap counterparties. This technique merges the credit intermediary and broker functions. The intermediary bears no market risk but does assume credit risk, that is, if one counterparty to a matched transaction fails, the principal must continue to service the other counterparty.
- *Dealers* make continuous two-way markets and hedge open swap positions in the cash securities or futures market. These positions are later matched with opposite

swaps and placed in the dealer's matched book. The dealer merges a market making function with the credit intermediation role.

- *Arbitrage swaps* involve a long or short swap position versus an opposite position in another financial instrument, for example, a bond or bond futures contract. Here, the motivation is to exploit inefficiencies between markets.

Principal trading or market making/warehousing in swap derivatives, options as well as commodity and equity instruments follows a similar pattern.

A significant difference which should be noted relates to options. In the early stages of development of option markets, there has been a reluctance for end users to *write* or *grant* options. This reflects the fact that the risk profile of the grantor potentially exposes it to unlimited losses. In this context, market makers have often provided essential liquidity to potential purchasers of options through the use of synthetic option replication techniques: see Chapter 36. The capacity of financial institutions to act as suppliers of options, through their capacity to assume and manage the risk of granting options, has been an important catalyst in the growth of these markets.

Virtually every major institution involved in the swap market, with minor, although notable, exceptions, participates in the swap and derivative markets as market makers or dealers. This analysis of swap and derivative market making and warehousing, therefore focuses primarily on this type of principal trading in these transactions without matching counterparties.

THE RATIONALE FOR SWAP AND DERIVATIVE MARKET MAKING

The emergence of market making reflects a response to a number of developments in the swap and derivative market, including:

- the increased range of applications of swap and derivative transactions;
- the increased desire for prompt execution on the part of users;
- the requirement of structural flexibility in swap and derivative transactions;
- the profit potential from market making in swaps and derivatives;
- the development of adequate hedging technology;
- the potential synergy of swap and derivative product with other activities such as new issues and sales and distribution of securities.

The cause and effect relationship in the emergence of market making is not easily discernible. The relationship is symbiotic. The development of market makers assisted in the actual further development of the swap and derivative market, while these developments, in turn, required participants who would act as market makers.

One of the major factors prompting the emergence of market makers was the evolution of the swap market from a market emphasising new issue arbitrage to a market focusing on asset liability management. This increased emphasis on asset liability management required the development of a relatively liquid swap market. The emergence of market makers providing two-way prices on swap transactions allows users of the swap market the requisite flexibility to reverse or unwind swap transactions at the current market rate, facilitating the increased use of swaps as an asset liability management technique.

As the swap market evolved, the users of the swap market came increasingly to expect, demand and receive instantaneous pricing and transaction structures tailored to their needs. The original structure of the market, essentially a broker market predicated upon arranging counterparties, was not capable of meeting these demands. This is because the intermediary in question could not guarantee that it would be able to locate and instantaneously price a perfectly matched swap with a counterparty. This resulted in the swap market becoming increasingly dominated by market makers.

The market makers provided both the required prompt execution and structural flexibility. The availability of intermediaries willing to commit to a swap without necessarily having a counterparty in position made possible a prompt execution capability which eliminated the delay where it was necessary to have a precisely matched counterparty to complete a transaction.

The market makers also provided enormous structural flexibility. As new issue structures grew more complex, usually to exploit identified arbitrage opportunities, the required swap structures grew correspondingly more complex. In addition, swaps utilised in asset liability management situations increasingly needed to be tailored to the cash flow characteristics required by the client. This lead to the increasing necessity of swap structures which departed significantly from the generic swap structure. The existence of market makers who were willing, for a cost, to absorb slight cash flow mismatches and to tailor the swap to specifically match client requirements thus provided the basis for the further development of the swap market.

Market makers also allowed complex multiparty swap transactions to be structured in a way which allowed each counterparty to exactly achieve their required objectives without the necessity of undertaking multiple swap transactions or entering into a number of swaps. The emergence of multiparty swaps, or cocktail swaps, greatly expanded the number of counterparties that could potentially be involved in any one transaction. The difficulty in persuading each counterparty to transact on perfectly matched terms as at the relevant dates meant that the interposition of a market maker to warehouse the various components of the swap, usually, for short periods, allowed such transactions to be undertaken.

An added impetus to the shift to principal trading or market making in swap and derivative products has been the increasing trend to multi-product combinations. Increasingly, engineered combinations of forwards, options, swaps, and more rarely, commodity and equity instruments are created in response to specific asset liability management requirements. The highly individualised nature of the products being dealt with necessarily means that matching counterparties with exactly offsetting requirements are extremely difficult, if not impossible, to locate. This necessitated an increasing role for principal traders or market makers structuring, pricing and hedging such transactions.

The emergence of swap market makers also reflected the changing remuneration basis in the swap market. Originally, swaps were structured on the basis of substantial arrangement fees with some ongoing "drip" income in the form of an annuity (from the difference between the cash flows on both sides of a matching swap trade). As the market developed and competition increased, the market rapidly evolved to a spread market with intermediaries earning the spread between the rate they paid on one side of the swap and the rate they received on the matching counterparty trade, usually, the fixed rate component of the swap.

This change in the pricing of swap transactions became evident with the emergence of the first market makers. With the emergence of these market makers, other intermediaries not willing to act as principals or market makers were placed in a position of significant competitive disadvantage.

An organisation's policy not to position swaps resulted in two fundamental constraints in the organisation's swap operations. The intermediary effectively became a *price taker*, that is, buyers at the offered side of the market and sellers at the bid side of the market. The intermediaries were further disadvantaged as they were dependent on locating market makers who had to be persuaded to trade instantaneously and to match the specifications of their client.

These prerequisites for entering into swap transactions severely impacted on the non-market making intermediary's price levels, price turnaround time, etc. This naturally inhibits volume and confines the intermediary's swap activities to delivering its client to another intermediary to get the order filled. An added problem, in this type of operation, is that it practically hands over the intermediary's client to a swap market maker, virtually inviting the client to go directly to the swap market maker for future transactions. The brokering fee earned in such transactions is significantly lower than one that could have been earned from entering into the swap as a principal, for example, 0.03 to 0.15% *flat* versus 0.05 to 0.125% *pa* for principal trades on interest rate swaps (for currency swaps the amounts are slightly higher).

In this situation, the non-market making intermediary could book the swap with the swap market maker as principal and then deal as principal with its clients. This would serve to disguise the identity of the ultimate swap provider from its client. However, the intermediary would be required to mark up its price to cover balance sheet usage. This effectively would add a credit intermediation fee of say 0.05% to 0.10% pa to the swap market maker's bid-offer price. This would mean that the actual swap quote is significantly above the actual dealer market price. The result is usually low volume and client dissatisfaction with the non-market making intermediary's swap prices and turnaround time. Increasingly, many end users of the swap market refuse to be brokered through, either directly or indirectly, to another swap market maker.

Consequently, once a small group of market makers in swap transactions emerged, it effectively forced other participants in the swap market to also commence market making in such transactions to avoid placing themselves at a competitive disadvantage.

The move to market making by intermediaries was also prompted by the potential to earn significant profits. This profit was primarily generated by changing the position of the intermediary from that of a *price taker* to a *price maker*. The basic profit strategy was for the intermediary to opportunistically position and execute round lots trades (usually US$50m to US$100m), which can be transacted at the most advantageous prices, at the time of its choice and to subsequently re-offer or bid the opposite side of the transaction on a continuous basis in smaller parcels (say US$5 to US$10m). This capacity to break down large positions into retail size and to distribute these smaller parcels combined with the opportunity to trade at the time of the intermediary's choice allows the intermediary to influence the market by letting the market come to it. This usually facilitates buying at the bid side of the market and selling at the offer side greatly increasing the volume of profitable transaction put through its swap book.

Opportunities to buy swaps at the bid side tend naturally to occur through new securities issues which are then re-offered to market participants seeking to synthetically create fixed rate liabilities. This pattern of activity is largely true for a wide range of markets.

The profit potential from this type of activity can be viewed as earning the spread between the buy and sell side of the market, supported by adequate hedging technology to manage the risks of booking open positions. Alternatively, the profit potential of the operation can be sought to be enhanced by operating the book, at least partially, in a speculative manner designed to take advantage of swap spread, interest rate and currency movements.

The development of an adequate hedging technology was crucial in the emergence of swap market makers. Recognition, over a period of time, of the fact that the risks entailed in booking open swap positions were not substantially different to the risks entailed in the management of bank treasury or securities dealing operations allowed institutions to adapt existing technology to the management of swaps operations.

In addition, the realisation that a large swap book with a locked in earnings spread and resulting income stream would, on an actuarial basis, allow a swap warehousing operation to operate on a profitable basis, after adjustment for risk, prompted a number of financial institutions to enter the market as principals.

The emergence of swap market makers can also be traced to potential synergies arising from the natural linkages of swap transactions with new issues of securities and the sales of securities. Increasingly, intermediaries were attracted to act as market makers in view of the fact that swaps were an essential complement to their new issue securities business. Alternatively, for institutions lacking a strong new issue business, such as commercial banks, swaps represented an opportunity to further develop their new issue business.

Intermediaries were also quick to realise that the ability to continuously make markets in swaps of all sizes and maturities greatly enhances the marketability of seasoned securities contributing to the liquidity of their security sales and distribution activities. As discussed in Chapter 18, asset swaps are increasingly utilised to transform securities, in terms of currency and/or interest rate basis, greatly expanding the universe of potential investors. In the US$ market, this type of technique has been instrumental in expanding the investor base for mortgage backed securities in particular. In addition, both US$ and currency swaps have been utilised to package seasoned Eurobonds for sale to suitable investors.

The impetus to develop principal trading or market making/warehousing capacities in swap and derivative instruments was largely uniform. The factors identified were present in relation to each of the various types of instruments identified. In the case of principal trading/market making in option-based instruments, commodity and equity based instruments, a number of additional factors were also relevant.

As noted above, the asymmetric risk profile of options in a number of cases dictated a shortage of option grantors. This facilitated a role for select financial institutions to utilise available hedging technology (primarily, synthetic option creation through replication techniques) to assume and manage the risk of options trading.

The move to principal trading/market making and commodity and equity derivatives is predicated on an identical logic to that prevailing in respect of interest rate and currency derivatives generally. The development of hedging technology and warehousing techniques in the context of interest rate and currency instruments facilitated the move by financial institutions to similar approaches to commodity and equity products. The fact that swap warehouses active in pricing, trading and managing portfolios of interest rate and currency instruments were well established provided the basic theoretical and practical framework for principal trading in commodities and equities.

An added impetus to entering into commodity and equity derivative transaction on a principal basis was the presence, in certain markets, of inbuilt structural patterns which, in the absence of the presence of principal trader/market makers, would impede liquidity in those markets. For example, in the oil market consumers generally, typically look to buy oil forward at what is historically attractive pricing levels to them. Conversely, producers are willing to sell forward production at historically high price levels, which are typically higher than the prices or which consumers are willing to buy forward. This creates market imbalances which can be absorbed by market makers who can provide one or other side of the transaction, hedge the position and ultimately move to match (in a specific or general sense) their internal exposure as market prices change whilst protecting its own outright risk through hedging mechanisms in the intervening period. Similar factors are also identifiable in a variety of equity derivative products.

In part, development of principal trading/market making capabilities in swaps and derivative product should, in reality, be regarded as part of a broader move to an increased principal/proprietary trading approach by financial institutions *generally*.

This tendency reflects an increased willingness by financial institutions to risk equity capital in order to:

- generate a significant earnings stream;
- facilitate servicing client product requirements.

This tendency to enhance and emphasise principal/proprietary trading approaches extends across all product groupings. At a macro level, this encompasses broad balance sheet asset liability mismatches and the resultant interest rate risk positions. In contrast, at the micro level, this relates to positions assumed seeking to benefit from movements in financial market variables such as interest rates, currencies, commodity and equity market prices. Within each risk category, there may be different dimensions of exposure which are sought to be created. For example, in interest rate risk, specific exposures may be sought to be created to absolute or yield curve shape movements, spread movements between various indexes, or changes in spreads between yield curves in different currencies. Exposure may also be sought to be created to changes in the volatility of various financial market variables, primarily, through asymmetric risk instruments such as options or instruments embodying option elements, or to changes in volatility between variables.

A major element underpinning this increased emphasis on principal/proprietary trading is the increased pressure on earnings as a result of declining profitability from more traditional financial institution activities, such as relatively risk-free financial services products such as, arranging, broking or lending activities. Pressure on earnings and the needs to build new and substantial earnings streams has been assisted by developments in risk management technology. These developments in risk management technology, typically allowing more accurate identification, analysis, quantification and management of risks has allowed financial institutions to quantify risk-reward relationships in various types of activities better and allowed these institutions to, effectively, increase the potential for added earnings, with, they would argue, only a relatively limited increase in overall organisational risk profile.

The relationship between the development of principal trading/market making in swaps and derivative products and the increased appetite for proprietary risk positions in these instruments is somewhat symbiotic. The entry by financial institutions into swap and derivative products forced increased investment in risk analysis and risk management technology. This investment allowed a better understanding of the risk parameters within which financial institutions operate and assists in the identification of proprietary trading opportunities.

An added element which has encouraged entry by financial institution into principal trading/market making in a variety of swap and derivative instruments is that, at the very least, it assists the relevant financial institutions *in its own risk management*. The technology acquired can, in the first instance, be applied to the internal risk management of the institution (who are, in their own balance sheet etc activities, end users of these products). At a secondary level, the capacity to trade in and, at a given point in time, to have positions in a variety of markets which are not perfectly correlated may, in fact, assist in the reduction of the overall risk profile institution and assist in its management.

SWAP AND DERIVATIVE MARKET MAKING APPROACHES

Different types of institutions have significantly different approaches to swap market making. The principal differences in approach have developed as between commercial banks and the investment or merchant banks. These differences reflect both the different client bases and also differences in the purpose for which these types of institutions utilise swaps.

Investment banks view swaps as a natural adjunct to their strong position in the new securities issues and security sales and distribution businesses. In addition, investment and merchant banks seek to exploit their historical client basis. For example, United States investment banks have based part of their swap business on their historically strong relationships with financial and thrift institutions, which use swaps primarily to create fixed rate liabilities which are difficult for them to raise in the capital markets directly. In the United Kingdom, merchant banks have, at least historically, dominated the building society sector of the swap market, based on their natural and historically strong relationship with these institutions.

In contrast, commercial bank swap dealers depend on the flow of swap transactions from the following sources:

- the liability management needs of corporations;
- general bank balance sheet management;
- swap and Eurobond combinations, usually introduced by an investment bank.

In each case, the swap activity is seen to naturally and profitably complement the entity's other businesses.

The difference between commercial and investment banks also reflects very different philosophies. The investment banks see swaps as another trading and arbitrage vehicle in their trading portfolios while commercial banks view swaps as akin to longer term commitments such as an extension of credit.

This difference can be graphically illustrated by examining market practice in the US$ swap market. Traditionally, the US$ swap market tends to operate as follows. When rates fell, United States corporates, for example, usually sought to fix the cost on their debt. These corporates would enter into swaps which the swap market makers would simply place on their books, hedged by shorting treasuries. The basic strategy by the swap market maker would be to take on the position at a relatively high spread as against the appropriate government bond. The market maker would then move to square its position by swapping out against a fixed rate securities issue, usually one in the Eurobond or US$ Yankee market and usually with a bank, financial institution or sovereign borrower seeking to generate sub-LIBOR floating rate funds. The swap market maker would seek to time the issue to take advantage of a spread window in the new issue market to allow it to satisfactorily close out its open swap position whilst satisfying all client needs and, hopefully, ensuring a successful bond issue.

The major difference would be that once both sides of the transaction were in place, the commercial banks would usually choose to stand in the middle of the swap transaction until its maturity. In contrast, the investment banks would generally, although there are a number of exceptions, commit to the swaps on a right of assignment basis allowing them to step out of the middle of the swap transaction and allowing the ultimate counterparties to directly deal with each other. In our example, this would be achieved by the investment bank assigning the original swap with the United States corporate to the issuer of the securities in the bond transaction.

The difference in approaches reflects the perspective of the investment bank which seeks to trade the spreads on swaps and new issues as against a commercial bank which sees the swap as a service to its corporate client in achieving a fixed rate cost on its debt.

The difference in approach between various types of financial institutions while important particularly in the early stages of development of the swap and derivative market, are less relevant to the current institutional structure of participants in these markets. This change and differences in approach reflect a variety of factors including:

- The change in the character of the participants themselves, including the entry of specialist swap and derivative operations, sponsored/supported by insurance/other financial services concerns.
- The expansion of derivative market into a wide range of products, including commodities and equities. The fact that neither commercial or investment banks have underlying risk positions in commodities and, to a limited extent, in equities dictates that positions of competitive advantage cannot necessarily be secured through matters of approach to principal trading/market making.
- Capital constraints confronting all types of financial services industry participants which dictate that sheer balance sheet capacity and capital availability cannot be utilised to secure competitive advantages, at least, unless an appropriate return can be generated on the capital/balance sheet capacity committed: see discussion in Part 8.

Increasingly, individual preferences of approach to swap and derivative market making/warehousing are dictated by:

- client preferences and requirements (product distribution issues);
- internal proprietary trading, including geographic arrangements, considerations (principal trading considerations).

Client requirements, which are increasingly influential in dictating the organisational approach of financial institutions and the manner of operating proprietary trading/market making activities in swap and derivative products, is focused on the following considerations:

- overall risk management approaches;
- specific financial engineering designed to manage corporate risk exposures.

As with financial institutions, corporations have increasingly focused on risks resulting from changes in financial market variables impacting upon their operations. Corporations have created integrated approaches to generalised risk management. These integrated risk management frameworks seek to create definitive linkages between activity in a particular product (for example, an interest rate swap) to its impact on the overall risk profile of the corporation. In addition, it is increasingly evident that corporations are seeking to understand the linkages between the various *types of risk*. For example, the linkages between interest rate and currency risk that may effect a particular corporation's risk profile.

This approach to risk management has implications for the instrument of product focus of financial institutions. Corporations increasingly require a wide range of products solutions to its specific risk management problems ranging from generic product types (which are traded as commodities, in much the same way as foreign exchange or other standardised product structures) to highly engineered products combining various derivative elements designed to manage specific corporate risks.

This change in focus within the swap and derivative markets, driven by client requirements, has increasingly made the traditional distinction in approaches between commercial and investment bank approaches to swap and derivative business irrelevant. The capacity for capital commitment and credit risk assumption, while continuing to be an important component, are increasingly considered in addition to factors such as product structuring, pricing and analytical techniques.

As the market in swaps changed, a large number of financial intermediaries started to operate what came popularly to be referred to as *swap warehouses*. These warehouses were merely the market making units within organisations which entered into the swap hedging the risk until a counterparty could be located. The advent of warehousing saw significant changes in the way swap business was conducted. The shift was one away from large swap origination teams located throughout the globe seeking to identify matching counterparties to smaller teams managing a number of warehouses in different currencies with the origination function being shifted to the corporate finance or general banking staff of financial institutions.

A number of institutions operate a large number of warehouses in a wide range of currencies including US$, C$, A$, NZ$, yen, GBP, deutschmark, Swiss franc and Dutch guilder. A number of other participants also run swap books in a number of currencies, although most participants tend to specialise in one or a few currencies. The largest number of market makers are in US$ while a number of banks specialise in particular market niches. For example, a number of Australian banks run swaps books in A$ reflecting their client base and their operational strengths.

In actual fact, it is difficult to accurately determine the number of market makers in swaps as it is not always possible to determine whether or not a participant is a true market maker or is merely acting as an intermediary broking through the trade to another swap trader.

A number of factors are identifiable as prerequisities to enable a participant to act as a market maker in swaps. These include:

- a strong distribution system to locate and market swaps to counterparties;
- a presence in the new issue markets to create wholesale swap positions;
- an active trading operation in the relevant government securities market, giving the swap book ready and efficient access to, and funding for, large securities positions needed to hedge and unwind swap positions;
- reasonable inventories of securities which can be sold in combination with swaps providing liquidity for both the securities and swap traders;
- a substantial capital base allowing the institution to deal, in a credit sense, with other swap counterparties.

The majority of major market makers in swaps have most, if not all, of the above qualifications.

The emergence of a select group of institutions willing to act as principals in interest rate and currency swap transactions, while important, is often overstated. While adding flexibility in terms of execution of transactions and while undertaking complex cocktail swaps entailing a series of cross-currency, fixed-to-floating, amortising permutations, the additional costs of hedging and warehousing as well as the necessity to commit capital and earn acceptable returns on risk where the institution acting as principal in a swap transaction effectively assumes a term commitment means that intermediated swaps are often uneconomic. In particular, the erosion of arbitrage margins dictates that intermediation in swap transactions, at least where the institution acting as a principal is adequately compensated for the risk assumed, does not always add value to the transaction.

Consequently, an active agency market in swaps where financial institutions arrange swap counterparties and design the transactions has continued to exist. Where the counterparties are mutually acceptable, the institution merely structures and arranges the swap acting as principal and intermediating the transaction only for credit enhancement reasons or where it otherwise makes economic sense. The emergence of a number of swap brokers, usually traditional Euromarket broking firms, with extensive data bases on potential swap counterparties has also helped ensure the continuance of direct counterparty transactions (see discussion below).

The emergence of market making in swap derivatives follows an identical pattern. However, there are also some minor differences.

LTFX market making was a natural extension of making two-way prices in the spot and short-dated forwards in the foreign exchange market. Given that the relevant hedging technology was already understood and capable of extension, albeit with greater risks as the maturity of contracts became longer, a number of financial institutions developed LTFX market making capabilities. As the currency swap markets developed, the fact that currency swaps and LTFX contracts could be utilised to replicate very similar economic consequences forced the market making function in these instruments to be combined.

Market making in FRAs to some extent predated the advent of swap warehouses. The fact that commercial banks could effectively replicate FRAs through borrowing and lending activities allowed these institutions to begin making prices as principal to clients. The emergence of warehouses, however, had an impact on FRAs as the portfolio of swaps allowed the institution to create FRAs either as a by-product of swaps or, alternatively, to hedge risks, particularly, mismatches within the swap portfolio.

Market making in caps, floors and collars developed relatively more slowly. Initially, only a few market makers of substance emerged reflecting the smaller size of the market for over-the-counter interest rate options, the problems with pricing and hedging technology and the higher risk associated with these activities. However, as option hedging technology developed, reflecting additional investment by financial institutions in both technology and human resources (with strong quantitative skills), market making in these types of instruments grew rapidly, paralleling the strong development in the market for caps, floors and collars.

Market making in swap hybrids does not necessarily entail establishments of specific portfolios making markets in these transactions. Typically, such hybrids are *unbundled* into their component elements which are then managed within the traditional portfolios themselves.

The development of market making/principal trading capabilities and commodity and equity products developed in response to similar, but in some ways, different factors which are considered below.

MARKET MAKING IN COMMODITY AND EQUITY DERIVATIVES

As noted in Chapter 1, the development of commodity and equity derivatives, to varying degrees, represents an extension of some of the basic concepts of swap financing to different market settings.

In the initial phase of development of the market for commodity and equity derivatives (excluding equity options on individual stocks in which substantial markets already existed), transactions were conducted on a matched basis with financial institutions arranging and intermediating the credit exposure between offsetting end user requirements. This pattern of activity was very similar to that prevailing in the market for interest rate and currency swaps in its initial phases.

However, paralleling the development of market making/warehousing capacities in interest rate and currency swaps and similar products, client demand for prompt execution and structural flexibility encouraged a trend towards principal trading/market making in these products.

A key element facilitating the development of these commodity and equity derivative portfolio and principal trading capacity in these products was the existence of a well developed technology for hedging interest rates and currency swaps which are capable of being adapted to hedging exposures encountered in commodity and equity derivative transactions.

The fact that commodity and equity swaps, in particular, functioned basically as over-the-counter forward contracts on the relevant commodity or equity market index greatly simplified the process of risk management. In essence, these transactions were not dissimilar to interest rate swaps or strips of FRAs hedged against forward or futures contracts in the underlying interest rate index market. For example, most commodity swaps were hedged by buying or selling futures contract in either the *same* commodity or in a commodity exhibiting a high degree of correlation in terms of price movements to the commodity in the swap. Similar factors are applicable in respect of equity market index swaps. This meant that the basic hedging technology underlying FRAs and interest rate swaps could be adapted relatively easily managing portfolios of commodity and equity swaps.

Similarly, commodity and equity market index options were, to a substantial degree, similar to options on interest rates as embodied in caps, floors and collars (in a number of respects, options on commodities and equity market indexes are simpler to price and hedge than interest rate options—see discussion in Chapter 11). This, again, facilitated the development of portfolios in these products.

The development of principal trading capacities in commodity and equity derivatives was, however, impeded by a different factor. Unlike interest rates and currencies, financial institutions typically have minimal exposures to commodity and equity market indexes (to a lesser extent) *directly*. Financial institutions may have indirect exposure through credit exposure on particular industries to these types of risks. Consequently, the financial institutions themselves, with limited exceptions, did not have underlying positions in their balance sheet, against which such commodity and equity market index derivative transactions could be structured. In addition, financial institutions were, in the main, less experienced in commodities and equities than in interest rate and currency risk management. The only exception to this was financial institutions with active bullion and precious metal franchises or with substantial metal trading capacities.

This impeded the entry of financial institutions into market making in these areas through a variety of factors including the absence of substantial inventories of the relevant commodity, positions in the underlying equity market index or the relevant trading skills in the underlying commodity or equity market. This was to some extent alleviated by the fact that most transactions in commodities or equity market indexes were effectively portfolios of forward contracts or options which could be hedged through the relevant futures or options market, albeit with significant residual mismatches and basis risks.

These factors were however significant in that it facilitated the entry into the commodity and equity derivatives markets of a variety of institutions with specialised expertise *in the commodity and equity market*. For example, a number of commodities trading firms, with significant commodities trading expertise, were able to expand into management of the underlying commodity risk.

ECONOMICS OF SWAP AND DERIVATIVE MARKET MAKING

The impetus to establish principal trading/market making capabilities and swap and derivative product was the potentially significant earnings believed to be available from this particular business. Frequent extravagant claims regarding the profitability of swap and derivative business operation are common. Belief that significant earnings can be generated in this type of activity continues to attract new participants to this market.

However, economics of swap and derivative operations are not generally well understood. While measurement of profitability in respect of all financial services businesses is necessarily a complex undertaking, the measurement of profitability of swap and derivative product activity is *particularly complex*. This complexity results in either failure to measure the profitability of this type of operation *at all* or techniques of measurement which are seriously flawed.

Exhibit 30.1 sets out an attempt to quantify the economics of global swap and derivative operations. The analysis examines the profitability of a medium sized global swap and derivatives operation within a financial institution operating in London, Tokyo and New York, active in approximately five major currencies and capabilities in most swap and derivative products.

Exhibit 30.1
Economics of Global Swap and Derivative Operation

1. ***Basic Parameters***

Assume a medium sized global swap and derivative operation within a financial institution structured as follows:

- Operations are headquartered in London with a substantial presence in New York and Tokyo.
- The operation is active in:

Currencies: US$, DEM, ECU, GBP, JPY

Products: FRAs, interest rate swaps
LTFX currency swaps
Swaption and other swap/option combinations
Caps, floors and collars

- The portfolio of transactions is:

—US$40 billion (in notional principal amount terms) in total terms, which is equivalent to a portfolio of US$20 billion in matched or paired transaction terms.

—The portfolio mix is:

US$30 billion in interest rate related products.

US$10 billion in exchange rate related products.

—Average transaction maturity is 3 years.

—Average transaction size is US$25m.

2. ***Profit and Loss Statement***

An estimated profitability analysis of the operation is summarised below:

Economics of Global Swap Operation

		US$	%
Income			
Interest Rate Products		7,500,000	45.5%
Exchange Rate Products		4,000,000	24.2%
Proprietary Trading		5,000,000	30.3%
Total		16,500,000	100.0%
Expenses			
Salaries		2,360,000	30.2%
Salary Add-on Costs @	30.0%	708,000	9.1%
Premises		316,400	4.0%
Marketing/Travel		750,000	9.6%
Equipment			
—Computers		150,000	1.9%
—Furniture		60,000	0.8%
—Information Services		300,000	3.8%
Information Systems		500,000	6.4%
Telecommunciation Charges		500,000	6.4%
Overhead Allocation			
As % of Salaries at	12.50%	295,000	3.8%
Sub Total		5,939,400	76.0%
Credit Reserve Against Future Losses (0.25% of Current Mark to Market Value)		1,875,000	24.0%
Total		7,814,400	100.0%
Pre-Tax Net Income		8,685,600	

Individual items are derived as follows:

Exhibit 30.1—continued

Income Items

- Income is separated into portfolio "bid-offer" spread earning and income from proprietary trading.
- All spread earnings are estimated *net* of hedging costs, including cost of funding hedges, hedge "slippage" costs, brokerage fees, cost of funding deposits and margin calls on future hedges etc.
- Average net spreads assumed are:

  0.05% pa on interest rate products;
  0.08% pa on exchange rate products.

  The spread relates to the bid-offer margin on a matched pair of transactions (that is, they should be halved for one side of a transaction).
- The spreads on individual transactions as between products, currencies or counterparties will vary significantly. As noted above, the spreads assumed are average spreads.
- Proprietary trading earnings relate to income from favourable impact of anticipated movements in interest rates, currencies etc on deliberate risk positions assumed. It has been assumed that such income, which is by its inherent nature difficult to forecast, runs at 30% of total earnings.

Expense Items

- Salary (covering all remuneration exclusive of bonus payments) costs are estimated as follows:

Staffing Arrangements

Location	London	New York	Tokyo	Total	%	Average Salary (US$)	Total Cost (US$)	%
Staffing Level								
Director	1	1	1	3	10.7%	150,000	450,000	19.1%
Trading	2	2	2	6	21.4%	120,000	720,000	30.5%
Sales/Marketing	3	2	2	7	25.0%	90,000	630,000	26.7%
Analytical Support/Systems	2	1	1	4	14.3%	75,000	300,000	12.7%
Back-Office	2	1	1	4	14.3%	40,000	160,000	6.8%
Secretarial	2	1	1	4	14.3%	25,000	100,000	4.2%
Total	12	8	8	28	100.0%	84,286	2,360,000	100.0%

Premises				Total
Avge Square Foot/Person	100	100	100	
Total Area Required	1,200	800	800	
Rent pa Per Square Foot	95	45	208	
Total Annual Cost	114,000	36,000	166,400	316,400

Salary add-ons, covering insurance, workers compensation, insurance etc, are based on a fixed percentage of salary.

- Marketing/travel expenditure is self-explanatory covering sales related travel/entertainment as well as marketing material and advertising.
- Equipment costs are based on estimated operating leases expenses covering computers and furniture. Lease cost for information services cover payments for subscription to Reuters, Telerate etc screen based information systems.
- Telecommunication expenses relate to normal telephone, fax and telex charges as well as the costs related to dedicated communication links necessary to support the computerised processing systems.
- Overhead allocations covers all other general corporate cost and is estimated as a percentage of salaries.

Credit Reserve

The credit reserve charge is designed to provide for losses in the event of counterparty default. The provision is calculated as a percentage (0.25%) of the estimated current mark-to-market exposure on the portfolio.

Exhibit 30.1—continued

3. ***Capital Requirements***

The capital required to be committed to support the operation is constituted of two specific components:

- to cover BIS Capital Requirements covering credit risk;
- to cover market risk positions.

The capital required in respect of BIS Capital Adequacy guidelines is estimated as follows:

Calculation of Earnings and Capital Committed

Product Type	Interest Rate	Exchange Rate	Total
Average Outstanding Notional Principal (US$m)	30,000	10,000	40,000
Average Term to Maturity (Years)	3	3	
Average Spread (on Each Side of the Transaction)	0.0250%	0.0400%	
Spread Earnings (US$m pa)	7.500	4.000	11.500
Capital Requirement Under BIS Guidelines			
Average Mark to Market Exposure (%)	1.500%	3.000%	
Average Mark to Market Exposure (US$ m)	450	300	750
Future Exposure Add-on (%)	0.500%	5.000%	
Future Exposure Add-on (US$m)	150	500	650
Counterparty Exposure			
—OECD Banks/Government Entities (20% Risk Weight)	60.0%	60.0%	
—Corporations (50% Risk Weight)	40.0%	40.0%	
Average Weighting	32.00%	32.00%	
Total Credit Equivalent Exposure (US$m)	192.000	256.000	448
Capital Ratio	8.00%	8.00%	
Total Capital Requirement (US$m)	15.360	20.480	35.840

The major assumption requirements include:

- *Average* mark-to-market exposure on the *gross* portfolio is estimated as:

  1.5% of notional principal on interest rate contracts;
  3.0% of notional principal on exchange rate contracts.
- Full add-ons are assumed for the *entire* portfolio.
- An average counterparty risk weighting of 32% is assumed reflecting the following mix of business:

  OECD banks/government entities (20% risk weighting)—60%; Corporation (50% risk weighting)—40%.
- A capital ratio of 8% is assumed.

The capital committed to cover market risk position is estimated at US$10m. This would be related to a variety of factors:

- size of limits;
- trading approach/degree of risk assumed within portfolio;
- type of products covered.

4. ***Return on Capital***

The overall return on capital from the operation is estimated below:

Return on Capital from Operations

	US$
Capital Required	
—Credit Exposure	35,840,000
—Market Risk	10,000,000
Total	45,840,000

Exhibit 30.1—continued

Pre-Tax Net Income	8,685,600
Return on Capital (Pre Tax)	18.948%
Return on Transaction Volume	0.0217%

NB: Please note that the above represents an estimate of the profitability/returns on a hypothetical swap operation, based on the author's assumptions.

The analysis indicates that on a portfolio of US$40 billion in notional principal amount terms (US$30bn in interest rate related products and US$10bn in exchange rate related products), based on the assumptions made, the return from the operation was:

Pre-tax net income—US$8.69m;
Capital required—US$45.8m;
Return on capital—18.95% pa pre tax;
Return on transactional volume (in terms of notional principal amount) 2.17bps pa.

This return compares to:

- a required return on equity capital for banks in the range of 15 to 18% pa *post-tax*;
- a return on a fully risk weighted loan asset bearing a margin of 0.75% pa of approximately 9.38% pa pre tax on bank equity capital required. (This return is based on a *net* margin, after adjustment for expenses, overheads and provision for loan losses.)

Increasingly, the key to above average performance and survival in the swap and derivatives trading/market making business will be, as discussed in Chapter 1, the capacity to adapt to a changing market environment which is more competitive. Approaches that will need to be adopted include:

- an understanding of the profit dynamics of individual institution's operations;
- identification of market segments, including the profitability of products, that are available;
- capacity to create innovative products and to modify existing products to match the requirement of clients;
- design of an organisation which provides an effective distribution capability to its particular target market.

As noted in more detail in Chapter 1, the period of growth in the swap and derivative markets has, to a substantial degree, obscured individual product profitability as substantial profit margins and the proliferation of products has ensured some level of profitability for most organisations active in the market. However, in the future, increased focus is necessary to ensure adequate return from these products. Possible approaches to swap and derivative business units include:

- focus on proprietary trading and speculative activity;
- focus on commodity transactions, emphasising large substantial market presences and a lower cost structure supported by accurate marginal pricing mechanisms for individual transactions;
- focus on complex structured transactions emphasising product innovation, research and market responsiveness.

SIGNIFICANT MARKET MAKERS IN SWAP AND DERIVATIVE PRODUCTS

Major participants

By the middle of the 1980s, principal trading/market making in swap and derivatives had become an established practice. The swap market makers that have evolved are capable of classification into three separate categories:

- US$ swaps;
- reserve currency swaps and derivatives;
- other currency swaps and derivatives.

The US$ swap market is by far the largest swap market and, correspondingly, has the largest number of traders/market makers, with a large number of commercial and investment banks participating. Market makers in other major reserve currencies (yen, deutschmarks, ECU, Swiss francs etc) are also numerous, although peculiarities and hedging difficulties of individual markets constrains the level of market liquidity.

In other currencies, market making in swaps and derivatives in varying degrees takes place. In currencies like A$ and NZ$, C$ etc active and often highly liquid markets of derivatives are maintained, but entail a limited group of financial institutions. In the remaining swap currencies, liquidity is relatively limited with transactions being undertaken on a substantially matched basis with market making being limited to very short-term positioning or, alternatively, the booking of positions purely for speculative purposes.

The individual swap market makers and the respective markets reflect the following pattern:

- The diversity of market makers in the US$ market is significantly greater than in other markets.
- In the reserve currencies, the principal market makers are typically major banks or financial institutions resident in the domestic market place of the currency supplemented by limited number of foreign institutions.
- In non-reserve currencies, swap and derivative market making tends to be dominated by major local banks predominant position in financial instruments in the relevant currency.
- Very few financial institutions are active traders/market makers in more than three to four currencies.

Exhibit 30.2 identifies a number of major organisations (in alphabetical order) active in the global swaps and derivatives market. The list is based on standings in an annual poll conducted by Euromoney and is based on standardings in the "best overall category".

Exhibit 30.3 identifies major swap and derivative market makers in *individual currencies*.

These "beauty contests" are statistics not wholly reliable and must as a result be treated with considerable caution. However, they do provide a basic indication as to the major and most active participants of these products.[1]

1. See also *Derivatives Survey 1993* (Euromoney Research, London, 1993).

Exhibit 30.2

Standing in Euromoney—Swaps/Derivatives Poll

Organisation*	"Best Overall" Category Year					
	1987	1988	1989	1990	1991	1992
AIG Financial Products					19	
Bank of America				11		
Bank of Montreal					20	
Bankers Trust	1	2	3	2	2	3
Banque Paribas	7	5		5	8	
Barclays/BZW				13	6	5
Chase Manhattan	10	7				
Chemical		6	8			
CIBC				15	9	
Citibank	6	3	1	3	4	7
Credit Lyonnais					15	
CSFP/CSFB/First Boston	8		9		1	2
Deutsche Bank/Morgan Grenfell		8		9	5	7
Dresdner Bank					20	
First Chicago			7	7	13	
Goldman Sachs						10
JP Morgan	2	4	4	4	3	1
Lehman Brothers						10
Manufacturers Hanover				10		
Merrill Lynch					12	
Midland Bank				12		
Morgan Stanley	9					
Prudential Bache	10					
Royal Bank of Canada			5		16	
Salomon Brothers	4	8	6	8	17	
Security Pacific	2	1	2	1	7	
Societe Generale					11	
Swiss Bank Corporation		10			14	6
Sumitomo Bank						9
Union Bank of Switzerland			10	6	10	4
Westpac				14	18	

* The listing of organisations is purely alphabetical.

Source: Euromoney.

Exhibit 30.3

Major Swap and Derivative Market Makers in Individual Currencies

Currency	Financial Institution*
North American	
US Dollars	AIG; Bank of America/Security Pacific; Bankers Trust; Barclays; Chase Manhattan; Chemical; Citibank; CSFP; General Re; JP Morgan; Merrill Lynch; Royal Bank of Canada; Sumitomo Bank Capital Markets
Canadian Dollars	Bank of Nova Scotia; Bank of Montreal; Bankers Trust; CIBC Wood Gundy; Citibank; Royal Bank of Canada; Toronto Dominion

Exhibit 30.3—continued

Europe	
Sterling	Barclays; Citibank; Midland Montagu; National Westminster; Royal Bank of Canada;
Deutschmark	Chemical; Citibank; Commerzbank; CSFP; Deutsche; Dresdner; JP Morgan; Morgan Stanley; Paribas; Royal Bank of Canada; Societe Generale; Swiss Bank Corporation; West LB
European Currency Units	ABN—AMRO; Bankers Trust; Credit Lyonnais; CSFP; Deutsche; JP Morgan; Paribas; San Paolo; Societe Generale; Sumitomo Bank
Swiss Francs	CSFP; JP Morgan; Paribas; Swiss Bank; UBS
French Francs	BNP; Credit Agricole; Credit Lyonnais; CCF; Indosuez; Paribas; San Paolo; Societe Generale
Dutch Guilders	ABN—AMRO; Rabobank
Lira	BCI; Casa di Rirparmio di Torino; Credit Lyonnais; CSFP; JP Morgan; Paribas; San Paolo
Pesetas	Banco Santander; Bank of America; Bankers Trust; Chase Manhattan; JP Morgan
Scandinavian Currencies	Den Danske Bank; Enskilda Corporate; KOP; Merrill Lynch; Se Banken; Svenska Handelsbank; Unibank
Asia/Far East	
Yen	AIG; Bank of Tokyo; Bankers Trust; IBJ; LTCB; Mitsubishi Bank; Paribas; Nomura; Salomon Brothers; Sakura Global Capital; Sumitomo Bank; Westpac
Hong Kong Dollars	Chemical; Hongkong Bank/Wardley; Paribas
Australasia	
Australian Dollars	ANZ; Bankers Trust; Commonwealth Bank; Citibank; National Australia; Westpac
New Zealand Dollars	Bank of New Zealand; Bankers Trust; Citibank; Westpac

* All listings within a currency are alphabetical.

Source: Compiled from *Corporate Finance*, Euromoney Publications; Euromoney; *Risk*. Alternatively, based on author's research.

Role of swap brokers

Complementing the role of principal traders/market makers in swaps, a number of specialised swap brokers have emerged. These include:

- Tullet and Tokyo (active in most major swap currencies);
- Euro brokers (particularly active in US$);
- Gottex (active in European currencies);
- Finacor (active in French francs);
- Intercapital brokers (active in European currencies);
- Other brokers active include Tradition, Exco, Harlow-Butler and CM Capital Markets Brokerage (particularly in pesetas).

The extension into swap and derivative business is a natural development for traditional money broking firms complementing existing core businesses entailed in broking money deposits and spot foreign exchange. Increasingly, broking firms have extended the range of their intermediation activities to cover a variety of products ranging from government bonds, repurchase agreements, LDC debt as well as swap and derivatives products. In addition, a few brokers are increasingly becoming active in commodity and equity products.

Brokers in the swap and derivative market provides the following advantages:

- capacity to deal anonymously;
- capacity to assess flow of transactions in a market from a relatively disinterested perspective (as brokers do not have proprietary positions);
- the ability to obtain the best price for a particular transaction.

Despite these advantages, the relationship between financial institutions and brokers is necessarily a relatively uneasy one. However, increasingly there is greater tolerance of the role of brokers in the swap and derivatives markets. A development which is assisted by the increasing investment by brokers in greater analytical capabilities adds significantly to their pure counterparty location and pricing advantages.

The role of swap brokers has to some extent been effected with instability among the broking firms themselves with team migrations from one firm to another as well as the liquidation of KBW in London, following its failure to meet Bank of England United Kingdom Capital Adequacy Requirements.

In addition, competition between brokers in a market categorised by slower growth, deteriorating bank credit ratings (swap and derivative brokers operate almost exclusively interbank) etc, have created severe pressures on commissions. The price war between brokers has forced all brokers to give bigger volume discounts.

However, the increased role of swap and derivative brokers is apparent as highlighted by the success of intercapital winning the mandate for a US$1.5bn swap programme for African Development Bank: see discussion in Chapter 12.

Chapter 31

Risks in Swap and Derivative Portfolio Management

RISKS IN MARKET MAKING IN SWAP PRODUCTS[1]

Risk dimensions

Risk and its impact on portfolio value as a result of movements in various financial market variables is an integral part of market making in swap and derivative products. In essence, the market maker earns a margin (the bid-offer spread and/or fees) in return for the assumption of various types of risks.

In this chapter, the types of risks that must be managed by market makers in these products are outlined.

It is possible to differentiate between two distinct categories of risk:

- *Short-term risk*—this is the risk assumed where entry into a transaction is hedged with the intention of matching the transaction entered into with an offsetting position. The two transactions are only differentiated in terms of time of entry. A temporary hedge is constructed to protect against adverse movements in the relevant financial market variable to protect against changes in market prices during this interim period.
- *Portfolio risk*—this entails an *ongoing* series of risks assumed in managing a portfolio of offsetting but not matched transactions. The portfolio is generally *immunised* against movements in the relevant financial market variables but the process of matching is not undertaken on a transaction-by-transaction basis but rather on an aggregation concept. The aggregation of individual transactions into the portfolio necessarily creates a series of *mismatches* or portfolio risk positions which must be managed.

It is also possible to differentiate as between the specific risk characteristics of individual products. In particular, a clear difference based on classification as to symmetric versus asymmetric instruments, that is, forwards versus option based instruments is necessary.

In the following sections, the risk aspects of swap and derivative products are considered in three specific groupings:

- *Interest rate swaps, FRAs, currency swaps and LTFX*—the major relevant risks include interest rate risk, currency risk and mismatch risk.
- *Risks on option based instruments (primarily, caps, floors etc)*—the major areas of risk include interest rate risk, volatility risk and hedging (or delta-gamma) risk.
- *Commodity and equity price risks*—the major risk dimension here is exposure to the movement in the underlying commodity price or equity market index level.

1. The discussion of swap market making risks draws on William P Lawton and Douglas Metcalf, "Portfolio Approach to Interest Rate Swap Management" in Antl (1986), Vol 2.

Swap and derivative warehouses are operated on the basis that the intermediary can enter into a contract without a matching counterparty being available. In entering into unmatched transactions, in the case of FRAs or interest rate swaps, the intermediary incurs an exposure to movements in interest rates and, in the case of currency swaps and LTFX, exchange rates and interest rates in *two* currencies. The principal purpose of swap portfolio management is to preserve the value of the swaps booked on the bid or offer side by hedging against the risk of loss from interest rate and/or currency movements created by temporary open swap positions in the portfolio.

It is useful in this context to differentiate between the *pre-closeout* period and the *post-closeout* period.

The pre-closeout period is typically a relatively short period, depending on the size and liquidity of the swap market, during which the open position is maintained and hedged until it is closed out by an equal and opposite transaction. The post-closeout period (typically up to ten years) is the period until maturity of the two matched transactions.

The risks as between the pre- and post-closeout period differ significantly. The primary risk in the pre-closeout period may be characterised as market risk, that is, the risk to movements in interest or currency rates, while the post-closeout period is characterised principally by counterparty default or credit risk.

The distinction while conceptually tenable is less clear in practice. For example, it is possible, although unlikely, for a default on credit grounds to take place during the pre-closeout period. Similarly, certain types of market risk are evident in the post-closeout period, including certain mismatch risks which must be assumed for the full term of the swap.

The differentiation between pre- and post-closeout risk has, over time, become less relevant. This reflects the increased utilisation of a portfolio approach to the management of exposures incurred in transacting in these products. The move to a portfolio approach necessarily implies that the risk assumed as part of market making in these products alters from a short-term risk management to a portfolio risk management problem (as discussed above).

In this part, the focus is primarily on market risk. Credit or default risk considerations in swap transactions are considered in detail in Chapter 37.

The market risk in swap warehousing operations can itself be classified into:

- interest rate risk;
- currency risk;
- mismatch risk.

The interaction of the various risk dimensions is relevant. For example, the interest rate risk incurred in transacting in these products to exposures to movements in rates in one currency are related to exposures to movements in interest rates in multiple currencies. For example, in relation to currency swaps and/or LTFX transactions, the risk assumed is in relation to the *relative* movements in yield curves as between two currencies. Similarly, the interest rate risk for a portfolio is related to and interacts substantively with the mismatch risk on a portfolio. Mismatches in payment timing, effectively, create borrowing or lending positions within the portfolio which must be funded or invested creating exposures to interest rate movements.

Each category of risk, as discussed in greater detail below, may have within it further sub-categories of risk. For example, interest rate risks can be differentiated as between base rate and spread risk or, alternatively, exposures to absolute rate movements and to yield curve shape changes.

These individual types of market risk are considered in detail below.

Interest rate risk

Interest rate risk in swap or derivative market making usually encompasses any actual exposure related to changes in interest rates as well as the risk associated with hedging that exposure.

In booking an open swap position, the intermediary creates interest rate exposures which are similar to exposures that can be created in the cash market for these instruments. The typical exposures are as follows:

- Receiving fixed rate and paying floating rate is equivalent to being long fixed rate bonds and short floating rate bonds.
- Paying fixed rate and receiving floating rate is equivalent to being short fixed rate bonds and long floating rate bonds.

It is usual in analysing the risks on swap transactions to decouple the fixed rate flows from the floating rate flows since these, in general, belong to different markets and must be managed separately. It is also common to focus attention on the management of the fixed rate flows rather than the floating rate flows as the value of the latter is more stable because it reprices more frequently and consequently trades at a level closer to par than the fixed rate component of the swap.

It is also customary to separate the interest rate risk component into two separate elements:

- the base interest rate risk;
- the spread risk.

The base risk usually refers to movements in the base rate off which swaps are priced. This is usually a government bond interest rate, such as US$ treasuries or the relevant government bond rates. The base risk is usually hedged by undertaking cash or financial futures transactions in the relevant securities.

The spread risk on swaps relates to the fact that swaps are priced as a margin relative to the fixed rate base or government bond. The risk in this context is that, for unmatched swap positions, the market spread will move against the intermediary and result in originating a matching position at a spread lower or higher than originally anticipated.

The swap market operates largely as a spread risk market since a common objective in swap market making is to lock in a positive spread on matched transactions. For example, a position may be booked to receive fixed rate at a spread of 60bps over a relevant five year government security, and hedged in anticipation of finding another counterparty to receive at the five year government bond rate plus 50bps. Assuming the *base rate* hedge is efficient, the intermediary's exposure is to changes in the spread and, in our example, an increase in the bid rate in the market or an increase in the overall spread structure could potentially produce a negative spread for the life of a matched transaction.

Spread risk cannot usually be hedged and since positions may be in inventory before matching, swap market makers are sensitive to volatility in swaps spreads. In essence, swap portfolios are essentially managed as spread portfolios with market makers seeking to identify potential shifts in swap spreads before they occur to minimise potential losses and take maximum advantage of spread shifts to benefit the swap portfolio.

Swap spread movements largely reflect the underlying arbitrage factors and changing supply and demand factors. The changing supply and demand in the swap market in turn reflects changes in anticipated volumes, directions, types of counterparties, levels of interest rates, new issue volumes, activity in parallel markets and maturity preferences.

Swap spreads can be notoriously volatile. The risk of changes in spread levels is greatest for shorter rather than longer maturity positions. Longer swap spreads are *relatively* more stable because transactions are normally linked to new issues and changes in swap spreads reflect changes in new issue spreads. Shorter maturity swap spreads are significantly more volatile, primarily reflecting the fact that these swap spreads are determined by swap and futures arbitrage, with changing prices of short-term interest rate futures contracts and particularly futures strip prices causing swap price changes. While the outer limits of a spread range may be approximately predictable, the swap spread is still relatively volatile.

The behaviour of swap spreads in individual swap markets is analysed in Part 6.

As noted above, spread risk cannot be hedged adequately. Protection against changes in the value of warehouse swap positions is a particularly vexed issue. Shorter positions are more vulnerable and are consequently usually taken on more cautiously, although this varies between markets, with very short swaps, such as positions in the US$ market, only being positioned at extremes of historical bid-offer range. Swap market makers seek to compensate for spread risk by maintaining an appropriate bid-offer spread in the relevant maturity. However, the fact remains that the best method to minimise spread risk, across all maturities, is to limit hedge positions by maturity and match them out relatively quickly.

Both base and spread interest rate risk incorporates an element of risk to *changes* in the shape of the yield curve. Interest rate risk includes both an exposure to absolute rate movements as well as an exposure to changes in the relationship between rates at different points of the yield curve. This yield curve risk can be viewed as an exposure to the absolute shape of the curve—a flat, positively or upwardly sloping or negatively or downwardly sloping. More specifically it can be considered to the exposure to the steepness or the degree of curvature in the yield curve.

As discussed in more detail below, the shape of the yield curve has the potential to change the value of both exposed positions within the portfolio or to impact upon portfolio value in a less direct manner, primarily through changes in reinvestment rates within the structure of the portfolio.

The effect of interest changes is also evident in another less obvious way. As discussed in the context of the pricing of forward contracts, the pricing of future contracts is based on the carry cost to the settlement date of the agreement. In this regard, absolute movements in interest rates as well as yield curve changes have the potential to alter the following cash to futures relationships:

- the cash to near month futures contract price;
- inter-month spreads between futures contracts with different maturities.

The impact of interest rate movements on the pricing of futures contracts is particularly important where futures contracts are used as the basic hedge for open swap positions. This is particularly evident in the hedging of interest rate swaps in a variety of currencies.

Currency risk

Currency swap transactions entail interest rate risks, as described above, as well as exposures to movements in currency rates. Booking currency swap positions exposes the intermediary to movements in the currency as the swap entails effectively being short or long the relevant currencies.

Typical exposures from currency swaps can be seen from the following example:

- Receiving fixed A$ and paying floating rate US$ is equivalent to being long A$ fixed rate bonds and short US$ floating rate bonds.
- Paying A$ fixed rate and receiving US$ floating rate is equivalent to being short A$ fixed rate bonds and long US$ floating rate bonds.

The currency exposures entailed in currency swap transactions are conceptually straightforward. It is important, however, to note that currency risk and interest rate risk are clearly interwoven. This requires that a combined hedge for the interest rate and currency risk be structured. This, in practice, entails either borrowing or lending the appropriate currency as well as seeking the appropriate interest rate risk cover through buying or selling a fixed or floating rate instrument.

A particularly important source of currency risk is coupon mismatches in currency swaps. As outlined in Chapter 8, currency swap structures invariably require one party to make payments above or below the relevant interest rate index, most typically the floating rate index, in the particular currency. These spreads relative to the index entail clearly identifiable exposures to movements in exchange rates and must be hedged accordingly.

Mismatch risk

Swaps have a number of factors which, if they are not matched or managed properly within the portfolio, have the potential to inflict substantial economic loss. It is incumbent on the portfolio manager to measure and manage this mismatch risk. The management of mismatch risk is arguably the single most important aspect of swap portfolio risk management.

Mismatches usually occur from the market maker's attempt to accommodate customer preferences. In practice, if a market maker insists on matching every swap in all its aspects, compensation will have to be paid to the other counterparty as an incentive to accept the required structure, which may be significantly different from its precise requirements. In addition to this reduction in margins, the institution must be willing to carry a large hedged inventory position for potentially longer periods while searching for the identical match thereby incurring hedging and spread risk.

The major areas of mismatch risk include:

- notional principal;
- maturity;
- floating index;
- floating rate index reset dates and payment frequencies;
- payment dates;
- coupon.

Mismatching notional principal and maturity is identical to having excess long or short swap positions. For example, if an US$20m five year swap is matched with an US$10m five year swap the effect is simply that of an open US$10m five year position. Similarly, if an US$20m five year is matched with an US$20m 10 year swap, the result is greater price volatility on the longer position and a five year open position starting five years in the future.

Notional principal mismatches are particularly common where a practice known as curve hedging is utilised. In markets where there are limitations on available hedging instruments, for example, the Japanese yen market where the hedging risk between the available interest rate instruments and swap rates is particularly significant, a common hedging strategy is to hedge a position of a particular maturity with a duration weighted or volatility matched offsetting transaction in another maturity. For example, a five year swap may be hedged with an equivalent amount of three year swaps or a duration weighted equivalent of three and ten year swaps. This type of hedging practice creates significant notional principal mismatches within the portfolio.

A major area of mismatch relates to the index used to calculate the floating rate payments. It may be desirable for the market maker to consider mismatching the index in order to create an arbitrage between the two floating rates. A common example of this type of practice in the US$ market is to receive six month LIBOR while paying three month LIBOR, or to receive three month LIBOR while paying one month CP.

Another major mismatch area is the reset dates. Even a one day mismatch on the floating rate index dates potentially exposes the principal to large daily changes in the index. As the size of a portfolio increases though, diversification may reduce the significance of small reset date mismatches as the gains and losses may tend to offset each other out. In contrast, if the swap book has only one mismatched transaction, it may have a loss with no prospect of an offsetting gain.

Payment dates represent another important area of potential mismatch. A payment date mismatch results from either payment cycle mismatches, that is, annual to semi-annual or when the cycle is the same, semi-annual to semi-annual, but the date of payment is different.

There are two risks with payment mismatches. The first risk is that a payment will be made and there is no reciprocal receipt, thus creating a credit exposure for the payment amount. This is reduced by specifying net payments when applicable. However, netting payments is not applicable when the payment cycle is different. The semi-annual payer has credit exposure to the annual payer for the entire semi-annual payment for six months.

In addition to any credit risk there is the reinvestment risk incurred in mismatching payments. At the time of the transaction the assumption is made that the semi-annual coupon received will be reinvested at the yield to maturity of the swap, or some other assumed reinvestment rate. If the coupon is reinvested at a lower reinvestment rate than assumed, then the semi-annual receiver suffers a loss.

The final significant area of mismatch risk is the coupon mismatch on two swaps. One of the objectives of putting together a matched swap may be to realise the spread between the two fixed coupons. However, if the swaps do not have similar coupon structures an assumption needs to be made on reinvestment rates or funding costs. For example, the coupon mismatch after adjusting for the result of hedging gains or losses which are being amortised against the swaps, or fees paid or received in a premium or discount swap, incurs potentially significant reinvestment or funding rate risk. Where money is paid or received (be it from hedges or coupon mismatches) the assumption is made that the money received will be reinvested at an assumed but unknown rate, and money paid is borrowed at an assumed but unknown rate.

The interaction of portfolio mismatches and interest rate risk has been noted previously. Portfolio mismatches essentially create portfolio cash surpluses or deficits which must be invested or borrowed creating exposures to interest rate movements. This exposure is not only to the absolute interest rate movements but also to yield curve shape.

An interesting feature of this exposure is that it can be present even where there is no movement in the yield curve from the time the transaction is undertaken. For example, a portfolio where cash flows are received prior to offsetting cash payments being required to be made will have an exposure to a positive yield curve. This reflects a fact that unless reinvestment assumptions are adjusted, cash surpluses will be reinvested at lower rates than the term rates that might have been utilised in transacting the swaps reflecting the lower rates payable for shorter maturities. Conversely, such a portfolio would benefit where the yield curve shape was negative. The reverse would apply to a portfolio where cash receipts occur *after* cash payments effectively reversing the pattern of exposure.

The currency risk assumed in the case of spread below or above a floating rate index in currency swaps is a special case of mismatch risk.

Each potential mismatch, in practice, must be evaluated carefully, as to the potential risk of the mismatch and the return expected. The risk analysis should incorporate the impact of cumulative portfolio mismatches. For example, a date mismatch on one transaction may be offset by the exact but opposite mismatch in another transaction. The market maker may also want to investigate possible offsetting or compounding effects of mismatches among different classes of mismatches.

Swap portfolio risk: an example

The risks inherent in swap portfolio management are best illustrated utilising an example. *Exhibit 31.1* sets out a hypothetical series of transactions and the overall final position of this portfolio. *Exhibit 31.2* sets out the detailed portfolio cash flows.

Exhibit 31.1

*Example of Swap Portfolio**

Assume the following sequence of swap transactions are booked by financial institution, Bank A (A), over a period of less than three weeks. The sequence assumes that the institution is able to maintain a spread of 20bps, that is, B + 40/B + 60 (where B = Australian Commonwealth government securities of the relevant maturity).

15/2/X5—Swap 1

Three year A$50m A$ fixed and US$ LIBOR swap off a EuroA$ bond issue commencing 12/3/X5 and maturing 12/3/X8 is booked. The specific terms are as follows:

- A pays A$ 13.00% pa (A) in arrears commencing 12/3/X6 and ending 12/3/X8.
- A receives six month US$ LIBOR—60bps (S/A) commencing 12/9/X5 and ending 12/3/X8.

Bonds = 13.00% pa (S/A) and the swap pricing incorporates all appropriate yield adjustment to the base price of 13.40% pa (S/A). Exchange rate on 12/3/X5 = US$0.7120/A$1.00.

16/2/X5—Swap 2

Three year A$20m A$ fixed and US$ LIBOR swap commencing 18/2/X5 and maturing 18/2/X8:

Exhibit 31.1—continued

- A receives A$13.30% pa (S/A).
- A pays six month US$ LIBOR (S/A).

Bonds = 12.70% pa (S/A). Exchange rate on 18/2/X5 = US$0.7040/A$1.00.

24/2/X5—Swap 3

Three year A$20m interest rate swap commencing 25/2/X5 and maturing 25/2/X8:
- A receives 13.67% pa quarterly.
- A pays three month BBR quarterly.

Bonds = 13.30% pa (S/A).

27/2/X5—Swap 4

Three year A$10m interest rate swap commencing 28/2/X5 and maturing 28/2/X8:
- A receives 13.80% pa (S/A).
- A pays six month BBR (S/A).

Bonds = 13.20% pa (S/A).

5/3/X5—Swap 5

Three year A$30m A$ BBR and US$ LIBOR currency swap commencing 7/3/X5 and maturing 7/3/X8:
- A pays six month US$ LIBOR (S/A).
- A receives six month BBR (S/A).

Exchange rate on 7/3/X8 = US$0.6950/A$1.00.

The overall swap portfolio is as follows:

Bank pays	**Bank receives**
A$ fixed rate	
13.00% pa annually on A$50m	{ 13.30% pa semi-annually on A$20m 13.67% pa quarterly on A$20m 13.80% pa semi-annually on A$10m
A$ floating rates	
{ three month BBR quarterly on A$20m six month BBR semi-annually on A$10m	six month BBR semi-annually on A$30m
US$ floating rate	
{ six month LIBOR semi-annually on US$14.08m six month LIBOR semi-annually on US$20.85m	six month LIBOR minus 60bps semi-annually on US$35.6m

Note: All swaps in this sequence are identified by a unique number which is used to identify specific cash flows in *Exhibit 31.2*.

* An A$ portfolio is utilised as this facilitates the incorporation of currency swaps with interest rate swaps.

The A$ Eurobond swap is ultimately matched off against one currency swap, two interest rate swaps and one floating-to-floating currency swap. However, the final portfolio position is *not* exactly matched for two reasons:

- the differences in the time of entry into the various swaps create exposures which would have had to be hedged to ensure profitability was maintained;
- the residual mismatches which will remain because of the slightly different terms of each swap.

Exhibit 31.2
Swap Portfolio Cash Flows (US$m or A$m)

Period	Bank pays[1]		Bank receives[1]	
	Principal	Interest	Principal	Interest
Year X5				
18/2/X5	(2) + US$14.08		(2) – A$20	
25/2/X5				
28/2/X5				
7/3/X5	(5) + US$20.85		(5) – A$30	
12/3/X5	(1) – US$35.6		(1) + A$50	
25/5/X5		(3) – (90 BBR × A$20 × 0.25)		(3) + (13.67% × A$20 × 0.25)
18/8/X5		(2) – (LIBOR × US$14.08 × 0.50)		(2) + (13.30% × A$20 × 0.50)
25/8/X5		(3) – (90 BBR × A$20 × 0.25)		(3) + (13.67% × A$20 × 0.25)
28/8/X5		(4) – (180 BBR × A$10 × 0.50)		(4) + (13.80% × A$10 × 0.50)
7/9/X5		(5) – (LIBOR × US$20.85 × 0.50)		(5) + (180 BBR × A$30 × 0.50)
12/9/X5				(1) + (LIBOR – 60bps × US$35.6 × 0.50)
25/11/X5		(3) – (90 BBR × A$20 × 0.25)		(3) + (13.67% × A$20 × 0.25)
Year X6				
18/2/X6		(2) – (LIBOR × US$14.08 × 0.50)		(2) + (13.30% × A$20 × 0.50)
25/2/X6		(3) – (90 BBR × A$20 × 0.25)		(3) + (13.67% × A$20 × 0.25)
28/2/X6		(4) – (180 BBR × A$10 × 0.50)		(4) + (13.80% × A$10 × 0.50)
7/3/X6		(5) – (LIBOR × US$20.85 × 0.50)		(5) + (180 BBR × A$30× 0.50)
12/3/X6		(1) – (13.00% × A$50)		(1) + (LIBOR – 60bps × US$35.6 × 0.50)
25/5/X6		(3) – (90 BBR × A$20 × 0.25)		(3) + (13.67% × A$20 × 0.25)
18/8/X6		(2) – (LIBOR × US$14.08 × 0.50)		(2) + (13.30% × A$20 × 0.50)
25/8/X6		(3) – (90 BBR × A$20 × 0.25)		(3) + (13.67% × A$20 × 0.25)
28/8/X6		(4) – (180 BBR × A$10 × 0.50)		(4) + (13.80% × A$10 × 0.50)

Exhibit 31.2—continued

Period	Bank pays[1] Principal	Bank pays[1] Interest	Bank receives[1] Principal	Bank receives[1] Interest
7/9/X6		**(5)** − (LIBOR × US$20.85 × 0.50)		**(5)** + (180 BBR × A$30 × 0.50)
12/9/X6				**(1)** + (LIBOR − 60bps × US$35.6 × 0.50)
25/11/X6		**(3)** − (90 BBR × A$20 × 0.25)		**(3)** + (13.67% × A$20 × 0.25)
Year X7				
18/2/X7		**(2)** − (LIBOR × US$14.08 × 0.50)		**(2)** + (13.30% × A$20 × 0.50)
25/2/X7		**(3)** − (90 BBR × A$20 × 0.25)		**(3)** + (13.67% × A$20 × 0.25)
28/2/X7		**(4)** − (180 BBR × A$10 × 0.50)		**(4)** + (13.80% × A$10 × 0.50)
7/3/X7		**(5)** − (LIBOR × US$20.85 × 0.50)		**(5)** + (180 BBR × A$30 × 0.50)
12/3/X7		**(1)** − (13.00% of A$50)		**(1)** + (LIBOR − 60bps × US$35.6 × 0.50)
25/5/X7		**(3)** − (90 BBR × A$20 × 0.25)		**(3)** + (13.67% × A$20 × 0.25)
18/8/X7		**(2)** − (LIBOR × US$14.08 × 0.50)		**(2)** + (13.30% × A$20 × 0.50)
25/8/X7		**(3)** − (90 BBR × A$20 × 0.25)		**(3)** + (13.67% × A$20 × 0.25)
28/8/X7		**(4)** − (180 BBR × A$10 × 0.50)		**(4)** + (13.80% × A$10 × 0.50)
7/9/X7		**(5)** − (LIBOR × US$20.85 × 0.50)		**(5)** + (180 BBR × A$30 × 0.50)
12/9/X7				**(1)** + (LIBOR − 60bps × US$35.6 × 0.50)
25/11/X7		**(3)** − (90 BBR × A$20 × 0.25)		**(3)** + (13.67% × A$20 × 0.25)
Year X8				
18/2/X8	**(2)** − US$14.08	**(2)** − (LIBOR × US$14.08 × 0.50)	**(2)** + A$20	**(2)** + (13.30% × A$20 × 0.50)
25/2/X8		**(3)** − (90 BBR × A$20 × 0.25)		**(3)** + (13.67% × A$20 × 0.25)
28/2/X8		**(4)** − (180 BBR × A$10 × 0.50)		**(4)** + (13.80% × A$10 × 0.50)
7/3/X8	**(5)** − US$20.85	**(5)** − (LIBOR × US$20.85 × 0.50)	**(5)** + A$30	**(5)** + (180 BBR × A$30 × 0.50)
12/3/X8	**(1)** + US$35.6	**(1)** − (13.00% of A$50)	**(1)** − A$50	**(1)** + (LIBOR − 60bps × US$35.6 × 0.50)

Note:

1. The term pay and receive is used in this Exhibit as the bank both pays and receives. The term pay and receive is used to group cash flows under each swap, for example, the fixed rate A$ flows are regarded as "bank pays" and the corresponding principal flows are linked to it. For convenience, principals' reversals at maturity are not switched from pay to receive or vice versa to avoid confusion. The bold number in parentheses refers to the swap identified in *Exhibit 30.2*.

The initial swap exposes the institution to a risk of A$ interest rates falling and the US$ depreciating against the A$. This risk is initially hedged by purchasing A$ three year government bonds and borrowing US$ to fund the purchases (the hedging methodology is described in detail in Chapter 32). The A$ bonds are sold and the US$ borrowing repaid as the offsetting swaps are entered into.

The hedges set up create two problems: hedge efficiency and funding (reinvestment) of hedge losses (profits). In the example utilised, the swap market maker's hedges yield the following cash flows:

- When Swap 2 is entered into, the sale of the A$ bonds creates a profit and the repayment of the US$ borrowing results in a loss.
- The unwinding of the *interest rate* hedges when Swaps 3 and 4 are entered into result in a loss.
- When Swap 5 is entered into, the repayment of the US$ borrowing results in a further loss.

The rate at which the loss is funded and the profit reinvested, and the accompanying coupon mismatches will significantly affect the swap's profitability. This, of course, also assumes that the hedge was in the first place efficient.

The final portfolio position while matched in a general sense, upon closer examination of *Exhibit 31.2*, reveals a series of major mismatches.

The swaps all have slightly different maturities which has the effect of distorting reset dates for the floating rate indexes. For example, it is necessary to pay out the LIBOR flows before actual receipt of the offsetting LIBOR inflow. This creates a problem that, unless managed and hedged, in a declining interest rate environment the portfolio will suffer losses. In addition, the actual cash payment must be funded which, if the funding cost is higher than LIBOR itself, will result in a further loss.

The portfolio also embodies a floating index mismatch as the swap market maker receives six month BBR semi-annually and pays three month BBR quarterly. This would result in a loss to the portfolio if the yield curve was negative as the absolute cash inflows would potentially be lower than the offsetting cash inflows. This would be compounded by the need to fund the quarterly payment if six month BBR is lower than the relevant funding cost.

The differing payment frequencies on the A$ fixed rate flows create a reinvestment problem as semi-annual and quarterly payment received must be reinvested to make the offsetting annual payments. The absolute interest rate levels and the slope of the yield curve, particularly relative to that assumed when the swap was priced and entered into, will affect the portfolio's earnings.

The most striking coupon mismatch in the sample portfolio is in the US$ floating rate flows where the margin under LIBOR creates a US$ shortfall which is presumably offset by surplus A$s elsewhere in the portfolio. This exchange risk element in the portfolio must be managed throughout the life of the transaction.

The mismatches identified in the example are relatively simple. Where the portfolio is managed using more complex hedging technology, for example, using duration or generalised cash flow concepts entailing significant mismatches in amount and maturity (see Chapter 33), the risks within the portfolio would necessarily be more complex as the date and amount mismatches would be exaggerated.

It is useful in reviewing this sample portfolio to keep in mind the absolute economic impact of changes in the numerous variables. *Exhibit 31.3* summarises the A$ value effect of fluctuation in a few of the risk dimensions discussed on an A$10m swap transaction.

Exhibit 31.3
Economic Impact of Changes in A$ and US$ Swap Variables

Variable	**Change measured**	**Profit/loss impact of change**
A$/US$ spot rate	US$0.0001	A$1,398
A$ swap rates		
• three year	1bps	A$2,537
• five year	1bps	A$3,860
• ten year	1bps	A$6,228
A$ BBR		
• three month	1bps	A$243
• six month	1bps	A$471
US$ swap rates		
• three year	1bps	US$2,664
• five year	1bps	US$4,157
• ten year	1bps	US$7,103
US$ LIBOR rate		
• three month	1bps	US$248
• six month	1bps	US$490

Notes:

The above assumes:

A$1.00 = US$0.7150
A$ swap rates = 10.00% pa (S/A)
US$ swap rates = 7.00% pa (S/A)
A$ BBR = 6.00% pa
US$ LIBOR = 4.00% pa

All profit/loss impact is calculated on an amount of A$10m or US$10m.

RISKS IN MARKET MAKING IN OPTION PRODUCTS

Market making in option and related products covers trading in instruments such as caps, floors and collars, swaptions and the various hybrid structures, incorporating interest rate and currency option elements.

The differences in risks entailed in market making in these products reflect the impact of the following factors:

- symmetric versus asymmetric risk profiles of the instrument;
- the presence of an additional risk dimension, namely volatility;
- the inherent nature of options as a wasting asset;
- the risk impact of hedging utilising replication techniques.

The fundamental source of differences in risk relates to the fact that unlike the instruments considered above, options have an asymmetric profile as between purchaser and seller. The asymmetric risk profile, with its commensurately higher risk exposure for the seller, necessarily entails different types of risk to those encountered in managing portfolios of symmetric instruments.

A fundamental element of this difference in risk profile relates to volatility risk. Management of portfolios of options, as discussed below, exposes portfolio managers to the risk of changes of volatility levels which are a critical element in the valuation of option instruments.

An added factor which has an impact on the risk profile is the fact that options are wasting assets. Essentially, the value of an option, provided all other variables are held constant, decreases with the passage of time. This change in the value of the option benefits a seller, but acts against the purchaser.

The final difference relates to the fact that because of the asymmetric risk profile and the nature of the asset, portfolios of options are hedged utilising option replication technique (discussed in detail in Chapter 36) whereby the payoff profile for the option is sought to be replicated by trading in a portfolio of assets, consisting of the underlying commodity and cash which is adjusted continuously. Slippage and errors in the replication process introduces an added dimension of risk to the management of such portfolios.

The risk dimensions encountered in market making in option products include a variety of risks which are also present in relation to general swap products. These include:

- Interest rate risk which affects both the price of the option (see discussion below) as well as the central role of interest rate movements in affecting the price of the underlying security on which the derivative is based. For example, the impact of interest rate on the price of deposits/borrowings which form the basis of interest rate cap or floor transactions.
- Mismatch risk which includes portfolio mismatches as a result of offsetting but not precisely matched transactions in the option portfolio.

Market making in option product also entails a variety of specific risks, not directly present in swap portfolios. These include:

- volatility risk;
- delta-gamma risk;
- theta risk;
- rho risk.

As detailed in Chapter 11, the volatility in the value of the underlying asset is an important determinant of option values. Consequently, portfolios of options are sensitive to changes in the volatility levels of the underlying asset. This sensitivity to changes in volatility is often identified as the options' vega or volatility delta. An alternative term for the change in the option value caused by change in volatility is the Greek letter kappa - hence, kappa risk.

As noted in Chapter 11 in the context of volatility estimation, the term structure of volatility for most assets exhibits a characteristic "cone" structure. Consequently, changes in the *term structure* of volatilities also has the capacity to impact upon the value of a portfolio of options.

Delta is integral to the application of option valuation theory in that it provides a valuable measure of the options exposure to price fluctuations of the underlying asset. The major impact of delta on an option portfolio risks is that such portfolios are typically operated on a "delta neutral" basis, positions in the underlying asset being utilised to hedge the option position held.

As alternated in Chapter 11, gamma measures changes in delta for a given change in the asset price. Gamma effectively measures the quantum adjustment necessary in the delta hedge for a given change in the asset price. In effect, it measures the rebalancing that will need to be done to maintain a delta neutral position within a hedged portfolio and provides an indication of the risk to which the portfolio is exposed should the asset price move and the hedge adjustment be effected on a delayed basis.

Theta risk refers to the rate of time decay for an option. As noted above, options as a wasting asset suffer a depreciation value with the effluxion of time. Theta essentially measures the time sensitivity of an option portfolio and the impact on the portfolio value of the passage of time.

Rho measures the interest sensitivity of the option. The time value of a call option comes, at least partly, from the interest that can be earned by investing the strike price until the expiration date of the option. Consequently, the value of a call option is higher for a higher level of interest rate while the opposite is true for a put. This reflects the fact that a put holder loses interest while waiting until option maturity to receive the strike price. Changes in interest rates consequently have the potential to significantly impact upon the value of an option portfolio through its impact on the prices of individual options.

Interaction of these various risk elements within an option portfolio is complex. Management of the individual risks as well as the interaction of risks to maximise portfolio value is considered in detail in Chapter 36 in the context of risk management techniques applicable to managing cap and floor portfolios.

RISKS IN MARKET MAKING IN COMMODITY AND EQUITY RELATED DERVIATIVES

The risks entailed in market making/trading in commodity and equity related derivatives are broadly similar to those identified in relation to swap and option instruments.

The risk dimensions relevant in relation to commodity and equity swaps are broadly similar to those applicable in respect of interest rate swaps, particularly those applicable to FRAs/interest rate swaps hedged against futures strips. Commodity and equity options or option related instruments have risk characteristics which have similarities to the risks applicable to option related instruments.

The mismatch risks applicable to commodity and equity product portfolios is somewhat different to that described above in the context of swap products. This reflects, substantially, the current practice whereby commodity and equity swaps are hedged, principally, by assuming offsetting position in futures markets in the relevant commodity or a related commodity or equity market index.

The key risk dimensions applicable to market making and commodity and equity related derivatives include:

- the risk on underlying commodity price or equity market index value;
- cash futures/forward or intercontract spread relationships;
- impact of interest rates;
- currency risk in currency hedged structures.

The exposure to the basic commodity price or equity market index value is self explanatory. An added dimension is the risk of changes in the relationship between the price of the commodity being hedged and the commodity being utilised *as a hedge* where one commodity is used as a surrogate for another. For example, the use of heating oil to hedge aviation as jet fuel swaps. In the context of equity market index swaps, an added risk dimension where the market index is replicated through a holding of physical securities constituting the index is potential tracking error as well as rebalancing risks.

As noted above, changes in interest cost or convenience yields may impact upon the relationship between cash market prices and futures/forward prices as well as the prices between futures contracts maturing at different dates. Changes in these relationships have the capacity to significantly affect the market value of a portfolio given the prevalent use of futures contracts to hedge portfolios of commodity and equity market index swaps. Major factors underlying changes in the interest rate environment as well as changes in the various factors effecting demand and supply for the underlying commodity which manifests itself by way of change in the convenience yields, are relevant.

As in the case of swap and option product portfolios, a major impact of changes in interest rates is its impact on reinvestment and borrowing costs created by portfolio mismatches. In addition, as noted above interest rates through changes in carry costs or intermarket spreads effectively engineer changes in the shape of the forward curve of a commodity or an equity market index thereby impacting upon the value of positions held.

This risk basically relates to commodity or equity market indexed products where the currency risk is eliminated for the investor or hedger. Currency risk in this context is not substantially different than that encountered in relation to currency swaps. Such risk is typically transferred through the use of compensating forward/option contracts or quanto hedges to the currency option portfolio or foreign exchange risk management function within the institution.

INTEGRATED RISK MANAGEMENT APPROACHES

Concept of portfolio risk

In recent times, the management of risk within portfolios of swap and derivative products has been increasingly oriented towards aggregating risk management functions into an integrated framework. Under this approach, the risks of *all* derivative products are sought to be managed within an overall integrated conceptual framework.

The major impetus for this move towards integration of portfolio risk management reflects the following pressures:

- The need for consistency of valuation approaches to ensure full pricing consistency and comparability between various products.
- Perceived improvement in pricing and hedging efficiency through an integrated approach. This greater hedging and pricing efficiency is usually attributed to the following factors:
  - —structured transactions involving combinations of various individual products do not need to be separately priced by several risk management units within an institution, thereby avoiding transfer pricing and a series of bid-offer spreads which would inflate the price of the whole structure;
  - —presence of offsetting exposures within portfolios of individual products which can be effectively reduced to the net exposure of the aggregated portfolios and thereby minimise the number of hedging transactions required.

- An integrated approach to risk management facilitates a total understanding of the exposures within the swap and derivative product range.
- The fact that an integrated approach to risk management is theoretically more correct.

The integrated framework for risk management also overcomes obvious disadvantages of an approach which emphasises independent hedging of individual transactions or product portfolios because of its superiority in modelling and valuing complex transactions, include transactions combining various product elements, the capacity to handle non-horizontal term structure movements in interest rates and the greater correspondence between practice and the reality of how portfolios are increasingly managed.

More recently, the release, initially for discussion purposes, pending implementation, of Market Risk Guidelines by the BIS which will determine capital requirements to be held against trading portfolios has created an impetus for implementing portfolio-based risk management approaches (see Chapter 39). This reflects the fact that the guidelines are predicated on this approach to risk management.

Modern portfolio theory

A number of constructs of modern portfolio theory underpin integrated approaches to risk management currently in vogue in managing the risk of swap and derivative portfolios.

Modern portfolio theory (MPT) has its origins in the work of Markowitz. In a famous article published in 1952, Markowitz drew attention to the common practice of portfolio diversification and showed exactly the capacity for an investor to reduce the risk of a portfolio return by choosing equity stocks that did not move exactly together.[2]

Under MPT, risk is defined as a variability of asset return, as measured by standard statistical measures of dispersion, such as variance and standard deviation. MPT demonstrates that risk is best judged in a portfolio context and that diversification reduces the risk of the overall portfolio, at least where returns on the assets within the portfolio are not perfectly correlated. MPT dictates diversification reduces risk only when the correlation is less than one with the greatest diversification benefit coming when the returns on the two assets are negatively correlated. However, as long as there is less than perfect correlation, diversification yields benefits.

Central to MPT is the classification of risk into two distinct categories:

- *Systematic risk*—which can be equated to market risk and cannot be reduced by diversification.
- *Unsystematic risk*—which represents unique risk aspects associated with the particular asset which can be reduced substantially through diversification.

Implications of these findings of MPT for the management of swap and derivative portfolios include:

- Exposures to similar market factors should be aggregated and managed on an integrated basis.

2. H M Markowitz, "Portfolio Selection" (1952) 7 (March) *Journal of Finance* 77.

- Risk factors have to be identified and, if possible, separated into systematic and unsystematic risk dimensions, with unsystematic risk dimensions being reduced through diversification practices.
- The covariance, that is the correlation relationship between risk factors, has to be determined. For example, interest rate risk, particularly yield curve risk, can be regarded as a covariance risk related to correlation in movements in interest rates at various points of the term structure. Similarly, correlation relationship between movements in various currencies and/or movements in interest rates as against currencies should be determined to establish a risk profile of the portfolio.
- The portfolio of swaps and derivative assets should be managed on a *net* basis with the net aggregated exposure position being hedged.

Integrated risk management approaches[3]

Traditional approaches

Traditional approaches to swap and derivative risk management have, generally, focused on series of separate product portfolios which are managed independently. Some integration may be encompassed with similar products, for example, interest rate swaps and FRAs, being managed within one portfolio.

Under this traditional approach, currency and interest rate risk have been separated and managed independently.

The management of currency risk is relatively straightforward. However, techniques for management of interest rate risk differ sharply as between different approaches to portfolio management.

One of the earliest approaches to measurement and management of interest rate risk was gap analysis. This technique, which derived from traditional bank asset liability management practices, required construction of cash flow "ladders" by either due date or rate refixing date (whichever was earlier). Within the cash flow ladders, receipts and payments within (arbitrary) time periods were summed to give total net position for a given time period. Impact of interest rate changes, as reflected under various yield curve scenarios, was then utilised to simulate the interest rate risk of the portfolio.

The major weakness of this type of approach was that specific exposures were often hidden within the arbitrary time bands and this approach could not provide information such as the actual impact of the immediate 1bps rise in a specific rate.

The gap analysis was supplanted, in the early 1980s, by duration analysis techniques which were originally utilised in bond portfolio management: see discussion in Chapter 33. Duration facilitates the measurement, represented by changes in net present value, of a given portfolio of instruments for a rise or fall in interest rates. The duration techniques were subject to the weakness that it generally depends on parallel shifts in the yield curve which, as an empirical fact, was not justified. A further difficulty was duration techniques did not exclude risky hedges, for example, hedging ten year bond positions with 30 day discount securities.

3. This discussion draws on Dr Simon Babbs, "Measuring Market Risks on Interest Rate Derivatives Portfolios" and Dr Colin Lawrence, "A Portfolio Approach to Risk Management" (conference papers presented at *Financial Risk Measurement and Management of Derivatives*, IIR Conference London, 28-29 April 1992).

Duration analysis of interest rate risk was complemented by convexity analysis (that is, how duration changes with yields). Use of convexity, to complement duration measures, was useful but did not assist in overcoming some of the deficiencies identified.

A major problem with these traditional approaches to interest rate risk management was the difficulty in incorporating symmetric risk instruments, such as options, within this framework.

Current approach

The deficiencies identified in traditional approaches to risk management, as noted above, led to institutions examining more integrated approaches to risk management of swap and derivative portfolios.

Central to this concept is management of risk on an aggregate basis. This aggregation effectively amalgamates similar instruments as follows:

- all non-option interest products in a given currency;
- all option products in a given currency;
- currency exposures.

Under this approach, all cash flows within each portfolio are partitioned by their dates into time periods (often referred to as "buckets" or "vectors").

In a number of systems, the use of cash flow partitioning is also associated with expressing positions as the equivalent of hypothetical instruments, for example as ten year bond equivalents. The exact utility of such an approach is not clear.

The cash flow portfolio, as derived by this partitioning process, is then subject to analysis to determine its sensitivity to identified risk factors. The key risk factors utilised are:

- interest rate risk (in a single currency) which includes exposure to absolute rate movements, yield curve changes, and spread movements;
- option risk (in a single currency) which effectively measures exposure to volatility changes and to delta-gamma risk;
- cross-currency instrument exposures, primarily foreign exchange risk;
- portfolio covariance or correlation risk.

The principal measurement technique utilised is the present value of a basis point (PVBP). The cash flows identified and partitioned are, in each currency, discounted utilising zero coupon rates, derived from the par yield curve by "stripping" the yield curve: see discussion in Chapter 8. Utilising zero coupon curves and the PVBP concept, measurement of the exposure to *individual* market interest rates at any point in the yield curve is feasible. This allows analysis of portfolio risk to non-parallel shifts in the yield curve, as well as spread movements in the relationship between various instruments.

The PVBP calculated can be restated as equivalent positions in common hedging instruments to identify possible hedging strategies.

A special problem in this regard relates to exchange traded instruments which are marked-to-market directly. In practice, increasingly, exchange traded instruments, such as Eurodollar futures, are incorporated into the basic yield curve. This means that the zero coupon curve derived agrees with the market price of these instruments and allows valuation utilising the zero coupon curves generated. In the event that the futures curve is not utilised, a spread relationship must be defined between the cash market curve and the exchange traded curve to reconcile the two valuations.

The basic framework can be adapted quite readily to calculate the PVBP of options. Given that PVBP simply expresses the sensitivities at the value of the underlying instrument to market rates, the PVBP of an interest rate option is, quite simply, its delta in respect to market rates. In addition to its delta or PVBP, the option portfolio is analysed for its gamma risk as noted above.

In essence, non-option instruments have very stable PVBPs as rates move, that is to say, such instruments have negligible gammas. In contrast, option instruments have unstable PVBPs, that is, they have high gamma exposure. Gamma is typically measured by calculating the second derivative of the option value, which measures the curvature of value changes as rate changes. The derivative approach is only reliable in relation to relatively small movements in interest rates. Increasingly, portfolio managers measure gamma where the yield curve is subject to one or more appreciable shifts to measure the change in PVBPs or gamma for the option portfolio to provide a more reliable measure of this exposure.

An additional risk factor incorporated in relation to option products is a measure of volatility exposure, measured by calculating the derivative value for vega or kappa.

In relation to volatility exposures, it is important to note that different option pricing models utilise slightly different concepts of volatility: see discussion in Chapter 11. Interaction of volatility, in this context, with interest rate movement dynamics has the potential to significantly impact upon the measured volatility exposure of the portfolio.

The single currency framework outlined above is capable of extension to a multi-currency setting. In practice, simple non-option, cross currency instruments (such as currency swaps/LTFX) can be decomposed into notional single currency deals combined with spot and forward currency transaction. The currency risk evident is relatively easily identified and managed along traditional currency risk management lines.

In the case of option instruments entailing currencies or more complex hybrid structures, such as options on currency swaps or index differential swaps, the currency risk element is considerably more complex. This risk is typically a function of a variety of factors including:

- yield curve in the relevant currency;
- spot FX rate;
- the yield curve volatilities in the relevant currencies;
- volatility of the spot FX rate.

In practice, the identified factors will be significantly correlated and will create complex risk interactions.

In practice, these risks are absorbed into the currency risk management unit, such as an FX options portfolio, and managed accordingly. The analysis of risk exposures in cross currency instruments highlights the role of correlation in integrated risk management.

As is evident, a variety of the financial market variables identified will be significantly correlated. For example, yield curve movements between currencies, movements in different parts of the yield curve in the same currency, and movements in different foreign exchange rates will all exhibit certain degrees of correlation. Increasingly, portfolios are managed to take advantage of the correlation relationships to, either, diversify and reduce risk, or facilitate the creation of surrogate hedges to manage existing risk exposures.

The management of portfolios based on these correlations introduces an additional risk dimension relating to the non-stability or change of the relationships. This reflects the fact that changes in the correlations or relationships will impact upon the efficiency of the various hedges utilised.

SWAP AND DERIVATIVE PORTFOLIO RISK—IN PRACTICE

The key issues in swap and derivative portfolio risk management, in practice, are: first, the identification of risk factors affecting portfolio value; secondly, the management of these risks; and, finally, pricing to cover the cost of hedging and risk management.

Significant differences exist in individual institution's approaches to their swap portfolios. Some institutions regard it as a servicing function to support other areas of business such as new issues or the underwriting and sales of securities. Other institutions treat swaps and derivatives as part of their overall treasury activity. However, the majority of institutions, currently, operate their swap and derivative activities as an identifiable and separate profit centre. Depending on the framework utilised, swap portfolios are operated in slightly different ways and within each framework individual transactions must be reconciled with the overall operational objectives.

An additional issue relates to the differences in the risk-return trade-offs within individual swap and derivative portfolios. For example, some institutions utilise their swap transactions to position to take advantage of anticipated movements in financial market variables while other swap market participants are restricted to operating their portfolios on a fully hedged basis, within very limited risk limits.

In general, swap and derivative portfolios, in the current market environment, are operated on a partial or fully hedged basis. Limit structures allow a certain degree of positioning activity to be undertaken. This is generally confined to trading basis and spread relationships, yield curve shapes and hedge risk relationships rather than positioning for absolute rate movement.

In considering the use of swaps and derivatives for the purpose of positioning, it is important to note that other markets are available which provide greater liquidity in opening and closing positioning trades and which better allow participants to more efficiently capture anticipated movements in the relevant variable.

In essence, portfolios are generally operated on a hedged basis, where institutions substitute absolute risk for hedging risk. This relates to the fact that hedging portfolio risk positions with surrogate instruments as a proxy for transactions being hedged, exposes the portfolio to a risk of gain or loss from the imperfect correlation in the movement of the hedge value as against the underlying transaction sought to be hedged.

The current approach adopted replaces the traditional product-by-product approach to portfolio management with an integrated risk management framework. Under this framework, a number of portfolios are operated. In a fully fledged, integrated risk management operation, the following portfolios might be utilised:

- interest rate exposure portfolios (by currency);
- interest rate option portfolios (by currency);
- cross-currency portfolio, usually incorporating currency option portfolios;
- commodity risk portfolios, incorporating both commodity swaps and, usually, separate commodity options portfolio;
- equity market index portfolio, including separate portfolios for equity swaps and equity market index options.

The exact structure of portfolios operated vary significantly as between institutions. For example, Chase Manhattan is reported to operate five separate books covering interest rate risk alone: a spread book, a volatility book, a basis book, yield curve book and a directional book. The bank runs the various risk books independently in order to provide flexibility to originators although risk is aggregated to some degree.

In practice, the portfolio structure adopted will, typically, reflect balance between maximising the benefits of integrated portfolio management and hedging efficiency of the organisation's requirements.

The remaining five chapters in this section of the book cover specific risk management practices as they pertain to individual types of products. Chapters 32, 33 and 34 focus on management portfolio risks in relation to managing interest rate swaps, currency swaps and LTFX transactions. Chapters 32 and 33 focus, primarily, on the management of the risk of the fixed rate payment flows in relation to these transactions. Chapter 34 focuses mainly on the management of the floating rate portfolio generated by such transactions which create significant and quite different risks requiring different management approaches.

Chapter 35 examines the specific issues in relation to hedging FRAs while Chapter 36 focuses on the management of portfolios of caps, floors and collars.

The management of portfolios of commodity and equity market index related derivatives are not specifically considered. As noted above, the management of portfolios of commodity price and equity market index swaps is analogous to the management of portfolios of interest rate swaps/FRAs hedged to futures transactions. The various factors discussed in this regard in Chapters 32, 33 and 35 are applicable to the hedging of these instruments. The management of portfolios of commodity and equity market index options is broadly similar to the management of portfolios of caps and floors. The basic option-hedging technology utilised is identical. The hedging of commodity and equity market related derivatives was considered, in part, in Chapters 16 and 17.

Chapter 32

Swap Portfolio Risk Management Techniques: Basic Hedging Approach

OVERVIEW

The preferred method of controlling exposure to market risks on a swap transaction is to match it by entering into an offsetting swap. Where swap transactions are matched in this way, if inflows match outflows, apart from spreads taken by the intermediary as income, the intermediary should, theoretically, be fully hedged against *market* risks. Mismatches and payment dates, reset periods, etc, lessen the effectiveness of the hedge created by matching out the two swaps.

Under current market conditions, very few intermediaries match each swap as it is booked. The structure and competitive pressures in the swap market now dictate that most intermediaries enter into each swap independently, that is, most intermediaries are ready to commit themselves to one leg of a swap transaction before the offsetting leg has been arranged. This activity is undertaken on the assumption that the matching swap transaction can be completed without an adverse change in the market during the interim period.

This market risk entailed in booking open swap positions can be approached in two different ways:

- It is possible to open swap positions to speculate on swap spread and interest rate movements.
- The swap position is booked and hedged against market risk pending arrangement of the matching part to the transaction.

Under current market practice, the vast majority of intermediaries utilise a variety of swap portfolio risk management techniques to, at least partially, hedge against the risk of market movements in the period between the entry into the first swap and the entry into the offsetting transaction. In essence, intermediaries do not seek to utilise their swap activities to take positions in interest rate markets or currency markets but operate their swap portfolios on a risk averse basis.

A number of approaches to swap portfolio risk management exist. These include:

- the hedging approach, entailing *individual* hedges for *each* swap transaction undertaken; or
- portfolio approaches, based on the practice of hedging *entire* swap portfolios.

In addition, specific approaches to hedging portfolios of FRAs and option based instruments, such as caps and floors, also exist.

The basic hedging approach, described in detail in this chapter, represents the original approach to swap portfolio risk management. It is predicated on a number of factors:

- Swap portfolio management entails hedging of *temporary* risk positions.
- A swap is the best hedge for another swap, hence any hedge is, necessarily, of a transient nature.

However, over time the relative inflexibility of the basic hedging approach combined with the evolution of the swap market itself with the development of non-generic swap structures and large portfolios of swap transactions entailing complex mismatches has necessitated the adoption of portfolio management approaches. These portfolio management approaches are considered in Chapter 33.

Specific issues relating to the hedging of FRAs and caps and floors are considered in Chapters 35 and 36 respectively.

HEDGING INTEREST RATE SWAP TRANSACTIONS

Basic concept

Hedging strategies, where interest rate swap transactions are booked without a matching counterpart transaction, are based on the fact that the exposure underlying unmatched swaps is directly analogous to cash market positions. Consequently, transactions involving physical cash market instruments or financial futures on the relevant cash market instrument can be utilised to offset the market risk assumed until the swap is matched with an offsetting transaction.

As discussed in Chapter 31, in an interest rate swap transaction in any currency, the physical market positions corresponding to swap positions are as follows:

- receiving fixed rate and paying floating rate is equivalent to being long fixed rate bonds and short floating rate bonds;
- paying fixed rate and receiving floating rate is equivalent to being short fixed rate bonds and long floating rate bonds.

Given these cash market equivalent positions, it is possible to hedge the market risk by effectively reversing the cash market position to provide a hedge against fluctuations in the value of the swap. Utilising this technology, the hedges are structured as follows:

- Where an intermediary receives fixed rate and pays floating rate it can hedge its exposure by shorting fixed rate bonds and purchasing or going long floating rate bonds.
- Where an intermediary pays fixed rate and receives floating rate the appropriate hedge is to go long fixed rate bonds and short floating rate bonds.

This type of hedging technique is best illustrated by example.

For example, assume an intermediary commits itself to a five year swap with a corporation when the yield on five year bonds is 8.00% pa. Under the terms of the swap, the intermediary pays bonds plus 40bps in return for receiving six month US$ LIBOR. The intermediary, not having a matching counterparty, hedges the swap temporarily by buying five year treasury bonds. Subsequently, a few days later, the intermediary matches out its original swap exposure by entering into a matching offsetting swap.

In the pre-closeout period, between the original swap and the matching swap, the spread on swaps has remained constant at bonds plus 40bps (bid) and bonds plus 50bps (offer). However, the yield on five year government bonds has fallen to 7.50% pa. This effectively means that in *absolute rate* terms the intermediary is paying 8.40% pa and receiving 8.00% pa on the fixed rate side of the swaps. It is assumed, in this case, that the floating rate sides, that is, the payment and receipt of floating rate BBR, are matched.

In terms of the matched swap positions, the bank loses 40bps on the notional principal at every payment date. However, this periodic loss is offset by the gain on the holdings of bonds. The bonds bought to hedge the swap position would have increased in price when government bond rates fell from 8.00% to 7.50% pa. This gain is realised when the intermediary sells the bonds at the time it enters into the matching swap transaction to close out its exposure. Once the value of the profit on the government bonds is factored into the transaction, the intermediary will approximately earn 10bps pa, representing the spread between the bid and offer rates, on the matched swap positions.

In the reverse situation, where the intermediary had received a fixed rate under the swap, it would have hedged by selling bonds and buying back those bonds when the offsetting swap was arranged. Under this transaction, the fall in rates would have resulted in a gain on the swap offset by a loss on the short bond position.

Examples of this type of hedge for interest rate swap portfolios are set out in *Exhibit 32.1* and *Exhibit 32.2*.

Exhibit 32.1 sets out an example of hedging a US$ interest rate swap. *Exhibit 32.2* sets out examples of this type of basic hedging approach in relation to A$ interest rate swaps.

Exhibit 32.1

Example of US$ Interest Rate Swap Hedge

As at 3/1/X5, ABC bank (ABC) enters into the following swap (commencing 5/1/X5):

ABC to pay fixed rate US$ at treasury bonds plus 45bps for three years against receipt of six month US$ LIBOR.

Swap terms are as follows:

Amount:	US$100m
Maturity:	5/1/X8
Swap fixed rate:	7.45% pa (S/A) or B + 45bps where B = 7.00% pa

Assume the three year swap market is pricing of the 7.50% 11/X7 treasury note, although the bond maturity is less than three years. Assume that the 7.50% 11/X7 is trading at 7.00% pa and that short-term overnight rates are 4.50% pa and six month US$ LIBOR is 5.00% pa.

ABC hedges through the purchase of 7.50% 11/X7. The hedge amount is US$103.5m reflecting weighting of the hedge due to differing price volatilities of the swap and bond arising from different maturities.

Calculated as:

$$N = \frac{(A_1 - A_2) \times FV}{(B_1 - B_2) \times FV} = \frac{(99.073 - 98.548)}{(100.367 - 99.860)} = 1.035$$

Where

N = hedge ratio

A_1 = price of swap as 7% coupon bond equivalent maturing 5/1/X8 at 7.35% pa (S/A) = 99.073

A_2 = price of swap as 7% coupon bond equivalent maturing 5/1/X8 at 7.55% pa (S/A) = 98.548

B_1 = price of 7.50% 15/11/X7 bond used as a hedge at 7.35% pa (S/A) = 100.367

B_2 = price of 7.50% 15/11/X7 bond used as a hedge at 7.55% pa (S/A) = 99.860

Please note the following points in respect of matching the volatilities of the swap and bond used as a hedge:

- In stating the swap as a bond equivalent it is structured as a 7.00% coupon three year bond, that is, 7.45% (the swap rate) adjusted for the spread. This reflects the fact that the hedge is designed to insulate against movements in the *base* rate not the spread. This is a matter

Exhibit 32.1—continued

for individual institutions. Some may prefer to *include* the spread component, requiring the swap to be restated with the *swap rate* as the coupon equivalent. This would result in small changes in the hedge ratio.

- The "clean" (that is, the ex-interest) price of the treasury bond is utilised in matching volatilities.
- The rates used to calculate the hedge is ± 10bps pa the swap rate.

The details of the hedge are as follows:

Amount:	US$103.5m
YTM:	7.00% pa
Price:	101.263 or US$104,806,707
Accrued interest:	1.057m or US$1,093,612
Total price:	102.319 or US$105,900,319

The swap is closed off on 19/1/X5 with ABC receiving fixed rate US$ versus six month LIBOR at B + 55bps.

The closeout swap terms are:

Amount:	US$100m
Maturity:	5/1/X8 (with a short first interest period)
Swap fixed rate:	7.20% pa on B + 55bps where B = 6.65% pa

As the closeout swap is entered into, ABC sells its bond position. Assume that the 7.50% 11/X7 is trading at 7.20% pa and six month US$ LIBOR is 4.80% pa.

The sales proceeds are as follows:

Amount:	US$103.5m
YTM:	6.65% pa
Price:	102.140 or US$105,714,386
Accrued interest:	1.347 or US$1,393,819
Total price:	103.486 or US$107,108,205

The result overall of the swap is as follows:

Fixed Rate Hedge

	US$m
Cash profit on hedge:[1]	907,679
Interest income:[2]	300,207
Funding cost:[3]	(182,787)
Net:	1,025,099

Notes:

1. US$105,714,386–US$104,806,707.
2. US$1,393,819–US$1,093,612.
3. 4.50% pa on US$105,900,319 for 14 days.

Swap Flows

At first settlement (on 5/7/X5)	**US$m**
Fixed rate side	
Fixed rate amount received:[1]	3,294,247
Fixed rate amount paid:[2]	3,694,384
Net (fixed side):	(400,137)
Floating rate side	
Floating rate amount received:[3]	2,513,889
Floating rate amount paid:[4]	2,226,667
Net (floating side):	(287,222)
Total difference:	(112,915)

Exhibit 32.1—continued

After first settlement

Fixed rate side

Fixed rate amount received:[5]	3,600,000
Fixed rate amount paid:[6]	(3,725,000)
Net:	(125,000)

Notes:

1. 7.20% on US$100m for 167 days, that is, 19/1/X5 to 5/7/X5.
2. 7.45% on US$100m for 181 days, that is, 5/1/X5 to 5/7/X5.
3. 5.00% on US$100m for 181 days, that is, 5/1/X5 to 5/7/X5 (based on 360 day year).
4. 4.80% on US$100m for 167 days, that is, 19/1/X5 to 5/7/X5 (based on 360 day year).
5. 7.20% on US$100m for six months.
6. 7.45% on US$100m for six months.

All floating rate flows are assumed to match after the first period as they reprice on identical dates.

The transaction overall produces the following cash flows:

- a profit on the hedge of US$1,025,099;
- a net difference at first settlement of US$(112,915);
- a net difference at each subsequent settlement date of US$(125,000).

Assuming that the hedge profit is reinvested at the bond rate (6.65% pa), the transaction yields a present value profit of US$364,352 which is equivalent to US$67,985 every six months or 0.136% pa. This compares to a bid-offer spread of 0.10% pa and reflects hedging costs such as the carry on the hedge and also the shift in the short-term US$ LIBOR rates.

Exhibit 32.2

Example of Interest Rate Swap Hedge (1)

As at 5/1/X7, ABC bank (ABC) enters into the following swap: ABC to pay fixed rate A$ at bonds plus 65bps for three years against receipt of six month BBR.

Swap terms are as follows:

Amount:	A$50m
Maturity:	5/1/X0
Swap fixed rate:	15.00% pa (S/A) or B + 65bps where B = 14.35% pa

Assume the three year swap market is pricing off the 13.00% 11/X9 Commonwealth bonds, although the bond maturity is less than three years. Assume that the 13.00% 11/X9 is trading at 14.35% pa and that short-term overnight rates are 18.20% pa and six month BBR is 16.30% pa.

ABC hedges through purchase of 13.00% 11/X9. Hedge amount is A$52,977,695 reflecting weighting of the hedge due to differing price volatilities of the swap and bond arising from different maturities and coupons.[1]

The details of the hedge are as follows:

Amount:	A$52,977,695
YTM:	14.35% pa
Price:	96.877 or A$51,323,172
Accrued interest:	A$970,282
Total price:	A$52,293,454

The swap is closed off on 19/1/X7 with ABC receiving fixed rate A$ versus six month BBR at B + 85bps.

Exhibit 32.2—continued

The closeout swap terms are:

Amount:	A$50m
Maturity:	5/1/X7 (with a short first interest period)
Swap fixed rate:	14.85% pa on B + 85bps where B = 14.00% pa

As the closeout swap is entered into, ABC sells its bond position. Assume that the 13.00% 11/X9 is trading at 14.00% pa and six month BBR is 16.40% pa.

The sales proceeds are as follows:

Amount:	A$52,977,695
YTM:	14.00% pa
Price:	97.683 or A$51,750,387
Accrued interest:	A$1,236,634
Total price:	A$52,987,021

The overall result of the swap is as follows:

Fixed rate hedge

	A$m
Cash profit on hedge:[2]	427,215
Interest income:[3]	266,352
Funding cost:[4]	(365,051)
Net:	328,516

Swap flows

At first settlement date (on 5/7/X7)	**A$m**
Fixed rate side	
Fixed rate amount received:[5]	3,397,192
Fixed rate amount paid:[6]	(3,719,178)
Net:	(321,986)
Floating rate side	
Floating rate amount received:[7]	4,041,507
Floating rate amount paid:[8]	(3,751,781)
Net:	289,726
Difference:	(32,260)
At subsequent settlement dates	
Fixed rate side	
Fixed rate amount received:[9]	3,712,500
Fixed rate amount paid:[10]	(3,750,000)
Net:	(37,500)

All floating rate flows are assumed to match after the first period as they reprice on identical dates.

The transaction overall produces the following cash flows:

- a profit on the hedge of A$328,516;
- a net difference at first settlement of A$(32,260);
- a net difference at each subsequent date of A$(37,500).

Assuming that the hedge profit is reinvested at the bond rate (14.00% pa), the transaction yields a present value profit of A$154,668 which is equivalent to A$32,449 every six months or 0.1298% pa. This compares to a bid-offer spread of 0.20% pa and reflects hedging costs such as the negative carry on the hedge and also the shift in the short-term BBR rate.

Notes

1. Calculated as:

$$N = \frac{(A_1 - A_2) \times FV}{(B_1 - B_2) \times FV} = \frac{(100.595 - 99.410)}{(97.438 - 96.320)} = 1.060$$

Exhibit 32.2—continued

where N = hedge ratio
A_1 = price of bond 14.35% maturing 5/1/X0 at 14.10% pa = 100.595
A_2 = price of swap 14.35% maturing 5/1/X0 at 14.60% pa = 99.410
B_1 = price of bond 13.00% maturing 15/11/89 at 14.10% pa = 97.438
B_2 = price of bond 13.00% maturing 15/11/89 at 14.60% pa = 96.320

Please note that numbers are subject to rounding error. Also note that the hedge structure in this case makes compensation for the higher swap coupon (excluding the swap spread) and therefore different price behaviour of the swap vis-à-vis the bond.

2. A$51,750,387–A$51,323,171.
3. A$1,236,634–A$970,282.
4. 18.20% pa on A$52,293,454 for 14 days.
5. 14.85% on A$50m for 167 days, that is, 19/1/X7 to 5/7/X7.
6. 15.00% on A$50m for 181 days, that is, 5/1/X7 to 5/7/X7.
7. 16.30% on A$50m for 181 days, that is, 5/1/X7 to 5/7/X7.
8. 16.40% on A$50m for 167 days, that is, 19/1/X7 to 5/7/X7.
9. 14.85% on A$50m for six months.
10. 15.00% on A$50m for six months.

Example of Interest Rate Swap Hedge (2)

As at 5/1/X7, ABC bank (ABC) enters into the following swap: ABC to receive fixed rate A$ at bonds plus 85bps for three years against payment of six month BBR.

Swap terms are as follows:

Amount:	A$50m
Maturity:	5/1/X0
Swap fixed rate:	15.25% pa (S/A) or B + 90bps where B = 14.35% pa

Assume the three year swap market is pricing off the 13.00% 11/X9 Commonwealth bonds, although the bond maturity is less than three years. Assume that the 13.00% 11/X9 is trading at 14.35% pa and that short-term overnight rates are 18.20% pa and six month BBR is 16.30% pa.

ABC hedges through short sale of 13.00% 11/X9. Hedge amount is A$52,977,695 reflecting weighting of the hedge due to differing price volatilities of the swap and bond arising from different maturities.

The details of the hedge are as follows:

Amount:	A$52,977,695
YTM:	14.35% pa
Price:	96.877 or A$51,323,172
Accrued interest:	A$970,282
Total price:	A$52,293,454

The swap is closed off on 19/1/X7 with ABC receiving fixed rate A$ versus six month BBR at B + 65bps.

The closeout swap terms are:

Amount:	A$50m
Maturity:	5/1/87 (with a short first interest period)
Swap fixed rate:	14.65% pa on B + 65bps where B = 14.00% pa

As the closeout swap is entered into, ABC buys back its short bond position. Assume that the 13.00% 11/89 is trading at 14.00% pa and six month BBR is 16.40% pa.

The purchase price is as follows:

Amount:	A$52,977,695
YTM:	14.00% pa
Price:	97.683 or A$51,750,387
Accrued interest:	A$1,236,634
Total price:	A$52,987,021

Exhibit 32.2—continued

The overall result of the swap is as follows:

Fixed rate hedge

	A$m
Cash loss on hedge:[1]	(427,215)
Interest income:[2]	(266,352)
Investment earnings:[3]	365,051
Net:	(328,516)

Swap flows

At first settlement date (on 5/7/X7)	**A$m**
Fixed rate side	
Fixed rate amount received:[4]	3,781,164
Fixed rate amount paid:[5]	(3,351,438)
Net:	429,726
Floating rate side	
Floating rate amount received:[6]	3,751,780
Floating rate amount paid:[7]	(4,041,507)
Net:	(289,726)
Difference:	140,000
At subsequent settlement dates	
Fixed rate side	
Fixed rate amount received:[8]	3,812,500
Fixed rate amount paid:[9]	(3,662,500)
Net:	150,000

All floating rate flows are assumed to match after the first period as they reprice on identical dates.

The transaction overall produces the following cash flows:

- a loss on the hedge of A$328,516;
- a net difference at first settlement of A$140,000;
- a net difference at each subsequent settlement date of A$150,000.

On the basis the hedge loss is funded at the swap rate (14.65% pa), the transaction yields a present value profit of A$370,030 which is equivalent to A$78,411 semi-annually or 0.314% pa (amortised at the bond rate). The discrepancy from the bid/offer spread reflects the positive earnings on the reinvestment of the proceeds of the short and also the favourable movement in BBR rate.

Notes:

1. A$51,323,171–A$51,750,387.
2. A$970,282–A$1,236,634.
3. 18.20% pa on A$52,293,454 for 14 days.
4. 15.25% on A$50m for 181 days, that is, 5/1/X7 to 5/7/X7.
5. 14.65% on A$50m for 167 days, that is, 19/1/X7 to 5/7/X7.
6. 16.40% on A$50m for 167 days, that is, 19/1/X7 to 5/7/X7.
7. 16.30% on A$50m for 181 days, that is, 5/1/X7 to 5/7/X7.
8. 15.25% on A$50m for six months.
9. 14.65% on A$50m for six months.

The basic technology described forms the basis of all swap portfolio risk management.

HEDGING CURRENCY SWAPS

The basic technique of hedging currency swaps is similar to that utilised with interest rate swaps. The major difference lies in the fact that two interest rates and the currency exchange rate must theoretically be hedged on open currency swap positions.

The basic hedging concepts can be illustrated by identifying a number of common swap transactions and their analogous cash market positions in the relevant currencies:

- Receiving fixed rate A$ and paying floating rate US$ is equivalent to being long A$ bonds and short US$ floating rate bonds. This type of position can be hedged by reversing the cash market positions, that is, by shorting A$ fixed rate bonds and investing the proceeds in US$ floating rate bonds. The relevant amounts in each currency are determined by the total notional principal amount of the swap and the spot currency rates as between the US$ and A$.
- Paying fixed A$ rates and receiving US$ floating rate is equivalent to being short A$ bonds and long US$ floating rate bonds which is hedged by buying fixed rate A$ bonds and funding the position by selling US$ floating rate bonds.

The hedging of a cross-currency floating-to-floating swap is similar with floating rate securities in both markets being bought and sold to hedge the currency risk positions booked.

The major differences in hedging currency swaps arise from the difficulty in hedging interest rates in both currencies. While the currency fluctuations can be hedged by simply going long and short the appropriate currencies, hedging of the interest rate levels as between the two currencies can be difficult and/or expensive depending on the efficiency and liquidity of the relevant securities markets.

The high cost of hedging and the fact that the hedging instruments provide poor surrogate cover has led to some currency swap market makers covering only the currency risk by taking open positions on the interest rate differential as between the two currencies. Hedging of the floating rate flows on a cross-currency swap is also relatively approximate in practice. For example, the long or short positions in the currencies are basically taken on a short-term, usually overnight, basis with the funding and/or investment in the relevant currency being rolled each day until the position is closed out. This means that while the spot exposure on the currency is largely covered, there is still exposure in the changes in the first period floating rate interest set which must be separately managed, for example, by utilising financial futures in the relevant short-term interest rates.

The exposure to currency rate fluctuations inherently creates greater risk from mismatches than in corresponding interest rate swaps. Cash flow surpluses or deficits arising from these mismatches, for example, as a result of margins above or below the relevant index can create interest rate and/or currency exposures which can lead to significant economic losses within the swap portfolio if not properly matched.

The existence of these difficulties means that there are fewer currency swap market makers than interest rate swap market makers. It also means that the bid-offer spread in currency swap transactions is significantly greater to cover the added costs and risks of running currency swap portfolios. The absence of consistent relationships between swap rates and the relevant government bond rates in a number of swap currencies means booking open currency swap positions requiring more complex exposure management techniques making the currency swap market more related to the LTFX market and less towards the classic arbitrage model of the interest rate swap market.

Exhibit 32.3 sets out an example of hedging a currency swap.

Exhibit 32.3
Example of Currency Swap Hedge

Assume ABC bank (ABC) enters into the following swap on 8/3/X6.

Under the terms of the swap therefore:

- At commencement (assuming a spot exchange rate of US$0.70/A$1.00), ABC will receive issue proceeds of A$49.50m from swap counterparty; in return, ABC will pay US$34.65m. ABC will also pay US$0.35m being reimbursement of fees of 1.00% or A$0.5m.
- Over the life of the swap:
  —every six months, ABC will receive six month LIBOR less 55bps upon US$35m;
  —every year on the coupon payment date, ABC will pay a payment of A$7m representing 14.00% on A$50m.
- At maturity, ABC will pay its counterparty A$50m to make the principal repayment to the bondholders; ABC will receive US$35m from the swap counterparty.

Assume that the swap is priced off the 13.00% 8/Y1 bond and ABC is quoting B + 60/B + 80 versus six month LIBOR. The current bond yield is 14.00% pa (S/A) and, therefore, the corresponding all-in swap rate is 14.60%/14.80% pa (S/A). The specific swap pricing reflects the adjustments described in more detail in Chapter 8 *(Exhibit 8.32)*.

Also assume: A$ short-term rates are 16.00% pa; US$ interest rates are 7.00% pa for overnight; six month US$ LIBOR is 8.00% pa (S/A); and US$ five year rates are 10.00% pa (S/A).

The swap is initially hedged by buying the 13.00% 8/Y1 bond and borrowing US$ on an overnight basis.

The specific details of the hedge are as follows:

- ABC buys A$48,342,581 face value of the 13.00% 8/Y1[1] on the following terms:

Amount:	A$48,342,581
YTM:	14.00% pa
Price:	96.255 or A$46,532,175
Accrued interest:	0.754 or A$364,573
Total price:	A$46,896,748

- ABC borrows US$35m on an overnight basis.
- In an overall cash flow basis, ABC's position is:

A$

Receipts from swap exchange:	+A$49,500,000
Payment for bond:	−A$46,896,748
Net:	+A$ 2,603,252

This balance is invested in the overnight cash market.

US$

US$ borrowing:	+US$35.0m
Payment under swap exchange:	−US$35.0m
Net:	—

As a separate matter, the sub-LIBOR margin has to be hedged. This hedge is separate from the pricing adjustment described in Chapter 8 (*Exhibit 8.32*) although it follows the same logic. This hedge operates as follows:

- ABC has an A$ surplus of 68bps pa or A$340,000 annually and a corresponding US$97,587 shortfall semi-annually being 55bps on US$35m.
- ABC therefore borrows the present value at 15.25% pa (A) of the A$ surplus that is A$1,133,019.

Exhibit 32.3—continued

- This A$ borrowing is exchanged in the spot market or US$793,113 (at US$0.70/A$1.00) and the US$ are invested at an average rate of 8.00% pa (S/A).
- Every six months, the US$ investment matures to produce a US$ cash flow which offsets the US$ shortfall under the swap structure.
- Every year, annually the A$ surplus is allocated to reducing the A$ borrowing incurred.

Under this structure, the A$ borrowing and the US$ investment declines over the life of the transaction. Please note in practice, precise borrowing and lending transaction may not be executed to hedge the margin exposure with the exposure being absorbed into the institution's overall treasury currency position.

The open, albeit hedged, swap position is closed off on 15/3/X6 with ABC receiving fixed A$ versus six month LIBOR at the original spread of B + 80. The precise closeout terms are:

Amount:	A$50m
Maturity:	8/3/Y1 (with a short first interest period)
Swap fixed rate:	14.00% pa (S/A) or 14.49% pa (A) based on B + 80 where B = 13.20% pa.

As at 15/3/X6, the spot exchange rate has moved to US$0.6940/A$1.00 while six month LIBOR has remained unchanged at 8.00% pa.

Under the terms of the closeout swap:

- On 15/3/X6, ABC will pay A$50m and receive US$34.7m.
- Over the life of the swap:
  —every six months, ABC will pay six month LIBOR on US$34.7m.
  —every year, on 8/3/X7 through to 8/3/Y1, ABC will receive the equivalent of 14.49% pa on A$50m.
- On 8/3/Y1, the intial exchange will be reversed.

As the closeout swap is entered into, ABC will unwind its hedges as follows:

- ABC sells its A$48,342,581 face value of the 13.00% 8/Y1 on the following terms:

Amount:	A$48,342,581
YTM:	13.20% pa
Price:	99.215 or A$47,963,311
Accrued interest:	1.006 or A$486,097
Total price:	A$48,449,408

- ABC repays its US$35m borrowing with interest.
- ABC's overall cash position is:

A$	
Payment under closeout swap:	−A$50,000,000
Sale of bond:	+A$48,449,408
Proceeds of maturing cash surplus:[2]	+A$ 2,611,240
Net:	+A$ 1,060,648

US$	
Receipts from swap exchange:	+US$34,700,000
Repayment of US$ borrowings:[3]	−US$35,046,986
Net:	−US$ 346,986

- At current exchange rates, this creates a cash surplus of A$560,668 after offsetting the A$499,980 shortfall (US$0.347m at US$0.6940/A$1.00).

The actual swap after that will be as follows:

Fixed rate A$ side

On first settlement date (on 8/3/X7)	**A$m**
Fixed amount received:[4]	7,106,055
Fixed amount paid:[5]	(7,000,000)
Repayment of A$ borrowing:[7]	(340,000)
Net:	(233,945)

Exhibit 32.3—continued

On subsequent settlement dates

Fixed amount received:[6]	7,245,000
Fixed amount paid:[5]	(7,000,000)
Repayment of A$ borrowing:[7]	(340,000)
Net:	(95,000)

Floating rate US$ side

On first settlement date (on 8/9/X6)	**US$m**
Floating amount received:[8]	1,332,722
Floating amount paid:[9]	(1,364,867)
Maturing US$ investment:[10]	97,784
Net:	65,639

On subsequent settlement dates

Floating amount received:	+ (LIBOR − 55bps × US$35m)
Floating amount paid:	− (LIBOR × US$34.7m)
Maturing US$ investment:[10]	97,784
Net:	+ (LIBOR × US$0.30m)

The transaction overall produces the following cash flows:

- A hedge profit of A$560,668.
- A net difference on the fixed A$ payments of:
  —A$(233,945) on the first settlement;
  —A$(95,000) on subsequent settlements.
- A net difference on the floating rate US$ payment of:
  —US$65,639 on the first settlement;
  —US$12,000 on subsequent settlements (assuming LIBOR of 8.00% pa).

The overall transaction profit can be determined as follows:

- Discount back the A$ loss at the appropriate rate, say 15.25% pa (A), giving a current value of approximately A$437,128.
- Discount each of the US$ profits at the appropriate rate say 8.00% (S/A), giving a current value of approximately US$148,907 or, at US$0.6940/A$1.00, A$214,563.

The total profit is therefore A$270,913 which amortised (at the bond rate) yields a profit margin of approx 0.129% pa, slightly different from the original bid/offer spread.

Notes:

1. The hedge amount is calculated as:

$$N = \frac{(A_1 - A_2) \times FV}{(B_1 - B_2) \times FV} = \frac{(100.883 - 99.127)}{(97.169 - 95.353)} = 0.967$$

where N = hedge ratio
A_1 = price of 14.00% swap maturing 8/3/X1 at 13.75% pa = 100.883
A_2 = price of 14.00% swap maturing 8/3/X1 at 14.25% pa = 99.127
B_1 = price of 13.00% bond maturing 15/8/X1 at 13.75% pa = 97.169
B_2 = price of 13.00% bond maturing 15/8/X1 at 14.25% pa = 95.353

2. A$2,603,252 (principal) + A$7,988 (interest @ 16.00% for seven days).
3. US$35m (principal) + US$46,986 (interest @ 7.00% for seven days).
4. 14.49% on A$50m for 358 days, that is, 15/3/X6 to 8/3/X7.
5. 14.00% on A$50m for 365 days, that is, 8/3/X6 to 8/3/X7.
6. 14.49% on A$50m for 365 days.
7. Repayment of A$0.340m pa on borrowing to hedge sub-LIBOR margins.
8. 7.45% pa (LIBOR − 55bps) on US$35m for 184 days, that is, 8/3/X6 to 8/9/X6 (based on 360 days).
9. 8.00% pa on A$34.7m for 177 days, that is, 15/3/X6 to 8/9/X6 (based on 360 days).
10. Maturing US$ investment to hedge sub-LIBOR margin.

ISSUES IN HEDGING SWAPS

Risk management objectives

The unifying principle underlying swap risk management is the desire on the part of the intermediary to maximise its earnings on a risk adjusted basis, which can be restated as:

$$\text{PV (net)} = \text{PV (asset inflows)} - \text{PV (liability outflows)}$$

where PV signifies the present value of the relevant cash flows

The application of this type of approach to conventional trading activities, such as trading in securities, is relatively straightforward as the market value of the securities usually implies their true economic value. However, in the case of swaps, as it is necessary to establish the economic value for inflows and outflows of both fixed and floating rates of interest at dates in the future, the application of this approach is less obvious.

Fixed versus floating rate flows

It is necessary to first decouple the fixed rate flows under a swap transaction from the corresponding floating rate flows. This separation is predicated on the fact that these, in general, belong to different markets and must, of necessity, be managed separately.

The fixed rate flows under a swap behave in a manner analogous to a fixed rate security or bond. In contrast, the floating rate flows behave like short-dated (six months or less) securities. As such, they closely approximate the behaviour of short-term money market securities and are usually managed accordingly.

In managing the risk of a swap portfolio, the portfolio manager of necessity seeks to substitute hedging risk for the market risk of an open swap position. The basic presumption is that by buying and selling securities of the appropriate maturity or financial futures on such securities, the risk on the fixed and floating rate flows under a swap transaction can be managed.

Hedging risk arises because hedging of the swap position is difficult because there is no single perfect hedging instrument for a swap other than a directly matching but offsetting swap transaction.

Fixed rate flows are usually hedged by utilising fixed rate securities of the appropriate maturity. It is customary to use government bonds in the relevant currency. This reflects the fact that the pricing behaviour in most swap markets implies pricing as a spread (often volatile) relative to the fixed rate government bond yield curve.

The efficiency of the hedge is determined by the degree of correlation between price movements of the hedge instrument and the swap pricing benchmark instrument. The lower the correlation between the two, the greater the hedging or basis risk. Where a security with differential pricing characteristics to the swap pricing benchmark is utilised, this additional hedging or basis risk must be managed. There appears to be two approaches in managing this basis risk. Some intermediaries view this as the opportunity to add value to the portfolio utilising elaborate proprietary hedging techniques. In contrast, other intermediaries seek to minimise this basis risk.

Risk management on the floating rate side entails the purchase or sale of instruments, physical securities or futures, which replicate the price behaviour of the floating rate index.

Traditionally, management of the floating rate side of a swap portfolio has attracted limited attention. This is because the floating side was regarded as being less volatile because the floating rate resets periodically at the new market rate which implies relative stability at or about par value even where there are substantial movements in rates. However, increased realisation that even minor mismatches on floating rate reset dates exposes the portfolio to large potential economic losses has forced swap portfolio managers to manage these floating rate exposures.

The management of the floating rate portfolio within a swap market making function presents unique problems which are considered in detail in Chapter 34.

Hedging efficiency and pricing

As noted above, swaps risk management essentially entails substituting hedging risk for market risk. The strategy of utilising hedging techniques to immunise portfolio value from changes in market rates is never perfect. Limitations in the hedging mechanisms, imperfections and illiquidity in the relevant bond and interest rate swap markets, generally prevent this. However, the hedging methodology usually utilised allows quantification of the residual risk after hedging and permits a high degree of control over the risks incurred.

The factors that affect the efficiency of the hedging process include:

- *Hedge transaction costs*—which represent costs incurred in establishing and then unwinding or adjusting the hedge.
- *Hedge carry or investment costs*—depending on the relationship between the swap yield curve and the relevant government yield curve, hedges will entail either a carry cost or generate investment income. This loss or gain on the hedge must be factored into the overall swap transaction requiring assumptions about reinvestment rates or alternatively funding costs. In addition, there may be costs of shorting a bond; usually the cost of borrowing the bond to maintain a hedge in a short position.
- *Changes in the shape of the yield curve*—hedge efficiency is usually affected by non-uniform movements of the yield curve. Where such changes in the shape of the yield curve occur, equality of the price change as between the swap and the hedge cannot be assured. A number of hedging strategies exist to adjust for these risks, provided there is no basis risk, but these are usually expensive and represent a trade-off between risk and cost avoidance.
- *Basis movements*—additional slippages in hedge efficiency occur in situations where movements in the swap market are imperfectly correlated with movements in the government bond market. In particular, as discussed above, the swap spread itself cannot, unlike the benchmark pricing instrument, be hedged and this intrinsically precludes an efficient hedging strategy.
- *Reinvestment and funding assumptions*—an inherent problem in the hedging technology developed is that the hedge will usually generate a cash profit or loss at the time the hedge is unwound. This profit or loss must then be amortised over the full life of the swap reflecting either recovery of the loss or subsidy to a deficit on matched swap payments. This requires assumptions on reinvestment rates and funding rates which are inherently subjective and, in particular, as they are forward looking, may, in actuality, not be realised thereby lowering hedge efficiency.

Although swap pricing is driven by the basic arbitrage in the market and also by supply and demand factors, the change in the market from matched counterparty transactions to a market driven by swap market makers, creates the need to have greater interaction between hedging costs and the pricing on the swap.

However, within most institutions uncertainty prevails with regard to the adequacy of returns, and minimum risk return criteria are far from clear. In this regard, it is increasingly evident that swap pricing reflects some of the risks and costs of swap portfolio management. The swap market maker has no other option but to seek compensation for the costs and risks assumed from entering into transactions on an unmatched basis. The costs of hedges, being reasonably deterministic, can be more or less determined, although, the risks of swap market making are less easily captured.

Risk control

The essential process of management of the hedge swap portfolio includes certain risk control measures. This usually takes the form of daily revaluations of both the swap and the hedge portfolio with the total risk being sought to be controlled by established limit systems. In this regard, the swap hedging system is part of most institutions' formal risk control and risk limit allocation and administration processes allowing the financial risk of such transactions to be estimated and managed (see discussed in Chapter 40).

FINANCING SWAP HEDGE POSITIONS

As discussed above, swap hedges entail the use of either physical securities or futures on the physical securities. Where physical securities are utilised, the purchase of bonds to hedge open swap risk positions requires holdings of securities to be financed. Conversely, short selling of securities to hedge a portfolio necessitate first, borrowing the necessary physical securities to short sell and secondly, investing the proceeds of the sale.

The financing or investment requirements required by the management of the swap hedge portfolio can be undertaken either in the short-term cash/money market, entailing purchasing or placing overnight or short-term deposits to offset the liquidity requirements of the hedge portfolio, or the use of the bond repurchase markets which performs a similar function.

The market used to manage the liquidity requirements of the swap hedge portfolio varies significantly between currencies. In US$ swaps, for example, the bond repurchase market is utilised predominantly. This reflects the highly developed nature of the repurchase market that operates in US$ treasury notes and bonds.

In other currencies, the cash market may be utilised reflecting the absence of well developed bond repurchase markets. However, increasingly, repurchase markets in a variety of currencies are developing quite rapidly.

A brief discussion of bond repurchase or "repo" market as it is used for financing swap hedge positions is set out in the appendix to this chapter.

The use of short-term financing and investment markets to manage the liquidity requirements of swap hedges creates a variety of problems. These markets are, predominantly, variable rate markets with interest rates fixed for short periods, overnight to one/two weeks. This creates exposures to interest rate movements in relation to hedging activities designed to insulate swap portfolios from interest rate exposures by purchasing and selling securities.

As described in detail above, assumptions are made in respect of the cost of financing hedge positions or investing the proceeds of short sales of securities. In reality, the combination of uncertainty as to time period for which the hedges are likely to be required to be maintained together with the inability to lock in interest rates for the required period necessarily means that some slippage may occur in relation to cost of financing a hedge or investing proceeds of a short securities position. Given that the assumed earnings or cost must be factored into the pricing of the swap, at the time of entry into the transaction, the uncertain outcome regarding these costs or income creates an extra dimension of risk in managing swap hedges.

This financing or reinvestment exposure is in addition to financing or reinvestment exposure in respect of interest rate movement which effects portfolio as a whole or an ongoing basis, in particular, in relation to cash flow mismatches: see discussion above.

CHOICE OF HEDGING INSTRUMENT—PHYSICAL OR FUTURES

General issues

In choosing hedging instruments, the principal consideration is to seek a security or derivative which has a relatively high correlation as between the hedge instrument and the benchmark swap pricing instrument to eliminate, as far as possible, hedging or basis risk.

The basic choices of hedging instruments are as follows:

- cash market instruments, usually physical securities such as government bonds or floating rate securities;
- financial futures on the relevant security.

The two instruments have different characteristics, including:

- *Balance sheet impact*—use of cash market instruments is usually reflected directly on the balance sheet. In contrast, futures contracts are usually off-balance sheet.
- *Carry cost*—in the case of futures contracts, the carry cost is built into the actual futures price, with the discount or premium relative to the spot cash security price reflecting the positive or negative carry. In the case of a physical security, the carry cost will usually reflect the difference between the coupon accrual on the security and the interest cost of funding the position which will result in actual cash surpluses or deficits.
- *Institutional considerations and flexibility*—the greater institutional flexibility of futures markets which in particular allow short selling may be relevant.
- *Liquidity considerations*—the differential liquidity as between the physical and futures markets may dictate one or other would be preferred.
- *Hedge structuring*—in practice, a hedge involving both physical securities as well as futures would necessitate hedge structuring to match out the relative volatilities of the swap and the hedging instrument.
- *Lack of earnings and accrual*—the fact that there is no interest accrual or earning on a futures position, other than effective change in carry cost, can be a disadvantage relative to using actual physical securities.

Current practice

In practice, the swap market tends to favour the use of physical securities vis-à-vis futures in hedging open swap position (with the exceptions outlined below). This reflects concern over the basis risk incurred in using futures to hedge swap positions as well as the rollover risk in using futures dictated by the need to closeout a futures contract if the swap is not closed out prior to the futures settlement date with its potential cash flow impact and the risk in maintaining hedge efficiency at the point of rollover. However, futures are sometimes used to hedge swap positions, particularly in circumstances where it is difficult to go short in the physical market or there are balance sheet constraints.

There are in effect different segments of the swap market and the choice of hedging instrument differs significantly as between the segments. The swap market, in US$ for example, can be separated into two very different segments:

- short-term interest rate swaps, usually of up to three to five years in maturity;
- long-term interest rate swaps, usually in excess of three to five years in maturity.

The short-term swaps are traditionally hedged using strips of futures. This entails the purchase or sale of a series of futures contracts to hedge the swap position. The futures trades are subsequently reversed where a matching swap counterparty is located. However, in some cases, the swap position may be left open for the full maturity of the trade with the futures positions being settled to coincide with interest settlement dates on the interest rate swap. In the US$ market, the futures contract utilised is usually the Eurodollar futures contract.

In contrast, swaps of longer maturity are traditionally hedged utilising physical securities.

Problems with using futures contracts to hedge swap positions

A key issue in utilising futures on government bonds and other physical securities to hedge swap position is to optimise the correlation between the futures contract and the swap being hedged at two separate levels: the correlation in price movements between the swap transaction being hedged and the price movements in the futures contract to be utilised as the hedge.

A number of identifiable problems exist in relation to utilising futures contracts as a hedge against swap risk positions:

- limited types of futures contracts available;
- the cash-futures pricing relationship;
- the non-convex nature of futures contracts.

The first difficulty relates to the fact that futures contracts are typically only available on limited and highly specific types of securities.

For example, futures contracts on government securities which are sufficiently liquid to be utilised as a hedge are usually confined to futures contracts on long-term government securities (usually with the maturity of ten years or more). In selected other currencies, futures contracts on shorter maturity government securities, say three years, may be available. There are very few currencies in which more than two relevant futures contracts, at least of sufficient liquidity, are available for use as a hedge against swap risk positions.

As a consequence, use of these futures contracts to hedge swaps of varying maturities inevitably creates exposure to changes in the yield curve shape. This reflects the fact that using these futures contracts to hedge swap positions entails an intrinsic assumption regarding the stability of the yield curve relationships assumed or existing at the point of time at which the swap hedge is established.

A number of institutions utilise mixtures of short-term futures contracts (usually on money market rates such as Eurodollars or the relevant index in each currency) and futures on longer-term bond rates in an effort to manage these yield curve exposures. However, in practice, they create quite complex risk positions requiring careful management.

The exposure to the yield curve shape as a result of the limited availability of futures contracts is most significant where the period for which hedge is to be maintained is of a significant duration in time. Futures contracts on term government bond rates can usually provide a short-term surrogate hedge of some accuracy in the short-term, but its efficacy usually decreases with the effluxion of time and inevitable changes in the shape of the yield curve.

The exposure to yield curve shape exists in another form, that is, through the cash-futures pricing relationship. As described in detail in Chapter 10, pricing of futures contracts reflects the cost of carry or interest rate differential between the time of entry into the futures or forward contract and the expiry of delivery date of the contract. Consequently, where a futures contract is utilised as a hedge within the swap portfolio, changes in short-term interest rates which will change the pricing of the futures contract may lessen the correlation between movements in the price of the futures contract relatively to the swap being hedged. This effectively represents the impact of changes in the yield curve shape. A further problem in this regard is that changes in short-term rates may change the path of convergence between the cash and futures markets which may also cause deterioration in the efficiency of the hedged transaction.

Convexity problem relates to the fact that the present value of a basis point (PVBP) for futures contracts is usually fixed, regardless of the level of absolute rates. PVBP of a swap will vary depending on the level of rates as well as the time to maturity. Consequently, where futures are utilised to hedge swap positions, the amount of futures contracts utilised will only be appropriate for the swap rate at the time the trade is done. As absolute yields change and the period to maturity of the swap changes, the PVBP relationship between the futures contract and the swap will change. Consequently, the number of contracts and the hedge will need to be constantly adjusted to reflect the change duration of the underlying swap which will, typically, cause further slippages in hedge efficiency.

Utilising swap futures contracts to hedge swap transactions

The concept of an interest rate swap futures contract has been actively discussed since the middle 1980s.[1]

An interest rate swap futures contract is a contract with delivery effected by entry into an interest rate swap contract on the delivery date of the futures contract. The swap futures contract is priced at the fixed rate that market participants expected to prevail in the swap market on the delivery date, based on the current market swap yield curve. For example, a futures contract maturing in December 19X4 off a five year interest rate swap would be priced at the *forward* five year rate that is expected to prevail on the relevant delivery date as embodied in the current swap yield curve.

Major users of a swap futures contract would be swap market makers and, to a more limited extent, end users of the swap market.

For the market makers, the major advantage would be the ability to hedge swap spread risk and some improvements in the cost of hedging. Major advantages in relation to hedging cost would be the capacity to use the swap futures contracts, in preference to physical securities thereby avoiding balance sheet utilisation costs. An additional benefit which might be applicable to weaker swap market participants

1. See for example James Kurt Dew (1987) (Winter).

would be that the implied financing or investment rates would be priced at the margin and therefore would be the same for most market participants.

For the end user, the swap futures contract would allow creation of forward swaps by trading in the futures rather than directly transacting forward swap financial institutions.

The significant, at least theoretical, potential of swap futures contract has created an impetus for a number of futures and options exchanges seek to introduce such a contract. Major developments in this context have been in relation to US$ swaps.

The major initiatives in this regard have come from the Chicago Board of Trade (CBOT) with its US$ interest rate swap futures contracts. The contracts covering three and five year swap futures and futures options compete to a substantive degree against the Chicago Mercantile Exchange (CME) three month Eurodollar futures contract.

The Eurodollar futures contract has, traditionally, been utilised to hedge short-dated US$ interest rate swaps. Strips of Eurodollar futures contracts have been traded as the offsetting component to interest rate swaps transacted by financial institutions with relevant counterparty: see discussion in Chapter 35. Utility of the CME Eurodollar contracts has increased significantly with extension of contract dates up to five years.

The CBOT contract is designed to offer some significant advantages over the CME Eurodollar futures contract by:

- reduction in commissions, reflecting the reduced number of contracts needing to be transacted;
- lack of liquidity in the CME Eurodollar contracts beyond first two to three years.

In a parallel development, the financial instrument exchange (FINEX), a division of the New York Cotton Exchange, has introduced two year and five year treasury notes futures contracts, originally to specifically assist swap hedgers. More recently, FINEX offerred an exchange for physical (EFP) mechanism from swaps to five year or two year interest rate futures or vice versa.

Exhibit 32.4 sets out details of CBOT swap futures and options contracts specifications.

Given the obvious advantages and benefits of an interest rate swap futures contract, it is surprising that the efforts to introduce such a facility have not encountered more success. The major factors militating against an increased role for interest rate swap futures appear to be:

- the lack of liquidity in these contracts, which reflects the lack of institutional support for the concept which would create the necessary liquidity to provide the basis for future growth;
- suspicions regarding the accuracy of cash/futures convergence in these products and some concern about the mechanism for setting closing rates, which some market participants fear is open to manipulation;
- the non-convex nature of the interest rate swap futures contracts (see discussion above) which requires constant adjustment of the hedge position reduce hedge slippage.

On the credit side, the interest rate swap futures should provide a means to hedge swap spread risk and also, in the case of options on the futures contracts, the spread volatility component option on swap products which is currently difficult to manage. An additional advantage is that, under current capital adequacy guidelines, futures contracts are zero risk weighted for capital purposes which should significantly improve the cost of hedging where these futures contracts are utilised in preference to holding physical securities.

Exhibit 32.4

CBOT Swap Futures and Option—Contract Specifications

Three and five-year futures

Underlying instrument: The fixed rate on a generic three year or five year US$25m interest rate swap over six month LIBOR.

Price quotation: 100 minus the swap yield.

Tick size: US$25 per one half basis point.

Contract months: March, June, September, December.

Last trading day: Monday before third Wednesday of month.

Daily price limit: 100 basis points (US$5,000 per contract) above or below the previous day's settlement.

Trading hours: 7.20 am to 2.00 pm (Chicago time). On the last day of an expiring contract closes at 9.30 am.

Options

Tick size: One quarter of a basis point or US$12.50 per contract.

Strike prices: Strike prices will be listed in multiples of 25 basis points to bracket the current CBOT interest rate swap futures price.

Exercise procedures: Option buyers may exercise the option before 6.00 pm (Chicago time) on any business day prior to expiration. Exercised options are randomly assigned to option sellers. All in-the-money options on the last day of trading are automatically exercised.

Expiration: Unexpired options expire 6.00 pm on last trading day.

Settlement Rate: For final settlement, CBOT will survey seven swap dealers, randomly chosen from a list of at least ten, to determine yields on three and five year swaps. These will be averaged out and rounded off to the nearest basis point. CBOT will then take the median of these averages and subtract the result from 100 for the final settlement price.

HEDGING LTFX

The risk entailed in LTFX transactions is usually managed in one of two ways:

- as fixed-to-fixed zero coupon currency swaps;
- as outright forward contracts.

As discussed previously, LTFX contracts are identical to zero coupon fixed-to-fixed currency swaps. Consequently, one approach to pricing and managing the risks inherent in booking an open LTFX position is to incorporate these transactions into the overall cross currency swap portfolio. In this regard, LTFX contracts can be incorporated very readily in swap portfolios operated on a portfolio basis as one period single cash flows.

The structuring of an LTFX hedge is complex. The currency swap structure, as it entails an exchange of principal at both the beginning and end of the swap at the current swap rate at the outset of the transaction, creates a series of cash flows in which the interest differentials between the two currencies are spread over the life of the swap as differentials in the value of the interest flows being exchanged. These interest flows can be characterised as a series of LTFX contracts with implied forward currency exchange rates. This allows the currency swap to be divided into a series of forward-to-forward contracts. By treating each settlement separately, a number of LTFX contracts can be created by fixing the foreign currency cash flows in one of the swap currencies for an equivalent amount of the other currency calculated at the current LTFX rate. This type of structure creates either a funding requirement or alternatively creates reinvestment risks for the intermediary as illustrated in *Exhibit 32.5*.

Exhibit 32.5

Currency Swap versus LTFX Trade

Assume the following market scenario:

Currency and interest rate swap market

A standard five year A$ fixed and US$ floating currency swap is quoted at 14.75/14.55% pa (A) versus six month LIBOR.

The US$ interest rate swap market is showing prices of 7.70/7.65% pa (A) versus six month LIBOR.

LTFX market

The A$ and US$ LTFX market is showing the following prices:

Spot forward	US$ per A$1.00
	0.70
1 year	0.6412
2 year	0.6018
3 year	0.5649
4 year	0.5326
5 year	0.5067

Under these circumstances, A bank (A) enters into the following two swaps:

- A$10m currency swap whereby A is to pay A$ fixed at 14.75% pa (A) versus receipt of six month LIBOR.
- US$7.0m interest rate swap whereby A is to receive US$ fixed at 7.65% pa versus payment of six month LIBOR.

The two swaps produce the following net cash flows:

Year	US$m	A$m
1	0.5355	– 1.475
2	0.5355	– 1.475
3	0.5355	– 1.475
4	0.5355	– 1.475
5	7.5355	– 11.475

The six month US$ LIBOR flows net out.

The A$ flows are now covered using the LTFX market:

Year	Exchange rate	A$m purchased	US$m
1	0.6412	1.475	0.9458
2	0.6018	1.475	0.8877
3	0.5649	1.475	0.8332
4	0.5326	1.475	0.7856
5	0.5067	11.475	5.8144

Exhibit 32.5—continued

This produces the following net US$ position:

Year	Swap flow	LTFX flow	Net US$ position
1	0.5355	−0.9458	−0.4103
2	0.5355	−0.8877	−0.3522
3	0.5355	−0.8332	−0.2977
4	0.5355	−0.7856	−0.2501
5	7.5355	−5.8144	+1.7211

The net cash flow position shows a surplus of US$0.4108m. Assuming a US$ cost of funding the US$ deficit of 7.50% pa, the transaction yield is net present value of US$0.0855m. As long as the funding cost is under 10.37% pa, the trade is profitable to A.

As mentioned previously, almost all currency swaps are based on a fixed rate in the currency against a floating rate in US$. The first step is, therefore, to combine a typical currency swap with an interest rate swap in US$ which results in known flows in both US$ and the relevant currency.

The difficult problem is to evaluate properly the resulting net US$ position, since its value is highly dependent on funding rates for the shortfall in the first four years, which will be offset by the surplus of US$1.2m in year five. This is a matter for the individual bank treasury.

In the example in *Exhibit 32.4*, the net US$ position implies a break-even reinvestment rate of 10.37% pa. If the intermediary expects the reinvestment rates to be lower than this level or alternatively can lock in all or part of the funding rate risk through FRAs or interest rate futures, it can create a profitable arbitrage by essentially creating a vector of LTFX contracts at margins away from interest rate parity.

The alternative hedging technology for LTFX entails treating the LTFX contract in a manner akin to normal foreign exchange outright forward forward transactions. This approach, until relatively recently, entailed LTFX trades beyond one year to be perfectly matched against a counterparty. The transactions were not usually executed until both counterparties were in position although the bank usually intermediated the transaction. A number of major commercial banks now routinely transact LTFX trades without having a counterparty. In these circumstances, the currency exposure is usually hedged against positions in the swap currency with the interest rate risk being left unhedged on the basis that the forward points, reflecting the interest rate differential between the two currencies, will remain relatively stable. Where LTFX trades are hedged in this way, the dealing spread is structured to protect against minor movements in interest rate differentials and consequently the forward points.

A variation on this technique is to utilise forwards mismatched as to maturity to hedge LTFX positions. Utilising this technique, the intermediary may not match the offsetting LTFX contract as to the cash flow maturities. For example, a bank may sell US$ forward for value in five years' time and purchase US$ forward for value in one year's time. The mismatch in value dates represents a gap which is managed within gap position limits until a counterparty can be found or the transaction squared in a different way. These gap mismatches in maturity are managed through futures and options contracts or through the institution's swap portfolio.

APPENDIX

Bond Repurchases Markets and Swap Hedging[1]

Introduction

The repurchase agreement or repo market is, in effect, a collateralised money market in which individual institutions borrow cash and lend a liquid, marketable security as collateral against the loan.

The repo market's economic function is based on its role in financing securities dealers' inventory of bonds as well as covering its short positions by facilitating the lending and borrowing of securities.

Given that in maintaining hedges against swap positions, financial institutions need to fund securities or, alternatively, borrow bonds to cover short positions held against swap risk positions, the repo market has come to play a significant role in swap portfolio management. This is particularly so in currencies, such as US$, where substantial repurchase agreement markets exist.

Bond repurchase structures

There are basically two types of repo agreements:

- *Repos*—where institutions lend the collateral and borrows cash, that is, the institution is set to "repo" the collateral.
- *Reverse repo*—where the financial institutions borrow the collateral security and lends the cash, that is they reverse the repo.

Generic Repo

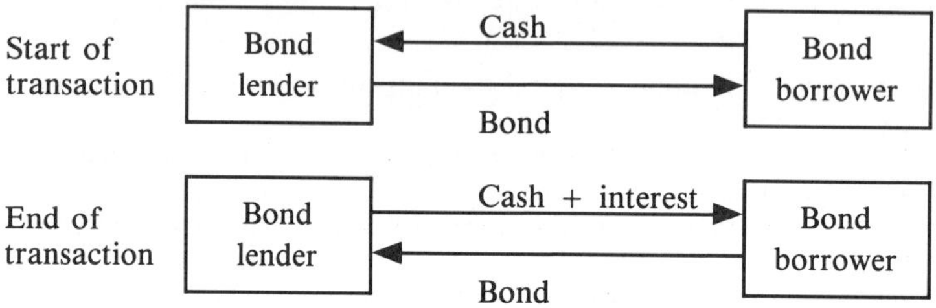

Start of transaction	Bond lender	← Cash ← / → Bond →	Bond borrower
End of transaction	Bond lender	→ Cash + interest → / ← Bond ←	Bond borrower

Source: Terry Shanahan (1991) (Summer).

The transaction can be structured in, at least, three ways:

- a repo agreement;
- sale and buy-back;
- bond lending.

While the term repo is used generically to cover all types of repurchase agreements, it is specifically utilised to describe a repurchase agreement where the bond lender sells the bond and prearranges to repurchase it *at the same price* it was

1. This appendix is based on Terry Shanahan, "The Repo Market" (1991) (Summer) *Journal of International Securities Market*.

sold at, together with an interest payment reflecting interest cost of borrowing funds for the relevant period. A repurchase agreement is structured so that the original bond owner receives any coupons paid on the bond.

Repurchase Agreement

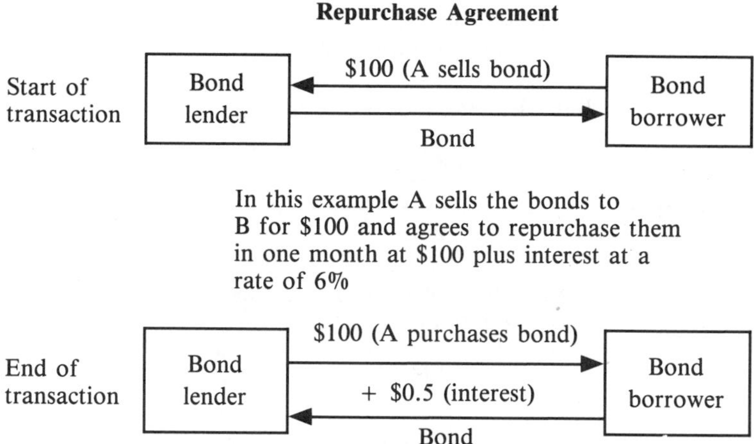

Source: Terry Shanahan (1991) (Summer).

Sale and buy-back transaction requires the bond lender to agree to sell the bonds today and repurchase them at a later date. Sale price of the bonds will include the accrued coupon interest to the sell date. The buy-back price will also be adjusted to include accrued coupon interest to the buy-back date. In order to ensure that the borrower of the funds pays appropriate rate of interest, the repo interest rate, the clean price of the buy-back (the price of the bond including no accrual) is set at a level which on an internal rate of return basis provides the relevant interest rate in the transaction.

Sale and Buy-Back

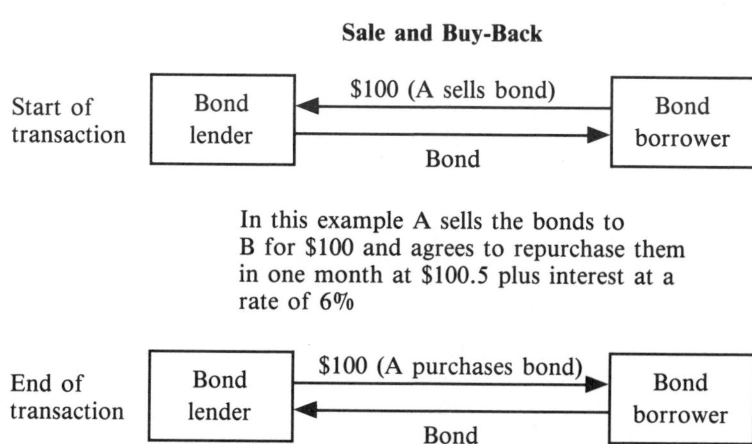

Source: Terry Shanahan (1991) (Summer).

In a bond lending transaction, the cash borrower agrees to to borrow the cash for a fixed period of time at a fixed rate of interest with the bonds being lodged as collateral to lower the overall risk of the transaction. At maturity of the transaction, the cash borrower pays back the loan with interest and receives the bond back. The original bond owner receives all coupons paid on the bond over the loan period. Bond lending transactions can be structured whereby the bonds are lodged for several days or weeks the rate of interest on the cash loan being reset daily.

Bond Lending ("Term" Repo)

Start of transaction | Bond lender | $100 (loan) ← | → Bond | Bond borrower

A agrees to borrow $100 for three months at a 6% rate of interest

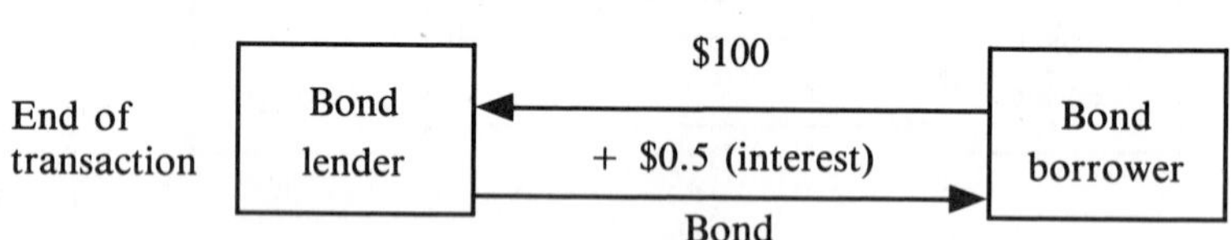

Source: Terry Shanahan (1991) (Summer).

The different structures are utilised usually to take advantage of different tax treatments of the cash flows and differing legal treatment of bond ownership. However, in substantive terms, the economic effect of the transactions are identical.

In financing securities inventories held as hedges against swap portfolios or borrowing bonds to create short positions, financial institutions will typically use repurchase agreements or sale and buy backs to finance a long position. In contrast, financial institutions will borrow bonds, usually as an open trade, that is for an uncertain period, to cover short positions held as a portfolio hedge.

Key issues

Several aspects of the operation of the repo markets should be noted. These include:

- the types of bonds utilised;
- the coupon effect;
- pricing and rate structure;
- basis trades; and
- credit risk aspects.

The typical bonds utilised in relation to the repurchase agreements as they impact upon swap portfolios are government securities. In practice, repo markets exist across a wide variety of securities, including Eurobonds.

In most markets, it is customary, where it is necessary to create a short treasury position, to create a short in the current "on-the-run" government security. This reflects the fact that the swap market typically prices "off" the most liquid government stock of the relevant maturity. However, a danger that needs to be carefully managed in regard to such short positions is that cost of borrowing such bonds to cover the short position can often escalate to very high levels. This reflects the fact that bond borrowers in the repo market tend to be market professionals and use the securities to short the bond market, either hedging portfolio positions or positioning against increases in interest rates. Where large short positions exist in a particular security, bonds may be difficult to borrow resulting in very high cost of borrowing which can adversely effect the efficiency of the hedge.

Repo market makers try to avoid repo bonds which have an intervening coupon payment during the term of the repo transaction.

The fundamental reason for utilising the repo market is that financing positions to such structures provides a cheaper alternative as well as diversifying the institutions funding sources. Depending on maturity, repos can be utilised to reduce the cost of financing inventory by anywhere between 0.125% pa and 0.75% pa, depending on currency the term of financing.

Similarly, cost of borrowing bonds is considerably cheaper through the repo market than alternative sources such as Cedel and Euroclear which usually charge between 2.5% and 3.75% to lend bonds, depending on currency.

Even for highly rated financial institutions (AA/AAA), use of financing and repurchase agreements allowed them to raise funds opportunistically at rates significantly better than the money market. For example, where institutions carry inventory of a particular security which is sought after to cover bond shorts, it may be possible to raise funds at levels often 100bps pa below interbank rates.

Other advantages of raising funds to repo transactions include the capacity to arrange funding from overnight to one year, although market is deepest for shorter-rated repos. The repo market also facilitates borrowing odd sums of cash which may be difficult to arrange by means of more formal money market transactions.

The formulas utilised for calculating the implied repo rate are summarised in *Table 1*.

TABLE 1

Pricing Repos

Formula for implied repo rate with zero or one interim coupon:

$$(P + A_1)(1 + rD_1/360) = C(1 + rD_2/360) + DP + A_2$$

Cost to purchase and finance bond	Interim coupon and reinvested earnings	Amount received from contract delivery

rearranging terms:

$$r = \frac{DP + A_2 - (P = A_1 + C)}{(P + A_1)(D_1/360) - C(D_2/360)}$$

Where:

P = bond purchase price (flat price)
A_1 = accrued interest at time of purchase
r = implied repo rate (as a decimal $r = 0.05 = 5\%$)
D_1 = days from purchase settlement to futures deliveries
C = actual interim coupon received (equals 0 if no coupon received)
D_2 = days from interim coupon receipt to futures delivery
DP = delivery price = (factor × futures quote for factor contracts) (price using futures yield for yield contracts)
A_2 = accrued interest on the bond on futures delivery day

Formula for the net basis:

NB = (P + A) (R − r) D/360

Where:

NB = Net basis
P = bond purchase price (clean price)
A = accrued interest at time of purchase
R = repo rate
r = implied repo rate
D = days from bond purchase to futures delivery

Source: Terry Shanahan (1991) (Summer).

The linkages between the repo market and the futures market allow market professionals to utilise what are known as "basis trades" to create cash and carry or reverse cash and carry positions. This is typically utilised to arbitrage cash futures relationships.

Repo markets are utilised on a "full accrual" pricing for valuing collateral. This means a bond user would be valued at market price plus accrued interest minus a reasonable margin (known as a "haircut") to allow for adverse bond market movements. If a coupon is payable prior to the repo maturity, the ultimate owner of the security gets the benefit of the coupon payment in an offsetting adjustment made in the value of the repo loan.

The credit risk on a repo transaction is akin to that applicable to any collateralised loans.

In general terms, the risk on a repo agreement is relatively low. A significant concern in this regard is the value of the collateral, particularly as its price will be affected by interest rate movements in financial markets causing potentially significant deviations of the value of the repo cash loans resulting in a risk exposure to either party to the transaction.

Structure of repurchase markets

Markets for repo transactions have, traditionally, only been a prominent part of US$ capital markets. However, increasingly active repo markets are developing in most reserve currencies including DEM, FFR, JPY as well as smaller markets in Dfl, ECU, LIT, PTA and even Scandinavian currencies.

A factor underlying the growth in international repo transactions is the corresponding growth in derivative product markets. The growth in derivative products stimulates both trading in the very large cash bond markets in the relevant currencies and in arbitrage between the cash and derivative markets. The repo market has become an essential component assisting the liquidity of both types of trading as it is capable of facilitating both of financing long positions and permitting short selling to assist in arbitrage between the physical and derivative markets.

A further factor giving impetus to the growth of repo markets in all currencies has been the increased risk of banks and financial institutions generally which has forced institution investors to seek other sources of investment.

The market in most major currencies is now reasonably liquid the number of dealers operating with a number of brokers active in matching borrowers and lenders.

The development of repo markets has assisted portfolio managers to finance holdings of securities and in procuring bonds to cover engineered short positions in securities designed to hedge portfolio risk positions. In currencies such as US$, the prevailing repo rate is typically utilised as the relevant bond borrowing or investment yield to adjust swap prices as described in Chapter 8. Increasingly, repo markets are beginning to play an important role in the management of swap portfolios.

Chapter 33

Swap Portfolio Risk Management Techniques: Portfolio Hedging Techniques

SWAP PORTFOLIO MANAGEMENT APPROACHES

As noted previously, there are basically two general approaches to swap portfolio management:

- a basic hedging approach, entailing individual hedges for *each* swap transaction undertaken; or
- a portfolio approach, based on the practice of hedging entire swap portfolios on an aggregated basis.

The basic hedging approach, described in detail in Chapter 32, usually entails the following steps:

- When a swap position is booked, the corresponding hedge is established.
- Once a matching swap is arranged, the hedge is unwound by reversing the original hedge, consisting of securities or futures, to coincide with the entry into the matching or offsetting swap.

The basic hedging approach requires the original swap to be matched relatively closely by the offsetting swap in terms of maturity, interest rate levels (adjusted for hedge profits and losses) as well as notional principal amounts. In essence, a five year swap is matched *with another five year swap*. The hedging approach is predicated on matching transactions with similar yields and, preferably identical, maturities and notional principals.

However, while relatively simple, the basic hedging approach is relatively inflexible and does not readily accommodate non-generic swap transactions within its framework.

In order to overcome some of the difficulties associated with the basic hedging approach, the portfolio approach to swap portfolio management has evolved. This approach entails hedging the *entire* portfolio of swap transactions on an aggregated basis.

Portfolio approaches model the existing portfolio of swaps by aggregating the individual fixed and floating rate cash flows. Portfolio value is determined by calculating the net present value of the cash flows within the portfolio. Present value of the portfolios are calculated utilising discount factors based on, typically, zero coupon or spot interest rates based on the existing swap yield curve.

The net present value difference, which is positive representing the profit of the portfolio, is then sought to be hedged to preserve portfolio value. As new positions are added, the impact of the marginal transaction on the overall portfolio is calculated with appropriate adjustments to portfolio hedges being implemented to continue the objective of preserving the value of the swap portfolio.

The portfolio approach to swap book management has, itself, evolved over time. The earliest portfolio approaches were based on a duration based hedging approach. Under this approach, the *net duration* of the cash flows in the portfolio was calculated with hedges being implemented to counteract the duration of the portfolio itself. Duration, in this context, functioned as a measure of the interest rate risk within the portfolio required to be managed.

The earlier duration-based approaches required a number of assumptions which, in practical terms, were difficult to justify (see discussion below). This created an impetus to newer approaches to portfolio management including what can be termed the generalised cash flow approach. Under the generalised cash flow approach, portfolio risk is measured in terms of the change in portfolio value as a result of movements in key variables and hedged utilising a regression-based minimum variance hedging methodology, which seeks to address the problems of basis risk in interest rate risk management.

The relative inflexibility of the basic hedging approach with its focus on individual swap transactions and the related problems of hedge transaction costs as *each* transaction had to be hedged has meant that almost all swap portfolios are now managed under some sort of portfolio approach to hedging. The portfolio approach has the advantage of being flexible as well as reducing transaction costs. The portfolio approaches emphasis on *cash flows* rather than transactions is also advantageous in that it accords with the evolution of the swap and derivatives business itself which is increasingly about managing and transmuting characteristics of streams of cash flows. A central element in the portfolio approach is that it allows the portfolio manager to determine the risk of the swap or derivative portfolio and then establish the impact of adding various hedge instruments or new transactions to the existing portfolio in terms of profit and loss and risk characteristics. This allows, to a greater degree than previously possible, decisions as to the degree of residual risk that the portfolio carries and the portion of this risk to be hedged and also facilitates a more accurate evaluation of the impact on the portfolio of every potential new transaction.

In the remainder of this chapter, portfolio hedging techniques, including duration based approaches and generalised cash flow approaches, are considered in detail.

In examining portfolio hedging techniques, it is important to note that to some extent, the valuation technology utilised to measure value, at a given instance in time, of a portfolio of swap and derivative transactions, is to an extent object specific. In this regard, an increasingly important aspect of valuation is the valuation of swap and derivative transaction portfolios with a view to purchase of the portfolio by an institution. Some specific issues relating to the valuation of swap and derivative portfolios for the purpose of purchase are considered in *Appendix A* to this chapter.

PORTFOLIO HEDGING

The key feature of utilising the portfolio approach is to undertake hedging of swap transactions as a portfolio of *fungible* cash flows. The basic principles underlying the operationalising of the portfolio approach are those outlined in the context of discussing the risks of swap portfolio management in Chapter 31.

The key measure of portfolio value utilising this approach is identical to that applicable under the basic hedging approach:

Present value (net) = present value (asset inflows) − present value (liability outflows)

Present value in this context signifies the discounted value of the portfolio using the relevant discount factors of all cash inflows and outflows. As discussed in Chapter 8, determination of the interest rate to be utilised to discount future cash flows is not an unambiguous exercise, nor is it without its own complexities.

The portfolio manager's objective is to maximise the net present value of the portfolio and to maintain this value.

The application of the portfolio approach necessitates the following steps:

- aggregation of portfolio cash flows;
- valuation of portfolio cash flows;
- determination of portfolio risk;
- hedging of portfolio risk.

The first step in implementing the portfolio approach is to establish what cash flows to be considered. As noted previously, cash inflows and outflows are, typically, aggregated into points of time ("buckets", "vectors" or "maturity points"). All known transaction cash flows are included in the portfolio.

The value of the portfolio is then determined by discounting the cash flows using:

- par coupon rates; or
- zero coupon or spot yield rates.

The issues related to selection between the two available interest rates and, by implication, discount factors have been considered in detail in Chapter 8. In practice, most portfolio managers utilise zero coupon rates using the swap yield curve, which incorporates the relevant futures contracts on short-term interest rates in the initial portion of the yield curve. In US$, for example, the Eurodollar futures curve would be used out to, say, three to five years with swap rates being utilised thereafter. In practice, mid rates are typically utilised.

The portfolio risk is determined by measuring the change in portfolio value for significant changes in financial market variables. For interest rates, the portfolio value is measured for parallel yield curve movements as well as non-parallel yield curve movement (that is, changes in the shape of the yield curve). Additional sensitivities such as to changes in spread relationships between swaps and underlying government bonds or in the cash-futures relationships where these are utilised as hedging instruments may be measured to estimate portfolio risk.

Valuation of the cash flows can be undertaken utilising alternative measures of value. For example, under the duration approach, portfolio risk would be measured by calculating asset and liability duration using either a single factor duration model or a multi-factor duration model.

Analysis of portfolio risk will yield an indication of the portfolio sensitivity to movement in the relevant variables, most significantly currency and interest rates. This risk represents the *marginal* risk position of the portfolio. The portfolio approach is predicated on the analysis of the risk position *of the portfolio in aggregate*. The theory underlying this approach is that various cash flows within the portfolio, at least partially, offset *other* cash flows within the portfolio effectively creating offsets and internal hedges. The marginal risk measured provides an indication of the aggregated risk of the portfolio, that is, a summation of the net positive and negative changes in value in individual cash flows.

The basic hedge strategy is:

Change in value of hedge portfolio = (negative) change in value of swap portfolio.

This implies that the portfolio manager will buy or sell currency or interest rate instruments which create the *opposite* exposure in the hedge portfolio to that measured in the swap portfolio. The consequence of the hedge strategy is to preserve the value of the portfolio by ensuring the changes in value of the swap portfolio are offset by equal but opposite changes in value in the hedge portfolio.

As in the case of the basic hedging approach (outlined in Chapter 32), a variety of instruments can be utilised to hedge portfolio risk. These include:

- cash/physical securities;
- futures on physical securities;
- other swaps (including swaps of different maturity in curve hedging practices).

The issues relating to the use of one or other category of instrument are not significantly different as between the basic and portfolio approaches to swap book management.

DURATION HEDGING APPROACH

Duration

One approach to swap portfolio management entails hedging the interest rate component of the portfolio utilising duration techniques. A brief explanation of duration as it applies to swap hedging technology is outlined in *Appendix B* to this chapter.

Duration can be defined as the weighted average of times in the future when interest and principal payments are to be received. It is a measure of the sensitivity of the price of the instrument to changes in interest rates.

The price of any security is an inverse non-linear function of the yield to maturity and the impact on the price of the security of a given change in the yield to maturity depends on the level of the yield to maturity at the relevant point in time, the coupon rate of the security and the term to maturity of the security. Duration, which is in some sense an *index* number, is utilised to calculate percentage price changes in the value of the security for a given change in interest rates or yield to maturity regardless of the characteristics of the security.

The principal utility of duration as a measure of interest rate risk derives from the following:

- The modified duration of a stream of cash flows, which can be calculated using the basic Macauley's duration, provides an accurate representation of the percentage price change corresponding to a given change in yield.

- Durations are additive, that is, the duration of a set of assets or liabilities is equal to the weighted average of the duration of each component asset and liability (the weights being equal to the proportion that each asset or liability represents of the total asset or liability portfolio).
- The equivalence of instruments, streams of cash flows or portfolios with equivalent durations. This implies that instruments with the same duration will experience identical changes in portfolio value for a given change in yields to maturity, provided the assumptions underlying the concept of duration itself are satisfied.

These features allow duration concepts to be utilised in swap portfolio management.

Utilising duration techniques

The duration approach to swap portfolio management is operationalised as follows:

- The aggregated portfolio cash flows are determined.
- The portfolio duration of the cash inflows and cash outflows are determined separately.
- Utilising the property of additivity of durations, the net duration of the portfolio is determined.

The net portfolio duration represents the interest rates risk profile of the swap portfolio.

In order to insulate the portfolio from the risk of changes in value as a result of interest rate movements, a hedge portfolio is created through the purchase and sale of physical securities, futures contract or other swap/derivative products. This hedge portfolio created with the specific objective of having the *same* duration as the net duration of the portfolio with the sole exception that it moves in an opposite direction to the swap portfolio for a given movement up or down in interest rates.

An example of utilising duration concepts to immunise a swap portfolio is set out in *Exhibit 33.1*.

Management of a duration hedge will require periodic rebalancing. This reflects the fact that the duration of the portfolio will alter over time reflecting changes in interest rates, changes in the absolute level of rates and the passage of time. Adjustment of the hedge is further complicated by the fact that changes in the duration of the portfolio of swaps will not necessarily be the same as the change in the duration of the hedge. This will result in the hedge portfolio being required to be adjusted by sales and purchases of the hedge instruments. This process of rebalancing will inevitably entail transaction costs as well as costs from buying and selling securities at loss generating levels creating a degree of slippage in the efficiency of the hedge.

Exhibit 33.1
Duration-Based Swap Hedge

1. *Portfolio structure*

Assume the following swaps constitute a portfolio of interest rate swaps:

- Pay US$ fixed at 10.00% pa (annual)/receive US$ six month LIBOR on notional principal of US$100m for one year.
- Receive US$ fixed at 10.20% pa (annual)/pay US$ six month LIBOR on notional principal of US$50m for one year.
- Receive US$ fixed at 10.20% pa (semi-annual)/pay US$ six month LIBOR on notional principal of US$50m for one year.

The structure of the portfolio together with its discounted value (at both current par and zero coupon discount rates) is summarised in *Table 1.*

2. *Portfolio interest sensitivity*

The portfolio duration is then calculated as follows:

(1) *Using par yields*

	Receipts	Payments	Net
Macauley's Duration (years)	0.9876	1.0000	0.0124
Modified Duration	0.9405	0.9524	−0.0118
% Price Volatility (for 1bps pa movement in yields)	0.009405	0.009524	−0.000118

(2) *Using zero coupon yields*

	Receipts	Payments	Net
Macauley's Duration (years)	0.9876	1.0000	−0.0124
Modified Duration	0.9405	0.9524	−0.0118
% Price Volatility (for 1bps pa movement in yields)	0.009405	0.009524	−0.000118

(3) *Hedging interest rate risk*

Utilising the modified duration measure (calculated using zero coupon yields), immunisation of the portfolio requires a transaction with a positive modified duration of 0.0118 years to offset the negative modified duration of the portfolio of the same amount.

Assume the following bond is to be used to hedge the position:

Coupon: 10% pa (annual in arrears).
Maturity: 1 year.
Yield to Maturity: 10% pa (semi-annual).
Modified Duration: 0.9524 years.

In order to immunise the portfolio risk, it would be necessary to purchase $1,238,975m of one year bonds: (calculated as 100,000,000 × 0.0118/0.9524).

(4) *Hedge performance*

Assume yields rise uniformly across the yield curve by 0.01% pa. The value of the portfolio will alter as set out in *Table 2.*

The change in value of the portfolio and hedge is as follows:

Value of Portfolio	Original	Current	Change
—Using par yields:	357,024	357,106	82
—Using zero coupon yield	359,626	359,708	82
Value of Hedge	1,238,975	1,238,860	(115)

Exhibit 33.1—continued

TABLE 1

Initial Portfolio

Period	Date	No of Days to Settlement	Cash Flow Amount ($)	Par Rates Discount Rate (% S/A)	Par Rates Discount Rate (% A)	Par Rates Discount Factor	Present Value ($)	Zero Coupon Rates Discount Rate (% S)	Zero Coupon Rates Discount Rate (% A)	Discount Factor	Present Value ($)
0	1-Jan-X2	0									
1	1-Jul-X2	182	2,550,000	5.000%	5.062%	0.9757	2,487,973	5.000%	5.062%	0.9757	2,487,973
2	1-Jan-X3	366	52,550,000	10.000%	10.250%	0.9068	47,651,658	10.128%	10.384%	0.9057	47,593,463
2	1-Jan-X3	366	55,100,000	10.000%	10.250%	0.9068	49,963,965	10.128%	10.384%	0.9057	49,902,946
2	1-Jan-X3	366	(110,000,000)	10.000%	10.250%	0.9068	(99,746,572)	10.128%	10.384%	0.9057	(99,624,755)
			200,000			Total	357,024				359,626

TABLE 2

Impact of Change in Yields

Period	Date	No of Days to Settlement	Cash Flow Amount ($)	Par Rates Discount Rate (% S/A)	Par Rates Discount Rate (% A)	Par Rates Discount Factor	Present Value ($)	Zero Coupon Rates Discount Rate (% S)	Zero Coupon Rates Discount Rate (% A)	Discount Factor	Present Value ($)	PVBP ($)	Cumulative PVBP ($)
0	1-Jan-X2												
1	1-Jul-X2	182	2,550,000	5.010%	5.073%	0.9756	2,487,852	5.010%	5.073%	0.9756	2,487,852	(121)	(121)
2	1-Jan-X3	366	52,550,000	10.010%	10.261%	0.9067	47,647,108	10.138%	10.395%	0.9056	47,588,921	(4,542)	203
2	1-Jan-X3	366	55,100,000	10.010%	10.261%	0.9067	49,959,194	10.138%	10.395%	0.9056	49,898,183	(4,762)	
2	1-Jan-X3	366	(110,000,000)	10.010%	10.261%	0.9067	(99,737,047)	10.138%	10.395%	0.9056	(99,615,248)	9,508	
						Total	357,106				359,708		82

Key issues

The major benefits of utilising duration to manage the interest rate risk profile of the swap portfolio include:

- reduction in portfolio basis risk;
- overcoming imperfections regarding the availability of hedge instruments;
- lowering of transaction hedging costs.

The major issues relating to the utilisation of duration approaches relates to problems in duration itself as a measure of interest rate risk.

Duration calculations rely on a number of assumptions:

- duration measures hold for only *small* changes in interest rates;
- it assumes a flat term structure of interest rates;
- it assumes parallel yield curve shifts.

The fact that duration only holds for very small changes in interest rates necessitates frequent rebalancing or adjustment of the hedge as interest rates change. The relationship between changes in price in the swap portfolio and also in the hedge instruments relative to interest rates is non-linear.

In fact, the function is convex. Convexity measures the curvature of the slope of the curve of the function of price plotted against yield. In essence, convexity is a measure of how much an instrument's or portfolio's price-yield curve deviates from a straight line. If the yield on the instrument increases by one basis point, the price will drop, however, the price will rise when the yield on a bond decreases by one basis point. However, because of convexity, the two price changes may not be exactly equal in magnitude. The convexity of a bond can be measured by subtracting the magnitude of the price drop from the magnitude of the price rise. One major advantage of the generalised cash flow approaches described in the following section is that it seeks to specifically create convexity adjusted hedges.

The problem in relation to yield curve shape changes is more problematic. In a sense, duration approaches to hedging because of the assumption of perfect substitutability across the yield curve, implies the capacity to hedge any portion of the yield curve with another portion of the yield curve. However, in practice attempting to hedge a portfolio of swap cash flows with a few instruments creates the probability of severe mismatches of cash flows between the swap and hedge portfolio creating significant residual risk to non-parallel changes in the yield curve.

In an effort to overcome this deficiency, multiple factor duration models have been developed and are frequently utilised: see discussion in *Appendix B*.

Two alternative ways to deal with the yield curve problem are:

- partitioning the portfolio in terms of maturity bands;
- utilising covariances across various points of the yield curve.

Under the partitioning approach, the duration of the portfolio is calculated both for the portfolio as a whole and for specific maturity blocks within the portfolio—say, one year and under, greater than one year less than three years, between three years and seven years, between seven and ten years, longer than ten years. Utilising this partitioning approach, the specific risk component in each portion of the yield curve is determined and an appropriate mixture of hedge instruments, representative of the yield curve as a whole, is utilised to minimise the portfolio risk to yield curve changes.

An alternative method of handling changes in the term structure of interest rates is to consider the cash flow at each of the relevant points in the swaps portfolio as zero coupon securities and to assess their individual volatilities. Simultaneously, correlations between rates at different maturities on the yield curve are determined (in essence, a parallel yield curve movement assumes that movements between various points of the yield curve are perfectly correlated).

Given established covariances between various points in the yield curve based on historical data, a covariance matrix of price volatilities can be established. Utilising this approach, the volatility of a portfolio of swaps can be measured incorporating likely relationships across the term structure of interest rates. This approach can be refined by adjusting the amount of any hedge instrument held to take into account its correlation with the estimated yield curve shape change risk within the portfolio as a whole.

In utilising duration as a means of measuring the interest rate risk within a swap portfolio, it is useful to classify market interest rate movements into two categories:

- *Systematic movements*—that is, consistent with statistically determined relationships.
- *Non-systematic movements*—that is, residual interest rate movement.

It should be noted that duration hedge matching immunises the portfolio from systematic movements in interest rates. For duration hedge matching to be efficient, it is necessary to assume that non systematic movements in market interest rates are random or are normally distributed. These are assumptions which, in practical terms, are difficult to realise.

GENERALISED CASH FLOW APPROACH[1]

Overview

The generalised cash flow approach to swap portfolio management represents an extension of the portfolio approach. It seeks to overcome some of the difficulties identified with duration based approaches.

The key features of the generalised cash flow approach include:

- it is predicated on a complete aggregated portfolio approach and is not based on matching up or offsetting particular swaps;
- it focuses on identifying specific risk characteristics of portfolio (measured as portfolio delta, gamma and theta—see discussion below);
- it utilises a regression based minimum variance hedging methodology.

The aggregation or portfolio approach underlying generalised cash flow techniques is similar to that applicable to duration-based hedging approaches. The focus on specific risk characteristics of the portfolio seeks to overcome some difficulties with utilising duration as a measure of interest rate sensitivity of swap portfolios. In particular, it seeks to address the issues relating to convexity (see above). Similarly, the regression-based minimum variance hedging methodology seeks to overcome some of the problems of non-parallel yield curve shift and basis risk entailed in hedging.

1. This section is based on Bernd P Luedecke, "Measuring, Displaying and Hedging the Market Risk on a Swap" in Satyajit Das (1991).

The generalised cash flow approach is sometimes referred to as the present value of a basis point (PVBP) approach. This reflects the fact that the delta of an instrument or cash flow, usually reflecting the value impact of changes in the underlying asset price, can be estimated using PVBP measure (rather than calculating the partial derivative of the instrument value function).

Utilising generalised cash flow approaches

In practice, utilising the generalised cash flow approach entails a number of specific steps:

- As with duration-based approaches, portfolio cash flows are aggregated in accordance with the principles outlined previously.
- It is necessary then to identify the value functions of individual instruments and inputs such as financial market variables (interest rates and currency values), time and contractual features of specific instruments. Additional inputs include volatility and other inputs specific to options where the portfolio includes these types of instrument.
- The portfolio cash flows are valued by discounting back both cash inflows and outflows utilising zero coupon rates (refer Chapter 8).
- As well as establishing value of the portfolio, its risk profile is measured calculating portfolio sensitivity to movement in key financial variables. This risk profile is measured utilising delta, gamma and theta concepts (which have a similar meaning to that utilised in relation to options—see discussion in Chapters 11, 31 and 36).
- The portfolio management objective under the generalised cash flow approach is to preserve or increase portfolio present value. Consequently, hedging strategies are developed to protect portfolio present value.
- The objective in undertaking hedging transactions is to create a portfolio of transactions with an equal and opposite potential for changes in value to that of the swap portfolio itself.
- Typical hedge instruments utilised under the generalised cash flow approach are identical to those utilised in the case of duration based approaches and, for that matter, basic hedging approaches. The only major difference in hedging practice is to determine hedging coefficients designed to protect the portfolio and improve hedging efficiency through the capture of the impact of non-parallel shifts in the yield curve.

Key aspects of the generalised cash flow approach and its implementation are considered below.

Portfolio risk measures

Value function basis

The value function of any instrument is merely the mathematical technique utilised to value that instrument. The value function is the formula or algorithim which gives a dollar value of the instrument. For example, in the case of a bond it would be the normal bond price formula. Value functions for derivative products vary in complexity. For example for option products, an option valuation formula such as Black-Scholes, is the relevant value function. The value function for interest rate and currency swaps are somewhat more complex. This reflects the fact that such transactions involve two components, being the simultaneous purchase and sale of a fixed or floating rate security. In addition, there is no broad standardisation of the valuation function.

The inputs into the valuation function include:

- currency rates;
- interest rates, including the complete yield curve for the relevant security;
- the effluxion of time;
- specific contractual features of the instrument including face value, coupon rates, settlement practices etc.

For asymmetric risk management instruments such as options, additional inputs include strike price and volatility of asset prices.

The most important thing to note about the inputs into the value function is that with the exception of time they are determined by market forces. Two features of the inputs should be noted:

- Time represents a special type of input as it is only capable of progressing in a single direction.
- The contractual features of instruments do not necessarily change significantly, although certain instruments such as interest rate swaps will have a specific contractual feature (such as the floating rate level) which must be reset periodically.

Delta-gamma risk

In the context of option pricing and risk measurement, the concept of delta is utilised to signify the sensitivity of the price of the option to changes in the price of the underlying asset.

Under the generalised cash flow approach, delta is similarly used as a risk measure to facilitate monitoring the effect of changes in various interest rates. Delta, in this context can be defined as "the change in value function resulting from a one basis points rise in an interest rate at a specific point on the yield curve". Mathematically, delta is the partial derivative of the instrument value function with respect to interest rates.

A specific feature of delta, given that it is the partial derivative of the instrument value function, is that it provides a measure of the convexity of the instrument price movements. This overcomes one of the major difficulties with utilising duration to measure interest rate risk.

The major significance of delta as a risk measurement construct is that it provides information about specific profits or losses to the portfolio for specific interest rate movements *at a given point in the yield curve.*

The key characteristics of delta are as follows:

- Zero delta signifies the portfolio is immune to interest rate movements, that is, it neither profits nor loses value as a result in movements in interest rate.
- Cash inflows have a negative delta while cash outflows have a positive delta. This is because long or purchased positions in the relevant security decrease in value as interest rates rise or increase in value as interest rates fall. Conversely, short or sold positions in securities increase in value as interest rates rise and decrease in value as interest rates fall.

- In utilising delta, it should be noted that any portfolio has *multiple* deltas. The multiple deltas corresponds to each point in the yield curve, as specified, signifying that the value of the portfolio changes in response to movements in the specific points in the interest rate yield curve.

It is evident that the delta of any portfolio of cash flows is dynamic and is characterised by:

- changes in value with changes in maturity (as a result of time decay—see discussion below);
- changes with absolute levels of interest rate as well as changes in the shape of the yield curve.

As noted above, in practice, the delta of any portfolio can be estimated by calculating the PVBP of the relevant cash flows.

The concept of gamma risk was discussed (in Chapter 31) in the context of the risk of asymmetric risk management products such as options. Management of gamma risk is a specific component of the management of option portfolios: refer Chapter 36.

Gamma measures the *change in delta* for a given change in the underlying asset price for any instrument. Mathematically, gamma is the second partial derivative of the instrument value function with respect to interest rates. As noted previously, gamma measures the degree to which portfolio delta will change. A large gamma of a portfolio indicates the potential for a portfolio delta to change rapidly when the relevant interest rate changes. In essence, gamma is a measure of how much risk or exposure the portfolio is subject to from a sudden and, possibly, discontinuous move in interest rates.

The gamma of symmetric risk management instruments is relatively stable. This reflects the fact that the delta of a symmetric instrument does not change significantly, at least for reasonable movements in interest rates. In contrast, for asymmetric instrument, given certain conditions, the gamma of a portfolio can be extremely large signifying potentially significant movements in portfolio delta.

The major significance of gamma within the generalised cash flow approach to portfolio management is that the portfolio may be thought to be immunised from interest rate risk by achieving delta neutrality. Delta neutrality in this context is usually achieved by creating a hedge portfolio which offsets the interest rate risk characteristics of the swap portfolio. Under these conditions, gamma measures the fact that for a given change in interest rates, the portfolio delta may change prior to the hedge being rebalanced to neutralise portfolio risk. In this sense, it measures the potential inefficiency or slippage of the hedge itself.

Theta/time decay risk[2]

Time decay also has the potential to significantly alter the value of a portfolio. The concept of changes in the value of an instrument as a result of the passage of time is well understood in the context of option pricing theory and option portfolio management: refer Chapters 31 and 36. Theta, which is the measure of time decay, can be defined as "the change in value function as a result of the effluxion of time assuming no change in interest rates". Mathematically, theta is the partial derivative of the instrument value function with respect to time.

Theta is analogous to the portfolio's carry cost or a daily portfolio accrual. The major characteristics of theta include:

2. This section is based on Bernd P Luedecke (1991) (May).

- Future cash inflows have positive theta while future cash outflows have, correspondingly, negative thetas. This reflects the fact that the passage of time increases the value of cash inflows, in part because of the declining effect of discounting. Similarly, cash outflows have negative thetas representing increasing present value of cash outflows as they become closer in terms of time.
- Theta is a function of:

  —the slope of the yield curve (that is, changes in zero coupon discount rates);

  —the time to maturity.

The slope effect on theta is particularly important to grasp. Changes in the slope of the yield curve can alter portfolio theta/cash flow characteristics, that is, cash inflows can have negative thetas while outflows can have positive thetas as the shape of the yield curve changes.

As noted above, under normal circumstances, a future cash outflow will have a negative theta and a future cash inflow will have a positive theta, reflecting the intuition that as time decays the present value of both assets and liabilities increase. However, if the zero coupon yield curve is sufficiently negative, future cash outflows may begin to exhibit positive theta and, vice versa, future cash inflows show negative theta. This will happen when a yield curve, or a section of the yield curve, rotates or flexes. This reflects the fact that the increase (decrease) in value of the relevant cash inflow (outflow) as a result of the passage of time is offset and exceeded by the higher discount rate applicable for the shorter maturity. While the sign of future cash flows, in this situation, may not have altered, the behaviour over time of the present value of those cash flows may change.

Generalised cash flows approaches—in practice

In practice, utilising the generalised cash flow approach to portfolio management necessitates a number of distinct steps:

- determination of the portfolio delta, gamma and theta risk measures;
- identifying portfolio risk characteristics from the measured portfolio risk characteristics;
- the establishment of hedges or addition of new transactions to reduce portfolio risk.

Portfolio deltas and gammas are calculated consistent with the methodology outlined above. Deltas are calculated for each instrument within the portfolio. The deltas are then summed to produce a delta profile for the entire portfolio.

The global delta profile will provide information to the portfolio risk manager at *two* distinct levels:

- The total portfolio delta will show the *overall* sensitivity of the portfolio to a one basis point increase in interest rates across the yield curve (effectively, a parallel yield curve shift). This information will be, effectively, the summation of the deltas of all instruments within the portfolio for changes in value corresponding to simultaneous and uniform changes in each of the relevant interest rates which are inputs into the portfolio value functions.
- Delta profiles for the entire portfolio for movements in interest rates at a specific point in the yield curve can also be determined. This would be calculated by summing the changes in value of each instrument in the portfolio for an increase of 1bps in interest rate at a specific point in the yield curve. This allows a precise measurement of the impact on portfolio value of movements at particular points

of the yield curve, providing information on the impact of non-parallel yield curve shifts within the portfolio.

This approach to portfolio delta measurement and analysis highlights the significant advantages of this approach to portfolio risk management:

- The technique of delta analysis highlights the residual risk in the portfolio. This reflects the fact that, intuitively, the global delta profile of the portfolio effectively nets transactions within the portfolio with offsetting value changes for a given interest rate move.
- A significant advantage of computing each delta individually for each instrument within the portfolio is that it does not require assumptions about yield curve movements. This facilitates the capacity of the delta profile analysis to provide information on portfolio risk from non parallel yield curve shifts. In fact, this type of analysis very specifically identifies the precise risk in the portfolio for *a given change in any one of the relevant interest rates utilised in valuing the portfolio*. The calculation of delta at each point in the yield curve facilitates analysis of every type of yield curve movement including specific dangers in each individual point in the yield curve.
- The combination of the above two advantages is that global portfolio delta allows the risk manager to, at a glance, grasp the overall portfolio risk as it has evolved as a result of series of individual transactions undertaken within the portfolio.
- A major advantage of this approach is that as it displays the specific risk characteristics of the portfolio to interest rate movements, it is feasible to utilise the portfolio delta analysis as the basis for determining specific hedging strategies required to neutralise portfolio risk (see discussion below).

An example of the global delta profile of a portfolio, utilising hypothetical data, is set out in *Exhibit 33.2*.

Exhibit 33.2
Portfolio Global Delta Profile

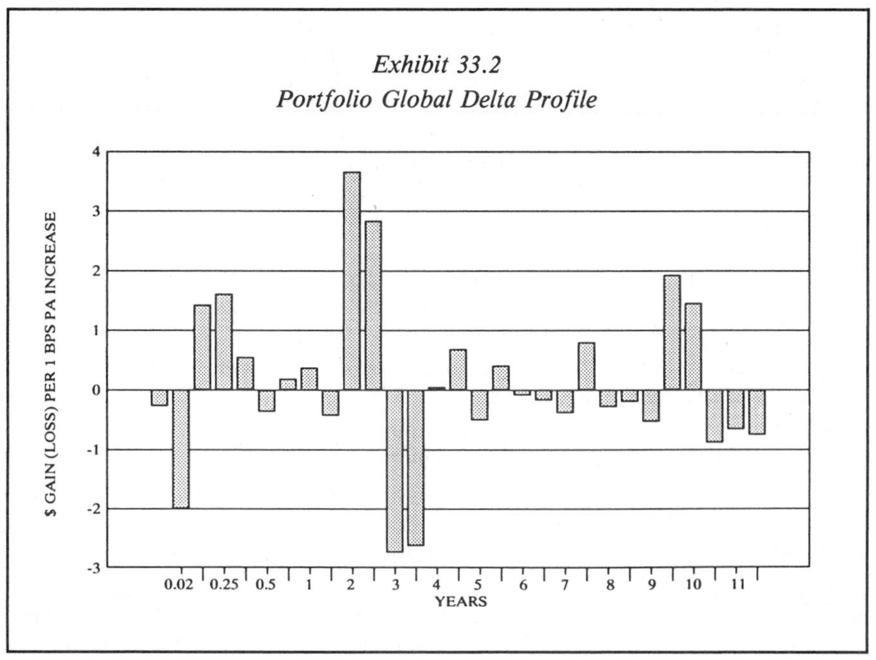

In addition to determining portfolio delta and, by implication, gamma, it is necessary for the portfolio risk manager to determine the portfolio's theta. Theta can be determined by utilising sophisticated computer software utilising partial derivative functions. In practice, theta can also be estimated utilising the following technique:

- The computer system's internal time clock is set one day in advance (this assumes the relevant time period internal for theta is one day).
- The portfolio is then revalued. This revaluation includes generation of all relevant zero coupon interest rates based on a one day time decay in maturity with portfolio present values of all cash flows occurring after the relevant day being included.
- Theta is then estimated utilising the following equation:

  Estimate of theta = present value (t + 1) − present value of portfolio (t) + net cash settlement (t + 1)

  Where

  t = today
  t + 1 = tomorrow.
  Net cash settlement (t + 1) = the net cash flow settlements on existing transactions taking place tomorrow.

Management of a portfolio theta risk requires an understanding of the two components of portfolio theta—namely the slope effect and, the simpler, time effect. Dynamic variations in the slope of the yield curve, particularly at the point in time at which the zero coupon yield curve switches from being positively sloped to negatively sloped (or vice versa) can lead to significant changes in portfolio value. In order to hedge the portfolio against risk of changes as a result of time decay, the portfolio manager will need to add hedges or new transactions to the portfolio to offset the portfolio's theta characteristics.

For example, portfolios occasionally can be characterised by very large negative thetas with the consequent loss of portfolio value, often, at a very rapid rate. Under these circumstances, the portfolio manager may seek to preserve portfolio values by entering into new transactions with *positive theta*. The new transactions themselves may well have *negative present value*, that is they may be loss making transactions. However, such transactions may help minimise the portfolio's overall theta and preserve the *total* value of the portfolio.

Identification of the risk characteristics of the portfolio can only be completed at a *specific point in time*. This reflects the fact that the risk characteristics of the portfolio are, by their very nature, dynamic. In this context, interaction of delta and theta is clearly pivotal. Portfolio risk management will, in practice, almost certainly require some trade-offs between the two.

In summary, the portfolio risk characteristics determined from the type of analysis discussed will be as follows:

- *portfolio delta*—which provides information on the *specific* interest rate movements that will effect portfolio value;
- *portfolio gamma*—which will identify specific interest rate movements that will effect the portfolios delta;
- *portfolio theta*—which measures the impact of time decay on the portfolio.

Once the portfolio risk characteristics have been determined, the portfolio risk manager will add hedges or new transactions to minimise the portfolio risk. Where new transactions are proposed, these transactions will be assessed according not only to their individual present value or profit potential but in accordance with its potential impact on the existing portfolio risk profile. The interaction between the existing portfolio and the new transaction will be reflected in the pricing of the transaction. For example, from a portfolio perspective, a relatively low value transaction may be able to be priced extremely attractively as it may impact positively on the value of the portfolio as a whole.

Exhibit 33.3 sets out a simplified example of utilising the generalised cash flow approach to measuring and managing swap portfolio risk.

Exhibit 33.3
Generalised Cash Flow Hedge

1. *Portfolio structure*

Assume the same portfolio of swaps as in *Exhibit 33.1*

The structure of the portfolio together with its discounted value (using both par and zero coupon rates) is summarised in *Table 1*, p 1035.

2. *Portfolio risk structure*

2.1 *Portfolio deltas on PVBPs*

The interest rate sensitivity of the portfolio is measured by the portfolio delta or PVBP for a 1bps pa increase in the zero coupon rate for each point along the yield curve.

The change in portfolio value is set out in *Table 2*, p 1035, and *Graph 1*, p 1038.

The analysis indicates that portfolio should be hedged for a parallel 1bps pa yield curve rise by:

- going short in six month interest rates;
- going long in 12 month interest rates.

See further discussion of hedging strategies below.

2.2 *Portfolio exposure to changes in yield curve shape*

The sensitivity of the portfolio can be estimated by varying the shape of the yield curve. This is done by "toggling" the zero rates to alternatively steepen and flatten the yield curve.

The change in portfolio values for a 1bps pa steeper yield curve is set out in *Table 3*, p 1036, and *Graph 2*, p 1038.

The change in portfolio values for 1bps pa flatter yield curve is set out in *Table 4*, p 1036, and *Graph 3*, p 1039.

The analysis indicates that the portfolio gains (loses) value from a steeper (flatter) yield curve.

2.3 *Portfolio time elapse on theta exposure*

The sensitivity of the portfolio to the effluxion of time is measured by re-setting the valuation timing one day forward.

The change in portfolio values are set out in *Table 5*, p 1037, and *Graph 4*, p 1039.

The analysis indicates that the portfolio loses significant value with the passage of time.

3. *Portfolio immunisation strategies*

3.1 *Risk profile*

The risk profile of the existing portfolio reflects its structure of deferred cash outflows and earlier cash inflows. This gives the portfolio its risk profile (on a ceteris paribus basis):

Exhibit 33.3—continued

- The portfolio value increases (decreases) for a rise (fall) in rates.
- The portfolio value increases (decreases) for a steeper (flatter) yield curve.
- The portfolio value decreases with time as the effect of discounting on the future cash outflows decreases.

3.2 *Hedge strategy*

The hedge strategy adopted would be structured to offset the impact of the factors identified above.

Assume that the following hedge instruments are available:

Cash deposits for six months (interest at maturity):*

PVBP per US$1m (@ 5.00% yield) = US$48.65
Theta for one day time decay = US$133.67

Cash deposit for one year (interest at maturity):#

PVBP per US$1m (@ 10.00% yield) = US$90.90
Theta for one day time decay = US$249.13

* Based on 182 day run and actual/actual day count.
# Based on 10% pa annual on 10.00% annual yield, 365 day run and actual/actual day count.

A number of hedge strategies can be posited:

(1) Make $1,685,509 cash deposit (lend cash) for six months—

The amount of the deposit is arrived at as follows:

Portfolio Net PVBP/Instrument PVBP = 82/48.65 = 1.6855

For a 1bps uniform increase in the yield curve the long position will depreciate approx $82 offsetting the gain in portfolio value.

The hedge however provides no protection against the changes in the shape of the yield curve. If the yield curve steepens, then the one year position will gain value, increasing overall portfolio value. If the yield curve flattens, the hedge will incur losses which will compound the losses in value in the one month position, decreasing the value of the overall portfolio value.

The hedge has positive time value of around $225.30 per day. This represents the accreting interest value of the position. This will offset the loss due to time decay in the original portfolio.

(2) Make $902,090 cash deposit for 12 months—

The amount of the deposit is arrived at as follows:
Portfolio Net PVBP/Instrument PVBP = 82/90.90 = 0.9021

For a 1bps uniform increase in interest rates, the hedge will depreciate by approx $82 offsetting the portfolio gain.

The hedge does not provide protection against changes in the yield, particularly a flattening of the yield curve.

The hedge has positive time value of around $224.74, representing the accreting interest value of the position which will offset the loss due to time decay in the original portfolio.

(3) Composite hedge—

Borrow $2,487,153m of six month cash deposit.
Make $2,233,223m of 12 month cash deposit.

For a 1bps uniform rise in interest rates, the portfolio will increase in value by $82.

The hedge portfolio will change in value as follows:

six month cash deposit— $ 121
12 month cash deposit— $(203)
Net $ (82).

The composite hedge will provide protection against yield curve shape changes as individual components of the hedge will offset changes in portfolio value as the yield curve flexes.

The hedge has position *net* time value of $223.90 ($556.36-$332.46) which will offset the time decay of the portfolio.

Exhibit 33.3—continued

TABLE 1

Initial Portfolio

Period	Date	No of Days to Settlement	Cash Flow Amount ($)	Par Rates Discount Rate (% S/A)	Par Rates Discount Rate (% A)	Par Rates Discount Factor	Par Rates Present Value ($)	Zero Coupon Rates Discount Rate (% S)	Zero Coupon Rates Discount Rate (% A)	Zero Coupon Rates Discount Factor	Zero Coupon Rates Present Value ($)
0	1-Jan-X2	0									
1	1-Jul-X2	182	2,550,000	5.000%	5.062%	0.9757	2,487,973	5.000%	5.062%	0.9757	2,487,973
2	1-Jan-X3	366	52,550,000	10.000%	10.250%	0.9068	47,651,658	10.128%	10.384%	0.9057	47,593,463
2	1-Jan-X3	366	55,100,000	10.000%	10.250%	0.9068	49,963,965	10.128%	10.384%	0.9057	49,902,946
2	1-Jan-X3	366	(110,000,000)	10.000%	10.250%	0.9068	(99,746,572)	10.128%	10.384%	0.9057	(99,624,755)
			200,000			Total	357,024				359,626

TABLE 2

Portfolio Deltas or PVBPs

Period	Date	No of Days to Settlement	Cash Flow Amount ($)	Par Rates Discount Rate (% S/A)	Par Rates Discount Rate (% A)	Par Rates Discount Factor	Par Rates Present Value ($)	Zero Coupon Rates Discount Rate (% S)	Zero Coupon Rates Discount Rate (% A)	Zero Coupon Rates Discount Factor	Zero Coupon Rates Present Value ($)	PVBP ($)	Change in PVBP ($)
0	1-Jan-X2												
1	1-Jul-X2	182	2,550,000	5.010%	5.073%	0.9756	2,487,852	5.010%	5.073%	0.9756	2,487,852	(121)	(121)
2	1-Jan-X3	366	52,550,000	10.010%	10.261%	0.9067	47,647,108	10.138%	10.395%	0.9056	47,588,921	(4,542)	203
2	1-Jan-X3	366	55,100,000	10.010%	10.261%	0.9067	49,959,194	10.138%	10.395%	0.9056	49,898,183	(4,762)	
2	1-Jan-X3	366	(110,000,000)	10.010%	10.261%	0.9067	(99,737,047)	10.138%	10.395%	0.9056	(99,615,248)	9,508	
						Total	357,106				359,708		82

Exhibit 33.3—continued

TABLE 3

Portfolio Sensitivity to Yield Curve Changes—Steeper Yield Curve

Period	Date	No of Days to Settlement	Cash Flow Amount ($)	Discount Rate (% S/A)	Discount Rate (% A)	Par Rates Discount Factor	Present Value ($)	Zero Coupon Rates Discount Rate (% S)	Discount Rate (% A)	Discount Factor	Present Value ($)	PVBP ($)	Change in PVBP ($)
0	1-Jan-X2												
1	1-Jul-X2	182	2,550,000	5.000%	5.062%	0.9757	2,487,973	5.000%	5.062%	0.9757	2,487,973	0	0
2	1-Jan-X3	366	52,550,000	10.010%	10.261%	0.9067	47,647,108	10.138%	10.395%	0.9056	47,588,921	(4,542)	203
2	1-Jan-X3	366	55,100,000	10.010%	10.261%	0.9067	49,959,194	10.138%	10.395%	0.9056	49,898,183	(4,762)	
2	1-Jan-X3	366	(110,000,000)	10.010%	10.261%	0.9067	(99,737,047)	10.138%	10.395%	0.9056	(99,615,248)	9,508	
						Total	357,227				359,829		203

TABLE 4

Portfolio Sensitivity to Yield Curve Changes—Flatter Yield Curve

Period	Date	No of Days to Settlement	Cash Flow Amount ($)	Discount Rate (% S/A)	Discount Rate (% A)	Par Rates Discount Factor	Present Value ($)	Zero Coupon Rates Discount Rate (% S)	Discount Rate (% A)	Discount Factor	Present Value ($)	PVBP ($)	Change in PVBP ($)
0	1-Jan-X2												
1	1-Jul-X2	182	2,550,000	5.010%	5.073%	0.9756	2,487,852	5.010%	5.073%	0.9756	2,487,852	(121)	(121)
2	1-Jan-X3	366	52,550,000	10.000%	10.250%	0.9068	47,651,658	10.128%	10.384%	0.9057	47,593,463	0	0
2	1-Jan-X3	366	55,100,000	10.000%	10.250%	0.9068	49,963,965	10.128%	10.384%	0.9057	49,902,946	0	
2	1-Jan-X3	366	(110,000,000)	10.000%	10.250%	0.9068	(99,746,572)	10.128%	10.384%	0.9057	(99,624,755)	0	
						Total	356,903				359,505		(121)

Exhibit 33.3—continued

TABLE 5

Portfolio Theta

Period	Date	No of Days to Settlement	Cash Flow Amount ($)	Discount Rate (% S/A)	Discount Rate (% A)	Par Rates Discount Factor	Present Value ($)	Discount Rate (% S)	Zero Coupon Rates Discount Rate (% A)	Discount Factor	Present Value ($)	PVBP ($)	Change in PVBP ($)	Changes in Deltas PVBP ($)
0	2-Jan-X2													
1	1-Jul-X3	181	2,550,000	5.000%	5.062%	0.9758	2,488,310	5.000%	5.062%	0.9758	2,488,310	337	337	458
2	1-Jan-X3	365	52,550,000	10.000%	10.250%	0.9070	47,664,399	10.128%	10.384%	0.9059	47,606,347	12,884	(576)	−779
2	1-Jan-X3	365	55,100,000	10.000%	10.250%	0.9070	49,977,324	10.128%	10.384%	0.9059	49,916,455	13,510		
2	1-Jan-X3	365	(110,000,000)	10.000%	10.250%	0.9070	(99,773,243)	10.128%	10.384%	0.9059	(99,651,725)	(26,970)		
						Total	356,791				359,387		(240)	(322)

Exhibit 33.3—continued

GRAPH 1: PORTFOLIO DELTAS

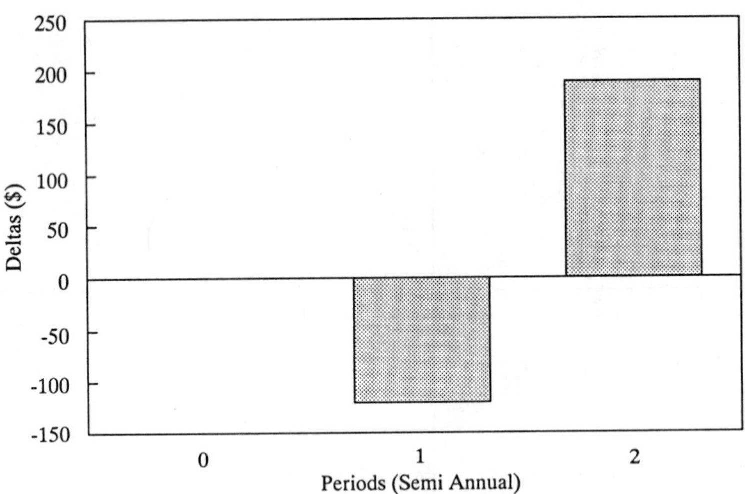

GRAPH 2: PORTFOLIO DELTAS

Yield Curve Steeper

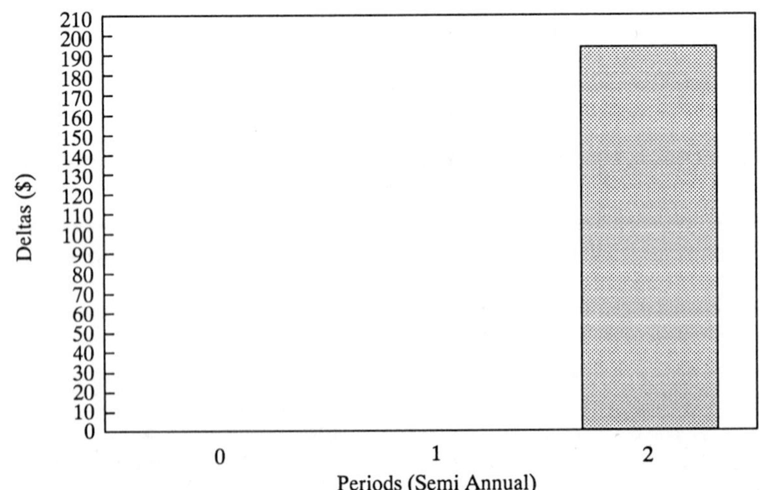

Exhibit 33.3—continued

GRAPH 3: PORTFOLIO DELTAS
Yield Curve Flatter

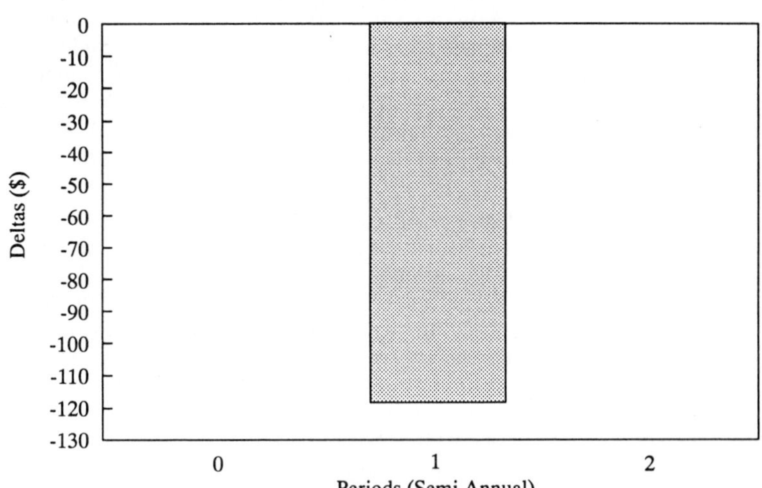

GRAPH 4: PORTFOLIO THETA
Impact of 1 Day

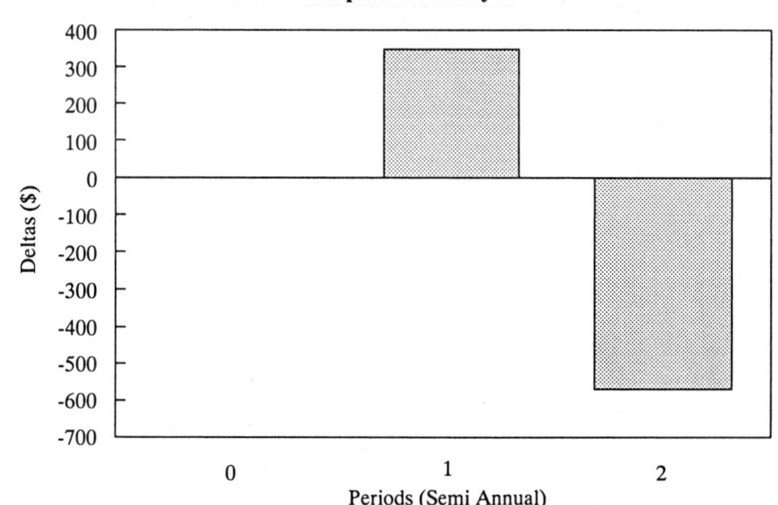

Hedging methodology

The basic hedging methodology implied by the generalised cash flow approach to swap portfolio management is that the portfolio risk as measured by its global delta and theta are sought to be offset by the purchasing or selling of portfolios of instruments with equal but exactly opposite deltas and thetas. This overall dictate of risk management under this approach is not different to that applicable in respect of either the basic hedging approach or duration-based portfolio approaches. However, an interesting feature of the generalised cash flow approach is its capacity to incorporate a regression-based minimum variance hedging methodology designed to overcome some of the difficulties of hedging swap portfolios encountered under those approaches.

The approach to global delta measurement effectively, as noted previously, provides a detailed mechanism to hedging the overall swap portfolio. As the present value of the existing swap portfolio depends on the interest rates defined in the swap yield curve as identified, a perfect hedge of a portfolio, devoid of basis or yield curve risk, can be constructed by holding a mixture of instruments with different maturities. In essence, the hedge is constructed by utilising instruments which are valued off an *identical* set of interest rates as the portfolio itself. Under this approach, the swap portfolio manager trades in a wide variety of instruments to create a relatively risk free hedge to immunise the portfolios risk characteristics.

Major difficulties with this approach include:

- high transaction costs as a wide variety of instruments need to be traded;
- such an approach also utilises significant balance sheet capacity;
- in practice, these problems can be overcome to an extent by the approach, described above, of partitioning the yield curve into bands and trading in selected instruments to provide the required hedging with lower transaction costs but minimal loss of hedge efficiency.

In practice, risk managers minimise the number of hedging instruments utilised and, for balance sheet utilisation reasons, prefer to utilise futures contracts on physical instruments. Where this approach is favoured, the generalised cash flow approach to portfolio management can be extended to encompass a regression based minimum variance hedging methodology. This methodology is quite similar to the covariance approach described above in the connection of duration based hedging approaches.

The problem of hedging, under these conditions, is the lack of perfect correlation (either positive or negative) between changes in the interest rate of the instruments being hedged and changes in the interest rate *of the hedging instrument.* Statistically, basis risk can be expressed as the absence of a perfect linear relationship between movements in interest rates as between different instruments. This deficiency can be overcome by determining correlations between each of the individual interest rates in the swap yield curve and the hedging instruments that are to be utilised. The objective is to exploit the degree of correlation that exists to derive the correct number of hedging contracts to maximise hedge efficiency and minimise basis risk.

This approach entails implementing the following steps:

- Historical data, preferably on a daily basis, on every rate utilised to value the swap portfolio is collected and organised into time series matrixes.
- Historical data, again on a daily basis on the relevant hedging instruments is also similarly collated into time series matrixes.

- Daily changes (that is, today's value minus yesterday's value) in each time series is determined.

Simple regressions for each of the variables constructed is performed. Regressions performed include simple single explanatory variable regressions but also possible combinations of two explanatory variable as well as multiple explanatory variable regressions. (Please note that there should be no constant term intercept in any of these regressions.)

The regressions performed have to be undertaken regularly. Some risk managers perform these regressions daily, reflecting the fact that one day's additional information has been added to the information set. This recomputation is designed to counter the fact that the relationships between the various rates is not characterised by stationarity, that is, the relationship varies. Frequent recomputation designed to re-estimate the relationships, whenever a new observation is available, is designed to counteract this problem of non stationarity. In practice, depending on the size of the time series, each additional day information will have minimal impact on regression results. Consequently, some portfolio managers perform these recomputations at less frequent intervals—say, monthly or weekly.

The technique outlined above allows construction of several linear basis relationships relating changes in the value of the hedging instrument to changes in each of the rates to be hedged. The portfolio manager then reviews the model equation and, generally, selects the most highly correlated hedging instruments to hedge individual interest rates. The hedging coefficients implied are then utilised to determine the number of hedge instruments required to hedge identified risk positions.

This approach to hedge management has a number of advantages:

- The technology is extremely flexible as the portfolio manager can exercise his or her discretion in choosing both the most accurate and best correlated model equation to establish and maintain the hedge. A particular feature, in this context, is that the re-estimation of the relationships allows the portfolio manager to adopt the best hedging instrument *at any given point in time.*
- The portfolio manager can minimise transaction costs by choosing between hedge instruments with similar correlation properties but different transaction costs and balance sheet utilisation considerations.
- This hedging approach is perfectly consistent with the overall objective of managing the total risk profile of the swap portfolio at *the margin* with hedges being constructed, on the basis at the highest degree of efficiency available to manage the residual risk of the portfolio.

A most useful feature of the regression-based hedging methodology is that, in practice, it provides a consistent and accurate method for pricing *new* transactions off the cost of the hedge. Based on available hedging coefficients, swap rates can be predicted to relatively high degrees of tolerance. In fact, this is a useful check upon and affirmation of the basic methodology as it allows frequent recalibration of the basic methodology.

The major difficulty with this particular technology is that relationships that exist between various interest rates are not stable over time. However, the linear relationships derived by the regression procedure have a certain minimum residual variance property, that is, tomorrow's relationships are accurately reflected in the sample over which the regressions have been computed (a necessary assumption common to most statistical analysis). Using any other set of coefficients would add more variability to the value of the combined position than the minimum variance technique outlined. In practice, hedge managers will typically "trade" the hedge by maintaining delta neutrality taking positions in respect of anticipated movements in the hedging coefficients. However, in effect, a strength of the generalised cash flow approach is that such a positioning approach to hedge management is not precluded and, moreover, the availability of model implied hedging coefficients allows quantification of the degree of additional risk assumed in trading the hedge.

RISK MANAGEMENT APPROACHES—ASSESSMENT

The three methods of managing swap portfolios identified (the basic hedging approach, the duration-based hedging approach and the generalised cash flow approach) have significant differences and correspondingly different advantages and disadvantages.

The basic hedging approach requires close matching of the offsetting swaps in terms of maturity, interest rate levels (after adjustment for hedge profits and losses) as well as notional principal amounts. Originally, basic hedging approaches were based on the par yield valuation methodology. However, the problems implicitly in utilising par yields can and have, more recently, been overcome by utilising a zero coupon valuation methodology.

The advantage of the basic hedging approach is that it is relatively low risk. Individual swaps can be identified and profitability can be determined for each transaction as basically the swap cash flows and the hedge flows are capable of being determined objectively. The main disadvantage with the basic hedging approach is its relative inflexibility making it difficult to undertake non-generic swaps.

The basic hedging approach is particularly relevant and useful in the context of transactions which are booked by swap market makers on an assignment basis. Under these transactions, the positioning intermediary would commit to one part of the swap with the intention of assigning the swap to the eventual counterparty when this counterparty was located. In the interim pre-closeout period, the intermediary would maintain an individual hedge which would be unwound at the time of the assignment. Consequently, the hedging approach is likely to continue to exist and find favour with institutions who prefer to operate on an assignment basis.

The duration-based portfolio hedging approach has the advantage that it is predicated on a pure cash flow approach and is based on theoretically sounder precepts such as zero coupon discount rates and on duration as a measure of interest rate risk.

The major advantages of the duration-based portfolio approach is that it gives the swap market maker the flexibility in taking on non-generic swap structures. This reflects the fact that the portfolio-based approach does not focus on a set of individual cash flows, focusing rather than on a stream of cash flows which means that each new cash flow booked in the swap portfolio can be aggregated with other swap flows and the residual risk managed. This means that the swap market maker is not concerned about matching equal, but opposite, partners on both sides of the swap transaction thereby allowing it to incur greater mismatches and to manage the risks encountered in terms of these mismatches.

Duration-based hedging approaches also have the advantage of improving risk management practices and minimising transaction costs through the practice of hedging marginal risk positions only. However, the improvement in management of portfolio risk is achieved only at the expense of assuming the risk of the assumptions underlying duration itself as a measure of interest rate risk.

The advantages of added flexibility and (potentially) improved risk management must be considered against the fact that the profitability of individual transactions under a portfolio approach is considerably more difficult to establish. Profitability can only be meaningfully calculated on the basis of overall portfolio performance rather than for individual components of the portfolio.

The generalised cash flow approach, which combines some elements of the duration based approach with pure statistically based risk management techniques, shares some of the same advantages and disadvantages as the duration based hedging approach.

A major advantage of the generalised cash flow approach is its flexibility. In addition, it allows hedging to be undertaken within a unified risk management framework and facilitates continuous dynamic hedging of portfolio risk.

A common criticism of the generalised cash flow approach is the entailed assumption of higher levels of basis risk over other techniques for portfolio management. In reality this is not correct. All techniques of hedging essentially require, as previously noted, substitution of outright risk to movements in financial market variables for basis risk.

While the generalised cash flow approach relies on the assumption that the experience of the recent past is a reasonable basis for predicting future relationships between interest rates, a similar problem exists in relation to other hedging techniques. For example, duration-based measures of interest rate risk only hold for small movements in interest rates. Similarly, where basic hedging approaches are utilised, portfolio risk is matched by purchasing or selling relevant hedge instruments with the amount of the hedge being determined based on a hedge ratio calculated by equating the present value of basis point movements in the portfolio and the hedge instrument. This approach basically assumes that the present value of basis points of the two instruments move identically which, in practice, is only infrequently the case.

In addition, the generalised cash flow approach has a significant advantage in that it is based on modelling involving estimation of the relationship between multiple time series of financial market variables. This is in marked contrast to most available hedging techniques which typically concentrate on a single time series. The difference in approach is, from a statistical view point, the substitution of multivariate time series analysis for univariate time series analysis.

The problems of determination of individual versus aggregate profitability also exists in the case of generalised cash flow approaches.

A significant feature of both duration-based hedge approaches and generalised cash flow approaches is that they tend to show a significantly different perspective of risk and profitability relative to that measured by the normal financial accounting process for the portfolio. An advantage in this regard is that it enables the sensitivity of the portfolio to be tested to changes in pricing and portfolio structure. Another important advantage is that assumptions about reinvestment rates are eliminated as under these approaches the discount rates used for present valuing of all cash flows are based on zero coupon rates for single period cash flows. However, the potential impact of relatively small changes in discount rates on overall portfolio value as well as the difficulty estimating the profitability or otherwise of individual transactions once undertaken is, to some extent, problematic.

The altered perception of swap portfolio profitability and, consequently, measurement of portfolio earnings requires additional comment. Performance measurement in this context can be defined as the decomposition of total portfolio returns over a given period of time into components of the return. Traditionally, the basic concept underlying measurement of swap earnings has been traditional accounting accrual concepts. This would entail accruing fixed and floating components of swap transactions and bringing earnings to account within an accrual accounting framework. However, duration based hedging approaches and generalised cash flow approaches to swap portfolio management effectively preclude application of such techniques for portfolio performance measurement and analysis.

Performance measurement under these approaches to swap portfolio management require a return over a given period to be defined as the net change in the present value in all portfolio assets and liabilities. This can be expressed as:

R(t1-t0) = [PV(At1) – PV(At0)] – [PV(Lt1) – PV(Lt0)] where:

R(t1-t0) = return over period from time t0 to t1;

PV(At1) = present value of all portfolio assets at time t1;

PV(At0) = present value of all portfolio assets at time t0;

PV(Lt1) = present value of all portfolio liabilities at time t1;

PV(Lt0) = present value of all portfolio liabilities at time t0.

An example of utilising this type of present valuing concept to measure portfolio earnings is set out in *Exhibit 33.4*. To a large extent, performance measurement techniques vary between portfolios reflecting the fact that institutions have developed a particular approach to performance measurement and attribution.

Exhibit 33.4

*Swap Portfolio Earnings and Performance Measurement**

1. *Swap portfolio earnings measurement*

The return on a swap portfolio over a given period can be stated as follows:

R(t1-t0) = [PV(At1) – PV(At0)] – [PV(Lt1) – PV(Lt0)]

where

R(t1-t0) = return over period from time t0 to t1

PV(At1) = present value of all portfolio assets at time t1

PV(At0) = present value of all portfolio assets at time t0

PV(Lt1) = present value of all portfolio liabilities at time t1

PV(Lt0) = present value of all portfolio liabilities at time t0

The practical implementation of this technique is set out in the examples below.

2. *Example 1—matched interest rate swaps*

Assume a portfolio of two matched interest rate swaps as follows:

(1) US$1,000,000 principal one year receive fixed at 10.00% pa S/A and pays US$ six month LIBOR.

(2) US$1,000,000 principal one year pay fixed at 9.00% pa S/A and receive US$ six month LIBOR.

The portfolio cash flows are summarised below:

Exhibit 33.4—continued

Swap 1 Receive Fixed/Pay Floating				**Swap 2 Pay Fixed/Receive Floating**		
Principal 1,000,000				Principal 1,000,000		
		Cash Flows			Cash Flows	
		Fixed	Floating		Fixed	Floating
	Rate	10.0000%	5.0000%	Rate	9.0000%	5.0000%
Day						
0		0.00	0.00		0.00	0.00
183		50,136.99	(25,416.67)		(45,123.29)	25,416.67
365		49,863.01			(44,876.71)	

In order to estimate the portfolio earnings over a period of seven days, the portfolio value is measured as at T0 and T7 in *Table 1* (see p 1047).

The return on the portfolio is $17.04. The return is attributable to a favourable change in value in the portfolio fixed payments which the floating rate payments did not contribute to portfolio earnings.

3. *Example 2—unmatched interest rate swap with portfolio hedges*

Assume the following variation on the above portfolio:

- Swap 1 is entered into at T0. It is hedged with the short sale of $1,000,000 of 9.00% coupon one year bonds, the proceeds of which are invested at 4.50% pa on an overnight basis.
- Swap 2 is dealt at T7 but for a notional principal of $500,000. As rates have moved down, the fixed rate payable on the swap is now 8.00% pa S/A and the first six month LIBOR set is 4.50%.
- 50% of the hedge is closed at a yield of 8% pa. The hedge results in a loss of $4,715.24 which must now be funded. The hedge loss is amortised over one year at 8.00% pa or two payments of $2,445.15.
- The remaining 50% of the hedge is assumed to be maintained.

* This exhibit draws heavily on William P Lawton, "Swap Portfolio Attribution and Analysis" in Boris Antl (ed) (June, 1988).

The portfolio cash flows are summarised below:

Swap 1 Receive Fixed/Pay Floating				**Swap 2 Pay Fixed/Receive Floating**		
Principal 1,000,000				Principal 500,000		
		Cash Flows			Cash Flows	
		Fixed	Floating		Fixed	Floating
	Rate	10.0000%	5.0000%	Rate	8.0000%	4.5000%
Day						
0		0.00	0.00			
7					0.00	0.00
14						
183		50,136.99	(25,416.67)			
190					(20,054.79)	11,437.50
365		49,863.01				
372					(19,945.21)	

		Hedge 1	**Closed**			**Hedge 2**	**Open**
		Cash Flows				Cash Flows	
		Fixed	Floating	Hedge		Fixed	Floating
Day	Rate	9.0000%	4.5000%	Gain (Loss)	Rate	9.0000%	4.5000%
0		(500,000.00)	500,000.00			(500,000.00)	500,000.00
7		(863.01)	431.51	(4,611.78)			
14							
183						(22,561.64)	11,280.82
190							
365						(22,438.36)	11,219.18
372						(863.01)	431.51

Exhibit 33.4—continued

In order to estimate the portfolio earnings over a period of seven days (between T7 and T14), the portfolio value is measured as at T7 and T14 (see *Tables 2* and *3*, pp 1048, 1049).

The return to the portfolio is $30.62. The return is attributable to positive changes in the fixed rate portfolio and negative change in the values of the floating rate and hedge portfolio. Please note the adjustment made for the cash flow settlement (on the hedge portfolio) as at T7.

4. *Currency swap*

The technique for measuring earnings on a currency swap portfolio are very similar. The major additional factor is the exchange rates (spot and the relevant forward rates) which must be utilised to convert foreign currency cash flows into the relevant bank currencies. Similarly, two different yield curves must be utilised.

As will be evident from a review of the basic approach, the passage of time and the addition of transactions to the portfolio increasingly complicates the problem of obtaining an accurate present value estimate of portfolio earnings and detailed analysis of changes in portfolio value are made more difficult. This difficulty is further complicated as additional instruments are encompassed by the portfolio.

The development of improved performance measurement and attribution techniques is likely to occur as increased focus is directed at the profitability and analysis of earnings from swap and derivative portfolios.

Exhibit 33.4—continued

TABLE 1

Matched Interest Rate Swaps

Portfolio Valuation—Time T0

Day	Discount Rate	Discount Factor	Fixed Payments Receipts	Fixed Payments Payments	Fixed Payments Net	Fixed Payments Present Value	Floating Payments Receipts	Floating Payments Payments	Floating Payments Net	Floating Payments Present Value
0			0.00	0.00	0.00	0.00	0.00	0.00	0.00	0.00
183	10.0000%	0.9533	50,136.99	(45,123.29)	5,013.70	4,779.75	25,416.67	(25,416.67)	0.00	0.00
365	10.0000%	0.9091	49,863.01	(44,876.71)	4,986.30	4,533.00	0.00	0.00	0.00	0.00
					Total	9,312.75			Total	0.00

Portfolio Valuation—Time T7

Day	Discount Rate	Discount Factor	Fixed Payments Receipts	Fixed Payments Payments	Fixed Payments Net	Fixed Payments Present Value	Floating Payments Receipts	Floating Payments Payments	Floating Payments Net	Floating Payments Present Value
7			0.00	0.00	0.00	0.00	0.00	0.00	0.00	0.00
183	10.0000%	0.9551	50,136.99	(45,123.29)	5,013.70	4,788.49	25,416.67	(25,416.67)	0.00	0.00
365	10.0000%	0.9108	49,863.01	(44,876.71)	4,986.30	4,541.29	0.00	0.00	0.00	0.00
					Total	9,329.79			Total	0.00

Portfolio earnings—Period T0 to T7

Net Change in Portfolio Values	
Fixed Payments	17.04
Floating Payments	0.00
Total	17.04

Exhibit 33.4—continued

TABLE 2

Unmatched Interest Rate Swaps

Portfolio Valuation—Time T7

Day	Discount Rate	Discount Factor	Fixed Payments Receipts	Fixed Payments Payments	Fixed Payments Net	Fixed Payments Present Value	Floating Payments Receipts	Floating Payments Payments	Floating Payments Net	Floating Payments Present Value
7	10.0000%	1.0000	0.00	0.00	0.00	0.00	0.00	0.00	0.00	0.00
14	10.0000%	0.9982	0.00	0.00	0.00	0.00	0.00	0.00	0.00	0.00
183	10.0000%	0.9551	50,136.99	0.00	50,136.99	47,884.95	0.00	(25,416.67)	(25,416.67)	(24,275.01)
190	10.0000%	0.9533	0.00	(20,054.79)	(20,054.79)	(19,119.00)	11,437.50	0.00	11,437.50	10,903.80
365	10.0000%	0.9108	49,863.01	0.00	49,863.01	45,412.95	0.00	0.00	0.00	0.00
372	10.0000%	0.9091	0.00	(19,945.21)	(19,945.21)	(18,132.00)			0.00	0.00
					Total	56,046.89			Total	(13,371.20)

Day	Discount Rate	Discount Factor	Hedge Cash Flows Receipts	Payments	Hedge Gains (Losses)	Net	Present Value
7	10.0000%	1.0000	(863.01)	431.51		(431.51)	(431.51)
14	10.0000%	0.9982	0.00	0.00		0.00	0.00
183	10.0000%	0.9551	(22,561.64)	11,280.82		(11,280.82)	(10,774.11)
190	10.0000%	0.9533	0.00	0.00	(2,445.15)	(2,445.15)	(2,331.05)
365	10.0000%	0.9108	(22,438.36)	11,219.18		(11,219.18)	(10,217.91)
372	10.0000%	0.9091	(863.01)	431.51	(2,445.15)	(2,876.66)	(2,615.14)
						Total	(26,369.73)

Portfolio Values at T7

Fixed Payments	56,046.89
Floating Payments	(13,371.20)
Hedge Portfolio (Incl Net Settlements at T7)	(25,938.22)
Total	16,737.46

Exhibit 33.4—continued

TABLE 3

Unmatched Interest Rate Swaps

Portfolio Valuation—Time T14

Day	Discount Rate	Discount Factor	Fixed Payments: Receipts	Fixed Payments: Payments	Fixed Payments: Net	Fixed Payments: Present Value	Floating Payments: Receipts	Floating Payments: Payments	Floating Payments: Net	Floating Payments: Present Value
14	10.0000%	1.0000	0.00	0.00	0.00	0.00	0.00	0.00	0.00	0.00
183	10.0000%	0.9568	50,136.99	0.00	50,136.99	47,972.55	0.00	(25,416.67)	(25,416.67)	(24,319.42)
190	10.0000%	0.9551	0.00	(20,054.79)	(20,054.79)	(19,153.98)	11,437.50	0.00	11,437.50	10,923.75
365	10.0000%	0.9124	49,863.01	0.00	49,863.01	45,496.03	0.00	0.00	0.00	0.00
372	10.0000%	0.9108	0.00	(19,945.21)	(19,945.21)	(18,165.18)	0.00	0.00	0.00	0.00
					Total	56,149.43			Total	(13,395.67)

Day	Discount Rate	Discount Factor	Hedge Cash Flows: Receipts	Payments	Hedge Gains (Losses)	Net	Present Value
14	10.0000%	1.0000	0.00	0.00		0.00	0.00
183	10.0000%	0.9568	(22,561.64)	11,280.82		(11,280.82)	(10,793.82)
190	10.0000%	0.9551	0.00	0.00	(2,445.15)	(2,445.15)	(2,335.32)
365	10.0000%	0.9124	(22,438.36)	11,219.18		(11,219.18)	(10,236.61)
372	10.0000%	0.9108	(863.01)	431.51	(2,445.15)	(2,876.66)	(2,619.93)
						Total	(25,985.68)

Portfolio Values at T14		**Net Change in Portfolio Values**	
Fixed Payments	56,149.43	Fixed Payments	102.54
Floating Payments	(13,395.67)	Floating Payments	(24.46)
Hedge Portfolio	(25,985.68)	Hedge Portfolio	(47.45)
Total	16,768.08	Total	30.62

APPENDIX A

VALUATION OF SWAP PORTFOLIO FOR THE PURPOSE OF PURCHASE[1]

Background

An increased feature of the global swap market is the reassessment of individual institutions' participation in swap and derivative activities. Increasingly, a number of institutions are reassessing their position in the swap and derivative market and, consequent upon this reassessment, reducing their involvement in swap and derivative activities generally or in particular sectors of this market.

Where an institution decides to exit a particular segment or all of its swap and derivative activities, it has two alternatives:

- Under the first alternative, new business in the relevant products is not transacted, but the existing portfolio continues to be maintained and managed to realise its value.
- The second approach entails sale of the entire portfolio or the relevant part thereof to other swap or derivative market participants to realise its value.

While both techniques coexist increasingly for the reasons identified below, sales of portfolios of swap and derivative products have become more prevalent.

The practice of sale and corresponding purchase of swap and derivative portfolio creates specific valuation problems. While the general principles determining valuation of swap transactions and portfolios of products are consistent with that described elsewhere, a number of additional factors are relevant and are considered in this Appendix.

Advantage of portfolio sales

The major impetus for disposing of swap and derivative portfolios as a set of continuing obligations is the potential benefits to both the seller and purchaser.

From the seller's perspective, the sale of the portfolio can reduce ongoing costs of running down the portfolio. These ongoing costs include costs of maintaining the book, as well as costs of systems, settlement and administration. Given that a given portfolio can have transactions in it with remaining maturities of (up to) ten years, these ongoing costs are not insignificant. Major problems in terms of ongoing cost where a portfolio is to be "run down" is the fixed nature of a variety of costs and the loss of economies of scale and scope as the portfolio contracts in size.

A related problem is that of managing the ongoing market risk of the portfolio. As noted previously, all swap portfolios have ongoing risk dimensions which require management. Where the portfolio is to be maintained, a significant problem that often emerges is that portfolio value may be difficult to preserve without the capacity to add transactions to the existing portfolios of transactions. In this connection, the portfolio may require high levels of hedging to allow the existing value of the portfolio to be preserved.

A significant additional factor requiring consideration is the ongoing credit risk of the portfolio. Where the portfolio is sold, the swaps are typically novated to the purchaser. Hence, all ongoing credit risk on swap counterparties is assumed by the

1. This appendix is based on Malcolm Coleman, "Purchasing an Interest Rate Portfolio" in Satyajit Das (1991).

purchaser. Where the portfolio is to be maintained and run down, the credit risk of the portfolio continues to be assumed by the original counterparty requiring commitment of capital to the transactions.

A significant but intangible and, by implication, unquantifiable difficulty with running down a swap portfolio is the difficulty of attracting and maintaining quality staff to undertake such activities.

These difficulties typically lead most institutions seeking to exit their swap or derivative businesses, in part or in its entirety, to decide on a sale of the portfolio to realise a sum certain equal to, at least, an approximation of the present value of the portfolio.

From the perspective of the purchaser, in addition to the commercial or economic value, being the potential income stream from the portfolio, purchase may enable a growing swap operation to rapidly expand its portfolio, gaining market share and achieving the benefits of developing the appropriate critical mass with its concomitant advantages of greater efficiency in pricing and hedging.

This potential advantage of achieving critical mass through purchase can, on occasion, dictate that an entrant to a particular market segment will pay a higher price for the swap portfolio compared to the intrinsic value of the portfolio as well as that would be paid by other potential buyers.

Purchasers of portfolios may also allow a purchaser to gain exposure to a client base which is significantly different to its existing market position allowing further development of the purchaser's swap and derivatives business.

Valuation issues

The valuation of a swap portfolio from the perspective of purchase entails two distinct steps:

- the valuation of the present value of the swap cash flows (and hedging instruments) within the portfolio;
- the value placed on the portfolio based on the purchaser's estimation of the risks of the portfolio including, credit risk, market risk and the ongoing cost of running the portfolio.

The first phase of valuation is relatively straightforward. In effect, the "mark-to-market" value of the portfolio is determined. The valuation is undertaken on a portfolio basis with portfolio cash flows being revalued at the mid price (between the bid and offer) on the swap yield curve.

Major causes of discrepancy in valuation between sellers and buyers as well as different purchasers include:

- disagreements about the actual swap curve to be used for revaluation;
- differences, which in practice can be quite significant, in discounting future cash flows within the portfolio.

In estimating the value of the portfolios, all hedges maintained in the portfolio (such as physical securities as well as futures contracts) have to be valued. Hedges within the portfolio are usually valued at the normal liquidation value of the instruments at a given point in time.

In practice, portfolios are typically purchased inclusive of the hedges. The main benefit is that outright risk is minimised during the purchase and sale process. In practice, once the transaction is agreed and completed, the portfolio is incorporated with the purchaser is existing portfolio and the hedges rebalanced. At that time, the hedge portfolio, including the hedges purchased, are adjusted.

An issue which is often debated in the context of valuation of the hedge portfolio is the appropriateness of pricing hedge instruments at the mid rate as this valuation favours the seller. In practice, if the purchaser wished to purchase the portfolio *without the hedges*, the seller would be forced to liquidate the hedge portfolio at the bid or offer side of the market (as appropriate). This potential benefit to the seller must be weighed against the risk assumed in the process of completing the purchase and sale transaction.

The overall value of the portfolio as determined must then be adjusted for the market risk and credit risk of the portfolio. The adjustment for market risk is necessarily intensely subjective. A part of the assessment of the portfolio risk would be to seek to analyse the marginal impact of incorporating the purchased portfolio into the purchaser's existing portfolio and its impact on risk and earnings.

The adjustment for credit risk can also, in practice, be extremely complex. The purchaser will generally classify the swap counterparties into two classes;

- acceptable credit risks;
- unacceptable credit risks.

Acceptable credit risks do not represent any problem and specific swap contracts are novated as described below.

Where a swap counterparty's credit risk is considered unacceptable, the purchaser will pursue one or other of the following courses of actions:

- Seek a credit counter indemnity from the seller (if it is of an acceptable credit standing) in respect of unacceptable counterparties.
- Seek some form of credit enhancement in respect of the specific counterparty, through third party guarantees, letters of credit or collateralisation provisions (see discussion in Chapter 37).
- Agree with the seller that the contract with the unacceptable counterparties be terminated with resulting cash payments or receipts reflecting the market value of the transaction. This can be undertaken prior to the sale or immediately after sale. In the latter case, agreement from the counterparty is usually sought before the purchase is consummated.

Attempts to deal with unacceptable counterparty credit exposure by pricing for this risk is rare. This reflects the difficulty of determining an appropriate price adjustment for the added credit risk.

Adjustments for ongoing maintenance costs are also extremely subjective. In reality, given that one of the motivating factors for purchase of such product portfolios is the economies of scale and scope, subjective estimates must be made of the ongoing cost of management and present value of these expenses deducted from the portfolio's pure economic value. Added costs are particularly significant where the portfolio being purchased entails currencies or geographical locations not currently serviced by the purchaser.

The adjustments for market and credit risk as well as ongoing costs are, generally, built into the premium or discount relative to the pure economic value of the portfolio. This premium and discount can, in practice, vary quite significantly between institutions.

Mechanical issues

A number of mechanical issues in relation to the purchase and sale of swap and derivative portfolios require consideration. These include:

- documentation issues;
- negotiating points;
- process and timing factors.

The sale of swap and derivative portfolios are usually structured as a novation of existing contracts from the seller to the purchaser whereby the old contract between the counterparty and the seller is terminated and a new contract between the counterparty and the purchaser created.

The purchaser effectively inherits any defects in the documentation necessitating detailed and thorough review of all swap and derivative documentation. This may necessitate, in certain cases, implementing new revised documentation with the existing counterparty, which must be agreed to between the potential purchaser and the counterparty prior to transaction being completed. The use of standard contracts, such as the ISDA Master Swap Agreement, is helpful in that where such contracts are utilised, there is a greater degree of documentary consistency and greatly reduces the time frame needed to review the seller's swap documentation.

Sellers typically are required to give a number of warranties regarding the swap and derivative portfolio including:

- the accuracy of all swap transactions as disclosed to the purchaser;
- that no events of default on any swap or derivative transaction within the portfolio has occurred;
- that no swaps have been amended.

Purchasers will also insist that the seller agree to assist in the event that there is a dispute regarding a specific transaction with a counterparty.

The seller and purchaser will usually agree on an adjustment to the swap price in the event that a counterparty specifically refuses to novate its contract. In this regard, there are two possible approaches. Under the first approach, all counterparties are approached prior to the transaction being completed requesting their agreement. This approach entails entering into heads of agreement followed by period in which appropriate consents are sought with the sale being completed upon receipt of appropriate consents. Alternatively, the transaction can be closed with novations with the counterparty to be concluded subsequently with agreement between the parties regarding adjustment to the sale price based on pre-agreed criteria in the event that counterparties refuse to undertake the novation.

The negotiation of the sale or purchase of swap and derivatives portfolio is complex. Typically, where an institution decides to sell all or part of its swap and derivatives portfolio, it will seek to negotiate with interested purchasers on either a bilateral or, increasingly, through a tender process. Where the institution itself is not experienced in the swap and derivative markets, it may retain the services of a financial institution with established expertise in swap and derivative products to assist in the process of sale. The advising institution should be precluded from bidding from the portfolio to avoid conflicts of interest.

Potential purchasers of a swap portfolio will typically include:

- institutions with strong relationships with the seller;
- institutions seeking to expand their swap and derivative portfolios in the relevant market sector;

- established institutions with significant market position in the relevant products and market who may benefit by purchasing a portfolio to reinforce dominant market positions.

Financial institutions with existing exposure to the market may also find a purchase an inexpensive mechanism for offsetting existing market exposures of positions.

Typically, a list of potential buyers is established. Bilateral negotiations are undertaken with potential purchasers. Tender documents are prepared and circulated to the potential purchasers. Information provided includes the relevant details of the portfolio including the hedging instruments maintained. Details about swap counterparties are not normally disclosed at this stage.

Potential purchasers are requested to submit their preliminary bids for the portfolio *as at a given point in time*. In seeking to maximise the benefit of the sale, sellers will typically focus on a number of factors:

- That the purchaser has an acceptable credit rating, strong systems and back-up and is regarded in the market place as a professional institution with a commitment to the particular product. The presence of a strong credit rating in particular, will assist in maximising the likelihood that existing swap counterparties will agree to novate existing agreements.
- Counterparty with whom the seller has a large number of existing transactions may be prepared to pay a premium as their credit exposure would be reduced as a result of the fact transactions within the portfolio are terminated through the process of purchase as it effectively would result in an unwinding of a portion of the combined swap portfolio.

Once indicative bids have been received for the portfolio, irrespective of whether a tender process or a bilateral negotiation approach has been adopted, the seller and potential purchaser would enter into series of negotiations. At this particular stage, the seller of the portfolio may provide details of swap counterparties in the portfolio to the potential purchaser to enable the evaluation of the credit risk of the counterparties to be undertaken following this round of negotiations.

Timing and process of the sale can be quite critical. Where the portfolio has substantive mismatches, purchasers may prefer to bid and receive information on the result of tendering process during market trading hours so that any appropriate hedging action can be implemented. Where a portfolio is relatively well matched and has minimal market risk positions, the transaction may be designed to be closed at the end of the business day. In the case of a purchase of a very large swap or derivative portfolio, the transaction may be completed as at close of business as at the end of the week to allow additional time to transfer transactions and to incorporate the portfolio into the purchaser's existing portfolio to allow the transfer to be effected rapidly.

Where significant discrepancies in portfolio valuation between the purchaser and the seller are identified a process of due diligence may be undertaken whereby the purchaser and the seller go through the portfolio and check each individual swap revaluation to reconcile the differences.

APPENDIX B

DURATION AND SWAP HEDGING TECHNOLOGY

Concept of duration

Duration

While term to maturity is widely utilised as a measure of the length or maturity of securities, it is a highly deficient measure in that it only indicates when the final payment falls due ignoring the time pattern of any payment received in the intermediate time span preceding the final payment. This deficiency of the concept of term to maturity can be overcome utilising the duration measure. Duration, as proposed in 1938 by Frederick R Macaulay, is the weighted average of the times in the future when interest and principal payments are to be received. Mathematically, duration can be measured as follows:

$$D = \frac{\sum_{t=1}^{n} \frac{C_t \times t}{(1+r)^t}}{\sum_{t=1}^{n} \frac{C_t}{(1+r)^t}}$$

where C_t = interest and/or principal payments at time t
t = length of time to the interest and/or principal payments
n = length of time to final maturity
r = yield to maturity.

For example, assume a four year bond with an 8.00% coupon rate and yielding 10.00% pa to maturity. Assume also that interest payments are received at the end of each of the four years and that the principal payment is received at the end of the fourth year. The duration of the bond would be:[1]

$$D = \frac{\frac{\$80(1)}{(1.10)} + \frac{\$80(2)}{(1.10)^2} + \frac{\$80(3)}{(1.10)^3} + \frac{\$1{,}080(4)}{(1.10)^4}}{\frac{\$80}{(1.10)} + \frac{\$80}{(1.10)^2} + \frac{\$80}{(1.10)^3} + \frac{\$1{,}080}{(1.10)^4}} = 3.56 \text{ years}$$

If the coupon rate were 4.00%, its duration would be:

$$D = \frac{\frac{\$40(1)}{(1.10)} + \frac{\$40(2)}{(1.10)^2} + \frac{\$40(3)}{(1.10)^3} + \frac{\$1{,}040(4)}{(1.10)^4}}{\frac{\$40}{(1.10)} + \frac{\$40}{(1.10)^2} + \frac{\$40}{(1.10)^3} + \frac{\$1{,}040}{(1.10)^4}} = 3.75 \text{ years}$$

1. The example is based on Van Horne (1984), pp 138, 139.

If the coupon rate were zero, however, duration would be:

$$D = \frac{\dfrac{\$1{,}000(4)}{(1.10)^4}}{\dfrac{\$1{,}000}{(1.10)^4}} = 4 \text{ years}$$

If there is only a single payment, duration must equal maturity. For bonds with interim coupon payments, however, duration is always less than maturity.

The relationship between duration, maturity and coupon is set out in the following table:

Duration (in years) for bonds yielding 8.00%[2]
(S/A coupons)

	Coupon rate			
Years to maturity	**2%**	**4%**	**6%**	**8%**
1	0.995	0.990	0.985	0.981
5	4.742	5.533	4.361	4.218
10	8.762	7.986	7.454	7.067
20	14.026	11.966	10.922	10.292
50	14.832	13.466	12.987	12.743
100	13.097	13.029	13.006	12.995
Perpetual	13.000	13.000	13.000	13.000

Typically, there is an inverse relationship between coupon and duration. High coupon bonds effectively have shorter durations than lower (or zero) coupon bonds of the same maturity. As the term to maturity extends, the disparity between duration and maturity for a given coupon also increases. Generally, duration falls when market yields rise because the present value of distant future payments falls relatively more than those closer to the present. As would be expected, when interest rates fall, duration rises for exactly the opposite reason.

Modified duration

Modified duration, which was independently developed by Hicks in 1939 without any reference to Macaulay duration, provides a particularly useful measure of the interest rate sensitivity or volatility of a given security. Mathematically, modified duration can be expressed as:

$$D_{mod} = \frac{D}{1 + y/f}$$

where D = Macaulay duration
y = yield to maturity (in decimal form)
f = frequency of cash flow payments per year
y/f = periodic yield (in decimal form).

For semi-annual coupon bonds, this formula becomes:

$$D_{mod} = \frac{D}{1 + y/2}$$

2. The source of the table is Lawrence Fisher and Roman L Weil (1971).

Modified duration can be used to estimate the percentage price volatility of a fixed income security. The relationship follows:

$$\frac{\Delta P}{P} \times 100 = -D_{mod} \times Y$$

Percentage price change = −modified duration × yield change (in absolute percentage points).

Qualifications to duration: single versus multiple factor duration

Given that duration can be utilised to measure the interest rate risk of a particular asset or liability, it would then appear possible to immunise against that interest rate risk by assuming an offsetting liability or asset with an equivalent duration. However, there are a number of qualifications to the duration measure which must be recognised in any such immunisation practice:

- Duration assumes a flat term structure of interest rates and parallel shifts of the yield curve.
- Regardless of the properties of the particular duration measure utilised, duration is a proxy for price risk only for relatively small changes in interest rates. Therefore, as market interest rates change, the duration of the relevant security also changes requiring adjustment of any offsetting hedge.

In the situation where the first assumption of flat term structure of interest rates and parallel shifts is violated, it would not be usually possible to effect immunisation of interest rate risk by simply holding an offsetting asset or liability with equivalent duration. In response to this qualification to the duration measure, a number of multiple factor duration models have been developed to provide a more complex mapping of the stochastic processes governing interest rate movements. For example, Schaefer (1984), has proposed a multi-factor duration model where duration is a measure of two factors, namely, the long-term interest rate and the short-term interest rate. This approach implicitly seeks to model changes in the yield curve shape and the resultant effect on the duration of the relevant security.

The difference between a single factor model and a two factor model is set out below:

Single factor model—level shift only

Movement in all intermediate and short rates = A × Movement in Long Rates + Error Term

Rates + Error Term

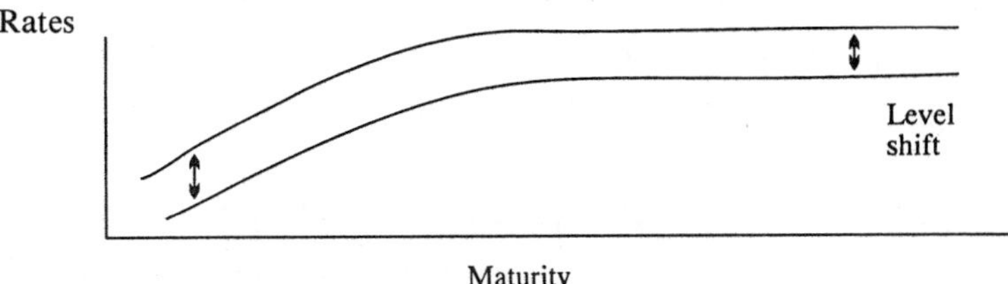

Two factor model—shift level + (yield curve change)

Movement in all intermediate and short rates = A × Movement in Long Rates + B × Movement in Spread + Error Term

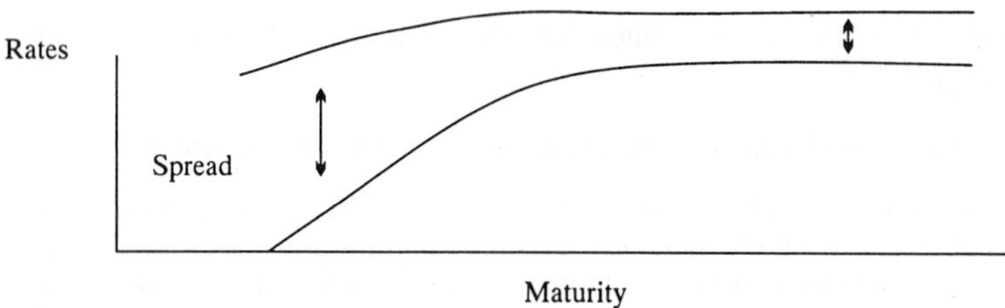

Duration and the zero coupon rate yield curve

It is clearly feasible in theory to calculate duration utilising either normal conventional par or coupon yields or zero coupon interest rates for pure discount securities. For example, the original Macaulay formulation rather than estimate interest rates for each future period and use them to discount the security payments to present value, for reasons of computational convenience, uses yield to maturity as the discount rate throughout. However, it is not reasonable to assume that yields to maturity on different assets or liabilities will always change by the same amount given that yields to maturity are complex averages of the underlying zero coupon yields. Consequently, in general a given shift in the zero coupon rate curve will result in the yields to maturity on different assets changing by different amounts.

To understand the interaction between duration and the zero coupon rate yield curve, it is necessary to define the following terms:

- zero coupon rate which is the rate of exchange between a cash flow now and a cash flow at a *single date in the future*, that is, the yield on a pure discount bond or zero coupon security;
- coupon or par yield to maturity which is the standard internal rate of return formula which discounts *all payments* on a *coupon* bond at the same rate.

The difference between the two interest rates lies in the fact that actual realised returns only equal the normal redemption par yield to maturity if reinvestment rates on intermediate cash flows, typically the coupon, are actually equal to the redemption yield. In practice, reinvestment rates on coupon cash flows will rarely equal the redemption yield as forward rates (see Chapter 10) are the only true measure of the reinvestment rates, and even then, the forward rates implicit in the yield curve at any point in time do not guarantee that these reinvestment rates are *actually achieved*. In contrast, determining present values using zero coupon rates, which are implicit in normal par redemption yields, do not involve any assumptions as to the reinvestment rate as no intermediate cash flows are involved.

The actual computation of the zero coupon rate yield curve is set out in Chapter 8.

Duration and swap hedging

The interest rate risk on the fixed rate component of the swap can be measured utilising duration. The duration of the fixed rate on a swap provides a measure of price volatility with respect to interest rate movements. It is feasible to hedge open interest rate or currency swap positions, at least the interest rate risk component, utilising duration as a measure of sensitivity of a position to movements in interest rates. Under this strategy, physical securities or futures contracts are held to offset potential changes in value on the swap position the level of hedge being determined by the duration factor. The basic duration hedging strategy is as follows:

Change in PV of Hedging Portfolio = – Change in PV of Swap Portfolio

Single factor model

Book value × adjusted duration	Must be equal for both portfolios

Two factor model

Book value × adjusted (long-term) duration	
and	Must be simultaneously equal for both portfolios
Book value × adjusted (short-term) duration	

The concept of duration-based swap hedging assumes that cash flows generated by the swaps booked by a financial institution form a portfolio of assets and liabilities which will vary with interest rates and with maturity. The use of duration-based hedging seeks to solve the problem of ensuring solvency, irrespective of interest rate movements, by matching the durations of the asset and liability cash flow streams. The underlying assumption is that irrespective of interest rate movements, and despite the fact that the cash flows are not perfectly matched, changes in values in the asset and liability portfolio would substantially offset each other.

The use of duration matching implicitly divides underlying market interest rate movements into two components:

- systematic movements whereby rates for all maturities move in some statistically determine constant proportion to one or two index rates, such as the long and short interest rates depending on whether single or multi-factor duration measures are utilised;
- non-systematic movements, which is the residual interest rate movement, unexplained by movements in the indexes utilised, and this is assumed to be randomly or normally distributed.

Duration matching only provides a formula to hedge away systematic market movements. Inefficiencies in hedge performance may result from the non-systematic risk component which cannot be effectively hedged under this approach.

Duration matching is utilised in preference to maturity matching because it is usually felt to reduce basis risk and to overcome imperfections in the hedge market, such as unavailability of securities of the appropriate maturity, as well as reducing the actual expense of hedging as, generally, significantly lower levels of hedges will need to be maintained.

The floating rate component of the swap is also capable of being hedged on a duration basis. It is possible to calculate the duration of a floating rate security. As a swap is essentially a combination of a long and short position in a fixed rate instrument and a floating rate instrument, the volatility or interest rate risk component of the total swap can be calculated as the net value of the different price risk of each component. This volatility can then be aggregated with the volatility of the portfolio to derive the total duration of the portfolio including the new swap.

The use of duration matching techniques in swap hedging requires some practical problems to be overcome. For example, to deal with the practical difficulties of matching durations and present values within a large portfolio, it is typically necessary to concentrate all cash flows to certain maturity points within the portfolio. For example, cash flows may be concentrated at monthly intervals over the life of outstanding transactions. Duration of the net cash flow at each allocation point for the portfolio can then be netted out against the present values for the hedge portfolio as a simple additive manipulation.

Although this type of cash flow concentration or allocation to particular maturity point greatly simplifies the management of risk, it is necessary to ensure that it allows sufficient precision of duration matching to eliminate the desired quantum of interest rate risk within the portfolio.

Chapter 34

Swap Portfolio Risk Management Techniques: Managing the Floating Rate Component of a Swap Portfolio[1]

INTRODUCTION

Swap portfolios are operated on the basis that the exposure underlying unmatched swaps is directly analogous to cash market positions, whereby transactions involving physical cash market instruments or financial futures on the relevant cash market instrument can be utilised to offset the market risk assumed until the swap is matched with an offsetting transaction.

Traditionally, in managing such portfolios, institutions have decoupled the management of the fixed rate payment flows from the floating rate payment flows under a swap transaction. This separation is predicated on the fact that, first, in general, these flows belong to different markets/market segments and must be managed separately, and secondly, differences in the perceived risk level of the different flows.

The initial assumption made by swap portfolio managers was that the longer maturity of the fixed rate flows made this aspect of the book more risky and, predictably, most research was directed to valuing the term cash flows and enhancing the methods available to hedge these risks. Management of the floating rate component of the swap portfolio attracted limited attention because of the implicit assumption that the floating rate resets periodically at the new market rate implying relative stability at or about par value, even where there are substantial movements in rates.

However, experience with the operation of swap portfolios has highlighted the fact that substantial mismatches on floating rate reset dates expose portfolios to the risk of large potential losses/gains. A particularly important feature of this risk aspect is that it is extremely volatile and dynamic. The fact that each transaction in the floating rate portfolio is reset at least six monthly coupled with the speed at which the short end of the yield curve can move and change shape exacerbates the risk profile. Management of the floating rate component of a swap portfolio under these circumstances becomes a daily positioning function with the objective of maximising the difference between cash receipts and cash payments on floating rate payments under transactions within the swap portfolio.

RISK COMPONENTS WITHIN THE FLOATING RATE PORTFOLIO

There are two basic categories of risk associated with floating rate swap portfolio:

- *Timing mismatches*

  This refers to the exposure resulting from differences in repricing dates; for example, a swap portfolio could be receiving/repricing three month LIBOR on 15 May 19X1 and paying/repricing three month LIBOR on 19 May 19X1.

1. This chapter is based substantially on Satyajit Das and Colin McKeith, "Managing the Floating Rate Component of a Swap Portfolio" in Satyajit Das (1991).

A swap portfolio always has a timing mismatch unless each floating rate swap payment within the portfolio is precisely matched by another floating rate swap payment under a different transaction, the second payment being exactly equal and opposite to the first. In order to provide an "exact" hedge, the second transaction must be the same as the first in the following respects:

— **Repricing date:** the transactions must reprice on the same day at the same time, utilising identical rate setting mechanisms (including the same side of the bid/offer spread).

— **Face value amounts:** the exact face value amounts must be equivalent.

— **Index/interest rate period:** the two transactions must reprice "off" the same index for the same interest rate period or frequency (that is, three or six months etc).

The maturity dates of the two transactions can vary. However, this creates an inherent problem within the portfolio because when one of the matching paired swaps terminates, a replacement swap will be required to be entered into in order to neutralise the floating rate exposure.

- *Index mismatches*

There are two levels of index mismatch:

— Receiving six monthly and paying three monthly will, of course, result in "mismatches" or portfolio "gaps" even if both fixed legs are completely matched. If the second three month rate set is hedged through a forward contract (like a futures or FRA contract), then the compounded cash flow payment on the six monthly date may vary significantly from the receipt under the six monthly reset.

In certain markets, the compounded three month rate plus the forward may consistently differ from the prevailing six month rate set. On large transaction, a 0.1 basis point per annum cost caused by a mismatch can be very expensive. As the only known cash flows are those that can be present valued now, there is no way to value these mismatches, at least exactly.

— Different indexes in the same currency will, of course, trade at *variable* margins relative to each other, that is, LIBOR vs Commercial Paper (CP). An added complication may be differences in the methods by which rates are calculated. CP swaps are generally quoted as an average of 30 day CP compounded each month and paid semi-annually. As most CP borrowers would issue 30 day CP on one day in each month there are potential discrepancies caused by yield curve moves between the average and the day they issue and re-price their CP borrowings.

The existence of these "mismatches" or "gaps" within the floating rate component of the swap portfolio exposes the portfolio to the risk of economic gain or loss from two sources:

- *Absolute rate changes*—for example, if the portfolio systematically reprices its receipts prior to payments, the portfolio will gain (lose) if interests fall (rise).
- *Yield curve shape changes*—for example, if the portfolio structure is such that the majority of receipts are priced off three month LIBOR while its payments are priced off six month LIBOR, the portfolio will gain (lose) under an inverse (positive) yield curve (provided certain conditions regarding movements in the absolute rate levels hold).

The nature of a typical floating rate portfolio is generally complex with a mixture of timing and index mismatches. Portfolios may not demonstrate a *systematic* pattern of risk. Under those circumstances, the exact impact of either an absolute rate or yield curve shape change may be difficult to separate.

The risk components inherent within the floating rate component of a swap portfolio are generated by a number of institutional and market factors:

- Customer demand for transaction structures.
- The institutional structure of the market which may dictate a particular pattern of transactional flow which creates these portfolio mismatches.
- The process of re-balancing hedges and the availability and the attendant cost of offsetting transactions may necessitate the absorption of some of these risks into the portfolio.
- The hedge efficiency between the fixed rate and the floating rate component of the swap portfolio must be balanced.

The last factor noted above is particularly interesting. Management of a swap portfolio necessitates a continual and dynamic series of choices whereby hedge efficiency in respect of the fixed rate component of the portfolio must be balanced continually against the risk profile of the floating rate component within the same portfolio. The portfolio manager is constantly confronted with the choice of reducing the exposure on one component of the portfolio at the risk of increasing the exposure in the other component of the portfolio.

For example, a portfolio manager may have a position whereby the portfolio has a substantial position where it has paid fixed rates against receipt of floating rate payments. The position is hedged with a long position in underlying government bonds. However, the volatility of the swap spread prompts the portfolio manager to liquidate the hedge position simultaneously with entry into a hedging swap where it receives fixed and pays floating rates. However, the floating rate it receives reprices on three month resets, while the rate it pays under the offsetting swap reprices at six monthly intervals. In this case, the swap portfolio manager must select between the spread exposure on the fixed rate side or the index timing mismatch on the floating rate portion of the portfolio.

FLOATING RATE PORTFOLIO RISK MANAGEMENT APPROACHES

Exposure identification

The information required to allow evaluation of portfolio risk is as follows:

- The floating cash flows must be separated from the fixed cash flows. These can be hedged later as an integrated portfolio but must be segregated to enable exposures to be identified and analysed in a manageable format.
- The portfolio must be separated further into the different indexes that is, US$ LIBOR versus US$ CP, three month US$ LIBOR versus six month US$ LIBOR etc.

When the portfolio exposures have been appropriately segregated the overall portfolio position is valued and analysed.

Valuation issues

The valuation of the floating rate portion of the swap portfolio utilises standard present value techniques to discount receipts and payments within the portfolio structure.

The valuation of the floating rate portfolio typically entails the following:

- *Cash flows to be discounted*

  At any one point in time, only known cash flows can be valued. Within the floating rate portfolio, these cash flows are a combination of the interest payable on the next repricing date plus the principal amount of the transaction. The actual principal is included at this point, rather than at the actual maturity date of the transaction because at this point the future floating rates that will occur cannot be determined. However, it is possible to apply forward rates from the existing yield curve but the present value determined by the forward rates will match that at the present value of the principal at the next repricing date.

  Margins on floating coupons should be treated and valued on a similar basis, that is, if the portfolio is paying LIBOR plus ten basis points then the ten points per period should be present valued back to determine its value. The margins are included and valued in the fixed rate portfolio rather than in the floating rate portfolio by some institutions. This is especially true when valuing margins on floating rates in different currencies.

- *Time buckets or vectors*

  While it is desirable and increasingly possible with increasing computing power to value the floating rate cash flows on a *daily* basis, in practice cash flows may be segregated into a number of convenient weekly or monthly vectors which are then managed.

- *Discount rates*

  Each component of the floating rate portfolio is discounted utilising the yield curve of the relevant floating rate index. The relevant yield curve can be derived from physical or cash market securities or alternatively, in certain cases, by combining futures with physical transactions to determine the yield curve. It is also often necessary to interpolate between reference rates for the dates that lie between months quoted on the cash and/or futures curve.

  An interesting issue arises in respect of bid-offer spreads (which could be relevant where positions must be hedged). A number of practitioners utilise mid-points to cover this contingency.

Valuation and risk

The identified cash flows are discounted using the zero coupon yield curve for the relevant floating rate index. The economic value of the floating rate portfolio is the present value of receipts less the present value of payments. The portfolio management objective is to ensure that receipts are greater than payments.

The discounting process provides the basis for the analysis of how the portfolio will react to changes in yield curve structures. An essential element of this valuation process is the sensitivity of the portfolio to, firstly, changes in interest rates and, secondly, the time decay.

The floating rate portfolio is volatile and dynamic with the nature of the exposures being sensitive to new transactions being added and old transactions being rolled over and being repriced at current market rates. In addition, the portfolio present values are affected by changes in interest rates and yield curve shapes with the slope of the yield curve becoming relevant as the payment pattern alters with time decay as payment days approach.

Risk management approaches

The approach to floating rate portfolio management is dictated to an extent by the objective of the institution. A number of institutions manage the floating rate portfolio on a "break-even" or loss minimisation basis with the portfolio profit being sought to be generated from the fixed rate portfolio. Other institutions actively manage the floating rate portfolio seeking to generate earnings from this component of the portfolio.

Approaches currently available for the management of the floating rate flows within a swap portfolio include:

- positioning approaches;
- diversification strategies;
- hedging techniques.

A number of portfolio managers utilise positioning strategies whereby floating rate mismatches are managed aggressively to take advantage of anticipated movements in the yield curve. The portfolio is managed in a manner analogous to a short-term securities trading portfolio with the portfolio manager either seeking to engineer transaction flows which create the optimal portfolio position consistent with interest rate expectations or, more commonly, overlaying physical and/or futures contracts in the relevant short-term interest rates on the existing portfolio to optimise the portfolio structure.

Positioning strategies can be designed to take advantage of absolute and yield curve movements as well as spread movements between indexes. For example, under the latter type of strategy, a portfolio manager could receive six month LIBOR while paying CP rates on the basis that six month LIBOR rates will average a level greater than one month CP rates.

An alternative strategy is to basically diversify the floating rate swap portfolio. This can be conceptualised in one of two ways:

- Management of the fixed and floating rate components of the swap portfolios can be integrated with both being valued utilising the same yield curve to ensure that the exposure in the fixed portfolio offsets, at least, part of the exposure in the floating rate component of the portfolio. The combined "net" exposure is then managed. This type of strategy would usually entail a high degree of exposure to changes in the shape of the yield curve.
- An alternative basis might be to seek to diversify risk through the size and structure of the portfolio. This approach seeks to diversify and thereby reduce the significance of small reset date mismatches on the basis that gains and losses on individual transactions will be mutually offsetting. A number of intermediaries utilise the term "date insensitive portfolio" to such diversified floating rate portfolios. Such diversification practices are often accompanied by elaborate simulation models which sample the portfolio to determine risk estimates associated with date mismatches with hedging transactions being undertaken at the margin to avoid excessive mismatches within such large portfolios.

The majority of swap portfolio managers seek to manage mismatches within the floating rate portfolio. The hedges required are affected through a variety of mechanisms:

- The floating rate component of the swap portfolio may be integrated with the institution's cash/short-term securities trading portfolio as exposures within these two operations may be offsetting.
- Basis swaps may be utilised to match or eliminate mismatches within the portfolio. The use of basis swaps can be costly unless the market structure facilitates the basis swap itself. An additional disadvantage is the utilisation of additional credit lines.
- The gaps within the floating rate portfolio can be hedged utilising short-term interest rate futures contracts, FRAs or short-dated forward securities transactions. Identified mismatches are then offset by equal and opposing positions taken in these forward contracts.

Hedging requires slight adjustments to be made to hedge equivalencies to overcome problems associated with different dollar value movements for basis point changes in various instruments. Large exposures or significant concentrations of transactions on particular repricing dates (the "lumpy" exposures) are often segregated and hedged individually under this approach. As an alternative to the use of forwards, options may be utilised. The decision to use symmetric instruments (that is, forwards) as against asymmetric instruments (options) is purely a trading decision based on the portfolio manager's expectations of interest rate movements.

The risks and benefits of individual portfolio management strategies are largely related to the structure of a portfolio and the currency of the swap portfolio itself. An additional factor is the organisation's tolerance for risk.

Increasingly, swap portfolio managers are combining approaches in the management of these floating rate exposures. Two approaches are increasingly common:

- *Portfolio simulation*—whereby statistical methods (such as Monte Carlo simulation techniques) are utilised to quantify the risk profile of the portfolio and to determine the minimal number and structure of hedge transactions designed to optimise the portfolio's exposure profile.
- *Layered approach*—whereby the manager focuses on the *net* portfolio mismatch which is then managed utilising the following "layers" of transactions:

  —Layer 1

  Actual swap transactions, priced attractively to induce participants to transact under particular structures, are utilised to reduce portfolio exposures.

  —Layer 2

  Basis swaps are utilised, where possible, to smooth out major timing or index mismatches.

  —Layer 3

  Forward or option-based hedges are utilised to minimise residual exposures. Alternatively, the residual portfolio exposures are positioned as acceptable risks.

FLOATING RATE PORTFOLIO MANAGEMENT—EXAMPLES

The following examples are based on the hypothetical portfolio in the table below. The portfolio is based on the following assumptions:

- The currency is in US$ and the floating index is US$ LIBOR (with interest being calculated on actual/360 days).

- 90 day Eurodollars futures contracts are used to hedge the portfolio.

The following series of examples examine the impact on the portfolio of:

—interest rate movements, including absolute rate movements and changes in yield curve shape;

—the effect of time on the portfolio.

Initial Portfolio (as at 21/9/X2)

Date	No of Days to Settlement	Pricing Amount ($)	Floating Rate (%)	Days in Interest Period	Settlement Amount ($)
21-Sep-X2	0				
25-Oct-X2	34	50,000,000	6.250%	91	50,789,931
15-Nov-X2	55	10,000,000	7.000%	183	10,355,833
08-Dec-X2	78	(100,000,000)	6.000%	92	(101,533,333)
14-Dec-X2	84	40,000,000	5.750%	91	40,581,389

Parallel shift in yield curves

By valuing the portfolio at the current market rates the net present value of the portfolio can be determined.

Portfolio NPV (at current rates)

Date	No of Days to Settlement	Pricing Amount ($)	Floating Rate (%)	Days in Interest Period	Settlement Amount ($)	Discount Rate (%)	Discount Factor	Present Value ($)
21-Sep-X2	0							
25-Oct-X2	34	50,000,000	6.250%	91	50,789,931	5.000%	0.9955	50,559,622
15-Nov-X2	55	10,000,000	7.000%	183	10,355,833	5.125%	0.9925	10,278,134
08-Dec-X2	78	(100,000,000)	6.000%	92	(101,533,333)	5.188%	0.9893	(100,441,905)
14-Dec-X2	84	40,000,000	5.750%	91	40,581,389	5.250%	0.9883	40,106,317
			Portfolio NPV					502,169

To determine the sensitivity of the portfolio to parallel shifts in the yield curve the same dates are utilised with an adjustment in the yield curve by 1bps.

Portfolio Sensitivity to Parallel Yield Curve Movement

Date	No of Days to Settlement	Pricing Amount ($)	Floating Rate (%)	Days in Interest Period	Settlement Amount ($)	Discount Rate (%)	Discount Factor	Present Value ($)
21-Sep-X2	0	0	0.000%	0	0	0.000%	1.0000	0
25-Oct-X2	34	50,000,000	6.250%	91	50,789,931	5.010%	0.9955	50,559,174
15-Nov-X2	55	10,000,000	7.000%	183	10,355,833	5.135%	0.9925	10,277,987
08-Dec-X2	78	(100,000,000)	6.000%	92	(101,533,333)	5.198%	0.9892	(100,439,864)
14-Dec-X2	84	40,000,000	5.750%	91	40,581,389	5.260%	0.9883	40,105,440
			Portfolio NPV					502,736
			Portfolio Sensitivity (to 1bps rise)					568

The value of the portfolio has increased from $502,169 to $502,736 when discounted at higher rates. Therefore, the portfolio sensitivity to interest rate moves is $568 per basis point in yield.

Various methods are available for eliminating any changes in value for yield curve movements as previously discussed. The most common would be the use of futures contracts to counteract the effects of changes in the yield curve. In this example, September or December Eurodollar futures contracts are utilised as the hedge because this is the next deliverable contract.

On the basis that for each movement in interest rates, up or down, the value of the portfolio will gain/lose $568, the number of futures contracts required to eliminate this sensitivity is calculated as follows (on the basis that the price sensitivity of the Eurodollar futures contract is $25.00 per bps):

$$\$568/\$25 = 22.7 \text{ contracts}$$

As the value of the portfolio decreases when interest rates fall by 1bps, to counteract this loss of value to a fall in interest rates it is necessary to buy the Eurodollar futures contracts.

Shifts in the shape of yield curve

This example examines the effect on the portfolio of a change in the shape of the yield curve.

Valuing the original portfolio at the same date as the example above and moving the yield curve into a "steeper" positive shape it is possible to analyse the change in value that occurs.

Portfolio Sensitivity to Parallel Yield Curve Movement

Date	No of Days to Settlement	Pricing Amount ($)	Floating Rate (%)	Days in Interest Period	Settlement Amount ($)	Discount Rate (%)	Discount Factor	Present Value ($)
21-Sep-X2	0							
25-Oct-X2	34	50,000,000	6.250%	91	50,789,931	5.000%	0.9955	50,559,622
15-Nov-X2	55	10,000,000	7.000%	183	10,355,833	5.135%	0.9925	10,277,987
08-Dec-X2	78	(100,000,000)	6.000%	92	(101,533,333)	5.208%	0.9892	(100,437,824)
14-Dec-X2	84	40,000,000	5.750%	91	40,581,389	5.280%	0.9882	40,103,686
			Portfolio NPV					503,472
			Portfolio Sensitivity (to 1bps change in yield curve shape)					1,303

The value of the portfolio is now $503,472—a change of $1,303. The effect of the positive change in shape is a gain to the portfolio.

The futures position (assuming a hedge is placed in the December contract and the contract rate charges by approximately 96bps consistent with the curve steepening) shows a loss of $1,725 on the 23 futures contracts. The net effect is a loss of $422 by combining the floating rate portfolio and the futures used to hedge the portfolio.

Other methods of hedging the portfolio may counteract the movement in the shape of the yield curve more efficiently. In this example, the futures delivery date does not correspond with the portfolio exposure. The use of FRAs, with a risk profile opposite to the portfolio, would cover the portfolio position more accurately avoiding the problems with change in the convexity.

Effect of time on the portfolio

The NPV of the portfolio will gradually increase or decrease to the value due on the settlement date. The effect of changes in interest rates, or the degree of sensitivity to time of the portfolio, will also change as the time period to the settlement dates diminishes.

In contrast, the hedges taken which in the case of futures contract have a fixed value to changes in yield and time.

Moving the original portfolio forward one day allows the effect of time on the value of the portfolio to be understood.

Portfolio Sensitivity to Time Decay

Date	No of Days to Settlement	Pricing Amount ($)	Floating Rate (%)	Days in Interest Period	Settlement Amount ($)	Discount Rate (%)	Discount Factor	Present Value ($)
22-Sep-X2	0							
25-Oct-X2	33	50,000,000	6.250%	91	50,789,931	5.000%	0.9956	50,566,381
15-Nov-X2	54	10,000,000	7.000%	183	10,355,833	5.125%	0.9926	10,279,542
08-Dec-X2	77	(100,000,000)	6.000%	92	(101,533,333)	5.188%	0.9894	(100,445,823)
14-Dec-X2	83	40,000,000	5.750%	91	40,581,389	5.250%	0.9884	40,111,939
					Portfolio NPV			502,040
					Portfolio Sensitivity (for elapse of 1 day)			(129)

The value of the portfolio has moved to $502,040 from the original value of $502,169. As the yields have remained constant, the portfolio value has decreased as a result of the effluxion of time rather than the result of any adverse movement in interest rates.

The portfolio's sensitivity to movements in interest rates will also be altered. Determining the sensitivity as calculated above allows the effect of time on interest sensitivity to be examined.

Portfolio Sensitivity to Time Decay Interest Rate Changes

Date	No of Days to Settlement	Pricing Amount ($)	Floating Rate (%)	Days in Interest Period	Settlement Amount ($)	Discount Rate (%)	Discount Factor	Present Value ($)
22-Sep-X2	0							
25-Oct-X2	33	50,000,000	6.250%	91	50,789,931	5.010%	0.9956	50,565,946
15-Nov-X2	54	10,000,000	7.000%	183	10,355,833	5.135%	0.9926	10,279,397
08-Dec-X2	77	(100,000,000)	6.000%	92	(101,533,333)	5.198%	0.9894	(100,453,808)
14-Dec-X2	83	40,000,000	5.750%	91	40,581,389	5.260%	0.9884	40,111,073
					Portfolio NPV			502,608
					Portfolio Sensitivity (for elapse of 1 day and parallel yield curve shift)			439

The portfolio sensitivity can be determined by a comparison of the two NPV amounts. This indicates that for the elapse of one day on the portfolio sensitivity is $439 per 1 basis point increase in interest rates versus $568 per 1 basis point currently.

Consequently, as the maturity of the portfolio decreases, the effect of interest rate changes also decreases. This has a significant impact on the efficiency of a hedge. It requires that the number of contracts utilised in the hedge will need to be adjusted to match the changing duration and, therefore, interest rate volatility of the portfolio. In the example, as the sensitivity of the portfolio reduces to $439 per basis point, the number of hedge contracts will need to be adjusted from the original 22.7 contracts to 17.6 contracts. Ideally, the adjustment to the hedge should be undertaken gradually as the portfolio maturity alters.

SUMMARY

Swap portfolio managers have increasingly become aware of the significant degree of risk within the floating rate component of swap portfolios. The volatility of short-term interest rates and the periodic resets of floating rates within the portfolio combine to make management of this exposure complex. This chapter outlines a framework for the identification of risk and a variety of techniques for the management of this risk. A combination of portfolio diversification and hedging techniques, primarily derivative products such as basis swaps, futures/FRAs and options, provide the fundamental basis for portfolio risk neutralisation.

Chapter 35

FRA Portfolio Risk Management Techniques

FRA HEDGING APPROACHES

There are two basic approaches to managing exposures under FRA transactions:

- cash market transactions involving mismatches in borrowing and lending;
- utilising futures transactions.

The risk management approaches closely reflect the pricing methodology for FRAs detailed in Chapter 10.

This chapter also includes discussion regarding co-ordinated purchases or sales (often referred to as "strips") of short-term interest rate futures contracts to replicate interest rate swaps, either by financial institutions to hedge interest rate swaps entered into with clients or by end users as a substitute for transacting interest rate swaps.

HEDGING BY UTILISING BORROWING AND LENDING TRANSACTIONS

FRA transactions can be hedged by the intermediary providing the FRA by creating mismatched borrowing and lending transactions on its own balance sheet. For example, an intermediary may provide an FRA to hedge a drawdown on a loan for one of its clients by borrowing for a maturity coinciding with the maturity of the FRA contract but investing for a shorter period, the maturity of the investment coinciding with the commencement date of the FRA. The mismatched investment and borrowing transaction is engineered to cover the risk under the FRA transaction created. In contrast, the intermediary could borrow for a short period and invest for a longer period to create an FRA position for an investor seeking to lock in rates on a future investment.

An example of an FRA hedge utilising borrowing and lending transactions is set out in *Exhibit 35.1*.

This type of hedging technique utilises the intermediary's balance sheet. This balance sheet utilisation can be justified where the intermediary would have undertaken the borrowing or lending transaction in any case as part of their general asset liability management activities but merely has restructured either the borrowing or investment decision to encompass the FRA transaction written for its client. However, where the FRA position cannot be engineered as part of its general treasury activities, it can be priced as an arbitrage to create a synthetic borrowing or investment away from implied forward rates earning the institution an arbitrage profit which compensates it for its balance sheet utilisation.

Another alternative may be to offset the risk exposure under an FRA against a mismatch in the institution's overall swap portfolio. For example, where the intermediary is matching a normal, immediate start swap against a deferred or forward swap, it might be possible to characterise the deferral period or delayed start as a string of FRA contracts to effectively match out the risk positions within the swap portfolio.

Exhibit 35.1

FRA Hedge Utilising Borrowing and Lending Transactions

Assume that a bank (B) is approached by a client to quote for and provide an FRA to hedge a loan drawdown for three months commencing in three months' time for an amount of US$10m, that is, B is selling a 3 × 6 FRA.

Current interest rates are:

Three months	11.00/11.20% pa
Six months	11.80/12.00% pa

B would price and hedge its FRA as follows:

- B borrows US$10m for six months at 12.00% pa and lends it for three months at 11.00% pa (note that it lends (borrows) at the market bid (offer) rates).
- B then sells the US$10m 3 × 6 FRA to essentially provide it with a replacement for the investment which matures in three months' time.
- B seeks to earn a spread of 0.25% pa on the FRA, that is, it must earn 12.25% pa over the six months. Therefore, B quotes an FRA rate of 13.51% pa.

After the transaction is executed, at the end of three months, B would need to re-lend the maturing US$10m for three months. The FRA would be settled and the cash payment by or to the client would have the effect of locking in the rate of 13.51% pa. The FRA could also be structured as a physical transaction whereby B actually provided funding for its client at the FRA rate.

If B had been asked to hedge an investment, by buying an FRA, B would have lent US$10m for six months at 11.80% pa and funded the loan for three months at 11.20% pa with the FRA locking in its refinancing cost. Using the same profit margin as above, the FRA rate quoted would be 11.90% pa. Notice the compounding effect of the different bid-offer spreads.

HEDGING BY UTILISING FUTURES

Basic concept

FRAs can be hedged by utilising financial futures on short-term interest rates as these futures markets offer a means to hedge the risk of unexpected price changes in that they permit the future purchase or sale of an asset at a price determined today. The basic hedge structure utilising futures entails the intermediary selling futures to hedge itself against the price risk of writing an FRA designed to protect a borrower and, conversely, buying futures to hedge its risk where it books FRAs to protect investment yields.

An example of using futures to hedge FRAs is set out in *Exhibit 35.2*.

Where the structure of the FRA coincides perfectly with the specification of the futures contract and the dates, including the commencement date of the FRA and futures contract, as in the example in *Exhibit 35.2*, the futures contract can be used as a perfect substitute for the FRA and a perfect or, at least, highly efficient hedge can be created. However, in practice, the terms of the FRA will depart significantly from the specifications of the futures contract used to hedge the FRA requiring considerable structuring of the hedging process.

Exhibit 35.2
FRA Hedge Utilising Futures

Assume a borrower approaches a bank (B) seeking to purchase a FRA to hedge a US$ loan drawdown for 90 days only, drawing down in early December 19X8. Assume it is *now* mid September and December Eurodollar futures are quoted as:

Sale	Bid	Offer
88.95	88.94	88.95

B will *sell* contracts to hedge its FRA position, so it must look to the opposite party, the buyer, that is, 88.94. A price of 88.94 *plus* a margin of 0.05% pa means a quote of 11.11% to the client.

In early December, the client draws down its loan and settles the FRA with B at the agreed yield rate of 11.11% pa. At the same time, B closes out the futures position by buying contracts at or about the same yield that the client can sell the physical securities.

If, in the example, the client was an investor, B would need to *buy* contracts (sellers at 88.95) and *deduct* its margin. The rate would be 11.00% pa.

Structuring the hedging process

Hedging and basis risk

The objective of utilising futures to hedge an FRA position is to construct positions in the futures market which offset the intermediary's position in the FRA such that the dollar price change for a given movement in interest rates will be identical but opposite in direction on the hedge.

However, the efficiency of the hedge will be affected by the changing relationship between the value of the security being hedged and the price at which the corresponding futures contract trades and how this relationship evolves over time. The difference between the cash and futures price is referred to as the "basis". Utilising futures to hedge FRAs essentially entails substituting basis risk for absolute market risk on changes in interest rates.

Utilising futures to hedge FRA positions, therefore, requires considerable structuring of the hedge itself, including:

- adjusting and anticipating basis fluctuations;
- determining the appropriate hedge ratios;
- selecting the appropriate contract and delivery month.

Appropriate hedge management requires determination of possible gains and losses due to basis fluctuation.

The effect of basis changes on the efficiency of the hedge can be viewed as the basis either increasing in value (strengthening) or decreasing in value (weakening). This necessarily means that a short hedger who buys the basis will have a net gain as the basis strengthens (that is, the basis becomes increasingly more positive or less negative), while a long hedger will have a net gain as the basis has weakened (that is, where the basis has become increasingly more negative or less positive).

Where these basis changes occur, the net profit or loss on the futures positions will not exactly offset the gain or loss in the cash position. This will effectively create a cash flow mismatch with resulting economic gains or losses between the settlement on the FRA contract and the settlement on the futures contract. Consequently, intermediaries when they are using futures to hedge FRAs must seek to adjust the hedge for the anticipated changes in basis by slightly over- or under-hedging.

Hedge ratio determination

The hedge ratio, that is, the number of futures contracts required to hedge the FRA position, must be determined to ensure that the hedge performs as expected. The hedge ratio must be determined to equate the price changes of the FRA and the futures contract which often will not be of the same magnitude because of differences in the contract specifications as between the FRA and the futures contract. The hedge ratio represents the principal face value of the futures contract held relative to the principal face value of the FRA position.

There are a number of techniques for calculating the hedge ratio. These include:

- volatility matching or the basis point model whereby the hedge is structured to match the change in the dollar value of the FRA to be hedged with the change in the dollar value of the futures contract;
- regression model whereby a regression relationship between the FRA contract price movements and the futures contract price movements is established on the basis of historical data with the hedge being structured as the value of the futures position that reduces the variability of price changes of the hedged position to the lowest possible level;
- duration model whereby the number of futures contracts utilised over the life of the hedge are designed to ensure changes in the value of the futures position will offset the changes in the value of the cash position by equating the duration of the FRA and the futures contract.

There are a number of other models for calculating the hedge ratio, each of which has implicit assumptions, and will be appropriate in one or other situation.

In the case of FRAs, basis point equivalency is commonly utilised to make the necessary hedge adjustments. An example of hedge ratio determination using this technique is set out in *Exhibit 35.3*.

Exhibit 35.3

FRA Hedge Ratio Determination

Refer to the situation described in *Exhibit 35.2*. Assume, however, that the borrower wishes to hedge a drawdown for 60 days. Given that the instrument underlying the futures contract is 90 day Eurodollar contract, the number of contracts utilised will need to be adjusted as follows:

$$N = \frac{(A_1 - A_2) \times FV_A}{(B_1 - B_2) \times FV_B}$$

where: N = hedge ratio

A_1 = the price of the underlying loan to be hedged (60 day term) at market yield minus 0.10% pa (11.05 − 0.10 = 10.95% pa)

A_2 = the price of the underlying security to be hedged at market yield plus 0.10% (11.15% pa)

FV_A = face value of underlying security to be hedged (US$10m)

B_1 = price of future contract at market yield minus 0.10%

B_2 = price of future contract at market yield plus 0.10%

FV_B = face value of futures contract (US$1m)

Exhibit 35.3—continued

$B_1 - B_2$ is taken to equal US$25 per 1bps consistent with the fixed PVBP of the Eurodollar Contract or US$300 for a 20bps.

In this example:

$$N = \frac{(100.0164 - 99.9836) \times US\$10m}{(500)} = 6.56$$

Therefore, B should utilise approximately seven contracts to match the respective price volatilities of the two securities.

Note that as a 60 day security is less volatile than a 90 day security, less contracts are utilised than would be suggested by the respective face values (US$10m/US$1m = 10). If the underlying FRA had a run longer than the underlying future contract, then *more* future contracts than face value securities would be dictated.

Delivery month and contract selection

A critical decision for the intermediary utilising futures to hedge FRAs is to:

- select the contract to be utilised to effect the hedge;
- select the delivery month in which the hedge will be placed.

Selection of the contract is usually based on the correlation between movements in the prices of the relevant futures contract and the price of the FRA. For example, Eurodollar futures will be utilised to hedge LIBOR based FRAs.

The selection of contract month is more problematic. FRAs written to meet client requirements will rarely exactly match the traded futures delivery dates. The selection of the delivery month to be utilised generally depends on the following factors:

- the time horizon over which the hedge is designed to be maintained;
- the liquidity of the particular delivery month, both at the time the position is established and at the time the position must be closed;
- the relative pricing of contracts across delivery months or the basis relationship between contract dates.

A variety of hedging strategies are available in regard to delivery month selection. These range from placing the hedge in the nearest liquid contract month to the relevant FRA to utilising a basket of delivery months and contracts, appropriately weighted, to effect the hedge. Two types of special hedging techniques (stack hedging and structured arbitrage and strip hedging) require special mention.

Stack hedging and structured arbitrage

Stack hedging refers to front loaded hedges where most of the futures positions are concentrated in certain contract months in an attempt to improve overall hedge performance. Front loading seeks to take advantage of the higher available liquidity in the nearby futures contract months. Utilising a stack hedge, an FRA contract starting some time in the future is hedged by entering into futures contracts which will expire prior to the commencement date of the FRA with the futures position being rolled at each settlement date until the commencement of the FRA.

An example of a stack hedge is set out in *Exhibit 35.4*.

Exhibit 35.4

Example of Stack Hedge

A company decides to use a stack hedge to hedge 91 day CP issuances for two years. On 6/6/X6, it issues US$250m face value of 91 day CP and establishes a futures hedge which is fully stacked in the front month contract. The initial and subsequent transactions necessary to keep the stack hedge in place are shown below:

16/6/X6	Sell 1708 September X6 Eurodollar contracts (1708 = seven future CP issuances to be hedged × 244 contracts per CP issuance).
15/9/X6	Close out the September X6 position and sell 1464 (6 × 244) December X6 contracts.
15/12/X6	Close out the December X6 position and sell 1220 (5 × 244) March X7 contracts.
16/3/X7	Close out the March X7 position and sell 976 (4 × 244) June X7 contracts.
15/6/X7	Close out the June X7 position and sell 732 (3 × 244) September X7 contracts.
14/9/X7	Close out the September X7 position and sell 488 (2 × 244) December X7 contracts.
14/12/X7	Close out the December X7 position and sell 244 (1 × 244) March X8 contracts.

Of course, the hedge could be stacked in other futures contract months. For example, the company could have strip hedged the first three CP issuances and stacked the remainder of the hedge in the fourth contract month.

Note: The number of contracts is based on an assumed hedge ratio of 0.9760 and a Eurodollar futures contract with face value of US$1m.

The risk of a stack hedge is that the basis between the months could alter, that is, the yield curve could change its shape such that deferred contract months will either become more expensive or cheaper relative to nearby contracts exposing the stack hedger to altered inter-contract month price spreads when rolling the stack hedge. This can result in a marked decline in hedge efficiency. Some additional aspects of stack hedging are discussed below in the context of strip hedging.

The structured arbitrage option is an alternative to stack hedging where there is little or no trading in a particular futures month, particularly in the more distant months. In this situation, the structured arbitrage trade entails an intermediary taking both sides of the futures transactions and incorporating the side that would usually have been taken by a counterparty into its futures portfolio.

The rationale in such structured arbitrages is that it is always possible to enter into a futures trade at a price but usually the counterparty will trade, particularly in the more distant lightly traded months, at a price designed to give the other party an arbitrage or a particularly attractive price. Accordingly, the structured arbitrage is predicated on taking that arbitrage internally and rolling out of that arbitrage by either creating a synthetic security or alternatively maintaining the position until such time as it can be liquidated.

Strip hedging

On occasions, the intermediary will be asked to hedge not a single FRA but a series of FRAs commencing at some point in the future involving the rolling of say short securities either from the perspective of a borrower or investor. For example, a borrower may wish to drawdown funding in nine months time and maintain the funding for a period of 12 months involving four rolls, each with a maturity of 90 days. In the extreme, the client could wish to enter into a series of FRAs over a period of two or three years. As will be readily apparent, this type of transaction is similar to an interest rate swap, particularly, the short-term (two years and under) interest rate swaps discussed above.

These types of transactions are hedged utilising a technique known as strip hedging whereby each roll of the FRA is hedged with a series of futures contracts whose settlement dates closely follow the relevant rollover dates of the FRAs.

The strip hedge operates in two phases:

- Initially, a series of futures contracts are bought and sold to hedge the rollovers on the FRAs. In essence, the strip is bought or sold.
- After the hedge is established, where the FRAs are not matched up against counterparties, the hedge must be rolled periodically, usually every 90 days. This involves lifting the futures leg by buying or selling the appropriate futures contract month and settling the corresponding leg of the FRA.

An example of a strip hedging operation is set out in *Exhibit 35.5*.

Exhibit 35.5

Example of Strip Hedge

An investor wants to enter into a series of FRAs, with a bank (B) to lock in investment rates for just under a year through to September X8, drawing down early October in X7. B does not need to hedge the first leg in the futures, as drawdown is today. Instead, the first leg is priced at where either the investor or B can *buy* an Eurodollar deposit on the spot market. The subsequent legs of the strip of FRAs are hedged in the futures market.

Assume the following rates prevail:

70 day Eurodollar deposit, maturing early December	10.60
Buy December futures	11.05
Buy March futures	12.45
Buy June futures	13.30

B now takes a weighted average of the rates and offers the investor one rate for the complete term, that is:

$$\frac{(10.6 \times 70) + (11.05 \times 91) + (12.45 \times 91) + (13.3 \times 91)}{343} = 11.926\% \text{ pa}$$

Deduct B's profit margin (0.05% pa) = 11.876% pa.

At each rollover, fresh deposits would be purchased by the investor and the FRA contracts closed out. B would simultaneously close out its futures position with the gain or loss on the futures more than offsetting the FRA settlement amount to provide B with its profit.

The above technique which is based on weighted average interest rate is not technically correct, particularly where the relevant interest rate periods are of uneven length. A more accurate price of the strip is provided by utilising the rate compounding method which is outlined below.

Using the same rates as outlined above the strip rate is determined as follows:

- The interest rates are first converted to an annual effective basis:

  10.60% pa quarterly = 11.0288% pa annual
  11.05% pa quarterly = 11.5164% pa annual
  12.45% pa quarterly = 13.0434% pa annual
  13.30% pa quarterly = 13.9782% pa annual

- The strip rate is determined as follows:

  $[(1 + 0.110288)^{70/360} \times (1 + 0.115164)^{91/360} \times (1 + 0.130434)^{91/360} \times (1 + 0.139782)^{91/360}] - 1$
  $= 0.11847$ or 11.847% pa.

As will be evident, stack hedges can be viewed as a substitute to strip hedging techniques. For example, instead of purchasing or selling a strip of futures, a stack hedge could be executed with the stack hedge being gradually rolled out as futures contracts expire with the amount of contracts maintained being adjusted as at each settlement date.

Strip hedging has a number of advantages over stack hedging including:

- fewer transactions and therefore lower commission costs;
- more certainty about the final performance of the hedge;
- lower hedge management requirements.

In contrast, a front loaded stack hedge has a number of advantages over a strip hedge including:

- The fact that a stack hedge involves trading in the more liquid contracts may minimise lower transaction costs, as reflected by the lower bid-offer spreads in the more liquid months.
- By maintaining the hedge in the liquid nearby contract months, the hedger has increased flexibility in adjusting the hedge position in response to changing market conditions and corporate objectives.

UTILISING SHORT-TERM INTEREST FUTURES STRIPS TO HEDGE INTEREST RATE SWAPS

As noted previously, interest rate swaps are, effectively, portfolios of forward contracts. The functional capacity to replicate interest rate swaps by entering into a series of short-term interest rate futures contracts on the relevant interest rate index is a direct result of this relationship.

Functional equivalence between strips of short-term interest rate futures contracts (or FRAs) in interest rate swaps has allowed these two separate types of transactions to be used as substitutes or as equivalence of the other.

Interest rate futures strips (which are identical to the strip hedges described above) represent co-ordinated sales (in the case of borrowers) or purchases (in the case of investors) of series of short-term interest rate contracts with successive expiration dates. Such transactions are designed to fix an interest rate for a term equal to the length of the strip. For example, a strip consisting of four, eight and twelve successive contracts would lock in, respectively, interest rates for periods of one, two and three years etc.

In this chapter, Eurodollar futures are utilised to illustrate the use of futures strips as surrogate interest rate swaps. Eurodollar futures are traded in a number of markets. The primary market for Eurodollar futures is the Chicago Mercantile Exchange (CME). Other markets include the Singapore International Monetary Exchange (SIMEX)—the SIMEX contracts are fungible with CME contracts—and the London International Financial Futures Exchange (LIFFE). *Exhibit 35.6* summarises the primary specifications of the CME Eurodollar futures contracts.

The principles applicable to Eurodollar futures can be utilised in other currencies in which short-term interest rate futures contracts are traded, for identical purposes. Consistent with this capacity of the technique to be translated across currencies, strips are used in all currencies where short term interest rate futures contracts are available.

Exhibit 35.6

Eurodollar Futures Contracts—Specifications

Commodity:	Three month Eurodollar Time Deposits.
Ticker Symbol:	ED.
Contract Size:	$1,000,000.
Contract Months:	March, June, September, December Quoted out to ten years.
Strike Price Intervals:	N/A.
Minimum Price Change:	1bp = $25.
Price Limit:	None.
Trading Hours (Chicago Time):	7.20 am-2.00 pm (last day-9.30 am).
Last Day of Trading:	Second London business day prior to the third Wednesday of the delivery month.
Delivery:	No delivery for Eurodollar futures. Final cash settlement on last day of trading.

The functional equivalence of futures strips and interest rate swaps facilitate their use in two regards:

- Financial institutions often utilise strips to hedge interest rate swap transactions entered into with end users.
- End users can directly utilise futures strips *as an alternative* to entering into interest rate swaps with financial institutions.

Market environment

Until recently, corporations have typically favoured interest rate swaps relative to futures strips. This preference is particularly marked outside the United States. A number of American corporations are active in directly using interest rate futures in the management of both short and intermediate maturity interest rate exposures.

This practice has led to a "tiered" market structure. Under this structure, corporations and other end users utilise OTC products (such as interest rate swaps and FRAs) to hedge interest rate exposures. These transactions were entered into with banks/financial institutions who, in turn, hedged or "laid off" their risk positions utilising ET products—primarily, interest rate futures on organised futures markets.

The primary basis for this particular market structure included:

- *Corporate preference for "customised" contracts*

  OTC products allow exact matching of the underlying interest rate exposures. In contrast, use of futures contracts are limited by:

  —lack of liquidity in futures contracts with distant delivery dates;

  —traded futures contracts were not available for periods beyond two years.

- *Credit availability*

  The availability of credit lines from the banking system for OTC hedge products and the acceptance of banks as credit-worthy counterparties favoured the use of OTC products.

This preference for OTC products over ET products was particularly marked for interest rate hedge products of maturities beyond 12/18 months with most corporations preferring to use FRAs/interest rate swaps (the phrase "interest rate swaps" is used throughout) to manage exposures for such intermediate maturities.

However, in recent times, significant changes in financial markets have altered the position significantly.

Technical difficulties in utilising interest rate futures contracts for hedging intermediate maturities have diminished. For example, the Eurodollar interest rate futures contract now trades for maturities (up to) five years. In addition, the liquidity levels in distant months has also improved significantly to the point where futures strips represent a realistic option to OTC products such as interest rate swaps.

Credit line availability and the level of counterparty risk has also changed significantly.

The introduction of BIS capital adequacy standards (encompassing, for the first time, previously off-balance sheet interest rate hedge products) has forced banks to seek higher returns on these transactions to meet required rates of return on capital employed. This has resulted in an increase in the cost of dealing in OTC hedge products (higher bid-offer spreads).

In addition, the deterioration in the credit quality of many corporations and the limited capacity of financial institutions to increase risk weighted assets has reduced the level of credit lines available for interest rate swap transactions. Simultaneously, the decline in the credit standing of the banking system itself has dictated that a number of corporations are no longer willing to accept certain banks as counterparties to hedge transactions.

The confluence of these various factors has significantly reduced the bias in favour of interest rate swaps relative to interest rate futures transactions.

Pricing issues

Given the equivalence of futures strips and interest rate swaps, economic theory would dictate that:

- The effective yields generated by both transactions should be closely correlated.
- The yield on a futures strip would be lower than that on the comparable interest rate swap.

The difference between the futures strip and the interest rate swap price would reflect the following factors:

- the financial institution's margin to generate return on capital invested in the transaction;
- an added "risk premium" to compensate for the credit risk assumed;
- the cost of hedging/assuming the risk of mismatches required to facilitate customisation.

In order to analyse the performance of a futures strip versus an interest rate swap the likely cash flows and net gains (losses) on a three year interest rate swap and a corresponding three year Eurodollar futures strip are simulated. The results of the analysis were as follows:

- *Yield comparison*

  Exhibit 35.7 sets out comparative yields on a three year futures strip and three year interest rate swap for the period January 1988 to February 1991. Yields on the futures strip and interest rate swaps were found to have a high degree of correlation (around 99%) confirming that the futures strip could be utilised to replicate an interest rate swap and vice versa.

  The yield on the futures strip (in this period) was found to be, on average, 7-9 basis points per annum (bps pa) lower than the yield on the comparative interest rate swap (refer *Exhibit 35.6*).

- *Effective cost analysis*

  The yield of a futures strip needs to be adjusted for cash flows arising from margin requirements, deposit funding costs, commission charges etc. *Exhibit 35.8* sets out the "all-in" net borrowing costs of utilising the futures strip after adjusting for these various costs. The analysis indicates that the "cost" of using futures strip is typically relatively low—less than 3-5bps pa.

The overall pricing analysis indicates that futures strips result in a significant cost saving (which in the specific transaction considered) totals around 2-6bps pa. This is equivalent to US$20,000 to US$60,000 pa or approx US$51,542 to US$154,626 (in present value terms) on a transaction for a face value amount of US$100 million.

Exhibit 35.7

Distribution of Yields on Three Year Eurodollar Futures Strip versus Three Year Interest Rate Swaps

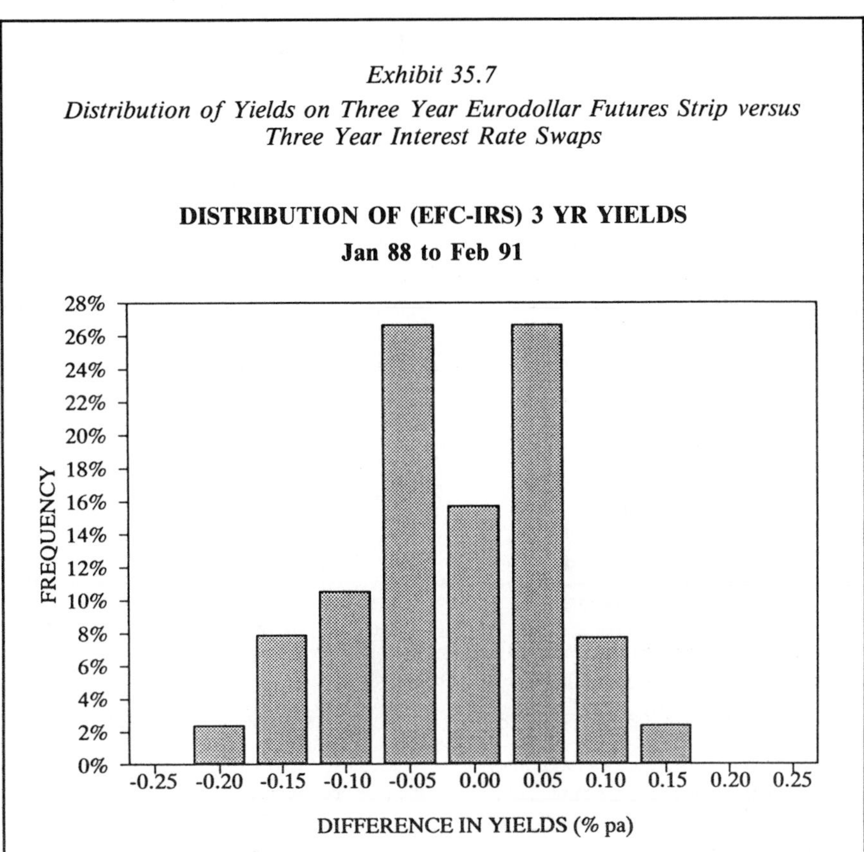

Exhibit 35.7—continued

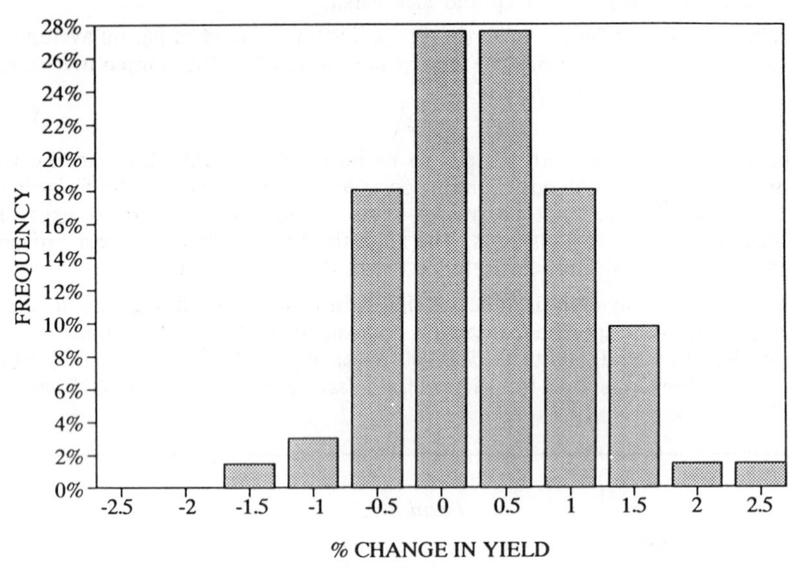

Exhibit 35.8

Effective Cost of Eurodollar Futures Strip

	(% pa)
Futures Strip Yield:[1]	8.0000
Cost of Funding Deposit:[2]	0.033
Cost of Funding Margins Calls:[3]	0.013
Brokerage Commissions:[4]	0.006
Effective Cost of Futures Strip	8.052

Note:

1. The yield at which the three year strip was entered into.
2. The deposit is $500 per contract. The cost is assumed to be 1%, which is the difference between borrowing the funds and investing in T-Bills, ie a "negative investment".
3. Cash flow is $25 per basis point move in the Eurodollar futures contract yield. Assume the cost of borrowing is 8% and yields fall 10 basis points for the life of the contract (12 quarters). Thus after three years, the contract yields are 6.8%. This represents a substantial adverse movement in the position and highlights the relatively minor impact of margin funding costs on the transaction.
4. Commission is $15 per contract, or a total cost of $18,000 over the life of the contract (three years).

It should be noted that Eurodollar strips provide a less effective hedge the further out the maturity is extended.

The main difference between the two instruments is that Eurodollars are non-convex whereas interest rate swaps are convex. The present value of a basis point (PVBP) for a Eurodollar contract is US$25, irrespective of the level of absolute rates. An equivalent swap will have its PVBP vary depending on the discount rate.

When a swap is initially offset with a Eurodollar strip, the amount of contracts in the futures hedge will only be appropriate for the swap rate at the time the trade is done. As absolute yields change, the number of contracts in the hedge will need to change to reflect the change in duration of the underlying swap. As an example, if a swap dealer pays fixed on a $100m two year swap at 8% (semi-annual bond) and hedges with a strip of Eurodollar futures at 8.03%, the true gain to the dealer is unlikely to be three basis points, because the dealer has taken on negative convexity by entering into this trade.

With a yield of 8%, one would need to buy a total of 726 contracts in order to match the duration of the swap.[1] If swap yields dropped the next day to 7%, a gain of $1,815,000 would be by 100bps. At these lower yields, however, the PVBP of the swap increases to $18,581 from $18,150. Consequently, the 100bps move in yield results in a loss of $1,836,500. The net loss due to a rate movement is $21,500, which equates to slightly over 1bps per annum over the life of the swap.[2]

The convexity cost of a swap versus strip position can be estimated using the expected swap interest rate volatilities. The longer the maturity of the position, the greater the convexity impact will be since the impact of the discounting will be felt over a greater time period.

As a result of the liquidity provided in the futures market, swap pricing has become highly influenced by the yields implied by the Eurodollar strip. The correlation between swap and strip prices is very high for one and two year swaps. The correlation is reduced the further out one goes along the maturity spectrum. Increased futures execution risk, interest rate volatility and liquidity concerns are all factors that result in the reduced pricing relationship.

Several dealers have started to use strips to price swaps beyond the traded Eurodollar contract maturities. It is theoretically feasible to price contracts out beyond these maturities by extending the linear relationship in the back contracts. These theoretical contracts would be hedged by stacking the contracts in the furthest traded Eurodollar contract. Although this pricing methodology and hedging strategy is only used by a small group of dealers, it is an emerging factor influencing the pricing of longer-term deals. To a large extent this practice relates to the period when Eurodollar futures were traded out to five years. With the extension in late 1993 for Eurodollar trading to initially seven years and subsequently for ten years, the actual ability to trade the underlying futures for more distant maturities eliminates the need for the theoretical pricing process.

Cash requirements

A feature of Eurodollar futures strips is the requirement that the contracts be marked-to-market on a daily basis and immediately cash margined if the position

1. The modified duration of a two year swap yielding 8% is 1.8149, resulting in the PVBP of $18,142 on a $100m notional value. Since Eurodollars have a PVBP of $25, it would take 726 contracts to match the PVBP of the swap.
2. See Richard Leibovitch, "The US Dollar Swap Market" in Satyajit Das (1991).

is out-of-the-money. This margin requirement means that the hedging corporation may be required to make substantial margin payments.

An important point to note is that cash requirements as between a futures strip and an interest rate swap should not vary substantially in terms of amount but only timing.

This reflects the fact that with the futures contract, as the position goes out of the money, margin calls would have to be posted and immediately cash settled. In contrast, with an interest rate swap, the cash flow (representing the difference between the fixed and floating interest rate) would not be realised until the relevant payment date (which would typically be either quarterly or semi-annually).

An additional difference is that with an interest rate swap the settlement payment as at any payment date relates *only to the immediate interest period* (three or six months). In contrast in the case of a futures strip, the margin settlement would relate to *all* futures contracts that are open—that is, all potential cash settlements *over the full term of the transaction*.

This cash margining requirement impacts on two levels:

- the potential requirement to fund large margin payments from available liquidity sources;
- funding costs in respect of such margin payments.

This cash requirement and cost of funding such margin variations can be analysed utilising the following simulation methodology. The transaction assumed is a US$100m face value hedge for a term of three years requiring an initial purchase of 1,200 contracts. At the end of each quarter, as futures contracts mature, 100 contracts expire and are closed out.

Exhibit 35.9 summarises cash flow requirements of this position on a particular day in each quarter if Eurodollar futures yields move by 1, 5 or 10bps. Note how the effect of a movement yield is felt most dramatically in the early period of the hedge when the number of contracts open is larger.

Exhibit 35.9

Cash Margin Requirement of US$100m 3 year Eurodollar Futures Strip

Purchase Month	Number of Contract	Deposit (Paid/ Received)	Interest on Deposit	Cash flow if futures' yields fall 1 basis point	5 basis points	10 basis points
June 1991	1200	($600,000)	($1,500)	($30,000)	($150,000)	($300,000)
Sept 1991	1100	($550,000)	($1,375)	($27,500)	($137,500)	($275,000)
Dec 1991	1000	($500,000)	($1,250)	($25,000)	($125,000)	($250,000)
Mar 1992	900	($450,000)	($1,125)	($22,500)	($112,500)	($225,000)
June 1992	800	($400,000)	($1,000)	($20,000)	($100,000)	($200,000)
Sept 1992	700	($350,000)	($875)	($17,500)	($87,500)	($175,000)
Dec 1992	600	($300,000)	($750)	($15,000)	($75,000)	($150,000)
Mar 1993	500	($250,000)	($625)	($12,000)	($62,500)	($125,000)
June 1993	400	($200,000)	($500)	($10,000)	($50,000)	($100,000)
Sept 1993	300	($150,000)	($375)	($7,500)	($37,500)	($75,000)
Dec 1993	200	($100,000)	($250)	($5,000)	($25,000)	($50,000)
Mar 1994	100	($50,000)	($125)	($2,500)	($12,500)	($25,000)

Exhibit 35.10 analyses the cash requirements on futures strip for larger moves in future yields. This study (which covers the period January 1985 to February 1991) indicates that there is 95% confidence (based on statistical methodology) that the *maximum* cash flow requirement to fund margin variations would total US$4.987m (or approximately 5% of the face value of the position). This assumes, in the case of a borrowing hedge, that following entry into the sold future strip, interest rates fall immediately and stay at this level throughout the life of this transaction.

Exhibit 35.10
Analysing the Potential Cash Requirements of a Futures Strip

Methodology

In order to simulate the potential cash requirement of margin calls resulting from large interest rate movements the following transaction was examined:

Face Value Amount:	US$100 million
Term:	3 years
No of Contracts:	1,200 Eurodollar futures contracts
Initial Yield:	8.00% pa.

The futures position requires lodgement of a deposit of US$600,000 (based on current deposit provision of US$500 per contract).

Interest Rate Assumptions

Three year Eurodollar futures strip yields ("strip yields") were calculated over the period January 1985 to February 1991.

Graph 1 sets out Eurodollar strip yields over the relevant period. *Graph 2* sets out the historical *changes* in the level of Eurodollar strip yield rates over a three month period. The data indicates that for the period January 1985 to February 1991, changes in Eurodollar strip yield rate changes had the following characteristics:

Average Change:	0.58%% pa
Range of Changes:	– 1.59% to 2.04%% pa
Standard Deviation:	0.43%% pa.

Assuming a normal distribution curve, based on the above information, there is a 95% probability that US$ Eurodollar strip yields would not move up or down by more than approx 166.25bps over a period of three months. In the transaction being analysed, this means that there is a 95% probability that the *maximum* change in Eurodollar strip yields over a three month period will be 166.25bps which assuming that the futures strip yield achieved initially was 8.00% pa means that rates should not be outside the range 6.34% pa and 9.66% pa. As a fall in interest rates will generate a negative margin payment requirement, the simulation focuses on a fall in interest rates to 6.34% pa.

Cash requirements

If Eurodollar rates fall to 6.34% pa, then the following cash requirements will need to be met:

Margin Call:	US$	4,987,563
Margin Funding Cost for three months (at 8.00% pa):	US$	99,751
Initial deposit:	US$	600,000 *
Deposit Funding Cost for three months (at 1.00% pa):#	US$	1,500 *
Commission (US$15/contract):	US$	1,500 *
Total	US$	5,090,314

* indicates cash flow that would have had to be committed irrespective of interest rate movements.

\# represents the difference between the funding cost and the rate earned on the deposit by lodging in the form of government securities.

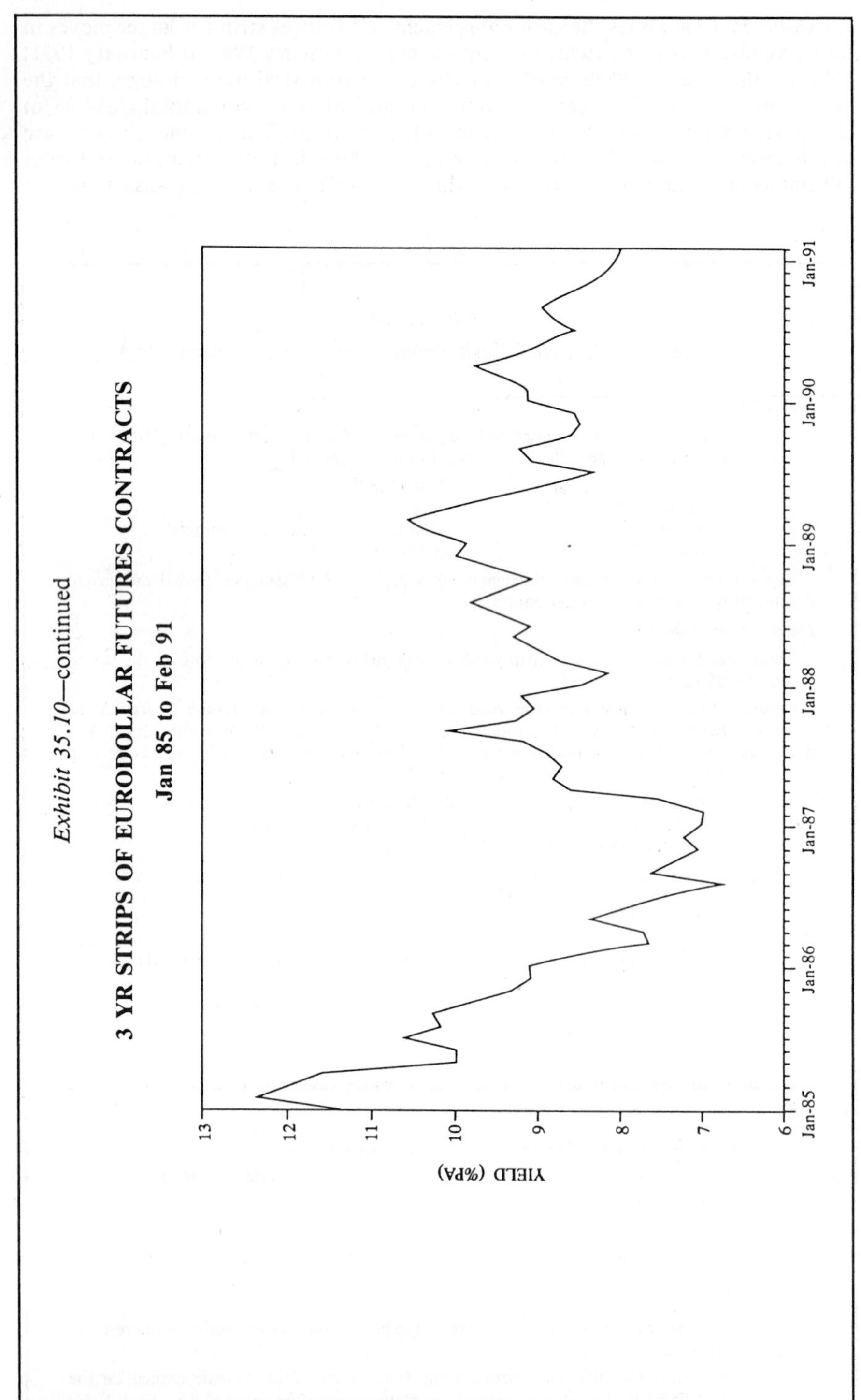

Exhibit 35.10—continued

3 YR STRIPS OF EURODOLLAR FUTURES CONTRACTS

Jan 85 to Feb 91

Exhibit 35.10—continued

COMPARISON OF EFC AND IRS 3 YEAR YIELDS

Jan 88 to Feb 91

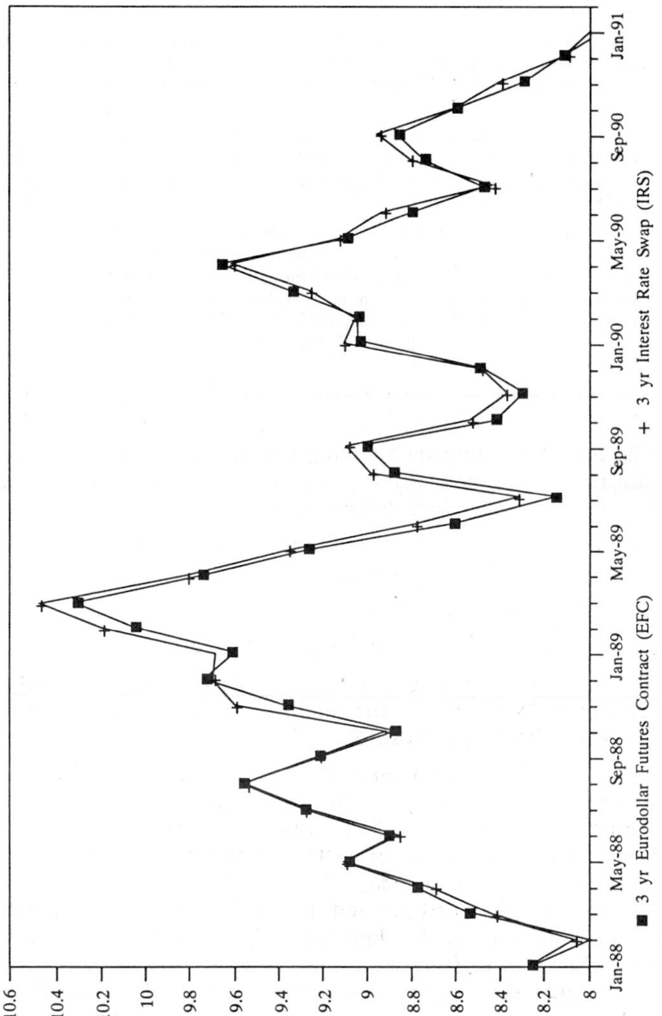

Exhibit 35.10—continued

The maximum cash flow requirement is based on holding 1,200 contracts in the first three month period of a three year US$100 million hedging transaction.

If interest rates fall to 6.34% pa and remain at this level, then the need to maintain and fund substantial margin requirements adds to the cost of the position. In this example, assuming a funding cost of 8.00% pa, the *additional* cost would be approx 20bps pa. This would make the futures strip approx 13bps pa more expensive than the equivalent interest rate swap.

Summary

The analysis indicates that in the case of a large movement in interest rates a hedger may be required to meet substantial cash margin requirements. In the transaction analysed, the *maximum* cash requirement identified was approx US$5 million on a three year US$100 million transaction.

However, the actual cash requirement of establishing and maintaining such a futures position is likely to be substantially lower. A major factor in this regard is likely to be the absolute rate achieved under the transaction and its relativity to the historical interest rate cycle.

For example, in the present market environment, a three year swap would achieve a rate of approx 8.00% pa. Although the statistical analysis indicates that there is a 5% chance that the hedger will have to meet margin calls of more than US$5 million during the first three months, this would require US$ three year rates to fall to and remain at 6.34% pa. An examination of US$ rates indicates that since late 1983, US$ LIBOR rates have been at or below these levels only 5% of the time—in the period August 1986 to February 1987.

The cost of funding such a margin payment over the full three year life of the transaction would have increased the cost of the hedge to (approx) 13bps pa above the cost of the equivalent interest rate swap.

Two specific aspects of the cash flow impact utilising futures to hedge interest rate swap positions should be noted:

- the concept of "tailing";
- the financing bias that may be present in futures.

The concept of tailing is used to describe a technique utilised, commonly in futures markets, to protect the funding cost of any adverse movement in margins required on the futures position.

In utilising short-term interest rate futures to hedge interest rate swap positions, substantial positions in the futures markets may be required to be maintained resulting in significant funding costs on margins required to be posted by the clearing house. The notion of a "tail" is that an opposing position is taken in the futures contract to protect against adverse movements in the average principal hedge required within the portfolio and the resultant increase in margins as a result of a subsequent increase in funding costs. The futures position taken is designed to protect the tail position. Important variables in determining the efficiency of the tailing include: the overnight cost of funds, the length of time the funding is required and the size of the interest rate futures position held.

For example, if interest rates rise in the principal bought futures position requiring a substantial margin payments to be made, then the cost of funding the margin will be offset by positive cash flow on the short interest rate futures tail position.

Tailing is an extremely important concept in large FRA/short-term interest rate swap books where interest rate futures are utilised as a major hedging technique. It is conceivable that the tail becomes substantial enough to require *its own tail*. As opposing positions are booked in and out of the portfolio, the size of the tail typically stabilises although substantial tails can develop where the portfolio acquires a significantly positive or negative bias in the nature of the underlying futures positions held.

The financing bias of using interest rate futures is particularly interesting. This results, primarily, in the margining of futures, as is the case with tails, but focuses on the more significant impact of margining for longer dated positions.

The concept of the financing bias is best illustrated by example. For example, if a portfolio is short interest rate futures and interest rates rise in all maturities, the portfolio will receive variation margins which can be invested at comparatively high short-term rates. As interest rates fall, the trader has to pay variation margins but this can be funded at comparatively lower short-term interest rates. This benefit may be cumulative as rates rise and fall over the life of a particular futures contract and even where the contract itself settles at the original price at which the contract was traded, the portfolio may have benefited from price oscillation.

An additional factor in the financing bias is that short-term rate movements are not perfectly correlated with forward rate changes, which reflect the change in the *total yield curve*. The changes in pattern between movements in spot interest rates versus forward interest rates can create significant cash flow investment and funding requirements within the interest rate portfolio.

Maturity liquidity and depth—Eurodollar interest rate futures

A vital factor in the use of interest rate futures strips as an alternative to interest rate swaps, either for the purpose of hedging directly or managing the exposure on interest rate swap transactions, is the depth in liquidity of the relevant interest rate futures markets. The degree of market liquidity and depth impacts upon the ease with which positions can be established and closed as well as determining the cost establishing positions (that is, the bid-offer spread).

Depth and liquidity of the Eurodollar futures markets is considerable. *Exhibit 35.11* summarises volumes and spreads of the CME Eurodollars futures contracts.

The data indicates that the Eurodollar futures market has good liquidity particularly in the front months and is relatively liquid, albeit less so, in more distant months. Liquidity also decreases with maturity of the futures contract.

However, in practice, in the back months, it is possible to establish substantial positions (up to US$100-300m with relative ease with a number of established price makers—either locals (20-50 lot parcels) or banks (100-300 lot parcels)). In the case of banks/financial institutions the capacity to find price makers is determined by the willingness of the banks to trade the treasury Eurodollar (TED) spread (see discussion in Chapter 23).

The average spread in the Eurodollar futures, particularly for the back months, compares favourably to the spread on interest rate swaps of similar maturity.

A number of banks and financial institutions quote the rates for the Eurodollar futures strip. Broker pages for such futures strips are also available (refer *Exhibit 35.12*).

The success of the back month Eurodollar contracts has drawn the attention of competing exchanges which are trying to capture the swap hedging business. In early 1990, the SIMEX introduced a strip contract, aiming at improving the ability to execute the various contracts by trading them simultaneously. To date, this development has had only modest success as the liquidity in Singapore hours for Eurodollars is somewhat limited.

Exhibit 35.11
Eurodollar Futures Contract—Market Depth & Liquidity

IMM EURODOLLARS BID AND OFFERS FOR 8 DECEMBER 1993

Quarter Number	Year	Month	Prices Bid	Prices Offer	Spread (bps)	Volume Daily	Volume Open	Strip Name
1	1993	Dec	96.58	59	1	27,303	264,471	)
2	1994	Mar	96.41	42	1	60,608	371,365	) Front
3		Jun	96.11	12	1	80,664	304,319	) Months
4		Sep	95.81	82	1	50,712	235,932	)
5		Dec	95.40	41	1	13,966	147,587	)
6	1995	Mar	95.31	32	1	10,245	173,515	) Red
7		Jun	95.10	11	1	6,876	116,061	) Months
8		Sep	94.92	93	1	5,958	102,024	)
9		Dec	94.62	64	2	2,840	80,715	)
10	1996	Mar	94.58	60	2	2,686	75,039	) Green
11		Jun	94.42	44	2	3,688	58,322	) Months
12		Sep	94.28	30	2	2,085	53,650	)
13		Dec	94.01	03	2	1,268	43,005	)
14	1997	Mar	94.00	02	2	1,509	42,101	) Blue
15		Jun	93.86	88	2	1,226	33,825	) Months
16		Sep	93.76	78	2	1,022	30,696	)
17		Dec	93.54	56	2	1,015	24,039	)
18	1998	Mar	93.56	58	2	839	20,444	) Gold
19		Jun	93.46	48	2	684	14,761	) Months
20		Sep	93.39	41	2	718	8,239	)
21		Dec	93.19	21	2	439	2,534	)
22	1999	Mar	93.23	25	2	503	1,984	) Pink
23		Jun	93.16	19	3	513	2,345	) Months
24		Sep	93.12	15	3	695	2,757	)
25		Dec	92.95	98	3	427	1,919	)
26	2000	Mar	92.99	02	3	563	1,602	) Orange/
27		Jun	92.93	96	3	470	2,053	) Purple
28		Sep	92.89	92	3	298	1,543	) Months
29		Dec	92.73	77	4	15	110	)

Please note that from Dec 1997 the market is very illiquid and mostly dominated by locals.

Based on data as of 8 December 1993.

Source: Bain Refco Commodities.

The liquidity in other currencies varies significantly. Almost uniformly, near month liquidity (which typically in non-Eurodollar contracts is limited to two/three years) is significant with the back months declining sharply. This necessitates the use of hedge stacking techniques (described above). However, liquidity in back months is improving gradually over time in these currencies.

Exhibit 35.12
Capital Markets Information Service

05/04 15:13 EDT (C)93 MKT DATA CORP DATA SOURCES: TULLETT, IMM PAGE 19915

[SPOT RUN $ STRIPS, 0-18 MONTH]

BEGIN	3 MO	6 MO	9 MO	1 YEAR
0	3.184	3.216	3.311	3.416
1	3.174	3.226	3.351	3.459
2	3.195	3.280	3.407	3.525
3	3.227	3.350	3.468	3.601
4	3.253	3.415	3.528	3.676
5	3.342	3.489	3.608	3.757
6	3.452	3.564	3.699	3.853
7	3.551	3.636	3.785	3.944
8	3.614	3.714	3.866	4.040
9	3.657	3.795	3.956	4.147
10	3.690	3.868	4.038	4.242
11	3.785	3.957	4.145	4.351
12	3.902	4.069	4.270	4.457
15	4.206	4.416	4.603	4.770
18	4.588	4.759	4.912	5.081

[SPOT RUN $ STRIPS, 21-36 MONTHS]

BEGIN	3 MO	6 MO	9 MO	1 YEAR
21	4.892	5.023	5.191	5.375
24	5.107	5.281	5.471	5.635
27	5.402	5.590	5.744	5.884
30	5.718	5.846	5.970	6.105
33	5.913	6.020	6.153	6.300
36	6.058	6.190	6.341	6.469

[IMM*]	3 MO	6 MO	9 MO	12 MO
JUN 93	3.170	3.228	3.365	3.472
SEP 93	3.260	3.435	3.545	3.704
DEC 93	3.580	3.657	3.817	3.979
MAR 94	3.700	3.896	4.072	4.273
JUN 94	4.040	4.212	4.423	4.603
SEP 94	4.350	4.586	4.753	4.922
DEC 94	4.790	4.900	5.057	5.226
MAR 95	4.940	5.118	5.297	5.494

[SPOT STARTS]

18 MO	3.638
21 MO	3.794
24 MO	3.925
27 MO	4.053
30 MO	4.188
36 MO	4.467
3M CASH	3.188

18 MO	24 MO	36 MO
3.722	4.030	4.572
3.983	4.292	4.824
4.278	4.581	* VS
4.557	4.873	IMM
4.866	5.158	3M E$

[NY 208-2160]
[LND 827-2345]
[TOK 241-8771]

Telerate Page 19915

Flagship IMM Strips Page

Futures strips based on IMM 90 day Eurodollar futures:

- Monthly starts, spot through 18 months, quoted for three, six, nine and 12 month maturities.
- Quarterly starts, 21 through 36 months, quoted for three, six, nine and 12 month maturities.
- Eurodollar strips with starts tied to IMM dates for first eight contracts, strip maturities of three months to 36 months.
- Three month cash Eurodollar deposit rate.

Source: Market Data Corporation, One Wall Street, 37th Floor, New York.

05/04 15:13 EDT (C)93 MKT DATA CORP DATA SOURCES: TULLETT, IMM PAGE 19916

STRIPS	9M	12M	15M	18M	2Y	30M	3Y	42M	4Y
IMM	[3.314	3.419	3.515	3.640	3.926	4.189	4.468	4.689	4.926]
3M	[3.314	3.418	3.515	3.640	3.926	4.189	4.468	4.698	4.926]
5M	[3.378	3.467	3.554	3.673	3.951	4.209	4.485	4.713	4.939]
JUNE 93	3.368	3.475	3.594	3.723	4.031	4.295	4.573	4.796	5.020
SEP 93	3.545	3.704	3.830	3.983	4.292	4.566	4.824	5.041	
DEC 93	3.187	3.979	4.128	4.278	4.581	4.837	5.085	5.284	
MAR 94	4.072	4.273	4.413	4.557	4.873	5.101	5.340		
JUN 94	4.423	4.603	4.727	4.866	5.158	5.368	5.588		
SEP 94	4.753	4.922	5.040	5.186	5.441	5.637			
DEC 94	5.057	5.226	5.351	5.457	5.696	5.868			
MAR 95	5.297	5.494	5.577	5.682	5.916				
JUN 95	5.618	5.756	5.832	5.924	6.136				
SEP 95	5.851	5.991	6.052	6.149					
DEC 95	6.064	6.195	6.265	6.329					
MAR 96	6.215	6.375	6.410						
JUN 96	6.431	6.541							

CASH IMM	3.148
RATES 3M	3.188
OFFER 6M	3.313

[IMM EURODOLLAR STRIP]
[DERIVATIVE CALCULATION]
[VS 90-DAY EURO$ CONTRACT]

* FOR DEALING PRICES CALL TULLETT *
SYD 223-3500 SIN 225-7688
TOK 241-6771 NY 208-2160 LND 827-2345

Telerate Page 19916

In-Depth IMM Eurodollar Strips

Futures strips based on IMM 90 day Eurodollar futures.

- Spot strips quoted for nine month through four year maturities, based on three different cash deposit rates:

  IMM: cash deposit rate to first IMM futures date.
  3M: three month cash Eurodollar deposit rate.
  6M: six month cash Eurodollar deposit rate.

- Eurodollar strips other than spot start on IMM Furutes dates, and are quoted for maturities of nine months to four years.

Exhibit 35.12—continued

05/04 15:13 EDT (C)93 MKT DATA CORP DATA SOURCES: TULLETT, LIFFE PAGE 19917

LDN 827-2345 NY 208-2160 [LIFFE STRIPS*] TOK 241-8771 SYD 223-3500

STG	9M	12M	15M	18M	DMK	9M	12M	15M	18M	3M CASH
CTR	6.232	6.341	6.415	6.543	CTR	6.884	6.685	6.468	6.346	[STG]
3M	6.248	6.354	6.425	6.552	3M	6.962	6.745	6.516	6.387	6.156
J 93	6.231	6.374	6.469	6.607	J 93	6.624	6.441	6.254	6.152	[DMK]
S 93	6.379	6.584	6.704	6.845	S 93	6.074	6.003	5.923	5.928	7.625
D 93	6.634	6.862	6.982		D 93	5.791	5.803	5.815		[US$]
M 94	6.963	7.184			M 94	5.664	5.771			3.188

US$	9M	12M	15M	18M
CTR	3.327	3.433	3.529	3.652
3M	3.328	3.434	3.530	3.653
J 93	3.382	3.488	3.604	3.730
S 93	3.562	3.717	3.838	3.988
D 93	3.830	3.987	4.132	
M 94	4.072	4.271		

	3M [STG]	5M	3M (DMK]	6M	3M [US$]	6M
SPT	6.132	6.162	7.430	7.145	3.190	3.224
1X	6.089	6.148	7.269	6.922	3.183	3.236
2X	6.098	6.169	7.039	6.713	3.207	3.297
3X	6.121	6.198	6.764	6.504	3.239	3.371
4X	6.123	6.214	6.463	6.286	3.265	3.438
5X	6.161	6.271	6.292	6.137	3.365	3.514
6X	6.201	6.338	6.163	6.010	3.481	3.589
9X	6.405		5.784		3.678	

* FOR DEALING PRICES CALL TULLET,
CTR--CASH RATE TO 1ST CONTRACT DATE

Telerate Page 19917

LIFFE Strips

- Sterling, deutschmark and US dollar futures strips pegged to LIFFE futures dates, quoted for nine, 12, 15 and 18 month maturities.
- Spot run strips quoted for sterling, deutschmark and US dollar, spot through nine month start dates, for three and six month maturities.
- Three month cash Eurodeposit rates for sterling, deutschmark and US dollar.

05/04 15:13 EDT (C)93 MKT DATA CORP DATA SOURCES: TULLETT, SIMEX, TIFFE PAGE 19918

3M US$ CASH = 3.250 [SIMEX US$ & TIFFE YEN STRIPS*] 3M YEN CASH = 3.270

[SIMEX US$]	9M	12M	15M	18M	[TIFFE YEN]	9M	12M	15M	18M
SPOT CTR	3.684	3.886	3.975	4.123	SPOT CTR	3.246	3.253	3.252	3.313
SPOT 3M	3.686	3.903	3.989	4.145	SPOT 3M	3.246	3.253	3.252	3.313
MAR 93	3.809	3.963	4.077	4.237	MAR 93	3.233	3.247	3.279	3.353
JUN 93	4.146	4.280	4.419	4.565	JUN 93	3.212	3.283	3.364	3.468
SEP 93	4.504	4.663	4,780		SEP 93	3.287	3.412	3.521	
DEC 93	4.657	4.852			DEC 93	3.467	3.616		

* FOR DEALING PRICES CALL TULLETT, CTR-CASH RATE TO 1ST CONTRACT DATE.

[LDN 827-2345] [NY 208-2160] [TOK 241-8771] [SYD 223-3500]

[US DOLLAR]

START	3 MO	6 MO	START	3 MO	6 MO
SPOT	3.297	3.381	4 M	3.525	4.036
1 M	3.315	3.434	5 M	3.869	4.176
2 M	3.380	3.639	6 M	4.215	4.313
3 M	3.440	3.843	9 M	4.375	

[JAPANESE YEN]

START	3 MO	6 MO	START	3 MO	6MO
SPOT	3.276	3.258	4M	3.190	3.189
1 M	3.269	3.242	5 M	3.185	3.195
2 M	3.248	3.227	6 M	3.175	3.198
3 M	3.221	3.208	9 M	3.201	

Telerate Page 19918

SIMEX and TIFFE Strips

- SIMEX US dollar futures strips pegged to SIMEX futures dates, quoted for nine, 12, 15 and 18 month maturities.
- TIFFE yen futures strips pegged to TIFFE futures dates, quoted for nine, 12, 15 and 18 month strips.
- Spot run strips in US dollar and yen, spot through nine month start dates, for three and six month maturities.
- Three month cash US dollar and Euroyen deposit rates.

Chapter 36

Cap/Floor Portfolio Risk Management Techniques

HEDGING CAPS: THE ALTERNATIVES

Caps, collars and floors are, as detailed in Chapter 5, essentially a series of options on debt instruments. The exposures incurred in creating these instruments for clients are identical, conceptually, to exposures incurred in writing or granting debt options.

Providers of cap, collar and floor facilities, as writers of options, seek to manage the exposure on the options written utilising active hedge management techniques involving cash and/or options markets.

There are basically two alternative types of strategies available in hedging debt options:

- purchasing matching options;
- creating synthetic options through option replication techniques (utilising delta or gamma hedging).

Both these strategies are considered below. In addition, risk management of a portfolio of caps and floors entails a number of special risks which are also considered.

PURCHASING DEBT OPTIONS

The only certain way to completely hedge an option is through the purchase of an equivalent option, identical with respect to all relevant terms of exercise price, face value and expiration date. The premium cost of an option purchased as a hedge is roughly equal to that received for an option written. Therefore, if options written are hedged with identical options purchased, the profit will, in principle, be limited to the bid-offer spread between the two.

The supply of options available for utilisation to hedge cap portfolios is limited to:

- exchange traded options;
- options created through capital market transactions.

Exchange traded options may be available to assist cap providers to hedge their portfolio exposures. However, the exchange traded options markets do not, generally, extend beyond two to three years thereby limiting their role in absorbing the risk assumed by cap providers.

Options created or engineered through capital market transactions are an increasingly important source of supply of options for intermediaries acting as providers of caps. The main source of this type of debt option has been issues of capped FRNs and CDs. The issues of caps, FRNs and CDs were primarily in and around 1985/86. In 1992, the issue of collared FRNs provided an additional source of debt options. Supply for caps and floors from these particular capital market transactions is generally spasmodic. Such capital market issues depend on prevalence of particular conditions in the relevant currencies and the availability of investors for these types of securities. The detailed structure of these options created through capital market instruments is discussed in Chapter 15.

Despite the increased supply of debt options with longer maturities, intermediaries acting as principal providers of caps frequently need to resort to synthetic option creation techniques to manage the exposures on their cap portfolios.

OPTION REPLICATION TECHNIQUES

Concept

One of the most common techniques for managing the risk entailed in cap portfolios is to utilise synthetic option technology to replicate the price characteristic of options on the relevant asset. A synthetic option is created from a portfolio of existing traded instruments which with proper management over time can replicate the return characteristics of an option. This is also referred to as delta or gamma hedging.

A synthetic option is created by using a portfolio consisting of two instruments:

- the instrument into which the option can be exercised, whether it be a cash market instrument or futures and forwards on the underlying asset; and
- a risk-free asset, usually cash or high quality securities.

The key to creating a synthetic call option is to determine the proportion of cash and asset to maintain in the portfolio. This proportion is adjusted through time in a very specific way to replicate the price behaviour of a call option. In practice, such a portfolio can be created and properly managed to give approximately the same premium and outcome as a traded call option on the underlying asset.

The intuition for synthetic options derives from the fact that the price behaviour of a call option is similar to that of a portfolio with combined positions involving the underlying asset and cash. Although the price of a call option and the price of the underlying asset change in the same direction, the effect on the price of the call option of a given change in the asset price, depends on the current price level of the asset. This is because the number of units of the asset held in the replicating portfolio must be sufficient to equate to the slope of the call option price curve at that particular price level or the particular option's delta.

Delta is a measure of the sensitivity of the option value to changes in the price of the underlying asset. For example, a call option with a delta of 0.5 will increase in value by $5 for an $10 increase in the underlying asset value.

The delta of an option has a value between 0 and 1. A delta of 1 means that the value of the option increases in proportion to the price of the underlying asset: one dollar for every one dollar increase in the value of the underlying asset. A deeply in-the-money option will have a delta close to or equal to 1, since the intrinsic value of the option will increase in proportion close or equal to the increase in the price of the underlying asset, while the time value will become very small. A deeply out-of-the-money option will have a delta close to 0, since it will have no intrinsic value and low time value owing to the small chance that it will become profitable.

Deltas for call options are positive and deltas for put options are negative. Put deltas are negative because put prices move in the opposite direction to the underlying asset price. The underlying asset delta is always 1 with positive 1 indicating a long asset position and negative 1 a short position.

Delta hedging basically operates on the basis that a writer of a call option can cover its price risk by purchasing an amount of the underlying asset in proportion to the delta, for any given price of the underlying instrument. For example, a call option written on US$1m against A$ with a delta of 0.60%, an at-the-money option, will rise or fall in value by about 0.60% for each 1.00% fall or rise in the value of the US$. Therefore, the option writer can purchase US$0.6m in the forward market and in theory the value of the cash position will move in exactly offsetting fashion to the value of the option written. The US$0.6m in our example is referred to as the equivalent delta position being the delta of the option multiplied by the par value of the option. An option which is hedged by an offsetting cash position according to this approach is said to be delta hedged or delta neutral.

The replicating portfolio must be adjusted as the asset price changes. This will usually entail selling assets as the asset price falls and buying assets as the asset price rises. As the portfolio is never fully invested when the asset price increases, nor fully disinvested when the asset price falls, this process of portfolio adjustment will reduce the initial investment. Theoretically, by the expiration of the call option, the cumulative depreciation should approximately equal the initial theoretical value of the call option.

The technique for replicating put options is similar. It entails maintaining a portfolio consisting of cash and a short position in the underlying asset which is adjusted as the price of the asset changes.

The concept of utilising option replication techniques is illustrated in *Exhibit 36.1*. Four examples are included: replication of a call option which expires in-the-money, expiration of a call option which expires out-of-the-money, replication of a put option which expires in-the-money, and replication of a put option which expires out-of-the-money.

Exhibit 36.1

Option Replication/Delta Hedging Techniques—Example

1. Call Option Example (Option Expires In-The-Money)

Inputs—		Hedge Profit and Loss	
Asset Price:	$100.00		
Strike Price:	$100.00		
Trade Date:	05-Oct-X2	Premium Receipt:	$21,935
Expiry Date:	02-Nov-X2	Interest on Premium:	$168
Time to Expiry (Days):	28.00	Hedge Costs:	($18,090)
Volatility:	20.00%	Net	$4,014
Interest Rate:	10.00%		
Holding Cost:	0.00%		

No of Assets:	10,000	10,000	10,000	10,000	10,000
Date:	05-Oct-X2	12-Oct-X2	19-Oct-X2	26-Oct-X2	02-Nov-X2
Time to Expiry (Days):	28.00	21.00	14.00	7.00	0.00
Asset Price:	$100.00	$101.00	$99.00	$100.50	$102.50
Option Value:	$2.1935	$1.9032	$1.5568	$1.1029	
Delta:	0.5073	0.5883	0.4048	0.5758	
Gamma:	0.0715	0.0797	0.0997	0.1404	

Exhibit 36.1—continued

Theta:	0.0386	0.0439	0.0532	0.0773	
Vega:	0.1096	0.0936	0.0749	0.0544	
Rho:	(0.0017)	(0.0014)	(0.0004)	(0.0003)	
Delta Hedge—					
Hedge Requirement:	5,073.25	5,882.65	4,048.45	5,758.29	10,000.00
Hedge Portfolio:					
1 Purchase Assets 5,073 @ $100.00	$507,325	$507,325	$405,402	$405,402	$405,402
2 Purchase Assets 809 @ $101.00		$81,749			
3 Sell Assets (1,834) @ $99.00					
4 Purchase Assets 1,710 @ $100.50				$171,838	$171,838
5 Purchase Assets 4,242 @ $102.50					$434,776
Value of Hedge Portfolio—					
No of Assets	5,073	5,883	4,048	5,758	10,000
Average Value of Assets	$100.00	$100.14	$100.14	$100.25	$101.20
Total	$507,325	$589,074	$405,402	$577,241	$1,012,016
Gain (Loss) on Hedge Adjustment:			($2,086.56)	$0.00	($12,016)
Interest (@ 10.0000%):		($972.95)	($1,129.73)	($777.48)	($1,107.04)
Cumulative Cost:		($972.95)	($4,189.24)	($4,966.73)	($18,089.99)

2. Call Option Example (Option Expires Out-Of-The-Money)

Inputs—

Asset Price:	$100.00	Hedge Profit and Loss	
Strike Price:	$100.00		
Trade Date:	05-Oct-X2	Premium Receipt:	$21,935
Expiry Date:	02-Nov-X2	Interest on Premium:	$168
Time to Expiry (Days):	28.00	Hedge Costs:	($16,123)
Volatility:	20.00%	Net	$5,980
Interest Rate:	10.00%		
Holding Cost:	0.00%		
Model Spec:	1.00		

No of Assets:	10,000	10,000	10,000	10,000	10,000
Date:	05-Oct-X2	12-Oct-X2	19-Oct-X2	26-Oct-X2	02-Nov-X2
Time to Expiry (Days):	28.00	21.00	14.00	7.00	0.00
Asset Price:	$100.00	$101.00	$99.00	$100.50	$98.50
Option Value:	$2.1935	$1.9032	$1.5568	$1.1029	
Delta:	0.5073	0.5883	0.4048	0.5758	
Gamma:	0.0715	0.0797	0.0997	0.1404	
Theta:	0.0386	0.0439	0.0532	0.0773	
Vega:	0.1096	0.0936	0.0749	0.0544	
Rho:	(0.0017)	(0.0014)	(0.0004)	(0.0003)	
Delta Hedge—					
Hedge Requirement:	5,073.25	5,882.65	4,048.45	5,758.29	0.00
Hedge Portfolio:					
1 Purchase Assets 5,073 @ $100.00	$507,325	$507,325	$405,402	$405,402	
2 Purchase Assets 809 @ $101.00		$81,749	$0		
3 Sell Assets (1,834) @ $99.00					
4 Purchase Assets 1,710 @ $100.50				$171,838	
5 Purchase Assets (5,758) @ $98.50					
Value of Hedge Portfolio—					
No of Assets	5,073	5,883	4,048	5,758	0
Average Value of Assets	$100.00	$100.14	$100.14	$100.25	$0.00
Total	$507,325	$589,074	$405,402	$577,241	$0
Gain (Loss) on Hedge Adjustment:			($2,086.56)	$0.00	($10,049)
Interest (@ 10.0000%):		($972.95)	($1,129.73)	($777.48)	($1,107.04)
Cumulative Cost:		($972.95)	($4,189.24)	($4,966.73)	($16,123.14)

3. Put Option Example (Option Expires In-The-Money)

Inputs—

Asset Price:	$100.00	Hedge Profit and Loss	
Strike Price:	$100.00		
Trade Date:	05-Oct-X2	Premium Receipt:	$21,935
Expiry Date:	02-Nov-X2	Interest on Premium:	$168
Time to Expiry (Days):	28.00	Hedge Costs:	($6,548)
Volatility:	20.00%	Net	$15,555
Interest Rate:	10.00%		
Holding Cost:	0.00%		

Exhibit 36.1—continued

No of Assets:		10,000	10,000	10,000	10,000	10,000
Date:		05-Oct-X2	12-Oct-X2	19-Oct-X2	26-Oct-X2	02-Nov-X2
Time to Expiry (Days):		28.00	21.00	14.00	7.00	0.00
Asset Price:		$100.00	$99.00	$100.00	$98.50	$98.00
Option Value:		$2.1935	$1.9032	$1.5568	$1.1029	
Delta:		(0.4854)	(0.5705)	(0.4904)	(0.7013)	
Gamma:		0.0715	0.0821	0.1015	0.1267	
Theta:		0.0386	0.0435	0.0552	0.0668	
Vega:		0.1096	0.0926	0.0778	0.0472	
Rho:		(0.0017)	(0.0014)	(0.0006)	(0.0004)	
Delta Hedge—						
Hedge Requirement:		(4,853.90)	(5,704.51)	(4,903.91)	(7,012.95)	(10,000.00)
Hedge Portfolio:						
1 Sell Assets	(4,854) @ $100.00	($485,390)	($485,390)	($489,660)	($489,660)	($489,660)
2 Sell Assets	(851) @ $99.00		($84,210)			
3 Purchase Assets	801 @ $100.00					
4 Sell Assets	(2,109) @ $98.50				($207,740)	($207,740)
5 Sell Assets	(2,987) @ $98.00					($292,731)
Value of Hedge Portfolio—						
No of Assets		(4,854)	(5,705)	(4,904)	(7,013)	(10,000)
Average Value of Assets		$100.00	$99.85	$99.85	$99.44	$99.01
Total		($485,390)	($569,600)	($489,660)	($697,400)	($990,131)
Gain (Loss) on Hedge Adjustment:				($119.38)	$0.00	($9,869)
Interest (@ 8.0000%):			$744.71	$873.91	$751.26	$1,069.98
Cumulative Cost:			$744.71	$1,499.24	$2,250.50	($6,548.41)

4. Put Option Example (Option Expires Out-Of-The-Money)

Inputs—		Hedge Profit and Loss	
Asset Price:	$100.00		
Strike Price:	$100.00		
Trade Date:	05-Oct-X2	Premium Receipt:	$21,935
Expiry Date:	02-Nov-X2	Interest on Premium:	$168
Time to Expiry (Days):	28.00	Hedge Costs:	($9,200)
Volatility:	20.00%	Net	$12,903
Interest Rate:	10.00%		
Holding Cost:	0.00%		

No of Assets:		10,000	10,000	10,000	10,000	10,000
Date:		05-Oct-X2	12-Oct-X2	19-Oct-X2	26-Oct-X2	02-Nov-X2
Time to Expiry (Days):		28.00	21.00	14.00	7.00	0.00
Asset Price:		$100.00	$99.50	$101.00	$100.50	$102.50
Option Value:		$2.1935	$1.9032	$1.5568	$1.1029	
Delta:		(0.4854)	(0.5292)	(0.3908)	(0.4223)	
Gamma:		0.0715	0.0829	0.0968	0.1404	
Theta:		0.0386	0.0444	0.0538	0.0775	
Vega:		0.1096	0.0944	0.0757	0.0544	
Rho:		(0.0017)	(0.0012)	(0.0004)	(0.0002)	
Delta Hedge—						
Hedge Requirement:		(4,853.90)	(5,291.71)	(3,907.58)	(4,223.45)	0.00
Hedge Portfolio:						
1 Sell Assets	(4,854) @ $100.00	($485,390)	($485,390)	($390,597)	($390,597)	
2 Sell Assets	(438) @ $99.50		($43,562)			
3 Purchase Assets	1,384 @ $101.00					
4 Sell Assets	(316) @ $100.50				($31,745)	
5 Purchase Assets	4,223 @ $102.50					
Value of Hedge Portfolio—						
No of Assets		(4,854)	(5,292)	(3,908)	(4,223)	
Average Value of Assets		$100.00	$99.96	$99.96	$100.00	
Total		($485,390)	($528,952)	($390,597)	$422,341)	
Gain (Loss) on Hedge Adjustment:				($1,441.39)	$0.00	($10,562)
Interest Cost (@ 8.0000%):			$744.71	$811.54	$599.27	$647.98
Cumulative Cost:			$744.71	$114.86	$714.14	($9,200.23)

The concept of synthetic options permits option granters to replicate not only call options, but many other option positions. Using replicating portfolios the granter of options can, where it has created a risk position by writing options, cover these open positions creating synthetic options which hedge the existing exposure.

Option replication—risk dimensions[1]

The use of option replication techniques entails significant risks which require management. These risks were alluded to in Chapter 11, in the context of the discussion of option pricing, and Chapter 31, in the context of discussing risks of swap and derivative portfolio management.

The major risk dimensions include:

- delta/gamma risk;
- vega/kappa or volatility risk;
- theta or time decay risk;
- rho or interest rate risk.

These Greek letters provide a measure of the behaviour of option value as market conditions change and allow evaluation and management of the risk within an option portfolio.

One additional measure which is sometimes used is referred to as lambda. While delta gives the dollar change in the option value caused by a change in the price of the underlying assets, lambda measures the percentage changes. Lambda, which in a sense measures the leverage or elasticity of an option, gives the percentage change in the option value due to a 1% rise in the underlying assets. Lambda is calculated by effectively scaling delta which is equal to delta times the asset price divided by the option price. Lambda is not typically an important factor in cap/floor portfolio risk management.

Delta-gamma risk

As previously outlined, the delta for derivative securities can be defined as the rate of change of its price with respect to the price of the underlying asset. Delta, as a construct, emerges quite clearly from the Black-Scholes option pricing approach which implies the possibility of establishing an instantaneous riskless portfolio consisting of a position in the derivative security and a position in the underlying asset.

The option's delta, as is evident from the discussion above, is essential to managing its risk within a hedge portfolio, in which the option is hedged by purchasing or selling delta units of the underlying asset. The risk management function (at least, as noted below, for small price changes) is determined by delta neutrality whereby the overall portfolio of options and hedges has a delta of zero, thereby immunising the portfolio for changes in value from both price increases and decreases.

The characteristics of delta are discussed in detail in Chapter 11. However, some additional features of delta should be noted:

- The concept of delta enables one option to be hedged with another option on the same underlying asset by creating delta neutral positions. As both options are affected by movements in the price of the underlying asset, to ensure that it is

1. This section draws on John Hull (1989) and Stephen Figlewski, "Theoretical Valuation Models" in Figlewski et al (ed) (1990).

necessary to hold the options in the right proportions, in the resulting changes in value to offset.

- The delta of the underlying asset is, by definition, 1.0. In practice, delta hedging utilises a *futures or forward contract* on the underlying asset rather than the asset itself. The principles of delta hedging are equally applicable where a futures or forward position in the underlying asset is utilised. The futures or forward contract utilised as the hedge does not, necessarily, have to have the same maturity as the derivative security.
- Deltas have the property of additivity. The delta of a portfolio of options and other derivative securities on an asset is the sum of the deltas of the individual options and other assets in the portfolio. This facilitates the use of delta to summarise the price sensitivity of even a very complex portfolio of assets and derivative products.

However, delta only holds for very small changes in the asset price. Therefore any movement in the asset price outside a small range leads to diminished hedge efficiency. This change in the asset price exposes the portfolio to what is commonly referred to as gap/jump risk or gamma risk.

Gamma is the change in delta as the underlying asset price changes. As changes in delta produce exposure in a portfolio, the level of gamma can be utilised to quantify the risk of an option portfolio. The gamma of an option is not stationary but changes as the asset price changes. Gamma is highest when the option is at-the-money and lowest when the option is deep in- or out-of-the-money.

The basic problem of delta hedging, therefore, is that while the delta of an option varies substantially through its life, the delta of the cash markets is always fixed. Consequently, in theory, continual rehedging is required to keep the portfolio perfectly delta neutral. This problem is sometimes sought to be averted by a technique known as gamma hedging whereby the intermediary seeks to match the rate at which the deltas themselves vary with changes in interest rates.

The concept of gamma neutral hedging recognises that adjusting the portfolio to delta neutrality after each market move does not give adequate protection to a portfolio. A gamma hedge is a hedge strategy that attempts to reduce the exposure of the portfolio by reducing total portfolio gamma.

A portfolio which is perfectly hedged will have both a zero delta and a zero gamma. The only means of creating a zero gamma position is to match each option with the offsetting position in that option series. Consequently, gamma is sought to be minimised, but never reduced to zero, by changing the composition of the option side of the portfolio. Changing the underlying asset side of the portfolio has no impact on gamma. For example, the gamma impact of selling at-the-money puts can be minimised by buying out-of-the-money puts.

Against this background, the notion of delta and gamma neutrality can be stated more simply. A delta neutral option or book of options (at least partially hedged with offsetting positions in the underlying asset) is one whose *value* is unaffected by (small) changes in the price of that underlying asset. A gamma neutral option portfolio is one that *remains delta neutral* as the price of the underlying asset changes (by small amounts).

There are three important characteristics of gamma:

- the shorter the time to expiration the higher the gamma will be;
- at-the-money options have the highest gammas in relation to other options in the same expiration period; and
- gammas vary with volatility, but in a complex way.

Gammas tend to decrease on medium to long-term options (that is, options with 60 days or more to expiration). For short-term options (with 45 days or less to expiration), the gammas of out-of-the-money options increase as volatility increases, but decrease as volatility increases for at-the-money options. These features of the gamma are important considerations for delta hedging management as they address the need for active rehedging of option positions.

In practice, gamma indicates the extent of portfolio rebalancing that will be needed in a delta neutral position. A large gamma position indicates that a portfolio hedge will become rapidly unbalanced when the asset price alters. In essence, gamma is a measure of the risk exposure of a hedge position that will emerge when the price of the underlying asset changes, particularly where it changes rapidly, and the portfolio hedge is not or is unable to be adjusted instantaneously. This is particularly the case where the price movement in the underlying asset is non-stochastic, commonly referred to as a price jump.

As noted above, the gamma risk of a portfolio can only be reduced by purchasing options. An alternative measure of managing the gamma exposure on a portfolio is to restructure the portfolio configuration of options to replicate synthetic positions in the underlying asset itself. That is, create purchased/sold positions in the relevant series of call and put options to create purchased or sold position equivalents in the underlying asset which by definition have limited gamma exposure.

Vega/kappa or volatility risk

As previously noted, option values are particularly sensitive changes in the volatility of the underlying asset. This is referred to as vega or, more correctly in the Greek alphabet, kappa, or volatility risk.

Kappa is uniformly positive for both calls and puts. In the case of an option combination within a portfolio, the sensitivity to change in volatility for the portfolio will be the difference between the two kappas, which may have either sign. In practice, kappa is expressed as a change in option value for a 0.01 change in standard deviation of the underlying option price.

Volatility risk is a particularly important factor in option portfolio management. This reflects the fact that portfolio management, is, in part, an exercise in management of volatility positions. Portfolio managers converse in terms of being short or long volatility. The underlying premise is that the portfolio manager's task is to attempt to position the portfolio volatility exposure to seek to profit from changes in volatility level within pre-specified limits.

An important aspect of managing volatility risk is that it can be only neutralised by taking positions in the same or a difference series of options. Volatility is not a determinant of value of the underlying asset and consequently cannot be neutralised through positions in the asset market itself.

Theta or time decay risk

The option theta measures the rate of change in the value of the portfolio with respect to time where all other value parameters are held constant. In effect, theta measures the rate of time decay for the options or the degree to which it loses its inherent value as a "wasting asset".

Theta measures the cost of holding an option and, conversely, the reward of selling an option.

As described in Chapter 11, the greater the time value in the option, initially, the larger the rate of time decay of that value. Theta is greatest in dollar term for at-the-money options, although as a percentage of value, theta is larger for out-of-the-money options.

A factor to note is that a deep in-the-money European put may be worth less than its intrinsic value. This reflects the opportunity loss for not being able to exercise it immediately and begin earning interest on the exercise price that will be received. As the option approaches maturity, the value of the put must rise to equate to its intrinsic value. Under this circumstance, theta is, conversely, positive in contrast to its negative value for most situations.

As discussed below, management of theta is particularly important and its interaction with gamma and vega risks constitute a major determinant of option portfolio value.

Rho or interest rate risk

Rho measures option portfolio risk with respect to changes in the riskless interest rate. As previously outlined, the time value for a call option comes partly from the interest that can be earned investing the strike price from the present until the expiration date. Conversely, the purchaser of put loses interest while waiting until option maturity to receive the strike price. Consequently, changes in interest rates will have an impact on the value of the option. This impact will be higher for options with longer periods to run to expiration and will also be greater for options that are in-the-money, reflecting the fact that the exercise price is more likely to be paid increasing the importance of the discounting process.

In practice, the rho or riskless interest rate risk of the portfolio can be managed assuming positions in the underlying interest rate market by traditional interest rate risk management measures.

Interaction of risks[2]

As might be expected, individual risk dimensions identified are substantively interrelated. This necessitates a constant process of trade-offs between the various risk dimensions and the management of an option portfolio. In this section, some key aspects of the trade-offs entailed in option portfolio management are examined.

For the market maker, offsetting the price risk of the portfolio of options by delta-based purchases and sales of the underlying asset reduces the risk of the delta neutral portfolio whereby the value of the portfolio is insulated from the effects of small price changes in the underlying assets, be it increases or decreases.

However, such a position still exposes the portfolio manager to significant risks. Delta neutral positions entailing a net *purchase* of options will have a positive theta, that is the option position will decline in value over time reflecting the nature of the option as a wasting asset. The value of the option evolves towards its intrinsic value as expiration approaches. In contrast, a delta neutral position which entails sold options will *gain* in value as expiration approaches.

Interaction of delta and theta, in this context, dictates that market makers prefer delta neutral positions that are net sold options to enable them earn the erosion in the value of the option, that is, benefit from the option portfolio theta.

2. This section draws on William L Silber, "Marketmaking in Options: Principles and Implications" in Figlewski et al (ed) (1990), and A L H Smith (1986).

Structuring a portfolio to benefit from theta, entails the portfolio manager assuming gamma and vega/kappa risk.

A portfolio which is delta neutral and short options will require the portfolio manager to rebalance the hedge by buying futures when the price of the underlying asset increases and selling futures on the underlying asset where the price falls. Similarly, the portfolio is exposed to increases in value from falls in volatility but loses value from increases in volatility.

To an extent, some of these risks are offsetting. For example, theta and gamma tend, at least to some degree, to offset the other. A net purchased option portfolio which is delta neutral simultaneously loses value because of time decay or theta with the passage of time, but improves in value as a result of the movement in price because of the position's gamma risk. Conversely, a delta neutral position entailing a net sold position in options increases in value because of theta each day, but, generally speaking, decreases in value when the market moves up and down because of the portfolio's gamma risk.

However, the risks are not necessarily entirely offsetting. Theta erosion in option values occurs relatively smoothly over the period to expiration. In contrast, the gains and losses from gamma rebalancing can be large and discontinuous, reflecting the fact that larger gains and losses from gamma occur when there is a sharp change in the price of the underlying asset which prevents the portfolio manager from adjusting or rebalancing the delta hedge appropriately.

The interaction of these risks forces, typically, portfolio managers to seek to generate earnings/value from an options portfolio by one or other of the following strategies:

- maintain delta neutral/net short options portfolio positions where it is anticipated that the underlying price movements will not be discontinuous (that is, the portfolio has low gamma risk) and volatility of the underlying assets are not expected to change substantially (that is, low vega/kappa risk);
- operate the portfolio on the basis that portfolio value/earnings derived from the bid-offer spread on purchasing and selling options. By implication, the portfolio manager would, under this strategy, seek to balance the portfolio by purchasing some option and selling others, in contrast to being a net purchaser or seller of options;
- managing the option portfolio as a volatility risk management functions where portfolio managers seeks to benefit from changes in volatility levels in the underlying asset.

The first strategy is fairly self explanatory and is consistent with the factors described above.

The second approach is also relatively straightforward and is predicated on the notion that portfolio managers view delta hedging in the underlying asset or option replication techniques as a temporary substitute for an offsetting option transaction. In effect, the portfolio manager plans to earn the bid-offer spread without seeking to worry about the erosion in value of the option portfolio or the management of the complex risks entailed.

The last approach, essentially taking views on volatility, is both complex and interesting. Volatility trading in the context of portfolio management seeks to generate profits according to the portfolio manager's capacity to anticipate price volatility changes for the underlying asset market, without taking a large market risk.

The opportunities for trading volatilities varies significantly between markets. However, the extent of fluctuations in the level of volatility in the US$ and other currency cap markets can be gauged from *Exhibit 36.2.*

In practice, volatility trading reflects a need to manage a problem with delta hedging that is the difficulty of defining, at least, in unique terms, the volatility of a particular option series. This reflects the fact that the hedge ratio or delta of an option is a function of a specific volatility level. Some of the problems of estimating volatility are discussed in Chapter 11.

In practice, portfolio managers use the implied option volatility of an option series to calculate a delta factor rather than an average figure calculated from the class as a whole or from analysis of price movements of the underlying instrument. However, this, in itself, creates a number of difficulties:

- The option series selected for the hedge may well be affected by special factors.
- There appear to be systematic differences in volatility levels in particular option series.

These factors dictate that a move in the underlying market volatility levels may not result, for a particular series, in a volatility change equal to that of the class as a whole.

The observed pattern of volatilities differing across strike prices is particularly interesting. From the viewpoint of portfolio managers, the differences are not particularly significant as long as the structure of implied volatilities across various strike prices are stable. However, the pattern is not stationary and is itself subject to some movements.

In practice, attempts to understand observe pattern for implied volatility is, in part, the basis of volatility trading itself.

One possible explanation is that the volatility component of option pricing techniques such as Black-Scholes Option Pricing Models is predicated on the simplifying assumption that asset prices follow a smooth, continuous diffusion process. In practice, asset prices, on occasions, exhibit discontinuous price movements which are particularly beneficial to purchasers of out-of-the-money options or, conversely, detrimental to sellers of these options. For the sellers of such options, such price movements are particularly concerning as there is no chance to rebalance the hedge and the deltas on such out-of-the-money options changes dramatically with such sharp jumps in price.

Consequently, for deep out-of-the-money puts, high implied volatilities reflect the purchasers willing to pay higher volatilities and the sellers demanding higher volatilities than those implied by simple diffusion processes for price movements in the underlying assets. Similar explanations are applicable to out-of-the-money call options.

An additional factor in regard to both puts and calls is the fact that smaller speculators in asset markets typically prefer to have highly leveraged positions in anticipation of substantial moves in the price of the underlying assets. As a consequence, such buyers tend to pay higher volatility but reflecting the fact that the options are out-of-the-money, *lower premiums* resulting in higher implied volatility for these series of options.

Exhibit 36.2
Fluctuations in Cap Volatility

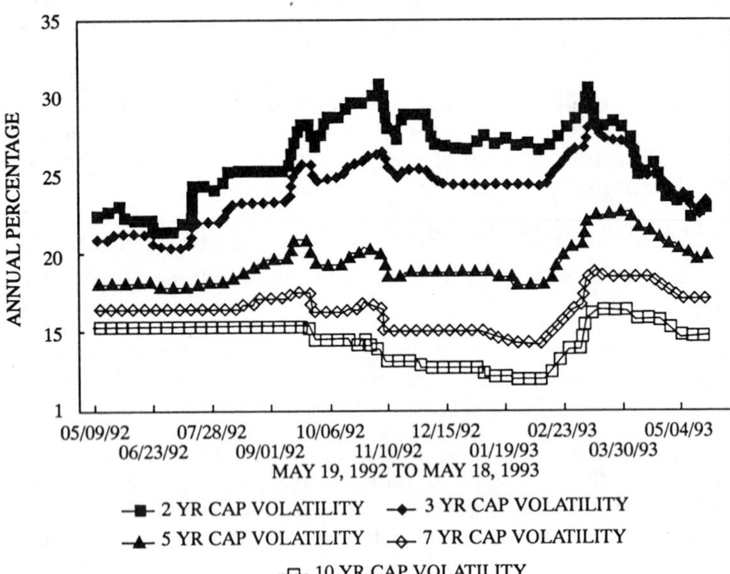

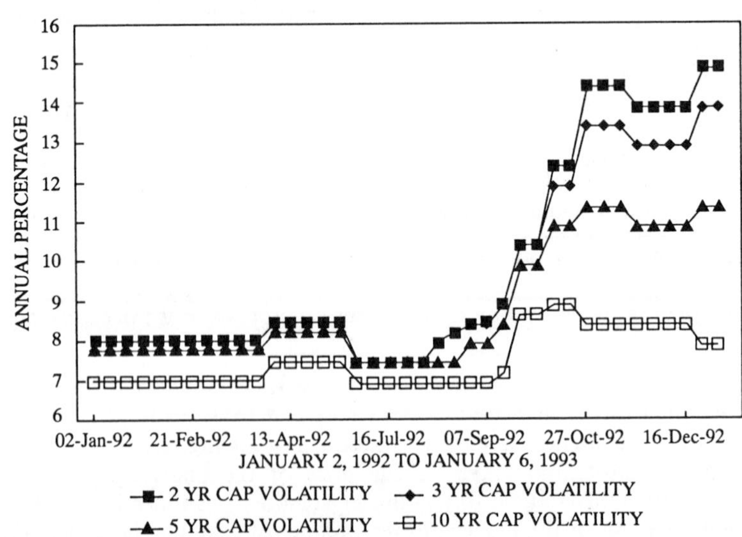

Exhibit 36.2—continued

FRENCH FRANC CAP VOLATILITY

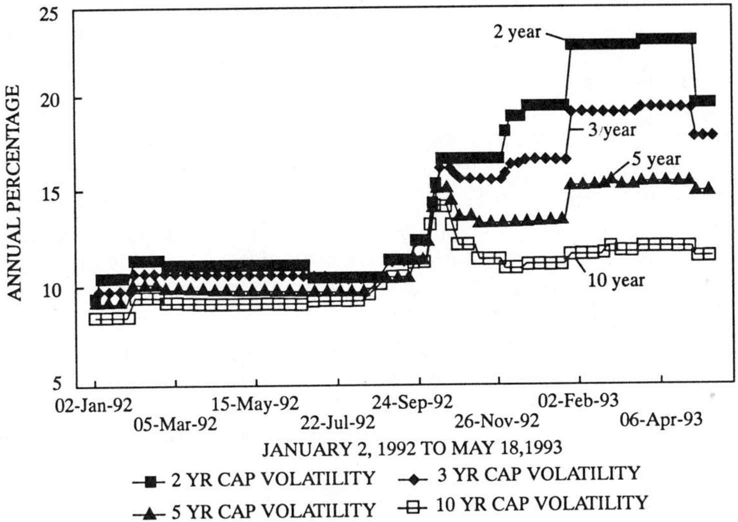

POUND STERLING CAP VOLATILITY

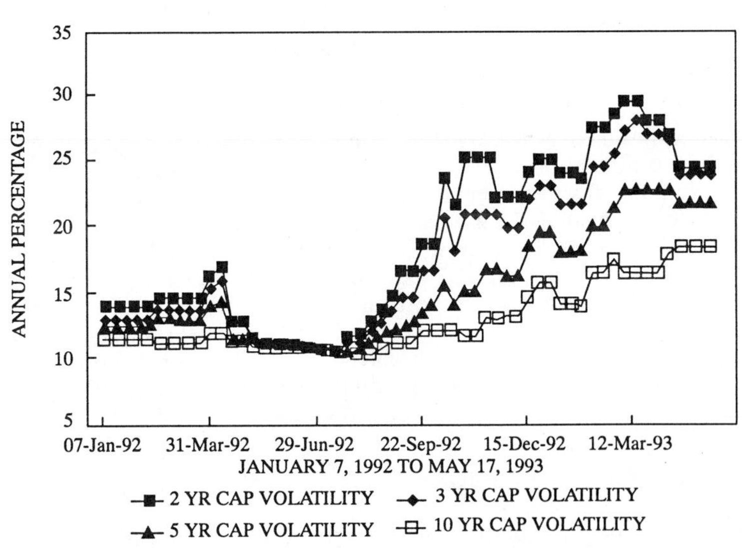

Source: JP Morgan.

In seeking explanations of the pattern of implied volatilities, individual markets have significant institutional and structural peculiarities which must be considered.

For example, in the crude oil market, out-of-the-money call options do not usually have significantly higher volatilities than at-the-money call options. This reflects the market assessment of the probability of price jumps as being asymmetric. This reflects a view that OPEC, as the price controlling cartel, may collapse, making the probability of sharp collapse in oil prices much greater than the probability of a sharp increase. This is manifested in-out-of-the-money put prices being higher, in implied volatility terms, relative to out-of-the-money call prices, the latter reflecting more normal probabilities associated with a smooth evolution of the price of the underlying asset.

In practice, this pattern of volatility implies that the volatility pattern reflects a variety of factors including institutional structure of the underlying market, market forecast of price volatility, estimates of the size and direction of price jumps, degree of risk aversion and other related factors.

The major problems for any option portfolio manager is that the volatility of the underlying asset, at least, as it is utilised to calculate option values, has a significant level of uncertainty associated with its estimation. Consequently, the *expected or true* volatility of the asset can change over the life of the option, resulting in changes in portfolio valuation.

The portfolio is affected by fluctuations in volatility at a number of levels:

- changes in the quoted bid and offer price of options;
- the changes in the value of the existing portfolio of options.

The adjustment of *current* quoted prices for options is relatively straight forward. Portfolio managers will adjust the bid and offers quoted in accordance with changes in views and volatility as well as the order flow in particular option series.

The impact of volatility changes on portfolio value is more problematic. Volatility risk—vega/kappa exposure—can only be hedged by taking positions in the relevant option series.

In practice, this dictates that portfolio managers may seek to balance the portfolio to earn the bid-offer spread, in volatility terms, whilst managing their portfolio to be delta, gamma, theta and kappa neutral. This is particularly the case where volatility levels in the underlying asset are subject to uncertainty or are experiencing rapid and sudden shifts. In contrast, in a market where volatility is "trending" in one or other direction, the portfolio manager may choose to take portfolio positions designed to facilitate increases in portfolio value in the event of the anticipated change in portfolio volatility occurring. Such positions regarding changes in volatility can be both for outright movements in volatility for a particular class of assets or positions for changes in the implied pattern of volatilities or its term structure.

Cap floor replication—in practice[3]

An example of option replication as it applies to a cap transaction is outlined in *Exhibit 36.3*. The example examines the use of option replication techniques to hedge a Eurodollar cap. The example covers both where the cap expires in and out of the money.

3. This section draws on M Desmond Fitzgerald (1987).

Exhibit 36.3
Synthetic Cap Portfolio Hedge

Assume a bank is asked to enter into a cap agreement on Eurodollar interest rate with a client. The bank utilises delta hedging or option replication technology to hedge its risk position.

The cap has the following terms:

Amount:	US$10,000,000
Interest Rate Index:	three month US$ LIBOR
Cap Level:	7.00% pa
Term to Expiry:	35 days.

The current forward rate on US$ LIBOR (91 day run 35 days forward) is 6.75% pa. Volatility is 1.00% in price terms. Riskless interest rate for 35 days is 6.50% pa.

The theoretical option premium is US$9,441 on 9.44bps. (In practice, the bank may charge a "mark-up" on the theoretical option price.)

The bank now proceeds to hedges its risk by trading in Eurodollar futures.

Two scenarios are considered:

The Cap Expires Out Of The Money

US$ LIBOR Cap/Floor Pricing (Using Black Option Pricing Model)
Cap Expires Out-of-the-Money

Inputs—		Hedge Profit (Loss)	
Amount:	10,000,000	Premium Receipt:	9,441
Cap Rate (% pa):	7.000%	Interest on Premium:	55
Interest Period (Days):	91	Hedge Costs:	(5,560)
Final Time to Expiry (Days):	35.00	Net	3,936
Holding Cost:	0.00%		

US$ LIBOR Cap/Floor Pricing (Using Black Option Pricing Model)
Cap Expires Out-Of-The-Money

No of Days:	35	28	21	14	7	0
Years:	0.096	0.077	0.058	0.038	0.019	0.000
Volatility:	1.0000%	1.0000%	1.0000%	1.0000%	1.0000%	1.0000%
Interest Rate:	6.500%	6.000%	5.750%	6.125%	6.000%	6.000%
Forward Rate:	6.750%	6.550%	6.050%	6.375%	6.130%	6.050%

Exhibit 36.3—continued

Strike Price:	$10,000,000	$10,000,000	$10,000,000	$10,000,000	$10,000,000	$10,000,000
Forward Asset Price:	$10,006,213	$10,011,190	$10,023,652	$10,015,548	$10,021,656	$10,023,652
Cap Option Value:						
Premium (US$):	$9,441	$6,322	$2,052	$2,379	$352	
Premium (%):	0.0944%	0.0632%	0.0205%	0.0238%	0.0035%	
Delta:	(0.4174)	(0.3412)	(0.1615)	(0.2130)	(0.0590)	
Gamma:	0.00001254	0.00001319	0.00001017	0.00001480	0.00000847	
Theta:	170.3496	180.1467	139.6760	203.0218	116.4364	
Vega:	12,038.4967	10,144.7321	5,879.5969	5,695.4570	1,630.8959	
Rho:	(9.0534)	(4.8495)	(1.1808)	(0.9124)	(0.0674)	
Delta Hedge Requirements:						
Delta Requirement	(4,173,764)	(3,411,501)	(1,615,203)	(2,130,387)	(589,852)	
No of Eurodollars Contracts:	−4	−3	−2	−2	−1	0
	No Price	No Price	No Price	No Price	No Price	No Price
1 Sell Futures	−4 93.25					
2 Purchase Futures		1 93.45				
3 Purchase Futures			1 93.95			
4 No Action				0 93.63		
5 Sell Futures					1 93.87	
6 Close Hedge						1 93.95
Hedge Portfolio						
No of Contracts	−4	−3	−2	−2	−1	0
Average Price	93.25	93.25	93.25	93.25	93.25	0.00
Current Price	93.25	93.45	93.95	93.63	93.87	93.95
Mark-to-Market	0	− 1500	− 3500	− 1875	− 1550	0
Gain (Loss) on Hedge Adjustment		(500)	(1,750)	0	(1,550)	(1,750)
Interest Income (Expense)		0	(1)	(2)	(3)	(4)
Cumulative Gains (Losses)	0	(500)	(2,251)	(2,253)	(3,806)	(5,560)

Exhibit 36.3—continued

The Cap Expires In The Money

The commencing forward rate is assumed to be 7.00% and the riskless interest rate is assumed to be 6.75% implying a theoretical option price of US$12,277 or 12.28bps.

US$ LIBOR Cap/Floor Pricing (Using Black Option Pricing Model)
Cap Expires In-The-Money

Inputs—		Hedge Profit (Loss)	
Amount:	10,000,000	Premium Receipt:	12,277
Cap Rate (% pa):	7.000%	Interest on Premium:	84
Interest Period (Days):	91	Hedge Costs:	(7,942)
Final Time to Expiry (Days):	35.00	Net	4,419
Holding Cost:	0.00%		

US$ LIBOR Cap/Floor Pricing (Using Black Option Pricing Model)
Cap Expires In-The-Money

No of Days:	35	28	21	14	7	0
Years:	0.096	0.077	0.058	0.038	0.019	0.000
Volatility:	1.0000%	1.0000%	1.0000%	1.0000%	1.0000%	1.0000%
Interest Rate:	6.750%	7.250%	7.200%	7.400%	7.250%	7.250%
Forward Rate:	7.000%	7.450%	7.280%	7.650%	7.450%	7.650%
Strike Price:	$10,000,000	$10,000,000	$10,000,000	$10,000,000	$10,000,000	$10,000,000
Forward Asset Price:	$10,000,000	$9,988,835	$9,993,050	$9,983,881	$9,988,835	$9,983,881
Cap Option Value:						
Premium (US$):	$12,277	$17,418	$13,386	$18,324	$12,792	
Premium (%):	0.1228%	0.1742%	0.1339%	0.1832%	0.1279%	
Delta:	(0.4963)	(0.6526)	(0.6111)	(0.7925)	(0.7888)	
Gamma:	0.00001280	0.00001323	0.00001590	0.00001451	0.00002081	
Theta:	173.1825	177.4837	214.9671	194.4779	282.0339	
Vega:	12,276.5667	10,126.1333	9,135.7087	5,545.7332	3,982.8168	
Rho:	($11.7721)	($13.3619)	($7.7016)	($7.0285)	($2.4532)	

Exhibit 36.3—continued

Delta Hedge Requirements:						
Delta Requirement	(4,962,642)	(6,526,236)	(6,111,241)	(7,924,925)	(7,888,088)	0
No of Eurodollars Contracts:	−5	−7	−6	−8	−8	0
	No Price	No Price	No Price	No Price	No Price	No Price
1 Sell Futures	−5 93.00					
2 Sell Futures		−2 92.55				
3 Purchase Futures			1 92.72			
4 Sell Futures				−2 92.35		
5 No Action					0 92.55	
6 Close Hedge						8 92.35
Hedge Portfolio						
No of Contracts	−5	−7	−6	−8	−8	0
Average Price	93.00	92.87	92.87	92.74	92.74	
Current Price	93.00	92.55	92.72	92.35	92.55	92.35
Mark-to-Market	0	5,625	2,271	7,821	3,821	
Gain (Loss) on cap						(16,119)
Gain (Loss) on Hedge Adjustment			375			7,800
Interest Income (Expense)		0	0	1	1	1
Cumulative Gains (Losses)	0	0	375	376	376	(7,942)

Please note that for simplicity the example makes a number of assumptions. Futures trade are assumed to be able to be transacted without bid-offer spreads. In addition, option volatility is assumed to remain constant.

In practice, financial institutions making markets in caps, floors and collars often utilise ET options to hedge risk positions in their cap/floor portfolios. As the OTC option (that is, the cap, floor or collar) is designed to suit the needs of the user resulting in a contract size, exercise prices and expiration dates which do not correspond to the limited ranges of values that characterise the ET options market, construction of the hedge requires determination of a traded option position which best approximates the cap, floor or collar position over time.

In designing the ET hedge for the OTC position, the following factors are relevant:

- Where the seller of the cap, floor or collar agrees with the end user to repurchase the option before expiration at a fair price, the ET market must be equivalent and opposite to the OTC option position matching movements in the fair price of the OTC option continuously in the period before expiration.
- In the event that the OTC option is only capable of being exercised, then the seller may construct a hedge to immunise the portfolio from *increases* in the intrinsic value of the option that exceeds the original fair price.

In practice, it is difficult to identify the two specific classes of options resulting in sellers designing the hedge as an equivalent, opposite and offsetting position for the cap, floor or collar that is created.

In designing the hedge, a number of specific factors need to be considered:

- size mismatches;
- exercise price mismatches;
- expiration date mismatches.

The size mismatch relates to the fact the size of the ET option is fixed and only unity multiples of the ET option can be utilised. This can result in size mismatches between the ET hedge and the cap, or floor option created. This problem cannot be overcome and, in practice, is not significant.

Exercise price mismatches result from the fact that the ET option strike prices may not correspond to the prices of the OTC option being hedged. Such an exercise price mismatch can be handled using a mixture of options from either side of the cap or floor exercise price to produce the combined position which behaves similarly to the option being hedged. The aim is to produce a weighted average exercise price approximating the OTC option exercise price.

In practice, such a hedge will, necessarily, be imperfect. This results from the fact that the price of the OTC option is, as a theoretical matter, not simply a linear combination of the option premiums on either side.

Expiration date mismatches reflect the fact that the maturity of the OTC option being hedged may not be capable of being matched by the corresponding expiration date of the ET options which are fixed. The difficulty that this mismatch gives rise to is that if a traded option with an expiration date longer than the expiration date of the OTC option is utilised, the time value of the traded option is greater than that of the OTC option. This difference will be lost if a major change in the underlying asset price occurs and the option expires out-of-the-money. In practice, this problem is handled, on a portfolio basis, to minimise such mismatches.

Where traded options are utilised to hedge OTC positions simple linear interpolation extrapolation produces effective hedge positions only within specific profit and loss boundaries. In the event that volatility of the underlying asset market changes significantly, interaction of volatility and time to maturity may greatly affect the efficiency of the hedge.

MANAGING CAP PORTFOLIOS[4]

Special considerations

There are a number of special considerations in managing the risk of cap portfolios.

Caps, collars and floors are usually modelled as a strip of European options on the relevant floating rate index with expiration date corresponding to the settlement frequency and strike prices corresponding to the interest rate cap or floor level under the agreement. Where the cap or floor level is done at a single interest rate, then the distant periods typically are either deep in-the-money or out-of-the-money depending on the shape of the yield curve. This, in certain circumstances, allows the distant periods to be hedged at nearly a one to one hedge ratio or delta with a relatively illiquid long-term instrument, such as a bond, as the low gamma of that section of the commitment should, in theory, require infrequent rebalancing of the hedge. In these circumstances, the shorter term portion of the cap is hedged separately.

This type of approach requires complex modelling techniques which split these types of agreements into various constituent elements which are analysed and hedged separately. The separation of the various elements of these agreements is important as typically each element reflects significant differences in market conditions and/or rate expectations. Consequently, for example, once a cap is decomposed it can be hedged using portfolio hedging techniques such as a strip of delta hedges, or option gamma matching techniques.

A special problem relating to long-term caps and floors is that their long maturities extend well beyond the usual hedging tools utilised to manage delta hedge portfolios in debt options such as futures contracts which are only available for periods generally up to two years. In these circumstances, it is increasingly common to construct hedges which combine standard option hedging strategies with interest rate swap transactions. This can be seen from the following example.

Assume a flat yield curve at 8.00% pa. A five year cap on six month US$ LIBOR is equivalent to a position in a five year floor plus long position in a par interest rate swap with a fixed semi-annual coupon of 8.00%, when both the cap and the floor are struck at the swap rate and if the fixed rate is paid on the same basis as the floating.

For all changes in rates, it can be shown that these positions will generate equivalent cash flows. For rates above the cap level, say 10.00%, the holder of the cap will be paid the difference between LIBOR and 8.00%, which is 2.00%. The floor and the swap combination generate the same cash flow. Since rates are above 8.00%, the floor by itself generates no income, while the swap entitles the holder to the difference between the 8.00% fixed outflow and the 10.00% floating index, also a net payment of 2.00%. For rates below the cap level, say 6.00%, the cap holder receives no payment. The floor generates a positive cash flow equal to the difference between 8.00% and the index level, that is, 2.00%, which covers the shortfall on the interest rate swap between the fixed payment outflow of 8.00% and the floating payment received, 6.00%. At exactly 8.00%, none of the securities generate cash flows.

4. This discussion and the later discussion on the risks of delta hedging draws on Cristobal Conde, "Risk Management Techniques for Writers of Caps and Floors" in *Interest Rate Caps, Floors and Collars* (1986).

Since these two positions are equivalent, the cost of the two portfolios should be the same. Thus, the cost of the cap will be the same as the cost of the interest rate swap plus the cost of the floor. Since an at-the-market swap is a par swap, no swap fee would pass between the two parties, and the cost of the floor would equal the cost of the gap.

Practical problems in cap portfolio management

The approach to cap portfolio management adopted by various intermediaries varies significantly depending, primarily, on the risk attitudes of the intermediary. There would appear to be two general approaches:

- a positioning approach to cap portfolio management;
- a hedged approach to cap portfolio management.

Under the positioning approach, the exposure in the cap portfolio is managed consistent with the intermediary's view on the direction of underlying interest rates. A variation on this type of positioning strategy is to operate a cap book with a good dispersion of exercise prices and maturities as well as caps and floors on the assumption that the book would be self-hedging. The essential theory behind this latter approach is that the various combinations of purchased and written puts and calls would be shown to be synthetic forward positions in the underlying asset market. Consequently, these synthetic forward positions could be managed against existing asset liability mismatches within the intermediary's balance sheet.

However, this type of approach has often proved to be unworkable as customer demand for options tended to cluster around certain exercise prices and maturities and there are frequent imbalances which tended to create portfolio exposures.

The alternative approach has been to operate cap portfolios on a hedged basis, traditionally using delta neutral hedging approaches. As noted above, delta or gamma neutral hedging does not completely eliminate risk. The risks include:

Volatility risk

Option positions hedged by utilising synthetic option technology are susceptible to losses upon an increase in the volatility of the market. Increases in volatility will boost theoretical premiums. This volatility risk can only be eliminated by hedging options with options.

This is because the cash and futures markets, however, are not, at least theoretically, affected by changes in volatility and the increase in value in the option granted position is not offset by any gain in value of the delta hedge.

Interest rate shifts

As interest rates move, different instruments in the portfolio will be affected differently. Shifts through time are particularly problematic as they require modelling the behaviour of forward-forward rates through time based on the underlying yield curve.

Jump or "gap" risk

A major problem relates to the fact that the delta hedge requires constant rebalancing which is not practically feasible. Where periodic rebalancing is used, the portfolio is adjusted after asset prices *have moved* which means that the wrong proportion of asset is held in the portfolio. This problem is accentuated where asset prices jump or gap significantly as the change in value of the hedge position is different from that which would be achieved with an option. This problem is complicated where the position is whipsawed. As rebalancing of the hedge is undertaken after the initial move in asset prices, any immediate reversal in the asset price, after adjustment of the hedge can lead to the option grantor sustaining losses as a result of holding the wrong number of contracts.

Hedging risks

The computation of the option position requiring hedging must properly be compared against the hedge instrument being utilised. When dealing with long-term instruments having intermediate cash flows, the reinvestment rates must be correctly adjusted when modelling yield curve shifts, especially when non-parallel shifts are employed.

Yield curve shifts

Assumptions must be made in relation to the basis relationship between instruments exhibiting different yield curves as well as the shape of various yield curves.

Settlement policies

Different settlement policies as between the option granted and the hedge instruments have to be accounted for in the computation of the hedged risk position for those instruments.

Transaction costs

Trading always has positive transaction costs. In volatile markets these transaction costs can become very large, as bid-offer spreads widen and markets become thin. Even if volatility remains fairly stable, strict delta hedging can be more costly than expected if a market becomes nervous and choppy. Delta hedging also requires the writer to monitor the position to continually adjust hedge positions, an approach which can be quite costly.

Despite these deficiencies, delta hedging is widely used in practice. Recent research[5] concludes that:

- the technique generates ex post option prices that approximate the ex ante theoretical value;
- the simulation study results were not sensitive to different adjustment gap sizes;
- the key to success in this type of hedging appears to be anticipating changes in volatility.

As the cap and debt options market grew rapidly in the early 1980s, intermediaries relied heavily on delta hedging of their option exposure, and several institutions created very sizeable books of options on this basis. However, the deficiencies of delta hedging large exposures resulted in a number of instances of large losses on cap books. The most aggressive banks have since sharply curtailed the amounts of options they were willing to write without cover in the form of an offsetting option.

5. Asay and Edelsburg (1986), pp 63-70.

Part 8

Credit Exposure in Swaps and Financial Derivatives

Chapter 37

Swap and Derivative Credit Exposure: Measurement and Management Issues

CREDIT EXPOSURE IN SWAP AND DERIVATIVE TRANSACTIONS: SPECIAL FEATURES

Swap and derivative transactions like other financial transactions are subject to default risk. Default risk in any particular swap is primarily a function of:

- credit risk; and
- market risk.

The overall default risk in any particular swap or derivative product is a function of the counterparty's credit risk (the probability of a counterparty defaulting) and market risk (the level of rates at the time of default).

There are a number of features that distinguish the credit exposure associated with swap and derivative transactions:

- limited initial exposure;
- the exposure is a function of the movement of exogenous variables (interest and currency rates);
- the exposure can be negative as well as positive; and
- the exposure is stochastic and cannot be determined, accurately, in advance.

A transaction typically does not initially result in any credit exposure to the counterparties as, by definition, the original exchange, if any, involves cash flows of equal value with no resulting net credit exposure at the time of commencement of the transaction. However, exposure can arise over time, reflecting changes in market conditions up to conclusion of the transaction, primarily, in exchange and interest rates, from those prevailing at the time of commencement of the transaction. These changes in exchange and interest rates affect the present value of the cash flow creating a net difference which represents the exposure of one counterparty to the other.

As the exposure under a swap or derivative product is the function of exogenous variables, it is axiomatic that swap exposure can take on negative or positive values for a particular party to a transaction. Negative exposures in this context refer to situations when movements in rates are such that the counterparties would suffer a loss if the intermediary defaulted, or to put it from the perspective of the intermediary, the intermediary would gain if the counterparty defaulted.

A key point to note, is that as exposures are determined by the movements of exogenous variables, the exposure cannot be determined *in advance*.

These features distinguish the credit exposure associated with swap and derivative transactions from credit exposure incurred under more traditional financial transactions, such as loan transactions. The exposure under these transactions has some similarity to exposures under a number of derivative instruments such as options and futures which also involve stochastic exposures.

The issue of credit risk in swap and derivative transactions is usually considered primarily with reference to financial intermediaries who, regularly, intermediate swaps and derivatives through until maturity of the transaction. However, the issue of credit exposure is also relevant to end users who must assess the credit standing of financial intermediaries to control any potential loss from default *by the intermediary* under the swap or derivative product.

The issues in relation to the credit exposure assumed by end users in entering into transactions with financial institutions has become increasingly important. This reflects, in part, the decline in the overall credit quality of the banking system. The impact of declining credit ratings on the capacity of some financial institutions to complete swaps and derivative with credit sensitive counterparties has prompted the establishment of high credit quality (AAA rated) special purpose derivative vehicles (see discussion below).

MEASUREMENT OF CREDIT EXPOSURE: THE THEORETICAL BASIS

Basic concepts

The basic methodology used to measure credit exposure involves *matched* pairs of *identical* but mirror opposite transactions entered into by the intermediary. The credit exposure is then measured where the counterparty under one of the matched swaps defaults in the performance of its obligations under the agreement.

Credit exposure under a transaction arises because swap or derivative product agreements between an intermediary and the two counterparties are independent agreements. Consequently, the intermediary must fulfill the terms of the contract with a remaining counterparty, even if the other counterparty defaults.

The basic concept used to measure credit exposure is "replacement cost". The replacement cost method of analysis estimates the economic impact on the intermediary of a default as a function of the original contract fixed rate and the market or replacement rate that would be used when finding a substitute counterparty. The loss or gain is effectively the difference between the original contract fixed rate and the replacement rate discounted to the termination date. This method of analysis implicitly assumes that the intermediary is unable to recover damages from a defaulting counterparty as specified in the swap agreement and closes out its exposure arising from a defaulting swap by writing a replacement swap or selling the now unmatched swap in the secondary market.

It is important to note that this approach, which focuses on the fixed rate component in swap transactions, assumes that the rate loss in replacing the floating rate side of a swap will be minimal as the swap payments are based on a market rate which readjusts periodically. Consequently, it is assumed that the replacement floating rate side will generally pay the same rate at any date, regardless of how long ago it was negotiated.

A number of swap transaction structures, depending on the pattern of cash inflows in relation to the pattern of cash outflows, result in settlement risk elements as payments to the intermediary are made in advance of receipt of payments from the counterparty. This creates a risk arising from the fact that default may occur prior to the next inflow. A common structure incorporation settlement risk occurs with annual, fixed rate cash inflows offset by semi-annual floating rate outflows. An extreme case of this problem is a zero coupon swap where semi-annual floating rate payments out are made in exchange for a single lump sum interest payment at final maturity.

Swap and derivative product transactions also give rise to delivery risk arising from the fact that in many foreign exchange transactions, because of the difference in the timing of currency settlement between the two jurisdictions, it is frequently impractical to verify the receipt of items or cash from the counterparty prior to paying out or delivering the item exchanged. This creates a settlement risk which can be equated to the maximum loss in such circumstances which is the total value of the cash or items to be received from the counterparty on any one day or series of days depending on when receipt can be verified.

The measurement of credit exposure in the various types of transactions is discussed below. However, before examining the mechanical aspects of quantifying the credit exposure in individual transactions, a number of boundary conditions, based on an overall analysis of swap and derivative transactions, should be mentioned. The essential considerations governing exposure from swaps and related transactions include:

- the exposure is stochastic in nature;
- the exposure is critically dependent on movements in the currency and interest rates in question;
- the magnitude of this exposure will normally be substantially less than 100.00% of the original par value of the swap.

Interest rate swaps

The credit risk of interest rate swaps is a function of the movement in fixed interest rates over the life of the transaction.

For example, assume a bank enters into a swap with a company which agrees to pay 11.00% pa for three years in exchange for receiving six month LIBOR. After one year has elapsed, the company has gone bankrupt. In order to cover its exposure, the bank undertakes a swap contract to receive a fixed rate for the remaining two years of the transaction. If rates have risen, for example, to 13.00% pa for two years, then the bank can crystallise a gain of 2.00% pa over the remainder of the term of the swap; conversely, if rates had fallen to 9.00% pa, the bank would have incurred a 2.00% pa loss.

This exposure under an interest rate swap is computed as the difference between the fixed rate of interest of the swap and the market fixed rate to the same maturity at the time of default or closeout, multiplied by the notional principal amount and discounted back at the prevailing rate of interest from each settlement date to the close-out date. In quantifying the exposure, the principal amounts are ignored, as the principal amounts are not exchanged in an interest rate swap. *Exhibit 37.1* sets out an example of the calculation of credit exposure in an interest rate swap.

Exhibit 37.1

Calculating Credit Exposure—Interest Rate Swaps

Assume the following transaction: Bank B (B) enters into an interest rate swap with Company A (A) whereby it receives 9.00% pa against payment of six month LIBOR for a period of 5 years.

Exhibit 37.1—continued

The potential replacement cost of the swap from the viewpoint of B (and consequently the credit exposure of B to a default by A) is calculated assuming forecast swap rate highs and lows over the forecast period of 7.00% pa and 11.00% pa.

Credit Exposure—Interest Swap Transaction

Interest Rate Swap Initial Interest Rate (S/A): 9.000%

Period (Semi-Annual)	Fixed Rate Payments	Fixed Rate Payments Replacement Swap Swap Rate		Cash Flow Differential on Default Swap Rate		Swap Exposure (At Start of Period) Swap Rate	
		7.000%	11.000%	7.000%	11.000%	7.000%	11.000%
0							
1	4.500	3.500	5.500	(1.000)	1.000	(7.608)	6.952
2	4.500	3.500	5.500	(1.000)	1.000	(6.874)	6.335
3	4.500	3.500	5.500	(1.000)	1.000	(6.115)	5.683
4	4.500	3.500	5.500	(1.000)	1.000	(5.329)	4.996
5	4.500	3.500	5.500	(1.000)	1.000	(4.515)	4.270
6	4.500	3.500	5.500	(1.000)	1.000	(3.673)	3.505
7	4.500	3.500	5.500	(1.000)	1.000	(2.802)	2.698
8	4.500	3.500	5.500	(1.000)	1.000	(1.900)	1.846
9	4.500	3.500	5.500	(1.000)	1.000	(0.966)	0.948
10	4.500	3.500	5.500	(1.000)	1.000	0.000	0.000

All exposures are stated as a percentage of face value of the swap. The negative (positive) number indicates a loss (gain) to B in the event of a default by A.

As would be anticipated, B's credit exposure under the swap occurs where swap rates fall (to 7.00% pa) resulting in B having to replace the existing swap *at lower rates*. The analysis indicates that B's credit exposure on the swap is initially zero and increases to a maximum of 7.608% of face value and declines as the transaction approaches maturity.

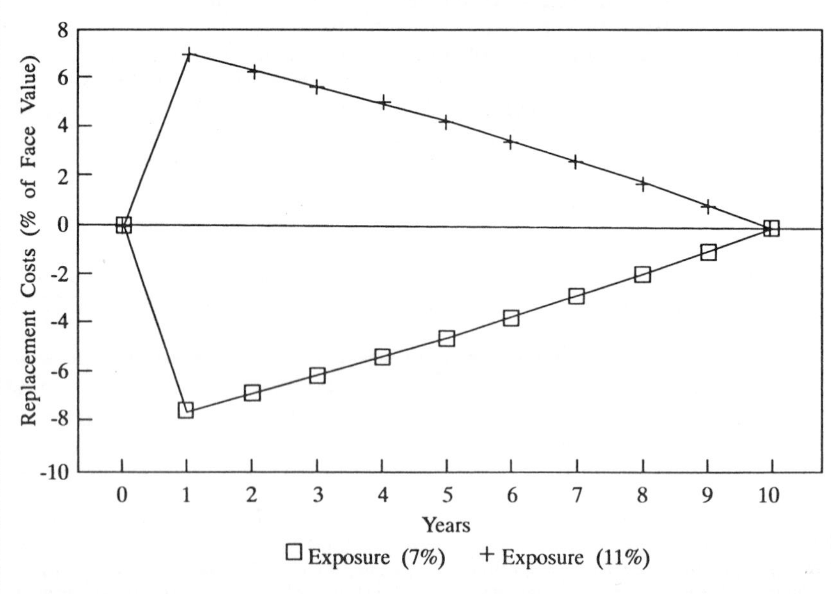

The general impact on the intermediary of a default in an interest rate swap is determined by the direction of rate changes and by which party defaults:

Interest rate environment	**If counterparty A (fixed payer) defaults**	**If counterparty B (fixed receiver) defaults**
Rate same as contract rates	No effect	No effect
Rates higher than contract rates	Intermediary gains	Intermediary incurs loss
Rates lower than contract rates	Intermediary incurs loss	Intermediary gains

The exposure under an interest rate swap typically decreases over time. The exposure is also at a higher level, irrespective of the outstanding maturity of the transaction, at or just prior to each settlement period. Typically, the exposure of interest rate swaps represents 5.00% to 20.00% of the notional principal amount, depending on the forecast interest rates and the maturity of the swap.

Currency swaps

The quantification of exposure under currency swaps is similar to that under interest rate swaps. The major difference is that the exposure under a currency swap is affected by interest rates in the two currencies involved as well as fluctuations in the currency exchange rate as between the two currencies.

Exposure in currency swaps is quantified as the difference between the present values of the two payment streams, discounted as at default, translated into a single currency. As the principal amounts are denominated in different currencies and are repayable at maturity, they are incorporated in the exposure analysis and affect the size of the intermediary's exposure under the currency swap. *Exhibit 37.2* sets out an example of the calculation of credit exposure in a currency swap.

Exhibit 37.2

Calculating Credit Exposure—Currency Swaps

Assume the following transaction: Bank B (B) enters into a currency swap with Company A (A) whereby it pays US$8.75% pa against receipt of A$11.50% pa for 10 years.

The potential replacement cost of the swap from the viewpoint of B (and consequently the credit exposure of B to a default by A) is calculated assuming the following variations in swap rates in the relevant currencies and the A$/US$ exchange rate over the forecast period:

A$ Swap Rate— 15.00% variation implying a range of 9.775% pa to 13.225% pa.
US$ Swap Rate— 15.00% variation implying a range of 7.438% pa to 10.063% pa.
A$/US$ Rate— 1.00% per period.

The exposure under the swap is set out in *Table 1*, p 1122.

All exposures are stated as a percentage of face value of the swap.

As would be anticipated, B's credit exposure under the swap occurs where A$ swap rates fall (to 9.775% pa) and the A$ appreciates relative to the US$ resulting in B having to replace the existing swap *at lower A$ swap rates and an unfavourable exchange rate*. The analysis indicates that B's credit exposure on the swap is initially zero and increases to a maximum of 14.578% of face value and declines as the transaction approaches maturity reflecting the reduced number of cash flows remaining. However, the exposure does not reduce to zero reflecting the currency exposure on the final swap payment (notional principal and interest). (See Graph, p 1123.)

Exhibit 37.2—continued

TABLE 1

Credit Exposure—Currency Swap Transactions

				Assumed Variations
Currency Swap	US$ Initial Interest Rate (S/A):	Rec	8.750%	15.000%
	A$ Initial Interest Rate (S/A):	Pay	11.500%	15.000%
	Commencement US$/A$ Rate:		0.7680	1.000%/Period

Period (Year)	Swap Flows A$	Swap Flows US$	NPV of A$ Payments Swap Rates 9.775%	NPV of A$ Payments Swap Rates 13.225%	NPV of US$ Payments Swap Rates 7.438%	NPV of US$ Payments Swap Rates 10.063%	Exchange Rate Forecasts High	Exchange Rate Forecasts Low	Maximum US$ Exposure of A$ Payments	Maximum Swap Exposure US$ Terms
0.0			−110.852	−90.581	83.823	70.536	0.7680	0.7680	0.000	0.000
0.5	(5.750)	3.360	−110.520	−90.821	83.580	70.724	0.7718	0.7642	−85.303	−14.578
1.0	(5.750)	3.360	−110.171	−91.076	83.329	70.923	0.7757	0.7603	−85.458	−14.535
1.5	(5.750)	3.360	−109.806	−91.348	83.067	71.131	0.7795	0.7565	−85.599	−14.468
2.0	(5.750)	3.360	−109.423	−91.639	82.797	71.350	0.7834	0.7527	−85.726	−14.376
2.5	(5.750)	3.360	−109.021	−91.948	82.515	71.580	0.7873	0.7489	−85.837	−14.257
3.0	(5.750)	3.360	−108.599	−92.279	82.224	71.821	0.7913	0.7452	−85.932	−14.110
3.5	(5.750)	3.360	−108.157	−92.631	81.922	72.075	0.7952	0.7415	−86.008	−13.934
4.0	(5.750)	3.360	−107.693	−93.006	81.608	72.341	0.7992	0.7377	−86.067	−13.726
4.5	(5.750)	3.360	−107.207	−93.406	81.283	72.620	0.8032	0.7340	−86.105	−13.485
5.0	(5.750)	3.360	−106.697	−93.832	80.946	72.914	0.8072	0.7304	−86.123	−13.209
5.5	(5.750)	3.360	−106.161	−94.287	80.596	73.223	0.8112	0.7267	−86.118	−12.896
6.0	(5.750)	3.360	−105.600	−94.772	80.233	73.547	0.8152	0.7231	−86.090	−12.543
6.5	(5.750)	3.360	−105.011	−95.288	79.857	73.887	0.8193	0.7194	−86.037	−12.150
7.0	(5.750)	3.360	−104.394	−95.839	79.466	74.244	0.8234	0.7158	−85.958	−11.713
7.5	(5.750)	3.360	−103.746	−96.427	79.062	74.620	0.8275	0.7122	−85.850	−11.231
8.0	(5.750)	3.360	−103.066	−97.053	78.642	75.014	0.8316	0.7087	−85.714	−10.699
8.5	(5.750)	3.360	−102.354	−97.720	78.206	75.428	0.8358	0.7051	−85.545	−10.117
9.0	(5.750)	3.360	−101.606	−98.432	77.754	75.863	0.8400	0.7016	−85.344	−9.481
9.5	(5.750)	3.360	−100.822	−99.191	77.286	76.320	0.8441	0.6981	−85.108	−8.788
10.0	(105.750)	80.160	−105.750	−105.750	80.160	80.160	0.8483	0.6946	−89.713	−9.553

Exhibit 37.2—continued

CREDIT EXPOSURE CURRENCY SWAP

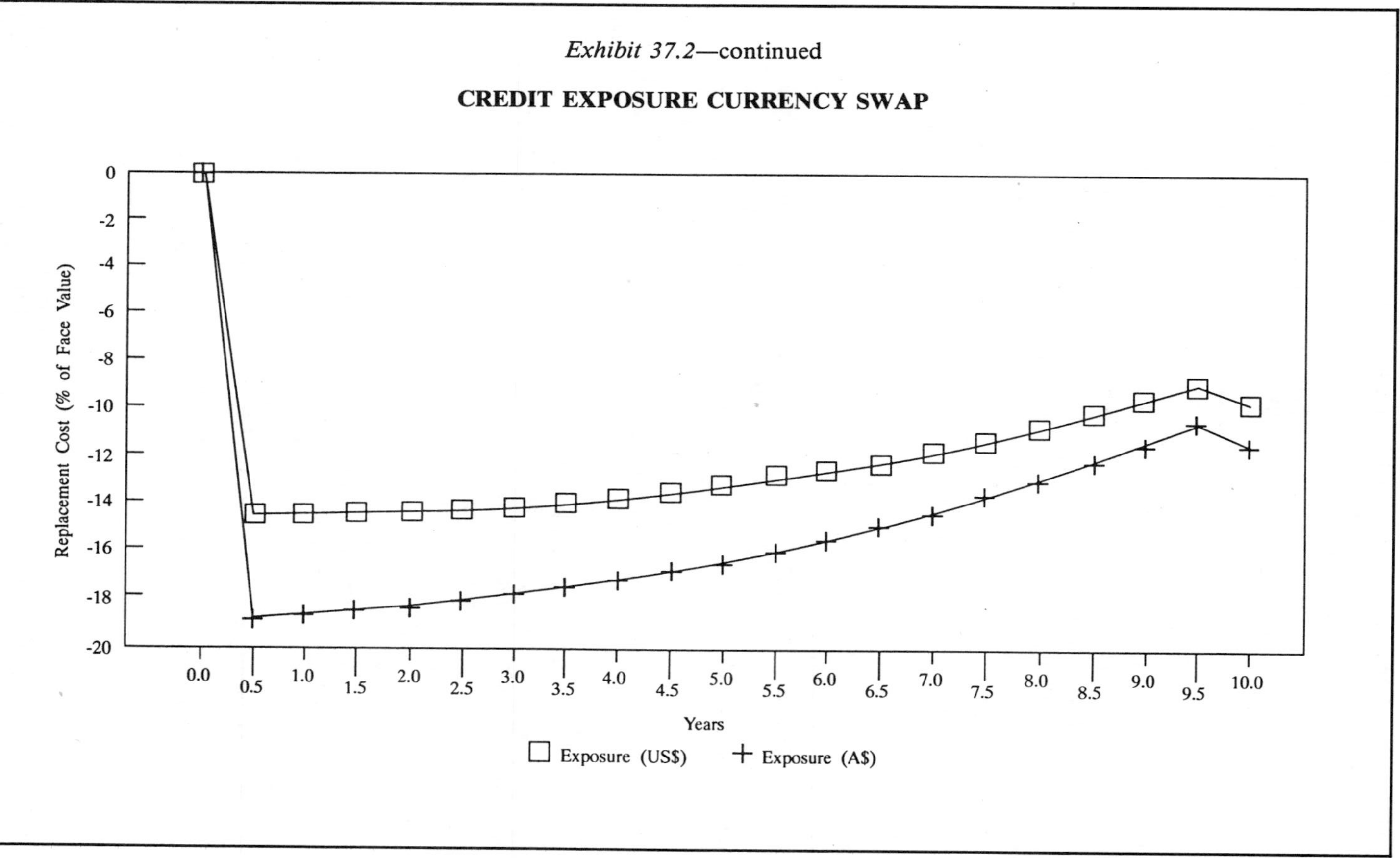

The general impact on the intermediary for a default in a fixed A$ to fixed US$ currency swap is summarised below:

	If counterparty A (fixed A$ payer and fixed US$ receiver) defaults	**If counterparty B (fixed A$ receiver and fixed US$ payer) defaults**
Interest rate environment		
Rates same as contract rate	No effect	No effect
A$ rate higher than contract rate	Intermediary gains	Intermediary loses
A$ rate lower than contract rate	Intermediary loses	Intermediary gains
US$ rate higher than contract rate	Intermediary loses	Intermediary gains
US$ rate lower than contract rate	Intermediary gains	Intermediary gains
Currency rate environment		
Rate same as contract rate	No effect	No effect
A$ appreciates against US$	Intermediary loses	Intermediary gains
A$ depreciates against US$	Intermediary gains	Intermediary loses

The quantum of exposure under a currency swap tends to depend on the types of instruments utilised. The fixed-to-fixed currency swaps are exposed as to interest rates on both currencies and the exchange rate. In contrast, fixed-to-floating currency swaps are exposed only on the fixed rate currency interest together with the exchange rate, while the floating-to-floating currency swaps are exposed only in terms of currency amounts.

The nature of exposures on currency swaps can be summarised as follows:

- The exposure of currency swaps tends to remain relatively constant or even increase with time, depending on currency fluctuations.
- Unlike interest rate swaps, the exposure under a currency swap will not, generally, tend towards zero as the maturity of the swap approaches. This reflects the fact that as the term to maturity decreases the number of remaining cash flows fall but the notional principal amounts must be exchanged at maturity. The impact of exchange rate fluctuations on the final re-exchange will mean that there is substantial credit exposure until maturity of such swaps.
- The exposure under a currency swap typically represents up to 50.00% of the principal amount, depending upon the currency and the maturity of the transactions.

LTFX

The exposure in the case of LTFX contracts is largley identical to those discussed in connection with a fixed-to-fixed currency swap as the LTFX contract pricing is based on the interest rate differential between the two currencies and will be affected by changes in the interest rates as between the two currencies and movements in the spot exchange rate.

FRAs

The exposure under a FRA contract is similar to that under an interest rate swap. The exposure represents the cost of replacement of the FRA counterparty, in the case of default, which will be determined by movements in short-term interest rates between the time of entry into the transaction and the default. As the maturity of FRAs are generally short, despite the often significant volatility of short-term interest rates, the exposure in such contracts is generally relatively small.

Caps, collars and floors

The approach to calculating exposures under cap, collar and floor agreements is similar to that utilised with interest rate swaps. However, where the intermediary writes the option in question, that is, it provides the cap or floor, it usually incurs *no* credit exposure to the counterparty. This is because as the grantor of the option, generally the *intermediary* has the performance obligation under the contract. Providing the option premium is paid at the time of entry into the transaction, the purchaser of the cap or floor does not have any further performance obligations and therefore the intermediary has no credit exposure to the purchaser. Where the premium is amortised and paid in instalments over the life of the transaction, it is equivalent to a loan transaction and credit exposure thereupon should be treated in a manner identical to that of a loan.

The basic exposure of an intermediary arises where it purchases an option from the counterparty. This occurs where, for example, the counterparty enters into a collar with an intermediary which entails the counterparty agreeing to make payments to the intermediary in case rates fall below the floor level of the collar.

The purchaser of an option, in all cases, assumes a credit risk in respect of the intermediary as it implicitly assumes that the intermediary will be capable of fulfilling its obligations under the contract if called upon to do so.

The exposure under such agreements can be equated to the replacement cost of substituting another intermediary should the counterparty fail to perform under the agreement. This replacement cost is equal to the cost of purchasing a substitute series of options. The cost of the substitute options will depend on the remaining time to maturity of the contract, and the changes in interest rate levels between the time of entry into the original contract and the time of default. In addition, the replacement cost of the options will be affected by changes in expectations as to the volatility of future interest rates in the relevant currency. The replacement cost can be estimated utilising option pricing methodology. Within this framework, the credit exposure in such contracts can be equated to the pricing of compound options or options on options.

Non-generic swaps and swap hybrids

The determination of credit exposure in relation to variations on the basic swap structures utilises an identical approach to that described above.

In each case, it is necessary to determine the replacement cost of the relevant transaction. The calculation of the replacement cost is complicated by the following:

- The replacement transaction must be structured to equate the cash flows of the original defaulted transaction. For example, in the case of a forward swap, the replacement transaction will be, initially, a forward swap until the underlying swap comes into operation when the replacement transaction is the equivalent swap. Similarly, in the case of instruments with option elements such as swaptions or the various swap hybrids, the replacement cost is calculated as the price of the equivalent option at the relevant time.

- The pattern of replacement cost and corresponding credit exposure is necessarily more complex reflecting the various factors impacting on the value of the instrument. In this context, there is arguably greater scope for divergence in replacement cost values in relation to these instruments reflecting the often lack of unambiguous valuation techniques and the potential for competing valuation methodologies.
- The issue of liquidity (see discussion below) is particularly relevant in relation to these instruments as the liquidity of structured and/or hybrid transactions are likely to be, often very significantly, lower than for more conventional structures. This may make it difficult to replace such transactions, in practice, or add markedly to the replacement cost and, hence, the credit exposure on the transaction.
- Depending upon the specific structure of the instrument, unique risk aspects may need to be considered. For example, where a deferred or accelerated cash flow structure is embodied in the transaction, the credit exposure of the swap will increasingly begin to resemble that of a deposit (low credit exposure) or loan (high credit exposure approximating the full face value of the transaction).

Commodity and equity swaps

The determination of the credit exposure of commodity and equity swap as well as related instruments utilises a similar replacement cost logic.

The pertinent factors in the determination of credit exposures on these instruments include:

- the relative stage of development of the market in each instrument, which impacts upon the liquidity and consistency of valuation methods;
- the higher volatility of some commodity prices and equity index values and the complex impact of the changing relationship between spot and forward prices in these markets on the replacement cost of transactions.

INTERACTION BETWEEN REPLACEMENT COST AND DEFAULT RISK

The measurement process described above can be utilised to determine *the replacement cost* of an identified transaction. In theory, the credit exposure under a swap transaction is related to the replacement cost of the transaction *adjusted for the risk of default* as well as a variety of other relevant factors.

Based on this insight, a number of similar models for assessing swap credit exposure have been proposed. The *expected* replacement cost of a swap can be specified as follows:[1]

$$\text{ERC} = \text{Pcd}\,[\text{ERV} + \text{ERFC} + \text{Plrc}\,(\text{ECLRC})]$$

where

1. The model described is that specified in Raj Aggarwal (1991) (May/June).

ERC = expected replacement cost

Pcd = probability of counterparty default

ERV = expected replacement value of transaction

ERFC = expected replacement fees and costs

Plrc = probability of legal or regulatory risks in the case of default

ECLRC = expected costs of legal or regulatory problems in case of default

The various elements of the calculation would generally be derived as follows:

- Probability of counterparty default for each counterparty could be derived through:
  —subjective estimates based on experience in credit intermediation and assessment of counterparty credit-worthiness; or
  —historical data (available from credit rating agencies) on default experience of corporations within specific rating classes (AAA, AA, A etc).

  In the event that historical default experience data is utilised, average default rates that is default rates adjusted for special events, should be used. In addition, it is necessary to use time-dependent data as it is apparent that default rates for companies within a specified rating category at the commencement of the study period will increase as the period of time elapsed increases—that is, the default rate of any corporation, irrespective of credit rating, increases with the tenor of the exposure.

  The probability of default for a specific counterparty should encompass country risk considerations where the transaction is cross-border.
- The expected replacement value of the swap is calculated utilising the replacement cost methodology described above.
- The estimate of expected replacement fees and other costs will be based on experience of defaults on similar transactions.
- The probability of legal or regulatory risks in the case of default will also have to estimated subjectively based on the jurisdiction involved, the degree of sophistication of the relevant capital markets, the regulated or deregulated nature of the capital market, experience with counterparties based in the jurisdiction etc.

Based on this model, the credit exposure under a swap transaction is positively correlated to the probability of default, the expected replacement cost (which is dependent on the worst case expected decline in the value of the swap), the expected costs associated with replacing the swap, the probability of legal and regulatory problems and the cost of such regulatory and legal problems.

MEASUREMENT OF CREDIT EXPOSURE: SOME ISSUES

A number of special issues relating to the measurement and quantification of credit exposure and swap transactions require additional comment. These issues include:

- timing considerations;
- liquidity issues;
- individual transaction versus portfolio approaches;
- option pricing approaches to swap exposures.

Timing issues

A major consideration in quantifying swap exposures is that credit risk under such transactions is not static over time. At the time of commencement of a transaction, its replacement value is by definition nil. However, as time elapses, if there is any deviation between the contract rates, both interest rate and currency rates (if applicable), and market rates, the replacement cost changes from zero. At the same time, as the outstanding life to maturity of the swap becomes shorter, and required contractual payments are made, the number of payments which remain exposed to any adverse movement in rates decrease. These two offsetting effects suggest the credit exposure of a swap transaction over its term may alter significantly. Importantly, the actual economic impact (the potential gain or loss) on a swap transaction held until maturity by an intermediary can only be determined definitively *at the maturity* of a swap.

The impact of time on credit exposure in swap transactions is also evident in two other ways:

- the path dependency of exposures;
- the time dependency of counterparty default experience.

The calculation of credit exposure as represented by replacement cost utilising the methodology described above was based on determining the present value of the swap assuming an immediate adverse movement in swap rates. In reality, the movement in rates is more gradual and, in particular, depends on the starting rate level and the path taken. In addition, as the remaining term to maturity of the swap is constantly decreasing the interest rate yield structure applicable to the transaction alters creating an exposure to not only the absolute rate movements but to *the shape of the yield curve.*

For example, let us assume that US$ five year swap rates are at 8.00% pa. As time expires, swap rates will move, either up or down, from this level. The applicable rate will also change; for example, the rate applicable after six months will be the four year six month rate and so on. This means that the rate applicable will reflect both the change in *absolute* rate levels as well as the *shape of the yield curve (whether it is positive or negative).*

Future rates will depend to a substantial degree on the *path* of interest rate movements. For example, if rates move up from their starting level of 8.00% pa to, say, 8.75% pa across the whole yield curve, then it is likely that the probability of a move to lower rates to, say, 6.00% pa will be somewhat lower. In effect, if the swap goes deeply in or out-of-the-money, then the probability of this reversing is lower in circumstances where path dependency of rate movements is assumed.

Similar arguments are applicable in relation to currency, commodity or equity index price movements.

The interaction of these factors is complex and makes it difficult to estimate swap credit exposure *in advance*. In an effort to capture these elements in determining swap credit exposure levels, a variety of statistical models have emerged. These models are based on constructs focused on *volatilities* rather than subjective measures of probable worst case interest rate and currency movements. The more sophisticated models utilised for these purposes also seek to capture the yield curve effect through the use of multiple interest rates (two factor models using a short-term and a long-term rate are commonly utilised).

The time dependency of default experience has been alluded to above. Default rates for companies within a specified rating category at the commencement of the study period will predictably increase as the period of time elapsed increases—that is, the default rate of any corporation, irrespective of credit rating, increases with the tenor of the exposure.

Liquidity issues

In utilising the concept of replacement cost in quantifying the credit exposure in swap and derivative transactions the existence of a liquid secondary market is implicitly assumed. While it is clear that the secondary market in swaps and some derivatives has developed, a number of considerations relevant to utilising the secondary market must be considered.

The problems in dealing in secondary market swaps and derivatives include:

- documentation;
- counterparty approval;
- payment of compensation.

In dealing in secondary market swaps, at least, on an assignment basis the documentation must often be accepted as originally entered into. In addition, counterparty approval must be obtained before an assignment can be completed. Finally, a payment (often substantial) between the parties must be effected in order to adjust the swap's fixed coupon to current market levels. Consequently, it is necessary to price swaps in the secondary market at a level attractive to conventional de novo transactions. This discount to market, to the extent that it deviates from normal pricing, has to be factored into the credit exposure assessment under swap transactions. This is because the liquidity premium will work against the party seeking to sell or buy a swap in the secondary market.

Consequently, it is necessary to make an assessment of the liquidity of the particular market when utilising the replacement cost concept to value the credit exposure. In markets where the relative liquidity is such that a replacement contract may not be capable of being easily arranged, the replacement cost may have to be calculated with reference to the purchase or sale of an asset to match the exposure on the transaction on which default has occurred. In this case, the cost of the particular physical transaction, including carrying costs and balance sheet utilisation costs, must be included in determining the credit exposure in entering into such a transaction.

An additional problem in the case of interest rate swaps which are structured as net settlement contracts may be that because of the particular yield curve shape prevailing, it may be desirable not to close out the defaulted position by entering into a replacement swap at all. For example, at one level, the exposure in an interest rate swap is a function of the probability that the rate being paid will average more than the rate being received over the life of the swap. For example, where an intermediary is receiving the fixed rate and paying a floating rate index, in an upward sloping or positive yield curve environment, no actual cash flow loss would be incurred until such time as short-term rates move above the fixed rate. Consequently, if the matching counterparty defaults, the intermediary may choose, given its view of interest rates, not to close up the position and to run the risk of changes in the yield curve shape.

Transactional versus portfolio approach to measurement

A major issue relating to quantification of credit exposure is whether exposure should be calculated on a transactional or portfolio basis. Initially, the risk associated with swap and derivative transactions was assessed independently of the intermediary's other activities. However, as intermediaries have created portfolios of transactions, risk measurement processes based on the marginal increase in overall risk as a new transaction is added to the portfolio have emerged.

Where each swap or derivative transaction is treated individually, and the total intermediary exposure is taken to be the sum of the exposures on individual transactions, an extremely conservative assessment of risk is produced as the analysis assumes that each counterparty defaults at the worst possible point in time for the intermediary. It is, however, intuitively plausible that in a portfolio, diversified with respect to counterparties, the required return for the portfolio could well be less than that which would be suggested from the pricing of individual transactions, depending on the extent of portfolio diversification. This implies that the nature of credit exposures alters as intermediaries acquire larger portfolios of transactions.

For an intermediary with a significant portfolio the risk of a marginal transaction is not simply the maximum worst case loss in the context of that particular transaction but rather is its marginal contribution, estimated at the expected replacement cost if a default occurs, to the overall risk of the portfolio. The approach recognises that the expected replacement cost if there is a default could equal any one of a range of values rather than a single worst case value and that the probability of each of these values occurring will vary.

Utilising this approach, the expected cost of a transaction is treated as the weighted average of all possible replacement costs, using the probability of adverse rate movements as weights. Statistically, this measure gives the best estimate of actual replacement cost if a default occurs. This will almost certainly be less than the worst case measure of individual swap credit exposure.

Exhibit 37.3 sets out an example of utilising a portfolio approach to the measurement of credit exposure utilising interest rate swap transactions.

Exhibit 37.3

Swap Credit Exposure—Portfolio Approach

Assume a bank has the following swaps in its portfolio:

- US$50 million five year swap where it receives 8.00% pa and pays US$ six month LIBOR;
- US$25 million seven year swap where it pays 8.00% pa and receives US$ six month LIBOR;
- US$25 million three year swap where it pays 8.00% pa and receives US$ six month LIBOR.

The potential replacement cost of the swaps (and consquently the credit exposure of counterparty default) is calculated assuming forecast swap rate highs and lows over the forecast period of 6.00% pa and 10.00% pa.

The credit exposure under the individual swaps are summarised below:

Exhibit 37.3—continued

Interest Rate Swap 1 Initial Interest Rate: 8.000% pa
US$50m 5 Year Swap

Year	Fixed Rate Payments	Fixed Rate Payments Replacement Swap Swap Rate		Cash Flow Differential On Default Swap Rate		Swap Exposure (At Start of Period) Swap Rate	
		6.000%	10.000%	6.000%	10.000%	6.000%	10.000%
0							
1	4.000	3.000	5.000	(1.000)	1.000	(3.717)	3.546
2	4.000	3.000	5.000	(1.000)	1.000	(2.829)	2.723
3	4.000	3.000	5.000	(1.000)	1.000	(1.913)	1.859
4	4.000	3.000	5.000	(1.000)	1.000	(0.971)	0.952
5	4.000	3.000	5.000	(1.000)	1.000	0.000	0.000

Interest Rate Swap 2 Initial Interest Rate: 8.000% pa
US$25m 7 Year Swap

Year	Fixed Rate Payments	Fixed Rate Payments Replacement Swap Swap Rate		Cash Flow Differential On Default Swap Rate		Swap Exposure (At Start of Period) Swap Rate	
		6.000%	10.000%	6.000%	10.000%	6.000%	10.000%
0							
1	2.000	1.500	2.500	(0.500)	0.500	(2.709)	2.538
2	2.000	1.500	2.500	(0.500)	0.500	(2.290)	2.165
3	2.000	1.500	2.500	(0.500)	0.500	(1.859)	1.773
4	2.000	1.500	2.500	(0.500)	0.500	(1.414)	1.362
5	2.000	1.500	2.500	(0.500)	0.500	(0.957)	0.930
6	2.000	1.500	2.500	(0.500)	0.500	(0.485)	0.476
7	2.000	1.500	2.500	(0.500)	0.500	(0.000)	0.000

Credit Exposure Measurement—Portfolio
Interest Rate Swap 3 Initial Interest Rate: 8.000% pa
US$25m 3 Year Swap

Year	Fixed Rate Payments	Fixed Rate Payments Replacement Swap Swap Rate		Cash Flow Differential On Default Swap Rate		Swap Exposure (At Start of Period) Swap Rate	
		6.000%	10.000%	6.000%	10.000%	6.000%	10.000%
0							
1	2.000	1.500	2.500	(0.500)	0.500	(0.957)	0.930
2	2.000	1.500	2.500	(0.500)	0.500	(0.485)	0.476
3	2.000	1.500	2.500	(0.500)	0.500	0.000	0.000

All exposures are stated as a percentage of face value of the swap.

The credit exposure of the *portfolio* as a whole is summarised below:

Year	Swap 1 Replacement Cost Swap Rate		Swap 2 Replacement Cost Swap Rate		Swap 3 Replacement Cost Swap Rate		Portfolio Total Replacement Cost Swap Rate		Individual Swap Replacement Cost
	6.000%	10.000%	6.000%	10.000%	6.000%	10.000%	6.000%	10.000%	
0	0.000	0.000	0.000	0.000	0.000	0.000	0.000	0.000	0.000
1	(3.717)	3.546	2.709	(2.538)	0.957	(0.930)	(0.052)	0.078	(7.185)
2	(2.829)	2.723	2.290	(2.165)	0.485	(0.476)	(0.053)	0.082	(5.470)
3	(1.913)	1.859	1.859	(1.773)	0.000	0.000	(0.055)	0.086	(3.686)
4	(0.971)	0.952	1.414	(1.362)			0.443	(0.409)	(2.332)
5	0.000	0.000	0.957	(0.930)			0.957	(0.930)	(0.930)
6			0.485	(0.476)			0.485	(0.476)	(0.476)
7			0.000	0.000			0	0	0

The credit exposures under the individual swap approach and the portfolio approach are set out in the graph below.

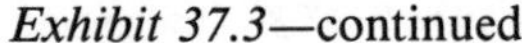
Exhibit 37.3—continued

PORTFOLIO EXPOSURE INTEREST RATE SWAPS

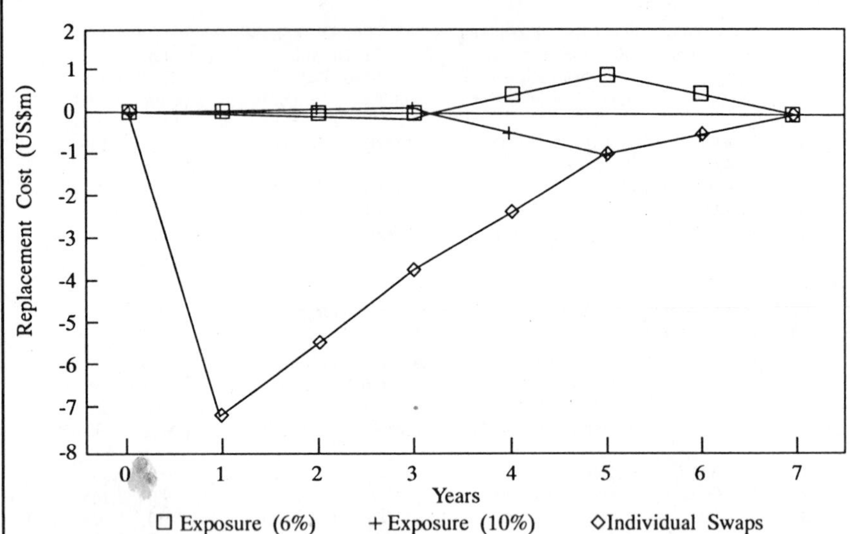

The analysis highlights the much lower exposure to default risk where the swap is treated on a portfolio basis.

However, the portfolio approach necessarily assumes the following:

- All swaps are with the same counterparty. Where the swaps are with *different* counterparties, for the portfolio approach to credit exposure to be tractable, it has to be assumed that all the relevant swap counterparties will default *simultaneously* or, at a minimum, there is strong correlation between counterparty defaults—an unlikely scenario.
- A default under one swap triggers default under the other swap—that is, there are cross-default provisions as between the swaps.
- The swap documentation provides for netting of replacement costs as between the swaps.
- The documentation and law governing the swaps are identical.

The example utilised illustrates quite clearly that the credit exposure of a swap or derivative portfolio, when considered on a portfolio basis, is significantly lower than that determined utilising a transactional approach to credit exposure measurement. However, a number of aspects of the portfolio approach must be noted:

- The portfolio approach assumes that all transactions are consummated with the same counterparty. In practice, even where the transactions are consummated with the same *economic entity*, different legal vehicles may be entailed which create potential legal problems in applying a portfolio approach to the measurement of credit exposure.
- Portfolio approaches are predicated on a reasonable mix of offsetting transactions. For example, where the particular counterparty only transacts a particular type of derivative (for example, only paying fixed and receiving floating

under interest rate swaps) the portfolio approach is of limited use. This, in practice, makes portfolio approach more suitable to transactions between financial institutions active in derivative markets as market makers than to end users of products.

- The portfolio approach assumes that a default on any one transaction in the portfolio is a default on *all transactions* between the relevant counterparties. This is necessary to enable all positions to be closed and marked-to-market to arrive at the net close-out amount at the same point in time.
- The portfolio approach also assumes that the legal documentation governing each transaction and, indeed, the specific law applicable to each of the transactions is identical or, at the very least, very similar.
- More specifically, documentation must provide for:

—Full netting and set-off rights as between the transactions to enable a *net* close out amount for all the transactions to be arrived.

—The documentation should provide for full two-way payment whereby, in the event of default, the net value of the position is recognised, even if it is in favour of the defaulting party.

This should be distinguished from limited two way payment provision whereby the non-defaulting party is permitted, in the event of a termination triggered by default by the other party, to terminate its obligations under the swap contract even if it would have had an obligation to pay a net amount to the defaulting party (often referred to as a "walkaway clause". (In theory, if the documentation only includes a limited two-way payment provision, it is possible that the theoretical exposure under the portfolio will be *lower* than with a full two-way payment provision.)

Issues relating to limited versus full two-way payment provisions are discussed in detail later in this chapter and also in Chapter 44 in connection with legal and documentation issues relating to swap transactions.

In addition, it should be noted that in *Exhibit 37.3*, benefits of the portfolio approach may be overstated because it was assumed that the swap yield curve is flat and all swaps are transacted at the same time. In practice, the fact that the swap transactions forming part of the portfolio are entered into at various times with different coupons (reflecting both the movement in absolute rates as well as changes in yield curve shapes) and the impact on replacement values changes in the shape of the yield curve as well as absolute rate movement (affected by time in the manner discussed above) means that benefits of a portfolio approach will vary significantly from one portfolio to another. However, in general terms, the portfolio approach will yield lower *net* credit exposure than simple summation of the exposure under individual transactions.

The basic premise underlying the portfolio approach to measurement of credit exposure with individual counterparties is capable of extension to the management of overall credit exposure within total swap portfolio, involving multiple counterparties. In measuring credit exposure, financial institutions, typically, assume that all counterparties will default *simultaneously*—hopefully an unrealistic assumption. In practice, applying some measures of *probable* default experience in relation to different categories of counterparties (utilising, for example, relative credit ratings as a surrogate for relative default experience on a projected basis), provides a more realistic measure of portfolio credit exposure.

Alternative approaches to exposure measurement

The procedure for determining the expected replacement cost involves a specification of a probability distribution for, for example, future interest rates and is mathematically similar to the procedure for calculating the value of interest rate options or currency options (in the case of currency swaps). Increasingly, intermediaries are using an option pricing model to generate market risk estimates based upon interest rate volatility at current market rates and the remaining life of the swap. This type of model implies that the longer the maturity of the swap, or higher the volatility of interest rates, the greater the amount of risk.

Utilising option pricing models to estimate the credit exposure under swap and derivative transactions is predicated on the simple assumption that, in the event of default by the counterparty, the non-defaulting counterparty will need to transact to replace the defaulted transaction. In essence, for example in the case of an interest rate swap, the non-defaulting counterparty can protect itself by purchasing an option on a swap identical to the transaction entered into.

In practice, this is necessarily more complicated. A simple option on a swap will not suffice as the transaction itself will, with the effluxion of time, change its characteristics. For example, in protecting itself against default under a five year swap, counterparty would need to buy a series of swaptions—a six month option on a 4.5 year swap, 12 month option on a four year swap, 18 month option on a 3.5 year swap etc.

The premium payable for these swaptions can be utilised as a surrogate measure of the credit exposure on the transaction. This reflects the fact that it is, at least theoretically, possible for the counterparty to insulate itself from the risk of default of the other party almost perfectly utilising this particular strategy.

An alternative technique for measuring swap exposures entails the use of various simulation techniques, particularly Monte Carlo and similar techniques, to simulate the possible credit exposure under a swap. This type of technique is predicated on probabilistic simulation of anticipated swap rate movements conforming to a specified distribution of future market rates and utilising this to derive a sequence of credit exposures that could occur over the life of the swap. Expected exposure at any time, utilising this approach, would be the average of a large number of exposures across simulations. Where netting is *not* assumed, the expected exposure of a portfolio of swaps would equal the sum of the expected exposures of all the swaps, while where netting is allowed, the expected exposure would be the net of the positive and negative replacement costs *with each counterparty.*[2]

It is important to note that the expected value approach to swap exposures is appropriate only in the case of intermediaries with a substantial portfolio of outstanding swaps. With smaller portfolios, a more conservative approach may be appropriate although this may place the institution in question at a competitive disadvantage since it would have to price its intermediation function for a higher assumed risk.

There is an interrelationship between the measurement of exposure under swap transactions and the termination provisions of swaps. It is desirable that these termination provisions represent accurately the available methods of neutralising any default exposure under a swap transaction in case of default.

2. See, for example, Benjamin Iben and Rupert Brotherton-Ratcliffe, (1991-1992); or M Ferron and G Handginicolaou, "Understanding Swap Credit Risk: Simulation Approach" in Robert J Schwartz and Clifford W Smith Jr (1991).

MEASUREMENT OF CREDIT EXPOSURE IN PRACTICE

Measurement of credit exposure under swap and derivative transactions in practice requires the operationalising of the theoretical principles outlined above. The major problem in this regard is that exposures cannot be determined in advance and are in this regard significantly different from other financial transactions such as loan transactions where the amount of exposure is immediately discernible.

There are basically two approaches, in practice, to the quantification of credit exposure in swap and derivative transactions on an ex ante basis:

- exposure measurement utilising statistical evaluation technology;
- exposure valuation utilising a mark-to-market technique.

The statistical methodology, commonly used by banks, bases exposure on assumptions of interest rate, currency, or equity or commodity price movements calculated from analyses of historical data combined with some subjective judgments. The approach requires an assessment of the potential exposure in a worst case scenario within given confidence limits over the life of the transaction. One potential approach is to evaluate actual exposure over a certain historical period and use this as a proxy for future exposure. An alternative approach is to assume that markets can be characterised by a predictable distribution of outcomes (for example, a normal or log normal distribution). Under the second method, the mean and standard deviations of these distributions are then evaluated and used to project exposure at the desired level of confidence.

The statistical methodology utilised to define swap and derivative credit exposures are summarised in *Exhibit 37.4*.

In contrast, the mark-to-market technology continually evaluates current exposure by effectively revaluing each swap transaction utilising current market rates.

The advantage of the statistical technique is that it is possible to calculate an absolute number representing the *anticipated* exposure under the transaction. The disadvantage of this approach is that the exposure determined is based on historical data which may not accurately reflect the actual fluctuations in rates over the life of the transaction.

The mark-to-market methodology has the advantage that the exposure calculated does not overstate or understate the risk of a transaction. The mark-to-market methodology does not require a complex set of assumptions for risk assessment and essentially creates a self-regulatory system with the intermediary required to expand or contract its exposures with market forces. However, the mark-to-market methodology does not provide an institution with a single indicia of the exposure under the swap on an ex ante basis. This means that the intermediary does not know in advance the amount of capital required to support its swap and derivative operations, the extent to which the transaction is likely to exceed the credit limits it has extended to the particular counterparty, and, most importantly, it does not allow the pricing of intermediation fees for the particular transaction.

These difficulties with the mark-to-market approach mean that the statistical valuation methodology is currently the most commonly utilised technique.

The approach to quantification of swap exposures is highly subjective, ultimately reflecting the objectives and risk profile of the participant. For example, it is entirely possible that regulators as against intermediaries will seek to place signficantly different exposure limits on swap transactions (see Chapter 39). For example, at one

Exhibit 37.4

Statistical Methodology for Swap Credit Exposure Measurement

In practice, use of statistical approaches entails a number of distinct steps:*

- Estimates of change in interest rates are derived. This would entail, most commonly, examining *changes* in the relevant swap rates over a reasonable period of time.

  For example, in the case of a three year swap, historical data on movements in three year swap rates would be derived. As the actual exposure would depend on movements not only in three year but in two and, ultimately, one year swap rates the absolute level of and changes in these rates must also be analysed.

- Based on this analysis, distributions of possible swap rates are derived utilising standard measures of data analysis, such as mean and dispersion measures, such as standard deviation.

- The level of mathematical confidence to be utilised is then selected. For example, the credit exposure may be calculated by using:

  —Mean plus or minus one standard deviation equivalent to 68.27% confidence criterion;

  —Mean plus or minus two standard deviation equivalent to 95.45% confidence criterion;

  —Mean plus or minus three standard deviation equivalent to 99.73% confidence criterion.

  In general terms, institutions typically utilise to 95% confidence criterion, that is two standard deviations from mean.

- Based on the selected confidence criterion, swap rates are projected to appropriate intervals over the life of the swap. For example, for a three year swap, appropriate intervals might be 2.5, 2.0, 1.5, 1.0 and 0.5 years.

- Utilising statistically determined forecast swap rates at each of the relevant maturity points, the replacement swap present value is calculated.

- Credit exposure under the transaction is determined as being equal to the largest potential exposure for any date.

- The statistical model outlined can be amended to incorporate a variety of yield curve moves such as parallel yield curve shifts or, utilising two factor models, changes in yield curve shape or to model path-dependent outcomes.

* The methodology identified relates to interest rates but is very similar to that which would be utilised for measuring the impact of movements in currency rates, commodity prices and equity market indexes.

extreme, an ultra-conservative approach to measurement of exposures on swap and derivative transactions would be to ignore the statistical origins of a swap transaction and value the swap as a loan requiring that the various risk ratios be computed using 100.00% of the par value of the swap.

The difficulty in practice entails specifying the worst case scenario for potential exposure for an individual transaction or for a portfolio. Initially, swap and derivative exposures were measured on the basis of conservative worst case levels for exchange and interest rates. This led to excessively conservative assessments on exposures and relatively large credit fees. However, because of the increasingly portfolio approach to credit risk adopted by intermediaries, as well as the fact that in a diversified portfolio interest rate and exchange rate movements can partially offset each other (that is, they are less than perfectly correlated), intermediation fees on transactions have declined. This decline also reflects the increased competitive nature of the market and the expansion of the volume of transactions which has also reduced the cost of each transaction as overheads are now distributed over more transactions allowing intermediaries to realise economies of scale in the administration of these transactions.

An interesting issue in the estimation of credit exposures is the impact of interest rate cycles and the pattern and institutional structure of the market itself which may significantly influence the exposures under such transactions.

In practice, total diversification of a portfolio is difficult because there is a built-in market bias against swap and derivative transactions being booked at the extremes in interest rate cycles. For example, when rates are very high, there are few counterparties willing to pay fixed rates, and when rates are very low, counterparties may be reluctant to receive fixed rates. Similarly, market biases may exist in currency swaps at the high and low points of currency cycles.

A further complication is that fact that counterparties traditionally most vulnerable to higher interest rate environments are most likely to be payers of the fixed rate which could, ironically, result in a gain to the intermediary if default occurs in a higher rate environment.

In practice, most intermediaries utilise a predetermined percentage of the nominal amount of a swap transaction as the relevant exposure in determining the amount to be used for credit approval purposes. Typically these percentages are as follows:

- For interest rate swaps, the percentages range from 3.00% to 20.00% depending upon maturity of the transaction. In the case of floating-to-floating interest rate or basis swaps, the relative minor risk means that either no credit risk percentage is computed or alternatively a relatively low figure such as 5.00% to 10.00% is utilised.
- For currency swaps and LTFX, percentages ranging from 20.00% to 50.00% of the notional principal of the transaction, depending upon maturity, are utilised.
- For FRAs, percentages range from 1.00% to 3.00% for transactions maturing within one year. For longer dated FRAs, percentages similar to those applicable to interest rate swaps are utilised.
- For cap, floor and collar rate agreements, no credit exposure is recorded where the counterparty is a purchaser, while for a grantor percentages ranging from 10.00% to 40.00% depending upon the maturity of the agreement are utilised.
- For commodity and equity swap transactions, percentages ranging from 10.00% to 40.00% face value are utilised depending upon the maturity of the agreement as well as specific structure. For example, the credit exposure under a variable notional principal, cross-currency equity swap is, generally, quite low reflecting the adjustment to principal reflecting changes in currency parities which are made periodically.

The actual percentages utilised will clearly vary as between products reflecting differing underlying volatilities in currency and interest rates or commodity and equity index prices.

A number of institutions have, in recent years, abandoned internal guidelines in favour of utilising the credit equivalents specified by regulatory authorities under the methods described in detail in Chapter 39 (typically, using the original exposure method). Under this method, central banks prescribe the credit equivalent of a swap depending on the number of years until maturity of the contract. A number of banks have begun to utilise these credit equivalents, in some cases with minor adjustments, for calculating internal credit exposure equivalents against counterparties. This is so whether or not the institution adopts the original exposure method for the purpose of calculating credit equivalent amount of the overall swap portfolio for the purposes of central bank capital adequacy calculations (see detailed discussion in Chapter 39).

Credit officers in some institutions merely approve or disapprove credit extensions on swaps and derivatives, charging the exposure against the institution's overall credit line to the counterparty. Others approve the transaction only if the institution receives a certain number of basis points for credit risk. In some cases the dealer actually pays the credit officer "shadow" income for the exposure. Typically, however, the dealer does *not* pass this charge explicitly into the quoted price of the transaction. If the trader cannot cover this charge at the prevailing swap price in the market, he or she does not enter into the transaction.

An estimate of the minimum spread required between two offsetting swaps for profitability can be obtained by charging such a premium on the estimated credit exposure. A shadow charge of 6bps to a particular customer might be arrived at in the following fashion. A loan to a customer would normally incorporate a spread of 0.375% pa over the bank's cost of funding the loan. For a swap where the credit exposure is calculated to be 16.00% of notional amount, the charge to cover the credit risk is 0.375% pa of the 16.00%, or 6bps (0.0006% pa). This covers the exposure to the failure of one counterparty.

In addition to setting aside credit lines for expected exposure, most dealers also monitor actual exposure as prices change. Management is periodically informed of the potential exposure if some or all counterparties were to default.

Practice differs among dealers on whether they monitor their credit exposure to a counterparty with which they have swaps in opposite directions. Some examine their exposure on a gross basis on the assumption that the counterparty could default on each swap only when interest rates have moved in the wrong direction. Others monitor exposure on a net basis, assuming that if the counterparty fails, the bank gains on some swaps and loses on others. Rights of netting offset provided by the swap contracts and the governing law under which the contracts are made are important factors in making this choice (see discussion in Chapters 39 and 44).

In most institutions, credit lines available for a particular customer are finite, and dealers must compete with other divisions of the bank for credit approval on the basis of earnings generated relative to limit utilisation.

MANAGEMENT OF CREDIT EXPOSURES

Overview

There are essentially three approaches to the management of credit exposure under swap transactions:

- acceptance and management of the credit exposure;
- passing the credit risk to another intermediary;
- enhancement of the credit exposure through various techniques.

The approach utilised by different organisations reflects their different business operations, objectives, and their respective capacities to assume and bear risk.

Management of credit exposure

The acceptance and management of credit exposure in swap transactions entails the following separate tasks:

- risk assessment;
- risk pricing.

Risk assessment entails quantification of the credit exposure under the transaction itself and an assessment of the counterparty's financial status and, thereby, its capacity to meet its financial obligations under the transaction. The assessment of counterparty risk in a transaction is not significantly different from general credit assessment involved in financial transactions. Once an overall limit for the particular counterparty has been established, the risk of the particular swap or derivative product is quantified utilising the techniques discussed and, if the overall limit to the counterparty is sufficient to enable the transaction to be entered into, the transaction is then booked thereby reducing the available credit that the intermediary can extend to the counterparty.

The process of pricing of the risk, that is, the setting of the intermediation fees, is considerable more complex. Generally, the difference between the interest paid and the interest received on the fixed rate component of a swap, the bid-offer spread, represents income to the intermediary. This income must be sufficient to compensate for the risk incurred and to provide a sufficient level of earning relative to the capital utilised.

In practice, the intermediation fee is calculated as the earnings required to provide the intermediary with the required rate of return on the transaction for a counterparty of comparable risk based on the calculated exposure under the transaction. Elaborate models exist to accurately measure the required rate of return on such a transaction. An illustration of calculating swap intermediation fees utilising return on risk criteria is set out in *Exhibit 37.5*.

Exhibit 37.5

Calculating Swap Intermediation Fees Utilising Return on Risk Criteria

Credit intermediation fees for an interest rate swap can be determined, utilising return on risk criteria, using the following method:

- Calculate the risk asset (that is, the exposure under the swap).
- Apply to the risk asset the required rate of return to calculate the dollar income sought.
- Calculate the equivalent annual fee in dollars which gives the same net present value as that of the dollar income.

Using the same scenario utilised in illustrating the credit exposure in interest rate swaps, the following risk asset can be generated:

Year	Maximum loss if fixed rate payer defaults (% of notional principal)	Maximum loss if floating rate payer defaults (% of notional principal)
0.0	6.25	6.78
0.5	5.48	5.87
1.0	4.60	4.89
1.5	3.63	3.81
2.0	2.55	2.65
2.5	1.35	1.35
3.0	—	—

Exhibit 37.5—continued

The minimum earning rate on risk assets will vary between one institution and another and will also reflect the credit standing of the counterparty. For illustration purposes assume that:

- the payer of the floating rate in the swap is a strong credit for which a bank might provide a three year letter of credit or guarantee for a fee of the order of 0.25% pa;
- the payer of the fixed rate in a swap is a weaker credit for which a three year letter of credit or term bank guarantee might be priced at say 1.00% pa.

The letter of credit or guarantee fees are used as a proxy or benchmark of the credit risk premium to be charged because the swap is not a fully funded balance sheet obligation and therefore funding margins are not relevant.

The earning required (per US$100m) will be as follows:

Year	Risk asset (fixed rate payer)	Required return (@ 1.00% pa)	Risk asset (floating rate payer)	Required return (@ 0.25% pa)
0.0	6.25	—	6.78	—
0.5	5.48	0.0313	5.87	0.0085
1.0	4.60	0.0274	4.89	0.0073
1.5	3.63	0.0230	3.81	0.0061
2.0	2.55	0.0182	2.65	0.0048
2.5	1.35	0.0128	1.35	0.0033
3.0	—	0.0068	—	0.0017
NPV of required return @ 14.00% pa		0.0993		0.0265
Equivalent % pa (on notional principal)		0.0417		0.0111

This requires a credit intermediation fee in this transaction of 0.0528% pa (S/A).

In the above approach, the likelihood of default as between the parties to the swap is "built in" to the differential required return for the two counterparties. An alternative method would entail the potential risk exposure being multiplied by the probability of default (as determinable from actual default experience on, for example, securities issued by an issuer of the relevant credit standing). This would provide a projected cost of default on the swap which could be used as the risk asset level on which to base an absolute earning level on risk.

The above example focuses on interest rate swaps but the methodology of calculating swap intermediation fees for currency swaps and other derivatives is identical.

Swap transactions are priced to give a return on risk which is consistent with the required return for comparable off-balance sheet items, such as letters of credit and guarantees. Intermediation fees are also charged against income earnings according to a graduated scale which depends upon the credit-worthiness of the counterparty resulting in a tiering of prices.

The essential technique in the management of the credit exposure of a swap or derivatives portfolio is diversification. Diversification can be achieved at a number of different levels.

Diversification by counterparty will reduce the default risk associated with the default of any one counterparty. In addition, a portfolio can be diversified in such a manner as to maturity and levels of interest rates as to minimise the risk of economic loss upon default. A further type of diversification entails the entry into transactions with the *same* counterparty at different times and in different markets to achieve different transactional objectives. The objective is to create *parallel* transactions to the extent that the transactions are opposite but equal such that the positive and negative exposures net to zero. In practice, it is not possible to transact identical transactions but entry into similar transactions can be utilised to manage exposures on the overall portfolio. Further dimensions of diversification within a portfolio is to reduce risk by structuring by country, industry, maturity and floating rate index on a selective basis.

The process of management of the exposures on a portfolio is dynamic and may require amendments from time to time as new information becomes available.

Passing on credit exposure

An alternative means of managing credit exposure is to pass on the exposure to a third party willing to assume the default risks entailed.

The credit exposure on a swap or derivative transaction may be passed on in a number of ways. A number of institutions seek to take on already completed transactions for an intermediation fee. The second approach, somewhat similar, entails the assignment of transactions from one counterparty to another. The basic difference between the two approaches is that the first does nothing to reduce the total amount of credit required to support the total market as an intermediating role is still being performed while the second approach reduces the credit demands on the market.

Credit constraints within the market have forced both financial institutions, active as market makers, as well as end users to focus on assignments as a means of reducing credit exposure. This has been a particularly strong feature of activity between financial institutions as they seek to aggressively reduce utilisation of credit lines as between dealers to facilitate trading activity.

Where an institution has two matching or near matching transactions, increasingly, the trend is to seek to assign one or other transaction in an effort to reduce credit exposure.

An interesting feature of the swap market in recent years has been the willingness of highly rated non-financial institutions to accept *direct* credit exposure on each other. For example, in August 1991, Goldman Sachs arranged a three-legged back-to-back swap involving the Province of Ontario (Ontario), the Inter-American Development Bank (IADB) and Finish Export Credit (FEC). Under the transaction, Ontario issued a US$390m Eurobond which was swapped into a fixed rate Canadian dollar liability with IADB and FEC who undertook simultaneous C$ issues in the Eurobond market. The swaps involved matched each of the counterparties cash flows, with the Bank of Montreal playing a part in smoothing out some transaction payment flows. Under the transaction structure, Ontario took the direct credit risk of both the IADB and FEC and vice versa.

A major factor in these direct counterparty-to-counterparty transaction is the savings as a result of avoiding the necessity of interposing a financial institution to absorb the credit exposure of both counterparties. In the transaction described above, it is estimated that each borrower saved approximately 5-10bps pa through the direct rather than intermediated swap structure. An essential factor in the resurgence in direct counterparty driven transactions is the narrowing arbitrage opportunities where the cost of intermediation would make it uneconomic to transact such swaps.

Credit enhancement

In certain circumstances, an intermediary may accept the credit exposures in booking swaps directly on the basis of enhancing the underlying credit of the counterparty utilising one of a number of available techniques, including:

- netting exposures;
- collateralisation; and
- insurance.

Netting

The approach of netting of exposures between counterparties is designed to reduce the exposure recorded for individual counterparties. Netting as between counterparties active in the interbank market can dramatically reduce interbank credit line utilisation assuming that business is written in both directions. Netting as a technique is primarily restricted to institutions who are using the swap and derivative market not as end users (which traditionally means an inbuilt bias to be either one side or the other) but as intermediaries acting on behalf of clients with diverse needs and who may be using the interbank market to close out positions.

The concept of netting is based on the portfolio approach to measurement of credit exposure as it can be applied to individual counterparties. As discussed above, combination of a portfolio approach and netting of exposures can dramatically reduce credit exposure with an individual counterparty. The conditions necessary for netting to be effective in the reduction of counterparty credit exposure is identical to those specified above in the context of portfolio approaches to credit measurement.

The dramatic impact that netting can have on credit risk of financial institutions is evident from *Exhibit 37.6*. This exhibit sets out the off-balance sheet credit risk of Bankers Trust New York Corporation as at 31 December 1991. As is evident, the use of netting in the specific case of Bankers Trust, has the impact of significantly reducing that financial institution's off balance sheet credit risk.

Exhibit 37.6

Bankers Trust New York Corporation Off-Balance Sheet Credit Risk (US$billion) (As at 31 December 1991)

	Notional	Credit Risk		
	FAS105	FAS105	Adjusted	Adjustment
Interest Rate				
Swaps	221.8	6.1		Netting
Options	123.8	1.0		Notl Amt of WI/TBAs
F&F	74.7	4.3		Notl Amt of WITBAs and Forwards
Foreign Exchange			15.3	
Swaps	74.3	5.0		Netting
Options	88.3	1.2		Netting
F&F	220.9	6.2		Netting
Equity Derivs/ Other	57.9	1.8		Netting
Total	861.7	25.6	15.3	

Source: Elizabeth H Ruml (Managing Director, Department Credit Officer, Global Markets, Bankers Trust, New York Corporation) "Derivatives 101" (Presentation to the Bank and Financial Analysts Association, 22nd Annual Banking Symposium, 26 March, 1992).

The use of netting to reduce credit exposure has broader implications. The BIS capital adequacy standards were amended in April 1993 to introduce bilateral netting schemes, to reduce the net credit exposure within the swap and derivative markets generally. The various issues related to such netting arrangements are discussed in detail in Chapter 39.

Collateralisation

Collateralisation of the obligations of a party under a swap is a more recent development. Collateralisation has its origins in the participation in the swap market of such United States financial institutions as saving and loan associations and smaller regional banks. The basic rationale in collateralisation is to secure the performance of a party's obligations under a swap agreement to protect the capital gain of the counterparty should interest or exchange rates move in a direction favourable to that party.

Collateralisation usually operates in one of two ways:

- In certain swaps, weaker counterparties are required to post collateral at the inception of the swap. The exposure on the swap is constantly monitored and if the level of collateral falls below a certain level of the termination exposure, the counterparty would be required to post further collateral to maintain the cover. The failure to produce further collateral is itself an event of default and consequently exposure under the swap on termination can never exceed the value of the collateral posted.
- An alternative approach is to provide for either party to require the other to provide collateral against the exposure under a swap agreement in the event that the exposure increases dramatically and/or the credit quality of either institution changes significantly.

The types of collateral traditionally utilised include:

- a pledge of government securities;
- a pledge of other marketable assets such as loans secured by mortgages or deed of trust or mortgage backed securities;
- standby letters of credit from an acceptable financial institution;
- a guarantee from a creditworthy third party.

The basic types of collateral utilised are government securities and marketable mortgage backed securities which are types of collateral readily available to United States thrift institutions which were originally the primary participants in the collateralised swap market.

A typical collateralised swap arrangement would operate as follows:

- The swap counterparty would be required to lodge collateral equivalent to 0 to 5% of the face value of the swap at the commencement of the transaction.
- Over the life of the transaction, the swap would be marked-to-market, typically, at monthly, quarterly or semi-annual intervals. The mark-to-market calculation would be undertaken to determine the replacement cost of the swap as at the relevant date and where the swap has a positive replacement cost, the swap counterparty would lodge additional collateral with the financial institution equal to the replacement cost. This mark-to-market procedure would be repeated as at each of the relevant dates over the life of the transaction.

The exact structure of the collateralisation arrangement is negotiated on a bilateral basis between the counterparty and financial institution. The function of the deposit collateral amount is to effectively protect the financial institution from the inability of the counterparty to mark the swap to market at any time over the life of the transaction. As a consequence, the collateral amounts specified to be deposited at the commencement of the transaction should be equal to the potential short term changes in the exposure under the swap.

The structure of collateralisation arrangements is almost identical to the operation of organised futures and options exchanges entailing the posting of deposits and margin calls on open futures or options contracts.

The party entering into the transaction and lodging collateral receives interest on the initial collateral and subsequent mark-to-market collateral payments at a negotiated rate. This rate is typically based on prevailing short term money market rates, such as US$ LIBOR.

It is important to note that where the counterparty has more than one swap with the financial institution, the mark-to-market calculation is generally performed on a *portfolio* basis. This ensures that the counterparty gets the benefit of negative as well as positive replacement costs, thereby reducing the amount of total collateral that may need to be maintained.

Additional features of the collateralisation arrangement include:

- A "trigger" mechanism whereby the financial institution can require the swap counterparty to post collateral *in between mark-to-market dates* where the potential replacement cost and therefore swap credit exposure exceeds a prespecified bench mark or trigger amount. For example, in the case of a five year swap with quarterly mark-to-market arrangements, it may be a term of the contract that in the event that the swap credit exposure to the financial institution exceeds a fixed amount (say, of notional principal 2% or, a monetary amount, US$1m) then the financial institution has the right to ask the counterparty to post collateral equivalent to the mark-to-market value at that time.
- An additional feature utilised by some institutions requires the swap counterparty to make settlements under the swap transaction *in advance*. Under this structure, the swap counterparty would, where it is required to make a swap settlement payment to the counterparty at the end of any interest rate period based on the interest rate calculations at the start of the period, be required to make the payment *at the time of calculation* on a discounted present value basis. This type of structure is designed to further reduce the financial institution's exposure to the default of the counterparty.

The proceeds for estimation of the cost of collateralisation arrangements are analysed in *Exhibit 37.7*.

Exhibit 37.7

Cost of Transacting a Collateralised Swap

Assume Company A (A) enters into an US$ interest rate swap for US$100m for a term of five years under which it receives fixed rates at 5.956% pa quarterly and pays US$ three month LIBOR.

Because of the non-investment grade credit standing of A, the swap is required to be collateralised on the following basis:

- initial cash collateral equal to 2.50% of the notional principal amount of the swap;
- a requirement to mark-to-market on a quarterly basis with A being required to lodge collateral where the replacement value of the swap is positive for the counterparty as a result of market rate movements;

Exhibit 37.7—continued

- a provision whereby the swap counterparty has the ability to call for additional collateral to be posted, in between quarterly mark-to-market dates, where the market value of the swap changes (negatively for A) by 1% of notional principal amount, effectively reducing the amount of collateral cover to 1.50%.

The counterparty agrees to pay interest at overnight LIBOR flat to A on all collateral required to be lodged.

The cost of A of the collateralisation arrangement is the "negative spread" between its cost of funding and the rate at which interest is received on collateral funds.

Assuming a cost of funds to A of LIBOR plus 2.00% pa, this negative spread is 200bps pa. (Note that this analysis ignores yield curve effects. A would typically borrow over three or six month LIBOR whereas it is receiving *overnight* LIBOR. This means it would suffer an additional cost under a positively sloped yield curve.)

The cost of collateralisation covers two components:

- financing the deposit; *and*
- financing the periodic mark-to-market variation margins.

The cost of financing the deposit can be estimated with accuracy. The cost of financing of the variation margins is more difficult reflecting the fact that it requires assumptions to be made about the following:

- future swap rate movements;
- changes in the shape of the swap curve (to adjust for the fact that the actual maturity of the swap declines);
- the timing of swap rate changes.

In this case, A will need to make margin calls where rates rise which will increase the replacement cost of the swap to the counterparty. Assume that swap rates are estimated to increase to 10% pa over the term of this swap in equal increments over the 20 quarters.

Based on this assumption, the cost of collateralisation can be estimated as follows:

Cost of Swap Collateralisation

Notional Principal Amount (M):	100.0		
Term (Years):	5		
Periods Per Year:	4		
Swap Rate:	6.000% pa Semi-Annual	6.090% pa	Annual
		5.956% pa	Qtly

Collateralisation Terms:		Swap Rate Expectations	
Deposit (% of Notional Principal):	2.50%	Swap Rate (At end of Swap Term):	
Margining Frequency:	Quarterly	10.000% Semi	10.250% Annual
Margin Trigger (% of Notional Principal):	1.00%		9.878% Qtly

Deposit/Margin Funding Cost:

Borrowing Cost:	LIBOR + 2.000%	
Interest Received:	LIBOR	
Net Cost:		2.00%

Period	Deposit Amount	Deposit Interest	Swap Rate	Mark-to-Market Margin Swap Value	Margin Requirement	Margin Interest
0	2.5000	0.0125	5.956%	100.0000	0.0000	0.0000
1		0.0125	6.152%	99.1975	0.8025	0.0040
2		0.0125	6.348%	98.4751	1.5249	0.0076
3		0.0125	6.544%	97.8324	2.1676	0.0108
4		0.0125	6.740%	97.2695	2.7305	0.0137
5		0.0125	6.936%	96.7864	3.2136	0.0161
6		0.0125	7.132%	96.3836	3.6164	0.0181
7		0.0125	7.328%	96.0617	3.9383	0.0197
8		0.0125	7.525%	95.8215	4.1785	0.0209
9		0.0125	7.721%	95.6642	4.3358	0.0217
10		0.0125	7.917%	95.5911	4.4089	0.0220

Exhibit 37.7—continued

Period	Deposit Amount	Deposit Interest	Swap Rate	Mark-to-Market Margin Swap Value	Margin Requirement	Margin Interest
11		0.0125	8.113%	95.6038	4.3962	0.0220
12		0.0125	8.309%	95.7043	4.2957	0.0215
13		0.0125	8.505%	95.8948	4.1052	0.0205
14		0.0125	8.701%	96.1777	3.8223	0.0191
15		0.0125	8.897%	96.5560	3.4440	0.0172
16		0.0125	9.094%	97.0326	2.9674	0.0148
17		0.0125	9.290%	97.6113	2.3887	0.0119
18		0.0125	9.486%	98.2958	1.7042	0.0085
19		0.0125	9.682%	99.0905	0.9095	0.0045
20		0.0125	9.878%			

Cost of Deposit
BPS Equivalent (pa):
5.00 Quarterly

Cost of Mark-to-Market Margins
NPV of Margin Payments: 0.2506
BPS Equivalent (pa): 5.83 Quarterly

Based on these assumptions, the cost of collateralisation is:

Cost of Deposit	5.00	bps pa
Cost of Expected Variation Margin	5.83	bps pa
Total	10.83	bps pa

This equates to an effective net rate received under the swap of 5.8477% pa quarterly.

The maximum cash required to be committed under the collateralisation arrangement is estimated at US$6.9m (6.9089% of notional principal).

The cost of variation margins is only an estimate as the pattern of future swap rates cannot be known with certainty. The sensitivity of the cost of variation calls (in bps pa) to the pattern of future rate movements is summarised below:

	Pattern of Rate Rise	
Maximum Swap Rate Expected (% pa)	Even Over Term	75% Rise in first 2.5 years
8	2.9	4.06
10	5.83	7.98
12	8.64	11.77
14	11.37	15.44

Collateralisation is primarily a feature of the US$ swap market. Additional credit support, primarily by way of bank letter of credit, is, however, utilised in other swap markets as well.

Option to terminate/non-standard cash flow structures

A number of alternative forms of credit enhancement which have developed over recent times merit discussion:

- Options to terminate which are also referred to as break rights or early termination provisions.
- The use of non-standard cash flows or off-market pricing to reduce credit exposure under swaps.

Under the option to terminate structure, the swap documentation involves an early termination provision or right to break clause which provides both parties with the agreement of the unconditional right to terminate a swap on:

- an agreed break date or dates; *or*
- at any time.

The termination payment as between the parties is set at the then mark-to-market value of the transaction.

The typical wording of this clause is as follows:

"(a) each party has the right by 30 days' notice to the other to terminate specified swap transactions on any break date (defined below).

(b) the party exercising this early termination clause (the terminating party) has the right to transfer the swap transaction to a third party during the period of [ ] days from delivery of a notice under paragraph (a). Any transfer by the terminating party under this paragraph will be subject to and conditioned upon the prior written consent of the other party (the non-terminating party), which consent will not be withheld if the non-terminating party's policy in effect at such time would permit it to enter into swap transactions with the transferee on the terms proposed and would be at not extra cost or loss to the non-terminating party.

(c) If this swap transaction is not transferred to a third party under paragraph (b) the relevant break date shall be an early termination date and the payments on early termination dates shall be determined under section 6(e) (i) (2) of the agreement on the basis of the terminating party in the effected party.

(d) 'Break date' means . . .

[This provision is usually incorporated in the Schedules to the Standard ISDA Master Swap Agreement.]"

The wording of paragraph (c) means that the non-terminating party has the swap closed out at their side of the market thereby preserving the "economic equivalent" of their payment obligations when the deal is terminated. This is specifically dealt with this definition for "market quotation" in the ISDA Master Swap Agreement. Paragraph (d) deals with the date on which the transaction can be terminated and depends on the term both parties want the deal restricted to.

Such provisions are primarily designed to allow either party to terminate the transaction where credit exposure in the transaction reaches unacceptable levels or the credit quality of the counterparty declines below acceptable level.

The major difficulty with this type of arrangement is the uncertainty faced by both counterparties as to whether the swap transaction will remain in place throughout its anticipated life. This problem is particularly acute for end users of the swap market who may be relying on the swap transaction to hedge specific exposures to achieve particular economic objectives and, therefore, are not indifferent (as would be the financial institution) to the termination of the transaction at replacement values.

An alternative structure which has gained some acceptance is the creation of off-market swaps or structuring of swaps with non-standard cash flows to minimise credit exposure of a counterparty in such transactions. This type of arrangement can take a number of forms.

Under one structure, it is possible for the financial institution to price transactions in a manner designed to lower its credit exposure. This is best illustrated by example.

For example, assume a low credit quality company wishes to hedge its interest exposure by entering into an interest rate swap where it pays fixed and receives floating. In order to reduce its credit exposure, the financial institution could agree to write the swap at a rate significantly above that currently prevailing in the market. This would be allied to an arrangement that the above market rate would be compensated for by payment of lump sum amount *at the maturity of the swap* to adjust the economics of the transaction to its fair value levels. Assuming that market rates for US$ interest rate swaps are, say, 7.5% pa, the swap would, under these arrangements, be written at, say, 10.00% pa.

This type of strategy has the effect of reducing the financial institution's risk as its cash flows under the swap transaction would be increased reflecting the above market coupon creating effectively a reserve fund which could be utilised to offset any replacement cost of the transaction in the event of default of the counterparty.

An alternative to this type of structure would be to in fact use a lower than current market swap coupon and have the corporation pay an upfront amount to adjust the swap economics to market levels. This upfront payment would represent essentially a deposit by the corporation with the financial institution which would again create a reserve fund against possible loss under the transaction in the event of default.

In another variation, it would be possible for the financial institution to arrange for the counterparty to pay all its swap fixed rate coupons or a significant proportion thereof *in advance* while not making any payments itself until the normal payment dates and arranging to make an adjustment payment at the end of the transaction. This type of structure is again designed to create a reserve fund which effectively acts as collateral reducing the mark-to-market value of the swap to the point where, typically, the bank has no exposure to the counterparty or the exposure is relatively small.

Insurance

An interesting development in the credit enhancement of swaps has been the development of swap insurance programmes, implemented initially in March 1986, between the World Bank and Aetna Insurance Company providing for the insurance of direct counterparty swaps between the World Bank and A or AA rated corporations. Under the agreement, the World Bank was able to expand the number of counterparties beyond the AAA rated corporations to which it has been restricted as well as financial institutions with a credit quality equivalent to those with whom the World Bank places its funds.

The swap insurance scheme operates as follows. The World Bank pays variable insurance fees to Aetna calculated with reference to the credit exposure under a nominated set of swaps which are marked-to-market each week. The fee scale may run from a nominal commitment fee based on no credit exposure to higher amounts based on an exposure ceiling of 30.00% to 50.00% of the par value for the swap. The insurance programme is designed to provide a backstop to the World Bank in the event of default to provide the funds needed to reconstitute the swap at the then prevailing market levels. The World Bank apparently decided to implement the swap insurance scheme to expand its universe of swap counterparties because the number of its potential counterparties was too limiting. This limitation had led to a fairly high concentration of counterparties within the World Bank portfolio. For example, approximately 40.00% of its swaps had apparently been done with only five institutions at the time the programme was implemented.

The swap insurance arrangement as structured provides three main benefits:

- It allows diversification of the World Bank swap portfolio.
- It is considered more cost effective than comparable bank intermediation.
- It is likely that swap insurance will provide even better credit quality than swaps with only AAA rated corporations as the probability of both a counterparty and

the insurer failing is more remote than the probability of potential failure of a AAA counterparty.

The swap insurance programme effectively allows the World Bank to completely segregate the credit aspects of the swap from the trading aspects.

The World Bank more recently negotiated a facility with Deutsche Bank, a AAA rated institution, whereby in return for receiving a fee the bank insures the World Bank against counterparty default. The agreement appears to have been designed to expand the World Bank's potential counterparties in Europe and Japan where ratings from the major United States ratings agencies are not common, given that the World Bank is restricted by its board to accepting only AAA rated corporations although it can in limited circumstances accept AA rated banks. An unusual feature of the Deutsche Bank facility is that the World Bank has the choice of requiring payment of a defaulting counterparty's swap coupon and/or principal stream or of taking the up-front termination value of the swap.

It is understood the World Bank has a number of swaps outstanding under the guarantee arrangements with Aetna totalling around US$250m. The Deutsche Bank facility has similarly been utilised by the World Bank with some US$170m of swaps outstanding under this facility.

The World Bank and its subsidiary, the International Finance Corporation (IFC), effectively themselves act as insurers to weaker counterparties and have commenced a programme to act as guarantor/insurers of swaps entered into developing nations who would otherwise be unable to access the swap market.

For example, the IFC as at middle 1991 had intermediated a variety of swaps for borrowers as diverse as Mexican commercial banks and an Egyptian steel company. More recently, the IFC have been involved in commodity derivative transactions, including one for a Ghanian gold mine.

A number of United States insurance companies, primarily monoline insurers active in providing financial guarantees, have provided credit enhancement in support of swap transactions. These institutions which include the Financial Guarantee Insurance Company (FGIC), owned by General Electric Capital Corporation, and Capital Markets Assurance Corporation (CAPMAC), owned until recently, by Citicorp, have both guaranteed derivative instruments in return for the payment of an upfront fee. However, both FGIC and CAPMAC generally guarantee swaps or other derivatives as part of larger transactions involving asset-backed security transactions or, in the case of CAPMAC, through its enhancement for Delta Government Option Corporation, a clearing organisation set up for over-the-counter options on United States treasuries.

SWAP AND DERIVATIVE MARKET—RECENT DEFAULT EXPERIENCE

In recent years, a number of significant insolvencies have provided the global market with *actual* experience in swap and derivative product credit exposure and default management. These include the insolvency of Development Finance Corporation of New Zealand (DFC), Drexel Burnham Lambert (DBL), British and Commonwealth Merchant Bànk (BCMB) and Bank of New England. More recently, the financial difficulties experienced by Olympia and York, particularly their Canadian subsidiaries, have also impacted upon the swap market. In addition, a number of institutions have for a variety of reasons, including declining credit standing, been forced to dispose of their swap and derivative portfolios on a voluntary basis.

In October 1989, DFC was put under statutory management. At that time, DFC had more than 100 swap transactions with over 70 counterparties involving a notional principal of about NZ$2bn. DFC management and the court-appointed statutory manager sought to preserve the value of the swap portfolio by transferring it in its entirety to Barclays Bank. DFC, in conjunction with its advisor, JP Morgan, was able to affect the transfer at fair market valuation adjusted for a credit spread.

Under the arrangements, DFC's counterparties allowed the assignment of the swaps from DFC to Barclays Bank. DFC sought to keep some of the swaps for its internal balance sheet hedging purposes. As Barclays Bank would not accept DFC credit, these transactions were credit enhanced, initially, by the Reserve Bank of New Zealand and were, subsequently, replaced by fresh swaps with the New Zealand Treasury Debt Management office.

The transactions took approximately six months to complete and was finalised in March 1990. After the swap book was transferred in March 1990, DFC took an additional nine months to reschedule other claims. JP Morgan utilised a variety of currency swaps and other enhancement for future cash flows to make these more acceptable to the rescheduled creditors.

In February 1990, DBL made a Chapter 11 filing. DBL immediately sought to transfer a swap portfolio totalling some US$25bn in notional principal. A major difficulty with the DBL portfolio was that unlike DFC many of its in excess of 250 counterparties were of lower credit quality. Following attempts to initially transfer the whole book to another institution, swaps within the portfolio were closed on a transaction by transaction basis. DBL was successful in settling almost all outstanding transactions by the end of the second quarter of 1990, the final transactions being completed by December of that year. DBL was unable to realise some US$10m in cash value from swaps its counterparties unwilling to give up windfall gains as a result of cash *owed to DBL* under limited two-way payment default clauses (see discussion below).

In June 1990, BCMB was forced to call in an administrator to avoid a liquidity crisis. BCMB had a swap portfolio of about GBP1.5bn in notional principal, involving 130 transactions with approximately 40 counterparties. The total swap portfolio was transferred to Barclays Bank at fair market value.

In early 1992, Canadian property group Olympia and York encountered severe financial difficulties. Following the company obtaining a general stay on its Canadian entities' liabilities, swap creditors of these companies approached the general division of Ontario court to exempt swaps. Ultimately, an out of court agreement was reached to preserve the value of the Olympia and York Canadian swap portfolio.

Under the agreement, Olympia and York's swaps were terminated to fix the counterparties exposures. The claims, representing the net exposure of Olympia and York, will be added to the body of the Canadian property companies' liabilities.

One Olympia and York counterparty, Canadian Imperial Bank of Commerce (CIBC), had an out-of-the-money swap position with Olympia and York and, theoretically, had an obligation to pay the counterparty a present value sum. The CIBC's transaction was included in the agreement to terminate all swaps without prejudice to CIBC's right to offset the position against other claims it might have on Olympia and York.

The above cases are discussed in the context of the legal issues posed in Chapter 44.

To date, in all major insolvencies, the transfer of the derivatives portfolio in its entirety or the termination of individual transactions at market value allowed avoidance of a major disruption to the global market. In all cases, prompt action to ensure that payment flows continued to be made in full while new counterparties were found for the swaps avoided any major disruption. Discreet assistance from regulators and a generally co-operative approach by counterparties were key factors in allowing these restructurings of swap portfolios to be completed.

The major problem to emerge in all these transactions related to the presence in some documents of limited two-way payment provision.

In most swap documents, default by a counterparty triggers termination of its swap agreement under the ISDA Swap Master Contract. Under some contracts, there is an optional clause that allows the non-defaulting party, upon termination being triggered by a default, to terminate all further obligations in relation to swaps under that contract. Under this provision, the non-defaulting counterparty can terminate its obligation even if it would have owed a net replacement cost sum to the defaulted party on a closeout (this is referred to as a limited two way payment (LTP) provision). In contrast, other agreements have full two-way payment (FTP) provisions whereby, even in the case of default by a party, the net value of the swap position is recognised and is a sum due and payable and owing to the defaulted party.

The difficulty with LTP provisions is that in the event of default the non-defaulting party, where it actually owes money to the defaulted swap counterparty, has the opportunity to secure a windfall gain by terminating all its obligations under the swap under the LTP provision. Such action under an LTP clause makes netting of swap obligations and the transfer of swap portfolios from financially distressed swap counterparties extremely difficult.

In the insolvencies noted above, the vast majority of counterparties chose not to terminate their future obligations, recognising the benefit to the market as a whole of assigning value to both the positive and negative positions of the defaulted counterparty.

However, this was not without exception. For example, Security Pacific Australia Limited, the Australian subsidiary of Security Pacific National Bank (subsequently merged with Bank of America), terminated a swap with the defaulted DFC to secure a windfall profit. Similarly, in both the DBL and BCMB cases, some counterparties also exercised their right under the LTP clause.

Subsequent to these developments, the new ISDA Master Agreement was amended to offer full two-way payments as an option and market practice currently tends towards use of full two-way payment provision. The impact of this provision in the case of default and the swap agreements is discussed and detailed in the context of the documentation of swaps in Chapters 39 and 44.

To date, the market has been successful in avoiding the potential disorder and disruption that would have been caused by counterparties unilaterally terminating contracts in the case of financial distress of major swap and derivatives counterparties before a global solution can be worked out.

Chapter 38

Special Purpose Derivative Vehicles

CONCEPT

A special purpose derivative vehicle (SPDV) or an enhanced derivative products company (DPC) is a subsidiary, typically of a financial services firm, that is established as a counterparty to derivatives transactions with the sole objective that the rating of the SPDV is higher than that of its parent. The credit standing of the separately capitalised SPDV is enhanced, typically, through a variety of mechanisms central to which is the segregation of its capital in a separate subsidiary and the absence of reliance on support from its parents to meet the financial obligations on its derivative contracts.

Credit-enhanced special purpose derivative counterparty vehicles represent a special case of swap credit exposure enhancement (additional to those discussed in Chapter 37). These types of special purpose vehicles have emerged in response to a number of special factors:

- Deterioration in the credit quality of financial institutions, particularly United States money centre banks and also securities companies, reflecting the impact of a variety of factors including declining profitability as a result of loan losses from lending to LDC countries, highly leveraged borrowers, real estate transactions and to saving and loans institutions, over capacity in the banking system resulting in reduced profit margins and reduced availability and the higher cost of bank capital.
- The increased credit sensitivity of end users where risk averse end users of swap transactions have increasingly concentrated their dealings with highly rated counterparties. This trend has emerged in response to the credit downgrading of a number of banks as well as a number of celebrated defaults amongst financial institutions (see discussion in Chapter 37).
- The entry into the swap market of a number of non-bank financial institutions (insurance companies) and highly rated banks (primarily, European and Japanese banks) competing for market share on the basis of their superior credit quality.

Against this background, a number of established swap market makers found their capacity to transact swaps limited. In order to protect their swaps and derivative business franchises, a number of institutions examined the possibility of creating special purpose vehicles which were designed to have AAA credit ratings through which they transact their swap and derivative business. The primary objective in this regard was to:

- allow swap and derivative houses with weaker credit ratings to compete with more highly rated competitors; and
- open up a range of credit sensitive counterparties, particularly, sovereign, supranational entities as well as large corporations.

In this chapter, the structure, ratings issues as well as examples of SPDVs are outlined.

STRUCTURAL ISSUES

SPDVs are a response to the increased credit sensitivity of the derivative markets. As OTC derivative instruments are negotiated and entered into between counterparties, the financial performance of the contractual obligations is based solely on credit quality. If a counterparty does not pay in accordance with the contract, then the other non-defaulting counterparty who is utilising the derivative contract to hedge or neutralise financial risk effectively is re-exposed to the actual exposure sought to be managed with the derivative contract.

The structure of OTC instruments, generally, contrasts with that of listed exchanges in which the performance of counterparties is supported by the capital or performance guarantee of the exchange. In one sense, the development of SPDVs obscures the difference between OTC and ET markets as the SPDV itself has as part of its credit enhancement structure features derived from exchange traded products.

The credit enhanced SPDV is typically a subsidiary of the relevant financial services provider. The SPDV is rated higher than the parent entity through the application of structured financing principles designed to create credit risk protection of the underlying portfolio.

As noted in Chapter 37, the credit risk of a derivatives portfolio is a function of:

- default risk; and
- market risk.

In particular, the market risk of derivatives portfolios can vary substantially and the exposure can be both positive and negative.

This basis of risk in such instruments creates significant complexity in structuring of the SPDV. In particular, it requires the use of complex risk modelling and statistical techniques to assess the varying exposures of the portfolio itself.

The higher rating of the SPDV is achieved by a combination of:

- the capital structure required for the vehicle;
- the separateness of bankruptcy proof nature of the vehicle; and
- understanding of the characteristics of the portfolio and the specification of particular management and operating guidelines designed to insulate the portfolio from the risk of credit loss.

SPECIAL PURPOSE DERIVATIVE VEHICLES—RATING ISSUES

Overview

The structure of SPDVs is, to a substantial degree, dictated by the attitude of rating agencies, particularly Moody's Investor Services and Standard and Poor's.

The rating agencies have, to date, applied a blend or hybrid rating philosophy to such vehicles. This approach combines elements of structured and operating company analysis. The rating approach, which dictates the requirements to establish such a vehicle, include:

- the capital adequacy of the structure;
- portfolio credit quality;
- counterparty credit risk;
- appropriate management and operating guidelines; and
- controls on the parent/subsidiary relationship.

The capital adequacy of the SPDV is the central element designed to provide it with a rating above that of its parent. The capital level required to be maintained in the SPDV is determined through the development of a risk model which assesses the combined effects of default and market risk on the likely portfolio of the SPDV. The capital adequacy levels are usually measured through probabilistic models that conservatively analyse a broad range of potential exposures. The risk model provides the means of examining the changing derivatives portfolios under dynamic market conditions. The risk model is essential to the rating of an SPDV and is discussed in detail in the following section.

The portfolio credit quality criteria is analogous to the determination of the credit quality of portfolios utilised for normal credit analysis. This seeks to determine the default risk of the credit risk relationship based on empirical studies of default experience utilising the counterparty credit quality criteria nominated for the vehicle. The rating agencies typically design risk models to test the impact of various default probabilities based on the universe of possible counterparties' unsecured debt ratings.

Counterparty credit risk controls are placed by restricting the range of counterparties with which the SPDV can enter into transactions. These are designed to limit exposures to less credit-worthy counterparties and to limit excessive concentration of exposures to particular classes of counterparties within the portfolio.

A unique aspect of rating SPDVs is the need to develop appropriate management and operating guidelines. This reflects the fact that unlike the relatively static portfolios of normal traditional structured transactions, SPDVs are characterised by dynamic trading portfolios where volatile asset values and changing portfolio characteristics create considerable volatility in the value of the portfolio itself.

Operating guidelines cover a variety of aspects of the operation of the SPDV:

- Management and operating guidelines designed to maintain the capital adequacy of the portfolio at all times are also important. These will usually take the form of operating guidelines to limit the unmatched or open positions an SPDV can take to ensure that the portfolio is substantially matched. This ensures each matched pair of transactions in the portfolio is immunised against movements in the value of the relevant financial market variable underlying the contract. This is designed to isolate the only cause of mismatches to counterparty defaults.
- As noted above, operating guidelines would limit the type of counterparty credit exposure assumed by the SPDV. This can include operating guidelines which embody absolute dollar or percentage of capital limitations on counterparties, together with industry or country limitations to assist in further diversifying the portfolio.
- Operating guidelines designed to limit the legal/documentation risk are also paramount. For example, the standardisation of documents and the nature of key documentary issues to be agreed between counterparties and the SPDV such as those relating to netting must be nominated at the outset.
- Similarly, operating guidelines on the level of liquidity to be maintained to enable the SPDV to meet short-term contractual obligation are usually specified. This is usually done by specifying an amount of capital to be invested in cash equivalents of high quality rated liquid assets maturing within 30 days.
- Management and operating guidelines focusing on management's risk appetite and strategy, including systems and controls, as well as documented operating guidelines.

The rating agencies' main concern regarding the parent/subsidiary relationship is to ensure the separateness of the SPDV and to ensure the insulation of the capital of the vehicle from a legal, operational and regulatory standpoint. The issues in this regard are similar to those applicable to other types of structured financings and special purpose vehicles. The major difference relates to the fact that the SPDV will continue to originate new business and manage a dynamic portfolio of instruments.

The rating agencies will typically consider such legal issues as the separateness and non-consolidation in bankruptcy of the SPDV with its parents. Other issues that may be relevant, depending on the specific structure of the SPDV and the nature of its protection from its ultimate parent, can involve analysis of issues such as true sale, fraudulent conveyance, preference and security interest perfection in collateral.

Other issues to be nominated include dividend policy and other covenants to protect the SPDV's assets and capitals from the parent. In this regard, it is designed so that only "true excess capital" should be allowed to be "leaked" to the parent. An independent board of directors and separate management is also seen as an important aspect of ensuring the separateness of the SPDV required for the enhanced rating.

Risk modelling approach[1]

The risk model, as noted above, is central to the whole process of rating of an SPDV. The central purpose of the risk model is to establish a base level of required capital for the vehicle. This is not to say that qualitative factors are not also relevant to the establishment of the capital adequacy level. However, the risk model analysis of quantitative factors provides the basis of the capital level for the SPDV.

The basic principles applied are similar to those that are utilised for normal structured financing cash flow models entailing determination of the nature of the assets, asset payment behaviour, liability behaviour and the priority of payments. The asset cash flow is tested under a variety of circumstances to determine its capacity to meet the liabilities. The shortfall of payment on any security, which represents debt to the transaction, creates a default allowing analysis of the credit and liquidity requirement of a transaction for any given rating category.

In an SPDV risk model the asset payment behaviour, that is, the terms and the payments of the assets and liabilities, are preset. In normal structured financing transactions, economic variables are generally held constant for defined periods of time with the vehicle being subjected to a series of stresses to understand the sensitivity of the portfolio. However, in modelling the risk characteristics of an SPDV, the high volatility of the value of the portfolio implies a fluctuating and highly volatile capital requirement. The dynamic nature of the vehicle's portfolio also makes it difficult to determine worst case stress test for a given rating category forcing the use of stochastic modelling techniques.

Additional complexity derives from the following factors:

- The claims under derivative contracts are contingent in that the amount and timing of the obligation varies, being determined by movements in the value of a certain index against a static value set at the time of entry into the transaction.
- The use of these instruments as a vehicle for risk transfer makes these obligations difficult to model in terms of the credit quality of the obligors and counterparties.

In practice, two types of models are used: probabilistic or deterministic models.

1. This discussion is based on Lisa M Raiti (1992).

The general risk model to test sufficiency of cash flow within a vehicle usually generates model credit exposures using one of a variety of techniques including:

- randon number generator;
- Monte Carlo simulation;
- modelling capacity to define the underlying index; and
- direct or simulated dichotomous variables to model defaults.

Under the random number generator approach, a stream of random numbers are generated, taking either discrete values or continuous values. The underlying distribution generated is uniform with the generated numbers of different drawings being completely uncorrelated. The portfolio value is then determined against a sequence of random events as generated.

The Monte Carlo simulation involves simply running a number of event sequences or paths using a random number generator to simulate the behaviour of an underlying group of variables and then computing an outcome based on the variables in a static financial model. Each individual path is deterministic but repeating path creation provides a distribution of outcomes which, assuming the asset price behaviour has been properly identified, provides a reasonable estimation of the potential range and likelihood of particular outcomes occurring.

An issue with using Monte Carlo simulation techniques is the number of paths and runs necessary to generate the desired level of confidence that the distribution created represents all outcomes at their real frequency of occurrence. This is usually achieved through specification of an acceptable level of tolerance for error and a level of confidence in that tolerance. The distribution generated is then utilised to test the cash flow profile of the model portfolios.

Modelling the behaviour of an underlying index can be viewed as a balance between two extremes. This approach assumes that the index behaviour is neither completely random nor completely determinable. Under this approach, a range of values that the variables can take on is established and, utilising information about the nature of the assets and liabilities, several worst case scenarios of the variables are created and tested to establish that the transactions can survive the stresses created. The difficulty with using this approach with derivative portfolios is that the contingent nature of the underlying instrument can cause the transaction to be at risk at any level of the underlying index. An alternative approach is to model the behaviour of the relevant indexes and create a large number of index paths which are then utilised to test the transaction outcomes through a range of potential values.

Modelling the behaviour of an underlying index has certain advantages for the analyst:

- The analyst does not have the responsibility of determining the definitive worst case.
- Based on the integrity of the model as a whole, it can provide a reasonable estimate of potential outcomes.

This approach requires assumptions to be made as to whether modelling of the index is posssible as well as assuming the means of predicting the level of the relationship of the variable being modelled will not change. The change in that variable can be modelled. For example, empirical work in financial economics has been utilised as the basis for generating the relevant distributions of variables for the purposes of this approach.

The final element of each of the models is to directly or indirectly simulate defaults. This is done in two ways:

- Under the first approach, defaults are simulated by utilising two stage variables. The variable is divided into two parts where the first is an indicator of default and the second provides the likelihood of default in the period in question. A random number generator then provides the likelihood of default. The value of the random number is less than or equal to the likelihood that default has occurred in the transaction.
- Under the second approach, instead of a single probability of default, a table is created given the likelihood of a change in a rating over a period of time. For example, there may be certain probability of an A rating changing to a BBB rating over a specified period. All ratings are included on the basis that a rating that is defaulted during the period has a 100% certainty of remaining defaulted in all successive periods. Under this approach, the effect of default is calculated as the probability of all possible default combinations with their corresponding exposures allowing construction of a table displaying the different levels of exposure and their probabilities.

SPECIAL PURPOSE DERIVATIVE VEHICLES

History

To date, a number of SPDVs have been created. The original SPDV was Merrill Lynch Derivative Products (MLDP) which has since been followed by GS Financial Products International LP (associated with Goldman Sachs) and Swapco (associated with Salomon Brothers). Each of these structures is considered in the following sections. A number of other structures which are conceptually similar to the SPDVs identified have emerged. Several other SPDV applications are understood also to be pending.

While non-bank financial institutions have been successful in implementing a number of SPDV structures, commercial banks have encountered a number of difficulties in implementing these arrangements. This is particularly true for US banks.

Citibank and Continental Bank sought permission to establish SPDVs in February and June 1992 respectively. However, in November 1992, both institutions withdrew their applications when it became apparent that these were likely to be rejected by the US Treasury's Office of the Comptroller of the Currencies. Other banks to have considered implementing SPDVs include Chase Manhattan and First Chicago, although it is not clear that they formally submitted applications.

It is not clear that the Office of the Comptroller of the Currencies had rejected the applications. There is speculation that the regulatory authorities, including the Federal Reserve and Federal Deposit Insurance Corporation (FDIC) were instrumental in effectively rejecting the applications based on concerns that SPDVs would, in effect, be circumventing market forces and would divert better quality assets away from the main banking vehicle in order to enhance the credit standing of the SPDV. This process would, the regulators argue, leave only lower quality assets in place to support existing bank liabilities, including those supported by the FDIC insurance provisions for depositors.

It is also understood that regulators in other countries, such as the Bank of Japan, have voiced similar concerns. However, Banque Paribas (a French bank), Abbey National (a UK bank) and Westpac (an Australian bank) have established SPDVs. In the case of Abbey National, the derivatives vehicle is not strictly an SPDV as it relies on the bank's credit rating directly.

However, the difference in treatment between securities/investment houses and commercial banks is problematic.

Merrill Lynch Derivative Products

The first significant credit enhanced derivative counterparty vehicle to be established was MLDP.

Prior to the establishment of MLDP in late 1991, Merrill Lynch had transacted swaps, since its entry into the swap market as a principal in 1982, through a subsidiary called Merrill Lynch Capital Services (MLCS). MLCS was fully guaranteed by its parent, Merrill Lynch & Co, and had a rating of A1 from Moody's Investor Services and A from Standard and Poor's.

The rating of MLCS was acceptable to most counterparties other than a number of major swap counterparties, primarily, sovereign governments, supranational agencies and very large corporations who would only transact swaps with counterparties rated AA or better.

In response to these pressures, Merrill Lynch developed a AAA rated special purpose vehicle—MLDP—to transact its swap and derivative business through.

Exhibit 38.1 sets out the detailed structure of MLDP.

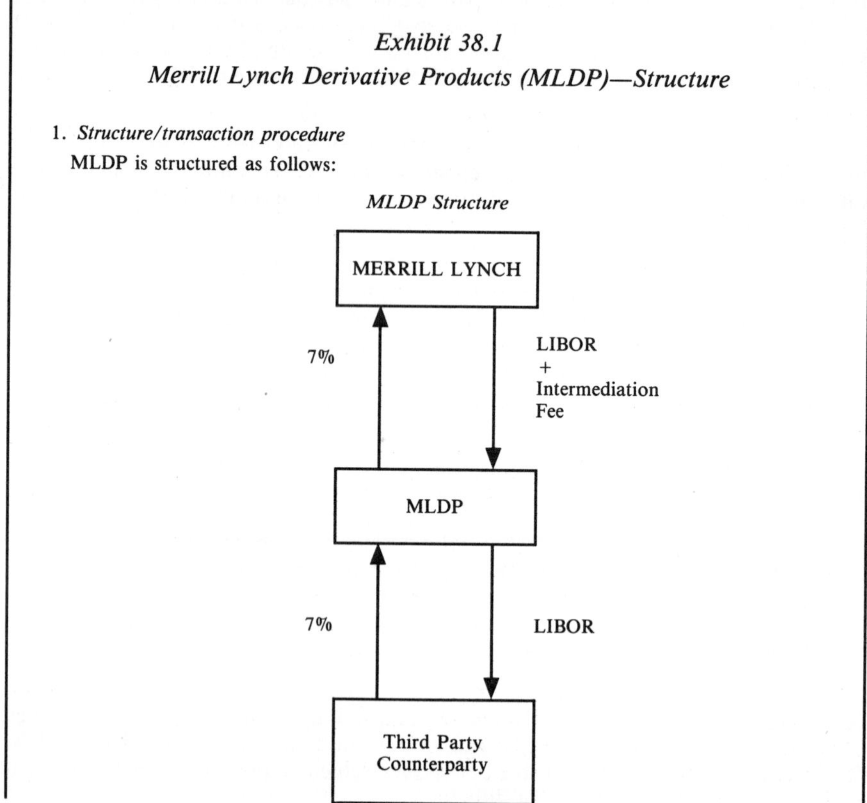

Exhibit 38.1

Merrill Lynch Derivative Products (MLDP)—Structure

1. *Structure/transaction procedure*

MLDP is structured as follows:

Exhibit 38.1—continued

The transaction chain is as follows:

- MLDP enter into swap with counterparty.
- MLDP simultaneously enters into swap with Merrill Lynch Capital Services (MLCS), the internal Merrill Lynch derivative operation.

The structure operates as follows:

- MLCS covers *market* risk of MLDP.
- MLDP bears *credit* exposure, effectively acting as a credit intermediary for MLCS.

2. *MLDP financial structure*

The principal features of MLDP's financial structure are as follows:

- MLDP has US$350m capital made up as follows:

—US$300m common stock subscribed by ML.

—US$50m 8.75% pa preferred stock subscribed by insurance companies.

- MLDP is not permitted to have any debt.
- MLDP's operating expenses are less than US$1m/year.
- MLDP has a (implied) fixed charge coverage of around three times calculated as follows:

Fixed charges:

8.75% pa on US$50m = US$4.375m
Pre-tax equivalent = US$7.0m (say).

MLDP income:
US$350m @ 6.0% pa = US$21.0m.

Fixed charges coverage: 3X.

3. *Counterparty restrictions*

MLDP is subject to a number of restrictions on its counterparties:

- Counterparties must be AA or higher rated by Moody's.
- If counterparties are rated below AA, then:

—MLDP will have to reassign the swap to another counterparty; or

—arrange to have the transaction collateralised to equate rating to AA.

- There are also the following restrictions on exposure to *individual* counterparties:

Rating	Gross Exposure (US$m)	Net Exposure (US$m)
Aaa	200	100
Aa1	150	75
Aa2	120	60
Aa3	100	50

4. *MLDP exposure to Merrill Lynch*

In order to control MLDP's exposure to Merrill Lynch through MLCS, the following controls apply:

- MLDP net exposure to MLCS must not exceed US$300m.
- MLDP's exposure to Merrill Lynch is covered by the requirement for Merrill Lynch to post collateral.
- The required amount of collateral is the sum of the following:

—MLDP's net positive exposure to MLCS;

—10% of MLDP's net exposure to MLCS or US$25m;

—Amount based on aggregate notional amount of MLCS's swaps with MLDP, consisting of a cash reserve and embedded ongoing intermediation fee;

—Amount based on sensitivity of MLDP's net exposure to MLCS from potential interest rate and currency movement.

Exhibit 38.1—continued

This structure of posting collateral means that MLDP is always collateralised to 110%—For example, if MLDP's exposure to MLCS reaches the maximum of US$300, then Merrill Lynch, under the first two categories listed above, would have to post US$330m.

According to Moody's assuming US$50bn notional principal of transaction with a three year average life, additional collateral needed would total US$66m. Assuming no extra collateral was needed under the fourth category listed, this would equate to total collateral of US$396m for a mark-to-market exposure of US$300m (a 132% over-collateralisation level).

Source: Gavin Gray (1992) (January).

The MLDP structure requires Merrill Lynch to commit US$300m in capital to its special purpose derivative vehicle. In addition, the company must be prepared to lodge extra collateral in proportion to the exposure under swaps entered into with MLDP.

The economics of special purpose vehicles, based on the MLDP structure, is examined in *Exhibit 38.2*. The analysis indicates that MLDP will have to generate significant earnings from transactions to which it is a counterparty to cover the capital cost to Merrill Lynch of the structure.

Exhibit 38.2

Merrill Lynch Derivative Products (MLDP)—Analysis of Economics

The economics of the MLDP structure can be inferred by determining the return required on Merrill Lynch's capital investment in the special purpose vehicle. The required return is based on:

- the imputed capital cost of the investment.
- the funding cost of collateral required to be lodged.

1. *Imputed capital cost*

Merrill Lynch are required to commit US$300 million to MLDP. The required rate of return on this investment can be calculated utilising Merrill Lynch's cost of capital.

Merrill Lynch's estimated cost of capital is as follows:

Cost of equity

Utilising the Capital Asset Pricing Model (CAPM), the cost of equity capital of an organisation can be specified as follows:

$$ke = rf + B*[E(rm) - rf]$$

where

ke =	cost of equity to the firm, that is, the expected return from investment in the firm
rf =	risk-free rate
B =	the firm's beta, that is, the firm-specific risk
[E(rm) − rf] =	the expected excess return from the market portfolio or the risk premium.

Assuming the following parameters for the individual imputs, the cost of equity capital to Merrill Lynch can be derived:

rf =	30 year treasury bond yield, 7.50% pa
B =	1.5
[E(rm) − rf] =	8.00% pa

$$ke = 7.50\% + 1.5*8.00\%$$
$$ke = 19.50\% \text{ pa.}$$

Exhibit 38.2—continued

Based on the above calculations, Merrill Lynch's cost of equity capital is estimated at 19.50% pa.

Weighted average cost of capital (WACC)

As the firm utilises a mix of equity and debt funding, the effective return on capital required by Merrill Lynch on its investment will need to be determined with reference to its WACC calculated as follows:

WACC = ke*(S/V) + kd*(1 – t)*(D/V)

where

ke = the cost of equity to the firm
kd = the cost of debt to the firm
t = the effective tax rate of the firm
S = the market value of the firm's equity
D = the market value of the firm's debt
V = the market value of the firm's assets.

The following assumptions are made regarding Merrill Lynch's debt costs, leverage and tax rate:

kd = 7.80% pa, based on a ten year treasury rate of 6.70% pa plus a spread of 110bps (for a single A risk)
t = 40%
S/V = 8.00%, being the assumed level of capital held by the firm as a % of total risk assets.

Based on the above, Merrill Lynch's WACC can be calculated:

WACC = the cost of equity to the firm

WACC = 19.50%*.08 + 7.80%*(1 – 0.40)*(1 – 0.08)
WACC = 5.8650% pa.

Based on the above calculations, Merrill Lynch's WACC is estimated at 5.8650% pa (after tax) which is equivalent to a pre-tax equivalent of 9.7760% pa (based on a 40% effective tax rate).

2. *MLDP—required return*

Based on the imputed cost of capital and the principle that the firm must receive an adequate return on its investment to reward its equity and debt capital providers at their required return on investment levels, Merrill Lynch would require a return of 9.776% pa before tax on its US$300 million investment in MLDP.

This equates to a pre-tax earning level for MLDP of:

US$300m @ 9.776% = US$29.33m

The return required on swap and derivative transactions in MLDP is determined by adjusting the required pre-tax earning requirement by *MLDP's existing earnings stream.* MLDP has operating income as follows:

Interest Income US$350m @ 6.50% pa	US$22.75m
Operating Expenses	US$(1.00)m
Preference Dividends US$50m @ 8.75% pa	US$(4.38)m
Net Income	US$17.37m.

Therefore, MLDP earning from swap and derivative transactions would need to be approximately US$11.96 million.

This equates to the following return levels based on the level of transaction volume:

Transaction Volume (US$ billion)	*Required Return (bps pa)*
5.0	23.93
10.0	11.96
25.0	4.79
50.0	2.39

Exhibit 38.2—continued

3. *Collateralisation costs*

The cost of collateralisation is the difference between the return earned on the collateral and the cost to Merrill Lynch of, at the margin, funding the deposit. This approach ignores the cost of balance sheet/capital utilisation and the fact that the actual economic financing cost of the collateral is the firm's WACC.

Based on a negative spread on moneys lodged as collateral of 1.00% pa, the return required (bps pa) on MLDP transactions to cover these additional costs is:

Collateral Amount (US$m)	100	200	300
Cost (US$m)	1.0	2.0	3.0
Transaction Volume (US$bn)			
5.0	2.0	4.0	6.0
10.0	1.0	2.0	3.0
25.0	0.4	0.8	1.2
50.0	0.2	0.4	0.6

4. *Total return required*

The total return required from MLDP is as follows:

Imputed Capital Charge	US$11.96m
Collateralisation Cost	US$1-3.0m.

The exact return required will depend on the actual amount of collateral required to be posted. The required return *per transaction* will depend on the overall volume of transactions booked through MLDP.

It should be noted that the identified required returns are *additional* to the return required by Merrill Lynch to cover for the usage of capital in Merrill Lynch Capital Services (as the swaps will appear in its books), the cost of hedging and risk, administrative costs, and the intermediation fee payable to MLDP.

The MLDP structure appears to have been successful in attracting significant swap and derivative business to Merrill Lynch. Based on information available in mid 1993, as at the end of the first quarter 1993, MLDP had a portfolio totalling US$34.4 billion (equivalent) in notional principal terms made up of 925 transactions with 148 counterparties. This was up from US$6.6 billion one year earlier.

The portfolio consisted of 59% interest rate swaps, 33% currency swaps and 8% interest rate option products. The average maturity of the portfolio was 5.2 years. Transaction currencies included all major global currencies as well as a number of more minor ones.

MLDP's notional credit exposure was 26% to AAA rated counterparties and 13% to AA rated counterparties.

As at the end of the first quarter 1993, MLCS has been required to post US$530.5m in collateral to MLDP.

Information available more recently indicated that by end of June 1993, MLDP's portfolio had increased to US$42.6 billion (equivalent). This consisted of 1,100 transactions with 180 counterparties (83% of which were AA1 or better).

In early 1993, MLDP was granted approval by the rating agencies to deal in any instrument, with the exception of commodity derivatives. In addition, the rules governing MLDP were relaxed allowing MLDP to maintain the swap transaction where a counterparty's credit rating falls below AA. This avoids the necessity for MLDP to assign the swap when a counterparty is downgraded.

GS Financial Products International LP

GS Financial Products International LP (GSFPI), a vehicle associated with the US investment bank Goldman Sachs, emerged in March 1992.

The vehicle emerged in connection with the issue by GSFPI of JPY30bn in debt to acquire a portfolio consisting of put and call warrants and options on the Nikkei 225 stock average. GSFPI is also authorised to act as an AAA rated counterparty to derivative transactions generally.

Public information available indicates that GSFPI's structure is as follows:

- It has capital of approximately JPY9.3bn, being approximately 20% of the initial portfolio's fair market value.
- The portfolio credit quality was high, reflecting the fact that the options purchased were all written by investment grade counterparties.
- Excess funds were invested by GSFPI in A1 + liquid assets.
- The vehicle was to operate under guidelines that encouraged diversification across counterparties by credit quality and country as well as maintenance of sufficient capital against credit, market and liquidity risks.
- GSFPI and its capital is separate from the Goldman Sachs group.

The GSFPI structure was significantly different to the MLDP structure outlined above as it appeared to represent an attempt by Goldman Sachs to effectively securitise and raise funds against its Nikkei option positions.

It is not clear whether Goldman Sachs intend to use GSFPI as its SPDV covering the full range of derivative products. The structure clearly contemplates this, although it is probable that the capital structure of GSFPI would need to be modified in line with growth in the size of the portfolio and its risk profile. In late 1993, Goldman Sachs established Goldman Sachs Mitsui Marine Derivative Products (GSMMDP), a joint venture between Goldman Sachs and Mitsui Marine and Fire Insurance, Japan's third largest non-life insurer, and its derivatives vehicles are largely superseding GSFPI. Some aspects of GSMMDP are discussed later in this chapter.

Salomon Swapco Inc

In February 1993, Salomon Brothers debuted their SPDV—Salomon Swapco Inc (Swapco).

Swapco is closer to the structure of MLDP than GSFPI and was intended to act as the AAA rated counterparty for Salomon Brothers derivative activities.

The Swapco structure was based on a number of specific elements:

- the classical bankruptcy proof vehicle, ensuring separation between Salomon Brothers' activities and that of Swapco;
- initial capital of US$175m;
- a dynamic variable capital structure which requires the company to maintain capital in an amount based on the size and credit quality of the exposures in its derivatives portfolio;
- structural incentives to maintain a diversified portfolio of high credit quality counterparties;
- a number of special termination features.

A feature of the Swapco structure was that it permitted Swapco to guarantee transactions entered into by other Salomon entities.

The Swapco capital structure is particularly interesting. The structure incorporates a dynamic capital rule that requires Swapco to maintain capital based on the size, concentration and credit quality of the customer exposures in its derivatives portfolio.

The minimum required capital formula incorporates a number of computations designed to address specific aspects of portfolio risk.

The required capital of Swapco must be equal to at least a fixed amount of US$175m. However, beyond this specified minimum, the capital level is a function of:

- portfolio size; and
- concentration and credit quality of customer exposures.

Under the dynamic capital rule, the capital requirement is calculated daily. If Swapco's actual capital does not exceed that day's minimum required capital, a termination event is triggered following a two day cure period. Accordingly, if Swapco suffers a credit loss that causes its actual capital to fall below the minimum required capital level or, alternatively, if changes in market levels cause the minimum required capital to increase above the actual capital lodged, Swapco has two days to receive the additional capital or to reduce customer exposures to avoid triggering a termination event.

The dynamic collateral formula entails Salomon Brothers posting collateral to Swapco daily in an amount equal to Swapco's exposure to Salomon Brothers plus market exposure cushion. If Salomon Brothers fails to post the required collateral, a termination event will occur following a two day cure period. The collateral posted effectively brings the capital level for Swapco up to the required minimum. The collateral cushion is designed to cover the potential increase in exposure between the last good valuation date and the date contracts are determined. The required collateral cushion is variable with the cushion level increasing if Salomon Brothers' rating falls below specified levels.

The dynamic collateral formula is mutual. In the event that Swapco has a negative exposure to Salomon Brothers, Swapco will post collateral to Salomon Brothers. The collateral posted by Swapco is an amount equal to the actual exposure that the SPDV has to Salomon Brothers less the cushion amount.

All of Swapco's invested capital in collateral is required to be invested in securities rated AAA and is assessed at market values, including standard market value discount factors to account for potential decreases in the securities' values between the last good valuation date and the date securities would be liquidated in a termination scenario.

An additional feature of the Swapco structure is the controls on portfolio credit quality.

The Swapco vehicle is subject to the requirement that counterparties must be at least investment grade. As noted above, the amount of capital required increases for a lower rated counterparty. This is designed in a manner to create a natural incentive for Swapco to maintain a high credit quality portfolio as a fall in credit quality of counterparties increases the cost of the vehicle through higher capitalisation requirements.

Where a counterparty is downgraded below investment grade, there are a number of alternative steps available:

- Swapco will not assign or terminate transactions with previously eligible counterparties upon its downgrade, but will not be allowed to enter into new transactions with the relevant counterparty unless the new transactions reduce exposure.
- All exposure to non-investment grade counterparties are required to be fully capitalised.

This specific feature of the Swapco structure allows the vehicle to be used to deal with a non-investment grade counterparty on the basis that the exposures are fully capitalised by Salomon Brothers.

As noted above, the Swapco structure has a unique termination feature.

Under this structure, there is a requirement that all Swapco's derivative contracts are cash settled within a predetermined period of time if certain termination events occur. If such a termination occurs, then counterparties will either pay or receive a net termination amount (based on mid-market values).

Nominated termination events include:

- failure by Salomon Brothers to post required collateral within the two day cure period;
- failure by Swapco to maintain actual capital in excess of the minimum required capital levels;
- failure by Swapco to maintain minimum required liquidity amounts in cash equivalents;
- downgrade of Swapco below AA;
- the bankruptcy of Salomon Inc, Salomon Brothers Holding Corporation or any other Salomon affiliate that has outstanding guaranteed transactions.

The special termination event effectively means that all contracts with Swapco will terminate in certain circumstances and be valued on that date unless a market disruption event occurs or unusual chaotic market conditions exist, as determined by a random poll of Swapco counterparties. On each valuation date for termination purposes, Swapco will poll market participants or otherwise ascertain the mid-market inputs to be used in its valuation models to price the terminated contracts. Following evaluation, Swapco will notify each counterparty with contracts valued on the date of its net termination payable or receivable. All counterparties with net termination amounts that are payable to Swapco will be required to make the payments within five business days of the valuation date. All counterparties with net termination amounts that are receivable from Swapco will be paid within ten business days of the valuation date.

The introduction of the termination event has created controversy. In the event that the termination provisions are triggered, counterparties face the spectre of their derivative contracts with Swapco being terminated. This has the effect of causing counterparties to lose the benefits of the derivative contracts and therefore have exposures to the underlying risks sought to be hedged through these transactions. The assumption in this regard is that the counterparties can then replace these transactions at current market rates. However, the termination at mid-market values will typically disadvantage all counterparties.

The advantage for rating purposes of the termination event is that the sufficiency of the capital of the Swapco vehicle is reinforced by the fact that in the case of the nominated events occurring, a higher degree of assurance exists that the capital will be sufficient to cover the contractual obligations of the vehicle.

It is not clear, at least at this time, whether the termination feature is an advantage or a disadvantage for Swapco.

Other structures

A number of structures modelled on the MLDP and Swapco precedents have emerged. The Swapco model with its lower threshold capital requirement and special termination feature has increasingly become the favoured structural model.

Two structures especially merit comment:

- the Banque Paribas SPDV—Paribas Dérivés Garantis (PDG);
- Westpac Derivative Products Limited (WDPL).

PDG, announced in late 1993, is an AAA rated SPDV which is modelled on the Swapco structure but with a number of unique characteristics. The key features of PDG are:

- An initial capital structure of FFR800m (approximately US$140m), which is dynamically variable.
- The vehicle, unlike other SPDVs, will *not* be the direct counterparty to transactions but *will act as a guarantor of a portion of Banque Paribas' derivative activities*.
- PDG will have assigned to it as security the receivables from Paribas' derivative contracts.
- The capital requirement will vary as a function of the size and nature of PDG's commitments, conforming to the rating agencies' overcollateralisation requirements.
- The capital calculation will be undertaken weekly unless Paribas' rating falls below BBB in which case it will be daily.
- If Paribas is upgraded to AA, the minimum capital requirement falls to FFR600m.
- Items qualifying as capital are defined as:

  —equity and subordinated debt;

  —cash invested in high-grade instruments rated A1+;

  —net receivables from guaranteed contracts.

  The net receivables provision is unusual. Permitted inclusions are receivables rated A− or above, aggregated by counterparty and adjusted by specific counterparty credit limits (for example, PDG cannot rely on receivables from any counterparty in excess of FFR800m).

PDG will operate by supporting Paribas' obligations under the relevant derivatives contracts in the following circumstances:

- if Paribas or its parent becomes insolvent; or
- if PDG itself is downgraded below A−; or
- if PDG fails to maintain the minimum required capital.

In these circumstances, a termination event will have occurred and a termination date (not exceeding eight calendar days after the termination event) is designated and the value of outstandings is calculated under nominated procedures to establish contract values. Importantly, PDG can only perform on *net* obligations.

The termination provision is similar to Swapco.

WDPL is a more classical AAA rated SPDV structure with two special features:

- The vehicle has a two-tier capital structure:
  —US$100m of paid up capital;
  —US$100m surety bond provided by AAA rated US monoline insurer Capital Markets Assurance Corporation.
- WDPL's capital and collateral is held in US$ in a trust in Britain to avoid the impact of the Australian sovereign ratings cap (currently AA).

Other features of WDPL such as the dynamic capital structure and termination provisions are similar to Swapco.

The structure of PDG and WDPL both increasingly highlight the dominancy of a dynamic capital approach to SPDV design. The major advantage is that it allows a company to allocate capital based on the risk level assumed rather than assigning a fixed quantum of capital and determining the risks to be assumed.

SUMMARY

The development of SPDVs represents an interesting feature of the derivative market generally in response to the competitive need for some counterparties to enhance their credit status. It is likely that the existing structures will evolve over time as the SPDV concept is further enhanced. Alternative solutions to the credit enhancement dilemma being examined include the possibility of joint ventures between derivatives operations and highly rated bank or non-bank financial institutions with no derivatives capacity.

Several models of this joint venture structure exist. The major examples include: Credit Suisse Financial Product (CSFP) and SBC O'Connor (the joint venture, at least initially, between Swiss Bank and O'Connor Partners). More recent examples include GSMMDP (see above) and Abbey National Baring Derivatives (ANBD)—a joint venture between Abbey National and Baring Derivatives.

In each case, a technically skilled derivatives operation with relatively limited capital resources and consequently modest ratings (below AA –) through the joint venture secured access to a higher rating facilitating access to credit sensitive counterparties. Other operational and business synergies may also be present including:

- market position in complementary segments—ET versus OTC;
- access to a potentially captive parent client, for example, ANBD's relationship to Abbey National; CSFP's relationship to Credit Suisse etc.

A major advantage of this approach is the lower separate capital claim for the joint venture which relies on the stronger joint venture partner's credit rating and the lower administrative burden relative to an SPDV structure.

Part 9

Regulatory Aspects of Swaps and Financial Derivatives

Chapter 39

Credit Exposure—Regulatory Framework

IMPETUS FOR REGULATION

The swap market developed originally under negligible regulatory attention. However, the increased importance of swaps and derivatives, together with other off-balance sheet commitments (such as letters of credit, guarantees etc) have increasingly attracted regulatory attention, particularly by bank regulators in OECD countries.

The primary areas of regulatory concern, in relation to swaps and other derivatives, have included:

- credit exposure assumed under swap and other derivative transactions; and
- market risks (including interest rate and currency risks) associated with market making/trading of swaps and other derivatives.

Bank regulatory authorities focused initially on the credit exposures incurred as a result of swaps and other derivative transactions. As noted in Chapter 40, increasing attention is now being focused on market risk aspects of swaps and other derivative instruments as they impact on bank activity.

The regulatory authorities have recognised that financial institutions who act as principals in swaps incur credit exposures to the counterparties involved for the term of the transaction. Furthermore, where they are intermediating a swap or trading swaps, they effectively take on the credit exposure of at least two counterparties; that is, the risk to the banks concerned doubles. In addition, the regulatory authorities have recognised that many institutions under their supervision take on large market risks, primarily interest rate and currency exposure, in making markets and trading in swaps.

An associated concern has been that market prices for swaps do not accurately reflect the actual risk involved in undertaking these transactions. The concern amongst regulators, in relation to pricing of swaps, was based on a number of factors:

- banks involved did not sufficiently understand the risks of swaps;
- more importantly, competitive pressures have not allowed banks to generate returns on capital commensurate with the risk of swaps.

Typically, intermediaries make a yes or no credit decision on a counterparty. Consequently, there is usually only one price in the swap market with minimal price tiering for differential credit quality. This price reflects only the average expected exposure of all counterparties in the swap market and not the specific risk of counterparties being dealt with.

The regulators concern over the pricing of swaps and allocation of capital to cover the risks has been exacerbated by evidence of deliberately mispriced swaps to secure mandates for securities transactions.

BIS CAPITAL ADEQUACY REQUIREMENTS

History

In March 1987, the Bank of England and the United States Federal Reserve issued a consultative document outlining risk based capital requirements in connection with off-balance sheet items, including swap and derivative transactions, designed to ensure stronger capital bases for regulated banks. Following an extensive process of consultation and (often heated) negotiations, the BIS and the Basle Committee on Banking Regulations and Supervisory Practices (the Basle committee—constituted by the central banks/supervisory authorities of the group of ten (G-10) countries plus Luxembourg) published a paper entitled "Proposal for International Convergence of Capital Measures and Capital Standards" defining a unified framework for determining the capital adequacy of banks, covering both minimum increased capital ratios and the treatment of instruments including swaps and derivatives, from the perspective of bank assumption of credit risk (the 1988 Capital Adequacy Accord).

Subsequently, the BIS Capital Adequacy Requirements, as they have come to be known, have been adopted by most OECD countries as well as a number of other countries, in its basic form with relatively minor amendments.

BIS approach

The BIS capital adequacy standards have a number of major features differentiating these from previous bank regulations:

- The BIS guidelines increased the level of capital required to be held by banks to 8% of *risk weighted assets*.
- A key element of the guidelines was the inclusion, for the first time, of a wide variety of off-balance sheet activities, including swaps and other derivatives, in the measurement of capital adequacy.
- The guidelines also established a series of five specific risk weights (between 0 and 100%) to be applied to the principal amounts of asset and selected off-balance sheet items. These weights vary according to the type of counterparty, essentially according recognition to different types or degrees of counterparty default risk.

The latter two features are of particular relevance to swap and other derivative transactions.

Under the BIS guidelines, the method for determining the amount of capital required to be held against a particular off-balance sheet transaction is the same for all off-balance sheet items including swap and derivative transactions which are classified as either interest rate or exchange related contracts.

The BIS guidelines require banks to undertake a three step process in converting swap and derivative transactions into a balance sheet equivalent amount against which an appropriate capital amount (currently 8%) must be held. These steps are as follows:

- The notional amount for swap is converted into a *credit risk equivalent* utilising, either, the current exposure method or the original exposure method (see discussion below).
- The credit risk equivalent is then weighted by a factor ranging 0-50% based on the credit quality of the counterparty, in accordance with pre-specified guidelines.
- The counterparty adjusted credit risk equivalent produces a risk weighted asset against which the specified capital ratio is applied to determine the level of capital to be held against the particular transaction.

Calculating credit risk weighting

Current exposure method

The credit risk equivalent amount is calculated as follows:

Credit risk equivalent amount = mark-to-market value plus potential future exposure.

The mark-to-market value is taken into account only if it is positive. If a transaction has *negative* replacement value (that is, the bank would gain by a default), then the mark-to-market value is taken to be zero. No specific procedure for calculating mark-to-market value is specified.

The potential credit exposure is calculated in accordance with the following factors.

Remaining Term to Materials	Interest Rate Contract	Exchange Rate Contract
<1 year	0	1.0%
>1 year	0.5%	5.0%

For basis swaps (in same currency) the add-on factor is zero.

Original exposure method

Under this method credit conversion factors are applied to the principal amount of the contract based on maturity.

The credit conversion factors are as follows:

Maturity	Interest Rate Contract	Exchange Rate Contract
1 Year	0.5%	2.0%
1-2 Year	1.0%	5.0% (2% + 3%)
Each Additional Year	1.0%	3.0%

For interest rate contracts individual regulatory authorities have discretion as to whether original or residual maturity is used.

For exchange rate contracts, original maturity is required to be used.

Selection of credit risk equivalent

The current exposure method is recommended for active participants in the swap and derivative product markets. The Basle Committee guidelines also recommended that banks not be able to switch between the two methods.

Counterparty risk weighted asset amount

The BIS guidelines for overall risk weighting for counterparties are as follows:

0% Cash, gold; claims on the central bank/government securities with maturities of one year or less.

10% Certain public sector entities located in the *same* country as the bank in question.

20% OECD banks; obligation on non-OECD banks with maturities less than one year; all OECD public sector entities (other than those in the category above); multilateral development banks.

50% Housing finance; foreign exchange and interest rate transactions (see below).

100% All other counterparties and assets.

The BIS guidelines provided that while the credit equivalent amounts would be risk weighted within the general framework according to the specified counterparty risk weighting, the *maximum* risk weighting for interest rate and foreign exchange contracts was 50%. This represented a specific exception to the 100% weight applicable to non-bank counterparties generally. This was in recognition of the "high quality" of swap counterparties.

Therefore, the specific levels of counterparty risk weightings for all swap transactions are as follows:

0% Central governments of the OECD countries.

Although all contracts with central governments which have a maturity of one year or less will attract the 0% risk weighting, national supervisory authorities may elect to assign contracts with a maturity of more than one year to the 10% risk category, to account for potential interest rate or currency risk associated with longer-term contracts.

10% Certain public sector entities (other than the central government, such as State governments, local authorities and government agencies) located in the same country as the bank in question.

20% Banks incorporated within OECD countries.

All public sector entities located within the OECD (with the possible exception of those within the same country as the bank in question).

Multi-lateral development banks (such as the World Bank and the European Investment Bank).

Banks outside of the OECD provided that the maturity of the contract is one year or less.

50% All other counterparties (including corporate users, non-bank financial institutions and banks incorporated outside of the OECD).

Calculation of swap credit exposure

In practice, the credit exposure under a swap transaction (utilising the current exposure method) is as follows:

$$\left[\left(\begin{array}{l}\text{Notional}\\ \text{Principal}\\ \text{of Off-}\\ \text{Balance}\\ \text{Sheet Asset}\end{array} \times \begin{array}{l}\text{Credit}\\ \text{Conversion}\\ \text{Factor}\end{array}\right) + \begin{array}{l}\text{Mark-to-}\\ \text{Market}\\ \text{Value}\end{array}\right] \times \text{Counterparty Risk}$$

$= \text{Risk Adjusted Asset}$

For example, in the case of a US$10m fixed/floating swap with three years to maturity which has a mark-to-market value of US$25,000, the swap credit exposure is as follows:

$$[(\text{US\$}10{,}000{,}000 \times 0.5\%) + \text{US\$}25{,}000] \times 50\% = \text{US\$}37{,}500$$

The above calculation would be adjusted (in terms of the counterparty risk weighting) where the counterparty had a lower risk weight, such as a bank or government body.

The swap credit exposure is then used as a basis for determining the level of capital required to be maintained.

The capital required against a swap transaction is calculated with reference to the risk-weighted asset amount and the minimum capital ratio. The general minimum capital ratio prescribed by the Basle Committee was 8% which was phased in by the end of 1992.

In the above example, the amount of capital required to be held is:

8% of US$37,500 = US$3,000.

Calculating swap intermediation fees

Swap intermediation fees can be calculated, utilising the 8% capital requirement, based on assumptions in relation to the following factors:

- required return on capital;
- applicable tax rate;
- *average* mark-to-market exposure of swap.

Exhibit 39.1 sets out an example of calculating intermediation fees.

Exhibit 39.1

Calculation of Intermediation Fee—Example

Assume the following swap transaction:

Type:	Interest Rate Swap
Notional Principal:	US$100m
Remaining Maturity:	five years
Mark-to-market Exposures:	US$1.5m
Counterparty Risk Weighting:	50%

The swap credit exposure calculation is as follows.

[(US$100m × 0.5%) + US$1.5m] × 0.50 = US$1.0m

The following additional assumptions are made in order to facilitate calculation of the intermediation fee:

Required Pre Tax Return On Capital (ROC):	20% pa
Capital Ratio:	8%

The pre-tax intermediation fee calculation is as follows:

ROC × (capital ratio × exposure) = dollar intermediation fee

20% × (8% × US$1.0m) = US$16,000.

The dollar intermediation fee is converted into a basis point equivalent as follows:

Dollar intermediation fee/notional principal = BP intermediation fee (pa).

Therefore:

0.016/100.0 = 1.6 bps pa.

The swap counterparty would need to change 1.6bps pa (an implied bid-offer of 3.2bps pa) to generate sufficient return to compensate for capital utilisation to cover *for swap credit exposure* on this transaction.

Utilising this methodology, it is feasible to generate minimum intermediation fees for various types of swap transactions. *Exhibits 39.2*, *39.3* and *39.4* set out minimum intermediation fee levels (based on 50% counterparty risk weights and a range of pre-tax returns on capital and assumed mark-to-market exposure) for interest rate swaps with maturities in excess of one year, currency swaps with maturities less than one year and currency swaps with maturities in excess of one year.

It should be noted that the intermediation fees identified are applicable *to each counterparty*. Consequently, the minimum bid-offer spread, required to meet the specified return criteria, would be *double* the intermediation fee.

BIS CAPITAL ADEQUACY REGULATIONS—MARKET IMPLICATIONS

Overview

The incorporation of credit risk associated with swap and derivative transactions in the measurement of risk assets has implications for banks and in turn for the market as a whole. While the term "bank" is utilised, to the extent that risk asset capital requirements will be extended to most financial intermediaries engaged in swaps and derivatives, the term should be read as synonymous for financial intermediaries in general.

The major impact of the capital adequacy regulations is to force internal capital allocation to cover the credit exposure associated with swap activity. In reality, the major participants in the swap market had, prior to the imposition of the BIS capital adequacy guidelines, effectively allocated a portion of their capital to swap and derivative activity to cover not only the risk of credit default but also market risks entailed in these businesses.

To the extent that these institutions already committed capital to these activities, the BIS capital adequacy regulation did not have a major impact. However, the increase in the actual *level* of capital (from the previous level of 5% to 8%) allied with the requirement to hold capital against a whole range of other off-balance sheet activities placed pressure on the banks capital resources. This pressure was exacerbated by the fact that the banks, with minor exceptions, were experiencing significant pressure on their capital ratios as a result of reduced profitability, higher levels of loan losses and loss of capital, in the case of some institutions, from a staged withdrawal from previous investments as part of a retrenchment of global expansion plans.

The major market implications of the BIS capital adequacy regulation can be categorised as follows:

- the implications for swap pricing and market structure;
- the impetus for adopting structural innovations seeking to minimise the impact of BIS Capital Adequacy regulations;
- the development of netting arrangements as well as a swap clearing house to *reduce* the overall credit risk exposure of swap and derivative activity.

Each of these aspects are considered below.

Exhibit 39.2

Interest Rate Swap Transaction

Principal:	$100
Capital Ratio:	8.00%
Maturity:	>1 Year
Credit Conversion Factor:	0.50%
Counterparty Risk Weight:	50.00%

Minimum Intermediation Fee (Basis Points per annum)

Pre-Tax Return on Capital (% pa)	Average Mark-to-Market Exposure (% of Principal)	0.00%	2.00%	4.00%	6.00%	8.00%	10.00%	12.00%	14.00%	16.00%	18.00%	20.00%
	Exposure ($)	$0.25	$1.25	$2.25	$3.25	$4.25	$5.25	$6.25	$7.25	$8.25	$9.25	$10.25
15.00%		0.30	1.50	2.70	3.90	5.10	6.30	7.50	8.70	9.90	11.10	12.30
20.00%		0.40	2.00	3.60	5.20	6.80	8.40	10.00	11.60	13.20	14.80	16.40
25.00%		0.50	2.50	4.50	6.50	8.50	10.50	12.50	14.50	16.50	18.50	20.50
30.00%		0.60	3.00	5.40	7.80	10.20	12.60	15.00	17.40	19.80	22.20	24.60
35.00%		0.70	3.50	6.30	9.10	11.90	14.70	17.50	20.30	23.10	25.90	28.70
40.00%		0.80	4.00	7.20	10.40	13.60	16.80	20.00	23.20	26.40	29.60	32.80
45.00%		0.90	4.50	8.10	11.70	15.30	18.90	22.50	26.10	29.70	33.30	36.90
50.00%		1.00	5.00	9.00	13.00	17.00	21.00	25.00	29.00	33.00	37.00	41.00

Exhibit 39.3

Currency Swap Transaction (1)

Principal:	$100
Capital Ratio:	8.00%
Maturity:	<1 Year
Credit Conversion Factor:	1.00%
Counterparty Risk Weight:	50.00%

Minimum Intermediation Fee (Basis Points per annum)

Pre-Tax Return on Capital (% pa)	Average Mark-to-Market Exposure (% of Principal)	0.00%	5.00%	10.00%	15.00%	20.00%	25.00%	30.00%	35.00%	40.00%	45.00%	50.00%
	Exposure ($)	$0.50	$3.00	$5.50	$8.00	$10.50	$13.00	$15.50	$18.00	$20.50	$23.00	$25.50
15.00%		0.60	3.60	6.60	9.60	12.60	15.60	18.60	21.60	24.60	27.60	30.60
20.00%		0.80	4.80	8.80	12.80	16.80	20.80	24.80	28.80	32.80	36.80	40.80
25.00%		1.00	6.00	11.00	16.00	21.00	26.00	31.00	36.00	41.00	46.00	51.00
30.00%		1.20	7.20	13.20	19.20	25.20	31.20	37.20	43.20	49.20	55.20	61.20
35.00%		1.40	8.40	15.40	22.40	29.40	36.40	43.40	50.40	57.40	64.40	71.40
40.00%		1.60	9.60	17.60	25.60	33.60	41.60	49.60	57.60	65.60	73.60	81.60
45.00%		1.80	10.80	19.80	28.80	37.80	46.80	55.80	64.80	73.80	82.80	91.80
50.00%		2.00	12.00	22.00	32.00	42.00	52.00	62.00	72.00	82.00	92.00	102.00

Exhibit 39.4

Currency Swap Transaction (2)

Principal:	$100
Capital Ratio:	8.00%
Maturity:	>1 Year
Credit Conversion Factor:	5.00%
Counterparty Risk Weight:	50.00%

Minimum Intermediation Fee (Basis Points per annum)

Average Mark-to-Market Exposure (% of Principal)

Pre-Tax Return on Capital		0.00%	5.00%	10.00%	15.00%	20.00%	25.00%	30.00%	35.00%	40.00%	45.00%	50.00%
(% pa)	Exposure ($)	$2.50	$5.00	$7.50	$10.00	$12.50	$15.00	$17.50	$20.00	$22.50	$25.00	$27.50
15.00%		3.00	6.00	9.00	12.00	15.00	18.00	21.00	24.00	27.00	30.00	33.00
20.00%		4.00	8.00	12.00	16.00	20.00	24.00	28.00	32.00	36.00	40.00	44.00
25.00%		5.00	10.00	15.00	20.00	25.00	30.00	35.00	40.00	45.00	50.00	55.00
30.00%		6.00	12.00	18.00	24.00	30.00	36.00	42.00	48.00	54.00	60.00	66.00
35.00%		7.00	14.00	21.00	28.00	35.00	42.00	49.00	56.00	63.00	70.00	77.00
40.00%		8.00	16.00	24.00	32.00	40.00	48.00	56.00	64.00	72.00	80.00	88.00
45.00%		9.00	18.00	27.00	36.00	45.00	54.00	63.00	72.00	81.00	90.00	99.00
50.00%		10.00	20.00	30.00	40.00	50.00	60.00	70.00	80.00	90.00	100.00	110.00

Swap pricing and market structure

The most immediate impact of the BIS guidelines on the swap market was in relation to the pricing of swap and derivative transactions and the structure of the swap market itself. While the effect of the proposed regulations varied between individual institutions, overall a number of major effects are identifiable:

- Banks were forced to specifically commit a designated level of capital to swap and derivative activities and seek returns on this investment.
- The capital requirements impacted on the pricing of swap transactions.
- The institutional market structure altered with participants focusing upon:
  - —the type of swap business undertaken;
  - —counterparties with whom business was undertaken;
  - —the exit from and entry of participants into the swap markets.
- The implications for liquidity and volumes in the swap market.

As noted above, the majority of participants in the swap market, prior to the introduction of the BIS capital adequacy guidelines, made specific allowance for credit risk on swap transactions and, implicitly, reserved capital against such commitments. In a number of cases, the capital commitment required to be made under internal credit guidelines often exceeded, in some cases by a considerable margin, the credit exposures required to be booked under the BIS capital adequacy regulations.

However, the need to explicitly hold capital against swap credit exposures forced even these institutions to seriously assess the commitment of capital, which was both scarce and expensive, to swap and derivative activities and, as an additional matter, to assess the return accruing on this capital commitment.

In the case of more marginal participants in the swap market, the requirement to hold capital against swap and derivative activity forced a more fundamental reassessment of their participation, resulting in some of these more marginal participants withdrawing from the swap market altogether: see discussion below.

The deemed credit equivalent value applied had an impact on the pricing of swaps. This was particularly marked in the case of swaps which carried a high capital charge, for example, long-term currency swaps. Some widening of spreads, as would have been anticipated, was experienced. However, the widening was neither as marked nor as consistent as might have been expected.

For example, spreads on US$ interest rate swaps have widened to around 5 to 10bps pa. Spreads on currency swaps have widened to 10 to 20bps, depending on tenor.

A major factor underlying the less than anticipated increase in dealing spreads is the competitive pressures in the swap market which has limited the ability of banks dealing in swaps to raise prices.

However, swap bid-offer spreads have probably reached a sensible minimum and the evidence indicates that the current spreads, at least, on interest rate swaps are adequate to cover for capital requirements. For example, research undertaken[1] indicates that for swaps with an average maturity of 2.5 to 3.5 years, a 5bps pa spread is adequate. The research indicated that a bid-offer spread of 8 to 10bps is required for a longer-term interest rate swaps to generate adequate returns on capital.

1. Refer Steve Myers (1990).

The increase in the pricing for long-dated currency swaps—to around 20bps pa for ten year transactions—has reflected a number of additional factors. The declining credit standing of a number of counterparties has limited the range of institutions with whom end users are willing to transact such long-term business. This reduction in the level of competition for long-dated transactions has allowed some increases in pricing to compensate for the higher capital utilisation of such transactions.

For other banks, the effect of the BIS regulations has been to force a reassessment as to the extent and nature of their participation in the swap and derivative markets generally. These banks have reassessed their commitment to the swap business, either in general terms, or in specific types of swaps.

This process of reassessment has led to three distinct developments:

- focus on the type of swap and derivative business transacted;
- the counterparties with whom such business is entered into;
- the implementation of exit and entry strategies in relation to swap and derivative businesses generally.

The BIS capital adequacy guidelines have an inherent bias in that the credit equivalent values placed effectively penalise transactions with either long tenors or involving more than one currency. Similarly, the tiered counterparty risk weightings favour a variety of counterparties (primarily, OECD banks, multi-national agencies, sovereign bodies) and discriminates against other classes of counterparties (primarily, non-OECD banks, non-bank financial institutions and corporations).

This regulatory framework allows individual institutions to maximise the advantage of the regulations by adopting strategies which minimise the level of capital for a specific volume of transactions.

For example, concentration on shorter maturity transactions and single currencies or transactions involving less than 50% weighted counterparties reduces the amount of capital required to be held against the relevant swap or derivative portfolio.

This process of assessment has been undertaken by a variety of institutions leading to a higher degree of specialisation than previously experienced as individual organisations try to maximise the level of return for particular classes of transaction either by specialisation by type of transaction or counterparty.

A major element of this process of specialisation has been a marked reduction in the number of institutions willing to enter into long-dated transactions, cross-currency transactions and accommodate 50% weighted counterparties. As noted above, this is manifested itself by the relatively higher degree of price adjustment in relation to these transactions.

In extreme cases, the BIS capital adequacy regulations have forced institutions to reassess their participation in the swap and derivative business generally, leading to these marginal participants withdrawing from the swap market altogether. These institutions, typically smaller banks, have withdrawn from the swap market in all respects except where they utilise swaps as part of their own balance sheet management/hedging requirements or transact matched swaps on behalf of counterparties, usually acting as an intermediary for credit purposes for the ultimate end user of the transaction.

However, the new BIS capital adequacy guidelines have also facilitated the entry by a variety of institutions into the swap market. These new entrants fall into two general categories:

- The entry by *non-bank financial institutions* who are unaffected by the BIS capital adequacy regulations. These include primarily insurance companies—Prudential Global Funding, AIG Financial Products, Mercadian, and General Reinsurance.
- Highly rated (AA/AAA) banks seeking to capitalise on their high credit ratings, sound capital adequacy and risk assumption capabilities etc. These institutions were attracted into the swap and derivative market to fill the vacuum left by the withdrawal of lower credit rated and more weakly capitalised competitors. Institutions in this category include—Deutsche Bank, Credit Suisse Financial Products and a number of Japanese banks. (The background to the entry of these institutions is discussed in detail in Chapter 1.)

A major initial concern in the implementation of the BIS guideline was the potential impact on the liquidity and volumes in the global swaps market. Market observers feared that the capital costs and the resultant changes in swap prices may, in fact, make swap arbitrage uneconomic resulting in a substantial drop in the volume of swap business. In effect, the implementation of the bank's proposal would result in a less liquid and inefficient swap market.

The impact on the liquidity and volumes in the swap market have, in fact, been negligible. The much feared reduction in liquidity has not occurred, although reductions in liquidity in specific sectors, such as long-dated currency swaps, is evident.

However, while the overall liquidity and volumes in the swap market (see Chapter 1) have remained strong, there have been subtler changes in the pattern of activity in the swap market.

For example, activity on organised futures and options exchanges in interest rates and foreign currency instruments has increased. This reflects, in part, the fact that interest rate and foreign exchange futures and options contracts traded on organised exchanges (which are subject to daily mark-to-market provisions and payments of variation margins) are excluded from the BIS capital adequacy guidelines. This exclusion allied to the fact that exchanges themselves sought to capture business volumes lost to the over-the-counter market by product innovation has seen some transfer of activity from the swap market to the organised futures and options markets.

For example, the Eurodollar futures contract has recently been extended and trades out to ten years. This allowed market participants to replicate interest rate swap transactions in US$ by trading strips of Eurodollar futures (see discussion in Chapter 35). The availability of this alternative to transacting a (up to ten year) US$ swap with no BIS capital commitment, albeit at the cost of deposits and variation margin calls has encouraged some market participants to use the contract in preference to the swap market itself.

The use of futures markets has been particularly utilised as a substitute for *interbank* or *inter-financial institution* activity in the relevant currencies, such as US$ interest rate swaps. This reflects in part differential capital requirements as well as factors such as the declining credit standing of some of these institutions and the unavailability of interbank credit lines due to the high volume of already outstanding transactions.

Structural innovations

Predictably, the introduction of the BIS capital adequacy regulations has prompted a variety of structural innovations in the swap market. These structural innovations fall into two categories: product developments designed to reduce the credit exposure on individual transactions (discussed in this section); and innovations, such as netting and development of swap clearing houses, designed to reduce credit exposure *within the swap market as a whole* (this is discussed in the sections following).

The two major structural innovations applicable to individual swap transactions are:

- development of a variable intermediation fee concept;
- the development of a mark-to-market swap structure.

A major difficulty with pricing swap transactions is that the exact quantum of the credit exposure for the transaction is not known until maturity. This has prompted a number of banks to consider changes to the manner in which swap intermediation is priced. These banks have promoted a *variable* intermediation fee instead of the current fixed intermediation margin. Conceptually, this entails charging a price for intermediation which is either fixed (based on average cost pricing utilising some statistical valuation of *expected* average exposure under the swap) *or* a variable fee (based on marginal cost pricing using *actual* exposure plus some potential exposure factor).

The theory underlying the shift is that under the fixed fee the counterparty pays an amount irrespective of the actual exposure, which can be lower than that assumed. In effect, the swap counterparties are paying for a conservative level of assumed exposure on the swap transaction. In contrast, under the variable fee structure, the counterparty pays only on the actual exposure. This would allow swap traders to price swaps more competitively as they would not have to build allowances for unexpected increases in the average exposure on a swap where there is no mechanism to adjust the intermediation margin.

Unfortunately, this concept of a variable intermediation fee has not proved popular with swap end users who have preferred the certainty of a fixed fee to the uncertainty, albeit at the cost of foregoing potential savings, of a variable fee structure.

The second structural innovation entails the development of a notional mark-to-market swap. This type of structure is predicated on the principles underlying the margining concept in futures and also in collateralised swaps: see discussion in Chapter 37.

The concept, originated by a number of primarily United States money centre banks, including Manufacturers Hanover (subsequently merged with and renamed Chemical Bank), Chase Manhattan, JP Morgan, Bankers Trust and Citicorp, was designed to ease the capital requirements of substantial interbank transactions.

Under the system, all swaps are periodically marked-to-market with cash payments being made between counterparties to effectively "zero" the credit exposure on the contract. This process can potentially eliminate or at least greatly reduce the capital requirement of swaps entered into under this arrangement under the capital adequacy guidelines. This is because the mark-to-market provision eliminates current exposure under the contract and the potential exposure beyond one year (irrespective of the outstanding maturity of the contract) as the contract provides for transaction to be marked-to-market every three or six months. The concept was originally applied to interest rate swaps and has been extended to currency swaps. A sizeable market in notional mark-to-market currently exists.

Netting

The concept

The concept of netting in the context of the swap market refers to the process of reducing a number of positive and negative payments between two parties to a single payment. For example, if Bank A has a stream of payments to Bank B on a certain date and Bank B has an offsetting stream of payments to Bank A on the same date, the cash flows can be represented by a single payment, representing the *net* payment due from one party to the other. This process of netting has the potential to reduce the overall credit exposure of the counterparties to each other, thereby reducing the credit exposure of the counterparty and therefore capital required to be committed in support of the exposure.

The concept of netting is predicated on the portfolio approach and measurement of swap credit exposures as between two counterparties: see discussion in Chapter 37.

The Basle Committee, as well as the United States Federal Reserve and Bank of England, recognised that netting arrangements may reduce credit risk on swap transactions. However, the 1988 Capital Accord did not allow netting of opposing swap contracts undertaken with the single counterparty, that is treating multiple contracts with a single counterparty as a single contract or the net of the exposures. The regulatory authorities reluctance to accept netting was based on concerns over rights of offset as provided for by the swap contracts themselves and/or national or international law under which the contracts are made. The regulatory authorities were further concerned as to whether the relevant corporations law and/or bankruptcy laws governing these transactions would permit netting to occur: see discussion below.

The regulatory authorities have stated, on a number of occasions, that they would accept netting in certain specific circumstances:

- Market participants developed standardised master agreements with general market wide application.
- There was unambiguous legal opinions that such agreements would act to reduce credit risk and would be recognised by the relevant judicial authorities.

The major impetus to netting in the swap market has come from financial institutions active in trading and market making in swap and derivatives. These institutions have, in recent times, found their interbank dealing capabilities reduced as the *gross exposure* under such contracts has reached trading limits. The impetus for netting has come from the fact that while the gross exposure under such contracts is substantial, the *net risk* under the outstanding contract is substantially lower. Accordingly, the use of net rather than gross exposure would assist in freeing up interbank trading lines facilitating liquidity within the swap market.

It should be noted that netting as a concept extends beyond the specific confines of the swap or derivatives market. For example, for a number of years, FX Net, a consortium of 12 banks providing foreign exchange bilateral netting by novation, has existed in London.

Central banks, throughout the world, have sought to encourage the development of netting systems, particularly for international payments and foreign exchange, to reduce the systemic risk in the international banking system arising from the settlement of cash flow obligations.

Consequently, the issue of netting is wide ranging and is aimed at ultimately arriving at a process allowing netting across instruments on a preferably multi-lateral basis. However, implementation of such a comprehensive netting system remains some time away.

BIS Lamfalussy Report

In February 1989, the Angel Report on netting schemes for the BIS gave support to netting for both the purpose of transaction payment and settlement as well as in the netting of market exposures for the purposes of credit and capital adequacy. In November 1990, the BIS issued a discussion document on behalf of the G-10 countries (the Lamfalussy Report).[2]

The Lamfalussy Report concluded the following:

- The committee agreed that central banks have a common interest in reducing systemic risk and encouraging improvements in settlement systems.
- The committee recognised advantages that netting can have in terms of improving both the efficiency and stability of interbank settlements, reduction in costs and risks, provided that certain conditions are met (see discussion below).
- The committee indicated that the development of multi-lateral netting systems called for the establishment of an oversight function by central banks.
- The committee indicated that the "host country" central bank would take primary responsibility for overseeing netting systems in operation in its country, in terms of reviewing operation and design of the system and consulting with other central banks who supervise the authorities which may have an interest in the systems prudent operation.

The Lamfalussy Report recommended six minimum standards for netting schemes (refer *Exhibit 39.5*).

Exhibit 39.5

Minimum Standards for Netting Schemes Set Out by the Lamfalussy Report

I. Netting schemes should have a well founded legal basis under all relevant jurisdictions.

II. Netting scheme participants should have a clear understanding of the impact of the particular scheme on each of the financial risks affected by the netting process.

III. Multi-lateral netting systems should have clearly defined procedures for the management of credit risks and liquidity risks which specify the respective responsibilities of the netting provider and the participants. These procedures should also ensure that all parties have both the incentives and the capabilities to manage and contain each of the risks they bear and that limits are placed on the maximum level of credit exposure that can be produced by each participant.

IV. Multi-lateral netting systems should, at a minimum, be capable of ensuring the timely completion of daily settlements in the event of an inability to settle by the participant with the largest single net-debit position.

V. Multi-lateral netting schemes should have objective and publicly disclosed criteria for admission which permit fair and open access.

VI. All netting schemes should ensure the operational reliability of technical systems and the availability of back-up facilities capable of completing daily processing requirements.

2. The summary of the Lamfalussy Report is based in part on Peter Bartko (1991).

The Lamfalussy Report considered alternative methods of netting:

- *The netting of bilateral forward credit exposures*—this entailed replacement of the forward revaluation costs of a number of individual transactions with a single counterparty, with a single legal agreement providing for a single net credit exposure. The obligation of each party to such a netting agreement would be to perform all of the identified transactions, which are typically expressed as the sum of the discounted present values of the unrealised gains and losses on all transactions.
- *The bilateral payment flow netting*—this is designed solely for the netting of payment orders in a single currency and do not impact at all on forward credit exposures. Each payment might represent the settlement of a variety of transactions and, as payment orders are exchanged, they are replaced by a single cumulative balance due to or from each counterparty, representing the single sum remaining to be settled on a given day. This type of netting scheme effectively reduces liquidity demand and credit risk in each country associated with the settlement of included payment orders.
- *Netting by novation arrangements*—this type of system combines the risk reduction of the two other schemes mentioned above in that it achieves a reduction in the level of forward revaluation cost risk and also cross-currency settlement and liquidity risks by placing forward value contractual commitments with new obligations under a single netting agreement in which a running balance between the counterparties becomes due in each currency for each value date.

The Lamfalussy Report was generally supportive of systems of *bilateral* netting for the purpose of capital measurement under the BIS capital adequacy guidelines. The committee argued that such arrangements would operate as follows in relation to the *current exposure method*:

- netting would be on a counterparty-by-counterparty basis;
- the replacement cost for individual transactions (effectively the mark-to-market value) subject to the bilateral netting arrangement would be netted to produce a single credit on debit position for each counterparty;
- there would be no allowance for netting add-ons (effectively the estimate of future credit exposure) and the existing system of gross credit exposures for future exposure based on the add on percentages of gross notional principal amounts would be maintained.

Given that the current replacement cost amount would, typically, be a significant component (say, 50-80%) of the total exposure, the absence of a system of netting *future* exposure would not prevent a substantial reduction in exposure level.

Netting under the original exposure method was not considered appropriate because the lack of separate assessment of current and potential future exposure made it unsuitable for netting.

The Lamfalussy Report highlighted the complexities inherent in creating any multi-lateral netting system where the netting provider (effectively, some type of clearing house) would assume all risks and undertake all risk management functions would necessitate the netting provider placing *its own* counterparty limits on each participant in the netting scheme to ensure its exposure to each participant was within the participant's overall financial resources.

The Lamfalussy Report considered the principal object of netting was to reduce the following risks:

- *Revaluation risk*—which is defined as the cost in the event of a counterparty default of replacing non-settled amounts. Revaluation risk is measured by marking contracts to market.
- *Settlement risk*—which is defined as the risk undertaken by each party on the value date to make payment of the relevant currencies creating a full exposure to the principal amount of the underlying transactions.
- *Temporal risk*—this is defined as risk entailed in the timing difference in settlements across different time zones which creates exposure to the full principal value of the transaction.

Netting schemes were considered to have the potential to substantially reduce not only individual revaluation risk but to have a cumulative affect on all netting counterparties, thereby reducing the risk of the market as a whole.

Netting was also viewed as reducing settlement and temporal risk by reducing average settlement amounts, the number of payments processed and the number of times the party is obligated to make payments in a currency in a different time zone.

The Lamfalussy Report considered that, for all forms of netting, a multitude of complex legal and regulatory issues required for its effective operation must be resolved. Importantly, the report, while recognising the potential for multi-lateral netting schemes, expressed some reservations on such arrangements indicating even where actual exposures are reduced, the nature of multi-lateral systems is such that risk could be shifted and concentrated to the extent that systemic risk is actually increased.

Netting agreements—the legal position

As is evident from the above discussion, the critical element in implementing netting arrangements is the status of such contracts under national bankruptcy regulations.

Since the adoption of the 1988 Capital Accord, the enforceability of netting provisions under the insolvency laws of the G-10 countries has been substantially clarified.

In the United States, as a result of an amendment made in June 1990 to the United States Bankruptcy Code, a United States corporation can now be certain that its swap exposures can be netted with a defaulting counterparty. The *Financial Institutions Reform, Recovery and Enforcement Act* 1989 (FIRREA) provides the same netting ability for United States commercial banks and thrifts.

These two changes in legislation have enabled banks to view their swap exposure to any single United States counterparty as the "net" of the mark-to-market value of their total swap portfolio with that counterparty. As a result of these changes, banks have moved from measuring swap credit exposure by notional principal amounts outstanding to counterparties within various maturity bands, to the more sophisticated approach of evaluating the "netted" expected and actual mark-to-market credit exposures. Expected exposures incorporate the potential impact due to time and interest rate volatility on the mark-to-market value.

In addition, ISDA has obtained legal opinions from counsel in Belgium, Canada, France, Germany, Italy, Japan, the Netherlands, Sweden and the United Kingdom indicating that netting provisions contained in *bilateral* master agreements will be upheld in each of those countries.

However, there are two additional issues which will require resolution to facilitate full-scale implementation of bilateral netting arrangements:

- netting arrangements applied to affiliates;
- the adoption of full two-way payment provisions in the event of default.

In order to give full effects to *bilateral* netting, it is essential that the netting arrangements encompass subsidiaries and affiliates of counterparties through which it may choose to deal. Under this expanded version of netting, in the case of default, the right of set off would allow a party owing money under the swap to set it off against other claims on its counterparty and *on the counterparty's subsidiaries and affiliates*.

The debate regarding full two way payment (FTP) and limited two way payment (LTP) was alluded to in Chapter 37. As noted in that context, the LTP provision allows the non-defaulting party in a swap contract that is terminated to abandon its obligation even though close out calculations would have required it make a payment to the defaulting party. In contrast, FTP allows a defaulted party in a forced termination to receive the full value of its in-the-money swaps.

As discussed in Chapter 37, in practice most counterparties have treated termination in FTP terms, even where their contracts have allowed for LTP. Increasingly, major swap market participants specify FTP in contract, but a significant group, although they support the principal of FTP, maintain LTP provisions in their documents as a deterrent against wilful termination by counterparties in order to realise the cash value of the contract.

These counterparties favour LTP as providing the non-defaulting party with bargaining power to its capacity to set off what it owes on swaps against other claims it has on a defaulting counterparty and its affiliates. ISDA along with other interested parties are currently seeking to limit the scope of LTP contractual provision in order to prevent it negating the impact of bilateral netting between derivatives counterparties. It is understood that ISDA is exploring a means of modifying the LTP provision but with a capacity to allow the right of set off with affiliates.

BIS guidelines for netting for capital adequacy purposes

In April 1993, in the culmination of the process described above, the Basle Committee released a consultative proposal entitled "The Supervisory Recognition of Netting for Capital Adequacy Purposes". In effect, the BIS adopted, substantively, the conclusions of the Lamfalussy report, proposing that the 1988 Capital Accord be revised to recognise, in addition to netting by novation, other forms of bilateral netting of credit exposures to the extent that such arrangements are effective under relevant laws and comply with the other minimum standards set forward in the Lamfalussy report (see *Exhibit 39.5* above).

The specific amendments to the 1988 Capital Accord are set out in *Exhibit 39.6*.

Exhibit 39.6

Proposed Amendment to the 1988 Capital Accord for Bilateral Netting

In the last sentence of the first paragraph on page 28 (Annex 3) of the 1988 Capital Accord the word "are" would be replaced with "may be".

The language below would replace page 30 (Annex 3) of the 1988 Capital Accord in respect of the recognition of bilateral netting for the purpose of calculating capital requirements. The footnote numbers are as they would appear in the revised Capital Accord.

Exhibit 39.6—continued

"Careful consideration has been given to the issue of bilateral netting, that is, weighting the net rather than the gross claims arising out of swaps and similar contracts with the same counterparties.[1] The Committee is concerned that if a liquidator of a failed counterparty has (or may have) the right to unbundle netted contracts, demanding performance on those contracts favourable to his client and defaulting on unfavourable contracts, there is no reduction in counterparty risk.

Accordingly, it has been agreed that:

(a) Banks may net transactions subject to novation under which any obligation between a bank and its counterparty to deliver a given currency on a given value date is automatically amalgamated with all other obligations for the same currency and value date, legally substituting one single amount for the previous gross obligations.

(b) Banks may also net transactions subject to any legally valid form of bilateral netting not covered in (a), including other forms of novation.

(c) In both cases (a) and (b), a bank will need to satisfy its national supervisor that it has:[2]

   (1) a netting contract or agreement with the counterparty which creates a single legal obligation, covering all included transactions, such that, in the event of a counterparty's failure to perform due to default, bankruptcy or liquidation, the bank would have a claim or obligation, respectively, to receive or pay only the net value of the sum of unrealised gains and losses on included transactions;

   (2) written and reasoned legal opinions that, in the event of a legal challenge, the relevant courts and administrative authorities would find the bank's exposure to be such a net amount under:

   — the law of the jurisdiction in which the counterparty is chartered and, if the counterparty is a branch of a foreign bank, then also under the law of the jurisdiction in which the branch is located;

   — the law that governs the individual transactions; and

   — the law that governs any contract or agreement necessary to effect the netting.

   The national supervisor, after consultation when necessary with other relevant supervisors, must be satisfied that the netting is enforceable under the laws of each of the relevant jurisdictions;[3]

   (3) procedures in place to ensure that the legal characteristics of netting arrangements are kept under review in the light of possible changes in relevant laws.

Contracts containing walk-away clauses will not be eligible for netting for the purpose of calculating capital requirements pursuant to this Accord.

For banks using the current exposure method, credit exposure on bilaterally netted forward transactions will be calculated as the sum of: the net marked-to-market replacement cost, if positive, plus an add-on based on the notional underlying principal.[4] The scale of add-ons to apply will be the same as those for non-netted transactions as set out in this Annex. The Committee will continue to review the scale of add-ons to make sure they are appropriate. In the case of foreign exchange contracts and other similar contracts, in which notional principal is equivalent to cash flows, total notional principal would be determined by reference to the pays or receipts with the netting counterparty on each value date, after taking account of netting of amounts falling due on each value date in the same currency. The reason for this is that offsetting contracts in the same currency maturing on the same date will have lower potential future exposure as well as lower current exposure.

The original exposure method may also be used for transactions subject to netting agreements which meet the above legal requirements until market risk-related capital requirements are implemented, at which time the original exposure method will cease to be available for netted transactions. The conversion factors to be used during the transitional period when calculating the credit exposure of bilaterally netted transactions will be as follows:

Maturity	Interest rate contracts	Exchange rate contracts
Less than one year	0.35%	1.50%
One year and less than two years	0.75%	3.75% (i.e. 1.5% + 2.25%)
For each additional year	0.75%	2.25%

Exhibit 39.6—continued

These factors represent a reduction of approximately 25% from those on page 29 of the Accord."

Notes:

1. Payments netting, which is designed to reduce the operational costs of daily settlements, will not be recognised in the capital framework since the counterparty's gross obligations are not in any way affected.
2. In cases where an agreement as described in (a) has already been recognised prior to the effect of this amendment to the Accord, the supervisor will determine whether any additional steps consistent with the requirements below are necessary to satisfy itself of the legal validity of the agreement.
3. Thus, if any of these supervisors are dissatisfied about enforceability under its laws, the netting contract or agreement will not meet this condition and neither counterparty could obtain supervisory benefit.
4. Supervisors will take care to ensure that the add-ons are based on effective rather than apparent notional amounts.

In effect, the BIS proposal had the following impact

- For banks using the current exposure method, the credit exposure on bilaterally netted forward transactions would be calculated as the sum of the net mark-to-market replacement costs, if positive, plus an add-on based on the notional underlying principal.
- For banks using the original exposure method, a reduction in the credit conversion factors applied to bilaterally netted transactions is to be permitted on a temporary basis until the market risk capital requirements are implemented when the original exposure method would cease to be available for netting transactions.

The BIS consultative proposal raised a number of issues:

- A sound legal basis for the recognition of netting was seen to be the basis of the proposal. The Committee was of the view that no single form of netting arrangement could be identified as appropriate in all jurisdictions and sought to lay down minimum standards which national supervisors would apply.
- The Committee was concerned about the impact of LTP and FTP clauses (referred to as "walk-away clauses"). The element of instability and uncertainty introduced by such provisions was seen by the Committee as unsuitable for netting and any netting arrangement that contained such clauses would not be considered as a qualifying arrangement.
- The Committee left open the issue of cross-product netting. In the Committee's view, cross-product netting added a level of technical complexity and raised legal issues which were jurisdiction specific. The Committee left open the way for individual national authorities to consider whether a range of instruments could be entitled to a supervisory benefit from netting.

The Committee gave significant consideration to the issue of multi-lateral netting. *Exhibit 39.7* sets out the discussion by the Basle Committee on the issue of multi-lateral netting. Several issues related to multi-lateral netting which are relevant to the issue of clearing houses are considered in detail in the section on clearing houses.

Exhibit 39.7
Multi-lateral Netting: Possible Approach for Supervisory Treatment at Some Future Date

(a) General considerations

Multi-lateral netting is designed to extend the benefits of netting to cover contracts which originate with any of a group of counterparties that participate in the netting arrangement, instead of with just a single counterparty as in bilateral netting. This can be achieved in practice by netting all transactions that originate bilaterally through a central counterparty—a clearing house. The legal techniques for achieving this netting may vary, but the result will be that for every eligible transaction agreed by a pair of members, the clearing house would be interposed as the common legal counterparty to each member, and the members would have no obligations towards each other under the deal. For each member, the clearing house would maintain a running, legally binding net position in each currency and each value date eligible for netting, all subject to a binding netting agreement between the member and the clearing house. Thus, for each member of the clearing house, multiple transactions that originate with many counterparties can be amalgamated and netted. As a result, in a well designed multi-lateral netting scheme, exposures would generally be a fraction of those that would arise in a non-netting environment.[1]

If a clearing house member defaults, a foreign exchange clearing house would have to replace the cash flows that the defaulting member's portfolio of foreign exchange contracts would have produced. It would establish immediately how much it should pay to, or claim from, the defaulting member, which would be the replacement value of the member's portfolio. In the event of a claim on the defaulter, clearing house members would have to cover the shortfall, since the clearing house may have very limited resources of its own.

Losses could be recovered from the membership in different ways. In a defaulter-pays (or centralised) clearing house, each member would be obliged to post collateral equal to its own net debit with the clearing house. In the event of a member's default, the clearing house would seize the defaulting member's collateral to cover the amount in default. In a survivors-pay (or decentralised) clearing house, a loss allocation rule would apply to the non-defaulting, surviving members. For example, losses could be allocated in proportion to a measure of the surviving members' bilateral relationship to the defaulting member, such as notional bilateral exposures to the defaulting member.[2]

However, as a practical matter, it could be misleading to make a strong distinction between the survivors-pay and the defaulter-pays models. In practice, multi-lateral netting schemes could be a hybrid of these models. That is, members would be obliged to reimburse the clearing house for losses according to a predetermined loss allocation rule, but losses to be allocated to survivors would be reduced in the first instance by collateral posted by the defaulting member. In addition, even nominal defaulter-pays schemes must include an allocation rule for losses in the event that a defaulter's posted collateral is inadequate to cover its net debit, for whatever reason.

The Lamfalussy Report sets out six minimum standards for netting schemes (see Annex 1). For example, multi-lateral netting arrangements will be expected to have, among other things, safeguards to address settlement risk in a responsible manner, including risk controls such as internal limits, adequate and reliable liquidity support, and appropriate technical back-up facilities. The adherence of multi-lateral schemes to these standards will be monitored by central banks and other relevant authorities. However, each national supervisor whose banks belong to a multi-lateral netting arrangement should be satisfied that the standards are met before extending supervisory recognition to the netting performed under the scheme.

(b) Capital requirements under multi-lateral netting

(i) Capital requirements for current exposure

Under any multi-lateral netting arrangement, there must be an agreed formula whereby any losses suffered by the clearing house from the default of any of the members would be allocated to other members, even if the possibility of loss for the clearing house is remote as a result of comprehensive collateral arrangements. This formula will provide the current exposure for each member. It appears that the multi-lateral foreign exchange netting

Exhibit 39.7—continued

arrangements now being developed will rely on procedures that would allocate the sharing of a loss pro rata according to the pattern of notional bilateral claims on the defaulting member. That is, if a member's default (or close-out) caused a replacement loss to the clearing house, a bank would be allocated a loss share in proportion to its notional bilateral exposure to the defaulting (or closed-out) member. If the clearing house requires collateral the loss to be allocated would be the residual loss (the amount by which the replacement loss exceeded the value of the collateral).

A starting point would be to regard a bank's current exposure as the sum of the loss shares that it would be allocated in the event of the default (or close-out) of each clearing house member to which it had a notional bilateral exposure, after factoring in the use of collateral available to the clearing house.[3] The sum of the loss shares provides an analogous treatment with non-netted contracts. In the case of non-netted contracts, the exposure is the sum of the exposure to the potential default of each counterparty. Of course, the effect of multi-lateral netting will tend to lower this exposure.

At this time, the Committee has not reached conclusions about the level of the capital requirements that should be attached to this measure of current exposure. This question will be kept under review in the light of the continuing development of the multi-lateral foreign exchange netting initiatives and their supervision by central banks and other relevant authorities. In due course, further consultation will be needed.

(ii) Capital requirements for potential future exposure

The capital requirements under consideration by the Committee would also require a charge for potential future exposure. However, potential future exposure for a member of a multilateral netting facility would be determined by a combination of the evolution of underlying rates and prices, the changing pattern of clearing house exposure to other members, and the loss allocation procedure in place. A highly simplified approximation will be required to determine the add-ons needed to cover the resulting exposure.

(c) Risk weights for the clearing house

Banks will have exposure to the clearing house, for example, through funding and liquidity back-up, to which a risk weight would need to be applied. Consistent with the Accord, the weight applicable to claims on a clearing house would be the normal 100% private sector weighting, unless the clearing house is incorporated as a bank and becomes subject to bank supervisors' rules, in which case a 20% weight would be appropriate, or the host government or central bank has given a clear and unequivocal guarantee for all of its obligations, in which case a zero weight would be justified.

(d) Summary questions

(i) If multi-lateral netting arrangements are recognised, the Committee would intend to apply the same legal requirements as is proposed for the recognition of bilateral netting arrangements. If market participants think different standards should apply, please explain why.

(ii) The Committee would welcome comments and suggestions regarding the capital requirements for current exposure under multi-lateral netting discussed in Section (b)(i) above.

(iii) The Committee would welcome comments and suggestions regarding the capital requirements for potential future exposure under multi-lateral netting discussed in Section (b)(ii) above.

Notes:

1. For example, according to market participants, simulations suggest that multi-lateral foreign exchange netting would reduce replacement costs by about 80% to 85% for a given set of transactions conducted in the absence of netting, and would reduce settlement flows by about 75% compared with the payments that would be needed to settle the corresponding gross obligations. (Estimates of the benefits of multi-lateral netting can vary somewhat depending on the specific aspects of the simulations, such as the nature of the transactions netted, the number of clearing house members and the patterns of trading.)

Exhibit 39.7—continued

Consistent with the Accord, this paper is concerned only with capital requirements for exposures related to replacement costs.

2. Notional bilateral exposures arise from the bilateral transactions that originating members submit to the clearing house for netting, and represent the bilateral positions that would have resulted in the absence of multi-lateral netting. They are notional (and have no legal standing) since once the transaction is accepted for netting by the clearing house, it becomes the legal counterparty to each member.
3. In the case of a clearing house that on a daily basis marks all outstanding contracts to market and collects from its members daily losses and pays out to its members daily gains (that is, collects and pays variation margin), the capital treatment would be consistent with that of exchange traded instruments in footnote 3 of Annex 3 of the Accord. Specifically, no capital would be required. In cases where a clearing house requires its members to collateralise fully or partially potential losses, but does not collect or pay variation margin, the present treatment of collateral in Section II(iv) of the Accord would apply.

Swap clearing house[3]

Concept

The development of a swap clearing house, like netting arrangements, represents a structural innovation designed to reduce *the overall level of risk in the swap market*. A swap clearing house, which is based on the concept of organised futures and option exchanges, would take the form, presumably, of a centralised exchange which would be interposed as a credit intermediary as between the end counterparties in any swap transaction. The clearing house will ensure the credit integrity of the swap market by an appropriate system of margins and deposits designed to insulate the clearing house and its members and, most importantly, the swap counterparties from the risk of default.

The net impact of a swap clearing house to essentially aggregate minimise swap exposure is considerable. *Exhibit 39.8* sets out an example of how the swap clearing house would operate to reduce the *overall market* credit exposure.

As in the case of netting, the major beneficiaries of a clearing house would be financial institutions active as dealers in swaps. The clearing house would serve to reduce the pressure on inter-dealer credit lines and assist in facilitating liquidity in the swap market.

Exhibit 39.8

Impact of Swap Clearing House on Swap Market Credit Exposures

Assume the following five year US$ interest rate swap where A pays 10% pa against receipt of floating rate US$ LIBOR and D undertakes the exact reverse transaction. In this case, A enters into the swap with B while D enters into its swap with C. Bank C and D then move to square their respective positions with each other. (Note that for the sake of simplicity, all rates are assumed to be the same.)

On the basis that each swap was for a notional principal of US$100m, the total market position is as follows:

3. The discussion of the formation of a swap clearing house draws on Michael G Rulle Jnr, "Is a Swap Clearing House More Likely Now?" in Satyajit Das (1991).

Exhibit 39.8—continued

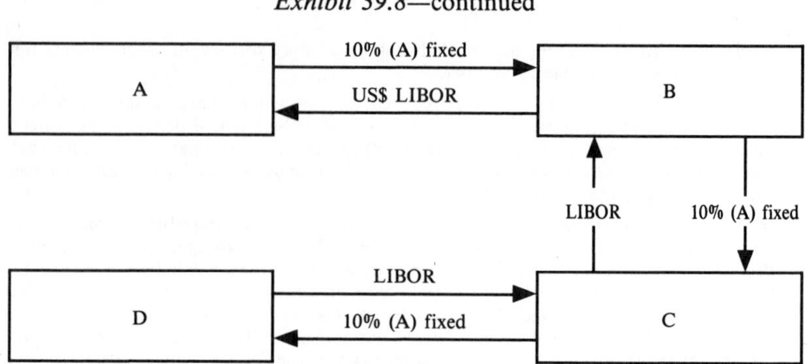

There are now a total of US$400m of swaps outstanding. A and D have open positions while C and D have matched swaps on their books.

If swap rates rise by 1% pa to 11% pa, then the gross exposure on the US$100m swap is US$3.696m (equivalent to 1.00% pa present valued over five years). The exposure in the market is as follows:

- A has an exposure of US$3.696m on B;
- B has an exposure of US$3.696m on C;
- C has an exposure of US$3.696m on D.

Market aggregate exposure in the market totals US$11.088m.

Let us assume that instead of transacting directly with each other the parties *all* enter into their respective transactions with a clearing house.

The position then is as follows:

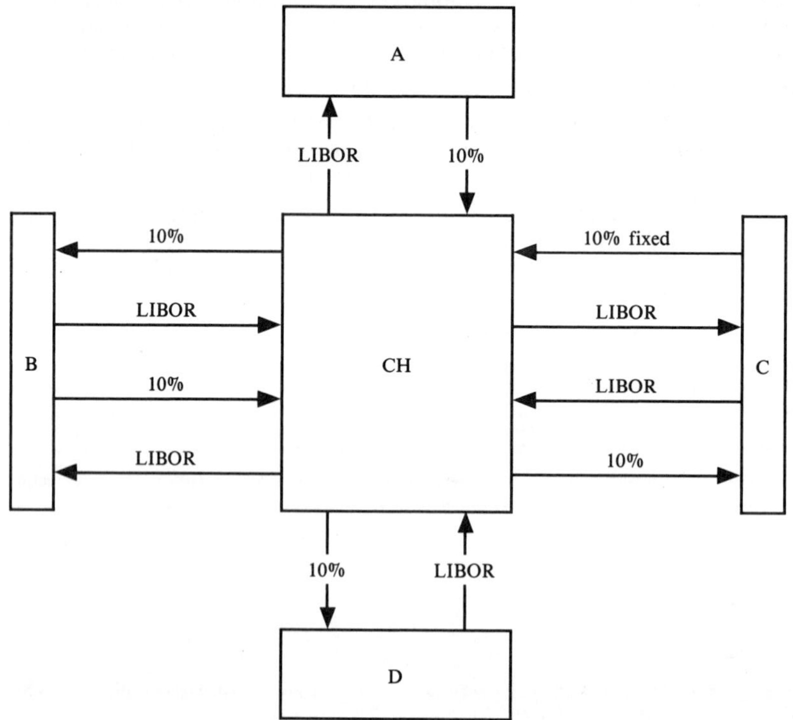

Exhibit 39.8—continued

The market exposure position is as follows:

- A has no exposure *to the clearing house* as the swap is in-the-money.
- B and C have *no* exposures as their payment streams cancel.
- D has an exposure of US$3.696m *to the clearing house* as the swap is out-of-the-money.

The above assumes that the swap clearing house is itself of high credit standing. This implies that the clearing house is appropriately capitalised and all transactions entered are supported by relevant deposit and mark-to-market margining arrangements.

As is evident, the market swap exposure in this case falls dramatically with the interposition of the clearing house.

Mechanics

From a mechanical perspective, a swap clearing house would operate in a manner analogous to organised future and options exchanges, but with significant differences.

Types of transactions

Classical clearing houses and other financial markets perform two functions:

- location of offsetting counterparties;
- acting as credit intermediaries.

Under this structure, the clearing house "clears" contracts by matching transactions submitted by buyers with those submitted by sellers and, upon matching, acts as a principal between the two offsetting parties.

The swap clearing house would, in all probability, *only perform the role of credit intermediation*. The actual swap contract would be agreed upon between two members which would then interpose the clearing house to act as credit intermediary to the transaction. This reflects that fact that the swap market features a significant proportion of non-standard contracts.

An alternative would be to create a two-tier clearing process:

- The first tier would be concerned with standardised generic interest rate and currency swaps (as specified by the clearing house) where it would perform both the functions identified above.
- A second tier for non-standard transactions where the swap clearing house would merely act as credit intermediary.

Deposits and margin requirements

The swap clearing house would operate a system of initial deposits and mark-to-market variation margins.

Upon transferring a contract to the clearing house, each counterparty would be required to post initial capital to establish both a net worth and a fund to subsidise potential losses. Similarly, each counterparty would be required to post variation margins, based on a mark-to-market of each swap daily in order to ensure that the clearing house is protected from default should interest rates or currency rates move significantly.

Counterparties would additionally be subject to a charge that would cover clearing house operating expenses.

Documentation

The clearing house would operate under a single form of swap contract agreement with each member seeking to transact with the clearing house. Matters to be covered in this agreement would include computation of required deposit and mark-to-market variation margins as well as the methodology for computing the mark-to-market amount and the mechanics for determining rates and spreads used in calculation.

It is likely that the clearing house would operate as a bilateral (rather than multilateral) netting system as master agreements would be between the clearing house and the member dealer only.

Default

In the event of a member default, the clearing house would close out all that member's positions either through the transfer of the contracts to other members of the clearing house or liquidating them. Both transfers and liquidation would be undertaken at mark-to-market values. Where losses exceeded the initial capital and subsequent margins supplied to the corporation by the defaulting party, the clearing house would need to bear the cost as a charge against its capital and assess the clearing house members for a certain share of the losses. However, presumably the deposit and mark-to-market variations in conjunction with its own capital base should provide sufficient buffer to prevent the clearing house incurring losses in the event of default.

Identity of the clearing house

The swap clearing house would clearly need to be of high credit standing. Existing commodities clearing houses are owned substantially by major international banks and other financial institutions. It is probable that the swap clearing house would need to be structured in a similar manner.

Another issue in this regard is whether a single global swap clearing house would be created or, in contrast, a series of individual national clearing houses would be created. The choice between the two is likely to be dictated by securities laws, bankruptcy regulations and taxation factors. Taxation factors in particular may favour national rather than international clearing house structures.

An important issue in regard to the structure of the swap clearing house would be its interaction with the BIS capital adequacy requirements.

The clearing house could be structured as solely a vehicle to insulate clearing house members from credit risk on each other. Under this arrangement, the clearing house would *not* alleviate BIS capital adequacy requirements. Swaps with the clearing house would have the same risk weight as swaps with individual members of the clearing house. Alternatively, the clearing house could be treated as a separate counterparty, presumably with full 50% risk weighting. This would diminish the attraction of a clearing house as it would increase the counterparty risk weighting in the case of OECD banks for example.

An alternative structure would be to seek to have regulatory authorities accept the swap clearing house as an organised exchange and as a result of the deposit and margining provisions, treat swaps undertaken with the swap clearing house as zero credit risk weighted for capital adequacy purposes.

The latter structure would provide additional impetus to the concept of a swap clearing house as it would then have advantages relative to alternative risk reduction systems such as netting because of its multi-lateral structure.

Examples

A number of clearing houses, primarily for foreign exchange contracts, are at various stages of development. A major example of these types of structures is a system called Echo netting developed by a group of 13 European banks which is designed to allow member banks to settle each transaction on a lump sum basis that will be proportioned by the current recipient by a clearing house.

More recently, two proposals for swap clearing houses have emerged:

1. *OMF proposal*

   The privately owned French futures and options exchange. Optionsmarknad France (OMF) announced in 1989 that it was finalising a system that would clear French franc interest rate swaps between members. The system is designed to net swaps with maturities up to 12 years against the French floating rate bases Pibor, TAM and T4M. Members' positions would be marked-to-market each day, and daily net positions would be covered by a deposit and margin calls. However, as the need for member commitment approaches, the OMF is finding difficulty in gaining support from the major French banks.

   Subsequently, MATIF, which inherited the defunct OMF, has experienced difficulty with implementing the clearing house concept. A major factor has been the reluctance of the Bank of France to sanction a system of net rather than gross payments.

2. *OM proposal*

   In early 1992, the Stockholm Options Market (OM) introduced a clearing service for the Swedish kronor swap market. The clearing service was designed to remove counterparty risk on swaps between fixed and floating rate kronor. The proposal was not received enthusiastically and the OM clearing house has not been well supported.

Assessment

While a swap clearing house has intuitive appeal as a means of reducing swap credit risk, the concept has a number of difficulties:

- While the clearing house may reduce inter-dealer credit exposures, the non-standardisation of swap transactions could prevent the clearing house from facilitating the liquidity of the swap market as a whole. The failure of the Finex swap futures contract to generate volume and liquidity seems to be a testament to this difficulty.
- Unless the clearing house mechanism, under the BIS capital adequacy regulations, is zero risk weighted on the basis of margin and deposit provisions, it would appear to offer little in the way of additional benefits to effective bilateral netting arrangements between counterparties.
- As banks already allocate a certain proportion of capital to swap transactions, it is arguable that the introduction of a properly capitalised clearing house would simply duplicate what the market currently has already allowed for.

A major problem with the introduction of a swap clearing house relates to market divisions as between large well capitalised, highly rated counterparties and weaker, less well capitalised participants. A swap clearing house would benefit smaller banks and investment banks, which have smaller balance sheet capacity, and is therefore resisted by the larger better capitalised competitors who would see such a development as undermining their competitive advantage.

Chapter 40

Market Risk: Regulatory Framework

REGULATORY DEVELOPMENTS

The BIS Capital Adequacy Guidelines (discussed in Chapter 39) represented, until recently, the most significant regulatory initiative in relation to swap and other derivatives. However, as the discussion above identifies, its scope is limited to credit exposure issues. In recent times, increasing focus has been directed towards certain deficiencies in the regulatory framework governing swap and derivative activities. These include:

- Regulations, such as the BIS guidelines, only affect *banks*. Other financial institutions, including investment banks and securities company as well as financial products affiliates of insurance companies, are, to varying degrees, outside the scope of these regulatory measures.
- The regulations, to date, exemplified by the BIS capital adequacy regulation, focus exclusively on *credit risk* in such transactions. Regulators have, in recent times, been increasingly concerned about the market risk (exposure to variations in interest rates and currency values etc) within portfolios of swaps and other derivative instruments.
- The lack of regulations governing the more complex variations on basic interest rate and currency derivative products which have proliferated. For example, the BIS guidelines were framed against a background of a limited range of instruments. In addition, expansion of derivative activity to commodities and equities, which were not designed to be dealt with under existing regulatory guidelines, have created problems.

The impetus for additional regulatory scrutiny of the swap market and its practices derives from a variety of factors:

- continuing rapid growth in the size of the market for swaps and financial derivatives generally;
- the increasing complexity of instruments and their inherent risk profiles;
- concern about the non-credit risk aspects of portfolio risk, such as interest rate, currency, commodity or equity market price risk which must be managed in modern swap and derivative portfolios;
- concern about management control of the swap and derivatives businesses currently operated by a wide range of financial institutions;
- the increased levels of default by counterparties experienced in the swap market.

The sheer size of the market, its continued rapid rate of growth, and the important contribution that these activities make to the profitability of institutions active in these products have all focused regulatory attention on this market.

An added concern in the regard is concern about a market which allowed approximately US$10 billion in notional principal of swaps, for what proved to be ultimately purely speculative purposes, to be entered into by a United Kingdom local municipal authority—Hammersmith and Fulham—focusing attention on the size and potential exposures in the swap market generally.

Overlaying the increase in size is the corresponding increase in complexity in the types of instruments that are now commonly priced, structured and hedged. Increasingly, single transactions contain different instrument elements creating a complex network of credit and market risk exposures which must be managed. Increasingly, regulators are concerned about *their* capacity to understand and to assess capacity of the individual institution to manage these exposures.

Opponents of increased regulation argue that, perversely, the development of derivative products has in fact had precisely the opposite impact. Proponents of this view argue that swaps and derivatives have *facilitated* the efficient transfer of risks between markets and as a by-product enabled better understanding of currency, interest rate and credit risks which has strengthened bank internal control of these exposures.

Nevertheless, regulators are increasingly concerned about the market risk positions assumed by banks and other financial institutions and have focused on expanding the regulatory framework to require these institutions to hold capital specifically against assessed market risk (this would be in addition to capital required to be committed through credit exposure on such transactions).

Regulators also continue to be concerned about the capacity of the senior management of banks active in these markets to control such activities. Increasingly, regulators are concerned that despite establishment of counterparty credit limits, trading limits and risk reporting systems, the level of control of exposures in such portfolios is relatively undeveloped.

A major concern in this regard is the reliance on a relatively few skilled individuals to manage such complex portfolios. Regulators increasingly question whether the control mechanisms and risk management skills are adequate. The increasing number of new entrants into the swap and derivatives market who, almost habitually, engage an existing team from another institution in an effort to short cut the process of establishment exacerbates this excessive reliance on a few skilled specialists who are, in turn, managed by senior managers who are themselves not experienced in the swap or derivative markets.

In early 1993, the Bank of England released a report—"Derivatives: Report of an Internal Working Group"—on the London Derivative Market. The report found derivatives to be an important means of managing risk but concluded that senior managers in organisations using derivatives need to be more rigorous in monitoring and controlling the risk of derivative operations. The report which had a survey group consisting of ten banks, seven non-bank financial institutions and two corporations, had as one of its main recommendations that senior managers in financial institutions and in non-financial corporations who are active in the use of such instruments, acquire a greater understanding of derivatives. The Bank of England recommended that, in order to monitor and control risk, at least two members of the Board of Directors (including the Finance Director) should have sufficient knowledge to supervise their firm's derivative operations.

Increased default experience in the swap market in recent years has also caused concern. A spate of recent failures (see Chapter 37) has led regulators to question the 50% ceiling on counterparty risk weighting as an exception to the normal 100% risk weighting for certain counterparties, such as corporations.

These regulators increasingly question whether the assumption underlying the original proposal on capital measurement and capital standards that most counterparties in swap markets, particularly for long-term contracts, are of very high credit standing, is in fact true.

ISDA, in August 1992, published its risk default survey which showed that cumulative losses over the history of the surveyed institutions involvement in swaps totalled only US$358.4m or 0.0115% of the notional principal outstanding at the surveyed firms. ISDA argued that this compares favourably with other sectors of the finance industry and utilised this risk default experience to resist suggestions of further regulatory initiatives in regard to swaps and derivatives.

Increasingly, in recent times, major regulatory bodies have voiced concern regarding the risks inherent in the swaps and derivatives market.

In December 1991, New York Federal Reserve Bank President Gerald Corrigan, who also heads the supervisors committee at the BIS, hinted at the necessity to review the regulation of off-balance sheet activities, particularly the derivatives market. Subsequently, at the Paris meeting of ISDA, Richard Farrant, Deputy Head of Banking Supervision at the Bank of England, reiterated a warning to ISDA members voicing concern about the risks inherent in the derivatives market.

Farrant, in his speech, articulated the range and depth of regulatory anxieties:

- that regulators were no longer qualified to regulate;
- the nature of derivative markets themselves have increased the riskiness of bank's activities;
- derivatives have increased systemic risk across financial market and, furthermore, the potential for shock in one market to be transmitted to others in ways that may not yet be fully understood.

The anxieties voiced by the Bank of England and the Federal Reserve have been reflected in similar concerns expressed by the BIS.

This increased concern of regulators is paralleled by increasing focus on a variety of new regulatory measures aimed at the swap and derivative market.

In 1992 and 1993, a diverse range of bodies undertook major new studies of the derivatives markets. The major study was the G-30 Global Derivatives Study Groups, under the chairmanship of Sir Dennis Weatherstone, Chairman of JP Morgan. This study, which was released in July 1993, is discussed in Chapter 41 was a hallmark study of the practices and principles of derivatives activity and the management of such activity within financial institutions.

Other studies completed include:

- Bank of England—internal working group on derivatives;
- Moody's Investors Services;
- Various US agencies including: the CFTC; Federal Reserve System; Federal Deposit Insurance Corporation (FDIC); the Office of the Comptroller of the Currency; General Accounting Office (GAO), the auditing arm of Congress; National Association of Insurance Commissioners (NAIC); Securities and Exchange Commission (SEC); Office of Thrift Supervision (OTS); and Congress itself (the Leach Report);
- European Community;
- BIS/Basle Committee.

The European Community's proposed capital adequacy directive and the more recent BIS Market Risk Guidelines currently represent the most advanced proposal for additional regulation of the swap market.

THE EUROPEAN COMMUNITY (EC) CAPITAL ADEQUACY DIRECTIVE[1]

Background

The EC Capital Adequacy Directive seeks both a harmonisation of capital requirements for all types of financial institutions operating within the European Community as well as extending regulatory coverage to a variety of non-credit market risks.

The EC Capital Adequacy Directive is issued against a background of the community's proposal to grant non-bank investment firms of single licence through the so called investment services directive. It follows on the 1989 decision by the EC to grant banks a single licence to conduct all banking activities throughout the community, including the right to conduct all types of securities activities.

As a condition for this single licence, the EC harmonised capital requirements for banks operating in the community, effectively adopting Basle Committee Capital Adequacy Guidelines as its directive. However, against a background of continuing need to harmonise requirements for banks and non-investment firms, as they increasingly provide the same products in the same market in particular, the underwriting and distribution of securities and trading foreign exchange and derivatives, the EC Capital Adequacy Directive seeks to harmonise prudential standards applicable to all such firms.

The International Organisation of Securities Regulators (IOSCO) is also considering harmonising capital acquirement for non-bank investment firms.

Scope

The EC capital directive does not differentiate between bank and non-bank forms of organisation. It recognises that a firm may engage in trading activities through a variety of organisational structures (refer *Exhibit 40.1*).

Common structures include:

- as a stand alone universal bank (most common in Germany and Switzerland) or as a stand alone non-bank investment firm;
- in a parent-subsidiary format whereby the bank conducts its securities activities through a non-bank investment firm subsidiaries (a common form of structure in the United Kingdom);
- as part of a financial holding company where both the bank and the non-bank investment firm are subsidiaries of a financial holding company (a common form of structure in the United States);
- as part of a mixed activity holding company in a variety of non-financial activities in addition to banking in investment activity are carried out through various subsidiaries of the parent firm (for example, American Express).

The EC Capital Adequacy Directive recognises the increasing similarity between bank and non-bank investment firm activity in that they increasingly provide the same products in the same markets. Accordingly, the Capital Adequacy Directive is designed to cover all firms, irrespective of type.

1. This discussion on the EC Capital Directive draws on Dr Thomas Heurtas (1992) (July).

Exhibit 40.1
Bank/Non-Bank Investment Institutions—Organisation Structures

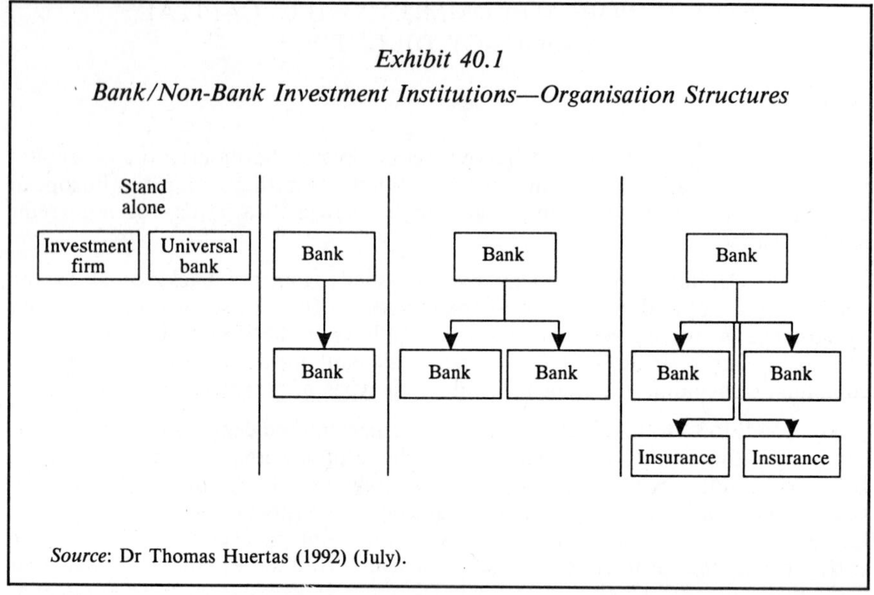

Source: Dr Thomas Huertas (1992) (July).

Capital requirements

The proposed capital requirements are summarised in *Exhibit 40.2*.

Exhibit 40.2
EC Capital Adequacy Directive—Framework

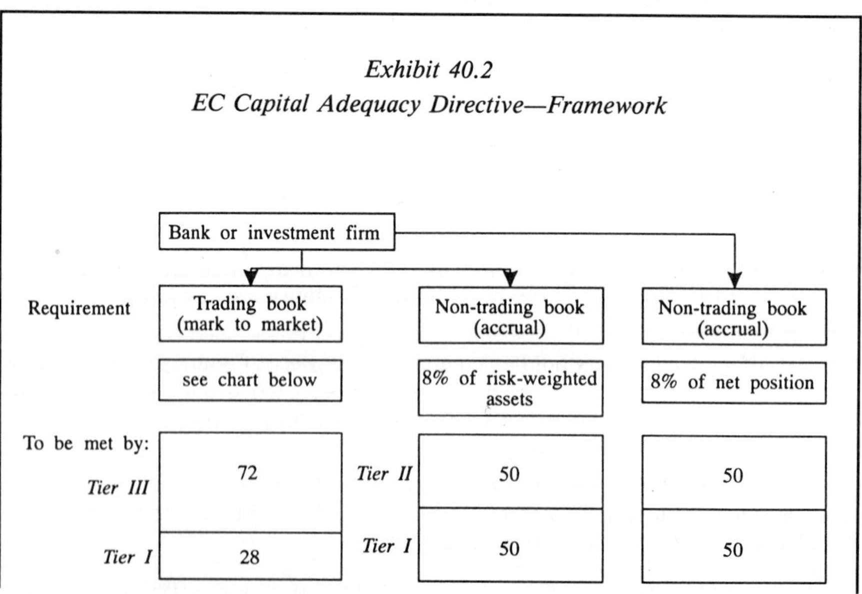

Exhibit 40.2—continued

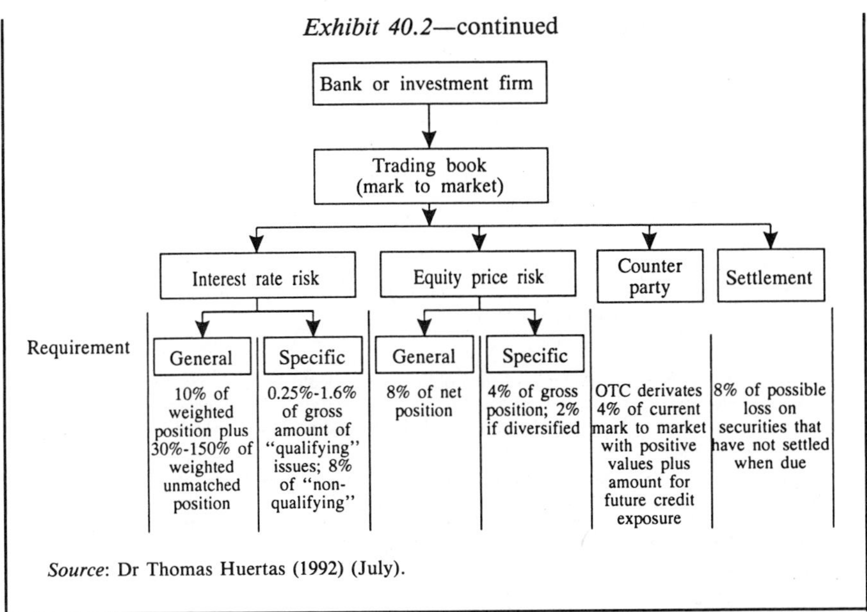

Source: Dr Thomas Huertas (1992) (July).

The major features of the regulatory framework include:

- The principal of the same capital for the same types of risk.
- This approach requires separation of the activities of the institution into two components—a *trading* book and a *non-trading* book.
- The proposal specifically requires capital to be committed to cover market risk on trading activities, although not on non-trading activities.
- An additional type of primary bank capital is introduced. This is short-term subordinated depth (so called Tier III) to complement equity (Tier I) or reserves or long term subordinated debt (Tier II capital).

Details regarding the regulatory structure, including how to define trading books, the degree to which firms may use short-term subordinated debt to satisfy requirements on the trading book etc are still far from settled.

The EC Directive proposes formulas to determine capital charges on interest rate and equity positions. The proposal utilises eight maturity bands, ranging from less than three months to over 20 years which are then weighted according to the credit quality of the exposure (government, other public sector and the rest). Similarly, for underwriting, exposure that exceeds 25% of the total issue must be fully covered by additional capital. If total exposure to one issuer exceeds 25% of the firms capital it must be fully covered by additional capital, which may not be subordinated debt.

IOSCO are considering a similar two tier approach to be used for market and issuer risk for both debt and equity securities: refer *Exhibit 40.3*. Under the proposed IOSCO guidelines, supervisors in individual banking systems will be able to use either the minimum levels that will be calculated under the guidelines (the so called "building block approach") or their own "comprehensive measure", provided they can demonstrate that it consistently demands at least as much capital as the building block approach.

Exhibit 40.3

The Basle Committee/IOSCO—Preliminary Understandings

After the meeting between IOSCO's technical committee and the Basle Committee, the chairmen of the two bodies set out the "preliminary understandings" that had been reached. Below is an extract from the joint statement.

Debt securities

In establishing a proposed standard for holdings of traded debt securities, the discussions led to development of a single methodology for computation of both general market and specific issuer risks. This methodology, called the "building block approach", would be utilised by all supervisors.

Minimum levels of capital and maximum permissible allowances for potentially offsetting positions were defined by the committees, subject to reservation by one country. At the same time, the committees also agreed to allow use of an alternative "duration" methodology that would utilise a somewhat different technique where a supervisor can demonstrate the equivalence of resulting capital charges.

Equity securities

In addressing the measurement of capital for equity positions, the committees recognised that two alternative approaches would be utilised. For bank supervisors and for some securities supervisors, the "building block" methodology for debt would be adapted to equity positions. A general consensus was reached on the respective percentages to be used for the "x" and "y" factors (general and specific risks) applied to gross and net portfolio values, subject to certain reservations by a small number of supervisors.

However, many securities supervisors that have long successfully applied a "comprehensive" methodology would continue to do so. Any supervisor utilising the comprehensive approach would undertake to demonstrate that its specific application of the comprehensive methodology would yield capital requirements that were consistently equal to or greater than the capital that would be required under the building block approach.

Definition of capital

Substantial progress was also made in reaching mutually acceptable definitions of capital. The securities regulators have agreed that securities firms' use of short term subordinated debt, with a "lock-in" clause for capital purposes should be limited to 250% of equity capital. A clear majority of the Basle Committee is prepared to entertain an approach to a definition of capital for market risk purposes of a bank's trading portfolio that would, in economic terms, closely approximate the approach followed by the securities regulators.

Source: David Shirreff (1992) (March).

Discussion

The approach described has the objectives of providing a framework in which banks and securities firms can compete fairly across markets and borders and to ensure that banks hold an appropriate level of capital relative to the risk of their activities.

Financial institutions, whether bank or non-bank, have generally been supportive of the move to harmonise prudential standards that this would ensure the much sought after "level playing field". However, the EC Directive has been criticised, particularly, in relation to the following aspects of the proposal:

- the differentiation between a trading and banking book;
- the approach to risk measurement adopted.

Differentiation between a trading and banking book, while logically tractable, may in practice present significant difficulties. For example, opponents of the directive argue that an underwriting position may become an investment.

Criticism of the measurement of risk is based on the fact that the approach to risk measurement is not related to how such risks are priced and the current capital market conditions.

Major criticisms relate to the fact that the regulatory proposal with their overall division into different types of risk—interest rate risk (which is split into general interest rate risk and specific interest rate risk), foreign exchange risk, equity price risk etc—a so-called building block approach is at variance with the way major market participants, banks, as well as non-bank investment firms, manage market risk. It is argued that these market participants manage market risk in line with modern portfolio theory, giving due recognition to hedging, correlation and diversification.

The portfolio approach would recognise that the value of individual instruments may be influenced by *a number* of different market factors. Conversely, a single market factor can influence the price of many different instruments: see *Exhibit 40.4*. These critics argue that a proper basis for risk measurement would recognise practice and incorporate the following:

- Risk requirements should be based on net exposures rather than gross exposures. For example, firms would determine sensitivity of their portfolios to each of the market factors by netting their exposures across products.
- Correlation as between market factors must be taken into account. In practice, many market factors are correlated and positions are often based on the correlation between market factors which, it is argued, should be recognised in any market risk system.

Exhibit 40.4

Product-Risk Factor Relationship

	Risk Factors				Volatility			
Products/Markets	Spot Forex Level	Interest Rate Domestic	Interest Rate Foreign	Equity Level	Interest Rate	Spot Forex	Interest Rates	Equity
Spot Forex	X							
Forward Forex	X	X	X					
Money Market		X						
FRAs		X						
Interest Rate Swaps		X						
Cross-Currency Swaps	X	X	X					
Caps/Collars		X			X		X	
Swaptions		X			X		X	
Currency Options	X	X	X			X		
Equity				X				
Equity Options		X		X				X

Source: Dr Thomas Huertas (1992) (July).

The most significant element of criticism of the risk measurement system is that it must be set to protect against a consistent and realistic norm for the probable movement in market factors. Critics argue that the proposed directive is predicated on a theory that capital requirements should be high enough to protect the firm against extremely large adverse moves in market factors. This, in turn, implies capital requirements far in excess of what market participants would consider prudent practice. Most market participants, they argue, would set the norm at two standard deviations moves in daily rates, recognising that even this is an overestimate of probable loss, as it assumes that the firm does nothing to change its position, even in the event that market prices move against their existing positions. Critics argue that EC capital adequacy directive measures are based on protecting against moves of six or more standard deviations—an extremely rare event.

An additional criticism of the capital adequacy directive is that requirements for counterparty risk are based on gross amounts of exposure rather than net, even where valid netting agreements are in place.

BIS MARKET RISK GUIDELINES

Framework

In April 1993, the Basle Committee on banking supervision issued a package of supervisory proposals. The package consisted of three separate proposals:

- the supervisory treatment of market risk;
- the supervisory recognition of netting for capital adequacy purposes; and
- measurement of bank's exposure to interest rate risk.

The proposal for recognition of netting is dealt with in Chapter 39.

The proposal on measurement of bank interest rate risk addresses the issue of overall interest rate risk within banking institutions generally. This is distinct from the specific interest rate risks incurred by banks in the context of trading portfolios which are addressed by the market risk guidelines. The primary risk being addressed is the risk that a change in interest rates might adversely affect a bank's financial condition through its effect on all interest-related assets, liabilities and off-balance sheet items, including securities which are not held for trading purposes.

The objective of this paper is to develop a measurement system for bank interest rate risk. The Basle Committee indicated that existing capital requirements are, generally, to be regarded as adequate protection for the degree of interest rate mismatches which the Committee regarded as a normal feature of the business of banking. However, the Committee's proposal provided national authorities with explicit discretion to impose larger capital charges where institutions incur large levels of interest rate risk.

The market risk guidelines which were the centrepiece of the supervisory proposal are fully integrated with the Capital Accord finalised in July 1988 (see discussion in Chapter 38). The objective of the market risk guidelines include:

- Requiring capital to be held against the risk of losses in on- and off- balance sheet positions arising from movements in market prices, interest rates, foreign exchange rates and equity values.
- The proposed capital charge is to constitute a minimum prudential standard for regulated institutions.

- The guidelines are predicated on the basis that capital charges for each class of instruments should be economically equivalent to avoid artificial incentives for one or other class of instrument.

The BIS proposal is similar to the EC Capital Adequacy Directive discussed above and the IOSCO proposals.

The EC Directive is significantly broader covering banks and securities firms predicated on the EC's attempt to create a level playing field between banks and non-banks in Europe. However, in general terms, the methodology of the BIS market risk guidelines are similar to the EC Directive. Where there are significant differences, primarily in the area of foreign exchange risk and equity securities, the BIS standards are stricter than those proposed by the EC Capital Adequacy Directive. The BIS and the EC are working, currently, to achieve closer convergence in these regulatory initiatives.

The BIS has undertaken joint work with IOSCO with a view to developing common minimum charges for banks' and security firms' positions in traded debt secutities, equity securities and related derivative instruments. However, as a result of IOSCO not being able to reach internal agreement, these discussions have not provided the basis for a joint proposal.

The timetable for the BIS market risk guidelines is as follows:

- The guidelines were released for comment in April 1993.
- Comments are anticipated by December 1993.
- Final revised proposal is expected sometime in 1994.
- The guidelines are expected to be introduced and effective end 1996.

General principles

Trading versus banking books

The guidelines differentiate between "trading" and "banking" books. The capital charges proposed for debt securities and equity securities would apply to the current market value item *in the bank's trading books only*. It is important to note that the proposals in respect of foreign exchange risks are designed to apply to the bank's *total* currency position.

Trading positions are defined to encompass the institution's proprietary positions in financial instruments assumed with the intention of:

- speculation;
- hedging trading books;
- securities held for resale;
- positions assumed in order to execute a trade with a customer.

In contrast, the banking book is defined as the non-trading book. The financial/derivative instruments used explicitly to hedge the banking book are also excluded from the scope of the capital charges proposed.

The major issues relating to this segregation include:

- monitoring the allocation of positions between trading books and other accounts;
- the need for supervisors to prevent "gains trading" whereby banks through switching transactions between portfolios can improve their short-term profitability by realising gains and deferring the realisation of losses.

In practice, the distinction between a trading and banking book should, at least in the majority of cases, be non-problematic. Some of the issues related to this distinction are discussed in the context of the EC capital adequacy, directive above. It is probable that specific national supervisory authorities will clarify, over time, the appropriate distinction between the trading and banking books.

Market risk versus credit risk

The interaction of the proposed capital charge for market as distinct from credit risk should be carefully noted. In the case of debt securities and equities held in the trading book, the proposed market risk charges would *substitute* for the credit risk weights presently applied to the business sheet assets.

In contrast, for debt and equity derivatives and for foreign exchange risk, there is no compensating reduction in credit risk charge. Consequently, in respect of these items, a capital charge for market risk would be additive to the existing charge for credit risk in the sense that no offsetting reduction in the credit risk capial charge is proposed.

Building block approach

The proposals for debt securities and equities are based on the so-called "building block" approach.

The central feature of this approach is a differentiation between:

- *Specific risk*—that is, the risk of loss caused by an adverse price movement of a security due principally to factors related to the issuer.
- *General market risk*—that is, the risk of loss caused by an adverse price movement unrelated to any specific security, in other words, a market-wide movement.

Treatment of derivative instruments

A major issue confronting the regulators is the treatment of derivative instruments. The basic approach adopted by the BIS has been to seek the conversion of derivative instruments into positions in the underlying asset, that is, the relevant debt or equity security or currency.

Within this framework, two specific approaches are offered:

- delta weighted basis; or
- alternative, more sophisticated approaches.

Under the delta weighted approach, the delta equivalent of the option position in the underlying asset is to be treated as a position within the basic building block approach.

However, the regulators were aware that this neglects the gamma and volatility risk evident in option positions. The regulators did not outline any formal proposal for additional a capital charge for these risks. One possibility canvassed was a fixed add-on for open option positions and/or high disallowances within the building block methodology for hedge positions (say, a 60% disallowance). The regulators are currently seeking alternative proposals from market participants.

Under the second approach, approved option pricing models could be used to calculate the risks in option positions and related positions in the underlying assets or in other derivatives, according to parameters to be nominated by the regulators. Under this approach, for example, the parameters could be designed to cover interest rate changes up to 1.00% at the short end and 0.6% at the long end (in line with the risk weights used for debt securities) as well as measures of changes in implied volatility of + or − 25% from the current level. The problem with this approach is that it would not be consistent with the building block methodology and would require institutions, utilising this approach, to "carve out" this position from the framework.

An exception to the above framework relates to exchange rated options where the exchange itself sets margin requirements. The BIS Committee noted that some securities regulators set the capital requirement at a level equal to the margin set by the Exchange in circumstances where the supervisor was fully satisfied that this accurately reflects the risk.

For exchange rated options, participants are required to put up initial original margin (5-10% of contract price) plus mark the contract to market on a daily basis posting variation margins. The initial margin is explicitly based on price risk measured according to historical volatility and is regularly reassessed with a view to covering expected market exposure over subsequent trading days.

The BIS Committee expressed concern about linking a capital standard intended for prudential purposes to margin requirements designed to protect exchanges from member default on three grounds:

- That this approach would not ensure equal treatment and could lead to pressure on exchanges to soften margining rules.
- It would create systemic biases as between over-the-counter and exchange traded products as a result of different capital charges applying.
- The potential systemic effects if capital requirements are free to rise sharply in periods of high market volatility.

Exhibit 40.5 summarises the BIS Committee's discussion of options. *Exhibit 40.6* summarises the proposed treatment of interest rate derivatives. *Exhibit 40.7* summarises the proposed treatment of equity derivatives.

Exhibit 40.5

Debt Securities and Equities: Alternative Treatment for Options

1. The Committee believes that there needs to be both a simplified approach for institutions which use purchased options largely to hedge other positions and a more sophisticated approach to be used by those who write options and the major players in the market.

2. It is proposed that institutions doing a limited amount and range of options business could use a simplified approach, as set out below, for particular trades.

Cash position	Option position	Treatment
Long None	Long put or Long call	Position risk would be the market value of the underlying security multiplied by the sum of specific and general market risk charges or the underlying less the amount the option is in the money (if any)[1]
None	Long call or Long put	Position risk would be the lesser of: (i) the market value of the underlying security multiplied by the sum of specific and general market risk charges for the underlying (ii) the market value of the option

3. The more sophisticated approach for use by institutions involved in more complex strategies than those set out above would give allowance for options-hedging for a variety of different trading book instruments. Comments from market participants would be especially welcome

Exhibit 40.5—continued

on how this can be done in a manner which is both sufficiently accurate and acceptable to supervisors and market participants for the purposes of minimum international standards. Two possible methods are being considered.

4. In the first of these, described in paragraph 29 of Section II and paragraph 16 of Section III, options positions would be delta weighted to convert them into positions in the underlying, which would then be treated as normal positions in the basic building block approach. However, because this would neglect the gamma and volatility risk it is proposed that there should be an additional capital charge. One possibility would be to have a fixed add-on for open options positions and/or higher disallowances than assumed in the building block methodology for hedged positions, for example, a 60% disallowance. However, consideration would be given to alternative proposals from the industry.

5. In the second approach, approved options pricing models could be used to calculate the risks in options positions and related positions in the underlying or other derivatives, according to parameters set by the regulators. For example, these parameters would be designed to cover interest rate changes up to 1% at the short end and 0.6% at the long end (in line with the scale set out in Column B of Annex 2) and changes in implied volatility of +/− 25% from the current level. This approach would not be consistent with the building block methodology and would mean institutions having discretion to "carve out" positions from the framework.

6. Currently, for measuring the overall market risk in *exchange traded options*,[2] some securities regulators set the capital requirement at a level equal to the margin set by exchange in circumstances where the supervisor is fully satisfied that this accurately reflects the risk. On most exchanges participants are required to put up initial or original margin (typically in the range 5% to 10% of the contract price) plus any variation margin which results from marking to market the firm's position daily. The margin requirements are explicitly based on price risk measured according to historic volatility and are reassessed daily or sometimes more frequently with a view to covering expected market exposure over the subsequent trading day.

7. The Committee has concerns about tying a capital standard intended for prudential purposes to margin requirements designed to protect exchanges from member defaults. It notes that this would not ensure equal treatment and could lead to pressure on exchanges to soften their margining rules. It also wonders what effects might result from using different systems for OTC and exchange traded products, and from applying different capital charges to different exchanges. Finally, some Committee members are concerned about the systemic effects if capital requirements are free to rise sharply in periods of high market volatility, expressing a strong preference for setting capital at a level which is considered adequate for all market situations.

Notes:

1. For example, if a holder of 100 shares currently valued at $10 each holds an equivalent put option with a strike price of $11, the capital charge would be: $1,000 × 16% (eg, 8% specific plus 8% general market risk) = $160, less the amount the option is in the money ($11 − $10) × 100 = $100, ie, the capital charge would be $60.
2. The same would also apply to exchange traded futures.

Source: (April 1993) The Supervisory Treatment of Market Risks: Consultative Proposal by the Basle Committee on Banking Supervision.

Exhibit 40.6

Summary of Proposed Treatment of Interest Rate Derivatives

Instrument	Specific risk charge	General market risk charge	Possible alternative treatments
Exchange traded future			
—Government security	No	Yes, as two positions[1]	Margin set by exchange

Exhibit 40.6—continued

Instrument	Specific risk charge	General market risk charge	Possible alternative treatments
—Corporate debt security	Yes	Yes, as two positions[1]	Margin set by exchange
—Index on short-term interest rates (eg, LIBOR)	No	Yes, as two positions[1]	Margin set by exchange
OTC forward			
—Government security	No	Yes, as two positions[1]	
—Corporate debt security	Yes	Yes, as two positions[1]	
—Index on short-term interest rates	No	Yes, as two positions[1]	
FRAs	No	Yes, as two positions[1]	
Swaps	None	Yes, as two positions	Sensitivity models
Exchange traded option			
—Government security	No	Yes	Either (a) Simple strategy requiring carve-out of purchased options and their hedges
—Corporate debt security	Yes	Yes	(b) The use of options pricing models to be applied to the whole options book and associated positions
—Index on short-term interest rates	No	Yes	(c) Margin set by exchange
OTC options			
—Government security	No	Yes	Either
—Corporate debt security	Yes	Yes	(a) Simple strategy requiring carve-out of purchased options and their hedges
—Index on short-term interest rates	No	Yes	(b) The use of options pricing models to be applied to the whole options book and associated positions.

Note:
1. Or as a single position in the underlying.

Source: (April 1993) The Supervisory Treatment of Market Risks: Consultative Proposal by the Basle Committee on Banking Supervision.

Exhibit 40.7

Summary of Proposed Treatment of Equity Derivatives

Instrument	Specific risk (x)	General market risk (y)	Possible alternative treatments
Exchange-traded future			
—Individual equity	Yes	Yes, as underlying	Margin set by exchange
—Index	2%	Yes, as underlying	Margin set by exchange

Exhibit 40.7—continued

Instrument	Specific risk (x)	General market risk (y)	Possible alternative treatments
OTC forward			
—Individual equity	Yes	Yes, as underlying	
—Index	2%	Yes, as underlying	
Exchange-traded option			
—Individual equity	Yes	Yes	Either
—Index	2%	Yes	(a) Simple strategy requiring carve-out of purchased options and their hedges (b) The use of options pricing models to be applied to the whole options book and associated positions (c) Margin set by exchange
OTC option			
—Individual equity	Yes	Yes	Either
—Index	2%	Yes	(a) Simple strategy requiring carve-out of purchased options and their hedges (b) The use of options pricing models to be applied to the whole options book and associated positions.

Source: (April 1993) The Supervisory Treatment of Market Risks: Consultative Proposal by the Basle Committee on Banking Supervision.

In practical terms, the treatment of derivative instruments would be as follows:

- *Debt derivatives*
  - — futures/forwards are to be treated as combinations of short and long positions;
  - — interest rate swaps are to be treated as two notional positions in securities, one fixed rate and one floating rate;
  - — currency swaps are to be treated as two notional positions, one in each relevant currency;
  - — commodity/equity/hybrid swaps are to be unbundled and to be treated as two notional positions in the relevant currency and in the relevant commodity and equity;
  - — for exchange traded and over-the-counter options, the position risk is to equate to the delta of the option position or a fixed add-on or specific risk parameters (in the case of over-the-counter options) and/or exchange margins (in the case of exchange traded instruments).
- *Equity derivatives*
  - — forwards on equities are to be treated as notional equity positions reported at:
    - * forwards on individual equities at current market prices
    - * for futures on market indexes at the mark-to-market value
  - — equity swaps are to be treated as noted above;

— equity options, whether exchange traded or over-the-counter are to be treated the same as debt options.

- *Foreign exchange derivatives*
  — forward foreign exchange positions are to be valued at spot rates, utilising forward exchange rates or by taking the net present value of forward positions;
  — currency swaps are to be treated as noted above;
  — currency options will receive the same treatment as debt and equity options.

Capital charge

Minimum capital requirement

Under the proposed BIS regulatory scheme, each regulated bank would need to monitor and report the position outstanding for each category of risk against which a capital requirement is applicable. The minimum capital requirements would be made up as follows:

- credit risk requirements for the banking business (loans, investments, etc) and the counterparty risk on over-the-counter derivatives (this would be based on the July 1988 BIS Capital Accord);
- capital charge for debt and securities in the trading portfolio (as prescribed by the BIS Market Risk Guidelines); and
- the capital charge for foreign exchange risk (as prescribed by the BIS Market Risk Guidelines).

In satisfying the capital requirements of the overall capital charge as calculated above, the BIS Market Risk Guidelines introduce a new concept of capital—"Tier III Capital".

The concept of Tier III Capital is not favoured by the BIS which would prefer the retention of the current definition of "capital" in the BIS Capital Accord to cover all bank capital requirements. The concept of Tier III Capital is required for a number of complex reasons:

- BIS acknowledges the capital requirements for market risk are more volatile than traditional bank capital.
- Securities firms are allowed to include a high proportion of short-term subordinated debt and inclusion of Tier III Capital assists in convergence between capital requirements of banks and securities houses.
- The fact that many banks affected by the BIS proposal would also be operating under the provisions of the EC Capital Adequacy Directive which permits Tier III Capital dictates that the inclusion of this concept in the BIS Market Risk Guideline facilitates convergence of regulations for banks active in this important geographical area.

Tier III Capital can be defined as "term subordinated debt permitted, at the discretion of national supervisors, to meet capital requirements for market risk". Tier III Capital will be eligible, if circumstances demand, to become part of an institution's permanent capital and, therefore, be available to absorb losses. These characteristics are, for practical purposes, satisfied where the instruments meet a number of minimal qualifications:

- It is unsecured, subordinated and fully paid up.
- It has an original maturity of at least two years.

- It is not repayable before the agreed repayment date unless the supervisor agrees.
- It is subject to a "lock-in" clause whereby it is stipulated that no interest or principal is payable under the instrument if capital allotted to the trading book for debt and equity securities would fall below a threshold 20% above the minimum required capital laid down in the BIS Market Risk Guidelines.

Tier III Capital complements existing Tier I and Tier II Capital. The major differences between Tier III subordinated debt and subordinated debt currently permitted as a subset of Tier II Capital in the 1988 Accord are:

- The minimum original maturity is shorter (two years as against five years).
- The debt is valued at par whereas in the 1988 Accord it is amortised over the last five years of the life of the subordinated issue.
- Tier III Capital has the lock-in feature with the restriction on payment if allotted capital falls below an early warning level of 20% above the minimum capital charge.

The BIS has also proposed that a number of limitations be applicable to the use of Tier III Capital:

- Tier III Capital can only be used to support market risk for debt and securities trading books. Tier I and II Capital must still be available to support market risk for foreign exchange and credit and counterparty risk.
- Tier III Capital is to be limited to 250% of Tier I Capital allocated to support securities trading book risks (this implies that a minimum of about 28.5% of trading book risks would need to be supported by Tier I Capital not required to support risk for the remainder of the book).
- Tier II Capital can be substituted for Tier III insofar as overall 1988 Accord provisions are not breached. That is, total Tier II Capital is less than or equal to Tier I Capital and long-term subordinated debt cannot exceed 50% of Tier I Capital.
- Reflecting conflicting views within the BIS, a further restriction is under consideration whereby Tier II plus Tier III Capital would not be able to exceed Tier I Capital.

Importantly, national supervisors have the discretion to refuse the use of short-term subordinated debt to individual banks or for their banking systems generally.

Miscellaneous issues

Two other general principles require comment:

- reporting cycle
- the issue of consolidated supervision.

Under the proposed guidelines, regular reporting would take place at specified intervals (quarterly). However, regulated banks would be expected to manage the market risk of their trading portfolio to meet the minimum capital requirement on a continuous basis, in practice, at the close of business each day. In addition, supervisors would be vigilant to ensure that the banks did not "window dress" by showing significantly lower market risks on reporting dates and would also be expected to ensure that intra-day exposures were not excessive.

The BIS has recommended that all transactions be captured on a trade day basis, although national authorities have the discretion to allow reporting on the basis of settlement dates, at least, where this is on a continuous basis if it was convinced that the use of settlement date basis would not produce a material difference.

The proposed supervisory framework will apply on a consolidated group-wide basis. Under this approach, group exposures will be the focus of regulation with national supervisors having the discretion to permit global consolidated risk reporting irrespective of which location the transaction is booked.

The consolidation principles will need to be adjusted for the following:

- obstacles to repatriation of profit from a foreign subsidiary;
- potential local tax liability; and
- operations where a bank's ownership is less than 100%.

Where these factors exist, consolidation would not be permitted with individual positions having to be separately taken into the measurement system.

In addition, all supervisory authorities would retain the right to continue to monitor the market risk of individual entities on a non-consolidated basis to ensure that significant imbalances within a larger group did not exist on an unsupervised basis.

The BIS Committee acknowledged the potential to reduce risk positions by passing positions to affiliates in later time zones. However, the Committee cautioned that it would require supervisors to be particularly vigilant to ensure that banks do not pass positions on reporting dates to affiliates whose positions escape measurement or cross the international date line.

Debt securities

Overview

The BIS Market Risk Guidelines as they affect securities cover the risk of holding fixed and floating rate instruments as well as other financial instruments which demonstrate similar price behaviour, such as non-convertible fixed rate preference shares or convertible debt, in certain circumstances.

The BIS Committee acknowledged that traded mortgage securities and mortgage derivative products possess unique characteristics because of the risk of prepayment and propose that, at least for the time being, no common treatment be applied with the securities to be dealt on a national basis by individual supervisors.

Securities subject to repurchase of securities lending agreements are to be treated as if it was still owned by the lender of the security, that is, consistent with other securities positions.

Under the proposed framework for debt securities, the minimum capital requirement embodies two separately calculated charges:

- a specific risk charge applicable to each security;
- a general market risk which attempts to measure the interest rate risk in the portfolio.

Specific risk charge

The specific risk charge is based on three categories of instruments:

- government;
- qualifying;
- other.

Exhibit 40.8 sets out the specific risk for each of the three categories together with precise definitions of each of the terms.

Exhibit 40.8
Specific Risk

It is proposed that the specific risk would be graduated in five broad categories as follows:

government	0.00%
qualifying	0.25% (residual maturity six months or less) 1.00% (residual maturity between six and 24 months) 1.60% (residual maturity exceeding 24 months)
other	8.00%

The category "government" would include all forms of government[1] paper including bonds, treasury bills and other short-term instruments, but national authorities would reserve the right to apply a specific risk weight to securities issued by certain foreign governments, especially to securities denominated in a currency other than that of the issuing government.

"Qualifying" would apply to issues which meet the criteria set out in the following paragraph.[2] Three different weights are proposed depending on the residential maturity of the issue in question. This is because the uncertainty about credit-worthiness increases with the life of the security, as reflected in the fact that spreads between corporate and government securities tend to widen along the maturity spectrum.

Qualifying items would include securities issued by public sector entities and multilateral development banks, plus other securities that are:

- rated investment grade[3] by at least two credit agencies specified by the relevant supervisor; or
- rated investment grade by one rating agency and not less than investment grade by any other rating agency specified by the supervisor (subject to supervisory oversight); or
- unrated, but deemed to be of comparable investment quality by the bank or securities firm, *and* the issuer has securities listed on a recognised stock exchange (subject to supervisory approval).

The supervisors would be responsible for monitoring the application of these qualifying criteria, particularly in relation to the last criterion where the initial classification is essentially left to the reporting institutions.

8. National authorities would also have discretion to include within the qualifying category debt securities issued by banks in countries which are implementing the Basle Accord, subject to the express understanding that supervisors in such countries would undertake prompt remedial action if a bank fails to meet the capital standards set forth in the Accord. Similarly, national authorities would have discretion to include within the qualifying category debt securities issued by securities firms that are subject to equivalent rules.

9. The "other" category would receive the same specific risk charge as a private sector borrower under the Basle Accord, that is, 8%. No maturity breakdown is proposed within this category of specific risk.

Notes:

1. Including, at national discretion, local and regional governments subject to a zero credit risk weight in the Basle Accord.
2. One country has expressed a general reserve on the definition of the qualifying category.
3. Eg, rate Baa or higher by Moody's and BBB or higher by Standard and Poor's.

Source: (April 1993) The Supervisory Treatment of Market Risks: Consultative Proposal by the Basle Committee on Banking Supervision.

The definitional framework creates a three tier structure:

- government;
- qualifying (that is, public sector entities, multi-lateral development banks, rated or deemed investment grade securities); and

- other securities.

Two controversial issues were:

- high yield issues (or junk) bonds;
- convertible securities.

In the case of high yield securities, the BIS Committee acknowledged the possibility of determining a specific higher risk charge for these types of securities which often have equity-like characteristics. The BIS proposed that:

- a specific high risk charge can be applied to high yield securities at the discretion of national supervisors; and/or
- no rights of offset for the purposes of general market risk be allowed between such securities and other debt securities.

In the case of convertible bonds, the BIS proposed that they would be treated as debt securities if they trade like debt securities (presumably, where the equity option element has little value) and as equities if they trade like equities.

In respect of the specific risk charge, rights of offset are allowable under specific conditions. Offsetting is restricted to matching positions in the *identical issue* (including positions in derivatives). However, even if the issuer is the same, no offsetting is permitted between different issues given differences in coupon rates, call features etc which dictate that prices may diverge in the short run.

General market risk

Basis

Capital requirements for general market risk are designed to capture the risk of loss arising from changes in market interest rate. The measures are based on modified duration of an 8% pa bond utilising two standard deviations of one month volatility. The basis requires that zero coupon securities (less than 3% coupon) must be converted into equivalent normal coupon (that is, 8%) bond equivalents.

Within this framework, the BIS guidelines proposed two possible measures of risk measurement: the standard method and alternative customised approaches.

Standard method

There are three components to this particular approach:

- the maturity ladder;
- provision for vertical offsetting;
- provision for horizontal offsetting.

The standard method requires long or short positions in debt securities and debt-related derivative instruments to be inserted into a maturity ladder comprising 13 maturity bands. *Exhibit 40.9* sets out the time bands and the risk weights applicable to each.

Fixed rate instruments are to be allocated according to the residual term to maturity and floating rate instruments according to the next repricing dates. Opposite positions of the same amount in the same issues (but not different issues by the same issuer), whether actual or notional, incur no interest rate risk and could therefore be omitted from the reporting framework. Similarly, closely matched swaps, forwards, futures and FRAs which meet certain conditions set out below are also omitted.

Separate reporting maturity ladders are required for each currency in which the regulated institution has positions.

Exhibit 40.9
Debt Securities: Risk Weights

The table below sets out the general risk weights which are proposed for the net open positions (long or short) in each time band under the standard method.

Coupon 3% or more	Coupon less than 3%	Duration weight (A)	Assumed change in yields (B)	Risk weight (A) × (B)
up to 1 month	up to 1 month	0.00	1.00	0.00%
1 to 3 months	1 to 3 months	0.20	1.00	0.20%
3 to 6 months	3 to 6 months	0.40	1.00	0.40%
6 to 12 months	6 to 12 months	0.70	1.00	0.70%
1 to 2 years	1.0 to 1.9 years	1.40	0.90	1.25%
2 to 3 years	1.9 to 2.8 years	2.20	0.80	1.75%
3 to 4 years	2.8 to 3.6 years	3.00	0.75	2.25%
4 to 5 years	3.6 to 4.3 years	3.65	0.75	2.75%
5 to 7 years	4.3 to 5.7 years	4.65	0.70	3.25%
7 to 10 years	5.7 to 7.3 years	5.80	0.65	3.75%
10 to 15 years	7.3 to 9.3 years	7.50	0.60	4.50%
15 to 20 years	9.3 to 10.6 years	8.75	0.60	5.25%
over 20 years	10.6 to 12 years	10.00	0.60	6.00%
	12 to 20 years	13.50	0.60	8.00%
	over 20 years	21.00	0.60	12.50%

For those who wish to apply the alternative method, slightly different time bands based on duration would apply:

Zone 1	Zone 2	Zone 3
up to 1 month	1.0 to 1.8 years	3.3 to 4.0 years
1 to 3 months	1.8 to 2.6 years	4.0 to 5.2 years
3 to 6 months	2.6 to 3.3 years	5.2 to 6.8 years
6 to 12 months		6.8 to 8.6 years
		8.6 to 9.9 years
		9.9 to 11.3 years
		11.3 to 16.6 years
		over 16.6 years

Source: (April 1993) The Supervisory Treatment of Market Risks: Consultative Proposal by the Basle Committee on Banking Supervision.

Once interest rate risk positions are inserted in the maturity ladder, long and short positions within each time band can be offset resulting in a single short or long position for each band. This process is referred to as "vertical offsetting".

However, the BIS guidelines call for vertical disallowance in order to adjust the degree of offset for:

- non-identical maturities *within the time band*; and
- different instruments with the same maturity (that is, basis risk).

The vertical disallowance factor to be applied is 10%. This vertical disallowance factor is applied to one side of the weighted matched position within each time band. For example, if the sum of the weighted longs in a time band is \$100m and the sum of the weighted shorts \$90m, the vertical disallowance for that time band would be 10% of \$90m (that is, \$9m).

The outcome of this process of vertical offsetting and vertical disallowance is to produce two sets of weighted positions:

- vertical offset, that is, net short or long position in each time band; and
- a vertical disallowance amount (which has no sign).

Once the process of vertical offsetting and vertical disallowance factors have been determined, it is necessary to undertake two specific tiers of "horizontal offsetting".

The concept of horizontal offsetting seeks to recognise offsets across the maturity spectrum based on the observed correlation of interest rate movements across the yield curve. However, full offsets are not allowed reflecting the fact that this correlation is less than perfect. This non-allowable horizontal offsetting adjustment is known as the horizontal offset disallowance factor.

Horizontal offsetting is undertaken in two stages:

- At the first stage, the net positions within each of three nominated time bands are offset. The relevant time bands are 0-1 year, 1-4 years and longer than four years.
- At the second stage, the net positions in different time bands are offset.

Exhibit 40.10 sets out the process of horizonal offsetting and nominates the time bands and the horizontal disallowance factors both within the time zone between adjacent zones and between non-adjacent zones.

Exhibit 40.10

Debt Securities: Horizontal Offsetting

The proposal groups time bands into three zones as indicated below.

Partial offsetting would be permitted between weighted long and short positions in each zone, subject to the matched portion attracting a disallowance factor that is part of the capital charge. The disallowance proposed within zone 1 is 40%, applied to one side of the matched amount. Within zones 2 and 3 the disallowance would be 30%.

The remaining net position in each zone would be carried over and offset against opposite positions in other zones, where the process is repeated. The proposed disallowance factor between adjacent zones is 40%. The disallowance between non-adjacent zones would be 150%, meaning that 25% of a matched position would be regarded as hedged.

	Time band	**Within the zone**	**Between adjacent zones**	**Between zones 1 and 3**
	0-1 month			
Zone 1	1-3 months	40%		
	3-6 months			
	6-12 months		40%	
	1-2 years			
Zone 2	2-3 years	30%		150%
	3-4 years			
	4-5 years		40%	
	5-7 years			
Zone 3	7-10 years			
	10-15 years	30%		
	15-20 years			
	over 20 years			

Source: (April 1993) The Supervisory Treatment of Market Risks: Consultative Proposal by the Basle Committee on Banking Supervision.

The horizontal offset disallowance factors are expressed as a fraction of the smaller of the offsetting positions. Disallowances proposed result in a greater recognition of hedging for offsets taking place within the same zone than for offsets between different zones.

The resulting horizonal offset disallowances are added to the disallowances for vertical offset already identified and to the absolute amount of the residual net short or long position within the total portfolio. The total generated is the market risk charge for the portfolio which, in conjunction with the specific risk charges for each issue, total the institution's overall capital requirement under the standard measurement method. An example of the calculations required is set out in *Exhibit 40.11.*

Exhibit 40.11

Debt Securities: Sample Market Risk Calculation

Time band	Issuer	Position	Specific risk Weight(%)	Specific risk Charge	General market risk Weight(%)	General market risk Charge
0-1 month	Treasury	5,000	0.00	0.00	0.00	0.00
1-3 months	Treasury	5,000	0.00	0.00	0.20	10.00
3-6 months	Qual Corp	4,000	0.25	10.00	0.40	16.00
6-12 months	Qual Corp	(7,500)	1.00	75.00	0.75	(52.50)
1-2 years	Treasury	(2,500)	0.00	0.00	1.25	(31.25)
2-3 years	Treasury	2,500	0.00	0.00	1.75	43.75
3-4 years	Treasury	2,500	0.00	0.00	2.25	56.25
3-4 years	Qual Corp	(2,000)	1.60	32.00	2.25	(45.00)
4-5 years	Treasury	1,500	0.00	0.00	2.75	41.25
5-7 years	Qual Corp	(1,000)	1.60	16.00	3.25	(32.50)
7-10 years	Treasury	(1,500)	0.00	0.00	3.75	(56.25)
10-15 years	Treasury	(1,500)	0.00	0.00	4.50	(67.50)
10-15 years	Non Qual	1,000	8.00	80.00	4.50	45.00
15-20 years	Treasury	1,500	0.00	0.00	5.25	78.75
> 20 years	Qual Corp	1,000	1.60	16.00	6.00	60.00
Specific risk				229.00		
Residual general market risk						66.00

Calculation of capital charge

1. Specific risk

	Charge
	229.00

2. Vertical offsets within same time bands

Time band	Longs	Shorts	Residual*	Offset	Disallowance	Charge
3-4 years	56.25	(45.00)	11.25	45.00	10.00%	4.50
10-15 years	45.00	(67.50)	(22.50)	45.00	10.00%	4.50

3. Horizontal offsets within same time zones

	Longs	Shorts	Residual*	Offset	Disallowance	Charge
Zone 1						
0-1 month	0.00					
1-3 months	10.00					
3-6 months	16.00					
6-12 months		(52.50)				
Total						
Zone 1	26.00	(52.50)	(26.50)	26.00	40.00%	10.40

Exhibit 40.11—continued

Zone 2						
1-2 years		(31.25)				
2-3 years	43.75					
3-4 years	11.25					
Total						
Zone 2	55.00	(31.25)	23.75	31.25	30.00%	9.38

* Residual amount carried forward for additional offsetting as appropriate

	Longs	**Shorts**	**Residual#**	Offset	Disallowance	Charge
Zone 3						
4-5 years	41.25					
5-7 years		(32.50)				
7-10 years		(56.25)				
10-15 years		(22.50)				
15-20 years	78.75					
> 20 years	60.00					
Total						
Zone 3	180.00	(111.25)	68.75	111.25	30.00%	33.38

4. Horizontal offsets between time zones

	Longs	**Shorts**	**Residual***	**Offset**	**Disallowance**	**Charge**
Zone 1 & Zone 2	23.75	(26.50)	(2.75)	23.75	40.00%	9.50
Zone 1 & Zone 3	68.75	(2.75)	66.00	2.75	150.00%	4.12

5. Total capital charge

Specific risk	229.00
Vertical disallowances	9.00
Horizontal disallowances	
(offsets within same time zones)	53.16
(offsets between time zones)	13.62
Residual general market risk after all offsets	66.00
Total	370.78

Residual amount carried forward for additional offsetting as appropriate.

Source: (April 1993) The Supervisory Treatment of Market Risks: Consultative Proposal by the Basle Committee on Banking Supervision.

The alternative method

Under this approach, institutions with superior capabilities could, with the relevant national supervisor's consent, utilise a more accurate method of measuring duration by calculating the price sensitivity of each position separately, taking into account the exact coupon of the bond (as distinct from the assumed 8% rate) and calculate duration according to the precise residual maturity of the instrument rather than the midpoint of a time band. The BIS Committee indicated that it would be acceptable for this alternative method to be utilised at least where it could be demonstrated that it produced results which are consistently equivalent with the standard method.

The BIS Committee nominated that the following processes should be followed to avoid production of any systematic biases:

- The institution would first calculate the price sensitivity of each instrument in terms of a change in interest rates of between 0.6 and 1.0% depending on the maturity of the instrument (using the same scale as that nominated in *Exhibit 40.9*).

- The resulting sensitivity measures would then be slotted into a duration-based ladder with 15 time bands as set out in *Exhibit 40.9.*
- Long and short positions in each time band would be subject to the 10% vertical disallowance.
- The net positions in each time band would be carried forward for horizontal offsetting subject to the disallowances applicable under the standard method.

The BIS Committee acknowledged that there may be some justification for using a lower vertical disallowance at 10% for the alternative method in recognition of the greater accuracy of this approach, although the vertical disallowance was also designed to capture basis risk which would still be present despite the more accurate maturity ladder.

Debt derivatives

As noted above, the basic concept underlying the treatment of debt derivatives is the creation of equivalent positions in the underlying asset. However, three specific issues require comment:

- allowable offsetting of matched positions;
- specific risk;
- general market risk.

The BIS guidelines allow offsetting of matched positions under specific circumstances:

- Matched positions in a futures contract and its underlying assets can be offset except where the futures contract comprises a range of deliverable instruments.
- Opposite positions in the same category of instrument can be matched and offset. The specific tolerances of maturity matching are specified.
  - *Futures contracts*: identical products which mature within seven days of each other.
  - *Swaps/FRAs*: matching an offset position requires that the reference rate be identical with the coupon rate closely matched (10-15 basis points allowance).
  - *Swaps/FRAs/forwards*: the next interest fixing date or, for fixed coupon positions or forwards, the residual maturity would need to correspond within the following limits:
    - less than one month—same day
    - between one month and one year—within seven days
    - over one year—within 30 days.

The BIS Committee acknowledged alternative approaches for sophisticated institutions with large derivatives portfolios could use a sensitivity model to calculate the positions to be included in the maturity models. Under this approach, a large swap book may be treated as an internally offset portfolio with only the *net position* being inserted into the maturity ladder within the building approach.

While the BIS Committee believes this would more closely capture the true risk in large derivative portfolios, it indicated that such models could only be allowed if:

- the relevant national supervisor was fully satisfied with the accuracy of the system being used;

- the positions calculated were fully reflective of the sensitivity of the cash flows to interest rate changes;
- the positions were denominated in the same currency.

The guidelines, as presently structured, do not include a specific risk charge for debt derivatives. The only specific risk charge is the normal credit/counterparty capital charge applicable under the 1988 Capital Accord. However, in the case of futures and options contracts where the underlying asset is a debt security or an index representing a basket of debt securities, a specific risk charge is applicable according to the credit risk of the issuer, consistent with the specific risk charges nominated in *Exhibit 40.8*.

The general market risk of debt derivatives is treated in the same manner as for cash position, subject only to an exemption for fully or very closely matched positions in identical instruments as noted above.

Equity securities

Specific versus market risk

The minimum capital standard in respect of equity securities covers the risk of holding or taking positions in equities in the trading account. All securities which exhibit market behaviour similar to equities are included. Instruments covered include common stocks, whether voting or non-voting equity warrants, convertible securities that behave like equities, commitments and other rights to buy or sell equity securities in limited partnership interests. Equity derivatives are also covered as discussed below. Non-convertible preferred shares or other instruments which bear characteristics similar to debt instruments are specifically excluded.

The BIS in stating its guidelines specifically invited proposals from market participants regarding the framework of regulation because of the "difficulty of structuring common rules that would adequately cover the price risk in different equity markets".

The overall regulation is consistent with the overall building block approach. It seeks to cover both specific risk, that is, the risk associated with holding a long or short position in an individual equity, and general market risk, that is, holding a long or short position in the market as a whole.

The minimum capital standard is expressed as follows:

$$x + y$$

where x is equal to the specific risk and y refers to the general market risk.

The capital charge is determined as follows:

- x is applied to the reporting institution's gross equity position, that is the sum of all long and/or short equity positions, and is applied at the rate of 8%.
- y is applied to the difference between the sum of long and the short position, that is, the overall net position in equity market, also at the rate of 8%.

The BIS Committee acknowledged that the criteria for the determination of the x factor for specific risk needs to reflect the diversification of the portfolio and the extent to which it contains liquid and marketable stocks.

The proposals acknowledge that a lower x factor could be applicable for major institutions whose portfolios are liquid and diversified. However, it is difficult to define liquidity and diversification in a manner establishing a common minimum standard. The BIS Committee has invited comment on specifying adequate common criteria for liquidity and diversification.

However, the Committee has cautioned that it is important to ensure that a relatively high x factor applies unless the portfolio is both liquid and well diversified. Accordingly, in the absence of any such assurances, the appropriate x factor will be 8%.

National supervisors will be allowed discretion to determine their own criteria for liquid and diversified portfolios. However, even where such criteria are met, x will be set not lower than 4% with a minimum of 8% applicable to portfolios of stocks that fail to meet the liquidity and diversification test.

Exhibit 40.12 illustrates the calculation of capital acquired for a range of hypothetical equity portfolios which qualify for a 4% (x factor) and 8% (y factor) capital charge.

Exhibit 40.12

Equities: Illustration of x plus y Methodology

Under the proposed two-part calculation described in Section 3 there would be separate requirements for the position in each individual equity (that is, the gross position) and for the net position in the market as a whole. The table below illustrates how the system would work for a range of hypothetical portfolios, assuming a capital charge of 4% for the gross positions and 8% for the net positions.

Sum of long positions	Sum of short positions	Gross position (sum of cols 1 & 2)	4% of gross	Net position (difference between cols 1 & 2)	8% of net	Capital required (gross + net)
100	0	100	4	100	8	12
100	25	125	5	75	6	11
100	50	150	6	50	4	10
100	75	175	7	25	2	9
100	100	200	8	0	0	8
75	100	175	7	25	2	9
50	100	150	6	50	4	10
25	100	125	5	75	6	11
0	100	100	4	100	8	12

Source: (April 1993) The Supervisory Treatment of Market Risks: Consultative Proposal by the Basle Committee on Banking Supervision.

Equity derivatives

As noted above, the treatment of equity derivatives is predicated on converting the derivative instruments into the delta equivalent of the underlying asset. The detailed classification of such instruments is considered above.

In calculating the capital charge and specifically measuring the specific and general market risk factors, matched positions in each indentical issue in each market may be fully offset, resulting in a single net short or long position on which the x and y charge will be applicable. This encompasses derivative positions such that a future in a given equity may be offset against an opposite cash position in the same equity.

However, where the derivative relates to an index, specific risk, that is, the risk of divergence from the general equity market movements, is less than for a random sample of equities and a lower x factor is justifiable. The Committee proposed that a standard x factor of 2% should be applied to the net position in an index comprising a diversified portfolio reflecting the fact that main stocks traded can move against the market. National supervisory authorities were delegated the task of determining criteria such that the treatment applied only to well diversified indexes and not to sectoral indexes.

Special factors apply to equity arbitrage. Equity arbitrage would take one of the following forms:

- *Intracontract spreads*—where an institution takes opposite positions in exactly the same index as at different dates.
- *Index spreads*—where an institution takes opposite positions in different but similar indexes at the same date.
- *Cash/futures positions*—where an institution arbitrages the index futures against a cash basket of securities.

The BIS guidelines proposed that deliberate arbitrage strategies can be removed from the building block process provided the following criteria can be satisfied.

- The transaction has been deliberately entered into and separately controlled.
- The basket of stocks represents at least 90% of the market value of the index.
- There is a minimum capital requirement of 4%, that is, 2% of the gross value of the positions on each side to reflect divergence and execution risks. This is applicable even if all securities comprising the index were held in identical proportions.
- Any excess values of securities over the value of the basket is treated as a normal long or short equity position.

Foreign exchange risk

Overview

The Market Risk Guidelines in respect of foreign exchange risk deal with open foreign exchange risk positions. The guidelines do not deal with supervisory requirements for defining and limiting undue concentrations of currency positions or counterparty exposures.

The foreign exchange risk capital requirements cover the following types of transactions:

- The net spot currency position—all asset items less all liability items, including accrued interests, denominated in the relevant currency.
- The net forward position—that is, all amounts to be received less all amounts to be paid under forward foreign exchange transactions, including currency futures and the principal on currency swaps not included in the spot position.
- Guarantees and other similar instruments—where there is certainty that the obligation will be called and is likely to be unrecoverable.
- Net future income/expense not yet accrued but already fully hedged (at the discretion of the reporting institution).
- The net delta or delta based equivalent of the total book of foreign currency option (or an alternative measure of the risk of the currency option positions).
- Any other items representing a profit or loss in foreign currencies.

The BIS Committee considered trading by banks in gold and precious metals as an extension of foreign exchange trading and, pending future development of specific capital requirements for commodities, precious metal positions are to be included within the scope of foreign exchange capital requirements. Where precious metal positions are included, existing credit risk related requirements in respect of long positions under the 1988 Capital Accord are not applicable.

In the case of composite currencies such as the ECU the position can be separately reported, although, for measuring the bank's open positions, it may either be treated as a currency in its own right or split into its component parts on a consistent basis. Two specific aspects of the overall foreign exchange risk capital scheme require comment:

- Treatment of interest, other income and expenses:

  Interest accrued, that is, earned, but not yet received, would be included as a position as would accrued expenses. Unearned but expected future interest would be excluded unless the amounts are certain and the banks have taken the opportunity to hedge them.

- The measurement of forward currency positions:

  Forward currency positions would normally be valued in one of three ways:

  — at current spot market exchange rates;

  — utilising forward exchange rates to measure positions reflecting current interest rate differentials which would normally be taken into account in measuring a bank's interest rate exposure; or

  — the forward positions would be discounted to net present value to allow recognition that cash flows occurring at different future dates have different values if measured in terms of their present value to the bank.

Treatment of structural positions

A specific regime in respect of "structural positions" is introduced.

The BIS Committee recognised that a matched currency position, while it protects a bank against loss from movements in exchange rates, does not necessarily protect its capital adequacy ratios. If a bank has its capital denominated in a domestic currency and has a portfolio of matched foreign currency assets and liabilities, its capital adequacy ratio tends to decline if the domestic currency depreciates.

Consequently, by running a short position in the domestic currency, the bank can protect its capital adequacy ratio, although the position shows a loss as the domestic currency appreciates.

The BIS Committee proposed that supervisors be permitted to allow banks to protect their capital adequacy ratio through deliberate hedging action, provided each of the following conditions are satisfied:

- The position is structural, that is non-dealing, under precise definitions to be set by individual national supervisors.
- The national supervisor would need to be satisfied that the structural position does no more than protect the bank's capital adequacy ratio.
- Any exclusion of the position would need to be applied in a consistent manner with the treatment of the hedge remaining the same with the life of the assets or other items.

The same treatment can be applied to positions related to items that are deducted from a bank's capital when calculating its capital base.

Measurement of foreign exchange risk

The BIS capital guidelines on foreign exchange risk entail a trade-off between simplicity and accuracy. The BIS acknowledged that there was a case for taking into account the correlations between exchange rate relationships and differing volatilities between currencies but that this would require a complex measurement system which might be unduly burdensome. Accordingly, the BIS proposes a choice between two alternative measures at supervisory discretion:

- a shorthand method;
- a more complex simulation method.

The simulation method would only be available to banks which can satisfy their national supervisors as to the adequacy of their measurement and control systems and their access to the necessary data. An overriding concern is the two methods are intended to deliver broadly equivalent capital requirements for a well diversified portfolio of foreign exchange positions of average riskiness.

The shorthand method

Under this approach, the net open position is measured as follows:

net open positions = sum of the short positions or sum of the long positions, whichever is the greater; plus the total of each net position (short or long) in any precious metal, regardless of size.

A capital requirement of 8% of the net open position as calculated above is charged.

The underlying assumptions of this approach include:

- Some, albeit not perfect, correlation between currencies. Cross-currency positions taken are not unduly penalised nor given undue preference.
- No correlation is recognised across precious metals reflecting the price volatility of these commodities which to the BIS Committee justified a more conservative treatment.

Exhibit 40.13 sets out an example of utilising the shorthand measure to calculate the capital requirement in respect of foreign exchange risk.

Exhibit 40.13

Example of the Shorthand Measure of Foreign Exchange Risk

Once a bank has calculated its net position in each foreign currency, it would convert each position into its reporting currency and calculate the shorthand measure as in the following example, in which the position in the reporting currency has been excluded:

JPY	DEM	GBP	FFR	US$	GOLD	PLATINUM
+50	+100	+150	−20	−180	−30	+5
	+300			−200		35

The capital charge would be 8% of the higher of the longs and shorts (that is, 300) plus gross positions in precious metals (35) = 335 × 8% = 26.8.

Source: (April 1993) The Supervisory Treatment of Market Risks: Consultative Proposal by the Basle Committe on Banking Supervision.

The simulation method

Under the simulation method, actual exchange rates are utilised to revalue the bank's present foreign exchange position to calculate simulated gains and losses. The capital requirement is to be set in relation to the worst or near to the worst simulated loss which would have arisen during that period.

The simulation technique is particularly complex and requires a number of parameters to be specifically identified:

- Period for which a bank is assumed to hold a position (a holding period).
- The period of observations of exchange rates necessary to capture the evidence of currency volatility (the period of observation).
- The level of confidence required in measuring the risk for the purpose of setting capital requirements (the level of confidence required).
- The scaling factor used to set the capital charge, depending on what is seen as an appropriate buffer against possible losses (the scaling factor).

The choice of holding period depends on the speed with which banks can be expected to terminate positions. This reflects the bank's objective as well as the liquidity and volatility of markets. The BIS proposed a holding period of two weeks or ten working days. This would be on an ongoing rolling basis such that each succeeding day the holding period would cease to include the earliest day included in the last holding period.

The length of the observation period should adequately capture relationships between currencies. A five year period has been chosen as sufficiently long to avoid over-reliance on recent exchange rate movements while still being sufficient time to provide a reasonable estimate of true currency market volatility. The BIS Committee was of the view that it was less necessary that the observation periods be rolled daily but as a minimum, it should be updated at regular reporting dates. Under this approach, the period of observation would be 1,300 observations (five working days × 52 weeks × five years).

The level of confidence required would be 95% which would identify the level of confidence required in measuring the risk for the purposes of setting capital requirements. This is equivalent to two standard deviations which is consistent with the approach utilised within the whole market risk guidelines.

From a conceptual point of view, placing complete weight on the most extreme situation causes the simulation to be very sensitive to the choice of observation period. In emphasising the importance of abnormal events, it would also maximise the problem of asymmetry of the result the simulation period could deliver depending on whether a short or long position is held in one particular currency where the exchange rate has consistently appreciated or depreciated in the past. It has the unfortunate attribute of placing a very high stress on data series quality. The disadvantages are lessened if the level of confidence required is lowered but that benefit is offset by the greater chance of missing an exchange rate movement which may recur in the future. The 95% quartile, which corresponds to the 65th largest loss out of 1,300 observations is proposed.

The scaling factor to be utilised is somewhere between 2% and 4% of the overall net position and is measured under the shorthand method which would deliver the approximate equivalent in terms of standard of capital requirement for a portfolio of average riskiness between the shorthand and simulation methods. The BIS Committee, while continuing to test bank portfolios, was of the view that this should be set at 3%. Accordingly, the scaling factor would dictate that the minimum capital requirement would never be less than 3%.

Treatment of currency options

Consistent with the treatment of derivatives in respect of other asset classes, currency options are to be restated as the delta equivalent of the underlying currencies.

However, acknowledging the use of options to hedge other positions as a form of insurance, the BIS nominated alternative risk capital standards where options are used as a hedge. Under this regime, the capital charge is as follows:

- *a combined forward and option position*—8% of position being hedged, less the amount by which the option is in-the-money (if any);
- *outright purchase of options*—lesser of:
  —8% of market value of underlying; or
  —market value of option.

As noted above, BIS has delegated to national supervisors the task of considering more advanced approaches to capturing the risks in option positions and related spot or forward positions which sophisticated trading institutions may wish to propose.

The overriding parameters in such alternative approaches must be that they cover the highest potential loss in the bank's foreign exchange options and related spot or forward positions portfolio assuming certain changes on a currency pair by currency pair basis in foreign exchange rates and implied volatilities.

BIS market risk guidelines: discussion

The BIS market risk guidelines, as an overall package, represent a comprehensive and, to a substantial extent, intellectually consistent framework for regulation. This is not to say that the regulations are ideal or without fault.

While at a fundamental level, the need for regulation may be questioned, the inevitability of a market risk based capital requirement derives substantially from the Capital Accord of 1988. The Capital Accord, which specifies capital requirements for credit and counterparty risk, in effect created an environment conducive to an adverse selection problem whereby institutions could trade credit risk off against market risk.

There is some anecdotal evidence to suggest that this has indeed been the case in the early 1990s. However, the origins of this behavioural pattern is complex and reflects the banking environment particularly, the withdrawal by banks from lending to corporations due to concerns about credit quality, as well as the particular regulatory framework in operation. Consequently, the Market Risk Guidelines, to a substantial degree, correct an anomaly created by the original Capital Accord.

However, at a more general level, the BIS Market Risk Guidelines continue to fail in two essential areas:

- creation of the much sought after "level playing field" between bank and non-bank financial institutions;
- coverage of all asset classes, particularly commodities.

The BIS Market Risk Guidelines, predictably given the jurisdiction of the BIS, does not attempt a uniform regulatory skein which covers banks and non-banks. In this regard, the approach of the EC Capital Adequacy Directive, discussed above, has important advantages.

A more disappointing aspect of the BIS Market Risk Guidelines in the omission of the coverage, at least specifically, of commodities. Precious metals are treated as foreign exchange risk equivalents for the purposes of capital requirements. It is disappointing, given the increased levels of activity in the area of commodities, that the BIS did not take this opportunity to propose a regulatory framework for dealings in commodities by banks. From an intellectual perspective, a framework not dissimilar to that applicable to foreign exchange trading should have been included. It is to be hoped that by the time the Market Risk Guidelines become mandatory, this oversight is corrected.

At a specific level, the major criticisms of the BIS Market Risk Guidelines in terms of approach is in relation to failure of the BIS guidelines in two areas:

- Its failure to fully address the actual means by which market participants manage these types of risks in line with modern portfolio theory, utilising concepts of hedging and diversification. In this regard, the failure by the BIS, except in a very rudimentary sense, to take into account correlation as between market factors is problematic.
- The second failure is that the overriding approach for seeking protection against extremely large adverse moves in market factors rather than consistent and realistic norms for the probable movement in market factors is also problematic.

Both of these criticisms are equally applicable to the EC Capital Adequacy Directive and are discussed in detail in that context (see above).

Specific areas of criticism include:[2]

- The vertical disallowance in the computation of capital for interest rate risk should be eliminated as it duplicates risk elements already captured more directly by the credit capital requirement, the specific risk charge and horizontal disallowances.
- Amending the guidelines to allow aggregation of rate risk across currencies where the relevant currencies are correlated. This would align the regulation with actual market practice.
- In exposure aggregation, the simple sum of exposures used is inconsistent with recent experience that major factors are largely uncorrelated. Given that each specific exposure—general and specific risk—is independent, the cumulative exposure should equal the square root of the sum of the squares of the exposure. This would be as follows:[3]

Overall: credit risk capital (CRC) and market risk capital (MRC)

Should total capital $= CRC + MRC$

or $= \sqrt{[(CRC)^2 + (MRC)^2]}$?

Within market risk: debt security risk (DSR), equity risk (EQR), and foreign exchange risk (FXR)

Should MRC $= DSR + EQR + FXR$

or $= \sqrt{[(DSR)^2 + (EQR)^2 + (FXR)^2]}$?

Within debt or equity risk: general market risk (GMR) and specific risk (SR)

Should DSR $= GMR + SR$

2. This discussion is based on Robert Gumerlock (1993) (September).
3. Robert Gumerlock (1993) (September), p 88.

or = $\sqrt{[(GMR)^2 + (SR)^2]}$?

Should EQR = GMR + SR

Or = $\sqrt{[(GMR)^2 + (SR)^2]}$?

- Consideration should be given to altering the credit exposure calculation to allow "negative" net replacement values to offset the future exposure add-on. The present formulation is overly conservative where a counterparty owes significant net replacement value to specific counterparties.
- Consideration should also be given to introducing a more precise system of credit risk weights based on credit ratings (investment versus non-investment grade).

The exact impact of the BIS capital requirements for market risk is difficult to estimate. This is particularly so, given the differences in practice and approach to market risk management amongst institutions.

An insight into the impact of the BIS Market Risk Guidelines can be gauged from a penetrating analysis undertaken by Robert Gumerlock[4] of Swiss Bank Corporation using a fictional US bank based on the average statistics of the top US banks (see *Exhibit 40.14*). The analysis indicates that depending on the degree of market risk assumed by the bank the additional capital required could be substantial.

Exhibit 40.14

Impact of BIS Market Risk Guidelines

Banks' reluctance to release data on positions and capital makes it difficult to show the impact of the new Basle requirements on an institution's aggregate capital charge. Nevertheless, it is possible, using public data and some imaginative assumptions, to investigate the pre- and post-capital charges for a fictional "BankUS" created from the average statistics of the top six US banks submitting data to the Federal Reserve (data from end June 1992). BankUS's outstanding off-balance sheet contracts have the following notional amounts and gross replacement values (GRVs):

($ bn)	**1 year and under**		**Above 1 year**		**Total**	
	Notional	**GRV**	**Notional**	**GRV**	**Notional**	**GRV**
Interest rate contracts (1.5%)						
Forwards	215	3.2			215	3.2
Swaps			250	3.8	250	3.8
Options	31	0.5	31	0.5	62	1.0
Exchange rate contracts (2.5%)						
Forwards	439	11.0			439	11.0
Swaps			49	1.2	49	1.2
Options	15	0.4	15	0.4	30	0.8
Equity/commodity contracts (10%)						
Forwards, swaps, options			10	1.0	10	1.0
Total	700	15.1	355	6.9	1,055	22.0

Capital under the 1988 Accord ($1,104 million)

Using the 1988 add-ons (with 5% applied to both equity/commodity and long-term exchange rate categories), and assuming that half of the engagements are with Organisation for Economic Co-operation & Development (OECD) banks (risk weight 1.6%) and one third with corporates (risk weight 8%), and one sixth with sovereigns (risk weight 0%), the computed capital under the accord is $1,104 million.

4. See Robert Gumerlock (1993) (September), pp 82, 83.

Exhibit 40.14—continued

Capital under the 1993 proposals ($784 million-1,978 million)

Capital under the 1993 proposals is very sensitive to assumptions about the level of market risk the bank is willing to assume, the composition of positions hedged against market risk and the interpretations that the Basle Committee will ultimately adopt. Within the latitude of realistic assumptions, capital for BankUS could be anywhere from roughly equal to capital under the 1988 Accord ($784 million) to twice that amount ($1,978 million).

Practitioners concerned about the sudden, large impositions are best advised to press for the reduced counterparty risk weightings for off-balance sheet exposures (savings of $600 million) and for smaller specific risk charges in rates and equities (savings of $400 million), particularly the punitive vertical disallowances in rates (savings of $250 million).

Capital for market risk ($626 million-1,075 million)

Because market risk is not related to the notional value of a position in even the loosest way, several more assumptions are required to arrive at market risk capital. Although the attempt has been to start from broad, workable assumptions, firms are welcome to substitute their own assumptions.

Interest rates ($286 million-548 million)

Assume BankUS has minimal cash positions. (This ensures that the credit exposure is met by the credit capital charge and does not require a supplementary "specific risk" charge.) Assume that half of the swaps, options and forwards meet the Basle Committee's stringent definition of "matching". Assume that the entire notional amount of $527 billion ($215 billion + $250 billion + $62 billion) is spread over the time buckets in the following proportions. (Note that since each rate instrument has two legs, the time band notional amounts sum to twice $527 billion.)

Maturity	$ billion	Risk weight (%)
0-1 month	88	0
1-3 months	157	0.2
3-6 months	182	0.4
6-12 months	190	0.7
1-2 years	212	1.25
2-3 years	60	1.75
3-4 years	50	2.25
4-5 years	40	2.75
5-7 years	30	3.25
7-10 years	20	3.75
10-15 years	10	4.5
15-20 years	10	5.25
More than 20 years	5	6

To see the effect of the vertical disallowance, assume the position in each time band is duration-neutral; then there will be no general charge and no horizontal offsets. Because half of each band's notional position is assumed to be "matching", and because the vertical disallowance is assessed against pairs of offset amounts, the vertical disallowance is one quarter of each band's notional amount multiplied by 10% and by its risk weight, totalling $286 million in capital requirements. (This would be the total market risk capital for a position with no horizontal risk and no general market risk—confirming the discussion in the text about the prohibitive size of the vertical disallowance.) Since most portfolios will not be completely offset within time bands, assume that 10% of the notional amount in each band is not offset; similarly, assume that 1% is not offset horizontally and constitutes general market risk. The vertical disallowance reduces to $228 million, but the horizontal disallowances total $206 million (assuming an average horizontal disallowance of 40%), with a final $114 million for residual general market risk. Total capital for BankUS's rate risk is between $286 million and $548 million.

Equities ($270 million-320 million)

Assume that BankUS has no commodity positions. Of the $10 billion in nominal equity positions, assume that half are index spreads (same index, different dates), one quarter are index arbitrage positions (forwards against "tracking" baskets), and one quarter are index forwards hedging liquid and diversified shares (but not "tracking" baskets). Assume $500 million unhedged shares, half of which are liquid and half of which are illiquid. The capital charge on the index spreads, the index arbitrage, and the hedging forwards will not have any

Exhibit 40.14—continued

''y'' component since the positions net to zero. The ''x'' component for the index spreads is 2% (with commentary invited about applying it to one side only), resulting in a charge of $100 million (possibly lowered to $50 million). The ''x'' component of the index arbitrage is 2%, leading to a $50 million capital requirement for that portfolio segment. The ''x'' component for the hedging forwards is 4%, with a requisite capital charge of $100 million. The unhedged shares would attract a ''y'' component of 8% and ''x'' components of 4% for half and 8% for half, triggering to a $70 million capital requirement. Total capital for the equity market risk of BankUS is between $270 million and $320 million.

Foreign exchange ($70 million-207 million)

Assume between $1 billion and $2.59 billion in gross long positions, against a total notional value of $518 billion. Further, assume that gross long positions dominate gross short positions. The shorthand method, applying 8% to the larger of the gross longs or the gross shorts, results in a capital charge of between $70 million and $207 million against this dimension of risk for BankUS.

Capital for credit risk ($158 million-903 million)

In moving to net replacement value (NRV), it is unrealistic to think that BankUS will have executed valid master agreements with each of its counterparties. Assume that agreements are executed with counterparties representing 50% of the outstanding replacement value and assume that NRV is on average half of GRV. As long as BankUS is required to use a risk weight of 8% for all corporate counterparties, the capital is not reduced significantly; it becomes $903 million. If BankUS is allowed to use, for all counterparties, the risk weights allowed for the specific risk of debt securities, namely 0.25%, 1% or 1.6%, then reductions are realised; capital becomes $262 million. If, in the best of all cases, BankUS has master agreements with all counterparties and if it is allowed to use the reduced risk weights, capital becomes $158 million.

Source: Robert Gumerlock (1993) (September).

Summary

The swaps/derivatives market existed free of any significant regulation for a substantial period of its early life. Since about 1987, regulators have increasingly focused their attention on such instruments as they seek to bring the prudential/regulatory framework for banks and other financial institutions in line with modern financial services practices.

The framework for capturing credit and counterparty risks and the capital requirements related thereto are now well established and understood. The discussion on the revised regulatory framework for the market risk in relation to market swaps and derivative products and banking generally is still evolving.

However, it is now inevitable that capital requirements against market risk will, in the near future, be introduced on a global basis. The proposals to date have sound objectives and it is to be hoped that the final structure of regulation adopted will ensure that the capital requirements for market risk are based on proper principles of portfolio risk management and recognise contemporary risk management practice.

Part 10

Operational, Control, Accounting, Taxation and Legal Aspects of Swaps and Financial Derivatives

Chapter 41

Swaps and Financial Derivatives—Operational and Control Aspects

BACKGROUND

The processes of structuring, pricing, hedging and trading swaps are typically the centre of focus in relation to such instruments. However, entry into a swap transaction, whether by a financial institution with a portfolio of hundreds or thousands of such transactions or for an end user with a relatively small portfolio of swaps, triggers the necessity to undertake a wide range of tasks related to the ongoing management of the transaction over its life.

These tasks cover, as described below, a wide range of activities which are essential to the performance and management of the total transaction. These operational and control aspects relating to swaps and derivative products are often referred to as "back office" matters. This term, often used disparagingly, grossly underestimates the importance and centrality of the tasks covered and their capacity to both create value for the institution or to derogate from the profitability of such transactions.

The key issues relating to operational aspects of swap and derivative transactions include:

- the complexity and diversity of products;
- the substantial number and size of cash flows that are required to be received or made under such transactions;
- the context in which such transactions are traded;
- the volume of swap transactions and the required speed of response;
- the costs entailed with operations supporting swap and derivative products;
- the impact on operations of often globalised trading in such products; and
- the risk and consequences of operational and control failures.

A key element in relation to operational and control aspects of swaps and derivative products is the complexity and diversity of the products themselves. As is evident from the review to date, the products themselves, while simple in overall concept, are, in their detailed configuration, often complex. This, in turn, requires operational staff to both comprehend and establish systems and techniques to encompass operational aspects of pricing, trading and managing portfolios of such transactions.

A significant complexity in this regard is the diversity of products. As is evident from the discussion in Part 4 of this book, a variety of non-generic swaps exist, each with its particular peculiarity or variation on standard structures, requiring the existence of flexible operational systems to cope with the myriad product variations that must be booked, settled and managed.

Individual swap transactions can give rise to a large number of cash flows. For example, a five year interest rate swap with semi-annual settlements gives rise to:

- ten settlement payment flows;
- ten rate resets to establish the floating rate payment flow and calculate the net settlement amounts due.

As at each settlement date, it must be established which party is required to make or receive the relevant payment.

In the case of a corresponding currency swap, there would be additional principal exchanges and both sets of interest payment flows would be made gross.

Under more complex structures, such as collateralised swaps, the transaction may need to be marked-to-market to establish its value *on a daily basis* to establish whether margin calls are required to be made.

Individual cash flows can be sizeable. For example, in a large currency swap, an initial exchange requiring the payment of several hundred million US$ equivalent with the receipt of a corresponding sum in another currency must be undertaken.

The large number of sizeable cash flows requires:

- the actual making of the payment, entailing provision of the appropriate settlement instructions;
- arrangement of appropriate banking facilities including transaction banking accounts to receive and make the appropriate payments;
- forecasting and financing or investing the liquidity in each relevant currency generated as a result of the receipt of payment of these cash flows.

As is evident, *absolute* accuracy in respect of the cash flows under these transactions is required.

The context in which such transactions are entered into and consummated plays an important part in determining the operational and support requirements. Typically, swap and derivative product transactions are concluded orally and documented subsequently. The oral completion of the transaction is typically followed by exchanges of confirmatory telexes or facsimiles. In some cases, significant cash flows will be paid away and received prior to formal legal documentation being completed. The possibility exists of errors in relation to the process of formally recording transactions completed and potential discrepancies in transaction details, and operational procedures to control the risk must be maintained.

An overriding factor in operational aspects of swap and derivative operations relates to the volume of transactions that must be processed. This is a major factor for financial institutions, who are active in trading in such instruments, although it is less of a factor for end users of the market. Financial institutions may complete tens and, in rare cases, hundreds of such transactions during a single day necessitating operational procedures capable of meeting the processing requirements dictated by the volume of transactions and the required speed of response.

A central element of operational aspects of such transactions is the cost incurred in processing and managing portfolios of such transactions. Costs incurred in this regard must be covered by earnings generated which must, in addition, cover other cost elements such as capital utilisation, hedging costs, earnings relative to market risk incurred as well as overheads.

An added dimension of operational requirements is the increasing tendency to trade a variety of these products on the basis of a 24 hour global trading day. Such globalisation places added pressures on the processing efficiency and timeliness of operations capabilities.

An overriding factor in relation to operational requirements is the need for accurate, preferably real time information on transactions and portfolio positions. For example, for accurate portfolio risk management as well as prudential control, it is desirable to have real time information on the portfolio as new transactions are added to the existing portfolio to allow an up-to-date perspective of portfolio risk and performance.

A major element shaping the increased emphasis on operational aspects of swap and derivative transactions is the risk and consequences of operational failures. Operational failures in terms of inaccuracies in payments and settlement can result in the institution incurring added costs. Operational failures also have the potential to expose the institution to unknown market and credit risks as trading, hedging or counterparty risk decisions are based on inaccurate information.

The consequence of these operational failures is either financial loss or breach of prudential controls which exposes the institution to the *risk of loss*.

A less well understood consequence of operational failure is that the high cost of processing, maintaining and managing swap or derivative portfolios has the capacity to significantly erode overall earnings from the operations to the point where the earnings stream from client or trading business is dissipated to unacceptable levels.

The factors identified have, in recent years, received increased focus. This reflects a growing emphasis within the banking industry on measurement of earnings and identifying processing costs and productivity improvements.

OPERATIONAL ASPECTS

Scope/range of activities

Exhibit 41.1 sets out in diagrammatic form the range of activities forming the operational and control aspects of swap and derivative portfolio management.

The diagram highlights the wide variety of activities which are encompassed within this general area of activity.

It is customary to differentiate between the so-called "front office" and "back office" functions. The differentiation relates largely to the fact that the front office, which covers sales/marketing and trading/risk management, is customer related and interfaces with counterparties and is directly involved in trading and the risk management portfolios of financial instruments. In contrast, the back office is concerned with processing, documentation, financial accounting/reporting and control aspects of such transactions. In this regard, the back office can be seen as a support function.

It is increasingly common to further differentiate functions to incorporate a "middle office". This "middle office" is designed to bridge what is perceived to be a gap or divide between the back office and front office. One possible configuration of the middle office and its interrelationship as between the front and back office is set out in diagrammatic form in *Exhibit 41.2*.

In effect, the middle office encompasses the trading/risk management and control aspects of the more traditional differentiation between front and back office. A key issue, related to, but not an integral part of, this middle office configuration issue, is the increasing trend to staff the middle office with support personnel who are quite capable of independently valuing portfolios, analysing risk positions and verifying earnings and market risk positions independent of traders and marketing staff.

The various elements encompassed within the scope of operational and control activities are discussed in detail below.

Sales/marketing and trading/risk management function

The so-called "front office" functions are largely focused on sales/marketing and trading/risk management.

The focus within sales/marketing is:

- transaction structuring;
- sales support.

Exhibit 41.1

Operational and Control Aspects of Swap and Financial Derivative Transactions

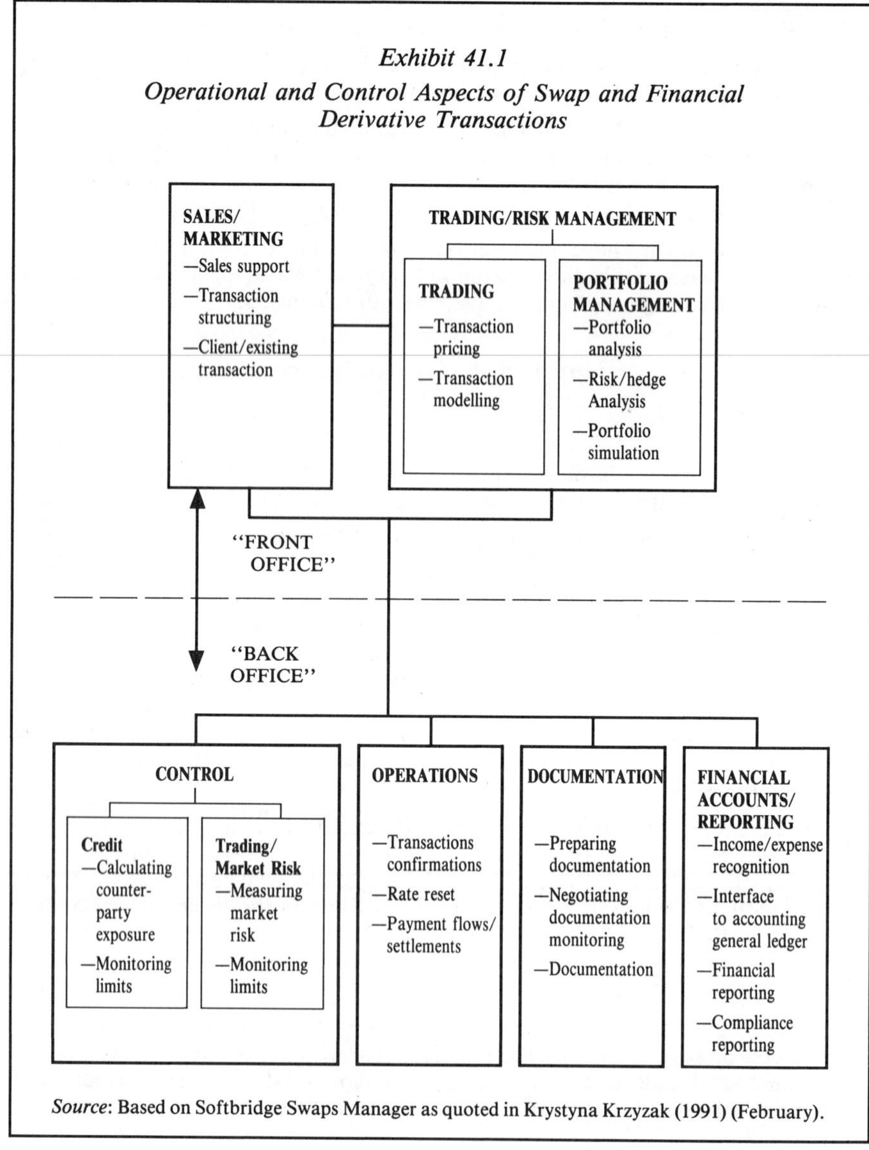

Source: Based on Softbridge Swaps Manager as quoted in Krystyna Krzyzak (1991) (February).

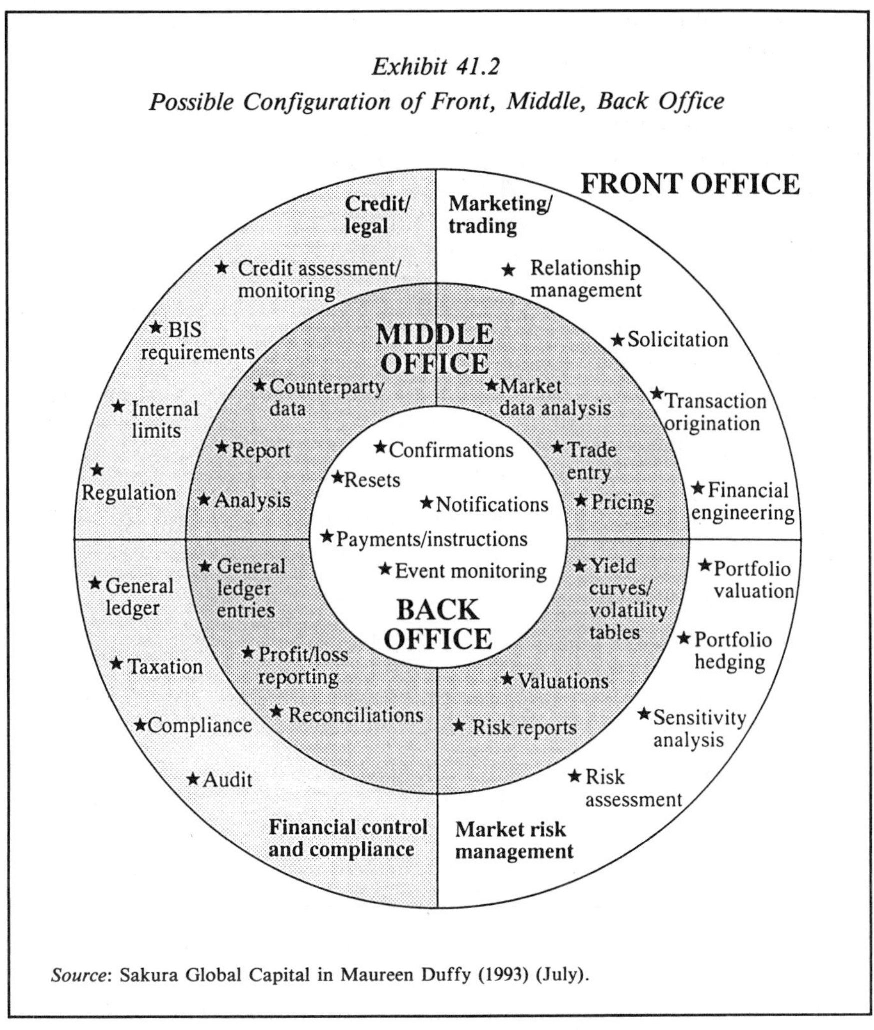

Exhibit 41.2
Possible Configuration of Front, Middle, Back Office

Source: Sakura Global Capital in Maureen Duffy (1993) (July).

The activity emphasises the work undertaken by corporate derivatives dealers/sales or marketing staff who are involved in the identification of counterparties, marketing to counterparties and structuring of transactions (usually in conjunction with trading/risk management personnel).

The sales/marketing personnel work closely with and, to some degree, overlap with the derivative traders and risk managers whose function it is to:

- undertake proprietary trading activities in the relevant instruments;
- price client transactions;
- hedge market risk exposures assumed as a result of entry into transactions; and
- manage the swap or derivative portfolio risks within prespecified guidelines.

The key operational requirements of these activities include:

- Availability of pricing and valuation models to structure and price transactions, as required.

- Information, in the form of a data base, on:
  - — existing transactions with various counterparties
  - — exchange rates, interest rates and swap and derivative rates.

  The information on existing transactions with counterparties is essential to enable derivative sales staff to focus on existing transactions to identify opportunities to reverse or restructure existing positions. In addition, transactions entered into with counterparties often provide a strong insight into the underlying exposures to currency, interest rate and commodity prices and therefore allow assessment of the applicability of particular transaction structures or market opportunities for the particular client.

  The availability of extensive databases on a variety of financial market variables is useful as an adjunct to marketing efforts and to allow rapid analysis of changing relationships, such as swap spread movements, which may be pertinent to identified trading and transaction generating opportunities.

- Trading/risk management systems which encompass both trading (transaction pricing and transaction modelling) and portfolio risk management (including portfolio analysis, hedge analysis, analysis of portfolio risks, and portfolio simulation capabilities).

The transaction pricing and modelling capabilities are not dissimilar to those required by sales/marketing staff. In practice, trading staff generally price transactions, utilising this system, for sales/marketing offices. The portfolio risk management requirements are, necessarily, more complex.

The ultimate objective of the portfolio risk management system is to provide the portfolio manager with an overview of the risk profile of transactions. This risk profile is usually undertaken at two specific levels:

- individual transactions, to facilitate hedging of transactions as they are entered into;

- analysis, identification and management of the risks *of the total derivatives portfolio* on an aggregate basis.

Traders and risk managers require, generally real time, information on the impact of each additional transaction on the overall portfolio as well as the potential impact of changes in exchange rates, interest rates etc on the risk profile and profitability of the portfolio. In addition, portfolio managers require the capacity to analyse the impact of implementing a particular hedge on the overall portfolio risk and earnings profile as well as the capacity to simulate portfolio characteristics and responses to changes in financial market variables or, quite simply, the passage of time.

The operational requirements of the front office are quite distinct from the operational requirements of the back office (see discussion below). In fact, it is not essential that the front and back office systems be integrated, although this is highly desirable. The advantages of integration derive largely from commonalities of data and information as well as consistency in the techniques utilised throughout the portfolio in performing various functions. For example, a major advantage is that portfolio risk management and reporting, including hedging action, should be able to be reconciled with the financial accounting and reporting of results of the derivatives portfolio.

Operations

Scope

The operations function encompasses the following range of activities:

- *Confirmation of transactions*—Transactions, as noted above, are entered into orally and are subsequently required to be confirmed. In general terms, the trader completing the transaction will fill out a deal slip or transaction record which will be utilised by the operations staff to prepare and transmit a confirmation. Confirmation will be acknowledged by the counterparty and the acknowledgment cross-checked against transaction details transmitted. For control purposes, it is imperative that the process of confirming the transaction be separated from the trading/dealing function to minimise potential problems of fraud or dealer error.

- *Rate resets*—Over the life of a typical swap transaction, one or both sets of payment flows will be variable and will require interest rates to be set at various points over the life of the transaction. Similar activities need to be performed in respect of FRAs, caps etc. The requirement that interest rates be reset necessitates that the counterparty, with the responsibility for setting interest rates, undertaking the following tasks:
  - Determine the relevant rate benchmark on a given day. This is more complex than immediately apparent simply because of the diversity of benchmarks that exist and slight variations that may apply to individual transactions. The problem is particularly acute in markets where the degree of standardisation of interest rate benchmarks is low.
  - Utilise the interest rate reset to calculate settlement amounts. This is complicated by the fact that depending upon the interest rate level, the payment flow directions may be reversed from one payment date to another.
  - The rate set and settlement amounts have to be advised and confirmed with the other party.

- *Payment flows/funds transfers/cash settlements*—As noted above, an integral part of the operations supporting swap and derivative product operations is the process of identifying and facilitating the funds transfers required under these contracts. This includes arrangement of the payment flows and the actual funds transfers allowing the cash amounts receivable and payable to be settled. As also noted above, the funds flows can be particularly large and absolute accuracy in both amounts and funds transfer instructions are essential. Failure to make payments or payments made to incorrect bank accounts can incur substantial financial costs and, in extreme cases, may result in default under the relevant contracts.

  The operations group in this regard must provide information regarding anticipated liquidity flows to the financial institution's liquidity management unit to ensure appropriate funding or investment actions are implemented to cover the liquidity requirements or cash generation of the swap/derivative operations.

An added level of complexity in the operational aspects derives from the geographic structure of operations. As increasingly swaps and derivatives businesses operate globally (as mentioned above), the location of operational bases are increasingly at issue. A number of financial institutions active in swaps and derivative products have moved to *centralise* their operational basis, either in one location or in three or four locations which process all operational aspects relating to portfolio. This process of centralisation is designed to provide better, more up-to-date information and facilitate control of these activities.

Alternatively, a number of institutions continue to run decentralised operational support units linked to each geographic entity active in swaps and derivatives. Informational and control requirements here are met by undertaking a variety of internal *intragroup* transactions to neutralise positions. The latter option, on the whole, increases the administrative tasks related to the operation of the overall portfolio.

Cost issues

The operational and administrative processes outlined represent a significant cost which must be covered by the earnings generated from the overall swaps and derivatives transactions entered into.

In recent years, consistent with the growing emphasis within the banking industry on cost and productivity improvements, increased attention has been focused on: firstly, fully costing operational and administrative processes; and, secondly, seeking to minimise these costs.

An indication of the costs of processing transactions can be obtained from a survey of treasury transaction costs undertaken by BDO Consulting.[1]

The BDO survey over the period from January 1991 to June 1991 an entailed participation from 15 London treasury operations, representing a mix of clearing banks, merchant banks and securities houses, and one large corporate treasury operation.

Cost categories considered included:

	Staff	**Systems**	**Premises**	**Other**
Front Office	dealers telex operators (quotes and deals)	telephone/telex/ direct voice lines information services IT equipment (deal recording pricing, information display)	dealing rooms	brokerage commission
Back Office	settlement confirmation clerks/runners document production	telex/telephone BACS, SWIFT etc confirmation settlement risk and position monitoring	settlement confirmation filing	nostro charges

Four basic instrument types were considered:

- foreign exchange;
- sterling and Euro money market products;
- derivative products (including currency and interest rate options, currency and interest rate futures, FRAs, currency and interest rate swaps, and commodity futures).

1. BDO Binder Hamlyn, *BDO Banking Survey 1991: Treasury Transaction Cost—Management Summary* (February 1992).

The BDO Consulting survey results are summarised in the table below:

	Total Transaction Cost (GBP)		
Instrument Category	**Average**	**Upper Quartile**	**Lower Quartile**
Foreign exchange	23.53	38.47	9.84
Local money markets	34.02	55.45	14.99
Euro markets	59.54	128.70	26.95
Derivatives	199.47	494.58	37.24

In relation to derivative products, the survey highlights the following:

- the wide discrepancy in transaction processing costs (which may reflect some problems relating to the emphasis on different types of products);
- the significant level of costs incurred in processing a single transaction.

It should be noted that it is not clear whether the estimates cover ongoing costs incurred in maintaining and undertaking the activities related to a transaction which stays within the portfolio for an extended period of time.

The four major findings from the 1991 BDO survey were as follows:

- There is scope for reducing transaction costs (on a per unit basis). The survey found that the large differences in per transaction cost were *not* related to transaction volume. This tends to highlight the fact that there appeared to be no standard costs for these activities, indicating reasonable scope for cost reduction.
- The survey did not support the assumption that investment in technology or automation of settlement activities has been matched by reductions in back office staff costs. This is based on the lack of correlation found between high systems technology expenditures and low expenditures in other categories, particularly staff. The survey found that the ratio of staff plus systems costs to total costs *increases* as the systems proportion of total costs increases. Consequently, it appears that actual benefits from technology or automation are dependent upon the individual operations product mix, product volumes, customer relationships and settlement methods.
- The survey indicated that decreasing unit costs did not correlate with increasing transaction volumes. That is, there appeared to be *no* discernible economies of scale. In theory, for an individual financial institution, per transaction cost improvements can be achieved with increasing transaction volumes over some range, reflecting the fact the additional throughput does not require additional investment to be incurred to support increased capacity. This may reflect the fact that, depending upon the product mix and transaction volumes, infrastructure is more accurately reflected by a series of increasing cost steps corresponding to stages and capacity levels.
- The BDO survey indicated that there appeared to be relatively low entry barriers for new entrants. Excluding clearing bank branch operations, large volume treasury operations with high investment in systems and technology were shown to be no more competitive than smaller operations. The survey found that smaller more focused operations achieved competitive costs reflecting a focused product, more restricted customer base and the benefits for utilisation of packaged cheaper technology solutions.

The findings of the survey, interestingly, challenge a number of commonly held assumptions about the dynamics of costs and the impact of technology on operational aspects of financial services.

Documentation

As noted above, the economic commitments agreed to under a swap or derivative transaction is confirmed in a number of ways:

- the agreement, usually oral, reached between the parties over the phone;
- confirmations (usually sent by operation staff) stating the terms of the transaction; and
- the actual legal documentation governing the terms of the transaction.

Increasingly, under the terms of the Master ISDA agreement governing swap and derivative transactions, the confirmation sent, subsequent to oral agreement of the transaction, is incorporated into the final documentation.

The process of documentation is extremely important as it represents the actual legal agreement between the parties. As noted above, the document itself does not come into being until some time after the transaction is consummated and, in some cases, may be completed after a number of payment flows have taken place under the terms of the agreement.

The documentation process entails a variety of activities:

- preparing documentation;
- negotiating documentation;
- monitoring documentation.

The detailed legal issues relating to documentation of these types of transactions is discussed in detail in Chapter 44.

The preparation and negotiation of the documentation can be undertaken either by a specialised swap and derivative documentation unit or an overall treasury or capital markets documentation unit. In certain cases, responsibility for documentation lies with the institution's separate legal departments, credit offices or may be undertaken by external legal advisers. Increasingly, the trend is to have a small documentation unit attached to treasury/swaps or financial derivatives unit responsible for documenting such transactions.

Nevertheless, the process of documentation requires very close liaison with credit officers to ensure that documentation reflects the terms of credit approvals that might need to be incorporated in the documentation governing the swap or derivative transaction.

The monitoring of documentary terms is particularly important. A critical aspect in this regard is to ensure that documentary conditions relating to credit matters are monitored closely to ensure that indications of weakening financial condition of the counterparty are registered and appropriate action taken. This process of monitoring, which is often neglected, can provide useful early warnings of financial distress and also allows institutions to take corrective action in respect of credit exposures within their derivative portfolios.

The increasing standardisation of swap and derivative documentation has assisted in the process of documenting swap and derivative transactions, although horrendous stories of backlogs of documentation (often ranging up to six to 12 months) abound.

Financial accounting/reporting

The swap and activities undertaken by any financial institution are required to be incorporated into the financial accounting and reporting framework of the institution. This would cover:

- income and expense recognition;
- an interface to the accounting general ledger;
- financial management reporting;
- prudential or compliance reporting requirements.

The detailed accounting issues relating to swap and derivative operations are covered in detail in Chapter 42.

A major issue relating to financial accounting and reporting of swap and derivative operations is the complexity of income and expense recognition in relation to such portfolios. In particular, a central issue is the need for a consistent valuation and income recognition methodology applicable to pricing, hedging, portfolio management and financial/management reporting.

The absence of a unified framework leads to significant discrepancies in trader-reported earnings on activities and those recorded by the financial/management accounting systems. This necessitates complex reconciliations as well as significant disputes and internal tensions within organisations. The process of income recognition and performance measurement is complicated by the need to integrate various portfolios and to incorporate hedges which are being maintained against portfolio economic risk positions.

In addition, information provided must facilitate an appropriate interface to the accounting general ledger including trading inventory, daily ledger general statements, account balances, etc. In addition, information facilitating recording of appropriate contingent liabilities incurred in the process of trading and managing derivative portfolio must be recognised.

Appropriate systems for, firstly, internal management reporting, and, secondly, incorporation of derivative portfolio activities into the reported financial statements of the company must exist. Additional reporting requirements, primarily in relation to regulatory standards, must also be encompassed. Demands in this regard focus on the following:

- statistical information on volumes and trading positions required by financial institution regulators; and
- capital adequacy reporting across the range of instruments required under prudential control mechanisms implemented by bank regulators.

The financial accounting/reporting system needs to be able to satisfy these requirements.

CONTROL ASPECTS

Background

All operations and administrative aspects of swap and derivative products are, to varying extents, related to control. However, two aspects of operations focus specifically and explicitly on control and risk minimisation. These operational aspects encompass credit and market risk control aspects which are incorporated into the operational framework of these types of transactions. Each of these aspects of control are considered in detail below.

Maintenance of appropriate controls covers a number of specific areas including: organisational structure; front office control; trade initiations; ongoing operational procedure; ongoing accounting process; risk management; and disaster recovery.

Appendix A to this chapter sets out a management checklist for derivatives finance. This checklist developed by C.ATS Software was designed for senior managers responsible for derivatives business units summarising a number of key internal control measures that are desirable to allow full assessment and control of risk without impeding the conduct of business.

Credit risk controls

The scope of the operational support for a swap and derivative trading unit must, as a priority, be able to facilitate monitoring consolidated credit risks against counterparties as a result of entry into swap or derivative transactions against the institutions limit structure.

Ideally, this information will be provided in real time to allow up-to-date information on counterparty credit exposures to be available, if required. In practice, real time processing may not be available and credit risk information is available after a delay of, say, one day which is usually adequate.

Several aspects of the credit risk exposure control system require comment:

- It is important that the system encompasses all products and also all trading entities. This reflects the fact that the exposure to a single customer may be fragmented across different products and may also be fragmented as a result of transactions undertaken with various units or different legal entities of the financial institution. In addition, lending risks, counterparty risks, risks of issuers of securities and off-balance sheet products must, in reality, be consolidated to facilitate management of risk on an effective basis. An additional fact in this regard is the capacity to monitor country/geographic risk dimensions.
- Individual institutions will have their own limit structures, including multi-level group/branch organisations and internal guidelines as to specific limits required by undertaking different types of transactions (this will vary between instruments). Counterparty/client limits will also need to be fully integrated with country/geographical area limits which will simultaneously be affected as a result of the transaction.
- Daily reporting of limits utilisation must be available to allow close monitoring counterparty credit exposures.
- Systems should ensure that any breach resulting from an excess limit utilisation is immediately flagged as an exception. Appropriate review and, if appropriate, authorisation procedures must exist.

Market risk controls

Entry into a derivatives transaction, generally, exposes institutions to varying degrees of market risk. Market risk, in this context, refers to the risk of favourable or unfavourable movements in the value of a portfolio of transactions as a result of movements in key financial market variables:

- In the case of currency and interest rate swaps, LTFX, FRAs and caps, floors/collars:
  - — currency rates;
  - — interest rates;
  - — changes in interest rate and currency volatility;
  - — liquidity risk;
  - — settlement risk.

- Commodity and equity swaps and related derivatives entail similar risks as above but, in addition, including:
  - — commodity price risk;
  - — commodity volatility risk;
  - — equity market index risk;
  - — equity market index volatility risk.

In the case of hybrid instruments, incorporating interest rate, currency, equity or commodity elements or some combination of these, the measurement of market risk and the establishment of appropriate controls is necessarily more difficult. The most appropriate approach, in this regard, is to unbundle the instrument into its constituent element (that is, interest rates, currencies, etc) and each constituent element is then absorbed into the relevant risk category and controlled accordingly.

Exhibit 41.3 outlines the basic limits that would need to be implemented to cover the major exposures likely to be encountered in managing this type of operation.

Exhibit 41.3
Market Risk Management Systems

A comprehensive market risk management system will encompass most of the following:

INTEREST RATE AND CURRENCY SWAPS, LTFX, FRAs

Currency risk

For a given change in currency rates (measured in % terms), the change in the portfolio value should not exceed a nominated monetary amount.

Generally, the tolerable levels of movement is defined for particular currency groupings. For example, for a US$-based institution:*

DEM, Dfl, GBP, JPY	—	[1.50%]
FFR, LIT, other ERM currencies	—	[1.25%]
A$, NZ$, C$	—	[1.20%]
Other minor currencies	—	[1.00%]
Exotic	—	[0.75%]

This banding process is designed to group currencies on the basis of assumed volatility levels and relative liquidity (which will govern the capacity to establish and unwind positions).

Interest rates, particularly interest rate differentials, have the capacity to impact on currency positions. The impact of interest rate movements on currency positions are usually encompassed within the interest rate component of the risk measurement system.

Interest rate risk

This will be measured utilising a range of measures:

Absolute rate movement

For a given change in *all* interest rates in each currency a parallel yield curve shift (usually measured in bps pa), the change in the portfolio value should not exceed a nominated monetary amount. As in the case of currencies, the tolerable level of movement is defined for particular currency groupings.

Yield curve shape movements

For a given change in the shape of the yield curve in each currency (measured in bps pa increase and decreases in the steepness and/or curvature of the yield curve, based on an assumed "pivot" point in the yield curve, say three or five years), the change in the portfolio value should not exceed a nominated monetary amount.

* Please note that all numbers are purely illustrative and are not designed to recommend appropriate tolerance levels.

Exhibit 41.3—continued

Spread movement

For a given change in spread relationships in each currency (measured in bps pa), the change in the portfolio value should not exceed a nominated monetary amount.

The spread relationship is usually defined as the differential between swap rates and the underlying benchmark interest rate (generally, the government bond rate or other relevant reference rate in the relevant currency or, in synthetic currencies such as the ECU, the theoretical benchmark yield).

It is theoretically feasible to set limits for changes in the *shape* of spread curve but this is rarely utilised.

Basis movements

For a given change in basis relationships (cash near-month futures or inter-month futures contract spreads) in a given instrument in a currency (measured in bps pa), the change in the portfolio value should not exceed a nominated monetary amount.

This limit is utilised in currencies where the institution utilises:

- futures contracts to hedge risk positions (for example, bond futures are used to hedge swap positions);
- futures contracts as a hedge and, due to the structure of the relevant futures market, they cannot be matched closely to the position being hedged (for example, a futures stack hedge for an interest rate swap).

This limit is designed to measure exposures to changes in the cash futures basis and/or inter-contract spreads or basis. To some extent measurement of exposure to absolute rate and yield curve shape movements captures this type of basis risk. Difficulties in implementing this type of risk limit have meant that few institutions utilise this limit. However, in markets where futures contracts are used as a major hedging instrument, it is useful to establish this category of limit.

Liquidity risk

The portfolio (particularly, defined to include hedging instruments) should not have an undue concentration in a particular instrument. Operationally, this limit can be specified as follows:

- an absolute monetary amount limitation (expressed in face value terms) on holdings of any particular security or series of futures or options contracts;
- a limitation expressed as a stated percentage (say 5%) of the current market outstandings of the relevant security or series of futures or options contracts;
- a requirement that, at least, a nominated percentage (say 85%) of hedges (securities or futures/options contracts) be held in "liquid" contracts. Liquidity in this context is defined differently as between markets (for example, "on-the-run" securities, near-month futures contracts etc).

This limit is designed to ensure that the hedge portfolio is highly liquid and rapidly tradeable.

Settlement risk

The portfolio structure should not have an undue concentration (expressed as a monetary amount) of payments/cash flows in any currency on any given settlement date. This limit is designed to minimise exposure to market disruption or failure in a particular currency and to minimise the liquidity impact of settlement failures.

This operates quite independently of and in addition to counterparty settlement risk limits which are credit risk driven.

COMMODITY AND EQUITY SWAPS DERIVATIVES

Commodity price risk

For a given change in commodity prices (measured in percentage or absolute monetary terms), the change in the portfolio value should not exceed a nominated monetary amount.

Exhibit 41.3—continued

As in the case of currencies and interest rates, the tolerable level of movement is defined for particular commodity groupings.

Equity market index risk

For a given change in equity market index prices (measured in percentage terms), the change in the portfolio value should not exceed a nominated amount. As above, the tolerable level of movement is defined for particular equity market groupings based on liquidity and relative volatilities.

Other risk

For both commodity and equity products, currency risks, interest rate risks, financial instrument liquidity risks and settlement risk may be relevant depending on the type of instrument utilised.

However, the following additional limits are also relevant:

Commodity/equity market price curve risk

For a given change in the shape of commodity or equity market forward price curve, that is, changes in the degree of backwardation or contango of the prices—effectively, changes in the convenience yields—the change in the portfolio value should not exceed a nominated monetary amount.

Commodity basis risk

For a given change in price basis as between nominated related commodities (for example, crude oil and products), the change in the portfolio value should not exceed a nominated monetary amount.

This is designed to measure the basis risk in commodity swaps where cross-hedges based on the correlation between related commodities are utilised as hedges.

Futures/forward basis risk

For a given change in cash futures or inter-month futures or forward contract spreads in a given commodity or equity index, the change in the portfolio value should not exceed a nominated monetary amount.

This is very similar to the basis movement limit for interest rate risk identified above and is designed to measure the risk of changes in futures/forward prices on the portfolio given their importance as a hedge in commodity and equity swaps and derivatives.

CAPS, FLOORS OR INSTRUMENTS WITH OPTION COMPONENTS

For instruments with option components, *in addition* to the types of limits noted above, the following limits are required.

Volatility risk

For a given change in the volatility of the relevant interest rate, currency, commodity or equity index price (measured in bps pa or % *change* in volatility), the change in portfolio value should not exceed a nominated monetary amount.

The change in volatility measured should be both an absolute increase or decrease in volatility as well as a change in the shape of volatility yield curve or volatility curve.

Gamma risk

For a given change in the spot price of the relevant variable (measured in bps pa or % change in price), the change in the *relative value* of the option portfolio and the delta hedges held should not exceed a nominated monetary amount. This measures the effective hedging slippage as a result of exposure on the accuracy of the delta hedge maintained on the portfolio.

Interest rate risk

For a given change in interest rates (both absolute and yield curve in the relevant currency), the change in the value of the portfolio should not exceed a nominated monetary amount. This measures the impact of interest rates on option premiums.

Theta risk

For a given change in the time to maturity, the change in the value of the portfolio should not exceed a nominated monetary amount. This is typically used to measure the impact of time

Exhibit 41.3—continued

decay on the portfolio. While traditionally used in the context of options, it can be used for other instruments.

MISCELLANEOUS

The limits identified above are stated in absolute monetary terms. In practice, some organisations prefer to nominate limits in terms of present value of a basis point (PVBP) or ten year bond equivalents.

Under this approach, portfolio managers merely calculate the dollar value of a PVBP or 0.01% pa yield movement on the price ten year bond and restate the portfolio risk in the required terms.

The only advantage of this approach is that it provides a common uniform measure of risk across instruments or portfolios and may be more easily comprehended. The major disadvantage of this method is the inappropriateness of restating certain portfolio exposures in other terms, for example, short-term exposure is ten year bond equivalents, etc.

Exhibit 41.4 sets out the basic methodology utilised to establish appropriate market risk limits.

The primary purpose of such market limits systems is to ensure market exposures, assumed as a result of hedging in or entering into transactions with counterparties, are maintained within acceptable bounds. The objective is to ensure that the impact on profit and loss amount of any movement in financial market variables capable of effecting the portfolio is known and understood. The explicit risk limits, usually based on conservative worst case scenarios defined by senior management, are designed to control the overall impact on the profitability of the institution resulting from a worst case movement in market variables.

These risk limits must be monitored to ensure that traders do not exceed authorities. Constant review and enforcement of market risk limits is essential to ensuring that the risk aspects of a swap or derivative operation are rigorously controlled.

As is evident from *Exhibits 41.3* and *41.4*, there is an inevitable tension between maintaining limits that are sophisticated enough to capture all potential risk eventualities and allowing risk limits to be simple and capable of providing full information which can be comprehended rapidly by a relatively wide audience, including non-specialists and senior management.

Exhibit 41.4

Generalised Methodology for Establishing Market Risk Management Systems

Designing and implementing a market risk management system entails, in general terms, the following steps:

1. Calculating tolerances

Tolerances for changes in financial market variables (such as interest rates, etc) are based on analysis of historical, time series data. The data used usually extends over a reasonable period—say up to five years. Typically, daily observations (for example, closing prices) are utilised, although it may be relevant to utilise intra-day (hourly or open-to-close) prices where *intra-day* rather than overnight limits are being sought to be developed.

Exhibit 41.4—continued

Daily changes (for calculation of overnight limits) are determined and the distribution properties of the population of measurements is calculated. In particular, population means and dispersion measures, such as standard deviations, are calculated.

The mathematical confidence level to be utilised is then selected. Typically, institutions utilise either:

two standard deviations—95.4% confidence criterion

three standard deviations—99.73% confidence criterion

Based on the nominated confidence criterion, the maximum tolerable movement in the relevant variable is specified—that is, mean ± 2 or 3 standard deviations.

2. Setting the monetary risk limit

The monetary risk limit essentially defines the amount of capital that would be lost as a result of all positions having to be liquidated at a given point in time following the maximum anticipated adverse movement in market variables as defined by the specified tolerances.

The specific limit, which will vary significantly between institutions, should be specified as an absolute amount which is related to the capital committed to that activity—say, 5-10% of the unit's capital can be put at risk at any one time.

3. Operationalising limits

In practice, the overall limits established must be operationalised at a number of levels within the organisation. In implementing the limits hierarchy, several factors need to be considered:

- The limits must, from a pragmatic viewpoint, be relatively easy to understand and simple to use.
- The simplicity of the limits is essential to allow traders and risk managers to determine their risk position relative to limits quickly and easily.
- A significant consideration is that detailed risk reports would usually not be available on a real time basis, being processed overnight. This means that a series of heuristics are needed to allow rapid evaluation of risk positions.

Against this background, the market risk limits may be restated as:

- open position limits (currency, interest rate, commodity or equity market index price)—specified on a security equivalent basis for example, ten year bond equivalent;
- curve risk position (primarily, for interest rates)—specified as a limit on portfolio gaps/mismatches, specified in terms of time period buckets (0-1 year; 1-3 years; 3-7 years; ten year etc), with a maximum open position allowed in any one "bucket";
- gamma and volatility risk positions (for options) specified as limits on portfolio gamma and vega risks.

The more comprehensive risk reports are then run overnight to provide a more complete perspective of the portfolio for the institution's risk managers.

4. Assumptions

The efficiency of the market risk management system, as specified above, is predicated on the maximum overnight movement in rates not exceeding the assumed tolerance levels and that, in the event of a required portfolio liquidation, positions can be terminated at or close to the values implied by the assumed "worst case" movement.

Two major factors which require consideration in designing and operating a market risk monitoring system include:

- The need to develop and review systems to ensure that the system captures all essential risk elements and does not allow traders to essentially maintain a risk position which is not captured by the limit framework. This is a particularly vexed issue, more apparent in complex products, which lend themselves to a form of limits "arbitrage" where traders are able to take substantial risks, which are outside the spirit of the limit system but not outside its literal definition.

- The degree of integration within the risk management system is also a major issue. For example, the institution may force traders to *each* operate within tightly defined limits or place an *overall limit for the total derivatives operation.*

  For example, should an open position in the interest rate swap book be netted against an offsetting position in the FRA or cap book? A similar issue relates to the degree of integration of risk management in terms of assumed correlation between various financial market variables. A simple example of this might be a derivative portfolio which has a long/net bought position in DEM and a short/net sold position in SFR. If it can be demonstrated that there is a high degree of correlation between the two currencies, should the positions be netted or, at the very least, some allowance be made through qualified aggregation of the positions?

Market risk management systems are highly individual to organisations, reflecting institutional strategies, organisation, risk assumption capabilities and attitudes to risk. However, irrespective of the individual institutional focus, it is imperative that the market risk management system facilitates access to immediate information on the potential magnitude, direction and impact on the profit and loss account of the total swap and derivative portfolio at any point in time.

SYSTEMS AND TECHNOLOGY ISSUES

Background

Technology has increasingly become a crucial element in facilitating the operational aspects of swap and derivative businesses. It is considered a strategic element which assists in assuring and maintaining the success of the swap derivative operations of financial institutions. The technology requirements of an institution active in the global derivative market, in terms of both scale and complexity, are extremely significant.

The necessity of having access to state-of-the-art pricing/valuation software as well as sophisticated portfolio risk analysis systems as financial institutions increasingly undertake complex financial instrument structures, incorporating a variety of elements, is now accepted. The complexity of the instruments and the volume of transactions undertaken dictate that significant investments in information technology are a prerequisite for a successful derivatives operation. In addition, the necessity of maintaining appropriate operational support and control over such operations dictates additional investments in technology to support the various "back office" functions identified.

Increasingly, institutions have increased their investment in advanced systems technology, assisted, in part, by the declining cost of the technology as well as the quantum leaps in technological capabilities, to seek to address these requirements. The strategy pursued by a number of institutions, although not supported necessarily by research (refer the BDO Consulting survey above), has been to *leverage* human resources with added investments in investment technology to facilitate the following:

- *Front office*—proprietary pricing, valuation and risk management technology which provides an edge in product innovation, improves hedging performance and improved portfolio earnings.
- *Back office*—improves the cost, efficiency and productivity of operational and support areas of the swap and derivatives unit in maintaining the requisite

administrative procedures and provides the requisite management information necessary to control the operations at minimal cost.

Types/scope of system

There are two main types of swap and derivative systems:

- front office systems;
- back office systems.

This follows the functionality and range of activities as defined in previous sections in this chapter.

Front office systems concentrate on activities such as pricing, risk management and sales and marketing support. As noted above, a number of commentators now utilise the term "middle office" covering portfolio management, including risk analysis and portfolio hedging aspects.

The front or middle office systems concentrate on pricing and valuation methodology, transaction pricing and structuring capabilities. From a risk management perspective, the focus is on identification, assessment of portfolio risk characteristics and hedging facilities. The system's capacity to perform sensitivity analysis on portfolio risk and facilitate analysis of portfolio hedging strategies, including simulation and modelling techniques, are the prerequisites for good middle office systems to support trading and risk management activity.

The focus of back office systems is somewhat different, covering:

- operations aspects, as defined above;
- accounting and reporting aspects; and
- capacities for implementing effective control procedures.

Substantial processing and administrative requirements in running a large derivative operation necessitates availability of efficient and time-sensitive back office systems.

As the focus on reporting of derivative activities to regulatory authorities increases in importance, the capacity to generate reports which meet regulatory requirements such as those for capital adequacy purposes are increasingly important elements of such systems. In addition, increased emphasis on control of derivatives trading and risk management activities has forced a focus on appropriate financial and management reporting capabilities within such systems.

A major issue, increasingly, relates to integration. The pressures for integration relate to two, quite different, aspects:

- integration of front and back office functionality;
- integration across various different derivative products.

Traditionally, front and back office systems have not been integrated in all cases. Because of the view maintained by a variety of institutions that competitive advantage can be gained from superior pricing, valuation and hedging knowledge, financial institutions have invested significantly in developing proprietary front office systems. Back office systems have also been developed and may be consistent with the chosen front office system, although, in a large number of cases, it takes the form of off-the-shelf software which is not necessarily consistent or integrated with the front office system.

Increasingly, systems integrating both front and back office function are favoured. The major advantages of such integration include:

- Significant cost savings, primarily as a result of avoiding double handling and double inputting. For example, completion of a deal slip which provides all essential information regarding a transaction can be the base document which "triggers" a variety of activities, including automatic confirmation of the transaction as well as updating transaction data portfolios.
- Integration generally ensures adoption of consistent revaluation methodologies and models both front and back office requirements.
- Integration also facilitates superior control for improved risk management, compliance, capital adequacy and limits reporting across all instruments.

A related aspect of integration is the capacity to manage portfolios in various derivative products on a joint/integrated basis as distinct from stand-alone product-by-product basis. As discussed in detail in Chapters 1 and 45, there is an increasing trend to integration of derivative operations within financial institutions to achieve perceived advantages in improved risk management and lower cost hedging opportunities. This is currently reflected in an increased focus on ensuring systems are capable of handling a variety of products and portfolio risk management can encompass cross-hedging strategies that may be a by-product of the integration of their derivative businesses.

Key issues in system design and selection

A major issue in relation to swap and derivatives systems is the "buy versus build" decision. Originally, many financial institutions developed their own systems as a matter of policy, on the basis that market systems available did not satisfy their unique requirements, or the opportunity to gain potentially competitive advantages from developing its own system. However, increasingly the purchase of off-the-shelf software (both for front/middle office and back office systems) was favoured. Major factors underlying this decision include:

- the increased availability of high quality software for derivative products;
- the lack of time or resources to develop in-house systems (there have been a number of celebrated systems failures with horror stories of escalating costs, deferred deadlines and over-staffing);
- the high risk entailed in systems development and the often acute dependence on the systems development staff for the proper operation of the system where the loss of key programmers etc create major disruptions to operations; and
- cost issues.

Increasingly, few financial institutions develop proprietary systems with the central focus being on selecting adequate information systems technology to support operational requirements. The major effort in information technology continues to be in respect of pricing, valuation and risk management technology which is still seen to provide competitive advantages, albeit short-lived, in the valuation and structuring of complex transactions. This requirement is increasingly negated by structuring off-the-shelf system to allow incorporation of customised valuational pricing algorithms to allow standard systems to be customised to a degree. This negates to some extent the advantages of proprietary pricing and trading technology.

A wide variety of systems are available and a number of surveys of available swap and derivative software have been published.[2]

2. See for example Boris Antl (1989) (August); "Swap Software" (1990).

A key aspect in acquiring appropriate technology/software to support derivative operations is to identify factors determining choice between competing systems. *Exhibit 41.5* sets out a brief summary of some of the major issues that are considered relevant to system selection.

Exhibit 41.5
System Selection Criteria

1. Product coverage

- What products (currency swaps, interest rate swaps, FRAs etc) are covered?
- Within each product range what types of variations on standard transactions are capable of being handled by the system (for example, are there flexible frameworks for creation, manipulation, cash flow generation create unique transaction structures)?
- Is there capacity to combine various instruments (for example, embed an option within a swap to create a hybrid and cross-market structures)?
- The range of markets or currencies handled (including whether there are standard templates or formats for major markets, products and currencies)?

2. Pricing issues

- Type of valuation method utilised (par, zero coupon, synthetic, blended, user-defined, type of interpolation technique utilised)?
- What is the method utilised to capture market data such as exchange rates, interest rates, etc (that is, are they required to be manually input or can direct feeds from external information services—Reuters, Telerate screens etc—be encompassed)?
- How is the market data incorporated into valuation methodology? Are the prices, rates etc generated and utilised in transaction calculations transparent to the user to facilitate analysis and verification of each calculation process?
- Is market data stored to create an extensive data base of information which can be quickly and easily tapped?
- Can a particular transaction structure be created and stored and priced or repriced against a variety of rate structures to rapidly assist sales and marketing of a product?
- How does the user interface operate: for example, are transaction details input using standard menu driven screens with automatic default settings (which may be able to be customised); can rapid movements between screens/menus be achieved (for example windows/multi-tasking environment)?

3. Portfolio revaluation/risk management

- How does the portfolio revalue existing transactions? What is the processing time?
- Can revaluations/analysis be performed on a part of the portfolio (selected by a discriminant such as currency, type of product, counterparty or groups of counterparties)?
- As with pricing, what types of valuation methods are utilised? Can customised/proprietary valuation risk analysis techniques be utilised?
- What risk analysis is performed (for example, parallel and non-parallel yield curve movements, types of duration analysis, gap analysis, payment analysis, principal stripping, convexity analysis, cash analysis, accrual analysis, reinvestment analysis, cash flow gridding, average life, future value, partial differential sensitivity, time decay analysis, multi-currency correlated standard deviation analysis, equivalent risk profile and cash flow, money market futures, cash bonds generic swaps, debt futures terms, blended, user-defined)?
- Can portfolio risk across products be integrated to provide for management of the derivatives portfolios in conjunction? Can this incorporate assumed correlation relationships between related variables?
- Can risk profiles be analysed graphically and displayed, preferably, in three-dimensional graphic structures?

Exhibit 41.5—continued

- Can particular hedge structures be modelled and analysed? Can hedge structures be optimised? If so, by what optimisation routine (user-defined or other prenominated algorithm)?

4. Operations issues

- Are transaction confirmations automatically created from deal inputs?
- Is there facility to automatically update existing transactions in respect of variable transaction data, such as floating rate resets?
- Does the system produce full standard confirmations and periodic rate and payment advice providing comprehensive information to the counterparty? Are these documents editable? What controls are imposed on these edits?
- Does the system generate automatic payment advice/settlement instructions based on pre-specified standard payment instructions?
- Does the system encompass a diary reporting structure giving adequately detailed information regarding upcoming events/cash flow payments etc?

5. Control/limits issues

- Does the system automatically calculate customer exposure for the purposes of internal and external (including regulatory) reporting requirements? Can multiple methods be defined?
- Can specific customers/transactions be identified within the given method of exposure management?
- Does the system automatically calculate market risk and provide comparisons covering all types of risks?

6. Accounting/reporting

- Does the system provide daily revaluations, profit (on a per period—daily, weekly etc and year-to-date basis), profit and loss and full accounting information?
- Does the system cover dual accounting streams for differentiated tax and financial accounting?
- Does the system provide for flexible, multi-currency accounting?
- Does it provide full hedge accounting and profit and loss amortisation?
- Does it provide information on specific broker commissions, fees, statements?
- Is there an automatic interface with nominated general ledger?
- How extensive is the management reporting facility within the system (can this be standardised for each client)?
- What audit capabilities (audit trails etc) are available within the system?

7. Regulatory information

- Does the system generate reports required by regulating authorities covering credit and market risk?
- Does it allow analysis of capital requirements in terms of credit and market risk?
- Are there capital utilisation optimisation routines available?

8. Data base and system issues

- What is the type of data base available? Which number of transactions can be stored and handled? What is the manipulation speed, for example, particularly with reference to portfolio revaluation and risk analysis?
- How much counterparty information can be stored (for example, can all information relating to individual contracts, multiple settlement instructions, documentation status, special documentation requirements, credit limits, market exposure, product coverage etc be stored on a single file)? What is the database design and hierarchy?
- What is the access structure to relevant files, including access to transaction values and accrual data for historical purposes, as well as interface to other systems to facilitate file transfer etc?

Exhibit 41.5—continued

- Types of hardware on which the system operates, including hardware and operating system requirements? Is it networkable, with multi-user, multi-site (including remote connecting) capabilities?
- What is the source code language?
- What type of interface capabilities are available, including interface with other systems, and other communications technologies such as telex and facsimile networks?
- Can the system allow on-line inquiries to be made of data stored using one of several data elements within a data file?
- What are the security arrangements within the system? For example, what access rights can be nominated, are individual files date stamped on entry/amendment including identifying individual making the changes etc?

9. Vendor issues

- Details of vendor including financial standing and affiliations.
- Individual(s) within vendor who will be involved in project.
- What type of installation support, including staff training, is available.
- What are the maintenance arrangements, including terms of any maintenance contract available?
- Are systems enhancements planned and on what terms are they available to existing users?
- Will the vendor customise the system, if required, to user requirements?
- Details of other users of the system.
- What type of system documentation is provided.

Note: The above list is based in part on Chris Phillips (1990).

The list is by no means comprehensive but indicates a variety of issues that must be addressed in selecting an appropriate swap or derivatives support system.

In practice, the following factors, which are necessarily more subjective, are also important:*

- *Provability*—a system must be able to prove that all calculations are done correctly.
- *Reliability*—systems failure must not cause loss of data or file.
- *Expandability*—the system can be amended or expanded to meet future needs.
- *Maintainability*—adequate maintenance provisions, not overly dependent on expert staff, are available.
- *Integration*—the system provides for possible integration with other internal systems.
- *Upgradability*—both hardware and software are adaptable to evolving technological factors.
- *Multi-user capacities*—the system allows openness, flexibility and efficient resource management.

---

* These criteria are identified in John Howland Jackson (1992) (Summer).

OPERATIONAL AND CONTROL ASPECTS—BEST PRACTICES

In middle 1993, the Group of Thirty released its global derivative study group results, entitled "Derivatives: Practices and Principles". *Appendix B* to this chapter summarises the key recommendations for dealers and end users of the study.

APPENDIX A

MANAGEMENT CHECKLIST FOR DERIVATIVES FINANCE

Checklist one: organisational/marketing structure

Does the organisation provide adequate oversight of derivatives trading?

- Does the overall derivatives trading operation report to a senior manager within the company?
- Is there adequate supervision and independent monitoring of trading personnel?
- Is there a risk-monitoring mechanism in place that is independent of trading personnel and reports to a senior manager?
- Do the accounting and operations functions report to a senior financial or operational manager? If not, are they responsible to a senior manager other than the business manager?

Is there a plan that outlines the process for implementing new derivatives products?

- Is there an approval process that evaluates risks before new products can be traded?
- Are operational and accounting procedures established before a new product can be traded?
- Can new products be traded on a trial basis?
- Is a cost-benefit analysis performed to insure that operational costs do not exceed profits?
- Is the marketing staff informed of new products?
- Are there avenues for marketing representatives to obtain information about the complexities of new products?

Are there organisational charts?

Checklist two: front office controls

Are all trades executed within well defined limits structures?

- Is there a process for determining that a counterparty has available credit and market limits before a trade is executed?
- Is there daily reporting of exceptions to trading and counterparty credit limits to an independent monitoring function?
- Does the trading manager have a real time method of monitoring exposure?
- Are externally determined trading limits in place by both geographical location and trader?

Are pricing models available and secure?

- Are pricing models reviewed by an independent function within or outside the organisation?

Checklist three: trade initiation procedures

Is access to the trading system limited to authorised personnel?

- Is access to trading systems password controlled?
- Must passwords be changed frequently?

Is the trade entry process formalised?

- What is the order process flow from the dealer's verbal commitment to the final booking of a deal?
  —Is there a queuing mechanism in operation to insure all deals are processed in a timely fashion?
  —What is the length of time from when a dealer commits until deals (both OTC and exchange traded) are officially entered into the system?
- Are confirms processed rapidly?
  —Are confirms sent in a timely fashion?
  —Is there an aging mechanism for outstanding confirms?
  —What are the average days elapsed from the time that an OTC derivatives trade is verbally committed before it is legally confirmed?
- Is there a feedback loop for traders to sign off on the terms of the deal once operations have completed processing?
- Is there a structured trade change process?
  —Do traders have the ability to change the terms of a deal once it is committed?
  —Do traders have to approve changes to booked deals?
  —Are there formal dispute resolution procedures for deals that one of the counterparties does not recognise?
  —Are all trading room conversations recorded? Are the recordings stored long enough to be used in resolving disputes that may arise?
  —Is there a system to track the dispute resolution process?

Is there a document tracking system in place?

- Are follow-up procedures in place to obtain missing documents?
- Is there timely reporting of missing documentation?
- Are legal agreements for derivatives trades current?

Checklist four: ongoing operational procedures

Is the payments processing system well controlled and efficient?

- What percentages of payments are late on derivatives trades?
  —Are trends increasing for either incoming or outgoing payments?
  —Is there a process in place to monitor late payments?
  —Is compensation always claimed for late incoming payments?
  —What is the trend of late penalties collected in the past?
  —What is the trend of late penalties paid in the past?
- What percentages of payments are handled manually?
  —Is the number of manually processed payments increasing?
  —Are there tickler files for manual payments?

Are resets handled automatically?

- What is the source of the quotes? Is it specified at time of trade?
- Does the system automatically prompt resets each day?
- How frequently are there disagreements over reset rates? How are they resolved?

Is there a process to control collateral?

- Is its location tracked?
- Is the collateral value compared to the valuation of the deal periodically?
- Is there a process to obtain additional collateral if the value of the deal rises or the collateral falls?

Checklist five: ongoing accounting process

Does the accounting process provide an independent check on the success of the business?

- How frequently are the books closed?
- What market price data are used? Is the collection process automatic or manual?
- Are rates, volatilities and prices obtained independently? How many observations are obtained?
- Is access to the prices and volatilities used by accounting password controlled and restricted to the accounting department?
- How are deals committed but unconfirmed accounted for?
- Are there procedures for handling data that appear to be incorrect?
- Are any proprietary models used for accounting mark-to-market valuations?
  —Under what circumstances would a proprietary model be acceptable for accounting purposes?
  —Is there a formal approval process for models that is independent of the business unit?
  —How different are the values than those that are produced by market-accepted models?
  —Are there adequate controls over the security of and changes in pricing models?
- How often are front office/back office reconciliations handled?
  —How large are the reconciliation differences?
  —Are formal approval processes in place for sign-off on reconciliation differences?
  —Do senior managers sign off if reconciliation differences are large?
- Does the accounting department have the ability to recreate previous closes?
- Are traders evaluated based on the accounting results? Are long-term goals considered?
- Are there effective controls to insure that deals used to hedge are segregated from trading positions?
- Do hedge accounting guidelines, documentation requirements and amortisation rules exist?

Checklist six: risk management process

Is management fully informed of the business risks?

- How frequently is top management informed of credit and product exposures and excesses?
- Is top management involved in decisions about amounts of acceptable credit and product exposures?

- Is top management aware of the sensitivity of the book to changes in rates, volatilities, etc?

Is an effective risk management process in place?

- How often is the complete derivatives portfolio marked to market? How long does it take?
- How is the price change in the derivatives portfolio analysed?

—Can various risk measures (including such items as time decay (theta), market price change (delta, gamma and vega), new transactions, expired transactions, etc) be explained?

—Is a catastrophe analysis performed? How far are the rates and volatilities used in the catastrophe analysis from current rates and volatilities?

- What other risk measures are monitored (for example, volatility) and how often?
- What risk limit systems are in place?
- How is exposure per counterparty analysed?

—How often are counterparty risk levels calculated?

- Are credit limits maintained by counterparty?

—How often are they updated?

—Is there an automated process to monitor and report positions against credit limits?

—Do monitoring procedures weigh customer exposures for both derivative and funded products?

- Are loss limits maintained and enforced by trader?

What would happen if the biggest counterparty went out of business tomorrow?

- How long (hours, days, weeks) would it take to fully measure the impact?
- What are the exact positions with that party, that is, what is the exposure?
- What would be the loss?
- Are there procedures for winding down business with troubled counterparties?

Are systems designed to minimise risk?

- How many separate software packages are used to determine the mark-to-market values?
- How many of these software packages are:

—Spreadsheets?

—Micro applications written by dealers?

—Applications internally developed by MIS?

—Applications developed by consultants?

—Commercial software packages used by other firms?

—Audited and by whom?

- Which systems were internally developed? Why?

—Have they been verified by a third party (an independent function within the company or an auditing firm)?

- What external systems are used?

—Have they been verified by a third party (another company or auditing firm)?

- How are these various systems integrated?

—By hand?

—By spreadsheet?

—Within a central data repository?

Checklist seven: disaster recovery process

Is there a disaster recovery plan?

- Has it been tested?
- Are records stored off-site?
- How frequently are back-ups made?
- How frequently are records moved off-site?

Does the disaster recovery plan cover both the front and back offices?

How often are simulations or fire drills run to test the recovery plan?

Source: C.ATS Software Inc.

APPENDIX B

Group of Thirty Recommendations

On the following pages, we have summarised the recommendations and, for dealers and end users, the extent to which each recommendation relates to

- the culture of the organisation, in terms of the appetite for risk and the way in which it is managed;
- the systems (management and technology) used;
- the expertise at all levels, from board through management to those who originate and process the business.

We would stress that this is a summary and would commend readers to look at the full recommendations in detail in order to draw more conclusions on the implications for specific institutions.

The Group of Thirty—Global Derivatives Study

Recommendations for Dealers and End Users	Culture	Systems	Expertise
1. Dealers and end users should use derivatives in a manner consistent with the overall risk management and capital policies approved by their boards of directors. Policies governing derivatives use should be clearly defined, including the purposes for which these transactions are to be undertaken. Senior management should approve procedures and controls to implement these policies and management at all levels should enforce them.	**H**	**M**	**M**
2. Dealers should mark their derivatives positions to market on at least a daily basis, for risk management purposes.	**M**	**H**	**L**
3. Derivatives portfolios of dealers should be valued based on mid-market levels less specific adjustments or an appropriate bid or offer level. Mid-market valuation adjustments should allow for expected future costs such as unearned credit spread, close-out costs, investing and funding costs, and administrative costs.	**L**	**H**	**M**
4. Dealers should measure the components of revenue regularly and in sufficient detail to understand the sources risk.	**M**	**H**	**M**
5. Dealers should use a consistent measure to calculate daily the market risk of their derivatives positions and compare it to market risk limits. • Market risk is best measured as "value at risk" using probability analysis based upon a common confidence interval (for example, two standard deviations) and time horizon (for example, a one day exposure).	**H**	**H**	**H**

Key: **L** Low implication **M** Medium implication **H** High implication

Recommendations for Dealers and End Users	Culture	Systems	Expertise
• Components of market risk that should be considered across the term structure include: absolute price or rate change (delta); convexity (gamma); volatility (vega); time decay (theta); basis or correlation; and discount rate (rho).			
6. Dealers should regularly perform simulations to determine how their portfolios would perform under stress conditions.	M	H	M
7. Dealers should periodically forecast the cash investment and funding requirements arising from their derivatives portfolios.	L	H	M
8. Dealers should have a market risk management function, with clear independence and authority, to ensure that the following responsibilities are carried out: • The development of risk limit policies and the monitoring of transactions and positions for adherence to these policies. (See recommendation 5.) • The design of stress scenarios to measure the impact of market conditions, however improbable, that might cause market gaps, volatility swings, or disruptions of major relationships, or might reduce liquidity in the face of unfavourable market linkages, concentrated market making, or credit exhaustion. (See recommendation 6.) • The design of revenue reports quantifying the contribution of various risk components, and of market risk measures such as value at risk. (See recommendations 4 and 5.) • The monitoring of variance between the actual volatility of portfolio value and that predicted by the measure of market risk. • The review and approval of pricing models and valuation systems used by front and back office personnel, and the development of reconciliation procedures if different systems are used.	H	M	H
9. As appropriate to the nature, size and complexity of their derivatives activities, end users should adopt the same valuation and market risk management practices that are recommended for dealers. Specifically, they should consider; regularly marking to market their derivatives transactions for risk management purposes; periodically forecasting the cash investing and funding requirements arising from their derivatives transactions; and establishing a	H	H	M

KEY: **L** Low implication **M** Medium implication **H** High implication

Recommendations for Dealers and End Users	Culture	Systems	Expertise
clearly independent and authoritative function to design and assure adherence to prudent risk limits.			
10. Dealers and end users should measure credit exposure on derivatives in two ways: • Current exposure, which is the replacement cost of derivatives transactions, that is, their market value. • Potential exposure, which is an estimate of the future replacement costs of derivatives transactions. It should be calculated using probability analysis based upon broad confidence intervals (for example, two standard deviations) over the remaining terms of the transaction.	**M**	**H**	**M**
11. Credit exposures on derivatives and all other credit exposures to a counterparty, should be aggregated taking into consideration enforceable netting arrangements. Credit exposures should be calculated regularly and compared to credit limits.	**L**	**H**	**L**
12. Dealers and end users should have a credit risk management function with clear independence and authority and with analytical capabilities in derivatives, responsible for: • approving credit exposure measurement standards; • setting credit limits and monitoring their use; • reviewing credits and concentrations of credit risks; • reviewing and monitoring risk reduction arrangements.	**M**	**M**	**H**
13. Dealers and end users are encouraged to use one Master Agreement as widely as possible with each counterparty to document existing and future derivatives transactions, including foreign exchange forwards and options. Master agreements should provide for payments netting and close-out netting, using a full two-way payments approach.	**M**	**H**	**L**
14. Dealers and end users should assess both the benefits and costs of credit enhancement and related risk reduction arrangements. Where it is proposed that credit downgrades would trigger early termination or collateral requirements, participants should carefully consider their own capacity and that of their counterparties to meet the potentially substantial funding needs that might result.	**H**	**H**	**H**
15. Dealers and end users should work together on a continuing basis to identify and recommend solutions for issues of legal enforceability, both within and	**M**	**M**	**H**

KEY: **L** Low implication **M** Medium implication **H** High implication

	Recommendations for Dealers and End Users	Culture	Systems	Expertise
	across jurisdictions as activities evolve and new types of transactions are developed.			
16.	Dealers and end users must ensure that their derivatives activities are undertaken by professionals in sufficient number and with the appropriate experience, skill levels and degrees of specialisation. These professionals include specialists who transact and manage the risk involved, their supervisors, and those responsible for processing, reporting, controlling and auditing the activities.	**M**	**L**	**H**
17.	Dealers and end users must ensure that adequate systems for data capture, processing, settlement and management reporting are in place so that derivatives transactions are conducted in an orderly and efficient manner in compliance with management policies. Dealers should have risk management systems that measure the risks incurred in their derivatives activities including market and credit risks. End users should have risk management systems that measure the risks incurred in their derivatives activities based upon their nature, size and complexity.	**M**	**H**	**L**
18.	Management of dealers and end users should designate who is authorised to commit their institutions to derivatives transactions.	**M**	**H**	**L**
19.	International harmonisation of accounting standards for derivatives is desirable. Pending the adoption of harmonised standards, the following accounting practices are recommended: • Dealers should account for derivatives transactions by marking them to market, taking changes in value to income each period. • End users should account for derivatives used to manage risks so as to achieve a consistency of income recognition treatment between those instruments and the risks being managed. Thus, if the risk being managed is accounted for at cost (or, in the case of an anticipatory hedge, not yet recognised) changes in the value of qualifying risk management instrument should be deferred until a gain or loss is recognised on the risk being managed. Or, if the risk being managed is marked to market with changes in value being taken to income, a qualifying risk management instrument should be treated in a comparable fashion. • End users should account for derivatives not qualifying for risk management treatment on a mark-to-market basis.	**H**	**L**	**M**

KEY: **L** Low implication **M** Medium implication **H** High implication

Recommendations for Dealers and End Users	Culture	Systems	Expertise
• Amounts due to and from counterparties should only be offset when there is a legal right to set off or when enforceable netting arrangements are in place. Where local regulations prevent adoption of these practices, disclosure along these lines is nevertheless recommended.			
20. Financial statements of dealers and end users should contain sufficient information about their use of derivatives to price an understanding of the purposes for which transactions are undertaken, the extent of the transactions, the degree of risk involved and how the transactions have been accounted for. Pending the adoption of harmonised accounting standards, the following disclosures are recommended: • information about management's attitude to financial risks, how instruments are used, and how risks are monitored and controlled; • accounting policies; • analysis of positions at the balance sheet date; • analysis of the credit risk inherent in those positions; • for dealers only, additional information about the extent of their activities in financial instruments.	H	H	L

Recommendation for legislators, regulators and supervisors

21. Regulators and supervisors should recognise the benefits of netting arrangements where and to the full extent that they are enforceable, and encourage their use by reflecting these arrangements in capital adequacy standards. Specifically, they should promptly implement the recognition of the effectiveness of bilateral close-out netting in bank capital regulations.

22. Legislation, regulations, and supervisors, including central banks should work in concert with dealers and end users to identify and remove any remaining legal and regulatory uncertainties.
    - the form of documentation required to create legally enforceable agreements;
    - the capacity of parties, such as governmental entities, insurance companies, pension funds and building societies, to enter into transactions;
    - the enforceability of bilateral close-out netting and collateral arangements in bankruptcy;
    - the enforceability of multibranch netting arrangements in bankruptcy;
    - the legality/enforceability of derivatives transactions.

23. Legislators and tax authorities are encouraged to review and, where appropriate, amend tax laws and regulations that disadvantage the use of derivatives in risk management strategies. Tax impediments include the

KEY: **L** Low implication **M** Medium implication **H** High implication

inconsistent or uncertain tax treatment of gains and losses on the derivatives, in comparison with the gains and losses that arise from the risks being managed.

24. Accounting standards-setting bodies in each country should seek, as a matter of priority, comprehensive guidance on accounting and reporting of transactions in financial instruments, including derivatives, and should work towards international harmonisation of standards on this subject.

Source: Price Waterhouse Client Memorandum—*Group of Thirty Report on Derivatives* (Price Waterhouse: Sydney, Australia, 1993).

Chapter 42

Accounting for Swaps and Financial Derivatives

KPMG Peat Marwick, Chartered Accountants

INTRODUCTION

The proliferation of financial instruments has outpaced the accounting profession. The international accounting bodies are cognisant of the need for authoritative guidance on the accounting treatment for the latest financial instruments and a number of accounting statements and exposure drafts have been released in recent years. However, in many countries definitive accounting standards on accounting for financial instruments have not been released.

Relevant accounting statements which exist include:

- E40, "Financial Instruments" (exposure draft—International Accounting Standards Committee);
- SFAS 105, "Disclosure of Information about Financial Instruments with Off-Balance Sheet Risk and Financial Instruments with Concentrations of Credit Risk" (United States);
- SFAS 107, "Disclosures about Fair Value of Financial Instruments" (United States);
- Statement of Recommended Accounting Practice, "Off-Balance Sheet Instruments and Other Commitments and Contingent Liabilities" (United Kingdom);
- ED59, "Financial Instruments" (exposure draft—Australia).

The standard setting process in this area is still developing and it is to be hoped that accounting practitioners in all countries will soon be provided with accounting standards to assist them in accounting for financial instruments.

In the absence of comprehensive accounting standards, accounting practitioners have developed a body of generally accepted accounting practice which seeks to reflect the "substance" of the transactions.

This chapter examines the basic components of interest rate and currency swaps, FRAs and caps, collars and floors from the accounting perspective and provides general guidance on the accounting treatment and disclosure requirements in relation to these financial instruments.

For each instrument the accounting principles are established at the outset. This is followed by an analysis of the accounting treatment likely to be adopted by both financial institutions and corporate sector entities in recording the instruments. The disclosure requirements and prudential supervision considerations in relation to each instrument concludes each section.

ACCOUNTING FOR INTEREST RATE AND CURRENCY SWAPS

General accounting principles

The accounting treatment to be applied to interest rate and currency swaps must follow the economic substance of the transactions to produce a true and fair view of an organisation's activities.

When accounting for swaps, there are two constituent parts that need to be dealt with:

- the principal amounts, which may be notionally or physically exchanged; and
- the interest flows, which may be in the same or different currencies.

Principal

The principal amounts exchanged, whether they are actual or notional, are not in the legal form of loans or deposits and since a swap does not involve the provision or receipt of finance, it is not appropriate to record the amounts exchanged in the balance sheet. However, the principal amounts should be recorded in general ledger memorandum accounts. Therefore, in a cross-currency swap where there may be an actual exchange of principal, there is no grossing up of the balance sheet, the amounts merely pass through the bank or nostro accounts.

Assume company A and company B have entered an interest rate swap based on a notional principal of A$10m under which company A receives floating rate interest and pays fixed rate interest. The arrangement is depicted diagramatically in *Exhibit 42.1*.

Exhibit 42.1
Interest Rate Swap

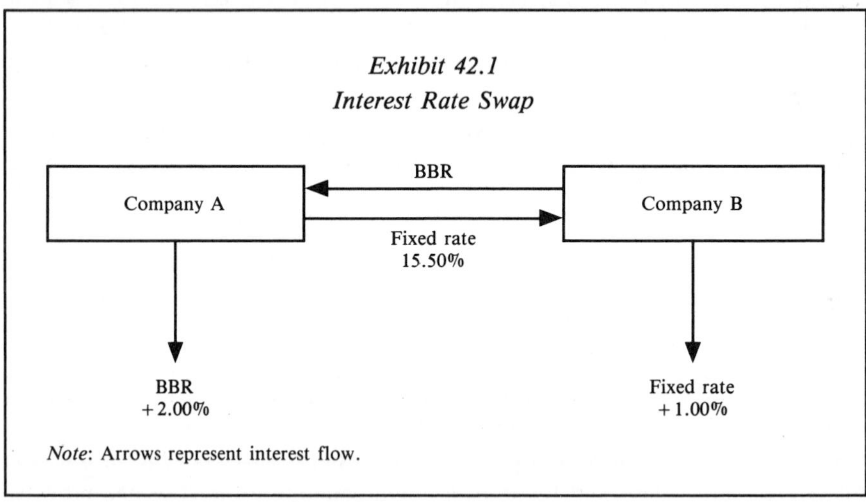

Note: Arrows represent interest flow.

The accounting entries to recognise the notional principal balances in the books of company A are:

At deal date	**A$**	**A$**
DR floating interest rate swap receivable (memo)	XXX	
CR fixed interest rate swap swap payable (memo)		XXX

To record notional principal balances in memorandum accounts

At maturity date

DR fixed interest rate swap payable (memo)	xxx	
CR floating interest rate swap receivable (memo)		xxx

To reverse the notional principal balances recorded in the memorandum accounts above.

Interest flows

There are two alternative treatments for recognising the interest flows associated with a swap: accrual or revaluation.

Accrual

The accrual treatment is based on the traditional "matching" concept which seeks to apportion the income or expense associated with a transaction into the periods to which it relates. As swap payments and receipts are in the nature of interest they should also be treated in a similar manner as interest income or expense. Intuitively this treatment is most suited to swaps which are driven by the provision or receipt of finance. It is also appropriate for swaps that are used to hedge financial assets and liabilities where the revenue and expense associated with those assets and liabilities is recognised on an accruals basis.

Again with reference to *Exhibit 42.1* assume company A is receiving floating rate interest based on BBR and paying fixed rate interest.

The accounting entries to recognise the interest accruals in the books of company A are:

At balance date	**A$**	**A$**
DR floating interest rate swap receivable (B/S)	xxx	
CR swap interest (P/L)		xxx
DR swap interest (P/L)	xxx	
CR fixed interest rate swap payable (B/S)		xxx

To record swap interest accruals

At interest settlement date

DR swap interest (P/L)	xxx	
CR floating interest rate swap receivable (B/S)		xxx
DR fixed interest rate swap payable (B/S)	xxx	
CR swap interest (P/L)		xxx

To record reversal of swap interest accrual entries above

DR nostro (B/S)	xxx	
CR swap interest (P/L)		xxx

To record floating rate swap interest received

DR swap interest (P/L)	xxx	
CR nostro (B/S)		xxx

To record fixed rate swap interest paid.

Revaluation

The concept of revaluation stems from the fact that a swap is a financial instrument with a value. The value may be calculated by discounting the future swap cash flows to their net present value. When the flows are actually paid or received they should be taken directly to the swap trading account in the profit and loss account. This treatment is normally only appropriate for an entity that is trading in swaps and is discussed below. Where an entity uses a swap as a hedging instrument it would not be appropriate to account for the swap on a revaluation basis unless the underlying hedged position/instrument itself was recognised in the profit and loss on a revaluation basis. Financial institutions should make the distinction between swaps that are held as hedges against their own balance sheet and swaps that are trading instruments.

The accounting entry to recognise a profit on the revaluation of a trading swap is:

	A$	**A$**
DR revaluation suspense (B/S)	xxx	
CR swap revaluation (P/L)		xxx

The revaluation of swaps is discussed in detail below.

Foreign exchange implications

A currency swap in isolation does not create a foreign exchange exposure in respect of the principal amount underlying the deal. This exposure is eliminated due to the agreement of the parties to re-exchange the same amount of principal at the conclusion of the swap. The principal exchange and re-exchange of an A$ and US$ currency swap can be illustrated as:

	A$	**US$**
Exchange of principals at deal date	xxx	(xxx)
Re-exchange of principals at maturity	(xxx)	xxx
Foreign exchange exposure	Nil	Nil

Currency swaps, however, do create an exposure in respect of the forward cash flows representing the interest payments and receipts. The effect of currency fluctuations on this exposure should be included in the revaluation of the foreign currency leg of a cross-currency swap. If the accruals method is being followed, the effect of currency fluctuations will only be taken into account to the extent that they affect the interest accrued to date. Any further gains or losses arising from currency fluctuations should be offset by gains or losses on the underlying hedged position.

Swap accounting decision model

The issue of whether a swap is a hedge or a trade is a crucial one in determining the most appropriate accounting treatment. The decision model set out in *Exhibit 42.2* will assist in determining whether accrual or revaluation is the most appropriate accounting treatment.

Accounting treatment—financial institutions

The motive for entering the swap market is the best indication as to the most appropriate accounting treatment to be adopted with respect to that transaction, that is, either accrual or revaluation treatment.

Hedging with swaps

Both financial institutions and corporate sector entities may use swaps as part of an asset and liability management strategy.

Typically corporations enter hedging swaps to transfer funds received from the issue of a medium-term bond or note, into another currency and/or to convert fixed rate finance into floating rate finance or vice versa. The accounting treatment for these transactions is the same whether or not that entity is a financial institution or a corporate sector entity.

Exhibit 42.2
Swap Accounting Decision Model

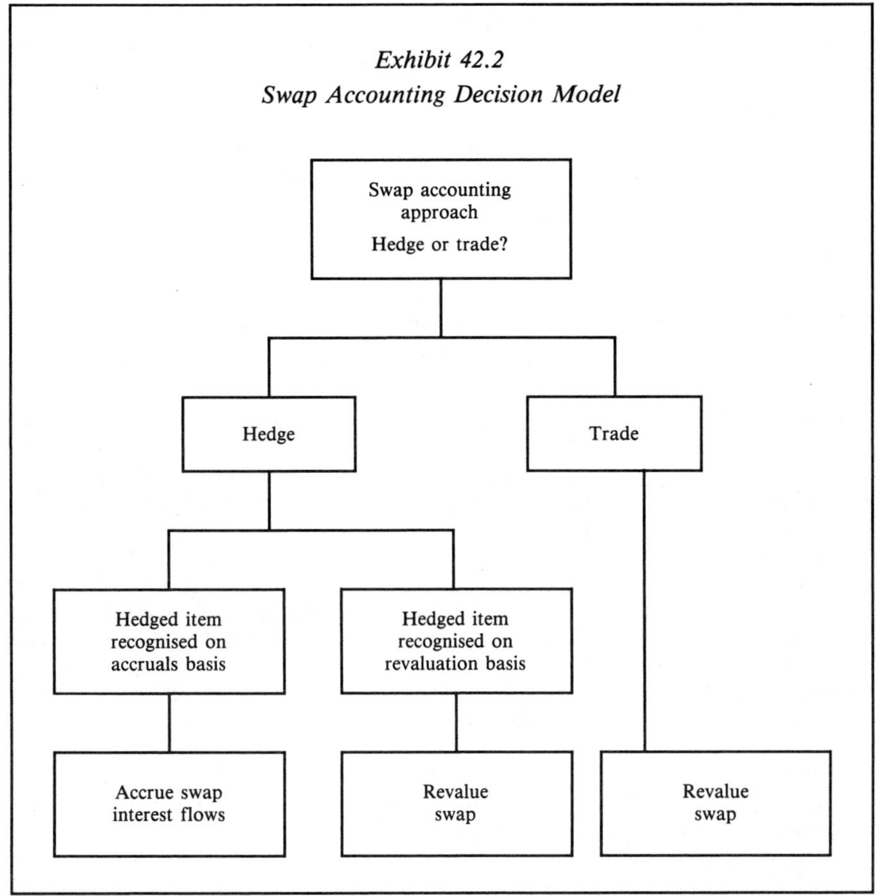

Principal

In an interest rate swap, the notional principal is *not* exchanged. The only flow of funds relates to interest on the notional principal amount. However, it would be appropriate to record the notional principal amounts in memorandum accounts in the general ledger.

In a currency swap, any initial exchange of principals will be recorded through the bank or nostro accounts. The forward commitment to re-exchange principals should be recorded as forward deals but separately identified in off-balance sheet swap memorandum accounts. As noted above, a currency swap in isolation does not create a foreign currency exposure in respect of the principal amount underlying the transaction. This is because the amounts exchanged at the commencement of the transaction are re-exchanged at maturity. Accordingly no profit or loss should arise on revaluing the principal balances. However if the foreign currency asset or liability hedged by the currency swap is revalued (as it is required to be under most foreign currency accounting standards, for example, Australia's AASB 1012, "Accounting for Foreign Currency Transactions"), the forward exchange under the currency swap must also be revalued.

The revaluation amount should be shown as a deferred foreign exchange gain or loss, that is, swap debtor or creditor. The entry in the profit and loss account will net off against the entry required to restate the asset or liability being hedged.

Interest flows

To reflect the substance of the transaction, the interest payments and receipts should be accounted for on an accruals basis, as a net adjustment to the interest expense on the borrowing.

Fees

Financial institutions acting as intermediaries may receive fees in the form of cash payments as opposed to adjustments to the interest rate pricing levels.

Broker's fees should be recognised on deal date because they are remuneration for bringing the parties together.

Fees received for intermediation services need to be reviewed in the light of the overall profitability of a deal. Where a large fee is received on deal date and no return (in the form of an interest spread) is generated, consideration should be given to amortising the fee over the life of the deal to match income with the expense of administering the deal and absorbing the credit risk. In the situation where the intermediary acts as broker as well as intermediary, the distinction between the constituent parts of the fee becomes blurred. Some of the fee could be recognised on deal date to recognise the work done in bringing the parties together, the rest being amortised over the life of the deal. In such a situation it would be preferable for the financial institution to determine a formal policy for accounting for fees, in particular the basis for calculating the amount of fee that can be recognised on deal date, and to apply this consistently.

Accounting entries

The accounting entries to recognise both interest rate and currency (unless indicated) hedging swaps are as follows:

- At deal date:
  - —record notional principal balances in memorandum accounts (interest rate and currency swaps);
  - —record exchange of principals in bank or nostro accounts (currency swap);
  - —record commitment to re-exchange principals at maturity in memorandum accounts (currency swap).
- At balance date:
  - —record swap interest accruals (pay and receive);
  - —revalue the asset or liability being hedged to the current spot rate taking the difference to the profit and loss account (currency swap);
  - —revalue the forward commitment to re-exchange principals at the current spot rate and take the difference to the profit and loss account. The revaluation surplus and deficit arising from the above revaluations will contra against each other in the profit and loss account (currency swap);
  - —recognise the deferred foreign exchange gain or loss created as a result or a revaluation of the forward commitment as a sundry debtor or creditor in the balance sheet (currency swap).
- At interest payment date:
  - —reverse swap interest accruals;

—record swap interest payments and receipts.

- At maturity date:
  —reverse notional principal balances recorded in memorandum accounts (interest rate swap);
  —record re-exchange of principals in nostro accounts (currency swap);
  —reverse commitment to re-exchange principals recorded in memorandum accounts (currency swap);
  —reverse swap interest accruals;
  —record swap interest payments and receipts.

An example of the accounting entries in respect of hedging currency swaps is illustrated below in *Exhibit 42.3*.

Exhibit 42.3
Hedging—Currency Swap

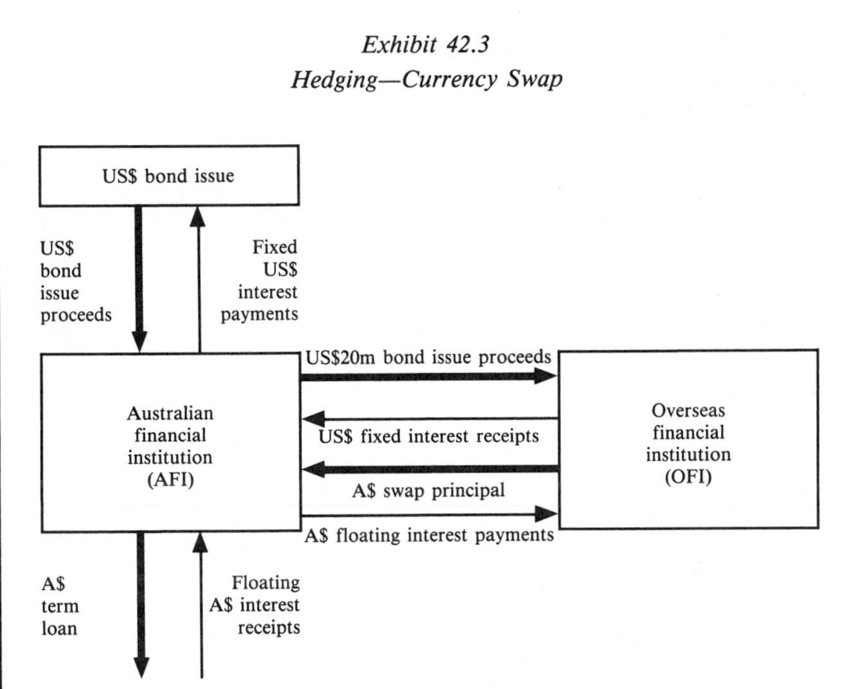

Note: Bold arrows represent principal flows whilst thin arrows represent interest flows.

ACCOUNTING ENTRIES—HEDGING WITH CROSS-CURRENCY SWAPS

Assume an Australian financial institution (AFI) has raised US$20m from a bond issue. To meet a term loan commitment in A$ AFI has entered a swap whereby the proceeds of the US$20m issue are swapped for A$. Over the term of the swap AFI will receive US$ interest on the US$20m and will pay A$ interest on the A$ balance it receives under the swap.

Additional information

Bond issue:

Term:	three years from 31 December 19X8
Coupon rate:	12.00% pa paid annually in arrears
Interest calculation:	CD basis (actual/360)
Interest paid:	31 December

Exhibit 42.3—continued

Term loan:

Term:	three years from 31 December 19X8
Interest rate:	BBR + 1.00% set semi-annually in advance
Interest received:	31 December

Currency swap:

Term:	three years from 31 December 19X8
Interest rate:	fixed rate (receive): 12.00% floating rate (pay): BBR + 1.00%
Swap fee:	A$200,000

Interest rates:

BBR set at:	13.00% at 31 December 19X8 14.00% at 30 June 19X9

Exchange rates:

31 December 19X8	A$1/US$0.625
30 June 19X9	A$1/US$0.650
31 December 19X9	A$1/US$0.725

The following accounting entries are required in the books of AFI to account for the bond issue, term loan and currency swap:

Entries at 31 December 19X8

Bond issue

1. DR US$ nostro (B/S)	US$20,000,000	
CR bond issue (B/S)		US$20,000,000
To record Euronote issue and receipt of proceeds		

Term loan

2. DR term loan (B/S)	A$32,000,000	
CR A$ nostro (B/S)		A$32,000,000
To record term loan advance		

Currency swap

3. DR prepaid swap fees (B/S)	A$200,000	
CR A$ nostro (B/S)		A$200,000
To record payment of swap fee		
4. DR A$ nostro (B/S)	A$32,000,000	
CR swap positions (memo)		A$32,000,000
DR swap position (memo)	US$20,000,000	
CR US$ nostro (B/S)		US$20,000,000
To record initial exchange of amounts under currency swap		
5. DR swap position (memo)	A$32,000,000	
CR forward swap payment (memo)		A$32,000,000
DR forward swap receipt (memo)	US$20,000,000	
CR swap position (memo)		US$20,000,000
To record commitment to re-exchange principal amounts under currency swap at maturity		

Entries at 30 June 19X9

Bond issue

6. DR bond interest (P/L)	US$1,216,666	
CR accrued bond interest (B/S)		US$1,216,666
To record accrued interest payable on the Euronote issue, that is, US$20,000,000 × 12.00% (365/2)/360 = US$1,216,666		

Term loan

7. DR accrued interest receivable (B/S)	A$2,240,000	
CR term loan interest (P/L)		A$2,240,000
To record accrued interest receivable on term loan		

Exhibit 42.3—continued

Currency swap

		Debit	Credit
8.	DR swap interest (P/L)	A$2,240,000	
	CR A$ nostro (B/S)		A$2,240,000
	DR US$ nostro (B/S)	US$1,200,000	
	CR swap interest (P/L)		US$1,200,000

To record interest entitlements and obligations under currency swap, that is, (A$32,000,000 × 14.00% (BBR + 1.00%))/2 = A$2,240,000
(US$20,000,000 × 12.00%)/2 = US$1,200,000

		Debit	Credit
9.	DR swap fee expense (P/L)	A$33,333	
	CR prepaid swap fees (B/S)		A$33,333

To record amortisation of swap fee, that is, 1/6 of A$200,000 = A$33,333

		Debit	Credit
10.	DR swap interest (P/L)	US$1,200,000	
	CR bond interest (P/L)		US$1,216,666
	DR spot position (memo)	US$16,666	
	CR swap interest (P/L)		A$1,846,154
	DR bond interest (P/L)	A$1,871,794	
	CR spot position (memo)		A$25,640

To "deal out" US$ profit and loss account into A$ which recognises the position created by the currency swap receipt against bond interest payable

Entries at 31 December 19X9

Bond issue

		Debit	Credit
11.	DR bond interest (P/L)	US$1,216,667	
	DR accrued interest (B/S)	US$1,216,666	
	CR US$ nostro (B/S)		US$2,433,333

To record payment of bond interest

Term loan

		Debit	Credit
12.	DR A$ nostro (B/S)	A$4,640,000	
	CR accrued interest receivable (B/S)		A$2,240,000
	CR term loan interest (P/L)		A$2,400,000

To record receipt of term loan interest

Currency swap

		Debit	Credit
13.	DR swap interest (P/L)	A$2,400,000	
	CR A$ nostro (B/S)		A$2,400,000
	DR US$ nostro (B/S)	US$1,200,000	
	CR swap interest (P/L)		US$1,200,000

To record interest entitlements and obligations under currency swap

		Debit	Credit
14.	DR swap fee expense (P/L)	A$33,333	
	CR prepaid swap fees (B/S)		A$33,333

To reflect amortisation of swap fee, that is, 1/6 of A$200,000 = A$33,333

		Debit	Credit
15.	DR swap interest (P/L)	US$1,200,000	
	CR bond interest (P/L)		US$1,216,667
	DR spot position (memo)	US$16,667	
	CR swap interest (P/L)		A$1,655,172
	DR bond interest (P/L)	A$1,678,160	
	CR spot position (memo)		A$22,988

To "deal out" US$ profit and loss account into A$ which recognises the position created by the currency swap receipt against bond interest payable

Closing entry

		Debit	Credit
16.	DR spot position (memo)	A$2,652	
	CR FX revaluation (P/L)		A$2,652
	DR forward swap payment (memo)	A$32,000,000	
	CR forward swap receipt (memo)		A$27,586,206
	CR swap creditor (B/S)		A$4,413,794

To close out memorandum accounts and consolidate results

Exhibit 42.3—continued

A$		31 December 19X8		30 June 19X9		31 December 19X9	Net balance
Balance sheet							
A$ nostro	2.	32,000,000 CR	8.	2,240,000 CR	12.	4,640,000 DR	40,000 CR
	3.	200,000 CR			13.	2,240,000 CR	
	4.	32,000,000 DR					
Term loan	2.	32,000,000 DR					32,000,000 DR
Prepaid swap fee	3.	200,000 DR	9.	33,333 CR	14.	33,333 CR	133,334 DR
Accrued term loan interest receivable			7.	2,240,000 DR	12.	2,240,000 CR	Nil
Profit and loss							
Term loan interest			7.	2,240,000 CR	12.	2,400,000 CR	4,640,000 CR
Bond interest			10.	1,871,794 DR	15.	1,678,160 DR	3,549,954 DR
Swap interest			8.	2,240,000 DR	13.	2,240,000 DR	978,674 DR
			10.	1,846,154 CR	15.	1,655,172 CR	
Swap fee expense			9.	33,333 DR	14.	33,333 DR	66,666 DR
Memorandum accounts							
Forward swap payment	5.	32,000,000 CR					32,000,000 CR
Spot position			10.	25,640 CR	15.	22,988 CR	48,628 CR
Swap position	4.	32,000,000 CR					Nil
	5.	32,000,000 DR					
		Nil		Nil		Nil	Nil

Exhibit 42.3—continued

US$		31 December 19X8		30 June 19X9		31 December 19X9	Net balance
Balance sheet							
US$ nostro	1.	20,000,000 DR	8.	1,200,000 DR	11.	2,433,333 CR	33,333 CR
	4.	20,000,000 CR			13.	1,200,000 DR	
Bond issue	1.	20,000,000 CR					20,000,000 CR
Accrued Euronote interest payable			6.	1,216,666 CR	11.	1,216,666 DR	Nil
Profit and loss							
Bond interest			6.	1,216,666 DR	11.	1,216,667 DR	Nil
			10.	1,216,666 CR	15.	1,216,667 CR	
Swap interest			8.	1,200,000 CR	13.	1,200,000 CR	Nil
			10.	1,200,000 DR	15.	1,200,000 DR	
Memorandum accounts							
Forward swap receipt	5.	20,000,000 DR					20,000,000 DR
Spot position			10.	16,666 DR	15.	16,667 DR	33,333 DR
Swap position	4.	20,000,000 DR					Nil
	5.	20,000,000 CR					
		Nil		Nil		Nil	Nil

Exhibit 42.3—continued

Worksheet	US$	Equivalent A$ @ 0.725	A$	Total A$	Closing journal	A$ consolidated
Balance sheet						
Nostro	33,333 CR	45,976 CR	40,000 CR	85,976 CR		85,976 CR
Term loan			32,000,000 DR	32,000,000 DR		32,000,000 DR
Bond issue	20,000,000 CR	27,586,206 CR		27,586,206 CR		27,586,206 CR
Prepaid swap fee			133,334 DR	133,334 DR		133,334 DR
Swap creditor					4,413,794 CR	4,413,794 CR
Profit and loss						
Term loan interest			4,640,000 CR	4,640,000 CR		4,640,000 CR
Bond interest			3,549,954 DR	3,549,954 DR		3,549,954 DR
Swap interest			978,674 DR	978,674 DR		978,674 DR
Swap fee expense			66,666 DR	66,666 DR		66,666 DR
Foreign exchange revaluation					2,652 CR	2,652 CR
Memorandum accounts						
Forward swap payment			32,000,000 CR	32,000,000 CR	32,000,000 DR	Nil
Forward swap receipt	20,000,000 DR	27,586,206 DR		27,586,206 DR	27,586,206 CR	Nil
Spot position	33,333 DR	45,976 DR	48,628 CR	2,652 CR	2,652 DR	Nil
	Nil	Nil	Nil	Nil	Nil	Nil

Note: The aggregate of the swap creditor and debtor and bond issue should always equal the balance disclosed as term loan, that is, A$32m being the amount swapped in the currency swap.

Trading in swaps

For financial institutions active in the swap market swaps are seen as more than tools to hedge existing exposure. Swaps are financial instruments with value and as such qualify as legitimate trading instruments. The value of a swap contract is most commonly calculated by discounting the swaps cash flows. In the development years of the swap market a vast majority of swaps had cash flow characteristics similar to a bond. That is, the institution paid or received a fixed payment every six months. Hence, a revaluation methodology was developed based on a bond equivalent yield. This method assumed a constant stream of interest payments which could be invested and allowed for a single discount rate to be applied to all payments.

As the market developed, there was an increase in non-standard transactions such as delayed starts, zero coupons, step-ups and step-downs (in which the notional principal amount changes over time) and non-coterminous payments where the fixed and floating payments are not paid at the same time.

In light of this, dealers and traders made changes to their valuation methodology.

The principal methods of valuing interest rate swaps are as follows:

- par yield;
- zero coupon curve pricing;
- "bootstrapping" or implied forward coupons.

The dominant practice for revaluation of swaps for accounting purposes is zero coupon curve pricing. The critical elements of each method are discussed below.

Par yield

This approach adopts the bond formula to determine the present value of the fixed rate cash flows. All the cash flows are discounted at a constant discount rate derived from the yield on a coupon-based instrument, for example, the yield on a treasury bond paying semi-annual interest, or the inter-bank swap rate for a swap of the appropriate maturity.

As such a par (or coupon) yield is in essence a weighted average. It is not appropriate to apply such a yield to discount a single cash flow in isolation. This factor gives rise to the problems inherent in the par yield method of valuation, that is:

- It assumes a constant re-investment rate that may be inconsistent with the re-investment rates implied by the yield curve.
- It relies on a pre-determined coupon (or cash flow) frequency. Where cash flows under the swap do not occur in the same regular pattern as those inherent in the instrument which is the source of the discount factor, the par yield method will not provide an accurate net present value.

In addition to discounting the cash flows under the fixed leg of the swap, the floating rate cash flows are also valued using the discount formula. It is only necessary to value the first tranche of the floating rate side on which the rate has already been set (as subsequent floating leg cash flows will be set at "market rate" and applying a "market" discount factor to these cash flows should, by definition, yield a present value of zero). The discount factor used to calculate the net present value of the floating leg should be a rate applicable to the term to next rollover.

Take, for example, a swap for $10 million which has two remaining periods, with a fixed rate of 14.58% and annual cash flows. On 30 March 1993, the floating rate for the next period is set at 15.0%. However, the yield curve is inverted, and the yield to maturity on a two year swap with annual coupons is 14%. The two legs would be valued as follows:

Fixed Leg (Valuation Date: 30 March 1993)

Coupon Date	Cash Flow Amount	Discount Rate	Present Value
30 March 1994	1,458,000	14.00%	1,278,947
30 March 1995	1,458,000	14.00%	1,121,884
30 March 1995	10,000,000	14.00%	7,694,675
			10,095,506

Floating Leg (Valuation Date: 30 March 1993)

Coupon Date	Cash Flow Amount	Discount Rate	Present Value
30 March 1994	1,500,000	15.00%	1,304,348
30 March 1994	10,000,000	15.00%	8,695,652
			10,000,000
Net Present Value			95,506

Zero coupon curve pricing

This approach uses the same conceptual framework as bond pricing, but discounts each cash flow at the specific *zero coupon rate* applicable to that cash flow. In theory, the zero coupon rate is the rate which will bring the NPV of a series of "coupon" cash flows to their "par" value. This is illustrated in the following example:

Notional principal	=	\$100
one year swap rate (annual)	=	15% (that is, an annual coupon rate of 15% for one year)
two year swap rate (annual)	=	14% (that is, an annual coupon rate of 14% for two years)

- The first period zero coupon discount factor would be calculated as follows:

$$100 = \frac{100 + 15}{1 + i}$$

$$1 + i = 1.15$$

$$i = 15\%$$

- The zero coupon discount factor for the second year would be calculated as follows:

$$100 = \frac{14}{1.15} + \frac{100 + 14}{1 + i}$$

$$1 + i = 1.29802$$

i = 29.802%, which equates to an annual interest rate of 13.93%

In practice, the zero coupon curve is derived from market rates for bills, futures, swaps, and bonds. The rates are derived for the "coupon" dates in the then-current market, and are interpolated to derive the appropriate discount rates for specific swap cash flow dates.

Using the same example, with the zero coupon rates derived above, gives the following valuation:

Fixed Leg (Valuation Date: 30 March 1993)

Coupon Date	**Cash Flow Amount**	**Discount Rate**	**Present Value**
30 March 1994	1,458,000	15.00%	1,267,826
30 March 1995	1,458,000	13.93%	1,123,249
30 March 1995	10,000,000	13.93%	7,704,042
			10,095,117

Floating Leg (Valuation Date: 30 March 1993)

Coupon Date	**Cash Flow Amount**	**Discount Rate**	**Present Value**
30 March 1994	1,500,000	15.00%	1,304,348
30 March 1994	10,000,000	15.00%	8,695,652
			10,000,000
Net Present Value			95,117

Note that this method approximates the result obtained for the par yield method for this swap. However, significantly different results will be obtained for swaps with irregular cash flows and, as a result, zero coupon curve pricing is the valuation method most commonly used in the market place.

Bootstrapping

This approach uses the zero coupon curve to derive "implied forward rates" (that is, future investment rates). These rates are, in turn, used to estimate floating rate cash flows over the life of the swap. Fixed and estimated floating cash flows are both discounted by the appropriate zero coupon rates to generate the NPV of the swap.

In the example below, the implied floating rate for the next coupon date (30 March 1994) is 12.8713%. You will note also that the principal values drop out; insofar as offsetting cash flows occur in the same period and are discounted by the same factor, they will net out.

Fixed Leg (Valuation Date: 30 March 1993)

Coupon Date	**Cash Flow Amount**	**Discount Rate**	**Present Value**
30 March 1994	1,458,000	15.00%	1,267,826
30 March 1995	1,458,000	13.93%	1,123,249
			2,391,075

Floating Leg (Valuation Date: 30 March 1993)

Coupon Date	**Cash Flow Amount**	**Discount Rate**	**Present Value**
30 March 1994	1,500,000	15.00%	1,304,348
30 March 1995	1,287,130	13.93%	991,610
			2,295,958
Net Present Value			95,117

You will note that this method gives the same result as the less complex formula using only first period floating rate flows.

While this method has certain advantages for purposes of the initial pricing of swaps, it is not often used for portfolio valuation, as the system time requirements are substantial.

Accounting entries

The following accounting entry is required in the books of the financial institution to account for the zero coupon curve revaluation of the interest rate swap.

Entry at 30 March 1993

DR Revaluation suspense (B/S)	$95,117	
CR Swap revaluation (P/L)		$95,117

Other valuation issues

- *Cross-currency swaps*

  Each leg of a cross-currency interest rate swap should be revalued in the currency in which it is denominated, using discount factors derived from interest rates in the appropriate currency. The present value of each leg is converted to the home currency at the prevailing spot rate.

- *Other cash flows*

  In some transactions the floating rate leg includes a basis difference in its pricing. For example, the floating leg may be priced at LIBOR plus ten basis points. This is best brought into the valuation calculation by notionally adjusting the fixed rate coupon.

  Additionally, a swap transaction may include fees receivable or payable in the future. These cash flows should also be included in the revaluation calculation.

- *Credit risk*

  The mark-to-market calculation recognises up-front the present value of any profit or loss arising from the swap transaction. Where it is a profit being recognised, care must be taken to ensure that it is not imprudent to do so. Accordingly the effect of the counterparty credit risk should be included in the valuation.

  Sophisticated models may be used to calculate credit provisions taking account of the remaining life of the transaction, the mark-to-market value (as a measure of replacement cost), the volatility of the underlying interest or exchange rates and the credit rating of the counterparty. However, many market participants simply calculate a credit provision as a factor of the notional principal.

- *Market liquidity*

  The concept of marking-to-market is predicated on the concept that the institution could "close out" their swap portfolio at the current market rates. If the market is illiquid, or the position is so large that it is unlikely to be able to be closed out without moving the market rate against the institution, consideration should be given to factoring this into the valuation calculation.

- *Administration costs*

  Institutions should consider making provision for the ongoing administration costs associated with the portfolio. The method for calculating the provision should be based on reasonable assumptions and should be applied consistently.

Hedging a trading portfolio

Financial institutions that run a sizeable swaps book generally experience problems of hedge identification. This is exacerbated as many institutions manage their swap book on a portfolio basis whereby hedging action is taken against the overall portfolio exposures, rather than by identifying a perfect match for each swap. Accordingly for major institutions with an active and sizeable swap book the only appropriate method is to mark all positions to market.

Accounting entries

The accounting entries to recognise trading swaps are as follows:

- *At deal date*—record notional principal balances in memorandum accounts.
- *At maturity date*—reverse the notional principal balances recorded in the memorandum accounts above.
- *At date of interest receipt or payment*—recognise interest received or paid in profit and loss account.
- *At revaluation date*—recognise the profit or loss on the revaluation of the swap cash flows.

Accounting treatment—corporate sector

Corporate sector entities utilise the swap market principally to access sources of finance at interest rates more favourable than those available in the open market or as a risk management instrument.

The accounting treatment for swaps undertaken by corporate sector entities will normally be identical to the treatment advocated for financial institutions in the section "Hedging with swaps". The accounting treatment to be adopted is not dependent upon the status of the counterparty, that is, corporate sector versus financial institution, but rather the reason for the transaction.

Corporate sector entities will generally not be involved in trading swaps.

When accounting for swaps undertaken by corporate sector entities it is important to remember the underlying purpose of the swap, that being to manage the entities' overall funding costs. The swap transaction can be considered a secondary or ancillary transaction undertaken to mitigate the exposure generated by the core borrowings transaction. Accordingly the interest payments and receipts made under the swap should be offset against the borrowings costs of the corporate sector entity when performing a cost of borrowing calculation.

Disclosure requirements

International disclosure requirements and disclosure requirements in Australia, the United States, the United Kingdom and Japan with respect to swaps are compared below.

International

Exposure Draft 40, "Financial Instruments" (E40) was issued by the International Accounting Standards Committee in late 1991. E40 provides three alternatives for measuring interest rate and currency swaps depending on how the swaps are categorised. The three categories and the different measurement principles under each category are discussed below:

- *Investing and financing activities*

  These activities are defined as those which result in the acquisition of assets or the assumption of liabilities which are intended to be held for the long term or to maturity. It is unlikely that swap transactions would fall into this category and they are more appropriately recognised in the remaining two categories.

- *Hedging activities*

  The financial instrument can be accounted for as a hedge when the position to be hedged can be specifically identified and exposes the enterprise to risk of loss from price changes. In this case the swap is accounted for on the same basis as the underlying asset or liability being hedged. Therefore, if the asset or liability is accounted for on an accruals basis then the swap hedging that asset or liability is also accounted for on an accruals basis.

- *Operating activities*

  Financial instruments that do not meet the requirements of either of the above two categories are classified as operating activities. These items are to be measured at their fair value with gains and losses arising from changes in the fair value being charged to the profit and loss account as they arise. Swaps transacted for trading purposes would fall into this category. Accordingly, they should be accounted for on a revaluation basis.

  From the above it is evident that E40 does not require deviation from the generally accepted accounting principles outlined earlier.

Disclosure under E40

E40 allows set-off of principal amounts under interest rate and currency swaps. Therefore there is no requirement to recognise the principal on the face of the balance sheet.

Information that would be required to be disclosed in the notes to the accounts is as follows:

- The extent of and the nature of the swaps and their significant terms and conditions, distinguishing between investing and financing items, hedging items and operating items.
- Information about the exposure to interest rate risk arising from the swaps including information on repricing or maturity dates and the "effective interest rate" (that is, the rate that, when used in a present value calculation, results in the carrying value of the instrument).
- Information about the exposure to credit risk including the amount that represents the maximum credit exposure.
- Information on the fair value including disclosure of the method adopted in obtaining the fair value of the swaps and any significant assumptions made in applying this method.

Australia

There are currently no specific disclosure requirements with respect to interest rate and currency swaps for Australian statutory reporting purposes. However, in March 1993 the Australian Accounting Research Foundation released Exposure Draft Accounting Standard ED59, "Financial Instruments".

ED59, as it affects interest rate swaps, is largely consistent with the requirements of the International Exposure Draft E40. Similarly to E40, ED59 allows set-off of principal amounts on the face of the balance sheet.

ED59 gives two alternatives for measuring interest rate and currency swaps:

- *Net market value*—under this method changes in the net market value of the swap are recorded in the profit and loss. This is in line with current accounting practice for trading swaps.
- *Purpose-led basis*—this method requires classification between investing and financing instruments, hedging instruments and trading instruments. Swaps classified as trading instruments are to be accounted for on a mark-to-market basis. Swaps classified as hedging instruments shall be accounted for on the same basis as the position being hedged.

ED59 allows set-off of principal amounts under interest rate and currency swaps on the face of the balance sheet. However the amounts set off must be disclosed in a note to the accounts.

Additionally, the notes to the accounts should provide disclosures similar to those noted above under E40.

ED59 is only an exposure draft and has not been applied by any Australian financial institutions at the time of writing. As a result, disclosures about financial instruments such as swaps have varied between institutions. However the following observations can be made:

- The existence of swap contracts should be disclosed if their omission would impact the overall truth and fairness of the financial statements.
- In Australia it has been general practice to treat swap principal obligations as off-balance sheet. However there has been much debate in recent years on the acceptability of this treatment. It would appear that the release of ED59 confirms that the generally accepted practice is appropriate.
- Many Australian financial institutions refer to the existence of swap contracts in a commitments and/or contingent liabilities note and in the accounting policy note. The United States practice of quantifying the notional principal amounts and the net open risk position with respect to swaps has rarely been followed in Australia except by those banks who have securities listed in the United States and who do so to satisfy SEC listing requirements.
- Schedule 5 of the *Companies Regulations* requires the disclosure of interest both credited and debited to the profit and loss account. Technically swap receipts and payments are not interest as they do not represent a cost of funding. However, it is still considered an acceptable policy to include swap interest streams in the amount disclosed as interest.
- Swap interest accruals receivable and payable calculated under the accruals method of swap accounting (that is, for hedging swaps) for single currency interest rate swaps may be set off in the balance sheet provided they meet the requirements set out in AASB 1014, "Set-Off and Extinguishment of Debt". However swap accruals for cross currency interest rate swaps will generally not meet the AASB 1014 criteria for set-off and, accordingly, should be shown gross on the balance sheet. Note that this position may be altered by ED59 which permits set-off of assets and liabilities arising from an individual financial instrument.
- AASB 1012, "Foreign Currency Translation" issued by the Australian Accounting Standards Board in September 1987 makes specific reference to the accounting for hedging swaps at para (xxiv) of the commentary section. The standard requires that both the underlying foreign currency asset or liability and the swap should be revalued to current exchange rates with the revaluation amounts offsetting in the profit and loss account.

United States

Generally speaking, all swaps are revalued to market unless they are linked to specific assets, liabilities or commitments. Those swaps linked to specific positions are accounted for by applying accrual accounting to the cash flows arising from the swaps.

The US Financial Accounting Standards Board is presently addressing the recognition and measurement of all off-balance sheet financial instruments. However, due to the complexity of the issues involved, it is expected to take considerable time to release comprehensive guidelines. As an interim step two accounting standards have been released which provide disclosure requirements for reporting off-balance sheet financial instruments. These are SFAS 105, "Disclosure of Information about Financial Instruments with Off-Balance Sheet Risk and Financial Instruments with Concentrations of Credit Risk", and SFAS 107, "Disclosures about Fair Value of Financial Instruments" which apply to both banking and non-banking entities.

In relation to swaps, the following items are required to be disclosed by SFAS 105 and 107 in the notes to the financial statements:

- the notional principal of swap agreements;
- nature and terms of the swaps including information on credit and market risk and the accounting policies adopted for recording the swaps;
- quantification of the losses which would be incurred if counterparties failed to fulfil their obligations under the agreement;
- collateral required by the entity upon entering into swaps;
- any concentration of credit risk arising from the swaps. Examples of concentration could be exposures to particular industries or swaps with highly geared companies; and
- the "fair" value of the total swaps book. If the swaps are linked to specific assets, liabilities or commitments, the fair value would be the estimated amount that the entity would receive or pay to terminate the swap agreements at balance date. For a trading swap the fair value would be its mark-to-market value.

United Kingdom

Under United Kingdom company law and accounting standards there are currently no specific disclosure requirements in respect of interest rate and currency swaps for statutory reporting purposes. Disclosure may be required, however, for a set of accounts to show a true and fair view, as is required by the *Companies Act* 1985 (UK).

A Statement Of Recommended Practice (SORP) was issued in November 1991 by the British Bankers Association and the Irish Bankers Federation on "Off-Balance Sheet Instruments and Other Commitments and Contingent Liabilities". (The SORP is "intended to be authoritative and persuasive" and has been "approved" by the Accounting Standards Board. However, compliance with the SORP is not compulsory.)

In relation to swaps the SORP states that, "Swaps taken out to hedge existing income and expenditure (or to hedge assets and liabilities) should be accounted for on an equivalent basis to the relevant income and expenditure (or the assets and liabilities)." Further, "where swaps are entered into as part of a trading portfolio or for speculative purposes, they should be marked-to-market by determining the net present value of future cash flows expected to arise under the swap at the current market interest rate." Accordingly, the guidance is in accordance with the generally accepted accounting practice set out earlier. The SORP recommends the following disclosures:

- where swaps are marked-to-market any resulting profits (or losses) will be recognised in the profit and loss account and the offsetting entry will form part of Other Assets/(Other Liabilities) in the balance sheet;
- the total notional principal of off-balance sheet instruments and other contingent liabilities should be disclosed on the face of the balance sheet as memorandum items, following the assets and liabilities;
- a note to the accounts should provide an analysis of the total off-balance sheet instruments between different transaction groupings, for example, swaps, foreign exchange and forward rate agreements. The credit risk weighted amount and the replacement cost should also be disclosed for swap agreements. The replacement cost is the cost of replacing all contracts which have a positive value when marked-to-market;
- a note to the accounts should state whether the swaps are transacted for hedging or trading purposes;
- a note to the accounts should disclose significant concentrations of swap (or other off-balance sheet) agreements; and
- an accounting policy note which, as a minimum, should explain the accounting practices followed for valuation and income recognition.

Japan

There are no accounting standards or specific disclosure requirements in respect of interest rate and currency swaps in Japan. Swaps are generally accounted for on an accruals basis rather than a revaluation or "mark-to-market" basis.

Disclosure examples

Exhibit 42.4 sets out extracts from the financial statements of one of the leading banks in Australia, the United States and the United Kingdom insofar as they concern the swap activities of the bank.

Exhibit 42.4

Note Disclosure—Examples

AUSTRALIA

Australia and New Zealand Banking Group Limited—September 1992

NOTE 1 ACCOUNTING POLICIES

(xix) Off-Balance Sheet Transactions

The Economic entity enters into a significant volume of off-balance sheet transactions. These include foreign exchange contracts, forward rate agreements, interest rate and currency swaps, futures and options.

Off-balance sheet transactions taken up as hedges against underlying asset/liability exposures are accounted for on the same basis as the underlying exposures. Off-balance sheet transactions taken up as part of trading activities are recorded at market value and all gains and losses, whether realised or unrealised, are taken to the profit and loss account.

Exhibit 42.4—continued

NOTE 36 CONTINGENT LIABILITIES AND OFF-BALANCE SHEET EXPOSURES

Market Related Items

The Economic entity deals in interest rate and foreign exchange futures, forward contracts, options and swaps which enable customers and the Economic entity to transfer, modify or reduce their interest rate and foreign exchange exposures. Futures and forward contracts are commitments to deliver financial instruments to the seller on a future date at a specified price or yield. Swap contracts are commitments to settle in cash on a future date or dates, interest rate commitments or foreign currency amounts based upon a notional principal amount. Option contracts give the acquirer the right to buy or sell a financial instrument or currency amount at a specified price within a specified time period. The Economic entity manages the exposures related to these instruments as part of its overall interest rate and foreign exchange risk management.

The credit risk has been based upon the credit equivalent amount determined in accordance with the Reserve Bank of Australia's capital adequacy guidelines.

	CONSOLIDATED				**THE COMPANY**			
	1992		1991		**1992**		1991	
	Contract or Notional amount $M	**Effective Credit or Market Risk $M**	Contract or Notional amount $M	Effective Credit or Market Risk $M	**Contract or Notional amount $M**	**Effective Credit or Market Risk $M**	Contract or Notional amount $m	Effective Credit or Market Risk $M
Currency swap agreements	**3,872.9**	**295.5**	4,150.5	255.5	**2,770.5**	**253.2**	3,147.7	209.3
Currency options purchased	**4,841.4**	**136.8**	3,424.1	64.1	**4,603.5**	**124.2**	1,907.5	43.4
Currency futures contracts	**2,394.6**	**—**	389.7	—	**2,394.6**	**—**	389.7	—
Forward rate agreements	**162,186.7**	**362.7**	82,108.2	132.8	**157,537.6**	**355.6**	78,232.4	125.4
Interest rate swap agreements	**61,877.2**	**1,050.2**	50,460.8	796.5	**56,923.2**	**926.4**	37,495.1	499.4
Interest rate futures contracts	**24,657.2**	**—**	29,155.8	—	**23,757.5**	**—**	28,456.7	—
Interest rate options purchased	**3,025.4**	**22.5**	2,703.9	16.5	**2,800.7**	**22.4**	2,703.9	16.5
Foreign exchange transactions	**143,679.2**	**3,953.1**	96,537.1	2,770.0	**123,340.6**	**3,461.4**	81,883.0	2,372.0
Other	**19.1**	**3.0**	3.9	0.1	**19.1**	**3.0**	3.9	0.1
	406,553.7	**5,823.8**	268,394.0	4,035.5	**374,147.3**	**5,146.2**	234,219.9	3,266.1

UNITED STATES

Citicorp—December 1992

STATEMENT OF ACCOUNTING POLICIES

Financial futures and forward contracts, interest rate swaps, options and similar derivative products are valued at market, with both realised and unrealised gains and losses included in trading account revenue, except for those designated as hedges. Gains and losses related to such positions that are designated as hedges are deferred and reflected as adjustments to the bases of the related assets and liabilities. Foreign exchange trading positions, including spot and forward contracts, are valued monthly at prevailing market rates on a net present value basis, and the resulting gains and losses are included in foreign exchange revenue.

NOTE 18 OFF-BALANCE SHEET FINANCIAL PRODUCTS AND CREDIT CONCENTRATIONS

Interest Rate and Foreign Exchange Products

Citicorp offers interest rate and foreign exchange futures, forwards, options, and swaps, which enable customers to transfer, modify or reduce their interest rate and foreign exchange risks. Futures and forward contracts are commitments to buy or sell at a future date a financial instrument or currency at a contracted price, and may be settled in cash or through delivery. Swap contracts are commitments to settle in cash at a future date or dates, based on differentials between specified financial indices, as applied to a notional principal amount.

Exhibit 42.4—continued

Option contracts give the acquirer, for a fee, the right, but not the obligation, to buy or sell within a limited time a financial instrument or currency at a contract price that may also be settled in cash, based on differentials between specified indices.

In most cases, Citicorp manages the exposures related to these products as part of its overall interest rate and foreign exchange trading activities, which include both funded (asset and liability) and non-funded positions. For example, Citicorp may hold a security in its trading portfolio and, at the same time, have futures contracts to sell that security. The losses on one position may substantially offset gains on the other position. Citicorp also uses these products to reduce exposure outside the trading portfolios as hedges of interest rate and foreign exchange positions.

The price and credit risks inherent in traditional banking services are also present in these specialised financial products, as are the various operating risks that exist in all financial activities.

Price risk is the exposure created by fluctuations in interest and foreign exchange rates, and is a function of the type of product, the volume of the transaction, the tenor and terms of the agreement, and the volatility of the underlying interest rate or exchange rate. Price risk is affected by the mix of the aggregate portfolio and the extent to which positions have offsetting exposures. The price risk of an interest rate swap, for example, will be reduced by the presence of securities, financial futures, or other interest rate swap positions with offsetting exposure. Citicorp manages its trading activities in these specialised financial products on a market basis that recognises in earnings the gains or losses resulting from changes in market interest or exchange rates. Trading limits and monitoring procedures are used to control the overall exposure to price risk.

Citicorp uses a variety of techniques to measure and manage its risk exposure in interest and foreign exchange rates. While the complexity of Citicorp's operations necessitates customised risk management techniques for the various businesses it engages in, the monitoring procedures generally entail an objective measurement system, various risk limits at appropriate control levels, and timely reports to line and senior management in accordance with prescribed policy. These comprehensive techniques enable Citicorp to prudently manage the maximum and probable impacts of price risk on its projected earnings based on historical and current implied interest and foreign exchange rate volatilities.

Credit risk is the exposure to loss in the event of non-performance by the other party to a transaction and is a function of the ability of the counterparty to honour its obligations to Citicorp.

For these specialised financial products, the amount due from or due to the counterparty will change as a result of movement in market rates, and the amount subject to credit risk is limited to this fluctuating amount. Credit risk is controlled through credit approvals, limits, and monitoring procedures, and the recognition in earnings of unrealised gains on these transactions is dependent on management's assessment as to collectibility.

Citicorp has a significant presence in the interest rate and foreign exchange markets. The following table presents the aggregate notional principal amount of Citicorp's outstanding interest rate and foreign exchange contracts at December 31, 1992 and 1991:

	Interest Rate Products		**Foreign Exchange Products**	
In Billions of Dollars at Year end	**1992**	1991	**1992**	1991
Futures Contracts	**$ 91.2**	$ 57.0	**$ 0.1**	$ 0.1
Forward Contracts	**162.0**	127.1	**788.1**	584.7
Swap Agreements	**217.0**	206.2	**37.6**	50.8
Purchased Options	**79.9**	53.7	**43.1**	40.7
Written Options	**61.3**	55.7	**41.1**	40.2

Notional principal amounts are often used to express the volatility of these transactions and do not reflect the extent to which positions may offset one another. These amounts do not represent the much smaller amounts potentially subject to risk.

Citicorp's credit exposure related to interest rate and foreign exchange products included in the trading portfolio, can be estimated by calculating the present value of the cost of replacing at current market rates all outstanding contracts; this estimate does not consider the impact that future changes in interest and foreign exchange rates would have on such costs. The gross

Exhibit 42.4—continued

aggregate unrealised gains based on current market values were $6.2 billion and $6.1 billion for all interest rate contracts and $23.3 billion and $23.2 billion for foreign exchange contracts at December 31, 1992 and December 31, 1991, respectively. Additionally, commitments to purchase when-issued securities were $0.9 billion and $0.1 billion at December 31, 1992 and 1991, respectively. Credit losses in 1992 related to these interest rate and foreign exchange products were higher than in prior years, reflecting commercial real estate related exposures. Apart from these, credit losses have not been material, however, there can be no assurance that this experience will continue in the future.

UNITED KINGDOM

National Westminster Bank Plc—December 1992

NOTE 1 PRINCIPAL ACCOUNTING POLICIES

(xii) Forward Foreign Exchange Contracts and Other Off-Balance Sheet Instruments

These are used in trading activities and are carried at market value; profits and losses on instruments which are being used to hedge exposures are recognised in a manner that reflects the accounting treatment of the assets or liabilities hedged.

NOTE 30 GENERAL

(ii) Off-Balance Sheet Financial Instruments

Companies in the Group enter into various off-balance sheet financial instruments as principal either as a trading activity or to manage balance sheet interest rate and foreign exchange rate risk. At the year end the notional or contract amounts of the instruments, which are not included on the Group's or the Bank's balance sheet, were:

	1992 Principal Amount £m	**1992 Risk Weighted Amount £m**	1991 Principal Amount £m	1991 Risk Weighted Amount £m
The Group:				
Interest rate related contracts	**182,743**	**749**	120,010	417
Exchange rate related contracts	**169,929**	**2,112**	112,174	1,287
Exchange traded and other instruments	**32,225**	—	7,445	—

The contract or notional principal amounts of these instruments are not indicative of the amounts at risk which are the smaller amounts payable under the terms of these instruments and upon the basis of the contract or notional principal amount. The amounts at risk are also reduced by entering into offsetting positions. Risk weighted amounts have been calculated in accordance with the Bank of England's guidelines implementing the Basle agreement on capital adequacy.

Prudential supervision

Technological and increased financial market sophistication have encouraged the development and growth of new financial instruments and techniques. Many off-balance sheet financing techniques are complicated and expose unsuspecting bankers to undue risk. For this reason central banks the world over are paying much closer attention to monitoring off-balance sheet business.

The approach employed by the central banks to monitoring and supervising the off-balance sheet activities of banks gained global uniformity following the adoption by the world's major central banks of the Basle Supervisors Committee statement "International Convergence of Capital Measurement and Capital Standards".

Under the Basle Committee guidelines, banks are required to report to their central bank on their capital adequacy. Off-balance sheet instruments are included in assessing the bank's minimum capital requirements. Swap transactions are converted to balance sheet equivalents in one of two ways: the "current exposure" method or the "original exposure" method.

Current exposure method (mark-to-market approach)

Credit equivalent amounts are represented by the sum of current and potential credit exposure.

- *Current credit exposure*—This is calculated as the mark-to-market valuation of all contracts with a positive replacement cost.
- *Potential credit exposure*—This is calculated as a percentage of the nominal principal amount of a bank's portfolio of interest rate and exchange rate related contracts split by residual maturity as follows:

Term to Maturity of Contracts	Interest Rate Contracts	Exchange Rate Contracts
Less than one year	nil	1.0%
One year or longer	0.5%	5.0%

Original exposure method (rule-of-thumb approach)

Credit equivalent amounts would be calculated by applying credit conversion factors to the principal amounts of contracts according to the nature of the instrument and its original maturity.

Original Maturity Contracts	Interest Rate Contracts	Exchange Rate Contracts
Less than one year	0.5%	2.0%
One year and less than two years	1.0%	5.0% (ie 2% + 3%)
For each additional year	1.0%	3.0%

Additionally, many central banks also require regular reporting of off-balance sheet transactions, including details of the "gross exposure", or face value and "assessed risk" as calculated under the Basle Committee guidelines set out above.

Proposed changes to prudential supervision

In April 1993 the Basle Committee on Banking Supervision issued a consultative proposal dealing with market risk. The proposals raise a variety of issues relating to the conceptual and technical methodology for assessing market risk, as well as the scope of the supervisory role in determining the capital requirements of such risk.

Under the Basle proposal all derivative instruments transacted for trading purposes and which react to changes in interest rates are included in the measurement of market interest rate risk. Unlike the existing Basle Committee guidelines, no provision is made for "specific" credit risk in relation to interest rate swaps or forward rate agreements (except for those held outside the trading book). Each trading derivative is converted into positions in the relevant underlying instrument and those positions are subject to complex proposals for requiring capital to cover "general market (interest rate) risk". These proposals would replace the present requirement to hold capital against the credit risk arising on these instruments.

Derivative transactions which fall outside the trading book are not subject to capital requirements in relation to interest rate risk. However, the market interest rate risk in relation to these transactions would be reported to the relevant banking supervisor. The present requirement to hold capital against the credit risk arising on these instruemnts would remain in place.

The Federal Reserve Board in the United States has also issued a proposal on the supervision of interest rate risk. Their proposal does not distinguish between trading trnsactions and other transactions. Capital is required to be set aside in relation to interest rate risk as calculated by an interest rate risk assessment model. The capital requirement arising out of this calculation will simply be added to the capital presently required to be held against credit risk.

ACCOUNTING FOR COMMODITY SWAPS

Commodity swaps are not specifically addressed by any of the accounting statements referred to in this chapter. However the broad accounting principles applied are consistent to those applied in relation to other instruments.

A fundamental distinction should be made between those transactions entered as hedges of underlying positions, and those transactions entered as trading and speculative transactions. In practice these transactions may be entered for a number of reasons, including:

- entities with an underlying exposure to the commodity price may wish to hedge their exposures;
- entities may wish to obtain an exposure to the price of the underlying commodity (speculators); and
- institutions may make a market in the commodity swaps to earn margins.

In each case the accounting should give effect to the substance of the entities interest in the transaction.

Accordingly an entity entering a commodity swap to hedge an underlying position should account for the commodity swap in a manner consistent with the accounting method applied to the underlying position. Therefore, a gold producer who transacts a commodity swap as a way of hedging future sales of its production should account for the commodity swap in a manner which results in any gain or loss on the swap offsetting gains or losses on the sales of the underlying production. (This analysis assumes that the production quantities are sufficiently certain for the commodity swap to be classified as a hedge.)

On the other hand, an entity entering a commodity swap for speculative purposes should account for the transaction on a revaluation basis. This requires that the entity must be able to determine the market value of the commodity swap.

Revaluation techniques are based on ascertaining the prevailing market price or calculating the net present value of future cash flows associated with the transaction. (Note that, by definition, the prevailing market price should approximate the net present value of future cash flows.) However, it may be very difficult to estimate the prevailing market price or the future cash flows in thinly traded markets. Accordingly, an entity should exercise prudence when revaluing thinly traded commodity swaps, particularly in relation to recognising unrealised profits.

ACCOUNTING FOR FRAs

General accounting principles

The accounting statements and exposure drafts referred to earlier in this chapter apply equally to FRAs as they do to interest rate and currency swaps. In addition, many of the principles set out in SFAS 80, "Accounting for Futures Contracts" can be applied to FRAs. As with swaps, the absence of comprehensive accounting standards resulted in the development of generally accepted accounting practices which seek to reflect the "substance" of the transactions.

The methodology to be adopted in accounting for these instruments is dependent on the intention underlying the transaction, that is, whether they are for hedging or trading purposes.

Accounting treatment—financial institutions

Hedging with FRAs

In general, for a FRA to qualify as a hedge the following conditions would have to be met:

- the institution must have net assets or liabilities which are subject to interest rate risk and in determining this condition the company must first take into account commitments and anticipated transactions which offset or reduce the exposure;
- the FRA must reduce that exposure and be designated as a hedge. The FRA must be designed in such a way (with regard to maturities, etc) that the result of the FRA will substantially offset the effect of interest rate changes on the exposed item.

Intention is important in determining whether a hedging state exists. Since it is frequently rather subjective, internal procedures should provide for the identification of hedging transactions at the outset, and for the documenting of such decisions. Mere existence of positions is not enough; the accounting should reflect the results of management decisions, and if a conscious decision was not taken, then the FRA should be treated as a trading FRA. However, as FRAs can be closely tailored it should often be easier for an FRA to qualify as a hedge than it is for a financial future.

When an FRA qualifies as a hedge in accordance with the above criteria, the amount paid or received by the company on settlement day should be deferred and amortised to profit and loss over the fixed rate period on a straight line basis (the discount element can usually be ignored as immaterial) to match and offset the effect of the hedged item.

Accounting entries

The accounting entries to recognise a hedging FRA are as follows:

- *At deal date*—record the principal sum of the FRA transaction in memorandum accounts.
- *At settlement date*
  —record the cash impact of the transaction, that is, the bank balance and a deferred asset/liability in the general ledger;
  —reverse memorandum account entries raised on deal date.

The deferred asset/liability should then be amortised on a straight line basis to the profit or loss account over the period for which the hedge was obtained.

An example of the accounting entries in respect of hedging FRAs is illustrated below in *Exhibit 42.5*.

Exhibit 42.5
Accounting Entries—Hedging with FRAs

Assume that at 31 December 19X8 a financial institution has A$100m in assets yielding an average of 15.00% (with rate adjustment after one year) funded by A$100m in liabilities costing 13.00% (with rate adjustment after nine months). To eliminate its exposure to an increase in BBR when its liabilities are subject to rate adjustment on 30 September 19X9, the financial institution enters into an FRA (at 31 December 19X8) at 13.00%. The contract amount of the FRA will be A$103,312,329 since at the contract rate of 13.00% the proceeds will be A$100m, the amount being hedged. Assume that at 30 September 19X9 the three month BBR is 17.00%.

Before recording the FRA transaction, the financial institution's profit and loss account for the year to 31 December 19X9 would be as follows:

Interest income

A$100,000,000 × 15.00% = A$15,000,000

Interest expense

$$\text{A\$100,000,000} \times \left(\frac{13}{100} \times \frac{272}{365} + \frac{17}{100} \times \frac{93}{365} \right) = \text{A\$14,019,178}$$

Net income A$ 980,822

On 30 September 19X9 the financial institution will receive A$976,865 from the counterparty under the FRA, calculated using the settlement sum formula as follows:

$$\frac{36{,}500 \times 103{,}312{,}329}{(93 \times 13) + 36{,}500} - \frac{36{,}500 \times 103{,}312{,}329}{(93 \times 17) + 36{,}500}$$

$$= 100{,}000{,}000 - 99{,}023{,}135$$

$$= \text{A\$976,865}$$

This amount should be deferred and released to income over the period 30 September to 31 December 19X9. Including the FRA transaction, the financial institution's profit and loss account for the year to 31 December 19X9 would be as follows (assuming that the cash received in settlement of the FRA is invested to yield BBR):

	A$
Interest income	15,000,000
Interest expense	(14,019,178)
Settlement income from FRA	976,865
Interest income on FRA settlement	42,313
	2,000,000

Or, in other words, a net spread of 2.00% for the entire period of one year.

The following accounting entries are required in the books of the financial institution to account for the hedging FRA:

Entries at 31 December 19X8	**A$**	**A$**
DR FRA hedge—borrowing (memo)	103,312,329	
CR FRA hedge—position (memo)		103,312,329
To record FRA commitment in memorandum accounts		
Entries at 30 September 19X9		
DR nostro (B/S)	976,865	
CR FRA—interest in advance (B/S)		976,865
To account for receipt of FRA settlement sum		

Exhibit 42.5—continued

DR FRA hedge—position (memo)	103,312,329	
CR FRA hedge—borrowing (memo)		103,312,329

To reverse FRA commitment following FRA settlement

Entries required each day during the hedge period—1 October to 31 December 19X9

DR FRA—interest in advance (B/S)	10.504	
CR FRA—interest received (P/L)		10.504

Being amortisation of FRA interest received in advance on straight line basis, over the 93 days.

Trading in FRAs

Financial institutions may enter into FRAs as part of their trading activities. In such cases, those FRAs outstanding at the end of the reporting period should be marked-to-market. In marking the FRA portfolio to market interest rates, settlement rate quotations for the relevant period should be obtained from an independent source.

Accounting entries

The accounting entries to recognise trading FRAs are as follows:

- *At deal date*—record the principal sum of the FRA transaction in the memorandum accounts.
- *At revaluation date*—recognise the unrealised gain or loss in the balance sheet and profit and loss account. These entries should be reversed at the beginning of the next period.
- *At settlement date*
  —record the realised gain or loss on the transaction, that is, the cash impact on the bank account and the corresponding impact on the profit and loss account;
  —reverse memorandum account entries raised on deal date.

An example of the accounting entries in respect of trading FRAs is illustrated below in *Exhibit 42.6*.

Exhibit 42.6

Accounting Entries—Trading in FRAs

Assume that on 31 October 19X8 a financial institution enters into a three against six FRA at 15.00% on A$1m. The FRA is part of its portfolio.

At 31 December 19X8 the financial institution must estimate its probable gain or loss under the FRA and therefore must estimate three month BBR on 31 January 19X9. If the estimated three month BBR for 31 January 19X9 was 16.00% the estimated loss would be A$2,288 as follows:

$$\frac{36{,}500 \times 1{,}000{,}000}{(90 \times 15) + 36{,}500} - \frac{36{,}500 \times 1{,}000{,}000}{(90 \times 16) + 36{,}500}$$

$$= 964{,}333 \quad - \quad 962{,}045$$

$$= \text{A\$}2{,}288$$

This loss would be provided for in the 31 December 19X8 financial statements.

Exhibit 42.6—continued

The following accounting entries are required in the books of the financial institution to account for the trading FRA:

	A$	A$
Entries at 31 October 19X8		
DR FRA trade—borrowing (memo)	1,000,000	
CR FRA trade—position (memo)		1,000,000
To record FRA commitment in memorandum accounts		
Entries at 31 December 19X8		
DR FRA trade—unrealised profit and loss (P/L)	2,288	
CR FRA trade—payable (B/S)		2,288
Being revaluation of FRA on mark-to-market basis. The revaluation entry should be reversed on first day of following month		
Entries at 31 January 19X9		
DR bank (B/S)	xxx	
CR FRA trade—settlement profit (P/L)		xxx
To record FRA profit and loss on settlement		
DR FRA trade—position (memo)	1,000,000	
CR FRA trade—borrowing (memo)		1,000,000
To reverse FRA commitment recorded in memorandum accounts.		

Accounting treatment—corporate sector

The accounting treatment for FRAs undertaken by corporate sector entities will normally be identical to the treatment outlined for financial institutions in the section "Hedging with FRAs".

Corporate sector entities will generally not be involved in trading FRAs.

Disclosure requirements

The disclosure requirements in relation to FRAs are set by the accounting statements referred to earlier in relation to interest rate swaps. The disclosures will take the same format as those outlined in relation to swaps. Examples of the disclosures are included in the excerpts from the accounts of the leading Australian, United States and United Kingdom banks, provided earlier in this chapter.

Prudential supervision

Prudential reporting requirements in relation to FRAs are effectively the same as the requirements imposed in relation to interest rate swaps, which are discussed earlier in this chapter.

ACCOUNTING FOR CAPS, COLLARS AND FLOORS

General accounting principles

Accounting for caps, collars and floors should follow the economic substance of the relevant party's interest in the transaction. Accordingly, the accounting treatment to be adopted is dependent on whether the party is a buyer or seller of the instrument and their purpose in entering the transaction (trading or hedging).

As a general rule, it is not possible to hedge a position by outright selling of options of any kind (although the sale of options can form a valid part of an option trading strategy and a collar, involving the purchase of a cap and the sale of a floor, or vice versa, can create a hedge of an interest rate exposure).

Accounting treatment—financial institutions

Hedging with caps, collars and floors

Purchase of an interest rate cap

The risk when borrowing floating rate funds is that interest rates will escalate and force a rise in borrowing costs. The purchase of an interest rate cap protects against this escalation and effectively places a ceiling on the interest rate the borrower will pay.

Accordingly the cost of the cap premium becomes an integral part of the overall borrowing cost calculation. The cost of the cap premium should be deferred and charged to profit and loss over the term of the cap.

An example of the accounting entries in respect of an interest rate cap transacted to hedge an underlying interest rate exposure which is accounted on an accruals basis is illustrated below in *Exhibit 42.7*.

Alternatively, where the underlying liability is accounted for on a revaluation basis, the cap should also be accounted for on a revaluation basis. This will require the use of an option valuation model and raises complex valuation issues. These issues are discussed further below.

Purchase of an interest rate collar

The purchase of an interest rate collar should be accounted for in a similar manner to the interest rate cap. However, as the collar also includes the sale of an interest rate floor this may result in the borrower having to pay amounts to the writer of the collar if the interest rates fall below the specified floor rate. If the collar is purchased to hedge floating rate borrowings then any payment to the writer should be treated in a similar way to any receipt received in the event the interest rate rises above the cap rate, that is, to include it as part of the total cost of funding.

As discussed above, in relation to the purchase of a cap, where the underlying asset or liability is accounted for on a revaluation basis, the collar should also be accounted for on a revaluation basis.

Purchase of an interest rate floor

Similar principles are applied to the accounting for an interest rate floor acquired as a hedge of an underlying asset position.

Where the underlying asset has been acquired for investment purposes it will normally be carried at cost in the balance sheet. The floor premium should be considered an integral part of the yield and therefore should be spread over the term of the floor. Receipts from the floor should be taken to income in a manner which offsets the reduction in income generated by the underlying asset.

Where the underlying asset is acquired for trading purposes and is accounted for on a revaluation basis, the floor should also be accounted for on a revaluation basis.

Exhibit 42.7
Accounting Entries—Interest Rate Cap

Assume that on 1 January 19X7 company A issued US$10m of FRNs maturing in five years' time, on 31 December 19X1. The interest rate on the FRNs is set at London LIBOR plus 10bps, which is fixed semi-annually on 30 June and 31 December.

Company A is concerned at the recent volatility in United States interest rates and decides to hedge against excessive upward movements by purchasing a strip of interest rate caps covering each rollover period. The cost of the cap is set at 0.50% for each six monthly rollover (that is, 1.00% pa). The total cost of the cap is therefore US$500,000 which is paid on 1 January 19X7 (for purposes of the example the pricing ignores the time value impact on the premium).

At the start of the contract, US$ six month LIBOR is standing at 8.00%. The strike rate on each of the caps is 9.00%.

Average LIBOR and actual funding costs over the first two periods are as follows:

	LIBOR	**Funding costs**
30 June 19X7	10.00%	10.10%
31 December 19X7	7.50%	7.60%

The following accounting entries are required in the books of company A to account for the interest rate cap:

Entries for six months to 30 June 19X7

	US$	**US$**
DR premium suspense	500,000	
CR cash		500,000

Being payment of cap premium

DR profit and loss—interest expense	505,000	
CR cash		505,000

Being interest on US$10m at 10.10% for six months (provided on a straight line basis over the six month period)

DR sundry debtors	55,000	
CR profit and loss		55,000

Being the anticipated receipt under the interest rate cap

$$(10.10\% - 9.00\%) \times \$10{,}000{,}000 \times \frac{180}{360}$$

DR cash	55,000	
CR sundry debtors		55,000

Being receipt of the intrinsic value under the cap

DR profit and loss	50,000	
CR premium suspense		50,000

Being amortisation of one tenth of the cap premium

Entries for six months to 31 December 19X7

DR profit and loss—interest expense	380,000	
CR cash		380,000

Being interest on US$10m at 7.60% for six months

DR profit and loss	50,000	
CR premium suspense		50,000

Being amortisation of one tenth of the cap premium

In summary:

Exhibit 42.7—continued

	US$ FRNs issued	Premium suspense	Cash	Profit and loss
Issue of FRNs	(10,000,000)		10,000,000	
Purchase of cap		500,000	(500,000)	
six months to 30 June 19X7				
Interest expense			(505,000)	505,000
Recovery under cap			55,000	(55,000)
Amortisation of cap premium		(50,000)		50,000
	(10,000,000)	450,000	9,050,000	500,000
six months to 31 December 19X7				
Interest expense			(380,000)	380,000
Amortisation of cap premium		(50,000)		50,000
	Nil	(50,000)	(380,000)	430,000
	(10,000,000)	400,000	8,670,000	930,000

The accrual method of accounting results in the following effective funding costs being shown in the accounts of the company:

	Average borrowing	Total "interest" cost	Funding rate
six months to 30 June 19X7	US$5,000,000	500,000	10.00%[1]
six months to 31 December 19X7	US$5,000,000	425,000	8.60%[2]

Notes:

1. Since the cap rate is set at 9.00% and the annualised cost of the cap is 1.00%, the maximum total cost of borrowing is 10.00%. When the cap is in-the-money the accrual method of accounting produces the correct result.
2. When the cap is out-of-the-money, as in this case, the effective funding cost is the actual rate (7.60%) plus the cost of the premium (1.00%); again, as reflected by the accruals method of accounting. As the cap was acquired out-of-the-money, the premium represented wholly time value, which is also the position at 31 December. Although time value does not decay evenly over the life of the cap, straight line amortisation is usually a good enough approximation for accounting purposes.

Writing caps and floors

Financial institutions are often active in writing caps and floors. This exposes the institution to the risk of adverse interest rate movements. In return for taking on this risk, the institution receives premium income.

In order to reflect this situation it is appropriate to account for the caps or floors on a revaluation basis. This will result in the effect of any adverse movements in interest rates being reflected in the results for the period.

However, the revaluation approach may be difficult to implement where there is a lack of depth in the market from which to derive fair market values for the option. In this case it is necessary to derive a value for the option using an option valuation model, which will be complex and may be expensive to acquire.

As a result, some institutions have accounted for sold option positions by amortising the premium received on a straight line basis over the life of the instrument. However, this will not result in recognition of any losses that may be incurred as a result of adverse interest rate movements, but which may be unrealised at that point in time. Accordingly, the revaluation method is the appropriate accounting treatment for a seller of options.

In this regard, one should consider that an institution would generally not (and arguably should never) write outright options unless they profess some expertise in the area of option valuation. Accordingly, a writer of options should be able to value their position at any point in time.

Trading caps, collars and floors

As discussed in relation to other financial instruments, an entity which actively trades caps, collars and floors should account for their activities on a revaluation basis. However, as a result of the lack of liquidity in many markets and the complexities of option valuation, it is important that the revaluation methodology should be applied in a prudent manner.

The most conservative method of applying the revaluation methodology is to only recognise realised gains and recognise both realised and unrealised losses arising on revaluation. However, a more common revaluation methodology is to build a margin into the revaluation to allow for a lack of market liquidity.

Accounting treatment—corporate sector

Corporate sector entities are most likely to enter into caps where they are floating rate borrowers and floors where they are floating rate investors. The purchase of the option allows them to hedge their underlying positions. Accordingly, the accounting treatment for caps, collars and floors undertaken by corporate sector entities should be identical to that described above for financial institutions who purchase options as hedging instruments.

Corporate sector entities will generally not be involved in trading caps, collars or floors.

Disclosure requirements

The disclosure requirements for caps, collars and floors are set by the accounting statements referred to earlier in relation to interest rate swaps. The disclosures will take the same format as those outlined in relation to interest rate swaps. Examples of the disclosures are included in the excerpts from the accounts of the leading Australian, United States and United Kingdom banks, provided earlier in this chapter.

Prudential supervision

The provisions of the Basle Committee discussed in relation to the other financial instruments earlier in this chapter also apply to caps, collars and floors. However, note that a writer of options has no further credit exposure once they have received the option premium. Accordingly, written options are not required to be included in the calculation of capital adequacy (note, however, that any unrealised losses on the option would normally indirectly affect the capital adequacy position by way of their effect on the profit and loss).

Chapter 43

Taxation Aspects of Swaps and Financial Derivatives

KPMG Peat Marwick, Chartered Accountants

GENERAL FRAMEWORK

This chapter provides a general overview of the taxation implications, in a number of countries, of the following financial instruments:

- interest rate swaps;
- currency swaps;
- commodity swaps and equity swaps;
- LTFX;
- FRAs;
- caps, collars and floors.

The countries surveyed are the United States, Canada, Japan, the United Kingdom and Australia.

Proposals for specific legislation concerning the taxation of financial instruments are currently under consideration in both the United Kingdom and Australia. However, it can generally be said that at present the income tax legislation and a substantial body of the case law in the countries surveyed does not specifically address the tax consequences of the abovementioned financial instruments. Accordingly, recourse must usually be made to the general statutory provisions and established taxation principles. In many cases, the income tax legislation is being interpreted and applied to financial instruments which were not specifically contemplated by the legislators.

Accordingly, the application of the income tax legislation to specific financial instruments often gives rise to areas of uncertainty and generally each case involves an analysis of the facts that are specific to the taxpayer's situation.

There are a number of major taxation issues currently surrounding these financial instruments. The characterisation of the payments and receipts arising from the various financial instruments is of fundamental importance. The first step in identifying the appropriate taxation treatment of payments and receipts involves determining whether the payments and receipts are considered to be of a revenue or capital nature. Generally, resolution of this threshold issue determines whether payments and receipts are deductible and assessable.

Once it has been determined that payments are on revenue account, the next step involves determining the timing of deductibility or assessability; that is, the time they are included in the computation of income subject to tax. The choices in this matter include an accruals basis, a due and payable/due and receivable basis and a mark-to-market basis.

Similar issues surround the appropriate taxation treatment of fees that are associated with the entry into and/or the continuing administration of the swap. It is necessary to determine whether these fees are deductible/assessable to the payer/payee. If they are, it is then necessary to determine the timing of deductibility/assessability; that is, are they deductible/assessable in full when paid/received or must they be amortised over the term of the particular agreement.

The development of an international market for financial products has made it inevitable that swap payments will be made between residents of different countries. In many tax jurisdictions this fact raises the possibility of a liability to pay income tax or a liability to pay withholding tax. This issue is dealt with differently by the various tax regimes.

It is also important to determine whether revaluations of the financial instruments for financial reporting purposes result in a taxable event as well as considering whether exchange gains or losses are brought into the tax computation.

TAXATION CONSIDERATIONS IN THE UNITED STATES

Interest rate swaps

Swap payments do not involve a sale or exchange. As a result, periodic payments pursuant to a swap will be considered ordinary income. Although analogous in many respects to interest, they are not to be treated as interest. Furthermore, while economically similar to futures contracts, interest rate swap contracts are not classified as s 1256 contracts under the Internal Revenue Code of 1986, as modified (hereinafter, all Section references are to this source unless otherwise indicated). Section 1256 contracts generally receive mark-to-market and capital gain/loss treatment while interest rate swap contracts generally do not.

It is worthwhile noting however, that the IRS has issued Proposed Regulations that provide an election for dealers and traders, in certain circumstances, to account for all of their derivative financial instrument positions on a mark-to-market basis for tax purposes. This election would apply to such instruments as interest rate swaps, caps, floors, and collars. The election is meant to address the timing of the swap income only; no inference is to be drawn concerning the character and source of the income. (Note that as of August 1993, the Proposed Regulations are not effective and thus merely reflect the IRS current position on the issues addressed).

In addition, under new s 475, enacted 10 August 1993 and effective for taxable years ending on or after 31 December 1993, "securities" held by a "dealer" generally must be marked-to-market for tax purposes: there are exceptions for securities properly identified as "held for investment" or "not held for sale" and certain hedges. Gains and losses thus recognised are treated as ordinary in character. The term "securities" for these purposes includes interest rate, currency and equity notional principal contracts (for example, swaps, caps and collars) although not commodity notional principal contracts.

Under current law, periodic payments pursuant to an interest rate swap will generally be taxable to the recipient and deductible to the payor in accordance with the taxpayer's method of accounting (cash or accrual). Note, however, that the Proposed Regulations mentioned above would require a rateable daily inclusion or deduction with respect to periodic payments, regardless of the taxpayer's method of accounting.

Additionally, existing law provides for rateable inclusion or deduction of lump sum payments made pursuant to a swap. The exact methodology for this amortisation is unsettled, but any reasonable method generally should be allowed. Some common amortisation methods include the straight-line method and the constant-yield method. The Proposed Regulations provide for amortisation based on the value of a series of cash settlement forward contracts using a reasonable method of amortisation. Examples of "reasonable methods" are included in the Proposed Regulations.

Termination or assignment of interest rate swaps

The termination or assignment of an interest rate swap involves an agreement between or among parties to terminate or assign their rights and obligations under the contract. One party will usually receive or make a cash payment in settlement of their obligation under the swap. It is the IRS position that these payments should be treated as capital in character.

Currency swaps

The general tax analysis above applicable to interest rate swaps also applies to periodic payments pursuant to a currency swap. An additional complexity concerning currency swaps is the tax treatment of exchange gains and losses arising on the periodic payments and principal re-exchange at maturity.

The US tax treatment of exchange gains and losses is provided in s 988. Section 988 transactions include futures contracts, forward contracts, options and similar financial instruments. Under s 988, the foreign exchange element of a s 988 transaction is given ordinary income or loss treatment. However, the taxpayer may elect to treat gain or loss from a currency forward, future or option as a capital gain or loss if the contract is a capital asset (for example, non-dealer property) in the hands of the taxpayer. A currency swap would typically fall under s 988. Generally any gain or loss recognised from a currency swap is treated as an exchange gain or loss (but generally *not* as interest income or expense) and thus as ordinary in character.

In certain circumstances, s 988 enables the taxpayer to integrate a currency swap with an underlying debt instrument and treat it as a single transaction. The Internal Revenue Service is also empowered to compel integration of a currency swap with an underlying transaction.

In summary, a s 988 analysis is necessary if any payment on the swap can be characterised as containing a foreign currency element.

Payments or receipts in a currency swap are treated as though they were made under a hypothetical loan denominated in the same currency in which the payments are made (or received). Exchange gain or loss on the swap principal amount is realised when the swap principal is exchanged at the swap's maturity. If the currency swap is disposed of or terminated, any resulting gain or loss is treated as an exchange gain or loss.

Equity swaps and commodity swaps

The tax treatment of equity swaps and commodity swaps is broadly the same as that of interest rate swaps outlined above. However, there are a number of issues which have not, as yet, been addressed by the Internal Revenue Service.

Equity swaps

- *Character*—Periodic swap payments are treated as ordinary income or expenses. In the case of an equity swap such payments typically reflect appreciation or depreciation in the value of the underlying equity. Although such appreciation or depreciation would be treated as capital gain or loss (upon realisation), the periodic swap payments retain their ordinary characterisation.
- *Dividends received deduction*—To mitigate the effect of double taxation, a corporation in receipt of dividends may be entitled to a dividends received deduction (DRD) equal to 70%, 80% or 100% of the dividends received. However, a corporation in receipt of dividends which, in effect, it is obliged to pay to another party under the terms of an equity swap is probably not entitled to a DRD in respect of the dividends received. Furthermore, parties to an equity swap are not entitled to DRDs as receipts under equity swaps do not actually constitute dividends.
- *Source/withholding tax*—Since February 1991, swap payments are sourced by reference to the residence of the recipient. Thus, by entering into an equity swap, a foreign investor can replicate, to some extent, an investment in a United States equity without being subject to United States dividend withholding tax. However, the IRS have noted in commentary on proposed regulations issued in January 1992 requiring withholding on substitute payments in cross-border securities lending transactions, that it was "considering whether the proposed regulations should apply to dividend equivalent payments made in connection with certain notional principal contracts, such as an equity index swap designed to replicate the cash flows that would arise from an instalment purchase of one or more equity securities". The IRS has not yet issued any further guidance.

Commodity swaps

- *Classification*—Periodic payments under commodity swap agreements are treated as ordinary income or expense. However, an oil company, for example, which has hedged the value of its oil reserves by entering into an appropriate swap agreement, may wish to include any swap payments and receipts in cost of goods sold or offset them against its allowance for depletion. It is unclear whether it is permissible for it to do so.

Associated swap costs

Such costs would normally be deductible for tax purposes and are not likely to be amortised over the term of the swap.

Swap revaluations

The Internal Revenue Service has ruled that currency swaps need not be marked-to-market under the rules of s 1256. Although securities dealers can generally adopt a mark-to-market valuation method for inventory, the use of such a method for swaps is highly questionable, as swaps do not generally constitute property but rather agreements to exchange property in the future. As mentioned above, the IRS has issued Proposed Regulations that would, when finalised, permit traders and dealers to mark-to-market interest rate swaps and other derivatives under certain circumstances.

Withholding tax

Interest rate swap income includable in taxable income after February 13 1991 will be sourced according to the residence of the taxpayer. Thus, where an interest rate swap payment is made to a non-United States resident there will be no withholding tax issues because the payment will not be sourced within the United States. If certain requirements are met, the source of the interest rate swap income will be the residence of a "qualified business unit" (that is, a foreign branch) of a United States corporation. Generally, the qualified business unit must engage in an active trade or business and the swap must be properly reflected on its books and records. An election is available to apply these post-13 February 1991 rules retroactively with respect to the withholding responsibility.

As with interest rate swaps, gain or loss from foreign currency swaps usually is sourced to the residence of the taxpayer or its qualified business unit.

Long-term foreign exchange forwards (LTFXs)

LTFXs entered into through the interbank market prior to 22 October 1988 are generally subject to the mark-to-market and capital gain or loss rules of s 1256 if the underlying currency is traded in the regulated futures markets. LTFXs that do not meet these criteria are subject to the rules of s 988 and the taxpayer's method of accounting for recognition of income. Section 1256 contracts that are part of an identified hedge or for which a "mixed straddle" election is made are not subject to s 1256 and are taxed in the same manner as non s 1256 contracts. LTFX contracts entered into after 21 October 1988 are subject to the s 988 ordinary characterisation and residency sourcing rules, regardless of whether marked-to-market under s 1256.

Forward rate agreements (FRAs)

FRAs resemble interest rate swaps, except that the interest rate is set at the beginning rather than at the end of the relevant period. Although not free from doubt, the tax treatment of forward rate agreements should be similar to the treatment of interest rate swaps. Thus, generally the character of the interest income or expense differential which arises on the settlement date should be ordinary, but the differential should not be considered interest income or expense because a forward rate agreement does not entail an exchange of principal. In addition, the source of the interest rate differential income should be determined by reference to the taxpayer's country of residence.

Interest rate caps, floors and collars

As with other countries, there are no definitive rules in effect specifically on point regarding the tax treatment of caps, floors, and collars. However, the Proposed Regulations referred to above with respect to interest rate swaps are applicable to caps, floors and collars.

Characteristics of payment

The Internal Revenue Service issued a notice in 1989 which provides for lump sum payments for caps, collars, floors and off-market swaps to be amortised as ordinary income over the term of the contract. Until further guidance is issued, any reasonable amortisation method will be allowed, including the straight-line method and constant yield method. The Proposed Regulations referred to above provide for an amortisation based on the values of a series of cash-settled option contracts. Upon the issuance of these regulations in final form, straight-line and accelerated methods will not be permissible.

Interest differential payments received by the purchaser of a cap, floor or collar will generally be considered ordinary income, not capital, since there is no sale or exchange. For a taxpayer in the business of providing caps, floors or collars, the payment of the excess interest should be considered an ordinary and necessary business expense.

Timing of assessability and deductibility of payments

Under current law, up-front payments to enter into caps, floors or collars should be amortised over the life of the agreement by both the payer and receiver. Interest differential payments under these agreements should be included as ordinary income or deducted as an ordinary expense in accordance with the taxpayer's method of tax accounting. (See the above section concerning the treatment under the Proposed Regulation.) In addition, the current IRS position is that termination or assignment gains and losses on caps, floors, and collars are capital in character.

Withholding tax on interest rate caps, floors and collars

The above comments concerning the US withholding tax implications of interest rate swaps also apply to interest rate caps, floors, and collars.

Note on the tax character of hedging losses

In what it is hoped will not be the first case in a long line of litigation, the United States Tax Court has upheld the position of the Federal National Mortgage Association that ordinary loss deductions should be allowed for certain hedging losses: *Federal National Mortgage Association v Commissioner* 100 TC No 36 (17 June 1993). The decision offers hope and encouragement to taxpayers in many different businesses that have been subjected to the Internal Revenue Service's aggressive attack on the characterisation of gains and losses on a broad range of transactions (for example, the character of swap termination or assignment gains and losses and the character of gains and losses on hedges of assets subject to s 582(c)). The decision should be viewed by the Internal Revenue Service and treasury as an invitation to end this conflict with taxpayers. Many taxpayers hope that the government accepts the Tax Court's invitation and uses the decision as the basis for issuing definitive guidance on the ordinary treatment of business hedging gains and losses.

TAXATION CONSIDERATIONS IN CANADA

Interest rate swaps

In determining the income tax implications of payments pursuant to swap contracts, regard must be had to the legal substance of the transactions as well as the intentions of the parties entering into the swap.

The application of Canadian tax legislation to swaps may give rise to areas of uncertainty to the parties to the swap, depending on their circumstances and motivation, the nature of the Canadian parties and the structures adopted.

Canadian taxation legislation adopts or contains no specific statutory provisions that specifically address swap transactions. Accordingly, for the most part recourse must be had to the general statutory provisions and to a substantial body of case law. However, none of the case law is specifically on point but only serves to establish certain general income tax principles. Thus, each case involves an analysis of the facts that are specific to the taxpayer's situation.

For a business, a taxpayer's income for tax purposes is its profit therefrom for the year determined in accordance with ordinary business and accounting practices but subject to modification by various provisions contained in the *Income Tax Act*. Generally, amounts payable and receivable under an interest rate swap agreement by a Canadian participant should be fully deductible or included in the income under the general rules for computing business profits. This follows either because they typically arise from transactions undertaken in the normal course of business or as adventures in the nature of trade, or because the net profit or loss is regarded as arising from a transaction entered into to hedge what is an income or revenue item. Revenue Canada's current administration position would appear to be consistent with this interpretation.

Currency swaps

Currency swaps may be motivated by a variety of objectives. The Canadian tax implications of currency swaps are similar to those for interest rate swaps although they are complicated by the fact that currency swaps involve two currencies.

The Canadian participant will recognise a foreign exchange gain or loss on re-exchange under the currency exchange agreement which should, in almost all cases, be equal but opposite to the foreign exchange loss or gain realised on the repayment of the foreign currency borrowings. It is only where both the gain or the loss are either on capital account or on income account that no issue arises.

Financial institutions and certain other corporates entering into currency swaps against trade assets or liabilities will normally be able to recognise both foreign exchange transactions on revenue account. However, the result is less certain where the original borrowing of the foreign currency by the corporate is on capital account as would normally be the case where the end use of the funds raised in the foreign currency is the acquisition of capital assets for the expansion of a permanent working capital base. In order to characterise a foreign exchange gain or loss on repayment of an outstanding debt, the Canadian courts have, as a rule, looked to the nature of the obligation. Where the corporate borrower's purpose in raising funds is to obtain capital, the foreign exchange gain or loss on repayment will be on capital account.

Accordingly, it will be important that the offsetting foreign exchange loss or gain on re-exchange of the currencies under the currency swap agreement is also on capital account.

Commodity swaps and equity swaps

Canada does not have legislation dealing with the taxation of commodity or equity swaps. At the present time, accounting guidelines are being developed to deal with income measurement in relation to various financial instruments. The income reported for taxation purposes is the same as that reported in the financial statements.

Timing of assessability and deductibility of swap payments

Interest rate swaps

The deduction for income tax purposes of a netting payment arising from a conventional swap occurs when an amount becomes payable under the terms of the contract. Thus, when an enforceable obligation of a payment has arisen the amount is an expense which is deductible in computing income for tax purposes. In practice, however, the amount is deducted in computing income for income tax purposes on the same accruals basis as is used in Canadian accounting practices and to date the Canadian tax authorities have not challenged this treatment.

Similarly, where an amount becomes due and receivable then that amount is included in income for tax purposes although in practice the amounts are recorded on an accruals basis.

Currency swaps

Under cross-currency swaps the same conclusions can be derived with respect to the netting payments relating to interest. With respect to any gains or losses arising on the repayment of the currency under current Canadian administrative practice, where the foreign exchange gains or losses are on account of income they may be accounted for on an accruals basis or a realised basis. However, where the foreign exchange gains or losses are on account of capital, then the taxpayer must record for income tax purposes the foreign exchange gains or losses on a realisation basis.

Accelerated or deferred payment swaps

Questions arise as to whether it is appropriate to recognise the accelerated swap income as having been earned where there is a requirement to make future payments and whether it is appropriate to recognise that the accelerated swap costs can be said to be fully incurred when they are referable to deferred income. For the most part, recourse must be had to the general statutory provisions contained in the *Income Tax Act* which uses accounting profit as a starting point in determining income for tax purposes. The accounting principles would indicate that the accrual method be used to include the payments in income on a basis that provides the best matching of income and expense.

In considering accelerated payments it is difficult to see how expenditure has been incurred for income tax purposes before the actual liability to pay that amount has become due under the terms of the contract. In respect of accelerated income the amount will be included in income for tax purposes pursuant to specific sections contained in the *Income Tax Act* but a reserve may be claimed in respect of services that it is reasonably anticipated will have to be rendered after the end of the fiscal period. This raises the question as to what services have been rendered and what portion, if any, of the total payment is refundable if the services are not provided.

In respect of deferred expenditures the absence of any forcible right of payment suggests that an accrual approach is not appropriate as an outlay or expense has not been incurred until the amount becomes payable. However, since Canadian income tax law is not specific, general income tax concepts must be used in examining these issues.

Associated swap costs

Fees and other costs of the swap should also be fully deductible on the same basis as amounts payable and receivable under an interest rate swap. Although, depending on the terms of the transaction, there may be a debate over the proper timing of the deduction.

Withholding taxes

Where the counterparty or arranger of the swap is a non-resident of Canada, the question of withholding tax will also arise. If the amount paid to the non-resident is found to be interest, withholding tax would be applicable. The rate of withholding tax with respect to interest is 25% of the amount paid or payable to a non-resident of Canada unless reduced by a double taxation agreement, in which case the rate is generally 15%. Swap payments themselves are not generally regarded as legally constituting interest in that there is no exchange for a principal obligation and, as such, the Canadian domestic tax legislation should not otherwise catch swap payments whether paid on a gross or on a net basis (that is, there would normally be no Canadian withholding tax concern).

Fees and other costs, to the extent that they are incurred in the normal course for services performed at arm's length outside Canada, will similarly not be subject to withholding tax.

An issue arises where, for one reason or another, the parties have agreed to a mismatching schedule of payments, and as a result, the Canadian participant to the swap will receive payments in advance of its liability to pay. The revenue authorities take the view that the portion of the outbound payment made by the Canadian must be regarded as interest on the one or more short-term advances received by the Canadian during the course of the year against its promise to pay a future liability. The interest portion is then dissected from a swap payment made by the Canadian participant and, as no Canadian domestic withholding exemption exists for interest on short-term funds, it is chargeable to Canadian withholding tax.

LTFXs

The Canadian income tax considerations arising in respect to foreign exchange gains and losses involves an examination as to whether there is an underlying transaction which has been hedged and whether the underlying transaction is on account of income or on account of capital.

In general terms, foreign exchange gains or losses arising from foreign exchange contracts which have been entered into as a hedge against underlying transactions will take on the characterisation of the item being hedged. For instance, if the item being hedged is on account of capital then normally the gain or loss arising on the foreign exchange contract is also on account of capital. It appears that a reasonably good argument can be made to support this position. However, case law indicates that taxpayers have had difficulty in obtaining the concurrence of the Canadian taxation authorities that a particular transaction is a hedge rather than a foreign currency speculation where the transaction is not an isolated transaction.

With respect to traders of foreign exchange contracts who value their inventory at market, the gain or loss is usually recognised for income tax purposes in the same period in which they are accounted for. There may be some opportunity, using the inventory valuation provisions, to value LTFXs for income tax purposes in a manner different from the value used for accounting, although this may be subject to challenge by the tax authorities.

Where a taxpayer has entered into an isolated foreign exchange contract on a speculative basis, the taxpayer may choose to utilise the Canadian taxation authorities administrative policy to consistently report these transactions either being on account of income or on account of capital.

If the foreign exchange contract is on account of income, then the gain or loss is recognised on an accruals basis except where the taxpayer chooses to follow the administrative practice of the taxation authorities and include the amounts on a realised basis. Where the gain or loss is on account of capital, it may be recognised for income tax purposes on a realised basis.

FRAs

Characterisation of settlement amounts

A taxpayer's income for tax purposes is the "profit" from a business determined in accordance with commercially accepted accounting practices subject to various adjustments required by the *Income Tax Act*. At the present time there are no provisions contained in the *Income Tax Act* and no cases have been litigated dealing specifically with the tax treatment of payments made or received on settlement of an FRA. For Canadian financial statement purposes an amount paid or received on settlement of an FRA would generally be treated on an accruals basis as a component of interest expense or interest income in computing financial statement income. The income tax treatment in Canada of these amounts would appear to follow the financial statement treatment and thus forward rate settlement payments should be considered to be on income account to the extent the amount is reasonable and the interest is deductible, which is usually the case where the underlying borrowed funds have been borrowed for the purpose of earning income.

Since forward rate settlement amounts are considered to be part of the trading activities of a financial institution, they are treated as being on account of income. For a non-financial institution the position might be taken that the transaction represents an "adventure in the nature of trade", which is included in the definition of "business" for Canadian income tax purposes. Amounts paid or received with respect to an adventure in the nature of trade are treated as being on account of income and fully deductible or included in determining income for Canadian income tax purposes.

Where the taxpayer has taken an isolated speculative position which is not related to the business he or she may take an income or a capital position with respect to any gain or loss realised.

Timing of recognition of settlement amounts

The recognition of forward rate settlement amounts for Canadian income tax purposes is based on Canadian financial statement accounting. Where the contract date and settlement date straddle the fiscal year end of a taxpayer, an amount is recorded in income for Canadian financial statement purposes to reflect the accrued gain or loss. This financial statement accrual has generally been recognised for Canadian income tax purposes although some doubt continues to exist that the amount should not be recognised for income tax purposes until the settlement date.

Canadian non-resident income tax

Where a payment on settlement of a forward rate agreement is made to a non-resident person by a resident of Canada, Canadian withholding tax is generally not exigible. This results from the fact that the amount of the payment under an FRA does not represent interest since a creditor and debtor relationship does not exist between the parties to the agreement. Accordingly, the Canadian withholding tax provisions do not have application in these circumstances.

Interest rate options—caps, floors and collars

Characterisation of settlement

Similar to FRAs, provisions do not exist in the *Income Tax Act* governing the taxation of interest rate caps, collars and floors and therefore the taxation in Canada of amounts arising from a cap, collar or floor generally follows the Canadian financial statement accounting. Amounts paid or received are accounted for on an accruals basis as part of the interest component of the underlying hedged assets.

For financial institutions such amounts represent the trading profit of the institution which is reflected in financial statement income. A concern may exist for non-financial institutions but the payment under the transaction may be considered to be on account of capital. If the Canadian taxation authorities were to take this position, any gain or loss arising on settlement would be a capital gain or loss. Only a portion of a capital gain is included in income for tax purposes while capital losses may only be deducted against capital gains.

However, the Canadian taxation authorities may take the position that for these taxpayers an interest rate cap, collar or floor represents an adventure in the nature of trade and accordingly any payments are on account of income.

Timing of recognition of settlement amounts

The recognition of an amount paid or received on the settlement of an interest rate cap, collar or floor would generally follow its recognition for Canadian financial statement purposes. The Canadian taxation authorities have accepted this treatment to date although it would appear that recognition for income tax purposes should not occur until the settlement date.

However, should the transactions be considered to be on capital account, then amounts paid or received may be recognised at the settlement date when the gain or loss is crystallised from a legal point of view.

Canadian non-resident income tax

Generally, the provisions dealing with Canadian withholding tax on interest are not applicable since the payment does not represent "interest" as a debtor and creditor relationship does not exist.

TAXATION CONSIDERATIONS IN JAPAN

Interest rate swaps

For interest rate swaps net payment or receipt of interest is recorded on an accruals basis. The tax treatment follows the accounting treatment.

Currency swaps/cross-currency interest rate swaps

Currency swaps and cross-currency interest rate swaps are generally recorded on an accruals basis. The spot position and the forward position are valued on a mark-to-market basis. Since the revaluation amounts offset each other, there is no resulting effect on earnings. The periodic interest payments are recognized as interest income/expense on an accruals basis.

The tax treatment is the same as the accounting treatment.

Commodity swaps and equity swaps

There are currently no commodity swaps or equity swaps in the Japanese market.

Forward rate agreement

Forward rate agreement (FRA) transactions are prohibited by the Ministry of Justice (MOJ) and the Ministry of Finance (MOF). However, these transactions exist under different names and are accounted for on a settlement basis. The tax treatment follows the accounting treatment.

Caps, collars, and floors

Generally, currency options are recorded on a mark-to-market basis, while interest rate options are recorded on a settlement basis. Premiums received are held as an asset/liability until settlement. If the option expires or if exercised, income is recognised at that time.

However, special treatment exists for caps, collars and floors (not called options). For banks, the settlement basis is used where the initial premium is recognised as income/expense at the time the option is exercised or at the end of the option period if the option is not exercised. For commercial companies, the initial premium is amortised over the life of the option.

TAXATION CONSIDERATIONS IN THE UNITED KINGDOM

Interest rate swaps

At present, the United Kingdom legislation does not specifically address the tax consequences of swaps, and the current taxation treatment is largely based on Inland Revenue practice which is not in all respects consistent. However, the Inland Revenue have announced their intention (when legislative priorities permit) to introduce legislation to implement proposals, subject to certain amendments, made in a Consultative Document issued in August 1991. Enactment of these proposals, discussed below, will result in significant amendment to the existing law.

Under existing law, swap payments do not constitute interest whenever there is no underlying debt obligations between the parties. This is generally not an issue for trading companies where the swap is entered into in the course of the trade as usually a deduction will be obtained for swap payments as a trading expense (and swap receipts taxed as trading income). However, where the swap is not entered into in the course of the company's trade or alternatively where the company does not trade, for example an investment company, it has to rely on concessionary relief from the Inland Revenue which allows the payments to be deducted as a "charge" on income (on a cash basis). There is no obligation to withhold tax provided the counterparty is a bank recognised by the Inland Revenue as carrying on a bona fide banking business in the United Kingdom (this generally includes United Kingdom branches of foreign banks), or is a "recognised swaps dealer". A "recognised swaps dealer" is a company listed by the Bank of England as an exempted person for the purposes of the *Financial Services Act* 1986 (UK) or authorised as a member of the Securities and Futures Association to carry on investment business; and confirmed by the Bank of England or the Securities and Futures Association to be entering into swaps as part of its regular business activity.

Swap payments can generally be made to and by United Kingdom recognised banks or swap dealers acting as principals (whether as counterparty or intermediary) without deduction of United Kingdom tax at source. For the remainder of this analysis of the United Kingdom position relating to swaps, references to banks and banking business should be taken to include recognised swap dealers and their dealing business, unless otherwise stated.

Under United Kingdom tax law, there is a general requirement to deduct income tax on annual payments except where paid in respect of an advance from a bank carrying on a bona fide banking business in the UK. Annual payments are, in broad terms, payments of income which cannot be deducted as trading expenses.

The Inland Revenue concession provides that there is no obligation to withhold income tax from annual swap payments when paid to or by a recognised bank or swaps dealer. Where the counterparty is not a recognised bank or swaps dealer, there will be an obligation to deduct income tax if the swap payments are regarded as annual payments rather than trading expenses (subject to clearance to pay the interest gross or at a reduced rate of withholding under the "business profits" or "other income" article of a relevant double tax treaty).

Swaps undertaken by banks may not necessarily be entered into in the ordinary course of their banking business. For example, a swap may relate to a borrowing undertaken by a bank on capital account as part of its funding strategy. Previously, it was understood that the Inland Revenue regarded seven years as a significant period in determining whether a borrowing was on revenue or capital account. However, in 1991 the Inland Revenue issued a Statement of Practice relating to the exemption from deducting basic rate tax from interest payments by banks carrying on bona fide banking business where the interest is paid "in the ordinary course" of its banking business. The statement provided that a liability of the bank would be treated as having been entered into "in the ordinary course" of banking business unless it conforms to any of the Tier I or Tier II definitions set out by the bank for international settlements (irrespective of whether the borrowing actually counts toward Tier I or Tier II capital for regulatory purposes), such liabilities being regarded as the capital structure of the bank. Although this Statement of Practice only specifically relates to the exemption from the requirement to deduct basic rate tax from interest payments, it is regarded as indicative of the Inland Revenue's current view as to the distinction between borrowing in the ordinary course of the banking business and on capital account.

Where a bank has entered into a swap agreement in connection with a capital borrowing, the Inland Revenue are likely to argue that, unless the payment was made to another recognised United Kingdom bank, such payments should be made after deduction of basic rate income tax.

Currency swaps

Where a trading company makes recurring payments under a currency swap to a United Kingdom bank the payments will generally be treated as trading expenses of the company. An investment company can obtain relief for recurring swap payments as a charge on income under the concessionary relief discussed above.

Where a currency swap is on capital account, a capital gain or loss may arise not on the swap itself but from the currency associated with the swap. Broadly speaking, capital gains or losses arise only on the disposal of chargeable assets. Accordingly, no chargeable gain or allowable loss occurs in respect of translation differences on a capital asset reflected in the accounts of the company prior to disposal. Some assets are not chargeable assets, for example trade debts, and no capital gain or loss arises on the discharge of a liability. Thus, although a currency swap may constitute a perfect economic hedge, the taxability of capital gains and losses can result in a mismatched position.

Commodity swaps and equity swaps

Existing United Kingdom legislation does not specifically deal with the tax treatment of commodity swaps and equity swaps. Furthermore, these swaps do not fall within the concessionary treatment extended to currency and interest rate swaps. Specific legislation does, however, exist for the taxation of commodity and financial futures. Transactions falling within this legislation (which may include commodity and equity swap transactions as discussed below) are afforded capital gains treatment.

The precise tax treatment of a commodity or equity swap will depend on the legal substance of the transaction. These types of swaps are generally notional principal contracts; that is, the payments under the swap are by reference to a notional amount of the commodity or equity (or equity index) concerned.

For banks and other financial traders, receipts and payments under commodity and equity swaps would be taxable or deductible on an accruals basis. For other companies (unless the company is regarded as "dealing" in such swaps), there is no basis for obtaining an income deduction for the swap payments. However, swap receipts may be taxable as income unless the swap is afforded capital gains treatment as a commodity or financial future.

"Commodity or financial futures" refers to futures dealt with on a recognised future exchange, although the same treatment also applies to transactions with institutions authorised under the *Financial Services Act* 1986. "Financial futures" have been stated to include contracts that are settled by payment of cash differences determined by movements in a financial index. Although the capital gains treatment may appear beneficial in that swap receipts are not taxable as income, there may be limited expenditure to set against the capital receipt. Swap payments will, at best, only result in capital losses.

The proposed legislation which will establish a new regime for the taxation of interest rate and currency risk instruments will not cover commodity swaps and equity swaps. Thus they will continue to be taxed under general principles.

Transactions in commodities, including precious metals, are potentially subject to VAT at positive rates and thus a commodity swap could attract VAT. However, as mentioned earlier, these transactions would normally be structured as notional principal contracts and thus be treated in the same way as other swaps for VAT purposes.

Timing of assessability and deductibility of swap payments

The timing of recognition of swap payments for tax purposes depends on whether the swap payments and receipts are categorised as annual payments and Schedule D Case III receipts or as trading payments and receipts.

Annual payments are, broadly, payments which are both recurrent and are "pure income profit" in the hands of the recipient (as Schedule D Case III income). Income is taxed when it arises (generally when received) whilst tax relief on the payment is obtained when payment is made. Charges on income are payments which are deducted from total profits rather than in computing profits chargeable under a particular schedule or case.

Trading expenses and receipts are generally computed on an accruals basis.

For a trading company, swap payments will be deductible as a trading expense if the swap is entered into on trading account and the expense is incurred wholly and exclusively for the purpose of a trade carried on by the company. Swap receipts will be taxable as trading income provided the swap is entered into in the course of the company's trade. For a company carrying on a banking or financial trade the swap is likely to be regarded as entered into in the course of that trade unless it is regarded as on capital account as part of its funding strategy, which for banks, generally, would only be the case where it is capable of being treated as such for regulatory purposes. Where a company carrying on a non-financial trade enters into a swap on trading account there is, in broad terms, a general presumption that swap payments will be wholly and exclusively for the purposes of the trade, and so deductible as trading expenses.

For non-trading companies (that is, investment companies), swap payments will be deductible as annual payments under the Inland Revenue concession. Swap receipts will generally be taxable under Schedule D Case III.

Accelerated or deferred payment swaps

For a bank or financial trader the position in relation to accelerated or deferred payment swaps would be similar to a conventional swap as the payments would be accrued and tax assessed on the profit recognised for accounts purposes.

For a non-bank entity there may be no recurrent element in the payments in which case they would not seem to be annual swap fees within the concession published by the Inland Revenue. A trading company might claim relief for the payment as a trading expense which, if accepted by the Inland Revenue, would probably be allowed on the same basis as for accounting purposes. An investment company, however, is unlikely to be able to obtain tax relief for a one off or lump sum payment. However, any receipts would probably be taxable when received.

Associated swap costs

Swap arrangement fees should normally be trading receipts or expenses of banks or other financial traders. For non-banks the position is less satisfactory.

The incidental costs of raising loan finance are not usually regarded as trading expenses, being capital in nature, although s 77 of the *Income and Corporation Taxes Act* 1988 (ICTA 1988) provides a special relief. Relief under s 77 of the ICTA 1988 does not extend to fees and expenses incurred in arranging swaps as no new loan is created as a result of the swap. In order to avoid losing taxation relief for swap fees and expenses altogether, where commercially possible, these costs should be subsumed into the margins on the recurring payments over the period of the swap.

Payments to terminate swap agreements will generally also not be tax deductible. This is clearly the case where a non-trading company makes the payment, but arguably it may be deductible as an expense to trading companies by reference to case law.

Swap revaluations

The concept of marking-to-market is an accepted accounting policy in the United Kingdom for a bank or financial trader with a swap book. The Inland Revenue are generally reluctant to bring unrealised gains and losses into account for tax purposes, but have agreed to accept marking-to-market in certain specific cases which have been discussed with them.

International tax issues

The general requirement to deduct basic rate income tax from annual swap payments (unless paid to a United Kingdom Bank or paid by a bank or financial trader) may be reduced or eliminated on payments made to recipients not resident in the United Kingdom under the provisions of a double taxation agreement. Such relief (if any) that is available is normally given under the "other income" or "business profits" article of the relevant agreements. As the payments are not interest, the "interest" article is not relevant. As with all United Kingdom treaty reliefs, specific application needs to be made and authorisation obtained before relying on it. If relief is available, it should be possible to make payments gross or at a reduced rate, in accordance with the terms of the relevant double taxation agreement. The gross payments will be relievable on a cash basis.

If the non-United Kingdom resident recipient trades in the United Kingdom through a permanent establishment, relief under a double taxation agreement may apply if the swap transaction is not effectively connected with that permanent establishment. Further, the effects of foreign withholding tax should be considered when dealing with overseas counterparties.

The booking of banking business is an area where there is often significant dispute between the Inland Revenue and taxpayers. In a head office to branch relationship, the Inland Revenue do not consider it possible for one office to book business generated by another.

Value added tax (VAT)

Under currency or interest rate swap agreements supplies are made for VAT purposes to the extent that payment is received. If payments are made gross by each party then two supplies are made. If amounts due are netted off and only one payment is made, then only one supply is made (by recipient of the payment). The value of the supply for VAT purposes is the amount received.

A United Kingdom business receiving a payment from a United Kingdom or Isle of Man counterparty in respect of a swap agreement has made an exempt supply. VAT is not charged on such supplies but none of the VAT on related expenditure can be reclaimed.

Proposed legislative framework for corporation tax

Following a series of earlier consultations the Inland Revenue published draft legislation in August 1993 which will establish a new regime for the taxation of interest rate and currency rate instruments. This legislation is likely to be included in the Finance Bill published in early 1994 and should be law by mid 1994. The new provisions will not take effect until a commencement date yet to be announced by the United Kingdom government. These new provisions are designed to correlate with the legislation enacted during 1993 that established a statutory framework for the taxation of exchange gains and losses.

Instruments covered by the proposals

The proposals cover interest rate swaps, currency swaps, forward rate agreements, currency and interest rate options and options to enter into such financial instruments (for example, swaptions).

Relief for swap payments

Under the proposed legislation all payments, including lump sums, in respect of instruments used to hedge against future interest rate movements will be taxed or relieved for United Kingdom corporation tax as income (this has been described as "assimilation to income"). However, only qualifying payments, broadly payments that do not artificially transfer value, will qualify for relief.

In general, it is proposed that companies would recognise payments and receipts for tax purposes on the same basis as their accounts, where either an acceptable mark-to-market basis or an acceptable accruals basis is used. (Banks and other financial traders will be expected to use a mark-to-market basis for their dealing contracts and an accruals basis for their other contracts.) Where such a method is not used the taxpayer's inspector of taxes will be able to specify the method to be used.

Two anti-avoidance measures are proposed. First, tax relief would be denied, or restricted, on payments under transactions entered into otherwise than at arm's-length. There would also be application of a withholding tax in limited circumstances, namely on payments to countries identified as low taxation territories (or alternatively, countries where there is no "Interest" article in force under a double taxation agreement) except where paid by or to a UK bank or financial trader acting as principal in the ordinary course of its business as a bank or financial trader.

LTFXs

The treatment of LTFXs is in principle no different from normal foreign exchange contracts, although for non-financial companies they are more likely to be on capital account. For banks, forward foreign exchange contracts are normally marked-to-market for taxation purposes except where associated with loan and deposit transactions when the profit or loss would be amortised over the life of the contract. For long-term contracts the market value is harder to determine and there is an argument that because the market is thin, unrealised profit or losses should not be taxed. In practice, a bank is unlikely to have substantial unhedged long forward positions.

FRAs

Again, in the United Kingdom the tax treatment of FRAs is an area of some uncertainty. Because there is no exchange of principal, any payment will not be interest for tax purposes. Moreover, FRAs do not come within the concessionary relief on swap payments which could otherwise allow a deduction for payment as a charge on income.

Characterisation of settlement sum

Where the FRA is entered into by a bank or financial trader as part of their business activities any income or expense from the FRA should be taken into account in computing its profit as part of its existing trade.

Timing of assessability and deductibility of settlement sum

Under the Inland Revenue's stated practice, profit and losses on FRAs entered into for speculative purposes or to hedge trading transactions may be taken into account in computing taxable trading profits. Trading companies making payments under FRAs may obtain relief from them, as trading expenses, if they enter into the FRAs in the course of their trades; receipts under such FRAs would similarly be taxable as trading income.

Where FRAs are entered into by investment companies, or non-financial trading companies other than in the course of their trade, capital gains treatment will apply, provided undertaken with authorised persons or listed institutions for purposes of the *Financial Services Act*. Payments made (but excluding any initial premium paid) are relieved as capital losses, and receipts are taken into account in computing chargeable gains.

Prospective legislative changes

As discussed above, the proposals in the Consultative Document for managing interest rate risk are intended to cover FRAs. Accordingly, payments and receipts under FRAs would generally be deductible or taxable as income.

VAT

Income received from entering into an FRA is treated as consideration for a supply of dealing in money.

If payment is received by a United Kingdom business from a counterparty outside the UK and the Isle of Man, then the United Kingdom business has made a supply which is outside the scope of UK VAT. If, however, the counterparty is also outside the EC, the UK business can reclaim the VAT incurred on expenditure related to the transaction.

A United Kingdom business receiving a payment under an FRA from a United Kingdom or Isle of Man counterparty has made an exempt supply. VAT is not charged on such supplies but none of the VAT on related expenditure can be reclaimed.

Interest rate options, caps, floors and collars

Characterisation of payments

The Inland Revenue consider that neither initial nor periodic payments to purchase a cap, floor or collar, nor payments and receipts under a cap, floor or collar constitute interest for tax purposes. The reason is that there is no underlying debt obligation between the payer and the recipient.

For a bank or financial trader, receipts or payments made under a cap, floor or collar agreement would normally be trading items taxable or allowable as trading receipts or expenses. Similarly, lump sum payments for the purchase or sale of a cap, floor or collar by a bank should fall within the computation of trading profits.

Premiums paid by companies carrying on a non-financial trade, where the cap hedges interest payments made for the purposes of the trade, is governed by Inland Revenue published stated practice which allows relief as a trading expense. A non-trading company will be unable to obtain a revenue deduction for a cap premium, unless exceptionally it can argue that it was a necessary cost of obtaining associated loan finance.

Where it cannot be relieved as an income deduction, the premium is likely to be treated as expenditure on a capital asset (namely the agreement); but if the asset is not a qualifying option, it is a wasting asset, whose deductible cost is amortised over its life. It follows that unless the cap is sold before expiry, there may well be no deduction at all for the premium. Such difficulties have led to the popularity of nil premium collars, combining a cap and a floor.

TAXATION CONSIDERATIONS IN AUSTRALIA

At the time of writing, the Australian government has announced its intention to introduce a comprehensive legislative regime dealing with the taxation of financial arrangements. A consultative document outlining the legislation is anticipated in the near future but no detail of the proposed legislation is currently available. Current indications are that the legislation is intended to be extremely broad and will apply to as many financial instruments as possible. It is expected that loans, bills of exchange, promissory notes, convertible notes, redeemable preference shares, interest rate and currency swap contracts, forward rate agreements, caps, collars and floors will all be within the legislation. Consequently, although the discussion below reflects the position at the time of writing, it must be remembered that it may be subject to change in the near future.

Interest rate swaps

The characterisation of payments under interest rate swap contracts has generally been analysed having regard to the taxation treatment of the financing commitments of the underlying borrowing transaction which the interest rate swap seeks to impact, and to the purpose of entering into the relevant swap contract.

Where a party has entered into an interest rate swap contract it generally indicates that the party has adopted a certain position in regard to its exposure to interest rates. The swap payments are seeking to impact the party's financing commitments so that its interest rate exposure is consistent with that position.

The unavoidable relationship with the underlying borrowing transaction and the financing commitments of the party to the lender in respect of that borrowing give considerable support for the conclusion that the characterisation of the swap payments would normally be determined by the underlying transaction test.

Thus, the netting payments under the interest rate swap to a counterparty would usually be considered deductible for income tax purposes pursuant to s 51(1) of the *Income Tax Assessment Act* (the ITAA) where the underlying interest obligations are deductible. Where the purpose of the underlying borrowing is to utilise the funds in connection with the production of assessable income, then the netting payments under the swap should be deductible given the fact that interest obligations on the underlying borrowing should be deductible. This general proposition appears to be accepted by the Australian Taxation Office in its Income Tax Ruling IT 2050 (*Exhibit 43.1*) dealing with interest rate swaps.

Furthermore, whilst the netting payments are referable to the underlying financing commitments, they do not represent a cost in borrowing the underlying loan principal. They are a cost in connection with the financing commitments attaching to the loan principal. Accordingly, the netting payments should not be considered borrowing expenses for the purposes of s 67 of the ITAA as a netting payment is not expenditure incurred in borrowing the principal.

In respect of swap receipts the above reasoning should be equally applicable such that receipts are assessable for income tax purposes pursuant to s 25(1) of the ITAA (or possibly s 26(j)).

Exhibit 43.1

IT 2050 "Interest Swapping" Transactions

Date of Ruling: 13 July 1983

TEXT OF RULING

Preamble

1. Consideration has recently been given to the income tax implications of a form of interest hedging arrangement known as "interest swapping".

2. An Australian resident borrower of moneys from overseas at a floating rate of interest, say London Inter-Bank Offered Rate (LIBOR) + 1.00%, would ordinarily seek to limit its exposure to fluctuations in interest rates. As an alternative to conventional hedging arrangements involving, as they would usually do, interest rate futures contracts there have developed "interest swapping" transactions.

3. In its simplest form, a foreign banking concern would provide a "swapping" facility to the borrower by itself raising a loan, at a fixed interest rate readily available to it, of an amount equivalent to the amount of floating rate funds which were originally obtained by the borrower from other foreign sources. The Australian resident borrower and the foreign banking concern would then exchange their respective interest commitments, quite independently of the relevant loans with third parties and without affecting those contracts in any way, by undertaking to pay to each other from time to time amounts equal to the other's interest obligations before payment of fees, commissions, margins, etc. to the bank for the facility. The arrangement would usually provide for the corresponding payments to be offset against each other so that only a single net payment would be made by one party to the other.

4. There may also be situations in which one party is unwilling to accept the risk of the other party to the swap arrangement fulfilling its obligations for payment and a third party intermediary, also usually a bank or other financial institution, would be interposed between the parties and would bear the risk of default by either party. In this way performance of all commitments by the parties to each other is effectively guaranteed. This variation does not otherwise alter the swapping techniques nor the income tax consequences.

Ruling

5. An "interest swapping" arrangement is a form of interest hedging facility and is a transaction quite independent of any loan obligations of the parties to which the arrangement might be referable. It does not involve any additional loans between the parties or any disturbance of existing loans and obligations to pay interest as it falls due.

6. The payments made by the parties to each other in accordance with the terms of the agreement are not amounts of interest as the term is defined for withholding tax purposes in s 128A(1).

7. An "interest swapping" arrangement involving an Australian resident borrower would not, in the circumstances which have been described, involve any interest withholding tax liability additional to that which might otherwise exist in respect of the borrower's existing interest obligations.

8. It is also accepted as a general principle that payments made by the parties in accordance with the interest swapping agreement are attributable to existing interest expenses and are themselves revenue in nature. As a consequence the payments would be assessable to the

Exhibit 43.1—continued

recipient and deductible to the payer as the case may be. The involvement of an intermediary would not alter the character of the payments.

9. It is necessary to say that the advice in the preceding paragraph operates as a general principle. As the arrangements are presently understood it would seem usual for the parties to have raised loans at rates of interest which are more or less comparable, though one is variable and the other fixed. If there were substantial differences between the two at the time that the parties enter into the interest swapping arrangement the particular circumstances would require examination to decide whether they were truly of a revenue nature.

10. Because the various incidental expenses which are associated with an interest swapping transaction relate to an existing interest expense they would ordinarily be deductible in accordance with s 51(1) of the ITAA 1936 in the same way as the incidental costs associated with a conventional interest hedging arrangement. Any payments which might be made by the parties upon early termination of the whole of the arrangements would also be of a revenue nature in the usual case, that is, assessable or deductible to the parties as the case may be.

11. In the event that interest was to be charged on overdue swap payments, any interest which might be paid to a non-resident would be subject to withholding tax.

Currency swaps

It is useful to view a typical currency swap as an interest rate swap augmented by an exchange of loan principal amounts with a mutual commitment to re-exchange principal loan amounts on maturity of the loans. Accordingly, it is necessary to consider both the tax treatment of recurrent payments under the swap and the treatment of exchange differences on the principal loan amounts. The currency swap participants will recognise a foreign exchange gain or loss on re-exchange of the principal amounts which may well hedge an equal but opposite foreign exchange gain or loss in respect of the underlying foreign currency borrowings.

The taxation consequences for the interest netting payments or receipts in respect of currency swaps should broadly follow the analysis set out above in respect of interest rate swaps.

Where the cross-currency swap is entered into to protect the exchange risks of foreign currency receivables and payables, the underlying transaction approach is to be preferred. There should be no difference in the treatment of the regular netting payments relating to interest swaps even though the interest rate divergencies may be greater. The characterisation should arguably still follow the underlying commitments.

An additional question arises as to the taxation treatment of any payment or receipt in regard to the exchange fluctuation on the principal component underlying the counterparty's obligations. Prior to the introduction of legislation governing foreign currency exchange gains and losses, it was arguable that, consistent with the underlying transaction approach, such payments should be viewed as having a similar taxation treatment to an exchange gain or loss on the party's principal obligations.

Pursuant to Pt III, Div 3B of the ITAA, the foreign currency exchange gain and loss legislation introduced with effect from 18 February 1986 has application to gains and losses realised on capital account that are attributable to currency exchange rate fluctuations (the general income and deduction provisions still apply to those on revenue account).

The legislation operates in respect of post-18 February 1986 contracts and where the contract is a hedging contract (which should encompass a currency swap) entered into after 18 February in relation to another contract which is also post-18 February, then any gain or loss should be assessable or deductible provided the other provisions of the legislation are satisfied. It should however be noted that deductibility may be denied by the Commissioner of Taxation unless certain notification requirements are satisfied.

Unfortunately, the Australian Taxation Office's own views on cross-currency swaps have yet to be made public, and indeed Income Tax Ruling IT 2050 suggests that where substantial interest rate differentials occur (which may well be the case in cross-currency swaps) the assessability or deductibility of any netting receipts or payment is uncertain. This uncertainty may, however, have arisen due to the fact that Pt III, Div 3B of the ITAA had not been enacted when IT 2050 was released and accordingly there may have been some concern that substantial netting payments under the cross-currency swap would have been deductible, whilst any currency adjustment receipt may have been tax free.

Limitations of underlying transaction approach

By definition, the approach of characterising the netting payments under swap contracts is only appropriate where the payments are referable to some underlying commitment.

It should not mean that this approach is only valid where there is a specific underlying interest-bearing borrowing similar to the notional principal amount in the swap contract. Rather, where it can be seen that the swap contract has been entered into so as to adjust the party's financing commitments, whether wholly or in part, then the netting payments should be assessable or deductible where the underlying financing commitments are assessable or deductible. Moreover, the fact that the timing of the netting payments may not exactly match the timing of the underlying financing commitments should not in itself alter the characterisation of the netting payments. For example, an Australian borrower with fixed financing commitments may have a preference to pay on the basis of floating rates. However, rather than receive a fixed amount on a periodical basis, the borrower may also have some preference to receive such payments on an accelerated or deferred basis.

This adds another dimension to the underlying transaction approach because presumably there are additional factors which the party considered in opting for a stream of swap payments which diverges from the stream of underlying financing commitments. In general, however, it is considered that the characterisation of the netting payments should not alter merely because of a mismatch in the cash streams. A mismatch would normally be utilised by the party in its management of its current and future financing commitments and its particular cash flow requirements. These additional factors are unlikely to change the characterisation of the payments merely because a decision was taken to receive the payment in advance or in arrears of underlying obligations.

It is, however, much more difficult to determine the appropriate taxation treatment for the netting payments where there is an absence of any underlying financing commitments or where the swap is only partly explicable by underlying financing commitments.

The absence of any underlying obligations requires the swap to be analysed at face value in order to characterise the netting payments. The substance of the transaction is that the parties to the swap are agreeing to exchange certain cash streams.

However, the amounts to be paid by each party may or may not be quantifiable at inception of the swap; the timing of the payments by each party may or may not match; and the cash payments may be made either as a lump sum or periodically.

In the absence of any underlying transaction, an analysis of the business of the relevant taxpayer and the structure of the cash flows is required to assist in the characterisation of the netting payments.

Thus, for an institution which as part of its ordinary business activities provides financial intermediary services or conducts swap warehousing activities, it should be appropriate to characterise the netting payments as being part of its regular receipts and outgoings from its financial operations. It should therefore be appropriate to regard the netting payments on revenue account.

However, for an entity which does not have such business activities, an analysis of the party's intentions for entering into the swap will be paramount. In this regard the cash payments themselves could be indicative of those intentions. For example, a swap transaction with one or both legs being floating indicates that one or both parties have entered into a speculative transaction as to future movements in the floating rates. This may give some indication that there is a profit making motivation in existence in which case the provisions of ss 25(1) and 25A of the ITAA should be considered in seeking to bring to account as assessable income any profit pursuant to the transaction. Indeed, it may be more appropriate to recognise the net profit or loss from such a swap rather than seeking to reflect gross receipts and payments as being income and deductions.

The appropriate taxation treatment is also uncertain where there is an identification of dual purposes for entering into the swap contract. It may be that an entity in seeking to alter its financing obligations may also wish to adopt a speculative position which can be accommodated in a single swap transaction.

The underlying transaction approach may therefore only have limited application in respect of such swap transactions and it would appear necessary to place greater emphasis on the party's business activities and the cash flows relating to the swap in seeking to characterise the netting payments under the swap.

Commodity swaps

It is generally accepted that payments made and received by a financial institution under interest rate swap contracts are revenue in nature. On the basis that the commodity swap transaction would be entered into by a counterparty in the ordinary course of its trading business with a view to deriving assessable income, it seems likely that the receipts and payments under these contracts should also be considered to be of a revenue nature.

Timing of assessability and deductibility of swap payments

Interest rate swaps

The timing of assessability and deductibility of swap payments under interest rate swaps is the subject of Taxation Ruling IT 2682 issued by the Australian Taxation Office on 21 May 1992.

The ruling outlines the Taxation Office's view on the rules concerning the timing of assessability and deductibility of swap payments made pursuant to a "bona fide interest rate swap".

Prior to the issue of IT 2682, there was doubt surrounding the timing of the assessability and deductibility of swap receipts and payments.

It is now accepted by the Taxation Office that where a series of payments of a similar nature flow between counterparties over a period of time under a single agreement, the generally accepted accounting practice of apportioning payments on a daily accruals basis fairly reflects the extent to which a swap counterparty receives/makes payments in a particular year of income. That is, where swap payments are made/received in arrears the daily accruals basis will be the most appropriate method to apportion the liability/receivable.

However, the Commissioner of Taxation has expressed the view in Taxation Ruling IT 2682 that there is no scope for spreading swap payments received in advance over the period to which the receipt relates and that the prepaid expense legislation does not apply to swap payments made in advance.

Where a taxpayer previously adopted a method of income recognition other than that outlined above, Taxation Ruling IT 2682 provides that the following transitional arrangements must be taken into account:

(a) all swap contracts entered into on or after 21 May 1992 must adopt the daily accruals basis of assessability and deductibility of swap payments made and received;

(b) where a taxpayer has previously adopted the due and payable/due and receivable basis, the taxpayer must elect to either continue to do so for all bona fide swaps entered into prior to 21 May 1992 or to recalculate payments and receipts under all swaps entered into prior to 21 May 1992 on a daily accruals basis; and

(c) where a taxpayer has previously adopted the mark to market basis or any other method(s) other than the daily accruals basis or due and payable/due and receivable basis, the taxpayer must recalculate payments and receipts under all swaps entered into prior to 21 May 1992 on a daily accruals basis; and

(d) paragraph (a) above applies to taxpayers who have been subject to audit action where the audit has been settled on a basis which included a requirement to adopt a due and payable/due and receivable method of accounting for interest rate swaps. Where those taxpayers have continued to tax account for swaps on a due and payable/due and receivable basis following the audit, they may adopt either of the two alternatives set out in paragraph (b) above from the first year of income following the last year audited. Under no circumstances should audit settlements be disturbed.

Where a taxpayer elects or is obliged to recalculate swap payments for the above reasons, amendments to previous assessments may be required. In such cases the provisions of Section 170 concerning amended assessments must be considered.

Where a taxpayer is required by the operation of these principles to request an amended assessment and the taxpayer's tax liability is increased as a result of the recalculation, there is a potential that additional tax by way of penalty may be imposed.

In general terms, where a taxpayer has previously adopted the due and payable/due and receivable basis (that is, the circumstances described in paragraph 90(b) of Taxation Ruling IT 2682) it would be rare that the taxpayer would exercise its election in a manner that leads to an increase in its tax liability. Accordingly, a question of additional tax is unlikely to arise in such circumstances.

Where a taxpayer has previously adopted the mark-to-market basis or any other method other than the daily accruals basis or due and payable/due and receivable basis (that is, the circumstances described in paragraph 90(c) of Taxation Ruling IT 2682) there is a greater likelihood that a taxpayer will be in a position where, as a result of the required recalculation, its tax liability may increase in relation to prior years. Additional tax by way of penalty will, prima facie, be payable in these circumstances.

However, the Commissioner of Taxation has a discretion to remit such additional tax in whole or in part. The Commissioner has issued Taxation Determination TD93/9 on 21 January 1993 outlining the guidelines to be adopted by the Taxation Office when considering whether, and if so in what manner, this discretion will be exercised.

Currency swaps

Taxation Ruling IT 2682 is expressly limited in its application to payments made and received under bona fide interest rate swaps. However, it is understood that taxpayers are applying the same principles (that is, the daily accruals basis) to periodic payments made and received under currency swaps.

Commodity swaps

Taxation Ruling IT 2682 only applies to payments and receipts under "bona fide interest rate swaps". A commodity swap would not be considered to be a bona fide interest rate swap. Although commodity swap agreements are similar in nature to interest rate swaps, IT 2682 cannot be directly relied upon to determine the appropriate timing of assessability and deductibility of payments and receipts under commodity swaps.

Nevertheless, it appears unlikely that the Australian Taxation Office would wish to treat commodity swaps on a different basis from interest rate swaps. Accordingly, it seems more likely than not that the Australian Taxation Office would accept an accruals basis for recognising the gross payments made and received under commodity swap contracts.

Accelerated or deferred payment swaps

Taxation Ruling IT 2682 applies to all bona fide interest rate swap contracts entered into by a taxpayer for hedging or trading purposes, *including accelerated and deferred interest rate swaps*. However, the concept of bona fide interest rate swap has been introduced to prevent taxpayers taking advantage of the rules for swap payments where the particular transaction is not in substance a swap contract.

Therefore, agreements which, although referred to by the parties as swap contracts are in substance the provision of finance or an investment, may potentially be excluded from the treatment prescribed by Taxation Ruling IT 2682 on the basis that they are not bona fide swap contracts.

Deferred interest securities

In considering the timing of the assessability and deductibility of swap payments, consideration also needs to be given to the provisions of Div 16E of the ITAA dealing with deferred interest securities.

Broadly, these provisions statutorily dictate an accruals income or expense recognition method in respect of qualifying securities.

A qualifying security is any "security" (which is defined to include any contract under which a person is liable to pay any amount), the term of which exceeds one year and has an eligible return.

In determining whether the security has an eligible return, it must be reasonably likely that at the time the security is issued, the sum of all payments (other than periodical interest payments) under the security will exceed the issue price of the security.

In many swap contracts it may not be reasonable to conclude, at the time of issue, whether an eligible return exists given the uncertainty as to future movements in interest rates and their effect on swap payments. Consequently, the exact terms of any swap contract will need to be carefully considered to determine the application or otherwise of Div 16E of the Act.

It can be seen from the definition of "security" that the potential scope of the provisions is very wide and it is likely that certain swap contracts (particularly some accelerated or deferred payment swaps) could fall within the definitions. If so, then provided the swap payments would otherwise have been assessable or deductible, an accruals method of income or expense recognition would appear necessary (although it is doubtful as to whether the legislation intended for the provisions to apply to swap contracts).

Associated swap costs

Income Tax Ruling IT 2050 concludes that where the netting payments are on revenue account then expenses incurred in respect of the swap contract should be considered to be on revenue account and deductible pursuant to s 51(1) of the ITAA. Again, such costs should be considered referable to the new financing obligations which are being undertaken rather than costs in connection with borrowing money. Thus the costs should be deductible pursuant to s 51(1) rather than s 67 of the ITAA.

Such expenses would include swap arrangement fees, documentation costs, credit risk fees and also the counterparty's borrowing costs borne by the higher credit risk party. For the higher credit risk party the bearing of the borrowing costs of the counterparty should still be characterised as a cost of altering the higher credit risk party's underlying financing commitments rather than as a borrowing cost. Taxation Ruling IT 2682 confirms that swap fees are deductible when they are due and that the actual time at which they are due depends on the terms of the particular contract. This ruling also confirms that if the fees are charged for the administration of a swap contract that extends for a period of more than 13 months, the fee will be subject to apportionment over the period of the swap agreement.

On the other hand, the recipient would normally be required to recognise the fee income at the time it was due and receivable. However, it should be noted that some of the fees may in fact constitute a receipt in advance for services rendered over the duration of the swap agreement and accordingly, it may be possible to bring such income to account on an accruals basis. Much depends on the characterisation of the fees and the relevant surrounding documentation.

Swap revaluations

The concept of marking-to-market at the end of the reporting period is generally viewed for taxation purposes as the recognition of unrealised gains and losses. Such revaluations are inappropriate for taxation purposes where there is an inability to treat swap contracts as being trading stock for the purposes of the ITAA. Until the market develops to an extent to which the relevant rights and obligations pursuant to the swap contract can be actively purchased and sold then no revaluation to market (or indeed to any other value) is probably available for taxation purposes. The gains and losses only arise for taxation purposes as they are derived or incurred.

International tax issues

Generally, a non-resident recipient of a netting payment should only suffer Australian income tax where the swap gain has an Australian source; and

- If the recipient is a resident of a country with which Australia has concluded a double tax treaty, the gain can be said to be attributable to a permanent establishment in Australia.
- If the recipient is a resident of a country with which Australia has not concluded a double tax treaty, the existence of a permanent establishment will be irrelevant and Australian tax will be suffered.
- The non-resident recipient is not specifically exempt from Australian income tax. Obviously, in these circumstances no Australian tax would be suffered.

It would generally be unlikely for a non-resident recipient to have a permanent establishment in Australia. However, with the increased activity of foreign banks in Australia there is a possibility that foreign banks may utilise their Australian operations to organise any Australian leg of a swap transaction and yet seek to book that swap outside Australia. The extent of any activities conducted in Australia therefore needs to be carefully considered.

The source of any swap gain or loss is not only important to a non-resident recipient but also to an Australian counterparty to a cross-border swap by reason of the provisions of Australia's foreign source income and foreign tax credit legislation. The current foreign tax credit legislation seeks to quarantine foreign sourced losses against foreign income. Thus, Australian parties to swap transactions will also need to give careful consideration to a question of the sourcing of swap income. In general, it would appear that the source of any swap gain or loss is most appropriately referable to where the negotiation and execution of the swap contract is conducted, and the mere booking of a contract in a particular country is unlikely to be determinative in identifying the appropriate source. Of course, if the swap does not give rise to foreign source income for the Australian counterparty for the purposes of Australian tax law, the Australian counterparty will not be entitled to a foreign tax credit in respect of any foreign tax paid.

Withholding taxes

In Income Tax Ruling IT 2050, the Australian Taxation Office has stated that the netting payments under an interest rate swap agreement are not amounts in the nature of interest for the purposes of Australia's withholding tax provisions.

Accordingly, the netting payments to a non-resident recipient should not be subject to Australian interest withholding tax. The payment should not be considered as interest or an amount in the nature of interest which is a prerequisite for the application of the interest withholding tax provisions.

The question of what constitutes interest or an amount in the nature of interest has long been a contentious subject. It is generally considered that to be in the nature of interest there must be some form of financial accommodation between the parties, interest being characterised as the return or price for the use of money.

It is difficult to identify in most swap contracts any financial accommodation between the parties and thus it is generally considered that there is an absence of any payment which could be characterised as being in the nature of interest. It is, however, recognised that swap contracts are extremely flexible instruments and it may be possible to structure certain swap contracts so as to achieve what in reality is a provision of finance. In such circumstances, it may be easier to characterise certain netting payments as being in the nature of interest.

Moreover, should the swap contracts fall within the definition of "qualifying securities" for the purposes of Australia's deferred interest security legislation, then there also exists in the ITAA provisions which may statutorily cause certain amounts to consist of interest for the purposes of the withholding tax regime. These provisions could give rise to a withholding tax exposure, although it is noted that there are certain limitations within the withholding tax regime which may preclude an application to swap contracts. In particular, the provisions require a *transfer* of a qualifying security and this may be absent in many swap contracts.

The views of the Australian Taxation Office concerning interest withholding taxes on currency swaps have not been made public. In practice, however, it would appear that the payment of withholding taxes on cross-currency swaps is not required.

LTFXs

The determination of the taxation treatment of a LTFX requires consideration of the nature of the transaction in the context of the taxpayer's business (that is, whether on revenue or capital account) and the application of statutory provisions as well as established taxation principles dealing with the tax consequences of gains and losses attributable to currency exchange movements.

In broad terms, gains or losses arising from LTFXs which have been entered into as a hedge against underlying revenue transactions would normally be assessable or deductible for tax purposes under the general income and deduction provisions. The recognition of any such gain or loss for tax purposes should occur at realisation.

Similar conclusions should arise for traders in LTFXs. The marking to market of LTFXs for traders represents the recognition of unrealised gains or losses and, given the fact that LTFXs probably do not constitute trading stock (as defined for income tax purposes), the timing of income and deductions should be at realisation.

The statutory provisions of Div 3B of the ITAA are broadly concerned with the tax treatment of currency exchange gains or losses under contracts which are on capital account. In general, the legislation has sought to treat exchange gains and losses on capital account on a similar basis to those on revenue account. That is, gains or losses on capital account are assessable or deductible on a realisation basis.

It should also be appreciated that a LTFX may merely comprise one leg of a more complex series of events. In such circumstances it is possible that the correct reflection of a taxpayer's income may require that tax should be paid having regard to the entire transaction rather than considering each leg of the transaction in isolation.

FRAs

Characterisation of settlement sum

Typically, for taxation purposes the characterisation of any payments under a contract which may be viewed as being in the nature of forward cover or a hedge has involved an analysis of the underlying transaction being hedged.

In circumstances where the taxpayer has entered into the FRA to minimise its future interest exposure on an underlying principal amount which is being used in the production of assessable income, any settlement sum receivable or payable would normally be viewed as being on revenue account and therefore assessable or deductible.

Where the taxpayer's business activities include the taking of speculative provisions in the financial futures markets, then any gains or losses from FRA contracts are likely to be viewed as forming part of the taxpayer's ordinary business income. Future development of an active secondary market in FRA contracts may give rise to questions as to whether such contracts can be classified as trading stock for tax purposes. Currently, however, this would seem unlikely.

Where a taxpayer takes isolated speculative positions under FRA contracts it may be that such gains or losses may not be characterised as being of an income nature. In this case the provisions of the taxation legislation dealing with capital gains and losses may need to be considered.

Timing of assessability and deductibility of settlement sum

Normally, at settlement date the present value of the net interest differential between the agreed and actual interest rate is paid in a lump sum to the counterparty which must be compensated under the terms of the FRA.

Prior to settlement date, any gain or loss from the FRA could not be said to have been realised for taxation purposes and accordingly any revaluation of the FRA (for example, FRA held for trading purposes) during the period up to settlement date would not represent a taxable gain or loss.

However, at settlement date it is likely that the settlement sum can be said to have been derived or incurred by the respective parties and accordingly it is at settlement date that the income or deduction has crystallised. Whilst the quantum of the payment does have a direct relationship with interest rates, it is not a payment that can be said to be interest. In these circumstances adoption of an "accruals approach" to the recognition of the settlement sum is unlikely to be acceptable (refer however to previous comments in connection with the income recognition methods for financial institutions).

It is noted that the deferred interest security legislation has been introduced to give legislative effect to the adoption of an accruals approach to income and expense recognition in respect of certain securities. However, notwithstanding the very broad definitional provisions in this legislation, it would normally be difficult to argue that FRAs come within the ambit of the deferred interest security regime.

The prepaid expense legislation may however impact the timing of the deduction for a settlement payment in certain FRA contracts and may in fact dictate an accruals deduction. This legislation should not however impact the timing of the recognition of income under the FRA.

Withholding tax issues

In transacting cross-border FRAs, consideration needs to be given to the question of whether the settlement sum constitutes interest or an amount in the nature of interest for the purposes of the withholding tax provisions.

In this regard, it is noted that the terms and conditions for FRAs often characterise the counterparties as "borrower" and "lender"; the settlement sum is quantified by reference to interest differentials; and a settlement sum may be accounted for in the books of the parties as interest income or expenses.

However, notwithstanding the above, the legal relationship between the counterparties is not that of borrower and lender. There is no loan transaction between the parties nor any financial accommodation which could be said to give rise to a payment which is the return for the use of money or is in the nature of such a return. It is therefore considered that the payment of a settlement sum to a non-resident party should not give rise to a withholding tax liability, assuming of course the transaction is on an arm's length basis.

Interest rate options—caps, floors and collars

The taxation consequences of interest rate option contracts entered into as a means of hedging underlying financing commitments should follow the underlying transaction approach.

Where the underlying financing commitments being hedged are on revenue account and relate to the generation of the taxpayer's assessable income, gains and losses arising from interest rate option contracts should be on revenue account and subject to tax pursuant to the ordinary income and deduction provisions of the ITAA.

Cap, floor and collar rate agreements are merely interest rate option contracts designed to achieve specific hedging objectives. That is, options can be written so as to give the hedger the ability to establish a maximum predetermined borrowing rate, a minimum investment yield, or a combination of both.

Characterisation of settlement sums

Profits and losses derived by taxpayers whose business includes trading in or writing such option contracts should also have their gains or losses treated as being on revenue account and fully subject to taxation. In the absence of a developed market in which option contracts can be readily bought and sold, as opposed to merely being closed out, the ability to characterise option contracts as trading stock is limited. Thus, option traders who seek to value options by marking-to-market are in effect recognising unrealised gains and losses, which from a taxation viewpoint are unlikely to constitute a taxable event.

For taxation purposes, it is likely that the gains or losses only become subject to taxation at the time the option contract is closed out. However, this general conclusion will be subject to the specific terms of the contract and the acceleration or deferral of any settlement sum may alter the timing of income and deductions. It would be necessary to review the particular contract to determine when the liability to make the settlement sum payment crystallises.

Timing of assessability and deductibility of fees

Fees or premiums paid in consideration for the granting of the option should similarly be on revenue and capital account having regard to the characteristics of the underlying transaction. Premiums on revenue account should be deductible at the time the obligation to make the payment arises, although the prepaid expense legislation may impact the timing of such deductions for option contracts extending over 13 months.

The option writer is also likely to be assessable at the time the premiums are due and receivable and it is doubtful that premiums received in advance can be brought to account on an accruals basis, although again the terms of the contract and the particular features of the writer's business need to be reviewed.

Structured caps, collars, floors

A separate analysis of the taxation consequences detailed above will be required where there are option contracts without any underlying transactions, or where off-market rates are utilised. The above analysis will not necessarily apply as a matter of course to such transactions.

Such contracts need to be reviewed in the context of the taxpayer's business and intentions in entering into such contracts. For taxpayers entering into isolated and speculative contracts it may be more appropriate to bring to account a net profit or loss at the conclusion of such transactions as being the proper reflection of the taxpayer's income. Alternatively, the contract may be on capital account which may require consideration of the capital gains tax provisions of the ITAA.

Withholding tax issues

The settlement sums and premiums arising pursuant to any cross-border caps, collars and floors should generally not be subject to Australian interest withholding tax. These amounts should not be considered as interest or amounts in the nature of interest which is a prerequisite for the application of the interest withholding tax provisions.

The legal relationship between the counterparties is not that of borrower and lender. There is no loan transaction between the parties nor any financial accommodation which could be said to give rise to a payment which is a return for the use of money or in the nature of such a return.

Exhibit 43.2: Taxation Aspects of Swap Transactions

SUMMARY TABLE

Interest rate swaps	**United States**	**Canada**	**Japan**	**United Kingdom**	**Australia**
Character of netting payments.	Periodic swap payments are generally considered ordinary income.	Regard must be had to the legal substance of the transaction as well as the intentions of the parties entering into the swap.	Income is characterised as ordinary income.	Under strict law, the legal substance of the swap transaction (in particular whether any debt obligation arises between the parties) will determine the taxation treatment. This treatment has been extended by concessionary treatment which, broadly, is anticipated to form the basis for new legislation.	Generally analysed by having regard to the taxation treatment of the financing commitments of the underlying borrowing transaction which the interest rate swap seeks to impact.
	Companies	*Companies*	*Companies*	*Companies*	*Companies*
Timing of inclusion of netting receipts or payments in the computation of taxable income for companies and financial institutions.	All taxpayers must recognise the rateable daily portion of a periodic payment for the taxable year to which that portion relates.	At law, the deduction of netting payments occurs when an amount becomes payable under the terms of the contract. Similarly, it is considered that netting income is earned when an amount becomes due and receivable.	Net payment/ receipt of interest is recorded in the accrual basis.	Generally deductible or assessable on a cash basis although an accruals basis may apply to trading companies.	Netting receipts and payments made in arrears pursuant to bona fide interest rate swaps should be recognised as income or deductions on a daily accruals basis.

Exhibit 43.2—continued

Interest rate swaps	**United States**	**Canada**	**Japan**	**United Kingdom**	**Australia**
	Financial institutions	*Financial institutions*	*Financial institutions*	*Financial institutions*	*Financial institutions*
	All taxpayers must recognise the rateable daily portion of a periodic payment for the taxable year to which that portion relates.	In practice, payments or receipts are included in the computation of taxable income on the same basis as used in Canadian accounting practice.	Net payment/ receipt of interest is recorded on the accrual basis.	Payments or receipts in the ordinary course of trade would normally be deductible or assessable as trading expenses (that is, on an accrual basis).	The above-mentioned principles apply equally to financial institutions.
Currency Swaps					
Netting payments	Tax analysis is applicable to interest rate swaps will apply where the periodical payments do not contain a foreign currency element.	The same conclusions can be derived with respect of the netting payments or receipts as interest rate swaps.	Similar to interest rate swaps.	Similar to interest rate swaps.	There are no specific rules in relation to payments made or received under currency swap agreements. However, as a matter of practice, the tax consequences for the payments made or received in respect of currency swaps broadly follow the analysis set out above.

Exhibit 43.2—continued

Currency swaps	United States	Canada	Japan	United Kingdom	Australia
Currency gains and losses	Under s 988 the foreign exchange element in a s 988 transaction is given ordinary income or loss treatment. Numerous special rules apply.	Financial institutions and certain other corporates entering into currency swaps against trade assets or liabilities will normally be able to recognise both foreign exchange transactions on revenue account. The treatment on capital account is less certain. In the case of a corporate, the Canadian courts have, as a rule, looked to the nature of the obligation. With respect to any gains or losses arising on the repayment of the currency under current Canadian administrative practice, where the foreign exchange gains or losses are on account of income they may	This spot position and the forward position are valued on a mark-to-market basis where the revaluation amounts offset each other. The periodic interest payments are recognised on an accrual basis.	Under existing law, the treatment of currency gains and losses will depend on the legal substance of the transaction. Where the transaction is undertaken as a hedge it is likely to take the character of the underlying transaction. Unless the swap transaction can be regarded as a trading transaction, a capital gain or loss may arise from the assets and liabilities associated with the swap rather than the swap itself.	Specific legislation provides that most currency exchange gains would be assessable at the time they are realised and most currency exchange losses would be deductible for income tax purposes at the time they are incurred.

Exhibit 43.2—continued

Currency swaps	**United States**	**Canada**	**Japan**	**United Kingdom**	**Australia**
Currency gains and losses		be accounted for on an accruals basis or a realised basis. However, where the foreign exchange gains or losses are on account of capital then the taxpayer must record the foreign exchange gains and losses on a realisation basis.			
Associated swap costs	Would normally be deductible for tax purposes and amortised over the life of the swap.	Should be fully deductible on the same basis as amounts payable and receivable under an interest rate swap. Although depending on the terms of the transaction there may be a debate over the proper timing of the deduction.	Usually deductible as an expense, amortised over the life of the swap.	Should normally be trading receipts or expenses for banks. For non-banks the position is less clear.	Where the netting payments are on revenue account the incidental expenses incurred in respect of the swap contract should be considered to be on revenue account and deductible. They should be deductible when due to be paid and the recipient would normally recognise the fee income at the time it was due and receivable. Where the

Exhibit 43.2—continued

	United States	Canada	Japan	United Kingdom	Australia
Associated swap costs					payment made relates to a swap which extends for a period of greater than 13 months the swap fee may have to be amortised.
Withholding tax	The source of the interest rate swap will be directed to the residence of the recipient. Thus where an interest rate swap agreement is made with a non-resident there will be no withholding tax issues as the payment will not be sourced within the United States.	Swap payments themselves are not generally regarded as legally constituting interest and should not be subject to withholding tax.	Swap payments are not considered "interest" and are not subject to withholding tax.	There is a general requirement to deduct basic rate income tax on swap payments which are regarded as annual payments, but under concessionary treatment this does not apply where paid to a United Kingdom bank or recognised swap dealer. In addition, the general withholding requirement may be eliminated or reduced on payments to non-UK residents under a double tax agreement.	The Australian Taxation Ofice has stated that the netting payments under an interest rate swap agreement are not amounts in the nature of interest and should not be subject to Australian interest withholding tax.
VAT	Not applicable.	VAT is not a major issue in swap transactions.	Not applicable.	VAT is not a major issue in swap transactions.	Not applicable.

Chapter 44

Legal and Documentation Issues of Swaps and Financial Derivatives

By Ian Wallace, Partner,
Allen Allen & Hemsley, Solicitors & Notaries

INTRODUCTION

The derivatives market has expanded at a rate which defies description both in absolute volume and, perhaps more importantly from a legal perspective, in the number of variants from the base swap model. This growth and diversification has resulted from many factors including:

- the increased de-regulation of financial markets world-wide;
- the volatility of interest and exchange rates and commodity and equity prices during the 1980s; and
- the increasing sophistication of the computer technology utilised to design and support these instruments.

It has also been assisted by the ability of lawyers in many jurisdictions to creatively apply their skills in a positive way in responding to their clients needs.

The constant innovation that has and still does characterise the swaps market in its various permutations has meant that swaps lawyers have been continually challenged to correctly analyse and document the contractual arrangements to which their clients wish to agree.

In any particular transaction a lawyer will need to consider at least the following:

1. Are all the essential elements for an enforceable contract present?
2. Are there any general law problems posed by the proposed transaction (for example, public policy in its various manifestations)?
3. Are there any specific statutory restrictions or prohibitions which are relevant (for example, gaming and wagering legislation, insurance legislation, exchange controls, securities industry laws or futures industry laws)?
4. Where the transaction involves more than one jurisdiction, are there any conflict of law issues which require resolution?
5. Are there any taxation issues which present potential problems for the transaction (not just income tax/withholding tax but also stamp taxes, turnover taxes, etc)?
6. What is the appropriate form of documentation for the transaction?
7. Are there any particular transaction risks which are accentuated by the proposed transaction structure (particularly insolvency risks)?

Frequently, consideration of these issues must take place in the pressurised environment of an imminent transaction. On other occasions it takes place after the event where there is, understandably, considerable pressure on lawyers not to discover problems.

All of this means that legal practice in this area is always challenging.[1]

In this chapter we will explore the following interrelated themes:

- documentation issues;
- legal lessons from the 1980s;
- regulatory developments.

DOCUMENTATION ISSUES

Elements of a swap agreement

The elements of a swap agreement are no different in their characterisation to the elements of any other contract involving an obligation to pay money or deliver property. Three broad categories of provision can be identified:

- *fundamental obligations and necessary mechanics*—these are the provisions detailing each party's respective payment obligations under the swap agreement and any conditions precedent to those obligations arising. They include the necessary definitional and mechanical provisions—for example, definition of how interest rate or other indicators which determine the quantum of periodic payment obligations are calculated—and also include any provisions dealing with circumstances where the payment obligations may vary—for example, allocation of withholding tax risk and any other yield protection provisions such as bank capital adequacy protection provisions.

  It is only provisions within this first category which are truly essential to the workings of a swap agreement. In a swap contract governing a single transaction between entities in the same jurisdiction, these provisions are likely to be quite brief. However, if the swap contract is a master agreement drafted to cover a broad range of individual transactions and is between parties in different jurisdictions then these provisions will be substantially longer and, potentially, require substantially more negotiation unless standard form documents are being used.

  An examination of the 1991 ISDA Definitions demonstrates the range of important terms which need to be defined in order to permit a master swap agreement to function properly. A comparison of the 1992 ISDA Master Agreement for multi-currency cross-border transactions with the 1992 ISDA Master Agreement for local currency single jurisdiction transactions also demonstrates the complexities which are introduced by transactions which cover different currencies and different jurisdictions.

- *fundamental contractual and credit provisions*—these provisions include representations and warranties, undertakings relating to the parties (as opposed to any undertakings relating to the transaction itself), credit support provisions (for instance requirements for collateralisation and/or guarantees), events of default/termination events and provisions dealing with the consequences of such events.

  Credit provisions are inevitable to a greater or lesser extent in any swap agreement other than, perhaps, swaps within corporate groups. Typically, credit

1. For detailed discussions of the legal and regulatory issues in various jurisdictions see: S Somer, "A Survey of Legal and Regulatory Issues Relevant to Interest Rate Swaps" *Depaul Business Law Journal* 385 (United States); "The Regulations Governing Derivatives—An International Guide" International Financial Law Review Special Supplement January 1992 (covering Canada, France, The Netherlands, United Kingdom, United States).

provisions are the source of the greatest amount of negotiation between counterparties as each counterparty considers the credit support, if any, that it requires, in what circumstances it wishes to have the ability to terminate the contract and the consequences which it wishes to flow from such termination.

- *contractual boilerplate*—this category includes provisions such as the governing law clause, the notices clause, provisions limiting assignability and the expenses clause.

  Boilerplate provisions are also important to varying degrees but ordinarily their absence would not mean that the transaction would fail. It may simply mean that some matters are more difficult to determine because they are left to the general law—for example, if an agreement has no governing law clause, general law of the relevant jurisdiction will apply settled principles to determine the appropriate governing law of the contract.

Development of master agreements

As swaps moved from being a novelty in the early 1980s to being widely used and understood (at least in their basic form) market participants sought to avoid the need to fully document each swap on a case by case basis in order to, amongst other things:

- standardise terms and conditions so as to aid liquidity and certainty (particularly in back-to-back deals);
- reduce costs;
- reduce and eventually eliminate any delay between commercial "agreement" and the entry of a binding legal agreement.

The spectacular expansion of the international capital markets through the 1980s was greatly assisted by the evolution of the swaps market to the point where many, perhaps a considerable majority of, capital markets issues were dependent on their associated swaps for success. In this context, for there to be any sort of delay for a financial institution in being certain that a counterparty was committed to a particular swap rapidly came to be unacceptable.

The first response to this problem was the development of codes of standard terms and conditions by industry associations which could be incorporated by reference into new transactions (for example, BBAIRS in the United Kingdom and AIRS in Australia).

At the same time various institutions developed their own "master agreements" to be executed with counterparties which would allow actual transactions to be documented by no more than a simple exchange of letters/telexes setting out the financial details of the transaction. These early master agreements either worked in the same way as the industry codes (that is, their terms were imported by reference into individual transaction contracts) or adopted the approach of establishing a permanent contract which was then supplemented by each individual transaction.

The former approach produces multiple contracts, the latter a single contract growing over time. As potential advantages flowing from netting of multiple transactions were realised the latter approach became the generally accepted one.

Predictably, these "in-house" masters, while an improvement, did not completely overcome the problems of delay in finalising documentation—particularly in situations where each counterparty had its own form of master.

From 1985 the International Swap Dealers Association began to produce standard documents which were recommended for general industry use. A brief chronology of ISDA's output is as follows:

- *1985 and 1986*—ISDA Codes of Standard Wording, Assumptions and Provisions for Swaps. These were not master agreements but contained terms which could be imported into agreements negotiated between counterparties.
- *1987*—ISDA published two master agreements and a set of definitions:
  - Interest Rate Swap Master Agreement—this was designed for single jurisdiction US$ transactions only and depended on the 1986 Code;
  - Interest Rate and Currency Exchange Master Agreement (1987 Master)—this document which quickly achieved widespread market use covered multi-currency, multi-jurisdiction transactions;
  - 1987 ISDA Interest Rate and Currency Exchange Definitions designed for use with the 1987 Master.
- *1988*—Tax Provisions for ISDA Agreements—designed for use with the 1987 Master.
- *1989*—Caps Addendum for incorporation into the 1987 Master and containing provisions required for interest rate caps, collars and floors.
- *1990*—Options Addendum containing provisions required for option transactions.
- *1991*—1991 ISDA Definitions issued to replace 1987 Definitions.
- *1992*
  - up-dated and expanded version of the 1987 Master (the 1992 Master);
  - updated single currency/single jurisdiction Master Agreement;
  - Form of OTC Equity Index Option Confirmation;
  - 1992 US Municipal Counterparty Definitions;
  - 1992 FX and Currency Option Definitions.
- *1993*—User's Guide to the 1992 Master.

ISDA published the 1993 ISDA Commodity Derivative Definitions during the course of 1993 (see *Appendix C*). It is also expected that further material in relation to equity derivatives will be published by ISDA.

The 1992 Master is set out in *Appendix A*. In *Appendix B* there is a brief clause by clause analysis of the 1992 Master and commentary on the principal differences between the 1987 and 1992 versions (together with a chart showing the interaction of the various ISDA documents).

It should be remembered that the ISDA Master Agreements are structured so that they contain only the basic mechanical and operational provisions and so that the parties have considerable flexibility both in selecting various optional parts of the document but more significantly in adding to and amending the base document through the Schedule. Similarly the Definitions and the Addenda contain, almost exclusively, provisions dealing with necessary mechanics of calculation. Neither they nor the Masters seek to deal in any detail with credit issues which may arise between particular counterparties. Those issues are left for the counterparties to resolve on a case by case basis.

In the 1992 Master significant matters which the parties must complete or where a decision must be made between various options include the following:

- Are there any "specified entities"?
- Are the cross default provisions to apply? If so, what is the relevant "threshold amount" and what is the "specified indebtedness"?
- Are the "credit event upon merger" provisions to apply to either or both parties?
- Is "automatic termination" to apply?
- How are payments on early termination to be calculated?
- What is to be the termination currency?
- Are there to be any "additional termination events"?
- Which of the "tax representations" are to apply to which party?
- What documents are to be delivered by which party and when?
- Are there any "credit support documents"?
- Are there any "credit support providers"?
- What is the governing law?
- When is "payment netting" to apply?

Whilst the ISDA Master Agreements have become industry standard documents for interest rate and currency swaps other forms of transaction are typically documented under other standard documents. For example, forward rate agreements are typically documented under the FRABBA terms in the United Kingdom and the ABAFRA terms in Australia (although in the latter case market participants are being encouraged to switch to the 1992 ISDA Master with appropriate amendments).

Limitations of Master Agreements

No documentation before dealing

Although the ISDA Master Agreements, the standard Codes and other standardised documents which have developed have substantially achieved the aims set out above there remain drawbacks and dangers which must be recognised by market participants.

It remains true that many transactions are initiated before a Master Agreement has been negotiated and executed between the counterparties. This practice is recognised in the Bank of England's London Code of Conduct issued in 1992 at paragraph 84:

> "In more complex transactions like swaps, institutions should treat themselves as bound to a deal at the point where the commercial terms of the transactions are agreed. Making swap transactions subject to agreement on documentation is not best practice. Principals must make every effort to progress the finalisation of documentation. The Bank believes it should be possible for this to be accomplished within two months of the deal being struck; and regards longer than three months as excessive."

This practice involves certain risks from a legal perspective particularly if one counterparty or the other wishes to add to the terms of, for instance, a standard ISDA Master Agreement.

In particular, because the ISDA Master Agreements require various important provisions to be completed even if a court would imply an agreement along the lines of, say, the 1992 Master between the parties beyond the mere financial terms typically contained in a Confirmation the implied agreement would of necessity be missing some provisions which a counterparty may regard as crucial.

There is an important distinction here between swaps and exchange-traded instruments where the terms of the contract are precisely formulated. The ability to tailor the terms of the swap agreement to fit the needs of a particular transaction is one of the greatest strengths of the swaps market. However, if the tailoring process is poorly handled or, worse, ignored then this strength can become a weakness.

Excessive adherence to Master Agreement

As with any precedent or standard form there is a natural tendency amongst market participants to simply complete an ISDA Master, for instance, without giving detailed consideration to the appropriateness of the terms.

Bearing in mind that the ISDA Master was drafted as an even-handed document which assumes an equal credit standing between the two counterparties its unamended applicability to a transaction between two parties of substantially different credit standing should be carefully questioned. Equally the ISDA Master does not necessarily deal appropriately with some of the sorts of actions which corporations regularly undertake.

This is not meant as a criticism of the ISDA Master. Both the 1987 and the 1992 versions are excellent documents which provide a very useful starting point for documenting transactions between counterparties. However, they should be seen as just that, that is, a starting point, not as the complete answer in all cases.

Depending on the particular characteristics of a proposed transaction a counterparty should assess some of the same matters which would be assessed by a bank in a loan transaction and then complete the Master Agreement appropriately or if a Master Agreement already exists, amend it as a condition of completing the proposed transaction.

A practical example may illustrate the point. An aggressive entrepreneurial company has large borrowings and has entered into a number of swaps with both lenders and non-lenders. The company runs into trouble short of an actual default on its borrowings but sufficiently serious that it is effectively being guided in an assets sale programme by its lenders under an informal arrangement.

The lenders decide that as a condition of rolling over their facilities they will take security from the company which has previously borrowed unsecured on a negative pledge basis.

This substantially disadvantages the non-lender swap counterparties as their claims against the company on a liquidation would rank behind the secured lenders. The non-lender counterparties examine their standard ISDA Master Agreements to determine what action they are able to take. The conclusion—none.

There is no negative pledge undertaking therefore the giving of security does not breach any undertaking. None of the "insolvency" events are triggered. There is no "material adverse change" event.

All swap counterparties, particularly those who are financial institutions, no doubt realise that interest rate and currency volatility is such that swap contracts can generate substantial termination payments and they should therefore apply the same sorts of analytical skills which are applied to assessing and documenting loan credits.

Corporate swap counterparties should recognise the same reality and realise that the credit standing of a bank or a bank subsidiary dealing in derivatives may decline substantially over the term of a transaction.

The answer to these types of problems is for the Master Agreement to be amended to include appropriate additional undertakings and termination/default events (for example, negative pledge undertakings and a termination event which is triggered if the rating of a counterparty falls to, for instance, below investment grade).

The provisions which will be appropriate will vary depending on both the parties involved and the particular transaction.

Non-standard transactions

There is an understandable tendency for market participants to try to squeeze into standard Master Agreements all sorts of non-standard transactions. There is nothing particularly dangerous about this and in fact there are positive advantages which may accrue in a default situation by virtue of the wider operation of the termination netting provisions of the 1992 Master. However appropriate consideration must be given to the nature of the proposed transaction and to whether any documentation adjustments are advisable.

For example, a transaction where one counterparty prepays in one lump sum a fixed rate payment stream while the other counterparty retains a floating rate payment obligation raises very different credit issues to an ordinary interest rate swap.

The following issues, at least, should be considered where non-standard transactions are being entered into, particularly where they are to be entered into under an existing Master Agreement:

(a) Is it necessary to incorporate the terms of an ISDA Addenda or additional ISDA Definitions for the purpose of the transaction?

(b) Will the new transaction be covered by the terms of any Credit Support document originally given in relation to the Master Agreement?

(c) Is there anything in any legal opinion originally obtained for the Master Agreement which may indicate that the new transaction may give rise to legal difficulties? Even if the answer to this is no, is the legal opinion so old that it would be prudent for it to be updated to ensure that there has been no relevant change of law in the interim?

(d) Given the nature of the non-standard transaction, is it safe to assume that various rules applicable to normal swaps (for example, taxation treatment) will also apply to the new transaction?

Mark-to-market arrangements

Where credit issues have been recognised as giving rise to difficulties the response frequently is for the swap to be "marked-to-market" under an arrangement which ties the amount of the payment required to a small percentage of notional principal amount. Normally there is an ability for either party to adjust the aggregate of the payments made over time by reference to the actual mark-to-market valuation of the swap so as to ensure that the security buffer is maintained.

This adjustment process is typically the most troublesome issue when these arrangements are being documented. It is very easy to state the concept of mark-to-market valuation but far harder to document it in a form satisfactory to both counterparties. The calculation procedure set out in the definition of "Market Quotation" in the 1992 ISDA Master Agreement (see *Appendix A*) provides a mechanism which addressed the majority of the issues—it requires reference to third party "reference market makers" and it requires those quotes to take into account existing Credit Support Documents.

However, as a practical matter, where adjustments may be required or permitted on a quarterly, monthly, weekly or even daily basis, such a procedure is generally regarded as being administratively unworkable and some other arrangement is preferred. For instance, the documentation may provide for the mark-to-market calculation to be performed by one party with the other party being given a residual right to query any determination made by requesting reference to external parties.

The other complicating factor in this process is the perhaps obvious one that the more complicated or exotic the transaction which is being marked-to-market the more difficult it may be to actually obtain market quotations for equivalent transactions. It may simply be impossible to find reference market makers who are prepared to invest the time and resources required to understand a complicated transaction to the point where they are in a position to quote a rate for replicating it.

Mark-to-market arrangements may be structured either as:

- payments by way of security (or "collateral"); or
- absolute payments.

In each case "interest" will accrue on payments made which means that for cross-border transactions interest withholding tax considerations become relevant.

The advantages and disadvantages of payments by way of security compared to absolute payments need to be considered on a case by case basis.

While there is a tendency for these sorts of quasi-margining arrangements to be documented on an informal basis market participants should note the following where the arrangement involves the provision of security:

- substantial stamp duty liabilities may be incurred in some jurisdictions when security is taken;
- the validity/priority of the security may depend upon registration;
- it would be normal for basic company searches to be conducted to ascertain the existence of any competing security which could adversely affect priority;
- in some jurisdictions (for example, the United Kingdom, Australia) the *Charge Card* case[2] means that it is not possible for a bank effectively to take security from a counterparty over a bank account of the counterparty with that bank; and
- the question of legal capacity to validly provide security should also be addressed. The same bodies where the issue of capacity to enter into swap agreements is acute (local authorities, building societies, statutory authorities and utilities) may also be either restricted or prohibited from granting security.

Where the arrangement involves absolute payments the following factors should be considered.

- What are the taxation effects of the absolute payments? Are they deductible/assessable?
- Is there any risk that the governing law of the transaction will "look through" the documentation and characterise the payments as payments by way of security?

2. *Re Charge Card Services* [1987] Ch 150 and affirmed in [1989] Ch 497.

LESSONS FROM THE 1980s

Defaults and insolvencies

The end of the 1980s boom resulted in problems in many areas of the world-wide financial markets. The swaps market was not immune from these problems and situations arose where active market participants were forced to cease operations as a result of the financial difficulties of the corporate groups of which they were members.

Particular examples were:

- Development Finance Corporation (New Zealand);
- Bank of New England (United States);
- British and Commonwealth Merchant Bank (United Kingdom);
- Drexel Burnham Lambert (United States).

It should be emphasised that in none of these cases was the swap business responsible for the wider problems of the relevant group. This fact no doubt significantly assisted the ultimately substantially successful outcomes.

In addition substantial end users of swaps have also failed (for example, Olympia and York (Canada)).

As a result we are now seeing, although only to a limited extent, court cases involving swaps being decided in various jurisdictions.

Development Finance Corporation (DFC)

In October 1989 statutory managers were appointed to DFC thereby implementing a moratorium preventing creditors acting under New Zealand law. At the time DFC held a swap portfolio of approximately NZ$4 billion notional amount. Documentation for the majority of the swap contracts included limited two-way payment provisions.

The statutory managers and the Reserve Bank of New Zealand quickly announced that DFC would maintain payments on its swap portfolio and began negotiations to transfer the entire portfolio to another institution.

A number of counterparties with contracts where DFC was "in-the-money" purported to terminate their contracts thereby realising windfall gains on the basis of the application of the limited two-way payment provision.

As a result of the ensuing negotiations, all but one of these counterparties either agreed to reinstate its contract or paid out to DFC all or substantially all of the termination amount which would have been payable but for the limited two-way payment provision. Litigation was commenced with the sole recalcitrant, Security Pacific. That litigation was settled in late 1992 on terms which are confidential but are understood to favour DFC. It is perhaps unfortunate that the case was settled as it would have involved consideration of a number of the arguments which are typically raised in common law jurisdictions when the efficacy of limited two-way payment provisions are in question.

The balance of the portfolio was successfully transferred to Barclays Bank Plc with new documentation being negotiated by Barclays and each counterparty.

Bank of New England (BNE)

BNE's financial difficulties were well known for at least a year before it was declared insolvent in January 1991. They stemmed, primarily, from imprudent real estate lending. During this 12 month period, despite considerable difficulties, BNE's swap traders under the close supervision of banking regulators, were able to reduce BNE's derivative portfolio from approximately US$30 billion notional amount to under US$7 billion notional amount. In the process they realised a profit for the year and left a residual portfolio with a net positive value of some US$185 million.

Following the declaration of insolvency, the entire residual portfolio was transferred by the Federal Deposit Insurance Corporation to the bridge bank created to assume BNE's assets and liabilities.

British and Commonwealth Merchant Bank (BCMB)

When an administrator was appointed to BCMB in early June 1990 it held a derivative portfolio of approximately 200 transactions with 50 plus counterparties ranging from other financial institutions to local authorities and corporates. The majority of the relevant documentation contained limited two-way payment termination provisions.

The administrators ceased payment on all ISDA documented swaps on the basis that the automatic termination provision in the 1987 Master Agreement was effective. However, the administrators moved very quickly to organise a transfer of the portfolio to a new counterparty (again Barclays). By 20 June 1990 the vast majority of the portfolio had been transferred under documentation with individual counterparties which, amongst other things, provided for:

- the reinstatement of the terminated ISDA contracts; and
- the making good of any payments that had fallen due but were unpaid due to the appointment of the administrators.

Again, in this case as in DFC, many counterparties who could have relied on the limited two-way payment provision to realise windfall gains did not, due it would seem to a combination of:

- business and regulatory pressure;
- legal doubts on the efficacy of the limited two-way payment provision.

Drexel

In February 1990 the parent of the Drexel Group filed for Chapter 11 protection. The derivative trading subsidiary (Drexel) of the Drexel Group was not directly affected by the Chapter 11 proceedings but as the parent was guarantor of certain of its swaps, the filing meant a default had occurred under those swaps. Drexel had a portfolio of 1500 plus swaps with more than 200 counterparties. Again, limited two-way payment provisions dominated in the documentation.

Between mid-February and the end of May 1990 when Drexel itself filed for Chapter 11 protection, the portfolio was unwound by negotiation with individual counterparties after initial attempts to sell the entire portfolio had failed.

The majority of counterparties agreed not to pursue windfall gains which would have arisen out of the application of limited two-way payment clauses and settled for full value.

It is understood that litigation has been pursued against some of the parties who refused to disgorge windfall gains. In a recent decision in a New York court Drexel failed to overturn a counterparty's reliance on the limited two-way payment clause.

The court concluded (without any detailed reasoning) that:

(a) the limited two-way payment clause constituted a valid liquidated damages clause and was therefore enforceable in accordance with its terms;

(b) the clause was not unconscionable or contrary to public policy as "the amount liquidated bears a reasonable relationship to the probable loss"; and

(c) requiring Drexel to forgo an unrealised investment gain was neither a penalty, a forfeiture nor an unjust enrichment.[3]

Lessons

1. The principal lesson that can be drawn from these situations is echoed in other sectors of the financial markets and that is that the larger the scale of the default, the more likely it is that the strict legal position which applies between the relevant parties will not be the major determinant of the outcome.

   Equally, or in many cases more, important will be the influence of commercial and regulatory pressures which may be brought to bear on the relevant parties in an attempt to ensure that those involved behave in a manner which is regarded as rational in terms of a wider market perspective rather than clinging grimly to perceived legal rights.

   The situations described above may have ended very differently both for the parties directly involved and financial markets generally if these pressures had not been brought to bear.

2. It is also evident that the limited two-way payment provision is a source of constant difficulty. Legally there are doubts as to its efficacy in many jurisdictions. It is argued that a court may hold that the limited two-way payment provision constitutes an unenforceable penalty or an unacceptable forfeiture of property or is contrary to public policy. The nature of these concerns will vary between jurisdictions but they will not be removed in any jurisdiction where they arise until there is an authoritative superior court decision or legislation is adopted to clarify the matter (the latter seems unlikely). They will not be removed by academic argument, no matter how closely reasoned.[4]

   Commercially the clause is offensive in the sense that it delivers windfall gains to parties on a purely chance basis to the detriment of other creditors of an insolvent counterparty. Any court case where a counterparty was seeking to justify retention of such windfall gain would be likely, at least in a public relations sense, to be very damaging to the counterparty. Even where contracts have contained limited two-way payment clauses the overwhelming market practice has been for parties who could have sought to retain the windfall gain to give it up to the defaulting party.

   These realities have been, at least partially, recognised in the 1992 ISDA Master Agreement where limited two-way payment is now an option along with a full two-way payment provision. It is also true that even before the issue of the 1992 Master an increasing number of market participants had adopted full two-way payment provisions in their documentation by making appropriate amendments to the 1987 Master.

3. *Drexel Burnham Lambert Products Corporation v Midland Bank Plc*, United States District Court, Southern District of New York, 92 CIV 3098, 9 November 1992.
4. See Ebo A Coleman, "Swaps, FX and the 'Full Two-Way Payments' Fallacy" (1993) (May) *Butterworths Journal of International Banking and Finance Law* 229 for an example of such an argument.

Perhaps the final death knell of the limited two-way payment clause is sounded in the April 1993 Consultative Proposal on Netting by the Basle Committee on Banking Supervision which, while recognising the acceptability of bilateral netting arrangements for calculation of capital adequacy requirements, proposes to exclude from the regime any netting arrangement that contains a limited two-way payment clause (or a "walk away" clause as it is described in the proposal).[5]

3. Automatic termination provisions are also troublesome given their potential to impact on attempts to dispose of a swap portfolio in an orderly manner.

   In many jurisdictions there is no benefit accruing to a non-defaulting party from automatic termination and there are positive advantages gained from maintaining control of the termination process.

   Again, this has been recognised in the 1992 ISDA Master where automatic termination is now an option available for selection by counterparties thus accommodating those jurisdictions where automatic termination may be beneficial in protecting the non-defaulting counterparty from the impact of insolvency legislation.

Hammersmith

Initial case

The facts of the *Hammersmith and Fulham* case[6] have sufficient notoriety that we need only summarise them in the briefest detail.

During the 1988 and 1989 financial years, the London borough of Hammersmith and Fulham (Hammersmith) entered into some 592 swaps and swap derivatives with an aggregate notional amount of over GBP 6 billion. Hammersmith was not hedging its debt obligations (other than perhaps to a limited extent)—it was gambling on interest rate movements. It lost its gamble. Hammersmith's auditor, acting through the Audit Commission for local authorities, began proceedings to have the transactions declared void on the basis that they were beyond the power of local authorities.

The case was argued in detail from May 1989 in the Divisional Court through the Court of Appeal to the House of Lords which handed down its judgment in January 1991. The Divisional Court ruled that all of the swaps were beyond power and therefore invalid. The Court of Appeal allowed the counterparty banks' appeal in part (the swaps were valid to the extent that they were used for the purpose of interest rate risk management). The House of Lords affirmed the Divisional Court judgment.

The ultimate outcome of the case, that is, that the swaps were beyond power and therefore void, was, obviously, devastating for the counterparties, particularly given that the swap portfolio was heavily out of the money (by some hundreds of millions of pounds).

Subsequent developments

Hammersmith was not the only local authority which had been active in the swaps market and so the decision effectively invalidated many other transactions.

5. "The Supervisory Recognition of Netting for Capital Adequacy Purposes", consultative proposal by the Basle Committee on Banking Supervision, April 1993.
6. *Hazell v Hammersmith and Fulham LBC* [1992] AC 1.

Subsequent submissions to the United Kingdom government to overcome the court result by legislation so as to avoid damage to London's reputation as a financial centre proved unsuccessful and further litigation is now in progress by the affected banks in an attempt to recover moneys paid under the swaps.

The first judgments in this follow-up litigation were delivered in February and March 1993 in separate cases involving the South Tyneside Metropolitan Borough Council and the Borough Councils of Islington and Sandwell. The judgments in these cases are complex as the arguments involved in the cases covered a range of difficult and esoteric areas of law.[7] However, in essence, the judgments provide that the bank plaintiffs were entitled to restitution of money paid under the void swap contracts (making due allowance for moneys actually paid by the local authorities under the swaps prior to the time when the *Hammersmith* case prompted all local authorities to cease payments).

Although this is no doubt an encouraging development for the banks, it is only a further shot in the battle, not the end of the war. The local authorities have appealed the decisions and the particular cases are only some of the many actions commenced and still on foot. It is understood that over 200 restitution actions have been commenced, although a considerable number of those have been settled without going to trial. It is undoubtedly true that the only winners in this litigation have been the lawyers not just in England but also in many other jurisdictions where the *Hammersmith* case has resulted in a flurry of requests for advice in relation to questions of capacity.

Lessons

The *Hammersmith* case is a clear example of the continuing importance of observing the fundamentals and of involving lawyers to ensure the fundamentals are present. As noted in the introduction to this chapter one of the first things that a lawyer will do in assessing a new transaction will be to ascertain whether the fundamentals for an enforceable contract are present. One of the most basic elements of this exercise in any jurisdiction is to ascertain whether the intended counterparty has the requisite legal power to enter into the transaction.

This is not to suggest that all of the counterparties to Hammersmith had failed to seek legal advice before entering into the relevant swaps. It is understood that many had and that that advice was to the effect that a swap entered into for the purpose of managing interest rate risk on borrowings was within the capacity of local authorities on the better view although there was room for argument.

There is an object lesson here for financial institutions. Receipt of a legal opinion which reaches a conclusion only on "the better view" should be treated with great caution. It means that there is at least a substantial argument to the contrary of the conclusion expressed. While there may be a considerable number of specific issues on which it is perfectly appropriate to accept the risk inherent in "better view" advice, the *Hammersmith* case demonstrates vividly the dangers of proceeding with a transaction where a party's power to enter into the transaction is the subject of such advice.

Such power cannot be assumed even amongst financial institutions. For instance, in Australia building societies and credit unions are specifically prohibited from entering into domestic currency denominated derivatives for other than proper hedging purposes. Even more stringent restrictions apply to any form of foreign

7. See A Burrows, "Restitution of Payments under Swap Contracts" (1993) 143 *New Law Journal* at 480-482.

currency derivative. Similarly, building societies in England have limited power to enter swaps.

Whilst, in many jurisdictions, the power issue has been either completely or substantially overcome for corporates so that it is simple for lawyers to satisfy themselves that a corporate has power, the same is not true for semi-government and other statutory bodies or classes of institution (such as building societies) which are regulated under specific statutory regimes. Semi-government bodies have been particularly heavy users of swaps (due in part to their generally high credit ratings) and, as a result, it is crucial for a careful examination of the authorised purposes and powers of the relevant entity to be undertaken before a transaction is effected. Depending on the nature of the legislation governing the particular body, it may be necessary for such an enquiry to be undertaken before every swap transaction is entered into. For instance, a particular form of authorisation or a certificate from a particular official may be required for the transaction to be binding on the counterparty. This of course is an unpalatable result from a swap dealer's perspective and would seem, frequently, to be ignored in practice.

REGULATORY DEVELOPMENTS

General

In the early stages of the development of the swaps market, swaps were "regulated" by accident, if at all. In some jurisdictions, existing general law or statutory rules impacted adversely on swap transactions although only unintentionally—those laws or rules having been developed or enacted prior to the existence of swap transactions and without swap transactions in mind. For instance, in some jurisdictions, gaming and wagering legislation created uncertainty, sometimes significant uncertainty, as to the validity of swap contracts and forced counterparties to transact their business in other jurisdictions. The international scope of the swap market was and is of great assistance in overcoming this type of problem. In other words, parties may overcome certain types of legal restrictions on swap transactions by entering into the transactions in a jurisdiction with favourable laws and by making an appropriate choice of governing law for the transactions.

In other jurisdictions technical legal rules required modification, sometimes only minor, to standard practice for swap transactions. For example, the Canadian *Interest Act* has the effect that interest rates must be disclosed in a contract on a 365/366 day basis as appropriate otherwise the Act requires a 5% interest rate to be applied.

Since the early 1980s it is possible to discern two broad streams of regulatory development. The first is those changes—some minor, others major—which have resulted from agitation by swap market participants and have been aimed at assisting the development of the swaps market by removing areas of legal doubt and/or introducing new concepts or legal regimes specifically applying to swap transactions.

Perhaps the most significant example of this process to date is the enactment in the United States of the *Financial Institutions Reform, Recovery and Enforcement Act* 1989 and the concurrent amendments to the United States Bankruptcy Code in June 1990 (discussed in more detail below).

There are other examples including: the development of consistent guidelines for the taxation treatment of swap payment flows, legislation to clarify the power of different entities—particularly statutory corporations—to enter into swap transactions and the removal of stamp duties and other transaction taxes from application to swap transactions.

The second stream of development in many respects flows in the opposite direction as it represents the efforts of different groups of regulators to come to grips with the swap market in its various forms and to devise regulations to address areas of concern. The most notable examples in this area have been the development by banking regulators of capital adequacy rules requiring capital to be allocated to swap portfolios (discussed in detail in Chapters 39 and 40) and the development by securities regulators in some jurisdictions of rules regulating the conduct of "over the counter" markets generally (discussed below).

These two streams almost inevitably conflict at different points as the desire of regulators to control and limit the market clashes with the desire of market participants to trade freely and to continue to innovate without restriction.

Self regulation or external regulation?

Swap market participants are understandably extremely keen on the general concept of self-regulation.

Regulators on the other hand have been increasingly concerned about aspects of the swap market and are seeking to develop and institute controls. Their concerns focus on different areas. Banking regulators are concerned about the credit risks to banks and the systemic risk to the international financial system of large derivative portfolios held by the banks and bank subsidiaries and also about the perceived lack of detailed understanding of the nature of and risks involved with the products being traded amongst senior bank management.[8]

Securities regulators are concerned about the spread of derivative products into retail or near retail levels where investor protection issues become significant. Commodities regulators are concerned about the movement of business from the exchanges they control into the over-the-counter market.

Regulators, inevitably, are struggling to keep up with market developments as new products are constantly developed and old products are refined and, in some cases, transformed by new techniques. One of the greatest risks inherent in any attempt by regulators to regulate the market restrictively is that the innovation which, to date, has been one of the swap markets most notable characteristics would be stifled.

A substantial difficulty facing regulators is the international nature of the swap market. For any restrictive regulation to be effective, it would need to be co-ordinated and consistent on an international level and not simply introduced in a single jurisdiction. Due to the highly portable nature of the market, restrictive regulation in a single jurisdiction would almost certainly result in business previously carried on in that jurisdiction being transferred to another, more amenable, jurisdiction.

The process leading to introduction of the Basle Accord Capital Adequacy Rules in 1988 is a clear example of the importance of a concerted international effort. Although the Federal Reserve in the United States and the Bank of England were the originators of the risk-based capital adequacy approach which, for the first time, sought to deal with off-balance sheet items generally and derivatives in particular, those central banks realised that the imposition of the new rules in their own

8. S Brady,"The Ref Gets Rough" (1992) (April) *Euromoney* 25.

jurisdictions alone would simply place their own country's banks at a substantial competitive disadvantage and result in banking business moving to banks established in other jurisdictions. Accordingly, the imposition of the new rules was co-ordinated with the adoption of the Basle Accord generally by banking regulators in all of the major economies.

Securities and commodities regulators face similar issues if they seek to restrict the swap market, although the likelihood of concerted international action amongst securities or commodities regulators is perhaps more unlikely.

Developments in the United States

It is no doubt the case that these types of consideration played a significant role in determining the outcome of the recent comprehensive revision of the commodities futures laws in the United States. In October 1992 the *Future Trading Practices Act* 1992 became law. This Act, amongst many other important provisions, granted the Commodities Future Trading Commission (CFTC) broad discretionary powers to exempt any agreement, transaction or contract from the provisions of the Commodity Exchange Act. The CFTC was directed to develop regulation to exempt certain classes of swap agreements and other derivatives from the Commodity Exchange Act and also provided for the overriding of State gaming and "bucketshop" laws for exempted transactions.

The CFTC issued the "swap rules" in February 1993. Their effect is to completely exempt the "professional" derivatives market from the provisions of the *Commodity Exchange Act* (with the exception of anti-fraud provisions) where the relevant agreement has certain characteristics, namely:

- the agreement is not part of a fungible class of standardised agreements;
- the counterparty's credit-worthiness is a material consideration in entering into the contract and/or in determining the terms of the contract;
- the agreement is not entered into and traded on or through a multi-lateral transaction execution facility.

In other words, a sharp distinction is drawn between exchange traded instruments and "over-the-counter" derivatives which are tailored to the needs of the particular transaction or the particular counterparty.

By restricting the exemption to a "professional" market, the regulators have avoided the need to address in detail questions of investor protection which become relevant when products are offered at a retail level.

The CFTC swap rules and indeed the whole thrust of the *Futures Trading Practices Act* represent a significant defeat for the futures/commodities/stock exchanges, all of whom would have been keen for the over-the-counter market to be more heavily regulated in order to remove some/all of the competitive advantages enjoyed by that market.

Developments in other jurisdictions

Similar processes are underway in other jurisdictions as an awareness of the size and growth rate of the over-the-counter market increases, particularly amongst regulators. For instance, in Australia the current unsatisfactory provisions in the Corporations Law are under review. The current law provides that all "futures contracts" must be traded on an exchange. The definition of "futures contracts" is extremely broad and arguably catches a substantial proportion of over-the-counter derivatives. The definition specifically excludes interest rate and currency swaps, forward interest rate agreements and forward exchange rate agreements. Whilst these "plain vanilla" contracts are excluded, others (for example, commodity derivatives, equity derivatives, etc) are caught. The only method of avoiding the prohibition is for the party to apply to the Australian Securities Commission for approval for it to conduct an "exempt" market. Partly as a result of an increasing number of such applications, the ASC has recently undertaken a review of the regulation of derivatives and suspended the granting of exemptions. Submissions to the ASC have been unanimous in agreeing that the present system of regulation is unsatisfactory but have, predictably, differed in their suggestions for the form regulations should take in future. The banking industry/derivative market participants have endorsed the United States model and played down the level of retail or near retail involvement in the derivatives market.

The futures and stock exchanges on the other hand have suggested that additional regulation is desirable.

The ASC has released a draft report which adopts a system similar to the United States approach. However the "safe-harbour" exemption to be made available to professional investors will require, as an initial step, declaration as an "exempt futures market". Accordingly there is an administrative step involved rather than the exemption being self-executing.

The ASC is considering further submissions on the subject and a final policy is expected towards the end of 1993.

Similar reviews are under way in other jurisdictions (for example, Japan) and also internationally through the Bank for International Settlements.

Netting

As discussed in Chapter 39 the issue of netting has assumed great importance in the swap market over the last eight years or so not only because of its potential significance in the context of capital adequacy rules but also in the context of the assessment of credit risk by swap market participants for internal purposes, particularly within banks.

Until April 1993 (see below), no banking regulator had been persuaded to recognise close-out netting, as embodied in the ISDA Master Agreements for the purposes of capital adequacy rules despite continuing efforts by market participants. Although ISDA had obtained legal opinions in most leading jurisdiction which confirmed (with varying certainty) that netting would be upheld on an insolvency, doubts remained, particularly in regulators' eyes.[9] ISDA's views were confirmed by the Lamfalussy Report published in November 1990 by the Bank for International Settlements. This report concluded that bilateral netting was likely to be effective in each G-10 country.

The doubts vary between jurisdictions and are strongest in common law jurisdiction (such as the United Kingdom, Australia and Canada) where the conclusions depend upon the application of general legal principles to novel fact situations and where there is a complete absence of any authoritative case law dealing directly with the relevant issues in the context of swap transactions. The doubts include the following:

9. R Derham, "Set-off and Netting of Foreign Exchange Contracts in the Liquidation of a Counterparty—Part II Netting" (1991) (November) *Journal of Business Law*. For contrary view see R Ayling and J Welch, "Netting in Australia" (1992) (March) *Butterworths Journal of International Banking and Finance Law* 105.

- the effect of bankruptcy laws on the enforceability of the termination provisions found in swap contracts (that is, are automatic termination provisions which seek to terminate contracts prior to the time of the relevant insolvency event effective and also, in the absence of automatic termination provisions, does a non-defaulting party have the ability post insolvency to exercise the contractual rights of termination?);
- whether the netting provisions offend against insolvency principles requiring equal treatment of creditors in a bankruptcy;
- whether the netting provisions offend against specific legislative rules applying to different classes of institutions, particularly banks (for example s 16 of the Australian *Banking Act*);
- whether contracts providing for limited two-way payments on termination are effective (as discussed above);
- whether a liquidator is able to "cherry pick" profitable contracts out of a swap portfolio.

Given the nature of these doubts, it is unlikely that any of them will be completely dispelled by academic legal argument between lawyers—it is always easy to raise doubts but much more difficult to remove them. Accordingly, without either authoritative judicial determination or, more likely, explicit statutory adoption of the validity of netting provisions in swap contracts in a bankruptcy the doubts will persist.

The United States has led the way in moving down the path of explicit statutory adoption of the relevant principles.

The *Financial Institutions Reform Recovery and Enforcement Act* 1989 (FIRREA) and the related Bankruptcy Code amendments provide a model for other countries. The effect of the legislation is to provide the certainty sought by swap participants in a number of crucial areas in relation to the insolvency of a United States incorporated counterparty (whether a bank or a non-bank corporation).[10] In particular:

(a) swap contracts are removed from the provisions of the automatic stay of exercise of rights against the insolvent party thus preserving the non-defaulting swap counterparty's rights to exercise termination provisions (in relation to banks there is a very brief—one day—period during which the FDIC may elect to transfer the insolvent bank's business to a new entity without the non-defaulting counterparty being able to terminate);

(b) rights to access collateral held as security for performance by the insolvent counterparty are specifically recognised;

(c) the right to exercise netting or set-off provisions in the swap documentation is expressly recognised.

It is unfortunate that other jurisdictions have not taken recent opportunities to achieve equivalent certainty. For instance, in Australia substantial amendments have recently been made to corporate insolvency rules, in particular to introduce a regime similar to the Chapter 11 procedure in the United States. Those amendments do not expressly confirm the efficacy of netting agreements on insolvency under Australian law, despite strong encouragement by sections of the Australian legal community to the legislators during the drafting process. Although the generally

10. D P Cunningham and W P Rogers Jr, "Netting is the Law" (1990) (August) *Butterworths Journal of International Banking and Finance Law* 354; S Tucker, "Interest Rate Swaps and the 1990 Amendments to the US Bankruptcy Code" (1991) 3 *Utah Law Review* 581.

held view in Australia is that netting agreements are effective, some commentators have raised doubts which could have been laid to rest once and for all quite simply in the recent amendments.

April 1993 proposal by the Basle Committee on Banking Supervision

In April 1993 the Basle Committee on Banking Supervision published a series of reports proposing amendments to the 1988 Basle Accord on Bank Capital Adequacy. Separate papers dealt with the issues of:

- netting;
- market risk; and
- interest rate risk.

The recommendations in the proposal dealing with netting represent a landmark. For the first time it is proposed that bilateral netting arrangements be recognised for the purpose of calculating capital adequacy requirements for bank swap portfolios. It is, however, important to note that this treatment will be extended on a country by country basis by the relevant national supervisor only if the relevant bank satisfies the supervisor that it has "written and reasoned legal opinions" that, in the event of a legal challenge, the relevant courts and administrative authorities would find the bank's exposure to be such a net amount under:

- the law of the jurisdiction in which the counterparty is chartered and, if the counterparty is a branch of a foreign bank, then also under the law of jurisdiction in which the branch is located;
- the law that governs the individual transactions; and
- the law that governs any contract or agreement necessary to effect the netting.

The national supervisor, after consultation when necessary with other relevant supervisors, must be satisfied that the netting is enforceable under the laws of each of the relevant jurisdictions.

Plainly, in the implementation period these proposals will result in a considerable amount of work for bank lawyers in providing the necessary opinions. It is not clear from the proposal whether a particular bank may be able to rely on a general legal opinion which has been obtained by an industry association (for example, ISDA) in sufficiently broad terms or whether opinions would need to be transaction or at least counterparty, specific. One thing which is clear is that the opinions will need to address the full range of instruments which may be entered into under a Master Agreement which permits cross-product netting. The proposal specifically contemplates that individual national supervisors may impose additional requirements or more restrictive conditions, for example in the cross-product netting context. ISDA will be playing a major role in seeking to co-ordinate the provision of relevant opinions in order to facilitate the prompt implementation of the netting proposal. It is likely that, at least in some jurisdictions, this will require some degree of statutory amendment.

APPENDIX A

ISDA MASTER AGREEMENT[1]

(Multicurrency—Cross Border)

ISDA®

International Swap Dealers Association, Inc.

MASTER AGREEMENT

dated as of ....

.... and ....

have entered and/or anticipate entering into one or more transactions (each a "Transaction") that are or will be governed by this Master Agreement, which includes the schedule (the "Schedule"), and the documents and other confirming evidence (each a "Confirmation") exchanged between the parties confirming those Transactions.

Accordingly, the parties agree as follows:—

1. Interpretation

(a) ***Definitions.*** The terms defined in Section 14 and in the Schedule will have the meanings therein specified for the purpose of this Master Agreement.

(b) ***Inconsistency.*** In the event of any inconsistency between the provisions of the Schedule and the other provisions of this Master Agreement, the Schedule will prevail. In the event of any inconsistency between the provisions of any Confirmation and this Master Agreement (including the Schedule), such Confirmation will prevail for the purpose of the relevant Transaction.

(c) ***Single Agreement.*** All Transactions are entered into in reliance on the fact that this Master Agreement and all Confirmations form a single agreement between the parties (collectively referred to as this "Agreement"), and the parties would not otherwise enter into any Transactions.

2. Obligations

(a) ***General Conditions.***

(i) Each party will make each payment or delivery specified in each Confirmation to be made by it, subject to the other provisions of this Agreement.

(ii) Payments under this Agreement will be made on the due date for value on that date in the place of the account specified in the relevant Confirmation or otherwise pursuant to this Agreement, in freely transferable funds and in the manner customary for payments in the required currency. Where settlement is by delivery (that is, other than by payment), such delivery will be made for receipt on the due date in the manner customary for the relevant obligation unless otherwise specified in the relevant Confirmation or elsewhere in this Agreement.

(iii) Each obligation of each party under Section 2(a)(i) is subject to (1) the condition precedent that no Event of Default or Potential Event of Default with respect to the other party has occurred and is continuing, (2) the condition precedent that no Early Termination Date in respect of the relevant Transaction has occurred or been effectively designated and (3) each other applicable condition precedent specified in this Agreement.

(b) ***Change of Account.*** Either party may change its account for receiving a payment or delivery by giving notice to the other party at least five Local Business Days prior to the scheduled date for the payment or delivery to which such change applies unless such other party gives timely notice of a reasonable objection to such change.

(c) ***Netting.*** If on any date amounts would otherwise be payable:—

(i) in the same currency; and

(ii) in respect of the same Transaction,

by each party to the other, then, on such date, each party's obligation to make payment of any such amount will be automatically satisfied and discharged and, if the aggregate amount that would otherwise have been payable by one party exceeds the aggregate amount that would otherwise have been payable by the other party, replaced by an obligation upon the party by whom the larger aggregate amount would have been payable to pay to the other party the excess of the larger aggregate amount over the smaller aggregate amount.

The parties may elect in respect of two or more Transactions that a net amount will be determinied in respect of all amounts payable on the same date in the same currency in respect of such Transactions, regardless of whether such amounts are payable in respect of the same Transaction. The election may be made in the Schedule or a Confirmation by specifying that subparagraph (ii) above will not apply to the Transactions identified as being subject to the election, together with the starting date (in which case subparagraph (ii) above will not, or will cease to, apply to such Transactions from such date). This election may be made separately for different groups of Transactions and will apply separately to each pairing of Offices through which the parties make and receive payments or deliveries.

(d) ***Deduction or Withholding for Tax.***

(1) ***Gross-Up.*** All payments under this Agreement will be made without any deduction or withholding for or on account of any Tax unless such deduction or withholding is required by any applicable law, as modified by the practice of any relevant governmental revenue authority, then in effect. If a party is so required to deduct or withhold, then that party ("X") will:—

(1) promptly notify the other party ("Y") of such requirement;

(2) pay to the relevant authorities the full amount required to be deducted or withheld (including the full amount required to be deducted or withheld from any additional amount paid by X to Y under this Section 2(d)) promptly upon the earlier of determining that such deduction or withholding is required or receiving notice that such amount has been assessed against Y;

(3) promptly forward to Y an official receipt (or a certified copy), or other documentation reasonably acceptable to Y, evidencing such payment to such authorities; and

(4) if such Tax is an Indemnifiable Tax, pay to Y, in addition to the payment to which Y is otherwise entitled under this Agreement, such additional amount as is necessary to ensure that the net amount actually received by Y (free and clear of Indemnifiable Taxes, whether assessed against X or Y) will equal the full amount Y would have received had no such deduction or withholding been required. However, X will not be required to pay any additional amount to Y to the extent that it would not be required to be paid but for:—

(A) the failure by Y to comply with or with or perform any agreement contained in Section 4(a)(i), 4(a)(iii) or 4 (d); or

(B) the failure of a representation made by Y pursuant to Section 3(f) to be accurate and true unless such failure would not have occurred but for (I) any action taken by a taxing authority, or brought in a court of competent jurisdiction, on or after the date on which a Transaction is entered into (regardless of whether such action is taken or brought with respect to a party to this Agreement) or (II) a Change in Tax Law.

(ii) ***Liability.*** If:—

(1) X is required by any applicable law, as modified by the practice of any relevant governmental revenue authority, to make any deduction or withholding in respect of which X would not be required to pay an additional amount to Y under Section 2(d)(i)(4);

(2) X does not so deduct or withhold; and

(3) a liability resulting from such Tax is assessed directly against X,

then, except to the extent Y has satisfied or then satisfies the liability resulting from such Tax, Y will promptly pay to X the amount of such liability (including any related liability for interest, but including any related liability for penalties only if Y has failed to comply with or perform any agreement contained in Section 4(a)(i), 4(a)(iii) or 4(d)).

(e) ***Default Interest; Other Amounts.*** Prior to the occurrence or effective designation of an Early Termination Date in respect of the relevant Transaction, a party that defaults in the performance of any payment obligation will, to the extent permitted by law and subject to Section 6(c), be required to pay interest (before as well as after judgment) on the overdue amount to the other party on demand in the same currency as such overdue amount, for the period from (and including) the original due date for payment to (but excluding) the date of actual payment, at the Default Rate. Such interest will be calculated on the basis of daily compounding and the actual number of days elapsed. If, prior to the occurrence or effective designation of an Early Termination Date in respect of the relevant Transaction, a party defaults in the performance of any obligation required to be settled by delivery, it will compensate the other party on demand if and to the extent provided for in the relevant Confirmation or elsewhere in this Agreement.

3. Representations

Each party represents to the other party (which representations will be deemed to be repeated by each party on each date on which a Transaction is entered into and, in the case of the representations in Section 3(f), at all times until the termination of this Agreement) that:—

(a) ***Basic Representations.***

(i) ***Status.*** It is duly organised and validly existing under the laws of the jurisdiction of its organisation or incorporation and, if relevant under such laws, in good standing;

(ii) ***Powers.*** It has the power to execute this Agreement and any other documentation relating to this Agreement to which it is a party, to deliver this Agreement and any other documentation relating to this Agreement that it is required by this Agreement to deliver and to perform its obligations under this Agreement and any obligations it has under any Credit Support Document to which it is a party and has taken all necessary action to authorise such execution, delivery and performance;

(iii) ***No Violation or Conflict.*** Such execution, delivery and performance do not violate or conflict with any law applicable to it, any provision of its constitutional documents, any order or judgment of any court or other agency of government applicable to it or any of its assets or any contractual restriction binding on or affecting it or any of its assets;

(iv) ***Consents.*** All governmental and other consents that are required to have been obtained by it with respect to this Agreement or any Credit Support Document to which it is a party have been obtained and are in full force and effect and all conditions of any such consents have been complied with; and

(v) ***Obligations Binding.*** Its obligations under this Agreement and any Credit Support Document to which it is a party constitute its legal, valid and binding obligations, enforceable in accordance with their respective terms (subject to applicable bankruptcy, reorganisation, insolvency, moratorium or similar laws affecting creditors' rights generally and subject, as to enforceability, to equitable principles of general application (regardless of whether enforcement is sought in a proceeding in equity or at law)).

(b) ***Absence of Certain Events.*** No Event of Default or Potential Event of Default or, to its knowledge, Termination Event with respect to it has occurred and is continuing and no such event or circumstance would occur as a result of its entering into or performing its obligations under this Agreement or any Credit Support Document to which it is a party.

(c) ***Absence of Litigation.*** There is not pending or, to its knowledge, threatened against it or any of its Affiliates any action, suit or proceeding at law or in equity or before any court, tribunal, governmental body, agency or official or any arbitrator that is likely to affect the legality, validity or enforceability against it of this Agreement or any Credit Support Document to which it is a party or its ability to perform its obligations under this Agreement or such Credit Support Document.

(d) ***Accuracy of Specified Information.*** All applicable information that is furnished in writing by or on behalf of it to the other party and is identified for the purpose of this Section 3(d) in the Schedule is, as of the date of the information, true, accurate and complete in every material respect.

(e) ***Payer Tax Representation.***Each representation specified in the Schedule as being made by it for the purpose of this Section 3(e) is accurate and true.

(f) ***Payee Tax Representations.*** Each representation specified in the Schedule as being made by it for the purpose of this Section 3(f) is accurate and true.

4. Agreements

Each party agrees with the other that, so long as either party has or may have any obligation under this Agreement or under any Credit Support Document to which it is a party:—

(a) ***Furnish Specified Information.*** It will deliver to the other party or, in certain cases under subparagraph (iii) below, to such government or taxing authority as the other party reasonably directs:—

(i) any forms, documents or certificates relating to taxation specified in the Schedule or any Confirmation;

(ii) any other documents specified in the Schedule or any Confirmation; and

(iii) upon reasonable demand by such other party, any form or document that may be required or reasonably requested in writing in order to allow such other party or its Credit Support Provider to make a payment under this Agreement or any applicable Credit Support Document without any deduction or withholding for or on account of any Tax or with such deduction or withholding at a reduced rate (so long as the completion, execution or submission of such form or document would not materially prejudice the legal or commercial position of the party in receipt of such demand), with any such form or document to be accurate and completed in a manner reasonably satisfactory to such other party and to be executed and to be delivered with any reasonably required certification,

in each case by the date specified in the Schedule or such Confirmation or, if none is specified, as soon as reasonably practicable.

(b) ***Maintain Authorisations.*** It will use all reasonable efforts to maintain in full force and effect all consents of any governmental or other authority that are required to be obtained by it with respect to this Agreement or any Credit Support Document to which it is a party and will use all reasonable efforts to obtain any that may become necessary in the future.

(c) ***Comply with Laws.*** It will comply in all material respects with all applicable laws and orders to which it may be subject if failure so to comply would materially impair its ability to perform its obligations under this Agreement or any Credit Support Document to which it is a party.

(d) ***Tax Agreement.*** It will give notice of any failure of a representation made by it under Section 3(f) to be accurate and true promptly upon learning of such failure.

(e) ***Payment of Stamp Tax.*** Subject to Section 11, it will pay any Stamp Tax levied or imposed upon it or in respect of its execution or performance of this Agreement by a jurisdiction in which it is incorporated, organised, managed and controlled, or considered to have its seat, or in which a branch or office through which it is acting for the purpose of this Agreement is located (''Stamp Tax Jurisdiction'') and will indemnify the other party against any Stamp Tax levied or imposed upon the other party or in respect of the other party's execution or performance of this Agreement by any such Stamp Tax Jurisdiction which is not also a Stamp Tax Jurisdiction with respect to the other party.

5. Events of Default and Termination Events

(a) ***Events of Default.*** The occurrence at any time with respect to a party or, if applicable, any Credit Support Provider of such party or any Specified Entity of such party of any of the following events constitutes an event of default (an ''Event of Default'') with respect to such party:—

(i) ***Failure to Pay or Deliver.*** Failure by the party to make, when due, any payment under this Agreement or delivery under Section 2(a)(i) or 2(e) required to be made by it if such failure is not remedied on or before the third Local Business Day after notice of such failure is given to the party;

(ii) ***Breach of Agreement.*** Failure by the party to comply with or perform any agreement or obligation (other than an obligation to make any payment under this Agreement or delivery under Section 2(a)(i) or 2(e) or to give notice of a Termination Event or any agreement or obligation under Section 4(a)(i), 4(a)(iii) or 4(d)) to be complied with or performed by the party in accordance with this Agreement if such failure is not remedied on or before the thirtieth day after notice of such failure is given to the party;

(iii) ***Credit Support Default.***

(1) Failure by the party or any Credit Support Provider of such party to comply with or perform any agreement or obligation to be complied with or performed by it in accordance with any Credit Support Document if such failure is continuing after any applicable grace period has elapsed;

(2) the expiration or termination of such Credit Support Document or the failing or ceasing of such Credit Support Document to be in full force and effect for the purpose of this Agreement (in either case other than in accordance with its terms) prior to the satisfaction of all obligations of such party under each Transaction to which such Credit Support Document relates without the written consent of the other party; or

(3) the party or such Credit Support provider disaffirms, disclaims, repudiates or rejects, in whole or in part, or challenges the validity of, such Credit Support Document;

(iv) ***Misrepresentation.*** A representation (other than a representation under Section 3(e) or (f) made or repeated or deemed to have been made or repeated by the party or any Credit Support Provider of such party in this Agreement or any Credit Support Document proves to have been incorrect or misleading in any material respect when made or repeated or deemed to have been made or repeated;

(v) ***Default under Specified Transaction.*** The party, any Credit Support Provider of such party or any applicable Specified Entity of such party (1) defaults under a Specified Transaction and, after giving effect to any applicable notice requirement or grace period, there occurs a liquidation of, an acceleration of obligations under, or an early termination of, that Specified Transaction, (2) defaults, after giving effect to any applicable notice requirement or grace period, in making any payment or delivery due on the last payment, delivery or exchange date of, or any payment on early termination of, a Specified Transaction (or such default continues for at least three Local Business Days if there is no applicable notice requirement or grace period) or (3) disaffirms, disclaims, repudiates or rejects, in whole or in part, a Specified Transaction (or such action is taken by any person or entity appointed or empowered to operate it or act on its behalf);

(vi) ***Cross Default.*** If "Cross Default" is specified in the Schedule as applying to the party, the occurrence or existence of (1) a default, event of default or other similar condition or event (however described) in respect of such party, any Credit Support Provider of such party or any applicable Specified Entity of such party under one or more agreements or instruments relating to Specified Indebtedness of any of them (individually or collectively) in an aggregate amount of not less than the applicable Threshold Amount (as specified in the Schedule) which has resulted in such Specified Indebtedness becoming, or becoming capable at such time of being declared, due and payable under such agreements or instruments, before it would otherwise have been due and payable or (2) a default by such party, such Credit Support Provider or such Specified Entity (individually or collectively) in making one or more payments on the due date thereof in an aggregate amount of not less than the applicable Threshold Amount under such agreements or instruments (after giving effect to any applicable notice requirement or grace period);

(vii) ***Bankruptcy.*** The party, any Credit Support Provider of such party or any applicable Specified Entity of such party:—

(1) is dissolved (other than pursuant to a consolidation, amalgamation or merger); (2) becomes insolvent or is unable to pay its debts or fails or admits in writing its inability generally to pay its debts as they become due; (3) makes a general assignment, arrangement or composition with or for the benefit of its creditors; (4) institutes or has instituted against it a proceeding seeking a judgment of insolvency or bankruptcy or any other relief under any bankruptcy or insolvency law or other similar law affecting creditors' rights, or a petition is presented for its winding-up or liquidation, and, in the case of any such proceeding or petition instituted or presented against it, such proceeding or petition (A) results in a judgment of insolvency or bankruptcy or the entry of an order for relief or the making of an order for its winding-up or liquidation or (B) is not dismissed, discharged, stayed or restrained in each case within 30 days of the institution or presentation thereof; (5) has a resolution passed for its winding-up, official management or liquidation (other than pursuant to a consolidation, amalgamation or merger); (6) seeks or becomes subject to the appointment of an administrator, provisional liquidator, conservator, receiver, trustee, custodian or other similar official for it or for all or substantially all its assets; (7) has a secured party take possession of all or substantially all its assets or has a distress, execution, attachment, sequestration or other legal process levied, enforced or sued on or against all or substantially all its assets and such secured party maintains possession, or any such process is not dismissed, discharged, stayed or restrained, in each case within 30 days thereafter; (8) causes or is subject to any event with respect to it which, under the applicable laws of any jurisdiction, has an analogous effect to any of the events specified in clauses (1) to (7) (inclusive); or (9) takes any action in furtherance of, or indicating its consent to, approval of, or acquiescence in, any of the foregoing acts; or

(viii) ***Merger Without Assumption.*** The party or any Credit Support Provider of such party consolidates or amalgamates with, or merges with or into, or transfers all or substantially all its assets to, another entity and, at the time of such consolidation, amalgamation, merger or transfer:—

(1) the resulting, surviving or transferee entity fails to assume all the obligations of such party or such Credit Support Provider under this Agreement or any Credit Support Document to which it or its predecessor was a party by operation of law or pursuant to an agreement reasonably satisfactory to the other party to this Agreement; or

(2) the benefits of any Credit Support Document fail to extend (without the consent of the other party) to the performance by such resulting, surviving or transferee entity of its obligations under this Agreement.

(b) ***Termination Events.*** The occurrence at any time with respect to a party or, if applicable, any Credit Support Provider of such party or any Specified Entity of such party of any event specified below constitutes an Illegality if the event is specified in (i) below, a Tax Event if the event is specified in (ii) below or a Tax Event Upon Merger if the event is specified in (iii) below, and, if specified to be applicable, a Credit Event Upon Merger if the event is specified pursuant to (iv) below or an Additional Termination Event if the event is specified pursuant to (v) below:—

(i) ***Illegality.*** Due to the adoption of, or any change in, any applicable law after the date on which a Transaction is entered into, or due to the promulgation of, or any change in, the interpretation by any court, tribunal or regulatory authority with competent jurisdiction of any applicable law after such date, it becomes unlawful (other than as a result of a breach by the party of Section 4(b)) for such party (which will be the Affected Party):—

(1) to perform any absolute or contingent obligation to make a payment or delivery or to receive a payment or delivery in respect of such Transaction or to comply with any other material provision of this Agreement relating to such Transaction; or

(2) to perform, or for any Credit Support Provider of such party to perform, any contingent or other obligation which the party (or such Credit Support Provider) has under any Credit Support Document relating to such Transaction;

(ii) ***Tax Event.*** Due to (x) any action taken by a taxing authority, or brought in a court of competent jurisdiction, on or after the date on which a Transaction is entered into (regardless of whether such action is taken or brought with respect to a party to this Agreement) or (y) a Change in Tax Law, the party (which will be the Affected Party) will, or there is a substantial likelihood that it will, on the next succeeding Scheduled Payment Date (1) be required to pay to the other party an additional amount in respect of an Indemnifiable Tax under Section 2(d)(i)(4) (except in respect of interest under Section 2(e), 6 (d)(ii) or 6(e)) or (2) receive a payment from which an amount is required to be deducted or withheld for or on account of a Tax (except in respect of interest under Section 2(e),6(d)(ii) or 6(e) and no additional amount is required to be paid in respect of such Tax under Section 2(d)(i)(4) (other than by reason of Section 2(d)(i)(4)(A) or (B));

(iii) ***Tax Event Upon Merger.*** The party (the "Burdened Party") on the next succeeding Scheduled Payment Date will either (1) be required to pay an additional amount in respect of an Indemnifiable Tax under Section 2(d)(i)(4) (except in respect of interest under Section 2(e), 6(d)(ii) or 6(e)) or (2) receive a payment from which an amount has been deducted or withheld for or on account of any Indemnifiable Tax in respect of which the other party is not required to pay an additional amount (other than by reason of Section 2(d)(i)(4)(A) or (B)), in either case as a result of a party consolidating or amalgamating with, or merging with or into, or transferring all or substantially all its assets to, another entity (which will be the Affected Party) where such action does not constitute an event described in Section 5(a)(viii);

(iv) ***Credit Event Upon Merger.*** If "Credit Event Upon Merger" is specified in the Schedule as applying to the party, such party ("X"), and Credit Support Provider of X or any applicable Specified Entity of X consolidates or amalgamates with, or merges with or into, or transfers all or substantially all its assets to, another entity and such action does not constitute an event described in Section 5(a)(viii) but the creditworthiness of the resulting, surviving or transferee entity is materially weaker than that of X, such Credit Support Provider or such Specified Entity, as the case may be, immediately prior to such action (and, in such event, X or its successor or transferee, as appropriate, will be the Affected Party); or

(v) ***Additional Termination Event.*** If any "Additional Termination Event" is specified in the Schedule or any Confirmation as applying, the occurrence of such event (and, in such event, the Affected Party or Affected Parties shall be as specified for such Additional Termination Event in the Schedule or such Confirmation).

(c) **Event of Default and Illegality.** If an event or circumstance which would otherwise constitute or give rise to an Event of Default also constitutes as Illegality, it will be treated as an Illegality and will not constitute an Event of Default.

6. Early Termination

(a) ***Right to Terminate Following Event of Default.*** If at any time an Event of Default with respect to a party (the "Defaulting Party") has occurred and is then continuing, the other party (the "Non-defaulting Party") may, by not more than 20 days notice to the Defaulting Party specifying the relevant Event of Default, designate a day not earlier than the day such notice is effective as an Early Termination Date in respect of all outstanding Transactions. If, however, "Automatic Early Termination" is specified in the Schedule as applying to a party, then an Early Termination Date in respect of all outstanding Transactions will occur immediately upon the occurrence with respect to such party of an Event of Default specified in Section 5(a)(vii)(1), (3), (5), (6) or, to the extent analogous thereto, (8), and as of the time immediately preceding the institution of the relevant proceeding or the presentation of the relevant petition upon the occurrence with respect to such party of an Event of Default specified in Section 5(a)(vii)(4) or, to the extent analogous thereto, (8).

(b) ***Right to Terminate Following Termination Event.***

(i) ***Notice.*** If a Termination Event occurs, an Affected Party will, promptly upon becoming aware of it, notify the other party, specifying the nature of that Termination Event and each Affected Transaction and will also give such other information about that Termination Event as the other party may reasonably require.

(ii) ***Transfer to Avoid Termination Event.*** If either an Illegality under Section 5(b)(i)(l) or a Tax Event occurs and there is only one Affected Party, or if a Tax Event Upon Merger occurs and the Burdened Party is the Affected Party, the Affected Party will, as a condition to its right to designate an Early Termination Date under Section 6(b)(iv), use all reasonable efforts (which will not require such party to incur a loss, excluding immaterial, incidental expenses) to transfer within 20 days after it gives notice under Section 6(b)(i) all its rights and obligations under this Agreement in respect of the Affected Transactions to another of its Offices or Affiliates so that such Termination Event ceases to exist.

If the Affected Party is not able to make such a transfer it will give notice to the other party to that effect within such 20 day period, whereupon the other party may effect such a transfer within 30 days after the notice is given under Section 6(b)(i).

Any such transfer by a party under this Section 6(b)(ii) will be subject to and conditional upon the prior written consent of the other party, which consent will not be withheld if such other party's policies in effect at such time would permit it to enter into transactions with the transferee on the terms proposed.

(iii) ***Two Affected Parties.*** If an Illegality under Section 5(b)(i)(l) or a Tax Event occurs and there are two Affected Parties, each party will use all reasonable efforts to reach agreement within 30 days after notice thereof is given under Section 6(b)(i) on action to avoid that Termination Event.

(iv) ***Right to Terminate.*** If:—

(1) a transfer under Section 6(b)(ii) or an agreement under Section 6(b)(iii), as the case may be, has not been effected with respect to all Affected Transactions within 30 days after an Affected Party gives notice under Section 6(b)(i); or

(2) an Illegality under Section 5(b)(i)(2), a Credit Event Upon Merger or an Additional Termination Event occurs, or a Tax Event Upon Merger occurs and the Burdened Party is not the Affected Party,

either party in the case of an Illegality, the Burdened Party in the case of a Tax Event Upon Merger, any Affected Party in the case of a Tax Event or an Additional Termination Event if there is more than one Affected Party, or the party which is not the Affected Party in the case of a Credit Event Upon Merger or an Additional Termination Event if there is only one Affected Party may, by not more than 20 days notice to the other party and provided that the relevant Termination Event is then continuing, designate a day not earlier than the day such notice is effective as an Early Termination Date in respect of all Affected Transactions.

(c) ***Effect of Designation.***

(i) If notice designating an Early Termination Date is given under Section 6(a) or (b), the Early Termination Date will occur on the date so designated, whether or not the relevant Event of Default or Termination Event is then continuing.

(ii) Upon the occurrence or effective designation of an Early Termination Date, no further payments or deliveries under Section 2(a)(i) or 2(e) in respect of the Terminated Transactions will be required to be made, but without prejudice to the other provisions of this Agreement. The amount, if any, payable in respect of an Early Termination Date shall be determined pursuant to Section 6(e).

(d) ***Calculations.***

(i) ***Statement.*** On or as soon as reasonably practicable following the occurrence of an Early Termination Date, each party will make the calculations on its part, if any, contemplated by Section 6(e) and will provide to the other party a statement (1) showing, in reasonable detail, such calculations (including all relevant quotations and specifying any amount payable under Section 6(e)) and (2) giving details of the relevant account to which any amount payable to it is to be paid. In the absence of written confirmation from the source of a quotation obtained in determining a Market Quotation, the records of the party obtaining such quotation will be conclusive evidence of the existence and accuracy of such quotation.

(ii) ***Payment Date.*** An amount calculated as being due in respect of any Early Termination Date under Section 6(e) will be payable on the day that notice of the amount payable is effective (in the case of an Early Termination Date which is designated or occurs as a result of an Event of Default) and on the day which is two Local Business Days after the day on which notice of the amount payable is effective (in the case of an Early Termination Date which is designated as a result of a Termination Event). Such amount will be paid together with (to the extent permitted under applicable law) interest thereon (before as well as after judgment) in the Termination Currency, from (and including) the relevant Early Termination Date to (but excluding) the date such amount is paid, at the Applicable Rate. Such interest will be calculated on the basis of daily compounding and the actual number of days elapsed.

(e) ***Payments on Early Termination.*** If an Early Termination Date occurs, the following provisions shall apply based on the parties' election in the Schedule of a payment measure, either "Market Quotation" or "Loss", and a payment method, either the "First Method" or the "Second Method". If the parties fail to designate a payment measure or payment method in the Schedule, it will be deemed that "Market Quotation" or the "Second Method", as the case may be, shall apply. The amount, if any, payable in respect of an Early Termination Date and determined pursuant to this Section will be subject to any Set-off.

(i) ***Events of Default.*** If the Early Termination Date results from an Event of Default:—

(1) *First Method and Market Quotation.* If the First Method and Market Quotation apply, the Defaulting Party will pay to the Non-defaulting Party the excess, if a positive number, of (A) the sum of the Settlement Amount (determined by the Non-defaulting Party) in respect of the Terminated Transactions and the Termination Currency Equivalent of the Unpaid Amounts owing to the Non-defaulting Party over (B) the Termination Currency Equivalent of the Unpaid Amounts owing to the Defaulting Party.

(2) *First Method and Loss.* If the First Method and Loss apply, the Defaulting Party will pay to the Non-defaulting Party, if a positive number, the Non-defaulting Party's Loss in respect of this Agreement.

(3) *Second Method and Market Quotation.* If the Second Method and Market Quotation apply, an amount will be payable equal to (A) the sum of the Settlement Amount (determined by the Non-defaulting Party) in respect of the Terminated Transactions and the Termination Currency Equivalent of the Unpaid Amounts owing to the Non-defaulting Party less (B) the Termination Currency Equivalent of the Unpaid Amounts owing to the Defaulting Party. If that amount is a positive number, the Defaulting Party will pay it to the Non-defaulting Party; if it is a negative number, the Non-defaulting Party will pay the absolute value of that amount to the Defaulting Party.

(4) *Second Method and Loss.* If the Second Method and Loss apply, an amount will be payable equal to the Non-defaulting Party's Loss in respect of this Agreement. If that amount is a positive number, the Defaulting Party will pay it to the Non-defaulting party; if it is a negative number, the Non-defaulting Party will pay the absolute value of that amount to the Defaulting Party.

(ii) ***Termination Events.*** If the Early Termination Date results from a Termination Event:—

(1) *One Affected Party.* If there is one Affected Party, the amount payable will be determined in accordance with Section 6(e)(i)(3), if Market Quotation applies, or Section 6(e)(i)(4), if Loss applies, except that, in either case, references to the Defaulting Party and to the Non-defaulting Party will be deemed to be references to the Affected Party and the party

which is not the Affected Party, respectively, and, if Loss applies and fewer than all the Transactions are being terminated, Loss shall be calculated in respect of all Terminated Transactions.

(2) *Two Affected Parties.* If there are two Affected Parties:—

(A) if Market Quotation applies, each party will determine a Settlement Amount in respect of the Terminated Transactions, and an amount will be payable equal to (I) the sum of (a) one-half of the difference between the Settlement Amount of the party with the higher Settlement Amount ("X") and the Settlement Amount of the party with the lower Settlement Amount ("Y") and (b) the Termination Currency Equivalent of the Unpaid Amounts owing to X less (II) the Termination Currency Equivalent of the Unpaid Amounts owing to Y; and

(B) if Loss applies, each party will determine its Loss in respect of this Agreement (or, if fewer than all the Transactions are being terminated, in respect of all Terminated Transactions) and an amount will be payable equal to one-half of the difference between the Loss of the party with the higher Loss ("X") and the Loss of the party with the lower Loss ("Y").

If the amount payable is a positive number, Y will pay it to X; if it is a negative number, X will pay the absolute value of that amount to Y.

(iii) ***Adjustment for Bankruptcy.*** In circumstances where an Early Termination Date occurs because "Automatic Early Termination" applies in respect of a party, the amount determined under this Section 6(e) will be subject to such adjustments as are appropriate and permitted by law to reflect any payments or deliveries made by one party to the other under this Agreement (and retained by such other party) during the period from the relevant Early Termination Date to the date for payment determined under Section 6(d)(ii).

(iv) ***Pre-Estimate.*** The parties agree that if Market Quotation applies an amount recoverable under this Section 6(e) is a reasonable pre-estimate of loss and not a penalty. Such amount is payable for the loss of bargain and the loss of protection against future risks and except as otherwise provided in this Agreement neither party will be entitled to recover any additional damages as a consequence of such losses.

7. Transfer

Subject to Section 6(b)(ii), neither this Agreement nor any interest or obligation in or under this Agreement may be transferred (whether by way of security or otherwise) by either party without the prior written consent of the other party, except that:—

(a) a party may make such a transfer of this Agreement pursuant to a consolidation or amalgamation with, or merger with or into, or transfer of all or substantially all its assets to, another entity (but without prejudice to any other right or remedy under this Agreement); and

(b) a party may make such a transfer of all or any part of its interest in any amount payable to it from a Defaulting Party under Section 6(e).

Any purported transfer that is not in compliance with this Section will be void.

8. Contractual Currency

(a) ***Payment in the Contractual Currency.*** Each payment under this Agreement will be made in the relevant currency specified in this Agreement for that payment (the

"Contractual Currency"). To the extent permitted by applicable law, any obligation to make payments under this Agreement in the Contractual Currency will not be discharged or satisfied by any tender in any currency other than the Contractual Currency, except to the extent such tender results in the actual receipt by the party to which payment is owed, acting in a reasonable manner and in good faith in converting the currency so tendered into the Contractual Currency, of the full amount in the Contractual Currency of all amounts payable in respect of this Agreement. If for any reason the amount in the Contractual Currency so received falls short of the amount in the Contractual Currency payable in respect of this Agreement, the party required to make the payment will, to the extent permitted by applicable law, immediately pay such additional amount in the Contractual Currency as may be necessary to compensate for the shortfall. If for any reason the amount in the Contractual Currency so received exceeds the amount in the Contractual Currency payable in respect of this Agreement, the party receiving the payment will refund promptly the amount of such excess.

(b) ***Judgments.*** To the extent permitted by applicable law, if any judgment or order expressed in a currency other than the Contractual Currency is rendered (i) for the payment of any amount owing in respect of this Agreement, (ii) for the payment of any amount relating to any early termination in respect of this Agreement or (iii) in respect of a judgment or order of another court for the payment of any amount described in (i) or (ii) above, the party seeking recovery, after recovery in full of the aggregate amount to which such party is entitled pursuant to the judgment or order, will be entitled to receive immediately from the other party the amount of any shortfall of the Contractual Currency received by such party as a consequence of sums paid in such other currency and will refund promptly to the other party any excess of the Contractual Currency received by such party as a consequence of sums paid in such other currency if such shortfall or such excess arises or results from any variation between the rate of exchange at which the Contractual Currency is converted into the currency of the judgment or order for the purposes of such judgment or order and the rate of exchange at which such party is able, acting in a reasonable manner and in good faith in converting the currency received into the Contractual Currency, to purchase the Contractual Currency with the amount of the currency of the judgment or order actually received by such party. The term "rate of exchange" includes, without limitation, any premiums and costs of exchange payable in connection with the purchase of or conversion into the Contractual Currency.

(c) ***Separate Indemnities.*** To the extent permitted by applicable law, these indemnities constitute separate and independent obligations from the other obligations in this Agreement, will be enforceable as separate and independent causes of action, will apply notwithstanding any indulgence granted by the party to which any payment is owed and will not be affected by judgment being obtained or claim or proof being made for any other sums payable in respect of this Agreement.

(d) ***Evidence of Loss.*** For the purpose of this Section 8, it will be sufficient for a party to demonstrate that it would have suffered a loss had an actual exchange or purchase been made.

9. Miscellaneous

(a) ***Entire Agreement.*** This Agreement constitutes the entire agreement and understanding of the parties with respect to its subject matter and supersedes all oral communications and prior writings with respect thereto.

(b) ***Amendments.*** No amendment, modification or waiver in respect of this Agreement will be effective unless in writing (including a writing evidenced by a facsimile transmission) and executed by each of the parties or confirmed by an exchange of telexes or electronic messages on an electronic messaging system.

(c) ***Survival of Obligations.*** Without prejudice to Sections 2(a)(iii) and 6(c)(ii), the obligations of the parties under this Agreement will survive the termination of any Transaction.

(d) ***Remedies Cumulative.*** Except as provided in this Agreement, the rights, powers, remedies and privileges provided in this Agreement are cumulative and not exclusive of any rights, powers, remedies and privileges provided by law.

(e) ***Counterparts and Confirmations.***

(i) This Agreement (and each amendment, modification and waiver in respect of it) may be executed and delivered in counterparts (including by facsimile transmission), each of which will be deemed an original.

(ii) The parties intend that they are legally bound by the terms of each Transaction from the moment they agree to those terms (whether orally or otherwise). A Confirmation shall be entered into as soon as practicable and may be executed and delivered in counterparts (including by facsimile transmission) or be created by an exchange of telexes or by an exchange of electronic messages on an electronic messaging system, which in each case will be sufficient for all purposes to evidence a binding supplement to this Agreement. The parties will specify therein or through another effective means that any such counterpart, telex or electronic message constitutes a Confirmation.

(f) ***No Waiver of Rights.*** A failure or delay in exercising any right, power or privilege in respect of this Agreement will not be presumed to operate as a waiver, and a single or partial exercise of any right, power or privilege will not be presumed to preclude any subsequent or further exercise, of that right, power or privilege or the exercise of any other right, power or privilege.

(g) ***Headings.*** The headings used in this Agreement are for convenience of reference only and are not to affect the construction of or to be taken into consideration in interpreting this Agreement.

10. Offices; Multibranch Parties

(a) If Section 10(a) is specified in the Schedule as applying, each party that enters into a Transaction through an Office other than its head or home office represents to the other party that, notwithstanding the place of booking office or jurisdiction or incorporation or organisation of such party, the obligations of such party are the same as if it had entered into the Transaction through its head or home office. This representation will be deemed to be repeated by such party on each date on which a Transaction is entered into.

(b) Neither party may change the Office through which it makes and receives payments or deliveries for the purpose of a Transaction without the prior written consent of the other party.

(c) If a party is specified as a Multibranch Party in the Schedule, such Multibranch Party may make and receive payments or deliveries under any Transaction through any Office listed in the Schedule, and the Office through which it makes and receives payments or deliveries with respect to a Transaction will be specified in the relevant Confirmation.

11. Expenses

A Defaulting Party will, on demand, indemnify and hold harmless the other party for and against all reasonable out-of-pocket expenses, including legal fees and Stamp Tax, incurred by such other party by reason of the enforcement and protection of its rights under this Agreement or any Credit Support Document to which the Defaulting Party is a party or by reason of the early termination of any Transaction, including, but not limited to, costs of collection.

12. Notices

(a) ***Effectiveness.*** Any notice or other communication in respect of this Agreement may be given in any manner set forth below (except that a notice or other communication under Section 5 or 6 may not be given by facsimile transmission or electronic messaging system) to the address or number or in accordance with the electronic messaging system details provided (see the Schedule) and will be deemed effective as indicated:—

(i) if in writing and delivered in person or by courier, on the date it is delivered;

(ii) if sent by telex, on the date the recipient's answerback is received;

(iii) if sent by facsimile transmission, on the date that transmission is received by a responsible employee of the recipient in legible form (it being agreed that the burden of proving receipt will be on the sender and will not be met by a transmission report generated by the sender's facsimile machine);

(iv) if sent by certified or registered mail (airmail, if overseas) or the equivalent (return receipt requested), on the date that mail is delivered or its delivery is attempted; or

(v) if sent by electronic messaging system, on the date that electronic message is received,

unless the date of that delivery (or attempted delivery) or that receipt, as applicable, is not a Local Business Day or that communication is delivered (or attempted) or received, as applicable, after the close of business on a Local Business Day, in which case that communication shall be deemed given and effective on the first following day that is a Local Business Day.

(b) ***Change of Addresses.*** Either party may by notice to the other change the address, telex or facsimile number or electronic messaging system details at which notices or other communications are to be given to it.

13. Governing Law and Jurisdiction

(a) ***Governing Law.*** This Agreement will be governed by and construed in accordance with the law specified in the Schedule.

(b) ***Jurisdiction.*** With respect to any suit, action or proceedings relating to this Agreement ("Proceedings"), each party irrevocably:—

(i) submits to the jurisdiction of the English courts, if this Agreement is expressed to be governed by English law, or to the non-exclusive jurisdiction of the courts of the State of New York and the United States District Court located in the Borough of Manhattan in New York City, if this Agreement is expressed to be governed by the laws of the State of New York; and

(ii) waives any objection which it may have at any time to the laying of venue of any Proceedings brought in any such court, waives any claim that such Proceedings have been brought in an inconvenient forum and further waives the right to object, with respect to such Proceedings, that such court does not have any jurisdiction over such party.

Nothing in this Agreement precludes either party from bringing Proceedings in any other jurisdiction (outside, if this Agreement is expressed to be governed by English law, the Contracting States, as defined in Section 1(3) of the Civil Jurisdiction and Judgments Act 1982 or any modification, extension or re-enactment thereof for the time being in force) nor will the bringing of Proceedings in any one or more jurisdictions preclude the bringing of Proceedings in any other jurisdiction.

(c) ***Service of Process.*** Each party irrevocably appoints the Process Agent (if any) specified opposite its name in the Schedule to receive, for it and on its behalf, service of process in any Proceedings. If for any reason any party's Process Agent is unable to act as such, such party will promptly notify the other party and within 30 days appoint a substitute process agent acceptable to the other party. The parties irrevocably consent to service of process given in the manner provided for notices in Section 12. Nothing in this Agreement will affect the right of either party to serve process in any other manner permitted by law.

(d) **Waiver of Immunities.** Each party irrevocably waives, to the fullest extent permitted by applicable law, with respect to itself and its revenues and assets (irrespective of their use or intended use), all immunity on the grounds of sovereignty or other grounds from (i) suit, (ii) jurisdiction of any court, (iii) relief by way of injunction, order for specific performance or for recovery of property, (iv) attachment of its assets (whether before or after judgment) and (v) execution or enforcement of any judgment to which it or its revenues or assets might otherwise be entitled in any Proceedings in the courts of any jurisdiction and irrevocably agrees, to the extent permitted by applicable law, that it will not claim any such immunity in any Proceedings.

14. Definitions.

As used in this Agreement:—

"***Additional Termination Event***" has the meaning specified in Section 5(b).

"***Affected Party***" has the meaning specified in Section 5(b).

"***Affected Transactions***" means (a) with respect to any Termination Event consisting of an Illegality, Tax Event or Tax Event Upon Merger, all Transactions affected by the occurrence of such Termination Event and (b) with respect to any other Termination Event, all Transactions.

"***Affiliate***" means, subject to the Schedule, in relation to any person, any entity controlled, directly or indirectly, by the person, any entity that controls, directly or indirectly, the person or any entity directly or indirectly under common control with the person. For this purpose, "control" of any entity or person means ownership of a majority of the voting power of the entity or person.

"***Applicable Rate***" means:—

(a) in respect of obligations payable or deliverable (or which would have been but for Section 2(a)(iii)) by a Defaulting Party, the Default Rate;

(b) in respect of an obligation to pay an amount under Section 6(e) of either party from and after the date (determined in accordance with Section 6(d)(ii)) on which that amount is payable, the Default Rate;

(c) in respect of all our obligations payable or deliverable (or which would have been but for Section 2(a)(iii)) by a Non-defaulting Party, the Non-default Rate; and

(d) in all other cases, the Termination Rate.

"***Burdened Party***" had the meaning specified in Section 5(b).

"*Change in Tax Law*" means the enactment, promulgation, execution or ratification of, or any change in or amendment to, any law (or in the application or official interpretation of any law) that occurs on or after the date on which the relevant Transaction is entered into.

"*Consent*" includes a consent, approval, action, authorisation, exemption, notice, filing, registration or exchange control consent.

"*Credit Event Upon Merger*" has the meaning specified in Section 5(b).

"*Credit Support Document*" means any agreement or instrument that is specified as such in this Agreement.

"*Credit Support Provider*" has the meaning specified in the Schedule.

"*Default Rate*" means a rate per annum equal to the cost (without proof or evidence of any actual cost) to the relevant payee (as certified by it) if it were to fund or of funding the relevant amount plus 1% per annum.

"*Defaulting Party*" has the meaning specified in Section 6(a).

"*Early Termination Date*" means the date determined in accordance with Section 6(a) or 6(b)(iv).

"*Event of Default*" had the meaning specified in Section 5(a) and, if applicable, in the Schedule.

"*Illegality*" has the meaning specified in Section 5(b).

"*Indemnifiable Tax*" means any Tax other than a Tax that would not be imposed in respect of a payment under this Agreement but for a present or former connection between the jurisdiction of the government or taxation authority imposing such Tax and the recipient of such payment or a person related to such recipient (including, without limitation, a connection arising from such recipient or related person being or having been a citizen or resident of such jurisdiction, or being or having been organised, present or engaged in a trade or business in such jurisdiction, or having or having had a permanent establishment or fixed place of business in such jurisdiction, but excluding a connection arising solely from such recipient or related person having executed, delivered, performed its obligations or received a payment under, or enforced, this Agreement or a Credit Support Document).

"*Law*" includes any treaty, law, rule or regulation (as modified, in the case of tax matters, by the practice of any relevant governmental revenue authority) and "*lawful*" and "*unlawful*" will be construed accordingly.

"*Local Business Day*" means, subject to the Schedule, a day on which commercial banks are open for business (including dealings in foreign exchange and foreign currency deposits) (a) in relation to any obligation under Section 2(a)(i), in the place(s) specified in the relevant Confirmation or, if not so specified, as otherwise agreed by the parties in writing or determined pursuant to provisions contained, or incorporated by reference, in this Agreement, (b) in relation to any other payment, in the place where the relevant account is located and, if different, in the principal financial centre, if any, of the currency of such payment, (c) in relation to any notice or other communication, including notice contemplated under Section 5(a)(i), in the city specified in the address for notice provided by the recipient and, in the case of a notice contemplated by Section 2(b), in the place where the relevant new account is to be located and (d) in relation to Section 5(a)(v)(2), in the relevant locations for performance with respect to such Specified Transaction.

"*Loss*" means, with respect to this Agreement or one or more Terminated Transactions, as the case may be, and a party, the Termination Currency Equivalent of an amount that party reasonably determines in good faith to be its total losses and costs (or gain, in which case expressed as a negative number) in connection with this Agreement or that Terminated Transaction or group of Terminated Transactions, as the case may be, including any loss of bargain, cost of funding or, at the election of such party but without duplication, loss or cost incurred as a result of its terminating, liquidating, obtaining or re-establishing any hedge or related trading position (or any gain resulting from any of them). Loss includes losses and costs (or gains) in respect of any payment or delivery required to have been made (assuming satisfaction of each applicable condition precedent) on or before the relevant Early Termination Date and not made, except, so as to avoid duplication, if Section 6(e)(i)(l) or (3) or 6(e)(ii)(2)(A) applies. Loss does not include a party's legal fees and out-of-pocket expenses referred to under Section 11. A party will determine its Loss as of the relevant Early Termination Date, or, if that is not reasonably practicable, as of the earliest date thereafter as is reasonably practicable. A party may (but need not) determine its Loss by reference to quotations or relevant rates or prices from one or more leading dealers in the relevant markets.

"***Market Quotation***" means, with respect to one or more Terminated Transactions and a party making the determination, an amount determined on the basis of quotations from Reference Market-makers. Each quotation will be for an amount, if any, that would be paid to such party (expressed as a negative number) or by such party (expressed as a positive number) in consideration of an agreement between such party (taking into account any existing Credit Support Document with respect to the obligations of such party) and the quoting Reference Market-maker to enter into a transaction (the "Replacement Transaction") that would have the effect of preserving for such party the economic equivalent of any payment or delivery (whether the underlying obligation was absolute or contingent and assuming the satisfaction of each applicable condition precedent) by the parties under Section 2(a)(i) in respect of such Terminated Transaction or group of Terminated Transactions that would, but for the occurrence of the relevant Early Termination Date, have been required after that date. For this purpose, Unpaid Amounts in respect of the Terminated Transaction or group of Terminated Transactions are to be excluded but, without limitation, any payment or delivery that would, but for the relevant Early Termination Date, have been required (assuming satisfaction of each applicable condition precedent) after that Early Termination Date is to be included. The Replacement Transaction would be subject to such documentation as such party and the Reference Market-maker may, in good faith, agree. The party making the determination (or its agent) will request each Reference Market-maker to provide its quotation to the extent reasonably practicable as of the same day and time (without regard to different time zones) on or as soon as reasonably practicable after the relevant Early Termination Date. The day and time as of which those quotations are to be obtained will be selected in good faith by the party obliged to make a determination under Section 6(e), and, if each party is so obliged, after consultation with the other. If more than three quotations are provided, the Market Quotation will be the arithmetic mean of the quotations, without regard to the quotations having the highest and lowest values. If exactly three such quotations are provided, the Market Quotation will be the quotation remaining after disregarding the highest and lowest quotations. For this purpose, if more than one quotation has the same highest value or lowest value, then one of such quotations shall be disregarded. If fewer than three quotations are provided, it will be deemed that the Market Quotation in respect of such Terminated Transaction or group of Terminated Transactions cannot be determined.

"***Non-default Rate***" means a rate per annum equal to the cost (without proof or evidence of any actual cost) to the Non-defaulting Party (as certified by it) if it were to fund the relevant amount.

"***Non-defaulting Party***" has the meaning specified in Section 6(a).

"***Office***" means a branch or office of a party, which may be such party's head or home office.

"***Potential Event of Default***" means any event which, with the giving of notice or the lapse of time or both, would constitute an Event of Default.

"***Reference Market-makers***" means four leading dealers in the relevant market selected by the party determining a Market Quotation in good faith (a) from among dealers of the highest credit standing which satisfy all the criteria that such party applies generally at the time in deciding whether to offer or to make an extension of credit and (b) to the extent practicable, from among such dealers having an office in the same city.

"***Relevant Jurisdiction***" means, with respect to a party, the jurisdictions (a) in which the party is incorporated, organised, managed and controlled or considered to have its seat, (b) where an Office through which the party is acting for purposes of this Agreement is located, (c) in which the party executes this Agreement and (d) in relation to any payment, from or through which such payment is made.

"***Scheduled Payment Date***" means a date on which a payment or delivery is to be made under Section 2(a)(i) with respect to a Transaction.

"***Set-off***" means set-off, offset, combination of accounts, right of retention or withholding or similar right or requirement to which the payer of an amount under Section 6 is entitled or subject (whether arising under this Agreement, another contract, applicable law or otherwise) that is exercised by, or imposed on, such payer.

"***Settlement Amount***" means, with respect to a party and any Early Termination Date, the sum of:—

(a) the Termination Currency Equivalent of the Market Quotations (whether positive or negative) for each Terminated Transaction or group of Terminated Transactions for which a Market Quotation is determined; and

(b) such party's Loss (whether positive or negative and without reference to any Unpaid Amounts) for each Terminated Transaction or group of Terminated Transactions for which a Market Quotation cannot be determined or would not (in the reasonable belief of the party making the determination) produce a commercially reasonable result.

"***Specified Entity***" had the meaning specified in the Schedule.

"***Specified Indebtness***" means, subject to the Schedule, any obligations (whether present or future, contingent or otherwise, as principal or surety or otherwise) in respect of borrowed money.

"***Specified Transaction***" means, subject to the Schedule, (a) any transaction (including an agreement with respect thereto) now existing or hereafter entered into between one party to this Agreement (or any Credit Support Provider of such party or any applicable Specified Entity of such party) and the other party to this Agreement (or any Credit Support Provider of such other party or any applicable Specified Entity of such other party) which is a rate swap transaction, basis swap, forward rate transaction, commodity swap, commodity option, equity or equity index swap, equity or equity index option, bond option, interest rate option, foreign exchange transaction, cap transaction, floor transaction, collar transaction, currency swap transaction, cross-currency rate swap transaction, currency option or any other similar transaction (including any option with respect to any of these transactions), (b) any combination of these transactions and (c) any other transaction identified as a Specified Transaction in this Agreement or the relevant confirmation.

"Stamp Tax" means any stamp, registration, documentation or similar tax.

"Tax" means any present or future tax, levy, impost, duty, charge, assessment or fee of any nature (including interest, penalties and additions thereto) that is imposed by any government or other taxing authority in respect of any payment under this Agreement other than a stamp, registration, documentation or similar tax.

"Tax Event" has the meaning specified in Section 5(b).

"Tax Event Upon Merger" had the meaning specified in Section 5(b).

"Terminated Transactions" means with respect to any Early Termination Date (a) if resulting from a Termination Event, all Affected Transactions and (b) if resulting from an Event of Default, all Transactions (in either case) in effect immediately before the effectiveness of the notice designating that Early Termination Date (or, if "Automatic Early Termination" applies, immediately before that Early Termination Date).

"Termination Currency" has the meaning specified in the Schedule.

"Termination Currency Equivalent" means, in respect of any amount denominated in the Termination Currency, such Termination Currency amount and, in respect of any amount denominated in a currency other than the Termination Currency (the "Other Currency"), the amount in the Termination Currency determined by the party making the relevant determination as being required to purchase such amount of such Other Currency as at the relevant Early Termination Date, or, if the relevant Market Quotation or Loss (as the case may be), is determined as of a later date, that later date, with the Termination Currency at the rate equal to the spot exchange rate of the foreign exchange agent (selected as provided below) for the purchase of such Other Currency with the Termination Currency at or about 11:00 a.m. (in the city in which such foreign exchange agent is located) on such date as would be customary for the determination of such a rate for the purchase of such Other Currency for value on the relevant Early Termination Date or that later date. The foreign exchange agent will, if only one party is obliged to make a determination under Section 6(e), be selected in good faith by that party and otherwise will be agreed by the parties.

"Termination Event" means an Illegality, a Tax Event or a Tax Event Upon Merger or, if specified to be applicable, a Credit Event Upon Merger or an Additional Termination Event.

"Termination Rate" means a rate per annum equal to the arithmetic mean of the cost (without proof or evidence of any actual cost) to each party (as certified by such party) if it were to fund or of funding such amounts.

"Unpaid Amounts" owing to any party means, with respect to an Early Termination Date, the aggregate of (a) in respect of all Terminated Transactions, the amounts that became payable (or that would have become payable but for Section 2(a)(iii) to such party under Section 2(a)(i) on or prior to such Early Termination Date and which remain unpaid as at such Early Termination Date and (b) in respect of each Terminated Transaction, for each obligation under Section 2(a)(i) which was (or would have been but for Section 2(a)(iii) required to be settled by delivery to such party on or prior to such Early Termination Date and which has not been so settled as at such Early Termination Date, an amount equal

to the fair market value of that which was (or would have been) required to be delivered as of the originally scheduled date for delivery, in each case together with (to the extent permitted under applicable law) interest, in the currency of such amounts, from (and including) the date such amounts or obligations were or would have been required to have been paid or performed to (but excluding) such Early Termination Date, at the Applicable Rate. Such amounts of interest will be calculated on the basis of daily compounding and the actual number of days elapsed. The fair market value of any obligation referred to in clause (b) above shall be reasonably determined by the party obliged to make the determination under Section 6(e) or, if each party is so obliged, it shall be the average of the Termination Currency Equivalents of the fair market values reasonably determined by both parties.

IN WITNESS WHEREOF the parties have executed this document on the respective dates specified below with effect from the date specified on the first page of this document.

....	....
(Name of Party)	(Name of Party)
By:	By: ....
Name:	Name:
Title:	Title:
Date:	Date:

(Multicurrency—Cross Border)

ISDA®

International Swap Dealers Association, Inc.

SCHEDULE
to the
Master Agreement

dated as of ....

between .... ("Party A") and .... ("Party B")

Part 1. **Termination Provisions.**

(a) "***Specified Entity***" means in relation to Party A for the purpose of:—

Section 5(a)(v), ...

Section 5(a)(vi), ...

Section 5(a)(vii), ...

Section 5(b)(iv), ...

and in relation to Party B for the purpose of:—

Section 5(a)(v), ...

Section 5(a)(vi), ...

Section 5(a)(vii), ...

Section 5(b)(iv), ...

(b) "***Specified Transaction***" will have the meaning specified in Section 14 of this Agreement unless another meaning is specified here ....

....

....

(c) The "***Cross Default***" provision of Section 5(a)(vi)
will/will not* apply to Party A
will/will not* apply to Party B

If such provisions apply:—

* Delete as applicable.

"Specified Indebtedness" will have the meaning specified in Section 14 of this Agreement unless another meaning is specified here ....

....

"Threshold Amount" means ....

....

(d) The *"Credit Event Upon Merger"* provisions of Section 5(b)(iv)
will/will not* apply to Party A
will/will not* apply to Party B

(e) The *"Automatic Early Termination"* provision of Section 6(a)
will/will not* apply to Party A
will/will not* apply to Party B

(f) ***Payments on Early Termination.*** For the purpose of Section 6(e) of this Agreement:—

(i) Market Quotation/Loss* will apply.

(ii) The First Method/The Second Method* will apply.

(g) *"Termination Currency"* means ...., if such currency is specified and freely available, and otherwise United States Dollars.

(h) *Additional Termination Event* will/will not apply*. The following shall constitute an Additional Termination Event:— ....

....

....

....

....

....

For the purpose of the foregoing Termination Event, the Affected Party or Affected Parties shall be:— ....

Part 2. **Tax Representations.**

(a) ***Payer Representations.*** For the purpose of Section 3(e) of this Agreement, Party A will/will not* make the following representations and Party B will/will not* make the following representations:—

It is not required by any applicable law, as modified by the practice of any relevant governmental revenue authority, of any Relevant Jurisdiction to make any deduction or withholding for or on account of any Tax from any payment (other than interest under Section 2(e), 6(d)(ii) or 6(e) of this Agreement) to be made by it to the other party under this Agreement. In making this representation, it may rely on (i) the accuracy of any representations made by the other party pursuant to Section 3(f) of this Agreement, (ii) the satisfaction

* Delete as applicable.

of the agreement contained in Section 4(a)(i) or 4(a)(iii) of this Agreement and the accuracy and effectiveness of any document provided by the other party pursuant to Section 4(a)(i) or 4(a)(iii) of this Agreement and (iii) the satisfaction of the agreement of the other party contained in Section 4(d) of this Agreement, *provided* that it shall not be a breach of this representation where reliance is placed on clause (ii) and the other party does not deliver a form or document under Section 4(a)(iii) by reason of material prejudice to its legal or commercial position.

(b) ***Payee Representations.*** For the purpose of Section 3(f) of this Agreement, Party A and Party B make the representations specified below, if any:

(i) The following representation will/will not* apply to Party A and will/will not* apply to Party B:—

It is fully eligible for the benefits of the "Business Profits" or "Industrial and Commercial Profits" provision, as the case may be, the "Interest" provision or the "Other Income" provision (if any) of the Specified Treaty with respect to any payment described in such provisions and received or to be received by it in connection with this Agreement and no such payment is attributable to a trade or business carried on by it through a permanent establishment in the Specified Jurisdiction.

If such representation applies, then:—

"***Specified Treaty***" means with respect to Party A ....

"***Specified Jurisdiction***" means with respect to Party A ....

"***Specified Treaty***" means with respect to Party B ....

"***Specified Jurisdiction***" means with respect to Party B ....

(ii) The following representation will/will not* apply to Party A and will/will not* apply to Party B:—

Each payment received or to be received by it in connection with this Agreement will be effectively connected with its conduct of a trade or business in the Specified Jurisdiction.

If such representation applies, then:—

"***Specified Jurisdiction***" means with respect to Party A ....

"***Specified Jurisdiction***" means with respect to Party B ....

(iii) The following representation will/will not* apply to Party A and will/will not* apply to Party B:—

(A) It is entering into each Transaction in the ordinary course of its trade as, and is, either (1) a recognised U.K. bank or (2) a recognised U.K. swaps dealer (in either case (1) or (2), for purposes of the United Kingdom Inland Revenue extra statutory concession C17 on interest and currency swaps dated March 14, 1989), and (B) it will bring into account payments made and received in respect of each Transaction in computing its income for United Kingdom tax purposes.

(iv) Other Payee Representations:— ....

....

....

* Delete as applicable.

N.B. The above representations may need modification if either party is a Multibranch Party.

Part 3. **Agreement to Deliver Documents.**

For the purpose of Sections 4(a)(i) and (ii) of this Agreement, each party agrees to deliver the following documents, as applicable:—

(a) Tax forms, documents or certificates to be delivered are:—

Party required to deliver document	Form/Document/ Certificate	Date by which to be delivered
....	....	....
....	....	....
....	....	....
....	....	....
....	....	....

(b) Other documents to be delivered are:—

Party required to deliver document	Form/Document/ Certificate	Date by which to be delivered	Covered by Section 3(d) Representation
....	....	....	Yes/No*
....	....	....	Yes/No*
....	....	....	Yes/No*
....	....	....	Yes/No*
....	....	....	Yes/No*

Part 4. **Miscellaneous.**

(a) ***Addresses for Notices.*** For the purpose of Section 12(a) of this Agreement:—

Address for notices or communications to Party A:—

Address: ....

Attention: ....

Telex No.: .... Answerback: ....

Facsimile No.: .... Telephone No.: ....

Electronic Messaging System Details: ....

Address for notices or communications to Party B:—

Address: ....

Attention: ....

Telex No.: .... Answerback: ....

* Delete as applicable.

Facsimile No.: .... Telephone: ....

Electronic Messaging System Details: ....

(b) ***Process Agent.*** For the purpose of Section 13(c) of this Agreement:—

Party A appoints as its Process Agent ....

Party B appoints as its Process Agent ....

(c) ***Offices.*** The provisions of Section 10(a) will/will not* apply to this Agreement.

(d) ***Multibranch Party.*** For the purpose of Section 10(c) of this Agreement:—

Party A is/is not* a Multibranch Party and, if so, may act through the following Offices:—

....

....

Party B is/is not* a Multibranch Party and, if so, may act through the following Offices:—

....

....

(e) ***Calculation Agent.*** The Calulation Agent is ...., unless otherwise specified in a Confirmation in relation to the relevant Transaction.

(f) ***Credit Support Document.*** Details of any Credit Support Document:— ....

....

....

....

(g) ***Credit Support Provider.*** Credit Support Provider means in relation to Party A,

....

....

....

Credit Support Provider means in relation to Party B, ...

....

....

(h) ***Governing Law.*** This Agreement will be governed by and construed in accordance with English law/the laws of the State of New York (without reference to choice of law doctrine)*.

(i) ***Netting of Payments.*** Subparagraph (ii) of Section 2(c) of this Agreement will not apply to the following Transactions or groups of Transactions (in each case starting from the date of this Agreement/in each case starting from ....*)

....

....

* Delete as applicable.

(j) "***Affiliate***" will have the meaning specified in Section 14 of this Agreement unless another meaning is specified here ....
....

Part 5. **Other Provisions.**

APPENDIX B

COMMENTARY ON 1992 ISDA MASTER AGREEMENT (MULTI-CURRENCY—CROSS-BORDER)

Initial recital and section 1: interpretation

Description

"Transactions" are entered into upon the basis that the Master Agreement (including the Schedule) (the Agreement) and all Confirmations constitute a "single agreement" reached by the parties. If inconsistency arises between the constituent documents (Master, Schedule and Confirmations), interpretative priority is held by the Confirmations, followed by the Schedule and then the remaining provisions of the Master Agreement.

The wording aims to accommodate Statute of Frauds requirements concerning the identification of the documentary evidence constituting the agreement reached by the parties. It upholds the integrity of the Agreement in those jurisdictions requiring "expression of single-agreement intent".

Significant differences from 1987 Master

The 1992 Master has a wider coverage of transactions than the 1987 Master—the term "transaction" is used generally as opposed to the previous term "swap transaction".

Section 2: obligations

Description

General

The section identifies the nature of the parties' payment obligations. A distinction is made between payments and settlement by delivery.

Netting

The section provides for automatic netting of amounts payable in the same currency and in respect of the same transaction on the same day through a "netting by novation" mechanism. Parties may elect to net payments arising in respect of two or more transactions having the same payment date and to be made in the same currency. Exercise of the election is indicated in the Schedule. The election may be exercised in relation to all or any specified group of transactions. This netting election helps reduce the settlement risk borne by each party as regards the other party's ability to pay when payments are due.

Withholding taxes

The payer is obliged to "gross up" in respect of any withholding tax if the tax is an "indemnifiable tax" (that is, any tax other than a tax imposed as a result of a present or former connection between the jurisdiction imposing the tax and the recipient of the payment). The payer escapes the "gross-up" obligation if the payee has not given true tax representations, unless the failure of the payee's tax representations is the result of a "change in tax law" or a change in official or judicial interpretation of tax law.

Default interest

Default interest is imposed on overdue amounts (payee's cost of funds plus 1%). Default interest applies only prior to designation of an early termination date. Where the transaction involves settlement by delivery, compensation for late delivery must be noted in the relevant Confirmation if it is to apply.

Significant differences from 1987 Master

The 1992 Master has a more flexible treatment of same day/same currency netting under different transactions.

Section 3: representations

Description

The Agreement contains a number of fundamental representations which are stated to be given as of the date of the Agreement and repeated on each date on which a transaction is entered into. The payee tax representations constitute an exception—they are expressed to be continuing representations (in order to counter balance the imposition of continuing gross-up risk on the payer under the Agreement).

Significant differences from 1987 Master

The "absence of litigation" representation is slightly narrower—otherwise the two Masters are substantially identical.

Section 4: agreements

Description

Basic covenants include delivering documents or notices which have been specified in the Schedule or any Confirmation, using reasonable efforts to maintain authorisations, complying with applicable laws, notifying any failure of a payee tax representation to the other party and payment of stamp duty liabilities.

Significant differences from 1987 Master

The two Masters are substantially identical although the 1992 Master adds the requirement to provide tax forms.

Section 5: events of default and termination events

Description

Events of default

Events of default cover the following areas:

(i) failure to pay within three business days after notice of failure to pay;

(ii) failure to perform other obligations under the Agreement within 30 days of notice (except obligation to deliver tax forms and to give notice of the failure of a payee tax representation which are dealt with under termination events);

(iii) defaults relating to credit support documentation;

(iv) misrepresentation (does not apply to failure of payer and payee tax representations);

(v) default by a party, any credit support provider or any specified entity under a "specified transaction";

(vi) optional cross-default provision (elected by the parties in the Schedule). Default is triggered by the acceleration of one or more obligations relating to "specified indebtedness" in an amount greater than the "threshold amount" specified in the Schedule or the failure to pay one or more such obligations at maturity or to make interest or sinking fund payments. The obligations can be those of a party, any credit support provider of such party or any specified entity relating to such party;

(vii) acts pertaining to bankruptcy, insolvency, dissolution or liquidation of, the appointment of a official manager to, or the exercise of security against, a party, credit support provider or specified entity; and

(viii) merger of a party or credit support provider without its successor entity assuming the obligations of the party under the Agreement or credit support document and the failure of any credit support document to extend to the successor entity.

Termination events

Termination events cover the following areas:

(i) a change in law which makes performance by a party or credit support provider under the Agreement or a credit support document illegal;

(ii) a "change in tax law" or any action by taxing authorities making it substantially likely that a party will be obliged to gross up on the next payment date or that a party will receive a payment net of a deduction where there is no obligation on the payer to gross up;

(iii) a tax gross-up obligation arising as a result of the merger of a party;

(iv) an optional termination provision (elected in the Schedule)—a materially weaker credit-worthiness of any successor entity brought into being by the merger or consolidation of a party, credit support provider or specified entity;

(v) "additional termination events"—parties may indicate in the Schedule or by Confirmation any additional termination events which are to apply.

Significant differences from 1987 Master

The 1992 Master introduces the concept of a "credit support provider" in some places replacing references to "specified entities" and in other places the new concept is used in addition to the old concept.

Both the swap and general cross default clauses are widened.

Concept of "official manager" is now referred to in the insolvency clauses.

Termination events have been amended in minor respects.

"Additional termination events" concept has been added to allow extra events to be specified in a Confirmation or the Schedule.

Section 6: early termination—right to terminate

Description

Event of default

If an event of default occurs, the non-defaulting party has the option to give from one to 20 days notice of early termination of the entire Agreement. If however a party elected in the Schedule for the "automatic early termination" option to apply, then on the occurrence of one of a selected menu of bankruptcy events the Agreement is terminated on a net basis before becoming subject to a bankruptcy regime.

Termination event

The consequences flowing from termination events are distinguished from those flowing from events of default. If a termination event occurs the affected party must give notice to the other party of such event and the transactions affected.

In the case of an illegality or tax event where there is only one affected party, or if a tax event upon merger occurs and the burdened party is the affected party, the affected party as a condition to its right to designate an early termination date must use reasonable efforts to transfer its obligations within 30 days to a branch office or affiliated office in another jurisdiction that would eliminate such an event without causing the party to incur a material loss.

If an illegality or a tax event occurs and there are two affected parties, they must use reasonable efforts to reach agreement on action to eliminate such an event.

Failing the above or if an illegality under section 5(b)(i)(2), a credit event upon merger or an additional termination event occurs, or a tax event upon merger occurs and the burdened party is not the affected party, section 6(b)(iv) identifies the specific party which may give notice setting an early termination date within 20 days of such notice for all transactions affected by such termination event.

Compensation on termination—events of default

There are different termination payment calculations for events of default and termination events.

For events of default, parties may elect limited two-way ("first method") or two-way ("second method") as payment methodology and market quotation or loss as the determinants of damages. If an election is not made in the schedule by the parties, then compensation will be by the second method where the non-defaulting party obtains market quotations for all transactions and then aggregates the result with any net unpaid prior period amounts ("unpaid amounts").

Compensation on termination—termination events

In the case of termination events, compensation is calculated on a no-default basis. If there is only one affected party, the amount due is determined in accordance with the second method and either market quotations or loss depending on the parties' election.

If there are two affected parties, both parties calculate their gains and losses on the terminated transactions (using either market quotation or loss depending on their initial election) and the difference is halved in calculating the final net payment due.

Parties delaying in making termination payments are liable to pay additional interest. Payments are also subject to any necessary bankruptcy adjustments. Payments are described as a "reasonable pre-estimate of loss" and not a "penalty".

Significant differences from 1987 Master

Automatic termination in the event of bankruptcy related events is now elective rather than mandatory. In other words when the master is executed parties must decide whether they wish automatic termination to apply. This allows parties additional flexibility depending on the nature of the bankruptcy regime which would apply to the party.

The "automatic" events are narrowed excluding:

- inability to pay debts;
- party taking action indicating consent to any of the bankruptcy proceedings.

Non-automatic termination also gives the non-defaulting party the ability to be certain that it is able to re-hedge its exposure simultaneously with the termination.

As with the 1987 Master parties must elect between limited two-way payments on termination or full two-way payments.

1992 Master now gives parties the option to elect at the outset whether termination payments are to be calculated on the basis of market quotations (as in the 1987 Master) or on the basis of "loss" suffered.

The possibility that rights of set-off will exist is now recognised in the drafting but no contractual set-off right has been included.

Section 7: transfer

Description

A party may only transfer its rights under the Agreement:

- with consent;
- in the course of a merger/consolidation; or
- if the other party has defaulted.

Significant differences from 1987 Master

The 1992 Master clarifies that the granting of security constitutes a transfer. It also specifically permits transfer of rights by a non-defaulting party.

Section 8: contractual currency

Description

This Section specifies rights which apply if parties receive payment in a non-specified currency or judgments/awards are granted in a non-specified currency. The indemnities given under this Section are noted as "separate indemnities" to avoid the risk of a claim based on the indemnity being held to have been merged in the initial judgment.

Significant differences from 1987 Master

The 1987 and 1992 Masters are substantially identical in this provision.

Section 9: miscellaneous

Description

Contains standard boilerplate provisions.

Significant differences from 1987 Master

The declaration that the parties are to be legally bound from the moment of agreement to the terms of any transaction (orally or otherwise) is new and can be seen as attempting to override existing statute of frauds provisions.

Section 10: multibranch parties

Description

Through appropriate elections in the Schedule a party may enter into transactions through any nominated office.

Significant differences from 1987 Master

This Section now provides, if the requisite election is made in the Schedule, that where a party enters into the Agreement through one of its branches or other offices, that party's full credit can be called upon under the Agreement to meet its obligations and not just the credit of the relevant branch.

Section 11: expenses

Description

The defaulting party is obliged to pay reasonable out-of-pocket expenses of the other party.

Significant differences from 1987 Master

None.

Section 12: notices

Description

Standard notice provisions.

Significant differences from 1987 Master

Provision for facsimile notices has been added. Facsimile notices are effective upon receipt (but cannot be given for default/early termination).

Section 13: governing law and jurisdiction

Description

The parties are required to specify the governing law in the Schedule. Parties are given a choice between New York or English courts for submission to jurisdiction. The selection is to be indicated in the Schedule.

Significant differences from 1987 Master

None.

Section 14: definitions

Description

The operation of a few important definitions is highlighted in this section of the discussion. The meaning of most definitions is self-evident.

- *Affected party*—this definition is important in determining the consequences which flow from a termination event. Affected parties are those identified in Section 5(b). Basically, they are a party that cannot perform because of an illegality, a party that must gross-up because of a tax event and the surviving entity of a party in the case of a tax event upon merger or credit event upon merger.

- *Indemnifiable tax*—payers are obliged to gross-up in respect of such a tax. It is defined as any tax other than a tax imposed as a result of a present or former connection between the jurisdiction imposing the tax and the recipient of the payment being taxed.
- *Loss*—this definition is important in the calculation of compensation payments under section 6 following an event of default or a termination event. It is broadly defined and includes any loss of bargain and costs of funding. Additionally, it may be determined with respect to a portfolio of transactions or a whole Master Agreement, it may include the cost of liquidating or replacing hedges. This extended definition is intended to permit damages calculations to be made for products not typically priced on a market quotation basis or for swaps so unique that market quotations are not available.
- *Market quotation*—this definition also plays an important role in the calculation of the section 6 compensation payments. The operation of this definition reflects a development in the swap market whereby calculation of damages is by reference to the replacement value of the terminated transactions as indicated by available market quotations.

In the event of an early termination, the non-defaulting party (or the non-affected party in a one affected party situation) must attempt to obtain quotations from four leading market-makers in the relevant swap market for each outstanding swap, to replace the remaining payments due under such swap from the defaulting (or affected) party. If four quotations are obtained, the market quotation for the swap is the average of such quotations disregarding the highest and lowest. If three quotations are obtained, the market quotation is the middle quote. If less than three quotes are obtained, the general indemnity method is used to calculate the non-defaulting (or non-affected) party's gain or loss.

- *Settlement amount*—is the third important definition in the calculation of the compensation payments under section 6 when market quotation is the calculation method selected by the parties. Settlement amount equals the sum of market quotations, except that the sum of losses will be substituted where Market Quotation cannot be determined and loss can be chosen at the outset of the calculation process by the party making the determination if the market quotation method would not produce a "commercially reasonable" settlement amount.

Significant differences from 1987 Master

- *Credit support provider*—new definition.
- *Loss*—expanded definition—may be positive or negative number.
- *Market quotation*—now permits a portfolio of transactions to be priced rather than individual transactions. Credit support to be considered in pricing and the definition is more flexible on the timing of quotations—"as soon as practicable" after termination date.
- *Settlement amount*—even where "market quotation" method is adopted loss is an alternative to determination of the settlement amount if "in the reasonable belief" of the party making the determination "market quotation" would not produce a "commercially reasonable result".

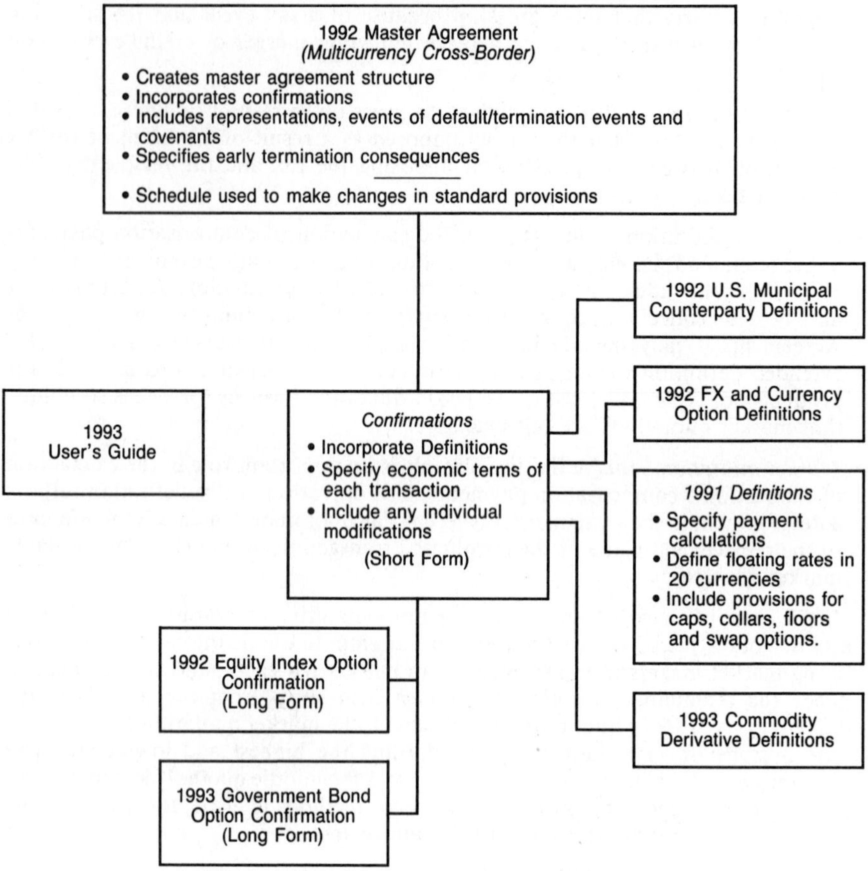

1992 Master Agreement
(Multicurrency Cross-Border)
• Creates master agreement structure
• Incorporates confirmations
• Includes representations, events of default/termination events and covenants
• Specifies early termination consequences
• Schedule used to make changes in standard provisions
1993 User's Guide
Confirmations
• Incorporate Definitions
• Specify economic terms of each transaction
• Include any individual modifications
(Short Form)
1992 U.S. Municipal Counterparty Definitions
1992 FX and Currency Option Definitions
1991 Definitions
• Specify payment calculations
• Define floating rates in 20 currencies
• Include provisions for caps, collars, floors and swap options.
1993 Commodity Derivative Definitions
1992 Equity Index Option Confirmation (Long Form)
1993 Government Bond Option Confirmation (Long Form)

1992 ISDA Master Agreement (Local Currency—Single Jurisdiction)
1992 Commodity Derivative Definitions (For Cash-Settled Transactions)
Confirmations
1992 U.S. Municipal Counterparty Definitions

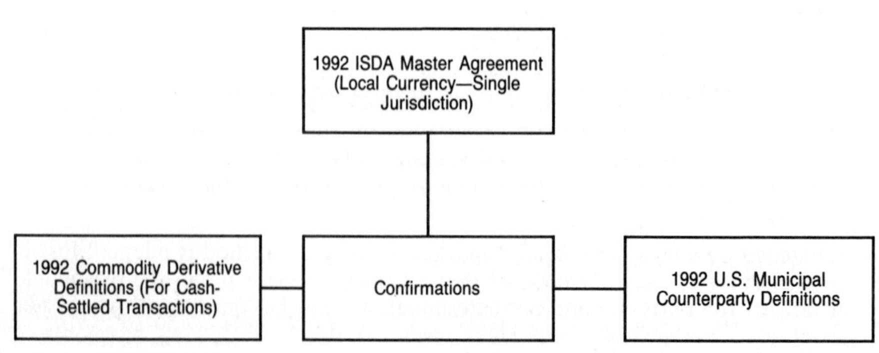

APPENDIX C

1993 ISDA COMMODITY DERIVATIVES DEFINITIONS[1]

TABLE OF CONTENTS

ARTICLE 6

FLOATING AMOUNTS

ARTICLE 7

CALCULATION OF PRICES FOR COMMODITY REFERENCE PRICES

ARTICLE 8

COMMODITY OPTIONS

ARTICLE 9

ROUNDING

EXHIBIT I

EXHIBIT II

INTRODUCTION TO THE 1993 ISDA COMMODITY DERIVATIVES DEFINITIONS

The 1993 ISDA Commodity Derivatives Definitions are intended for use with agreements, such as the 1992 ISDA Master Agreements (the "ISDA Master Agreements") published by the International Swaps and Derivatives Association, Inc. ("ISDA"), and in Confirmations of individual transactions governed by those agreements. Copies of the ISDA Master Agreements are available from the executive offices of ISDA. A sample form for a letter agreement or telex constituting a Confirmation is attached as Exhibit I to these Definitions. Sample forms of specific provisions for inclusion in a Confirmation to document different types of commodity derivative transactions are attached as Exhibits II-A through II-D to these Definitions.

These Definitions are designed for use by participants in the markets for commodity derivative transactions to document cash-settled commodity swaps, options, caps, collars, floors and swaptions or such other cash-settled commodity derivative transactions as the parties desire. These Definitions can be incorporated into Confirmations governed by an agreement such as either of the ISDA Master Agreements.

These Definitions do not contain settlement or other provisions designed to permit the documentation of transactions that settle by physical delivery of the underlying commodity. Accordingly, parties should carefully consider any necessary modifications and consult with their legal advisors before using these Definitions when documenting such a transaction.

The 1991 ISDA Definitions served as the basis for certain of the definitions and provisions contained in these Definitions. In many cases, these Definitions have been modified from the 1991 ISDA Definitions as a result of input from participants in working groups sponsored by ISDA. The definitions and provisions in these Definitions that are not part of the 1991 ISDA Definitions were developed by the working groups based, in large part, on market practice and a studied consideration of the relevant issues. These working groups included representatives from ISDA member institutions as well as representatives from institutions that are not ISDA members but specialize in commodity derivative transactions.

These Definitions may be updated periodically to include additional definitions and provisions. While the definitions and provisions contained in these Definitions may be modified in any update, it is not anticipated that they will be changed substantively unless then prevailing market practice supports such a change. At any time a copy of the then current version of these Definitions can be obtained from the executive offices of ISDA.

ISDA has no relationship with the organizations that have created or publish or provide the information that serves as a basis for the prices referred to in these Definitions. ISDA does not assume any responsibility for the non-availability or miscalculation of, or any error or omission in, any of the prices referred to in these Definitions. ISDA assumes no responsibility for any use to which these Definitions may be put or for any use of any price in connection with a commodity derivative transaction.

ISDA has not undertaken to review all applicable laws and regulations of any jurisdiction in which these Definitions may be used, and therefore parties are advised to consider the application of any relevant jurisdiction's regulatory, tax, accounting, commodity exchange or other requirements that may exist in connection with the entering into and documenting of a commodity derivative transaction.

1993 ISDA COMMODITY DERIVATIVES DEFINITIONS

Any or all of the following definitions and provisions may be incorporated into a document by wording in the document indicating that, or the extent to which, the document is subject to the 1993 ISDA Commodity Derivatives Definitions (as published by the International Swaps and Derivatives Association, Inc.). All definitions and provisions so incorporated in a document will be applicable to that document unless otherwise provided in that document, and all terms defined in these Definitions and used in any definition or provision that is incorporated by reference in a document will have the respective meanings set forth in these Definitions unless otherwise provided in that document. Any term used in a document will, when combined with the name of a party, have meaning in respect of the named party only.

ARTICLE 1

CERTAIN GENERAL DEFINITIONS

Section 1.1. Transaction. "Transaction" means (a) any transaction that is a commodity swap transaction, cross-commodity swap transaction, commodity cap transaction, commodity floor transaction, commodity collar transaction, commodity option transaction or any other similar transaction (including any Option with respect to any of these transactions), (b) any combination of these transactions and (c) any other transaction identified as a Transaction in the related Confirmation.

Section 1.2. Confirmation. "Confirmation" means, with respect to a Transaction, one or more documents or other confirming evidence exchanged between the parties which, taken together, confirm all of the terms of a Transaction.

Section 1.3. Business Day. "Business Day" means a day on which commercial banks and foreign exchange markets settle payments in the local currency in the place(s) specified for that purpose in the relevant Confirmation and, if a place is not so specified, a day on which commercial banks and foreign exchange markets settle payments (a) in U.S. Dollars in New York if the payment obligation is in U.S. Dollars or (b) in Sterling in London if the payment obligation is in Sterling.

Section 1.4. Commodity Business Day. "Commodity Business Day" means (a) in respect of a Transaction for which the Commodity Reference Price is a price announced or published by an Exchange, a day that is (or, but for the occurrence of a Market Disruption Event, would have been) a trading day on that Exchange and (b) in respect of a Transaction for which the Commodity Reference Price is not a price announced or published by an Exchange, a day in respect of which the relevant Price Source published (or, but for the occurrence of a Market Disruption Event, would have published) a price.

Section 1.5. Business Day Convention; Commodity Business Day Convention. (a) "Business Day Convention" means the convention for adjusting any relevant date if it would otherwise fall on a day that is not a Business Day. "Commodity

Business Day Convention'' means the convention for adjusting any relevant date if it would otherwise fall on a day that is not a Commodity Business Day. The following terms, when used in conjunction with the term ''Business Day Convention'' or ''Commodity Business Day Convention'' and a date, will mean that an adjustment will be made if that date would otherwise fall on a day that is not a Business Day or a Commodity Business Day, as the case may be, so that:

(i) if ''Following'' is specified, that date will be the first following day that is a Business Day or a Commodity Business Day, as the case may be;

(ii) if ''Modified Following'' or ''Modified'' is specified, that date will be the first following day that is a Business Day or a Commodity Business Day, as the case may be, unless that day falls in the next calendar month, in which case that date will be the first preceding day that is a Business Day or a Commodity Business Day, as the case may be;

(iii) if ''Nearest'' is specified, that date will be the first preceding day that is a Business Day or a Commodity Business Day, as the case may be, if the relevant date otherwise falls on a day other than a Sunday or a Monday and will be the first following day that is a Business Day or a Commodity Business Day, as the case may be, if the relevant date otherwise falls on a Sunday or a Monday; and

(iv) if ''Preceding'' is specified, that date will be the first preceding day that is a Business Day or a Commodity Business Day, as the case may be.

(b) The Business Day Convention or Commodity Business Day Convention applicable to a date that is specified in these Defintions or in a Confirmation to be subject to adjustment in accordance with an applicable Business Day Convention or Commodity Business Day Convention will be (i) the Business Day Convention or Commodity Business Day Convention, as the case may be, specified for that date in these Definitions or in that Confirmation and (ii) if such a convention is not so specified for that date but is specified for a Transaction, the Business Day Convention or Commodity Business Day Convention, as the case may be, specified in the Confirmation for that Transaction.

Section 1.6. Currencies. (a) **Sterling.** ''Sterling'', ''£'', ''GBP'', ''STG'' and ''pence'' each means the lawful currency of the United Kingdom.

(b) **U.S. Dollar.** ''U.S. Dollar'', ''U.S.$'', ''$'', ''USD'', ''U.S. cent'' and ''cent'' each means the lawful currency of the United States of America.

ARTICLE 2

PARTIES

Section 2.1. Fixed Price Payer. ''Fixed Price Payer'' means, in respect of a Transaction, a party obligated to make payments from time to time in respect of the Transaction of amounts calculated by reference to a fixed price or to make one or more payments of a Fixed Amount.

Section 2.2. Floating Price Payer. ''Floating Price Payer'' means, in respect of a Transaction, a party obligated to make payments from time to time in respect of the Transaction of amounts calculated by reference to a Commodity Reference Price or to make one or more payments of a Floating Amount.

ARTICLE 3

Term and Dates

Section 3.1. Term. "Term" means the period commencing on the Effective Date of a Transaction and ending on the Termination Date of the Transaction.

Section 3.2. Effective Date. "Effective Date" means the date specified as such for a Transaction, which date is the first day of the Term of the Transaction.

Section 3.3. Period End Date. "Period End Date" means, in respect of a Transaction and a party, each day during the Term specified as such or otherwise predetermined in the relevant Confirmation.

Section 3.4. Settlement Date; Payment Date. "Settlement Date" or "Payment Date" means, in respect of a Transaction and a party, each date specified as such or otherwise predetermined in the relevant Confirmation, subject to adjustment in accordance with the Following Business Day Convention unless another Business Day Convention is specified to be applicable to Settlement Dates or Payment Dates in respect of the Transaction or that party.

Section 3.5. Termination Date. "Termination Date" means the date specified as such for a Transaction, which date is the last day of the Term of the Transaction. The Termination Date will not be subject to adjustment in accordance with any Business Day Convention or Commodity Business Day Convention unless the parties specify in a Confirmation that the Termination Date will be adjusted in accordance with a specified Business Day Convention or Commodity Business Day Convention.

Section 3.6. Trade Date. "Trade Date" means, in respect of a Transaction, the date on which the parties enter into the Transaction.

ARTICLE 4

Certain Definitions Relating to Payments

Section 4.1. Fixed Amount. "Fixed Amount" means, in respect of a Transaction and a Fixed Price Payer, an amount that, subject to any applicable condition precedent, is payable by that Fixed Price Payer on an applicable Settlement Date or Payment Date and is specified in a Confirmation or is determined as provided in Article 5 of these Definitions or as provided in a Confirmation.

Section 4.2. Floating Amount. "Floating Amount" means, in respect of a Transaction and a Floating Price Payer, an amount that, subject to any applicable condition precedent, is payable by that Floating Price Payer on an applicable Settlement Date or Payment Date and is determined by reference to a Commodity Reference Price as provided in Article 6 of these Definitions or pursuant to a method specified in a Confirmation.

Section 4.3. Notional Quantity. (a) "Notional Quantity" or "Notional Quantity per Calculation Period" means, in respect of a party, a Transaction or, if applicable, any Calculation Period for a Transaction, the quantity, expressed in Units, specified as such for that party, that Transaction or that Calculation Period.

(b) "Total Notional Quantity" means, in respect of a Transaction or a party, the sum of the Notional Quantities per Calculation Period for all the Calculation Periods in respect of that Transaction or that party.

Section 4.4. Calculation Period. "Calculation Period" means, in respect of a Transaction and a party:

(a) if one or more periods are specified as such in the relevant Confirmation (without reference to Period End Dates), each period from and including the first date specified as being included in that Calculation Period to and including the last date specified as being included in that Calculation Period (without reference to any Effective Date or Termination Date); and

(b) if a Calculation Period is not specified in the relevant Confirmation, but an Effective Date, one or more Period End Dates and a Termination Date are specified, each period determined by reference to those dates as follows:

(i) if "(ERMA)" is specified in the relevant Confirmation, each period from, but excluding, one Period End Date to, and including, the next following applicable Period End Date during the Term of the Transaction, except that (A) the initial Calculation Period will commence on, and include, the Effective Date and (B) the final Calculation Period will end on, and include, the Termination Date; and

(ii) otherwise, each period from, and including, one Period End Date to, but excluding, the next following applicable Period End Date during the Term of the Transaction, except that (A) the initial Calculation Period will commence on, and include, the Effective Date and (B) the final Calculation Period will end on, but exclude, the Termination Date.

Unless otherwise provided for a Transaction or a party, where the Fixed Amount or Floating Amount is calculated by reference to a Calculation Period, the Fixed Amount or Floating Amount applicable to a Settlement Date or Payment Date will be the Fixed Amount or Floating Amount calculated with reference to the Calculation Period ending closest in time to that Settlement Date or Payment Date.

Section 4.5. Calculation Agent. "Calculation Agent" means the party to a Transaction (or a third party) designated as such for the Transaction and responsible for (a) calculating the applicable Floating Price, if any, for each Settlement Date or Payment Date, (b) calculating any Floating Amount or Cash Settlement Amount payable on each Settlement Date or Payment Date, (c) calculating any Fixed Amount payable on each Settlement Date or Payment Date, (d) giving notice to the parties to the Transaction on the Calculation Date for each Settlement Date or Payment Date, specifying (i) the Settlement Date or Payment Date, (ii) the party or parties required to make the payment or payments then due, (iii) the amount or amounts of the payment or payments then due and (iv) reasonable details as to how the amount or amounts were determined, (e) if, after notice is given, there is a change in the number of days in the relevant Calculation Period and the amount or amounts of the payment or payments due for that Settlement Date or Payment Date, promptly giving the parties to the Transaction notice of those changes with reasonable details as to how those changes were determined and (f) determining, as provided in Section 7.4(e), whether a Market Disruption Event exists on any Pricing Date and, if applicable, the price for that Pricing Date pursuant to Section 7.5(c). Whenever the Calculation Agent is required to act, it will do so in good faith, and its determinations and calculations shall be binding in the absence of manifest error. When the Calculation Agent is required to select dealers or a quotation for the purpose of making any calculation or determination, the Calculation Agent will make the selection in good faith after consultation with the other party (or the parties, if the Calculation Agent is a third party), if practicable, for the purpose of obtaining a representative price that will reasonably reflect conditions prevailing at the time in the relevant market.

Section 4.6. Calculation Date. "Calculation Date" means, in respect of any Settlement Date or Payment Date, the earliest day on which it is practicable to provide the notice that the Calculation Agent is required to give for that Settlement Date or Payment Date, and in no event later than the close of business on the Business Day next preceding that Settlement Date or Payment Date (unless that preceding Business Day is a Pricing Date, then in no event later than the latest time that will permit any payment due on that Settlement Date or Payment Date to be made on that Settlement Date or Payment Date).

ARTICLE 5

FIXED AMOUNTS

Section 5.1. Calculation of a Fixed Amount. The Fixed Amount payable by a party on a Settlement Date or Payment Date will be:

(a) if an amount is specified for the Transaction as the Fixed Amount payable by that party for that Settlement Date or Payment Date, such amount; or

(b) if that party is a Fixed Price Payer and an amount is not specified for the Transaction as the Fixed Amount payable by that party for that Settlement Date or Payment Date, an amount calculated on a formula basis for that Settlement Date or Payment Date as follows:

$$\text{Fixed Amount} = \frac{\text{Notional Quantity per}}{\text{Calculation Period}} \times \text{Fixed Price}$$

Section 5.2. Fixed Price. "Fixed Price" means, for purposes of the calculation of a Fixed Amount payable by a party on any Settlement Date or Payment Date, a price, expressed as a price per relevant Unit, equal to the price specified as such for the Transaction or that party.

ARTICLE 6

FLOATING AMOUNTS

Section 6.1. Calculation of a Floating Amount. The Floating Amount payable by a Floating Price Payer on a Settlement Date or Payment Date will be an amount calculated on a formula basis for that Settlement Date or Payment Date as follows:

$$\text{Floating Amount} = \frac{\text{Notional Quantity per}}{\text{Calculation Period}} \times \text{Floating Price}$$

Section 6.2. Certain Definitions Relating to Floating Amounts. For purposes of the calculation of a Floating Amount payable by a party:

(a) "Floating Price" means, in respect of any Settlement Date or Payment Date, a price, expressed as a price per relevant Unit, for the related Calculation Period equal to:

(i) if the Confirmation (or the agreement between the parties governing the Transaction) specifies a cap price or a floor price:

(A) if a cap price is specified, the excess, if any, of a price determined pursuant to subparagraph (ii) below over the cap price so specified; or

(B) if a floor price is specified, the excess, if any, of the floor price so specified over a price determined pursuant to subparagraph (ii) below; and

(ii) in all other cases and for purposes of subparagraphs (A) and (B) above:

(A) if a price is specified for the Transaction or that party to be the Floating Price applicable to the Calculation Period, the Floating Price so specified;

(B) if only one Pricing Date is established for the Transaction or that party during (or in respect of) the Calculation Period or in respect of the Settlement Date or Payment Date, the Relevant Price for that Pricing Date; or

(C) if more than one Pricing Date is established for the Transaction or that party during (or in respect of) the Calculation Period or in respect of the Settlement Date or Payment Date, the unweighted arithmetic mean (or such other method of averaging as is specified) of the Relevant Price for each of those Pricing Dates.

(b) "Pricing Date" means each date specified as such (or determined pursuant to a method specified for such purpose) for the Transaction, which date is a day in respect of which a Relevant Price is to be determined for purposes of determining the Floating Price. Unless otherwise provided, the Pricing Date will be in respect of (i) a European style Option, the Expiration Date, (ii) an American style Option, the Exercise Date and (iii) an Asian style Option, each Commodity Business Day during the Calculation Period.

(c) "Relevant Price" means, for any Pricing Date, the price, expressed as a price per Unit, determined with respect to that day for the specified Commodity Reference Price as provided in Article 7 of these Definitions.

ARTICLE 7

CALCULATION OF PRICES FOR COMMODITY REFERENCE PRICES

Section 7.1. Commodity Reference Prices. Subject to Sections 7.3, 7.4 and 7.5, for purposes of determining a Relevant Price:

(a) **Energy**.

(i) **Diesel Fuel**.

(A) "DIESEL FUEL—NO. 2 BILLINGS—PLATT'S OILGRAM" means that the price for a Pricing Date will be that day's Specified Price per gallon of no. 2 diesel fuel, stated in U.S. Dollars, published under the heading "U.S. Tank Car Truck Transport: PAD 4: Billings: Diesel No. 2 Fuel" in the issue of Platt's Oilgram that reports prices effective on that Pricing Date.

(B) "DIESEL FUEL—NO. 2 SALT LAKE—PLATT'S OILGRAM" means that the price for a Pricing Date will be that day's Specified Price per gallon of no. 2 diesel fuel, stated in U.S. Dollars, published under the heading "U.S. Tank Car Truck Transport: PAD 4: Salt Lake: Diesel No. 2 Fuel" in the issue of Platt's Oilgram that reports prices effective on that Pricing Date.

(ii) **Fuel Oil**.

(A) "FUEL OIL—1 PERCENT NWE (CARGOES CIF)—PLATT'S EUROPEAN" means that the price for a Pricing Date will be that day's Specified

Price per metric ton of fuel oil with a sulphur content of up to one percent, stated in U.S. Dollars, published under the heading "Cargoes CIF NWE Basis ARA: 1 PCT" in the issue of Platt's European that reports prices effective on that Pricing Date.

(B) "FUEL OIL—1 PERCENT NWE (CARGOES FOB)—PLATT'S EUROPEAN" means that the price for a Pricing Date will be that day's Specified Price per metric ton of fuel oil with a sulphur content of up to one percent, stated in U.S. Dollars, published under the heading "Cargoes FOB NWE: 1 PCT" in the issue of Platt's European that reports prices effective on that Pricing Date.

(C) "FUEL OIL—180 CST SINGAPORE (CARGOES)—PLATT'S OILGRAM" means that the price for a Pricing Date will be that day's Specified Price per metric ton of fuel oil with a viscosity of up to 180 centistokes, stated in U.S. Dollars, published under the heading "Spot Price Assessments: Singapore/Japan Cargoes: Singapore: HSFO 180cst" in the issue of Platt's Oilgram that reports prices effective on that Pricing Date.

(D) "FUEL OIL—2.2 PERCENT RESIDUAL (BARGE)—PLATT'S OILGRAM" means that the price for a Pricing Date will be that day's Specified Price per barrel of no. 6 fuel oil with a sulphur content of up to 2.2 percent, stated in U.S. Dollars, published under the heading "Spot Price Assessments: New York/Boston: Barge: No. 62.2%S Max" in the issue of Platt's Oilgram that reports prices effective on that Pricing Date.

(E) "FUEL OIL—2.2 PERCENT RESIDUAL (CARGO)—PLATT'S OILGRAM" means that the price for a Pricing Date will be that day's Specified Price per barrel of no. 6 fuel oil with a sulphur content of up to 2.2 percent, stated in U.S. Dollars, published under the heading "Spot Price Assessments: New York/Boston: Cargo: No. 62.2%S Max" in the issue of Platt's Oilgram that reports prices effective on that Pricing Date.

(F) "FUEL OIL—3.5 PERCENT NWE (CARGOES CIF)—PLATT'S EUROPEAN" means that the price for a Pricing Date will be that day's Specified Price per metric ton of fuel oil with a sulphur content of up to 3.5 percent, stated in U.S. Dollars, published under the heading "Cargoes CIF NWE Basis ARA: 3.5 PCT" in the issue of Platt's European that reports prices effective on that Pricing Date.

(G) "FUEL OIL—3.5 PERCENT ROTTERDAM (BARGES FOB)—PLATT'S EUROPEAN" means that the price for a Pricing Date will be that day's Specified Price per metric ton of fuel oil with a sulphur content of up to 3.5 percent, stated in U.S. Dollars, published under the heading "Barges FOB Rotterdam: 3.5 PCT" in the issue of Platt's European that reports prices effective on that Pricing Date.

(H) "FUEL OIL—380 CST SINGAPORE (CARGOES)—PLATT'S OILGRAM" means that the price for a Pricing Date will be that day's Specified Price per metric ton of fuel oil with a viscosity of up to 380 centistokes, stated in U.S. Dollars, published under the heading "Spot Price Assessments: Singapore/Japan: Cargoes: Singapore: HSFO 380 cst" in the issue of Platt's Oilgram that reports prices effective on that Pricing Date.

(I) "FUEL OIL—380 CST WEST COAST (WATERBORNE)—PLATT'S OILGRAM" means that the price for a Pricing Date will be that day's Specified Price per metric ton of fuel oil with a viscosity of up to 380 centistokes, stated in U.S. Dollars, published under the heading "Spot Price Assessments: West Coast Waterborne: 380cst" in the issue of Platt's Oilgram that reports prices effective on that Pricing Date.

(J) "FUEL OIL—NO. 6 0.7 PERCENT U.S. GULF COAST (WATERBORNE)—PLATT'S OILGRAM" means that the price for a Pricing Date will be that day's Specified Price per barrel of no. 6 fuel oil with a sulphur content of up to 0.7 percent, stated in U.S. Dollars, published under the heading "Spot Price Assessments: U.S. Gulf Coast: Waterborne: No. 6 0.7%S" in the issue of Platt's Oilgram that reports prices effective on that Pricing Date.

(K) "FUEL OIL—NO. 6 3.0 PERCENT NEW YORK/BOSTON (CARGO)—PLATT'S OILGRAM" means that the price for a Pricing Date will be that day's Specified Price per barrel of no. 6 fuel oil with a sulphur content of up to 3.0 percent, stated in U.S. Dollars, published under the heading "Spot Price Assessments: New York/Boston: Cargo: No. 6 3.0%S Max" in the issue of Platt's Oilgram that reports prices effective on that Pricing Date.

(iii) **Gas Oil.**

(A) "GAS OIL—IPE" means that the price for a Pricing Date will be that day's Specified Price per metric ton of gas oil on the IPE of the Futures Contract for the Delivery Date, stated in U.S. Dollars, as made public by the IPE on that Pricing Date.

(B) "GAS OIL—0.2 PERCENT ROTTERDAM (BARGES FOB)—PLATT'S EUROPEAN" means that the price for a Pricing Date will be that day's Specified Price per metric ton of gas oil with a sulphur content of up to 0.2 percent, stated in U.S. Dollars, published under the heading "Barges FOB Rotterdam: Gasoil .2" in the issue of Platt's European that reports prices effective on that Pricing Date.

(C) "GAS OIL—0.5 SINGAPORE—PLATT'S ASIA-PACIFIC" means that the price for a Pricing Date will be that day's Specified Price per barrel of gas oil with a sulphur content of up to 0.5 percent, stated in U.S. Dollars, published under the heading "Singapore: Gasoil Reg 0.5 PCT" in the issue of Platt's Asia-Pacific that reports prices effective on that Pricing Date.

(D) "GAS OIL—1.0 SINGAPORE—PLATT'S ASIA-PACIFIC" means that the price for a Pricing Date will be that day's Specified Price per barrel of gas oil with a sulphur content of up to 1.0 percent, stated in U.S. Dollars, published under the heading "Singapore: Gasoil Reg 1.0 PCT" in the issue of Platt's Asia-Pacific that reports prices effective on that Pricing Date.

(E) "GAS OIL—L.P. SINGAPORE—PLATT'S ASIA-PACIFIC" means that the price for a Pricing Date will be that day's Specified Price per barrel of gas oil with a pour point below six degrees celsius, stated in U.S. Dollars, published under the heading "Singapore: Gasoil L/P 0.5 PCT" in the issue of Platt's Asia-Pacific that reports prices effective on that Pricing Date.

(F) "GAS OIL—0.5 SINGAPORE—PLATT'S EUROPEAN" means that the price for a Pricing Date will be that day's Specified Price per barrel of gas oil with a sulphur content of up to 0.5 percent, stated in U.S. Dollars, published under the heading "Singapore: Gasoil Reg 0.5 pct" in the issue of Platt's European that reports prices effective on that Pricing Date.

(G) "GAS OIL—1.0 SINGAPORE—PLATT'S EUROPEAN" means that the price for a Pricing Date will be that day's Specified Price per barrel of gas oil with a sulphur content of up to 1.0 percent, stated in U.S. Dollars, published under the heading "Singapore: Gasoil Reg 1.0 pct" in the issue of Platt's European that reports prices effective on that Pricing Date.

(H) "GAS OIL—L.P. SINGAPORE—PLATT'S EUROPEAN" means that the price for a Pricing Date will be that day's Specified Price per barrel of gas oil with a pour point below six degrees celsius, stated in U.S. Dollars, published under the heading "Singapore: Gasoil L/P 0.5 pct" in the issue of Platt's European that reports prices effective on that Pricing Date.

(iv) **Gasoline.**

(A) "GASOLINE—GULF COAST—NYMEX" means that the price for a Pricing Date will be that day's Specified Price per gallon of Gulf Coast unleaded gasoline on the NYMEX of the Futures Contract for the Delivery Date, stated in U.S. Dollars, as made public by the NYMEX on that Pricing Date.

(B) "GASOLINE—NEW YORK—NYMEX" means that the price for a Pricing Date will be that day's Specified Price per gallon of New York Harbor unleaded gasoline on the NYMEX of the Futures Contract for the Delivery Date, stated in U.S. Dollars, as made public by the NYMEX on that Pricing Date.

(v) **Heating Oil.**

(A) "HEATING OIL—GULF COAST (PIPELINE)—PLATT'S OILGRAM" means that the price for a Pricing Date will be that day's Specified Price per gallon of Gulf Coast no. 2 heating oil, stated in U.S. Dollars, published under the heading "Spot Price Assessments: U.S. Gulf Coast: Pipeline: No. 2" in the issue of Platt's Oilgram that reports prices effective on that Pricing Date.

(B) "HEATING OIL—NEW YORK—NYMEX" means that the price for a Pricing Date will be that day's Specified Price per gallon of New York Harbor no. 2 heating oil on the NYMEX of the Futures Contract for the Delivery Date, stated in U.S. Dollars, as made public by the NYMEX on that Pricing Date.

(C) "HEATING OIL—NEW YORK (BARGE)—PLATT'S OILGRAM" means that the price for a Pricing Date will be that day's Specified Price per gallon of New York Harbor no. 2 heating oil, stated in U.S. Dollars, published under the heading "Spot Price Assessments: New York/Boston: Barge: No. 2" in the issue of Platt's Oilgram that reports prices effective on that Pricing Date.

(D) "HEATING OIL—NEW YORK (CARGO)—PLATT'S OILGRAM" means that the price for a Pricing Date will be that day's Specified Price per gallon of New York Harbor no. 2 heating oil, stated in U.S. Dollars, published under the heading "Spot Price Assessments: New York/Boston: Cargo: No. 2" in the issue of Platt's Oilgram that reports prices effective on that Pricing Date.

(vi) **Jet Fuel.**

(A) "JET FUEL—ITALY (CARGOES FOB)—PLATT'S EUROPEAN" means that the price for a Pricing Date will be that day's Specified Price per metric ton of jet fuel, stated in U.S. Dollars, published under the heading "Cargoes FOB Med Basis Italy: Jet" in the issue of Platt's European that reports prices effective on that Pricing Date.

(B) "JET FUEL—ITALY (CARGOES FOB)—PLATT'S OILGRAM" means that the price for a Pricing Date will be that day's Specified Price per metric ton of jet fuel, stated in U.S. Dollars, published under the heading "Spot Price Assessments: European Bulk: Cargoes FOB Med Basis Italy: Jet Kerosene" in the issue of Platt's Oilgram that reports prices effective on that Pricing Date.

(C) "JET FUEL—NEW YORK/BOSTON (BARGE)—PLATT'S OILGRAM" means that the price for a Pricing Date will be that day's Specified Price per gallon of jet fuel, stated in U.S. Dollars, published under the heading "Spot Price Assessments: New York/Boston: Barge: Jet Fuel" in the issue of Platt's Oilgram that reports prices effective on that Pricing Date.

(D) "JET FUEL—NWE (CARGOES CIF)—PLATT'S EUROPEAN" means that the price for a Pricing Date will be that day's Specified Price per metric ton of jet fuel, stated in U.S. Dollars, published under the heading "Cargoes CIF NWE Basis ARA: Jet" in the issue of Platt's European that reports prices effective on that Pricing Date.

(E) "JET FUEL—NWE (CARGOES CIF)—PLATT'S OILGRAM" means that the price for a Pricing Date will be that day's Specified Price per metric ton of jet fuel, stated in U.S. Dollars, published under the heading "Spot Price Assessments: European Bulk: Cargoes CIF NWE Basis ARA: Jet Kerosene" in the issue of Platt's Oilgram that reports prices effective on that Pricing Date.

(F) "JET FUEL—ROTTERDAM (BARGES FOB)—PLATT'S OILGRAM" means that the price for a Pricing Date will be that day's Specified Price per metric ton of jet fuel, stated in U.S. Dollars, published under the heading "Spot Price Assessments: European Bulk: Barges FOB Rotterdam: Jet Kerosene" in the issue of Platt's Oilgram that reports prices effective on that Pricing Date.

(G) "JET FUEL—U.S. GULF COAST (PIPELINE)—PLATT'S OILGRAM" means that the price for a Pricing Date will be that day's Specified Price per gallon of jet fuel, stated in U.S. Dollars, published under the heading "Spot Price Assessments: U.S. Gulf Coast: Pipeline: Jet Kerosene" in the issue of Platt's Oilgram that reports prices effective on that Pricing Date.

(H) "JET FUEL—U.S. GULF COAST (WATERBORNE)—PLATT'S OILGRAM" means that the price for a Pricing Date will be that day's Specified Price per gallon of jet fuel, stated in U.S. Dollars, published under the heading "Spot Price Assessments: U.S. Gulf Coast: Waterborne: Jet Kerosene" in the issue of Platt's Oilgram that reports prices effective on that Pricing Date.

(vii) **Kerosene**.

(A) "KEROSENE—SINGAPORE—PLATT'S ASIA-PACIFIC" means that the price for a Pricing Date will be that day's Specified Price per barrel of kerosene, stated in U.S. Dollars, published under the heading "Singapore: Kero" in the issue of Platt's Asia-Pacific that reports prices effective on that Pricing Date.

(B) "KEROSENE—SINGAPORE—PLATT'S EUROPEAN" means that the price for a Pricing Date will be that day's Specified Price per barrel of kerosene, stated in U.S. Dollars, published under the heading "Singapore: Kero" in the issue of Platt's European that reports prices effective on that Pricing Date.

(C) "KEROSENE—SINGAPORE—PLATT'S OILGRAM" means that the price for a Pricing Date will be that day's Specified Price per barrel of kerosene, stated in U.S. Dollars, published under the heading "Spot Price Assessments: Singapore/Japan: Cargoes: Singapore: Kerosene" in the issue of Platt's Oilgram that reports prices effective on that Pricing Date.

(viii) **Natural Gas**.

(A) "NATURAL GAS—INSIDE FERC" means that the price for a Pricing Date will be that day's Specified Price per one million British thermal units of natural gas for delivery on the Delivery Date, stated in U.S. Dollars, published under the heading "Prices of Spot Gas Delivered to Pipelines (per MMBtu dry): Tennessee Gas Pipeline Co.: Louisiana (zone 1): Index" in the issue of Inside FERC that reports prices effective on that Pricing Date.

(B) "NATURAL GAS—NATURAL GAS WEEK" means that the price for a Pricing Date will be that day's Specified Price per one million British thermal units of natural gas for delivery on the Delivery Date, stated in U.S. Dollars, published under the heading "Gas Price Report ($/MMBtu): Louisiana: Gulf Coast, Onshore: Delivered to Pipeline" in the issue of Natural Gas Week that reports prices effective for that Pricing Date.

(C) "NATURAL GAS—NYMEX" means that the price for a Pricing Date will be that day's Specified Price per one million British thermal units of natural gas on the NYMEX of the Futures Contract for the Delivery Date, stated in U.S. Dollars, as made public by the NYMEX on that Pricing Date.

(ix) **Oil—Brent**.

(A) "OIL—BRENT—ARGUS" means that the price for a Pricing Date will be that day's Specified Price per barrel of Brent blend crude oil for delivery on the Delivery Date (at the location and time specified in the relevant Confirmation or otherwise), stated in U.S. Dollars, published under the heading "Key Crude Assessments: Brent" in the issue of Argus that reports prices effective on that Pricing Date.

(B) "OIL—BRENT (DTD)—ARGUS" means that the price for a Pricing Date will be that day's Specified Price per barrel of Brent blend crude oil, stated in U.S. Dollars, published under the heading "Key Crude Assessments: Brent: London 18:30 hrs: DTD" in the issue of Argus that reports prices effective on that Pricing Date.

(C) "OIL—BRENT (DTD)—PLATT'S OILGRAM" means that the price for a Pricing Date will be that day's Specified Price per barrel of Brent blend crude oil, stated in U.S. Dollars, published under the heading "Spot Crude Price Assessments: International: Brent (DTD)" in the issue of Platt's Oilgram that reports prices effective on that Pricing Date.

(D) "OIL—BRENT—IPE" means that the price for a Pricing Date will be that day's Specified Price per barrel of Brent blend crude oil on the IPE of the Futures Contract for the Delivery Date, stated in U.S. Dollars, as made public by the IPE on that Pricing Date.

(E) "OIL—BRENT—PLATT'S OILGRAM" means that the price for a Pricing Date will be that day's Specified Price per barrel of Brent blend crude oil for delivery on the Delivery Date, stated in U.S. Dollars, published under the heading "Spot Crude Price Assessments: International: Brent" in the issue of Platt's Oilgram that reports prices effective on that Pricing Date.

(x) **Oil—Tapis**.

(A) "OIL—TAPIS—APPI" means that the price for a Pricing Date will be that day's Specified Price per barrel of Tapis crude oil, stated in U.S. Dollars, published under the heading "Crude Oils: Code/Crude: 2(B) Tapis" in the issue of APPI that reports prices effective on that Pricing Date.

(B) "OIL—TAPIS—PLATT'S OILGRAM" means that the price for a Pricing Date will be that day's Specified Price per barrel of Tapis crude oil, stated in U.S. Dollars, published under the heading "Spot Crude Price Assessments: Pacific Rim: Tapis" in the issue of Platt's Oilgram that reports prices effective on that Pricing Date.

(xi) **Oil—Dubai**.

(A) "OIL—DUBAI—PLATT'S OILGRAM" means that the price for a Pricing Date will be that day's Specified Price per barrel of Dubai crude oil for delivery on the Delivery Date, stated in U.S. Dollars, published under the heading "Spot Crude Price Assessments: International: Dubai" in the issue of Platt's Oilgram that reports prices effective on that Pricing Date.

(xii) **Oil—WTI**.

(A) "OIL—WTI—ARGUS" means that the price for a Pricing Date will be that day's Specified Price per barrel of West Texas Intermediate light sweet crude oil for delivery on the Delivery Date, stated in U.S. Dollars, published under the heading "Key Crude Assessments: Houston 17:00 hrs: Cash WTI" in the issue of Argus that reports prices effective on that Pricing Date.

(B) "OIL—WTI MIDLAND—PLATT'S OILGRAM" means that the price for a Pricing Date will be that day's Specified Price per barrel of West Texas Intermediate Midland light sweet crude oil, stated in U.S. Dollars, published under the heading "Spot Crude Price Assessments: U.S.: WTI Midland" in the issue of Platt's Oilgram that reports prices effective on that Pricing Date.

(C) "OIL—WTI—NYMEX" means that the price for a Pricing Date will be that day's Specified Price per barrel of West Texas Intermediate light sweet crude oil on the NYMEX of the Futures Contract for the Delivery Date, stated in U.S. Dollars, as made public by the NYMEX on that Pricing Date.

(D) "OIL—WTI—PLATT'S OILGRAM" means that the price for a Pricing Date will be that day's Specified Price per barrel of West Texas Intermediate light sweet crude oil for delivery on the Delivery Date, stated in U.S. Dollars, published under the heading "Spot Crude Price Assessments: U.S.: WTI" in the issue of Platt's Oilgram that reports prices effective on that Pricing Date.

(b) **Metals.**

(i) **Aluminium.**

(A) "ALUMINIUM—LME" means that the price for a Pricing Date will be that day's Specified Price per metric ton of high grade primary aluminium on the LME for delivery on the Delivery Date, stated in U.S. Dollars, as made public by the LME on that Pricing Date.

(B) "ALUMINIUM—METAL BULLETIN" means that the price for a Pricing Date will be that day's Specified Price per metric ton of high grade primary aluminium for delivery on the Delivery Date, stated in U.S. Dollars, published under the heading "Daily metal: Aluminium $ High Grade" in the issue of Metal Bulletin that reports prices effective on that Pricing Date.

(ii) **Copper.**

(A) "COPPER—LME" means that the price for a Pricing Date will be that day's Specified Price per metric ton of grade A copper on the LME for delivery on the Delivery Date, stated in U.S. Dollars, as made public by the LME on that Pricing Date.

(B) "COPPER—METAL BULLETIN" means that the price for a Pricing Date will be that day's Specified Price per metric ton of grade A copper for delivery on the Delivery Date, stated in U.S. Dollars, published under the heading "Daily metal: Copper Grade A" in the issue of Metal Bulletin that reports prices effective on that Pricing Date.

(C) "COPPER—COMEX" means that the price for a Pricing Date will be that day's Specified Price per pound of high grade copper on the COMEX for delivery on the Delivery Date, stated in U.S. cents, as made public by the COMEX on that Pricing Date.

(iii) **Gold.**

(A) "GOLD—BULLION—FINANCIAL TIMES" means that the price for a Pricing Date will be that day's Specified Price per troy ounce of gold, stated in U.S. Dollars, published under the heading "World Commodities Prices: London Bullion Market" in the issue of the Financial Times that reports prices effective on that Pricing Date.

(B) "GOLD—COMEX" means that the price for a Pricing Date will be that day's Specified Price per troy ounce of gold on the COMEX for delivery on the Delivery Date, stated in U.S. Dollars, as made public by the COMEX on that Pricing Date.

(C) "UNALLOCATED GOLD—LOCO LONDON DELIVERY" means that the price for a Pricing Date will be that day's Specified Price per troy ounce of unallocated gold bullion for delivery in London through a member of the LBMA authorized to effect such delivery, stated in U.S. Dollars, as calculated by the LBMA and displayed on page "GOFO" of the Reuters Monitor Money Rates Service on that Pricing Date.

(iv) **Lead**.

(A) "LEAD—LME" means that the price for a Pricing Date will be that day's Specified Price per metric ton of standard lead on the LME for delivery on the Delivery Date, stated in U.S. Dollars, as made public by the LME on that Pricing Date.

(B) "LEAD—METAL BULLETIN" means that the price for a Pricing Date will be that day's Specified Price per metric ton of lead for delivery on the Delivery Date, stated in U.S. Dollars, published under the heading "Daily metal: Lead" in the issue of Metal Bulletin that reports prices effective on that Pricing Date.

(v) **Nickel**.

(A) "NICKEL—LME" means that the price for a Pricing Date will be that day's Specified Price per metric ton of nickel on the LME for delivery on the Delivery Date, stated in U.S. Dollars, as made public by the LME on that Pricing Date.

(B) "NICKEL—METAL BULLETIN" means that the price for a Pricing Date will be that day's Specified Price per metric ton of nickel for delivery on the Delivery Date, stated in U.S. Dollars, published under the heading "Daily metal: Nickel $" in the issue of Metal Bulletin that reports prices effective on that Pricing Date.

(vi) **Platinum**.

(A) "PLATINUM—METAL BULLETIN" means that the price for a Pricing Date will be that day's Specified Price per troy ounce of platinum, stated in U.S. Dollars, published under the heading "Daily metal: Platinum: London" in the issue of Metal Bulletin that reports prices effective on that Pricing Date.

(B) "PLATINUM—NYMEX" means that the price for a Pricing Date will be that day's Specified Price per troy ounce of platinum on the NYMEX of the Futures Contract for the Delivery Date, stated in U.S. Dollars, as made public by the NYMEX on that Pricing Date.

(vii) **Silver**.

(A) "SILVER—COMEX" means that the price for a Pricing Date will be that day's Specified Price per troy ounce of silver on the COMEX for delivery on the Delivery Date, stated in U.S. Dollars, as made public by the COMEX on that Pricing Date.

(B) "SILVER—METAL BULLETIN" means that the price for a Pricing Date will be that day's Specified Price per troy ounce of silver for delivery on the Delivery Date, stated in U.S. Dollars, published under the heading "Daily metal: Silver" in the issue of Metal Bulletin that reports prices effective on that Pricing Date.

(C) "UNALLOCATED SILVER—LOCO LONDON DELIVERY" means that the price for a Pricing Date will be that day's Specified Price per troy ounce of unallocated silver bullion for delivery in London through a member of the LBMA authorized to effect such delivery, stated in U.S. cents, as published under the heading "World Commodities Prices: London Markets" in the issue of the Financial Times that reports prices effective on that Pricing Date.

(viii) **Tin**.

(A) "TIN—LME" means that the price for a Pricing Date will be that day's Specified Price per metric ton of tin on the LME for delivery on the Delivery Date, stated in U.S. Dollars, as made public by the LME on that Pricing Date.

(B) "TIN—METAL BULLETIN" means that the price for a Pricing Date will be that day's Specified Price per metric ton of tin for delivery on the Delivery Date, stated in U.S. Dollars, published under the heading "Daily metal: Tin $" in the issue of Metal Bulletin that reports prices effective on that Pricing Date.

(ix) **Zinc**.

(A) "ZINC—LME" means that the price for a Pricing Date will be that day's Specified Price per metric ton of zinc on the LME for delivery on the Delivery Date, stated in U.S. Dollars, as made public by the LME on that Pricing Date.

(B) "ZINC—METAL BULLETIN" means that the price for a Pricing Date will be that day's Specified Price per metric ton of zinc for delivery on the Delivery Date, stated in U.S. Dollars, published under the heading "Daily metal: Zinc $ Special High Grade" in the issue of Metal Bulletin that reports prices effective on that Pricing Date.

(c) **General**.

(i) "COMMODITY—REFERENCE DEALERS" means that the price for a Pricing Date will be determined on the basis of quotations provided by Reference Dealers on that Pricing Date of that day's Specified Price for a Unit of the relevant Commodity for delivery on the Delivery Date, if applicable. If four quotations are provided as requested, the price for that Pricing Date will be the arithmetic mean of the Specified Prices for that Commodity provided by each Reference Dealer, without regard to the Specified Prices having the highest and lowest values. If exactly three quotations are provided as requested, the price for that Pricing Date will be the Specified Price provided by the relevant Refence Dealer that remains after disregarding the Specified Prices having the highest and lowest values. For this purpose, if more than one quotation has the same highest value or lowest value, then the Specified Price of one of such quotations shall be disregarded. If fewer than three quotations are provided, it will be deemed that the price for that Pricing Date cannot be determined.

(ii) COMMODITY REFERENCE PRICE FRAMEWORK. The parties may specify for any Transaction a Commodity Reference Price that is not set forth above by specifying in the relevant agreement or Confirmation:

(A) if that Commodity Reference Price is a price announced or published by an Exchange, (1) the relevant Commodity (including, if relevant, the type or grade of that Commodity, the location of delivery and any other details), (2) the relevant Unit, (3) the relevant Exchange, (4) the relevant currency in which the Specified Price is expressed and (5) the Specified Price and, if applicable, (6) the Delivery Date, in which case the price for a Pricing Date will be that day's Specified Price per Unit of that Commodity on that Exchange and, if applicable, for delivery on that Delivery Date, stated in that currency, as announced or published by that Exchange on that Pricing Date; and

(B) if that Commodity Reference Price is not a price announced or published by an Exchange, (1) the relevant Commodity (including, if relevant, the type or grade of that Commodity, the location of delivery and any other details), (2) the relevant Unit, (3) the relevant Price Source (and, if applicable, the location in that Price Source of the Specified Price (or the prices from which the Specified Price is calculated)), (4) the relevant currency in which the Specified Price is expressed and (5) the Specified Price and, if applicable, (6) the Delivery Date, in which case the price for a Pricing Date will be that day's Specified Price per Unit of that Commodity and, if applicable, for that Delivery Date, stated in that currency, published (or shown) in the issue of that Price Source that reports prices effective on that Pricing Date.

Section 7.2. Certain Definitions Relating to Commodity Reference Prices.

(a) **Price Sources.**

(i) "APPI" means the Asian Petroleum Price Index, or any successor report, prepared by Sea Pac Services, Ltd. or its successor and reported on the Energy Market Information Service or its successor.

(ii) "Argus" means the Argus Crude Report, or any successor publication, published by Petroleum Argus Ltd. or its successor.

(iii) "Financial Times" means the Financial Times, or any successor publication, published by The Financial Times Ltd. or its successor.

(iv) "Inside FERC" means Inside F.E.R.C.'s Gas Market Report, or any successor publication, published by McGraw-Hill Inc. or its successor.

(v) "Metal Bulletin" means Metal Bulletin, or any successor publication, published by Metal Bulletin Journals Ltd. or its successor.

(vi) "Natural Gas Week" means Natural Gas Week, or any successor publication, published by The Oil Daily Inc. or its successor.

(vii) "Platt's Asia-Pacific" means Platt's Asia-Pacific/Arab Gulf Marketscan, or any successor publication, published by McGraw-Hill Inc. or its successor.

(viii) "Platt's European" means Platt's European Marketscan, or any successor publication, published by McGraw-Hill Inc. or its successor.

(ix) "Platt's Oilgram" means Platt's Oilgram Price Report, or any successor publication, published by McGraw-Hill Inc. or its successor.

(x) "Platt's U.S." means Platt's Oilgram U.S. Marketscan, or any successor publication, published by McGraw-Hill Inc. or its successor.

(xi) "World Crude Report" means the LOR World Crude Report, or any successor report, published by the ICIS-LOR Group Ltd. or its successor.

(b) **Exchanges and Principal Trading Markets.**

(i) "COMEX" means the Commodity Exchange Inc., New York or its successor.

(ii) "IPE" means The International Petroleum Exchange of London Ltd. or its successor.

(iii) "LBMA" means The London Bullion Market Association or its successor.

(iv) "LME" means The London Metal Exchange Limited or its successor.

(v) "NYMEX" means the New York Mercantile Exchange or its successor.

(vi) "SIMEX" means The Singapore International Monetary Exchange, Inc. or its successor.

(c) **General.**

(i) "Commodity" means, in respect of a Transaction, the commodity specified in the relevant Commodity Reference Price or in the relevant Confirmation.

(ii) "Commodity Reference Price" means, in respect of a Transaction, any of the commodity reference prices specified in Section 7.1(a) or (b) or determined pursuant to Section 7.1(c)(i) or (c)(ii).

(iii) "Delivery Date" means, in respect of a Transaction and a Commodity Reference Price, the relevant date or month for delivery of the underlying Commodity (which must be a date or month reported or capable of being determined from information reported in or by the relevant Price Source) as follows:

(A) if a date is or a month and year are specified in the relevant Confirmation, that date or that month and year;

(B) if a Nearby Month is specified in the relevant Confirmation, the month of expiration of the relevant Futures Contract; and

(C) if a method is specified for the purpose of determining the Delivery Date, the date or the month and year determined pursuant to that method.

(iv) "Exchange" means, in respect of a Transaction, the exchange or principal trading market specified in the relevant Confirmation or Commodity Reference Price.

(v) "Futures Contract" means, in respect of a Commodity Reference Price, the contract for future delivery in respect of the relevant Delivery Date relating to the Commodity referred to in that Commodity Reference Price.

(vi) "Nearby Month", when preceded by a numerical adjective, means, in respect of a Delivery Date and a Pricing Date, the month of expiration of the Futures Contract identified by that numerical adjective, so that: (A) "First Nearby Month" means the month of expiration of the first Futures Contract to expire following that Pricing Date; (B) "Second Nearby Month" means the month of expiration of the second Futures Contract to expire following that Pricing Date; and, for example, (C) "Sixth Nearby Month" means the month of expiration of the sixth Futures Contract to expire following that Pricing Date.

(vii) "Price Source" means, in respect of a Transaction, the publication (or such other origin of reference, including an Exchange) containing (or reporting) the Specified Price (or prices from which the Specified Price is calculated) specified in the relevant Commodity Reference Price or in the relevant Confirmation.

(viii) "Reference Dealers" means, with respect to any Transaction for which the relevant Commodity Reference Price is "COMMODITY—REFERENCE DEALERS", the four dealers specified in the relevant agreement or the Confirmation or, if dealers are not so specified, four leading dealers in the relevant market selected by the Calculation Agent.

(ix) "Specified Price" means, in respect of a Transaction and a Commodity Reference Price, any of the following prices (which must be a price reported or capable of being determined from information reported in or by the relevant Price Source), as specified in the relevant Confirmation (and, if applicable, as of the time so specified): (A) the high price, (B) the low price, (C) the average of the high price and the low price, (D) the closing price, (E) the opening price, (F) the bid price, (G) the asked price, (H) the average of the bid price and the asked price, (I) the settlement price, (J) the morning fixing, (K) the afternoon fixing or (L) any other price specified in the relevant Confirmation.

(x) "Unit" means, in respect of a Transaction, the unit of measure of the relevant Commodity, as specified in the relevant Commodity Reference Price or Confirmation.

Section 7.3. Corrections to Published Prices. For purposes of determining the Relevant Price for any day, if the price published or announced on a given day and used or to be used by the Calculation Agent to determine a Relevant Price is subsequently corrected and the correction is published or announced by the person responsible for that publication or announcement within 30 calendar days of the original publication or announcement, either party may notify the other party of (i) that correction and (ii) the amount (if any) that is payable as a result of that correction. If, not later than 30 calendar days after publication or announcement of that correction, a party gives notice that an amount is so payable, the party that originally either received or retained such amount will, not later than 3 Business Days after the effectiveness of that notice, pay, subject to any applicable conditions precedent, to the other party that amount, together with interest on that amount (at a rate per annum that the Calculation Agent determines to be the spot offered rate for deposits in the payment currency in the London interbank market as at approximately 11:00 a.m., London time, on the relevant Payment Date or Settlement Date) for the period from and including the day on which a payment originally was (or was not) made to but excluding the day of payment of the refund or payment resulting from that correction.

Section 7.4. Market Disruption Events; Additional Market Disruption Events. (a) "Market Disruption Event" or "Additional Market Disruption Event" means an event that, if applicable to a Transaction, would give rise in accordance with an applicable Disruption Fallback to an alternative basis for determining the Relevant Price in respect of a specified Commodity Reference Price or the termination of the Transaction were the event to occur or exist on a day that is a Pricing Date for that Transaction (or, if different, the day on which prices for that Pricing Date would, in the ordinary course, be published or announced by the Price Source).

(b) A Market Disruption Event or an Additional Market Disruption Event is applicable to a Transaction if it is specified in the relevant agreement or Confirmation or if, pursuant to Section 7.4(d), it is deemed to have been specified for that Transaction.

(c) For purposes of specifying that it is applicable to a transaction (by using it in conjunction with the term "Market Disruption Event" or "Additional Market Disruption Event") and for purposes of Section 7.4(d), each of the following is a Market Disruption Event or Additional Market Disruption Event, as the case may be, with a meaning as follows:

(i) "Price Source Disruption" means (A) the failure of the Price Source to announce or publish the Specified Price (or the information necessary for determining the Specified Price) for the relevant Commodity Reference Price, (B) the temporary or permanent discontinuance or unavailability of the Price Source or (C) if the Commodity Reference Price is COMMODITY—REFERENCE DEALERS, the failure to obtain at least three quotations as requested from the relevant Reference Dealers.

(ii) "Trading Suspension" means the material suspension of trading in the Futures Contract or the Commodity on the Exchange or in any additional futures contract, options contract or commodity on any exchange or principal trading market as specified in the relevant agreement or Confirmation.

(iii) "Disappearance of Commodity Reference Price" means (A) the failure of trading to commence, or the permanent discontinuation of trading, in the relevant Futures Contract on the relevant Exchange or (B) the disappearance of, or of trading in, the relevant Commodity.

(iv) "Material Change in Formula" means the occurrence since the Trade Date of the transaction of a material change in the formula for or the method of calculating the relevant Commodity Reference Price.

(v) "Material Change in Content" means the occurrence since the Trade Date of the Transaction of a material change in the content, composition or constitution of the Commodity or relevant Futures Contract.

(vi) "*De Minimis* Trading" means that the number of contracts traded on the relevant Exchange on the day that would otherwise be a Pricing Day is fewer than the Minimum Futures Contracts.

(vii) "Tax Disruption" means the imposition of, change in or removal of an excise, severance, sales, use, value-added, transfer, stamp, documentary, recording or similar tax on, or measured by reference to, the relevant Commodity (other than a tax on, or measured by reference to, overall gross or net income) by any government or taxation authority after the Trade Date, if the direct effect of such imposition, change or removal is to raise or lower the Relevant Price on the day that would otherwise be a Pricing Date from what it would have been without that imposition, change or removal.

(viii) "Trading Limitation" means the material limitation imposed on trading in the Futures Contract or the Commodity on the Exchange or in any additional futures contract, options contract or commodity on any exchange or principal trading market as specified in the relevant agreement or Confirmation.

The parties may specify in the relevant agreement or Confirmation other Market Disruption Events or Additional Market Disruption Events that they agree will apply to a Transaction. Such an event should only be characterized as an Additional Market Disruption Event if it is intended that it will apply to the Transaction in addition to the events deemed to have been specified pursuant to Section 7.4(d)(i). The term "Inapplicable" when specified in conjunction with the term "Market Disruption Event" means that the calculation of a Relevant Price will not be adjusted as a result of any Market Disruption Event (in which case there would also be no cause to specify any Additional Market Disruption Event).

(d) Unless the parties provide in the relevant agreement or Confirmation that the calculation of a Relevant Price will not be adjusted as a result of any Market Disruption Event,

(i) if the parties do not specify any Market Disruption Event in the relevant agreement or Confirmation, the following Market Disruption Events will be deemed to have been specified for a Transaction: (A) "Price Source Disruption", (B) "Trading Suspension", (C) "Disappearance of Commodity Reference Price", (D) "Material Change in Formula" and (E) "Material Change in Content";

(ii) if one or more Market Disruption Events are specified in the relevant agreement or Confirmation, then only the Market Disruption Events specified will apply to the Transaction; and

(iii) if one or more Additional Market Disruption Events are specified in the relevant agreement or Confirmation, then each such Additional Market Disruption Event, together with the Market Disruption Events deemed to have been specified pursuant to Section 7.4(d)(i), will apply to the Transaction.

(e) if the Calculation Agent, after consultation with the parties or the other party, determines in good faith that a Market Disruption Event or an Additional Market Disruption Event applicable to a Transaction has occurred or exists in respect of that

Transaction on a day that is a Pricing Date for that Transaction (or, if different, the day on which prices for that Pricing Date would, in the ordinary course, be published or announced by the Price Source), the Relevant Price for that Pricing Date will be determined in accordance with the first applicable Disruption Fallback (applied in accordance with its terms) that provides the parties with a Relevant Price or, if there is no such Relevant Price, provides for the termination of the Transaction.

Section 7.5. Disruption Fallbacks. (a) "Disruption Fallback" means a source or method that, if applicable to a Transaction, may give rise to an alternative basis for determining the Relevant Price in respect of a specified Commodity Reference Price or the termination of the Transaction when a Market Disruption Event or an Additional Market Disruption Event occurs or exists on a day that is a Pricing Date for that Transaction (or, if different, the day on which prices for that Pricing Date would, in the ordinary course, be published or announced by the Price Source).

(b) A Disruption Fallback is applicable to a Transaction if it is specified in the relevant agreement or Confirmation or if, pursuant to Section 7.5(d), it is deemed to have been specified for that Transaction.

(c) For purposes of specifying that it is applicable to a Transaction (by using it in conjunction with the term "Disruption Fallback") and for purposes of Section 7.5(d), each of the following is a Disruption Fallback with a meaning as follows:

(i) "Fallback Reference Price" means that the Calculation Agent will determine the Relevant Price based on the price for that Pricing Date of the first alternate Commodity Reference Price, if any, specified in the relevant agreement or Confirmation and not subject to a Market Disruption Event or an Additional Market Disruption Event.

(ii) "Negotiated Fallback" means that each party to a Transaction will, promptly upon becoming aware of the Market Disruption Event or Additional Market Disruption Event, negotiate in good faith to agree with the other on a Relevant Price (or a method for determining a Relevant Price), and, if the parties have not so agreed on or before the fifth Business Day following the first Pricing Date on which that Market Disruption Event or Additional Market Disruption Event occurred or existed, the next applicable Disruption Fallback shall apply to the Transaction.

(iii) "No Fault Termination" means that the Transaction will be terminated in accordance with any applicable provisions set forth in the relevant agreement or Confirmation as if a "Termination Event" and an "Early Termination Date" (each as defined in the relevant agreement or Confirmation) had occurred on the day No Fault Termination became the applicable Disruption Fallback and there were two "Affected Parties" (as defined in the relevant agreement or Confirmation).

(iv) "Postponement" means that the Pricing Date will be deemed to be the first succeeding Commodity Business Day on which the Market Disruption Event or Additional Market Disruption Event ceases to exist, unless that Market Disruption Event or Additional Market Disruption Event continues to exist (measured from and including the original day that would otherwise have been the Pricing Date) for consecutive Commodity Business Days equal in number to the Maximum Days of Disruption. In that case, (A) the last such consecutive Commodity Business Day will be the Pricing Date and (B) the next Disruption Fallback specified in the relevant agreement or Confirmation will apply to the Transaction. If, as a result of a postponement pursuant to this provision, a Relevant Price is unavailable to determine the Floating Price for a Floating Amount payable on any Settlement Date or Payment Date, that Settlement Date or Payment Date will be postponed to the same extent as the Pricing Date and, if a corresponding Fixed Amount or Floating Amount would otherwise have been payable in respect of the same Transaction on the same date that the postponed Floating Amount would have been payable but for the postponement, the Settlement Date or Payment Date for that corresponding Fixed Amount or Floating Amount will be postponed to the same extent.

(v) "Calculation Agent Determination" means that the Calculation Agent will determine the Relevant Price (or a method for determining a Relevant Price), taking into consideration the latest available quotation for the relevant Commodity Reference Price and any other information that in good faith it deems relevant.

(vi) "Average Daily Price Disruption" means that the price for the Pricing Date will not be included in the calculation of the Floating Amount, but if a Market Disruption Event or an Additional Market Disruption Event occurs or exists on more than the Maximum Days of Disruption during the relevant Calculation Period, then, for each Pricing Date during that Calculation Period on which a Market Disruption Event or an Additional Market Disruption Event occurred or existed, a price will be determined using the first alternate Commodity Reference Price, if any, specified in the relevant agreement or Confirmation.

The parties may specify in the relevant agreement or Confirmation other Disruption Fallbacks that they agree will apply to a Transaction.

(d) Unless the parties otherwise provide in the relevant agreement or Confirmation,

(i) if the parties do not specify any Disruption Fallback in the relevant agreement or Confirmation, the following Disruption Fallbacks will be deemed to have been specified (in the following order) for a Transaction: (A) "Fallback Reference Price" (if the parties have specified an alternate Commodity Reference Price), (B) "Negotiated Fallback" and (C) "No Fault Termination"; and

(ii) if one or more Disruption Fallbacks are specified in the relevant agreement or Confirmation, then only the Disruption Fallbacks specified will apply to the Transaction (in the order so specified).

(e) If a Market Disruption Event or an Additional Market Disruption Event occurs or exists on a day that would otherwise be a Pricing Date for the Transaction (or, if different, the day on which prices for that Pricing Date would, in the ordinary course, be published or announced by the Price Source) and none of the applicable Disruption Fallbacks provides the parties with a Relevant Price, the Transaction will terminate in accordance with "No Fault Termination".

Section 7.6. Certain Definitions Relating to Market Disruption Events and Additional Market Disruption Events. (a) "Maximum Days of Disruption" means, in respect of a Transaction, the number of Commodity Business Days specified as such in the relevant agreeement or Confirmation.

(b) "Minimum Futures Contracts" means, in respect of a Transaction, the number of futures contracts specified as such in the relevant agreement or Confirmation.

ARTICLE 8

Commodity Options

Section 8.1. Option. (a) "Option" means any Transaction that is identified in the related Confirmation as an Option and provides for the grant by Seller to Buyer of (i) the right to cause Seller to pay Buyer the Cash Settlement Amount, if any, in respect of that Transaction on a Settlement Date, (ii) a Swaption or (iii) any other right or rights specified in the related Confirmation. An Option may provide for the grant of one or more of the foregoing rights, all of which can be identified in a single Confirmation.

(b) "Swaption" means the right to cause (i) an Underlying Transaction to become effective or (ii) Seller to pay Buyer the Cash Settlement Amount, if any, in respect of an Underlying Transaction on the Settlement Date.

Section 8.2. Parties. (a) "Buyer" means, in respect of an Option, the party specified as such in the related Confirmation.

(b) "Seller" means, in respect of an Option, the party specified as seller or as writer in the related Confirmation.

Section 8.3. Certain Definitions and Provisions Relating to Options. When used in respect of an Option, the following terms have the indicated meanings:

(a) "American" means a style of Option pursuant to which the right or rights granted are exercisable during an Exercise Period that consists of more than one day.

(b) "Asian" means a style of Option pursuant to which the right or rights granted are exercisable only on the Expiration Date (unless otherwise specified) and the Floating Price for which is the unweighted arithmetic mean (or such other method of averaging as is specified) of the Relevant Price for each Pricing Date during the Calculation Period.

(c) "Call" means an Option entitling, but not obligating, Buyer to receive upon exercise the Cash Settlement Amount if the Floating Price exceeds the Strike Price.

(d) If "Cash Settlement" is specified to be applicable to the Option, it means that Seller grants to Buyer pursuant to that Option the right to cause Seller to pay Buyer the Cash Settlement Amount, if any, in respect of the Transaction (or, if that Option is a Swaption, the Underlying Transaction) on the Settlement Date.

(e) "Cash Settlement Amount" means, in respect of an Option to which Cash Settlement is specified to be applicable, an amount, if any, that, subject to any applicable condition precedent, is payable by Seller on the applicable Settlement Date and is determined as provided in Section 8.7 of these Definitions or by a method specified in or pursuant to the relevant agreement or Confirmation governing such Option.

(f) "European" means a style of Option pursuant to which the right or rights granted are exercisable only on the Expiration Date.

(g) "Put" means an Option entitling, but not obligating, Buyer to receive upon exercise the Cash Settlement Amount if the Strike Price exceeds the Floating Price.

(h) "Strike Price" or "Strike Price Per Unit" means the amount specified as such in a Confirmation.

Section 8.4. Certain Definitions and Provisions Relating to Swaptions. When used in respect of a Swaption, the following terms have the indicated meanings:

(a) If "Cash Settlement" is specified to be applicable to the Swaption, it means that Seller grants to Buyer pursuant to the Swaption the right to cause Seller to pay Buyer the Cash Settlement Amount, if any, in respect of the Underlying Transaction on the Settlement Date.

(b) If "Physical Settlement" or "Contract Settlement" is specified to be applicable to the Swaption, it means that Seller grants to Buyer pursuant to the Swaption the right to cause the Underlying Transaction to become effective.

(c) "Underlying Transaction" means a Transaction, the terms of which are identified in the Confirmation of the Swaption, which Underlying Transaction will not become effective unless (i) "Physical Settlement" or "Contract Settlement" is specified to be applicable to the Swaption and (ii) the right to cause that Underlying Transaction to become effective has been exercised.

Section 8.5. Terms Relating to Exercise. (a) "Exercise Period" means (i) in respect of a European or (unless otherwise specified) an Asian style Option, the one day period consisting of the Expiration Date and (ii) in respect of any other Option, each of the periods specified in or pursuant to the related Confirmation.

(b) "Exercise Date" means, in respect of an Option, the Seller Business Day during the Exercise Period on which that Option is or is deemed to be exercised.

(c) "Notice of Exercise" means, in respect of an Option, irrevocable notice given by Buyer to Seller (which may be given orally (including by telephone) unless the parties specify otherwise in the related Confirmation) of its exercise of the right or rights granted pursuant to the Option during the hours specified in the relevant Confirmation on a Seller Business Day during the Exercise Period. If the Notice of Exercise is received on any Seller Business Day after the latest time so specified, the Notice of Exercise will be deemed to have been received on the next following Seller Business Day, if any, in the Exercise Period. Buyer may exercise the right or rights granted pursuant to the Option only by giving a Notice of Exercise unless Automatic Exercise is specified to apply and the Option is deemed exercised.

(d) If "Written Confirmation" is specified to be applicable to the Option or if demanded by Seller (which demand, notwithstanding any provisions regarding notice applicable to the Option, may be given orally (including by telephone)), Buyer will (i) execute a written confirmation (including by facsimile transmission) confirming the substance of the Notice of Exercise and deliver the same to Seller or (ii) issue a telex to Seller setting forth the substance of the Notice of Exercise. Buyer will cause such executed written confirmation or telex to be received by Seller within one Seller Business Day following the date that the Notice of Exercise or Seller's demand, as the case may be, becomes effective.

(e) "Automatic Exercise" means, in respect of an Option to which Automatic Exercise is applicable, that, if at the close of the Exercise Period the Option has not been exercised, the Option will be deemed exercised as of that time. Unless the parties specify otherwise, Automatic Exercise will be deemed to apply to any Option (other than a Swaption to cause an Underlying Transaction to become effective).

(f) Any notice or communication given, and permitted to be given, orally (including by telephone) in connection with an Option will be effective when actually received by the recipient.

(g) "Expiration Date" means, in respect of an Option, the date specified as such in a Confirmation (or, if no such date is specified, the last day of the Exercise Period) or, if that date is not a Commodity Business Day, the first following day that is a Commodity Business Day.

(h) "Seller Business Day" means any day on which commercial banks are open for business (including dealings in foreign exchange and foreign currency deposits) in the city in which Seller is located for purposes of receiving notices.

Section 8.6. Terms Relating to Premium. (a) "Total Premium" means, in respect of an Option, an amount, if any, that is specified as such in or pursuant to the related Confirmation and, subject to any applicable condition precedent, is payable by Buyer on the Premium Payment Date or Dates.

(b) "Premium Per Unit" means, in respect of an Option, the amount specified as such in or pursuant to the related Confirmation, which, when multiplied by the relevant Notional Quantity, will be equal to the Total Premium.

(c) "Premium Payment Date" means, in respect of an Option, each date specified as such in or pursuant to the related Confirmation, subject to adjustment in accordance with the Following Business Day Convention or, if another Business Day Convention is specified to be applicable to the Premium Payment Date, that Business Day Convention.

Section 8.7. Calculation of a Cash Settlement Amount. Unless the parties otherwise specify, the Cash Settlement Amount in respect of an Option payable by a party on a Settlement Date will be:

(a) in respect of an Option other than a Swaption, an amount, if any, calculated on a formula basis for that Settlement Date as follows:

$$\text{Cash Settlement Amount} = \text{Notional Quantity} \times \text{Strike Price Differential}$$

(b) in respect of a Swaption, an amount in respect of the Underlying Transaction, if any, determined by a method specified in or pursuant to the relevant agreement or Confirmation.

Section 8.8. Strike Price Differential. "Strike Price Differential" means, in respect of an Option to which Cash Settlement is specified to be applicable, a price, expressed as a price per Unit, equal to (i) if the Transaction is a Put Option, the excess, if a positive number, of (A) the Strike Price over (B) the Floating Price and (ii) if the Transaction is a Call Option, the excess, if a positive number, of (A) the Floating Price over (B) the Strike Price.

ARTICLE 9

ROUNDING

Section 9. Rounding. For purposes of any calculations referred to in these Definitions (unless otherwise specified), (a) unless "Rounding of Payments Only" is specified (i) all percentages used in or resulting from such calculations will be rounded, if necessary, to the nearest one ten-thousandth of a percentage point (with five one-hundred thousandths of a percentage point being rounded up), (ii) all U.S. Dollar amounts resulting from such calculations will be rounded to the nearest cent (with one half cent being rounded up) and (iii) all Sterling amounts resulting from such calculations will be rounded to the nearest pence (with one half pence being rounded up) and (b) if "Rounding of Payments Only" is specified, only Fixed Amounts, Floating Amounts and Cash Settlement Amounts will be rounded, so that (i) all such amounts stated in U.S. Dollars will be rounded to the nearest cent (with one half cent being rounded up) and (ii) all such amounts stated in Sterling will be rounded to the nearest pence (with one half pence being rounded up).

EXHIBIT I
to 1993 ISDA Commodity Derivatives Definitions

Introduction, Standard Paragraphs and Closing for a Letter Agreement or Telex Confirming a Transaction

---

Heading for Letter[1]

[Letterhead of Party A]

[Date]

Commodity [Swap] [Option] [Cap/Collar/Floor] [Swaption]—Cash-Settled

[Name and Address of Party B]

Heading for Telex[1]

Date:

To: [Name and Telex Number of Party B]

From: [Party A]

Re: Commodity [Swap] [Option] [Cap/Collar/Floor] [Swaption]—Cash-Settled

---

Dear :

The purpose of this [letter agreement/telex] is to confirm the terms and conditions of the Transaction entered into between us on the Trade Date specified below (the "Transaction"). This [letter agreement/telex] constitutes a "Confirmation" as referred to in the ISDA Master Agreement specified below.

The definitions and provisions contained in the 1993 ISDA Commodity Derivatives Definitions[2] (as published by the International Swaps and Derivatives Association, Inc.) are incorporated into this Confirmation. In the event of any inconsistency between those definitions and provisions and this Confirmation, this Confirmation will govern.

1. This Confirmation supplements, forms part of, and is subject to, the ISDA Master Agreement dated as of [date], as amended and supplemented from time to time (the "Agreement"), between you and us. All provisions contained in the Agreement govern this Confirmation except as expressly modified below.

[INSERT RELEVANT ADDITIONAL PROVISIONS FROM EXHIBITS II-A THROUGH II-D.]

3. Calculation Agent[3]:

4. Account Details:

Payments to party A:

Account for payments:

---

[1] Delete as applicable.

[2] If the Transaction contemplates only one party paying a price based on a Commodity Reference Price and the other party paying a price based on another floating price or rate, such as LIBOR, the parties may also wish to incorporate the 1991 ISDA Definitions and specify the priorities in the event of any inconsistency between the definitions.

[3] If the Calculation Agent is a third party, the parties will want to consider any documentation necessary to confirm its undertaking.

Payments to Party B:

Account for payments:

[5. Offices:

(a) The Office of Party A for the Transaction is ; and

(b) The Office of Party B for the Transaction is .]

[6. Broker/Arranger:]

Closing for Letter[4]

Please confirm that the foregoing correctly sets forth the terms of our agreement by executing the copy of this Confirmation enclosed for that purpose and returning it to us or by sending to us a letter or telex substantially similar to this letter, which letter or telex sets forth the material terms of the Transaction to which this Confirmation relates and indicates agreement to those terms.

Yours sincerely,

[PARTY A]

By: ______________________

Name:
Title:

Confirmed as of the date
first above written:

[PARTY B]

By: ______________________

Name:
Title:

Closing for Telex[4]

Please confirm that the foregoing correctly sets forth the terms of our agreement by sending to us a letter or telex substantially similar to this telex, which letter or telex sets forth the material terms of the Transaction to which this Confirmation relates and indicates agreement to those terms, or by sending to us a return telex substantially to the following effect:

"Re:

We acknowledge receipt of your telex dated [ ] with respect to the above-referenced Transaction between [Party A] and [Party B] with [an Effective] [a Trade] Date of [ ] and [a Termination] [an Expiration] Date of [ ] and confirm that such telex correctly sets forth the terms of our agreement relating to the Transaction described therein. Very truly yours, [Party B], by [specify name and title of authorized officer]."

Yours sincerely,

[PARTY A]

By: ______________________

Name:
Title:

---

[4] Delete as applicable.

Exhibit II-A
to 1993 ISDA Commodity Derivatives Definitions

Additional Provisions for a Confirmation of a Commodity Swap

[See Exhibit I for the introduction, standard paragraphs and closing for the letter agreement or telex.]

2. The terms of the particular Transaction to which this Confirmation relates are as follows:

Notional Quantity per Calculation Period:[1]	[Specify quantity in relevant units of commodity (*e.g.*, barrels)] (Total Notional Quantity:)
Commodity:	
Trade Date:	
Effective Date:	
Termination Date:	
Calculation Period(s):	
[Period End Date(s):]	
[Settlement] [Payment] Dates:[2]	[, subject to adjustment in accordance with the [Following/Modified Following/Nearest/Preceding] Business Day Convention]
Fixed Amount Details:	
Fixed Price Payer:	[Party A/B]
Fixed Amount [or Fixed Price]:	
Floating Amount Details:	
Floating Price Payer:	[Party B/A]
Commodity Reference Price:[3]	
[Commodity: Unit: Price Source/Reference Dealers: Currency:][4]	

[1] The parties may specify a different Notional Quantity for each party. In addition, the parties may specify a different Notional Quantity (or a formula for determining that Notional Quantity) for each Calculation Period.

[2] If it is contemplated that the Settlement or Payment Dates for the Fixed Price Payer and the Floating Price Payer will not match, include such dates for the parties in the Fixed Amount Details and the Floating Amount Details.

[3] The parties may either (i) specify one of the Commodity Reference Prices defined in the 1993 ISDA Commodity Derivatives Definitions or (ii) create a Commodity Reference Price by specifying a Commodity, a Unit, a Price Source and a currency.

[4] Delete if a Commodity Reference Price (other than COMMODITY—REFERENCE DEALERS) is specified above.

Specified Price:	[Specify whether the price will be the bid price, the asked price, the average of the high and low prices, the morning fixing, etc.; if appropriate, indicate the time as of which the price is to be determined]
[Delivery Date:]	[Specify whether the price will be based on the spot market, the First Nearby Month, the Second Nearby Month, etc.]
Pricing Date(s):[5]	[, subject to adjustment in accordance with the [Following/Modified Following/Nearest/Preceding] Commodity Business Day Convention]
[Method of Averaging:]	
[Market Disruption:]	
[Market Disruption Event(s):]	
[Additional Market Disruption Event(s):][6]	
[Disruption Fallback(s):]	
[Fallback Reference Price:][7]	
[Rounding:]	[Rounding of Payments Only]

[5] The parties must specify the date or dates, or the means for determining the date or dates, on which a price will be obtained for purposes of calculating the Floating Amount, *e.g.*, each Commodity Business Day during the Calculation Period or the last three Commodity Business Days in each Calculation Period.

[6] The parties should specify Market Disruption Events if they wish to modify, or Additional Market Disruption Events if they wish to add to, the Market Disruption Events set forth in Section 7.4(d)(i) of the 1993 ISDA Commodity Derivatives Definitions.

[7] The parties should specify an alternate Commodity Reference Price if they are relying on the Disruption Fallbacks set forth in Section 7.5(d)(i) of the 1993 Commodity Derivatives Definitions or if they have otherwise specified "Fallback Reference Price" as applicable.

Exhibit II-B
to 1993 ISDA Commodity Derivatives Definitions

Additional Provisions for a Confirmation of a Commodity Option

[See Exhibit I for the introduction, standard paragraphs and closing for the letter agreement or telex.]

2. The terms of the Transaction to which this Confirmation relates are as follows:

General Terms:	
Notional Quantity:	[Specify quantity in relevant units of commodity (*e.g.*, barrels)]
Commodity:	
Trade Date:	
Option Style:	[American] [European] [Asian][1]
Option Type:	[Put] [Call]
Seller:	[Party A/B]
Buyer:	[Party B/A]
Commodity Reference Price:[2]	
[Commodity: Unit: Price Source/Reference Dealers: Currency:][3]	
Specified Price:	[Specify whether the price will be the bid price, the asked price, the average of the high and low prices, the morning fixing, etc.; if appropriate, indicate the time as of which the price is to be determined]
[Delivery Date:]	[Specify whether the price will be based on the spot market, the First Nearby Month, the Second Nearby Month, etc.]
[Pricing Date(s):][4]	
[Method of Averaging:]	
Strike Price per Unit:	
Total Premium:	(Premium Per Unit:)

[1] If an Asian style option, the parties should specify the Calculation Period or, if more than one Settlement Date, Calculation Periods.

[2] The parties may either (i) specify one of the Commodity Reference Prices defined in the 1993 ISDA Commodity Derivatives Definitions or (ii) create a Commodity Reference Price by specifying a Commodity, a Unit, a Price Source and a currency.

[3] Delete if a Commodity Reference Price (other than COMMODITY—REFERENCE DEALERS) is specified above.

[4] The parties must specify the date or dates, or the means for determining the date or dates (including any applicable Commodity Business Day Convention), on which a price will be obtained for purposes of calculating the Floating Price and determining the Cash Settlement Amount only if they wish to modify the presumptions set forth in the Pricing Date definition.

Premium Payment Date(s):	[, subject to adjustment in accordance with the [Following/Modified Following/Nearest/Preceding] Business Day Convention]
Procedure for Exercise:	
Exercise Period:	[From and including to and including][5] between a.m. and p.m. (local time in).[6]
[Expiration Date:][7]	
Automatic Exercise:	[Applicable/Inapplicable]
[Written Confirmation:]	[Applicable/Inapplicable]
Seller's telephone, telex or facsimile number for purpose of giving notice:	
[Market Disruption:]	
[Market Disruption Event(s):] [Additional Market Disruption Event(s):][8]	
[Disruption Fallback(s):]	
[Fallback Reference Price:][9]	
Cash Settlement Terms:[10]	
Cash Settlement:	Applicable
Settlement Date(s):	[ ] Business Days following the last Pricing Date
[Rounding:]	[Rounding of Payments Only]

[5] Include if American style option.

[6] Specify city in which Seller is located for purposes of receiving notices.

[7] Include if option is exercisable only on the Expiration Date.

[8] The parties should specify Market Disruption Events if they wish to modify, or Additional Market Disruption Events if they wish to add to, the Market Disruption Events set forth in Section 7.4(d)(i) of the 1993 ISDA Commodity Derivatives Definitions.

[9] The parties should specify an alternate Commodity Reference Price if they are relying on the Disruption Fallbacks set forth in Section 7.5(d)(i) of the 1993 ISDA Commodity Derivatives Definitions or if they have otherwise specified "Fallback Reference Price" as applicable.

[10] If a currency conversion is contemplated, parties may wish to provide for how, when and by whom the relevant exchange rate is to be determined.

Exhibit II-C
to 1993 ISDA Commodity Derivatives Definitions

Additional Provisions for a Confirmation of a Commodity Cap, Collar or Floor

[See Exhibit I for the introduction, standard paragraphs and closing for the letter agreement or telex.]

2. The terms of the particular Transaction to which this Confirmation relates are as follows:

Notional Quantity per Calculation Period:[1]	[Specify quantity in relevant units of commodity (*e.g.*, barrels)] (Total Notional Quantity:)
Commodity:	
Trade Date:	
Effective Date:	
Termination Date:	
Calculation Period(s):	
[Period End Date(s):]	
Fixed Amount Details:[2]	
Fixed Price Payer:	[Party A/B]
Fixed Price Payer [Settlement] [Payment] Date(s):	[, subject to adjustment in accordance with the [Following/Modified Following/Nearest/Preceding] Business Day Convention]
Fixed Amount [or Fixed Price]:	
Floating Amount Details:	
Floating Price Payer:	[Party B/A]
[Cap/Floor] Price:	
Floating Price Payer [Settlement] [Payment] Dates:	[, subject to adjustment in accordance with the [Following/Modified Following/Nearest/Preceding] Business Day Convention]
Commodity Reference Price:[3]	
[Commodity:	
Unit:	

[1] The parties may specify a different Notional Quantity for each party. In addition, the parties may specify a different Notional Quantity (or a formula for determining that Notional Quantity) for each Calculation Period.

[2] For a collar transaction there would be no Fixed Amount Details. Instead, one party would pay a Floating Amount based on a cap price and the other party would pay a Floating Amount based on a floor price. Separate Floating Amount Details would need to be included for each party.

[3] The parties may either (i) specify one of the Commodity Reference Prices defined in the 1993 ISDA Commodity Derivatives Definitions or (ii) create a Commodity Reference Price by specifying a Commodity, a Unit, a Price Source and a currency.

Price Source/Reference Dealers:	
Currency:][4]	
Specified Price:	[Specify whether the price will be the bid price, the asked price, the average of the high and low prices, the morning fixing, etc.; if appropriate, indicate the time as of which the price is to be determined]
[Delivery Date:]	[Specify whether the price will be based on the spot market, the First Nearby Month, the Second Nearby Month, etc.]
Pricing Date(s):[5]	[, subject to adjustment in accordance with the [Following/Modified Following/Nearest/Preceding] Commodity Business Day Convention]
[Method of Averaging:]	
[Market Disruption:]	
[Market Disruption Event(s):]	
[Additional Market Disruption Event(s):][6]	
[Disruption Fallback(s):]	
[Fallback Reference Price:][7]	
[Rounding:]	[Rounding of Payments Only]

---

[4] Delete if a Commodity Reference Price (other than COMMODITY—REFERENCE DEALERS) is specified above.

[5] The parties must specify the date or dates, or the means for determining the date or dates, on which a price will be obtained for purposes of calculating the Floating Amount, *e.g.*, each Commodity Business Day during the Calculation Period or the last three Commodity Business Days in each Calculation Period.

[6] The parties should specify Market Disruption Events if they wish to modify, or Additional Market Disruption Events if they wish to add to, the Market Disruption Events set forth in Section 7.4(d)(i) of the 1993 ISDA Commodity Derivatives Definitions.

[7] The parties should specify an alternate Commodity Reference Price if they are relying on the Disruption Fallbacks set forth in Section 7.5(d)(i) of the 1993 ISDA Commodity Derivatives Definitions or if they have otherwise specified "Fallback Reference Price" as applicable.

Exhibit II-D
to 1993 ISDA Commodity Derivatives Definitions

Additional Provisions for a Confirmation of a Commodity Swaption

[See Exhibit I for the introduction, standard paragraphs and closing for the letter agreement or telex.]

2. (a) The particular Transaction to which this Confirmation relates is an Option, the terms of which are as follows:

Trade Date:	
Option Style:	[European/American]
Option Type:	Swaption
Seller:	[Party A/B]
Buyer:	[Party B/A]
Total Premium	
Premium Payment Date(s):	[, subject to adjustment in accordance with the [Following/Modified Following/Nearest/Preceding] Business Day Convention]
[Physical/Contract Settlement:]	[Applicable/Inapplicable]
[Cash Settlement Terms:]	
[Cash Settlement:]	[Applicable/Inapplicable]
[Settlement Date:]	[Business Days following the Exercise Date]
[Cash Settlement Amount:]	[Specify means for determination]
Procedure for Exercise:	
Exercise Period:	[From and including to and including][1] between a.m. and p.m. (local time in).[2]
[Expiration Date:][3]	
Automatic Exercise:	[Applicable/Inapplicable]
[Written Confirmation:]	[Applicable/Inapplicable]
Seller's telephone, telex or facsimile number for purposes of giving notice:	

(b) The terms of the Underlying Transaction to which the Option relates are as follows:

---

[1] Include if American style option.

[2] Specify city in which Seller is located for purposes of receiving notices.

[3] Include if option is exercisable only on the Expiration Date.

Notional Quantity per Calculation Period:[4]	[Specify quantity in relevant units of commodity (*e.g.*, barrels)] (Total Notional Quantity:)
Commodity:	
Effective Date:	
Termination Date:	
Calculation Period(s):	
[Period End Date(s):]	
[Settlement] [Payment] Date(s):[5]	[, subject to adjustment in accordance with the [Following/Modified Following/Nearest/Preceding] Business Day Convention]
Fixed Amount Details:	
Fixed Price Payer:	[Party A/B]
Fixed Amount [or Fixed Price]:	
Floating Amount Details:	
Floating Price Payer:	[Party B/A]
Commodity Reference Price:[6]	
[Commodity: Unit: Price Source/Reference Dealers: Currency:][7]	
Specified Price:	[Specify whether the price will be the bid price, the asked price, the average of the high and low prices, the morning fixing, etc.; if appropriate, indicate the time as of which the price is to be determined]
[Delivery Date:]	[Specify whether the price will be based on the spot market, the First Nearby Month, the Second Nearby Month, etc.]
Pricing Date(s):[8]	[, subject to adjustment in accordance with the [Following/Modified Following/Nearest/Preceding] Commodity Business Day Convention]

---

[4] The parties may specify a different Notional Quantity for each party. In addition, the parties may specify a different Notional Quantity (or a formula for determining that Notional Quantity) for each Calculation Period.

[5] If it is contemplated that the Settlement or Payment Dates for the Fixed Price Payer and the Floating Price Payer will not match, include such dates for the parties in the Fixed Amount Details and the Floating Amount Details.

[6] The parties may either (i) specify one of the Commodity Reference Prices defined in the 1993 ISDA Commodity Derivatives Definitions or (ii) create a Commodity Reference Price by specifying a Commodity, a Unit, a Price Source and a currency.

[7] Delete if a Commodity Reference Price (other than COMMODITY—REFERENCE DEALERS) is specified above.

[8] The parties must specify the date or dates, or the means for determining the date or dates, on which a price will be obtained for purposes of calculating the Floating Amount, *e.g.*, each Commodity Business Day during the Calculation Period or the last three Commodity Business Days in each Calculation Period.

[Method of Averaging:]	
[Market Disruption:]	
[Market Disruption Event(s):]	
[Additional Market Disruption Event(s):][9]	
[Disruption Fallback(s):]	
[Fallback Reference Price:][10]	
[Rounding:]	[Rounding of Payments Only]

[9] The parties should specify Market Disruption Events if they wish to modify, or Additional Market Disruption Events if they wish to add to, the Market Disruption Events set forth in Section 7.4(d)(i) of the 1993 ISDA Commodity Derivatives Definitions.

[10] The parties should specify an alternate Commodity Reference Price if they are relying on the Disruption Fallbacks set forth in Section 7.5(d)(i) of the 1993 ISDA Commodity Derivatives Definitions or if they have otherwise specified "Fallback Reference Price" as applicable.

INDEX OF TERMS

Part 11

Future Prospects for the Global Swaps and Financial Derivatives Market

Chapter 45

The Market for Swaps and Financial Derivatives—Future Developments

INTRODUCTION

The swap and derivative market in its modern configuration has existed since the early 1980s. During this period, the market has been characterised by dramatic growth. This growth reflects a variety of factors:

- the capacity of swaps and derivatives to be utilised in a variety of roles;
- broad cross-section of end users who can and have utilised these products;
- the capacity of swaps and derivatives to encompass structural variations which have spawned a variety of related instruments further extending their applicability; and
- the adaptation of basic swap and derivative concepts to other financial markets (for example, commodities and equities) which has created a variety of related financial instruments further extending the range of potential users and applications.

The growth in the market has a fundamental economic basis. Swaps and related derivative products have acted as instruments facilitating market integration linking various national and international money, foreign exchange, commodity and equity markets. The growth of these instruments has not coincidentally parallelled a period of profound change in financial markets in general. A major characteristic of this change has been deregulation of many national markets and the gradual internationalisation of individual domestic markets and currencies. In addition, swap and financial derivative instruments have allowed the economics of comparative advantage to be extended from commodity and service markets to the capital markets. This fundamental economic basis of the swap market necessarily means that its potential for future development and growth is sound.

The fact that the swap and derivative market has been able to resolve a variety of issues which had the potential to impede its development, as well as the fact that it has withstood a number of external and internal crises or potential crises, provides further assurance of its continued potential for growth.

Over the last three to five years, the market for swaps and derivative instruments has, to varying degrees, shown itself capable of dealing with a number of factors that had the potential to impede its development including:

- regulations;
- liquidity;
- accounting and tax treatment of swap and derivative instruments;
- back office procedures and systems for recording swap transactions.

The swap and derivative market has been able to resolve both internal and external regulatory pressures. Internal pressures for the need for standardisation of conventions in relation to documentation, quoting of swaps, yield mathematics valuation techniques and trading conventions have been recognised. The necessary standardisation has, to a substantial degree, been achieved.

The emergence of bodies, most notably the International Swap and Derivatives Association (ISDA) (formerly the International Swap Dealers' Association) and parallel bodies in a variety of jurisdictions have assisted significantly in achieving the necessary standardisation of practices necessary to create a truly global, integrated swap and derivatives market.

External regulatory pressure has been exerted for the most part by bank regulators concerned at the risk aspects of swap and derivative instruments. The principal focus of bank regulators, at least to date, has been the credit risk inccurred by financial institutions in transacting swap and derivative business. However, more recently, an increased focus on market risk aspects of these operations has also emerged.

The swap and derivative market has shown itself to be capable of coping with regulatory pressures of this type. The BIS capital adequacy directives have been in operation for some time and the market has adapted, relatively rapidly and successfully, to these requirements. It seems likely that the market will also be capable of adapting to any market risk regulations introduced by regulators.

Liquidity is essential to the development of any market in traded financial instruments. The swap and derivatives market is no exception. A number of fundamental problems relating to enhancing liquidity in the swap and derivatives markets have been addressed. These include standardisation of documents and conventions in relation to most swap and derivative products. The achievements of ISDA, in this context, in developing the ISDA standard documentation for swap and, increasingly, all derivative products has been one of the principal factors in assisting in improving liquidity.

The other major factor in improving trading liquidity remains credit risk. The term nature of swap and derivative obligations dictates that availability of credit limits between major participants in the swap market restricts the growth of a truly liquid secondary market. As discussed in Chapters 37 and 38, the development of swap clearing houses, netting arrangements between financial institutions, as well as developments in swap assignment technology remain essential to the further development of a secondary market in such products. However, liquidity has undoubtedly improved over the last five years and the development of the secondary market remains important as it is the key to improving potential applications of swaps as a generalised financial management instrument.

Problems arising from different and often inconsistent accounting and tax treatments of swap and derivative transactions in different jurisdictions continues to be a problem, albeit a lessor one than previously, for the growth of the market. The fact that these transactions must usually be accommodated within existing accounting and tax frameworks often resulting in anomalous balance sheet, earnings or expense treatment is increasingly being recognised by fiscal authorities in a variety of jurisdictions. While a relatively uniform system of global accounting and tax treatment for these types of transaction remains unlikely to be achieved in the foreseeable future, a greater degree of consistency will emerge.

Increasingly, individual fiscal authorities are seeking to define *specific* accounting and tax frameworks consistent *with the economic basis of such transactions.* However, this process remains painfully slow and subject to often complex negotiations between market participants and fiscal authorities. However, the progress to date is encouraging. Certainly, the absence of defined frameworks for accounting or the taxation treatment of such transactions no longer represents a barrier to participants seeking to transact in such instruments.

The systems, procedural and control aspects of swap and derivative instruments, at least initially, lagged significantly behind the development of such products. However, increased management concern regarding profitability and risk of such operations and the demand for improved management information and reporting has provided a catalyst for improvements in these areas. Sophisticated "off-the-shelf" systems for recording and managing portfolios of transactions and swaps and derivative product are now available. These products complement inhouse software developments directed at the same objective. Allied to the significant advances in computing technology and power and the improvements in the cost of such technology, the front and back office systems for trading and managing portfolios of such products has improved immeasurably.

However, despite these significant advances in systems technology, the problems of reconciliation of the underlying economics of transactions with its accounting and tax treatment continues. In particular, disagreements about the actual earnings of a particular transaction are evident as no one answer is particularly meaningful and the adoption of complex portfolio risk management systems has greatly complicated the process of performance measurement and attribution.

The maturity of the swap market is demonstrable by the fact that it has withstood a number of "shocks", which have been both market and externally imposed.

The swap and derivatives market has withstood the potentially significant market disruptions of the October 1987 crash and the mini crash of October 1988. The market has also continued to operate in periods of significant disruption such as the collapse of the stock market in Japan in the early 1990s and the collapse of the European Rate Mechanism in 1992/93.

The market has also withstood the potential disruptions from the celebrated collapses of a number of major swap dealers and the general credit problems of the banking systems.

External regulatory action, most notably the introduction of the BIS capital adequacy directives, have been absorbed by the market. The capacity of the market to adapt to these regulatory moves is an impressive indicia of its maturity and its evolution into the mainstream of capital market activity.

The capacity of the swap and derivatives market to function and continue to adapt is an important aspect of the market's development.

FUTURE DEVELOPMENTS[1]

Swap/derivative products—life cycles

The evolution of the swap market can be separated into three fairly distinct phases:

- *Phase 1*—(the period to 1982/83)—the new product phase;
- *Phase 2*—(the period between 1983 and 1988/89) the period of growth;
- *Phase 3*—(the period from 1989 to the present) period of maturity.

1. The text draws on Ronald E Reading, "Opportunities and Challenges for the Derivatives Market", a presentation to conference "Financial Risk Measurement and Management of Derivatives" (IIR Limited) London, 28 and 29 April 1992.

The evolution of the swap and derivative market has been considered in detail in Chapter 1.

In terms of its product life cycle, it is arguable that swaps and derivative products are still in the early/middle stages of their product life cycle.

Exhibit 45.1 sets out product life cycle stage of individual swap/derivative product categories.

Exhibit 45.1
Swap/Derivatives Individual Product Life Cycle

Type of Risk Management Product	**Stage of Life Cycle**
Interest Rate Swaps/FRAs Caps and Floors	Mature
Currency Swaps/LTFX	Mature
Swap/Option Hybrids	Growth
Commodity Risk Products (eg Commodity Swaps)	Introduction
Equity Risk Products (eg Equity Swaps)	Introduction
Other Risks: —Credit —Non-Financial	Conceptual

As is evident, while the overall swap/derivative products may be in the middle stages of their life cycle, there are significant differences as between individual products.

Traditional swap instruments, such as interest rates swaps, FRAs, caps and floors, currency and interest rate swaps and LTFX are relatively mature products. Options on swaps and swap/option hybrids, in contrast, are in the early stages of growth. Commodity and equity risk management products, such as commodity and equity swaps are also in a relatively early stage of their individual product life cycles. Risk management products for other credit or non-financial risks are still only at the conceptual stage of product development.

Analysis of swap and derivative products in terms of product life cycle evolution indicates potential for significant growth. The key factors underlying this potential for growth includes:

- The process of decomposition of a variety of financial risks and the attendant processes of analysis and management of these risks is still evolving.
- The fact that risk decomposition approaches are still not completely developed suggests that product innovation is likely to continue in response to improved risk analysis and management requirements.
- New users and new applications for *existing* products continue to be developed. In addition, applications for products that are increasingly capable of being developed are also relatively unexploited.

Corporate interest rate and currency risk management principles are now generally well understood and accepted. However, the processes of identification, analysis and management of a variety of other risks are relatively undeveloped. These include management of a variety of risks:

- interest rate and currency volatility risk;
- debt prepayment/funding risk;
- basis risks;
- economic risks;
- commodity and equity price risks.

Each of these categories of risk encompasses a variety of other more specific types of risk the understanding and analysis of which are still in their infancy.

Market research indicates that end user applications of swaps and derivative products are also still developing. For example, while traditional risk management instruments such as interest rate and currency swaps, FRAs and LTFX are accepted, the use of more complex variations on these products is still relatively low. In addition, the acceptance and understanding of the applications of commodity and equity related products is still low.

A further area of opportunity continues to be that the use of swaps and derivative products by asset managers remains low, although increasing.

Against the background of this market environment, there are a number of key areas of development in the market for swaps and derivative instruments. These include: new product innovations; likely development of new applications and user groups; the interaction of OTC and ET product markets; and general developments affecting the market.

Product developments

Direction of development

Product development and innovation has been the cornerstone of the swap and derivative markets. It is probable that the process of creation of new financial derivatives, in response to market opportunities and client requirements, will continue. However, it is difficult to predict, with any degree of certainty, the direction of these developments.

It is probable that product development will focus on two distinct types of activities:

- the development of "new" products; and
- extension of existing product structures to new asset classes.

New product

The creation of new products, that is, pure product development, is likely to focus on:

- the development of new generations of options products. The development of so-called "exotic options" (such as the products already developed including average rate, look-back, barrier, chooser, quanto and digital options) promises to continue.
- additional cross-market and hybrid products, such as index differential swaps and the spread warrant structure identified, are likely to proliferate. In addition, complex combinations of products with currency, interest rates, equities and commodity elements being combined are also probable.

- development of correlation-based products, for example, the index differential and other quanto structures as well as spread products, are likely to increase in availability reflecting the requirement of investors and liability managers to structure complex hedges based on covariance/correlation relationships between various financial market variables.

New asset classes

The development of new products, in terms of new instruments, will be complemented by extension of existing and developing instruments to *new asset classes*. The development in this area is likely to be at least as important as the development of new products.

Currently, financial derivatives exist in relation to the following asset classes:

- interest rates;
- currencies;
- commodities;
- equities.

There is scope for further penetration and extension of existing instruments within the existing asset classes, such as the new currency markets, such as those in Asia, Eastern Europe, South America and Africa. Similarly, there is scope to extend the availability of financial derivatives into commodities and equity indexes and individual stocks in which they are currently not available.

New asset classes to which financial derivative instruments are likely to be extended in the near future include:

- macroeconomic variables;
- property/real estate indexes;
- credit;
- insurance;
- taxation.

The extension of financial derivatives to new asset classes requires the existence of certain conditions in each market sector including:

- the presence of offsetting counterparties;
- the transparency of pricing of the relevant asset;
- the availability of (universal) market driven price indexes;
- the availability of hedging instruments, being the physical asset itself or futures or synthetic products on the physical asset, which facilitate hedging and market making in these products.

The development of macro-economic derivatives is already evident. As discussed in Chapter 16, the emerging market for inflation derivatives represents the first tentative signs of an evolving market in transactions involving this asset class. The increased interest in macroeconomic hedging as corporations and investors extend their hedging activities to cover fundamental economic exposures is likely to create opportunities for further development of these types of derivatives.

Similarly, a tentative market in property/real estate indexed derivatives is emerging. Conceptually identical to commodity swaps, a number of this type of transaction have already been completed—see discussion in Chapter 16. The use of property derivatives to alter asset allocation within portfolios, hedge existing exposures or arbitrage (through selection of properties to outperform the index) is likely to become increasingly available.

Other potential classes to which derivative concepts can be extended are at the early stages of development.

Credit derivatives

The market for credit derivatives is seen as particularly promising. This reflects the fact that the level of credit risk within the global capital markets is substantial.

The basic underlying concept of credit derivatives is the design of instruments designed to:

- hedge loan values;
- hedge against deterioration of credit quality generally;
- arbitrage risk-reward relationships, effectively trading off loan margins or spreads against the risk of default.

A key factor underlying potential growth of credit derivatives is the United States Accounting Standards FASB107 under which United States banks are to be required to mark loan portfolios to market.

While the market is still at a development stage, from a theoretical perspective, it is possible to identify two potential structures for credit derivatives:

- indirect hedges; and
- direct hedges.

Indirect hedges for credit quality risk and therefore credit derivative structures can be based on the correlation between loan defaults or deterioration/improvement in credit quality and other financial market variables, such as interest rates, currencies, commodity prices etc. For example, if high (low) interest rates are strongly correlated with declining (improving) credit quality, then it would be feasible to create credit derivatives based on this underlying relationship. For example, short and long positions in interest rate assets could be established to create the desired exposure to credit quality changes.

Alternative types of indirect hedges could be based on:

- equity market indexes and their correlation to loan quality;
- spreads between securities of different credit quality.

The concept of using equity market indexes and their correlation to loan quality underlie a number of hedging practices that were developed, originally, to immunise portfolios against the risk of fluctuations in the value of high yield securities in the late 1980s. This was based on the fact that such (often) deeply subordinated and high-risk securities exhibited characteristics closer to equity and were strongly correlated to broad equity market index movements.

Hedges based on spreads between traded securities of different credit quality—effectively, taking offsetting short and long positions in securities having identical characteristics other than issuer quality—also offer opportunities for structuring credit derivative positions.

Complementary to these indirect approaches to creating credit derivatives which entail difficulties in regard to stability of relationships between credit quality and the relevant index is a total class of direct credit derivatives. These entail transactions on specific loan assets either on a bilateral or a multi-lateral basis, through the mechanism of a secondary market in loan assets.

At the extreme, the market for Latin American debt derivatives is, substantively, a market in credit quality with prices reflecting changed perceptions of credit quality as well as more fundamental economic factors such as currency and interest rate values.

The further development of direct credit derivatives would be enhanced by the development of credit value indexes. These could take the form of:

- secondary market loan asset trading; or
- a total credit quality index.

Tentative attempts to create a secondary market loan asset trading index are already evident. Citibank has developed a corporate loan index which covers 1,000 loans to 600 publicly listed and rated United States companies. The total value of loans covered by the index is US$400bn. Intended for use by banks as a framework for asset allocation, a performance measurement tool, or to allow price comparisons, the index has potential as the basis for credit derivative transactions where one component of the derivative is changes in the value of this index.

Similarly, development of broader-based indexes, ideally by major global rating agencies, based on movement in the universe of rated borrowers (increases in ratings or decreases in ratings), may also provide impetus in the creation of true index-linked credit derivatives.

The existence of these indexes would logically encourage the creation of futures markets in these indexes facilitating the creation of a liquid market in such asset classes as well as a transparent and true market set price. The emergence of futures and related derivative instruments on such indexes would, in turn, facilitate the further development of the OTC credit derivative markets with traders and market makers utilising the futures market as a means for hedging temporary risk positions as well as arbitraging between their own portfolios and the traded futures markets.

Insurance derivatives

The emergence of insurance derivatives is predicated on different concepts. It is based on asset liability management problems in:

- protecting asset yields;
- creating inflation-indexed products;
- liability hedging vehicles for underwriters to manage loss ratios in general insurance.

The first two potential applications are similar to normal asset and liability applications of swaps and other derivatives (for example, see the discussion in Chapters 20 and 21 regarding asset management utilising derivatives and the coverage of utilising inflation linked derivatives to create inflation index products in Chapter 16).

There is, as discussed below, considerable potential for development of the market for derivatives amongst asset managers who continue to be relatively modest users of such instruments.

A more specialised use of derivatives in the context of insurance is the use of traditional instruments to hedge insurance company capital reserves. The use of derivatives, in this context, reflects the need for insurance companies to manage their balance sheet risk to hedge capital reserves as well as reduce asset liability mismatches.

A purer case of insurance derivatives relates to those instruments designed as liability hedging vehicles for underwriters. The major example of this type of instrument is the catastrophe risk insurance futures contract introduced by the Chicago Board of Trade in December 1992. The Chicago contracts are designed to track quarterly insured losses resulting from national and regional catastrophes and are based on a loss index provided by the Insurance Services Office (ISO). Quarterly loss figures are fed to the ISO by at least ten insurers and include losses caused by wind, hail, earthquake, riot and flood.

The CBOT's futures prices based on the quarterly data provided by the ISO in relation to the same quarter's estimated annual insurance premium is known as the loss ratio. The premium amount derived from the reporting company's annual statements is also provided by the ISO and remains constant during the life of the futures contract. The loss and premium figures used to calculate the loss ratio are lagging indicators as the ISO considers losses reported to the insurers as of the end of the quarter following the catastrophe quarter.

There is interest in establishing a European contract on a similar basis. A working party has been established jointly by LIFFE and insurance brokers to design a suitable index roughly equivalent to that provided by the ISO in the US.

Based on the catastrophe risk insurance futures contracts, a variety of OTC insurance derivative products are slowly emerging.

Tax derivatives

The concept of tax derivatives is perhaps more closely related to the original concept of swap transactions. Tax derivatives entail financial exchanges designed to create value by reallocating tax benefits between counterparties to equalise after tax returns. Such derivatives are often not true derivatives but pure exchange transactions which work on multiple levels.

The first type of tax derivative is effectively the maximisation of hedging efficiency on an after-tax basis *utilising existing derivatives*. For example, the use of equity derivatives, where there are differential tax rules dictating different treatments of various components of equity income across jurisdictions, to arbitrage tax regimes is designed to increase the efficiency of asset allocation on an after-tax basis. This type of structure allows the optimisation of after-tax returns on each class of assets based on jurisdiction and the taxation treatment of different streams of income in those jurisdictions.

The second type of tax derivative involves exchange of tax benefits between counterparties. This would be designed to:

- exchange or reallocate tax benefits or credits, for example, pollution credits, foreign tax credits, etc;
- hedge tax change risks between counterparties willing to take positions regarding the value of benefits or tax costs through such exchange transactions.

The potential new asset classes for financial derivatives are, unlike the existing asset classes, diverse. This diversity brings with it an added level of complexity. The markets for these new asset class derivatives are still in the very early stages of development. In part, development of these markets is dependent on development of new applications and user groups for financial derivatives generally.

Development of new applications and user groups

A key factor in the growth and evolution of the market for swap and derivative instruments has been the broad nature of the underlying user base and the wide range of applications of swap and derivative products. The increased penetration of existing user groups as well as the development of new user groups and the creation of new potential applications of existing and newly created products remains central to the future of the market.

The further and continued development of existing users of derivatives is reliant on a combination of improved understanding of financial risk as it impacts on asset and liability managers, the development of new and improved products or variations on products to better enable these managers to hedge identified risks and more focused and penetrative marketing efforts by financial institutions.

While knowledge and understanding, albeit at different levels, of swap and derivative instruments is high, there continues to be scope to develop the market. For example, as noted elsewhere, a number of groups continue to be relatively modest users of derivative products, in some cases for historical and regulatory reasons.

Groups which continue to be targeted as potentially more substantial users of derivative products include asset managers as well as liability managers in specific locations, such as Europe and Japan.

A key user group that is increasingly targeted as a potential substantial participant in the global derivatives market are:

- the less developed and emerging economies; and
- the retail markets in developed economies.

The increased participation of the International Finance Corporation (and development agencies generally) as credit-enhancing intermediaries to transactions involving less developed and emerging economies is increasingly opening up derivative markets for these users.

The expansion of global derivative markets to retail participants provides the opportunity for a potential incremental increase in the size of the market. Involvement of the retail sector is being sought at two levels:

- through derivative funds and specially created derivative investment products sold through investment management groups and private banks;
- through the creation of derivative-based retail banking products.

The first category of innovation involves, for example, creation of investment instruments which are capital guaranteed but where the return is linked to the performance of several equity indexes. These may be packaged and sold as a low denomination security such as a certificate of deposit or as an investment account. Such developments are increasingly evident in the major reserve currencies.

The alternative structure involves normal deposits and loan products with derivative elements. Examples of these types of structures include:

- deposits with a floor interest rate level whereby the deposit interest rate will fluctuate in accordance with a nominated market index but will never be lower than the stated floor level;
- deposit accounts with tiered interest rates utilising the value evident in an upward sloping yield curve through higher forward rates;
- floating rate mortgage and personal finance loan transactions with an embedded cap, which may, in some instances, be purchased separately, to ensure that the interest rate on the loan does not exceed the specified maximum level;
- mortgage and personal financed loans where the interest rate is "collared" with an effective embedded cap and floor level; and

- facilities to lock in floating mortgage interest rates, effectively forward interest rate agreements or interest rate swaps, with a capacity—in return for an unwind fee (the termination value)—to revert to a floating rate basis.

The development of retail demand for derivative products is driven, simultaneously, by client demand for more flexible personal finance products as well as intense competition between providers of retail financial services.

The effort to increase the user groups generally are increasingly allied to efforts to shift the focus of marketing derivative products away from product-specific issues to application-based approaches.

The predominant approaches to providing derivative solutions to client's requirements are predicated on:

- an increasingly integrated approach to financial risk management;
- the integration of derivative/risk management technology with corporate finance applications.

In the shift from a product to an application-based marketing approach, providers of derivative instruments are increasingly emphasising the role of these instruments as a means for managing financial risk within corporations and investment organisations.

This entails the development of integrated risk management approaches designed to determine the appropriate risk profile of individual entities. The derivative instrument solution is then tailored to align its risk profile to these risk management objectives.

The second approach is merely a further extension of this shift from a product to an application-based marketing focus. A number of major providers of derivative products have strengthened the relationship between derivative/risk management product units and corporate finance operations. Organisations such as Bankers Trust and CSFP are increasingly emphasising the linkage between corporate finance and derivative operations.

For example, in relation to equity derivatives, the linkage is designed to create new applications for equity instruments related to corporate equity funding practices. This would include capital raising through quasi-equity structures, repurchase of outstanding stock or stock protection transactions as well as corporate restructuring applications including mergers and hostile takeovers.

Additional linkages arise from incorporating interest rate, currency or commodity elements with financing transactions in the form of structured loans designed to combine a capital raising with an integrated risk management solution.

The realignment of marketing approach and focus is still evolving as the rearrangement organisational responsibilities and structures within major derivative providers are implemented.

Relationship between over-the-counter and exchange traded instruments

As identified, the over-the-counter financial derivative market *complements* the exchange traded derivative markets at various levels. This linkage relates to the fact that market makers in OTC products typically rely on the availability of ET markets to create temporary or more permanent hedges to the risk positions assumed in concluding transactions with end users. As also noted, increasingly the credit issues confronting the OTC market has made the ET market more directly competitive with the exchanges seeking to attract new users of futures and options contracts *as a substitute* for OTC products.

The competitive positioning of the OTC and ET participants has occasionally spilled over into acrimonious debate such as those regarding the exclusion of swaps and other OTC financial derivates from the CFTC rules in the United States (refer Chapter 23).

However, it is probable that the complementary, albeit competitive, relationship between the two markets will continue.

The interrelationship at the level of risk transfer whereby traders and market makers in OTC markets rely on the liquidity of the ET markets to construct hedges for client-driven transactions is likely to continue and expand. Credit considerations may allow exchanges to attract increasing participation from corporations and investment managers to futures and options markets, particularly where futures/options products are particularly innovative and the user is sophisticated. However, demand from clients for customised solutions to risk management problems will ensure a substantial role of OTC products.

The symbiotic relationship between the two competing institutional structures will be most evident in product development. The development of new futures and options contracts, particularly on macroeconomic variables, property/real estate index, credit quality indexes and insurance contracts, is vital as a means for allowing liquid markets in these types of derivatives to be developed for end users.

General development

Credit risk issues

Markets for swap and derivative instruments evolved without specific focus on the capital requirements or the counterparty credit limit needs for these instruments. However, in recent years, the continued development of this market has been in a market environment where financial institutions' capital and counterparty credit capacity are increasingly viewed as expensive and scarce resources.

The BIS capital adequacy directives, the depletion of bank capital and its increasing cost have forced financial institutions increasingly to identify the capital committed in these businesses to seek to ensure that an adequate return on capital is generated from these activities (see discussion on product profitability below).

While the early stages of the swap and derivative market were characterised by a relatively low rate of counterparty default, more recent experience (described in Chapter 37) has focused increasing attention on counterparty credit risk. An added element in this focus has been increased strains placed on counterparty credit exposures, particularly, *as between financial institutions* where large volumes of outstanding transactions increasingly constrain the capacity to undertake further business. This development is particularly important as interbank trading is essential to risk management and market liquidity and constraints on these activities have the capacity to restrict overall market growth.

An added dimension of the problems of credit risk management has been that credit ratings have proved to be unstable. A number of institutions with relatively high credit ratings (such as United States money centre banks) saw their credit ratings decline through the 1980s and early 1990s.

The problems of credit risk exist at two levels:

- the acceptance by financial institutions of end user counterparty risk;
- acceptability of the financial institutions themselves as counterparties, reflecting the increased preference by end users for high credit quality counterparties

(typically, at least A and preferably AA or better, particularly for longer-term transactions).

The market approach to the management of credit risk issues has been undertaken on two levels: individual institutions and collective market responses.

Responses by individual institutions to the problems of credit risk and its management include:

- Enhancement of overall bank credit ratings, including restructuring of bank operations contracting the scope of its business or mergers designed to improve its credit standing.
- Establishment of credit enhanced derivative counterparty vehicles, for example, development of Merrill Lynch Derivative Products and similar special purpose derivative vehicles.
- The creation of joint ventures between weaker, lowly capitalised organisations with excellent derivative technology and larger better capitalised financial institutions to provide basis for expansion of swap and derivative activity. In extreme cases, this is taken by the form of a takeover of the specialist derivative operation by financial institution.
- A more systematic approach to the efficient use of credit capacity, including focusing activities on particular types of transactions or counterparties and the use of assignments etc to manage utilisation of credit and capital resources.

The collective market responses to these issues have included:

- the increased use of collateralised swap structures and mark-to-market techniques;
- the search for an acceptable netting system, designed primarily to reduce existing interbank exposures and provide additional credit capacity;
- the continuing search for a swap clearing house mechanism.

Regulatory issues

An increased factor in recent years which is likely to increase in its influence is the impact of financial institution regulators on the pattern of development of the swap and derivatives markets.

The BIS capital adequacy directives represent an *initial* attempt at regulatory action in relation to this market. Major issues that continue to be implemented include:

- adoption of bilateral and multilateral netting arrangements and regulatory sponsored means of managing counterparty credit exposure;
- perfection of collateral and its acceptance by bank regulators as reducing counterparty credit exposures;
- bankruptcy proof new structured derivative counterparty vehicles.

Additional regulatory initiatives in the area of market and trading risk are currently under consideration. The EC Directive and the BIS Guidelines (discussed in detail in Chapter 40) seek to expand the process of regulations to cover market risk elements assumed in trading and managing portfolios of swaps and derivative instruments.

The impact of regulatory development is difficult to anticipate. However, it is probable that these developments will ultimately result in the adoption of some method of at least bilateral netting between major market participants as well as perfection of collateral which will significantly increase the available credit capacity within the swap and derivative market. However, the adoption of some form of market risk measure and the need to hold capital in proportion to the level of market risk assumed will require additional capital to be committed to swap and derivative trading operations which will increase the cost, explicitly or implicitly, of maintaining such operations.

Product profitability

Concern about product profitability in relation to swap and derivative instruments focuses on the following factors:

- A perception that pricing of these instruments does not reflect appropriate credit risk or market risk assumed in posititioning such transactions.
- Concern that market/hedging risk in managing such portfolios are not well understood.
- Fears that the process of measurement of earnings from such activities is inadequate. This factor is compounded by fact that it is difficult to reconcile the economic basis of such operations with the reported accounting and taxation earnings of such portfolios.

The key approaches which are currently evolving to the problems of profit and performance measurement include:

- The development of risk adjusted information systems which measure performance and profitability covering:
  - return on capital measured as earnings compensating the capital utilisation in support of credit and market risk;
  - credit exposures, including creation of an appropriate credit reserve for potential future losses;
  - proper expense (including hedging cost) allocation;
  - allocation of all overhead costs relating to such operations.
- Development of appropriate income/expense recognition policies.
- Improving the efficiency and productivity of operational aspects of these businesses (covering back office/settlement/documentation etc) through investment in technology to "leverage" existing human resource commitments as well as selective outsourcing of certain functions.
- Significant investment in improving management and control strategies:
  - to ensure measurement, monitoring and management of all risk aspects of these operations;
  - to maintain proper management control of these businesses.

Traditional performance measurement has increasingly been found to be inadequate. A number of types of risk adjusted performance measures are increasingly being implemented. These include:

- return on risk adjusted capital (RORAC);
- risk adjusted return on capital (RAROC);
- return on risk adjusted assets (RORAA);
- risk adjusted return on assets (RAROA).

The basic objective of all these types of measurement techniques is to ensure that the return on specific businesses fully compensates the organisation for the level of capital commitment and risks assumed in individual activities (see discussion in Chapter 30).

Product development/delivery

A key aspect of the development and continuing growth of the market for swaps and derivative instruments has been the capacity to adapt basic transaction structures to accommodate specific market opportunities and end user requirements. This capacity to develop and deliver new products is likely to continue to be a significant feature of the market of the future.

The key issues in this regard include:

- creation of an appropriate structure for new product development and appropriate risk management;
- appropriate sales/distribution mechanisms for marketing new products to potential users;
- the development of appropriate product support facilities.

It is almost impossible to predict the nature or course of new product innovations. However, it is likely that the following factors will be important in product development:

- market opportunities as a result of specific developments in financial market variables;
- identification of specific client requirements and the adaptation of existing products to create specific structures with risk characteristics matching client requirements;
- an increased trend to cross market products, effectively combining elements from various market sectors—a process which will be assisted by the increasing trend to the integration of trading of swaps and derivative instruments.

Major areas of growth in respect of new products appear likely to be in relation to commodity and equity risk as well as general economic or macroeconomic risk management.

Vital elements in new product development approaches will be:

- the ability to *price* new products;
- the corresponding ability to design efficient hedges, which allow products to be traded within acceptable risk parameters.

The challenge in respect of product distribution revolves around the design and operation of a system which integrates, to the maximum degree possible, the following activities:

- pricing/risk management;
- sales/distribution to clients;
- product support.

Organisations continued to experiment with alternative forms of organisation. These cover:

- product versus client focus;
- centralised or global versus geographically decentralised approaches.

The principal form of current organisation appears to revolve around specific product groups, with some degree of geographical decentralisation. Some commentators predict the appropriate form of organisation in the future will be in terms of *risk types* with distribution being structured on the basis of customers being assigned to groups with similar risk management requirements.

An appropriate structure for the provision of product support is regarded as vital to facilitating appropriate product development and delivery capability. Product support, in this regard, will focus on maintaining flexible, reliable and accurate capabilities covering:

- credit risk analysis;
- documentation/legal risk analysis;
- assessment of regulatory exposures;
- rapid development of appropriate operational and support systems for new products.

MANAGING SUCCESSFUL SWAP/DERIVATIVES BUSINESSES[2]

As the market for swaps and derivative instruments matures and consolidates, competition between providers of these services also intensifies. While in periods of rapid growth weaker and less efficient providers of products operate profitably, the likely consolidation that has been foreshadowed will increasingly marginalise the less professional and inefficient providers of these instruments.

Keys to success in the swap and derivative business in the future would appear to be predicated on:

- possessing the appropriate technology;
- high credit standing;
- an appropriate organisational structure;
- appropriate support systems.

The possession of appropriate technology to price, trade and hedge the exposures assumed will be critical to success. To a substantial degree, this technological capacity will have to be allied to the availability and willingness to risk often substantial amounts of capital in support of trading activities in relation to swap and derivative instruments.

Possession of high credit rating, at least AA, will be essential to maintaining a position in the swaps and derivatives market. Allied to this high credit standing must of necessity be sound approaches to the efficient use of credit capacity and to counterparty exposure management.

Appropriate forms of organisation, which will almost certainly vary significantly between successful organisations, will be required to facilitate continual modification of products to satisfy demand as well as facilitate distribution of products to end users.

Central to success will be appropriate systems and operational support capacities to measure risk and profitability and ensure efficient and cost-effective settlements and operations on complex swap portfolios. Efficient performance of subsidiary tasks such as documentation in relation to swap and derivative transactions will be of importance in the future.

The capacity, in particular, to support product activities in a cost efficient manner to enable institutions to be at least comparable, if not the lowest, cost producers is seen as vital.

2. See John Howland Jackson (1992).

As the swap market matures, the process of *managing* swap and derivative instrument operations *as a business* is increasingly evident. For much of its history, the swap market has been the preserve of traders, risk managers and product specialists. However, as the market has matured, profitability has diminished and the nature and complexity of risks resulting from participating in such product market segments has increased, necessitating management understanding and control of activity in swap and derivative instruments *as a business*.

Sound management of successful swaps/derivatives businesses will focus on:

- a clear understanding of the type and scope of derivatives business the institution wishes to operate;
- understanding the nature of risks entailed and the implementation of appropriate systems for the measurement and reporting of risks incurred in trading and hedging such products on an independent basis;
- the need to balance cost and profit centres within swaps and derivatives operations, with a particular focus on ensuring full costing, appropriate methods of revenue/earnings recognition, control of operational expenses and systems costs; and
- balancing the need to control and measure business risks with the need to facilitate product innovation.

CONCLUSION

The market for swaps and derivative instruments, as a whole, is entering a period of consolidation. However, the basic rationale of swap and derivative transactions continues to remain the same:

- the trading of economic advantages within capital markets;
- the creation of surrogate or synthetic transaction structures by linking swaps to underlying, borrowing or investment decisions.

The prognosis for the market as a whole is for continuing growth. The rate of growth may, reflecting the maturity of the market, decrease. In addition, the rate of growth between various product and market segments will vary substantially.

The proliferation of product innovations will continue, with a strong focus on combinations of various product types as well as innovations in the management of cross-market commodity, equity and macro-economic risks.

Penetration of end users and the development of additional applications of swap and derivative products is also set to continue.

Fundamentally, swap and derivative instruments represent perhaps the most significant financial innovation in capital markets in the latter half of the 20th century. As catalysts for integration of various markets, swaps and financial derivatives have been a major factor in developing more efficient global intermediation processes. Swaps serve to foster more rapid growth in international trade and capital flows, allowing the channelling of excess savings in one market to another. These are all fundamental changes which will ensure the continuing and increasing role of swap and financial derivative products in global capital markets in the future.

Index